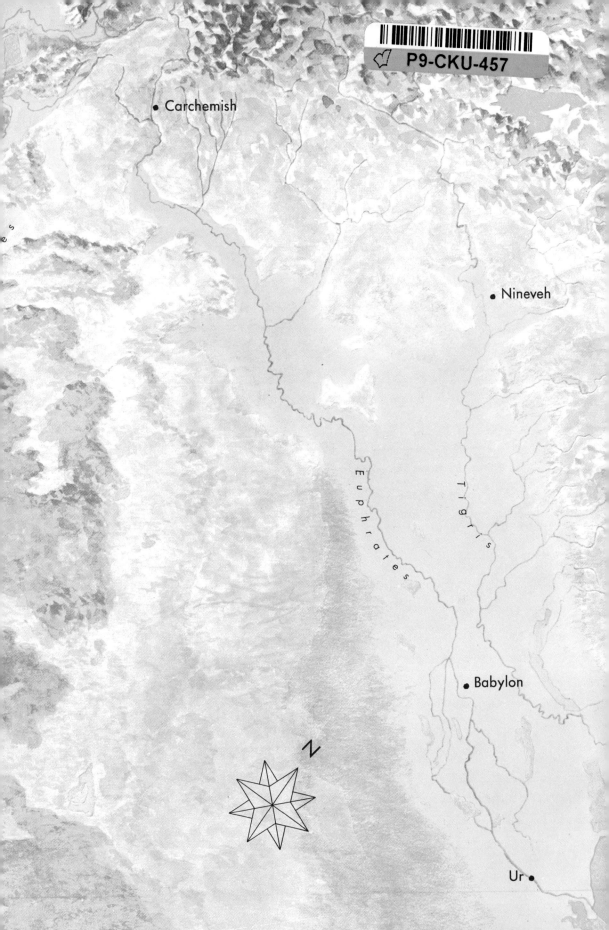

• Carchemish

• Nineveh

Euphrates

Tigris

• Babylon

Ur •

N

E. LOWENSTEIN

THE INTERPRETER'S BIBLE

THE INTERPRETER'S BIBLE

IN TWELVE VOLUMES

VOLUME V

THE BOOK OF
ECCLESIASTES

THE SONG OF SONGS

THE BOOK OF
ISAIAH

THE BOOK OF
JEREMIAH

THE
INTERPRETER'S BIBLE

—

The Holy Scriptures

IN THE KING JAMES AND REVISED STANDARD VERSIONS

WITH GENERAL ARTICLES AND

INTRODUCTION, EXEGESIS, EXPOSITION

FOR EACH BOOK OF THE BIBLE

IN TWELVE VOLUMES

VOLUME
V

דבר־אלהינו יקום לעולם

Abingdon

NASHVILLE

Standard Book Number: 687-19211-0

Library of Congress Catalog Card Number: 51-12276

Thirty-sixth Printing 1982

MANUFACTURED BY THE PARTHENON
PRESS AT NASHVILLE, TENNESSEE,
UNITED STATES OF AMERICA

ABBREVIATIONS AND EXPLANATIONS

ABBREVIATIONS

Canonical books and bibliographical terms are abbreviated according to common usage

Amer. Trans. — *The Bible, An American Translation,* Old Testament, ed. J. M. P. Smith
Apoc.—Apocrypha
Aq.—Aquila
ASV—American Standard Version (1901)
Barn.—Epistle of Barnabas
Clem.—Clement
C.T.—Consonantal Text
Did.—Didache
Ecclus.—Ecclesiasticus
ERV—English Revised Version (1881-85)

Exeg.—Exegesis
Expos.—Exposition
Goodspeed—*The Bible, An American Translation,* New Testament and Apocrypha, tr. Edgar J. Goodspeed
Herm. Vis., etc.—The Shepherd of Hermas: Visions, Mandates, Similitudes
Ign. Eph., etc.—Epistles of Ignatius to the Ephesians, Magnesians, Trallians, Romans, Philadelphians, Smyrnaeans, and Polycarp

KJV—King James Version (1611)
LXX—Septuagint
Macc.—Maccabees
Moffatt—*The Bible, A New Translation,* by James Moffatt
M.T.—Masoretic Text
N.T.—New Testament
O.L.—Old Latin
O.T.—Old Testament
Polyc. Phil.—Epistle of Polycarp to the Philippians
Pseudep.—Pseudepigrapha
Pss. Sol.—Psalms of Solomon

RSV—Revised Standard Version (1946-52)
Samar.—Samaritan recension
Symm.—Symmachus
Targ.—Targum
Test. Reuben, etc.—Testament of Reuben, and others of the Twelve Patriarchs
Theod.—Theodotion
Tob.—Tobit
Vulg.—Vulgate
Weymouth—*The New Testament in Modern Speech,* by Richard Francis Weymouth
Wisd. Sol.—Wisdom of Solomon

QUOTATIONS AND REFERENCES

Boldface type in Exegesis and Exposition indicates a quotation from either the King James or the Revised Standard Version of the passage under discussion. The two versions are distinguished only when attention is called to a difference between them. Readings of other versions are not in boldface type and are regularly identified.

In scripture references a letter (*a, b,* etc.) appended to a verse number indicates a clause within the verse; an additional Greek letter indicates a subdivision within the clause. When no book is named, the book under discussion is understood.

Arabic numbers connected by colons, as in scripture references, indicate chapters and verses in deuterocanonical and noncanonical works. For other ancient writings roman numbers indicate major divisions, arabic numbers subdivisions, these being connected by periods. For modern works a roman number and an arabic number connected by a comma indicate volume and page. Bibliographical data on a contemporary work cited by a writer may be found by consulting the first reference to the work by that writer (or the bibliography, if the writer has included one).

GREEK TRANSLITERATIONS

$\alpha = a$	$\varepsilon = e$	$\iota = i$	$\nu = n$	$\rho = r$	$\varphi = ph$
$\beta = b$	$\zeta = z$	$\kappa = k$	$\xi = x$	$\sigma(\varsigma) = s$	$\chi = ch$
$\gamma = g$	$\eta = \bar{e}$	$\lambda = l$	$o = o$	$\tau = t$	$\psi = ps$
$\delta = d$	$\theta = th$	$\mu = m$	$\pi = p$	$\upsilon = u, y$	$\omega = \bar{o}$

HEBREW AND ARAMAIC TRANSLITERATIONS

I. HEBREW ALPHABET

א = '	ח = h	ט = ṭ	מ(ם) = m	פ(ף) = p, ph	שׂ = s, sh
ב = b, bh	ו = w	י = y	נ(ן) = n	צ(ץ) = ç	ת = t, th
ג = g, gh	ז = z	כ(ך) = k, kh	ס = ṣ	ק = q	
ד = d, dh	ח = ḥ	ל = l	ע = '	ר = r	

II. MASORETIC POINTING

Pure-long	Tone-long	Short	Composite *shᵉwa*
ָ = â	ָ = ā	_ = a	ֲ = ᵃ
.. = ê	.. = ē	·· = e	⁚ = ᵉ
. *or* ִ = î		. = i	⁚ = ᵒ
ֹ *or* ˙ = ô	˙ = ō	ָ = o	
ֻ = û		·. = u	ֳ = ᵒ

NOTE: (*a*) The *páthah* furtive is transliterated as a *ḥateph-páthah.* (*b*) The simple *shᵉwa,* when vocal, is transliterated ᵉ. (*c*) The tonic accent, which is indicated only when it occurs on a syllable other than the last, is transliterated by an acute accent over the vowel.

TABLE OF CONTENTS

VOLUME V

THE BOOK OF ECCLESIASTES

THE SONG OF SONGS

THE BOOK OF ISAIAH

CHAPTERS 1-39

CHAPTERS 40-66

THE BOOK OF JEREMIAH

MAPS

The Book of

ECCLESIASTES

Introduction and Exegesis by O. S. RANKIN
Exposition by GAIUS GLENN ATKINS

ECCLESIASTES

INTRODUCTION

In the Hebrew Bible the book of Ecclesiastes is called קהלת, that is, as transliterated, *Qôhéleth* or "Koheleth." The opening verse, which reads, "The words of Koheleth, the son of David, king of Jerusalem," is usually considered to be an editor's superscription to the book. But in 1:12 the author himself announces, "I, Koheleth, have been king over Israel in Jerusalem." The exact content of meaning attaching to the word Koheleth may never be determined.

I. Title

Speculating exegetes have suggested that the word "Koheleth" might be a cryptogram, perhaps a kind of abbreviation formed by the initial letters of a longer name and title, such as "Rambam," from Rabbi Moses ben Maimon, and "Rashi," from Rabbi Shelomo (ben) Isaac. But the word Koheleth does not bear the aspect of such a formation. It represents a participial feminine singular form of the verb קהל, otherwise unused in the Qal, which appears to be derived from the noun קהל, meaning "assembly," ἐκκλησία. This is apparently the way it was understood by the Greek translators of the Septuagint, who rendered it Ἐκκλησιαστής —Vulgate: *Ecclesiastes*. Hence, for the most part, the term Koheleth has been explained either as: (*a*) one who addresses an assembly (cf. Jerome: *Concionator*), that is, a preacher or a speaker (cf. Moffatt's translation), or (*b*) one who collects or gathers. In this latter case it is possible to think of persons being assembled together for instruction, or of epigrammatic sentences of wisdom or aphorisms being gathered together (cf. 12:9-10) for the purposes of teaching. In 12:8 we are further en-

lightened as to the author's use of the word. Here it is given the definite article—"Vanity of vanities, says the Koheleth"—which shows that it is not intended to be used as a personal name but as a description, in some aspect, of Solomon, who must be understood to be the king mentioned in 1:1, 12.

But the feminine gender of the word presents a difficulty. Had it had reference to personified Wisdom, who in Prov. 8–9 calls out "beside the gates, at the entry of the city" (Prov. 8:3), that is, in places of assembly (cf. Prov. 1:20), inviting the sons of men to turn in to her house and listen to her voice (Prov. 9:4), we might readily acknowledge the word form to be appropriate. For, as applied to Solomon, a feminine gender appears incongruous. Nevertheless, since the book refers to a king in Jerusalem, the feminine form of the word may be justified as denoting an activity, office, or function. The book of Ezra contains two words similar to Koheleth in structure, *ṣophéreth* (Ezra 2:55) and *pôkhéreth* (Ezra 2:57), which refer to persons in a list or register of names. Originally they may have signified respectively the office of scribe and the office of gazelle tender. Thus, commending itself to modern scholars, is the explanation that Koheleth signifies "the office of speaker in an assembly." If this is the meaning, it might represent no appreciable advance upon the old rendering "preacher," who has usually some official standing, except that it permits us to view the book of Ecclesiastes not so much as a sermon but as an address, discourse, or lecture.

The character of the book is not sermonic but sapiential. It sets forth certain viewpoints

3

on the value of life and may refer critically to other wise sayings which seem to contradict its conclusions. The Solomon of the book should thus be regarded not as a preacher, but as the ideal teacher or exponent of wisdom. The author was probably, like Jesus ben Sirach, who lived somewhat later (180 B.C.), a professional teacher of wisdom. The words in the epilogue (12:9-11) are usually taken to be the contribution of a pupil, although they might be the author's own postscript of self-commendation "in the gnomic style." [1] Ben Sirach has a similar piece of a self-appreciatory nature (Ecclus. 51: 13-22) at the end of his work, and advertises his school with the words,

Turn in unto me, ye unlearned
And lodge in my house of instruction (Ecclus. 51:23).

He also invites disciples to learn from "Wisdom,"

Bring your necks under her yoke,
And her burden let your soul bear (Ecclus. 51:26).

In I Kings 8:1 (cf. vs. 55) the Hebrew verb of which Koheleth represents a participial form is used of Solomon assembling the people of Israel to himself at the time of the dedication of the temple. Whether the choice of the word Koheleth had any connection in the thought of the author of Ecclesiastes with Solomon's part as assembler, leader, and speaker on that occasion we are unable to tell. In the environment of Greek culture which highly esteemed the rhetor, the figure of Solomon, renowned for his judicial decisions and proverbial lore, was probably turned by Judaism into the patron of the orator or speaker.

II. Canonicity

Of the book of Ecclesiastes Ernest Renan spoke words of high praise. He called it "a charming book, the only pleasant book that has been composed by a Jew." [2] Judaism reads it on the third day of the feast of Booths (Tabernacles), apparently in order to qualify the cheerfulness of that day with the thought that life and its joys are fleeting and that everything has its time. The work is not, however, a product of orthodox Judaism. It has been termed "the most heretical book of the third century B.C." [3]

[1] Otto Eissfeldt, *Einleitung in das Alte Testament* (Tübingen: J. C. B. Mohr, 1934), p. 552. The author of Koheleth, following the model of Egyptian wisdom writers, may have himself provided the superscription (1:1), and the laudatory postscript (12:9-11). Cf. Adolf Erman, *The Literature of the Ancient Egyptians* (tr. A. M. Blackman; New York: E. P. Dutton & Co., 1927), pp. 72-74.

[2] *L'Antichrist* (Paris: M. Lévy Frères, 1873), p. 101.

[3] Johannes Hempel, *Die althebräische Literatur* (Potsdam: Akademische Verlagsgesellschaft, 1930), p. 191.

Its acceptance into the canon of Scripture was preceded by long controversy and the school of Hillel did not concur in the judgment of the school of Shammai, to whom the work was obnoxious. Finally the Synod of Jamnia, about A.D. 100, decided in favor of its canonical standing. The work was given this status not on account of any of its religious ideas, but rather because it bears a pseudonym which suggests Solomon as its author. Even today there are Jewish scholars who accept and defend the tradition of Solomonic authorship. [4] While the religious conceptions of Ecclesiastes were for some the stone of stumbling to its canonization, the book was defended by others on strictly religious grounds. According to a Talmudic tradition (Shabbath 30b), it was admitted to canonical rank because "its beginning is religious teaching and its end is religious teaching." It is true that at the end it stresses belief in God and in divine judgment, as well as obedience to God's commandments, while it contains at the beginning a poem of sad beauty on the vanity of human existence. In the aesthetic quality of its pessimistic strain lies the secret of its attraction and of its spiritual significance. It was probably a latent sense of this significance which effected its retention among the "sacred writings." The purest and highest religions—highest because of their depth of thought—are not characterized by a naïve optimism in regard to the world of man. Judaism and Christianity both acknowledge that our life is as grass—"in the morning it flourisheth, and groweth up; in the evening it is cut down, and withereth" (Ps. 90:6) —and that man's duty is to number his days and acquire a heart of wisdom (Ps. 90:12). To whatever height of hope and faith the soul may rise, it cannot forget that "here have we no continuing city" (Heb. 13:14). The faith of Christianity is founded not only upon a belief in the Incarnation but also on the historical event of the Crucifixion. This event is intimately related to the evil in man's nature, and the profound conception of sin which is inherent in biblical thinking leaves no room for optimism so far as man by himself is concerned. The Christian optimism is attached to the doctrine that God has revealed himself in Christ as redeemer. It may be profitable to contrast the spirit of Koheleth's reflections with the spirit of the evangelists, whose teachings, when the new age dawned, were aglow with faith, hope, and love. But we cannot remove Koheleth from the place in history which he occupied. In that place he is a link in the chain of thought and divine revelation of which the Old and New Testa-

[4] Abraham Cohen, "Ecclesiastes," *The Five Megilloth* (Hindhead: Soncino Press, 1946), p. 106.

ments are the records. We must appreciate Koheleth's integrity of mind, the clarity of the critical judgment with which he reviews all the things "under the sun," as he sees them, which seem to him to be worthy of consideration by men. The placing of his book in Scripture pays honor to a work which is alone of its kind in Israel's wisdom literature and which in its "tragic sense of life" throws a searching light upon our human nature and, indirectly, upon the need of that nature for reconciliation with the divine.

III. Contents

An examination of the contents of Ecclesiastes should involve an exegetical study of the text line by line. Only thus can be clearly revealed what gaps, if any, exist in the logical sequence of the author's thought, or if there is any intrusion into the text of heterogeneous ideas or teaching which disturb the unity of the book.

To begin with a summary of the thought of the book on the basis of the chapters into which the work is divided in the English versions may not seem to be a fruitful method of inquiry into the question of the book's structure. Yet a synopsis of the contents will be useful in presenting in a brief form the subjects with which the book deals, and how the author deals with them. Also, certain general impressions, which can be verified or controlled by reference to the actual text, may be formed and found useful. But we must remember that a summary tends to knit together thoughts that are less closely associated in the complete text, and obscures the contradictions and dissonances which appear therein.

Chaper 1. Koheleth asserts that the course of nature does not alter itself. The present is as the past; nothing is new, and this eternal sameness continues to be the nature of man's existence. Koheleth has had a very ample experience of life and has learned that it leads to no lasting gain. The wisdom which he possesses does not make any difference to his condition, except that it deepens the sorrow caused by his comprehension of the uselessness of life.

Chapter 2. The answer is given to the questions: How can you say that life is profitless? Why can you not enjoy living? Koheleth has tested whether this might be possible. He has occupied himself with great enterprises, the raising of majestic buildings, the planting of gardens and parks, the amassing of wealth. He has known the delight of the love of women. He has tasted all that could be regarded as good. He has denied himself nothing. But he has perceived that there is no real gain or permanent value in all this. Has he then experienced the benefit and pleasure of learning? Has he discovered the value of the improving of the mind? There is much to be said on behalf of wisdom, he replies, but in the end the wise man dies, just as the fool does. He does not really gain anything more out of life than the fool does. Anything obtained in life by toil has to be left at death to other persons who did not toil for it. Toil in any case brings only sorrow. Vss. 24-26 state that it is a good thing for a man to enjoy himself in his toil, that God gives this enjoyment to persons who please him and allows those who do not please him, that is, "the sinners," to gather for them that please him.

Chapter 3. A process of opposites is perceived in the human situation—life and death, doing and not doing, weeping and laughing, and so forth—for there is a season for everything. But this makes existence only more perplexing, for man cannot find out what God's purpose is in this endless chain of opposites. Nothing is better for man than that he should be happy, and happiness is a gift of God. But life is just an eternal round of events. "That which is, already has been" (vs. 15). The lack of any apparent purpose in things is the worst feature of life. Where one might well expect to find righteousness, there is wickedness. God doubtless will judge both the righteous and the wicked, but his plan seems to be to employ the experience of life to test men and demonstrate that they are beasts. Man has no advantage over the beast. Both have the same fate—death and the return to the dust. Certainly, in view of this end, man should try to "enjoy his work, for that is his lot" (vs. 22).

Chapter 4. The world presents a long history of oppression and of the miseries of the oppressed. Those who have not yet been born and have not seen what sufferings men have endured are more fortunate than those who have experienced the world's woes. Successful toil raises up envy among a man's neighbors, though it is foolish to abstain from work. Quietness has twice the value of toil. He who toils for riches and leaves them to others is doing a vain thing. Those who combine together in their work secure a greater reward for it. Unity is strength. Vss. 13-16, which follow, are a digression contrasting a poor and wise youth with an old and foolish king.

Chapter 5. In the worship of God be humble and listen. Do not talk much. Do not be rash in speech. God is in heaven, remember, and you upon the earth. Do not make rash vows. Pay the vows which you have made (vss. 1-7). Do not be surprised at injustice and corruption among officials, for all officials are encouraged by the example of those above them to make what gain they can from their vocations (vss. 8-9).

Man is never satisfied, for he is always trying to gain more. He occasionally makes bad ventures which lead to poverty. At death he departs from life's scene as empty and naked as he came into it (vss. 10-17). What man should do therefore, since life is short, is "to accept his lot" and enjoy what wealth God gives him in contentment and joy of heart, particularly in his vocation (vss. 18-20).

Chapter 6. Sometimes God bestows his gifts bountifully on a man who has not the power to enjoy them. A long life and a large family are good gifts from which the goodness vanishes if they are joined to poverty. The reason for a man's toiling is to stay his hunger and to find satisfaction, but the wise man and the poor man of worth often lack the power to find this satisfaction. Man cannot dispute with the will of God on this matter, "For who knows what is good for man while he lives the few days of his vain life?" (vs. 12).

Chapter 7. The spirit of mirth and levity becomes fools. But since the day of death is better than the day of birth, the wise man will feel himself more at home in the house of mourning than in the house of mirth. The wise man can be made foolish through oppression and be corrupted by bribery. The wise man will be patient and eschew anger. "Wisdom is good with an inheritance" (vs. 11). Like money, learning has a protective value (vss. 1-12). God has made some things straight and some things crooked, and the world shows that the righteous may have misfortune, while the wicked may have prosperity. But the wise man will avoid all extremes in conduct and will fear God. Wisdom is of great help to a man. Even the righteous are not free from sin. Do not try to learn what people are saying to each other lest you hear your own servant curse you. But it is very difficult for a man either to know what wisdom is or to "know the wickedness of folly" (vs. 25). Among the worst evils that can befall a man is that which comes from "the woman whose heart is snares and nets" (vs. 26). The sinner is taken by her.

Chapter 8. Wisdom even changes the look of a man's countenance. When the wise man receives a king's command, he will know the time and method of fulfilling it. He recognizes that the king's authority is supreme. There are certain things over which man has no power (vss. 1-9). The wicked behave as if they were pious and are praised by their fellow men, but it will not be well with them. It happens in life that the wicked prosper and the righteous fare badly. This appears to be senseless. Therefore Koheleth commends man to eat and drink and enjoy himself. Man cannot solve the riddle of life.

Chapter 9. The bad and the good are subject to God, "and one fate comes to all" (vss. 1-2). This sameness of fate is an evil inherent in existence. Nevertheless, to be alive is better than to be dead. While one lives one has hope. But the dead know nothing and have nothing. Make therefore the most of life while you have it. Drink your wine with a merry heart, let your garments be white, enjoy life with the woman you love, take an interest in your work. For there is no capacity for thought and knowledge in Sheol where the dead go. "Time and chance happen . . . to all" (vss. 11-12). Men are as fish on whom the net that captures them falls in evil times. Wisdom can do mighty things, yet the possessors of wisdom are not rewarded, not even with gratitude. Though the poor man's wisdom is despised, wisdom has its merits and is better than weapons of warfare.

Chapter 10. A little folly may frustrate wisdom. Folly often appears in a high position and is given honor, but wisdom lightens man's tasks and removes his difficulties. The wise man's mouth wins him favor, while the fool manifests himself to men as a fool (vss. 1-15). A country's fortune or misfortune is reflected in the person of its king and the conduct of its princes (vss. 16-17). Here follow proverbs on (*a*) indolence, (*b*) bread, wine, and money, and (*c*) the need of care in expressing thoughts that are unfavorable to others, since what we say or even think becomes known and is carried abroad.

Chapter 11. Take life as it is, grasping its opportunities, being neither too fearful nor hesitant when decisions have to be made. As you do not know everything and are ignorant of what actions will succeed, you have to assume a risk in doing what you deem suitable. Make what you can of the pleasant light of life, for it will fade into darkness. Especially value the days of youth. Satisfy the desires of your youth, keeping in mind that God's judgment rests on all your doings.

Chapter 12. In the days of your youth remember your Creator, while your vitality is yet unimpaired by the infirmities of age. At vss. 8-9 follows the epilogue.

From this summary it may be seen that Ecclesiastes is not a closely argued treatise. The thought progresses, in spite of what appear to be interruptions or asides, in the manner in which a conversation progresses. It has been said that the logical conclusion of Koheleth's thinking has already been reached at the end of ch. 2,[5] but while this may be so there are various aspects of existence and of human experience— for example, life's opposites in ch. 3, its oppressions in ch. 4, what befell the poor man whose

---

[5] H. W. Hertzberg, *Der Prediger* (Leipzig: Werner Scholl, 1932; "Kommentar zum Alten Testament"), p. 14.

wisdom delivered the city in ch. 9, the opportunities of youth in chs. 11–12—which support the conviction which the author has stated early in his work and strengthen his argument by illustration. Is there an advance in the book from a deeply pessimistic view to what seems to be a more positive outlook upon life? From the beginning Koheleth is of the opinion that there is a relative good to be found in existence, a relative gain to be had through wisdom, but his pessimism never disappears. Toward the end his mood becomes, or seems to become, lighter and less oppressive. The poem on the advantages of life before the infirmities of age draw nigh affirms at least that something, however temporary, may be gained by man, something of value. What is positive, however, in the *carpe diem* exhortation, is limited by the thought of the brevity of life. The picture of youth's privileges does not dispel the author's consciousness of the darker side of reality out of which the picture arises.

The summary which has been given discloses to a certain but slight degree several digressions or interruptions of thought. It does not show the very loose connection of the aphorisms which appear in the long passage 9:17–10:20, aphorisms which in their relationship one to the other are reminiscent of the style of the book of Proverbs.

IV. Composition and Structure

The history of criticism has revealed, on patient study of the text, great divergence of opinion concerning the structure and unity of the book.

A. The Main Hypotheses. 1. Minor Additions. —According to this view, the book is a literary unit which has received editorially a few minor additions: Gerrit Wildeboer explained in 1898 what seem to be incongruities within the book by saying that although "not the product of systematic thinking [Koheleth] is the honest confession of an earnest man who doubts much that others readily believe, but who refuses to renounce the faith of his childhood." [6] Wildeboer did not think that even the epilogue had been added by another person.

A later commentator, Hertzberg,[7] while considering the epilogue as not being from the author's pen, agreed otherwise with Wildeboer on the book's unity, and stated that from the point of view of the convictions expressed in Koheleth, its language, style, meter, structure, and thought, 1:2–12:8 is a literary unit. The uniformity of style throughout Ecclesiastes, Hertzberg thinks, is unfavorable to the assump-

tion that various writers have had a part in its composition.

Paul Volz[8] was of less rigid opinion than Wildeboer and Hertzberg. The supposition that the book has remained free of insertions would indeed be extraordinary when comparison is made with other biblical books and when the strongly provocative nature of Ecclesiastes is taken into account. Volz admitted that certain passages are justly regarded as additions made by an interpolator who deemed them necessary to support the doctrine of divine judgment and retribution and to induce in the heart of the reader the fear of God. These passages, intended to be corrective of Koheleth's teaching, are, in Volz's judgment, 3:15b; 5:6b, 18-19; 7:18b, 29; 8:5-6, 12-13; 9:7b; 11:9b; 12:1a, 13-14. They appear to have been made either entirely or mostly by the pious contributor to the epilogue who wrote the admonition, "Fear God, and keep his commandments; for this is the duty of all men. For God will bring every deed into judgment" (12:13-14). Volz also suggested that additions may have been made here and there to Koheleth's aphorisms. But apart from these few insertions, which were made probably in a dogmatic interest, Volz held that the book is a literary whole, a work practically of one piece.

2. Major Additions.—According to this view, the book as it now exists does not possess unity but embraces major additions. Certain scholars have seen in Ecclesiastes the activity of more than one writer. The lack of orderly arrangement of thought so impressed Gustav Bickell[9] that he sought to account for it by supposing that an accident had befallen a manuscript upon which our present Hebrew text is based. This manuscript, he assumed, was in codex form and its sheets accidentally came to be misplaced. Before the dislocation an opponent of the original writer's opinions had effected textual alterations, and afterward further retouching took place. Such a theory, which is too drastic to appeal to many, reveals at least how disconnected the thought and how inharmonious the book of Ecclesiastes may appear.

The most radical solution of the problem has been presented by Carl Siegfried.[10] This scholar perceived the existence of an original

[6] *Die fünf Megillot* (Leipzig: J. C. B. Mohr; "Kurzer Hand-Commentar zum Alten Testament"), p. 115.

[7] *Op. cit.*

[8] *Weisheit* (Göttingen: Vandenhoeck & Ruprecht, 1911; "Die Schriften des Alten Testaments"), pp. 232-33, 257.

[9] *Der Prediger über den Wert des Daseins* (Innsbruck: Wagner, 1884). Bickell's theory received a very full account in G. A. Barton, *A Critical and Exegetical Commentary on the Book of Ecclesiastes* (New York: Charles Scribner's Sons, 1908; "International Critical Commentary"), pp. 25-26; see also pp. 28-29 for a description of Paul Haupt's (1905) equally radical theory, which reckons barely more than half of Ecclesiastes as genuine.

[10] *Prediger und Hoheslied* (Göttingen: Vandenhoeck & Ruprecht, 1898; "Handkommentar zum Alten Testament").

document written by a philosopher influenced by Greek thought. To this original were added in the course of time the comments of a Sadducean Epicurean who tendered the precept to enjoy life while it lasted. This latter writer was followed by a wisdom writer (a ḥākhām) who added proverbial sentences in defense of the advantages of wisdom. Then came a pious orthodox Jew (a ḥāṣîdh) who interpolated some precepts on divine judgment as a corrective to the original writer's reflections on the prosperity of the unrighteous. Furthermore, Siegfried observed additions of a lesser amount made by glossators interested in wisdom, by two redactors and by three contributors to the epilogue. All these elements represent the various voices that one may hear in the completed book.

Siegfried's analysis is not rightly described when it is called an attempt to disclose the sources of Koheleth, for, as he says in his preface, the parts of the book to which he draws attention are not sources in the Pentateuchal sense, but corrective glosses that have been made to an original literary unit by individual writers. In general, those who have addressed themselves to the question of the integrity of Ecclesiastes have regarded Siegfried's view as extreme. Nevertheless, two important exegetes, A. H. McNeile,[11] who spoke of Siegfried's analysis as a ruthless dissection, and Barton,[12] who thought that Siegfried failed to reckon with the capacity of the human mind to entertain a variety of conceptions, both agreed with him in a very substantial measure. And this agreement must to some extent be inevitable whenever Ecclesiastes in its present condition cannot be regarded as a consistent unity. If accretions are admitted, the question presents itself, To what extent do they occur and of what nature are they? McNeile and Barton dismissed Siegfried's Sadducean Epicurean from the scene, and also those who were credited by Siegfried as making sundry minor glosses on wisdom; but both commentators retained Siegfried's wisdom writer (ḥākhām) and his pious interpolator (ḥāṣîdh). The parts of Ecclesiastes which were attributed by Siegfried, McNeile, and Barton to the ḥākhām and the ḥāṣîdh may be seen in a comparative table as follows:

Passages allotted to the ḥākhām

By Siegfried	By McNeile	By Barton
2:13, 14a; 4:5;	4:5, 9-12; 6:7,	4:5; 5:3, 7a; 7:
6:8, 9a; 7:11,	9a; 7:1a, 4-6,	1a, 3, 5, 6-9,
12, 19; 8:1; 9:	7-12, 19; 8:1;	11, 12, 19; 8:1;
13-18; 10:1-3,	9:17-10:3; 10:	9:17, 18; 10:1-
12-15	8-11, 12-15, 18,	3, 8-14a, 15, 18,
	19; 12:11, 12	19

[11] An Introduction to Ecclesiastes (Cambridge: Cambridge University Press, 1904).
[12] Op. cit.

Passages allotted to the ḥāṣîdh

By Siegfried	By McNeile	By Barton
2:24b-26a; 3:	2:26ab; 3:14b,	2:26; 3:17; 7:
11, 13, 14, 17;	17; 4:17-5:6;	18b, 26b, 29;
4:17-5:1; 5:3-	7:18b, 26b, 29;	8:2b, 3a, 5, 6a,
5, 6b, 7; 6:10-	8:2b, 3ab, 5,	11-13; 11:9b;
12; 7:13, 17,	6a; 8:11-13; 11:	12:1a, 13 (from
23-25, 29; 8:2-	9b; 12:1a, 13,	the words
8, 11-13; 9:1;	14	"fear God"), 14
11:5, 8b, 9b;		
12:1a, 7b		

McNeile said of the ḥākhām's insertions that they were

more or less isolated apophthegms bearing on life and nature . . . . Some of these seem to be suggested by Koheleth's words, and correct or enlarge upon his remarks, but many are thrown in at random with no kind of relevance. In every case their frigid didactic style is in strong contrast to the heat and sting of Koheleth's complaints.[13]

In regard to the passage 9:17-10:20, a very long stretch of loosely connected maxims, it is interesting to observe how much of it McNeile ascribed to the wisdom glossator: 9:17-10:3; 10:8-11, 12-15, 19. According to McNeile, the theory of the unity of authorship of Ecclesiastes "affords no explanation of the miscellaneous proverbs wedged into chaps. iv-x."[14] In a clearly argued essay on the composition of Ecclesiastes, Edouard Podechard[15] has taken the same line as McNeile and Barton. He attributes additions to the ḥākhām and the ḥāṣîdh, and holds that the section 12:9-12 in the epilogue, which in the third person speaks admiringly of Koheleth, derives from a disciple of Koheleth. According to Podechard, this disciple is also responsible for the personal references in the third person which appear in the text (viz., 1:2; 7:27; 12:8).

3. Independent Aphorisms.—According to this view, the book presents thirty-seven independent sentential pieces—aphoristic units—each of which treats of a topic from its own particular angle. Kurt Galling stated in various studies[16] that Ecclesiastes is no well-planned

[13] Op. cit., p. 22.
[14] Ibid., p. 28.
[15] "La composition du livre de l'Ecclésiaste," *Revue Biblique*, IX (1912), 161-91. See also his monumental commentary, *L'Ecclésiaste* (Paris: J. Gabalda, 1912), pp. 142-70. Podechard allots to the ḥāṣîdh 2:26ab; 3:17; 7:26b; 8:2b, 5-8, 11-13; 11:9c; 12:1a, 13-14; and to the ḥākhām 4:5, 9-12; 5:2, 6a; 6:7; 7:1-12, 18-22; 8:1-2a, 3-4; 9:17-10:4; 10:10-14a, 15-20; 11:1-4, 6. Podechard's ḥākhām is a convenient symbol for one or more wisdom writers. He also contends that 4:17-5:6 is a separate wisdom gloss, and that 12:2-6 is by a young wisdom writer.
[16] "Kohelet-Studien," *Zeitschrift für die alttestamentliche Wissenschaft*, L (1932), 276-99; Review of Hertzberg's *Der Prediger*, in *Theologische Literaturzeitung*, LVIII (1933), 271-75; "Stand und Aufgabe der Kohelet-Forschung," *Theologische Rundschau*, VI (1934), 355-73; see also Max Haller and Kurt Galling, *Die fünf Megilloth*

philosophical treatise but a collection or arrangement of single proverbs (*Sprüche*). Galling meant by a proverb (*Spruch*) a sentence or aphoristic literary unit which is from two to fifteen lines in length and which sets forth its own viewpoint on a definite subject. Koheleth, the poet, we must suppose, made thirty-seven different poems at various times, and then Koheleth, the editor of "the book," strung these poems together.

No one will perceive in the present "book" a senseless conglomerate of aphorisms, but we must hold responsible for the arrangement [of the aphoristic units] the editor Koheleth, not the poet Koheleth. In other words, we must always be conscious of the fact that it is in a secondary stage in which the thoughts of Koheleth present themselves in the form of this book." [17]

Koheleth the editor and Koheleth the poet, Galling explained,[18] are one and the same person, but must nevertheless be sharply distinguished, for the poet did not turn out his poems on a production line, nor design them from the first as organic elements of a book, nor, while he was composing a new poem, did he consult the manuscript which contained the poems that he had already created.

In support of this view of the structure of Ecclesiastes, Galling[19] contended that the requirement according to which a book be written in logical or historical order corresponds to a mode of thought which Europeans adopted from the Greeks, but to a document that is prior to the Greek period and has nothing to do with the Greek spirit, we must not expect this mode of thought to apply. Koheleth stood on the frontier of two periods, and the redactors, the man who wrote in the epilogue the section 12:8-11 (cf. Podechard above) and he who wrote the section 12:12-14, are the first "Greek" interpreters of the yet pre-Grecian book, both of whom understood the "book" as treating of a single theme (cf. 12:8).[20] Galling (as against Volz) did not observe in Koheleth any progress of thought toward a positive outlook on life, for in his view the book has no uniform theme, no logical structure, and each aphoristic piece stands by itself.

Hertzberg, who accepted the idea of separate divisions in Ecclesiastes, yet, in Galling's judgment, offends against this principle of independence by explaining a passage in one section on the basis of a sentence in another,[21] thus assuming the existence of a literary connection between the two. The section 8:1–9:12, which Galling regarded as the largest passage with the semblance of a thematic arrangement, is divided by Hertzberg into five separate aphoristic pieces, each of which speaks on the subject of injustice, but with its own special application or point. In these single aphoristic pieces throughout "the book" of Ecclesiastes various attitudes of the author toward wisdom are displayed: his reliance upon it, the discovery of its failure, or the rejection of its validity. These phases of thought represent—and Hertzberg shares this view with Galling—Koheleth's dispute with the tradition of the wisdom schools. But there is no clue in this dispute to an evolution of thought, since each aphoristic piece, though the pieces are placed side by side, is of different content and attitude. The person of Koheleth is the unity in which the various pieces repose and in which their contradictions likewise reside. But since the conflict in Koheleth's mind does not express itself in the sequence which the aphoristic pieces have, and does not come to a final result within them, the attempt to express the teaching of Koheleth leads only to "a hypothetical reconstruction,"[22] which however must be made if we are to assess the spiritual contribution of the book.

Views regarding the composition of Ecclesiastes which are similar to that of Galling have been held by C. Schmidt,[23] Albert Condamin,[24] and Vincenz Zapletal.[25] Schmidt believed that at different dates and in different moods the author of Ecclesiastes wrote out certain pieces, but, not having had time to elaborate his work, left behind only a rough draft. Condamin thought that Ecclesiastes is not a treatise that represents a whole, written at one time, but is, especially in its middle chapters, a collection of thoughts expressing momentary impressions written probably at intervals more or less remote. Zapletal observed the absence of logical sequence in the book's arrangement. The author wrote down his thoughts as they presented themselves to him, and the contradictions which are seen in them may in part be due to the fact that it is customary to appreciate the same things in different ways at different times.

4. Psychological Unity.—According to H. J. Blieffert,[26] the literary problem of Ecclesiastes

(Tübingen: J. C. B. Mohr, 1940; "Handbuch zum Alten Testament"), p. 49.

[17] Review of Hertzberg, *Der Prediger*, p. 272.
[18] "Stand und Aufgabe der Kohelet-Forschung," p. 360.
[19] "Kohelet-Studien," pp. 278-79.
[20] Galling (*ibid.*, p. 279) regarded 12:12-14 as a polemic against 12:8-11.

[21] Cf. Hertzberg, *Der Prediger*, p. 86.
[22] Cf. "Kohelet-Studien," p. 281.
[23] *Salomos Prediger* (Giessen: 1792), p. 82.
[24] "Études sur l'Ecclésiaste," *Revue Biblique*, VIII (1899), 508.
[25] *Das Buch Koheleth* (Freiburg i. S.: O. Gschwend, 1905), p. 32.
[26] *Weltanschauung und Gottesglaube im Buch Koheleth* (Rostock: R. Beckmann, 1938).

can only be solved theologically. The contradictions within the book are explained by the quality of the mind of the author, which retained elements of traditional Judaism together with a lively secular world outlook. The expression "secular world outlook" (*Weltanschauung*) is a modern term but in a high degree appropriate as a description of the spiritual temper of Ecclesiastes. In order to show how this term applies to the book, Blieffert points out that in the Old Testament the event of death is considered as ordained by God, but in Ecclesiastes death is a *mikreh,* which (even if this word means no more than "happening" or "occurrence") has not the definite significance of an event ordained by God. A secular world outlook is associated with the attempt of man to direct his life without reference to God, with the effort of "the natural man" to rely upon his own mental and other resources to meet the world's exigencies, and with the resolve to answer life's problems and difficulties by purely rational and worldly means. This combination of the religious and the nonreligious aspects of belief is revealed in the mind of Koheleth by the disparity of thoughts within the book, but in spite of this disparity the book is a unity. At this juncture Blieffert found support in the statement made by Hermann Gunkel [27] that in Ecclesiastes the inconsistency and lack of symmetry should not be resolved by literary critical analysis. In Blieffert's view the correct conception of the quality of Ecclesiastes' thought renders unnecessary the theory of interpolations. Blieffert furthermore held that Galling did not give enough importance to the personal factor, namely, that Koheleth, the man, is the unity in which the diversity of thought resides. Moreover Galling's division of Ecclesiastes into a series of isolated aphoristic pieces would only make more contradictions come to light than actually appear when the work is read as an indivisible whole. Blieffert thus found in the book a man whose thought is both within and without the circle of Old Testament piety, the quality of whose mind explains those features that are evident in his writing: namely, the low esteem in which life and the world are held, and yet the positive valuation of life; the praise of wisdom, and yet the sense that wisdom also is vanity.

B. Critical Appraisal.—Further discussion on the problem of the book's literary structure must be concerned chiefly with the change most recently effected in the question by the criticisms offered by Galling.

(*a*) The decision as to what are the aphoristic pieces is the result of a subjective process which introduces a factor not amenable to control. As Galling himself remarked,[28] less injury is done to the meaning of a literary source by regarding certain sections of it as independent—though they are too small to make such a judgment conclusive—than is done by uniting portions that do not belong to one another. But it cannot be held with any approach to certainty that Ecclesiastes consists of thirty-seven aphoristic pieces. To give one example—in the aphoristic unit which Galling ranks as No. XII, namely, 4:7-12, vss. 7-8 describe a man without a family who labors to amass riches which, before he can experience any joy of living, he must leave at death to others. Vss. 9-12 are a meditation on the subject of "two are better than one" or "unity is strength." With quite as much reason, if not indeed with better reason, these two groups of verses in aphoristic piece No. XII might be regarded as two separate aphoristic pieces, or they might have been included with the section Galling numbers as XI, namely 4:4-6, since the subject of toil and work is common or relevant to all the verses in 4:4-12, that is, in Nos. XI and XII.

(*b*) Within the aphoristic pieces which Galling discerned as single literary units the feature of loose connection of sentences still persists, and in this respect the problem of Ecclesiastes is yet unsolved. For example, in 10:18-20 (=Galling's No. XXXV) vs. 18 speaks about slothfulness, vs. 19 about bread, wine, and money, and vs. 20 about exercising care in expressing one's thoughts. It would need some time and inventive power to find a principal concept that would hold all these verses together. In a unit so small as 10:18-20, looseness and inconsistency of thought are felt to be infinitely more awkward than would be the case when they are viewed within the connection of a larger literary unit. According to Galling, there are seven aphoristic pieces (Nos. XXIX–XXXV) in 9:17–10:20. Yet all of these pieces are more closely united under the idea "wisdom versus folly" than are the single verses in the section 10:18-20 (i.e., No. XXXV) connected with one another.

(*c*) If the aphoristic pieces were collected by Koheleth himself, we can hardly think that he put them together in a haphazard way, without regard to the ideas which they contained. Galling's careful distinction between Koheleth the poet and Koheleth the collector of the poetic pieces seems to be necessary to his theory, but it does not make it more convincing. It is not likely that a collector put the poems together which he himself had made, piece on piece, without any more thought than a man exercises when he puts cherries into a basket.

[27] "Predigerbuch," *Die Religion in Geschichte und Gegenwart* (Tübingen: J. C. B. Mohr, 1930), IV, 1405-8.

[28] "Stand und Aufgabe der Kohelet-Forschung," p. 360.

(d) It is true that Koheleth is an Oriental wisdom writer, not a Greek philosopher, but this fact alone cannot explain the unordered character of large portions of the book. It is not lack of logic which is distinctive of his mentality. He is so logical, so full of the urge to probe and investigate, that this characteristic endangered the canonization of his work.

(e) Galling's theory is really a large-scale attack on the critical school, represented mainly by Siegfried, which attributed to others than Koheleth the noncoherent elements of the book. By his supposition of aphoristic pieces, Galling sought to dissolve these elements through a process of fragmentation. But he had to admit [29] that even this conjecture was not a complete solution since the refractory elements to which reference has been made still persist in the isolated units. Moreover, when confronted with the question of the author's ideas, Galling said that all that can be offered is a "hypothetical reconstruction" which theology must make in the interest of assessing Koheleth's spiritual contribution. This conclusion is almost Ecclesiastian in its quality.

(f) In an attempt to explain the disorder or the lack of cohesion within single aphoristic pieces, one may remark that in the soul of Koheleth there exists a conflict with the traditional wisdom school. Galling applied this point of view in his treatment of the so-called aphoristic piece No. XI, namely, 4:4-6: "Then I saw that all toil and all success in work brings a man the envy of his neighbor. This also is vain and a striving after wind" (vs. 4). "The fool folds his hands, and eats his own flesh" (vs. 5). "Better is a handful of quietness than two hands full of toil" (vs. 6).

Galling considered vss. 5-6 to be citations from the school tradition [30] and therefore placed these verses each within inverted commas. That they are citations is evident, he said, from the fact that there is no immediate connection between the critical attitude to life expressed in vs. 4 and the practical considerations which follow in vss. 5-6. In vs. 4 Koheleth sees the tragic character of human effort, and in the following verses "finds safety" in quoting the school tradition. But how were readers to know that vss. 5-6 were quotations, unless they were told? The text gives no such information. The logical hitch in the sequence of thought between vs. 4 and vs. 5 would of course be felt by most readers. Whether vs. 5 is regarded as an interpolation (McNeile) or as needing the introduction "But does not the proverb say . . ." (Hertzberg), vss. 4-6 gain more, and that more naturally, from their place in the context of the

book than they do from the commentary imposed upon them from without, under the supposition that they form an independent poem. For the verses preceding 4:4-6 are a complaint about the miseries and oppressions of man's existence (vss. 1-3), and the verses which follow (viz., vss. 7-9) continue to refer to the various aspects of toil which man's existence entails. Thus Hertzberg very reasonably placed 4:4-6 within the larger portion 3:1–4:16.

The independent pieces theory, when aided by the idea of an inner conflict of Koheleth with the school tradition, appears to be a revival, so far as the single pieces are concerned, of the theory of the "two voices" proposed by Herder, who saw in the book of Ecclesiastes a kind of dialogue between a doubting seeker after truth and a teacher who interrupts the seeker to instruct him.

C. A Possible Solution.—If the literary problem of Ecclesiastes is not regarded as solved by Galling, there remains the task of stating those conclusions which, as a result of the history of the discussion of the problem, would seem to have established themselves as necessary to the criticism of the book and to its exegesis.

(a) The book of Ecclesiastes is not a collection of independent pieces, but an account of the author's wisdom which left the author's hand as a whole, however loosely connected parts of his work may be.

(b) In the consideration of sentences of a dissonant or contradictory character, full account must be taken of the quality of the author's mind—a quality which is adequately described by Blieffert as the result of a secular world outlook existing alongside remnants of traditional Jewish religious belief.

(c) Koheleth, however, should not be represented, in a way suggested by Wildeboer, as a man who, venturing too far afield in speculating on life's problems, turns back ever and again tremulously to the faith of his childhood. For his secular world outlook is more fully developed than are the elements of religious tradition which he retains. The deity of his belief has largely become depersonalized. Living before the Maccabean revolt, he represents the spirit of a "reformed" Judaism which was by no means "a-religious" or without its martyrs, but which was swept away by the new orthodox enthusiasm of the second century. He is boldly critical of the traditional orthodoxy of the wisdom schools. The tenor of his disquisitions is not faith but discovery, the testing of the truth of a matter by reference to the evidence of life and experience.

(d) In view of the religious and "a-religious" nature of Koheleth's mind, we must expect to find in the book elements that seem difficult to

[29] "Kohelet-Studien," p. 281.
[30] *Ibid.*, p. 283.

harmonize, and a spirit as latitudinarian as possible must be cultivated in judging whether a sentence in any passage is or is not authentic.

(e) Nevertheless, there can be little doubt that the text has been much worked over. Provocative of comment and rejoinder, the book appears to have received additions from persons who represent the traditional wisdom school which Koheleth criticized (cf. Wisd. Sol. 2). Hardly all the loosely connected aphorisms in the book can be original, but to pronounce any one of them an insertion depends to a greater or lesser degree upon a subjective judgment. The additions which McNeile and Barton (see above) ascribed to the ḥākhām or wisdom writer provide an estimate which, whether reduced or not, may serve as a basis for determining what elements in the book are extraneous.

(f) There are furthermore some additions of a definite character antagonistic to, and corrective of, Koheleth's type of religious thought. Gunkel [31] suggested that 2:26; 3:15a, 17; 5:19; 7:18b, 26b, 29; 8:5, 11, 12b, 13a; 11:9b; 12:1a, 7b are additions made by a pious soul who wished to make the book suitable to tender consciences. This pious soul is equated with the orthodox redactor who wrote 12:12-14 in the epilogue regarding the divine judgment and the duty of fearing God. Those passages which Gunkel specified as additions are in the main those which Moffatt in his translation included in double brackets (e.g., 2:26; 3:17; 5:7; 7:18b, 19, 26b; 8:11-13; 11:9d; 12:1a) as indicating "either editorial additions or later interpolations."

(g) On the basis of the Exegesis which follows, it is held that there are within the work three divisions of thought which may be described as the plan of the author's work. (i) 1:2–4:3: Koheleth's world outlook; the general principles which he perceives as governing man's existence "under the sun"; the limitations of human knowledge and its inability to probe to the meaning of life. (ii) 4:4–9:16: Particular situations or difficulties which occur in man's life and the response which the wise man will make to them. (iii) 10:4–12:7: Concluding advice of Koheleth to his young pupils.

(h) Furthermore, the book is affected by additions. These for the most part have been made by a pious glossator, and are: 3:17; 4:5; 6:7; 7:6 (the words, "this also is vanity"); 7:29; 8:11-13; 9:17–10:3; 10:8-14a, 15, 18, 19; 11:9b; 12:1a, 8-11 (first epilogue), 12-14 (second epilogue). That these additions are reckoned as fewer than those which McNeile judges to be present in the book is due to two factors, namely, an attempt to appreciate both the specific qualities of Koheleth's own "piety" (e.g.,

see Exeg. on 5:7; 7:18), and the effect which the contact with Egyptian wisdom literature had upon the expression of Koheleth's thought (see below).

(j) The question of the circumstances in which the original work, which had a real unity without possessing an irreproachable progression of thought, received the additions that have been made to it, remains to be considered. Podechard [32] regarded the writer of the book as a teacher held in high esteem by his contemporaries. Those people thought of him in the same way as the disciple who celebrated his master's genius in 12:9-10. However, the book was not written in the first place for the general public, but for the wisdom schools themselves, those schools to which the children of the aristocracy and the future officials of the state were sent for instruction. There the work which Koheleth had composed was used as presenting subjects for discussion. It was preserved from mutilation or deletions by the renown of its author, but it was enriched by disciples' remarks and observations. This augmentation was made in the interests of orthodox piety and correction of possible misrepresentation. With these additions Ecclesiastes went forth, after it had served the purpose of the schools throughout the generations and the memory of the author had faded, to serve as instruction for the people. It was probably through some such process as this which Podechard describes that Ecclesiastes has come to us in its present form.

V. Language and Date

Ecclesiastes was written in a late form of Hebrew which is akin to the language of the Mishnah (ca. A.D. 200) and is much affected with Aramaisms. Franz Delitzsch remarked that "if the Book of Koheleth were of old Solomonic origin, then there is no history of the Hebrew language." [33] As judged by its language, the book of Ecclesiastes is much later than the work of the Chronicler and later than the book of Esther (ca. 300 B.C.). At one time critics were prone to detect numerous Grecisms in the book, but in recent years that number has been much reduced. McNeile [34] almost went so far as to deny their presence. Barton [35] saw but one example of a Grecism, namely עשׂה ימים=ποιεῖν χρόνον, used of the passing or spending of days (6:12). Eissfeldt [36] however has been less hesitant in affirming the presence of Grecisms in Ecclesiastes and has offered as examples עשׂה

[31] Religion in Geschichte und Gegenwart, Vol. IV, col. 1408.

[32] L'Ecclésiaste, p. 187.

[33] Commentary on the Song of Songs and Ecclesiastes (tr. M. G. Easton; Edinburgh: T. & T. Clark, 1877), p. 190.

[34] Intro. to Ecclesiastes, p. 43.

[35] Ecclesiastes, pp. 33, 138.

[36] Einleitung in das A.T., p. 557.

טוב=εὖ πράττειν="to do oneself well" (3:12) and מקרה=τύχη="chance" (2:14; 3:19; 9:2-3). Galling holds that the first of Eissfeldt's examples, where the verb is used of reflexive action, cannot be shown to be a Greek usage, and that in regard to the second example, the Hebrew word "can have nothing to do with τύχη." [37]

Opinions concerning the style and language of Koheleth are of a contrary nature. According to McNeile, the author's "intense originality raised him far above the literary level of his day." Under the stress of keen disappointment and indignation at the wrongs of the world he gave to his style "a stinging sarcasm, a tendency to epigram, a *moan* in it, which is unique in Hebrew literature." [38] Hertzberg is no less enthusiastic in his judgment. For him Ecclesiastes had "a highly individual and thoroughly original style, in a likewise thoroughly individual language constructed with deliberation and often with consummate skill." [39] Yet side by side with these appreciations may be placed the judgments of others who have been very much otherwise impressed. According to Adolf Schlatter, the language of Koheleth "by its obscurity and heaviness proves that the author did not any longer speak Hebrew but only read it and wrote it." [40] F. C. Burkitt's view is even more trenchant. According to him the style of Ecclesiastes is neither "correct" nor "natural"; it has "the awkward stiffness of a translation." Its language is a crabbed and unnatural lingo, and the book appears to be a translation from the Aramaic. [41]

Burkitt's supposition may yet be worked out more convincingly; he argued his case with only two passages. (a) 7:14b: "God also hath set the one [viz., the day of prosperity] over against the other [viz., the day of adversity] to the end that man should find nothing after him." Since in Syriac (Eastern Aramaic) "to find a thing after so-and-so" means to find him guilty or responsible for it, Burkitt translated, with the support of the version of Symmachus, "God has made one thing against the other in such a way that no man should find any occasion of complaint against him." The Hebrew text in this sentence Burkitt deemed therefore to be "an over-literal translation from an Aramaic original." [42] But it is unfortunate for this conclusion that exactly the same expression as occurs in 7:14b, namely,

אחריו, "after him," in the sense of "after the death of the man in question," or more generally, "in the future," occurs also in 3:22; 6:12, and in this sense 7:14 would declare that God has so arranged the incidence of joy and sorrow in life that man is never able to know or to divine the nature of the future that lies ahead. A. Lukyn Williams [43] called 7:14 "the only strong example" which Burkitt adduced in support of the translation theory, and indeed this passage would have been strong evidence for the theory had not the phrase "after him" appeared elsewhere in Ecclesiastes as referring to the future.

(b) The second trace of a translator's activity is observed by Burkitt in 4:15 in the Hebrew word, hashshēnî="the second"—which occurs in the phrase hayyéledh hashshēnî="the youth, the second" (ERV)—which Burkitt considers to be an attempt to render the Aramaic word tinyānā', which often implies the notion of "second in command." Burkitt would therefore translate vs. 15 thus: "I saw all the living under the sun going along with the youthful generation now occupying the second place, who will one day supplant their elders." But as in vs. 13 "a poor youth" (yéledh miṣkēn) is spoken of, it is impossible in vs. 15, with the same story, to render hayyéledh hashshēnî, which means literally "the second youth," as "the youthful generation now occupying the second place." The expression "the second youth" (if genuine) may be taken—as Hertzberg and Galling, for example, took it—to mean the youth now second in position in the state after the old king (cf. vs. 13); but in this case we are not even compelled to admit a quite possible Aramaic influence upon late Hebrew, far less to suppose that a translator of an Aramaic manuscript has faltered in his translating.

Since the view that Ecclesiastes is translated from the Aramaic was first tentatively suggested by F. C. Burkitt, it has been more thoroughly argued and energetically maintained by Frank Zimmerman. [44] Zimmerman is supported by C. C. Torrey [45] and by H. L. Ginsberg, [46] but Robert Gordis [47] very convincingly shows that the assumption of a translation of Ecclesiastes

[37] "Stand und Aufgabe der Kohelet-Forschung," p. 362.

[38] *Op. cit.*, p. 32.

[39] *Der Prediger*, p. 10.

[40] Article, "Prediger Salomo," in Paul Zeller, ed., *Calwer Bibellexikon* (4th ed.; Stuttgart: Calwer, 1924), pp. 585-86.

[41] "Is Ecclesiastes a Translation?" *Journal of Theological Studies*, XXIII (1922), 22-28.

[42] *Ibid.*, p. 24.

[43] *Ecclesiastes* (Cambridge: Cambridge University Press, 1922; "Cambridge Bible"), p. 1. Williams (p. 80) held the expression "after him" (cf. Old Syriac of Luke 23:14) to be simply an Aramaism in Eccl. 7:14.

[44] "The Aramaic Provenance of Koheleth," *Jewish Quarterly Review*, XXXVI (1945-46), 17-45; cf. "The Question of Hebrew in Qohelet," *ibid.*, XL (1949-50), 79-102.

[45] "The Question of the Original Language of Qoheleth," *ibid.*, XXXIX (1948-49), 151-52.

[46] *Studies in Koheleth* (New York: Jewish Theological Seminary of America, 1950).

[47] *Koheleth: the Man and His World* (New York: Jewish Theological Seminary of America, 1951).

from an Aramaic original cannot be sustained. The view according to which the book was written in Hebrew by a writer who in daily life used Aramaic freely meets the literary situation with which Ecclesiastes confronts us.

Two factors are adverse to the theory that the book is a translation from the Aramaic. In the first place this view could hardly be held of the whole; for even if the form of the book is not poetical throughout, as Hertzberg [48] and Gunkel [49] maintain it to be, there are at least certain poetical portions (1:2-8; 3:1-8; 11:8–12:7) which seem to have within them the poet's original sense of rhythm and assonance and do not appear to have passed through the stage of translation. Again, it is probable that the Hebrew in which Koheleth wrote is the form of that language which was in use in the schools of the time and which had been subject to much influence from Aramaic. In the post-exilic period the Hebrew speech was preserved by the cult and was in literary use. "But the common folk when gossiping, exchanging their views and their wares or doing their shopping, used the Aramaic speech." [50] We must think of Koheleth, at least if he were an inhabitant of Palestine, as speaking that language. In this case it is most likely that the Aramaic expressions found in his book are there because the Hebrew as written at that time had adopted them.

Ecclesiastes was certainly written before 180 B.C. Ecclesiasticus, composed about that year, made use of Koheleth's teaching. Both Barton and Hertzberg utilized the so-called "historical" allusions in an attempt to reach a more accurate date—4:13-16; 10:16-17 (Barton); 8:2-5; 10:16-17 (Hertzberg)—but such allusions, even if they are more than mere moral pattern examples of the wisdom tradition, are too general in character to permit any precise dating. If we think of the book as belonging to the Greek period to which, quite apart from any problematical connections with Greek literature, the author's power of consequent and abstract thought points,[51] we may place its writing between 250 and 200 B.C. Its geographical background seems to be Jerusalem or Alexandria. On the whole, the references to rain and cisterns (11:4; 12:2c, 6) would seem to indicate a Palestinian rather than an Egyptian setting.

VI. Foreign Influences

A. Greece.—Various attempts have been made to show that Ecclesiastes was dependent upon Greek philosophy. Otto Pfleiderer (1886) held

that he was indebted to Heraclitus for elements of teaching and language; while the commentaries of Thomas Tyler (1874) and E. H. Plumptre (1881) have regarded the Stoic philosophy as contributing to Koheleth's thought. Tyler was also of the opinion that Koheleth aimed at setting Stoicism and Epicureanism over against each other in order to discredit both.[52] The most impressive of the efforts to prove that Ecclesiastes was influenced by Greeks has been made by Harry Ranston [53] who, judging that Koheleth would more probably be dependent on popular aphoristic writers than on philosophical works, has found in the work of Theognis (ca. 520 B.C.) many general parallels of thought and similarities of language which, he maintained, prove their influence on Ecclesiastes. Hertzberg has agreed with Ranston's view so far as to say that "Koheleth knew the work of Theognis, at least indirectly." [54]

The trend of modern criticism is to maintain that in no case has it been proved that Ecclesiastes is dependent on any Greek writing, but that the Jewish book appears to be pervaded by the popular Greek spirit. Barton [55] has pointed out that the motif of *carpe diem*, which has caused some to think of influence upon Ecclesiastes from Epicureanism, occurs in ancient Semitic literature—for instance, in the Babylonian Gilgamesh epic (which provides a very close parallel to 9:7-9). He also shows that the differences between Stoicism and Ecclesiastes are fundamental. And as to the claim of Ranston that Theognis has exercised an indirect but very sustained influence upon Ecclesiastes, Galling [56] has put forward the view that the parallels of thought which Ranston cited as existing between Theognis and Ecclesiastes are in no single case particularly close, and that the aphorisms selected for comparison have in both books a different setting.

But if the attempts to prove Koheleth dependent on Greek literature have not been conclusive, what are the grounds upon which it may be said that Ecclesiastes shows traces of the Greek spirit? Does this conclusion rest upon the realism of the author's mind? McNeile [57] appears to have held that Koheleth has not come into contact with the Greek mind at all; yet he recognized a close affinity of thought between Koheleth and Xenophanes of Colophon (ca. 570 B.C.), whom Gilbert Murray described as "al-

[48] *Op. cit.*, p. 10.
[49] *Religion in Geschichte und Gegenwart*, pp. 1405-6.
[50] Albert Vincent, *La religion des Judéo-araméens d'Eléphantine* (Paris: P. Geuthner, 1937), p. 319.
[51] Cf. Hempel, *Althebräische Literatur*, p. 191.

[52] Cf. Adolphe Lods, *The Prophets and the Rise of Judaism* (tr. S. H. Hooke; London: Kegan Paul, Trench, Trubner & Co., 1937), pp. 15, 344-45.
[53] *Ecclesiastes and the Early Greek Wisdom Literature* (London: Epworth Press, 1925), p. 61.
[54] *Op. cit.*, p. 51.
[55] *Op. cit.*, pp. 34-39.
[56] "Stand und Aufgabe der Kohelet-Forschung," p. 365.
[57] *Op. cit.*, pp. 44-53.

most the only outspoken critic of religion preserved to us from Greek antiquity." [58] According to McNeile, Koheleth occupies "the debatable ground between Semitic and Greek thought," and lived at a time when Greek thought and Hebrew thought were of themselves beginning to converge. Thus, "Koheleth's affinities with Greek thought are close and significant" [59] and Ecclesiastes contains many of the "seed-thoughts" from which Stoicism sprang. Therefore, although McNeile [60] dated Ecclesiastes as later than 300 B.C., he approached the opinion held by Galling, namely, that Koheleth lived on the frontier between two periods of history.

A characteristic of that epoch was its individualistic and cosmopolitan spirit. And this spirit, though it characterizes the wisdom literature as a whole, is especially prominent in Ecclesiastes. In every part of the book appeal is made to the individual's reason and judgment, and throughout is the universalistic outlook which is concerned with man and with what man experiences everywhere under the sun—an outlook in conformity with that mingling of peoples caused by the campaigns of Alexander the Great. This mark of the Hellenistic age, which may be accounted the Greek contribution to the spirit of that age, along with Koheleth's realism and logical type of thought [61] may well be all that Ecclesiastes shows of Greek origin or influence. As noted by Blieffert,[62] the thoughts of the Greek philosophers were popularized in the Hellenistic period and became part of general culture, so that knowledge of the ideas was acquired without any acquaintance with books. Lukyn Williams well described Koheleth's contact with Greek thought when he wrote: "Stoicism must have been in the air; its phrases would be current coin. But that is all." [63] Each one therefore is presented with the task of deciding whether Koheleth was aloof from all contact with Greek thought, or whether he was merely breathing a Hellenistic atmosphere. The facts that would seem to emerge from weighing the question are that Koheleth was an original thinker, that he was distinctly affected by the Greek spirit, and that his originality of thought is the quality which makes it uncertain whether his book, which gives no unequivocal evidence of borrowing from the Greek literature, is at all influenced by Greek thought. This may seem to be a meager result, but its meagerness accords with findings that have been made regarding the question of

Greek influence in the East during the period in which Koheleth lived. Volz [64] pondered the resemblance of Stoicism and Ecclesiastes in respect of their common deterministic outlook, and he refrained from ascribing any influence of one upon the other, but he connected the determinism in Ecclesiastes with the spirit of the age and the political conditions which produced the all-disposing sovereign states, first the Macedonian and later the Roman. This explanation, however, is far too general. The source of the deterministic belief of Koheleth is probably to be found in the popular stellar religion of the ancient Mesopotamians, according to which the astral divinities—sun, moon, and stars—exercised an influence on the earth and on man, and determined their destiny.[65] A true perspective is not won by thinking only of the possibility of Greek influence upon Koheleth. For in the latter's time a reverse process was taking place, namely, the influence of Oriental thought upon the Greek world.

In Palestine the thought of the Hellenistic period was a mingling not only of Greek but also of Oriental conceptions, under which we must include, besides Chaldean and Iranian, also Egyptian ideas. The influence of Egypt upon Hebrew gnomic teaching is evident from the fact that a considerable section of the book of Proverbs, namely, 22:17–23:11, is a careful adaptation of the Egyptian book, The Wisdom of Amen-em-ope.[66] Besides this one instance of sustained borrowing there are striking parallels of thought between the Hebrew and the Egyptian wisdom writings.

Paul Humbert described the kind of Egyptian influence which the Hebrew wisdom writings reveal thus:

"The foreign and especially Egyptian influence is traceable in the use of certain literary forms—the king as fictive author; maxims and a more or less philosophical dialogue with a narrative framework; satires on callings; praise of the wise . . . ; descriptions of the feebleness of old age . . . ; exhortation to enjoyment of life in view of the certainty of death.[67]

Elsewhere [68] he examined the biblical wisdom literature for traces of Egyptian influence, and in particular pointed out many resemblances

[58] *A History of Ancient Greek Literature* (London: W. Heinemann, 1898), p. 74.

[59] *Op. cit.*, pp. 46, 45.

[60] *Ibid.*, p. 33.

[61] Cf. Hempel, *Althebräische Literatur*, p. 191.

[62] *Weltanschauung und Gottesglaube*, p. 89.

[63] *Ecclesiastes*, p. xxxiii.

[64] *Weisheit*, p. 239.

[65] See Hugo Gressmann, *Die hellenistische Gestirn-religion* (Leipzig: J. C. Hinrichs, 1925), and O. S. Rankin, *Israel's Wisdom Literature* (Edinburgh: T. & T. Clark, 1936), pp. 136-45.

[66] See Rankin, *op. cit.*, pp. 6-7.

[67] "Weisheitsdichtung," *Religion in Geschichte und Gegenwart*, Vol. V, col. 1808.

[68] *Recherches sur les sources égyptiennes de la littérature sapientale d'Israël* (Neuchâtel: Secrétariat de l'Université, 1929).

between Ecclesiastes and the Egyptian gnomic writings. A few of these parallels follow:

1. *The Picture of Old Age:* From The Instruction of Ptahhotep (third millennium B.C.).

Old age hath come and dotage hath descended. The limbs are painful and the state of being old appeareth as something new. Strength hath perished for weariness. The mouth is silent and speaketh not. The eyes are shrunken and the ears deaf. . . . The heart is forgetful and remembereth not yesterday. The bone, it suffereth in old age, and the nose is stopped up and breatheth not. To stand up and to sit down are alike ill. Good is become evil. Every taste hath perished.[69]

Cf. 12:3-7, where the account of old age and its infirmities is highly allegorical. The point of comparison is, however, the theme of old age as affecting the members of the body.

2. *Life's Paradoxes:* From *The Admonitions of an Egyptian Sage.*

In truth, the poor now possess riches and he who was not even able to make sandals for himself possesses treasures. . . . He who had not any servants is now become master of (many) slaves and he who was a nobleman has now to manage his own affairs.[70]

Cf. 9:11: "I saw that . . . the race is not to the swift, nor the battle to the strong, nor bread to the wise, nor riches to the intelligent." Cf. 10:7: "I have seen slaves on horses, and princes walking on foot like slaves."

3. *Carpe diem:* From the Song of the Harpist. This song was sung at funerary banquets by the friends of a deceased person gathered in the tomb, partaking there of a meal which was enlivened by wine, music, flowers, singing, and perfumes. This custom enshrined the two phases—death and the enjoyment of life—which are combined in the reflections of Koheleth (see 2:24; 3:12-13; 5:17; 9:7-9; 11:7-9). The singer of the song declares:

None cometh from thence [i.e., from the place of the dead] that he may tell us how they fare, that he may tell us what they need, that he may set our heart at rest (?), until we also go to the place whither they are gone.
Be glad. . . . Follow thy desire, so long as thou livest. Put myrrh on thine head, clothe thee in fine linen, and anoint thee. . . .
Increase yet more the delights that thou hast, and let not thine heart grow faint. Follow thy desire, and do good to thyself (?) [71]

Also from the inscription on the tomb of Petosiris (*ca.* 300 B.C.):

Drink and be drunken, do not cease to [make] festival. Follow [the desires of] your hearts in the time [you are] on the earth. . . . When a man goes hence, his goods go from him. He who shall inherit them will satisfy his desires as he wishes. For the rich there is no more sun. . . . He departs quickly as a dream. There is no one who knows the day when [death] will come. It is the work of God to make the heart forgetful (?) . . . . God it is who puts . . . into the heart of him whom he hates, in order to give his goods to another whom he loves, for he is the disposer (?) of [man's] goods.[72]

With these Egyptian texts may be compared the Babylonian parallel with Koheleth (9:7-9), which the latter may also have known, namely, the passage from the Gilgamesh epic (*ca.* 2000 B.C.):

Since the Gods created men
Death they ordained for man,
.   .   .   .
Day and night be thou joyful,
Daily ordain gladness,
Day and night rage and be merry,
Let thy garments be bright,
Thy head purify, wash with water,
Desire thy children which thy hand possesses,
A wife enjoy in thy bosom.[73]

4. *God is the Giver:* From The Instruction of Ptahhotep.

Reverence [the man of repute] in accordance with what hath happened unto him, for wealth cometh not of itself. . . . It is God that createth repute . . . . The vestibule [of the great] hath its rule . . . . It is God who assigneth the foremost place.[74]

(Cf. 3:13: "Also . . . it is God's gift to man that every one should eat and drink"; 5:18-19, "Every man also to whom God has given wealth"; see also 6:2. Naturally the various similarities that are brought to light have different degrees of closeness, and some may seem to have little importance as proof of the dependence of Ecclesiastes on Egyptian gnomic works; but it is clear that the Hebrew writer was acquainted with the Egyptian wisdom and that the resemblances mentioned are more tangible and less problematical than those adduced from the Greek sphere. The author of Ecclesiastes did not borrow en bloc. His originality is not impaired by the phrases and pictures which recall the Egyptian background, any more than a speaker's originality is diminished by using expressions

[69] Erman, *Literature of the Ancient Egyptians*, p. 55.
[70] A. H. Gardiner, *The Admonitions of an Egyptian Sage* (Leipzig: J. C. Hinrichs, 1909); cf. Humbert, *Recherches*, p. 121.
[71] Erman, *op. cit.*, p. 133.
[72] Gustave Lefèbvre, *Le tombeau de Pétosiris* (Le Caire: Imprimerie de l'Institut Français d'Archéologie Orientale, 1924), I, 161.
[73] Tablet X, Col. III, ll. 2-13.
[74] Erman, *op. cit.*, pp. 58-59.

that have a biblical context. The knowledge of the source might contribute to the depth and meaning of the speaker's words.

VII. Ideas

A. Theological Background.—It was Koheleth's purpose not to convey teaching about God but rather to tell what he had discovered regarding life and what a man might gain from life. His conception of God is nevertheless fundamental to his conclusions about the world and "life's profit under the sun." Therefore it is of advantage to consider first of all Koheleth's conception of God. His mind was radically different from that of the prophets who received a word of God and declared it, who because of their faith in God sought to strengthen among their fellow men faith in God's purpose and promote obedience to the divine commands. The keynote of Koheleth's teaching was neither faith nor obedience. He claimed only to present as a result of reflection and research that which man must accept as truth for the guidance of life. He announced not a divine oracle given him from without, but the lessons of life and experience. In his book there is no reference to the divine name Yahweh with its nationalistic implications, nor to a Messiah. He used the general name, God—*Elohim*. His outlook was universalistic. The name Israel occurs only once (1:12). His purpose in writing was "to seek and to search out by wisdom all that is done under heaven" (1:13). He spoke of himself as testing what he saw by wisdom (7:23), and said that what he found he laid to heart and examined (9:1). This attitude is characteristic of all wisdom teaching. But Koheleth is much more rationalistic than any other Hebrew wisdom writer.

Koheleth did not look upon nature from that angle of religious faith from which the Old Testament in general saw it. He did not describe the glory and marvel of the Creator's handiwork, nor did he praise the God

who by his power made the earth,
　who by his wisdom founded the world,
　　and by his knowledge spread heaven out;
when he thunders, the heavens are in tumult,
．　．　．　．　．　．　．　．　．　．
he flashes lightning through the rain,
　and brings wind from his storehouses (Jer. 10:12-
　　13 Moffatt; cf. Prov. 3:19-20; Job 38:1–39:30).

For Koheleth the regularity of the processes of nature was no longer depicted as worthy of wonderment, but as giving rise in the human breast to the feeling of weariness, disappointment, and despair. It appeared as a "soulless mechanism which is regardless of human woes and human wishes and is without any discern-

ible purpose." [75] Ecclesiastes observed—and his observation was a complaint—how each day

The sun rises and the sun goes down,
　and hastens to the place where it rises (1:5);

how the wind returns on its appointed course and how "all things are full of weariness" (1:8). Thus Koheleth, unlike any Old Testament writer before him, "succeeded in depersonalizing the forces of the natural order and in this way his thought approached nearest to the modern concept of the law of nature, although he did not recognize his viewpoint as signalizing a triumph but rather as indicating a limitation of the human spirit which in consequence was cast back upon itself." [76]

In the world as Koheleth saw it every possible occurrence or event is followed by an event of a contrary character, since "for everything there is a season, and a time for every matter under heaven" (3:1). The author's account of illustrative opposites as these occur in man's experience is one of the most impressive parts of the book (3:1-8). So far as we may judge from what the author himself said, he advanced this conception of opposites in order to teach that God has "made everything beautiful in its time" (3:11), and to ask the question (3:9) whether any satisfaction can accrue to a man toiling in a world which is marked by this eternal recurrence of events and their opposites, where "that which is, already has been; that which is to be, already has been; and God seeks what has been driven away" (3:15). Koheleth seems to have said all he meant to on this when he stated that the world is thus ordered by God; and he evidently felt that human freedom is strictly limited by this system of opposites that prevails everywhere. God's will is the cause of this ordinance, which is of a strongly fatalistic, deterministic character.

In his essay on Ecclesiastes D. B. Macdonald has maintained that the doctrine of opposites in Ecclesiastes implies much more:

If there was wickedness now regnant in the place where righteousness should be, by this very law of opposites righteousness would come and in its turn would go. That is what Ecclesiastes calls "judgment" —the change from A to not-A and back again. Otherwise life would be impossible (iii, 17; viii, 6, and often). So he can call the change from youth to age "judgment." The context shows that there is no moral condemnation. [77]

If we were to accept this interpretation, then the statements of 3:17 and 11:9 which are com-

---

[75] Walther Eichrodt, *Theologie des Alten Testaments* (Leipzig: J. C. Hinrichs, 1933-39), II, 83.

[76] *Ibid.*

[77] *The Hebrew Literary Genius* (Princeton: Princeton University Press, 1933), p. 207; see also pp. 197-215.

monly ascribed to the pious glossator (ḥāṣîdh), who is zealous for the doctrine of God's retributive judgment on evil and compensation for goodness, would have to be given back to Koheleth as original to his work. But can we accept the view of Macdonald that in these two verses the words "judge" (3:17) and "judgment" (11:9) do not involve any moral condemnation but merely signify a changing over from one state or condition to its opposite?

The doctrine of monotheism in the postexilic period produced a deep consciousness of the transcendent nature of God and "gave birth, in the Book of Job, not only to the sense of man's moral limitations before God, whose very angels are convicted of error (4¹⁷f.), but of the inability of human reason to reconcile the facts of experience with the idea of divine righteousness." [78] From ch. 38 onward the poem of Job expressed the thought that man's mind cannot measure the wisdom of God or understand the design of the Deity in his world government. Ecclesiastes was also deeply conscious of the gulf between the infinite and the finite, between God and the world of humanity. "God is in heaven, and you upon earth; therefore let your words be few" (5:2). In the development of thought that springs from the idea of the transcendence of God, Koheleth is more thoroughgoing than the author of Job, and his idea of the relationship of God to the world finds expression in deterministic beliefs. "Whatever happens has been determined long ago, and what man is has been ordained of old; he cannot argue with One mightier than himself, and lavish talk about it only means more folly" (6:10-11 Moffatt; cf. 9:1). Man, in other words, cannot question the fittingness of the divine action even when he cannot understand how a world supposed to be under the divine sovereignty should exhibit the characteristics which it manifests. What is the use of questioning the justice and wisdom of the divine providence? "Who can make straight what he [God] has made crooked?" (7:13.) All things are predestined by God; he makes both the good and the evil day (7:14). For Koheleth, God is a person, but his personality is much attenuated in comparison with the active moral personality whom the prophets of the eighth and seventh centuries knew. The Deity is now remote. He is the determining power. It is this doctrine of predestination which makes it impossible to connect Koheleth with the Sadducees; although they held views similar to his in many other respects, they were opponents of the notion of divine predestination and strong advocates of free will.

[78] Rankin, *Israel's Wisdom Literature*, p. 17.

B. Man's Life.—As life is transitory there can be no permanent gain or advantage attaching to existence. The fact which affects all Koheleth's thinking is that death befalls all that lives under the sun. He is very well aware that the belief in an afterlife is entertained by some, but he dismisses this belief summarily (3:21). The traditional belief in Sheol stands firmly, so firmly indeed that not the slightest assistance is sought or desired from a belief in a future world as a help to alleviating the sorry spectacle of this world's inequalities and of the oppression and sufferings of the righteous. At death "all go to one place" (3:20), both man and beast, and turn to dust. Koheleth's inductions from what he has tested and pondered do not go beyond the area of man's experience. It is upon the shadow of the universal incidence of death—death inexorable and everlasting—that there strikes such light of hope and cheer as Koheleth's teaching affords. The joy and happiness which may fall to a man's portion, shortlived though they will be, are the full measure of life's worth. Typical of those passages in which at intervals throughout the book (3:22; 8:15; 9:7; 10:19; 11:9) Koheleth expresses this view is the following: "There is nothing better for a man than that he should eat and drink, and find enjoyment in his toil. This also, I saw, is from the hand of God; for apart from him who can eat or who can have enjoyment?" (2:24-25.)

Besides prosperity and well-being, of which eating and drinking are the symbol, Ecclesiastes makes a special point of indicating man's work or toil ('āmāl) as a source of happiness and satisfaction. The author is also careful to emphasize that this happiness is not a thing that man can acquire for himself; it is a gift of God. Both the possession of the goods to be enjoyed and the ability to enjoy them are God's gift (cf. 6:3).

C. Value of Wisdom.—Possibly Koheleth regarded what he had to say about wisdom as his book's major contribution. There were two aspects of wisdom upon which he felt moved to put his opinion on record: first, that man's knowledge, so far as it might help him understand the meaning of life and the purpose of God as reflected in the world, is not, and never will be, sufficient for this purpose; and second, that in the practical sphere of man's daily duties and associations wisdom has a certain value, though in a relative way. The writer of the hymn on wisdom in Job 28 had the same lesson to teach as Ecclesiastes in regard to the impossibility of ever solving by human knowledge the ultimate problems of existence. Traces of profound wisdom, says the writer of Job 28, are to be found with men; but wisdom itself, the knowledge wherewith the works and forces of creation were devised and fashioned, is with God alone. It is man's highest wisdom (Job 28:28) to accept this fact with reverence and piety. "This dethronement of self-proud wisdom," suggested Eichrodt, "is also that which Koheleth seeks to accomplish when he acknowledges wisdom, limited as it is, to be of great value but, at the same time, through his reflection on the creative power of God, lays bare the fruitlessness —the 'vanity'—of wisdom in regard to the ultimate questions." [79] The skepticism which occurs in Hebrew literature in Job 28 thus appears later in Ecclesiastes, but is here deepened by the author's particular conception of God. Without doubt the suggestion is correct that Koheleth criticizes those wisdom teachers of his time who showed the same spirit of confidence with which the friends of Job tendered their theodicies. Speculation on the riddles of existence, according to Koheleth, will never be able to present answers that are true solutions, for, "When I applied my mind to know wisdom, and to see the business that is done on earth, . . . then I saw all the work of God, that man cannot find out the work that is done under the sun. However much man may toil in seeking, he will not find it out; even though a wise man claims to know, he cannot find it out" (8:16-17).

When Koheleth turned to assess wisdom on its practical side, his words did not have the optimism of the proverb collectors. He was alive to the limited value of wisdom as an aid to man. The advantage which the wise man may have over the fool is only brief and temporary, since death distinguishes neither the one from the other and in the underworld there is "no . . . thought or knowledge or wisdom" (9:10; cf. 9:5; 6:8). Nevertheless, the advantage which the wise man has over the foolish person is a real one since "wisdom excels folly as light excels darkness" (2:13), and whereas "the fool walks in darkness" the wise man "has his eyes in his head" (2:14). Yet the more a man learns of the world, the more his sympathy will go out to the oppressed and unfortunate, and Koheleth was aware that "he who increases knowledge increases sorrow" (1:18). Thus wisdom has its disadvantages as well.

Though the book of Ecclesiastes commends happiness as life's *summum bonum*, it is also able to say that life has its solemn and somber periods when "it is better to go to the house of mourning, than to go to the house of feasting" (7:2), and when "sorrow is better than laughter" (7:3). The motive of *carpe diem* which the author stressed is no mere thoughtless plucking of the flower of today. He was sufficiently clear-visioned to see that the advantage of possessing wisdom is not only limited by the fact of death but also by the conditions of life, its duties and sorrows. Besides, the world in which we live does not honor wisdom for its own sake. A poor man's wisdom may rescue a whole community in its hour of danger, but afterward no one remembers the poor man. The world does not always give "riches to the intelligent, nor favor to the men of skill" (9:11), but a knowledge of the world will keep a man safe from the destruction that attends the rash and impetuous. That is why Koheleth gave the advice to shun extremes, excesses, and enthusiasms. His wise man is a conformist who will be nothing overmuch, neither overrighteous nor overwise (7: 16). As Macdonald said of Koheleth himself:

He was an explicit conformist and had no use at all for the non-conformist conscience, running out into its lunatic fringe of kickers, reformers, and uplifters. He had a conscience, but it was a well-trained conscience; he knew the unescapable rules of life and that it is absurd for man to "batter the wheels of heaven, if they roll not rightly by." [80]

The attitude to the state which Koheleth's wisdom recommends a man to adopt (8:2-6) is thoroughly conformist in character.

D. Christian Significance.—The pessimism of Koheleth in regard to the value of what the world has to offer to man is not alien to Christian thought. If nothing of that optimism which is found elsewhere in the Old Testament and in the New Testament in regard to God's purpose with man appears in Ecclesiastes, this book is at least at one with Christianity in its rejection of a confident humanism. Koheleth reads with an uncanny psychological insight the hearts and thoughts of his fellow men. Jesus also, according to John 2:25, "knew what was in man." Along with the poet of Job, Koheleth has the distinction of investigating a problem which besets mankind in general and for which there is no easy solution—indeed no solution offered by human resources. He has been justly praised for the candor and honesty with which he pursues his quest.

It has to be admitted that there is a very wide and deep contrast between the message of Ecclesiastes and that of the Gospels. The conception of God which is fundamental to the Gospels is altogether different from the notion of the Deity which Koheleth presents. But central both to Ecclesiastes and to the teaching of the New Testament is the question: What is the worth of life, what content of real value has it or can it be made to have? Here Ecclesiastes is as relevant to Christianity as were the prophets whose ethics and ideals the Jesus of the Gospels accepted and fulfilled. Though Christianity does

---

[79] *Op. cit.*, II, 43.   [80] *Op. cit.*, p. 213.

not accept Koheleth's conclusions, to this rationalist wisdom teacher belongs the credit of setting forth with a compelling realism the problem of existence and of attempting to supply an answer with a fearless honesty.

In view of the importance of the question to which Koheleth and Christianity address themselves, it cannot appear accidental that both the Old Testament sage and Christian thinkers insist upon the urgency with which the goal or the prize of life should be pursued. Koheleth's doctrine of opportunism—take your opportunity today—is the consistent, logical concomitant of his thought. A kindred though more deeply founded opportunism is reflected (for a similar reason, i.e., an awakened sense of values) in the New Testament writers when they speak of "redeeming the time" (Eph. 5:16) and of working while it is day, since "night comes, when no one can work" (John 9:14). Koheleth is a skeptic. But the subject of his contendings—life and how best to use and appraise it—lies at the heart of all religions, for each of them to provide in its own way an answer. Pious glosses suitable to Jewish tradition were made within the Old Testament writer's work, and it became at length canonical. But the man Koheleth without the glosses provided for him remains, for reflective Jew and Christian alike, a challenging and likable personality. It was a wise providence that gave this man's work a place in Scripture.

VIII. Outline of Contents

IX. Selected Bibliography

COMMENTARIES

BARTON, G. A. *The Book of Ecclesiastes* ("International Critical Commentary"). New York: Charles Scribner's Sons, 1908.

HALLER, MAX, and GALLING, KURT. *Die Fünf Megilloth* ("Handbuch zum Alten Testament"). Tübingen: J. C. B. Mohr, 1940.

HERTZBERG, H. W. *Der Prediger* ("Kommentar zum Alten Testament"). Leipzig: Werner Scholl, 1932.

ODEBERG, HUGO. *Qohaelaeth, A Commentary on the Book of Ecclesiastes*. Uppsala: Almqvist & Wiksells, 1929.

PODECHARD, EDOUARD. *L'Ecclésiaste*. Paris: J. Gabalda, 1912.

WILLIAMS, A. LUKYN. *Ecclesiastes* ("Cambridge Bible"). Cambridge: Cambridge University Press, 1922.

GENERAL

GORDIS, ROBERT. *The Wisdom of Ecclesiastes*. New York: Behrman House, 1945.

————. *Koheleth: the Man and His World*. New York: Jewish Theological Seminary of America, 1951.

MACDONALD, D. B. *The Hebrew Literary Genius*. Princeton: Princeton University Press, 1933.

RENAN, ERNEST. *L'Ecclésiaste*. Paris: C. Lévy, 1882.

FOREIGN INFLUENCES

CAUSSE, A. "Sagesse égyptienne et sagesse juive," *Revue d'Histoire et de Philosophie Religieuses* (1929). Pp. 149-69.

HUMBERT, PAUL. *Recherches sur les sources égyptiennes de la littérature sapientale d'Israël*. Neuchâtel, Secrétariat de l'Université, 1929.

RANSTON, HARRY. *Ecclesiastes and the Early Greek Wisdom Literature*. London: Epworth Press, 1925.

ECCLESIASTES

TEXT, EXEGESIS, AND EXPOSITION

A Preliminary Survey.*—The introduction to a book of the Bible places it as to authorship, date, sources, and relation to the whole. The exegesis examines the text, subjects it to exhaustive analysis, cites alternative translations, and explores the author's possible meanings. The exposition attempts in a sense to put together again what the exegesis has dissected. It explores meanings and messages and their bearing upon faith, character, and conduct. It suggests, as best it can, the content and value of the book for the student, for the Christian teacher or preacher. The expositor is therefore allowed more latitude than his fellow craftsmen. He is, or should be, a liaison officer between the text and the teacher.

The homiletical value of Ecclesiastes is determined to an unusual extent by its critical introduction and exegesis. They reveal how profound a gulf is fixed between its dominant motif, "Vanity of vanities," and the gospel. Yet no book in the O.T. so challenges Christian faith to meet the questions it asks: questions as old as our human perplexities; as old as our search for the meaning of life. It voices, as few books in any literature, the "still, sad music of humanity." [1]

A Problem Book.—The questions the book raises are part of its perpetual allure. No book in the O.T., for all its deceptive brevity, faces vaster frontiers. No book in the O.T. is so insistently a problem book, and the range of the problems it presents has evoked a literature which supplies material for almost endless study. The Intro. and Exeg. make the Expos. possible and subordinate it to their authority, but the text cannot contain the interpretation, for the text itself confronts the mystery of life and the hidden ways of God with man: as though Koheleth were sending out from his station appeals for understanding and maybe deliverance to which no answers come back, only echoes of his own voice from summits lost in clouds, like

voices of the wandering wind,
Which moan for rest and rest can never find. [2]

Few books in the O.T. are more difficult to summarize. This is not entirely due to its confused organization. From first to last its motif is simple: the futility of all effort. The harvests of life are Dead Sea fruit, only dust and ashes upon lips soon to become dust themselves. All this is plain to read. There is an often offered prayer which seeks divine approval in some enterprise of life on what is begun, continued, and ended, thus wrapping it up neatly in one bundle with no loose ends. But Ecclesiastes itself leaves too many loose ends. Its strands never reach far enough. They are left broken and hanging as though the lines of communication leading out from a great city, if followed long enough, led nowhere—when by all their implications they should be part of a system charged with authentic tidings.

1. *Against Whom—and What?* Ecclesiastes, almost more than any other O.T. book, must be read and interpreted with a constant and baffling reference to what is never fully cited in the book itself. If Koheleth is making a case, the defendants are not in court. The phrase shadowboxing has possible applications beyond its uses in sports columns. Paul said very much the same thing in reverse, "So fight I, as not beating the air" (I Cor. 9:26). The Preacher has opponents enough, yet most literally he is in action against shadows, shadows in his own soul, shadows which lie deeply across his world, shadows in the mystery of life itself.

But it is quite as much the task of those who try to interpret him to find out and to state plainly what he was after, as to find out and to state plainly what he was against. The writer was busy with no trivial engagement. He was at odds in his own soul with the belief that there is a moral order in which the relation—the reciprocal relation—between conduct and recompense is precise and unfailing. Right conduct is rewarded with good fortune, amply conceived. Wrong conduct incurs penalties, also amply

---

*Pp. 21-25 include the expositor's introduction. Text and Exegesis begin on p. 26. Editors.

[1] Wordsworth, "Lines Composed a Few Miles Above Tintern Abbey."

[2] Edwin Arnold, "The Deva's Song."

conceived. In the moral balances of life God holds the scales and measures out rewards and punishments according to moral deserving, and his scales are accurate.

2. *His Fathers Had Told Him.* One needs to take care of his words here, for no one word is right. Koheleth was not a rebel or a revolutionary, but he was bringing up for examination all that his fathers had told him. There was, to begin with, the covenant relationship between Yahweh and his chosen people. They owed him sacrifice, worship, and obedience. He promised them in return security, kind skies and good harvests, victory over enemies, and what else they might desire. When these were lacking, as they mostly were, the prophet told his fathers that the fault was theirs. The travail of Hebrew prophecy is the reconciliation of invasion, exile, and famine with the promises of Yahweh, whose word cannot be broken.

All this was part of Koheleth's inheritance, though for the most part he makes little direct reference to it. Personal elements come in with the psalmists. They too are confident of a just moral order: those that trust in the Lord are secure. Even through the valleys of shadow the Lord will be with them. The psalmist had longings for the still unattained, but he had never seen the children of the righteous begging bread. He trusted in divine healing for his sicknesses, he believed that the Lord would hold an overflowing cup to the lips of the faithful, and he saw the repentant sinner wrapped in a mantle of divine forgiveness. Beyond everything else there is in the psalms an awareness of personal relationship with the Lord which has made them across millenniums the comfort of the sorrowing and the assurance of the perplexed. All this Koheleth's fathers had told him. And all this he denies or questions.

3. *The Old Order Changeth.* It must of course be remembered that for all their seeming certainties, Koheleth's fathers had never been quite sure themselves. There are questions in the psalms—"Where is your God?" (Ps. 42:3, 10)—and the prophets were honest with their own perplexities. Their whole pattern, consistent as it seemed, was vulnerable to all the shadowed side of life—its pain, its tears, its frustration, its vast and tragic mischances. To these Koheleth was sensitive, and he was willing to let his questions lead him where they would. The book of Job never breaks so completely with the Hebrew past as does Ecclesiastes; but Job too knew that his comforters had no formula competent to explain the pains and sorrows of the human estate. The problem was too vast. Job thus became almost the first questing voice—solitary, voice and nothing more—asking of a pitiless sky "Why"—"Why"—"Why?"

Then the Hebrew became a citizen of the world. He had never been isolated, though he was long an isolationist. But when Alexander marched into Asia, Hellenism came with him, bringing its philosophies and its dramas—so largely dramas of doubt—and its strange power to possess the human mind. Koheleth belongs to this melting pot. The stimulus of Greek thought activated his fluid and questioning mind. His penetrating observation of, and his wide acquaintance with, all sorts and conditions of life confirmed his distrust of inherited patterns and easy conclusions, and he said of the prophet's vision and the psalmist's trust as though in stress himself: "This will not do. Life is not like that." The race is not to the swift, nor the battle to the strong. The good do suffer and the wicked do prosper. God does not mantle us with kindness or even justice. Along all these lines Koheleth's break with the Hebrew past is complete.

4. *What Then?* What does Koheleth offer to take the place of his Hebrew inheritance from the prophets and the psalmists? A most considerable literature seeks to answer that question. D. B. Macdonald places Ecclesiastes in the structure of Hebrew philosophy, relates it to its historic context, and summarizes the author's beliefs with convincing insight. No background reading in any study of Ecclesiastes is more rewarding. Koheleth, he says,

like Paul, was a Hebrew of the Hebrews. But he was also an independent thinker, facing and questioning life for himself. . . . The reality of life was his strength and joy and the mystery of the background of life was his problem. . . . His heart was full of the pathos of life . . . ; his mind was eager to work out some consistent statement of the essential facts of life.[3]

Moreover, though Macdonald does not say so, he was a poet, with a gift for crossing an abyss with a flight of words—a man of many and often tremulous moods.

He does not doubt the existence and sovereignty of God, but his God is absentee, lost in the distance, not only apparently careless of mankind, but at variance with it. The writer never denies the fundamental difference between right and wrong, between wisdom and folly, but he cannot see any consistency of consequence in the conduct of life. To use current phrases, his almost heartbreaking concern was with "sanctions" and "values" (Emerson would have said "compensations"). He searched the whole front of human existence—the wisdom sector; the power and possession sector; the sectors of self-indulgence and toil: and found

[3] *The Hebrew Philosophical Genius* (Princeton: Princeton University Press, 1936), p. 85.

nowhere any adequate balance between life's longings and its fugitive and shadowed harvests. "For he was," says Macdonald, "in a strait between two worlds: Life with its value and glory and reality and the background of life with its rigid scheme." [4]

Abraham in the very dawn of Hebrew history stood up to Yahweh with a forthright question to plead for a doomed city. "Shall not the Judge of all the earth do right?" (Gen. 18:25.) In a very true sense that question is the motif of the O.T. Genesis asked it, believing that the Judge of all the earth would do right. Malachi postpones the answer: "Then shall ye return, and discern between the righteous and the wicked, between him that serveth God and him that serveth him not" (Mal. 3:18). Koheleth could not see any difference, and left the question suspended—an interrogation point between earth and sky, between faith and negation, between the O.T. and the N.T.

5. *Comrades in the Shadows*. There are background regions in any study of Ecclesiastes which demand exploration. To begin with, its relationship to the wisdom literature of the O.T., with which it is usually classified: [5] "Religion," says James G. Frazer, "is what passed for wisdom when the world was young." [6] It is still the final wisdom now that the world has grown old, or there is no wisdom at all. Even in its most speculative forms religion must bear upon the wise conduct of life. In some religions, such as Brahmanism, the corpus of ethical instruction is vague and illusive. In Confucianism it is solid as jade, Confucianism being almost entirely a wisdom religion.

Parallels between Gautama's teaching, as reported in the earliest and least speculative form of Buddhism, and many passages in Ecclesiastes are so striking as to lead E. J. Dillon [7] to believe that Koheleth was profoundly influenced by some diffusion of Gautama's teaching. Gautama and Koheleth have the same sense of the weariness of life, and the slow vast turning of the wheel of existence. Otherwise there is little in common between them. Gautama's concern was with the way of escape from the sorrows of our tear-bathed human order. For that he offered only the denial of desire, the low bed, the yellow robe, the beggar's bowl, and the peace of Nirvana. What resignation there is in Ecclesiastes is an irritated resignation. The spiritual climates of the two teach-

ers are as far apart as Palestine and the "Four Rivers" of India.

All commentators stress the relationship of Ecclesiastes to Greek, Egyptian, even Chaldean, inquiries and conclusions upon the meanings of life, or else its dependence upon them. The resemblances cited prove at least how the shadows which lie across so many quests and so many conclusions are confined to no region and darken all time. Koheleth did not need Gautama to teach him the weariness of life, or the Greek tragedies to teach him the inexorableness of fate.

6. *Inheritors*. But Koheleth did become almost the first of a long line. We have noted, for all his lightness of touch, the deeps he sounds. He said himself that God had put mystery at the heart of life. How thought and action confront that mystery is both revealing and creative. Paul, Augustine, and John Calvin subdued all mystery to the sovereign will of God, and said to all its puzzles and restlessnesses, "Peace, be still." Dante likewise found the answer to his pilgrimage through fire and purging in one timeless line, "And His will is our peace." [8] There is a strange kinship of seekers across the ages. Pascal and Koheleth would in some regions have understood each other. A most unexpected relationship between Ecclesiastes and Montaigne has been suggested. And so on.

There have been many since Ecclesiastes who have seen the seas of mystery which wash the shores of time from the coasts of disillusionment, and have thus created a literature of melancholy, brooding at the best, and with downright despair at the worst. Schopenhauer found life as meaningless and purposeless as Koheleth found it. It was, he thought, a kind of spume thrown up by the waves of existence, fugitive and inconsequential, known only by its pains and frustrations. Arthur Balfour's profound pessimism is noted in the Expos. on 2:13-17, and in essence Omar Khayyam is only Koheleth plus a "Jug of Wine" and "Thou" under the bough.

7. *No Sense of Sin?* Finally, and by no means a footnote, there is little of what we would call a sense of the reality and consequence of sin in Ecclesiastes, or in wisdom literature generally. That literature equates "wisdom" and "folly" with right (fearing the Lord) and wrong (ignoring the Lord). It considers the unhappy estate of the "fool," and not specifically the wretched estate of the sinner; the fortunate estate of the "wise," rather than the secure estate of the righteous. There is bewilderment enough in and between the lines of Ecclesiastes, but no confession. William James called "healthy-mindedness" one of the varieties of religious experi-

[4] *Ibid.*, p. 68.
[5] For material for such a study see W. A. Irwin, "The Wisdom Literature," Vol. I, pp. 212-19, and Intro. and Exeg. of Proverbs, Vol. IV.
[6] See *The Magic Art* (London: Macmillan & Co., 1911), pp. 222-43.
[7] *The Sceptics of the Old Testament* (London: Isbister & Co., 1895), p. 122.

[8] *Paradise*, Canto III, l. 85.

ence.[9] Ecclesiastes is a variant of that variety—in reverse; i.e., healthy-mindedness in very sore need of a doctor!

The mental and spiritual dislocations which followed World War II were variously diagnosed; fundamentally, the conclusion was that the breaking point of personality is much nearer the surface than we have supposed. After World War I, the emotionally displaced went to the spiritualist; after World War II, in the United States at least, they went to the psychiatrist. When the world begins to fall in, it carries everything with it, unless those who are caught in the fall are undergirded by faith. Koholeth was by no means a neurotic, and he never heard of a psychiatrist; otherwise he would have added that specialist to his vanity of vanities! But the stuff of which psychoses are made is in his book.

Sources and Characteristics.—Ecclesiastes begins, continues, and ends upon the levels of mortality. Levels? Yes, for the most part; there are depths in Ecclesiastes, but few heights. The accounts of life are balanced here and now—or not at all. There must be a "why" for all this; and the "why" is the enigma of the book. The Intro. points out the possible sources upon which the author has drawn: Chaldea, Greece, Egypt, and his own inherited but sadly diluted religious faith. E. H. Plumptre [1] puts him more deeply in debt to the Greeks than to any others, and cites a wealth of similarity in Greek poetry and philosophy. Instead of paying him the compliment of such a wide acquaintance with literature, it would perhaps be easier to assume that his "wisdom" was in the very atmosphere of the time and the region—and in his own spirit and moods.

For here is not fundamentally book wisdom, though books enough have been written about it. It is observation and experience, mediated through the author's temperament and colored by his moods. It is at least an attempt to reconcile what is with what ought to be, and its deeper meanings are between its lines. There should be, the writer thinks, a pattern of justice to which life ought to conform; but he cannot find that pattern anywhere, and so concludes that there is none. Existence for him has no discoverable meaning—not at least on any earthly level.

These are the things men must have talked about then, men of leisure and culture: in pillared porticoes, in the public squares, under the shadows of city gates; as they reclined by low tables after the feast was over; on the

housetops under the stars, or when the caravans were halted for the night, or the galleys crossed seas spread with history. For these are timeless questions. They have created literatures and evoked philosophies and haunted the thoughtful always and everywhere. They have no chronology, save the mystery of life; that is one reason why the book is in many ways so amazingly modern. Aldous Huxley might have written it; in one phase of his brilliant career he has. Life, he held, has no discernible point or bearing. Nothing makes any difference; do what you please. No book in the Bible reflects more sensitively, allowing for all the differences, the moods and phases of our always deeply shadowed time. We are doomed to moral confusion unless we find an answer to the old, old question, "Shall not the Judge of all the earth do right?" (Gen. 18:25.)

The Writer's Temperament.—The book that bears for us the title of Ecclesiastes moves in these regions with a curious touch. There are agony and travail of spirit in Job. There is a suffused sadness in many of the passages here, but less apparent travail in Koheleth's soul. He concludes that everything (bright or shadowed) is only a vapor blown down the corridors of time; and being only a vapor himself, it does not too bitterly disturb him. The book reflects on its surface his moods; whatever agonies there are, lie deep below the passing scene. Ecclesiastes, one may say with a certain measure of truth, voices the combination of a decadent religion with a decadent philosophy. It is Judaism rather too lightly held and a kind of Oriental Epicureanism which has been challenged by moral standards and by the persuasion that after all life is an affair with God and duty.

It is therefore difficult to reach dogmatic conclusions about the author or authors (see Intro., pp. 7-12). In a way the book is a tissue of meditations about life, its meanings, it values, its destiny. It is, if one wishes an analogy, a river fed by many sources. It takes no straight course, but twists and winds, and always it is flecked by light and shadow. There are depths and shallows in it; pools of meditation and questing currents. It flows over maxims and proverbial sayings as any river flows over time-worn stones. Or else it is as an ancient symphony modulating endlessly one motif—"Vanity of vanities! All is vanity." But there is nothing in it of Beethoven's *Eroica Symphony;* more of Tchaikovsky's *Symphonie Pathétique,* yet without the final resolution of pain into peace.

And all of it, or most of it, seems mediated through a fascinating personality. It is done with an anonymous pride of craftsmanship, as though the writer thought his name no business of posterity and so, as the fashion was, signed

[9] *The Varieties of Religious Experience* (New York: Longmans Green & Co., 1902), p. 78.

[1] *Ecclesiastes* (Cambridge: Cambridge University Press, 1890; "Cambridge Bible").

24

himself "son of David, king in Jerusalem" (1:1), with no thought at all that his parchments or papyri would become a part of the Hebrew canon and subject of concern for the folk of lands and times far, far beyond his horizons.

If we could recover Koheleth's life we might discover the key to the whole book. One of the most entrancing attempts a reader could make would be to re-create from its revelations the man who wrote it. There are commentators who have suggested that he may well have been a teacher in a Jerusalem school of wisdom, or a man who, having drunk deep from an ample cup of life, not always wisely, ends his lonely life in a sort of Alexandrian club where old men argue together, having nothing else to do. Robert Gordis, in a brilliant and illuminating work, speaks of his style as "rich in nuance and eloquent in its reticence," [2] as he stands, like Matthew Arnold, between two worlds, one dying and another still unborn.

The Christian believer does not need to accept Koheleth's conclusions. On the contrary, he will need to question many of them, deny others, qualify and interpret; above all, interpret. Yet they have profound significance for every disillusioned and frustrated spirit; not because there is a gospel in them, but because they reveal the sources of disillusionment and, by implication at least, by pushing men to the very edge of the abyss of un-faith, point up humanity's desperate need of that gospel which waited for the fullness of time, and of which there is, of course, in Ecclesiastes, neither intimation nor anticipation. Otherwise Koheleth would never have written, "Vanity of vanities! All is vanity."

Reading his book is like taking hold of the poles of a battery—result: a series of shocks. Koheleth thought in terms of concrete situations and facts as he observed them. He is always vivid and often dramatic. His writing has the epigrammatic quality of the Hebrew proverb. The number of really self-contained apothegms is outstanding. They are self-contained, i.e., as far as their context goes, because they have some quality of the universal. But the broken and sometimes tangled association lines make the expository sequence of passages unusually difficult. There is little cumulative ascent either of argument, insight, or conviction; few if any such passages as lend more than rhetorical splendor to Isaiah, to Paul's letters, and to Revelation. Nor is there anywhere here the divinely illumined tableland of the Gospels.

By way of compensation, Ecclesiastes offers for meditation and development marginal topics too numerous to mention: e.g., "Masters of Our

Moods" (Ecclesiastes more than most Bible books reflects the writer's moods); "Masters of Time and Chance"; "The Loneliness of High Station"; "Making the Past a Success"; "The Real Profit System"; "Dividends of Satisfaction"; "Goodness and Happiness"; "Shall Not the Judge of All the Earth Do Right?" "The Balanced Scales of the Eternal"; "The Goodness of Being Good"; "What Despair Leaves Out"; and so on and on.

This one word more. The book touches so many points as to make what seems an excess of minor movement almost a necessity of exposition. Whatever seems repetitious does no more than follow the text, which the reader will be told more than once is itself repetitious. If the Expos. is perhaps overparsimonious in its citation of supporting passages, the Exeg. will be found to supply the lack. We trace here for the most part the bold contour of the different chapters as they move straight on or turn back upon themselves. Certainly no expositor can live long with them and fail to acknowledge their spell—or his inadequacies in dealing with them.

Ecclesiastes as Literature.—The KJV has been called the noblest monument of English prose. The Hebrew genius supplied vivid narration, rhythmic qualities to which the English language most happily responded; and in the great passages, richly imaginative, there was beside what Matthew Arnold called the test of all great literature—noble seriousness. The translators were still under the remembered spell of the sonorous Latin liturgies and inherited the Elizabethan joy, by that time restrained and disciplined in noble speech and writing. Moreover, their mother tongue was still plastic enough in form and rhythm for them to achieve a new creation. All this is reflected in the standard translations of Ecclesiastes. The book lacks the rhythmic balance of the Psalms, the vivid simplicity of such narrations as Elijah's journey toward his chariot of fire, and the great majesty of, say, Isa. 40; but the spell of it grows with reading and rereading.

Its thought paths are confusedly obscure; the current of it hesitates, turns and returns upon itself; there are quietnesses of meditation depth; the shadows of frustration and mortality darken it; but from time to time there are haunting gleams of light.

Many of its phrases are unforgettable, e.g., 8:5-6, which is the requiem of all that is fugitive. One hears the winds blowing across waste spaces or else in its overtones and intimations a music which baffles words. Its great passages are part of the still sad music of humanity.

Ecclesiastes and Christian Faith.—There is generally no suggestion of redemption in wisdom literature, as Christian theology defines it,

[2] *The Wisdom of Ecclesiastes* (New York: Behrman House, 1945), p. 37.

1 The words of the Preacher, the son of David, king in Jerusalem.

1 The words of the Preacher,[a] the son of David, king in Jerusalem.

[a] Heb *Koheleth*

I. KOHELETH'S WORLD OUTLOOK (1:1–4:3)
A. SUPERSCRIPTION (1:1)

1:1. The superscription identifies "Koheleth" (see Intro., p. 3) with Solomon. This literary convention, loosely held, is dropped in 2:12. Yet Solomon's name is not inappropriately invoked in the book, for this king was the traditional patron of wisdom, and he afforded a significant example of wisdom culminating in foolishness, of business energy and toil of a lifetime terminating in futility, and of a culture holding the promise of exceptional development that was shattered at his death.

---

though there are gleams of hope along its low horizon. There is no hope of real redemption in any literature of despair, else it would not be literature of despair. Nor in general do those who have spoken for the disillusioned in the literature of the ages offer much hope of escape, save perhaps Gautama, and he offered only idealized nothingness. In ways demanding an elaboration here impossible, this is the front along which the Christian must not only oppose Koheleth and all who are akin to him, but supply victorious alternatives. There are minor perplexities as to how Ecclesiastes ever got into the canon. A. S. Peake has the answer for the Christian. "It puts the logic of a non-Christian position with tremendous force, to all who feel keenly the misery of the world. More vividly than anything else in the Old Testament, it shows us how imperious was the necessity for the revelation of God in Christ." [3] The attitudes and tempers of Ecclesiastes cannot be dated. They also grow old without ceasing, and they are always spiritual hydrogen.

Arnold J. Toynbee's study of the decline of civilizations offers as the final cause of despair the schism in the soul.[4] When disillusionment says, "Who knoweth what is good for a man all the days of his vain life, which he spendeth as a shadow?" the schism in the soul goes very deep. The Christian, whose office it is to supply an authentic voice to redress the balance of a shaken world and to reassure the despairing, will find in Ecclesiastes an approach and a challenge of outstanding value. The questions he asks are as old as Koheleth's forgotten yesterdays, as persistent as human experience. Their phrasing may be recast, but they remain identical in their substance. They are accents of the incessant quest for the meanings, values, and sanctions of life. In seasons of good fortune

[3] *The Problem of Suffering in the Old Testament* (London: Robert Bryant, 1904), p. 135.

[4] See *Civilization on Trial* (New York: Oxford University Press, 1948), pp. 253-63.

they are only muted whispers. In the crises of the soul or society they will not let us go. They began to be asked in the historic period of the eclipse of Hebrew faith, and the breaking up of an inherited order. When like periods recur in any order, they bring with them the travail of Ecclesiastes, strangely unchanged.

There has been since the beginning of the twentieth century a growing interest, not only in wisdom literature generally, but in Ecclesiastes specifically; some of it due to the freer approach which criticism of the O.T. has made possible, some due to the literary charm of the book. But most of all, because Koheleth's amazing modernity has a way of reasserting itself and its kinship with the time and spirit of a world war-worn, disillusioned, and weary. An adequate paraphrase of about the same length, capturing his moods and formulating his doubts in terms of contemporary thought patterns, would, if it could be done, show how great a company of the frustrated and perplexed are thinking as he thought and seeking what he sought.

The answers, the healings, the reconciliations, are in the Christian gospel. These are spacious words. They include Christianity's own wisdom about life. They include the divine wisdom of Jesus Christ about life. They include Christian ethics. They include the promise and potency of the Christian order. They include a faith which like Paul's denies death any victory. They include the whole way of the truth and life of Jesus Christ, and they include the outstretched arms of the Cross, which is the terminal of them all. If, as has been said, the lines of quest and perplexity which go out from Ecclesiastes are left broken and hanging in the void, the Christian gospel accepts the task of carrying them through to triumphant assurance.

1:1-11. That Which Has Been Is That Which Shall Be.—The book opens with what would seem in English, if not in the Hebrew, a dirge-like passage on the monotony of nature and the

2 Vanity of vanities, saith the Preacher, vanity of vanities; all *is* vanity.

3 What profit hath a man of all his labor which he taketh under the sun?

2 Vanity of vanities, says the Preacher, vanity of vanities! All is vanity.

3 What does man gain by all the toil at which he toils under the sun?

B. NATURE'S CEASELESS AND AIMLESS TOIL (1:2-11)

2. G. A. Barton regards **says the Preacher** as an addition, on the ground that elsewhere the author speaks of himself in the first person. Paul Volz and Kurt Galling think that this whole verse is an insertion, introducing the poem that follows by the well-known dictum which summed up Koheleth's thought. Yet though the verse is abrupt it appears to have poetic rhythm, a feature which argues somewhat, if not absolutely, for its originality. **Vanity** (*hébhel*="vapor," "breath") indicates the fruitlessness, aimlessness, emptiness, and transitoriness of all that happens upon earth (cf. 2:26*d*). The earth itself, as central point of this happening, **remains for ever** (vs. 4). **Vanity of vanities** expresses the superlative degree (cf. "holy of holies"). Hertzberg's view that in *hébhel* (vanity) there is an allusion to *Hébhel* (Abel), the first of the human race to suffer death, does not seem probable, although in Ecclesiastes there are echoes of the early chapters of Genesis.

3-8. These verses are in poetic form. The substance of their thought is that nature reveals an eternal monotonous activity. There is a coming and going of generation after generation of men. The sun's journey is repeated day by day. The wind follows a regular round. All rivers flow to the sea, and the stream, renewed from the source, flows where the waters flowed before, to the same goal. The processes of nature show a

---

futility of initiative. Koheleth's first indictment against existence is that it is only repetition, an endless turning upon a timeless wheel. We are but atoms in a cycling flux upon which we ourselves are borne. This has been the motif of meditative souls since men began in somber moments to brood upon the brevity of life.

> Time, like an ever-rolling stream,
> Bears all its sons away.[5]

Bossuet, in his orations over the "great" dead of France, sees even kings swept down into nothingness, and in his noblest passages one seems to hear the movement of irresistible tides. Ecclesiastes agrees, but adds something else, vast as those tides returning upon themselves: it is the earth itself, forever unchanged, that turns and returns in its own master cycles. There is that about the Preacher which is reminiscent of Egypt and Babylonia, some have thought, wrongly no doubt, even of the Stoic philosophy. All of it he phrases magnificently. The sun pants across the sky, the winds repeat their directions. "Rivers to the ocean run, nor stay them in their course"; yet the sea is never full. Monotony numbs both nature and life. We have a hunger which is never satisfied. **There is nothing new under the sun.**

Few have not known what it means to be brought under the spell of the tides which first

[5] Isaac Watts, "O God, our help in ages past."

flood the marshes, making of them inland seas; then ebb again, leaving the tall grasses bare and all the little channels empty. James Martineau has a noble sermon on "The Tides of the Spirit." Life is like that; we live in alternating cycles of waking and sleeping, of working and resting; in the words of the psalmist, of going out and coming in—though with this difference: When the psalmist takes up the theme, the ever-recurring movement is toward a goal which stands within the framework of God's revelation in nature and history. Here experience and time apparently do no more than lengthen the radii by which the lines of life and nature are controlled, as they swing purposelessly around. All this Koheleth says with grave music. Through all these returnings the sun and our souls keep toiling on.

There is weariness in it of course; as if the world, while still young, has already grown tired. For the most part, parallel passages in the poets and dramatists are based upon limited observation and the experiences of the sensitive or personally disillusioned. There is more than that in this instance: a broader and speculative background. Koheleth does not suggest specifically how human history does repeat itself, but surely in spacious ways it supports his conclusion. Never in detail, but again and again in attitudes and tempers which dismiss the past too reluctantly and welcome the future too slowly. Arnold J. Toynbee found such attitudes undo-

27

4 *One* generation passeth away, and *another* generation cometh: but the earth abideth for ever.

5 The sun also ariseth, and the sun goeth down, and hasteth to his place where he arose.

6 The wind goeth toward the south, and turneth about unto the north; it whirleth about continually, and the wind returneth again according to his circuits.

7 All the rivers run into the sea; yet the sea *is* not full: unto the place from whence the rivers come, thither they return again.

4 A generation goes, and a generation comes,
  but the earth remains for ever.
5 The sun rises and the sun goes down,
  and hastens to the place where it rises.
6 The wind blows to the south,
  and goes round to the north;
round and round goes the wind,
  and on its circuits the wind returns.
7 All streams run to the sea,
  but the sea is not full;
to the place where the streams flow,
  there they flow again.

ceaseless motion but no progress—and where there is no progress there is no aim. Man's work too, the toil wherein **he toils under the sun**—an expression contained in Phoenician inscriptions of the fifth century B.C. and which therefore need not be a Grecism—is bound up with the perpetual coming and going of generations of men; and their activity becomes lost and profitless.

5. The sun **hastens** (lit., "pants"; cf. Gordis "breathlessly rushing"). F. C. Burkitt ("Is Ecclesiastes a Translation?" *Journal of Theological Studies,* XXIII [1922], 26) suggested that the word for "pants" should be emended because "elsewhere in the O.T. [there is] no trace of the idea that the Sun goes on his course with fatigue or effort, so that an unexplained allusion to the Sun 'panting' is really a difficulty." Burkitt's observation is of interest, in view of the signs of contact between Ecclesiastes and Egyptian literature. The sun is described in that literature (in "The Deliverance of Mankind"; see Adolf Erman, *Literature of the Ancient Egyptians* [tr. A. M. Blackman; New York: E. P. Dutton & Co., 1927], p. 47) as having become old and exhibiting signs of agedness.

ing civilization after civilization. One cannot entirely deny the Preacher's contention. But something of inestimable value escapes him.

4-7. The Comfort of the Constant.—One must allow something for the author's rhetorical flair. He must have known that he was writing well. Some allowance must also be made for exaggeration. Perhaps other and more suitable analogies were not chosen because they did not fit his purpose. In any case, he overstates the truth. It is the very constancies in nature and experience that make ordered life possible. Ancient and established habits of earth and sky are our safeguards. Viscount Grey once wrote of the support he found in nature's ordered ways in World War I. Everything else seemed shaken to the breaking point, but springtime and bird song never failed. If we have no other quarrel with earth order and sky order than their constancies, we have little ground for complaint.

Nor, if life is well ordered, have we any ground of complaint against the routines of our own individual lives. How could we go on at all if every dawn rose upon the wholly unfamiliar, and the faces we love and the tasks we perform were not there? We should be hopelessly lost and the dawn would be darkness.

Besides, there is always something new under the sun. The paths along which we come back at night are never quite the same as the paths by which we went out in the morning. The most familiar tasks are never quite the same in business, in the household, or in the conduct of life. The variations within the vast encompassing frame of the constant and seemingly recurrent are beyond telling. Every day is a fresh beginning in an order which in detail is never twice the same.

So do new forces and forms emerge in history, and though the great world spins, it spins down the ringing grooves of change. Turning wheels grip the road or the rail and move on. Though tides rise and fall, their floodtime never washes exactly the same beach. There is more in the rhythm than endless repetition. Christian faith sees a directing purpose in what otherwise is self-defeating confusion.

Koheleth, commentators say, lived in a world static in many ways, at least in its mechanism. Architecture, clothes, tools, had not greatly changed along the eastern Mediterranean coast for centuries. Conquerors had come—and gone—but those who survived the endless wars saw little change in their own conditions. Nor was

8 All things *are* full of labor; man cannot utter *it:* the eye is not satisfied with seeing, nor the ear filled with hearing.

9 The thing that hath been, it *is that* which shall be; and that which is done *is* that which shall be done: and *there is* no new *thing* under the sun.

10 Is there *any* thing whereof it may be said, See, this *is* new? it hath been already of old time, which was before us.

---

8 All things are full of weariness;
  a man cannot utter it;
the eye is not satisfied with seeing,
  nor the ear filled with hearing.
9 What has been is what will be,
  and what has been done is what will be
    done;
  and there is nothing new under the
    sun.
10 Is there a thing of which it is said,
  "See, this is new"?
It has been already,
  in the ages before us.

---

8. The first two words are translated by a number of commentators as "all words" (cf. LXX and the use elsewhere in Ecclesiastes of the Hebrew plural form *debhārîm* = "words"). Hence Hertzberg renders, "All speech is a wearying of oneself, no man can utter it"—a justifiable interpretation. But the rendering **all things,** which means all that man can observe of the toiling, aimless movement of the natural world, fits the context of thought much better. The major difficulty of the verse is the lack of logical connection between the reference to the **eye** and the **ear** and the words that precede this reference. Two explanations given are: (*a*) the eye and the ear cannot take in the weary toil of the natural processes; (*b*) man's spirit becomes weary at the sight of the endless monotonous rounds of nature, so that the eye and ear enter upon endless courses of seeing and hearing that never satisfy (Barton). This latter interpretation is the better, though it is rather finely spun. Justice would appear to be done to what seems to be the author's meaning if the latter part of the verse is rendered as an interrogation, with the omission of the interrogative particle, as occurs at times in animated speech. The sentence would then run, "All things are wearied [in their course], no man can describe it [or "put it into words"]. Is not the eye sated with beholding it? and is not the ear surfeited with hearing of it?"

9-11. The author now concludes from what he has described in vss. 3-8 of nature's plodding monotonous round that all things, apparently not only in nature but in human history, repeat themselves. What appears to be new is only the return of phenomena already old. **What has been done is what will be done.** The verb נעשה, **has been done,** refers in Ecclesiastes not only to human action but to the divine activity (cf. 8:17). Vs. 10 should be understood rather as a statement: "If there is a thing whereof men say,

---

the era fertile in such inventions as give us—often misleadingly—the persuasion of progress. It may well be that our own sense of change and novelty is too largely in externals. Whether we fly or walk, we are not so changed as we think we are. For all of man's inventions and unbelievably augmented power, our author, contemplating what we have done and left undone, might still reach his hand across the millenniums and hail us as his brethren.

8-10. Reconciliation.—The reconciliation between Ecclesiastes' contention that there is nothing new under the sun and our own sense of an always changing order is in the recognition that both are true and each has its value. Without the constancies of earth and sky, planting would be a game of chance, foresight impossible, plan-

ning a farce, and so on and on. But we plant grains Koheleth never knew, in fields of which he had never heard, in ways he could not imagine. Without variations, inward and outward, imagined to begin with, and carried through in venture and experiment, uniformity would become stagnant and toil defeat itself. The protest against the always recurrent without lift or fruition, the protest which accentuates the minor music of these verses, is really the adventurer in the human spirit always seeking new frontiers, the "divine discontent" which, though it forbids us the lesser peace, calls us to the heights. That is why **the eye is not satisfied with seeing, nor the ear filled with hearing.** The human spirit seeks the unseen and listens for the inaudible voice.

11 *There is* no remembrance of former *things;* neither shall there be *any* remembrance of *things* that are to come with *those* that shall come after.
 	
12 ¶ I the Preacher was king over Israel in Jerusalem.
	11 There is no remembrance of former things,
	    nor will there be any remembrance
	of later things yet to happen
	    among those who come after.
	12 I the Preacher have been king over

'See, this is new.'" Men do not know that the so-thought new thing is old because former generations of men and what they did and experienced are forgotten by those who come after. **There is no remembrance of former things:** The reference is most probably, however, to former times or to the generations of men (cf. ERV, "former generations"). The exegesis of this verse is of some weight in regard to the interpretation of 3:11. The forgetfulness is not merely a lack of remembrance of men's fame—a subject which is not mentioned here—but of events which, when they reappear, are mistakenly accounted to be new.

C. Purposelessness of Human Life (1:12–2:26)

12-18. After his preface (1:2-11) on the world's processes as eternally fixed and repetitive, Koheleth appears in the role of Solomon to give his judgment on the value of life. There had been none so rich in experience as this monarch, none so full of wisdom, none more fitted for the task of giving guidance in regard to life's conduct and of assessing life's worth.

12. The phrase **have been king** is strikingly peculiar, since Solomon continued to be king until his death. Even if **was king** is read, this peculiarity is not removed. It has

---

11. Disillusion.—*Remembrance:* The structure of the Hebrew at times adds length to Ecclesiastes without adding substance. Its rhythmic repetitions give literary charm but tend to inflate and to invite exaggeration. Koheleth cannot have known all that happened in the past; nor could he assume that the future would keep no records. Too easily he equates the fugitive with the futile, both doomed to oblivion. Malachi knew better. He knew not only that God remembers but that the generations remember, and that each of us has his "book of remembrance." Some of its pages are dim, some glow with light; we live out of it increasingly and part of our wisdom is what it teaches us. Ecclesiastes itself is written in part out of Koheleth's book of remembrance.

Perspective: Life and labor, so runs the conclusion, are like a section of road one might find in a wilderness; where it came from and where it leads equally lost in the fog. And it carries no new traffic. Everything has passed before, over and over again. Precisely this lack of perspective is one of the fundamental causes of the somber judgments of the book upon life and history. It does not see either steadily or as a whole. It has no far horizons. Its vision of issues and consequences is strangely limited.

Detachment: We have a word which the Preacher did not know, and with which, had he known it, he would not have labeled himself. He seems to us a pessimist; but the word does

not apply. One feels a strange serenity between his lines, with here and there a fleeting hint as to its source. Life for him is a spectacle, curious, interesting, whose confused moments are beyond his power to understand, from which he has at last achieved detachment. And the secret of that detachment lies beyond the orb of the world. The traditional interpreters call him "the Preacher." Plumptre calls him "the Debater."[6] He has really named himself: "The Observer"—"I have seen"—"I have seen"—"I have seen." Count them as you read.

Interpretation: His observations are integrated, and he is sincere. He draws upon them, and upon his own wisdom and the lore of the ages, with vivid and often poetic analogies. "Life," he says, speaking of the winds and the vapors, "is like that." The one thing lacking is interpretation. In *The Pilgrim's Progress* Bunyan stopped Christian at Mr. Interpreter's house. The seeming facts of life support Koheleth's conclusions; but they are only the *seeming* facts. There is no situation which, seen in the light of a fuller and profounder faith than his, will not reveal qualities and possibilities that doubt cannot discern or despair conceive. There is always an alternative to the "facts." There is always in Christian faith another interpretation of their meaning.

12-18. Borrowed Robes.—The prologue to the book ends with vs. 11. Indeed, the substance of

[6] *Ecclesiastes,* p. 17.

13 And I gave my heart to seek and search out by wisdom concerning all *things* that are done under heaven: this sore travail hath God given to the sons of man to be exercised therewith.

Israel in Jerusalem. 13 And I applied my mind to seek and to search out by wisdom all that is done under heaven; it is an unhappy business that God has given to the

been suggested that Koheleth-Solomon means, "I have been king (and still am)," or that we must picture the old king as looking back on the energy of his youth and saying, "I was king then—now I regard it all from another point of view" (A. Lukyn Williams, *Ecclesiastes* [Cambridge: Cambridge University Press, 1922; "Cambridge Bible"], p. 10). In support of this view commentators quote the story of Louis XIV, who in the last days of his life renounced all earthly concerns and was often heard to say, "When I was king. . . ." But there is not the slightest indication given in our book that either Koheleth or Solomon was ever in a state of mind similar to that of the French king. The explanation given by Franz Delitzsch (*Commentary on the Song of Songs and Ecclesiastes* [tr. M. G. Easton; Edinburgh: T. & T. Clark, 1877], p. 226) is less oblique, viz., that "Solomon, resuscitated by the author of the book, . . . looks back on his life as king." That Solomon should look back upon his life's experience is of course the purpose of the author who identifies himself with the king, but this admission does not remove the difficulty of the expression **have been king.** Possibly we must regard the phrase as carelessly expressed; the author has assumed the role of a personage of past history, while at the same time he is well aware that his readers know him to be who he is, that his identity with Solomon is but a literary disguise. The same carelessness in regard to details of history is seen in 2:7, 9; cf. 1:16, where **all who were over Jerusalem before me** would imply that Solomon had had several predecessors in Jerusalem. Volz translates, "I was once king"; he thinks it possible that Koheleth believed that his spirit had once been the spirit of Solomon. This curious interpretation at least appreciates the difficulty presented by the text. Kurt Galling ("Kohelet-Studien," *Zeitschrift für die alttestamentliche Wissenschaft*, L [1932], 298) holds that in 1:12 the book reveals another point of contact with the Egyptian wisdom writings, where it is typical of the royal "admonitions" (cf. Erman, *op. cit.*, pp. 72, 75) that the king gives his instruction on the day of his relinquishing the throne. Thus Galling says, "If we compare with the Egyptian wisdom, the phrase 'I have been king' loses its peculiar character."

13-15. By wisdom: Lit., in the M.T., "by [or with] the wisdom," which must mean by reason of the wisdom which he has or was reputed to have. H. W. Hertzberg (*Der Prediger* [Leipzig: Werner Scholl, 1932; "Kommentar zum Alten Testament"], *ad. loc.*) translates, "to seek for wisdom," i.e., for the sense or purpose of what is done on earth.

it is all there. The motif is now heard, a motif almost as simple as that of Beethoven's *Fifth Symphony*, grave, sustained, with a final falling note, like the dropping of the "tears of things." The motif? That all labor is vain because at the best it does no more than rebuild a vanished past, retrace deep worn roads; and even so, this vain labor is itself foredoomed. Did the author feel that such conclusions as these needed an authority his name could not supply? Is there a faint suggestion that the authority of Solomon, who so excelled in splendor and wisdom, should possess finality? The Intro. (see p. 4) considers this use of a borrowed name. The Exeg. specifies the difficulties attending a too literal acceptance of the author's device. But what if even a king should find life a vain **striving after**

wind? Surely then nothing is left for common folk. **What is crooked cannot be made straight,** and it is an **unhappy business that God has given to the sons of men to be busy with.** There are theologies which hold that man is a disappointment to God—and with good reason. Koheleth's audacity reverses that: God does not deal justly with men. This, too, Job pondered over; and many before and since.

We know a little of the long and costly processes through which human life must come into its own—if it ever does. Of this Koheleth knew less than we. Whether such fuller knowledge would have changed his point of view, who can tell? There is too much in the conduct of our affairs which indicates that we ourselves do not sense the high obligations of our shared

14 I have seen all the works that are done under the sun; and, behold, all *is* vanity and vexation of spirit.

15 *That which is* crooked cannot be made straight: and that which is wanting cannot be numbered.

sons of men to be busy with. 14 I have seen everything that is done under the sun; and behold, all is vanity and a striving after wind.*b*

15 What is crooked cannot be made straight, and what is lacking cannot be numbered.

b Or *a feeding on wind.* See Hos 12. 1

The judgments which Solomon-Koheleth gives on **all that is done under heaven**— by which reference is made both to the processes of nature (cf. Exeg. on vs. 9), as described in the preface, and to the strivings and doings of men—come swiftly and with decision. The **unhappy business that God has given to the sons of men** is well defined by Ernest Renan (*L'Ecclésiaste* [Paris: C. Lévy, 1882], p. 21): "In short God takes little interest in man, since he has put him in a false position by giving him the task of concerning himself with wisdom but has allotted to him a finite destiny which is the same for fool and sage, man and beast, and this within a society where what happens is opposed to justice and reason." The God-given task imposed on men **to be busy** there- with is a sorry business because their wisdom is too insufficient an instrument. The impossibility of solving the problems of life is also given by God, which to the mind of Koheleth means little more than given by life. All the activity that is observable in humanity, and in nature exterior to man, leads to nothing of permanent worth. It is an aimless activity, futile, **a striving after** [or "a feeding upon"] **wind.** All that man can do is to accept the conditions of life as these are, for

> **What is crooked cannot be made straight**
> **and what is lacking cannot be numbered.**

The root of these judgments and of their pessimism is the view that all things are ordained and cannot be otherwise than they are.

humanity. By every test life is not meant to be **an unhappy business,** even if we do make it so. It should indeed be the greatest business in which God and man together can be engaged.

> . . . Life is not as idle ore,
>
> But iron dug from central gloom,
>   And heated hot with burning fears,
>   And dipt in baths of hissing tears,
> And batter'd with the shocks of doom,
>
> To shape and use.[7]

The fallacy of Koheleth's mood, therefore, is more than a fallacy; it is the result of a fatal oversight. There is neither yet nor later any adequate recognition of the "hero in the soul," the God-given power to subdue circumstance to high purpose: to build, of what seems most dis- couraging, steps, hard hewn, to climb by; to recast what seems least kind into victorious qualities of character and conduct. What should be a challenge to that "hero in the soul" be- comes for Koheleth an occasion for a Miserere

[7] Tennyson, *In Memoriam,* Part CXVIII, sts. v-vii.

instead of a Te Deum. Here is no music like the music of Isa. 40 to march by, nor is there anywhere heard even the most distant echo of any summoning trumpet. Only this quiet and somber word, "In the multitude of dreams . . . fear thou God" (5:7).

15. *The Glory of Going On.*—Life is never a finished business; least of all are we given a finished product, either in our own souls or in any society. Besides, are there not Satanic forces at work? We do, however, possess the power by the grace of God and the mystery of our own creative personalities to take the raw material of experience and our own always unfinished selves, and make of life an enterprise worthy of its cost and promise. The **crooked** can be **made straight,** in highways, in society, and in the soul; not always easily or soon, and always at a price. But we have no choice save to try. It is better—and braver—to say of seeming failure, "I have tried to make a straight way, a highway in the wilderness, for truth and goodness, but I must leave it unfinished," than to surrender before the challenge, as so many are wont to do, pleading a fatalistic philosophy in justification.

16 I communed with mine own heart, saying, Lo, I am come to great estate, and have gotten more wisdom than all *they* that have been before me in Jerusalem: yea, my heart had great experience of wisdom and knowledge.

17 And I gave my heart to know wisdom, and to know madness and folly: I perceived that this also is vexation of spirit.

18 For in much wisdom *is* much grief: and he that increaseth knowledge increaseth sorrow.

16 I said to myself, "I have acquired great wisdom, surpassing all who were over Jerusalem before me; and my mind has had great experience of wisdom and knowledge." 17 And I applied my mind to know wisdom and to know madness and folly. I perceived that this also is but a striving after wind.

18 For in much wisdom is much vexation,
and he who increases knowledge increases sorrow.

16-18. The wise man must not restrict himself to the observation of one side of life. Having already acquired much knowledge, "Solomon" seeks to gain more wisdom by a study of wisdom's opposites, **madness**—a phase of which is no doubt recklessness—and **folly.** The Hebrew word for **madness** in vs. 17 does not appear to refer mainly or only to conduct, but rather to errors of thought. Theod. renders this word by παράφορας (="derangements"), Aq. by πλάνας, and the Vulg. by *errores*. Thus Delitzsch (*op. cit.,* p. 231) comments that Solomon "wished to be clear regarding the real worth of wisdom and knowledge in their contrasts." But the thought of vs. 17 is deeper than this. Solomon's investigation was an attempt to determine the principles which distinguish what is wise and what is unwise or foolish (so Hertzberg and Siegfried); as this quest proves fruitless, the solution of the problem shows itself to be beyond his reach. The attempt to extend his knowledge only brings him a sense of frustration and painful disappointment; it **increases sorrow**—the word for **sorrow** is the same as the word translated "pain" by the American Jewish Translation of Lam. 1:12, and means suffering of a mental or spiritual sort. There is no absolute standard by which to differentiate what is truth and what is error and delusion. That which is divine wisdom may appear to be the maddest folly (cf. I Cor. 1:22-25; 3:18-20).

Vss. 15 and 18 are couched in the form of maxims, and they appear to be closely related in thought. The wise man in his study of life becomes aware that some conditions cannot be corrected but have to be accepted as they are; and when he turns to search for an infallible guide as to what is true and wise, or false and mad, he finds that there is none. This increment of knowledge brings with it a sense of weakness and defeat as well as a sense of sympathy and pity for his fellow men who are left with the sorry, because wholly uncertain, business of applying wisdom to life.

At least one will have gained a wisdom beside which even Koheleth's wisdom will seem sadly incomplete.

16-18. *The First Quest.*—Something must be allowed in Ecclesiastes, as in all the wisdom literature of the O.T., for the rather specialized meanings of the word **wisdom.** With a capital letter it is a personification, a divine agent furthering God's creative purposes in ways difficult to understand. From that, through many intervening stages, one moves back and forward, to **wisdom** without a capital letter—the technique of dealing well with situations, conducting oneself wisely. It has overtones of knowledge, suggests insights and understanding. A famous passage in Ecclesiasticus (38:24-34) confines it to the learned and cultured with leisure

to debate and talk—endlessly. They sit in high places of honor and administration. The passage allows to craftsmen at the forge, or at the potter's wheel, only the wisdom of their crafts; but for all that, "they maintain the fabric of the world." Koheleth stresses repeatedly the futility of such a quest. That too is **a striving after wind.**

It is of course a fact that as we extend the frontiers of knowledge we face always more spacious frontiers of mystery. Science, for example, raises more questions than it answers. The two-hundred-inch reflector telescope on Mount Miromar will add incalculable light years to the dimensions of the universe, but it will only add mystery to mystery and leave the astronomer humbled, as Job was humbled before the God of stars and nebulae, which are

2 I said in mine heart, Go to now, I will prove thee with mirth; therefore enjoy pleasure: and, behold, this also *is* vanity.

2 I said of laughter, *It is* mad: and of mirth, What doeth it?

2 I said to myself, "Come now, I will make a test of pleasure; enjoy yourself." But behold, this also was vanity. 2 I said of laughter, "It is mad," and of pleasure,

---

2:1-11. Perceiving that man's knowledge and wisdom, i.e., his intellectual powers, must always be so limited by the conditions of existence that their cultivation cannot provide an adequate measure of attainment, "Solomon" turns to the task of testing whether perchance pleasure may be a worth-while object of human effort, the good which is completely satisfying. Wine, women, and song, the gathering of riches, the enjoyment of luxury, the acquisition of rare and special products and commodities derived from foreign rulers and countries through trade, gift, or tribute, the prosperity fostered by successful projects of agriculture and afforestation, the magnificence of his buildings, of his gardens and parks and vineyards—all this "Solomon" briefly indicates in describing the means he used to find out by test and trial whether pleasure provided a soul-satisfying purpose of life. **My mind still guiding me with wisdom,** or "my heart behaving itself in wisdom" (*A Hebrew and English Lexicon of the Old Testament,* ed. Francis Brown, S. R. Driver, and C. A. Briggs [Boston: Houghton Mifflin Co., 1906], *s.v.* נהג) , may mean that he did not allow indulgence to overcome his judgment, or merely that he conducted the experiment with particular discernment and attention to its thoroughness. What he did discover was that pleasure actually was attainable and did yield a reward (lit., "portion") for his toil; but as he considered this reward and the efforts he had put forth to secure it, he concluded that the pursuit of pleasure had yielded him no *yithrôn,* i.e., no remaining result, no permanent profit, no real gain. Koheleth recognizes that pleasure can be gained, and especially that work is for man a source of joy, but he reflects that as soon as we look upon such gains with regard to their place in the eternal stream of events, times, and generations, they appear to be so small and disappointing that to strive for them is **a striving after wind** (cf.

---

only the trailing of his garments, "the outskirts of his ways."

There is, however, a wisdom other than this wisdom, not "under the sun," a wisdom of faith and courage won from life because illumined by revelation. It is neither vanity nor vexation of spirit. Would not Koheleth agree? It is the final harvest of life. And it needs no jeweled robes of vanished kings to make it royal. It has thrones of its own.

2:1-12. *I Got Me.*—Roger Williams, toward the end of his life, having suffered many things, grew weary of being called by any of the names with which the free religious groups of his time designated themselves. He was, he said, only a "seeker" and thereafter rested content so far as his restless spirit could ever be content. This spacious title Koheleth would willingly have accepted. Commentators are generally agreed in finding in his book a framework which can be used for the organization of their studies. One by one he calls up for examination the values of life and the terminals of action (see Exeg. for a representative classification) . If Koheleth himself had possessed a more orderly mind, the commentator's task would be greatly simplified.

So far the Preacher has confined himself to generalities, variations of one over-all theme: Life is a complex of futilities which dulls the nerve of all endeavor. There are always significant omissions to which we shall often return. There is little or no mention of duty or moral obligation. Beyond debate the writer assumes them, but they are in his remote and ancestral backgrounds. The only references to hope assume nothing to hope for. Gordis discovers a sublimated courage between the lines, but there is in the lines themselves no exhortation to courage. Beyond a pious reference to God, little is left to believe in. Actually the author is not fair to himself. The book is set in the framework of the Hebrew faith of his time, but power to sustain and illumine has gone out of it.

He has already made King Solomon, the wisest of men, confess the futility of his quest for wisdom, and so dismisses wisdom as the seeker's support. He turns next to pleasure and possession and draws upon a classic source, the power of a king to do anything he pleases and have anything he wants. His king is a fairy story kind of king, who has only to ask in order to have, has only to command in order to be

3 I sought in mine heart to give myself unto wine, yet acquainting mine heart with wisdom; and to lay hold on folly, till I might see what *was* that good for the sons of men, which they should do under the heaven all the days of their life.

4 I made me great works; I builded me houses; I planted me vineyards:

5 I made me gardens and orchards, and I planted trees in them of all *kind of* fruits:

"What use is it?" 3 I searched with my mind how to cheer my body with wine — my mind still guiding me with wisdom — and how to lay hold on folly, till I might see what was good for the sons of men to do under heaven during the few days of their life. 4 I made great works; I built houses and planted vineyards for myself; 5 I made myself gardens and parks, and planted in

---

Hugo Odeberg, *Qohaelaeth, a Commentary on the Book of Ecclesiastes* [Uppsala: Almqvist & Wiksells, 1929], p. 20).

3. The word rendered **to cheer—to cheer my body with wine**—means in Hebrew "to draw," "to attract." The sense of the verse, however, requires some such meaning as **cheer,** "stimulate," or "refresh." Delitzsch translates a Talmudic passage (Hagigah 14*a*) where the word occurs, "Refresh the heart of a man as with water," and cites it in favor of translating the Hebrew verb in question as "refresh" (*op. cit.,* p. 234). But in this Talmudic passage too the verb means to "draw" or "attract": "Draw the heart of a man as [one conducts] water" (cf. Williams, *op. cit.,* p. 17; and Lazarus Goldschmidt, *Der babylonische Talmud* [Berlin: Jüdischer Verlag, 1931], IV, 280). The LXX also in vs. 3 renders "attract." The sense "attract" is not a very happy one—"attract my body with wine"—but the Hebrew verb cannot, if it is allowed to remain, be given a meaning for which there is not sufficient evidence. The Hebrew text might be translated "to sustain [or stay] my body with wine" if the word למשך ("to draw") is emended into לסמך ("to sustain"; cf. Song of S. 2:5).

5. **Parks:** So the RSV and ERV. The Hebrew *pardēṣîm* is sometimes considered as a loan word from the Persian, whence παράδεισος and "paradise" (however, cf. Akkadian *pardīsu,* "park").

---

obeyed. It is all, confessedly, an experiment: **Come now, I will make a test of pleasure.** And he cannot wait to pronounce his verdict. **But . . . this also was vanity.** The laughter of feasters was mockery, and the fruits of pleasure were Dead Sea apples, bitter dust upon the lips. And in the most paradoxical of passages he employed wisdom **to lay hold on folly** (vs. 3), which in a sense is precisely what Erasmus did in his *Encomium Moriae.*

There is no need to comment upon his diversions, or what his pleasure and his possessions cost his subjects. That was the habit of the state and the tyranny of Oriental kings. He would have Solomon surpass them all. The supposititious king has the grace to be ashamed of himself. It was all, he is made to say, only a wayside halt in his quest for wisdom, and so —? The terseness of the old translations supplies something which the versions we are using lack, a quality like a sword thrust: "I got me"—"I got me"—"I got me." What he got sounds like Hollywood, but no matter.

4. *Prophets and Kings.*—The significant thing is that a quest so motivated and so achieved was foredoomed. Life was never meant to be

lived between "I" and "me," "I" for the subject and "me" for the object. Our powers are too spacious thus to be employed. Here are words arresting enough to be put upon any bulletin board and to challenge any student of human motivation. "I got me" is a philosophy of life, tyrannical, insidious, and far too largely the dominant technique of Western civilization in its economic and international aspects.

The Hebrew, it is generally held, was not primarily a philosopher. He did not generally think in abstract terms. He was imaginative, rather than speculative—though it must be added that philosophy has asked few questions for which there are not answers in the O.T. and the N.T. Neither underestimates the authority of reason or the value of argument. "Come now, and let us reason together, saith the Lord" (Isa. 1:18). Yet the great biblical assurances, like a poet's song, reach their resting places by sure and swift flight which veil the depths they have crossed.

The Hebrew thought rather in terms of situations, and for that he had a matchless faculty. We turn still to his prophets for their description of the luxury which lies upon ivory beds

6 I made me pools of water, to water therewith the wood that bringeth forth trees:

7 I got *me* servants and maidens, and had servants born in my house; also I had great possessions of great and small cattle above all that were in Jerusalem before me:

8 I gathered me also silver and gold, and the peculiar treasure of kings and of the provinces: I gat me men singers and women singers, and the delights of the sons of men, *as* musical instruments, and that of all sorts.

9 So I was great, and increased more than all that were before me in Jerusalem: also my wisdom remained with me.

10 And whatsoever mine eyes desired I kept not from them, I withheld not my heart from any joy; for my heart rejoiced in all my labor: and this was my portion of all my labor.

them all kinds of fruit trees. 6 I made myself pools from which to water the forest of growing trees. 7 I bought male and female slaves, and had slaves who were born in my house; I had also great possessions of herds and flocks, more than any who had been before me in Jerusalem. 8 I also gathered for myself silver and gold and the treasure of kings and provinces; I got singers, both men and women, and many concubines,[c] man's delight.

9 So I became great and surpassed all who were before me in Jerusalem; also my wisdom remained with me. 10 And whatever my eyes desired I did not keep from them; I kept my heart from no pleasure, for my heart found pleasure in all my toil, and this

[c] The meaning of the Hebrew word is uncertain

---

6. Pools has been regarded as referring to the "Solomonic" reservoirs southeast of Bethlehem, but according to Hertzberg these pools belong to the Roman period (cf. article, "Wasserversorgung," in Kurt Galling, *Biblisches Reallexikon* [Tübingen: J. C. B. Mohr, 1937; "Handbuch zum Alten Testament"], pp. 534-36).

8. The peculiar treasure renders the single word *ṣegullāh,* which conveys the ideas of possession (property), preciousness, and speciality, e.g., the gold from Ophir, the artistic work and skill of the Phoenician builders. **And many concubines:** The Hebrew words so rendered are obscure. The LXX translates "cupbearers, male and female."

---

and the heartlessness which sells the needy for a pair of shoes; of the civilizations which waste a kingdom to adorn a woman's dressing table, and of the deepening and portentous shadows which have always, since history began, lain across them. Ecclesiastes has something of this quality, and commentators have found in that fact some intimation of the writer's acquaintance with the prophets. At the best such acquaintance is vague, though in his description of the foolish and costly luxury of the kings' courts the writer might have been mindful of Amos—with the difference, however, that the prophet reaches through doom to repentance and promises a dawn beyond the dark.

Ecclesiastes dismisses the question of issues as immaterial. There is no issue beyond the tomb; death sees to that. There is no issue in hard-won wealth of character; that apparently is nowhere in Koheleth's mind. There is material here for the moralist, not only that he may correct Koheleth's conclusion and add what Koheleth leaves out, but in the gleams of wisdom which shine through the Preacher's gentle melancholy. Whoever our writer may be, he knows that the jeweled robes in which a self-

centered life is wrapped do but hide a self-consuming emptiness. He does not moralize, which is in some ways the secret of his strange fascination. Self-seeking, he wrote, was self-consuming. That was enough.

6. Sand or Spring?—An order of go-getters which furnishes magazines with success stories, motivates competing groups, and arms nations on sea and land and in the sky, is all as costly as it is tragic, as tragic as it is fallacious. Self-interest is a deeply rooted and defensible motivation, depending, however, upon what true self-interest is. The wise have long noted that we have more power to act and to produce than we need in order to keep us physically alive. Rabindranath Tagore, quoting from his ancient literature, speaks of this as the "surplus," the margin of action and realization above our strictly biological needs. It is the explanation of what we have done or left undone, the secret of our restlessness, the source of our hopes and our dreams. The right use of it furnishes our most creative challenge; the wrong use of it is the doom of souls and civilizations.

The birds which flutter among the trees need to do about everything they can to survive and

11 Then I looked on all the works that my hands had wrought, and on the labor that I had labored to do: and, behold, all *was* vanity and vexation of spirit, and *there was* no profit under the sun.

12 ¶ And I turned myself to behold wisdom, and madness, and folly: for what *can* the man *do* that cometh after the king? *even* that which hath been already done.

13 Then I saw that wisdom excelleth folly, as far as light excelleth darkness.

was my reward for all my toil. 11 Then I considered all that my hands had done and the toil I had spent in doing it, and behold, all was vanity and a striving after wind, and there was nothing to be gained under the sun.

12 So I turned to consider wisdom and madness and folly; for what can the man do who comes after the king? Only what he has already done. 13 Then I saw that wisdom excels folly as light excels darkness.

12-17. "Solomon" now ponders the contrast of wisdom and its opposite, madness or folly, these qualities being now regarded in their practical aspects. He admits that wisdom has in principle the advantage over foolishness, since the fool always suffers from the inability to perceive what is plain and obvious to the wise man. But on the other hand this gain does not amount to much, since it is only temporary; and death, which befalls both the wise man and the fool, makes no distinction between them. It is this lack of discernment and discrimination on the part of life, its neglect and forgetfulness of human worth, which in particular fills Koheleth with dislike (vs. 17) and calls forth the protest of his whole being, as in the exclamation, **So I hated life.**

12. Hertzberg suggests that the original text read, "So I turned to consider wisdom: but it is stupidity and folly" (cf. Gordis, "I saw that wisdom is but madness and folly"). But without any support of MSS or versions, this emendation would seem to be arbitrary. The only exegetical difficulty occurs in vs. 12b, where the Hebrew text runs, "For what [can or will] the man [do] who will come after the king? That which they have [many MSS, LXX, Vulg. read "he has"] already done." The rendering **for what can the man do who comes after the king?** would appear to understand **the man** (hā'ādhām) as referring to men in general. This generalization accords with the view (cf. Abraham Cohen) that Koheleth asks what use it is that men (the common man) should conduct again the experiment which Solomon the king has already conducted, since they can only come to the same results. So in effect is Gordis' translation, "For of what value is a man coming after the king, who can only repeat what he has already done?" But the question is, Can the clause, **the man . . . who comes after the king,** be thus generalized in view of the fact that practically the same expression, viz., "the man who will come after me," appears a few lines farther down (vs. 18) in an obvious reference to

---

raise their nestlings, though even a bluebird has a surplus for song in an old apple tree and an oriole a surplus for rapture in the pendant branches of an elm; but we have almost unimaginable surplus. There is then this paradox: Life can be either sand, soaking up one's own surplus and the surpluses of others, or it can be a spring and source of blessing inexhaustible in its flow. "I got me" makes life a sandy waste, the strange issue of which is that thirsts are always unassuaged. "The water that I shall give him," said Jesus, "shall be in him a well of water springing up into everlasting life," which in blessing others blesses us. There is no other wisdom of Life. "I got me" is not a good policy for kings. They thus bleed nations white and the end is revolution. Nor is it a good policy for societies and industries. Koheleth's Solomon had

wisdom enough to see the futility of his quests. He had not wisdom enough to see why they were futile.

The king's gardens and palaces have long since become dust, wind-blown down the corridors of time. The lesson remains that "I got me" is a foredoomed way of life. There is a better way to use the surplus, a blessed power to share it for the good of others. Life transformed by the spirit of Jesus may become an overflowing fountain, and do what waters do for the desert. Those who have been transformed in this fashion never say that life is a striving after vapor and that there is nothing worth while under the sun.

13-17. *The Quest for Wisdom Is Vanity.*— "Koheleth," says Gordis, "is . . . adopting the role of King Solomon as a literary device, in

14 The wise man's eyes *are* in his head; but the fool walketh in darkness: and I myself perceived also that one event happeneth to them all.

15 Then said I in my heart, As it happeneth to the fool, so it happeneth even to me; and why was I then more wise? Then I said in my heart, that this also *is* vanity.

16 For *there is* no remembrance of the wise more than of the fool for ever; seeing that which now *is* in the days to come shall all be forgotten. And how dieth the wise *man?* as the fool.

17 Therefore I hated life; because the work that is wrought under the sun *is* grievous unto me: for all *is* vanity and vexation of spirit.

14 The wise man has his eyes in his head, but the fool walks in darkness; and yet I perceived that one fate comes to all of them. 15 Then I said to myself, "What befalls the fool will befall me also; why then have I been so very wise?" And I said to myself that this also is vanity. 16 For of the wise man as of the fool there is no enduring remembrance, seeing that in the days to come all will have been long forgotten. How the wise man dies just like the fool! 17 So I hated life, because what is done under the sun was grievous to me; for all is vanity and a striving after wind.

---

the king's successor on the throne? The view that the words of vs. 12*b* refer to the king's successor (see Barton, Hertzberg) can thus hardly be overcome. Koheleth makes "Solomon" ask what his successor will do. If we read **what** [the king] **has already done,** the answer supplied is that Solomon's successor can do no more than pursue the transitory gains and profitless aims which the king himself pursued. If we retain the M.T. and read, "what has already been done," which is exactly the same as "what they [an indefinite pronoun, meaning people in general] have already done," the thought is that under Solomon's successor all will sink into the *status quo ante* in consequence of the principle of the eternal repetition of events that lies at the heart of the scheme of things (Wildeboer).

14. **One event** or **one fate** translates *miqreh 'ehādh. Miqreh* can have the meaning of "accident," "chance," "fortune," but here the significance is of a neutral quality, since it refers merely to the happening or incidence of death, without reference either to the incalculable character of the time or manner of death, or to death as a mischance, or to the time of death being foreordained. No doubt Koheleth does think of the time

---

order to drive home his point on the futility of wealth and wisdom." [8] But it is as hazardous to play a great king's role as it is to succeed him. As the Exeg. shows, one cannot say how many of these rather bitter moralizations are the reflections of a disillusioned king—there have been disillusioned kings enough since Solomon —and how many are the writer's own moralizations. At any rate, Koheleth's bill of indictment against life is already drawn. From now on he does little more than amplify and précis it. He is, so to speak, always closing his cases and opening them again. A lawyer would insist that his pleas are not well drawn; that he introduces too much matter which is irrelevant and incompetent; that his briefs are inconsistent; that he seems to plead only in the lower courts, and fails to carry his cases to any supreme court.

In substance, however, all this is but the evidence of a brilliant mind haunted by its own unanswered questions. He has now made his case for wisdom, borrowing King Solomon's

[8] *Wisdom of Ecclesiastes,* p. 14.

robe to plead in; and wisdom he pronounces futile. For all its vaunted excellence it only assures the wise that they too will die. They walk in the **light**—yes; while folly stumbles in **darkness. But one event happeneth to them all.** Nor was Koheleth either the first or the last to say that. Arthur Balfour was sometime prime minister of England. He had everything; high birth and breeding, a brilliant mind, possessions and power. The light which shines upon a throne does not compare with the light which falls upon No. 10 Downing Street, and Solomon's empire was petty and fugitive compared with the empire Balfour administered. He also, power-weary and disillusioned, wrote:

We sound the future, and learn that after a period, long compared with the individual life, but short indeed compared with the divisions of time open to our investigation, . . . the earth, tideless and inert, will no longer tolerate the race which has for a moment disturbed its solitude. Man will go down to the pit. . . . Imperishable monuments, and immortal deeds, . . . and love stronger than

18 ¶ Yea, I hated all my labor which I had taken under the sun: because I should leave it unto the man that shall be after me.

19 And who knoweth whether he shall be a wise *man* or a fool? yet shall he have rule over all my labor wherein I have labored, and wherein I have showed myself wise under the sun. This *is* also vanity.

20 Therefore I went about to cause my heart to despair of all the labor which I took under the sun.

21 For there is a man whose labor *is* in wisdom, and in knowledge, and in equity;

18 I hated all my toil in which I had toiled under the sun, seeing that I must leave it to the man who will come after me; **19** and who knows whether he will be a wise man or a fool? Yet he will be master of all for which I toiled and used my wisdom under the sun. This also is vanity. **20** So I turned about and gave my heart up to despair over all the toil of my labors under the sun, **21** because sometimes a man

---

of death in each man's case as predetermined, but this thought is not relevant to this passage.

18-26. These verses take up the thought of vs. 12*b*, where "Solomon" puts to himself the question what the man who comes after him will do. This man, he reflects, whether a wise man or a fool, will inherit the result of the king's labors. All that Solomon has gathered with foresight and toil will become the property of a person who expended not the slightest effort in acquiring it. In vss. 21-22 this personal consideration is contemplated in the broader light of general experience which corroborates the prevalence everywhere

---

death, will be as though they had never been. Nor will anything that is be better or be worse for all that the labour, genius, devotion, and suffering of man have striven through countless generations to effect.[9]

Balfour might have been reading Koheleth. No wonder he and his brief administration begin to be forgotten. An empire, inner or outer, cannot be administered in a spirit like that.

18-23. You Can't Take It with You.—Koheleth has made his case against wisdom. Knowledge does no more than extend the frontiers of our ignorance. The wise man dies as the fool dies. Life itself is therefore hateful. Whereupon he proceeds to examine the case for what he sometimes calls **labor** and sometimes calls **toil**, both of them words shadowed by weariness, though spacious and in Ecclesiastes ill-defined. Somewhere in the background are the social, economic, and industrial conditions of Koheleth's world, predominantly of slave labor, though there were free and skilled craftsmen along the narrow streets of the cities he knew. The products of their handicraft have become the treasures of our museums. The writer may have had them in mind, so certain passages indicate. But the labor he indicts was mostly the merchant's and banker's labor, the toil for accumulated possessions. The passages in which he dismisses such labor are melodious with the music of sadness, capable of vast dilation, but adequate in themselves.

No one, he now says, king or commoner, takes the results of his toil with him, or has any assurance that what he leaves, whether a realm or an estate, will be wisely administered by his successor. Some commentators argue from this that Koheleth had ample estates but no children, and knew that what he had toiled for with wisdom, i.e., with knowledge or success, would be enjoyed—maybe wasted—by someone who had never lifted a hand for it. The suggestion at least reveals some knowledge of human nature. It takes considerable grace for men of possessions to look upon their heirs with complete confidence. Consider how many estates are left "in trust." The heirs too often begin to appraise the family property before the incumbent is dead. The concentration of life effort upon gains and possessions is often terribly devastating. Too often the possessor bequeaths to his heirs only litigations and estrangements, even though the "dead hand" may extend its administrative controls beyond the grave.

George Frederic Watts painted a king upon his bier with the baubles of his pride and his power on the floor beside him, and above him in dim letters: "What I spent I had, what I saved I lost, what I gave I have"[1]—and that says it all.

21. Enduring Bequests.—There are, of course, dimensions in which all this is changed. Wisdom, knowing that material possessions end at the grave, will make use of them in such a way

[9] Quoted by André Maurois, *The Edwardian Era* (New York: D. Appleton-Century Co., 1933), p. 116.

[1] M. S. Watts, *George Frederic Watts* (London: Macmillan & Co., 1912), II, 190.

yet to a man that hath not labored therein shall he leave it *for* his portion. This also *is* vanity and a great evil.

22 For what hath man of all his labor, and of the vexation of his heart, wherein he hath labored under the sun?

23 For all his days *are* sorrows, and his travail grief; yea, his heart taketh not rest in the night. This is also vanity.

who has toiled with wisdom and knowledge and skill must leave all to be enjoyed by a man who did not toil for it. This also is vanity and a great evil. 22 What has a man from all the toil and strain with which he toils beneath the sun? 23 For all his days are full of pain, and his work is a vexation; even in the night his mind does not rest. This also is vanity.

---

of this **great evil** in human affairs. There is no law of exact and balanced justice, giving to each person, and securing for him only, that which he **has toiled** [for] **with wisdom and knowledge and skill.** Life reveals that the fruits of a man's hard work, of the **strain**— lit., "the striving of his heart," or perhaps "the cogitation of his mind"—of restless days and sleepless nights, fall into the lap of another as **his portion.** "Then whose shall those things be, which thou hast provided?" (Luke 12:20.) This disconcerting thought, the discovery that an irrational and arbitrary element lies at the very basis of human life, brings to the highly individualistic mind of Koheleth a feeling of deep despair.

---

as to help and bless others. The really wise make what they own subservient to their spiritual needs, and loving and trusting their children will be glad that something of what they have gained has been won for those who will succeed them.

Happily, Koheleth was spared the necessity of moralizing on inheritance taxes. Had he contemplated a society in which so much of what a man earns with a reasonable wisdom would be taken by the state for the cost of past, present, and future wars, even his capacity for sardonic statement would have been strained.

There are bequests the wise and good leave behind them which cannot be appraised. Many whose estates were otherwise negligible have left the world its songs, its treasures of art, the wealth of its literature. They knew that what they did was too precious for monopoly. They knew the secret of the treasures which increase by being shared, and though they often "toiled terribly," as genius does, they never thought their labor **vanity.** These have been the elect, the richly gifted. But there have also been the loving and the good, who, though they leave no memorial behind them, leave tender memories. Their influence has become part of our general human treasure, and so endures. It is the wise order of our mysterious lives that we cannot take with us what belongs to an order we are born to transcend.

"Lay not up for yourself treasures upon earth," said Jesus. For Koheleth death is final. All that he says is limited by the horizons of mortality. A faith in immortality would have changed all his evaluations. Then he would have known that there are treasures of the soul which can be stored where moth and rust do not

consume nor thieves break through and steal (Matt. 6:19-20).

22-24. The Resource of Labor.—Our tasks, Emerson thought, are our life preservers. Koheleth is not so sure. Dr. Richard C. Cabot called labor one of the four resources of life.[2] But apart from implications in the book of Proverbs, there would seem to be comparatively little recognition in the O.T. of the creative role which our daily work plays. For Ecclesiastes it is always **toil,** with its accompanying weariness and frustration. Even if we succeed, everything eventually slips from our nerveless hands. There is one little gleam in vs. 24: **There is nothing better . . . than that he should . . . enjoy good in his labor**—get a little pleasure out of it; apparently, however, largely because it makes him hungry enough to eat, thirsty enough to drink, tired enough to sleep. There is nowhere at all any recognition of its social value.

Here is a challenge which the Christian should and can meet. The shadow of the old sentence that a man should earn his bread by the sweat of his brow still lies darkly across our whole conception of labor, social and economic. The subject is almost hopelessly complicated. Divisions of responsibility which doom a workman to do no more than tighten a nut or two which the assembly line carries past him have done too much to make the task monotonous, to take away the joy of craftsmanship. No wonder labor demands shorter hours and higher pay, too often turning from daily work to the excitement of sterile pleasures. How many men and women do what they must, without ever finding the joy of congenial work, which is surely

[2] See *What Men Live By* (Boston: Houghton Mifflin Co., 1914).

24 ¶ *There is* nothing better for a man, *than* that he should eat and drink, and *that* he should make his soul enjoy good in his labor. This also I saw, that it *was* from the hand of God.

25 For who can eat, or who else can hasten *hereunto,* more than I?

26 For *God* giveth to a man that *is* good in his sight, wisdom, and knowledge, and joy: but to the sinner he giveth travail, to gather and to heap up, that he may give to *him that is* good before God. This also *is* vanity and vexation of spirit.

24 There is nothing better for a man than that he should eat and drink, and find enjoyment in his toil. This also, I saw, is from the hand of God; 25 for apart from him*d* who can eat or who can have enjoyment? 26 For to the man who pleases him God gives wisdom and knowledge and joy; but to the sinner he gives the work of gathering and heaping, only to give to one who pleases God. This also is vanity and a striving after wind.

d Gk Syr: Heb *apart from me*

24-26. In facing and recognizing the facts of life, Koheleth adjusts his mind to them and for the first time enunciates the view that the best response a man can make to the circumstances of existence is to accept life's conditions and to take what **enjoyment** he can out of it. This enjoyment is temporary and fugitive, but in the time to which it belongs it is present and real (cf. vs. 10). It is a gift of God, and **apart from him** no man can have it. The gift does not depend upon any moral qualities a man may possess, but entirely upon the favor of God. Koheleth concludes on a highly ironic note by saying that God indeed gives to the man whom he favors the power and means of enjoyment, while to others he gives the business of **gathering and heaping** for his favorites.

24. The M.T., along with the best MSS of the LXX, reads, "It is not good on man's part that he should eat. . . ." The KJV and RSV emendation accords with 3:12, 22; 8:15; and with the supposition, generally accepted, that the Hebrew letter ם was accidentally dropped after באדם.

25. **Can have enjoyment:** This verb may be related to the Arabic word *hassa,* meaning "to experience" or "to feel," and is preferable to **hasten. Apart from him** (so LXX) emends the M.T., "apart from me," "except myself" (cf. **more than I**).

26. The interpretation of this verse is of much importance for the understanding of the thought of the author. Koheleth contrasts with **the sinner** "the man who is good [*ṭôbh*] before [God]," i.e., **who pleases him,** and this comparison has been held to imply a moral distinction between the persons contrasted. Odeberg, who takes this view, further explains that the sinner must pass on his "good" to the "good," for only the latter can enjoy it. Koheleth-Solomon, however, has described himself as heaping up for the benefit of another the fruits of his labor, and has thus put himself into the sinner class—but not on moral grounds, because were this the case he could not have represented the particular feature of life of which he complains as a **great evil** or a great wrong. The word חוטא,

one of the high resources of life. Much of the fundamental discontent of our industrial civilization grows out of just this. Koheleth's feeling about toil is all around us.

The Christian church must find an answer, reinterpret the resource of labor. There was a time, a poet thought, when men sang as they labored. We need to hear that music again.

24-26. *What Is Left?*—In striving to find the meanings and values of life, the writer has examined wisdom, pleasure, power, and toil. His conclusions are here, plain to read. Life is "an unhappy business" (1:13) in which every road is a dead-end street. What then shall a man do? For the first time he raises that crucial

question, upon the answer to which so much depends. We wait almost breathlessly for what he has to say. To a degree, it has already been anticipated. There has been so far no call to the "hero in the soul," or any summons to change a sorry for a better business. There is no intimation of any real road of escape from his fog of futilities, save two: The first is acceptance of it all with a maximum of resignation and a minimum of complaint. There may be undertones of resignation in Koheleth's mournful numbers; there is certainly no parsimony of complaint. Otherwise we should not have his book. The other alternative is a quest for compensation. Perhaps one may call it that,

3 To every *thing there is* a season, and a time to every purpose under the heaven:

3 For everything there is a season, and a time for every matter under heaven:

---

sinner, bears in vs. 26 a sense directly opposed to the other term in the comparison—the man who **is good before God**—which is by most understood as meaning "the man whom God favors." Hence **the sinner** signifies the man with whom God is displeased (so Volz and Hertzberg; also Galling), a sense which the word bears in 7:26, where the same contrast again occurs. In regard to the phrase, **good before God,** it must be observed that *ṭóbh* (**good**) seldom has an ethical meaning in the O.T. (see G. A. Barton, *A Critical and Exegetical Commentary on the Book of Ecclesiastes* [New York: Charles Scribner's Sons, 1908; "International Critical Commentary"], p. 96). Koheleth therefore does not employ the contrast as expressing a moral judgment. As death does not distinguish between the just and the unjust, neither does life in the distribution of its gifts. D. B. Macdonald (*The Hebrew Literary Genius* [Princeton: Princeton University Press, 1933], p. 204) relates the Exeg. of vs. 26 to the conception of Koheleth regarding God by the statement, "For Ecclesiastes, then, there are two norms as to conduct: an absolute moral norm which he [Koheleth] himself has and applies, and a very relative norm as to what pleases or displeases God." In his use of the absolute norm Koheleth finds, says Macdonald, "that 'God' does not pay any attention to it," but that the rule for success in life is that man should conform to the caprice of this Being, and change when that caprice changes.

Vs. 26 has been held to be an addition made by the *ḥāṣídh,* i.e., the pious glossator, who has elsewhere added to the book words or sentences in defense of the doctrine of divine retribution. But if the above interpretation is correct, the teaching of a moral retribution is not contained in the verse. The irony of Koheleth's verdict on life must not be missed. In this verse in particular it is obvious that he has his tongue in his cheek. Furthermore, vs. 26 exhibits very close contact with the Egyptian wisdom teaching. The same thought in practically the same words appears in the inscription on the tomb of Petosiris (see Intro., p. 16), and this contact suggests that vs. 26 is not from a glossator's hand but belongs to the original fabric of the book.

D. Futility of Human Effort (3:1-15)
1. A Season for Everything (3:1-8)

3:1. Volz translates the words **for everything there is a season** as, "everything is under inexorable law." This is an appropriate rendering since the Hebrew verb, to which the late word *zemān* (**season**) corresponds, and which is used passively in Ezra 10:14 and Neh. 10:35, signifies "to be fixed," "to be appointed." The term *'ēth,* translated **time** throughout the poem, has as its root meaning the significance of "occurrence" (H. Wheeler Robinson, *Inspiration and Revelation in the Old Testament* [Oxford:

---

though it is really more. Here for the first time is the appearance of what many scholars have believed to be Koheleth's philosophy. They call it a kind of Epicureanism. In a sentence, the object of life is a sensible and moderate enjoyment of whatever one can enjoy. Since all this is literally woven through the whole book, comment may be reserved; but here is the first and rather colorless statement of it. Blocked down the high road, one is to take the low road, **eat and drink,** and though toiling, enjoy oneself as best one can—which is quite different from finding joy in one's task.

Food and drink are homely blessings, but they are good. The man whose bread is consecrated by the labor of earning it may say, "Give

us this day our daily bread," and thank God for hunger and for food. They too are from God's hand. As are also the pleasures of sense. Paul said as much centuries later: "Whether you eat or drink, . . . do all to the glory of God" (I Cor. 10:31). So is sense lifted above the dust, and food becomes a sacrament. This Koheleth sees for a moment; but then the vision is lost.

3:1-8. *To Everything Its Season.*—These verses are a kind of chant, whose rhythm is probably partially lost in translation, famous and often quoted. Its meanings are what commentators make them—or else the reader. They are as spacious as life, as entangled as experience. Their music may be a dirge or a muted Te Deum. They may urge us to wisdom in the

2 A time to be born, and a time to die; a time to plant, and a time to pluck up *that which is* planted; **3** A time to kill, and a time to heal; a time to break down, and a time to build up; **4** A time to weep, and a time to laugh; a time to mourn, and a time to dance;	**2** a time to be born, and a time to die; a time to plant, and a time to pluck up what is planted; **3** a time to kill, and a time to heal; a time to break down, and a time to build up; **4** a time to weep, and a time to laugh; a time to mourn, and a time to dance;

Clarendon Press, 1946], pp. 106-22). So if there is any distinction intended, as seems probable, between the words *zemān* and *'ēth*, the author implies by the use of the former term that whatever occurs has been determined or fixed by God.

It is not the purpose of Koheleth in this poem to encourage the cultivation of a wise and prudent opportunism, to declare that there is a proper time when a man should perform certain actions, that he should "buy up the time" or utilize the right moment for doing particular things. That is a thought to which Koheleth gives due importance elsewhere (cf. 8:5-6; 11:9; 12:1); but the poem itself is not at all concerned with the practical prudence of taking advantage of the hour when the sun shines.

As a record of Koheleth's teaching, the theme of the poem is as significant as 1:2-11, to which it is closely related in thought. World history is a cycle of events and of their opposites which occur in endless repetition. Against this stream of events of a dual order, ordained by God, man can do nothing. He is hedged around and bound in everywhere by a stern necessity. Man of course can toil and have pleasure in his toil (2:10, 24), and accept the glint of joy which God gives him in its time, but on the whole his work is ineffectual, profitless (vs. 9), as he is powerless over against the fixed and prescribed happenings of existence. It must also be noted that the poem does not refer to the works of God in creation or in the maintenance of the world order, but to the various activities with which human life is concerned. This has the further effect of exhibiting

timing of our enterprises, that we may know when to seize the opportunity, feel for the opening door; or when to conclude that the door will not open, that there is nothing to do but to wait or to knock elsewhere. They may supply a basis for patient courage—"Do not be discouraged, the right time will come"; or they may involve us in a web of fatalism, since every issue and every action is controlled by a Power beyond ourselves who has fixed us in a vast and rigid pattern.

Let all that go for the moment. Consider first the fascinating variety of strings upon which Koheleth plays his music. This, from a literary point of view, is part of the fascination of his book. They are all within the range of human endeavor and response. Here is what men do or leave undone. The passage pulses with the writer's joy in his own composition. He is captured by his own fecundity, and possibly by his own ingenuity. It was not easy to think of all these things and their proper antitheses. The obscurity of some of the lines is puzzling.

Vss. 1-8, says the Exeg., "represent the things that have constantly to be done in the round of life's duties"; one might well add, "as Koheleth saw them." The omissions are as significant as

the things written. Nevertheless, the passage has a restrained majesty of movement, as though the river of life were two currents flowing between the same banks. There is a current of permission, so to speak, and a stream of prohibition. It is a part of the wisdom of life to know where to catch the flowing tide and not to waste hope and effort on what cannot—at that time at least—be done.

> There is a tide in the affairs of men,
> Which, taken at the flood, leads on to fortune;
> Omitted, all the voyage of their life
> Is bound in shallows and in miseries.[3]

Less rhetorically said, good timing is one of the sovereign conditions of success, from golf to a *coup d'état,* from planting potatoes to charting a course for the ship of state.

One may, if he pleases, find here also some suggestion of the rich varieties of experience; that there is a time in life for loss as well as gain, for tears as well as laughter. So warned, the wise will, in accepting the shining side of life, anticipate the inevitability of its shadows.

2-8. Events Fixed and Predetermined?—But all this, they tell us, was not in Koheleth's mind

[3] Shakespeare, *Julius Caesar,* Act IV, scene 3.

5 A time to cast away stones, and a time to gather stones together; a time to embrace, and a time to refrain from embracing;

6 A time to get, and a time to lose; a time to keep, and a time to cast away;

7 A time to rend, and a time to sew; a time to keep silence, and a time to speak;

8 A time to love, and a time to hate; a time of war, and a time of peace.

5 a time to cast away stones, and a time to gather stones together;
  a time to embrace, and a time to refrain from embracing;
6 a time to seek, and a time to lose;
  a time to keep, and a time to cast away;
7 a time to rend, and a time to sew;
  a time to keep silence, and a time to speak;
8 a time to love, and a time to hate;
  a time for war, and a time for peace.

how helpless and hopeless man is, since in the very things in which he is a participant he can do nothing against the necessity which governs him and his life. **For every matter under heaven** there is an occasion. Everything occurs when it must occur. There appears to be no place where man's freedom may exercise itself. Not only man's planting (vs. 2) and other operations, but even his very inmost emotions, his loves and his hatreds (vs. 8; cf. 9:1), are products of a universal necessity. Man is not a free agent. He is not master even of his life within. There is no thought in Ecclesiastes that history (e.g., the Exodus) has or had a redemptive purpose. Indeed, the personality of the Deity appears to be reduced almost to the vanishing point.

The list of activities mentioned represents the things that have constantly to be done in the round of life's duties. Each action is associated with its antithesis.

5. The Midrash Qoheleth Rabbah explains **a time to cast away stones** as a metaphor implying the act of marital intercouse, and **a time to gather stones** as meaning that there is a time for refraining from this act. The rest of the verse would seem to support this interpretation, and Williams, among others, accepts it as probably correct.

7. **To rend** is thought by some to refer to the ritual act of tearing the clothing in times of sorrow or mourning (cf. Gen. 37:29-34). Hence, in the parallel line, **to keep**

at all. The Exeg.—and there is no reason to question it—sees life, according to the Preacher, as a series of mixed and predetermined events. They are already there, as waymarks, along the roads we travel. As we go on we meet them at the appointed hour. The problem of the fatalist —if this is fatalism—has always been to correlate what is waiting for us with our being there, at the right place and at the right time. If Koheleth is right, there is a sequence of occasions perfectly timed to the paces of our life journey. How far we individually agree with all this depends. But as with the lengthening years a man travels in retrospect the roads of life, often he has a strange, a haunting sense, of having met the appointed, stage by stage. When the time had come, it was there and waiting, and he himself, being how and what he was, accepted it and wrought it into the texture of his life. He had no alternative.

For one school of philosophy this is indeed fatalism, with all its implications and all its difficulties; but fatalism may do many things to the fatalist. He may abandon hope and accept supinely what he believes he cannot escape. He may make his fatalism an alibi—"I had no other choice." Or he may accept its challenge and keep proud step with destiny. It may even furnish him with a paradoxical courage. "If my name is on the bullet, it will find me; if not, I am safe"; and so he flies his plane into the jaws of death. The theologian calls it predestination, the complete subordination of all the ways of life and the issues of destiny to the sovereign will of God. The awesome splendor of that conception captured Paul and Augustine and John Calvin. Multitudes have rested in its assurances and wrestled with its problems. Some have found in it a courage to sustain them against embattled opposition; others, among them women and children, the temerity to face martyrdom with psalms on their lips.

Tennyson said of his exquisite cantos in *In Memoriam*, that they were like the flight of swallows which dipped their wings in tears—and were gone. But there were always depths beneath his singing lines. Ecclesiastes, one can never stop noting, has the same quality. If in this passage he is saying that the rhythm of life is predetermined, then by what or whom? Is "everyman's life a plan of God"? The book never says in so many plain words that it **is.**

9 What profit hath he that worketh in that wherein he laboreth?

10 I have seen the travail, which God hath given to the sons of men to be exercised in it.

9 What gain has the worker from his toil?

10 I have seen the business that God has given to the sons of men to be busy with.

---

silence has been regarded as referring to silent sorrow (cf. Lev. 10:3) but, as Hertzberg rightly points out, silence is by no means a general sign of sorrow. The actions mentioned in the poem are more suitably viewed as purposely representing activities of the most general character, not as emphasizing any particular aspect of their application.

2. FUTILITY OF HUMAN STRIVING (3:9-15)

9. If the actions of a man are bereft of freedom because his every act or thought is dictated by a will power that is outside him, what value can those actions have, what is the use of human striving? To this question the answer that man's toil is of no real worth is implied. Koheleth then draws five conclusions from the doctrine which he has stated, and these are set forth respectively in vss. 10, 11, 12-13, 14, and 15.

10. The activities mentioned in the preceding poem have the merit, or at least the effect, of keeping man occupied. H. H. Graetz (*Kohelét* [Leipzig: C. Winter, 1871], p. 70) rightly observes that the words **I have seen the business** ["occupations"] **that God has given** are an inversion for such a sentence as "I have seen that God has given to the sons of men this business that they may be busied [Graetz and Hertzberg understand "plagued"] therewith." The author may, however, only intend to say that he has seen (or examined) the task (*'inyān*) which God has given man to be occupied with, viz., that of considering the problem which vss. 1-8 set. Practically the same sentence appears in 1:13, where man has the "unhappy business" or task of searching out by wisdom "all that is done under heaven."

It does say over and over that the travail of life is God imposed. We live and move and have our being in an appointed pattern too vast and entangled for us to understand, in which

> Our little systems have their day;
> They have their day and cease to be.[4]

Wisdom says in substance that our adjustment to the pattern is the test of our wisdom or our folly; which assumes, though the wisdom literature does not raise the question, a sufficient freedom of choice and consequent responsibility. That, however, seems beyond the province of Ecclesiastes. Koheleth is always more sure of entanglement than he is of deliverance. For him constantly a fog blows in from the sea and the far horizons never clear and his expositors do not escape them. The attempt to resolve the problem of human freedom and accountability, set over against the divine sovereignty, has engendered vast controversy and never reached finality. The true reconciliations are in life itself. We know our freedom and our limitations.

> Our wills are ours, we know not how;
> Our wills are ours, to make them thine.[5]

[4] Tennyson, *In Memoriam*, Prologue, st. v.
[5] *Ibid.*, st. iv.

Without a divine "thine" in life, its fogs are impenetrable. Without an "ours" in life, we have no place in a moral order, we hear no call from the heights of love and goodness.

Christian faith transcends philosophies and theologies. It rests in the "will of God." It sings "my life is portioned out to me," and therein finds peace and victorious resignation, because it believes that the portioning is love's assignment, and that in all things God does work together for good with them that love him—always reserving the one essential fact which so easily escapes us, that we too possess a power to make all things work together for good by the spirit in which we deal with them. For they are also plastic beneath our touch, and of them, God appointed if you will, we make the splendor or the shame of life. We do, Christian faith believes, keep step with a vaster purpose than our own, but it leaves us free enough to choose or to avoid. It affirms what entirely escapes Koheleth, *that in the alembic of the soul there is a power to transform experience.* The Christian may therefore with the Preacher stress the wisdom which knows the right occasion, moralize upon the swift passage of time, and warn with discretion that when the opportunity is past it may not come again, almost certainly not in the same form. But he will maintain, as he must,

11 He hath made every *thing* beautiful in his time: also he hath set the world in their heart, so that no man can find out the work that God maketh from the beginning to the end.

11 He has made everything beautiful in its time; also he has put eternity into man's mind, yet so that he cannot find out what God has done from the beginning to the

---

11. Each event in life "comes in a setting into which it fits" (Macdonald, *Hebrew Literary Genius,* p. 214), but God has, by a limitation of man's power, made it impossible for men to comprehend the whole of his purpose. This is the most disputed verse in Ecclesiastes. Its interpretation depends on the meaning of the word העלם, vocalized by the Masoretes as *hā'ôlām.* God, states Koheleth, **has made everything beautiful**—an allusion to Gen. 1:3, 12, 25, 31—in its time. The exact quality of the word translated **beautiful** may range from the idea of good to that of excellence, of that which is proper to that which is appropriate. Each event fits into its appointed place. "Also," continues the writer, God "has put *hā'ôlām* into man's [Hebrew, into their] heart [or mind]." What does *hā'ôlām* mean? The following explanations have been given:

(*a*) The world: The meaning given by Ewald and a number of scholars was that man's heart or mind is a microcosm in which the great world is reflected. Volz also translates, "God has set the whole world in their mind." Against this interpretation it is often urged that *hā'ôlām* does not appear anywhere else in the O.T. in the sense of **world,** and is first found in this sense in postbiblical Hebrew (Pirke Aboth 4:7). But since the Hebrew of Ecclesiastes differs very sharply from that of the other O.T. books, and since several words in Ecclesiastes are found nowhere else in the O.T.—e.g., *'inyān=* "task," "business," a common expression in Koheleth's language and in postbiblical speech—this argument has no weight whatever. But it must be confessed that the notion of putting or setting the world in man's mind is harsh in expression and difficult to conceive. The amplifications of the word "world" which seek to remove this difficulty are "worldliness," "love of the world" (see H. L. Ginsberg, *Studies in Koheleth* [New York: Jewish Theological Seminary of America, 1950], *ad loc.,* and Robert Gordis, *The Wisdom of Ecclesiastes* [New York: Behrman House, 1945], p. 52). The Vulg. translation is most interesting as it shows that the Hebrew MS on which it is based differed from the M.T. It renders thus: *et mundum tradidit disputationi eorum=*"also [God] has handed over the world to their [man's] contention," which means that instead of reading (as M.T.) בלבם, **in their** [man's] **heart,** it read לרבם—cf. Job 31:13, "for their strife or contention."

The Hebrew MS or MSS which the Vulg. used had a text which at least makes good sense and suits the sardonic quality of Koheleth's mind. God has made every single event fit its occasion and has given, or handed over, to the sons of men the world, which is the sum total of all events and of all God's works, for their contending, in order that they may never grasp God's purpose (cf. the similar motif in Gen. 3:22). The strife

---

that we have the power to weave out of the checkered warp and woof of life a pattern of faith and courage, and he will know that the weaver may profit from his toil.

11. Eternity in the Heart.—There are texts in the Bible which have the right through certain great qualities to stand alone. They have their contexts; they are proper parts of the pattern of their writers' minds, and it is the proper business of the biblical scholar so to relate them. But they dominate all the approaches to them. They are like mountain peaks which rest upon some continental divide, but which, seen against the skyline, detach themselves from all that supports them. Such texts have an unsurpassed

value, as much for their majesty as for their mystery. **He has put eternity into man's mind** is one of these texts—one of the greatest. It has a sovereign power to stand alone, and so taken, is sufficient in itself.

The context carries on. The occupations chanted in the recitative of vss. 1-8 are God-given occupations. Each one is right in its time, no one is sufficient in itself. They are in their sequences parts of a vaster order. They belong to the successions of time. They are the beats of the pendulum, measuring out the ways and will of God; fugitive as the moments, they measure and still measure out eternity. Behind a time to speak and a time to keep silence, and

among men we must conceive of as being about God's purpose in history and nature, which man can never discover in its entirety, **from the beginning to the end.** Or possibly the last phrase is intended to signify that man can never know God's purpose at all (cf. 8:17).

(b) Eternity: In Hebrew thought, says Johannes Pedersen (*Israel, Its Life and Culture I-II* [London: Oxford University Press, 1926], pp. 490-91), history consists of all the generations of men and their experiences fused into a great whole and "this concentrated time, into which all generations are fused, and from which they spring, is called eternity." To this Robinson (*op. cit.*, p. 121) adds that the predominant sense of 'ôlām is "of the permanent or continuous in contrast with the fragmentary 'times.' " This being so, Koheleth may have said that God has made everything excellent in its own proper time and has placed in man's heart (i.e., mind) a conception of the sum total of the "times," but in such a way that man cannot understand the work which God does from beginning to end (Grimm's interpretation, adopted by A. H. McNeile, *An Introduction to Ecclesiastes* [Cambridge: Cambridge University Press, 1904], pp. 62, 99). This view thus expressed is better than that of Wildeboer and Hertzberg, who do not define **eternity** in terms of time but give it a spiritual quality. According to Gerrit Wildeboer (*Die fünf Megillot* [Leipzig: J. C. B. Mohr, 1898; "Kurzer Hand-Commentar zum Alten Testament"], *ad. loc.*), Koheleth here speaks of "the divine quality which God has placed in man, [and] probably thinks of the image of God in which man is made in Gen. 1:26-27." This latter thought would be highly inconsistent with the rest of Koheleth's thinking. But even against the explanation given by Grimm and McNeile, in which eternity is not given a false content, the objections may be brought that (i) **eternity** is explained as the conception or notion of eternity which God has put into man's mind, i.e., the word requires an amplification to make it acceptable; and (ii) since the notion of **eternity** would not incapacitate man's mind in any way, the conjunction which introduces the final clause—*mibbelî 'asher lô*'; Vulg., *ut non;* LXX, ὅπως μὴ; i.e., "so that [in order that] not"—is interpreted as meaning "yet [or only] so that not" or "yet in such a way that [man can] not." Both these objections considerably weaken this interpretation. But both are removed if the Vulg. reading "for their strife" is accepted. The sentence would then mean either that God has given men eternity, i.e., all time, for their strife or has given them as subject for their strife the aggregate of the "times" and of the experiences of the generations of men. In this last significance it makes little difference whether we interpret *hā'ôlām* as "eternity" or as "the world." As Pedersen (*loc. cit.*) says, 'ôlām is "history and thus the world as a compact whole."

---

all the other times, there is the intimation of the timeless—man's intuition and God's revelation. **He has put eternity into man's mind.**

We are the latest born children of time, but its allotments have never been enough for us. From the dim dawn of religious faith life has sought beyond our seen and temporal horizons the unseen horizons of the eternal. It is a quest as old as the sepulchers in which the dead were buried with their faces turned to greet the dawn of another life. It is as old as the first altars of sod or stone, where the sacrifices were shared by the departed. Why? Whence the faith?

There are endless answers. But the answer which includes them all is that we have never accepted our time-limited estates as final, as enough. Something within us wants more time and presses against the limits of the finite to reach the infinite, something which claims as its birthright "the wages of going on." Faith in im-

mortality thus evoked is more than a desire for continued existence—which might become a wearing weariness. It is the desire for another dimension of existence, a dimension of fulfillment and assuagement; a dimension sufficient for the needs of love and the challenge of truth; sufficient for us to become the selves we were meant to be, for the continuity of dear comradeship, and the prophetic hunger of human hearts. The sense of the eternal is ours from the sources from which our very being is drawn; God **has put eternity into man's mind**—and **heart.**

This it is which lifts us above the dust, invests all the enterprises of life with their right significance, saves us from surrender to the unworthy, assures us in seasons of distress, and washes life with a light from beyond the hills of time. When the sense of eternity, with all its implications, has faded out of the minds of men,

(c) An aspect of eternity: (i) The future (Siegfried); (ii) hidden time, i.e., past and future (Blieffert); (iii) eternity as "the permanence or continuity of God's work . . . in contrast with the transitory beauty of the time-content" (Robinson, *op. cit.*, p. 122; Robinson suggests that **in their heart** may mean not in the heart of men but "in their midst"; cf. Exod. 15:8; etc.).

(d) Other interpretations rest upon slight emendations of the M.T.: (i) God put in man's heart (mind) knowledge (*'elem* from Arabic *'ilm,* suggested by Hitzig, *et al.,* but it is doubtful whether in Hebrew this word existed); (ii) mystery (*ta'alûmāh* or *'élem,* Allgeier, Moffatt); (iii) that which veils (*hā'ôlēm,* Haupt); (iv) the sign (from Arabic *'alam,* J. E. C. Schmidt); (v) to refrain from searching (*lehith 'allēm,* Ehrlich); (vi) the desire to search out all that is hidden (*hā'ālûm,* Bickell); (vii) toil (*he'āmāl,* Macdonald [*Hebrew Literary Genius,* pp. 202, 206]: "God put 'toil' in man's mind in order that man might not be able to understand God's working as a whole. [Man] must keep on working, at one thing or another, and so God has secured that He Himself and His doings . . . should remain a mystery." This suggestion finds support in vs. 10, especially as interpreted above); (viii) ignorance, forgetfulness (*hā'élem,* Coverdale, Graetz, Barton).

In favor of *hā'élem,* especially in the sense of forgetfulness, several arguments may be adduced: (a) This reading represents no change in the form which the Hebrew text had before it received, in the course of the centuries, the Masoretic vocalization. (b) It allows the conjunction of the final clause to be understood in what is without doubt its true meaning, viz., "so that [or in order that] not." (c) In the inscription on the tomb of Petosiris (see Intro., p. 16) a sentence speaks of the action of God upon the human heart to make it forgetful, "There is no one who knows the day when [death] will come. It is the work of God to make the heart forgetful" (Gustave Lefèbvre, *Le tombeau de Petosiris* [Le Caire: Imprimerie de l'Institut Français d'Archéologie Orientale, 1924], I, 161). Also in the "Instruction of Ptahhotep" (Erman, *Literature of the Ancient Egyptians,* p. 55), which describes the infirmity of old age as this affects the various members of the body. It is said that the heart "is forgetful and remembereth not yesterday." Thus there appears in two wisdom passages, with which the affinity of thought with Ecclesiastes is very marked, this association of forgetfulness with the heart. (d) Koheleth himself (1:11) speaks of forgetfulness—the lack of remembrance—which is a severe limitation of man's powers and of life's value in that it destroys the link binding the generations of the past, the present, and the future. (e) If the expression **in their heart** is retained (as against the evidence of the Vulg.), the emendation *hā'élem* gives

---

they have lost their birthright and may well sink to lower levels than the beasts which never had it.

So much the passage seems to say, if one sees it as a mountain peak against the sky—standing alone. As the Exeg. explores alternative translations or tries to fit it into the context, it becomes unexpectedly difficult. At any rate, in the translation here used, Koheleth sets up a warning sign. We possess only a limited sense of eternity—yet so that [we] **cannot find out what God has done from the beginning to the end.** Persuasion of the eternal is still veiled with mystery. The ways of God, though timeless, are beyond our knowing. Surely that should keep us humble. This in substance is also Moffatt's translation; and it seems more than defensible: true to Koheleth's text, truer still to his mind, as he seeks to find some answer to the riddles of life and is baffled by them; most of all, true to our

pilgrimage through time. We have only to reach out our hands and touch the trailing veils of mystery. Even a piece of wood is not what it seems. In our seasons of profoundest insight we are mysteries to ourselves. It is better so. The charm of any far horizon, whether on land or sea, is in what still lies beyond it. Where there is no mystery, where we see the end from the beginning, there is no challenge, nor any place for the imagination, nor—to put it more nobly —any room for faith or hope.

We know more now of God's ways than Koheleth knew. We have in stone the record of geological epochs whose beginnings, durations, and endings stagger the imagination. We have charted the skies and measured celestial distances in light years. We have traced a little the long, long ascent of man; but there are undeciphered pages enough to fill us with awe, veiled in mystery.

12 I know that *there is* no good in them, but for *a man* to rejoice, and to do good in his life.

13 And also that every man should eat and drink, and enjoy the good of all his labor, it *is* the gift of God.

14 I know that, whatsoever God doeth, it shall be for ever: nothing can be put to it, nor any thing taken from it: and God doeth *it*, that *men* should fear before him.

15 That which hath been is now; and that which is to be hath already been; and God requireth that which is past.

end. 12 I know that there is nothing better for them than to be happy and enjoy themselves as long as they live; 13 also that it is God's gift to man that every one should eat and drink and take pleasure in all his toil. 14 I know that whatever God does endures for ever; nothing can be added to it, nor anything taken from it; God has made it so, in order that men should fear before him. 15 That which is, already has been; that which is to be, already has been; and God seeks what has been driven away.

---

the most probable interpretation. The thought in this case is that God has made everything excellent in its time, but as he has placed in man's heart the inability to remember and record all the generations of human history as well as the events and experiences pertaining thereto, God's work and purpose from beginning to end—i.e., in their entirety—remain to man forever incomprehensible and inexplicable.

12. The only good thing in human experience is the element of enjoyment such as comes to a man from his food, his drink, and his work. (The true emphasis of vs. 12 is obtained from the literal translation: "I know that there is no good thing for [men] except . . . .")

13. The means of enjoyment and the ability to enjoy are also God's gift (cf. 5:19), i.e., God's working, not anything that man can do for himself.

14. Man cannot alter anything in the eternal laws of God's world government and providence. The fixed and predestined character of all that happens serves the purpose of keeping man humble and in awe of God. The clause **God has made it so, in order that men should fear before him** is not to be regarded as an addition made by the pious glossator (McNeile), since it does not exhibit any concern for orthodox religious belief or for that reverence often described in the O.T. by the phrase "fear of Yahweh." The words express here an actual **fear**—if not indeed terror (Williams)—which compels acceptance and resignation.

15. Not only are all things determined by God, but all things are recurrent (Hertzberg). The last sentence, which runs, lit., "God seeks that which is pursued," has perplexed commentators and evidently was not understood by the LXX. But if the underlying idea is that each event pursued the other in a revolving circle (Barton), the sense

---

I dimly guess what Time in mists confounds;
Yet ever and anon a trumpet sounds
From the hid battlements of Eternity:
Those shaken mists a space unsettle, then
Round the half-glimpsèd turrets slowly wash again.[6]

But we have seen them, and we can go on.

12-15. *Two Answers to the Mystery of Life.*—What shall we do, we who have seen, "half-glimpsèd," the "hid battlements of Eternity"? Koheleth had his answer. Paul had another. Life is a mystery, says Ecclesiastes, its scales unbalanced, its issue futile. It has its laws and occasions, its seemingly rigid framework within

[6] Francis Thompson, "The Hound of Heaven." From *Collected Works*, ed. Wilfred Meynell. Used by permission of Burns Oates & Washbourne, Ltd., and The Newman Press, publishers.

which we live and move. The framework itself is like a wheel spinning on its axis with no tangential track to lay hold on. The past is always returning; we are forbidden fullness of knowledge. We do not know the harbors from which we set sail or "in what ports our frail barques are due." Eternity is in our hearts to haunt us with an incurable homesickness; but we have for action and understanding only the too brief present. Take therefore what happiness you can. Food and drink, labor and rest, are God's gifts to men. Forget the haunting sense of the eternal and seize the day. All this is as old as the sword of Damocles or the feasts of Egypt—with a skull on the table.

Paul also had eternity in his heart, and an equal sense of the veils of mystery which trail

16 ¶ And moreover I saw under the sun the place of judgment, *that* wickedness *was* there; and the place of righteousness, *that* iniquity *was* there.	16 Moreover I saw under the sun that in the place of justice, even there was wickedness, and in the place of righteousness, even there was wickedness. 17 I said in my heart,
17 I said in mine heart, God shall judge the righteous and the wicked: for *there is* a time there for every purpose and for every work.	God will judge the righteous and the wicked, for he has appointed[e] a time for
	e MT *there is a time there*

is that as given by the RSV. In stating his belief in the recurrence of events, Koheleth reverts to what he has said in 1:9-10, with more special reference to the recurrence of the acts and events of human history.

E. The Amorality of Natural Order (3:16–4:3)

"The proof that there is no moral world order but merely an order of nature to which both man and beast are subject" (Carl Siegfried, *Prediger und Hoheslied* [Göttingen: Vandenhoeck & Ruprecht, 1898; "Handkommentar zum Alten Testament"], p. 42).

16-18. In this world **justice** and **righteousness** are frustrated, and God manifests to man through man's experience of human injustice and **wickedness** that man is on the level of the beast.

17. Probably a gloss from the hand of a pious scribe who is zealous for the orthodox doctrine of divine retribution. This doctrine is not consistent with the thought of Koheleth, which is thoroughly deterministic. Also vs. 17 is an interruption of the sequence of thought in vss. 16, 18. The author of vs. 17, who announces judgment on the **righteous** and the **wicked,** can hardly be the same person who in vs. 18 says that men are **beasts** (Siegfried). Macdonald (*Hebrew Literary Genius*, p. 207) tries (see Intro., pp. 17-18) to save vs. 17 as Koheleth's property by affirming that it contains no moral condemnation, and that the idea of "judgment" as it appears in 3:17; 11:9 has nothing

---

around us. But he had a persuasion of its meaning for life that Ecclesiastes does not have. For him Jesus Christ had revealed the eternal, and Paul knew the qualities which belong to lives that have eternity in their hearts. "If ye then be risen with Christ, seek those things which are above" (Col. 3:1), which fit into the dimensions of the timeless—"whatsoever things are true, . . . lovely, . . . of good report, . . ." and so on to the end (Phil. 4:8). There is no vision in Ecclesiastes of an order in which our homesickness for the eternal can or will be satisfied. Paul and Koheleth had a common basis of observation, but their ways of dealing with experience are farther apart than are the east and the west.

There are certain summaries of Koheleth's "wisdom" which can be made here as well as anywhere else. His statements of that wisdom are recurrent throughout his book. We live in an ordered world, and have an appointed place in it. The defect is that this place is never ample enough. Everything is timeworn, but it cannot be renewed; for all its returnings, it never changes. All life's roads are dead-end streets. The key is always in the changing and inconsistent play of his sad spirit. One must not read too much between the lines. How far had the

writer shared the frustrations of which he writes? Was he only a shrewd observer, disillusioned by experience and age? It is not easy to say. On the whole, there is too much detachment in the book to suggest a writer who was at the time suffering very deeply, or whom the years had taught to see life steadily and whole. Job and Koheleth asked the same questions, but Job's questions are tremulous with the travail of his soul; and he found his answers in submission to the will of God, his hand to his mouth and his mouth to the dust. Koheleth found no answers; they lay beyond and above his horizons. But more incisively than Job he supplies the data for the problems with which both of them wrestled. There was to be a rising Light which neither of them foresaw.

16-22. *Muted Music.*—The element of repetition in Ecclesiastes, already noted, may be partially due to want of final organization in the writing, or to qualities of the writer's mind. But most of all, it is due to the limitations of the motif itself. If everything is futile, the effort to make a brave and heartening music of saying so is equally futile. Isaiah has his ch. 40; the Psalms praise the goodness of God in unforgettable strophes; Paul challenges all the heights

18 I said in mine heart concerning the estate of the sons of men, that God might manifest them, and that they might see that they themselves are beasts.

19 For that which befalleth the sons of men befalleth beasts; even one thing befalleth them: as the one dieth, so dieth the other; yea, they have all one breath; so that a man hath no preeminence above a beast: for all *is* vanity.

20 All go unto one place; all are of the dust, and all turn to dust again.

every matter, and for every work. 18 I said in my heart with regard to the sons of men that God is testing them to show them that they are but beasts. 19 For the fate of the sons of men and the fate of beasts is the same; as one dies, so dies the other. They all have the same breath, and man has no advantage over the beasts; for all is vanity. 20 All go to one place; all are from the dust,

---

of a moral character but signifies only the change involved in one event being followed by, and being canceled by, its opposite. But if Koheleth had drawn the conclusion that each event in the cycle of life was a "judgment" on its opposite—and this would also mean that unrighteousness was a "judgment" on righteousness—he would scarcely have left others to draw so important an inference into the light of day. Besides, the impression which 3:17 and 11:9 make upon the reader is that in these verses a religious moralist is uttering an earnest caveat.

19-20. Moreover, man has no superiority over the beast in respect of destiny since man and beast have the same fate—death and the dust which is their winding sheet (cf. Ps. 49:20; Gen. 2:7, 19; 3:19).

---

and depths which separate us from the love of God, and goes out victorious to meet the executioner's sword; and in Revelation those who come out of great tribulation are before the throne of God with palms in their hands. There is nothing of this in Ecclesiastes; only **All is vanity.**

If God brings back that which has passed away, Koheleth, who so continuously repeats what he has already said, is in no position to reproach divine Providence for its want of originality. Conduct and character, he feels, should make a difference in the issues of life. He cannot find that they do. Christian faith looks beyond the inequalities and seeming injustices of our temporal estate to the healings and recompenses of the life to come. The little span of earthly life is not spacious enough for what both love and justice demand. Browning's "Cleon" and Koheleth have this at least in common: Cleon, who also had so much, finds that the best life can give is not enough. But Cleon dares to hope for time and room beyond the sepulcher.

Koheleth had thought—may one read at least this much between his lines?—that there might be adjustments beyond the sepulcher, and he had too acute a mind not to see how completely that would compel him to recast his philosophy of futilities; but his faith was not winged enough to carry him over the grave. There is no difference between man and beast. Dust to dust for each. **Dust** in the O.T. is most often a symbol

of brevity and mortality, and so Koheleth uses it. The threnody of the Christian committal service does but echo Gen. 3:19: "Dust thou art, and unto dust shalt thou return." Ecclesiastes repeats it. Dust is equally the symbol of the fugitive and the inconsequential. Mourners scattered dust upon their heads and their garments, the humbled bowed themselves to the dust, and so on and on. For us dust is no longer only dust. It is promise and potency, something for a wheat field to turn into bread, or a rose into fragrant beauty. It may pulse with atomic energy, binding with its strong locks the mysteries of creation.

20-22. *The Corrections and Completions of Christian Faith.*—Christian faith does not believe that life is only a pilgrimage between two dusts. It may be, should be, a journey to "other heights in other lives, God willing," and the earthly stage of that pilgrimage may be invested with rare and radiant qualities. One of Koheleth's omissions—if it can be so called, for it is fundamental—is really the answer to his despair: what men may become as they go on. He never adequately considers the possible reactions of experience upon character and upon the soul; or most of all, what the soul can make of experience.

On some level or other every experience has meaning beyond itself; but that final meaning is never automatic or unconditioned: it is what by the grace of God and the interpreting and transmuting power of the human spirit we make

21 Who knoweth the spirit of man that goeth upward, and the spirit of the beast that goeth downward to the earth?

22 Wherefore I perceive that *there is* nothing better, than that a man should rejoice in his own works; for that *is* his por-

and all turn to dust again. 21 Who knows whether the spirit of man goes upward and the spirit of the beast goes down to the earth? 22 So I saw that there is nothing better than that a man should enjoy his work,

---

21. The LXX and other versions read this as a question, **Who knows whether the spirit of man goes upward?** But the KJV follows the Masoretic pointing of the text which (cf. also Hebrew of vs. 19) cannot be regarded as other than a dogmatic alteration of the sense. In vs. 21 there appears for the first time within a Jewish writing—besides the archaic stories of the translation of Enoch and Elijah—the idea of the ascent of the soul (or spirit) of man to heaven, apparently immediately after death, without intermediate resting in Sheol. For the influence at work here we must look not so much to Greek thought as to Mesopotamian astral religion, which held that the soul of man, partaking of the fiery nature of the stars, had come from the heights of heaven and thither would ascend after man's death. Koheleth rejects this view of immortality in favor of the ordinary Jewish belief of his time, which denied a personal existence after death. Koheleth accepted the fatalistic thought of the Oriental astral religion but rejected its hope (see O. S. Rankin, *Israel's Wisdom Literature* [Edinburgh: T. & T. Clark, 1936], pp. 138-41). In 12:7 Koheleth states that the spirit of man at death returns to God who gave it, while the body returns to the dust. But this return of the spirit to God must not be regarded as intending any such thing as a continuance of personality (cf. Paul Volz, *Weisheit* [Göttingen: Vandenhoeck & Ruprecht, 1911; "Die Schriften des Alten Testaments"], p. 241).

22. Thus human life as seen in this aspect leads Koheleth again to the verdict that the best which existence has to offer to man is the enjoyment to be found in **his own**

---

it. Only the supine ask if there is any, and failing to find the answer, surrender to the impulses and the currents of life. Tears may be turned into tenderness, a present defeat into an access of courage; the "patience of unanswered prayer" may enrich the spirit, the seemingly defeated may come from contested fields like a king returning from his wars.

> Only the actions of the just
> Smell sweet and blossom in their dust.[7]

The difference between a **man** and a **beast**, or between a Christian man and a beastly man, is not in the dust to which they both return, but in those qualities so far and far and far apart from the dust that Koheleth must have been blind not to see them. His feeling about life is essentially pagan, hence his sense of futility. Sophocles chanted Koheleth's creed in four lines:

> Never to be at all
> Excels all fame;
> Quickly, next best, to pass
> From whence we came.[8]

[7] James Shirley, *Contention of Ajax and Ulysses*, scene iii.

[8] *Oedipus at Colonus.*

William Knox said the same thing in a poem which Lincoln is reported to have quoted often:

> Oh why should the spirit of mortal be proud?
> . . . .
> For we are the same things that our fathers have been,
> We see the same sights that our fathers have seen,
> We drink the same stream, and we feel the same sun,
> And we run the same course that our fathers have run.[1]

Knox also might have been reading Ecclesiastes. The continuity of these attitudes across millenniums and lands testifies to deep and persistent rootings. Such moods may evoke humility. They are more likely to paralyze action. They must be met with a more penetrating vision, a nobler creative faith. To all this the Christian will oppose the affirmations of the gospel and the testimony of the communion of the saints.

Alternative translations of the last verses of the chapter change the overtones, but do not resolve the writer's perplexities. The destiny of the human spirit is for him in these passages involved in mystery. He will in the end affirm that the spirit returns to the God who gave it; but that access of faith is not here in evidence.

[1] "Mortality."

tion: for who shall bring him to see what shall be after him?

4 So I returned, and considered all the oppressions that are done under the sun: and behold the tears of *such as were* oppressed, and they had no comforter; and on the side of their oppressors *there was* power; but they had no comforter.

2 Wherefore I praised the dead which are already dead, more than the living which are yet alive.

3 Yea, better *is he* than both they, which hath not yet been, who hath not seen the evil work that is done under the sun.

for that is his lot; who can bring him to see what will be after him?

4 Again I saw all the oppressions that are practiced under the sun. And behold, the tears of the oppressed, and they had no one to comfort them! On the side of their oppressors there was power, and there was no one to comfort them. 2 And I thought the dead who are already dead more fortunate than the living who are still alive; 3 but better than both is he who has not yet been, and has not seen the evil deeds that are done under the sun.

---

works—i.e., in the wide and general sense of activities. This is his reward (portion), for what lies beyond his particular life has in the nature of the case—life's limitation by death and destruction—no interest at all for him.

4:1-3. These verses connect naturally (Gordis) with those which precede them, viz., the section opening at 3:16 with the theme of man's inhumanity to man. As 3:16 is followed by a comparison of man with beast and a reflection on the common destiny of both in death, so 4:1-3 points to the misery that springs from man's oppression of his fellows and to the advantage which the dead have over the living. The author's pessimism here contrasts with his conviction expressed in 9:4, that a live dog has it better than a dead lion. In 4:1 the repetition of **no one to comfort them** is effective and forceful—a trait of style which 3:16 in repeating the word "wickedness" seems also to reveal.

We possess only the present tenses of life; the past is oblivion, the future beyond our ken. A single clause recognizes that what men do may bring them happiness, not frustration; then the gleam is gone.

Finally, the wise and good may and must anticipate the future, and though they do not return to see it may yet march to one heartening strain of music. There will be somewhere and sometime a blessed issue of our toil. Even that perhaps is assurance enough to go on with.

4:1-16. *With None to Comfort Them.*—In his next movement—and it would be better if there were no chapter division—the writer turns from the individual to society. The social and governmental backgrounds of his world show through these brief passages. Somewhere, far off, was probably a Persian emperor; much nearer there were his satraps, greedy, loosely controlled; and always and everywhere there were heartless pride and power. Koheleth views all this with detachment, and with the numbing persuasion that nothing can be done about it. A cynic, the wise have said, sees the wrong but makes no effort to mend it, only to write clever, acid-etched things about it. But one must not deny our author a sad sensitiveness. Mark Twain, it is suggested, wrote often so bitterly

because he felt so deeply. Koheleth may have been like that. But he is fundamentally an isolationist: "I" and "I" and "I."

Gautama Buddha said that "if all the tears by sorrow shed" were confluent, they would fill the seas. There was no escape, Gautama taught, save through cessation of desire. Koheleth saw no cure at all—save the dust—for the pain of the lonely, the helplessness of the oppressed, the heartlessness of pride and power. This he did see with a strange insight. Oppressors need comfort as well as the oppressed. Their heartless deeds are the issues of their frustrations and discontents. They have found no right way to use their power; it baffles them, leads to caprice and excess. All this the Christian expositor and the psychologist may well consider. High places are lonely and often sad.

Vss. 2-3 plumb the depth of despair. Better, the writer thinks, never to have been born. Job in his blackest moments felt the same way. Some faint shadow of that attitude falls, perhaps more often than we think, across the most fortunate: the wish that they had been spared the burden of life. And yet, life is a trust; and though there is no promise that it will be easy, enough is given to make it not only a brave adventure, but in its nobler accomplishments a challenge worth the labor and the cost, both for

4 ¶ Again, I considered all travail, and every right work, that for this a man is envied of his neighbor. This *is* also vanity and vexation of spirit.

5 The fool foldeth his hands together, and eateth his own flesh.

6 Better *is* a handful *with* quietness, than both the hands full *with* travail and vexation of spirit.

7 ¶ Then I returned, and I saw vanity under the sun.

8 There is one *alone,* and *there is* not a second; yea, he hath neither child nor brother: yet *is there* no end of all his labor;

4 Then I saw that all toil and all skill in work come from a man's envy of his neighbor. This also is vanity and a striving after wind.

5 The fool folds his hands, and eats his own flesh.

6 Better is a handful of quietness than two hands full of toil and a striving after wind.

7 Again, I saw vanity under the sun: 8 a person who has no one, either son or brother, yet there is no end to all his toil, and his eyes are never satisfied with riches,

---

II. A WISE MAN'S EXPERIENCES (4:4–9:16)

A. THE WISE CONDUCT OF LIFE (4:4–5:20)

1. COMPETITION AND CO-OPERATION (4:4-12)

Wisdom displays itself not so much in the successful competition of man with man as in co-operation with one's fellows.

4. "I saw all toil and all success in work that it is the קנאה [i.e., the rivalry, envy, or jealousy] of a man with his neighbor." Industry and success in work spring from the competition of man with man.

5. It is foolish to be lazy, since thus a man **eats his own flesh,** i.e., reduces himself to penury, or, as perhaps the meaning is, would have to live off his own relations. This remark appears to be a gloss intended to correct Koheleth's view in vs. 4. Vss. 5-6 are doubtless current proverbs, but they cannot be reconciled except by inserting words which the author himself would have perhaps added had vs. 5 been original to his work. It is mistaken to think of Koheleth as illogical or careless, or that he had the habit of simply placing (cf. Macdonald, *Hebrew Literary Genius,* p. 211) two or more heterogeneous proverbs together without troubling about their cohesion.

6. A modest quantum of peace and **quietness** is more desirable than a life full of the toiling that is inspired by rivalry and after all is but a **striving after wind.**

7-8. A man without any dependents may have the fever of working and of moneymaking so deeply seated in his mind that he may never stop to ask himself the question for whom he is slaving and wearing himself out.

---

this shadowed world and for an enduring and spiritual order.

All commentators are agreed that logical unity is not Koheleth's strong point. He has a discursive mind, returning, as has already been said, to the same conclusion, **This also is vanity and a striving after wind.** There are gleams of the proverbial wisdom of the immemorial East, and one lovely phrase, **a handful of quietness.** Generals rest a marching army at intervals, for, say, fifteen minutes: only a handful of quietness, but it keeps the army marching. The faculty to seize a handful of quietness out of the stresses and strains of the world has healing and sustaining power. We call it relaxation. It is more than that. It is letting life rebaptize itself in the blessed and enduring, and so find rest. It quiets the perturbed spirit and anticipates the

ultimate healing when "the wicked cease from troubling, and . . . the weary are at rest" (Job 3:17).

7-16. *The Futility of Success.*—Ecclesiastes says success brings only envy and loneliness, an echo from earlier passages. Many years ago there was a funeral which Henry Ford attended. At the interment, "earth to earth and dust to dust," he stood apart, and one sensed the loneliness of great wealth. Possession and power are insulators. They may shelter and enclose, but they also shut out much. And, say life and Koheleth together, they stimulate a hunger which is never satisfied; they raise a haunting question, "Whose shall all this be when I am gone?"

Only one gleam of light dispels here the shadows of the writer's moralizations: **Two are better**

neither is his eye satisfied with riches; neither *saith he,* For whom do I labor, and bereave my soul of good? This *is* also vanity, yea, it *is* a sore travail.

9 ¶ Two *are* better than one; because they have a good reward for their labor.

10 For if they fall, the one will lift up his fellow: but woe to him *that is* alone when he falleth; for *he hath* not another to help him up.

11 Again, if two lie together, then they have heat: but how can one be warm *alone?*

12 And if one prevail against him, two shall withstand him; and a threefold cord is not quickly broken.

13 ¶ Better *is* a poor and a wise child, than an old and foolish king, who will no more be admonished.

so that he never asks, "For whom am I toiling and depriving myself of pleasure?" This also is vanity and an unhappy business.

9 Two are better than one, because they have a good reward for their toil. 10 For if they fall, one will lift up his fellow; but woe to him who is alone when he falls and has not another to lift him up. 11 Again, if two lie together, they are warm; but how can one be warm alone? 12 And though a man might prevail against one who is alone, two will withstand him. A threefold cord is not quickly broken.

13 Better is a poor and wise youth than an old and foolish king, who will no

---

9-12. Far better than the successful rivalry that places a man above his fellows and keeps him aloof from them are the advantages which come from co-operation. Warmth, comfort, security, and protection flow from association with others.

2. USELESSNESS OF SEEKING AFTER FAME (4:13-16)

Wisdom may come to fame and even secure a kingdom. But favor depends on popular esteem, which is unenduring. In seeking fame as the reward of wisdom a wise man is but **striving after wind.** This passage contains several obscurities that arise from too highly abridged expressions and from a lack of clarity in regard to the persons to whom the pronouns refer. Vss. 13-16 read as follows: "Better a poor and wise youth than an old and foolish king who could no longer be warned that one can come forth [historic present] from a prison to be a king, yea, can have been by birth a poor man even in his own kingdom [i.e., in the kingdom that was one day to be his]. I have seen all that live beneath the sun accompany the youth who had been 'the second' [i.e., in the state; cf. Intro., p. 13] and was to stand in his [i.e., the old king's] stead: people innumerable, at the head of all of whom he was to be. Yet those who were to come later were to have [frequentative imperfect in Hebrew] no pleasure in him."

13-14. Probably a parable which tells how a poor youth through his wisdom rises to kingship. Such narratives may have been common as school examples in the instruction imparted by the wisdom schools; cf. Ecclus. 11:5-6:

Many downtrodden have sat upon a throne,
And those who were never thought of have worn a crown.
Many exalted have suffered great abasement.

---

than one. Kipling in "Tomlinson" says that "the race is run by one and one and never by two and two"; but that is a futile race. The blessings of companionship compensate the wearinesses of toil, and comradeship is itself a reward. All commentators note Koheleth's longing for friendship and his comfort in the one friend he found (vss. 11-12). Here is a theme inexhaustible in its suggestion: the sense of solidarity, with all its implications, which working together evokes. This, for good or evil, is

the product of modern industrialism. The craftsmen Koheleth may have watched worked alone. One wonders what he would have said of Willow Run, but he never saw an assembly line. He knew the perils of traveling alone, the needs of mutual defense, the scant shelters where men lie more warmly together; and if two are good, three, the symbol of completeness, are better. **A threefold cord is not quickly broken.**

The final verses of the chapter are enigmatical. They may reflect the legend of a king who

14 For out of prison he cometh to reign; whereas also *he that is* born in his kingdom becometh poor.

15 I considered all the living which walk under the sun, with the second child that shall stand up in his stead.

16 *There is* no end of all the people, *even* of all that have been before them: they also that come after shall not rejoice in him. Surely this also *is* vanity and vexation of spirit.

5 Keep thy foot when thou goest to the house of God, and be more ready to hear, than to give the sacrifice of fools: for they consider not that they do evil.

---

longer take advice, 14 even though he had gone from prison to the throne or in his own kingdom had been born poor. 15 I saw all the living who move about under the sun, as well as that[f] youth, who was to stand in his place; 16 there was no end of all the people; he was over all of them. Yet those who come later will not rejoice in him. Surely this also is vanity and a striving after wind.

5 [g] Guard your steps when you go to the house of God; to draw near to listen is better than to offer the sacrifice of fools; for they do not know that they are doing

[f] Heb *the second*
[g] Heb Ch 4. 17

But as vss. 15-16 speak of the career of the poor youth having been witnessed by Koheleth himself, the preceding verses cannot be held to be merely parabolic. The personal interest of Koheleth in the youth can hardly be represented as being mere literary form, even though what is told of the youth is too slender in substance to draw from it any historical or chronological conclusion (see Intro., pp. 13-14).

16. Those who come later refers to those of a later generation who were not present when the youth acceded to the throne with such popular acclamation.

3. CIRCUMSPECTION IN PIETY (5:1-7)

The wise man will be cautious in the practices of religious devotion. His prayers to God will be brief, for God dwells high above the sphere of human interests. The wise man will perform his vows.

5:1. To draw near to listen or **be more ready to hear:** These renderings correspond with the view that there was in the temple worship an opportunity of listening to an exposition of the law. Possibly the meaning is "be ready to obey" (cf. I Sam. 15:22; so Vulg. and Galling). The M.T. reads, lit., "is better than that fools should give a sacrifice." Probably the last words of the verse originally read "for they know not but to do wrong." Renan remarks that the man who cannot distinguish between true piety and false piety displeases God by those very acts which he believes to be most pleasing to God.

---

lived in vanity and died unmourned, like so many kings. Of record, Oriental despots have often been jealous of their possible successors; the heir would come out of prison to rule, only to manage as miserably as his predecessor. Koheleth might have agreed with Emerson: "God said, I am tired of kings." [2]

5:1–8:17. Observations and Admonitions.— Chs. 1–4 say in substance all the writer has to say. What follows is scarcely more than a modulation on his theme. There is much variety of observation and admonition, and he has a highly gifted way of writing it down: but everything is subject to his inevitable conclusion— "Vanity of vanities." There are always overtones in his music: one secret of his power. The book is also notable for its isolated texts, over

[2] "Boston Hymn," st. ii.

---

and above its arguments or meditative moments. But once the expositor has dealt as best he can with its dominants, his own observations may be speeded up without essential loss.

5:1-2. When Thou Goest to the House of God. —The religious background of chs. 1–4 is both dim and distant. There stands God, but he stands within the shadows. He bestows the doubtful blessing of life, "an unhappy business" (1:13), but the justice of his administration is far to seek. Still he must receive due worship and recognition. **The house of God,** whether synagogue or temple, must be reverently entered. Silence is the true sacrifice, more acceptable to the Most High than any patterned form worn smooth by repetition. The impulses of the heart must be guarded. All this echoes the prophets and the psalmists.

2 Be not rash with thy mouth, and let not thine heart be hasty to utter *any* thing before God: for God *is* in heaven, and thou upon earth: therefore let thy words be few.

3 For a dream cometh through the multitude of business; and a fool's voice *is known* by multitude of words.

4 When thou vowest a vow unto God, defer not to pay it; for *he hath* no pleasure in fools: pay that which thou hast vowed.

5 Better *is it* that thou shouldest not vow, than that thou shouldest vow and not pay.

6 Suffer not thy mouth to cause thy flesh to sin; neither say thou before the angel, that it *was* an error: wherefore should God be angry at thy voice, and destroy the work of thine hands?

evil. 2[h] Be not rash with your mouth, nor let your heart be hasty to utter a word before God, for God is in heaven, and you upon earth; therefore let your words be few.

3 For a dream comes with much business, and a fool's voice with many words.

4 When you vow a vow to God, do not delay paying it; for he has no pleasure in fools. Pay what you vow. 5 It is better that you should not vow than that you should vow and not pay. 6 Let not your mouth lead you into sin, and do not say before the messenger[i] that it was a mistake; why should God be angry at your voice, and destroy the work of your hands?

[h] Heb Ch. 5. 1
[i] Or *angel*

---

3. This proverb is to the effect that as excessive business leads to a night of dreams, so verbosity leads a man into talking nonsense (Hebrew **a fool's voice**).

4. The making of rash vows is a particular phase of rash speech.

5. Cf. Deut. 23:21-23.

6. **Flesh** means here no more than self or person (cf. 4:5) ; hence, **Let not your mouth lead you into sin.** This should not be explained as inferring that God will exact a penalty upon the sinner's body. When a man does not pay his vows, God will **destroy the work of** [his] **hands,** i.e., frustrate his undertakings, and so diminish his property or success. The words *liphnê hammal'ākh* signify **before the messenger** or **before the angel,** and are best interpreted on the basis of Mal. 2:7, where the priest is described as "the messenger of the LORD of hosts." The priesthood was ultimately responsible for the collection of temple dues. The Mishnah (Bikkurim 3:3) tells that the rulers and the prefects (i.e., the chiefs of the priests and Levites) and the treasurers of the temple went forth from Jerusalem to meet and welcome those who brought first-fruit offerings. The LXX here differs from the M.T. by rendering "before God," a phrase we should understand as meaning "at the sanctuary," the sense which "unto God" has in Exod. 21:6, where Moffatt translates "to the local sanctuary." In effect, this is the same as **before the messenger** (i.e., priest). But the LXX variant should not be regarded merely as a "paraphrase" of the M.T.

But we are earthbound, and God is high and far in the heavens. There is no music here of

Speak to Him thou for He hears, and Spirit with Spirit can meet—
Closer is He than breathing, and nearer than hands and feet.[a]

Had Koheleth known that, everything would have changed.

3. *Troubled Dreams.*—All through the book there is something half seen and half lost, tantalizingly difficult to trace, the web, literally, of the writer's association lines. The general conclusions are evident, the minor movements part of the seeming disorder of the book. Why the writer passes so abruptly from restraint in

words, for example, to the dreams of the worried is lost in his own mental processes. But there is truth in his obiter dicta. He finds it hard to let dreams alone. They were in his time mystic messages needing to be interpreted, and that was the business of the soothsayer. They still need to be interpreted, but the psychologist and psychiatrist are now our soothsayers. At any rate, restless and anxious days cause troubled sleep, and dreams in a twisted way may echo foolish or intemperate speech. There is sound psychology in many of Koheleth's disconnected observations, though he never heard the word.

4-7. *Concerning the Sanctity of Words.*—Vows in the O.T. sense are mostly dated, but they continue in less formal ways. They are in es-

[a] Tennyson, "The Higher Pantheism," st. vi.

7 For in the multitude of dreams and many words *there are* also divers vanities: but fear thou God.

8 ¶ If thou seest the oppression of the poor, and violent perverting of judgment and justice in a province, marvel not at the matter: for *he that is* higher than the highest regardeth; and *there be* higher than they.

7 For when dreams increase, empty words grow many:*j* but do you fear God.

8 If you see in a province the poor oppressed and justice and right violently taken away, do not be amazed at the matter; for the high official is watched by a higher, and there are yet higher ones over them.

j Or *For in a multitude of dreams there is futility, and ruin in a flood of words*

---

7. The text of this concluding proverb appears to have suffered in transmission and should be emended as in the RSV mg., or read, "In the multitude of business are [i.e., come] dreams, and vanities in many words." **Fear God** does not mean what is generally known as "godly fear," but, as D. B. Macdonald (*The Hebrew Philosophical Genius* [Princeton: Princeton University Press, 1936], p. 70) points out, it indicates "caution not to irritate [that] amoral Personality" which was Koheleth's conception of the Deity.

4. Vanity of Wealth (5:8-20)

This section deals with acquisitiveness: (*a*) the wrongs it occasions (vss. 8-9); (*b*) the getting and gaining of wealth does not satisfy man's desires but increases his cares (vss. 10-12); (*c*) a man may not be able to retain the wealth which he has gained, and thus dire poverty may succeed abundance (vss. 13-17); (*d*) the best rule is to take what enjoyment this short life offers and take it as God's gift (vss. 18-20).

8-9. Vss. 8-20 all relate to the same theme, viz., man's acquisitiveness as everywhere apparent in his striving to fill life with content and value. From this standpoint vss. 8-9 should not be separated from what follows. The oppression of the poor, the wresting of justice, as these manifest themselves in the government of a province (or state), need cause no surprise, for these injustices are a direct result of the insatiable disposition to acquire wealth. Each official in the state service watches (M.T., *shômēr*) the official beneath him in expectation of receiving from him some part of the money which has been gathered in taxes, rentals, dues, etc., from the citizens. The method of collecting, or of accounting for what has been collected, leads to overcharging, expropriation, or other dishonesties, but at every point along the whole line of the administrative staff the same corruption appears, and the takings of the officer who is highest are the largest of all. Vs. 8*b* is, lit., "For high one watches over high one, and high ones [are] over them," which must signify that official watches over (in M.T. a present participle of a verb which has the same or much the same sense as it has in I Sam. 19:11; Pss. 59:1; 56:7; 71:10; Jer. 20:10; etc.) official and that there are still higher officials above them. The

---

sence a contract with God. "Save me from this peril, cure me of this sickness, grant me this petition, and I will do better and be better." They continue in self-commitments to God and duty, and it is still perilous to play fast and loose with them. Right resolutions have a strong sustaining power as long as they are carried through; but a broken pledge to God, oneself, or others weakens the very structure of character.

Let not your mouth lead you into sin. The context focuses upon vows, but there is a vaster context, the sanctity of words: "Man's word is God in man." [4] Words have a power beyond

[4] Tennyson, *Idylls of the King*, "The Coming of Arthur."

our knowing. They are the bridges of all fellowship. They heal or wound. They mobilize armies, launch battleships, and lift bombing planes to the stratosphere. So often the air is full of confusing and confused words, intemperate, provocative, which tighten the tension between classes and nations, and fill the world with suspicions and estrangements. **Why should God be angry at your voice?** has in it some quality of the Judgment Day; for we are also judged by our words. James knew that (cf. Jas. 1:26; 3:5-6, 8).

8. Concerning the Prudent Conduct of Life.
—The prudential admonitions of Koheleth and the wisdom literature are too repetitious for

9 ¶ Moreover the profit of the earth is for all: the king *himself* is served by the field.

10 He that loveth silver shall not be satisfied with silver; nor he that loveth abundance with increase: this *is* also vanity.

11 When goods increase, they are increased that eat them: and what good *is there* to the owners thereof, saving the beholding *of them* with their eyes?

12 The sleep of a laboring man *is* sweet, whether he eat little or much: but the abundance of the rich will not suffer him to sleep.

9 But in all, a king is an advantage to a land with cultivated fields.[k]

10 He who loves money will not be satisfied with money; nor he who loves wealth, with gain: this also is vanity.

11 When goods increase, they increase who eat them; and what gain has their owner but to see them with his eyes?

12 Sweet is the sleep of a laborer, whether he eats little or much; but the surfeit of the rich will not let him sleep.

[k] Or *The profit of the land is among all of them; a cultivated field has a king*

---

words "high ones" are not to be explained as a "plural of majesty," denoting "God." Hertzberg's rendering, "For one official protects the other from the higher ones above them" (*Der Prediger,* p. 107), rests upon another interpretation of *shômēr* and a transposition of words which hardly seems justified. Much divergence of interpretation has been caused by vs. 9, but the most intelligible translation would seem to be: "And the profit of the land is among the whole [of them]; a cultivated field has a king" (cf. RSV mg.). In other words, the author, after describing the hierarchy of officials, states that the profit of the country's produce is shared by all the officials (M.T., lit., "among the whole"; cf. the idiom of common speech "among the lot"), and that there is no cultivated territory without its king. Koheleth means that there is no cultivated area which is not regarded as dutiable to the crown and therefore subject to the attention of those who collect duty in the king's name. **A king is an advantage to a land with cultivated fields** is more or less supported by Hertzberg ("An advantage for the land would be, in all this, a king who serves the arable land") and by Barton ("But an advantage to a country on the whole is a king," i.e., to an agricultural land). Barton believes that the author wishes to say that a monarchy has some advantages. But the assumption that Koheleth has anything complimentary to say about monarchy is not warranted by what he says in his book. The last words of the verse read, lit., "a king for a cultivated field." Williams (*Ecclesiastes,* p. 62) regards them as meaning that "even the wild land when cultivated has a king," i.e., it "falls under the exactions of the state directly it is cultivated." This thought no doubt suits the situation described, but the word *sādheh*

---

detailed comment. They are all middle level—shrewd directions for the shrewd conduct of life. They are the accepted morality of the time and the place. They do indicate, however, the extent to which long-vanished generations examined the ways and means of life. Good government, if it can be had—Koheleth had reason to doubt that it could—is a blessing. This obscure verse assumes a series of overlordships with authority to correct provincial injustice. Wise administration (vs. 9) takes care of the land, for there are the sources of true prosperity. Job's "oath of clearance" recognizes as much:

If my land has cried out against me,
  and its furrows have wept together (Job 31:38).

Current literature dealing with our abuse of the resources of a continent give substance to the doctrine of the sanctity of the soil.

5:11–6:12. Anxieties Multiply with Possession.—Unless there is wealth in the soul, men go down to their graves with empty hands. Right pleasures are simple. Contentment in them is a gift of God; but all contentments are fugitive. We live and die with unsatisfied desires. Omar Khayyám also made his sad music of this:

We are no other than a moving row
Of Magic Shadow-shapes that come and go.[5]

For Koheleth, as for Omar, there was a door for which he found no key.

[5] *The Rubáiyát,* st. lxviii.

13 There is a sore evil *which* I have seen under the sun, *namely,* riches kept for the owners thereof to their hurt.

14 But those riches perish by evil travail: and he begetteth a son, and *there is* nothing in his hand.

15 As he came forth of his mother's womb, naked shall he return to go as he came, and shall take nothing of his labor, which he may carry away in his hand.

16 And this also *is* a sore evil, *that* in all points as he came, so shall he go: and what profit hath he that hath labored for the wind?

17 All his days also he eateth in darkness, and *he hath* much sorrow and wrath with his sickness.

18 ¶ Behold *that* which I have seen: *it is* good and comely *for one* to eat and to drink, and to enjoy the good of all his labor that he taketh under the sun all the days of his life, which God giveth him: for it *is* his portion.

19 Every man also to whom God hath given riches and wealth, and hath given him power to eat thereof, and to take his portion, and to rejoice in his labor; this *is* the gift of God.

20 For he shall not much remember the days of his life; because God answereth *him* in the joy of his heart.

13 There is a grievous evil which I have seen under the sun: riches were kept by their owner to his hurt, 14 and those riches were lost in a bad venture; and he is father of a son, but he has nothing in his hand. 15 As he came from his mother's womb he shall go again, naked as he came, and shall take nothing for his toil, which he may carry away in his hand. 16 This also is a grievous evil: just as he came, so shall be go; and what gain has he that he toiled for the wind, 17 and spent all his days in darkness and grief,[l] in much vexation and sickness and resentment?

18 Behold, what I have seen to be good and to be fitting is to eat and drink and find enjoyment in all the toil with which one toils under the sun the few days of his life which God has given him, for this is his lot. 19 Every man also to whom God has given wealth and possessions and power to enjoy them, and to accept his lot and find enjoyment in his toil — this is the gift of God. 20 For he will not much remember the days of his life because God keeps him occupied with joy in his heart.

[l] Gk: Heb *all his days also he eats in darkness*

---

does not always mean **field,** nor does it even usually signify the wild land, and hence it is best to understand that Koheleth is referring to any or every field or parcel of ground that is cultivated. It seems hardly necessary to introduce the notion that the field had been reclaimed from a state of wilderness. Should vs. 9, as some interpret, express by way of concession a favorable opinion upon the office of king as in some respects an advantage to a land, then perhaps the emendation offered by Galling—"An advantage to a land is above all this, that a king is there for both prince and peasant" (reading לשר ולעבד for the last two words of the M.T.) —should be commended. The interpretation of vs. 8 and vs. 9 in the Vulg. is of much interest (see Ronald A. Knox, tr., *The Old Testament* [New York: Sheed & Ward, 1948-50]) .

14-15. **As he came:** The pronoun (vs. 15) refers to **father** (vs. 14) .

17. The LXX (cf. RSV mg.) probably represents the original text.

18-20. He who enjoys what his life offers, having both the wherewithal and the power to enjoy, will find that his days flit pleasantly past, since **God keeps him occupied** [Vulg., *Deus occupet*] **with joy in his heart.** This latter phrase is explanatory of the words **enjoyment in his toil** in vs. 19. Koheleth's teaching is not that of an unthinking hedonist, for he appreciates the zest for life which a man's work yields. The translation of the Hebrew word ענה as "occupy" (LXX, Vulg., Barton, *et al.*) in vs. 20 accords with the sense of this word elsewhere in Ecclesiastes (1:13; 3:10) and may well be taken as more in harmony with Koheleth's type of thought than is the translation "answer," which is represented by the KJV, ERV, McNeile, Williams, *et al.*

6 There is an evil which I have seen under the sun, and it *is* common among men:

2 A man to whom God hath given riches, wealth, and honor, so that he wanteth nothing for his soul of all that he desireth, yet God giveth him not power to eat thereof, but a stranger eateth it: this *is* vanity, and it *is* an evil disease.

3 ¶ If a man beget a hundred *children,* and live many years, so that the days of his years be many, and his soul be not filled with good, and also *that* he have no burial; I say, *that* an untimely birth *is* better than he.

6 There is an evil which I have seen under the sun, and it lies heavy upon men: 2 a man to whom God gives wealth, possessions, and honor, so that he lacks nothing of all that he desires, yet God does not give him power to enjoy them, but a stranger enjoys them; this is vanity; it is a sore affliction. 3 If a man begets a hundred children, and lives many years, so that the days of his years are many, but he does not enjoy life's good things, and also has no burial, I say that an untimely birth is better

---

B. THE FRUSTRATION OF DESIRES AND HOPES (6:1-12)

In the foregoing section Koheleth believes that life presents a real, even if temporary, good, when God has given wealth and possessions together with the "power to enjoy them" (5:19). In ch. 6 he speaks of life under the contrary aspect, i.e., when the power of enjoyment has been withheld.

Better than this frustration of longing and desire, particularly when the means of satisfaction are otherwise abundant, would be to experience nothing at all, to forfeit existence, to be as the **untimely birth** that has never received a name or seen the light of day (vss. 1-5).

The woefulness of this condition of thwarted fulfillment is met by the author with considerations that are of the nature of comfort, even if of a lugubrious kind: (a) Death concludes the experience of all men alike; the wise man and the fool have the same end (vss. 6-9). (b) Everything that happens to a man is determined long ago. Thus man cannot argue with God about the happenings and contents of life, for to do so would be to dispute with one stronger than himself and therefore would be only a waste of words (vss. 10-11). (c) In the light of this determinism which governs life, and of death which ends man's short life altogether, to speak of anything as being **good for man** is to speak without weighing words (vs. 12a). For determinism is the negation of worth, and man's life—**his vain life**—is empty of value. Not only so, but man himself has in such case a certain unreality; he passes his days **like a shadow**, where the comparison is more than a picture only of swiftly passing days. Omar Khayyám (*The Rubáiyát,* st. lxviii), from the same deterministic thought arrives at the same assessment of life. (d) Moreover, the fact that all of life is determined makes a man's thought as to what will happen on earth after his death a profitless speculation (vs. 12b). In ch. 6 Koheleth applies to a specific situation the general principles of his world outlook (1:1–4:3).

6:2. A stranger enjoys them: The sense is "will enjoy them" or "some stranger is destined to consume it," as Gordis well renders it (cf. Gen. 15:1-4).

3. No burial: That the dead should be without burial was in Hebrew thought the summit of misfortune (cf. Isa. 14:19; Jer. 22:19). To bury the dead was a pious duty (Tob. 1:18; 2:4-5). A man with many children and yet with none willing or able to provide burial for him might be regarded as a most pitiable example of human woe.

Yet it cannot be denied that in the context of vs. 3 **and also has no burial** presents us with no very clear sense. But if we interpret the Hebrew, with Abraham Cohen ("Ecclesiastes," *The Five Megilloth* [London: Soncino Press, 1946], *ad loc.*), as meaning "and even were he to have no burial," i.e., "were he never to die," or "though he is still among the living" (cf. the Hebrew, which reads, lit., "And also burial has not been to

4 For he cometh in with vanity, and departeth in darkness, and his name shall be covered with darkness.

5 Moreover he hath not seen the sun, nor known *any thing:* this hath more rest than the other.

6 ¶ Yea, though he live a thousand years twice *told,* yet hath he seen no good: do not all go to one place?

7 All the labor of man *is* for his mouth, and yet the appetite is not filled.

8 For what hath the wise more than the fool? what hath the poor, that knoweth to walk before the living?

9 ¶ Better *is* the sight of the eyes than the wandering of the desire: this *is* also vanity and vexation of spirit.

10 That which hath been is named already, and it is known that it *is* man: neither may he contend with him that is mightier than he.

11 ¶ Seeing there be many things that increase vanity, what *is* man the better?

off than he. 4 For it comes into vanity and goes into darkness, and in darkness its name is covered; 5 moreover it has not seen the sun or known anything; yet it finds rest rather than he. 6 Even though he should live a thousand years twice told, yet enjoy no good — do not all go to the one place?

7 All the toil of man is for his mouth, yet his appetite is not satisfied. 8 For what advantage has the wise man over the fool? And what does the poor man have who knows how to conduct himself before the living? 9 Better is the sight of the eyes than the wandering of desire; this also is vanity and a striving after wind.

10 Whatever has come to be has already been named, and it is known what man is, and that he is not able to dispute with one stronger than he. 11 The more words, the more vanity, and what is man the better?

---

him"), the author's thought becomes plain. In this case the idea is that if a man has every conceivable fortune but not the means to enjoy it, though he may still have a good hold upon life, he is worse off than the untimely birth. Commentators have found this sentence about burial a difficult one. Thus the translation of the Swiss Church, the so-called Zürich Bible, completed *ca.* 1931, supposes the sentence to have become misplaced and therefore detaches it from the description of the rich man who has not been given the power to enjoy (vs. 3) and joins it to the description (vs. 5) of the untimely birth which "sees no sun and knows of nothing and to it no burial is given; yet it has peace and he—the rich man—has none."

4. **For he cometh** refers (wrongly) to the unfortunate **man** of vs. 3.

5. Some translate "has never seen or known the sun." But the idea would appear to be "has never come to consciousness at all." Hence, **nor known any thing.**

7. McNeile (*Intro. to Ecclesiastes,* p. 22) perceives this is a gloss, but says it is inserted with no apparent reason. The reason, however, is fairly obvious. The glossator seeks to counter Koheleth's conclusions on frustrated desire by saying man's longings are the very essence of life, that man's insatiable hunger and his work to satisfy his mouth are essential parts of his existence. Vs. 7 interferes also with the sequence of thought between vs. 6 and vs. 8.

8. Burkitt (reading מבלעדי instead of M.T. מה־לעני; cf. Vulg., *nisi ut*) translates, "What advantage hath the wise man over the fool, except that he knows how to walk (i.e., to behave) before his contemporaries?" The phrase **to walk before the living,** which is a literal translation of the Hebrew, is taken by Galling to mean "to live without thought of the morrow" (*in den Tag leben*). He therefore thinks that the original text ran, "What advantage has the wise man over the fool, the man of understanding over him who lives thoughtlessly?"

9. In effect, the meaning is that satisfaction is better than perpetual longing, **than the wandering of desire,** lit., "than the [out-]going of desire."

10. An alternative translation is, "What happens has long since been named, and known [i.e., determined] what a man will be."

12 For who knoweth what *is* good for man in *this* life, all the days of his vain life which he spendeth as a shadow? for who can tell a man what shall be after him under the sun?

7 A good name *is* better than precious ointment; and the day of death than the day of one's birth.

12 For who knows what is good for man while he lives the few days of his vain life, which he passes like a shadow? For who can tell man what will be after him under the sun?

7 A good name is better than precious ointment;
and the day of death, than the day of birth.

---

12. Delete אשר, or (with Galling) transpose it, reading אשר יעשם, meaning, **which he passes.** (For this latter [Greek?] phrase cf. Intro., p. 12, and see Odeberg, *Qohaelaeth,* p. 54.)

C. Enjoyment of Relative "Good" (7:1-22)

In the preceding section the words "what is good for man while he lives" (6:12) appear in connection with the belief that all things are determined—a belief which denies the possibility of moral good altogether. But Koheleth admits that there are relative "goods" which a man may enjoy and which a wise man will seek to have. Thus a good reputation has a real, if relative, value for a man who lives among his fellow men (vs. 1). In vss. 1-9, 11-12, 19 the author employs aphorisms in poetic form—after the style of the book of Proverbs—to set forth certain qualities of mind and character which a wise man should cultivate and other qualities which he should avoid. Whether these aphorisms are of Koheleth's own shaping after current models, or are merely citations by him, is not certain. But in favor of the latter one may argue that for the most part they have a loose rather than a strict cohesion with Koheleth's distinctive views. This looseness of cohesion is the basis of the judgment of Siegfried, McNeile, Haupt, and Barton that the bulk of the aphorisms are glosses; e.g., Barton holds that the thought of vs. 3 is foreign to Koheleth, since the latter never seems to grasp the moral purpose in suffering, and likewise that vs. 5 is out of harmony with the spirit of the author. In Barton's opinion few of the maxims should be considered to be genuine. But Koheleth in this section must be interpreted as employing aphorisms well known in the schools of wisdom, in order to convey the traditional standpoint of these schools in their delineation of the character of the good (i.e., the wise) man. Koheleth agrees generally with the teaching of the schools, but for him—and here the gap between the author and the schools is a wide one—the good qualities which are commended by the traditional wisdom literature are only relative goods. The wise man has a sense and sanity which the fool has not, but his wisdom is limited and as to the solving of ultimate questions is powerless. One "good" may be better than another (vss. 1, 2, 3, etc.), but there is no absolute good. Koheleth presents the traditional picture of the good man sympathetically—though perhaps in the presentation there is a slight hint of condescending irony—in order that he may have a background upon which to draw the more strikingly his own particular and contrasting conclusions, which follow in the next section. Possibly there may be slight glosses (cf. vs. 4, which Galling thinks is a gloss upon vs. 2), but in consideration of the purpose which the maxims serve it is not possible, in the absence of positive evidence of the versions, to view these proverbs as a concentration of additions. They represent the wisdom school, but Koheleth intended them to do so.

7:1-29. The Lore of Proverbs.—Specifically, the use in Ecclesiastes of proverbial wisdom is the concern of the specialist in the general field of wisdom literature rather than of the expositor. These varied, more or less disconnected, proverbs which the writer quotes with agree-

ment or disagreement are in substance the deposits of long experience worn smooth by the tides of time and minted by repetition. Their brevities are none the less pregnant. Many of them are still current, and they carry across the centuries extremely good advice, moralities

2 ¶ *It is* better to go to the house of mourning, than to go to the house of feasting: for that *is* the end of all men; and the living will lay *it* to his heart.

3 Sorrow *is* better than laughter: for by the sadness of the countenance the heart is made better.

4 The heart of the wise *is* in the house of mourning; but the heart of fools *is* in the house of mirth.

5 *It is* better to hear the rebuke of the wise, than for a man to hear the song of fools.

6 For as the crackling of thorns under a pot, so *is* the laughter of the fool: this also *is* vanity.

7 ¶ Surely oppression maketh a wise man mad; and a gift destroyeth the heart.

2 It is better to go to the house of mourning
　　than to go to the house of feasting;
　for this is the end of all men,
　　and the living will lay it to heart.
3 Sorrow is better than laughter,
　　for by sadness of countenance the heart
　　　is made glad.
4 The heart of the wise is in the house of mourning;
　　but the heart of fools is in the house of mirth.
5 It is better for a man to hear the rebuke of the wise
　　than to hear the song of fools.
6 For as the crackling of thorns under a pot,
　　so is the laughter of the fools;
　this also is vanity.
7 Surely oppression makes the wise man foolish,
　　and a bribe corrupts the mind.

Some disarrangement of the text has taken place. The prosaic sentence in vs. 10 has its proper position before vs. 13, not with the metric maxims; and vs. 19 has its place both in regard to form and logic among these maxims, after vs. 12. Furthermore, the words **this also is vanity** (vs. 6) are a prose comment and a later addition.

7:1-2. The wise man is described as valuing a good reputation (**name**)—the verse exhibits wordplay upon *shēm* (**name**) and *shémen* (**ointment**)—and as preferring to associate with those who are in sorrow rather than to spend his time in **feasting**. The reason for this preference is that a wise appreciation of life must rest upon the fact that death ends all.

3. The Hebrew verb rendered **made glad** is found in this sense in Judg. 19:6, 9; etc., but it has also the general sense of "being well with." Through his earnest outlook the wise man's mind is given a proper poise.

6. Burning **thorns** give forth a **crackling** noise without engendering enduring heat. In the Hebrew there is a wordplay upon *ṣîr* (**pot**) and *ṣirîm* (**thorns**).

7b. This verse begins very abruptly. Therefore Williams (*Ecclesiastes*, p. 76) joins to it the last words of vs. 6, reading, "This also is vanity, that oppression . . ." (so also Odeberg). But the added words interfere with the meter of vs. 7. Thus the suggestion that a metric line—such as "Better a handful with justice than two hands full of oppression" (cf. 4:6)—has by error been omitted is probable, but what the exact words were cannot now be determined. The Hebrew word rendered **oppression** may also mean

---

standard then and still standard, and a sublimated philosophy of life. They witness to the fact that the contemplative East thought more deeply about life wisdoms than the action-driven West. There was, a penetrating thinker has contended, an epochal reorientation from the contemplation of excellence to the drive of action somewhere in the Middle Ages, and it has changed the very nature of civilization.

The proverbs which Koheleth quotes he has tested by his own wisdom; but their far issues escape him. Here they constitute a fabric of wisdom. Parallel observations and admonitions may be found in Proverbs and in non-Hebrew literatures. Such subjects occupy him as the worth of a good name; the need to pay attention to the rebuke of the wise; the more than folly of a fool's laughter; the greed that undoes the greedy; the patience that outlasts pride; the wisdom that is better than an inheritance; the wisdom which is strength; etc. But all this more or less proverbial wisdom, mediated through the

8 Better *is* the end of a thing than the beginning thereof: *and* the patient in spirit *is* better than the proud in spirit.

9 Be not hasty in thy spirit to be angry: for anger resteth in the bosom of fools.

10 Say not thou, What is *the cause* that the former days were better than these? for thou dost not inquire wisely concerning this.

11 ¶ Wisdom *is* good with an inheritance: and *by it there is* profit to them that see the sun.

12 For wisdom *is* a defense, *and* money *is* a defense: but the excellency of knowledge *is, that* wisdom giveth life to them that have it.

13 Consider the work of God: for who can make *that* straight, which he hath made crooked?

14 In the day of prosperity be joyful, but in the day of adversity consider: God

8 Better is the end of a thing than its beginning;
and the patient in spirit is better than the proud in spirit.

9 Be not quick to anger,
for anger lodges in the bosom of fools.

10 Say not, "Why were the former days better than these?"
For it is not from wisdom that you ask this.

11 Wisdom is good with an inheritance,
an advantage to those who see the sun.

12 For the protection of wisdom is like the protection of money;
and the advantage of knowledge is that wisdom preserves the life of him who has it.

13 Consider the work of God;
who can make straight what he has made crooked?

14 In the day of prosperity be joyful,
and in the day of adversity consider; God

---

gain of extortion, i.e., ill-gotten gain (*unrecht Gut,* Hertzberg). Both the LXX and Vulg. render it "calumny," a sense which the word has in Syriac.

8. This verse reflects the thought of vs. 1*b* but is capable of wider reference.

10. The question "How is it that the former days were better?" is not reasonable. Koheleth has already developed the thought that from nature and human experience there evolves nothing that is new (1:9-10), that the world's course of events is repetitive, and that each event and its opposite has its appointed time (3:1-8). Without doubt comparison can be made between good and evil experiences, but both occur in their place in the meaningless cycle of events (cf. Intro., pp. 17-18). Koheleth acknowledges a utilitarian morality whereby the wise man learns to make the best of life's circumstances as they are, but he does not think that there is any goal or good toward which the world or the individual can progress.

11. This verse, together with vss. 12 and 19, is in accord with the general trend of Koheleth's thought. The combination of knowledge and wealth is a double line of defense against life's difficulties and assaults.

12. The M.T. says, lit., "In the shadow of wisdom [a man is] in the shadow of money." The content of **life,** as this is understood in the Wisdom Literature, is in all its aspects—including a good name, well-being, longevity—promoted by wisdom.

13. This world—**the work of God**—shows that all that occurs is predestined so that no one can change, with a view to improving, what God has determined should be (1:15*a*; 3:15; 6:10).

14. In the days of prosperity a man should rejoice in his condition, and when adversity comes he should remember that life has a dual aspect, so that the pattern of life

---

writer's mind, is colored or challenged by his own observation, as though he were saying of it, "All this is too simple and too final." **That which is, is far off, and deep, very deep; who can find it out?**

11-18. *It Is Better.*—The most that Koheleth dares to conclude is that some attitudes, tempers,

lines of conduct, are **better** than others (note the repetition of **better**). Beyond that he does not dare to go. Any conclusion is open to qualification, so the exceptions prove. The only rule is moderation in all things. One may recall the Greek admonition, "Nothing too much." The application of it has cost the expositors of life

also hath set the one over against the other, to the end that man should find nothing after him.

15 All *things* have I seen in the days of my vanity: there is a just *man* that perisheth in his righteousness, and there is a wicked *man* that prolongeth *his life* in his wickedness.

16 Be not righteous over much, neither make thyself over wise: why shouldest thou destroy thyself?

17 Be not over much wicked, neither be thou foolish: why shouldest thou die before thy time?

18 *It is* good that thou shouldest take hold of this; yea, also from this withdraw not thine hand: for he that feareth God shall come forth of them all.

has made the one as well as the other, so that man may not find out anything that will be after him.

15 In my vain life I have seen everything; there is a righteous man who perishes in his righteousness, and there is a wicked man who prolongs his life in his evil-doing. **16** Be not righteous overmuch, and do not make yourself overwise; why should you destroy yourself? **17** Be not wicked overmuch, neither be a fool; why should you die before your time? **18** It is good that you should take hold of this, and from that withhold not your hand; for he who fears God shall come forth from them all.

---

is confused, its content rendered incalculable, and nothing certain can be read from it as to what the future will hold. (On the objection to Burkitt's interpretation of the words **that will be after him** see Intro., p. 13.)

15-17. Experience does not support the view (cf. Ps. 1:3-4) that God rewards and defends the righteous and punishes the wicked (cf. 8:14). With regard to the choices of good and evil which confront all men, a wise man will conduct his life in such a way that he is neither overpious nor extremely wicked. He will take a middle course. **Why should you destroy yourself? . . . Why should you die before your time?** These two questions, though the first refers to the rigidly pious and the second to the man who knows no restraint in evil-doing, teach the same thing, viz., that extremes of conduct lead to disaster, ruin a man's life, spoil his prospects, indeed sometimes even have fatal results. Both the religious idealist and the criminal may find the same violent end. History affords many examples vindicating Koheleth's thought, e.g., the Covenanters' tombstone (in Greyfriars' Churchyard, Edinburgh) records that these faithful martyrs here lie buried,

> . . . mixt with murderers, and other crew,
> Whom justice did justly to death pursue.

The righteous and the transgressors found here the same common grave. It is more probable that by **die before your time** Koheleth is thinking of the action of society upon the wrongdoer than that he is referring to ill-health as a result of wrongdoing.

18. The world has not only a righteous but also an unrighteous aspect, and of both a man must take account and must have to do with both, for he must take the world as he finds it. Williams thinks that **of this** and **from that** refer to the two persons mentioned in vs. 15, but there is no need to revert in thought to that passage. Koheleth does not advise indulgence in wickedness, but his view is that in certain situations in which life places a man it is advisable and right for him to compromise in his actions and decisions, and he should conform when circumstances make conformity the only safe—and wise—course. Koheleth does not encourage martyrdom (cf. 8:2-5 and see Intro., pp. 18-19).

---

book much more or less speculative comment. **Be not righteous overmuch . . . ; why should you destroy yourself? Be not wicked overmuch . . . ; why should you die before your time?** If the author's righteousness is self-righteousness, the caution is defensible, or if it is the ritual righteousness which Jesus indicated. Otherwise one may explain it only by Koheleth's philosophy: that conduct should be balanced in its self-denials and indulgences. "Just be safe."

19 Wisdom strengtheneth the wise more than ten mighty *men* which are in the city.

20 For *there is* not a just man upon earth, that doeth good, and sinneth not.

21 Also take no heed unto all words that are spoken; lest thou hear thy servant curse thee:

22 For oftentimes also thine own heart knoweth that thou thyself likewise hast cursed others.

23 ¶ All this have I proved by wisdom: I said, I will be wise; but it *was* far from me.

24 That which is far off, and exceeding deep, who can find it out?

25 I applied mine heart to know, and to search, and to seek out wisdom, and the reason *of things,* and to know the wickedness of folly, even of foolishness *and* madness:

---

19 Wisdom gives strength to the wise man more than ten rulers that are in a city.

20 Surely there is not a righteous man on earth who does good and never sins.

21 Do not give heed to all the things that men say, lest you hear your servant cursing you; 22 your heart knows that many times you have yourself cursed others.

23 All this I have tested by wisdom; I said, "I will be wise"; but it was far from me. 24 That which is, is far off, and deep, very deep; who can find it out? 25 I turned my mind to know and to search out and to seek wisdom and the sum of things, and to know the wickedness of folly and the

---

For he who fears God shall come forth from them all: The M.T. reads יצא את־כלם, lit., "shall come forth with them all." These words suggest that the God-fearer escapes the consequences of taking, or the temptation to take, extreme modes of conduct. But the sentence is best explained as resting on an idiom found in the Mishnah (יצא, "fulfill an obligation") , and as meaning that the God-fearer will fulfill his duties in every case or "will preserve a worthy attitude" (Odeberg) to all men. McNeile takes the words as a gloss of the *ḥāṣîdh.* But since for Koheleth a man who fears God is a man who applies "caution not to irritate this amoral Personality" (Macdonald, *Hebrew Philosophical Genius,* p. 70) , no objection can be taken to the words on the ground that they are incompatible with Koheleth's thought. The extremist was the very sort of person who would irritate Koheleth's Deity.

19. The institution of "the ten chief men" (δέκα πρῶται) who formed the city government in the Hellenistic age may have been in the author's mind.

20. There is no sense in not compromising with the world, in not meeting it halfway, for there is no such thing as an absolutely good man, a man without moral fault.

21-22. Anyone who listens to his servants' conversation will be liable to hear them curse him, and his conscience will tell him that he has often cursed others. Blameworthiness is universal. No man attains to perfection. Galling is right in regarding these verses as a proverb of the school tradition cited to illustrate vs. 20. The words in the citation which are intended to have relevance are only those that present cursing as an example of a sin that is commonly or generally indulged.

D. Source of Wisdom (7:23-29)

"Thou, O God, existeth but thy counsel is hidden and who shall attain to it? Deep, deep it is—who shall discover it?" (Solomon ibn Gabirol, A.D. 1021-1058, in *The Royal Crown.*)

23. All this, i.e., that which he is about to say, Koheleth put to the test of wisdom. He resolved to **be wise** but discovered that wisdom is as a goal too far off for a man to reach; **that which is,** "all that has come into being" (Gordis) , "the reality below all changing phenomena" (Barton) —all this is beyond the capacity of man to comprehend and explain. The same thought is taken up again in 8:16-17.

25. Turning to the subject of the practical realm of conduct, the author now applies his mind to seek for a reasoned judgment (**wisdom, and . . . reason**), and finds it to

26 And I find more bitter than death the woman, whose heart *is* snares and nets, *and* her hands *as* bands: whoso pleaseth God shall escape from her; but the sinner shall be taken by her.

27 Behold, this have I found, saith the Preacher, *counting* one by one, to find out the account;

28 Which yet my soul seeketh, but I find not: one man among a thousand have I found; but a woman among all those have I not found.

29 Lo, this only have I found, that God hath made man upright; but they have sought out many inventions.

8 Who *is* as the wise *man?* and who knoweth the interpretation of a thing?

foolishness which is madness. 26 And I found more bitter than death the woman whose heart is snares and nets, and whose hands are fetters; he who pleases God escapes her, but the sinner is taken by her. 27 Behold, this is what I found, says the Preacher, adding one thing to another to find the sum, 28 which my mind has sought repeatedly, but I have not found. One man among a thousand I found, but a woman among all these I have not found. 29 Behold, this alone I found, that God made man upright, but they have sought out many devices.

8 Who is like the wise man?
And who knows the interpretation of a thing?

---

reside in the proposition that "wickedness is foolishness and folly is madness" (so literally the M.T.).

26. From this meager and negative conclusion which describes wisdom in terms of its opposite (cf. Job 28:28, "to depart from evil is understanding") Koheleth proceeds further to say that a supreme example of folly and evil is a woman into whose hands a man who is displeasing (cf. 2:26) to God is destined to fall.

27-28. Another conclusion reached is that a good (wise) man is a rarity and a good woman scarcer still. Upon establishing this fact Koheleth has spent much thought, **adding one thing to another** to find a reason for it—a reason (*ḥeshbôn*) which still he has not found.

29. This verse is probably a glossator's protest against vss. 16-18, 20 (where Koheleth urges compromise and where he states that there is no such thing as a righteous man). God made mankind **upright** (straightforward) but men **have sought out many inventions,** i.e., have taken, like Koheleth, to subtle and clever reasonings or **devices.** The word **inventions** (*hishshebhônôth* in II Chr. 26:15, "engines") is a play upon the word which Koheleth uses for "reason," *ḥeshbôn* (Vulg., *rationem*) in vss. 25, 27.

E. Necessity of Compromise (8:1-9)

Koheleth draws a picture of a wise man who serves a king whose will is often arbitrary and unjust. In the course of his service conflict arises in the servant's mind on questions of right and wrong. But compromise is the essence of a wise man's conduct. The king must be obeyed, and the oath of obedience to the king gives a sanction to actions

---

26-29. More Bitter Than Death.—The writer does not for some reason think highly of women; neither does the Orient generally. He has found one true friend **among a thousand**—and that a man. This alone he concludes: **God made man upright,** but man has defeated himself by his own devices. We go to so much trouble to make trouble for ourselves.

8:1-17. The Religious Feeling Deepens.—The religious bearing of the book grows more definite as the chapters go on, as though from the depths of his frustrations the author saw from time to time a rising light; but intermittent

shadows veil it. This is one of the shorter chapters, and of varied content. The relation between **wisdom** and **interpretation** is suggested. Wisdom may know, but interpretation sets a thing forth. Almost parallel passages in Job contrast wisdom and the insight which finds hidden meanings, as though all experience were only symbol and suggestion. Wisdom and the gift to find those deeper meanings are rare and invaluable qualities. "They illumine [the better translation] the face" (vs. 1).

1. The Message of a Face.—Jacob saw the forgiving face of Esau as though it were the

a man's wisdom maketh his face to shine, and the boldness of his face shall be changed.

2 I *counsel thee* to keep the king's commandment, and *that* in regard of the oath of God.

3 Be not hasty to go out of his sight: stand not in an evil thing; for he doeth whatsoever pleaseth him.

A man's wisdom makes his face shine, and the hardness of his countenance is changed.

2 Keep[m] the king's command, and because of your sacred oath be not dismayed; 3 go from his presence, do not delay when the matter is unpleasant, for he does what-

[m] Heb inserts an *I*

---

which the servant would not otherwise have countenanced. But the wise servant is no mere subservient weakling, for he is master both of the time and mode of action.

8:1. Some exegetes join to the previous section this verse, which, however, belongs to the following description of a wise man as Koheleth sees him. He is a man who knows how to solve a difficult problem: "he knows the solution of a thing" (so, literally, the M.T.). The Hebrew word for "solution," *pēsher* (an Aramaic loan word), means also **interpretation**, but "solution" is more suitable in the context. Williams' translation, "insight into the meaning of each difficult matter before him" is too general. The particular meaning is, as Graetz points out, that the wise man knows a way out (*Ausweg, Ausgleich*) of difficult situations. It is significant that *pēsher,* though in this verse it has the sense of "solution," gains in rabbinical Hebrew the meaning "compromise." **Wisdom makes his face shine:** His face has a kind and gracious expression; the opposite of this is **hardness,** a word which conveys the idea of severity and the determination to have one's own way.

2-3. Your sacred oath: The M.T. (lit., the [an] oath of God) has been explained as (*a*) an oath made before God and affirming fidelity to the king, or (*b*) an oath sworn by God himself, promising support to the king (cf. "king by divine grace"), or (*c*) an oath made to the divine king, i.e., to the king as a divine person or deity, in accordance with the beliefs and tradition of ancient Egypt and with the legal practice of the Ptolemaic period. (For discussion on this question see Hertzberg, *Der Prediger,* pp. 142-43, Galling, "Kohelet-Studien," pp. 294-95, and Paul Humbert, *Recherches,* p. 119.) If (*c*) is accepted, then the word **God** refers to the king himself. Possibly, however, the first words of the verse should be rendered "Keep the king's command even in the manner of an oath sworn to God."

Many critics, following the LXX, join the two first words of vs. 3 to vs. 2. These words may bear the meaning of **be not dismayed** or "be not frightened," or "be not precipitate" or "rash" or **hasty.** But if this phrase is to be detached from vs. 3, the next words must be translated **go from his presence,** which, as expressing ill will on the part of the wise man, does not seem to accord with Koheleth's presentation of wise conduct. Besides, in 10:4 the wise man is told, in circumstances similar to those in which he is found in 8:1-9, to be deferential to the ruler, "do not leave your place." Therefore the better translation is "Keep the king's command, and [this] because of your sacred oath. Be not hasty to go from his presence; [and] do not persevere ["continue," "insist," lit., "stand"] when the matter is unpleasant." The wise man will not rashly resign his office or continue arguing "in a difficult matter" (lit., "in an evil thing"), i.e., **when the matter is unpleasant.**

---

face of God. His disciples read in the face of Jesus the determinations which led him to the Cross. Every heart knows how the faces of those we love bless and content us, and how beautiful any face may be if the soul shines through.

2-9. No Discharge.—Koheleth seems to have dealt with kings; at least he meditates upon their capricious ways. They were best obeyed

without question. There must be in all this some relation to the writer's world, ill-governed and seamed with discontents. Loyalty was safest; but the administration of the king and his satraps lay within the framework of a vaster moral order. Authority ends with the grave, even the authority of kings. Kipling made a poem out of one phrase of the passage: **There is no**

4 Where the word of a king *is, there is* power: and who may say unto him, What doest thou?

5 Whoso keepeth the commandment shall feel no evil thing: and a wise man's heart discerneth both time and judgment.

6 ¶ Because to every purpose there is time and judgment, therefore the misery of man *is* great upon him.

7 For he knoweth not that which shall be: for who can tell him when it shall be?

8 *There is* no man that hath power over the spirit to retain the spirit; neither *hath he* power in the day of death: and *there is* no discharge in *that* war; neither shall wickedness deliver those that are given to it.

9 All this have I seen, and applied my heart unto every work that is done under the sun: *there is* a time wherein one man ruleth over another to his own hurt.

ever he pleases. 4 For the word of the king is supreme, and who may say to him, "What are you doing?" 5 He who obeys a command will meet no harm, and the mind of a wise man will know the time and way. 6 For every matter has its time and way, although man's trouble lies heavy upon him. 7 For he does not know what is to be, for who can tell him how it will be? 8 No man has power to retain the spirit, or authority over the day of death; there is no discharge from war, nor will wickedness deliver those who are given to it. 9 All this I observed while applying my mind to all that is done under the sun, while man lords it over man to his hurt.

4. He will obey the royal command as a divine ordinance, and since the king's word is law the wise man's conscience is salved. The teaching of Koheleth here is as Macdonald (*Hebrew Literary Genius*, p. 211) delineates it: "When, out of the fear of God, you conform to the situation into which God has brought you, *pecca fortiter;* you may be immoral but conform and be safe." (Cf. 7:16-17.)

5. Who keeps to the rule **will meet no harm,** i.e., he will experience (Vulg., *experietur*) no unpleasantness (lit., **evil thing**).

6-7. A wise man knows two important accompaniments of every action, viz., the time and the manner of acting, **although**—and here Koheleth makes a characteristic caveat—there lies upon man a sorely felt misfortune (**trouble, misery**). His knowledge is entirely valueless in regard to the future, which cannot be known at all. The Hebrew word rendered "manner" (**way**) has been explained less aptly as meaning "decision" (Williams), and by others as **judgment** (so KJV). On the view that the meaning is **judgment** McNeile regarded vss. 5-6a as additions of the pious glossator.

8-9. There are powers that defy man to restrain them. The first of these to be mentioned is the *rûaḥ,* the **spirit** of man or, as some prefer, "the wind" (cf. John 3:8). Then there is **death,** which on the appointed day claims its victim. There is also **war,** which in the area of its raging engulfs and carries all away, and from which there is no *mishláḥath* (**discharge** or getting off). Kuhn *et al.* suggest the emendation *meluḥésheth* (amulet): "There is no amulet against war." But the M.T. is preferable. The war exemptions recorded in Deut. 20 are too narrow in scope to affect the author's view of war as sweeping aside all attempts to evade its consequences. Finally, the most tenacious of all powers is that of moral evil, which will not free any **who are given to it.** All these powers are indestructible. The wise man will recognize them to be so, bow to necessity and conform to it when safety demands. Koheleth says that he has based his conclusions upon his observation of human affairs at such times as **man lords it over man to his hurt.**

discharge in that war (vs. 8). Exegetes argue whether **that** belongs to the text. Otherwise the passage might mean that there is no escape from the imperial draft; or else that wars are inevitable; or else, as Kipling meant, that there are engagements in life from which there is no

discharge. All the millenniums of history sadly confirm vs. 9: **Man lords it over man to his hurt.** "Power," said Lord Acton, "tends to corrupt, and absolute power corrupts absolutely."[6]

[6] *Essays on Freedom and Power* (Boston: Beacon Press, 1948), p. 364.

10 And so I saw the wicked buried, who had come and gone from the place of the holy, and they were forgotten in the city where they had so done: this *is* also vanity.

11 Because sentence against an evil work is not executed speedily, therefore the heart of the sons of men is fully set in them to do evil.

12 ¶ Though a sinner do evil a hundred times, and his *days* be prolonged, yet surely I know that it shall be well with them that fear God, which fear before him:

13 But it shall not be well with the wicked, neither shall he prolong *his* days, *which are* as a shadow; because he feareth not before God.

14 There is a vanity which is done upon the earth; that there be just *men*, unto whom it happeneth according to the work of the wicked; again, there be wicked *men*, to whom it happeneth according to the work of the righteous: I said that this also *is* vanity.

10 Then I saw the wicked buried; they used to go in and out of the holy place, and were praised in the city where they had done such things. This also is vanity. 11 Because sentence against an evil deed is not executed speedily, the heart of the sons of men is fully set to do evil. 12 Though a sinner does evil a hundred times and prolongs his life, yet I know that it will be well with those who fear God, because they fear before him; 13 but it will not be well with the wicked, neither will he prolong his days like a shadow, because he does not fear before God.

14 There is a vanity which takes place on earth, that there are righteous men to whom it happens according to the deeds of the wicked, and there are wicked men to whom it happens according to the deeds of the righteous. I said that this also is vanity.

F. Aimlessness of History (8:10-17)

There is no moral purpose working itself out in human history.

10. The M.T. is not very coherent; it reads, lit., "And then I saw the wicked buried and they came and from the place of a holy [one] they went and were forgotten [LXX, Aq., **were praised**] in the city where they had done so [i.e., **done such things**]." Since the word here rendered "so" (כֹן) may mean also "right," it is possible to translate the last words of the sentence, "where they had done rightly [i.e., justly]." The M.T. here has suffered in transmission. Already in the Talmud (cf. Graetz) suggestions are given for its emendation. The following attempts at restoration, out of the many that have been made, may seem to be the most worthy of consideration: (*a*) "And I saw that wicked men were brought to the grave [קברים מובאים] at a holy place, but they who had done what was right had to depart and be forgotten in the city" (Galling, Volz). Since strict Judaism regarded a burial place as impure, Galling sees in the reference to a burial place as a holy place some additional evidence of non-Jewish (Egyptian) influence on Koheleth's thought. (*b*) "And furthermore, I saw wicked men draw nigh to worship [קרבים] and enter; but from the holy place they who had done what was right had to depart and be forgotten in the city" (Hertzberg). (*c*) "And further I have seen wicked men at worship [קרבים], and they who have done so come in and go off on their ways from the Holy Place and boast of it" (Burkitt).

11-13. These verses, quite clearly in contradiction to Koheleth's thought, may represent the orthodox statement by a glossator of the Deuteronomist theory of reward

---

10-17. *Long-range Sins.*—All commentators acknowledge the difficulties of this section. Where and what was the holy place? And were the wicked in their burial exiled from consecrated burying grounds? No matter. The richest suggestion is in vss. 11-12: **Because sentence against an evil deed is not executed speedily, the heart of the sons of men is fully set to do**

evil. The lag in retribution is the secret of many of our follies and our faults. It lulls us into a false sense of security. If evil, like fire, scorched us at once, we would take care; but when its issues are hidden by time—?

There was once a wise little book which dealt, among other vital things, with "long-range sins," sins whose consequences whether

15 Then I commended mirth, because a man hath no better thing under the sun, than to eat, and to drink, and to be merry: for that shall abide with him of his labor the days of his life, which God giveth him under the sun.

16 ¶ When I applied mine heart to know wisdom, and to see the business that is done upon the earth: (for also *there is that* neither day nor night seeth sleep with his eyes:)

17 Then I beheld all the work of God, that a man cannot find out the work that is done under the sun: because though a man labor to seek *it* out, yet he shall not find *it;* yea further; though a wise *man* think to know *it,* yet shall he not be able to find *it.*

9 For all this I considered in my heart even to declare all this, that the right-

15 And I commend enjoyment, for man has no good thing under the sun but to eat, and drink, and enjoy himself, for this will go with him in his toil through the days of life which God gives him under the sun.

16 When I applied my mind to know wisdom, and to see the business that is done on earth, how neither day nor night one's eyes see sleep; 17 then I saw all the work of God, that man cannot find out the work that is done under the sun. However much man may toil in seeking, he will not find it out; even though a wise man claims to know, he cannot find it out.

9 But all this I laid to heart, examining it all, how the righteous and the wise

and retribution, and are intended to be corrective of vss. 10, 14 (McNeile, Barton, *et al.;* attempts to save some fragments of vss. 11-13 as Koheleth's thought—e.g., by Budde— lack all power of conviction, since this passage forms a consistent whole).

16b. Lit., "although even [or "for also"] by day and by night he does not see sleep with his eyes." These words appear in the KJV properly as a parenthesis, apparently to qualify the word **business,** but even so they have no good connection. When placed in vs. 17 (cf. Moffatt) the sentence makes excellent sense: **However much man may toil in seeking** [though even day and night his eyes should see no sleep], **he will not find it.**

17. Koheleth stresses one of his main conclusions. It is impossible, so far as man can study **the work of God,** to discover what the purpose of life is. Indeed, man cannot discover any purpose. The evidence which the author brings from human history and experience in vss. 10, 14 is that in this sphere there is no moral purpose at all in life. Life as tested at this critical point is proved to be vain and empty of purpose.

G. DEATH AS A COMMON FATE (9:1-16)

This section is closely related to the preceding, where Koheleth speaks of life's lack of purpose. His theme now is that (*a*) man cannot reckon that good fortune will be the reward of good character (vss. 1-6), or (*b*) that skill and ability will secure life's

in space or time are beyond our immediate vision, like a shell timed to explode fifty miles away. A wrong done in North America may accomplish its evil work in Asia; the folly of dead statesmen yields the red harvest of wars to come. Always and always the wrongdoings of the vanished past finally find their sad issues.

Though the mills of God grind slowly, yet they grind exceeding small;
Though with patience he stands waiting, with exactness grinds he all.[7]

Koheleth believed that—and yet he could not see how. The wicked do prosper, the days of the

righteous are not prolonged. It must be well with those who fear God; else life is like a shadow gone when the sun goes down. But the balancing of the scales of divine justice are beyond his knowing. He had spent sleepless nights in asking, and had found but one answer. "The finite cannot grasp the infinite." "Dangerous it were for the feeble brain of man to wade far into the doings of the Most High." So he returns to the shallow philosophy, eat, drink and be merry—if you can. The Christian knows that there is a better answer than that.

9:1-6. The Travail of the Heart.—"For to all this I gave my heart to dig through."[8] Ch. 9 is Koheleth's *De Profundis:* "Out of the depths

[7] Longfellow, "Poetic Aphorisms: Retribution." From the *Sinngedichte* of Friedrich von Logau.

[8] Plumptre, *Ecclesiastes,* p. 183.

eous, and the wise, and their works, *are* in the hand of God: no man knoweth either love or hatred *by* all *that is* before them.

2 All *things come* alike to all: *there is* one event to the righteous, and to the wicked; to the good and to the clean, and to the unclean; to him that sacrificeth, and to him that sacrificeth not: as *is* the good, so *is* the sinner; *and* he that sweareth, as *he* that feareth an oath.

and their deeds are in the hand of God; whether it is love or hate man does not know. Everything before them is vanity,[n] 2 since one fate comes to all, to the righteous and the wicked, to the good and the evil,[o] to the clean and the unclean, to him who sacrifices and him who does not sacrifice. As is the good man, so is the sinner; and he who swears is as he who shuns an oath.

[n] Syr Compare Gk: Heb *Everything before them is everything*

[o] Gk Syr Vg: Heb lacks *and the evil*

---

prizes (vss. 11-12), or (c) that wisdom in its own right will come to honor and fame (vss. 13-16). In vss. 7-10 the writer again stresses that over against the facts of existence all that is left for a man to do is to take from life what enjoyment is possible.

9:1. This verse is textually difficult. The RSV (examining it all) follows the emendation לתור ("to explore") proposed by Graetz instead of the dubious לבור of the M.T., which has been rendered **declare**, "explain," "prove." The LXX reads ולבי ראה, "And my heart saw all this, that the righteous," etc. Opinions on the original text vary greatly, but the sense of the verse is on any reading little affected. **In the hand of God:** I.e., entirely at his disposal. **Love or hate** should be taken with most exegetes as referring to God's loving and hating (cf. Mal. 1:1-3; Rom. 9:13) and as describing God's will in favoring some and rejecting others. The **righteous and the wise** and their actions are subject, along with the evil and unreligious, to this predestinating will which **no man knoweth.** Moral character gives a man no advantage, so far as fortune is concerned, over those who are immoral. **Everything before them:** These words might mean, "All has been determined before their time," but preferable is Podechard's emendation, הכל לפניהם הבל, which signifies "all [of life] is before them [i.e., in their sight] vanity," hence, **Everything before them is vanity** (cf. LXX).

2-6. Besides the particular predetermined lot which is given to each apart from any question of character, there is **one fate,** death, which befalls all without distinguishing good from bad. The veil which rests upon the drama of existence does not permit of any glimpse of a plan which might yield a clue to the meaning of life.

---

have I cried." Give him credit for sincerity; for all his seeming cynicism his pen is dipped "in the tears of things," his book written out of the heart. The Hebrew made an invaluable contribution to psychology in his uses of the word **heart:** they are beyond easy definition; they were born of ignorance and insight. No one had traced for him the mysterious pathways of thought through the seemingly inert matter of the brain, or told him their significance. The heart was the vital organ of life; that he did know, and when its red tides ebbed, life was over.

So he made the heart the designation and symbol of all human force, the source of desire, the secret of personality. Therefore poets have sung of its longings and satisfactions, and by a multitude of uses the word has become indispensable. We know now that thought is never uncolored by emotion; even in the most abstract processes of the mind, and when great

causes are at stake, "Out of [the heart] are the issues of life" (Prov. 4:23). "Le coeur a ses raisons," Pascal said in a famous passage;[9] the heart has not only its reasons, but its rights. Faith itself, he held, is an affair of the heart, not of the reason. That, one may question; but when the seeker gives his heart to the travail of thought, he can do no more to penetrate the secret of the great enigma of life.

2-3. The Crucial Problem of the Book.—For Koheleth, as for Job and all the great seekers—and the great doubters—the enigma of life, given the sovereignty of God, is its apparent inequities, the baffling relationship between character and compensation, between deserving and receiving. Ch. 9 is seamed with the tensions between faith and the too-pregnant issues of life. This, for Ecclesiastes, is the mystery of life. The book is like a landscape seen on a day

[9] *Pensées*, tr. H. F. Stewart (London: Routledge & Kegan Paul, 1950), No. 626.

3 This *is* an evil among all *things* that are done under the sun, that *there is* one event unto all: yea, also the heart of the sons of men is full of evil, and madness *is* in their heart while they live, and after that *they go* to the dead.

4 ¶ For to him that is joined to all the living there is hope: for a living dog is better than a dead lion.

5 For the living know that they shall die: but the dead know not any thing, neither have they any more a reward; for the memory of them is forgotten.

6 Also their love, and their hatred, and their envy, is now perished; neither have they any more a portion for ever in any *thing* that is done under the sun.

7 ¶ Go thy way, eat thy bread with joy,

3 This is an evil in all that is done under the sun, that one fate comes to all; also the hearts of men are full of evil, and madness is in their hearts while they live, and after that they go to the dead. 4 But he who is joined with all the living has hope, for a living dog is better than a dead lion. 5 For the living know that they will die, but the dead know nothing, and they have no more reward; but the memory of them is lost. 6 Their love and their hate and their envy have already perished, and they have no more for ever any share in all that is done under the sun.

7 Go, eat your bread with enjoyment,

---

3. Human beings in their lifetime show themselves to be weak creatures morally, unstable mentally (Hebrew, "madness is in their minds"), and the nothingness of death is an appropriate end for them.

4. The precious spark of life has all the attraction of which vs. 4 speaks, but after all, it amounts only to this, that the living have the advantage of knowing that they will die, while the dead are not even aware of it.

---

whose wind-swept clouds wash it with alternate lights and shadow. "The righteous and the wise and their deeds are in the hand of God" (vs. 1). Koheleth believed that, nor did he ever surrender his conviction. But what he saw, and had seen, did not seem to undergird his faith.

One fate comes to all. So wrote Isaac Watts:

> Time, like an ever-rolling stream,
> Bears all its sons away.[1]

There is a tide, said Bossuet over the biers of dead kings, which carries pomp and power into oblivion; Ecclesiastes said it first, with a somber eloquence which even Bossuet could not match. Vss. 1-6 are among the saddest in any literature—and the most hopeless. Since these passages are in a way the deeply shadowed substance of Koheleth's verdict upon life, it is proper to consider, at the risk of repetition, where his fallacies are and the corrective message with which the Christian can meet them.

Of this Preacher one may say once and for all that his pride and profession of wisdom lacked understanding, and most of all, insight. He is too much concerned with what happens to us, too little concerned with what we are— or may become. He would have profited by reading Emerson's essay on "Compensation" if he had had it to read. He would have gained

by Henry van Dyke's "What we are is what becomes of us,"[2] and character *is* eternal destiny. In Ecclesiastes there is no examination of the tangled and often distant causes and sources —distant both in time and space—of evil fortune, of sorrows, pains, frustration, and the like subjects of Koheleth's complaints.

There are indictments of social wrongs, but no assumption of social responsibility. Amos and Micah possessed social visions and understandings entirely beyond Koheleth's range. The book, to repeat the oft-repeated, does present the Christian with an arresting succession of observations, proverbs, epigrams, mottoes. It asks questions, for answers to which there always has been and still is a most pressing need. Christian wisdom and faith have the answers, and the only answers. Our indebtedness to this O.T. sage may well be chiefly at the point where he puts into words, after his own fashion, those half-hidden reasons why religion has lost power and meaning in all too vast regions of our own troubled world. Secularism is in the saddle, and now there is written across the façade of what had once been the seats of the mighty in a historic church order, "Religion is the opium of the people."

7-10. Seize the Day.—There is no suggestion anywhere in the book even of George Eliot's

[1] "O God, our help in ages past."

[2] *Six Days of the Week* (New York: Charles Scribner's Sons, 1924), p. 253.

and drink thy wine with a merry heart; for God now accepteth thy works.

8 Let thy garments be always white; and let thy head lack no ointment.

9 Live joyfully with the wife whom thou lovest all the days of the life of thy vanity, which he hath given thee under the sun, all the days of thy vanity: for that *is* thy portion in *this* life, and in thy labor which thou takest under the sun.

10 Whatsoever thy hand findeth to do, do *it* with thy might; for *there is* no work, nor device, nor knowledge, nor wisdom, in the grave, whither thou goest.

11 ¶ I returned, and saw under the sun, that the race *is* not to the swift, nor the battle to the strong, neither yet bread to the

and drink your wine with a merry heart; for God has already approved what you do.

8 Let your garments be always white; let not oil be lacking on your head.

9 Enjoy life with the wife whom you love, all the days of your vain life which he has given you under the sun, because that is your portion in life and in your toil at which you toil under the sun.

10 Whatever your hand finds to do, do it with your might; for there is no work or thought or knowledge or wisdom in Sheol, to which you are going.

11 Again I saw that under the sun the race is not to the swift, nor the battle to

---

11-12. Doubtless Koheleth had seen industry rewarded and genius crowned, but he was more impressed by the numberless examples of ability unrecognized, of excellence that had failed to make its mark; for life is no less indiscriminative than death. The

---

"immortality of influence." "The memory of them is lost" (vs. 5). This is the nadir of despair. Therefore—? Koheleth's "therefores" are always the same: seize the day, seek what happiness you can. The "enjoyments" commended are, for his time and most times, normal and blameless. They are today pleasant aspects of the normal life of every quiet and prosperous land, what its people want and are trying, for the most part successfully, to get. Hebrew religion was never ascetic. There are similar permissions and exhortations in the writings of other Jewish teachers. Koheleth did not need to go to school to the Greek Epicureans to learn them. Here is something as old as human nature. Passages from Chaldean clay tablets say the same thing: seek the bright paths of pleasure, though they are not long at their best, and end in the underworld of dust and darkness from which there is no return. These are not the highest levels of life; that is their limitation. But the Preacher is right when he says that happiness is the gift of God, to be sought and not to be feared, if only we seek the right happiness and the right conditions of it. But there is another level than all this: the level of the Christian Beatitudes. Ecclesiastes has no vision of that.

11-12. *Koheleth Rests His Case.*—Vs. 11 is classic in its negations, a summary in which Koheleth rests his case. He takes his analogies from the Greek stadia and from contested battlefields, and sees no fairness in any of them. **The race is not to the swift, nor the battle to the strong.** The wise are poor, and the learned are

without honor. Then one devastating sentence: **Time and chance happen to them all.** We are like netted birds beating our wings in vain. The implications of this passage are searching and far-reaching. The corrections of it lie in another dimension.

To begin with, this is to evaluate life on its lower levels, almost fatally to confuse means and ends, actually to misrepresent factual experience. These are all relative terms. What **race?** What **battle?** What wages for wisdom and knowledge? There are so many races, so many battles on so many fields, so many wisdoms—and so many follies. It all depends. In the main, the swift do win the race for which they are fitted and trained; the strong do win the battle for which they are properly armed. Breadwinning wisdom does get bread, money-making intelligence does make money. It is a part of the wisdom of life to know for what race one should enter himself, and whether it is worth the running, what are one's appointed battlefields, what wealth one should seek and whose favor one should court. There are, said Paul, "diversities of gifts"; and they are, he believed, God's gifts. Browning's Pompilia knew to her sorrow that "God plants us where we grow." [3] Equally, in way of long sequence, he apportions gifts. There is nothing of this in Ecclesiastes.

Neither is there any sense of the worth of the struggle. Browning's grammarian, who finished the business of a Greek particle, "dead from the waist down," [4] knew something Koheleth never

[3] *The Ring and the Book,* "Pompilia."
[4] "A Grammarian's Funeral."

wise, nor yet riches to men of understanding, nor yet favor to men of skill; but time and chance happeneth to them all.

12 For man also knoweth not his time: as the fishes that are taken in an evil net, and as the birds that are caught in the snare; so *are* the sons of men snared in an evil time, when it falleth suddenly upon them.

13 ¶ This wisdom have I seen also under the sun, and it *seemed* great unto me:

14 *There was* a little city, and few men within it; and there came a great king against it, and besieged it, and built great bulwarks against it.

the strong, nor bread to the wise, nor riches to the intelligent, nor favor to the men of skill; but time and chance happen to them all. **12** For man does not know his time. Like fish which are taken in an evil net, and like birds which are caught in a snare, so the sons of men are snared at an evil time, when it suddenly falls upon them.

13 I have also seen this example of wisdom under the sun, and it seemed great to me. **14** There was a little city with few men in it; and a great king came against it and besieged it, building great siegeworks

---

words עת ופגע mean **time and chance** (KJV, RSV, Hertzberg, *et al.*), or rather "time and adverse fate" (Odeberg, Kautzsch; cf. Galling, "time-appointed fate"). Man is thwarted continually in life's struggle.

13-16. A poor wise man gains no fame however wise he may be.

---

seems to have suspected; nor is there an adequate sense of the ultimate, time-needing results of the battle and the race. The great issues, the final citations, do need time. One must sweep vast circles to include the divine adjustments. The grammarian knew that also.

> Oh, if we draw a circle premature,
>   Heedless of far gain,
> Greedy for quick returns of profit, sure
>   Bad is our bargain![5]

11-12. *Masters of Time and Chance.*—Time and chance do happen to all; but they are not by any right of their own our masters. Time is given to be used—the tritest of commonplaces. "Give me health and a day," said Emerson, "and I will make the pomp of emperors ridiculous."[6] The Bible makes much of time. Life, in a way, is a traffic in time. We exchange—or may—the sequent days and years for duties and wisdoms, comradeships and goodnesses, and through the seasons reap the harvests of the soul.

Chance, commentators say, is "occurrents" in the Hebrew. We breast a stream of occurrents, often enough not of our choosing. This gives to life a double texture: what happens, and what we make of happenings; or the pattern we seek to weave, and another pattern woven for us by a power not ourselves. Thus as weavers, out of the warp of the occurring and the woof of our own creative power, we weave strangely different fabrics. One man, out of sorrow, pain, or loss, weaves resentment and despair; another, tenderness and sympathies. And so on and on through all the circumstances of life.

[5] *Ibid.*
[6] *Nature,* ch. iii.

Nor are the occurrents themselves unrelated to what wisdom or vision we possess. The wise anticipate them, and what occurs is often of our own seeking or causing. But by the grace of God the wise and the good have made of **time and chance** a spiritual conquest, and pass on to the music which Tennyson heard, as of "some wise prince of this world [returning] from his wars."[7] Christian faith knows that with our work still unfinished we pass from the temporal to the enduring, to where there is again "time enough." Had Koheleth even glimpsed that vision, or been even in the least sustained by that faith, his whole sad philosophy would have been changed.

In the end, as always, he falls back on two supports: take and enjoy the fugitive good; seek what undergirding wisdom you can find. There is no need to linger further upon this aspect of Koheleth's wisdom—or lack of wisdom. It is old, tenacious, and has found multitudinous voices. He is right in his insistence that happiness is the gift of God. He did not know, nor do any like-minded know, that if happiness is denied one may harvest blessings from its denials. The Beatitudes say that over and over; and they endure, being divinely addressed to our human estate, while soft philosophies perish.

13-18. *A Little City.*—The chapter ends with either a parable or some now-forgotten historical incident. Some have made an allegory of it, as in Bunyan's *Holy War* Satan was defeated under the walls of the city of Mansoul. Koheleth says only that the **poor wise man** was forgotten—he so often is—but that the city was saved. An epigram concludes the matter. Quiet wisdom is best, and too much good lies at the mercy of

[7] *Becket,* Act V, scene 2.

15 Now there was found in it a poor wise man, and he by his wisdom delivered the city; yet no man remembered that same poor man.

16 Then said I, Wisdom *is* better than strength: nevertheless the poor man's wisdom *is* despised, and his words are not heard.

17 The words of wise *men are* heard in quiet more than the cry of him that ruleth among fools.

18 Wisdom *is* better than weapons of war: but one sinner destroyeth much good.

10 Dead flies cause the ointment of the apothecary to send forth a stinking savor: *so doth* a little folly him that is in reputation for wisdom *and* honor.

---

against it. 15 But there was found in it a poor wise man, and he by his wisdom delivered the city. Yet no one remembered that poor man. 16 But I say that wisdom is better than might, though the poor man's wisdom is despised, and his words are not heeded.

17 The words of the wise heard in quiet are better than the shouting of a ruler among fools. 18 Wisdom is better than weapons of war, but one sinner destroys much good.

10 Dead flies make the perfumer's ointment give off an evil odor;

so a little folly outweighs wisdom and honor.

---

15. Deliver the city: If this is the meaning, then vs. 16 is a general statement about poor men's wisdom being unheeded and has only a loose connection with vs. 15, where the poor man's wisdom was heeded. Possibly the proper translation is "would have delivered the city" (McNeile, Hertzberg, Volz, Galling). The wise man could have saved the city, but no one thought of (**remembered**) him, because he was poor. If this is adopted, the translation of vs. 16 should be as in the KJV, **Then** [or And] **said I.**

III. CONCLUDING ADVICE TO DISCIPLES (9:17–12:7)

A. VARIOUS MAXIMS (9:17–10:20)

In this section several small groups of maxims in the style of the book of Proverbs enclose and penetrate a passage (10:4-7, 14b, 16-17, 20) which has the distinctive marks of Koheleth's thinking. The surrounding maxims are rightly regarded by McNeile, Barton, *et al.,* as interpolations. Commentators who hold that the whole of 9:17–10:20 is from Koheleth commonly do so on the ground that it is not possible to require of him a thoroughly logical sequence of thought. But to argue thus is to forget that readers in general are impressed with the sundry and inconsequent nature of 9:17–10:20, for the very reason that this section is in such palpable contrast with the character of the rest of the book. Up to 9:16 the course of thought is a path which is clear enough, although at times uneven, but in 9:17–10:20 the road has become blocked by a sturdy crop of loosely associated proverbs, whose presence is probably to be accounted for in such a way as Podechard (see Intro., p. 12) has suggested. The bulk of original material is probably found in 10:4-7, 14b, 16-17, 20, while the maxims are in 9:17–10:3; 10:8-14a, 15, 18, 19.

17. The quiet words of a wise man receive a better hearing than does the loud speaking of a fool haranguing his followers.

10:1. The sense is quite clear. The M.T., however, is not beyond the suspicion of corruption. Galling emends: "A fly dies [זבוב ימות] and makes the perfumer's ointment

---

sinners who have no mercy. All this also our own time would be wise to remember.

10:1–11:10. *A Teacher's Notebook.*—If Koheleth had been a wisdom school teacher, much that is enigmatic and more or less apparently displaced in Ecclesiastes would explain itself. Such passages as chs. 10–11 might be transcripts from his notebooks, meant to be amplified in

the lecture room, dilated in the give and take of discussion. Now at the best they are seen as through a glass—darkly. Translators do not agree; the passages are debated. There is a wealth of scholarly material upon the sources, the form, and the content of the proverbial wisdom upon which Koheleth drew. "It knows," says T. T. Perowne, "no distinction of race or

2 A wise man's heart *is* at his right hand; but a fool's heart at his left.

3 Yea also, when he that is a fool walketh by the way, his wisdom faileth *him,* and he saith to every one *that* he *is* a fool.

4 If the spirit of the ruler rise up against thee, leave not thy place; for yielding pacifieth great offenses.

5 There is an evil *which* I have seen under the sun, as an error *which* proceedeth from the ruler:

6 Folly is set in great dignity, and the rich sit in low place.

---

2 A wise man's heart inclines him toward the right,
but a fool's heart toward the left.
3 Even when the fool walks on the road,
he lacks sense,
and he says to every one that he is a fool.
4 If the anger of the ruler rises against you,
do not leave your place,
for deference will make amends for great offences.
5 There is an evil which I have seen under the sun, as it were an error proceeding from the ruler: 6 folly is set in many high places, and the rich sit in a low place.

---

give off an evil odor; so a little folly destroys [מאבד] the choicest of wisdom." Cohen quotes Rashi in favor of the words **dead flies** meaning "flies about to die," i.e., in their sickly condition in wintertime.

2. Cf. Matt. 25:33, where right and left symbolize good and bad. The wise man's mind is adroit, the mind of a fool is gauche (so Odeberg).

3. He proclaims himself through his manner and conduct as a fool, or he calls everybody whom he meets a fool, or "all the world says [lit., "and one says to all"]: 'that is a fool.'"

4. Kurt Galling ("Prediger Salomo," in Max Haller and Kurt Galling, *Die fünf Megilloth* [Tübingen: J. C. B. Mohr, 1940; "Handbuch zum Alten Testament"], p. 49) thinks that Koheleth's farewell to his pupils starts with 11:1, but the concluding remarks of the author would seem rather to begin here. The passage is in the strain of 8:1-9, but now Koheleth admonishes not so much to compromise as to exercise self-control. The students in the wisdom schools were to a large extent the youth who were training for government service.

The word מרפא (Vulg., *curatio;* RSV, **deference**—cf. Moffatt) means "equanimity," "composure." Hence, "for composure allays gross blunders" or, if יניא is read for יניח, "for composure prevents gross blunders."

5-7. Upheavals in the composition of councils of state may occur, changes for the worse, reflecting something amiss **(an error)** at the source of authority itself. Koheleth has experienced a turn of events of this kind.

---

country." [8] It covers the spacious fields of life. It achieves literary excellence, and has so become a treasured inheritance.

10:2. *The Frontages of Life.*—This verse is representative: A wise man's heart [note **heart** again] **inclines him toward the right, but a fool's heart toward the left.** The distinction between **right** and **left** is as old as the sense of direction. The terms have become symbolic of dominant trends in conduct, in society, and in the soul. They have been used to designate political and economic attitudes, and radio commentators have filled the air with them. They are the frontages of life along which we move; the ways in which we lay out and follow our schemes and

[8] *The Proverbs* (Cambridge: Cambridge University Press, 1899; "Cambridge Bible"), p. 12.

patterns. They are strategic and commanding; they carry the detail of life with them; their issues are characters and dispositions. Down these frontages we move not only toward what we become, but toward what becomes of us.

All wisdom literature, in substance, contrasts the frontage of wisdom with the frontage of folly. Ecclesiastes takes the same line, case by case, trenchant, unforgettable. Here are admonitions against folly and its consequences which repeat themselves across the millenniums. Their apparent simplicities are misleading. They are like bird flights over deep places. Their compactness is tantalizing; their vague allusions are windows opening upon a vanished world.

6, 8-9, 12, 18-19. *Unanswered Questions.*—The proverbs shrewdly characterize wisdom and

7 I have seen servants upon horses, and princes walking as servants upon the earth.

8 He that diggeth a pit shall fall into it; and whoso breaketh a hedge, a serpent shall bite him.

9 Whoso removeth stones shall be hurt therewith; *and* he that cleaveth wood shall be endangered thereby.

10 If the iron be blunt, and he do not whet the edge, then must he put to more strength: but wisdom *is* profitable to direct.

11 Surely the serpent will bite without enchantment; and a babbler is no better.

12 The words of a wise man's mouth *are* gracious; but the lips of a fool will swallow up himself.

13 The beginning of the words of his mouth *is* foolishness: and the end of his talk *is* mischievous madness.

14 A fool also is full of words: a man cannot tell what shall be; and what shall be after him, who can tell him?

15 The labor of the foolish wearieth every one of them, because he knoweth not how to go to the city.

7 I have seen slaves on horses, and princes walking on foot like slaves.

8 He who digs a pit will fall into it;
and a serpent will bite him who breaks through a wall.

9 He who quarries stones is hurt by them;
and he who splits logs is endangered by them.

10 If the iron is blunt, and one does not whet the edge,
he must put forth more strength;
but wisdom helps one to succeed.

11 If the serpent bites before it is charmed,
there is no advantage in a charmer.

12 The words of a wise man's mouth win him favor,
but the lips of a fool consume him.

13 The beginning of the words of his mouth is foolishness,
and the end of his talk is wicked madness.

14 A fool multiplies words,
though no man knows what is to be,
and who can tell him what will be after him?

15 The toil of a fool wearies him,
so that he does not know the way to the city.

8-9. "May fall," "may bite," "may be hurt": such renderings are better than those given in the KJV, ERV, or RSV. The thought is that every occupation has its particular danger. Possibly the glossator wished to imply that it is not only the king's service which has drawbacks. In vs. 8 there is no suggestion that the **pit** is dug for someone to fall into.

10. What sharpness is to a tool, so are wits to him who has them.

14-15. Vs. 15 has given much trouble to interpreters. The conjunction **because** (KJV) is correct; **so that** (RSV) is possible but unconvincing. The verse must be taken with vs. 14a and reads, lit., "A fool multiplies words; fool's labor wears him out, for he does not know how to go to town." Vs. 14b seems to follow up the thought of vs. 7. No one can tell when adversity may come for "man does not know what may happen and none can say what the future has in store." (For Egyptian parallels see Erman, *Literature*

folly, and tabulate concisely their contrasted consequences; but they leave unanswered the master questions: What are the sources of our follies? Why, knowing better, do we yield to them? Where, in the entangled complexes of personality, are the relationships between folly and sin, or sin and folly? Why, having been taught so long and so much in costly schools, do we still by follies (too slight a word) "hold the earth from heaven away"?[9] Why so frequently is there such sore need of a prayer not often enough found in the treasuries of prayer, "Lord,

[9] Edward Rowland Sill, "The Fool's Prayer."

be merciful to me, a fool"?[1] It is not so simple as the proverb coiners seemed to think.

Here are only prudential considerations, with no strong foundation to sustain the imperiled society or soul; no healing for their sicknesses save inexorable consequence. Nevertheless, these verses are filled with treasure; they are pregnant and arresting. Their interpretation is not so easy as it seems, but one may "read, mark, learn, and inwardly digest them"[2] for himself. If

[1] *Ibid.*
[2] Book of Common Prayer, Collect for the Second Sunday in Advent.

16 ¶ Woe to thee, O land, when thy king *is* a child, and thy princes eat in the morning!	16 Woe to you, O land, when your king is a child, and your princes feast in the morning!
17 Blessed *art* thou, O land, when thy king *is* the son of nobles, and thy princes eat in due season, for strength, and not for drunkenness!	17 Happy are you, O land, when your king is the son of free men, and your princes feast at the proper time, for strength, and not for drunkenness!
18 ¶ By much slothfulness the building decayeth; and through idleness of the hands the house droppeth through.	18 Through sloth the roof sinks in, and through indolence the house leaks.
19 ¶ A feast is made for laughter, and wine maketh merry: but money answereth all *things*.	19 Bread is made for laughter, and wine gladdens life, and money answers everything.
20 ¶ Curse not the king, no not in thy thought; and curse not the rich in thy bedchamber: for a bird of the air shall carry the voice, and that which hath wings shall tell the matter.	20 Even in your thought, do not curse the king, nor in your bedchamber curse the rich; for a bird of the air will carry your voice, or some winged creature tell the matter.
11 Cast thy bread upon the waters: for thou shalt find it after many days.	11 Cast your bread upon the waters, for you will find it after many days.

of the Ancient Egyptians, pp. 109, 239.) The way to the city was visible to practically everybody. The fool in his verbosity labors on without coming to a conclusion, can never make his point plain or reach his goal.

16-17. A land whose **king is a child** (נער, interpreted by some, perhaps rightly, as "slave" or "low born") is compared with a land ruled by **the son of free men,** a son of **nobles.**

19. Apparently a gloss on vs. 16. The princes who feast in the morning are those for whose merriment bread and wine are prepared at lavish expense—**money** answering for, i.e., providing for, **everything.**

20. A precept inculcating discretion. Birds are able to reveal secrets (cf. Schiller's poem "Die Kraniche des Ibykus," and note G. H. Box on IV Ezra 5:6 in R. H. Charles, *The Apocrypha and Pseudepigrapha of the Old Testament in English* [Oxford: Clarendon Press, 1913], II, 569: "Birds . . . were regarded in antiquity as possessing supernatural knowledge. They could foresee impending events").

B. NEED FOR ACTION (11:1-8)

Though no one can know what the result of any of his ventures will be, for all things are predestined and the method of God's working as seen in creation is beyond man's knowledge, yet man must not be irresolute in acting or overcautious in regard to the time of action.

wisely applied, they will speak with practical directness to every wayfarer down the mysterious ways of life. They seem on the face of them to be a résumé of Koheleth's observations and admonitions as he draws his book to a close. He recognizes the uncertainties of existence, the contingencies to which all effort is subject, how dim the future is to human vision, what finalities attend the pilgrimage.

Therefore commit your enterprises generally to the tides of time. **For you do not know which will prosper, this or that** (11:6). There | is a wealth of suggestion here on "the ventures of life." One may deal with it upon many levels, and most of all upon the level Ecclesiastes never reaches, the level of Christian faith. For faith itself is an adventure, a stepping out upon the yet unproved, to find, as Hopeful in *The Pilgrim's Progress* told Pilgrim when the waters began to carry him down, "I feel the bottom, and it is good."

11:1-10. *Hold Your Course.*—There are warnings here against an excess of caution. **He who observes the wind will not sow.** The great con- |

2 Give a portion to seven, and also to eight; for thou knowest not what evil shall be upon the earth.

3 If the clouds be full of rain, they empty *themselves* upon the earth: and if the tree fall toward the south, or toward the north,

2 Give a portion to seven, or even to eight, for you know not what evil may happen on earth.

3 If the clouds are full of rain, they empty themselves on the earth; and if a tree falls to the south or to the north,

---

11:1-2. This passage has had many explanations, foremost among which are: (a) A reference to maritime trade; after long voyages the merchant's venture may be rewarded by a rich profit. (b) A reference to the practice in Egypt of sowing rice upon the sodden ground when the inundation of the Nile subsides (see John Kitto, *The Illustrated Commentary on the Old and New Testaments* [London: Charles Knight, 1840], III, 305). (c) According to Harry Ranston (*Ecclesiastes and Early Greek Wisdom Literature* [London: Epworth Press, 1925], p. 40), Koheleth, controverting Theognis' advice against "sowing the waters"—i.e., against helping the ungrateful—means, "Be generous, do not be narrow in your liberality; even on the thankless waters scatter broadcast the seeds of kindness; be sure that sooner or later you will be rewarded." (d) The verse exhorts to practice charity from which a reward at long last may be reaped (traditional Jewish view). (e) According to Hertzberg, the Hebrew conjunction כי, which generally means **for**, "that," or "when," and is usually translated in vss. 1-2 as **for (for you will find it . . . for you know not)**, should here be regarded as having the sense of "yet" or "nevertheless" (cf. KJV in Exod. 5:11; I Sam. 15:35; γὰρ in Matt. 15:27; Mark 7:28; Rom. 5:7 as rendered by KJV). The translation therefore is "yet you may find it . . . yet you know not . . . ," and the meaning is as follows: Cast your bread on the face of the waters; yet (though it is highly unlikely) you may find it again, for strange things have occurred. Put your capital for safety's sake (vs. 2) in seven or even eight concerns; yet, though it is not likely that all of them will fail, you never know what evil, what disaster, may happen; you may lose the entire sum. However unwise or wise your action may seem, there is no certainty about the result.

Hertzberg's interpretation appears to have solved the problem, but it may further be asked whether **cast your bread upon the waters** is a mere figure of speech indicating apparently useless efforts, or if it has a more substantial background. Such a background might be found in the popular practices of the Adonis festival, still prevalent in Palestine in Koheleth's day. Adonis was a deity of vegetation, especially of the corn; the so-called Gardens of Adonis were baskets or pots filled with earth in which wheat, barley, lettuces, etc., were sown till they shot up, and then the baskets and their contents were flung into the sea or into the springs. This action was considered to be a charm affecting the growth of crops and securing a good harvest. The casting of bread upon waters appears to be the means of obtaining a rich return (see James G. Frazer, *Adonis Attis Osiris* [London: Macmillan & Co., 1907], pp. 137-38; Rankin, *Israel's Wisdom Literature*, p. 186).

3. Nature's laws cannot be altered. The clouds, when full, **empty themselves.** Where the tree has fallen, there it will remain. McNeile renders "stick" (i.e., divining rod)

---

stancies of nature must be trusted. Vs. 3 has been given a theological authority which certainly the writer never intended. It has nothing to do with the doom of the impenitent dead; rather with the impartial and inexorable sequences of life. Vs. 7, **Light is sweet, and it is pleasant for the eyes to behold the sun,** may be a little window into Koheleth's perturbed spirit. His puzzles and forecastings had, he says, cost him sleepless nights; so he welcomed the morning, as only the sleepless can; or else some

inner light began to dawn for him. Plumptre thinks so: "The pessimism of the thinker is passing away." [3] He has begun to see the light.

But never clearly. Koheleth's metaphorical uses of **light** and **darkness**—he uses darkness oftener than light—are more than poetic diction. They are a part of the texture of his mind and spirit, and even where he does not use them himself we may use them for him and about him. Painters make much of the contrast

[3] *Ecclesiastes,* p. 208.

in the place where the tree falleth, there it shall be.

4 He that observeth the wind shall not sow; and he that regardeth the clouds shall not reap.

5 As thou knowest not what *is* the way of the spirit, *nor* how the bones *do grow* in the womb of her that is with child: even so thou knowest not the works of God who maketh all.

6 In the morning sow thy seed, and in the evening withhold not thine hand: for thou knowest not whether shall prosper, either this or that, or whether they both *shall be* alike good.

7 ¶ Truly the light *is* sweet, and a pleasant *thing it is* for the eyes to behold the sun:

in the place where the tree falls, there it will lie.

4 He who observes the wind will not sow; and he who regards the clouds will not reap.

5 As you do not know how the spirit comes to the bones in the womb*?* of a woman with child, so you do not know the work of God who makes everything.

6 In the morning sow your seed, and at evening withhold not your hand; for you do not know which will prosper, this or that, or whether both alike will be good.

7 Light is sweet, and it is pleasant for the eyes to behold the sun.

? Or As you do not know the way of the wind, or how the bones grow in the womb

---

instead of **tree**, for man can alter the position of a fallen tree. But on this very strict reasoning it might also be objected to Koheleth's saying, "What is crooked cannot be made straight" (1:15), that man frequently succeeds in making straight what is crooked.

4-6. After vss. 1-3 have stated that there are conditions of life which are beyond man's reckoning or control, vss. 4-6 counsel to take life as it is and not to kill all effort by waiting for ideal conditions that may never arrive.

4-5. Man cannot have absolute assurance of safety and success before he begins to act. Besides, man's knowledge of the works of creation—e.g., the growth of the embryo in the womb—is small and insignificant. The original text probably read, "And you do not know the way of the spirit in the womb . . ." (Galling). The Hebrew word rendered "as-the-bones" appears to be an explanatory gloss. The thought evidently is that although man has not the knowledge of the mystery of life, yet he does not on that account refrain from the act of procreation.

6. No man can tell whether the earlier (**morning**) or the later (**evening**) sowing will be the more fruitful.

7. The thought here supplements that of 9:4. Macdonald (*Hebrew Philosophical Genius*, p. 70) suggests that Koheleth's favorite phrase "under the sun" is touched with the spirit of this verse.

---

of light and shading in pictures and have a term for it, chiaroscuro, borrowed from the Italian, "dark light." Skill in such combinations is one test of a painter's technique. He cannot paint in light alone, but unless the light is dominant where there must be light something irreparable is lost. Koheleth knows that life is light and shadow, but he never quite finds light enough, i.e., faith and hope and courage enough, to dispel the shadows. At the best he writes and thinks and feels in "dark light." The shadows to which he was so deeply sensitive were waiting to be dispelled by a Light which had not yet risen. But it did rise, with its shadow-scattering proclamation, "I am the light of the world" (John 8:12).

This "dark light" quality, or if Plumptre is

right, "light dark" quality, strongly colors vss. 8-10. A man may rejoice in the gifts and blessings of maturity and length of life, but they are always touched and chilled by the presages of the coming night. All this Koheleth may have said as though thinking aloud, while his silent class wondered at an old man casting up the accounts of his fugitive years. Then he seems to collect himself, and looking into the faces before him, seeing them touched with the radiance of youth, counsels them sadly and maybe enviously, conscious of his own late afternoon, to cherish their youth and live in the glow of it. The context seems to bear out that interpretation. Youth, he seems to say, is a trust. You have so much in just being young.

Expositors now would be grateful if the

8 But if a man live many years, *and* rejoice in them all; yet let him remember the days of darkness; for they shall be many. All that cometh *is* vanity.

9 ¶ Rejoice, O young man, in thy youth; and let thy heart cheer thee in the days of thy youth, and walk in the ways of thine heart, and in the sight of thine eyes: but know thou, that for all these *things* God will bring thee into judgment.

10 Therefore remove sorrow from thy heart, and put away evil from thy flesh: for childhood and youth *are* vanity.

12 Remember now thy Creator in the days of thy youth, while the evil days come not, nor the years draw nigh, when thou shalt say, I have no pleasure in them;

8 For if a man lives many years, let him rejoice in them all; but let him remember that the days of darkness will be many. All that comes is vanity.

9 Rejoice, O young man, in your youth, and let your heart cheer you in the days of your youth; walk in the ways of your heart and the sight of your eyes. But know that for all these things God will bring you into judgment.

10 Remove vexation from your mind, and put away pain from your body; for youth and the dawn of life are vanity.

12 Remember also your Creator in the days of your youth, before the evil days come, and the years draw nigh, when you will say, "I have no pleasure in them";

---

8. This verse urges the diligent use of time by reminding us of **the days of darkness,** i.e., death, and that all that comes—i.e., all life's events and opportunities—is fleeting. "Work, for the night is coming."

C. *Carpe Diem* (11:9–12:7)

The theme of this section is "Let us therefore rejoice while we are young."

9. Walk in the ways of your heart and the sight of your eyes: This advice is closely akin to "follow thy desire so long as thou livest" in the harpist's song (see Intro., p. 16). **But know that for all these things . . . judgment:** Clearly an addition of the pious glossator.

10. Dawn of life: Hertzberg *et al.* translate "black hair." The Hebrew word suggests both the **dawn of youth** and the "blackness" of the hair of the young man.

12:1. Remember also your Creator in the days of your youth does not correspond with the style of Koheleth's thought. Certain exegetes therefore have regarded the word בוראיך (a so-called plural of majesty, hence, **your Creator**) as being an alteration of an original בורך, "thy cistern," or of בארך, "thy well"; both terms are often applied to a wife (Prov 5:15-18). The precept would thus run, "Remember also your wife in the days of your youth." A parallel thought appears in the Egyptian wisdom literature, "Love thy wife at home. . . . Gladden her heart, so long as she liveth: she is a goodly field for her lord" (Erman, *op. cit.,* p. 61). Galling thinks that the *memento mori* motif

---

writer had been more explicit about how **youth** [should] **walk in the ways of** [its] **heart** and in **the sight of** [its] **eyes;** these are questions which have perplexed the young, their teachers and advisors, always and always. For "the thoughts of youth are long, long thoughts."[4] The passage condenses into a single phrase what the wisdom books and the wisdom teachers expanded at length. Koheleth says but one covering thing, **For all these things God will bring you into judgment.** Therefore guard against provocations and evil desires. If youth is a trust, do not stain or shadow it.

Then the writer's mood changes. Perhaps the twilight began to invade the room in which he

was speaking, and his words are as the tolling of a vesper bell, **For youth and the dawn of life are vanity.**

12:1. *Remember—So Soon It Grows Later than You Think.*—The exhaustive Exeg. of the final passages of Ecclesiastes supplies a sufficiency of detail and illustrates the difficulties which attend a critical examination of the text. But we must not allow the grave music of one of the noblest passages in any literature to become "like sweet bells jangled, out of tune and harsh."[5] Here perhaps imagination is the better guide. Afternoon speaks to morning with wisdom, pathos, and warning. All this might have been, before the writer gave it its final perfect

---

[4] Longfellow, "My Lost Youth."

[5] Shakespeare, *Hamlet,* Act III, scene i.

2 While the sun, or the light, or the moon, or the stars, be not darkened, nor the clouds return after the rain:

3 In the day when the keepers of the house shall tremble, and the strong men shall bow themselves, and the grinders cease because they are few, and those that look out of the windows be darkened,

2 before the sun and the light, and the moon, and the stars are darkened and the clouds return after the rain; **3** in the day when the keepers of the house tremble, and the strong men are bent, and the grinders cease because they are few, and those that look through the windows are dimmed,

---

is more appropriate and believes that the original text read, "Remember thy grave" [בּוּרֶךָ], etc. But while a reference to a wife cannot be considered out of place or out of taste in a *carpe diem* passage (cf. 9:9), it is more satisfactory to consider vs. 1a not as the result of a corrupted text but rather as an addition from the same orthodox interpolator who wrote 11:9b and similar corrective notes. The section 11:9–12:7 reveals a close sequence of thought where the word **before** (עַד אֲשֶׁר לֹא), appearing in three places (vss. 1b, 2a, 6a), is more naturally governed by the word "rejoice" and its equivalents in 11:9-10 than by the precept **remember,** etc., which, on this account also, has the character of being a later intrusion.

2. Old age is depicted as a time of fading light and is compared with winter, when storms darken the horizon. Even after the rain has ceased, clouds again gather and obscure the luminaries in the skies. Luster and joy, warmth and sunshine, have gone.

3. Allusion is no longer made to the winter storms; man's body, afflicted by old age, is likened to a household which has entered upon hard times and has the service of only very inefficient domestic help. The **keepers of the house** are the arms and hands. **The strong men** are the legs. **The grinders** (lit., "grinding women") are the teeth; and **those that look through the windows** are the eyes.

---

form, his final counsel to a graduating class; or else his valedictory to the school he was leaving; or else the late harvest of his own life made moving and rhythmic; or else— No matter. The occasion is what it was; the message is timeless. "Remember, remember, so soon it grows later than you think."

There is, then, a wisdom of anticipation. "Seize the day" was fundamental in Koheleth's wisdom; but you cannot hold the day, and one would better take thought for the days which will succeed it, that they are not haunted by regrets, or pursued by might-have-beens. For unless one is ready for the day, either he cannot seize it, or it wounds him as he grasps it.

All meditative literature has lingered long upon the brevity of life. Job bemoans his fugitive days, swifter than the weaver's shuttle, though they bring him nothing but pain. "My days," said the psalmist, "are like a shadow that declineth" (Ps. 102:11). It is at the best a mournful music, but how it echoes across the millenniums! The final strophes of Ecclesiastes take their time from Time itself; and physical failure beats out their measures. They are a threnody, not for a departed friend, but for the lost faculties of physical force and enjoyment, a Miserere of self-pity.

The arresting thing is what they leave out:

that old age has its compensations, its own funded wealth of wisdom, resource, and recollection. It is attended by hazards and anxieties, it may be deeply shadowed by economic insecurity. The current phrase "old-age security" recognizes that, and recognizes society's obligation to provide such security. But if old age is unhaunted by too many regrets and fears, it may well be a gracious period of tranquillity, with treasures of memory, the compensations of children's children, blessed comradeship of mind and spirit—and rest. Like the late afternoon of a summer's day, when the shadows have grown long but the light lingers, and there are still bird notes in the treetops, and twilight is peace. It may indeed be more; it may be the season for reaping and storing the final harvest of life. Eliphaz the Temanite made out a better case than Koheleth, though no doubt somewhat naïvely oversimplified: a godly man comes to his grave like corn to the harvest (Job 5:26).

1-14. The Noblest Music of Mortality.—Koheleth's warning that what youth forgets to its later loss will deepen the afternoon shadows, and that a restraining sense of responsibility to God and his always-balancing scales is needed—so much is enduringly true.

Commentators make much of the words for

4 And the doors shall be shut in the streets, when the sound of the grinding is low, and he shall rise up at the voice of the bird, and all the daughters of music shall be brought low;

5 Also *when* they shall be afraid of *that which is* high, and fears *shall be* in the way, and the almond tree shall flourish, and the grasshopper shall be a burden, and desire shall fail: because man goeth to his long home, and the mourners go about the streets:

4 and the doors on the street are shut; when the sound of the grinding is low, and one rises up at the voice of a bird, and all the daughters of song are brought low; 5 they are afraid also of what is high, and terrors are in the way; the almond tree blossoms, the grasshopper drags itself along*q* and desire fails; because man goes to his eternal home, and the mourners go about the

q Or is a burden

---

4. The doors (in Hebrew a dual form meaning "double doors," i.e., two-leaved doors) might refer to the jaws or to the lips, but here more fittingly to the ears. Deafness cuts a man off very largely from the world outside. **The sound of the grinding** (lit., "of the mill") indicates the ordinary stir of the household, but here in particular the conversation of other persons. To the deaf man this becomes **low** and subdued. His own voice becomes thin and high-pitched, resembling the **voice of a bird.** Musical notes (in the Hebrew idiom **the daughters of song**) seem softer to him than they really are, and become indistinct. The translation **and one rises up at the voice of a bird** (RSV) and the rendering of the KJV are literal, and have been taken as meaning that an old man awakes at dawn. With slight emendation (ויקום לו קול) one may render, "and there arises for him the voice of a bird," i.e., the old man gets a high, tremulous voice.

5. Even small ascents are a strain on aged persons. Even the ordinary streets of an Eastern town, narrow as they are, and unregulated as the traffic upon them is, provide dangers and terrors enough for frail people. Having described the helplessness of the aged, Koheleth now enters upon his peroration which speaks of **the almond tree,** the locust **(grasshopper),** and the caper berry (cf. **desire**). Hertzberg translates: "The almond tree blossoms and the locust burdens itself [i.e., with food] and the caper bursts into bloom (ותפרח)." According to this interpretation, Koheleth expresses a contrast between nature at the height of its beauty and fullness, in spring and early summer, and the feebleness of the old man. Indeed, the world outside is in all its brightness when he is on his deathbed "when [כי] the man goes to his eternal home" and the professional **mourners** loiter in the streets nearby, expecting soon to be engaged to mourn him.

Another view is that of McNeile, who, following Ginsburg, renders: "And he rejecteth the almond, and the locust fruit is [too] heavy and the caper-berry becomes ineffectual." This translation sees in the **almond,** etc., the mention of luxuries which are

---

God in Ecclesiastes. He is never Yahweh, the covenant God of the Hebrews. He is universal, omnipotent, meting out evil and good as though he were a personalized and deified version of the Greek word whose very sound is like the clanking of a chain by which all life is bound and dragged: ἀνάγκη, "necessity." There is now and then, as the writer's moods change, some sense of a God more tender and considerate, gleams which glow—and vanish. Yet God is fundamental in the writer's mind. Koheleth was never an atheist. He was between two worlds, one dead, the other not yet born. Here his God is the "creating"—a rarely used Hebrew word. "It is he that hath made us, and not we ourselves" (Ps. 100:3).

What follows is classic, highly figurative, sometimes enigmatical; but the movement of it is majestic and sonorous in any translation. It is for the music of mortality what I Cor. 15 is for the music of immortality. It lends itself to cadenced reading, and without being set to music sings itself. Its figures of speech have become part of English literature; its analogies, the delight of the commentator. The imagery in detail is confused, but in substance it is plain for anyone to read. Old age is like so many things. It is like a stormcloud veiling the horizon; sun, moon, and stars go out, and there is no later clearing of the skies. Or else its heralds are failing faculties—again, no matter. Here, as in so many other passages, the

6 Or ever the silver cord be loosed, or the golden bowl be broken, or the pitcher be broken at the fountain, or the wheel broken at the cistern.

7 Then shall the dust return to the earth as it was: and the spirit shall return unto God who gave it.

8 ¶ Vanity of vanities, saith the Preacher; all is vanity.

9 And moreover, because the Preacher was wise, he still taught the people knowledge; yea, he gave good heed, and sought out, *and* set in order many proverbs.

streets; 6 before the silver cord is snapped,[r] or the golden bowl is broken, or the pitcher is broken at the fountain, or the wheel broken at the cistern, 7 and the dust returns to the earth as it was, and the spirit returns to God who gave it. 8 Vanity of vanities, says the Preacher; all is vanity.

9 Besides being wise, the Preacher also taught the people knowledge, weighing and studying and arranging proverbs with great

[r] Syr Vg Compare Gk: Heb *is removed*

---

no longer capable of reviving the old man's appetite. Of the many other explanations which have been given, these should be noted: (*a*) The **almond tree** in blossom is a symbol of the white hair of old age. (*b*) Even such a light thing as a locust **is a burden** (RSV mg.) to an old man who cannot bear the smallest weight. (*c*) The locust itself is a metaphor for an old man who is a burden to himself and can hardly drag himself along (cf. the fable of Tithonus who, living to an extreme old age, was at last turned into a locust). (*d*) The caper berry as an aphrodisiac loses its power. Against this it is said that there is no available evidence of any such use of the caper bud prior to medieval times. Evidence, however, might not be easy to establish.

The term *beth 'ōlāmô* (**his eternal home**) is found only in Ecclesiastes but corresponds to an Egyptian expression meaning the tomb. Humbert (*Recherches*, p. 123) thinks that although the term appears in Palmyrene and Punic its presence in Ecclesiastes reveals Egyptian influence.

6. It has been held that this verse presents only one picture, that the **cord**, the **bowl**, the **pitcher**, and the **wheel** all belong to the apparatus of water-drawing. But the terms **golden** and **silver** are against this opinion. There are two pictures, that of the lamp attached to the ceiling by a silver cord and that of the broken pitcher and the broken wheel. **Broken** as applied to the lamp is doubtless a hyperbole describing the crashing of the **bowl** to the ground and the spilling of the oil. Light and water are well-known symbols of life. The cessation of life is here represented by the perishing of those vessels which contain oil and water and aid man to see and to slake his thirst.

7. The spirit returns to God: The **spirit** is the breath of life which goes back to the source from which it came (cf. Ps. 104:29; Job 34:14-15). Koheleth does not mean that man's personality continues to exist.

D. First Epilogue: A Disciple's Praise (12:8-11)

9. The word עוֹד has been translated "still," **and moreover, besides,** "also," "continually," "continued [to teach]." All these are possible. The rendering "And besides

---

association lines are in the writer's own mind. He is a poet now, and who can forecast the ways of a poet's thought? Else how could a nightingale's song lead Keats to Ruth "in tears amid the alien corn"?[9]

The imagery is confused, but all the toil of the passing years is subdued to the music of it. It will be millenniums before Tennyson will write "Crossing the Bar"; but the overtones of the twilight and evening bell, echoing against the horizons, are "remember, remember, remem-

[9] "Ode to a Nightingale," st. vii.

ber." So much is pathetically true. Weakness and wakefulness do attend old age: sight fails, light burdens grow heavy, the back stoops, and the hands grope. That which is high becomes a peril. The lamp of life has no longer any oil to feed it; its golden bowl is broken. The tired heart ceases beating, and the hired mourners are waiting in the street.

We still repeat "Earth to earth, dust to dust" in the interment of our dead, a requiem old as mortality; and yet— Yet there is—Koheleth recognized it as a final gleam of hope—that

10 The Preacher sought to find out acceptable words: and *that which was* written *was* upright, *even* words of truth.

11 The words of the wise *are* as goads, and as nails fastened *by* the masters of assemblies, *which* are given from one shepherd.

12 And further, by these, my son, be admonished: of making many books *there is* no end; and much study *is* a weariness of the flesh.

care. 10 The Preacher sought to find pleasing words, and uprightly he wrote words of truth.

11 The sayings of the wise are like goads, and like nails firmly fixed are the collected sayings which are given by one Shepherd. 12 My son, beware of anything beyond these. Of making many books there is no end, and much study is a weariness of the flesh.

---

that Koheleth was a *ḥākhām* [i.e., a professional teacher of wisdom], he continued to teach [or "also taught"] knowledge to the people" brings out the meaning more fully. The book of Ecclesiastes was not written for the people. But after having written it, Koheleth continued to write, this time for a wider public, pondering, examining, and **arranging proverbs with great care.** The Hebrew word here rendered **proverbs** can mean maxims, parables, or allegories.

10. **Uprightly:** Koheleth never sacrificed his moral integrity in his search for what was **pleasing.**

11. The words, as in the RSV, down to **firmly fixed,** are clear. The meaning of the rest of the verse will perhaps never attain certainty. The best that can be made of it is: "[And as nails firmly fixed] are the members [i.e., the constituent sayings] of collections [i.e., collections of proverbs]; they are given by one shepherd" (cf. Barton; Hertzberg). The comparison of maxims with **goads** and **nails** is very apt, since maxims both stimulate thinking and connect ideas. The expression **one Shepherd** refers not to Koheleth or Solomon but to God, who is the fountainhead of wisdom. The Hebrew phrase rendered above as "members of collections" received in rabbinical exegesis (Siegfried, *Prediger und Hoheslied,* p. 77) the meaning **masters of assemblies,** an expression which has been explained as signifying "schools of wise men from which teaching was issued to the people" (Cohen, *The Five Megilloth,* p. 190). But the American Jewish Translation departs from this tradition, for it renders, "as nails well fastened are those that are composed in collections." Moffatt's translation, "like nails driven home; they put the mind of one man into many a life," rests upon the conjecture (see Burkitt, "Is Ecclesiastes a Translation?") that מרעה אחד (**from one shepherd**) is a corruption of מדע האחד ("the mind of one [man]").

E. SECOND EPILOGUE: A DISCIPLE'S WARNING (12:12-14)

These verses are either from the hand of the pious glossator who interpolated within the book the sentences safeguarding the doctrine of divine retribution, or they derive from someone of the same quality of mind.

12. The opening words have generally been regarded as a reference to the **sayings of the wise** mentioned in vs. 11. More probably they refer to the contents of the whole

---

which the sepulcher could not contain nor the clay dissolve. For God had breathed upon the clay, man had become a living spirit, and that which drew from out the boundless deep returns again home (vs. 7).

Who of us does not cherish the memory of some morning, some afternoon in a little burying ground, when the sunlight washed the very bottom of an open grave, and father, mother, brother, sister, husband, or wife was buried not in darkness but in light? "Twilight and evening

bell," but not the dark. There is a quenchless light beyond the hills of time. "O grave, where is thy victory?" (I Cor. 15:55.) Dust falling upon dust is not the requiem of earth's pilgrimage. There can be trumpets sounding on the other side.

The final verses are apparently an epilogue written later by another to facilitate the inclusion of the book into the Hebrew canon, or to appraise its final values. Koheleth can hardly have written them himself. One thing is sure:

13 ¶ Let us hear the conclusion of the whole matter: Fear God, and keep his commandments: for this *is* the whole *duty* of man.

14 For God shall bring every work into judgment, with every secret thing, whether *it be* good, or whether *it be* evil.

13 The end of the matter; all has been heard. Fear God, and keep his commandments; for this is the whole duty of man.*

14 For God will bring every deed into judgment, with[t] every secret thing, whether good or evil.

* Or *the duty of all men*
[t] Or *into the judgment on*

---

book. **My son,** a common form of address in the wisdom literature (cf. Prov. 1:8, 10) when a writer addresses his reader after the manner of a teacher addressing his pupil, must be taken as a reference to the general reader. The first epilogue may have been written several generations before the time of the writer of the second epilogue, and we can hardly think of the later writer addressing the earlier as **my son.** Galling renders: "Beyond this there is yet this to be added, my son: be admonished." Cf. "And furthermore, my son, be admonished" (ERV). The writer has in mind Koheleth as a student and thinker, whose views require some corrective emphasis. Williams (*Ecclesiastes,* pp. 161-62) thinks that "those things" refers to what the writer is about to say concerning **books** and **study.** Accordingly he renders: "And further, against those (two things), my son, be warned, of making many books there is no end, and much devotion (to study) is a weariness of the flesh." This is a possible but strained translation.

---

there is no end of the making of many books about Ecclesiastes. It may even be appropriate to add, as we look back over the Expos. of this, one of the most fascinating and in some ways the most difficult of O.T. books, that much

study is a weariness of the flesh. The final verse might be Koheleth himself in a humble mood of clearer vision, speaking still from his dust: **Fear God, and keep his commandments.** You have light enough to go on by!

THE SONG OF SONGS

Introduction and Exegesis by Theophile J. Meek

Exposition by Hugh Thomson Kerr *and*

Hugh Thomson Kerr, Jr.

THE SONG OF SONGS

INTRODUCTION

Of all the books in the Old Testament none is so difficult to interpret as the Song of Songs. About no other book has so much been written, and concerning no other are there such differences of opinion and such a variety of interpretations.

I. Title

The title is manifestly from the hand of an editor because it uses the relative particle אשׁר, which is never used in the Song itself. The phrase "The Song of Songs" would seem to be a superlative, "the best of songs," like "the Lord of lords" and kindred expressions. Hence Rabbi Akiba (early second century), according to the Mishnah (Yedaim 3:5), called it "the holy of holies," and said that "no day outweighed in glory the one on which Israel received the Song of Songs." The editor treated the book as a single poem and apparently ascribed its authorship to Solomon, although the preposition ל in the title can have a variety of meanings—"by Solomon," "belonging to Solomon," "to Solomon," "for Solomon," and "concerning Solomon"—and there is insufficient evidence in the context to determine definitely which of these meanings was intended. The same preposition appears also in titles in Ugaritic (a language closely related to Hebrew) where it definitely does not indicate authorship.[1]

II. Canonicity

From the Mishnah (Yedaim 3:5; cf. Tosephta Yedaim 2:14, and Aboth of Rabbi Nathan I) we know that there was considerable discussion regarding the canonicity of the Song. The Palestinian school of Shammai opposed it, while the less stringent Babylonian school of Hillel sup-

ported it. Eventually, however, it came to be accepted by all, and anathema were those who dared any more to sing it as a wine song in the banqueting halls,[2] as some had been accustomed to do. Its erotic character manifestly caused it to be so used, and doubtless also this feature caused its canonicity to be questioned.

III. Place in the Canon

The Song of Songs is found in the third division of the Hebrew canon, the Writings, which are a miscellaneous collection. Most of these are late in origin, but it does not follow that all are late. Traditionally the Song was regarded as early; hence it must have been its character that put it in the third division. From Masseketh Sopherim 14:3, 18, we know that when that was written in the eighth century, the Song was used liturgically by being read on the eighth day of the Passover celebration at the beginning of the new year. Exactly when this custom had its origin we cannot say, but there is every indication that it harks back to time immemorial. The Pesiqta (seventh century and later) contains a series of homilies on the Song, and this implies that the book was read publicly, as does also the fact that it has a Midrash known both as Rabbah and Hazitha. It is still prescribed that the book shall be read at the conclusion of the morning service on the intermediate sabbath of Passover, or on the seventh or eighth day if Passover begins on a sabbath. In most synagogues, however, outside of north Poland and Lithuania, it is read not publicly but by each individual privately in connection with the Passover celebration. It was doubtless this practice that Theodore of Mopsuestia (360-429) had in mind when he said that the book

---

[1] Julian Obermann, *How Daniel Was Blessed with a Son* (New Haven: American Oriental Society, 1946), p. 1.

[2] See Tosephta Sanhedrin 12:10; cf. also the parallel passage, Babylonian Talmud: Sanhedrin 101a.

was not read publicly in his day by either Jews or Christians.

IV. Peculiar Features of the Book

The Song is unique in Hebrew literature; there is nothing even remotely like it anywhere else in the Bible. Its peculiar features may be summarized as follows:

1. It is lyric poetry of exquisite beauty, full of sensuous symbols.

2. It is the only book in the Bible to have all its content put into the mouth of speakers, but it is monologue with practically no dialogue. The speakers are not identified nor are their speeches introduced. The book has certain dramatic characteristics, but it is not drama.

3. It is marked by frequent repetitions, by refrains and antiphonal responses.

4. It lacks structure. There is no movement to a conclusion; matters are as far advanced in 1:4 or 2:4 as they are in 8:4.

5. It is manifestly folk poetry, not belles-lettres. It is simple and naïve, not the studied work of a littérateur. The many repetitions in the poem and its lack of structure preclude that.

6. It is full of elaborate imagery, with extravagant, sometimes overbold, metaphors. There is a remarkable appreciation of the beauties of nature in the poem and nature is prominent throughout.

7. There is an elusive geographical background—sometimes Judean, sometimes Israelite, or Trans-Jordanian, or Syrian. It is Palestinian rather than Hebraic. It has a wider range than just the Hebrew people.

8. In its present form it is purely secular in character, with no apparent theological, religious, or moral attributes. God never once appears in it.

9. In no other book of the Old Testament do we have the exclusive use of the relative particle ‎ש or the personal pronoun אני.

10. In no other book are there so many *hapax legomena* (49 in 117 verses) or so many unusual words (at least 70 in all). The Song has a vocabulary all its own, and a very difficult one, as every translator knows.

11. Much of the syntax is unusual: for example, the frequent substitution of masculine for feminine forms in pronouns, verbs, and suffixes; the pleonastic use of the personal pronoun with the finite verb; and the use of an anticipatory suffix followed by the relative particle and the possessive ‎ל.

This is a considerable array of peculiarities for a short book like the Song of Songs, and they all need to be taken into account when the book is being interpreted.

V. Interpretations

The interpretations of the song are legion.[3]

A. Allegorical Interpretation.—This is the earliest interpretation and it prevailed throughout Jewish and Christian circles for many centuries. It is found in the Talmud (*ca.* A.D. 150 to 500), but reached its most extravagant presentation in the Targum to the Song of Songs in the sixth century, the earliest Jewish commentary on the entire book that has come down to us. The bridegroom is interpreted as Yahweh, the bride as the Jewish nation, and the book itself as an allegory depicting in great detail the experiences of the nation in its relations with its God from the Exodus down to the coming of the Messiah and the building of the third temple. This in general is also the interpretation of the Midrash Rabbah and such famous scholars as Saadia ben Joseph, Rashi, and Ibn Ezra, although they differ considerably among themselves in details. Another expression of the allegorical interpretation was the mystic type, represented best by Immanuel ben Solomon, who maintained that the Song represents the union of the active intellect with the passive. Presently, however, the allegorical interpretation lost its popularity with the Jews and has now practically disappeared from Jewish scholarship, although it remains as the orthodox interpretation.

It persisted much longer in Christian circles and was marked by even greater vagaries. Origen did admit that the Song might be an epithalamium on the marriage of Solomon with Pharaoh's daughter, but beneath this he found a deeper meaning that was to be reached only by interpreting the book allegorically. The bridegroom was Christ and the bride, according to Origen's homilies, was the church, but in his commentaries, the individual believer. With most, however, it was the first interpretation that was followed; so Jerome, Augustine, Theodoret, John Wesley, and the authors of the chapter headings in some editions of the King James Version. With others the second interpretation was followed; so Gregory of Nyssa, Bernard of Clairvaux, and Moses Stuart. In certain Roman Catholic circles the bride came to be identified with the Virgin Mary, and this for a time became a favorite line of interpretation. To the scholastics of the Middle Ages the book was full of mystic meaning. Others followed the example of the Targum and saw

[3] For more details see C. D. Ginsburg, *The Song of Songs* (London: Longman, Brown, Green, Longmans, & Roberts, 1857), pp. 20-102; Harry Ranston, *The Old Testament Wisdom Books and Their Teaching* (London: Epworth Press, 1930), pp. 191-219; H. H. Rowley, "The Interpretation of the Song of Songs," *Journal of Theological Studies,* XXXVIII (1937), 337-63; also the literature cited there.

in the book a history of the past and a prophecy of the future. According to Thomas Brightman, for example, 1:1–4:6 describes the condition of the legal church from the time of David to the death of Christ, while 4:7–8:14 describes the state of the evangelical church from A.D. 24 to the second coming of Christ. On the other hand, such scholars as C. F. Keil and Paul Joüon followed the Targum more closely and interpreted the book throughout in terms of Israel's history. According to Martin Luther, the bride was the symbol of the state, and the book was a paean in which Solomon thanked God for the loyalty of his people. Others identified the bride with Wisdom, and this has a modern advocate in Gottfried Kuhn. The allegorical interpretation could make the book mean anything that the fertile imagination of the expositor was able to devise, and in the end its very extravagances [4] were its undoing, so that it has now all but disappeared.

B. Two-Character Dramatic Interpretation.— Since the drama had its beginning with the Greeks, the origin of the dramatic interpretation should be looked for in Hellenistic circles. The first indications are found in two Greek translations, Codex Sinaiticus and Codex Alexandrinus (from the fourth and the fifth century respectively), which have marginal notes indicating the speakers and the persons addressed. The Ethiopic translation, which is based on the Greek, goes a step farther and divides the book into five parts, corresponding in a way to five acts. However, it is not until after the Protestant Reformation that we find the dramatic theory fully developed. There are two chief characters (Solomon, sometimes in the guise of a shepherd, and the Shulammite), and the book consists substantially of mutual expressions of love on the part of these two. Various scholars tried their hand at distributing the speeches and in supplying the scenic directions, but the most popular presentation was that of Franz Delitzsch (1875), who divided the book into six acts, with two scenes in each.[5] The two-character interpretation had been the popular one from the beginning, but with its adaptation to the dramatic theory there seemed to be a contradiction in terms. The book was a drama, but there was no dramatic development, as there could not be with only two characters. Furthermore, if the book exhibits only two principal characters, it is destitute of ethical purpose. To supply these deficiencies there developed the three-character theory.

C. Three-Character Dramatic Interpretation. —Ibn Ezra was apparently the first to find three principal characters in the book, the king and two lovers (a country maiden and a shepherd), but it was not until J. F. Jacobi (1771) that this interpretation became at all popular. Then it was taken up by a host of writers and put new life into the dramatic theory. It is most elaborately presented by Heinrich Ewald (1826), who divides the book into five acts, with one or more scenes in each.[6] Solomon abducts a beautiful Shulammite maiden and attempts to win her love, but she resists all his blandishments and remains true to her shepherd lover; thus the theme of the book is not conjugal love, as in the two-character interpretation, but fidelity in love. This interpretation, however, puts Solomon in such an unfavorable light that it cannot be correct because such a book would never have been admitted into the canon by the rabbis. For this reason Leroy Waterman [7] introduces a Judean editor who by transposing the introduction, reinterpreting דודי, and other devices, turned what was a disparagement of Solomon by a northern writer into something very different; but why any Judean would have wanted to preserve such a writing is not apparent. Interpreted literally, the book has definitely three leading characters: Solomon, a maiden, and a shepherd. When this is combined with the dramatic interpretation, it makes the role of Solomon utterly impossible for a canonical book, and the whole theory has to be rejected. In any case, the drama was so foreign to Jewish orthodoxy as to preclude this interpretation. If by any chance the author did intend a drama of some sort, he would have used dialogue rather than monologue, and he would assuredly have been more explicit about the identity of the speakers, the distribution of the speeches, the time sequence, the change of locale, and the plot.

D. Wedding Cycle Interpretation.—According to J. G. Wetzstein's description (1873) of the seven-day wedding festivities among Syrian peasants, the bridegroom and bride are treated as king and queen, and poems describing their physical beauty, called wasfs, are recited in their honor, with the bride at one point performing a sword dance. This suggested to Karl Budde in 1894 that the Song of Songs was a collection of Judean wedding songs like those of Syria, and he presented his theory [8] so forcibly and persuasively that it dominated the interpreta-

[4] Summarized in graphic form by Ginsburg, op. cit., pp. 101-2.

[5] Summarized by S. R. Driver, An Introduction to the Literature of the Old Testament (rev. ed.; New York: Charles Scribner's Sons, 1913), pp. 438-40.

[6] Ibid., pp. 440-43.

[7] The Song of Songs (Ann Arbor: University of Michigan Press, 1948).

[8] "The Song of Solomon," The New World, III (1894), 56-77; "Das Hohelied," Die fünf Megillot (Leipzig: J. C. B. Mohr, 1898; "Kurzer Hand-Commentar zum Alten Testament").

tion of the book for the next quarter century. However, the Syrians are a mixed people, and it is inconceivable that any Jewish wedding customs have survived with them when we find no trace of similar customs in Palestine itself. Furthermore, the girl is never named or treated as queen in the Song of Songs, and there is no satisfactory explanation for having the youth called King Solomon. Those who hold to this theory date the poem very late in the postexilic period. and it is inconceivable that the Jewish fathers would have admitted to their sacred canon a book consisting of secular love songs, composed not long before their own time and sung at their own weddings. There are poems in the Song somewhat akin to the Syrian *wasfs*, but descriptions of personal beauty are characteristic of lyric poetry in every land and every age.

E. Secular Love Song Interpretation.—Theodore of Mopsuestia (360-429) was one of the first to interpret the book as a collection of secular love songs, attributing them to Solomon. For this the church later anathematized him, but the secular interpretation survived in spite of the anathema and ultimately received its classical presentation by J. G. von Herder in 1778. Since then it has been advocated in various forms by numerous writers and remains one of the prevailing views today. It is best presented by Robert Gordis,[9] who argues that the book is an anthology of twenty-eight love poems, covering five centuries of time, all the way from Solomon's reign in the tenth century to the Persian period in the fifth. An earlier presentation was that by Morris Jastrow, Jr.,[10] who, however, has to take considerable liberty with the text to maintain his view. He sees in the book a collection of twenty-three poems from different authors, but other scholars see only one author. All the proponents of the secular interpretation see a great deal of symbolism in the book, but they often differ, as they must, in the interpretation of the symbols. Paul Haupt,[11] a prominent advocate of this interpretation, completely rearranges the book, with many emendations, and tends to emphasize its obscene features. Some of his predecessors, for example, Sebastion Castalion (1544) and Eduard Reuss (1879), went so far as to declare that the book was actually immoral and should be excluded from the canon. In fact, one wonders how it ever did get into the canon if it is merely a collection of secular love songs after the order of the

Arabic love songs collected by Gustaf Dalman[12] and St. H. Stephan,[13] the Druze songs collected by Aapeli Saarisalo,[14] and the Egyptian songs published by A. H. Gardiner.[15] The advocates of the theory claim that it was Solomon's supposed authorship that got the book into the canon, but it is not clear on this hypothesis how Solomon's name became attached to it; even so, his name was no open sesame to acceptance, because other writings attributed to him, much superior in content, such as The Wisdom of Solomon, were not accepted. Another serious objection to the secular interpretation is the fact that the youth is sometimes king, in fact King Solomon, and sometimes shepherd, and recourse to a supposed analogy in the Syrian wedding songs is no satisfactory answer. If the book is to be interpreted literally, there must be two beloveds, a king and a shepherd. Furthermore, it is difficult, if not impossible, to explain the presence of a chorus ("the daughters of Jerusalem"), which is never found in secular love poetry, and it is equally difficult to explain the other dramatic features of the book. It is not drama, but it does have certain dramatic features that are found nowhere in secular love songs. The adjuration "by the gazelles or the hinds of the field" (2:7; 3:5) is passing strange if the book is secular poetry. Also, it is the maiden who takes the initiative and presses her suit, and this is never the case in secular love. All in all, the secular interpretation is not without its defects; but since it is one of the prevailing views today, it will be presented in the Exegesis along with the liturgical.

F. Liturgical Interpretation.—According to this theory, the Song of Songs is the survival in conventionalized form of ancient Hebrew New Year liturgies that celebrated the reunion and marriage of the sun god with the mother goddess, which in the ancient world typified the revival of life in nature that came with the return of the growing season.[16] It is the literary residue of a myth, a liturgy of life; it harks back to the ancient fertility cult which in its many forms was found throughout the whole world and is not without its survivals even in our own day, as witness features in our Easter celebration. The frequent description in the prophetic writings of the relation between Yahweh and his

[9] *The Song of Songs: A Study, Modern Translation and Commentary* (New York: Jewish Theological Seminary of America, 1954).

[10] *The Song of Songs* (Philadelphia: J. B. Lippincott Co., 1921); see also Nathaniel Schmidt, *The Messages of the Poets* (New York: Charles Scribner's Sons, 1911).

[11] *The Book of Canticles* (Chicago: University of Chicago Press, 1902).

[12] *Palästinischer Diwan* (Leipzig: J. C. Hinrichs, 1901).

[13] "Modern Palestinian Parallels to the Song of Songs," *Journal of the Palestine Oriental Society*, II (1922), 199-278.

[14] *Songs of the Druzes* (Helsingfors: Academic Bookshop, 1932; "Studia Orientalia").

[15] *The Library of A. Chester Beatty* (London: Emery Walker, 1931), pp. 27-38.

[16] Of all such liturgies the Babylonian is best known; cf. Henri Frankfort, *Kingship and the Gods* (Chicago: University of Chicago Press, 1948), pp. 281-94, 313-33.

people as that of husband and wife indicates the existence of the sacred marriage as a feature of ancient Hebrew ritual. If this was not so, the prophetic reformers would scarcely have used so persistently a symbolic pattern which was connected in the minds of the people only with an alien cult. In trying to stamp out Baalism the prophets would surely have avoided mention of the nation's marriage to Yahweh if that concept originated in and belonged only to the Baalized forms of the Hebrew religion.[17] The transforming influence of later Yahwism has almost completely obliterated the elements of the dying and rising god, the sacred marriage, and the place of the king in the rites;[18] but enough traces remain to show that they were once there, although long since forgotten. The Hebrews had their New Year celebration like all other peoples; in fact, like others of the Near East, where nature provides two starting points in the solar year, they had two: one in the fall with the coming of the rains, the feast of Booths or Sukkoth (originally called Asiph), and one in the spring, the feast of Unleavened Bread or Mazzoth, which in time became fused with Passover. We have already noted the liturgical connection of the Song with Passover, and there is evidence also for its connection with the autumn celebration. The setting for most of the poems is in the spring, but some very clearly have their setting in the fall.[19]

According to the Mishnah (Taanith 4:8), it was customary at the Wood Festival on the fifteenth of Ab and at the close of the day of Atonement for "the daughters of Jerusalem" (cf. 1:5 et passim) to go out and dance in the vineyards. There was alternate singing between them and the youths, and the latter were wont to recite the words of 3:11. This would indicate that a part at least of the Song was used liturgically in these festivals, and Julian Morgenstern has shown conclusively that the festivals themselves hark back to pre-exilic times as features

of the New Year celebration connected with the fertility cult.[20] Both Mazzoth and Sukkoth came to be interpreted as celebrating the Exodus, and so did the early part of the Song (up to 3:7). It is now generally recognized that some of the New Year liturgies survive in the so-called Enthronement Psalms,[21] and others would seem to survive in the Song of Songs. There is a certain unreality about the Song which suggests that its action is symbolic and cultic rather than merely human. In course of time, however, the early connections of the book were forgotten, and it became so secularized that it appears today as a simple anthology of love poems without any religious connotation other than its connection with Passover and its inclusion in the canon.

The liturgical interpretation, like all others, is not without its difficulties, but on the whole it would seem to be more acceptable than any other. In its preliminary form, here considerably modified, it was presented at length in 1922,[22] and in a slightly different form by Salvatore Minocchi in 1924.[23] It is followed in large part by W. O. E. Oesterley,[24] in an extreme form by Wilhelm Wittekindt,[25] and it is favored by D. C. Margoliouth[26] and Harry Ranston,[27] and by Max Haller.[28] It has been criticized by Nathaniel Schmidt,[29] Umberto Cassuto,[30] and H. H.

---

[17] For the fertility cult as an integral part of the Hebrew religion see the article and extensive literature cited by Beatrice A. Brooks, "Fertility Cult Functionaries in the Old Testament," Journal of Biblical Literature, LX (1941), 227-53; see also O. S. Rankin, Israel's Wisdom Literature (Edinburgh: T. & T. Clark, 1936), pp. 185-210.

[18] As Richard C. Wolf says (Old Testament Commentary, ed. H. C. Alleman and E. E. Flack [Philadelphia: Muhlenberg Press, 1948], p. 637), "By origin religious, the fertility cult was lifted higher and higher as men mounted nearer and nearer to God."

[19] Cf. N. H. Snaith, "The Song of Songs: The Dance of the Virgins," American Journal of Semitic Languages and Literatures, L (1933-34), 129-42. Snaith would seem to carry his thesis too far and divide the book too mechanically between the fall and spring festivals. For the connection between the feast of Booths and the fertility cult see Hugo Gressmann, "The Mysteries of Adonis and the Feast of Tabernacles," The Expositor, Ser. 9, III (1925), 416-32.

[20] "Two Ancient Israelite Agricultural Festivals," Jewish Quarterly Review, N. S. VIII (1917-18), 31-54. That the day of Atonement here described could not be the postexilic day of fasting and humility is clear from its joyous character. It must be the pre-exilic forerunner, a New Year festival which fell on the same day, the tenth of the first month (Ezek. 40:1), later known as the seventh month. See also Julian Morgenstern, "The Despoiling of the Egyptians," Journal of Biblical Literature, LXVIII (1949), 5-18.

[21] See W. O. E. Oesterley, The Psalms (New York: The Macmillan Co., 1939), I, 44-55, and the literature there cited. Cf. also Elmer A. Leslie, The Psalms (New York and Nashville: Abingdon-Cokesbury Press, 1949), pp. 62-130.

[22] Theophile J. Meek, "Canticles and the Tammuz Cult," American Journal of Semitic Languages and Literatures, XXXIX (1922-23), 1-14; Wilfred H. Schoff, ed., The Song of Songs: A Symposium (Philadelphia: Commercial Museum, 1924), pp. 48-79.

[23] Le Perle della Bibbia: Il Cantico dei Cantici e L'Ecclesiaste (Bari: G. Laterza & Figli, 1924).

[24] The Song of Songs (London: Golden Cockerel Press, 1936).

[25] Das hohe Lied und seine Beziehungen zum Istarkult (Hannover: H. Lafaire, 1926).

[26] "The Song of Solomon (Canticles)," in Charles Gore, H. L. Goudge, and Alfred Guillaume, eds., A New Commentary on Holy Scripture (New York: The Macmillan Co., 1928), pp. 411-18.

[27] O.T. Wisdom Books and Their Teaching, pp. 202-9.

[28] "Hoheslied," Die fünf Megilloth (Tübingen: J. C. B. Mohr, 1940; "Handbuch zum Alten Testament").

[29] "Is Canticles an Adonis Litany?" Journal of the American Oriental Society, XLVI (1926), 154-64.

[30] Review of Schoff, op. cit., Giornale della Societa Asiatica Italiana, N. S. I (1925-26), 166-73.

Rowley,[31] though all of them, like most moderns, acknowledge some influence from the fertility cult; as for example Rowley, when he says that "many of the allusions in the Song may genuinely refer to elements of the Adonis-Tammuz cult, whether found in the practice of the poet's contemporaries, or inherited in speech from an earlier age." [32] The criticisms that have been advanced are not always fair to the theory, some of them are more ironical than argumentative, and many of them will not apply to the modified form of the theory presented here. On separate items the evidence may be slight, but the critics fail to note that it is cumulative, and the theory does help to solve problems that were previously insoluble.

In the liturgies of the fertility cult women always play a prominent role (there is a chorus of women, and the chief character is a goddess separated from her beloved, longing for reunion with him and aggressively forwarding her suit) ; the speakers are not named, and their speeches are more monologue than dialogue and are very repetitious; the goddess is sometimes bride, sometimes sister, sometimes mother; the beloved is sometimes king, but more often shepherd; the liturgy was acted out in part, with the king taking the role of the god, and it is the nearest approach to drama that has come to us out of the ancient Near East. In short, the peculiar characteristics of the Song, already listed, are more fully explained by this theory than by any other. It is true that Yahweh appears by name nowhere in the Song, but if Sukkoth and Mazzoth were a part of Yahwism, as everyone believes, and if the Song is a partial survival of the liturgies connected with these festivals, as we believe, it was of course unnecessary to introduce the name of Yahweh. The epithets alone were sufficient, particularly an epithet like *Dôdh*, which is applied to the youth and is used in the peculiar sense of the Song elsewhere only in Isa. 5:1, where it is manifestly a title of Yahweh,[33] as it is without question in the proper name Dodavahu, "Yahu is *Dôdh*" (II Chr. 20:37). It is this theory that explains most easily the connection of the Song with Passover, its admission into the canon, its allegorical interpretation, its linguistic peculiarities, its cultic terms, its adjurations by animals sacred to the fertility cult, its refrains and antiphonal responses, its repetitiousness, and its elusive geographical background, more in the north, where the cult flourished, than in the less agricultural south. The title of the youth throughout the poem is *Dôdh*, and this we know was the name of a fertility god. The name Solomon in Hebrew is almost identical with the name of another fertility god, Shelem or Shulman, and Shulammite is simply the feminine form.

If the book is an anthology of liturgies of folk origin, that would explain its lack of unity, order, and movement. Its purely secular, erotic character would be explained by the nature of its employment, namely, as the text sung by dancers whose subject was the portrayal of love and whose object, according to the Mishnah, was matrimony. Its inclusion in the canon would be explained by the fact that the singing and dancing belonged to festivals of good religious standing, Sukkoth and Mazzoth. To have got into the canon the book at some time must have had some religious function, and that was manifestly the promotion of new life in soil and womb. The earliest and most persistent interpretation, the allegorical, in itself is evidence for this. Just as the prophets, particularly Hosea and Jeremiah, took over the principles of the fertility cult but ethicized them by identifying the god with Yahweh and the goddess with the people,[34] so the rabbis and Christian fathers did the same for the Song of Songs by allegorizing it, and their interpretation could only have grown out of its cultic use. In fact, we actually have the technical word for ritual song in 2:12 (*zāmîr;* see Exeg., *ad loc.*), and the closest parallels are to be found in the Tammuz liturgies, particularly the *irtu* songs listed in a catalogue of hymns and liturgies.[35]

No matter what interpretation of the Song is followed, there are passages which seem to yield no very clear meaning at all. That is characteristic of folk poetry and to some degree of poetry in general, since its appeal is often to the aesthetic sense in imagery and sound rather than to the intellect in logical argumentation. The exegesis of the Song is also difficult because the context is often slight, and there are many unusual words whose meaning is not always clear.

VI. Authorship, Date, and Provenance

No serious scholar today believes that Solomon was the author, and there are few who believe that the book was the work of a single

---

[31] "The Song of Songs: an Examination of Recent Theory," *Journal of the Royal Asiatic Society for 1938,* pp. 251-76.

[32] *Ibid.,* p. 272; see also "Interpretation of the Song of Songs," *Journal of Theological Studies,* XXXVIII (1937), 361.

[33] See Wittekindt, *op. cit.,* pp. 111-12.

[34] See Theophile J. Meek, *Hebrew Origins* (rev. ed.; New York: Harper & Bros., 1950), pp. 224-25; Rankin, *Israel's Wisdom Literature,* pp. 191-97.

[35] Erich Eberling, *Keilschrifttexte aus Assur religiösen Inhalts* (Leipzig: J. C. Hinrichs, 1919), Vol. IV, No. 158, pp. 268-75; Theophile J. Meek, "Babylonian Parallels to the Song of Songs," *Journal of Biblical Literature,* XLIII (1924), 245-52; also in Schoff, *op. cit.,* pp. 70-79. In view of present-day knowledge of Akkadian the translation could be improved at a number of points.

hand. It is too repetitious for that and too disorderly in its content. It is accordingly not belles-lettres. Comparison with the idyls of Theocritus on a kindred theme, or with the erotic poems of Meleager and Philodemus, is sufficient evidence of that. The Song of Songs is clearly not the studied work of a littérateur, but folk poetry. It is simple and naïve—a group of poems on a common theme that grew up with the people over the centuries. Its refrains and its presentation as speeches of individuals who are unnamed suggest that it grew up as a liturgy. In any case, it is an anthology, and its unity is that of common theme and common function rather than of single authorship. If it is folk poetry, it cannot come from the third century B.C., as so many believe. In that case the book would have been written in Aramaic, the only language that the common people knew or used at the time. Furthermore, as Margoliouth has well said, "The freshness and charm of the language and at times of the thought, the depth of passion and the naïveté of the enjoyment, are quite unlike the formalistic Judaism which we associate with this age."[36] The book is altogether incongruous with the puritanical atmosphere of the third century. However, its present text may come from a date as late as that. This is suggested by the Persian word for "garden" in 4:13 (pardēs) and what is apparently the Greek word for "palanquin" in 3:9 ('appiryôn—Greek phoreion); also by such late-known spices as henna, spikenard, and saffron, but more particularly by such Aramaisms as the shift from צ to ט in the use of נמר (1:6; 8:11, 12) for נצר, the shift from שׁ to ת in the use of ברות (1:17) for ברושׁ, and especially the shift from שׁ to ס in the case of סתו (2:11), or, better, סוג (7:2 [Hebrew 7:3]), which is the latest of the phonological changes by which Aramaic became differentiated from Hebrew. On the other hand, שׁזף in 1:6 is the Hebrew form of Aramaic שׁדף. Many scholars regard the exclusive use of שׁ for the relative particle as a mark of late date, but שׁ is undoubtedly related to the Akkadian ša, and to say that every occurrence in early Hebrew (Gen. 6:3; Judg. 6:17; 7:12; 8:26; II Kings 6:11) is suspect on text-critical grounds is the purest assumption with no basis in fact. It is true that the particle is used more frequently in postexilic literature, but in none is it used exclusively or even as frequently as אשׁר. The use of אשׁר in the title of the book suggests that it must have been added when שׁ was not in such general use as it was in the postexilic period, and that would make the book itself pre-exilic. The reference to Tirzah in parallelism with Jerusalem in 6:4 carries at least that part of the book back to the

time when Tirzah was the capital of the Northern Kingdom as Jerusalem was of the south, namely, from the reign of Baasha to Omri's sixth year (ca. 900-871 B.C.). The references to Heshbon (7:4 [Hebrew 7:5]) and to Gilead (4:1; 6:5) also suggest an early date since the former was lost to the Hebrews before Isaiah's time (cf. Isa. 15:4) and the latter in the Syro-Ephraimitic War in 734 B.C. There are only six occurrences of wāw with verbal forms (2:3, 17; 4:6; 6:1, 9 [bis]), but in each instance the form follows Hebrew syntax, not the slovenly usage of the postexilic period. Most of the so-called Aramaisms are peculiar to the book and have little affinity with those in late writings.

The language of the Song is all its own, not that of Ecclesiastes or Chronicles or any other late book. It has all the marks of a dialect. Many of the words, phrases, and constructions, as noted in the Exegesis, are found nowhere else in Hebrew, but are found in other Semitic languages. Hence many scholars believe that the book is north Palestinian or Syrian in origin, and that would seem to be confirmed by the fact that the geographical references are predominantly northern. In that case the original poem or collection of poems was probably very early. There is a certain crudity about many of the figures of speech, comparing things that are only slightly, if at all, alike, which suggests an early literary stage of development as well as folk origin. As the poem drifted from the north to the south, it was naturally oriented to Jerusalem and King Solomon, and in the centuries that followed it kept attune with the language of the common people, as folk songs and such compositions as are in continued use by the people always do—witness the hymns of the church, the King James Version, and the plays of Shakespeare. This may be another argument in favor of the liturgical interpretation. In any case, whether secular songs or liturgies accompanying dances and masques, they were kept alive by continual recitation, which accounts for any marks of late style and for the splendid preservation of the text so that the whole book requires remarkably few emendations. One notes in contrast the many textual corruptions in such poetry as Proverbs or Judg. 5, which was never used liturgically.

VII. Metrical Structure

The meter is predominately that of the qînāh (see Vol. I, p. 227; Vol. VI, Intro. to Lam., "Metrical Structure"). The usual form is a line of 3+2 beats, as in 1:9-10. Occasionally we get a 2+3 line, as in 1:12, or a 2+2 line, as in 2:8b. More frequently than in any other book we have a tristich instead of the usual distich, for example, 1:7a (3+2+3) and 1:8b (3+2+2),

---

[36] Op. cit., p. 413.

with a whole series in 4:9–5:1a (see Exeg.). The only exception to the *qînāh* meter is 1:2-4, where the meter is 3+3, with its variant 3+3+3 in 1:3. It should be noted that the lines in the Revised Standard Version correspond generally to the stichs of the Hebrew text, with the secondary stich or stichs indented.

VII. Selected Bibliography

BETTAN, ISRAEL. *The Five Scrolls*. Cincinnati: Union of American Hebrew Congregations, 1950.

BUDDE, KARL. "Das Hohelied," *Die fünf Megillot* ("Kurzer Hand-Commentar zum Alten Testament"). Leipzig: J. C. B. Mohr, 1898.

CANNON, W. W. *The Song of Songs*. Cambridge: Cambridge University Press, 1913.

GINSBURG, C. D. *The Song of Songs*. London: Longman, Brown, Green, Longmans, & Roberts, 1857.

GORDIS, ROBERT. *The Song of Songs: A Study, Modern Translation and Commentary*. New York: Jewish Theological Seminary of America, 1954.

HARPER, ANDREW. *The Song of Solomon* ("Cambridge Bible"). Cambridge: Cambridge University Press, 1902.

JOÜON, PAUL. *Le Cantique des cantiques*. 2nd ed. Paris: G. Beauchesne, 1909.

LEHRMAN, S. M. "The Song of Songs," in Abraham Cohen, ed. *The Five Megilloth*. Hindhead: The Soncino Press, 1946.

MARTIN, G. C. *Proverbs, Ecclesiastes and Song of Songs* ("The New-Century Bible"). New York: Oxford University Press, 1908.

OESTERLEY, W. O. E. *The Song of Songs*. London: Golden Cockerel Press, 1936.

POUGET, WILLIAM, and GUITTON, JEAN. *Canticle of Canticles*. Tr. Joseph L. Lilly. New York: D. X. McMullin Co., 1948.

SCHOFF, WILFRED H., ed. *The Song of Songs: A Symposium*. Philadelphia: Commercial Museum, 1924.

WATERMAN, LEROY. *The Song of Songs*. Ann Arbor: University of Michigan Press, 1948.

WUTZ, F. X. *Das Hohelied*. Stuttgart: W. Kohlhammer, 1940.

THE SONG OF SONGS

TEXT, EXEGESIS, AND EXPOSITION[1]

The Song of Songs is an enigma. Its place in the canon has occasioned constant controversy. There is no agreement among scholars as to its author or its interpretation. Is it an allegory, as plainly set forth by the translators of the KJV; a drama, as printed in the Amer. Trans.; a series of secular love songs, as presented by Jastrow; a Syrian wedding ritual, as proposed by Wetzstein; a Hebrew poem, showing the influence of a Canaanitish liturgy of the god and goddess of fertility, as suggested by the exegete? Are there two, three, or more persons; the king, the shepherd, the Shulammite, the "daughters of Jerusalem"? What is the purpose of the Song? Sermons preached from this book, in early, medieval, and modern times, have been based in the main upon the allegorical method, which in our day has been discarded as out of keeping with reality and good scholarship.

When the Intro. and Exeg. have been studied, the expositor must reach his own conclusions.

Perhaps none is satisfactory. Yet this book is in our Bible, and to those who included it in the canon it had meaning. It suggested the love of God for Israel. Does it have meaning for us?

The theme of the book is love: pure, sensuous, youthful, passionate love; love that is "hungry as the sea." This theme, of course, is as old as the world, and as new as today. It is echoed in literature and finds expression in Scripture. It begins in the garden of Eden, when man says, "This is now bone of my bones, and flesh of my flesh." It appears in the teaching of Jesus. It is a mystery on the lips of Paul. It lingers on into the Revelation, where the New Jerusalem comes down out of heaven, "prepared as a bride adorned for her husband."

The original structure and purpose of the Song are hidden from us. One thing, however, is clear. It is a poem in praise of love. It is expressed in romantic and radiant language. It is love poetry, folk poetry telling in passionate language of the devotion of a man and a maid. Says Nathaniel Schmidt:

It sings the praise of the greatest force in the world, that which builds the universe, from atom to man, draws individuals together in fruitful union, forms the foundation on which alone their mutual

[1] Pages 98-102 of prefatory Exposition were written by Hugh Thomson Kerr, who died before he had completed his work for this Commentary. The supplementary Exposition written by Hugh Thomson Kerr, Jr., begins on p. 102. Text and Exegesis begin on page 103. Editors.

relations can profitably rest, rears families, organizes society, interprets nature, lifts aloft shining ideals, and gives the touch divine to all existence.[2]

Milton said that true poetry is "simple, sensuous, and passionate." [3] Tested by his dictum, this Song is poetry of a high order. Perhaps we should linger on this theme; for if we approach the Song as pure poetry, its meaning may be disclosed. In his essay *The Name and Nature of Poetry*, A. E. Housman, himself a poet of quality, says: "To transfuse emotion—not to transmit thought but to set up in the reader's sense a vibration corresponding to what was felt by the writer—is the peculiar function of poetry." [4] Poetry thus becomes an emotional rather than an intellectual experience. The Intro. says: "There are passages which seem to yield no very clear meaning at all. That is characteristic of folk poetry and to some degree of poetry in general, since its appeal is often to the aesthetic sense in imagery and sound rather than to the intellect in logical argumentation." If this is true, how far should the interpreter go in analyzing and expounding a love poem like the Song of Songs? In poetry there is often a vague, mystical, emotional awareness. There are thoughts "that break through language and escape." In all parts of the Bible, especially in its poetry and its prophets, as well as in much of the teaching of Jesus, there are passages where literalism holds no key. What can exegesis do with such passages as Isa. 6, with its seraphim, its smoke-filled temple, its antiphonal, heavenly singing? The interpretation of such symbolic literature requires imagination, insight, spiritual sensitivity. The question thus presents itself: Wherein does mystical poetry differ from allegory? Is there not an element of allegory in all deep-toned poetry? In allegory, as in poetry, the words mean other than they say. Bunyan's *Pilgrim's Progress* is an allegory, as is also the "parable" of the vine. In poetry this hidden meaning is frequently present. We speak of it as imagery, as figurative, as symbolic. It "bodies forth the forms of things unknown."

In dealing with poetry, therefore, we cannot escape the mystical and perhaps the allegorical. May it not be that the author of the Song had some hidden spiritual meaning in his mind? Speaking of poetry, especially the sonnet, Wordsworth exclaimed:

> Scorn not the sonnet;
> .   .   .   .   .   .
>   with this key
> Shakespeare unlocks his heart.[5]

[2] *The Messages of the Poets* (New York: Charles Scribner's Sons, 1911), p. 236.
[3] *On Education.*
[4] New York: The Macmillan Co., 1933, p. 8.
[5] "Scorn Not the Sonnet."

It may be that this is what the author of the Song has done. In his lyrics he has unlocked the human heart. The words of Andrew Harper are not without significance. He says:

When therefore we find, as we certainly do find, that the Song of Solomon was probably received into the Canon mainly in the sense which made it a text-book of the love of God to the Church or the individual soul, and of its reciprocal love to God; if we find that it has from the earliest times edified the Church by inspiring some of its finest minds and many of its most saintly lovers of God to the fullest expression of their highest thoughts; if we find that more than any other book of Scripture it has kept men in mind of the fact that their highest moments, the moments when earthly love has lost all its carnality and all its selfishness, and has become a pure flame of utter devotion, are typical of what the relation between the soul and God ought to be, then it does seem unduly bold to deny that the author may have intended the more recondite spiritual reference as well as the more obvious ethical one.[6]

Accepted then as poetry—mystical, lyrical poetry—may not familiar and oft-quoted lines, some of which have entered our hymnody, be used in presenting the message of the gospel? A few suggestions may be helpful:

First Things First.

They made me keeper of the vineyards;
but, my own vineyard I have not kept! (1:6.)

The primacy of personal religion is emphasized. Cf. "Take heed to yourselves" (Mark 13:9).

The Virtue of True Humility.

> I am a rose of Sharon,
>   a lily of the valleys (2:1).

Cf. "I am meek and lowly in heart" (Matt. 11:29).

The Banner of Victory.

> He brought me to the banqueting house,
>   and his banner over me was love (2:4).

No other banner can assure victory in personal and national life.

The Springtime of the Soul.

> For lo, the winter is past,
> .   .   .   .
>   the time of singing has come (2:11-12).

"When Jesus came, a breath of hope shivered throughout the world" (R. F. Horton).

[6] *The Song of Solomon* (Cambridge: Cambridge University Press, 1907; "Cambridge Bible"), p. xl. Used by permission.

The Subtle Influence of Little Things.

> Catch us the foxes,
> the little foxes (2:15).

Cf. "A little yeast leavens the whole lump" (Gal. 5:9).

The True Life of the Soul.

> I slept, but my heart was awake (5:2).

"There is a deep self that never sleeps and never dies" (George Tyrrell).

When Severity Speaks for Love.

> Terrible as an army with banners (6:4, 10).

Love is not to be identified with sentiment. Cf. "The goodness and severity of God" (Rom. 11:22) and the words of Jesus: "whited sepulchers"; "serpents"; "vipers"; "wolves"; "hypocrites." We must hate that which would destroy what we love.

The Strongest Thing in the World.

> Love is strong as death (8:6).

Shall we not say love is stronger than death? Did not Christ, who is love incarnate, triumph in the Cross? "Love is a violent and vigorous passion" (Matthew Henry).

Treated as poetry and without dropping into allegory, there are many verses in the Song that will render rich meanings to those who seek them. There are of course lines of sensuous passion that may not have sounded to Orientals as they do to us. But who will set limits to the passionate language of lovers?

The Ministry of Love.—What can love—"simple, sensuous, . . . passionate," as expressed in the poetry of the Song of Songs—teach us? We learn what we already know, that love casts a spell over the intimate relationships of man and woman. We call to mind the suggestive myth of Plato that is capable of mystical interpretation, to the effect that man and woman were at the beginning one, but being sundered, "love is an appetite" which is ever urging them to be reunited. This same love is the constant theme of the poets. In the *Oxford Book of English Mystical Verse* one is constantly in the atmosphere of the Song of Songs. In a way such an anthology provides a striking commentary on the biblical book.

If we are reluctant to enter the secret places of affianced or wedded love, two considerations should nerve our perhaps too sensitive consciences. First of all, we are aware that love is a recurring theme in Scripture. We begin with the story of the man and the woman in Eden,

"one flesh," made for each other and for God. "He for God only, she for God in him." [7] How familiar are the words, "Jacob served seven years for Rachel; and they seemed unto him but a few days, for the love he had to her" (Gen. 29:20). Here is the story again: "They called Rebekah and said unto her, Wilt thou go with this man? and she said, I will go. . . . And Isaac brought her into his mother Sarah's tent, and took Rebekah, and she became his wife; and he loved her." (Gen. 24:58, 67.) In the story of Ruth (3:18) we have the same note: "The man will not be in rest, until he have finished the thing this day." But "the thing" is never finished. The story of Hosea and his betrayed love touches a deep and tragic chord. "Go again, love a woman who is beloved of a paramour and is an adulteress, even as the LORD loves the people of Israel" (Hos. 3:1). Paul lifted wedded love into something beyond the flesh: "I have espoused you to one husband, that I may present you as a chaste virgin to Christ" (II Cor. 11:2). "This is a great mystery, but I speak concerning Christ and the church" (Eph. 5:32).

But there is a further consideration; for this, the deepest and finest instinct of the soul, has been despoiled. There have been many influences that have brought love and marriage into disrepute. The world of our day has popularized infidelity in regard to the marriage bond, and has too often identified lust with love. The divorce courts have crowned love-loyalty with dishonor. The Song of Songs, however interpreted, points the true road to paradise. It was a touch of insight on the part of the poet who said that Love, found wandering outside the ramparts of paradise, declared that she had never known until then where paradise was. This book, without mentioning it, frowns upon polygamy, upon infidelity, and sings of the ardor and unalloyed passion of a love that is "stronger than death." The Shulammite would confirm the words of Elizabeth Barrett Browning:

> I love thee with the breath,
> Smiles, tears, of all my life!—and, if God choose,
> I shall but love thee better after death. [8]

Did not John Keats write to his ladylove: "I could die for you. My Creed is Love and you are its only tenet"? [9] It were better had he added another word to his creed: "God is love."

Furthermore, love casts a spell over nature. In the presence of such a love as is revealed in the Song, we would expect nature to become

[7] Milton, *Paradise Lost*, Bk. IV.
[8] *Sonnets from the Portuguese* XLIII.
[9] Letter to Fanny Brawne, October 13, 1819.

resplendent. A new loveliness fills all the world. Speaking of his love, Tennyson exclaimed,

> Behold, I dream a dream of good,
> And mingle all the world with thee.[1]

That is exactly what happens. What a miracle it is! When love and light entered the empty and dark soul of Saul Kane, he saw beauty everywhere:

> O glory of the lighted mind.
> How dead I'd been, how dumb, how blind.[2]

In the eyes of love nature becomes all alive with significance. It is suggested in the Exeg. that it is the loveliness of the Northland that is reflected in the Song. We are introduced to flocks and vineyards, to kids and shepherds' tents, to myrrh and clusters of henna blossoms, to doves and little foxes, to fir trees and cedars, to the rose of Sharon and the lily of the valleys, to raisin cakes and apples, to young stags and gazelles, to the vineyards in blossom and to clefts of the rocks, to flocks of goats and to the hinds of the field, to the wood of Lebanon, to myrrh and frankincense and fragrant perfumes, to oils and spices and pomegranates, to saffron and calamus and cinnamon, to nectar and the flowing streams of Lebanon. Across the wide spaces of the world, we hear the call:

> Awake, O north wind,
>   and come, O south wind!
> Blow upon my garden,
>   let its fragrance be wafted abroad.
> Let my beloved come to his garden,
>   and eat its choicest fruits. (4:16.)

The beauty of nature is everywhere revealed.

> Arise, my love, my fair one,
>   and come away;
> for lo, the winter is past,
>   the rain is over and gone.
> The flowers appear on the earth,
>   the time of singing has come,
> and the voice of the turtledove
>   is heard in our land.
> The fig tree puts forth its figs,
>   and the vines are in blossom;
>   they give forth fragrance.
> Arise, my love, my fair one,
>   and come away. (2:10-13.)

In the Intro. it is suggested that the Song may celebrate "the reunion and marriage of the sun god with the mother goddess, which in the ancient world typified the revival of life in nature that came with the return of the growing season." The emphasis upon nature may be, from this point of view, a reflection of the ancient myth.

The Bible and the teaching of Jesus are constantly pointing us to nature as a revelation of God, for those who have eyes that see and ears that hear. "The heavens declare the glory of God" (Ps. 19:1); "Consider the lilies how they grow" (Matt. 6:28). We have not made enough of this spiritual ministry. We fail to see that

> Earth's crammed with heaven,
> And every common bush afire with God.[3]

If the Song of Songs opens our eyes to the glory of God in earth and sky, it has served a gracious purpose. It is love, and love alone, that gives us this new and glorious world.

Love, "simple, sensuous, . . . passionate," such as is displayed in the Song of Songs also interprets and glorifies God. Richard Garnett says: "Thou mayest bar thy door against Divine Love and yet leave it free for human love: but if thou deniest it to love human expect no visit from Love Divine." Do we then step from human love to the love of God? Says John, "We love him, because he first loved us" (I John 4:19). And that is a penetrating word. But suppose we ask, "Is the love that characterizes God something other than the love that has its home in the human heart? Is love fractional, or is it all of a piece?" Love, as has been said, is the essence of God, and when love comes to the weakest and poorest of his children, something takes place akin to a sacrament. "Do you know what you are to me?" Elizabeth Barrett wrote to Robert Browning. "We talk of the mild weather doing me good . . . of the sun doing me good . . . ! Have you done me no good, do you fancy, in loving me and lifting me up? Has the unaccustomed divine love and tenderness been nothing to me? . . . I see the dancing, mystical lights . . . and I think of you with an unspeakable gratitude." [4] What do these strange words "unaccustomed divine love" and "dancing, mystical lights" mean? There is little wonder that the allegorical interpretation laid hold of the saints. It is said that when Thomas Aquinas was dying the attendant monks asked him to interpret the Song of Songs to them. He replied, "Give me the spirit of Bernard and I will do what you ask." The spirit of Bernard of Clairvaux is indeed a key, and his *Eighty-Six Sermons on the*

---

[1] *In Memoriam*, Part CXXIX, st. ii.

[2] *The Everlasting Mercy.* Copyright, 1911, by John Masefield. Used by permission of The Macmillan Company, The Society of Authors, and Dr. Masefield.

[3] Elizabeth Barrett Browning, *Aurora Leigh*, Bk. VII, 1. 820.

[4] *The Letters of Robert Browning and Elizabeth Barrett Barrett 1845-1846* (New York: Harper & Bros., 1899), II, pp. 129-30.

Song of Solomon are not all allegory. They reach out into the O.T. and the N.T. They lay hold of the love of God in its length and breadth, its height and depth. In one of his last sermons he says, "Love is alone sufficient by itself; it pleases by itself, and for its own sake. It is itself a merit, and itself its own recompense." [5] Properly and ultimately there can be no separating chasm between love divine and love human; and because of this fact the marriage bond became, both in the O.T. and the N.T., the symbol of the divine love. The evangelical prophet did not hesitate to say: "As a young man marrieth a virgin, so shall thy sons marry thee: and as the bridegroom rejoiceth over the bride, so shall thy God rejoice over thee" (Isa. 62:5). It was said of Christ, "He that hath the bride is the bridegroom" (John 3:29). Before his tragic death in the blizzards of the antarctic, Edward Wilson, the heroic companion of Robert F. Scott, wrote to his wife: "Don't be unhappy—all is for the best. We are playing a good part in a great scheme arranged by God himself. . . . All is for the best to those that love God and . . . we have both loved Him with all our lives. . . . Life itself is a small thing to me now, but my love for you is for ever and a part of our love for God. . . . All is well." [6] Could there be a nobler demonstration of how human lovers may consecrate their love in the divine presence?

Love is the central message of the Song of Songs and is so stated in the closing verses of the book. What strong, true words they are!

> Set me as a seal upon your heart,
>   as a seal upon your arm;
> for love is strong as death.
>
> .   .   .   .
>
> Many waters cannot quench love,
>   neither can floods drown it (8:6-7).

While it is true that Bernard preached eighty-six sermons on two chapters and three verses of the Song, one could easily preach that many and more from this crowning courageous text. The Song of Songs, however, is not God's final word concerning love. We call to remembrance the great word about the love of God in the N.T., and we keep central the message "God is love." Let us also recognize the fact that there is a "song of songs" in the N.T.—I Cor. 13. It too is couched in rhythmic language and belongs to the finest poetry. It transcends our analysis. It makes no mention of God, yet it is of him that we think as, over against the crowning central verse in the O.T. Song, "Love is strong as death," we set the confident true words of the N.T. song, "Love never faileth." It is worth while to stress the language used. In the Song of Songs in the Vulg. the word "love" is twice translated *amor* (2:5; 5:8); twice by the word *dilectio* (8:6, 7); and three times by the word *caritas* (2:4; 3:10; 8:7). The Latin is rich in words for love. So is the Greek. In English we have only one word that carries such a load of diverse interpretations as to confuse the minds of many people, both young and old. Out of several words for love in the Greek language, the LXX uses the word ἀγάπη to translate the "love" of the Song of Songs. This is significant. Richard Trench said that the word ἀγάπη was born in the bosom of revealed religion and the N.T. writers poured into the word the content of the Christian virtues. It is of ἀγάπη that the N.T. speaks. From this point of view love is not an emotion but a dynamic energy expressing itself in unselfish service. It is revealing that in translating the Song of Songs this unusual word is used. It is evidence that the translators were aware of dealing with high matters and were not thinking in terms of sensual passion. Of the best and highest that human life knows, the Song of Songs in the O.T. and the "song of songs" in the N.T. use a word that has been baptized into Christ.

The Song of Songs: Principles of Interpretation.—In many ways, as has been indicated, the Song of Songs is unique among the books of the Bible. The Exeg. contains a detailed examination of the problems of vocabulary, the frequently cryptic allusions, and the structure of the book. But if the Song of Songs is primarily love poetry, and this is virtually the only unanimous judgment about the book whatever interpretation is given it, then the method of exposition becomes a problem in itself.

To enter into the spirit of the poetry of love and to expound its meaning require that we know something of the author's background, the sources of his references, the peculiarities of his style, rhythm, and vocabulary, as well as some understanding of the intention and structure of his verses. But they require more than this. We must see the poem as an organic whole, not as a mere miscellany of words, phrases, and fragments.

If we take the Song of Songs as a poem in praise of love, the necessity for imaginative and sensitive interpretation is not precluded by insisting that the origin of the poetry is to be found in a secular fertility cult. To understand and appreciate a poem we do not perform an autopsy on it and dissect it under a microscope; we seek to see it as a living whole. Beyond the parsing of the sentences, the counting of rhythm

[5] Ed. John Mabillon and S. J. Eales (London: John Hodges, 1896), p. 509.

[6] George Seaver, *Edward Wilson of the Antarctic* (London: John Murray, 1933), pp. 293-94.

1 The Song of songs, which *is* Solomon's.

2 Let him kiss me with the kisses of his mouth: for thy love *is* better than wine.

3 Because of the savor of thy good ointments thy name *is as* ointment poured forth, therefore do the virgins love thee.

1 The Song of Songs, which is Solomon's.

2 O that you*a* would kiss me with the kisses of your*b* mouth!

For your love is better than wine,

3 your anointing oils are fragrant, your name is oil poured out; therefore the maidens love you.

a Heb *he*
b Heb *his*

Title (1:1)

1:1. Haller, following Kuhn, emends אשר to אשירה, making the verse read, "The Song of Songs I will sing to Solomon." The emendation gets rid of the troublesome אשר, but it is purely conjectural.

The Maiden (1:2-4)

2. The RSV, following most scholars, emends the text to make the first stich agree in person with the second, but oscillation in person, although awkward to our ears, is characteristic of Hebrew poetry (see Aubrey R. Johnson, *The One and the Many in the Israelite Conception of God* [Cardiff: University of Wales Press, 1942]).

3. The word טובים is an abstract plural, "sweetness," and the preposition ל with ריח is possessive; lit., "Sweetness belongs to the fragrance of your ointments," or in better English, "The fragrance of your ointments is sweet" (Amer. Trans.). It is also possible to take the preposition as the ל of specification; in that case טובים would be a predicate adjective: "Your ointments are sweet in the matter of fragrance." There is no reason to emend the text, as many do.

In the second stich תורק is an enigma. If it is a verbal form, it can be Hophal imperfect of ריק, "to pour out," either second person masculine or third person feminine, both

beats, and the identification of mysterious images, there lies the task of the interpreter who gratefully receives what piecemeal analysis renders but who must also put the parts together again and see the work as a whole.

It therefore seems desirable in the Expos. to disregard the usual method of verse-by-verse and paragraph-by-paragraph analysis in favor of a thematic device which may help to preserve the wholeness of the book and at the same time provide a way for accenting the main ideas and themes of this particular kind of love poetry. In dealing with the book of Esther, which has often been compared to the Song of Songs because neither mentions God, the Expos. consists of a series of character sketches. So here certain dominant themes which run through all the chapters of the Song will be made the basis for the interpretation. In this way full cognizance can be taken of the secular origin and the sensuous character of the Song, and at the same time an effort can be made to do justice to the undeniably poetic character of the book without becoming involved in the extremes of allegorical subjectivism.

The biblical interpreter has the responsibility of expounding any verse, any passage, any book, not only in the light of its own particular origin and purpose but also in the context of the total biblical record of revelation. Whether we like it or not, the Song of Songs is part of this biblical record. To isolate it and attempt to interpret it without any regard whatever for the biblical context is, as a principle of exposition, as unjustifiable as it is to spiritualize the text in such a way as to obscure completely its secular, profane origin. We must somehow avoid these two quite different perils of interpretation.

The isolating of sections and whole books of the Bible by exploring their literary and historical roots has been characterized by C. H. Dodd as the "centrifugal" tendency of biblical scholarship. But this movement, which has contributed so much by way of understanding the origins of the various biblical strata, "needs to be balanced by a centripetal movement which will bring these ideas, now better understood in their individual character, into the unity of the life which originally informed them."[7] This

[7] *The Present Task in New Testament Studies* (Cambridge: Cambridge University Press, 1936), p. 35.

4 Draw me, we will run after thee: the King hath brought me into his chambers: we will be glad and rejoice in thee, we will remember thy love more than wine: the upright love thee.

4 Draw me after you, let us make haste.
　　The king has brought me into his chambers.
We will exult and rejoice in you;
　　we will extol your love more than wine;
　　rightly do they love you.

---

difficult to understand here. Most scholars emend, with the LXX, Aq., O.L., and Vulg., to the participle מוּרָק, **poured out**, but the word is probably best understood as a noun, meaning perhaps "storax," or some other important source of ointments (cf. Syriac, "oil of myrrh"). The word שְׁמָנִים is **ointments**, rather than **oils**. Together with שֵׁם, it constitutes a paranomasia, a device used rather frequently by Hebrew poets. The latter word is, lit., "your name," a Semitic idiom for "your very self" (Amer. Trans.). **Therefore the maidens love you** may be a gloss, or better, the line is a tristich (3+3+3) instead of the usual distich. **Virgins** is quite incorrect for עֲלָמוֹת, since the word means simply **maidens**, or "young women," with no specific reference to their virginity. On the cultic interpretation, as originally understood, the **maidens** would be the female votaries; on the three-character interpretation, the women of Solomon's harem; on other interpretations, simply girls in general, as also on the cultic when the original significance of the Song came to be lost.

4. The RSV in the first stich is contrary to the accents (so Targ.), but is preferable to the M.T., which is followed by the KJV. Those who follow the secular interpretation see in **king** a title of the bridegroom, as in the Syrian wedding songs; but **king** is a common title of the fertility god in the Ras Shamra texts, as elsewhere, and it was common for the king to play the role of the god in the liturgy.

The change to the first person plural in the second line is best explained as another instance of oscillation; the maiden identifies herself with the whole group instead of

---

means that it is just as important to estimate the significance of context as of origin, and this is especially so in the case of the O.T., where the centrifugal technique promises such fruitful rewards.

At last we have realized that there are limits beyond which literary analysis cannot be pressed without doing more harm than good. Even the good order of J, E, D, and P may corrupt the scholarly world. We have been so very energetic in isolating each from other, and even within each, in separating stratum from stratum, that we have tended to forget that there might be method even in the madness which so thoroughly dovetailed them in together. Perhaps after all that madness was divine. In a similar way, our preoccupation with origins and development has blurred our eyes from seeing whither the development was making, and equally has tied our tongues from asking why this way and no other way. Nay more, we can be accused, and with considerable measure of justification, of being foolish enough to advance backwards, our faces always turned towards the point of our departure.[8]

[8] Norman H. Snaith, *The Distinctive Ideas of the Old Testament* (London: Epworth Press, 1944), p. 13. Copyright 1946 by W. L. Jenkins. Published by The Westminster Press. Used by permission. Cf. also A. G. Herbert, *The Throne of David* (New York: Morehouse-Gorham Co., 1941), especially pp. 31-32.

The danger of allegorizing, on the other hand, is that the original intent and meaning of the text are obscured by unwarranted, subjective flights of fancy. To interpret the Song of Songs as allegory may indeed result in edifying comments, but much of the original setting and purpose of the Song will necessarily be submerged or, as is more likely, actually distorted by what Adolf von Harnack termed the magic of "biblical alchemy." In repudiating the allegorical method Luther said:

Wiles and evasions for the distorting of the Scriptures St. Paul, in Ephesians iv, calls in Greek *kybia* and *panurgia*, that is, "sleight of hand," "jugglers' tricks," "gamesters' tricks," because they toss the words of God to and fro, as the gamesters throw their dice; and because, like the jugglers who give things new noses and change the whole appearance of them, they take from the Scriptures their single, simple, constant sense, and blind our eyes, so that we waver to and fro, hold fast to no sure interpretation, and are like men whom they have bewitched or tricked, while they play with us as gamblers with their dice.[9]

In arranging the Expos. of the Song of Songs in terms of certain dominant themes that run

[9] H. T. Kerr, Jr., ed., *A Compend of Luther's Theology* (Philadelphia: Westminster Press, 1943), p. 18.

5 I *am* black, but comely, O ye daughters of Jerusalem, as the tents of Kedar, as the curtains of Solomon.

6 Look not upon me, because I *am* black, because the sun hath looked upon me: my mother's children were angry with me; they made me the keeper of the vineyards; *but* mine own vineyard have I not kept.

---

5 I am very dark, but comely,
  O daughters of Jerusalem,
like the tents of Kedar,
  like the curtains of Solomon.
6 Do not gaze at me because I am swarthy,
  because the sun has scorched me.
My mother's sons were angry with me,
  they made me keeper of the vineyards;
  but, my own vineyard I have not kept!

---

thinking of herself individually (cf. vs. 11, an exact parallel). Some scholars get over the difficulty by assigning the words to the chorus, "the daughters of Jerusalem." Others assign the whole passage, vss. 2-4, to the chorus.

Most scholars emend נזכירה, **we will extol,** in vs. 4*d*, to נשכרה, "we will be drunk with," but the M.T. is quite acceptable. All the verbs in this line smack of cultic language (see W. O. E. Oesterley, *The Sacred Dance* [Cambridge: Cambridge University Press, 1923], *passim*). The word מישרים is an abstract plural noun adverbial accusative; hence **rightly.** The last stich, omitted in the O.L., is generally regarded as a gloss because it makes the line a tristich and reads like a moralizing gloss, but it may be original. The subject of the verb may be **the maidens** of vs. 3, as in the RSV, or the third plural may be taken as indefinite; hence "are you loved" (Amer. Trans.).

THE MAIDEN TO THE DAUGHTERS OF JERUSALEM (1:5-6)

5. Very dark: Better, "swarthy" (Amer. Trans.), i.e., blackened by exposure to the sun (cf. Theocritus, *Idyls* X. 26-29, where Bambyce is called beautiful though sunburned). Note that **the tents of Kedar** (a Bedouin tribe of north Arabia; cf. Gen. 25:13), woven of goat's hair, are black, while **the curtains of Solomon** are beautiful, the latter being tapestries hung on the walls of Oriental mansions. The reference makes this poem in its present form no earlier than the time of **Solomon,** who is named here because he was noted for his royal splendor. It is difficult to explain the presence of a chorus, **daughters of Jerusalem,** on any hypothesis other than the liturgical, according to which the original reference was to the female votaries of the fertility goddess. The secular hypothesis interprets them as companions of the bride.

6. The word ראה is used here with a double accusative: the suffix **me** and an object clause introduced by the particle ש, which is always used in this book in place of the usual אשר. The word שזפתני is not to be derived from שזף, "to look upon" (Job 20:9; 28:7), but with many of the ancient versions and most moderns from שזף, "to scorch," the Hebrew form of Aramaic שדף (Gen. 41:6, 23, 27), suggesting an early date for the

---

throughout the book as a whole, something of the sharpness and antithesis of the dilemma posed by the twin perils of interpretation just mentioned can be transcended. We will seek to understand the Song as the love lyrics, often earthy and sensual, of a maiden and a youth; and at the same time we will seek to relate by analogy, not by allegory, the peculiar love poetry of this book with the total biblical conception of love. The Song of Songs by itself cannot give us the gospel of God's redeeming love in Christ, but in the larger biblical context, where the Song now happens to be, it is inevitable to compare and contrast what it says about the love of youth and maiden with the unique love of God for mankind.

I. The Language of Love.—The Song of Songs, the best of all songs, the song traditionally attributed to the wisest of all men, Solomon, is a love song. Love is something to sing about. Love is a language all its own. It is the universal language which everyone understands. Whether we interpret the Song of Songs as the love of man and woman, or the love of God for the individual or the church, we cannot miss the lilting, exuberant accents of the language of love.

To love is to sing. The best songs, the most familiar songs, the songs we all love to sing are love songs. Love puts music in the heart, translates prose into poetry, and fills the mind with images and dreams and visions. That is

passage. **My mother's sons** may be a poetic way of saying "my brothers," or the expression may have its usual meaning of half brothers on the mother's side. Theod. reads the singular "son," in which case the final *yôdh* of בני would be the helping *yôdh* that is so common with the construct in Hebrew poetry (see Exeg. on Lam. 1:1). The word נחרו is difficult; it could be the Niphal perfect of חרה, "to burn," "to be angry," or of חרר, "to burn." The verb שמני is strictly singular, "he made me" (so Theod., agreeing with his reading of the preceding stich), but in the M.T. it is pointed to make it plural. The words כרמי שלי, lit., "my vineyard which belongs to me," are usually taken as emphatic, **my own vineyard.** The expression is not an Aramaism, as generally supposed, and must be dialectic.

The interpretation of the passage is anything but clear, and it does not agree with certain other passages. Instead of being swarthy, the maiden is compared to the white moon and shining sun in 6:10 and to ivory in 7:4 [Hebrew 7:5], and instead of having brothers she is "the only one of her mother" in 6:9. Also it is not clear why her brothers were angry, nor is it clear what **my own vineyard** is—perhaps the girl's person. The passage, if interpreted literally, is a fragment of a bucolic song rather than a love song, with too little context to determine its meaning. If בני and שמני are taken as singular, and נחרו emended to singular, following Theod., the passage could be given a cultic interpretation, referring to the drying up of vegetation under the scorching rays of the sun. In that case "my mother's son has burned me" (Amer. Trans) would be parallel to the preceding stich, "that the sun has scorched me" (Amer. Trans.), to make the line a tristich, 3+2+2, and the last line, as understood originally, would mean that she who

---

why the world's great music and poetry and art are inspired by love. That is why Christianity, the supreme religion of love, is the most singing religion in all the world. Some religions never break forth into song. They do not speak the language of love. They have no hymnals, no anthems, no "Hallelujah Chorus." But the Christian faith weds music and poetry, and the Bible, especially the N.T., is a treasury of love songs of all kinds. It is no accident that the gospel of God's love begins with the Magnificat which Mary sings, and then there is the angels' chorus, which the shepherds heard, and Simeon's Nunc Dimittis in the temple. The apostle Paul, who knew how to sing even in prison (Acts 16:25), and who himself composed the N.T. "song of songs" (I Cor. 13), admonished the early Christians to sing "in psalms and hymns and spiritual songs, singing and making melody to the Lord with all your heart" (Eph. 5:19; cf. Col. 3:16). And as it begins, so too the N.T. ends (Rev. 19:6-8) with a glorious triumphant love song:

> Hallelujah! For the Lord our God
>   the Almighty reigns.
> Let us rejoice and exult and give
>   him the glory,
> for the marriage of the Lamb has come,
> and his Bride has made herself ready;
> it was granted her to be clothed
>   with fine linen, bright and pure.

Love creates its own language, a language that is closer to poetry than to prose, for there is more of music in it than grammar. For love is a special way of speaking, a strange and wonderful medium of communicating truth. But there is something impressionistic and elusive about the language of love. It makes use of words, to be sure, but words seem so inadequate. Robert Browning, in expressing his love for Elizabeth Barrett Browning, tells of his search for "one word more" that would be "Fit and fair and simple and sufficient." [1] Anyone who has ever written a love letter knows what the poet means.

Consider some of the features of the language of love as it is found in the Song of Songs. For the grammarian, the etymologist, the lexicographer, the Song is both exasperating and intriguing. The Hebrew language expert tells us there is nothing quite like the words and phrases, the grammar and the rhythm of the Song of Songs. There are, for example, nearly 50 words in this short book of 117 verses which occur nowhere else in the Bible. That is one reason why the translation of the original Hebrew presents such a problem. We can never be sure that we know in every case what a word or a phrase means, so that a literal translation is frequently impossible. [2]

But the grammarian's problem of translation is itself a kind of parable of the uniqueness of the language of love. When love finds its voice

[1] "One Word More," st. viii.

[2] The Intro. gives the details of the peculiarities of language: "The Song has a vocabulary all its own, and a very difficult one."

7 Tell me, O thou whom my soul loveth, where thou feedest, where thou makest *thy flock* to rest at noon: for why should I be as one that turneth aside by the flocks of thy companions?

7 Tell me, you whom my soul loves,
     where you pasture your flock,
     where you make it lie down at noon;
for why should I be like one who wanders[c]
     beside the flocks of your companions?

[c] Gk Syr Vg: Heb *is veiled*

---

was the source of fertility and goddess of life is herself dried up and deprived of life. In the cult legends it is not always the god who dies, but sometimes the goddess, as in the case of Kore-Persephone, Eurydice, and Jepththah's daughter (Judg. 11:34-39; for the latter see C. F. Burney, *The Book of Judges* [2nd ed.; London: Rivingtons, 1920], pp. 321-24; also Julian Morgenstern, "The Chanukkah Festival and the Calendar of Ancient Israel," *Hebrew Union College Annual*, XX [1947], 82-83).

THE MAIDEN (1:7)

7. My soul is a Semiticism for "I" (Amer. Trans.). The usual meaning of איכה is "how," but here it means **where**, like the Akkadian *ēkā*, and may be dialectic. The word שלמה is regularly taken as an Aramaism, in which case the translation would be "lest," as in the LXX. Here it would seem to be dialectic, meaning **for why**, the prefix ש having the unusual meaning of "for" (cf. also 5:2; 6:5). Instead of בעטיה, **like one who is veiled** (RSV mg.), the RSV reads כטעיה, **like one who wanders**, with the Syriac, Symm., and Vulg., but this verb is found only in Ezek. 13:10, and there is no good reason to doubt the reading of the M.T., supported as it is by the LXX and O.L. and also by 4:1; 6:7, where the girl is described as veiled. The reference may be to veiling in mourning (cf. II Sam. 15:30; 19:4) or in shame (cf. Jer. 14:3; Mic. 3:7), or as a temple prostitute or votary (cf. Gen. 38:15, 19). Since the part of the body covered is invariably stated whenever veiling is used as a symbol of mourning or shame, the last meaning is the best. The goddess of fertility is regularly represented as veiled, and the motif of seeking is likewise suggestive of the cult, as is also the representation

---

and seeks to become articulate it scorns the usual, common, prosaic language of "basic English," and creates new words, new figures of speech, in its passionate search for "one word more." Bernard of Clairvaux says the Song of Songs "is not a cry from the mouth, but the gladness of the heart; not the sounding of the lips, but the impulse and emotion of joys within; not a concert of words, but of wills moving in harmony." [3]

As the youth and the maiden in the Song seek to tell each other of their love, they alternate between lengthy, sometimes highly involved, descriptions and brief all-inclusive exclamations. It is as if, having strained language to its utmost, the lovers realize how inadequate words are to express their love. This agonizing shuttle between verbose description and the realization of the insufficiency of words is part of the poignancy of love. The lover will use and manufacture all kinds of words in careless extravagance, and yet to put love into words can be an ultimately frustrating will-o'-the-wisp. Having said all that can be said, the lover in exasperation realizes that "I love you" is all that can be said.

The youth in the Song of Songs compares the maiden whom he loves "to a mare of Pharaoh's chariots" (1:9). That is not, as it might seem to us, a questionable compliment: it is the kind of hyperbole which all lovers conjure up in their imagination. But a few verses later the youth says simply, "Behold, you are beautiful, my love" (1:15a). This dialectic between fanciful exaggeration and straightforward affirmation is an essential characteristic of the language of love. Thomas Hood, who was a punster and writer of comic verses as well as a celebrated poet of more serious themes (cf. his social-conscious "The Song of the Shirt"), is only one of many who, in searching for ways of expressing his love, falls back on a simple declaration:

> I love thee—I love thee!
>   'Tis all that I can say;—
> It is my vision in the night,
>   My dreaming in the day.[4]

[3] *Eighty-Six Sermons on the Song of Solomon*, pp. 11-12.

[4] "I Love Thee."

8 ¶ If thou know not, O thou fairest among women, go thy way forth by the footsteps of the flock, and feed thy kids beside the shepherds' tents.

9 I have compared thee, O my love, to a company of horses in Pharaoh's chariots.

8 If you do not know,
   O fairest among women,
follow in the tracks of the flock,
   and pasture your kids
   beside the shepherds' tents.

9 I compare you, my love,
   to a mare of Pharaoh's chariots.

---

of the lovers as shepherdess and shepherd. The meaning then would be, "Why cannot I be with you rather than with your votaries?"—the question introducing the antiphonal response that follows; so also in 3:6; 5:9; 6:1; 8:8, and liturgies in general (cf. Ps. 24:7-10). On all interpretations the verse expresses the longing of one for her beloved.

THE DAUGHTERS OF JERUSALEM (1:8)

8. This verse contains the response of the chorus. The preposition in לך is reflexive, and the idiom is improperly called the ethical dative in most grammars; it occurs rather often in the book.

THE YOUTH (1:9-11)

9. The word ססתי is clearly the construct singular, **mare**, with a helping *yôdh*, and since רכב is nowhere found in the plural, being both singular and collective, רכבי is another occurrence of the same construction; hence "chariot" (so Syriac) rather than **chariots**. For **of** the original has **in**, meaning "attached to." The verb דמיתיך is the perfect of instantaneous action; hence **I compare you.** Stallions rather than mares were used with chariots, but the word is **mare** here because the subject of comparison is a woman. Comparison with a steed is highly flattering in the East, where both horses and women are excessively adorned. The term רעיתי, **my love**, is regularly applied to the maiden throughout the book and would seem to be of cultic origin, because it is used elsewhere only in Judg. 11:37 (*Kethîbh*) of the votaries who yearly bewailed the

---

The same problem of language presents itself also in the religious expression of love. Paul, who knew how to bend language to the service of the gospel, and who showed himself to be a poet in his hymn on love (I Cor. 13), also knew the inadequacies of language when speaking of the love of God in Christ. Such love is ultimately incomparable and calls forth not a description but an exclamation: "Thanks be to God for his inexpressible [unspeakable] gift!" (II Cor. 9:15.) In the same way one of the most familiar hymns, attributed to Bernard of Clairvaux and sometimes called "the sweetest and most evangelical" hymn of the Middle Ages, "Jesus, the very thought of thee," contains the lines:

> But what to those who find? Ah, this
>   Nor tongue nor pen can show:
> The love of Jesus, what it is
>   None but his loved ones know.[5]

This is not to say that love cannot be communicated through words at all, but only that it cannot be fully or completely expressed. The Song of Songs has made its impression upon

[5] Tr. Edward Caswall.

successive generations of readers by the sheer beauty and suggestiveness of its language. Regardless of its possible allegorical or religious interpretation, the music and poetry of love are given remarkable utterance.

To illustrate this distinctive quality of language would be to quote the whole book, but consider a few of only the most familiar lines. Take the descriptions which the lovers apply to each other.

> Your cheeks are comely with ornaments,
>   your neck with strings of jewels (1:10);

> As a lily among the brambles,
>   so is my love among maidens (2:2);

> He brought me to the banqueting house,
>   and his banner over me was love (2:4);

> You are all fair, my love;
>   there is no flaw in you (4:7);

> My beloved is all radiant and ruddy,
>   distinguished among ten thousand (5:10);

> You are beautiful as Tirzah, my love,
>   comely as Jerusalem,
>   terrible as an army with banners (6:4);

10 Thy cheeks are comely with rows *of jewels,* thy neck with chains *of gold.*	**10** Your cheeks are comely with ornaments, your neck with strings of jewels.
11 We will make thee borders of gold with studs of silver.	**11** We will make you ornaments of gold, studded with silver.
12 ¶ While the King *sitteth* at his table, my spikenard sendeth forth the smell thereof.	**12** While the king was on his couch, my nard gave forth its fragrance.
13 A bundle of myrrh *is* my well-beloved unto me; he shall lie all night betwixt my breasts.	**13** My beloved is to me a bag of myrrh, that lies between my breasts.

death of vegetation, typified by the death of Jephthah's daughter; but by the time the Song of Songs was written down, the term was probably one of endearment only.

10. Strings of jewels is one word in the Hebrew and is found only here; better, "beads" (Amer. Trans.), as its Arabic cognate indicates. Commentators have been puzzled to explain the cheek **ornaments**, but in the East jewelry is worn around the forehead, with bangles hanging over the cheeks. The verb נאוו is stative perfect Pilel of נאה, "to be comely."

11. Studded with silver is a paraphrase; the original reads **with studs of silver.**

THE MAIDEN (1:12-14)

12. The meaning of מסבו, a derivative from the Hiphil of סבב, "to go around," is uncertain. In Josh. 6:11 the verbal form is used of taking the ark in procession around Jericho, and in the verse here the word may originally have referred to the religious procession that was a feature of the fertility cult; but it came later to mean **couch** or "divan," on which one reclined at **table,** as the versions indicate. **Nard,** or more specifically **spikenard,** found only here and in 4:13-14, is strictly a product of India and probably did not reach Palestine until fairly late; hence an ointment made from native aromatic grasses may be intended here. In India **nard** was a love charm connected with the fertility cult.

13. The word דודי, **my beloved,** is an enigma. The regular meaning is "my uncle," "my near kinsman," and this is the translation in all the versions, except that the Syriac merely transliterates the word everywhere except here. In Isa. 5:1 and the Song of Songs,

How fair and pleasant you are,
   O loved one, delectable maiden! (7:6);

Make haste, my beloved,
   and be like a gazelle
or a young stag
   upon the mountains of spices (8:14).

But what kind of love is it that the Song of Songs exalts? We say it is magnificent poetry expressed in vivid words that sing and dance. But is the love of which it sings the same as the love which Paul praises in I Cor. 13?

What, then, is love? It is one of the vaguest of words. It is shopworn. It is like old money that has been worn smooth. It is used in Hollywood, in the newspaper, on the stage, over the radio, in the pulpit; and it means something different in each case. It is a synonym for the passion to give, and also for the passion to get. It is used in connection with deeds of heroism and with deeds of shame.[6]

[6] Hugh T. Kerr, *The Challenge of Jesus* (New York: Fleming H. Revell Co., 1939), p. 189.

We have suggested that the language of love as found in the Song of Songs is analogous in many ways to the religious or biblical way of speaking of God's love. But we may speak of two quite different kinds of love in very much the same way. There are many scholars who see in the Song of Songs nothing but romantic love, the passionate, physical attraction of two lovers who discover in each other their deepest longings and desires. On this level the Song at its best sings of the pure and natural love of man and woman, and at its worst is embarrassingly frank and suggestive in its praise of a sexual love that borders on lust.

We cannot, however, ignore the fact that this was decidedly not the level on which the Song of Songs was regarded by the Jewish rabbis or by Christian interpreters until fairly modern times. They saw the Song, rightly or wrongly, as a symbol of God's love. They were not concerned in the least to magnify romantic or physical love, though they may have had no

14 My beloved *is* unto me *as* a cluster of camphire in the vineyards of En-gedi.

14 My beloved is to me a cluster of henna blossoms
in the vineyards of Enge'di.

---

however, it must have a different meaning, somehow connected with love, and there is every reason to believe that it was originally the name of the Palestinian god of fertility, *Dôdh* (see Theophile J. Meek, "Canticles and the Tammuz Cult," *American Journal of Semitic Languages and Literatures*, XXXIX [1922-23], 4-6). The name appears in the proper name Dodavahu, "Yahu is *Dôdh*" (II Chr. 20:37) and in Amos 8:14, as regularly emended: "As your god lives, O Dan!" and "As your Dodh lives, O Beersheba!" In the original liturgy דודי, "my Dôdh," was a form of address quite like "my Tammuz," which appears often in the Tammuz liturgies. Later generations, however, lost sight of the original meaning of the expression as the Song became a conventionalized form for the celebration of the New Year; the phrase lost its earlier connection and came to be traditionally interpreted **my beloved**, but significantly always masculine, a synonym of the usual ידיד. The word דודים, "love," in vs. 4, *et al.*, manifestly goes back to the same root, and likewise דודאים, "mandrakes," in 7:13 (Hebrew 7:14), which were used as a fertility charm (cf. Gen. 30:14-17).

Myrrh (also 3:6; 4:6, 14; 5:5) is a perfume obtained from a shrub growing in south Arabia and Abyssinia and, according to the Mishnah (Shabbath 6:3), Hebrew women were accustomed to wear little bags of it, hanging from the neck between their **breasts**. It was the incense used at the festival of Adonis, and he himself was said to have been born from a myrrh tree. The second stich is strictly a relative clause, with the relative particle understood, as often in Hebrew poetry: **that lies between my breasts**.

14. The word הכפר, **henna**, found only here and in 4:13; 7:11 (Hebrew 7:12), where it is plural, is regarded by some as a loan word from Greek, but it is rather a loan word in Greek. The plant is native in Palestine and its powdered leaves are still used as a stain for the hair and various parts of the body. Its flowers grow in clusters. **Engedi** was an oasis west of the Dead Sea, famed for its **vineyards**. The preposition ב, **in,** can also be translated "from" (Amer. Trans.), as in Ugaritic, and this would seem to be preferable here.

---

reason to disparage or minimize its place and importance in human life. (The Bible is not prudish literature; it knows how to call a spade a spade; it is fully aware of sex and lust.) The Song of Songs was regarded by Jews and Christians as part of the canon of Scripture not because it was composed of striking language nor because it celebrated physical love, important and necessary as that may be.

Some importance, in other words, attaches to the fact that the Song of Songs has enjoyed a virtually uncontested place among the books of the Bible. This does not mean that we are necessarily bound to the traditional allegorical method of interpretation, but it does lay upon us the responsibility of discovering what the biblical view of love is, its content and the language in which it is expressed. We may also discover, incidentally, that the biblical view of love gives a deeper meaning to the Song of Songs even when it is taken to be no more than the passionate, sensual love associated with physical attraction—that the Bible here, as in other ways, redeems and baptizes what otherwise is vulgar, common, and prurient.

It is a significant fact that both the O.T. and the N.T. think of love as a distinctively theological word.[7] It is a God-centered word; its meaning and its content derive from God's revelation of himself as love. Whether we think of the O.T. word *'āhēbh* or the N.T. *agapē*, it is clear that for the biblical writers love is of God. It is true that the O.T. also uses the same word, and some others, to denote the love of man and woman, family love, friendship, etc. And it is no less true that in the Greek there are words like *erōs* and *philia*, from which we get our words "erotic" and "philanthropy," which have little if any religious or theological associations. But the distinctive N.T. word for love is *agapē*, which had little currency in clas-

[7] For discussions of the biblical view of love see Anders Nygren, *Agape and Eros* (tr. Phillips Watson and A. G. Hebert; London: Society for Promoting Christian Knowledge, 1932-39); Ethelbert Stauffer and Gottfried Quell, *Love,* in J. R. Coates, tr., *Bible Key Words from Gerhard Kittel's Theologisches Wörterbuch zum Neuen Testament* (New York: Harper & Bros., 1951); C. E. B. Cranfield, "Love," in Alan Richardson, ed., *A Theological Word Book of the Bible* (New York: The Macmillan Co., 1951), pp. 131-36.

15 Behold, thou *art* fair, my love; behold, thou *art* fair; thou *hast* doves' eyes.

16 Behold, thou *art* fair, my beloved, yea, pleasant: also our bed *is* green.

17 The beams of our house *are* cedar, *and* our rafters of fir.

15 Behold, you are beautiful, my love;
    behold, you are beautiful;
    your eyes are doves.

16 Behold, you are beautiful, my beloved,
    truly lovely.
    Our couch is green;

17   the beams of our house are cedar,
    our rafters*d* are pine.

d The meaning of the Hebrew word is uncertain

THE YOUTH (1:15)

15. This verse is repeated in 4:1, where it has the additional stich, "behind your veil," which the meter requires: 3+2, 2+2. The comparison with **doves** is frequent in the Song (also 2:14; 4:1; 5:2, 12; 6:9), and the dove, we know, was a common symbol of the fertility goddess. It is also the emblem of purity and constancy.

THE MAIDEN (1:16-17)

16. The last stich, with the emphatic particle אַף (not translated in RSV), requiring a preceding phrase parallel to its own, if dropped down one line to the end of vs. 17, would make better sense and the meter of the couplet would be 3+2, 3+2+3. The word רַעֲנָנָה, **green**, "leafy," "luxuriant," is regularly used to describe the sacred tree that was a feature of the Baal cult (e.g., Jer. 3:6, 13). One is also reminded of the bower of "fresh new grass, dewy lotus, crocus, and hyacinth, thick and soft," which "the divine earth" prepared as the nuptial couch of Zeus and Hera (Homer *Iliad* XIV. 347-51). The sacred marriage connected with the New Year festival was the subject of mystic drama all over the ancient Near East.

17. The expression קֹרוֹת בָּתֵּינוּ, lit., "the beams of our houses," with both elements of the compound pluralized, is a late form, meaning **the beams of our house.** The word רַחִיטֵנוּ is found only here, and its translation, **our rafters,** is a conjecture suggested by the parallelism. In late Hebrew and Arabic it means "furniture." The word בְּרוֹתִים,

sical Greek, but which was utilized by the N.T. writers as the special word for God's love in Christ. There is a clear correspondence between the Hebrew *'āhēbh* and the Greek *agapē*, and it is important to notice that in the LXX *agapē* (not *erōs* or *philia*) is almost always used as a translation of the Hebrew *'āhēbh*—and this is the case even in the Song of Songs.

The interesting feature about the biblical view of love is not that it thinks of many different kinds of love, but that it tends to locate love in the being and revelation of God himself, and that consequently all human expressions of love are related to that primary love, and are either reflections of the love of God or aberrations and perversions of it. The Bible therefore uses human love, even the love of man and woman, as part of its language when speaking of the love of God. But it does so not because human love is one of the best ways of speaking of God's love (anthropomorphism), but because of the conviction that human love derives from God's love. Evidence of this is plentiful in both the O.T. and the N.T. The whole book of Hosea, for example, makes use of the marriage motif as a means for speaking of the love of God (cf. also Jer. 2:2, 32-33; 3:1, 14; 31:22; Isa. 54:5; 62:4), and the N.T. also follows the same use of language (cf. Mark 2:19-20; Matt. 22:2; John 3:29; Eph. 5:22-23; Rev. 19:7-9; 21:2, 9; 22:17). The biblical association of man's love for woman (and its degenerative perversions, "whoredoms," "adulteries," etc.) with the love of God is not simply a human way of speaking about God, but a divine way of speaking about human relationships.

Whether the Bible speaks of man's love for God or for his fellow man or the love of man and woman for each other, they all are made dependent upon the love of God, i.e., we love not because there is something in us that makes us act that way, but because God is love, and our love is in response to his. It is God's initiative that creates love in us (cf. Deut. 4:5-40; Ps. 116; Matt. 5:43-48; Mark 12:29-31; John 5:42; 13:34; 14:15; 15:9, 12; 21:15-17; Eph. 5:2, 25; I John 4:10, 19). The biblical sequence is admirably and succinctly summarized in the words, "In this is love, not that we loved God

2 I *am* the rose of Sharon, *and* the lily of the valleys.

2 As the lily among thorns, so *is* my love among the daughters.

2 I am a rose[e] of Sharon,
   a lily of the valleys.

2 As a lily among brambles,
   so is my love among maidens.

[e] Heb *crocus*

---

found only here, is the Aramaic, or perhaps north Palestinian, equivalent of the Hebrew ברושים, pine, more likely "cypresses" (Amer. Trans., following LXX and Syriac), a better parallel to "cedars."

The description of the hut or booth in vss. 16-17 is very suggestive of the green bowers of Sukkoth or feast of Booths—further evidence in favor of the liturgical interpretation. Note too that in the Adonis festival booths were erected, and in each were placed the images of Adonis and his consort, Astarte, in representation of their marriage.

The Maiden (2:1)

2:1. The word חבצלת is found elsewhere only in Isa. 35:1, but it appears in Akkadian, meaning "meadow saffron" or **crocus**; it assuredly does not mean **rose**, but "saffron" (Syriac and Amer. Trans.), or **crocus** or "narcissus" (Targ. and Saadia). Since **Sharon** (the coastal plain between Mount Carmel and Joppa) is parallel to the **valleys** in the next stich, it is better taken with the LXX and Vulg. as a common noun, "the plain" (Amer. Trans.). The word שושנת is derived from the Egyptian *ššn*, Coptic *šošen*, "lotus," and it is of interest to note that the commonest type of Canaanite Astarte figurines represents the naked goddess carrying the lotus as her symbol. In ancient times the lotus grew in the Jordan Valley. From 5:13 it would appear to be red, since it refers there to the color of the lips. The RSV translates **lily**, following the KJV.

The Youth (2:2)

2. The preposition בין usually means "between," but here **among**, as, e.g., in Judg. 5:16; some regard the usage as north Palestinian. The word הבנות, **maidens**, lit., **the daughters**, but "son" or "daughter" in Hebrew can also denote "youth," i.e., "young man" or "maiden." The RSV takes the article as generic, but most take it as definite.

---

but that he loved us. . . . If God so loved us, we also ought to love one another" (I John 4:10-11).

This divine initiative is a truth the religious mind has always known. Augustine: "Thou hast formed us for thyself, and our hearts are restless till they find rest in thee." [8] Pascal: "I would not now be seeking thee, if I had not already been found of thee." [9] The anonymous hymn:

> I sought the Lord, and afterward I knew
>   He moved my soul to seek him, seeking me;
> It was not I that found, O Saviour true;
>   No, I was found of thee.
>
> .   .   .   .
>
> I find, I walk, I love, but, oh, the whole
>   Of love is but my answer, Lord, to thee!
> For thou wert long beforehand with my soul;
>   Always thou lovedst me.

[8] *Confessions* I. 1.
[9] Cf. *Great Shorter Works of Pascal*, tr. Emile Cailliet and John C. Blankenagel (Philadelphia: Westminster Press, 1948), p. 135.

Now there is no suggestion in the Song of Songs itself that the love of which it sings is in any way related to the love of God. Perhaps it is safe to say that if the various songs in the book originated in the midst of pagan fertility cults, then the view of love which it expresses so graphically very definitely does not have anything to do with God's love. But in any event, this was how the book was interpreted by those who put it alongside the psalms of David and the prophecy of Isaiah. For the Christian interpreter this was even more plausible than for the rabbinical scholar, since God's love in the N.T. was incarnated in a Person, so that the figure of the bride and the bridegroom became a natural way of speaking of the church and Christ himself.

It is highly suggestive to notice that many aspects of the N.T. use of love (*agapē*) find a parallel in the Song of Songs quite apart from an allegorical interpretation; e.g., God's love in the N.T. is spontaneous and uncaused (cf. Matt. 5:45; 20:1-16; Rom. 5:6-8). "God's love

3 As the apple tree among the trees of the wood, so *is* my beloved among the sons. I sat down under his shadow with great delight, and his fruit *was* sweet to my taste.

4 He brought me to the banqueting house, and his banner over me *was* love.

3 As an apple tree among the trees of the wood,
so is my beloved among young men.
With great delight I sat in his shadow,
and his fruit was sweet to my taste.

4 He brought me to the banqueting house,
and his banner over me was love.

THE MAIDEN (2:3-7)

3. The word הבנים, lit., **the sons,** is used in the Tammuz liturgies as a designation of the male votaries of the cult, and Ishtar is called "daughter." Trees like the apple, cedar, cypress, and palm are everywhere connected with the vegetation cult. The verb חמדתי, stative perfect, and hence "I long" (Amer. Trans.), is nowhere else Piel and perhaps should be pointed as Qal here. The expression וישבתי, lit., "that I may sit," with *wāw* conversive introducing an object clause, is a variant construction of the infinitive construct, by which it is translated in the Targ. The RSV and KJV take the two verbs as hendiadys and the *wāw* as simple, which would be a violation of classical Hebrew syntax and would be the one exception for a verbal form in the book. The second line of this verse as it stands is 3+3 metrically. Since this is not a variant of the 3+2 meter, the original may have had לי, "to me," in place of לחכי, **to my taste,** to make the regular 3+2 meter, or the poet may have made a slip here. Ancient writers were no more infallible than their modern counterparts and metrical slips are found in all literatures.

4. In parallelism with the following verse it is better to point הביאני and דגלו as imperatives, with the LXX, Symm., O.L., Syriac, and Arabic: "Bring me to the house of wine, and look upon me with love" (Amer. Trans.). This is further supported by the use of דגל as a verb in 5:10; 6:4, 10. The RSV follows the M.T., but **banqueting house** is really interpretative of "house of wine." Also it is a strange figure to say **his banner over me was love.**

---

is always spontaneous; it is not called out by anything outside itself. Hence, when it is said that God loves man, this is not a judgment on what man is like, but on what God is like." [1] It would be inconsistent with the N.T. interpretation of God's love to suggest that the Song of Songs belongs in the same category. The lovers who sing of their love for each other are clearly motivated and inspired by each other. Their love is not uncaused. But it may well partake of a spontaneous quality and actually appear to the lovers themselves to be uncaused. Unless we must say that the Song sings exclusively of physical desire, and we need not say this, then it is possible, and not sacrilegious, to relate the experience of true love of man and woman for each other to God's uncaused, spontaneous love. There are frequent suggestions of this very thing in the Song, and the book as a whole simply takes for granted the love of the youth and the maiden without intimating in any way what it is that has brought them together. Perhaps the descriptions of each other, to which reference has already been made, are in the nature of attempted answers to the perennial

question of lovers—"Why do I love thee?" But it is inevitably, as every lover knows, a rhetorical question, for love often comes unexpectedly and for no reason at all.

Like Dian's kiss, unasked, unsought,
Love gives itself, but is not bought.[2]

Thus love borders on the miraculous. There is something ineffable, unspeakable, even irrational about it. Love gives itself without measure and without counting the cost.

Love sacrifices all things
To bless the thing it loves! [3]

If thou must love me, let it be for nought
Except for love's sake only.[4]

"Love is alone sufficient by itself; it pleases by itself, and for its own sake. It is itself a merit, and itself its own recompense. It seeks neither cause, nor consequence, beyond itself. It is its

[1] Nygren, *op. cit.,* Pt. I, p. 52.

[2] Henry Wadsworth Longfellow, "Endymion," st. iv.
[3] Edward Bulwer Lytton, *The Lady of Lyons,* Act V, scene 2.
[4] Elizabeth Barrett Browning, *Sonnets from the Portuguese* XIV.

5 Stay me with flagons, comfort me with apples: for I *am* sick of love.
 	
6 His left hand *is* under my head, and his right hand doth embrace me.
 	
7 I charge you, O ye daughters of Jerusalem, by the roes, and by the hinds of the field, that ye stir not up, nor awake *my* love, till he please.
	5 Sustain me with raisins,
	    refresh me with apples;
	    for I am sick with love.
	6 O that his left hand were under my head,
	    and that his right hand embraced me!
	7 I adjure you, O daughters of Jerusalem,
	    by the gazelles or the hinds of the field,
	    that you stir not up nor awaken love
	    until it please.

5. Raisins, better, "raisin-cakes" (Amer. Trans.), are explicitly connected with the fertility cult in Hos. 3:1; also in Jer. 7:18; 44:19, with a different word of the same meaning; **flagons** follows the rabbinical interpretation, but is quite wrong. **For I am sick with love** expresses the intense longing of one separated from her beloved, equally applicable to an ordinary lover or to the goddess separated from her lord who is in the underworld.

6. Since תחת ל is quite un-Hebraic, we should delete ל, with the duplicate in 8:3 and the Syriac, or better, with Bruston, *et al.,* divide the letters differently: תחתל ראשי, let his left hand "encircle my head." This has the advantage of better parallelism with the second stich and requires no change in the C.T.

7. The song ends in an adjuration (repeated in 3:5; with some slight changes in 8:4) that would seem to be inexplicable on any hypothesis other than the liturgical. The whole passage is so full of cult terms and allusions, with the background neither shepherd life nor royal, but purely cultic, that Haller is fully convinced of its cultic character. This is apparently reflected in the Greek translation, "by the forces and by the powers of the field," i.e., the gods of the field, **gazelles** and **hinds** being sacred to Astarte. The adjuration not to arouse love prematurely suggests that this passage in its original setting indicated that the women were engaged in some rite of sympathetic magic which was intended to arouse love between god and goddess at the proper season, viz., at the time when the growing season should begin. Also **love** may be a divine name here, as Margoliouth suggests. **Or the hinds,** omitted in Codex Alexandrinus in the parallel passage (8:4), reads like a gloss that was inserted to indicate that the preceding word צבאות was to be understood as "gazelles," not as the common title of Yahweh, "Sabaoth," despite which, however, the Targ. so interpreted it. Another reason for taking the phrase as a gloss is the fact that the line seems to be too long, being apparently 3+3, when it ought to be 3+2. However, the M.T. could be read as a tristich, 2+2+3. The Syriac here and elsewhere corrects the masculine **you** to feminine, but the use of masculine for feminine, as already noted, is characteristic of our book and may be dialectic.

own fruit, and its own object and usefulness." [5] As J. C. Powys says: "Love . . . is always in the mood of believing in miracles." [6]

Of the essence of the N.T. view of love (*agapē*) is its boundless and all-encompassing outreach. God "makes his sun rise on the evil and on the good, and sends rain on the just and on the unjust" (Matt. 5:45). "Agape is the direct opposite of that love which is called out by the worthiness of its object and so may be said to be a recognition of the value and attractiveness of its object. The man whom God

loves has not any value in himself. His value consists simply in the fact that God loves him." [7] There is something of this spontaneous, creative love, which is largely indifferent to merit or worth, in the Song of Songs. To be sure, the youth and the maiden are in love because they see in each other something to love. There is an "object" for their affections. But it is worth noting that the one who is loved tends to deprecate his or her worth, as much as to say, "Why do you love me?" The maiden thinks herself unworthy and undeserving of the youth's love because she is "dark" and "swarthy" and no more than "a rose of Sharon" (1:5-6; 2:1). Yet the youth, because of his love, gives new

[5] Bernard of Clairvaux, *Eighty-Six Sermons on the Song of Solomon,* p. 509.

[6] *The Meaning of Culture* (New York: W. W. Norton & Co., 1929), p. 144.

[7] Nygren, *op. cit.,* Pt. I, p. 54.

8 ¶ The voice of my beloved! behold, he cometh leaping upon the mountains, skipping upon the hills.

9 My beloved is like a roe or a young hart: behold, he standeth behind our wall, he looketh forth at the windows, showing himself through the lattice.

10 My beloved spake, and said unto me, Rise up, my love, my fair one, and come away.

11 For, lo, the winter is past, the rain is over *and* gone;

8 The voice of my beloved!   Behold, he comes,   leaping upon the mountains,   bounding over the hills.   9 My beloved is like a gazelle,   or a young stag.   Behold, there he stands   behind our wall,   gazing in at the windows,   looking through the lattice.   10 My beloved speaks and says to me: "Arise, my love, my fair one,   and come away;   11 for lo, the winter is past,   the rain is over and gone.

The Maiden (2:8-17)

8. The voice of: Better, "Hark!" (Amer. Trans.), as in 5:2. Note the vividness and dramatic force of the opening words and the hyperbole, if the beloved is merely human and not a god.

9. In this one verse there are no less than four *hapax legomena*, but their meanings are fairly clear. The preposition מִן, twice in the last line, is, lit., "from," but **at** and **through** give the sense correctly.

10. Speaks and says: The RSV considers the verbs as perfects of instantaneous action, but it is preferable to take them as ordinary perfects and translate, "spoke up and said" (Amer. Trans.; cf. KJV). The second verb, in accordance with classical Hebrew syntax, is perfect with simple *wāw* rather than imperfect with *wāw* consecutive because the second verb follows closely after the first and has a similar meaning. The words are introductory to the poem that follows and constitute the only prose in the book outside the title (1:1).

11. This verse is metrically 3+3, suggesting that חָלַף, is over, which is set down with הָלַךְ, "is gone" (Amer. Trans.), without a connecting *wāw*, is a gloss due to dittography; or it is a variant reading, thus giving us a conflate text. The word הַסְּתָו, the winter, found only here, refers to the rainy season, at the end of which the growing season (March-April) starts in earnest. The ending ו represents the old nominative.

value and importance to the one who feels unimportant and lowly (cf. 1:9-11; 2:2). No one who has ever experienced a boundless love, whether of God or of man or woman, feels he deserves it.

The language of love, however, is infinitely more than words and phrases. Love expresses itself not so much in what it says as in what it is and does. This is clearly implied in the Song of Songs by the uniquely personal character of the book. It is the only book in the Bible composed completely of direct personal address. And although the lovers speak of their love in exquisite language, what they say to each other is that love is personal togetherness. Hence the maiden is distraught when she is separated from her lover, even though she may be assured of his love. This personal presence is likewise the heart of the Christian view of love. God com-

municates his love to us, for example, through the words of the prophets. But in the N.T. God's word becomes flesh and dwells among us (John 1:14).

II. The Redemption of the Commonplace.— What are we to do with the unmistakable sensual and erotic dimension of the Song of Songs? The traditional allegorical interpretation virtually eliminated the necessity of answering such a question, but modern scholarship insists, and rightly so, that we take seriously, not only symbolically, the physical and sexual imagery of the Song. Clearly the first step, if we are to be honest, is to recognize frankly and openly that much of the language has to do with love between the sexes. Jewish and Christian interpreters from the beginning have assumed that it has to do with more than physical love, but even the most farfetched allegory cannot avoid

12 The flowers appear on the earth; the time of the singing *of birds* is come, and the voice of the turtle is heard in our land;

13 The fig tree putteth forth her green figs, and the vines *with* the tender grape give a *good* smell. Arise, my love, my fair one, and come away.

---

12 The flowers appear on the earth,
    the time of singing has come,
and the voice of the turtledove
    is heard in our land.
13 The fig tree puts forth its figs,
    and the vines are in blossom;
    they give forth fragrance.
Arise, my love, my fair one,
    and come away.

---

12. The verb נראו, **appear,** "are seen," is a stative perfect. In זמיר we have a word that gives strong support to the liturgical interpretation. As Arnold B. Ehrlich has pointed out (*Randglossen zur hebräischen Bibel* [Leipzig: J. C. Hinrichs, 1914], VII, 7), derivatives from זמר in the sense of **singing** are used in the O.T. for ritual songs only. Since he believes that our book has nothing to do with ritual singing, he follows the versions, Targ., and many scholars in giving to זמיר here the meaning of "pruning." On the ancient Hebrew calendar found at Gezer (see W. F. Albright, "The Gezer Calendar," *Bulletin of the American Schools of Oriental Research,* No. 92 [Dec., 1943], pp. 16-26) the month of July-August is known as זמר, which seems to mean "pruning," but this is later than the month indicated in our poem; hence **singing** would seem to be better here because it is more in harmony with the context and the general character of the book, and **singing** is the meaning everywhere else in the O.T. The same word has this meaning in Akkadian and appears as the title of Tammuz ritual songs. **The turtledove** was a migratory bird in Palestine and its coming was the sign of spring (Jer. 8:7). The meter of the verse is 3+2, 2+2.

13. The verb חנטה, **puts forth,** is better translated "is ripening," as its Arabic cognate suggests. The noun סמדר is strictly a predicate, "grape blossom" (cf. KJV); hence **in blossom.** The verbs in the first line are in the perfect of experience. The RSV follows the accents in the division of the second line, but for metrical reasons the division should come after **my love** (so Amer. Trans.). The word לכי (*Kethibh*) is the archaic poetic form of לך (*Qerê*) and is another of the rather numerous instances of reflexive ל.

---

the sexual symbolism, and it is better surely to begin by acknowledging the fact that sex is inescapable in any view of the Song.

It would be foolish, for example, to gloss over the sexual allusions and implications of such phrases and passages as the following:

My beloved is to me a bag of myrrh,
    that lies between my breasts (1:13);

Your two breasts are like two fauns (4:5);

I will hie me to the mountain of myrrh
    and the hill of frankincense (4:6);

Let my beloved come to his garden,
    and eat of its choicest fruits (4:16);

Your rounded thighs are like jewels,
.   .   .   .
Your navel is a rounded bowl
.   .   .   .
Your belly is a heap of wheat (7:1-2);

I say I will climb the palm tree
    and lay hold of its branches (7:8);

Make haste, my beloved,
    and be like a gazelle
or a young stag
    upon the mountains of spices (8:14).

It is true, of course, that the meaning of such passages as these, and others that could be mentioned, is not always self-evident. The language of love is symbolical and poetical, but it does not follow that every word and figure must have a double meaning. It is possible to overdo the sexual symbolism of the Song. For those who are looking for hidden suggestions there is no end of possibilities, just as the prurient adolescent can find a double meaning where none is intended. Yet it is impossible to avoid altogether the physical side of love in the Song, and there is no reason why we should. The Bible is far from being silent on the subject of sex. In fact, there have been those who have sought to discredit the Bible simply because it is so frank and open. The biblical vocabulary is extensive and varied in sexual terms, and there

14 ¶ O my dove, *that art* in the clefts of the rock, in the secret *places* of the stairs, let me see thy countenance, let me hear thy voice; for sweet *is* thy voice, and thy countenance *is* comely.

15 Take us the foxes, the little foxes, that spoil the vines: for our vines *have* tender grapes.

16 ¶ My beloved *is* mine, and I *am* his: he feedeth among the lilies.

17 Until the day break, and the shadows flee away, turn, my beloved, and be thou like a roe or a young hart upon the mountains of Bether.

14 O my dove, in the clefts of the rock,
   in the covert of the cliff,
let me see your face,
   let me hear your voice,
for your voice is sweet,
   and your face is comely.
15 Catch us the foxes,
   the little foxes,
that spoil the vineyards,
   for our vineyards are in blossom."

16 My beloved is mine and I am his,
   he pastures his flock among the lilies.
17 Until the day breathes
   and the shadows flee,
turn, my beloved, be like a gazelle,
   or a young stag upon rugged*f* mountains.

f The meaning of the Hebrew word is unknown

14. In the Near East the dove nests in cliffs (Jer. 48:28). The expression מראיך, **your face**, is, lit., "your form" (Amer. Trans.), from the root ראה, "to see," which is a final *yôdh* verb; hence the *yôdh* in our word is part of the root, not the mark of the plural as generally believed.

15. The word שעלים can be **foxes** or "jackals"; just how such animals can despoil a vineyard is not clear—perhaps by burrowing. The verse reads like a snatch from a rustic dance song and seems to have no point here unless it is reminiscent of an ancient fertility rite like the Roman Cerialia or Robigalia, with foxes figuring in the former and puppies in the latter. Gordis suggests that the vineyard may be the maiden and the little foxes the young men who lay siege to her. The last clause is circumstantial: **for** (better, "since") **our vineyards are in blossom.**

16. The form הרעה is the article plus the participle; hence "who is pasturing" (Amer. Trans.), not **he pastures.**

17. The reference here is to the breezes that come up in the evening (cf. Gen. 3:8) and the disappearance of **the shadows** with nightfall (cf. Jer. 6:4). The phrase is repeated in 4:6 and means all day long. The word סב is from the root סבב, "to turn around," "to go around"; hence "gambol" (Amer. Trans.) rather than **turn,** following the LXX. The noun בתר is obscure; since the root means "to cut in two," **rugged** or "craggy" (Amer. Trans.) would seem to be the best translation, reproducing the noun

are stories and passages too numerous to catalogue which by themselves do not rise above the obscene and pornographic. Who does not remember first stumbling, with mixed feelings of surprise and shame, on Onan, David and Bathsheba, Tamar, Solomon and his concubines, Hosea and his prostitute wife, the woman taken in adultery, Paul's list of sexual vices? Nor does the Song of Songs have any monopoly on the kind of descriptive language already referred to (cf. Ps. 45; Ezek. 16; 23; Rev. 17–19; *et al.*). But the Bible is what it is, and it would be a mistake to censor it because it speaks out clearly on the subject of sex. Far from discrediting it, such passages illustrate the realism of the Bible,

for sex is inextricably interwoven in the fabric of human nature. In this sense there is no real conflict between the Bible and, say, Freud or Kinsey, insofar as sex is recognized as a dynamic and in many ways a dominant force in life.

One would expect therefore that the Christian church, on the basis of the biblical realism, would have something significant to say about sex. But it must be admitted that all too often this has not been so. The interpretation of the Song of Songs is a case in point. Instead of using the graphic imagery of the Song as a point of departure for expounding the biblical view of sex, interpreters in the past have shied away from this as being beneath the high, spir-

3 By night on my bed I sought him whom my soul loveth: I sought him, but I found him not.

2 I will rise now, and go about the city in the streets, and in the broad ways I will seek him whom my soul loveth: I sought him, but I found him not.

3 The watchmen that go about the city found me: *to whom I said,* Saw ye him whom my soul loveth?

4 *It was* but a little that I passed from them, but I found him whom my soul loveth: I held him, and would not let him go, until I had brought him into my mother's house, and into the chamber of her that conceived me.

---

3 Upon my bed by night
　　I sought him whom my soul loves;
　I sought him, but found him not;
　　I called him, but he gave no answer.*g*
2 "I will rise now and go about the city,
　　in the streets and in the squares;
　I will seek him whom my soul loves."
　　I sought him, but found him not.
3 The watchmen found me,
　　as they went about in the city.
　"Have you seen him whom my soul
　　loves?"
4 Scarcely had I passed them,
　　when I found him whom my soul loves.
　I held him, and would not let him go
　　until I had brought him into my moth-
　　　er's house,
　　and into the chamber of her that con-
　　　ceived me.

g Gk: Heb lacks this line

---

by an adjective. The figure in the verse is extravagant if a human being rather than a god is meant. The meter is 2+2, 2+2, 2+2, here a variant of the 3+2.

THE MAIDEN (3:1-5)

3:1. The word בלילות is plural to indicate that it was not one particular night, but night after night—**by night**; the girl's dream experience was a reflection of her waking hours. The final stich of the verse is lacking, but is found in the duplicate passage (5:6b) and in the LXX and O.L.: "I called him, but he did not answer me" (Amer. Trans.); the RSV omits "me." Here and in vss. 2-4 we have once again the motif of seeking and finding as well as the reference to **watchmen** impeding the way (see also the parallel passage, 5:2-8), reminding us of the watchmen that Ishtar had to pass to get into the underworld to bring back her dead lord to life and thus bring new life into the world. Interpreted as a secular song, the passage is expressive of the girl's intense love, imagining and fearful of separation from her beloved.

2. The imperfects in this verse are all in the emphatic form to express determination.

3. The meter is 2+2+3. **As they went about in the city** would be the translation of a circumstantial clause, whereas the Hebrew is relative: **that go about the city.**

---

itual message of God's love. It is thus common to find modern exponents of a freer discussion of sex matters blaming religion for thwarting open consideration of what is manifestly an important area of human existence. "There is no instinct that has been so maligned, suppressed, abused, and distorted by religious teaching as the instinct of sex. Yet sex-love is the most intense instinctive pleasure known to men and women, and starvation or thwarting of this instinct causes more acute unhappiness than poverty, disease, or ignorance." [8]

[8] Dora Russell (Mrs. Bertrand Russell), *The Right to Be Happy* (New York: Harper & Bros., 1927), p. 128. The Russells were popular advocates of the "new morality" of the 1920's.

Let us think of three ways in which the physical side of love which finds expression in the Song of Songs can be dealt with: (a) the natural or biological approach; (b) the romantic or true-love approach; and (c) the Christian or redemptive approach. Over against the Victorian embarrassed and prudish cloaking of sex, when the word and all it implies was hush-hush, when it was more polite to speak of a "limb" than a "leg," when one expositor of the Song of Songs, for example, suggested that 7:2 referred to the maiden's "lap"—over against all this, there has been a veritable revolution in our attitude toward sex. The effect of this revolution has been to bring sex out into the open where it may be regarded without shame

5 I charge you, O ye daughters of Jerusalem, by the roes, and by the hinds of the field, that ye stir not up, nor awake *my* love, till he please.

6 ¶ Who *is* this that cometh out of the wilderness like pillars of smoke, perfumed with myrrh and frankincense, with all powders of the merchant?

7 Behold his bed, which *is* Solomon's; threescore valiant men *are* about it, of the valiant of Israel.

---

5 I adjure you, O daughters of Jerusalem,
     by the gazelles or the hinds of the field,
   that you stir not up nor awaken love
     until it please.

6 What is that coming up from the wilderness,
     like a column of smoke,
   perfumed with myrrh and frankincense,
     with all the fragrant powders of the merchant?
7 Behold, it is the litter of Solomon!
     About it are sixty mighty men
     of the mighty men of Israel,

THE DAUGHTERS OF JERUSALEM (3:6-11)

6. The word מי regularly means **who**, but here **what**, as in Akkadian; it may be dialectic. The verb עלה, **coming up**, is feminine to agree with the feminine neuter זאת, **this**. **A column of smoke** should be plural (as in KJV), referring to the clouds of dust stirred up by the procession or to the clouds of incense profusely burned. The use of כ is pregnant, meaning "as in," not simply **like**. The last stich reads, "from all kinds of merchants' spices" (Amer. Trans.), where מן expresses source, "made from" (Amer. Trans.), and cannot mean **with**.

7. **The litter of Solomon**, lit., "his litter which belongs to Solomon," is an idiom found in Mishnaic Hebrew; it may be dialectic here. The following clause is circumstantial: "with sixty warriors around it." If **Solomon** in this passage is not playing the role of the god in a festal procession, it is difficult to see how his name got into the text, and to delete it, with Jastrow and many modern scholars, is too easy a way out. Also we have no indication anywhere that the bridegroom in secular weddings was ever carried in procession, whereas the god was. Solomon's name, שלמה, is manifestly derived

---

or embarrassment as a natural and biological function of the human body akin to hunger and thirst. The modern revolt against Victorian mock modesty is illustrated in the flood of books dealing with sex information and education, the instruction of young people beginning at the primary grades and running through high school and college, and the increasing use of sex as a theme for novel, stage, movie, radio, and television. Much of the force of this attempt to emancipate sex from the restrictions of older taboos is to suggest that it is a quite natural and biological phenomenon and that it can best be treated that way. Part of the significance of the Kinsey reports,[9] whatever else may be said of them, lies in the frank and statistical disclosure of actual sexual behavior among men and women without any conscious effort to moralize.

Now the Christian church in various ways has

shown that it is ready to make the best of this natural and biological approach. Perhaps there are still too many inhibitions about sex where the church and religion are concerned, but certainly there is little evidence that religious writers, preachers, counselors, chaplains, or teachers are trying to ignore the subject or hush it up as was once the case. No longer is it necessary to point in a facetious way to the theologian's lack of knowledge of anatomy in interpretations of the Song of Songs. Says a biblical interpreter:

We ought to be thankful that the weaknesses and contradictions in the traditional ecclesiastical view have been brought to light so that they can no longer be denied. The whole development has, further, helped to bring it about that we again have courage to speak of the sexual life without periphrases, without timidity and without concealment.[1]

[1] Otto Piper, "The Christian in the Sexual Disorder of the Present Day," in A. S. Nash, ed., *Education for Christian Marriage* (London: Student Christian Movement Press, 1939), p. 37; see also Piper, *The Christian Interpretation of Sex* (New York: Charles Scribner's Sons, 1951).

[9] Alfred C. Kinsey, *et al.*, *Sexual Behavior in the Human Male* (Philadelphia: W. B. Saunders Co., 1948); *Sexual Behavior in the Human Female* (Philadelphia: W. B. Saunders Co., 1953).

8 They all hold swords, *being* expert in war: every man *hath* his sword upon his thigh because of fear in the night.

9 King Solomon made himself a chariot of the wood of Lebanon.

10 He made the pillars thereof *of* silver, the bottom thereof *of* gold, the covering of it *of* purple, the midst thereof being paved *with* love, for the daughters of Jerusalem.

8 all girt with swords
    and expert in war,
  each with his sword at his thigh,
    against alarms by night.
9 King Solomon made himself a palanquin
    from the wood of Lebanon.
10 He made its posts of silver,
    its back of gold, its seat of purple;
  it was lovingly wrought within[h]
    by the daughters of Jerusalem.

[h] The meaning of the Hebrew is uncertain

---

from Shelem, שׁלם, the name of a fertility god; the name appears also in the word ירושלם, "Jerusalem," abbreviated as שׁלם, "Salem," in Gen. 14:18; Ps. 76:2 [Hebrew 76:3]. If our book is a liturgy, the name that stood here originally must have been Shelem, and it was changed to Solomon when the liturgy came to be adapted to the Jerusalem cultus.

8. The word אחזי, lit., "held," a passive participle in an active sense, is a deponent, best translated by **girt**. **Against alarms by night**, lit., "because of alarms by night," is difficult to understand if the reference is not to the god coming up (note the verb in vs. 6) from the underworld and its terrors.

9. The line as it stands is 2+2+2, but many scholars delete **Solomon** as redundant, to make the regular 3+2.

10. The RSV cannot be correct here either in translation or arrangement. Whatever the fourth stich means, it is parallel to the third. Unfortunately רצוף is found only here, but the cognates indicate the meaning "fitted out," and אהבה should not be translated **love**, but "leather," in accordance with its Arabic cognate (see G. R. Driver, "Supposed Arabisms in the Old Testament," *Journal of Biblical Literature*, LV [1936], 111): "its interior fitted out with leather." This is better than emending אהבה to הבנים, "ebony," as most scholars do. The last stich, "from the daughters of Jerusalem" (by is

---

The fact is, however, that mere knowledge of sex is not enough. Sex may be likened to hunger, but it is a much more subtle natural and biological function. We have more discussion and openness about sex than perhaps the world has ever known, but it does not follow that we have learned to master its mysteries or develop a "new morality" that would be better than the older codes because it would be enlightened and free. Sex knowledge by itself is no panacea for human ills.

Medical students, by reason of their studies, have to know the facts of anatomy, physiology and disease on which many of the teachings of what is called sex hygiene appear to depend . . . ; but I have never found that their knowledge of these facts made them any more chaste than other people, or any less so—rather it left them just about the average of men. Now, if the full knowledge of facts could hold people straight and make them behave themselves, medical students ought to be an ideal body of men. But they are not.[2]

"They'll tell you sex has become a mess because it was hushed up. But for the last twenty years it has *not* been hushed up. . . . Yet it is still in a mess. If hushing up had been the cause of the trouble, ventilation would have set it right. But it hasn't."[3]

It is one thing to see that sex is a natural and biological fact, but it is quite another thing to say that sex is love or that sex is life. So too the interpreter of the Song of Songs ought not to blink at the sexual bluntness of the book, but he need not be persuaded that sex and sex alone is all that matters here. What is natural and biological in animals may become repulsive and degrading in human beings simply because sex by itself or for itself is not enough to inspire or sustain love.[4] Let us freely admit that the Song of Songs has to do with the physical side of love, but let us also remem-

[2] Richard C. Cabot, *Christianity and Sex* (New York: The Macmillan Co., 1937), pp. 7-8.

[3] C. S. Lewis, *Christian Behavior* (New York: The Macmillan Co., 1944), p. 26.

[4] Referring to the possibility that sex by itself may lead to lust rather than love, Martin Luther is reported to have said: "The reproduction of mankind is a great marvel and mystery. Had God consulted me in the matter, I should have advised him to continue the generation of the species by fashioning them of clay." (*Table Talk*, tr. William Hazlitt [London: George Bell & Sons, 1902], No. DCCLII.)

11 Go forth, O ye daughters of Zion, and behold king Solomon with the crown wherewith his mother crowned him in the day of his espousals, and in the day of the gladness of his heart.

11 Go forth, O daughters of Zion,
    and behold King Solomon,
with the crown with which his mother
        crowned him
    on the day of his wedding,
    on the day of the gladness of his heart.

4 Behold, thou *art* fair, my love; behold, thou *art* fair; thou *hast* doves' eyes within thy locks: thy hair *is* as a flock of goats, that appear from mount Gilead.

2 Thy teeth *are* like a flock *of sheep that are even* shorn, which came up from the washing; whereof every one bear twins, and none *is* barren among them.

4 Behold, you are beautiful, my love,
    behold, you are beautiful!
Your eyes are doves
    behind your veil.
Your hair is like a flock of goats,
    moving down the slopes of Gilead.
2 Your teeth are like a flock of shorn ewes
        that have come up from the washing,
    all of which bear twins,
        and not one among them is bereaved.

---

impossible), probably belongs to the beginning of vs. 11; in that case "from" should be omitted; likewise, delete "daughters of Zion" in vs. 11, which appears only here, as a variant of "daughters of Jerusalem," and is omitted in the best LXX MSS and O.L. and was not in Origen's text.

11. The RSV takes the second ב as expressing accompaniment, but it is clearly locative, identical with the first. The last phrase in the verse is a compound, and in accordance with the rules of Hebrew grammar (see Exeg. on Lam. 1:7) it should be translated "on the day of his gladness of heart." The *wāw* at the beginning of the phrase is explicative, "namely," and so need not be translated; or the phrase may be a variant of the preceding stich, thus giving us a conflate text.

The Youth (4:1-15)

4:1. The expression שגלשו, **moving down,** is strictly a relative clause with its verb in the perfect of experience, "which trail down"; the verb is found only here and in 6:5, and its translation is purely an inference. **Gilead,** the northern part of Trans-Jordan, was famous for its pasturage. Most scholars omit **slopes,** with many MSS, the LXX, and the parallel in 6:5, but the RSV inserts it in 6:5.

2. The passive participle הקצובות here expresses imminent action (as the participle frequently does), "about to be shorn," not completed action; **shorn ewes** would be anything but **beautiful,** and sheep are washed before shearing, not afterward. The emphasis on the fecundity of the ewes is suggestive of the fertility cult.

---

ber that it is poetry and music, not a statistical report on sexual behavior.

An attempted step beyond the natural, biological approach is the romantic, true-love attitude, which does not deny the place or power of sex, but seeks to consecrate the physical with the loftier motives of mutual personal regard, respect, and devotion. It is this view that lies behind the traditional "dramatic" interpretation of the Song of Songs. Whether the "drama" includes two main figures, Solomon and the maiden, or three, Solomon, the maiden, and her shepherd-lover, the point of this interpretation was to stress the note of true love as something

more than physical attraction. In the three-character view the romantic element is enhanced by suggesting that the maiden resists the alluring temptations of Solomon and his court and remains faithful to her lowly shepherd-lover.

It is significant that this romantic or true-love attitude did not emerge much before the Middle Ages, "when knighthood was in flower," and sexual passion was overlaid with what C. S. Lewis calls "courtly love." [5] In our day Hollywood for reasons of its own has become the

[5] *The Allegory of Love* (London: Oxford University Press, 1936), pp. 14-17.

3 Thy lips *are* like a thread of scarlet, and thy speech *is* comely: thy temples *are* like a piece of a pomegranate within thy locks.

4 Thy neck *is* like the tower of David builded for an armory, whereon there hang a thousand bucklers, all shields of mighty men.

5 Thy two breasts *are* like two young roes that are twins, which feed among the lilies.

6 Until the day break, and the shadows flee away, I will get me to the mountain of myrrh, and to the hill of frankincense.

7 Thou *art* all fair, my love; *there is* no spot in thee.

---

3 Your lips are like a scarlet thread,
and your mouth is lovely.
Your cheeks are like halves of a pomegranate
behind your veil.
4 Your neck is like the tower of David,
built for an arsenal,[i]
whereon hang a thousand bucklers,
all of them shields of warriors.
5 Your two breasts are like two fawns,
twins of a gazelle,
that feed among the lilies.
6 Until the day breathes
and the shadows flee,
I will hie me to the mountain of myrrh
and the hill of frankincense.
7 You are all fair, my love;
there is no flaw in you.

[i] The meaning of the Hebrew word is uncertain

---

3. The word for **mouth** is found only here and means, lit., "that with which one speaks." The noun רקה, "the thin part of the skull," "the temple," from the root "to be thin," can scarcely mean **cheeks**, nor can the singular פלח, "slice," from the root "to cleave," mean **halves**; translate accordingly, "Your temple is like a slice of pomegranate" (Amer. Trans.). The **pomegranate** (again in vs. 13; 6:7, 11; 7:12 [Hebrew 7:13]; 8:2) owes its connection with the fertility cult to its numerous seeds, symbolic of fertility.

4. The **tower of David** is otherwise unknown; it was probably some well-known fortress built by David. The meaning of תלפיות, a feminine plural noun, is quite unknown and one guess is as good as another: **armory** or **arsenal**. The following stich is strictly a circumstantial clause, "with a thousand bucklers hung upon it" (Amer. Trans.). **All of them** would require כלם; the word כל here means "all kinds," as in 3:6; 4:10, 14; 7:13 (Hebrew 7:14); Lev. 19:23; *et al.* For **shields** hung around a tower, referring here to the elaborate jewelry around the neck of the girl, cf. Ezek. 27:11.

5. Two with **breasts** is superfluous and the line would be better metrically without it. The last stich, repeated from 2:16; 6:3, looks like a gloss and is lacking in the duplicate, 7:3 (Hebrew 7:4).

6. This verse, repeated in part from 2:17, breaks the thought and would come better after vs. 7. **The mountain of myrrh** and **the hill of frankincense** manifestly refers to the girl, the metaphors being very suggestive of the fertility goddess.

---

great interpreter and spokesman for a romantic love that borders on sentimentality. Sex, to be sure, is not underplayed in films, but the dominant accent is very much like the three-character dramatic view of the Song of Songs—true love will find a way. Thus a romantic glow may be given the obviously physical side of love in the Song of Songs, and attention may be directed rather to such expressions of true love as "love is better than wine" (1:2; 4:10); "his banner over me was love" (2:4); "my beloved is mine and I am his" (2:16; 6:3; 7:10); "love is strong as death" (8:6-7).

This, we say, is a step beyond mere sensuality and sex. As Sylvanus M. Duvall writes:

Love and sex are fundamentally different. A valid sex code would not confuse love needs with sex needs (as so many people do). It would recognize that the basic need of all people is for love. If love needs are met, sexual satisfactions will often become relatively unimportant. On the other hand, offering sex to the love hungry, whether within or outside of marriage, may result in making their condition worse instead of better.[6]

But it must be said that if sex itself is not enough, neither is romanticism or sentimentality. "The contemporary love-story," says H. G. Wells, "begins in illusions and goes on by way

[6] *Men, Women, and Morals* (New York: Association Press, 1952), p. 303.

8 ¶ Come with me from Lebanon, *my spouse*, with me from Lebanon: look from the top of Amana, from the top of Shenir and Hermon, from the lions' dens, from the mountains of the leopards.

9 Thou hast ravished my heart, my sister, *my* spouse; thou hast ravished my heart with one of thine eyes, with one chain of thy neck.

---

8 Come with me from Lebanon, my bride;
   come with me from Lebanon.
Depart[j] from the peak of Ama'na,
   from the peak of Senir and Hermon,
from the dens of lions,
   from the mountains of leopards.

9 You have ravished my heart, my sister,
      my bride,
   you have ravished my heart with a
      glance of your eyes,
   with one jewel of your necklace.

[j] Or *Look*

---

8. For the M.T. **with me** (twice) the LXX, Vulg., and Syriac read the imperative "come" by a different vocalization. The RSV follows the M.T., except that it inserts **come** at the beginning (without authority) and reads **my bride** instead of "O bride." The line as it stands is too long metrically. Hence the second **with me** should probably be dropped as due to dittography, or אחתי, "my sister," should be inserted with the Syriac before **bride**, as it is in vss. 9, 10, 12; 5:1, to make the line read 2+2+3. Since there are several roots שור in Hebrew, תשורי can be translated as **look**, "journey," or "leap." **Amana** is the Anti-Lebanon range of the Lebanon Mountains, of which the highest peak is Hermon, called by the Amorites Senir (Deut. 3:9); hence the translation here should be "Senir (that is, Hermon)," with explicative *wāw* before the gloss (so Amer. Trans.). The use of **Senir** for **Hermon** would seem to be another indication of north Palestinian or even Syrian origin for the book. Since no human bride could perform the feats named in this verse, the implication is, according to D. C. Margoliouth ("The Song of Solomon [Canticles]," in Charles Gore, H. L. Goudge, and Alfred Guillaume, eds., *A New Commentary on Holy Scripture* [New York: The Macmillan Co., 1928], p. 415*b*), that the person addressed was divine; and Alfred Bertholet was convinced of this as long ago as 1918 ("Zur Stelle Hohes Lied 4 8," in Wilhelm Frankenberg, ed., *Abhandlungen zur semitischen Religionskunde und Sprachwissenschaft Wolf Wilhelm Grafen von Baudissin, zum 26. September 1917 überreicht von Freunden und Schülern* [Giessen: A. Töpelmann, 1918], pp. 47-53), since Lebanon was so intimately connected with the Adonis cult. Note, e.g., the legend of the descent of Astarte upon a certain day in each year from the top of the Lebanon Mountains into the Adonis River at Aphaca.

9. The word לבבתני is the factitive Piel of a root derived from the noun **heart**, "mind"; hence "you have heartened me" (so Symm., Syriac, Arabic, and Targ.), rather than **you have ravished my heart**, taking the Piel as privative with the LXX. **My sister, my bride** should be "my sister, bride," a combination that is exceedingly suggestive of the fertility cult. If there is any one feature that is distinctive of the fertility cult in

---

of misunderstandings to conflict. It opens cheaply and ends in dispute or dull resignation." [7] Emil Brunner says: *"Where marriage is based on love all is lost from the very outset. . . . To base marriage on love is to build on the sand. It is this subjective individualism, more than anything else, which has caused the present crisis in marriage."* [8]

[7] *The World of William Clissold*, Bk. VI, ch. iii.

[8] *The Divine Imperative* (tr. Olive Wyon; Philadelphia: Westminster Press, 1947), pp. 344-45. Brunner's reason is that "the lover cannot guarantee that his emotion of love will be either permanent or directed solely to the one person."

Is it possible then to go still another step and speak of a specifically Christian or redemptive view of sex which goes beyond the natural, biological, and romantic true-love attitudes, retaining all that is good and worthy in them but eschewing all that is degrading and sentimental? We should be led to think so. Christianity has a way of making old things new (Rev. 21:5).

There is a difference between making new things and making things new. The influence of the Christian faith has been to make things new. It speaks, for example, of a rebirth, a regeneration, a renewal of life. It pours new meaning

10 How fair is thy love, my sister, *my* spouse! how much better is thy love than wine! and the smell of thine ointments than all spices!

11 Thy lips, O *my* spouse, drop *as* the honeycomb: honey and milk *are* under thy tongue; and the smell of thy garments *is* like the smell of Lebanon.

12 A garden inclosed *is* my sister, *my* spouse; a spring shut up, a fountain sealed.

---

10 How sweet is your love, my sister, my bride!
> how much better is your love than wine,
> and the fragrance of your oils than any spice!

11 Your lips distil nectar, my bride;
> honey and milk are under your tongue;
> the scent of your garments is like the scent of Lebanon.

12 A garden locked is my sister, my bride,
> a garden locked, a fountain sealed.

---

all its forms, it is the confusion as to the relationship between god and goddess: sometimes husband and wife; sometimes bridegroom and bride; sometimes brother and sister; and sometimes son and mother. In Egyptian love songs the girl is often addressed as sister, and some would see Egyptian influence here. **With a glance of your eyes,** lit., **with one of thine eyes.** In the last stich the numeral **one** should follow its noun and so is probably to be deleted as dittography on the preceding **one;** the last two words are of uncertain meaning, but seem to be connected with **neck** or **necklace.** The meter of the line without the second אחד would be 3+3+2.

10. This verse has an extra stich at the end and likewise vs. 11; if the two are joined, it brings parallels together and helps the meter: "How much better . . . and the fragrance of your ointment than any spices, with the fragrance of your garments like the fragrance of Lebanon" (a 3+2+2 line).

11. My bride should be "O bride" as in vs. 8, and **scent** is the same word that was translated **fragrance** in vs. 10. Every word which drops from the maiden's lips is like a drop of **nectar** (cf. Prov. 16:24). The meter is 2+2+3.

12. In the second stich the M.T. has גל, **spring,** in place of גן, **garden,** which is the reading of many MSS and all the important versions and is followed by the RSV; but the M.T. may be correct. The metaphor means that the maiden is exclusively her

---

into old forms. It fulfills rather than destroys. For that is what Jesus himself did. He took a despised taxgatherer, ostracized by his own people and hated by all, and made a disciple out of him. He took a woman, disgraced and rejected, and gave her a new lease on life. He took little children into his arms, and the gesture, as an early church father said, put a "sacred circle of safety around the head of childhood." Thus the N.T. speaks of a new commandment, a new creature, a new man, a new and living way, a new heaven and a new earth, a new name, a new song, and we must not forget that the gospel itself is a new testament. "If any one is in Christ, he is a new creation; the old has passed away, behold, the new has come" (II Cor. 5:17).

Why should we not expect that Christianity can redeem and transform the love of man and woman beyond the natural or romantic levels? Not, to be sure, in order to sublimate or avoid the biological urges with which we are all created or the romantic glow that all true lovers know. Why should not the Christian

faith consecrate the natural and romantic affections and give to love between the sexes a totally new orientation simply because "love is of God"?

When the poet Goldsmith died, Samuel Johnson prepared an epitaph which declared that he "touched nothing that he did not adorn" (*Nullum quod tetigit non ornavit*). That is an extravagant claim to make for anyone, especially Goldsmith. But it is true of Christ, and it is an authentic illustration of the way Christian faith works.

What is desperately needed in dealing with the whole problem of sex is a transforming dynamic that will redeem the commonplace, whether the merely physical or the romantically sentimental.

What society really needs is, not a new set of rules, but a new point of view; not a new code, but a new vision. We must clear our minds alike of the Manicheism which regards the physical side of sex as merely disgusting, and of the Romanticism which makes the thrill of "love's young dream" the supreme spiritual value in life. Having done this,

13 Thy plants *are* an orchard of pomegranates, with pleasant fruits; camphire, with spikenard,

14 Spikenard and saffron; calamus and cinnamon, with all trees of frankincense; myrrh and aloes, with all the chief spices:

---

13 Your shoots are an orchard of pomegranates
  with all choicest fruits,
  henna with nard,
14 nard and saffron, calamus and cinnamon,
  with all trees of frankincense,
  myrrh and aloes,
  with all chief spices —

---

beloved's. The meter is apparently 2+2, 2+2, but it is better to take the second נעול as due to dittography and make the meter 2+2+3, "A garden locked is my sister, bride, a spring, a fountain sealed."

13. Your shoots: Rather "your products" (Amer. Trans.), from the root "to send forth." The word פרדם is "park" (Amer. Trans.) rather than **orchard. With all choicest fruits** should be "with the choicest fruits," or "with choice fruits," lit., "with fruits of choiceness," the last word being an abstract plural. The meter is 3+2+2.

14. The Amer. Trans. is preferable to the RSV. The meter is 2+2+3 and 2+3, the only distich in a series of tristichs from vs. 9 to 5:1a. The whole context suggests luxuriousness and fertility.

---

we shall see clearly that there is a proper place both for the physical and for the romantic side of sex; and that in this proper place they are both good. . . . The richest range of love lies beyond the physical and the romantic. It must pass through these and include these, but it does not attain its maturity until these are felt to be beautiful and necessary incidents rather than essentials.[9]

It is surely significant that the prophet Hosea makes deliberate use of his own personal and intimate experience with the sexual and romantic aspects of his marriage to speak of a deeper love that is like the love of God for the sinful.

The notion of a divine marriage conceived in various ways was only too familiar (expressed in immoral worship, sacred prostitutes, etc.) both in the surrounding paganism and in Heb. syncretism, which tried to worship Yahweh by the methods of the fertility cult. In his attack on this syncretism Hosea was led (we cannot be sure how) to adopt as an effective metaphor the very relationship, which, understood in a crudely naturalistic sense as an actual reality, was central in what he was attacking. Perhaps it was because this was the most effective way of making his contemporaries aware of the tremendous contrast between the truth and their illusions.[1]

So too in the N.T. the figure of the bride and the bridegroom (Mark 2:19-20; John 3:29; II Cor. 11:2; Eph. 5:22-23; Rev. 19:7; 21:2, 9) tells us something not only about God's love but about the love of man and woman.

God's choice of this image brings out the fact that there cannot be any more intimate unity among human beings than that between man and woman, but also at the same time the fact that the meaning of that unity is missed where there does not exist between them the same love as that between the Saviour and His faithful people.[2]

May we not also look at the Song of Songs in this way? Perhaps that was not its original intention, and taken by itself we may not be justified in going beyond the natural or romantic view of love. But we should not take it by itself. It is, for good or bad reasons, in the whole context of the biblical view of love. The allegorists no doubt wrongly transgressed against the natural and romantic sides of love, but they were guided by a sure biblical instinct in suggesting that love—in the specifically Christian sense—redeems the commonplace.

Bernard of Clairvaux speaks of the Song of Songs as

that sacred and sublime discourse [which] is not to be listened to except by ears and hearts which are chastened and wise. For otherwise, unless the flesh has been mastered by discipline, and subjected to the Spirit . . . , the heart is impure and unworthy to peruse the sacred Song. Just as the pure light is poured, vainly and to no purpose, on blind eyes, or upon eyes that are closed, so "the natural man receiveth not the things of the Spirit of God."[3]

[9] B. H. Streeter, *Moral Adventure* (New York: The Macmillan Co., 1935), pp. 115-16; (London: Student Christian Movement Press, 1936), pp. 112-13. Used by permission.

[1] Cranfield, "Love," in Richardson, ed., *A Theological Word Book of the Bible*, p. 132; cf. Stauffer and Quell, "The twilight of the Mystery cults gives place to 'the mysteries of Agape'" (*Love*, p. 67).

[2] Piper, "The Christian in the Sexual Disorder of the Present Day," in Nash, ed., *Education for Christian Marriage*, p. 41.

[3] *Eighty-Six Sermons on the Song of Solomon*, p. 8.

15 A fountain of gardens, a well of living waters, and streams from Lebanon.

16 ¶ Awake, O north wind; and come, thou south; blow upon my garden, *that the* spices thereof may flow out. Let my beloved come into his garden, and eat his pleasant fruits.

5 I am come into my garden, my sister, *my* spouse: I have gathered my myrrh with my spice; I have eaten my honeycomb with my honey; I have drunk my wine with my milk: eat, O friends; drink, yea, drink abundantly, O beloved.

---

15 a garden fountain, a well of living water, and flowing streams from Lebanon.

16 Awake, O north wind,
and come, O south wind!
Blow upon my garden,
let its fragrance be wafted abroad.
Let my beloved come to his garden,
and eat its choicest fruits.

5 I come to my garden, my sister, my bride,
I gather my myrrh with my spice,
I eat my honeycomb with my honey,
I drink my wine with my milk.

Eat, O friends, and drink:
drink deeply, O lovers!

---

15. This verse belongs to vs. 12 and should be joined to it by transposing the one to the other. **A garden fountain:** Lit., **a fountain of gardens.** The meter is 2+3+2.

THE MAIDEN (4:16)

16. The reference may be to an Adonis **garden,** which was a pot filled with earth and sown with seeds that quickly sprouted. That the making of these gardens was practiced by the Hebrews is known from Isa. 1:29; 17:10. On the other hand, the **garden** here may be the maiden herself; in that case we should assign the first part of the verse to the youth (so Rashi, *et al.,* as against Rashbam, Ibn Ezra, and most scholars). The verse should be set up in two lines, 2+2+2 and 2+3+3, with the *'athnaḥ* pause transferred to גני, as parallelism and sense demand.

THE YOUTH (5:1)

5:1. The verbs in the first two lines are all in the perfect of instantaneous action and are accordingly translated by the English present. In figurative language the youth expresses his joy at reunion with his lover. The last line may be assigned to the youth or the chorus or the poet himself. The RSV translates דודים here as **lovers,** in parallelism with **friends,** but everywhere else as "love." The second line can be scanned only as 3+3, and like 2:3b must be another slip on the part of the poet.

Perhaps Bernard was too negative and too ascetic, but he was rightly concerned to set the theme of the Song of Songs alongside the dominant biblical love motif. "The Church has always consecrated the union of man and woman in matrimony, and taught that marriage is a divine ordinance, and it is not unfitting that a book which expresses the spiritual and physical emotions on which matrimony rests should be given a place in the Canon of Scripture." [4]

III. The Exclusiveness of Love.—The love which the Song of Songs sets to such exquisite music is deeply personal, selective, and exclusive. It is the love of a particular youth and a

[4] H. H. Rowley, "The Interpretation of the Song of Songs," *Journal of Theological Studies,* XXXVIII (1937), 363.

particular maiden who are completely wrapped up in each other, and more or less oblivious to everything around them. The Song is not a treatise on love in general or an abstract discussion of the idealism of love; it is the love story of two individuals, this person and that person. It is an exclusive story, personal, intimate, private.

As the lovers speak of their love, they say, "I am yours," "You are mine." They know that they "belong" to each other, that they were "made" for each other. The thrill of possession and commitment runs like a refrain: "My beloved is mine and I am his" (2:16); "I am my beloved's and my beloved is mine" (6:3); "I am my beloved's, and his desire is for me" (7:10). The youth likens his beloved **to a**

2 ¶ I sleep, but my heart waketh: *it is the* voice of my beloved that knocketh, *saying,* Open to me, my sister, my love, my dove, my undefiled: for my head is filled with dew, *and* my locks with the drops of the night.

3 I have put off my coat; how shall I put it on? I have washed my feet; how shall I defile them?

4 My beloved put in his hand by the hole *of the door,* and my bowels were moved for him.

5 I rose up to open to my beloved; and my hands dropped *with* myrrh, and my fingers *with* sweet smelling myrrh, upon the handles of the lock.

2 I slept, but my heart was awake.
Hark! my beloved is knocking.
"Open to me, my sister, my love,
my dove, my perfect one;
for my head is wet with dew,
my locks with the drops of the night."

3 I had put off my garment,
how could I put it on?
I had bathed my feet,
how could I soil them?

4 My beloved put his hand to the latch,
and my heart was thrilled within me.

5 I arose to open to my beloved,
and my hands dripped with myrrh,
my fingers with liquid myrrh,
upon the handles of the bolt.

The Maiden (5:2-8)

Another dream experience like 3:1-5, with the same motif of seeking against resistance.

2. My heart: Better, "my mind," because the heart was the seat of the intellect with the Hebrews. **Is filled with:** Preferable to the paraphrase **is wet with.**

4. The meaning is most obscure. The first clause reads, lit., "My beloved sent forth his hand from the hole." **Hole** must mean some opening in the **door** or the doorway itself and can scarcely mean **latch,** nor can מן, "from," be translated **to.** The second clause reads, lit., **and my bowels were moved for him,** best interpreted by the parallel in Jer. 31:20 as "my heart yearned for him," since the **bowels** were a seat of the emotions with the Hebrews, like the English **heart.** Many scholars follow numerous MSS and editions in reading עלי, "upon me," instead of the M.T. עליו, "upon him," in which case comparison with Ps. 42:5 (Hebrew 42:6) indicates the translation, "and my heart was perturbed within me."

5. The maiden had so much perfume on her hands that it **dripped** on the door as she opened it—an extravagant picture characteristic of the book.

garden, not a public garden for all to see and enjoy, but a private garden, a secret garden, set aside exclusively for him.

> A garden locked is my sister, my bride,
> a garden locked, a fountain sealed (4:12).

He calls her his "sister," and she imagines him to be her "brother" to whom she could show her affection publicly:

> O that you were like a brother to me,
> . . . .
> If I met you outside, I would kiss you,
> and none would despise me (8:1).

When the maiden becomes panicky in her search for her lover and asks "the daughters of Jerusalem" if they have seen him, they ask, "What is your beloved more than another beloved?" She replies:

> My beloved is all radiant and ruddy,
> distinguished among ten thousand (5:9-10).

The youth in turn singles out his beloved among all others. "There are sixty queens and eighty concubines" (6:8), he says, perhaps referring generally to the fact that there are lots of pretty girls to choose from, or perhaps he refers specifically to Solomon and his harem (which in I Kings 11:3, however, numbers "seven hundred wives, princesses, and three hundred concubines"). But what does it matter how many other beautiful women there are when you are in love with the only one in the world? "My dove, my perfect one, is only one" (6:9). And the maiden suggests that her own "Solomon" is preferred to the real Solomon, the great lover, the fabulously wealthy king. "Solomon had a vineyard at Baal-hamon," but she says, "My vineyard, my very own, is for myself" (8:11-12). It may not be worth much compared to Baal-hamon, but it is her own and she can bestow it all, without counting the cost, upon her beloved.

It is this personal, discriminating, **exclusive**

6 I opened to my beloved; but my beloved had withdrawn himself, *and* was gone: my soul failed when he spake: I sought him, but I could not find him; I called him, but he gave me no answer.

7 The watchmen that went about the city found me, they smote me, they wounded me; the keepers of the walls took away my veil from me.

8 I charge you, O daughters of Jerusalem, if ye find my beloved, that ye tell him, that I *am* sick of love.

9 ¶ What *is* thy beloved more than

6 I opened to my beloved,
    but my beloved had turned and gone.
My soul failed me when he spoke.
I sought him, but found him not;
    I called him, but he gave no answer.
7 The watchmen found me,
    as they went about in the city;
they beat me, they wounded me,
    they took away my mantle,
    those watchmen of the walls.
8 I adjure you, O daughters of Jerusalem,
    if you find my beloved,
that you tell him
    I am sick with love.

9 What is your beloved more than another beloved,
    O fairest among women?

6. The first line reads 3+3+3, which is not a variant of the 3+2 meter. Hence the asyndeton עבר, "he had passed on," **had . . . gone,** must be a gloss on the unusual חמק, "he had turned away," or a variant reading. In either case the meter would run correctly as 3+2+3. The last stich of the line reads, lit., "my soul went forth upon his speaking," or "upon his turning away," meaning apparently "I fainted when he spoke," or "I fainted when he turned away," with the latter fitting better into the context and supported by the root דבר, "to turn away."

7. The first line is a tristich, 2+2+2, and the second stich is a relative clause, "who go about the city," not circumstantial, as in the RSV. Also "they stripped me of" (Amer. Trans.) is closer to the Hebrew than **they took away,** which ignores מעלי, "from upon me."

8. This verse is a variant of the adjuration in 3:5, which likewise concluded the dream there. It expresses the intense longing of the girl for reunion with her beloved.

The Daughters of Jerusalem (5:9)

9. An enigma here is the interpretation of מן. The RSV takes it as comparative, with the attribute of comparison understood as in Ezek. 15:2; Isa. 10:10; *et al.* Comparison with Arabic suggests the rendering, "What kind of a beloved is your beloved?" Others

quality that is of the essence of what we call true love. It finds an echo in all the classic love stories, such as Romeo and Juliet, Tristan and Isolde, Abelard and Héloïse, Robert and Elizabeth Browning. It has been the theme of poets and musicians, and it lies deeply embedded in the literature of every people. To love is to choose and be chosen; to know and to be known; to be at one with one alone. Perhaps that is why the Song of Songs contains so many references to the physical "charms" of the youth and the maiden and the reason why they try to outdo each other in describing in detail the most intimate things. This is not eroticism. This is the way lovers discover each other, this is how they come to "know" each other, and what it means to be "one flesh," to use biblical language.

It is highly significant that this exclusiveness of love between lovers, of which the Song of Songs says so much, is precisely the quality of love which is found everywhere in the Bible.

The love which is commended in the Old Testament is the jealous love which chooses one object among thousands and holds it fast with all the strength of its passion and its will, brooking no relaxation of the bond of loyalty. It is just this jealousy which reveals the divine strength of such love. It is no accident by which in the Song of Songs (viii, 6) love strong as death is inseparably connected, in the poetic parallelism, with jealousy hard as Hell.[5]

Jacob, for example, has two wives, but he gives his love to one (Gen. 29) ; he has many

[5] Stauffer and Quell, *op. cit.,* p. 32.

another beloved, O thou fairest among women? what *is* thy beloved more than *another* beloved, that thou dost so charge us?

10 My beloved *is* white and ruddy, the chiefest among ten thousand.

11 His head *is as* the most fine gold; his locks *are* bushy, *and* black as a raven:

12 His eyes *are* as *the eyes* of doves by the rivers of waters, washed with milk, *and* fitly set:

13 His cheeks *are* as a bed of spices, *as* sweet flowers: his lips *like* lilies, dropping sweet smelling myrrh:

What is your beloved more than another beloved,
  that you thus adjure us?

10 My beloved is all radiant and ruddy,
  distinguished among ten thousand.

11 His head is the finest gold;
  his locks are wavy,
  black as a raven.

12 His eyes are like doves
  beside springs of water,
  bathed in milk,
  fitly set.[k]

13 His cheeks are like beds of spices,
  yielding fragrance.
His lips are lilies,
  distilling liquid myrrh.

[k] The meaning of the Hebrew is uncertain

---

suggest, "What is your beloved but Dod?" which may have been what the author originally intended, with its play on דוד. In any case, the meaning seems to be, "What is there that is so extraordinary about your beloved?"

THE MAIDEN (5:10-16)

The description of the youth in these verses is full of extravagant figures which must not be interpreted too literally; or the subject may be a god. The author was piling up figures for their total effect of gorgeous beauty.

10. There is no **all** in the original and מן is comparative; hence "above" rather than **among.**

11. The word תלתלים is found only here, but its cognate in Akkadian means "palm sprouts"; **wavy** is an interpretation rather than a translation.

12. The word רחצות in the M.T. is an active participle, "bathing" (Amer. Trans.), not passive, **bathed.** The last phrase is, lit., "sitting by a full place," perhaps "sitting by a pool" (Amer. Trans.), as suggested by Akkadian *mîlu*, "flood," and the LXX.

13. The noun ערוגת is singular in the M.T., but the RSV follows many MSS, the LXX, Vulg., Syriac, and M.T. in 6:2 in reading the plural **beds.** In the M.T. מגדלות is "towers," but differently pointed, as in the Targ., LXX, O.L., and Vulg., it is **yielding;** better, "exhaling" (Amer. Trans.).

---

sons, but he loves one more than the other (Gen. 37:3). So, too, God is the creator of heaven and earth, but he chooses one nation as his own (cf. Exod. 19:5; 20:3-5; Deut. 4:37; 6:5; 7:6; 10:15; 14:2; Ps. 135:4; Isa. 43:4; Hos. 2:16, 19; Amos 3:2; Mal. 3:17).

In the N.T. this same preferential love is an essential feature of the word *agapē* and serves to distinguish Christian love from the *erōs* love of Plato and classical Greek thought. "Eros is promiscuous and finds its satisfaction here, there and everywhere; but Agape is the love that makes distinctions, choosing its object and holding to it."[6]

The love of God is no abstract attribute but

[6] *Ibid.*, p. 28.

a personal self-disclosure, a "beloved Son" (Mark 1:11; 9:7; 12:6; John 3:16, 35; Rom. 8:32; Eph. 1:5-6; Col. 3:12-13). And we in turn are to love God in Christ with obedience and fidelity (Matt. 6:24; 10:37-38; John 21:15-17). It is the apostle Paul who gives the most suggestive treatment of what God's love in Christ means to the believer. It means, he said, to be in Christ as Christ is in us.

The heart of Paul's religion is union with Christ. . . . Paul beheld Christ summoning and welcoming him in infinite love into vital unity with Himself. If one seeks for the most characteristic sentences the apostle ever wrote, they will be found . . . where his intense intimacy with Christ comes to expression. Everything that religion meant for Paul is

14 His hands *are as* gold rings set with the beryl: his belly *is as* bright ivory overlaid *with* sapphires:

15 His legs *are as* pillars of marble, set upon sockets of fine gold: his countenance *is* as Lebanon, excellent as the cedars:

16 His mouth *is* most sweet: yea, he *is* altogether lovely. This *is* my beloved, and this *is* my friend, O daughters of Jerusalem.

14 His arms are rounded gold,
　　set with jewels.
His body is ivory work,[l]
　　encrusted with sapphires.[m]
15 His legs are alabaster columns,
　　set upon bases of gold.
His appearance is like Lebanon,
　　choice as the cedars.
16 His speech is most sweet,
　　and he is altogether desirable.
This is my beloved and this is my friend,
　　O daughters of Jerusalem.

[l] The meaning of the Hebrew word is uncertain
[m] Heb *lapis lazuli*

14. His arms: Lit., **his hands.** The word תרשיש, **jewels,** is more explicitly "Tarshish-stones" (Amer. Trans.) or "chrysolite," according to the LXX, Aq., Josephus, *et al.* The word מעים is used in the sense of **body** elsewhere only in the late Aramaic portion of Daniel (2:32); everywhere else it means the internal organs, the bowels. The word עשת can scarcely mean **work,** but is to be connected with the Akkadian *esētu,* "column" (so Amer. Trans.).

15. The word שוק means the leg from the knee downward. **Lebanon** was famous for its beauty and fertility, and its cedars.

16. His speech, lit., "his palate," which is used for the organ of speech and for speech itself (cf. Job 6:30; 31:30; Prov. 5:3).

focused for us in such great words as these: "I live, yet not I, but Christ liveth in me" [Gal. 2:20]. "There is, therefore, now no condemnation to them which are in Christ Jesus" [Rom. 8:1]. "He that is joined unto the Lord is one spirit" [I Cor. 6:17].[7]

The allegorical interpretation of the Song of Songs identified the lovers with Christ and his bride, the church. The first of the "headings" in some editions of the KJV reads: "Christ calleth the church: she glorieth in him." To make such an interpretation, of course, is to read back into the Song something that was not originally there. It would be more in keeping with the Song itself to stress the intimacy and exclusiveness of the love the youth and the maiden feel for each other. But in the biblical context of love, and that is where the Song happens to be now, the parallel between the preferential love of a youth and a maiden and the selective, electing love of God in Christ is inescapable.

The Christian faith after all is a matter of intimate, personal relationships. There is always a temptation to forget this and to think of Christianity in impersonal terms, as a system of doctrines or a code of ethics. But the gospel, the good news, is that God has made himself known as redemptive love in Jesus Christ. And Chris-

tianity asserts that faith is not simply a matter of proper beliefs or ethical standards, but a personal relationship of love, an "I-Thou" relationship.

Jesus, thy boundless love to me
　No thought can reach, no tongue declare;
O knit my thankful heart to thee,
　And reign without a rival there!
Thine wholly, thine alone, I'd live,
Myself to thee entirely give.[8]

IV. The Extravagance of Love.—In one of his sermons on the Song of Songs, Bernard of Clairvaux says: "To appear admirable to others, and to think humbly of yourself, this I judge to be the most marvelous among the virtues themselves." [9] The reason why it is marvelous is that this is invariably the effect which love, the greatest of the virtues, has upon the loved one and the one who loves. The language of love is heavily weighted with extravagances—the loved one feels unworthy and undeserving to the point of self-abasement, while the one who loves bestows superlatives and compliments with reckless devotion. This universal fact and experience, that love both humbles and exalts, is echoed and re-echoed in the great love music and poetry of the centuries, and it is a recurring theme in the Song of Songs.

[7] James S. Stewart, *A Man in Christ* (New York: Harper & Bros., 1935), p. 147.

[8] Paul Gerhardt, tr. John Wesley.
[9] *Eighty-Six Sermons on the Song of Solomon*, p. 69.

6 Whither is thy beloved gone, O thou fairest among women? whither is thy beloved turned aside? that we may seek him with thee.

2 My beloved is gone down into his garden, to the beds of spices, to feed in the gardens, and to gather lilies.

3 I *am* my beloved's, and my beloved *is* mine: he feedeth among the lilies.

6 Whither has your beloved gone,
O fairest among women?
Whither has your beloved turned,
that we may seek him with you?

2 My beloved has gone down to his garden,
to the beds of spices,
to pasture his flock in the gardens,
and to gather lilies.
3 I am my beloved's and my beloved is mine;
he pastures his flock among the lilies.

The Daughters of Jerusalem (6:1)

6:1. The question introduces an antiphonal response. According to the cultic interpretation, the words had reference in the original liturgy to the death of the vegetation god, being strikingly like a phrase from a Tammuz liturgy (*Cuneiform Texts from Babylonian Tablets in the British Museum*, Part XV [London: Oxford University Press, 1902], Pl. XX, ll. 24-25):

> Whither has your brother gone, the lamented one?
> Whither has Tammuz gone, the bewailed one?

The Maiden (6:2-3)

2. Garden is one of the many terms used for the underworld in the fertility liturgies (note the verb here, **has gone down**), and **beds of spices** are also connected with death in II Chr. 16:14. It is hard to see what the words mean if applied to a human being. Jastrow takes them as referring to the perfumed maiden.

3. The last stich is a relative clause, "who pastures" (Amer. Trans.), not **he pastures.**

Immediately as the Song begins, with the maiden's expression of the ecstasy of love, we hear her making self-effacing and deprecatory remarks about herself. "I am very dark, . . . like the tents of Kedar. . . . I am swarthy, because the sun has scorched me. . . . My own vineyard I have not kept!" (1:5-6.) She thinks she is anything but beautiful; she is as drab and colorless as the goat's-hair tents of Kedar; she is weatherbeaten from working in the fields, and her own vineyard, i.e., her own person, is unkempt and unlovely; and her love makes her all the more self-conscious of her unworthiness. But what says the youth?

> I compare you, my love,
> to a mare of Pharaoh's chariots.
> Your cheeks are comely with ornaments,
> studded with silver. (1:9-11.)

And elsewhere he speaks of the "dark," "swarthy" maiden as being "fair as the moon, bright as the sun" (6:10), and he says, "Your neck is like an ivory tower" (7:4).

The maiden's sense of unworthiness contrasts sharply with the youth's extravagant praise of her charms. She says she is "a rose of Sharon, a lily of the valleys" (2:1). Again this is a disparaging remark (cf. Moffatt, where she says she is "only a blossom of the plain, a mere lily of the dale"); but the youth says she is like "a lily among brambles, so is my love among maidens" (2:2). Here the youth accepts the maiden's description of herself but cleverly transforms it into a compliment. Later in one of his longer descriptions (4:1-15), the youth pretends to see "behind" her "veil" (4:1), and he itemizes her hidden perfections in his imagination, becoming more and more intoxicated with the "fragrance" of her "garden." To this intimate and flattering outburst the maiden can only respond:

> Awake, O north wind,
> and come, O south wind!
> Blow upon my garden,
> let its fragrance be wafted abroad.
> Let my beloved come to his garden,
> and eat its choicest fruits. (4:16.)

It is as if she knew well enough that she does not measure up to such superlatives, and so she calls upon the winds to enhance and accentuate her modest endowments.

131

4 ¶ Thou *art* beautiful, O my love, as Tirzah, comely as Jerusalem, terrible as *an army* with banners.

5 Turn away thine eyes from me, for they have overcome me: thy hair *is* as a flock of goats that appear from Gilead:

6 Thy teeth *are* as a flock of sheep which go up from the washing, whereof every one beareth twins, and *there is* not one barren among them.

7 As a piece of a pomegranate *are* thy temples within thy locks.

8 There are threescore queens, and fourscore concubines, and virgins without number.

---

4 You are beautiful as Tirzah, my love,
   comely as Jerusalem,
   terrible as an army with banners.
5 Turn away your eyes from me,
   for they disturb me —
Your hair is like a flock of goats,
   moving down the slopes of Gilead.
6 Your teeth are like a flock of ewes,
   that have come up from the washing,
all of them bear twins,
   not one among them is bereaved.
7 Your cheeks are like halves of a pomegranate
   behind your veil.
8 There are sixty queens and eighty concubines,
   and maidens without number.

The Youth (6:4-10)

4. Since **Tirzah** is parallel to **Jerusalem,** the reference must be to the city when it was a capital like Jerusalem, i.e., from the reign of Baasha to Omri's sixth year, *ca.* 900-871 B.C. The verb נדגלות is best taken as the Niphal participle of דגל, "to look up to"; the root is used also in 5:10; 2:4 (as repointed); hence "distinguished ones," rather than **an army with banners,** a denominative from דגל, "banner." Some scholars emend to כנרגל, "like Nergal" (an ancient name of the planet Mars), which fits rather well the thought of vs. 10, where the phrase reappears. The last stich may be a gloss, since it is repeated from vs. 10, which originally may have preceded vs. 4.

5b-7. These verses are repeated from 4:1b-3. The line in 4:3a is not repeated in the M.T., but it is in the LXX, Aq., Symm., O.L., Syriac, and Syro-Hexaplar.

8. It is not clear what this verse can mean on the secular interpretation. Some scholars insert לשלמה, "belonging to Solomon," but this is purely conjectural and in any case does not give Solomon the harem recorded in I Kings 11:3. The cultic interpretation sees a reference to the votaries of the cult, with all the words strongly suggesting this.

Assuming that the youth is a humble shepherd (cf. 1:7; 2:16; 6:2-3) and that the maiden is a country girl (cf. 1:6; 6:11; 7:11-12; 8:5), we hear the note of love's extravagance as they speak of each other as "king" and "queen." The maiden says, "The king has brought me into his chambers" (1:4), "the king was on his couch" (1:12), and the references to the real King Solomon (cf. 3:7-9; 8:11) are perhaps in contrast to her shepherd lover who, in the language of love, is her own special king, her own Solomon. In turn the maiden is called "the Shulammite" (6:13), which modern scholars take to be the feminine of Solomon, and the youth exclaims, "O queenly maiden!" (7:1).

If, as the Intro. suggests (see pp. 94-96), the Song of Songs belongs to an ancient fertility-cult liturgy, then this manner of speaking is highly symbolic. But apart from this observation, it is also true that lovers have always spoken of each other in some such fanciful way, and wedding customs throughout the centuries have preserved something of this regal, royal atmosphere.

Now we can hardly fail to observe that on a quite different level of experience the biblical view of love presents striking parallels to the Song of Songs. One does not need to allegorize the Song or stretch its obvious intention to notice that the biblical way of speaking of God's love involves both self-effacement and exaltation. God's love is a creative love. "That which in itself is without value acquires value by the fact that it is the object of God's love." [1]

The effect of God's love, as the Bible everywhere makes clear, is to call forth protestations of unworthiness on the part of the recipient and at the same time to lift up and exalt the one to whom God's love is given. The song of Mary, the Magnificat, is a beautiful and striking illustration of the effect of God's love. "My soul

---

[1] Nygren, *Agape and Eros*, Pt. I, p. 54.

9 My dove, my undefiled is *but* one; she *is* the *only* one of her mother, she *is* the choice *one* of her that bare her. The daughters saw her, and blessed her; *yea,* the queens and the concubines, and they praised her.

10 ¶ Who *is* she *that* looketh forth as the morning, fair as the moon, clear as the sun, *and* terrible as *an army* with banners?

11 I went down into the garden of nuts

---

9 My dove, my perfect one, is only one,
the darling of her mother,
flawless to her that bore her.
The maidens saw her and called her happy;
the queens and concubines also, and they praised her.
10 "Who is this that looks forth like the dawn,
fair as the moon, bright as the sun,
terrible as an army with banners?"

11 I went down to the nut orchard,
to look at the blossoms of the valley,

---

9. The only one of her mother reminds one that Persephone was the only one of her mother, and so with other fertility deities. The RSV translates אחת as **only one** in the first stich and as **the darling** in the second, which is very strange. The Amer. Trans. and its arrangement are to be preferred; the first line is 2+2 and the following verbs are better taken as in the perfect of experience. The RSV ignores the thrice-repeated היא and makes the first line prose. The second line is too long metrically; hence its second היא, which is quite unnecessary, should be deleted as due to dittography. The last line is 3+3, but ויחללוה, **and they praised her,** must be a variant reading of ויאשרוה, "and they blessed her." This reading also improves the parallelism and corrects the present awkwardness.

10. This verse would seem to be the words of the women of vs. 9, or it may be introductory to a song now lost, or it may be introductory to the present strophe, in which case it should precede vs. 4. The verse reads like the description of a divine rather than a human being.

THE MAIDEN (6:11-12)

11. This is another of the several references to the coming of the growing season; note also "the nut garden" associated with the Adonis cult at Aphaca in Syria. **Blossoms**

---

magnifies the Lord. . . . He has regarded the low estate of his handmaiden. . . . He has put down the mighty from their thrones, and exalted those of low degree" (Luke 1:46-55). Commenting on these verses, Martin Luther says of Mary:

Among the downtrodden people she was one of the lowliest, not a maid of high station in the capital city, but a daughter of a plain man in a small town. . . . And yet this was the one whom God chose. He might have gone to Jerusalem and picked out Caiaphas' daughter, who was fair, rich, clad in gold-embroidered raiment, and attended by a retinue of maids in waiting.[2]

And when Mary says, "He has regarded the low estate of his handmaiden," Luther remarks that "the stress should not be on the 'low estate,' but on the word 'regarded.' Her low estate is not to be praised, but God's regard, as, when a

prince gives his hand to a beggar, the meanness of the beggar is not to be praised, but the graciousness and goodness of the prince." [3]

Mary's song has its O.T. parallel in the Song of Hannah (I Sam. 2:1-10):

The Lord makes poor and makes rich;
he brings low, he also exalts.
He raises up the poor from the dust;
he lifts the needy from the ash heap,
to make them sit with princes
and inherit a seat of honor.

In the case of both Mary and Hannah, God's love comes to them in wonder and surprise, making them humble in his exaltation of them. Perhaps this is especially true of what we call "mother love." Mothers have a way of self-effacement as they dream and plan for their children, and the love which they lavish upon sons and daughters also produces humility and exaltation. There is a phrase in the Song of

[2] Roland H. Bainton, *The Martin Luther Christmas Book* (Philadelphia: Westminster Press, 1948), pp. 20-21.

[3] *Ibid.,* p. 28.

to see the fruits of the valley, *and* to see whether the vine flourished, *and* the pomegranates budded.

12 Or ever I was aware, my soul made me *like* the chariots of Ammi-nadib.

13 Return, return, O Shulamite; return, return, that we may look upon thee. What will ye see in the Shulamite? As it were the company of two armies.

---

to see whether the vines had budded, whether the pomegranates were in bloom.

12 Before I was aware, my fancy set me in a chariot beside my prince.[n]

13[o] Return, return, O Shu'lammite, return, return, that we may look upon you.

Why should you look upon the Shu'lammite, as upon a dance before two armies?[p]

[n] Cn The meaning of the Hebrew is uncertain
[o] Heb Ch 7. 1
[p] Or *dance of Mahanaim*

---

is better "verdure" (Amer. Trans.). The first line can only be scanned 3+3, and like 2:3*b*; 5:1*b*, it must be a slip on the part of the poet.

12. This is the one hopelessly corrupt verse in the Song; the corruption antedates the versions because they all had trouble with it and interpreted it in different ways. Any restoration is a guess, and although many have been offered there is none that is satisfactory. The first clause is manifestly circumstantial, "without my being aware of it," or **before I was aware.** If מרכבות can be taken as a terminative accusative after a verb of motion, the rest of the verse reads, lit., "my soul set me amid the chariots of my princely people," but that makes no sense and any emendation is purely conjectural. The KJV follows many MSS, the LXX, O.L., Vulg., and Arabic in reading the last two words together as a proper name, but such a reading makes no sense here, unless perchance this is the name of the youth, which is not likely.

THE DAUGHTERS OF JERUSALEM (6:13=Hebrew 7:1)

13. The second line is best rendered, "How you gaze on the Shulammite, like one in the Mahanaim dance!" taking מה to be exclamatory, as in the next verse, and כ to be pregnant, as in 3:6. If **Mahanaim** (a sacred place in Trans-Jordan, Gen. 32:2) is read as plural (so LXX, O.L., Symm., Syriac, and Vulg.) instead of dual, the last phrase would be "war dance." In any case, it was some special **dance,** apparently performed in the nude, as the following verses suggest, reminding one of the naked goddess of the fertility cult. The many different readings and interpretations of **the Shulammite** in the versions and among ancient and modern scholars are summarized by H. H. Rowley ("The Meaning of 'The Shulammite,' " *American Journal of Semitic Languages and Literatures,* LVI [1939], 84-91), and he has shown conclusively that the generally accepted connection

---

Songs which may reflect this—it speaks of King Solomon and "the crown with which his mother crowned him" (3:11). Perhaps it refers to his wedding, as the verse suggests, or the ancient fertility cult, but beyond that, every son and daughter is crowned with a mother's crown. One thinks of Abraham Lincoln's remark, "All that I am and hope to be I owe to my angel mother." Whether it is love of mother and children or the love of man and woman, there is inevitably a sense both of humility and ecstasy. "What honest man ever believed that he merited the love of a good woman? Is not his immediate reaction to the discovery that his love is returned a feeling of utter unworthiness, and a

---

confession that he is receiving more by far than his deserts?" [4]

In the N.T. God's love in Christ invariably suggests this double experience of unworthiness on the one hand, and exaltation on the other. When the Son of God came into contact with men and women they seemed to sense their littleness and their failings in the light of his pure love. John the Baptist said he was "not worthy to stoop down and untie" the sandals of him who would come (Mark 1:7); Peter began his discipleship with the confession, "Depart from me, for I am a sinful man, O Lord"

[4] H. R. Mackintosh, *The Christian Experience of Forgiveness* (New York: Harper & Bros., 1927), p. 142.

7 How beautiful are thy feet with shoes, O prince's daughter! the joints of thy thighs *are* like jewels, the work of the hands of a cunning workman.

2 Thy navel *is like* a round goblet, *which* wanteth not liquor: thy belly *is like* a heap of wheat set about with lilies.

3 Thy two breasts *are* like two young roes *that are* twins.

7 How graceful are your feet in sandals, O queenly maiden!
Your rounded thighs are like jewels, the work of a master hand.
2 Your navel is a rounded bowl that never lacks mixed wine.
Your belly is a heap of wheat, encircled with lilies.
3 Your two breasts are like two fawns, twins of a gazelle.

---

with Abishag of Shunem has no basis in fact whatever. The word is best interpreted as the feminine of Solomon, and in the original poem as the feminine of Shelem, another form of which was Shulman, thus accounting for *shûreq* in השולמית, although many MSS omit the *wāw*. The article may have been added when the word came to be interpreted as a gentilic, but it can also be original, for the name of the fertility god Tammuz is likewise written with the article (Ezek. 8:14). The cry **return, return** is the same one that was made by the chorus of women in the festival of Adonis as they cast their Adonis gardens and the images of Adonis and Astarte into the water.

THE YOUTH (7:1-9＝Hebrew 7:2-10)

7:1. Your rounded thighs: Lit., "the curves of your thighs." Like so many other words in this book, חלאים is uncertain in meaning; **jewels** perhaps. The last stich is, lit., "the work of the hands of a master craftsman."

2. Navel is apparently the lower abdomen, or the vulva, as the Arabic cognate suggests. **Rounded bowl,** lit., "bowl of roundness," with the generic use of the article. The second stich is a relative clause with the relative particle understood, as so often in Hebrew poetry. The unusual negative particle, אל, with the imperfect is emphatic, **never,** like the Akkadian *ul.*

3. This verse is repeated from 4:5 without the final stich, which, however, appears in the Syriac.

(Luke 5:8); the centurion whose servant was sick said, "I am not worthy to have you come under my roof" (Matt. 8:8). And throughout the Gospels we see how Christ's love exalts and magnifies the humble.

Of a scorned, renegade taxgatherer He said, "He also is a son of Abraham" (Luke 19:9). A woman whom all good people obstracized He treated with a dignity and courtesy that might have been given to a queen (Luke 7:37 ff.). And when He said, "Take heed that ye despise not one of these little ones" (Matt. 18:10), He was thinking, not only of the children, but of all the weak, defenseless, sensitive things of life.[5]

This is not just one facet of the teaching of Jesus, it is of the essence of the Incarnation. What we have called the extravagance of love is revealed not only in such sayings as "Whoever humbles himself will be exalted" (Matt. 23:12; Luke 14:11; 18:14), but in the life, death, and resurrection of Christ himself. Sometimes in theological language this is spoken of as the "humiliation and exaltation" of Christ.

St. Paul perceived the theological significance of the lowliness of the Son of God in his incarnation: he who was in the form of God emptied himself and humbled himself (Phil. 2.6-8): he who was rich became poor for our sake (II Cor. 8.9, 13.4). The wonder of the divine humility, revealed in the manger at Bethlehem, in the life of a working man in Nazareth and on the cross on Golgotha, has led men in every succeeding age to "pour contempt o'er all their pride."[6]

But he who was meek and lowly, "God has highly exalted . . . and bestowed on him the name which is above every name" (Phil. 2:9-11). He is "exalted at the right hand of God" (Acts 2:33); "all things" are "under his feet" (Eph. 1:22; cf. Mark 16:19; Luke 24:26; John 7:39; Rom. 8:17, 34; Eph. 4:10; I Tim. 3:16; Heb. 1:3; 2:8).

[5] James S. Stewart, *The Life and Teaching of Jesus Christ* (London: Student Christian Movement Press, 1935), p. 132.

[6] Richardson, "Pride," *A Theological Word Book of the Bible,* p. 176.

4 Thy neck *is* as a tower of ivory; thine eyes *like* the fishpools in Heshbon, by the gate of Bath-rabbim: thy nose *is* as the tower of Lebanon which looketh toward Damascus.
5 Thine head upon thee *is* like Carmel, and the hair of thine head like purple; the King *is* held in the galleries.

4 Your neck is like an ivory tower.
Your eyes are pools in Heshbon,
by the gate of Bath-rab'bim.
Your nose is like a tower of Lebanon,
overlooking Damascus.
5 Your head crowns you like Carmel,
and your flowing locks are like purple;
a king is held captive in the tresses.[q]

[q] The meaning of the Hebrew word is uncertain

4. The first line lacks a second stich, suggesting that we take the first stich from vs. 5 (Hebrew vs. 6), which has an extra stich, and add it here: "Your neck is like a tower of ivory; your head crowns you like Carmel." **Heshbon,** in Trans-Jordan, was originally a Moabite city which later came into the possession of the Amorites, and then into the hands of the Hebrews (Num. 21:25-26), who lost it before Isaiah's time (cf. Isa. 15:4). **The gate of Bath-rabbim,** apparently a city gate of Heshbon, is otherwise unknown. The comparison in the last line was probably intended to suggest a well-proportioned **nose** rather than a prominent one.

5. The first stich is, lit., **Thine head upon thee is like Carmel,** suggesting a head as proudly held as Mount Carmel, the summit of which overlooks the sea in solitary state midway up the coast of Palestine. **Your flowing locks** is, lit., "the locks of your

The extravagance of God's love, which knows both humiliation and exaltation, is the redemptive heart of the Christian gospel. Anyone who has ever come within range of the magnet of God's love in Christ knows what it means to be drawn irresistibly up and out of oneself into oneness with Christ.

But should we liken such a sublime spiritual experience to the love of the youth and the maiden in the Song of Songs? "It is a significant fact that in our age The Song of Solomon should not be appreciated as a book that speaks about God. It is significant that nowadays people think it quite natural to use language like this about love between the sexes, but consider it fantastic to apply this kind of language to our love of God." [7]

We were not once so cautious about speaking of the love of God in Christ for sinful mankind. Perhaps we need another Frances Ridley Havergal to put into extravagant language for our day, as she did for hers, the intimate personal relationship of love between the bride and the bridegroom:

I could not do without thee;
I cannot stand alone,
I have no strength or goodness,
No wisdom of my own;
But thou, beloved Saviour,
Art All in all to me,
And weakness will be power
If leaning hard on thee.[8]

[7] Norman F. Langford, *The Two-Edged Sword* (Philadelphia: Westminster Press, 1945), p. 129.
[8] "I could not do without thee," st. ii.

V. Lovesickness.—The Song of Songs is not all sweetness, romance, and melody. There is an unmistakable counterpoint of deep pathos that throbs and vibrates to the lilting rhapsodies on love. The lovers stand on the threshold of ecstasy, eager and impatient to enter into the consummation of their love; but there is something elusive and evanescent about love which keeps them poised on tiptoe in an anguish of expectancy and a torment of unfulfilled passion. Irresistibly drawn together, they yet find themselves groping for each other; transported into a paradise of delight by the prospect of being in each other's presence, they nevertheless feel the pang and heartache of separation.

The opening profession of the maiden's love for the youth—with the impatient plea, "Draw me after you, let us make haste" (1:4)—is followed by the frantic question:

Tell me, you whom my soul loves,
where you pasture your flock,
where you make it lie down at noon;
for why should I be like one who wanders
beside the flocks of your companions? (1:7.)

The lovers, eager to be together, are thwarted, and they find themselves involved in an exasperating game of hide and seek. There is something frustrating about their love for each other brought about by the intense agony of separation. As Browning put it:

Never the time and the place
And the loved one all together! [9]

[9] "Never the Time and the Place."

6 How fair and how pleasant art thou, | 6 How fair and pleasant you are,
O love, for delights! | O loved one, delectable maiden![r]
7 This thy stature is like to a palm tree, | 7 You are stately[s] as a palm tree,
and thy breasts to clusters *of grapes*. | and your breasts are like its clusters.

[r] Syr: Heb *in delights*
[s] Heb *This your stature is*

---

head," the first word strictly meaning "thrum." The dark hair is represented as having a **purple** tinge. The last clause is circumstantial, "with a king held captive in the tresses," a figure common in all love poetry. The last word is found elsewhere only in Gen. 30:38, 41; Exod. 2:16, where it means "watering troughs," so that **tresses** here is purely an inference from the context.

6. The last stich is, lit., "O love, among delightsome things!" but the RSV follows the Syriac, Vulg., and most scholars in repointing the first word as a passive participle, **loved one**, and it likewise follows Aq., Syriac, and most scholars in dividing the last word into two, lit., "daughter of daintiness"; hence **delectable maiden**.

The Youth (7:7-9 = Hebrew 7:8-10)

7. You are stately as: Lit., "this your stature is like," where the demonstrative זֹאת, **this**, is emphatic; hence "your very stature is like" (Amer. Trans.). **Its clusters:** Better,

---

"I am sick with love" (2:5; 5:8), sighs the maiden. So close and yet so far away! And three times she voices the "adjuration"—"Stir not up nor awaken love until it please" (2:7; 3:5; 8:4), which is like saying, "All or nothing." If lovers cannot be united, it is better not to love at all. "It is the special quality of love not to be able to remain stationary, to be obliged to increase under pain of diminishing." [1]

Lo all things wake and tarry and look for thee:
She looketh and saith, "O sun, now bring him to
 me.
Come more adored, O adored, for his coming's sake,
And awake my heart to be loved: awake, awake!" [2]

At the close of what is perhaps the most familiar passage in the Song of Songs, the springtime lyric,

Arise, my love, my fair one,
 and come away;
for lo, the winter is past,
. . . .
the time of singing has come,
and the voice of the turtledove
 is heard in our land (2:10-14),

there occur the puzzling lines:

Catch us the foxes,
 the little foxes,
that spoil the vineyards,
 for our vineyards are in blossom (2:15).

Exegetes have suggested that the verse seems to have no point here, and Moffatt puts the lines within parentheses. But perhaps it is one more example of the poignancy of love. Just when love seems on the verge of fulfillment, casting a romantic spell upon nature itself, the lovers sense the ominous possibility that subversive and destructive forces may threaten their love. The "foxes" (or "jackals") are "little," but they can burrow and gnaw at the roots of the vines.[3]

On two different occasions the racking pain of separation is appropriately set in the context of a reverie, a dream, or, perhaps more accurately, a nightmare (3:1-5; 5:2-8). "Upon my bed by night [night after night] I sought him whom my soul loves" (3:1); "I slept, but my heart was awake" (5:2). And as is so often the way in dreams, there is the vain and futile questing which is so painful. "I sought . . . I sought . . . I called"; "found him not . . . no answer . . . found him not"; "I opened to my beloved, but my beloved had turned and gone. . . . I sought him, but found him not; I called him, but he gave no answer." And in both dreams the maiden wanders aimlessly and desperately about the city searching for her beloved, asking the watchmen if they have seen him. It is a nightmare which the return to consciousness does not relieve, for it is the unrest caused by separation from the beloved, the sickening fear that love will not be consummated.

[1] André Gide, *The Counterfeiters* (tr. Dorothy Bussy; New York: A. A. Knopf, 1951), p. 252.
[2] "Awake, My Heart, to Be Loved, Awake, Awake!" From *Shorter Poems of Robert Bridges.* Used by permission of the Clarendon Press, Oxford.

[3] Cf. John Van Druten, *The Voice of the Turtle* (New York: Random House, 1944); Lillian Hellman, *The Little Foxes* (New York: Random House, 1939); George Victor Martin, *For Our Vines Have Tender Grapes* (Chicago: Argus Books, 1940).

8 I said, I will go up to the palm tree, I will take hold of the boughs thereof: now also thy breasts shall be as clusters of the vine, and the smell of thy nose like apples;

9 And the roof of thy mouth like the best wine for my beloved, that goeth *down* sweetly, causing the lips of those that are asleep to speak.

8 I say I will climb the palm tree
  and lay hold of its branches.
Oh, may your breasts be like clusters of
  the vine,
  and the scent of your breath like apples,
9 and your kisses[t] like the best wine
  that goes down[u] smoothly,
  gliding over lips and teeth.[v]

[t] Heb *palate*
[u] Heb *down for my lover*
[v] Gk Syr Vg: Heb *lips of sleepers*

"clusters," since the Hebrew has neither suffix nor article, one of which the first translation would require.

8. The RSV takes the first word as the perfect of instantaneous action, **I say** (better, "I think"), and the two following cohortatives as emphatic. The Amer. Trans. equates the simple imperfect plus the particle נא in the second line with the cohortatives and translates them all as desiderative. **Your breath:** Lit., **thy nose.** Many scholars emend ריח, **scent,** to רוח, reading "the breath of your nose."

9. Your kisses: Lit., **your palate,** interpreted as "speech" in 5:16. **That goes down** is strictly "going," "moving along," or "flowing" (Amer. Trans.). The word לדודי, **for my beloved,** is better deleted with the RSV as due to vertical dittography from the following line. The form למישרים is the ל of norm plus the same abstract plural noun that we had in 1:4, here meaning **smoothly** or "pleasantly" (Amer. Trans.). The last stich is difficult. The meaning of דובב, found only here, is uncertain, perhaps **gliding over.** The rest of the M.T., **lips of sleepers,** makes no sense and must be emended

The bittersweet character of love is suggested further in the Song of Songs by repeated references to "myrrh." Eight times mention is made of this Near Eastern perfume which was also used as a spice, a preservative, and an antiseptic (1:13; 3:6; 4:6, 14; 5:1, 5 [twice], 13). The use of the word is perhaps intentionally ambiguous and in keeping with the poetic and symbolic language of the Song. When the maiden says:

My beloved is to me a bag of myrrh,
  that lies between my breasts (1:13),

does she mean to emphasize the sweetness or the bittersweetness of her love? The comment of Bernard of Clairvaux on this verse reads: "Myrrh, which is bitter, signifies the hard and rigorous facts of trouble and sorrow."[4] On the basis of the Song itself it may be that myrrh is synonymous with perfume and exquisite fragrance. Yet elsewhere in biblical thought the bittersweet quality is clearly intended; e.g., myrrh was used in compounding Israel's holy anointing oil (Exod. 30:23-33); it was highly prized as a perfume (Ps. 45:8; Prov. 7:17; Esth. 2:12); and it was one of the three gifts presented by the magi to the Christ child (Matt.

[4] *Eighty-Six Sermons on the Song of Solomon,* p. 267.

2:11). But it was also given to Christ on the cross as an anodyne for pain (Mark 15:23), and later it was brought by Nicodemus and the women to prepare Christ's body for burial (John 19:39; Mark 16:1). It was this latter association which took hold of the Christian imagination, as is seen by the words of the third king in the familiar Christmas carol, "We three kings of Orient are":

Myrrh is mine: its bitter perfume
Breathes a life of gathering gloom:
Sorrowing, sighing, bleeding, dying,
  Sealed in the stone-cold tomb.

There is yet another symptom of the lovesickness of the Song of Songs. It is the aggravating intervention, sometimes the obtuse indifferentism and ineptitude, of the minor characters who figure in the Song, "the daughters of Jerusalem," the "watchmen," and perhaps the poet-author himself. They all seem to serve the sole purpose of hindering and obstructing the union of the lovers, and this is frequently accompanied by their inability to understand and appreciate the lovers' passion for each other.

Like the classical Greek chorus, these apparently incidental figures act as a foil to the main plot. They sometimes stand by as spectators, aloof, indifferent, unmoved; they sometimes en-

10 ¶ I *am* my beloved's, and his desire *is* toward me.

11 Come, my beloved, let us go forth into the field; let us lodge in the villages.

12 Let us get up early to the vineyards; let us see if the vine flourish, *whether the* tender grape appear, *and* the pomegranates bud forth: there will I give thee my loves.

13 The mandrakes give a smell, and at our gates *are* all manner of pleasant *fruits,* new and old, *which* I have laid up for thee, O my beloved.

---

10 I am my beloved's,
    and his desire is for me.

11 Come, my beloved,
    let us go forth into the fields,
    and lodge in the villages;

12 let us go out early to the vineyards,
    and see whether the vines have budded,
    whether the grape blossoms have opened
    and the pomegranates are in bloom.
There I will give you my love.

13 The mandrakes give forth fragrance,
    and over our doors are all choice fruits,
    new as well as old,
      which I have laid up for you, O my beloved.

---

with the LXX, Aq., and Syriac to read "my lips and teeth," or with the Vulg., "his lips and teeth," or **lips and teeth,** i.e., שפתים ושנים for שפתי ישנים. The Amer. Trans. reads "stirring my lips and teeth."

THE MAIDEN (7:10-13=Hebrew 7:11-14)

10. Repeated in part from 2:16; 6:3. Here, as frequently elsewhere in the book, the lovers are represented as separated, with the girl longing for her beloved—a situation reminiscent of the fertility cult.

11. The word כפרים may be **villages** or "henna flowers" (Amer. Trans.), but the context and its use in 1:14; 4:13 indicate the latter.

12. The second stich is an asyndeton clause, best taken as expressing purpose, "in order that we may see." It is difficult to take the Piel פתח as intransitive; perhaps we should read the Niphal נפתח, with נ lost by haplography. On the cultic interpretation the verse would refer to the revival of life in nature on the reunion of god and goddess.

13. Mandrakes were highly prized for their aphrodisiac and procreative properties (cf. Gen. 30:14-16). **Over our doors:** Better, "at our doors" (ERV), i.e., "in the neighborhood of our houses." **All:** Better, **all manner of,** or "all kinds of" (Amer. Trans.). In **new as well as old** there may be a reference to the Passover offering of fruits of the old

---

gage in exchanges of dialogue and proffer advice and remarks of their own. When the maiden asks where her lover pastures his flock, "the daughters of Jerusalem" respond:

> If you do not know,
>   O fairest among women,
> follow in the tracks of the flock,
>   and pasture your kids
>   beside the shepherds' tents (1:8).

This is a practical, or perhaps a cynical, answer to the maiden's consuming desire to be with her lover. In the dream sequences already referred to, the "watchmen" are asked for information as to the whereabouts of the youth, but in the first instance they offer no help (3:3), and in the second they beat and wound her, perhaps because they think her mad (5:7). In the long involved description of Solomon's "palanquin" (3:6-11), "the daughters of Jerusalem" describe a procession of armed men bearing a litter on

which King Solomon reclines. (The passage is placed between the maiden's hectic quest for her lover and the youth's extravagant description of the maiden. Is it placed there for any purpose, or is it merely an irrelevant interruption?) They see Solomon the king with his army, but the maiden is interested only in her own "Solomon" (cf. 8:11-12).

> All day long on the highway
> The King's fleet couriers ride;
>   You may hear the tread of their horses sped
> Over the country side.
>   They ride for life and they ride for death
>   And they override who tarrieth.
> With show of color and flush of pride
> They stir the dust on the highway.
>
> Let them ride on the highway wide.
> Love walks in little paths aside.[5]

[5] Louise Driscoll, "The Highway." Used by permission of the author.

8 O that thou *wert* as my brother, that sucked the breasts of my mother! *when* I should find thee without, I would kiss thee; yea, I should not be despised.

2 I would lead thee, *and* bring thee into my mother's house, *who* would instruct me: I would cause thee to drink of spiced wine of the juice of my pomegranate.

8 O that you were like a brother to me,
  that nursed at my mother's breast!
If I met you outside, I would kiss you,
  and none would despise me.
2 I would lead you and bring you
  into the house of my mother,
    and into the chamber of her that conceived me.[w]
I would give you spiced wine to drink,
  the juice of my pomegranates.

[w] Gk Syr: Heb *mother; she* (or *you*) *will teach me*

---

harvest to ensure the productivity of the new, or the phrase may simply mean "all kinds," as in Matt. 13:52.

THE MAIDEN (8:1-4)

8:1. The first stich reads, lit., "Who will give you as a brother to me?" a Hebrew idiom for "Oh, that you were really a brother to me," with the asseverative *kaph* (see Exeg., on Lam. 2:5). This again is suggestive of the fertility cult, with god and goddess sometimes thought of as brother and sister; on the other hand, the clause may express nothing more than the yearning of the girl for her beloved. The word גם, **and,** is used in place of ו for poetic and metrical reasons and also perhaps for emphasis.

2. The expression תלמדני, **who would instruct me,** which makes no sense here, is lacking in Origen's Greek O.T., the LXX, O.L., and Syriac, and in its place we have

---

After an exchange between the lovers, in which they delight in each other's love, there occurs the incidental remark:

> Eat, O friends, and drink:
>   drink deeply, O lovers! (5:1.)

Is this an editorial aside, a quip, a gibe by one who looks on with amusement and not a little skepticism? When "the daughters of Jerusalem" ask where the youth has gone so they can help to look for him, the maiden replies absently, as in a trance:

> My beloved has gone down to his garden,
>   to the beds of spices,
> to pasture his flock in the gardens,
>   and to gather lilies.
> I am my beloved's and my beloved is mine;
>   he pastures his flock among the lilies. (6:2-3.)

It is a pointless dialogue; they are using the same words, but they are talking about different things.

> Love has gone and left me and I don't know what
>   to do;
>   This or that or what you will is all the same to
>   me;
> But all the things that I begin I leave before I'm
>   through—
>   There's little use in anything as far as I can see.[6]

[6] Lines from "Ashes of Life" in *Renascence and Other Poems* published by Harper & Bros. Copyright 1915, 1943 by Edna St. Vincent Millay.

As the Song begins, so too it ends with an expression of the lovers' desire to be in each other's presence and their urgent plea to each other to come quickly. Separated and thwarted in their quest for each other, the maiden cries:

> O you who dwell in the gardens,
>   my companions are listening for your voice;
>   let me hear it (8:13),

with the emphasis on the "me" perhaps; and the youth replies in the same way:

> Make haste, my beloved,
>   and be like a gazelle
> or a young stag
>   upon the mountains of spices (8:14).

The lovesickness of the Song of Songs is a complex of intense desire for personal union and the tormenting ache of separation which baffles and obstructs the lovers, preventing them from enjoying to the full the wonder and the rapture of their love. This is not the sickness of unrequited or unreturned love; it is not the pain of infidelity or the loss of love. It is the lovesickness all true lovers know—"Love's alternate joy and woe."[7]

It is this element of pathos that distinguishes true love from mere sentimentality and infatuation. For love is not something to be manipulated or taken for granted. We do not so much lay hold of it as it lays hold of us. If we seek

[7] Byron, "Maid of Athens, Ere We Part."

3 His left hand *should be* under my head, and his right hand should embrace me. 4 I charge you, O daughters of Jerusalem, that ye stir not up, nor awake *my* love, until he please.	3 O that his left hand were under my head, and that his right hand embraced me! 4 I adjure you, O daughters of Jerusalem, that you stir not up nor awaken love until it please.

ואל־חדר הורתי, **and into the chamber of her that conceived me,** repeated from 3:4 and an excellent parallel to the preceding stich, making the line a tristich, 2+2+2. Or the asyndeton אביאך could be taken as a variant reading of אנהגך, thus giving us the regular 3+2, which is better. **Spiced wine:** Better, "some spiced wine" (Amer. Trans.), since the original has the partitive מן; so also "some juice" in place of **the juice. My pomegranates,** following the Syriac, O.L., and Vulg., is, lit., **my pomegranate,** but it is much better to read the simple plural, **pomegranates,** with many MSS and the Targ.

3-4. This passage is repeated from 2:6-7, with מה in vs. 4 in place of אם, and with "by the gazelles or the hinds of the field" omitted but supplied by four MSS, most LXX MSS, and Arabic. The word מה (=Arabic *mā*) is manifestly a dialectic variant here of אם and was so interpreted by many LXX MSS, the Syriac, Vulg., Arabic, and KJV.

to grasp it, it eludes us, and the more we would enjoy it, the more it causes heartache.

This element of pathos, this lovesickness which runs like a minor chord throughout the Song of Songs, is also a characteristic of the biblical conception of love. It is not surprising, for the Bible as a whole, and not only this one book, is a love story. From the beginning to the end, from the Garden of Eden in Genesis to the tree of life "for the healing of the nations" in Revelation, the Bible tells the love story of God's yearning for his creatures and mankind's restless quest for communion with the Creator.

The biblical love story is more complicated than the Song of Songs because of the sin of infidelity on man's part, his rebellion against the spontaneous, redemptive love of God, and in this sense the love story of the Bible is the story of God's unrequited love. But even in his sin mankind is aware of God's patient, unceasing wooing which, like Francis Thompson's "Hound of Heaven," pursues him "down the nights and down the days; . . . down the arches of the years." Man's willful, deliberate separation of himself from God occasions a lovesickness for both God and man that pains deeper than the separation of the youth and the maiden in the Song of Songs. That is why God's persistent courtship is "so amazing, so divine," for "God shows his love for us . . . while we were yet sinners" (Rom. 5:8).

The God of the Bible is a loving God. This is true of the Old Testament as well as the New. . . . It is in the New Testament, indeed, that we read "God is love" (I John iv. 8, 16), "God so loved the world" (John iii. 16), . . . and many another verse which emphasizes the thought that the greatness of God is matched with His graciousness, His

majesty with His mercy, His loftiness with His lovingkindness. But in the Old Testament we read: "It was not because you were more numerous than other peoples that the Lord set His heart on you and chose you . . . but because the Lord loved you" (Deut. vii. 7 f.); "With an everlasting love have I loved thee: therefore have I drawn thee with lovingkindness" (Jer. xxxi. 3); "When Israel was a child, I loved him, and called my son out of Egypt" (Hos. xi. 1); "The lovingkindness of the Lord is from everlasting to everlasting upon them that fear Him" (Ps. ciii. 17). . . . The revelation that love is of the essence of God's heart is given in all its fullness in Christ Himself. . . . He showed His love not alone in His restless seeking to lead men to the Father. He showed it in His yearning pity for Jerusalem, which coldly rejected Him: "O Jerusalem, Jerusalem, . . . how often would I have gathered thy children together, as a hen gathereth her brood under her wings, and ye would not!" (Luke xiii. 34); "Oh that thou hadst known in this day, even thou, the things which belong to thy peace" (Luke xix. 42). He showed it in His prayer for those who nailed Him to the Cross: "Father, forgive them, for they know not what they do" (Luke xxiii. 34). He showed it above all in His endurance of the Cross.[8]

It is because men rebel and sin against God, separating themselves from his love, that the Bible portrays God's love as a suffering love, a love that knows the pathos of unfulfilled possibilities. It is a love which suffers as the Father suffers in the departure of the prodigal son, and a love which goes out to meet the returning penitent, welcoming him back into the fellowship of the Father's home. It is a love which in its self-giving and its self-identification involves a cross. The passion of Christ with the agonizing

[8] H. H. Rowley, *The Relevance of the Bible* (London: J. Clarke & Co., 1942; New York: The Macmillan Co., 1944), pp. 129-32. Used by permission.

5 Who *is* this that cometh up from the wilderness, leaning upon her beloved? I raised thee up under the apple tree: there thy mother brought thee forth; there she brought thee forth *that* bare thee.

5 Who is that coming up from the wilderness,
   leaning upon her beloved?

Under the apple tree I awakened you.
There your mother was in travail with you,
   there she who bore you was in travail.

THE DAUGHTERS OF JERUSALEM (8:5*a*)

5a. According to the cultic interpretation, this would refer to the **coming up of** the god and goddess from the underworld. The question has no point on the secular interpretation and is deleted by Jastrow and Haupt.

THE MAIDEN (8:5*b*-7)

5b. These lines are also deleted by Jastrow and Haupt. In behalf of the cultic interpretation it should be noted that the fertility god is often connected with a **tree**, e.g., Adonis was said to have sprung from a myrrh tree. Many scholars follow the Syriac in pointing the second person suffixes as feminine and thus put the words into the mouth of the youth, but the M.T. is better.

plea, "Let this cup pass from me" (Matt. 26:39), and the Crucifixion, with that most poignant sigh of dereliction, "Why hast thou forsaken me?" (Matt. 27:46), are awesome reminders of the pathos of love. The torment of separation which thwarts the union of the lovers in the Song of Songs is re-enacted in the greatest drama ever staged, the drama of God's redemptive love in Christ.[9]

The note of pathos in the biblical conception of love, however, is not confined to the suffering love of God in Christ. From man's side too there is a restless quest and yearning for fellowship which is hindered and obstructed not only by the sin of willful separation, but by the disquieting apprehension that God is remote, withdrawn, hidden. Sometimes fellowship with God is prevented by force of circumstance, as when the psalmist in exile cries, "How shall we sing the Lord's song in a strange land?" (Ps. 137:4). Sometimes it is the mystery of God's purposes, as when Jeremiah bewails, "I have become a laughingstock all the day. . . . The word of the Lord has become for me a reproach and derision all day long" (Jer. 20:7-8). Sometimes it is the fear that God himself retires behind his unapproachable sovereignty, as when the disciples grow perturbed at Jesus' announcement of his imminent departure (John 13:31–14:7).

On a somewhat different level the pathos of God's love for mankind and man's response in love to God is frequently indicated in the Bible by the mockery and scorn which those who cannot know or appreciate such love pour upon the believer. As "the daughters of Jerusalem" and the "watchmen" in the Song of Songs act as a negative foil to the lovers, so elsewhere in the Bible there are bystanders and spectators who ridicule the love of God and man. "My tears have been my meat day and night, while they continually say unto me, Where is thy God?" (Ps. 42:3); "The chief priests, with the scribes and elders, mocked him, saying, 'He saved others; he cannot save himself' " (Matt. 27:41). Commenting on the maiden's dream (5:2-8), Norman F. Langford says:

The Church is under the impression that there is a kind of midnight prowler in the world, more fascinating and more to be desired than the things of the world. The Church has heard God knocking at the doors of human life, and she cannot refrain from going after him and making her desire for him the chief object of her life. But see what happens then! It is just as in this parable. The Church cannot, after all, prove that there is anything to life beyond the things which men see with their eyes and touch with their hands. She seems to be following a phantom voice, and many will not believe that she has experienced anything but a delusion that has made her superstitious.[1]

In the history of Christian thought it has been the "mystic" or "contemplative," who has understood and elaborated upon what we have been calling lovesickness. For one thing, the mystic invariably interprets the essence of religion in terms of love. Richard Rolle of Hampole says: "Oh merry love, strong ravishing, burning, willful, strong, unslaked, that all my

---

[9] Cf. the crucifixion scene in Marc Connelly's play *The Green Pastures* (New York: Farrar & Rinehart, 1929).

[1] From *The Two-Edged Sword*, p. 140. Copyright 1945 by The Westminster Press. Used by permission.

6 ¶ Set me as a seal upon thine heart, as a seal upon thine arm: for love *is* strong as death; jealousy *is* cruel as the grave: the coals thereof *are* coals of fire, *which hath* a most vehement flame.

6 Set me as a seal upon your heart,
as a seal upon your arm;
for love is strong as death,
jealousy is cruel as the grave.
Its flashes are flashes of fire,
a most vehement flame.

---

6. In ancient times, when few could write, one carried a **seal** suspended from the neck over the heart (Gen. 38:18, 25) or worn on the right hand (Jer. 22:24), with which to make his signature; hence the figure here. The word for **death** is the same as that for the god of Sheol or the underworld in the Ras Shamra texts, Mot. The word קנאה, **jealousy**, is better rendered "zealous love" or "passion" (Amer. Trans.), as the parallelism indicates; and because the line is too long metrically, it is better to take the word with the next line as a *casus pendens* and transfer the *'athnaḥ* pause to the preceding word (so Amer. Trans.). The expression שלהבתיה, **a most vehement flame** ("furious flames" Amer. Trans.), may be taken as one word with the

---

soul brings to thy service, and suffers to think on nothing but thee." Thomas a Kempis says: "The lover flies, runs, and rejoices: he is free, and cannot be restrained. He gives all for all, and has all in all; for he rests in One Supreme above all, from whom all good flows and proceeds." Jacob Boehme says: "I only sought the heart of love in Jesus Christ, and when I had attained that with great joy of my soul, then was this treasure of natural and Divine knowledge opened and given unto me." Tauler says: "Pierce, I pray Thee, this heart of mine with the sweet dart of Thy fiery love, that I may languish for love of Thee all the days of my life." Evelyn Underhill sums up the mystic's emphasis on love:

The mystic's outlook, indeed, is the lover's outlook. It has the same element of wildness, the same quality of selfless and quixotic devotion, the same combination of rapture and humility. This parallel is more than a pretty fancy: for mystic and lover, upon different planes, are alike responding to the call of the Spirit of Life. The language of human passion is tepid and insignificant beside the language in which the mystics try to tell the splendours of their love.[2]

The significant point to observe about the mystic's view of love, however, is not merely that it finds expression in a language very similar to the Song of Songs, or that it speaks of the "mystical union" of the soul with the Absolute —it is rather that in this quest for love and union the mystic invariably senses what is known as "the dark night of the soul." This is that lovesickness which results from the inability

to realize to the full the love and union which the lovers so much desire. "Impotence, blankness, solitude, are the epithets by which these immersed in this dark fire of purification describe their pains."[3] John of the Cross says: "The greatest affliction of the sorrowful soul in this state is the thought that God has abandoned it." Madame Guyon says: "Thou didst begin, oh my God, to withdraw Thyself from me: and the pain of Thy absence was the more bitter to me, because Thy presence had been so sweet to me, Thy love so strong in me." Meister Eckhart says of God: "He acts as if there were a wall erected between Him and us."[4]

When Christ, the Lord, was born,
It was starlight,
Not sunlight.

When the Christmas angels sang
The Gloria in Excelsis,
It was midnight.

When on Calvary, the Saviour of the world
Opened the Kingdom of Heaven to all believers,
There was darkness over the whole land.

My soul: Why is this? Why does God
Come in the shadows? Is it because
The whole world is still, and our eyes are clear?
Then let us at this Christmas time
When the old year turns to the new
"Be still and know that He is God."[5]

It is highly appropriate to remember in this connection that the Song of Songs has had a traditional liturgical association in Judaism with the feast of the Passover (see Intro., p. 91). This most sacred of all Jewish festivals

[2] *Mysticism* (New York: E. P. Dutton & Co., 1912), pp. 106-7. See also T. H. Hughes, *The Philosophic Basis of Mysticism* (Edinburgh: T. & T. Clark, 1937), pp. 70-78; and W. R. Inge, *Christian Mysticism* (New York: Charles Scribner's Sons, 1899), p. 8: "The true hierophant of the mysteries of God is love."

[3] Underhill, *op. cit.*, p. 454.
[4] *Ibid.*, p. 465.
[5] H. T. Kerr & W. Wentzell, "When Christ, the Lord, Was Born," A Christmas Anthem (Boston: The Boston Music Co., 1933). Used by permission.

7 Many waters cannot quench love, neither can the floods drown it: if a man would give all the substance of his house for love, it would utterly be contemned.

8 ¶ We have a little sister, and she hath no breasts: what shall we do for our sister in the day when she shall be spoken for?

---

7 Many waters cannot quench love,
  neither can floods drown it.
If a man offered for love
  all the wealth of his house,
  it would be utterly scorned.

8 We have a little sister,
  and she has no breasts.
What shall we do for our sister,
  on the day when she is spoken for?

---

emphatic *yāh* ending, or as two words, lit., "flame of Yah," which again is emphatic in accordance with the Hebrew idiom of using the divine name with superlative force (see J. M. Powis Smith, "The Syntax and Meaning of Genesis 1:1-3," and "The Use of Divine Names as Superlatives," *American Journal of Semitic Languages and Literatures,* XLIV [1927-28], 111-12; XLV [1928-29], 212-13).

7. This would seem to be the climax of the poem; love will find a way to bring the lovers together, the meaning being the same for all interpretations of the book. **Offered** is better rendered "were to offer," since the verb is imperfect, and איש is "one" rather than **a man.** The antecedent of the suffix of לו can be either איש or הון, **wealth,** and the clause can be read as a question or a statement, with the verb in the indefinite plural. Actually there is little difference in meaning among the various interpretations; they all affirm the pricelessness of love.

The Daughters of Jerusalem (8:8-9)

8-9. There seems to be no way to interpret this strophe other than symbolically, and its connection with the book as a whole is not clear. It would seem to be a fragment from another source. If it belongs to the book it must be assigned to the chorus of women

---

(Exod. 12) included the symbolism of both an agricultural and a pastoral background. "The agricultural feast of unleavened bread and bitter herbs was combined with the primitive nomadic feast of the firstborn of the flock sacrificed at the same vernal season." [6] The celebration of the Passover was a holy reminder of God's redemptive mercy in delivering the children of Israel from their Egyptian bondage. In this sense it was a festival of joy and victory, but it also involved the solemn note of "bitter herbs" and "sacrifice," and served to recall the agonies and heartaches of the Egyptian sojourn. Thus the Passover, like the Song of Songs itself, involves the element of pathos.

In the N.T. the Last Supper is related to the Passover. Though the connection is not altogether clear, "it is indisputable that the incident took place at the Passover season and that Paschal ideas and associations must have filled the mind of Jesus at such a time." [7] Thus Christ and his sacrificial death are interpreted as "our paschal lamb" (I Cor. 5:6-8; cf. John 1:29; Rev. 5:9). So in the most sacred sacrament of the

[6] F. J. Taylor, "Passover," in Richardson, ed., *A Theological Word Book of the Bible,* p. 163.
[7] *Ibid.,* p. 164.

Christian church, as also in the most significant festival of the Jewish faith, the element of pathos, the bittersweet quality of love, finds solemn and majestic expression.

VI. The Strongest Thing in the World.—The Song of Songs sings of a love that is all-consuming and overpowering. As we have seen, there is an element of pathos occasioned by the lovers' separation from each other, but the Song is not a dirge or a lament; it is not in a minor key, though there are minor chords. It is the song of an irresistible love, invincible and triumphant.

Here at least all interpreters are agreed. There is no mistaking the major theme regardless of the difficulties of translation and exegesis. We may be easily confused by the lack of structure in the book, the fact that there is so little movement and no plot to speak of, yet we cannot miss the dominant pervasive passion that gives unity to the whole.

Scholars tell us that it is folk poetry, simple and naïve. It is not belles-lettres or the studied composition of a littérateur. We hardly know who the speakers are, or when and where they speak. The lovers are clearly very much in love, yet there is no mention of marriage, home, or family life. There is something impressionistic

9 If she *be* a wall, we will build upon her a palace of silver: and if she *be* a door, we will inclose her with boards of cedar.

10 I *am* a wall, and my breasts like towers: then was I in his eyes as one that found favor.

9 If she is a wall,
  we will build upon her a battlement of silver;
but if she is a door,
  we will enclose her with boards of cedar.
10 I was a wall,
  and my breasts were like towers;
then I was in his eyes
  as one who brings[x] peace.

[x] Or *finds*

---

rather than to the girl's brothers, as many believe. The first clause reads, lit., "The sister belonging to us is young"; hence "Our sister [i.e., the heroine of the book] is young" (so LXX, Vulg., Amer. Trans.).

THE MAIDEN (8:10)

10. The suffix of עֵינָיו, his eyes, has no antecedent, but presumably the reference is to the beloved. The RSV takes the verb in the last clause as the Hiphil participle of יצא, lit., "like one who causes prosperity to go forth," a clear reference to the fertility cult. The verb may also be taken as the Qal participle of מצא—"like one who finds favor" (Amer. Trans.; cf. KJV). In either case *kaph* may be asseverative, as in 8:1.

---

and ethereal about the Song that borders on the unreal and irrational. It is an idyl, an eclogue, rather than an epic or a saga. Yet it is undoubtedly a song of love, a love that transcends the boundaries of space and time, a love that overcomes and vanquishes all that stands in its way.

Mention has been made of the intimate, personal declarations of love which the youth and the maiden repeatedly utter, their extravagant descriptions of each other's charms, the ecstasy which they feel in each other's presence, and the anguish of separation. There are in addition numerous more generalized statements in the Song about the power and value of love. Thus three times it is said that "love is better than wine" (1:2, 4; 4:10). Whether "wine" is to be interpreted as food and drink, the elemental sustainers of life (cf. Gen. 14:18; Judg. 19:19; Neh. 5:15), or as the intoxicating stimulant "to gladden the heart of man" (Ps. 104:15), in either case the superiority of love is acclaimed. Cf. the familiar lines of Ben Jonson's "To Celia":

> Drink to me only with thine eyes,
>   And I will pledge with mine;
> Or leave a kiss but in the cup
>   And I'll not look for wine.

When the maiden says:

> My beloved is to me a cluster of henna blossoms
>   in the vineyards of Engedi (1:14),

the reference is suggestive of love's uniqueness. Engedi was an oasis west of the Dead Sea in one of the wildest and most desolate spots in the whole of Palestine. Sometimes called Hazazon-tamar, Engedi is mentioned several times in the O.T. and there is a strange, eerie association of ideas and events connected with this isolated refuge and beauty spot in the midst of the desert (cf. Gen. 14:7; I Sam. 23:29; 24:1-22; II Chr. 20:2; Ezek. 47:10).

Especially for Near Eastern peoples, the desert was not only a natural phenomenon which confronted them on all sides, it was also symbolic of the tenuousness of life and the obstacles which constantly endangered their very existence. This is also true of biblical thought, where the Exodus through the Sinai desert figures so prominently, where John the Baptist is described as "the voice of one crying in the wilderness" (Matt. 3:3), where the temptation of Jesus is located in the wilderness of Judea (Matt. 4 and parallels), and where Paul, just after his Damascus road experience, is reported to have gone "into Arabia" (Gal. 1:17).

Coupled with this is the frequently recurring theme in the Bible that the desert and the wilderness will someday be redeemed and reclaimed. Thus in the book of Isaiah we read:

> The wilderness and the dry land shall be glad,
>   the desert shall rejoice and blossom (35:1).

> In the wilderness prepare the way of the Lord,
>   make straight in the desert a highway for our God (40:3).

11 Solomon had a vineyard at Baal-hamon; he let out the vineyard unto keepers; every one for the fruit thereof was to bring a thousand *pieces* of silver.
 	
12 My vineyard, which *is* mine, *is* before me: thou, O Solomon, *must have* a thousand, and those that keep the fruit thereof two hundred.
	11 Solomon had a vineyard at Ba′al-ha′mon;
	  he let out the vineyard to keepers;
	  each one was to bring for its fruit a
	    thousand pieces of silver.
	12 My vineyard, my very own, is for myself;
	  you, O Solomon, may have the thousand,
	  and the keepers of the fruit two hundred.

The Maiden (8:11-12)

This is another strophe that is hard to connect with its context and may have got into the book through its reference to **Solomon,** or **Solomon** originally may have been "Shelem."

11. Baal-hamon ("possessor of abundance") is otherwise unknown, but the name suggests a city sacred to the fertility cult. **A thousand pieces of silver:** Lit., "a thousand of silver," with "shekels" understood, as so often in Hebrew. For this amount as a symbol of opulence see Isa. 7:23.

12. The first stich reads, lit., **My vineyard, which is mine, is before me. Two hundred,** i.e., 20 per cent, was the usual rate of interest in the ancient Near East.

I will make a way in the wilderness
and rivers in the desert (43:19).[8]

In a somewhat different figure of speech love's supremacy is suggested in the Song of Songs when the maiden says, immediately after a profession of her love for the youth:

Our couch is green;
the beams of our house are cedar,
our rafters are pine (1:16-17).

Moffatt's translation is even more suggestive:

Our bed of love is the green sward,
our roof-beams are yon cedar-boughs,
our rafters are the firs.

A house, we say, is not a home, but love can transfigure and exalt the meanest abode. So too the lovers experience the thrill of the great outdoors which love captures and transforms for their own use and enjoyment. The same thought recurs when the maiden, again after a declaration of love, says:

Come, my beloved,
let us go forth into the fields,
and lodge in the villages (7:11).[9]

[8] For a modern treatment of this symbolic theme cf. T. S. Eliot, "The Waste Land" in his *Complete Poems and Plays* (New York: Harcourt, Brace & Co., 1952), pp. 37-50).

[9] In the novel by Pearl S. Buck, *Come, My Beloved* (New York: John Day Co., 1953), which takes its title from this verse, a quite different symbolic theme is presented. Concerned with the West's attitude toward the East, she portrays four successive generations of an American family and their views toward India, all the way from patronizing benevolence to self-identification with the people in the villages.

All interpreters agree that if the Song of Songs has a climax, it is to be found in the familiar and often quoted lines "Love is strong as death. . . . Many waters cannot quench love, neither can floods drown it" (8:6-7). Here is the Song's doxology to love, victorious, invincible, irresistible. And it is an affirmation that strikes a responsive chord in the human heart. "Love conquers all"; [1] "Love will conquer at the last"; [2] "Love is greater than illusion, and as strong as death." [3]

But there is something strange and ironic about this climactic panegyric in the Song of Songs. There is no mistaking the accent on love's victory, but "love" is compared to "death"; "jealousy" (or better, "passionate love") is said to be "cruel as the grave." Such love is like "flashes of fire, a most vehement flame" which "many waters" cannot "quench" nor can it be drowned by "floods." It is of inestimable value, but money "would be utterly scorned," for love is priceless and cannot be bought. The point is not merely that love is something beautiful and ineffable, but that it is a powerful force, as strong and irresistible as death itself, a consuming fire that withstands all efforts to quench its flame. The symbolism suggests that love's victory is set over against whatever threatens it—death, the grave, waters, floods, wealth, barter.

The victory of love of which the Song of Songs

[1] Vergil *Eclogues* X. 1. 79.

[2] Tennyson, "Locksley Hall Sixty Years After."

[3] Alberto Casella, *Death Takes a Holiday,* rewritten by Walter Ferris (New York: Samuel French, 1934), Act III.

13 Thou that dwellest in the gardens, the companions hearken to thy voice: cause me to hear *it*.	13 O you who dwell in the gardens, my companions are listening for your voice; let me hear it.

THE YOUTH (8:13)

13. My companions is an emended text, with the last letter dropped as due to dittography and the word repointed; or **my** is added to identify the companions as belonging to the youth. The clause is circumstantial, "with my companions listening." Since it is our belief, as noted in the Intro. to Lamentations (see Vol. VI), that a single

sings, therefore, has little to do with the sentimental, mawkish platitude of minor poets and writers of popular songs who proclaim smoothly that love is the sweetest thing in the world. The maiden and the youth in the Song do not indulge in banal or vapid truisms about the beauty or wonder of love; their love is a hard-won thing that emerges victorious and triumphant in spite of everything that would hinder and prevent it.

As a testimony to the invincible power and inestimable value of love the Song of Songs takes a high place, perhaps a unique place, in the literature of mankind. Its uniqueness, however, lies not merely in its enchanting imagery, its consummate literary composition, its appreciation of nature's charms, or its description of love's rapture. These are not inconsiderable merits, and the Song, to be sure, can be read and enjoyed on the basis of such intrinsic qualities. Yet on this level alone it is but one of innumerable examples, both ancient and modern, of exquisite love poetry.

For better or for worse the Song of Songs found its way into the canon of Scripture, and unless we are to say that it has no place there, we must reckon with this historical fact of context. We need not press its earthy figures into allegorical molds. From the biblical perspective itself there is no reason why its sensuous and sensual language cannot be taken at its face value. The Bible, as we have seen, does not minimize the love of man and woman. This indeed is a negative understatement, for, rightly viewed, the biblical conception of love can enhance and exalt what otherwise is merely human and mundane. The biblical perspective accordingly can appreciate the Song of Songs for what it is and rejoice in its eulogy of love. "All things are yours," says the apostle, "whether Paul or Apollos or Cephas or the world or life or death or the present or the future, all are yours" (I Cor. 3:21-22). Writing to the Philippian Christians who wondered what to do about the secular society in which they lived, Paul said: "Whatever is true, whatever is honorable, whatever is just, whatever is pure, whatever is

lovely, whatever is gracious, if there is any excellence, if there is anything worthy of praise, think about these things" (Phil. 4:8). From the Christian point of view therefore the facile distinction which is so often made between secular and sacred is transcended simply because we are to "take every thought captive to obey Christ" (II Cor. 10:5).

It is inevitable from the vantage point of the biblical context to set love's victory in the Song of Songs in juxtaposition with the N.T. song of songs: "Love bears all things, believes all things, hopes all things, endures all things. Love never ends. . . . So faith, hope, love abide, these three; but the greatest of these is love" (I Cor. 13:7-8, 13). Here too we have a hymn to love as the strongest thing in the world. The theme is the same, but the N.T. song interprets love in terms of God's redemptive power in Christ. It is a four-dimensional love: "That you, being rooted and grounded in love, may have power to comprehend with all saints what is the breadth and length and height and depth, and to know the love of Christ which surpasses knowledge, that you may be filled with all the fullness of God" (Eph. 3:17-19). God's love in Christ

is broader
Than the measure of man's mind.[4]

It goes to any length to achieve its purpose, "even death on a cross"; it reaches up to God himself, it stoops down in order to lift up.

Stronger his love than death or hell;
Its riches are unsearchable;
 The first-born sons of light
Desire in vain its depths to see;
They cannot reach the mystery,
 The length, the breadth, the height.[5]

It is at this point that we move beyond the highest reaches of the Song of Songs. "Love is

[4] Frederick W. Faber, "There's a wideness in God's mercy," st. ii.
[5] Charles Wesley, "O Love divine, how sweet thou art!" st. ii.

14 ¶ Make haste, my beloved, and be thou like to a roe or to a young hart upon the mountains of spices.	14 Make haste, my beloved,
	    and be like a gazelle
	or a young stag
	    upon the mountains of spices.

word may not constitute two feet, the punctuation of the line should be changed slightly to read the last two words together, "let me hear your voice" (Amer. Trans.). On the cultic interpretation the **companions** would be the male votaries.

The Maiden (8:14)

14. The comparison is also found in 2:9, 17. **The mountains of spices** is a rather extravagant figure characteristic of the book; it means "sweet-smelling mountains" (cf. 4:6).

strong as death," says the maiden; but God's love in Christ is stronger than death. T. R. Glover, in speaking of the Christian victory over Greece and Rome, said: "The Christian 'out-lived' the pagan, 'out-died' him, and 'out-thought' him. He came into the world and lived a great deal better than the pagan; he beat him hollow in living." [6]

A story is told about how the Communists came into a North China village and found a little group of Christians. Probably because the Christians refused to participate in the hate campaign against the landlords, the Communists lost their tempers. "We will take away your land," they said. And the Christians only replied, "That is all right. Our possessions belong to the Lord Jesus Christ." The Communists said, "We will beat you." And the Christians replied, "That is all right. Our bodies belong to the Lord Jesus Christ." The Communists said, "We can kill you." And the Christians replied, "Even our lives belong to the Lord Jesus Christ." [7]

For such faith God's love in Christ is not only as strong as death, it is stronger than death. It is the strongest thing in the world. "Who shall separate us from the love of Christ? Shall tribulation, or distress, or persecution, or famine, or nakedness, or peril, or sword? . . . No, in all these things we are more than conquerors through him who loved us. For I am sure that neither death, nor life, nor angels, nor principalities, nor things present, nor things to come, nor powers, nor height, nor depth, nor anything else in all creation, will be able to separate us from the love of God in Christ Jesus our Lord" (Rom. 8:35, 37-39).

[6] *The Jesus of History* (New York: Association Press, 1921), pp. 200-1.

[7] Samuel Hugh Moffett, *Where'er the Sun* (New York: Friendship Press, 1953), p. 38.

The Book of

ISAIAH

Chapters 1–39

Introduction and Exegesis by R. B. Y. Scott

Exposition by G. G. D. Kilpatrick

Chapters 40–66

Introduction and Exegesis by James Muilenburg

Exposition by Henry Sloane Coffin

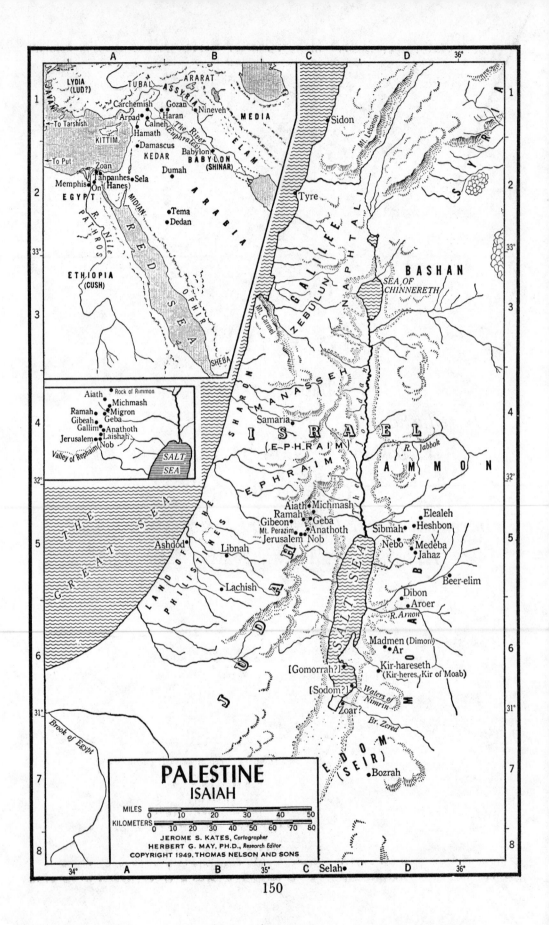

PALESTINE
ISAIAH

MILES 0 10 20 30 40 50

KILOMETERS 0 10 20 30 40 50 60 70 80

JEROME S. KATES, *Cartographer*
HERBERT G. MAY, PH.D., *Research Editor*
COPYRIGHT 1949, THOMAS NELSON AND SONS

ISAIAH

INTRODUCTION, CHS. 1-39

Isaiah falls into two clearly distinguishable parts: chs. 1-39 and chs. 40-66. The first of these alone contains the literary records of the major prophetic figure whose name the whole book bears, for the material in chs. 40-66 presupposes the very different situation of the sixth century or later. We are concerned here with "First Isaiah," which is, of course, the designation of a corpus of literary material, not that of the earlier of two prophets of the same name.

The material of First Isaiah is marked off from what follows by a series of narratives (chs. 36-39) concerning the activities of the prophet toward the end of the reign of Hezekiah, when his ministry was drawing to a close. It does not follow that all the material in chs. 1-35 is the work of the prophet, or even that it comes from his own period or that which immediately followed it. There are clear indications that material from long after Isaiah's day (e.g., the doom oracle on Babylon in ch. 13) has been included, and equally clear evidence that the growth of the present book around the core of authentic records of Isaiah's ministry was a long and complicated process. To the very end of that process (which may have been as late as the first half of the second century B.C.) it was still possible for additional matter to be added, or rather inserted, at what was felt by later custodians of the tradition to be appropriate points. This was in no sense a deliberate falsification of the record. In some instances it seems to have been merely the adding of something which had become associated in tradition with the prophet's name. In other cases it was the drawing out of what was felt to be implicit in Isaiah's message, in the altered circumstances of a later

day. There was as yet no fixed canon of prophecy, and the impact which Isaiah had made upon his contemporaries was transmitted to later generations in a living literary tradition.

In fact, the distinction between Isaiah the prophet and the book of Isaiah must be kept clearly in mind. The significance of the man and his prophetic ministry and the significance of the book are not the same. It will not do to assume that whatever in the book cannot be linked directly with the prophet of the eighth century is necessarily of little or even of lesser value on that account. The task of the interpreter therefore is to distinguish, not between the authentic and the spurious, but between what contributes to our knowledge and understanding of Isaiah and his message and what does not, although the latter may be significant for other reasons. What actually lies before us is a book containing a great variety of material from the period of Isaiah's ministry and later times. Almost all of it is of unusual interest and value, both literary and religious. But each part must be studied for itself, to see what it says, what it means, and what it implies—without presuppositions as to authorship beyond the undoubted fact that the core of the collection consists of literary records of Isaiah's ministry.

I. Contents

The usual analysis [1] distinguishes the following sections of the book by subject matter, the occurrence of titles (as in 1:1; 2:1), and literary characteristics:

[1] George Buchanan Gray, *A Critical and Exegetical Commentary on the Book of Isaiah I-XXXIX* (New York: Charles Scribner's Sons, 1912; "International Critical Commentary"), I, xlvii.

Ch.   1. A booklet of prophecies.
Chs. 2–12. A collection of prophecies, mainly concerning "Judah and Jerusalem," with some narratives.
Chs. 13–23. A collection of doom oracles on foreign peoples.
Chs. 24–27. A booklet of late eschatological prophecy.
Chs. 28–33. A collection of oracles beginning "Woe . . . !" with supplementary matter.
Chs. 34–35. Two eschatological prophecies.
Chs. 36–39. Narratives concerning Isaiah, taken over with modifications from II Kings 18:13–20:19.

Some scholars maintain that these or similar divisions of the present text mark off older and smaller collections which have been brought together in chs. 1–39. This is very doubtful, for reasons given below. The arrangement of the book is the result of a long and complicated process of collecting and editing, and the total literary evidence does not support so simple and clear-cut a solution. Other scholars have suggested that chs. 1–39, like Ezekiel and the Septuagint arrangement of Jeremiah, fall into three broad divisions: (a) Threats against the prophet's own people (chs. 1–12); (b) threats against foreign peoples (chs. 13–23); and (c) promises to the prophet's own people (chs. 28–35); chs. 24–27 are partly in (b) and partly in (c). This analysis is true to the facts only in a very general way, for chs. 28–31, for example, consist largely of reproaches addressed to Judah; the truth is that the bulk of Isaiah's own prophecies occur in chs. 1–11 (with a second, smaller group in chs. 28–31) and are chiefly reproaches of Judah, that later he spoke about foreign peoples, and finally that the non-Isaianic eschatological promises have been added chiefly, though by no means exclusively, in the latter part of chs. 1–35.

The following analysis of the subject matter of chs. 1–39 makes use of the descriptive titles from the Exegesis for the literary units and for the larger divisions and subdivisions. Some divergences from the "usual analysis" given above will be noted. The first division consists of the wholly oracular material in chs. 1–5, with 2:1-5 attached to ch. 1 as the first subdivision of this section. The second division (6:1–8:18) is marked off from what precedes and what follows as consisting principally of narrative. The third division consists of a further selection of oracles (8:19–10:4), some of which at least have been artificially or accidentally separated from the oracles in chs. 1–5. At 10:5 a new note is introduced with the pronouncement of judgment upon the Assyrian invader, and the oracles (including messianic promises), which now follow this up to the end of ch. 12 are grouped with it

in Section IV. At ch. 13 begins the long section of oracles which continues to ch. 23 and consists mainly of doom oracles ("burdens") on various foreign peoples. Section VI comprises chs. 24–27, an independent body of late eschatological prophecy interspersed with psalms. Section VII (chs. 28–32) is a collection of Isaiah's prophecies mainly concerned with the intrigue with Egypt (ca. 702), with some added matter. In chs. 33–35 are found three longer compositions, a prophetic liturgy and two eschatological poems, which have little or nothing in common with the preceding collection of relatively brief oracles, and hence are put in a separate division. About the distinction of the final Section (chs. 36–39), the considerably modified excerpt from II Kings 18:13–20:19, there can be no difference of view.

 I. "They have rebelled against me" (1:1–5:24a)
    A. Superscription (1:1)
    B. A booklet of oracles (1:2–2:5)
       1. Israel's ingratitude (1:2-3)
       2. Dire straits of Zion (1:4-9)
       3. God's primary concern (1:10-17)
       4. The alternative: repent, or be destroyed (1:18-20)
       5. Lament over Jerusalem (1:21-23)
       6. The Lord's judgment (1:24-26)
       7. An addendum (1:27-31)
       8. Turning of the peoples to Zion's God (2:1-5)
    C. The day of the Lord (2:6-22)
       1. Coming doom upon idolatry (2:6-11, 18-22)
       2. Humbling of human pride (2:12-17)
    D. The doom of rulers (3:1-15)
       1. Social anarchy (3:1-7)
       2. A ruined people (3:8-12)
       3. Rapacity of the rulers (3:13-15)
    E. The proud women of Jerusalem (3:16–4:1)
    F. Zion purged by judgment (4:2-6)
    G. A song of the Lord's vineyard (5:1-7)
    H. Those who neither fear God nor regard man (5:8-24a)
 II. "Bind up the testimony" (6:1–8:18)
    A. Isaiah's vision of God (6:1-13)
    B. Isaiah and the Syro-Ephraimite War (7:1–8:15)
       1. Sign of Shear-jashub (7:1-9)
       2. Sign of Immanuel (7:10-17)
       3. The coming invasion (7:18-25)
       4. Sign of Maher-shalal-hashbaz (8:1-4)
       5. Oracle of the two rivers (8:5-8a)
       6. Faith declares defiance (8:8b-10)
       7. The fear of man and the fear of God (8:11-15)
    C. Withdrawal of the prophet (8:16-18)
 III. "His anger is not turned away" (8:19–10:4; 5:24b-30)
    A. Two fragments of ominous prophecy (8:19-22)
    B. The messianic king (9:1-7 [Hebrew 8:23–9:6])

D. Isaiah's oracle of defiance (37:22-29)
E. A sign for the remnant (37:30-32)
F. A metrical oracle on the departure of Sennacherib (37:21, 33-35)
G. Destruction of the Assyrians and death of Sennacherib (37:36-38)
H. Hezekiah's illness and recovery (38:1-22)
J. The embassy from Merodach-baladan (39:1-8)

II. Literary Components

The literary units which have been distinguished in the above analytical outline fall into one of four categories: (a) "oracles," or declarations by the prophet of Yahweh's word (e.g., 1:10-17); (b) "memoirs," or narratives recounted by the prophet himself and incorporating certain oracles (e.g., 6:1-13); (c) "prophetic biography," or narratives about the prophet as told by another person (e.g., 7:1-17), and again incorporating oracles; and (d) various less characteristic forms such as psalms (e.g., 12:1-6; 38:10-20); prophetic poems (e.g., 14:4b-21); parables (e.g., 28:23-29); utterances of "wisdom" (e.g., 32:1-8); and prophetic liturgies (e.g., 33:1-24).

A. Oracles.—The basic literary record of prophecy is the published oracle. This is most clearly indicated in the account given in Jer. 36:1-4 of the recording by Jeremiah of "all the words of Yahweh" which he had declared over a period of twenty years. Each "word" was a distinct oracle. That they had been preserved heretofore without written record is not only an indication of the powers of memory which can be developed by those who do not customarily rely on notes, but it suggests also that the oracles had been put into memorable poetic form and had been linked in a catena for recital. There is a striking example in 1:9, 10 of the linking of two distinct oracles by the key words "Sodom" and "Gomorrah." Elsewhere oracles have been brought together by an association of ideas. Twice in chs. 1–39 there are indications that Isaiah, like Jeremiah, caused a series of oracles to be put in writing (8:16-18; 30:8).

The published or "public" oracle is the declaration by the prophet of a "word of the Lord" which he felt himself commissioned to speak (cf. 1:10). When he says, "Thus saith the Lord" (as in 10:24 or 37:6), he is the bearer of an authoritative message from his Sovereign, just as when the messengers of a human king preface an announcement with "Thus saith Hezekiah" (37:3) or "Thus saith the great king, the king of Assyria" (36:4). This ambassadorial utterance presupposes the private audience in which the envoy has been told what he must say, and we have a number of instances of such "private" oracles commanding Isaiah to speak or to record a particular "word" (5:9;

6:8, 9-10, 11-13; 8:1, 3b-4, 5-8, 11; 22:14-15; 30:8). Some of these in turn enclose in summary form the oracles which were to be published (e.g., 6:9b, 8:1d).

In Isa. 1–39, as elsewhere in the records of prophecy, the "public" oracles usually take one of four forms: reproach, threat, exhortation, or promise. The genuine prophecies of Isaiah are mainly reproaches and threats; the promises are chiefly post-Isaianic. These primary forms not seldom appear in combination, especially (as is natural) the reproach and the threat. It is not always easy to tell, however, whether the connection is original or editorial. There are also two composite oracles with refrains (2:6-22 and 9:7-20 plus 10:1-4, plus 5:26-29) which may represent a second stage of the prophet's own composition, combining in a larger unit distinct oracles previously spoken.

A reproach is a denunciation of moral or spiritual evil. Its opening is marked by the exclamation "Oh!" "Woe!" or "Shame!" or by a call for witnesses to hear the complainant's accusation, or by a series of mocking imperative verbs (cf. 5:8; 1:2; 29:9). A threat of punishment frequently follows upon a reproach, and is introduced by "therefore" (cf. 5:24); elsewhere it is introduced by a particle which is usually rendered "for," but which is better translated "Yea!" and understood as marking the emphatic assertion of an oath (cf. 1:29; I Sam. 14:44). The reproach sometimes, and the threat usually, come to an emphatic conclusion (cf. 5:8; 8:15). The promise normally begins with "In that day" (10:20) or a similar phrase, and has an emphatic conclusion (cf. 31:5). The exhortation has no special distinguishing marks, and in fact is the least frequently found of the four forms of the oracle (e.g., 7:4-6; 8:12-13).

It will be noted that these "public" oracles vary in length from one or two verses to eight or ten verses; where, as in 10:5-16, a longer unit appears, there are evident subdivisions within its structure. Although in the form of public pronouncements, these pregnant utterances with their rhythmic and (usually) polished form are clearly too short to be speeches or sermons. Apparently they were spoken on significant occasions when the prophet might be expected to be heard from, such as at an assembly for worship in the temple (cf. Jer. 26:2), in the presence of the king and his council (cf. I Kings 22:5-23), or in an assembly of the elders (cf. Jer. 19:1-3). The prophet declared his message in striking fashion; he did not teach or "expound" but announced a compact "word" which had been given him.

Nevertheless, the oracles usually have the appearance of careful and indeed brilliant composition for the purpose they had to serve. The choice of language, the effectiveness of the figures and imagery, the forcefulness with which the central theme is stated, the fine balance of the literary structure, all testify that these were not the spontaneous utterances of a moment. Yet we must remember that the prophets spoke not of their own volition, but because "the hand of the Lord" was upon them; his word was "as a burning fire" within them which they could not contain (cf. Jer. 20:7-9).

Two points should be noted if we are to do justice both to the evidence of "ecstatic" religious experience and to that of deliberate literary composition. The supreme moment when a man knew that God had commissioned him as a prophet—the occasion of his "call" as in ch. 6—was an experience which colored all his subsequent ministry and gave authority to his utterances (cf. Amos 7:15). Similar experiences doubtless occurred later. However, not all his oracles were necessarily preceded by them, for the prophet knew himself to have the status and understanding required of Yahweh's envoy. There was thus an enduring authority for prophesying which might embody a large measure of deliberate reflection.

The second point to be noted in this connection is that there are traces of a primary or "embryonic" form in which certain oracles existed in the prophet's consciousness before they had been worked out in full literary form. Here and there we come across brief, enigmatic phrases or sentences like "Shear-jashub," "[only] a remnant shall return" (7:3), "Maher-shalal-hashbaz," "swift the spoiling, prompt the plundering" (8:1), or "Magor-missabib," "terror all around" (Jer. 20:3). These contain the quintessence of longer oracles. In Amos 8:1-3 and in Jer. 1:11-12 the word-pairs *qáyiç . . . qēç,* "fruit . . . end," and *shāqēdh . . . shôqēdh,* "almond-tree . . . watch," with their similar sounds and contrasting meanings, provide the nucleus of the oracles in which they are quoted. The corresponding wordplay, *çedhāqāh . . . çe'āqāh,* "righteousness . . . a cry" (5:7), brings to emphatic conclusion an oracle of which it is the gist, and which may well have first presented itself to the prophet's mind in this compact form. There are several other examples in Isa. 1–39 of such brief, enigmatic phrases marked by verbal symmetry and wordplay. They apparently represent the first articulation of prophetic "words" which later were developed as oracles for public presentation.

B. Memoirs.—The narrative sections of the book are much less extensive. They are of two kinds: biographical and autobiographical. The latter may be called "memoirs," because in ch. 6 Isaiah recounts, in one of the most striking

and important passages in prophetic literature, the story of the experience through which he was commissioned as Yahweh's messenger. The story was set down long afterward, since it is clearly colored by subsequent experience. The purpose in mind when the account was written was apparently to round out a collection of oracles by disclosing the event which lay back of, and justified, them. At the same time the more recent circumstances of the publication of the oracles in 8:1-8, 11-15 are recounted by Isaiah before he draws the memoirs to a close with the announcement that he is now sealing up his message (see Exeg.).

It will be noted that some "public" as well as some "private" oracles are incorporated in the prophet's memoirs (cf. 6:8, 9-10, 11-13; 8:1, 3b-4, 5-8, 12-15). And at various points in the oracle collections there appear brief hints of autobiography, references to the "private" oracles which preceded public announcement (cf. 5:9; 18:4; 22:14-15; 28:22; 30:8; 31:4). In every case these are connected with oracles which on other grounds can be assigned to Isaiah, so that it seems that these oracles belong to one or other of the two groups recorded by the prophet himself (see Exeg. on 8:16-18; 30:8-17).

C. Prophetic Biography.—Another series of narratives of a type quite different from the memoirs appears in 7:1-17; 20:1-6; and 36:1–39:8. Some scholars think that the first of these passages, having been turned by slight textual changes into a third-person account, belongs to the memoirs which are found in chs. 6 and 8. In fact, this is a different type of writing, concerned with outward events in which Isaiah participated rather than with his inner experience. It is "prophetic biography" of essentially the same kind as that concerning Elijah which is incorporated in I Kings 17–19; 21, and that concerning Isaiah himself which is drawn upon by the Deuteronomic editors in II Kings 18:17–20:19. One can go further and suggest that 7:1-17 is from the same source as that from which II Kings 18:17–19:4c was taken (cf. 7:3; II Kings 18:17). These "prophetic biographies" contained oracles quoted in the historical context to which they belonged (cf. 7:3-9, 13-17; II Kings 19:20-28). With 7:1-17 is to be associated 20:1-6 (i.e., in type, not in date).

As in 7:1-17 there is inserted a narrative section concerning an important episode in the relations of the prophet Isaiah with King Ahaz (735-720 or 715), so in chs. 36–39 a similar prose section narrates certain of the prophet's dealings with Ahaz' successor Hezekiah (720 or 715-687). Whereas, however, the former is an extract made directly from a biography of Isaiah and does not appear elsewhere, the latter is taken with some modifications from II Kings

18:13–20:19, where material from several sources had already been combined. The modifications are (a) the omission in Isaiah of II Kings 18:14-16, which recounts Hezekiah's submission to Sennacherib; (b) the abridgment of II Kings 18:17, 32; 19:35; 20:4-6 (cf. Isa. 36:2, 17; 37:36; 38:4-6) and other minor changes; (c) the displacement of II Kings 20:7-8 to follow 20:11, somewhat altered (cf. Isa. 38:6-7, 21-22); the insertion following II Kings 20:11 of a psalm of entreaty ascribed to Hezekiah (Isa. 38:9-20). The priority of the Kings to the Isaiah version is accepted by almost all critics because the material common to both shows certain features of arrangement and phraseology characteristic of Kings.

The most significant difference between the two versions is (a). The omitted verses are unusually important since they correspond closely with Sennacherib's own account of the events of 701, where we are told that Hezekiah submitted after "forty-six of his strong walled cities" were taken, and "himself, like a caged bird, I shut up in Jerusalem, his royal city." The tribute paid, according to II Kings 18:14, was thirty talents of gold and three hundred talents of silver; according to Sennacherib it was thirty talents of gold, eight hundred talents of silver, and other valuables. The omission of this passage by the editor of Isaiah was doubtless due to its inconsistency with the following accounts of the elimination of Sennacherib's army (Isa. 37:36-37) and of the apparently untouched wealth shown to the envoys of Merodach-baladan (39:1-2).

There remain other difficulties in the material common to both versions. The "fourteenth year of King Hezekiah" (36:1) was certainly much earlier than 701; either this date is due to editorial calculation from II Kings 18:2; 20:6, or it properly belongs to the account of Hezekiah's illness. Other problems of chronology are raised by the references (a) to Tirhakah as king of Ethiopia (37:9), a position he did not hold until some years after 701; and (b) to the death of Sennacherib which did not occur until 681, although 37:38 implies that it took place shortly after the destruction of his army in Palestine.

The sequence of the narratives and oracles in chs. 36–37 also is perplexing. The account in 36:2–37:7 tells how Sennacherib sent a message to Hezekiah, by the hand of a high-ranking officer accompanied by a strong force, demanding Hezekiah's surrender. Hezekiah resorts to the temple, and sends word to Isaiah; the prophet responds with an oracle predicting the departure and death of the Assyrian king. Again, in 37:9-35, Sennacherib sends a message to Hezekiah—this time by letter and apparently

from Libnah—closely resembling the latter part of the previous message sent by the hand of the officer and his army; again Hezekiah resorts to the temple and prays, and as a consequence Isaiah responds with three distinct oracles. The first of these is a defiance addressed to the Assyrian king; the second is a promise to Hezekiah of survival; the third is a promise that the Assyrians will not take the city. To these two parallel narratives is appended in 37:36-37 a brief account of the miraculous destruction of the Assyrian army and the departure and murder of Sennacherib.

The unlikelihood that Hezekiah would be so distressed by a letter when he had already defied a threatening demand accompanied by a demonstration in force suggests either that the order of the two messages has been reversed, or that they are parallel accounts of the same incident. The latter seems the more likely, not only because of their striking parallelisms but because of the marked superiority of 36:2–37:4c as historical narrative. The problem is more complex than this, however, for the oracle now appended to the first narrative clearly belongs with the conclusion of the second (with 37:5-7, cf. vss. 36-37), and the oracle now found in 37:22-29 is more appropriate after 37:4d than in its present position. Moreover, in the first narrative as it now stands Hezekiah's messengers come twice to Isaiah (37:2-5), but in 37:21 Isaiah replies without having received a message from the king. In 37:3-4c Hezekiah asks for an oracle against the Assyrian, but in vs. 4d for a prayer for "the remnant"; the first points forward to vss. 22-29, the second to vss. 30-32, two oracles markedly different in spirit and style.

We have thus to reckon not only with the alterations by the editor of Isaiah in the text of his excerpt from Kings, noted above, but with the use made of his sources by the editor of Kings. These sources at this point appear to have been:

(a) The "Annals of the Kings of Judah" (II Kings 20:20) or perhaps a distinct book of temple records, since the point of this excerpt is as much concerned with the despoiling of the temple as with the submission of Hezekiah (cf. also II Kings 16:17-19). From this source were taken II Kings 18:14-16 and perhaps 18:13 (except the date), the latter verse alone being taken over in Isa. 36:1.

(b) An almost contemporary account of the "demonstration in force" with which Sennacherib demanded the surrender of Jerusalem while he was besieging Lachish in 701, and of Hezekiah's appeal to Isaiah for an oracle. This is the source of II Kings 18:17–19:4c, and probably also of the corresponding oracle in 19:20-28 (cf. Isa. 36:1–37:4c, 22-29). These may be selections from the same "prophetic biography" of Isaiah from which was taken the almost equally graphic account of Isaiah's relations with Ahaz under similar circumstances (Isa. 7:1-17).

(c) A later and less historical account of the dealings of Isaiah with Hezekiah, containing narratives in a chronological order which was disarranged by the editor of Kings. This contained:

(i) The story of Hezekiah's illness (II Kings 20:1-11; Isa. 38:1-6, 21-22, 7-8). To this probably belongs the reference to the "fourteenth year" (II Kings 18:13a; Isa. 36:1a; cf. II Kings 18:2; 20:6).

(ii) The story of Merodach-baladan's embassy (II Kings 20:12-19; Isa. 39:1-8).

(iii) The story of Sennacherib's threat and overthrow, somewhat disarranged and edited in the course of its combination with (b) above. This comprises:

The king of Assyria fighting against Libnah (II Kings 19:8b; Isa. 37:8b).

Messengers bring threat; Hezekiah's prayer (II Kings 19:9-19; Isa. 37:9-20).

Isaiah asked to pray, promises Sennacherib's departure and death, in a prose oracle (II Kings 19:4d-7; Isa. 37:4d-7).

Oracle introduction. Sennacherib in third person (II Kings 19:20; Isa. 37:21).

Oracle in verse of which a prose version is given in Isa. 19:6-7; 37:6-7 (II Kings 19:32-34; Isa. 37:33-35).

A "sign" for the remnant (II Kings 19:29-31; Isa. 37:30-32).

The miraculous fulfillment of the prophecy (II Kings 19:35-37; Isa. 37:36-38).

Thus rearranged, the excerpts from source (c) occur in a natural sequence and display common characteristics, such as interest in "signs" and in the protection of the city for the sake of David. It is this source which has developed, from the last words of Isaiah's oracle of defiance (37:29) and the subsequent abrupt departure of Sennacherib, the legend of the miraculous annihilation of Sennacherib's army, which flatly contradicts the acknowledgment in II Kings 18:14-16 that Hezekiah submitted and paid the tribute demanded. The action of the king, like that of his predecessor Ahaz in II Kings 16:7-9, must have been a profound disappointment to the prophet, whose oracle had declared that Yahweh would turn back the Assyrian threat (Isa. 37:22-29). Once more the counsel of faith was rejected by the weak victim of terror and despair. How long a time elapsed after the events recounted in 36:2–37:4c before Hezekiah gave in, we do not know. Sidney Smith says that "the prospect of a long siege caused Hezekiah to submit. . . . The campaign had been absolutely successful, and Pales-tine remained at peace and faithful to Assyria for the remainder of Sennacherib's reign."[2]

D. Other Materials.—The oracles, the memoirs, and the third-person biographical narratives are the principal component parts of the book. Nothing more need be said here of the various subsidiary literary forms—psalms, poems, parables, liturgical matter—which fill out the book, since these are dealt with in the Exegesis where they appear. It remains only to remind the reader that, in addition to the oracles of Isaiah preserved in the memoirs and narratives as well as in the independent oracle collections, there have been inserted a considerable number of anonymous oracles which cannot be attributed to Isaiah, but which belong to later stages in the composition of the book known by his name.

III. Composition

The process of composition whereby the book of Isaiah reached its present form was a long one. Chs. 1–39 certainly contain material from Isaiah himself written in the eighth century, no less certainly material from the period of the Exile, and very probably material from three or even four centuries later still. The task of analysis is a complex one, for we have only the final edition from which to work. The phenomena to be taken into account are so many and various that scholars inevitably differ at least to a degree in their conclusions. Particularly with respect to the problem of distinguishing the authentic words of Isaiah from those of later writers, one must be cautious about going beyond the evidence. Certainly one cannot claim that everything in the book known by Isaiah's name is his, even if the qualification is added, "failing conclusive proof to the contrary." For example, we find the same oracle in the books of Isaiah and Micah (Isa. 2:2-4; Mic. 4:1-3), and obviously it cannot be attributed to the authorship of either prophet merely because it has become associated with a collection of his oracles. Gray's words may be a truism, but they are worth repeating: "What clearly proceeds from Isaiah is to be regarded as his, all that clearly proceeds from other or later writers is not to be regarded as his, and all that is neither clearly his nor clearly not his must be regarded as uncertain."[3]

If anything in the book can be said clearly to be Isaiah's own composition, it is the narrative of his call in ch. 6. Here is the authentic note of profound personal experience, and with it a consecutive and convincing introduction to the man, his times, and his message. The event is

[2] *Cambridge Ancient History*, ed. J. B. Bury, S. A. Cook, and F. E. Adcock (New York: The Macmillan Co., 1923), III, 74.

[3] *Isaiah I-XXXIX*, I, lvii-lviii.

tied to a specific date; it shows us that Isaiah then felt himself to have been called to a prophetic ministry doomed to frustration from the first, and with no prospect for his people but desolation and exile.

Why should the prophet have felt called on to publish such an account? And if he did so, why was this narrative not placed in what would seem to be the logical position at the beginning of the collection of his oracles? An answer to both questions is suggested by the fact that, as we have seen above, the memoirs are continued in ch. 8 and conclude with the statement that the prophet now intends to withdraw from his active ministry, having "sealed up" his testimony (8:16-18). He and the sons referred to in chs. 7–8 are to be living "signs" of the messages he has proclaimed until Yahweh fulfills his declared purpose. The account of the call of Isaiah in ch. 6 thus stood (before the insertion of the biographical narratives of ch. 7) in conjunction with further memoir material which belongs to the time of the Syro-Ephraimite War (734 B.C.; cf. 8:3) and which concludes with a statement that Isaiah is going into retirement. The reason for this is the refusal of his hearers, specifically Ahaz, to heed his words. The inference is clearly that the "testimony" which is now sealed up consists of the oracles which have been proclaimed up to this time, but without effect. And in chs. 1–5, which precede the memoirs, is to be found a collection of oracles, mainly directed to "Judah and Jerusalem," which in its message and background is congruous with the circumstances of Isaiah's ministry up to the time of the Syro-Ephraimite War. The first recording in writing of Isaiah's oracles is thus a collection of the oracles of his early period, to which were appended the autobiographical memoirs now found in 6:1-13; 8:1-8a, 11-18.

This does not mean, however, that all the material now found in chs. 1–5 belonged to this first collection or, for that matter, that no oracles from the prophet's early period are found outside these chapters. The two eschatological oracles in 2:2-5 and 4:2-6 have been inserted in their present position at a later stage in the composition of chs. 1–39; there are also minor insertions in 1:27-31; 3:18-23; 5:24b. On the other hand, the "oracle complex" with refrains now found in 9:8 (Hebrew 9:7) –10:4 has certainly a connection of some kind with ch. 5, where the same refrain appears (5:25) and where the "Woe" of 10:1 is of the same type as the "Woes" of 5:8-12, 18-23. Other material in ch. 10 also appears to come from the time prior to, or at the time of, the Syro-Ephraimite War (viz., vss. 17-19, 22-23, 27d-32, 33-34). These brief oracles appear to have been unattached fragments which were linked later to two oracles concerning the Assyrians in 701; vss. 17-19 are connected by the key word "fire" to vss. 5-16, and vss. 22-23 by the key word "remnant" to vss. 17-19. By association of ideas, vss. 27d-32 and vss. 33-34 are linked with vss. 24-27c.

An important clue for distinguishing the collection of oracles to which ch. 6 was appended is the fact that in 6:11-13 the doom pronounced is the desolation of the land and the exile of its people. This is stated in general terms, without the naming of the invader or the description of the onslaught itself. With this corresponds the punishment threatened in a series of oracles which concern "Judah and Jerusalem" (cf. the titles in 1:1; 2:1), condemning chiefly the injustice and corruption of the upper classes. These are linked to each other by a series of key words:

"Children" ("sons"), "people" (1:2-3)
"People" ("children"), "Sodom," "Gomorrah" (1: 4-9)
"Sodom," "Gomorrah"; "fatherless," "widow" (1: 10-20)
"Fatherless," "widow"; "judges," "counselors" (1:21-26)
"Judge," "counselor"; "women" (3:1-15)
"Daughters of Zion," "war" (3:16-17, 24-26; 4:1)
"Break down the wall," "oppression" ("bloodshed") (5:1-7)
A series of "woes" on oppression and corruption (5:8-13, 17-24a with 10:1-2)

Apart from the omission of the two eschatological oracles and other minor passages noted above, it will be seen that one major unit of chs. 1–5 has been left out of this sequence, i.e., the oracle complex now found in 2:6-22. Not only does the series of key words skip this passage, but it differs from its context also in three important particulars: it is addressed to "the house of Jacob" rather than to Judah or Jerusalem; it denounces idolatry and arrogance before God; and the doom it announces is the terror of earthquake. In the genuine prophecies of Isaiah, "Jacob" or "the house of Jacob" seems to be used only of the Northern Kingdom (cf. 9:8; 17:4; possibly also 8:17); its application to Judah is found elsewhere only in passages which on other grounds appear to be post-Isaianic (cf. 2:3, 5; 10:20-21; 14:1; 27:6, 9; 29:22-23). Idolatry is not a complaint which Isaiah makes concerning Judah (31:7 is a fragment echoing 2:20). The punishment by earthquake reappears only in 5:25, a point significant in connection with the second oracle complex which concludes with 5:25-29(30). These facts point to the intrusion into the series of oracles on Judah and Jerusalem of 2:6-22, which is an older oracle concerning northern Israel. It comes from the time before Isaiah felt the threat of impending war, and therefore probably before the Assyrian armies appeared in the west in 738. Indeed, its message of the humbling of human pride before the majesty of God suggests a moment soon after the vision of Yahweh's exaltation. We know further that an earthquake in Uzziah's reign was remembered for centuries (cf. Zech. 14:5), and Isaiah himself may have lived through this, and thought of it at that time as the most dreadful image of Yahweh's judgment.

A second oracle complex with refrains is now found in 9:8 (Hebrew 9:7)–10:4, and what looks like its conclusion in 5:26-29(30). Here again the opening address is to "Jacob" (9:8 [Hebrew 9:7]), but the doom threatened is that of (Assyrian) invasion (5:26-29[30]), so that the occasion must have been closer to the publication date of the "Judah and Jerusalem" collection than was the case with respect to 2:6-22. This oracle complex was added at the end of chs. 1–5 and the final "Woe" of the series in 5:8-13, 17-24a incorporated in it (10:1-2). The resulting original conclusion to ch. 5 apparently was 10:1-2, 3-4; 9:8-17; 9:18-21; 5:24b-25; 5:26-29(30). At a later date 9:8-21 and 10:1-4 were accidentally omitted, but were appended to the collection after 8:18, together with other unattached fragments now found in 8:19-22 (which appear to follow on 5:30). There is another suggestion of disarrangement in ch. 5 with the intrusion into the series of "Woes" of a threat (vss. 14-16) which seems to have belonged at one time with one of the oracles now combined in 2:6-22.

The next stage in the preparation of the materials from which the book was composed was the issuance by Isaiah himself of a second collection of oracles, many years later but under similar circumstances. The "private oracle" in 30:8 clearly refers to the recording for posterity of the series of oracles in chs. 28–31 which denounces the intrigues with Egypt in 703 or 701. As with the message of Ahaz, these denunciations did not deter the rulers of Judah and they were put in writing as a witness, for the future, of the testimony the prophet had given. The original material of this collection comprises 28:1-4, 7-13, 14-22; 29:15-16; 30:1-7, 8-17; 31:1-3, and contains a series of "Woes" (28:1; 29:15; 30:1; 31:1) and consequent threats. To this were attached soon after 701 some further oracles dealing with the Assyrian invasion of that year which fulfilled Isaiah's inspired forebodings (29:1-8 [an additional "Woe"]; 30:27-33 [in part] 31:4-9).

In addition to these two collections of prophecies made by Isaiah himself in 734-733 and 703-702 as a standing witness against political leaders who ignored his words, there have been preserved a goodly number of his oracles given at various times between 734 and 701 or slightly later. These are now found scattered through the book from 10:5 to 39:8. One group has been used by Isaiah's disciples who wrote the first of the two prophetic biographies, of which selections appear in 7:1-17; 20:1-6, and (as used by the editor of Kings) in 36:2–37:4c, 22-29; the oracles here are 7:4-9, 13-17; 20:3-6; 37:22-29. That this biography was written soon after 701 is highly probable because of the impression given by ch. 36 that it is an eyewitness account. The second and less historical "prophetic biography" from which also the editor of Kings derived material (37:4d-7, 8b-21, 30-38; 38:1-8, 21-22; 39:1-8 [see Exeg. on chs. 36–39]) contains further oracles attributed to Isaiah; these may contain reminiscences of his words, but in their present form come from the author of the biography.

At the close of Isaiah's ministry there were, then, two collections of his oracles which had been published by himself, and a considerable number of unattached oracles, some of which had been or were about to be incorporated by the author of the first prophetic biography. That the two oracle collections were not immediately united is evident from the fact that they are so widely separated in the present arrangement of the book, and that each of them shows signs of independent growth by the inclusion of unattached oracles from the period of the Assyrian threat in 701 (10:5-16, 24-27c; 14:24-27; 29:1-8; 30:27-33 [in part]; 31:4-9).

The next stages in the growth of the first selection were the insertion within it of the two "messianic" or dynastic oracles (9:2-7 [Hebrew 9:1-6] and 11:1-9), which had apparently been composed by Isaiah for special occasions; the insertion of ch. 7 to fill the chronological gap between chs. 6 and 8; and the addition at the end of the collection of other oracles which he had uttered concerning foreign peoples (10:27d-32; 14:28-32; 17:1-6; 18:1-7; 19:1-15[?]; 22:1-14, 15-25, included apparently because Shebna was a foreigner).

The second oracle collection also shows evidence of further growth before it was finally combined with the first collection. There have been attached to it several Isaianic oracles having no clear connection (if any) with the events of 704 and 701 which are the main subjects of this group of prophecies (28:23-29; 29:9-12, 13-14; 32:9-14). The "wisdom" poem of 32:1-8 and the prophetic liturgy of ch. 33 may also have been added at this time, but the weight of probability is that they come from later times.

Three further main stages in the growth of the book around its two nucleuses (in addition to the attachment of minor elements) can be distinguished. The first is the insertion within the group of Isaianic prophecies about foreign peoples of similar oracles from later anonymous prophets (13:1-22; 14:1-23; 15:1–16:14; 21:1-10, 11-12, 13-17; 23:1-14). The second is the joining of the two oracle collections (as now expanded) before the interpolation in both of them of a long series of eschatological prophecies reflecting the outlook of late exilic or postexilic Judaism (2:2-5; 4:2-6; 11:10-16; 19:16-25; 23:15-18; 24:1–27:13; 29:17-21, 22-24; 30:18-26; 32:15-20). With this may be linked the insertion of ch. 12 (psalms). The third stage is the adding to the end of the book of chs. 34–39. Chs. 34–35 are closely related in some way to chs. 40–66, and it is at least possible that the bulk of chs. 34–35; 40–66 had been attached to chs. 1–33 before the insertion of the modified selection from II Kings found in chs. 36–39. The title in 1:1, however, suggests that the book ended with chs. 36–39 when the title was prefixed to it.

The many and complicated literary strands which lie behind the present form of Isa. 1–39 cannot easily be disentangled, but the attempt to separate them must be made if one is to take seriously the question of understanding the nature of the prophetic records. For purposes of reference the view outlined above and in corresponding sections of the Exegesis is now summarized as follows:

1. The first written collection of his prophecies, made by Isaiah for purposes of record immediately after Ahaz' refusal in 734 to heed his message:

    a) The "Judah and Jerusalem" oracles (1:2-3; 1:4-9; 1:10-20; 1:21-26; 3:1-15; 3:16-17, 24-26, 4:1; 5:1-7; 5:8-13, 17-24a plus 10:1-2).

    b) Two earlier oracle complexes inserted in a), with resulting disarrangement of the material in ch. 5, from which 10:1-2 was incorporated in the second oracle complex: (i) 2:6-22 with 5:14-16; (ii) 9:8 [Hebrew 9:7]–10:4 with 5:24b-29 (possibly 5:30; 8:19-20; 8:21-22 belong here).

    c) The "memoirs" (6:1-13; 8:1-8a, 11-18, and probably 8:8b-10).

2. The second written collection of his prophecies, made by Isaiah for purposes of record after his denunciation of the intrigues with Egypt, about 704, had proved of no avail (28:1-4, 7-13; 28:14-22; 29:15-16; 30:1-7; 30:8-17; 31:1-3).

3. The expansion of each collection by the addition or insertion of other oracles relating to the Assyrian threat in 701:

    a) In the first collection: 10:5-16; 10:24-27c; 14:24-27.

    b) In the second collection: 29:1-8; 30:27-33 (in part); 31:4-9.

4. The further expansion of each collection soon after the death of Isaiah by the addition of other authentic material concerning him or his message:

    a) In the first collection:

        (1) The dynastic oracles (9:2-7 [Hebrew 9:1-6]; 11:1-9).

        (2) The biographical narrative (7:1-7) and attached oracles (7:18-25; 20:1-6).

        (3) Minor oracles and fragments (10:17-19; 10:20-21[?]; 10:22-23; 10:33-34; 17:12-14).

        (4) Oracles on foreign peoples (10:27d-32; 14:28-32; 17:1-6; 18:1-7; 19:1-15[?]; 22:1-14; 22:15-25). Of these, the second, third, fifth, and sixth have the special title "doom oracle."

    b) In the second collection: Isaianic oracles of uncertain date (28:23-29; 29:9-12; 29:13-14; 32:9-14).

5. The further expansion of each collection by the addition of similar but non-Isaianic material:

    a) In the first collection:

        (1) Oracles on foreign peoples (13:1-22; 14:1-23; 15:1–16:14; 21:1-10; 21:11-12; 21:13-17; 23:1-14). The title "doom oracle" is given to all but the second of these.

        (2) Short oracles and fragments (1:27-31; 5:24b; 9:1 [Hebrew 8:23]; 17:7-8; 17:9-11).

    b) In the second collection:

        (1) A "wisdom" poem (32:1-8).

        (2) A "prophetic liturgy" (33:1-24).

    N.B. Some of the above material may have been inserted after the joining of the two collections (see 6. below).

6. The joining of the two collections; the subsequent insertion of a series of eschatological prophecies and some psalms, reflecting the outlook of late exilic or postexilic Judaism: (2:2-5; 4:2-6; 11:10-16; 12:1-6; 19:16-25; 23:15-18; 24:1–27:13; 29:17-21; 29:22-24; 30:18-26; 32:15-20).

7. The addition to chs. 1–33 of material from outside sources:

    a) Chs. 34–35.

    b) Chs. 36–39, an excerpt inserted after ch. 35 from II Kings 18:13–20:19 (modified), including selections from two prophetic biographies (36:2–37:4c with 37:22-29; and 37:4d-21, 30-38; 38:1-8, 21-22; 39:1-8).

IV. The Masoretic Text and the Dead Sea Scroll

The Hebrew text of Isaiah on which this commentary is based is derived from three manuscripts: one dated A.D. 895, now in Cairo; a second from the first part of the tenth century, in Aleppo; and a third dated 1008, in Leningrad. Until recently these could claim to be the oldest witnesses to the original text of Isaiah. They represent the culmination of nearly eight centuries of effort to produce a standard text from the various manuscripts and traditions in existence in the second century A.D.

It will at once be apparent that a long period of manuscript transmission links the standard text and its second-century forebears with the earliest publication of Isaiah's oracles in the eighth century B.C. and with the completion of the book in its present form (at the very latest) in the second century B.C. The text has been transmitted with great care and fidelity. Nevertheless, in the course of time the traditional text has acquired and transmitted some defects, originally due to errors in copying or to the deterioration of manuscripts. Attention is drawn to these at various points in the Exegesis, and suggestions are made for restoration of what seems to have been the original form of the text. These conjectural emendations are not wholly subjective, for they are based as far as possible on supplementary evidence from the ancient versions in Greek, Latin, Syriac, and Aramaic as to the form of the Hebrew text when these versions were made; and also on the usages of other parts of Isaiah and the Hebrew Bible generally where the reading of the text is clear.

Recently there has become available a further witness to the Hebrew text of Isaiah with the discovery in 1947 and the publication in 1950 of the manuscript known as the 'Ain Feshka or Dead Sea Scroll of Isaiah.[4] The date of this manuscript (and of other manuscripts found at the same time, including an incomplete second copy of Isaiah) is still in dispute at the time of this writing. The majority of scholars assign it to the first or second century B.C., while others hold that it was written between the third and eighth centuries A.D. In either case, it is the oldest witness in existence to the Hebrew text of Isaiah. It is therefore most significant that the newly found manuscripts support the consonantal Masoretic Text, except in a few particulars which are noted in the Exegesis.

V. The Man, His Times and His Message

The superscription of the book (1:1) tells us that Isaiah prophesied in the reigns of four kings of Judah—Uzziah, Jotham, Ahaz, and Hezekiah—and from 6:1 we learn further that his call to the prophetic office took place in the last year of Uzziah's reign. It is notoriously difficult to reconcile all the biblical and external evidence bearing on the regnal dates of these four kings of Judah, and the reader will find considerable discrepancies between the conclusions reached by different authorities. The dates given by George A. Barrois [5] seem the most probable: Uzziah, 783-742; Jotham, regent 750-742, king 742-735; Ahaz, 735-715; Hezekiah, 715-687.

A. Early Ministry (742-734).—If these dates are correct, Isaiah began his ministry in the year 742, the very year when the heavy hand of Assyria was first felt by Israel after a long period

during which she had been unmolested. According to II Kings 15:19, "Pul the king of Assyria" (i.e., Tiglath-pileser III, 745-727) invaded (or threatened to invade) northern Israel and exacted a heavy tribute from Menahem. This near approach of the Assyrian armies would give point to the doom announced in 6:11-13 in terms of the laying waste of the land and the exile of its people. The doom is pictured alternatively in the early oracles of 2:6-22 in terms of a terrible earthquake, such as had occurred in the reign of Uzziah (cf. Amos 1:1; Zech. 14:5), presumably not long before 742. The failure of this earthquake to disturb seriously the people of the Northern Kingdom is referred to in another oracle from Isaiah's early period (9:9-10 [Hebrew 9:8-9]). The oracles concerning "Judah and Jerusalem" in chs. 1–5, which confine their condemnation to internal conditions in Judah—religious disloyalty, social injustice, the depravity and rapacity of the upper classes—seem to have been spoken in the reign of Jotham. The "Shear-jashub" oracle, on the other hand (10:22-23), makes reference to a war situation; it may have been Isaiah's warning against the attack on the Ammonites recorded in II Chr. 27:5, "Only a remnant of them will return." From the fact that in 734 the son named Shear-jashub was old enough to accompany his father to a meeting with Ahaz (7:3), it is clear that this oracle had been spoken several years before when the child was born and named (cf. 8:1, 3).

B. The Withdrawal (734-715).—This first and most intense period of Isaiah's activity came to an end with the prophet's withdrawal and the recording of the first collection of his prophecies, after Ahaz had refused to heed his word from Yahweh and had appealed to the Assyrian king for support against the Syro-Ephraimite coalition. While it may be that some oracles of uncertain date are to be placed in the interval between 734 and the accession of Hezekiah in 715, there is no clear evidence of this. It appears rather that Isaiah spoke no more during the lifetime of Ahaz, in fulfillment of his purpose as announced in 8:16-18.

C. Middle Ministry (715-705).—With the death of Ahaz a new day dawned, and Isaiah felt himself free once more to prophesy. The oracle in 14:28-32 is specifically dated at this time, and the passages in 9:2-7 (Hebrew 9:1-6) and 11:1-9 are dynastic oracles, probably composed by Isaiah for use at religious ceremonies connected with the accession and coronation of Hezekiah. From this time until at least as late as 701, the year of Sennacherib's invasion of Judah, Isaiah from time to time pronounced his oracles. One oracle (20:1-6) definitely, and another (22:1-14) probably, belong to the year

---

[4] Millar Burrows, ed., The Dead Sea Scrolls of St. Mark's Monastery (New Haven: American Schools of Oriental Research, 1950), Vol. I.

[5] Interpreter's Bible, Vol. I, pp. 146-47.

711, "the year that Tartan came unto Ashdod, when Sargon the king of Assyria sent him" (20:1). The new Ethiopian (Twenty-fifth) Dynasty in Egypt had instigated this revolt, but the brunt of Sargon's punishment was felt by the Philistines, notably Ashdod. Shortly before this are to be dated two oracles (18:1-7; 22:15-25), and perhaps part of a third (19:1-15), which reveal Isaiah's attitude at that time to the intrigues of Egypt against Assyria.

These oracles, together with the prophet's remaining utterances to the close of his ministry, display a marked change in the nature of his message and the object of his concern. At the beginning of his prophetic work Isaiah denounced the willful pride and wickedness and the religious disloyalty of his people. He dwelt particularly on the corruption and oppression of their rulers. On these he pronounced a divine doom in terms of earthquake, war, and exile. Only at the close of this period, in the time of the external threat from the Syro-Ephraimite alliance, does he call for faith in Yahweh as the nation's sole security (7:4, 9; 8:12-13). But in Hezekiah's reign Isaiah lifts his eyes to a farther horizon. The working out of Yahweh's purpose in the area of historic events is that on which he now concentrates his attention. True, he denounces the intrigues of political leaders who scheme to alter the course of events (28:14-15; 29:15-16; 30:1-5; 31:1-3), and who are themselves proud, irreligious, and dissolute (22:15-25; 28:1-21; 29:9-14). But in the years 714-711, and later, he has little or nothing to say about social injustice and oppression.

D. Later Ministry (705-701?).—Another group of oracles—those which formed the nucleus of the second collection recorded by Isaiah himself as a testimony for the future—were uttered at a time when the Judean political leaders were taking the initiative in seeking support from Egypt (28:7-13, 14-22; 29:15-16; 30:1-7; 31:1-3). Following the death of the Assyrian Sargon II (722-705), the Chaldean prince Merodach-baladan tried to organize a general revolt against Sargon's successor Sennacherib; the story of his envoys' visit to Hezekiah is told in ch. 39. That Hezekiah agreed to participate in the revolt is clear from that story. When, however, Sennacherib took prompt action in 703 and decisively defeated Merodach-baladan in Babylonia, Hezekiah, who was implicated already, made urgent overtures to Egypt for help against the imminent threat of Assyrian vengeance. Isaiah denounced this "covenant with death" (28:15) and its false hope of finding security through military alliances. He declares once more that faith in her own God, the Lord of history, was Judah's only secure foundation. But though Hezekiah seems to have been uneasy about the outcome, it was

too late for him to draw back from a plot which by then involved not only Judah and Egypt, but also Tyre and Sidon, Arvad, Byblos, Moab, Ammon, and Edom. The revolt began with risings in the Philistine cities against the officers of the Assyrian overlord, and one of these, Padi of Ekron, was handed over in chains to Hezekiah.

Sennacherib moved quickly in 701 to crush the rebellion. First he subdued the Phoenician cities; then he recaptured Askalon and Ekron, turning aside for an easy victory over an advancing Egyptian army. The rest of the conspirators submitted without a fight—all except Hezekiah. The Judean king hung on while forty-six of his fortified cities fell one by one before the Assyrian onslaught, until he himself (as Sennacherib puts it) "like a caged bird" was shut up "in Jerusalem, his royal city." Under the hopeless prospect, Hezekiah eventually decided to submit and pay tribute, so that Jerusalem escaped destruction.

In those critical days Isaiah the prophet exemplified in his own person the resources of spiritual strength of which he spoke. He recognized in the Assyrian king the instrument of Yahweh's chastisement for the sins of Judah, but he saw also that the conqueror's pride must be humbled when he had served God's purpose (10:5-16; 37:22-29). The carrying forward of the divine purpose required that Jerusalem should survive and the burden of the invader depart (14:24-27; 29:7-8; 30:30-31; 31:4-5).

With this message Isaiah, so far as the records go, concluded his prophetic ministry. His was a long life. It was divided, as we have seen, into two periods of active and significant activity, separated by a long interval of withdrawal. His latest oracles show him to be still at the height of his powers, still acutely responsive to Yahweh's word, and still brilliant and powerful in composing its literary form for publication.

VI. Personality of the Prophet

Isaiah, indeed, was an aristocrat of the spirit. He moved like a prince among men. He spoke with the dignity and moral authority which he knew befitted an ambassador of the Most High, and it is evident that he was a product of the finest culture of Judah. Like Jeremiah, Ezekiel, and others, he may have been a priest, for his vision of God came to him as he stood where the priests stood "between the porch and the altar" (Joel 2:17) where he could hear the door-pivots vibrate in the sills at the sound of the shout (6:4). In this connection it may be significant that he was able to call on the chief priest at Jerusalem to attest a written oracle (8:2; cf. II Kings 16:10), and that only once did he associate priests with prophets and secular leaders in his denunciations (28:7; cf. 3:2; 9:15 [Hebrew 9:14]; 29:10). Here, and in 1:10-17; 29:13, he discloses an intimate acquaintance with what went on in the temple.

At the same time Isaiah shows that he is especially familiar with the way of life of the ruling classes. He accuses them of failing in their responsibility to maintain justice (1:23; 3:13-15; 5:7), of rapacity (3:14; 5:8), of moral depravity (5:11-12, 18-22; 28:7-8), of ostentation and self-indulgence at the expense of the poor (3:14-16; 5:23) and of brazen irreligion (5:19; 28:14-22). That he seems to have had easy access to the ruling king (7:1-17) suggests that he may have been a member of the king's council. He was apparently called on to compose the dynastic oracles for the accession ceremonies of Hezekiah. Again and again he concerns himself with questions of government and foreign policy (3:1-12; 7:1-17; 8:1-8*b*, 11-15; 10:24-27*c*; 14:24-32; 20:1-6; 30:1-17; 31:1-5).

Although himself a man of the city, Isaiah draws many of his most graphic images from close and sympathetic observation of rural life and conditions. He has watched the animals returning to their stable (1:3) and has observed the solitariness of the watchman's hut (1:8; 21:11-12). He knows what must be done to prepare a vineyard, and which are the best vines to plant (5:1-7). He can estimate the amount of grain a field should yield (5:10). Moreover, he knows the effects of a storm upon the crops (28:2; 29:5).

A few further details about Isaiah the man may be found in or inferred from his oracles and the narrative records. He must have been young, yet mature, when he was called to be a prophet, for nearly forty years later (or more, if a date as early as 742 is accepted for the death of Uzziah) he was still in full vigor. At the time of the Syro-Ephraimite crisis he was married (8:3). There are some rather slight indications that he may at times have acted as a physician (1:6; 3:7). That he gathered about him early in his ministry a group of disciples has often been inferred from 8:16, but the meaning of this verse is uncertain (see Exeg.). On the other hand, 8:18 implies that the prophet and his sons—along with the recorded message—are the sole continuing representatives at this time of his prophetic testimony.

VII. Theology of the Prophet

Something must now be said in conclusion about the theology of Isaiah, the principal themes of his prophetic message, and his place in the story of Old Testament prophecy. To his experience in the temple in the year that King Uzziah died can be traced the prophet's characteristic understanding of the nature of God, and of the divine relationship to man and his world, which constitutes his theology and provides the substance of his message.

To Isaiah, Yahweh is the inexpressibly exalted One, the sovereign Lord. His exaltation must be experienced in order to be realized, for it is not merely a dimension of infinite immensity and power confronting man but an absolute moral difference. The ethically neutral idea of "holiness" or divinity takes its quality from the goodness and the righteous purpose of Yahweh. The measure of his exaltation is the measure of his justice (5:16). In his presence righteousness itself is defined, and there can be no other. In addition, this sovereign righteousness is personal in its relationships with men. It lays its demand upon their conscience and makes its claim to their unquestioning obedience. The will of God declares itself to man and makes known a purpose for his life in the world of peoples. The "Holy One of Israel" is Israel's king, the sovereign power in her history and in that of the other nations with which she comes in contact. He is her "Maker" (17:7) and her life is in his hands. The divine acts may not be discernible by men, but they are the determinants of history (5:12, 19; 28:23-29; 29:14). God's manifest presence, his "glory," fills the whole earth. The "Holy One of Israel" is not like other "holy ones"; in his nature, in his universality and supremacy, in the declaration through his prophet of his will and far-reaching purpose, in the "strange acts" which carry that purpose forward, and finally in the claim he makes upon the response of a people for the fulfillment of that purpose, the God of Isaiah and of Israel is unique.

In the presence of such exaltation and sovereign righteousness Isaiah became intensely aware of his and his people's creatureliness and moral evil. He found that the sacrifices and ceremonial purifications of the temple rites were insufficient; God was weary of them, and of men who honored him with their lips while their hearts were far from him (1:14; 29:13). Isaiah's lips and the lips of his people were morally unclean, their minds were dulled by sensuality and materialism, their wills were infected by rebellious pride. What Yahweh demanded of them was that they should become clean, that they should cease to do evil and learn to do right (1:16). Their injustice to the innocent, their oppression of the poor, their trust in material things, their self-indulgence and pride (1:23; 2:7-8; 3:12-15) had reduced them to a condition in which they could not discern the presence and activity of God. They could not even distinguish any more between good and evil (5:19-20; 29:9-12). As a result, they relied upon unstable human supports for their community and sought frantically in foreign alliances the political security which could come only from reliance on the Governor of history himself (3:1-15; 7:9; 28:14-22; 30:1-7; 31:1-3).

Yet "this people"—the phrase is indignant—were Yahweh's own people, the sons of his home and upbringing (1:2-3), the vineyard he had prepared with loving care (5:1-7). Isaiah speaks of the choice of Israel only in general terms, and makes no reference to the Exodus tradition. Nevertheless Israel was for him the people of Zion, the sanctuary of the divine King, and a city with foundations unseen and eternal (28:16). But the walls were not built on these foundations and were further weakened by perverse refusal to abide by the laws of a sound architecture (30:9-14). The city of integrity had become a harlot among cities! (1:21.)

To Isaiah in his vision the realization of the fearful contradiction between sovereign holiness and human sin could mean only one thing—that he was "done for," and his people with him. For a people who are unclean and choose to remain unclean there can be no alternative to judgment. The working of the moral law of God is inexorable (1:18-20). A "day" is coming when the pride of man and his rebellion, which is idolatry, will be cast down utterly before the terror of the Most High (2:9-22). A destruction is decreed which will be the overflowing of the divine righteousness (10:23; 28:22). The Champion of the poor is entering into judgment with the elders and princes of his people (3:13-15).

The fire of judgment may destroy (5:24; 9:19 [Hebrew 9:18]) or, like the hot stone of the vision, it may cleanse (1:25-26). The Lord has not utterly forsaken his people so long as a solitary remnant remains to the "daughter of Zion" (1:4-9). His purpose is chastisement, that his people may turn again to him (9:13 [Hebrew 9:12]; 10:12). Only obdurate evil will make ultimate destruction inevitable (28:22). For God is able by divine cleansing to take away the sin of those who recognize it and repent. The original threat—"only a remnant shall return"—becomes a promise—"a remnant shall return unto the mighty God" (7:3; 10:20-23).

The transformation from threat to promise depends on faith, which is a response to the vision of the divine sovereignty, and marks the acceptance of the divine cleansing and readiness to obey. Isaiah tells Ahaz to pay heed to God and wait in quiet confidence, for trust in him is the foundation and cornerstone of life (7:4, 9; cf. 28:16; 30:15). What happens will not be the result of man's contriving and his doing; God also is wise and he will act (31:2-3); he will do mighty deeds, as in the days of old (29:14). This confidence means the setting at rest of man's anxieties and the refreshing of his spirit (28:12; 30:15). The movement of events is under God's control. The enemy cannot threaten God's people mortally unless it is his will (7:7). The Assyrians, as instruments of the divine chastisement, can go only so far and no farther (10:12-17). Faith can discern the "signs" of what Yahweh's purpose is and is to be (7:14; 20:3-4). The goal of that purpose is that Judah should become in truth as well as in name "his people" and should survive as his witness in the world (1:26). The Lord is both her judge and her defender (14:24-27; 31:5).

Isaiah shares with the other pre-exilic prophets much of his thought of God and of God's relationship to the life of man. He shares with them many of the particular themes of his prophesying. His distinctive emphasis and contribution lie in his vivid realization of the exaltation of God as being an ethical exaltation, and in his discovery of faith as quiet and active confidence in the unseen but conclusive participation of God in the affairs of men. No one can read the story of Isaiah's vision in the temple without a new understanding of what is meant by religious experience. No one can listen receptively to the matchless language of his oracles without hearing in them the word of the God who sent Isaiah to proclaim it. What this prophet has to say concerning sin, righteousness, and judgment, other prophets have said. But when he lays bare his soul's experience of the sovereign grace of God, when he looks on life with unveiled eyes and sees events shaped by a sovereign purpose, when he calls for that faith which is the resting of life upon a sovereign goodness, he makes his own distinctive contribution to prophecy and to religion. These are the words which he was sent to speak. They are revelation.

VIII. Selected Bibliography

Box, G. H. *The Book of Isaiah*. London: Isaac Pitman & Sons, 1908.

DUHM, BERNHARD. *Das Buch Jesaia* (Göttingen Handkommentar zum Alten Testament"). 4th ed. Göttingen: Vandenhoeck & Ruprecht, 1922.

GRAY, GEORGE BUCHANAN. *A Critical and Exegetical Commentary on the Book of Isaiah I-XXXIX* ("International Critical Commentary"). New York: Charles Scribner's Sons, 1912. Vol. I.

KISSANE, EDWARD J. *The Book of Isaiah*. Dublin: Browne & Nolan, 1941. Vol. I.

PROCKSCH, OTTO. *Jesaia I* ("Kommentar zum Alten Testament"). Leipzig: A. Deichert, 1930.

ROGERS, ROBERT W., "Isaiah," *The Abingdon Bible Commentary*, ed. F. C. Eiselen, Edwin Lewis, and D. G. Downey. New York and Nashville: Abingdon-Cokesbury, 1929.

SKINNER, JOHN. *The Book of the Prophet Isaiah* ("The Cambridge Bible"). Rev. ed. Cambridge: Cambridge University Press, 1915.

SMITH, GEORGE ADAM. *The Book of Isaiah*. New and rev. ed. London: Hodder & Stoughton, 1927.

ISAIAH

TEXT, EXEGESIS, AND EXPOSITION, CHS. 1-39

1 The vision of Isaiah the son of Amoz, which he saw concerning Judah and Jerusalem in the days of Uzziah, Jotham, Ahaz, *and* Hezekiah, kings of Judah.	**1** The vision of Isaiah the son of Amoz, which he saw concerning Judah and Jerusalem in the days of Uzzi'ah, Jotham, Ahaz, and Hezeki'ah, kings of Judah.

I. "They Have Rebelled Against Me" (1:1–5:24a)

The first section of the book consists of prophetic oracles directed to Judah and Jerusalem, mainly condemnations and threats from Isaiah's early period, but incorporating also promises, some of which at least are post-Isaianic.

A. Superscription (1:1)

1:1. This verse was the title of the book of Isaiah when it ended with the narratives of the reign of Hezekiah in chs. 36–39, before the anonymous prophecies of chs. 40–66 had become attached to it. It appears to be an expansion of a briefer heading—**The vision of Isaiah the son of Amoz, which he saw concerning Judah and Jerusalem**—which would be appropriate for one of the earlier and smaller collections of material now found in chs. 1–5 and later chapters but is not suitable for a volume now including oracles on northern Israel (9:8-21 [Hebrew 9:7-20]) and an extended section on foreign peoples (chs. 13–23). The lateness of the title in its present form is shown also by its identification of the kings named as **kings of Judah,** indicating that the days of the monarchy lay in the past.

The vision may indicate that the early collection of which this was the title included the narrative in ch. 6; but the word here, as in Obad. 1:1 and Nah. 1:1, may have the later weakened meaning of "recorded prophecy." **Isaiah the son of Amoz:** The prophet's name means either "Yahweh is salvation" or "Yahweh will give salvation (deliverance)"; the second meaning is to be preferred. The name of the prophet's father is spelled in Hebrew quite differently from the name of the prophet Amos; there is no connection between them.

1:1-31. The Heart of Isaiah's Message.—Here is a tremendous indictment of an apostate nation. The charge is the blindness, the insensibility, the brutish stupidity of a people steeped in sin. The prophet is witness against them. In a sense the chapter is an epitome of Isaiah's whole message and ministry. In this series of oracles he proceeds from accusation to judgment, and on to the divine promise of mercy in terms of repentance and obedience. Throughout the book the changes are rung on these themes.

For this was Isaiah called, that in the name and by the authority of God he might confront his people with their sin, declare the imminence of their judgment, awaken their penitence, and preach the gospel of redeeming mercy. No one who reads this chapter with a sensitive mind can escape the awful relevance of its message for our own age, or miss the evangel which redeems a word of judgment from despair, and lightens the predicament of men with a divine hope. Every section of it speaks to our condition.

2 Hear, O heavens, and give ear, O earth: for the LORD hath spoken; I have nourished and brought up children, and they have rebelled against me.	2 Hear, O heavens, and give ear, O earth; for the LORD has spoken: "Sons have I reared and brought up, but they have rebelled against me.

B. A BOOKLET OF ORACLES (1:2–2:5)
1. ISRAEL'S INGRATITUDE (1:2-3)

2-3. This brief and poignant poem is not strictly an oracle but the formal opening of an early collection of Isaiah's prophecies published by the prophet himself. It bears the stamp of Isaiah's mind and style, and just as clearly is introductory to a series of compositions of which it strikes the keynote. The literary form of the exordium is traditional, as exemplified in the opening verses of the early poems in Gen. 49; Deut. 32; Judg. 5. Just as in Amos 3:9 and Mic. 6:2 the scandal of Israel's behavior is published to the world, so here the hosts of heaven and earth's inhabitants are called upon to bear witness to her base ingratitude and obdurate rebellion.

The popular idea that the conception of the fatherhood of God is peculiar to the N.T. is sufficiently refuted by such passages as this and Hos. 11:1-4 from as early as the eighth century B.C. The Lord speaks here as a father deeply moved by grief and anger because his love and care have been rewarded by callous disregard and open rebellion. From helpless childhood to maturity he has cared for his sons with a love which still they do not discern, though even dumb animals recognize their master's care and find their way home to the place where they are fed. But the **people** of God are as unresponsive as inanimate objects; they do not think; they do not realize what has been done for them, and would not care if they did; they have no sense of belonging.

The LORD hath spoken, i.e., to the prophet, and has commissioned him to proclaim the divine plaintiff's grievous charge against his people. He is the mouthpiece of the divine word and shares its grief and indignation.

2-3. The Father's Sorrow.—In this brief and poignant poem there is a foreshadowing of the greatest article of our faith in God, viz., his fatherhood. The full disclosure of that divine truth we rightly ascribe to Jesus Christ, who has shown us the Father. But it belongs to the greatness of Isaiah's lonely soul that he saw, if only "through a glass, darkly" (I Cor. 13:12), what it took the Cross to confirm: that God is love, and that amidst the sin and shame of human life it is a father who pleads with his children. There is much in this chapter which suggests God is our accuser, but at the very outset the prophet shows us not the menace of judgment but the yearning of a father's heart. That is a sorrowful cry,

Sons have I reared and brought up,
but they have rebelled against me.

This is not the thunder which is yet to roll through Isaiah's pages; it is the sorrow of a father for the sons he has lost, the agony of a father whose concern that they might understand and give answer is mocked by the dull stupor, the fatal inertia, of unbelieving and uncaring hearts.

The modern world has reason to acknowledge the fact of the moral law and its inexorable operation in life; contemporary history proclaims the judgment of God on the sin of man. It is not difficult in such an age to preach the anger of a righteous God against a people who have rebelled and have flouted his law. The emphasis unescapably rests on God as judge and accuser; and rightly so, for the whole history of the twentieth century is a lurid vindication of the law that "whatsoever a man soweth, that shall he also reap" (Gal. 6:7) and that "the wages of sin is death" (Rom. 6:23). But in all that has befallen us, in the destruction and chaos which our own hands have wrought, we are not inclined to think of God as father: there is no place in our thinking for the injured love of God, but only for his wrath. It is profoundly significant that Isaiah, whose fate it was to pronounce a judgment against the people he loved, before he said a single word about the divine anger, pleaded with men to consider the suffering of a father's love over his lost children. Our world will begin to be saved when it recovers faith in the fatherhood of God and, like the prodigal coming to himself, cries, "I will arise and go to my father" (Luke 15:18).

Only a personal God can matter for religion; yet that is the very faith which the modern world finds most difficult to make its own. The

3 The ox knoweth his owner, and the ass his master's crib: *but* Israel doth not know, my people doth not consider.

4 Ah sinful nation, a people laden with iniquity, a seed of evildoers, children that are corrupters: they have forsaken the LORD, they have provoked the Holy One of Israel unto anger, they are gone away backward.

3 The ox knows its owner,
　and the ass its master's crib;
but Israel does not know,
　my people does not understand."

4 Ah, sinful nation,
　a people laden with iniquity,
offspring of evildoers,
　sons who deal corruptly!
They have forsaken the LORD,
　they have despised the Holy One of
　　Israel,
　they are utterly estranged.

Children: Better, **sons,** i.e., "The sons I have (begotten) and reared have rebelled against me." The LXX reads "have begotten" for the first of the two synonymous words meaning "to rear," and is perhaps to be preferred. While the relationship of Israel to Yahweh is by adoption, the adoptive formula, as in Ps. 2:7, is in the form of a declaration of paternity. **His owner:** Strictly, "his purchaser." **Knows** has here the sense of "comes to know through association." But from the more deeply intimate human-divine relationship of a Father's home, Israel has learned nothing. **Crib:** Better, "feeding place," "stable," i.e., the hard floor of the enclosure where domestic animals were kept; cf. Job 39:9, "Will the wild ox . . . stay in your stable?" (Moffatt) .

2. DIRE STRAITS OF ZION (1:4-9)

Although this oracle follows the preceding one in such good sequence that they often are taken as one oracle, vss. 4-9 form a distinct literary unit. It opens with the characteristic formula of the "reproach" or public denunciation, "Shame on . . . ." The historical background also is distinctive; the Judean towns and countryside have been ravaged by an enemy, so that Jerusalem is isolated. This happened in 701 when Sennacherib shut up Hezekiah in his capital "like a bird in a cage," but it may have happened also earlier in Isaiah's lifetime as an episode in one of the many wars of which we have little or no record.

Speaking in his own name rather than as the voice of Yahweh (as in vss. 2-3), the

disclosures of science as to the structure of our universe vastly increase the sense of man's insignificance. It is possible to think of God as caring for a world "not too big to be cozy," but that comfortable faith grows dim when one considers this wayside planet swinging in immeasurable space, in a universe vast beyond man's conceiving. How can God with the business of such a universe on his hands care for our pigmy world among the crowding giants of space? So it is that much of our literature is haunted with unhappiness and fear. By an intellectual compulsion men may concede the necessity of a First Cause, but belief in a God who cares is beyond them. Mechanistic philosophers, describing the nature of this self-acting universe, find no room for such a God. At best, those reluctant to abandon all faith may seek for God in the gaps which research has not yet explored; but for multitudes the old steadying faith in a God who has his hand on our world

has gone, leaving that world wounded, confused, broken, and afraid.

Yet observe that the humanistic doctrine of the adequacy of man for his own salvation has had bitter refutation. Neither the United Nations, the Atlantic Pact, nor any other scheme of man's devising can finally allay the fear or quicken the hopes of the human heart. Only faith in a God who has to do with this world, and with whom we have to do, faith in a sovereign power which is not the cold abstraction of infinite force but the omnipotence of love, only faith in a heavenly Father can redeem us from sin and the despair it begets. Isaiah's faith in such a God was a divine surmise; ours may be a great certainty because of Jesus Christ, through whom, as Peter said, we "do believe in God" (I Pet. 1:21) .

4-9. A Desperate Need.—In this reproach there is a clear reference to a definite historical situation. It is one of the oracles which may be

5 ¶ Why should ye be stricken any more? ye will revolt more and more: the whole head is sick, and the whole heart faint.

6 From the sole of the foot even unto the head *there is* no soundness in it; *but* wounds, and bruises, and putrifying sores: they have not been closed, neither bound up, neither mollified with ointment.

---

5 Why will you still be smitten,
    that you continue to rebel?
The whole head is sick,
    and the whole heart faint.
6 From the sole of the foot even to the head,
    there is no soundness in it,
but bruises and sores
    and bleeding wounds;
they are not pressed out, or bound up,
    or softened with oil.

---

prophet denounces the obduracy and unfaithfulness of Yahweh's people, with whom at the same time he identifies himself (vs. 9; cf. 6:5). He expostulates with them for the stubborn stupidity which has brought ever-new punishments for their contemptuous indifference to God. To such straits have they been reduced that only through an "uncovenanted mercy" have they escaped so far the complete obliteration which overtook the proverbial "cities of the plain."

4. **Ah:** A colorless rendering of the emotion-charged word *hôy*, which is an exclamation of censure or derision like "Shame!" **Nation . . . people, . . . seed, . . . children:** Four terms progressively concentrating on the idea of kinship. The masses have missed the mark, the Lord's people are burdened with guilt, whole clans are criminal, the sons of the home have become degenerate. The correlative clause explains why: they have contemptuously **forsaken the LORD. The Holy One of Israel,** i.e., the Deity proper to Israel. The phrase is a favorite of Isaiah's, with whom, so far as our records go, it originated. Holiness is the essential quality of deity and of persons, actions, and things to the degree that they are associated with deity. Originally a cultic term, it is itself ethically neutral in meaning and mirrors the ethical qualities of the god to whom it refers. The clumsy **they are gone away backward** (KJV) looks like a marginal note which has crept into the text; if retained, **utterly estranged** (RSV) is a smoother translation.

5. **Why?** Better, "where?" i.e., upon what (part of the body)? The picture is that of a servant cruelly beaten for repeated misdemeanors.

6. **No soundness in it:** "No spot is well," but only "bruises and welts and open wounds, uncleansed, unbandaged, and unsoothed with oil."

---

dated. In 701 Sennacherib invaded the land and Hezekiah's refuge in Jerusalem became his prison, while the enemy worked its cruel will on the hapless nation. Vss. 7-9 are Isaiah's memory of those terrible days. We cannot realize what an Assyrian invasion meant. There was about it a deliberation in slaughter and destruction unknown in modern mechanized warfare. A single shell or a burst of machine-gun fire may obliterate a score of men; but when the Assyrian "came down like a wolf on the fold" it took time to kill twenty. From village to village, from house to house, the invaders waded literally through blood to victory, and passed leaving a land blackened, destroyed, dead. There is no poetry but stark realism in these lines,

> Your country lies desolate
>   your cities are burned with fire;
> in your very presence
>   aliens devour your land.

That was the invader's "scorched earth" policy in eighth-century B.C. warfare.

Isaiah saw it all and put his own interpretation on it. Patriot as he was, feeling the sheer tragedy and heartbreak of it, his commission to speak for God for the moment silenced his sympathy. It is impossible to capture in the translation the force of that opening *hôy!* **Ah sinful nation.** There is indignation in it, even derision; not the gloating of a small soul over the suffering of those who have mocked his word, but a sense of the vindication of the divine warning in this judgment. The prophet wastes no words in condoling with the nation. They have brought this tragedy on themselves; he piles up the adjectives of his accusation: **sinful, laden with iniquity, offspring of evildoers, corrupters, forsaken, despisers of the Holy One of Israel.** One may well object that when a people are down, it is no time to kick them by reminding them that they themselves are responsible for

7 Your country *is* desolate, your cities *are* burned with fire: your land, strangers devour it in your presence, and *it is* desolate, as overthrown by strangers.
 	
8 And the daughter of Zion is left as a cottage in a vineyard, as a lodge in a garden of cucumbers, as a besieged city.
 	
9 Except the LORD of hosts had left unto us a very small remnant, we should have been as Sodom, *and* we should have been like unto Gomorrah.
	7 Your country lies desolate,
	   your cities are burned with fire;
	in your very presence
	   aliens devour your land;
	   it is desolate, as overthrown by aliens.
	8 And the daughter of Zion is left
	   like a booth in a vineyard,
	like a lodge in a cucumber field,
	   like a besieged city.
	
	9 If the LORD of hosts
	   had not left us a few survivors,
	we should have been like Sodom,
	   and become like Gomor'rah.

7. The devastation of war was almost as terrible then as now, especially after invasion by the Assyrians, who were specialists in the techniques of military terrorism. **As overthrown by strangers:** Lit., "like an overthrow by [of] strangers." Ewald's suggested reading, "like the overthrow of Sodom," has much to commend it.

8. The daughter of Zion: The city personified as a young woman; cf. Amos 5:2. Originally the name of the Jebusite stronghold captured by David (II Sam. 5:7), Zion became a poetic name for the city as associated with David and his dynasty. The name Jerusalem, like the city itself, is many centuries older than his time (cf. G. E. Wright and F. V. Filson, eds., *Westminster Historical Atlas to the Bible* [Philadelphia: Westminster Press, 1945], p. 97). In three deft illustrative phrases the prophet here emphasizes the complete isolation of the capital.

9. The LORD of hosts, i.e., of the heavenly court and armies (cf. Judg. 5:20; Josh. 5:14), a favorite prophetic term (especially with Isaiah, Amos, Jeremiah, Haggai, Zechariah, and Malachi) to emphasize the majestic authority of God. **A very small**

their own misery and reap only a just retribution. National morale is not likely to be recovered by denunciation. No! But if the nation is still without sense of guilt, if self-pity, not repentance, is all they feel, it belongs to their very salvation to have the truth about themselves thrust in their faces. It is of the mercy of God that sometimes for our redemption he must be merciless. So Isaiah, looking on a smoldering land, hearing the wailing of women mourning their dead, and yet failing to discern anywhere the tokens of a nation brokenhearted for all they have been and done, rounds on them with scorn. He shows them what they are, a people outwardly defeated, inwardly corrupt, sick unto death, in mortal agony, and yet still rebellious, still unaware of the necessity of penitence and their need of God, while over all the scene of desolation broods the figure of **the Holy One of Israel,** of whose outraged justice and flouted law this tragedy is the outcome. It would be the end of Israel, and finis would be written in blood and tears to the story of an apostate nation, but for one thing, one tremendous fact: the justice of a holy God is matched by his mercy and his love. The oracle closes with that.

One can discern a note of amazement in Isaiah's voice as he proclaims the divine mercy. Surely at this point he laid down his pen and wrote no more for a little, lost in wonder at the patience of him who, if the Lord of Hosts, is also the Father of his children.

There is a dreadful relevance in all this. Twice already in this century the world has been swept into the blasphemy and stupidity of war; every phrase of Isaiah's description of stricken Israel has been true of modern life. Had Isaiah come upon the scene, he would have gazed in horror on an infinitely vaster tragedy than he saw on the little battlefields of Israel; but his judgment would in no wise be other than that which he flung at his own nation.

They have forsaken the LORD,
   they have despised the Holy One of Israel.

That is the root cause of all that has befallen us. But it is *that* which we will not acknowledge. Historians will yet write their acute analysis of the causes of two world wars, they will trace the interplay of forces, national, political, economic, which finally lead to strife, they may name the agents who were the head and front of the

10 ¶ Hear the word of the Lord, ye rulers of Sodom; give ear unto the law of our God, ye people of Gomorrah.

10 Hear the word of the Lord,
    you rulers of Sodom!
Give ear to the teaching of our God,
    you people of Gomor'rah!

---

remnant: The word translated **very small** is omitted by the principal ancient versions; *sārîdh*, **remnant**, is not the same word as that found in 7:3; 10:19-22, *she'ār*, which had acquired special associations in Isaiah's early period, so that he may have deliberately avoided it here.

The picture given in this oracle of a people corrupt and irreligious, devastated by war both materially and spiritually and surviving at all only by the grace of God, has an obvious contemporary meaning. Only by the mercy of the God whose goodness we have spurned and whose moral law we have disobeyed do we survive to learn the lesson of history—that the desolation we lament is the direct result of our own moral failure. "Where further would you be smitten, that you continue to turn away?"

3. God's Primary Concern (1:10-17)

One of the most notable and original features of the teaching of the Hebrew prophets is their repeated insistence that the Lord is more concerned with men's behavior in their social relationships than with the formal worship offered to him. He is not pleased by gifts and praise and "religious" ceremonies and observances as such, but looks for the more sincere tribute of imitation in human conduct of his justice, goodness, truth, and mercy (cf., among others, Amos 5:21-24; Hos. 6:6; 8:11-14; Mic. 6:6-8; Jer. 7:22-23). It is not that formal worship has no place; rather, it must be the expression and symbol of reverence for the moral character of God and of the corresponding moral standards which should characterize his people. Otherwise worship and sacrifice become meaningless, or even a positive evil, since men may thereby deceive themselves and falsify the meaning of true religion, exhausting their religious impulse without real commitment of themselves to the service of God. Nor is it the sacrificial cultus which is rejected by the prophets, although prophetic religion really is independent of it. The

---

tragedy; but who will dare, as Isaiah did, to placard before men their corporate moral responsibility for the sin of war? The world has resounded with recriminations and accusations against men and nations. Every combatant has proclaimed the justice of his cause and laid claim to the divine reinforcement of his arms. The guilt has invariably been ascribed to another; only a handful of believers among enemies and allies alike have had the honesty or the moral sensitiveness to cry *Mea culpa*. It is not less than blasphemy so to read history as to plead the inevitability of war, or to suggest, if not to claim, that by slaughter and destruction the will of God is done. Repentance is the invariable condition of salvation. But instead of repentance, a race that has twice been reprieved from death redoubles its researches in methods of slaughter and puts its faith in an atomic bomb, or even in that last device of evil, biological warfare. To such a people the word is spoken again:

Why will you still be smitten
that you continue to rebel?

And smitten the world will be, if men continue to desert the Lord God, scorn the Holy One, and from his pleading and his warning turn away like strangers. When the philosophers, statesmen, or economists have spoken their minds on the world situation, the prophet has still to be heard; and his first word must, by the compulsion of God, be a judgment on sin. His first, but not his last word, for he who would speak for God has authority to proclaim the everlasting mercy. **Except the Lord of Hosts had left unto us a very small remnant** (vs. 9). There Isaiah, with the insight of a great and discerning faith, declares the presence of God in history. God has not given us up. War has taken its terrible toll. The youngest and fairest are gone, but God has still his **remnant**; the divine purpose of redemption is not to be frustrated by this passion for annihilation which has swept the world. By the mercy of God, not the victory of arms, we are spared to build anew and to find our peace in his will.

10-17. Unacceptable Worship.—This exhortation is a brilliant example of that insistent emphasis which Hebrew prophets have laid on

| 11 To what purpose *is* the multitude of your sacrifices unto me? saith the LORD: I am full of the burnt offerings of rams, and the fat of fed beasts; and I delight not in the blood of bullocks, or of lambs, or of he goats. | 11 "What to me is the multitude of your sacrifices? says the LORD; I have had enough of burnt offerings of rams and the fat of fed beasts; I do not delight in the blood of bulls, or of lambs, or of he-goats. |

form of worship may be elaborate or simple, the ritual that of the eye or of the ear, carefully regulated or formless; it is equally hateful to God if it has become a substitute for the life of moral obedience and the sincere goodness which imitates and reflects the goodness of God.

The passage here is one of the most striking utterances of this prophetic theme. In form it is an exhortation in rhythmic speech, addressed upon a public occasion to the ruling class and to the people. Very probably the occasion was an assembly in the temple court for a religious festival; there, rather than in the market place or street, the prophets most often found their audience. There is no definite indication of date, but the similarity to the messages of Amos suggests the early period of Isaiah's ministry, in the regency or reign of Jotham, when Judah, like Israel, was prosperous and undisturbed as yet by the Assyrians.

10. **Hear, . . . give ear:** The same form of address as in the first oracle (vss. 2-3), which this may have immediately followed in an earlier collection. The intervening oracle (vss. 4-9), which may be one of the prophet's later utterances, has been introduced here because both make striking use of the figure of **Sodom** and **Gomorrah,** in the first instance as a figure of destruction, in the second as a figure of wickedness. **The law:** *Tôrāh,* here used in its primary sense, **teaching,** the authoritative instruction given by a priest or a prophet; Isaiah is no iconoclast in attacking the distorted emphasis on the cultus, but speaks for the distinctive tradition of Israel.

11. "What good to me are your multiplied sacrifices? I am surfeited with burnt offerings of rams, and the grease of fat animals; the blood of bulls . . . gives me no

the relationship between worship and character. Isaiah, Amos, Micah, Hosea, Jeremiah, each in turn denounces forms of worship which have no influence on a man's handling of life. They labor to bring it home to the nation that God is far more concerned with right relations between men than with scrupulous regard for public worship. Isaiah draws a vivid picture of the violent contrast between what men do in church and what they are in daily life.

Imagine the scene. It is one of the great church festivals. The temple courts are filled with the jostling, clamorous crowd; the air is filled with the sound of the lowing of cattle, the bleating of sheep, thick with the smoke of burnt offerings, heavy with the scent of incense. The worshipers assume the postures of prayer, they have the appearance of piety, they show scrupulous attention to liturgical detail. It is a spectacle to move one to admiration, this, of a devout people who spare no pains to make their worship magnificent in its fervor as in its setting. Isaiah agreed that it was indeed a spectacle, but added the devastating judgment that in the

eyes of God it was all a hollow mockery. He says, in effect, no splendor of worship can compensate for a complete disregard of the moral demands of God in social relationship. He sees in the ostentation of the service, and the assumed piety of the people, sheer hypocrisy; for this congregation so vocal in praise, so fervid in response, is made up of men whose hands are bloodstained, whose eyes are hot with lust and greed, men whose fortunes are built on crimes, and who have hardened their hearts against justice, and shut their ears against the tears of little children and brokenhearted women. Against this, cries Isaiah, the anger of God is kindled. He is, to use the hearty language of the street, fed-up with this meaningless display of hypocrites aping piety.

It is fatally easy to read this passage and agree with Isaiah that that kind of thing is little short of blasphemy. So long as we keep our eyes fixed on the temple services of the eighth century B.C., we can join cordially with the prophet in scorn and denunciation of a hypocrisy so patent. It is always easy to be lavish in condemnation of

12 When ye come to appear before me, who hath required this at your hand, to tread my courts?	12 "When you come to appear before me, who requires of you this trampling of my courts?
13 Bring no more vain oblations; incense is an abomination unto me; the new moons and sabbaths, the calling of assemblies, I cannot away with; *it is* iniquity, even the solemn meeting.	13 Bring no more vain offerings; incense is an abomination to me. New moon and sabbath and the calling of assemblies — I cannot endure iniquity and solemn assembly.
14 Your new moons and your appointed feasts my soul hateth: they are a trouble unto me; I am weary to bear *them*.	14 Your new moons and your appointed feasts my soul hates; they have become a burden to me, I am weary of bearing them.

pleasure." The way to make the Lord willing to grant his servants' wishes is not (as they thought) more and costlier sacrifices but moral obedience, a sacrifice valued in a different currency.

12. When you come to appear before me should be taken, with the LXX, as the last clause of the preceding verse. The Hebrew consonants suggest the rendering, "to see my face," an old phrase meaning "to be admitted to the presence of someone" (cf. Gen. 43:3) ; but for reverential reasons the Masoretic editors of the text prescribed the reading adopted by the English versions. The meaning is simply "when you come to worship me." "Who demanded of you this [piling up of sacrifices]? Trample my courts [heedlessly] no more!" (This translation follows the verse division of LXX.)

13. Translate, "to bring offerings is worthless[ness]." The vehemence of the prophet's language is seen in his application to normal features of Israelite worship of epithets elsewhere applied to idolatrous practices: "worthlessness" (cf. Jer. 18:15) , **abomination** (I Kings 14:23-24). **Calling of assemblies:** I.e., general assemblies of the people in connection with major festivals (Exod. 12:16) or on special occasions (Joel 2:15-17). **I cannot away with . . . iniquity:** There is something wrong with the text of the second half of the verse. The ellipsis after **assemblies** is unnatural, as is the appearance of the word **iniquity** in a list of religious festivals. The LXX reads "fasting" (*çôm*) instead of **iniquity** (*'âwen*), and takes this word and the next with vs. 14. T. H. Gaster (*Thespis* [New York: Henry Schuman, 1950], p. 12) justifies the translation "mortification" for *'âwen*. It is probably better to recognize these two words as a marginal note; **I cannot endure,** then, is to be construed with the preceding words, giving an excellent parallelism with vs. 14*a*.

14. Your new moons: *ḥodhshêkhem;* since this festival has been mentioned already, Friedrich Schwally's suggestion to read here "your pilgrimages" (*ḥaggêkhem*) is attractive.

another age. But the Word of God has a most perturbing way of disregarding dates and of making truth contemporary. What of the relationship between worship and social ethics now? What is the bearing of religion on character and conduct in our own day? One has only to look at contemporary society to see on every hand cruelties, injustices, sins, which give the lie to all public protestation of faith. It is perfectly true that many who are guilty of these evils make no pretense of religion; it is therefore unjust to attribute the moral condition of society to the failures of the Christian church, as many are quick to do. Nevertheless, though Christian people may not be guilty of hypocrisy in their worship, they must face the truth that to lift no voice in protest against evils in the social order, to consent by silence to the existence of injustice, to see men made victims of greed or cruelty and do nothing about it, is to leave a fatal gap between the worship we offer to a righteous God and the attitude we assume to tolerated wrong in social relationships. Passivity in the face of evil means complicity in evil. To the degree in which that is true, the things Isaiah said brutally to the religious people of his day have a disquieting relevance to the moral neutrality of many professing Christians today.

| 15 And when ye spread forth your hands, I will hide mine eyes from you; yea, when ye make many prayers, I will not hear: your hands are full of blood. | 15 When you spread forth your hands, I will hide my eyes from you; even though you make many prayers, I will not listen; your hands are full of blood. |
| 16 ¶ Wash ye, make you clean; put away the evil of your doings from before mine eyes; cease to do evil; | 16 Wash yourselves; make yourselves clean; remove the evil of your doings from before my eyes; cease to do evil, |

My soul is used, instead of the first person pronoun, with a verb expressing strong feeling; the prophet, like some of his psalmist brethren, makes bold use of anthropomorphic language with telling effect. "They have become to me a burden which I am weary of bearing."

15. Not only the sacrifices and festivals of cultic worship but prayer itself is rejected, for the **hands** stretched out toward heaven are covered with **blood**. The trouble is that, unlike Lady Macbeth, the temple worshipers are not conscious of their condition. Not that all those condemned had actually committed murder; the prophets were brutally frank in holding men responsible for the ultimate consequences of their acts and attitudes (cf. Amos 4:1-2; Mic. 3:1-3). **When ye spread forth your hands** (lit., "your palms"): In the gesture of petition. **Many** [or "long"] **prayers:** Cf. Mark 12:40. "I hide my eyes; . . . I am not listening," like an irritated judge or ruler. The Dead Sea Scroll of Isaiah (see Intro., pp. 160-61) completes the verse by adding "and your fingers with iniquity."

16. The tone and meter change as the prophet concludes his admonition with a series of abrupt imperatives. "Bathe," as before worship (II Sam. 12:20), "make yourselves pure," i.e., in heart (Ps. 73:13), not merely physically **clean.** The symbol must become a symbol of reality. **The evil of your doings:** Lit., "your crimes," which the Lord sees when men want him to see only their hands outstretched in prayer.

Say what one will in defense of the church, and there is much to be said, applaud as one may its awakened social conscience, so courageously vocal in contemporary life, there remains a deep inconsistency between the faith which we profess in the fatherhood, the justice, the holiness of God, and the ethical standards to which we consent in our handling of life and our relations with others.

Isaiah's exhortation, so devastating in its indictment, ends on a high note of summons and appeal. "Concern yourselves with justice, put right the wrong" (vs. 17). At the last, the only worship worthy of God, the only worship he seeks from men, is the praise of lives which in justice, righteousness, unselfishness, and purity, reveal his character and will. What we are must ratify what we say; alike in character and conduct, we must vindicate the faith we proclaim or stand accused of a religion which is meaningless because unrelated to life. It is the business of the church to make the love of God known and to confront men with their Lord and Savior. It cannot be done through worship alone, through preaching alone, or by any institutional method, but only through lives which reflect his spirit and do his will. The final witness to the truth of Christianity will be an order of life transfigured and transformed by the one perfect life of the ages. Then and only then shall men worship God "in spirit and in truth" (John 4:23) and faith stand justified.

While Isaiah's exhortation was addressed to the nation, the meaning for personal life has equal claim. It is not simply that true worship must issue in right relations between men, but rather that the character of worship, one might even say the right to worship a God of righteousness and love, depends on the quality of our relations to others. How can those who treat their fellows with contempt, who carry into church anger, greed, revenge, or any other distortion of his spirit, how can they in any sense worship the God who is, above all, merciful, just, and loving? Our Lord speaks with unmistakable clearness about this. He says that if on entering church we remember an unresolved quarrel with anyone, we had better delay our worship until we have cleared up the misunderstanding; because God can neither hear nor bless the man who comes to offer praise or claim a mercy, but at that moment has something on his conscience about a fellow man. It is at this point that the voice of Isaiah reaches us across

17 Learn to do well; seek judgment, relieve the oppressed, judge the fatherless, plead for the widow.

18 Come now, and let us reason together, saith the LORD: though your sins be as scarlet, they shall be as white as snow; though they be red like crimson, they shall be as wool.

17 learn to do good;
  seek justice,
    correct oppression;
  defend the fatherless,
    plead for the widow.

18 "Come now, let us reason together,
  says the LORD:
though your sins are like scarlet,
  they shall be as white as snow;
though they are red like crimson,
  they shall become like wool.

---

17. "Learn [as they have not yet done, the real requirement of the service of God] to do what is good" in his sight. **Seek** [as you seek God himself] **justice,** the rule of right. **Relieve the oppressed:** Better, with ASV mg., "set right the oppressor." The morality of the prophets, as Bernhard Duhm says, is "a morality of action, . . . which concerns men as citizens, and seeks first of all the *salus rei publicae (Das Buch Jesaia* [4th ed.; Göttingen: Vandenhoeck & Ruprecht, 1922; "Göttinger Handkommentar zum Alten Testament"], p. 31). **Judge** ["do justice by"] **the fatherless; plead for** ["champion"] **the widow:** In the old tribal society widows and orphans were cared for by their kin, but under the later conditions of village and city life they were helpless unless a powerful person could be persuaded to intervene on their behalf (cf. II Sam. 14:4-7; II Kings 4:1; Ruth 3:1-4).

4. THE ALTERNATIVE: REPENT, OR BE DESTROYED (1:18-20)

In form and content this brief oracle is distinct from the foregoing, although related to the same situation and probably from the same period. The Lord speaks as a judge before whom Israel stands accused. The guilt of the prisoner is certain, but he will receive from the judge a second chance as if he were an innocent man. He is on probation and must now make his own decision and choose his fate. This is his judgment.

18a. Reason together: "Argue," "correct one another"; each is to state his case, as at a trial. The same stem of the verb is used in Job 23:7a, and the meaning is clear from the context there.

18b-20. At this point there follow four conditional sentences, the first pair in synonymous parallelism (vs. 18bc), the second in antithetical parallelism (vss. 19-20).

---

the centuries and bids us look into our own heart before we come to God.

Wash yourselves clean
  Take out of my sight your evil deeds (vs. 16).

"Leave there thy gift before the altar, and go thy way; first be reconciled to thy brother, and then come and offer thy gift" (Matt. 5:24). If that word were obeyed, there would be a sudden exodus from our churches, for so many lives are burdened with unconfessed wrongs done to others. But if it were indeed heeded, there would be a new note in our praise, a new expectation in our petitions, because by being right with our brethren we would have authority to speak to our Father.

18-20. *A Conditioned Salvation.*—As translated in the KJV, vs. 18 has probably been the basis of more evangelistic sermons than almost any word in the O.T. How the changes have been rung on the divine mercy which meets the sinner and his sin with this unconditional assurance of forgiveness, **Though your sins be as scarlet, they shall be as white as snow.** That has been preached as a message of the sheer grace of redeeming love; and that, indeed, in a deep sense is and always will be the evangel, the good news of God for sinful men. But even the N.T., with the cross of Christ as its message, does not declare unconditional forgiveness. The assurance of mercy must always be preceded by a penitent's cry for mercy. Forgiveness is the divine possibility. It is only "if we confess our sins," that "he is faithful and just to forgive us" (I John 1:9). So Isaiah inserts his crucial "if": **If you are willing and obedient.** The great vs. 18

19 If ye be willing and obedient, ye shall eat the good of the land:

20 But if ye refuse and rebel, ye shall be devoured with the sword: for the mouth of the LORD hath spoken *it*.

19 If you are willing and obedient,
    you shall eat the good of the land;
20 But if you refuse and rebel,
    you shall be devoured by the sword;
    for the mouth of the LORD has spoken."

The second pair is clearly the Lord's statement of the case, and appears to be a rejoinder. The first pair, then, is the claim of the accused as summed up by the judge, speaking in scorn:

> Though your sins are like scarlet
>   they shall be as white as snow[!]
> though they are red like crimson,
>   they shall become like wool[!]

Not so! The judge will have none of such hypocrisy, nor condone glaring sin. There is a choice to be made, the choice between "life and good, and death and evil" (Deut. 30:15). The modern interpretation of vs. 18 as an unconditional promise of forgiveness is out of keeping with Isaiah's teaching, and can be maintained only by deliberately ignoring the context in which it appears. The date of the oracle is uncertain.

---

may have to lose something of its glow and rapture if we are to be true to Isaiah's profound reading of the mind of God. Speaking for God, he says in effect: Come, let us state the case to each other, and let us be clear about this. **Though your sins be as scarlet, they shall be as white as snow; though they be red like crimson, they shall be as wool.** Is that what you say? Is that how you think of the Holy One of Israel, you whose hypocrisy has made a mockery of your worship? Such brazen confidence that of course all will be forgiven is a measure of your ignorance of eternal justice and righteousness. God is not to be mocked by the avowal of a faith which completely ignores his moral demands. You have forgotten something, or rather, in the stupor with which sin has bemused you, you never saw it at all, never considered that God cannot forgive an unrepentant people. Your flaming sin will not, cannot, be **white as snow** until you see yourselves as you are, see what you have done to your Father's love, and are ready, if in his mercy he gives you another chance, to show your repentance in obedience to his will. But if not, if you go on refusing and rebelling, that is the end; you will write your own death sentence.

And when he has thus confronted his nation with this gospel—and it is a gospel, this word of a God whose mercy is greater than his wrath, this offer of forgiveness and a chance to live— when he has done that, Isaiah seals his message with the authority of God—God's ultimatum: **For the mouth of the LORD hath spoken it.**

It is a tremendous message. There have been days when men have heard it and trembled, days when they realized the power and the guilt of sin. They did not treat it as an abstract noun, they did not view it as mere immaturity or regrettable error; they saw it as it is, rebellion against a righteous and loving God. In that mood they were afraid, for they had in their conscious and presumptuous sin forfeited all claim to mercy; on the grounds of bare justice they had no defense to make. In that mood, too, they were utterly penitent; for they saw what they had done to the love of God, and they knew what they were. Then like the sound of a bell there fell on their troubled spirit that tender, that incredible evangel, **Though your sins be as scarlet, they shall be as white as snow, though they be red like crimson, they shall be as wool.** "For God so loved the world, that he gave his only begotten Son, that whosoever believeth in him should not perish" (John 3:16).

The N.T. is full of this divine assurance of mercy, indeed it has no other word for men than this of a love which goes "after that which is lost" (Luke 15:4) until ———? Until the lost one is found in his unhappiness, shame, and need, and taken home again, forgiven. Whereupon, as we are told, they suspend all the blessed business of heaven to celebrate the return of a soul and the glory of redeeming love. Have we lost the evangel of vs. 18? No, rather we have found it enriched and deepened by the truth that God has honored the soul of man by giving him a part to play in his own salvation, that love may win its victory through penitence, and forgiveness find its perfecting in obedience.

21 ¶ How is the faithful city become a harlot! it was full of judgment; righteousness lodged in it; but now murderers.

22 Thy silver is become dross, thy wine mixed with water:

21 How the faithful city
   has become a harlot,
   she that was full of justice!
Righteousness lodged in her,
   but now murderers.
22 Your silver has become dross,
   your wine mixed with water.

5. Lament over Jerusalem (1:21-23)

The lament, with its limping meter, is a well-known literary form in the O.T. Used originally to express sorrow over the death of individuals (cf. the superb elegy in II Sam. 1:17-27), it came to be used also by prophets and poets to lament the corruption (cf. Amos 5:2) or desolation of the nation (cf. Lam. 1). Here it provides a variant literary form to express essentially the same message as the positive admonition of vss. 16-17 and the accusing challenge of the people's champion in 3:13-15.

21. Harlot: The figure here is not, as in Hosea, that of an unfaithful wife, but of evil character in general; it is probably chosen by association of ideas, corresponding to the **murderers,** renegades, and thieves against whom the oracle is directed. **Faithful:** "Trustworthy," "loyal." **Justice** and **righteousness:** "*Righteousness* [*çedheq*] is the principle of right action . . . , *judgement* [*mishpāṭ*] the embodiment of that principle" (John Skinner, *The Book of the Prophet Isaiah* [Rev. ed.; Cambridge: Cambridge University Press, 1915; "Cambridge Bible"], I, 11), but "righteousness" means also the concrete "righteous acts." **Lodged:** Frequentative imperfect, "used to stay ['visit'] there"; the virtues named are not abstract virtues but qualities of social life in the idealized past, when they pervaded **the faithful city** and were at home there. Hebrew thought is concrete and pictorial; it does not easily handle abstract ideas; **justice** is what just men **do;** **righteousness** is the expression of what is right.

22. Two illustrations of the spoiling of a valuable substance by the mingling with it of an alien element; **dross** (waste matter) is not a good translation of *ṣighîm,* which means metal (usually silver) mixed with dross or a glaze of lead oxide which looks like silver. What justice there is, is so mingled with injustice as to be spoiled and no longer trustworthy. **Wine:** Lit., "liquor."

21-23. The Corruption of Jerusalem.—When this lament was first uttered, Jerusalem in all probability was outwardly unscathed: the sun shone upon her towers and battlements, her streets were thronged with busy people, hers was the traffic of peace, not war; yet Isaiah saw the beloved city as fallen. He compares it to a woman of the streets, not because of the shame of her profession but because of the sorrow of her lost purity. So is it with Jerusalem, once inviolate in integrity and justice, now invaded, captured by the forces of moral evil. He uses figures of contamination, debased silver, adulterated liquor, to spell out the shame of it. "Bribery and corruption," that familiar phrase, has a long history. Here it is in the eighth century B.C., the charge of a patriot against his nation's capital. No accusation could be more damning; for where justice is polluted at its source, there is the end of all law, all honor, and all compassion. What could be a clearer disclosure of the greatness of Isaiah's spirit, his native chivalry, than the fact that again and again when he inveighs against the crass selfishness of men, he names, as he does here, the orphans and the widows as the victims of their greed? Law and order, economic stability, social justice, are gone from the corrupt city; but the head and front of the evil is the degradation of human values. In that Isaiah surely anticipated Christ's unsparing denunciation of any man or any society which ignores or scorns the sacred worth of human personality. Our Lord never pronounced a more terrible judgment than that which he directed against those who neglect or profane the lives of little children. Woe to them! They are better dead (Luke 17:2).

One cannot read this lament, born of the prophet's grief rather than of his anger, over the city he loved, without remembering that far down the ages another voice was lifted in sorrow over the same city, and Another who loved it with a deeper love than Isaiah's wept over a people deaf, blind, and obdurate in sin. "O

23 Thy princes *are* rebellious, and companions of thieves: every one loveth gifts, and followeth after rewards: they judge not the fatherless, neither doth the cause of the widow come unto them.

24 Therefore saith the Lord, the LORD of hosts, the Mighty One of Israel, Ah, I will ease me of mine adversaries, and avenge me of mine enemies.

23 Your princes are rebels
  and companions of thieves.
Every one loves a bribe
  and runs after gifts.
They do not defend the fatherless,
  and the widow's cause does not come
    to them.

24 Therefore the Lord says,
  the LORD of hosts,
  the Mighty One of Israel:
"Ah, I will vent my wrath on my enemies,
  and avenge myself on my foes.

---

23. Thy princes are rebellious: With a play on the similar sounds of words Isaiah begins to apply his illustrations; *sārîm* (princes, officials) have become *ṣôrerîm* (rebels, renegades), "keen for bribes, running after favors." But the helpless members of the community, the orphan and the widow who should be their special charge, cannot obtain their attention (cf. Luke 18:2-5).

6. THE LORD'S JUDGMENT (1:24-26)

Although vss. 21-23 may originally have been an independent reproach oracle, vss. 24-26 were undoubtedly composed by Isaiah as a sequel making use of the figure of the removal of dross as a figure of divine judgment. The threat is like other threats of judgment from the earliest period of Isaiah's ministry, without specific reference to punishment by invasion and exile. The figure of the refining of silver carries a promise within the threat and gives us Isaiah's first formulation of his conviction that a "messianic" age of righteousness will follow the impending judgment.

24. The solemnity of the sentence to be pronounced is emphasized by reciting the majestic traditional titles of the Judge: "The Supreme Lord," **the Lord of hosts, the Mighty One of Israel. Ah:** The Hebrew word in the M.T. is *hôy*, "Shame!" (see Exeg. on vs. 4), which usually introduces a reproach rather than a threat; on the other hand, the introductory particle *hinnēh*, "Behold," is a normal opening for a threatening announcement (cf. 10:33; 17:1) and probably should be read here (the Dead Sea Scroll lends some support to this proposal). Again there is a play on similar words: *'ennāḥēm*, **I will ease me** (lit., "pant," i.e., in a struggle) ; *'innāqemāh*, **I will . . . avenge me.**

Jerusalem, Jerusalem, . . . how often would I have gathered thy children, . . . and ye would not! (Luke 13:34.)

Whether by chance or by the deliberate work of the ancient editors, the fact that the lament is followed by judgment is not only fitting but in a deep sense inevitable.

24-26. A Judgment.—Certainly these verses reflect the movement of Isaiah's mind from the exposure and denunciation of evil to the certainty of judgment and on to the greater certainty of redemption. None of the prophets of Israel had a deeper faith in the sovereignty of God than he. Isaiah knew that all life was not only under the scrutiny of God but under the control of God. Faced as he was by the spectacle of rampant evil, he was impressed far less by its supremacy than by the inevitability of judgment.

These people in Jerusalem, playing fast and loose with the moral law, had too small an idea of God to realize the enormity of their offense. Therefore Isaiah confronts them with the God with whom they had yet to reckon. He launches this threat of doom with the great titles of the Almighty. At the opening of a law court the crier demands silence as he announces the entry of the judge, the law incarnate; so Isaiah cries to his nation "He is coming, the supreme Lord, the Lord of hosts, the Mighty One of Israel." This is no tribal God to be either cozened or defied; it is no mere tradition they are violating, no priestly legislation or religious convention, but the immutable law of the Eternal Righteousness and Justice. **I will . . . avenge myself on my foes.** Above the clamor of the market place, where honor was for sale and

25 ¶ And I will turn my hand upon thee, and purely purge away thy dross, and take away all thy tin:

26 And I will restore thy judges as at the first, and thy counselors as at the beginning: afterward thou shalt be called, The city of righteousness, the faithful city.

25 I will turn my hand against you
    and will smelt away your dross as with lye
    and remove all your alloy.
26 And I will restore your judges as at the first,
    and your counselors as at the beginning.
    Afterward you shall be called the city of righteousness,
    the faithful city."

---

25. Pureiy purge (KJV), **smelt away . . . as with lye** (RSV): The verb means "to smelt" (metals), and figuratively "to test," "to purify"; but as Mal. 3:2 makes clear, **lye** or soap belongs to the process of washing, as fire to that of smelting, and we should therefore read *kakkûr,* "as in the smelting pot [or furnace]" rather than *kabbôr,* **as with lye. Dross:** *ṣighîm,* the ore or unpurified metal; **tin:** *bedhîl,* what is separated from the metal, dross or (as appropriate here) "impurities."

26. I will restore: By the cleansing of fire Zion shall be made like new, her rulers and counselors as in the ideal days of David (cf. II Sam. 8:15), when Jerusalem first became the center of Judean life. "Afterward ["thereafter"] thou shalt deserve the name [with Ehrlich] the city of righteousness [*ṣedheq*]," a traditional name of Zion (cf. Gen. 14:18; Ps. 110:2, 4) associated with the Davidic dynasty. Whether or not *ṣedheq* was originally the proper name of a deity worshiped in pre-Israelite Zion, by this time it had the clear meaning "that which is morally right in the sight of God." The prophet infers that it is a word which too glibly passes the lips of Jerusalemites. **The faithful city:** With moral force and poetic effectiveness Isaiah reverts to the name used of Jerusalem in vs. 21. נאמנה, **faithful,** has a second meaning which gives point to its use here: "firmly established," "enduring," used of David's dynasty (cf. II Sam. 7:16; Ps. 89:37 [Hebrew 89:38]) and is synonymous with the verb used of "the city of our God" in Ps. 48:8. Men spoke familiarly of Jerusalem as "the Enduring City," as today of Rome "the Eternal City." But the name, says Isaiah, is only a sentimental one and is used unworthily, for the enduring city must be also the **faithful,** trustworthy city (cf. 7:9 where the same idea reappears).

---

souls were cheap, that menacing word is spoken.

It is noteworthy that at this point—and it was probably early in his ministry—Isaiah does not identify the judgment of God with such national disasters as war, famine, or exile, which he was later so luridly to foretell. As his warning went unheeded, as the nation became still more defiant in its repudiation of God, he became ever more convinced of the imminence of destruction; in the human situation he came to see no hope, and the note of doom sounded in his words. But at this moment, it would seem, he saw in the corruption of the nation not only the certainty of a divine visitation in judgment, but of a disciplining, purifying, restoring act of God.

I will purify you of dross as in a smelter . . . .
I will restore to you rulers like those you had at first. . . .
Afterward, you shall be called the city of righteousness (vss. 25-26).

This is our first glimpse of Isaiah's ever-deepening confidence that beyond the punishment lay a messianic age of righteousness. Even more than his unyielding conviction of the justice of God, this hope is the great, the distinctive faith of the prophet. God's judgment is never retributive only; it is always redemptive. And it begins with cleansing. Here is one aspect of divine omnipotence, the power to use as means to the end of redemption the very disasters which men themselves occasion. God does not send war; men make it. Whereupon God uses it for the cleansing of human life. That is a truth for every age to ponder.

"I will purify you as in a smelter." The modern world has suffered many convulsions. Have they cleansed national life of those evils, those distortions of the spirit which are the final cause of war? There is little evidence of it, to judge by the policies of the nations. Can covenants and treaties ever bring peace if the funda-

27 Zion shall be redeemed with judgment, and her converts with righteousness.

28 ¶ And the destruction of the transgressors and of the sinners *shall be* together, and they that forsake the Lord shall be consumed.

29 For they shall be ashamed of the oaks which ye have desired, and ye shall be confounded for the gardens that ye have chosen.

30 For ye shall be as an oak whose leaf fadeth, and as a garden that hath no water.

31 And the strong shall be as tow, and the maker of it as a spark, and they shall both burn together, and none shall quench *them.*

2 The word that Isaiah the son of Amoz saw concerning Judah and Jerusalem.

27 Zion shall be redeemed by justice,
   and those in her who repent, by righteousness.
28 But rebels and sinners shall be destroyed together,
   and those who forsake the Lord shall be consumed.
29 For you shall be ashamed of the oaks
   in which you delighted;
   and you shall blush for the gardens
   which you have chosen.
30 For you shall be like an oak
   whose leaf withers,
   and like a garden without water.
31 And the strong shall become tow,
   and his work a spark,
   and both of them shall burn together,
   with none to quench them.

2 The word which Isaiah the son of Amoz saw concerning Judah and Jerusalem.

---

7. An Addendum (1:27-31)

27-31. A quite different situation, a different theology, and a distinct use of terms mark off this short passage from the foregoing. **Zion shall be redeemed** ("ransomed," "set free"), and her survivors (lit., "those of her who return" or **repent**), by the **justice** and **righteousness,** i.e., of God (cf. 35:10; 51:11). Zion here represents the pious Jews in contrast to sinners and apostates, as in late psalms (cf. Pss. 1:1-6; 119:53; cf. the "publicans and sinners" of the Gospels). In vss. 29-31 the apostates are identified in particular with the devotees of the ancient cult of sacred trees and "groves" (Moffatt). The change from third to second person in the verbs indicates that vss. 27-28 and vss. 29-31 were originally distinct compositions. Ideas and vocabulary show that both come from the circle of writers who made many additions to Second Isaiah in the fifth century B.C. or later (cf. 57:3-8; 59:1-8; 65:1-7).

8. Turning of the Peoples (2:1-5)

2:1. The occurrence here of a second heading, similar in some respects to that in 1:1, raises several possibilities: (*a*) that this is the heading to chs. 2–12, following which a

---

mental attitudes of men remain unchanged? It is both strange and tragic to consider how obdurate is the human heart. At the end of World War I, men were chastened and humbled. They were resolved that it would never happen again. It seemed as if the smelter of war had cleansed them. In the mood and emotion of the hour they turned from the defense of arms to the security of a great ideal, and the League of Nations was born. Subsequent history revealed how superficial was the cleansing. Gradually, but soon with increasing pace, they returned to the old levels of pride and selfishness; so slowly at first that no one noticed it, and then precipitately they were drawn again into the maelstrom of another war. Is there to be no end of strife? Surely history does teach the inevitability of war so long as the passions which beget it sway human life. No horrific devices of science can outlaw war, no national or international pacts finally prevent it; only religion can put an end to it, because only religion can put a new spirit into human relationships. The secret of peace is spiritual. By thy cleansing fire, "Create in me a clean heart, O God; and renew a right spirit within me" (Ps. 51:10).

27-31. *Redemption Through Justice.*—Notes on the distinctive features of this passage are given in the Exeg. Against a different historical situation they reiterate the assured judgment of God against apostasy. Redemption can come only through justice.

2 And it shall come to pass in the last days, *that* the mountain of the Lord's house shall be established in the top of the mountains, and shall be exalted above the hills; and all nations shall flow unto it.

2 It shall come to pass in the latter days
    that the mountain of the house of the
        Lord
    shall be established as the highest of the
        mountains,
        and shall be raised above the hills;
    and all the nations shall flow to it,

---

new section begins with the title in 13:1; in this case ch. 1 was prefixed to chs. 2–12 after having circulated separately; (*b*) that 2:1 is the heading of one of the smaller collections now incorporated in chs. 2–12, since the latter is not solely concerned with **Judah and Jerusalem;** (*c*) that the heading refers to the eschatological oracle immediately following, in vss. 2-4, claiming for Isaiah an oracle also claimed for Micah (cf. Mic. 4:1-3), and bringing to a conclusion the section 1:1–2:5. The "burden" (doom oracle) on Babylon in 13:1 certainly has reference only to the first of the series of oracles in chs. 13–23. (For **the word** as referring to a following oracle, cf. Jer. 7:1; 11:1; contrast Jer. 1:1.)

2-5. This justly famous passage appears also in Micah, where the addition of a final line (Mic. 4:4*a*) rounds out the poem. That the final editors of both books included it in their collections shows that the piece, like much else in the prophetic books, was in fact anonymous and may well date from a later time than the eighth century B.C. There is some ground for believing that the oracle first appeared in the book of Isaiah, and was taken over into the book of Micah, carrying with it some of its context from what is now Isa. 2, where the text is broken off after vs. 4. The restoration of Mic. 4:4 to its place after Isa. 2:4 not only completes the final strophe of the oracle but brings with it the phrase "for the mouth of the Lord of hosts has spoken," which otherwise is peculiar to Isaiah (cf. 1:20; 40:5; 58:14). Vs. 5 also is related to Mic. 4:5 (see Exeg. below).

Neither in Isaiah nor in Micah does this passage fit well its context. Whatever its authorship, it must have been inserted where it is now found in one of the later stages of the long and complicated process of compilation. The future exaltation of the temple as a center of pilgrimage and religious instruction for all peoples (vss. 2-3) is a strangely different picture from that in ch. 1, and the transition to what follows in ch. 2 is equally abrupt. If this oracle-poem is from Isaiah it is from his old age, when, following the deliverance from Sennacherib's armies, he appears to have seen the future role of Zion as the seat of a new kind of world empire; from all peoples would its citizens come eagerly to learn the ways of Zion's God and find justice, peace, and freedom from fear.

2. In the latter days: I.e., "in a later time" or "in the distant future." The phrase, which does not appear again in Isaiah, is not at first (cf. Deut. 4:30) what it later becomes (cf. Dan. 10:14), a technical term for the messianic age. **The mountain of the house of the Lord:** The Jerusalem temple on its hill; the usual phrase (as in vs. 3) omits **of the**

2:2-5. *A Prophecy of Peace.*—This noble passage is in all probability a quotation from some unknown author, since both Isaiah and Micah make use of it. How it came to be inserted here in the record need not occupy us. Whoever first wrote it, Isaiah has made it his own as the very word of God for men. Here it is, one of the great prophetic visions of all time, making articulate the immemorial longing of the human heart for peace. The man who prides himself on his realism will dismiss it as mere wishful thinking; few will read it as anything but poetry, which by a strange blindness they will relegate to the sphere of dreams unrelated to life. The truth, on the contrary, is that the faith uttered

in this prophecy is indispensable for the hope of the world. Here is a conviction born of Isaiah's reading of the mind of God, that there shall yet be a day when mankind shall live together and walk together in faith and righteousness and brotherhood. How desperately our world needs such a faith! Without its inspiration and its power to sustain our search for a way of peace, we are condemned to the dreadful prospect of wars succeeding wars until the human race destroys itself. We have in each generation the strange, tragic spectacle of men endowed with genius, yet wholly unable to learn the art of living together in peace. Even with bitter experience of the horrors of war, every proposal

3 And many people shall go and say, Come ye, and let us go up to the mountain of the LORD, to the house of the God of Jacob; and he will teach us of his ways, and we will walk in his paths: for out of Zion shall go forth the law, and the word of the LORD from Jerusalem.	3 and many peoples shall come, and say: "Come, let us go up to the mountain of the LORD, to the house of the God of Jacob; that he may teach us his ways and that we may walk in his paths." For out of Zion shall go forth the law, and the word of the LORD from Jerusalem.

house, as the LXX does here and in Mic. 4:1, adding as a parallel "the house of God." The Isaiah Dead Sea Scroll omits **to the mountain of the LORD** in vs. 3. The unusual phrase in vs. 2 appears to be a conflation of the two parallel designations of the temple. **Established as the highest:** "Set first," "made most prominent." **Shall flow:** Like a river (cf. Jer. 51:44).

3. **Many peoples:** This picture of Zion as a goal of pilgrimage and the religious center of mankind has analogies but no close parallel in late eschatological prophecies like 11:10; 60:1-14; Zech. 8:20-23. The real point of contact is with the first of the "Servant Songs" of Second Isaiah (42:1-4); i.e., we have here the promise of the peoples' response to Hebrew prophecy (*tôrāh*, "teaching") as a missionary message to mankind. **Let us go up,** as "the tribes of the LORD" (Ps. 122:4). **Walk in his paths:** This familiar biblical idiom (cf. "the Way," Acts 9:2) connotes both a religious belief and the moral behavior according with that belief; it appears to combine two pictorial ideas, (*a*) the path as a customary route, and (*b*) the right path to choose where paths diverge, leading to the temples of different gods (cf. Exod. 32:8).

for peace is basically related to the use of brute force. It is a question to ponder, how long the patience of Almighty God will be shown to a people apparently bent on self-annihilation. It may well be that we are rapidly coming to the place in history where a last chance is offered to humanity to consider the terms God has laid down for life on this earth; to consider, to accept and obey, or to perish miserably.

For such a moment the prophecy of Isaiah about world peace has a supreme and crucial relevance. He paints in glowing colors the picture of a united world, a true league of nations, made one not by treaty but by common faith, and no more afraid. This is not mere wishful thinking; it is a projection on the screen of history of life lived in keeping with the will of God for his children. This is what the weary hearts of men have longed to see. What is the secret? What will make it come true? Analyze the vision of the prophet and you see that there is first, the supremacy of faith in God. The preeminence of religion is the key to all that follows. It is because the sovereignty of God is acknowledged, and men no longer pay lip service to it, but are prepared to organize life in keeping with it, that the whole face of the world is changed. There is second, the response of mankind, all nations streaming toward the sanctuary of faith, the willingness, yes, the eagerness of men to learn the new way of life.

There is third, an entirely new spirit in international relationships, because God is brought into all the issues of life. The court of appeal is not that of war but of divine arbitration, and the problems are faced in the light of God's will for men. This does not necessarily imply the direct intervention of God in human affairs, but rather that his spirit will guide the negotiations of men. Man's attempts at arbitration are continually foiled by mutual suspicion and fear of hidden purposes. Isaiah sees the day when the distrust of men will be overcome by trust in God. When misunderstandings are laid out before a judge whose righteousness is absolute, and whose wisdom is infinitely greater than man's, when the councils of the nation are overseen by one who is almighty in goodness and love, then, as Isaiah says, it is God who settles the issues; as a result of trust in the great Judge, the suspicions, hatreds, and fears of men are dispelled, and they trust one another. Finally, and as consequence of faith operative in life, there is the great transformation, the forces of destruction become the agencies of construction, and as Micah adds, fear no longer besets mankind; there is peace on earth because there is good will among men.

No serious mind can dismiss such a vision as unrelated to life. At every point it touches the contemporary situation. It is perfectly true the conditions for the fulfillment of the vision are

4 And he shall judge among the nations, and shall rebuke many people: and they shall beat their swords into plowshares, and their spears into pruning hooks: nation shall not lift up sword against nation, neither shall they learn war any more.

5 O house of Jacob, come ye, and let us walk in the light of the LORD.

6 ¶ Therefore thou hast forsaken thy people the house of Jacob, because they be replenished from the east, and *are* sooth-sayers like the Philistines, and they please themselves in the children of strangers.

---

4 He shall judge between the nations,
  and shall decide for many peoples;
and they shall beat their swords into
  plowshares,
  and their spears into pruning hooks;
nation shall not lift up sword against
  nation,
  neither shall they learn war any more.

5 O house of Jacob,
  come, let us walk
  in the light of the LORD.

6 For thou hast rejected thy people,
  the house of Jacob,
because they are full of diviners*a* from
  the east
  and of soothsayers like the Philistines,
  and they strike hands with foreigners.

a Cn: Heb lacks *of diviners*

---

4. He shall judge, . . . decide: "settle the disputes, . . . decide the issues." The biblical pictures of the messianic age link the coming of peace with the establishment of a just rule among men (cf. 9:7; 11:1-9). **Plowshares, . . . pruning hooks:** Weapons and implements of iron had not always been available to Israel (cf. I Sam. 13:19-22). A later prophet uses the same figure in reverse when summoning the nations to prepare for the last battle (Joel 3:10). To complete the poem Mic. 4:4 should be inserted here: "And every man shall sit under his vine, or under his fig tree, and no one shall make him afraid: for the mouth of the LORD of hosts has spoken."

5. This short verse is in a fragmentary condition, as it apparently was when the editor of Micah took it over with the preceding verses and freely paraphrased it (Mic. 4:5). It appears to be simply a textual variant of part of vs. 3.

C. The Day of the Lord (2:6-22)

In this section two distinct oracles from Isaiah's early period have been brought together in a larger literary unit with refrains, similar to that now found in 9:8–10:4, plus 5:24b-29(30). The text is in some confusion, as will be evident to anyone who attempts to trace the sequence of thought and to relate the recurrent refrains. The problem is not made easier by the fact that the opening of the first of the two oracles in vs. 6 has been jumbled in transmission, as has the concluding vs. 22, which the LXX omits altogether. Vss. 9b-10 are missing in the Dead Sea Scroll. It is not surprising that Duhm (*Das Buch Jesaia,* p. 39) declares that this section is the worst preserved in the entire book.

---

still lacking; but that does not discredit the dream or dispose of its claim on the minds of men. Here is the plain declaration of God, that only on such terms can we know peace. This world will not run on any other lines than those laid down by God for men. It is not the high idealism but the everlasting sanity of the prophecy which should strike us. Surely we have learned enough of life to know that at the last all human relationships are spiritually conditioned. Leave God and his will for men out of account and we get the kind of world we have.

Put God in the only place he can rightfully occupy, at the center of our thinking and our planning, and every single problem that now vexes the nations will move toward solution. History will reveal whether we have suffered enough to believe that. Abandon the faith which created this vision of a world under the rule of God, and we shall have but an uneasy leisure in which to see our plans disintegrate and to make preparations for the next war.

6-22. *The Judgment on Idolatry.*—This passage is full of difficulties for the exegete because

7 Their land also is full of silver and gold, neither *is there any* end of their treasures; their land is also full of horses, neither *is there any* end of their chariots:	7 Their land is filled with silver and gold, and there is no end to their treasures; their land is filled with horses, and there is no end to their chariots.

The two oracles appear to have been combined as elements of a larger literary unit on account of their general similarity in tone, because the climactic verses of the first oracle refer to **that day** (vs. 20), and because the same verbs, שחח and שפל, are used to describe the humbling of man (vss. 9, 17). The oracle on the day of the Lord (vss. 12-17) is inserted into the middle of the oracle against idolatry (vss. 6-11, 18-21), and becomes the second of three strophes, each of which now ends with the refrain of its conclusion (vss. 11, 17, 22 [see below]). Vs. 10, an adaptation of the concluding threat of the first oracle (cf. vss. 19, 20-21) is inserted before the first refrain apparently because of the association in the later strophes of vss. 17 and 19, and vss. 21 and 22.

The curious, ungrammatical verse, vs. 22, omitted by the LXX altogether, and looking like a clumsy annotation in which some persons unknown are admonished to profit by the lesson of the preceding oracles, has resulted apparently from a very early misreading by a copyist of the words of the same refrain which appears in vss. 11, 17. If, with the substitution of the synonym גאון for גבהות, the consonants of vs. 17 had been written crowded into the margin of a MS in short irregular lines which had become partly illegible, it is possible to see how the next scribe might have read them in the form which vs. 22 now has in the M.T. Twenty-five of the thirty-one consonants of vs. 22 are found in vs. 17, fifteen of them in the same order. The fourth and final words are the same in both verses, and a third common word, אנשים, appears in the correct position in the verse when the common consonants are marked. It seems probable, therefore, that the words of vs. 17 should be read again as a final refrain in vs. 22, instead of the meaningless (or at least unsuitable) sentence which the copyist extracted from a partly illegible text.

1. Coming Doom upon Idolatry (2:6-11, 18-22)

The first oracle is a reproach directed against the idolatry which accompanies material prosperity as Israel eagerly assimilates the way of life of neighboring peoples. It is followed by a threat of judgment when the Lord will declare his majesty in the terrors of an earthquake (vss. 6-8*a*, 9*c* as emended, 8*bc*, 9*ab*, 18-21).

6. Probably to be emended: "Because they have forsaken the Lord, even his people, the house of Jacob." The context shows clearly that it is Israel who has abandoned her God, not vice versa (cf. 1:4); moreover, the LXX reads "his people"; and "the Lord" is the final word in the fragmentary vs. 5. **Because they are full of diviners** [like those] **from the east, . . . they strike** [clap] **hands:** The latter phrase may refer to the striking of bargains (Duhm, Gray), but O.T. usage suggests rather a gesture of defiance (Job 34:37; Ezek. 25:6) or a gesture used in worship (Ps. 47:1); in either case the phrase refers to an association with foreigners.

7. The traditional terms for royal wealth (cf. Deut. 17:16-17; I Kings 10:14-29). The situation envisaged is that at the end of Uzziah's reign or shortly thereafter (cf. II Chr. 26:6-15).

of the corruption of the text. It is clear however that we have here two distinct oracles which have been brought together as a literary unit because they both deal with the one theme of the terrors of God's judgment on sin. The cadences of the exquisite vs. 4 have hardly died before there is an abrupt and dramatic change in the tone of Isaiah's words. He turns his eyes,	as it were, from the glow and rapture of the distant day of peace and looks squarely at the earthly scene. So far from finding a people concerned about God's ways, he sees a nation enslaved by superstition. It is significant that he fastens on that feature of life; it is to him *the* deadly sin precisely because it means a repudiation of God. He has shown us that the pre-

8 Their land also is full of idols; they worship the work of their own hands, that which their own fingers have made:

9 And the mean man boweth down, and the great man humbleth himself: therefore forgive them not.

10 ¶ Enter into the rock, and hide thee in the dust, for fear of the LORD, and for the glory of his majesty.

11 The lofty looks of man shall be humbled, and the haughtiness of men shall be bowed down; and the LORD alone shall be exalted in that day.

8 Their land is filled with idols;
  they bow down to the work of their hands,
  to what their own fingers have made.
9 So man is humbled,
  and men are brought low —
  forgive them not!
10 Enter into the rock,
  and hide in the dust
  from before the terror of the LORD,
  and from the glory of his majesty.
11 The haughty looks of man shall be brought low,
  and the pride of men shall be humbled;
  and the LORD alone will be exalted
  in that day.

8, 9c. As in the long-remembered time of Solomon, the quest for material wealth and power led the way to cultural and religious assimilation with "the world" (cf. the warning in Deut. 17:15-17). The final clause of vs. 9 (we'al tissā' lāhem, **forgive them not**), which is meaningless in its context, can be emended to read wayyinnātheshû 'elōhîm, "and the gods are rooted up" (cf. vs. 18; Mic. 5:13).

9ab, 18. Read: "Therefore man shall be abased, and each man brought low, and [continuing with vs. 18] the idols shall utterly pass away."

19. **And men shall enter the caves**, or "get you into . . . ," imperative (cf. vs. 10); so men hid from the Philistines in the days of Saul (cf. I Sam. 13:6). Palestine and adjacent regions have always been subject to earthquakes, which biblical writers took to be immediate manifestations of the awful power of God and marks of his presence in self-revelation or judgment (cf. Exod. 19:18; II Sam. 22:8; Amos 4:11; 8:8). **Terror:**

requisite of peace is the reference of all life to the guidance of God, and here is a people who have turned from God to traffic with spirits which they have imported from pagan cults. God is not in their minds at all; it is not his judgment they seek, but "How do the omens read? What has the oracle to say? Give us a magic spell." This craze for the occult is just the reverse side of a prevailing secularism, for men are money-mad.

> Their land is filled with silver and gold,
>   and there is no end to their treasures.

It is the continual penalty of material success to beget in men a self-confidence and pride which to their minds makes God unnecessary; but since all men must have a God, and a righteous God asks awkward questions as to how the wealth was made, they turn to more amenable divinities, elevate their own prowess, create a pantheon of their own achievements, and worship their own successes.

A modern prophet with Isaiah's insight, courage, and faith might well repeat this oracle to Western civilization. Secularism, the confidence of men in their own powers and the gains of their own labor—that and not any other ism is the real peril. The judgment in which men parody the old answer of the Shorter Catechism to read, "The chief end of man is to glorify prosperity and enjoy it forever," is far too true to be laughed off as a clever saying. The land is full, not of images, but of idols, of ambitions, of passions, of aims erected as the ends of life. Profit is an idol, power is an idol, prosperity is an idol, and multitudes literally abase themselves before these false gods. No preacher has far to look for evidence of prevailing materialism, while he will search in vain for a prevailing faith.

From the exposure of the moral condition of a nation which has abandoned God, the prophet passes to a lurid portrayal of the coming judgment. The logic is inexorable if you believe in the sovereignty of God, as Isaiah did. God is not mocked, and out of the eternities he comes to blast with the flame of his wrath the pitiful pretensions of human arrogance and conceit. The indictment is detailed and complete. The evils which the lightning of divine judgment will strike are named one by one. G. K. Chesterton is reported to have said, "If you want to make

12 For the day of the LORD of hosts *shall be* upon every *one that is* proud and lofty, and upon every *one that is* lifted up; and he shall be brought low:

13 And upon all the cedars of Lebanon, *that are* high and lifted up, and upon all the oaks of Bashan,

14 And upon all the high mountains, and upon all the hills *that are* lifted up,

12 For the LORD of hosts has a day
 against all that is proud and lofty,
 against all that is lifted up and high;[b]
13 against all the cedars of Lebanon,
 lofty and lifted up;
 and against all the oaks of Bashan;
14 against all the high mountains,
 and against all the lofty hills;

[b] Cn Compare Gk: Heb *low*

Terrifying presence, numinous awe (as in Job 4:14; I Sam. 11:7). **The glory of his majesty:** "The splendor of his exaltation," the absolute, irresistible power of the divine sovereign. The prophet speaks in the light of his own tremendous experience of the Lord as righteous, sovereign power (ch. 6). The oracle undoubtedly belongs to the earliest period.

20. In that day: This opening phrase of the climactic conclusion to the first oracle led to the combination with it of the second oracle on the day of the Lord (vss. 12-17). In Isaiah's own oracles it is commonly used in connection with a threat, whereas in the editorial supplements it usually introduces a promise relating to the messianic age (cf. 11:10-11; etc.). **Men will cast forth their idols . . . to the moles and to the bats,** whose caves and holes they now share. The words omitted are a prosaic insertion into the rhythmic lines of the oracle. The word used for **idols,** *'elîl,* is not descriptive, like "graven image," but epithetical; it means "worthlessness," "nothingness," but resembles the word *'ēl,* "god." Thus it provides the play on words of which the prophets were so fond when pointing a contrast.

2. HUMBLING OF HUMAN PRIDE (2:12-17)

The second oracle—one of Isaiah's earliest messages—which has been combined with the first in a longer literary unit with refrains, is found in vss. 12-17. It too is a threat, directed not against cultural assimilation and idolatry but against man's proud self-exaltation which ignores the authority of that one "throne, high and lifted up" (6:1).

12. And he shall be brought low: The RSV emends this, with the LXX, to read **all that is lifted up and high.** The Dead Sea Scroll has a shorter line which suits the meter better: "Upon everything that is proud and high and exalted."

13-14. Cedars of Lebanon, . . . oaks of Bashan, . . . mountains, . . . hills: Features of the natural world which from time immemorial have awed man with the dimension of height.

---

a thing living, make it local." Isaiah localizes the sin of Israel.

It is pride which is peculiarly the sin of worldly success; secularism is its breeding ground. Where there is wealth, there invariably is pride. The finest spirits have always been the most sensitive to its dangers. In their conjectures about the nature of evil they attribute to pride the fall of the very angels. According to Milton, the outstanding feature in the character of their leader was arrogance. "Better," cried Lucifer, "to reign in Hell, than serve in Heav'n." [2] Dante sets pride first in the list of the seven deadly sins. The word of God attributes to it the fall of man. "Ye shall be as Gods" (Gen. 3:5), whispered the tempter, and the fear of God

[2] *Paradise Lost,* Bk. I, l. 263.

melted before the prospect of power. It is significant that human pride in its visible expression is continually associated with size. A proud nation boasts of the size of its army, navy, air force, exults in astronomical statistics, and declares its greatness through architecture, the biggest auditorium, the tallest building. So, from the Tower of Babel to the skyline of New York, pride has declared itself in wood and stone.

On this sin so manifest in Israel Isaiah fastens and proclaims its doom.

The haughty looks of man shall be brought low and the pride of men shall be humbled.

There follows the list of "high" things which are to be brought down—men of high station, high hills, high trees, high towers, tall ships, all

15 And upon every high tower, and upon every fenced wall, 16 And upon all the ships of Tarshish, and upon all pleasant pictures. 17 And the loftiness of man shall be bowed down, and the haughtiness of men shall be made low; and the LORD alone shall be exalted in that day. 18 And the idols he shall utterly abolish. 19 And they shall go into the holes of the rocks, and into the caves of the earth, for fear of the LORD, and for the glory of his majesty, when he ariseth to shake terribly the earth.	15 against every high tower, and against every fortified wall; 16 against all the ships of Tarshish, and against all the beautiful craft.[c] 17 And the haughtiness of man shall be humbled, and the pride of men shall be brought low; and the LORD alone will be exalted in that day. 18 And the idols shall utterly pass away. 19 And men shall enter the caves of the rocks and the holes of the ground, from before the terror of the LORD, and from the glory of his majesty, when he rises to terrify the earth. [c] Compare Gk: Heb uncertain

15-16. "Upon every great tower and every fortress wall, upon all the [tall] ships of Tarshish, upon [their] every splendid canopy": Those creations of man's soaring ambition to express himself in the great and the magnificent, "Building proud towers which shall not reach to heaven" (Laurence Housman, "Father Eternal, Ruler of Creation," st. iii) as in the dawn of time (Gen. 11:1-9).

Ships of Tarshish: Vessels able to make the voyage of two thousand miles to the smelting center of Tartessos in Spain, and so all ocean-going vessels. **All the beautiful craft:** "Every splendid canopy." The noun שביות occurs nowhere else, and has been emended in the RSV to ספינות, **ships.** The best description of such a ship is in Ezek. 27:5-11, where we find in vs. 7 reference to the purple "awning," מכסה; a synonym for this is כסות, plural, כסיות, "coverings," "canopies," an emendation closer to the existing Hebrew text and inherently suitable.

17. That day: A judgment, the form of which is unspecified in the early prophecies of Isaiah, will expose the hollow pretensions and real weakness of man and declare the inaccessible supremacy of God. Man's self-sufficient pride is the mark of his impossible ambition to overcome his littleness and finitude and make himself like God.

18-22. See Exeg. on 2:6-11, 18-22.

flaunting their pride before the world. But the God whose presence they ignore and whose power they deny is not awed by human pretensions. He has only to appear, only to touch with the finger of his judgment the works of man to have them crumble to dust, and the pride which begot them shrivel in the white heat of his anger.

> Lo, all our pomp of yesterday
> Is one with Nineveh and Tyre! [3]

We are left with the picture of a nation once "drunk with sight of power" now stripped of

[3] From "Recessional," from *The Five Nations*, by Rudyard Kipling. Copyright 1903 by Rudyard Kipling, reprinted by permission of Mrs. George Bambridge; Methuen & Co.; and Doubleday & Co., Inc.

every pretension, its pride literally flattened, and men gone to ground from the terror of him who shakes the earth in his wrath. Nothing is left but God in his exalted glory standing in the midst of the wreckage of human pride.

So periodically God visits on man, by the operation of his immutable moral laws, a divine judgment. The way of history is strewed with the wreckage of destroyed civilizations which went down in flaming ruin or rotted in the stagnation of moral corruption because they had no place in their piled-up glories for God. It has come again, this terror of judgment, and man stands in his stricken world with fear in his heart. Thus far, in the mercy of God, there has always been for him another chance. "Thus far," for we cannot presume to say it will always be so. But the end is not yet. Still the infinite

20 In that day a man shall cast his idols of silver, and his idols of gold, which they made *each one* for himself to worship, to the moles and to the bats;

21 To go into the clefts of the rocks, and into the tops of the ragged rocks, for fear of the LORD, and for the glory of his majesty, when he ariseth to shake terribly the earth.

22 Cease ye from man, whose breath *is* in his nostrils: for wherein is he to be accounted of?

3 For, behold, the Lord, the LORD of hosts, doth take away from Jerusalem and from Judah the stay and the staff, the whole stay of bread, and the whole stay of water,

20 In that day men will cast forth
   their idols of silver and their idols of
      gold,
which they made for themselves to wor-
      ship,
   to the moles and to the bats,
21 to enter the caverns of the rocks
      and the clefts of the cliffs,
   from before the terror of the LORD,
      and from the glory of his majesty,
      when he rises to terrify the earth.
22 Turn away from man
      in whose nostrils is breath,
   for of what account is he?

3 For, behold, the Lord, the LORD of
   hosts,
is taking away from Jerusalem and from
      Judah
stay and staff,
   the whole stay of bread,
      and the whole stay of water;

D. THE DOOM OF RULERS (3:1-15)

This passage falls into three sections which may originally have been independent, but which are so closely related in tone and substance that they now form a literary unit. Vss. 1-7 are a threat of social anarchy, to follow when the Lord snatches away the men in key positions in Judah's social structure. Vss. 8-12 are a similar threat of society's collapse, linked with a reproach giving, as the reason for the collapse, the nation's rebellion against the supreme authority of God. Vss. 13-15 are a reproach directed to the rulers themselves and accusing them of plundering the people committed to their charge. A feature common to the three sections is that Yahweh speaks in the first person, after having been introduced in the third person.

The passage as a whole is distinguished from 2:6-22 by the specific references to Jerusalem and Judah and by the threat of the deportation of the leading members of the community, which is almost tantamount to prediction of an Assyrian invasion. In the latter respect its viewpoint resembles that of 6:11-12 rather than that of 2:19, 21, where the terror of the Lord is to be manifested by an earthquake. The naming of Jerusalem and Judah relates 3:1-15 to 5:1-7; these are the only two passages, curiously enough, which recall the wording of the headings in 1:1; 2:1. It seems probable that the title in 1:1 (in its shorter form) stood originally at the head of a collection of Isaiah's prophecies from his early period which included these and other passages in the early chapters of the present book (see Intro., pp. 158-60). The only indications of date in these two passages are: the prosperity and self-confidence of the upper classes (3:2-3, 14, 16, 24; 5:8); the association of Judah with Israel in the prophet's mind (5:7); the recognition of the Assyrian menace as imminent (3:1, 25; 5:5-6, 13); and possibly a reference to the youth of Ahaz when he succeeded to the throne (3:4, 12; cf. II Kings 16:2). These

---

patience of God suffers us to rebuild. How it shall fare with us depends altogether on the place we shall give God and his laws in our rebuilding.

3:1-15. The Corruption of Society.—These are dark chapters; the prophet's warnings have become open threats; he piles horror on horror as he depicts what is going to happen. It is no longer a conjecture as to what *may* happen; it is a lurid and brutal picture of the chaos that awaits a state which in its corruption is beyond salvation. The process of disintegration is swift.

2 The mighty man, and the man of war, the judge, and the prophet, and the prudent, and the ancient,	**2** the mighty man and the soldier,
	    the judge and the prophet,
	    the diviner and the elder,

3 The captain of fifty, and the honorable man, and the counselor, and the cunning artificer, and the eloquent orator.	**3** the captain of fifty
	    and the man of rank,
	the counselor and the skilful magician
	    and the expert in charms.

4 And I will give children *to be* their princes, and babes shall rule over them.	**4** And I will make boys their princes, and babes shall rule over them.

indications together point to a period prior to the alliance of "Ephraim" with Damascus against Judah (cf. 7:1-2) in 734 B.C., and perhaps to the time of Tiglath-pileser's demonstration in force against the western states, which led to the payment of tribute by Menahem of Israel in 738.

With profound insight Isaiah points out the dependence of a human society upon its key members, how quickly it will collapse into chaotic and helpless anarchy when left leaderless, especially if there is no common conviction of social purpose to fall back upon. These people have not looked beyond the familiar rulers and functionaries of their society to the divine Ruler and to the principles of his rule. When the leaders who have betrayed them are removed like rotten timbers, they have no foundation on which to rebuild. A society where those in authority have no feeling of responsibility to God, and to justice and right, is dangerously unstable. The people have no longer the ability to govern themselves because they have depended utterly on the passing leadership of the day. Whether in politics or in religion, men may lose their security the moment they rely on functionaries and have no real relationship of their own to the sovereign power.

1. Social Anarchy (3:1-7)

3:1. The Lord, the Lord of hosts: "The sovereign Lord of hosts," as in 1:24; 10:16, 33; etc. The almighty, overruling power of God is emphasized by the formal title, *hā'ādhôn*, "the supreme Lord," when a solemn judgment is to be pronounced. **Is taking away:** "Is on the point of taking away." The prophet sees what is happening in the broad sweep of events as seen by the eye of God; the men of Judah, on the other hand, are immersed in the present moment and the immediate situation and see nothing. **Stay and staff:** The alliteration attempts to reproduce the effect of the Hebrew use of the same word, in masculine and feminine forms, to suggest "every kind of prop and stay," everything on which man rests the weight of his life. **Bread . . . water:** The introduction of the idea of economic resources as distinct from key persons in the structure of society (vss. 2-3) is probably a later though legitimate extension of the thought of the prophet here.

2-3. Cunning artificer, . . . eloquent orator: The quite different rendering of the RSV, **skilful magician, . . . expert in charms,** which parallels the words **prophet . . . diviner** of vs. 2, is to be noted. The **prophet** here is the professional soothsayer or "false prophet" (cf. Mic. 3:5; Hos. 9:7), and is grouped with the other representatives of popular superstition and magic religion.

When the foundations are destroyed the structure collapses. Without leadership society becomes a mob, hunger and thirst make men desperate, all the decencies of life go by the board, no one will accept responsibility, it is every man for himself, civil strife breaks out, and there is blood in the streets. There is no law or order left, save the inexorable law of God. That stands. What men sow they reap, and the wages of sin is still death. As is always the case when a civilization goes to pieces, the corruption begins at the top, especially among two classes, the rulers, business and political, and the women.

It would be untrue to conditions in Western civilization to attempt to establish any close

5 And the people shall be oppressed, every one by another, and every one by his neighbor: the child shall behave himself proudly against the ancient, and the base against the honorable.
 	
6 When a man shall take hold of his brother of the house of his father, *saying*, Thou hast clothing, be thou our ruler, and *let* this ruin *be* under thy hand:
 	
7 In that day shall he swear, saying, I will not be a healer; for in my house *is* neither bread nor clothing: make me not a ruler of the people.
 	
8 For Jerusalem is ruined, and Judah is fallen: because their tongue and their doings *are* against the LORD, to provoke the eyes of his glory.
 	
9 ¶ The show of their countenance doth witness against them; and they declare their sin as Sodom, they hide *it* not. Woe unto their soul! for they have rewarded evil unto themselves.
	5 And the people will oppress one another,
	    every man his fellow
	    and every man his neighbor;
	  the youth will be insolent to the elder,
	    and the base fellow to the honorable.
	
	6 When a man takes hold of his brother
	    in the house of his father, saying:
	  "You have a mantle;
	    you shall be our leader,
	  and this heap of ruins
	    shall be under your rule";
	7 in that day he will speak out, saying:
	  "I will not be a healer;
	    in my house there is neither bread nor
	      mantle;
	  you shall not make me
	    leader of the people."
	8 For Jerusalem has stumbled,
	    and Judah has fallen;
	  because their speech and their deeds are
	    against the LORD,
	  defying his glorious presence.
	
	9 Their partiality witnesses against them;
	    they proclaim their sin like Sodom,
	    they do not hide it.
	  Woe to them!
	    For they have brought evil upon themselves.

5. Oppress (*niggas*): Better, "fall upon," *nāghash,* with some Hebrew MSS, the LXX, Vulg., Targ. The picture is not that of the setting up of new tyrants but of the violence which will result when there is no ruler and no restraint.

6-7. A vivid glimpse of the destroyed and leaderless community. **I will not be a healer,** or "I am no healer," one who bandages a wound, and so, figuratively, a physician of the spirit, as in 30:26; 61:1.

2. A RUINED PEOPLE (3:8-12)

8. Jerusalem is ruined or **has stumbled:** Better taken as a prophetic perfect, "shall stumble," "shall totter in ruins." This is a threat of what is about to happen (cf. vs. 1), because the people are **defying his glorious presence.** This last phrase is the verbal link with 2:21 and is a reminiscence of Isaiah's experience of the Lord's presence as one of exalted majesty (cf. 6:1-5).

9. The show of their countenance or **their partiality:** Lit., "their recognition of faces." A better parallel with the next clause is obtained if, with Arnold B. Ehrlich

parallel between the situation in Israel as Isaiah saw it and that which exists in the Western Hemisphere. Our social order, despite its need for reform, is still basically sound. Nevertheless, the evils which Isaiah denounced as the cause of the nation's collapse can destroy any civilization, for they are not the sins of any one age but of	all ages, not the effects of economic or political forces, but themselves the causes of ruin. Nor can it be denied that they are present in our order of life. Corrupt politicians, unscrupulous demagogues, merciless exploiters of the poor, businessmen without conscience, who take "all the traffic will bear," moneylenders who bleed

10 Say ye to the righteous, that *it shall be* well *with him:* for they shall eat the fruit of their doings.

11 Woe unto the wicked! *it shall be* ill *with him:* for the reward of his hands shall be given him.

12 ¶ *As for* my people, children *are* their oppressors, and women rule over them. O my people, they which lead thee cause *thee* to err, and destroy the way of thy paths.

13 The LORD standeth up to plead, and standeth to judge the people.

14 The LORD will enter into judgment with the ancients of his people, and the princes thereof: for ye have eaten up the vineyard; the spoil of the poor *is* in your houses.

10 Tell the righteous that it shall be well with them,
    for they shall eat the fruit of their deeds.

11 Woe to the wicked! It shall be ill with him,
    for what his hands have done shall be done to him.

12 My people — children are their oppressors,
    and women rule over them.
O my people, your leaders mislead you,
    and confuse the course of your paths.

13 The LORD has taken his place to contend,
    he stands to judge his people.[d]

14 The LORD enters into judgment
    with the elders and princes of his people:
"It is you who have devoured the vineyard,
    the spoil of the poor is in your houses.

[d] Gk Syr: Heb *judge peoples*

(*Randglossen zur hebräischen Bibel* [Leipzig: J. C. Hinrichs, 1912], p. 14), we read *pîhem,* "their mouth(s)," for *penêhem,* "their face(s)," and translate "their own mouths witness against them." **Like Sodom:** Either "as brazen as" or "as vile as" Sodom (cf. Gen. 19:4-5).

10-11. These two verses, with their contrast of the **righteous** and the **wicked** as groups within the community, stand apart from the context and recall the language of postexilic psalms like Ps. 1.

12. The repetition of **my people** suggests that the first line of this verse, like the second, is exclamatory, and that the pronouns should be second person throughout. The word translated **children** is found elsewhere not with this meaning, but with the meaning "gleaner," adopted by the LXX and more suitable here: "Thy oppressors glean thee, take thy last copper." The LXX and other ancient versions also read *nôshîm,* "exactors," "creditors," instead of *nāshîm,* **women.** The Masoretic interpretation, followed by the English versions, has been unduly influenced by vs. 4.

3. RAPACITY OF THE RULERS (3:13-15)

13. Once more a reproach adopts the favorite figure of a complaint as made in a court of justice. "The LORD has risen to accuse, he stands to judge." As he gives judgment against the guilty he makes his own the accusers' complaint (cf. I Sam. 24:15).

14. "It is the LORD himself who comes to execute judgment"; the word order of the sentence emphasizes the subject of the verb. **Elders** were the rulers under the old clan structure of society, and still had the prestige of leading citizens. **Princes** were state officials, not members of the royal family; they were magistrates, court officials, or army officers. **It is you:** Once more the subject is emphasized as the leaders are indignantly accused of having betrayed and exploited those committed to their care. **Eaten up** or **devoured** ["destroyed," "plundered"], as in 5:5, when the fence of the vineyard is removed. The LXX reads "my vineyard," as in 5:3-5; cf. "my people" in 3:15. **The spoil of the poor,** who have been plundered like a defeated enemy (cf. Mic. 2:8-9). The prophets tear aside the veil of custom and appearance to disclose the real situation (cf. Amos 2:6; 4:1; and the "whited sepulchres" of Matt. 23:27).

15 What mean ye *that* ye beat my people to pieces, and grind the faces of the poor? saith the Lord GOD of hosts.	15 What do you mean by crushing my people,
	     by grinding the face of the poor?" says
	       the Lord GOD of hosts.

16 ¶ Moreover the LORD saith, Because the daughters of Zion are haughty, and walk with stretched forth necks and wanton eyes, walking and mincing *as* they go, and making a tinkling with their feet:	16 The LORD said:
	 Because the daughters of Zion are
	     haughty
	   and walk with outstretched necks,
	     glancing wantonly with their eyes,
	 mincing along as they go,
	     tinkling with their feet;

---

15. Beat . . . to pieces: "Crush" or "overwhelm." As in Ps. 72:4, God is said to overwhelm the oppressor. **Grind:** As between millstones.

E. THE PROUD WOMEN OF JERUSALEM (3:16–4:1)

This passage is a reproach and threat addressed to the vain, proud women of the leading families of Jerusalem who are to share the judgment of the day when "the haughtiness of man shall be humbled" (2:17). The connection between vs. 17 and vs. 24 is broken by the later insertion of a long list of articles of dress and ornament. At vs. 25 there is an abrupt change to an address to Zion personified as an individual woman (cf. 1:8; 10:32), and many commentators have held that 3:25–4:1 is a fragment of a distinct oracle. But 4:1 is necessary as the conclusion of 3:16-17, 24, while at the same time it is a direct continuation of the thought of vss. 25-26. The change of figure at vs. 25 is to be explained as an example of the easy transition in Hebrew prophetic and poetic thought from the idea of a group of individuals to that of a representative figure in which the individuals are incorporated (cf. 43:10; Deut. 26:5-9). Here the prophet begins with **the daughters of Zion** and ends with the feminine personification of the city itself.

It is a striking fact that three of the greatest of the Hebrew prophets found themselves in sharp opposition to the thoughtless and luxury-loving women of their people (cf. 32:9-12; Amos 4:1-3; Jer. 44:15-30). "Feminine morality is the surest criterion of the morality of a people and of an age; if that is lax, morality itself is decaying and breaking down" (Otto Procksch, *Jesaia I* [Leipzig: A. Deichert, 1930; "Kommentar zum Alten Testament"], p. 78). The pride of men showed itself in the building of great towers and tall ships, in the arrogance which sought to master the world in forgetfulness of God (cf. 2:15-17). The same pride showed itself in the luxury and ostentation which had become the sole objective and standard of fashionable women, contemptuous of others and indifferent to the human cost of the privileges they enjoyed. Isaiah (vs. 17) and Amos (4:1-3) are almost brutal in the language they use to describe punishments suitable for such feminine arrogance. They do not speak in general terms but describe with realism the fate which awaits these proud women when their whole world will be overturned in the agonies of war.

16. "They walk with chin in air and roving eye, with mincing steps and jangling their bangles as they go." The phrases **wanton eyes** (KJV) and **glancing wantonly with**

---

their victims white—they are to be found in every great city, poisoning its life and eating into the very foundations of the social order. Such forces of evil, whether in personal life or organized in trusts or "rings," are the real enemies of society; they are openly at war with it, and if unchecked can destroy it.	**16-26. A Degenerate Womanhood.**—It may not be as obvious, but it is equally true, that a degenerate womanhood can corrupt a nation. Isaiah's scorn of the society women of Israel is savage. In eleven blistering verses he pillories their empty vanity, their ostentation, their vulgarity, and with a certain savage satisfaction

17 Therefore the Lord will smite with a scab the crown of the head of the daughters of Zion, and the LORD will discover their secret parts.

18 In that day the Lord will take away the bravery of *their* tinkling ornaments *about their feet,* and *their* cauls, and *their* round tires like the moon,

19 The chains, and the bracelets, and the mufflers,

20 The bonnets, and the ornaments of the legs, and the headbands, and the tablets, and the earrings,

21 The rings, and nose jewels,

22 The changeable suits of apparel, and the mantles, and the wimples, and the crisping pins,

23 The glasses, and the fine linen, and the hoods, and the veils.

---

17 the Lord will smite with a scab
    the heads of the daughters of Zion,
    and the LORD will lay bare their secret
      parts.

18 In that day the Lord will take away the finery of the anklets, the headbands, and the crescents; 19 the pendants, the bracelets, and the scarfs; 20 the headdresses, the armlets, the sashes, the perfume boxes, and the amulets; 21 the signet rings and nose rings; 22 the festal robes, the mantles, the cloaks, and the handbags; 23 the garments of gauze, the linen garments, the turbans, and the veils.

---

their eyes (RSV) translate a word not found elsewhere; a very similar word meaning "deceiving" is read by some MSS. The short, quick footsteps (lit., "walking like a child") were necessitated by the wearing of ornamental ankle chains; the jingling of anklets attracted attention, as many feminine adornments are intended to do.

17. With an almost savage abruptness Isaiah pronounces the divine judgment; **smite with a scab,** a loathsome sore, not necessarily that of leprosy as in Lev. 13:2. The verb may mean instead "undo" (i.e., the covering of). **Their secret parts:** The word is not used elsewhere with this meaning; it is better to translate "their foreheads." For cutting off the hair as a sign of shame cf. 7:20.

18-23. The identification of many of the items of feminine finery is at best uncertain, since most of the terms used occur only here in the O.T. The etymology of the words, the renderings in the ancient versions, and the study of the many objects for personal adornment found in Palestinian excavations of remains dating from this period are the best guides. The translations of the RSV are preferable to the KJV, but for some of them alternatives are here suggested. **Headbands:** "Buckles," with circular faces of bright metal, "little suns" (cf. Ugaritic *shapash,* "sun"; cf. Edmond Jacob, "Les textes de Ras Shamra-Ugarit et l'Ancien Testament," *Revue d'Histoire et de Philosophie Religieuses,* XXVII [1947], 246). **Crescents:** Broaches or **pendants. Scarfs:** "Wimples," "shawls," possibly the long garment covering the head and hanging down the back, pictured in Sennacherib's Lachish relief (see illustration in Kurt Galling, *Biblisches Reallexikon* [Tübingen: J. C. B. Mohr, 1937; "Handbuch zum Alten Testament"], p. 335). **Sashes:** Possibly "beaded belts"; in Neo-Hebrew the word means "band," "beads." **Perfume boxes:** Lit., "soul houses," and therefore probably "charms." **Garments of gauze:** "Filmy shawls." **Linen garments:** "Linen shawls."

---

describes their fate. The very form of the penalty which is to overtake them reveals Isaiah's contempt for them; for it is not the ruin of their homes, or their sons, or any of the values which make true life they are to lament, but merely the loss of their finery, their jewels, their cosmetics, and the security of "kept" women. Isaiah is the more bitter about the women be-

cause he has such deep appreciation of their influence. There he is profoundly right. To a degree seldom realized, the moral quality of womanhood determines the character of society. These are the mothers of men, they set the ideals of men and, by what they are, either inspire or corrupt their sons. Modern women have claimed equality with men, they have invaded the realms

24 And it shall come to pass, *that* instead of sweet smell there shall be stink; and instead of a girdle a rent; and instead of well set hair baldness; and instead of a stomacher a girding of sackcloth; *and* burning instead of beauty.

25 Thy men shall fall by the sword, and thy mighty in the war.

26 And her gates shall lament and mourn; and she *being* desolate shall sit upon the ground.

4 And in that day seven women shall take hold of one man, saying, We will eat our own bread, and wear our own apparel; only let us be called by thy name, to take away our reproach.

24 Instead of perfume there will be rotten-ness;
and instead of a girdle, a rope;
and instead of well-set hair, baldness;
and instead of a rich robe, a girding of sackcloth;
instead of beauty, shame.[e]

25 Your men shall fall by the sword
and your mighty men in battle.

26 And her gates shall lament and mourn;
ravaged, she shall sit upon the ground.

4 And seven women shall take hold of one man in that day, saying, "We will eat our own bread and wear our own clothes, only let us be called by your name; take away our reproach."

[e] One ancient Ms: Heb lacks *shame*

---

24. At this point the oracle is resumed. The stern judgment of vs. 17 is continued with a picture of the complete transformation of circumstances which the fashionable women will experience when they are carried away as captives in war; each item of the description drives home the thought that the punishment will fit the crime. **Instead of perfume there will be rottenness,** i.e., the stench of decay. For a **girdle** or "belt" there will be a **rope,** i.e., an encircling rope, a "halter." **Well-set hair:** Lit., "dressed like artistic metalwork," an elaborate coiffure, hair curled or braided. **Baldness, . . . sackcloth:** Customary signs of mourning (cf. Amos 8:10), originally intended as a disguise for protection against the spirits of the dead; here, as in I Kings 20:31; 21:27, adopted as a mark of abject submission. **Burning instead of beauty:** A good example of the forced translations which occasionally result from the rule that the English versions must render the text as it stands, even when it is obviously defective. The first word, כי, from its position in the sentence and its accentuation must be the common conjunction "for," probably with the force of the asseverative "yea!" The existence of a noun identical in form and meaning **burning** has had to be inferred from a rare verbal root to give a possible, though unsuitable, translation here. Actually there is a gap in the Hebrew text, and as it stands it can only be rendered "Yes— (for) instead of beauty. . . ." The Dead Sea Scroll of Isaiah supplies the missing word, בשׁת (there shall be) **shame** (so RSV).

25. Your men: "Thy menfolk"; the possessive pronoun is singular (see KJV, **thy men**), for the city is being addressed (see above).

26. Her gates: Places of assembly (cf. Ps. 69:12). Addressing now the women, the prophet reverts to the third person in speaking of the city. **Desolate** or **ravaged:** Lit., "cleaned out"; "she shall sink exhausted to the ground."

4:1. The extremity to which the proud, self-confident women will be reduced will be seen when, contrary to nature and custom, they will go to any lengths to come under

---

once exclusively ruled by men, and have done it with brilliant success in almost every field of activity. It is not, however, the public women who put a stamp on national life; it is still the women of the factory, the office, or fashionable society, who by their taste, their standards, their character, determine whether the ideals of purity, integrity, unselfishness, and faith are to prevail or to fall. The old sentimentality, that

. . . the hand that rocks the cradle
Is the hand that rules the world,[4]

if quoted today, meets with derisive laughter; but the truth stands that the womanhood of a nation, more than any other single agency, determines the character and destiny of men.

[4] William Ross Wallace, "The Hand that Rules the World."

| 2 In that day shall the branch of the LORD be beautiful and glorious, and the fruit of the earth *shall be* excellent and comely for them that are escaped of Israel. | 2 In that day the branch of the LORD shall be beautiful and glorious, and the fruit of the land shall be the pride and |

the protection of the few surviving men. A man normally was required by law to provide his wife with food and clothing (Exod. 21:10). **Reproach:** "Disgrace," i.e., of childlessness (cf. Gen. 30:23; I Sam. 1:6), and still more, of bearing no man's name and so being without standing in the community (cf. Ruth 2:10; 4:10).

F. ZION PURGED BY JUDGMENT (4:2-6)

This is one of the eschatological passages which have been inserted in contexts where they stand out in marked contrast and which, in their present form at any rate, come from a period later than Isaiah. Some scholars hold that vss. 2-3 (perhaps preceded by vs. 4) are Isaianic and that the remainder consists of later supplements. It is better to recognize that literary prophecy in the later period was largely derivative and that we have here such a composition, making use of ideas and language found in Isaiah and developing them with a new emphasis. The promise of the fruitfulness of the land for the survivors of the catastrophe is found in 7:15-16, 21-22; 37:30-31; in the last passage the same words as here are used for **survivors** (פליטה) and **he who is left** (הנשאר). The washing of the filth of Jerusalem recalls the language of 1:16; 28:8, and "daughter(s) of Jerusalem" is derived either from 3:16-17 or (more probably) from 1:8; 10:32. The application to individuals of the epithet **holy** is a far cry from the thought of Isaiah (6:3), and much closer to that of Ezekiel (44:23) and Zechariah (14:20-21). The idea of the "book of life" is a favorite one in late eschatological writings (cf. Mal. 3:16; Dan. 12:1; Rev. 3:5); so also is the picture of the visible, **flaming glory** of the Lord as the mark of his overshadowing presence (cf. Ezek. 43:1-4).

At the same time no reader should depreciate unduly the literary quality and spiritual value of a passage such as this simply because it is probably the work of a writer later than Isaiah, who has drawn his inspiration in part from that prophet. This is a song of that hope by which men may live when all that they have built and have rejoiced in has been taken from them and their spirits are threatened with despair. It is hope for the future which is more than wishful thinking, because it is grounded in faith in God and in confidence that the historic process will yet demonstrate his goodness and his power.

2. The branch of the LORD: The word צמח (lit., "that which sprouts") is used in Jer. 23:5; Zech. 3:8; etc., of the messianic king as sprouting from the stock of David; but here the parallel expression **the fruit of the earth** shows that it has its primary meaning, "new growth," "vegetation." One manifestation of the creative power of God in the time of deliverance will be that where now there is only barren desolation, the earth will again be "fair and radiant" with growing things. **Them that are escaped** or **the survivors:** The word פליטה, "escape," eventually became almost a technical term for the Jews who had survived exile and had returned from Babylonia to Judah (cf. Neh. 1:2). Here it

---

4:2-6. The Promise of Restoration.—This passage seems a sudden intrusion into the oracles of doom which precede it. It is held to be of other than Isaianic authorship, probably of a date much later than his. Be that as it may, the editors who placed it here were true to the faith of Isaiah that judgment is never God's last word. Suddenly the scene shifts from the sight and sounds of destruction to a land clad in the greenery of spring "lovely and glorious," the habitation of people who have been through great tribulation but have been spared to come home. Jerusalem stands again restored to its lost glory; its people, purged by pain, won back to faith by experience of God's redeeming power, are a dedicated race; every man is set apart as

3 And it shall come to pass, *that he that is* left in Zion, and *he that* remaineth in Jerusalem, shall be called holy, *even* every one that is written among the living in Jerusalem:

4 When the Lord shall have washed away the filth of the daughters of Zion, and shall have purged the blood of Jerusalem from the midst thereof by the spirit of judgment, and by the spirit of burning.

5 And the Lord will create upon every dwelling place of mount Zion, and upon her assemblies, a cloud and smoke by day, and the shining of a flaming fire by night: for upon all the glory *shall be* a defense.

6 And there shall be a tabernacle for a shadow in the daytime from the heat, and for a place of refuge, and for a covert from storm and from rain.

glory of the survivors of Israel. 3 And he who is left in Zion and remains in Jerusalem will be called holy, every one who has been recorded for life in Jerusalem, 4 when the Lord shall have washed away the filth of the daughters of Zion and cleansed the bloodstains of Jerusalem from its midst by a spirit of judgment and by a spirit of burning. 5 Then the Lord will create over the whole site of Mount Zion and over her assemblies a cloud by day, and smoke and the shining of a flaming fire by night; for over all the glory there will be a canopy and a pavilion. 6 It will be for a shade by day from the heat, and for a refuge and a shelter from the storm and rain.

---

appears to be used in a promise to the exiles that they *will* return. **Israel**, as vs. 3 shows, is not the Northern Kingdom of Isaiah's day but "the Israel that survives" in Judah.

3. Each individual citizen of that new Jerusalem **shall be called holy.** The "holy people" of Deut. 7:6; etc. (itself an ideal later than Isaiah), is individualized; every one, as in Zech. 14:20-21 every thing, will always be in a state of ritual purity. **That is written among the living** or **who has been recorded for life:** "Listed as living"; life and death being in God's hands, the names of the living are written in his book (cf. Exod. 32:32; Mal. 3:16), and hence David's taking of a census was punished as sacrilege (II Sam. 24).

4. Daughters of Zion: The parallelism with **Jerusalem** makes it highly probable that the word should be in the singular; vss. 4-6 refer not only to the women but also to the city as a whole. **Spirit of judgment** or **spirit of burning:** There is a play here on the double meaning of רוח, "wind," **spirit;** the hot, suffocating wind from the desert is both the means and the symbol of the Lord's judgment (cf. Jer. 4:11-12; 51:1).

5. Will create, ובּרא, is not the right word here; the LXX and the Vulg. read ובא, "and he will come." But reference to passages describing the events of the wilderness wanderings (to which this certainly refers) makes it almost certain that the text here read originally ונראה, "and [the Lord] shall appear." The whole verse may be rendered: "Then the Lord shall appear over the whole site of Mount Zion and over her (sacred) assemblies (in) a cloud by day, and in flame-lit smoke by night, and over all the glory (of the Lord) shall be a canopy." The word for **canopy** is used elsewhere only of the bridal tent (cf. Ps. 19:5; Joel 2:16).

6. Tabernacle or **pavilion,** is an approximate synonym of **canopy** and belongs to vs. 5, as in the RSV.

---

one bought with a price; and the city itself, cleansed as by fire, is a holy place. This is a song of hope, the old undying faith in God's restoring love, something far deeper than the unconquerable optimism of the human heart. The furious storm of God's righteous judgment must some day pass, for he does not "keep his anger for ever" (Ps. 103:9). Some sanctified soul, believing where he could not see, thus sang of the mercy yet to be shown; and we are left with the vision of the beloved city, its battlements clear in the evening light, the home of a redeemed people, and over all the brooding compassion of God which is the **canopy** of his **glory.**

5 Now will I sing to my well-beloved a song of my beloved touching his vineyard. My well-beloved hath a vineyard in a very fruitful hill:

5 Let me sing for my beloved
a love song concerning his vineyard:
My beloved had a vineyard
on a very fertile hill.

G. A Song of the Lord's Vineyard (5:1-7)

This striking passage is unique in the prophetic canon. It is a reproach and threat cast in the form of a parable and culminating in the interpretation of the parable. At the same time it is introduced like a popular ballad, and vss. 1-4 have the sprightly rhythm and quick movement of a song. The vintage festivals were times of feasting and singing (cf. 16:10; Judg. 9:27), and Isaiah here adopts the role of the ballad singer introducing a new song. By so doing he beguiles the attention of those who otherwise might not have given him a hearing, as Amos beguiled the men of Israel (Amos 1–2) and Nathan inveigled David into pronouncing judgment on himself (II Sam. 12:1-12).

The poem falls into two parts, vss. 1-4 and vss. 5-7, distinguished by a marked change of meter, each introduced by a line in prose announcing what is to follow. Each part in turn has two subdivisions: vss. 1b-2 describe the favorable conditions of the planting of the vineyard and the disappointing results; vss. 3-4 challenge the hearers to say where the fault lies; vss. 5-6 declare the owner's intention to destroy the vineyard, a fate which the hearers have been led into approving; and the climax comes in vs. 7 when the vineyard of the parable is identified as Israel, and its bad fruits as her evil ways.

The occasion when the prophet addressed his song-parable to the **inhabitants of Jerusalem and men of Judah** was in all probability one of the great gatherings at the temple to celebrate the feast of Tabernacles, following completion of the harvest (cf. Deut. 16:13-15). Vintage songs were in the air, and the crowd would listen with interest as the well-known prophet undertook to sing one in the informal atmosphere of the temple court before the sacrifices had begun. There are only vague indications of the period when the song was first published, since **the house of Israel** is a reference not to the Northern Kingdom (which Isaiah calls "Ephraim"; cf. 7:5, 9; contrast 8:14), but to the whole people as a religious community with its distinctive history as the Lord's people. At the same time, this phrase and its synonym "the house of Jacob" are characteristic of Isaiah's earlier oracles (cf. 2:6; 8:14, 17), as is the demand for social justice. In his later prophecies during the reign of Hezekiah the characteristic (though not exclusive) designation of the people is "the daughter [or inhabitants] of Zion" (cf. 1:8; 10:24, 32; 14:32; 37:32; etc.), the concern of the prophet is with the fate of Judah among the nations, and his appeal to his people is for faith in their God as Lord of history. The most cogent evidence that this oracle belongs to the period prior to the Syro-Ephraimite attack on Judah, however, is the expectation of complete disaster (as in 6:11-13); and also the resemblance to the message of Amos in this respect and in the presentation of Israel's sin as the greater because of the favors she had received (cf. Amos 2:9-11).

5:1. Let me sing ["Now hear me sing" or "I wish to sing"] **for my beloved a love song:** It is not easy to discern the exact shade of meaning of these words, which in the Song of Songs have an erotic sense unsuitable here. In accordance with the Oriental fondness for grandiloquent language, the words could be used with the weakened sense

---

5:1-24. The Song of the Vineyard.—This chapter, opening with a song followed by a series of graphic exclamatory reproaches and closing with a brilliant pen picture of an army on the march, is so full of ideas of timeless force that it is possible to mention only the chief of these which clamor to be heard. Isaiah displays an astonishing versatility in his methods of

teaching. He despises nothing which can be a vehicle for his message: an acted parable, a signboard, a costume; he uses anything which will make his word articulate or visible. So here he employs one of the oldest customs of men: he sings a song. It is a clever song; it paints a picture, elicits a sympathetic response, asks a question, and leaves the hearers condemned

2 And he fenced it, and gathered out the stones thereof, and planted it with the choicest vine, and built a tower in the midst of it, and also made a winepress therein: and he looked that it should bring forth grapes, and it brought forth wild grapes.

3 And now, O inhabitants of Jerusalem, and men of Judah, judge, I pray you, betwixt me and my vineyard.

4 What could have been done more to my vineyard, that I have not done in it? wherefore, when I looked that it should bring forth grapes, brought it forth wild grapes?

5 And now go to; I will tell you what I will do to my vineyard: I will take away the hedge thereof, and it shall be eaten up; *and* break down the wall thereof, and it shall be trodden down:

6 And I will lay it waste: it shall not be

2 He digged it and cleared it of stones,
　and planted it with choice vines;
he built a watchtower in the midst of it,
　and hewed out a wine vat in it;
and he looked for it to yield grapes,
　but it yielded wild grapes.

3 And now, O inhabitants of Jerusalem
　and men of Judah,
judge, I pray you, between me
　and my vineyard.
4 What more was there to do for my vineyard,
　that I have not done in it?
When I looked for it to yield grapes,
　why did it yield wild grapes?

5 And now I will tell you
　what I will do to my vineyard.
I will remove its hedge,
　and it shall be devoured;
I will break down its wall,
　and it shall be trampled down.
6 I will make it a waste;
　it shall not be pruned or hoed,
　and briers and thorns shall grow up;

---

of "friend" (cf. Procksch, *Jesaia I,* p. 88). It is almost inconceivable that Isaiah, of all people, would use an erotic term for his God, even in a parable; moreover, by no stretch of the imagination can the song be called a love song. It is probably best to take ידיד and דוד as synonyms, and to translate: "Now hear me sing on behalf of my friend, my friend's song about his vineyard." **Fruitful hill** or **fertile hill:** Lit., "a horn, son of oil"; a hill summit, very fat or rich (cf. "valley of oils, fat things" in 28:1).

2. Choice vines: Hebrew שרק, from a root meaning "to be red," i.e., either red grapes or grapes of Sorek, a valley in the foothills west of Jerusalem (where the village of Timnah was), known for its vineyards (cf. Judg. 14:5). **Watchtower . . . wine vat:** This was no casual experiment but a costly undertaking intended to be permanent; Palestinian vineyards still have stone watchtowers as protection against thieves. **Looked:** "Waited eagerly." **Wild grapes:** "Bitter fruit," lit., "stinking fruit."

4. What more was there to do? "What more could have been done?"

5-6. "So now let me tell you what I am going to do to my vineyard." With the removal of the fence and the breaking down of the wall, the vineyard will be **devoured**

---

by their own answer. By it Isaiah indirectly, but nonetheless clearly, confronts his people with the infinite pains God had taken for them and his expectation that they would respond to his love. Because they failed his trust and forfeited his favor, because they return evil for his good, they are to be cast out and become like the deserted vineyard, gone to seed, a nation choked with evil growths and arid with a multitude of sins.

It is a perturbing experience for any who are sensitive to the lovingkindness of God to reflect what they have done with his gifts, and how poor a thing they have made of a life so crowned with mercies.

Thy life was given for me;
　Thy blood, O Lord, was shed
That I might ransomed be,
　And quickened from the dead:
Thy life was given for me;
　What have I given for thee? [5]

Isaiah does not reproach men for failure to become what it was in them to be; it is not for that they are judged, but because they had suffered

[5] Frances R. Havergal.

pruned, nor digged; but there shall come up briers and thorns: I will also command the clouds that they rain no rain upon it.

7 For the vineyard of the LORD of hosts *is* the house of Israel, and the men of Judah his pleasant plant: and he looked for judgment, but behold oppression; for righteousness, but behold a cry.

8 ¶ Woe unto them that join house to house, *that* lay field to field, till *there be* no place, that they may be placed alone in the midst of the earth!

I will also command the clouds
　　that they rain no rain upon it.

7 For the vineyard of the LORD of hosts
　　is the house of Israel,
and the men of Judah
　　are his pleasant planting;
and he looked for justice,
　　but behold, bloodshed;
for righteousness,
　　but behold, a cry!

8 Woe to those who join house to house,
　　who add field to field,
until there is no more room,
　　and you are made to dwell alone
　　in the midst of the land.

---

and **trampled** by animals; it will become "a waste, unpruned, unweeded, and choked with briers and thorns," and the very **clouds** will be forbidden to drop **rain** upon it. The final clause suggests for the first time who is the "friend" in whose name the prophet speaks.

7. The hint becomes explicit: Israel is the vineyard of the Lord, and Judah "the planting of his delight" or "what he planted with such delight." He **looked for** ("expected") *mishpāṭ* (justice), but instead there was *mispāḥ* (**bloodshed**); and *çedhāqāh* (**righteousness**), but instead there was *çeʻāqāh* (**a cry**). This play on words similar in sound but sharply contrasting in meaning provides a powerful conclusion to the oracle; it is used, however, not merely as a literary device but because of the Hebrews' vivid sense of the power inherent in words, especially in words which, like these, seem mysteriously related by similarity and contrast. G. H. Box (*The Book of Isaiah* [London: Isaac Pitman & Sons, 1908], p. 41) attempts to convey the assonance of the Hebrew by translating:

> For measures He looked—but lo massacres!
> For right—but lo riot.

It seems probable that these two word pairs were the oracle in germ as it first emerged in the prophet's mind with the conviction that the Lord was prompting him to speak a message of which they were to be the essential content. Man's sin is not merely failure to rise to his best in response to God's call; it is the perversion of the good, and rebellion, not against arbitrary authority, but against love.

H. THOSE WHO NEITHER FEAR NOR REGARD MAN (5:8-24a)

The distinctive feature of this section is the series of exclamatory reproaches beginning **Woe unto . . .** (vss. 8, 11, 18, 20, 21, 22) and picturing the pride and self-indulgence, the callousness, moral bankruptcy, and religious indifference which could result only in disaster in a world ruled by a just and holy God. Linked with these (in vss. 9-10, 13 plus 17, 24) are threats of doom unmitigated by any hope. Enclosed within this section

---

the good which God implanted in them to be corrupted. Conscience does not rebuke us chiefly because we are less than we might have been. The root sin is what we have done with God's love; it is the perversion of good which is our shame—not the refusal to obey a law, but the selfishness which scorned a divine appeal and

which, as the author of Hebrews says (Heb. 6:6), is not less than a new crucifixion of love.

From the exposure of what is really the sin of ingratitude and contempt of God's love, Isaiah passes to denunciation of personal and social sins. He never loses himself in generalities; the analysis of the moral and spiritual state of the

9 In mine ears *said* the LORD of hosts, Of a truth many houses shall be desolate, *even* great and fair, without inhabitant. 10 Yea, ten acres of vineyard shall yield one bath, and the seed of a homer shall yield an ephah.	9 The LORD of hosts has sworn in my hearing: "Surely many houses shall be desolate, large and beautiful houses, without inhabitant. 10 For ten acres of vineyard shall yield but one bath, and a homer of seed shall yield but an ephah."

is another and distinctive threat (vss. 14-16) which clearly is related in some way to the oracle complex of 2:6-22 (with vs. 15 cf. 2:9; with vs. 16 cf. the refrain in 2:11, 17, 22). Either this section (5:14-16) is the conclusion of the first of the two poems from which 2:6-22 was put together or it is an independent threat in which the prophet made use of similar language and ideas.

The tenor of these denunciations recalls much that is found in the other eighth-century prophets, especially Amos and Micah. All confronted a society where a period of prolonged prosperity for the ruling classes had absorbed their interest and established new standards of luxury and social power; as a corollary, the old sense of kinship among members of the community was lost, the poor were exploited and oppressed, and justice was no longer administered in accordance with the old standards of right. At the same time, the meaning of religion itself was changed; worship became an occasion of display, and the worth of sacrifices was measured by their costliness. The forms and ceremonies adopted from Canaanite religion had become dominant, and the living relationship to the Lord as the covenant God peculiar to Israel was now a fading tradition.

This section, like the foregoing, declares that a day of reckoning is at hand, when those who have produced in their lives the bitter fruit of irreligion and moral depravity will know a devastation like that of a vineyard abandoned to the wild beasts of the wilderness. The most probable background is the reign of Jotham or the early part of the reign of Ahaz, since the doom (as in the story in ch. 6 of Isaiah's commission) is absolute, and since the worship of foreign gods which marked the later reign of Ahaz is not one of the sins denounced. At the same time, the disaster is no longer pictured (as in ch. 2) as brought by earthquake. The reference in vs. 13 to the carrying of the people into exile suggests a time when this possibility was brought to Isaiah's attention by the appearance in the west of Assyrian armies, as in 738 when Tiglath-pileser (Pul) cowed the western states into paying tribute (cf. II Kings 15:19), or in 733-32 when he devastated Damascus and turned the greater part of the territory of northern Israel into Assyrian provinces (cf. II Kings 15:29).

8-10. Woe unto . . . : "Shame on . . . ," or in view of vs. 9, "A curse on . . . ." These verses should be compared with Mic. 2:1-2, 8-9, where is denounced the same sin of covetousness (with Mic. 2:2 cf. the Tenth Commandment, Exod. 20:17) in the building up of vast estates without regard to the cost to fellow Israelites and to the community as a whole. The doom is appropriate: in depriving his neighbors of their land, the powerful man deprives himself of neighbors and the land of cultivators. The Dead Sea

nation is always in terms of visible evil. So here he fastens on specific and associated sins.

First, the rapacity of the wealthy, especially in the matter of real estate. "Shame on those who add house to house and field to field until they have got it all, and are left neighborless on their estates" (vs. 8). This might have been said yesterday, so true it is. It is the curse of luxury that it can lead to loneliness; every property purchased, every acre added, withdraws a man a little farther from brotherhood, until he sits among his piled-up possessions, unenvied and unloved—in the solitude of wealth. It is all wrong. No man has the right to acquire vast tracts of land if in so doing he denies to his fellows their chance of home and field. It is one thing for a man to own his parcel of ground and rejoice in his own cottage; so far, private prop-

11 ¶ Woe unto them that rise up early in the morning, *that* they may follow strong drink; that continue until night, *till* wine inflame them!

12 And the harp and the viol, the tabret and pipe, and wine, are in their feasts: but they regard not the work of the LORD, neither consider the operation of his hands.

13 ¶ Therefore my people are gone into captivity, because *they have* no knowledge: and their honorable men *are* famished, and their multitude dried up with thirst.

14 Therefore hell hath enlarged herself, and opened her mouth without measure: and their glory, and their multitude, and their pomp, and he that rejoiceth, shall descend into it.

11 Woe to those who rise early in the morning,
    that they may run after strong drink,
who tarry late into the evening
    till wine inflames them!
12 They have lyre and harp,
    timbrel and flute and wine at their feasts;
but they do not regard the deeds of the LORD,
    or see the work of his hands.

13 Therefore my people go into exile
    for want of knowledge;
their honored men are dying of hunger,
    and their multitude is parched with thirst.
14 Therefore Sheol has enlarged its appetite
    and opened its mouth beyond measure,
and the nobility of Jerusalem*f* and her multitude go down,
    her throng and he who exults in her.

f Heb *her nobility*

Scroll of Isaiah and the versions support the rendering of the RSV: **And you are made to dwell alone. The LORD of hosts has sworn in my hearing** supplies the words **has sworn** which have dropped out of the Hebrew text; this is supported by the LXX and the Vulg. **Bath:** A liquid measure approximately of six gallons, equivalent to the dry measure **ephah,** or bushel, ten of which made a **homer.** The yield would be so small that the farmer would lose nine tenths of his seed; cf. Amos 5:3, where the same figure of decimation is applied to the population.

11-12. The shame of those who have no other thought from dawn to midnight than one carousal after another. For והיה, "and it shall be" (see KJV **are,** RSV **they have**), at the beginning of vs. 12, we should probably read a second הוי, "Shame on their drunken revels" (feasts); cf. 28:1-4, 7-8; Amos 6:4-6. **They regard not the work of the LORD:** "They do not discern what the LORD is doing." Their spiritual senses are atrophied by disuse (cf. 6:9-10). That God is an active Doer rather than a static Being, and that he reveals himself in what is happening to men by injecting into the maelstrom of human wills his dominating will, is a fundamental doctrine of the theology of the prophets. Thus God makes history in giving meaning, direction, and purpose to human experience.

13. For want of knowledge: "Through their failure to perceive" the active presence of the Lord; cf. 6:9-10; Hos. 4:1, 6, 12.

14-16. As noted above, these verses are out of place and may well be part of the first of the two oracles which have been combined in a larger composition in 2:6-22. Where it stands, the **therefore** has no preamble but hangs in the air. Moreover, the possessive pronouns translated **their** in the KJV are in Hebrew the feminine singular

erty is the inalienable right of free men, but it is quite another thing when a man corners the available real estate for his own profit and pleasure, and condemns others to the fate of the dispossessed. No wonder the great estates of devastated lands in Europe were the target of men's wrath. Greed is never more heartless

than when it infects men with the passion for possessions and the power they bestow. Ultimately, as Isaiah says, it is self-defeating, and ends with empty hearts and empty homes (vss. 9-10).

Second (vss. 11-12), Isaiah deals with the sin of drunkenness. The use and abuse of liquor

15 And the mean man shall be brought down, and the mighty man shall be humbled, and the eyes of the lofty shall be humbled:

16 But the LORD of hosts shall be exalted in judgment, and God that is holy shall be sanctified in righteousness.

17 Then shall the lambs feed after their manner, and the waste places of the fat ones shall strangers eat.

15 Man is bowed down, and men are brought low,
  and the eyes of the haughty are humbled.

16 But the LORD of hosts is exalted in justice,
  and the Holy God shows himself holy in righteousness.

17 Then shall the lambs graze as in their pasture,
  fatlings and kids*g* shall feed among the ruins.

g Cn Compare Gk: Heb *aliens*

"her," which has no antecedent feminine noun; the RSV supplies the word **Jerusalem.** But in 2:7-8 occurs the word "land," which is equally suitable; the correspondence of 2:9 and 5:15 is explained if these verses have been detached from their original context following 2:8.

Hell or **Sheol:** The abode of the dead, where men are mere shadows of their former selves, as in 14:9-18; here pictured figuratively as a monster waiting to devour men in her gigantic mouth. **The LORD of hosts is exalted in justice:** That which exalts God above man is not merely the mysterious power of deity but the **justice** which is of the essence of his being, and the **judgment** by which that justice is vindicated; either translation of *mishpāṭ* is suitable here. **The Holy God shows himself holy:** "Displays his divinity." Holiness is the quality of divinity, that which distinguishes God from a man; the idea has no necessary ethical content in itself, but corresponds in this respect to the nature of the god in question. What Isaiah declares with resounding emphasis is that justice and righteousness belong to the very nature of Israel's God and hence are fundamental in the quality of holiness associated with him and with his worship.

17. The completion of the threat in vs. 13. **As in their pasture** (RSV) is better than the KJV; and **kids,** גדיים, as in the LXX, not **strangers,** גרים, **shall feed among the ruins.**

---

always have been and always will be a social problem. Probably there were in Israel men who could take it or leave it, occasional drinkers, moderate drinkers, people who illustrated the possibility of being temperate in the use of alcohol. But there were others—there always are—who had debauched themselves with liquor; they were drunk from breakfast till dawn. Their so-called parties were nothing but occasions for getting drunk to music. Their successors are in all our cities, chronic alcoholics paying in lost power and moral blindness the old price of drink. The Exeg. shows that vss. 13-16 are out of place, but it is a happy interpolation, for the evil of drunkenness has disastrous social and economical results. "Their nobility will die of hunger and their masses be parched with thirst." Money squandered on liquor affects the whole economy of a people. Our national drink bills not only accuse us but they have much to do with the tragedy of literal starvation for thousands. The drunkard is the glaring instance of the sin Isaiah here denounces, the perversion of the good in a man; every gift of mind and spirit, every noble capacity dies with fearful

rapidity in the slave to drink. "Hell gapes for him," says Isaiah (vs. 14), and that once proud figure, so splendidly endowed, now a thing both of pity and contempt, is living proof of a judgment and a judge.

The third evil on which Isaiah fastens (vss. 18-23) is a flippant skepticism about God and a perversion of the moral sense, with a consequent perversion of justice. He uses a vivid agricultural figure to depict the condition of men who have become accustomed to sin, made it their own, so that it goes with them as easily as the unresisting farm beast on the end of a rope. These are those who question the very existence of God. "You prate of God," they say; "let's see him if he is, let him prove his power; as for judgment, we have to be shown." There is a legitimate skepticism in all quest for truth, but flippancy utterly disqualifies a man; it condemns him to the darkness of his own cynicism, a darkness to be shot through with the flame of the judgment he scorns. It is only a step from such flippancy to complete moral blindness. He who continually trifles with the ultimates, and can jest about the reality of God, comes to a

18 Woe unto them that draw iniquity with cords of vanity, and sin as it were with a cart rope:

19 That say, Let him make speed, *and* hasten his work, that we may see *it:* and let the counsel of the Holy One of Israel draw nigh and come, that we may know *it!*

20 ¶ Woe unto them that call evil good, and good evil; that put darkness for light, and light for darkness; that put bitter for sweet, and sweet for bitter!

21 Woe unto *them that are* wise in their own eyes, and prudent in their own sight!

22 Woe unto *them that are* mighty to drink wine, and men of strength to mingle strong drink:

23 Which justify the wicked for reward, and take away the righteousness of the righteous from him!

---

18 Woe to those who draw iniquity with
    cords of falsehood,
  who draw sin as with cart ropes,
19 who say: "Let him make haste,
    let him speed his work
    that we may see it;
  let the purpose of the Holy One of Israel
    draw near,
    and let it come, that we may know it!"
20 Woe to those who call evil good
    and good evil,
  who put darkness for light
    and light for darkness,
  who put bitter for sweet
    and sweet for bitter!
21 Woe to those who are wise in their own
    eyes,
  and shrewd in their own sight!
22 Woe to those who are heroes at drinking
    wine,
  and valiant men in mixing strong
    drink,
23 who acquit the guilty for a bribe,
  and deprive the innocent of his right!

18-19. A vivid figure from rural life illustrates the obstinate attachment of men to their sins: they "drag their guilt after them, like a bullock on a rope, and their sin, like a heifer on a lead" (reading *hashshôr,* "bullock," for *hashshāw',* "worthlessness"; and *'eglāh,* "heifer," for *'aghālāh,* **cart**). Vs. 19 has a different meter and refers to a different sin; perhaps הוי, "Shame on . . . ," has dropped out. This is the language of a flippant skepticism, which implies disbelief in God's reality and revelation while it mocks the language of religion.

20. The depravity of those who no longer make moral distinctions, which are as real as any noted by the senses.

21. The pride of self-sufficient reason which denies any need of understanding given by God is a recurrent theme in the Bible (cf. 28:9-13; 29:14; 31:1-2; Jer. 9:23; Prov. 1:7; I Cor. 1:18-25).

22-23. With striking irony the prophet pictures the foolish boasting of men under the influence of liquor; these bibulous **heroes** (!) are the very ones who **acquit the guilty for a bribe,** and "rob the innocent of his innocence."

---

place where he does not know the difference between good and evil, darkness and light—a condition which our Lord describes as the unforgivable sin (Luke 12:10). The sin against the Holy Ghost is not the blasphemy of the spoken word, but the state of soul so saturated with evil that for it there exists nothing else than evil. There is no longer a moral alternative; it knows the dreadful peace of one exempt from strife. Isaiah does not elaborate on such a condition; he simply adds what is invariably true, that the lack of moral sense inevitably results in the corruption of justice. They **acquit the guilty.** Of course they do, for in their blind-

ness and cynicism there is no guilt. History has shown unanswerably that when a nation permits justice to be perverted at its source, when its administration is bought and sold, that nation is on the way out.

They have rejected the law of the LORD of hosts,
   and have despised the word of the Holy One
   (vs. 24).

Let it not be concluded that only those who have corrupted themselves with gross sins can reach this state of spiritual death. It ought to be noted that a proud intellectualism can also lead to a condition immune against the instiga-

24 Therefore as the fire devoureth the stubble, and the flame consumeth the chaff, *so* their root shall be as rottenness, and their blossom shall go up as dust: because they have cast away the law of the Lord of hosts, and despised the word of the Holy One of Israel.

25 Therefore is the anger of the Lord kindled against his people, and he hath stretched forth his hand against them, and hath smitten them: and the hills did tremble, and their carcasses *were* torn in the midst of the streets. For all this his anger is not turned away, but his hand *is* stretched out still.

26 ¶ And he will lift up an ensign to the nations from far, and will hiss unto them from the end of the earth: and, behold, they shall come with speed swiftly:

27 None shall be weary nor stumble among them; none shall slumber nor sleep; neither shall the girdle of their loins be loosed, nor the latchet of their shoes be broken:

28 Whose arrows *are* sharp, and all their bows bent, their horses' hoofs shall be counted like flint, and their wheels like a whirlwind:

29 Their roaring *shall be* like a lion, they shall roar like young lions; yea, they shall roar, and lay hold of the prey, and shall carry *it* away safe, and none shall deliver *it*.

30 And in that day they shall roar against them like the roaring of the sea: and if *one*

---

24 Therefore, as the tongue of fire devours the stubble,
and as dry grass sinks down in the flame,
so their root will be as rottenness,
and their blossom go up like dust;
for they have rejected the law of the Lord of hosts,
and have despised the word of the Holy One of Israel.

25 Therefore the anger of the Lord was kindled against his people,
and he stretched out his hand against them and smote them,
and the mountains quaked;
and their corpses were as refuse in the midst of the streets.
For all this his anger is not turned away and his hand is stretched out still.

26 He will raise a signal for a nation afar off,
and whistle for it from the ends of the earth;
and lo, swiftly, speedily it comes!

27 None is weary, none stumbles,
none slumbers or sleeps,
not a waistcloth is loose,
not a sandal-thong broken;

28 their arrows are sharp,
all their bows bent,
their horses' hoofs seem like flint,
and their wheels like the whirlwind.

29 Their roaring is like a lion,
like young lions they roar;
they growl and seize their prey,
they carry it off, and none can rescue.

30 They will growl over it on that day,
like the roaring of the sea.

24a. The doom to follow is described with mixed metaphors, the burning of **chaff** and the withering of plants. **Go up:** "Be blown away." The second half of the verse is in a different mood and meter, and is an editorial supplement from the time (of Manasseh ?) when the prophetic message, written and spoken, was deliberately rejected; cf. the insertion of Amos 2:4-5 in the oracle complex of Amos 1–2. Even if vs. 24b is held to be from Isaiah, it does not belong to its present context.

24b-29 (30). These verses contain the threat which concludes the oracle complex in 9:8–10:4 (see Exeg., p. 234) .

---

tions of God. One can find men in university chairs, among literary cliques and the blasé sophisticates of the lecture platform, so wise in their own conceit that they are superior to the idea of God. They are not evil men, but they are godless; and so, morally blind, bespattering with their cynical sophistries every fair ideal of the human spirit.

24b-30. The concluding verses are apparently an editorial supplement from a later age and a different author. They belong to the conclusion of 9:8–10:4 (see pp. 234-39) .

| look unto the land, behold darkness *and* sorrow; and the light is darkened in the heavens thereof. | And if one look to the land, behold, darkness and distress; and the light is darkened by its clouds. |

| 6 In the year that king Uzziah died I saw also the Lord sitting upon a throne, high and lifted up, and his train filled the temple. | 6 In the year that King Uzzi'ah died I saw the Lord sitting upon a throne, high and lifted up; and his train filled the tem- |

II. "BIND UP THE TESTIMONY" (6:1–8:18)

This section is marked off from what precedes and what follows by the fact that it consists largely of narrative, with oracles enclosed within the narrative or attached to it. The division is here made according to the nature of the content in the present structure of the book; it implies no necessary conclusions as to the original connection of the narratives with the oracular matter. Ch. 6 and 8:1-8, 11-18 comprise personal memoirs of Isaiah, narrated in the first person singular. In 7:1-17 we have a fragment of a biography of Isaiah as told by someone else. As in other prophetic books (cf. Amos 7:10-17), such narrative sections are part of the record of a prophet's work and message, preserved along with collections of oracles as his "testimony." The autobiographical sections seem to have been composed to accompany the publication by Isaiah of a collection of oracles from his early period.

A. ISAIAH'S VISION OF GOD (6:1-13)

This chapter is one of the best known in the prophetic literature, and although it has been much studied and more often quoted, it still requires close attention in any consideration of Hebrew prophecy in general and of the life and message of Isaiah in particular. Here we have the most vivid and detailed account given in the Bible of the making of a prophet. The interpretation of the chapter is of crucial importance for the understanding of Isaiah's teaching as a whole, and its literary relationships to the remainder of chs. 1–39 are an important clue in the attempt to reconstruct the process by which these chapters came to be arranged as they are.

There is no reason to doubt the vivid impression of authentic experience which the chapter conveys, nor the authorship of the one whose experience it was. That this account was not composed until some time had passed, however, is shown by the opening reference to its date, and also by the way in which Isaiah's subsequent experience of prophesying has colored his recollection of the original command to speak. The question then arises as to when and for what purpose the narrative was composed. The answer must take account of the fact that the autobiographical narrative is continued in 8:1-8,

---

6:1-13. The Making of a Prophet.—This chapter stands apart in literature as a unique record of how the call of God reached a man and a prophet was born. It is a piece of pure autobiography, the record of an experience so indelibly impressed on Isaiah's mind that to the end of his days every least detail was vividly before him. Men are not wont to expose to others the most sacred moments of life, but Isaiah had a clear purpose in recording this experience. He had reached the parting of the ways in his ministry. In 734 B.C. King Ahaz finally rejected the prophet's appeal to trust in God and turned to seek security in Assyrian protection. It would seem that at this Isaiah felt, for the time being at least, the futility of his ministry, and so withdrew from the political scene to let things

take their course; and his voice was heard no more in the councils of men. In solitude he looked back over the years of warning, reproach, and threatened judgment, and as testimony against the obdurate nation and witness to his own fidelity to his commission to speak for God, he set down the substance of the oracles he had pronounced, that to all who read it might be clear that these words were given, not composed, that he indeed had been sent by God to speak them, so that refusal to hear was not less than rejection of God himself. Here he adds to the record of his oracles the account of how he was claimed and commissioned by God.

The conjectured circumstances of the vision itself are these: At some great religious festival held during **the year that king Uzziah died**

11-18, which concludes with a statement implying that Isaiah has for the time being suspended his pronouncement of oracles. This carries us down to 734, when Ahaz rejected Isaiah's urging to put his trust in the Lord and appealed instead to the Assyrian king (cf. 8:6; II Kings 16:7). It seems probable, then, that Isaiah took the opportunity, as Jeremiah did under somewhat similar circumstances (cf. Jer. 36:1-8), to put into writing the oracles he had delivered since the beginning of his ministry. To this he appended, as explanation and justification of the oracles, the account of his original commission to prophesy and the concluding oracles in their autobiographical setting now found in 8:1-8, 11-18 (see Intro., pp. 158-59).

In presenting this firsthand account of the ecstatic vision which had initiated and authenticates his mission, Isaiah passes from narrative (vss. 1-8) to recorded oracles (vss. 9-13). Vss. 9-10 are a "private" oracle, addressed (in the second person singular) to the prophet and enjoining him to address the people in the form of a "public" oracle (in the second person plural) which is incorporated in vs. 9bc. This "public" oracle is both enigmatic and incomplete in itself; it resembles the opening of the reproach form of extended oracles (cf. 29:9; 32:9) and represents the keynote speech from which a longer oracle would be developed in actual delivery. Vss. 11b-13 are a second "public" oracle in form, this time a threat, and again incomplete since there is no antecedent in the oracle iself for the opening "until."

For the most part the text of this important chapter has been well preserved. Unfortunately this is not true of the final verse, on the elucidation and interpretation of which depends the answer to a question of importance: Is there here a reference to the survival of a "remnant," or is the prophet's message at first to be one of unrelieved disaster? The grounds for accepting the second alternative are given in the Exeg. on vs. 13. A second major question of interpretation is the meaning of the command to Isaiah to harden the hearts of the people (see Exeg. on vss. 9-10). The third question which arises concerns the nature of the visionary experience itself and the significance of the occasion and circumstances under which it came to the prophet.

There can be no doubt that Isaiah here describes a profoundly real psychological and spiritual experience through which he passed on a particular occasion. While it is true that in late written prophecy, like Zech. 1–8, and in apocalyptic books the vision-description has become a literary form, this is only because visions had been recorded by the classical prophets (cf. Amos 7:1-9; 8:1-3; Jer. 24:1-3). They in turn had inherited the tradition of the more ancient "seers" (cf. I Sam. 9:9). In the great prophets the

---

Isaiah was present in his official capacity as a prophet. Standing with the priests between the porch and the altar, he watched the play and movement of the ancient ceremony, so rich in symbolism, in color, and in music. To the worshipers it was a drama, familiar but still enthralling, that and nothing more. But to Isaiah, who had walked with God and grown ever more sensitive to spiritual and eternal values, suddenly there came an awareness of the divine reality behind the symbolism. The vision is described in terms of the ceremony, but the interpretation Isaiah put upon things visible is proof of his spiritual perception. There is an ultimate solitude about all great spiritual experiences. In that supreme moment Isaiah was alone with God. The earthly scene faded, the sound of singing died away, and he saw the Lord sitting upon a throne. While he dares to be detailed in recounting the setting and content of the vision, Isaiah is utterly restrained in words about God.

He can describe the shining ones, but he cannot frame in speech the vision of the One on the uplifted throne.

> No face: only the sight
> Of a sweepy garment, vast and white.[6]

By what Isaiah does not try to say, our sense of the overwhelming glory and holiness of the Lord God is deepened. **His train filled the temple,** and awareness of the divine presence flowed like deep waters over his servant's soul. There he stands, solitary before the throne of God. Who can wonder that when he came to himself he saw what he was, a sin-stained creature in the white radiance of the divine purity, and there broke from him that cry of self-discovery. **Woe is me! . . . a man of unclean lips, . . . for mine eyes have seen the King, the LORD of hosts.** It was that realization of sin, that over-

[6] Browning, "Christmas-Eve," Part VIII.

ecstatic experience is far oftener an audition than a vision, or, as here, a visionary experience in the course of which the prophet hears the word of the Lord. It is noteworthy, too, that Isaiah, like Amos and Jeremiah, describes what he sees in terms of the familiar world of the senses and not, like the apocalyptic writers, in grotesque imagery which defies graphic representation (cf. Dan. 7:7-8). The ecstasy of the great prophets differed profoundly from the crude psycho-physical manifestations of the older and contemporary professional "holy men" (cf. I Sam. 19:23-24; Mic. 3:5); it was the intensified spiritual perception of noble minds. This is not to say that the visions and oracles originated with these men; they themselves were sure that God had spoken to them and would speak through them. In the last analysis the whole Hebrew and Christian religion rests upon our acceptance of this claim.

Something must now be said of the special significance of the occasion and the circumstances of Isaiah's vision. That it took place "in the year that King Uzziah died" is probably no more than an indication of date; the suggestion that the king's death was related to Isaiah's vision of the King who does not die has little to recommend it, since the clause does not necessarily mean that Uzziah had already died. It is true that the occasion may well have been one of special religious emotion related to the idea of the divine kingship, as is held by those scholars who see here the characteristic marks of the Israelite counterpart of the Babylonian New Year's Day festival (cf. Ivan Engnell, *The Call of Isaiah* [Uppsala: A.-B. Lundeqvistska, 1949], p. 31, and the references there to the works of Lindblom, Mowinckel, Pedersen, Morgenstern, and May). On this day the cultic ceremonies represented the divine king as returning to his temple in a processional triumph, victor over the forces of chaos; and as being there enthroned as king, creator, and judge, to fix the fate of his people for the coming year. That such a festival ceremony on New Year's Day (the day of the Lord?) once existed in Israel has yet to be proved, but strong support is given to this theory by such passages as Pss. 24:7-10; 47; 93; 97; 98; 99. The relevance of it for Isa. 6 is that the prophet, present in the temple on this supreme occasion, in the intensity of his spiritual absorption *saw* the reality symbolized by its ritual and ceremonial. But his experience does not end there; the divine king calls for a messenger, and that distinctively Hebrew phenomenon—a prophet of divine righteousness—is created.

This chapter is one of the outstanding passages of the Bible which justify a doctrine of revelation in and through recorded spiritual experience. The story of Isaiah's call to be a prophet has been a powerful formative influence in the Hebrew and Christian

---

whelming sense of unworthiness, which was the first step in the making of a prophet. God can do something with those who see what they are and know their need of cleansing. He can do nothing for the man who can stand before what is holy and not feel himself unclean. There is no use preaching a gospel of forgiveness to those who feel no need of forgiveness. But how swift is the answer of divine mercy to a sinner's cry! Isaiah's confession is hardly uttered before forgiveness is on its way, and the shining one has touched his stained lips with the fire of God's cleansing. That is the second step in the making of a prophet: the experience of forgiveness. Henceforth Isaiah was to speak much to men about their sin, and one who had stood for a moment bathed in the holiness of God could not do that without the terror of judgment in his words. But there is no gospel in denunciation: thunder and lightning do not cause growth; only the life-giving touch of sun and

rain can do that; only the assurance of divine mercy can bring hope to sinful men. He who would speak for God must know forgiveness, not as a doctrine, but as an experience. It was a forgiven man who was to leave the temple court that day and plead with his people, plead with the authority of one whose own sin had been blotted out by the touch of God.

So follows the third step, the dedication of a life redeemed. There have been many whose experience of forgiveness has taken them back to life rejoicing in regained peace, but with eyes still blind to others' need and hearts uncommitted to love's unending quest. They heard no voice, God's question never reached them; but to Isaiah it came with intense and personal reality, **Whom shall I send, and who will go for us?** He did not pause to debate the obligations of forgiveness; he answered a call. This was more than obedience; it was the response of the man's whole being to an overwhelming sense of

religious traditions, and we have the story in his own words. We learn that his ministry was initiated by a soul-shaking experience of the reality of God, as of One inexpressibly exalted, whose ethical "holiness" marked the most significant distinction between God and man. This experience is an authentic datum of religion, because its reality was validated by its results in the prophet's life and work.

In reading this chapter we participate imaginatively in Isaiah's vision and feel the same pang of conscience in the presence of the unutterable and sovereign glory of the goodness of God. It was brought home to the prophet with startling clarity that however well he might have purified himself according to cultic requirements, however well he might have kept the customary rules of morality, in the presence of a holiness exalted in righteousness he and all men were unclean. But with this recognition of creatureliness and unworthiness there came also a cleansing by a sovereign act of grace, and a commission to speak a word which was not his but God's. The truth spoken was to be both a summons to obey and a judgment upon the inevitable disobedience of those who were satisfied to be "unclean." The degenerative process cannot arrest itself; to the question "How long?" there can be but one answer, "To the end, in the collapse and ruin which stubborn rebellion must bring upon itself."

6:1. The year that King Uzziah died is uncertain, as indeed are the years of many reigns; the date 742 is approximate. This king is called also Azariah; indeed, both names are used indifferently by the same writer (cf. II Kings 15). Azariah may have been the original name (II Kings 14:21) and Uzziah a throne name adopted on his accession but never quite displacing the other; the latter means "my strength is Jah," and it recalls the opening words of the royal Ps. 21 as well as the name (Boaz, "in the strength of . . .") of one of the two pillars in front of the temple which had some symbolic significance in the coronation ceremony (cf. I Kings 7:21; II Kings 11:12-14). **I saw the LORD:** It is only a glimpse, a sudden overpowering realization that he is in the presence of the Majesty on high; the **throne,** the royal robe, and the attendant beings are described, but not the appearance of the One upon the throne. The effect is far more powerful than such attempts to describe the appearance of God as are found in Ezek. 1:26-27; Dan. 7:9: "Seated upon a high, exalted throne," with **his train** (the skirts of the royal robe, cf. II Chr. 18:9) filling the temple. The vision came to Isaiah apparently when he was participating as an official prophet in the ceremonies of the cult, standing with the priests "between the porch and the altar" (cf. Joel 2:17; II Chr. 20:4-19) and gazing through the open portals of the sanctuary, now filled with the swirling smoke of incense,

---

God's mercy. In forgiveness God claimed him; under that constraint he spoke the quiet words, **Here am I; send me,** and a prophet was born.

Nothing in Isaiah's ministry can be truly understood apart from this transforming experience. The terrible words of doom which he must hereafter speak broke from the heart of a man who had glimpsed the eternal holiness and knew that sin in its rebellion spells out its own death. Those urgent appeals, the passionate summons—what are they but the outreach of a soul which had caught the whisper of a divine love, agonizing over the dull indifference of blind spirits, a love which was someday to endure a cross that men might turn and be saved? Those exquisite oracles of hope, those tender pictures of a people coming home to the welcome and peace of a father's love—they were given to the man who in all the tumult and travail of his ministry never forgot, and never lost the peace of God's forgiveness. That is why the vision is

in the book; it explains both the man and his message.

1-8. The Call of God.—This is a phrase generally associated with the vocation of the ministry. But why should it be limited to one profession in life? Surely it is possible for any man so to resolve what he will do with his life as to be able to say that in his chosen work he is answering God's call to him. There is nothing of necessity mystical about it. Isaiah saw a vision and heard a voice. Paul was confronted with a presence and had speech with the living Christ. Such instances of an encounter with God have marked the call of thousands to his service. Nevertheless they are not to be taken as the norm. They are special cases and generally occur when the summons involves a sudden diverting of life to an entirely new channel. The call is really a sense of vocation brought to a focus in a decision. That need not be either sudden or dramatic. It may be, and generally is,

2 Above it stood the seraphim: each one had six wings; with twain he covered his face, and with twain he covered his feet, and with twain he did fly.

3 And one cried unto another, and said, Holy, holy, holy, *is* the LORD of hosts: the whole earth *is* full of his glory.

ple. 2 Above him stood the seraphim; each had six wings: with two he covered his face, and with two he covered his feet, and with two he flew. 3 And one called to another and said:

"Holy, holy, holy is the LORD of hosts; the whole earth is full of his glory."

---

toward that innermost chamber where the Lord dwelt in "thick darkness." Isaiah does not refuse the title of *nābhi'* ("prophet"), as does Amos; indeed, by calling his wife "the prophetess" (8:3) he accepts it. There were multitudes of *nebhi'îm* connected with the cultic worship who left no mark on history (cf. I Kings 18:4; Mic. 3:5; Jer. 26:11). Those who did so and whom we know as the "Hebrew prophets" were, like Isaiah, men "called to be apostles," who might or might not have had the title "prophet" in their own day.

2. **Above him,** not **above it,** i.e., the throne; but both are too literal; "attendant on him" (LXX, "around him") is what is meant, as can be seen by reference to Gen. 18:2, 8, where the phrase is used of those standing in the presence of one seated. **The seraphim:** Attendants on the heavenly throne, comparable to the four "living creatures" of Ezek. 1:5-25; Rev. 4:6-8, and the members of the "heavenly host" (cf. Dan. 7:10). The word means "burning ones" in the transitive sense; the fact that it is used to describe the serpents in the wilderness (cf. Num. 21:6, 8) has led some commentators here to the illogical conclusion that the seraphim of the vision were serpentine in form. Actually, like the cherubim and "living creatures," they belong to the category of unearthly beings— human only in part—which in the art and literature of the ancient world are commonly represented as attendants upon the gods and their sanctuaries (cf. Galling, *Biblisches Reallexikon,* pp. 384-86). The seraphim (mentioned only here and in vs. 6; but see Num. 21:6, 8; Deut. 8:15; Isa. 14:29; 30:6) have the hands, faces, and voices of men, and stand upright; and they have three pairs of wings. But the primary characteristic lies in their name, and Procksch (*Jesaia I,* p. 54) suggests that they symbolized lightning, as the cherub symbolized the thundercloud (cf. Ps. 18:8-15). **Covered his face:** The glory and majesty of the God they attend is emphasized by this attitude of the unearthly beings, who themselves are enough to strike the prophet with awe. **Covered his feet:** His nakedness.

3. **One called to another:** In antiphonal song; the clause does not necessarily mean that there were two only. As in his trance the visual elements of a familiar scene are transfigured, so the anthem of the temple ritual is heard by the prophet as if sung by heavenly creatures. That the occasion is the annual enthronement festival is again

---

the culmination of a growing awareness of what one may and ought to do with life. To everyone God has given certain gifts and capacities, and the secret of the good life is the use of these to the highest ends. One may quite reasonably say that when a man has skill with his hands or a mind unusually logical in its processes or endowed with rare imaginative power, the gift indicates the intention for that life and is the guiding clue to what we significantly term its "calling"; i.e., a man will best realize the powers within him when he is doing work which gives opportunity for these to be expressed. Unquestionably he is happiest when he is doing what he is particularly equipped to do. The misfits in life, the men who have no sense of vocation, are those unhappy ones thrust by circumstances or

by a domineering parent into a vocation for which they have neither liking nor aptitude. The institution of guidance counselors in modern education is entirely sound. It may avert some of the tragedies of lives frustrated by being denied the chance of doing what they were meant by nature and capacity to do. It may help young lives to answer the most crucial question of all, "How am I to make the best use of my life?" Too many have missed their vocation because they have not realized that a gift is given to be used, and an aptitude ought to be wedded to a task. One of the chief concerns in any great industry today is to see that square pegs are put into square holes, which is one way of saying that business realizes that a man is most efficient and most contented when his work gives

4 And the posts of the door moved at the voice of him that cried, and the house was filled with smoke.

5 ¶ Then said I, Woe *is* me! for I am undone; because I *am* a man of unclean lips, and I dwell in the midst of a people of unclean lips: for mine eyes have seen the King, the LORD of hosts.

6 Then flew one of the seraphim unto me, having a live coal in his hand, *which* he had taken with the tongs from off the altar:

4 And the foundations of the thresholds shook at the voice of him who called, and the house was filled with smoke. 5 And I said: "Woe is me! For I am lost; for I am a man of unclean lips, and I dwell in the midst of a people of unclean lips; for my eyes have seen the King, the LORD of hosts!"

6 Then flew one of the seraphim to me, having in his hand a burning coal which he had taken with tongs from the altar.

---

suggested by the similar thought and phrasing of Pss. 47:6-8; 93:1, 5. The threefold repetition of **holy** is for great emphasis; the Hebrew language has no way to express the superlative except by repetition. Holiness is the essential quality of deity, **glory** the manifestation of deity in the natural world. Thus the first line of the hymn declares the divine exaltation amid the **hosts** of heavenly beings like the seraphim; the second line, "the whole earth overflows with his glory," "that the world has become the world of God, as when He created it and made Himself its king" (Aage Bentzen, *Jesaja I* [Kopenhagen: G. E. C. Gad, 1944], p. 47, tr. in Engnell, *op. cit.*, p. 36).

4. The foundations of the thresholds shook ["the door pivots vibrated in the sills with the noise of the shout"] **and the house was filled with smoke:** The trembling and the smoke manifest the powerful presence of the God of heaven, as in Pss. 18:7-8; 97:2-5; the **smoke** is the same as the "cloud" of glory which filled the tabernacle (Exod. 40:34) and the **house** (Ezek. 10:4), both hiding and revealing the divine presence. Lev. 16:13 suggests a thought connection between the visible smoke of incense which filled the sanctuary before Isaiah's eyes and this element in the vision.

5. As the momentary sight of the throne of God is hidden again by the smoke, Isaiah suddenly becomes conscious of himself and of the awful consequences of his having seen a sight forbidden to mortal men (cf. Exod. 33:20). He has intruded while **unclean,** i.e., "unconsecrated," into the holiest of all sanctuaries; he cries, "Woe to me! I am done for!" His human lips are not fit to join in the ritual song. He realizes that he and all his people, even though they may have fulfilled the cultic requirements of the earthly temple, are debarred from the highest worship by the moral uncleanness of their nature (cf. vs. 7); the gulf between God and man, between the holy and the unclean, is created by an ultimate distinction between supreme ethical holiness and the corruption of human nature. **The King:** Not of Israel alone, but of **the whole earth** (vs. 3).

6. Again his surroundings appear in the prophet's vision; from the smoking incense altar a firestone is taken by one of the seraphim, **with the tongs** used to arrange these heated stones on the fireless altar. **A live coal** and **a burning coal** wrongly suggest that the object was a glowing ember; rather, it was a heated flat stone such as was in domestic

---

him the chance to express what is in him. It is not straining language to say that a well-adjusted life, a life using its endowment for constructive ends, is fulfilling God's intention, and in that sense has answered his call.

It must be admitted that the conditions of modern industrial production make it increasingly difficult for men to retain their sense of vocation in their work. It was different in those days when man was dependent for so much on his own skill in craftmanship. Creative work gave him the opportunity to express himself,

and he could feel that in it he was fulfilling a purpose.

> 'Tis God gives skill,
> But not without men's hands: He could not make
> Antonio Stradivari's violins
> Without Antonio.[7]

But in what measure is a man expressing his native capacity or fulfilling the purpose of his nature if his job consists only of mechanical repetition? How can he redeem such work from

[7] George Eliot, "Stradivarius."

7 And he laid *it* upon my mouth, and said, Lo, this hath touched thy lips; and thine iniquity is taken away, and thy sin purged.

8 Also I heard the voice of the Lord, saying, Whom shall I send, and who will go for us? Then said I, Here *am* I; send me.

7 And he touched my mouth, and said: "Behold, this has touched your lips; your guilt is taken away, and your sin forgiven." 8 And I heard the voice of the Lord saying, "Whom shall I send, and who will go for us?" Then I said, "Here I am! Send me."

---

use for baking (cf. I Kings 19:6). It is implied that the seraph was sent by the divine King to perform this priestly act.

7. He touched my mouth: Better, with Edward J. Kissane (*The Book of Isaiah* [Dublin: Browne & Nolan, 1941], I, 75), "When this has touched thy mouth." Engnell (*op. cit.,* pp. 40-41) sees here a clear parallel to the "mouth purification" rites of Akkadian and Egyptian royal rituals which came to be applied also to the priests. The symbol is cultic; the stone conveys the holiness of the altar and, so to speak, purifies the unclean lips. The reality behind the symbol is the divine act of forgiveness, made possible by Isaiah's awakened consciousness of the nature and power of God's holiness and of the real and dreadful condition of moral uncleanness in which he himself stood. **Iniquity** or **guilt:** The state of his present uncleanness will pass away. "Your guilt is gone." **Your sin:** The outward manifestation in word and deed of **iniquity** as a condition. **Purged** or **forgiven:** "Blotted out," "atoned for," (*a*) by the touch of the firestone representing contact with the holiness of God, and (*b*) by the divine act of forgiveness in sending the seraph (as is implied) to sanctify the prophet so that he could be admitted to audience.

8. Also: Better, "then"; for the hearing is consequent upon the act of purification, which affects not only the lips but (cf. vs. 10) the ears and the heart. So Jeremiah was "sanctified," or cleansed, by contact with holiness when he was made a prophet (Jer. 1:5). The result is a new capacity to hear the Lord's word and an immediate spontaneous response of willing obedience. Isaiah now stands on the outskirts of the heavenly company about the throne; when the Lord, in a rhetorical question which perhaps implies previous embassies and a feeling of frustration (cf. vss. 9-10), asks those about him, **Who will**

---

being literally soul-destroying? This is a question which claims the most serious study of the church. We have passed from the enriching era of craftsmanship, wherein the genius of the human spirit had its most noble expression, to the day of mechanized industry. We shall never return to the time when human hands fashioned most of the goods in use. Nothing we can possibly do can make serving a machine comparable in value to the creation of things by one's own skill. It might be said of modern production, "Ichabod," the glory is departed. If we are to save men from becoming themselves mere machines, we must somehow give them a sense of being involved in something greater than the job, something more significant than the physical act required of them. If a man can see that his part in the whole involved process is vital, that on his skill and fidelity others depend, that the thing being produced cannot be perfected without him, then at least he can be saved from contempt of his job, and a sense of vocation, though it falls far short of that which crowns the craftsman's labor, may give him pride

of work and beget in him a feeling that what he does has its own value, that he himself is to be reckoned with in the service of a cause greater than his own life.

There is more, however, in this matter of the call than simply finding one's proper niche in life. There is the question of the ends served by the vocation. No man, whatever his capacities, can expect to have a sense of call if he is using these for evil purposes. It would be a mockery approaching blasphemy to say that a burglar or a dope peddler could have a sense of call. Given however a legitimate work, serving the welfare of others, there still remains for the Christian the question of how in his environment he can relate his skill or his knowledge to the service of God. It is only when he is consciously using his situation and its opportunities for the good of others that he can know the peace of answering God's call. Here the modern employee or professional man greatly needs guidance. A study of vocational Christianity is long overdue. People need to be shown how their religious faith can be expressed in their

9 ¶ And he said, Go, and tell this people, Hear ye indeed, but understand not; and see ye indeed, but perceive not.

10 Make the heart of this people fat, and make their ears heavy, and shut their eyes; lest they see with their eyes, and hear with their ears, and understand with their heart, and convert, and be healed.

9 And he said, "Go, and say to this people:
'Hear and hear, but do not understand;
see and see, but do not perceive.'
10 Make the heart of this people fat,
    and their ears heavy,
    and shut their eyes;
lest they see with their eyes,
    and hear with their ears,
and understand with their hearts,
    and turn and be healed."

---

go for us? Isaiah responds simply and humbly, **Send me.** The great prophets were men who stood in the counsel of God (cf. Amos 3:7), who could hear his word, and felt themselves commissioned and empowered to proclaim it.

9-10. **Hear ye indeed** or **Hear and hear:** i.e., "Hear again and again." The highly condensed and enigmatic form of the "primary" oracle addressed to the prophet in vs. 9 is paraphrased and expanded in vs. 10. **Hear ye** marks the opening of such public reproach oracles as 1:2-3; 7-13; so a series of imperative verbs begins an exhortation in 7:4. What we have in vs. 9bc, then, is in form (note the second person plurals) a "public" oracle; but it is quoted and enclosed within an oracle addressed privately to the prophet in vss. 9-10. The importance of this is that the idea of repetition and persistence has been transposed from vs. 9a to the public form of the oracle in vs. 9bc, in a way which can be brought out only by paraphrasing: "Go, and say again and again to this people, Hear ye!—but understand not if you will not. See!—but perceive nothing since you choose to be blind." The hearing is of the divine word (1:10), the seeing refers to the Lord's self-disclosure in events (5:19; 28:21). **This people:** An expression of exasperation as used by Isaiah; the reference usually is to Judah (cf. 28:14), but in 9:16 it is used of Ephraim; in each case it is the social entity as separated from the God to whom it properly belongs. **Make the heart . . . fat:** "You will dull the mind." The imperative is used here idiomatically to express a future certainty; the **heart** in the Bible is not the symbol of the emotions but of the mind and will; **fat** in this connection means "insensitive," "stupid," like cattle (cf. Deut. 32:15). **Shut** ["blear"] **their eyes. Lest they see:** "So that they shall not see." The negative purpose clause follows the imperative referred to above to express the consequence. The literal translation of this verse, here and where it is quoted in Mark 4:12 and its parallels, has caused much perplexity. The prophet is commanded to declare the will of the Lord, even though the result will be that men's unwillingness to respond will develop into a stubborn opposition, eventually making

---

work. What unrealized possibilities, for example, await the Christian teacher, the Christian doctor, the Christian business executive, the Christian foreman, if only they see clearly that their work is their opportunity for the service of God and man, that it is not merely a livelihood but in truth a calling of God. A layman may receive and answer a call just as truly as any minister. It is possible for a man facing the opportunity of some honest labor or great profession and ready to give his life to it to hear, as Isaiah did, a summons, and to answer as he did, **Here am I; send me.**

9-13. *A Note of Doom.*—The textual problems involved in these verses make it difficult to speak with assurance of their precise meaning. It is evident, however. that the condensed

oracle in vss. 9-10 implies the doom of the obdurate nation. Isaiah is instructed so to speak that the insensibility of men toward the truth may be increased, thus blotting out the last hope of repentance. Against this the prophet in effect protests, for his question **Lord, how long?** implies a refusal to believe that God will go the length of exterminating the nation. The answer is uncompromising; the judgment is to be complete and final, and if Israel is not to be obliterated, at least exile awaits her. The reference in vs. 12 is unmistakable: **And the Lord have removed men far away, and there be a great forsaking in the midst of the land.** It would be a prospect of unrelieved tragedy but for the ray of light in vs. 13, **But yet in it shall be a tenth, and it shall return.** This veiled reference

11 Then said I, Lord, how long? And he answered, Until the cities be wasted without inhabitant, and the houses without man, and the land be utterly desolate,	11 Then I said, "How long, O Lord?" And he said:

11 Then said I, Lord, how long? And he answered, Until the cities be wasted without inhabitant, and the houses without man, and the land be utterly desolate,

12 And the LORD have removed men far away, and *there be* a great forsaking in the midst of the land.

13 ¶ But yet in it *shall be* a tenth, and *it* shall return, and shall be eaten: as a teil tree, and as an oak, whose substance *is* in them, when they cast *their leaves: so* the holy seed *shall be* the substance thereof.

11 Then I said, "How long, O Lord?" And he said:
"Until cities lie waste
    without inhabitant,
and houses without men,
    and the land is utterly desolate,
12 and the LORD removes men far away,
    and the forsaken places are many in the midst of the land.
13 And though a tenth remain in it,
    it will be burned again,
like a terebinth or an oak,
    whose stump remains standing
    when it is felled."
The holy seed is its stump.

their response impossible. As men's ears are deafened by loud continuous noise, so the very clarity and insistence of the revelation will increase their unbelief and rebelliousness, because of their initial opposition to the divine message (cf. Jer. 1:7-10, 17-19).

11-12. There is a note of protest in Isaiah's question, as always where this phrase is used elsewhere (cf. Ps. 74:10; Jer. 4:14); he at first cannot accept the finality of the judgment and the stultification of his work. But the Lord's answer (here cast into the form of a "public" oracle in which the LORD is spoken of in the third person), is that the doom will be final and complete: "Until abandoned cities and deserted houses crash in ruins, and the country is left [so LXX] desolate, and the LORD has carried men far away, and the land is utterly deserted." The sentence ends here, and it is as plain as anything could be that Isaiah's original commission was to proclaim the utter doom of a faithless and obdurate people.

13. The text and the translation of this verse are in places difficult, and the uncertainty of its interpretation has made it possible for some of the best commentators to find in the inaugural vision reference to the later doctrine of the Remnant. (But on a priori grounds, cf.: "Isaiah's characteristic doctrine of the Remnant, which we should certainly expect to find in his inaugural vision" [Skinner, *Isaiah*, I, 51]; "the verse expresses nothing but *the consistent theme of the prophetic teaching*, its kernel: apostasy, doom—a purification, not an annihilation doom—and a remnant, linked up with the Davidic Messiah" [Engnell, *op. cit.*, p. 51]; "Isaiah from the first believed in the escape of a Remnant. This hope he cannot have found made fruitless by the Call Vision" [Procksch, *op. cit.*, p. 60].) That the verse is a supplementary expansion and qualification of vss. 11-12 is surely evident from the contradiction between the complete depopulation pictured in the earlier verses and the survival of a tenth, which recalls the similar subsequent qualification of utter doom found in Amos 9:8. Moreover, the form of the verse, opening with a conditional clause, itself suggests that it is a modification of what immediately precedes. The historic fact is that in the course of Isaiah's ministry the "ten tribes" of northern Israel were exiled, and the remaining tenth, as Karl Marti points out (*Das*

to Isaiah's conviction that a remnant shall be saved may be only a postscript to an oracle of doom; but it tempers the inflexibility of the judgment he must proclaim, and at least raises a suggestion of hope—though in the next moment even that is eclipsed as Isaiah declares that the remnant itself must pass through the fire: the tree is felled and the slash is burned; there is nothing left. It is a dark saying, a death knell, a sentence of final rejection.

Homiletically this passage may seem to be barren ground; but it contains the germ of much that needs to be said to modern society. The subject is the danger of becoming accustomed to the gospel. Modern psychology will confirm the claim that minds continually subjected to an appeal, or to a warning which they do not propose to hear, develop a fatal immunity to truth. It is the same warning which our Lord gives in the parable of the soil which

7 And it came to pass in the days of Ahaz the son of Jotham, the son of Uzziah, king of Judah, *that* Rezin the king of Syria,

7 In the days of Ahaz the son of Jotham, son of Uzzi'ah, king of Judah, Rezin the

---

Buch Jesaja [Tübingen: J. C. B. Mohr, 1900; "Kurzer Hand-Commentar zum Alten Testament"], p. 68), could well refer in these circumstances to Judah, or otherwise to the remaining population after Nebuchadrezzar's first deportation in 597 B.C. (II Kings 24:14). In any case, the verse is an attempt to explain, in the light of vss. 11-12, the fact that the predicted exile had taken place but that it had not been complete. **And though a tenth remain** recognizes the conditional clause, as the KJV fails to do. **It will be burned again** seems to be the meaning, although there is some doubt about the word לבער, "for burning." **Shall be eaten** makes nonsense, unless it is understood that this implies "by grazing animals" (cf. 5:5); "be consumed" is the best rendering in this context. In the remainder of the verse neither the KJV nor the RSV is satisfactory; and it is to be noted that the last clause, **the holy seed is its stump,** is missing in the LXX. The word **stump** or **substance** is in Hebrew מצבה, which normally means "upright (stone)" or "pillar"; it is quite different from the word for the stump or trunk of a tree, גזע. The Dead Sea Scroll, with one word transposed, gives a possible reading: "As an oak when it is thrown down, and as the terebinth by the sacred column of a high place" (cf. William H. Brownlee, "The Text of Isaiah VI 13 in the Light of DSIa," *Vetus Testamentum,* I [1951], 296-98). The final clause, identifying the obscure מצבה with **the holy seed,** is a late gloss; this belongs to the language of postexilic Judaism and has its only close analogy in Ezra 9:2.

B. ISAIAH AND THE SYRO-EPHRAIMITE WAR (7:1–8:15)

A new and distinct section of narrative is found in 7:1-17, falling into two parts which may be designated from outstanding features as the sign of Shear-jashub (vss. 1-9) and the sign of Immanuel (vss. 10-17). Not only is this narrative concerned with events which took place several years after the death of Uzziah, but it is marked off from ch. 6 by a change in the character of the narrative, from a personal memoir of inward experience (with allusions to outward circumstances) to a third-person account of outward events in which Isaiah participates, along with Ahaz. The view (cf. George Buchanan Gray, *A Critical and Exegetical Commentary on the Book of Isaiah I-XXXIX* [New York: Charles Scribner's Sons, 1912; "International Critical Commentary"], I, 112) that this section was once continuous with the autobiographical narratives in chs. 6 and 8, and that the references to Isaiah can be changed from the third person to the first person, is to be rejected because (*a*) this change alone cannot transform 7:1-17 into the kind of personal memoirs found in chs. 6 and 8; and because (*b*) this section is comparable rather with the further biographical narratives of chs. 20; 36–39 (see Intro., pp. 155-56). The stylistic similarities with ch. 8, pointed out by Gray, concern exclusively the oracular matter enclosed within the narrative of 7:1-17.

---

is so hardened by the traffic of familiar ideas that it becomes impenetrable to any instigation of truth.

7:1-25. God's Message to King Ahaz.—The Exeg. makes clear the historical situation to which the prophet speaks. Judah was threatened by neighboring states, invasion was imminent, and panic swept both court and nation. Enter the prophet, with a plain word to the hysterical king. They meet in the open, while Ahaz and his staff are inspecting the defenses. Notice how Isaiah continually reinforced his spoken word by using the outward circumstance of the moment.

Here he meets a man frantic about defense, to tell him where the real defense lies. Here he brings his little son, who is a kind of living oracle, for his name is "Only a Remnant Shall Return." When and why the child was given that sinister name we do not know, but Ahaz did, and as he looked at the boy, a warning and a hope sounded wordlessly in his ears. "Only a remnant"—the price has to be paid in blood and sorrow; but a "remnant shall return." No matter how the battle goes, the issue is in God's hands and he has a purpose for his people. Everything conspired to make this a decisive

and Pekah the son of Remaliah, king of Israel, went up toward Jerusalem to war against it, but could not prevail against it.	king of Syria and Pekah the son of Remali'ah the king of Israel came up to Jerusalem to wage war against it, but they could

This oracular matter in fact comprises the bulk of the section, and the narrative provides its setting and explanation. A "private" oracle in vss. 3-4aα instructs Isaiah to speak to Ahaz the "public" oracle in vss. 4aβ-8a, 9. Again, after a preliminary exchange between the prophet and the king, a further "public" oracle follows in vss. 13-16(17).

For the historical circumstances of the Syro-Ephraimite attack on Judah in 734 B.C. we have, in addition to what is recorded or hinted in this chapter, the accounts of the reign of Ahaz in II Kings 16 and II Chr. 28 and also the Assyrian records of Tiglath-pileser's forceful dealings with the small states on the western border of the empire. II Kings 15:37 affirms that the alliance of northern Israel with Damascus against Judah began in the reign of Jotham; the statement may be explained by the fact that years of plotting among the western states are to be inferred from Tiglath-pileser's successive campaigns in that area in 740, 738 (when Menahem of Israel and also Rezin of Damascus paid tribute), 734, and 733-32 (when Damascus was destroyed). That Ahaz appealed to Tiglath-pileser for help and introduced a form of Assyrian worship at Jerusalem (cf. II Kings 16:7-16) shows that he was unwilling or afraid to join an alliance against Assyria; this explains the attack made upon him by his neighbors. Since the king—**the son of Tabeel**—whose rule was to be forced on Judah (Isa. 7:6) was evidently an Aramaean, it seems that Judah was to be subjugated and included in the domains of Damascus in order to eliminate a defaulter from the ranks of the anti-Assyrian alliance. The terror which prevailed in Jerusalem when word came of the advancing armies is sufficient indication that the hostility of her neighbors and the insecurity of her position were already too well known in Judah.

1. Sign of Shear-Jashub (7:1-9)

7:1. An editorial introduction effecting the transition from the days of Uzziah to those of Ahaz (vs. 1*a*), and quoting (vs. 1*b*) from II Kings 16:5 the summary account of the attack on Jerusalem, which in vss. 2-17 is still in its early stages. The verse in Kings adds the information that Ahaz was actually besieged, and this gives point to the statement that they were unable "to engage him in battle" (not **prevail against** or **conquer**). But even behind his walls Ahaz was in such terror that he emptied the treasuries of court and temple to obtain help from the Assyrians (II Kings 16:7-8) and offered a sacrifice of his own son (II Kings 16:3; cf. 3:26-27). Thus he completely rejected the plea of Isaiah for courage and faith, as well as his message of deliverance.

moment for the unhappy king, and Isaiah's appeal for faith in God had its allies in the setting and circumstance of the meeting.

1-9. A Great Reassurance.—The substance of the first oracle is the assurance that any attack which might be made by those whom Isaiah contemptuously called **smoldering stumps of firebrands** would break on the rock of God's purpose for Israel. But there is not going to be any invasion, for Syria and Ephraim are on the way out, and within a few years will themselves be shattered. Let Ahaz trust in God, for faith is the true source and secret of security. The appeal fell on the ears of a man beside himself with fear; Ahaz was past speaking to, and it is doubtful whether he really heard what Isaiah was saying. In modern slang, he "had the wind-

up" so badly that he bankrupted himself to buy Assyrian help and sacrificed his own children to the gods who seemed more real to his panic-stricken mind than Yahweh. If we cannot condone the king's action, we can at least understand his mood. If in 1940-41, when Great Britain was threatened with invasion, Hitler's armies poised on the shores of the English Channel, and she herself alone against that terrible and victorious force, Winston Churchill had cried to the people of Britain, "Trust in God; it shall not happen," they would hardly have been comforted by so unrealistic an assurance. But Isaiah more than once said that very thing to his nation in some desperate moment. Are we to wonder that their faith was not equal to such a test? That subsequent events invari-

2 And it was told the house of David, saying, Syria is confederate with Ephraim. And his heart was moved, and the heart of his people, as the trees of the wood are moved with the wind.

3 Then said the LORD unto Isaiah, Go forth now to meet Ahaz, thou, and Shear-jashub thy son, at the end of the conduit of the upper pool, in the highway of the fuller's field;

4 And say unto him, Take heed, and be quiet; fear not, neither be faint-hearted for the two tails of these smoking firebrands, for the fierce anger of Rezin with Syria, and of the son of Remaliah.

not conquer it. 2 When the house of David was told, "Syria is in league with E′phraim," his heart and the heart of his people shook as the trees of the forest shake before the wind.

3 And the LORD said to Isaiah, "Go forth to meet Ahaz, you and She′ar-jash′ub[h] your son, at the end of the conduit of the upper pool on the highway to the Fuller's Field, 4 and say to him, 'Take heed, be quiet, do not fear, and do not let your heart be faint because of these two smoldering stumps of firebrands, at the fierce anger of Rezin and

[h] That is *A remnant shall return*

---

2. The house of David: The monarchy, which was specifically threatened (cf. vs. 6) ; it is possible that the king is not named because this threat was of long standing and existed under Ahaz' predecessor (cf. II Kings 15:37) , or the phrase may simply be a circumlocution for "the king," like "Pharaoh," i.e., "the Great House." **Is confederate with** or **in league with:** These renderings follow the LXX in interpreting the Hebrew נחה, which means lit., "rests upon"; **Syria** (Aram) has reached and joined forces with **Ephraim** (northern Israel). **Was moved** or **shook:** The noise and confusion of a forest in a violent windstorm is a vivid figure for the panic in Jerusalem.

3-4. Isaiah is instructed to confront Ahaz at a point outside the walls, "at the end of the aqueduct of the upper reservoir," where it is natural to suppose that the king was inspecting the reservoir and considering its defenses. The aqueduct from the spring Gihon was at this time outside the city walls; in Hezekiah's reign a tunnel was made through the hill on which stood the east wall, to bring the water into the city without its being exposed to an enemy. The exhortation to courage and faith was in some way to be emphasized by the presence at the interview of the prophet's son Shear-jashub, as a "sign" which Ahaz would recognize. The name has the oracular ambiguity of the Maher-shalal-hashbaz of 8:1, 3; it can mean "a remnant shall return" or, more probably because of the emphatic position of the subject, "*only* a remnant shall return." In 10:20-21, 22-23 this enigmatic oracle is expanded in opposite senses as a promise and as a threat. Since a child was named at birth (cf. vs. 14; 8:3) , and since the boy was now old enough to go (i.e., on foot) with his father, it seems clear that he had been so named on a previous occasion as a "living oracle," in the sense of 10:22-23. What the occasion was we do not know, but Ahaz had known a series of military disasters (cf. II Kings 16:6; II Chr. 28:17-18) in addition to his present troubles with Syria. The message of Shear-jashub, then, was originally a threatening one, in accordance with Isaiah's commission (cf. 6:11-12) . The reappearance of the boy with this ominous name was a "sign" and a reminder to Ahaz, as Isaiah exhorted him to faith while at the same time confronting him with a further conditional threat (vs. 9b). **Take heed** [Watch out, but be tranquil! Fear not, nor let your courage fail] **because of these two smoldering stumps of firebrands.**

---

ably proved that Isaiah was right does not alter the fact that when he made his demand to wait on the Lord, all the instincts of men were to find a way to meet the threat; action was what they wanted, not piety. If we had been with Ahaz when Isaiah gave his bland assurance that nothing would happen, it is certainly more than

doubtful that we would have gone back to the day's work assured everything was all right.

There is a very real problem here. What is the relationship between the demand for faith in God and the entirely human impulse to do something practical in an emergency? Does faith cancel the need for action? Experience em-

5 Because Syria, Ephraim, and the son of Remaliah, have taken evil counsel against thee, saying,

6 Let us go up against Judah, and vex it, and let us make a breach therein for us, and set a king in the midst of it, *even* the son of Tabeal:

7 Thus saith the Lord GOD, It shall not stand, neither shall it come to pass.

8 For the head of Syria *is* Damascus, and the head of Damascus *is* Rezin; and within threescore and five years shall Ephraim be broken, that it be not a people.

9 And the head of Ephraim *is* Samaria, and the head of Samaria *is* Remaliah's son. If ye will not believe, surely ye shall not be established.

Syria and the son of Remali'ah. 5 Because Syria, with E'phraim and the son of Remali'ah, has devised evil against you, saying,
6 "Let us go up against Judah and terrify it, and let us conquer it for ourselves, and set up the son of Ta'be-el as king in the midst of it," 7 thus says the Lord GOD:

It shall not stand,
    and it shall not come to pass.
8 For the head of Syria is Damascus,
    and the head of Damascus is Rezin.
(Within sixty-five years E'phraim will be broken to pieces so that it will no longer be a people.)
9 And the head of E'phraim is Samar'ia,
    and the head of Samar'ia is the son of Remali'ah.
If you will not believe,
    surely you shall not be established.' "

5-7. The evil designs of her enemies on Judah call forth what is perhaps the first enunciation by Isaiah of a message other than unconditional doom; it is the Lord's will, not the malice of men, which will determine the outcome of events. **The son of Tabeel:** Presumably a Syrian nominee as puppet king of Judah; the Hebrew text has vocalized the name **Tabeel** to make it mean "no good" instead of "God is good."

8-9. The plan of the invading kings to displace the Davidic monarchy will fail; each is by divine appointment head only of his own country and capital city. But the survival of David's dynasty is dependent on trust in Yahweh (note the plural verbs in vs. 9*b*). Vs. 8*b*, which so obviously interrupts the sequence of vss. 8*a*, 9*a*, is either a gloss inserted after 668 B.C., when a deportation of the last remaining Ephraimites appears to have taken place (cf. Jer. 41:5; Ezra 4:2), or this line should follow vs. 9*a* and be read as emended by Kissane, "Yet six, nay, five years more, and Syria shall be shattered, Ephraim diminished" (*Isaiah,* I, 78-79, 82). The concluding sentence is particularly noteworthy; it is a conditional threat enforced by the sign of the presence of Shear-jashub, and has the play on two stems of the same root (*tha'amînû–thē'āmĕnû*) which suggests that it is the "embryonic" form of the enlarged oracle (see Intro., p. 155). Theologically and historically it is important as marking the emergence in prophecy of the idea of faith as an activity of soul, and by its form throwing light on the meaning of that idea. The verbal root *'mn* means "to be steady, firm, certain"; of words and promises, "true"; of a state or condition, "lasting," "secure"; of persons, "trustworthy." **If ye will not believe, surely ye shall not be established** may be paraphrased: "If you are not steady of soul, completely confident of the trustworthiness of God, and certain that his word will be fulfilled, you are [i.e., your physical existence is] not firm and enduring." The paranomasia

---

phatically denies that it does, and history abundantly confirms the truth that God helps those who, believing in him, help themselves. There is nothing contradictory between faith in God and the utmost man can do for his own salvation. Whether we agree or disagree with the ethics, there is a lot of sound theology in such sayings as "Trust in God and keep your powder dry," [8] and "Praise the Lord and pass

the ammunition." [1] Yet fundamentally Isaiah was right: faith in God is the basis of life "lucid, poised, and whole"; and whether it is the case of a besieged city or a mind beleaguered with fears, as the prophet said, without belief there is no relief. Faith in the love and power of God may not alter the circumstance; but it enables a man to endure and not give way. And it lights his suffering and his death, if die he must, with

[8] Attributed to several sources, including Oliver Cromwell.

[1] Attributed to a U. S. Navy chaplain during World War II.

10 ¶ Moreover the Lord spake again unto Ahaz, saying,

11 Ask thee a sign of the Lord thy God; ask it either in the depth, or in the height above.

12 But Ahaz said, I will not ask, neither will I tempt the Lord.

10 Again the Lord spoke to Ahaz, 11 "Ask a sign of the Lord your God; let it be deep as Sheol or high as heaven." 12 But Ahaz said, "I will not ask, and I will not put the

---

of the original can be brought out by the rendering "If you will not be sure, you cannot be secure," or "If you will not affirm, you will not be confirmed." Faith is both a moral relationship and the resolve to commit oneself unreservedly and firmly to that relationship, because of confidence in the trustworthiness of the object of faith. Moreover, it is in a real sense the only source of that inner security which gives to men the strength and steadiness needful amid "the changes and chances" of this mortal life.

2. Sign of Immanuel (7:10-17)

The circumstances of this episode are in general the same as those of the preceding, but vs. 10 suggests that it took place a little later, and vs. 13 (possibly) that the scene was the court or council chamber. Whereas in vss. 4, 11, and 16 the king is addressed in the singular, in vss. 9b, 13-14 the plural is used. The king and his counselors are still wavering; they have not yet finally rejected the prophet's word and appealed to Tiglath-pileser. So Isaiah goes further and offers them a **sign,** i.e., an event which will soon happen and prove to them that the Lord has indeed spoken by his prophet. The sign is thus firmly anchored to the historical situation in which it was given. Its use (by the author of Matt. 1:23, alone in the N.T.) as evidence of a prophetic expectation of the virgin birth of Jesus Christ, is based on a mistranslation of vs. 14 (see Exeg. below), and on a mystical or allegorical interpretation of prophecy which divorces it from history.

10-12. A sign: A "signal," "communication." In the Lachish Letters the word (אות) is used of beacon fires; in biblical usage it is a token or memorial (Gen. 9:12), either declaratory as in 20:3, or confirmatory, as here. It may be a natural event which becomes a **sign** because it is predicted (cf. I Sam. 2:34), or an extraordinary or miraculous happening, a "wonder," מופת (cf. Exod. 7:9). Isaiah and his sons are living signs which will be recognized as such when his prophecies are fulfilled (cf. 8:18; 20:3). Here Ahaz is given the unusual option of naming the sign from anywhere, even from areas normally outside human experience, **deep as Sheol** [the world of the dead] **or high as heaven.** The king cloaks his unwillingness to obey by pious cant, professing that he does not doubt and hence will not **test** the Lord, even at the Lord's command. But his real attitude was evident not only from his well-known idolatry but from his fearfulness, unbelief, and disobedience to the divine word.

---

a confident hope that the best shall yet be, and God will have the last word. Nothing else than faith in the sovereign love of God can enable one to meet with fortitude the frustrations and defeats of life, endure its discipline, accept even what seem unanswered prayers, and still believe, still trust and obey.

10-14. A Challenge to the King.—When and where this oracle was spoken is not known; but it is clearly a supplement to the appeal to Ahaz to put his trust in God. The Hebrew prophets repeatedly reinforced the spoken word with a sign which confirmed the message of God. So here Ahaz is invited, or rather dared, to name the thing in heaven or earth or hell itself which

to him would be proof of God's word. He refused, as we would expect a man to refuse who did not want to be convinced by that which would either commit him or discredit him. With pretended piety he says he **will not put the Lord to the test.** "No!" answers the prophet, "you will not test him, but you will flaunt him and deny him and weary him till even divine patience is at an end. To that point you have come. Therefore a sign you will have." The oracles which follow are a compound of hope and disaster.

First, the promise of God stands; Israel will be saved from attack by Syria and Ephraim. Somewhere in Israel a little son will be born,

13 And he said, Hear ye now, O house of David; Is it a small thing for you to weary men, but will ye weary my God also?

14 Therefore the Lord himself shall give you a sign; Behold, a virgin shall conceive, and bear a son, and shall call his name Immanuel.

LORD to the test." 13 And he said, "Hear then, O house of David! Is it too little for you to weary men, that you weary my God also? 14 Therefore the Lord himself will give you a sign. Behold, a young woman[i] shall conceive and bear[j] a son, and shall

[i] Or virgin
[j] Or is with child and shall bear

---

13. "Is it not enough that you exhaust the patience of man [i.e., the prophet] that you must exhaust the patience even of my God?" In his indignation Isaiah no longer acknowledges that the Lord is Ahaz' God (cf. vs. 11).

14. **Therefore** normally introduces a threat, as is to be expected after the reproach in vs. 13; the **sign** will demonstrate the fulfillment of the promise already given of immediate deliverance which the Lord has willed; but because of Ahaz' refusal to believe, a greater disaster will follow (vs. 17). **Behold, a** [or "the"] **young woman shall conceive and** [or "has conceived and shall"] **bear a son. Young woman,** "maiden," is the only correct translation of the Hebrew *'almāh*, as is recognized by Aq., Symm., and Theod., who render it by *neanis*. **Virgin** is taken from the Greek word *parthenos*, found here in the LXX, although this corresponds rather to the Hebrew word *bethûlāh*. The quotation in Matt. 1:23 is taken from the LXX, not from the Hebrew, and is one of a number of such quotations used by the author of that Gospel to show that the O.T. foreshadowed the life of Jesus Christ. That he uses these without particular regard to their meaning in their original context is clear from the quotation of Hos. 11:1 in Matt. 2:15. This later "messianic interpretation" is derived from the conviction that the messianic hope had been fulfilled in Jesus. This conviction we may firmly retain, while recognizing that the N.T.'s use of Isa. 7:14 is based on an inaccurate translation of the Hebrew text, which must not prejudice our interpretation of this verse in its original setting. The word *'almāh* means "a young woman of marriageable age," possibly a virgin (cf. Gen. 24:43; Exod. 2:8; Prov. 30:19); if Isaiah had wished to make clear that he had in mind a miraculous virgin birth, he would have had to use the specific term *bethûlāh*. Who, then, was the maiden referred to? "The maiden" may be general—"a

---

and his mother, rejoicing in the deliverance of her nation, will call him **Immanuel,** i.e., **God is with us.** The salvation offered and refused will, despite the king's unbelief, become a fact, and before the child is three years old, Syria and Ephraim will have met their doom. The controversy which has waged for generations about vs. 14 is not our immediate concern. It is clear, however, that in the judgment of most exegetes the translation given in the KJV is inexact, and has been made the basis for views which the Hebrew text cannot support. Modern criticism may protest against the use of this verse in support of the doctrine of the Virgin Birth; it may deny that this is a prophecy of the Messiah: but nothing can dissociate it in the minds of devout believers from the birth of our Lord, and the beautiful and beloved name Immanuel is forever the title of Jesus Christ to his disciples.

14. *Immanuel.*—How perfectly the name fits our Lord! Before he came God had his spokesmen, and among them were some of the greatest souls who ever lived. But none of them could

measure up to the name **Immanuel.** It was too big for them. Then Jesus Christ was born, and because of all he was and did for men we know that to him alone belongs the name. Only he fulfilled its glowing meaning **God is with us.** It fortifies our faith to consider the right of our Lord to bear the great title. Immanuel—the word slips easily from our tongue, for centuries of use have dulled men's sense of its wonder. It means what it says, **God is with us.** A mortal body, a human soul, became for a little the habitation of the Spirit of God. It is a stupendous and almost inconceivable thought. To peoples of earlier days there was nothing incredible in the idea. Greek mythology is full of stories of the gods on earth, and very unlovely stories some of them are. But to sober reason the thought of God dwelling among us is not easy. Yet daring as it is, there is something about God and something about man which make such a coming of the divine not incredible, indeed almost inevitable.

Something about God. If God is a person, we

certain maiden"—but since the sign would have to be one which would come to the attention of Ahaz, either this means that young women will be bearing children and calling them "Immanuel," or it refers to a young woman well known to both king and prophet, the wife of either (perhaps a new wife of Ahaz, since the LXX, Aq., Symm., and Theod. read here "thou shalt call his name"). **Immanuel** or **God is with us:** For the naming of a child by its mother in token of deliverance, cf. Ishmael, "God hears" (Gen. 16:11).

It should be added that many exegetes, Protestant as well as Roman Catholic, prefer a messianic interpretation of the Immanuel saying to that given above. Some of these, e.g., Hugo Gressmann (*Der Messias* [Göttingen: Vandenhoeck & Ruprecht, 1929], pp. 235-42), interpret it in the light of the expectation, widespread in the ancient world, that a divine mother would give birth to a redeemer babe who would supplant the reigning king (cf. Matt. 2:1-12). Mic. 5:2-3 is cited as evidence that such a belief was held in some Judean prophetic circles. The fatal objection to this view is that the child is to be named in token of a deliverance (**Immanuel, God is** [or "be"] **with us**) but is not himself represented as the deliverer.

The traditional messianic interpretation, on the other hand, proceeds from the premise that this passage must predict the virgin birth of a Messiah because Matt. 1:23 so interprets it; e.g., although Kissane (*op. cit.*, I, 89) admits that '*almāh* "does not *necessarily* mean 'virgin,'" he goes on to say: "The use of the word *parthenos* in the Septuagint probably indicates that that further revelation had come before that Version was formed; the fulfilment of the revelation in the person of Christ has proved that in fact the word referred to a virgin in the strict sense (*cf.* Matt. i, 18-23)." This method of reasoning is not convincing, if for no other reason than that a prediction of the miraculous birth of a Messiah more than seven centuries later could hardly have served as a sign to Ahaz.

---

would expect that he would make himself known. If he is indeed Love, nothing could keep him from his children. The Incarnation becomes a necessity. Therefore God took the one way in which to reveal his love: he became one of us. Through the life of Jesus Christ he spoke to us by human lips, and looked on us with human eyes. It is of him and him alone that we say, **Immanuel, God is with us.**

Something about man. A son of Adam he may be, a frail and sinful creature, but a son of God too, with a capacity for faith and eternal things, an unquenchable spark of the divine in him, so that we dare to say that he is "made in the image of God." Surely that fact justifies his right to hope that the yearnings of his soul for knowledge of God would finally be answered. It is not reasonable to think that God created us for himself only to mock us. J. D. Jones once said, "An instinct is an argument, and a desire is equal to a demonstration." [2] "The Word was made flesh, and dwelt among us" (John 1:14).

Because God was in Christ he is known. How utterly mistaken men can be in their thought of God, who have no other witness concerning him than the nature of the world about them. Apart from the revelation of Christ, Huxley's word is quite true, "The highest altar man can raise is to the unknown and unknowable God." But if you have seen Jesus Christ, you cannot say that. Because of his life and death and victory, we believe that all he was, God is. Our Lord himself in the full consciousness of revealing God said, "He that hath seen me hath seen the Father" (John 14:9). No longer can we who know that story raise an altar "To an unknown god" (Acts 17:23).

> For Mercy has a human heart;
> Pity, a human face;
> And Love, the human form divine:
> And Peace, the human dress.[3]

God is with us, and therefore known to us.

Immanuel—God is with us to seek and to save. That is the crown of Christ's word to men, and if it is true, once again the necessity of the Incarnation is shown. Salvation in its full magnitude as forgiveness, healing, comfort, moral strength, cannot be given from afar or in impersonal fashion. Sin is not forgiven by the stroke of a pen, and pain is not removed from the heart by a word of sympathy from one who knows nothing of its anguish. Therefore God to be our Savior entered into our life, faced our temptations, carried our sorrows, and bore our sins on the cross that we might know the length his love would go for our redemption.

Immanuel—unto us is born a Savior! For love of us he came, and for love he still abides. "Lo,

---

[2] *The Hope of the Gospel* (New York: Hodder & Stoughton, 1911), p. 160.

[3] William Blake, "The Divine Image."

15 Butter and honey shall he eat, that he may know to refuse the evil, and choose the good.

16 For before the child shall know to refuse the evil, and choose the good, the land that thou abhorrest shall be forsaken of both her kings.

17 ¶ The LORD shall bring upon thee, and upon thy people, and upon thy father's house, days that have not come, from the day that Ephraim departed from Judah; *even* the king of Assyria.

18 And it shall come to pass in that day, *that* the LORD shall hiss for the fly that *is* in the uttermost part of the rivers of Egypt, and for the bee that *is* in the land of Assyria.

call his name Imman'u-el.[k] 15 He shall eat curds and honey when he knows how to refuse the evil and choose the good. 16 For before the child knows how to refuse the evil and choose the good, the land before whose two kings you are in dread will be deserted. 17 The LORD will bring upon you and upon your people and upon your father's house such days as have not come since the day that E'phraim departed from Judah — the king of Assyria."

18 In that day the LORD will whistle for the fly which is at the sources of the streams of Egypt, and for the bee which is in the

[k] That is *God is with us*

15-16. It appears that the order of these verses has been reversed. Vs. 16 is the continuation of the promise of deliverance in vs. 14, whereas vs. 15 (in the light of vss. 21-22) appears to be part of the threat to Ahaz in vs. 17. Because Ahaz has refused to believe that Judah will be saved from the present attack by Syria and Ephraim, this deliverance which the Lord has promised will be followed by a far greater disaster. **Before the child knows:** Probably the reference is not to the awareness of ethical distinctions, but simply (as in vs. 15) to the child's learning to know which foods he likes, after being weaned at the age of two or three. **The land before whose two kings you are in dread will be deserted** (RSV) is much more accurate than the KJV. **Butter, curds and honey:** The best food available to nomadic wanderers, but not the food of Ahaz' court. The word **honey** can refer to bee honey, or to a sweet made from dates. The child, whose weaning will be a reminder that the first deliverance has taken place, will yet see days when the proud city dwellers will be thankful for the simpler fare of their ancestors.

17. The day that Ephraim departed from Judah: "Severed herself from Judah"; the disruption of the kingdom of David into its component parts (I Kings 12:1-20; cf. II Sam. 5:1-5) had undone the work of Judah's greatest king and left her permanently reduced in political significance. **The king of Assyria** is a marginal note here, in vs. 20, and in 8:7; it is to be attributed to a later reader, for the prophets do not mar their poetic sentences, as these sentences are marred even in the English versions, by inserting prosaic notes on their meaning.

3. THE COMING INVASION (7:18-25)

These four threats, of which the first two predict invasion in striking figures of speech, and the second two describe the resulting ruin of the land, are distinct from the preceding biographical narrative, although they may be from the same period as that

---

I am with you alway, even unto the end of the world" (Matt. 28:20).

15-25. *Other Signs.*—If at Isaiah's word Ahaz, his skepticism silenced by God's assurance, had cried, like the distraught father in the N.T., "Lord, I believe; help thou mine unbelief" (Mark 9:24), all that follows in this chapter might have remained unsaid. But because the king was obdurate in his unbelief, Isaiah proceeds to other signs, not of deliverance but of destruction. There is a day coming which would be as disastrous for Israel as that tragic moment

when God's people were split asunder and the two kingdoms went their sorrowful ways, to meet the doom their own hands had wrought (I Kings 12:1-20). Isaiah uses two metaphors to indicate the agents of the destructions so soon to fall: a plague of flies and bees, and a **razor.** The veterans of the 1944 North African campaign in World War II would appreciate the description of the land black with flies. It should be noted that both instruments of disaster are to come from beyond the borders of Israel. Only the rare soul can truly interpret events as they

19 And they shall come, and shall rest all of them in the desolate valleys, and in the holes of the rocks, and upon all thorns, and upon all bushes.

20 In the same day shall the Lord shave with a razor that is hired, *namely,* by them beyond the river, by the king of Assyria, the head, and the hair of the feet: and it shall also consume the beard.

21 And it shall come to pass in that day, *that* a man shall nourish a young cow and two sheep;

22 And it shall come to pass, for the abundance of milk *that* they shall give, he shall eat butter: for butter and honey shall every one eat that is left in the land.

land of Assyria. 19 And they will all come and settle in the steep ravines, and in the clefts of the rocks, and on all the thornbushes, and on all the pastures.

20 In that day the Lord will shave with a razor which is hired beyond the River — with the king of Assyria — the head and the hair of the feet, and it will sweep away the beard also.

21 In that day a man will keep alive a young cow and two sheep; 22 and because of the abundance of milk which they give, he will eat curds; for every one that is left in the land will eat curds and honey.

---

of the concluding threat in vss. 15, 17. It is not certain whether they refer to Judah or to Israel; if the former, they would find their place either *ca.* 740-738, or between 734 (the threat to Ahaz) and 721, when Samaria was destroyed and Isaiah saw that the historic purpose of the Lord required the survival of Judah. If northern Israel is in view, the prediction would not have such force after the invasion and loss of territory in 733-32 had taken place. In any case, the underlying idea is the same: the Lord is a God who directs the movements of history, whose power extends beyond the borders of his own land, and who can and will bring doom upon his own people since they are in rebellion against him (cf. 6:9-12).

18-19. Hiss or whistle: Rather "call shrilly," as a shepherd summoning his sheep (cf. Judg. 5:16; John 10:3); the word is often used of a shout of derision (cf. Jer. 19:8), hence the mistaken rendering hiss. The fly . . . and . . . the bee: The hostile armies are likened to swarms of insects, stinging flies, and wild bees (cf. Exod. 8:16-24; Ps. 118:12). The identifications may be marginal notes, since Isaiah does not elsewhere speak of Egypt as the invader, although in the same period Hosea does so (cf. Hos. 9:3).

20. Shave with a razor, lit., "knife," with a double reference, to razor and to sword; the figure is not that of complete depopulation but of utter ignominy (cf. II Sam. 10:4). Hair of the feet: A euphemism. Hired or "which has been hired," i.e., by Ahaz, whose land will suffer from the flood he has set loose by appealing to the Assyrian king (cf. 8:5-8). Alternatively, the meaning may be that the Lord will pay their wages to the instruments of his wrath (cf. 45:1-3; Ezek. 29:19-20). Beyond the river: The Euphrates, which makes the meaning so clear that here the marginal note the king of Assyria (cf. vs. 17) would have seemed unnecessary.

21-22. The first impression that these verses contain a promise arises from the word abundance (and, in the KJV, butter). But a man with only one heifer and two sheep was a poor peasant (cf. II Sam. 12:1-3). Those who will eat the food of nomadic

---

occur. Most men need the perspective of time to evaluate them. Alone in the nation, Isaiah saw the hand of God in the affliction of the people. To be invaded by foreigners must have appeared to the suffering Jews the final proof of their abandonment by God. They had no mind for the future; all they knew was that their land was ruined and they were starving. The faith on which they had been nurtured, that God would save his people, was utterly discredited. But Isaiah, with the God-lighted vision, seeing

as it were *sub specie aeternitatis,* dares to assert that God is the author of a disaster which is permitted not for revenge but for the ultimate salvation of a nation which must be brought to its knees before it can stand before God. Whether one is prepared to read history as the scene of God's direct action, or to take it as the stage whereon through frustration, rebellion, and even defeat, the eternal will of God is wrought out, one cannot deny, and it is surely one aspect of divine omnipotence, that God has

23 And it shall come to pass in that day, *that* every place shall be, where there were a thousand vines at a thousand silverlings, it shall *even* be for briers and thorns.

24 With arrows and with bows shall *men* come thither; because all the land shall become briers and thorns.

25 And *on* all hills that shall be digged with the mattock, there shall not come thither the fear of briers and thorns: but it shall be for the sending forth of oxen, and for the treading of lesser cattle.

8 Moreover the LORD said unto me, Take thee a great roll, and write in it with a man's pen concerning Maher-shalal-hash-baz.

---

23 In that day every place where there used to be a thousand vines, worth a thousand shekels of silver, will become briers and thorns. 24 With bow and arrows men will come there, for all the land will be briers and thorns; 25 and as for all the hills which used to be hoed with a hoe, you will not come there for fear of briers and thorns; but they will become a place where cattle are let loose and where sheep tread.

8 Then the LORD said to me, "Take a large tablet and write upon it in common characters, "Belonging to Ma'her-shal'-baz.

---

wanderers, **curds and** [wild] **honey** (cf. Mark 1:6) are survivors. We should translate, "In that day a man who has kept alive a heifer and two sheep, from the amount of milk they give, will eat curds—yea, every survivor in the land will eat curds—and honey."

23-25. The richest vineyards, where each vine had been worth a silver shekel, will quickly become a thicket so dense that men will have to revert to hunting there; the hillsides which had been brought under cultivation by endless hand labor will be abandoned to wandering cattle.

The rather prosaic style of vss. 21, 25 throws some doubt on their Isaian composition, usually so brilliant and finished. Since there is no reason to question that the subject matter is in accord with the prophet's thought in this period, it may be that these passages represent a disciple's recollection of his message rather than his own words.

4. SIGN OF MAHER-SHALAL-HASHBAZ (8:1-4)

8:1-4. In vss. 1-8*a*, 11-18 we have the second and final installment of Isaiah's personal memoirs, apparently completed, along with the story of his call, at the time when Ahaz had turned his back on the prophet and appealed instead to the Assyrians for help. In so doing the king made himself a client of the heathen empire, not only politically but in matters of religion; he paid over the treasures of the Jerusalem temple and introduced there an altar of the Assyrian god. In consequence of this, it seems from vss. 16-18 that Isaiah withdrew for the time being from an active prophetic ministry to await the fulfillment of his predictions, which at the same time he put on record in writing.

The theme of the doubly attested oracle in vss. 1-4 is the same as that of 7:7-9 and 7:14, 16, viz., that the doom of Syria and Ephraim is certain. The new feature is the

---

the power to use the very disasters of life, the work of malignant forces, and to weave them into his purposes for men. The story has yet to be written by some Christian historian, of how God employed incarnate evil in Adolf Hitler, and bloody revolution in communism, to discipline a world that could be saved only through suffering; for indeed salvation can come through judgment.

8:1-4. A Placarded Warning.—Here is the first of a series of abrupt oracles directed against a rapidly changing political situation. The whole chapter gives an impression of confusion, and thereby reflects the character of the day.

The air was alive with rumor, and as a result fear was abroad.

Since Ahaz had refused to heed the divine warning, and so had failed both God and the nation, Isaiah turned to the people to reiterate the same message. He did not speak it in words, but literally placarded it before their eyes on a signboard. Month after month the noisy hissing word, **Maher-shalal-hashbaz**, "swift the spoiling, prompt the plundering," painted without comment on a plank, confronted them with its dark warning. Within the year Isaiah repeated the message in another way, this time in a living form; for he called his newborn son by the same

2 And I took unto me faithful witnesses to record, Uriah the priest, and Zechariah the son of Jeberechiah.

3 And I went unto the prophetess; and she conceived, and bare a son. Then said the LORD to me, Call his name Maher-shalal-hash-baz.

4 For before the child shall have knowledge to cry, My father, and my mother, the riches of Damascus and the spoil of Samaria shall be taken away before the king of Assyria.

5 ¶ The LORD spake also unto me again, saying,

6 Forasmuch as this people refuseth the waters of Shiloah that go softly, and rejoice in Rezin and Remaliah's son;

al-hash'baz.' " *l* 2 And I got reliable witnesses, Uri'ah the priest and Zechari'ah the son of Jeberechi'ah, to attest for me. 3 And I went to the prophetess, and she conceived and bore a son. Then the LORD said to me, "Call his name Ma'her-shal'al-hash'baz; 4 for before the child knows how to cry 'My father' or 'My mother,' the wealth of Damascus and the spoil of Samar'ia will be carried away before the king of Assyria."

5 The LORD spoke to me again: 6 "Because this people have refused the waters of Shilo'ah that flow gently, and melt in fear before*m* Rezin and the son of Remali'ah;

l That is *The spoil speeds, the prey hastes*
m Cn: Heb *rejoices in*

---

naming of the instrument of the Lord's intervention as **the king of Assyria**. In the first instance, Isaiah is commanded to take, not **a great roll**, but **a large tablet** or "board," and to inscribe on it in **common characters** (or "in plain letters"; cf. Hab. 2:2) an ambiguous message: "Swift the spoiling, prompt the plundering." **Concerning** and **belonging to** should be omitted in translation, since these imply that the tablet refers to the boy who is to bear this name (vs. 3), whereas the tablet and the boy's name are distinct publications of the oracle (the prefix ל is the sign of the accusative case). The message is to be attested by **reliable witnesses,** so that when the prediction is fulfilled it can be shown that Isaiah had indeed brought a sign from God (cf. Deut. 18:22). **The prophetess** appears only here as designating the wife of a prophet; elsewhere it means a female seer (cf. II Kings 22:14). The son born some time after the making of the enigmatic inscription is to have as his name the same words. But this time their meaning and application are to be explained, as in vs. 4. Since the overthrow of the Syro-Ephraimite alliance lies still in the future, after the interval between the two episodes plus the period of pregnancy, it may be that the oracle was first given several years earlier, following Tiglath-pileser's demonstration in force in 738. Isaiah saw that the instrument was being prepared for the chastisement of his recalcitrant people; the specific application to Ephraim and its ally became clear to him only later as the situation developed.

5. ORACLE OF THE TWO RIVERS (8:5-8a)

5-8a. This oracle is not only additional to the foregoing but an extension of it: "The LORD spoke to me again, saying further. . . ." The prophet declares that the flood which Ahaz has let loose by his appeal to Assyria will not stop short with Damascus and

---

sinister name. Incidentally, one feels that it was most unfair to the child to inflict on him such a handicap. The word was a prophecy of the overthrow of Syria and Ephraim by Assyria and a warning against the folly of any alliance with that nation. It is immediately followed by the prediction of the invasion of Judah itself by Assyria, given in the image of the two streams, **the waters of Shiloah** and the Euphrates. Because the nation has scorned the one, it shall be scoured by the other. The waters of Shiloah, the gentle unhurrying water supply of Jerusalem, represent trust in God. To the

flustered people, however, so meager a resource was not enough. The waters of Shiloah were a mere trickle, and trust in Yahweh an impalpable defense; they wanted deep waters and visible reinforcement. So, cries the prophet, because you despise that quiet flow, you will get the raging flood, the land will be inundated with Assyrian power, Assyrian oppression, Assyrian idolatry. You will be figuratively "up to the neck in it," and all but perish. The alliance you thought would save you will ruin you.

Behind this figure of speech lies an enduring moral principle vividly illustrated in national

7 Now therefore, behold, the Lord bringeth up upon them the waters of the river, strong and many, *even* the king of Assyria, and all his glory: and he shall come up over all his channels, and go over all his banks:

8 And he shall pass through Judah; he shall overflow and go over, he shall reach *even* to the neck; and the stretching out of his wings shall fill the breadth of thy land, O Immanuel.

9 ¶ Associate yourselves, O ye people, and ye shall be broken in pieces; and give ear, all ye of far countries: gird yourselves, and ye shall be broken in pieces; gird yourselves, and ye shall be broken in pieces.

7 therefore, behold, the Lord is bringing up against them the waters of the River, mighty and many, the king of Assyria and all his glory; and it will rise over all its channels and go over all its banks; 8 and it will sweep on into Judah, it will overflow and pass on, reaching even to the neck; and its outspread wings will fill the breadth of your land, O Imman'u-el."

9 Be broken, you peoples, and be dismayed;
  give ear, all you far countries;
  gird yourselves and be dismayed;
  gird yourselves and be dismayed.

Ephraim, but **it will sweep on into Judah.** Since the king has surrendered to doubt and fear, he will have real cause for fear, for the God he has distrusted will strike him down with the weapon with which Ahaz had thought to defend himself. The oracle probably ends with **even to the neck;** vs. 8*b* is to be taken with vss. 9-10 (with Marti, *Das Buch Jesaja*, pp. 84-85, and Gray, *Isaiah I-XXXIX*, I, 148-49; see Exeg. on vss. 8*b*-10). **The waters of Shiloah that flow gently:** The canal which conducted the water from the spring Gihon to "the pool of Siloam," or its earlier counterpart, before the construction of Hezekiah's tunnel (cf. II Kings 20:20). This is probably "the conduit of the upper pool" (7:3; cf. II Kings 18:17). The figure is an effective one in contrasting Jerusalem's tiny stream with the mighty Euphrates, and at the same time suggesting the "quietness" and "confidence" (30:15) which Ahaz had rejected in favor of material power. For **rejoice in,** משוש, which destroys the sense, the RSV rightly reads **melts in fear before,** מסוס, which provides a play on words with **have refused,** מאס. This is a "public" oracle, of which the "embryonic" primary form seems to have emerged in the prophet's consciousness summed up in these two words similar in sound but different in meaning.

The river Euphrates is not only a great river, but here it is pictured as in flood, overflowing the **channels** and **banks** which Ahaz expected to retain its force, changing its course disconcertingly and flooding even distant Judah up **to the neck.** For the overwhelming onslaught of the Assyrian hordes this again is an apt figure; in 30:28 it is used of the overflowing wrath of God, which is the undertone here too.

6. FAITH DECLARES DEFIANCE (8:8*b*-10)

8*b*-10. Ps. 46 is the best commentary on these verses, which express a very different mood from that of the foregoing and reflect a different background. The separation of

---

and personal life, viz., that compromise with evil initiates a process which cannot be stayed. What begins as dalliance ends in doom. A man negotiates with evil: it may have its risks, but it gratifies a desire, and he can always quit. But can he? The vast multitude of men enslaved by the sin with which they trifled is the answer. Almost before they knew it, their lives were flooded with the evil to which they turned for relief or pleasure. It is the same with nations. In the first half of the twentieth century this law of spiritual life twice worked destruction on a great power. Germany, birthplace of the Reformation and its religious freedom, home of

science and art, philosophy and music, dallied first with the idea of world power, yielding to the pressure of ambitious men and movements; then defeated, gradually surrendered the very principles which made her great, and ended a slave to militant evil. In all history there is no more lurid illustration of how a strong nation by its own compromise with evil can be submerged in the tyranny of sin.

9-10. *An Unsurrendered Faith.*—These two verses strike an entirely different note. It is as though Isaiah, looking on the dark prospect he has foretold, felt a surge of the undying patriotism of the Jews, and broke out in defiance

| 10 Take counsel together, and it shall come to nought; speak the word, and it shall not stand: for God *is* with us.

11 ¶ For the LORD spake thus to me with a strong hand, and instructed me that I should not walk in the way of this people, saying, | 10 Take counsel together, but it will come to nought;
speak a word, but it will not stand,
for God is with us.

11 For the LORD spoke thus to me with his strong hand upon me, and warned me not to walk in the way of this people, say- |

vs. 8b from vs. 8a is made almost necessary (a) by the abrupt change of figure to that of a great bird with **wings** outstretched, hostile (cf. Jer. 48:40) or protecting (cf. Ps. 17:8), and (b) by "the difficulty, never satisfactorily met, of explaining an appeal to Immanuel, [since] he was not yet born if this passage is continuous with 8:1-4" (Gray, *op. cit.,* I, 149, 145). It is probably best, with Gray, to see in these verses a fragment of a prophetic liturgical poem having the refrain **For God is with us** (cf. Ps. 46:7, 11). This, if it is Isaiah's, must belong to his later period when he looked for deliverance rather than destruction (cf. 37:21-35), and when Judah was recurrently threatened by armies under Assyrian command but composed of contingents from many **peoples** from **far countries.** The **outspread wings** are the protecting wings of the Lord (cf. 31:5; Ps. 91:4), and vs. 8b is of course not the beginning of the poem. **O Immanuel** is to be read as in vs. 10: **for God is with us. Associate yourselves** or **be broken,** רעו, is rather to be read as the imperative "know," דעו, with the LXX and the Vulg., providing a normal parallel with **give ear** in the next line. For other examples of a series of taunting imperative verbs cf. 23:1-7; 29:9; the sense is, "Know this, O peoples, though you gird on your arms, you shall be terrified; though you make plans, they shall be frustrated." The thought is Isaiah's (cf. 2:10-11; 7:7; 10:5-15).

7. THE FEAR OF MAN AND THE FEAR OF GOD (8:11-15)

This important passage is sufficiently ambiguous to have given rise to quite different interpretations. The chief difficulty arises from the fact that the alternative attitudes described in vss. 12-13 are contrasted in language closely parallel except for the key words **conspiracy,** קשר, and **sanctify, regard as holy** (from the same root as קדש, "holiness"). Since these words are similar in appearance, it has been widely held that they have been confused, and that these verses should read (completing the parallelism) either (a) "Do not [you, plural] call conspiracy all that this people calls conspiracy, . . . but the LORD of hosts, make a conspiracy [or "alliance"] with him"; or (b) "Do not [you, plural] call holy all that this people calls holy, . . . but . . . call him holy." The second alternative harks back to ch. 6, and the single change to "calls holy" can be explained more easily than the double substitution of **conspiracy.** For this reason the first alternative is preferable. (It should be added that some scholars hold that the same sense can be extracted without altering the Hebrew text.) Another reason for retaining the word conspiracy is that this section follows immediately upon vs. 10, where a similar idea is prominent, although in a distinct oracle; since in the putting together of the book the oracles have been so largely arranged on the principle of the association of ideas or key

against the hostile powers closing in on Judah. It is not the challenge of earthly power, for the Jews had none, but the assertion of an unsurrendered faith in the sovereignty of Almighty God. It is really an incredible picture, this, of a man standing in a squalid little provincial town and defying the world. But the daring of Isaiah's faith in God has been and always will be vindicated. We have the cross of Christ and the Resurrection to justify our conviction that God's love is stronger than sin, mightier than death;

our faith is grounded on God's historic deed. Isaiah had no such unanswerable argument. He "ventured all at a clap" that God would not forsake his people, and against the marshaling might of a great empire, lifted the battle cry of his faith, "Emmanuel, . . . God with us" (Matt. 1:23).

11-15. The Conspiracy of Faith.—Despite the ambiguity of these verses the meaning of the oracle is clear enough. Conspiracy is in the air, the conspiracy to dethrone Ahaz, and the king's

12 Say ye not, A confederacy, to all *them to* whom this people shall say, A confederacy; neither fear ye their fear, nor be afraid.

ing: 12 "Do not call conspiracy all that this people call conspiracy, and do not fear what

---

words (see Intro., p. 158), it is more than probable that the word conspiracy was read in the text of vs. 12.

The question remains as to what conspiracy or alliance was referred to. The answer is bound up with that to the further question: Who are those addressed in vss. 12-13, since they are singled out from **this people?** The previous verse leads the reader to expect a message addressed to Isaiah himself; this fact, together with the use of the plural, and the apparent reference in vs. 16 to "disciples," has led to the conclusion that the oracle is directed to Isaiah in association with his inner circle of followers. But why should not those within range of the prophet's voice at any time have been exhorted to reject the prevailing attitude of the nation? And why should disciples of Isaiah need to be urged to follow him rather than the king? This is apparently the first summons to men in the history of biblical religion to separate themselves in spirit from their social group in obedience to God. It was a moment pregnant with significance for the future histories of Judaism and of the Christian church.

There is a hiatus between vs. 11 and vs. 12, and also an unusual circumstantial clause within vs. 11 which gives in indirect narration a "private" oracle cautioning the prophet. The sense is clear if one supplies at the end of vs. 11 what apparently has been accidentally dropped out, "Go and say to . . . , 'Thus says the Lord.'"

The word קֶשֶׁר, conspiracy, is used normally of an attempt to usurp royal authority (cf. II Kings 15:30), or of rebellion of a vassal king against his overlord (cf. II Kings 17:4). Once it is used of Judah's rebellion against her God (Jer. 11:9). Here it can hardly mean that Isaiah was being denounced as a conspirator, as Procksch suggests (*Jesaia I*, p. 136); it must refer, rather, to the conspiracy of the Syrians and Ephraimites to dethrone Ahaz, since it is this attack which the people dread (cf. 7:2, 6). The point of the oracle is simply that men must not fall into panic because of any human conspiracy, however dangerous, since if they will but "conspire" with God and "fear" him, they will be secure (7:9). But refusal to do so can result only in a disaster greater and more certain than that which now overhangs Judah.

11. With a strong hand: "With compelling power"; the reference is not necessarily to a special incidence of ecstasy, as in Ezek. 8:1. The prophets always spoke under a sense of the masterful will of God compelling them to utter his word (cf. Amos 7:14-15; Jer. 20:7-9).

12. Saying: On the hiatus here see above.

---

proposal to conspire with Assyria. Nobody knows what to think, and therefore everybody is afraid. Speaking to that mood, Isaiah under the prompting of God cries, "Conspire with God, fear him and nobody else." There is a suggestion, borne out by the reference to disciples in vs. 16, that the prophet, realizing that the nation is past hearing, and that he is wasting words on the masses, makes his appeal to the handful of those who are still prepared to trust God, the minority group of the faithful. If this is so, it marks a turning point. This is the first time in Jewish history that a man speaking for God turns from the nation to pin his hope on an elect following within the nation, and calls on them to dare to stand against their fellows

for God and the truth. From this point on, the story of faith is the record of God's saving remnant. In almost every great movement of the spirit the majority has been consistently wrong, while the minority, in Winston Churchill's words, has been gloriously vindicated, through "blood, toil, tears, and sweat," and has saved the cause. Nowhere has that been more heroically illustrated than in the history of the church. In every century the church has been kept spiritually alive by the quiet but unsurrendered faith of the few, living and moving, not by the pretensions of the unthinking majority, but by the fidelity and devotion of the elect community whose lives were a sustained conspiracy of faith.

13 Sanctify the LORD of hosts himself; and *let* him *be* your fear, and *let* him *be* your dread.

14 And he shall be for a sanctuary; but for a stone of stumbling and for a rock of offense to both the houses of Israel, for a gin and for a snare to the inhabitants of Jerusalem.

15 And many among them shall stumble, and fall, and be broken, and be snared, and be taken.

16 Bind up the testimony, seal the law among my disciples.

they fear, nor be in dread. 13 But the LORD of hosts, him you shall regard as holy; let him be your fear, and let him be your dread. 14 And he will become a sanctuary, and a stone of offence, and a rock of stumbling to both houses of Israel, a trap and a snare to the inhabitants of Jerusalem. 15 And many shall stumble thereon; they shall fall and be broken; they shall be snared and taken."

16 Bind up the testimony, seal the teach-

---

14. A sanctuary: Since מקדש means "place of worship," but has not the secondary meaning, "place of refuge," which it has in English, the word here is more probably מוקש, snare, as in the Targ. **Stone of offence:** A stone against which a man strikes his foot and stumbles. **Both houses of Israel:** This is an inexact parallel or antithesis to **inhabitants of Jerusalem;** important Greek MSS read simply "the house of Jacob."

C. WITHDRAWAL OF THE PROPHET (8:16-18)

With these verses the autobiographical memoirs of Isaiah, composed to accompany the first recording of his oracles, are concluded. The occasion is the rejection by king and people of Isaiah's message at the time of the Syro-Ephraimite attack (cf. vss. 1-8*a*). Now the prophet announces that he will speak no more, but will wait for the fulfillment of the prophecies of which his own and his sons' portentous names are the "signs."

16. Bind up, . . . seal: A scroll of parchment or papyrus was tied with cord and sealed when it was not currently used (cf. 29:11) but was to be preserved, like a deed (cf. Jer. 32:10), for future reference. The verbs as vocalized are imperatives, but the C.T. permits their interpretation as infinitives absolute, to be translated, with vs. 17, as future indicatives: "I will tie up the evidence; I will seal the admonition." The Hebrew adds "in my disciples," but if this means "in the minds of my disciples," it is vaguely expressed, and the LXX, Syriac, and Targ. find no reference here to **disciples.** The LXX reads the preposition "from," and, particularly in the light of 29:11, this suggests that we should read here *millimmūdh*, "from the learned," i.e., so that even the learned cannot read it. Up until now his message has been proclaimed for all to hear and

---

In vs. 14 there is a memorable example of what might be termed the inevitability of paradox in religious thinking: God **will become a sanctuary, and a stone of offence.** This is perhaps a theme for the theologian rather than for the people; and yet all believers should be brought to see that there are conflicting elements in our thought of God, that his nature is beyond definition and his truth cannot be finally analyzed and docketed. Granted there is a divine revelation; yet mystery remains, and must always remain, as finite minds strive with the Infinite. Paradox is inescapable—proof not of the inconsistency of God but of the limitations in man.

16-18. *Withdrawal of the Prophet.*—This passage brings to a close the personal memoirs of Isaiah. He has spoken for God, and the message

has been finally rejected by king and people alike. He therefore declares his purpose to become a spectator of the debacle which must ensue. He will file away the spoken oracles, and when they have been vindicated in history they will be available as witnesses of the integrity of God's Word, while Isaiah and his sons, the living oracles, will stand justified.

16-18. *The Strategy of Silence.*—Isaiah's decision to stop speaking was not an acknowledgment of defeat, it was not prompted by either petulance or despair, but was deliberate. In God's strategy there is a place for silence and the pause is one of his devices. There comes a time in his dealing with us when words are unavailing. The message has been delivered, the warning sounded, the appeal to honor and faith has been made, and still men, obdurate in evil,

17 And I will wait upon the LORD, that hideth his face from the house of Jacob, and I will look for him.

18 Behold, I and the children whom the LORD hath given me *are* for signs and for wonders in Israel from the LORD of hosts, which dwelleth in mount Zion.

19 ¶ And when they shall say unto you, Seek unto them that have familiar spirits, and unto wizards that peep and that mut-

ing among my disciples. 17 I will wait for the LORD, who is hiding his face from the house of Jacob, and I will hope in him.

18 Behold, I and the children whom the LORD has given me are signs and portents in Israel from the LORD of hosts, who dwells on Mount Zion. 19 And when they say to you, "Consult the mediums and the wizards who

---

placarded (vs. 1) for all to read; now it is to be written and sealed until verified by the fulfillment of the signs.

17. I will wait for the LORD: In the patience of complete faith (cf. Hab. 2:3). **Who is hiding his face:** The opposite of "lifts up his countenance"; the figure is that of a king's favor or disfavor, as indicated by his recognition or nonrecognition of one in his presence (cf. Prov. 16:15; Dan. 5:6). **Look for:** Better, **hope in.**

18. I and the children ... are signs and portents: Isaiah's own name means "Yahweh is salvation." The meaning of Shear-jashub's name is ambiguous, but its primary sense is ominous (see on 7:3). Maher-shalal-hashbaz (vs. 3) also has a certain ambiguity, but is interpreted in vs. 4 as referring to the spoiling of Judah's enemies. These are the "living epistles," and when the time has come for the Lord to bring to pass what the names represent the written oracles will be unsealed and read with understanding (cf. Dan. 12:4). **The LORD of hosts, who dwells on Mount Zion:** The meaning is not that the Deity is localized or confined to the earthly temple, for his glorious presence fills the earth (6:3); rather it is that he is there as a real presence which Isaiah himself had experienced. Zion was the name of the Jebusite stronghold on the southeastern hill which was captured by David and thereafter was known as "the city of David" (II Sam. 5:7); **Mount Zion** was the higher hill immediately north of the old city, where Solomon erected his temple; hence it was called also "the hill of the LORD" (Ps. 24:3).

III. "HIS ANGER IS NOT TURNED AWAY" (8:19–10:4; 5:24*b*-30)

There follows here on the autobiographical sections and the material now associated with them a further selection of oracles, mainly concerned with the wickedness and punishment of Judah (and incidentally of Ephraim). This has the appearance of having been separated artificially from ch. 5 by the intervening material (with 8:19-22 cf. 5:30, and with 9:12, 17, 21 [Hebrew 9:11, 16, 20] and 10:4 cf. 5:25). The oracle of the messianic King (9:2-7 [Hebrew 9:1-6]) strikes a wholly different note, but is an insertion here like the similar insertion of 11:1-9 in the next section, and does not alter the fundamental similarity of the subject matter in sections I and III. With 10:5 a new note, that of judgment upon Assyria, is introduced and marks the end of the messages of reproach and doom to Judah in the earlier chapters of the present book.

---

go their own ways unheeding, uncaring. There is no use saying any more; the moral law must take its course. God's purpose of redemption is constantly thwarted by the indifference of men. He cannot compel obedience without invading the freedom he has given them. The irresistible and indisputable are weapons God cannot use to save us. Therefore he must needs let us go our own stubborn and foolish ways until life brings us up short and we, beaten to our knees and realizing our own misery and helplessness, are at last ready to hear his word. God at times

seems to withdraw from the human scene in order that we may learn our need of him. So Isaiah retired from the court and market place to watch with God what happens to a people who deliberately refused his counsel, and to wait until sorrow and suffering should spell out for them the truth that in God alone was their hope.

19-22. *Recourse to Superstition.*—Here are two fragmentary oracles which have somehow found their way into this chapter. They seem to have little or no relationship to what pre-

ter: should not a people seek unto their God? for the living to the dead?

20 To the law and to the testimony: if they speak not according to this word, *it is* because *there is* no light in them.

21 And they shall pass through it, hardly bestead and hungry: and it shall come to pass, that when they shall be hungry, they shall fret themselves, and curse their king and their God, and look upward.

chirp and mutter," should not a people consult their God? Should they consult the dead on behalf of the living? 20 To the teaching and to the testimony! Surely for this word which they speak there is no dawn. 21 They will pass through the land,[n] greatly distressed and hungry; and when they are hungry, they will be enraged and will curse[o] their king and their God, and

[n] Heb *it*
[o] Or *curse by*

A. Two Fragments of Ominous Prophecy (8:19-22)

The interpretation of these verses is made difficult by the fact that they appear fragmentary and unrelated either to each other or to their present context, except for one thing: both refer to times of distress and darkness, and so form a dark background against which the great messianic prophecy of 9:2-7 (Hebrew 9:1-6) stands as in a spotlight. It is noteworthy also that if the distinctive narrative sections with their oracular enclosures now found in 6:1–8:18 are removed, they follow a similar verse in 5:30 (see Intro., p. 159). Whatever this may mean as an indication of a different arrangement of the material in earlier stages of the composition of the book, the exegesis of the fragments themselves is not seriously affected.

19-20. A condemnation of superstition as a substitute for religion. Especially in times of acute distress, then as now, many resorted to practitioners of the ancient superstitions of the human race (cf. I Sam. 28:3-25). The prophets fought a constant battle to substitute faith in a living God for the tyranny of demons and the pretensions of magic (cf. Deut. 18:9-12; II Kings 17:17; Jer. 14:14). **Them that have familiar spirits** or **the mediums:** the word אוֹב is the "spirit" or "control" (cf. 29:4; I Sam. 28:7), and only in a derived sense the medium. **Wizard:** "The knowing one," also refers primarily not to the practitioner but to **the dead,** who were believed to have supernatural knowledge desired by the **living** (cf. I Sam. 28:15). Vs. 20 appears to be the sequel of vs. 19, but the meaning is obscure. Apparently it was obscure even to the editor or to an early reader, who noted in the margin, "This is with reference to the teaching and to the testimony" mentioned in vs. 16. The remainder of the verse should be translated, not as a conditional sentence (see KJV), but as an emphatic affirmative (see RSV). For the meaningless שַׁחַר (**dawn**) read שָׂכָר ("reward"), with the LXX and Syriac, "Surely they speak after this fashion, which will have no reward," i.e., "which is profitless."

21-22. The fragmentary nature of these verses is evident from the lack of an antecedent to the opening words, **they shall pass through it; it** is feminine and must refer to

cedes them, except in so far as they suggest the devices to which men have recourse when the voice of God's spokesman falls silent. The prophet will no more be heard, but the people who have had the doubtful privilege of rejecting his message find the silence more unbearable than his warning. So, lapsing into the sphere of superstition, they turn from the living to the dead, hiring mediums and spiritualists to tell them what to do.

It is significant that when men give up true religion they always become victims of superstition. By their very nature as essentially spiritual, with an instinct for faith and a capacity for God, they must have something beyond themselves in

which to believe; if it is not God, then it will be demons or ghosts. Superstition is thus at once a tribute and a revelation. It reveals a moral condition which because of unbelief or sin cannot live neighbor to God. A rabbit's foot in a man's pocket declares that here is one who, reluctant to face the truth or accept the demands of God, still feels he must take precautions against the unknown. Superstition is not intellectual but practical atheism. That is why to the prophets it was the deadly sin; it denied God, and yet by its tawdry devices sought a substitute for God. The prophets had no hope for a man or a nation who would prostitute the implanted instinct for the divine to traffic with spirits. As

22 And they shall look unto the earth; and behold trouble and darkness, dimness of anguish; and *they shall be* driven to darkness.

9 Nevertheless the dimness *shall* not *be* such as *was* in her vexation, when at the first he lightly afflicted the land of Zebulun, and the land of Naphtali, and afterward did more grievously afflict *her by* the way of the sea, beyond Jordan, in Galilee of the nations.

turn their faces upward; 22 and they will look to the earth, but behold, distress and darkness, the gloom of anguish; and they will be thrust into thick darkness.

9 *p* But there will be no gloom for her that was in anguish. In the former time he brought into contempt the land of Zeb'ulun and the land of Naph'tali, but in the latter time he will make glorious the way of the sea, the land beyond the Jordan, Galilee of the nations.

p Heb Ch 8. 23

---

the land. The necessary connection may be found after 6:12 or after 7:25. The picture is that of a country empty and desolate, in which the few desperate survivors will curse the king who has betrayed them and the God who has punished them. "Whether they turn their faces heavenwards or look to the earth, they will see only" **distress and darkness, the gloom of anguish; and they will be thrust into thick darkness.**

B. The Messianic King (9:1-7 [Hebrew 8:23–9:6])

1. A Transitional Verse (9:1 [Hebrew 8:23])

9:1. As in Amos 9:8, a sharp transition from a word of doom to one of promise is marked by a short editorial sentence qualifying and even contradicting the word of doom: "Yet there shall not be [i.e., continue] gloom to her [i.e., the land] that has known anguish." Then follows an oracle promising that the ancient territory of **Zebulun** and **Naphtali,** which had been overrun by Tiglath-pileser in 733-32 and incorporated into the Assyrian empire, would once more be "brought to honor." **The way of the sea** was the ancient caravan route to the sea from Damascus; we should read, with Procksch (*op. cit.,* p. 144), "from the land beyond Jordan to Galilee of the nations." The territory traversed by this road, broadly speaking, corresponds to that taken by the Assyrians in 733-32, which included Zebulun and Naphtali (II Kings 15:29). That the Assyrian-held territory is thus described shows that the oracle antedates the final onslaught on northern Israel in 724-21.

Isaiah says, they get what they deserve: disillusionment, bitterness, unappeased hunger of spirit, and a great enveloping darkness of soul.

9:1-7. *A Prophecy of the Messiah.*—While this glorious messianic oracle was first uttered by Isaiah, and stands forever as his word to his people, Christendom has claimed it for its own, and it has come to be not less than a hymn of faith. Never a Christmas dawns but the cadences of this lovely song are heard wherever Christ's people are met, for to Christian faith the great prophecy has had its fulfillment in the birth of Jesus of Nazareth. The exegesis of the passage has been the occasion of long debate, and there is even now no unanimity of opinion on its exact meaning. Had Isaiah a living monarch in mind when he cried, **Unto us a child is born? Is** this a dynastic oracle spoken on the occasion of a coronation? Or is it a prophecy of a "far-off divine event"? These questions are of living interest to scholarship; but when the Christian

church reads or sings these words, it is to exult in the gift of God's love in Jesus Christ. It is his song, and we sing it in thanksgiving for the fulfillment of that hope which burned in the weary human heart through centuries of darkness and pain, that God would yet visit and redeem his people. It has all come true: **The people that walked in darkness have seen a great light,** on them has "the light of the knowledge of the glory of God in the face of Jesus Christ" (II Cor. 4:6) flashed out. It is amazing how every detail of the song fits our case and meets our needs. Across the centuries it leaps; spoken to the despairing hearts of a handful of Jews more than twenty-five hundred years ago, it gives voice to the thanksgiving of all the sons of men for a great deliverance and a divine Savior. Timeless and universal, it is the song of the Redeemer and his kingdom. How perfectly it mirrors the hopes of men! In it are the light and joy of freedom. Over the last verse of the pre-

| 2 The people that walked in darkness have seen a great light: they that dwell in the land of the shadow of death, upon them hath the light shined. | 2*a* The people who walked in darkness have seen a great light; those who dwelt in a land of deep darkness, on them has light shined. |

a Heb Ch 9. 1

2. Oracle of the Messianic King (9:2-7 [Hebrew 9:1-6])

This great utterance of exultant faith bursts like the first light of Creation upon the darkness and chaos of the earth as pictured in the closing part of ch. 8. Distress is turned into unspeakable rejoicing, with the overthrow of the oppressor, and the coming to the throne of David of a king whose lofty titles betoken a new age of peace and justice. The passage is famous not only because of its intrinsic merit, but because its opening verse and the preceding verse with its reference to Galilee are quoted in Matt. 4:15-16 as a prophecy of Jesus' Galilean ministry. The association has been further strengthened by the use of the whole oracle as an O.T. lesson for Christmas Day.

For Christians the messianic hope of Judaism is fulfilled in Jesus of Nazareth; but not in the way expected by the Jews of his time on the basis of the description in messianic psalms and prophetic oracles. In the passage before us the king whose coming is celebrated is to mount the throne of David amid general rejoicing, consequent upon the overthrow in war of a foreign oppressor. Two questions arise in connection with the interpretation of this passage in its context in Isaiah: Is the reference to a contemporary king, or to an ideal king in the future? Is the oracle to be attributed to Isaiah, or does it in reality express a hope for the restoration of the Davidic monarchy, which arose only after the last king of Judah had been carried into exile by the Babylonians?

These questions have been answered in many different ways, because the evidence is not decisive. The custom of designating a future ideal king as "the Messiah," i.e., "the Anointed One," arose from the fact that a man became king through a religious rite of anointing (II Sam. 2:4; II Kings 11:12), and henceforth was known during his lifetime as "the (Lord's) Messiah" (I Sam. 24:10; II Sam. 19:21; Ps. 2:2). The highest titles were given to the king. After his anointing he was a sacred person, with whose life the welfare of the nation was involved (II Sam. 21:17). He stood then in a unique relation to the nation's God, who on the day of the king's anointing had become his Father (II Sam. 7:13-14; Pss. 2:6-7; 89:26-27).

In the light of this, 9:1-6 appears to be a dynastic oracle uttered on the occasion of the anointing of a new king, or at the anniversary celebration of this event. (Cf. Margaret B. Crook, "A Suggested Occasion for Isaiah 9₂₋₇ and 11₁₋₉," *Journal of Biblical Literature*, LXVIII [1949], 213-24.) The author holds that the former is a liturgy of enthronement, the latter a coronation liturgy, used on the accession of Jehoash. The idea is suggestive, but Ps. 2:7 shows that the oracles of Isa. 9:2-7; 11:1-9 have no necessary

---

ceding chapter lies a pall of darkness. Suddenly—

> Out of the night that covers [it]
> Black as the Pit from pole to pole,[4]

comes a ray of light; it brightens and broadens until the land is flooded with sunshine and the winds of a radiant dawn carry the sounds of exultant singing to the farthest corners.

On November 11, 1918, the sun rose on the delivered city of Mons. All night long the dark-

[4] William Ernest Henley, "Invictus."

ness had been shot through with the lurid flashes of gunfire, and the staccato chatter of the machine guns had echoed through deserted streets. But at dawn the last German outpost withdrew, and from the barred and shuttered homes of men the people streamed. Down the street sped the cry, "Hang out your flags." When the sun rose, it shone on a city of banners, and on the delirious joy of those who, having for four and a half years dwelt in a land of darkness, now walked free. So Isaiah in his moment of vision saw his beloved nation. He projects on the screen of the future the great deliverance.

3 Thou hast multiplied the nation, *and* not increased the joy: they joy before thee according to the joy in harvest, *and* as *men* rejoice when they divide the spoil.

3 Thou hast multiplied the nation,
　　thou hast increased its joy;
they rejoice before thee
　　as with joy at the harvest,
　　　as men rejoice when they divide the
　　　　spoil.

---

reference to a child-king; the king, as son of Yahweh, is metaphorically begotten on the day of his anointing. The language passes the bounds of ordinary human qualities in its description, because the monarch is no longer, in the thought of the poet, an ordinary man but is the chosen and anointed son of Yahweh. It is striking to note the occurrence of motifs characteristic of psalms related to the Davidic dynasty and its place in the temple cult: the dawn of a great light (II Sam. 23:4; Pss. 110:3; 118:24, 27) ; the exultant rejoicing of the people (Pss. 118:15, 24; 132:9, 16; cf. I Kings 1:40) ; the overthrow of the king's enemies (Pss. 2:2, 8, 9; 72:4, 14; 89:23; 110:1, 5-6; 132:18) ; the burning with fire (II Sam. 23:7; Pss. 21:9; 118:12) ; the gift of a divine Son (Pss. 2:7; 89:26-27; cf. 110:1) ; the proclamation of the royal qualities (Pss. 2:6-7; 21:5; 72:17; 89:27; 110:4; II Sam. 23:3; cf. II Sam. 5:2) ; the establishment of the throne in peace and justice forever (Pss. 2:8-9; 21:4; 61:6-7; 72:1-8, 17; 89:3-4, 28-29, 36-37; 132:11-12) .

It seems probable, then, that this oracle was composed to celebrate the accession of an actual Judean king. Too much weight must not be put on the apparent circumstances of recent delivery from foreign oppression, since this is almost a standard formula for such an occasion. There is nothing in the language which requires a date later than Isaiah, especially if the final sentence (vs. 7, found also in 37:32) is recognized as editorial. Isaiah appears to have been a prophet officially associated with both the temple and the monarchy, and was thus a likely person to be given the responsibility of composing a cult oracle for a coronation ceremony. It is not possible to say definitely whether the king in question was Ahaz or Hezekiah. The persistent Jewish tradition linking the oracle with Hezekiah may have no other basis than its present position following oracles connected with Ahaz, but it is the more probable as well as the more congenial supposition.

The structure of the poetic oracle is straightforward: vss. 2-3 announce the transformation of darkness to light and the resultant rejoicing; vss. 4-6 give three reasons for this, in an ascending scale—the overthrow of the oppressor, the blotting out of the symbols of war, and the gift of a divinely endowed king; vss. 7 proclaims the promised permanence of his rule of peace, justice, and right.

2. The tenses are simple perfects, as in KJV, not prophetic perfects. Translate, "who have been living in darkness have seen . . . ; who have been dwelling . . . has shone. . . ." "To walk" is idiomatic for "to live."

3. The flat contradiction found in the KJV is due to corruption in the text, and must be resolved either (*a*) with the RSV, by following the Masoretic tradition, Syriac, and

---

The enemy has gone, the captains and the kings departed; gone the threat of slavery, gone the agents and instruments of destruction, blood-stained tunics, broken swords, the very boots that trampled roughshod over a shaking land, all are in the fire, and the smoke of their burning proclaims the blessed peace which has fallen on the delivered country.

But the glory of the vision is in its king. There are few things in the Jewish faith more pathetic, and at the same time more heroic, than the refusal to surrender the hope of the ideal king who should come at the behest of God to rule his people. At every coronation festival it stirred again in loyal hearts. Is this he, the God-anointed one? Is this the Messiah? And though no prince of the house of David ever fulfilled the hope, and king after king brutally disillusioned the believing people, yet they went on hoping, praying, trusting; he will come; if not today, then some other day. That is the courage of faith. Here it is again, breaking out in singing in Isaiah's prophecy, **Unto us a child is born, unto us a son is given.** It is true that if the Jews had cherished anything but a high spiritual ideal of the divine monarch, they might have hailed

4 For thou hast broken the yoke of his burden, and the staff of his shoulder, the rod of his oppressor, as in the day of Midian.

5 For every battle of the warrior *is* with confused noise, and garments rolled in blood; but *this* shall be with burning *and* fuel of fire.

6 For unto us a child is born, unto us a son is given: and the government shall be upon his shoulder: and his name shall be called Wonderful, Counsellor, The mighty God, The everlasting Father, The Prince of Peace.

4 For the yoke of his burden,
   and the staff for his shoulder,
   the rod of his oppressor,
   thou hast broken as on the day of
     Mid'ian.

5 For every boot of the tramping warrior
    in battle tumult
   and every garment rolled in blood
   will be burned as fuel for the fire.

6 For to us a child is born,
   to us a son is given;
  and the government will be upon his
    shoulder,
   and his name will be called
  "Wonderful Counselor, Mighty God,
    Everlasting Father, Prince of Peace."

Targ., and reading **its joy;** or (*b*) by reading הגילה, "the rejoicing," for הגוי לא, "the nation, not." The second alternative is less awkward and restores the parallelism: "Thou hast made great the rejoicing, thou hast increased the joy." For the celebrations at harvesttime, and when victors divided the spoils, cf. Pss. 126:6; 119:162.

4. Better, "His burdensome yoke," a figure of oppression as in I Kings 12:4-14. **The staff for his shoulder** appears synonymous with **the rod of his oppressor;** but מטה may be a participle rather than a noun, "that which bows down his shoulder" (cf. Ps. 144:5). For the **rod** of the slaveowner cf. Exod. 21:20. **The day of Midian:** The famous day of Gideon's complete victory over the invading Midianites (Judg. 6–8).

5. For **rolled in blood** read "stained with blood," by a slight change in the text (מגלולה for מגאלה).

6. The government: A rare Hebrew word meaning either "the burden of authority" (cf. "the key . . . upon his shoulder," 22:22) or, more probably, some symbol of majesty such as a rosette embroidered on the royal robe (cf. Edwin R. Goodenough, "Kingship in Early Israel," *Journal of Biblical Literature*, XLVIII [1929], 190; and I Kings 22:10, 30) or the scepter (cf. Ps. 45:6). **His name will be called** or "His name is proclaimed": The lofty titles and qualities of the divinely endowed king follow; they are four, so that the comma between **Wonderful** and **Counselor** (KJV) is a mistake. The first two declare that the king participates in the divine attributes of wisdom and might, while the third and fourth proclaim the nature of his rule. **Wonderful Counselor:** I.e., the supreme fount of wisdom or "Wonderful in Purpose" (cf. 14:24). **Mighty God:** "Divine in might." **Everlasting Father:** Better, "A Father forever," since it is not the king's continued existence but his constant care for his people that is in question. **Prince of Peace** or "Prince beneficent": This last phrase in the KJV and the RSV has become universally

---

many a messiah, for they had great and good kings. But in the very purity of their ideal they doomed themselves to disappointment, until in the fullness of time a king came, not with panoply and splendor but "lowly, and riding upon an ass" (Zech. 9:9). By faith Isaiah saw him. To him are given the titles no earthly king could hope to justify: a **Counselor** more wonderful than any sage of the century; a **Hero** strong with the strength of the Eternal; a **Friend** and **Father** with a love for men that neither time nor death could destroy; a **Prince** in whose reign every fair hope of the human heart would

have its perfecting. The pretentious titles of Oriental monarchs are empty words, but the names of the Messiah belong to his very nature as one sent by God and standing in a unique relationship to God. The type of the kingdom is to be determined, as it always is, by the character of the king. Isaiah makes no mention of enlarged borders, invincible armies, thriving trade, and the like. The glory of the Messiah's reign and the strength of the nation are to be **justice and . . . righteousness.**

It is a far cry from Isaiah's day to ours, but the prophet has discerned and declared the

7 Of the increase of *his* government and peace *there shall be* no end, upon the throne of David, and upon his kingdom, to order it, and to establish it with judgment and with justice from henceforth even for ever. The zeal of the LORD of hosts will perform this.

8 ¶ The Lord sent a word into Jacob, and it hath lighted upon Israel.

7 Of the increase of his government and of
   peace
   there will be no end,
upon the throne of David, and over his
   kingdom,
   to establish it, and to uphold it
with justice and with righteousness
   from this time forth and for evermore.
The zeal of the LORD of hosts will do this.

8 The Lord has sent a word against Jacob,
   and it will light upon Israel;

familiar as an epithet of Jesus, who came to bring "peace on earth," and is too firmly fixed in the traditional translation of this passage to be altered to the more accurate rendering suggested. But it must be remembered that the Hebrew word for **peace**, שׁלוֹם, means not merely the cessation of war but a condition of rich, harmonious, and positive well-being.

7. Of the increase of his government: Better, with a slight change in the text, "Great shall be his dominion." **Justice** and "right" are the indispensable accompaniments of any sovereignty which is to endure. The Davidic kings were not absolute monarchs but stood in a covenant relationship both with their God and with the people over whom they ruled (cf. II Sam. 5:3; II Kings 11:17; Jer. 22:15-16). The last sentence of this verse is editorial.

C. THE JUDGMENT ON EPHRAIM AND ITS LESSON FOR JUDAH
(9:8 [Hebrew 9:7]–10:4; 5:24b-30)

In this section, as in 2:6-22 and in Amos 1–2, we find an oracle complex with refrains, which may represent a longer address, put together by the prophet out of previously existing messages of his own for use on some special occasion, or when committing it to writing for the first time. In each of these three instances distinct oracle units are brought together in a larger composition and marked off by the repetition of a refrain. Here and in Amos 1–2 the iniquities and doom of neighboring peoples prepare the way for a climactic condemnation and threat addressed to the prophet's immediate audience. To this the refrains point forward, with their picture of Yahweh's hand still outstretched to strike.

How the conclusion of the oracle complex in 5:24b-29 came to be detached from it is part of the difficult problem of the sources from which the book of Isaiah was put together (see Intro., pp. 158-59). That 5:24b-29 is the (probably incomplete) conclusion of the section 9:8–10:4 is fairly certain (a) because of the occurrence of the identical refrain in 5:25, and (b) because it is entirely suitable as the climax demanded by the successive refrains in 9:12, 17, 21; 10:4, and is otherwise missing.

9:8-12. The three strophes in 9:8-21 point to facts well known to the Judeans concerning their northern neighbor Ephraim, viz., the successive disasters and the present

unchanging secret of national greatness. Justice and righteousness! Give us these in personal life, in the social order, and in international relationships, and the atomic bomb, the hydrogen bomb, and all the instruments of death will be remembered as creations of a barbaric age. Unescapably to a Christian, this whole great passage is bound up with faith in Jesus Christ as the Son of God; phrase by phrase, line by line, all that Isaiah proclaimed about the coming Mes-

siah has been fulfilled in the person and mission of our Lord, and for two thousand years the Christian church has taken up and sung in thanksgiving the good news from God: **Unto us a child is born, unto us a son is given,** Jesus Christ, the Prince of Peace, the "unspeakable gift."

9:8-10:4; 5:24b-30. The Judgment on Ephraim. —If, as suggested in the Exeg., there has been deliberate editorial work in the framing of this

9 And all the people shall know, *even* Ephraim and the inhabitant of Samaria, that say in the pride and stoutness of heart,

10 The bricks are fallen down, but we will build with hewn stones: the sycamores are cut down, but we will change *them into* cedars.

11 Therefore the Lord shall set up the adversaries of Rezin against him, and join his enemies together;

9 and all the people will know,
   E'phraim and the inhabitants of Sa-
      mar'ia,
   who say in pride and in arrogance of
      heart:
10 "The bricks have fallen,
   but we will build with dressed stones;
   the sycamores have been cut down,
   but we will put cedars in their place."
11 So the Lord raises adversaries[r] against
      them,
   and stirs up their enemies.

[r] Cn: Heb *the adversaries of Rezin*

---

anarchy which have followed on pride and wickedness unrepented. In the first (9:8-12) the Ephraimites, their boastful pride unhumbled by one disaster, now find themselves by Yahweh's command crushed between two adversaries, Syrians and Philistines. The book of Kings does not by itself enable us to identify the occasion referred to, but by piecing out the information it gives with that found in the Assyrian annals, we can make a probable suggestion. Menahem of Israel paid tribute to Tiglath-pileser in 738. Two years later his son Pekahiah was assassinated and replaced by the anti-Assyrian Pekah. In 734 Tiglath-pileser attacked the Philistines, and in 733-32 Syria (Damascus) and Ephraim. It seems therefore that the Philistines and Syrians about the year 737 were bringing the same kind of pressure on Pekahiah of Israel to join an anti-Assyrian alliance as was brought on Ahaz of Judah in 734 (cf. 7:1), and were "devouring Israel with open mouth." The murder of Pekahiah by Pekah, a tool of Syria, fits into this pattern. Although the figure is that of an earthquake, vs. 10 could well describe the devastating effects of the immense tribute paid by Menahem (cf. II Kings 15:19-20), which Isaiah says failed to break the vainglorious pride of the people of northern Israel.

8. The **word** is the utterance of Yahweh's will and embodies his intention and his power; once spoken, it continues to operate as an effective factor in history, for judgment (as here) or for blessing (as in 55:10-11). **Jacob . . . Israel:** The whole people, both Ephraim and Judah (cf. 1:3; 2:3). This verse is thus introductory to the entire oracle complex, with its references to Ephraim and its culminating judgment upon Judah. The verbs are co-ordinate perfects, "has sent forth, . . . has fallen," not **will light upon.**

9. "And all the people know it" or "have known it," in the sense "have felt its effects"; this clause belongs with vs. 8. Now comes the first application, to **Ephraim,** whose vain self-sufficiency and materialism were unshaken by the first blow of Yahweh's judgment.

10. Brick, mud, and sycamore timbers were the material of ordinary houses; hewn stone and cedar that of palaces.

11. For **the adversaries of Rezin** we must read "his adversaries" (i.e., Israel's), parallel with **his enemies,** since in vs. 12 it is the countrymen of Rezin who attack Israel.

---

passage, it has been magnificently done. The four oracles succeed one another with a mounting sense of the dramatic. They are lighted with lurid fires of judgment; the note of doom tolls menacingly in the reiterated words:

> Yet his wrath is not abated,
>   his arm is stretched out still to strike.
>   (9:12, 17, 21; 10:4 Moffatt.)

Four times the voice speaks, and a shudder passes through the reader. What further horror

of judgment is yet to fall on unrepentant man? In three of the oracles the object of God's anger is the Northern Kingdom, victim of invasion, defeat, and the horrors of civil war. The judgment of God, however, has beaten and broken them unavailingly. With an obduracy which would be noble were it inspired by faith, they rise upon the ruins of their broken homes, boasting that they will show the enemy, whether God or man, that they can "take it." But theirs is not the courage of a good conscience or a great cause;

12 The Syrians before, and the Philistines behind; and they shall devour Israel with open mouth. For all this his anger is not turned away, but his hand *is* stretched out still.

13 ¶ For the people turneth not unto him that smiteth them, neither do they seek the LORD of hosts.

14 Therefore the LORD will cut off from Israel head and tail, branch and rush, in one day.

15 The ancient and honorable, he *is* the head; and the prophet that teacheth lies, he *is* the tail.

16 For the leaders of this people cause *them* to err; and *they that are* led of them *are* destroyed.

12 The Syrians on the east and the Philistines on the west
　　devour Israel with open mouth.
　For all this his anger is not turned away
　　and his hand is stretched out still.

13 The people did not turn to him who smote them,
　　nor seek the LORD of hosts.
14 So the LORD cut off from Israel head and tail,
　　palm branch and reed in one day —
15 the elder and honored man is the head,
　　and the prophet who teaches lies is the tail;
16 for those who lead this people lead them astray,
　　and those who are led by them are swallowed up.

12. "From the east, . . . from the west," lit., "Before and behind," because the observer was thought of as facing the sunrise (see above). "They devoured," a perfect tense referring to a past episode. With the refrain **For all this . . . still** cf. Amos 1:3; Zeph. 1:4.

13-17. The second strophe gives as the reason for further judgment the stubborn refusal of Israel to learn her lesson; leaders and people had persisted in their folly and had brought a common ruin upon themselves and the innocent. Since the ruin is so general, the event referred to can hardly be merely one of the dynastic revolutions which marked the closing years of the Northern Kingdom, unless it is the conspiracy against Pekah, an episode connected with the Assyrian invasion in 733-32. The sequence of thought in this strophe has led some scholars to suspect disarrangement, but we must beware of imposing on Hebrew literary artists any rigid logical scheme.

13-15. Because the people had not recognized and accepted their sufferings as Yahweh's punishment, he had proceeded to cut them down, first and last: **head and tail** (cf. Deut. 28:43-44). Lofty **palm branch** and lowly **reed** are figures of rulers and ruled, so vs. 15 is almost certainly a later reader's mistaken note.

16. The language is almost the same as that of 3:12b. For **destroyed** and **swallowed up,** read "bewildered." Failure of its leadership in vision and integrity can quickly bring a society to confusion and disaster.

it is the defiance of a people who far from being repentant, glory in their iniquity. Crazed like the beasts of the forests in a fire, they turn in maniacal rage on their fellows until the streets are a shambles and the stench of the unburied dead fills the air. It is a ghastly picture of the condition of an invaded nation, leaderless and in utter chaos. And again the bell tolls:

Yet his wrath is not abated,
　his arm is stretched out still to strike.

Why this unappeasable wrath of God? Must his anger continue forever? Isaiah, inflexible as the judgment he pronounces, has no word of hope for an unrepentant people. In that mood

they are beyond salvation, and the measure of their degradation can be discerned in the fact that the merciful and all-loving God finds in them nothing worthy of redemption.

So the Lord spares not their soldiers,
　pitiless even to orphans and widows;
for they are all profane and wicked,
　impiety is on every lip (9:17 Moffatt).

Here the thunder of judgment rolls away, rumbling in the distance, only to return with a crash on the people of Judah; what they had seen others suffer, they too must bear. Did they gloat over the judgment on their northern neighbors? But what will they do when the same

17 Therefore the LORD shall have no joy in their young men, neither shall have mercy on their fatherless and widows: for every one *is* a hypocrite and an evildoer, and every mouth speaketh folly. For all this his anger is not turned away, but his hand *is* stretched out still.

18 ¶ For wickedness burneth as the fire: it shall devour the briers and thorns, and shall kindle in the thickets of the forest, and they shall mount up *like* the lifting up of smoke.

19 Through the wrath of the LORD of hosts is the land darkened, and the people shall be as the fuel of the fire: no man shall spare his brother.

20 And he shall snatch on the right hand, and be hungry; and he shall eat on the left hand, and they shall not be satisfied: they shall eat every man the flesh of his own arm:

21 Manasseh, Ephraim; and Ephraim, Manasseh: *and* they together *shall be* against Judah. For all this his anger is not turned away, but his hand *is* stretched out still.

---

17 Therefore the Lord does not rejoice over
  their young men,
    and has no compassion on their father-
    less and widows;
for every one is godless and an evildoer,
  and every mouth speaks folly.
For all this his anger is not turned away
  and his hand is stretched out still.

18 For wickedness burns like a fire,
    it consumes briers and thorns;
  it kindles the thickets of the forest,
    and they roll upward in a column of
    smoke.

19 Through the wrath of the LORD of hosts
    the land is burned,
  and the people are like fuel for the fire;
  no man spares his brother.

20 They snatch on the right, but are still
    hungry,
    and they devour on the left, but are not
    satisfied;
  each devours his neighbor's[s] flesh,

21 Manas'seh E'phraim, and E'phraim Ma-
    nas'seh,
    and together they are against Judah.
  For all this his anger is not turned away
    and his hand is stretched out still.

[s] Tg Compare Gk: Heb *the flesh of his arm*

---

17. The reference is to war, in which the "red, sweet wine of youth" is poured out in quarrels not of youth's making, and suffering falls on the helpless. "The whole nation was godless and given over to evil deeds, and every mouth spoke folly," i.e., moral folly (cf. 32:6).

18-21. In the third strophe the final destructive power of evil in society is pictured as a forest fire, and its consequence is seen in the collapse of society into the lawless violence of jungle beasts. A similar account of the years of the Northern Kingdom's moral and political disintegration is given in Hos. 4:2; 6:8-9; 7:1.

20. The RSV emends the text to read, with LXX and Targ., **devours his neighbor's flesh**, instead of **his own arm** (KJV), i.e., רעו for זרעו. The C.T. can mean alternatively "his offspring" (cf. Lam. 4:10).

21. The reference apparently is to the overthrow and murder of Pekahiah by Pekah, a Gileadite from the territory of Manasseh, east of Jordan, and to Pekah's subsequent

---

storm breaks on them? They are one with the very people whose lands it has blackened, one in their ruthless stupidity, their conscienceless greed, their merciless selfishness. "To whom," cries Isaiah, "will you run for help? And where will you put your plunder?" There is no cover for evildoers when the anger of God is loose in the land. And again the menacing word sounds:

Yet his wrath is not abated,
  his arm is stretched out still to strike.

At this point, according to the Exeg., there should be inserted 5:24b-30. These verses form the conclusion of the oracle complex, and are apparently an editorial supplement from a later age and a different author. The judgment here foretold is described in terms of an approaching army. It is a piece of magnificent realism—only an eyewitness of a mobile desert force could have so vividly portrayed these disciplined and seasoned warriors—and we are left with a sense of imminent menace. The storm is coming, **and**

10 Woe unto them that decree unrighteous decrees, and that write grievousness *which* they have prescribed;
 	
2 To turn aside the needy from judgment, and to take away the right from the poor of my people, that widows may be their prey, and *that* they may rob the fatherless!
 	
3 And what will ye do in the day of visitation, and in the desolation *which* shall come from far? to whom will ye flee for help? and where will ye leave your glory?
	10 Woe to those who decree iniquitous decrees,
	   and the writers who keep writing oppression,
	2 to turn aside the needy from justice
	   and to rob the poor of my people of their right,
	that widows may be their spoil,
	   and that they may make the fatherless their prey!
	3 What will you do on the day of punishment,
	   in the storm which will come from afar?
	To whom will you flee for help,
	   and where will you leave your wealth?

attack, in company with Rezin of Damascus, against Ahaz of Judah. The mention here of **Judah** is only incidental, since it is the suffering of the northern Israel in the days of anarchy and dynastic struggle which is being illustrated.

10:1-4. The fourth strophe marks the transition from the presentation of past events illustrating the sins and punishments of Ephraim to the present condition and threatened doom of Judah, **my people** (vs. 2). The way is prepared for this by the mention of Judah at the end of the third strophe. The sequence is interrupted also by the abrupt "Shame on" or "Accursed be" which usually marks the commencement of a reproach oracle. It may be that we have here an oracle originally taken from the series found in 2:8-12, 18-23, to be given prominence in a new context on some special occasion. Certainly the threat addressed in the second person to a particular group in the community, viz., those who make decrees which rob the helpless of their rights, does not parallel the more general accusations addressed to a whole people in the preceding part of this section. It is possible that this originally independent oracle was substituted for the one which survives in a truncated form in 5:24b-25.

1-2. Arbitrary **decrees** made by rulers and judges, and written or registered by the scribes, are **iniquitous** because they "deny justice to the lowly" and "rob the poor among my people of justice." Widows and orphans are treated as if they were the spoil of battle.

3. "What will you do on the day of retribution [the "day of the Lord," cf. 2:12] and in the gale that is coming in the distance?" Read **your wealth** for **your glory.**

---

the light is darkened under the lowering clouds (5:30).

It is all intensely dramatic but somewhat remote. It belongs to

> . . . old, unhappy, far-off things,
> And battles long ago.[5]

But does it? If the sins named in these oracles are indeed the cause of the anger of a just and righteous God, we had better pause before we close the book. For these things are not of yesterday; godlessness, inhumanity, injustice—they are in our midst, tolerated if not condoned. Are there not in our social and economic life

> those who issue harsh decrees,
>   planning orders that oppress (10:1 Moffatt)?

[5] Wordsworth, "The Solitary Reaper."

Are there not "big" men robbing the weak of their rights and defrauding the poor of their dues? Have we not seen the widow's pittance fall to them as spoil, and orphans made victims of their greed? These are commonplaces of modern life. It is not the big sins, the guilt of which is obvious, which corrupt a nation; or the lurid crimes, for which men can be brought to account; it is social injustice, the contempt of human values, the barter of souls; it is these evils that sap the moral strength of a nation, and against these the anger of the eternal justice is still hot. His judgment may be deferred, but it is never canceled. In a thousand ways the protest of righteousness is heard in our midst. If the divine word goes unheeded, there must come a day of reckoning—whether by revolution, or because God signals to a foreign power,

4 Without me they shall bow down under the prisoners, and they shall fall under the slain. For all this his anger is not turned away, but his hand *is* stretched out still.	4 Nothing remains but to crouch among the prisoners
	  or fall among the slain.
	For all this his anger is not turned away
	  and his hand is stretched out still.

5 ¶ O Assyrian, the rod of mine anger, and the staff in their hand is mine indignation.	5 Ah, Assyria, the rod of my anger, the staff of my fury!*t* *t* Heb *a staff it is in their hand my fury*

4. Both the KJV and the RSV give forced translations of the ungrammatical opening of this verse, which has suffered in transmission. It seems best to emend בלתי כרע to כי תכרעו, "when you shall crouch," following the suggestion of Kissane (*Isaiah*, I, 117, 121).

5:24b-30. We turn back now to 5:24b-29(30) for the conclusion of the oracle complex. The refrain is found at the conclusion of 5:25, and the earlier part of this verse appears to be the conclusion of yet a fifth strophe, of which the remainder has been lost. The substance of the lost material may be given in vs. 24b, which is in a meter quite different from the rest of the poem, and in any case is much too short by itself to fill in the gap. On **the law** and **the word** cf. Exeg. on 1:10; the thought and phraseology are Isaiah's. In vs. 25a the reference is again to a past event, the blow struck against his people by the Lord's sending one of Palestine's not infrequent earthquakes: "the mountains trembled, and (men's) corpses were like refuse in the open streets."

Now follows the announcement of the doom which is at hand for Judah; Yahweh, the Lord of history, signals for an avenging army. The oncoming (presumably Assyrian) soldiery are pictured in one of the most vivid pieces of descriptive verse in the O.T. The army approaches with relentless speed, alert and ready for battle; the noise of the horses and chariots grows to a roar suggesting the roar of a lion as it pounces upon the helpless prey.

26. He will raise a signal, lit., "a flag," on a height where it would be visible from a distance; cf. 30:17; Jer. 6:1. **Whistle** is better than **hiss**; it is a summons (cf. 7:18; Zech. 10:8). Read **nation,** singular: "See! at once and swiftly it comes!"

28. Like flint: I.e., striking sparks, like flint.

29. And none can rescue: Lit., "and there is no deliverer," a favorite concluding expression to mark the completeness of a disaster (cf. 42:22).

30. This verse is not the sequel to vs. 29 but a fragment brought in here because of the verb **they will growl,** which occurs in vs. 29 with reference to **young lions** and in vs. 30 with reference to **the sea.** The second part of the verse closely resembles 8:22, and the whole verse may well belong in that context.

IV. "BE NOT AFRAID OF THE ASSYRIAN" (10:5–12:6)

After 10:4 there is another break in the sequence of the book in its present form, with the introduction of the Assyrians as the object of Yahweh's wrath rather than as his instrument for the punishment of Judah (as in chs. 7–8). This is the principal theme in 10:5-34, and with this the oracle now found in 14:24-27 was doubtless originally associated. Chs. 11–12 contain a second dynastic oracle like that in 9:2-7 (this time with a more definitely eschatological note), together with other eschatological oracles and short psalms which are certainly post-Isaianic and which have been inserted by later editors

whistling for it from the ends of the earth, matters not. By the immutable moral law of God evil shall be judged.

10:5-34. *The Great Alternative: Force or Faith.*—Both in its literary power and its religious insight this is one of the great passages of the book. The vivid picture of a great power on the march, harrying the nations, dividing to conquer, and filling the air with bombast, must be positively alive for any who have lived through the experience of war. Dictators and their tyrannies do not change; they behave in exactly the same way, whether their campaigns are fought in the eighth century B.C. with sword

6 I will send him against a hypocritical nation, and against the people of my wrath will I give him a charge, to take the spoil, and to take the prey, and to tread them down like the mire of the streets.	**6** Against a godless nation I send him, and against the people of my wrath I command him, to take spoil and seize plunder, and to tread them down like the mire of the streets.
7 Howbeit he meaneth not so, neither doth his heart think so; but *it is* in his heart to destroy and cut off nations not a few.	**7** But he does not so intend, and his mind does not so think; but it is in his mind to destroy, and to cut off nations not a few;

as a counterpart to the words of Isaiah concerning the doom of Assyria and the deliverance of Judah.

A. The Assyrian Threat (10:5-34)

1. Boasting of the Assyrian (10:5-16)

This is one of the most striking prophecies of Isaiah. In it his view of God as the lord of history is set out with great distinctness. God uses the king of Assyria and his army to carry out the sentence which has been pronounced against Judah. But as the rod with which a master chastises his servant is unconscious that it is but an instrument, so the Assyrian is unaware of the overruling divine purpose which his conquests serve. He becomes intoxicated with conquest and presumes not only to bestride the world in pride but to assert that the God of Israel is a helpless idol like the rest. Thus, when Assyria has served God's purpose, she will suffer the penalty of her impiety and arrogance and it will be made clear who it is that determines the course of history.

Although this prophetic poem is in the main clear in import and vivid in expression, it has suffered somewhat by the insertion of two supplementary notes in vss. 10 and 12; and part at least of the conclusion is missing. The doom pronouncement to which it all points forward can hardly have consisted originally of the mixed metaphors and confused ideas now found in vss. 16-19. Either the concluding threat is now found in 14:24-27; or it remains in fragmentary form in vs. 16, with the addition perhaps of part of vs. 18; or it is missing altogether. The second possibility seems the most likely.

5-6. The opening word of the reproach, הוי, is almost impossible to represent in English: "Oh!" "Ah!" or "For shame!" hardly conveys the force of this indignant denunciation, "Accursed be." **Rod of my anger:** "The rod which I have used in my anger to chastise Judah." The second part of the line provides a good example of the lengths to which translators will go in trying to make sense of a Hebrew phrase which is certainly corrupt (see RSV mg.). The RSV omits two words, shortening the line unduly. Procksch (*Jesaia I*, p. 163) corrects the Hebrew very slightly and reads, "The staff of my anger is he in my hand."

7. "But *he* [the pronoun is emphatic] has no such intention." **His heart:** Better **his mind,** for the **heart** in Hebrew usage is the seat of intelligence rather than of emotion. **He** is the Assyrian king, not the personified nation. Rather, **it is in his mind to destroy** no small number of nations. The unbridled lust for conquest is used and limited by Yahweh, but comes under his judgment.

and spear, or in the twentieth century with tanks and airplanes; they scream the same threats and make the same boasts whatever their language. It is all in this chapter. Who said, "I did it all with my genius for strategy. I shifted national boundaries and remade the map; I plundered their treasures; I reduced them to ashes and went through them like a mad bull; the wealth of the nations I rifled like a bird's nest; I ransacked the world and not a cheep out of them"? Sennacherib or one of the modern dictators? No matter; they all said it; for thus does man, when "drunk with sight of power," vaunt himself and defy his creator.

The whole passage ought to be read as a commentary on the modern world situation. Here is an exposé of what has been called "the atheism of force." No intelligent man would cut

8 For he saith, *Are* not my princes altogether kings?	8 for he says: "Are not my commanders all kings?
9 *Is* not Calno as Carchemish? *is* not Hamath as Arpad? *is* not Samaria as Damascus?	9 Is not Calno like Car'chemish? Is not Hamath like Arpad? Is not Samar'ia like Damascus?
10 As my hand hath found the kingdoms of the idols, and whose graven images did excel them of Jerusalem and of Samaria;	10 As my hand has reached to the kingdoms of the idols whose graven images were greater than those of Jerusalem and Samar'ia,
11 Shall I not, as I have done unto Samaria and her idols, so do to Jerusalem and her idols?	11 shall I not do to Jerusalem and her idols as I have done to Samar'ia and her images?"

8-9. The proud monarch boasts of the vassal kings he has as his army commanders, of the famous cities he has conquered, and of the helplessness of their gods. Four famous cities of northern Syria are named, beginning with those most remote from Jerusalem, and to these are added Judah's immediate neighbors, which also by this time had been incorporated into the Assyrian Empire. The Assyrian tide had risen and receded many times, and now (apparently during Sennacherib's invasion in 701) it was lapping the walls of Jerusalem. The conquests of his predecessors are subsumed in those of the latest king.

10. It is anomalous to find **Samaria** linked here with **Jerusalem**, since in vss. 9, 11 it is included with the conquered cities; and the verse as it stands cannot be translated literally, is metrically distinct from its context, and interrupts the series of rhetorical questions. Most scholars consider it a later gloss. Kissane (*op. cit.*, I, 124, 127-28), however, proposes to repair the text by reference to the LXX, so as to read:

> As my hand has subdued
> These kingdoms,
> Shall [Judah's] images succeed?
> Shall they protect Jerusalem?

11. The Assyrian speaks contemptuously of the **idols** (better, "godlets," "no-gods") of **Jerusalem** and the **images** of Samaria; he assumes, and with some justification, that the religion of these cities is similar to that of the other places he has conquered; even if Samaria and Jerusalem have a distinctive deity, he has not saved Samaria. But Isaiah quotes the king in irony; in spite of the prevalent idolatry, Israel is still the people of the only real God. The fate of Samaria and the different fate he expects for Jerusalem are explained from the fact that Yahweh is both a God of wrath and a God of grace, as he overrules the forces of history to fulfill his purposes.

scientific research out of modern education, but all sane men must stand aghast at the possibility of unlimited destructive force in the hands of men not equal to its moral control. It raises an issue decisive for human destiny. Are we to stake everything on the rule of force, and gamble with the possibility of obliterating the world itself? Or are we to turn belatedly, to recover a saving faith in spiritual power for the re-creation of life? There is no question comparable to this: is it to be force or God? Circumstances have conspired to make of it not a matter of abstract speculation but literally of life and death. Our scientists have warned us in uncompromising words that to go on depending for security on the use of incredible destructive power threatens the existence of man himself. On which will the world's bet be placed, the forces of nature or the power of the spirit?

But the problem is far deeper than any question concerning foreign policy or defense strategy; it has to do with our ultimate philosophy of life, our faith. The devastating possibility suggested by physical science has only brought to one particular focus the whole question of our understanding of the meaning of life and of God. The atheism of force is quite as discernible in the economic realm as in the military, and the issue is raised as specifically for personal life as for international. Were he to come again

12 Wherefore it shall come to pass, *that,* when the Lord hath performed his whole work upon mount Zion and on Jerusalem, I will punish the fruit of the stout heart of the king of Assyria, and the glory of his high looks.

13 For he saith, By the strength of my hand I have done *it,* and by my wisdom; for I am prudent: and I have removed the bounds of the people, and have robbed their treasures, and I have put down the inhabitants like a valiant *man:*

14 And my hand hath found as a nest the riches of the people: and as one gathereth eggs *that are* left, have I gathered all the earth; and there was none that moved the wing, or opened the mouth, or peeped.

15 Shall the axe boast itself against him that heweth therewith? *or* shall the saw magnify itself against him that shaketh it?

12 When the Lord has finished all his work on Mount Zion and on Jerusalem he[u] will punish the arrogant boasting of the king of Assyria and his haughty pride. 13 For he says:

"By the strength of my hand I have done it,
   and by my wisdom, for I have understanding;
I have removed the boundaries of peoples,
   and have plundered their treasures;
   like a bull I have brought down those who sat on thrones.
14 My hand has found like a nest
   the wealth of the peoples;
and as men gather eggs that have been forsaken
   so I have gathered all the earth;
and there was none that moved a wing,
   or opened the mouth, or chirped."

15 Shall the axe vaunt itself over him who hews with it,
   or the saw magnify itself against him who wields it?

[u] Heb *I*

12. A prosaic note summarizing vss. 5-11, 13-16, and more suitably placed at the beginning than in its present position in the middle of the Assyrian king's speech. Read **he will punish** (with LXX). The expectation of a great judgment to come upon the nations who attack Jerusalem becomes a major theme in later prophetic and apocalyptic eschatology (cf. Ezek. 38:17 ff.; Zech. 14:1 ff.; Joel 3 [Hebrew 4]:9-16).

13-14. The Assyrian speaks not only with the pride of a victor, but as self-sufficient and autonomous man, master of his fate and of the world, and responsible to no power higher than himself. **I have removed the boundaries of peoples:** It was Assyrian imperial policy to incorporate conquered lands as Assyrian provinces and to displace whole populations in order to destroy local patriotism which might prompt rebellion (cf. II Kings 17:23-24). **Like a bull,** or "like a mighty one," i.e., a divine being. Or Kissane's (*ibid.,* I, 126, 129) suggestion to read כאביב for כאביר may be adopted: "Like ripe grain I have laid low the inhabitants." **Inhabitants** is to be preferred to the reading of the RSV. **My hand has [clutched] like a [full] nest.** The inhabitants were so terrified that they did not try to protect their treasures, as a mother bird tries to protect her nest: "No one flapped a wing or uttered a squeak."

15. The prophet introduces the concluding threat by a rhetorical question harking back to the opening vs. 5. The Assyrian is only an instrument, powerless in himself:

to earth, Isaiah would say to us precisely what he said to his nation twenty-seven hundred years ago. The ultimate power in the universe is God: the powers of nature which we have so tragically misused are the instruments of his will. Men and nations are the agents of his purpose. They are free to do what they like, free to defy him and even for the time being to frustrate him; but

the sovereignty of justice and righteousness is not at the last to be mocked by men. It belongs to the omnipotence of God that he can and does use the movement of human history for the accomplishment of divine ends. Therefore Isaiah can describe **Assyria** as a club wielded by the hand of God, and therefore, without any sense of contradiction, Isaiah can go on to say that

as if the rod should shake *itself* against them that lift it up, *or* as if the staff should lift up *itself, as if it were* no wood.

16 Therefore shall the Lord, the Lord of hosts, send among his fat ones leanness; and under his glory he shall kindle a burning like the burning of a fire.

17 And the light of Israel shall be for a fire, and his Holy One for a flame: and it shall burn and devour his thorns and his briers in one day;

18 And shall consume the glory of his forest, and of his fruitful field, both soul and body: and they shall be as when a standardbearer fainteth.

19 And the rest of the trees of his forest shall be few, that a child may write them.

As if a rod should wield him who lifts it,
   or as if a staff should lift him who is
     not wood!
16 Therefore the Lord, the Lord of hosts,
   will send wasting sickness among his
     stout warriors,
  and under his glory a burning will be
     kindled,
   like the burning of fire.
17 The light of Israel will become a fire,
   and his Holy One a flame;
  and it will burn and devour
   his thorns and briers in one day.
18 The glory of his forest and of his fruitful
    land
   the Lord will destroy, both soul and
    body,
   and it will be as when a sick man
    wastes away.
19 The remnant of the trees of his forest
   will be so few
   that a child can write them down.

an **ax**, better, a "pickax" or "chisel," used in hewing, i.e., digging or cutting stone; a **saw**, which a man "plies," lit., "moves to and fro."

16. His fat ones or **his stout warriors:** Better, "his fatness" (an intensive plural; cf. 28:1), i.e, "his prosperity." For **send . . . leanness** and **wasting sickness** read "send a wasting," "cause to waste away." **Under his glory** may mean "in his inward parts" (cf. Ps. 7:5), or "his honor (which he has heaped up) will be set all ablaze as when a fire is kindled." Probably the words "and (the Lord) will make an end of him, body and soul" in vs. 18 should follow upon vs. 16 as the conclusion of the threat and of the oracle as a whole.

2. The Forest Fire (10:17-19)

17-19. This brief oracle of judgment on Israel has been brought in here by the key word **fire** (on the linking together of oracles by key words to facilitate memorization in the period of oral transmission, see Intro., p. 158). The distinction from the foregoing oracle is evident from the change of figure; there the Lord sent the fire; here he *is* the fire; there the fire is to destroy Assyria's glory; here a land is to be burned over, and the land is described in terms used elsewhere of the land of Israel (cf. vss. 33-34; 5:6; 7:23-25; 9:18 [Hebrew 9:17]; 29:17). And the key word **remnant**, which links this with the next oracle in vss. 20-21, shows that when the oracles were associated **the remnant of the trees** was understood to refer to Israel, not to Assyria. This is apparently one of the oracles of doom belonging to Isaiah's early period. **The light of Israel** (cf. Ps. 27:1) is "the glory of [the Lord's] majesty" as in the judgment of the day of the Lord in 2:10, 19, 21, manifested as a devouring flame in 29:6 (cf. Amos

the power which can make the wrath of man to praise him can also turn to judge the very people whose ruthless brutality he employed for the scourging of a delinquent nation. Thus does Christian faith read history, as the disclosure of the presence and action of God within the movements of men and nations. It would be possible to begin a tenth chapter of a modern prophecy of Isaiah, "Cursed be Hitler and damned be Mussolini, twin clubs of my wrath wielded in mine anger"; for someday, looking back, men of insight and faith will be able to see how God's will for men was advanced by the cruel surgery of world war.

It is said that men have crowded God out of their calculations; but even at that, men's

20 ¶ And it shall come to pass in that day, *that* the remnant of Israel, and such as are escaped of the house of Jacob, shall no more again stay upon him that smote them; but shall stay upon the LORD, the Holy One of Israel, in truth.

21 The remnant shall return, *even* the remnant of Jacob, unto the mighty God.

22 For though thy people Israel be as the sand of the sea, *yet* a remnant of them shall return: the consumption decreed shall overflow with righteousness.

23 For the Lord GOD of hosts shall make a consumption, even determined, in the midst of all the land.

20 In that day the remnant of Israel and the survivors of the house of Jacob will no more lean upon him that smote them, but will lean upon the LORD, the Holy One of Israel, in truth. 21 A remnant will return, the remnant of Jacob, to the mighty God. 22 For though your people Israel be as the sand of the sea, only a remnant of them will return. Destruction is decreed, overflowing with righteousness. 23 For the Lord, the LORD of hosts, will make a full end, as decreed, in the midst of all the earth.

7:4). The **thorns and briers** of the waste land and the rich **forest** and "fruit lands" will be consumed **in one day,** the day of the Lord (cf. 2:12). **As when a standardbearer fainteth** and **as when a sick man wastes away** are unsatisfactory attempts to make sense of a difficult line; by reading נמס for נסס, we get, "and it shall be like the melting of the molten" (on vs. 18*b* see Exeg. on vs. 16).

3. The Escaped Remnant and the Destroyed Remnant (10:20-23)

20-23. The name of Isaiah's son Shear-jashub (see Exeg. on 7:3-4) was an oracular utterance in germ; as in the case of the second son mentioned in 8:1-4, this utterance would also be written down and proclaimed in expanded form. The phrase is ambiguous; it can be interpreted as a promise, **a remnant shall return,** or as a threat, "only a remnant shall return." Because of the emphatic position of the subject, the latter is probably the correct interpretation of the oracle in the first instance. In the passage now before us we have in vss. 20-21 the later, and in vss. 22-23 the earlier, form in which this enigmatic oracle was expanded. The phrase *she'ār yāshûbh,* which is the name of the prophet's son in 7:3, occurs in both, but is interpreted in opposite senses. Vss. 22-23 constitute the doom oracle uttered at the time of the birth and naming of Shear-jashub, which of course is some time before the lad's appearance with his father at the interview with Ahaz. It is thus from the prophet's earliest period and corresponds to the ominous tone of the message given him in his original commission (cf. 6:9-13). **Thy people:** Apparently addressed to the king, as in 7:17. A **destruction is decreed** which will be the **overflowing** of the divine **righteousness.**

In vss. 20-21, on the other hand, the remnant are those who have survived disaster and whose return is repentance, a return to their God, the One "divine in might"; the phrase is the same as that applied to the messianic king in 9:6 (Hebrew 9:5). **No more lean upon him that smote them:** It is needless to look for circumstances in which a Judean king put his trust in a foreign state, only to be smitten by it. The point is much more likely that of 31:1 where the nation is condemned for putting its reliance in

---

thoughts of the God thus deposed were not big enough for the crisis. It is not a new God we need for the twentieth century, but a greater thought of the Eternal who surmounts all things in wisdom, power, and love. When men really believe in the sovereignty of God, when they put him in the only place he rightfully can occupy, at the heart of their planning and their living, then, and only then, shall we know the peace we have unavailingly sought, and the sons

of men shall dwell together in friendship under the rule of Love.

Though the absolute supremacy of God in human affairs is the regnant idea of this passage, there is other material which claims us, particularly vss. 16-19. Isaiah lived in an era of incessant strife; the tramp of invading forces echoes through his pages. Inevitably he sees the judgment of God wrought out in catastrophe: invasion, famine, fire, and pestilence—to the

24 ¶ Therefore thus saith the Lord GOD of hosts, O my people that dwellest in Zion, be not afraid of the Assyrian: he shall smite thee with a rod, and shall lift up his staff against thee, after the manner of Egypt.

25 For yet a very little while, and the indignation shall cease, and mine anger in their destruction.

26 And the LORD of hosts shall stir up a scourge for him according to the slaughter of Midian at the rock of Oreb: and *as* his rod *was* upon the sea, so shall he lift it up after the manner of Egypt.

27 And it shall come to pass in that day, *that* his burden shall be taken away from off thy shoulder, and his yoke from off thy neck, and the yoke shall be destroyed because of the anointing.

24 Therefore thus says the Lord, the LORD of hosts: "O my people, who dwell in Zion, be not afraid of the Assyrians when they smite with the rod and lift up their staff against you as the Egyptians did. 25 For in a very little while my indignation will come to an end, and my anger will be directed to their destruction. 26 And the LORD of hosts will wield against them a scourge, as when he smote Mid′ian at the rock of Oreb; and his rod will be over the sea, and he will lift it as he did in Egypt. 27 And in that day his burden will depart from your shoulder, and his yoke will be destroyed from your neck."

He has gone up from Rimmon,ᵛ

ᵛ Cn: Heb *and his yoke from your neck, and a yoke will be destroyed because of fatness*

---

armaments and warfare rather than in God; here they have trusted in war only to suffer by war. They shall learn through experience that for the weight of life God is the only support which will not give way (cf. 3:1).

4. THE ENCOURAGEMENT OF ZION (10:24-27c)

This brief oracle of exhortation and promise provides a suitable conclusion to the reproach and threat directed to the Assyrian (king) in vss. 5-16, 18b, but it has not been preserved entirely in its original metrical form. It resembles the short word of encouragement which in 37:6-7 is addressed to Hezekiah in similar if not identical circumstances, and which has been preserved in prose. Whether or not we are to infer that 10:24-27c also belonged once in a biographical narrative, it is certain that the substance of prophetic oracles was not infrequently cast into prose (cf. Jer. 22:10 in verse, with vss. 11-12 in prose).

24. The prophet calls on his people not to yield to fear. If they will but recognize that they are suffering chastisement as their forefathers did in Egypt, and that Yahweh is the same God as of old, they will know that the day of deliverance is coming. For they are still **my people.**

25. "Very soon my indignation and anger will be spent." The remaining words of the verse are obscure.

26. **Wield against them a scourge:** "Brandish a lash over them." On **The rock of Oreb,** cf. Judg. 7:25. With a slight rearrangement of the text, read "He will lift up his rod over them [i.e., the Assyrians] as he did over the Egyptians."

27a-c. **His burden will depart:** Better, "shall be removed." **Destroyed from thy neck:** For וחבל read with the LXX יחדל "shall cease," "shall no longer be upon thy neck." **The yoke . . . because of the anointing** is meaningless; the RSV reads the Hebrew differently and takes it as the opening line of the following poem.

5. THE APPROACH OF THE INVADER (10:27d-32)

In this remarkable poetic fragment describing the approach of an invader toward Jerusalem and the alarm of the countryside, the prophet adopts the stirring, impres-

---

prophet they are all visitations of God. It is therefore the more striking to come on a passage which suggests that not all judgment is violent; it may be unseen, silent, unknown, and

yet as inexorable as the hammer blows of war. "The Lord of Hosts," he cries, "will send a wasting disease on a flourishing life, and under the glow of health shall be a destroying fever

28 He is come to Aiath, he is passed to Migron; at Michmash he hath laid up his carriages:

29 They are gone over the passage: they have taken up their lodging at Geba; Ramah is afraid; Gibeah of Saul is fled.

30 Lift up thy voice, O daughter of Gallim: cause it to be heard unto Laish, O poor Anathoth.

31 Madmenah is removed; the inhabitants of Gebim gather themselves to flee.

32 As yet shall he remain at Nob that day: he shall shake his hand *against* the mount of the daughter of Zion, the hill of Jerusalem.

33 Behold, the Lord, the LORD of hosts, shall lop the bough with terror: and the

28 he has come to Ai'ath;
    he has passed through Migron,
      at Michmash he stores his baggage;
29 they have crossed over the pass,
    at Geba they lodge for the night;
  Ramah trembles,
    Gib'e-ah of Saul has fled.
30 Cry aloud, O daughter of Gallim!
    Hearken, O La'ishah!
    Answer her, O An'athoth!
31 Madme'nah is in flight,
    the inhabitants of Gebim flee for safety.
32 This very day he will halt at Nob,
    he will shake his fist
    at the mount of the daughter of Zion,
    the hill of Jerusalem.

33 Behold, the Lord, the LORD of hosts
    will lop the boughs with terrifying power;

---

sionistic style of the war ballad (cf. Judg. 5). In vss. 27d-29b the rapid progress of the foe is recounted as if by a succession of breathless messages, reporting the points he has passed as he moves down from the north upon Jerusalem. Vss. 29c-31 picture the panic in the towns and villages which lie immediately in his path. Vs. 32 brings the climax, with its picture of the enemy about to stand within sight of Jerusalem, shaking his fist at the city.

If this passage is complete in itself, as seems improbable, it must be taken as a threat. Most commentators adopt from its present context the view that the enemy is the Assyrian army; but the passage itself gives no indication of this. On the other hand, the movement of the Syrian-Ephraimite forces from the vicinity of Samaria toward Jerusalem in 734 produced similar terror (cf. 7:2), and the route described is much more suitable if the invader is so identified. In that case these verses are a fragment of a poetic description of the Syro-Ephraimite war. The tense of the verbs is thus not future but the historic present.

27d. He has gone up from Rimmon: Better, "from before Samaria" (which is closer to the Hebrew); the phrase may mean "from the vicinity of Samaria" or even "from the frontier of Samaria."

29. Lodge: "Bivouac."

32. As yet . . . that day or **This very day:** Better, "While it is still today" (cf. Ehrlich, *Randglossen zur hebräischen Bibel,* p. 45, who compares Gen. 29:7): "Before this day ends, standing at Nob he will shake his fist." **Nob** is probably to be located on Mount Scopus, a ridge just north of Jerusalem from which, coming from the north, the first sight of the city is obtained. Titus encamped here with his legions in A.D. 70.

6. HUMBLING OF THE FOREST (10:33-34)

33-34. The editor has introduced as a counterpoise to the picture of the enemy arrogantly threatening Zion a threat of judgment under a very different figure—that

---

consuming soul and body." It takes little imagination to lift these words from their context and find in them an image of that unspectacular moral deterioration which attacks a life grown careless about things unseen and eternal. Life is

full of poignant illustrations of what happens to a man who begins to trifle with conscience, who abandons his standards, and gives up faith in anything which makes demands on self. Outwardly there is no change; indeed, the man

high ones of stature *shall be* hewn down, and the haughty shall be humbled.	the great in height will be hewn down, and the lofty will be brought low.
34 And he shall cut down the thickets of the forest with iron, and Lebanon shall fall by a mighty one.	34 He will cut down the thickets of the forest with an axe, and Lebanon with its majestic trees[w] will fall.
11 And there shall come forth a rod out of the stem of Jesse, and a Branch shall grow out of his roots:	**11** There shall come forth a shoot from the stump of Jesse, and a branch shall grow out of his roots.

w Cn Compare Gk Vg: Heb *with a majestic one*

---

of the divine Forester who will humble the pride of the forest. For the necessary antecedent (since vss. 18-19 use the different figure of a forest fire) we must go back to 2:12-13, "the day of the Lord against all that is proud and lofty, . . . cedars of Lebanon and oaks of Bashan." Although 10:33-34 is an independent oracle, perhaps fragmentary, it is cognate in idea and mood with the earlier passage, and has no original connection with its present context.

Lop the boughs with terrifying power: All three Hebrew words are found only here in the O.T., and the meaning of the last is doubtful; it is from the verbal root ערץ, "to shake terribly" found in 2:19, 21 (another link between this passage and 2:12-22). **With iron,** or "with an iron tool," is more accurate than **with an ax,** which is too specific. The emendation adopted in the RSV, **with its majestic trees** or "its majestic ones," is justified by the ancient versions and gives better sense.

B. The Messianic Age (11:1-16)
1. The Davidic Messiah (11:1-9)

This oracle is a companion piece to 9:2-7 (Hebrew 9:1-6), and the reader should refer to the Exeg. on that passage. Here too the king is "messianic" only in the sense that every monarch of the Davidic dynasty was an anointed representative of Yahweh, and a sacred, even semidivine, person. The superlative terms in which his endowment and the prospects of his reign are spoken of are thus not necessarily to be interpreted as referring to an ideal and remote messianic age, but as the proper terms to describe the kingship of one who on his accession was adopted as Yahweh's son. Every king was thus designated as a messiah, and at his accession his reign was spoken of as a prospective golden age. Needless to say, this faith was often cruelly mocked and its language falsified by events. But it resulted, when the last king of Judah had died in exile, in the emergence of the undying hope that God would yet restore his people under a Davidic king worthy to rule as his vicegerent.

The oracle was thus, in the first instance, related like 9:2-7 to one of the royal accession ceremonies described in II Kings 11:12-19. It may well have been composed by Isaiah for the occasion of the anointing of Hezekiah. It has three strophes or stanzas,

---

| may greatly prosper. **But** within, unseen, the process of decay has set in, and all that is fine and generous and honorable is slowly being consumed, wasting away, till the once strong character is a mere shell, supported by a few conventions, a character ready to collapse under strain, like a pier standing on piles rotten from within, eaten away by the worms of the sea. Such candor will win no acclaim, for men shrink from disclosures about themselves. It is, | however, part of a prophet's commission, and part of the price to be paid for its fulfillment, that he will, in the name of the God he serves, be not afraid to speak the odious truth. **11:1-5. The Ideal King.**—When a twentieth-century Christian reads this oracle, he sees at once its fulfillment in the person and work of our Lord. That is understandable; but it is to be noted that Isaiah had in mind not some dim and distant figure, but a living king. With a |

2 And the Spirit of the LORD shall rest upon him, the spirit of wisdom and understanding, the spirit of counsel and might, the spirit of knowledge and of the fear of the LORD;	2 And the Spirit of the LORD shall rest upon him, the spirit of wisdom and understanding, the spirit of counsel and might, the spirit of knowledge and the fear of the LORD.
3 And shall make him of quick understanding in the fear of the LORD: and he shall not judge after the sight of his eyes, neither reprove after the hearing of his ears:	3 And his delight shall be in the fear of the LORD. He shall not judge by what his eyes see, or decide by what his ears hear;

---

of which the first seems to have lost its opening lines: vss. 1-3a, the appearance and anointing of the king; vss. 3b-5, the pledged characteristics of his reign; and vss. 6-8 (Hebrew vs. 9), the resulting state of peace, under the figure of a return to the conditions of Eden. Here is the ideal and hope of kingship in Judah—the gift of superhuman wisdom and the consequent rule of justice in society, producing positive good, restraining evil, and ensuring the personal integrity in the ruler himself. Today, when the personal rule of monarchs has long been abolished in Western society, our elected governments have need of the same endowment and should have the same objectives.

11:1-2. There shall come forth: In the Hebrew text the verb is preceded by "and," which presupposes an immediately antecedent sentence in poetry, though not in prose; it thus appears that an opening couplet has been lost. If the interpretation of the oracle given above is correct, the tense of the verbs in vs. 1 is present, not future: "comes forth, . . . grows." **Shall rest** (vs. 2) is declaratory, not predictive. **A shoot from the stump of Jesse** has suggested to many commentators the inference that the dynasty of David has been, or will be, cut down like a tree. But the word גֵּזַע, translated **stump,** may mean rather "stalk," "trunk," as in 40:24, and the meaning of the figure be simply that the tree with its trunk and roots, the dynasty, has produced a new branch. The second word for **branch** or "twig," נֵצֶר, is perhaps used to suggest by assonance נֵזֶר, the crown marking the king's consecration (cf. II Kings 11:12). For the gift of **the Spirit of the LORD** as the source of the divine wisdom required by kings, cf. II Sam. 23:2; I Kings 3:28; Zech. 4:6. **The fear of the LORD:** Reverence, piety, religion. **Knowledge:** I.e., of God (cf. Hos. 4:1). **Spirit** is divine energy with which men may be specially endowed.

3a. This line appears to be a dittograph of the preceding one, and even in the English translation it can be seen to stand outside the regular structure of the poem. Literally it is "His smelling [incense or sacrifice] shall be in the fear of the LORD." Crook ("Occasion for Isaiah 9₂-₇ and 11₁-₉," pp. 214, 220) finds here a reference to the anointing oil, but it is doubtful if the text can be made to justify this interpretation. The rendering of the RSV is impossible; the line should be omitted.

3b-5. The infusion of the divine spirit will ensure the fulfillment of the king's vows to rule justly, in accordance with the covenant (cf. II Kings 11:17; Ps. 72:1-2); the

---

hopefulness which repeated disillusionment failed to put out, the Jew hailed every new king as the Lord's anointed who would usher in a golden age. It was only when the last of the Davidic kings died in exile that faith in the divine character of the monarch was transferred to the Messiah, who, coming from God, would fulfill in his life and reign the ideal so long and heroically cherished. Therefore something is lost	from the original if we limit the application of this oracle to Jesus Christ. It was realized in him, but it is meant to be realized in all who govern. The figure which stands out in Isaiah's oracle is not simply an ideal; it is a character, the living embodiment of the qualities which are to be expected of one worthy to govern. In vss. 2-5 we are shown the virtues which God requires in those set apart for leadership. They are named

4 But with righteousness shall he judge the poor, and reprove with equity for the meek of the earth: and he shall smite the earth with the rod of his mouth, and with the breath of his lips shall he slay the wicked.

5 And righteousness shall be the girdle of his loins, and faithfulness the girdle of his reins.

6 The wolf also shall dwell with the lamb, and the leopard shall lie down with the kid; and the calf and the young lion and the fatling together; and a little child shall lead them.

---

4 but with righteousness he shall judge the poor,
　and decide with equity for the meek of the earth;
and he shall smite the earth with the rod of his mouth,
　and with the breath of his lips he shall slay the wicked.
5 Righteousness shall be the girdle of his waist,
　and faithfulness the girdle of his loins.

6 The wolf shall dwell with the lamb,
　and the leopard shall lie down with the kid,
　and the calf and the lion and the fatling together,
　and a little child shall lead them.

---

substance of the royal pledge is thus cast into the third person. There is some correspondence between the qualities enumerated in vs. 2 and the different aspects of the king's rule: through **wisdom** and "discernment" he will uncover the truth beneath appearances, as God does (cf. I Sam. 16:17); with **counsel and might** ["with discretion and authority"] **he shall judge** the cases of the poor "according to what is right," and "render decisions in equity for the humble of the land." Moreover, "he shall strike down the bully [or, "tyrant," reading עָרִיץ for אֶרֶץ] and the wicked," by the stern judgments of his authority. Because he truly shall know and reverence God, righteousness and integrity shall be his armor (cf. Eph. 6:14); or (with Ehrlich, *op. cit.*, p. 47) be as inseparable from him as his **girdle**.

6-8. The state of peace and well-being to follow is symbolized by the idyllic picture of wild beasts and dangerous reptiles in harmonious companionship with domesticated animals and children. **Shall lie down**, as one of the flock. מְרִיא, **fatling**, may represent מֵרֵעִים, "friends": "the calf and the lion shall be friends together." The last line of vs. 6 is

---

in three pairs: First, **wisdom and understanding**, which are the essential intellectual qualities of a judge or ruler; second, **counsel and might**, which represent the practical application of wisdom, the gift of decisiveness in judgment and moral energy to carry it out; third, **knowledge and the fear of the LORD**, which is the religious characteristic of leadership. He who would rule others must himself be ruled by knowledge of God, must himself be under constraint to live according to God's moral demands. It is significant that the princely figures of our race, the statesmen and judges who have been accounted great by men, have all approximated in some measure to Isaiah's conception of the ideal ruler. If the electorate of the nations would demand of those who seek office intellectual power, moral force with practical sagacity, and religious faith, we should be better governed. For mark what follows when such character is at the nation's

head. Vss. 3-5 give us the picture of a perfect, just, and equitable government.

He will not judge by appearances,
　nor decide by hearsay,
but act with justice to the helpless,
　and decide fairly for the humble.
He will strike down the ruthless with his verdicts,
　and slay the unjust with his sentences.
Justice shall gird him for action,
　he shall be belted with trustworthiness (Moffatt).

The ideals of democracy can be vindicated only through character. Men do not sufficiently consider that where democracy has failed it has not been because of constitutional weaknesses or faults in administrative procedure, but because of moral defects in the governors and the governed.

6-9. *Reconciliation with Nature.*—This picture of a social order, wholesome and content be-

7 And the cow and the bear shall feed; their young ones shall lie down together: and the lion shall eat straw like the ox.

8 And the sucking child shall play on the hole of the asp, and the weaned child shall put his hand on the cockatrice' den.

9 They shall not hurt nor destroy in all my holy mountain: for the earth shall be full of the knowledge of the LORD, as the waters cover the sea.

7 The cow and the bear shall feed;
　their young shall lie down together;
　and the lion shall eat straw like the ox.

8 The sucking child shall play over the
　hole of the asp,
　and the weaned child shall put his
　hand on the adder's den.

9 They shall not hurt or destroy
　in all my holy mountain;
　for the earth shall be full of the knowl-
　edge of the LORD
　as the waters cover the sea.

---

a circumstantial clause, "while a little boy leads them," i.e., is in charge of them as herdsman. "A babe at the breast, . . . a newly weaned child" shall play unharmed by the holes of venomous snakes: The prophet may be alluding to the perpetual enmity between man and serpents, which resulted from the loss of the original conditions of Eden (cf. Gen. 3:15).

9. The two parts of this verse are found respectively also in 65:25 and Hab. 2:14, and for this reason its genuineness has been questioned. But examination of these passages suggests that they have been derived from this verse, not vice versa. At the same time vs. 9, or at least its second line, seems inappropriate as part of the royal accession liturgy, since it gives a different reason for the ending of hostility and strife, viz., the universality of the true knowledge of Yahweh (cf. Jer. 31:34), rather than the just rule of the anointed king. **My holy mountain:** The hill country of Judah, with its center in the "temple mount" of Jerusalem; the possessive pronoun shows that the prophet is declaring a divine oracle, and it is probable that it originally concluded with "saith the LORD," as in the summary quotation of this passage in 65:25. The remainder of the verse, where the reference to Yahweh is in the third person, is thus an addendum. In 6:3 it is Yahweh's "glory" which fills the earth; in Ps. 33:5 his "mercy," i.e., faithful love; in Hab. 3:3, his "praise." So here, "The land shall be filled" with **the knowledge of the LORD,** as if flooded by the waters of the sea.

---

cause justice rules, is followed by a vision which passes all bounds of probability, but which in itself testifies to the depth of Isaiah's conviction that the "work of righteousness shall be peace and the fruit of it quietness and assurance forever" (32:17). There is, he declares, to be reconciliation in the world of nature, and the ancient enmity between man and beast shall be done away. It is an idyllic picture, this of wild beasts and little children playing together absolutely unafraid, and a wee laddie herding them.

It is to our minds, however, quite unrealistic. Our idea of utopia does not include this sentimentality. We have our own methods of dealing with wild beasts. The high-powered rifle is our answer, which is just another indication of how modern man identifies his golden age with materialism. The ideal he has set before himself is almost wholly a matter of physical condition, a higher standard of living, social security, old-age pensions, state medicine, unemployment in-

surance, etc. He has heard, but does not believe, that to seek "first the kingdom of God" (Matt. 6:33), the kingdom of right relationships, will result in these blessings. He proposes to seek economic and social reform first, confident that improvement in material circumstances will induce a change of heart and a new spirit among men.

In all history there is not a shred of evidence to support that view. It is in flat contradiction to the wisdom of Jesus Christ. The implications of his gospel certainly involve a reorganization of life. They have to do with the practical affairs of industry and economics; but they are implications of a gospel which declares that until the spirit of man himself has changed, no shifting of the scenery will avail for human need. Accept or reject, as one may, the details of Isaiah's picture of the golden age, the ground of his confidence none can challenge. All this will happen, and can happen only when the earth is full of the knowledge of the Lord, when the

10 ¶ And in that day there shall be a root of Jesse, which shall stand for an ensign of the people; to it shall the Gentiles seek: and his rest shall be glorious.

11 And it shall come to pass in that day, *that* the Lord shall set his hand again the second time to recover the remnant of his people, which shall be left, from Assyria, and from Egypt, and from Pathros, and from Cush, and from Elam, and from Shinar, and from Hamath, and from the islands of the sea.

12 And he shall set up an ensign for the nations, and shall assemble the outcasts of Israel, and gather together the dispersed of Judah from the four corners of the earth.

10 In that day the root of Jesse shall stand as an ensign to the peoples; him shall the nations seek, and his dwellings shall be glorious.

11 In that day the Lord will extend his hand yet a second time to recover the remnant which is left of his people, from Assyria, from Egypt, from Pathros, from Ethiopia, from Elam, from Shinar, from Hamath, and from the coastlands of the sea.

12 He will raise an ensign for the nations,
    and will assemble the outcasts of Israel,
  and gather the dispersed of Judah
    from the four corners of the earth.

---

2. The Messiah and the Future Restoration of Israel (11:10-16)

Here, as in 19:16-25 and 27:12-13, one of the later editors of the Isaianic corpus has introduced supplementary material representing the burning faith of fifth- or fourth-century Judaism that their enemies would be overthrown and the dispersed of Israel restored to their own land and temple. The themes of this passage occur again and again in the anonymous additions to pre-exilic prophecy: the world dominion of the Davidic Messiah (cf. Mic. 5:4 [Hebrew 3]; Zech. 9:9-10) ; the restoration of the Jews from the Dispersion (Jer. 31:8-9; Hos. 11:11; Zech. 10:10) ; the reconciliation of Ephraim and Judah (Jer. 3:18; Hos. 3:5; Zech. 10:6-7) ; revenge on Judah's neighbors, on Edom especially (34:1-17; 63:1-6; Obad. 1-21; Amos 9:12; Zeph. 2:4-11; Zech. 9:1-7) ; the doom of Egypt (19:16-17; 27:12; Zech. 10:11) ; the highways from Assyria and Egypt (19:23; 35:8-10; Zech. 10:10; Mic. 7:12) .

10. A brief independent oracle, inserted here because of the key words **root of Jesse,** derived from vs. 1. The sense, however, is different, for the **root** here is no longer the dynasty but its offshoot the Messiah (cf. Rev. 22:16) . Standing up like a flagstaff, he will be a rallying point for the nations, like the restored temple in 2:2. **His dwellings** (lit., "resting-place") are also Yahweh's dwellings, Zion and its temple (cf. 4:5; 60:13) .

11-16. A second oracle, partly in prose and partly in verse; it appears to have been worked over and modified, as by the words following **from Egypt** in vs. 11. In this verse also a verb is missing, and we undoubtedly should read שׂאת, "raise" **(his hand),** for שׁנית, a second time. The latter should be omitted in translation. **Recover:** Better, "to possess," "repossess"; the reference is to Yahweh's having taken possession of his people in the first instance at the Exodus (cf. Exod. 15:16; Ps. 74:2) . Translate, "The Lord will again raise his hand to take possession of the remnant" (for **the remnant,** שׁאר, see Exeg. on 10:20-21) . **Pathros** was Upper Egypt, **Elam** lay east of Babylonia or **Shinar, Hamath** was in north Syria. **Coastlands** is better than **islands;** the reference is to the indented coast and islands of the Aegean.

12. **Ensign** here is a signal, but not the Messiah. **Outcasts,** נדחי, and **dispersed,** נפצות, are the "banished and scattered" tribes and cities, or men and women (since the second

---

sons of men know "him with whom they have to do," and when his will is their law. It is one way of saying that a planned economy presupposes a divine plan; to realize this is the work of all who believe in Jesus Christ and his kingdom.

10-16. *God's Triumph.*—Here is a passage which is clearly an addendum from the hand of some devout editor, who in the ardor of his faith and patriotism must needs add this assurance of a glorious restoration from exile and a triumph over the enemy. While it implies a

13 The envy also of Ephraim shall depart, and the adversaries of Judah shall be cut off: Ephraim shall not envy Judah, and Judah shall not vex Ephraim.

14 But they shall fly upon the shoulders of the Philistines toward the west; they shall spoil them of the east together: they shall lay their hand upon Edom and Moab; and the children of Ammon shall obey them.

15 And the Lord shall utterly destroy the tongue of the Egyptian sea; and with his mighty wind shall he shake his hand over the river, and shall smite it in the seven streams, and make *men* go over dry-shod.

16 And there shall be a highway for the remnant of his people, which shall be left, from Assyria; like as it was to Israel in the day that he came up out of the land of Egypt.

13 The jealousy of E'phraim shall depart,
    and those who harass Judah shall be
      cut off;
E'phraim shall not be jealous of Judah,
    and Judah shall not harass E'phraim.
14 But they shall swoop down upon the
    shoulder of the Philistines in the
    west,
    and together they shall plunder the
      people of the east.
They shall put forth their hand against
    Edom and Moab,
    and the Ammonites shall obey them.
15 And the Lord will utterly destroy
    the tongue of the sea of Egypt;
and will wave his hand over the River
    with his scorching wind,
and smite it into seven channels
    that men may cross dryshod.
16 And there will be a highway from Assyria
    for the remnant which is left of his peo-
      ple,
    as there was for Israel
      when they came up from the land of
      Egypt.

---

word is feminine). These words are commonly used in postexilic prophecy with reference to the exiles.

13-14. For **those who harass Judah** read with Procksch and Kissane, "the enmity of Judah." **The shoulder of the Philistines:** I.e., "on the Philistine foothills"; Ehrlich (*ibid.*, p. 49), however, takes the meaning to be "they shall swoop down shoulder to shoulder upon the Philistines" (cf. Zeph. 3:9); this gives good parallelism with **together** in the next line.

15. The tongue of the sea of Egypt: I.e., the Gulf of Suez (Procksch), the "Reed" Sea of the Exodus (Marti, Gray, Kissane), or the Nile (Duhm, cf. 19:5-6; Zech. 10:11). The reference in any case is to the deliverance of the Jews through the smiting of Egypt. **The river** usually refers to the Euphrates, but here as in 19:5 it almost certainly means the Nile. For **with his scorching wind,** which gives a doubtful translation of the obscure word עים, read "and he will divide the sea with his wind," ובקע ים ברוחו (cf. Exod. 14:21), which accords with the next line.

16. The remnant here, as in vs. 11, has become a standard term for the Jews dispersed throughout the world. This verse is the complement of vs. 15 (cf. vs. 11, **from Assyria, from Egypt**), so that it may be read, "There will be a highway also from Assyria, as for Israel on the day when they come up" (not *"came* up").

---

historical situation far down the years from Isaiah's day, it does represent the prophet's unmoved faith in the final victory of God. It is part of our legacy from Hebrew faith, this unshakable confidence in the power and purpose of God. Centuries later another seer, facing a chaotic and disintegrating world, struck the same note, crying, "The kingdoms of this world are become the kingdoms of our Lord, and of his Christ" (Rev. 11:15). That was not a brave surmise; it was a prophecy and a faith based on the decisive act of God, who in the cross of Christ accepted the challenge of sin and death and triumphed over them. Because of the Cross and the Resurrection we know how things will fall out in this dark world. "This is the victory that overcometh . . . , even our faith" (I John 5:4).

12 And in that day thou shalt say, O Lord, I will praise thee: though thou wast angry with me, thine anger is turned away, and thou comfortedst me.

2 Behold, God *is* my salvation; I will trust, and not be afraid: for the Lord Jehovah *is* my strength and *my* song; he also is become my salvation.

12 You will say in that day:
"I will give thanks to thee, O Lord,
    for though thou wast angry with me,
thy anger turned away,
    and thou didst comfort me.

2 "Behold, God is my salvation;
    I will trust, and will not be afraid;
for the Lord God is my strength and my
        song,
    and he has become my salvation."

C. An Outburst of Thanksgiving (12:1-6)

Two brief psalms of thanksgiving of unknown origin and date—vss. 1-2 and 3-6—are inserted here as a suitable conclusion to the messianic pictures of ch. 11. The presence of many such inserted psalms in the prophetic books has been noted. Some, like those in Jonah 2 and Hab. 3, are full-fledged psalms; others, like Jer. 20:13; 31:7, are represented by one or more selected verses. For the liturgical rubrics of vs. 1*a* and vss. 3-4*a*, cf. Deut. 26:5*a*, and the similar psalm introductions in Isa. 25:9*a*; 26:1*a*.

12:1-2. An individual thanksgiving for deliverance, comparable to Ps. 116 and used as the verbal ritual accompanying a sacrifice in payment of a vow. The Dead Sea Scroll inserts a second אל, "Behold, God is the God of my salvation"; the second part of vs. 2 appears also in Exod. 15:2; Ps. 118:14.

12:1-6. *A Song of Thanksgiving.*—It was a true instinct which led the editors to insert a song of thanksgiving after the prophecy of the return of the exiles, with which ch. 11 closes. Any great deliverance is an occasion for praise and the O.T. is full of songs of deliverance. Ch. 12 forms a "lyrical epilogue" to the first main division of the book (chs. 1–12). It is of unknown authorship and date. Clearly the mind of the poet was filled with the thought of the goodness and the power of God in the care of his people. The two hymns which make up the chapter echo the mood and indeed some of the very phrases of Moses' great song of deliverance (Exod. 15:1-18). Whatever the occasion which inspired them, they are timeless and universal in giving voice to the gratitude of the human heart for every experience of the mercy of God.

And they have a peculiar religious value for an age which needs continually to be confronted with its debt to that goodness. The more confident men become in their own powers the less inclined they are to remember and give thanks to God. A materialistic generation is not much given to thanksgiving; pride always silences the praise of God. Any revival of religion which may yet come to the world will be marked by a new outburst of thanksgiving; a singing church is spiritually alive, for the praise of God bespeaks experience of his saving power. It is when men have been brought out of darkness into light, when they have been set free, when forgiven they have found again their lost peace, that by an inner compulsion they lift their hearts and voices in praise.

The key to the gladness which rings through ch. 12 is in that exquisite verse, **Therefore with joy shall ye draw water out of the wells of salvation.** The poet had often heard the village girls singing at the wells. It is significant that in all the simple forms of social life singing is associated with labor. The songs of the Hebrides, the western isles of Scotland, for example, are nearly all concerned with daily tasks, weaving, cattle herding, potato lifting, and milking. However much modern man has increased his productive capacity, however much he has shortened his hours and eased his toil, the fact remains that the mechanization of industry has taken the song out of life, and melody has been replaced by rhythm. What one hears in much modern music is not the echo of gladness, but rather the beat of the machine. Among all the problems of the modern social order this surely is not least, how to recover the lost music. It will be one of the tokens of a new relationship between men, and of a new understanding of the dignity and the value of labor, when we once more sing at our work.

But the beautiful verse has other and deeper meanings and the expositor has not dealt with it truly until he has held out to thirsty souls the offer and promise of the "living water" (John

3 Therefore with joy shall ye draw water out of the wells of salvation.

4 And in that day shall ye say, Praise the LORD, call upon his name, declare his doings among the people, make mention that his name is exalted.

5 Sing unto the LORD; for he hath done excellent things: this is known in all the earth.

6 Cry out and shout, thou inhabitant of Zion: for great is the Holy One of Israel in the midst of thee.

13 The burden of Babylon, which Isaiah the son of Amoz did see.

3 With joy you will draw water from the wells of salvation. 4 And you will say in that day:

"Give thanks to the LORD,
    call upon his name;
make known his deeds among the nations,
    proclaim that his name is exalted.

5 "Sing praises to the LORD, for he has done gloriously;
    let this be known[x] in all the earth.
6 Shout, and sing for joy, O inhabitant of Zion,
    for great in your midst is the Holy One of Israel."

13 The oracle concerning Babylon which Isaiah the son of Amoz saw.

[x] Or this is made known

3-6. A second psalm of thanksgiving, to be used when "with joyous singing you draw water from the springs," whose life-giving water was a mark and symbol of Yahweh's saving power. Cf. Judg. 5:11, "Hark to the maidens laughing at the wells! There they recount the righteous acts of Yahweh" (C. F. Burney, *The Book of Judges* [2nd ed.; London: Rivingtons, 1930], p. 163). The phraseology has many echoes in the Psalms (105:1; 148:13; 66:2; 67:2 [Hebrew 67:3]; cf. Zech. 2:10). See also "the Song of the Well" in Num. 21:17-18 and the references to vintage songs in Isa. 65:8; Jer. 25:30. The common tasks of daily life became for the ancient Israelites occasions of religious celebration and praise.

V. "The Uproar of Many Peoples" (13:1–23:18)

In this section are grouped a series of oracles directed to foreign peoples, some of them by Isaiah and some from other hands but attributed to him by later editors. Similar collections of such oracles are found in the books of Jeremiah (chs. 46–51) and Ezekiel (chs. 25–32). In Isaiah this collection is further distinguished from its context by ten occurrences of a distinctive oracle designation, "Burden of" or "Doom Oracle concerning . . ." (13:1; 14:28; 15:1; 17:1; 19:1; 21:1; 21:11; 21:13; 22:1; 23:1).

A. The Doom of Babylon (13:1-22)

This prophetic poem comes from a time long after that of Isaiah, for the great world power is no longer Assyria but Babylon. Babylon is threatened by the Medes,

4:10), which is the gift of God to men. When they **draw water out of the wells of salvation,** a new joy will mark the lives of men, and the song of faith will be heard on the lips of those who know the gladness of redemption.

It has always been so. The Christian church has come singing through the ages. The source of its joy has been the gospel of God's love in Jesus Christ and the new life which opens to those who accept the offer of salvation. Among the things which moved, amazed, and finally won the hearts of men in the first century was the radiance of the Christian faith revealed

among common people. This was a new thing in that age hag-ridden by fear, and men wondered what made these Christians different. It is still so. "What makes you so shining faced, Memsahib?" asked an old woman of one of our missionaries in an Indian village. She got her answer from a life claimed and won by Jesus Christ. If the modern church is to recover the lost radiance of faith it will do so only by drawing anew from **the wells of salvation** that water of life which is the gift of God's love in Christ.

13:1-22. The Doom of Babylon.—This is a chapter of sheer terror; all is a welter of confu-

2 Lift ye up a banner upon the high mountain, exalt the voice unto them, shake the hand, that they may go into the gates of the nobles.

3 I have commanded my sanctified ones, I have also called my mighty ones for mine anger, *even* them that rejoice in my highness.

4 The noise of a multitude in the mountains, like as of a great people; a tumultuous noise of the kingdoms of nations gathered together: the LORD of hosts mustereth the host of the battle.

2 On a bare hill raise a signal,
　cry aloud to them;
wave the hand for them to enter
　the gates of the nobles.
3 I myself have commanded my consecrated
　ones,
　have summoned my mighty men to
　　execute my anger,
　my proudly exulting ones.

4 Hark, a tumult on the mountains
　as of a great multitude!
Hark, an uproar of kingdoms,
　of nations gathering together!
The LORD of hosts is mustering
　a host for battle.

---

a circumstance which appears to date vss. 17-22 of this chapter shortly after the death of Nebuchadrezzar in 562 B.C. The rest of the poem, vss. 2-16, has no necessary connection with the doom of Babylon, but provides the setting for it with an awe-inspiring picture of the terrors of the approaching day of the Lord. The description of that day, however, does not correspond to Isaiah's in 2:10-22, but rather to the later eschatological expectations of universal judgment and catastrophe as found in characteristic form inserted in several prophetic books: cf. 24:1-12, 17-23; 34:1-4, 10-15; Joel 2:1-11, 30-32 (Hebrew 3:3-5); 3:9-16 (Hebrew 4:9-16); Zeph. 1:14-18; 3:8; Zech. 14:2, 6; for other doom oracles on Babylon in similar settings cf. 21:1-9; Jer. 50:1–51:58.

13:1. The burden or **The oracle:** The first of a series of ten such headings in chs. 13–23 which distinguish this section of the book. The word משא means "that which is lifted up," a **burden** (cf. Exod. 23:5) or, as here, an oath or curse uttered with uplifted hand (cf. Ps. 106:26; Ezek. 36:7), and so a doom oracle. The ascription to Isaiah, like that in 2:1, claims for this prophet one of the anonymous oracles in circulation in the time of the editor; perhaps because there are echoes of Isaiah's language in vss. 2, 5 (cf. 5:26) and vss. 6, 11 (cf. 2:12). The similarities in thought and language to the oracle in Jer. 51:27-32 should be noted.

2-4. The summons to Yahweh's avenging armies. **Cry aloud to them:** Perhaps "Sound the call to battle," reading מלחמה for להם, which is a pronoun lacking an antecedent. **Enter the gates of the nobles:** If the text is right, the meaning is apparently that the Babylonians should take refuge in their city. But פתחי, **gates**, may represent פתחו, "draw"; hence read "let the nobles unsheath (the sword)," cf. Ezek. 21:28, where the **nobles** are the commanders of the summoned forces. **My consecrated ones:** Soldiers were set apart for a battle or campaign, and were under certain taboos related to the sacrifices and vows

---

sion and death as the judgment of God falls on the world. It belongs to an age long after that of Isaiah, but the nameless one who wrote it was one with the prophet in his certainty of the judgment and his sense of the awfulness of the divine visitation. The day of the Lord breaks, his signal is run to the masthead on the hilltop. At that instant his poised and waiting forces begin to close in. There follow breathless sentences which depict the panic which sweeps the world. Not man alone but all nature is shaken, the stars are blotted out, the very heavens quiver. On earth there is wild panic as the

terror-stricken inhabitants rush blindly for shelter only to be cut down in their tracks. The chapter ends with a grim picture of the sack of Babylon by the Medes. The spectacle of the vast metropolis in ruins, shunned by the living, tenanted only by the dead, with jackals skulking among the rubble heaps, busy at their obscene scavengering, while demons dance and the scream of the night bird echoes through the ruins, leaves one with a sense of horror and fear.

What is there in such a chapter to claim the modern mind? Little is said among us about the day of judgment. It might be well if there were

5 They come from a far country, from the end of heaven, *even* the LORD, and the weapons of his indignation, to destroy the whole land.

6 ¶ Howl ye; for the day of the LORD *is* at hand; it shall come as a destruction from the Almighty.

7 Therefore shall all hands be faint, and every man's heart shall melt:

8 And they shall be afraid: pangs and sorrows shall take hold of them; they shall be in pain as a woman that travaileth: they shall be amazed one at another; their faces *shall be as* flames.

9 Behold, the day of the LORD cometh, cruel both with wrath and fierce anger, to lay the land desolate: and he shall destroy the sinners thereof out of it.

10 For the stars of heaven and the constellations thereof shall not give their light: the sun shall be darkened in his going forth, and the moon shall not cause her light to shine.

11 And I will punish the world for *their* evil, and the wicked for their iniquity; and I will cause the arrogancy of the proud to cease, and will lay low the haughtiness of the terrible.

---

5 They come from a distant land,
  from the end of the heavens,
the LORD and the weapons of his indignation,
  to destroy the whole earth.

6 Wail, for the day of the LORD is near;
  as destruction from the Almighty it will come!

7 Therefore all hands will be feeble,
  and every man's heart will melt,
8   and they will be dismayed.
Pangs and agony will seize them;
  they will be in anguish like a woman in travail.
They will look aghast at one another;
  their faces will be aflame.

9 Behold, the day of the LORD comes,
  cruel, with wrath and fierce anger,
to make the earth a desolation
  and to destroy its sinners from it.
10 For the stars of the heavens and their constellations
  will not give their light;
the sun will be dark at its rising
  and the moon will not shed its light.
11 I will punish the world for its evil,
  and the wicked for their iniquity;
  I will put an end to the pride of the arrogant,
  and lay low the haughtiness of the ruthless.

---

made in hope of victory (cf. Joel 4:9 [Hebrew 3:9]; Deut. 23:9-14; II Sam. 11:11). **Nations gathering,** as contingents were supplied by vassal states to the Assyrian and Babylonian armies (cf. 10:8).

5-8. The approach of the army and of **the day of the LORD.** From beyond the farthest horizon come the hosts who are **the weapons of Yahweh's indignation, to destroy the whole earth,** the world-wide empire of Babylon. **Their faces will be aflame:** Better, reading חבלים, "pains," for להבים, "flames," "with agony written on their faces."

9-12. The terrors of **the day. The sinners,** not enemies, are the objects of Yahweh's destroying wrath; this is a picture of the Last Judgment (cf. vs. 11). **Constellations:** Lit., "their Orions"; one of the most striking of star groups gives its name to all. The darkening of the heavenly bodies becomes a characteristic feature in descriptions of the final cataclysm (cf. Joel 2:30-31 [Hebrew 3:3-4]; Luke 21:25; Rev. 6:12). **Ophir is in** southwest Arabia.

---

more; certainly if men are silent on this it cannot be because there is no occasion for judgment. The apocalyptic note is only seldom heard; perhaps in part at least because the modern mind views judgment as a continuous process within history, rather than as a catas-

trophic visitation—though twice in this century the world has been scourged and judged in the fires of war. It is another question how one shall interpret war. Isaiah depicts God as the direct instigator of it. The Christian mind today does not charge God with it. Our indict-

12 I will make a man more precious than fine gold; even a man than the golden wedge of Ophir.	12 I will make men more rare than fine gold, and mankind than the gold of Ophir.

12 I will make a man more precious than fine gold; even a man than the golden wedge of Ophir.

13 Therefore I will shake the heavens, and the earth shall remove out of her place, in the wrath of the LORD of hosts, and in the day of his fierce anger.

14 And it shall be as the chased roe, and as a sheep that no man taketh up: they shall every man turn to his own people, and flee every one into his own land.

15 Every one that is found shall be thrust through; and every one that is joined *unto them* shall fall by the sword.

16 Their children also shall be dashed to pieces before their eyes; their houses shall be spoiled, and their wives ravished.

17 Behold, I will stir up the Medes against them, which shall not regard silver; and *as for* gold, they shall not delight in it.

18 *Their* bows also shall dash the young men to pieces; and they shall have no pity on the fruit of the womb; their eye shall not spare children.

19 ¶ And Babylon, the glory of kingdoms, the beauty of the Chaldees' excellency, shall be as when God overthrew Sodom and Gomorrah.

12 I will make men more rare than fine gold,
    and mankind than the gold of Ophir.
13 Therefore I will make the heavens tremble,
    and the earth will be shaken out of its place,
at the wrath of the LORD of hosts
    in the day of his fierce anger.
14 And like a hunted gazelle,
    or like sheep with none to gather them,
every man will turn to his own people,
    and every man will flee to his own land.
15 Whoever is found will be thrust through,
    and whoever is caught will fall by the sword.
16 Their infants will be dashed in pieces
    before their eyes;
their houses will be plundered
    and their wives ravished.

17 Behold, I am stirring up the Medes against them,
    who have no regard for silver
    and do not delight in gold.
18 Their bows will slaughter the young men;
    they will have no mercy on the fruit of the womb;
    their eyes will not pity children.
19 And Babylon, the glory of kingdoms,
    the splendor and pride of the Chalde'ans,
will be like Sodom and Gomor'rah
    when God overthrew them.

13-16. The dreadful consequences of Yahweh's wrath. Man's proud social structures will be broken down and it will be "every man for himself," as in the legend of an older Babel-Babylon (cf. Gen. 11:8-9).

17-19. The onslaught of the Medes on Babylon. The actual historical situation is viewed in the lurid light of Yahweh's universal judgment. The Medes had the reputation of being interested only in war, rather than in empire building or commerce. **The glory of kingdoms:** Better, "Most glorious of kingdoms."

---

ment is directed against the unchecked evils which make strife inevitable. It is man, not God, who is responsible for the ravaged lands, the slaying of the nations, and the broken hearts of millions; man who in the pride of his own achievements extends his truculence from one realm to another till he sets the world on fire. And then so often he is prone to charge God with misgovernment! "What kind of God is this?" he cries, pointing to the ruin his own hands have wrought. "Why doesn't he stop it?" How even God could do that without making moral imbeciles of us is not considered.

The Christian position differs from that of Isaiah in its view of the relationship of God to history, but it does not deny the relationship. It too holds that human life is the scene of the presence and action of God. Therefore it de-

20 It shall never be inhabited, neither shall it be dwelt in from generation to generation: neither shall the Arabian pitch tent there; neither shall the shepherds make their fold there.

21 But wild beasts of the desert shall lie there; and their houses shall be full of doleful creatures; and owls shall dwell there, and satyrs shall dance there.

22 And the wild beasts of the islands shall cry in their desolate houses, and dragons in *their* pleasant palaces: and her time *is* near to come, and her days shall not be prolonged.

14 For the LORD will have mercy on Jacob, and will yet choose Israel, and set them in their own land: and the strangers shall be joined with them, and they shall cleave to the house of Jacob.

---

20 It will never be inhabited
　or dwelt in for all generations;
no Arab will pitch his tent there,
　no shepherds will make their flocks lie
　　down there.
21 But wild beasts will lie down there,
　and its houses will be full of howling
　　creatures;
there ostriches will dwell,
　and there satyrs will dance.
22 Hyenas will cry in its towers,
　and jackals in the pleasant palaces;
its time is close at hand
　and its days will not be prolonged.

14 The LORD will have compassion on Jacob and will again choose Israel, and will set them in their own land, and aliens will join them and will cleave to the

---

20-22. The utter desolation of Babylon. Vs. 20*a* is found also in a similar oracle in Jer. 50:35-40; cf. also the doom of Edom in Isa. 34:1-15. Not even an **Arab** nomad (first mentioned in Jer. 3:2) will **pitch his tent** there; the only living things will be wild creatures of the desert, and **satyrs;** better "goat-demons." The latter word means also "he-goats"; it appears that he-goats as well as calves were worshiped as theriomorphic deities in Israel down to the time of Josiah's reform (cf. II Kings 23:8; II Chr. 11:15; Lev. 17:7). Later the goat-god was degraded to the role of a demon in popular superstition, and was thought to inhabit waste and desolate places.

B. DOWNFALL OF A TYRANT (14:1-23)

One of the most remarkable poems of the O.T. celebrates in the form of a mocking dirge the overthrow and death of a mighty monarch who had terrorized the world. The poem itself (vss. 4*b*-21) has been given a prose introduction (vss. 1-4*a*) and conclusion (vss. 22-23) by one of the postexilic annotators and editors who had a hand in the later stages of the composition of the book. He it is who has identified the fallen tyrant with **the king of Babylon,** though it is not clear whether an actual king or a personification of the Babylonian imperial power is intended. A third and not improbable alternative is

---

clares that war is always a judgment on the sin that causes it, that war is itself sin, and brings its own retribution in its wake, precisely because God is on the throne and the moral laws of his government are inescapable and inexorable. The day of battle is indeed **the day of the LORD,** "for the wages of sin is death" (Rom. 6:23). Isaiah declares that God employs heathen powers as agents of his wrath. The Christian declares that God can and does use the very disasters caused by human sin for the ultimate good of men. We discover our sin through suffering and learn our weakness and our helplessness in the misery which we ourselves have occasioned. Isaiah did not know about the Incarna-

tion, therefore he must needs depict God as hurling the bolts of his judgment on men. Ours is the vision of the God who condemns sin in the cross of his own Son. There is more judgment of evil in that cross than in any flame and thunder of war. Where a thousand may be crushed by their own suffering, a multitude no man can number may respond to the love which suffered for them. Christ lifted up on the cross will yet draw all men to himself.

14:1-21. *Ironic Oracle on the Death of the King of Babylon.*—This tremendous chapter, with its incomparable poetry and imaginative power, ranks among the great passages of all literature. Between the prose introduction and

2 And the people shall take them, and bring them to their place: and the house of Israel shall possess them in the land of the house of Jacob. 2 And the peoples will take them and bring them to their place, and the house of Israel will possess them in the

---

that "Babylon" has become a symbolic term for the dominant world power whose fall must precede the promised restoration of the Jews; in this case it would represent the Persian Empire, since the indications are that this introduction is to be dated in the fifth or fourth century B.C. (cf. Rev. 14:8). The language and viewpoint are similar to those of late supplements to Second Isaiah, such as 49:22-23; 56:1-8; 61:4-9 (cf. also Zech. 2:6-13 [Hebrew 2:10-17]) and do not provide any certain indications of date; it is possible, but not probable, that Isaiah was the author.

The poem itself, vss. 4b-21, is called a *māshāl*, a word which means primarily "a comparison," then a mocking comparison or taunt, and eventually a proverb or parable. There is a correspondence between the object of the משל as seen on the surface and its hidden or deeper meaning. Here, as in Num. 23:7, it is a kind of prophetic spell or invocation of fate. The tenses of the verbs are prophetic perfects; this has happened in a future already realized in the mind of the speaker. The prophet's announcement of the overthrow of the tyrant as an accomplished fact is to him a mysterious force effective for the accomplishment of the fact.

The use of mythological material has special importance in this connection. Myths (except in the Platonic sense) are pictorial presentations of enduring and essential truth about the unseen forces with which man has to do, and of his relations with them. In 10:5-16 the arrogant boasting of a world conqueror is exhibited and its doom pronounced in historical terms, as here in representational, mythological terms. Each is a prophetic oracle, declaring the reiterated biblical message that no man and no people can with impunity ignore the divine supremacy and scale the heights of heaven (cf. Gen. 3:22; 11:4-8; Dan. 4:32).

The dramatic power of the poem is notable. The first strophe (vss. 4b-8) secures a striking effect by the dissonance of thought and form—the oppressor's end joyously celebrated in the limping meter of the dirge. At the same time the general terror is made a measure of the universal relief as the storm passes and there is a great calm. The whole earth and the very trees of the forest break forth into a paean of joy. With the second strophe (vss. 9-11) the scene is shifted to Sheol, where the shades of dead kings stir feebly to greet the mighty despot whose strength has been extinguished in death, as with any other man. In the third strophe (vss. 12-15) the poet mocks the fall of one who had sought to penetrate beyond the stars to the forbidden place of the Most High, and now has been cast down to the lowest depths of the **Pit** (of death). Next, in vss. 16-19c, 19e (the second to last line of vs. 19 belongs with vs. 20) the scene is shifted again to earth, where the wondering observers ponder the dishonored corpse of one who had mastered the world. The concluding strophe (vss. 19d, 20-21) is shorter than the others and may not have been preserved complete. Its theme is the legacy of hatred, the curse which the fallen tyrant has left behind.

The message of this vivid and powerful poetic oracle, with its dramatic movement and completeness, is primarily that of the certain overthrow of the proud will to mastery of the world, which is at the same time an assault upon the throne of God. Israel, which had no material and political strength of her own, had to live in the faith that all oppressor kings and empires would dash themselves to pieces in attempting to scale the heights unto which no man can approach. With this principal theme there are also at least three subordinate ones: (a) the empty failure of a life, however ambitious and outwardly successful, whose ending prompts an outburst of rejoicing and whose only legacy is an execration; (b) the equal humbling of all men by death; and (c) the perpetual astonishment of men that one whose power had seemed unassailable could so quickly be overtaken by nemesis.

LORD for servants and handmaids: and they shall take them captives, whose captives they were; and they shall rule over their oppressors.

3 And it shall come to pass in the day that the LORD shall give thee rest from thy sorrow, and from thy fear, and from the hard bondage wherein thou wast made to serve,

4 ¶ That thou shalt take up this proverb against the king of Babylon, and say, How hath the oppressor ceased! the golden city ceased!

5 The LORD hath broken the staff of the wicked, *and* the sceptre of the rulers.

6 He who smote the people in wrath with a continual stroke, he that ruled the nations in anger, is presecuted, *and* none hindereth.

7 The whole earth is at rest, *and* is quiet: they break forth into singing.

8 Yea, the fir trees rejoice at thee, *and* the cedars of Lebanon, *saying*, Since thou art laid down, no feller is come up against us.

LORD's land as male and female slaves; they will take captive those who were their captors, and rule over those who oppressed them.

3 When the LORD has given you rest from your pain and turmoil and the hard service with which you were made to serve, 4 you will take up this taunt against the king of Babylon:

"How the oppressor has ceased,
　the insolent fury[y] ceased!
5 The LORD has broken the staff of the wicked,
　the scepter of rulers,
6 that smote the peoples in wrath
　with unceasing blows,
that ruled the nations in anger
　with unrelenting persecution.
7 The whole earth is at rest and quiet;
　they break forth into singing.
8 The cypresses rejoice at you,
　the cedars of Lebanon, saying,
'Since you were laid low,
　no hewer comes up against us.'

[y] One ancient Ms Compare Gk Syr Vg: The meaning of the Hebrew word is uncertain

---

14:1-4a. Again choose Israel: Reaffirming his mighty act whereby at the first the Israelites became his "prized possession" (cf. Deut. 14:2), delivering them from exile, as formerly from Egypt, and bringing them again into **their own land. Aliens** or **the strangers:** The accession of proselytes to Judaism is referred to not infrequently in postexilic prophecy (cf. 2:3; Zech. 8:20-22). It was an unlooked for result of the calamity of the burning of the temple and the dispersion of the Jews, that their religion became known in many parts of the world. A less attractive element in the expectation of deliverance is the anticipated reversal of the roles of captives and captors (cf. 60:10-14). **Hard service** or **bondage:** Better, "harsh slavery"; the phrase is an echo of Exod. 1:14.

4b-8. How . . . ! The standard opening of a lament (cf. II Sam. 1:19). "How still the oppressor has become! How the uproar has ceased!" **The wicked . . . of rulers:** Plural because what has happened to this wicked despot is but an example of Yahweh's authority when he "breaks" the power of tyrannical kings and empires, "raining ceaseless blows on them" and "unrelenting in pursuit" (reading מרדף). The plundered earth breaks **forth into singing,** especially the **fir trees** and **cedars of Lebanon,** a silent, unresisting host which had been ruthlessly destroyed for the building and commerce of the imperial city.

---

the conclusion, inserted by some editor to give a framework for the oracle, there are five scenes.

4-8. *The Gladness of Liberation.*—Scene One: This is the picture of the earth rejoicing in liberation from its persecutor. Those who have seen a great storm sweep over a summer landscape will understand perfectly this little lyric of peace. The thunder has crashed, the lightning split the heavens, the gale has raged, devastating the forests, the torrential rain has changed the quiet stream to a raging flood. But as swiftly as it came the attack dies away, the thunder withdraws and, like a drunken god, stumbles off among the hills, the sun breaks through the clouds, the beaten grasses rise, the bowed flowers lift their faces, the tortured trees, released from strain, renew the song of rustling leaves. **The whole earth is at rest, and is quiet.** So it is, says the prophet, with the nation delivered from the torment of incarnate evil.

9 Hell from beneath is moved for thee to meet *thee* at thy coming: it stirreth up the dead for thee, *even* all the chief ones of the earth; it hath raised up from their thrones all the kings of the nations.

10 All they shall speak and say unto thee, Art thou also become weak as we? art thou become like unto us?

11 Thy pomp is brought down to the grave, *and* the noise of thy viols: the worm is spread under thee, and the worms cover thee.

12 How art thou fallen from heaven, O Lucifer, son of the morning! *how* art thou cut down to the ground, which didst weaken the nations!

13 For thou hast said in thine heart, I will ascend into heaven, I will exalt my throne above the stars of God: I will sit also upon the mount of the congregation, in the sides of the north:

9 Sheol beneath is stirred up
  to meet you when you come,
 it rouses the shades to greet you,
  all who were leaders of the earth;
 it raises from their thrones
  all who were kings of the nations.

10 All of them will speak
  and say to you:
 'You too have become as weak as we!
  You have become like us!'

11 Your pomp is brought down to Sheol,
  the sound of your harps;
 maggots are the bed beneath you,
  and worms are your covering.

12 "How you are fallen from heaven,
  O Day Star, son of Dawn!
 How you are cut down to the ground,
  you who laid the nations low!

13 You said in your heart,
  'I will ascend to heaven;
 above the stars of God
  I will set my throne on high;
 I will sit on the mount of assembly
  in the far north;

9-11. Sheol: The abode of the shades, not **hell,** which has different associations for us, derived largely from Rev. 9:2; 20:10, and Dante's *Inferno.* Its meaning is "the grave." There all alike will rest in silence (cf. Job 3:13-19), unremembered (cf. 26:14) and no longer able to praise God (cf. Ps. 115:17). There ghostly kings sit on ghostly thrones, weak shadows of living men, amid worms and dust (cf. Dan. 12:2). Sometimes Sheol is pictured as a monster with open mouth and ravenous appetite (cf. 5:14; Hab. 2:5), a pagan goddess of destruction. It is called also "the Pit" and Abaddon (cf. Job 26:6), and is equated with the Canaanite god of the underworld, Mot or "Death" (cf. 28:15, 18).

12-15. The use in these verses of material derived from Canaanite myths is unmistakable, and the point is made that the meaning of what the tyrant has done is set forth in the myth of Helal, the **Day Star** or "Lightgiver" (cf. Vulg. "Lucifer"), son of Shahar, **Dawn.** It is a manifestation on earth of the ultimate conflict set forth in the myth in timeless terms. We know that there was a god Shahar in Canaanite (Ugaritic) mythology, the god of dawn or of the morning star (cf. Theodore H. Gaster, "A Canaanite Ritual Drama," *Journal of the American Oriental Society,* LXVI [1946], 49), and "Helal, son

---

9-11. *A King Arrives in Sheol.*—Scene Two: There is a swift transition from the sunlit land to Sheol, the dusty prison house of the ghostly dead, where through the eternities they sit immobile in vacuous contemplation. Suddenly there is a stir in that insubstantial company, and spectral kings rise from spectral thrones to stare at the figure which glides among them. Enter another monarch stripped of earthly splendor, unannounced by trumpet call. Their greeting is a passionless whisper, "You too, your glory gone, come to dust." And once again the silence settles on the halls of the dead.

12-15. *The Sin of Presumption.*—Scene Three: The accusation which the ghosts of Sheol cannot, dare not, frame finds a voice.

**How you are fallen from heaven,
O Day Star, son of Dawn!**

He thought to rise to divine sovereignty over the dead bodies of his enemies, he beat with bloodstained hands on the gates of God, clamoring for a throne; and in his presumption perished, cast out like an unclean thing from the courts of heaven, to the derisive laughter of the God he mocked.

14 I will ascend above the heights of the clouds; I will be like the Most High.

15 Yet thou shalt be brought down to hell, to the sides of the pit.

16 They that see thee shall narrowly look upon thee, *and* consider thee, *saying, Is* this the man that made the earth to tremble, that did shake kingdoms;

17 *That* made the world as a wilderness, and destroyed the cities thereof; *that* opened not the house of his prisoners?

18 All the kings of the nations, *even* all of them, lie in glory, every one in his own house.

19 But thou art cast out of thy grave like

---

14 I will ascend above the heights of the clouds,
    I will make myself like the Most High.'
15 But you are brought down to Sheol,
    to the depths of the Pit.
16 Those who see you will stare at you,
    and ponder over you:
'Is this the man who made the earth tremble,
    who shook kingdoms,
17 who made the world like a desert
    and overthrew its cities,
    who did not let his prisoners go home?'
18 All the kings of the nations lie in glory,
    each in his own tomb;
19 but you are cast out, away from your sepulchre,
    like a loathed untimely birth,[z]

[z] Cn Compare Tg Symmachus: Heb *a loathed branch*

---

of Shahar" is mentioned apparently in one of the texts from Ugarit. Another clearly mythological element is **the mount of assembly** [of the gods] **in the far north,** the point around which the constellations turned, where was located the summit of the heavenly mountain and the throne of **the Most High** (cf. Ezek. 28:14; Pss. 48:2 [Hebrew 48:3]; 82:1, 6; cf. Procksch, *Jesaia I,* p. 197). The passage before us preserves the Canaanite form of a nature myth, telling of the attempt of the morning star to scale the heights of heaven, surpassing all other stars only to be cast down to earth by the victorious sun (cf. Hermann Gunkel, *Schöpfung und Chaos in Urzeit und Endzeit* [2nd ed.; Göttingen: Vandenhoeck & Ruprecht, 1921], pp. 133-34). This became in turn the story of the aspiring of a minor deity to reach the highest heaven where the supreme god dwelt in remote and lonely splendor, and finally the symbol of the ambition and downfall of an earthly monarch. He who has climbed so high will be cast down to **the depths,** better, "the uttermost depths" of **the Pit** of Sheol.

16-19c, 19e. Away from your sepulchre: Better, "with no sepulcher." **Like a loathed untimely birth:** The text is corrupt; the word נצר, **branch,** in the archaic script resembles פגר, "corpse," which gives the suitable meaning "like a horrid corpse." **Clothed with the slain** is meaningless; we may emend לבוש to לבאש "with the stench of those slain by the sword." Perhaps "slain" is a gloss on the rare word מטעני, **pierced.**

19d, 20-21. The Pit here is not Sheol, but the grave of **stones,** or cairn, in which men were hurriedly entombed on the battlefield (cf. II Sam. 18:17). But this dishonored

---

16-19. *Repudiated.*—Scene Four: Back to earth and to the judgment of men. With a vast incredulity the spectators gaze at the defaced image of the man who dared to rival God. "Is this the man, this poor mangled thing, is this he who strode the world like a Colossus, and looked pitilessly on the lands he ruined and the hearts he broke? No marble tomb panoplied in splendor, no mourning throng for him! Like refuse on the dunghill he lies, the stench of rotten death befouling the air." No modern man can read this passage and not remember the infamy of Hitler's death, and Mussolini's, two dictators who also **made the earth to tremble,**

and at the last were flung aside in the ignominy of a universal execration.

19-21. *The Epitaph of Tyranny.*—Scene Five: This is the damnation of an evil life, that at its end all men should rejoice and pray to God that never again shall any of its cursed line trouble the sons of men.

This tremendous passage has much to say to us. In particular three truths stand out.

First, here is depicted the judgment of pride. This is a favorite theme of biblical writers. The Hebrews were not speculative thinkers, but they had an eye for truth revealed in life. They had no need to theorize on the sin of pride, for on

an abominable branch, *and as* the raiment of those that are slain, thrust through with a sword, that go down to the stones of the pit; as a carcass trodden under feet.

20 Thou shalt not be joined with them in burial, because thou hast destroyed thy land, *and* slain thy people: the seed of evildoers shall never be renowned.

clothed with the slain, those pierced by
   the sword,
who go down to the stones of the Pit,
   like a dead body trodden under foot.
20 You will not be joined with them in
   burial,
because you have destroyed your land,
   you have slain your people.

"May the descendants of evildoers
   nevermore be named!

---

corpse will not be joined with them in burial, for the tyrant has brought his people to ruin with him. **Evildoers** should be read as a singular, as in the Greek, "the evil-doer"; similarly, "their father." **Fill . . . with cities:** "And spread across the face of the world," omitting **with cities,** which appears to be a textual variant.

---

every hand they saw the judgment meted out to the presumption which ignored or even patronized God. The Bible abounds in illustrations, solemn and lurid, of the fate of those who by their insolence provoked his anger. The Church Fathers in their lists of the seven deadly sins put pride first. So would the Hebrews, because the essence of this sin is to treat God with disdain or actually to defy him. That being so, it is not difficult to make out a case for pride, as the peculiar evil of modern civilization. As humanity increasingly realized its own powers, man took such pride in the work of his own hands that multitudes felt no necessity for God. The philosophy of Humanism was born of an age of scientific achievement. It proclaimed the inherent greatness of man, and denied the need of any power other than his own for salvation. Such a philosophy does not command the respect one may feel for intellectual atheism. Not to believe in God at all is something of an achievement; Humanism simply dismisses God as irrelevant. Pride reaches a pitch of audacity when it reveals contempt for the Almighty. Read modern history in the light of this glorification of man, and all our wars become not regrettable failures in diplomacy, but the judgment of God on human pride. To dismiss God, to leave him out of account in the handling of life, means a steady deterioration in human relationships; arrogance engenders hatred and fear, till the world is full of suspicion, the armaments are piled up, the fatal "incident" occurs, and the earth is on fire. So man in his pride is "brought down to hell" (vs. 15).

Second, in a world which so covets success, the question of what success does to men's souls and to their relationships to others is worth considering. Is the successful man liked? Does he gather friends? Is he feared? Envied? Hated?

Success can be too dearly bought. Our Lord asked a question which still echoes to our world, "What shall it profit a man, if he shall gain the whole world, and lose"—his friends? his faith? his soul? (Mark 8:36). There is a charming verse in the Psalms: "They that fear thee will be glad when they see me" (Ps. 119:74). Contrast the pure joy of being wanted and welcome with the fate of the dead king in this chapter. He won the supremacy of his world; he had everything—unlimited treasure, absolute power, undisputed possession of human lives. But at what a cost! On a bloodstained throne he sat, friendless, feared, forlorn, and when he died the world echoed with thanksgiving that he was gone, and all men celebrated his death with curses. That is not likely to be our fate, yet it confronts every man with the question of what he is paying for his success in the capital of the spirit and the treasures of human friendship.

Third, occasionally we ought to talk about death, especially since Christ has given us something to say about it. Vss. 10-11 remind us that death abolishes all pretensions of rank and station. Sir Walter Raleigh wrote these magnificent words:

O eloquent, just, and mighty Death! whom none could advise, thou hast persuaded; what none hath dared, thou hast done; and whom all the world hath flattered, thou only hast cast out of the world and despised;—thou hast drawn together all the far-stretched greatness, all the pride, cruelty, and ambition of men, and covered it all over with these two narrow words, *Hic jacet.*[6]

Dying is one experience all men share, and

   Golden lads and girls all must,
   As chimney-sweepers, come to dust.[7]

[6] *History of the World,* Bk. V, ch. vi, sec. 12.
[7] Shakespeare, *Cymbeline,* Act IV, scene 2.

21 Prepare slaughter for his children for the iniquity of their fathers; that they do not rise, nor possess the land, nor fill the face of the world with cities.

22 For I will rise up against them, saith the Lord of hosts, and cut off from Babylon the name, and remnant, and son, and nephew, saith the Lord.

23 I will also make it a possession for the bittern, and pools of water: and I will sweep it with the besom of destruction, saith the Lord of hosts.

24 ¶ The Lord of hosts hath sworn,

---

21 Prepare slaughter for his sons
    because of the guilt of their fathers,
lest they rise and possess the earth,
    and fill the face of the world with
    cities."

22 "I will rise up against them," says the Lord of hosts, "and will cut off from Babylon name and remnant, offspring and posterity, says the Lord. 23 And I will make it a possession of the hedgehog, and pools of water, and I will sweep it with the broom of destruction, says the Lord of hosts."

24 The Lord of hosts has sworn:
    "As I have planned,

22-23. The prose conclusion added by the editor to underline the application of the poem to Babylon; the form is that of an oracle in which Yahweh is the speaker. **Remnant,** *she'ār,* should be read *she'ēr,* "blood relative." With this picture of the abandoned and desolate site of the city cf. 13:20-22; 34:10-15. What creature is meant by קפד, translated **bittern** and **hedgehog** is uncertain; it is mentioned only in connection with desolate places (cf. 34:11; Zeph. 2:14; English translators perforce make approximate identifications of Palestinian fauna and flora with forms familiar to their readers).

C. The Divine Purpose in Assyria's Overthrow (14:24-27)

With this short doom oracle we are back again in the time and circumstances of the Assyrian attack on Judah referred to in 10:5-16, 24-27. Although it may not have reached us in quite its original form, the substance of the oracle is undoubtedly Isaiah's.

Do we ever take time to consider what life would be like if that were the final truth about us? The pathos of the O.T. is in its despair over death; for apart from a few gleams of light, there is a great pervading darkness. If the O.T. does not pronounce death as obliteration, the best it can surmise is some insubstantial existence in a shadowy land. Save for some elect souls who dared to believe that death is not the end, the O.T. writers have no hope. At the last they have to bid farewell to God himself and go down to the gray and dismal land. And we should have no reason to think otherwise of death but for Jesus Christ. The Christian church has come down the ages singing not alone for forgiveness, but for eternal life. There is no greater word for men who in their own homes have known the visitation of death, and must someday face it themselves, than this, "Jesus Christ . . . hath abolished death, and hath brought life and immortality to light" (II Tim. 1:10). Now we can believe that "No work begun shall ever pause for death."[8] Now we can gird ourselves to face its dreaded dissolution, knowing that it will be but a little darkness before a

[8] Browning, *The Ring and the Book,* "Pompilia."

great light, a short pause in an immortal energy. Whatever the conditions of life in the better country, we know and are persuaded that it will be forever with the Lord, and with those who for a little have been parted from us; not the dreary stagnation of Sheol but the glory of going on, all the stir and business of the city of God where "there shall be no more death, neither sorrow, nor crying" (Rev. 21:4). *Sursum corda!* There is to be a homecoming of the children of God, and from the peace of that place we shall not go out any more. Blessed be God, who "hath begotten us again" to this living hope! (I Pet. 1:3).

22-23. The Fall of Babylon.—These verses constitute the editor's prose conclusion to the oracle. They make it unmistakably clear that the application is to Babylon. The royal line is to be cut off root and branch, and the proud city itself reduced to utter desolation. When God's besom of destruction has done its work, there will be nothing left but ruin, stagnant pools, and furtive creatures of the wild.

24-32. The Lord Reigneth.—In vss. 24-27 is a short doom oracle referring to the time and circumstance of the Assyrian attack, which is

saying, Surely as I have thought, so shall it come to pass; and as I have purposed, *so* shall it stand:

25 That I will break the Assyrian in my land, and upon my mountains tread him under foot: then shall his yoke depart from off them, and his burden depart from off their shoulders.

26 This *is* the purpose that is purposed upon the whole earth: and this *is* the hand that is stretched out upon all the nations.

27 For the LORD of hosts hath purposed, and who shall disannul *it?* and his hand *is* stretched out, and who shall turn it back?

28 In the year that king Ahaz died was this burden.

so shall it be,
and as I have purposed,
so shall it stand,
25 that I will break the Assyrian in my land,
and upon my mountains trample him
under foot;
and his yoke shall depart from them,
and his burden from their shoulder."
26 This is the purpose that is purposed
concerning the whole earth;
and this is the hand that is stretched out
over all the nations.
27 For the LORD of hosts has purposed,
and who will annul it?
His hand is stretched out,
and who will turn it back?

28 In the year that King Ahaz died came
this oracle:

It comes from the same situation as 10:5-16, 24-27, and is probably the conclusion of the former passage. Here Isaiah's message that Yahweh is Lord of history, and that his purpose is the finally determining factor in what happens, comes to clear expression. It is not the will of God that any conqueror should permanently enslave mankind, for not Judah's deliverance only is in question. And it is altogether appropriate that the clash of the conqueror's will with the fixed purpose and invincible might of the Lord should take place **in my land, and upon my mountains.** Here the issue which concerns all mankind is joined, for the Assyrians in threatening Jerusalem have reached the climax of their arrogant purpose to dominate the world, and have challenged the Lord of the hosts of heaven.

24-25. The LORD . . . has sworn: A threat oracle introduced by a solemn oath else-where in the prophetic books always refers to an immediately preceding condemnation (cf. 5:9; Amos 4:2; 6:8; Jer. 22:5); this makes it highly probable that this passage has been accidentally separated from 10:5-16, to the thought of which it is so closely related. **Planned** is better than **thought. Purposed:** The verb is the same as that used in 9:6 (Hebrew 9:5) as an epithet of the messianic king, "Wonderful in purpose." **Stand:** Better, "happen" or "come to pass." **His yoke . . . his burden:** Cf. 9:4 (Hebrew 9:3); 10:27. The Assyrian rule had been oppressive.

26-27. The emphasis, as Procksch remarks (*op. cit.,* p. 180), lies on the double **this;** Yahweh's plan is not only that Assyria should be punished, but that the peoples of the earth should find freedom. Neither the imperialist dreams nor the physical might of any world power can finally subjugate mankind, for they will break themselves against the divine purpose and the strength which undergirds it. It is a message peculiarly relevant in the twentieth century.

D. PREMATURE REJOICING OF PHILISTIA (14:28-32)

This is an unusual and unusually difficult oracle. It is unusual in that it is one of the only three oracles of Isaiah to be precisely dated (cf. 6:1; 20:1), and that it concludes

the subject of 10:5-16, 24-32. The passage itself may be out of place, but not its message. No-where in the book does Isaiah's faith in the Almighty as the Lord of history find clearer expression. The truth proclaimed is of extraordi-

nary relevance to a century which has seen the rise of dictators and governments with world ambitions. Isaiah declares that these have to reckon with God. He takes Assyria as the representa-tive of all conquerors, for the issue is not of one

apparently with a brief dependent oracle to be given to **the messengers of the nation** as a result of the foregoing. The difficulties lie in determining the relationship of the heading and the conclusion to the main body of the oracle, in identifying the historical circumstances and interpreting the symbolism, and in dealing with one possibly crucial corruption of the text.

The interpretation has always turned largely on the reference to the **messengers of the nation**, "an odd expression," Gray calls it, and possibly "the result of corruption" (*Isaiah I-XXXIX*, I, 270). The Greek, Syriac, and Targ. read "nations"; the Greek also reads "kings of," מלכי, for **messengers of,** מלאכי, and omits the last word of the previous verse. The verb **answer** lacks a subject, and the line is unduly short. The text and meaning of vs. 32a are thus too uncertain to justify the interpretation of the oracle as prompted by the arrival at Jerusalem of Philistine envoys. It is best to take vs. 32 as the concluding couplet of the oracle, affirming the security of Judah through reliance upon Yahweh in contrast to the approaching doom of Philistia set out in vs. 31. In any attempt to restore vs. 32a to its original form—an attempt at best conjectural—the language of 28:16 must be taken into account.

The next problem is to determine the relationship of the heading in vs. 28 to the oracle which follows. One must not jump to the conclusion that it is the death of Ahaz which led to the rejoicing of the Philistines at the breaking of **the rod which smote you,** since (*a*) vs. 28, like 6:1, does not necessarily mean that the king named had already died, but may be only an indication of date; (*b*) there is no evidence that Ahaz had in fact smitten the Philistines, whereas the Assyrians certainly did so; and (*c*) the point of vss. 31-32 is that a common foe from the distant **north** will bring disaster to Philistia but not to Judah. Moreover, this foe in vs. 29 is the same as that which had struck down the Philistines before.

There is considerable uncertainty as to whether the year of Ahaz' death was 720 or 715 (cf. Kemper Fullerton, "Isaiah 14:28-32," *American Journal of Semitic Languages,* XLII [1925-26], 105; Procksch, *op. cit.*, p. 202; cf. Barrois, Vol. I, p. 146). About 720 news had come of a serious check to Assyrian power following the death of Shalmaneser V in 722; the new king, Sargon II, had not yet been able to establish his authority in Syria and Palestine. It looked as if **the rod which smote** might indeed be broken, and about this time the Philistines did join in a coalition organized against Assyria by the king of Hamath. In this oracle Isaiah declares that their rejoicing is premature, for the Assyrians will return to destroy their enemies—as indeed they did. The Philistines have mistaken a temporary reprieve for deliverance; they are a standing example of the folly of wishful thinking in political affairs and of human unwillingness to face squarely the facts of approaching disaster. But even the helpless poor of Judah have a deeper security, for theirs is a "city which has foundations, whose builder and maker is God" (Heb. 11:10).

28. This [doom] **oracle:** The second of the ten oracles designated משא in chs. 13–23 (see Exeg. on 13:1).

---

land or age but of all times. Is history made and controlled by the ambitions of men or by the purpose of God? For a people who have lived through or are living in a period in which men or nations are out to rule the world, it is a steadying thing to hear the great prophet's conviction that no imperialistic dream, no martial might of any world power, can finally subdue or enslave a race which God has created for freedom. The arrogance of men challenging the authority of God will be broken on his divine purpose. He is not on the side of the big bat-

talions, but with those prepared to do his will and serve his cause. At the last it will not be any political ism which is to work its will on mankind, for "the Lord reigneth."

> **For the Lord of hosts has purposed**
>   **and who will annul it?**
> **His hand is stretched out,**
>   **and who will turn it back?**

The chapter closes on that note of unmoved confidence in God. "What," the prophet asks,

29 ¶ Rejoice not thou, whole Palestina, because the rod of him that smote thee is broken: for out of the serpent's root shall come forth a cockatrice, and his fruit *shall be* a fiery flying serpent.

30 And the firstborn of the poor shall feed, and the needy shall lie down in safety: and I will kill thy root with famine, and he shall slay thy remnant.

31 Howl, O gate; cry, O city; thou, whole Palestina, *art* dissolved: for there shall come from the north a smoke, and none *shall be* alone in his appointed times.

32 What shall *one* then answer the messengers of the nation? That the LORD hath founded Zion, and the poor of his people shall trust in it.

15 The burden of Moab. Because in the night Ar of Moab is laid waste, *and* brought to silence; because in the night Kir

---

29 "Rejoice not, O Philistia, all of you,
  that the rod which smote you is broken,
  for from the serpent's root will come
    forth an adder,
  and its fruit will be a flying serpent.

30 And the first-born of the poor will feed,
  and the needy lie down in safety;
  but I will kill your root with famine,
  and your remnant I*ᵃ* will slay.

31 Wail, O gate; cry, O city;
  melt in fear, O Philistia, all of you!
For smoke comes out of the north,
  and there is no straggler in his ranks."

32 What will one answer the messengers of
    the nation?
  "The LORD has founded Zion,
    and in her the afflicted of his people
    find refuge."

15 An oracle concerning Moab.
  Because Ar is laid waste in a night
  Moab is undone;

ᵃ One ancient Ms Vg: Heb he

29-30. Rejoice not, O Philistia, all of you: There is a certain awkwardness in the use of the name of the country for its citizens, which explains the clumsy literal rendering of the KJV (cf. the similar 22:1). **Root . . . fruit:** The figure of a tree applied to a people or dynasty (cf. 11:1; Amos 2:9). The **adder** is one species of the genus **serpent,** and the fabulous **fiery flying serpent** is spoken of as another (cf. 6:2; 30:6). **The first-born of the poor:** Better, "the poor shall feed in my pasture," reading *bekhārî* for *bekhôrê* (with Koppe; cf. Procksch, *op. cit.*, p. 204). The founder of Zion is the shepherd of his people (cf. vs. 32; Ezek. 34:11-16).

31-32. Smoke comes out of the north (cf. Jer. 1:13-15; Ezek. 38:15-16). **Smoke** is here synonymous with "storm cloud" (cf. Ezek. 38:16; Ps. 18:8 [Hebrew 18:9]). The coming of the Assyrians from the ominous and distant north is meant. **No straggler in his ranks:** Cf. the very different translation of KJV. The text is doubtful. On vs. 32 see above.

E. DEATH THROES OF MOAB (15:1–16:14)

There are few passages in the O.T. which convey so little meaning to the modern reader as do these two chapters, beyond the general picture of the people of Moab over-

---

"will one say to the messengers of the oncoming power? How in the face of the enemy's overwhelming strength is a man to bear himself?" This is his answer,

The Lord has founded Zion,
  and in her the afflicted of his people find refuge.

It is the old faith of the martyrs and confessors of all the ages. "God is our refuge and strength,

a very present help in trouble. Therefore will not we fear" (Ps. 46:1-2).

15:1–16:14. An Elegy on Moab.—This obscure oracle directed against Moab is one of a series dealing with foreign nations. Thus far in the book the prophecies have been concerned with the Jewish nation; they have issued from a known historical situation on which God through his servant has pronounced a verdict. It has been in a sense plain sailing; there has

of Moab is laid waste, *and* brought to silence:

2 He is gone up to Bajith, and to Dibon, the high places, to weep: Moab shall howl over Nebo, and over Medeba: on all their heads *shall be* baldness, *and* every beard cut off.

3 In their streets they shall gird themselves with sackcloth: on the tops of their houses, and in their streets, every one shall howl, weeping abundantly.

4 And Heshbon shall cry, and Elealeh; their voice shall be heard *even* unto Jahaz: therefore the armed soldiers of Moab shall cry out; his life shall be grievous unto him.

5 My heart shall cry out for Moab; his fugitives *shall flee* unto Zoar, a heifer of three years old: for by the mounting up of Luhith with weeping shall they go it up; for in the way of Horonaim they shall raise up a cry of destruction.

because Kir is laid waste in a night
    Moab is undone.
2 The daughter of Dibon[b] has gone up
    to the high places to weep;
    over Nebo and over Med'eba
    Moab wails.
On every head is baldness,
    every beard is shorn;
3 in the streets they gird on sackcloth;
    on the housetops and in the squares
    every one wails and melts in tears.
4 Heshbon and Elea'leh cry out,
    their voice is heard as far as Jahaz;
therefore the armed men of Moab cry
    aloud;
    his soul trembles.
5 My heart cries out for Moab;
    his fugitives flee to Zo'ar,
    to Eg'lath-shelish'iyah.
For at the ascent of Luhith
    they go up weeping;
    on the road to Horona'im
    they raise a cry of destruction;

[b] Cn: Heb *the house and Dibon*

---

whelmed by some great disaster. Scholars are in little better case, as is evident from the major commentaries. Text and translation are in many places uncertain, the literary structure (especially its relationship to a second form of the poem in Jer. 48) is perplexing, and the historical circumstances referred to are obscure.

From the fact that much of 16:6-11, plus 15:2-7, reappears in Jer. 48:29-38 (but not the intervening section 15:8–16:5), and from the further fact that 16:1-5 differs in tone from what precedes and follows it, it appears that we have in both books recensions of the same anonymous elegy over Moab. In Isaiah this elegy is preserved in three strophes (15:1-5a, 5b-9; 16:7-11). The third strophe has been enclosed, as it were, in quotation marks, 16:6 and 16:12, and is thus treated as a prophetic "word," referred to in vs. 13 as having been uttered at some time prior to a new doom oracle in vs. 14. The interpolated section (16:1-5) contains what appears to be an appeal by Moabite refugees for sanctuary in Judah, concluding with a verse of messianic promise which juts out of the context like a rock out of the sea.

The uncertainty of the text and the inconclusiveness of the linguistic and historical indications have resulted in the ascription of the elegy to periods ranging from the ninth century (Hitzig credited it to the prophet Jonah) to the second. If the concluding verses (16:13-14) are by Isaiah, as is quite possible, the earlier oracle referred to may also be his own, although 16:13 suggests rather that he is quoting an earlier prophet.

15:1-9. The first two strophes of the elegy over the sudden overwhelming of the Moabite kingdom. **Because:** Rather, "Yea." For the naming of particular localities to

---

been little obscurity about the references, and certainly none as to the message. Now, however, we come on a perfect jungle of oracles, obscure to the point of being meaningless to us. The Exeg. must needs plow its laborious way through

corrupt text, linguistic anomalies, and baffling references. Any man bold enough to attempt an exposition of these chapters can look for little help from the exegetes, many of whom are frank enough to say, "We don't know what this

6 For the waters of Nimrim shall be desolate: for the hay is withered away, the grass faileth, there is no green thing.

7 Therefore the abundance they have gotten, and that which they have laid up, shall they carry away to the brook of the willows.

8 For the cry is gone round about the borders of Moab; the howling thereof unto Eglaim, and the howling thereof unto Beer-elim.

9 For the waters of Dimon shall be full of blood: for I will bring more upon Dimon, lions upon him that escapeth of Moab, and upon the remnant of the land.

6 the waters of Nimrim
   are a desolation;
the grass is withered, the new growth
   fails,
   the verdure is no more.
7 Therefore the abundance they have
   gained
   and what they have laid up
they carry away
   over the Brook of the Willows.
8 For a cry has gone
   round the land of Moab;
the wailing reaches to Egla'im,
   the wailing reaches to Beer-e'lim.
9 For the waters of Dibon[c] are full of
   blood;
   yet I will bring upon Dibon[c] even
   more,
a lion for those of Moab who escape,
   for the remnant of the land.

16 Send ye the lamb to the ruler of the land from Sela to the wilderness, unto the mount of the daughter of Zion.

2 For it shall be, *that,* as a wandering bird cast out of the nest, *so* the daughters of Moab shall be at the fords of Arnon.

3 Take counsel, execute judgment; make thy shadow as the night in the midst of the noonday; hide the outcasts; bewray not him that wandereth.

16 They have sent lambs
   to the ruler of the land,
from Sela, by way of the desert,
   to the mount of the daughter of Zion.
2 Like fluttering birds,
   like scattered nestlings,
so are the daughters of Moab
   at the fords of the Arnon.
3 "Give counsel,
   grant justice;
make your shade like night
   at the height of noon;
hide the outcasts,
   betray not the fugitive;

[c] One ancient Ms Vg Compare Syr: Heb *Dimon*

give a general picture cf. 10:28-32. The poet's eye moves from south to north, but this need not imply that the invasion came from the south. **Over the Brook of the Willows:** The desperate refugees with their pitiful loads of possessions flee across this deep valley, usually identified with the Wadi el-Ḥesā or Brook Zered, which long formed the boundary between Moab and Edom. **The waters of Dibon:** An improbable correction of the KJV, since Dibon did not stand on any large stream, and this city has already been named in vs. 2. Even beyond their borders destruction will pursue the Moabites. For lion, 'aryēh, read, "I will drench," 'arawweh, i.e., with blood (cf. 16:9).

16:1-5. The refugees send an appeal to Judah for sanctuary from their temporary refuge at **Sela** in Edom. The appeal is supported by a present of **lambs**, the principal

means." The expositor will therefore be well advised to abandon the hope of dealing in any detail with these strange oracles, and devote himself to such passages as suggest some truth which has a validity quite apart from its immediate context; e.g., in 16:3-4 there is the cry of the outcast which forever echoes through this world. Whether one thinks of the vast and tragic

4 Let mine outcasts dwell with thee, Moab; be thou a covert to them from the face of the spoiler: for the extortioner is at an end, the spoiler ceaseth, the oppressors are consumed out of the land.

5 And in mercy shall the throne be established: and he shall sit upon it in truth in the tabernacle of David, judging, and seeking judgment, and hasting righteousness.

6 ¶ We have heard of the pride of Moab; *he is* very proud: *even* of his haughtiness, and his pride, and his wrath: *but* his lies *shall* not *be* so.

7 Therefore shall Moab howl for Moab, every one shall howl: for the foundations of Kir-hareseth shall ye mourn; surely *they are* stricken.

8 For the fields of Heshbon languish, *and* the vine of Sibmah: the lords of the heathen have broken down the principal plants thereof, they are come *even* unto Jazer, they wandered *through* the wilderness: her branches are stretched out, they are gone over the sea.

9 ¶ Therefore I will bewail with the weeping of Jazer the vine of Sibmah: I will

---

4 let the outcasts of Moab
  sojourn among you;
be a refuge to them
  from the destroyer.
When the oppressor is no more,
  and destruction has ceased,
and he who tramples under foot
  has vanished from the land,
5 then a throne will be established in stead-
    fast love
  and on it will sit in faithfulness
  in the tent of David
one who judges and seeks justice
  and is swift to do righteousness."

6 We have heard of the pride of Moab,
  how proud he was;
of his arrogance, his pride, and his in-
    solence —
  his boasts are false.
7 Therefore let Moab wail,
  let every one wail for Moab.
Mourn, utterly stricken,
  for the raisin-cakes of Kir-har'eseth.

8 For the fields of Heshbon languish,
  and the vine of Sibmah;
the lords of the nations
  have struck down its branches,
which reached to Jazer
  and strayed to the desert;
its shoots spread abroad
  and passed over the sea.
9 Therefore I weep with the weeping of
    Jazer
  for the vine of Sibmah;
I drench you with my tears,

---

product of Moab and the form of tribute formerly paid to Judah (cf. II Kings 3:4). **Scattered nestlings:** "As if emptied out of a nest." Read "from the fords," the place of origin—not the present location—of **the daughters of Moab.** Vss. 4c-5 form the conclusion of the appeal, on the ground that mercy shown now will establish more firmly the authority of the dynasty of David. The language is so markedly that of Jewish messianism (cf. 9:7 [Hebrew 9:6]; Ps. 89:19-37 [Hebrew 89:20-38]) that the appearance of an appeal by Moabites is forgotten.

6-12. The third strophe of the elegy, vss. 7-11, picturing the disaster in terms particularly of the desolation of the vineyards, is here enclosed by the introductory vs. 6 and the concluding vs. 12, declaring that the pride of Moab is the cause of her

---

multitudes of displaced persons in a postwar age who plead for sanctuary in lands unravished; or of the unnumbered throng of weary and embittered men, victims of an order of life which has not done justly or loved mercy; or of

spiritual exiles, fugitives from their own pursuing shame, this passage confronts those who call themselves Christians with the duty of compassion toward all homeless and friendless folk, in the name of One who goes "after that which

water thee with my tears, O Heshbon, and Elealeh: for the shouting for thy summer fruits and for thy harvest is fallen.

10 And gladness is taken away, and joy out of the plentiful field; and in the vineyards there shall be no singing, neither shall there be shouting: the treaders shall tread out no wine in *their* presses; I have made *their vintage* shouting to cease.

11 Wherefore my bowels shall sound like a harp for Moab, and mine inward parts for Kir-haresh.

12 ¶ And it shall come to pass, when it is seen that Moab is weary on the high place, that he shall come to his sanctuary to pray; but he shall not prevail.

13 This *is* the word that the LORD hath spoken concerning Moab since that time.

14 But now the LORD hath spoken, saying, Within three years, as the years of a hireling, and the glory of Moab shall be contemned, with all that great multitude; and the remnant *shall be* very small *and* feeble.

O Heshbon and Elea'leh;
for upon your fruit and your harvest
   the battle shout has fallen.

10 And joy and gladness are taken away
   from the fruitful field;
and in the vineyards no songs are sung,
   no shouts are raised;
no treader treads out wine in the presses;
   the vintage shout is hushed.[d]

11 Therefore my soul moans like a lyre for
      Moab,
   and my heart for Kir-he'res.

12 And when Moab presents himself,
when he wearies himself upon the high place, when he comes to his sanctuary to pray, he will not prevail.

13 This is the word which the LORD spoke concerning Moab in the past. 14 But now the LORD says, "In three years, like the years of a hireling, the glory of Moab will be brought into contempt, in spite of all his great multitude, and those who survive will be very few and feeble."

[d] Gk: Heb *I have hushed*

---

trouble and that prayer to the gods of Moab will not bring deliverance. **Let Moab wail:** Better, "must Moab wail." In vs. 11 add "like a flute," from the parallel verse in Jer. 48:36. With vs. 12, cf. I Kings 18:25-29.

13-14. This is the word must refer to what immediately precedes, since it is contrasted with what follows (cf. 30:12). Vs. 14 says that just as formerly Moab's prayer for deliverance was not to be answered, so now in a time of her prosperity a further disaster is at hand. **Like the years of a hireling:** Better, "a wage-laborer," who works for a previously specified time and no longer (cf. 21:16).

---

is lost, until he find it" and brings it to the shelter of his love (Luke 15:4-7).

16:12. Worship—an Affront?—Under the figure of Moab, worn out with unavailing worship, there is presented the truth that while God is the hearer of prayer, not all prayers can be answered. Indeed, the Bible makes it clear that the spiritual condition of a man may be such as actually to result in his prayer being an abomination to God (Prov. 28:9). In Ps. 66:18 it is written, "If I regard iniquity in my heart, the Lord will not hear me." Our Lord in the Sermon on the Mount declared that until a man was right with his fellows, he could never be right with God (Matt. 5:23-24). No wonder Moab wrestled in vain on the hilltop.

We have heard of the pride of Moab,
   how proud he was;
of his arrogance, his pride, and his insolence—
   his boasts are false (vs. 6).

People in that condition need not expect to have their prayers answered; their worship is an affront to God. Christian faith proclaims that all true prayer is heard and answered by God. That does not mean, however, that all our petitions are to be granted. God will deal with us as his love deems best, and we may pray in vain for some things, because God has something else in mind for us. Nevertheless true prayer, the prayer of the believing heart and the obedient spirit, is always answered. Therefore, when like Moab we fling out our importunate supplications, the heavens are as brass and there is no sign from God, then is the time not to rail against the God who does not care, or to become cynical about prayer itself. Then is the time to look into our own hearts, to discover there the sin which accounts for our unanswered prayer. Prayer is always spiritually conditioned. The man who declares defiantly that he has given up prayer because it never works proves nothing about God but reveals much about himself.

17 The burden of Damascus. Behold, Damascus is taken away from *being* a city, and it shall be a ruinous heap.

2 The cities of Aroer *are* forsaken: they shall be for flocks, which shall lie down, and none shall make *them* afraid.

3 The fortress also shall cease from Ephraim, and the kingdom from Damascus, and the remnant of Syria: they shall be as the glory of the children of Israel, saith the LORD of hosts.

4 And in that day it shall come to pass, *that* the glory of Jacob shall be made thin, and the fatness of his flesh shall wax lean.

5 And it shall be as when the harvestman gathereth the corn, and reapeth the ears with his arm; and it shall be as he that gathereth ears in the valley of Rephaim.

6 ¶ Yet gleaning grapes shall be left in it, as the shaking of an olive tree, two *or* three berries in the top of the uppermost bough, four *or* five in the outmost fruitful branches thereof, saith the LORD God of Israel.

17 An oracle concerning Damascus.
Behold, Damascus will cease to be a city,
and will become a heap of ruins.
2 Her cities will be deserted for ever;[e]
they will be for flocks,
which will lie down, and none will make them afraid.
3 The fortress will disappear from E'phraim,
and the kingdom from Damascus;
and the remnant of Syria will be
like the glory of the children of Israel,
says the LORD of hosts.

4 And in that day
the glory of Jacob will be brought low,
and the fat of his flesh will grow lean.
5 And it shall be as when the reaper gathers standing grain
and his arm harvests the ears,
and as when one gleans the ears of grain
in the valley of Reph'aim.
6 Gleanings will be left in it,
as when an olive tree is beaten —
two or three berries
in the top of the highest bough,
four or five
on the branches of a fruit tree,
says the LORD God of Israel.

e Cn Compare Gk: Heb *the cities of Aroer are deserted*

F. DOOM OF THE SYRO-EPHRAIMITE ALLIANCE (17:1-6)

This passage should be studied in conjunction with 7:1–8:4, where Isaiah similarly affirms that the threat to Judah by her allied neighbors, Damascus and Ephraim (northern Israel), will be brought to nothing. The date is *ca.* 734 B.C. Most, but not all, commentators regard vss. 7-11 or vss. 9-11 as part of the oracle or oracles in vss. 1-6. This is improbable, because in no other instance does Isaiah address himself directly in the second person to Ephraim, and the twin oracles in vss. 1-6 are complete without what follows. Moreover, the language of vss. 7-11 has points of contact with other oracles addressed to Judah and Jerusalem (cf. 31:1; 22:11; 1:29).

17:1-3. The fourth "doom oracle." That these headings are editorial is evident from the fact that only the city first named in the oracle, Damascus, is named here. **Fortress ... kingdom:** Concrete terms for the abstract ideas "military strength" and "sovereignty." **Cities of Aroer** is a corruption, as the Greek shows, of **cities ... for ever.** For **and the remnant ... like the glory,** read, "like the remnant [כשאר] shall be the glory."

4-6. **As when an olive tree is beaten:** Better "shaken" (cf. KJV).

17:1-14. *Two Oracles of Doom.*—The first oracle (vss. 1-11) is on the approaching doom of the Syro-Ephraimite alliance. The unity of this passage is broken by the insertion in vss. 7-8 of a fragment of another oracle which has no real connection either with what precedes or follows

it. The second oracle (vss. 12-14) foretells the sudden annihilation of the Assyrians.

1-6. *The Doom of Damascus.*—There is a wealth of imagery in the prophet's description of the fate of Damascus and Ephraim. Those who heard Isaiah could never complain that they

7 At that day shall a man look to his Maker, and his eyes shall have respect to the Holy One of Israel.

8 And he shall not look to the altars, the work of his hands, neither shall respect *that* which his fingers have made, either the groves, or the images.

9 ¶ In that day shall his strong cities be as a forsaken bough, and an uppermost branch, which they left because of the children of Israel: and there shall be desolation.

7 In that day men will regard their Maker, and their eyes will look to the Holy One of Israel; 8 they will not have regard for the altars, the work of their hands, and they will not look to what their own fingers have made, either the Ashe'rim or the altars of incense.

9 In that day their strong cities will be like the deserted places of the Hivites and the Amorites,*f* which they deserted because of the children of Israel, and there will be desolation.

f Cn Compare Gk: Heb *the wood and the highest bough*

G. Idolatrous Worship (17:7-11)

1. A Turning from Idols (17:7-8)

7-8. A fragment of an oracle, the opening of which has been lost, since there is no connection in thought with what precedes. It has been introduced here because of a loose connection in idea with the following and quite distinct oracle. The language, with its reference to God as man's **Maker** and to **men** as "mankind," points to a time later than Isaiah. **The Asherim** or **groves:** Cult symbols of the goddess Asherah, probably wooden poles appropriately carved, or idols representing her (cf. William L. Reed, *The Asherah in the Old Testament* [Fort Worth: Texas Christian University Press, 1949]). **Altars of incense,** not **images,** is correct.

2. The Adonis Cult, a False Security (17:9-11)

Desolation will come to the cities of Judah because they have abandoned the worship of Yahweh for the fertility cult of Adonis. This widespread cult of the vegetation god, who died and rose to life each year, had as one of its rites the forced growth of seedlings in pots or baskets, as a form of sympathetic magic intended to bring back to life the dead god and to stimulate the general growth of vegetation. The point of the passage is that man is incurably religious, and if he forsakes a real faith he will develop a substitute religion or lapse into the grossest superstition. But the harvest will correspond to the sowing (cf. Gal. 6:7).

9. Their strong cities: Read "thy," following Greek and corresponding to the second person in vss. 10-11. **The Hivites and the Amorites:** The reading preserved in Greek makes

could not understand him, for all his images were drawn from the life of the common people. Here we have such pictures as a deserted village, with sheep among the ruins (vs. 2); a wasting disease (vs. 4); a farmer reaping (vs. 5); the gathering of olives (vs. 6). Each conveys in vivid fashion the idea of irretrievable ruin.

7-8. *The Consternation of Men.*—These two verses constitute a kind of aside in which Isaiah speaks of the profound impression made on men by the demonstration of God's righteous anger. There is a general abandonment of idolatry and a wistful turning to God, the hope of the world. As already noted, however, the verses break the continuity of the oracle.

9-11. *The Failure of the Gods.*—These verses deal with the inevitable disillusionment which results from trusting in foreign gods. In particular the Adonis cult and certain practices

associated with it are mentioned. The apostasy of his nation affected Isaiah in various ways. Sometimes it evoked his contempt, sometimes his hot anger, or again the sorrow of an anguished spirit. In this oracle there is singularly little passion. With a serene faith in the righteousness of God, he simply declares in unmistakable imagery the inevitable outcome of any alliance which involves giving up faith in Yahweh and becoming involved in heathen religions. Two verses in the oracle rise above the local and the contemporary to speak to our generation.

(a) **Because thou hast forgotten the God of thy salvation, and hast not been mindful of the Rock of thy strength, therefore . . . .** Let the reader conclude the sentence. What has happened in this century? What must always happen at the last when men leave God out of account? As has been repeatedly urged by

10 Because thou hast forgotten the God of thy salvation, and hast not been mindful of the Rock of thy strength, therefore shalt thou plant pleasant plants, and shalt set it with strange slips:

11 In the day shalt thou make thy plant to grow, and in the morning shalt thou make thy seed to flourish: *but* the harvest *shall be* a heap in the day of grief and of desperate sorrow.

12 ¶ Woe to the multitude of many people, *which* make a noise like the noise of

10 For you have forgotten the God of your salvation,
    and have not remembered the Rock of your refuge;
therefore, though you plant pleasant plants
    and set out slips of an alien god,
11 though you make them grow on the day that you plant them,
    and make them blossom in the morning that you sow;
yet the harvest will flee away
    in a day of grief and incurable pain.

12 Ah, the thunder of many peoples,
    they thunder like the thundering of the sea!

---

sense where the Hebrew does not; these are representatives of the peoples displaced by Israel in Canaan (cf. Judg. 3:5; Amos 2:9-10).

10-11. For should be **because,** introducing a protasis. **Rock of your refuge:** A well-known figure to express the impregnable strength of God (cf. Deut. 32:31); the word means not a boulder but a height or cliff of rock. **Pleasant plants:** Lit., "gardens of the desirable one." Doubtless the fertility deity is intended; Adonis was his Hellenized form; his name in Israel was more probably Dod (cf. Song of S. 1:13, 14, 16, *et passim*). **An alien god:** Lit., "a strange one." No matter how successful is the forced growth of the plants, **the harvest** will "be blown away" in a storm of **grief.**

H. RISING AND PASSING OF THE STORM (17:12-14)

This brief but vivid oracle may well have followed originally upon 14:24-27, since it shares the atmosphere of, and is a suitable sequel to, that pledge of the overthrow of

---

serious minds, the truth is that the crucial problems of modern civilization are all basically religious. It is the neglect of God, indifference to his proclaimed will, unbelief in his power and purpose, which lie behind our wars, our economic strife, our national distrust, our confusion, and our fear.

(*b*) **But the harvest shall be a heap** [shall disappear] **in the day of grief and of desperate sorrow.** The emphasis is not on the inescapable moral law of sowing and reaping, but rather on the truth that the final test of life is **in the day of grief and of desperate sorrow.** Such a day comes to all men; none can evade it. The crucial question is whether a man has a faith which can stand up to it. To meet sorrow victoriously makes far deeper demands on faith than do adversity, frustration, or physical pain. Sorrow raises questions to which there is no answer this side of death; questions about what lies beyond the grave, about the condition of those we have "loved long since, and lost awhile," questions about the love of God. It is the supreme tragedy of the soul if the harvest of all its striving,

planning, hoping, should disappear in the day of desperate sorrow, leaving that soul to face death's separation embittered, forsaken, and alone. "Where shall wisdom be found?" asks the book of Job (28:12); our question is "Where shall faith be found? Faith equal to the strain of life's cruelties and griefs, faith to furnish courage, quicken hope, and give us peace?" The answer has everything to do with the love that will not let us go, and with Jesus Christ who has made it known. Those who trust in the love of God are not immune to grief; for them also there is a **day . . . of desperate sorrow.** But its darkness is lighted by an immortal hope, and the harvest of their faith, so far from disappearing, comes to its glory in their being able to say, "I know whom I have believed, and am persuaded that he is able to keep that which I have committed unto him against that day" (II Tim. 1:12).

12-14. *The Tide of Terror.*—These verses are notable not for their didactic value but for their poetic power. In the whole book of Isaiah there is no finer illustration of what is termed ono-

the seas; and to the rushing of nations, *that* make a rushing like the rushing of mighty waters!

13 The nations shall rush like the rushing of many waters: but *God* shall rebuke them, and they shall flee far off, and shall be chased as the chaff of the mountains before the wind, and like a rolling thing before the whirlwind.

14 And behold at eveningtide trouble; *and* before the morning he *is* not. This *is* the portion of them that spoil us, and the lot of them that rob us.

Ah, the roar of nations,
   they roar like the roaring of mighty
     waters!
13 The nations roar like the roaring of
   many waters,
   but he will rebuke them, and they will
     flee far away,
chased like chaff on the mountains before
     the wind
   and whirling dust before the storm.
14 At evening time, behold, terror!
   Before morning, they are no more!
This is the portion of those who despoil
     us,
   and the lot of those who plunder us.

18 Woe to the land shadowing with wings, which *is* beyond the rivers of Ethiopia:

18 Ah, land of whirring wings
   which is beyond the rivers of Ethiopia;

---

the Assyrian hosts which threatened Jerusalem in 701. At the same time it must be said that the **many peoples** may refer, not to the national contingents making up the Assyrian army, but to the restless vassals of Assyria in the west who more than once sought to force Judah to join them in rebellion. The date and precise occasion of the passage must remain uncertain, but there is no sound reason to doubt that its author was Isaiah. Like a gale upon the alien sea the enemy threaten, but as by a storm on the familiar hills they will be dispersed. Literally overnight the situation will change completely; in 37:36 a later chronicler describes the discomfiture of the hosts of Sennacherib in similar terms. It was in the night, traditionally, that Yahweh had smitten the first-born of Egypt (cf. Exod. 12:29-31); and like "a vision of the night" the assailants of Ariel would vanish (cf. 29:7-8).

12-14. Ah and **Woe** are equally unsuitable for the cry of derision, הוֹי. "Shame!" will hardly do here, since the **peoples** are not reproached for any specific wrongdoing; indeed, since this oracle is a threat rather than a reproach, הוי may represent an original הנה, "Lo!" or "Hark!" as in 1:24 (cf. הנה in 17:1). The first line of vs. 13 is a mistaken repetition of all but the first word of vs. 12*b*; it should be omitted, with eight Hebrew MSS and the Syriac. **Whirling dust** is better than the vague **rolling thing** of the KJV. "In the evening, there is terror! Before morning, they are no more!" **The portion:** I.e., "the fate."

J. CONCERNING EGYPT (18:1–20:6)
1. REPLY TO THE CUSHITE ENVOYS (18:1-7)

In spite of the many perplexities which beset the interpreter of this passage, there is a magnificence of language and imagery and a depth of perception and faith which accord

---

matopoeia, i.e., the wedding of sound to sense. Isaiah compares the chaos of the nation to the onward rush of the surf. The Hebrew words reverberate with the boom and roar of the waters. The use of sibilants is particularly effective, and in vs. 13 the long-drawn *yishshā'ûn* vividly suggests the hiss of a great wave withdrawing from the beach. One can actually hear the sound of a comber, sweeping on in a smother of foam, to crash with boiling tumult

on the sand. In the midst of all the welter of human passion, Isaiah declares, the rock of Yahweh's strength stands unmoved, and the noisy strife of men will break on it in vain. **God shall rebuke them, and they shall flee far off.** It is well to remember in any day of confusion that amid the crash of human forces there is still that rock of ages, that sovereign God.

18:1-7. *The Watching and Waiting God.*— The occasion of this splendid oracle was the

2 That sendeth ambassadors by the sea, even in vessels of bulrushes upon the waters, *saying,* Go, ye swift messengers, to a nation scattered and peeled, to a people terrible from their beginning hitherto; a nation meted out and trodden down, whose land the rivers have spoiled!	2 which sends ambassadors by the Nile, in vessels of papyrus upon the waters! Go, you swift messengers, to a nation, tall and smooth, to a people feared near and far, a nation mighty and conquering, whose land the rivers divide.

well with the noblest of Isaiah's utterances. These verses set forth under dramatic circumstances the sublime faith of the prophet that the Lord is the ultimate arbiter of the issues between nations, and that men must wait in faith until he gives the signal for the final overthrow of the (Assyrian) tyranny. To the Cushite or Ethiopian envoys who have come, apparently, to seek Judah's participation in a general revolt (vss. 1-2a), he gives a message to be conveyed to their people whom he describes in the flattering language of diplomacy (vs. 2bcd). The message (vs. 3) is addressed to them and to all peoples under the Assyrian yoke; it is that they are to wait for the signal which Yahweh will give when the time comes for the great revolt. The message given is prompted by a "private oracle" which has come to the prophet, telling him that Yahweh is watching as in the stillness of summer on the eve of harvest (vs. 4). And so when he is ready, the harvesting will begin; it is pictured first figuratively (vs. 5) and then literally (vs. 6). To the oracle proper a later editor has added an assurance, curiously out of keeping with it, that in days to come the people of Cush—like other peoples in 19:21; 60:4-14; Zech. 14:16-19—will bring tribute to Yahweh and to his sanctuary in Zion.

The occasion of the oracle may be inferred from the two circumstances that a new Ethiopian dynasty (the twenty-fifth) was established in Egypt about 714 B.C., and that shortly afterward the intrigues of Egypt led to a revolt against Assyria by Philistia, Judah, Moab, and Edom. The revolt collapsed when Sargon in 711 took stern action against the Philistine cities, notably Ashdod (cf. 20:1). Judah does not appear to have been touched. It may be that, due to Isaiah's influence, her part had not gone beyond what Sargon would regard as treasonable correspondence, the reception of envoys from Egypt's new Ethiopian dynasty which is pictured in ch. 18.

18:1-2a. The הוי of the typical reproach oracle appears here in a weakened sense, simply as a striking form of address, "Ho!" **Land shadowing with wings** or **land of whirring wings:** A presumed reference to the insect-ridden Nile Delta. But the rare word צלצל more probably means "boat," "ship," as in LXX and Targ. (cf. G. R. Driver, "Difficult Words in the Hebrew Prophets," in *Studies in Old Testament Prophecy,* ed. H. H. Rowley [New York: Charles Scribner's Sons, 1950], p. 56): "land of the winged ship." Egyptian river craft used sails as well as oars from an early date. **Beyond the rivers:** I.e., stretching beyond the upper reaches of the Nile. **By the sea** is parallel with **upon the waters;** doubtless the Nile is in the speaker's mind, but that does not justify the prosaic identification of the RSV. **Vessels of papyrus:** The paper made from reeds or **bulrushes;** timber was scarce in the Nile Valley, and light boats of basketwork covered with pitch, "papyrus canoes," were much used.

2bcd. Tall and smooth is at least more comprehensible than **scattered and peeled;** Herodotus (*History* III. 20) describes the Ethiopians as "tallest and fairest of men" and the epithets here are certainly intended as compliments. **Smooth:** I.e., with bodies burnished with oil. **Whose land the rivers divide:** A poetic plural for the Nile (cf. 7:18).

arrival in Jerusalem of ambassadors from Ethiopia to confer on the Assyrian menace. Only such a master of style as Isaiah could contrive to give in so few words so vivid a picture of a land and its people. We see them come, noble bronzed warriors from the land of many waters	and of winged ships; there is a dignity and authority in their bearing as befits the messengers of a victorious king. All Jerusalem must have taken heart to know that these people were with them in their defense. Isaiah's eye, however, is never held by the earthly scene, but is

3 All ye inhabitants of the world, and dwellers on the earth, see ye, when he lifteth up an ensign on the mountains; and when he bloweth a trumpet, hear ye.

4 For so the LORD said unto me, I will take my rest, and I will consider in my dwelling place like a clear heat upon herbs, *and* like a cloud of dew in the heat of harvest.

5 For afore the harvest, when the bud is perfect, and the sour grape is ripening in the flower, he shall both cut off the sprigs with pruning hooks, and take away *and* cut down the branches.

6 They shall be left together unto the fowls of the mountains, and to the beasts of the earth: and the fowls shall summer upon them, and all the beasts of the earth shall winter upon them.

3 All you inhabitants of the world,
  you who dwell on the earth,
when a signal is raised on the mountains,
  look!
When a trumpet is blown, hear!
4 For thus the LORD said to me:
"I will quietly look from my dwelling
  like clear heat in sunshine,
like a cloud of dew in the heat of
  harvest."
5 For before the harvest, when the blossom
  is over,
  and the flower becomes a ripening
  grape,
he will cut off the shoots with pruning
  hooks,
  and the spreading branches he will hew
  away.
6 They shall all of them be left
  to the birds of prey of the mountains
  and to the beasts of the earth.
And the birds of prey will summer upon
  them,
  and all the beasts of the earth will winter upon them.

---

3. The world: The whole expanse of the world then subject to Assyria.

4. The picture is of the immeasurably exalted One, calm and watchful above the turmoil of earth. The two similes emphasize the exaltation of the divine **dwelling place** by reference to a dazzling glow in Yahweh's abode beyond the light of day, and to the cloud, so lofty as to be unseen, from which comes the **dew** [so the poet surmises] **in the heat of harvest.**

5-6. Harvest: The general term meaning primarily the reaping of field crops, but sometimes used, as here, of the vintage. **Before** the fruit of Assyria's power is ripe—but

---

lifted to another and mightier throne; always when he had heard the words of man, he speaks the Word of God.

The oracle which follows is addressed not alone to the Ethiopian court but to all the nations threatened by Assyrian power. It is a picture of the watching and waiting God. Over against the human plans of defense, the strategy, the combined operations of armies, there are the wisdom, the power, and the patience of God. Above the feverish activity of human forces there broods the figure of the Almighty. Still as a land shimmering under the noonday blaze, high and serene as a summer cloud, he bides his time. The oracle breathes a magnificent confidence in God's control of life. It is not man who decides the issue, but that invisible presence in the inaccessible height of his splendor. In his own time he strikes; the ripening harvest of human aims is suddenly smitten, the oncom-

ing hosts of Assyrians decimated, the land is strewed with the dead, and the carrion birds and beasts gather for their dreadful carnival.

So again Isaiah reminds his people that God rules. The purposes of God are inexorably wrought out. Up to a point he can suffer men to fashion their own destiny, using the devices they contrive; after that he acts on his own initiative. A man with such a faith can face anything, and only such a faith can deliver us from final despair. The optimism of faith has no ground other than the nature and purpose of Almighty God, himself the divine watchman. To this age, confused, groping, and afraid, Isaiah speaks his quiet strong word.

> . . . Behind the dim unknown
> Standeth God within the shadow, keeping watch
>   above his own.[1]

[1] James Russell Lowell, "The Present Crisis," st. viii.

7 ¶ In that time shall the present be brought unto the Lord of hosts of a people scattered and peeled, and from a people terrible from their beginning hitherto; a nation meted out and trodden under foot, whose land the rivers have spoiled, to the place of the name of the Lord of hosts, the mount Zion.

19 The burden of Egypt. Behold, the Lord rideth upon a swift cloud, and shall come into Egypt: and the idols of Egypt shall be moved at his presence, and the heart of Egypt shall melt in the midst of it.

7 At that time gifts will be brought to the Lord of hosts
from a people tall and smooth,
　from a people feared near and far,
a nation mighty and conquering,
　whose land the rivers divide,
to Mount Zion, the place of the name of the Lord of hosts.

19 An oracle concerning Egypt.
Behold, the Lord is riding on a swift cloud
and comes to Egypt;
and the idols of Egypt will tremble at his presence,
and the heart of the Egyptians will melt within them.

---

not yet—Yahweh will intervene. **Flower:** Better, "green berry." **Will summer . . . will winter:** Better, "In summer they will be the prey of birds, and in the winter of beasts."

7. In this supplementary verse the language of vs. 2 becomes a peroration declaring that the day will come when the proud Ethiopians, like all mankind, will bring **gifts** or "tribute" to Yahweh and his temple at Jerusalem (cf. Ps. 68:29, 31 [Hebrew 68:30, 32]) .

2. The Doom of Egypt (19:1-15)

This poem falls into three parts, vss. 1-4, 5-10, 11-15, of which the second may not belong to the poem in its original form. In vss. 1-4 Yahweh is about to descend in wrath upon Egypt, bringing upon her the horrors of civil war and tyranny, and overwhelming the Egyptian gods. In vss. 5-10 are pictured the drying up of the life-giving Nile and the consequent social distress; this is a distinct disaster, having no apparent connection with the foregoing. Vss. 11-15 taunt the Egyptians for the failure of their boasted wise men to discern Yahweh's hostile purpose and to give good counsel for the salvation of their land.

So far as the subject matter goes, the first and third strophes at least can be given a meaningful relationship to the history of Egypt during Isaiah's ministry, in the internal disorders which culminated in the establishment of an alien Ethiopian dynasty about 714 B.C. But it is curious that no reason is given for Yahweh's judgment on Egypt, and while the language has some affinities to that of Isaiah, it has also several features which are more compatible with exilic or postexilic usage. It is best to acknowledge that the historical context and date of the poem are uncertain.

There is, however, food for thought in the picture of social disintegration and civil strife, the failure of courage and resolution, the frantic turning to impotent forms of religion and superstition, and the final triumph of a dictator (cf. the similar picture of what might happen in Judah, 3:1-8) . The social catastrophe resulting from the failure of Egypt's "stay and staff," the Nile, is a reminder of man's dependence on economic resources which he did not create and cannot command, which the Lord gives and may take away. The final strophe is a vivid statement of the limitations of human wisdom.

19:1-4. The Lord . . . riding on a swift cloud is a figure derived from the thought of God's power manifested in a storm (cf. Ps. 18:10 [Hebrew 18:11]) ; it came to have

---

19:1-25. The God Who Bringeth Down and Lifteth Up.—For the exegete this chapter is full of difficulties; there are obscure words, debatable references capable of more than one interpretation, and problems of history on which there is

no general agreement. Nevertheless the great oracle on Egypt presents a vivid and dramatic picture of a nation brought to its knees in judgment, and thereafter lifted up in mercy by the same hand which smote it. It closes with a burst

2 And I will set the Egyptians against the Egyptians: and they shall fight every one against his brother, and every one against his neighbor; city against city, *and* kingdom against kingdom.

3 And the spirit of Egypt shall fail in the midst thereof; and I will destroy the counsel thereof: and they shall seek to the idols, and to the charmers, and to them that have familiar spirits, and to the wizards.

4 And the Egyptians will I give over into the hand of a cruel lord; and a fierce king shall rule over them, saith the Lord, the Lord of hosts.

5 And the waters shall fail from the sea, and the river shall be wasted and dried up.

6 And they shall turn the rivers far away; *and* the brooks of defense shall be emptied and dried up: the reeds and flags shall wither.

7 The paper reeds by the brooks, by the mouth of the brooks, and every thing sown by the brooks, shall wither, be driven away, and be no *more.*

8 The fishers also shall mourn, and all they that cast angle into the brooks shall lament, and they that spread nets upon the waters shall languish.

9 Moreover they that work in fine flax, and they that weave networks, shall be confounded.

2 And I will stir up Egyptians against Egyptians,
  and they will fight, every man against his brother
  and every man against his neighbor,
  city against city, kingdom against kingdom;
3 and the spirit of the Egyptians within them will be emptied out,
  and I will confound their plans;
  and they will consult the idols and the sorcerers,
  and the mediums and the wizards;
4 and I will give over the Egyptians into the hand of a hard master;
  and a fierce king will rule over them,
      says the Lord, the Lord of hosts.

5 And the waters of the Nile will be dried up,
  and the river will be parched and dry;
6 and its canals will become foul,
  and the branches of Egypt's Nile will diminish and dry up,
  reeds and rushes will rot away.
7 There will be bare places by the Nile,
  on the brink of the Nile,
  and all that is sown by the Nile will dry up,
  be driven away, and be no more.
8 The fishermen will mourn and lament,
  all who cast hooks in the Nile;
  and they will languish
  who spread nets upon the water.
9 The workers in combed flax will be in despair,
  and the weavers of white cotton.

---

associations with the idea of his coming to judge (cf. Nah. 1:3; Dan. 7:13). **The spirit of the Egyptians:** I.e., their mind or purpose; contrast the meaning of "spirit" in 31:3. **Be emptied out:** Better, "be divided, confused." Procksch (*Jesaia I,* p. 245) calls Egypt "the classical land of magic and witchcraft." **A hard master, . . . a fierce King:** Possibly but not necessarily a foreign invader; in Isaiah's day these might be either the Ethiopian invader Piankhi, or his successor Shabaka, who returned to found the Twenty-fifth Dynasty of Pharaohs.

5-10. Waters of the Nile: Lit., **from the sea,** the presumed source of the Nile waters (cf. Gen. 2:10-14). **Will be parched and dry:** Two synonymous verbs, used for emphasis: "will dry up completely." For the first line of vs. 7 read with the Greek, "All vegetation

---

of prophecy unique in its scope and its brilliant vision of a day when ancient enmity will be blotted out, and nations once at each other's throats will be at God's feet in faith and worship.

1-17. The Doom of Egypt.—First there is the judgment on Egypt executed by God himself, who, riding on a swift cloud, suddenly strikes. The nature of the judgment is not described but the effect is devastating. The nerve of Egyptian

10 And they shall be broken in the purposes thereof, all that make sluices *and* ponds for fish.

11 ¶ Surely the princes of Zoan *are* fools, the counsel of the wise counselors of Pharaoh is become brutish: how say ye unto Pharaoh, I *am* the son of the wise, the son of ancient kings?

12 Where *are* they? where *are* thy wise *men?* and let them tell thee now, and let them know what the Lord of hosts hath purposed upon Egypt.

13 The princes of Zoan are become fools, the princes of Noph are deceived; they have also seduced Egypt, *even they that are* the stay of the tribes thereof.

14 The Lord hath mingled a perverse spirit in the midst thereof: and they have caused Egypt to err in every work thereof, as a drunken *man* staggereth in his vomit.

15 Neither shall there be *any* work for Egypt, which the head or tail, branch or rush, may do.

16 In that day shall Egypt be like unto women: and it shall be afraid and fear because of the shaking of the hand of the Lord of hosts, which he shaketh over it.

---

10 Those who are the pillars of the land
     will be crushed,
   and all who work for hire will be
     grieved.

11 The princes of Zo'an are utterly foolish;
     the wise counselors of Pharaoh give
     stupid counsel.
How can you say to Pharaoh,
   "I am a son of the wise,
   a son of ancient kings"?

12 Where then are your wise men?
     Let them tell you and make known
   what the Lord of hosts has purposed
     against Egypt.

13 The princes of Zo'an have become fools,
     and the princes of Memphis are deluded;
   those who are the cornerstones of her
     tribes
   have led Egypt astray.

14 The Lord has mingled within her
     a spirit of confusion;
   and they have made Egypt stagger in all
     her doings
   as a drunken man staggers in his vomit.

15 And there will be nothing for Egypt
     which head or tail, palm branch or
     reed, may do.

16 In that day the Egyptians will be like women, and tremble with fear before the hand which the Lord of hosts shakes over

---

shall disappear," ועבר כל ירק, **on the brink of the Nile. Be driven away:** "Be blown away" (like chaff). **Pillars . . . all who work for hire:** The meaning of these terms is quite uncertain, as seen in the completely different rendering of vs. 10 in the KJV.

11-15. Zoan: In the Hellenistic period Tanis, near Palestine, and more than once the Egyptian capital. The ancient lineage of Egyptian "wise men" is attested in I Kings 4:30 and in surviving Egyptian wisdom literature. In vs. 12 they are challenged to show that they can discern Yahweh's plans; the verse recalls Second Isaiah (cf. 41:21-23; 44:25). **Memphis,** called Moph or **Noph** in the O.T., was the ancient capital of lower Egypt and was situated at the apex of the delta. **Cornerstones** is figurative for "chieftains" (cf. I Sam. 14:38). **Mingled:** Better "mixed"; the figure is that of preparing a stupefying drink (cf. 5:22). The concluding vs. 15 recalls Isaiah's phraseology in 9:14.

3. A Further Threat to Egypt (19:16-17)

The first of the five eschatological pieces in prose which complete the chapter, all reflecting the view common to many late supplements to the prophetic books, that Judah

---

life is cut when the national religion collapses. The idols tremble, and immediately with the breakdown of faith a state of anarchy and civil war follows. Recourse to sorcery and magic is futile, and the ensuing chaos is checked only by the rise of a pitiless dictatorship. Next, as if to match the human debacle, nature fails. An appalling drought begins, the Nile itself and its

17 And the land of Judah shall be a ter-ror unto Egypt, every one that maketh mention thereof shall be afraid in himself, because of the counsel of the LORD of hosts, which he hath determined against it.

18 ¶ In that day shall five cities in the land of Egypt speak the language of Canaan, and swear to the LORD of hosts; one shall be called, The city of destruction.

them. 17 And the land of Judah will become a terror to the Egyptians; every one to whom it is mentioned will fear because of the purpose which the LORD of hosts has purposed against them.

18 In that day there will be five cities in the land of Egypt which speak the language of Canaan and swear allegiance to the LORD of hosts. One of these will be called the City of the Sun.

---

would one day dominate the world and her religion be universally acknowledged (cf. 11:10-16; Mic. 7:16-17). The negative aspect is found here in vss. 16-17; the positive in vss. 18-25.

16-17. The land of Judah: A phrase resembling Ezekiel's "land of Israel" (11:17) rather than the speech of Isaiah. **Become a terror to:** Rather, "reduce to confusion." The hostile purpose of Yahweh will show itself in the aggressiveness of Judah. Whereas in the previous oracle the wise men of Egypt could not discern this purpose, here every Egyptian will know and fear it. The difference in outlook and the nationalistic tone of his later eschatology are evident.

4. FUTURE WORSHIP OF YAHWEH IN EGYPT AND ASSYRIA (19:18-25)

Whereas the attitude toward Egypt in vss. 16-17 was hostile, we find here two predic-tions of the worship of Yahweh in Egypt (vss. 18-22) and two of the inclusion of both Egypt and Assyria in the universal community of Jewish religion (vss. 23-25). It is difficult to resist the conclusion that the first two were inserted in the scroll of Isaiah's prophecies in order to provide justification for existing situations described in vss. 18-19. At least as early as the sixth century B.C. there were Jewish colonies in Egypt (cf. Jer. 43:7; 44:1), and by the time of Christ there were, according to Philo, a million Jews here. As we know, not only from Jer. 44:15-19 but also from the Elephantine papyri, many of these combined the worship of Yahweh with that of other gods; and even the purer Yahwism of the later Ptolemaic period did not conform strictly to the tenets of Palestinian Judaism (as witness the wider content of the LXX, the Egyptian Jews' Greek version of the O.T.). Although, after the Deuteronomic reform in 621 B.C., the Jews of Palestine claimed that the Jerusalem temple was the sole legitimate place of sacrificial worship, not all the Jews of Egypt were in agreement. We know that the garrison of Jewish mercenaries at Elephantine in Upper Egypt had their own temple of Yahweh as early as 525 B.C., and that ca. 160 a second temple was built at Leontopolis by the exiled high priest Onias, who appealed for justification, so Josephus tells us (*Antiquities* XIII. 3. 1; *Jewish War* VII. 10. 2), to the present passage in Isaiah (cf. A. E. Cowley, ed., *Aramaic Papyri of the Fifth Century B.C.* [Oxford: Clarendon Press, 1923], pp. xx, 113). It is just possible that this second temple is intended by the mysterious

---

tributaries dry up, the crops wither, the very topsoil is blown away. Economic life collapses; the industries which were the very life of the nation are wiped out—fishing, textiles, construc-tion. Finally the last hope of recovery dies as the boasted wisdom, the secret of Egypt's great-ness, utterly fails and a once proud people are reduced to the state of a filthy, stumbling drunkard.

18-25. Egypt and Assyria Turning to God.— At this point there comes a sudden change of note in the oracle. In their desperate plight the

Egyptians begin to recognize the hand of Yahweh in their calamity; the very name of this implacable judge sent terror through the land. If "the fear of the Lord is the beginning of wisdom" (Ps. 111:10), Egypt's salvation became a possibility when she shrank under the scourge of God. The process of deliverance is indicated as follows: (a) **five cites** are mentioned as adopt-ing the **language of Canaan,** i.e., they turned to the Hebrew religion. This is borne out by (b) the erection of **an altar to the LORD** in the heart of the land and **a pillar at its border,**

19 In that day shall there be an altar to the Lord in the midst of the land of Egypt, and a pillar at the border thereof to the Lord.	19 In that day there will be an altar to the Lord in the midst of the land of Egypt,

city of destruction or City of the Sun, since Leontopolis was in the district of Heliopolis. However, if vs. 18 had been written in connection with Onias' undertaking in the second century, the reference to the speaking of Hebrew by Egyptian Jews would be an anachronism—unless, indeed, the reference is to the conduct of worship in the sacred tongue.

The same objection does not rest against the identification of the **altar** of vs. 19 with that of Onias at Leontopolis (near modern Cairo), which could be said to be **in the midst of the land of Egypt**. The **pillar . . . at its border** is more difficult to explain. The sacred pillars of the Palestinian temples were specifically condemned in Deuteronomy (16:22), but this provision need not have troubled exiled Jews who had decided to ignore the fundamental Deuteronomic rule of the single sanctuary. The suggestion that a memorial stele rather than a temple symbol is intended is quite out of keeping with the content of the oracle (Gray, *Isaiah I-XXXIX*, I, 338). Tahpanhes or Daphnae, one of the centers of Jewish settlement mentioned in Jer. 43:7; 44:1, was on the Asiatic **border** of Egypt, and the reference here may be to a contemplated or actual local temple there also, of which we have no knowledge. The **altar** and **pillar** will mark the presence of Yahweh with his people now again in Egypt; when they cry to him for help, he will deliver them and, in so doing, make himself known not only to them but to the Egyptians (cf. Exod. 7:5). This time the Egyptians will come to worship Yahweh (hence a temple in Egypt will be required).

The final pair of promises breathes a more generous air than almost any other picture, in the eschatology of postexilic prophecy, of the relationship of Judah to foreign peoples. Egypt, the ancient oppressor, and Assyria, the cruel conqueror, will share the highway of Zion's restoration (cf. 11:16) and will be united with Israel as equal members of the chosen people.

18. The language of Canaan: I.e., Hebrew, the language which was spoken in Canaan and neighboring lands and so was not peculiar to Israel; here, however, it is the ancestral and sacred language whose use marked off the Egyptian Jews from their neighbors. **Swear allegiance to:** Better, "make oath by the name of," thus acknowledging Yahweh as their god. **City of the Sun** and **city of destruction:** The Greek reads "city of righteousness," thus affirming that the city in question shared in the Greek period the claim of Jerusalem (cf. 1:26). There is textual evidence in support of each of the similar words הרס, destruction, and חרס, sun; it seems likely that the former (found in most Hebrew MSS) is an alteration of the latter by Palestinian scribes, who thus expressed their resentment against Onias' schismatic temple. On the other hand, if Heliopolis was intended, it is strange that it was not called, as elsewhere in the O.T., On or Beth-shemesh. The meaning remains uncertain.

19-22. Will smite . . . smiting and healing: This is not a judgment of enmity but the treatment of Egyptian proselytes as Israel has been treated, with both chastisement and mercy.

---

tokens of God's claim and the nation's acknowledgment (vs. 19). (c) Further, a highway to Assyria is opened, i.e., a way to the heart of the enemy (vs. 23). Over it pass not the armed forces of contending foes, but the peaceful ambassadors of trade. The oracle closes with the picture, almost unique in ancient prophecy, of a great reconciliation: Assyria, Egypt, Israel—the triple alliance of faith.

There could be no surer witness to the spiritual genius, the inspired insight of Isaiah, than this discernment of the vital relationship between peace and religion. More than two thousand years ago this man of God saw clearly what the modern world is only now glimpsing, that peace is spiritually conditioned. Humanity has been compelled by its own triumphs in physical science to face the fact that it is now quite pos

20 And it shall be for a sign and for a witness unto the LORD of hosts in the land of Egypt: for they shall cry unto the LORD because of the oppressors, and he shall send them a saviour, and a great one, and he shall deliver them.

21 And the LORD shall be known to Egypt, and the Egyptians shall know the LORD in that day, and shall do sacrifice and oblation; yea, they shall vow a vow unto the LORD, and perform *it*.

22 And the LORD shall smite Egypt: he shall smite and heal *it:* and they shall return *even* to the LORD, and he shall be entreated of them, and shall heal them.

23 ¶ In that day shall there be a highway out of Egypt to Assyria, and the Assyrian shall come into Egypt, and the Egyptian into Assyria, and the Egyptians shall serve with the Assyrians.

24 In that day shall Israel be the third with Egypt and with Assyria, *even* a blessing in the midst of the land:

25 Whom the LORD of hosts shall bless, saying, Blessed *be* Egypt my people, and Assyria the work of my hands, and Israel mine inheritance.

and a pillar to the LORD at its border. **20** It will be a sign and a witness to the LORD of hosts in the land of Egypt; when they cry to the LORD because of oppressors he will send them a savior, and will defend and deliver them. **21** And the LORD will make himself known to the Egyptians; and the Egyptians will know the LORD in that day and worship with sacrifice and burnt offering, and they will make vows to the LORD and perform them. **22** And the LORD will smite Egypt, smiting and healing, and they will return to the LORD, and he will heed their supplications and heal them.

23 In that day there will be a highway from Egypt to Assyria, and the Assyrian will come into Egypt, and the Egyptian into Assyria, and the Egyptians will worship with the Assyrians.

24 In that day Israel will be the third with Egypt and Assyria, a blessing in the midst of the earth, **25** whom the LORD of hosts has blessed, saying, "Blessed be Egypt my people, and Assyria the work of my hands, and Israel my heritage."

23-25. Read, "A blessing which the Lord of hosts utters," lit., "blesses." The promises to, and titles of, Israel will now belong to the larger community of the wider covenant. It is thus that Christianity appropriates the language of the O.T.

---

sible to destroy the human race. The problem of peace is no longer a question of attaining a moral ideal, but a stark necessity for the continued existence of man. The history of the twentieth century thus far is littered with the wreckage of peace plans that failed. Why has the genius of man been unequal to making peace? It is not a question of brains. Every covenant from the League of Nations to the Locarno Pact was theoretically the guarantee of peace. Yet in this era of international covenants one world war after another brought civilization to the edge of the abyss. It is clear that man has the capacity to solve every problem except the problem of self-control. That victory still awaits him, and must continue to elude him until he acknowledges the need of power other than his own to change the human spirit. Isaiah saw it long ago, and this is the message of his prophecy of reconciliation. Peace is not basically a matter of treaties but of a new spirit in human relationships, and that new spirit is possible only through a shared faith, trust, and obedience to God. It is so easy to write this or say it, but

little short of an agony to bring men to accept it as God's condition for peace on earth. The alternative is before us, a godless civilization moving to its own doom and damnation, or a race which has found its salvation and its peace in a common faith and obedience to Almighty God. Is there yet to be a day when the oracle shall read,

Blessed be Russia, my people,
And America, the work of my hands,
And the Commonwealth of Nations, my inheritance?

The answer is ours to give.

There is one phrase in this chapter which more than others ought to quicken the mind. **And the LORD will smite Egypt, smiting and healing.** If there is any light on the dark mystery of suffering, it is in such a promise. The golden harvest comes only from furrows pain has cut. Life's **smiting** we cannot escape; the sorrowful thing is that so many miss God's **healing.** At the heart of the gospel of Jesus Christ is the divine love which heals the wounds sin has made, the hurt of life's frustration and cruelty,

20 In the year that Tartan came unto Ashdod, (when Sargon the king of Assyria sent him,) and fought against Ashdod, and took it;

2 At the same time spake the LORD by Isaiah the son of Amoz, saying, Go and loose the sackcloth from off thy loins, and put off thy shoe from thy foot. And he did so, walking naked and barefoot.

3 And the LORD said, Like as my servant Isaiah hath walked naked and barefoot three years *for* a sign and wonder upon Egypt and upon Ethiopia;

20 In the year that the commander in chief, who was sent by Sargon the king of Assyria, came to Ashdod and fought against it and took it, — **2** at that time the LORD had spoken by Isaiah the son of Amoz, saying, "Go, and loose the sackcloth from your loins and take off your shoes from your feet," and he had done so, walking naked and barefoot — **3** the LORD said, "As my servant Isaiah has walked naked and barefoot for three years as a sign and a

---

5. An Acted and Spoken Prophecy Against Egypt (20:1-6)

This short passage belongs by its content among the doom oracles on foreign peoples; but it is not called משא, "doom oracle," and is in fact a section of biographical narrative giving the circumstances of the oracle it contains, as in 7:1-17. It is remarkable also as an example of the symbolic acts with which sometimes the prophets drew attention to and declared the "word" which they felt called upon to utter (cf. I Kings 11:29-31; 22:11). The date is given specifically by the narrator as the year in which the Assyrians crushed the rebellion centered in the Philistine city of Ashdod—711 B.C. The new Ethiopian dynasty in Egypt had instigated this revolt (hence **Egypt and Ethiopia** as the designation here). Isaiah declares that Egypt will be crushed; the hope misplaced in her by the small states such as Judah and the Philistines can lead only to disillusionment and disaster. Isaiah's oracle, although dated in the same year, must have been published before the actual attack on Ashdod, since he expected the brunt of the attack to fall upon Egypt rather than, as it turned out, on the Philistines. The Egyptians failed to send help, and Sargon contented himself with making an example to his vassals of Ashdod and two other Philistine cities. Judah apparently hastened to submit, and thus Isaiah's conviction that the time had not yet come for the Assyrian overthrow (cf. ch. 18) was vindicated.

20:1. Tartan is not a proper name, but an official title, **commander in chief** or "governor general"; the holder was a military officer ranking next to the king (cf. II Kings 18:17).

2-4. Had spoken: I.e., at the beginning of the three-year period of the conspiracy; the message in vss. 3-6 is what is dated in 711. **By Isaiah:** Lit., "by the hand" or agency

---

the sorrow death has caused. **Smiting!** It is the mark of the world's treatment. **Healing!** It is the ministry and mercy of God's love.

20:1-6. *An Acted Parable.*—To the prosaic mind the acted parable set forth in this chapter may appear ridiculous. The picture of a silent half-clad figure walking the streets of Jerusalem fits ill with our idea of a prophet of God. Certainly no dignitary of the modern church would so expose himself to ridicule. We have, however, to recognize two facts. (*a*) There is a complete lack of self-consciousness about Isaiah, and indeed about any true servant of God. A man with a mission does not hesitate to accept scorn or derision in doing his duty. The Salvation Army violated all the conventions of the day when it first began street preaching, but its servants did not hesitate to be "fools for Christ's

sake" (I Cor. 4:10). If the modern church were as morally in earnest, there might be a fine upsetting of the religious proprieties in some city churches. (*b*) There is a limit to the effectiveness of the spoken word if there is only one to declare it. Between 1939 and 1945 the world had a terrific demonstration of the power of words; they enslaved the mind of a nation and changed the course of history. But the words were spoken by scores and hundreds of voices from the platform, over the air, and in the press. Not a soul in Germany escaped the barrage of propaganda. But Isaiah stood in Jerusalem the sole messenger of God; only the merest handful of people ever heard him speak. Therefore, on occasion, he was not above making a spectacle of himself to compel attention. Even in the unconventional East a man who for three years walked the

4 So shall the king of Assyria lead away the Egyptians prisoners, and the Ethiopians captives, young and old, naked and barefoot, even with *their* buttocks uncovered, to the shame of Egypt.

5 And they shall be afraid and ashamed of Ethiopia their expectation, and of Egypt their glory.

6 And the inhabitant of this isle shall say in that day, Behold, such *is* our expectation, whither we flee for help to be delivered from the king of Assyria: and how shall we escape?

portent against Egypt and Ethiopia, 4 so shall the king of Assyria lead away the Egyptians captives and the Ethiopians exiles, both the young and the old, naked and barefoot, with buttocks uncovered, the shame of Egypt. 5 Then they shall be dismayed and confounded because of Ethiopia their hope and of Egypt their boast. 6 And the inhabitants of this coastland will say in that day, 'Behold, this is what has happened to those in whom we hoped and to whom we fled for help to be delivered from the king of Assyria! And we, how shall we escape?' "

21 The burden of the desert of the sea.
As whirlwinds in the south pass

21 The oracle concerning the wilderness of the sea.
As whirlwinds in the Negeb sweep on,

---

of Isaiah, in acting as he did. The prophet at this time had been wearing a simple long shirt of **sackcloth,** perhaps temporarily while calling for repentance (cf. 37:2). But this, or a "hairy mantle," may have been the customary garb of prophets (cf. Zech. 13:4; Mark 1:6). Now he is to strip off shirt and sandals and go about clad only in the apron or loin cloth of a war prisoner or slave; this is to be a sign that it is now too late for penitence and entreaty, for the doom has been decreed. **A sign and a portent:** A symbol and token of an event to come. (For an illustration of a pitiful procession of prisoners, see J. H. Breasted, *A History of Egypt from the Earliest Times to the Persian Conquest* [2nd ed.; New York: Charles Scribner's Sons, 1909], Pl. CXIX.)

5-6. Those who hoped would include all the peoples in the conspiracy, but Isaiah's particular reference is to those in Judah who had favored participation. **This coastland, not this isle;** the Philistine plain and coastal cities are clearly what is in the prophet's mind (cf. Jer. 47:4).

K. The Appalling Vision of Babylon's Fall (21:1-10)

In this strange passage with its enigmatic title "Doom Oracle of a Sea Wilderness," an anonymous seer of *ca.* 540 B.C. attempts to set down in writing a description of his

---

streets clad only in a slave's loincloth was bound to create a stir. Questions were asked as to why the man made a fool of himself, and the answer was given. So Isaiah got his message across. It was a word of doom to any hope from alliance with Egypt, and a prophecy of the further extension of Assyrian triumphs.

The chapter may appear barren ground for the expositor; but in the light of the apathy of the "sermon-saturated heathen of the pew" it might be well to challenge the modern ministry to consider whether the conventional sermon, spoken to a handful of church members from the safe elevation of the pulpit, is the only or the most effective method of confronting men with the Word of God. That it is one way which under God has been a mighty instrument of truth none can deny; but is it for these times the most realistic way of compelling a hearing?

And what of the people who do go to church? Are they witnessing for Christ? It is enough to note the dreary silence which has fallen upon the modern church membership, insomuch that the burden and responsibility of proclaiming the Word of God is left entirely to the professional preacher. That picture of Isaiah, the sensitive soul with the vision and mind of a poet, content to be an object of derision, if by any means men might be brought to hear and see, ought to shame a people so conscious of their own dignity, so zealous to observe the conventions that they hardly dare mention the name of Christ to another, let alone do anything for his sake which might make them conspicuous. The chapter is not so barren after all for the man whose passion it is to make Christ known.

21:1-17. *The Fall of Babylon.*—If Isaiah pronounced these oracles—which as the Exeg. shows

through; *so* it cometh from the desert, from a terrible land.	it comes from the desert, from a terrible land.
2 A grievous vision is declared unto me; The treacherous dealer dealeth treacherously, and the spoiler spoileth. Go up, O Elam: besiege, O Media: all the sighing thereof have I made to cease.	2 A stern vision is told to me; the plunderer plunders, and the destroyer destroys. Go up, O Elam, lay siege, O Media; all the sighing she has caused I bring to an end.
3 Therefore are my loins filled with pain: pangs have taken hold upon me, as the pangs of a woman that travaileth: I was bowed down at the hearing *of it;* I was dismayed at the seeing *of it.*	3 Therefore my loins are filled with anguish; pangs have seized me, like the pangs of a woman in travail; I am bowed down so that I cannot hear, I am dismayed so that I cannot see.

subjective experience while in a state of prophetic ecstasy. Without introduction or comment he launches into an account of his state of mind and of his emotions as he perceives, through vision and audition, "the word of Yahweh." Amid the disjointed outcries which exhibit his agitation two germinal oracles are impressed on his mind— "The robber robbed, the destroyer destroyed" (vs. 2), and "my threshing and my son of a threshing floor" (vs. 10). The message of these clarifies itself in the words **Fallen, fallen is Babylon.** The historical situation presupposed is that of the sixth century, for in Isaiah's day Babylon had not yet succeeded to the world empire of Assyria, and the association of Elam with Media in an attack on Babylon was subsequent to 550 B.C.

The passage falls into two parts, differing in meter and mood and presenting two distinct scenes in the vision. Vss. 1-5 describe the intense emotion with which the prophet catches glimpses of the siege of Babylon, and vss. 6-10 depict how he waits for the definitive word of the messengers that all is over. The text is difficult in vss. 1, 2, 10, and this has contributed to the apparent obscurity of the oracle as a whole. The slight restorations of the text proposed below remove the obscurity almost entirely.

21:1. The oracle concerning the wilderness of the sea cannot be the "sea land" near the Persian Gulf, for this was marsh land rather than wilderness steppe. The LXX preserves the original title "Oracle of the Wilderness"; the Dead Sea Scroll omits **wilderness** and reads only דבר ים, which gives us the missing opening word of the oracle, *debhārîm,* "words." The M.T. is clearly explained as the result of haplography. Translate, "Words like storm winds sweeping through the Negeb, coming [*bā'îm,* a second case of haplography] from the desert, from a terrible land." The **stern vision** rushes through the prophet's mind like a storm of words.

2-5. The gist of the oracle emerges in an alliterative line which is to be read with passive participles: "The plunderer is plundered, the destroyer destroyed" (cf. 33:1; Jer. 51:11, 25). The rallying cry to Elam and Media echoes in the prophet's consciousness.

is very doubtful—he appears in a new light, and uses a form and style of utterance strangely unlike anything we have yet heard. There is none of the characteristic lucidity which marks his speech; the measured beat of his style gives place to a rapid staccato rhythm, and the straightforward word to the weird device of question and answer between the prophet and his own spirit, the watchman.	First (vss. 1-10), under the image of a terrible sandstorm sweeping up from the south, Isaiah sees the advance of Elam and Media against Babylon. He is filled with horror at the spectacle, and in curious detail he describes his feelings. He writhes **with anguish,** he **cannot see** for the shock, his **mind reels,** the **horror has appalled him.** Far off in Babylon they eat and drink, all unconscious that tomorrow they die.
The chapter contains three oracles, all concerned with the fall of Babylon and its consequences.	The tables are ready in the banquet hall, and the carpet is spread. Suddenly the revelry is broken by the call to arms. Then follows what

4 My heart panted, fearfulness affrighted me: the night of my pleasure hath he turned into fear unto me.

5 Prepare the table, watch in the watchtower, eat, drink: arise, ye princes, *and* anoint the shield.

6 For thus hath the Lord said unto me, Go, set a watchman, let him declare what he seeth.

7 And he saw a chariot *with* a couple of horsemen, a chariot of asses, *and* a chariot of camels; and he hearkened diligently with much heed:

8 And he cried, A lion: My lord, I stand continually upon the watchtower in the daytime, and I am set in my ward whole nights:

9 And, behold, here cometh a chariot of men, *with* a couple of horsemen. And he answered and said, Babylon is fallen, is fallen; and all the graven images of her gods he hath broken unto the ground.

10 O my threshing, and the corn of my floor: that which I have heard of the LORD of hosts, the God of Israel, have I declared unto you.

4 My mind reels, horror has appalled me;
　the twilight I longed for
　has been turned for me into trembling.

5 They prepare the table,
　they spread the rugs,
　they eat, they drink.
Arise, O princes,
　oil the shield!

6 For thus the Lord said to me:
"Go, set a watchman,
　let him announce what he sees.

7 When he sees riders, horsemen in pairs,
　riders on asses, riders on camels,
let him listen diligently,
　very diligently."

8 Then he who saw⁹ cried:
"Upon a watchtower I stand, O Lord,
　continually by day,
and at my post I am stationed
　whole nights.

9 And, behold, here come riders,
　horsemen in pairs!"
And he answered,
"Fallen, fallen is Babylon;
and all the images of her gods
　he has shattered to the ground."

10 O my threshed and winnowed one,
　what I have heard from the LORD of hosts,
the God of Israel, I announce to you.

⁹ One ancient Ms: Heb *a lion*

Vss. 3-4 describe the mental stress of the experience. For **so that I cannot hear . . . see** read "By what I hear . . . see." Vs. 5 pictures the Babylonian warriors as feasting when the sudden call to arms is heard; the story of Belshazzar's feast develops the same theme (cf. Dan. 5).

6-10. The second scene is introduced as an audition or "private oracle," **the Lord said to me;** the description is consecutive, not emotional. The prophet himself is to be the **watchman,** as is clear from vs. 8 and Hab. 2:1, and **what he sees** in the vision he is to **declare** as prophecy. **And he answered** (vs. 9): better, "one answered." Vs. 10 is completely obscure in the KJV, and only slightly less so in the RSV, which takes the opening words to refer to the afflicted Israel, long **threshed and winnowed** by Babylon. But "my threshing and my son of a threshing floor" (literally) is much better taken as referring to Yahweh's threshing of his enemies, in this case of Babylon (cf. Jer. 51:33): "The daughter of Babylon shall be like a threshing floor at the time when it is trodden" (cf.

---

is an audition rather than a vision. The prophet is instructed to **set a watchman** to wait for a sign, which is to be the passing of an army on the march. His own spirit takes the post, and from its unseen vantage point sends back the word: "They are coming—the retreating, broken remnants of a battle. Babylon is fallen! Babylon is fallen!" (Vs. 9.) Whereupon Isaiah apostrophizes his own nation in words which echo

their suffering. "My own crushed countrymen, my downtrodden folk, this is God's word for you." It is as if he said: "I would to God I could speak otherwise, but the enemy still triumphs. Assyria is still on the march; your deliverance is not yet."

The second oracle (vss. 11-12) bears out this word, for in it Isaiah hears voices asking how far gone is the night of oppression. He answers:

11 ¶ The burden of Dumah. He calleth to me out of Seir, Watchman, what of the night? Watchman, what of the night?

12 The watchman said, The morning cometh, and also the night: if ye will inquire, inquire ye: return, come.

13 ¶ The burden upon Arabia. In the forest in Arabia shall ye lodge, O ye traveling companies of Dedanim.

14 The inhabitants of the land of Tema brought water to him that was thirsty, they prevented with their bread him that fled.

15 For they fled from the swords, from the drawn sword, and from the bent bow, and from the grievousness of war.

---

11 The oracle concerning Dumah.
   One is calling to me from Se'ir,
      "Watchman, what of the night?
      Watchman, what of the night?"
12 The watchman says:
   "Morning comes, and also the night.
      If you will inquire, inquire;
      come back again."

13 The oracle concerning Arabia.
   In the thickets in Arabia you will lodge,
      O caravans of De'danites.
14 To the thirsty bring water,
      meet the fugitive with bread,
   O inhabitants of the land of Tema.
15 For they have fled from the swords,
      from the drawn sword,
   from the bent bow,
      and from the press of battle.

---

also Isa. 41:15; Mic. 4:13; Hab. 3:12). The enigmatic phrase is the "doom" on Babylon as it first formed itself in the prophet's mind, and was appended to the vision description in vss. 6-9 when that was published (cf. vs. 10*bc*).

L. A Cry from Edom (21:11-12)

11-12. This striking little passage seems to be a second account of prophetic experience by the author of the foregoing section. It is clearly not a doom oracle, and its title has arisen from corruption of the text; for the words משא דומה we should probably read *nôśē' mē'edhôm*, "One is lifting up the voice from Edom." The prophetic watchman is appealed to by Judah's neighbor, Edom, to say how much of the **night** (of oppression ?) remains. The answer is enigmatic; it may mean either that though **morning** is coming, another **night** will follow, or that though morning has come, it is still dark. The seer is not yet ready to announce that the night has really passed, but he expects this, for he invites further inquiry.

M. Doom of Dedan and Kedar (21:13-17)

The obscure and perhaps fragmentary oracle in vss. 13-15 pictures the Arabian tribe of Dedan (Gen. 10:7) fleeing before an unnamed enemy to **the land of Tema,** an oasis in the Arabian Desert, southeast of Palestine. The concluding prose oracle suggests that Kedar, a powerful tribe of north Arabia in Jeremiah's day (2:10), was the enemy.

13-15. The title is missing in the LXX, and probably has been inferred by an editor from vs. 13*b*; but **in Arabia** should be read "in the steppe" (so Duhm, Marti, Procksch).

"The morning is not far off, there is light in the sky; but there is more to endure, and it is always darkest before the dawn." The oracle is deliberately obscure. The seer has no clear vision of the fate of Edom and his answer is not final. That is why he invites further inquiry. He says in effect, "If you would know when the dark night has passed, come back later."

The third oracle (vss. 13-17) describes an aftermath of a great battle. A caravan of the merchant tribe of Dedan, driven from the old,

safe routes by war, has taken refuge in the open and sought covert in thicket and wadi. They are at the last gasp for food and water. Isaiah calls on the people of Tema to send help, and the oracle ends with the prophecy that within three years all the north Arabian tribes will be in the same straits, scattered and broken.

Inasmuch as these three strange oracles deal with a local and dated situation, they have really no relevance for our day. Treating them metaphorically, one might compel them to yield

16 For thus hath the Lord said unto me, Within a year, according to the years of a hireling, and all the glory of Kedar shall fail:	16 For thus the Lord said to me, "Within a year, according to the years of a hireling, all the glory of Kedar will come to an end;
17 And the residue of the number of archers, the mighty men of the children of Kedar, shall be diminished: for the LORD God of Israel hath spoken *it*.	17 and the remainder of the archers of the mighty men of the sons of Kedar will be few; for the LORD, the God of Israel, has spoken."
22 The burden of the valley of vision. What aileth thee now, that thou art wholly gone up to the housetops?	22 The oracle concerning the valley of vision. What do you mean that you have gone up, all of you, to the housetops,

The word translated **in the thickets** or **in the forest** is totally unsuitable, and is to be explained as a scribal variant.

16-17. Within a year: The Dead Sea Scroll reads "within three years" (cf. 16:14), corresponding to the plural, **years of a hireling**, apparently the usual term of an agreement with hired labor. **The glory of Kedar:** Cf. 60:7; Ezek. 27:21.

N. Reckless Revelry on the Eve of Disaster (22:1-14)

This oracle is in two parts, vss. 1-8*a* and vss. 8*b*-14, of which the second is a sequel to the first and refers back to it in vs. 12. The first part opens with an indignant reproach of a city given over to revelry upon some occasion unspecified (vss. 1-2). But the prophet has an inward vision of the same people scattered and made captive (vs. 3), and he weeps for their fate amid their noisy celebration (vs. 4). The vision is that of the day of the Lord and the terrors of invasion it will bring (vss. 5-8*a*). At vs. 8*b* there is a transition from poetry to prose; the writer recalls that Judah's response has been to look to material defenses rather than to discern Yahweh's purpose and its realization (vss. 8*b*-11). Instead of the fear and self-abasement which the situation has called for, there has been only reckless revelry (vss. 12-13). So now the Lord utters a solemn sentence of doom upon his heedless and unrepentant people (vs. 14).

The historical situation against which the passage is to be interpreted cannot be established with certainty. The exultation described in vss. 1-2 seems at first sight appropriate to the occasion of Jerusalem's remarkable deliverance from Sennacherib in 701, but this date is not compatible with an expected attack by forces from Elam and Kir, nor with Isaiah's attitude to that deliverance (cf. 37:33-35). It seems that a similarly unexpected if less spectacular escape from the horrors of siege took place in 711, when Sargon struck down Ashdod (cf. ch. 20) but left Jerusalem unmolested, although she had taken part in the conspiracy. Word of the retirement of the Assyrian armies at that time would give rise to rejoicing by the citizens, who, as Isaiah says in looking back on it (vss. 8*b*-11), had made desperate preparations for defense. The vision of a future attack by Elam and Kir did not contemplate that these peoples would be serving in the Assyrian forces, but rather that these enemies of Assyria and friends of Merodach-baladan

expository material; but that is not good exposition. Such suggestive values as may be discerned in them will be found in a single phrase or verse, e.g.,	most obvious text, however, is the famous cry, **Watchman, what of the night?** At any moment of history God's watchmen should be prepared to declare how it fares with men, to detect the light on the skyline, or to warn of the threatening darkness.
the twilight I longed for **has been turned for me into trembling** (vs. 4).	
It is the retribution of an evil life that it can know neither peace nor security; its twilight is filled with the voices of pursuing shame. The	**22:1-14.** *A Premature Rejoicing.*—There is no agreement among critics as to the exact historical situation which called forth this oracle of doom. If, however, the view is accepted that

2 Thou that art full of stirs, a tumultuous city, a joyous city: thy slain *men are* not slain with the sword, nor dead in battle.

3 All thy rulers are fled together, they are bound by the archers: all that are found in thee are bound together, *which* have fled from far.

4 Therefore said I, Look away from me; I will weep bitterly, labor not to comfort me, because of the spoiling of the daughter of my people.

5 For *it is* a day of trouble, and of treading down, and of perplexity by the Lord GOD of hosts in the valley of vision, breaking down the walls, and of crying to the mountains.

6 And Elam bare the quiver with chariots of men *and* horsemen, and Kir uncovered the shield.

7 And it shall come to pass, *that* thy choicest valleys shall be full of chariots, and the horsemen shall set themselves in array at the gate.

2 you who are full of shoutings,
   tumultuous city, exultant town?
Your slain are not slain with the sword
   or dead in battle.
3 All your rulers have fled together,
   without the bow they were captured.
All of you who were found were captured,
   though they had fled far away.[h]
4 Therefore I said:
"Look away from me,
   let me weep bitter tears;
do not labor to comfort me
   for the destruction of the daughter of
      my people."

5 For the Lord GOD of hosts has a day
   of tumult and trampling and confusion
      in the valley of vision,
a battering down of walls
   and a shouting to the mountains.
6 And Elam bore the quiver
   with chariots and horsemen,[i]
   and Kir uncovered the shield.
7 Your choicest valleys were full of chariots,
   and the horsemen took their stand at
      the gates.

[h] Gk Syr Vg: Heb *from far away*
[i] The Hebrew of this line is obscure

(cf. ch. 39) would in turn come against unrepentant Judah on the day of the Lord. Now, in recalling the former prophecy, perhaps under the circumstances of a new conspiracy which developed on the death of Sargon in 705, Isaiah announces that Judah has greater regard for material defenses than for Yahweh's purposes in history. Her continued unrepentant and reckless spirit has called forth an immutable sentence of doom (vs. 14).

22:1-4. The valley of vision: An obscure phrase, borrowed for the title from vs. 5; the reference is probably to divination at an altar in the "Valley of Hinnom" at Jerusalem (cf. Jer. 7:31-34). **Not slain with the sword,** but "overcome with wine" (28:1). **Without the bow they were captured:** Better, "without use of the bow."

5-8a. Vs. 5b is obscure; Procksch (*Jesaia I*, p. 280), following Klostermann, reads, "In the vision-valley Koa makes an uproar, and Shoa against the mount"; these two subject peoples of Assyria are mentioned in Ezek. 23:23. **With chariots and horsemen:** Better, reading ארם for אדם, with Procksch (*ibid.*, p. 276), "Syria mounted horsemen."

the prophecy belongs to the period of Sennacherib's invasion in 701 B.C., then sentence after sentence becomes luminous with dreadful meaning. It is known that when the Assyrian forces swept south to deal with Egypt, King Hezekiah ignominiously accepted Sennacherib's terms. This lifted for the moment the threat of siege, and the entire population went mad with joy. Amid the frenzied celebration Isaiah walked alone in bitterness of soul. To his grief-stricken spirit came a vision of another day when the enemy would close in on a doomed city, and the cheering would give place to wailing and the parades to panic. There would be not even the dignity of defeat, but a craven rout; no honorable wounds, no dead in the streets, for the cowards had broken and run. That was the fate which awaited the city now tumultuous in its revelry. At this point the mind of Isaiah flashes back to a very different day, when in the

8 ¶ And he discovered the covering of Judah, and thou didst look in that day to the armor of the house of the forest.

9 Ye have seen also the breaches of the city of David, that they are many: and ye gathered together the waters of the lower pool.

10 And ye have numbered the houses of Jerusalem, and the houses have ye broken down to fortify the wall.

11 Ye made also a ditch between the two walls for the water of the old pool: but ye have not looked unto the maker thereof, neither had respect unto him that fashioned it long ago.

12 And in that day did the Lord GOD of hosts call to weeping, and to mourning, and to baldness, and to girding with sackcloth:

13 And behold joy and gladness, slaying oxen, and killing sheep, eating flesh, and drinking wine: let us eat and drink; for to-morrow we shall die.

8 He has taken away the covering of Judah.

In that day you looked to the weapons of the house of the forest, 9 and you saw that the breaches of the city of David were many, and you collected the waters of the lower pool, 10 and you counted the houses of Jerusalem, and you broke down the houses to fortify the wall. 11 You made a reservoir between the two walls for the water of the old pool. But you did not look to him who did it, or have regard for him who planned it long ago.

12 In that day the Lord GOD of hosts,
  called to weeping and mourning,
  to baldness and girding with sackcloth;
13 and behold, joy and gladness,
  slaying oxen and killing sheep,
  eating flesh and drinking wine.
"Let us eat and drink,
  for tomorrow we die."

For **took their stand at,** read "set their faces toward." For *māṣakh,* "covering," "screen," read *muṣṣēk,* "thy melting," "thy terror," and point the verb as Niphal, "And thy terror, O Judah, was revealed."

8b-11. The house of the forest: One of Solomon's buildings (I Kings 7:2), so called because of the many pillars supporting the roof; since the time of Solomon it had been used as an armory (cf. I Kings 10:17). The reference to **the waters of the lower pool** has been displaced from the beginning of vs. 11. **Planned:** Better, "determined," lit., "fashioned." The hastily improvised defenses show that Judah had no conception of the irresistible forces of divine judgment set in motion by her faithlessness.

12-14. The reckless words of those who celebrate their commitment to the revolt against Assyria are taken out of their own mouths in the dreadful sentence of doom which follows.

frenzied preparation for defense the people had given all they had, and at least evinced a spirit ready to suffer and die. The details of that plan of defense are vividly told. The arsenal was strengthened (vs. 8), the breaches in the walls repaired (vs. 9), the water supply channeled into the city itself (vss. 9-11), the field of fire opened up by the tearing down of obstructing houses (vs. 10). So they had taken all necessary precautions save the one essential—the remembrance of God, the true and only defense of his people. It was that blindness which in Isaiah's eyes doomed the nation, that insensibility to the things of faith which led them to blind orgies when they should have been on their knees before God. Only a people who are atheists in spirit, if not in creed, could in a moment of great deliverance or of dire peril sink to the depth of irreverence in which they could say, "Time is short; let's get drunk" (vs.

13). In that mood men are not forgivable; they have made their own judgment inescapable. On deaf ears Isaiah pronounces sentence,

Surely this iniquity will not be forgiven you till you die.

Though this dreadful oracle was spoken against a people in time of war, when neither men nor things are normal and all the moral values are in jeopardy, there is that in it which is not bound by temporal conditions but is true for all men and all times: the solemn warning that the life, whether of the individual or of society, which leaves God out of account finally reaches a point at which its world goes to pieces about it. The Jews of Isaiah's day were at the same moment scrupulously religious and fundamentally irreligious. They performed the motions of worship, but without belief; they bowed at the name of God, but never trusted him. In

14 And it was revealed in mine ears by the LORD of hosts, Surely this iniquity shall not be purged from you till ye die, saith the Lord GOD of hosts.

15 ¶ Thus saith the Lord GOD of hosts, Go, get thee unto this treasurer, *even* unto Shebna, which *is* over the house, *and say*,

16 What hast thou here, and whom hast thou here, that thou hast hewed thee out a sepulchre here, *as* he that heweth him out a sepulchre on high, *and* that graveth a habitation for himself in a rock?

17 Behold, the LORD will carry thee away with a mighty captivity, and will surely cover thee.

14 The LORD of hosts has revealed himself
    in my ears:
"Surely this iniquity will not be forgiven
    you
till you die,"
says the Lord GOD of hosts.

15 Thus says the Lord GOD of hosts, "Come, go to this steward, to Shebna, who is over the household, and say to him: 16 What have you to do here and whom have you here, that you have hewn here a tomb for yourself, you who hew a tomb on the height, and carve a habitation for yourself in the rock? 17 Behold, the LORD will hurl you away violently, O you strong man.

O. DOWNFALL OF SHEBNA THE KING'S STEWARD (22:15-25)

We have several examples in prophecy of oracles which are in effect solemn curses upon individuals who were spearheads of opposition to the word the prophet was declaring (cf. Amos 7:16-17; Jer. 20:1-6; 28:15-17). Here Isaiah proclaims the downfall of Shebna, a royal official of importance, who apparently was held responsible by the prophet for instigating the policy of revolt against Assyria. It has been suggested that the immunity of Judah at the time of Sargon's punishment of Ashod (711) was due to a reversal of her policy following Shebna's fall from power. In 36:3; 37:2 Shebna is in a subordinate position and the promotion of Eliakim has apparently taken place.

There are some difficulties in interpreting the passage as a unity; (a) in vss. 15-18 Shebna is denounced for aspiring to an honor to which he has no right, and is (apparently) threatened with exile, whereas in vss. 19-23 he is to be deposed and replaced by Eliakim; from the sequel (cf. 36:3) it seems that this is what actually happened; (b) the promise to Eliakim in vs. 23 is taken back in vs. 25. The second difficulty can be eliminated at once by noting that vss. 24-25 are in prose, and are almost certainly a supplement added when the hopes placed in Eliakim had faded; as Gray says (*Isaiah I-XXXIX*, I, 375), "It is certainly improbable that a prophet should at the same moment, *in an address to the person to be deposed,* predict both the promotion and the disgrace of his successor." The first difficulty also disappears when it is noted that the language of vs. 18 does not necessarily imply exile from Palestine, but only the hurling of Shebna from his post in the capital into the "wide open country." In fact, the picturesque figure of speech is specifically interpreted of deposition rather than of exile in vs. 19, the concluding verse of the first section.

15-19. To Shebna . . . household: Read "concerning Shebna" and insert the clause after **hosts.** The one **over the household,** the major-domo, was one of the principal

perturbing fashion the questions are thrust on us: "Are we any better? How far is religion real for our people? Is it the true security of the nation?" We say, "In God we trust." Is that true? Social security! This slogan of the welfare state poses a far deeper question than that of the legislation or taxation necessary to provide old-age pensions. When one reads with wonder of the economic and scientific advances of the age, when one sees men adding dollars to dollars and piling up financial resources, when the press announces the production of new and incredible

armaments, and the government publishes the latest strategy in foreign policy, then breaking in on men's comfortable sense of security comes the echo of Isaiah's voice: "But ye look not unto him, the Lord of history; ye have no mind for the God whose will is to be wrought out in the movements of men and nations." Where does God come into our planning? The answer will be decisive for our destiny.

15-25. An Upstart Exposed.—From the judgment of the people Isaiah turns to pillory a man whom he accounted the chief enemy of his

18 He will surely violently turn and toss thee *like* a ball into a large country: there shalt thou die, and there the chariots of thy glory *shall be* the shame of thy lord's house.

19 And I will drive thee from thy station, and from thy state shall he pull thee down.

20 ¶ And it shall come to pass in that day, that I will call my servant Eliakim the son of Hilkiah:

21 And I will clothe him with thy robe, and strengthen him with thy girdle, and I will commit thy government into his hand: and he shall be a father to the inhabitants of Jerusalem, and to the house of Judah.

22 And the key of the house of David will I lay upon his shoulder; so he shall open, and none shall shut; and he shall shut, and none shall open.

23 And I will fasten him *as* a nail in a sure place; and he shall be for a glorious throne to his father's house.

24 And they shall hang upon him all the glory of his father's house, the offspring and the issue, all vessels of small quantity, from the vessels of cups, even to all the vessels of flagons.

25 In that day, saith the LORD of hosts, shall the nail that is fastened in the sure

He will seize firm hold on you, 18 and whirl you round and round, and throw you like a ball into a wide land; there you shall die, and there shall be your splendid chariots, you shame of your master's house. 19 I will thrust you from your office, and you will be cast down from your station. 20 In that day I will call my servant Eli'akim the son of Hilki'ah, 21 and I will clothe him with your robe, and will bind your girdle on him, and will commit your authority to his hand; and he shall be a father to the inhabitants of Jerusalem and to the house of Judah. 22 And I will place on his shoulder the key of the house of David; he shall open, and none shall shut; and he shall shut, and none shall open. 23 And I will fasten him like a peg in a sure place, and he will become a throne of honor to his father's house. 24 And they will hang on him the whole weight of his father's house, the offspring and issue, every small vessel, from the cups to all the flagons. 25 In that day, says the LORD of hosts, the peg that was fastened in a sure

---

ministers of state (cf. I Kings 4:6) ; **this steward** is contemptuous, implying that Shebna, for all his airs, was only a glorified personal servant. **What . . . whom have you here?** The inference is that Shebna is a parvenu, using his present position to prepare for himself **a tomb** among those of the nobles. **Whirl you round** suggests too plausibly the modern figure of a baseball pitcher; "wind you round" (thus making a ball) is better.

20-25. On his shoulder the key: The heavy key of the palace carried on a loop slung over the shoulder gave both symbolic and actual sole power to lock and unlock the principal door (cf. Matt. 16:19; Rev. 3:7) . **Nail** and **peg:** Made of wood (cf. Ezek. 15:3) and driven into the wall for hanging domestic utensils; it can mean also a "tent peg."

---

message and the leading advocate of the fatal policy of alliance with Egypt. That there are difficulties and inconsistencies in this passage the Exeg. makes clear; but nothing can mitigate the scorn and anger of the prophet for this upstart foreigner who had bartered and bribed his way to power. With undisguised contempt for the man, Isaiah declares God will deal with him. He is to be thrown out as a man tosses a ball, and that will be the end of **Shebna**, his pretensions and his famous **tomb**. It is significant that Shebna's chief ambition was to have a tomb to rival that of the nobility. It was not his name that would endure, but only his grave; which is true of many a man who has won a position of power, and for a little has

been a force to reckon with, and then suddenly gone out like a light. Shebna's case raises the question of any man's memorial. Where is it? In the cemetery or in men's lives? It is a poor immortality that is bought from the stonemason; but a man has not lived in vain if he is remembered gratefully for what he did and was to his fellows.

25. *The Support that Failed.*—Shebna's successor, Eliakim, is hailed by the prophet as a man with a future. All the glory that had been Shebna's, all the authority, the emoluments are to be his. Eliakim had character, he was to be the father of his people, a man to be trusted, strong with a strength of a clinched nail or a tent peg driven home. It is a sad commentary on

place be removed, and be cut down, and fall; and the burden that *was* upon it shall be cut off: for the LORD hath spoken *it.*

23 The burden of Tyre. Howl, ye ships of Tarshish; for it is laid waste, so that there is no house, no entering in: from the land of Chittim it is revealed to them.

2 Be still, ye inhabitants of the isle; thou whom the merchants of Zidon, that pass over the sea, have replenished.

place will give way; and it will be cut down and fall, and the burden that was upon it will be cut off, for the LORD has spoken."

23 The oracle concerning Tyre.
Wail, O ships of Tarshish,
    for Tyre is laid waste, without house
      or haven!
From the land of Cyprus
    it is revealed to them.
2 Be still, O inhabitants of the coast,
    O merchants of Sidon,
    your messengers passed over the sea*j*
     and were on many waters;

j One ancient Ms: Heb who passed over the sea, they replenished you

---

A throne [better, "seat"] **of honor:** Presumably a heavy stone used to brace the tent peg was thus regarded. With the change of figure in vs. 24 there is the suggestion that nepotism has led in turn to Eliakim's downfall.

P. CONCERNING TYRE (23:1-18)

1. A DOOM ORACLE ON TYRE AND SIDON (23:1-14)

The text, translation, and meaning of this passage are in many places uncertain. The unity of the poem has been suspect because, although the title and epilogue (vss. 15-18) refer only to Tyre, vss. 2, 4, 12 are addressed to Sidon, and only one city, Tyre, appears in vss. 7-9 to be the object of Yahweh's wrath. Actually the general tenor of the oracle is clear enough if it is recognized that it is concerned with the Phoenician people under various designations—the **inhabitants of the coast** (vs. 2) and of **Canaan** (vs. 11), whose principal cities were **Tyre** and **Sidon,** whose trading colonies were in **Tarshish** and **Cyprus,** and who had a large trade also with Egypt. Yahweh has declared the doom of this proud maritime power (cf. Ezek. 26–28). Her fame as the home of seafarers, merchants, and colonizers will make her fate the more appalling to those who know her (vss. 5-7; cf. Rev. 18:9-19). The extraordinary vs. 13 seems to be a marginal note by a reader seeking to correct the impression that a prophecy ascribed to Isaiah must refer to the Assyrian period. Vs. 14 is a doublet of vs. 1a, inserted as a note of reference for the following supplementary promises, vss. 15-18; it is valuable as preserving a reading which has become corrupt in vs. 1a.

23:1-4. Ships of Tarshish: Ocean-going ships engaged in trade with Phoenician settlements in the western Mediterranean. **Tyre is laid waste:** Better, as in vs. 14, "your

---

human weakness, and an interesting light on the fallibility of Isaiah's judgment of the man, that apparently Eliakim betrayed his trust: the securely fastened nail pulled out, and all the family and relations who had hung upon it fell with it; his downfall is told in a footnote, clearly added by someone who had the facts.

It would be easy to address our legislators, judges, and those who are in power on the subject of Eliakim and the dangers of men in high places. It is not so easy, however, to take to ourselves the same warning that no man is secure in position unless he is secure in character. Why do so many who begin with every promise

of success disappoint the hopes of their friends? How is it that the man who has apparently "arrived" begins to slip, or suddenly crashes, bringing down in his fall all who leaned on him? In every such case one comes on some hidden moral weakness, the gradual abandonment of spiritual values, the estrangement from God. Any carpenter knows that the nail not driven home will pull out. So it is in life. Character not stayed on the eternal and immutable always gives way under the strain, whether of success or disaster.

23:1-16. *The Doom of Tyre and Sidon.*— This great oracle on the fall of Tyre has more

3 And by great waters the seed of Sihor, the harvest of the river, *is* her revenue; and she is a mart of nations.

4 Be thou ashamed, O Zidon: for the sea hath spoken, *even* the strength of the sea, saying, I travail not, nor bring forth children, neither do I nourish up young men, *nor* bring up virgins.

5 As at the report concerning Egypt, *so* shall they be sorely pained at the report of Tyre.

6 Pass ye over to Tarshish; howl, ye inhabitants of the isle.

7 *Is* this your joyous *city*, whose antiquity *is* of ancient days? her own feet shall carry her afar off to sojourn.

8 Who hath taken this counsel against Tyre, the crowning *city*, whose merchants *are* princes, whose traffickers *are* the honorable of the earth?

9 The LORD of hosts hath purposed it, to stain the pride of all glory, *and* to bring into contempt all the honorable of the earth.

10 Pass through thy land as a river, O daughter of Tarshish: *there is* no more strength.

---

3 your revenue was the grain of Shihor,
  the harvest of the Nile;
  you were the merchant of the nations.

4 Be ashamed, O Sidon, for the sea has spoken,
  the stronghold of the sea, saying:
  "I have neither travailed nor given birth,
  I have neither reared young men
  nor brought up virgins."

5 When the report comes to Egypt,
  they will be in anguish over the report about Tyre.

6 Pass over to Tarshish,
  wail, O inhabitants of the coast!

7 Is this your exultant city
  whose origin is from days of old,
  whose feet carried her
  to settle afar?

8 Who has purposed this
  against Tyre, the bestower of crowns,
  whose merchants were princes,
  whose traders were the honored of the earth?

9 The LORD of hosts has purposed it,
  to defile the pride of all glory,
  to dishonor all the honored of the earth.

10 Overflow your land like the Nile,
  O daughter of Tarshish;
  there is no restraint any more.

---

stronghold is laid waste." **Tyre** is not mentioned in the Hebrew text here. The word "stronghold" has been corrupted into the words translated **without house or haven.** On arriving at Cyprus, homeward bound, the seamen hear the news. **The sea has spoken** (omit **the stronghold of the sea** as a gloss); the poet scorns the poetic—and perhaps mythological—claim that the Phoenicians were children of the sea.

5-8. The consternation in Egypt calls forth the cry in vss. 6-8. For **pass over** (imperative) the Dead Sea Scroll reads "you who pass over" or "flee."

9-12. Vs. 10 is corrupt; it may be emended to read עברו מארצך אניות תרשיש אין מנח עוד, "Sail away [lit., "cross over"] from your land, O ships of Tarshish; there is no harbor any more."

---

of lamentation in it than judgment. It is like a highland coronach celebrating the glory that is gone. There is the sound of the sea in it, and the wail of the wind. Only in vs. 9 of the first section is there any note of judgment at all. Isaiah seems to have been profoundly moved over the passing of this mighty sea power. It is only in the second part, the authorship of which is in doubt, that the ugly reference to Tyre as a discarded prostitute occurs. While the oracle names **Tyre** and **Sidon** specifically, it is clearly intended for the whole Phoenician people. It is an unforgettable picture Isaiah draws of how

the word spread, "Tyre is fallen!" It sweeps along the coastline, leaps the sea to Cyprus, goes echoing south to Egypt, and everywhere the dread news brings grief and sorrow to men. There are many occasions on which Isaiah speaks for God with indignation and a sense of the justice of the verdict; but here there is a suggestion of tears. So great was Tyre! The world had brought its treasures to her door, her fearless sailors had dared the seven seas, her galleys had grounded on the beaches of nameless shores, her market places displayed the wealth of nations. Isaiah was great enough of spirit to

11 He stretched out his hand over the sea, he shook the kingdoms: the Lord hath given a commandment against the merchant *city,* to destroy the strongholds thereof.

12 And he said, Thou shalt no more rejoice, O thou oppressed virgin, daughter of Zidon: arise, pass over to Chittim; there also shalt thou have no rest.

13 Behold the land of the Chaldeans; this people was not, *till* the Assyrian founded it for them that dwell in the wilderness: they set up the towers thereof, they raised up the palaces thereof; *and* he brought it to ruin.

14 Howl, ye ships of Tarshish: for your strength is laid waste.

15 And it shall come to pass in that day, that Tyre shall be forgotten seventy years, according to the days of one king: after the end of seventy years shall Tyre sing as a harlot.

16 Take a harp, go about the city, thou harlot that hast been forgotten; make sweet melody, sing many songs, that thou mayest be remembered.

11 He has stretched out his hand over the sea,
   he has shaken the kingdoms;
the Lord has given command concerning Canaan
   to destroy its strongholds.
12 And he said:
  "You will no more exult
   O oppressed virgin daughter of Sidon;
arise, pass over to Cyprus,
   even there you will have no rest."

13 Behold the land of the Chalde'ans! This is the people; it was not Assyria. They destined Tyre for wild beasts. They erected their siege-towers, they razed her palaces, they made her a ruin.[k]
14 Wail, O ships of Tarshish,
   for your stronghold is laid waste.
15 In that day Tyre will be forgotten for seventy years, like the days of one king. At the end of seventy years, it will happen to Tyre as in the song of the harlot:
16 "Take a harp,
   go about the city,
    O forgotten harlot!
Make sweet melody,
   sing many songs,
   that you may be remembered."

[k] The Hebrew of this verse is obscure

---

2. Restoration of Tyre After Seventy Years (23:15-18)

15-18. One of the late supplementers of the prophetic books has added this postscript as a contemptuous comment on the revival of Tyrian power and prosperity, probably under the Seleucid kings, following its destruction by Alexander in 332. In a new day, after a full lifetime of seventy years, and "in the days of another king" (so Procksch,

---

salute the achievements and mourn the fall of a people who had accomplished so much and had sent their name to the fringes of earth. Why was the judgment pronounced? Isaiah declares it in two lines:

> To abase man's pride,
> to humble human splendour (Moffatt).

This will provide any thinker with material for a grave exposure of the peril of the commercial spirit, and the doom that hovers over it. Many possibly will be inclined to go further and become lavish in accusation of the capitalistic system. It is suggested that whatever use a man may choose to make of a chapter rich in material for denunciation, he should first seek to stand alongside Isaiah and acknowledge the greatness of man's achievements. Before he turns

to be eloquent in condemnation of the sins, injustices, and cruelties which have marked the economic progress of civilization, let him purge his spirit of jealousy, and admit that it is a story rich in courage, sacrifice, and toil. Before he becomes an advocate of a change which will replace the ancient structure, he has a moral duty to consider whether the new will give equal opportunity for the development and exhibition of those qualities of personal and social life which brought greatness to the past. Certainly the heroic story of the pioneer and builder of life in this Western Hemisphere would never have been written if our fathers' first concern had been for security, or if they had been dependent upon government subsidies. Say what one may of the evils bound up with the profit system, its record stands as one of magnificent

17 ¶ And it shall come to pass after the end of seventy years, that the LORD will visit Tyre, and she shall turn to her hire, and shall commit fornication with all the kingdoms of the world upon the face of the earth.	17 At the end of seventy years, the LORD will visit Tyre, and she will return to her hire, and will play the harlot with all the kingdoms of the world upon the face of the earth. 18 Her merchandise and her hire will be dedicated to the LORD; it will not be stored or hoarded, but her merchandise will supply abundant food and fine clothing for those who dwell before the LORD.
18 And her merchandise and her hire shall be holiness to the LORD: it shall not be treasured nor laid up; for her merchandise shall be for them that dwell before the LORD, to eat sufficiently, and for durable clothing.	
24 Behold, the LORD maketh the earth empty, and maketh it waste, and turneth it upside down, and scattereth abroad the inhabitants thereof.	24 Behold, the LORD will lay waste the earth and make it desolate, and he will twist its surface and scatter its inhabitants.

op. cit., p. 302), Tyre will recover something of her old position, courting attention like an old harlot returning to her trade. The figure is not, as in Hosea, Micah, and Ezekiel, that of faithlessness or uncleanness but that of prostituting everything to commercial gain (cf. Rev. 17:5; 18:3, 11-13). Vs. 18 goes to extraordinary lengths in suggesting that even this "harlot's hire" will be included in the wealth to be **dedicated to the LORD** in the day of Zion's dominance (cf. 45:14; 60:4-14; Zech. 14:14).

VI. "AWAKE AND SING, YE THAT DWELL IN THE DUST (24:1–27:13)

This collection of eschatological prophecy, psalms, and prayers dating from the later postexilic period was appended to an earlier edition of the book of Isaiah which comprised the bulk of the material now found in chs. 1–23. Appendixes of similar material are found in chs. 33–34 of the further collection comprising chs. 28–34, and in chs. 63–66 of Second Isaiah, as well as at the end of Amos, Micah, Zephaniah, Zechariah, Joel, and Obadiah. There is no real justification for the designation of chs. 24–27 as "an apocalypse" with interpolated "songs" (Duhm, Marti, Gray, Procksch). Certain motifs of eschatological prophecy which were taken over in later apocalyptic writings do indeed appear; e.g., universal judgment, signs in the heavens, imprisonment of members of the heavenly host, the eschatological banquet, the resurrection of the dead, the mythological figure of Leviathan. But most of these are found also elsewhere in late prophecy or poetry. The distinctive features of such books as Dan. 7–12 and Revelation are missing: pseudonymity, weird symbolism, heavenly visions interpreted to the seer by an angel,

achievement, the source of such initiative, daring, and heroic striving as in part redeems the shame of its abuse. There is no denying the evils which mark the past and the present. The one deadly peril to the soul of man is secularism, the gross materialism which measures its goods in terms of cash, and in its passion for things denies to God any place in human life. Against that any Christian can inveigh with the moral passion of the prophets, though if he is truly prophetic he will do more than denounce; he will confront men with God's plan for his children, and declare the hope of the world in the principles of his kingdom.

17-18. The Dedicated Life.—The second section of the great oracle closes with an astonishing conception, viz., that the wages of the **harlot** are to be consecrated to God's service. We need not press the figure of speech, but rather see the magnificence of the thought it clothes. Commerce, trade, business, dedicated to the service of God and man! That is the glory of the kingdom. It is our Lord's own faith that when men seek first that kingdom, all these things shall be added to them, and the glory of Tyre shall be surpassed in the splendor of a peace and prosperity dedicated not to gain but to service.

24:1–27:13. A Collection of Eschatological Prophecies.—In these chapters we have, in the judgment of the critics, a distinct section of the book of Isaiah. It is different in character, and certainly in authorship. Inspired as it must have

dualistic cosmology, reinterpretation of older prophecies, and calculation of times and seasons. These features of apocalyptic as a literary genre are quite distinct from the themes which apocalyptic derives from prophetic eschatology, especially from the eschatological supplements to the prophetic books.

The whole section, chs. 24–27, is composed of originally independent pericopes of eschatological prophecy interspersed with psalms which seemed to the editor appropriate to their contexts. The eschatological prophecy is of three types: (a) pictures of a general desolation of the earth, with special mention of an unnamed city and of Moab, 24:1-12, 16b-18b; 25:10-12; 27:7-11; (b) predictions making use of traditional mythological terms and ideas, 24:18c-23; 25:6-8; 26:20–27:1; (c) promises of Israel's future restoration, 24:13-16a; 27:2-6, 12-13. The psalms are: (a) thanksgivings for deliverance from oppression, 25:1-5, 9; 26:1-6; and (b) an entreaty, 26:7-19. The almost universal judgment of scholars is that all of chs. 24–27 is postexilic in date, but the attempts of Duhm and others to find allusions to particular circumstances cannot be justified on the basis of the vague and general references in the text.

Although the several pericopes of these chapters as analyzed above have the appearance of original independence, their arrangement in sequence is not haphazard. There is a clearly marked alternation between the moods of woe and weal, but it must remain doubtful how far this is due to the editor of the collection and how far to the previous linking in pairs of sections here distinguished; e.g., 24:1-12 is a complete poem in a mood of unrelieved gloom; it is followed in vss. 13-16a by a promise introduced by a connecting particle, which yet has no inner relation of content to the foregoing.

A. First Cycle (24:1-23)
1. The Land Desolate Because of Sin (24:1-12)

This poem describes the desolation (vss. 4-6) of Judah as the fulfillment of a prediction (vss. 1-3), and the consequence of the transgression of the covenant (vs. 5b). The first two strophes of equal length are followed by a longer strophe (vss. 7-12) describing the desolation of the vineyards and the city. This interpretation runs counter to that of most commentators as well as of the translators of the KJV and the RSV, who render the ambiguous הארץ as **the earth** rather than "the land" (i.e., of Judah), resting their case almost entirely on the parallelism in vs. 4 of הארץ and תבל, **the world**. But the parallelism may as well be "extended" as synonymous, i.e., "not only the land but the whole world." And it is highly unlikely that the inhabitants of the whole earth are held responsible for transgressing **the laws, . . . the statutes and . . . the everlasting covenant** of Israel; the covenant with Noah (Gen. 9:1-17) is not a sufficient explanation of these terms as applied to all mankind. Rather, the desolation is that of the same or a similar time referred to in 64:10-11, and the cause of it is ascribed to conditions reflected also in 59:1-15; 65:1-7.

24:1-3. Twist its surface: Rather, "distort its surface," i.e., by an earthquake. **The people . . . the priest:** Hosea's proverb (4:9) is extended and used differently to emphasize the universality of the effects of the desolation. The pairing of **people** with

---

been by some definite historical situation, there is no agreement as to what that was, saving that it was far down the centuries from Isaiah's time. The theme of these chapters is "The Day of the Lord," that terrible reckoning with a race whose piled up sin made doom inevitable. The darkness is strangely and beautifully shot through with gleams of light, lyrical passages of hope, the outpouring of a believer's heart. Despite these breaks in the sequence of thought, there is a certain underlying unity in the whole section

as this servant of God faces the worst and yet, clutching at the skirts of God, dares to believe the best.

24:1-23. The Scourge of God.—Here is a lurid and appalling picture of the world scourged by the wrath of God. Under this visitation all distinctions of rank and class are swept away. When it comes to judgment, "God is no respecter of persons" (Acts 10:34). Experience has taught us that. The impersonality shown by nature in the disasters of flood, fam-

2 And it shall be, as with the people, so with the priest; as with the servant, so with his master; as with the maid, so with her mistress; as with the buyer, so with the seller; as with the lender, so with the borrower; as with the taker of usury, so with the giver of usury to him.

3 The land shall be utterly emptied, and utterly spoiled: for the LORD hath spoken this word.

4 The earth mourneth *and* fadeth away, the world languisheth *and* fadeth away, the haughty people of the earth do languish.

5 The earth also is defiled under the inhabitants thereof; because they have transgressed the laws, changed the ordinance, broken the everlasting covenant.

6 Therefore hath the curse devoured the earth, and they that dwell therein are desolate: therefore the inhabitants of the earth are burned, and few men left.

7 The new wine mourneth, the vine languisheth, all the merry-hearted do sigh.

8 The mirth of tabrets ceaseth, the noise of them that rejoice endeth, the joy of the harp ceaseth.

2 And it shall be, as with the people, so
   with the priest;
  as with the slave, so with his master;
  as with the maid, so with her mistress;
as with the buyer, so with the seller;
  as with the lender, so with the borrower;
as with the creditor, so with the debtor.

3 The earth shall be utterly laid waste and
   utterly despoiled;
  for the LORD has spoken this word.

4 The earth mourns and withers,
  the world languishes and withers;
  the heavens languish together with the
   earth.

5 The earth lies polluted
  under its inhabitants;
for they have transgressed the laws,
  violated the statutes,
  broken the everlasting covenant.

6 Therefore a curse devours the earth,
  and its inhabitants suffer for their
   guilt;
therefore the inhabitants of the earth are
   scorched,
  and few men are left.

7 The wine mourns,
  the vine languishes,
  all the merry-hearted sigh.

8 The mirth of the timbrels is stilled,
  the noise of the jubilant has ceased,
  the mirth of the lyre is stilled.

---

priest rather than with "king" is a clear indication of postexilic circumstances. **This word:** The foregoing oracle.

4-6. "The land" (not **the earth**) is the center of the desolation, but it extends also to **the world** and to "the heights of [so LXX] the earth," i.e., **the heavens. Laws, . . . statutes, . . . covenant:** Cf. Neh. 9:13-14. With these verses cf. 42:22-25.

7-12. The vintage festivals, a figure of joy, are no more. **The city of chaos** or **confusion:** Not an epithet for the city which **is broken down,** but a description of the result,

---

ine, or plague abolishes in an instant all artificial classifications. Reduced to the lowest common denominator of their humanity, people suffer and die. Even so God deals with evil. A king may be as great a sinner as a peasant. The divine judgment disregards all accidents of birth or station and falls upon the sin wherever it is found. If we are "bound in the bundle of life" (I Sam. 25:29), we are also one in the contagion and contamination of sin.

The language here used is that of house-

cleaning. It is not of sinners the prophet speaks, but of sin itself, as having so infected the earth that God must needs literally clean it up. It is a terrible process, nothing is spared, nor is the hand of God stayed till he has dealt with the very heavens, gathering in the sweep of his judgment all rebellious spirits, and imprisoning them in darkness. The chapter closes with a vision of the splendor of God surmounting his cleansed and re-created world.

What can modern man make of such an escha-

9 They shall not drink wine with a song; strong drink shall be bitter to them that drink it.

10 The city of confusion is broken down: every house is shut up, that no man may come in.

11 *There is* a crying for wine in the streets; all joy is darkened, the mirth of the land is gone.

12 In the city is left desolation, and the gate is smitten with destruction.

13 ¶ When thus it shall be in the midst of the land among the people, *there shall be* as the shaking of an olive tree, *and* as the gleaning grapes when the vintage is done.

14 They shall lift up their voice, they shall sing for the majesty of the LORD, they shall cry aloud from the sea.

15 Wherefore glorify ye the LORD in the fires, *even* the name of the LORD God of Israel in the isles of the sea.

9 No more do they drink wine with singing;
　　strong drink is bitter to those who drink it.
10 The city of chaos is broken down,
　　every house is shut up so that none can enter.
11 There is an outcry in the streets for lack of wine;
　　all joy has reached its eventide;
　　the gladness of the earth is banished.
12 Desolation is left in the city,
　　the gates are battered into ruins.
13 For thus it shall be in the midst of the earth
　　among the nations,
　as when an olive tree is beaten,
　　as at the gleaning when the vintage is done.

14 They lift up their voices, they sing for joy;
　　over the majesty of the LORD they shout from the west.
15 Therefore in the east give glory to the LORD;
　　in the coastlands of the sea, to the name of the LORD, the God of Israel.

i.e., the city becomes a **city of chaos**, it is **broken down. Joy has reached its eventide:** An unlikely figure; the obvious reading is עברה, "has vanished" (for similar pictures of a desolate Jerusalem from the later postexilic period cf. 63:18; 64:10-11; Neh. 1:3; Ps. 74:1-11).

2. A Shout of Expectant Triumph (24:13-16a)

13-16a. Appended to the description of desolation is this promise of a harvest of rejoicing like the rejoicing at the harvest of the olive trees and the vineyards. The language resembles that of Second Isaiah (cf. 49:12-13; 51:3). The poet hears in spirit the songs of those whose sorrow has been turned into joy. **Give glory** should be read, like the other verbs, as an indicative. Read עלזו for על־כן, "therefore" (cf. Procksch, *Jesaia I*, p. 311), and render vss. 14-15 more smoothly than in the RSV: "They lift up

tological prophecy with its mysterious and symbolic language? It is entirely foreign to modern thought; the concept of the Last Judgment which so profoundly affected our fathers has almost completely disappeared from contemporary thinking. We do not regard fear as the highest motive for a good life; we put the emphasis on the constraint of the good, rather than on the terror of judgment. Our Lord, it is pointed out, did not win men by a doctrine of hell-fire, but by the doctrine of the loving mercy of the heavenly Father. Yet you cannot have

love without judgment, and you cannot inculcate morality while silent about a reckoning. No one who would present the gospel of divine love in its full magnitude can maintain complete silence about the wrath and judgment of love scorned and flouted. Modern history warrants a return to the old emphasis on the inescapable judgments of God. Leave aside the eschatological reference, and there is still contemporary life which is the scene of the operation of moral law; and nearer still, personal life, where the wages of sin are still paid. No gospel

16 ¶ From the uttermost part of the earth have we heard songs, *even* glory to the righteous. But I said, My leanness, my leanness, woe unto me! the treacherous dealers have dealt treacherously; yea, the treacherous dealers have dealt very treacherously.

17 Fear, and the pit, and the snare, *are* upon thee, O inhabitant of the earth.

18 And it shall come to pass, *that* he who fleeth from the noise of the fear shall fall into the pit; and he that cometh up out of the midst of the pit shall be taken in the snare: for the windows from on high are open, and the foundations of the earth do shake.

16 From the ends of the earth we hear songs
  of praise,
  of glory to the Righteous One.
But I say, "I pine away,
  I pine away. Woe is me!
For the treacherous deal treacherously,
  the treacherous deal very treacherously."

17 Terror, and the pit, and the snare
  are upon you, O inhabitant of the
  earth!
18 He who flees at the sound of the terror
  shall fall into the pit;
and he who climbs out of the pit
  shall be caught in the snare.
For the windows of heaven are opened,
  and the foundations of the earth
  tremble.

their voice, they shout for the majesty of the Lord. They cry aloud from the west, they exult in the east, they glorify the Lord on the shores of the sea." **Righteous One** should not be capitalized as in the RSV; the reference is not to God but to restored Israel, **righteous** in the sense of "vindicated" (cf. 26:2; Ps. 37:28) ; "the righteous one has been made glorious."

3. The Terror of the Lord (24:16*b*-18*b*)

16*b*-18*b*. The opening line of this fragment is obscure. For other pictures of man's flight from the terror of the day of the Lord cf. 2:19-21; Amos 5:19-20. The alliterative words of vs. 17 reappear in Jer. 48:43, applied to Moab.

4. The Final Cataclysm, the Judgment, and the New Age (24:18*c*-23)

This is the first of the three short sections which make use of traditional mythological ideas transferred to the realm of eschatology, and which are the only parts of chs. 24–27 resembling apocalyptic writing. It pictures a cataclysm overwhelming the natural world with storm and earthquake, accompanied by the eclipse of sun and moon, the imprisonment and subsequent punishment of the rebellious "host of heaven" and earthly kings, and the final establishment of Yahweh's sovereignty in a universe centered in Jerusalem. The religious significance of this lies in the conviction that God, simply because he is God, must in the end "reign until he has put all his enemies under his feet" (I Cor. 15:25) . There can be no rival and independent authority, spiritual or political, to his sovereignty.

The manifestation of Yahweh's power in storm and earthquake is a familiar element in the O.T. (cf. Judg. 5:4-5; Ps. 18:7-15) . But the ancient myth of the combat of a god

for the twentieth century which evades the dark doctrine of divine judgment can be true either to the facts of history or to the nature of God. Isa. 24 deals with a truth which the modern Christian dare not ignore if he would keep his intellectual and spiritual integrity.

One feature of this chapter is the startling and arresting thought that sin corrupts not man alone, but the very earth on which he dwells. "The earth," says the writer, "is profaned by

the sins of men" (vs. 5) . The contamination of evil permeates even the structure of the world. The Bible knows nothing of the theory that matter is itself evil. The great disasters which ravage nature and destroy life are not depicted as the work of evil spirits, but always as the judgment on human sin. The scientific mind may be reluctant to consider such a theory, but it is worth pondering. Is there some kind of moral sympathy between man and nature? Is man

19 The earth is utterly broken down, the earth is clean dissolved, the earth is moved exceedingly.	19 The earth is utterly broken, the earth is rent asunder, the earth is violently shaken.
20 The earth shall reel to and fro like a drunkard, and shall be removed like a cottage; and the transgression thereof shall be heavy upon it; and it shall fall, and not rise again.	20 The earth staggers like a drunken man, it sways like a hut; its transgression lies heavy upon it, and it falls, and will not rise again.
21 And it shall come to pass in that day, *that* the LORD shall punish the host of the high ones *that are* on high, and the kings of the earth upon the earth.	21 On that day the LORD will punish the host of heaven, in heaven, and the kings of the earth, on the earth.
22 And they shall be gathered together, *as* prisoners are gathered in the pit, and shall be shut up in the prison, and after many days shall they be visited.	22 They will be gathered together as prisoners in a pit; they will be shut up in a prison, and after many days they will be punished.
23 Then the moon shall be confounded, and the sun ashamed, when the LORD of hosts shall reign in mount Zion, and in Jerusalem, and before his ancients gloriously.	23 Then the moon will be confounded, and the sun ashamed; for the LORD of hosts will reign on Mount Zion and in Jerusalem and before his elders he will manifest his glory.

with rebellious powers, his subduing of them and subsequent enthronement as supreme king (cf. Marduk in *Enūma eliš*, Tablets IV, VI; Baal in The Poem of Baal, III AB, A; II AB; cf. Gaster, *Thespis*, pp. 74-75, 153-82) is clearly seen in the background of this, as of other O.T. passages like 14:12-15; Pss. 29; 82; 89:2-19; Ezek. 28:12-17. **The host of heaven** (vs. 21) are astral deities, rebellious "sons of Elyon" (Ps. 82:1, 6-7), to be imprisoned in the **pit** (cf. 14:15; Rev. 20:1-3; I Enoch 18:12-16).

18c-20. The windows of heaven: Source of torrential rainfall, as at Noah's flood (cf. Gen. 7:11); the phrase occurs also in The Poem of Baal, II AB, for rifts in the clouds through which rain came. **Foundations:** Not "the waters under the earth" but the base of the solid earth itself. **Cottage** or **hut:** Better, "shelter," temporary and flimsy.

21-23. In heaven: Better, "in the height," "the north pole or zenith of the Ecliptic . . . , the abode of Deity" (C. F. Burney, "The Three Serpents of Isaiah XXVII I," *Journal of Theological Studies,* XI [1909-10], 446). **After many days:** The interval which in later apocalyptic imagery became the "thousand years" of Rev. 20:3, 7. For the darkening of the sun and moon which became a standard feature of such descriptions, cf. 13:10; Joel 2:10; Matt. 24:29. **Reign:** Mount his throne in triumph. **Will manifest his glory:** Either we should read with the LXX "he will be glorified," or we should see here a reference to the "Gloria" or doxology uttered by those assembled to acclaim God (cf. Pss. 29:9; 86:9).

merely a temporary manifestation of a type of life, which for a little infests the earth and then passes, leaving to time the healing of the scars and disfigurements of his habitation? Or is he, as the Bible claims, of such moment to God that the earth is at his service, and responds to his development, either in evil or in good? Isa. 24 declares that the judgment fell on a world made evil by men who have **transgressed the** [divine] **laws, changed the** [eternal] **ordinance, broken**

the everlasting covenant (vs. 5). It would seem to be the same deep thought which led the N.T. to speak of "a new heaven and a new earth" (Rev. 21:1). Something had to be done with a world profaned and an earth poisoned by human sin. But the new heaven and the new earth of Christian faith have more to do with a cross on a lonely hill, and a risen Christ, and the spirit of his kingdom, than with the flame and thunder which echo through Isa. 24.

25 O Lord, thou *art* my God; I will exalt thee, I will praise thy name; for thou hast done wonderful *things; thy* counsels of old *are* faithfulness *and* truth.

2 For thou hast made of a city a heap; *of* a defensed city a ruin: a palace of strangers to be no city; it shall never be built.

3 Therefore shall the strong people glorify thee, the city of the terrible nations shall fear thee.

4 For thou hast been a strength to the poor, a strength to the needy in his distress, a refuge from the storm, a shadow from the heat, when the blast of the terrible ones *is* as a storm *against* the wall.

5 Thou shalt bring down the noise of strangers, as the heat in a dry place; *even* the heat with the shadow of a cloud: the branch of the terrible ones shall be brought low.

---

25 O Lord, thou art my God;
　I will exalt thee, I will praise thy
　　name;
for thou hast done wonderful things,
　plans formed of old, faithful and sure.
2 For thou hast made the city a heap,
　the fortified city a ruin;
the palace of aliens is a city no more,
　it will never be rebuilt.
3 Therefore strong peoples will glorify
　　thee;
　cities of ruthless nations will fear thee.
4 For thou hast been a stronghold to the
　　poor,
　a stronghold to the needy in his dis-
　　tress,
　a shelter from the storm and a shade
　　from the heat;
for the blast of the ruthless is like a storm
　　against a wall,
5　like heat in a dry place.
Thou dost subdue the noise of the aliens;
　as heat by the shade of a cloud,
　so the song of the ruthless is stilled.

B. Second Cycle (25:1-9)

1. A Thanksgiving for Victory (25:1-5)

This short hymn of thanksgiving for the overthrow of an enemy city might have been found in the Psalter (cf. Ps. 145). Pss. 60:9; 108:10 point to a fortress in Edom (Sela ?) as possibly the city referred to (cf. Obad. 3); or, since a world power seems indicated, the reference may be to Nineveh (Nah. 2–3), to Babylon (Isa. 13), or to the capital or fortress of a later oppressor. The dependence on the language of prophecy suggests the later Persian or the Hellenistic period. The psalm reflects the deepening faith that the preservation of the politically helpless Jews was to be explained by the persistent purpose of God, in order that through them all nations would come to serve him.

25:1-5. Plans formed of old: Lit., "from afar," stressing the limitless range in time or space of Yahweh's power in history. Or, with a change of accent, the line may read, "Thou hast carried out thy wondrous plans." **A heap:** A pile of rubble (cf. Mic. 3:12). **Palace of aliens:** Better, "the castle of the insolent," reading with LXX זדים for זרים. **Strong peoples:** The KJV is correct in reading the singular here and in the next line, "the city of dreadful nations"; the reference is to an imperial power which will be forced to acknowledge Yahweh's supremacy. **The poor** or "helpless" are here the Jewish community (cf. Pss. 113:7; 132:15). **A storm against a wall:** Better, reading קר for קיר, "a winter storm."

25:1-5. A Hymn of Praise.—The chapter opens with a psalm of thanksgiving for deliverance. It is vibrant with praise for the goodness of God to his people. The stronghold of the enemy has been overthrown; God's poor have been brought through their tribulation; they have seen what all the world must see, that the immutable purposes of God are fulfilled, however wild the rebellion of men. This is every man's psalm, as true of life today as when a nameless poet wrote it long ago in the rapture of liberation. Those who have been through things, and have in the dark days been conscious that God's care was about them, can make this their own song. Line by line it is true for them, and looking back they too can say, **Thou hast done wonderful things.** The experience of suffering or sorrow is never in vain if afterward

6 ¶ And in his mountain shall the LORD of hosts make unto all people a feast of fat things; a feast of wines on the lees, of fat things full of marrow, of wines on the lees well refined.

7 And he will destroy in this mountain the face of the covering cast over all people, and the veil that is spread over all nations.

8 He will swallow up death in victory; and the Lord GOD will wipe away tears from off all faces; and the rebuke of his people

6 On this mountain the LORD of hosts will make for all peoples a feast of fat things, a feast of wine on the lees, of fat things full of marrow, of wine on the lees well refined. **7** And he will destroy on this mountain the covering that is cast over all peoples, the veil that is spread over all nations. **8** He will swallow up death for ever, and the Lord GOD will wipe away tears from all faces, and the reproach of his

2. THE FEAST OF TRIUMPH AND THE END OF SORROW (25:6-9)

This is the second of the eschatological pericopes making use of traditional mythic material. The brief psalm in vs. 9 speaks in the usual language of the Psalter; but in relation to the foregoing verses it finds "an echo in the ritual cry which greeted the reappearance of Attis in the Asianic mysteries" (Gaster, *op. cit.*, p. 208). The theme of a feast for all (nations) celebrating the destruction of God's enemies and the commencement of a new era of peace and salvation is already found in north Canaanite mythology (cf. *ibid.*, pp. 207-16). It is reflected also in later apocalyptic literature proper (cf. Baruch 29:3-8; II Esdras 6:52; Rev. 19:9, 17). It can hardly be accidental that the swallowing up of Death (Hebrew *mâweth, môth*) is paralleled in the Canaanite myth by Baal's victory over Mot, god of death and the underworld (cf. *ibid.*, pp. 124, 204). And the destruction of the **covering** and the **veil** which is over all peoples, and the wiping away of tears, correspond in The Poem of Baal to the triumphant warrior's command to Anat to "banish warfare from the earth, . . . weave no longer on the earth tissues of lies, . . . a mesh of guile" (Tablet V AB, iv, *ibid.*, p. 213).

The discovery of antecedents in mythological language and ideas to this and other biblical passages does not discount their value as expressions of Hebrew thought and feeling. Here we have again the deep conviction that the Lord of hosts—not Baal—will do all that was ever said of Baal, and more. The feast described will make his triumph at the end of history, and he will bring to an end the reality of sorrow and suffering which have marked **the reproach of his people.** The idea that God's ultimate triumph over his enemies will be also a victory over death and pain takes on a new and deeper meaning here, because the thought of God was more true and worthy in Israel than in north Canaan centuries before. And when in Rev. 21:4 the words of this passage were quoted, it was in the light of a new certainty which was theirs who knew that Christ was risen.

6-9. For all peoples: Because his sovereignty had been declared universal. **Fat things:** Rich food. **Wine on the lees:** Well matured. **Swallow up death:** As the grave swallows

a man is able to see something of God's purpose in it, and can face life with new and deeper knowledge of his love and care.

6-8. A Festival of Joy.—This section ought logically to follow immediately on ch. 24. The reign of God over his re-created world is to be ushered in with a feast, a coronation festival. It is for all men, for the covenant of his mercy is all-inclusive. By an amazing leap of faith the poet transcends all national bounds, and sees the nations of earth "bound by gold chains about the feet of God."[3]

[3] Tennyson, "The Passing of Arthur," *Idylls of the King.*

7-8. The End of Tears.—There follow the immortal words which have echoed the hope of the sons of men down through the ages: **He will swallow up death in victory; and the Lord GOD will wipe away tears from off all faces.**

The splendor of the prophet's faith can be appreciated only when one remembers that for the greater part of their history the Jews had no real hope of immortality. Here and there some elect soul voices a divine surmise that death is not the end; but for the most part the Jews labored, suffered, sorrowed, and died without any expectation of the glory of going on. What pathos and what courage, that men should

shall he take away from off all the earth: for the LORD hath spoken *it*.

9 ¶ And it shall be said in that day, Lo, this *is* our God; we have waited for him, and he will save us: this *is* the LORD; we have waited for him, we will be glad and rejoice in his salvation.

10 For in this mountain shall the hand of the LORD rest, and Moab shall be trodden down under him, even as straw is trodden down for the dunghill.

11 And he shall spread forth his hands in the midst of them, as he that swimmeth spreadeth forth *his hands* to swim: and he shall bring down their pride together with the spoils of their hands.

12 And the fortress of the high fort of thy walls shall he bring down, lay low, *and* bring to the ground, *even* to the dust.

people he will take away from all the earth; for the LORD has spoken.

9 It will be said on that day, "Lo, this is our God; we have waited for him, that he might save us. This is the LORD; we have waited for him; let us be glad and rejoice in his salvation."

10 For the hand of the LORD will rest on this mountain, and Moab shall be trodden down in his place, as straw is trodden down in a dung-pit. **11** And he will spread out his hands in the midst of it as a swimmer spreads his hands out to swim; but the LORD will lay low his pride together with the skill[l] of his hands. **12** And the high fortifications of his walls he will bring down, lay low, and cast to the ground, even to the dust.

[l] The meaning of the Hebrew word is uncertain

up men (cf. Ps. 124:3; Prov. 1:12). **In victory** is a mistaken rendering of **for ever;** it is used by Paul in I Cor. 15:54, with Aq. and Theod., but not the LXX. Read in vs. 9, "Behold our God for whom we have waited"; the verse is a hymn of praise for victory, like Ps. 9.

C. THIRD CYCLE (25:10–27:1)
1. DOOM OF MOAB (25:10-12)

10-12. It is strange to find a single enemy selected in this context for vituperation, and some emend מוֹאָב, **Moab,** to אֹיֵב, "enemy." The figure of the enemy as a man struggling to escape from a dung pit is unusually coarse, and the connection is obscure. Vs. 10*a* may be taken more suitably with vs. 9 as the conclusion of the psalm, since **the hand of the LORD** is protective, and **this mountain** (as in vs. 6 and 24:23) refers to Zion.

face life with unsurrendered loyalty to the best they knew, and at the end of the day bid farewell even to God himself, and go out into the night! But here is a God-lighted soul daring to proclaim that in God's kingdom the two great enemies of the human heart shall have no place, death and sorrow being vanquished. That hope, struck off in darkness, never waned, but rather continued to glow and brighten until in a burst of glory the words were written, "And there shall be no more death, neither sorrow, nor crying, neither shall there be any more pain: for the former things are passed away" (Rev. 21:4); passed away in the victory of "Jesus Christ, who hath abolished death, and hath brought life and immortality to light" (II Tim. 1:10). For the dying, for the mourner; aye, and for the living faced with the contradictions of life and the denials of death, that is Christianity. He who long ago heralded the light and proclaimed the hope had nothing but his faith to support his message. With his face to God he could only hold that it ought to be true, that

with such a God it was "too good not to be true." But we have Jesus Christ, his life, his death, his victory to transmute the hope into the promise of his love. Wherefore, "Bless the Lord, O my soul."

9-12. *The Doom of Moab.*—The final section of the chapter deals with the humiliation of Moab. Why at this point one nation is singled out for denunciation we do not know. It can only be assumed that for some unrecorded deed of horror Moab receives this dishonorable mention. It is a coarse, brutal figure the writer gives us, of a man submerged in a **dung-pit,** and actually trying to swim in its foulness. The passage is redeemed by its opening lines (vs. 9). Again and again in history men who have endured, clinging to their hope in God, and been suddenly brought out of darkness to light, have taken on their grateful lips these words, and flung them out in thanksgiving. **Lo, this is our God; we have waited for him, . . . we will be glad and rejoice in his salvation.** There is no surer test of character than a man's reaction to

26 In that day shall this song be sung in the land of Judah; We have a strong city; salvation will *God* appoint *for* walls and bulwarks.

2 Open ye the gates, that the righteous nation which keepeth the truth may enter in.

3 Thou wilt keep *him* in perfect peace, *whose* mind *is* stayed *on thee:* because he trusteth in thee.

4 Trust ye in the LORD for ever: for in the LORD JEHOVAH *is* everlasting strength.

5 ¶ For he bringeth down them that dwell on high; the lofty city, he layeth it low; he layeth it low, *even* to the ground; he bringeth it *even* to the dust.

6 The foot shall tread it down, *even* the feet of the poor, *and* the steps of the needy.

26 In that day this song will be sung in the land of Judah:
"We have a strong city;
  he sets up salvation
  as walls and bulwarks.
2 Open the gates,
  that the righteous nation which keeps faith
  may enter in.
3 Thou dost keep him in perfect peace,
  whose mind is stayed on thee,
  because he trusts in thee.
4 Trust in the LORD for ever,
  for the LORD GOD
  is an everlasting rock.
5 For he has brought low
  the inhabitants of the height,
  the lofty city.
He lays it low, lays it low to the ground,
  casts it to the dust.
6 The foot tramples it,
  the feet of the poor,
  the steps of the needy."

2. A HYMN OF THANKSGIVING FOR VICTORY (26:1-6)

This is the first part of the composite psalm, vss. 1-19, but it is taken separately because at vs. 7 the note of praise changes to that of supplication, Yahweh is spoken of in the second person instead of in the first, and there is a change of meter. Similar changes within a single psalm are common in the Psalter and may indicate (though not necessarily) composition from originally independent units. Vss. 1-6 are a liturgy for use by a ceremonial procession entering Jerusalem to celebrate a victory; the best commentary on it is Ps. 24:7-10. In its present position after 25:10*b*-12 the opening rubric, vs. 1*a*, appears to prescribe it for use on the occasion of the overthrow of Moab. The psalm opens with proud praise of Zion's strength (cf. Ps. 48:13-14 [Hebrew 48:12-13]), followed by the call to open the gates that **the righteous nation** [i.e., the nation vindicated by victory—cf. 24:16; Zech. 9:9] **may enter.** The nation's trust which has brought her to triumph is declared in vs. 3, and in vs. 4 follows a call to faith in the God who has laid low the enemy (vs. 5) under the feet of his people.

26:1-6. Salvation, or "victory": He makes victory to be "the walls and rampart" (cf. 60:18). If the Dead Sea Scroll is right in reading "thy gates," the psalm begins, "O our strong city . . . ." Vs. 3 continues to speak of the **nation:** "Steadfast in purpose, her welfare thou dost guard, for she trusts in thee." **The lofty city** recalls Edom in Obad. 3.

deliverance. Does he congratulate himself on having "stuck it out"? Does he accept it as part of the way things work out? Or does he see God's hand in it, and so give thanks, and turn again to life, debtor to his love? God with us!

26:1-21. The Song of the City of God.—This great psalm of thanksgiving and faith can be lifted out of its historical context and used in Christian worship as the expression of the church's devotion; for the centuries have con-

firmed its truth, and the experience of men has vindicated its faith. Such a verse as **Thou wilt keep him in perfect peace, whose mind is stayed on thee: because he trusteth in thee** contains a gospel for multitudes of perplexed and anxious souls. Modern psychology testifies to its truth and declares it in the consulting room and clinic. There are multitudes who can bear witness that their first discovery of peace of mind came to them when, weary with struggle and

7 The way of the just *is* uprightness: thou, most upright, dost weigh the path of the just.

8 Yea, in the way of thy judgments, O LORD, have we waited for thee; the desire of *our* soul *is* to thy name, and to the remembrance of thee.

9 With my soul have I desired thee in the night; yea, with my spirit within me will I seek thee early: for when thy judgments *are* in the earth, the inhabitants of the world will learn righteousness.

7 The way of the righteous is level;
thou[m] dost make smooth the path of
the righteous.
8 In the path of thy judgments,
O LORD, we wait for thee;
thy memorial name
is the desire of our soul.
9 My soul yearns for thee in the night,
my spirit within me earnestly seeks
thee.
For when thy judgments are in the earth,
the inhabitants of the world learn
righteousness.

[m] Cn Compare Gk: Heb *thou* (*that art*) *upright*

3. A PRAYER OF ENTREATY AND FAITH (26:7-19)

This psalm is a liturgy of entreaty similar to Pss. 44; 60; 74, as used in time of calamity at a solemn assembly like that described in Joel 2:15-17 (cf. I Kings 8:33-34). The opening cry of complaint and appeal has apparently been lost (cf. Pss. 60:1; 74:1); what remains in vs. 7 is its accompanying assertion of confidence in the ways of God. In vss. 8-9, 12-15 the community proclaims its loyalty to God (cf. Ps. 44:17-22), and in vss. 16-18 draws attention to its great distress (cf. Ps. 44:9-16, 25). In vss. 10-11 and the concluding vs. 19 there is the same urgent appeal for succor from the enemies of the moment (cf. Ps. 44:4-5, 26). The distinctive feature of the psalm here is that the appeal is not only for the overthrow of the enemy but for Yahweh's aid to be shown in a startlingly new way—the resurrection of those who have died at the enemy's hands (vs. 19). This points to a date for this psalm not far removed from that of Dan. 12:2-3, in the second century B.C.

8. Omit **for thee,** as conjectured by Lowth and others, now confirmed by the Dead Sea Scroll. **Thy memorial name:** The name which has acquired meaning from what Israel remembers Yahweh to have done; the Dead Sea Scroll reads instead "thy name and thy law," which may be original.

9. My soul: As so often in the Psalms, the first person singular is used in common prayer by the congregation (cf. Ps. 44:4, 6 [Hebrew 44:5, 7]).

baffled in their quest, they cast their burden on God and were sustained. Rupert Brooke, who in World War I found peace in death, wrote these words which are a perfect commentary on our text:

We have gained a peace unshaken by pain for ever.
War knows no power. Safe shall be my going,
Secretly armed against all death's endeavour;
Safe though all safety's lost; safe where men fall;
And if these poor limbs die, safest of all.[4]

Vs. 9 suggests the theme of "Light Through Judgment": **When thy judgments are in the earth, the inhabitants of the world will learn**

[4] "Safety," from *The Collected Poems of Rupert Brooke.* Copyright 1915 by Dodd, Mead & Co., Inc., and used by their permission, together with that of Sidgwick & Jackson and McClelland & Stewart.

righteousness. In one sense history seems to refute that claim; for God's judgments have continuously fallen upon the race, and yet at this latest point of time righteousness is about the last word to apply to international relationships. But this at least is true: the retribution which has fallen on human sin has progressively made clear how God looks on life, and what he requires of men. Far more effectively than the spoken word, a judgment experienced reveals the mind and will of God. No one can deny that the twentieth century has been a period of world judgment. We have reason to know as never before the conditions God lays down for peace. We have not learned righteousness, but we are learning. We have not made peace, but we know something of the conditions which make it possible. Out of the dark judgment of war has come light on our own failures and

10 Let favor be showed to the wicked, *yet* will he not learn righteousness: in the land of uprightness will he deal unjustly, and will not behold the majesty of the LORD.

11 LORD, *when* thy hand is lifted up, they will not see: *but* they shall see, and be ashamed for *their* envy at the people; yea, the fire of thine enemies shall devour them.

12 ¶ LORD, thou wilt ordain peace for us: for thou also hast wrought all our works in us.

13 O LORD our God, *other* lords besides thee have had dominion over us: *but* by thee only will we make mention of thy name.

14 *They are* dead, they shall not live; *they are* deceased, they shall not rise: therefore hast thou visited and destroyed them, and made all their memory to perish.

15 Thou hast increased the nation, O LORD, thou hast increased the nation; thou art glorified: thou hadst removed *it* far *unto* all the ends of the earth.

---

10 If favor is shown to the wicked,
    he does not learn righteousness;
in the land of uprightness he deals perversely
    and does not see the majesty of the LORD.

11 O LORD, thy hand is lifted up,
    but they see it not.
Let them see thy zeal for thy people, and be ashamed.
Let the fire for thy adversaries consume them.

12 O LORD, thou wilt ordain peace for us,
    thou hast wrought for us all our works.

13 O LORD our God,
    other lords besides thee have ruled over us,
    but thy name alone we acknowledge.

14 They are dead, they will not live;
    they are shades, they will not arise;
to that end thou hast visited them with destruction
    and wiped out all remembrance of them.

15 But thou hast increased the nation, O LORD,
    thou hast increased the nation; thou art glorified;
    thou hast enlarged all the borders of the land.

---

11. Read with the LXX, "Let the fire consume thy adversaries."

12-15. **Thou hast wrought . . . works:** "In everything that we have done thou hast wrought for us." **Ruled over:** "Mastered." The alien rulers are as good as dead, under Yahweh's judgment, and for them (contrast vs. 19) there will be no resurrection; Procksch (*Jesaia I*, p. 328) thinks of the impotent gods of the heathen (cf. 41:23-24).

---

on God's terms. Whether we will follow the gleam and, learning righteousness, come at last to peace on earth and good will among men, the future is yet to declare.

10-11. Spiritual Inertia.—While vs. 10 specifically mentions the insensibility of the **wicked**, it suggests a danger to which we are all exposed, viz., the blinding effect of prosperity. It is not the wicked only who fail to learn **righteousness** when favor is shown to them. A high standard of living always tends to make people complacent. Unconsciously they begin to feel that they deserve success. If favor is shown to them, they take it as token that they themselves are righteous. There are thousands who have never suffered financial or other straitening who apparently assume that the man who does the right thing and lives a decent life is assured of prosperity. Preoccupation with things, a comfortable and undisturbed standard of living, can slowly but surely blot out from a man's mind all sense of gratitude to or dependence upon God. People comfortably off seldom evince any awareness of "the majesty of God." The good home, the automobile, all the amenities which are taken for granted beget in them a sense of well-being which is essentially self-righteous. The churches are full of people who while they would not say it in so many words, really feel that they have a right to be well off, and that the honesty they display, all the moral virtues they possess, largely account for their prosperity. There is even a touch of condescension in their going to church at all. They do not feel that they need to go, but it is well to support the

16 LORD, in trouble have they visited thee; they poured out a prayer *when* thy chastening *was* upon them.

17 Like as a woman with child, *that* draweth near the time of her delivery, is in pain, *and* crieth out in her pangs; so have we been in thy sight, O LORD.

18 We have been with child, we have been in pain, we have as it were brought forth wind; we have not wrought any deliverance in the earth; neither have the inhabitants of the world fallen.

19 Thy dead *men* shall live, *together with* my dead body shall they arise. Awake and sing, ye that dwell in dust: for thy dew *is as* the dew of herbs, and the earth shall cast out the dead.

16 O LORD, in distress they sought thee,
  they poured out a prayer[n]
  when thy chastening was upon them.
17 Like a woman with child,
  who writhes and cries out in her pangs,
  when she is near her time,
 so were we because of thee, O LORD;
18 we were with child, we writhed,
  we have as it were brought forth wind.
 We have wrought no deliverance in the earth,
  and the inhabitants of the world have not fallen.
19 Thy dead shall live, their bodies[o] shall rise.
  O dwellers in the dust, awake and sing for joy!
 For thy dew is a dew of light,
  and on the land of the shades thou wilt let it fall.

[n] Heb uncertain
[o] Cn Compare Syr Tg: Heb *my body*

16-18. In vs. 16 read "we" for **they,** with the LXX and vss. 17-18. In vs. 16b read, "We cried out when the trouble of thy chastening was upon us" (צעקנו לחץ . . . לנו).

19. Read, "Those who dwell in the dust shall awake and sing for joy," with the Dead Sea Scroll and the LXX. As the **dew** brings life to parched vegetation, so "thy dew shall be like the dew of dawn" (or "the glistening dew"). It should be added that although the reference to a literal resurrection is the more probable meaning, it is also possible that this is a figure of speech for the restoration of the life and fortunes of the nation, as in Ezekiel's vision (ch. 37) of the valley of dry bones.

institution. There is nothing like the spiritual inertia of a complacent middle-class church.

> **O LORD, thy hand is lifted up,**
> **but they see it not.**

How true that is! It matters not whether God's hand has been lifted in mercy or in judgment. They are unaware of it. They find sufficient explanation of events in economic law or political theory. It is a matter of history that eras of prosperity have been consistently periods of worldliness, godlessness, and refined selfishness. These have not been the ages of social reform or religious revival, or the ages of deepening righteousness and greater faith in God. On the contrary, they have been marked by a mounting pride in human achievement and a waning sense of gratitude to God.

The awakening from this stupor of complacency is always a sore business. It may take a war or a depression or a profound personal sorrow to do it. But if as a result men become aware of God, if at last they see him, then not less than their salvation is in their suffering. When they see through to their shame as the prodigal did, there is at least a possibility that like him also they will say, "I will arise and go to my father" (Luke 15:18).

19. *The Resurrection Hope.*—This is the most moving and wonderful section of the psalm. It is quite clear that the poet has no idea of a general resurrection, for in vs. 14 he exults in the thought that the dead enemies are gone forever, and he finds relief in the knowledge that never again will these "other lords" trouble Israel. The source of the poet's hope, which was for the faithful among his own people, is, to say the least, unusual; for it seems to be born of the fact that the land of Israel was well-nigh depopulated. It is as if, musing on the nation's history, he sees the hand of God guiding the people to the hour of deliverance. At last the day dawns when the land is free; but how few there are to glory in it! By the mercy of God Israel has been saved; but what of the thousands

20 ¶ Come, my people, enter thou into thy chambers, and shut thy doors about thee: hide thyself as it were for a little moment, until the indignation be overpast.

21 For, behold, the LORD cometh out of his place to punish the inhabitants of the earth for their iniquity: the earth also shall disclose her blood, and shall no more cover her slain.

20 Come, my people, enter your chambers,
and shut your doors behind you;
hide yourselves for a little while
until the wrath is past.
21 For behold, the LORD is coming forth out of his place
to punish the inhabitants of the earth for their iniquity,
and the earth will disclose the blood shed upon her,
and will no more cover her slain.

---

4. SLAYING OF LEVIATHAN (26:20–27:1)

This is a prophetic oracle in response to the foregoing psalm of entreaty, and here the dependence upon traditional mythological material is very obvious. There are numerous references in the O.T. (as well as in Rev. 12:3-17; 20:10) to the overthrow by Yahweh of the dragon variously known as Leviathan (27:1; Pss. 74:13-14; 104:26), as Rahab, "the Rager" (30:7; 51:9; Ps. 89:10; Job 9:13; 26:12-13), as Tannin, "the Dragon" or "the Monster" (51:9; Ezek. 29:3; 32:2; Ps. 74:13; Job 7:12); as the serpent (27:1; Amos 9:3; Job 26:13); or as the Sea (51:10; Hab. 3:8; Ps. 74:13; Job 7:12; 26:12; 38:8; cf. Rev. 21:1). The myth is in the first instance the story of the slaying or imprisonment by the Creator of the dragon of chaos, and when projected into eschatology, as here, it becomes the symbol of the final overthrow of God's enemies and the establishment of his unquestioned sovereignty. The theme appears in many ancient mythologies (cf. Gaster, *op. cit.*, pp. 140-51), of which the biblical forms most resemble, as might be expected, the Babylonian and Canaanite versions.

20-21. God's word to his people is that they can do nothing but wait until—very soon—he overthrows finally his enemies and theirs. The day is at hand! In the light of Israel's long history of oppression, mankind is to be judged for the sin of Cain (Gen. 4:8-12; cf. Luke 11:51).

---

who endured, suffered, and died before their prayers were answered? Is it really salvation if they have no part in it? Then the faith of the poet takes wings. Unsupported by argument, with nothing but the instinct of his own great heart, he breaks into the song of resurrection. The dead heroes, God's and Israel's together, shall come back. It will be the final miracle of God's power and the perfecting of his great salvation.

Some men argue themselves into belief in immortality; others reach it through an agony of hope and longing. This nameless poet stands at the height of a progressive revelation that the final redemption of man is not to be wrought out through natural or evolutionary process, for always death intervenes and writes finis to an uncompleted chapter. It will take nothing less than a miracle to deal with death's obstructing power. The final venture and victory of human faith are celebrated in this voice which is sent ringing over the wasted land, thick with the graves of the fallen: **Awake and sing, ye that dwell in dust.** Here is one who dares to proclaim the miracle. He hazards all

his faith and love on the response and the action of God.

The N.T. echoes with the rapture of that same faith; but it is no longer a brave guess: it takes its stand on the historic facts that Christ was not held by death, that in him God's power wrought the miracle and once for all revealed the sovereignty of divine love over sin and death. There is certainty in the Christian faith only because we are persuaded "that neither death, nor life, . . . nor any other creature, shall be able to separate us from the love of God, which is in Christ Jesus our Lord" (Rom. 8:38-39). Certainty—but not such courage as marked the faith of that man who put the trumpet to his lips and pealed out the notes of promise, **Thy dead shall live,** when he had nothing to go on but the outreach of his own faith that somehow God must deal with death's denial. Only a voice crying to a lonely land; but the hope kindled never died, and in God's own time another voice spoke to the people of Israel, and to all the sons of men, "I am the resurrection, and the life. . . . Because I live, ye shall live also" (John 11:25; 14:19).

27 In that day the LORD with his sore and great and strong sword shall punish leviathan the piercing serpent, even leviathan that crooked serpent; and he shall slay the dragon that *is* in the sea.

2 In that day sing ye unto her, A vineyard of red wine.

3 I the LORD do keep it; I will water it every moment: lest *any* hurt it, I will keep it night and day.

4 Fury *is* not in me: who would set the briers *and* thorns against me in battle? I would go through them, I would burn them together.

5 Or let him take hold of my strength, *that* he may make peace with me; *and* he shall make peace with me.

27 In that day the LORD with his hard and great and strong sword will punish Leviathan the fleeing serpent, Leviathan the twisting serpent, and he will slay the dragon that is in the sea.

2 In that day:
"A pleasant vineyard, sing of it!
3   I, the LORD, am its keeper;
      every moment I water it.
  Lest anyone harm it,
      I guard it night and day;
4   I have no wrath.
  Would that I had thorns and briers to
      battle!
  I would set out against them,
      I would burn them up together.
5 Or let them lay hold of my protection,
      let them make peace with me,
      let them make peace with me."

27:1. His . . . sword: With which he "hewed" and "pierced" the dragon (cf. 51:9; Job 26:13); in the Babylonian and Canaanite versions the principal weapon was a club, and this version seems to lie behind Ps. 74:13-14. **Leviathan:** From a root meaning "turn," "twist"; the closeness of the biblical to the Canaanite myth can be seen from the Ras Shamra tablet I AB (as translated in Alexander Heidel, *The Babylonian Genesis* [Chicago: University of Chicago Press, 1942], p. 91; used by permission):

> When thou hast smitten L-t-n, the fleeing serpent,
> (And) hast put to an end the tortuous serpent,
> The mighty one with seven heads. . . .

The reference to the multiple heads of the monster is interesting in view of Ps. 74:13. Sometimes the dragon is equated with the sea (Ps. 74:13; Job 26:12); sometimes as here it is thought of as imprisoned at the bottom of the sea (Amos 9:3).

D. FOURTH CYCLE (27:2-13)
1. THE LORD'S VINEYARD (27:2-6)

A brief poem using the same figure as in 5:1-7, but in an opposite sense—that the Lord will protect his vineyard from the briers and thorns which are its enemies, and that he promises to make it abundantly fruitful in contrast to its present condition. The text is corrupt, and the version in the LXX differs considerably from the Hebrew.

2-6. The opening is abrupt, but apparently means "Sing for it the chorus 'A lovely vineyard.' Would that I had [or "should there be"] thorns and briers, I would march to battle against them." The last line of vs. 5 is missing, "when they have made peace

---

27:1-13. God's Vineyard.—This is a very difficult chapter. The Exeg. reveals the fragmentary and confused condition of the text. However, it is possible to discern the general movement of thought. The oracle responds to the entreaty of ch. 26. It really begins at 26:20, where the people are advised to hide themselves till the coming storm of judgment passes. There follows in 27:1 the announcement of the divine verdict on the world powers: they are to be destroyed. Using the figures of mythology, the

prophet depicts these as monsters, Leviathan, the serpent, the dragon, all to be slain by the sword of the Lord.

Vss. 2-6 seem to bear little relationship to vs. 1. They consist of a song about God's vineyard which is under his protection and very precious to him. Vss. 7-11 set out the conditions of final deliverance for Israel. God has been lenient in his punishment of his disobedient people, he has been patience plus; but forgiveness can follow only when the last vestige of idolatry

6 He shall cause them that come of Jacob to take root: Israel shall blossom and bud, and fill the face of the world with fruit.

7 ¶ Hath he smitten him, as he smote those that smote him? or is he slain according to the slaughter of them that are slain by him?

8 In measure, when it shooteth forth, thou wilt debate with it: he stayeth his rough wind in the day of the east wind.

9 By this therefore shall the iniquity of Jacob be purged; and this is all the fruit to take away his sin; when he maketh all the stones of the altar as chalkstones that are beaten in sunder, the groves and images shall not stand up.

10 Yet the defensed city shall be desolate, and the habitation forsaken, and left like a wilderness: there shall the calf feed, and there shall he lie down, and consume the branches thereof.

6 In days to come⁹ Jacob shall take root,
    Israel shall blossom and put forth shoots,
    and fill the whole world with fruit.

7 Has he smitten them as he smote those who smote them?
    Or have they been slain as their slayers were slain?

8 Measure by measure,ʳ by exile thou didst contend with them;
    he removed them with his fierce blast in the day of the east wind.

9 Therefore by this the guilt of Jacob will be expiated,
    and this will be the full fruit of the removal of his sin:
when he makes all the stones of the altars like chalkstones crushed to pieces,
    no Ashe'rim or incense altars will remain standing.

10 For the fortified city is solitary,
    a habitation deserted and forsaken, like the wilderness;
there the calf grazes,
    there he lies down, and strips its branches.

⁹ Heb Those to come
ʳ Compare Syr Vg Tg: The meaning of the Hebrew word is unknown

with me. . . ." In vs. 6, as at the conclusion of 5:1-7, the identification with Israel is made clear, although the figure is changed to that of a giant vine spreading through the earth, a blessing to mankind.

2. Meaning of Israel's Suffering (27:7-11)

7-11. This obscure fragment seems to have no connection with the foregoing. Israel has not suffered to the same degree or for the same end as those who oppressed her and whom Yahweh will punish (vs. 7). The meaning of vs. 8a is quite uncertain, including the reference to **exile.** Apparently vs. 8a suggests a mild judgment on Israel in contrast to the severe one of vs. 8b which has come or is to come on her enemies. **The guilt of Jacob will be expiated,** not by her suffering, but **by this,** i.e., the complete abolition of idolatrous worship. There follows in vss. 10-11 a disconnected picture of a city, presumably Jerusalem, in desolation and still under judgment because her people are **without discernment** (cf. 1:3).

has gone from the national life. Vss. 12-13 close the chapter with a prophecy of the recall of the banished and the outcast.

The whole makes heavy weather of it; there is little poetry and less rapture in it. It has not much relevance to our day. Only by seizing on a phrase here and there can the expositor make it yield any clear message; e.g., a man of sensitive spirit could take the song of the vineyard

and speak on God's care of his church. After all, the Christian church is living witness to the guidance and protection of God. There is no accounting for its continuance apart from the truth that it is God's agent, and that his Spirit works through it. No institution of earth could have survived the betrayals and treachery of which in certain eras the people of the church have been guilty. If God had not kept **it night**

11 When the boughs thereof are withered, they shall be broken off: the women come, *and* set them on fire; for it *is* a people of no understanding: therefore he that made them will not have mercy on them, and he that formed them will show them no favor.

12 ¶ And it shall come to pass in that day, *that* the LORD shall beat off from the channel of the river unto the stream of Egypt, and ye shall be gathered one by one, O ye children of Israel.

13 And it shall come to pass in that day, *that* the great trumpet shall be blown, and they shall come which were ready to perish in the land of Assyria, and the outcasts in the land of Egypt, and shall worship the LORD in the holy mount at Jerusalem.

28 Woe to the crown of pride, to the drunkards of Ephraim, whose glorious beauty *is* a fading flower, which *are* on

---

11 When its boughs are dry, they are broken;
women come and make a fire of them.
For this is a people without discernment;
therefore he who made them will not have compassion on them,
he that formed them will show them no favor.

12 In that day from the river Eu-phra′tes to the Brook of Egypt the LORD will thresh out the grain, and you will be gathered one by one, O people of Israel. 13 And in that day a great trumpet will be blown, and those who were lost in the land of Assyria and those who were driven out to the land of Egypt will come and worship the LORD on the holy mountain of Jerusalem.

28 Woe to the proud crown of the drunkards of E′phraim,
and to the fading flower of its glorious beauty,

---

3. DAY OF HARVEST AND THE LAST TRUMP (27:12-13)

12-13. The booklet made by chs. 24–27 concludes appropriately with an eschatological promise of deliverance in these two verses. In vs. 12 the figure of a final harvest day (cf. Joel 3:13 [Hebrew 4:13]; Matt. 13:39; Rev. 14:15) proclaims the separation not of the righteous from the wicked, but of the Jews from their heathen environment, and their reunion as the **children of Israel.** In vs. 13 **the great trumpet** summons men to worship (cf. Joel 2:15; Ps. 81:3) rather than to war (cf. I Sam. 13:3, calling them from exile beyond the ideal boundaries of Israel's land, which were **the river Euphrates** (cf. Gen. 15:18) and the **Brook of Egypt,** the Wadi el-ʿArîsh, fifty miles southwest of Gaza.

VII. "BE NOT SCOFFERS, LEST YOUR BONDS BE MADE STRONG" (28:1–32:20)
A. NO REFUGE FROM THE STORM (28:1-22)
1. A LESSON THE DISSOLUTE MUST LEARN (28:1-13)

The construction of this oracle is unusual in that it is introduced by the quotation of a word spoken previously under similar circumstances concerning Samaria (vss. 1-4). The sequence is interrupted by the interpolation of a brief oracle of promise from a

---

and day, it would long ago have passed as a discredited organization. It is a thing to humble Christ's people, that looking on the modern church with its dissensions, its jealousies, its fitful loyalty and measured devotion, the Lord of it should say, **I have no wrath.** It is not anger that is in the heart of Jesus Christ as he looks on his people, but yearning for their unity, the deeper fellowship, the wider service, which is theirs who are truly one in Christ.

It is but a step from that thought to the conclusion of the chapter, with its sound of the trumpet and the great ingathering of the people

of God. The prophecy of the homecoming has been heard in every age. So deeply implanted is the love of home, and so great is our final need of one another, that among the hopes of the human heart none is dearer than this: that at the last men will return from the far country of their sin, from the estrangements of unreal social distinctions, from the exile of national hates and jealousies, to find their home and their peace in the love of God.

28:1-29. *A Covenant with Death.*—There are four distinct parts of this chapter, each with its own theme. It is marked by the vigorous style

the head of the fat valleys of them that are overcome with wine!

2 Behold, the Lord hath a mighty and strong one, *which* as a tempest of hail *and* a destroying storm, as a flood of mighty waters overflowing, shall cast down to the earth with the hand.

3 The crown of pride, the drunkards of Ephraim, shall be trodden under feet:

4 And the glorious beauty, which *is* on the head of the fat valley, shall be a fading flower, *and* as the hasty fruit before the summer; which *when* he that looketh upon it seeth, while it is yet in his hand he eateth it up.

5 ¶ In that day shall the LORD of hosts

---

which is on the head of the rich valley of those overcome with wine!

2 Behold, the Lord has one who is mighty and strong;
   like a storm of hail, a destroying tempest,
   like a storm of mighty, overflowing waters,
   he will cast down to the earth with violence.

3 The proud crown of the drunkards of E'phraim
   will be trodden under foot;

4 and the fading flower of its glorious beauty,
   which is on the head of the rich valley,
   will be like a first-ripe fig before the summer:
   when a man sees it, he eats it up
   as soon as it is in his hand.

5 In that day the LORD of hosts will be a crown of glory,

---

later hand (vss. 5-6), and is resumed in vss. 7-10 with a denunciation of the dissolute and defiant leaders of Judah. The concluding threat in vss. 11-13 is of overthrow before a people of foreign speech. The opening threat directed against Samaria clearly has in view an onslaught by Assyria, but just as clearly the siege of 724-721 has not yet begun. A date *ca.* 726 or 725, when Hoshea withheld the Assyrian tribute (II Kings 17:4), is the most probable one, corresponding as it does with the arrogant recklessness pictured in vs. 1. The date of the main section of the oracle, vss. 7-13, must be one when a similar situation had come to prevail in Judah; this might be just prior to the revolt of Ashdod in 711, but is more probably to be found in the period of disturbance which followed the death of Sargon in 705.

There is nothing obscure about the prophet's message. Just as the proud and dissolute leaders of Ephraim had been overthrown as by a tempest sent by Yahweh (vss. 1-4), so the befuddled authorities of Judah, who refuse to listen as Isaiah underlines the lesson (vss. 7-10), will learn it perforce from the barbaric speech of an invader.

28:1-4. The **walls** which encircled the hill of Samaria are likened to the quickly dilapidated wreath on a reveler's head. The words **of those overcome with wine** should follow **Ephraim** (so Kissane, *Isaiah*, I, 313). **Behold** (introducing a threat) has here the sense, "Beware! the Lord has [ready] a mighty force. Like a heavy, engulfing downpour, he will flatten [it] violently to the ground." **A first-ripe fig**, a prized delicacy, is quickly disposed of; so with Ephraim.

5-6. The language of vs. 1 is drawn on by the writer of vs. 5, but the figure is changed radically; the **crown**, which in vs. 1 suggests proud folly, is here a symbol of divine

---

and vividness of speech so characteristic of Isaiah when something of God's anger has kindled his spirit.

The chapter begins with a quotation from an older oracle which was pronounced against Samaria some years before, but which Isaiah

---

feels is equally applicable to conditions in Jerusalem. In four verses of great power and beauty he gives us a picture of Samaria queening it in her fertile valley; but her **glorious beauty is a fading flower,** because her rulers are a set of dissolute **drunkards.** This snatch from an oracle

be for a crown of glory, and for a diadem of beauty, unto the residue of his people,

6 And for a spirit of judgment to him that sitteth in judgment, and for strength to them that turn the battle to the gate.

7 ¶ But they also have erred through wine, and through strong drink are out of the way; the priest and the prophet have erred through strong drink, they are swallowed up of wine, they are out of the way through strong drink; they err in vision, they stumble *in* judgment.

8 For all tables are full of vomit *and* filthiness, *so that there is* no place *clean*.

9 ¶ Whom shall he teach knowledge? and whom shall he make to understand doctrine? *them that are* weaned from the milk, *and* drawn from the breasts.

and a diadem of beauty, to the remnant of his people;

6 and a spirit of justice to him who sits in judgment,
and strength to those who turn back the battle at the gate.

7 These also reel with wine
and stagger with strong drink;
the priest and the prophet reel with strong drink,
they are confused with wine,
they stagger with strong drink;
they err in vision,
they stumble in giving judgment.

8 For all tables are full of vomit,
no place is without filthiness.

9 "Whom will he teach knowledge,
and to whom will he explain the message?
Those who are weaned from the milk,
those taken from the breast?

---

blessing. Moreover, a promise to **the remnant** (always elsewhere of Judah) appears strangely between a threat to Ephraim and a threat to Judah; the thought is much like that of the late passage 4:2-6. It is a promise to the remnant, when only a remnant remained. In the coming day of blessing the same spirit will empower the administration of justice and the heroic defenders who in a critical moment **turn back the** [tide of] **battle at the** [very] **gate.** Justice and peace are the deep desires of the mass of men everywhere; they were central in the hope of a messianic age (cf. 2:4; 9:7; 11:1-9; 32:16-18).

7-10. The prophet here couples with his denunciation an account of an altercation which he had with the priests and prophets attached to the temple, as a result of which the "word" of vss. 11-13 came to him in terms reflecting this altercation (for similar experiences of other prophets cf. Amos 7:10-17; Hos. 4:6-8; Jer. 26:8-16). **These also,** like the rulers of Ephraim, are sunk in drunkenness and folly. Isaiah points in temple court or council chamber to the evidence that the spiritual and political advisers of Judah are incapacitated by self-indulgence, and hence the advice they have given is wrong. Presumably that advice was that Judah should rebel against Assyria and look to Egypt for help. The men accused retort indignantly that they are not children to be lectured by Isaiah. **Err in vision:** I.e., the very visions the prophets declare as oracles of

---

of doom is followed in vss. 5-6 with a momentary glance at another day when the Lord of unfading splendor, wearing **a diadem of beauty,** shall bring justice to the land and strength to its defenders. In that is the glory of a nation.

7-13. The Prophet and the Drunken Court.— These are highly dramatic verses. What was true of Samaria before its fall is true now of Judah, and there follows a vivid picture of the prophet's encounter with the men whose drunken counsel it is to trust in Egyptian support. Isaiah breaks in on one of the periodic orgies which

marked court life. They are all drunk, priest and politician alike. The hall is heavy with the fumes of liquor, loud with the bravado and profanity of drunken men. Enter God's servant, to stand looking with contempt and wrath on these leaders of the nation. For a moment there is silence and then an insolent voice is raised. "Here he is, the great teacher! And whom do you think you are going to teach? Children? Babes? You and the everlasting repetition of your same infantile lesson, your stuttering *çaw laqaw, çaw laqaw!*" Whereupon with a gale of

10 For precept *must be* upon precept, precept upon precept; line upon line, line upon line; here a little, *and* there a little:

11 For with stammering lips and another tongue will he speak to this people.

12 To whom he said, This *is* the rest *wherewith* ye may cause the weary to rest; and this *is* the refreshing: yet they would not hear.

13 But the word of the LORD was unto them precept upon precept, precept upon precept; line upon line, line upon line; here a little, *and* there a little; that they might go, and fall backward, and be broken, and snared, and taken.

---

10 For it is precept upon precept, precept
   upon precept,
line upon line, line upon line,
here a little, there a little."

11 Nay, but by men of strange lips
   and with an alien tongue
the LORD will speak to his people,
12   to whom he has said,
"This is rest;
   give rest to the weary;
and this is repose";
   yet they would not hear.
13 Therefore the word of the LORD will be
   to them
precept upon precept, precept upon precept,
line upon line, line upon line,
here a little, there a little;
that they may go, and fall backward,
   and be broken, and snared, and taken.

God are confused by liquor, while the priests **stumble** as they give **judgment** on religious questions referred to them (cf. Hag. 2:11-13). The **tables** are for the feast accompanying the offering of sacrifice (cf. I Sam. 9:12-13). In vss. 9-10 the leaders whom Isaiah has reproved retort contemptuously that he is talking to them like a schoolmaster teaching small children. This much is clear, but the meaning of what follows is uncertain. The monosyllables *çaw* and *qaw,* each repeated four times in vs. 10*ab*, may suggest (*a*) meaningless babble (cf. vs. 11); (*b*) children learning the alphabet, in which ק succeeds צ; (*c*) a drunken man's muttering of the words "command" and "measuring line" (cf. vs. 17); or (*d*) the prophet's slow spelling out of the verbal root צוק, "distress," which appears in the nouns צוקה and מוצק in 8:22-23. Here ..., there a little may mean "a little at a time," or may, as Procksch suggests, represent the words of the teacher calling on "the little one here, the little one there" to repeat the lesson.

11-13. The prophet takes the words out of the mouths of his mocking opponents (vs. 13). "For [**Nay, but** or "Yea, truly"] with stammering lips and [in] another tongue will he speak to this people who said to them. . . ." The strange and apparently stammering speech of barbarians will speak a word of doom to those who would not find **rest**

---

laughter the whole company takes up the jibe, "*Çaw laqaw, çaw laqaw!*" Unmoved, and with a face of doom, Isaiah hears them out; then replies—and there is menace in the words—"You will hear it again, God's lesson. You will hear it in the speech of strangers, and learn it at the hands of aliens." There is such a thing as the divine reiteration. "*Çaw laqaw, çaw laqaw!*" they will stammer in the uncouth Assyrian tongue; but it will mean the same thing, the intolerable, inescapable judgment of God.

The secret of good teaching is repetition and review. According to the capacity of men to receive and to understand it, the lesson is taught. Revelation is itself a continual process of reit-

eration on the theme of sin and salvation. For how long has God been repeating to the nations the conditions of peace on earth? **Precept upon precept; line upon line; . . . here a little and there a little** he has taught us, and always this lesson: that the hope of men is in the fellowship of a common faith in God, the good will of brethren. For how long has God been repeating to every one of us that "the wages of sin is death" (Rom. 6:23)? From the first disobedience to the last betrayal of honor, the same inexorable truth has been driven home, **line upon line.** How desperately man has sought to prove God wrong and has, up to a point, succeeded marvelously in making sin pay; but always at

14 ¶ Wherefore hear the word of the LORD, ye scornful men, that rule this people which *is* in Jerusalem.

15 Because ye have said, We have made a covenant with death, and with hell are we at agreement; when the overflowing scourge shall pass through, it shall not come unto us: for we have made lies our refuge, and under falsehood have we hid ourselves:

14 Therefore hear the word of the LORD,
　you scoffers,
who rule this people in Jerusalem!
15 Because you have said, "We have made a
　covenant with death,
　and with Sheol we have an agreement;
when the overwhelming scourge passes
　through
　it will not come to us;
for we have made lies our refuge,
　and in falsehood we have taken
　shelter";

---

and "repose" in Yahweh. The climactic series of synonyms in vs. 13*ef* is an effective characteristic of Isaiah's style in concluding a threat oracle (cf. 29:6; 30:30).

2. THE COVENANT WITH DEATH (28:14-22)

Again in circumstances similar to those of the foregoing oracle, the prophet confronts the rulers of Jerusalem with the assertion that their policy and behavior are bringing inevitable ruin. This time the fault is that they have deliberately entered into a covenant to serve, in return for protection, a god or gods other than their own. **Death**, *mâweth*, is here the god of the underworld, **Sheol** or **hell**. Perhaps the Canaanite god of the underworld, Mot, is intended, or the reference may be to the Egyptian Osiris. It was customary for the prophets to speak of the alien deities as **lies** and **falsehood** (cf. Amos 2:4; Jer. 10:14). In contrast to this act of panic by the rulers, Isaiah declares that faith in her own God is the only secure **foundation** of Zion's security, and that his **justice** and **righteousness** alone can erect a building that will stand. Those who in fright have sought to secure themselves by worshiping other gods as well, will experience in **sheer terror** the effects of Yahweh's **decree of destruction**.

14-15. Agreement: Lit., "vision," חֹזֶה, or as in vs. 18, חָזוּת. If the text is right, the particular shade of meaning is obscure, although the general sense is clear from the context. For **scourge** read "flood" (with Procksch, *Jesaia I*, p. 361, following Barth).

---

the last, amid the ruins of his home, his fortune, his health, his peace, only to find himself confronted with the same truth: the wages—death!

And for how long has God sought to teach us the lesson of his love? From the very beginning this has been his great word for men. Once again, little by little, **precept upon precept**, here a word spoken, there a life radiantly transformed, here a mighty deliverance, there a great consolation, all telling the same thing: that God cares and God is love. The very Incarnation, wherein the lesson blazed once and for all in the life of Jesus Christ, is itself a continuous reiteration as those whom the love of God has claimed and won reveal in their lives the saving love of God. Every Christian life is meant to be another syllable in the reiteration of God's love.

14-22. The Secret Alliance.—These threatening words are spoken to the leaders of the political party in power who are plotting a secret alliance with Egypt, in open defiance of Isaiah's warning that only in God is there a sure defense. What the terms of the proposed treaty are the prophet does not know, for this is a matter of top secret diplomacy; but he sees from their smug looks and their contempt of himself that they feel secure against the worst. He calls their plan a pact with death, a treaty with hell, and warns them that it will not stand. Their covenant is not, like certain famous modern pacts, to be torn up as a "scrap of paper," but to be swallowed up in a rising tide of judgment, obliterated, canceled by God himself. The one sure foundation of salvation in the day of trouble is Israel's covenant with God. That they have scorned; and because they have left God out of account they will find the bed of their own choosing too short, and the blanket they have provided too narrow, when the storm breaks and the Almighty turns to the strange business of punishing his own people through their enemies—this unheard-of-thing, that by the barbarity of the barbarians the people of the covenant should be judged.

16 ¶ Therefore thus saith the Lord God, Behold, I lay in Zion for a foundation a stone, a tried stone, a precious corner *stone,* a sure foundation: he that believeth shall not make haste.

17 Judgment also will I lay to the line, and righteousness to the plummet: and the hail shall sweep away the refuge of lies, and the waters shall overflow the hiding place.

18 ¶ And your covenant with death shall be disannulled, and your agreement with hell shall not stand; when the overflowing scourge shall pass through, then ye shall be trodden down by it.

16 therefore thus says the Lord God,
"Behold, I am laying in Zion for a foundation
a stone, a tested stone,
a precious cornerstone, of a sure foundation:
'He who believes will not be in haste.'
17 And I will make justice the line,
and righteousness the plummet;
and hail will sweep away the refuge of lies,
and waters will overwhelm the shelter."
18 Then your covenant with death will be annulled,
and your agreement with Sheol will not stand;
when the overwhelming scourge passes through
you will be beaten down by it.

16-17a. A parenthesis which may not originally have belonged in this context, but is certainly genuine. The Lord will erect a building "not made with hands," its **cornerstone** will be faith, and its walls will be built true with justice and right. Omit the first **stone** (with LXX). The word translated **tested** or **tried** is not found elsewhere; it is apparently a loan word from the Egyptian designating the special type of stone used for carved objects. On the stone is an inscription: "The believer is not anxious," or "alarmed" (cf. Matt. 6:25; Kissane, *op. cit.,* I, 318, and Ludwig Koehler, ed., *Lexicon in Veteris Testamenti Libros* [Leiden: E. J. Brill, 1948-], pp. 117, 284). With vs. 17a cf. Amos 7:7-9.

17c-22. Hail . . . and waters: Better, "a hailstorm . . . and a flood." For **be annulled,** וכפר, read "be broken," ותפר, in accordance with the usual idiom; and for **scourge** read

---

16. *The Composure of Faith.*—The words of the verse mean what they say. Some translators have thought to improve the rendering to convey the idea of the fortitude of faith. But Isaiah must have deliberately chosen the word that means an alarmed haste. What he seeks to convey is the thought that those who trust in God are not flustered; theirs is the composure of faith. When a man is frightened he is, as we say, "jumpy." Soldiers have a curious expression for panic; they talk about having "the wind up" or being "windy," and they mean that condition of alarm which may lead a man at any moment to break and run. There is a haste which betokens urgency, but there is also a haste which reveals fright. Modern man is always in a hurry. If this verse suggests inversely that haste is a token of unbelief, it raises a question of the condition of the crowd in the subway rush hour. There is no doubt about it; the speed of modern life bespeaks a state of tension, and the tension in turn suggests men not sure either of themselves or of God. A life with poise has always sure foundations. It is unperturbed because it is

lived with faith in God's care for his people, it is persuaded of the meaning and purpose of life, it has a final trust in a love that in every way is infinite. A poised life is really an achievement; it is not to be accounted for by nature but by the possession of a quiet confidence in God. There are people who are phlegmatic in temperament, they are not easily put out, their very movements may reveal a monumental deliberation. But such composure may be explained by a lack of sensitivity rather than by convictions about life and God. How different is the life "lucid, poised, and whole." There never was anyone so subject to tension as our Lord. He bore on his heart the sins and sorrows, the pain and despair of men; he endured the contradiction of sinners, but he moved through it all with unbroken peace. Any other thus beset might well have given way. But because he had given his life to God and received it again for his service, our Lord bore himself with the dignity, the composure, and the authority of one who walks in an unseen companionship, and drew his strength from the resources of the

19 From the time that it goeth forth it shall take you: for morning by morning shall it pass over, by day and by night: and it shall be a vexation only *to* understand the report.

20 For the bed is shorter than that *a man* can stretch himself *on it:* and the covering narrower than that he can wrap himself *in it.*

19 As often as it passes through it will take you;
  for morning by morning it will pass through,
  by day and by night;
  and it will be sheer terror to understand the message.
20 For the bed is too short to stretch oneself on it,
  and the covering too narrow to wrap oneself in it.

"flood," as in vs. 15. **As often as it passes through** . . . should be "It will be more than enough in its passing to overtake you, [and the news will be nothing but] sheer terror" (the bracketed words are the rendering of *The Bible in Basic English* [Cambridge: Cambridge University Press, 1949]). Vs. 20 is a proverbial saying in parentheses "describing a predicament for which there is no remedy" (Kissane, *op. cit.,* I, 319). Though the Assyrians may be Yahweh's instruments, he himself will be the unseen antagonist,

---

Eternal. In contrast to such peace, consider the fussiness of multitudes of people driven here and there by conflicting impulses, always in a hurry, determined not to get left, though they have no clear objective, anxious and perturbed because they have little inner strength with which to meet life's demands. Such people weary themselves, exhausting their nervous energy in the endeavor to keep up with others or to surpass them in the race of life. We find them thronging the psychiatrist's office, seeking a peace they have never known. A living faith could transform life for all such flustered souls. **He that believeth shall not make haste.** Isaiah's word echoes the counsel which the Bible keeps thrusting upon men: "Thou wilt keep him in perfect peace, whose mind is stayed on thee: because he trusteth in thee" (26:3). "Be still, and know that I am God" (Ps. 46:10). "Wait on the LORD: be of good courage, and he shall strengthen thine heart" (Ps. 27:14). "Rest in the LORD and wait patiently for him: fret not thyself" (Ps. 37:7). "O men, how little you trust him! Do not be troubled, then, and cry, 'What are we to eat?' or 'what are we to drink?' or 'how are we to be clothed?' . . . Your heavenly Father knows" (Matt. 6:30-33 Moffatt).

20. *Inadequate Religions.*—Isaiah evidently knew what it was to put in some cold and sleepless nights on a short bed with blankets too narrow to tuck in. Under the graphic and humorous figures of the bed with the skimpy covering there is suggested the inadequacy of some current views of religion which neither cover the facts nor meet the needs for life. The modern world is full of them: ethical cults, humanistic philosophies, the half-truths of eccentric sects; all inadequate because, while they concede to God a place, they will not acknowledge that the ultimate source and hope of salvation is in his love. In fair weather a man can make shift to live by such religions; but when the dark night falls and the storm begins to howl about his life, he has nothing to fall back upon, and the little faith that met his small demands when all was well offers him neither protection nor covering. The prophet saw in his own nation a ritual conducted by degenerate priests, and a voluptuous ceremonial without moral content. Such a religion might serve when men sunned themselves in the warmth of a momentary prosperity, but when the night fell and the cold wind of adversity struck life it would be pitiably inadequate.

Everyone should consider whether his religion is equal to the demands of life. One can meet anywhere the man who, defending his indifference to the church or organized religion, says, "To do your duty and play the game is religion enough for me." Duty and decency! Are these two ideals sufficient in themselves to enable one to stand up to life? Is it enough to reduce religion to such a minimum and, so to speak, boil it down to a few ethical principles? Reduction can never be the last word about religion. When we talk of music, we do not ask how much we can get rid of and still be counted musical. When we speak of the family, we never dream of considering how many of a parent's duties we can evade and still be reckoned a father. So is it with religion. It is not a question of how little we can do with, but rather of how much that is true and vital we can make our own. The man who can reduce religion to duty and decency

21 For the Lord shall rise up as *in* mount Perazim, he shall be wroth as *in* the valley of Gibeon, that he may do his work, his strange work; and bring to pass his act, his strange act.

22 Now therefore be ye not mockers, lest your bands be made strong: for I have heard from the Lord God of hosts a consumption, even determined upon the whole earth.

21 For the Lord will rise up as on Mount Pera'zim,
    he will be wroth as in the valley of Gibeon;
to do his deed — strange is his deed!
    and to work his work — alien is his work!
22 Now therefore do not scoff,
    lest your bonds be made strong;
for I have heard a decree of destruction
    from the Lord God of hosts upon the whole land.

---

as in David's famous victories over the Philistines recorded in II Sam. 5:20, 25. But this time Yahweh will be his people's enemy, for he comes in judgment **to do his deed,** which will be like the deed of a stranger and a foreigner. The words vividly express the prophetic conception of God as a "Doer" rather than a static "Being"; it follows that important events have moral meaning because the just and righteous God is at work in them. In vs. 22 the oracle is summed up with a solemn warning, **lest your bonds be made strong,** i.e., be firmly tied so that there is no escape. It still remains true that if

---

has been too drastic; in the crises of life he will find that **bed . . . too short** and that **covering too narrow.**

Such a minimum religion is not enough because the deepest conception of life is not summed up in a duty to be done, but in a trust to be kept. For duty Jesus Christ put love, and in so doing infinitely extended the sphere of opportunity and responsibility. When it is said of a man, "He does his duty by his family," something is missing, viz., the love which takes one farther than duty. There are limits to duty, but there are no frontiers to love. It is the voluntary going on beyond the requirements of duty which brings graciousness and beauty into life. In the citation for the American Medal of Honor the key phrase, the basis of the honor, is that the recipient had shown a fidelity and courage "beyond the call of duty." Duty is not the ultimate standard of true manhood.

To reduce religion to one's duty and to "playing the game" is not adequate because while it confronts one with an ideal, it has nothing to say of the resources of power needed to realize the ideal, i.e., it is a moral precept, not a religious faith. To confront a man with an ideal he cannot possibly attain is only to deepen in him a sense of frustration. But it is the glory of Christianity that with the high ideal it promises strength to attain it. The N.T. rings with a note of gratitude over the discovery of resources. "Strengthened with might through his Spirit in the inner man" (Eph. 3:16); "Strengthened with all power, according to his glorious might" (Col. 1:11); "I can do all things through Christ

which strengtheneth me" (Phil. 4:13). These are the accents of one who glimpsed the high duty of the call of God, and who found in the companionship of Christ the power to do it.

The inadequacy of the conception of duty or decency as the substance of religion is, however, most clearly seen when the moral problem is faced. What is the use of telling a man to do his duty or to "play the game" when he is the slave to an evil habit? There is no gospel for a broken heart in the call of duty. Magnificent as the ideal of duty may be, it falls far short of the constraint of love as the motive of life. Our Lord said that he did not call his disciples servants—i.e., those of whom duty was demanded—but friends, who served him for love's sake. No religion is equal to the strain of life unless it is able to make us sure of God's love so that we can meet sorrow without rebellion, loss without self-pity, adversity without whining, temptation without surrender, death without fear.

21. *God's Strange Work.*—The supremely difficult but always timely subject of the problem of pain is hinted at in these three words, **his strange work.** From time immemorial, out of the unconsoled grief of the human heart, the cry has broken, "Why?" At the hands of a God of love, sorrow, suffering, undeserved adversity, are unexplained mysteries. A young life cut off on the threshold of promise; a young widow left with little children; a great leader gone at the very moment when his presence seemed vital: they belong to the "strange" acts of God. If there is any light at all on this dark question, it falls from the love in Christ's life and death.

23 ¶ Give ye ear, and hear my voice; hearken, and hear my speech.	23 Give ear, and hear my voice; hearken, and hear my speech.
24 Doth the plowman plow all day to sow? doth he open and break the clods of his ground?	24 Does he who plows for sowing plow continually? does he continually open and harrow his ground?
25 When he hath made plain the face thereof, doth he not cast abroad the fitches,	25 When he has leveled its surface, does he not scatter dill, sow cummin,

scoffing should give way to faith, the **decree of destruction** would not apply. But it is clear that the prophet sees no sign of repentance, so he says in effect, "Since you are defiant in your unbelief, the sentence of doom I have heard uttered by the Lord will be carried out." The verb **I have heard** suggests that the oracle was recorded by Isaiah himself.

B. A PARABLE OF THE FARMER (28:23-29)

This parable differs from that in 5:1-7 in that it has no direct interpretation appended to it as in 5:7; nor is it, as in that passage and in Nathan's parable (II Sam. 12:1-6), a device to compel the hearers to pass judgment upon themselves. In fact, it more closely resembles the "riddles" or proverbial "dark sayings" of the sages and traditional heroes like Lamech (Gen. 4:23, with its interpretation in 4:24) and Samson (Judg. 14:12-18; cf. also Prov. 1:6; 7:1-23; 30:11-31). Just as in 5:1-7 the prophet has adopted the literary form of the love song and has turned it to parabolic use, so here, as is clear from the opening and closing verses, he speaks in the manner of his contemporaries, the wisdom teachers (cf. Jer. 18:18).

The poem falls into two parts, the first drawing attention to the methods of the farmer in plowing and **sowing** grain, the second to the careful distinction he makes in his methods of threshing different crops. The farmer's skill is God-given wisdom (vss. 26, 29), and the inference is that God's activities in the field of history are similarly purposeful, orderly, and discriminating. "He also is wise" (31:2), and when men scoff at his prophets (28:9, 14; 30:9-11) and demand to see evidence of his part in events (5:19) let them understand that, like the farmer, God is working out a long-term plan and adapts his methods to its successive stages and to differing situations. He plows only for a time, then sows different crops in appropriate places, and finally harvests and threshes each crop in the way suited to its nature. The farmer's methods are not haphazard; still less are God's ways. His judgments are like the overturning and harrowing of the ground, and one must see in them a purpose beyond mere destruction. The promise lies in the seed that is sown. In the second strophe the judgments appear under a new figure, that of **threshing**, which seems to suggest three things about the action of God: (a) the purposiveness of the process, in the separation of the grain from the chaff; (b) the meaning of suffering as the necessary condition of the emergence of good; and (c) the care of the divine Harvester in dealing with the more precious kinds of grain.

23-29. The word לְזֹרֵעַ, **for sowing**, is omitted by the LXX and the Syriac, and takes away the force of the second rhetorical question. Kissane (*ibid.*, I, 313, 319) reads here לְרֶגַע, "every moment": "Is the plowman continually plowing, every moment breaking

| The God who "so loved the world" (John 3:16) must be able to weave our sorrow and our pain into our salvation. There surely is the omnipotence of love, that it should be able to take our afflictions and in ways past our understanding use them for the perfecting of that which concerns us. It is the Christian faith that when we see no longer "through a glass, darkly," when | we "know . . . as also" we are known (I Cor. 13:12), then the strange acts of God shall be seen as steps up the steep ascent, the very means whereby his love makes us "perfect through sufferings" (Heb. 2:10). |
| | **23-29. A Lesson from the Farmer.**—The conclusion of the chapter is a parable of the farmer, who has his own knowledge and skill in prepar- |

and scatter the cummin, and cast in the principal wheat and the appointed barley and the rye in their place?

26 For his God doth instruct him to discretion, *and* doth teach him.

27 For the fitches are not threshed with a threshing instrument, neither is a cart wheel turned about upon the cummin; but the fitches are beaten out with a staff, and the cummin with a rod.

28 Bread *corn* is bruised; because he will not ever be threshing it, nor break *it with* the wheel of his cart, nor bruise it *with* his horsemen.

29 This also cometh forth from the LORD of hosts, *which* is wonderful in counsel, *and* excellent in working.

29 Woe to Ariel, to Ariel, the city *where* David dwelt! add ye year to year; let them kill sacrifices.

---

and put in wheat in rows
and barley in its proper place,
and spelt as the border?

26 For he is instructed aright;
his God teaches him.

27 Dill is not threshed with a threshing sledge,
nor is a cart wheel rolled over cummin;
but dill is beaten out with a stick,
and cummin with a rod.

28 Does one crush bread grain?
No, he does not thresh it for ever;
when he drives his cart wheel over it
with his horses, he does not crush it.

29 This also comes from the LORD of hosts;
he is wonderful in counsel,
and excellent in wisdom.

29 Ho Ariel, Ariel,
the city where David encamped!
Add year to year;
let the feasts run their round.

---

up and harrowing his land?" There seems to be an intended contrast between the scattering of the less valuable **dill** and **cummin** and the "planting" of the wheat and barley with **spelt as the border.** The latter was the practice, says R. H. Kennett (*Ancient Hebrew Social Life and Customs* [London: British Academy, 1933], p. 67), "so that the wheat and the barley when in ear might escape being plucked by passers-by." The words translated **in rows** and **in its proper place** in the RSV are of doubtful meaning, and are probably to be taken as dittography from adjacent words. The softer grains could not be threshed, as were wheat and barley, by driving over the pile on the threshing floor a **threshing sledge** or **cart wheel.**

28. There is no justification for turning the opening words into a rhetorical question as in the RSV; though quaintly archaic, the KJV is more accurate. "Bread ['grain'] is ground," unlike dill and cumin, but this is not accomplished in the threshing process. **Horses:** Lit., horsemen, *pārāshāw*, is apparently a textual error for "bullocks," *pārāw*, since horses were used only as riding animals and to draw chariots.

C. A MARVELOUS WORK OF GOD (29:1-14)

1. DISTRESS AND DELIVERANCE OF ARIEL (29:1-8)

Just as in 28:1-13 an oracle from an earlier period is repeated by Isaiah with supplementary material suitable to a later situation, so here an earlier threat that **Ariel** (Jerusalem) will be besieged is quoted when the siege threatens in 701. The prophet now believes that the triumph of Yahweh's plan requires the deliverance of Jerusalem

---

ing the soil for various seeds and the threshing of the grain. It seems to have been added in justification of the "strangeness" of God's action. As the depth and width of a plowed furrow are adapted to the kind of seed sown, so God's treatment is meted out in accordance with the purpose in view. His dealing is a preparation for the harvest; it is not a meaningless plowing. And when the harvest comes, the method of threshing fits the grain, rough usage for coarse grain,

less bruising for the finer. So in judgment the divine husbandman has a mind for those who are his hope, and judgment is tempered with mercy.

29:1-5. Quiet Before Storm.—Vss. 1-14 contain another oracle of doom, with a clear statement of why it was inevitable; vss. 15-24 are a prophecy of the messianic age. Jerusalem is addressed by the strange and beautiful name **Ariel.** The best of its possible derivations seems

2 Yet I will distress Ariel, and there shall be heaviness and sorrow: and it shall be unto me as Ariel.

3 And I will camp against thee round about, and will lay siege against thee with a mount, and I will raise forts against thee.

4 And thou shalt be brought down, *and* shalt speak out of the ground, and thy speech shall be low out of the dust, and thy voice shall be, as of one that hath a familiar spirit, out of the ground, and thy speech shall whisper out of the dust.

2 Yet I will distress Ariel,
　　and there shall be moaning and lamentation,
　　and she shall be to me like an Ariel.
3 And I will encamp against you round about,
　　and will besiege you with towers
　　and I will raise siegeworks against you.
4 Then deep from the earth you shall speak,
　　from low in the dust your words shall come;
　　your voice shall come from the ground like the voice of a ghost,
　　and your speech shall whisper out of the dust.

from her enemies; that his former prediction of a siege has come to pass is confirmation to him that Yahweh has now disclosed to him his further purpose of deliverance. Reverting to the figure of the previous section, the threshing is part of the process of harvest. It is her God who is punishing Judah, but her enemies will not be allowed to obliterate her; they will vanish like a bad dream, for it is Yahweh's will that a remnant shall survive in Jerusalem (cf. 37:6-7, 32-35).

The original oracle of threat comprises vss. 1-4, 5c-6; the opening lines of vs. 5 have been displaced from their obvious position after the mention of the tempest in vs. 6. The latter is the culminating threat of the first oracle, but this is modified in the longer revised oracle by the addition of vs. 5ab, which says that the tempest which was to fall upon Judah will now blow away her foes like dust.

29:1-2. That **Ariel** here indicates Jerusalem is certain from what is said in vss. 1, 7-8. The etymology of this word is mysterious, but it may well be an ancient form of the city's name in which the word '*ēl*, "god," is substituted for the proper name of the deity "Shalem," after whom the city was called (cf. Gen. 14:18). It is used here to provide a play on the word '*ar'ēl* or '*arî'ēl* in vs. 2, meaning "altar hearth," the highest tier of the altar (cf. Ezek. 43:15) on which the fire was kindled. The city "against which David encamped" (cf. II Sam. 5:6-7) is now the great center of religious **feasts** or "festival pilgrimages," for which men come up zealously year by year (cf. I Sam. 1:3). In reproachful irony like that of Amos (4:4-5) the prophet bids them keep up the traditional round of religious observances. But God in his wrath will make of Ariel an altar hearth, a place of flame (vs. 6), blood and death (vss. 4-5).

3. Round about: Lit., "like a circle"; but this word כדור should be read כדוד, "like David," as in the LXX (cf. vs. 1).

4. The city shall be like a man prostrate in the dust, gasping for help with the weak whisper of a ghost.

to be that of the altar hearth, where the sacrifice was offered, the blood flowed, and the fire burned. Things are quiet in Jerusalem, though every man of sense knows that the storm raging in the north is likely to creep south. But why worry? Assyria has her hands full with Babylon, and as always with the careless, out of sight is out of mind. So life goes on as usual in the city, the buying and selling, the feasting and gaiety, and always, of course, the worship, punctiliously

attended. To the heedless crowd Isaiah calls, "The time is short; another year or so of the old routine, and then death and destruction." Then Jerusalem shall indeed be **Ariel,** the altar hearth lurid with flame, red with the blood of victims. Beyond the walls the enemy will be entrenched, each new earthwork nearer to the gates, while inside the city consternation and despair, terror-stricken whispers, and the muffled words of beaten men.

5 Moreover the multitude of thy strangers shall be like small dust, and the multitude of the terrible ones *shall be* as chaff that passeth away: yea, it shall be at an instant suddenly.

6 Thou shalt be visited of the LORD of hosts with thunder, and with earthquake, and great noise, with storm and tempest, and the flame of devouring fire.

7 ¶ And the multitude of all the nations that fight against Ariel, even all that fight against her and her munition, and that distress her, shall be as a dream of a night vision.

8 It shall even be as when a hungry man dreameth, and, behold, he eateth; but he awaketh, and his soul is empty: or as when a thirsty man dreameth, and, behold, he drinketh; but he awaketh, and, behold, *he is* faint, and his soul hath appetite: so shall the multitude of all the nations be, that fight against mount Zion.

9 ¶ Stay yourselves, and wonder; cry ye out, and cry: they are drunken, but not with wine; they stagger, but not with strong drink.

5 But the multitude of your foes[s] shall be like small dust,
    and the multitude of the ruthless like passing chaff.
And in an instant, suddenly,
6   you will be visited by the LORD of hosts
    with thunder and with earthquake and great noise,
    with whirlwind and tempest, and the flame of a devouring fire.
7 And the multitude of all the nations that fight against Ariel,
    all that fight against her and her stronghold and distress her,
    shall be like a dream, a vision of the night.
8 As when a hungry man dreams he is eating
    and awakes with his hunger not satisfied,
  or as when a thirsty man dreams he is drinking
    and awakes faint, with his thirst not quenched,
  so shall the multitude of all the nations be
    that fight against Mount Zion.

9 Stupefy yourselves and be in a stupor,
    blind yourselves and be blind!
Be drunk, but not with wine;
    stagger, but not with strong drink!

[s] Cn: Heb *strangers*

5c-6. But suddenly there shall burst upon it the furious storm of Yahweh's wrath. The piling up of words to describe the storm is characteristic of the conclusion of a threat oracle (cf. 28:13; 30:30).

5ab, 7-8. The figure of "chaff blowing away" before the storm is found also in 17:13. For **all that fight against her and her stronghold** read "all that besiege her [so Kissane, *op. cit.*, I, 322-23] and press hard upon her [צריה ומצריה; so Ehrlich, *Randglossen zur hebräischen Bibel*, p. 104]." The simile of the dream suggests either or both the sudden awakening of Jerusalem from the nightmare and the equally sudden disillusionment of the Assyrians.

2. WHY MEN CANNOT PERCEIVE GOD'S WORK (29:9-12)

This pericope may be related either to the preceding or to the following oracle, but it is essentially an independent piece. It resumes the thought of the passage in the

---

6-8. *Deliverance.*—These verses are in dramatic contrast to the oracle of doom, for they promise the lifting of the siege and the confounding of the Assyrians. Suddenly God will strike the enemies of his people. The thing that actually happened, and for which there has never been a natural explanation, Isaiah foresaw. Overnight the enemy, who had dreamed their dream of spoils, melted away—foiled, embittered, empty-handed.

9-14. *The Unseeing Multitude.*—Here Isaiah turns again to the people who are too stupefied with the prophecy of doom to take in the promise of relief, and in scathing words he de-

10 For the LORD hath poured out upon you the spirit of deep sleep, and hath closed your eyes: the prophets and your rulers, the seers hath he covered.

11 And the vision of all is become unto you as the words of a book that is sealed, which *men* deliver to one that is learned, saying, Read this, I pray thee: and he saith, I cannot; for it *is* sealed:

12 And the book is delivered to him that is not learned, saying, Read this, I pray thee: and he saith, I am not learned.

13 ¶ Wherefore the Lord said, Forasmuch as this people draw near *me* with their

10 For the LORD has poured out upon you
    a spirit of deep sleep,
and has closed your eyes, the prophets,
    and covered your heads, the seers.

11 And the vision of all this has become to you like the words of a book that is sealed. When men give it to one who can read, saying, "Read this," he says, "I cannot, for it is sealed." 12 And when they give the book to one who cannot read, saying, "Read this," he says, "I cannot read."

13 And the Lord said:
"Because this people draw near with
    their mouth

---

inaugural vision (6:9-10), where Isaiah is told to speak even though his hearers cannot perceive the meaning of his message. Here again the solemn truth is declared, that willful disobedience to moral and spiritual claims upon his life finally destroys man's capacity to hear and respond. With bitter irony the prophet bids his hearers **stupefy** and **blind** themselves, so that they **stagger** like a drunken man in their moral confusion. For the inevitable result—which is at the same time an act of God—is that they have fallen into that **deep sleep** from which men cannot be awakened or, in another figure, have by their attitude sealed the book in which the message is written.

10-12. The prophets . . . the seers: Glosses by a later annotator which are inconsistent with the thought of vss. 9-10*a* that the stupor is self-induced by the people addressed (cf. 6:9-10). **When men give it . . . :** A prose addendum to the oracle; the book is sealed for the scribes by their self-confident human "wisdom," and for the illiterate laity by the ignorance in which they rest content.

3. OVERTHROW OF CONVENTIONAL RELIGION (29:13-14)

13-14. The discomfiture of self-sufficient human wisdom is again the theme of this brief reproach and threat (cf. I Cor. 1:17-19, where Isa. 29:14 is quoted). **Wisdom** here is

---

clares they are drugged by their own sin. Because it is God they have insulted, and his law they have flouted, Isaiah can quite rightly assert that he has blinded them. Their spiritual insensibility is the result of the sheer hypocrisy of their religion. To such a people God's words are unintelligible, the book is closed to them, they are spiritually illiterate. They go through the motions of worship, they have memorized the liturgy, but it is all meaningless to them, and God is a name and nothing more. Therefore he must speak through deeds of which there shall be no misunderstanding. Where words are unavailing, the sword shall give tongue to God.

In this section of the chapter there are at least two subjects which claim the reader. The first is suggested by vss. 10-12, in which Isaiah points out that a nation immersed in material concerns inevitably grows less and less sensitive to the presence of God in life, until it becomes blind to all warning and appeal. At that point the prophet declares God must needs make his presence felt by other than spiritual means. The

history of the twentieth century in Western civilization, to go no farther back, is a commentary on that truth. The commercial and scientific success of these years produced a materialism which literally blinded men to the signs of the times. The historian of the future will marvel at the stupidity of those generations which were so intent on getting and spending that they never saw, or if they did, never cared for the impending judgment of war. "In God we trust" is a famous motto of colleges and of coinage, but it was not true of the first half of the twentieth century. God was not in men's minds; his book was "sealed," his portents meaningless to a spiritually insensitive people. They brought war on themselves, and God used it to thunder in their ears the moral demands of his rule, and men were **drunken, but not with wine; they [staggered], but not with strong drink.** It is, and always will be, the duty of the Christian church to expose while yet there is time the danger of a prevailing secularism. The second subject, the dark indictment of formalism in

mouth, and with their lips do honor me, but have removed their heart far from me, and their fear toward me is taught by the precept of men:

14 Therefore, behold, I will proceed to do a marvelous work among this people, *even* a marvelous work and a wonder: for the wisdom of their wise *men* shall perish, and the understanding of their prudent *men* shall be hid.

15 Woe unto them that seek deep to hide their counsel from the LORD, and their works are in the dark, and they say, Who seeth us? and who knoweth us?

16 Surely your turning of things upside down shall be esteemed as the potter's clay: for shall the work say of him that made it, He made me not? or shall the thing framed say of him that framed it, He had no understanding?

and honor me with their lips,
while their hearts are far from me,
and their fear of me is a commandment
of men learned by rote;
14 therefore, behold, I will again
do marvelous things with this people,
wonderful and marvelous;
and the wisdom of their wise men shall
perish,
and the discernment of their discerning
men shall be hid."

15 Woe to those who hide deep from the
LORD their counsel,
whose deeds are in the dark,
and who say, "Who sees us? Who knows
us?"
16 You turn things upside down!
Shall the potter be regarded as the
clay;
that the thing made should say of its
maker,
"He did not make me";
or the thing formed say of him who
formed it,
"He has no understanding"?

identified with the traditional forms of a religion in which the officials put on the lips of the worshipers words which have no vital meaning for them, so that men simply say and do what they are told. The oracle can be applied in rather different ways to the situation of all branches of Christendom in our time. But essential to the faith of Israel was a continual and living response to the **marvelous** act of God in taking this people to be his "personal possession" (cf. Exod. 34:10; 19:5-6). Since he is the living God, he will **again do marvelous things** in deliverance and self-revelation and will restore the religious relationship to a basis of reality, with an authority other than that of the priestly scribes and professional "wise men" (cf. Matt. 7:29).

D. REJECTION OF FAITH'S SECURITY (29:15–30:17)

1. CONSPIRATORS REPROACHED (29:15-16)

15-16. The occasion of this reproach, from which the normal concluding threat is missing, is to be found in the plotting of the Judean leaders to form an alliance with Egypt for revolt against Assyria, a theme which also underlies 28:7-22; 30:1-5; 31:1-3. They have hidden their schemes from the Lord in hiding them from his prophet, who steadfastly maintains that such action is not in accordance with Yahweh's plan. They try to manipulate the course of events and thus pre-empt the authority of God, whose sphere

religion, is brought out in vss. 13-14. **Their [piety] is taught by the precept of men.** How often is it true that men honor God with their lips, but their minds are not on him? There are thousands in our churches word-perfect in the responses; they have memorized the phrases of a devout life, and that is the end of it. There is little or no relationship between what is said in worship and what is done in the market

place. There is no evidence of the moral passion of a vital faith. Until religion becomes personal, it must of necessity remain conventional—if it remains at all. Formal worship never saved any man or any society. Honoring God with the lips is the constant habit of multitudes, but it is blasphemy when it is denied in the structure and spirit of society.

15-16. See Expos. below.

17 *Is* it not yet a very little while, and Lebanon shall be turned into a fruitful field, and the fruitful field shall be esteemed as a forest?	17 Is it not yet a very little while until Lebanon shall be turned into a fruitful field, and the fruitful field shall be regarded as a forest?
18 ¶ And in that day shall the deaf hear the words of the book, and the eyes of the blind shall see out of obscurity, and out of darkness.	18 In that day the deaf shall hear the words of a book, and out of their gloom and darkness the eyes of the blind shall see.
19 The meek also shall increase *their* joy in the LORD, and the poor among men shall rejoice in the Holy One of Israel.	19 The meek shall obtain fresh joy in the LORD, and the poor among men shall exult in the Holy One of Israel.
20 For the terrible one is brought to nought, and the scorner is consumed, and all that watch for iniquity are cut off:	20 For the ruthless shall come to nought and the scoffer cease, and all who watch to do evil shall be cut off,

is supremely the arena of history. In vs. 16 the RSV makes sense where the KJV does not, but the translation **You turn things upside down!** is a dubious rendering of the M.T., which is defective. The Dead Sea Scroll may have preserved the true text, הפך מכם, "Things are upside down because of you."

2. Two Eschatological Supplements (29:17-24)

The sudden change from condemnation to promise and the dependence in thought and language of these passages upon parts of chs. 35; 40–66 suggest that we have here the work of later supplementers inserted, as elsewhere, into the text of an Isaianic collection. For the dependence on Second and Third Isaiah, with vs. 17 cf. 35:2; 41:19; with vs. 18 cf. 35:5; 42:16, 18; 43:8; with vs. 19 cf. 41:17; 51:1-3; with vss. 20-21 cf. 59:18; with vs. 22 cf. 41:8; 48:1; 49:26; with vs. 23 cf. 41:17; 44:21; 60:21; 64:8; and with vs. 24 cf. 48:17. At the same time, vs. 17 seems to refer to vs. 16 in the previous oracle, vs. 18 to vss. 11-12, and vss. 20-21 to 28:14, 17, so that the passage was probably composed for its present context by one of the later supplementers of the Isaianic writings.

The first section, vss. 17-21, declares—without any suggestion that the change is the result of repentance or of purification through suffering—that Yahweh's mighty power will in **a very little while** (this is a note of later apocalyptic) transfigure the earth and deliver **the deaf** and **the blind, the meek** and **the poor,** i.e., the remnant of his people. **The ruthless** evildoers are not identical with external foes as in vs. 5, but are oppressors among the Jewish people. In the second section the promise is of a new deliverance by

17-24. *Two Eschatological Supplements.*—The second section of the chapter is a messianic forecast. These verses are apparently the work of later editors, who added them as supplements to match the dark words of Isaiah with hope and promise. The section begins in vss. 15-16, with a condemnation of the political intrigue that is going on with Egypt. It is "secret and highly confidential," and Isaiah rightly had a deep suspicion of any policy which could not bear the light. Secret diplomacy was to him a sure token that God was being either ignored or defied; and there is much in the history of diplomacy to support his view. He charges the politicians with an attempt to bemuse God and to assume the power which belongs to him	alone. As a result of their conspiracy of silence, the national life is utterly confused, and "things are up-side down." It is here the later editors inserted the vision of another day when God's power would be manifest in a complete transformation of men and society. In that glorious age the neglected poor will come to their own, while the tyrant and the conspirators of evil, the slanderers and corrupters of justice, will be silenced forever (vs. 21). Religion will no more be a man-made discipline but the glad response of a people who through obedience learned the liberating truths of God. Ancient Jewish eschatology does not seem to have much reality to the modern mind. It belongs to another age and speaks in thought

21 That make a man an offender for a word, and lay a snare for him that reproveth in the gate, and turn aside the just for a thing of nought.

22 Therefore thus saith the LORD, who redeemed Abraham, concerning the house of Jacob, Jacob shall not now be ashamed, neither shall his face now wax pale.

23 But when he seeth his children, the work of mine hands, in the midst of him, they shall sanctify my name, and sanctify the Holy One of Jacob, and shall fear the God of Israel.

24 They also that erred in spirit shall come to understanding, and they that murmured shall learn doctrine.

21 who by a word make a man out to be an offender,
and lay a snare for him who reproves in the gate,
and with an empty plea turn aside him who is in the right.

22 Therefore thus says the LORD, who redeemed Abraham, concerning the house of Jacob:
"Jacob shall no more be ashamed,
no more shall his face grow pale.
23 For when he sees his children,
the work of my hands, in his midst,
they will sanctify my name;
they will sanctify the Holy One of Jacob,
and will stand in awe of the God of Israel.
24 And those who err in spirit will come to understanding,
and those who murmur will accept instruction."

---

the God who redeemed Abraham, the friend of God and the father of his people, a thought first found in Second Isaiah. As a result of this deliverance the children of Jacob (Israel) will accept the prescribed standards of holiness and **accept instruction,** i.e., at the hands of the priests (cf. Ezek. 36:23; Hag. 2:11-13; Joel 3:17 [Hebrew 4:17]; Zech. 14:20-21). The mood and ideas of late postexilic Judaism clearly mark this passage.

17-21. Lebanon: The coastal range of mountains north of Palestine, famous for its forests of cedar and fir. **A fruitful field:** Better, "fruit country." **Watch** [their chance] **to do evil. Who . . . make a man . . . an offender,** or "who destroy a man's character." **Reproveth:** Better, "claims justice." **With an empty plea . . . right** is clumsy; better, "with specious argument deny redress to the innocent."

22-24. Concerning, 'el, should probably be read 'ēl, "God of." **His children** may be a gloss to provide a plural antecedent for the following verbs.

---

forms utterly strange to us. Quite true, all that is foretold of the messianic age can be claimed for the kingdom of God. If, however, we are going to think about the things that are to be, one would far more naturally do so in terms of Christ's teaching than of messianic prophecy. Nevertheless, this section contains words which suggest things to be said with personal and gripping force to any modern group. Take vs. 15,

> Woe to the men who hide
> their plans from the Eternal,
> working in the dark, and thinking,
> "No one sees or knows" (Moffatt).

Life abundantly justifies that judgment. There is no corner of this morally governed universe where the sinner can escape the eye of God. The whole theme of "the unescapable God" is magnificently treated by Francis Thompson in "The Hound of Heaven," and the heart of the matter is, "All things betray thee, who betrayest Me."

Naming and indicting sins may seem an easy and perhaps profitless task. It has, however, to be done, and vss. 20-21 contain references to sins of the common day which are entirely modern:

All that watch for iniquity, i.e., the kind of person alert for the chance to do or say the mean, the cruel, the selfish thing; these are they who make out a man to be at fault, with a lie. The world is full of people eager to believe the worst, and to seize on what is not true to blacken a man's character and "make a trap for fools."

"Who lay traps for the upholder of justice" (Amer. Trans.), and by false evidence or a bribe, or by any means however low, undertake to defeat the law. There is actually in modern

30 Woe to the rebellious children, saith the Lord, that take counsel, but not of me; and that cover with a covering, but not of my Spirit, that they may add sin to sin:

2 That walk to go down into Egypt, and have not asked at my mouth; to strengthen themselves in the strength of Pharaoh, and to trust in the shadow of Egypt!

3 Therefore shall the strength of Pharaoh be your shame, and the trust in the shadow of Egypt *your* confusion.

4 For his princes were at Zoan, and his ambassadors came to Hanes.

5 They were all ashamed of a people *that* could not profit them, nor be a help nor profit, but a shame, and also a reproach.

30 "Woe to the rebellious children," says the Lord,
"who carry out a plan, but not mine;
and who make a league, but not of my spirit,
that they may add sin to sin;
2 who set out to go down to Egypt,
without asking for my counsel,
to take refuge in the protection of Pharaoh,
and to seek shelter in the shadow of Egypt!
3 Therefore shall the protection of Pharaoh turn to your shame,
and the shelter in the shadow of Egypt to your humiliation.
4 For though his officials are at Zo'an
and his envoys reach Ha'nes,
5 every one comes to shame
through a people that cannot profit them,
that brings neither help nor profit,
but shame and disgrace."

3. An Ill-omened Embassy to Egypt (30:1-7)

As a result of the "covenant with death" (28:14-22), when the die was cast for rebellion against Assyria on the death of Sargon in 705, and of the subsequent secret scheming to which the prophet refers in 29:15-16, a Judean embassy is now en route to Egypt to seek her backing. Isaiah denounces this as rebellion, not against Assyria but against Yahweh. Because this scheme does not fit in with Yahweh's ongoing and comprehensive purpose in history, it can end only in failure and disgrace.

30:1-2. "Shame on the rebellious sons"; cf. 1:2, where this graceless conduct of those whom Yahweh has reared as sons is underlined. **Make a league:** Lit., "pour out a libation" in honor of the deity invoked at the making of a convenant. Isaiah had been kept in the dark in view of his known opposition to the contemplated action. Once more the political leaders had acted in defiance of Yahweh's plan, "so that they" (not **that they may**) **add sin to sin. Who set out:** The prophet is speaking as the embassy departs. **My mouth:** The prophet (cf. Exod. 4:16).

3-5. His officials . . . his envoys: Pharaoh's. The mention of **envoys** of **Pharaoh** in an oracle concerned with a Judean embassy makes for confusion. The point apparently is

society such a prostitution of justice that some men live by their cleverness in thwarting it, and criminals walk free because of astute and unscrupulous lawyers.

"Who thrust aside the innocent on an empty plea" (Amer. Trans.), i.e., the kind of man who in business will defraud with a quibble.

Even if such types are not commonly found among church members—who can say?—nevertheless it is part of the function of the church to create a public conscience about the evils which poison society. Certainly this age needs to be continually confronted with the ethical demands of the Christian life.

30:1-7. *The Folly of Trusting Egypt.*—This chapter contains a series of oracles dealing with the politicians and their Egyptian policy, the revelation of the spiritual condition of the nation, the prospect for the future, and the doom of Assyria. The divisions of the chapter are quite clear. In these verses Isaiah pours out scorn and anger on the Jewish embassy to Egypt. Apparently the prophet's previous denunciation of secret diplomacy brought things into the open. The leaders ceased to meet behind closed doors, they made known their brilliant stratagem and sent off their delegation freighted with gifts for Pharaoh. Isaiah declares

6 The burden of the beasts of the south: Into the land of trouble and anguish, from whence *come* the young and old lion, the viper and fiery flying serpent, they will carry their riches upon the shoulders of young asses, and their treasures upon the bunches of camels, to a people *that* shall not profit *them*.

7 For the Egyptians shall help in vain, and to no purpose: therefore have I cried concerning this, Their strength *is* to sit still.

8 ¶ Now go, write it before them in a table, and note it in a book, that it may be for the time to come for ever and ever:

6 An oracle on the beasts of the Negeb.
Through a land of trouble and anguish,
    from where come the lioness and the
      lion,
    the viper and the flying serpent,
they carry their riches on the backs of
    asses,
    and their treasures on the humps of
      camels,
to a people that cannot profit them.
7 For Egypt's help is worthless and empty,
    therefore I have called her
    "Rahab who sits still."

8 And now, go, write it before them on a
    tablet,
    and inscribe it in a book,
that it may be for the time to come
    as a witness for ever.

that the power of the Ethiopian dynasty in Egypt had reached as far north as **Zoan** or Tanis (almost on the border of Palestine) and **Hanes** or Anusis in middle Egypt, and thus had given the Judeans hope that Egypt was strong enough to face Assyria. In point of fact, the issue was as Isaiah anticipated, and the Egyptians were quickly defeated by Sennacherib. **Every one comes to shame:** Better, "all shall be shamed."

6-7. These verses appear to be marked off from vss. 1-5 by a heading: **An oracle** [lit., **burden**] **on the beasts of the Negeb.** Since what follows is not a "doom oracle" either on beasts or on Egypt, since this is the only occurrence of the title in Isaiah outside the series of "doom oracles" on foreign peoples in chs. 13–23, and finally since vss. 6-7 continue the thought of vss. 1-5 and repeat as a refrain the almost identical phrase **to a people that cannot profit them,** it seems clear that the opening words are not the title of an independent oracle. The Targ. has recognized this, and reads ישאו, "they carry," instead of משא, "doom oracle"; the object of the verb is unexpressed. The word בהמות, **beasts,** should then be read בחמת, "in the heat of," providing an excellent introduction to the verse: "They carry, through the heat of the Southland, through a land of trouble and anguish. . . ." The Dead Sea Scroll adds וציה, "and drought," a possibly correct textual variant of צרה, "trouble." **Rahab,** the mocking appellation of Egypt, was the name of the mythological serpent or dragon destroyed in combat by Yahweh at the Creation (see Exeg. on 26:20–27:1). For the impossible **who sits still,** lit., "they, a-sitting," read (following Gunkel) *hammoshbāth,* i.e., "Rahab, who shall be destroyed."

4. A Summation and a Testament (30:8-17)

Once before, in the days of the Syro-Ephraimite War, Isaiah had recorded his message as a witness for the future (see Exeg. on 8:16-18). Now long afterward, when again his word from God had been ignored by political leaders intent on finding their security through calling upon a foreign power, the prophet once more puts his message in writing as a testament. So far as the introduction to the oracle (vs. 8) goes, this may

it is stupid politics and worse religion, for it puts its trust in a shadow. Egypt will promise anything and do nothing. The best thing Egypt does, Isaiah says, is to talk. **Rahab,** the big braggart, he calls her. Moreover, the policy is worse than stupid, it is contempt of God and his will. The national temper is reflected in a

move which leaves God completely out of account. **Woe to the rebellious children,** rebels not against Assyria but against God.

8-11. *A Domesday Book.*—Isaiah is instructed to publish a summary of God's judgment on the Egyptian policy, both as a permanent record and as a witness against leaders and people

9 That this *is* a rebellious people, lying children, children *that* will not hear the law of the LORD:

10 Which say to the seers, See not; and to the prophets, Prophesy not unto us right things, speak unto us smooth things, prophesy deceits:

11 Get you out of the way, turn aside out of the path, cause the Holy One of Israel to cease from before us.

9 For they are a rebellious people,
lying sons,
sons who will not hear
the instruction of the LORD;
10 who say to the seers, "See not";
and to the prophets, "Prophesy not
to us what is right;
speak to us smooth things,
prophesy illusions,
11 leave the way, turn aside from the path,
let us hear no more of the Holy One
of Israel."

---

comprise simply vss. 8-17. But since, when Jeremiah was similarly commanded to record his message he included a whole series of oracles, and since related oracles denouncing the scheme for alliance with Egypt appear as a group in chs. 28–31, and finally since this group of oracles addressed to Judah is separated from the other oracles similarly addressed by two distinctive collections of material in chs. 13–23 and 24–27, it is tempting to regard vs. 8 here as marking the publication of a further collection of oracles. This would comprise in the first instance only the messages in chs. 28–31 denouncing the Egyptian alliance, in which there is no sign of the immediate threat to Jerusalem by Sennacherib in 701.

As in his message to Ahaz under somewhat similar circumstances, the prophet in vss. 8-17 declares that Judah's security lies not in military action and political alliances but in humble and quiet faith in God (with vss. 15-16 cf. 7:4, 9). Isaiah is not, however, counseling the quietism which withdraws from responsibility; with his overwhelming sense of the activity of God in historic events and his certainty that the divine plan is being carried out behind the scenes, he sees that Judah's panicky and shortsighted efforts to affect the course of events are foolish. The nation is at cross-purposes with her God. She makes her plans without regard to his will, and refuses to listen to his messengers. Thus Judah brings judgment upon herself; she will collapse like a weakened wall and will find that her trust in military adventures has worked her undoing.

The first part of the passage, vss. 8-11, is a private oracle instructing the prophet to make a permanent record of his warning words, because **they are a rebellious people** who refuse to hear them. There follow in vss. 12-14 and 15-17 two versions of a solemn sentence of judgment in the form of public proclamation. If the order of these is reversed the sequence is better, since **this word** in vs. 12 is undefined in vss. 12-14, and can hardly refer to vs. 9, which is addressed to the prophet by Yahweh; if, however, vss. 15-17 are inserted before vss. 12-14 the despised **word** is to be found in the pregnant sentence of vs. 15.

8-11. A tablet: Presumably a wooden writing tablet such as was used in Egypt, about the size of a child's slate. **A book:** A scroll of papyrus or skin. Read, "That it may be a perpetual testament for a later day." For **lying children** a freer but more accurate translation would be "sons who deny their sonship," i.e., by the disobedience which

---

alike. They have deliberately closed their minds to the truth, they have lied to themselves and to God. When the leaders snarled at Isaiah, "Get out of the way," and the voice of the nation said "No" to God, it was the ironical fate of a people who did not want truth, but only fair promises, to be caught in the lure of Egypt, the great promiser, purveyor of **smooth things**, "prophet of deceit."

9-11. *Refusing to Face Reality.*—Life is not all plain sailing; it is not "roses, roses, all the way." [5] The craven spirit in some lives demands an easy religion. It is not the truth they want; it is assurance that all will be well. These are the people who can grow eloquent about the joy of living and indignant over a gospel of sin and judgment. To them the cross of Christ is a

[5] Browning, "The Patriot."

12 Wherefore thus saith the Holy One of Israel, Because ye despise this word, and trust in oppression and perverseness, and stay thereon:

13 Therefore this iniquity shall be to you as a breach ready to fall, swelling out in a high wall, whose breaking cometh suddenly at an instant.

14 And he shall break it as the breaking of the potters' vessel that is broken in pieces; he shall not spare: so that there shall not be found in the bursting of it a sherd to take fire from the hearth, or to take water *withal* out of the pit.

15 For thus saith the Lord God, the Holy One of Israel; In returning and rest shall

---

12 Therefore thus says the Holy One of Israel,
"Because you despise this word,
　and trust in oppression and perverseness,
　and rely on them;
13 therefore this iniquity shall be to you
　like a break in a high wall, bulging out, and about to collapse,
　whose crash comes suddenly, in an instant;
14 and its breaking is like that of a potter's vessel
　which is smashed so ruthlessly
that among its fragments not a sherd is found
　with which to take fire from the hearth,
　or to dip up water out of the cistern."

15 For thus said the Lord God, the Holy One of Israel,
"In returning and rest you shall be saved;

---

dishonors their father. **Smooth things:** The word has the double sense of "agreeable" and "false." The true prophet was one who spoke the unpleasant truth, but men were ever eager to be deluded by false prophets who spoke what they wanted to hear (cf. I Kings 22:5-28; Jer. 28:8-9). "Get out of the way! Step aside from [our] path!"

12-14. Despise ["reject"] **this word:** The promise of vs. 15. **Trust in oppression and perverseness,** or "in force and deceit." **This iniquity** (or "guilt") will be a fatal weakness which may not show itself at once but will be **like a [crack] in a high wall, bulging out and about to collapse. Potter's vessel:** A pottery jar. **To take fire from the hearth** would require more than a tiny fragment of potsherd; the meaning seems to be rather "to rake together [cf. Koehler, *Lexicon in Veteris Testamenti Libros*, p. 343] the fire from what was kindled," i.e., "to poke [or "to bank"] the fire."

15-17. The pregnant and somewhat enigmatic words of vs. 15bc, each parallel line containing a compact exhortation and promise, looks like the "embryonic" form of an

---

hideous thing, and they echo the cry of the scribes and elders, "Come down from the cross, and we will believe" (Matt. 27:42). We cannot have life on such terms. At the heart of it is still a cross; no one can explain or escape the fact of pain. Our hope is that we may meet it and bear it without whimpering and despair. The victory has been won by him who "endured the cross, despising the shame" (Heb. 12:2), and will be won by those who in his fellowship and by his strength have accepted the discipline and suffering of life and have not ceased to believe and trust God.

12-14. *Collapse of the Egyptian Treaty.*— This is God's answer to such rebellion. The Egyptian alliance will break down. That is as inevitable as the crashing ruin of a badly built wall. The moral law is no less sure than the

natural; things not "straight," whether in bricks or in character, cannot stand.

15-17. *The True Secret of Security.*—In God's name Isaiah reiterates the only policy of security and strength, trust in the power and purpose of God. It is the statesmanship of faith and obedience. To make light of it, to devise something better, like this Egyptian alliance, means but one thing—defeat. Vss. 16-17 are both ludicrous and humiliating. The military advisors insist on cavalry. Isaiah remarks that it would be well to have good horses if they are to get away in the rout. Then follows the final debacle: a voice is raised and a thousand take flight, a few shout and the nation panics.

15. *The Lord of History.*—This verse is the greatest text of the chapter, and perhaps the

ye be saved; in quietness and in confidence shall be your strength: and ye would not.

16 But ye said, No; for we will flee upon horses; therefore shall ye flee: and, We will ride upon the swift; therefore shall they that pursue you be swift.

17 One thousand *shall flee* at the rebuke of one; at the rebuke of five shall ye flee: till ye be left as a beacon upon the top of a mountain, and as an ensign on a hill.

in quietness and in trust shall be your strength."
And you would not, **16** but you said,
    "No! We will speed upon horses,"
        therefore you shall speed away;
and, "We will ride upon swift steeds,"
        therefore your pursuers shall be swift.
17 A thousand shall flee at the threat of one,
    at the threat of five you shall flee,
till you are left
    like a flagstaff on the top of a mountain,
    like a signal on a hill.

---

oracle which would later be expanded for publication. Here it is repeated in the abbreviated form and included as a quotation within the public reproach. It is not impossible that the quotation is as old as the time of Ahaz, in view of the affinity with the thought of 7:3-9; 10:20-21. **In returning** [to God] **and in rest** [or "surrender" to him] **you shall be saved** [as a remnant]; **in quietness** [of mind] **and in trust shall be your strength.** Here in classic words are set out the constituents of that faith which is at once strength of soul and the victory which overcomes the world—a turning to God, surrender to his will, the quiet mind which will not yield to anxiety and fear, and perfect confidence in his wisdom, justice, and power. But Judah would have none of this: **No! we will speed** [not flee] **upon horses**—"so indeed you shall fly!" (in defeat). **At the threat of five . . . shall** ["a myriad"] **flee** (so Kissane, *Isaiah,* I, 338, 345, following the LXX). "Till what is left of you shall be like a flagpole," the abandoned standard of a vanished army. It should be noted that there is reference here to the original threatening sense of Shear Yashub, "only a remnant shall survive" (see Exeg. on 7:3-4; 10:20-23).

---

most difficult. On the face of it, Isaiah's counsel to stop making alliances and to trust in God would seem utterly fatuous to the modern age. At all the great junctures of history diplomacy apparently knows no other means of security than pacts, covenants, and armaments. Anybody who will advocate the kind of pacifism which trusts in God, and refuses to lift a hand in the defense of faith and freedom, must be prepared to lose his audience. That in itself does not of course prove him to be wrong. Most of the world's great leaders have known what it was to stand alone. But Isaiah was no pacifist; to base on this text any policy of disarmament is completely to misunderstand both the man and the message. All that Isaiah is saying to the national leaders is in effect this: "You are putting the first emphasis on the wrong thing; in your feverish negotiations to buy Egyptian support, in your frantic planning to increase your military strength, you are acting as if God has nothing to do with history, and as if men had literally to work out their own salvation or perish. The truth is that God is the Lord of history, and until you recognize that, until you believe that his power is greater than man's,

and that the defeat of the enemies of his purpose is his concern, your clever diplomacy is futile."

Can that not be said to the modern world? Does it not need to be said to an age which bets its life on physical science and economic pressure as the means to peace? The outlook of the world for the last hundred years gives no evidence that men believe God has anything to do with history, except to judge it after men have made it. They have persistently acted without any reference to God's existence, let alone his presence among men. A century of strife is witness to what comes of human diplomacy without faith. Isaiah said to his nation, "Trust God and act accordingly; trust him and use the means to do his will." He would say that today. What might not the world become if man really believed in God and ordered life accordingly? It is a trite thing to say that if we were to use our intellectual power and material resources to get God's will done, we could transform the earth; but there is at the last no other way to peace. **Quietness and confidence,** which are the real strength of a people, come only to those who in trust and obedience, serve God.

18 ¶ And therefore will the Lord wait, that he may be gracious unto you, and therefore will he be exalted, that he may have mercy upon you: for the Lord *is* a God of judgment: blessed *are* all they that wait for him.

19 For the people shall dwell in Zion at Jerusalem: thou shalt weep no more: he will be very gracious unto thee at the voice of thy cry; when he shall hear it, he will answer thee.

20 And *though* the Lord give you the bread of adversity, and the water of affliction, yet shall not thy teachers be removed into a corner any more, but thine eyes shall see thy teachers:

18 Therefore the Lord waits to be gracious to you;
  therefore he exalts himself to show mercy to you.
For the Lord is a God of justice;
  blessed are all those who wait for him.

19 Yea, O people in Zion who dwell at Jerusalem; you shall weep no more. He will surely be gracious to you at the sound of your cry; when he hears it, he will answer you. 20 And though the Lord give you the bread of adversity and the water of affliction, yet your Teacher will not hide himself any more, but your eyes shall see your

---

E. The Power of the Unseen God (30:18–31:9)
1. A Promise to Those in Adversity (30:18-26)

The break in continuity at vs. 18 is unusually abrupt; Judah is here no longer a rebellious people threatened with disaster but an afflicted people to be encouraged with a promise. **Therefore** in vs. 18 does not establish a logical connection with the preceding oracle; like other occurrences of "therefore" in 10:24; 29:22, it seems in later style to have little more force than "Behold" when introducing a promise. The passage begins with a text in the parallelism of poetry (vs. 18) ; thenceforward it is in prose, and the prose is practically a homiletical Midrash on the poetic introduction. The Jews of a time long after Isaiah's, who suffer **affliction** and feel themselves abandoned by their God, are exhorted to wait in patient faith for the moment for which Yahweh himself is waiting, when according to his plan he will intervene on their behalf. **Your [teachers KJV] will not hide** [themselves] **any more,** and the now silent **word** of prophecy will be spoken again (vs. 21). This time the idolators will hear and abandon their idolatry. Then follows one of the hyperbolic pictures of the blessings of the new age which are characteristic of late eschatological prophecy (cf. 65:17-25; Amos 9:13-15; Joel 3:18 [Hebrew 4:18]) .

18-22. Some commentators take vs. 18 as a kind of explanatory threat: God delays to be gracious because he is a God of justice, and the peoples' sin is not yet expiated!

18-26. The Everlasting Mercy.—Here is a gracious and tender passage. Isaiah for the moment is done with anger and sarcasm. He returns to the old and deep conviction that God has a purpose for his people, and it shall yet be well with his remnant. Despite their folly and rebellion, God's love of them, unstable and stubborn as they are, never changes. After the purging fire of defeat, theirs will be a great restoration. This section is entirely given over to the vision of the day when earth shall be fair and human life be purged of sin and sorrow by the healing touch of God. Every line has its own beauty, breathing the immemorial hope of the soul of man.

18. Divine Delays.—The key to the meaning of this verse is the phrase **The Lord is a God of judgment.** The word **judgment** is not used in the familiar sense of a sentence, a doom, but

rather as meaning a continued process of justice. God is not subject to fits of anger. He has laid down eternal principles for life. He has established his laws, and he governs history and his own actions by them: **The Lord is a God of judgment.** Very simply, that means he knows best. With infinite patience he waits for the right hour of deliverance. Whether in the affairs of nations or of men, God's timing is that of omniscience and love. We think of frustrated purposes, of deferred hopes, and weary souls waiting for an answer to their prayers; we do not often think of the delays imposed by wisdom and love on God himself, who with yearning for our redemption, must needs wait that he may be gracious unto us. It would take the perspective of eternity to see the perfect timing of God's deliverances. But we must not forget meanwhile that often it is

21 And thine ears shall hear a word behind thee, saying, This *is* the way, walk ye in it, when ye turn to the right hand, and when ye turn to the left.

22 Ye shall defile also the covering of thy graven images of silver, and the ornament of thy molten images of gold: thou shalt cast them away as a menstruous cloth; thou shalt say unto it, Get thee hence.

23 Then shall he give the rain of thy seed, that thou shalt sow the ground withal; and bread of the increase of the earth, and it shall be fat and plenteous: in that day shall thy cattle feed in large pastures.

24 The oxen likewise and the young asses that ear the ground shall eat clean provender, which hath been winnowed with the shovel and with the fan.

25 And there shall be upon every high mountain, and upon every high hill, rivers *and* streams of waters in the day of the great slaughter, when the towers fall.

26 Moreover the light of the moon shall be as the light of the sun, and the light of

Teacher. 21 And your ears shall hear a word behind you, saying, "This is the way, walk in it," when you turn to the right or when you turn to the left. 22 Then you will defile your silver-covered graven images and your gold-plated molten images. You will scatter them as unclean things; you will say to them, "Begone!"

23 And he will give rain for the seed with which you sow the ground, and grain, the produce of the ground, which will be rich and plenteous. In that day your cattle will graze in large pastures; 24 and the oxen and the asses that till the ground will eat salted provender, which has been winnowed with shovel and fork. 25 And upon every lofty mountain and every high hill there will be brooks running with water, in the day of the great slaughter, when the towers fall. 26 Moreover the light of the moon will be as the light of the sun, and the light of the

---

But this is an unnatural reading of the verse, for vs. 18c and vs. 18d go together, with what follows: "Because the Lord is a God of justice" he will bring justice to those who with patience wait for it (cf. Ps. 33:20). With vs. 19, cf. 65:24. Vs. 20a interrupts the sequence, and the sudden change to a second plural subject and back again throws doubt on its originality in this context. **Thy teachers** (KJV) is better than **your Teacher** (RSV), since it could not be said that men's eyes would see God; the Dead Sea Scroll reads the verb **hide** as a plural. The teachers are the prophets of the **word** (vs. 21).

23-26. **Rain for the seed,** and not, as occasionally happens, insufficient rain in December-January, following sowing. Pasture quickly becomes a problem in a year of below normal rainfall; it is to be remembered that almost no rain at all falls for the four summer months in Palestine. **Salted provender:** A kind of silage mash, made from grain **which has been winnowed** [by tossing it into the air] **with shovel and fork;** i.e., good grain will be so abundant that it can be made into cattle food. Even the normally waterless hillsides will be irrigated with "ditches running with water." **In the day of the great slaughter, when the towers fall** is incongruous here and appears to have been displaced from before vs. 29. **As the light of seven days:** Better, "seven days' light in one"; the words are omitted by the LXX but are in keeping with the writer's heaping up of superlatives.

25de. See Exeg. on vss. 25de, 29, 32c, p. 337.

---

we who impose the delay. God has to let us go our own way till we "come to ourselves" and realize our own ultimate need and helplessness. The door to experiencing the full measure of God's grace and mercy is the awareness of how lost we are. It may take a lifetime for a man to come to that condition of humility and need, but God is waiting; and always, when the prodigal turns again home, there is for him the welcome of the Father's forgiving grace.

21. *Instigations of God.*—This verse invites meditation on guidance. Whether a man believes in luck, chance, or an overruling purpose depends on whether he has any faith in God as concerned with or involved in his life. It is the firm conviction of Christian experience that guidance is offered. It may be and often is refused, but there are instigations of God for any man who will look for them. Guidance is not often as obvious as the voice of which the verse

the sun shall be sevenfold, as the light of seven days, in the day that the LORD bindeth up the breach of his people, and healeth the stroke of their wound.

27 ¶ Behold, the name of the LORD cometh from far, burning *with* his anger, and the burden *thereof is* heavy: his lips are full of indignation, and his tongue as a devouring fire:

28 And his breath, as an overflowing stream, shall reach to the midst of the neck, to sift the nations with the sieve of vanity: and *there shall be* a bridle in the jaws of the people, causing *them* to err.

sun will be sevenfold, as the light of seven days, in the day when the LORD binds up the hurt of his people, and heals the wounds inflicted by his blow.

27 Behold, the name of the LORD comes from far,
   burning with his anger, and in thick rising smoke;
his lips are full of indignation,
   and his tongue is like a devouring fire;
28 his breath is like an overflowing stream
   that reaches up to the neck;
to sift the nations with the sieve of destruction,
   and to place on the jaws of the peoples a bridle that leads astray.

---

2. Deliverance Through the Storm of Yahweh's Anger (30:27-33)

The general sense of this passage is clear, but some dislocations in the text have introduced a degree of confusion. The general theme is the destruction of the Assyrians (in 701) by the storm of Yahweh's anger. But vs. 29 in the present text is introduced into the middle of the description of this storm of judgment, and the mention of **timbrels and lyres** in vs. 32 could hardly be more incongruous with its context. Moreover, the two final clauses of vs. 25 in the previous passage belong rather in vss. 27-33 and provide a suitable transition from the picture of judgment to that in vs. 29 of the festival celebration of deliverance. If the latter belongs at all to the original composition, its place—with the intrusive words in vs. 32—is at the end; the order of the verses would then be vss. 27-28, 30-32*a*, 33; then vss. 25*de*, 29, 32*b*. It can only be surmised that at some stage in the transmission of the text, vss. 25*de*, 29, 32*b* were written in the margin of a MS and were subsequently copied mechanically in sequence with the verses opposite which they were written. While the evidence is not conclusive, the threat of judgment on the Assyrians has the appearance of being Isaiah's, and the picture of the temple celebration that of a later hand (with the latter cf. Jer. 33:10-11; Zech. 3:14-20).

27-28, 30. The might, majesty, and wrath of Yahweh are pictured here, as often in the O.T., in the imagery of a thunderstorm (cf. Pss. 18:7-15 [Hebrew 18:8-16]; 29:3-9; Hab. 3:3-11). **The name of the LORD:** A manifestation of power recognizable as that of Yahweh. **Comes from far:** Like the thunderstorm whose approach from the distance can be watched; but the phrase suggests also the distant seat of Yahweh's power (cf. Judg. 5:4; Hab. 3:3). **In thick rising smoke** is a dubious translation; "glorious in his exaltation," *kebhēdh massā'ôh,* suits the line better. **His breath:** Lit., "his wind," with the double suggestion of an angry person and a storm. The **overflowing stream** is a brook in spate

---

speaks. It requires at least a hearing ear and a responsive spirit. Given that, however, life is shot through with light for our pilgrimage. An open mind does not need to look far for signposts of God's purpose: in nature, history, books, human character, the Bible, the life and words of Jesus Christ, and the "still small voice" of the Holy Spirit. To the man who wants to know the way, the promise is abundantly fulfilled, "Thou shalt guide me with thy counsel" (Ps. 73:24).

27-33. The Wrath of God.—In violent contrast to the song of blessed days are the verses of doom that follow. Before God's purpose for Israel can be wrought out, not only must the nation be purged by pain but the enemies of God must be stricken. Isaiah therefore once more sounds the trumpet note of war and destruction. There is a flaming magnificence in his description of God's assault on Assyria. The oracle closes with a lurid and awful picture of the fiery hell prepared for the king of Assyria,

29 Ye shall have a song, as in the night *when* a holy solemnity is kept; and gladness of heart, as when one goeth with a pipe to come into the mountain of the LORD, to the Mighty One of Israel.

30 And the LORD shall cause his glorious voice to be heard, and shall show the lighting down of his arm, with the indignation of *his* anger, and *with* the flame of a devouring fire, *with* scattering, and tempest, and hailstones.

31 For through the voice of the LORD shall the Assyrian be beaten down, *which* smote with a rod.

32 And *in* every place where the grounded staff shall pass, which the LORD shall lay upon him, *it* shall be with tabrets and harps: and in battles of shaking will he fight with it.

33 For Tophet *is* ordained of old; yea, for the king it is prepared; he hath made *it* deep *and* large: the pile thereof *is* fire and much wood; the breath of the LORD, like a stream of brimstone, doth kindle it.

29 You shall have a song as in the night when a holy feast is kept; and gladness of heart, as when one sets out to the sound of the flute to go to the mountain of the LORD, to the Rock of Israel. 30 And the LORD wili cause his majestic voice to be heard and the descending blow of his arm to be seen, in furious anger and a flame of devouring fire, with a cloudburst and tempest and hailstones. 31 The Assyrians will be terror-stricken at the voice of the LORD, when he smites with his rod. 32 And every stroke of the staff of punishment which the LORD lays upon them will be to the sound of timbrels and lyres; battling with brandished arm he will fight with them. 33 For a burning place[t] has long been prepared; yea, for the king[u] it is made ready, its pyre made deep and wide, with fire and wood in abundance; the breath of the LORD, like a stream of brimstone, kindles it.

[t] Or *Topheth*
[u] Or *Molech*

---

following a downpour; here it is a simile of the wind against which men cannot maintain their footing and which will carry away **the nations** like grain and chaff together when one tries to **sift** or "winnow" them in too strong a wind. The verb **sift** in its primary sense, "jerk to and fro," governs the final clause with its changed figure: "and with a halter that misleads on the jaws of the peoples."

30. Cloudburst: Lit., "a shattering" (i.e., tempest) ; translate, "with tempest, downpour, and hailstorm."

31. Read, "when with the rod he is smitten."

32. The KJV is meaningless. Procksch (*Jesaia I,* p. 399) emends מוסדה to מוסרה and translates "every blow shall be by the rod of his chastisement."

33. A burning place or **Tophet:** A place of sacrifice by fire is ready for the Assyrians, like the infamous altar where children were made to "pass through the fire" to the god Moloch or Malik (cf. W. F. Albright, *Archaeology and the Religion of Israel* [Baltimore: Johns Hopkins Press, 1942], pp. 162-64) .

25*de,* 29, 32*c.* In the day of the great slaughter, when the towers fall, . . . you shall have a song as in the night when a holy "pilgrimage festival" is kept; and gladness of

---

and God waiting to blow the coals into searing flames.

Isaiah's exposure of the weakness and inevitable failure of godless diplomacy has not lost its force or relevance. The pulpit should never be used as a sounding board for political opinion, but the minister is nevertheless commissioned to examine all national policy in the revealed light of God. A sermon on foreign policy, if it expresses the preacher's personal judgment, has no greater value or authority than the view of any other educated man. Isaiah did not condemn the Egyptian alliance

because he belonged to the opposition. He examined it and denounced it in the light of the declared will of God. The only justification for the minister's judgment of national policy is the fact that he speaks in the name of God, and examines the proposal not to declare whether it is good policy or good economics, but whether it is good religion. The final authority of the modern prophet is the ancient "thus saith the Lord," which through the ages has prefaced the verdict of faith on the affairs of men. The danger in a minister's preaching on national issues is the likelihood of a too-ready agreement

31 Woe to them that go down to Egypt for help; and stay on horses, and trust in chariots, because *they are* many; and in horsemen, because they are very strong; but they look not unto the Holy One of Israel, neither seek the Lord!

2 Yet he also *is* wise, and will bring evil, and will not call back his words: but will

31 Woe to those who go down to Egypt for help
and rely on horses,
who trust in chariots because they are many
and in horsemen because they are very strong,
but do not look to the Holy One of Israel
or consult the Lord!

2 And yet he is wise and brings disaster,
he does not call back his words,
but will arise against the house of the evildoers,

heart, as when one sets out to the sound of the flute . . . to the Rock of Israel ["with"] timbrels and lyres ["and dancing," reading ובמחלות with Procksch, *loc. cit.*] to go to the mountain of the Lord. The night festival of Passover celebrated the deliverance from Egypt (cf. Exod. 12:42), and now there is to be a similar celebration of the new deliverance.

3. The Strength of Armies or the Power of the Spirit (31:1-3)

This oracle is a companion piece to 30:1-7, with its references to the Judean embassy seeking Egyptian help, to the illusory strength of Egypt, to the wisdom and the spirit of God, and to the inevitable discomfiture of a plan to seek foreign aid rather than to rely on God. The propensity of human beings in time of danger to grasp for material support at whatever moral cost, and to neglect the priority of spiritual realities because they are intangible, is here vividly set out. The grandiose dreams of the Judean leaders will come to nothing; instead, they will invoke the nemesis of history. For this the prophet gives two reasons: (*a*) their policy flouts the wise purpose of Yahweh, which alone governs the course of events; and (*b*) they are putting their trust in something as weak and transitory as themselves, which will perish with them.

31:1-3. Woe to: "Shame on . . . ." **Horses . . . chariots:** An arm in which Judah was deficient, partly owing to her poverty and partly to the hilly nature of her territory;

on the part of the congregation. They so seldom realize that national policy is the reflection of their own spirit. They persuade themselves that the preacher is talking about the politicians, and they agree with what he approves or condemns, according to their own political viewpoint. It will be quite otherwise if the expositor will use this passage to speak about planning in personal life, and to raise the question of the place of God in man's business, his ambitions, his relations to others. Every one of us has a plan, an ideal, an objective in living. The value of any man's life aim, therefore, should be measured by the place God can have in it. There can be no final happiness or success in the program which leaves him out of account. On those that take counsel, but not of God, who weave their web, ignoring or denying the claims of the spirit, who set their faces to go down to their Egypt, and have neither sought nor asked the blessing of God, the **woe to the rebellious children** is still to be spoken.

31:1-9. The Failure of Force.—This brief chapter is a supplement to the oracle against Egypt in 30:1-7. In addition to the denunciation of the folly of relying on the human aid of a people strong in cavalry but without faith in God, the prophet declares that the alliance will involve Israel in Egypt's defeat; the two allies will go down together. Nevertheless, since God's purpose includes the salvation of his chosen people, he will yet rescue them from their own folly. They will see the stupidity and wickedness of their idolatry as the majesty and power of the one true God is revealed in the overthrow of Assyria. Isaiah adds nothing to his previous prophecy in this chapter. He reiterates and reinforces the great conviction of his faith, that human history is the scene of God's action. In the clash and play of the human factors God is at work; the final issue is spiritual, not material, and the decision is in God's hands, not man's.

2. Yet He Also Is Wise.—These are sarcastic words uttered in scorn against the politicians

arise against the house of the evildoers, and against the help of them that work iniquity.

3 Now the Egyptians *are* men, and not God; and their horses flesh, and not spirit. When the Lord shall stretch out his hand, both he that helpeth shall fall, and he that is helped shall fall down, and they all shall fail together.

4 For thus hath the Lord spoken unto me, Like as the lion and the young lion roaring on his prey, when a multitude of

and against the helpers of those who work iniquity.

3 The Egyptians are men, and not God;
    and their horses are flesh, and not spirit.
When the Lord stretches out his hand,
    the helper will stumble, and he who is helped will fall,
    and they will all perish together.

4 For thus the Lord said to me,
    As a lion or a young lion growls over his prey,
    and when a band of shepherds is called forth against him

---

there is only one reference to the possession of a force of chariots by a Judean king (II Kings 8:21) subsequent to the disruption of Solomon's kingdom. "[They] do not look to [in confidence] or consult the Lord [before embarking on serious enterprises], though it is he who [alone] is wise." These men are **evildoers,** not because of transgression against social morality, but because there was in them "an evil heart of unbelief."

4. The Lord, Jerusalem's Defender (31:4-9)

Again in this passage we are faced with difficulties of interpretation due to dislocations in the text and the insertion of extraneous matter. From vs. 5 and vss. 8-9 it is clear that the setting and purpose of the oracle are quite different from those of the preceding; the time is 701, and now, as in 37:21-35, Yahweh undertakes to defend the

---

who boasted of their wisdom in making an alliance with Egypt. It is as if the prophet said: "God also has a plan, and you are involved in it. You have devised a clever strategy, you are betting on the power of Egypt to save you; it is a gamble with death which you will lose, because you have left God out of account. He has planned your salvation, but as long as you think you can do better than he, you must take the consequences. Sign the compact with Egypt and go to your doom. You have not done with God; his divine purpose for his people is not to be defeated by Egyptian cavalry."

Living as we are in an age of planning and of long-range policy, Isaiah's words have tremendous force for us. What place is there in men's thoughts for God's plan? Is there room for him at the council table of the nations? We call on the finest minds of the race for leadership, we commit our destiny to their wisdom, but do we consider that God **also is wise?** Granted that those who seek to establish righteousness, justice, freedom, are in a deep sense serving God, there is little evidence that in our planning, whether in matters of economics or of foreign policy, God or his purpose is the point of reference. What modern nation has ever dared to fashion its policy in terms of his will for men? Of

modern diplomacy it might be written as of Jewish diplomacy in Isaiah's day, "They look not unto the Holy One of Israel, neither seek the Lord!" Is not that the final defect in modern planning? It is unrelated to the purpose of God, and therefore unavailing to secure the peace for which men yearn.

God's plan is for the redemption of the world, but his methods are utterly different from those of men. The human plan depends on armed might, economic forces, power politics; but God commits his purpose to such means as the birth of a child in a manger, a carpenter's life, a ministry of love, a stark cross on a lonely hill, an empty tomb. In the face of pride and greed and fear these things seem both foolish and futile. An alliance with Egypt appears far more realistic than declaring a gospel of the power of love. Still, "The preaching of the cross is to them that perish, foolishness. . . . But God hath chosen the foolish things of the world to confound the wise; and God hath chosen the weak things of the world to confound the things which are mighty, . . . because the foolishness of God is wiser than men; and the weakness of God is stronger than men" (I Cor. 1:18, 27, 25) .

4-5. The Goodness and Severity of God.—In these verses, under the images of the **birds** and

shepherds is called forth against him, *he* will not be afraid of their voice, nor abase himself for the noise of them: so shall the LORD of hosts come down to fight for mount Zion, and for the hill thereof.

5 As birds flying, so will the LORD of hosts defend Jerusalem; defending also he will deliver *it; and* passing over he will preserve *it.*

6 ¶ Turn ye unto *him from* whom the children of Israel have deeply revolted.

7 For in that day every man shall cast away his idols of silver, and his idols of gold, which your own hands have made unto you *for* a sin.

is not terrified by their shouting
  or daunted at their noise,
so the LORD of hosts will come down
  to fight upon Mount Zion and upon its
    hill.

5 Like birds hovering, so the LORD of hosts
  will protect Jerusalem;
he will protect and deliver it,
  he will spare and rescue it.

6 Turn to him from whom you[v] have deeply revolted, O people of Israel. 7 For in that day every one shall cast away his idols of silver and his idols of gold, which your hands have sinfully made for you.

[v] Heb *they*

city of his sanctuary against the arrogant Assyrians. The main problems are (*a*) in vs. 4 Yahweh fights against Jerusalem, but in vs. 5 he protects her; (*b*) the obscurity of the figures of Yahweh as a lion coming down, and as flying birds (plural); (*c*) the abrupt summons to repentance which breaks the sequence of the oracle at vs. 6.

There can be no doubt that לצבא על in vs. 4 means "to fight against" rather than to fight for (KJV) or to fight upon (RSV; cf. 29:7-8; Num. 31:7). The solution is to recognize that לצבא is a variant of the preceding word צבאות, and to omit it. The two figures of the lion and the birds are confused as they stand; Yahweh will come down like a "flight of birds," and like the lion . . . will protect what he holds, undismayed by the uproar of those who would drive him away. A later reader has sought to explain the abrupt change from condemnation in vss. 1-3 to the promise of protection in vss. 4-5, 8-9, by writing in the margin a prediction of repentance of idolatry, which was then incorporated in the body of the oracle in vss. 6-7.

4-5. Growls is more accurate than roaring, since the word indicates a low, muttering sound. Lions straying into the hills from the semitropical jungle in the Jordan Valley were a serious problem to shepherds (cf. I Sam. 17:34-37; Amos 3:12); one method of dealing with them apparently was to summon all shepherds in the vicinity to try to frighten off the lion by making a great din. Passing over is better than he will spare, because it preserves the allusion to the deliverance commemorated by the Pesach (Passover) festival; the verb appears in the O.T. only here and in Exod. 12.

6-7. For turn (imperative), שובו, read "they will return," ישובו.

the lion, two aspects of God's power are set forth, viz., his goodness and his severity (Rom. 11:22). Isaiah puts the severity first, as is natural for a man living in an age of storm. The figure of the lion snarling defiance over its kill is a daring one to apply to God. Those who have been brought up hearing the accents of a gospel of love may shrink from it, but in its graphic way it is true. There is that in love which faces evil with implacable anger. Paradoxically, there is such a thing as the merciless judgment of love. Isaiah depicts God as coming to the defense of Jerusalem like an enraged lion. The king of beasts is not to be driven off by the shouting of a handful of shepherds, nor is God to be deterred by the scorn or anger of his enemies.

There is a truth with both terror and comfort in it.

Terror because "It is a fearful thing to fall into the hands of the living God" (Heb. 10:31). History records many a time when under the lash of divine judgment mankind could only cower in terror, and everyone whose conscience is not dead has known the misery and fear of standing in discovered guilt before the gaze of God. Love without severity could not save us. We are so made that we could neither respect nor receive a love which could make light of sin and condone its guilt. When men are stricken and bowed beneath the judgment of God, something within them rises up, not merely to bear it, but to see in it the divine justice and righteous-

8 ¶ Then shall the Assyrian fall with the sword, not of a mighty man; and the sword, not of a mean man, shall devour him: but he shall flee from the sword, and his young men shall be discomfited. 9 And he shall pass over to his stronghold for fear, and his princes shall be afraid of the ensign, saith the Lord, whose fire *is* in Zion, and his furnace in Jerusalem.	8 "And the Assyrian shall fall by a sword, not of man; and a sword, not of man, shall devour him; and he shall flee from the sword, and his young men shall be put to forced labor. 9 His rock shall pass away in terror, and his officers desert the standard in panic," says the Lord, whose fire is in Zion, and whose furnace is in Jerusalem.

8-9. Flee from the sword: The Dead Sea Scroll reads "flee, but not from the sword [of man]." **A mighty man, . . . a mean man** is an unjustified distinction of the synonyms for man. **His rock** is difficult; it has been interpreted of the Assyrian god or king, but it is more probably a figure of security. **Fire** and **furnace,** or "firepot," represent both the sanctity and the destructiveness of the altar of Zion.

---

ness. So the severity of God is used for our salvation, and the way to penitence and forgiveness lies through the valley of humiliation.

But there is also comfort in this thought of God closing in on life in wrath; for it means that those evils which invade life are marked down for judgment. Again and again faith is dismayed at the power and the progress of the organized forces of wickedness. A godless movement sweeps a nation, it captures the government, it enslaves the multitude, it reaches out and engulfs other lands, its aim is world dominion. By every device of evil, without scruple or conscience, it eats its way like a canker into the hearts of men or, resorting to force, beats down all opposition and triumphs. For the time being justice and righteousness are powerless, and faith in goodness and truth is staggered. What is the believer to do in such a time? He will strengthen himself in God, fighting, enduring, dying if need be, in the confidence that the divine purposes at the end are to be accomplished and the evil which defied them is to go out into everlasting night. "This is the victory that overcometh the world, even our faith" (I John 5:4).

Over against the severity of God, therefore, and at the very heart of it, stand his eternal goodness and love.

> Like a bird fluttering above its nest
> shall the Eternal ward Jerusalem,
> shielding her and saving her (Moffatt).

From the ferocity of the hunting lion the prophet turns to the protective instinct of the mother bird. "He will not always chide: neither will he keep his anger forever" (Ps. 103:9). It

is one of the tender and beautiful things in nature to see a tiny bird hovering over its nest in the grass, or trailing a wing in pretended injury, seeking to lead the intruder away from her fledglings. If the creatures of the wild protect their own, will not God come between his people and their peril?

There are no lovelier passages in the world than those which dwell on God's keeping and saving love. "How excellent is thy loving-kindness, O God! therefore the children of men put their trust under the shadow of thy wings" (Ps. 36:7). "I will trust in the covert of thy wings" (Ps. 61:4). From every age voices reach us declaring the peace of trusting in the protecting love of God.

> O spread thy covering wings around,
> Till all our wanderings cease,
> And at our Father's loved abode
> Our souls arrive in peace.[6]

> All my trust on thee is stayed,
> All my help from thee I bring,
> Cover my defenseless head
> With the shadow of thy wing.[7]

The figure of the hovering bird suggesting the care by God of his own has not lost its force and beauty; but for the Christian there is another image which proclaims the far deeper power of the love which will not let us go. It is that of the Cross. It is there that we see "the breadth, and length, and depth, and height, and . . . know the love of Christ which passeth knowledge" (Eph. 3:18-19).

[6] Philip Doddridge, "O God of Bethel."
[7] Charles Wesley, "Jesus, Lover of My Soul."

32 Behold, a King shall reign in righteousness, and princes shall rule in judgment.
 	
2 And a man shall be as a hiding place from the wind, and a covert from the tempest; as rivers of water in a dry place, as the shadow of a great rock in a weary land.
	32 Behold, a king will reign in righteousness,
	    and princes will rule in justice.
	2 Each will be like a hiding-place from the wind,
	    a covert from the tempest,
	  like streams of water in a dry place,
	    like the shade of a great rock in a weary land.

F. An Appendix (32:1-20)

1. Justice in Rulers and Wisdom in Society (32:1-8)

At first sight the opening lines of this poem suggest the promise of a messianic reign, and they have been so interpreted. But the parallelism of **a king . . . and princes** is unexampled elsewhere in predictions of the messianic age, when the ruler is to be God himself or his vicegerent. As the poem proceeds it becomes apparent that its subject is the more abstract one of the good fruits of the just rule—the defense of the needy and oppressed, the increase of wisdom, and the discomfiture of the fool and the knave. In a previous passage (28:23-29) Isaiah has shown himself able to adapt the method and manner of the wisdom teachers to his prophetic message. While it is not impossible that we have here a further example of the same thing, the lack of any real contact of this poem with the thought of Isaiah and its marked resemblance not only to the language but to the thought of the later wisdom writers make it more probable that this passage is a product of their hands. The theme is that of Prov. 16:10-15; 20:8, 26, 28; 25:5; and especially of the passage beginning "By me [wisdom] kings reign, and princes decree justice" (Prov. 8:15-21).

32:1-2. Behold, a king will reign: Better, "when a king reigns . . . and princes rule . . . , they are like . . . ." The supreme pictorial quality of Hebrew verse is illustrated by the

---

32:1-20. Erewhon.—It is characteristic of Isaiah and the editors who compiled his work generally to follow the specific judgment on the national condition with a glimpse of the ideal which is denied by the human situation. Thus having in chs. 30–31 leveled his accusation against the character and the policy of the nation's leaders, he proceeds in this chapter to show us what men and society become when the Spirit of God permeates life. The Exeg. casts doubt on the Isaianic authorship of certain sections of the chapter, but the tone and the emphasis are certainly in keeping with the prophet's teaching.

1-8. Society Transformed.—These verses contain Isaiah's vision of a reformed society. He does not deal here, as he does in vss. 15-19, with the physical and material effects of a new spirit in men, but solely with the moral qualities which transform life. The source of the change is in the character of the ruling classes. When righteousness and justice mark their lives, the whole of society feels the purifying influence. In considerable detail Isaiah describes the new quality in life. The rulers cease to be tyrants and become friends and protectors of men; there is an immediate quickening of the moral

perception of the people, rash judgments are restrained and moral timidity gives place to confidence; artificial class distinctions disappear, and the true aristocracy of character reigns. It is no longer a question of wealth or poverty, of power or servitude, but of right or wrong, of noble personality or of evil. The whole section is one of the noblest expressions of the prophet's unchanging conviction that the nature and the circumstance of society depend on the character of the people.

2. The Shadow of a Great Rock.—George Adam Smith,[8] in interpreting this verse, sees in it three truths.

1. *A philosophy of history.* Great men, he points out, are not the whole of life, but they are the condition of all the rest. The first requisites of religion and civilization are outstanding characters. Isaiah knew the desert. He had muffled his face against the sandstorm, he had seen it pile the dunes like waves of the sea. The encroaching sand blotted out all growing things. The only thing that could stay the drift was a great rock. In its lee brave shoots appeared, behind its bulwark life was possible, safe from

[8] *The Book of Isaiah* (New & rev. ed.; London: Hodder & Stoughton, 1927), pp. 257-62.

3 And the eyes of them that see shall not be dim, and the ears of them that hear shall hearken.

4 The heart also of the rash shall understand knowledge, and the tongue of the stammerers shall be ready to speak plainly.

5 The vile person shall be no more called liberal, nor the churl said *to be* bountiful.

6 For the vile person will speak villainy, and his heart will work iniquity, to practise hypocrisy, and to utter error against the LORD, to make empty the soul of the hungry; and he will cause the drink of the thirsty to fail.

7 The instruments also of the churl *are* evil: he deviseth wicked devices to destroy the poor with lying words, even when the needy speaketh right.

8 But the liberal deviseth liberal things; and by liberal things shall he stand.

---

3 Then the eyes of those who see will not be closed,
　and the ears of those who hear will hearken.

4 The mind of the rash will have good judgment,
　and the tongue of the stammerers will speak readily and distinctly.

5 The fool will no more be called noble,
　nor the knave said to be honorable.

6 For the fool speaks folly,
　and his mind plots iniquity:
to practice ungodliness,
　to utter error concerning the LORD,
to leave the craving of the hungry unsatisfied,
　and to deprive the thirsty of drink.

7 The knaveries of the knave are evil;
　he devises wicked devices
to ruin the poor with lying words,
　even when the plea of the needy is right.

8 But he who is noble devises noble things,
　and by noble things he stands.

---

four figures for the protection of the needy in vs. 2, and nowhere is the music of the KJV more notable. The word translated **tempest** means more exactly a torrential rainfall; and **rivers** or **streams** are irrigation channels which bring **water in a dry place. A weary land:** Parched and lifeless in the torrid heat (cf. Ps. 63:1 [Hebrew 63:2]).

3-4. The just ruler will attend to the need which he sees and of which he hears, and because of new confidence the voluble complainants will learn restraint, while those who stammered through nervousness **will speak readily.**

5-8. In the well-ordered society moral wisdom and nobility of character on the one hand, and wickedness and folly on the other, will be seen for what they are. This contrast of the wise man and the fool is one of the dominant themes of the wisdom books (cf. Prov. 13–15; Eccl. 7:4-9; 9:17-18); the difference lies in moral quality rather than in intelligence. **The fool** is a **knave** in thought and speech; he is an oppressor because he is a godless man; his evil-doing is deliberate. But the **liberal, noble,** or "magnanimous" man "is magnanimous in purpose, and it is he who takes a stand for generous deeds [lit., "arises concerning noble things"]."

---

the smothering sand. Smith shows that this is how great men benefit human life. They serve the world by arresting the deadly forces which sweep across it. History is full of illustrations of that truth. Lincoln stayed the drift of slavery; Shaftesbury put his own life between commercial greed and the children of England; between 1939 and 1945 Winston Churchill was the rallying point of the free nations of the earth, and in his fearless defiance of the enemy, in his unflinching confidence and courage, was to tens of thousands **a hiding place from the wind, and a covert from the tempest.** Again and again what has saved humanity has been the rise of some great man who set his will against the drift of evil.

2. *The promise of a divine life to stay the drift of sin and death.* Against evil, man raised his barriers of government, education, and philosophy, but none could stay the drift. It overwhelmed them all. Then into human defeat came Jesus Christ. He set his life between men and encroaching evil, he resisted unto the death and saved the world.

3. *A summons to every life to be a shelter and a strength to others.* The work of salvation is not left to the great ones of earth. Indeed, that better, kinder world for which we long is to be

9 ¶ Rise up, ye women that are at ease; hear my voice, ye careless daughters; give ear unto my speech.

10 Many days and years shall ye be troubled, ye careless women: for the vintage shall fail, the gathering shall not come.

11 Tremble, ye women that are at ease; be troubled, ye careless ones: strip you, and make you bare, and gird *sackcloth* upon *your* loins.

12 They shall lament for the teats, for the pleasant fields, for the fruitful vine.

13 Upon the land of my people shall come up thorns *and* briers; yea, upon all the houses of joy *in* the joyous city:

14 Because the palaces shall be forsaken; the multitude of the city shall be left; the

9 Rise up, you women who are at ease,
     hear my voice;
   you complacent daughters, give ear to
     my speech.

10 In little more than a year
   you will shudder, you complacent
     women;
  for the vintage will fail,
     the fruit harvest will not come.

11 Tremble, you women who are at ease,
     shudder, you complacent ones;
  strip, and make yourselves bare,
     and gird sackcloth upon your loins.

12 Beat upon your breasts for the pleasant
     fields,
     for the fruitful vine,

13 for the soil of my people
     growing up in thorns and briers;
  yea, for all the joyous houses
     in the joyful city.

14 For the palace will be forsaken,
     the populous city deserted;
  the hill and the watchtower
     will become dens for ever,

2. Frivolous Women Warned of Disaster (32:9-14)

A second time Isaiah threatens the women of his people, not, as in 3:16–4:1, the fashionable women of Jerusalem for their arrogance and worldliness, but the women who danced at a harvest festival for the heedlessness of their gaiety. The oracle comes from the prophet's early ministry when he was proclaiming unconditional disaster (cf. 5:5-6; 6:11-13). The only visible connection with its present context is the "wisdom" mannerism of the opening verse (see Exeg. on 28:23-29).

The point of the oracle turns upon the threat that, in contrast to the present situation, the **fruit harvest** and **vintage will fail,** lit., "in days unto [or "upon"] a year." The latter phrase must be an idiom like "a year and a day," "when a year comes around." Those who now gaily celebrate the harvest festival (cf. Judg. 21:19-21) are summoned instead to the ritual mourning for the coming desolation of city and country alike (cf. 58:3-7; Jer. 14:12; Joel 1:8-15; 2:12-17) which will be next year's harvest of destruction.

9. Complacent daughters: Better, "confident maidens."

10. "The confident ones will be trembling, for the vintage will have failed, and the autumn harvest will not arrive."

13. The joyous houses, . . . the joyful city: As at the moment when the prophet speaks.

14. "The bustling city will be deserted, its acropolis and tower shall be destroyed [reading לבער for בער], a place to be trampled down henceforward [reading מרמס for

built not by our leaders but by ourselves, the common people, who will show the saving spirit of love. In one pungent sentence Smith declares, "Some righteous people have a terribly northeastern exposure; children do not play about their doors, nor the prodigal stop there." [9] There are many who fail in the struggle of life because they never meet anyone who is a living embodi-

ment of the good they seek. "The spectacle of one pure, heroic character would be their salvation." [1] It is at least open to all men so to live that it will be easier for others to believe in God.

9-14. *A Judgment on the Frivolity of Women.* —Another of Isaiah's judgments on the women of the nation. He here accuses them of sheer frivolity and reckless indifference in the face

[9] *Ibid.,* p. 262.

[1] *Ibid.*

forts and towers shall be for dens for ever, a joy of wild asses, a pasture of flocks;	a joy of wild asses, a pasture of flocks;
15 Until the Spirit be poured upon us from on high, and the wilderness be a fruitful field, and the fruitful field be counted for a forest.	15 until the Spirit is poured upon us from on high, and the wilderness becomes a fruitful field, and the fruitful field is deemed a forest.
16 Then judgment shall dwell in the wilderness, and righteousness remain in the fruitful field.	16 Then justice will dwell in the wilderness, and righteousness abide in the fruitful field.

מערות]." For these emendations of the obscure words translated by the RSV **will become dens for ever,** cf. 5:5.

3. The Transforming Gift of the Spirit in the Age to Come (32:15-20)

This is another of the supplements to the book of Isaiah, comparable to those in 29:17-24, and setting forth the eschatological hope. Vs. 15 is in part an exact repetition of 29:17. In both passages there is a sudden shift from threat to promise, and the opening הלא־עוד, in the former, confirms Duhm's proposal to point 'adh as 'ōdh in the latter [Das Buch Jesaia, p. 238]. The writer was familiar with the main constitutents of the present book, but because of his subject he draws more largely on the latter part (with vs. 15, cf. 10:18; 44:3; with vs. 16, cf. 45:8; 61:11; with vs. 17, cf. 30:15; 54:13; 60:17; with vs. 18, cf. 33:20; 60:21; with vs. 19, cf. 10:18; with vs. 20, cf. 7:25; 30:23-25).

The pentecostal outpouring of the Spirit of God which the first Christians recognized as a sign that the new age had dawned (Acts 2:1-18, 33) is a feature of the eschatological hope found also in 44:3; Joel 2:28-29; Zech. 12:10. Its result is to be a new creation in nature (vs. 15) and in the moral and spiritual realm (vs. 16). Moreover—and here the writer shows that he has entered into the inheritance of prophetic understanding—the well-being and security on which men then and now set their hearts can be found only as **the effect of righteousness. When the Spirit is poured** out it will create the conditions which alone make it possible for men to find what they deeply desire. As in the promise of a "new covenant" in Jer. 31:31-34, God's new act of grace in the last days will open the way for his people to meet the moral demands which are indispensable to their achievement of true happiness.

15-17. "There shall yet be poured upon us the Spirit ["of Yahweh," added by Procksch, Jesaia I, p. 415, for metrical reasons] from on high." Note in vs. 16 the concrete,

of God's solemn warning. In his previous indictment, 3:16–4:1, he had attacked their pagan luxury and ostentation. In this passage he is concerned with their complete irresponsibility. They are in a gay fever of indifference from which he tries to bring them to reality by prophesying the utter destruction of Jerusalem. So vivid is his sense of the imminent doom of the city that he calls the women to begin even now the wailing and lamentation of the mourner.

15-20. A World Renewed.—After the dark comes the dawn. The prophet paints a vignette of the re-created earth that will one day result from an outpouring of God's Spirit. It is a vision of the fruitful earth in quiet beauty, and of a righteous people rejoicing in the security and peace of those who do the will of God. The section ends with a homey little pic-

ture of the farmer in a well-watered land, so free from danger that he can let his cattle out to graze wherever they like.

On the basis of the inspired insight of this great chapter, a study of the character and structure of an enduring social order might well be made. It is significant that the basic principles laid down are moral and spiritual. Isaiah and all the great prophets offer a valuable corrective to the prevalent tendency to put the first emphasis on social legislation and economic reform as the mainspring of a re-created society. They declare with one voice that prosperity in agriculture and trade and all the physical blessings for which men strive result from a new spirit in human relationships. They anticipate in their teaching the words of our Lord, "Seek ye first the kingdom of God, and his righteous-

| 17 And the work of righteousness shall be peace; and the effect of righteousness, quietness and assurance for ever.

18 And my people shall dwell in a peaceable habitation, and in sure dwellings, and in quiet resting places; | 17 And the effect of righteousness will be peace,
  and the result of righteousness, quietness and trust for ever.
18 My people will abide in a peaceful habitation,
  in secure dwellings, and in quiet resting places. |

pictorial imagery which the Hebrew poet uses for abstract ideas (cf. 60:17; 61:11; Ps. 85:10-11 [Hebrew 85:11-12]).

18-20. The first line of vs. 19 is corrupt and must be emended as in the RSV; the verse clearly is misplaced in this context. In vs. 20 the farmer is congratulated that he

ness; and all these things shall be added unto you" (Matt. 6:33). God and his righteousness come first. That message, which through the centuries has been the witness of the Christian church, men have consistently ignored. They have refused to believe that religion is related to economics, despite the fact that the history of human enterprise, the story of competitive private business, the unavailing quest for peace, all testify to the impossibility of creating a just and enduring order of life while greed, pride, selfishness, and such distortions of the spirit prevail in the relations of men. The old proverb, that you cannot make a silk purse out of a sow's ear, puts in its own coarse way the truth Isaiah never ceased to declare, that good character is the indispensable condition of good society. It is here that the supreme relevance of the Christian gospel to the problems of humanity is to be seen; for good character is not a natural endowment of man, but something attained, not by human device, but by the recreative power of God's Spirit. The modern humanistic philosophy, with which so much psychology and social science are infected, dismisses this claim of faith, or at most concedes to it a merely subordinate influence. The church today has no graver duty, no greater message, than to declare to men the truth of the Word of God, that faith in God and response to him in personal and social life are the final conditions of peace on earth. The church has indeed much more to say, for there is not a single problem now vexing society on which the Word of God has not light to throw; but the first duty of those who will speak for God is to confront the world with his declared purpose and revealed will. There will be no immediate response; men will still object to what they term "the unrealistic idealism" of the Christian message. Nevertheless, there are not lacking signs that slowly the truth is beginning to dawn on us: this world can never know peace till life is organized on the principles laid down by God for his children. It is to be remembered that

Jesus Christ came not merely to proclaim a new life, but to produce it. The Christian gospel holds out to men the ideal, and at the same time offers the power to attain it; its message is of a divine hope and a divine dynamic. There could be nothing more practical for a distracted and confused generation than the offer of God to do for us and through us what we have never been able to do without him. This chapter paints the picture of life as all men would fain have it: the wilderness become a fruitful field, righteousness the foundation of the nation and the source of peace, sure dwellings, and men at their work with fear lifted from their hearts. The phrases utter the deepest longings of mankind. So fair a dream! But only a dream till men in their need open their lives to that Spirit from on high which God has poured upon the world, and are enabled and persuaded to allow him to make all things new.

17. The True Security.—George Adam Smith [2] points out that the cause of the blessed condition described here is the outpouring of the Spirit of God (vs. 15). All the great prophets place their hope of new life for men on the transforming power of the Spirit of God. They do not however deny that man has a part to play in his own redemption. The material blessing promised is conditioned by the moral response of men to the visitation of the Spirit. One could wish that Smith had laid a greater emphasis on this truth. The twentieth century has been compelled as no other to face the fact that peace is a necessity for the survival of the race. To put all the emphasis on the outpouring of the Spirit as man's hope may reduce our sense of responsibility to accept and obey the guidance of the Spirit. If as Smith says, "righteousness and peace are to come to earth by a distinct creative act of God," then some may conclude our part is simply to wait for God's action. The correction of that defective view of how peace is to be secured is suggested in this verse, **The**

[2] *Ibid.*, pp. 254-76.

19 When it shall hail, coming down on the forest; and the city shall be low in a low place.

20 Blessed *are* ye that sow beside all waters, that send forth *thither* the feet of the ox and the ass.

33 Woe to thee that spoilest, and thou *wast* not spoiled; and dealest treach-

---

19 And the forest will utterly go down,[w]
 and the city will be utterly laid low.
20 Happy are you who sow beside all waters,
 who let the feet of the ox and the ass range free.

33 Woe to you, destroyer,
 who yourself have not been destroyed;
you treacherous one,
 with whom none has dealt treacherously!

[w] Cn: Heb *And it will hail when the forest comes down*

"will sow beside all waters," i.e., without fear of their failing (cf. 35:7), and will be able to let his animals find their own pasture.

VIII. "The Recompense of God" (33:1–35:10)

These chapters are marked off from chs. 28–32 by both style and content. Instead of the relatively brief oracles of that section, the majority of which are Isaiah's, we have here three longer compositions which belong to the later strata of the book and which have no direct connection with the eighth-century prophet. Ch. 33 is a "prophetic

---

work of righteousness shall be peace; and the effect of righteousness, quietness and assurance for ever. But righteousness is not something imposed by God on life; rather is it the manifestation of his Spirit in human conduct and relationships. Righteousness is given; it is also achieved as men respond to the leading of God's Spirit.

We may leave aside for the moment consideration of the other possible danger in Isaiah's suggestion that righteousness produces material blessings. In a broad way that is true. A world truly at peace would know a prosperity such as has never been man's. In a particular and personal way, however, life denies that the good are invariably well off. Many a righteous man has suffered privation and gone hungry. It is difficult to understand how the psalmist could seriously claim that he had never seen a righteous man "forsaken, nor his seed begging bread" (Ps. 37:25). Nevertheless, there is a fundamental relationship between morality and welfare. It is the teaching of our Lord that when we seek first the kingdom, things will be added unto us (Matt. 6:33).

The main emphasis in Isaiah's teaching, however, lies on the spiritual fruit of faith. It is that peace of which material blessings are a by-product. The lesson for us is inescapable. If we are to know peace we have to show a new concern for righteousness, a new understanding of the spiritual conditions of peace. No one can claim that in all modern man's unavailing labors for peace there has been a first concern for righteousness. We have not aimed high enough;

we have set our sights on a balance of power, on compromise between competing ambitions, on mutual pacts, and on all the manipulations of human resources which might prevent war. Limiting our conceptions of peace to a state of armed preparedness, we have hoped that fear would restrain strife. In no sense is that truly a quest for peace, and until we make right relationships between nations, friendship, mutual trust, and brotherhood our aim, we shall never know a condition other than that of a precarious cease-fire. A true peace cannot be arranged at the council table. As Isaiah declares, it can never be "until the spirit be poured upon us from on high" (vs. 15). When shall that be? The answer in part at least lies with man. God is always ready to come to those who will receive him. "Therefore will the LORD wait, that he may be gracious unto you" (30:18). He must wait, for it is not love's way to invade our freedom. He

Has waited long, is waiting still:
You treat no other Friend so ill.[3]

When God sees that we in our misery and suffering are ready to receive him, to accept his will and go his way, then in all the plenitude of his mercy will the Spirit be poured out from on high. "And it shall be said in that day, Lo, this is our God. . . . We will be glad and rejoice in his salvation" (25:9). And in his peace!

33:1-24. *The Deliverance of Jerusalem.*—The Expos. of this chapter is made difficult by un-

[3] Joseph Grigg, "Behold! a Stranger's at the door!"

erously, and they dealt not treacherously with thee! when thou shalt cease to spoil, thou shalt be spoiled; *and* when thou shalt make an end to deal treacherously, they shall deal treacherously with thee.	When you have ceased to destroy, you will be destroyed; and when you have made an end of dealing treacherously, you will be dealt with treacherously.

liturgy" (see below); chs. 34–35 are part of (or closely dependent upon) the work of the nameless poet-prophet(s) whose distinctive characteristic messages of hope and promise are found in chs. 40–66. Between ch. 35 and ch. 40 now stands the narrative section concerning Isaiah and Hezekiah, marking off the first half of the book, which had grown up around collections of genuine Isaian oracles and memoirs, from the second half, which is entirely exilic or postexilic in date.

A. A Prophetic Liturgy of Entreaty (33:1-24)

The sudden breaks in sequence which characterize this chapter (cf. vss. 2, 3, 7, 10, 14, 17) are quite different from those which mark the transition from one oracle to the next in the previous chapters. Here a series of prophetic oracles related to the same situation is interspersed with prayers of entreaty (vs. 2) and lamentation (vss. 7-9), and (in vss. 14-16) with a liturgical dialogue which recalls Pss. 15; 24:3-5. Evidently we have here an example of the alternating prayers and prophetic oracles which were uttered at such a service of entreaty in the temple as is referred to in Jer. 14:12; 36:6; Joel 2:15-17; II Chr. 20:3-19. Similar liturgies of entreaty linked with prophetic oracles are to be found in Mic. 7:7-20; Pss. 12; 20; 60; 85; and elsewhere.

The enemy against whom the complaint is made is unnamed and this, together with the obscurity of some of the figures and the seeming dependence upon various prophetic books, points to a period considerably later than Isaiah's. The desolation of the land described in vss. 8-9 might be the result of any of the numerous invasions from that of Sennacherib in 701 to that of Bacchides in 160. But the more specific references in vss. 7-8 to **the envoys of peace** and to one who **hath broken the covenant** seem particularly suitable to either of two episodes of the Maccabean struggle: (*a*) the destruction of the temple fortress in 162 by Lysias, the Syrian commander, in violation of the terms of capitulation which Judas Maccabaeus had accepted (cf. I Macc. 6:51-62; so Duhm, *op. cit.*, p. 242; Marti, *Das Buch Jesaja*, p. 238); or (*b*) the slaughter of the Hasidim in 160 by Alkimus and Bacchides in violation of their oath, and the subsequent struggle ending in the disastrous battle at Elasa (cf. I Macc. 7:5-20; 9:1-18). The reference in I Macc. 7:17 to the words of Ps. 79:2-3, and the further quotation in 7:36-38 of a prayer of entreaty on an occasion such as that suggested for Isa. 33, should be noted.

1. First Movement (33:1-6)

This section might be complete in itself, as it includes a statement of the theme in the form of a prophetic reproach (vs. 1), followed by the congregation's prayer of

certainty both as to authorship and to the historical situation to which it refers. Since there is no agreement among critics upon these points, it is at least legitimate to accept the conjecture that Isaiah wrote this poem to celebrate the miraculous deliverance of Jerusalem from Assyrian attack. Against such a background, or a similar one, the chapter is luminous with meaning.

It begins with a woe pronounced against the enemy (vs. 1). After a moment's pause, in which the prophet breathes a prayer both with and for his people (vs. 2), he passes to declare his confidence in the God who had acted to save the nation and make Jerusalem a city of righteousness and peace (vss. 3-6). In vss. 7-9 he recalls that dark day on which the envoys returned with the news that an emissary of Assyria had contemptuously repudiated his treaty, torn up the covenant, and demanded surrender. Nature herself, Isaiah adds, shuddered at this treachery. But God took up the challenge, and in vss. 10-13 he speaks and acts for the deliverance of Israel; the fire flames, blasting and de-

2 O Lord, be gracious unto us; we have waited for thee: be thou their arm every morning, our salvation also in the time of trouble.

3 At the noise of the tumult the people fled; at the lifting up of thyself the nations were scattered.

4 And your spoil shall be gathered *like* the gathering of the caterpillar: as the running to and fro of locusts shall he run upon them.

5 The Lord is exalted; for he dwelleth on high: he hath filled Zion with judgment and righteousness.

6 And wisdom and knowledge shall be the stability of thy times, *and* strength of salvation: the fear of the Lord *is* his treasure.

---

2 O Lord, be gracious to us; we wait for thee.
Be our^x arm every morning,
our salvation in the time of trouble.

3 At the thunderous noise peoples flee,
at the lifting up of thyself nations are scattered;

4 and spoil is gathered as the caterpillar gathers;
as locusts leap, men leap upon it.

5 The Lord is exalted, for he dwells on high;
he will fill Zion with justice and righteousness;

6 and he will be the stability of your times,
abundance of salvation, wisdom, and knowledge;
the fear of the Lord is his treasure.

^x Heb *their*

---

entreaty (vs. 2), and a prophetic oracle of promise responding to the latter (vss. 3-6). It is quite possible that the prayer—as well as the oracles—was uttered by the prophet as spokesman for the congregation, for we know that this was on occasion a part of the prophet's responsibility (cf. 37:4; Amos 7:2, 5; Jer. 18:20; 27:18).

33:1. The same terms **destroyer,** "betrayer" are used of Babylon in 21:2. The anomalous form כנלתך in the M.T. represents ככלתך, **when you have made an end,** as assumed by the translators and now confirmed by the Dead Sea Scroll.

2. The people's cry for help (cf. Pss. 44:3 [Hebrew 44:4]; 79:9). **Be our arm every morning:** Lit., "be thou their arm in the morning," a curious expression. Reference to Ps. 4:1 (Hebrew 4:2) suggests that for בקרים, "the mornings," we should perhaps read בקראם, "when they call," and translate the line, "Be thou the arm of thy people when they call [upon thee]."

3-6. The prophetic voice declares the impending doom of the enemy, because **the Lord is exalted.** This is the supreme fact which his people must never forget, for its ultimate consequences are certain—the overthrow of his enemies and the establishment in Zion of those things she is called to treasure most. The renderings of the KJV and the RSV in vs. 6 are both doubtful; **thy times** and **your times,** עתיך, seem to represent a word corresponding to חסן, **strength, abundance,** and אוצר, **treasure,** viz., עתיד, "stores," "possessions" (cf. 10:13). The verse may then be translated: "And that which is cherished shall be made sure, there shall be abundant deliverance; wisdom and knowledge (and) the fear of the Lord shall be (her) treasure."

---

vouring. In vss. 14-16 the effect of the judgment, not on the Assyrian, but on Israel itself, is described. The sinners are appalled at the manifestation of God's power; they see not only the holocaust of divine judgment on the enemy, but they see themselves as they are, in the light of God's flaming anger, and they break out in the cry, "Who can live with him who is a consuming fire?" Isaiah answers: "When God's fire is abroad, nothing can escape save the believing soul, the life unstained by cruelty and greed. For all such there is a security which the anger of man cannot, and the judgment of God will not, invade." From that thought of the safety with which goodness is invested, the prophet passes to a glowing vision of the golden age. The Messiah, the King in his beauty, is on the throne, ruling a spacious and extending kingdom. In violent contrast were the days of Israel's humiliation, when the people were under the heel of the conqueror. In the glorious freedom of God's reign there will be no foreign officials exacting tribute, no brutal officers out to detect the weakness of the defense, no con-

7 Behold, their valiant ones shall cry without: the ambassadors of peace shall weep bitterly.

8 The highways lie waste, the wayfaring man ceaseth: he hath broken the covenant, he hath despised the cities, he regardeth no man.

9 The earth mourneth *and* languisheth: Lebanon is ashamed *and* hewn down: Sharon is like a wilderness; and Bashan and Carmel shake off *their fruits.*

10 Now will I rise, saith the LORD; now will I be exalted; now will I lift up myself.

11 Ye shall conceive chaff, ye shall bring forth stubble: your breath, *as* fire, shall devour you.

---

7 Behold the valiant ones[y] cry without;
   the envoys of peace weep bitterly.
8 The highways lie waste,
   the wayfaring man ceases.
Covenants are broken,
   witnesses[z] are despised,
   there is no regard for man.
9 The land mourns and languishes;
   Lebanon is confounded and withers
      away;
   Sharon is like a desert;
   and Bashan and Carmel shake off their
      leaves.

10 "Now I will arise," says the LORD,
   "now I will lift myself up;
   now I will be exalted.
11 You conceive chaff, you bring forth stub-
      ble;
   your breath is a fire that will consume
      you.

[y] The meaning of the Hebrew word is uncertain
[z] One ancient Ms: Heb *cities*

---

2. SECOND MOVEMENT (33:7-16)

In vss. 7-9 the congregation pathetically bewails its situation; in vss. 10-13 the very words of Yahweh, announcing his purpose to intervene, are declared in a prophetic oracle; in vss. 14-17 the promise of salvation is made to the faithful.

7. Their valiant ones, אראלם, an obscure word, best connected with אריאל and translated "the priests of the altar" (see Exeg. on 29:1). On **the envoys of peace** see Exeg. on 33:1-24. The **cry** is for help, as in 5:7; entreaty accompanies the ceremonial wailing of the priests between the altar and the porch, **without** the shrine itself.

8. Highways were deserted as too dangerous, as they had been long before in the time of the judges (cf. Judg. 5:6); the reopening of communications was a sign that peace had come (cf. 62:10). **Covenants are broken** transforms the more literal rendering of the KJV, **he hath broken the covenant,** into a general statement of the collapse of society (cf. Hos. 4:1-2). But it is more likely that some definite betrayal by the enemy lies behind these words (see Exeg. on vss. 1-24). **Witnesses** עדים, has been proposed as an emendation of the meaningless **cities,** ערים, and is strikingly confirmed by the Dead Sea Scroll.

10-11. As in Ps. 12:5 (Hebrew 12:6) the response to a passionate cry for help is **"Now will I arise,"** says the LORD, i.e., to intervene (cf. Ps. 3:7 [Hebrew 3:8], etc.). Vs. 11 shows a curious mixture of metaphors.

---

querors with guttural speech (vss. 17-19). Instead of these memories of the dark days, there will be the sight of the beloved city made safe and glorious, not as other capitals, by defending rivers and armed ships, but by the presence of the Lord himself, the Judge, the King and Savior. In his patriot's love and pride Isaiah invests Jerusalem, the little provincial town set on its barren rock, with the majesty of a world capital, because his faith sees it glorified by God's presence (vss. 20-22). Then suddenly

there is another of those abrupt transitions which continually mark Isaiah's prophecies. It all depends on where his eyes are fixed: if on God, the vision may be of judgment or mercy; if on man, almost invariably the words are dark and accusing. So here, continuing the metaphor of the armed ships, he turns to compare the nation to an unseaworthy galley, with cordage slack, guy ropes so rotten that the mast is apt to fall, and tackle so weak they could not hoist the sails. Such, says the prophet, were you

12 And the people shall be *as* the burn-ings of lime: *as* thorns cut up shall they be burned in the fire.

13 ¶ Hear, ye *that are* far off, what I have done; and, ye *that are* near, acknowledge my might.

14 The sinners in Zion are afraid; fear-fulness hath surprised the hypocrites. Who among us shall dwell with the devouring fire? who among us shall dwell with ever-lasting burnings?

15 He that walketh righteously, and speaketh uprightly; he that despiseth the gain of oppressions, that shaketh his hands from holding of bribes, that stoppeth his ears from hearing of blood, and shutteth his eyes from seeing evil;

12 And the peoples will be as if burned to lime,
    like thorns cut down, that are burned in the fire."

13 Hear, you who are far off, what I have done;
    and you who are near, acknowledge my might.

14 The sinners in Zion are afraid;
    trembling has seized the godless:
"Who among us can dwell with the de-vouring fire?
    Who among us can dwell with everlast-ing burnings?"

15 He who walks righteously and speaks uprightly;
    he who despises the gain of oppres-sions,
    who shakes his hands, lest they hold a bribe,
    who stops his ears from hearing of bloodshed,
    and shuts his eyes from looking upon evil.

---

12. **The peoples** (not singular as in KJV) are those of the pagan world, to be overthrown by Yahweh in the last days, as in late eschatological prophecy (cf. 24:1; 34:2; Zech. 14:2-3). Here the immediate enemy is thought of as included.

13. The whole world is called on to acknowledge the might which Yahweh has displayed on behalf of his people (cf. 34:1). This assurance is given in the oracle as a fact—something which has already been done in the counsels of God, although to his people it lay still in the future.

14-16. The terror of the Lord will consume not only the external enemy but also the faithless and disloyal among his own people. Duhm (*op. cit.*, p. 244) is probably

---

or are you, a people absolutely unfit. But as quickly as he takes up the figure he drops it, and closes the chapter with one word of the final glory of the Messiah's reign, viz., the forgiveness of sin.

14. *The Fires of God.*—As in other of his prophecies, Isaiah in this chapter is dealing with a concrete historical situation, and we can-not expect to find in all its references truth to match our need or our condition. Nevertheless, because the prophet always deals with the hu-man situation in terms of the divine purpose, there is in all his oracles some element of the timeless and the universal. In this chapter one living truth is given in the concept of God as a consuming fire. This figure of speech has in the past been lavishly used to depict the horrors of hell. However effective it may have been then to confront sinners with the awful prospect of eternal flame, that is not an emphasis which

will prevail with men today. But what shall we employ instead? Far too lightly we have dropped from modern thought the concept of hell as a place of torment. If we have any moral convic-tions at all, there must be room in our thinking for the inevitable judgment of sin, the retribu-tion which justice will exact from the guilty. We may need neither the vision of unappeasable flame nor Dante's horrific picture of the damned, frozen in eternal ice; but we have stopped short of the full moral truth if we do not declare that sin shall be judged. It may well be that the discovery of guilt, the realization of what we have done to God's love, and have become in ourselves, is hell enough. A literal hell of fire is a horrible concept which fits ill with Christ's revelation of the nature of God. Nevertheless, the metaphor of the fire has un-escapable force. Moreover, the fire of God need not involve any crude insistence on literal flames

16 He shall dwell on high; his place of defense *shall be* the munitions of rocks: bread shall be given him; his waters *shall be* sure.

17 Thine eyes shall see the King in his beauty: they shall behold the land that is very far off.

18 Thine heart shall meditate terror. Where *is* the scribe? where *is* the receiver? where *is* he that counted the towers?

19 Thou shalt not see a fierce people, a people of a deeper speech than thou canst

16 He will dwell on the heights;
   his place of defense will be the fortresses of rocks;
   his bread will be given him, his water will be sure.

17 Your eyes will see the king in his beauty;
   they will behold a land that stretches afar.

18 Your mind will muse on the terror:
   "Where is he who counted, where is he who weighed the tribute?
   Where is he who counted the towers?"

19 You will see no more the insolent people,
   the people of an obscure speech which you cannot comprehend,

---

right in finding here a reference to the "ungodly Israelites" (I Macc. 6:21) who made common cause with the Syrians against Judas Maccabaeus. They are pictured as asking, **Who among us can dwell with the devouring fire** of Yahweh's presence? The question is a variant of "Who shall ascend into the hill of the Lord?" (Ps. 24:3), and the answer given is in the form of the threshold liturgies, Pss. 15; 24:3-5; he who would be Yahweh's guest and enjoy the security of his house must accept the ways of his household.

3. CONCLUSION: A WORD OF PROMISE (33:17-24)

This concluding section falls into two parts, vss. 17-20 and vss. 21-24. The first is a prophetic promise of the coming time when a messianic king shall reign and the beloved Zion shall be at peace, while the present terror has become but a painful memory. In the second part, as the text now stands, a strange figure of rivers and ships is introduced, having no evident connection with the foregoing; in the middle of it is inserted a congregational shout of acclamation (vs. 22), and to it is appended a prosaic conclusion (vss. 23c-24), which seems not to have been part of the original composition.

17. A (not the) king in his beauty: Once more in the new age a king would reign as anointed vicegerent of the divine King (cf. Ps. 2:1-8), over "a land of far horizons," and **your eyes** will see it.

18. Your mind will muse on the vanished taxgatherers of a foreign power. For **the towers,** המגדלים, Gunkel (*Zeitschrift für die alttestamentliche Wissenschaft*, XLII [1924], 177) reads המגדים, "precious things."

---

of judgment; for fire has other uses than that of destruction, and judgment is only one aspect of the work of love. Let a man review the function of fire, and he will find that there is comfort and hope, as well as dread, in the thought of the fire of God. Fire purges: that is true, and it can be made both personal and social in its application. Fire refines: and we have seen men and women emerge from trial, discipline, suffering, as pure gold; for a man shall be saved, "yet so as by fire" (I Cor. 3:15). Fire warms and comforts: untold multitudes of cold and lonely spirits have known John Wesley's experience of the heart "strangely warmed" by the fire of God's love. Fire illumines: sometimes in lurid light, as a great conflagration reveals the dis-

integrating structure of a building; sometimes in softer beauty, as when the flaming glory of a sunset sky lights the earth with its radiance. In the modern world the fire of war has thrown into stark relief the sin of man and the brutality and stupidity of strife, even as it has lighted with unearthly light the valor and unselfishness of the human spirit.

So manifold are the applications of the metaphor of fire that a man might well work out a series of expositions on "The Fires of God," to bring home the wonder, the awfulness, and the glory of divine love.

Isaiah's vision of fire, says George Adam Smith, suggests two thoughts. First, he raises the question, Are we right in confining "our hor-

perceive; of a stammering tongue, *that thou canst* not understand.

20 Look upon Zion, the city of our solemnities: thine eyes shall see Jerusalem a quiet habitation, a tabernacle *that* shall not be taken down; not one of the stakes thereof shall ever be removed, neither shall any of the cords thereof be broken.

21 But there the glorious LORD *will be* unto us a place of broad rivers *and* streams; wherein shall go no galley with oars, neither shall gallant ship pass thereby.

22 For the LORD *is* our judge, the LORD *is* our lawgiver, the LORD *is* our King; he will save us.

stammering in a tongue which you cannot understand.

20 Look upon Zion, the city of our appointed feasts!
Your eyes will see Jerusalem,
a quiet habitation, an immovable tent,
whose stakes will never be plucked up,
nor will any of its cords be broken.

21 But there the LORD in majesty will be for us
a place of broad rivers and streams,
where no galley with oars can go,
nor stately ship can pass.

22 For the LORD is our judge, the LORD is our ruler,
the LORD is our king; he will save us.

---

20. The sense requires an imperfect in place of the imperative, "You shall look on Zion, our festival city." The figure of the **tent** or **tabernacle** recalls the fact that the temple was only a more permanent substitute for the original tent-shrine (cf. II Sam. 6:17; 7:2).

21-24. Kissane (*Isaiah,* I, 371-72) has the best solution of the difficulties of the opening line of vs. 21, reading כי מושב אדיר יהיה לנו, "For a glorious abode shall be ours"; the KJV and the RSV are meaningless. The **rivers and streams** are to refresh the land (cf. Ps. 1:3; 46:4 [Hebrew 46:5]), not to serve as a highway for hostile fleets. Vs. 22

---

ror of the consuming fires of righteousness to the next life?"[4] There are here fires as fierce, as pitiless as ever gleamed across the grave to the eyes of a conscience-stricken sinner.

It was not hell that created conscience; it was conscience that created hell, and conscience was fired by the vision which fired Isaiah—of all life aglow with the righteousness of God—*God with us,* as He was with Jerusalem, *a spirit of burning and a spirit of justice.* . . . Isaiah has nothing to tell us about hell-fire, but a great deal about the pitiless justice of God in this life. . . . Our God *is* a consuming fire.[5]

Second, he points out that the metaphor of life as a battle does not take into account all the facts which contribute to defeat or victory. He does not deny the reality of the struggle for existence or that its results are enormous, but he urges us to consider that while we strive with each other and affect each other for good and for evil we do not fight in a vacuum.

We fight in an atmosphere that affects every one of us far more powerfully than the opposing wits or wills of our fellow-men. Around us and through us, within and without as we fight, is the all-pervading righteousness of God; and it is far oftener the effects of this which we see in the falls and the changes of life than the effects of our struggle with each other.[6]

It is his contention that in our conception of life as a battle we analyze the world situation in terms of economic, military, political strength, and by these we account for victory or defeat. In the matter of our personal struggle we find in such factors as our education, or lack of it, our heredity and environment, our privileges or handicaps, reasons for all that happens, and in particular the excuse for our own defeats. In both cases we leave out of account the invisible and immutable moral law, the righteousness of God active in life.

Righteousness is not an occasional spark; righteousness is the atmosphere. Though our dull eyes see it only now and then strike into flame in the battle of life, and take for granted that it is but the flash of meeting wits or of steel on steel, God's justice is everywhere, pervasive and pitiless, affecting the combatants far more than they have power to affect one another.[7]

Life, whether good or bad, cannot be explained by what we see of it. It is the invisible that contains the secret of what is seen.

When we behold fortune and character go down in the warfare of this world, we ought to remember that it is not always the things we see which are to blame for the fall, but that awful flame which, unseen by common man, has been revealed to the prophets of God.[8]

[4] *Op. cit.,* p. 351.
[5] *Ibid.,* pp. 352-53.
[6] *Ibid.,* p. 354.

[7] *Ibid.,* p. 355.
[8] *Ibid.,* p. 356.

23 Thy tacklings are loosed; they could not well strengthen their mast; they could not spread the sail: then is the prey of a great spoil divided; the lame take the prey.

24 And the inhabitant shall not say, I am sick: the people that dwell therein *shall be* forgiven *their* iniquity.

34 Come near, ye nations, to hear; and hearken, ye people: let the earth hear, and all that is therein; the world, and all things that come forth of it.

---

23 Your tackle hangs loose;
     it cannot hold the mast firm in its place,
   or keep the sail spread out.

Then prey and spoil in abundance will be divided;
   even the lame will take the prey.
24 And no inhabitant will say, "I am sick";
   the people who dwell there will be forgiven their iniquity.

34 Draw near, O nations, to hear,
   and hearken, O peoples!
Let the earth listen, and all that fills it;
   the world, and all that comes from it.

---

gives the words of the "shout" (תרועה) with which the congregation responded at an appropriate point in the liturgy (cf. Pss. 46:7, 11 [Hebrew 46:8, 12]; 24:8, 10; Ezra 3:11; the word "Selah" in the psalms marks the points where this shout of acclamation or entreaty is called for). Vs. 23 seems to continue the figure of the ship, but the words translated **mast** and **sail** appear in 30:17 as a "staff" and a "flag" on a hilltop, so the meaning here is ambiguous, and the connection with the context obscure.

B. The Fearful End of the Enemies of God (34:1-17)

This powerful eschatological poem may be too easily passed over by the reader who finds it printed as prose, as in the KJV, and who is repelled by its picture of Yahweh, sword in hand, wreaking vengeance on Edom. In Hebrew it is a striking literary composition, carefully worked out in arrangement and in details; something of its effectiveness can be felt in the verse translation of the RSV. If the picture it paints is terrible to contemplate, this is because the subject itself is awe-inspiring. Here, as in such other passages as chs. 13; 24; 63:1-6; Zech. 1, are seen the terrible consequences of the final intervention of God to deal with the implacable opponents of his righteous purpose. The language is passionate and the figures vigorous and vivid, for these are the qualities of Hebrew poetry seeking to convey the conviction that the righteous will of Yahweh must ultimately prevail on the earth. The clash between good and evil, between the Creator, the Lord of history, and the forces which defy him, must be resolved in the end. Such an issue can be nothing less than awful. The poet inevitably draws on mythological imagery as he portrays the Last Judgment on a cosmic scale.

It is true that the land of Edom is specified in vss. 5-6 as the immediate object of Yahweh's wrath, and that this suggests that the writer is only expressing once more the long-standing antipathy between Israel and Edom. This goes back to the story of Jacob and Esau, and reaches great intensity after the Edomites had sought to profit through Judah's destruction by the Babylonians (cf. Obad. 10-12). But in Obad. 15-16 the

---

Righteousness and retribution are an atmosphere: not lines or laws that we may happen to stumble upon, not explosives that, being touched, burst out on us; but the atmosphere always about us and always at work, invisible and yet more mighty than anything we can see. God in whom we live and move and have our being is a consuming fire.

34:1–35:10. Judgment and Salvation.—These two chapters belong to each other; the one is an oracle of judgment, the other a prophecy of salvation. According to the critics, they come from the postexilic period and therefore cannot be ascribed to Isaiah. In spirit and in beauty, however, the exquisite poem in ch. 35 might indeed be his, and one feels that he would have rejoiced in it.

Ch. 34 is entirely given over to a description of God's judgment on the nations, especially the kingdom of Edom, which had through its his-

2 For the indignation of the LORD *is* upon all nations, and *his* fury upon all their armies: he hath utterly destroyed them, he hath delivered them to the slaughter.

3 Their slain also shall be cast out, and their stink shall come up out of their carcasses, and the mountains shall be melted with their blood.

4 And all the host of heaven shall be dissolved, and the heavens shall be rolled together as a scroll: and all their host shall fall down, as the leaf falleth off from the vine, and as a falling *fig* from the fig tree.

2 For the LORD is enraged against all the nations,
  and furious against all their host,
  he has doomed them, has given them over for slaughter.
3 Their slain shall be cast out,
  and the stench of their corpses shall rise;
  the mountains shall flow with their blood.
4 All the host of heaven shall rot away,
  and the skies roll up like a scroll.
All their host shall fall,
  as leaves fall from the vine,
  like leaves falling from the fig tree.

judgment on Edom is again only a particular manifestation of "the day of Yahweh [which] is near upon all the nations," and Edom is thus a representative of the enmity to Judah and to her religion which to the Jews was the same thing as enmity against God.

The broad conception and careful literary artistry of the poem are most effective (on the latter cf. James Muilenburg, "The Literary Character of Isaiah 34," *Journal of Biblical Literature,* LIX [1940], 339-65). After the exordium addressed to the whole world (vs. 1), the composition is in two movements in striking contrast: vss. 2-8, the violent outpouring of the wrath of God, and vss. 9-17, the aftermath of ruin in the wake of the storm. In the first the fury of Yahweh rages through earth and heaven (vss. 2-4); then his reeking sword is turned on "Edom" to exterminate man and beast in a frightful sacrifice of appeasement (vss. 5-7); this is "the day" when accounts are settled (vs. 8). In the second movement a dreadful hush has fallen on a scene of desolation; the smoke rolls upward from the whole land as from an unquenchable fire (vss. 9-10), and amid the overgrown ruins of the city there is no sound or movement but that of the wild creatures who dwell where no man is found (vss. 11-17). The feeling of perpetual desolation is forcibly conveyed by the long-drawn-out description in the last named verses (on the relationship of this chapter to ch. 35, and to the other materials in the book, see Intro., p. 160).

34:1. The **nations** are summoned, not as witnesses as in Amos 3:9, but to hear their sentence pronounced, as in Mic. 1:2.

2-4. Yahweh's fury is the fury of battle. **He has doomed them:** I.e., to extermination, as a sacrifice (cf. Josh. 6:17, 21). The "prophetic perfect" tenses express a future which is certain. The earthly scene of carnage (vs. 3) is not all; the familiar heavens also, with the stars which men worshiped as gods, will be shattered by Yahweh in the unearthly combat (cf. 24:21; II Kings 17:16). The sky, thought of as a mysteriously inscribed scroll, will **roll up like a scroll** when its two ends are released. In the second figure it is

tory shown an implacable hatred of Israel. There is nothing to expound in this oracle. There it stands, unrelieved in its horror and desolation. The author exhausts his imagination to picture the stricken earth, shrouded in smoke from its smoldering ruins, haunted by wild beasts, empty of all human life, the stench of the slain clinging to the very soil "dunged with rotten death." One passes from it with a sense of thanksgiving to the beauty and the joy of ch. 35, the oracle of divine redemption, the homecoming.

The contrast to the scenes of horror we have just left is breath-taking; gone now the stench of death, gone the skulking beasts of night, gone the fearsome landscape of desolation. The air is crystal-clear, sweet with the scent of flowers; the heavy silence and torpor of death have given place to the music of a re-created world, the fields bright with blossom and "every common bush afire with God." [9] This garden land is the home which the Lord has prepared for his

[9] Elizabeth Barrett Browning, *Aurora Leigh,* Bk. VII, l. 821.

5 For my word shall be bathed in heaven: behold, it shall come down upon Idumea, and upon the people of my curse, to judgment.

6 The sword of the LORD is filled with blood, it is made fat with fatness, *and* with the blood of lambs and goats, with the fat of the kidneys of rams: for the LORD hath a sacrifice in Bozrah, and a great slaughter in the land of Idumea.

7 And the unicorns shall come down with them, and the bullocks with the bulls; and their land shall be soaked with blood, and their dust made fat with fatness.

8 For *it is* the day of the LORD's vengeance, *and* the year of recompenses for the controversy of Zion.

9 And the streams thereof shall be turned into pitch, and the dust thereof into brim-

5 For my sword has drunk its fill in the heavens;
behold, it descends for judgment upon Edom,
upon the people I have doomed.
6 The LORD has a sword; it is sated with blood,
it is gorged with fat,
with the blood of lambs and goats,
with the fat of the kidneys of rams.
For the LORD has a sacrifice in Bozrah,
a great slaughter in the land of Edom.
7 Wild oxen shall fall with them,
and young steers with the mighty bulls.
Their land shall be soaked with blood,
and their soil made rich with fat.

8 For the LORD has a day of vengeance,
a year of recompense for the cause of Zion.
9 And the streams of Edom*a* shall be turned into pitch,

a Heb *her streams*

said that the **host shall fall**: one mythological conception was that the stars were fruit on a heavenly tree. Instead of the first line of vs. 4, the Dead Sea Scroll reads "and the valleys shall be split open" (cf. Zech. 14:4).

5. For: Better, as introducing a new strophe, "Yea" or "When." Read חרב י' "the sword of Y." for חרבי, **my sword**, in keeping with the third person in vss. 6, 8. **Bathed** is unsuitable, unless this is interpreted as "anointed," i.e., for battle use (with C. C. Torrey, *The Second Isaiah* [New York: Charles Scribner's Sons, 1928], p. 283). **Has drunk its fill** is a second possible meaning. **The people of my curse** (**I have doomed,** RSV) again introduces the improbable first person singular in a forced translation of חרמי; if this is read as a Hophal participle, "the doomed people," the sentence is bettered with only a slight change in the text.

6. The sword of the LORD appears in 27:1, where it is used in conflict with his supreme enemy in a myth of origins which has become a myth of the end. **Sacrifice . . . slaughter** are correlative and almost synonymous terms; the animals named are those which usually were slain for sacrifice. **Bozrah:** A principal city, at that time perhaps the capital of Edom.

8. "Yea, it will be Yahweh's day of vengeance." For **the cause of** [**the controversy of,** KJV] **Zion,** it is better with Torrey (*ibid.*, p. 284) to take ריב as a verbal adjective, and to translate, "for the champion of Zion."

9-10. In the second movement of the poem, beginning here, not only has the storm passed but the mood has changed from violent activity to the relative stillness of prolonged

returning people. No wonder the poet cries hope to the fearful heart: "Lift up your eyes; look, behold your God; he comes to save you." Then follows the vision of what redemption means. Healed bodies, eyes to see the beauty God has fashioned, ears to hear the music of nature and the praise of man, feet swift to do God's bidding. A healed earth! The barren and arid land is bright with the sheen of many

waters, and loud with the singing of the streams. Best of all, there is an open way to home and the heart of God. It is an exquisite picture, this of the exiles' return, singing their hearts out, the tears forgotten, the joy of the Lord their strength.

There are many ways in which men have envisaged life: as a battle, a sea voyage, a quest, a race. The choice of the metaphor depends

stone, and the land thereof shall become burning pitch.

10 It shall not be quenched night nor day; the smoke thereof shall go up for ever: from generation to generation it shall lie waste; none shall pass through it for ever and ever.

11 ¶ But the cormorant and the bittern shall possess it; the owl also and the raven shall dwell in it: and he shall stretch out upon it the line of confusion, and the stones of emptiness.

12 They shall call the nobles thereof to the kingdom, but none *shall be* there, and all her princes shall be nothing.

13 And thorns shall come up in her palaces, nettles and brambles in the fortresses thereof: and it shall be a habitation of dragons, *and* a court for owls.

14 The wild beasts of the desert shall also meet with the wild beasts of the island, and the satyr shall cry to his fellow; the screech owl also shall rest there, and find for herself a place of rest.

15 There shall the great owl make her nest, and lay, and hatch, and gather under her shadow: there shall the vultures also be gathered, every one with her mate.

and her soil into brimstone;
her land shall become burning pitch.

10 Night and day it shall not be quenched;
its smoke shall go up for ever.
From generation to generation it shall lie waste;
none shall pass through it for ever and ever.

11 But the hawk and the porcupine shall possess it,
the owl and the raven shall dwell in it.
He shall stretch the line of confusion over it,
and the plummet of chaos over[b] its nobles.

12 They shall name it No Kingdom There,
and all its princes shall be nothing.

13 Thorns shall grow over its strongholds,
nettles and thistles in its fortresses.
It shall be the haunt of jackals,
an abode for ostriches.

14 And wild beasts shall meet with hyenas,
the satyr shall cry to his fellow;
yea, there shall the night hag alight,
and find for herself a resting place.

15 There shall the owl nest and lay
and hatch and gather her young in her shadow;
yea, there shall the kites be gathered,
each one with her mate.

[b] Heb lacks *over*

---

desolation. The picture is that of a ruined city surrounded by a land on fire, whose **smoke shall go up forever,** like that of Sodom. The city is not named (see KJV and RSV mg.) and the literary effect is increased by the repeated indefinite references to **her streams, her soil, her land.** It is not a particular city but the city of this world; it has no name except the mocking **No Kingdom There** (vs. 12).

11. The line of confusion . . . the plummet of chaos: The words are those used in Gen. 1:2 to describe the chaos of matter into which God introduced order by his creative word. "Her nobles," חריה, is incongruous here; probably חמתה, "[upon] her wall," is intended.

14. The demons of popular superstition, including Lilith, the storm demon or **night hag,** which haunt ruins and waste places, have taken possession of the former homes of men.

---

largely on our circumstances. There is, however, one figure of speech which has in all ages caught the imagination—that of the journey and the road. From the distant day when humanity followed its dim rough trails through a dangerous world down to the present age of four-lane highways and no speed limit, the road has been of increasing importance to mankind. History indeed might be written as the epic of the road.

As the highways were pushed on, man extended his domain. Over them flowed his traffic, by them his armies moved; they have been his lines of communication and the very arteries of his civilization. It is significant that he should have found in the road the symbol of his life, for to say that life is a journey is itself a confession of faith. We are not here to settle down; stagnation means death. We are so made that we must

16 ¶ Seek ye out of the book of the Lord, and read: no one of these shall fail, none shall want her mate: for my mouth it hath commanded, and his spirit it hath gathered them.

17 And he hath cast the lot for them, and his hand hath divided it unto them by line: they shall possess it for ever, from generation to generation shall they dwell therein.

16 Seek and read from the book of the Lord:
    Not one of these shall be missing;
    none shall be without her mate.
  For the mouth of the Lord has commanded,
    and his Spirit has gathered them.
17 He has cast the lot for them,
    his hand has portioned it out to them with the line;
  they shall possess it for ever,
    from generation to generation they shall dwell in it.

35 The wilderness and the solitary place shall be glad for them; and the desert shall rejoice, and blossom as the rose.

35 The wilderness and the dry land shall be glad,
  the desert shall rejoice and blossom;

16-17. This is Yahweh's decree; it is written in **the book of the Lord,** in which are the names and numbers of the stars (40:26) and of all his creatures (Mal. 3:16; Ps. 130:16). The word **seek** (vs. 16) belongs in the previous verse, i.e., "each one shall seek out her mates." **And read,** וקראו, is not to be taken as a present imperative but, as Torrey suggests (*ibid.*, p. 294), is the predicate belonging with the preceding words: "From the book of Yahweh their names shall be read" (נקראו).

C. A Transformed World and the Return to Zion (35:1-10)

"Upon the inferno [of ch. 34] follows the Paradiso" (Procksch, *Jesaia I,* p. 434). While it is doubtful if these two chapters are the work of the same hand, they probably appeared together at the opening of the great postexilic composite prophecy, chs. 40–66, which has become attached to the volume of Isaiah. It is certain that they have been associated deliberately, whatever their ultimate source. This exultant lyric of confidence and joy exhibits the other face of the same coin, the final intervention of God in judgment and deliverance.

Like ch. 34, this one falls into two parts: vss. 1-6a, the manifestation of God in his power and glory as the deliverer of his helpless people; vss. 6b-10, the joyful return of his people to Zion over an open highway, prepared by God through what has been an arid and trackless desert. The melodious language of the KJV, especially in the opening and closing verses, is unusually appropriate in this poem, for its mood and structure are those of a choral symphony. It begins with a joyous burst of song in a major key, as all nature breaks out in new life and beauty in the presence of God's creative power (vss. 1-2). The second movement is more subdued as the prophetic messengers are bidden to encourage the feeble and fear-ridden people with the announcement that their deliverance is at hand; but it ends with a return upon the opening theme of joy (vss. 3-6a). In the third movement, comprising the whole of the second part of the poem (vss. 6b-10), a subordinate theme of the first movement—the fertility of the desert— introduces the climactic scene. Beside the newly rushing streams and through the fresh

---

forever be moving to new objectives of knowledge and faith. Always before us is some unexplored vista calling us on; and when we reach the margin of the world faith declares that there is still "the glory of going on." Deeply implanted in the human spirit is the instinct for immortality; and the instinct is itself an argument. From the dawn of time man has lived and died a pilgrim.

No people have had greater cause than the Jews to make their own that metaphor of the road. They have been wanderers through all the centuries, and have left their bones on every highway of the world. No wonder then that to this travel-weary race the thought of a safe abiding place, the rest of an eternal home, has been their dearest hope. At the heart of their dream of a Messiah and his kingdom has been

2 It shall blossom abundantly, and rejoice even with joy and singing: the glory
of Lebanon shall be given unto it, the excellency of Carmel and Sharon; they shall
see the glory of the LORD, *and* the excellency
of our God.

3 ¶ Strengthen ye the weak hands, and
confirm the feeble knees.

4 Say to them *that are* of a fearful heart,
Be strong, fear not: behold, your God will
come *with* vengeance, *even* God *with* a
recompense; he will come and save you.

5 Then the eyes of the blind shall be
opened, and the ears of the deaf shall be
unstopped.

like the crocus ² it shall blossom abun-
    dantly,
  and rejoice with joy and singing.
The glory of Lebanon shall be given to it,
  the majesty of Carmel and Sharon.
They shall see the glory of the LORD,
  the majesty of our God.

³ Strengthen the weak hands,
  and make firm the feeble knees.
⁴ Say to those who are of a fearful heart,
  "Be strong, fear not!
Behold, your God
  will come with vengeance,
with the recompense of God.
  He will come and save you."

⁵ Then the eyes of the blind shall be
  opened,
  and the ears of the deaf unstopped;

---

greenery can be seen a highroad, a pilgrims' way, where there is no common traffic and
no threat of death. Nay—and here the choral voices rise in crescendo to the finale—it is
the ransomed people of the Lord who crowd that highway, singing with almost incred-
ulous joy as they draw near to Zion. The sun has risen, and like the shadows, **sorrow and
sighing shall flee away.**

35:1-2. Dry land, not **solitary place,** is correct, but the emphasis is on the adjective;
others translate "the parched land" (Amer. Trans.), "the steppe" (Kissane, *op. cit.,* I,
384), "the barren" (Torrey, *op. cit.,* p. 224). The words suggest the trackless Syrian
desert, which lay between the exiles and their homeland. **The desert:** Here almost
synonymous with **wilderness,** but more often applied specifically to the vicinity of the
Dead Sea. **As the rose** should be read as the first words of the next line, as in the RSV;
a "flower of the field" like **the crocus** or asphodel is meant. "It shall blossom abundantly
with the crocus." **With joy and singing,** as if praising God in his temple (cf. Ps. 132:9).
The glory of Lebanon ["the splendor"] **of Carmel and Sharon:** The luxuriant vegetation
for which these districts were famous.

3. "The drooping hands" (*ibid.,* p. 225), the ["stumbling"] **knees,** as of exhausted
prisoners herded by an enemy.

4. **Behold, your God:** As in 40:9. "Vengeance is coming (upon your oppressors) and
God's compensation (to you)."

5. **The blind . . . the dumb,** the most helpless of the exiles, will have the greatest
cause to praise God (cf. 61:1; Matt. 11:5).

---

the vision of the homeland and the return of
the exile. Greater than the passion for vengeance on their foes, deeper than the exultation
of victory has been the comfort of God's promise
that for them there would come at last a glad
home, the great ingathering of the ransomed
and redeemed. Ch. 35 is the perfect expression
of this undying faith. As perhaps no other chapter of the great prophecy it is understood of all
men; for it pictures what we have dreamed but
could not utter, and "deep calleth unto deep."

The modern expositor, therefore, need not

hesitate to lift it from its ancient setting and
hold it out to men, for time has not dimmed
its radiant color, and life has not altered its appeal. This is what we dream of, out of this brutal, cruel world—the earth at peace, its defaced
beauty restored, its wounds all healed, its sorrows lifted, and on the open road to home and
to God, the children of men, one in joy and
in praise. Are not these the very blessings which
our Lord declares are the marks of the kingdom
(Matt. 11:5)? The danger of a dream is that
we so often dismiss it as unreal. "Only a dream!"

6 Then shall the lame *man* leap as a hart, and the tongue of the dumb sing: for in the wilderness shall waters break out, and streams in the desert.

7 And the parched ground shall become a pool, and the thirsty land springs of water: in the habitation of dragons, where each lay, *shall be* grass with reeds and rushes.

8 And a highway shall be there, and a way, and it shall be called The way of holiness; the unclean shall not pass over it; but it *shall be* for those: the wayfaring men, though fools, shall not err *therein*.

9 No lion shall be there, nor *any* ravenous beast shall go up thereon, it shall not be found there; but the redeemed shall walk *there*:

6 then shall the lame man leap like a hart,
and the tongue of the dumb sing for joy.
For waters shall break forth in the wilderness,
and streams in the desert;
7 the burning sand shall become a pool,
and the thirsty ground springs of water;
the haunt of jackals shall become a swamp,*c*
the grass shall become reeds and rushes.

8 And a highway shall be there,
and it shall be called the Holy Way;
the unclean shall not pass over it,*d*
and fools shall not err therein.
9 No lion shall be there,
nor shall any ravenous beast come up on it;
they shall not be found there,
but the redeemed shall walk there.

c Cn: Heb *in the haunt of jackals is her resting place*
d Heb *it and he is for them a wayfarer*

7. **The parched ground** or **the burning sand**, not "the mirage," as some commentators have suggested. **The haunt of jackals** is preferable to **the habitation of dragons**; wilderness creatures, not mythological ones, are referred to. The word translated in the KJV as **where each lay**, רבצה, lit., "her lair," is grammatically impossible; the RSV emends this to (shall become a) **swamp**, לבצה. Another possibility is to read here מרעה "a pasture"; then, **grass, with reeds and rushes**.

8. **The Holy Way** is so called because it leads to the holy place, to Zion. The second part of vs. 8 has been mutilated in transmission, as is obvious from the attempt of the KJV to translate it literally (cf. RSV mg.). Torrey's emendation is preferable to the total omission of four words by the RSV: **The unclean** ["and the perverse," ונואל] **shall not pass over it**, and "the depraved will not lead astray him who treads it" (*ibid.*, pp. 225, 300).

9. **They shall not be found there** is apparently an old textual variant of **nor . . . come up on it**. The last line of vs. 9 belongs to vs. 10. **The redeemed . . . the ransomed**, i.e., from captivity and exile. As Procksch points out (*op. cit.*, pp. 437-38), these terms are not quite synonymous; the first implies the act of one who has a responsibility (such as kinship) to redeem (cf. Ruth 4); the second implies an act of free choice. Thus

we say, and turn to face what we call reality. The Christian ought never to call this chapter a dream. Call it rather God's promise; say not that it will yet be true, but that it is true now. **A highway shall be there** (35:8). And a highway there is: God in Christ has opened unto us "a new and living way" (Heb. 10:20). For those who in faith commit themselves to that way the world is even now transformed and all things are new. "If any man be in Christ, he is a new creature" (II Cor. 5:17): the eyes of faith are open, the ears once deaf to the call of God are

now quick to hear, the hesitant feet are now swift and sure in their going. Life is still dangerous, but the pilgrim himself is safe in God's hands, and over all, as the very atmosphere of life, is the gladness of a living faith. The life, the love, the victory of Jesus Christ, have transformed the prophet's dream into the great fact. It is no longer a poem, but an experience; for ours is a world redeemed by the love of God in Christ our Lord. The way is open, the voice still calls, "This is the way, walk ye in it" (30:21). Those who by faith will go that way shall know

10 And the ransomed of the LORD shall return, and come to Zion with songs and everlasting joy upon their heads: they shall obtain joy and gladness, and sorrow and sighing shall flee away.

36 Now it came to pass in the fourteenth year of king Hezekiah, *that* Sennacherib king of Assyria came up against all the defensed cities of Judah, and took them.

10 And the ransomed of the LORD shall return,
and come to Zion with singing,
with everlasting joy upon their heads;
they shall obtain joy and gladness,
and sorrow and sighing shall flee away.

36 In the fourteenth year of King Hezeki'ah, Sennach'erib king of Assyria came up against all the fortified cities

are emphasized both the loyal love of God for his people and his gracious act in delivering them though they had broken the covenant.

IX. ISAIAH AND HEZEKIAH: A NARRATIVE (36:1–39:8)

The literary analysis of this section will be found in the Intro., pp. 155-57.

A. SENNACHERIB DEMANDS THE SURRENDER OF JERUSALEM (36:1–37:4c)

This is a brilliant piece of historical writing, a vivid and circumstantial account of a memorable event. The reader is enabled to relive the experience and feel its tension as the spokesman of the mighty Assyrian monarch hurls his challenge in terrifying language and the defenders are struck dumb with consternation. For behind the Assyrian officer stood a detachment of the dreaded Assyrian armies encamped in full force not far away. Only the walls of Jerusalem lined by the listening defenders stood as their security, unless like Isaiah they were prepared to put their trust in a divine but invisible power.

The demand of the enemy is couched in clever and effective language, an argument so unanswerable and damaging that the Judean leaders ask that negotiations be conducted in another tongue. What are brave words in face of the realities like the presence of the dreaded Assyrian army (vs. 5)? What help can come from the undependable Egyptians (vs. 6)? How can you say you expect the help of your God, when your king has just now destroyed all your ancient sanctuaries except the royal shrine in the capital city (vs. 7)? How can you, without chariots, fight an army which has horsemen and chariots to spare (vss. 7-8)? How do you know your own God has not sent us as the instruments of your destruction (vs. 10)? If the defenders could find no answer, it was because there was force in every argument, and when he is asked to speak in Aramaic, the envoy sees that his words are striking home. He turns the full force of his eloquence to breaking down the authority of the defenders' king. Hezekiah, he cries, is deceiving you; neither he nor his God can save you from the dreadful doom of a city which the Assyrians besiege. Desert the hopeless cause and you shall be unmolested, until we take you away to a land better than this one!

But Hezekiah's soldiers maintained discipline and held their peace, while Hezekiah himself went to the temple to offer the sacrifices appropriate to a moment of emergency,

how true is the promise, **They shall obtain joy and gladness, and sorrow and sighing shall flee away** (35:10).

36:1–39:8. Prose Narrative.—These chapters bring to a close the first part of the book of Isaiah. They differ from those which precede them in that they present a prose narrative of three historical events. There is little of prophecy in them, nor was Isaiah their author. Critics have agreed that they are excerpts from II Kings 18–20, and a comparison with that passage re-

veals that they are practically identical. The only reason for their inclusion in the book is the light they throw on the place and influence of Isaiah in the national crisis, and the proof they present of the fulfillment of his warnings. The editors rightly felt that in the incidents described both the man and his message were vindicated.

36:1–37:38. Sennacherib's Challenge.—This is a vivid account of how Sennacherib sent his chief of staff, at the head of a large detachment

2 And the king of Assyria sent Rabshakeh from Lachish to Jerusalem unto king Hezekiah with a great army. And he stood by the conduit of the upper pool in the highway of the fuller's field.

3 Then came forth unto him Eliakim, Hilkiah's son, which was over the house, and Shebna the scribe, and Joah, Asaph's son, the recorder.

4 ¶ And Rabshakeh said unto them, Say ye now to Hezekiah, Thus saith the great king, the king of Assyria, What confidence *is* this wherein thou trustest?

5 I say, *sayest thou,* (but *they are but* vain words) *I have* counsel and strength for war: now on whom dost thou trust, that thou rebellest against me?

6 Lo, thou trustest in the staff of this broken reed, on Egypt; whereon if a man lean, it will go into his hand, and pierce it: so *is* Pharaoh king of Egypt to all that trust in him.

of Judah and took them. 2 And the king of Assyria sent the Rab'shakeh from Lachish to King Hezeki'ah at Jerusalem, with a great army. And he stood by the conduit of the upper pool on the highway to the fuller's field. 3 And there came out to him Eli'akim the son of Hilki'ah, who was over the household, and Shebna the secretary, and Jo'ah the son of Asaph, the recorder.

4 And the Rab'shakeh said to them, "Say to Hezeki'ah, 'Thus says the great king, the king of Assyria: On what do you rest this confidence of yours? 5 Do you think that mere words are strategy and power for war? On whom do you now rely, that you have rebelled against me? 6 Behold, you are relying on Egypt, that broken reed of a staff, which will pierce the hand of any man who leans on it. Such is Pharaoh king of Egypt

and sent a message to Isaiah asking for a "word" from Yahweh. Here this narrative breaks off (at 37:4c), and a connecting sentence or two is missing before the introduction of the expected oracle in 37:22.

36:1. The fourteenth year of King Hezekiah: This date belongs apparently to ch. 38; see Exeg. on 38:1-22. **All the fortified cities:** Forty-six walled towns as well as neighboring villages, according to Sennacherib. Jerusalem was isolated, and according to the Assyrian account was blockaded but not attacked.

2. Rabshakeh: Not a proper name but an official title, "chief steward" or "principal envoy"; this man was a civilian accompanied by high military officers (II Kings 18:17). **Lachish:** About twenty-five miles southwest of Jerusalem; the capture of this city is pictured in a relief now in the British Museum (with vs. 2b cf. 7:3).

3. The parley was conducted from the Jewish side by civilian ministers, two of whom appear again in 22:15, 20.

5. Do you think . . . ? Lit., "Dost thou say?" The KJV is unusually clumsy.

of both infantry and cavalry, to make a display in force outside Jerusalem. The king apparently argued that there was no necessity to waste men and material in an attack when a demonstration and a threat could break morale and secure surrender. The account is given with such vividness that nothing is gained by retelling it. The chapter closes with the picture of Jerusalem encircled by the Assyrians while the citizens, from the walls and turrets, listen in stunned silence to the lurid threats of the Assyrian officer.

Act II of the drama is given in ch. 37. It is deeply significant that on hearing the Assyrian message, Hezekiah immediately turns to Isaiah. He may with self-will and under political pressure have refused to listen to the prophet's warnings, but clearly he has never ceased to be uneasy in the presence of this stern figure with

the inexorable message from God. Instinctively in the hour of peril he turns to the man whom he has repeatedly ignored. It is a triumph for Isaiah, and an open confession that the Egyptian policy was a complete failure. A lesser man than the prophet might have taunted the king; but Isaiah rises above all personal consideration: enough that Hezekiah was praying, or rather beseeching him to pray, for the nation. That he had no need to do: the mind and the will of God were already known to him. The answer was more than the king deserved, and all he could desire, viz., the assurance that the Assyrians would meet the doom of the blasphemer, and the menace disappear overnight.

The next section of the chapter is puzzling. If a display of force failed to bring surrender, why should the king of Assyria think that a

7 But if thou say to me, We trust in the Lord our God: *is it* not he, whose high places and whose altars Hezekiah hath taken away, and said to Judah and to Jerusalem, Ye shall worship before this altar?

8 Now therefore give pledges, I pray thee, to my master the king of Assyria, and I will give thee two thousand horses, if thou be able on thy part to set riders upon them.

9 How then wilt thou turn away the face of one captain of the least of my master's servants, and put thy trust on Egypt for chariots and for horsemen?

10 And am I now come up without the Lord against this land to destroy it? the Lord said unto me, Go up against this land, and destroy it.

11 ¶ Then said Eliakim and Shebna and Joah unto Rabshakeh, Speak, I pray thee, unto thy servants in the Syrian language; for we understand *it:* and speak not to us in the Jews' language, in the ears of the people that *are* on the wall.

12 ¶ But Rabshakeh said, Hath my master sent me to thy master and to thee to speak these words? *hath he* not *sent me* to the men that sit upon the wall, that they may eat their own dung, and drink their own piss with you?

13 Then Rabshakeh stood, and cried with a loud voice in the Jews' language, and said, Hear ye the words of the great king, the king of Assyria.

14 Thus saith the king, Let not Hezekiah deceive you: for he shall not be able to deliver you.

to all who rely on him. 7 But if you say to me, "We rely on the Lord our God," is it not he whose high places and altars Hezeki'ah has removed, saying to Judah and to Jerusalem, "You shall worship before this altar"? 8 Come now, make a wager with my master the king of Assyria: I will give you two thousand horses, if you are able on your part to set riders upon them. 9 How then can you repulse a single captain among the least of my master's servants, when you rely on Egypt for chariots and for horsemen? 10 Moreover, is it without the Lord that I have come up against this land to destroy it? The Lord said to me, Go up against this land, and destroy it.' "

11 Then Eli'akim, Shebna, and Jo'ah said to the Rab'shakeh, "Pray, speak to your servants in Aramaic, for we understand it; do not speak to us in the language of Judah within the hearing of the people who are on the wall." 12 But the Rab'shakeh said, "Has my master sent me to speak these words to your master and to you, and not to the men sitting on the wall, who are doomed with you to eat their own dung and drink their own urine?"

13 Then the Rab'shakeh stood and called out in a loud voice in the language of Judah: "Hear the words of the great king, the king of Assyria! 14 Thus says the king: 'Do not let Hezeki'ah deceive you, for

---

7. Hezekiah's destruction of local sanctuaries (II Kings 18:4) would have come to the attention of the Assyrians as they overran the country, and they were determined to make the most of it.

11. In the Syrian language or **in Aramaic:** A language related to Hebrew, which spread from its original home in northwest Mesopotamia until by this time it had become an international second language of diplomacy.

---

letter could do it? Critics submit the possibility that 37:9b-36 is an alternative account of the whole incident. While it is essentially the same story, this version contains additional material of great interest: Hezekiah's prayer, two oracles from Isaiah, a poem on the pride of Sennacherib, so soon to fall, and a prediction of Jerusalem's liberation.

36:7. The Taunt.—The Rabshakeh's message of defiance from Sennacherib had a devastating effect on the defenders of Jerusalem. Psychological warfare is apparently no new thing, for the Assyrian challenge might well have broken the army's morale, and Jerusalem might have fallen without a blow being struck. It was at once so unanswerable and so calculated to break all resistance that the Jewish leaders begged that anything further to be said should be in Aramaic, which the troops would not understand. No charge that the Rabshakeh brought

15 Neither let Hezekiah make you trust in the LORD, saying, The LORD will surely deliver us: this city shall not be delivered into the hand of the king of Assyria.

16 Hearken not to Hezekiah: for thus saith the king of Assyria, Make *an agreement* with me *by* a present, and come out to me: and eat ye every one of his vine, and every one of his fig tree, and drink ye every one the waters of his own cistern;

17 Until I come and take you away to a land like your own land, a land of corn and wine, a land of bread and vineyards.

18 *Beware* lest Hezekiah persuade you, saying, The LORD will deliver us. Hath any of the gods of the nations delivered his land out of the hand of the king of Assyria?

19 Where *are* the gods of Hamath and Arphad? where *are* the gods of Sepharvaim? and have they delivered Samaria out of my hand?

20 Who *are they* among all the gods of these lands, that have delivered their land out of my hand, that the LORD should deliver Jerusalem out of my hand?

21 But they held their peace, and answered him not a word: for the king's commandment was, saying, Answer him not.

22 ¶ Then came Eliakim, the son of Hilkiah, that *was* over the household, and Shebna the scribe, and Joah, the son of Asaph, the recorder, to Hezekiah with *their* clothes rent, and told him the words of Rabshakeh.

37 And it came to pass, when king Hezekiah heard *it,* that he rent his clothes, and covered himself with sackcloth, and went into the house of the LORD.

he will not be able to deliver you. 15 Do not let Hezeki'ah make you rely on the LORD by saying, "The LORD will surely deliver us; this city will not be given into the hand of the king of Assyria." 16 Do not listen to Hezeki'ah; for thus says the king of Assyria: Make your peace with me and come out to me; then every one of you will eat of his own vine, and every one of his own fig tree, and every one of you will drink the water of his own cistern; 17 until I come and take you away to a land like your own land, a land of grain and wine, a land of bread and vineyards. 18 Beware lest Hezeki'ah mislead you by saying, "The LORD will deliver us." Has any of the gods of the nations delivered his land out of the hand of the king of Assyria? 19 Where are the gods of Hamath and Arpad? Where are the gods of Sepharva'im? Have they delivered Samar'ia out of my hand? 20 Who among all the gods of these countries have delivered their countries out of my hand, that the LORD should deliver Jerusalem out of my hand?'"

21 But they were silent and answered him not a word, for the king's command was, "Do not answer him." 22 Then Eli'akim the son of Hilki'ah, who was over the household, and Shebna the secretary, and Jo'ah the son of Asaph, the recorder, came to Hezeki'ah with their clothes rent, and told him the words of the Rab'shakeh.

37 When King Hezeki'ah heard it, he rent his clothes, and covered himself with sackcloth, and went into the house of

---

19. The mention of **Samaria,** then an Assyrian province, is a telling point.

37:1. Hezekiah went to the temple to offer the sacrifice accompanying a prayer of entreaty as in Neh. 9 (cf. Joel 1:13-14; 2:15-17).

---

was more damaging than the sarcasm about relying on religion. "What a mockery," he said, "to expect help from the God you have banished. Your king has ordered the destruction of all sanctuaries except the royal shrine. You fool nobody but yourselves, parading your faith in a God whom by your own action you have disowned." Against that the leaders had nothing to say, for it was true. As Hebrews they had a name as worshipers of Yahweh—that was their religion. But in a crisis it was not to their God they turned, but to the cavalry of Egypt.

Are we in the modern world in any other plight than were these discomfited Jews? We have claimed to be Christian and have so labeled our civilization. Has anything characteristic of Christian faith marked our proposals to solve international issues? Does modern history justify our repeating the motto of faith *In Domine confido?* Has it not been the bitter accusation leveled against us time and again by angry men: "You are Christian in name, Christian in conduct when it suits you, and for the rest of the time you play the world's game"? The apologist

2 And he sent Eliakim, who *was* over the household, and Shebna the scribe, and the elders of the priests, covered with sackcloth, unto Isaiah the prophet the son of Amoz.

3 And they said unto him, Thus saith Hezekiah, This day *is* a day of trouble, and of rebuke, and of blasphemy: for the children are come to the birth, and *there is* not strength to bring forth.

4 It may be the Lord thy God will hear the words of Rabshakeh, whom the king of Assyria his master hath sent to reproach the living God, and will reprove the words which the Lord thy God hath heard: wherefore lift up *thy* prayer for the remnant that is left.

5 So the servants of king Hezekiah came to Isaiah.

6 ¶ And Isaiah said unto them, Thus shall ye say unto your master, Thus saith the Lord, Be not afraid of the words that thou hast heard, wherewith the servants of the king of Assyria have blasphemed me.

the Lord. **2** And he sent Eli′akim, who was over the household, and Shebna the secretary, and the senior priests, clothed with sackcloth, to the prophet Isaiah the son of Amoz. **3** They said to him, "Thus says Hezeki′ah, 'This day is a day of distress, of rebuke, and of disgrace; children have come to the birth, and there is no strength to bring them forth. **4** It may be that the Lord your God heard the words of the Rab′shakeh, whom his master the king of Assyria has sent to mock the living God, and will rebuke the words which the Lord your God has heard; therefore lift up your prayer for the remnant that is left.'"

5 When the servants of King Hezeki′ah came to Isaiah, **6** Isaiah said to them, "Say to your master, 'Thus says the Lord: Do not be afraid because of the words that you have heard, with which the servants of the

---

B. A Prose Oracle: Sennacherib Will Depart and Be Slain (37:4d-7)

This brief section is part of the later historical account (iii) which has been broken up and redistributed by the editor of Kings (see Intro., p. 156). It seems originally to have followed 37:20, but there is a hiatus after that verse where the sending of the messengers to Isaiah was recounted; of this only the last sentence, vs. 4d, asking Isaiah to pray for "the remnant" has been preserved. The prose oracle is an equivalent of 37:33-35, which once it immediately preceded (if the analysis given in the Intro. is right), just as in Jer. 22:10-12 the prose and metrical forms of an oracle appear in conjunction.

4d. Remnant: *She'ērîth,* not *she'ār,* as in 7:3; 10:20-23 (cf. vss. 31-32). The word implies the situation of a later day when, after the fall of Jerusalem in 586, its people were "the remnant" (cf. Jer. 40:11).

---

cannot evade that challenge. Speak as he may of the influence of the church for good, name as he can victories of Christian faith, he cannot deny that after twenty centuries of Christianity we have not produced an economic or social order which is Christian in emphasis or spirit; we have not come within sight of achieving world unity, and we have acquiesced in conventions, practices, and aims which are at entire variance with the ideals and spirit of the religion we profess. The echo of the Rabshakeh's taunt reaches us across the centuries: "You have made your boast in God, but have denied him in what you have tolerated or accepted. You have your shrines, but what relation is there between what is said and sung in them and your conduct of life?"

The Christian may not be inclined to take

that lying down, but he will have a difficult time answering the indictment. There is too much truth in it. The powers that be have consistently staked everything on the modern counterpart to alliance with Egypt and have left God to the devout. They have said of physical science, industry, economic strength, military resources, money, **You shall worship before this altar.** And we have done just that. As a result, we have found no solution for the problems which beset us and make the world a place of conflicting fears and hatreds. The Rabshakeh went further. He matched his taunt with a bet. "Stake what you will on God," he cried, "our money is with the army. If you win, there are two thousand horses in it for you," adding with a sneer, "if you can find two thousand men to ride them." One could wish that King Heze-

7 Behold, I will send a blast upon him, and he shall hear a rumor, and return to his own land; and I will cause him to fall by the sword in his own land.

8 ¶ So Rabshakeh returned, and found the king of Assyria warring against Libnah: for he had heard that he was departed from Lachish.

9 And he heard say concerning Tirhakah king of Ethiopia, He is come forth to make war with thee. And when he heard it, he sent messengers to Hezekiah, saying,

10 Thus shall ye speak to Hezekiah king of Judah, saying, Let not thy God, in whom thou trustest, deceive thee, saying, Jerusalem shall not be given into the hand of the king of Assyria.

11 Behold, thou hast heard what the kings of Assyria have done to all lands by destroying them utterly; and shalt thou be delivered?

king of Assyria have reviled me. 7 Behold, I will put a spirit in him, so that he shall hear a rumor, and return to his own land; and I will make him fall by the sword in his own land.' "

8 The Rab'shakeh returned, and found the king of Assyria fighting against Libnah; for he had heard that the king had left Lachish. 9 Now the king heard concerning Tirha'kah king of Ethiopia, "He has set out to fight against you." And when he heard it, he sent messengers to Hezeki'ah, saying, 10 "Thus shall you speak to Hezeki'ah king of Judah: 'Do not let your God on whom you rely deceive you by promising that Jerusalem will not be given into the hands of the king of Assyria. 11 Behold, you have heard what the kings of Assyria have done to all lands, destroying them utterly. And

---

7. Put a spirit in him: An "impulse" (cf. I Sam. 18:10). **A rumor** or "report": A clear reference to the news of unrest in Babylonia which led to Sennacherib's hurried departure from Palestine, leaving most of his army to follow him later. **Fall by the sword:** The prophecy to be fulfilled by the patricide described in vs. 38; this did not happen, however, until twenty years later.

C. A Threatening Letter and Hezekiah's Prayer (37:8-20)

This section, as noted in the Intro., p. 156, is almost certainly a later version of 36:1–37:4c. The Assyrian king is at **Libnah** rather than at **Lachish,** ten miles away, when the message is sent; the editor adds to the words **the king of Assyria fighting against Libnah** the remainder of vs. 8, in order to link the two accounts. The great similarity of vss. 10-13 and the last three verses of the other account, 36:18-20, should be noted. The language of Hezekiah's prayer resembles that of Second Isaiah (cf. 44:6-8; 45:18-22) and of exilic psalms (cf. Ps. 80).

9. Tirhakah king of Ethiopia: Apparently an anachronism since Tirhakah did not become Pharaoh until 689; he may, however, have been king of Ethiopia in Sennacherib's day.

---

kiah had been the kind of man to take Sennacherib up on that, but it took the prophet to answer the blasphemy. It always requires a supreme faith to stand up to the world's challenge. The odds against God's poor minority are tremendous. On the one side are the vast resources of evil, its organized strength, its repeated victories, and all the allies of sin in the human heart. On the other side are Christ's church, its strength sapped in its divisions, the obscure multitude of believing souls themselves severed by race and creed. What chance has faith in such a situation? None at all if you leave out God. The mistake the world makes is to rely on the material and ignore the spiritual.

Communism has repeated the Rabshakeh's challenge. It is willing to bet that a purely materialistic conception of life can overwhelm any order that has room for God and the spiritual values. The conflict is on, and while the forces of atheism have captured nation after nation, the Christian cannot surrender his faith in the ultimate triumph of God. "The kingdoms of this world are become the kingdoms of our Lord" (Rev. 11:15).

But the wager is not yet won. We have to recognize that God's victory is delayed not alone by the opposition of evil, but by the failure of faith on the part of those who profess themselves Christians. "And he did not many mighty works

12 Have the gods of the nations delivered them which my fathers have destroyed, *as* Gozan, and Haran, and Rezeph, and the children of Eden which *were* in Telassar?

13 Where *is* the king of Hamath, and the king of Arphad, and the king of the city of Sepharvaim, Hena, and Ivah?

14 ¶ And Hezekiah received the letter from the hand of the messengers, and read it: and Hezekiah went up unto the house of the LORD, and spread it before the LORD.

15 And Hezekiah prayed unto the LORD, saying,

16 O LORD of hosts, God of Israel, that dwellest *between* the cherubim, thou *art* the God, *even* thou alone, of all the kingdoms of the earth: thou hast made heaven and earth.

17 Incline thine ear, O LORD, and hear; open thine eyes, O LORD, and see: and hear all the words of Sennacherib, which hath sent to reproach the living God.

18 Of a truth, LORD, the kings of Assyria have laid waste all the nations, and their countries,

19 And have cast their gods into the fire: for they *were* no gods, but the work of men's hands, wood and stone: therefore they have destroyed them.

20 Now therefore, O LORD our God, save us from his hand, that all the kingdoms of the earth may know that thou *art* the LORD, *even* thou only.

shall you be delivered? 12 Have the gods of the nations delivered them, the nations which my fathers destroyed, Gozen, Haran, Rezeph, and the people of Eden who were in Telas'sar? 13 Where are the king of Hamath, the king of Arpad, the king of the city of Sepharva'im, the king of Hena, or the king of Ivvah?' "

14 Hezeki'ah received the letter from the hand of the messengers, and read it; and Hezeki'ah went up to the house of the LORD, and spread it before the LORD. 15 And Hezeki'ah prayed to the LORD: 16 "O LORD of hosts, God of Israel, who art enthroned above the cherubim, thou art the God, thou alone, of all the kingdoms of the earth; thou hast made heaven and earth. 17 Incline thy ear, O LORD, and hear; open thy eyes, O LORD, and see; and hear all the words of Sennach'erib, which he has sent to mock the living God. 18 Of a truth, O LORD, the kings of Assyria have laid waste all the nations and their lands, 19 and have cast their gods into the fire; for they were no gods, but the work of men's hands, wood and stone; therefore they were destroyed. 20 So now, O LORD our God, save us from his hand, that all the kingdoms of the earth may know that thou alone art the LORD."

12-13. The cities mentioned were in Mesopotamia (vs. 12) and Syria (vs. 13). The Dead Sea Scroll adds "Samaria" (as in 36:19).

14. **The letter,** not mentioned until this point, was the text from which the messengers were to read aloud. Hezekiah **spread it before the LORD,** i.e., "displayed it" by unrolling the scroll (cf. Ezek. 2:9-10).

16. **Enthroned above the cherubim:** A reference to the winged creatures, guardians of the shrine, represented on the ark, with which Yahweh's presence was associated (I Kings 8:6-7), and also to their unseen prototypes in the skies (Ps. 18:10 [Hebrew 18:11]).

there because of their unbelief" (Matt. 13:58). Our unbelief has stayed the hand of God. The world has yet to have from Christ's people the witness of lives really committed to his service on every level. When we make faith in him and obedience to his will central in personal life, in economic planning, in foreign policy, and in all relationships, then at least we shall have prepared the way of the Lord and shall have created a condition in which his power can work. God himself waits for that day. When it comes,

"then shall be brought to pass the saying that is written, Death is swallowed up in victory" (I Cor. 15:54), and love so long despised and rejected will rule the hearts of men for their salvation and their peace.

37:14-20. Hezekiah's Prayer.—These verses contain the king's prayer. According to the first narrative, Hezekiah turned to the prophet and asked for his intercession; here he goes straight to God with the arrogant and dismaying message. It is an interesting psychological question

21 ¶ Then Isaiah the son of Amoz sent unto Hezekiah, saying, Thus saith the LORD God of Israel, Whereas thou hast prayed to me against Sennacherib king of Assyria:

22 This *is* the word which the LORD hath spoken concerning him; The virgin, the daughter of Zion, hath despised thee, *and* laughed thee to scorn; the daughter of Jerusalem hath shaken her head at thee.

23 Whom hast thou reproached and blasphemed? and against whom hast thou exalted *thy* voice, and lifted up thine eyes on high? *even* against the Holy One of Israel.

24 By thy servants hast thou reproached the Lord, and hast said, By the multitude of my chariots am I come up to the height of the mountains, to the sides of Lebanon; and I will cut down the tall cedars thereof, *and* the choice fir trees thereof: and I will enter into the height of his border, *and* the forest of his Carmel.

25 I have digged, and drunk water; and with the sole of my feet have I dried up all the rivers of the besieged places.

---

21 Then Isaiah the son of Amoz sent to Hezeki'ah, saying, "Thus says the LORD, the God of Israel: Because you have prayed to me concerning Sennach'erib king of Assyria, 22 this is the word that the LORD has spoken concerning him:

'She despises you, she scorns you —
  the virgin daughter of Zion;
she wags her head behind you —
  the daughter of Jerusalem.

23 'Whom have you mocked and reviled?
  Against whom have you raised your voice
and haughtily lifted your eyes?
  Against the Holy One of Israel!
24 By your servants you have mocked the Lord,
  and you have said, With my many chariots
I have gone up the heights of the mountains,
  to the far recesses of Lebanon;
I felled its tallest cedars,
  its choicest cypresses;
I came to its remotest height,
  its densest forest.
25 I dug wells
  and drank waters,
and I dried up with the sole of my foot
  all the streams of Egypt.

---

21. See Exeg. on 37:21, 33-35, p. 370.

D. ISAIAH'S ORACLE OF DEFIANCE (37:22-29)

This oracle should be compared with that in 10:5-16 which, like this passage, sets forth the impending doom of the overweening pride of the Assyrian king. It opens with a picture of Jerusalem the maiden mocking and taunting the enemy (vs. 22). Then the Assyrian is reminded that his arrogant boasts are a defiance of the Lord (vss. 23-25). The reproach is followed by the consequent threat (vss. 26-29); the monarch is told he has been given rein to wreak destruction only in fulfillment of Yahweh's plan, and now like a wild animal he will be caught and tamed.

24. Omit **by your servants**, which overloads the line and breaks the sequence; this is a gloss by the editor with the "messengers" of vs. 9 in view.

---

to determine which of the two accounts is the more true to human conduct. When a man has repeatedly refused to listen to a messenger of God, and therefore to God himself, to whom is he likely to turn in his desperate need? To the prophet, or to the God behind the prophet? One feels that a man with a sense of guilt would more readily ask the help of the prophet than dare the presence of the God he has flouted. However, we are given the actual prayer attrib-

uted to Hezekiah. One feels that it is far too fine a prayer for a man whose attitude to God had hitherto denied all he now says. Hezekiah may have been desperately sincere in beseeching God to save the nation, **that all the kingdoms of the earth may know that thou art the LORD, even thou only;** but such words sound strange on the lips of the man who has preferred to trust the nation's fate to Egypt, her cavalry and her gods. But we have no right to judge, and it may

26 Hast thou not heard long ago, *how* I have done it; *and* of ancient times, that I have formed it? now have I brought it to pass, that thou shouldest be to lay waste defensed cities *into* ruinous heaps.	26 'Have you not heard that I determined it long ago? I planned from days of old what now I bring to pass, that you should make fortified cities crash into heaps of ruins,
27 Therefore their inhabitants *were* of small power, they were dismayed and confounded: they were *as* the grass of the field, and *as* the green herb, *as* the grass on the housetops, and *as corn* blasted before it be grown up.	27 while their inhabitants, shorn of strength, are dismayed and confounded, and have become like plants of the field and like tender grass, like grass on the housetops, blighted*e* before it is grown.
28 But I know thy abode, and thy going out, and thy coming in, and thy rage against me.	28 'I know your sitting down and your going out and coming in, and your raging against me.
29 Because thy rage against me, and thy tumult, is come up into mine ears, therefore will I put my hook in thy nose, and my bridle in thy lips, and I will turn thee back by the way by which thou camest.	29 Because you have raged against me and your arrogance has come to my ears, I will put my hook in your nose and my bit in your mouth, and I will turn you back on the way by which you came.'
30 And this *shall be* a sign unto thee, Ye shall eat *this* year such as groweth of itself; and the second year that which springeth of the same: and in the third year sow ye, and reap, and plant vineyards, and eat the fruit thereof.	30 "And this shall be the sign for you: this year eat what grows of itself, and in the second year what springs of the same; then in the third year sow and reap, and plant

e With 2 Kings 19. 26: Heb *field*

27. Grass on the housetops: Growing in the cracks (cf. Ps. 129:6). For the dubious **blighted before it is grown** we should read "which is burned up [so the Dead Sea Scroll] by the east wind" (reading קדים for קמה).

28. Thy abode is better than **your sitting**.

29. The second line of vs. 28 and the first line of vs. 29 are doublets; the former is omitted in the LXX; the latter in the Dead Sea Scroll. **Tumult** and **arrogance** are substitutes for the impossible reading of the M.T., "thy ease"; the Targ. recognizes here the word **tumult,** "uproar." **My hook in your nose:** As when a lion (cf. Ezek. 19:3-4) or a crocodile (cf. Ezek. 29:4) was caught and mastered.

E. A SIGN FOR THE REMNANT (37:30-32)

The dislocation of this prose oracle is plain from the fact that there is an abrupt transition at vs. 30 from words addressed in threat to the Assyrian king to words addressed in promise to Hezekiah; and also from the totally different style and content of what follows. These verses belong between vs. 35 and vs. 36 of this chapter. The "sign" is a

be that the king was utterly humbled and truly penitent—ch. 38 is certainly a story of repentance—in which case the prayer assumes a new beauty and significance. When did Hezekiah learn so to pray? A man capable of such intercession is far from being spiritually hardened.

Isaiah makes the king's prayer the occasion of a lyrical passage of great power. Without questioning the authorship of the poem, one wonders if a man of his directness and common sense would have paused long enough in such a critical moment to write or deliver it. It suggests the hand of an editor. As it stands, it presents both a judgment and a taunt. It opens with derision. Anticipating the rout of the Assyrian forces, Isaiah declares that Jerusalem, still inviolate upon her rock, is laughing at Sennacherib. What kind of God did he think was hers? There follows another of the prophet's indictments of the sin of pride. It is the enemy's boast

31 And the remnant that is escaped of the house of Judah shall again take root downward, and bear fruit upward:

32 For out of Jerusalem shall go forth a remnant, and they that escape out of mount Zion: the zeal of the LORD of hosts shall do this.

33 Therefore thus saith the LORD concerning the king of Assyria, He shall not come into this city, nor shoot an arrow there, nor come before it with shields, nor cast a bank against it.

34 By the way that he came, by the same shall he return, and shall not come into this city, saith the LORD.

35 For I will defend this city to save it for mine own sake, and for my servant David's sake.

vineyards, and eat their fruit. 31 And the surviving remnant of the house of Judah shall again take root downward, and bear fruit upward; 32 for out of Jerusalem shall go forth a remnant, and out of Mount Zion a band of survivors. The zeal of the LORD of hosts will accomplish this.

33 "Therefore thus says the LORD concerning the king of Assyria: He shall not come into this city, or shoot an arrow there, or come before it with a shield, or cast up a siege-mound against it. 34 By the way that he came, by the same he shall return, and he shall not come into this city, says the LORD. 35 For I will defend this city to save it, for my own sake and for the sake of my servant David."

---

predicted event whose coming will be evidence that Yahweh indeed had spoken; not only will the city be saved (vss. 33-35), but by the third year conditions will again be normal after the devastation of the invasion. The "remnant," i.e., Judah (in the postexilic usage) will survive and take on new life.

30. What grows of itself, . . . what springs of the same or "what grows wild": The first word means that which grows in the fields and around threshing floors from kernels lost in reaping and threshing; the second word is of uncertain meaning but apparently refers to wild grains eaten only when the cultivated were not available. In the current year no sowing was possible, and the people must depend on what could be gleaned from the accidental growth. Since this would not provide both food and seed grain, in the next year they would have to use wild grains for food. But by the year after that, all would be normal.

32. The zeal of the LORD of hosts is the jealous ardor of the Champion of his people's cause (cf. 42:13); this last line is appropriate in the present context (material taken over from Kings) but is not so in 9:7, where an editor has copied it from this passage.

F. A METRICAL ORACLE ON THE DEPARTURE OF SENNACHERIB (37:21, 33-35)

21, 33-35. The **therefore** with which this oracle begins points back to its introduction now found in vs. 21, from which it has been separated in the rearrangement of the material of this chapter (see Intro., p. 157). It is preceded in vss. 6-7 by a prose oracle which is the same in essence but which is so composed as to point forward specifically to the narrative which concludes the series in vss. 36-37. Here it is said that the Assyrian king will depart before being able to besiege Jerusalem; nothing is said about the miraculous destruction of his army. The final verse takes up a theme prominent in Kings (cf. I Kings 11:13, 34; 15:4; II Kings 8:19), and is probably an addition to the oracle by the editor of Kings.

---

that with contemptuous ease he has disposed of Israel and her God. He has despoiled nature, and with bombast entirely unsupported by fact claims that he has even dried up the Nile. Whereupon Isaiah inserts his own reading of history, declaring that in all he has done Sennacherib has been the unconscious instrument of God's purpose. "Have you not learned," he makes God ask the king, "that I planned all

this, making you my instrument, prompting your going and coming, listening to your boasting and your blasphemy?" (vss. 26-28). But now the king's course is run; like an unmanageable beast he is to be brought to judgment, while the people whom he thought to destroy, God saves and blesses (vss. 29-32). At this point the poem passes abruptly into a blunt assurance that Sennacherib shall lay no hand on Jeru-

36 Then the angel of the LORD went forth, and smote in the camp of the Assyrians a hundred and fourscore and five thousand: and when they arose early in the morning, behold, they *were* all dead corpses.

37 ¶ So Sennacherib king of Assyria departed, and went and returned, and dwelt at Nineveh.

38 And it came to pass, as he was worshipping in the house of Nisroch his god, that Adrammelech and Sharezer his sons smote him with the sword; and they escaped into the land of Armenia: and Esar-haddon his son reigned in his stead.

36 And the angel of the LORD went forth, and slew a hundred and eighty-five thousand in the camp of the Assyrians; and when men arose early in the morning, behold, these were all dead bodies. 37 Then Sennach'erib king of Assyria departed, and went home and dwelt at Nin'eveh. 38 And as he was worshiping in the house of Nisroch his god, Adram'melech and Share'zer, his sons, slew him with the sword, and escaped into the land of Ararat. And E'sarhad'don his son reigned in his stead.

G. DESTRUCTION OF THE ASSYRIANS AND DEATH OF SENNACHERIB (37:36-38)

36-38. This famous legend as to the way in which Isaiah's prediction of the discomfiture and death of Sennacherib came about is apparently based on a vague suggestion in 31:8, in another oracle from the same time. The destruction of the army in a single night (the words "it came to pass that night" in II Kings 19:35 have been omitted accidentally) by **the angel of the LORD** recalls the smiting of the Egyptian first-born (cf. Exod. 12:29) and the pestilence in the time of David (cf. II Sam. 24:15-16). Herodotus (*History* II. 141) records an Egyptian legend that Sennacherib's army was made helpless before the Egyptians when mice in a single night gnawed the bowstrings of his soldiers, and many scholars have seen a connection between a plague of mice and an attack of pestilence. Whatever truth may lie behind the legend (and the account in Herodotus does not purport to tell of the same event), it is clear that here in vss. 36-38 the form *is* legendary. The prediction in the genuine oracle of Isaiah (vss. 22-29) was fulfilled; Sennacherib departed hurriedly and Jerusalem was delivered from a siege. But the evidence of II Kings 18:14-16, which corresponds closely to Sennacherib's own account of the campaign (see Intro., pp. 155-56), makes it certain that Hezekiah submitted and paid tribute in spite of Isaiah's reassuring oracle. This fact is incompatible with the literal truth of vs. 36. And while it is true that Sennacherib was murdered by his sons, this occurred twenty years afterward and not immediately, as is here implied. It is no

salem; without loosing an arrow, he is to go, never to return.

36-38. *A Divine Deliverance.*—These verses tell how that impossible word was fulfilled. It was a miracle of divine intervention. In the evening the smoke of an army's campfires hung in the air; at dawn the light struck on a scene of desolation, dead men everywhere, and the enemy gone. The chapter closes with a terse sentence telling how Sennacherib, victor of a thousand battles, fell by the sword, not in action but in his own temple, murdered by his own sons.

What happened to Sennacherib's army? Speculation on this may be interesting but it is futile. There is no means of finding out. It remains, however, a fact of history that the siege was raised literally overnight. The impression on the nation must have been profound. The skeptics and unbelievers who had united to deride Isaiah and his message must have been dismayed and silent. How magnificently the prophet was vindicated! Alone through the years he had stood for God among the heedless people. He had been treated with contempt; his message, God's own word, had been received with laughter or dismissed as the obsession of a fanatic; but never did he lose his unshakable faith or swerve from his duty. Then the thing happened, the swift miracle of salvation; God acted to prove his case. Behind the story lies this certainty, that somehow or other truth is always vindicated. Periodically God breaks in on life, publishing in a deed, demonstrating in a fact, all that his servants have proclaimed.

The supreme illustration is the Incarnation. After the centuries of witness, the constant testimony of the elect, the long process of educating the human race with regard to the divine purpose, "when the fulness of the time was

38 In those days was Hezekiah sick unto death. And Isaiah the prophet the son of Amoz came unto him, and said unto him, Thus saith the LORD, Set thine house in order: for thou shalt die, and not live.

2 Then Hezekiah turned his face toward the wall, and prayed unto the LORD,

38 In those days Hezeki'ah became sick and was at the point of death. And Isaiah the prophet the son of Amoz came to him, and said to him, "Thus says the LORD: Set your house in order; for you shall die, you shall not recover." 2 Then Hezeki'ah turned his face to the wall, and

---

service to the truth of religion to refuse to recognize a legend for what it is simply because it is picturesque and familiar.

H. HEZEKIAH'S ILLNESS AND RECOVERY (38:1-22)

This section is quoted from II Kings 20:1-11, but with more abbreviations than elsewhere in chs. 36–39. Perhaps this was to compensate to some degree for the insertion of Hezekiah's psalm of thanksgiving for his recovery, not found in Kings. The story is linked with the following one of the coming of Merodach-baladan's envoys (cf. 39:1) in connection with this Chaldean prince's attempt to organize revolt against the Assyrians after the death of Sargon in 705. The promised extension of Hezekiah's life for **fifteen years** is to be taken in connection with the statement in II Kings 18:2 that Hezekiah reigned twenty-nine years, giving the date in Isa. 36:1, which must have belonged originally to this story in ch. 38. The reference to the deliverance of the city from the Assyrians (vs. 6) introduces an element which has no connection with the rest of the chapter, and which has been inserted here by the editor of Kings to link this section with the preceding one (with vs. 6 cf. II Kings 20:6; 19:34).

There is no suggestion in the text that Hezekiah's illness was a punishment for wrongdoing, and the favorable response to his prayer of entreaty implies that his claim to have served Yahweh well (cf. II Kings 18:3-6) was accepted. The psalm inserted in vss. 9-20 is a liturgical thanksgiving for use at the presentation in the temple of a thank offering by a man who has recovered from grave illness (cf. Ps. 32); it was tradi-

---

come, God sent forth his Son" (Gal. 4:4). The truth proclaimed in word was gathered up, made visible in a life. The Incarnation is the final revelation of God's purpose. The O.T. prophecy proclaims the ethical and spiritual nature of God, but Jesus Christ has shown us the Father; the mercy and forgiveness of God are great themes in the Hebrew faith, but it took the cross of Christ to persuade men of redemption; the sovereignty of God is the great doctrine of the O.T., but it was the Resurrection which proved the omnipotence of love. Whether it is in national or personal life, truth at the last prevails, not by the spoken word, but by experience of the power of God. The highest revelation of God is not in the Bible but in those historic acts whereby he confronts men with his judgment and his redeeming love. Thus are the claims of God established, not by words but by deeds; and faith is justified, not through an argument but by experience.

38:1-22. The Difference Christ Has Made.— George Adam Smith has given the title "An Old Testament Believer's Sick-bed; or, The Difference Christ Has Made" to his exposition

of this chapter, confessing that he chose these words because they seemed to him to express "the predominant feeling left in Christian minds after reading the story."[1] Hezekiah's prayer is a noble expression of the sense of the frailty and brevity of life, of the awe and dread which a man who has no hope of life beyond the grave must feel as he faces death. We can share in the mood of the dying king, for we are one with him in our mortality; but the Christian has something which Hezekiah did not have, for between him and us stands the figure of Jesus Christ "who hath abolished death, and hath brought life and immortality to light" (II Tim. 1:10).

With graphic and imaginative power Smith describes the scene in the king's chamber. Hezekiah sees the shadow of the sundial, on top of the courtyard steps, creeping slowly downward. Silent and inexorable it draws nearer, like the beckoning finger of death. In the mercy of God it was stayed and Hezekiah was spared. What any man does with the life which is restored to him is always revealing. Hezekiah laid firmer

[1] *Isaiah*, p. 394.

3 And said, Remember now, O LORD, I beseech thee, how I have walked before thee in truth and with a perfect heart, and have done *that which is* good in thy sight. And Hezekiah wept sore.

4 ¶ Then came the word of the LORD to Isaiah, saying,

5 Go, and say to Hezekiah, Thus saith the LORD, the God of David thy father, I have heard thy prayer, I have seen thy tears: behold, I will add unto thy days fifteen years.

6 And I will deliver thee and this city out of the hand of the king of Assyria: and I will defend this city.

7 And this *shall be* a sign unto thee from the LORD, that the LORD will do this thing that he hath spoken;

prayed to the LORD, 3 and said, "Remember now, O LORD, I beseech thee, how I have walked before thee in faithfulness and with a whole heart, and have done what is good in thy sight." And Hezeki'ah wept bitterly.

4 Then the word of the LORD came to Isaiah: 5 "Go and say to Hezeki'ah, Thus says the LORD, the God of David your father: I have heard your prayer, I have seen your tears; behold, I will add fifteen years to your life. 6 I will deliver you and this city out of the hand of the king of Assyria, and defend this city.

7 "This is the sign to you from the LORD, that the LORD will do this thing that he has

---

tionally ascribed to Hezekiah, as the inscription in vs. 9 indicates. The reference to the medical treatment prescribed by Isaiah and to the king's request for a sign (II Kings 20:7-8) is transferred in a garbled form to the end of the chapter here.

38:3-5. The prayer for recovery from illness is of a type found in the Psalter (cf. Ps. 6). Vs. 5 is much abbreviated (cf. II Kings 20:4-6a), as are vss. 7-8 (cf. II Kings 20:9-11).

7-8. The **sign** of the return of **the declining sun** has an obvious appropriateness to the addition of years to the declining life of a man; that **ten steps**—not **ten degrees** (KJV)—are mentioned instead of the fifteen years to be added, may point to an alternative version. The **sun dial:** Lit., "the stairs" of Ahaz; not a sundial in our sense, but what served the purpose, viz., the steps of the "king's entry," presumably a private

---

grip on God, he made new discovery of the divine mercy and forgiveness, he saw deeper into the meaning and sacredness of life, and he rededicated himself to God. "This is the effect which every great sorrow and struggle has upon a noble soul." [2] They bring back into time a sense of eternity. "Sorrow's subjects, they are our kings; wrestlers with death, our veterans: and to the rabble hordes of society they set the step of a nobler life." [3]

But as ch. 39 reveals, Hezekiah did not remain true to his psalm of deliverance. There is always the danger that those who have come conquerors out of the struggle with death may fall a prey to common life. "How awful to have fought for character with death only to squander it upon life!" [4] Then follows the difference that Jesus Christ has made to our meeting with death. Hezekiah had no sure faith in life beyond the grave. To him to die was to leave all his friends, even God himself. **I said I shall not see the LORD . . . in the land of the living; I shall behold man no more with the inhabitants**

of the world. . . . **They that go down into the pit cannot hope for thy truth** (vss. 11, 18). Death for the king was postponed for fifteen years, but at the end of that respite lay the certainty of going out into darkness, and death would have the last word. He might face it with heroic resignation, but a faith that is good for this life alone, and not equal to the challenge of death, fails the soul at the crucial point.

It is the glory of the Christian faith that it holds for all time and eternity. Jesus Christ has taken the measure of sin and death, and is therefore able to save unto the uttermost. Because of his victory and his love we are persuaded that not even death "shall be able to separate us from the love of God" (Rom. 8:38-39). That faith has transfigured life for untold multitudes who have faced death clear-eyed and unafraid because of their trust in their King and Savior. This is the secret of the peaceful hearts, the unfaltering spirit of those who were persuaded that Christ was able to keep that which they committed unto him against the day of death.

The account of Hezekiah's mortal sickness is told with great vividness and detail in II

[2] *Ibid.*, p. 400.
[3] *Ibid.*, pp. 400-1.
[4] *Ibid.*, p. 402.

8 Behold, I will bring again the shadow of the degrees, which is gone down in the sun dial of Ahaz, ten degrees backward. So the sun returned ten degrees, by which degrees it was gone down.

9 ¶ The writing of Hezekiah king of Judah, when he had been sick, and was recovered of his sickness:

10 I said in the cutting off of my days, I shall go to the gates of the grave: I am deprived of the residue of my years.

promised: 8 Behold, I will make the shadow cast by the declining sun on the dial of Ahaz turn back ten steps." So the sun turned back on the dial the ten steps by which it had declined.*f*

9 A writing of Hezeki'ah king of Judah, after he had been sick and had recovered from his sickness:

10 I said, In the noontide of my days
    I must depart;
I am consigned to the gates of Sheol
    for the rest of my years.

f The Hebrew of this verse is obscure

stairway, built by Ahaz (cf. II Kings 16:18) on the west side of the temple enclosure, so that a horizontal shadow moved up the steps as the sun declined.

9. The so-called "psalm of Hezekiah" (vss. 9-20), like the "song of Hannah" (I Sam. 2:1-10) and the "prayer of Jonah" (Jonah 2:2-9), is a liturgical composition for use in the temple service at the private presentation of a sacrifice of thanksgiving for some personal deliverance; each is inserted in what was felt to be an appropriate context. The title, as in the Psalter, is not part of the poem, but was added by the compiler of the psalmbook from which the poem was derived (cf. the headings to Pss. 56; 90). A **writing**, מכתב, should be מכתם, the designation in their titles of Pss. 56–60, each of which is an appeal for divine help ending on a note of confidence.

10. The noontide: Lit., "the half."

Kings 20:1-11, a passage which stands as an illustration of the superb narrative power of Hebrew genius. Our chapter, however, is enriched by the inclusion of Hezekiah's hymn of thanksgiving on his recovery. There is here a wealth of material for the interpreter. We are confronted throughout with the solemn question, "What is a man's hope as he faces death?" Considering that no one can escape, it is the more strange that men so generally refuse to face that last sure fact. They are reluctant to think about it, much less talk about it. Yet probably the final revelation of man's character, his courage, his faith, is the way in which he meets it. Why should we be so unwilling to entertain the idea of dying, when it is the one experience common to the race? We need not become morbidly concerned about it. Morbidity is always unhealthy. But surely it would be a natural thing, and the part of wisdom, so to prepare ourselves for the great adventure that we could contemplate it with dignity and without fear. No man has thought his way through the implications of his faith till he has made quite clear to himself what his hope is when he looks toward that last threshold.

The chief impression left on the mind of a Christian when he reads this story of Hezekiah is the awesomeness of the thought that death is the end of everything. Unconsciously, and without considering its full import, the modern generation has largely taken for granted the Christian faith in immortality. Therefore to read of a man facing death, convinced that there is nothing beyond it, brings us up short. It brings into focus the amazing difference that the Christian faith makes. The ancient Hebrews saw no reason to believe in immortality; neither could they ignore it. Their conception of Sheol was, as it were, a compromise between the idea of extinction and the idea of life after death. They died and were ushered from the warm, rich contacts of life into an unsubstantial and meaningless existence. Death meant the end of anything that could be called life. The dead had no employment, no real fellowship, and worst of all, no touch with God. It was saying good-by to God, which to the Hebrew invested death with terror. They were not afraid to die, but they shrank from the thought of separation from God. Sheol was not a place of torment; its horror consisted in the fact that the soul was but a shadow of itself. To us it is an unbearable thought that all the goodness and truth for which we have striven, all the fair hopes which we have cherished, and above all, those dear souls we have loved, should be blotted out—eternally lost to us through death. The native courage of the human heart is nowhere more clearly shown than in those

11 I said, I shall not see the LORD, *even* the LORD, in the land of the living: I will behold man no more with the inhabitants of the world.

12 Mine age is departed, and is removed from me as a shepherd's tent: I have cut off like a weaver my life: he will cut me off with pining sickness: from day *even* to night wilt thou make an end of me.

13 I reckoned till morning, *that,* as a lion, so will he break all my bones: from day *even* to night wilt thou make an end of me.

11 I said, I shall not see the LORD
   in the land of the living;
I shall look upon man no more
   among the inhabitants of the world.

12 My dwelling is plucked up and removed
   from me
   like a shepherd's tent;
like a weaver I have rolled up my life;
   he cuts me off from the loom;
from day to night thou dost bring me
   to an end;[g]

13 I cry for help[h] until morning;
   like a lion he breaks all my bones;
   from day to night thou dost bring me
   to an end.[g]

[g] Heb uncertain
[h] Cn: Heb obscure

---

11. The final sting of death for the psalmists (until the late period) was that it would cut them off from the worship of God (cf. vs. 18 and Pss. 27:13; 115:17).

12. Not **mine age** or **my dwelling** but "my life span." **Plucked up:** Better, "is struck" (like a tent when one sets out on a journey). Read "thou hast rolled up, . . . thou hast cut off," and for **bring me to an end,** read "abandon me."

---

countless generations who faced life, and died valiantly, without any hope beyond the grave.

It is no wonder that through the ages certain elect of the race have protested against the finality of death, and in the face of received tradition have flung out their surmise that it will not have the last word. Faith in immortality is not an intellectual tour de force; it has laid hold of the human heart not by the compulsion of an argument, but through the agony which the alternative involved. Against all the evidence, without a vestige of proof, heroic souls have denied the omnipotence of death, daring to declare their unsupported conviction that there must be life beyond. That was the deduction of faith; their trust in God made it a necessity.

Brave as it was, however, it had no confirmation till Jesus Christ "brought life and immortality to light" (II Tim. 1:10). Even yet, with his victory and his word, belief in eternal life is always a matter of faith. It is what the writer of Hebrews calls "the assurance of things hoped for" (Heb. 11:1). The Christian has no proof, as such, of immortality; he can only say in the presence of death, "I am persuaded, that neither death, nor life, . . . nor any other creature, shall be able to separate us from the love of God, which is in Christ Jesus our Lord" (Rom. 8:38-39). Jesus said: "In my Father's house are many mansions: if it were not so, I would have told you. I go to prepare a place for you. And if I go and prepare a place for you, I will come

again, and receive you unto myself; that where I am, there ye may be also" (John 14:2-3). It is enough. It is better than proof; it is the pledged word of our Lord. The great hope has become his promise. Of all the world religions, Christianity alone has a fact on which to rest its assurance of eternal life: the fact of Christ's victory over death, and the truth that "God so loved the world, that he gave his only begotten Son, that whosoever believeth in him should not perish, but have everlasting life" (John 3:16). There the matter rests. We know the love that will not let us go. It is to that love we give our dear ones when they die; it is into our Father's hands that we commend our spirit as we ourselves launch out into death. In that faith untold multitudes have died triumphantly; the waters of death have been shallow to their feet because of their trust in Jesus Christ.

Eternal life! What that means no man can say. Our Lord was silent on the conditions of life in the many mansions of God. It is as if he said, as we say to our children about some great surprise, "Wait and see." In the meantime, nothing can keep us from wondering about it. Surely we have authority to let loose our imagination and see with the eyes of faith the condition and employment of our loved ones in that other country, with that great company of the redeemed which no man can number. None can deny us that right; and though we have nothing to guide our thoughts but love, and in a sense all our speculations are vain, yet it not only

14 Like a crane *or* a swallow, so did I chatter: I did mourn as a dove: mine eyes fail *with looking* upward: O LORD, I am oppressed; undertake for me.

15 What shall I say? he hath both spoken unto me, and himself hath done *it:* I shall go softly all my years in the bitterness of my soul.

16 O Lord, by these *things men* live, and

14 Like a swallow or a crane[i] I clamor,
     I moan like a dove.
My eyes are weary with looking upward.
     O Lord, I am oppressed; be thou my
        security!

15 But what can I say? For he has spoken to
     me,
     and he himself has done it.
All my sleep has fled[j]
     because of the bitterness of my soul.

16 O Lord, by these things men live,
     and in all these is the life of my spirit.[k]

[i] Heb uncertain
[j] Cn Compare Syr: Heb *I will walk slowly all my years*
[k] Heb uncertain

14. For עָגוּר, a crane, read עוּרָג, "yearning," "longing," i.e., "like an unhappy swallow," or "like a plaintive swift I twitter."

15. The third line **I shall go softly all my years** (all my sleep has fled, RSV) is obscure; Ehrlich's emendation נדדה כל־שׁנתי (*Randglossen zur hebräischen Bibel*, p. 140), which underlies the RSV, may better be rendered "sleep is quite fled from me."

16. The first two lines in both versions are a forced translation of the Hebrew which has suffered in transmission. With slight changes Kissane (*Isaiah*, I, 416, 418) restores the text:

O Lord, with Thee are the days of my life,
Thine alone is the life of my spirit.

brings comfort to our spirit just to talk about that place of peace, it also quickens our expectations of the best which is yet to be. And when we have done, when the gates of the heavenly city swing to, shutting from our longing eyes all the glory and the wonder, there comes to us this word, "Eye hath not seen, nor ear heard, neither have entered into the heart of man, the things which God hath prepared for them that love him" (I Cor. 2:9).

There are many verses in Hezekiah's hymn which open out vistas of truth, e.g., vs. 15: **What shall I say? he hath both spoken unto me, and himself hath done it: I shall go softly all my years in the bitterness of my soul.** Some critics have given us an entirely different translation. Moffatt renders it:

And yet what can I say to him,
     who himself does this to me?
I toss on through the hours of sleep
     in bitterness of soul.

Nevertheless, one is loath to let slip the opportunity given by the translation in the KJV for a word to those who have been through deep waters. How do men who have been down, hard by the gates of death, face life again? Some talk about "good luck," about "getting the breaks,"

or about the wonders of modern medicine. They seem to have absolutely no awareness of God. Others take for granted their recovery. That chapter is closed; they want to forget it. With renewed vigor they return to business, resolved to get something of their own back. The experience has left no mark on their hardened spirit. But there are still others who return to life as new men, for they found God, or rather were found by him, in their helplessness and need. These are those who carry into life rich gain from the fields of pain. In weakness they were utterly humbled, stripped of proud independence and brought by the very nearness of death to realize that there are values which no money can buy, but only God can give. Thousands of men have caught a glimpse of the dignity and meaning of life because they looked in the face of death. **I shall go softly,** they say; and it means with humility, because of the things learned in bitter hours. A man has not suffered in vain if he can carry into all that life shall thereafter hold for him a sense of the littleness of time and the greatness of eternity.

16. *The Things We Live By.*—Modern exegesis questions the accuracy of the KJV, **O Lord, by these things men live, and in all these things is the life of my spirit.** But God can use **even**

in all these *things is* the life of my spirit: so wilt thou recover me, and make me to live.

17 Behold, for peace I had great bitterness; but thou hast in love to my soul *delivered it* from the pit of corruption: for thou hast cast all my sins behind thy back.

18 For the grave cannot praise thee, death cannot celebrate thee: they that go down into the pit cannot hope for thy truth.

19 The living, the living, he shall praise thee, as I *do* this day: the father to the children shall make known thy truth.

Oh, restore me to health and make me live!
17 Lo, it was for my welfare
    that I had great bitterness;
but thou hast held back[l] my life
    from the pit of destruction,
for thou hast cast all my sins
    behind thy back.
18 For Sheol cannot thank thee,
    death cannot praise thee;
those who go down to the pit cannot hope
    for thy faithfulness.
19 The living, the living, he thanks thee,
    as I do this day;
the father makes known to the children
    thy faithfulness.

[l] Cn Compare Gk Vg: Heb *loved*

---

17. The psalmist realizes that his sufferings have been for his own good; forgiveness of sin and recovery from mortal illness have been two sides of the same experience of God's saving power.

---

mistranslations! And certainly these words suggest a truth that claims all who have suffered.

By these things. What things? The very things men passionately plead to escape—pain, weakness, death. But according to the faith of these words, it is by these very experiences that we lay hold of a deeper thought of life. According to modern standards there are literally hundreds of things necessary for a full life, and the chief of them is money. The world says confidently, **by these things men live.** The wisdom of the ages, and supremely Christian faith, denies that. Those who have sojourned in the valley of humiliation or tarried in Gethsemane are one in their witness that in the hour of suffering all earthly things lost meaning, and such confidence as they had in the things of the spirit, such faith as they could muster, alone mattered. The older one grows, the more one realizes that the essentials of life are few. We find that many things we once considered of first importance are really secondary. Moreover, we learn that the few things truly vital are inward, such as moral character, faith, love. More often than not it takes some sore discipline to teach us that. In the crises of life things are powerless to help us. Neither rank nor wealth can save a man in pain or shame or sorrow. Hezekiah declares, and he speaks for multitudes who have suffered, that it was in the hour of utter helplessness that he heard God, felt the constraint of divine love, and knew the peace of forgiveness. Looking back on those days of suffering, he realized that the greatest thing in life, the one thing that invests it with meaning and purpose, is to be sure of God. It is by the experience of his presence, his forgiveness and his love that a man really lives. He exists by material things; he lives by the great spiritual verities. Pain, loss, sorrow, all devastating experiences can make stoical heroes out of some men, they can reduce others to whimpering cowards, and still others they can make embittered rebels. But to those who can believe that even in the darkest hour God has not given them up, and who know that he is with them when they feel most forsaken, these experiences may become gateways to new and deeper knowledge of his mercy and his love. That surely is the meaning of Hezekiah's strange word that **by these things men live.**

17. *Out of the Pit.*—The KJV does not do justice to the pregnant construction of the Hebrew, which reads, lit., "Thou hast loved my soul out of the pit of destruction." It means, "Thou hast loved, and by thy love lifted me." That Hezekiah is not thinking only of deliverance from physical death is clear from the words he adds, **Thou hast cast all my sins behind thy back.**

For every man who is persuaded of the love of God by the beneficence of life, by beauty, by experience of joy and peace, there are a thousand who have found their certainty in forgiveness. The doxologies of heaven will be as many and as varied as man's experience of God's goodness, but one will take precedence of all the rest and it will be sung by a multitude no man can number, "Unto him that loved us, and washed us from our sins in his own blood, . . .

20 The LORD *was ready* to save me: therefore we will sing my songs to the stringed instruments all the days of our life in the house of the LORD.

21 For Isaiah had said, Let them take a lump of figs, and lay *it* for a plaster upon the boil, and he shall recover.

22 Hezekiah also had said, What *is* the sign that I shall go up to the house of the LORD?

20 The LORD will save me,
  and we will sing to stringed instruments[m]
all the days of our life,
  at the house of the LORD.

21 Now Isaiah had said, "Let them take a cake of figs, and apply it to the boil, that he may recover." 22 Hezeki'ah also had said, "What is the sign that I shall go up to the house of the LORD?"

[m] Heb *my stringed instruments*

---

20. "The Lord has become my savior" is to be the theme of the perpetual hymn of thanksgiving.

21-22. These verses were omitted from between vs. 6 and vs. 7 (cf. II Kings 20:6-9), and are given here in a different form from that of Kings. Apparently the borrower of the Kings passage found difficulty in the anticipatory statement of II Kings 20:7 that Hezekiah had recovered before he asked for a sign. Isaiah's prescription of a (hot) fig poultice to be applied to the boil is one of several slight indications that he may have known and practiced the arts of the physician (cf. 1:5-6; 6:10).

---

to him be glory and dominion for ever and ever. Amen" (Rev. 1:5).

20. *Experience of God.*—The Exeg. suggests the translation "The Lord has become my salvation." The change in the tense of the verb transforms the verse. The assurance that God could and would save Hezekiah passes into a grateful confession that he has done it. The source of the great thanksgiving that through the ages has risen to God from the lips of delivered and redeemed souls is in these words, "has become my salvation." There is a difference between theology and religion. Theology is the framing in words, the setting forth in doctrine, of man's thoughts of God. Religion is his experience of God. "The Lord has become my salvation."

Some can say that God is the interpretative center of all thinking, others that he is the unifying principle of experience, still others that he is the life force emerging in creation. These are profound philosophical theories. They may be the conclusions of detached speculation about the nature of the universe. They have no necessary bearing on the character of the thinker. But "the Lord has become my salvation" is the testimony of one who, having been saved from sin or fear, henceforth must think of God in terms of that liberating experience. God is no longer a first principle, an ultimate cause, or any other abstraction; he is known as Savior. That is the very heart of religion. That is why a faith born of experience is always jubilant with song. Supremely is it true of the Christian religion that it is vibrant with the joy of salvation. T. R. Glover says Jesus came to help men to rethink their thoughts of God.[5] That is true; but deeper far is Paul's declaration, "Christ Jesus came into the world to save sinners" (I Tim. 1:15). Our Lord has many titles, Son of man, Messiah, King of kings, Son of God, each of them framing some aspect of his glory. But he bears one name that is above every name. Because he has loosed men from their sins, they call him Savior. "The Lord has become my salvation." Until we can say that, we do not know what it really is to be a Christian, a saved soul.

Deliverance from the power and guilt of sin is the most obvious meaning of salvation, but we must not limit it to the experience of being forgiven. Salvation means the lifting of the whole personality to new life. It means new values, new purposes on every level of our being, physical, moral, and spiritual. For some it does mean first and foremost the striking off of the chains of sin. For others it is a new way of living that puts giving before getting, for others still a new understanding and adjustment to life. Every man must put his own interpretation on salvation. It is his own experience which will decide what it means to him. The glory of the gospel of Christ is that "he is able . . . to save them to the uttermost that come unto God by him" (Heb. 7:25). "The Lord has become my salvation"—that is the authentic voice of Christian faith.

[5] *The Jesus of History* (London: Student Christian Movement, 1917), p. 72.

39 At that time Merodach-baladan, the son of Baladan, king of Babylon, sent letters and a present to Hezekiah: for he had heard that he had been sick, and was recovered.

39 At that time Mer'odach-bal'adan the son of Bal'adan, king of Babylon, sent envoys with letters and a present to Hezeki'ah, for he heard that he had been

J. THE EMBASSY FROM MERODACH-BALADAN (39:1-8)

The event which this chapter recounts is linked in vs. 1*b* with the preceding account of Hezekiah's sickness. If Hezekiah's illness was fifteen years before his death in 687, it would provide the occasion for the embassy of Merodach-baladan which is to be dated about 703. This was undoubtedly part of the intrigue carried on by the Babylonian prince in connection with his revolt against Assyrian control after the death of Sargon in 705. It may be concluded, therefore, that the words in vs. 1*b*, connecting this chapter with the preceding one, are editorial and incorrect; in any case, they have no bearing on the substance of the chapter itself.

This narrative, like the others in chs. 36–39, is taken from the book of Kings (cf. II Kings 20:12-19), which brings the story of the Judean kingdom down to the Babylonian exile. It is written, therefore, in the light of that tragic climax, and this explains why Isaiah is here represented as having in effect reversed his promise that the Lord of hosts would defend Jerusalem. The tradition that Isaiah had denounced Hezekiah for opening his treasures to the sight of Babylonian envoys is not at all improbable; that he did so in words anticipating the account in II Kings 24:10–25:17, nearly a century before Babylon replaced Assyria as the supreme world power, is less likely. In other words, the account in this chapter is in substance historical, but is colored by the experience of the later generation when it was written down.

39:1. Merodach-baladan, or Marduk-apal-iddina, Chaldean prince of Bit-Yakin, who revolted against the Assyrians in 721, 710, and 704. The Hebrew text vocalizes the divine

39:1-8. *A Vow Soon Forgotten.*—The Exeg. reveals the difficulty of dating the events told in this chapter. It is a technical question, and of moment only to the scholar. To the ordinary reader the chapter presents no difficulties. An embassy from Babylon arrived at the court of Hezekiah, ostensibly to congratulate him on his recovery, but really with a view to negotiate an alliance. The moment Isaiah heard of it his suspicions were aroused. He had good reason to know how easily the royal house yielded to the proposals of the great powers, and he was inflexibly opposed to foreign entanglements. His book records his constant struggle to prevent the king from committing the nation to any treaty which would in effect mean abandoning trust in God. It did not on this occasion take Isaiah long to get to the palace. There he confronted the king with the accusing question, **What said these men? and from whence came they unto thee?** That Hezekiah was uneasy in mind is clear from his answer. Note that he ignores the vital point as to the proposal made, and declares that since he has been honored by a greeting from the Babylonian king, on the ground of his royal duty, hospitality had to be shown to these strangers. Probing the matter further, Isaiah asks what the embassy has seen. The king, whose vanity has been stirred by flat-

tery, replies that he has shown them everything: his court, his treasures, his store of merchandise, and his armory. Doubtless the embassy expressed themselves as profoundly impressed. Isaiah, however, is not impressed. Curtly he breaks in on the king's gratification with a sweeping judgment. The day is coming when all this treasure will be taken as spoil by Babylon, and the royal sons will be not princes, but slaves at a foreign court. That puts an abrupt end to Hezekiah's boasting, and he can only stammer the formal response of pious resignation (vs. 8).

The whole incident throws into relief a weakness in the king which is common to most men. He could not live up to his high resolutions; he forgot so soon. Following the sequence of the KJV, from ch. 38, with Hezekiah's moving pledge to God that thenceforth he would go humbly and gratefully because he had been reprieved from death, we pass in ch. 39 to this picture of the same man strutting before his visitors with ill-concealed conceit of his treasures. There is no humility here, no remembrance of the black shadow creeping down the steps of the sundial, or of the vows he flung out to God in his extremity. It is all so true to life! We too in our fickleness can promise anything to God in our bitter hour; we can say, and mean it too, that if only he will be merciful we

2 And Hezekiah was glad of them, and showed them the house of his precious things, the silver, and the gold, and the spices, and the precious ointment, and all the house of his armor, and all that was found in his treasures: there was nothing in his house, nor in all his dominion, that Hezekiah showed them not.

3 ¶ Then came Isaiah the prophet unto king Hezekiah, and said unto him, What said these men? and from whence came they unto thee? And Hezekiah said, They are come from a far country unto me, *even* from Babylon.

4 Then said he, What have they seen in thine house? And Hezekiah answered, All that *is* in mine house have they seen: there is nothing among my treasures that I have not showed them.

5 Then said Isaiah to Hezekiah, Hear the word of the LORD of hosts:

6 Behold, the days come, that all that *is* in thine house, and *that* which thy fathers have laid up in store until this day, shall be carried to Babylon: nothing shall be left, saith the LORD.

sick and had recovered. 2 And Hezeki'ah welcomed them; and he showed them his treasure house, the silver, the gold, the spices, the precious oil, his whole armory, all that was found in his storehouses. There was nothing in his house or in all his realm that Hezeki'ah did not show them. 3 Then Isaiah the prophet came to King Hezeki'ah, and said to him, "What did these men say? And whence did they come to you?" Hezeki'ah said, "They have come to me from a far country, from Babylon." 4 He said, "What have they seen in your house?" Hezeki'ah answered, "They have seen all that is in my house; there is nothing in my storehouses that I did not show them."

5 Then Isaiah said to Hezeki'ah, "Hear the word of the LORD of hosts: 6 Behold, the days are coming, when all that is in your house, and that which your fathers have stored up till this day, shall be carried to Babylon; nothing shall be left, says the

---

name "Marduk" with the vowels of "Adonai"—"LORD"—to avoid pronouncing it, just as was done with the divine name "Yahweh." **Letters and a present:** Doubtless a proposal in flattering terms that Hezekiah join Merodach-baladan in revolt.

2. Was glad of them, welcomed them: וישמח עליהם; cf. the similar sounding עליהם וישמע, "hearkened unto them," of II Kings 20:13. The Isaiah text is preferable here; the point is that Hezekiah's vanity was flattered. **His treasure house** was not so full after the tribute was paid to Sennacherib (cf. II Kings 18:14-16).

3-4. Isaiah suspects intrigue; it was his unchanging counsel that Judah should refrain from foreign entanglements, for these would compromise her reliance on the power of her own God (cf. 7:3-9; 30:3-5).

5-7. The punishment will fit the crime (cf. 3:16-17, 24).

---

will be different men and women. Nothing is too great to undertake when in desperation we importune God. But afterwards? Ah, that is another story! A month passes, and our self-confidence returns; a year passes, and we have lost all trace of the seriousness which fell upon us in our trouble; another year, and we have forgotten that meeting of our soul with God.

Such a theme as "Living Up to Our Resolutions" might have much to say to men. There should be rebuke in it, for there is no meaner vice than ingratitude, no greater weakness than inconstancy. All of us have reason to remember

Vows in the night, so fierce and unavailing!
Stings of my shame and passion of my tears! [6]

[6] Frederick W. H. Myers, *St. Paul*, st. xvi.

When we really consider what we have been and done, over against the amazing patience and constant goodness of God; when we recall our broken promises, our sheer presumption in trifling with his love, we know that we, like Hezekiah, deserve the judgment of God. But after conscience has thus brought us low it is the function of faith, and the work of God's spokesman, to lift up our hearts. The gospel of forgiveness is the religion of a new beginning. When we examine our own lives, we discover that our slackened purposes of good, our carelessness of spiritual values, our forgotten resolutions, are all due to our neglect of what our fathers called the "means of grace." The Christian life is an affair of unceasing discipline; to keep our faith strong and vital God has given

7 And of thy sons that shall issue from thee, which thou shalt beget, shall they take away; and they shall be eunuchs in the palace of the king of Babylon.

8 Then said Hezekiah to Isaiah, Good *is* the word of the LORD which thou hast spoken. He said moreover, For there shall be peace and truth in my days.

LORD. 7 And some of your own sons, who are born to you, shall be taken away; and they shall be eunuchs in the palace of the king of Babylon." 8 Then said Hezeki'ah to Isaiah, "The word of the LORD which you have spoken is good." For he thought, "There will be peace and security in my days."

---

8. The word . . . is good, i.e., "acceptable"; an expression of respect, not, as the editor suggests in vs. 8*b*, of relief that the punishment will not come in his lifetime.

---

us the means to secure ourselves against our own weakness, and at the same time to make us more sure of himself. He has given us his word, his church, the holy sacraments, prayer, and the example and fellowship of great souls. It is when we neglect these "means of grace" that religion becomes less and less real to us, and we trail after Christ spiritually shabby, wondering why something has gone dead within us. On the other hand, to make use of what God has provided is to discover not only that gratitude and hope are alive in our hearts, but that actually we grow in power to do his will, and to keep faith with the covenant which we made in some moment of awakening or decision. The truth is that no man can live up to his resolutions in the great things of faith unless he lives neighbor to Christ.

INTRODUCTION, CHS. 40-66

The poetic sequence in Isa. 40–55 represents the noblest literary monument bequeathed to us from Semitic antiquity. The literatures of the ancient Near East have now been recovered in substantial quantities,[1] and they reflect in a remarkable way the cultural mentality, world view, and interior aspirations of the peoples whence they came.[2] To these the O.T. bears many interesting affinities. Yet after due weight has been given to all that the O.T. and the other Near Eastern literatures have in common, it is the distinctiveness of the records of Israel which emerges as the single most impressive and revealing fact. In this collection of sacred books the poems of Second Isaiah occupy a position of pre-eminence both for their literary power and elevation and for the profundity of their thought.

Nowhere in the whole O.T. do we possess a continuous series of poems by a single author of a range comparable to these chapters in Isaiah, with the possible exception of the book of Job, to which, interestingly enough, they have many important relationships.[3] Both of these literary monuments have been characterized as epics; at least they have epic qualities.

Isa. 40–55 is a profoundly authentic product of the Hebraic mind and spirit. Its roots lie deep within the great tradition. The thought and theological perspective of the Yahwist is grasped and interpreted in a fashion unmatched by any other biblical book. Its prophetic thought and form move naturally from the great pre-exilic prophets, more especially Isaiah of Jerusalem, Jeremiah, and Ezekiel. The elevation of thought is matched by an intense lyricism. Moreover, in mood, style, and thought it is a superb reflection of its social environment. The Hebraic sense of time here achieves an amplitude and depth that does justice, not only to the classical tradition of Israel as it was enshrined in the literature of the past, but also to its later appropriation by the writers of the N.T. The theocentricity of Scripture rises to unprecedented heights, and the uniqueness of Israel's relationship to her God as it was understood in the classical tradition is bodied forth with a concreteness, perceptiveness, and imaginative insight which are paralleled only by the writings of Paul and Augustine.

[1] See especially J. B. Pritchard, ed., *Ancient Near Eastern Texts Relating to the Old Testament* (Princeton: Princeton University Press, 1950).

[2] See Henri and H. A. Frankfort, *et al.*, *The Intellectual Adventure of Ancient Man* (Chicago: University of Chicago Press, 1946) for an admirable discussion of the thought of these civilizations.

[3] See Vol. III, pp. 889-90.

I. Literary Problems in Chapters 1–66

Is the book of Isaiah the work of a single writer, the prophet Isaiah, whose prophetic oracles appear in chs. 1–39? This view has been held until relatively modern times. In the twelfth century, however, Ibn Ezra in somewhat guarded language expressed his doubts that chs. 40–66 were written by Isaiah. The hypothesis that they originated with a later poet was first formulated and defended by Johann Christoph Döderlein in 1775, popularized by Johann Gottfried Eichhorn in 1780-83, and is now widely accepted. The arguments for this position are based upon (*a*) the historical background reflected in the book; (*b*) the language, literary style, and form; and (*c*) the theological ideas.

A. Historical Background.—Isaiah of Jerusalem lived in the second half of the eighth century B.C. and addressed himself to the conditions existing at that time.[4] Judah and Israel were still in existence as independent kingdoms. Their kings are referred to by name (Uzziah, Ahaz, Hezekiah, Pekah), and the prophet's encounters with them are described in simple narrative discourse. Assyria was the oppressing power; Sargon and Sennacherib are clearly referred to. It is not difficult to discern the various Assyrian campaigns and the reactions of the kingdoms to each threat. The death of Uzziah, the Syro-Ephraimitic crisis, the fall of the Northern Kingdom, the siege of Ashdod, and the invasion of Sennacherib are among the central events. In chs. 40–55, however, the background is the middle of the sixth century B.C., the close of the neo-Babylonian period.[5] Israel has long ceased to be a kingdom, and Judah is languishing in Babylonian exile. Cyrus king of Persia is twice mentioned by name (44:28; 45:1), and there are a number of other passages where he is clearly in the writer's mind. His great military campaigns are mentioned, and the fall of Babylon is believed to be imminent.

B. Language, Literary Style, and Form.—The diction of the book has been subjected to exhaustive analysis by T. K. Cheyne.[6] Not all the words given in the lists have the same value as evidence, but a substantial number of them show the contrast in usage between chs. 1–39 and 40–66.[7] The differences in literary style

[4] See above, pp. 161-62.

[5] See article "The Old Testament World," Vol. I, pp. 267-68.

[6] *Introduction to the Book of Isaiah* (London: A. & C. Black, 1895), pp. 255-70.

[7] See especially S. R. Driver, *An Introduction to the Literature of the Old Testament* (9th ed.; Edinburgh: T. & T. Clark, 1913), pp. 238-40. In such studies it is essential to distinguish between Isaiah's own oracles and those of later writers (e.g., 13:1–14:23; 34–35).

between the two sections of the book are even more obvious.

Isaiah's style is terse and compact: the movement of his periods is stately and measured: his rhetoric is grave and restrained. In these chapters [40–66] the style is much more flowing: the rhetoric is warm and impassioned; and the prophet often bursts into a lyric strain.[8]

Especially notable is the contrast of literary types that are employed. Isaiah, like his prophetic contemporaries, is fond of the invective and threat; the writer of chs. 40–66 is sparing in his use of them and frequently employs such other forms as the oracle of salvation.

C. *Theological Outlook.*—It is true that there are affinities in thought between chs. 1–39 and 40–66, as indeed there are in language also. But the differences are much more striking and numerous than the similarities. The relationships to chs. 1–39 are important and must not be minimized. Yet one has also to take account of the literary relationships to Jeremiah and Ezekiel. Sometimes, indeed, passages from Jeremiah and Ezekiel are dependent on Isa. 40–66, but it is probable that these are later additions. The philosophy of history of chs. 40–66 is much more highly developed than that in chs. 1–39. The portrait of God as creator and redeemer has no close parallel in Isaiah of Jerusalem. The conception of the remnant is not the same. The difference between the Messiah of 9:1-6 and 11:1-9 and the portrait of the servant of the Lord in chs. 40–55 is so great that even if the servant is interpreted messianically, it is hard to believe that the two figures are the creation of a single mind.

Attempts to show that chs. 40–66 are the projection of the prophet's vision into the distant future have led to the most tortuous kind of reasoning and are at variance with the whole nature of Hebrew prophecy where the oracles, however predictive in character, are always related to the concerns and issues of the time in which the prophet is living. Yet it is possible to overstate the evidence. There was good reason why the late materials of the book were attached to Isaiah's name. It may be that they represent, at least in part, the perpetuation of an Isaiah tradition.[9] The view of Yahweh as the Holy One of Israel, the way in which the divine activity in history is grasped, the style and thought of messianic oracles in chs. 9 and 11, the intimate relationship between chs. 34–35 and 40–66, and the eschatological orientation of many of the poems suggest how a compiler

would collect them in one corpus. "The prophet could be called by that name (the second Isaiah) with the more justification because the spirit of the old Isaiah in fact celebrates its resurrection in him." [10]

II. Integrity of Chapters 40–66

In his epoch-making commentary [11] Bernhard Duhm undertook to defend two important positions: [12] (a) Four servant songs (42:1-4; 49:1-6; 50:4-9; 52:13–53:12), which belong to a different time and represent a different sphere of thought, have been inserted into the poems; (b) chs. 56–66 are the product of a later age, the last half of the fifth century B.C. The latter view has been accepted by the majority of scholars, although a strong minority has held out against it.[13] Certainly there are numerous striking affinities between chs. 40–55 and 56–66; indeed their number seems to increase with each successive reading. The language and style are frequently similar, and there are numerous resemblances in thought. Torrey attaches 56:1, 7-8 directly to ch. 55, and Kissane [14] makes 56:1-2 the conclusion of the poem. The degree of relationship between the two sections is incomparably closer than to anything found in the genuine oracles of Isaiah. On the other hand, it is important to recognize that some sections of chs. 56–66 are much closer to chs. 40–55 than others. For example, 57:14-21 and chs. 60–62 have much of the ecstatic fervor and brilliant style of chs. 40–55 and are believed by some scholars to be the work of the same poet. The weightiest argument against the literary integrity of chs. 40–66 is the difference in historical situation which they appear to presuppose. In chs. 40–55 the Jewish community is in exile in Babylon (see Exeg.); in chs. 56–66 it is in Jerusalem. The problems which confront the latter group are such as would arise after

---

[8] *Ibid.*, pp. 240-41.

[9] Sigmund Mowinckel, *Jesaja-diseplene* (Oslo: H. Aschenong, 1926).

[10] Rudolf Kittel, *Geschichte des Volkes Israel* (Gotha: Leopold Klotz, 1929), III, 205. Cited by Sidney Smith, *Isaiah, Chapters XL-LV* (London: British Academy, 1944), p. 113.

[11] *Das Buch Jesaia* (Göttingen: Vandenhoeck & Ruprecht, 1892; Göttinger Handkommentar zum Alten Testament").

[12] The first of these was adumbrated in his *Die Theologie der Propheten* (Bonn: A. Marcus, 1875).

[13] C. C. Torrey (*The Second Isaiah* [New York: Charles Scribner's Sons, 1928]) argues with great force and in detail for the integrity of chs. 34–35; 40–66. See also Eduard König, *Das Buch Jesaja* (Gütersloh: C. Bertelsmann, 1926); Ludwig Glahn, *Die Einheit von Kap. 40-66 des Buches Jesaja* (Giessen: A. Töpelmann, 1934); Louis Finkelstein, *The Pharisees* (Philadelphia: Jewish Publication Society of America, 1938), II, 627-31; Fleming James, *Personalities of the Old Testament* (New York: Charles Scribner's Sons, 1939), pp. 361-63. All of these scholars support the unity of chs. 40–66.

[14] *The Book of Isaiah* (Dublin: Browne & Nolan, 1941-43), II, 208-10.

the return, when the difficulties of reconstruction and restoration would be acute. The interest in the cult is different from anything we find in chs. 40–55. The preoccupation with sabbath observance and fasting is foreign to chs. 40–55. The representation of the blind leaders in 56:9–57:13 is quite different from the blindness of Israel in chs. 40–55, and the character of the apostasy is different too. The picture of factional strife and dissension is not that of chs. 40–55. The eschatology of chs. 65–66 is much more like that of chs. 34–35 than of chs. 40–55. Again, the literary forms, such as the "torah liturgy" of 56:1-8 and the long intercessory prayer of 63:7–64:12, are not in the manner of the earlier section. Further, the way other biblical passages are quoted almost verbatim, especially verses from chs. 40–55, does not display the kind of literary independence which characterizes the writer of the latter section. In chs. 56–66, the writer (or writers) employs these lines as points of departure, much in the fashion of a preacher developing a text.

One cannot deny categorically that chs. 56–66 contain no material from the author of chs. 40–55. Their literary quality is high, but uneven; at least it is not always on the same level as chs. 40–55. It is likely, then, that they are the work of followers of the prophet. The close relationship suggests a date not far from that of the prophet, though the temporal locus of each poem is not always easy to determine. Karl Elliger argues for the unity of chs. 56–66, which he calls Third Isaiah,[15] but his stylistic analysis points to such a degree of diversity that unity of authorship cannot be proved. The older school of critics, following Duhm, have assigned these poems to the middle of the fifth century. They believe that the conditions reflected in them belong to the time of Ezra and Nehemiah, and they think of the apostates in terms of the Samaritan schismatics. There is no convincing proof for this position, however. The similarities to chs. 40–55 in thought and style, and indeed the conditions which lie in the background, argue for an earlier period.

III. Second Isaiah

A. Unity.—The German poet Friedrich Rückert, in his work on the Hebrew prophets,[16] articulated the poems of Isa. 40–66 into three divisions of nine chapters each, and he called attention to the similarity of the rubrics which mark each section (48:22; 57:21; 66:24). The

division between chs. 40–48 and chs. 49–55 has been observed by nearly all commentators. W. H. A. Kosters[17] and T.K. Cheyne[18] denied chs. 49–55 to the writer of chs. 40–48, but their view has not been generally followed. The absence of any reference to Cyrus and of many of the themes of chs. 40–48 in the later chapters can be explained by the movement of the poems and the development in the precise situation in which the poet was writing. The continuity in style and thought far outweighs the differences. Elliger, following suggestions by Ernst Sellin, found evidence for the presence of Third Isaiah material in substantial sections of chs. 40–55 (e.g., the servant passages, 42:1-4; 49:1-6; 50:4-9; 52:13–53:12); also 42:19-23; 45:9-10; 46:12-13; 47:1-15; 48:8b-10, 16b-19; 49:22-26; 50:1-3; 51:4-5, 10b, 12-14; 52:3; 54:1–55:13), but this view has not commended itself to other scholars.

The unity of chs. 40–55 has been attacked in a somewhat different way by the majority of form critics (*Gattungskritiker*). These scholars have properly attempted to understand the poems in the light of literary type and form. The result of this investigation has been to resolve the materials into a large number of small units, many of them not more than a verse or two in length. Thus Hugo Gressmann finds forty-nine such independent units,[19] Ludwig Köhler, seventy,[20] Mowinckel, forty-one (excluding the servant songs),[21] Paul Volz, fifty (excluding the servant songs),[22] Joachim Begrich, seventy.[23] According to some of these scholars and many others, the poems do not stand in any perceptibly logical relationship to one another, and are therefore by no means to be interpreted in the light of each other. Each unit is said to exist independently by itself. In a detailed and thorough study Mowinckel has attempted to show that the order is to be determined on the external principle of the use of catchwords (*Stichworte*).[24] Aside from the inherent unlikelihood of an ordering of material in such a purely mechanical way, the

[15] *Die Einheit des Tritojesaja* (Stuttgart: W. Kohlhammer, 1928). W. S. McCullough ("A Re-examination of Isaiah 56–66," *Journal of Biblical Literature*, LXVII [1948], 27-36) holds a similar view, dating the work from 587 to 562 B.C.

[16] *Hebräische Propheten* (Leipzig: Weidmann, 1831).

[17] "Deutero- en Trito-Jesaja," *Theologisch Tijdschrift*, XXX (1896), 577-623.

[18] *The Book of the Prophet Isaiah* (Leipzig: J. C. Hinrichs, 1899; "Sacred Books of the Old Testament").

[19] "Die literarische Analyse Deuterojesajas," *Zeitschrift für die alttestamentliche Wissenschaft*, XXXIV (1914), 254-97.

[20] *Deuterojesaja (Jesaja 40–55) stilkritisch untersucht* (Giessen: A. Töpelmann, 1923), pp. 4-56.

[21] "Die Komposition des deuterojesajanischen Buches," *Zeitschrift für die alttestamentliche Wissenschaft*, XLIX (1931), 87-112, 242-60.

[22] *Jesaia II* (Leipzig: A. Deichert, 1932; "Kommentar zum Alten Testament").

[23] *Studien zu Deuterojesaja* (Stuttgart: W. Kohlhammer, 1938; "Beiträge zur Wissenschaft vom Alten und Neuen Testament"), p. 5.

[24] *Loc. cit.*

form and style of the poems themselves, and the way these words are repeated for stylistic reasons, argue strongly against this theory.

That the ancient Hebrew writers employed literary types and forms has been demonstrated by the important work of Hermann Gunkel and his followers. But the process of classification has been carried to such lengths as to raise serious doubts as to its validity. The sharp criticism of this method by Sidney Smith is not infrequently well deserved.[25] It is absurd to detect a new literary type in every instance that a new thought motif occurs. The literary problem of chs. 40–66 must be approached from the point of view of the literary revolution which took place in Israel and perhaps in the Near East as a whole toward the end of the seventh century. This movement is perceptible in such works as Deuteronomy, Jeremiah, Ezekiel, and Second Isaiah. Here we often have a fusion of literary types, a combination of several forms to make a whole. The units are often more extensive than has been generally supposed. What are construed as independent poems are in reality strophes or subordinate units in a longer poem. This literary situation has been understood by many of the form critics. It has been well stated by Hugo Gressmann in a notable passage.

If Deutero-Isaiah is to be assigned a place in the literary history of Israelite prophecy, it may be said . . . that the dissolution of the prophetic types begins with him. The fixed forms that had prevailed till then break up. While the types of speech which had been employed by the prophets before the exile are mostly quite sharply distinguished from one another, exact separation is often impossible in the case of Deutero-Isaiah; the supplementary reflections, with which the oracles are surrounded, have grown luxuriantly over everything, so that the lines of division between an utterance of God and an utterance of the prophet cannot always be clearly recognized.[26]

When the form and structure of the poems have been properly understood, and the subordinate units of strophes or stanzas seen in their relation to each other, it becomes easier to recognize the continuity of the poems—the way they follow one another from beginning to end. This is perhaps the reason why the older critics, such as Karl Budde, were quick to see the movement of the whole series. To be sure, we cannot expect to find the kind of continuity we see in Western literature, or even in such a book as Job, for again and again it will appear that verses and strophes break in without any apparent relation to the context. But when we perceive the dominant themes the progress of thought becomes more intelligible. In the first place, the relation of the initial poem (40:1-11) to the final poem (55:1-13) is unmistakable. The announcement of Yahweh's coming, the imminent return to Zion, the word of the Lord which stands forever, the transformation of nature, the relation of announcement to fulfillment, the motif of universality, and the divine reconciliation are among the central features which relate beginning and end, the focuses to which the prophet is sensitive in the composition of all his poems.

Again, despite the independence of the various poems and the difference in mood and occasion that may inspire them, there is a remarkable persistence of major motifs all the way through. Conspicuous among these is the pervasive concern with the nations, the promise of the return, the glorification of Yahweh, the redemption of Israel, the covenant of the peoples, the despair of Israel, and the servant of the Lord. The imagery of the poems reinforces the argument drawn from their thought. Most notable here are *the arm of the Lord,* the redemptive instrument of his great deliverance; *the way of the Lord,* on which the exiles will return; and the *mountains,* which characterize so much of the eschatological imagery. The intensity of the prophet's theocentricity continues from first to last, and this intensity is matched by a unique lyrical quality which, despite its vivid variety, bears witness to the fundamental unity of the whole series. The presence of the same literary forms—e.g., the use of the hymnic style, the oracles of salvation, the scenes of judgment—is noteworthy; so also the conspicuous absence of other forms.

Even more important is the continuity of the prophet's thought. The poems open with the great announcement in the heavenly council that God is about to appear. He will come on the great highway as conqueror and victor over Israel's enemies, as king to usher in his kingdom, as judge to adjudicate the inequities of the past, as shepherd to comfort and heal. The poem on the decisive event of the divine advent is followed by another on God as creator, and thus the major framework of the prophetic "drama" is established. But God's creative work is guarantee for his effectual work in history. Thus in the following poem the nations are called to an encounter with the Lord of history. The failure of the nations to meet the questions which God puts to them prompts him to turn to Israel, his chosen and called servant, in whom he has revealed himself from the beginning in Abraham, his friend. Israel is called to a high

[25] *Isaiah XL-LV,* pp. 1-23, 86-114.

[26] "Die literarische Analyse Deuterojesajas," p. 295. The passage is quoted at length in Sidney Smith, *op. cit.,* p. 9.

destiny, but she is blind and deaf. The ills that have befallen her are the consequence of this fatal blindness. Yet Yahweh is gracious and promises her his imminent redemption. The motif of redemption grows ever more clear until Cyrus is named and his great mission in the world is described in deeply moving language (44:24–45:13). Then follows the imminent conquest of Babylon. The servant of the Lord (49:1 ff.) enters the scene, calling upon the nations to hear (cf. 41:1 ff.; 42:1-4). These words are spoken *de profundis,* but the promise of redemption is renewed. The poignant confession of the servant follows (50:4-9), here in a more tragic cry of suffering, but the subsequent poem rises to the greatest heights of exultation as the coming of the king is envisioned and the cry breaks forth, "Yahweh has become king!" Yahweh then promises the exaltation of the servant (52:13-15), in response to which the nations make their confessional lament (53:1-9). Yahweh's vindication of the servant is repeated (53:10-12). The next poem (54:1-17) is a triumphant cry of joy, quite in keeping with the major context, and the final poem brings the collection to a superb climax in which numerous motifs are gathered into a singular unity.

B. Poetic Form, Structure, and Style.—In ancient Israel language possessed a primitive vitality that is relatively alien to the modern Western mind. The relation between sound and meaning was grasped with an immediacy and directness that are best understood by children and poets. The elemental situations in which words are spoken and heard are intuitively recognized. Exclamations, commands, direct address, dialogue, question and answer, the use of names, and climax—all reflect the functions which words perform in life. Much of the Old Testament has its origin in words that are spoken, rather than in written literature. Men participate in them and surrender themselves to them in an interior and responsible way. Words are alive. They have within them the power and vitality of the speaker, and they are transmitted to those who hear with ears attuned to their living sources. They tend to arrange themselves in all kinds of patterns. They succeed one another in series and thus produce a climactic effect. They balance each other in many different ways, whether as words or clauses or more extended units, and give rise to what is known as parallelism. They are repeated again and again in fresh contexts to give them emphasis and force. This attitude toward language was congenial to the production of poetic expression.

1. Oral or Written?—The poems of Second Isaiah exhibit numerous signs of literary craftsmanship; they are so elaborate in their composition and in the detail of technical devices that they must have been written rather than spoken. This does not mean that the poet had no place in the life of the people. Quite the contrary. Nor may we suppose that his work was designed primarily to be read, although this possibility must not be excluded. He may have delivered his poems to his fellow exiles, or he may have sent them to various groups among the exiles.

2. Poet and Prophet.—Poet and prophet meet in Second Isaiah. It is difficult to say whether he is more the one than the other; the distinction would not have occurred to him. He is both poet and prophet, and both in a pre-eminent degree. But he is so much the poet, so much a master in the art of poetic composition, that one can never be unaware of his literary genius. He is the proclaimer of the Word of God as the other prophets were. But he transfigures the prophetic forms into great artistic compositions. The elevation and urgency of his prophetic mood are matched by forms of expression commensurate with the thoughts which surged through his soul. He has been frequently accused of exaggeration and excess. But it must be remembered that he writes as an Oriental. Moreover, the significance of the events he proclaims justifies his use of superlatives. For his thought is always of God and of his imminent coming in world history, and his remarkable capacity for participation in the event that had been disclosed to him in the heavenly councils taxed all his powers of thought and feeling.

3. Lyrical Character.—The intensity of the prophet's thought and feeling is expressed in many ways. He lifts his voice in exulting triumph as he sees the approach of Israel's conquering Lord. He breaks into ecstatic hymns again and again as the event takes place before his enraptured eyes (cf. 42:10-13; 44:23; 45:8; 49:13). The theme of redemption almost invariably stirs him to songs of praise. He who calls upon Israel to sing is himself Israel's most exultant singer (52:7-12; 54:1-10). The contemplation of creation, as of redemption, kindles in him the impulse to praise and glorify God. When he lowers his eyes from his vision to the actual conditions among his people, he is stirred to words of vehement judgment. Yet his compassion creates some of the most moving lines in the whole of scripture (43:1-4; 44:21-22; 48:18-19; 49:14-16; 54:6-8). In the confessions of 50:4-9 and 53:1-9 he portrays a figure of inexpressible poignancy. He who sings the hymn of redemption, calling upon heavens and earth, the mountains and the deserts, to join in the great chorus, knows the depths of grief and alienation. Above all, his lyrical gifts are always undergirded by a profundity of religious faith and a self-identification with his time which give them the power they have.

4. Parallelism.—Second Isaiah uses poetic parallelism with great versatility. He employs many different forms, some of them quite elaborate.

A voice says, "Cry!"
And I said, "What shall I cry?"
All flesh is grass,
and all its beauty is like the flower of the field.
The grass withers, the flower fades,
when the breath of the Lord blows upon it;
surely the people is grass.
The grass withers, the flower fades;
but the word of our God will stand for ever (40:
6-8).

The poet is a master of form, but he is never bound to any single type.

Hear, you deaf;
and look, you blind, that you may see!
Who is blind but my servant,
or deaf as my messenger whom I send?
Who is blind as my dedicated one,
or blind as the servant of the Lord? (42:18-19.)

The parallelism of members, the variety of grammatical constructions, the repetitions, the climax, the rhetorical devices of exclamation and question—all serve to produce a superb effect upon the reader.

5. Meter.—In Second Isaiah the meter is seldom regular throughout a single poem. Many poems are, to be sure, dominated by the 3+3 or the 3+2, but even within these categories there is variety in the number of words for a single accent. In the opening poem (40:1-11) the first two lines are clearly 3+2, the next two 3+3, the following two 2+2 (or 4+4?). Vs. 6 is 3+3, vs. 7, 2+2+3. The mocking song over Babylon (47:1-15) is a fine example of the *qînāh* or lamentation meter (3+2). The poet has a special fondness for the tristich (e.g., 40:12cde, 15; 43:7; 44:24cde; 51:6cde, 11cde).[27]

6. Assonance.—The poetry of the prophet gains by being read aloud, for the sound effects of the successive words are often striking and moving. The best example of assonance is found in the confession of the nations in 53:1-9, where the u sound in the lament is stirring (e.g., vss. 4-6). The following classification of assonance in the poems illustrates a few of the ways sounds are employed:

a. Onomatopoeia (40:1a; 42:14cd; 47:2a, 14ab; 53:4-6)

b. Paronomasia (40:11; 41:5a; 43:24a; 45:9b; 53:10b; 54:6ab)

c. Alliteration (40:6; 47:1)

d. Approximations to rhyme (41:11-13; 49:10cd; 53:6ab)

e. Dominance of a single sound throughout a line (40:2cd; 54:1)

f. Two successive words with similar sounds (40:12ab; 41:1ab, 17a; 45:9c, 20e; 50:4e; 54:8a)

g. Lines beginning and ending with the same sound (49:13ab; 53:6ab)

7. Dramatic Style.—The religion of Israel was uniquely fitted to body itself forth in highly dramatic forms. Its preoccupation with God's action in history, with the persistence of his divine will and purpose, with the eventfulness of revelation, with the hostile forces which were in conflict with him, and with the dramatis personae who were involved in this conflict—all served to produce dramatic narratives and dramatic prophetic discourses. Second Isaiah brings this dramatic quality of biblical faith to a great culmination. He portrays vividly dramatic scenes, such as the council in heaven (40:1-11), the trial of the nations (41:1–42:4) and numerous other trial scenes (43:8-13, 26; 44:7; 45:20-24; 48:15-16; 50:8-9), the exodus of Babylon's gods (46:1-13), the dethronement of imperial Babylon to serfdom (47:1-15), the coming of Yahweh as king (52:7-10).

The dramatic style of the poems is well illustrated by the use of rhetorical devices of many kinds. A good example is the use of the word "behold" (הִנֵּה or הֵן). At the dramatic climax of the introductory poem on the coming of the Lord, God is presented upon the stage of world history with a threefold "behold" (40:9-10); the servant is introduced in a crucial context in a similar fashion (42:1), and again at the beginning of the great climactic poem of 52:13–53:12. The nations first appear with the use of this word (40:15). Often the word introduces judgments, sometimes in trial scenes (41:11, 15, 24, 29), at other times as climaxes (47:14; 51:22c-23). Most interesing of all is the remarkable use of the word in ch. 50, where it serves to outline the structure of the poem and gives it its moving effects (vss. 1e, 2e, 9a, 9b, 11). Notably, too, it introduces the announcement of the eschatological new events (42:9; 49:12-13, 22-23; 51:22c-23; 54:11c-15, 16-17; 55:4-5).

We stand in these poems on the verge of an eschatological drama in which creation, history, and redemption constitute the central themes. Each of these great themes is presented in dramatic ways. God is the central figure from beginning to end; Israel's life and destiny are dynamically involved in the events by which he manifests himself;[28] crucial episodes such as

---

[27] For further discussion see Torrey, *Second Isaiah*, pp. 151-72.

[28] See the discussion on the servant of the Lord, pp. 406-14.

the floodwaters of the time of Noah, the call of Abraham, the exodus from Egypt, the desert wandering, the covenant with David, are recalled and related to the vast pattern of the divine purpose. The purpose of God is a dominant motif in the poems, and they all lie under the tensions of its imminent fulfillment. Cyrus, the Persian king, plays a role of great importance, and not only are his conquests portrayed in very dramatic forms, but Yahweh's choice of Cyrus as his instrument becomes a dramatic issue in which Israel finds her uniqueness imperiled. The emphasis upon Israel's call and election, upon her mission in the world, upon her tasks as witness and servant, upon her blindness and deafness, upon judgment and supervening grace—indeed, the theology of Second Isaiah is from beginning to end a dramatic theology. It is worth noting, too, that this dramatic style pervades every poem, the so-called servant songs (42:1-4; 49:1-6; 50:4-9; 52:13–53:12) as well as the others. Yet nowhere do we have anything approximating a drama; all the materials are here except the architectonics of the drama itself. The scope of the poet's perspective, the literary forms and types, the imminence of a great divine event, decisive and redemptive, make these poems the supreme achievement of the Hebrew mind in history.

8. Stylistic Characteristics. a) Imagery.—The most revealing feature of the poet's style is his use of imagery. The predilection of Oriental poetry for visualizing imagery is present in an unusual degree. The distinction between the literal and figurative meaning of a symbol is not biblical. The symbolic meaning participates in the figure itself. God is pictured as a conqueror, a man of war prepared to enter the battle (42:13), as a woman in travail panting in her birth pangs (43:14), as the destroyer laying waste mountains and hills and all fertility (43:15), as the leader of the blind (43:16), as the king ushering in his kingdom (42:10; 52:7), as the judge adjudicating the inequities of the past (40:10; 41:1–42:4; 43:8-13; 48:14-16), as the husband (54:5) and father of Israel (50:1). He is the creator and fashioner of the universe and of Israel (40:22, 28; 43:1), as he is her covenant Lord and Redeemer and Holy One. But these lofty names are constantly developed in elaborate imagery. Jerusalem and Zion are similarly portrayed in a great variety of images: as Yahweh's bride (49:18; 54:5; cf. 62:5), barren (54:1) and forsaken (54:6-7) though not divorced (50:1), as blessed with many children (51:1-3), as a mother (49:17, 22-23; 51:18-20) bereft of her sons (49:20-21; 51:20), and now granted new sons more than before (49:20-21; cf. 60:4-5). Israel is blind and deaf (42:16, 18-20), intoxicated from the heavy draught of wine

(51:17-18, 21-22), refined and tested in the furnace of affliction (48:10). She is God's chosen one, his called one, his witness, his son, fashioned and called from the womb, the servant of the Lord. The eschatological pictures are extremely powerful. Nature is transformed at the divine advent. The hills and mountains participate in the event; the forests and trees lose their ancient silence, heavens and earth join in the universal witness. Similes, metaphors, apostrophes and personifications, hyperbole—all appear in great profusion. We see Yahweh seated high above the firmament, looking down upon his creatures far below (40:22),[29] the glorious spectacle of the heralds announcing his coming to Zion (52:7-10), Babylon as the slave girl grinding at the mill (47:1-2).

The theology of Second Isaiah is written in a highly lyrical mood; it is set forth in the form of a vast dramatic spectacle and numerous dramatic episodes; it is articulated in many pictures and comparisons.

b) Rhetorical Devices.—Characteristic again of the poet's Oriental mentality is his remarkable use of rhetorical devices. He uses strong contrasts, often in figurative form. Thus the worm Israel becomes Yahweh's threshing sledge. The queen of empire is degraded to grind at the mill. The peoples are like a drop in the bucket before God. Abraham was but one, yet God made of him a mighty nation; from the quarry of Sarah and Abraham, Israel grew to be a people. Even more notable is the use of the interrogative (some poems like 40:12-31 and 50:1-11 are questions almost throughout). There is an abundance of interrogative pronouns, like "who" (40:12, 13, 14, 18, 25, 26; 41:2-4, 26; 42:19 [twice], 23, 24; 43:9; 45:21; 48:14; 49:21; 50:8 [twice], 9; 51:12-19 [twice], 53:1, 8), or "what" (40:18; 45:9, 10 [twice]), or interrogative adverbs like "why" (40:27; 55:2) and "where" (40:13, 15). Often the questions appear in extended series, sometimes in triadic form (see below), sometimes as brief queries. These questions often provide an essential key to an understanding of the formal construction of many of the poems. The use of questions is also part of the dialogic style which characterizes our poet to an extraordinary degree. Here again we have an instance of how Second Isaiah apprehends a central characteristic of Hebraic mentality. He appropriates it for his own purposes in the proclamation of his eschatological word, employs it with intensity of passion, transforms it into all kinds of patterns, and gives it a deeply inward character (e.g., as

[29] Cf. the representation in Ezek. 1, where Yahweh sits enthroned above the firmament, also the Sippara stone and especially the Etana myth, where Etana rises to such heights that the earth below looks like a garden.

in the servant passages, but also elsewhere as in 49:14; etc.). Yahweh's questions again and again strike the very heart of the poem. Furthermore, notice must be taken of the poet's fondness for quotations. These are used in a great variety of ways; most notably they conclude strophes or poems. Sometimes they are only a single word (40:6a; 41:26b; 42:22e; 43:6a, 6b, 9-10; 44:5c), more often a brief clause (40:6b, 9g; 41:13cd; 42:17d; 44:5a, 26c, 26de, 27ab, 28ab; 45:9c, 9d, 10a, 10b, 19d, 24ab; 47:7a, 10b, 10e; 49:3, 4, 6; 51:16d); sometimes they contain two or three lines (40:27cd; 47:8def). On the other hand, they not infrequently become developed utterances. It is in these quotations that the dialogic style becomes most apparent. One more feature of the poet's rhetorical style deserves special consideration. It is his lavish use of imperatives. Here, too, we find certain poems controlled by these commands (e.g., 40:1-11). It is significant that the verb "call" or "proclaim" is employed more than thirty times in the collection. Indeed, it is the proclaiming style of the poetry which gives it much of its urgency, passion, and immediacy.

A stylistic feature which has been much misunderstood, but one of first importance for an understanding and appreciation of the poems, is the poet's use of repetition. This stylistic habit is characteristic of much of the Old Testament, and careful scrutiny will show that it is often employed as a literary device. The following list is not complete, but will illustrate the great variety of usages, a variety that is paralleled by the way questions, brief quotations, and imperatives are used.

1. Repetition of single words: "comfort, comfort" (40:1); "behold, behold them" (41:27); "I, I" (43:11, 25; 48:15); "for my own sake, for my own sake" (48:11); "awake, awake" (51:9; 52:1); "rouse yourself, rouse yourself" (51:17); "depart, depart" (52:11). Cf. also 57:6, 14, 19; 62:10; 65:1.

2. Repetition of particles, etc., in immediate context: "that," Hebrew *ki* (40:2cde [thrice]); "behold" (40:9g, 10a, 10c); "who, . . . who, . . . whom" (40:12-14); "scarcely" (40:24); "when," Hebrew *ki* (43:2-3); "no" or "none" (43:11-12; 51:1c, 2a, 9c, 10a); "for" (54:4-5); etc.

3. Repetition of single words or phrases in immediate context: "evangelist Zion, . . . evangelist Jerusalem" (40:9); "his arm, . . . his arms" (40:10-11); "lift up your voice . . . lift it up" (40:9); "I will carry" (46:4b, 4d); "sit in the dust, . . . sit on the ground" (47:1); "shall come to you . . . shall come upon you" (47:9); "perhaps" (47:12); "All we . . . of us all" (53:6);

"he opened not his mouth" (53:7); "to the peoples, . . . for the peoples" (55:4).

4. Repetition of several different words in immediate context: 40:13-14, 28-31; 46:3-4; 48:3-5, 6-8.

5. Repetition of words at the beginning of lines: "behold" (40:15); use of *he*-interrogative (40:21-23); "not" (43:22-24b); cf. 44:26c-28c; 51:2c-3b; 55:8-10b.

6. Threefold repetition of a single word within a strophe: "strengthen" (41:6-7); "declare" (41:25-27); "justice" (42:1-4; and many others.

7. Repetitions in chiastic arrangement: 43:19d, 20d, 25ab, 27; 44:1a, 2c; 46:1a, 2a; 51:6fg, 8cd.

8. Repetitions at the beginnings of successive or neighboring strophes: "A voice . . ." (40:3, 6); "Who has . . ." (40:12, 13); "To whom . . ." (40:18, 25); "Have you not known?" (40:21, 28); "Hearken to me" (51:1, 4, 7); cf. also 51:9, 17; 52:1.

9. Repetition of key words throughout a poem: "cry" or "proclaim" (40:1-11); "fear . . . strengthen . . . help" (41:5-16); "sit" and "come" (47:1-15).

10. Repetition of crucial clauses, etc.: "Fear not" (41:10, 13, 14; 43:1, 5; 44:2; 54:4); "I am the first, and I am the last" (41:4; 44:6; 48:12; cf. 43:10); "I am the LORD, and there is no other" (45:5, 6, 18, 22; 46:9); "Redeemer and Holy One" (41:14; 43:14; 48:17; 49:7; 54:5).

11. Repetition of major motifs throughout the collection: the arm of Yahweh; the way of Yahweh; Yahweh, creator of heaven and earth; the creator of Israel; Yahweh as Redeemer, as Holy One, as Holy One and Redeemer; the transformation of nature, the return of Yahweh to Zion, etc.

c) Literary Types and Forms.—There is a disposition in some quarters to ignore completely the presence of literary types, while in other quarters there is a tendency to exaggerate and overrefine them. In a number of instances they are incorporated into the poems in a rather fluid fashion, and the literary unit simply becomes a poem of various motifs and forms. But in others they are clearly present. Chief among these perhaps is the judicial proceeding (41:1–42:4; 43:8-13; 45:20-24; 48:15-16; 50:8-9). Joachim Begrich discovers no fewer than twenty-four examples of what he calls the oracle of salvation (*priesterliche Heilsorakel*),[30] a form also found in the Psalms. In the great

[30] *Studien zu Deuterojesaja*, pp. 6-19. Begrich mentions the following: 41:8-13, 14-16, 17-20; 42:14-17; 43:1-7, 16-21; 44:1-5; 45:1-7, 14-17; 46:3-4, 12-13; 48:17-19; 49:7, 8-12 (Hebrew 13), 14-21, 22-23, 24-26; 51:6-8, 12-16; 54:4-6, 7-10, 11-12 and 13b, 14a and 13a-17; 55:8-13.

majority of instances the poet's style may have been influenced by this liturgical form, for the liturgical style does seem to be present. But it is impossible to conceive all of these as separate literary units. Ch. 47 provides a fine example of the Hebrew mocking song. In 40:9-11 and 52:7-10 the style is clearly that of the herald's message.[31] The interpolated passage (44:9-20) is obviously a satire. Notable also is the presence of the confession as in 50:4-9; 53:1-9; and elsewhere.

Willy Stärk was much impressed by the hymnic style of the poet, and considered the hymn as the dominant literary influence.[32] There is much to be said for this, for the poet does use the characteristic forms of this type, especially in his introductions, following the oracular formula, "Thus saith the Lord," or the covenant asseveration, "I am Yahweh." For striking examples of the hymn style see 40:12-26, 27-31; 44:23; 48:20-21; 49:13, and especially the eschatological hymn of 42:10-13 on the order of the enthronement hymn (cf. Pss. 47; 93; 96–99). The invective and threat are almost absent, a striking contrast to the prophet's literary predecessors. For possible examples of the former see 42:18-25; 43:22-24; 45:9-13. The invective does not have the sharpness of the pre-exilic prophets and, more important, it occurs in a context in which it is followed by an assurance of grace rather than by the customary threat (Drohrede). Motifs of the lament are certainly present in 49:14-21 and 53:1-9, but here too it is clearly subordinate to promise, assurance, and exhortation.[33]

Another stylistic feature—the theophany—pervades many of the poems. One may observe, for example, the frequent use of the expression "I am Yahweh," the negative monition "Fear not," and above all, the unique word of disclosure (the *hieros logos*), which seems to be present in not a few momentous eschatological contexts. Parallels to the old theophanies (e.g., Jacob's at Bethel in Gen. 35:9-15) are never present in a pure form, not even in 40:1-11.

d) Triads.—Another indication of the rhetorical style of Second Isaiah is the copious use of words, phrases, sentences, and larger units in triadic form. The purpose of this device is to bring the thought to a climax or to give special emphasis to the culminating member. The

[31] Köhler, *Deuterojesaja*, pp. 102-9, presents a thorough analysis of this form and gives many examples of it from Second Isaiah. Here too it is possible that this style has influenced the writer, but that these examples represent fixed literary types seems unlikely. The composition is much more fluid and mixed.

[32] Willy Stark, *Lyrik* (Göttingen: Vandenhoeck & Ruprecht, 1911; "Die Schriften des Alten Testaments"), pp. 34 ff.

[33] See Begrich's fruitful discussion, *op. cit.*, pp. 12-13.

simplest form of this phenomenon is the repetition of a single particle such as "for" (40:2; 55:8-9), or "behold" (40:9-10), or the negative interrogative (40:21). See also 41:26cd; 43:2-3; 46:11cd; 48:8; 44:5; 49:12. In many instances key words are repeated three times, and it will be found that almost invariably the third word carries the climax (e.g., 41:21-23; 41:5-7; 42:1-4). There are a large number of instances where a single line contains a succession of three brief units. Sometimes these appear in the great Yahweh asseverations as in 47:3: "Our Redeemer, Yahweh of hosts is his name, the Holy One of Israel" (cf. 43:3ab, 15; 44:6 et passim). Similar are the not infrequent self-asseverations in the first person: "I am he; I am the first, I also am the last" (48:12cd; cf. 46:4, 11). Note also the triad within the larger complex of 42:2-4:

> He will not cry or lift up his voice,
>   or make it heard in the street.

For other examples of this type cf. 42:23-24b, 24cde; 43:1de; 43:4ab, 9ef, 10cd, 12a; 45:20, 21; 48:3; 51:5abc, 6cde; 52:7cde. These triads are used with a high degree of versatility and artistry. Almost as frequent, however, are the stichs or half lines which appear in threes. Note the following:

> Comfort, comfort my people
>   says your God.
> Speak tenderly to Jerusalem,
>   and cry to her (40:1-2b)

> that her warfare is ended,
>   that her iniquity is pardoned,
>   that she has received from the Lord's hand
>   double for all her sins (40:2cdef)

> "Behold your God!"
> Behold, the Lord God comes with might,
>   and his arm rules for him;
> behold, his reward is with him,
>   and his recompense before him (40:9g-10)

> This one [זה] will say, "I am the Lord's,"
>   another [וזה] will call himself by the name of Jacob,
>   and another [וזה] will write on his hand, "The Lord's"
>   and surname himself by the name of Israel (44:5).

Cf. also 54:4, 11; 52:7cde; 49:13abc. Note the triadic lines. These often appear in the participial hymnic style; at other times they are a part of the divine self-asseverations:

> For I am God, and there is no other;
>   I am God, and there is none like me,
> declaring the end from the beginning
>   and from ancient times things not yet done,

saying, "My counsel shall stand,
and I will accomplish all my purpose,"
calling a bird of prey from the east,
the man of my counsel from a far country (46:9b-11b).

The following passages provide further examples: 44:24bcd, 25a-26b, 26c-28b; 45:1c-2b; 47:11. Many strophes appear in triadic arrangement, as the literary analyses of the Exegesis clearly demonstrate. The following examples will suffice at this point: 40:1-11, 12-17; 42:5-17; 43:1-7, 8-13; 44:24–45:13; 53:1-9. Finally the question must be raised whether this triadic organization may extend even farther. It is obvious that some of the poems seem to fall in groups. If so, the first three poems (40:1-11, 12-31; 41:1–42:4) form an admirable introductory eschatological trilogy.

9. Structural Patterns.—A thorough discussion of the literary composition of the poems of Second Isaiah would require a detailed consideration of the relationship of words in the stich, the relation of various stichs to each other, the important matter of word order, word series (nominal and verbal), variation in diction, the different meanings the same word may have in the same context, etc. The Exegesis will present occasional discussions of this sort, but they are necessarily brief and incomplete. What is attempted here is an examination of strophic composition and then a study of the poems as literary units.

a) Preliminary Observations.—The poems are developed literary compositions. Most of them are longer than pre-exilic prophetic oracles. The current atomization of the poems into fragments and pieces has been one of the major difficulties in apprehending the true significance of the prophet in the history of Israel's thought. One of the effects of the decline and fall of Assyria and the social disintegration which followed was the transformation of literary form and expression.

The composition of the poems shows great variety. We have noticed that the poet uses many different literary types, that he employs them in a very free and creative fashion, and that the forms correspond to the theology which he seeks to set forth. The general eschatological situation which lies within and behind the thought is no doubt partly responsible for the mood of the poet and his method of writing. Like his predecessors he employs the oracular formula, "Thus says the LORD," but he adds to it extended participial phrases drawn from the hymn, which in turn are expressed in a great variety of ways. So, too, he uses the revelatory words "I am Yahweh," but these are usually included in larger patterns, some of them participles, some relative clauses, and some elaborate appositions. These contexts are especially important because they contain the great titles and names associated with God. Indeed, it is not too much to say that they contain the very essence and substance of the prophet's view of God. A list of such terms would be a theology *in parvo.*

As in Hebrew poetry generally, the development of the poems is episodic rather than rational, dramatic rather than expository, lyrical and poetic rather than prosaic. The strophes usually frame the episode. It is therefore nearly always quite easy to recognize the extent and form of this literary unit.

b) Strophes.—Second Isaiah uses a large number of devices to begin and end his strophes. Notable among these, of course, is the emphatic personal pronoun ("I," "thou," etc.), the oracular formula, exclamations like "Behold," imperatives like the call to hear, transitional devices like "But now," rhetorical questions, impressive vocatives like "O afflicted one, storm-tossed, and not comforted" (54:11), particles like "for" (*kî*), and shifts in speaker or those addressed. Perhaps the most common and in many ways the most impressive among these is the use of the imperative.

Observe, for example, the beginning of the second half of the poem in 42:18–43:7, a composition of most extraordinary craftsmanship (see below). The construction scarcely calls for comment. The transitional words "But now" (43:1) mark the passage from invective to oracle of salvation and introduce the oracular formula, which is expanded by two participial phrases. Then appears the important monition "Fear

But now thus says the LORD   your creator, O Jacob,
                               your fashioner, O Israel:
Fear not for [*kî*]   I have redeemed you,
                               I have called you by name,
                               You are mine.
When [*kî*] you pass through the waters I will be with you;
    and through the rivers they shall not overwhelm you;
When [*kî*] you walk through fire you shall not be burned,
    and the flame shall not consume you.
For [*kî*] I am Yahweh your God, the Holy One of Israel, your Savior.

not" in the style of the theophany. This is followed by the sacred disclosure, the *hieros logos*, containing (*a*) the three brief and momentous assurances, and (*b*) the two finely developed lines each opening with the usual *kî* (characteristic of contexts of this kind throughout the Old Testament). The third *kî* has the causal meaning here and introduces the great divine self-asseveration with the covenant formula, "I am Yahweh," expanded by two great titles, similar to the expansion of the oracular formula at the beginning.

The next example is chosen chiefly for its brevity, but also because it is one of the lyrical finales of which the poet is particularly fond. These lyrical outbursts almost invariably appear immediately following disclosures of a supremely fateful nature.

> Sing, O heavens, for the LORD has done it;
>   shout, O depths of the earth;
> break forth into singing, O mountains,
>   O forest, and every tree in it!
> For the LORD has redeemed Jacob,
>   and will be glorified in Israel (44:23).

Here we have a perfect hymn with all the characteristic features of that type. Observe the poet's fondness for imperatives, the impassioned address with its magnificent apostrophes, the intensity of the lyrical mood, and the way the conclusion, introduced by the usual "for," connects with the disclosure with which the previous strophe closes. The accent of the final lines falls superbly on Jacob and Israel. The poet is a master in the art of literary emphasis. There is scarcely a strophe in the whole collection of poems which does not merit literary analysis. The results of such a study will show the infinite variety of strophic composition. Neither Oriental antiquity nor the Bible has anything to match such sheer literary artistry.

c) *Strophic Settings.*—The strophes are linked to one another in a great number of different ways. One of these is by the similarity of the introductions (cf., e.g., 40:3*a*, 6*a*, 9; 40:18, 25; 40:21, 28; 43:14, 16 [cf. also 44:1-2]; 48:12*a*, 14*a*, 16*a*; 51:1*ab*, 4*ab*, 7*ab*; 51:17; 52:1; 52:11). Similarly, conclusions serve to unite the strophes (41:4*cd*, 10*cd*, 13 [cf. "the Holy One of Israel" in 41:16*d*, 20*d*]; 41:24, 29; 48:5*cd*, 7*c*; 51:6*fg*, 8*cd*). These conclusions bring the thought to a climax and therefore help to reveal the center of the poet's thought. The use of the solemn divine asseveration is especially frequent in these contexts. A third way of marking the continuity of the strophes is by the use of central key words. This is the significance of Mowinckel's important study on the subject.

The biblical theological preoccupation with beginning and end is also apparent in the mentality that went to the making of its literature. In many instances the end recapitulates or repeats the major motif of the introduction. The formal devices by which Second Isaiah begins and ends his poems are here illustrated.

Introductions:

1. Oracular formulae ("Thus says the LORD"), usually expanded, sometimes to the extent of a complete strophe (43:14; 44:6; 44:24; 50:1; 51:1).
2. General invocation or appeal to hear, to be silent, etc. (41:1; 42:18; 48:1; 49:1).
3. Exclamations like "Behold" (52:13; 55:1).
4. Interrogatives like "Who" (40:12-13; 53:1; the latter opens the confession of the nations, a device frequent in secondary introductions).
5. Vivid pictures or scenes (46:1; 47:1; 54:1).
6. Imperatives exclusive of invocations (cf. *b* above; 40:1; 51:17; 54:1).
7. Cohortatives (43:8, 9).
8. Addresses. These are usually associated with the imperatives. They are extremely common.

Conclusions:

1. Judgment (41:29; 42:17).
2. Appeal (45:22-24; 46:12-13).
3. Climactic series (44:5).
4. Short quotations (51:16).
5. Summary lines like "These are the things . . ." (43:7; 45:15; 50:11*ef*).
6. Climactic assurances, etc. (45:13, 24-25; 49:25-26; cf. also 40:31; 46:12-13; 52:12).
7. Pathetic motifs (40:11; 53:12).
8. Questions (43:13*c*).
9. Hymns (44:23).

d) *Illustrative Analysis.*—We may now turn to examine the literary composition of a complete poem (44:24–45:13). Many of the phenomena previously mentioned will find concrete illustration. The representation shown on p. 393 does not adhere closely in every case to the stichs of the Hebrew text, but the attempt is made to call attention to formal elements. The translation diverges from the Revised Standard Version only where it is necessary to point out more clearly the actual form of the text.

In the Exegesis the poem will be articulated into three major strophes. It is possible, however, that the foregoing analysis is the true one. In that event, three strophes are followed by a lyrical interlude. The interlude is followed by a twofold invective and a concluding oracle of salvation. The poem contains three major oracular formulas, at least four covenant asseverations ("I am Yahweh"), and a pervasive emphasis upon Yahweh's action in creation (note "Maker of all," and similar references throughout). The triads in the opening strophe are especially noteworthy. Observe how the concluding lines

Thus says Yahweh,

your Redeemer,
and your fashioner from the womb:

I am Yahweh,

maker of all,
stretcher forth of the heavens alone,
establisher of the earth—who was with me?

Frustrating the omens of liars,
Turning wise men back,
Confirming the word of his Servant,
Saying to Jerusalem,
  and to the cities of Judah,

and making fools of diviners;
and their knowledge he makes foolish;
and fulfills the counsel of his messengers;
"She shall be inhabited,"
"They shall be built,
  and their ruins I will raise up."

Saying to the deep,
Saying to Cyrus,

"Be dry, I will dry up your rivers."
"He is my shepherd,
  and he shall fulfill all my purpose." [34]

Thus says Yahweh
  to his anointed, to Cyrus,
to subdue nations before him,
to open doors before him
"I will go before you,
I will break in pieces the doors of bronze,
I will give you the treasures of darkness
that you may know that I am Yahweh,

whose right hand I have grasped,

and the loins of kings I will ungird,
that gates may not be closed:
and I will level the mountains, [35]
and I will cut asunder the bars of iron,
and the hoards in secret places,
who call you by name, the God of Israel.

For the sake of my servant Jacob,
I call you by your name,
I am Yahweh, and there is no other,
I gird you, though you do not know me,
that men may know, from the rising of the sun,
I am Yahweh, and there is no other.

and Israel my chosen,
I surname you, though you do not know me.
besides me there is no God;

and from the west, that there is none besides me;
Fashioner of light,
creator of darkness,
maker of weal,
creator of woe.

I am Yahweh, doer [maker] of all these things.

Shower, O heavens, from above,
let the earth open, that salvation may sprout forth,
I, Yahweh, have created it.

and let the skies rain down righteousness;
and let it cause righteousness to spring forth also;

Woe to him who strives with his Fashioner,
Does the clay say to him who fashions it,

an earthen vessel with the potter!
"What are you making?"
or "Your work has no handles!"

Woe to him who says to a father,
  or to a woman,
Thus says Yahweh,

"What are you begetting?"
"With what are you in travail?"
the Holy One of Israel
and his Fashioner:
or command me concerning the work of my hands?

"Will you question me about my children,
I made the earth,
I, my own hands, stretched out the heavens,
I have aroused him in righteousness,
He shall build my city,
not for price or reward,"

and created man upon it;
and I commanded all their host.
and I will make straight all his ways;
and set my exiles free,
says Yahweh of hosts.

---

recapitulate the opening. The quotations in this poem are very striking and are one of many stylistic phenomena demonstrating its unity. The large number of verbs is generally typical of Second Isaiah's style, but here they appear in great profusion. The theocentricity of the poem is strongly marked throughout, indicated chiefly by the oracular formulas and covenant words. The divine first person is another strik-ing feature. Finally, the motifs drawn from nature and history are superbly combined.

  C. Historical Situation.—Behind the thought and activity of Second Isaiah lie two major lines of historical development: the covenant history of Israel and the history of the ancient Near

[34] The next two lines are a later insertion; see Exeg. ad loc.
[35] See Exeg. ad loc.

East. The former was read in the light of the traditions from Abraham to the fall of the nation and the "events" which led to the emergence of Abraham; the latter was understood chiefly in terms of the sequence of events which had brought about the neo-Babylonian (Chaldean) empire and its growth and also in terms of the forces which contributed to its demise. For the prophet, to be sure, these two histories are dominated by a common sovereignty, but in this he was again influenced by a tradition which had taken radical account of the existence of other nations from the very beginning.

1. The Decline of Assyria.—In the century which comes under our immediate purview, extending from the death of the last of the great Assyrian kings in 631 B.C. to the conquest of Babylon by Cyrus II in 538 B.C., events occurred which were destined to influence profoundly not only the political fate of nations but also their thought and faith. Fresh ideas were stirring in the world. The same perplexities and concerns troubled the thoughts of all men. Breaking of ancient boundaries inspired them to look beyond the limits of their own heritage. "There was an interconnection of peoples, for a parallel to which we must go back to the Amarna age." [36] The old Semitic empires were nearing the end of their great historical career, and the coming of Cyrus had an electrifying effect far beyond the confines of the Fertile Crescent. Many peoples appear upon the stage: Assyrians, Babylonians, Egyptians, Medes, Persians, Greeks, and smaller peoples like the Phoenicians and Israelites. It was an age which quickened men's minds while it filled them with fears and dim forebodings. The records that have come down to us from this age bear eloquent testimony to the corrosive effects of vast historical and social movements: a new sense of humility, a search for world-embracing categories of thought, perplexity concerning the meaning of suffering and adversity, and a profound nostalgia for the past.

The death of Ashurbanipal in 631 B.C. gave the signal for change. Nabopolassar, the ruler of the Chaldean state, threw off the bonds of Assyrian vassalage. The Medes under Cyaxares asserted their independence. Scythian hordes from beyond the Caucasus added to the general melee. Herodotus reports that they invaded Media, "became masters of Asia," and dominated it for twenty-eight years. [37] Egypt was ex-

periencing a recrudescence of her ancient vitality under the energetic Psamtik I (663-609 B.C.) and engaged in the struggle for empire. Phoenicia gave notice that she would no longer take orders from Assyria. In Israel there arose a national movement under Josiah (640-609/8 B.C.), and the able king extended his territory to the north. [38] The Babylonian Chronicle [39] reports the history of the conflict between Assyria and the Medes and Babylonians from 616 to 610 B.C. In 612 B.C. Nineveh fell, an event which the book of Nahum memorialized in a triumphant and stinging cry of jubilation. Pharaoh Necho came to the support of the Assyrian king, who had taken refuge in the ancient city of Harran. On his way he called Josiah king of Judah to account at Megiddo for his bold assertion of independence and nationalistic ambition, and the king was put to death. Finally at ancient Carchemish the opposing forces of the Babylonians and the Egyptians met, and Nebuchadrezzar, the son of Nabopolassar, won a decisive victory.

2. The Neo-Babylonian Empire.—Nebuchadrezzar was the greatest of the Babylonian kings, the most brilliant monarch of his age (604-562 B.C.). The smaller nations soon recognized his rule. In Judah, Jehoiakim—whom Necho had placed on the throne in place of Jehoahaz, the choice of the anti-Egyptian party—made his peace with the Babylonian king, but after three years revolted. Troops were dispatched to quell the revolt. The second revolt culminated in the first captivity of 597 B.C. Jehoiakim died before the city was taken, but his son Jehoiachin, a mere youth, was put in chains and taken as prisoner to Babylon, to remain there for thirty-seven years. [40] Zedekiah succeeded Jehoiachin and ruled for eleven years (597-586 B.C.). In 588 B.C. the kingdom rebelled once more, and in 586 on the ninth of Ab the Babylonians entered the city. Zedekiah, who sought to escape,

[36] S. A. Cook, "The Fall and Rise of Judah," in *The Cambridge Ancient History*, ed. J. B. Bury, S. A. Cook, F. E. Adcock (New York: The Macmillan Co., 1925), III, 394.

[37] *History* I. 104. Despite a strong admixture of legend and exaggeration, Herodotus contains much trustworthy information. See George Cameron, *History of Early Iran* (Chicago: University of Chicago Press, 1936), p. 182.

[38] Albrecht Alt, "Judas Gaue unter Josia," *Palästina Jahrbuch*, XXI (1925), 100-16. Alt believes that Josh. 15 comes from the time of Josiah and reflects the expansion of his domination, a view accepted by Noth, Albright (with qualifications), *et al.* (see Vol. II, p. 542).

[39] Originally published by C. J. Gadd in 1923. Tr. A. Leo Oppenheim in Pritchard, *Ancient Near Eastern Texts*, pp. 303-5.

[40] In 1939 E. F. Weidner ("Jojachin, König von Juda, in Babylonischen Keilschriften," *Mélanges Syriens* [Paris: P. Geuthner, 1939], II, 923-27) published several of the three hundred administrative documents discovered in a vaulted building near the Ishtar gate in Babylon, which refer specifically to Jehoiachin (Yaukin). The texts date from the tenth to the thirty-fifth year of Nebuchadrezzar and register the deliveries of oil for the subsistence of prisoners and those dependent upon the royal household. Jehoiachin is called "king of the land of Yahud" (Judah). His five sons are referred to three times (cf. I Chr. 3:17-18). The implication of the texts is that the king was given considerable freedom (see Pritchard, *op. cit.*, p. 308).

was captured at Jericho and sent to Nebuchad-rezzar at Riblah. His sons were executed, and he was blinded and sent to Babylon where he died shortly afterward. A month after the conquest Jerusalem was completely destroyed, the temple burned, and a part of the population carried into exile. The royal line of David had come to an end, the sanctuary built by Solomon lay in ashes. A long chapter of history came to a close, and a new chapter opened.

The achievements of Nebuchadrezzar's reign are well known.[41] He laid siege to Tyre for thirteen years, engaged in other military undertakings, and showed himself a master builder and architect. He was succeeded by Amel-Marduk (Evil-merodach, 562-560 B.C.), who abandoned his father's antihierarchical policy and followed the priests. Jehoiachin was set free. After two years he was supplanted by Nergal-sharusur (Neriglissar), the son-in-law of Nebuchadrezzar, a man of some affluence it appears (560-556 B.C.). He in turn was followed by Labashi-Marduk, but revolution broke out soon after and Nabonidus was elected to the throne by his fellow conspirators.

Nabonidus reigned from 556 to 538 B.C. When Harran was taken by the combined forces of the Medes and Babylonians in 610 B.C., Nabonidus and his mother were made captive. The mother became the favorite wife of Nebuchadrezzar's harem, and the son acquired important political status as an officer of the king.[42] He appears to have been of priestly lineage, most probably through his grandmother.[43] The king's early years were occupied in war with Syria and with the construction of Ehulhul, the famous sanctuary to Sin at Harran. It was this enterprise that served to alienate him from the Babylonian priesthood, and if Lewy is right, was the cause for his years of residence at Teima, a city in Edom.[44] The "Verse Account of Nabonidus," though badly preserved, seems

clearly to refer to the king's heresy.[45] Nabonidus secured himself in comfort three hundred miles from the capital, while his son Belshazzar acted as regent in his absence. Like Ashurbanipal before him in a historically analogous situation, he showed a great interest in antiquities.

Nabonidus . . . surpassed them all [his predecessors] by his zeal for antiquity, which led him to make excavations in many of the then known temple-sites of Babylonia in order to determine the name and date of the first builders. His scholars were ordered to decipher all early inscriptions which came to light and to date their authors (which they were able to do with relative accuracy though not with absolute precision). Moreover, he endeavored to revive ancient cults and rituals which had long since been abandoned, and he thus incurred the bitter enmity of the priests of Marduk in Babylon, whose established prerogatives were threatened by his innovations.[46]

3. The Persian Conquest.—In the meantime the Near Eastern world was in ferment. Astyages was king of the Median Empire, which had divided the Near Eastern world with Babylonia at the fall of Assyria. Such a division could not last for long, and it was destined sooner or later to bring about conflict between the two powers. Nabonidus and Astyages seem to have been bound by a treaty during the former's

[41] See article "The Old Testament World," Vol. I, p. 268.

[42] See Sidney Smith, *Isaiah XL-LV*, p. 24.

[43] The common view that his mother was a high priestess (Dhorme, Thureau-Dangin, Doughterty, *et al.*) is vigorously attacked by Julius Lewy in a thorough and well-documented discussion ("The Late Assyro-Babylonian Cult of the Moon and Its Culmination at the Time of Nabonidus," *Hebrew Union College Annual*, XIX [1945-46], 405-89). Sidney Smith raises the possibility that his father was the priest of Sin (*op. cit.*, pp. 24, 116, n. 2). See especially B. Landsberger, "Die Basaltstele Nabonids von Eskin Harran" in *Halil-Edhem Hatira Kitabi* (Ankara: Türk Tarih Kurumu Basimevi, 1947-) I, 115-51.

[44] This view is not shared by Sidney Smith, who presents a strong case for the more common position that Nabonidus was motivated by interests of trade and commerce.

[45] See Pritchard, *op. cit.*, pp. 312-15.

(Nabonidus said): "I shall build a temple for him [the moon-god Sin], I shall construct his (holy) seat,
I shall form its (first) brick (for) him, I shall establish firmly its foundation,
. . . .
I shall lead him by his hand and establish him on his seat.
. . . .
I shall omit (all) festivals, I shall order (even) the New Year's Festival to cease!"

Cf. with this representation the repeated words of the Nabonidus Chronicle: "The king did not come to Babylon for the (ceremony of the) month Nisanu; the [image of the] god Nebo did not come to Babylon, the [image of the] god Bel did not go out (of Esagila in procession), the festival of the New Year was omitted" (*ibid.*, p. 306). Quite basic to the whole discussion is the account of the building of the temple to Sin at Harran (*ibid.*, pp. 311-12).

[46] W. F. Albright, *From the Stone Age to Christianity* (2nd ed.; Baltimore: Johns Hopkins Press, 1946), p. 242; cf. R. Campbell Thompson, "The New Babylonian Empire," in *Cambridge Ancient History*, III, 218; Jack Finegan, *Light from the Ancient Past* (Princeton: Princeton University Press, 1946), pp. 42-44. Sidney Smith is doubtful concerning this antiquarian interest of Nabonidus, but the records of his constructions at Harran, Ur, and elsewhere confirm it. It is probable, however, that in many of these undertakings he was motivated by religious interest, above all in Sin (cf. Lewy, *loc. cit*). It is illuminating to observe the various forms which nostalgia for the past assumes in Assyria under Ashurbanipal, Babylonia under Nabonidus, and Israel at the time of its greatest prophet.

early years.[47] But in 553 b.c. Cyrus, the king of the little principality of Elam, challenged the Median power, probably with the support of some of the Medes, if Herodotus is right. At first the struggle went against him, but by 550 b.c. he succeeded in defeating Astyages when the latter's own troops went over to him. In 547 b.c. Cyrus followed his victory over the Medes by a campaign in the north, where he overran the regions formerly held by Astyages. Croesus, the fabled king of Lydia, prepared to engage him in conflict. Cyrus met the enemy in the broad valleys near the ancient Hittite city of Pteria, but no decisive battle was fought. Croesus retired to Sardes where he disbanded his armies. Winter was approaching, and Croesus did not expect Cyrus to press the battle. But Cyrus urged on his troops, and Sardes fell. The Persian Empire now extended from the Persian Gulf to the Halys River. Babylon and Egypt were confederate with Lydia, and it was natural that these powers should fear that they would be the next to be challenged. Unfortunately there is no accurate information concerning the years following. According to Berossus, Cyrus reduced the rest of Asia in the interval. Xenophon states that Cyrus subdued the Phrygians in Great Phrygia, overcame the Cappadocians, and made the Arabs subject to him.[48] Sidney Smith thinks these "Arabs" were the people of the Damascus area and Palestine.

Nabonidus returned to the capital. In the fall of 539 b.c. Cyrus engaged in battle at Opis on the Tigris. Revolt among the Babylonians ensued. Nabonidus fled to Borsippa. He had evidently lost the support and confidence of the people. He had hopelessly alienated the Marduk priests by his failure to recognize the official cult, by refusing to participate in the annual New Year's festival, and by his devotion to the ancient moon-god Sin. It was too late to make amends.[49] With the fall of Opis and its fortifications, the way was open to Babylon. Events followed in swift succession. Sippar fell without resistance, and by a clever piece of strategy in which the flow of the river was reduced, the troops of Cyrus, under Gobryas, who had deserted Nabonidus, entered the ancient city.

On October 13, 539, Babylon fell. The propaganda went out that all was done at the will and behest of Marduk. The infidelities of Nabonidus had been judged, and Marduk called Cyrus for his service. "He scanned and looked (through) all the countries, searching for a righteous ruler willing to lead him (in the annual procession). . . . He pronounced the name of Cyrus, king of Anshan, declared him to be(come) ruler of all the world. . . . He made him set out on the road to Babylon going at his side like a real friend."[50] The words of the Cyrus Cylinder have so many affinities with Second Isaiah (e.g., 45:1 ff.) that some scholars have declared that the two cannot be independent. The accounts portray Cyrus as benevolent, but they betray a propagandistic penchant. Yet there is a certain consistency in the representation, and the edict of Cyrus (Ezra 6:1-5), though it has been edited and reworded, has doubtless a historical basis.[51]

4. The Exiles in Babylon.—The number of the Judeans who had been carried into exile was not large. In what appears to be an official document, the book of Jeremiah states that in the three exiles of 597, 586, and 581 a total of 4,600 persons was carried to Babylonia. Nor was their lot grievous. They apparently enjoyed considerable freedom. They seem to have had their own houses (Jer. 29:5) and were permitted to gather together (Ezek. 8:1; 14:1; 20:1). Land was assigned to them, and many of them became farmers, as the names they gave to their towns suggest: Tell-abib ("hill of corn") and Tell Charsa ("hill of the plow"). As time went on some of them engaged in trade, and by the fifth century many of them had acquired a reputation in business.

The practice of the regular cult was impossible, especially in view of such standards as the Deuteronomic reformers had set. The sacrificial cult was not practiced. But with the absence of institutions associated with the holy temple other practices received all the greater emphasis. The importance of the sabbath as a holy day was accentuated (Ezek. 20:12 ff.; 22:8, 26; 23:38). Doubtless the practice of circumcision was strictly observed. Ancient memories and traditions were cherished, and it is likely that the exiles gathered to listen to the reading of their venerable writings. In this period Israel's memory of the past received a fresh impulse, and the recollection of the fathers, of the Mosaic covenant, and of the prophets helped them to maintain continuity with their inherited faith. It is likely, too, that they were consoled and inspired by their hymns and other sacred songs (cf. Ps. 137). Prayer acquired new depth and meaning. It is possible that out of such gather-

---

[47] Sidney Smith, *op. cit.*, pp. 32-33.

[48] *Anabasis* I. 5. 1; see Sidney Smith, *op. cit.*, pp. 42-43 for details and evaluation of the account.

[49] The Babylonian Chronicle seems to refer to a New Year's procession. The text is badly damaged, but this seems a legitimate inference (see Pritchard, *op. cit.*, p. 306).

[50] *Ibid.*, p. 315.

[51] Torrey has launched an attack against its authenticity, but other scholars (e.g., Eduard Meyer, W. F. Albright, and H. Wheeler Robinson) are stanch in defense of it; see the Cyrus Cylinder for an account of the restoration of the inhabitants of the country to their homes (Pritchard, *op. cit.*, pp. 315-16). See also Vol. III, pp. 613-16.

ings the synagogue found its origin, but we have no direct evidence for this.

While there may have been occasions when the heavy arm of foreign authority asserted itself and some suffered under the yoke of foreign domination, in general the exiles seem to have been allowed considerable liberty. But precisely for this reason some of them may have been attracted to the pageantry and color and splendor of the native cult. The polemic of Second Isaiah suggests something of the sort. After all, Babylon was the mistress of kingdoms; its gods had wrought great victories and extended its power to remote regions. The great processions like those on New Year's Day, the display of the idols, the drama of the cult, the ancient myths, the impressive rituals, and the elaborate pantheon may easily have tempted not a few to abandon the ways of their fathers and to seek the help of such powerful gods as Marduk. Perhaps, too, cosmic interests assumed greater importance, such as is reflected in the *Enûma eliš,* which was recited on the occasion of the New Year's festival. There is much in Second Isaiah which leads us to suspect that such was the case.

5. Conditions in Palestine.—Judah had suffered heavily from the invasions of the Babylonians. Most of the fortified towns were destroyed, as is now confirmed by the excavations of such places as Debir, Lachish, and Bethshemesh. Tribes from the south pressed into Judah. The Edomites (Idumeans) occupied a portion of the land formerly belonging to her. The rich and the skilled had been carried off to exile, and the population was in general poor. Samaria became the center of the Babylonian province.[52] There were Israelites in the north, as in Galilee, and in Trans-Jordan. The judgment that fell upon Judah did not bring to an end the practices of the syncretistic cult. It was certainly not in Egypt alone that the Jews were attracted by the worship of Ishtar, the mother-goddess (Jer. 44, especially vss. 16-19). The picture of conditions in Palestine that we receive from Third Isaiah is of a cult that had absorbed many foreign elements, some of them very strange and reminiscent of the mysteries.

D. Author.—Next to nothing is known of the author of chs. 40–55 and the external facts of his life. Even his name is lost to us. He is commonly designated as "Second Isaiah" because his words found refuge in the book which contains the oracles of Isaiah of Jerusalem (*ca.* 738-697 B.C). We do not know who his father was, where he was born or when, or how he pursued his ministry. He has been called the most impersonal

of all the prophets, but there is no one whom we should less expect to be so impersonal as he. He has listened with such deep earnestness to the voices of the heavenly council (40:1-11) that he has himself become an incarnate voice preparing the way of his Lord. For him the word is a reality of such far-reaching extent, so vastly historical and cosmic in its range, so powerful in the achievement of its purpose, that it has made of him the kind of writer whom his poems reflect. He stands in lineal succession to the great pre-exilic prophets; indeed his is the only prophetic voice which could meet the disaster and the resulting dejection of 586 B.C. with a faith undimmed and a vitality undaunted. Despite his familiarity with the words and ways of his predecessors, and despite their influence upon him, he goes his own way with an almost sovereign independence. He is capable of profound inwardness, intimacy, and sensitivity, like Hosea and Jeremiah before him, but these qualities are not directed to himself. Like Isaiah, he has a deep sense of a divine reality at work through the movements of history, but there is a spaciousness and amplitude in his vision which Isaiah did not achieve. In many ways he stands closest to the writer of Israel's most glorious epic, the Yahwist, and he grasps the distances and guises of the epic with a fidelity and certitude equaled only by the apostle Paul.

Of the many places that have been proposed as the home of Second Isaiah, Babylon has the best claim. Marti and Hölscher place him in Egypt, Duhm in Phoenicia or the region of the Lebanons, Mowinckel and Torrey in Palestine. However, he seems to have a firsthand acquaintance with conditions in Babylonia. His description of idol manufacture sounds like that of an eyewitness. The vivid picture of the gods leaving Babylon has the verisimilitude of one who has seen the sacred processions. The details concerning astrology, divination, and magic (e.g., 44:24-25; 47:12-13) support the same conclusion. The literary affinities with extant Babylonian literature are so numerous as naturally to suggest Babylon as the prophet's home. To be sure, there is much in the poems with which any intelligent observer in the Near East would be familiar, but the repeated references to Babylon (e.g., ch. 47), the numerous allusions, and the literary relationships make Babylon the most likely possibility.

Max Haller[53] supposes that Second Isaiah was a member of the royal entourage of Cyrus, the Persian king. He believes a number of the poems are in actuality compositions written in honor of the great conqueror (41:1-13, 21-28;

[52] Albrecht Alt, "Die Rolle Samarias bei der Entstehung des Judentums" in *Festschrift Otto Procksch,* ed. Albrecht Alt, *et al.* (Leipzig: A Deichert, 1934), pp. 5-28.

[53] "Die Kyros-Lieder Deuterojesajas," in Hans Schmidt, ed., ΕΥΧΑΡΙΣΤΗΡΙΟΝ (Göttingen: Vandenhoeck & Ruprecht, 1923), pp. 261-77.

42:5-9; 43:1-7; 44:24-28; 45:1-8, 9-13; 46:1-13; 48:12-16). Others, impressed by the striking relationships between the Cyrus Cylinder and Isa. 45:1 ff., believe that the prophet must have been familiar with its contents.[54] Karl Budde [55] thinks of the compositions as prophetic flyleaves issued from time to time for the edification of the exiles, perhaps in the synagogue. Paul Volz sees the prophet as the spiritual leader of the Exile, the true founder of the synagogue. As the exiles gathered for worship on the sabbath, the prophet came to them with the word of the Lord for their comfort, hope, and instruction. This latter view has much to commend it, although the associations with the synagogue are of course only conjectural. In any case, the author was a great prophet, perhaps the greatest of all the prophets, certainly in the range of his vision, his grasp of the great tradition, and the exulting passion of his faith. He was a poet of remarkable lyrical gifts, a master of literary form, and a singer given to joy and praise. He was a man of a sympathy so inward and stirring that it extended itself to the whole realm of nature—heavens and earth, mountain, sea, and desert—to all things animate and inanimate, to mother and wife, to children, and to animals. When he says of the Lord's coming that all flesh shall see his glory, it is no empty phrase. He scales the heights of ecstatic praise and descends the abyss of darkest grief. He knows the Oriental capacity for scorn and contempt; at times his anger seems beyond restraint. But in reality it is not so. His compassion triumphs. His invectives are overcome by oracles of grace and promise. He is Israel's profoundest thinker. The drive of his enthusiasm and ardor tends to obscure this, but it is significant that his feeling always matches the content of his thought. Martin Buber calls him "the originator of a theology of world-history," and this is in reality the case.[56] Neither his particularism nor his universalism get out of leash, for each is understood and grasped in the light of the other.

Reference has been made to the writer's relation to the classical Hebrew tradition. He is steeped in it, knows where its central points lie, and how it bears relevantly upon the broken era in which he has been called to prophesy. The figures of Noah, Abraham and Sarah, Moses and David; the historical events of the call of Abraham, the Exodus, the desert wandering; the primordial events of the chaos struggle, the Creation and the Flood; the meaning of the divine revelation involved in these events and personages—all this and more have left a deep impression upon the writer's imagination and thought. "The style is the man himself," said Buffon in a famous utterance, and it is this which helps to open the door to an understanding of Second Isaiah. The poems are the record of the man.

E. Theology.—The religious thought of Second Isaiah is presented to us in the literary form and manner of ancient Semitic literature. A formal statement of his theology in modern terms therefore defies both the ecstatic feelings of the poet and the literary guise in which it is set forth. In Second Isaiah more than elsewhere in the Old Testament the form and pattern of expression articulate the writer's thought, since he is a consummate master in the art of literary style and rhetoric.

Of first importance for the understanding of these ancient compositions is their poetic guise. Here is the distilled essence of language. So much of a poet is Second Isaiah that he has been considered by some writers to be more the poet than the thinker or prophet. But form and thought cannot be separated so sharply. He is so supreme a poet because the message he proclaimed demanded the poetic form; no other form could bear the burden of his impassioned spirit.

In the second place, the thought of Second Isaiah is intensely dramatic; not a few of his poems are miniature dramas. The collection of poems as a whole has all the elements for the making of a vast drama in which heaven and earth, past, present, and future, Israel, the nation, and Yahweh become major participants. But the dominant unities which pervade the poems do not produce a drama; from the point of view of fixed dramatic structure the poems often seem inchoate. Their structure is Semitic, and they must be judged accordingly.

Again, the theology of Second Isaiah is a precipitate of an extremely dynamic period of human history, the period in which the Babylonian Empire is in radical decline and the Persian age is dawning, the end of the great Semitic empires, or, to use Arnold J. Toynbee's phrase, the end of the Syriac "time of troubles." [57] The depth of history is superbly marked by the way in which nature responds to the movement of events.

Another characteristic of the thought of Second Isaiah is explained by his prophetic herit-

[54] See, e.g., Rudolf Kittel, "Cyrus und Deuterojesaja," *Zeitschrift für die alttestamentlichen Wissenschaft,* XVIII (1898), 149-62.

[55] *Das Buch Jesaia Kap. 40-66* (3rd ed.; Tübingen: J. C. B. Mohr, 1909; "Die Heilige Schrift des Alten Testaments"), pp. 609-71.

[56] *The Prophetic Faith,* tr. Carlyle Witton-Davies (New York: The Macmillan Co., 1949), p. 208. The whole discussion is one of the most profound and penetrating interpretations of the prophet's theology.

[57] See *A Study of History,* Abridgement of Vols. I-VI by D. C. Somervell (New York: Oxford University Press, 1947), p. 451.

age. Five major forces went into the making of his message: God, the people, the event, the prophet, and the word. Each of these demands detailed treatment; only in the light of all of them in their dynamic interrelation to one another can we grasp the prophet's message. The "words" which the prophet uses to proclaim the word of God have been referred to. Here we shall enumerate certain other stylistic features which contain the essence of the theology: (a) the divine self-asseverations which appear in climactic contexts; (b) the participial phrases appearing either after the oracular formula, "Thus says the LORD," or the covenant disclosure, "I am Yahweh"; (c) the appositional words which also appear in great profusion (i) in relation to Yahweh and (ii) in relation to Israel; (d) the remarkable words of address, many of them in greatly extended form; and (e) the great abundance of verbs which express Yahweh's activity in judgment and salvation.

Finally, the thought of Second Isaiah is eschatological, and the primary matrix of all the poems is eschatological. When we speak of eschatology, we refer to the imminence of a great divine event which is to mark the decisive end of the age. Israel's time of service has come to an end; the old age is passing away and a new age is about to dawn. The new age will be ushered in by new events, and the new events are greeted with eschatological singing. The new Exodus which stands over against the old; the new covenant which will last forever and is a relationship of pure grace; the new creation which is at least adumbrated in 51:1-16 (though not of the apocalyptic kind as in 65:17; 66:22); the new age which is described in the glowing colors of eschatological imagery—these are but the central motifs which mark the difference between time past and time future. In this connection the theophanic language and imagery are especially noteworthy. The coming of Yahweh is marked by the manifestation of his glory (כבוד). Nature leaps forward in response: her ancient shackles are loosed at the divine appearing. The three major areas of eschatological thought which occupy the prophet's mind are redemption, creation, and history. Redemption is the central act which God performs at his appearing, but this redemption which marks the "end" is viewed from the vantage point of God's act in creation, for the end is related to the beginning. History is understood in the light of the epochal events associated with the rise of Cyrus but also in the light of the two primary focuses of redemption and creation. That which bridges the grievous plight of the present and the felicity of the new age is the faith of the prophet in the revelation that has

been disclosed to him in the celestial council where the imminent coming of God is first announced. He has witnessed the Lord sitting on his throne and the heavenly beings of his entourage; he has listened to the great announcement of the imminent advent of God, and he has finally participated in the councils by accepting the burden of prophetic responsibility. Thus he becomes the evangelist of the coming age.

1. Eschatological Perspective.—God's decision to enter upon the stage of world history is first announced in heaven (40:1-11). This decision exacts responsibility. The way of the Lord must be prepared, for upon it he will appear (40:3) to lead his exiles home (42:16; 45:13; cf. 48:17). This is the new event that he will perform (43:19). The mountains and hills will be leveled, the crooked roads made straight, the valleys raised (40:4-5; 45:2; 49:11). Again and again Yahweh's advent is described in language drawn from the Exodus (e.g., 43:19-20; 48:21; 52:11-12). Israel's first redemption will be repeated in even more marvelous fashion and with even greater wonders than at the beginning in the new Exodus from the whole of the wide-spreading Diaspora. The way of Yahweh is the primary image used to express Yahweh's return.

When God appears in his glorious theophany, his glory, the central Old Testament theologoumenon for Yahweh's self-manifestation, will appear. As in the priestly document the glory of Yahweh (כבוד יהוה) appeared on the mountain on the occasion of the Sinaitic revelation associated with the momentous covenant events (Exod. 24:15-17), so now he appears in a universal revelation in which all flesh shall see the glory. Ezekiel pictures the departure of the glory from the temple (Ezek. 1:28; 10:18; 11:22-23); now it returns for all men to see (cf. Isa. 6:3). The revelation of the glory calls into action many events, chief among which are the transformation of nature, the assertion of the divine sovereignty in history, and the inauguration of the kingship of God. The announcement of its imminent appearing is the occasion for the prophet's call (see 40:6) and provides the content of his gospel (see 40:9-10; 52:1-2, 7-10).

The imminence of God's coming is portrayed in language drawn from Oriental categories of imagery. Chief among these is the myth, which in Israel becomes a reflection upon first and last things (πρῶτα καὶ ἔσχατα). Buber describes it as "the spontaneous and appropriate speech of the expecting as of the remembering community." [58] Memory and expectation are the major elements in the mentality of prophetic Israel.

[58] *Das Kommende* (Berlin: Schocken, 1932), Vol. I, "Königtum Gottes," p. xi.

Indeed, these are the two major psychological dispositions of our prophet. He never wearies of calling upon his people to remember the events of its past sacred history and the persons who played a part in them. Chief of his sources is the Yahwist. Thus he recalls the idyllic life in Eden abounding in life and fertility (51:3; cf. 41:17-20), the solemn oath of Yahweh after the floodwaters of Noah's time (54:9); the promises to Sarah and Abraham and their miraculous fulfillment (51:2-3); the covenant sworn to David, now to become an everlasting covenant (55:3-5). It will be observed that each of these passages has strikingly common features, most notable of which is their eschatological orientation. The prophet sees all things from the point of view of the divine initiative and fulfillment. His prophecy is an Oriental drama of beginning and end, of former things and latter things, of memories and expectations. Yet it would be an error to think of him as retreating from the hazards and perils of the present in order to fashion for himself an imaginative world of felicity. Nothing could be less true. Rather, he sees the despair and darkness of his times in an all-inclusive framework of divine revelation.

It is a common practice in the interpretation of the prophet's theology to list the various divine attributes under the doctrine of God and the characteristics of man under the doctrine of man. But such interpretations are alien to the prophet. For convenience we shall examine several of the dominant emphases of Second Isaiah as they appear in the great appositions, but in each case it will be observed that the special title is invariably combined with other titles and expressions. Thus the prophet has frequently been chided for his repetitions. But strictly speaking, there are no repetitions because of the numerous fresh combinations and contexts in which the specific title appears.

2. Yahweh, the Holy One of Israel.—Holiness is the unique attribute of God. All that is holy is derivative from his holiness. He is the Holy One in an absolute sense (cf. 40:25*b*, "says *qādhôsh*"). It is only with Israel, his people, that he has entered into this relationship of holiness; therefore she is the holy people (Exod. 19:6[J]), and he is the Holy One of Israel (קדוש ישראל). Isaiah of Jerusalem was the first to make this term central in Israel's religion, and Second Isaiah is plainly dependent upon him. The word occurs no fewer than eleven times (41:14, 16, 20; 43:3, 14; 47:4; 48:17; 49:7 [twice]; 54:5; 55:5), each time in climactic contexts: in self-asseverations, in theophanic disclosures (*hieroi logoi*), in oracular formulas, or in other momentous pronouncements (e.g., 54:5; 55:5). In Isaiah the holiness of God stands over against all that is human, in con-

trast to everything worldly, and evokes the forlorn cry of the prophet (6:3-5). Yet he is Israel's Holy One. That is the wonder and uniqueness of her existence. But in Second Isaiah the conception is combined with others, most notably with Redeemer: "Your Redeemer is the Holy One of Israel" (41:14); "and the Holy One of Israel is your Redeemer" (54:5; see also 43:3, 14; 47:4; 49:7). It is possible that Second Isaiah is under the influence of Hosea: "The Holy One in your midst" (Hos. 11:9); "Judah . . . is faithful to the Holy One" (Hos. 11:12). It is Yahweh's utter holiness, with its terrible power, its distinction from all that is human, its exclusiveness and yet outgoing quality, that evokes the constantly reiterated command (drawn from the theophanies), "Fear not." These commands must always be read in their total contexts. This will show that there is a remarkable uniformity in the words that follow them (cf. 41:10-11, 13 [note the brief *hieros logos* "I will help you"], 14 [where the same promise is expanded]; 43:1*d*-3*b*, 5-7; 44:2-5, 8; 51:7, 7*c*-8; 54:4-10). Yahweh's holiness, while uniquely and peculiarly his, manifests itself in mighty acts and wonders, but supremely in the redemption of his people. Here, as elsewhere, the prophet is laying hold of the fundamental reality of Mosaic religion (cf. Exod. 19:5-6). Holiness demands responsibility. Israel is forever accountable to her holy Lord.

3. The Redeemer of Israel.—The theology of Second Isaiah is everywhere rooted deep in the sacred tradition. As at Sinai Israel became a holy people through Yahweh's initiative and her own response, so in the Exodus from Egypt and the liberation from bondage Israel became his chosen people, his possession, his son. The Exodus was therefore understood as an act of great redemption (Exod. 15:13 [J]; 6:6 [P]; Ps. 77:15). The term "redeemer" is drawn from family law. The redeemer as the nearest male relative is under obligation to guarantee the family solidarity. Thus when a kinsman has been sold into slavery, the redeemer pays a sum of money to purchase him back. Similarly, if the family's blood has been shed, the redeemer must avenge it. Redemption took other forms also, but these are the most common. The central importance of the term is reflected in its frequent use as a title (41:14; 43:14; 44:6, 24; 47:4; 48:17; 49:7, 26; 54:5, 8; cf. 59:20; 63:16), in its common association with "Holy One," and by the other remarkable contexts in which it appears. Because of these highly rhetorical and therefore crucially important contexts, it is not always clear what the redeeming act is, but the poems as a whole leave no doubt.

In the first place, the term is used in a juristic sense in which the physical aspects of the redemption are stressed. Yahweh performs the duties of the redeemer (gŏ'ēl) by paying the ransom for his people (43:3; cf. 50:2cd); he avenges himself upon those who have violated what belongs to him (41:14 ff.; 43:14; 47:4 ff.; 49:7; 54:5-6). The new feature in the prophet's understanding of redemption is its eschatological orientation. It is perhaps not too much to say that the whole eschatological event associated with Yahweh's coming, or the events preliminary to his advent, are included in redemption. These events may be summarized as follows:

a. Release from bondage a counterpart to the release from Egypt (43:5-7; 45:13; 48:20; 49:9, 11, 14; 52:2-3; 55:12-13);

b. Judgment of wrath upon Israel's enemies (41:11 ff.; 49:25-26; 51:23);

c. Return home to Palestine (40:9-10; 43:20; 49:11; 51:11; 55:12-13);

d. Rebuilding of Jerusalem (44:26; 45:13; 49:16-17; 51:3; 52:9);

e. The restoration of the holy city (52:1; 54:11-12);

f. The restoration of the land, a counterpart to the gift of the land (44:26; 49:8, 19);

g. The conversion of the nations (45:20-23; 51:4-5; cf. 49:6).

In the second place, however, the redemption is inward and spiritual. Yahweh acts for the comforting of his people. He wipes out their sins (43:25; 44:22; 54:8). As in Jeremiah's eschatological oracle of the new covenant (Jer. 31:31-34), the coming of God is the time of forgiveness. He acts not because Israel possesses any merit of her own; indeed, Israel did not deserve to be redeemed. Yahweh acts for his own sake (43:25; 48:11), that his name should not be profaned (48:9, 11), and for his glory and praise (42:8; 43:7; 48:9). He redeems because he is powerful to redeem; he is Israel's mighty One, the Lord of hosts, the coming conqueror.

The prophet is particularly fond of portraying God's work of redemption in military imagery. The new age is introduced by Yahweh's victory over his enemies (40:9-10; 42:13). Here, too, he goes back to the earliest traditions of Israel (Exod. 15:3 ff.; Num. 10:35-36; Judg. 5) and refashions them in eschatological contexts. Among the many verbs that are used to describe Yahweh's power is one that is drawn from the vocabulary of war. In the time of salvation Yahweh will "help" his people (44:2-3; 49:8); upon his help they can rely (41:10, 13, 14), and the servant of the Lord lives by the assurance that God is his helper (50:7, 9). "The arm of Yahweh" is the major symbol which the prophet employs to describe this divine might and power. It brings in his kingdom (40:10); by it he protects Israel (40:11), creates the heavens

and earth (48:12-13), judges the peoples (51:5), conquers the nations so that all may see his salvation (52:1). It is his arm to which the nations bear witness in 53:1, and in 51:9 ff. the prophet breaks out in an impassioned apostrophe of prayer imploring the arm of Yahweh to "awake" as in primeval times when he smote the chaos dragon and created the earth. One of the reasons that Second Isaiah employs the creation motif so often is that in the creation God showed himself a God of power, Lord of all nature, and therefore powerful to deliver Israel and defeat her enemies. It is Yahweh's great power which shows him to be God, the only God; there is none who can rival him or compete with him. The gods of the nations are powerless; they can do nothing (41:24, 28; 43:12; 46:1-2).

4. The Creator.—The purpose of God's coming into history is to effect redemption. As we have seen, this is primary in Second Isaiah's thought. But closely related to it is God's activity in creation. The God who redeems is the creator. The prophet employs many verbs to express this creative activity, notably the verb יצר, used by the Yahwist in Gen. 2:7, 19, etc., and, above all, the verb ברא, which appears no fewer than sixteen times (40:26, 28; 41:20; 42:5; 43:1, 7, 15; 45:7 [twice], 8, 12, 18 [twice]; 48:7; 54:16 [twice]). Wherever this latter verb appears in the Old Testament, God is always the subject, and it surely refers to a unique creative action which he alone can perform.

As in the case of God's redemptive activity and power, Second Isaiah not only plays upon the theme of creation again and again but transforms the idea to suit his purposes in the context of eschatology. Most obvious, of course, is the prophet's strong cosmic interest, more pronounced and more highly elaborated than at any previous time in the prophetic literature of Israel. It is God's cosmic power that triumphs over all the heathen gods with their theogonic stories and vast creation myths. God's creation of the stars is pointed to as the source of Israel's hope and consolation (40:26-27). Again creation is his revelation; in it are disclosed his might, his wisdom, his unaided initiative (40:13-14).

Yet the prophet's interest is by no means cosmogonic or cosmic alone. Invariably it is related to other concerns. First of these is the area of human history. Repeatedly the prophet appeals to God's creation as the background for history (e.g., 40:15, 17, 23-24; 42:5; 43:1-7; 54:15-16). The use of the chaos dragon myth in 51:9-10 is a good illustration of the way in which he employs the ancient cosmogonic myth of the Near East and orients it to the historical Exodus tradition of Israel. Thus the meaning of history acquires new depths and ranges heretofore unparalleled. In this connection it is most interesting to see the prophet using the verb ברא, "to create," in relation to history. God not only creates the universe but also the people of Israel (cf. Gen. 1:27) and the "new and hidden things" (48:6-8) ; the whole context shows clearly the unprecedented wonder of his unique creation.[59]

Finally and most important of all is Second Isaiah's transformation of his cosmogonic passages into contexts of salvation. Yahweh's creation is for the salvation of his people and for the world; he made the world to be inhabited (45:12, 18). Yahweh's purpose is the salvation and redemption of his people; creation is the initial act of which redemption is the finale.[60]

5. *Yahweh Is an Eternal God.*—Again the prophet connects his thought with an ancient tradition in which Yahweh is known as 'ēl 'ōlām (Gen. 21:33 [J]). "Yahweh is an everlasting God, Creator of the ends of the earth" (Isa. 40:28). He is the first to connect creation with eternity.[61] That God is Lord of nature and of time is the source of Israel's comfort (40:27-28). God creates space and stands above all time (Eissfeldt) ; he brings the beginnings of all things into existence, and is present to act in the *eschaton.* He is "the first and . . . the last" (44:6; etc.), "the hidden Alpha and Omega of things in which the first and last of temporality [*Zeitlichkeit*] is determined."[62] The prophet does not say God is timeless; rather, God initiates time (cf. Gen. 1:1-5) and fulfills his purpose in time (42:21; 44:28; 46:10; 53:10; 55:10-11). Here again the prophet rises to unprecedented heights. Nowhere else in the Old Testament do we encounter such constant stress on the divine purpose. It is the fundamental reality in God's being which moves from beginning to end, from creation to redemption, as it is the fundamental reality which underlies all history, the history of Israel in a unique fashion, to be sure, but the history of the nations also. God created the universe for a purpose.

[59] The sharp distinction between nature and history, so characteristic of the modern West, is hardly characteristic of the biblical mind. Both nature and history are God's activity. Creation brings the world into existence, and the world is always under the active divine sovereignty; precisely the same thing can be said of history.

[60] Gerhard von Rad, "Das theologische Problem des alttestamentlichen Schöpfungsglaubens" in *Werden und Wesen des Alten Testaments,* ed. Paul Volz (Berlin: A. Töpelmann, 1936), pp. 138-47. The prophet's faith in the divine creation is inextricably bound with his understanding of history, revelation, and salvation. They constitute the major realities of the *Heilsgeschichte.*

[61] See Otto Eissfeldt, *Geschichtliches und ubergeschichtliches im Alten Testament* (Berlin: Evangelische Verlagsanstalt, 1947), p. 28: "The mighty confession of Yahweh as the Eternal sounds first in Second Isaiah."

[62] Otto Procksch, *Theologie des Alten Testaments* (Gütersloh: C. Bertelsmann, 1950), p. 273.

It was his sure and steadfast purpose to magnify his revelation (*tôrāh*) and make it glorious (42:21). He sends Cyrus as his shepherd and fulfills his purpose through him (44:28). Above all things else he wills the sufferings of his servant; it was his purpose to afflict him with suffering that the sins of the nations might be thus expiated. It is not surprising that in the closing lines of the final poem this motif is given classic statement.[63]

Thus Second Isaiah interprets the purpose of God in the same many-sided and fluid way that he interprets God's holiness, redemption, and creation. They are not understood abstractly, but very concretely, and each reference casts a flood of light both forward and backward. Thus eschatology achieves its great ranges, its full-orbed amplitude, its mythological heights and depths, its dramatic proportions and dynamic, and its theological profundity.

6. *Judge, King, Savior, Comforter, and Teacher.*—The fundamental eschatological categories outlined in the foregoing discussion are combined with many other aspects of God's activity which are made manifest in the time of his appearing. One major aspect of the universal eschatological drama is God's judgment. Again Second Isaiah combines his conception with many others, especially the major categories of his eschatology. Moreover, it is portrayed with such variegated imagery and in such differing contexts that it is impossible to grasp the meaning fully unless all the other elements of his thought are taken into consideration. Significantly the climax of the three "beholds" in the climactic strophe of the opening poem falls on judgment:

> Behold, his reward is with him,
> and his recompense before him (40:10).

The whole realm of history and nature is involved in God's action: Jerusalem and Israel, the foreign nations (Babylon, "the ends of the earth," Egypt, Ethiopia, Seba) and their rulers, the servant of the Lord, the enemies of the servant, and even the heavens and earth (e.g., 51:3, 6). Israel is both judged and designated as the instrument of judgment. Her judgment is both negative and positive: she is God's mighty threshing sledge to thresh the mountains and make the hills as chaff; she brings her revelation to all the nations and imparts to them the divine statutes. Through Cyrus' military victories Yahweh exercises his sovereignty over the nations.

Judgment is the function of the king. The new age is introduced by the declaration of God's universal rule (40:10; 52:7), and all peo-

[63] See pp. 651-52.

ple will see him coming in all his glory. But he is Israel's king in a unique sense, just as he is Israel's Holy One, Redeemer, Mighty One, and Creator (44:6). These latter titles show him to be sovereign over the nations and nature; both respond to his bidding and participate in his salvation. In his use of the word "salvation" Second Isaiah is again indebted to tradition, but he also moves beyond it and transforms it to give it deeper and fuller meaning. God's coming is the time of salvation (52:7-10). Then he will come with his help and saving deeds (צדקות). He is "a righteous God and a Savior" (45:21). That is the strange and mysterious paradox which baffles the nations and makes them cry out in impassioned prayer,

> Truly, thou art a God who hidest thyself,
> O God of Israel, the Savior (45:15).

Yahweh is unique in his saving power; there is none other who can save (43:11; 45:21; 46:2, 4, 7, 13; 47:13, 15). His salvation is everlasting (45:17; 51:6, 8), and it manifests itself not only in deliverance and victory but also in other ways which are much more extensive. This is why the title "Savior" is related with the other great eschatological titles. All the nations are infolded within his saving acts (51:4-6; 52:10, where it is associated with Yahweh's holy arm). The many oracles of salvation containing the divine promises and assurances reflect the central importance of this emphasis.

One of the most striking features of the passages where Yahweh's great titles appear is the compassionate and even intimate attitude toward Israel. This interior relationship between God and his people is especially clear in the introductions, in the climactic self-asseverations, and in the intimate words of personal address. When God comes to redeem his people from their bondage, he comes as their comforter. With this note the poems begin, and it sounds like a major theme throughout (40:1; 49:13; 51:3, 12, 19; 54:11; cf. 57:18; 61:2; 66:13). The message of comfort is always expressed with great urgency; this is why the poems begin with the words of "comfort, comfort" (see also 49:13; cf. 1:2). After a remarkable passage in which the love of God for his people is expressed in most moving language (54:6-8, 9-10) Yahweh addresses his people:

> O afflicted one, storm-tossed, and not comforted,
> behold, I will set your stones in antimony,
> and lay your foundations with sapphires (54:11).

The eschatological imagery is apparent here, and the whole context is rich in the imaginative categories with which the divine salvation is portrayed. In this same poem we have another eschatological motif in which all the sons of Yahweh will be taught by him. Yahweh is Israel's teacher. He teaches them to profit and leads them in the way they should walk (48:17). He has delivered the *tôrāh* to his people, and it is part of their witness in the world to make it known among the nations.

7. Yahweh Alone Is God.—It is usual to begin the discussion of Second Isaiah's theology with his teaching concerning monotheism. But this is to mistake his mentality and to misinterpret the idea itself. Moreover, his teaching is sometimes called "theoretical monotheism." This is a misleading term, for his "monotheism" is far from theoretical; indeed, even the word "teaching" does not do justice to the poems themselves. Rather, Yahweh makes himself known in mighty self-asseverations as the only God, beside whom there is no other (44:6, 8; 45:5, 6, 21; cf. 41:26-27). The same thought is expressed in the oft-repeated "I am he," which is tantamount to "I am the only true God" (41:4; 43:15; 46:4; 48:12), and in the constant repetition of the first personal pronoun in the mouth of Yahweh and in the series of first person verbs.

Second Isaiah nowhere effaces the distinctiveness of Israel's faith. His universalism is balanced by a strong particularism, and is filled with the concrete content which has its source in historical moments like those at Sinai or the Exodus from Egypt. He does not say that all gods represent the one and same God; no, his meaning is rather that Yahweh is the only true God. His eschatological thought contributes to his formulation of "monotheism." Yahweh is "the first, and . . . the last" (44:6; etc.), the alpha and omega, the beginning and end. His purpose penetrates all history from its inception to its fulfillment. He knows events, creates them for his purpose, and is sovereign over history. He alone can recount the past and foretell the future. This emphasis upon prediction is one of the chief supports for the prophet's faith in the oneness of Yahweh. That he is in control of events and proclaims them before they happen shows him to be Lord of history and nature. Again, Yahweh's coming reveals him in glorious epiphany as the only God, for his glory is disclosed before the eyes of all flesh. His redemption is his alone; the gods of the nations can do nothing. He is incomparable. Other nations fashion their gods and make them like what they imagine gods to be; Yahweh tolerates no such representation. He is unique in his incomparability. Further, Yahweh alone created the universe, he alone sustains and conserves it. His unsearchable understanding and inexhaustible knowledge were responsible for it. The holiness of Yahweh is his alone; other religions have their taboos, mysteries, and secret cults, but Yahweh's holiness is revealed in the unique events of Israel's historical past. The description of the prophet's faith as monotheistic does scant justice to his thought; there was monotheism long before him and among other peoples. What is distinctive is the elements which go into its making, and it is these in their eschatological context, their dramatic guise, their urgent self-asseverations, and their hymnic outbursts that make the prophet the towering figure in human thought that he is.

8. God Reveals Himself in His Word.—Underlying all that the prophet has to say about the imminent coming of Yahweh, in which he will make himself known to all the world, is his deep, sure faith that God has revealed himself. So rich is the vocabulary of revelation that it penetrates into every conceivable situation and always with the great variety and fluidity that characterize all his thought. In this he is heir to his prophetic predecessors, but he transforms traditional prophetic language and thought to direct it to the eschatological situation which he describes. Already in the opening poem the speaking-hearing reality is magnificently expressed, and culminates in such climactic lines as "for the mouth of the LORD has spoken it" and "the word of our God shall stand for ever." Such lines as these dominate all the poems, but they receive a detailed documentation throughout. Observe, for example, the large number of speaking-hearing contexts and the crucial position in which the speaking-hearing words occur. The oracular formula is characteristically transformed to give it depth and range. The covenant words, "I am Yahweh," receive the same significant elaboration and intensification. But there are other words, all of them important, which show us what this speaking involves: "proclaim," "announce," "cry," "foretell" or "predict," "declare" or "tell," "shout," "call by name," "rebuke," etc. At times this vocabulary has great depth and inwardness, as in the servant's words in 49:1-6 and 50:4-9. Most important of all is the eschatological orientation of the word of the Lord which forms the framework for all the poems (40:5, 8; 55:10-11). In such passages (see also 45:18-19) the word of God fills all time and space, fulfills God's purpose from creation to redemption, and addresses itself to Israel, to the nations, to heaven and earth, and to the whole complex of events which constitute the eschatological drama. Thus the whole of nature and history come under the reign of God's speaking, and to it they respond with joy and praise. The word of God assumes numerous literary forms, such as the words of judgment in the judicial scenes, words of promise and comfort in the oracles of salvation, and words of prediction which give meaning to history. Especially powerful and moving are the direct and intimate words of address to Israel, whom God calls by name and to whom he proclaims his name.

9. Israel, the People of God.—It is in the words of address and the solemn words of assurance which follow them that the nature and meaning of the people of God are revealed. The most striking of the words of address is the emphatic use of the second person, e.g., "but you, Israel." God's mighty first person "I" is repeated again and again, and this first person is paralleled by his speech in intimate address. Among the many words which give content to this I-Thou relationship the following are notable: "I am your Holy One," "I have redeemed you," "I have created you," "I uphold you," "I strengthen you," "I help you," "I say to you, 'Fear not!'" "You are mine," "I have chosen you," "I have made you a covenant to the peoples," "I have put my words in your mouth," "I am your King," "I will comfort you," "I will save." In these words, and many like them, the whole tradition is comprehended and the eschatological ranges of Israel's life are grasped.

10. Israel, the Seed of Abraham.—The life of Abraham lives on in Israel. The call, promise, and blessing which were given to him persist in Israel's history. Significantly, when the servant of the Lord is first introduced, it is in terms of Abraham, "my friend." Israel is the extension of Abraham. When the poems move in rising crescendo to their great finale, the prophet makes a fervent appeal to her and bids her turn to her ancestral origins:

Look to the rock from which you were hewn,
and to the quarry from which you were digged.
Look to Abraham your father
and to Sarah who bore you;
for when he was but one I called him,
and I blessed him and made him many (51:1c-2).

This deep historical appeal is the ground for the eschatological promise which follows (51:3). In it beginning and end are brought into connection with each other, and the transformation of the desert into a primeval Eden evokes joy and gladness, thanksgiving, and the voice of song.

11. Israel, Led by Yahweh.—As in the wilderness he led Israel to Sinai, the mount of covenanting, and the Promised Land, so in the new age Israel will return to the land under his gracious leading. Thus Yahweh is Israel's leader, and as the procession advances nature awakens into new life to give glory to him and to join in the eschatological hymns. This leading of Yahweh is related to the motif of the way of the Lord which, as we have seen, becomes in Second

Isaiah a major eschatological symbol to characterize the event of Yahweh's coming and of his leading of the exiles home.

12. Israel, Chosen by Yahweh.—In her election Israel discerns the purpose which lies behind her history. One of the most characteristic words of address with which Yahweh speaks to his people is "my chosen." The Exodus from Egypt was the hour of her election. There was nothing to account for this gracious, unmotivated action of Yahweh. It was not that Israel deserved this deed in her behalf (cf. Deut. 7:7-8; 9:4 ff.). Second Isaiah knows that her life has its origin in God's unaccountable goodness; he develops the motif in many ways and deepens it both by its eschatological contexts and by the implications which he sees in the conception. For election meant for Israel not only privilege but accountability and obligation (see Exod. 19:5-6 and the *tôrāh* which follows upon the appeal to the deliverance from bondage in Exod. 20:1 ff.). Of all Old Testament doctrines election would seem to be the most particularistic of all, and yet Second Isaiah, as the Deuteronomist before him, combines it with a widehearted universalism that includes both Israel's responsibility and Yahweh's ever-renewed and available grace. Of the many covenant realities which are affirmed of both Israel and the servant (both within and outside of the songs), election is the most outstanding. Israel, the servant, is God's chosen one (41:8-9; 42:1; 43:10, 20; 44:1-2; 45:4; 49:7; cf. also, among others, 43:1-2; 44:21, 24; 45:11; 48:11; 48:12; 51:7; 55:5 ff.).

13. Israel, the Covenant People.—The prophetic interpretation of the idea of the covenant received its greatest deepening with Second Isaiah.[64] He has nothing to say of the Sinaitic covenant, and his only allusion to a historical covenant refers to David, the leader of the people (55:3-5). In this he seems to be influenced by the royal theology of II Sam. 7 and the royal psalms (e.g., Ps. 89). Like the idea of election, the covenant of Yahweh with Israel is viewed in the light of his coming and the eschatological events associated with it. It is a covenant of peace which will last to the remotest time (54:10; 55:3). And yet when he seeks to interpret the depths of its meaning, he appeals to the solemn oath he swore at the time of the Flood, that the waters should no longer cover the earth. Here, too, in the P version, the covenant is stated to be an everlasting covenant (Gen. 9:8-17). This provides the prophet with an adequate symbol for the interpretation of the meaning of the covenant in the eschatological hour of the redemption. Thus again, as

in the election and other characteristic ideas, the end is understood in relation to the beginning. The prophet does not say that this is a new covenant—a strange circumstance in view of his constant emphasis upon the newness of the new age and in view of the presence of the phrase in Jeremiah and Ezekiel (though the authenticity of these references is widely contested). Perhaps it is because he is so sensitive to the underlying continuities throughout the history of the great tradition. As for the Davidic covenant to which he appeals (cf. II Sam. 7:3-17), he may have considered it more suitable for eschatological formulation and for expressing his faith that the covenant is of grace alone.[65] Its greatest deepening, however, appears in the servant passages, where Israel is to be "a covenant to the people, a light to the nations" (42:6; 49:8). Thus the servant becomes the instrument for including other peoples within the embrace of the covenant relation and covenant promises, and the last poem magnificently affirms the consequences of this mission (see 55:1, 3-5).

14. Israel, Yahweh's Witness.—The motif does not appear often, but in the one poem where the idea is central, it is stated in a form which suggests its great importance for the prophet (43:8-13). Israel is addressed in the succinct words, "You are my witnesses," and the line is in parallelism with "my servant whom I have chosen." The nations cannot produce any such witnesses to justify them or to point to the great historical events of the age. But Israel is uniquely equipped to witness to the events (cf. 41:8 ff.). Her great task is to bear testimony that Yahweh alone is God, that there is no savior beside him. He—he alone—is God, and Israel is his witness. Here the missionary motif, so strong a feature of other poems, becomes almost incandescent in its intensity. Nowhere is the oneness of God more powerfully stated, and nowhere is Israel's relationship to his oneness more effectively portrayed.

Finally, Second Isaiah does justice to still another characteristic of Israel's life which runs throughout the sacred tradition. It is Israel's peculiar task to praise God, to glorify him, to give thanks to him for his great mercies, and to sing songs of gladness and rejoicing. Among all the central categories in her historical life which Second Isaiah employs for his eschatology, this motif of joy, praise, and song is one of the greatest and, indeed, one of the most disregarded. The praises of God sound throughout the earliest records and appear in the historical and prophetic books as well as the Psalter.

[64] Walter Eichrodt, *Theologie des alten Testaments* (3rd ed.; Berlin: Evangelische Verlagsanstalt, 1948), I, 20.

[65] To what degree the prophet's thought has been influenced by the royal theology of II Sam. 7; 23:1 ff., and especially the royal psalms, is difficult to say.

Many of these songs and hymns are late, but a large number still remain which witness to Israel's proclivity for singing from the earliest times (e.g., Exod. 15:1-18, 21; Judg. 5). To Yahweh's new event Israel responds with a new song (42:8-9, 10-12), and the most immediate response to Yahweh's coming is the outburst of joy and gladness (41:16; 48:20; 51:11). The former time of despair and darkness is transformed into joy and felicity. The advent of God to introduce a new time and to intervene in behalf of his chosen and covenanted people evokes the impassioned cry to nature to witness to his mighty work.

Sing for joy, O heavens, and exult, O earth;
break forth, O mountains, into singing!
For the LORD has comforted his people,
and will have compassion on his afflicted (49:13;
cf. 44:23; 51:3; 52:9; 55:12).

15. The Servant of the Lord. a) The Problem.

—The dramatic movement of the first three poems, which form a kind of eschatological trilogy (see pp. 447; 467), comes to a climax with the entrance of the servant of the Lord upon the stage of world history. The announcement in the celestial council of Yahweh's imminent advent (40:1-11), the change of scene from heaven to earth in the poem on Yahweh, the creator, whose climaxes fall invariably upon the events of history (40:12-31), and the great trial of the nations, where contemporary events are adduced by God for the nations' response, form a background against which the figure of the servant emerges, and it may not be premature to add, emerges again and again throughout the whole collection of poems. In the third poem, however, the trial is presented twice, particularly in the first three and the last three strophes. In the climactic strophe of each section the servant is introduced in extraordinarily dramatic fashion (41:8-10; 42:1-4). The true significance of the servant's entrance is grasped only when it is seen in its total literary context and "situation in life"—the dramatic trial scene.

Precisely at this point a problem is raised that has exercised the minds of scholars perhaps more than any other single Old Testament question. For in the first reference (41:8-10) the servant is equated with Israel in the most emphatic fashion, and the words addressed to her are of the greatest significance; in the second reference (42:1-4) the words are also singularly fateful and full of destiny, but no reference is made to Israel. This situation may serve to illustrate the major problem of the poems: in one series of passages the servant is clearly identified with Israel (41:8 ff.; 43:8-13; 43:14–44:5 [see 44:1-2]; 44:6-8, 21-23 [see vs. 21]; 44:24–45:13 [see 45:4]; 48 [cf. vss. 1, 7, 10-12, 17]); in a second series

(42:1-4; 49:1-6; 50:4-9; 52:13–53:12) there is only a single reference to Israel (49:3), and this is usually expunged by those who believe that the servant in these passages refers to an individual.

b) The Literary Relationship.—Duhm (1892) and those who follow him believe that the so-called servant songs represent intrusions into the text, that their deletion would never be noticed, and that the form and style of the songs are different from what we meet elsewhere in Second Isaiah. A vast literature has gathered about the problem, and the number of solutions that have been proposed, even among those who accept Duhm's view that the songs are the work of another and later writer, is legion.[66]

One of the first things to strike the reader of this literature is the want of unanimity as to the number and scope of the servant passages. Duhm reduced the first song from 42:1-7 to 42:1-4, and held vss. 5-7 to be a later addition. Gressmann discovered seven separate servant units: 42:1-4, 5-9; 49:1-6, 7, 8-13; 50:4-10; 53:1-12.[67] Many scholars think of 61:1-3 (or beyond) as a servant poem; Torrey includes 61:1-3, 10-11; 62:1-12; 63:7-14 as utterances by the servant.[68] Aage Bentzen adds 51:9-16.[69]

There is also disagreement as to the limits of the song in ch. 50, the majority following Duhm, but some ending the passage with vs. 10 (Budde, Gressmann). Lindblom finds four "allegorical oracles": 42:1-9; 49:1-7; 50:4-11; 52:13–53:12. North thinks of 42:5-9 as "an oracle originally relating to Israel, and subsequently transformed into a secondary Servant-Song."[70] Volz also takes 42:5-9 as a servant song. The limits of the poem in ch. 49 are as undetermined as those in ch. 42, some scholars ending it with vs. 7, others with vs. 9a, others with vs. 14, and still others with vs. 26.

An examination of the foregoing literature demonstrates quite conclusively that the excision of the four servant poems, far from resolving difficulties, has only added to them. Duhm and others have been compelled to delete contiguous verses; others have added verses to the poems or have made new poems of them. Now the significant feature about such changes is that once verses are added or believed to belong to

---

[66] See Christopher R. North, *The Suffering Servant in Deutero-Isaiah* (London: Oxford University Press, 1948), for an excellent history and critical discussion of modern investigation of the problem. See also A. S. Peake, ed., *The Servant of Yahweh* (Manchester: Manchester University Press, 1931), pp. 1-74, and H. H. Rowley, *The Servant of the Lord and Other Essays on the Old Testament* (London: Lutterworth Press, 1952), pp. 5 ff.

[67] *Der Messias* (Göttingen: Vandenhoeck & Ruprecht, 1929), pp. 287-339.

[68] *Second Isaiah*, pp. 264-70 and notes *ad loc.*

[69] *Introduction to the Old Testament* (Copenhagen: G. E. C. Gad, 1949), II, 110.

[70] *Op. cit.*, pp. 134-35.

42:1, "Behold my servant"

"my chosen"

"whom I uphold"
"I have put my spirit upon him"
42:4, "and the coastlands wait for his law [tôrāh]"

49:1, "Listen to me, O coastlands,
and hearken, you peoples from afar"

"The LORD called me from the womb,
from the body of my mother he named my
name (cf. vs. 5)
49:2, "He made my mouth like a sharp sword,
in the shadow of his hand he hid me"
49:3, "You are my servant
Israel, in whom I will be glorified"

49:5, "For I am honored in the eyes of the LORD"
49:6, "I will give you as a light to the nations"

40:9g-10 introduces God with three "behold's"; 41:
24, 29, the judgment against the nations with two
(cf. also 40:15); for style cf. 41:8
41:8, "Whom I have chosen"; vs. 9d, "I have chosen
you" (cf. 42:20; 45:4; 43:10; 44:1)
41:10d, "I will uphold you"
44:3, "I will pour my Spirit upon your descendants"
51:5d, "the coastlands wait for me." See especially
the preceding verse, "for a law will go forth from
me"
See 41:1; 51:1, 4, 7. The reference to the coastlands
is frequent in Second Isaiah, and the style is
characteristic
44:2, 24, "who formed you from the womb"
43:1, "he who formed you, O Israel . . .
I have called you by name"

51:16, "And I have put my words in your mouth,
and hid you in the shadow of my hand"
44:21, "You are my servant;
O Israel . . .
44:23, "For the LORD . . .
will be glorified in Israel"
43:4, "because you are . . .
honored, and I love you"
42:6, "I have given you as . . .
a light to the nations"
51:4, "and my justice for a light to the peoples"

---

the special group of songs, the situation changes completely. For it is in these contexts that we recognize the framework in which the poems must fall. One example will serve. It has always been recognized that 42:5 is a crucial verse and thus marks a new beginning. But the body of the poem must be longer than merely two verses (42:6-7). Moreover, vss. 8-9 connect perfectly with what precedes, as many scholars have been quick to see (observe the twofold "I am Yahweh"). Again, vs. 9 anticipates "the new song" which corresponds to "the new events"; besides, the parallelism of "glory" and "praise" in vss. 8, 12 shows the connection between the two strophes (vss. 6-9, 10-13). Vs. 13, in turn, introduces the great intervention of Yahweh in vss. 14-17. The poem is a model of composition, and detailed analysis only confirms this impression. Similarly, most if not all of ch. 49 is characterized by its dialogue style, and the history of investigation into the form of the chapter confirms this. Finally, it is becoming increasingly clear that vss. 10-11 in ch. 50 are required, and if this is accepted, then vss. 1-3 assume a more plausible status as part of the poem (see Exeg. ad loc.). Bertholet and Volz and others have assigned 52:13–53:12 to another author. But the continuity between 51:17–52:12 and ch. 54 is preserved in 52:13–53:12 when one recognizes the dominating mood given in the framework of the poem. Moreover, the poem contains a number of the major motifs of the surrounding context.

A partial list of relationships between the so-called servant poems and the rest of Second Isaiah appears above. The third song (50:4-9) has equally striking parallels, and the fourth (52:13–53:12) has a sufficient number to suggest identity of authorship. The impression gained from a literary comparison is confirmed by an examination of the pervasive motifs which are so characteristic a feature of Second Isaiah's poems. The following are far from a complete listing; they may be said to be typical, however: "justice" in 42:1-4 (note the many judgment scenes and the constant use of mishpāṭ in crucial contexts, e.g., 40:27; 51:4); "law" or "teaching" (42:4, 21, 24; 51:4); "nations" and "peoples"; "coastlands"; the weakness of Israel and the strength of God; the arm of Yahweh (40:10, 11; 48:14; 51:5, 9; 52:10; 53:1; cf. 59:16; 63:5, 12), the birth of the servant (49:1, 5; 44:21, 24); "salvation" (49:6; 51:5, 6, 8). Again, studies of the vocabulary of the servant songs confirm the results of literary comparison and examination of motifs.[71] Further, if the poems are the work of an interpolator, why is there no indication of it? There is no formal device anywhere suggesting that an interpolator has sought to introduce alien material, and this is the more striking since the representation of the servant in the poems is held to be so divergent from that of their con-

[71] Martin Schian, Die Ebed-Jahwe-Lieder in Jes. 40-66 (Teuchern: Otto Lieferenz, 1894); cf. North, op. cit., pp. 168-69.

texts. It is worth observing that the songs and the poems betray the same literary relationships, above all to Jeremiah, both in language and in literary type (e.g., the confessions). A final argument supporting Second Isaiah's authorship of the songs emerges from an examination of the literary structure of the poems. Such an examination shows that the first three songs are parts of larger literary units and that they fall into a clearly perceptible structure which is characteristic of the prophet's method of composition displayed elsewhere (see Exeg. *ad loc.*).

c) *The Servant and Israel.*—The results of this study thus far are of great consequence, for if the servant songs are the work of Second Isaiah and an integral part of his poetic compositions, then the servant of the Lord is certainly Israel. Moreover, it is possible to interpret the songs in the light of their present contexts and in the light of the prophet's thought revealed elsewhere in the poems. Yet there is one consideration, perhaps outweighing all others, which makes the problem exceedingly acute and difficult. This is the portrait of the servant in the songs as compared with the portrait in the poems. For the position of those who see in the songs a separate collection, either by another author or by Second Isaiah himself in a later stage of his prophetic career, is that the figure presented in the songs is an individual person. In the second and third poems he speaks in autobiographical fashion in the profoundly inward accents of such a one as Jeremiah, and above all in the supreme poem of the collection (52:13–55:12) the lines sketch the life story of an individual sufferer. There is a concreteness of detail and withal such a striking semblance to an actual person that a collective entity like Israel seems out of the question. Not only so, but the figure of the songs seems to stand in sharp contrast to the figure of the holy community of Israel. This position has been admirably stated by Johann Fischer:

The servant of Yahweh and the servant Israel are also basically different in their character. The servant Israel is despondent and faint-hearted [*versagt*] and must be admonished again and again to turn to trust in God (40:27; 41:8 ff.; 44:1-2, 21, etc.), the servant of Yahweh overcomes momentary despair through unshakable trust in God (49:4; 50:7-9). The servant of Yahweh is guiltless and sinless (50:5; 53:4-6, 12), the servant Israel on the contrary is a sinner from birth (48:4; cf. 43:27). The suffering of the servant of God is only explicable as suffering for the sins of others (53:4-6, 9, 11-12), the servant Israel suffers in exile for his own sins (42:18-25; 43:22-28; 47:6; 50:1; 54:7). The servant of Yahweh suffers patiently (53:7), the servant Israel in discouragement (40:27; 49:14; 50: 1-2); the servant of Yahweh suffers voluntarily, he interecedes for the sinners; the servant Israel suffers

unwillingly and his enemies are to be avenged (41:11-12, 15-16; 42:13-15, etc.). To this basically different characterization is to be added the fact that the servant of the pericopes has an active mission to Israel. . . . Finally the servant of Yahweh has a mission of suffering for Israel (52:13–53:12) and thus cannot be identical with Israel.[72]

These contrasts are given further weight by the fact that in 49:5-6 it is the task and mission of the servant

to bring Jacob back to him,
   and that Israel might be gathered to him

and

to raise up the tribes of Jacob,
   and to restore the preserved of Israel.

Here the servant seems to be set over against Israel so that it is difficult to identify the two.

d) *The Servant and an Individual.*—But who, then, is the individual referred to in the songs? Many identifications have been proposed. Duhm saw in the figure a prophet-teacher of the law who became afflicted with leprosy, and assigned the songs to the middle of the fifth century B.C. But in 1921 Sigmund Mowinckel[73] sought to identify the servant with the prophet (cf. Acts 8:34). According to Mowinckel, the servant of the songs is not a future (eschatological) figure, as elsewhere, but a contemporary whose work is described vividly and impressively as taking place in the present (42:6-7; 49:1-6; 50:4-11). He is an individual whose mission is directed to the conversion of the nations in contrast to the poems where he is a purely passive agent. He is a Jew and, above all, a prophet whose life and activity are those of the prophets. Indeed, the consciousness of the servant is like that which can be derived from inferences concerning the prophet in the poems. Thus the servant is equated with Second Isaiah. Mowinckel's publication received an acclamation second only to that accorded Duhm's famous commentary. Among the scholars who accepted his view were Hermann Gunkel, Max Haller, Emil Balla, and Hans Schmidt. Others accepted it in a somewhat modified form. Ernst Sellin, who had written three monographs on the subject, identifying the servant with Zerubbabel (1898), Jehoiachin (1901), and Moses (1922), now expressed the opinion (1930) that the servant of the first three songs was the prophet but that the fourth song was a funeral dirge composed by the

---

[72] *Das Buch Isaias* (Bonn: Peter Hanstein, 1939; "Die Heilige Schrift des Alten Testaments"), II, 10-11. Used by permission. Fischer's presentation of the argument is one of the most detailed and cogent of those who argue for two servants.

[73] *Der Knecht Jahwäs* (Kristiania: Gröhndahl & Sons, 1921).

prophet's pupil, Third Isaiah, in honor of his master, a view which was developed some time later by Karl Elliger. Paul Volz identified the servant with the prophet in the four songs (42:1-4, 5-9; 49:1-6; 50:4-9), but he isolated 52:13–53:12 from the rest as a composition from a much later period. Only in this last song is there an eschatological setting and orientation.

It was difficult to maintain Mowinckel's thesis in the form in which he submitted it, chiefly because it ascribed to the prophet the description of his own sufferings and death. For this reason Mowinckel himself found it necessary to restate and reformulate his views in various ways, but such scholars as Balla,[74] and more particularly Joachim Begrich, continued to support his earlier position.[75] Other identifications have been made with some historical character of the past: Moses (Sellin, 1922), Uzziah (J. C. W. Augusti), Hezekiah (K. F. Bahrdt), Josiah (Abarbanel), Jehoiachin (Sellin, 1901),[76] Zerubbabel (Sellin, 1898), Isaiah (C. F. Stäudlin, 1791), a martyr from the time of Manasseh, probably Isaiah (Ewald), Jeremiah (Saadia Gaon, F. A. Farley),[77] Meshullam, the elder son of Zerubbabel (J. L. Palache), Eleazar (Bertholet). Not all of the foregoing writers deny the authorship of Second Isaiah to the poems. Volz, for example, defends it for all except 52:13–53:12, and explains the difference by the transformation that came over the prophet at his call to be the servant.

The history of the attempts to identify the servant of the songs is illuminating. On the one hand, it shows how many different persons have been seized upon as possibilities, and how in turn each of these has been rejected by the majority of scholars. Again, scholars have repeatedly turned to historical characters about whom very little is known and for whom extant information gives little support. On the other hand, such figures as Moses, Jeremiah, and above all the prophet himself, bear upon them the features which are consistent with the servant's portrait. But when all is said, the fact remains that no single person is sufficient to bear the burden of what is disclosed in the songs. For the reality that lies within and be-

hind the songs is infinitely greater than any person could exemplify. The scope of the servant's mission is wider and more universal than that of Jeremiah (Jer. 1:5, 10 ff., or the Scythian-Babylonian oracles); the nature of the mission (42:1-4; 52:13–53:12) is not such as any historical Israelite could be expected to accomplish; the effects of his work are not such as to produce the extraordinary response from the nations; and the description of the servant's sufferings in 52:13–53:12 can hardly apply to any single person. Karl Budde scarcely overstates the case in pronouncing the usual identifications as "nothing short of fantastic, and the extreme of absurdity."[78] On the other hand, what cannot apply to an individual may apply to a community such as Second Isaiah conceives Israel to be.[79] The momentous character of the servant's mission within the servant songs is no greater than the momentous character of his mission without (cf., e.g., 40:9-10; 41:14-16; 43:8-13); moreover, the songs and the poems share the same quality of intimacy, inwardness, and sense of high destiny.

We have already noticed the similarity of phraseology and thought between the songs and the poems, In both, the servant is Yahweh's elected one, his called one, his "named one," his instrument of justice (*mishpāṭ*); in both he is comforted, given as a light to the nations (42:6; 49:6; 51:4); in both the purpose of Yahweh is the salvation of the peoples. But it is contended that the servant in the songs is clearly an individual, that the characterization is so personal and concrete that reference to a community is extremely unlikely. At this point it is essential to remember that Oriental ways of speaking about a community are not ours and that the Old Testament is itself its own best witness to this. Thus in Second Isaiah Israel is constantly addressed by the singular second personal pronoun "thou," perhaps more emphatically and constantly than any passage of similar scope in the Old Testament, and this form of address appears in both the songs and the poems. Again, Israel is given a name of endearment like "Jeshurun." It is doubtful whether the songs ever surpass such individualization as that found in 46:3-4; 54:1-8; or in 47:1-3, 5, 7-8 (cf. 41:13; 42:19; 44:1-2). Moreover, it is important to

[74] Balla, "Das Problem des Leides in der Geschichte der israelitisch-jüdischen Religion" in Schmidt, ed., ΕΥΧΑΡΙΣΤΗΡΙΟΝ, pp. 214-61.

[75] *Studien zu Deuterojesaja*, pp. 131 ff.

[76] For other theories which in one way or another detect the influence of the figure of Jehoiachin, see Rowley, *Servant of the Lord*, pp. 12-16; cf. North, *op. cit.*, pp. 50-52.

[77] Farley, "Jeremiah and 'The Suffering Servant of Jehovah' in Deutero-Isaiah," *Expository Times*, XXXVIII (1926-27), 521-24. Sheldon H. Blank ("Studies in Deutero-Isaiah," *Hebrew Union College Annual*, XV [1940], 1-46), thinks of the servant as Israel but sees many of the lines in the portrait drawn from Jeremiah.

[78] "The So-called 'Ebed Yahweh Songs,' and the Meaning of the Term 'Servant of Yahweh' in Isaiah, Chaps. 40-55," *American Journal of Theology*, III (1899), 507.

[79] Cf. H. Wheeler Robinson, *The Cross of the Servant* (London: Student Christian Movement, 1926), p. 24: "No obscure and private person could have been the Servant intended by the prophet, and those who seek an individual reference have not yet discovered with any unanimity any prominent and public personage of this age adequate to the effect on the world described in the Songs."

observe that such concrete, individualizing speech is coherent with the mood, manner, and language of Second Isaiah throughout all the poems. From the opening words ("my people . . . your God") to the end, Israel is addressed in a great variety of ways in a mood of great passion and urgency, with a remarkable realization of the divine love and compassion toward her, with an impassioned call to self-awareness, with a repeated appeal to memory of things past, and with a constant reminding of her uniqueness, which is rooted in her ancestors Abraham and Jacob. It is in this matrix that the servant of the Lord is fashioned, and the prophet merely utilizes such individualizing speech as characterized biblical thought and expression from earliest times. In this, it is worth observing, he betrays the same mentality that he exhibits in every other of his major ideas. Everywhere is displayed the same intense mood, the same propensity for laying hold of the living roots of an idea, and the same variegated and fluid manner of giving fresh nuances to the thought.

A more formidable objection to the collective view of the servant may be found in the contrast between the servant and Israel in 49:5-6. It must be admitted that here the most natural reading is to make the servant the subject of the infinitives which refer to the restoration of Israel. But this is not the only possible rendering, and a number of scholars have translated the words in such a way as to make Yahweh the subject (see Exeg. *ad loc.*). The alternative would be to see within Israel the faithful group which had not taken on the ways and worship of the conqueror. This group is not an "ideal Israel," as has been supposed by many (Skinner, *et al.*), but rather a strong minority of faithful men. Moreover, in this same song (49:3) the servant is clearly identified with Israel, and attempts to delete "Israel" on textual or metrical grounds are without any foundation. The alternative procedure to translate the word so as not to make the identification is awkward and unlikely. Yet it must be admitted that 49:5-6 constitutes the strongest argument for the individualistic interpretation.

But what answer can be given to those like Fischer, who point to the sharp contrast which exists between the contents of the songs and the poems? In the opening poem, which serves as a clue to the interpretation of so many others, Israel is said to have suffered twofold for all her sins (40:2). There was the judgment that was deserved and the judgment that was in excess of her deserts. Her sins were expiated, but there was a surplus of suffering and adversity beyond the measure needful for expiation. Again, while in the sight of God Israel's guilt was very deep and dark (the prophet nowhere minimizes this fact), yet in comparison with the nations, especially those who made her their victim, she might appear innocent. The prophet did not stand alone as the representative of the true Israel, though he did represent the true Israel in a very interior way. There were those who were loyal to the traditions of the ancestors, to the Mosaic covenantal tradition, and to the preaching of the prophets. It is precisely this awareness that prompts Second Isaiah to call his contemporaries to the faith of their fathers. As for the sharp contrasts drawn by Fischer and others, close scrutiny of both sections shows that they are much exaggerated. The servant in the songs is quite as discouraged as the servant in the poems; if in the former he overcomes "momentary despair" by his unshakable faith, the prophet, representing the true Israel, embodies this faith in at least as powerful a way. Those who equate the servant of the Lord with the prophet are following a right instinct, for it is the voice of the prophet speaking in the songs—as it is, moreover, in all the rest of the poems. If he does not appear at all times to be consistent with himself, this is no more than the fluctuation of the mood and temper of any man confronted with a similar task and situation; and from all that we can infer from the poems as to the prophet's personality, we should be surprised if he were so consistent as his modern interpreters expect him to be. The contrasts are present, but these contrasts are characteristic of his words and ideas throughout the poems; they are characteristic of a mind that is more intuitive and spontaneous, more quickly responsive to the immediacies of life, than it is logical and self-consistent. Finally, many of these sharp contrasts have been exaggerated because the judgment contexts have been read in isolation. Yet it may be doubted whether in any of the poems we have a message which is pure judgment; on the contrary, they all, or nearly all, stand in a framework where grace and compassion dominate.

e) The Mission and Destiny of Israel.— Rather than inquire into the identity of the servant in Second Isaiah, perhaps one should inquire first into the identity of Israel, the meaning of her life in the world, her history and destiny. It is obviously with these concerns that the prophet is preoccupied in the passages where the servant is clearly understood to be Israel. Such an inquiry would include all those passages where Israel is mentioned, even though the word "servant" does not appear. In the first place, we see that Israel is the offspring of Abraham (41:8), that from one ancestor she became a great people (51:1-2). In Hebraic mentality this means that the father lives on in his children.

Community goes deeper than to the one generation; it extends backwards as well as forwards through history. We see this whenever we consider the family. From fathers to sons the same soul grows through time; it is the same in preceding and succeeding generations, just as at any time it is common to the whole family. . . . The blessing which was given to Abraham keeps on acting in his successors, first in Isaac, then in Jacob and all his sons, and so in the whole of Israel.[80]

The promise made to Abraham (Gen. 12:1-3) is realized in those who follow him; this is the meaning of the Yahwist's family history. The blessing to Abraham lives on in all who are Abraham's seed (51:1; John 8:33). The progenitor lives on in those who are his descendants. The social group thus takes on the character of the ancestor. This relationship of ancestor to descendants is but one aspect of the psychic unity that pervades Israel's life. "The unity of the people rests upon a common being and a common history, or in other words, upon a psychic community."[81] Thus the tribe or the people can speak as though it were an individual (e.g., Lam. 3; etc.), and it can be addressed as an individual. The intensely individualistic passages in Isa. 1:5-6; Ezek. 16; Hos. 2:4 ff.; and the Psalms (e.g., Pss. 126; 130; etc.) are but a normal Semitic way of speaking. The heavy emotional burden of the prophet is explained by this psychic rapport he bears with his people; his intercessions for Israel avail because he speaks as their representative. Similarly, the priest in his cultic ministrations acts in behalf of Israel. The good and evil deeds of the king are accounted as the deeds of the people; they reap the rewards and punishments of the king's behavior. Second Isaiah is thus appropriating a major feature of Israel's psychical mentality: his personal vocabulary in all its intensity is characteristic of the way he deals with other aspects of Hebraic traditional mentality. Israel includes past, present, and future. The eschatological matrix of the Israel passages is primary, but eschatological thought includes within its range the whole of the past and the present.[82] *The primary relationship*

Israel bears to the Lord is that of servant. Her worship of Yahweh is a service (עֲבֹדָה) to him; the members of the faithful community are his servants (Neh. 1:10; Pss. 89:50; 90:13; etc.). The patriarchs in general are called his servants (Deut. 9:27), also in particular (Abraham— Gen. 26:24; Jacob—Ezek. 28:25); so too the prophets in general (Jer. 7:25; Amos 3:7) and in particular (Elijah—II Kings 9:36; Jonah—II Kings 14:25; Isaiah—Isa. 20:3). Most frequently the term is applied to Moses and David (more than thirty times). In Third Isaiah the term is applied frequently to the worshiping community (56:6; 63:17; 65:8-9, 13-15; 66:14). Again Second Isaiah lays hold of a central motif of biblical faith, and again he transforms it by filling it with deeper and broader content; indeed, this single word is the prophet's central designation for Israel.

But with this word he employs other categories which greatly deepen and enrich it: Israel's peculiar relationship to her Holy One, her unique creation and birth, her redemption, the help and strength which comes to her as Yahweh's servant, her witness to him as one God, her vast and varied mission to all the nations, her covenanthood;[83] indeed, all the major features of the prophet's theology are constantly understood in relation to the servant of the Lord. On the other hand, Israel is blind and deaf, disobedient, willful and apostate; she suffers under the judgment of God, yet the judgment is overcome by Yahweh's unmotivated grace. It is the servant's place to glorify God, to sing God's praises, and to respond with joy and gladness to God's mighty work of redemption.

Above all, the servant offers himself willingly as a vicarious sacrifice for the sins of the nations. The divine judgment which was the nations' due was voluntarily borne by him; he substituted his own life for theirs. All the affliction, pain, persecution, disdain, execution, and death —every imaginable kind of suffering—fell upon him. All this lay in the purpose of God (observe again the pervasiveness of this motif). And in the midst of his suffering he attached himself to the company of Israel's intercessors from Abraham on, and prayed for those who smote him.

Israel, and Israel alone, is able to bear all that is said about the servant of the Lord. For the fundamental fact outweighing all others is the repeated equation of the two in the poems. And with this incontrovertible fact belong two

[80] Johannes Pedersen, *Israel: Its Life and Culture I-II* (London: Oxford University Press, 1926), p. 276; see also Aubrey R. Johnson, *The One and the Many in the Israelite Conception of God* (Cardiff: University of Wales Press, 1942).

[81] Pedersen, *op. cit.*, p. 275.

[82] See H. Wheeler Robinson, "The Hebrew Conception of Corporate Personality," in Volz, ed., *Werden und Wesen des Alten Testaments*, pp. 49-62; see also the discussion of Israel, pp. 404-6.

[83] For the connection between covenant and the verb "to serve," etc., see the important discussion by Curt Lindhagen, *The Servant Motif in the Old Testament* (Uppsala: A.-B. Lundequistska, 1950), pp. 82-106, *et passim.*

other considerations scarcely less weighty: (a) on grounds of literary style and form the songs belong with the poems, and (b) far from marring their contexts, the songs fit into the framework of the poems, while their deletion has raised difficulties which have never been resolved. Between the servant of the songs and the servant of the poems there is a profoundly interior relation; they move on the same lofty plane and descend to the same depths. For this portrait the prophet utilizes the classical materials to which he was heir: protology, with its reflection upon the primordial deeps; eschatology, with its reflection upon the wonders of the fulfillment of the divine purpose in the holy, chosen, called, redeemed, and covenanted people; history, as it was understood in the sacred tradition, in the light of the great international movements of the sixth century B.C., and the contemporary events in which Cyrus, Yahweh's chosen deliverer, is the central figure; prophecy, as it was proclaimed by its greatest exemplars, above all, Jeremiah, whose prophetic ministry to the nations, personal sufferings and afflictions, and confessional cries were appropriated by a mind which stood in profound rapport with him; liturgy, as it was employed in the cultic life of the people, in Israel's hymns and prayers and laments and salvation oracles; judicial proceedings, both in the celestial realm where Yahweh holds council and on earth where the events of history are seen as divine judgments. All the resources of the prophet's fervent imagination and capacious memory are used to describe Israel, and each of these is employed with an interior apprehension and yet with an independence which transmutes and deepens all that is borrowed.

That the prophet is influenced by the prevailing modes of Near Eastern thinking is highly probable. The affinities with Babylonian and Ugaritic literature cannot be denied. To what extent he was influenced by the Tammuz liturgies it is difficult to say. He probably did not sketch his servant portrait after the model of Tammuz; indeed, he probably did not portray him as a dying and rising savior-god. Yet the language may well have been influenced by the liturgies of the Near East. Many of the parallels which have been adduced have little weight, but there are a sufficient number to suggest the possibility of outside influence.

In his use of Israel's traditions Second Isaiah turns to the patriarchs Abraham and Jacob, the two ancestors whose stories have been coalesced into a continuous narrative by the Yahwist; to Moses,[84] the leader of the Exodus and the desert

[84] Aage Bentzen, Messias, Moses redivivus, Menschensohn (Zürich: Zwingli, 1948).

sojourn; to David, the king to whom Yahweh granted his election and covenant promises; and to the prophets, above all (see p. 566) to Jeremiah, whose life story weaves itself into the fabric of the prophet's writing. The Exodus, the wandering, the conquest, the long periods of Egyptian and Assyrian oppressions, the history of Babylonian rule, and the destruction of the Holy City constitute the background against which he composes his poems. All the sacred past converges upon the present decisive moment in which the campaigns of Cyrus open a new era and prepare for the coming of the Lord. All the persons and events to which we have referred are present, and present in a unique degree. The prophet interprets their significance in an eschatological context; they all have a maximum meaning in the life history of the true Israel.

f) The Servant and the Messiah.—There still remains one problem of great importance and difficulty. How is the servant of the Lord to be related to Israel's messianic conceptions, and especially to the figure of the Messiah? Not a few scholars see in the servant the features of the divine king as he appears in the royal psalms and elsewhere (e.g., II Sam. 21:17; Lam. 4:20). On the basis of such passages as Pss. 2; 18; 89; 118:5 ff.; etc., Aubrey R. Johnson concludes:

> The Davidic king is the Servant of Jahweh; but . . . at the New Year Festival he is the suffering Servant. He is the Messiah of Jahweh; but on this occasion he is the humiliated Messiah. The fact is that we are here dealing with a ritual humiliation of the Davidic king which in principle is not unlike that suffered by the Babylonian king in the analogous New Year Festival.[85]

Other scholars (e.g., Engnell) have pressed this position much farther than Johnson. It is true that there are a number of interesting links between the psalms in question and the poems of Second Isaiah. The similarity in terminology is especially noteworthy. But that the Davidic Messiah is to be identified with the servant is hard to believe, for there is no credible evidence that the two were equated before the Christian Era.[86] Moreover, the attributes given to the

[85] "The Role of the King in the Jerusalem Cultus," in The Labyrinth, ed. S. H. Hooke (London: Society for Promoting Christian Knowledge, 1935), p. 100.

[86] See Rowley, Servant of the Lord, for a thorough and superbly documented discussion of "The Suffering Servant and the Davidic Messiah," pp. 61-88, especially p. 85: "There is no serious evidence, then, of the bringing together of the concepts of the Suffering Servant and the Davidic Messiah before the Christian era, or of the formulation of the doctrine of the Messiah ben Ephraim at so early a date, and the opinions of the leading authorities in this field cannot be overturned by any tangible evidence. On the other hand, there is tangible

servant by Second Isaiah are by no means confined to the Davidic king; indeed, as we have seen, they are to be found in many places in the Old Testament, and Second Isaiah is fond of ranging throughout the tradition. The late Targum, to be sure, identifies the servant with the Messiah, but in doing so it eliminates all traces of his suffering in ch. 53.

The traditional messianic interpretation is upheld with great learning by such eminent Roman Catholic scholars as Fischer, Feldmann, van der Ploeg, and Kissane. It must be admitted that the absence of the term "Messiah" constitutes no objection, since First Isaiah does not use it in his messianic oracles. Nor is the ascription of the term to Cyrus a serious obstacle. But it does remind us of the fact that the term Messiah nowhere in the Old Testament has the technical associations of later times. To interpret the Messiah in such language as is used of the servant would be out of harmony with anything else in the Old Testament. The affinities of the songs with the messianic passages in Isaiah and Jeremiah are by no means as close as is sometimes supposed; the contexts and terminology are quite different, and the provenance of the words to which reference is made can be easily quite other than has been assumed. Finally, account would have to be taken of the servant references where Israel is mentioned and where the language is equally impressive and momentous.

Yet the servant is a figure of the coming age. He must be understood in the total setting of the whole collection of poems and of the individual poems which make reference to him. The autobiographical utterances of 49:1-6; 50: 4-9 are no objection to this view; these passages appear in a wider setting which makes the future reference clear. The decisive point of time is historical and yet more than historical. The history of Israel is not enough to explain him, though the whole sacred history is somehow involved in the portrait as are the tumultuous events of the prophet's age.[87] The servant stands at the eschaton. It is precisely in this kind of setting that all that is said concerning him and all that he has himself to say have meaning and relevance. Because of this position in which he stands, the figure was susceptible of messianic interpretation. As the chosen servant of God from Abraham to Cyrus, from the old Exodus to the new, from the creation of the world to the

and positive evidence in the New Testament which is fatal to such a view."

[87] Cf. H. H. Rowley, *The Re-discovery of the Old Testament* (Philadelphia: Westminster Press, 1946), pp. 201-2: "This great idea was not the deduction from any historical suffering of Israel, for history knows of none that could sustain it"; see also *Servant of the Lord*, p. 51.

imminent appearing of Yahweh in all his glory, he was such a reality as might later be identified with "the coming One."

g) *The Servant and Jesus of Nazareth.*—It is on the foundation of Second Isaiah's eschatological poems that the authors of the Gospels write their accounts of Jesus of Nazareth. The earliest of them opens his Gospel with a quotation from the opening poem of Second Isaiah and sees its fulfillment in John's preaching (cf. 40:3 and Mark 1:1-3), and Matthew and Luke refashion the account each in his own dramatic way (Matt. 3:1-3; Luke 3:1-6). The writer of the Fourth Gospel makes the words even more dramatic and momentous (John 1:19-23). The infancy hymns in Luke's Gospel contain a number of clear echoes of Second Isaiah, and they appear in the kind of lyrical context which is characteristic of the prophet (Luke 1:51-52, 54-55, 76-77; 2:30-32). The messianic words of ordination at Jesus' baptism are drawn from 42:1 (Mark 1:11 and parallels), and when he returns to Nazareth, he unrolls the long roll to Isa. 61:1 ff., which was doubtless understood as a reference to the servant, and upon completing the passage, he says, "Today this scripture has been fulfilled in your hearing" (Luke 4:16 ff.). Matthew interprets the miracles of Jesus as a fulfillment of 42:1-4 (Matt. 12:15-21; see also 8:17). At the Transfiguration (Mark 9:2-8; Matt. 17:1-8; Luke 9:28-36) the words from 42:1 sound again from heaven, as at the baptism.

More important, and indeed more difficult, is the relation of Jesus' ministry to the suffering servant. Our answer to this question will depend at least in part upon the authenticity of the relevant verses, above all, the crucial verse of Mark 10:45: "For the Son of man also came not to be served but to serve, and to give his life as a ransom for many." Here the allusion to Isa. 53 seems unmistakable. Equally clear and significant are the words of Jesus in Luke 22:37: "For I tell you that this scripture must be fulfilled in me, 'And he was reckoned with transgressors'; for what is written about me has its fulfillment." The apostle Paul nowhere speaks of Jesus as the servant of the Lord, but the primitive tradition which he received already refers to the suffering servant (I Cor. 15:3: "Christ died for our sins in accordance with the scriptures"). The preaching of Philip in Acts 8:26-39 is based on Isa. 53:7-8. These passages are by no means all of those that allude to the suffering servant. Millar Burrows concludes his examination of a number of the references with the following judgment: "It is thus fair to say that from Acts on the identification of Jesus with the Suffering Servant of the Lord is constant in the New Testament, and there is no compelling reason to doubt that Jesus himself originated the idea." [88] H. Wheeler Robinson, who holds the same view as Burrows, remarks as follows:

It is no exaggeration to say that this is the most original and daring of all the characteristic features of the teaching of Jesus, and it led to the most important element in His work. . . . There is no evidence of a suffering Messiah in previous or contemporary Judaism to explain the conception in the consciousness of Jesus.[89]

IV. Third Isaiah

In chs. 56–66 the disciples (or disciple?) of Second Isaiah seek to perpetuate the prophetic message of their master, but they do so under different conditions. Again and again there sound the notes of expectancy of imminent deliverance and salvation (56:1, 7-8; 58:8-9*b*, 12; 59:15*c*-20; 60:1–62:12; 63:1-6; 66:21-22). The words and sentences of the prophet are remembered and repeated in the manner of a disciple. It is obvious almost throughout that the writers depend for their message not only upon what they have learned from Second Isaiah but also upon their familiarity with the prophetic tradition. On the other hand, there is a notable lack of missionary interest and concern, though there are passages which are as universalistic and widehearted as anything in the Old Testament. The servant of the Lord does not appear in the guise represented in Second Isaiah, although 61:1-3 is considered by many to be another servant utterance. The eschatology resembles that of chs. 34–35 more than that of chs. 40–55. It is more apocalyptic in character, more tragic in its pessimism, more dualistic, more cosmic in its depths. The new age will be ushered in by the creation of a new heaven and earth (65:17; cf. 66:22). While certain sections are much like Second Isaiah in the participation of all Israel in the coming salvation (57:14-19; 59:21; 60:1–62:12), others include only the pious community while the rebellious and apostates are punished (50:18; 63:1-6; 65:12 ff.; 66:16-17).

Very striking is the interest in the practices and observances of the cult. The syncretistic activities of the apostates are roundly condemned (57:3 ff.; 65:2 ff.) while Yahweh's affection for his loyal devotees is portrayed in profoundly moving words (63:16; 66:13). The sabbath is an institution whose observance is incumbent upon all of Yahweh's people (56:2, 4, 6; 58:13-14), yet its meaning is interpreted according to the deepest ethical insights of the pre-exilic prophets. Similarly, fasting is to be

practiced, but not as a mere form. The fasting which God "chooses" is inward and ethical (58:6 ff.). The reflections upon the temple and its cult are among the most remarkable in the Old Testament. The eunuch and the alien are not to be excluded, but God accepts their worship and sacrifices; he will make them joyful in his house of prayer, "For my house shall be called a house of prayer for all peoples" (56: 6-7). Yet the temple is not to be unduly venerated; God does not dwell in temples made with hands, and the true tabernacle of his dwelling is with the humble and contrite in spirit (66:1-2; cf. also the equally remarkable words of 57:15). As in Ezekiel, cultic and moral performances are linked together, both their faithful performance and their apostate violation (cf., e.g., 56:1-2, 4; 58:1-14, 59:1-9). Finally, the emphasis upon prayer and its efficacy is one of the noteworthy contributions of these poems to Israel's religious faith. The liturgical form of several of the poems, in which we hear the cries of penitence and confession, the response of the prophet, and the words of warning and assurance in the context of the act of worship, ushers us into the living faith of an emerging Judaism.

As the foregoing discussion indicates, chs. 56–66 do not have the dominating coherence of Second Isaiah's eschatological poems. The writers are familiar with the work of their great leader, but the practical problems of restoration and reconstruction, the disappointment and discouragement of the people, the presence of alien influences corrupting their common life, all these press for immediate answer. There are passages in these poems which rise to the very heights of prophecy, such as 57:15-16; 58:6-14; 61:8; 64:8; 66:1-2; there are others which resemble Haggai and Zechariah in the way they deal with the concrete issues of the time and the eschatological hope in relation to them (56:1-8; 59:1-21; 66:6-14). The prophecy as a whole gives us valuable insight into the conditions and religious life of Israel in the decades following 538 B.C.

V. Text

The Hebrew text of Second Isaiah has been transmitted exceptionally well. Its superior value is shown by the way in which it has preserved parallelism and metrical construction and also by the fact that it generally yields a satisfactory sense. It is not flawless, but the number of corruptions is small.[90]

The discovery of two scrolls of the book of Isaiah near the Dead Sea in 1947 has given fresh impetus to the study of the text. One of

---

[88] *An Outline of Biblical Theology* (Philadelphia: Westminster Press, 1946), p. 88.

[89] *Redemption and Revelation* (New York: Harper & Bros., 1942), p. 199.

[90] See Torrey's important discussion in *Second Isaiah*, pp. 206-7.

these, which has been published in its entirety,[91] contains the complete text, with the exception of a few lacunae. Divergences are numerous but deal chiefly with orthography. The date has been much controverted; it probably falls somewhere between 100 B.C. and A.D. 100. Thus it antedates our earliest Hebrew manuscript and the Masoretic Text by many centuries. Since, however, an early text is not necessarily superior to a late one, the Dead Sea Scroll must be judged solely on its own merits. The RSV adopts its reading in only thirteen instances, which is perhaps unduly conservative. The Exegesis takes account of some of the most important divergences.

The Septuagint represents the same type of text as the Masoretic, but its distinct inferiority is shown by its many loose renderings, its paraphrases, its many obscurities, and its additions and omissions. Torrey gives a reliable estimate of its value: "It is only by a single word here and there, more often by a single letter, that it enables us to emend the massoretic text; and in the majority of these instances the correction is so obvious that it could have been made by conjecture alone." [92] The general inferiority of the Septuagint is to be explained not only by the state of its Hebrew prototype but also by the corruptions which arose in the course of its transmission.[93] The Targum, the Syriac, and the Vulgate have their value chiefly in relation to other witnesses.

VI. Outline of Contents

---

[91] Millar Burrows, ed., *The Dead Sea Scrolls of St. Mark's Monastery* (New Haven: American Schools of Oriental Research, 1950-51), Vol. I. Of the second scroll, E. L. Sukenik has published two columns (Isa. 47:17–49:7 and 50:7–51:8) in his *Megilloth Genuzoth* (Jerusalem: Bialik Foundation, 1950), Vol. II.

[92] *Op. cit.*, p. 209. Torrey's discussion of the text in his introductions and notes to the poems is of the first importance.

[93] See especially Joseph Ziegler, *Untersuchungen zur Septuaginta des Buches Isaias* (Münster i.w.: Aschendorffs, 1934; "Alttestamentliche Abhandlungen").

VII. Selected Bibliography

COMMENTARIES

DUHM, BERNHARD. *Das Buch Jesaja* ("Göttinger Handkommentar zum Alten Testament"). Göttingen: Vandenhoeck & Ruprecht, 1892. 2nd ed., 1902. 3rd ed., 1914. 4th ed., 1922.

FELDMANN, FRANZ. *Das Buch Isaias* ("Exegetisches Handbuch zum Alten Testament"). Münster in Westfalen: Aschendorff, 1925-26.

FISCHER, JOHANN. *Das Buch Isaias* ("Die Heilige Schrift des Alten Testaments"). Bonn: Peter Hanstein, 1939.

KISSANE, EDWARD J. *The Book of Isaiah.* Dublin: Browne & Nolan, 1943. Vol. II.

LEVY, REUBEN. *Deutero-Isaiah.* London: Oxford University Press, 1925.

SKINNER, JOHN. *The Book of the Prophet Isaiah* ("Cambridge Bible"). Rev. ed. Cambridge: Cambridge University Press, 1915.

SMITH, GEORGE ADAM. *The Book of Isaiah.* New and rev. ed. New York: Doubleday, Doran, n.d.

TORREY, C. C. *The Second Isaiah.* New York: Charles Scribner's Sons, 1928.

VOLZ, PAUL. *Jesaia II* ("Kommentar zum Alten Testament"). Leipzig: A. Deichert, 1932.

WADE, G. W. *The Book of the Prophet Isaiah* ("Westminster Commentaries"). 2nd. ed. London: Methuen & Co., 1929.

TEXTUAL AND SPECIAL STUDIES

BEGRICH, JOACHIM. *Studien zu Deuterojesaja* ("Beiträge zur Wissenschaft vom Alten und Neuen
Testament"). Stuttgart: W. Kohlhammer, 1938.
BURROWS, MILLAR. "Variant Readings in the Isaiah
Manuscript," *Bulletin of the American Schools of
Oriental Research*, No. 111 (1948), pp. 16-24; No.
113 (1949), pp. 24-32.
———, ed. *The Dead Sea Scrolls of St. Mark's
Monastery*. New Haven: American Schools of Oriental Research, 1950-51. Vol. I, "The Isaiah Manuscript and the Habakkuk Commentary."

ELLIGER, KARL, "Der Prophet Tritojesaja," *Zeitschrift
für die alttestamentliche Wissenschaft*, XLIX
(1931), 112-41.
KÖHLER, LUDWIG. *Deuterojesaja (Jesaja 40–55) stil-
kritisch untersucht*. Giessen: A. Töpelmann, 1923.
LINDHAGEN, CURT. *The Servant Motif in the Old
Testament*. Uppsala: A.-B. Lundequistska, 1950.
NORTH, CHRISTOPHER R. *The Suffering Servant in
Deutero-Isaiah*. London: Oxford University Press,
1948.
SMITH, SIDNEY. *Isaiah, Chapters XL-LV*. London:
British Academy, 1944.

TEXT, EXEGESIS, AND EXPOSITION, CHS. 40-66

The Relevance of These Prophecies to Our Time.*

—The century and longer during which these poems were written and addressed to the exiles in Babylon, and to the returned community attempting to build again its ruined land, had a mood strangely similar to that of the mid-twentieth century.

The poet-prophets spoke to apprehensive people. After more than a generation of the exile in Babylon, a new military power rose suddenly on the scene under Cyrus, the Persian, and moved westward, sweeping everything before it. Empires were toppling. Commerce and trade were in chaos. The Hebrews in Babylon had followed the counsel of Jeremiah and had settled down in the communities where they had been placed. With the industry, thrift, and skill characteristic of their race, they had become a vigorous element in the body economic. Financial uncertainty now clouded the horizon. What was befalling their world? They looked with alarm upon this new conqueror from the east who was upsetting it.

There had followed a time of relief and eager anticipation when Babylon had fallen, and the opportunity to return to their homeland had arrived. But when some of them reached Jerusalem and began the arduous task of rebuilding their wrecked land, the difficulties loomed overwhelmingly. The small religious community found enemies both within and without Israel. The depressed and fearful mood which prevailed during the Exile settled on them once more. Other prophets took up the comforting ministry of the great unknown poet of chs. 40–55, and gave messages of God's judgment on his enemies and of glowing hope to the faithful.

A modern volume of verse bears the title *The Age of Anxiety*.[1] It portrays the mind of its generation all over the earth. Destructive wars have left many lands on the brink of economic collapse. Men follow with concern the meetings of statesmen, wondering whether powers as spiritually incompatible as those which dominate the current world can adjust to one another. Do they wish for stability and prosperity for every people? Or are some hoping that financial chaos will prove the undoing of the regimes of others? Many nations seem hopelessly divided within themselves. The worst result of the world wars has been widespread moral deterioration, together with a loss of nerve. Nations, once vigorous, lack the spiritual vitality needed to cope with existent problems. Fear of another global war which would portend the destruction of our civilization, and even more immediate dread of business depression with consequent unemployment and social upheaval, leave few men

> of cheerful yesterdays
> And confident to-morrows.[2]

The devout among the exiles were beset with religious perplexities. The destruction of Jerusalem and the captivity in Babylon had been recognized as punishment for national sin. But not all Israelites had been equally sinful. Why should the righteous suffer with the guilty? Why should one nation, patently not worse than others, suffer most? These poignant questions harassed the more serious-minded. A new generation had been born and had grown up in exile. They had not been involved in the evils so terribly visited with divine wrath. Was it

---

* Pp. 419-21 include the expositor's introduction. Text and Exegesis begin on p. 422. Editors.

[1] W. H. Auden, New York: Random House, 1947.
[2] Wordsworth, *The Excursion*, Bk. VII.

justice that these young people should be fated to pass their lives in a land not their own? A gloomy proverb was on men's lips: "The fathers have eaten sour grapes, and the children's teeth are set on edge" (Jer. 31:29). Ezekiel (18:2-3) challenged this as an untrue criticism of God's government of his world. He asserted that each man is accountable only for his own good or ill. But the pessimistic proverb appeared truer to the facts of life. More than fifty years went by after the Jewish community had been brought by their captors into Babylon, and they had proved tragic years. The more sensitively religious were in constant torment of soul in their heathen surroundings. They suffered more acutely than fellow Jews who accommodated themselves to their environment. This suffering of the best was a baffling problem. It underlies the great drama of an unfairly afflicted soul—the book of Job—some of the profoundest psalms, and is dealt with in the figure of the suffering servant in Isaiah (50:1-11; 52:13–53:12). The misery of the loyally devout appeared to reflect upon the faithfulness and justice of God. Did he forget and neglect his people? Had he given up his purpose, announced to their forefathers, of making their seed a blessing to mankind? They looked at imposing images of gods of force. Could it be that their God was less mighty and unable to deliver his worshipers? The scornful exposures of idolatry show the danger to his fellow religionists which this prophet saw (44:9-20; 46:1-13; 48:5-6). They felt themselves a doomed people, with an uncaring or perhaps an incapable deity.

And when those who returned from exile reached Jerusalem the realities that confronted them were so grim, compared with the hopes by which they had been buoyed up, that a host of questionings assailed them. Why were God's promises unfulfilled? Why was only a fraction of his dispersed people restored to their homeland? Why did numbers of their fellows fall into apostasy? Why had the discipline of the Exile borne such meager fruit? If Israel had suffered vicariously on behalf of the nations, where was the result of her travail? What hope could now sustain them when earlier expectations had proved fallacious?

Similar questions bedevil the minds of more thoughtful contemporary races. Problems which wrought havoc with believing Christians some decades ago are no longer major concerns. It is not the reconciliation of the views of physical scientists with religious beliefs or difficulties caused by psychology which hold the floor when students discuss religious issues. As in these sublime poems, it is the basic character of the universe and the meaning of human history which are in question. To most Christians in the West it seemed clearly the will of God to contend for the dignity and freedom of men when brutal despotisms were ruthlessly ending both. But what did toil and blood achieve, however victorious, if they resulted in slave states holding millions in terrified subjection? Where has been the peace so confidently looked forward to? Is not our "way hid from the Lord" and the justice due to our aims "passed over by our God"? Are we assured that the God of our faith is Lord of this apparently "nonchalant universe" and controller of the puzzling pageant of events which we label history?

This is no new mood even in the hopeful United States. In the middle of the optimistic nineteenth century two writers most engrossed in the profounder aspects of life, Nathaniel Hawthorne and Herman Melville, met. The former reported of the latter:

Melville, as he always does, began to reason of Providence and futurity, and of everything that lies beyond human ken, and informed me that he had "pretty much made up his mind to be annihilated"; but still he does not seem to rest in that anticipation, and, I think will never rest until he gets hold of a definite belief. He can neither believe, nor be comfortable in his unbelief; and he is too honest and courageous not to try to do one or the other. If he were a religious man, he would be one of the most truly religious and reverential.[3]

So might be many of a later generation. They have desperately urgent business on their hands—the settling under God of a world in such justice and liberty that nations may live together in friendship. This requires a host of changes within each country and in their relations with one another. The changes often appear impossible of attainment. But others before us have confronted similarly impossible tasks. When Granville Sharp and his hardy associates in the eighteenth century battled against the unscrupulous African slave-traders, firmly entrenched both economically and politically, and faced the indifference of the mass of church people, the octogenarian John Wesley wrote Sharp a letter which concludes:

In all these difficulties what comfort it is to consider (unfashionable as it is) that there is a God! Yea, and that (as little as men think of it!) He has still all power in heaven and on earth! To Him I commend you and your glorious Cause; and am, sir, Your affectionate servant.[4]

Second Isaiah's poems contain such a noble self-revelation of the gracious and sovereign God as bred the faith of a Wesley.

[3] *English Note-books*, November 30, 1856.
[4] *The Letters of the Rev. John Wesley*, ed. J. Telford (London: Epworth Press, 1931), VIII, 17. Letter dated October 11, 1787.

Nor was religious perplexity the main obstacle. Both in Babylon and in partially restored Jerusalem the devout community felt frustrated. Its leaders kept saying: "I have labored in vain, I have spent my strength for nought, and in vain" (49:4). Whatever faith and hope might tell them, they faced the harsh facts of history. The world had gone to pieces. Their own loved people were scattered over the known earth. Where could they look for help? They knew they could do nothing to wrest liberty from their captors, to retrieve the calamities of an earlier day, to reassemble their dispersed fellow countrymen, to reconstitute their people an independent nation and to speed it to the fulfillment of its destiny. They were "in the fell clutch of circumstance." What or who could master events? Likewise in the twentieth century, men once confident of advances won by education, by idealism, by religious faith, have found history raising walls in their path. The course of events seems against them. They are incapable of bringing to birth in nations the mind essential to peace. Their very gains in knowledge, their vast strides in science and technology, the rich accumulations of the centuries in culture only render more pitiable their impotence to establish relations between races and nations which assure a decent future for the children of today and tomorrow.

Such widespread sense of helplessness provides a welcome for a gospel of God such as the poet-prophets brought to Israel in the fifth and fourth centuries before Christ. John Buchan once said: "Religion is born when we accept the ultimate frustration of mere human effort, and at the same time realise the strength which comes from union with superhuman reality." [5]

Earlier prophets had dealt with the complacent, with those "at ease in Zion." Their messages had been startling announcements of imminent calamity. But these with whose words we are dealing now impart comfort to the unhoping. They are among God's most gracious messengers to his people. Their chief, the writer of chs. 40–55, felt a ministry laid upon him to "bruised reeds" and "dimly burning wicks." The man himself is so lost in his message that we can scarcely discern his personality. Other prophets speak in the first person; they give an account of God's call to them; but this modest poet effaces himself. The "I" in 40:6, as the Exeg. explains, is not in the original. The opening words of the prophecy are in the plural: "Comfort ye." The poet is content to be one in any company of heralds who proclaim the evangel of God's grace to his sorely bestead people. And he became, in a way he could

not have foreseen, the inspiration of such a company; for, unless most modern scholars are astray, he was followed in succeeding generations by prophets who produced the poems in chs. 56–66. These poets absorbed many of his major convictions and also his forms, his metaphors, and much of his language. This absorption of their mighty predecessor's thought and speech is so complete that they do not give an impression of being imitators.[6] The outstanding poet himself has left no name, although he is among the sublimest writers in any literature. This anonymity seems to be what he himself wished. We speak of him as "the prophet of the Exile," or as "Second Isaiah"; and his messages, together with those of his devoted successors, have been bound up in this book which bears the name of the great prophet of Jerusalem in the days of the kingdom of Judah. The self-effacement which this exilic poet urges upon Israel in the discharge of her ministry to the nations he has himself practiced. He does not "cry, nor lift up, nor cause his voice to be heard in the street" (42:2). He attracts no attention to himself. He is eager to remain hidden and unrecognized. Like the mysterious celestial voices in his opening poem, he remains merely "the voice of one crying." Enough for him if he could induce downhearted folk to behold their God.

In an age of publicity, when self-advertisement invades every calling, the ministry of the gospel not excepted, this willingness to remain obscure, and the ability to communicate to his attached followers a like modesty, have a lesson for those who would share his evangel of comfort with men. He who would make God prominent must keep himself out of sight. Preaching is "truth through personality"; but the personality of the messenger must be so translucent that it is unnoticed in the blaze of the truth of God.

A brilliant man—George Bowen—who, after a striking conversion, went out more than a century ago as a missionary to India, in a letter to his sisters in his old age confessed: "I told the Lord that I was content to be everlastingly insignificant." [7] This admission to the Lord is in marked contrast to earlier entries in his diary in which he aims to become a second Paul, or to move about the bazaars of Bombay as "Christ himself." His spiritual ambition was knocked out of him by the discipline of a missionary career. While to himself a failure, his devotional

[5] *The Pilgrim's Way* (Boston: Houghton Mifflin Co., 1940), p. 296.

[6] An instance of such absorption of language by another writer without loss of originality is Melville's assimilation of Shakespeare; cf. F. O. Matthiessen, *American Renaissance* (London: Oxford University Press, 1941), pp. 424 ff.

[7] Robert E. Speer, *George Bowen of Bombay* (New York: Private Printing, 1938), p. 280.

40 Comfort ye, comfort ye my people, saith your God. | **40** Comfort, comfort my people, says your God.

I. THE IMMINENT COMING OF GOD (40:1–48:22)
A. THE COMING OF THE LORD (40:1-11)

A prologue prepares the way for the poems which follow. It provides the setting, determines the point of vantage, and strikes the dominant mood for the entire collection. The scene opens in the council of Yahweh (*sôdh Yahweh;* cf. Jer. 23:18; H. Wheeler Robinson, "The Council of Yahweh," *Journal of Theological Studies,* XLV [1945], 151-57; *Inspiration and Revelation in the Old Testament* [Oxford: Clarendon Press, 1946], pp. 167-70). A supremely important decision is about to be announced. Such celestial assemblies are not infrequent in the Bible (I Kings 22; Isa. 6; Job 1–2; Pss. 82:1; 89:7; Dan. 7:9 ff.; Gen. 1:26 ff.; Rev. 4:1-11; cf. Julian Morgenstern, *Amos Studies* [Cincinnati: Hebrew Union College Press, 1941], I, 137 ff., 157 ff.; Hermann Gunkel, *Genesis* [3rd ed.; Göttingen: Vandenhoeck & Ruprecht, 1922; "Göttinger Handkommentar zum Alten Testament"], p. 111; Paul Humbert, "La relation de Genèse 1 et du Psaume 104 avec la liturgie du Nouvel-An israëlite," *Revue d'Histoire et de Philosophie Religieuses,* XV [1935], 1-27; Thorkild Jacobsen, "Primitive Democracy in Ancient Mesopotamia," *Journal of Near Eastern Studies,* II [1943], 159-72; G. Ernest Wright, *The Old Testament Against Its Environment* [Chicago: Henry Regnery, 1950], pp. 30-41. Jacobsen cites a number of Akkadian sources which have interesting parallels to Second Isaiah; the Ugaritic poems contain not infrequent references to the assembly of the gods; see also J. B. Pritchard, ed., *Ancient Near Eastern Texts Relating to the Old Testament* [Princeton: Princeton University Press, 1950], pp. 62 ff. for Akkadian references and pp. 130 ff. for Ugaritic). Some of these have been associated with the celebration of the New Year's festival (cf. Julian Morgenstern, "The Book of the Covenant," *Hebrew Union College Annual,* V [1928], 48 ff.; Jacobsen, *op. cit.,* 162 ff., 169. The judicial character of the divine assembly is generally recognized). It is possible that the council in the present poem is to be understood against that background. The entrance of the glory of the Lord (*kebhôdh Yahweh*) into the holy of holies (cf. Ezek. 43:2 ff.) with the rising of the sun as an expression of the divine favor for the ensuing year; the fateful decision of the intervention of God at a moment of acute historical crisis; the description of the great highway; the portrait of God as conqueror, king, judge, and shepherd; the hymnic style, and the place of nature in relation to the theophany suggest that the imagery may be drawn from the celebration of the Babylonian New Year's festival. The writer was doubtless familiar with the *akitu* festival, but the language and thought are characteristically Hebrew throughout. The poem on the creation (40:12-31) and on the trial of the nations (41:1–42:4) may be part of the same complex of thought. The sublime background of the heavenly council accounts for the atmosphere and mood of the poems. The bonds of nature are broken and an event of decisive significance is set in motion as a consequence of the divine decision. Already in the opening lines we hear

---

writings circulated with marked effect on several continents.

A saintly Scots layman, Thomas Erskine of Linlathen, whose conversations and letters were a potent spiritual influence, remarked: "Most men are so possessed by themselves that they have no vacuum into which God's deep water may rise."

The fellowship of nameless prophets to whom we owe chs. 40–66 lost themselves in their poems of the Lord, lofty and holy, who dwells with the lowly to revive the spirit of the contrite.

In literary form their writings are the high-water mark of the O.T., and in spiritual content they are most closely kin to the gospel of Christ.

40:1-11. Behold Your God.—This passage is an overture to the entire prophecy. It came at a turning point in history. Historians speak of it as the end of the Babylonian and the beginning of the Persian period. One contemporary of the startling crisis, this unknown prophet, saw it as a climactic hour when God was arriving on the human scene to establish an ultimate

Yahweh addressing the members of his council. The prophetic vista is heaven and earth (cf. Isa. 1:2). What is determined in heaven is to be fulfilled on earth (cf. I Kings 22:18-38; Isa. 6:9-13; Job 1:6–2:10). Yahweh does nothing without revealing his counsel "to his servants the prophets" (Amos 3:7). The word ṣôdh can mean both "council" and "counsel," both the meeting and what is determined. The prologue is all speaking and hearing, call and response, proclamation and answering responsibility to proclaim. The style of voice answering voice is a superb example of the pervasive dialogue quality of the O.T. Even in heaven the human situation as it is involved in dialogue is retained. The vocabulary of speech in the poem and throughout the collection of poems is a major reflection of Israel's psychological and religious mentality.

The poem is carefully constructed. A triad of stichs (half lines) with imperatives (**comfort, speak, cry**) and objects (**people, Jerusalem, her**) constitutes the proem. The climactic verb **cry** or "proclaim" introduces three solemn disclosures (vs. 2) and provides the framework for the three strophes that follow (vss. 3-5, 6-8, 9-11). Each strophe has its own beginning (vss. 3a, 6a, 9a) and ending (vss. 5c, 8b, 10). The third and climactic strophe culminates in a triad announcing the imminent advent of God in great theophany upon the stage of world history:

> **"Behold your God!"**
> **Behold, the Lord GOD comes with might,**
> **and his arm rules for him;**
> **behold, his reward is with him,**
> **and his recompense before him.**

The imperative mood dominates throughout the poem. Literary types are fused and transformed. In vss. 9-10 we have the instruction to the herald, which also contains the herald's announcement (*Botenspruch*); it is possible that vss. 1-2 are a transformed herald's cry. In that event the poem begins and ends in the same manner. Style and mood conform to contents. The language is kindled by a live Oriental imagination and an urgent prophetic faith. As the literary unity lies in its imperatives and exclamations, so the unity of thought lies in what is proclaimed. So elevated and sublime is the scene that personal details are not permitted to intrude (contrast Amos 7:1-9; 8:1-3; Jer. 1:4-10). The prophet himself is all but lost. The poem gains by being read aloud, for the sound brings out the emphasis and mood with striking effect. Repetitions serve a special purpose. Meter enforces both style and thought. The scenery is grandiose and impressive: the highway through the desert, the glory of the Lord revealed to all flesh,

---

divine order. It has not proved, as it appeared to him, the final event in history; but spiritually it inaugurated a new day with its good tidings of God. The glory of the Lord was revealed to this seer. Nowhere in the O.T. is there more of the Christian gospel: God, creator and sovereign of all nations; God at work in history, in judgment and redemption; God's gracious forgiveness of his sinful people; God educating them for the evangelization of mankind, and when they prove unresponsive, God choosing, training, and empowering from among them his servant church to win to him all peoples; God employing the vicarious suffering of his righteous servant to bring the nations to repentance and to life with him; God for his own love's sake initiating and carrying to completion the salvation of the world. This is "the gospel of God" according to this nameless prophet. The

word of the Lord, which was to him both enlightening and potent to accomplish its purpose, foreshadows "the word made flesh" revealing God's glory "full of grace and reality" (John 1:14 Moffatt).

The overture introduces the motifs which occur and recur throughout the poems. These motifs fitted the plight of apprehensive, perplexed, and frustrated exiles and are as relevant to us in this bewildered mid-twentieth century. They are three in number: (*a*) God at work redemptively in the events of history; (*b*) the frailty and impermanence of man; (*c*) the mission to mankind of Israel, God's chosen.

1-2. *God Fills the Center of the Stage.*— He is active in current happenings. Attention is focused on him in the council of heaven and upon the earthly scene. No summons is given to depressed and confused men to rouse them-

2 Speak ye comfortably to Jerusalem, and cry unto her, that her warfare is accomplished, that her iniquity is pardoned: for she hath received of the Lord's hand double for all her sins.

2 Speak tenderly to Jerusalem,
     and cry to her
that her warfare[n] is ended,
     that her iniquity is pardoned,
that she has received from the Lord's hand
     double for all her sins.

[n] Or time of service

---

the blasting heat of the sirocco withering grass and flower, the call of the herald from the mountain height. The portrait of God is of a mighty conqueror returning from his conquests, a king about to inaugurate his kingdom, a righteous judge adjudicating the inequities of the past, and a solicitous shepherd who gathers the lamb in his bosom.

1. Proem (40:1-2)

40:1. Comfort, comfort: The repeated imperative (cf. 51:9, 17; 52:1; also 57:14; 62:10; 65:1) strikes the note of compassion and urgency. The emphasis upon comfort pervades many of the poems (40:13; 51:6, 12, 19; 52:9; 54:11) and is consistent with the poet's message of an imminent redemption. The LXX renders the verb by παρακαλεῖτε and repeats it in the last verse (cf. Luke 2:25). The consolation forms a sharp contrast to the judgment which Isaiah is commissioned to speak as he participates in the divine council (6:9-13). **My people** is the object of the verb, not a vocative (cf. Vulg. *popule meus*). **My people . . . your God** are covenant words and thus express the basic reality of O.T. religion. Israel is the people of Yahweh, and Yahweh is the God of Israel. This cardinal faith is assumed throughout the whole prophecy. The imperfect tense is exceptional (cf. vs. 25; 41:25). "The call is not a single, momentary one, it is repeated, or at least continuing" (S. R. Driver, *A Treatise in the Use of the Tenses in Hebrew* [3rd ed. rev.; Oxford: Clarendon Press, 1892], p. 38). The number and variety of references to God reflect the theocentricity of the poet's thought (**your God** in vss. 1, 9; "Yahweh" in vss. 2, 3, 5; "Lord Yahweh" in vs. 10; **our God** in vss. 3, 8).

The LXX understands vss. 1-2 as addressed to the priests and begins the next line with a vocative, "Speak, priests!" The Targ., on the other hand, addresses the words to the prophets, "O prophets, prophesy consolation" (cf. also vs. 2). The latter has some claim since the prophet was actually present in the divine council (Jer. 23:18).

2. Speak tenderly to Jerusalem: Lit., "speak to the heart of" (cf. Gen. 34:31; Hos. 2:14, and especially Gen. 50:21; Ruth 2:13). To speak to the heart is to speak consolingly,

---

selves and break their bonds. Such "activistic" preaching is futile. In both the O.T. and the N.T. the gospel is first a message concerning God—what he has done, is doing, and is about to do. Only secondarily is it a call to men to respond to the good news of God. It would revolutionize the preaching and teaching of our churches did every message deal primarily with God.

The prophet's comfort starts with the announcement that his people's period of harsh discipline is over and God has forgiven them. Sin separates from him. If these dejected exiles are to be revived, their first need is for restoration to the source of life in God and the re-establishment of association with him. God it at hand to lead them back to their homeland;

but the gospel always declares, "Thy sins are forgiven thee," before it bids, "Arise and walk." Generously they are told that the nation has received **double for all her sins.** This is no calculation of debit and credit. It does not imply that what they have endured has overpaid their iniquities. A most poignant question was the punishment by captivity of those who had not been responsible for the nation's sin, and a sublime poem will portray the redemptive effects of vicarious suffering. Pardon is always an act of God's grace. Both the discipline and the vicarious sufferings of the righteous are of his appointment. His fatherly heart goes out to sinners; his arms are open to receive the penitent. His discipline serves to produce penitence and turn the rebellious to him. His

gently, kindly, tenderly. "Psychical and ethical functions are considered to be just as appropriate to the bodily organs as the physiological, with the result that there can be ascribed to the heart everything which popular thought today ascribes to the brain, a quite neglected organ in Semitic thought" (H. Wheeler Robinson, "Hebrew Psychology," in A. S. Peake, ed., *The People and the Book* [Oxford: Clarendon Press, 1925], pp. 353-54; cf. also Johannes Pedersen, *Israel, Its Life and Culture, I-II* [London: Oxford University Press, 1926], pp. 102, 104, *et passim*). **Jerusalem:** The city is often used to refer to the whole community of Judah. The prophet's thought begins and ends with the city (vss. 1, 9). Jerusalem, like Zion, is uniquely related to God, thus becoming the holy city (48:2; 52:1). For Isaiah too, Jerusalem has a unique status. It is the place where Yahweh of hosts dwells and where he has established the line of David. **And cry unto her:** Better, "call" or "proclaim." It is one of the prophet's favorite words, appearing more than thirty times in chs. 40–55, and is used with a variety of significant meanings. Moreover, he frequently employs synonyms like the causative forms of the verbs "to hear" (שמע) and "to tell" (נגד). His own mission as well as the mission of Israel is understood in terms of proclamation; this explains the passionate and exultant character of the language. For the prophet as for Israel the first great command is "Proclaim!" This is the burden of the first and the last strophes (vss. 1-2, 9-10). **That her warfare is ended:** A better rendering is **time of service.** The meaning of the verb is, lit., "filled" (מלאה); cf. Mark 1:15 (πεπλήρωται ὁ καιρὸς); Gal. 4:4; Eph. 1:10. The figure is military (cf. Job 7:1; 14:14). The Exile was like a soldier's time of service. This is the first momentous disclosure in the council of Yahweh. The decisive moment has come. But how is this "end" to be understood? Part of the answer is discovered in the historical situation: the Babylonian age, which is drawing to a close, and the Persian, which is about to dawn.

That her iniquity is pardoned: The announcement of the imminent "end" is followed by the announcement of expiation of guilt. The verb (נרצה) appears in the Niphal and may be rendered, lit., "is made acceptable" or "has been accepted." It occurs in Lev. 26:41, 43 in the sense of paying off a debt incurred by guilt: "accept the punishment of their iniquity" (ASV). The Targ. preserves this meaning: "her debts shall be forgiven her." The Greek λέλυται reflects the same idea of remission of sins. The Vulg. *dimissa est* bears a similar sense, although it can also mean paying a debt. The emphasis is upon forgiveness, though the idea of a payment is present as is clear from the Leviticus passage. The new age opens with forgiveness of sins (cf. 43:25; 44:22; 48:9). In Jeremiah the eschatological new covenant is motivated by God's forgiveness (Jer. 31:31-34). Now comes the climactic disclosure of the heavenly voice. The expression **double for all her sins** is characteristic Oriental exaggeration. God's punishment of Israel has been greater than she deserved. Reuben Levy refers to the provision in the Covenant Code (Exod. 23:7-8) where the thief is required to make twofold restitution

---

forgiveness is not to be set over against his righteousness: it is part of it. He is "a righteous God and [not "yet"] a Savior" (45:21).

God's redemptive advents take place in history. The Bible looks on all events as under his providential control; but man's willfulness throws God's design into disorder. So God comes upon the scene. This is a distinctive Hebrew and Christian conviction. In his essay on Montaigne, Sainte-Beuve complains that this semi-pagan "had no room in his system for that *coup de grâce,* that decisive striking-in of the divine, which is the foundation of true Christianity." [8] God mercifully strikes in upon

[8] *Causeries du Lundi* (Paris: Garnier Freres, n.d.), IV.

the career of a wayward man, as he did upon Saul of Tarsus, and upon a critical situation in the world's affairs, as he did in the startling rise and advance of the Persian Empire. He comes in judgment, bringing home the consequences of rebellion to his will. And he comes in grace to redeem men to his righteous purpose.

In these strophes mysterious voices are heard. They speak from the unseen, where the council of heaven is in session. They may be compared to the Presences in the realm of spirits in Thomas Hardy's *The Dynasts*—the Shade of the Earth, the Spirit of the Years, the Chorus of the Pities, etc. These comment on what is taking place in the historic events where Britain is battling to liberate the Continent from the

3 ¶ The voice of him that crieth in the wilderness, Prepare ye the way of the LORD, make straight in the desert a highway for our God.	3 A voice cries: "In the wilderness prepare the way of the LORD, make straight in the desert a highway for our God.

for what he has taken: "The thought here would then be that Israel has paid in full the statutory penalty for his delinquency" (*Deutero-Isaiah* [London: Oxford University Press, 1925], p. 114). Torrey refers to the parallels in the Koran (7:36; 33:68; 34:36). As the stress in the foregoing line belongs on forgiveness, so the stress here is on suffering. It was the prophets who first posed the crucial question of the relation of the divine justice to the divine mercy and love. The sufferings of Israel must be accounted for in the purpose and sovereignty of God, and along lines radically different from the simple moral coherence of the Deuteronomists (e.g., note the Deuteronomic frameworks in Judges and Kings). The resolution of the conflicts within her historical life must be consistent with the outreach of the prophet's thought in this crucial passage in which he views the destiny of Israel, and indeed of the whole world of nations, as it is determined in the divine council.

2. FIRST STROPHE: THE WAY OF THE LORD (40:3-5)

3. A voice cries, or "Hark! one proclaims": The instant response to the climactic command of vs. 1. Who the speaker is we are not told. The words must not be connected with the following as is done in the LXX, the Vulg., the N.T. (Matt. 3:3; Mark 1:3; Luke 3:4), the KJV, and Torrey. The literary form of the passage, the parallelism, and the Hebrew accentuation demand that they be taken as introduction to the strophe. The reference to **the wilderness** (which the LXX omits) is drawn partly from the experience of the desert waste between Babylonia and Palestine. **The way of the LORD:** The frequent mention of the *derekh Yahweh* (42:16; 43:16, 19; 48:17; 49:11; 51:10) and the return (vss. 10-11; 41:18-19; 42:6; 43:19-20; 48:21; 49:9 ff.; 55:12-13) are too constant a feature to be explained as an abstraction (contra Duhm). The practice of preparing roads

---

despotism of Napoleon, and upon the indifference of an unthinking Deity to the fate of human beings. The Pities are heard singing:

> Still thus? still thus?
> Ever unconscious!
> An automatic sense
> Unweeting why or whence?
> Be, then, the inevitable, as of old,
> Although that so it be we dare not hold! [1]

Similarly, as Cyrus is sweeping over empires in western Asia in the sixth century B.C., and Babylon is about to fall, this prophet in the council of heaven hears voices.

3-5. Celestial Voices Herald God's Advent.— The first of them (vs. 3) calls upon equally mysterious celestial agents to **prepare the way** for God's arrival. These exiles are confronted with insuperable difficulties. To them it appears impossible that they can be set free, much less restored to their homeland and national independence. The voice does not bid them make

---

[1] London: Macmillan & Co.; New York: The Macmillan Co., 1936, I, 1-2. Used by permission of the Trustees of the Hardy Estate and of the publishers.

---

ready the highway; nor is it a highway for their journey; nor is it their nation's glory which is to be revealed. Forces beyond their knowledge or control—the forces of history, ultimately God himself, the one supreme factor in the ongoings of the universe—are preparing a route along which God will arrive and lead them. Nothing which they can devise or do will remove the obstacles that loom on their horizon. But to their amazement these obstacles will vanish—valleys will be leveled up, mountains will be lowered, steep heights and rough ridges will become a smooth plain. This is poetry; the metaphors are not to be linked with topography. The poet foresees the way back across the desert with numberless difficulties for a miscellaneous company of refugees. A map discloses no towering ranges of mountains between Babylon and Jerusalem. Valleys and hills, uneven and rough places, represent difficulties—political, physical, psychological—which are filling their minds with forebodings. These will disappear as their wonder-working God marches to them and with them. The military successes of Cyrus, the downfall of their oppressors, the diplomatic negotia-

4 Every valley shall be exalted, and every mountain and hill shall be made low: and the crooked shall be made straight, and the rough places plain:	4 Every valley shall be lifted up,
	   and every mountain and hill be made
	   low;
	the uneven ground shall become level,
	   and the rough places a plain.

for the victorious advance of a conqueror or king by clearing them of obstacles is not unknown (see Robert Lowth, *Isaiah, A New Translation* [London: J. Dodsley & T. Cadell, 1779], *ad loc.*; John Skinner, *The Book of the Prophet Isaiah* [rev. ed.; Cambridge: Cambridge University Press, 1915; "Cambridge Bible"], p. 4; cf. Isa. 57:14; 62:10; Ps. 80:8-9; Mal. 3:1). Many scholars see an allusion to the great processional street of Marduk in Babylon; in view of the parallels this is probably correct. Friedrich Stummer cites the following: "From hostile Elam he took the street of joy, a path of jubilation, . . . of a favorable hearing to Sú-an-na (i.e., Babylon). The people of the land saw his lofty form, the ruler in his adornments." (Cf. "Einige keilschriftliche Parallelen zu Jes. 40–66," *Journal of Biblical Literature*, XLV [1926], 172.) But this must not preclude an allusion to the Exodus road from Egypt, since the prophet constantly refers to it elsewhere and it is a primary element in his eschatology. Such combinations are characteristic of the prophet. The **highway for our God** is built in preparation for his coming. "Es ist hier alles Wunder und Geheimnis: der Rufer, die Arbeiter, der Weg" (Paul Volz, *Jesaia II* [Leipzig: A. Deichert, 1932; "Kommentar zum Alten Testament"], p. 4). What is determined in heaven is to be executed on earth. History and eschatology meet in these lines, and the boundary between supernatural and natural must not be drawn (cf. Mal. 3:1). It is doubtful whether the poet had any definite road in mind, and yet the return was an actual historical event.

4. Uneven is preferable to **crooked**. It is not the winding road but the unevenness of the surface that is referred to. The word translated **rough places** occurs only here in the O.T. Its meaning is by no means certain, but the context makes this rendering plausible.

---

tions which will procure their liberty, the change in their own outlook and morale, have and will have spiritual causes. The sovereign disposer of events and mover of the hearts of men is the living God.

This is not our outlook upon contemporary happenings. Few think of an invisible factor. Many share Carlyle's gloomy view of God, when he grumbled to Froude, "He does nothing."[2] Others, more unbelieving still, view tragic events as did Zola who in his *La Bête Humaine*, likens the movement of human affairs to a railway train, drawn by a locomotive whose driver has been killed, dashing at headlong speed into midnight: "The train is the world; we are the freight; fate is the track; death is the darkness; God is the engineer—who is dead." It was in revolt against such stark materialism that a generation ago pragmatism, as taught by William James, was welcomed. In a metaphor, irrelevant to our time where a leisure class is almost unknown, James wrote: "The prince of darkness may be a gentleman, as we are told

he is, but whatever the God of earth and heaven is, he can surely be no gentleman. His menial services are needed in the dust of our human trials, even more than his dignity is needed in the empyrean."[3] But James's conception of the part in events taken by God—a conception still widely held—falls far short of the Bible's. James appears to leave the initiative with man, and to overlook what God is constantly doing altogether apart from man. James B. Pratt asked him: "Do you accept Him not so much as a real existent Being, but rather as an ideal to live by?" (Language typical of religious thought at the beginning of the twentieth century.) James replied: "More as a more powerful ally of my own ideals."[4] But neither these exiles in Babylon, nor we, faced with the obstructions to our hopes for mankind in the conflicting minds of men and nations, have the wit or energy to take the lead in breaking through the obstacles. We need not an ally of *our* ideals, but one who both initiates and

[2] John Nichol, *Carlyle* (New York: Harper & Bros., 1901), p. 231.

[3] *Pragmatism* (New York: Longmans, Green & Co., 1907), p. 72.

[4] Henry James, ed., *The Letters of William James* (Boston: Atlantic Monthly Press, 1920), II, 214.

5 And the glory of the Lord shall be revealed, and all flesh shall see *it* together: for the mouth of the Lord hath spoken *it*.

5 And the glory of the Lord shall be revealed,
and all flesh shall see it together,
for the mouth of the Lord has spoken."

---

5. Yahweh is to manifest himself in an unparalleled revelation. He had appeared in other unique moments of Israel's tradition in wonderful theophany: to the patriarchs, Abraham (Gen. 12:7-8 [J]; 18:1 ff. [J]) and Jacob-Israel (Gen. 28:10-19 [JE]); to Moses in the bush (Exod. 3:2-6 [JE]); to Israel on Mount Sinai (Exod. 24:9-11 [J], 15-18 [P]); to charismatic deliverers like Gideon (Judg. 6:11-24); and to the prophets in visions and calls (Amos 7:1-9; Isa. 6; Jer. 1:4-10; Ezek. 1); see also the remarkable account of Moses' request to see God's glory in Exod. 33:18-23 (J), the story of the capture of the ark, where the divine glory dwells (I Sam. 4:19-22), and Yahweh's entrance into the holy city as the *melekh kābhôdh* (Ps. 24). He was to appear on the great and terrible Day of the Lord in a decisive theophany in which he would show himself victor over all his enemies (Amos 5:18-20; Isa. 2:5-22; Zeph. 1:7, 14-18; cf. I Cor. 15:6-8). It was the common belief of the Exile that **the glory of the Lord** had left the temple at the destruction of the city of Jerusalem, but that it would return again in God's time (cf. Ezek. 1:28; 3:23; 10:18-19; 11:23; 43:1-5). **The glory** that once appeared on the sacred mount (Exod. 24:15-18 [P]), and later tabernacled in the sacred precincts of the holy of holies, is now to appear in a final epiphany. **And all flesh shall see it together:** This is not merely another theophany which belongs to a series of divine appearances in the O.T. It is final and decisive, universal and all-inclusive. It "fills" time and space. It is a world theophany and comes at the turn of the ages as the fulfillment of the divine purpose in history. In Isaiah's vision the seraphs cover their faces before the *kābhôdh;*

---

achieves. We find "comfort" in the conviction that

> Before man's First, and after man's poor Last, God operated and will operate.[5]

This is God as proclaimed in the gospel of our prophet. He is preparing his **highway** in the wilderness of current history. His **glory** he will himself reveal; no men's hands can tear aside the concealing curtains. His breath, like a parching sirocco (vs. 7), withers the proudest and most powerful. In contrast to transient and fragile human strength, his word stands fast forever (vs. 8). Such is the good news of God for a frustrate generation.

Like all prophets, this seer sets forth who God is. Again and again in suggestive symbols he places God before his listeners. Here (vss. 10-11) he employs two metaphors, the warrior and the shepherd, to depict God in his might and in his tenderness. "The All-great" is "the All-loving too." He comes upon the scene with strong arm, so that his efforts are never without result. His "reward" and "recompense" will be the restoration of his people to their national role in his gracious purposes for mankind. And he comes with considerate affection. The long journey back will be hard. The exiles recalled

[5] Browning, "A Camel-Driver."

the accounts which fathers and mothers had given of terrible experiences in the weary miles over which their captors had driven them. Now their good shepherd, with loving thoughtfulness, will "gently lead" and "carry" them back.

These two aspects of God must always be held together. To stress his love without his "might" renders his goodness futile in the face of overwhelming circumstances. The N.T., which declares that God is love, repeatedly asserts that "God is able." Who would trust himself or his nation to an incompetent? And there are many who acknowledge a power behind events, but are unsure whether it or he has a heart. An arm which both rules, so that purposes come to pass, and which gathers and carries frail children of men to a destiny beyond any they ask or think, is the God for a desperate world.

Just before the Russians took over the city of Breslau, on the last Sunday when the congregation was permitted to worship in the St. Elizabeth Church, their pastor told his people:

One and a half years ago, when the Russians arrived, the church had to stay in order to officiate as long as any of the people of the community remained here and were in need of the aid and comfort of the Gospel. And lo and behold! God richly blessed the hard work of the Evangelical Church in the period of siege and occupation. . . .

6 The voice said, Cry. And he said, What shall I cry? All flesh *is* grass, and all the goodliness thereof *is* as the flower of the field:

6 A voice says, "Cry!"
 And I said, "What shall I cry?"
All flesh is grass,
 and all its beauty is like the flower of the field.

---

in this appearing all flesh shall see it. Of all the superlatives which crowd the poems of Second Isaiah, this is the greatest and the most momentous. For the phrase **all flesh** cf. the priestly history (Gen. 6:12, 13, 17, 19; 7:15, 16; 9:11-17).

3. SECOND STROPHE: "THE WORD OF OUR GOD" (40:6-8)

6. A voice says, "Cry!" or "Hark! one saying, 'Cry.'" A second voice takes up where the first leaves off. The M.T., the Targ., and the Syriac read "and he said" in response to the demand, but the LXX, the Vulg., and the Dead Sea Scroll have the first person. The prophet never speaks of himself in the first person, however (48:16*d* is a gloss). If the Masoretic reading is retained, it is a member of the heavenly council who is referred to. If we read the first person, which is probably better, the prophet himself breaks forth into speech at this point (cf. Isaiah's response after his cleansing [6:8]), and we have an account of his prophetic call and his initial response to it (cf. Mohammed's call in the Koran, 96). To the disclosure that all flesh shall see the divine *kābhôdh,* the prophet comments disconsolately that **all flesh is grass** (cf. 37:27; 51:12; Pss. 90:5-6; 103:15). The prologue already reflects the deep pessimism which appears again and again in the poems (cf., e.g., 40:27). The prophet is here expressing the despondency of his contemporaries. **All its beauty:** The Hebrew word *ḥeṣedh* is nowhere else used with this meaning. The LXX translates δόξα ἀνθρώπου, "glory of man" (cf. I Pet. 1:24 δόξα αὐτῆς); O.L., *gloria hominis;* Vulg., *gloria eius.* But it is hard to see how this can be derived from the Hebrew. Many scholars therefore emend to *ḥemdô* (חמדו)) **its beauty;** others to *hᵃdhārô* (הדרו), "its glory." The Targ. interprets "their strength," and the context supports this meaning. The word has the connotation of steadfastness or reliability (the RSV renders it elsewhere by "steadfast love"), and is used in connection with the covenant; cf. also its association with truth (אמת), which

---

If, nevertheless, all human hopes which we cherished for our homeland are frustrated, if our community buildings and churches are taken from us, if one street after another is evacuated, . . . God doesn't take without giving at the same time. He doesn't demand the grave sacrifice of homelessness without ennobling us at the same time with a great task and endowing us with the promise of His blessing if we will but trust in His . . . eternal goodness. . . .

Thus being called, we are going to bid farewell to our beloved Silesia, if this is God's will; farewell as it must be also from our beloved Elizabeth Church which like a mother has nurtured our soul. We have to thank God for what he has entrusted to us. May He hold us in His arms and guide us.[6]

6-8. Transience and Frailty of Human Beings. —That is the burden of the second voice. The prophet hears it saying **Cry** and he records his response, **"What shall I cry?"**

Many a conscientious soul in critical times hears an imperative to speak. But when he con-

[6] The Rev. Dr. Konrad, "A Sermon to German Exiles," *Christianity and Crisis,* Vol. VII (1947), No. 16, pp. 4-6. Used by permission.

siders what he should say, uncertainty and confusion enshroud him: **What shall I cry?** This is a usual plight among ministers. Week after week the demanding situations and the expectation of their people say, **Cry.** Their baffled minds answer, **What shall I cry?** To this message-craving prophet, as often happens with modern preachers, a commonplace is suggested —a truth uttered again and again, not only in Israel but also in many faiths: **All flesh is grass, and all the goodliness thereof is as the flower of the field: the grass withereth, the flower fadeth.** A commonplace may in a particular situation become apposite and alive. It is not always the novel which is timely.

These dispirited exiles were overawed by the might and splendor of their oppressors. Babylon was a city goodly in its architecture, its sculpture, its commerce, in its confident and luxurious life. The political and financial prestige of its people might well overawe captives on whom its lordly inhabitants looked down with contempt. What was worship of companies of impoverished and exiled foreigners in their im-

7 The grass withereth, the flower fadeth;
because the spirit of the LORD bloweth upon
it: surely the people *is* grass.

8 The grass withereth, the flower fadeth:
but the word of our God shall stand for
ever.

7 The grass withers, the flower fades,
     when the breath of the LORD blows
       upon it;
surely the people is grass.

8 The grass withers, the flower fades;
     but the word of our God will stand
       for ever.

---

has the same root meaning of steadfastness (Norman H. Snaith, "The Exegesis of Isaiah xl. 5, 6," *Expository Times,* LII [1941], 394-96). In contrast to the frailty of grass and flower, God's word abides and stands steadfast and sure.

7. When the breath [or "the wind"] **of the LORD blows upon it:** The scorching east wind from the desert blasts all vegetation (cf. Ps. 103:16; Jer. 4:11; Ezek. 17:10; Luke 12:55). **Surely the people is grass:** Many scholars take these words as a gloss, but their presence is in conformity with the prophet's literary style. The somber reflection begins with **all flesh is grass** and ends with **surely the people is grass.** The LXX (I Pet. 1:24) and the Dead Sea Scroll have a somewhat shorter reading. The Dead Sea Scroll of vss. 7-8 reads, "The grass withers, the flower fades, but the word of our God shall stand forever. Surely the people is grass." But a correction "when the wind . . . blows over it" is inserted over the phrase "the word of our God shall stand forever." Before the transcendent majesty of the glory of God, man is transient and ephemeral, **like the flower of the field** (cf. Pss. 90:2-4; 103:14 ff.; Job 4:19 ff.; Isa. 34:4-8). This is the reply to the prophet's words.

8. The grass withers, the flower fades: The repetition is characteristic of the poet's style and increases the force of the concluding words; but **the word of our God shall stand for ever.** Here we have a vivid expression of Second Isaiah's view of the word of God. It is not the creature of a season like the grass, rather it abides forever. It stands as a power within history to achieve that for which it was sent. It is doubtless related to the prophetic word which Second Isaiah, like all the prophets, was commissioned to

---

provised synagogues, compared with the pomp and circumstance of the pageants which celebrated the triumphant gods of Babylon? To raise their spirits the prophet's first message is of the living and almighty God above and behind all things seen. His second is a reminder of the ephemeral nature of man and his works. **Flesh** is man in his weakness and mortality, contrasted with God who is spirit, potent and eternal. **All flesh** includes both the Gentile nations and Israel. Man's showy civilization with its art, science, amenities, and comforts may seem vigorous and fair as a meadow in bloom. A blast of the searing wind of history reduces it to a wasteland. Why then tremble before aught human?

Our generation is obsessed by fears similar to those which weighed on these captives: dread of scientific advances which have furnished the means of devoting masses to an appalling destruction, dread of the machinations of aloof and secretive powers, dread of enslavement by an economic tyranny contemptuous of our morals and derisive of our venerated pieties, or dread of economic collapse which might plunge our country and many others in chaos. Many

among us are frightened by more trivial fears: by what their neighbors may be thinking or saying of them. Young people are haunted with anxiety lest they be "queered" with their fellows. Custom, the fashion, good taste, what "is done" or "is not done," exercise a despotic sway. Mrs. Grundy or

The little laws that lacqueys make,
The futile decalogue of Mode,[7]

are for them the intimidating equivalents of imposing Babylon. More people are afraid of committing a gaucherie which might start a laugh at their expense than of disobeying the will of God. Subserviency to current wont and use is the most paralyzing hindrance to men's response to God when he claims them for his surprising purposes. A sight of his everlastingness and of the mutability of man's opinions and institutions is a deliverance from such inhibitions. "Who art thou, that thou shouldest be afraid of a man that shall die, . . . and for-

[7] William Watson, "The Things That Are More Excellent," st. vi. From *The Poems of Sir William Watson, 1878-1935* (London: George G. Harrap & Co., 1936). Used by permission.

9 ¶ O Zion, that bringest good tidings, get thee up into the high mountain; O Jeru-

9 Get you up to a high mountain,
O Zion, herald of good tidings;[o]
lift up your voice with strength,

[o] Or O herald of good tidings to Zion

---

proclaim. But it is more than this. It is proclamation and demand, prediction and realization of the prediction, promise and fulfillment; it expresses God's plan and purpose, but it also has the power of carrying his plan into effect and achieving his purpose. (The history of prophecy in relation to the temporal order—nation, temple, and national and religious institutions—illustrates the thought of the prophet.) It is not an abstract, divine teaching. Above all the flux and confusion of time and circumstance, the word of God abides sure—surer and more enduring than nature. Yet it is not static but living and dynamic for, as Duhm rightly observes, Israel's religion holds firmly to movement even in the superearthly spiritual world. The word is God's outgoing, active, living speech with which he is yet mysteriously identified. The little mashal on the word of God in 55:8-11 is a commentary on this word.

4. THIRD STROPHE: "BEHOLD, YOUR GOD" (40:9-10)

Everything from the very beginning has been a preparation for this final word. Both in form and content it is more impressive than the foregoing lines. The same imperatives are present, but they are more eager, more intense and impassioned, more imaginative and wide ranging. The scene shifts from heaven to earth, from the celestial council to Jerusalem. Zion-Jerusalem is addressed as a herald, and she is commissioned to proclaim the good news of the Lord's advent. She must ascend a high mountain that she may be seen of all men; she must shout with a loud voice that her words may be heard by all. She must announce the coming of God whose glory all the world is to see. She must announce his conquest and his victory, the bringing in of his kingdom and the institution of his sovereignty (vs. 10b), and above all his act of justice (vs. 10c). Thus the announcements and decisions of heaven descend to earth; the heavenly voices become the immediate demands of Israel's sacred history, and the way is prepared for the vast panorama of history and eschatology which is to follow.

9. O Zion, herald of good tidings: The alternative translation, "O thou that tellest good tidings to Zion" (RSV mg., with Vulg., Targ.), is possible in the light of the poet's

---

gettest the LORD thy Maker, that hath stretched forth the heavens, and laid the foundations of the earth?" (51:12-13.)

Not only is **all flesh . . . grass,** but so too are these downhearted captive Israelites—**surely the people is grass.** Even when self-assurance seems utterly remote, the prophet will allow no room for confidence in human abilities. The **people** in vs. 7 is contrasted with "my people" in vs. 2. The people, Israel, apart from God is as impotent and void of lasting significance as pagan peoples. "My people," Israel, in covenant with God, responsive to his word, is linked with his eternal purpose.

We and our contemporaries teeter between belief in man's almost limitless capacities to advance in knowledge and power, and disgust at the pettiness, stupidity, and cruelty of a race apparently heading for mass suicide. At one moment men are so self-sufficient that religion seems an irrelevance. They can manage their own affairs and carve out their own destiny.

At another moment they turn in bitter cynicism from man's lofty hopes and endeavors and denounce their futility. In the hugeness of the stellar universe how ridicuously small and trifling these seem! As the eons roll along, how completely man's schemes will be forgotten! Are man's religious convictions any less evanescent? "However we brave it out, we men are a little breed." [8] This prophet would have us recognize our creatureliness in its mortal frailty, and our enduring role in history in obedience to the word of its righteous Lord. His message is repeated with N.T. fullness in an apostle's assertion: "The world passeth away, and the lust thereof: but he that doeth the will of God abideth for ever" (I John 2:17).

9-11. Israel's Mission as Herald of the Good News of God.—This prophet's ministry of comfort is not that of a pastor to individuals. He is charged with a message to the nation: "Comfort ye my people." The name used for the nation

[8] Tennyson, "Maud," Pt. IV, st. v.

salem, that bringest good tidings, lift up thy voice with strength; lift *it* up, be not afraid; say unto the cities of Judah, Behold your God!

10 Behold, the Lord GOD will come with strong *hand,* and his arm shall rule for him: behold, his reward *is* with him, and his work before him.

O Jerusalem, herald of good tidings,[p]
　lift it up, fear not;
say to the cities of Judah,
　"Behold your God!"

10 Behold, the Lord GOD comes with might,
　and his arm rules for him;
behold, his reward is with him,
　and his recompense before him.

[p] Or *O herald of good tidings to Jerusalem*

elliptical style. But it is better to take the word (*mebhassēreth*) in apposition to Zion and Jerusalem, for (*a*) the feminine gender is consistent with the five feminine verbs of vs. 9 and (*b*) it is the cities of Judah who are to receive the herald's message, not Jerusalem herself. The root בשׂר occurs a number of times in the Ugaritic inscriptions (Cyrus Gordon, *Ugaritic Handbook* [Roma: Pontificium Biblicum, 1947], p. 220). See also the Lachish letters in Pritchard, *Ancient Near Eastern Texts,* p. 322. Cf. the Greek translation of *mebhassēreth* here, ὁ εὐαγγελιζόμενος. The N.T. connotation of gospel has its source in Second Isaiah, just as the language of the prophet profoundly influenced the Gospels (see Millar Burrows, "The Origin of the Term 'Gospel,'" *Journal of Biblical Literature,* XLIV [1925], 21-33). **Behold your God!** The advent of God is announced with a threefold exclamation. This is the good news which is proclaimed and announced in the council of Yahweh.

10. Behold, the Lord GOD comes with might (or "with power"): The introductory *hinnēh* may be an anacrusis, or it is possible that the two words in the divine name were counted as one beat. The **arm** of Yahweh is the instrument of redemption (vs. 11; 48:14; 51:5, 9; 52:10; 53:1; cf. 59:16; 62:8; 63:5, 12). Yahweh comes as conqueror and victor; as king to bring in his kingdom (cf. 52:7-10; 41:21; 43:15; 44:6). Cf. the Tell el-Amarna letters: "The arm of the mighty king conquers the land of Naharaim and the land of [lust]" No. 288; see Pritchard, *op. cit.,* pp. 488-89); also the statuette of Baal from Ras Shamra (*The Biblical Archaeologist,* II [1939], p. 5, Fig. 1). Second

is rich with meaning—**Jerusalem.** That city, miles distant, lay in ruins. Most of the exiles had never seen it. It lived as a hallowed symbol in their hearts. Its capture and devastation by enemies, followed by the bitter years in Babylon for its children, had fitted it to rise again transfigured in their souls. Jerusalem was now far more than the sacred capital of a once independent people cherishing a hope of its liberation and rebuilding. The name stood for the nation in covenant with God, with a chief role in his plan for the world. Jerusalem was all and more than the object of patriotic faith and aspiration of devout Israelites scattered all over the known world. She was God's chosen messenger to whom he had revealed himself, whom he was disciplining for a unique service to mankind, and to whom he was now affectionately speaking, entrusting her with this larger mission. The prophet hails her in this new role: **O Zion, herald of good tidings.** There might be little of the evangelist in most of these captives absorbed in making a living in unfriendly Babylon. But the prophet believed in a divine life in the nation beyond that which the mass of its people disclosed. He thought of Jerusalem as

Lowell in his "Commemoration Ode" hailed the United States:

　'Tis no man we celebrate,

•　　•　　•　　•　　•　　•
　But the pith and marrow of a nation
　Drawing force from all her men,

•　　•　　•　　•　　•　　•
　Pulsing it again through them,
　Till the basest can no longer cower,
　Feeling his soul spring up divinely tall,
　Touched but in passing by her mantle-hem.

The spiritual "pith and marrow" of the nation were the loyal minority, in fellowship with God, of whom the prophet was the outstanding example.

In this passage Jerusalem's mission is limited to her own land, **Say to the cities of Judah.** Her immediate task is home missions. But the prophet sets before her a far wider horizon. God's glory to be revealed in Israel's deliverance and restoration is to be seen of "all flesh . . . together." From the outset of these poems a world mission is envisaged for God's people.

This appears to be the earliest description in Scripture of a missionary. Others among

| 11 He shall feed his flock like a shepherd: he shall gather the lambs with his arm, and carry *them* in his bosom, *and* shall gently lead those that are with young. | 11 He will feed his flock like a shepherd, he will gather the lambs in his arms, he will carry them in his bosom, and gently lead those that are with young. |

Isaiah proclaims as the beginning of his gospel the coming of God as king of his people. The **reward** and **recompense** may be the booty and spoil which Yahweh has won from his victory (cf. Gen. 15:1; Jer. 31:15; Ezek. 29:18, 20). Kimhi and Ibn Ezra assert that it will be given to Israel as the reward for faithfulness during the Exile (Levy, *Deutero-Isaiah*, p. 118). It is the gift which Yahweh bestows upon his people in the day of his appearing.

5. CODA: THE CONQUEROR AS THE SHEPHERD (40:11)

11. Cf. Mic. 2:12; Jer. 31:10; Ezek. 34:11 ff.; Pss. 78:52; 80:1. Yahweh leads his exiles home as the shepherd leads his sheep; cf. the Admonitions of Ipu-wer in Pritchard, *op. cit.*, p. 443: "He is the herdsman of all men. Evil is not in his heart. Though his herds may be small, still he has spent the day caring for them." The arm raised in

Israel's prophets and teachers had believed that in her all the families of earth were to be blessed; but this prophet is the first to lay upon her the responsibility of heralding the gospel of her God. This marks a decisive development in religion. Israel is commissioned to evangelize. It is likely that at the time few among the exiles had either a missionary outlook or a missionary devotion. Indeed, despite the explicit command of the risen Christ, are there many in the Christian church? But the prophet confronts the nation with this supreme God-appointed task. Her crowning "comfort" is to be the proclaimer of the good news of God to the whole earth.

In Commonwealth England there were not many committed to search out and speak forth truth; but Milton in his *Areopagitica* holds up this national mission before the Parliament:

Methinks I see in my mind a noble and puissant nation rousing herself like a strong man after sleep, and shaking her invincible locks. Methinks I see her as an eagle mewing her mighty youth, and kindling her undazzled eyes at the full midday beam; purging and unscaling her long-abused sight at the fountain itself of heavenly radiance.

The conception of a national spiritual mission has special pertinence in this century when minds are focused on the world scene. Peoples with a Christian heritage, and with numbers of their inhabitants professing faith in the God and Father of all men, assuredly are trustees of a gospel desperately needed by mankind.

All nations have their message from on high;
Each the messiah of some central thought; [9]

[9] James Russell Lowell, "L' Envoi."

and a disintegrated and threatened world looks wistfully to those who claim knowledge of a reconciling God. This message must be demonstrated on a national scale. Christian missionaries—however resolutely they try not to be identified with the countries from which they came but to identify themselves completely with the people to whom they minister—can never in their listeners' minds be divorced from the land of their birth. Their color, their accent, their mode of thought, are constant reminders of their national origin. The life with God in Christ to which they invite men, the virtues and obligations which in his name they seek to commend, at once raise the question, "How are these illustrated in the social life and national aims of the missionary's homeland?" However he seeks to obliterate it, behind this ambassador of Christ rises the picture of his country. In this age of publicity newsreels, the press, the radio, report what goes on. A nation's foreign policy makes itself felt in far corners of the globe. If economic injustices, if racial discriminations, if schemes of aggression and exploitation characterize his own land, the unhappy missionary is sorely hindered. No great headway is likely to be made by the Christian faith today until there are evangelist nations which, in their corporate life and their relations with other peoples, show the mind of Christ. The Christian cause will not grip the attention of mankind until the glory of God is revealed in the righteousness of a nation.

Meanwhile these expressions, first held up to a nation, have been rightly applied to the functions of the Christian church. Israel as a whole did not respond to this divine call; only a small minority in the nation were impressible. They formed a spiritual community, a church,

12 ¶ Who hath measured the waters in the hollow of his hand, and meted out	12 Who has measured the waters in the hollow of his hand 　　and marked off the heavens with a span,

triumph is lowered in compassion. The shepherd gathers to his bosom the young lambs unable to follow where he leads; he guides to quiet waters the mother ewe which requires special care and is solicitous for her offspring. Thus the closing lines strike the note of comfort of the beginning (cf. vss. 28-31).

B. Creator of the Ends of the Earth (40:12-31)

The poem is as remarkable for its literary composition as for its theological thought. Majestic in its theme, clear in its construction, effective in its repetitions, moving in its imagery, stirring in its moods, gripping in its climaxes, it moves to its finale with sure and dramatic progress. The stylistic unity of the opening poem lies in the imperatives; that of the second poem lies in the interrogatives. This composition contains seven strophes: vss. 12, 13-14, 15-17, 18-20, 21-24, 25-27, 28-31. The first two are questions; the third is introduced by two exclamations (cf. vss. 9-10) and forms the first climax. The second climax appears in the fifth strophe (vss. 21-24), where the point of the first climax is expanded and made more definite. But it is the third climax (vss. 28-31) which brings everything to a focus. After the urgent interrogative, the last of all the questions, we are given the crucial line of the poem:

> The LORD is the everlasting God,
> the Creator of the ends of the earth.

Then follow the closing lines of consolation. The first and second strophes are parallel to each other, as are also the fourth and the sixth (**to whom then will you compare me?**) and the fifth and the seventh (**have you not known?**). The questions of the fourth and the sixth strophes are followed by mashals. The fifth and seventh carry the burden of the poet's thought: the divine sovereignty over nature and history, judgment, omnipotence, lordship over history, incomparability and uniqueness, holiness, wisdom, eternity. These are not presented in the form of theological statements but in the impassioned language of prophetic proclamation. The closing verse is the inevitable conclusion of all that has preceded it. The literary type represented in the poem is the hymnic monologue in the manner of a self-predication.

1. First Strophe: Who Created the Universe? (40:12)

12. Who has measured the waters . . . ? The questions of this five-line strophe have but one answer: "God." Observe the use of pronouns throughout and the absence of

of which the Christian church is the lineal successor. She is Zion, herald of God's good tidings, Jerusalem, mother of those wistful for life with God. The overwhelming nature of the church's task, and the fewness of her members grasped by its compulsion, render her hesitant. In her timidity and lethargy the church needs this prophet's summons, **Get you up to a high mountain,** boldly in the sight of all men asserting your gospel for them; **lift up your voice with strength,** affirming the presence of the redeeming God; **lift it up, be not afraid**—no apologetic tone will win the attention and lay hold of the conscience of a sin-enslaved world. And in every age, as in this prophet's, the church's good tidings are not chiefly a message

of what *men* may or should be and do. Let her say, **Behold your God!**—*he* comes, *he* rules, *he* feeds, *he* gathers, *he* carries, *he* gently leads.

12-31. *Creator of the Ends of the Earth.*—The overture came to its climax with the call to the exiles, "Behold your God!" This next poem sets forth God, the maker of the universe and therefore controller of all events in its history. It was events, such as the conquests of Cyrus, which had rendered the Jewish captives fearful. The prophet's aim is to raise them to a confident faith, and he begins not with God's mighty movements in human affairs, but with his creation of seas, earth, and skies.

12-17. *The Incomparable Greatness of the Creator.*—In Babylon the Jews may well have

heaven with the span, and comprehended the dust of the earth in a measure, and weighed the mountains in scales, and the hills in a balance?	enclosed the dust of the earth in a measure and weighed the mountains in scales and the hills in a balance?

the divine name. The reference is to the Creation as an actual event in the past. In the prologue the prophet announced the imminence of the "end"; here he turns to the beginning. The God who is about to come to reveal his glory and to redeem his people is the Creator. Beginning and end, creation and redemption, are the two poles of eschatological thought. The relation between the beginning of time and the end of time (however these are construed) has been recognized since the classical treatment of the subject in Hermann Gunkel's *Schöpfung und Chaos im Urzeit und Endzeit* (Göttingen: Vandenhoeck & Ruprecht, 1895). The end cannot be understood without the beginning, redemption without creation. In the Babylonian *akitu* festival the creation epic *Enûma eliš* was recited on the fourth day of the celebrations.

Those whom the prophet addresses are borne down with despondency and despair (vs. 27). To their doubts concerning God's sovereignty in history the prophet replies by pointing to the creation of the universe. History is sustained by the God who created the seas, the heavens, and the earth (cf. Job 26:5-14; Ps. 104). Many scholars (Duhm, Köhler, Kittel) emend מים (waters) to ימים ("seas"). The change would give an excellent triad, "sea," **heavens**, and **earth**, to which there are excellent Babylonian parallels (cf. Stummer, "Einige keilschriftliche Parallelen zu Jes. 40-66," pp. 171-89; L. W. King, *A History of Babylon* [New York: Frederick A. Stokes, 1915], pp. 291 ff.). According to the ancient view, "sea," "earth," and "heavens" are the three stories of the cosmos; "mountains" and "hills" are the bulwark to support the firmament and fortify the earth. See also Pritchard, *op. cit.*, p. 332, l. 241. The Akkadian liturgies have many interesting parallels to this poem (cf. vss. 18-20 below). The Dead Sea Scroll reads "waters of the sea" (מי ים). But in view of the word play (*máyim weshāmáyim*) the M.T. is probably original. **And marked off the heavens with a span:** The verb is absent from the LXX both here and in the following verse. **A span** is the distance between the extremities of the thumb and little finger when the fingers are fully extended. **Measure:** Sidney Smith points out that "the verbs and the objects are carefully balanced to cover the measurable

been influenced by the legend of the mighty Marduk's victory over Tiamat and his creation of the cosmos from her split body. Hebrew religion had not stressed God's creatorship; but Babylonian thought challenged Hebrew faith, and helped it to enlarge its conception of God's mighty acts. The essence of vital piety is such reliance on God as commits believers confidently to him. There can be no realm of existence in which his sovereignty is not realized. Luther, in his *Greater Catechism*, interpreting the First Commandment, asks: "What means it to have a God?" and answers, "To have a God is nothing else than to trust him with all our hearts." Much so-called religious faith is not thus alive. J. Middleton Murry said of John Henry Newman that "he believed in God, but he did not trust him." [1] That was true of many of these exiles, as it is true of numbers in our churches today. Faith is born and reborn in visions of God, and the gospel

has always to be "a gift to the imagination." [2] Preachers have to turn listeners' ears into eyes and make them see the Invisible, if they are to be grasped and moved by him. This poem, by a skillful use of suggestive questions (there are a dozen of them in the first three verses) places before the downhearted community a majestic conception of God as creator. If the poet can assure them of God's absolute sovereignty of the entire fabric of the cosmos, a fortiori they will be confident of his control of whatever occurs on the earthly scene. In metaphor and rhythm the poet lays hold of their imaginations, Here is "wisdom married to immortal verse." [3]

Our generation is akin to theirs to this extent that for nearly a century little has been taught of God as creator. A marked change took place in Christian thought with the advent of the

[1] *Things to Come* (New York: The Macmillan Co., 1923), p. 34.

[2] See Horace Bushnell's essay, "Our Gospel a Gift to the Imagination," *Building Eras in Religion* (New York: Charles Scribner's Sons, 1903), pp. 249-85.
[3] Wordsworth, *The Excursion*, Bk. VII.

| 13 Who hath directed the Spirit of the LORD, or *being* his counselor hath taught him? | 13 Who has directed the Spirit of the LORD, or as his counselor has instructed him? |

forms of matter, i.e., liquid, air, powder, solid, and all the types of measurement" (*Isaiah, Chapters XL-LV* [London: British Academy, 1944], pp. 12-13, 97 n. 85). The Babylonians also measured by "thirds" (cf. the discussion of François Thureau-Dangin, "Notes assyriologiques," *Revue d'Assyriologie et d'Archéologie*, XXXI [1934], 49-52, where it is suggested that the term arose from measuring in heaps with a bushel measure). The Hebrews called the measure itself a "third" (Smith, *op. cit.*, p. 97 n. 83). The literal meaning of the **measure** is "third" (*shālish*; cf. Ps. 80:5 [Hebrew 80:6]), probably a third of an ephah or about three gallons. The point of all these measures is their smallness. What is infinitely large to us is for Yahweh very small indeed. A thousand years to him are but as yesterday (cf. Ps. 90:4).

2. SECOND STROPHE: WHO WAS GOD'S HELPER AT CREATION? (40:13-14)

13. The answer expected to this second five-line strophe of questions is not "God" but "No one." God alone created the universe without counsel or counselor. The verb *tikkēn*, **directed**, is the same as that rendered by "marked off" in the preceding verse. It is a verb of measurement (cf. Job 28:25), but here Second Isaiah, while continuing his description of the Creation, shifts his meaning. Volz rightly prefers "regulate" or "adjust" (cf. Ezek. 18:25, 29; 33:17, 20; see C. C. Torrey, *The Second Isaiah* [New York: Charles Scribner's Sons, 1928], p. 307, and cf. Ps. 75:4 [Hebrew]; G. R. Driver, "Hebrew Notes," *Vetus Testamentum*, I [1951], 242-43). The LXX renders the line τίς ἔγνω νοῦν Κυρίου, "who has known the mind of the Lord," an interesting Greek interpretation of a

theory of evolution. In the beginning of the nineteenth century Thomas Chalmers had captivated the merchants of Glasgow with a series of "Chemical Lectures," which drew crowds to the Tron Kirk at a weekday service, and later, when published, sold in thousands.[4] But when the ruthless struggle in nature for survival—as depicted by evolutionists—filled the public mind, nature became a cross to faith. Darwin himself remarked: "What a book a Devil's-chaplain might write on the clumsy, wasteful, blundering, low and horribly cruel works of nature."[5]

In consequence, devout men no longer tried to go through nature to God, for the Deity reached by that route seemed morally ambiguous; he was not the Christian God. It became customary to seek him through man's loftiest ideals. But to withdraw him thus from the physical cosmos is pitifully to belittle him. In our time, as in this prophet's, we must employ current knowledge of the vast and intricate universe "to ascribe greatness to God." No limited Deity serves when men are pitted against overmastering powers in the world's ongoings.

With these verses we may compare a device employed in our time by a naturalist and a statesman to let the cosmos make its awesome impression upon them. Charles William Beebe used to visit Theodore Roosevelt at Sagamore Hill.

After an evening of talk, perhaps about the fringes of knowledge, or some new possibility of climbing into the minds and senses of animals, we would go out on the lawn, where we took turns at an amusing little astronomical rite. We searched until we found, with or without glasses, the faint, heavenly spot of light-mist beyond the lower left-hand corner of the Great Square of Pegasus, when one or the other of us would then recite:

That is the Spiral Galaxy in Andromeda.
It is as large as our Milky Way.
It is one of a hundred million galaxies.
It is 750,000 light-years away.
It consists of one hundred billion suns, each larger than our sun.

After an interval Colonel Roosevelt would grin at me and say: "Now I think we are small enough! Let's go to bed."

We must have repeated this salutary ceremony forty or fifty times in the course of years, and it never palled.[6]

Such a "rite" corresponds to this poem's appeal to the imagination. It brings home the over-

[4] William Hanna, *Memoirs of the Life and Writings of Thomas Chalmers* (New York: Harper & Bros., 1850), II, 97.

[5] Quoted in Sara Norton and M. A. DeWolfe Howe, *The Letters of Charles Eliot Norton* (Boston: Houghton Mifflin Co., 1913), II, 336.

[6] *The Book of Naturalists* (New York: Alfred A. Knopf, 1944), p. 234. Used by permission.

14 With whom took he counsel, and *who* instructed him, and taught him in the path of judgment, and taught him knowledge, and showed to him the way of understanding?

15 Behold, the nations *are* as a drop of a bucket, and are counted as the small dust of the balance: behold, he taketh up the isles as a very little thing.

14 Whom did he consult for his enlightenment,
   and who taught him the path of justice,
and taught him knowledge,
   and showed him the way of understanding?
15 Behold, the nations are like a drop from a bucket,
   and are accounted as the dust on the scales;
   behold, he takes up the isles like fine dust.

Hebraic idea which has exercised a strong influence upon most commentators. The verb "know" is not a good rendering of the Hebrew since it does not do justice to the activity of **the Spirit.** If mind were meant, the prophet would more likely have used *lēbh.* It is doubtful, therefore, whether the divine intelligence is referred to here. God sends forth his **Spirit** as an active and life-giving force to do his work and achieve his purpose. "Under prophetic influence (e.g., Isa. 30:1) the elements of will and wisdom were included above all in the spirit of God" (Volz, *Jesaia II,* p. 9). The wisdom vocabulary of the strophe is striking and witnesses to the presence of wisdom speculation in Israel much earlier than is generally supposed. (Note the use of this passage [LXX] in Rom. 11:34 and I Cor. 2:16).

14. The words **and taught him knowledge** seem awkward. The LXX does not have them, but too much must not be made of this. On the other hand, their presence conforms to a common stylistic mannerism of the prophet in employing important words chiastically in successive strophes. **The path of justice** is not clear; the true meaning is orderly procedure or the right way of doing things (cf. 28:26). Yahweh has his own *mishpāṭ;* he needs no direction, guidance, counsel, or instruction. All the understanding and enlightenment which creation reveals have their *fons et origo* in him alone (cf. vs. 28e).

3. THIRD STROPHE: THE NATIONS ARE AS NOTHING BEFORE HIM (40:15-17)

15. The climax reveals the major concern of the poet. Exalted in his majesty and power, God creates the universe as a man performs the simplest operations of measuring and weighing; the whole of creation is his work, and therefore all that exists is under his sole sovereignty. Small and insignificant were the measures he used; so are the nations

---

whelming magnitude and complexity of God's creation. It enhances his power and wisdom, and staggers minds to conceive "the Creator of the ends of the earth" (vs. 28). It is salutary in reducing men to their proper human dimensions before God.

15-17. *The Relative Insignificance of Human Powers.*—These verses portray the relative insignificance of the mightiest human powers. **accounted by him as less than nothing and emptiness.** The Jews in Babylon were panicky over what might be going to happen. Cyrus was shaking empire after empire. But viewed in the light of God, nations are **like a drop from a bucket,** falling without appreciably lessening its content, mere **dust on the scales,** negligible in computing weight; God **takes up the isles like fine dust.** In comparison with God's immensity, the most powerful force on the human scene

counts for naught. Before him nations avail no more than the waste nothingness of the primeval chaos.

Devout folk in every age, like these believing Jews who had set up their synagogues in the land of their captivity, need constant freshening of their thought of God by having their imaginations stirred by the vastness of his creation and the comparative pettiness of all things human. We find ourselves caught in trends of the time, in tidal movements of feeling which sweep over mankind, in economic pressures and cultural "lags," in flooding emotions of race, class, and nation. We are powerless before these seemingly irrational forces. Those of us in the churches who hear and speak oftenest of God, by our familiarity with religious ideas and words, are in peril of being robbed of the realities these try to express. One may compare Thackeray's

16 And Lebanon *is* not sufficient to burn, nor the beasts thereof sufficient for a burnt offering.

17 All nations before him *are* as nothing; and they are counted to him less than nothing, and vanity.

18 ¶ To whom then will ye liken God? or what likeness will ye compare unto him?

16 Lebanon would not suffice for fuel, nor are its beasts enough for a burnt offering.

17 All the nations are as nothing before him, they are accounted by him as less than nothing and emptiness.

18 To whom then will you liken God, or what likeness compare with him?

---

before him, **like a drop from a bucket,** like a speck of **dust on the scales.** They are "nothing at all." Why should men fear or despair before such a God? The control of history as of nature belongs to him and to him alone (cf. Amos 1:1–2:16; 4:6-12). The vast international forces which arouse the deepest perplexity among the prophet's contemporaries (vs. 27) are in reality nothing in comparison with God's work and purpose in history. The meaning is not that God has no concern for the nations, for all the poems deny that. On the contrary, the thought is that the nations are no threat; they have no power of their own; their pretensions have no weight with God.

16-17. The transition from nature (vss. 13-14) to history (vss. 15-17) is characteristic of the prophet (vss. 9-10; 44:24 ff.; 45:12-13; 51:9-10), as it is of most of the O.T. (cf., e.g., the Yahwist theology from creation to history in the emergence of Abraham). While the poem is about creation, its emphases fall on history (vss. 15, 17, 24, 28-31). Nature provides the theater for history: God created the earth that it might be inhabited (cf. 42:5; 45:12). Creation prepares the way for history: the power that is sovereign in creation is sovereign in history. Vs. 16, with its reference to sacrifice, occasions some difficulty. It breaks the continuity, and Volz therefore deletes it. The emphasis is not upon the value of the cult. All the forests of **Lebanon** would not be sufficient **fuel** for a sacrifice to Yahweh, nor would its **beasts** suffice as victims. The verse may be an addition. The twofold **behold** (vs. 15) has the sureness of the prophetic "therefore," but is stronger in its force and vaster in its cosmic-historical perspectives.

4. FOURTH STROPHE: IDOLS DO NOT MOVE (40:18-20)

18. The thought of the first strophe is developed. It is not primarily a polemic against idolatry, but rather a reflection upon the nature of the Creator portrayed in vss. 12-17. **To whom then will you liken God?** The Hebrew introduces the question with a conjunction, "but." In the first strophe the poet employed many anthropomorphisms; in the second his contemplation has deepened. God is God alone, and there was no one beside him to aid him in his creation, as later Jewish thought imagined, no hypostatized

---

outburst at some of the religious teaching of his day:

O awful, awful name of God! Light unbearable! Mystery unfathomable! Vastness immeasurable! Who are these who come forward to explain the mystery, and gaze unblinking into the depths of the light, and measure the immeasurable vastness to a hair? O name, that God's people of old did fear to utter! O light, that God's prophet would have perished had he seen! Who are these that are now so familiar with it? [7]

Devout thought and speech become divorced from the stupendous actualities with which they

[7] *The Paris Sketch Book,* "Madame Sand and the New Apocalypse."

deal. They lose the tone of awed wonder, the one sure token of their contact with the transcendent God. Current interpretations of the cosmos by physicists and astronomers do not tend to make its Creator less marvelous or less mighty. An occasional sermon which stretches the minds of hearers, by confronting them with the almost illimitable distances of solar space and astounding them by disclosures in the minutest particles of "matter," begets a reverent wonder in which God becomes actual. It humbles spirits before the Most High, and fortifies them in fellowship with one so infinitely great.

18-20. *The Folly of Idol Making.*—**To whom then will you liken God?** The prophet's point

19 The workman melteth a graven image, and the goldsmith spreadeth it over with gold, and casteth silver chains.	19 The idol! a workman casts it, and a goldsmith overlays it with gold, and casts for it silver chains.
20 He that *is* so impoverished that he hath no oblation chooseth a tree *that* will not rot; he seeketh unto him a cunning workman to prepare a graven image, *that* shall not be moved.	20 He who is impoverished*q* chooses for an offering wood that will not rot; he seeks out a skilful craftsman to set up an image that will not move.

q Heb uncertain

Memra or Wisdom or Spirit. The poet contemplates the infinite wonder and mystery of the Spirit of God. The third strophe brought the thought to a culmination; the nations are as nothing before him. Now in the fourth the poet asks what comparisons, what likenesses describe God. The word "El" is the generally diffused Semitic appellation of Deity, but there are no qualifying words (cf. "Holy One" in the parallel vs. 25). For such a one every measure is wanting; in the whole cosmos there is no point of contact from which one might hope to imagine or conceive him (Volz). Second Isaiah is articulating one of the cardinal tenets of Hebraic faith from Mosaic times: the God of Israel was imageless. He is pressing Mosaic religion to a magnificent culmination. This majestic and exalted Creator and Sovereign, before whom the nations are as nothing— to whom will you liken him? (Cf. Temple Program for the New Year's Festivals at Babylon in Pritchard, *Ancient Near Eastern Texts,* pp. 331-34; the literary style of the liturgy has many affinities with Second Isaiah; see also the hymn and lamentation to Ishtar, pp. 383 ff.) The poet then turns quite naturally to the idolmaking that he knows so well. This is the final attempt to make God like a thing. The description shows clearly that the prophet had observed their manufacture (see *ibid.,* p. 331, where the manufacture of two images is described in connection with the New Year's festival on the sixth day of Nisan). Paul's speech to the men of Athens is an excellent parallel (Acts 17:22-31).

Many scholars insert 41:6-7 at this point under the conviction that these verses are needed here and are out of place where they stand. In this event, vs. 19 and 41:6-7 would describe a metal, vs. 20 a wooden image. The difficulty with this view is that the verses are essential in their present position and are not required here when the passage is understood. Sidney Smith describes the process as follows: "On a metal figure, פסל, cast by the 'artificer,' חרש, the gold- and silver-smith, צרף, proceeds to hammer a gold overlay, בזהב ירקענו, 'smelting bonds of silver,' that is pouring molten silver alloy into sockets to hold the figure upright, רתקות כסף צורף" (*Isaiah XL-LV,* p. 171). The use of silver as solder, Smith admits, is unusual, but suggests that it is probably confused with lead.

20. This verse is a famous crux. The first words, **he who is impoverished . . . for an offering,** occasion the greatest difficulty. They are absent from the Vulg., but appear in

is that God is incomparable, and therefore all making of images of him is absurd. He is speaking both to his fellow religionists, who were being seduced to idolatry by imposing statues of deities all about them, and to the heathen themselves. He is satirical both here and in subsequent descriptions of idol manufacturing. It is not difficult to show how ludicrous are likenesses in metal, wood, or stone, of the God of the universe. But the poet's question,

To whom then will you liken God,
 or what likeness compare with him?

is not fully answered by exposing the folly of idolatry. A basic conviction of Christian faith is involved here.

It is through images that intercourse between persons becomes possible. We may say that we "see" one another. In fact, we see tiny images which rays of light refract upon the retina of the eye. Through these diminutive images we do business and form friendships. In men's intercourse with God they are impelled to form images of him. There is nothing wrong in such image making; but an unworthy or inadequate mental image is tragic, because it thwarts God's

21 Have ye not known? have ye not heard? hath it not been told you from the beginning? have ye not understood from the foundations of the earth?	21 Have you not known? Have you not heard? Has it not been told you from the beginning? Have you not understood from the foundations of the earth?

the LXX (contra Sidney Smith) at the close of the preceding sentence ὁμοίωμα κατεσκεύασεν, "he made it a likeness." Duhm, Kittel, and others emend to המכנן תמונה, "he that setteth up a likeness." Jerome explains the first word המסוכן as a kind of wood which Sidney Smith (*ibid.,* pp. 171-72) connects with the *musukanu* of the Assyrians, identified by R. Campbell Thompson with the mulberry (*The Assyrian Herbal* [London: Luzac & Co., 1924], p. 181). Levy (*Deutero-Isaiah,* p. 123) offers perhaps the most satisfactory solution. Beginning with the observation that "a wooden image might have formed the foundation of the molten image by having molten metal poured over it," he cautiously ventures the reading המסכה לתמונה (cf. LXX): lit., "He that causeth the casting thereof for a likeness." G. R. Driver ("Linguistic and Textual Problems: Isaiah XL-LXVI," *Journal of Theological Studies,* XXXVI [1935], 396-97) actually proposes a simpler solution, merely revocalizing the consonants to *hammiṣkēn terāmāh:* "The poor man (as) a costly idol," but the meaning is strained and awkward. Lorenz Dürr (*Ursprung und Ausbau der israelitisch-jüdischen Heilandserwartung* [Berlin: C. A. Schwetschke & Sohn, 1925], p. 147) cites a Babylonian parallel in the Texts IV, Ser. 40, No. 1 of the New Year's liturgy for the third of Nisan: "For 2½ double-hours . . . (he calls) a stone cutter, and he gives him precious stones and gold from the possession of Marduk for the completion of two images for the sixth day. He calls a carpenter, he gives him wood of the cedar and tamarisk; he calls a goldsmith and gives him gold." Volz, in quoting this parallel (*Jesaia II,* p. 7), comments relevantly that this inscription shows that the divine image consisted of a wooden core with gold overlay.

5. FIFTH STROPHE: LORD OF NATURE AND HISTORY (40:21-24)

A strophe of extraordinary literary construction. Continuing the interrogative form, the first three lines are introduced with the same expression **Have you not** (Hebrew, *halô'*). The poet then falls into the style of a hymn with a triad of participial double lines, **he that sitteth, . . . spreadeth, . . . bringeth** (vss. 22-23), followed by three verbs— each of which is introduced by **scarcely** (vs. 24*ab*); then comes the sharp *wegham,* **and . . . also,** with the vigorous conclusion (vs. 24*c*).

The elaborate introduction (vs. 21) leads to a lyrical triad, the first two members of which (like the first two strophes) describe God as creator and the third his activity in history (like the third strophe). Cf. 51:9-11; Pss. 33:6 ff.; 44; 136:1-26. In vs. 24 the judgment is vividly elaborated. Here again creation and history, the world of nature and the world of nations, meet to reveal the sovereignty and judgment of God.

21. From the foundations of the earth: The Hebrew lacks the preposition. Duhm, Köhler, Torrey, Kittel, and others rightly emend to *miṣudhath,* "from the founding of

desired fellowship with his children. Revelation is his effort to convey a correct impression of himself. The folly is in resting in man-made conceptions of God, instead of responding to his own disclosure of himself. It is not for us to devise a likeness, but to accept his own self-portrait. The prophet's question found its answer centuries later when, out of the church's experience of Christ, an apostle called him "the image of the invisible God" (Col. 1:15), and	another heard him saying, "He that hath seen me hath seen the Father" (John 14:9). **21-24. *The Unapproachable Exaltation of God.***—But while Christ is for us "the whole fullness of deity" (Col. 2:9), there are cosmic functions and relations of the godhead which cannot be revealed in man. Jesus is all of God that man can disclose. An entire ocean is not seen in a bay, and there are aspects of deity unrevealed in his incarnation in Jesus. John

22 *It is* he that sitteth upon the circle of the earth, and the inhabitants thereof *are* as grasshoppers; that stretcheth out the heavens as a curtain, and spreadeth them out as a tent to dwell in:

23 That bringeth the princes to nothing; he maketh the judges of the earth as vanity.

22 It is he who sits above the circle of the earth,
 and its inhabitants are like grasshoppers;
who stretches out the heavens like a curtain,
 and spreads them like a tent to dwell in;
23 who brings princes to nought,
 and makes the rulers of the earth as nothing.

---

the earth." The Yahwist begins his epic with the creation (Gen. 2:4*b*) which leads to the election of Israel in Abraham; in the priestly document the creation account serves as a solemn and sublime introduction to the succession of generations by which history is grasped. The historical revelation is grounded in the prior creation, although it is the reflection upon history that produced this deepening.

22-23. The earth is conceived as a dome. In Prov. 8:27 **the circle** (*ḥûgh*) is the "vault over the face of the abyss" (*tehôm*); in Job 22:14 Yahweh walks upon the vault of the heavens; cf. the legend of Adapa:

> As Adapa from the horizon of heaven to the zenith of heaven
> Cast a glance, he saw its awesomeness (Pritchard, *op. cit.*, p. 102).

See also the Temple Program for the New Year's Festivals at Babylon (*ibid.*, p. 331). **Like a curtain . . . like a tent:** Cf. 42:5; Pss. 104:2; 18:11; 19:4. **Princes . . . judges: Rulers** of the earth like the kings whom Abraham conquered (Gen. 14), like Pharaoh in the time of Moses, like the kings whom Israel overcame in the conquest, and like the great Assyrian and Babylonian monarchs.

14:28 should be read with John 14:9. There is a "greaterness" in the Father; that must always be in our minds to do justice to the spiritual life of Jesus with God. This incalculable "greaterness" of God, the Lord of the universe, the prophet proclaims:

> **It is he who sits above the circle of the earth,**
> **and its inhabitants are like grasshoppers;**
> **who stretches out the heavens like a curtain,**
> **and spreads them like a tent to dwell in.**

This transcendent creator is the disposer of men. The poet has deftly employed nature as a sacrament to lead his hearers' minds up to God, and stay them upon him. Why should they be frightened at anything a Cyrus might do? The ancient empires which are toppling, or this new power which is now beginning to dominate the scene, are like all things human, ephemeral. God, **the everlasting,** swiftly takes them off the stage. **They wither, and the tempest carries them off like stubble.**

We need to recover this conviction of God's abiding sovereignty. Our generation has witnessed systems of collective control come to power which confer on governments totalitarian authority. Even where such systems are democratic, majorities may become tyrannical and attempt to dominate men's spirits. Collectivist regimes tend to deify the state. Consciences may prove troublesome and interfere with the government's purposes. Religious men and women rightly refuse total subjection to any earthly authority in loyalty to one far above them. Fellow mortals, even those most exalted, are to them as nothing compared with the Lord of all worlds to whom they are directly accountable. Speaking of the unique role played by religious men in the struggle with totalitarian tyrannies, Walter Lippmann wrote: "By the religious experience the humblest communicant is led into the presence of a power so much greater than his master's that the distinctions of this world are of little importance." [8] Democracies no less than despotisms may attempt to enslave souls. Liberty is not safe unless it is anchored beyond the fabric of human systems in him who is creator and controller of all, from whom come his children's dignity and rights. The

[8] *An Inquiry into the Principles of the Good Society* (Boston: Little, Brown & Co., 1937), p. 382.

24 Yea, they shall not be planted; yea, they shall not be sown; yea, their stock shall not take root in the earth: and he shall also blow upon them, and they shall wither, and the whirlwind shall take them away as stubble.

25 To whom then will ye liken me, or shall I be equal? saith the Holy One.

24 Scarcely are they planted, scarcely sown,
    scarcely has their stem taken root in
    the earth,
when he blows upon them, and they
    wither,
and the tempest carries them off like
    stubble.

25 To whom then will you compare me,
    that I should be like him? says the
    Holy One.

---

24. They flourish for a time like the seed planted in thin soil, but then God intervenes and they wither and are carried off by the wind (a favorite figure of the prophet's).

6. Sixth Strophe: Yahweh Is Incomparable (40:25-27)

The opening words repeat those of the companion strophe of vss. 18-20. But their effect is not the same, for vs. 18 appears in the context of the first three strophes, while this strophe coming as it does after the momentous lines of vs. 24, prepares for the climax in vss. 28-31. The fourth strophe leaves one with a sense of the utter futility and poignant pathos of image-making; the sixth leaves one with a sense of great exaltation before the majesty of the Creator. Only one who has known the infinite majesty and the solemn mystery of the heavens could write lines like these (cf. Ps. 8; also Blaise Pascal, *Pensées* [London: J. M. Dent & Sons, 1913], No. 206: *"Le silence éternel de ces espaces infinis m'effraie"*).

Mowinckel believes that Yahweh is portrayed here as the shepherd of the stars. More likely the figure is military. The poet calls upon his listeners to lift their faces to the midnight heavens (cf. Gen. 15:5), and then with terrific force poses his final question: "Who created these?" God, the captain of the host, calls out his myriads upon myriads of stars, and each star takes its appointed place as its name is called. There they stand in their great battalions in response to the call of the captain. Not one is missing; each responds to the call of its own name. To Israel's "Why?" the prophet now turns abruptly at the most impressive point of his poem and addresses himself to his people (vs. 27).

25. Yahweh speaks and addresses the question to Israel (cf. Job 38:1 for a somewhat similar situation). Observe the title **Holy One** without pronoun or article in the Hebrew (cf. Hab. 3:3; Job 6:10). Holy is what God really is (Lev. 19:2; Josh. 24:19; I Sam. 2:2; Isa. 1:4; 5:16, 19, 24; 6:3; 10:17; 29:19; 30:11-12, 15; 31:1; cf. also Isa. 8:13 ff.; Pss. 22:3; 99:1-9). Holy is his name (cf. 57:15). The religion of the O.T. is a religion of the holiness of God (cf. Johannes Hänel, *Die Religion der Heiligkeit* [Gütersloh: C. Bertelsmann, 1931]). It is the unique word for the divine (Rudolf Otto, *The Idea of the Holy*, tr. J. W. Harvey [rev. ed.; London: Oxford University Press, 1928]). When God reveals himself, he reveals himself as holy. The theophany to Moses is a revelation of holiness (Exod. 3:5) and the only words the seraphim know before the presence of God are the words of the trisagion (6:3).

---

supremacy of conscience among men and nations derives from his supreme righteousness. Abraham Lincoln correctly placed democratic freedom under his sway when he concluded his Gettysburg Address: "That this nation, under God, shall have a new birth of freedom, and that government of the people, by the people, for the people, shall not perish from the earth." Free popular rule flourishes when people recog-

nize the supremacy of God. Without the acknowledgment of a moral judgment to which all must conform, there seems little likelihood of a stable world organization. The judgment of God is a standard not susceptible of a veto by any nation or of defeat by all nations combined.

25-26. God Incomparably Lofty and Mighty.
—The captives were fearful that their rem-

26 Lift up your eyes on high, and behold who hath created these *things*, that bringeth out their host by number: he calleth them all by names by the greatness of his might, for that *he is* strong in power; not one faileth.

26 Lift up your eyes on high and see: who created these? He who brings out their host by number, calling them all by name; by the greatness of his might, and because he is strong in power not one is missing.

---

26. The heavens are not named, neither are the stars. There they shine in their transcendent beauty, each orb in its piercing intensity, myriads upon myriads of them, silent and eternal, yet eloquent in their witness (cf. Ps. 19; Job 38:7). **Who created these?** Each word has its special emphasis. The pronoun **who** repeats the opening interrogatives of vss. 12-13. The verb *bārā'*, **created,** brings the entire poem to a focus. It is a very striking word, one which Second Isaiah employs more frequently than any other writer in the O.T. (vss. 26, 28; 41:20; 42:5; 43:7; 45:7, 8, 12, 18; 54:16; cf. 57:19; 65:17, 18), and to which he brings his own special contribution. Hitherto Israel had not occupied itself extensively with cosmogony; references earlier than Second Isaiah are conspicuous by their paucity and brevity, above all in comparison with the great cosmogonies of the other peoples of the Near East. Babylonian influence is probably present in these lines (see Martin Buber, *The Prophetic Faith,* tr. Carlyle Witton-Davies [New York: The Macmillan Co., 1949], p. 211). The annual recital of the creation epic in the New Year's festival was doubtless familiar to the writer. Here the prophet portrays Israel's God, one infinitely greater than Marduk, who engaged in primordial combat with Tiamat at the creation of the heavens and the earth. Observe how silent and majestic and sublime the description is in comparison with the *Enûma eliš.* The word **these** is almost breathless in its awe. He knows the stars, and **calls them all by name** (cf. Pedersen, *Israel, Its Life and Culture, I-II,* pp. 245-59). Of course they have **names**—that is essential, for name and existence are one in ancient thought, and it may be inferred that it is God who gave the names in the beginning. There is also the picture of God's great power and might. In all this infinite expanse of innumerable stars, stretching beyond all imagination and power to grasp, not one is missing. Such a God, the prophet is saying, is Lord of his universe and of your history; cf. the words of Ahiqar, "Many are the stars of heaven, and no man knows their names" (Pritchard, *op. cit.,* p. 429).

It is possible that we have here a polemic against Babylonian astral worship. The greater gods of Babylon had long since "become identified with the planets, and the lesser gods with the fixed stars, each deity having his special house or star in heaven in addition to his temple on earth" (King, *History of Babylon,* p. 292). The stars have no independent sovereignty. In a late apocalypse Yahweh brings judgment upon the host of heaven (24:21-23).

---

nant, scattered over the earth, would disappear as a nation. But he who both creates and commands the stars in their courses can be relied on to preserve his people and not allow them to be lost to his purposes for mankind. This is the sacrament of the skies.

The upward look has been the deliverance of many in the hour of sorrow. After the death of her sister Emily, and with another sister, Anne, dying of tuberculosis, Charlotte Brontë wrote to a friend:

I avoid looking forward or backward, and try to keep looking upward. . . . The days pass in a slow, dark march; the nights are the test; the sudden

wakings from restless sleep, the revived knowledge that one lies in her grave, and another not at my side, but in a separate and sick bed. However, God is over all.[9]

One often derives scant comfort from the human scene. To maintain poise and assurance we must turn our eyes on high. The dependable order of the heavens suggests the reliability of him who marshals the planets and the lives of men. It is tranquilizing to "stand amid eternal ways" and await serenely the fulfillment of God's times.

[9] Clement Shorter, *The Brontës, Life and Letters* (New York: Charles Scribner's Sons, 1908), II, 20.

27 Why sayest thou, O Jacob, and speakest, O Israel, My way is hid from the Lord, and my judgment is passed over from my God?
 	
28 ¶ Hast thou not known? hast thou
	27 Why do you say, O Jacob,
	    and speak, O Israel,
	"My way is hid from the Lord,
	    and my right is disregarded by my
	      God"?
	28 Have you not known? Have you not
	    heard?

27. Why do you say, O Jacob? A striking shift in thought, but it is this verse that lies behind the whole poem. Before such a God as has been portrayed in ever-increasing power and majesty, how can Jacob believe that his way is hid from the Lord? **Jacob** and **Israel** are favorite designations in the poem. "Second Isaiah is the true originator of the spiritual idea of the 'people of God,' of the 'true Israel'" (Volz, *Jesaia II*, p. 13). **My way is hid:** God does not see what has happened to me; my lot is hid from him. **My right:** The word usually translated "justice" or **judgment** means "the right that was due to me" (cf. vss. 2. 10). Observe the use of the same word in the Dead Sea Manual of Discipline: "As for me, my justification belongs to God" (ix. 2; cf. Isa. 49:4).

7. Seventh Strophe: An Everlasting God (40:28-31)

28abc. Immediately following the people's despondent cry, the prophet breaks forth with his final word: Yahweh, the historical God of the historical people, is an everlasting

27-31. The Absurdity of Fancying God Careless or Incapable.—The personal words, **Jacob and Israel,** stress the enduring unity of the nation before God. Behind every people is Providence, which out of the racial stock, geographical situation, historical occurrences, cultural heritage, has fashioned them into a nation. Each nation has a place in God's design for his world; each is a significant experiment in corporate living. Discouraged Jews would be heartened by this reminder that they belong in a people with a distinctive mission. Names such as **Jacob** and **Israel,** with memories and associations, recalled the nation's relationship to God. Circumstances may change, but his relationship with them continues. "It is on religion the inmost and deepest life of a nation rests."[1]

The exiles had many reasons for questioning God's justice toward them. Had Israel been a sinner above other nations? Ought innocent Israelites to suffer with the guilty? When men begin to doubt God's fairness, their minds become embittered. They are not so much thinking as feeling. A first step in the cure of such depression is to induce them to question their own reasons. We fling our "Why?" at God; but we should first challenge ourselves (cf. Ps. 42:5). The problem of Israel's suffering runs through these poems and comes to its sublime solution in the figure of the servant offered for the sins of the nations (ch. 53). It is typical of men's misinterpretation of God's dealings with them that what they term his disregard proves his

supreme choice of them for his unique task in the salvation of mankind. The Exile was Israel's Gethsemane, in which the prayer rose daily, "Let this cup pass from me"; but to this inspired poet it was the cup of the world's redemption, to be drunk vicariously by his chosen servant. To be sure, God's answer to his people's protests was not in the terms of their **right.** God's thoughts and ways are not on the human level (55:8-9). Redemption by vicarious suffering is far above human justice.

Have you not known? We have stressed that faith precedes knowledge, and the N.T. and subsequent Christian thought bear us out; witness Paul's "I know whom I have believed" and Anselm's *credo ut intelligam.* But it is also true that knowledge precedes faith: "We have known and believed the love that God hath to us" (I John 4:16). Great views of God are essential to call forth great hopes and great energies. The prophet is bent on supplying his people with an adequate theology. Benjamin Whichcote well said: "Religion begins with knowledge; it proceeds to temper; and ends in practice."[2] A conviction of God, creator of the universe and controller of history, leads to a courageous temper and issues in resolute and indefatigable effort.

> The Lord is the everlasting God,
>   the Creator of the ends of the earth.

These lines are central in the poem and announce its theme. The long grim years of the

---

[1] James Bryce, *The Holy Roman Empire* (new ed.; New York: The Macmillan Co., 1904), p. 93.

[2] See his sermon "The Work of Reason," on Phil. 4:8.

not heard, *that* the everlasting God, the LORD, the Creator of the ends of the earth, fainteth not, neither is weary? *there is* no searching of his understanding.	The LORD is the everlasting God, the Creator of the ends of the earth. He does not faint or grow weary, his understanding is unsearchable.

God, Creator of the ends of the earth. The God of Israel is Lord of beginning and end, and he is sovereign through the intervening ages. The words **everlasting** and **Creator** appear together purposely because both express the fundamental character of the divine sovereignty: God is Lord of time and Lord of space. Yet he does not dwell in isolation, self-sufficient, imperturbable, and unmoved. His eternity stands above the events of time, yet he manifests himself in all the events of history; his creation declares him Lord of the universe, but he gives power to those who have no strength. At a time when the tide of events exacts Israel's energy and vitality, God is the source of power. Israel is called upon to wait, to live by waiting for the Lord (cf. 49:23; 59:9, 11). This is not the first time in the history of Israel's religion that the emphasis upon waiting appears (8:16-18; Hab. 2:3[?]), but from here on it becomes one of the cardinal words of O.T. faith, above all in the psalms (see Pss. 25:3, 21; 27:14; 33:20; 37:7, 9; 40:1; 69:6; etc.). This emphasis provided the mentality which made of Israel the waiting community, par excellence. In this strophe the prophet is articulating clearly what is shadowed forth in vss. 12-14. Cf. "his unfathomable understanding" with vs. 14.

28d-31. The weakness of Israel and the strength of God are sharply focused. The picture of the eagle's flight is a marvelous figure of the reality and power of faith (cf.

captivity had been exhausting physically and nervously. There was a spiritual fatigue which was a most serious obstacle to venturing upon the homeward march. The prophet does not exhort his people to rouse themselves from their defeatism. That is like whipping a jaded horse. He proclaims a freshening gospel of their untiring and resourceful God, whose boundless energies the whole cosmos witnesses.

The middle years of the twentieth century, after the drain of two devastating wars, brought a heavy strain upon Christians. There appears little prospect that even the young will live to see the fulfillment of men's generous expectations for the race. Christians must be steeled for prolonged effort, for repeated checks, for exasperating delays. The *reductio ad absurdum* is apparently a favorite method with God in his education of mankind. He allows evils to work themselves out, and thus expose their true character. Only an **everlasting God** would have the patience to carry out such a process. He outwearies his antagonists. The enemies of righteousness may win many battles, but in the long duration of God's unflagging war they have no chance at all. Lessing's prayer is appropriate for our day: "Pursue thy secret path, everlasting Providence; only let me not, because thou art hidden, despair of thee. Let me not despair of thee if thy steps appear to retreat. It is not true that the shortest line is always straight." [3]

God's everlastingness suggests his constancy.

[3] *Die Erziehung des Menschengeschlechts.*

In our personal lives, as well as in public affairs, few of us escape periods of depression. Physical and mental fatigue have a deeper cause in a tired spirit. This is one of the trials of waning powers which come with advanced years. It requires spiritual treatment, and is part of the church's ministry to the elderly. Jowett, the master of Balliol, at seventy-five, wrote to a friend as old as he:

Age like youth is a blessed time. . . . It totters in its steps and also sometimes in its thoughts and words; but yet it may preserve a sort of continuity of mind by trusting in God. Judging from my own experience, I should say that the greatest difficulty was to get above moods of mind which vary from day to day and really arise from physical causes. When we feel ourselves weakest it is a new strength to think of the unchangeableness of God. [4]

Frustrations age us. Whether young or old in years, these Jewish captives and we twentieth-century men and women, caught and imprisoned by barriers to our hopes which we seem incapable of surmounting, need the aspects of **the everlasting God** stressed by this prophet:

**He does not faint or grow weary,
his understanding is unsearchable.**

To keep before our minds these qualities in God furnishes the active patience which bears up and marches onward.

[4] Evelyn Abbot and Lewis Campbell, *The Life and Letters of Benjamin Jowett* (New York: E. P. Dutton & Co., 1897), II, 455-56.

| 29 He giveth power to the faint; and to *them that have* no might he increaseth strength. | 29 He gives power to the faint, and to him who has no might he increases strength. |

Ps. 103:5). The LXX interprets the verb as meaning "shall put forth wings"; the Vulg. reads similarly, *assument pennas*. The Targ., on the other hand, appears to read "lift up their wings." The RSV takes the noun **wings** as an adverbial accusative of instrument or means (cf. Torrey, *Second Isaiah*, p. 309). The force of the lines lies in the verbs.

His understanding does not refer to God's omniscience, but to his sympathetic knowledge of his own people and their needs. They had been tempted to think their **way . . . hid from the LORD;** but all the while love watched over and felt with them. The word opens for us the heart of God. It is akin to Job's believing reflection when God had seemed to conceal himself from him, "He knoweth the way that I take" (Job 23:10).

Baffled men often exclaim, "God knows." It is their assertion that what has happened is too puzzling for them. But to say "God understands" is to rest upon a wisdom kinder and more discerning than man's. Such **unsearchable understanding** assures the prophet of God's solicitous provision for those without resources sufficient for the demands about to be made on them—**the faint** and those who **have no might.** And there must have been many such among these unhappy captives.

To **wait for the LORD** is contrasted in the prophet's mind with watching current events. The world was rocking under the campaigns of Cyrus. Their neighbors and the Jews themselves kept asking, "What next?" To this the Bible's invariable answer is "the living God." This answer, however, never comes from events in themselves. There may be bright spots on the horizon, but these are not of such size or brilliance as to lift spirits to the pitch of noble adventure. Those who turn expectantly toward God discover that occurrences are not "bare events," but advents of **the everlasting God.** They derive from them an access of force. Waiting for the Lord provided Israel, as the Exeg. comments, with the mentality which made the nation pre-eminently "the waiting community." The early church was possessed by the same mentality, which unhappily has ceased to be the mind of contemporary Christians. We are not looking hopefully for God's arrivals on the scene in gracious power in historic happenings. Yet it is to this waiting mentality that increases of strength are promised.

The prophet anticipates the effects of this increase of strength (vs. 31). The first response to the realization that their God was at hand in these shattering victories of the Persians, making possible their liberation, would be an enthusiastic upsurge; then would follow rapid preparations for the start home and an eager leaving; and then a steady march home, and no less unflagging effort day after day to repair their ruined land. Some have seen in this sequence a spiritual progress. Whether this is fanciful or not, all three responses occur in the life with God.

Men of faith know an exaltation as of wings. The African explorer, Henry M. Stanley, recorded in a notebook that prayer "lifted me hopefully over the one thousand five hundred miles of Forest tracks, eager to face the day's perils and fatigues." [5] Thomas Chalmers, when a divinity student at St. Andrew's, with thoughts of God akin to those of this poem, wrote of himself: "I spent nearly a twelvemonth in a sort of mental elysium, and the one idea which ministered to my soul all its rapture was the magnificence of the Godhead, and the universal subordination of all things to the one great purpose for which He evolved and was supporting creation." [6] Such winged spirits—and this prophet was surely one in his day—soar above the obstacles which impede and take the heart out of their fellows. With minds stayed on God, they advance in full flight. Others tirelessly storm their God-assigned tasks. John Wesley, at eighty-two, declared:

Mr. Henry said "I bless God that I am never tired *of* my work, yet I am often tired *in* my work." By the blessing of God, I can say more: I am never tired *in* my work. From the beginning of the day or the week or the year to the end I do not know what weariness means. I am never weary of writing or preaching or travelling; but am just as fresh at the end as at the beginning. Thus it is with me today, and I take no thought for to-morrow. [7]

Wesley was endowed with extraordinary physical vitality, and doubtless his faith had much to do with his health and spirits. Many ordinary Christians, too, discover that when they are moving swiftly, absorbed in their work, they have themselves in better control than when they slacken their pace. At a maritime inquiry

[5] *Autobiography*, ed. Dorothy Stanley (Boston: Houghton Mifflin Co., 1909), p. 519.
[6] Hanna, *Memoirs of Chalmers*, I, 28-29.
[7] *Letters*, ed. Telford, VII, 254. Letter dated February, 1785.

30 Even the youths shall faint and be weary, and the young men shall utterly fall:	30 Even youths shall faint and be weary, and young men shall fall exhausted;
31 But they that wait upon the Lord shall renew *their* strength; they shall mount up with wings as eagles; they shall run, and not be weary; *and* they shall walk, and not faint.	31 but they who wait for the Lord shall renew their strength, they shall mount up with wings like eagles, they shall run and not be weary, they shall walk and not faint.
41 Keep silence before me, O islands; and let the people renew *their* strength: let them come near; then let them speak: let us come near together to judgment.	**41** Listen to me in silence, O coastlands; let the peoples renew their strength; let them approach, then let them speak; let us together draw near for judgment.

C. The Trial of the Nations (41:1–42:4)

Redemption and creation are the two focuses of the prophet's eschatology. But just as redemption is the end of which creation is the beginning, so human history is the area which emerges from creation and closes with redemption. Thus redemption, creation, and history constitute the background for the prophet's thought. The unity of the first three poems is seen in their convergence upon history. Just as the poem on creation has its interest in its implications for history, so the poem on the nations has its importance for the way it points to Yahweh's chosen servant and the agent of his righteous sovereignty over the nations.

The literary character of the poem is determined throughout by its setting in the court of law, its formal construction, and its prevailing dramatic style. The want of transitions, the exclamations (**behold**, etc.), the imperatives (41:1, 21-23), the carefully wrought repetitions (e.g., **strengthen**, 41:6, 7, 13; **fear not**, 41:10, 13c, 14; cf. vs. 5; **I will help you,** 41:10c, 13d, 14c; cf. vs 6a; **behold,** 41:24, 29; 42:1), the directness of address to Israel (41:8 ff.) and the nations (41:1 ff., 21 ff.), the pronouncement of the verdict (41:11, 24, 29), and the climactic emphases, similar to those encountered in the preceding poem, all betray a dramatic style that binds the work into a literary unity. The proem (41:1; cf. 1:2; 34:1; 49:1; also 45:20; 51:4-5; Mic. 6:1) opens chiastically (a b b a), then follows a triad of verbs (vs. 1cd). All the verbs of vs. 1 are emphatic (cf. 40:1) and set the stage for the first main speech. The poem proper is composed of nine strophes,

---

upon a collision in which a small vessel was run down by a huge Atlantic liner, her captain testified that at a reduced speed his ship was less readily responsive to her steering gear. Those who **run** upon God's purposes are more sensitive to his guidance than the mass of Christians who stroll. It is the loiterers that go astray.

But the main company of God's people neither fly nor run: they **walk.** The largest part of the world's most useful work is accomplished by plodders. This is as true in the church as in science, government, and industry. "It's dogged as does it." [8] Ministers in their parishes, teachers in Sunday schools, workers in missionary enterprises, scholars in the church's institutions of learning, who trudge along undiscouraged, year in and year out, are those upon whom men

[8] Anthony Trollope, *The Last Chronicle of Barset* (New York: E. P. Dutton & Co., 1909), ch. lxi.

depend. The inspiration for such unremitting effort comes from waiting for the Lord. **The everlasting God, the Creator of the ends of the earth,** comes to believing men in seemingly commonplace and routine happenings no less than in the startling crises of history. Their "sufficiency is from God" (II Cor. 3:5).

41:1–42:4. The Trial of the Nations.—Ch. 40 began with a council in heaven; ch. 41 opens with a gathering of the nations for a trial. It is a dramatic scene, where God the judge poses the questions, and finally propounds the verdict by declaring his servant, Israel, the mediator of judgment, whose instruction is the standard by which all peoples will be judged and redeemed.

41:1-4. The Nations Cited to Appear Before God.—Vs. 1 is an introduction to the poem and contains the citation to the nations to appear.

grouped in triads (vss. 2-4, 5-7, 8-10; 11-13, 14-16, 17-20; 21-24, 25-29, 42:1-4). It will be observed that the climax falls in each case upon the third member of the triad. In the first instance the emphasis is upon Israel, the servant of the Lord (vss. 8-10), thus providing a clue as to where the interest of the poet lies; in the second case the climax is especially effective, appearing after a bitter judgment against the nations (vss. 11-13) and a remarkable address to Israel (vss. 14-16), and coming in the form of a lyrical interlude (vss. 17-20) which closes with the words:

> That men may see and know,
> may consider and understand together,
> that the hand of the LORD has done this,
> the Holy One of Israel has created it.

The final strophe is directed solely to Israel, the servant of the Lord. The emphases are everywhere the same, and the greatest emphasis falls precisely where it should be expected in the light of the other poems (cf. the threefold "behold" in 40:9-10 and the remarkable climax of 40:28-31).

The court of law has a special place in Hebraic tradition and thought. (For descriptions of Hebrew juristic procedures see Ludwig Köhler, "Die hebräische Rechtsgemeinde," *Jahresbericht der Universität Zürich,* 1930-31; Joachim Begrich, *Studien zu Deuterojesaja* [Stuttgart: W. Kohlhammer, 1938; "Beiträge zur Wissenschaft vom Alten und Neuen Testament"], pp. 19-32; Hellmuth Frey, *Das Buch der Weltpolitik Gottes* [Stuttgart: Calwer, 1937], pp. 143-45; Johann Fischer, *Das Buch Isaias* [Bonn: Peter Hanstein, 1939], II, 41. See Isa. 1:2-4; 3:13-15; Mic. 6:1-8; Dan. 7:9 ff.; Matt. 25:31 ff.) It was in the trial, which usually took place at the city's gate, that the ancient man of Israel was called to account (Deut. 21:19; 22:24; Isa. 29:21; Amos 5:10, 15. The excavations at Tell en-Naṣbeh, probably the biblical Mizpah, afford a vivid glimpse of the whole area of the city gate. See C. C. McCown *et al., Tell en-Naṣbeh, Archaeological and Historical Results* [Berkeley and New Haven: Palestine Institute of Pacific School of Religion and the American Schools of Oriental Research, 1947], I, 196). No social situation reminded him more strongly of his accountability as an Israelite. Here he was confronted as a responsible member of the community to answer for his conduct. Second Isaiah's little "drama" of the nations under trial is rich in the *termini technici* of the ancient Hebrew law court. The plaintiff, the defendants, the witnesses, the bystanders, the accusation, the demand for a reply to the accusation, and the verdict are all present. The nations are called before the bar of the Lord of history to answer to the great crisis evoked by the unprecedented victories of Cyrus. It was the end of the Semitic era and the rise of the Persian age. The clear relation between the beginning (41:1) and end (42:1-4) is to be observed.

1. THE SUMMONS TO TRIAL (41:1)

41:1. In the midst of the turbulence precipitated by the unprecedented victories of the non-Semitic Cyrus, the world of nations is transformed into a court of law. The dispute is between Yahweh, Israel's covenant Lord, and the nations with their gods. Yahweh enters history as Judge (cf. 40:10). The nations are admonished to silence (cf.

It is a vivid expression of faith in God's authority over all powers on the scene. In 40:12-13 the emphasis had been on God as creator of the cosmos; now it is upon him as sovereign over the peoples. In modern times the international situation occupies men's minds and causes their alarms. The gospel needed is this of God's control of history, and the consequent tranquil trust of his people in his disposal of events and their readiness to fulfill the mission which he may assign them. The Puritan vice-chancellor

of Oxford University under the Commonwealth, John Owen, wrote:

We are ready to be affected with the appearance of present power in creatures, and to suppose that all things will go according unto their wills, because of their power. But it is quite otherwise; all creatures are poor feeble ciphers that can do nothing: power belongs unto God; it is a flower of his crown imperial, which he will suffer none to usurp.[9]

[9] *The Grace and Duty of Being Spiritually Minded,* ch. ix.

2 Who raised up the righteous *man* from the east, called him to his foot, gave the nations before him, and made *him* rule over kings? he gave *them* as the dust to his sword, *and* as driven stubble to his bow.	2 Who stirred up one from the east whom victory meets at every step? He gives up nations before him, so that he tramples kings under foot; he makes them like dust with his sword, like driven stubble with his bow.

the impressive *haṣ*, "hush!" of Zeph. 1:7, Hab. 2:20, and especially Zech. 2:13 [Hebrew 2:17]). It is an hour tense with destiny. The **coastlands** (cf. vs. 5; 42:10, 12; 49:1; 51:5) have a wider reference than **islands** (KJV, ASV); they include the lands of the Mediterranean basin. **Let the peoples renew their strength:** The line seems strangely out of place and may be explained as dittography from 40:31. Duhm therefore follows the attractive proposal of Lagarde to emend יחליפו כח to יחלו נכחי, "await my argument," or as Bewer translates, "wait before me." But the appeal to strength cannot be considered entirely out of place in view of the presence of this motif in the lines following (vss. 6-7, 9-10, 13, 14-16). First silence, then the summoning of resources to meet the test, then the approach to **judgment**. After the initial imperative and jussive (**let [them] renew**) follow three emphatic verbs: **approach, then . . . speak, together . . . draw near.** They all converge upon one word (cf. the "proclaim" of 40:2), *mishpāṭ*, usually translated **judgment** or "justice." The meaning here is "judicial proceedings" (Judg. 4:5; Mal. 3:5; cf. Isa. 3:14; Job 9:23; 14:3; 22:4). This connects admirably with the crucial line in vs. 27 where Israel complains that her *mishpāṭ* has been passed over by her God. With this summons the stage is set for the trial.

2. First Strophe: Appeal to History (41:2-4)

Immediately following the summons, Yahweh challenges the nations with the events of contemporary history. Can the religions of the sixth century B.C., a period of radical religious transformation in the ancient Near East, answer these historical questions?

2. The interrogative pronoun here and in vs. 4 is interesting. The same word appears twice at the beginning of the preceding poem (40:12-13) and is repeated in the crucial vs. 26 (cf. similarly vs. 26 and vs. 28; cf. also vs. 19 and vss. 23-24). This interrogative has a significant stylistic function throughout the poems. To both the cosmogonic and the historical questions the answer is the same. The Targ., the Jewish exegetes (with the exception of Ibn Ezra), Calvin, and, among moderns, Torrey and Kissane interpret the reference to the conqueror from the east as Abraham (cf. Gen. 14). If the passage stood alone, there would be much to say for this, but it must be understood in relation to other similar contexts (especially 45:1 ff.; see C. C. Torrey, "Isaiah 41," *Harvard Theological Review*, XLIV [1951], 121-36). It is more likely that Cyrus is meant. Even the excision of his name from 44:28 and 45:1, and of Babylon-Chaldea from three other passages (43:14; 48:14, 20) does not eliminate him. The reference would be plain to all contemporaries. Cyrus had succeeded to the great empire of Astyages the Mede, had thrust his battalions far into the north and west, and had defeated the Lydians at Sardes. **Who stirred up** (RSV) or "aroused," not **raised** (KJV). The word rendered **victory** (צדק) is often translated "righteousness," although it may be an adverbial accusative, "in righteousness." Second Isaiah employs this word and its cognates in various senses, usually with the meaning of salvation, vindication, justification, deliverance, etc. Here it means something that has been brought to successful completion, which has fulfilled its true end. Torrey, following the Targ. and Jerome's *iustum*, takes the word with the

---

2-4. The Question of Cyrus' Conquests.— Cyrus was no worshiper of Israel's God, for in the Cyrus Cylinder he speaks of himself as beloved of Bel and Nebo. His religious utterances seem politically opportunist. But God's sover- eignty is not limited to those who consciously obey him. That would severely restrict his sway to a meager realm. Our faith is that whether or not men are aware of him, whether they regard or disregard his moral law, he directs their move-

3 He pursued them, *and* passed safely;
even by the way *that* he had not gone with
his feet.

4 Who hath wrought and done *it,* calling
the generations from the beginning? I the
LORD, the first, and with the last; I *am* he.

3 He pursues them and passes on safely,
by paths his feet have not trod.
4 Who has performed and done this,
calling the generations from the beginning?

I, the LORD, the first,
and with the last; I am He.

---

first stich and reads, "who has aroused from the east a righteous one" (צדיק), but
neither the Hebrew form nor the accentuation and the meter favor this. The Dead Sea
Scroll has the conjunction "and" before "he called" and thus gives some further support to
Torrey's view (cf. KJV). If *çedheq* is read with the first stich, it might be interpreted
"of set purpose" (cf. 45:13). Victory follows Cyrus wherever he goes, "at every step."
The verb *qārā'* (lit., "call") has also the meaning of "encounter," "befall," "meet." **He
tramples kings under foot:** The KJV rendering, **made him rule,** is an attempt to translate
the enigmatic form ירד; since Ewald it is generally read *yārôdh* from the verb רדד; cf. the
closely related passage in 45:1 (see the critical apparatus of Kittel's *Biblia Hebraica,*
3rd ed., *ad loc.*), "tread under foot, subdue." The Dead Sea Scroll reads יוריד, "lays
prostrate," which has much to be said for it; cf. the LXX ἐκστήσει, "terrifies" (יחריד). The
RSV, following Torrey, takes **sword** and **bow** as adverbial accusative. An alternative
and perhaps better rendering is to take them as subject, "his sword makes them like dust."

3. The Assyrian records refer to new paths blazed by conquerors through difficult
terrain. Cyrus is treading either new roads or roads he has not trod before. But many
think that it is the meteoric swiftness of Cyrus' armies that is meant: "he does not
tread a road with his feet." In 46:11 Cyrus is described as a bird of prey; cf. Dan. 8:5,
which refers to the advance of Alexander the Great; also the horses of Erichthonius in
Homer (*Iliad* XX, 226-30) and of the huntress in Vergil (*Aeneid* VII, 807 ff.).

4. The strophe closes by repeating the germane question "Who has performed and
done?" (so the Hebrew; LXX adds ταῦτα; Vulg., *haec*). **Calling the generations from
the beginning:** By emending הדרות to הקרות the line reads, "proclaiming from the
beginning things to come" (cf. vs. 22). But the emendation is not required. The phrase
is a fine commentary on the Yahwist's family epic which is dominated by the persistence
of the divine purpose through successive generations of the patriarchs and their descendants. The priestly historian fashions his work in Genesis on the structure of succeeding
generations (*tôlēdhôth;* cf. also I Chr. 1–9). The prophet Isaiah, too, in the midst of
the period of Assyrian military aggression, points again and again to the reality of a
mighty, divine purpose and inexhaustible wisdom in the orderliness of history (14:24 ff.;
22:11; 28:23 ff.; 29:14; 31:2; 37:26). Second Isaiah is standing on the shoulders of the
greatest of his predecessors. This same purposiveness of God is eloquently set forth in
the call of Abraham. It is easy to see how the Targumist and the rabbis saw a reference
to him here. The answer to the **Who** of world history is proclaimed by God with a mighty
word of self-revelation reminiscent of the supreme revelation at Sinai (Exod. 20:2):

---

ments for his purposes. Milton voiced this confidence when he made Beelzebub in his address
to the revolting angels declare:

for he, be sure,
In height or depth, still first and last will reign
Sole King, and of his kingdom lose no part
By our revolt, but over hell extend
His empire, and with iron scepter rule
Us here, as with his golden those in heaven.[1]

[1] *Paradise Lost,* Bk. II, ll. 323-28.

Most of the powers then, like many today, were
strangers to and scornful of Israel's religion.
This prophet could not foresee in detail the
results of Cyrus' spectacular victories; but he
knew that God was at work in them, and all
human plans would be overruled to conform to
the divine purpose.

**I, the LORD, the first,
and with the last; I am He.**

5 The isles saw *it*, and feared; the ends of the earth were afraid, drew near, and came.

5 The coastlands have seen and are afraid, the ends of the earth tremble; they have drawn near and come.

I, the LORD, the first,
and with the last; I am He.

Such impressive lines occur characteristically at the end of strophes. Yahweh brings both creation and history into existence; he governs his universe and directs the course of history. Neither Second Isaiah nor the O.T. as a whole know anything of the birth or origin of God. The myths of the Orient abound in theogonies (cf. the Ugaritic epics and the Babylonian creation epic; see Pritchard, *Ancient Near Eastern Texts*, pp. 129 ff., 60 ff.). But Yahweh is **the first**, and Israel does not speculate on his origin. And he who is first is present at **the last**. He is both beginning and end, alpha and omega (cf. 43:10; 44:6; 46:3-4; 48:12). **I the LORD . . . I am He.** The LXX reads simply, ἐγώ εἰμι, **I am**. The covenant words in Second Isaiah are often equivalent to "I am God" in an absolute sense, i.e., the universal God, the one eternal God, ruler of all nature and of all the ages. **I am He** is tantamount to saying "I am God." Levy aptly compares the Arabic *huwa* (cf. Hebrew *hû'*) in the Koran and Sufi literature. Morgenstern believes the meaning of the pronoun is "the eternally existent one" ("Deutero-Isaiah's Terminology for the 'Universal God,'" *Journal of Biblical Literature*, LXII [1943], 269-80; cf. Sheldon H. Blank, "Studies in Deutero-Isaiah," *Hebrew Union College Annual*, XV [1940], 1-46). The context suggests that the emphasis is not so much on being as on presence and activity and purpose.

3. SECOND STROPHE: THE NATIONS RESORT TO IDOLS (41:5-7)

For those who transfer vss. 6-7 to 40:19, vs. 5 is an acute embarrassment. Duhm, Marti, Begrich, and others are forced to delete it, a harsh procedure. The last line, **They have drawn near and come**, is sometimes explained as a gloss, but parallels both in the O.T. and in Akkadian and Ugaritic literature argue for its authenticity. The strophe presents the reaction of the nations to the historical appeal of God. Such a challenge they cannot answer. The nations are **afraid** and **tremble**. For the latter verb the Dead Sea Scroll reads "together." The **coastlands** naturally refers to the summons of vs. 1. The Hebrew poet is fond of repeating key words at the beginning of strophes.

5-7. *Busy Idol Factories.*—Here we are shown panicky nations busily manufacturing idols. After his conquest of the Medes, Cyrus attacked Croesus, king of Lydia. Herodotus [2] has left an account of this monarch's feverish activity in dispatching embassies to various oracles to learn heaven's will, and of his lavish gifts to the gods of Delphi and Amphiaraus. The prophet ironically pictures what went on inside an idol factory. Distraught men seek some strong support while their world goes down in ruins.

The contrast is between gods men have to strengthen—the changes are rung on **Take courage!**—and God who strengthens men. Man-made gods betray distrust of the character of the God of the universe. Biblical faith is assured acquiescence in his righteous will, whether it brings victory or defeat, whether it spares us or nails us to a cross. The fabrication of an idol is an effort to render God useful to

[2] *History* I. 46-48.

us. Such utilitarian religion is the foe of true faith. It places man's interests uppermost, and attempts to make God their servant.

Such utilitarian religion is prevalent in our churches. One sees advertisements of sermons upon "The Uses of Religion," "Faith, an Aid to Health," "Prayer, the Remedy for Fear," "Religion, a Morale-Builder," etc. Fellowship with God has many by-products of great worth; but to seek them first, and to view trust in God as a means to them, is fatal to true communion with him. Utilitarianism in personal relations wrecks them. If one "uses" a friend, he ruins the friendship. If marriage is entered with the motive of finding in wife or husband an asset to one's self, marriage is degraded. Friend, mate, and the living God must be sought for their own sakes. To crave God as a help to our aims is to deify these aims, and this is idolatry.

Inside the idol factory workmen are depicted in cordial comradeship (vss. 6-7). Here are en-

6 They helped every one his neighbor; and *every one* said to his brother, Be of good courage.
 	
7 So the carpenter encouraged the goldsmith, *and* he that smootheth *with* the hammer him that smote the anvil, saying, It *is* ready for the soldering: and he fastened it with nails, *that* it should not be moved.
	6 Every one helps his neighbor,
	    and says to his brother, "Take courage!"
	
	7 The craftsman encourages the goldsmith,
	    and he who smooths with the hammer
	    him who strikes the anvil,
	saying of the soldering, "It is good";
	    and they fasten it with nails so that it cannot be moved.

6-7. These verses are transferred to 40:19 by the great majority of scholars, but the transfer is neither necessary nor wise. The context of 40:19 does not require any addition either from considerations of literary form or of thought. Moreover, the lines are required in their present position. The response of the nations to Yahweh's challenge would be expressed in only two lines and would form no sufficient basis for the striking turn to Israel at the beginning of vs. 8 ("but you, Israel, my servant"). With a strophe devoted to the nations (vss. 11-12) and another to Israel (vss. 14-16), a balance is retained. More important is the argument from the poet's thought. Throughout this section he is exhibiting the weakness of the nations. Their gods give them no power. Their recourse to idolmaking is a pathetic and feverish endeavor to find security in the works of their hands. **Every one helps his neighbor** (vs. 6a) in the enterprise of idolmaking, but it is Yahweh who helps Israel (vss. 10, 13-14). Each one says to his brother, **Take courage!** (vs. 6b), and **the craftsman encourages the goldsmith** (vs. 7a), but it is Yahweh who strengthens his chosen people (vss. 9a, 10c, 13b, 14-16; the verb "to grow strong," or "to strengthen" is employed three times in vss. 6-7 and is repeated and paraphrased in succeeding strophes). Above all, they are afraid (vs. 5), but Yahweh dispels the fear of Israel by his command "Fear not!" (10a, 13c, 14a). The same literary method is present elsewhere (e.g., 46:1 ff.). Lastly, if vss. 6-7 are removed, we are not prepared for the final judgment on the idols, pronounced with such power in vs. 29, "Their molten images are empty wind."

All these perfervid religious performances will not avail. Not all the mutual encouragement, not all the smoothing and striking and soldering and fastening can save the nations in their hour of crisis. The end of the age is the twilight of the gods (Volz). It is the hour of the God of Israel and of his coming into world history.

In vs. 7 the Dead Sea Scroll reads for פטיש (**hammer**) the word פלטיש. The word rendered **anvil** (פעם) should probably be translated "club" or some synonym for **hammer.** It seems to have this meaning in the Ugaritic texts and is used in parallelism with *hrz.* With it Baal smashes the heads of his opponents (Alfred D. Haldar, *The Notion of the Desert in Sumero-Accadian and West-Semitic Religions* [Uppsala: A.-B. Lundequistska, 1950], p. 37; Haldar cites Judg. 5:26, where Jael kills Sisera with a hammer, but the Hebrew word is not the same; see the interesting figure accompanying Haldar's discussion of Baal's annihilation of his foes).

thusiasm and good fellowship in a pathetically futile enterprise—making false deities. A modern substitute for the sovereign God of Christian faith has been the religion of human brotherhood. A personal deity, presiding over the universe and history, was held incredible. Orphaned men sought to warm each other in the bleak void where he had once been. Thomas Hardy described a vanishing God complaining that man had created him: The truth should be told, and the fact be faced That had best been faced in earlier years:	The fact of life with dependence placed On the human heart's resource alone, In brotherhood bonded close and graced With loving-kindness fully blown, And visioned help unsought, unknown.[3] How tragic is mankind, huddled in mutual encouragement and earnestly toiling at some- [3] "A Plaint to Man," *Collected Poems* (London: Macmillan & Co.; New York: The Macmillan Co., 1940), p. 306. Used by permission of the Trustees of the Hardy Estate and of the publishers.

8 But thou, Israel, *art* my servant, Jacob whom I have chosen, the seed of Abraham my friend.	8 But you, Israel, my servant, Jacob, whom I have chosen, the offspring of Abraham, my friend;

4. THIRD STROPHE: "ISRAEL, MY SERVANT" (41:8-10)

The trial proceeds. The nations are in terror before the indictment of history. But now the Judge turns suddenly and unexpectedly to Israel and addresses her with all the maximum words drawn from covenant life:

Israel, my servant,
Jacob, whom I have chosen,
the offspring of Abraham, my friend.

As always in Second Isaiah, these intimate words of address are enforced by verbs which describe the content of Israel's life: **I have chosen you,** "I have grasped you" (החזקתיך; **RSV took;** cf. Vulg., *apprehendi*), "I have called you, I said to you." So prophetic Israel understood its life. Israel has no ground for fear in this age of tumult. She has the infinite resource of her God, who is ever present with her and with whom she has entered into a unique relationship of election, call, covenanthood, and revelation. Her God is not silent. He is eloquent and urgent in speech, one who triumphs over the chaos and "distraughtness" of the times. He speaks the words which the gods of nature could never speak. Fear haunts the religions of the ancient Near East, fear of hostile demons, divine caprice, and the coercions of nature. But in Israel, Yahweh speaks words of comfort and hope, and assurances which are based upon election and covenant.

8. The words of address (vss. 8-9) are impressive and extended: (*a*) **But thou Israel, . . . my servant:** The conjunction represents a sudden turning from the nations; then follows **thou,** often emphatic in Second Isaiah and, as here, at the beginning of the line. The "I-thou" relationship between Yahweh and his people, repeatedly expressed in the urgent asseverations of the divine first person and in the words of address, is a central feature of Second Isaiah's theology. The prophet's revelatory speech is bodied forth in the "I" (אני) of Yahweh and the **thou** (אתה) of Israel, and the verbs which are attached to them gain their force through the intensity with which the pronoun is uttered by God himself. But it is noteworthy that God gives to the **thou** its specific content by the names **Israel** and **Jacob** and **Abraham,** for these names give the pronoun its identity and historical reality. Yahweh's **thou** is embodied in the historical names (cf. Gen. 32:24-30 [J]; 17:1-8 [P]). The **Jacob Israel** parallelism (vs. 14; 40:27; 42:24; 43:1, 22, 28; 44:1, 5, 21, 23; 45:4; 46:3; 48:1-12) casts light on Israelite views of solidarity and thus on the **servant** of the Lord. The reference to the servant, which appears here for the first time in the poems, is the chief characterization of the covenant people. Israel is first of all servant because Yahweh is first of all Lord. The connotations of the term are not servile only, for the servant of the king was a man of some importance (cf.,

thing unconnected with ultimate reality—in an idol factory! How ironic to say of the soldering, **It is good,** when that which is soldered is a false deity! Suppose the community of nations were united in good will, what could it achieve if its aims did not accord with those of the universe? Man's loftiest accomplishments are like houses of sand built by children on the seashore. Nothing that human effort nails down is permanent. Invaders soon ripped out these carefully fastened statues of deities. We can say of nothing, **It is good,** or view it as immovable, unless it is in line with the purpose of the Creator and Lord of all.

8-10. *Israel, God's Chosen Servant From of Old.*—The Judge turns to Israel, standing among the assembled nations, and assures her that she is his **chosen,** whom he sustains. This forms a climax to the first part of the poem. The contemporary civilization is cracking up. The Babylonian epoch is tottering. Man-devised religion affords its devotees no stability or comfort. The God of history speaks confidently to his own people.

The allusion to Israel's past is a means of reviving the present drooping faith of the exiles. At this trial of the nations God testifies for himself. He adduces his grace toward his people.

9 *Thou* whom I have taken from the ends of the earth, and called thee from the chief men thereof, and said unto thee, Thou *art* my servant; I have chosen thee, and not cast thee away.

9 you whom I took from the ends of the earth,
  and called from its farthest corners,
saying to you, "You are my servant,
  I have chosen you and not cast you off";

e.g., the *'ebhedh-mélekh* seals; see Curt Lindhagen, *The Servant Motif in the Old Testament* [Uppsala: A.-B. Lundequistska, 1950], pp. 6-39, for many examples drawn from ancient Near Eastern literatures; for "Servant of El" [*'bd il*], see Pritchard, *op. cit.*, pp. 142-49 [Legend of Keret]; cf. too the "Ebed" compounds in personal names). The religion of Israel was service to God, and her truest representatives are the servants of God. In Second Isaiah, where Israel has a great mission to perform for the nations, the word servant is a peculiarly appropriate designation (cf. Jer. 30:10 ff.; Ezek. 28:25; 37:25).

(b) **Jacob, whom I have chosen:** Faith in the divine election marks the beginning of Israel's religion (cf. Kurt Galling, *Die Erwählungstraditionen Israels* [Giessen: A. Töpelmann, 1928]). That Yahweh should take the initiative by choosing for himself a people, and that this people should be Israel, is the source of wonder. This tradition goes back to our earliest sources, and it is likely that it preserves an authentic memory. The Deuteronomists in a time of international ferment and threat to Israel's tradition stress the election of Israel (Deut. 4:37; 7:7-8; 10:15; 14:2) as a holy and separate people (Deut. 7:6; 14:2, 21; 26:19; cf. Exod. 19:6), a covenant people in the world (Deut. 4:13,

---

The contemporary scene seemed disheartening. The exiles, like their heathen neighbors, were terrified as this new conqueror from the east swept westward. But the prophet is sure of God's faithfulness to his chosen, and in retrospect we see the vindication of his faith in the events which overthrew Babylon and made possible the return to Jerusalem.

In these poems both Cyrus and Israel are spoken of as God's **servant** (cf. vs. 2 with 44:28; vs. 8 with 45:1). But there is a vast difference between a pagan monarch, unwittingly God's agent, and his covenant people, admitted to his secret (cf. Ps. 25:14) and resolved to know and do his will. Israel is the descendant of **Abraham, my friend.** A friend is in such sympathetic fellowship that he senses another's mind. God's direction of heathen people is like that given a horse or a mule, "with bit and bridle" (Ps. 32:9). We can be thankful that

A gracious spirit o'er this earth presides,
[A] tendency benign, directing those
Who care not, know not, think not what they do.[4]

But those who wait upon God with attentive minds receive suggestions from countless sources. John Owen asserted: "There are a thousand ways, if I may so say, wherein an observing Christian may find God hinting and intimating duties to him." [5] The church is the company of

those supposedly friends of God. His purposes in our generation should be understood and carried out far more fully through her members than through outsiders.

And there is point in a troubled time of reminding God's people of his presence in their long history. Men draw strength from their continuity with their spiritual fathers. Retrospect convinces them of God's dependableness. It is not the new but the tried and tested to which in crises they confidently turn. It is significant that in our day the church fills a far larger place in Christian thought than she did in the more tranquil days of the nineteenth century. She is the historic institution in which are conserved the memories of the Christian generations. God's dealings with his people are stored in the Scriptures, the hymnal, the prayers of the ages. The church meets us saying:

. . . I am like a stream that flows
Full of the cold springs that arose
  In morning lands, in distant hills;
  And down the plain my channel fills
With melting of forgotten snows.[6]

In the midst of political turbulence, when nations were going down before a conqueror, it was heartening to recall that the base of the national life lay beyond the flux of history in the deliberate choice of God. Israel was an elect spiritual community—**Whom I have**

---

[4] Wordsworth, *The Prelude*, Bk. V.

[5] James Moffatt, *The Golden Book of John Owen* (London: Hodder & Stoughton, 1904), p. 188.

[6] Alice Meynell, "A Song of Derivations," *Poems* (New York: Charles Scribner's Sons, 1913).

| 10 ¶ Fear thou not; for I *am* with thee: be not dismayed; for I *am* thy God: I will strengthen thee; yea, I will help thee; yea, I will uphold thee with the right hand of my righteousness. | 10 fear not, for I am with you, be not dismayed, for I am your God; I will strengthen you, I will help you, I will uphold you with my victorious right hand. |

23, 31; 5:2; 8:18; cf. Gerhard von Rad, *Das Gottesvolk im Deuteronomium* [Stuttgart: W. Kohlhammer, 1929; "Beiträge zur Wissenschaft von Alten und Neuen Testament"]). The prophet is again carrying one of the persistent realities of his inherited faith to its culmination (cf. 42:1; 43:10, 20; 44:1-2; 45:4; 48:10).

(*c*) **Seed of Abraham my friend:** Second Isaiah presses the origin of Israel's faith back to her progenitor and father (cf. 51:1-2). Thus he grounds it in a more ultimate point in history. For him the election and covenant go back to the first Hebrew. Abraham lives on in his descendants. The word אהבי, "my beloved," is commonly rendered **friend,** though as Levy points out (*Deutero-Isaiah,* p. 134) "the idea of reciprocity contained in the latter does not exist in the Hebrew" (cf. the familiar *khalilu 'allah,* "the friend of God" of the Koran [4:124]; on Yahweh's love for his people cf. Isa. 43:4; 48:14-15; 49:15-16; 54:9-10; 63:9; Hos. 11:1-8; Deut. 7:7-11). The love between Yahweh and his people belongs to the most ancient traditions (Buber, *The Prophetic Faith,* pp. 8-12; for Ugaritic parallel cf. *nemn 'glm il,* "beloved lad of El" in the Legend of Keret; Pritchard, *op. cit.,* pp. 143 ff.). The long address to Israel ends as it began, but more intimately: "The one who says to you 'You are my servant.'" Israel belongs to Yahweh in a covenant bond. She has been **chosen** in an election of grace. Therefore she not only need not be overcome by fear as the nations are (vs. 7), but is to be equipped to perform her mission in the earth. For this great task God gives his promise and assurances (vs. 10).

The language seems to be drawn from the theophany. The words of address, the revelatory **I am your God,** the establishment of a relationship between God and man, the assurances of the *hieros logos,* and the command **Fear not** are among the most striking features (Ludwig Köhler, "Die Offenbarungsformel 'Fürchte dich nicht!' im

---

chosen—called of God to achieve his purpose (Exod. 19:3-8). God's calling remains unchanged. He may be obliged to discipline his people; he had done so in the Exile; but he does **not cast** them **off.**

The Christian church is God's elect community (I Pet. 2:9). Often it does not seem a "choice people." Speaking of the church throughout British history, Esmé Cecil Wingfield-Stratford writes: "No doubt the spirit of His Excellency Pilate and His Holiness Caiaphas were sometimes at least as much in evidence as that of the irrepressible Revolutionary from Nazareth." [7] Nonetheless, he speaks of the church in various centuries as "a mind-training society" on a vast scale. Not all Israelites belonged to spiritual Israel (Rom. 9:6); but the sense of national calling remained the heritage of the nation and bound her people in one, even when they had been scattered over the known world. Could we recover for the contemporary church this conviction of her election—and election to a unique divine mission—we might possess again a strong impulse to out-

[7] *The History of British Civilization* (London: G. Routledge & Sons, 1932), pp. 258-59.

ward unity. In the United States and in other nominally "Christian nations" there is a similar mixture of people more or less loyal to the nation's inheritance and mission. Yet the spiritual quality of their founders—their faith, conscience, and purpose—abides a living force, claiming the national allegiance and committing it to a distinctive role among the peoples of mankind.

Fear not—here the prophet takes up his gospel of comfort again. He heaps up expressions of God's companionship with his people: **I am with you; I am your God; I will strengthen you; I will help you; I will uphold you with my victorious right hand.** God never assigns a task or appoints an ordeal without personally accompanying his people in it. But it is noteworthy that nothing is said of his people's awareness of his presence. God's promise does not read, "Thou shalt feel me with thee." Feelings come and go; they are affected by many factors —health, circumstances, even the weather. Our Lord himself felt abandoned on the cross (Mark 15:34). The Bible is superbly objective. It does not ask men to look in, but to look up. It builds their confidence not on their changing

11 Behold, all they that were incensed against thee shall be ashamed and confounded: they shall be as nothing; and they that strive with thee shall perish.	11 Behold, all who are incensed against you shall be put to shame and confounded; those who strive against you shall be as nothing and shall perish.
12 Thou shalt seek them, and shalt not find them, *even* them that contended with thee: they that war against thee shall be as nothing, and as a thing of nought.	12 You shall seek those who contend with you, but you shall not find them; those who war against you shall be as nothing at all.
13 For I the LORD thy God will hold thy right hand, saying unto thee, Fear not; I will help thee.	13 For I, the LORD your God, hold your right hand; it is I who say to you, "Fear not, I will help you."

Alten Testament," *Schweizerische Theologische Zeitschrift,* XXXVI [1919], 33-39; cf. also Isa. 41:13-14; 43:1, 5; 44:2, 8; 51:12; examination of such passages as Gen. 15:1; 21:17; 26:24; Deut. 20:1; 31:6, 8; Josh. 8:1; etc., reveals striking parallels).

5. FOURTH STROPHE: JUDGMENT OF THE NATIONS (41:11-13)

11-13. This is a carefully composed oracle of judgment against the nations in the *qînāh* or lamentation meter. The preliminaries are now completed: the issue has been stated, the nations and Israel have both been addressed, and now the verdict is anticipated, first to the nations (vss. 11-13) and then to Israel (vss. 14-16). The judgment begins with **Behold** (cf. vs. 29; 3:1; 7:14 [?]; 8:7; 10:33; Amos 2:13; 4:2; 6:11; 8:11). Neither the KJV nor the RSV preserves the Hebrew order satisfactorily. The verbs all appear in the first lines, the subjects mostly in the second:

> Behold, they shall be ashamed and confounded,
>> all who are incensed against you;
> they shall be as nothing and shall perish,
>> the men who strive against you;
> you shall seek them but will not find them,
>> the men who contend with you;
> they shall be as nothing at all,
>> the men who war against you.

Then follows the conclusion directed to Israel, introduced by *kî* (**for**), and the covenant formula, **I** [am] **the LORD your God.** Second Isaiah often reserves his weightiest utterances for these covenant contexts. The three major emphases (vs. 13*bcd*) are precisely those

moods, but on God's fidelity. Public prayers should never allude to our consciousness of God's presence: they should affirm he is with us.

11-12. *Israel's Opponents Made Powerless.*— The prophet sympathizes with the fears the exiles have of enemies who will do their utmost to keep them in bondage and will oppose their attempt to return to Jerusalem. In the Exeg. these verses are translated to bring out the contrast between the verbs which set forth the impotence of these enemies in the clauses which portray them.

It is a well-proved fact of spiritual experience that when we start upon God's purpose difficulties take themselves out of the way (e.g., the iron door which "opened . . . of its own accord" when Peter obeyed the summons to leave prison, Acts 12:10). Our fears leave God out of the reckoning. We foresee perils and obstacles, and think it is ourselves who must overcome them. We forget that to those who love God, he in everything works with them for good (Rom. 8:28). It is this unsuspected divine activity which we fail to count on. Many a man has repeated Wordsworth's discovery:

> Yes, the realities of life so cold,
> So cowardly, so ready to betray,
> So stinted in the measure of their grace
> As we pronounce them, doing them much wrong,
> Have been to me more bountiful than hope,
> Less timid than desire.[8]

[8] *The Recluse,* Pt. I.

14 Fear not, thou worm Jacob, *and* ye men of Israel; I will help thee, saith the LORD, and thy Redeemer, the Holy One of Israel.

15 Behold, I will make thee a new sharp threshing instrument having teeth: thou shalt thresh the mountains, and beat *them* small, and shalt make the hills as chaff.

---

14 Fear not, you worm Jacob,
  you men of Israel!
  I will help you, says the LORD;
  your Redeemer is the Holy One of
    Israel.

15 Behold, I will make of you a threshing
    sledge,
  new, sharp, and having teeth;
  you shall thresh the mountains and crush
    them,
  and you shall make the hills like chaff;

---

which give vss. 1-21 their unity. They connect what has preceded with what is to follow. The concluding divine assurance brings the thought to a focus.

6. FIFTH STROPHE: ISRAEL A THRESHING SLEDGE (41:14-16)

Now for the third time (vs. 14) Yahweh speaks to his people, and Israel is admonished not to fear for her God will help her (cf. vss. 10c, 13d and contrast vs. 5), but above all, she is told that God will make her strong. This emphasis throughout the poem is fortified by the extraordinary figure of the threshing sledge as the instrument of divine judgment. One new word which Second Isaiah has not employed hitherto appears among the assurances. Yahweh, the Holy One of Israel, is her redeemer. The thought has been present from the beginning, but here it appears explicitly, and from now on constitutes one of the most frequent as well as one of the most important ideas (43:1, 14; 44:6, 23, 24; 47:4; 48:17, 20; 49:7, 26; 52:3, 9; 54:5, 8; cf. also 60:16; 63:9, 16).

14. You worm Jacob: Not "worm of Jacob." The two words are in apposition. The expression is one of endearment, as in modern German. The word מְתֵי, **men,** has the connotation of few or small, as the biblical references clearly show (cf. LXX ὀλιγοστός, which may be correct). Most commentators accept Ewald's emendation to רִמָּה, "maggot," which gives good parallelism. Driver ("Linguistic and Textual Problems: Isaiah XL-LXVI," p. 399) derives the word from the Akkadian *mutu*, "louse," thus "lice of Israel." The Exodus from Egypt came to be understood as redemption (Exod. 6:6; 15:3; Deut. 7:8; 13:5; 15:15; 24:18). The term *gō'ēl*, **redeemer,** described a function not uncommon in the social life of Israel. In various ways the *gō'ēl* witnessed to the solidarity of the Hebrew family, e.g., by avenging the blood of a relative or by buying back alienated property (Ruth 3:11-12; 4:1-6; Lev. 25:23-25, 29-30) or an enslaved person (Lev. 25:48-49).

15. A threshing sledge (*môragh*) was a heavy threshing board or drag, studded underneath with sharp stones or iron points; the word here translated **sharp** may be a variant of *môragh*, since it elsewhere has the meaning of a threshing instrument (Amos 1:3; cf. Isa. 28:27; see note and illustrations in S. R. Driver, *The Books of Joel and Amos*

14-16. *Abject Israel Transformed into a Potent Force.*—The supine dejection of the exiles is contrasted with the triumphant prospect God has in store for them. **You worm Jacob:** Devout folk often seem like crawling things. At a critical juncture in the affairs of the Church of Scotland, Samuel Rutherford preached two sermons on this text. It is a text for our time. The church goes underground before current threats and issues instead of standing up and facing them with daring. (But see Exeg.) God offers to help by holding our right hand, but that requires an erect posture on our part. In the well-known hymn, "The

God of Abraham praise," Thomas Olivers has the line "He calls a worm his friend." [9] But so long as his people continue "worms," they cannot respond to his friendship. His call requires upstanding and venturesome believers to go through with him his hazardous enterprises.

Behold, I will make of you a threshing sledge, new, sharp, and having teeth.

What a transformation—a worm become a heavy sledge studded on its under surface with knives or sharp stones! There were formidable ob-

[9] The full text is in John Julian, *A Dictionary of Hymnology* (London: John Murray, 1925), p. 1150.

16 Thou shalt fan them, and the wind shall carry them away, and the whirlwind shall scatter them: and thou shalt rejoice in the LORD, *and* shalt glory in the Holy One of Israel.	16 you shall winnow them and the wind shall carry them away,
	    and the tempest shall scatter them.
	And you shall rejoice in the LORD;
	    in the Holy One of Israel you shall glory.

17 *When* the poor and needy seek water, and *there is* none, *and* their tongue faileth for thirst, I the LORD will hear them, *I* the God of Israel will not forsake them.	17 When the poor and needy seek water,
	    and there is none,
	    and their tongue is parched with thirst,
	I the LORD will answer them,
	    I the God of Israel will not forsake them.

18 I will open rivers in high places, and	18 I will open rivers on the bare heights, and fountains in the midst of the valleys;

[Cambridge: Cambridge University Press, 1934; "Cambridge Bible"], pp. 232-33) ; but Haldar (*Notion of the Desert in Sumero-Accadian and West-Semitic Religions,* p. 36) calls attention to the presence of this word in the Ugaritic texts and describes it as a sharp weapon for stabbing the enemy. (See Baal smiting his foes, *ibid.,* p. 38, Fig. 2.) **New, sharp, and having teeth** (lit., "master" or "lord of teeth") , the instrument is strong and effective. **Mountains . . . and hills:** Symbols of Israel's foes, or more generally of the overwhelming difficulties which seem to face her. The mountains and hills appear often in Second Isaiah, sometimes as a symbol of strength (cf. 42:15) .

16. After the threshing the grain is winnowed by being hurled into the air, and the wind blows the chaff and straw away. Now that Israel's fear is dispelled and she has performed her work of judgment, she will finally **rejoice in** [her] **Lord** and glory in **the Holy One of Israel.** This designation appears often in Isaiah. Israel stands in a unique relationship to her Holy One, and her religion is a religion of holiness. In this relationship she discerns the ultimate meaning of her life; therefore she rejoices and glories in her Holy One.

7. SIXTH STROPHE: LYRICAL INTERLUDE (41:17-20)

17-20. Following the three strophes of comfort and assurance (vss. 8-10, 11-13, 14-16) , which may correspond to the literary form of the oracle of salvation (Begrich, *Studien zu Deuterojesaja,* pp. 19-42, *et passim;* "Das priesterliche Heilsorakel," *Zeitschrift für die alttestamentliche Wissenschaft,* LII [1934], 81-92) , Second Isaiah breaks into a lyrical

stacles to be faced—**mountains, hills.** A worm was impotent; but a people resolutely committed to God could be empowered to cope with anything. Mountains are crushed, hills become chaff, and God's winds in history carry them away. This odd combination of metaphors —**worm** and **threshing sledge**—describes what God can make out of his church in a critical hour. A **worm** before **mountains**—such the church feels herself in the presence of the hindrances to her work; a **threshing sledge, new, sharp,** and **having teeth**—such she is when she vigorously exerts her God-given powers. **And you shall rejoice in the LORD.** Again and again this prophet pictures God's people in jubilation. That is the result of his fellowship with them and the startling consequences which ensue. A

Jewish legend has it that Satan was once asked what he missed most when banished from heaven. He replied, "The trumpets in the morning." No biblical writer more often than this poet rejoices in God, and calls on men and nature to join him in exultation over what God has wrought in his mighty acts of redemption. It is an evidence of his assurance that he anticipates the triumph and hails with exuberant gladness what shall come to pass.

17-20. God's Gifts to His People.—This is a lyrical interlude. It seems to have little relation to the trial, and may have been suggested by the jubilation of the surprised people in vs. 16. It is a tenderly comforting promise to the exiles in their spiritual poverty in a heathen land and in the dreaded hardships of the desert journey

fountains in the midst of the valleys: I will make the wilderness a pool of water, and the dry land springs of water.

19 I will plant in the wilderness the cedar, the shittah tree, and the myrtle, and the oil tree; I will set in the desert the fir tree, *and* the pine, and the box tree together:

20 That they may see, and know, and consider, and understand together, that the hand of the LORD hath done this, and the Holy One of Israel hath created it.

I will make the wilderness a pool of
    water,
    and the dry land springs of water.
19 I will put in the wilderness the cedar,
    the acacia, the myrtle, and the olive;
I will set in the desert the cypress,
    the plane and the pine together;
20 that men may see and know,
    may consider and understand together,
that the hand of the LORD has done this,
    the Holy One of Israel has created it.

---

interlude (for other examples cf. 42:10-13; 44:23; 45:8). The imagery throughout—especially water and trees—is characteristic of the poet. The transformation of nature is a central feature of Second Isaiah's eschatology (43:18-21; 48:21; 49:9-11; 55:13). The strong emphasis upon the miraculous fertility of the land and the creative activity of God at the end (cf. vs. 20) is of a piece with God's work in creation at the beginning and his continuing work of conservation. How are these vivid pictures to be taken? The eschatological setting and orientation of the poems favors a literal interpretation. As Wheeler Robinson has written concerning Jer. 4:23-26 and by implication concerning this passage: "These pictures are to be taken realistically, not allegorically; if they seem strangely impossible to us, it is partly because we come to Nature with an inveterate prejudice in favour of its fixity and virtual independence of God. But, if we look closely at the details, we shall often find unmistakable hints of the underlying realism, proofs that the whole are to be taken as more or less literal expectation, and not merely as poetic imagery." (*Inspiration and Revelation in O.T.*, p. 29; see the more extended discussion, pp. 1-33.) The language of myth is used here, but it witnesses to events that

---

before them. A spiritual thirst would be acutely felt by the devout among them who were finding it hard to "sing the Lord's song in a strange land" (Ps. 137:4).

The middle years of the twentieth century brought penury to the church in a world impoverished by two wars. Her institutions were destroyed, her financial resources were pitiably straitened, and above all, many young men on whom she had counted were dead or crippled. There was, however, a more avid hunger for spiritual food. Writer after writer has insisted that the solution of mankind's desperate ills can be only in a new heart and a right spirit in men and peoples. Yet wistful seekers find food and drink for their spirits hard to come by. They wander in a wilderness a long way from the land of their hearts' desire. But the promise of this lovely little interlude holds that when God's people seek his purpose for themselves and for mankind, rivers flow from bare heights, springs appear in the arid valleys, and where only scrubby desert vegetation is looked for there is a planting of fruitful and shade-giving trees. Our poet may, as the Exeg. suggests, have been thinking of a physical miracle. But physical and spiritual blend in his verse. The lines describe God's wonder-working provision for his faithful

in unlikely situations. Such experiences of his care century after century leave his people amazed at his power and grace. They **see, know, consider,** and **understand together** that the hand of their unseen God was at work. This interlude belongs in this trial of the nations as Israel's witness to her God's faithfulness.

Arnold J. Toynbee's thesis that churches "represent the first experiments in a new and higher species of society," and that "the deepest spiritual lessons are learnt [in] the breakdown and disintegration of civilization," is borne out by Israel's enrichment in the desert of her captivity. It suggests that a similar gain for the contemporary church is coming from the collapse of our self-sufficient Western civilization.

We have relapsed from the worship of a One True God, who in virtue of the Incarnation is the brother as well as the father of all men, to the worship of our respective local human communities; for the real religion of the great majority of Western or Westernized men and women in our age is the worship of their national state. . . . In worshipping our community we are . . . indulging in a collective worship of ourselves, . . . dazzled by our own intellectual and technological prowess, without recognizing how humiliatingly unsuccessful . . . we have

| 21 Produce your cause, saith the LORD; bring forth your strong *reasons,* saith the King of Jacob. | 21 Set forth your case, says the LORD; bring your proofs, says the King of Jacob. |
| 22 Let them bring *them* forth, and show us what shall happen: let them show the former things, what they *be,* that we may consider them, and know the latter end of them; or declare us things for to come. | 22 Let them bring them, and tell us what is to happen. Tell us the former things, what they are, that we may consider them, that we may know their outcome; or declare to us the things to come. |

are to take place. To the ancient Hebrew, nature, like history, is the realm of eventfulness. It is the theater of God's activity.

8. Seventh Strophe: Renewed Appeal to History (41:21-24)

The trial is resumed after the interlude. The issues are sharpened and clarified, the challenge to the nations with their idols is pressed to the limit, and the consequences of their failure to meet it are drawn. The nations have nothing to say about history, past and future; they cannot foretell, and therefore know nothing about the goal of history. The verdict is inevitable (vs. 24).

But if the gods of the nations know nothing at all, it is quite otherwise with the King of Israel. He knows the past and the future, proclaims what is to happen, and speaks through his servants, the prophets (cf. vs. 4b). History is not a vast and turbulent sea filled with shipwrecked vessels for which there is no harbor. God is ruler of the waves and brings the vessels to their destined haven. His purpose lies behind and within all things. This knowing is a sole knowing; none other can fathom the depths of time past and time future (cf. also 43:9; 44:7; 45:21; 46:10; 48:3, 14; for parallel, see E. F. Weidner, "Die Feldzüge Šamše-Adads V gegen Babylonien," *Archiv für Orientforschung,* IX [1934], 89-104; the parallel gives the battle account of Shamshi-Adad V as a fulfillment of a divine oracle). The prophet here is adducing one of his great arguments for monotheism. God reveals that he alone is God because he alone knows the former and the latter things; he speaks the language of history. History has a unity, for it is under the control of the supreme and effectual purpose of One who is redeemer, creator, and now lord and king of the nations.

21. Set forth your case or "present your case": The word ריב is a *terminus technicus* for a legal proceeding or dispute (cf. the verbs in Mic. 6:1; Hos. 2:4). **Bring your proofs** or **strong reasons:** There is no necessity for emending to עצבותיכם, "your idols." The renewal of the legal action (cf. vs. 1) and the parallelism favor this interpretation (see LXX, αἱ βουλαὶ ὑμῶν; Vulg., *siquid forte habetis;* cf. Prov. 18:18). **King of Jacob:** As king, Yahweh is also judge. His unique relationship to Israel is maintained throughout the proceedings.

22. The word rendered **tell** (also "foretell," "predict," "declare," "make known") is emphatic, the key verb of the strophe. The threefold occurrence in a single strophe

been in dealing with human nature in ourselves and in our fellow men.[1]

Has not the mood of mankind been chastened? Is not the church being drawn into an enriching unity? May not this be part of God's dealing with a spiritually thirsty generation, and his provision for the needs of his people in the wilderness of a secular age? If under God's leading souls are refreshed and revived, and we

are brought to a rebuilt Jerusalem—a church "compacted together"—may this not be his miraculous method of enabling that church to proclaim and help create a new world-wide community of all races and nations?

21-24. *Let the Heathen Deities Account for Cyrus.*—The prophet summons the nations and their idols to produce their evidence, and this must be in the sphere of events. The prophet has in God's name explained the stirring up of Cyrus. Can any other deity interpret the course of events and thus demonstrate his godship?

[1] "Churches and Civilizations," from *The Yale Review,* XXXVII (1947-48), 5-8, copyright Yale University Press.

23 Show the things that are to come hereafter, that we may know that ye *are* gods: yea, do good, or do evil, that we may be dismayed, and behold *it* together.

24 Behold, ye *are* of nothing, and your work of nought: an abomination *is he that* chooseth you.

23 Tell us what is to come hereafter,
　　that we may know that you are gods;
　do good, or do harm,
　　that we may be dismayed and terrified.

24 Behold, you are nothing,
　　and your work is nought;
　an abomination is he who chooses you.

---

is a common stylistic device of the prophet and provides a valuable clue for deciding where the emphasis lies (cf., e.g., חוק in vss. 6-7 and משפט in 42:1-4). The third and fourth lines are striking in the Hebrew: "The former things, what they are, foretell, that we may take them to heart." This is one of the most frequently repeated ideas of the prophet. It is his witness to the meaningfulness of history as it is understood in prophetic Israel (42:9; 43:9, 18-19; 44:7; 45:11, 21; 46:9-11; 48:3, 6). **That we may know their outcome:** Events are not capricious. They move toward a goal and are involved in a destiny. They have an 'aḥarîth, an end or an outcome. The Dead Sea Scroll reads "latter things." Where history is viewed as filled with meaning, men will inquire about the outcome or issue of events.

23. That we may be dismayed and terrified: Both verbs are present in vs. 10. For the first the LXX has θαυμασόμεθα, "we may wonder," Vulg., *loquamur,* "we may speak." The Dead Sea Scroll reads "that we may hear and see," which gives good sense and involves the change of only one letter in the first verb. The RSV follows the *Kethîbh,* **be . . . terrified,** against the *Qerê,* **behold,** of the KJV. This rendering fits both the immediate and wider context best.

24. The nations' inability to respond leaves no alternative but doom. The word translated **nought** should be read מאפס instead of the present מאפע (omitted in the Dead Sea Scroll). Duhm, Cheyne, Marti, and others consider the last line a gloss, and Torrey retains it by emending to "He who chooses you goes astray," a mild statement in the context. Render: "In you one chooses an abomination." Cf. the Cyrus Cylinder: "The worship of Marduk, the king of the gods, he changed into abomination" (Pritchard, *Ancient Near Eastern Texts,* p. 315). The order of the words and the elliptical style are like Second Isaiah (see H. L. Ginsberg, "Some Emendations in Isaiah," *Journal of Biblical Literature,* LXIX [1950], 58, for an acute and attractive, but radical, restoration of the text: "Behold you are nothing, and your work is naught; chaos and wind are your images"; cf. vs. 29).

It has been customary to say that the prophets of Israel were forthtellers, rather than foretellers, preachers of God, rather than predictors of things to come. But he to whom God has revealed himself in past events can interpret what he is doing in current happenings and forecast what he will do.

A notable modern instance of such prediction is a sermon preached by F. W. Robertson on January 11, 1852. Britain, in the heyday of her commercial expansion, was glorifying the advances of civilization in the Crystal Palace Exhibition. Political leaders, the press, poets, and the pulpit were hailing a new era of peace brought about by the links of commerce. F. W. Robertson said:

We are told that that which chivalry and honor could not do, . . . personal interest *will* do. Trade is to bind men together into one family. When they feel it their *interest* to be one, they will be brothers.

Then he prophesied:

Brethren, that which is built on selfishness cannot stand. The system of personal interest must be shivered into atoms. Therefore, we, who have observed the ways of God in the past, are waiting in quiet but awful expectation until He shall confound this system, as He has confounded those which have gone before. And it may be effected by convulsions more terrible and more bloody than the world has yet seen. While men are talking of peace, and of the great progress of civilization, there is heard in the distance the noise of armies gathering rank on rank; east and west, north and south, are rolling towards us the crushing thunders of universal war.[2]

From an observation of God's ways in history this prescient herald announced the global

[2] "The Christian Church a Family," *Sermons Preached at Trinity Chapel, Third Series* (Boston: Ticknor & Fields, 1859), p. 252.

25 I have raised up *one* from the north, and he shall come: from the rising of the sun shall he call upon my name: and he shall come upon princes as *upon* mortar, and as the potter treadeth clay.

26 Who hath declared from the beginning, that we may know? and beforetime, that we may say, *He is* righteous? yea, *there is* none that showeth, yea, *there is* none that declareth, yea, *there is* none that heareth your words.

27 The first *shall say* to Zion, Behold, behold them: and I will give to Jerusalem one that bringeth good tidings.

25 I stirred up one from the north, and he has come,
  from the rising of the sun, and he shall call on my name;
he shall trample[r] on rulers as on mortar,
  as the potter treads clay.
26 Who declared it from the beginning, that we might know,
  and beforetime, that we might say, "He is right"?
There was none who declared it, none who proclaimed,
  none who heard your words.
27 I first have declared it to Zion,[s]
  and I give to Jerusalem a herald of good tidings.

[r] Cn Heb *come*
[s] Cn: Heb *first to Zion, Behold, behold them*

---

9. Eighth Strophe: Renewed Judgment on the Nations (41:25-29)

At the close Yahweh again descends to the world of contemporary history as in vss. 2-4. Vs. 26 occupies the same place and function in the poem as 40:26 in the preceding. **Who declared it from the beginning . . . ?** Certainly not the nations with their gods. **None . . . declared, . . . none proclaimed, none . . . heard** (cf. I Kings 18:26, 29). But in Israel the situation was different. The beginnings were already given to Zion, and to Jerusalem was given an evangelist (cf. 40:9-10). Vs. 27 is difficult but its ecstatic, exultant character is plain, "Behold them, behold them!"

25. Cf. vs. 2. Cyrus did in actuality come from the north and from the east. **He shall call on my name:** The fact that in the famous Cyrus Cylinder the Persian king recognizes Marduk, the god of Babylon, should occasion no difficulty. Long before this time the prophet is affirming his faith that Cyrus is in reality the instrument of Yahweh, that he comes as his servant, that though he does not know him, he will yet come to acknowledge him as the one true God (cf. 45:4-5). **He shall trample:** The Hebrew reads, ויבא, **and he shall come** (KJV), but the emendation to ויבם (cf. RSV) is slight, gives better sense (cf. Targ.), and improves the parallelism. H. L. Ginsberg emends to "he shall trample nations" (cf. 41:2; 45:1).

26. **He is right:** Better simply, "Right!" **There was none . . . none . . . none** (cf. 40:24). The pagan gods had nothing to declare concerning the future, no prophets to proclaim its meaning, and so there was no one who "heard" them.

27. The text is difficult and probably corrupt. The LXX reads ἀρχὴν Σειὼν δώσω καὶ Ἰερουσαλὴμ παρακαλέσω εἰς ὁδόν, "I will give to Zion a beginning, and I will comfort

---

conflicts decades later in which proud nineteenth-century industrial civilization was to meet disaster.

When the deities of the nations make no answer, there is apparently an embarrassed silence in the court. The auditors are pictured as waiting to be **dismayed and terrified** by oracles from the divinities of these many peoples. When no word is uttered, the Judge turns contemptuously on them (vs. 24).

These frequent exposures of the nullity of idols are evidence of the peril of apostasy in which this prophet thought his people stood. Babylon's gods and their festivals must have been impressive. They were surrounded by an aura as the deities of a conquering nation. Again and again the prophet piles upon them his disgust and scorn. They are "do-nothings," and their worshipers become odious in their stupidity.

25-29. *Address to the Discredited Idols.*—Over against these futilities that effect nothing in history, the Lord repeats his assertion that **Cyrus** was divinely called: **I stirred up one from the**

28 For I beheld, and *there was* no man; even among them, and *there was* no counselor, that, when I asked of them, could answer a word.

29 Behold, they *are* all vanity; their works *are* nothing: their molten images *are* wind and confusion.

42 Behold my servant, whom I uphold; mine elect, *in whom* my soul delighteth; I have put my Spirit upon him: he shall bring forth judgment to the Gentiles.

28 But when I look there is no one; among these there is no counselor who, when I ask, gives an answer.

29 Behold, they are all a delusion; their works are nothing; their molten images are empty wind.

42 Behold my servant, whom I uphold, my chosen, in whom my soul delights; I have put my spirit upon him, he will bring forth justice to the nations.

Jerusalem on the road." The Hebrew reads, lit., "First to Zion behold, behold them" (see Jer. 4:16 for use of הנה). The RSV emends the exclamation (הנה הנם) to *higgadhtihā,* I . . . **have declared,** which improves the parallelism. But the reference is obviously to 40:9-10 (note the threefold "behold") and the mood of exultancy is expected (cf. 42:9; 48:6). The restoration is not certain, but the meaning is probably that Yahweh was the first to announce the good news and to send a herald.

29. This verse forms an excellent conclusion to the judgment of the idols. While it is parallel to vs. 24 and serves the same purpose in the strophe, the repetition brings the judgment against the idols to a finale.

10. Ninth Strophe: The Mission of the Servant (42:1-4)

The strophe is a model of literary form and style. Each word registers its effect, each line adds something distinctive, each stroke contributes to the portrait of the **servant** of the Lord. Verbs and nouns of great import mingle and blend. The style is measured, quiet, terse, pregnant, and concentrated. From the opening words of introduction (**Behold my servant**) to the concluding **till** the thought marches forward. The last line produces a strong impression (cf. 40:11, 31). There is the usual repetition despite the economy of phrase. The sevenfold repetition of לא, "not," in vss. 2-4 is cast into characteristic Semitic forms and culminates in the servant's mission to the nations (cf. 43:22-24). The threefold *mishpāt* serves the purpose of centering the thought. Just as the emphasis falls on this word in the introductory summons, so here in the finale it

---

north, and he has come. We do not know the dates of the composition of the various poems in this prophecy. We should like to know when first this prophet identified Cyrus as summoned by God. At all events he alone interpreted this conqueror's significance (vs. 26). The opening verses of ch. 40 are apparently in mind here in vs. 27.

It is always easier to predict disastrous issues to present evils than to see God's gracious workings in frightening events. The prophet is concerned with **good tidings.** God's advent is both a judgment on Israel's oppressors and a creative act by which Jerusalem is to be restored. It is this arrival of the long hoped-for return which is vividly set forth in the words, **Behold, behold them.** It is as though the rebuilt city and the re-established nation were actually on hand and could be seen. Men like ourselves, in a shattered world, know God's judgments. They are trag-

ically patent "in the earth" (26:9). The church is awaiting evangelists of good tidings—men who discern what the King of Jacob is creating, and set forth clearly what now by his grace may be.

The Judge dismisses the divinities with disgust (vs. 29). We might place beside these discredited gods the divinities of modern man— science, education, technology, commerce, racism, nationalism, etc.—and proclaim their worthlessness to satisfy spiritual cravings and bring about a stable, friendly world. But such negative preaching, however true, has no appeal for wistful spirits. It ruins this magnificent drama to conclude it with the end of the chapter. Its climax comes in the Judge's pointing to Israel, his servant.

42:1-4. *The Verdict to Be Given by God's Servant Israel.*—The words go back to 41:8. Israel has been laid hold of by God for his task.

receives the major stress. As the nations are called to trial in 41:1 (cf. 49:1), their ultimate destiny is interpreted in the light of Israel's peculiar function as the instrument of divine judgment (41:8 ff.). Without this strophe the poem would not be complete either in structure or in thought. The style here is essentially the same as in 41:8-10. Such differences as exist are to be explained by the presentation of the servant and by the climactic position of the strophe. Yahweh is the speaker in both, and the literary mentality and theological thought belong to a single author. The party addressed is to be decided by the eschatological context of all the poems (cf. 52:13–53:12).

42:1. **Behold:** This exclamation follows the twofold judgment against the nations, likewise introduced by this word (41:24, 29); cf. the introduction of God in the herald's cry in 40:9 and of the servant in 52:13. The word appears seventeen times in Second Isaiah; elsewhere in the Prophets only thirteen. **My servant:** The LXX has "Jacob, my Servant" and "Israel, my chosen," an interpretation obviously derived from 41:8. Yahweh has already addressed Israel as **"my servant"** in 41:8-9, so we are prepared for the very direct address here. The word "servant" has numerous associations and connotations (see Lindhagen, *The Servant Motif in the Old Testament;* for the further servant terminology expressed in verbs see pp. 204-6; Begrich, *Studien zu Deuterojesaja,* p. 161). In Second Isaiah it not infrequently seems to be derived from court style where the official of the king was known as his servant (*'ebhedh-hammélekh;* see Hugo Gressmann, *Der Messias* [Göttingen: Vandenhoeck & Ruprecht, 1929], p. 60; Engnell, Lindhagen, *et al.* of the Scandinavian school think the language is characteristic of kingship ideology). As Begrich points out, it was the function of this official to make known the king's judicial decision. Yahweh is the King of Israel (cf. the crucial position of the term in 41:21; also 43:15; 44:6), and Israel is the Servant of the King. The possessive **my** has the same intimate association as in 41:8-9. For Israel it is given content in her election, covenant relation, and call. **I uphold:** Cf. the climax of Yahweh's words to Israel in 41:10*d*. The meaning here is rather "grasp," "lay hold of," as in Gen. 48:17; Amos 1:5, 8, and especially Prov. 3:18. Yahweh lays hold of Israel for his will and purpose; he appoints his servant to his work. **My chosen:** See 41:8*b*, 9*d*. Israel's sacred history begins with her election, the act of Yahweh's unmotivated grace. It is her supreme privilege to be chosen, but it is also her supreme obligation (Exod. 19:5-6 [J]; Amos 3:1-2; Deut. 7:7 ff.; 14:2). To be chosen is to be singled out for a purpose. When God has a work to do in the world, he chooses for himself patriarchs like Abraham and Jacob-Israel, mediators like Moses, military champions like Gideon, kings like David, prophets like Amos and Jeremiah. The title is assigned above all to Moses and David (cf. Enoch 45:3-4; 55:4, where it is used as a messianic title; also Luke 9:35; 23:35). Election and service go hand in hand (41:8-9; 43:10; 44:1-2). **In whom my soul delights:** Better, "in whom I delight." The intimate style is in keeping with God's love for his people (cf. 41:8; 49:15-16; 54:9-10). The words occur in the voice from heaven at Jesus' baptism (Mark 1:11 and parallels) and at his transfiguration (Matt. 17:5). **I have put my spirit upon him:** The election of the servant is followed by his endowment. The gift of the Spirit is permanent, like that of the messianic king in 11:2. It is not knowledge and will (contra Levy) but power and might; it is charismatic and equips its possessor with unusual powers. The Spirit is not generally the agency of inspiration among the pre-exilic

---

This passage was apparently in our Lord's mind at the time of his baptism, and possibly again at other critical junctures in his career. It is one of the strongest expressions of God's satisfaction in possessing on the earthly scene a selected agent **in whom** [his] **soul delights.** The servant nation is primarily a teacher, and this teaching is the standard by which all nations will be tested. Hence it forms the true conclusion of a trial.

I have put my Spirit upon him. The servant has a prophet's task and requires endowment with the Spirit who illuminates and empowers prophets. God never assigns a duty without also furnishing the requisite equipment. Our Lord asked his disciples, "When I sent you, . . . lacked ye any thing?" and their instant reply was, "Nothing" (22:35). Many a congregation and many a Christian longs for an outpouring of the Spirit. If a task is clearly seen, they need

2 He shall not cry, nor lift up, nor cause his voice to be heard in the street.

3 A bruised reed shall he not break, and the smoking flax shall he not quench: he shall bring forth judgment unto truth.

2 He will not cry or lift up his voice,
 or make it heard in the street;
3 a bruised reed he will not break,
 and a dimly burning wick he will not
 quench;
 he will faithfully bring forth justice.

---

literary prophets. After the Exile it is again invoked as in the period of the early monarchy (see Sigmund Mowinckel, " 'The Spirit' and the 'Word' in the Pre-exilic Reforming Prophets," *Journal of Biblical Literature*, LIII [1934], 199-227). Here the gift is bestowed upon Israel in the fateful hour of her destiny. **He will bring forth justice:** The word *mishpāṭ* is usually interpreted as meaning true religion, parallel to the Arabic *din*, which may mean true religion but also **judgment** or custom or law (cf. Bernhard Duhm, *Das Buch Jesaia* [4th ed.; Göttingen: Vandenhoeck & Ruprecht, 1922; "Göttinger Handkommentar zum Alten Testament"], p. 285). Modern commentators such as Begrich, Sidney Smith (*Isaiah XL-LV*, pp. 54-56), and Johannes Lindblom (*The Servant Songs in Deutero-Isaiah* [Lund: C. W. K. Gleerup, 1951], pp. 16-18) have inclined more to the judicial meaning of the term. In view of the terminology of the strophe, the relationship to 41:1 and the entire poem, and the usual meaning of the word, it is better to retain **judgment** (KJV) or **justice** (ASV, RSV) without excluding the wider connotations of the term. As Second Isaiah characteristically brings the prophetic movement to its loftiest expression and develops the main streams of prophetic thought to their highest point, so here he thinks of the servant as the mediator of judgment and justice in its highest sense.

2-3. The royal servant works silently, unobtrusively. **He will not cry:** This verb generally connotes the idea of distress or grief, but the parallelism suggests a more general meaning. If the references to the **bruised reed** and the **dimly burning wick** are to be taken literally, it is best to assume with Begrich, Sidney Smith, and Lindblom that they refer to symbolical legal practices. Otherwise they are simply figurative expressions describing the extraordinary methods of the servant (cf. 43:17). In his quiet, unostentatious, patient way he effects the will of his Lord and King. **He will faithfully bring forth justice:** Friedrich Giesebrecht, Kittel, and others have proposed emending *le'emeth*, **faithfully,** to *le'ummôth*, "to the peoples," but there is neither evidence nor felicity in favor of this conjecture. **Faithfully** underlines all that has been said in the preceding lines. (See J. C. C. Van Dorssen, *De Derivata van de Stam* אמן *in het*

---

wait for no further spiritual power. The message to them is rather, "Stir up the gift of God, which is in thee" (II Tim. 1:6). The servant's work lies in the future: **he will bring forth justice to the nations;** but the Spirit is represented as already his: **I have put my Spirit upon him.**

The nation in covenant with God is a missionary, and the methods and mood of this missionary community are prescribed to it. There is to be no self-advertising (vs. 2). What a nation or a church is and does speaks so loud men cannot hear what it says. God's servant must use "a still, small voice," as God himself uses in his most convincing speech. Noisy propaganda has only a brief effect, and often defeats itself. No iron curtain long conceals the quality of a people's life, or can shut out the impression of the lives of other nations. Boast-

fulness is never convincing. A nation's genuine service to mankind, and the modesty with which it is discharged, are the persuasive commendation of its God. Another prophet gave a description of Israel's quiet ministry in a suggestive metaphor, "The remnant of Jacob shall be in the midst of many people as a dew from the LORD" (Mic. 5:7).

There is to be no coercion (vs. 3). The nation will not impose its will or its manner of life upon others. It appreciates the pathos of the plight of the heathen peoples: they are like **a bruised reed** and **a dimly burning wick.** Its approach to them is not censorious but sympathetic. This is in rather startling contrast with the scornful verdicts on heathen deities in the preceding two strophes. However stupid the worship of idols, the prophet appears to recognize the continuance of conscience in all peo-

4 He shall not fail nor be discouraged, till he have set judgment in the earth: and the isles shall wait for his law.	4 He will not fail[t] or be discouraged[u] till he has established justice in the earth; and the coastlands wait for his law.

[t] Or *burn dimly*
[u] Or *bruised*

Hebreeuwsch van het Oude Testament [Amsterdam: Drukkerij Holland N. V., 1951], pp. 53-54, 108. Van Dorssen approves Delitzsch' interpretation of the word as the recognition of the true facts of the case in the manifold human situations; cf. also Ralph Marcus, "The 'Plain Meaning' of Isaiah 42.1-4," *Harvard Theological Review*, XXX [1937], 253: "He will introduce justice effectively.")

4. He will not fail or be discouraged (RSV mg., **burn dimly** or **be bruised**): The verbs obviously play upon the two expressions in vs. 3. The time may be long, the obstacles great, and the chances of success dim, but the servant continues to perform his mission, conscious of his election and calling and endowment. Here the true conqueror is no longer Cyrus, although there is no reason to believe that the poet had forgotten him and had not meant what he said in 41:2-4, 25. Cyrus performs his work also, but it is not the same as the servant's. Recent attempts to identify Cyrus with the servant confuse the missions of the two. It is the servant who occupies the center at the bar of history, not Cyrus (cf. 41:8 ff.). The final issue of history lies with him whom God has chosen for his purpose, his mediator and servant Israel, not with Cyrus, the conqueror of the Medes and Lydians. "For his teaching [*tôrāh*] the coastlands wait" (cf. 41:1). Covenant (*berîth*) and teaching (*tôrāh*) belong together; the covenant people have been entrusted with teaching or law (cf. Exod. 19–24; etc.).

ples. Without it no missionary appeal could be made. A. B. Davidson suggests that the prophet may be referring to

the human virtues expiring among the nations, but not yet dead; the sense of God, debased by idolatries, but not extinct; the consciousness in the individual soul of its own worth and its capacities, and the glimmering ideal of a true life and a worthy activity almost crushed out by the grinding tyranny of rulers and the miseries entailed by their ambitions.[3]

This may be colored by nineteenth-century feeling, but the spirit of the servant who does not destroy but fulfills remains the true spirit of the Christian missionary.

This missionary task must be pursued with indefatigable constancy (vss. 3c-4). The prophet foresaw a prolonged and exhausting campaign before his missionary people. The effort to establish a standard of judgment—respect for human dignity, liberty of thought, speech, and religion, friendly exchange of goods for mind, body, and soul, etc.—seems to encounter obstruction after obstruction. Nations commissioned to this task need endless endurance. The church, whose mission is reconciliation of all men with God in Christ, and the creation of a world community in him, has to be as undiscourageable as her God, who faints not, neither is weary (40:28). While it is tender toward crushed reeds and nearly extinguished wicks, it must not allow itself to **burn dimly** and be **bruised**. The verbs in vs. 4 play on the expressions in vs. 3 (cf. RSV mg.). The sense that he has been chosen and endowed with the Spirit sustains the servant and makes him— not Cyrus, on whom all eyes are set—the true victor in the world.

Masters of the life of the soul warn against becoming disheartened and flagging. The warnings apply both to the church and to her members. Bunyan confesses: "Oh, it is hard continuing believing, continuing loving, continuing resisting all that opposeth." [4] Jonathan Edwards, analyzing men's spiritual condition, says: "The degree of religion is . . . to be judged of by the fixedness and strength of habit that is exercised in affection." [5] It is such fixedness of devotion to the task of setting the mind of Christ as the ruling standard for all peoples, and bringing all human thought under its sway, which is essential in Christians, who severally and collectively are God's servants to mankind.

[3] "The Book of Isaiah: Chapters XL-LXVI. VI. The Servant of the Lord," *The Expositor*, Second Series, VIII (1884), 365. See also pp. 364-66.

[4] "Christian Behavior," in *Practical Works of John Bunyan* (Aberdeen: George King, 1842), p. 193.
[5] *A Treatise Concerning Religious Affections*, Part I.

5 ¶ Thus saith God the LORD, he that created the heavens, and stretched them out; he that spread forth the earth, and that which cometh out of it; he that giveth breath unto the people upon it, and spirit to them that walk therein:

5 Thus says God, the LORD,
　who created the heavens and stretched
　　them out,
　who spread forth the earth and what
　　comes from it,
　who gives breath to the people upon it
　　and spirit to those who walk in it:

D. THE NEW EVENT OF THE DIVINE INTERVENTION (42:5-17)

The first three poems have described the vast panorama of Second Isaiah's prophetic vision: the eschatological event of the coming of the Lord (40:1-11), the primordial event of the Creation (40:12-31), and the events of contemporary history which are seen in the context of beginning and end and in relation to Yahweh's covenant history with his chosen people. Now the covenant history emerges in all clarity and concreteness (vss. 6-7). It is viewed in the universal framework of creation (vs. 5) and the imminent divine intervention (vss. 9, 13, 14-16). The "new" event evokes a "new" song (vss. 10-13). The herald's message of the prologue is here bodied forth in words of intense realism and power.

The literary form of the poem is exceptionally regular. Three strophes of seven lines each are introduced by an oracular formula and concluded by a coda (cf. 40:11). The first strophe (vss. 6-9) is an oracle of call, the second (vss. 10-13) a hymn, the third (vss. 14-16) an oracle of salvation. The same economy of phrase, pregnancy of style, abundance of verbs, use of key words, and high seriousness are present here as elsewhere (cf. 42:1-4). The supreme significance of the new event is reflected in the hymnic interlude. The third strophe describes the eschatological event itself: the Lord, long silent and restrained, himself intervenes in behalf of his people. The mention of the **graven images** in vs. 8c and the coda connect well with the previous poem.

1. ORACULAR INTRODUCTION (42:5)

5. Thus says God, the LORD: The Hebrew reads *hā'ēl Yahweh;* LXX, Κύριος ὁ θεός; Vulg., *Dominus Deus;* the Dead Sea Scroll, interestingly, *hā'ēl hā'elōhîm.* Yahweh is the one universal God. The covenant Lord of Israel is God of the nations also (cf. 40:9g, 10a; 41:1–42:4). The rest of the verse is in apposition. The relative clauses are participial phrases in Hebrew (cf. 40:22-23 *et passim;* Ps. 104:2-4). This hymn style is appropriate at the beginnings of poems, especially where the theme of creation is present (Pss. 8; 19; 104; Amos 4:13; 5:8). Creation constantly forms the general matrix of the prophet's literary form and thought (40:12-13, 26, 28; 41:20; 43:1, 8, 12, 13, etc.). **Spread forth:** The verb רקע means "to beat out to a thin surface" (cf. the noun "firmament" [רקיע] in Gen. 1:6-8). **Gives breath:** Now comes the climax of the triad. God not only breathed

---

5-17. The Coming of the Lord.—This fourth poem continues the theme of its three precursors. The announcement of the Lord's coming has been made in 40:9. He has been set forth as "the Creator of the ends of the earth" (40:12 ff.). At the trial of the nations Israel has been declared his chosen servant to "bring forth justice to the nations" (vs. 1). This poem carries us forward to the immediate arrival of the Lord: The LORD goes forth like a mighty hero (vs. 13). This is the key line of the poem.

5. Who God Is.—Here is a prologue in which the prophet dwells on who God is. F. D. Maurice called it "the great disease of our time, that we talk about God and about our religion, and do

not confess Him as a living God." [6] That is even truer of our day than it was of Maurice's, a century ago. This prophet is vividly aware of the living God, and constantly confesses who he is, what he has done, and what he is doing.

In this confession there is a combination of God's transcendence,

who created the heavens and stretched them out,
who spread forth the earth and what comes from it,

and his special gift of his own **breath** and **spirit** to man. Neither element can be left out. We

[6] Frederick Maurice, *The Life of Frederick Denison Maurice* (New York: Charles Scribner's Sons, 1884), II, 359.

6 I the LORD have called thee in right-eousness, and will hold thine hand, and will keep thee, and give thee for a covenant of the people, for a light of the Gentiles;

6 "I am the LORD, I have called you in righteousness,
I have taken you by the hand and kept you;
I have given you as a covenant to the people,
a light to the nations,

---

into the nostrils of the first man and made him a living soul (Gen. 2:7); his **breath** gives life to all mankind, his "spirit" animates **the people** who **walk** his earth.

2. FIRST STROPHE: LIGHT TO THE NATIONS (42:6-9)

6. I am the LORD: The LXX repeats the Κύριος ὁ θεός. The usual rendering is **I the LORD have called,** but both the general context and the repetition in vs. 8a favor the predication. Then follow the events of Israel's covenant history: "I have called . . . , I have grasped . . . , I have kept . . . , I have given . . . , to open the eyes . . . , to release the prisoners" (cf. 41:8-10). The oracle opens with an address to the servant Israel. The universal God, creator of heaven and earth and giver of life, speaks covenant words to a people. It is Israel's ear that is attent (cf. 50:4-5). Israel is a "called" people (48:12); she has a divine mission and destiny. Those who are chosen to be God's servants are "called" men, and they are best understood through their calls (Gen. 12:1; Exod. 3:1-16 [JE]; Amos 7:1-9; Isa. 6:1-13; Jer. 1:4-10; Ezek. 1–3). **Righteousness** refers to the purpose of God, "a stedfast and consistent purpose" (Skinner, *Isaiah, ad loc.*). **I have taken you by the hand:** Better, "grasped" (cf. 8:11, בחזקת היד); see Exeg. on "uphold," vs. 1 (cf. 41:10d, 13b). **And kept you:** Some scholars derive the verb from יצר, "to fashion" or "to form," which is grammatically possible but violates the sequence of the verbs and should therefore be rejected. **A covenant of [to] the people:** A famous crux which has been much controverted. Lowth (*Isaiah, ad loc.*), on the basis of two MSS (?) proposes ברית עולם, "everlasting covenant," an admirable reading also supported by one of the Khirbet Qumran fragments which date probably from the first century B.C.; cf. 54:9-10; 55:3. Torczyner interprets *berîth* from the Akkadian *bararu*, "to shine," thus "splendor of the people," which would provide a parallel to "light of the nations." But the Hebrew Bible offers no adequate linguistic analogy for this meaning. It is best to approach the problem with the word **people** which has just been used in the introductory verse as applying to all mankind (vs. 5d). Levy argues that the word 'amm in Arabic sometimes means "general," "universal" and he adduces several parallels from the O.T. (Jer. 21:7;

---

must dwell on the sublimity of one "beyond the flaming ramparts of the world," and his kinship with man. God is "other," but not "wholly other" than ourselves. He is the lofty one vastly above us, but his spirit is in us. Were that not so, he could not enter into communion with us.

This presence of the divine spirit in sinful men is emphasized as an encouragement to the servant in undertaking his mission of good tidings to the nations. John Calvin stressed the total corruption of fallen man, but still insisted that he shows the Spirit's presence in his ca-pacity to learn truth and to show it forth in the arts and sciences.[7] We are often impressed with the spiritual quality in men in whom we had not looked for it. H. M. Tomlinson's hero in *Gallions Reach* escapes from a sense of the

[7] *Institutes* II. 2. 14, *et passim.*

meaninglessness of the cosmos by what he dis-covers in ordinary seamen:

His knowledge of Sinclair and that bunch of men of his old ship gave to an aimless and sprawling world the assurance of anonymous courage and faith waiting in the sordid muddle for a signal, ready when it came. . . . Those people gave to God any countenance by which he could be known.[8]

The servant of the Lord needed the reminder both of God's sufficiency as creator of the cosmos, and of his breath enlivening the lowliest heathen. There would be something in the non-Jewish world to respond to the proclama-tion of God's justice.

6-9. The Task of the Lord's Servant.—As the Exeg. suggests, the covenant at Sinai is recalled in the solemn opening line, **I am the LORD, I**

[8] New York: Harper & Bros., 1927, pp. 165-66.

7 To open the blind eyes, to bring out the prisoners from the prison, *and* them that sit in darkness out of the prison house.

8 I *am* the LORD; that *is* my name: and my glory will I not give to another, neither my praise to graven images.

7 to open the eyes that are blind,
   to bring out the prisoners from the dungeon,
    from the prison those who sit in darkness.
8 I am the LORD, that is my name;
   my glory I give to no other,
   nor my praise to graven images.

22:4). Torrey translates it "peoples"; Lindblom, "a confederacy of peoples"; Volz, *Menschheit* or *Menschenvolk* (so Marti, Kittel, Köhler). The presence of the word in vs. 5, the manner of Second Isaiah in picking up key words like this, the parallel to **nations,** and the universalism of the prophet's thought balance the evidence in favor of the plural. **Covenant** is the most likely meaning in view of the language and thought of this strophe and of the parallels in 54:10; 55:3. It is the gift of divine grace but also the basis of Israel's mission. God's gracious purpose for the nations of the world is embodied in Israel.

Like the Deuteronomists, Second Isaiah combines his universalism and particularism (note vs. 5a) in such a way as to deepen and reinforce both. Where the perspectives are widest, there Israel's election and uniqueness are most clearly and emphatically present. **A light to the nations:** In First Isaiah (9:2) it is the people walking in darkness who see a great light; here Israel is herself made the light which shines in the spiritual darkness of the surrounding world (cf. 49:6; 51:4; 60:1-3 and especially the Nunc Dimittis, Luke 2:31-32).

7. To open the eyes that are blind: The subject of the infinitive on purely grammatical grounds could be God, but it is obviously the servant. The release of the captives from prison is not to be taken as referring to liberation from exile but rather in a spiritual sense, a liberation of all the peoples from bondage. All of vs. 7 is a development of **light to the nations.**

8. I am the LORD: The strophe falls into two divisions, a common feature in Second Isaiah and many psalms; here the theophanic words are repeated to give them greater force. **That is my name:** Name and person are one; name signifies identity (Pedersen, *Israel, Its Life and Culture, I-II,* pp. 245-59). Israel knows the **name** of her God; therefore she stands in unique and concrete relationship with him (cf. 41:8). But the meaning is more universalistic here. The pronoun *hû'* is synonymous with the divine name. It is Yahweh's revelation to all the world that he alone is God. **My glory I give to no other:** Duhm and others take this verse and the following as a continuation of 41:21-29. It is to be understood, however, in relation to the preceding lines, as the structure plainly shows. The interpretation of Sheldon Blank that the words "I am Yahweh" in Second Isaiah mean "I am God," the one and true and only God, receives strong support here. His name must not be profaned or his **glory** shared by other gods. His glory is his alone.

---

have called you in righteousness. The **righteousness** is not Israel's moral character, but God's dependable purpose. It is the thought which the N.T. repeats in II Tim. 2:13. Israel was to be in her national life an incarnation of God's covenant. This would render her **a light to the nations.** Such attainment was not within her grasp, but was within God's grace. Thus is the gospel of the prophet wrapped up in his vision of God's righteousness. Israel's ministry of enlightenment to blind nations and liberation to the bound is all God's gracious doing through her (vs. 7).

There is a similar prophetic hope in the Russian novelist, Dostoevski. His Father Zossima declares:

The Christian society now is not ready and is only resting on some seven righteous men, but as they are never lacking, it will continue still unshaken in expectation of its complete transformation from a society almost heathen in character into a single universal and all-powerful Church. So be it, so be it! Even though at the end of the ages, for it is ordained to come to pass! [9]

[9] *The Brothers Karamazov,* tr. Constance Garnett (New York: Modern Library, n.d.), Bk. I, ch. v, p. 74.

9 Behold, the former things are come to pass, and new things do I declare: before they spring forth I tell you of them.

10 Sing unto the Lord a new song, *and* his praise from the end of the earth, ye that

9 Behold, the former things have come to pass,
   and new things I now declare;
before they spring forth
   I tell you of them."

10 Sing to the Lord a new song,
   his praise from the end of the earth!

His glory and his praise are the ultimate categories of revelation and response (cf. 6:1-3; Pss. 148–150). **Praise** is due to him and to no other, surely not to the idols (see 41:6-7, 29; cf. Pss. 29:1-2; 65:1). Note the emphasis on the first person: **I am the Lord, . . . my name, . . . my glory, . . . my praise** (cf. 43:11-13).

9. A literal rendering of vs. 9a is, "The former things! Behold, they have come." The events of the past are predicted and fulfilled (cf. 41:27). Their full meaning is disclosed in the light of the **new things**. What was hidden in them is now to be revealed. God is about to perform **new** events in the earth, and he is proclaiming them before they have happened, before even the first faint shoots have shown themselves. He is Lord of time, of past events and future events. History and eschatology are not to be taken as antithetical to each other. This is the truth in Ernst Sellin's statement that the movement of the whole O.T. is eschatological, and of Ludwig Köhler's remark that creation always implies a resolution in the "end." Redemption, creation, and history as it is interpreted in the covenant life of the servant Israel, meet in this poem, which characteristically follows the eschatological trilogy of 40:1–42:4. With these major categories the heavenly council is occupied. **I tell you** [אתכם] **of them:** The second person singular of vs. 6 here becomes plural, a characteristic suited to Israel as corporate personality. "This community cannot be anything but Israel" (Lindblom, *Servant Songs in Deutero-Isaiah*, p. 22).

3. Second Strophe: New Song of Redemption (42:10-13)

The eschatological hymn follows immediately upon the announcement of new events. It is in the style of the enthronement hymns (Pss. 47; 93; 96–97).

10. **Sing to the Lord a new song:** The song of redemption and praise (cf. vs. 8c) follows the twofold word of revelation **I am the Lord:** the covenant assurance (vss. 6-7)

The evangelization of the world by God's servant redounds to his glory (vs. 8). He, and he alone, is true God, controlling history and knowing the meaning of its events. How absurd to mention idols in the same breath with him and suppose that they too share his reign. The prophet, at the risk of repetition, harps on the futility of idols. We grant that many factors influence the course of history; the point for us to stress is that all of them are under God's direction, and he is the sovereign whom we must ever keep in mind.

Behold, the former things have come to pass. Cyrus' campaigns mark the passing of one epoch and the dawn of another. **New things** are announced and about to happen. To this prophet the final era was at hand, the consummation of history, as Dostoevski had "the end of the ages" in view. We look back over the stretches of centuries and think the prophet wrong, as we suppose the early church mistaken in its anticipation of the proximate return of

Christ and the end of this world. But both prophet and apostles were profoundly right in their conviction that what they believed in and saw arriving was God's ultimate order for his creation. We may connect the liberation of Israel through Cyrus, its exaltation as God's missionary servant, and the carrying of its gospel to mankind with the coming of God's kingdom. A correct reading of the past and of the present prepares us for God's further and final advent in victory.

For all the past, read true, is prophecy,
And all the firsts are hauntings of some Last,
And all the springs are flash-lights of one Spring.
Then leaf, and flower, and fall-less fruit
Shall hang together on the unyellowing bough.[10]

10-13. *All Nature Hails the Lord's Coming as a Warrior.*—The Lord appears to redeem his

[10] Francis Thompson, "From the Night of Forebeing." From *Collected Works*, ed. Wilfred Meynell. Used by permission of Burns, Oates & Washbourne, Ltd., and The Newman Press, publishers.

go down to the sea, and all that is therein; the isles, and the inhabitants thereof.

11 Let the wilderness and the cities thereof lift up *their voice,* the villages *that* Kedar doth inhabit: let the inhabitants of the rock sing, let them shout from the top of the mountains.

Let the sea roar[v] and all that fills it, the coastlands and their inhabitants.

11 Let the desert and its cities lift up their voice, the villages that Kedar inhabits; let the inhabitants of Sela sing for joy, let them shout from the top of the mountains.

[v] Cn Compare Ps 96. 11; 98. 7: Heb *Those who go down to the sea*

and the promise of the new event. As on the occasion of the first Exodus Miriam sang in praise of Yahweh's great and victorious deed (Exod. 15:21), so now in the hour of the new Exodus a new song is to be sung from one end of the earth to the other (cf. 40:5). The whole earth is to join in jubilation before the coming of the mighty Conqueror. The manifestation of God's glory awakens the voice to song. Second Isaiah himself illustrates this response. His poems are an exulting rhapsody at the revelation of the glory of God (40:5). The ritual celebrations of the New Year, in which the enthronement songs were sung, account for the style and language. It is significant that the heavenly council of the prologue, with its emphasis upon the *kebhôdh Yahweh* and the imminence of judgment, is followed by the poem on creation, which in turn is followed by the council of judgment in which the nations are brought to account, and in the present poem by the active intervention of Yahweh in armed conflict with his foes. It seems not impossible, then, that the prophet has been influenced by Babylonian prototypes. At the enthronement of the king songs of praise are sung (see Sigmund Mowinckel, *Psalmenstudien II* [Kristiania: Jacob Dybwad, 1922]). It is a perfectly constructed poem with seven great ascriptions of praise. The lines begin and end with **praise** (vss. 10*b*, 12*b*); vs. 12 connects closely with vs. 8 (**glory . . . praise**); and all the lines prepare the way for the word which gives the hymn its point and power: **The LORD goes forth like a mighty man. Let the sea roar:** The Hebrew text reads, **who go down to the sea** (RSV mg.), which seems out of place here and is out of keeping with the parallelism of the poem. Lowth (*Isaiah, ad loc.*) first proposed the emendation from ירדי to ירעם, although he did not adopt it. But it has commended itself to most commentators; cf. Ps. 98:7, where the present line (as emended) occurs.

11. Let the desert and its cities lift up: The Hebrew reads so, the verb being an elliptical term for "lift up the voice." The LXX translates εὐφρανθήσονται and the Targ., ישׁושׁו, "rejoice," a reading adopted by several scholars. It is not necessary to identify the desert with any special locale. The cities and the villages are the settlements of the oases, places like Tadmor and Petra. **Kedar:** Cf. 21:16; 60:7; Ps. 120:5; Jer. 2:10; 49:28-29. The stationary Arabs are called *hadariya* in contrast to the *wabariya,* the nomads (Delitzsch and Skinner). **The inhabitants of Sela:** Often identified with Petra. Levy (*Deutero-Isaiah,* p. 150) suggests that the prophet may have in mind some such cliff as that near Eridu, "which is said to give its name to 'Irāk = 'cliff' or 'mountain tract.' "

The point in all these lines is the universality of praise; even the most obscure and remote places join with the sea and the desert in the hymn of rejoicing. It is the

people and his world. A new thing (vs. 9) demands **a new song.** Since God is Lord both of the physical cosmos and of the pageant of human affairs, the destinies of nature and of man are linked (cf. Paul's similar conviction in Rom. 8:19 ff.). This is a conviction which recurs often in these poems. Behind Israel's mission is the Creator and Lord of the universe (vs. 5); when

God comes like a warrior to free her for this world-wide service, it is fitting that all his creation unite in hailing him with jubilation. So the ends of the earth, the sea, the coastlands, the desert with towns in its oases, villagers and crag dwellers, are swept by the poet's imagination into one exultant chorus shouting "Glory!" A supremely dramatic event is occurring—**The**

12 Let them give glory unto the LORD, and declare his praise in the islands.

13 The LORD shall go forth as a mighty man, he shall stir up jealousy like a man of war: he shall cry, yea, roar; he shall prevail against his enemies.

14 I have long time holden my peace; I have been still, *and* refrained myself: *now* will I cry like a travailing woman; I will destroy and devour at once.

12 Let them give glory to the LORD,
    and declare his praise in the coastlands.
13 The LORD goes forth like a mighty man,
    like a man of war he stirs up his fury;
he cries out, he shouts aloud,
    he shows himself mighty against his
      foes.

14 For a long time I have held my peace,
    I have kept still and restrained myself;
now I will cry out like a woman in travail,
    I will gasp and pant.

---

response of all the world before the coming of God in his triumph (cf. Pss. 113–118; 146–150).

12. Duhm regards the whole verse as a gloss, but this robs the poem of a great climax and divorces it from vs. 8 (an advantage to Duhm *et al.*). **Glory** and **praise** belong only to the one God of all the earth. The chief end of all creation is to praise, exalt, and magnify its Lord.

13. **The LORD goes forth like a mighty man:** The figure is military and theophanic (Henning Fredriksson, *Jahwe als Krieger* [Lund: C. W. K. Gleerup, 1945], pp. 10, 24, 63, 77, 87). As captains "go forth" (a technical military expression) to wage war, so Yahweh as *gibbôr* takes the field against his enemies (cf. the Arabic *baraza*, "he went out," and *mubaraza*, "a challenge to single combat" [Levy, *loc. cit.*]). There are numerous parallels to this passage in the Near Eastern texts, especially in the Akkadian and Ugaritic materials. As Yahweh triumphed in combat in the primeval abyss (cf. 51:9-10*b*) or in the combat at the time of the Exodus (Exod. 15:3 ff.), so he will triumph now. Whatever may be said of the context as a whole, vss. 10-13 certainly have a liturgical style. Yahweh, the conqueror, appears arrayed in all his panoply to do battle against the powers which resist him. **Like a man of war he stirs up his fury:** Cf. Exod. 15:3. It is possible that we have a literary reminiscence of an ancient war poem which lies at the basis of the present expansion in Exod. 15. The poet does not hesitate to employ the most realistic terms to describe the fury of God. He raises the terrible battle cry and shrieks (cf. Zeph. 1:14 ff.). **He shows himself mighty.** The verb *yithgabbar* has the same root as *gibbôr*, "hero," in vs. 13*a*. He shows himself a soldier or mighty man.

4. Third Strophe: Intervention of Yahweh (42:14-17)

Here we have the theophanic language of Yahweh's conquest in battle (Exod. 15; Judg. 5; cf. also Ps. 18; Hab. 3; Zech. 14:3). In fifteen verbs, all of them in the first person, Yahweh describes line upon line what he is about to do, from the final moment of breaking his long-kept silence to the summary at the close. The realism of the passage

---

LORD goes forth like a mighty man. No wonder that this universal welcome resounds!

This coming of the warrior-God, raising his battle cry, repeats the initial announcement in 40:10. It is his stern work in the campaigns which free his people from their oppressors that first fills the poet's thought (vs. 13). In the quieter days of recent generations, and surviving in pacifist circles, protests were heard against military metaphors. We know how tragically evil our world is. God's justice, truth, and love encounter obstinate antagonism. He

and his servants must endure the hardships of prolonged and desperate struggle if his gracious plans for mankind are to be achieved. Such metaphors in the N.T. and in Christian hymns recall us to share his courageous warfare. How heartening is the expression **he shows himself mighty!**

14-16. *The Self-restrained God Breaks Forth.* —God confesses his self-restraint, **For a long time I have held my peace.** His suffering and perplexed people had wondered at the silence and charged him with indifference. How little

15 I will make waste mountains and hills, and dry up all their herbs; and I will make the rivers islands, and I will dry up the pools.	15 I will lay waste mountains and hills, and dry up all their herbage; I will turn the rivers into islands, and dry up the pools.

is intense, but no more so than the thought behind it. It is ancient Oriental eschatological speech with all its rich mythological overtones, and it is poetry which describes in characteristic imagery the final issue of history.

14. For a long time I have held my peace: The poet is thinking in the more spacious perspectives of world history. The general context is universal: from creation (vs. 5) to redemption (vs. 14-16), from the former things to the latter things (vs. 9), for all nations (vss. 6-8) and for all who inhabit the earth (vss. 10-12). God stands at the last frontier of history; he can wait no longer for the moment of his going forth. In such fashion the poet describes the urgency of the divine act. The sudden shift from Yahweh as warrior to Yahweh as a woman in childbirth (vs. 14c) is in the manner of the poet; such imagery depicts the passion of God in his relation to history. The two triads of verbs (vss. 14ab, 14cd) express the contrast between "then" and "now." The figure of Yahweh's travailing has a profundity not easily discerned by modern minds. It did justice to the events that were about to occur: they were the birth pangs of God (cf. the messianic birth pangs in Rom. 8:22). The hour is desperate, the darkness and plight of men are sore. Ancient empires and past ages are drawing to a close. But now a new reality is dawning. God is in the midst of the world-wide turmoil; he is active in its events; his purpose is revealed in this time between the ages; and his victory in the conquest is certain.

15. The imagery is characteristically eschatological. First, the **mountains and hills,** for they were the bulwarks of God for holding the earth secure. When the mountains fall, the end is at hand (cf. Ps. 46:3). The transformation of the desert into a land of fertility is a major feature of apocalyptic eschatology. The word אִיִּים, **islands,** is very common

---

they suspected the pain he underwent in not interfering in their folly! Is anything harder than to keep hands off when those whom one loves make tragic blunders and must take the devastating consequences? A modern poet, compelled to watch a loved one suffer without being able to do anything to alleviate the pain, speaks of "the all-endured this nothing-done costs me."[1] The calm of the silent skies has frequently appeared to men amid calamities on earth evidence of an unfeeling God. How can there be a heart behind the stillness of the heavens?

In Israel Zangwill's *The Cockpit,* the queen bursts out: "The peace of God? As I lie sleepless I think of the eternal insomnia of God." Her maid, shocked, interrupts her: "Madam!" But the queen continues: "I only quote the Bible. God neither slumbers nor sleeps. Ah, it is the pain of God, not His peace that passeth understanding."[2] There is a suggestion of such pain, endured during centuries of his people's sinning and wrecking his and their land, when God says, **For a long time I have held my peace.**

Now, as shaken by convulsive emotion, he groans, he pants, he gasps **like a woman in travail.** These are the birth throes of a new

creation. In such O.T. passages, with their startling Oriental imagery, we catch sight of a cross in the heart of God centuries before the cross of wood stood upon the mound at Golgotha. It is the intensity of his suffering love which distinguishes his self-revelation to Israel from the loftiest contemporary religious thinking. Contrast the imperturbable tranquillity of the celestials in most faiths with this travailing God. Such O.T. metaphors render God's coming in Christ and offering himself for his sinning children congruous with his nature. "He grew likest God in being born."[3]

When the warrior-God comes on the scene, "like a man of war he stirs up his fury" (vs. 13). Wrath is love's instinctive reaction to all that injures the beloved. There is a

> . . . fierceness that from tenderness
> Is never far."[4]

One of the saintliest of British preachers spoke of his blood "running liquid fire" in the presence of despicable wrongs.[5] It is comforting to realize that things which injure God's people and enslave them are intolerable to God. His

[3] *The Ring and the Book,* "Pompilia."
[4] William Watson, "The Tomb of Burns."
[5] Stopford A. Brooke, ed., *Life and Letters of Frederick W. Robertson* (Boston: Ticknor & Fields, 1865), I, 186.

[1] Robert Lytton Bulwer-Lytton, "The Last Wish."
[2] New York: The Macmillan Co., 1921, p. 210.

16 And I will bring the blind by a way *that* they knew not; I will lead them in paths *that* they have not known: I will make darkness light before them, and crooked things straight. These things will I do unto them, and not forsake them.

17 ¶ They shall be turned back, they shall be greatly ashamed, that trust in graven images, that say to the molten images, Ye *are* our gods.

16 And I will lead the blind
   in a way that they know not,
in paths that they have not known
   I will guide them.
I will turn the darkness before them into light,
   the rough places into level ground.
These are the things I will do,
   and I will not forsake them.
17 They shall be turned back and utterly put to shame,
   who trust in graven images,
who say to molten images,
   "You are our gods."

in Second Isaiah, but it is strange here as a parallel to **pools.** C. F. Houbigant and Robert Lowth, and most scholars since, have favored emending to "dry places" (ציים), which is doubtless right.

16. In characteristic fashion the poet advances from nature to history. In the hour of his advance God will **lead the blind** to their home. They cannot see, it is so dark. But God will guide them along unknown paths, and will **turn the darkness . . . into light,** as once he guided the chosen people from Egypt to Sinai (Exod. 13:21-22). The lines are reminiscent of the prologue (40:3-5). What is adumbrated in the celestial council in general terms is articulated in the concreteness of eschatological (mythological) imagery. The reference to **the blind** is important, for it constitutes one of the major themes which are to follow. Volz finds the last two lines of vs. 16 "pale" and metrically disturbing. On the contrary, they are an impressive and climactic summary.

17. The conclusion connects well with the central thought. It is characteristic of the poet to end his poems with brief quotations. The coming of God in the time of his glorious conquest will bring an end to the worship of other gods. Those who trust in idols (cf. vs. 8) will be confounded, those who say to them, **You are our gods,** will be **put to shame,** for God has shown himself mighty. Beside him there is no other.

nature blazes at them. The redemption of an evil world is assured when "our God is a consuming fire" (Heb. 12:29).

God thus aroused is represented as destroying **mountains and hills.** These are the symbols of earth's firmness, the means of holding it together. But in his fury they go; and earth is left a chaos, with no familiar landmarks. This is part of the terror of his judgment. But God's people need not fear "though the mountains be carried into the midst of the sea" (Ps. 46:2), for God himself will lead his servant and, however **blind** Israel is, God is familiar with paths unknown to these exiles.

In the perplexities which confront nations and the church, if God were limited to alternatives which men see we might well be hopeless. It is because he leads the blind **by a way that they know not** that we can be confident. Christians often have hardly an inkling as to how the purposes which lay claim on them as God's will can come to pass. Obstructions seem insuperable. But our inability to see ways and

means by which the divine purpose can be accomplished should not discourage us or hinder us from advancing as though victory were sure. Martin Luther wrote to the hesitant Melanchthon: "Had Moses waited till he understood how Israel could elude Pharaoh's armies, they might have been in Egypt still."[6] When in sheer faith we embark on God's enterprises, **darkness** becomes **light.** The prophet could not point out in detail the road to freedom or the steps to be taken on the journey to the homeland. But he had no question as to the resourcefulness of the divine guide. He hears God saying with magnificent assurance:

> **These are the things I will do,**
> **and I will not forsake them.**

The poem shocks modern readers by its closing lines depicting the discomfiture of idol worshipers. Current sentimentality protests the doom of those who for whatever reason disobey

[6] Margaret A. Currie, ed., *Letters of Martin Luther* (New York: The Macmillan Co., 1908), Letter CCXXVI.

| 18 Hear, ye deaf; and look, ye blind, that ye may see. | 18 Hear, you deaf; and look, you blind, that you may see! |

E. The Blind and Deaf Servant Redeemed (42:18–43:7)

All the major themes which have thus far guided the movement of the prophet's thought appear in this poem in such form and such position as to show that the general outlines of his message are kept clearly and steadily before him. Creation (43:1bc, 7), redemption (43:1d-7), history (42:22-25), and the servant of the Lord (42:19) are all present, yet in such fashion as an Oriental poet like Second Isaiah would deal with them. But it is more than the major themes which are present here. Other motifs like blindness, hearing, the Torah, "fear not," glory, and love suggest that the same thoughts are stirring the prophet's mind. On the other hand, the poem presses on to a fresh dimension; its horizon is both expanded and deepened. In contrast to the earlier prophets, Second Isaiah hitherto has had no word of judgment or censure of Israel. In this poem he joins his predecessors. Yet the judgment appears in a context which is the prophet's own. A second theme, even more central in his mind, is redemption. Only once before, although in a most moving context, has this note been sounded (41:14). Here it controls his thought, for the judgment of 42:18-25 clearly anticipates the redemption of 43:1-7. The theological interest of the poem lies in these two aspects of the Lord's appearing.

The poem is divided into two parts: an invective (42:18-25) and an oracle of salvation (43:1-7). One section stands over against the other; each is to be read in the light of the other. Each section has its effective beginning (42:18; 43:1) and ending (42:25; 43:7), as do most of the strophes. The threefold *ki,* **when** or **for** (43:2-3b), the threefold repetition of **blind** and **deaf** (42:18-19), **spoil** and **robbery** (vss. 22-24), the "covenant-theophanic" word in 43:3a, the twofold **Fear not,** the presence of triads of verbs (42:23, 24cde; 43:7; cf. 43:1cd), the expanded oracular formula (43:1), and the vocabulary—all reveal the style and manner of the poet with whom we have become familiar. The problem of the strophic articulation is not simple, but if the present text is accepted in substantially its present form, then the division seems to be as follows: 42:18 (proem or appeal), 19-21, 22 (note the striking *wehû'*), 23-24, 25; 43:1-3a, 3b-4, 5-7; seven strophes in all, the last three forming a triad of their own design.

1. Proem or Appeal (42:18)

18. The opening call is to the **deaf** and the **blind,** and in this order. The common practice of inverting the lines is unhappy. Literary antecedents, the succeeding words in vs. 19, and the total impact of the first section of the poem (vss. 18-25) all argue for the text as it is. The imperatives with which the poem opens are frequent in the prophets, especially in Second Isaiah (cf. 41:1; 43:8, 9; 48:16; 49:1; 51:1; etc.). The mood of urgency and immediacy is present everywhere. But who are the deaf and the blind, and

---

the only true God. But life's alternatives are real issues. Our Lord did not content himself with proclaiming the blessed results of faith and fidelity; he was as plain-spoken as this poet in setting forth the consequences of neglect. One might extenuate it as due to thoughtlessness, but life's circumstances take no heed to excuses. Not only does the house built on a rock stand fast in a shattering storm, but also the house carelessly erected without foundation crashes "and the ruin of that house was great" (Luke 6:49).

42:18–43:7. *The Blind and Deaf Servant Judged and Redeemed.*—In the previous poem Israel had been called "blind" (42:16). How can

God employ such a nation to accomplish the salvation of mankind? Only by causing it to pass through the fire of his judgment and redeeming it by his grace. In this poem the prophet returns to the tradition of his predecessors, and dwells on God's discipline of his unperceptive people. This is the theme of the first half of the poem, 42:18-25. But this is not its final or even its chief message. The conclusion is a promise of redemption characteristic of this messenger of God's comfort.

History as we know it is a series of judgments. Men and nations reap as they sow. Only a realistic faith which sees in tragedies and disasters the hand of God renders him relevant to

19 Who *is* blind, but my servant? or deaf, as my messenger *that* I sent? who *is* blind as *he that is* perfect, and blind as the LORD's servant?

19 Who is blind but my servant,
    or deaf as my messenger whom I send?
Who is blind as my dedicated one,
    or blind as the servant of the LORD?

what is it that they do not hear and see? The succeeding lines answer these questions. The servant of the Lord is addressed (vs. 19), the same servant who has emerged with ever-growing clarity (vss. 1-4, 5-9; 41:8-10), whose mission it is to be the light to the nations, to open the eyes of the blind (vss. 6-7). "Pathetically enough, he is himself afflicted with the woes which he is to cure in others" (Levy, *Deutero-Isaiah*, p. 152). God himself will lead him by paths he has not known and will turn his darkness into light (vs. 16), a characteristic and strong preparation for the words of this poem. How different Second Isaiah is from Isaiah of Jerusalem here is seen by a comparison with the words in the vision of the latter. There deafness and blindness are the judgment upon Israel; here the prophet hears God commanding his contemporaries to **hear** and to **see**, for they, of all peoples, have much to hear and see. Blindness for Second Isaiah is the cardinal sin of Israel, as social injustice in Amos, infidelity in Hosea, rebellion in Isaiah, and apostasy in Jeremiah.

2. First Strophe: The Blind Servant (42:19-21)

The twofold **who** (cf. 40:12, 13; 41:2, 4), repeated in vss. 23-24 (cf. 40:26b; 41:26; 44:24; 50:8-10), does not require an answer. Who is so **blind** and who so **deaf** as Israel, the servant!

19. My servant: The LXX translates παῖδές μου, "my servants," a reading accepted by Duhm and many others but without sufficient reason. **My messenger whom I send:** The Vulg. reads, *nisi ad quem nuncios meos misi*, "as he to whom I have sent my messengers," an unwarranted and incorrect paraphrase. God has called Israel to service in the world, but she has not heeded the call; he has sent Israel on a great mission (vss. 1-4, 6-7), but she has not carried it out. The deaf and the blind are strongly emphasized and, with the proem, form an impressive climax in vs. 19cd. Originally, we may suppose, the words occurred in chiastic arrangement (reading "deaf" for **blind** in vs. 19c). Note the climactic force of vs. 19cd and the focus upon the **servant of the LORD**. **My dedicated one:** The LXX reads οἱ κυριεύοντες αὐτῶν, "they that rule over them" or "their rulers" (cf. משליהם), a reading accepted by Duhm and many others, but without justification. The presence of the servant is not removed so simply. The word משלם is translated in many different ways: "he that is at peace" (ASV), "made perfect" or "recompensed" (ASV mg.), "the purchased one" (Rosenmüller), "the devoted one" (Cheyne), "the confidant" or "submissive one" (cf. *muslim* and Job 5:23, Delitzsch *et al.*), "the befriended one" (Skinner), "one made whole" (Levy), "the perfected one" (Torrey and Buber). Graetz and Marti emend to *meshullāhî*, "my apostle." Others retain the Hebrew word *meshullām* as a proper name. Perhaps the best solution is that proposed by Kissane, "the covenanted one," derived from the verb meaning "to be in covenant of peace." The sequence of the central words is moving: **my servant, my messenger,** "the covenanted one," **the servant of the LORD.** These with the chiasmus of **blind, deaf, deaf, blind,** and

the whole of life. In this instance the judgment has happened in the destruction of the national independence and the captivity. But has this divine discipline really educated the nation?

In the proem (vs. 18) Israel is addressed as **deaf** and **blind.** Her mission is to open deaf ears and blind eyes; but she is suffering from the malady which afflicts the world to which she goes as physician. In the two immediately preceding poems the servant of the Lord has been shown his purpose (42:1-4) and has received the divine call (42:5-17). But has Israel seen and heard? The prophet is facing his people as he knows them.

19-21. God's Discipline of His People Seemingly Futile.—We often remark that experience is a great teacher. But is it? "Men are wise in proportion not to their experience, but to their capacity for experience. If we could learn from mere experience, the stones of London would

20 Seeing many things, but thou observest not; opening the ears, but he heareth not.	20 He sees[w] many things, but does not observe them; his ears are open, but he does not hear.
21 The LORD is well pleased for his righteousness' sake; he will magnify the law, and make *it* honorable.	21 The LORD was pleased, for his righteousness' sake, to magnify his law and make it glorious.

[w] Heb *you see*

the repeated question **who** reflect the importance of the verse in the writer's thought. The contrast between the messenger and his blindness and deafness is basic to an understanding of the prophet's portrait of the servant (see Buber, *Prophetic Faith,* pp. 222-23).

20. He sees many things: The C.T. reads "you have seen," which is also the reading of the Dead Sea Scroll. Torrey argues strongly for the participle "seeing," but the finite verb is more emphatic and smoother after the impressive questions. The LXX and the Targ. read the second person plural. **His ears are open.** The Dead Sea Scroll reads the third person plural of another verb also meaning **open** (פתחו). The Hebrew has **he does not hear,** but about sixty MSS have the second person, which is doubtless the true reading. Israel's blindness and deafness is the more terrible and inexplicable because no nation has seen and heard what she has. What nation had such a history? What people could boast such a succession of men of God as Abraham and Moses and David and the prophets? What nation had experienced such mighty events as the Exodus, the revelation at Sinai, the wonders of the Conquest, and the wonder of the prophets sent by God in the midst of these events? It was a history of revelation which was known by what was seen and apprehended by the hearing of faith (cf. Deut. 4:7-8, 32; 5:26; 20:3-4; Pss. 78; 105:5; 136).

21. To magnify his law: The LXX reads תודה, "thanksgiving" or "praise," for תורה, law, "teaching," or "revelation." The latter is surely the right reading. But does the verse belong here? The language and diction are certainly the writer's; the reference to the law or teaching recalls 42:4, which is also a climax to the strophe; and vs. 24e, another climax, supports it. Many scholars, however, reject the verse in its entirety. But the evidence is not decisive against it, and the meaning is clear. It was God's sure and steadfast purpose (למען צדקו) to reveal himself through his servant Israel to all the nations. His teaching through the Mosaic revelation, through his servants the prophets, and through his ministers in the cult was lodged deep within Israel and continued to exist in her. It was to this revelation that she was now so blind that she could not see.

be wiser than its wisest men."[7] All that befalls some men and nations seems only to add to the sum total of their inexperience, leaving them more confused and less perceptive. How little mankind appears to have learned from two devastating world wars! If exiled Israel lived through revealing events, if she saw **many things,** what of our generation? One wonders what future historians of the twentieth century will say that mankind observed and heard (vs. 20).

If the mass of mankind are unperceptive, what of the Christian church? It is the **servant** of the Lord whom the prophet addresses. That servant is spoken of as **my messenger** and **my dedicated one.** It was a saying of Pasteur's that "in the fields of observation, chance only favours the mind which is prepared."[8] The church is called to be the people prepared for God's advents in history (cf. Luke 1:17). Such preparation for observing God in past and present events comes through obedience to his will in so far as we grasp it. Jesus asserted that obedience is the organ of spiritual knowledge (John 7:17). This poet is confident that God is at work through Cyrus and the sequels of his campaigns. One supreme result is the liberation of Israel to become "a light to the nations" (vs. 6). But to this the mass of the people were unresponsive. They had neither ears to hear nor eyes to see. It is a similar obtuseness which we have most to fear. In every age God works mightily for his people; but how few of them

[7] G. B. Shaw, *Maxims for Revolutionists* (London: Constable & Co., 1930), pp. 225-26.

[8] R. Vallery-Radot, *The Life of Pasteur* (tr. Mrs. R. L. Devonshire; Garden City: Doubleday, Page & Co., 1924), p. 79.

22 But this *is* a people robbed and spoiled; *they are* all of them snared in holes, and they are hid in prison houses: they are for a prey, and none delivereth; for a spoil, and none saith, Restore.

23 Who among you will give ear to this? *who* will hearken and hear for the time to come?

22 But this is a people robbed and plundered,
  they are all of them trapped in holes
    and hidden in prisons;
  they have become a prey with none to rescue,
    a spoil with none to say, "Restore!"
23 Who among you will give ear to this,
    will attend and listen for the time to come?

3. Second Strophe: A People Plundered and Preyed Upon (42:22)

22. The strophe begins, as frequently in O.T. poetry, with an emphatic pronoun, וְהוּא, "but it," which forms a sharp contrast to what has just preceded. The people to whom the divine revelation came, whose way through history was illumined and guided by divine Providence, whose existence was described by the purpose of God, now lies languishing in exile, scattered throughout the earth in degradation and lostness. But it is Yahweh who has brought this judgment upon them because they would not listen to his teaching (vs. 24e). The picture is, of course, exaggerated. The prophet seems to be describing Israel's present condition under the figure of a caravan attacked by the Bedouin in the desert, plundered and robbed, held prisoner in holes of the ground, and forgotten by those who might have rescued them (Volz, Frey). Observe how the writer heaps up his words: **robbed, plundered, trapped, hidden, a prey, a spoil.** Notice, too, how the words **prey** and **spoil** are played upon in different ways to form a twofold triad (vss. 22a, 22de, and 24ab). The verb translated **trapped** (*hapheah*) appears as a Hiphil infinitive absolute, but should be emended with Lowth and many others to the Pual (*huphahu*), and "in the holes" (so M.T.) should be read without the article (see KJV, RSV).

4. Third Strophe: Israel Sent into Exile (42:23-24)

23. The third strophe returns to the opening of the first with a twofold **who.** The answer required to the second is the same as in 40:12; 41:2, 4 (also a twofold "who"). Here the emphasis is upon hearing rather than seeing: **give ear, attend, listen.** That the people who had ears to hear should not hear is the tragedy that appalls the prophet. Who among you, he asks pointedly, will now give heed for the future (לְאָחוֹר)? The ear is the instrument for the discernment of history and revelation, for words have the same movement and temporal reality that events do. God's purpose transcends the darkness of the present hour. Second Isaiah is speaking within the covenant community for whom past, present, and future are native categories, and here he turns from Israel's

have any inkling of it! Paul asked the Galatians, "Did you experience so many things in vain?" (Gal. 3:4). In Israel's case it has been the most painful discipline which God had given, and yet the nation is deaf and blind (vs. 20).

22. *Israel Like a Plundered Caravan.*—Israel has been trapped and imprisoned. How similar is the plight of our once proud and wealthy Western world! Our civilization was like a rich caravan going its careless way unaware of the robbers lying in wait for it. But it has been **plundered** by devastating wars. The standard of living has everywhere been lowered, and resources which might have been devoted to human welfare have been wasted in ruinous

strife. There is **none to say, "Restore!"** The losses are irreparable—in lives which might have enriched the culture and religion of the century, in irreplaceable architectural and artistic treasures, in the physical equipment for manufacturing goods, for education, for scientific investigation, for the work and worship of the church.

23-24. *The Unrecognized Educator.*—Do those who have suffered the tragedies of history know who has been judging them in wrath? Has our plundered generation grasped the meaning of what has befallen its world? Do we understand that behind events are moral factors?

24 Who gave Jacob for a spoil, and Israel to the robbers? did not the Lord, he against whom we have sinned? for they would not walk in his ways, neither were they obedient unto his law.

25 Therefore he hath poured upon him the fury of his anger, and the strength of battle: and it hath set him on fire round about, yet he knew not; and it burned him, yet he laid *it* not to heart.

24 Who gave up Jacob to the spoiler,
   and Israel to the robbers?
Was it not the Lord, against whom we
   have sinned,
in whose ways they would not walk,
   and whose law they would not obey?
25 So he poured upon him the heat of his
   anger
and the might of battle;
it set him on fire round about, but he did
   not understand;
it burned him, but he did not take it
   to heart.

precarious present to the future. What gives content to these "times" is law and grace, but it is grace, not law, which has the final word (for style cf. 43:9c).

24. For a spoil (KJV): Read with RSV, **to the spoiler** (so *Qerê* and the Dead Sea Scroll).

5. Fourth Strophe: The Fire of Judgment (42:25)

25. The might of battle: An alternative rendering is "the violence of war." The imagery of **fire** is common in O.T. scenes of judgment. Israel did not grasp the significance of what she was suffering as the work and intention of God. She **did not take . . . to heart** the events which were God's words of judgment against her.

At the turn of the century, William Watson, who complained (in his sonnet, "I think the immortal servants of mankind") of

> . . . Man's barren levity of mind,
> .   .   .   .
> The eye to all majestic meanings blind,[9]

pictured "Europe at the Play." He saw her, like ancient Rome, oblivious and callous to what her strivings for power were causing:

> High was her glory's noon: as yet
> She had not dreamed her sun could set!
> .   .   .   .
> Another's pangs she counted nought;
> Of human hearts she took no thought.[1]

Then he prophesied, employing a metaphor of Second Isaiah (vs. 25):

> Yet haply she shall learn, too late,
> In some blind hurricane of Fate,
> How fierily alive the things
> She held as fools' imaginings.[1]

Those who lived through the two world wars had reason to appreciate this seer's vision. But how many of our contemporaries even now have ears and eyes for the living God in the occurrences of history or in the experiences of their

[9] From *The Poems of Sir William Watson, 1878-1935* (London: George G. Harrap & Co., 1936). Used by permission.
[1] *Ibid.*

own lives? There is a Controller of events who speaks in and through them.

Writing of the disastrous defeat which the Scots suffered at Solway Moss, John Knox said:

> Worldly men may think that all this came but by misorder and fortune, as they term it; but whosoever hath the least spunk [i.e., spark] of the knowledge of God may as evidently see the work of his hand in this discomfiture, as ever was seen in any of the battles left to us in register by the Holy Ghost.[2]

If through the prophet's question **Who?** we are led to recognize God's presence in both public events and personal experiences, we may become God's servants with ears and eyes.

25. *Unperceiving Israel.*—This concluding strophe of the first part of the poem describes Israel in the midst of things "fierily alive," still obtuse and uncomprehending.

Modern Christians dislike such references to God's **anger**. It is part of our sentimentality and also of our superficiality. Unless God is capable of anger he cannot really love. He cares intensely. After hearing Daniel Webster speak, Emerson entered in his *Journal:* "His splendid wrath, when his eyes became fires, is as good to see, so intellectual it is, and the wrath of the fact and cause he espouses, and not at all personal to himself." [3]

[2] *History of the Reformation in Scotland,* Bk. I, 1542.
[3] Boston: Houghton Mifflin Co., 1911, VI, 431-32.

43 But now thus saith the LORD that created thee, O Jacob, and he that formed thee, O Israel, Fear not: for I have redeemed thee, I have called *thee* by thy name; thou *art* mine.

43 But now thus says the LORD,
he who created you, O Jacob,
he who formed you, O Israel:
"Fear not, for I have redeemed you;
    I have called you by name, you are
    mine.

6. FIFTH STROPHE: GRACE BEYOND JUDGMENT (43:1-3*b*)

43:1. The second part of the poem is a counterpart to the first. There the theme was predominantly one of judgment; here it is redemption. There it was the past and present, here the future. There the picture was Israel, here it is God. Yet these contrasts must not be stated too strongly, for the two sections of the poem are written in relation to each other, and God and Israel are present in both parts. Yet there is a break here as the opening words indicate: **but now** (cf. 44:1; 47:8; 49:5). Thereupon follows the oracular formula, **Thus says the LORD,** expanded in the usual manner of Second Isaiah. Such expansions always have a content suited to their contexts. As the opening words of revelation are followed by creation, so the oracular imperative **Fear not** is followed by redemption, the two focuses of the prophet's eschatology. Revelation comes first, then creation, then redemption. Israel lives between beginning and end, her creation and redemption, but both stand in the matrix of revelation. The rest is the interlude of history. They are the ground of her existence: of her understanding of who she is, of her origin and destiny.

He who created you: An alternative rendering is "your Creator . . . and your Fashioner" (cf. 44:2, 21, 24; 45:11; 49:1). God was and is Israel's creator. Israel does not view her creation as an event which constituted a permanent, immanent reality of her being; rather, it was a unique event which brought her into existence, by which Yahweh chose her to be his people, and yet in every moment of her life she was dependent upon his deeds, ever new and ever the result of his will and purpose and grace (cf. Walther Eichrodt, *Theologie des Alten Testaments* [2nd ed., Leipzig: J. C. Hinrichs, 1948], II, 78

Wrath in God is as redemptive as his love. We can rest confident that the world's evils will be cleansed away because "our God is a consuming fire" (Heb. 12:29)—words penned by one who entered most profoundly into our Lord's ministry of sympathy, and kept ever before him the sacrifice of the Cross.

And yet the effect of God's advent in anger had apparently been nil. Israel **did not understand, . . . did not take it to heart.** This is one of the most striking declarations of God's failure. One sees God doing his utmost and Israel untouched and unmoved. "How often would I, . . . and you would not!" (Matt. 23:37.)

43:1-3a. God's Amazing Grace.—In sharp contrast to the preceding strophes of judgment, this strophe begins with a momentous **But now.** God is never finally defeated, never at his last resort. It is not that Israel repents or shows the least sign of responsiveness. There is nothing in his people which encourages him. All that follows is his sheer grace. Robert Rainy, writing to a correspondent troubled with his own sinfulness and lack of vital religion, used this striking description: "Grace is goodness that

triumphs over all reasons to the contrary."[4] It is when the human situation appears utterly desperate that God graciously intervenes: **But now thus says the LORD.**

He comes to the rescue as the creator and fashioner of the nation. He will not forsake the work of his own hands (Ps. 138:8). That would be to confess the utter failure of his plan for the world's redemption. Israel falls back on her divine origin. God chose and formed her for a particular purpose. However unworthy she may prove, however unresponsive to him, he can be counted on not to abandon the purpose on which he has embarked. It is the apostle's confidence concerning Christians—"I am sure that he who began a good work in you will bring it to completion" (Phil. 1:6). There are occasions when we become discouraged with the church. She seems so dead, with no realization of her role in society or of God's exhaustless resources at her disposal. Then is the time to stay ourselves on the recollection that God created and formed the church. She may lack all signs of

[4] P. Carnegie Simpson, *The Life of Principal Rainy* (London: Hodder & Stoughton, 1909), I, 423.

2 When thou passest through the waters,
I *will be* with thee; and through the rivers,
they shall not overflow thee: when thou
walkest through the fire, thou shalt not be
burned; neither shall the flame kindle upon
thee.

2 When you pass through the waters I will
  be with you;
  and through the rivers, they shall not
  overwhelm you;
  when you walk through fire you shall not
  be burned,
  and the flame shall not consume you.

and references cited [Exod. 34:10; Num. 16:30; Isa. 43:1, 15; 45:7; 48:7; 54:16; 57:19; 65:18; Pss. 51:12; 102:19; Eccl. 12:1]). The address **O Jacob, O Israel** is thus very personal (see 41:8). The relationship is rooted in the election, the historical event of the Exodus from Egypt, and in the covenant event concluded on Sinai, which are always remembered and yet given enriched content by the experience of new "creations" in Israel's life. **Fear not:** The ancient theophanic word stands in the center of a great context. Israel's life is all of God's grace and is grasped by faith. **I have redeemed, . . . I have called you by name, you are mine:** The first two verbs are prophetic perfects. They do not record what has happened—although Israel had already known the meaning of the verbs in her own history—but rather what is about to happen. The time of Israel's redemption draws near. Redemption comes first—this the prophet always knows—then naming, then covenant. God's naming gives to Israel her identity, character, history, and uniqueness (cf. Gen. 32:24-30; Exod. 33:12, 16; Isa. 45:3, 4). Israel is Yahweh's special possession, a precious treasure (cf. Exod. 19:5; Moshe Greenberg, "Hebrew *segulla*: Akkadian *sikiltu*," *Journal of the American Oriental Society,* LXXI [1951], 172-74). She is conscious of belonging to him, and this belonging is the source of her confidence and hope. Observe the general structure of the verse: a transition, **but now;** an oracular formula of revelation; two participles in apposition with Yahweh, "your Creator" and "your Fashioner"; two vocatives; an opening cry, **Fear not,** expanded by an impressive triad introduced by *kî,* for, culminating in the covenant words, **you are mine.** The message of redemption is set in a universal eschatological framework.

2-3b. The next three double lines begin with the particle *kî,* **when.** The last of them (absent from the Dead Sea Scroll) with a different force from the other two **(for)** forms the climax of the strophe. The figures of **fire** and **waters** as symbols of danger are

being his handiwork; but he has gifted her with his Spirit, and "the gifts and the call of God are irrevocable" (Rom. 11:29).

The creation and fashioning are not a past act merely; they are continuing, even in the dire process of judgment which has taken the people into exile. One is reminded that modern men dwell on the continuance of God's creative work in nature:

> Ever fresh the broad creation,
> A divine improvisation,
> From the heart of God proceeds.[5]

God is no more finished with his church or with any of its members. It is his unfailing work which supplies assurance when nothing seems as it should be. And even beyond his creation of the nation, the exiles are reminded that God has **redeemed** them. This is the new and distinctive message of Second Isaiah. **I have called you by name, you are mine.** God's name, his

reputation, is at stake. He cannot allow it to be said that those who were called his people turned out such a disappointment that he had to abandon them. This is akin to the great argument for "a continuing city" in the N.T. "Therefore God is not ashamed to be called their God, for he has prepared for them a city" (Heb. 11:16).

This is an even stronger encouragement for the Christian church. We look back to Calvary. It was there that God created for himself a people to be his agents in the world's salvation. Is the passion of Christ to go for nought? This is the supreme plea of a sinner:

> *Quaerens me sedisti lassus,*
> *Redemisti crucem passus;*
> *Tantus labor non sit cassus!* [6]

It is all this—God's creation and redemption of the nation—which prompts the prophet to declare his distinctive gospel—**fear not.**

---

[5] Ralph Waldo Emerson, "Woodnotes II."

[6] Thomas of Celano, *Dies Irae,* st. x.

| 3 For I *am* the Lord thy God, the Holy One of Israel, thy Saviour: I gave Egypt *for* thy ransom, Ethiopia and Seba for thee. | 3 For I am the Lord your God, the Holy One of Israel, your Savior. I give Egypt as your ransom, Ethiopia and Seba in exchange for you. |

paralleled in the Psalms (66:12; cf. 32:6; 42:7). Some scholars see reminiscences of the Exodus here. The LXX and the Syriac omit the preposition **through** in vs. 2*b* and thus make the line parallel with vs. 2*d*. The people of God are under the constant protection of their God in the hour of his redemption. The strophe ends (contra RSV) with the expanded covenant word (vs. 3*ab*). Thus beginning and end form a framework of revelation: "Yahweh your Creator and your Redeemer" and "Yahweh, the Holy One of Israel and your Savior." In this theocentric context Israel has nothing to fear. For **your Savior** the Dead Sea Scroll reads "your Redeemer." There is no reason for suspecting the Hebrew text (cf. vss. 11; 44:2; 45:15, 21; 49:26; also 60:16; 63:8). The word bears a concrete sense: help, deliverance from distress, Yahweh's victory over his enemies. The language is probably derived from the theophany. In the heart of the revelation are the assurances and promises whose fulfillment is expected.

7. Sixth Strophe: Yahweh's Ransom for Israel (43:3c-5a)

3c. Here again history and eschatology meet. The mention of **Egypt, Ethiopia,** and **Seba** doubtless refers to their expected conquest by Cyrus. Actually, Egypt was first

The ordeal now confronting the people is described as a passage through **fire** and **waters** (cf. Ps. 66:12). God's gracious assurance is of his companionship throughout. No intimation is given that the circumstances will be made less terrible. The difference is his presence. The political scene was alarming and confusing. A small and defenseless people was exposed to mighty and ruthless military powers. They had nothing to sustain them but their God—that surely was all-sufficient. An eminent British surgeon, Lord Moynihan of Leeds, operating before a group of distinguished surgeons from many lands, was asked how he could do it apparently unperturbed.

"Well, it is like this: there are just three people in the theater when I operate—the patient and myself."
"But that is only two; who is the third?"
And Moynihan replied quietly, "God."

It is those who do their work as ever in the "great Taskmaster's eye," who are set free from inhibiting fears.

I will be with you—nothing is said of the people's awareness of God's presence. His presence is a conviction, not a feeling. A surgeon with knife in hand must concentrate upon his delicate task: he cannot be thinking of anything else. It is so with the experiences through which we pass. They require all our mental energies to cope with them. We cannot spare at the time

a thought even for God. But his presence is never to be estimated by our consciousness of it. In the ordeal by fire, vividly pictured in Dan. 3:25, where it is said that the spectators saw beside the three faithful Israelites in the flames of persecution a fourth "like the Son of God," there is no indication that the three had a sense of his fellowship. The Bible lays no stress upon our emotions or awarenesses. It asserts the fact of God's constant presence with his people. "Lo, I am with you" was the final promise of the Master (Matt. 28:20); but nothing is said of our sensation of his comradeship (cf. Expos. on 41:8-10). Few complaints from tried Christians are commoner than this, "I cannot feel God with me." In this poem the insensitiveness of Israel to the experiences of calamity (42:25) is dwelt on. Faith has always to make an effort and assert that in and behind happenings is the living God. When we assert our conviction, feelings, apparently dormant or dead, awake.

3b-5a. God's Disposition of Peoples for Israel.—The prophet turns to contemporary history as an added proof of God's fidelity to his own nation. He sees Cyrus sweeping westward and turning south toward Egypt and the lands in northeast Africa. Egypt, Ethiopia, and Seba are to be given him as a ransom for Israel. In fact not Cyrus but his son Cambyses II made these conquests; yet the prophet's conviction remains that God is Lord of all peoples, disposing of them for his gracious purpose. It is not said that Israel is to become a world power; these peoples

4 Since thou wast precious in my sight, thou hast been honorable, and I have loved thee: therefore will I give men for thee, and people for thy life.

4 Because you are precious in my eyes, and honored, and I love you, I give men in return for you, peoples in exchange for your life.

---

conquered by Cambyses, the son of Cyrus, but the prophet had every reason to expect that Africa would be next in Cyrus' plan of world conquest (cf. Herodotus *History* I. 153 and especially Xenophon's *Cyropaedia* VIII. 6. 20). The imagery is drawn from the negotiations in the act of redemption where the next of kin pays the ransom money for the release of the enslaved person. Here Yahweh is to give the wealthy peoples in exchange for his beloved people, and it is a heavy price he is to pay. This measures how precious a treasure Israel is to him. Literalistic interpretations do violence to the meaning.

4. Because you are precious, . . . and honored, and I love you: The clauses are co-ordinate and are not to be taken in the temporal sense of the KJV and the ASV. The triad of clauses presses even further the remarkable words of the previous strophe. The love of God serves as a motive throughout the poems, and here again Second Isaiah is true to traditions that reach back to the origins of Israel's faith. In the hour of redemption the love of God achieves its greatest work. The prophet exhausts every symbol at his disposal to express the depth and power of the divine love, and here it appears in a most spacious and universal context, drawn partly from contemporary history, partly from eschatological imagination, partly from the covenant tradition (cf., e.g., Exod. 19:5). There is nothing that God will not give—so the prophet seems to be saying—in exchange for Israel. **I give men:** The Dead Sea Scroll reads *hā'ādhām*, "man." Duhm and other scholars read אדמות, "lands"; Volz, אלפים, "thousands," on the basis of 60:22; Torrey, איים, "coastlands." Of these proposals Torrey's gives the best parallelism (cf. 41:1; 49:1). On **honored** cf. 49:5; on the **love** of God cf. 49:14 ff.; 54:6-8 *et passim*.

---

are not made her dependents; they are accorded to Cyrus, while the Lord of nations gives Israel her freedom that she may discharge her spiritual mission to them and to all mankind.

For Americans, long accustomed to regard themselves as a people remote from the struggles of the powers and destined to work out national life apart from others, it has been hard to be thrust into the midst of world conflicts, and more difficult to be confronted with responsibility for leadership due to unique wealth and power. No more than Israel is the United States destined to dominate other lands. That would ruin the ideal of liberty to which God has dedicated the country. Its mission, like hers, is to be his and their servant, embodying his justice and friendship, standing among them not to be ministered unto but to minister. It is a most difficult role, for in a self-seeking world a servant nation is misunderstood, and may easily misunderstand itself, uncritical of its own motives and policies. Unconsciously a well-meaning people may employ power to coerce others to its will, rather than to aid them in discovering God's distinctive purpose for themselves. If of God's mercy the United States employs its wealth and power for their relief and strength-

ening, the fatal temptation to smugness is ever at hand. Against that there is only one defense—the conviction of God's fellowship, and the reverent upward look toward the Holy One, abasing pride and keeping a nation humble before him.

When one recalls the harsh judgment on deaf and blind Israel, one is startled by the divine assertion:

> **You are precious in my eyes, and honored, and I love you.**

What was there in this people which rendered her precious, honorable, and lovable? We are thrown back upon the ultimate mystery of God's election. Another O.T. writer is puzzled by God's choice (Deut. 7:7). He can give no reason to account for it except God's inexplicable love and his fidelity to his covenant with the patriarchs. There is always this element of mystery in God's grace. Paul spoke of it in his own case, "I am the least of the apostles, unfit to be called an apostle" (I Cor. 15:9); "To me, though I am the very least of all the saints, this grace was given" (Eph. 3:8). Grace is love working in the face of everything which appears to render it impossible.

5 Fear not; for I *am* with thee: I will bring thy seed from the east, and gather thee from the west:

6 I will say to the north, Give up; and to the south, Keep not back: bring my sons from far, and my daughters from the ends of the earth;

5 Fear not, for I am with you;
I will bring your offspring from the east,
and from the west I will gather you;
6 I will say to the north, Give up,
and to the south, Do not withhold;
bring my sons from afar
and my daughters from the end of the earth,

5a. The strophe ends with a repetition of the exclamation **Fear not.** The assurance that God is with Israel in the turbulent years of her history must sustain her. The realization that in the midst of world events he is the universal God of all nations and of all history, and that he nevertheless stands in unique relation to her should remove all fear and help her to view all that is happening with courage and faith. The "I-thou" relationship in all its varying forms and contexts (subjects, objects, possessives, and the concluding **thy life** of vs. 4) culminates in the simple and final assurance **I am with thee** (see vs. 2a; cf. Pss. 23:4; 73:23). The next strophe articulates the relation magnificently.

8. Seventh Strophe: Return of the Diaspora (43:5b-7)

5b-6. The final strophe describes the home gathering of Israel. From every quarter of the globe they will come, **east** and **west** and **north** and **south** (see Gen. 28:14 [J]). None will **withhold,** but all will respond to the divine command to allow the dispersed people to return. As once they were freed from bondage in Egypt to journey to the Promised Land, so now in an even greater exodus they will come from the ends of the earth. The evidence of a fairly early dispersion "throughout the world" is now widely recognized. There is no attempt to explain how so large a population will be able to live in so small a land, as there is in Ezekiel and the later apocalyptical writers. The ardor and passion of faith in the time of redemption dissipates all mundane problems. **My sons . . . and my daughters:** Here the "I-thou" relationship of God and Israel is given

5b-7. The Reassembling of Dispersed Israel.— One of the disheartening circumstances which confronted the exiles was the scattering of their people all over the then known world. They were not a united community in Babylon, but had been sold into slavery in many lands or had dispersed themselves in their efforts to earn a living.

The instinct which made them feel incapable of their divine national mission unless their unity was restored was a correct instinct. Social organisms must be units spiritually in order to fulfill their functions. God's purpose for a nation or for his church involves them as wholes. To be sure, when God calls a community, national or ecclesiastical, the call is perceived and answered at first by a small minority with insight and faith. But if only a fraction of its members is alive to God, the inert majority thwart his aim and prove a drag on the dedicated few. Nation or church "moveth all together" when it moves forcefully. Indifferent segments in a nation's citizenry or a church's membership chill the ardor and frustrate the endeavors of their awakened fellows. An up-

surge of consecration, like a tidal wave, must sweep all elements in a people into a united effort. This is the work of the Spirit of God. It is he who must gather from east and west, and say to the north, **Give up,** and to the south, **Keep not back.**

Hegel defined tragedy as "the division of the spiritual substance against itself." Nations become tragic when spiritual tensions set their people in antagonistic groups. One thinks of France in World War II. This is more acutely tragic in spiritual communities like the Christian church. Class divisions and racial segregations wreck her spiritual solidarity. Contemporary Protestantism has no more serious impediment to its missionary work at home and abroad than the limitation of many of its congregations to those of one race or of one class. This is the nemesis of fellowship, the destruction of the communion of the Holy Spirit. The modern urge to reunite the church into one organized fellowship is akin to this prophet's wholesome instinct which felt Israel's reassembling essential for the fulfillment of her world mission. A divided church cannot integrate a world rent

7 *Even* every one that is called by my name: for I have created him for my glory, I have formed him; yea, I have made him.

8 ¶ Bring forth the blind people that have eyes, and the deaf that have ears.

7 every one who is called by my name,
    whom I created for my glory,
    whom I formed and made."

8 Bring forth the people who are blind, yet have eyes,
    who are deaf, yet have ears!

---

characteristic content (cf. 41:8). In the early tradition already Israel had known God as her Father (Exod. 4:22-23; Hos. 11:1; Isa. 1:2; cf. also Jer. 3:4, 19; 31:9; Hos. 1:10; Isa. 63:16; 64:8; Mal. 1:6).

7. The conclusion forms the close not only of the strophe but of the whole poem. United Israel, all the sons and daughters of God, all who bear his **name** (cf. 44:5) and are known as "Yahweh's people," will return. And the people's return, like everything else, is for the **glory** of God (cf. 42:8*b*, 12*a* and observe again how the closing lines connect with the previous poem; see 42:17). **Created, formed,** and **made:** In this closing triad the prophet forges the oracle of salvation into a perfect whole (cf. vs. 1). Redemption and creation are the two final notes as they are the first of the oracle (vss. 1-7) addressed to the people who are blind and deaf (42:18-25).

F. Yahweh and Israel (43:8-13)

The poem opens with a characteristic appeal or call (vs. 8; see Exeg. on 42:18). Then follow three strophes (vss. 9, 10, 11-13), each with its own opening and close. The first concerns the nations, the second Israel, the third the one God Yahweh. The parallelism of the lines is exceptionally clear and all the literary phenomena encountered in the preceding poems are present in this composition. The use of repetition is especially revealing. First we have that of the **blind . . . deaf** motif (cf. 42:18-19). Then there is the striking repetition of **who** at the beginning and end of Yahweh's address (vss. 9*c*, 13*e*). More impressive is the threefold reference to **the witnesses,** the second major theme of the poem (once in each strophe, vss. 9*e*, 10*a*, 12*c*), two of them the ordination words to Israel: **you are my witnesses** (cf. "you are my servant" in 41:8-9; 44:21 *et passim*). By far the most important, however, is the divine use of the first person (אֲנִי, אָנֹכִי, "I, even I"). Three double lines in the final strophe begin with the first personal pronoun (for the text of vs. 13*a* see Exeg. below) and in the first instance it occurs twice. Observe also the threefold **I am He** (vs. 10*d*), **I am God** (vs. 13*a* [Hebrew vs. 12*e*], **I am He** (vs. 13*a*), emphatic assertions by God himself of his oneness. Such divine self-asseverations are the classical expressions of Hebrew monotheism. The threefold negative (וְאֵין, "and there is no . . . ," vss. 11*b*, 12, 13*b*) accentuates God's exclusive deity. The prophet has purposely employed both the literary form of the judicial process (cf. 41:1 ff., 21 ff.) and

---

by racial, class, and national tensions. Her separated communions must hear God's **Give up,** spoken to their complacent self-sufficiency, and his **Do not withhold,** spoken to their unwillingness to share whatever gifts have come to them through their distinctive traditions. This is a noble text for church unity. When Christ's followers of all nations, races, economic classes, and cultural levels become "of one accord" under his lordship, the Spirit can descend and work through them in power.

The ingathering and unification of the people of God is not for their sakes alone (vs. 7). Their reassembling enables them to discharge their mission to mankind and to show forth God's

glory. His **glory** is the manifestation of what he is. It is his self-revelation. The nations will see what God is like in his people's renewed and unified life. In the N.T. the same end is sought in the genuine unification of the church: "And the glory which thou gavest me I have given them; that they may be one, even as we are one: I in them, and thou in me, that they may be made perfect in one; and that the world may know . . ." (John 17:22-23).

8-13. *The Lord Alone Is God, and Israel Is His Witness.*—This poem depicts another trial scene like that in ch. 41, where all nations and Israel are summoned into the divine presence. A major value in these prophecies is their fac-

9 Let all the nations be gathered together, and let the people be assembled: who among them can declare this, and show us former things? let them bring forth their witnesses, that they may be justified: or let them hear, and say, It is truth.

9 Let all the nations gather together,
   and let the peoples assemble.
Who among them can declare this,
   and show us the former things?
Let them bring their witnesses to justify
   them,
   and let them hear and say, It is true.

---

brevity of style to focus his message. The style is throughout eager and passionate, intense and urgent. And this passionate speech is God's.

Present again are the three major dramatis personae of the poems: God, the nations, and Israel. A strophe is devoted to each, with God the speaker throughout (vss. 9c-13). The meaning of prediction (cf. 41:21 ff.) ; the significance of history; the election of Israel; the activity, eternity, oneness, and saving power of God; and the servant of the Lord all receive emphasis. The two major emphases of the poem constitute a new element, new in the intensity with which they are asserted: the oneness of God and the mission Israel, as his witness.

1. PROEM OR SUMMONS (43:8)

The new poem connects admirably with the preceding.

8. Bring forth the people: Not from exile but before the court of justice as in 41:1, 21. The verb is in the Hiphil perfect, but should be pointed in the imperative, as there is no clear subject. In contrast to the negative judgment of the invective of 42:18-25, the attitude toward Israel, **blind** and **deaf,** is more affirmative because of the words which precede (vss. 1-7). It is true the people are **blind** and **deaf,** but they **have eyes** to see and **ears** to hear. They have been witness to events of the past, and they are still a witness to these events even though they do not grasp their meaning or heed their warning (cf. 42:20). They were custodians of a tradition which had been enshrined in narrative epics and interpreted in prophetic oracles. This is what their eyes have seen and their ears heard.

2. FIRST STROPHE: THE HISTORICAL ISSUE (43:9)

9. A six-line strophe devoted to the **nations.** All the nations are gathered together because the disclosures of the divine revelation concern them specifically. The KJV, the RSV, and others read the jussive in both verbs. The first, however, is Niphal perfect,

---

ing the church everywhere with God's expectation of her. It is easy for any congregation to become local in its horizons. But as part of the universal community of the people of God, Christians in every place must live in the presence both of God and of all nations. Without the personal relation to him, and the universal relation to the entire race, Christians cannot understand their commission.

8. The Citation to Appear.—This connects with the two preceding poems by addressing Israel as

> . . . the people who are blind, yet have eyes,
> who are deaf, yet have ears!

They had witnessed God's mighty acts for them in the past; they were witnessing his mighty acts in the present, although they did not grasp their significance or fully recognize his presence. Is this not a true description of the con-

temporary church? We are aware that we live in critical days when current events are changing the face of the world. Christians know that God who controls history has spoken to his people in days gone by, and that he is surely speaking in the present. But we have a confused sense of what events mean. Many of us are dimly conscious of his more personal dealings with us. We feel ourselves pushed and urged; we find situations demanding a change in our manner of thought and life; but while we are certain that something momentous is occurring all about us and claiming our attention and devotion, we are left vague and bewildered. We have eyes but are blind, hear but are deaf. We need this direct command to face God and our world and become clear as to our duty.

9. The Question Put.—The first strophe addresses the nations, who are as definitely concerned as is Israel in God's inclusive purpose.

"and the peoples are assembled." The situation is similar to the trial of the nations described in 41:1 ff., 21 ff. Here the issue is repeated: **Who among them can declare this?** (Cf. 41:2a, 4a; 42:23a, 26; 48:14b; etc.; for form cf. also 40:12-13, 26b.) Who can foretell the imminent redemption described in vss. 1-7? And who among them can **show** or proclaim (lit., "cause to hear") **the former things,** the events that have taken place in the past? The answer has already been given to these crucial queries (41:21 ff.). Yet the nations are appealed to again. If they can produce satisfactory **witnesses,** then **they may be justified.** The root of the verb is the same as that for "righteous," but here it belongs (as in 41:26b) to legal parlance (cf. also vs. 26). In the court of law the "guilty" person was declared rāshā‘, the "innocent," çaddîq. In the trial against the nations the verdict had been "guilty." Yet here the opportunity for witnesses is given so that their evidence may prove them "right" or "innocent." But this innocence before the court of God will not be neutral guiltlessness. If they are proved right, the issue for history and religion will be momentous. There will be validity in their claims and reality in their gods. The witnesses will listen to what the gods (and the nations) have to claim, and they will stand in court before the judge and confirm what the gods have had to declare; they will say **It is true.** They will speak what they have heard. Yahweh invited the encounter with the nations' gods, but of course there is no answer (so the prophet is

---

They with their gods, as in ch. 41, are marshaled before God. And they are posed again with the question of the meaning of history:

**Who among them can declare this,
and show us the former things?**

Anyone who studies the non-Christian faiths is impressed with their lack of all sense of the message of the past and of the present in human affairs. They deal with awesome aspects of nature, or they bid their devotees sink inward and indulge in mystic contemplation of the Infinite. But the pageant of mankind's life marches on, and they have nothing to tell men of its true significance. They do not think and feel and decide the issues in history.

One rival philosophy of life is a portent and factor in current history—communism. Its devotees believe that main trends in the human scene sustain their movement and its ideals. These trends are altogether materialistic—economic forces which direct and control men's minds. Communism is an heir, even though heretical, of the Hebrew-Christian tradition. Communism's dependence upon historic movements stems from this tradition. This fact renders it a serious antagonist for spiritual faith. It leaves no room for the direct activity of the God of righteousness. Its standards actually derive from its materialistic determinism, not from the character of the God revealed in the prophets and incarnate in Christ; but its fanatical assurance comes from the conviction that its aims have the backing of tidal forces in history. Its prophets have no hesitation in showing **the former things,** and in predicting what is to be. Faith's most serious rivals are always those who are heirs in part of God's self-revelation. One thinks of Mohammedanism, with its indebtedness to "the people of the Book." Communism, similarly, is partially Christian. To be "partially Christian" is to have truth but to have it in tragically distorted form. Its appeal to men's hearts and consciences lies in what it has borrowed from the gospel; part of this is its concern with the endeavor to understand and gain confidence from a reading of history. Many of its goals are Christian goals—brotherhood, equality, justice, etc. But its materialistic interpretation of man and his life, and its consequent ruthless and brutal methods of attaining these goals, are directly contrary to the Christian doctrine of man as the child of God and the Christian dependence upon faith and love to achieve with God his purposes for all his children.

Religions without the Hebrew-Christian heritage have no word to say on the meaning of history. This prophet asks the nations and their spiritual guides to produce witnesses to their ability to read the past and so observe the present that they can lead men sure-footedly in paths of righteousness. In the altered situation of a day faced with communism and its doctrines of materialistic determinism in human affairs, we must still appeal to history. Is this interpretation correct?

**Let them bring their witnesses to justify them,
and let them hear and say, It is true.**

We and all nations are in court. The trial is on. Can this partially true explanation of life and practical program in economics and politics prove its case? If not, can Christians with their conviction of God in Christ and of his redemptive purpose for all men produce in the church a community whose word and life are patently more convincing?

10 Ye *are* my witnesses, saith the LORD, and my servant whom I have chosen; that ye may know and believe me, and understand that I *am* he: before me there was no God formed, neither shall there be after me.

10 "You are my witnesses," says the LORD, "and my servant whom I have chosen, that you may know and believe me and understand that I am He. Before me no god was formed, nor shall there be any after me.

saying), for there is no reality behind them. With the central motif of **witnesses** established, the poet has prepared the way for the next strophe. Yahweh has his witnesses.

3. SECOND STROPHE: YAHWEH'S WITNESS AND SERVANT (43:10)

10. Yahweh addresses Israel forthwith: **You are my witnesses.** The pronoun is emphatic (cf. 41:8). Here the prophet is introducing another of his major themes. He is describing Israel's mission in the world, and he follows the solemn commission with the oracle formula. The succeeding line substantiates this interpretation. The **witnesses** (plural) are identified with the **servant** (singular). Duhm and others read "servants," but there is no evidence for this. Indeed, the plural **witnesses** and the singular **servant** are precisely what is needed, what the context demands, and what the prophet's thought concerning Israel throughout the poems requires. Israel does not exist for herself. She is not first of all a great nation, a great military power, an economic force, a cultural center, or any other secular order. Her mission is to be God's witness and elected servant. She exists to fulfill his purposes and to do his will. The words of address (vs. 10*ab*) are followed by *lemá'an,* "in order that," and are to be retained (contra Köhler *et al.*), for they connect closely with the three great verbs (to be kept in the second person): **know** (*tēdh'û*), **believe** (*ta'amînú*), **understand** (*tābhînû*), which culminate in the final object of all knowledge and faith and insight: **that I am He,** the one universal God. Through her witness and service she will come to know that Yahweh is God of all the nations. That God is God and the only God, this is Israel's witness, her mission as servant, and the meaning of her election. The strophe began, as we have seen, with an emphatic **you;** all the rest of the words flow from it to the final word **I am He.** Just as the word **witnesses** prepares the way for the second strophe, so the monotheistic witness of the servant *kî-'anî hû',* **that I am He,** prepares the way for the final strophe. The lines in vs. 10*ef* simply witness to the eternity of God (cf. 40:28*c*; 41:4*cd*). In the *Enûma eliš* the gods emerge from the watery chaos. There was no such a time for Yahweh, no **before**

10. *Witnesses.*—The church is composed of believers, each of whom is a witness; the corporate fellowship of Christians, the body of Christ, is the supreme witness. This prophet's word **witnesses** was taken up by the N.T. church (cf. Acts 1:8). Every Christian is called to be a witness to the worth of his Lord. But many feel a great reluctance to fulfill this obligation. At the turn of the century W. T. Stead, editor of the *Review of Reviews,* wrote to a number of prominent persons, inquiring what hymns helped them most. Among those thus solicited was Lord Rosebery, who declined to confess to the public in general on such a subject. Stead commented:

There is a curious and not very creditable shrinking on the part of many to testify as to their experience in the deeper matters of the soul. It is an inverted egotism—selfishness masquerading in disguise of reluctance to speak of self. Wanderers across the wilderness of Life ought not to be chary of telling their fellow-travellers where they found the green oasis, . . . or the shadow of a great rock in a desert land. It is not regarded as egotism when the passing steamer signals across the Atlantic wave news of her escape from perils of iceberg or fog, or welcome news of good cheer. Yet individuals shrink into themselves, repressing rigorously the fraternal instinct which bids them communicate the fruits of their experience to their fellows. Therein they deprive themselves of a share in the communion of saints, and refuse to partake with their brother of the sacramental cup of human sympathy, or to break the sacred bread of the deeper experiences.[8]

Perhaps Stead's journalistic aims may have led him to a too harsh judgment on those who find it immodest to see their most personal secrets in print, but it is a fact that tongue-tied Christians rob their fellows and themselves of com-

[8] *Hymns That Have Helped* (New York: Doubleday, Page & Co., 1904), pp. 16-17.

| 11 I, *even* I, *am* the Lord; and beside me *there is* no saviour. | 11 I, I am the Lord, and besides me there is no savior. |

Yahweh and **after** Yahweh, no time when he did not exist. He initiated history and will bring history to its close. But to use the language which the nations know: **no god was formed** before him, **nor shall there be any after** him. The Hebrew does not say that he is timeless.

4. Third Strophe: "I Alone Am God, and You Are My Witnesses" (43:11-13)

The literary pattern of the strophe shows the quality of the thought:

> I, I am Yahweh, and there is not a savior beside me;
> I declared, and I saved, and I proclaimed, and there is
>   not an alien god among you;
> I am God . . . I am He, and there is not any who can deliver . . . ;
> I work, and who can hinder it?

There are in the Hebrew twenty-nine words, and twelve of them are in the first person singular. It is monotheism at its most intense pitch. But it is not cast in any speculative or theoretical form. Second Isaiah does not say, "There is one God," or "Israel's faith is monotheistic." It is Yahweh who speaks, and in the first person. The first personal pronoun appears five times: twice at the beginning of the first double line, then at the beginning of the next line, and finally in the emphatic asseverations, **I am God** (*'anî 'ēl*) and **I am He** (*'anî hû'*). There are four verbs in the first person, and these are especially important because they show not only how Israel's monotheistic faith is filled with the content of action, but also the kind of action by which God reveals himself. Finally, there are two possessives: **my witnesses** and **my hand.**

11. With great urgency the prophet repeats the covenant words, "I am Yahweh" (cf. 43:25; 51:12), which here is the same as saying "I am God," but significantly the covenant or theophanic speech of revelation is retained (cf. 40:9g, 10a). The name "Yahweh" is not lost. Elohim is not meant as a more profound or universal term. The nations will come to know and hear the great asseveration, "I am Yahweh." **Besides me there is no savior.** What is expressed here is the living content of the word "God" in terms of what he does, of his relationship to men, and of his outgoing purpose. The word **savior** connects with the climax of the great covenant utterance at the close of 43:1-3a ("the Holy One of Israel, your Savior"), where Yahweh's redemption is described, and it

---

munion in the things of God. If this nameless poet-prophet had not brought to his deaf and blind people a witness to their Savior and the Savior of the whole world, a most valuable contribution to the religious message of Israel and to the faith of humanity would have been lost.

In addition to the witness of individual Christians there is the corporate witness of the church. In every service of public worship, in the testimony of the sacraments, in the mobilizing of Christian opinion on subjects of the day, above all in the life and activities of each congregation, the church proclaims her Lord, and commends—or unhappily, by insincerity or defects in her best acts, fails to commend—his worth. The ecumenical conferences of the twentieth century are increasingly supplying the opportunity for the larger fellowship of Christians in all the churches to bear its collective witness to God and to his present will for a disordered

world. Even the most tongue-tied Christian can without violence to his modesty bear his part in this corporate testimony.

11-13. God's Witness to Himself Through Israel.—This is biblical religion. Through the words of his servants, the living and self-disclosing God speaks directly to men (cf. II Cor. 5:20). The important title is **savior.** God's essence is revealed in his redemption of men. One cannot discover the character of God by investigating and discussing him; one must let him save; then one knows. In Christ he came saying that his mission is "to seek and to save." The prophet is here at the heart of the Christian gospel.

And there is an insistence on the sole godship of this saving God. Modern men do not think themselves in danger of lapsing into polytheism. The danger is secular humanism—the complete banishment of any deity and man's reliance

12 I have declared, and have saved, and I have showed, when *there was* no strange *god* among you: therefore ye *are* my witnesses, saith the Lord, that I *am* God. 13 Yea, before the day *was* I *am* he; and *there is* none that can deliver out of my hand: I will work, and who shall let it?	12 I declared and saved and proclaimed, when there was no strange god among you; and you are my witnesses," says the Lord. 13 "I am God, and also henceforth I am He; there is none who can deliver from my hand; I work and who can hinder it?"

continues throughout the poems as a description of God's redemption. "The will and power to 'save' is to II Isaiah the distinctive function and predicate of true deity" (Skinner, *Isaiah, ad loc.*). The exclusive deity of God is accompanied by such attributes as in the prophetic thought of Second Isaiah belong inextricably with it.

12. For **declared** translate "foretold." The verbs are a history of Israel's religious faith, a summary of what God has done in history, prophecy, and salvation. Hebrew history, prophecy, and psalmody record the content of Israel's witness. For **strange god** the Hebrew has simply "stranger." Israel had known gods many and lords many, but an alien god had never proffered a revelation. It is Yahweh, the God Israel knows, who performs these unique acts, not a stranger (god) like Marduk or Nebo or any other. His assertions concerning his oneness, his activity and revelation, are not proclaimed as a universal truth, but rather *en famille,* **among you.** So the next oracular words, repeated from the previous strophe (where they are central), appear in the heart of the great monotheistic utterance: "and you are my witnesses, the oracle of the Lord." The ordination of Israel is deepened and made momentous by the urgency, concreteness, and profound content of the new setting. The M.T. closes the verse with the climactic monotheistic proclamation, **I am God** (KJV), but many scholars attach them to what follows (so RSV).

13. Again we have the divine first person. Thus the prophecy gains its immediacy and powerful impact. Everything is centered in God's own words and the prophet in such contexts does not call attention to himself by proclaiming his faith in the third person. Not only in Israel's past, where prophecy and history had wrought together for her salvation, but in the future too, God is one and he is almighty. From now on and

upon himself to do everything. The First Commandment, if written for our time, might read, "Thou shalt have at least one God." But polytheism is by no means dead. Men worship one God in their homes, another in the competitive life of business and industry; one God in their dealings with those of their own nation, race, and class, and another in their dealings with outsiders; one God in personal relations, where forgiveness, generosity, sympathy, are adored, another God in social or group relations, where pride of race or nation, the self-assertion of a country in demanding its rights, the aggressiveness of a church in its attitude toward other churches, are regarded as virtuous and praiseworthy. It is open to discussion whether the God of nature is one with the God of our hearts and consciences, whether the God worshiped by poet and artist is one with the God of righteousness, and, practically, it is no easy matter to be ruled by one divine Spirit in the many and divers areas of life where one moves.

In a sorely divided world it is all-important that the nations and peoples of the earth revere one deity. One standard of truth, of honor, of justice is essential if international relations are to be stable. Of what value are treaties or agreements unless universal respect for the pledged word binds the powers which enter into them? Without a conviction that one Lord alone is God, there will be no common moral foundation uniting and holding firm and fast the often clashing interests of men and nations.

I declared and saved and proclaimed summarizes God's revelation of himself. Here is his work in history, redemption, and prophecy. The poet witnessed all three in his day. The Lord declared his purpose through the startling conquests of Cyrus. He was mysteriously using these conquests and the changes which followed them to *save* Israel from her captivity. He was *proclaiming* her earth-wide mission as his servant to make him known to mankind. One may see a similar work of God in our time. Through

14 ¶ Thus saith the LORD, your Redeemer, the Holy One of Israel; For your sake I have sent to Babylon, and have brought down all their nobles, and the Chaldeans, whose cry *is* in the ships.

14 Thus says the LORD,
　　your Redeemer, the Holy One of
　　　Israel:
"For your sake I will send to Babylon
　　and break down all the bars,
　　and the shouting of the Chalde'ans will
　　be turned to lamentations.ˣ

ˣ Heb obscure

---

forever (Hebrew, "from day"; LXX, "from the beginning," ἀπ' ἀρχῆς; Vulg., *et ab initio*) he continues to be the one true God in whose hands alone lie the destinies of Israel and the nations, and for whom there is no hindrance or reversal. For the final verb cf. Amos 1:1, 3, 6, 9, 11, 13, etc. The divine address ends in the fashion of its opening (vs. 9c).

G. REDEMPTION BY GRACE (43:14–44:5)

The poem contains three oracles introduced by the formula of revelation (43:14, 16; 44:2). Each is expanded in the manner characteristic of Second Isaiah. The first strikes the key of the whole poem, **your Redeemer, the Holy One of Israel,** a collocation of great significance (41:14; 47:4; 48:17; 49:7; 54:5). The concluding asseveration (vs. 15) sets the stage for the strophic triad which follows (vss. 16-17, 18-19, 20-21). The second (vss. 16-17) recalls the wonders of the redemption from Egypt and is expanded in the style of the hymn. The third (44:2-5) seizes upon the close relationship expressed in the other two oracles and brings them to a climax. The central thought of the poem is expressed in the third strophe (43:18-19): **Behold, I am doing a new thing** (cf. 40:9-10; 41:24, 27, 29), a message first proclaimed in the eschatological poem which follows the call and ordination of the servant (42:5-17, especially vss. 9-10). In the fourth strophe (vss. 20-21) the poet describes the response of the beasts and of Israel to the gift of waters in the desert. In the second exodus God is again acting in behalf of his chosen people, "for his own sake." It is to this thought that the two following strophes are devoted (43:22-24, 25-28). The third oracle (44:1-5) thus continues the argument brought to

---

disastrous wars and the break-up of our complacent nineteenth-century Western world he has made his church keenly sensitive to his presence in current events. God in history was little thought of in the nineteenth century, but now Christians recognize his coming in judgment on a social life which was unjust and unbrotherly. He has saved nations from their coveted isolation, irresponsibility, and self-interest. Everywhere people live in a larger world and must regard the concerns of other lands. Some nations, and assuredly his church in all countries, see a vaster and much more desperately urgent mission to bring all peoples under the reign of the righteous God. The task of being his **witnesses** is laid on the church and her members with a fresh insistency. The word stresses what our vocation is. Our calling is not to coerce but to commend. The many ministries of the Christian missionary propaganda have their role to play—ministries of healing, of education, of human welfare in a dozen realms, as well as the preaching and teaching of the gospel. In many a non-Christian land one discovers that it was the impression given by these auxiliary ministries of helpfulness which first led folk to listen to the Christian message. They had been attracted by its fruits, were eager to learn of its roots, and so came face to face with God in Christ.

You are my witnesses, . . . I am God. The connection reminds us who is behind and active in our testimony by deed or word. **And also henceforth I am He** faces us with an unlimited prospect of service for men under his energizing sway. **There is none who can deliver from my hand** furnishes assurance of his competency against the hostile factors in the thought, politics, and customs of our age, and against the ruthless opponents of the church. "The gates of hell shall not prevail against it" (Matt. 16:18). And the concluding statement on the Lord's lips rings out with the certain promise of ultimate triumph: **I work and who can hinder it?**

14-15. *God, Redeemer, Creator, King of Israel Overwhelms Babylon.*—In this significant poem the prophet announces at long last what his people have been eagerly anticipating—that God's hour for Babylon has come, and his hour

a climax in vss. 17-21. With an emphatic **But now** (44:1*a*) God turns to Israel, addressing her with the interior words of her existence, **Jacob my servant; and Israel whom I have chosen,** and calling her to hear his oracle. After the usual introduction of a prophetic oracle (vs. 2*a*) he admonishes her, "Fear not!" and repeats the words of address, but with an accent of even deeper intimacy, **Jacob, my servant, and thou Jeshurun, whom I have chosen.** Then with the usual introductory *kî,* "for" (44:3*a*), he gives new promises of redemption, the gift of **water** to the thirsty ground (cf. 43:20) and the even greater gift of the outpouring of the **Spirit.** Finally, in the last strophe (44:5), there is a remarkable description of new adherents to the community of Yahweh. "This one will say, 'I belong to Yahweh'; this one will call himself by the name of Jacob, and this one will write on his hand, 'To [or "belonging to"] Yahweh.'" The triad of demonstratives, the lengthening of the third line into a fourth, and the alternation of Yahweh in the first and third lines with **the name of Jacob** and **the name of Israel** in the second and fourth bring the poem to an impressive close.

The poem as a whole seems to be composed of seven strophes of approximately the same length (43:14-15, 16-17, 18-19, 20-21; 44:1-2, 3-4, 5) with an interlude of two longer strophes (43:22-24, 25-28) which proclaim that God will again come in grace and forgiveness in the time of redemption (43:22-28). The individual strophes possess a remarkable unity.

1. First Strophe: Liberation From Bondage (43:14-15)

14. Second Isaiah is unwilling that the expression **Thus saith the Lord** should lapse into a mere formula as was the tendency of later times (cf. Zech. 1:2-6). Therefore he adds two significant phrases in apposition to **Lord: your Redeemer, the Holy One of Israel.** Israel is called to be a holy people (*'am qādhôsh,* Exod. 19:6; Deut. 7:6; etc.). But Second Isaiah precedes the great title of Isaiah of Jerusalem, **the Holy One of Israel,** with **your Redeemer.** Yahweh, the holy God, acts redemptively in relation to his holy people. His holiness is not merely a metaphysical attribute; its content is made known by his ethical activity (cf. 5:16*b et passim*). In Second Isaiah this action of the Holy God of Israel is primarily redemption (41:14; 47:4; 48:17; 49:7; 54:5). Like the conception of the holy people, made holy by a holy God, the conception of redemption belongs to the central deposit of the biblical tradition. By the act of redeeming, Yahweh recognizes his unique relationship to Israel and acts in conformity with the duties of the "possessor." He vindicates his right of ownership which Israel had lost. Jacob confesses Yahweh's redemptive act in his behalf (Gen. 48:16 [E]), and the exodus from Egypt is constantly viewed as an act of redemption from bondage (Exod. 15:13; Deut. 7:8; 13:5; 21:8; 24:18; II Sam. 7:23; Mic. 6:4). When Yahweh chose Israel to be his own possession, he assumed the obligation of redemption and entered into a covenant relationship. It was in his redemptive acts that Israel knew him to be their God. Israel's Holy One is Israel's Redeemer, and her Redeemer is her Holy One (see Johann Jakob Stamm, *Erlösen und Vergeben im Alten Testament* [Bern: A. Francke A.-G., 1940], pp. 27-44; Buber, *Prophetic Faith,* pp. 206-8; Eichrodt, *Theologie des A.T.,* III, 90, 137; Johannes Hempel, *Gott und Mensch im Alten Testament* [2nd ed.; Stuttgart: W. Kohlhammer, 1926], pp. 83-84). It

---

for his people's deliverance. It is proclaimed with startling suddenness in the first strophe (vs. 14). The announcement is no more startling than the event itself. From Herodotus we know how easily Babylon fell. The Persian host slipped in by diverting the river into an old channel and, once inside the walls, resistance was negligible. So sudden was the fall of the proud city of mighty conquerors.

The titles applied to God both before and following the great news are significant. The prophet does his utmost to stress the relationship of God to his people—their **Redeemer, Creator, King.** The order of the titles is noteworthy. God had redeemed them from the slavery of Egypt, as now he redeems them by Cyrus from their captivity. Redemption created the nation at the Exodus, and now will re-create it. Over his own nation he is sovereign. Monarchs did much to make or mar their peoples. The reigning Babylonian sovereign was apparently impotent, but consider what Cyrus was

15 I *am* the LORD, your Holy One, the | 15 I am the LORD, your Holy One,
Creator of Israel, your King. | the Creator of Israel, your King."

---

is noteworthy that Second Isaiah employs the word **Redeemer** in reference to Yahweh more often than all the other writers of the O.T. Observe, too, that he employs it in new contexts of profound importance (cf. 44:6, 24; 47:4; 49:6; 54:8). The words **for your sake . . . Babylon** like the theophanic *hieros logos* disclose historical concreteness. The phrase **for your sake** follows superbly after the words of relationship in the introduction: **your Redeemer, the Holy One of Israel.** This intimate relationship is maintained throughout the poem (cf. vs. 15; 44:1-2). The meaning is not that Israel deserved this deed in her behalf but that Yahweh acts for the sake of Israel, with whom he stands in covenant relationship. The emphasis is on God's relationship to Israel, not on Israel's merit.

Torrey omits **to Babylon** and **the Chaldeans** and translates, "For your sake I will send, and cause all the fugitives to embark." The verb **send,** however, demands an object, most probably Cyrus, whom the prophet is not yet ready to name. He is preparing the way, however, in the mention of Babylon and Chaldea. Despite the fervor and exuberance of the poet, his method of gradually unfolding central ideas and words shows restraint. **And break down all the bars:** Both the verb and its object occasion difficulties. A literal rendering would be "I will cause to go down fugitives [?], all of them." The LXX reads, ἐπεγερῶ πάντας φεύγοντας, "I will stir up all that flee," and the Vulg., *detraxi vectes universos.* Some have emended בחירים into בחורים "in the holes" (of the earth; cf. 42:22). Duhm's final solution seems to be to read, הורידתי בריחי כלא, "I break down the bars of imprisonment." Volz, following one of Duhm's suggestions in part, reads בריחי כלאכם והרסתי, and translates, "I will break down the bars of your imprisonment." The RSV is influenced by these emendations in part. Ever since Ewald the vocalic reading of באניות, **in the ships**—always a vexatious word for commentators—as *ba'aniyyôth,* **into lamentations,** has commended itself. The reading of the RSV is perhaps the best that can be made of a difficult text. The Dead Sea Scroll agrees with the M.T. throughout. Yahweh is to liberate his people from captivity and Babylon's exulting shouts are to be turned to laments.

15. As the oracle opens solemnly, so it closes with the asseveration "I am Yahweh, . . ." **Holy one** is common to beginning and ending, quite properly; the additional words in apposition, **Creator of Israel** and **your King,** give concrete content to Yahweh's relationship to Israel, and reveal him as the one who originates and completes her life. The order of these divine titles is not fortuitous. Redemption, creation, and sovereignty are the sequence the prophet intends to emphasize. The words, **your King,** continue a major motif of the poems (40:10*b*; 41:21; 43:15) and focus the thought upon Israel's need in the contemporary world situation. The nations have their kings who are responsible for the welfare and protection of their people, kings like the pharaohs of Egypt, the great Assyrian conquerors, and Babylonian rulers like Nebuchadrezzar and Nabonidus. Israel in her present plight has her King, and he will reveal his power, his protection, and his universality in the present juncture of human history.

---

doing for his Persians. When this new world force was rising to power amid the chaos of falling empires, God, Israel's king, was leading her forth on her mission of world conquest until all peoples joined themselves in one divine community of righteousness. The opening of this poem links itself with its glorious missionary conclusion. This is the origin and mission of the Christian church—redeemed, created, reigned over by a divine Lord.

Cyrus is sent to Babylon **for your sake.** The

poem from first to last stresses God's gracious care of his people. He is not acting because they merit his efforts on their behalf. He acts for his own sake (vs. 25), in order to live up to his name as their creator and king. His church today does not appeal to him on the basis of its deserts; its record, like Israel's, is a shabby one (vss. 22-24). But God has redeemed her out of many nations by the blood of his Son, made her by the gift of his Spirit, and is inextricably bound to her as her living monarch. This is

16 Thus saith the Lord, which maketh a way in the sea, and a path in the mighty waters;

17 Which bringeth forth the chariot and horse, the army and the power; they shall lie down together, they shall not rise: they are extinct, they are quenched as tow.

16 Thus says the Lord,
    who makes a way in the sea,
    a path in the mighty waters,
17 who brings forth chariot and horse,
    army and warrior;
they lie down, they cannot rise,
    they are extinguished, quenched like a
      wick:

2. Second Strophe: Deliverance at the Sea (43:16-17)

The oracle of promise of imminent deliverance is followed by another oracle recalling the supreme event of Israel's past, the deliverance from oppression in Egypt. The whole strophe deals with a single event and is introductory to the two that follow. The elaborate introduction measures the momentous importance of what is to be disclosed. The prophet develops his oracle in the style of a hymn in participial construction. The three strophes (vss. 16-17, 18-19, 20-21) form a close-knit unity, but they are written against the background of the promise in vss. 14-15. In the recollection of the miracle of the Exodus, Second Isaiah is following his prophetic predecessors (cf. Amos 2:7, 10; 3:1; Hos. 11:1; 13:4; Mic. 6:4; Isa. 11:16; Jer. 2:2 ff.; Ezek. 20:7-9), but he is the first to relate it to an eschatological context.

Two features in the tradition are emphasized: the highway that Yahweh made in the sea and the destruction of the Egyptian pursuers (Exod. 14–15). Nature and history are under the control, rule, and purpose of God, and nature is overcome to serve his revelation in history. A path is made in the mighty waters that Israel may pass over dryshod; the waters return in order that the Egyptian foe may be overcome. Such a memory was relevant to the present moment. Faith in the divine revelation in the greatest event of Israel's past, in which God proved himself deliverer and Lord and one who fulfilled his word, is the faith the prophet seeks to inspire in his contemporaries.

16. Second Isaiah describes Yahweh "giving" (literally) **a way** in the water, a miracle for the sake of Israel in the moment of her darkest crisis. **Mighty waters:** A characteristic exaggeration reminding one of the Deuteronomists' characterization of the howling wilderness (Deut. 1:19; 8:15; 32:10; cf. Neh. 9:11). The order of the Hebrew is "in the mighty waters a path." The prophet feels the exultancy of Miriam's ecstatic hymn (Exod. 15:21) as he contemplates the event.

17. The imagery is military. Yahweh is portrayed as a conqueror over the Egyptians (cf. Jethro's blessing in Exod. 18:10-11; also Isa. 42:13-14; Fredriksson, *Jahwe als Krieger,* pp. 10, 24). The word rendered **warrior** literally means "strong one" (cf. ASV "the mighty man") and is used also in Ps. 24:8. **They lie down, . . . :** An unusually graphic description of the utter annihilation of the pursuing Egyptians (cf. Exod. 15:4-5). Second Isaiah is fond of such powerful contrasts as an army **quenched like a wick** (cf. 42:3). The alternation of tenses in the last two lines in the Hebrew is effective, two imperfects followed by two perfects.

---

the basis of our assurance that he will continue, despite all our defects and negligences, to abide with and employ his church.

16-17. God Works a New Exodus for His People.—The memory of God's mighty acts is reinforcement to present confidence. The prophet harps on God's presence in the nation's past. A skeptical Frenchman asked contemptuously, "Why should God use Moses to speak to Jean Jacques Rousseau?" But why not? In fact, it is through Moses, the prophets, and his word in Jesus of Nazareth that he speaks most tell-

ingly. Memory is the place where nations and individuals find God. Augustine put it: "Since then I learned Thee, Thou residest in my memory; and there do I find Thee, when I call Thee to remembrance, and delight in Thee." [9]

A devout retrospect gives hope in the critical present.

> Before me, even as behind,
>   God is, and all is well. [1]

[9] *Confessions* X. 24.
[1] John Greenleaf Whittier, "My Birthday."

| 18 ¶ Remember ye not the former things, neither consider the things of old.

19 Behold, I will do a new thing; now it shall spring forth; shall ye not know it? I will even make a way in the wilderness, *and* rivers in the desert. | 18 "Remember not the former things, nor consider the things of old.

19 Behold, I am doing a new thing; now it springs forth, do you not perceive it? I will make a way in the wilderness and rivers in the desert. |

---

3. Third Strophe: "Behold, I Do a New Thing" (43:18-19)

The strophe begins with a negative command (cf. vs. 1; 41:14; 44:2, 8; 54:4) and continues with the exclamatory oracular word, **Behold, I am doing a new thing,** which is reinforced in vs. 19c by the particle *'aph,* untranslated in the RSV but rendered **even** in the KJV. The opening admonition seems strange at first, since Second Isaiah is constantly calling upon Israel to remember (44:21; 46:8-9; 47:7). Moreover, no O.T. prophet remembers more or better than he, above all the very events which we are here told not to remember! Besides, he has himself just adduced the record of the miracle of the Red Sea crossing to fortify Israel's faith in the fresh revelation. The explanation for the command is obvious, however. The poet is speaking rhetorically. The new event that is about to occur is so much greater than the old, so much more wonderful and glorious, that by comparison the old is as nothing at all, and therefore to be forgotten (cf. Jer. 16:14; 23:7). The former things are the events of the Exodus and sojourn. In form the command corresponds to the usual exhortation "Fear not" (vs. 1b; 41:10, 14; 44:2b), and is followed by the assurance of intervention (vss. 19-20) in the regular style of the oracle of salvation. The prophet is calling upon Israel to turn from memory to hope, from the epochal events of the past to the even more decisive and redemptive events of the future.

19. The prophet is so certain of the truth of what he is saying, so sure of the imminence of redemption, that he sees it taking place before his very eyes (cf. 52:7 ff.). It springs forth **now.** Logically, this line stands in contradiction to 42:9, a passage which is dealing with the same theme of the "new events," but such inconsistencies are not to be pressed. **Do you not perceive it?** The prophet's faith gives him vision to see what only faith can see. As God had made a way in the sea, a path through the waters (vs. 16), so now he is to **make a way** through **the wilderness.** The motif of the way or road (*dérekh*) is prominent in Second Isaiah. It is already sounded in the first strophe of the Prologue and it continues to the end (55:12-13). Its imagery weaves itself into the accounts of the history of Israel (the road of the Exodus, the journey through the wilderness to Sinai and from Sinai to Palestine, the going away into exile and the return to Jerusalem). It was a figure eminently suited to Israel's geographical environment and to her historical consciousness. It becomes a primary figure to express the realities of history, of ethics, of eschatology, and of personal piety. The **new thing** that the Lord is doing is

---

18-19. *The New Exodus Wonderful.*—The third strophe seems to contradict the thought in the second (vs. 18). But this is precisely what the prophet has been doing in recalling the Exodus. It is, however, a vivid way of saying that they need not look back on a glorious past, for the present is to be even more full of divine glory. The Exodus had been startling in its path through a sea. The long, much-feared desert between Babylon and Jerusalem would see a new divine route over which the returning people would pass as safely as their fathers. The Exodus had surprised them with waters gushing from the smitten rock in the wilderness. Again

the miracle was to occur, and his people would see **rivers in the desert.** Vividly the poet asks:

> Behold, I am doing a new thing;
> now it springs forth, do you not perceive it?

Such perception was possible only to the eye of faith. It is that eye which the contemporary church most needs. On the horizon there appears no road for humanity toward the Jerusalem of a fraternal and just order. But even through most unlikely circumstances it is there. Men may see only the deep waters of the sea or the sands of a scorched wilderness. But he who leads the blind "by a way that they know

20 The beast of the field shall honor me, the dragons and the owls: because I give waters in the wilderness, *and* rivers in the desert, to give drink to my people, my chosen.	20 The wild beasts will honor me, the jackals and the ostriches; for I give water in the wilderness, rivers in the desert, to give drink to my chosen people,

the making of a way for his people to return from exile to Palestine. Observe how the strophe begins and ends on this motif. **And rivers in the desert:** The reading of the Dead Sea Scroll is not clear, but is probably נתיבות, "paths," the plural of the same word used in vs. 16c (see H. M. Orlinsky, "Photography and Paleography in the Textual Criticism of St. Mark's Isaiah Scroll, 43:19," *Bulletin of the American Schools of Oriental Research,* No. 123 [Oct., 1951], pp. 33-35). This would improve the parallelism, relate it more clearly to vs. 16, where דרך and נתיבה stand in parallelism. On the other hand, the rejoicing of the animals would have to be explained more by what follows vs. 20ab than by what precedes. It is perhaps precarious to make a change on the basis of the evidence of one MS, even so important a one, since the reference to **rivers** well fits the context following (vss. 20-21). Note too that the plural of the Dead Sea Scroll is in contrast to the singular of the parallel. The Hebrew word *yeshimôn* refers to the barren and dry regions (Deut. 32:10; Pss. 68:7; 78:40; etc.) in contrast to the *midhbār* ("steppe," "wilderness"), where it is possible for flocks to graze.

4. Fourth Strophe: Streams in the Desert (43:20-21)

20-21. Israel's sojourn through the desert was accompanied by many signs and wonders, but none was more memorable than the gift of **water.** The people thirsted, and Yahweh healed the bitter waters of Marah (Exod. 15:22-26 [J]) and at Rephidim made waters to gush from the rock (Exod. 17:1-7 [JE]; cf. the climax in Isa. 48:21). But now in this new and greater event the desert will cease to be a threat of destruction and death. Here again nature stands in the service of history (cf. 41:17-20; 42:10-17). Streams break forth in the path of the chosen people. It was cause for universal gladness: **that they might declare my praise.** The folk motif of the animals is part of a spacious world of reality. The animals are closer to the ancient Hebrew than they are to us. Their creation is almost in the same class as the creation of man (Gen. 2:7, 19; cf. also Gen. 1:24-26), and in the messianic age they participate in the wonders of the transformation (11:6 ff.). The wild beasts will honor Yahweh for the gift of plenteous waters not

not" (42:16) has already prepared his path, and is waiting to bring us into it. Nor in this spiritually arid world are most men aware of refreshing springs. These too are discerned only by the eye of faith; yet God has provided them in abundance. Those downhearted exiles who stayed on in Babylon or in the faraway "coastlands" would never discover them. But the believing who answered God's call and followed him in this new and vastly more glorious exodus toward a world-mission, would see **rivers** of spiritual inspiration more than sufficient for the needs of all. **A way** and a supply of water—these are the elementary essentials, and God, who knows well his people's needs, can be counted on not to fail them.

20-21. *Desert Animals Rejoice in God's Provision.*—This is a surprising conclusion. One might have expected the poet to envisage a grateful people on their journey. Instead, he pictures wild animals rejoicing in the trans-

formed desert, glad not alone for themselves in the abundant flow of waters, but more glad that God **gives drink to** [his] **chosen people.**

This is a devout poet's confident expectation. What we call "nature" is the servant of God's plans for man, and especially for redeemed man. It is man's sinful dominion which has broken the "social union" in which hills and valleys, trees, and especially the **wild beasts** were meant to be one harmonious family. One thinks of modern poets who have addressed verses to dogs, birds, cats, mice, horses, etc. In both the O.T. and the N.T., animals are viewed as God's creatures, with places in his order subordinate to man, but nonetheless the objects of his loving providence. They have claims upon man's consideration as fellow creatures, and he must recognize his obligations to them under God.

The naturalist John Muir, brought up on a farm with domestic animals and spending years in lonely places where he had intimate associa-

| 21 This people have I formed for myself; they shall show forth my praise. | 21 the people whom I formed for myself that they might declare my praise. |
| 22 ¶ But thou hast not called upon me, O Jacob; but thou hast been weary of me, O Israel. | 22 "Yet you did not call upon me, O Jacob; but you have been weary of me, O Israel! |

for their own sakes alone but for Israel's. Second Isaiah is not content with saying, lit., "animals of the field," but in his fondness for the concrete he must enumerate them, **the jackals and the ostriches,** just as he enumerates the trees (41:19-20; 55:13). In the lonely far-off places, in the hidden lairs of the wilderness fastnesses men will not hear the forlorn and eerie cries and howls of beasts (cf. 34:11-15), but the beasts, having lost their wildness, will break forth into song out of sheer joy and fellow feeling (cf. 42:10-12).

The closing line is a splendid reminiscence of 42:8, 10, a context similar to this one. In both, "glory" or "honor" (*kābhôdh*) and **praise** (*tᵉhillāh*) are associated. As Torrey comments, the praise of Israel is "the indispensable counterpart of the praise rendered by the beasts of the desert" (*Second Isaiah*, p. 341). Israel is the praising and worshiping community as she is the redeemed, elect, called, chosen, holy, and covenanted people. In these latter events Yahweh formed a people for himself, and therefore Israel's most native response is praise and worship. The pervasive emphasis upon singing belongs to the same complex of thought.

5. FIFTH STROPHE: YAHWEH'S INDICTMENT (43:22-24)

Abruptly the prophet turns to the thought of Israel as she really is. For this purpose he seems to employ again the form of a legal process (cf. vss. 8-13; 41:1–42:4; 44:6-8; 48:1-11; 50:1-3), but his language is like the invective (*Scheltrede*). We should expect a threat (*Drohrede*) to follow, but surprisingly in its stead there follows fervent assurance of redemption and forgiveness (cf. vss. 1-7; 42:18-25). The invective is meant, to be sure, for Second Isaiah does not discount the realities of Israel's sins, but the grace of God transcends the deserved judgment. Volz pictures the prophet, whom he believes to be a pastor and leader of the synagogue, addressing these words on a day of repentance.

tions with wild creatures, contended valiantly against the theory that they were "machines in fur and feathers." Against a mechanistic interpretation of animal behavior he insisted that they had individualities. He noted differences in intelligence and feeling in creatures of the same species. He denounced the attitude of many among the godly that as "lords of creation" they were without responsibility for their dumb fellow inhabitants of the earth. He wished children to grow up with a chance to acquire friendship with these lesser neighbors.

Thus godlike sympathy grows and thrives and spreads far beyond the teaching of churches and schools, where too often the mean, blinding, loveless doctrine is taught that animals have neither mind nor soul, have no rights that we are bound to respect, and were made only for man, to be petted, spoiled, slaughtered, or enslaved.[2]

[2] *The Story of My Boyhood and Youth* (Boston: Houghton Mifflin Co., 1913), pp. 109-10.

The poet-prophet finds in them a mystical relationship to God:

> **The wild beasts will honor me,**
> **the jackals and the ostriches.**

We must not lose sight of the fact that for him this is the consummation of history when God's people set up the final divine order in Jerusalem. So all creation participates in the coming glory. Not only will heathen nations be gathered in, but all creatures will share in God's provision for his people's glorious future.

22-28. God Inherently Forgiving.—The next strophes appear to be an interlude, but they contain the chief religious message of the poem, assuring the exiles of God's gracious forgiveness in the final period. The fifth strophe (vss. 22-24) opens with a series of negatives—the religious omissions of the people and the noninsistence of the Lord on ritual observances. The Exeg. explains the prophet's indifference to such

23 Thou hast not brought me the small cattle of thy burnt offerings; neither hast thou honored me with thy sacrifices. I have not caused thee to serve with an offering, nor wearied thee with incense.

23 You have not brought me your sheep for burnt offerings,
or honored me with your sacrifices.
I have not burdened you with offerings,
or wearied you with frankincense.

Despite her lofty mission to worship God, Israel had not called on him or worshiped him. Volz, on the basis of vs. 28, believes that the invective is meant to refer to the whole of Israel's past. But in view of the prophetic denunciations of Amos (5:22-25), Isaiah (1:12-14), Jeremiah (7:21-22), and the writer of Mic. 6:1-8, it is hard to believe that this is the case. On the other hand, Israel could hardly be censured for not offering sacrifices in a foreign land, for they were doubtless forbidden (cf. Deut. 12:13-14). The meaning seems to be: "You did not offer me sacrifices, and indeed I did not require them. But in their stead you offered me the gifts of your sins. You have been weary of me and have not called upon me in worship of any sort. You have cut yourself off from me. You have burdened me with your sins and wearied me with your iniquities."

22. The Hebrew order of the words is effective: "Not me did you call upon, O Jacob," the meaning being not that Israel had called on other gods, but rather that in the time of trouble she had not turned to Yahweh, her covenant Lord. The verb **call upon** refers to worship in prayer and petition. **But you have been weary of me:** This line contains the key word that runs through the strophe (vss. 22b, 23d, 24d; cf. Mic. 6:3b, where another word, however, is used).

23. Second Isaiah likes to build up a succession of clauses in order to produce a powerful climactic effect. The change of pronoun from the second to the first person in the third and fourth lines is striking. The last two lines repeat the verbs to produce a climax. The succession of negatives reinforce each other and help to give effect to the final particle 'akh, "No, but" (vs. 24c; cf. the adversative kî **but**, at the beginning [vs. 22b]).

G. W. Wade (*The Book of the Prophet Isaiah* [London: Methuen & Co., 1929; "Westminster Commentaries"], pp. 281-82) seems to suggest that condemnation is intended here for Israel's failure to offer sacrifices and that the Deuteronomic provision against such offerings in a strange land may not have been held obligatory by the prophet. He refers to the temple at Elephantine in Egypt in support of this view, but

acts, but the point is that the people have deserved nothing at God's hand, and his pardon is therefore clearly unmerited grace. Israel had not chosen him, but he had chosen them; he had not burdened them, but they had burdened him with their disobedience, distrust, and disloyalty. The sixth strophe (vss. 25-28) sets forth God's forgiveness, and summons the people to a judicial hearing when they can present their case, if they have any, and he will tell them why he punished them.

Thomas Erskine caught the basic conviction of this prophet when he insisted that forgiveness is a permanent condition in the heart of God.[3] It is part of God's nature as love. Nor does this passage contradict what the prophet will tell us later in ch. 53, that God's servant by his suffering offers a sacrifice for sin, for this too is of God's arranging, and his servant carries out his purpose. It is so also in the N.T., where the

propitiation for sin is furnished by God himself through his beloved Son. It is God who throughout reconciles sinful men to himself.

A modern religious thinker, David Cairns, has left a record of his struggles when he gave up an inherited evangelical faith and strove to obtain new ground on which to plant his feet. He read a book, which he had stumbled on in the library, by a popular preacher of the day,

which all at once opened my eyes to one simple elementary fact which, in spite of all the good teaching I had had, had never really come home to me. This was, that just as I was, and whether I loved Him or believed in Him or not, God loved me. . . . It made all the difference in the world to me. I have never in my life known more intense happiness than in the days that followed.[4]

Blotting out transgressions does not erase their consequences in national character at a

[3] See his *The Unconditional Freeness of the Gospel* (Boston: Crocker & Brewster, 1828).

[4] *David Cairns, An Autobiography* (London: Student Christian Movement Press, 1950), pp. 86-87.

24 Thou hast bought me no sweet cane with money, neither hast thou filled me with the fat of thy sacrifices: but thou hast made me to serve with thy sins, thou hast wearied me with thine iniquities.

25 I, *even* I, *am* he that blotteth out thy transgressions for mine own sake, and will not remember thy sins.

24 You have not bought me sweet cane with money,
    or satisfied me with the fat of your sacrifices.
But you have burdened me with your sins,
    you have wearied me with your iniquities.

25 "I, I am He
    who blots out your transgressions for my own sake,
    and I will not remember your sins.

the practice of the cultus there can hardly be considered normative. The more probable meaning throughout the passage is that the cult was not maintained at all. No pretense was made of serving God either in prayer or in sacrifice. Various kinds of sacrifices are mentioned only to elaborate the prophet's central thought. **Frankincense:** "A fragment gum-resin that exudes from certain trees of the genus *Boswellia,* which come originally from Western Asia" (Levy, *Deutero-Isaiah,* p. 166).

24. You have not bought me sweet cane: The Hebrew contains a paronomasia not infrequent in Second Isaiah: *qānîthā . . . qāneh.* Jer. 6:20, in a context not dissimilar to this, mentions frankincense that comes from Seba and sweet cane from a distant land. Exod. 30:23 [P] also mentions the sweet cane as one of the ingredients for the sacred anointing oil. By one "gift" Israel had served (**burdened**) Yahweh—by her **sins!** She was weary of him, but he too has been wearied—by her iniquities! The pronouns stress the relationship between Yahweh and Israel. The verbs are nearly all in the second person, and they all express Israel's failure in relation to Yahweh. The strophe begins with an emphatic **me** and this stress is continued throughout (in the Hebrew text) by prepositions (cf. vss. 22*b*, 23*a*, 24*a*), by pronominal suffixes (vss. 23*b*, 24*bcd*), or by shift in subject (vs. 23*cd*). In this fashion the way is prepared for the next strophe which is the counterpart of Israel's record of infidelity.

6. Sixth Strophe: Grace and Judgment (43:25-28)

25. Abruptly and unexpectedly the new strophe begins with the asseveration: **I, I am he,** i.e., "I, only I, am God," but to it is added a strong assurance of forgiveness (cf. vs. 11). When such phrases or relative clauses are joined to theophanic or covenant words such as these, the disclosure is always of great consequence (cf. Exod. 20:2). By

single stroke. But the relationship with God is immediately restored, and in fellowship with him the sinister damages of sin are repaired and the nation is restored to health and vigor. The emphasis in blotting out and not remembering is the banishment of any recalling of past offenses. One may contrast the pathetic plaint of Effie Deans, when she was taken back to the house of her pious father:

Since every look and word of her father put her in mind of her transgression, and was like to drive her mad,—that she had nearly lost judgment during the three days she was at St. Leonard's—her father meant weel by her, and all men, but he did not know the dreadful pain he gave her in casting up her sins.[5]

[5] Sir Walter Scott, *The Heart of Midlothian,* ch. xliv.

Sin is tiresome in its monotony (vs. 24*b*). It allures us as something novel, but there is no new way of "going to the dogs." Every iniquity in contemporary society can be found in the most ancient civilization.

Who shall doubt "the secret hid
Under Cheops' pyramid"
Is that some contractor did
    Cheops out of several millions? [6]

In Israel's history no monarch appeared to invent a fresh form of leading his people astray. Each sinning king followed the pattern set by

[6] "General Summary," st. iv, from *Departmental Ditties and Ballads,* and *Barrack-room Ballads,* by Rudyard Kipling. Reprinted by permission of Mrs. George Bambridge, Methuen & Co., Macmillan Co. of Canada, Ltd., and Doubleday & Co.

26 Put me in remembrance: let us plead together: declare thou, that thou mayest be justified.

27 Thy first father hath sinned, and thy teachers have transgressed against me.

28 Therefore I have profaned the princes of the sanctuary, and have given Jacob to the curse, and Israel to reproaches.

26 Put me in remembrance, let us argue together;

 set forth your case, that you may be proved right.

27 Your first father sinned,

 and your mediators transgressed against me.

28 Therefore I profaned the princes of the sanctuary,

 I delivered Jacob to utter destruction and Israel to reviling.

God's grace alone is Israel forgiven. The emphasis falls on the phrase **for my own sake.** The only motivation lies in God's nature, but his nature is grasped by Israel in the light of her election and covenanthood. **I will not remember your sins:** Eschatological time is the time of forgiveness (see 40:2; cf. the final words of Jeremiah's prophecy on the new covenant in Jer. 31:31-34).

26. Israel might remonstrate, as doubtless many of the prophet's contemporaries did, that her case before Yahweh was not quite so terrible, that the prophet did not take account of other facts of her religious life. In comparison with other nations, above all her captors, she could give some account of herself. Moreover, she was suffering grievously enough at the present time. So the prophet resorts to his favorite judicial situation where the dispute may be settled. Somewhat in the fashion of First Isaiah (1:18) God invites Israel to a legal encounter. Israel will have her opportunity to state her case, to make clear how she merits God's special consideration. If she can do this, she will have some ground for vindication, for being declared "innocent." **Put me in remembrance:** "Bring to mind," or "remind me," an ironic anthropomorphism. Perhaps there is evidence for Israel which Yahweh has forgotten!

27. The indictment against Israel goes back to her earliest beginnings. Already her **first father sinned.** The reference is not to Abraham, but rather to Israel's eponymous ancestor, Jacob (cf. Hos. 12:3). The later religious development of Israel traced the sin of man to Adam as in Rom. 5:12 (cf. also II Esdras 7:11 et passim). The LXX reads "your first fathers." **And your mediators:** Nils Johannson translates מליציך by Fürsprecher, "intercessors" (Parakletoi [Lund: Hakan Ohlssons, 1940], p. 47) and refers the expression here to Moses and the prophets, i.e., Israel's spiritual leaders. If even these could not refrain from sin, how much worse must be the situation of the people! Cyrus Gordon (Introduction to Old Testament Times [Ventnor, N. J., Ventnor Publishers, 1953], p. 199, n. 7) finds the word in the Karatepe inscriptions (Azitewadd's Phoenician text) where it has the meaning of "ancestral spirits": "And I filled the arsenals of Paar and I multiplied horse upon horse and shield upon shield and camp upon camp by the grace of Baal and the assemblage of lares."

28. The Hebrew has "and" instead of **therefore.** The LXX and the Syriac read "the rulers [princes] desecrated my holy things" (sanctuaries?). Houbigant, Klostermann,

---

Jeroboam "who made Israel to sin" and "did evil in the sight of the LORD, and walked in the way of his father" (I Kings 15:26 et passim). This poet sees contemporary Israel's iniquity in her ancestor Jacob (vs. 27). Paul labels the evil in us "the old man"; and "old" is the adjective associated in popular speech with wickedness—"Old Nick," "Old Boy," "Old Harry," etc. We speak of the evil as "the fast set"; but they are the retarded ones, reactionaries reverting to the outmoded ways of a re-

mote antiquity. Is it any wonder that sin bores God? The load it places on him is due not merely to its tiresome repetitiousness, but to the strain on his heart and conscience by the ill-doing and ill-being of dearly loved children. This is clear when his patient Son exclaims: "O faithless generation, how long am I to be with you? How long am I to bear with you?" (Mark 9:19). Here in Isaiah it is a load in the sins of all nations which the prophet felt placed on suffering Israel (cf. ch. 53). In the immediate pas-

44 Yet now hear, O Jacob my servant; and Israel, whom I have chosen:	44 "But now hear O Jacob my servant, Israel whom I have chosen!
2 Thus saith the LORD that made˚ thee, and formed thee from the womb, *which* will help thee; Fear not, O Jacob, my servant; and thou, Jeshurun, whom I have chosen.	2 Thus says the LORD who made you, who formed you from the womb and will help you: Fear not, O Jacob my servant, Jeshu'run whom I have chosen.

Cheyne, Whitehouse, Box, and G. A. Smith read substantially as follows, "Your princes have desecrated my sanctuary." Torrey emends שרי to עֲרֵי and translates, "Therefore I let my holy cities be profaned" (cf. 40:9; 44:26; 61:4; and especially 64:9). Yet the expression **princes of the sanctuary** is not unusual. It follows well upon vs. 27*b*, and may refer to the incidents recounted in II Kings 25:18-21.

Such passages as this should deliver the prophet from the charge of being divorced from the realities of history. He does not soar aloft on the wings of millenarian ecstasy, and even when he is most lyrical he is disciplined by thoughts such as those which characterize the foregoing developments.

7. SEVENTH STROPHE: "FEAR NOT, O ISRAEL" (44:1-2)

The seventh, eighth, and ninth strophes (vss. 1-2, 3-4, 5) match the second, third, and fourth (vss. 16-17, 18-19, 20-21). That the poet is about to announce some new and unprecedented disclosure is shown by the strong transition (**But now**), the same as the opening of 43:1-3*a*, with which the present strophe is closely related. Then follows the command to **hear**, the verb that most characteristically opens such prophetic introductions, and the intimate address to Israel, the chosen servant of the Lord. The second double line gives the prophetic oracular formula, **Thus says the LORD**, and is expanded in the style of the hymn (cf. 43:16-17). The third double line communicates the important admonition to his people, **Fear not**, and the words of address which follow repeat and deepen the opening line of 44:1.

44:1. The usual collocation of **servant** and chosen one (**whom I have chosen**) appears at the crucial point in the poem. It was through her election that Israel became the servant of the Lord. Yahweh *chose* Israel to be his servant. His purpose was to be fulfilled in the servant (cf. 41:8; 42:1).

2. The context of the oracular formula has a freshness and warmth and urgency which prevents it from becoming a stereotype form. So the prophet follows it with two participles of even greater intimacy: lit., "the one making you and the one forming you" (51:13; 54:5; cf. also 43:1, 15, where the verb is *bārā'*). Observe that election precedes creation. It is the reality and significance of the election that evokes the reflection upon creation. Second Isaiah is constantly seeking to ground Israel's unique character in something more ultimate than the Exodus. The two lines culminate in a single word in Hebrew, the one to which each of the impressive words of the strophe has been moving: [he] **will help you.** Yahweh's help is an important category of O.T. thought (Gen. 49:25; Exod. 18:4; Deut. 33:26; I Sam. 7:12; Ps. 33:20; etc.). It

sage (vs. 27) it is Israel's prolonged record of sinning which is the cause of God's fatigue. What an unbroken succession of sinning any man's or nation's career discloses!

44:1-2. *Fear Not, Jacob My Chosen.*—This strophe turns in characteristic abruptness with a **But now** to declare God's grace over against this black background of his undeserving people. The names by which God calls himself and his people are noteworthy: **The LORD who made you, who formed you from the womb and will** **help you; Jacob, my servant; Upright One whom I have chosen.** This is the poet's familiar insistence upon God's obligation for a nation whom he chose and made. The word **Jeshurun,** apparently coined by him, carries with it God's faith that unlikely Israel will startle the world by becoming righteous. We have had much to say of faith in God; but what of God's faith in us? That underlies his costly work of redemption: were he not confident that he could make a new man and a new people, he would leave us

3 For I will pour water upon him that is thirsty, and floods upon the dry ground: I will pour my Spirit upon thy seed, and my blessing upon thine offspring:

4 And they shall spring up *as* among the grass, as willows by the watercourses.

3 For I will pour water on the thirsty land,
　　and streams on the dry ground;
　I will pour my Spirit upon your descendants,
　　and my blessing on your offspring.
4 They shall spring up like grass amid waters,[y]
　　like willows by flowing streams.

[y] Gk Compare Tg: Heb *They shall spring up in among grass*

---

sometimes has the effect of a military *terminus technicus.* Yahweh is Israel's helper in battle. But the connotations of the word are broader and more extensive and are finally employed in an eschatological context, as we should expect in view of the motif of conquest and victory in battle on the day of Yahweh. Salvation and help are closely connected (cf. 41:10, 13, 14; 49:8; 50:7, 9). Israel's relation to Yahweh as one who has chosen and fashioned her in the womb ensures her of his help and salvation. **Jeshurun** is a poetic name for Israel, a diminutive of endearment derived from *yāshār*, "upright," and possibly of the prophet's own coinage (cf. Deut. 32:15; 33:5, 26). Second Isaiah is fond of hypocoristic names. Interestingly, the LXX reads "beloved Israel" (ὁ ἠγαπημένος Ἰσραήλ) instead of **Jeshurun.** Some Hebrew MSS, the Syriac, and the Targ. also read "Israel." The Vulg. has *rectissime.* Observe how the strophe begins and ends with references to the servant and the election.

8. Eighth Strophe: Water and the Spirit (44:3-4)

3. The introductory *kî* reinforces the admonition "Fear not." It is in the style of the assurance of the oracle of salvation. The **water on the thirsty land** continues the motif of 43:19-21. Here the thought is pressed into a more clearly eschatological context. The LXX reads, "For I will give water to the thirsty who walk in a dry land." The Hebrew has only "upon the thirsty" (cf. KJV), but the parallelism suggests that the land is meant. The transformation of nature is accompanied by the transformation of Israel's **descendants.** The physical and the psychical or spiritual are often combined in Second Isaiah. Yahweh pours out his gifts upon both, and both respond, since the land is viewed as alive and capable of response (see 32:15; Ps. 104:30). The **Spirit** of God imparts new life and vitality. Moses' intense longing that all of God's people might be prophets through the gift of God's Spirit upon them (Num. 11:29 [J]) becomes a promise for the new age (cf. Ezek. 37, where the Spirit infuses life into the dry bones). For a development of Second Isaiah's thought, see Joel 2:28 (Hebrew 3:1). For the relation of **water** and **Spirit,** see Mark 1:8-10 and parallels. The **blessing** which follows the gift is closely connected with it, for blessing contains within it power and vitality and life (cf. Pedersen, *Israel, Its Life and Culture, I-II,* pp. 182-212). The new age is ushered in with the Spirit.

4. Like grass amid waters: See the LXX. On the basis of the Arabic *ban* J. M. Allegro renders "as the green bay tree" (*Zeitschrift für die altestamentliche Wissenschaft* 64 [1952], 154-56).

---

in our sins. This strophe repeats the prophet's familiar **Fear not,** perhaps his most frequently used expression. He would agree with Thoreau: "Nothing is so much to be feared as fear; God himself likes atheism better."[7] Fear is atheism, utterly incompatible with trust in an all-sufficient and faithful God.

[7] Quoted by Emerson in *Lectures and Biographical Sketches,* "Perpetual Forces."

3-4. *An Unpromising People to Become Fruitful.*—Here a physical metaphor has a patently spiritual meaning. The **thirsty land** and **dry ground** are the people in their present plight in Babylon. They despaired of the future of their nation, but their **offspring** and **descendants** are to flourish. The prophet is not so much concerned with Israel the politically independent nation as with Israel the spiritual community,

5 One shall say, I *am* the LORD's; and another shall call *himself* by the name of Jacob; and another shall subscribe *with* his hand unto the LORD, and surname *himself* by the name of Israel.

5 This one will say, 'I am the LORD's,'
    another will call himself by the name
    of Jacob,
  and another will write on his hand, 'The
    LORD's,'
  and surname himself by the name of
    Israel."

---

9. NINTH STROPHE: NEW ADHERENTS TO THE COVENANT PEOPLE (44:5)

Who are these persons who, as a result of the gift of the Spirit and its attendant blessing, join themselves to the community of Israel? Are they apostate Israelites or those weak in faith who, as a result of seeing God's wonderful activity among his people, return to the covenant community of their fathers? Or are they foreigners who, witnessing the evidences of God's special concern for the chosen people, join themselves as proselytes to Israel? The answer is not easy. On the one hand, the foregoing context would seem to suggest that the reference is to Israelites (vss. 1-2); on the other, the return of disloyal Jews would not be nearly so much of a wonder as the conversion of aliens. If vs. 5 constitutes a new strophe, as seems probable, then it is likely that foreigners are meant and that an entirely new and surprising revelation is given here. Moreover, for an Israelite, even an apostate, to say, "I belong to Yahweh," does not make particular sense since he is already a member of Israel. The better solution is to think of proselytes. Then the climax is very effective and opens a wide door to the universality of Second Isaiah's thought.

5. This one will say, "I am the LORD's." An alternative translation is "I belong to Yahweh." A general religious movement was going on in the ancient Near East of the sixth century B.C. There was everywhere an openness and receptivity to other religions. As in a later period of history proselytes were attracted by Israel's monotheism and the ethical purity of her faith, so at a much earlier time men turned here and there to Israel as their spiritual home. The use of "Yahweh" as the divine name is especially interesting

---

which will be God's witness to all peoples. In the sequence of ideas, forgiveness with restoration to God's fellowship is followed by the gift of the **Spirit** and growth. This anticipates N.T. teaching. For some reason insufficient emphasis is laid today upon spiritual growth in Christians, in churches, and in nations. Among the books which John Henry Newman's mother gave him were those of the evangelical Biblical scholar, Scott, from whom, he tells us, he derived the principle that growth is the only evidence of life. Jowett, master of Balliol, wrote to Francis Turner Palgrave: "I hate to meet a man whom I have known ten years ago, and find that he is at precisely the same point, neither moderated, nor quickened, nor experienced, but simply stiffened: he ought to be beaten." [8] The same may be said of churches and nations. If there is spiritual life in them, there should be increasing evidences of spiritual maturity. Like Wordsworth's "happy Warrior," they should be "daily self-surpast."

The poem reaches a climax in an ingathering of new members of the community. These

[8] Abbott and Campbell, *Life and Letters of Jowett,* I, 414.

proselytes are lured by its spiritual excellence. If any religious community does not attract outsiders, something is wrong. It is meant "to declare the wonderful deeds of him who called [its members] out of darkness into his marvelous light" (I Pet. 2:9). In this instance the poet sees these heathen from the nations seeking incorporation in the spiritual Israel. It is worth noting that they assume not only the name of God —the LORD's—branded as a slave on the hand, but also the name of the community, **Jacob** or **Israel.** There is no purely personal religion, no attachment to God which does not involve fellowship with the company of the similarly devoted.

In recent decades the church was made little of. In Protestant circles a distinction was made between Christianity and "churchianity." Earnest and thoughtful Christians sometimes cherished a deep trust in Christ but felt no compelling impulse to become associated with the church. Even then, however, one may overhear confessions of their sense of lack. The poet Edward Rowland Sill, once set toward the ministry, but losing his faith under the impact of the Darwinian philosophy, wrote to a friend:

and emphasizes the covenant community of Israel who know God as he is revealed in the covenant relationship. **Another will call himself by the name of Jacob.** The M.T. reads "will call on the name of Jacob." However, it is better, with the RSV, to vocalize the word in the Niphal. So also the verb in vss. 5d (or in the Pual). They who call themselves by the name of Jacob do so because they see in the covenant people the community to which they would themselves belong. **And another** [lit., "this one"] **will write on his hand, "The LORD's"** or "belonging to Yahweh" (cf. the *lemélekh* seals on jar handles, etc., designating the owner to whom the object belonged; cf. 8:1). Volz aptly refers to the memorial signs bound on the hands, described in Exod. 13:16; Deut. 6:8-9; 11:18; Prov. 7:3. Levy refers to the branding of slaves with the owner's name or the branding practiced elsewhere in the religious cults of the East, though this was forbidden in Israel. This "writing" upon the hand will be a perpetual reminder and a physical sign that the proselyte belongs to Yahweh. Indeed, the words "belonging to Yahweh" on the body will ensure that the individual is in the possession of Yahweh. **And surname himself by the name of Israel:** The verb is cognate with the Arabic word *kunya*, a kind of household name which designates a person as being father of a particular child. The meaning is that the proselyte will add the name of Israel to his own name; he will be a member of the *bené 'isrā'ēl*, a *ben berîth* ("son of the covenant"). When Yahweh addresses Israel as "my people" or "sons," he will not feel himself an alien (cf. Ps. 87:4-5). All these considerations fortify the conviction that proselytes are referred to.

With the admission of foreigners to the community of the covenant people, the meaning of "Israel" acquires wider range and inclusiveness: not those who are Israel according to the flesh, but those who confess the God of Israel as Lord belong to the covenant community (cf. Rom. 8:14-17). To be sure, the prophet does not say this expressly, but the meaning exists in embryo. It is consistent with Israel's function as a

---

"For my part I long to 'fall in' with somebody. This picket duty is monotonous. I hanker after a shoulder on this side and the other." [9] The church has to embody herself in institutional forms, and these often appear to cramp her more ardent and inquiring members. She must learn in every generation to accord liberty in a fellowship which maintains loyalty to her Lord. This is always a difficult task and demands of her leaders a sympathetic spiritual insight. There are no unerring outward tests of Christian fidelity which may not become outworn or which do not prove unfit for all her members. Happily, amid the clash of current social forces a churchless Christianity has lost all appeal. We have returned to the N.T. position where faith in the church is an integral article of the Christian gospel. These proselytes in the prophet's vision were right in taking upon themselves the name of the historic fellowship, along with the name of God. Jacob and Israel doubtless always stood for much less than the fullness of the divine, and frequently appeared in glaring contradiction to God's character. But the faulty community was essential to his purposes and essential for the development and

effectiveness of those who were his servants and witnesses. Life with God is inherently social. The Spirit in the N.T. is the possession of the body of Christ, and in this poet's thought is poured out on Israel as the corporate community of God's people. It is in "the communion of the Holy Spirit" that the individual believer matures in power to serve God. Confronted with the battles and tasks of our difficult century, the ecumenical church may hear again the counsels of the Puritan leader, John Winthrop, addressed to his people about to undertake the settlement of a new land:

We must be knit together in this work as one man. We must entertain each other in brotherly affection, we must be willing to abridge ourselves of our superfluities, for the supply of others' necessities. We must uphold a familiar commerce together in all meekness, gentleness, patience and liberality. We must delight in each other, make other's conditions our own, rejoice together, mourn together, labor and suffer together, always having before our eyes our commission and community in the work . . . as members of the same body.[1]

God's redemption of his people, then and now, is never complete until he makes of them a

[9] William B. Parker, *Edward Rowland Sill, His Life and Works* (Boston: Houghton Mifflin Co., 1915), p. 129.

[1] *A Model of Christian Charity*, ed. S. E. Morison (Boston: Old South Association, 1916).

6 Thus saith the Lord the King of Israel, and his Redeemer the Lord of hosts; I *am* the first, and I *am* the last; and besides me *there is* no God.

6 Thus says the Lord, the King of Israel
and his Redeemer, the Lord of hosts:
"I am the first and I am the last;
besides me there is no god.

---

missionary people to the nations and with the prophet's constant concern for the nations. The passage prepares the way for such poems as 52:13–53:12 and especially ch. 55.

H. Yahweh Glorifies Himself in Israel (44:6-8, 21-23)

The exegete's primary problem here is to determine the extent of the poem, and the chief issue to be settled is the authenticity of vss. 9-20. If this section is original in its present context, then the poem is of substantial length, like several others which have been encountered heretofore. If it does not belong here, then the literary unit is much smaller, for students generally hold that vs. 24 begins a new poem. Those who belong to the school of literary form criticism (*Gattungskritik*) generally favor this position. It must be admitted that the question of the genuineness of vss. 9-20 is not yet finally settled. It is not hard to find a continuity between this composition and the rest of the poems. Not only is the polemic against idolatry a persistent motif (40:18-20; 41:6-7, 29), but the stress on monotheism in 43:8-13 and in 44:6-8 prepares the way for what is given in this section. The important verb in vs. 21, "I have fashioned you," seems to follow admirably upon the description of the fashioning of the idols in vss. 9-20 (note the first words of vss. 9-10 and cf. vs. 12; cf. also the synonyms like עשה, "made"). The emphases of the passage in vss. 15*de*, 17 are congenial to the general context. Moreover, much of the language and imagery is characteristic of Second Isaiah. On the other hand, there are discrepancies of style. But do they indicate a diversity of authorship? Again, to whom does the demonstrative pronoun these in vs. 21 refer? Kissane and others say that it most naturally applies to what has been said in vss. 9-20. But here the argument is clearly on the side of the *Gattungskritiker,* for as Wade and others who make nothing of this form of approach point out, the reference applies much better to vss. 6-8. More important is the general theme of all the poems in this section, the theme of redemption, which is uppermost in the prophet's mind as the introductions and conclusions of the strophes or poems clearly show. Vss 9-20 do not fit in well with this emphasis. In all probability it is the work of Second Isaiah, but it does not seem to belong here. If we remove the satire from its present position, then the literary situation is clear. The poetic section in vss. 6-8 is followed by vss. 21-23. The succeeding poem will make clear why the prophet comes to such a triumphant climax here. He is about to make a very important disclosure, which is here announced for the first time.

---

spiritual fellowship which fascinates and draws outsiders and incorporates them all into one community for the spread of his reign over the entire world. And all this is the manifestation of the might of his grace.

6-23. The Redeemer of Israel Is Alone God. —If vss. 6-8, 21-23 are considered a separate short poem—a confessedly difficult critical problem—it must also be granted that whoever divided it—the original poet himself or some editor—and employed its parts as the background for the satire on idol making in vss. 9-20, showed acute spiritual insight. The two divisions supply a contrasting introduction and a devout conclusion to a poem otherwise only a biting, negative polemic. Those employing the material in vss. 6-23 for teaching or preaching will do well to combine all of it as it now stands, remembering that (*a*) the poem in vss. 6-8, 21-23 offers scarcely anything which has not been dealt with already in the immediately preceding poems; it therefore will bring no new message to our contemporaries, and (*b*) the poem does, however, admirably set forth the prophet's sublime conviction of the only living God, Israel's Redeemer and King, and is a foil to the penetrating humor with which he exposes the absurdity of idolatry and the tragic religious plight of its devotees.

The Expos. will follow the Exeg., treating first the brief poem in vss. 6-8, 21-23, then the satire in vss. 9-20.

6-8. God a Rock to His People.—These verses contain one new word, Rock, applied to God.

7 And who, as I, shall call, and shall declare it, and set it in order for me, since I
appointed the ancient people? and the
things that are coming, and shall come, let
them show unto them.

7 Who is like me? Let him proclaim it,
  let him declare and set it forth before
  me.
Who has announced from of old the
  things to come?[z]
Let them tell us[a] what is yet to be.

[z] Cn: Heb *from my placing an eternal people and things
to come*
[a] Tg: Heb *them*

The poem is of two series of three strophes (vss. 6, 7, 8, 21, 22, 23), each group
having its own unity and climax (cf. 43:16-21; 44:1-5). The literary forms are not
difficult to detect. Vss. 6-8 have the style and form of the speech of a plaintiff (cf. 41:5, 26;
43:9), although it must be remembered that the plaintiff is also the judge. Vss. 21-22
are described as an exhortation (*Mahnwort*) by both Begrich and Gressmann, but vs. 22
is surely in the style of the oracle of salvation (cf. 43:25), and vs. 23 is certainly a hymn.

1. First Strophe: King, Redeemer, Lord of Hosts and Lord of Time (44:6)

6. The King of Israel: Cf. 41:21. The climax of 43:15*b* ("your King") here takes
a place of prominence, but not over the thought of redemption. Israel's **King** is her
Redeemer (see 43:14). Yahweh's sovereignty over history and over Israel, his people,
grows increasingly clearer. **The Lord of hosts:** Used here for the first time in Second
Isaiah (45:13; 47:4; 48:2; 51:15; 54:5; cf. 40:26 and especially 52:7*e*). It is not a verse-
filling epithet (Duhm), but a title of the greatest import, describing the exaltation of
God over all the hosts of heaven and earth. Such a lofty ascription prepares magnificently
for the words to follow (cf. 43:14). The Dead Sea Scroll reads, "The Lord of hosts
is his name" (cf. Amos 4:13; 5:8). **I am the first and I am the last:** Cf. the impressive
words of 41:4; 48:12*cd*; note also the usage of this form in Rev. 1:8, 17, and its expansion
in 22:13. The succession of divine titles is illuminating: "Yahweh," Israel's covenant
God; **the King of Israel,** sovereign over her life and destiny; **his Redeemer** from bondage
in the past and in the imminent future; **Lord of hosts,** omnipotent and exalted; **first
and . . . last,** Lord of beginning and Lord of end and an eternal God; the only
God beside whom there is none other.

2. Second Strophe: God of History and Prophecy (44:7)

Second Isaiah reverts to a theme which never ceases to stir his imagination and
wonder. To the covenant people of Israel, and to them alone, God reveals himself as
Lord of history. It is he who causes events to occur, he initiates them, determines their
course and sequence, makes them known through his servants the prophets, and brings
them to fulfillment. Only he proclaims them, none other; only he declares them and
sets them forth in order; only he announces them **from of old** and tells what is **yet to be.**
Dominating all three strophes is the proof that Yahweh alone is God.

7. The LXX reads the first line as follows: "Who is like me? Let him stand forth,
let him proclaim." The Vulg. follows the LXX in the independence of the first words,
as do many commentators and some modern translations. The Hebrew does not have
"let him stand forth" (στήτω), but Hebrew legal terminology favors it, for the verb
עמד is a typical *terminus technicus* of court speech. Moreover, the setting would then

---

It is a word used in Deut. 32:4, 15, 18, 30, 31,
37—a poem which has many affinities with those
of this prophet—and in other poetical passages.
It is used to assert God's unchangeable fidelity
to his people and his utter dependableness.

Idols of man's making show the fickleness of
human fashions. They are dated. One generation fabricates after one pattern, and its successor is governed by a changed taste. The invisible
God of Israel's faith knows no variableness.

8 Fear ye not, neither be afraid: have not I told thee from that time, and have declared *it?* ye *are* even my witnesses. Is there a God besides me? yea, *there is* no God; I know not *any.*

9 ¶ They that make a graven image *are* all of them vanity; and their delectable things shall not profit; and they *are* their own witnesses; they see not, nor know; that they may be ashamed.

10 Who hath formed a god, or molten a graven image *that* is profitable for nothing?

8 Fear not, nor be afraid;
    have I not told you from of old and
        declared it?
    And you are my witnesses!
    Is there a God besides me?
    There is no Rock; I know not any."

9 All who make idols are nothing, and the things they delight in do not profit; their witnesses neither see nor know, that they may be put to shame. 10 Who fashions a god or casts an image, that is profitable

---

approximate those of 41:21 ff.; 43:9. On the other hand, it would make the line rather heavy and destroy the triad of verbs. Perhaps it is safest to follow the Hebrew and read as the RSV, though the LXX reading is possible. The Hebrew in vs. 7c is unintelligible. The RSV adopts H. Oort's emendation מי השמיע מעולם אתיות, **Who has announced from of old the things to come?** Torrey's emendation is preferable (reading משמיע) but the result is the same. When was it Yahweh **announced** these things **from of old?** Duhm suggests happily that Second Isaiah may have the time of Noah in mind (Gen. 8:21-22; 9:25 ff.), or even Gen. 3. A more likely solution would be that he is thinking of the promises to the patriarchs, especially Abraham (Gen. 12:1-3; 18:18). The Dead Sea Scroll inserts "and he said" before the last line.

3. THIRD STROPHE: "FEAR NOT: I AM THE GOD OF HISTORY, I ALONE" (44:8)

8. The thought of the prophet culminates in a twofold call of encouragement, **Fear not, nor be afraid.** Neither of these verbs is the one usually employed, and the second word occurs only here in the O.T. Several scholars restore the word to the usual תירא. This is now confirmed by the reading of the Dead Sea Scroll, תיראו, which should be adopted. **And you are my witnesses:** See 43:10, 12. Israel is called to be God's prophet. She must witness to his character and activity and purpose in the world, but above all, she must proclaim that he alone is God (cf. Deut. 32:4; Isa. 17:10; 30:29; Ps. 18:31; etc.). **I know not any:** Some scholars, following Houbigant, emend to בלעדי, "apart from me" or **beside me,** which is not very happy in view of its presence in the previous line.

9-20. See Exeg., pp. 510-15.

Amid "the vast driftings of the cosmic weather," religious beliefs, like everything else, are affected. A believer in the one living and true God looks and sings:

Change and decay in all around I see;
O thou, who changest not, abide with me.

How different the products of men's thought and fabrication which bear the marks of human finitude and sin! They are as fleeting in form as their mortal producers.

For their rock is not as our Rock,
Our enemies being the umpires.[2]

[2] S. R. Driver, *A Critical and Exegetical Commentary on Deuteronomy* (New York: Charles Scribner's Sons, 1895; "International Critical Commentary"), p. 371.

Men, homeless in an alien universe, crave the permanent, something or someone to tie to. Beyond the fluid thoughts of deity in human minds, the First and the Last continues from generation to generation. Our individual conceptions of God vary as we mature and as we are played on by the shifting trends of current thinking, but his association with us remains.

Thou broadenest out with every year
Each breadth of life to meet.[3]

His people find him "a rock of habitation" whereunto century after century they "continually resort" (Ps. 71:3).

9-20. See pp. 510-15.

[3] Frederick W. Faber, "The God of My Childhood," st. xiv.

11 Behold, all his fellows shall be ashamed; and the workmen, they *are* of men: let them all be gathered together, let them stand up; *yet* they shall fear, *and* they shall be ashamed together.

12 The smith with the tongs both worketh in the coals, and fashioneth it with hammers, and worketh it with the strength of his arms: yea, he is hungry, and his strength faileth: he drinketh no water, and is faint.

13 The carpenter stretcheth out *his* rule; he marketh it out with a line; he fitteth it with planes, and he marketh it out with the compass, and maketh it after the figure of a man, according to the beauty of a man; that it may remain in the house.

14 He heweth him down cedars, and taketh the cypress and the oak, which he strengtheneth for himself among the trees of the forest: he planteth an ash, and the rain doth nourish *it*.

15 Then shall it be for a man to burn: for he will take thereof, and warm himself; yea, he kindleth *it,* and baketh bread; yea, he maketh a god, and worshippeth *it;* he maketh it a graven image, and falleth down thereto.

16 He burneth part thereof in the fire; with part thereof he eateth flesh; he roasteth roast, and is satisfied: yea, he warmeth *himself,* and saith, Aha, I am warm, I have seen the fire:

17 And the residue thereof he maketh a god, *even* his graven image: he falleth down unto it, and worshippeth *it,* and prayeth unto it, and saith, Deliver me; for thou *art* my god.

18 They have not known nor understood: for he hath shut their eyes, that they cannot see; *and* their hearts, that they cannot understand.

19 And none considereth in his heart, neither *is there* knowledge nor understanding to say, I have burned part of it in the fire; yea, also I have baked bread upon the coals thereof; I have roasted flesh, and eaten *it:* and shall I make the residue thereof an abomination? shall I fall down to the stock of a tree?

20 He feedeth on ashes: a deceived heart hath turned him aside, that he cannot deliver his soul, nor say, *Is there* not a lie in my right hand?

for nothing? 11 Behold, all his fellows shall be put to shame, and the craftsmen are but men; let them all assemble, let them stand forth, they shall be terrified, they shall be put to shame together.

12 The ironsmith fashions it[b] and works it over the coals; he shapes it with hammers, and forges it with his strong arm; he becomes hungry and his strength fails, he drinks no water and is faint. 13 The carpenter stretches a line, he marks it out with a pencil; he fashions it with planes, and marks it with a compass; he shapes it into the figure of a man, with the beauty of a man, to dwell in a house. 14 He cuts down cedars; or he chooses a holm tree or an oak and lets it grow strong among the trees of the forest; he plants a cedar and the rain nourishes it. 15 Then it becomes fuel for a man; he takes a part of it and warms himself, he kindles a fire and bakes bread; also he makes a god and worships it, he makes it a graven image and falls down before it. 16 Half of it he burns in the fire; over the half he eats flesh, he roasts meat and is satisfied; also he warms himself and says, "Aha, I am warm, I have seen the fire!" 17 And the rest of it he makes into a god, his idol; and falls down to it and worships it; he prays to it and says, "Deliver me, for thou art my god!"

18 They know not, nor do they discern; for he has shut their eyes, so that they cannot see, and their minds, so that they cannot understand. 19 No one considers, nor is there knowledge or discernment to say, Half of it I burned in the fire, I also baked bread on its coals, I roasted flesh and have eaten; and shall I make the residue of it an abomination? Shall I fall down before a block of wood? 20 He feeds on ashes; a deluded mind has led him astray, and he cannot deliver himself or say, "Is there not a lie in my right hand?"

[b] Cn: Heb *an axe*

21 ¶ Remember these, O Jacob and Israel; for thou *art* my servant: I have formed thee; thou *art* my servant: O Israel, thou shalt not be forgotten of me. 22 I have blotted out, as a thick cloud, thy transgressions, and, as a cloud, thy sins: return unto me; for I have redeemed thee.	21 Remember these things, O Jacob, and Israel, for you are my servant; I formed you, you are my servant; O Israel, you will not be forgotten by me. 22 I have swept away your transgressions like a cloud, and your sins like mist; return to me, for I have redeemed you.

4. Fourth Strophe: "Remember These Things, My Servant Israel" (44:21)

21. The reference to Israel in the introduction (vs. 6) and in the last strophe ("my witnesses") now receives its full scope and play. She is addressed with the prophet's most significant and characteristic title, **my servant. These things:** (See above, p. 505.) The things Israel must remember are the disclosures of vss. 6-8; if she is to be the Lord's witness and servant she will have to remember, for the faith of Israel, with its profound assertion of a historical revelation, communicates itself by its memorabilia. **You will not be forgotten by me:** The Hebrew has the Niphal with a first person pronominal suffix (lit., "thou will not be forgotten me"). The versions render as the RSV. Fischer explains the verb as the Hiphil of נשא: "you will not disappoint me." So, interestingly, the Dead Sea Scroll (cf. 49:15).

5. Fifth Strophe: Forgiveness and Repentance (44:22)

22. "The perfect tense . . . represents a triumphant flight of faith rather than an accomplished theological fact" (Torrey, *Second Isaiah,* p. 354). This is the true explanation of many similar perfects in Second Isaiah. Forgiveness is so sure a reality that he portrays it as prior to repentance. **Return to me, for I have redeemed you** is the perfect expression of the situation, but its explanation is discovered in the logic of personal experience, not in the logic of time. The lines are very similar to 43:25, and are consciously repeated here at the close of a succession of poems on God's redemptive activity. The figure of the **cloud** and the **mist** is most happy, one that would appeal to an Oriental. Sin hangs like a cloud or mist over Israel, but like the rising of the sun, Yahweh comes to drive it away.

21-23. The Gospel of Redemption.—In vs. 21 there is a mutual remembering: Israel is bidden to **remember,** for she encounters God in her history, and he assures her **you will not be forgotten by me.** The idols are disconnected from the events of history; they neither influence them nor interpret them. They speak not, see not, hear not (Ps. 115:5-6). They are mindless things. But the Lord is "mindful" of his people (Ps. 115:12). He "thinks on" the nation and the individual (Ps. 40:17).

I formed you. This idea of God's fashioning the nation here (if we use these verses after the satire in vss. 9-20) is in suggestive contrast with the manufacture of an idol. The poet has pictured a skillful and painstaking artisan at work on an idol, and despite the poet's scorn of the man's inanity, he cannot withhold admiration of his craftsmanship. Is God to be thought less expert or less laborious in his creative toil on men and nations? An idol will have a limited existence, especially in a turbulent world where conquerors destroy their victims' gods; but a nation goes its way through centuries, as Israel has done, and a man's spirit is formed for eternal fellowship with God. Christians do well to **remember these things.**

Vs. 22 is one of the richest utterances of the gospel. It is not so much his people's captivity that occupies God's concern, but their sin. And the order of the words is thoroughly evangelical: God first forgives, then calls on them to repent. We usually place the two in a different sequence, making pardon follow repentance. But God redeemed Israel from bondage in Egypt, and again in Babylon, independently of her penitence. Indeed, it was his "goodness" which led to her repentance. The sacrifice of Christ long precedes the return of sinning men to their Father, and forms the compelling inspira-

23 Sing, O ye heavens; for the LORD hath done *it*: shout, ye lower parts of the earth: break forth into singing, ye mountains, O forest, and every tree therein: for the LORD hath redeemed Jacob, and glorified himself in Israel.

23 Sing, O heavens, for the LORD has done it;
shout, O depths of the earth;
break forth into singing, O mountains,
O forest, and every tree in it!
For the LORD has redeemed Jacob,
and will be glorified in Israel.

6. Sixth Strophe: The Lord Has Redeemed Israel (44:23)

23. As the prophet contemplates the divine forgiveness and redemption, he breaks forth in an ecstatic cry of joy. The great news has come, and the heavens must confess and extol what God has done. **Sing, O heavens, for the LORD has done** [it]. The prophet was familiar with the folk belief of the singing of the heavens, the stars and the greater luminaries (cf. Exeg. on 40:26). The whole expanse of the firmament must resound with joy for this deed of God. **Shout, O depths of the earth:** Even the deepest abysses and hidden caverns will awaken to song and join the universal chorus. The **mountains** with their ancient security and strength will bear their joyous witness (cf. 41:19-20). The forest, too, and every tree in it must break silence (55:12-13). Nature yields her voice to history. Then with a final shout the prophet communicates the content of the great news which he has been proclaiming all along:

Yahweh has redeemed Jacob
and will glorify himself in Israel!

J. A Satire on the Making of Idols (44:9-20)

See Exeg. on 44:6-8, 21-23. The polemic against the manufacture of **idols** is surely no alien interest in Second Isaiah (40:19-20; 41:6-7, 29; 45:16; 46:5-7). It is consistent with the whole tenor of his thought and an inevitable part of his view and portrait of God.

Torrey, Kissane, Fischer, and Ziegler render the passage in poetic form, and careful reading of the Hebrew confirms their judgment in this matter. The parallelism is apparent almost throughout, and the presence of strophes can hardly be denied. That the writer has had difficulty in transmitting in poetry the description of what he has seen is apparent. Here he is setting forth a masterful portrayal of his own observation, and a regular or smooth rhythm does not come easily to him. There are exceptions, of course; some lines are fairly smooth, and the parallelism is effective (vss. 12-13, 15-17). But often the details seem to stand in his way and he does the best with the words as they rise before his memory and imagination. Second Isaiah is describing what he has seen. He has observed the idol makers at their work, and has stood there, watching the process step by step and

tion to leave the far country of self-will and go home to God. **Return to me, for I have redeemed you** is the announcement of the gospel in both the O.T. and the N.T.

Vs. 23 is a characteristic outburst of exultation. **The LORD has done it.** The people had not yet shown any impulse to return to him. The jubilation is not over sinners who repent, but over a God who redeems. Presumably Babylon had fallen, and this filled the poet's heart with exultation. He could not help singing, shouting, breaking forth. In such expressions we gain an inkling of the character of this nameless prophet. His joy runs over upon the world about him, and **heavens, depths of the earth, mountains** seem in sympathetic gladness. Such exuberance of spirit is a result of his faith.

G. K. Chesterton has reminded modern folk of the nexus between belief and hilarity: "If we are to be truly gay, we must believe that there is some eternal gaiety in the nature of things. . . . The thing called high spirits is possible only to the spiritual." [4]

Again, if we use this passage as it now stands, for the climax of the satire on idolatry contained in vss. 9-20, what a contrast between the pitiable idolater feeding his soul on ashes (vs. 20) and this buoyant and blithesome believer who "rejoices with the truth" and is a sharer in the joy of his Lord!

9-20. *A Satire on the Making of Idols.*—From the first dogmatic sentence this is a biting and contemptuous denunciation of idolatry. It is

[4] *Heretics* (New York: John Lane Co., 1912), p. 110.

missing nothing of the workman's craft, though not so sympathetic perhaps to his art and devotion. He is too good a Hebrew to contemplate the manufacture of idols with equanimity or objectivity. The conviction that Yahweh must not be seen by mortal eye is written so deep in the heritage that it may be accepted as essentially historical. The Elohistic narrative of Exod. 33:14-23, freed of its accretions, reveals an extraordinary experience of Moses himself in which the visibility of Yahweh is the great issue at stake. This one request which Moses makes with an intense urgency is denied him. Beyond the mists which hover over these records the faith in the invisibility of Yahweh emerges as a central reality. The representation of the Elohistic decalogue (Exod. 20:4a) may preserve a tradition long antecedent to the eighth century. Indeed, it is not too venturesome to assert that the tradition may go back to Moses himself.

1. FIRST STROPHE: THE FUTILITY OF IDOL MAKING (44:9)

9. Men who fashion images are bent upon a futile enterprise. The word for **nothing** means, lit., "chaos," as in Gen. 1:2a; Isa. 34:11; Jer. 4:23 (cf. Isa. 40:17; 41:29; 45:18-19). The opening line is a wholesale and outright denunciation of human attempts to make a likeness of God. The prophet admits the fascination that the idols cause their worshipers. But, he says, they have no value, for they accomplish **nothing** (cf. 41:22). He does not distinguish between the image and the numen or divinity which functions in and through the image. Whitehouse, Skinner, and Volz propose emending **witnesses** (עדיהם) to "servants" or "worshipers" (עבדים). This is doubtless the appropriate meaning here, but **witnesses** is probably meant to reflect it. **Neither see nor know:** The words are in contrast to Israel, who is called upon again and again that she may see and know what Yahweh has done for her (cf. 41:20). The inane, lifeless idol gives neither sight nor

typical of Hebrew religious thought at its loftiest. The prophets of Israel, with their passionate devotion to the invisible God of righteousness, had no interest in the aesthetic approach to religion characteristic of some other peoples. They had an aesthetic appreciation of nature, and there is no question of their sublime attainments in poetry; but any artistic representation of deity, however lovely and awesome, was to them a degradation of the Holy One. Doubtless they were right. Israel's unique witness to God, by far the richest contribution to the faith of mankind—indeed, worth far more than all others put together—would have been watered down had it compromised with the faiths which found inspiration in man-made images. But in contrast with this poet's sweeping condemnation of all idol makers, and his unqualified assertion that all images of the divine are without profit, we may recall what statues of deities have meant to those for whom they had numinous power and were symbols of the unseen.

Far more charming to us than the art of the Babylonians is that of Greece, whose most renowned sculptor, Phidias, carved the figure of Olympian Zeus at Elis. A philosopher-missionary, Dion Chrysostom, bent on the moral elevation of his people in the first century of our era, has left his testimony to the effect which this colossal statue had on him: "Whosoever among mortal men is most utterly toil-worn in spirit, having drunk the cup of many sorrows and calamities, when he stands before this image, methinks, must utterly forget all the terrors and woes of this mortal life." [5] No trace of this magnificent statue remains, save reproductions of it on coins, but in our modern world a chief religious statue of another highly artistic people, the figure of Buddha in bronze, dramatically placed at the end of a lovely valley in Kamakura, Japan, still fascinates and awes those who stand before its majestic serenity. Its half-opened eyes—suggestive of wisdom beyond man's, from some imperturbable realm—seem to penetrate the soul. There can be no question of the elevating and humbling impressions on men made by such works of devout art. One cannot say categorically that they **do not profit.** But their worth for such spiritual fellowship with God as Israel's prophets knew is another matter. One recalls a scene in the life of Heinrich Heine, heir of Israel's faith although often scornful of it, who during the Revolution of 1848, on the last day he was out before his long final illness, found himself flustered by the crowd, and took refuge in the Louvre. He sought out the Venus of Milo: "At her feet I lay a long time . . . and wept so as to move a stone to pity. And the blessed Goddess of Beauty, our Dear Lady of Milo, looked down on

[5] *Discourses* XII. 51.

knowledge. The Hebrew has an emphatic personal pronoun "they" following **their witnesses,** which the KJV and the ASV render by **their own.** The word is marked with *punctus extraordinarius* and is without accent in the M.T., suggesting that it is spurious. The effect or consequence of idol worship is expressed as the purpose of the worshipers, as though they are worshiping, intentionally closing their eyes and minds, in order to **be put to shame.** This substitution of purpose for consequence is not infrequent in the O.T. (cf. 6:10). Man acts thoughtlessly, as Volz finely observes, but the prophet makes human responsibility plain.

2. Second Strophe: Judgment upon the Idol Makers (44:10-11)

10. The idol maker intends to make **a god** (*'ēl*), but produces an ineffectual **image** instead (cf. Jer. 7:8).

11. *Hēn,* **behold,** introduces the judgment (cf. 41:11, 24, 29) upon the members of the idol's cult. The particle follows nicely upon the previous lines. **All his fellows:** The word is a passive participle "those who are united" or "joined"; cf. Hos. 4:17, "Ephraim is joined to idols," חבור עצבים (but see critical apparatus in Kittel's *Biblia Hebraica,* 3rd ed.). Kissane feels that the reference to the associates or fellows is the guild of craftsmen, not the worshipers. **And the craftsmen are but men:** The Hebrew is probably corrupt. The LXX reads, "and let all the deaf be gathered together," translating חרשים as "deaf," which is nonsense. Torrey emends the line to וחרשיו מהמה מאדם, "And as for those who fashion them, confusion is all they can accomplish" (cf. Deut. 6:5; II Kings 23:25). If the text is to be altered, this is an excellent solution. The meaning of the RSV is simply that the craftsmen are only human beings. A man cannot make a god. **Let them all assemble . . . :** Words and lines characteristic of the writer, yet not composed entirely in his customary manner. They are reminiscent of the terminology of the judicial scenes.

3. Third Strophe: The Ironsmith (44:12)

12. The ironsmith fashions it: A notorious *crux interpretum.* The Hebrew has the word **axe** following "worker in iron," which does not yield sense, as all commentators recognize. The RSV emends מעצד to יצרהו (cf. vs. 12c, where it is parallel as here to פעל). The LXX meets the difficulty by repeating the last word in vs. 11 (so Syriac) and translating it as "sharpen" (ὤξυνεν τέκτων σίδηρον: "the workman sharpens the iron"). Aside from the violence of this procedure, it destroys the parallelism with vs. 13 and

---

me with mingled compassion and desolation, seeming to say: 'Dost thou not see that I have no arms, and therefore cannot help thee?' " [6] It is an eloquent corroboration of the prophet's conviction.

10-11. Can Men Make God?—The men in the idol shop may associate together to bolster one another's confidence in their mutual work, but the net result is confusion and shame.

The essential element in revelation is that it originates in God. It is as idolatrous to grave an image in our thought as to carve it in stone. The distinctive factor is, Did it originate with us or with God? According to the O.T., man does not search for God and then make in his mind the best image of him of which he is capable. He lets God speak his word to him, and say who he is. To the Christian Jesus Christ

is God's self-portrait. Hence the necessity in all our religious thinking of starting with Christ and testing the result at every step by God's word made flesh in him. This was a chief recovery of faith made by Luther:

Begin by applying thy skill and study to Christ, there also let them continue fixed, and if thine own thoughts or reason or some one else guide and direct thee otherwise, only close thine eyes and say: I must and will know of no other God, save in my Lord Christ. . . . Anything that one imagines of God apart from Christ is only useless thinking and vain idolatry.[7]

12. Can Workers Who Tire Make an Untiring God?—The poet stresses again the unwearying God whom these exiles needed, as does our

[6] Lewis Browne, *That Man Heine* (New York: The Macmillan Co., 1927), p. 362.

[7] Quoted by Adolf Harnack, *History of Dogma* (tr. Neil Buchanan; Boston: Roberts Bros., 1895-1903), VII, 199 n.

encounters further difficulty with the succeeding words. Others omit the word as a gloss. But a gloss must have some explanation. Torrey emends מעצד to מעצב (Piel participle, *me'aççebh*) and translates, "the worker in iron cuts out" (cf. Job 10:8). In the Gezer calendar (1. 3) the word עצד seems to be present in the sense of cutting. If this is the right reading, it is best to retain the C.T.

4. FOURTH STROPHE: THE CARPENTER (44:13)

13. The carpenter or "worker in wood" is contrasted to the worker in iron of vs 12. The poet devotes a strophe to each. **The carpenter stretches a line** in order to measure the dimensions of the image he proposes to make, then draws an outline (תאר) of it with a pencil (שׂרד) or stylus. The word for **pencil**, as for **planes**, appears only here in the O.T. The meaning of the former word is derived from the context, the latter from its cognates (cf. Lev. 14:41). It is a scraping instrument or chisel designed to reduce the timber to the size and proportions of the image. **A compass**: From a root meaning "circle." The line seems out of order. The LXX omits vs. 13cd and reads instead "and fits it with glue." **He shapes it into the figure of a man**: Better, "He makes it like a human figure." Out of the crude timber a man! **With the beauty of a man**: Better, "Like a handsome man." **To dwell in a house**: In a temple or domestic shrine.

5. FIFTH STROPHE: WOOD FOR FUEL AND A GOD (44:14-15)

14. After describing the careful assiduity with which each step is carried out, the satirist presses his main point by reverting to the first stage in the process, the cutting of wood from the forest. It is as though he were saying, "Now look where this god comes from!" **He cuts down cedars**: The verb is an infinitive construct, but a finite verb is required. **Cedars . . . holm . . . oak**: With characteristic concreteness the writer identifies the various kinds of wood. It is possible that he has a special reason for doing so. Certain trees were sacred to different gods in Babylonia (e.g., the cedar). **Or he chooses a holm tree or an oak**: You can take various kinds of wood for the purpose! The idol maker does it all. If he cannot find the tree he wants, then he cultivates ("makes grow strong") one of the trees himself that it may serve his purpose. The word ארן occurs only here, but in many MSS the third letter is written as a minuscule, implying that the word was actually the word for **cedar**, ארז. Köhler (Ludwig Köhler and W. Baumgärtner, *Lexicon in Veteris Testamenti Libros* [Leiden: E. J. Brill, 1918-], *ad loc.*) identifies it with the laurel (*Lauria nobilis;* Immanuel Löw, *Die Flora der Juden* [Wien & Leipzig: R. Löwit, 1924-31], II, 119-23). The LXX reads κύριος (אדן), "lord"; hence, "which the Lord planted," or as some render it, "He planted a god."

15. Part of the tree he uses for fuel to keep himself warm, part he kindles into fire for baking bread, and part of it (introduced by the particle *'aph,* **yea**) "he makes into a

---

generation. How can a product of a workman who tires as he toils at his forge be the deity whom they can rely on?

13. *Painstaking Craftsmen Make a Comely Figure.*—The skill and pains of the workman claim the poet's admiration. He grants that the figure fabricated is a handsome man. But how he ridicules this so easily domesticated deity, **to dwell in a house!** The nineteenth century domesticated its conception of God. He became a Father, entirely like ourselves. One heard much of "the humanity of God." Protestant churches were constructed with the comfortable furnishings of the homes of the well to do. The element of homage disappeared from worship.

Men became "chummy" with God in sentimental hymns and prayers. They forgot that in religion that only helps us before which we bow. Sinful creatures became presumptuously at home with the lofty One who inhabits eternity, whose name is holy. In the twentieth century, theology has sought to stress the difference between God and man. He is not "wholly other," or we could not have fellowship with him; but he is certainly "other" with thoughts and ways far above ours and unlike ours, as this prophet insists (55:8-9).

14-15. *One Log for Fuel and Deity.*—Utility and comfort are not readily combined with passionate faith. That demands a complete

god and worships it" or "he fashions it into an idol and prostrates himself before it." The juxtaposition of the two pairs of verbs is effective: **he makes a god and worships it; he fashions an idol, and prostrates himself.** The parallel in Horace, *Satires* (I. 8. 1 ff.) is cited by most commentators:

> *Olim truncus eram ficulnus, inutile lignum,*
> *Cum faber, incertus scamnum faceretne Priapum,*
> *Maluit esse Deum.*

"Once I was a trunk of fig-wood, a worthless log, when a carpenter, doubtful whether to make a stool or a Priapus [the god of gardens], chose that I should be a god." Wisd. Sol. 13:11-13 is influenced by this and other passages in Second Isaiah. Observe the climax of vss. 15*de* and cf. vss. 13*ef*, 17*cd*, 19*fg*. The emphasis is everywhere the same from the opening line of vs. 9 on, and each emphasis heightens the ridicule. The succession of verbs in very short lines greatly enhances the effect of the final lines of the strophes.

6. Sixth Strophe: Out of the Residue a God (44:16-17)

The strophic division of the poem is not marked by any formal elements, but it seems likely that the writer is proceeding a step further in the biting detail of his irony. The strophe elaborates vs. 15, proceeding point by point, line by merciless line, as in preceding strophes, but here the writer breaks out in scorn mingled with laughter at the whole business.

16. Half of it . . . over the half: Two halves make a whole, so strictly speaking there is no residue left for the god. This has prompted many scholars to emend the second "half of it" (חֶצְיוֹ) to "its coals" (גֶחָלָיו). Codex B reads, "Upon half of it he bakes loaves on the coals," which is very close to vs. 19*d* (cf. Syriac). The Dead Sea Scroll reads, instead of "He roasts meat and is satisfied; also he warms himself," וְעַל נֶחָלָיו יֵשֵׁב וְיֵחַם, "he sits by the coals and warms himself." There is much to be said for this reading, but the case is not decisive. **He eats flesh, he roasts meat** (lit., "roasts roast"; cf. KJV): The order is strange, one expects just the reverse (cf. LXX). Many scholars therefore change the order of the two verbs. And now the man **warms himself** and luxuriates in the comfort of the heat. The brief quotation is characteristic of the prophet. **I have seen the fire:** The Dead Sea Scroll reads, "I am warm before the fire." The noun occurs only five times in the O.T., three of them in Second Isaiah (here, 47:14; 50:11).

17. Cf. vss. 15, 19. For **his graven image** the Dead Sea Scroll reads "block of wood" (cf. vs. 19*g*). Note the succession of verbs: **he . . . falls down, . . . worships, prays, . . . and says.** The closing quotation contains the climax of the strophe (cf. vs. 15*e*).

7. Seventh Strophe: Blindness of the Idol Worshipers (44:18-20)

18. This verse seems to repeat what is said in vs. 19*ab* and looks like a gloss. Yet the repetition may be intentional. **For he has shut their eyes:** Better, "he has smeared"

---

abandon. This smug idol maker cannily arranging for both fuel supply and soul satisfaction is a very mediocre religionist.

16-17. *A Remainder Deity.*—The residue **thereof he maketh a god** suggests that material interests come first and spiritual interests are served by what remains over. The primary necessities of life are warmth and food, and must first be planned for; then religion gets the leftovers. Such "remainder religion" is never effective. A N.T. writer puts these concerns in a different sequence, "Beloved, I wish above all things that

thou mayest prosper and be in health, even as thy soul prospereth" (III John 2). This woodworker's physical comfort is fully met: **Aha, I am warm, I have seen the fire!** But the poet suggests the grim contrast in the empty and unsatisfied soul whose prayer has no result. He has real food and real heat, but a man-made and do-nothing deity.

18-19. *Self-deceived Idolaters.*—Blindly following idolatrous custom, the idolater does not use his intelligence; he is the victim of a delusion and feels gratified. There is a parallel in the

(מֹה) ; or read, "their eyes are smeared" (מֹחוּ) . Their minds have grown insensate to what they have actually been doing (cf. 6:10) .

19. Nor is there knowledge or discernment: The nouns repeat vs. 18a. The following lines are the words of the idol maker (cf. vs. 16ac) . After the triad (vs. 19cde; cf. vss. 15-16) the prophet comes to the point of the satire (vs. 19fg; cf. vss. 15-16) by making the idol maker say, "Of the residue I shall make an abomination," which, of course, no idol maker would ever say.

To Jeremiah the gods are mere vapor or vanity (2:5; 10:8; 14:22) , "no gods" (2:11; 5:7) . They are the work of men's hands, "detested things" (שִׁקּוּצִים; Jer. 4:1; 7:30; 13:27; 16:18; Deut. 29:16) , shapeless blocks or "dung-idols" (גִּלּוּלִים; Francis Brown, S. R. Driver, and C. A. Briggs, eds., *A Hebrew and English Lexicon of the Old Testament* [Boston: Houghton, Mifflin & Co., 1906], *s.v.* גִּלּוּל; Eichrodt, *Theologie des A.T.*, I, 113) . The word **abomination** which Second Isaiah uses here belongs in this general class. To him an idol is **an abomination,** and so he renders it by what it is, and goes so far as to make the idol maker call it by its right name. But the idol maker has not the sense or knowledge to do so (vss. 18a-19b) . And in the last line he brings everything to a head by stating the issue of the whole poem, **Shall I fall down before a block of wood?**

The prophet seems nowhere to reveal any true understanding of the pagan mind on this subject. He does not sense the numinous quality in the idol, the thing that evoked wonder and awe and reverence and fear before it. It is only an ordinary piece of **wood,** no different from any other wood. This is the constant burden of his polemic. For it is a polemic that the prophet is writing, a biting satire, a prophetic utterance designed to warn Israel of the emptiness of this kind of man-made religion. Behind it all stands his invincible faith in one God, exalted and sovereign in the earth, present in the hearts and consciences of men, available to all who cry to him, yet invisible and holy, whom men apprehend not by the seeing of the physical eye but by the eye of faith and by the revelation of the word.

20. The final pronouncement of judgment upon the idol maker: **He feeds on ashes** or "a feeder on ashes." Instead of the idol giving vitality and sustenance, it not only offers nothing at all but feeds on loathsome, unpalatable pabulum. It is quite remarkable how the poet centers his thought throughout on the idol maker. The reason is obvious. He has seen the manufacture going on about him, and his people have witnessed the same scene. He begins his poem with "They who fashion an idol," and the climaxes fall again and again on these fabricators (vss. 11, 12ef, 13ef, 15de, 17, 20) . Then follows the elaboration: **A deluded mind has led him astray** (Hophal of תלל) . It has been turned away from its normal path (cf. II Sam. 19:14; I Kings 11:2, 4; Job 36:18; Prov. 7:21) . All this arduous and assiduous effort does not produce religion and the things religion gives: **And he cannot deliver himself.** He is too blind and deluded to make the proper judgment upon his own work. He cannot pause to inquire whether the whole thing is **a lie.** A superb ending, and in the style of the prophet.

---

effect of the promulgation of the dogma of papal infallibility upon the reigning pope. The ceremonial connected with images in Babylon, and the prostration of their devotees in worship, had a hypnotic effect and prevented straight thinking in their deification of a bit of wood. Pius IX, after the pageantry of the Vatican Council, is said to have remarked: "Before I was pope I believed in papal infallibility; now I feel it." A council had made a man the mouthpiece of God, and the man could not see the absurdity of his situation. How easily in religion critical faculties are put to sleep, and men believe what it pleases them to think true!

20. *The Poet's Judgment on the Idol Fabricator.*—The tragedy of false religion is that its devotees become incapable of facing reality. Metal and wood become their god, and they worship without using their minds to assess that before which they bow. One may compare with it the striking conclusion of one of the richest N.T. epistles: "This is the true God and eternal life. Little children, keep yourselves from idols." (I John 5:20-21.)

24 Thus saith the LORD, thy Redeemer, and he that formed thee from the womb, I *am* the LORD that maketh all *things;* that stretcheth forth the heavens alone; that spreadeth abroad the earth by myself;

24 Thus says the LORD, your Redeemer,
who formed you from the womb:
"I am the LORD, who made all things,
who stretched out the heavens alone,
who spread out the earth — Who was
with me?[c] —

[c] Another reading is *who spread out the earth by myself*

K. The Anointing of Cyrus (44:24–45:13)

The thought of redemption which has been present in the prophet's mind from the beginning has in recent poems become more pronounced and clear (42:18–43:7; 43:8-13; 43:14–44:5; 44:6-8, 21-23), and in the last poem was carried to a climax in the closing strophe (44:22-23). The prophet now presses forward to a more historical phase of his thought. The new shift is perfectly reflected in the construction of the poem and in its convergence upon the Persian king. Beyond Cyrus lies Babylon and its conquest. The section marks another definite stage in the prophet's work and culminates in a powerful lyrical effusion (48:20-21).

The poem is composed of three long strophes (44:24-28; 45:1-7, 9-13) with a hymnic interlude (45:8). Each of these might conceivably be resolved into three parts. As in 43:14–44:5, and in much the same fashion, the poem contains three oracular formulas (44:24; 45:1, 11). The first of these is followed by the word of revelation, "I am Yahweh," to which are attached the two crucial words, "your Redeemer" and "your Creator." These in turn are resolved into three triads (44:24*cb*, 24*d*, 24*e*; 25*ab*, 25*cd*, 26*ab*; 26*cd*, 27, 28*ab*), all of them modifying Yahweh. Each line opens with a participle in the style of the hymn. In each triad the climax falls upon the third member. The purpose of this long and impressive introduction is to bring everything to center upon Cyrus the Persian. The text of vs. 28 has been disturbed (see below), and the last two lines (vs. 28*cd*) must be deleted. There are no superlatives too strong for the poet, for he is concerned with a theme in which all that is ultimate is involved.

1. First Strophe: Yahweh Fulfills His Purpose in Cyrus (44:24-28)

All the major elements of the prophecy are present in the introduction: redemption, creation, history, monotheism, prophecy, sovereignty, and purpose. Redemption and creation are the two focuses of the prophet's eschatological thought. Creation and history are inextricably bound in a common matrix of meaning (cf. 40:12-31); nowhere in Second Isaiah does creation have a meaning distinct from its relevance for history. History and prophecy belong together, for God reveals his will and purpose in history;

44:24–45:13. The Anointing of Cyrus.—This poem and the following form a climax to those which have preceded, for the prophet, who has mentioned Cyrus incidentally, now proclaims him God's chosen agent for the achievement of Israel's release and restoration. It is interesting, with George Adam Smith [8] and others, to contrast the treatment of Cyrus by the Greek historians, Herodotus and Xenophon, with the treatment of him by this prophet. For the Greeks Cyrus was an admirable figure whose virtues they held up for emulation. Xenophon's *Cyropaedia* is a fictionalized biography, in which a very slight historical basis is worked up to present an ideal figure. Both Herodotus and

[8] *The Book of Isaiah* (New York: A. C. Armstrong & Sons, 1901; "Expositor's Bible"), pp. 162-76.

Xenophon therefore dwell on the character of Cyrus. Our prophet says nothing of his character. He does not pronounce him good or bad; he is an instrument of the Lord of history, the sole God on whom all attention is fixed. For the Greek, moral advancement was a primary concern. This could be furthered by setting before men those whom they should imitate. If they are shown the good life, it is assumed that they will attempt it. They can to that extent be their own saviors. For this Hebrew prophet, submission to and partnership with the one God of the universe and of history was the sole aim of man. Man cannot redeem himself, but must trust the only Savior. The sovereign God uses many tools to achieve his purposes. The men whom he selects may be

25 That frustrateth the tokens of the liars, and maketh diviners mad; that turneth wise *men* backward, and maketh their knowledge foolish;	25 who frustrates the omens of liars,
	     and makes fools of diviners;
	who turns wise men back,
	     and makes their knowledge foolish;

they belong together as event and word belong together. Not only does the prophet present the argument of the meaning of prophecy (vs. 26*ab*), but all that he has to say about the imminent redemption appears in the form of divine revelatory "words." The first triad deals with the divine activity in creation, the second with the divine activity in revelation, the third with the divine activity in history. He moves to the climax from the general to the concrete.

24. The note of living relationship is struck at once: **Your Redeemer, who formed you from the womb.** Redemption precedes creation (cf. vs. 23*e*). The two realities pervade the entire poem, but redemption dominates, and creation serves to provide an adequate context for redemption. As Yahweh fashions each child in the womb of its mother, so he has fashioned his people (see 49:1). It is a most interior way of expressing Yahweh's sovereignty over Israel's life (cf. vs. 2; also 43:1, 7, 21). "I am Yahweh": The word of revelation which the rest of the poem develops (cf. 45:3*cd*, 5*a*, 6*c*, 7*c*, 8*e*). Israel had first heard the revelatory words at Sinai. Other peoples know the theophanic formula, as in "I am Ishtar" or "I am Bel," etc. Israel alone has heard these words and through them has entered into covenant relation with Yahweh. **Who made all things:** Lit., "Maker of all," i.e., the universe. The conflict with the nature cults and their competing claims is over. In Jeremiah and Ezekiel Baalism is still a foe to be reckoned with; in Second Isaiah Yahweh is creator of all nature. **Who stretched out the heavens alone:** Cf. 40:22; 42:5. These words and the following emphasize the oneness of God; beside him there is no other. **Who was with me?** (RSV; *Kethîbh;* cf. Dead Sea Scroll, LXX, Vulg.). The KJV reads, **by myself** (*Qerê;* cf. Targ.). See 41:12-13.

The emphasis upon creation is one of the most remarkable in the O.T. (cf. Amos 4:13; 5:8-9; 9:5-6, which are possibly late). Whereas the theophanic revelation at Sinai was elaborated in terms of the deliverance from Egypt (Exod. 20:2), here it is followed by cosmogonic affirmations. Yet the significance of these is grasped only by the triads which follow. The prophet is perhaps influenced by Babylonian court style (Gressmann, *Der Messias,* p. 60; Eduard Norden, *Agnostos Theos* [Leipzig: B. G. Teubner, 1913], pp. 207 ff., 215 ff.; Morris Jastrow, Jr., *Die Religion Babyloniens und Assyriens* [Giessen: A. Töpelmann, 1912], II, 155 ff.; Sidney Smith, *Isaiah XL-LXVI,* pp. 59, 180) which was diffused throughout the Semitic world.

25. Who frustrates the omens of liars: Or "boasters," "babblers." The same word is found in Jer. 50:36. Paul Haput's emendation ("Babylonian Elements in the Levitic

---

entirely unconscious of the ends they serve and of God's use of them. They may be believers or unbelievers, Israelites or pagans, morally good or evil. The sole fact that matters is that the one Lord of history lays hold of and works through them. They are merely instruments in his hand. Every expression used by this poet concerning Cyrus says nothing whatsoever of his devoutness or of his character. He is pictured as an irresistible conqueror, and, without his knowing it, he achieves God's plan for the release of his people and their return to their homeland. The Greek places many heroes before men's eyes; the Hebrew knows but one hero— the sovereign Lord, in conformity with whose will men find their blessedness.

24-28. The All-sufficient Redeemer and Creator.—Here God, the Lord of creation and of history, is placed in the foreground and his purpose is shown coming to fulfillment in the conquering king, called the Lord's **shepherd.** The introductory lines sum up the functions and powers of the sovereign God which have already been dwelt on in previous poems. His particular relationship to Israel is stressed. The exiles are not spoken of as scattered individuals or small groups, but as a nation corporately one. For the moment they may be dispersed in many places, but God, their **redeemer** and fashioner **from the womb,** designed them to be one people and can be counted on to keep them one for the achievement of his world-wide plan.

26 That confirmeth the word of his servant, and performeth the counsel of his messengers; that saith to Jerusalem, Thou shalt
be inhabited; and to the cities of Judah, Ye
shall be built, and I will raise up the de-
cayed places thereof:

26 who confirms the word of his servant,
  and performs the counsel of his mes-
    sengers;
who says of Jerusalem, 'She shall be in-
    habited,'
  and of the cities of Judah, 'They shall
    be built,
  and I will raise up their ruins';

Ritual," *Journal of Biblical Literature*, XIX [1900], 57) of ברים to ברים, referring to the
Babylonian *baru* priests, is not necessary. The soothsayers who stood high in the Babylonian hierarchy give omens, indeed, but Yahweh "breaks" them so that they have no
effect. The events of the future are not under the control of foreign gods; hence the
signs mean nothing. Yahweh, the Lord of history, makes the diviners senseless, he
confuses the wise men, **makes their knowledge foolish** (cf. 47:1-15; Ezek. 21:21).

26. Many scholars read the plural "servants" to conform with the parallelism; others
change "messengers" to the singular. It is best to leave the text unchanged since the
servant appears later in the poem. The servant is prophetic Israel; to him Yahweh has
revealed his word, and he confirms what he reveals. Some believe that Jeremiah or the
prophet himself is referred to, but this is not likely. The whole context is more
general and spacious. Yahweh confounds the omens of the soothsayers, but he mediates
his will and purpose in a living, personal revelation to Israel and his messengers, the
prophets. Does the poet have any specific prophetic "words" in mind? Perhaps not,
although he witnesses to the existence of such words in prophecy, possibly of the nature
of the optimistic oracles original to the older prophets or later added to them (e.g.,
2:2-4; Mic. 4:1-5; etc.). Some scholars delete the verb **performs** for metrical reasons,
but the parallelism with the other members of the triad in vs. 25 outweighs this
consideration. Vs. 26b opens a third triad, which includes a threefold, "the one saying."
The last three stichs of vs. 26 seem overfull and are without the apodosis of vss. 27-28.
The prophet is fond of the triple line, but vs. 26d spoils the symmetry of the triad and
should be excised. For **cities of Judah** the LXX^B reads "cities of Idumea." Observe the

Creatorship involves obligations. God does
not fashion a nation or make men and women
without assuming responsibilities for them. The
nation can therefore assert with confidence:
"The LORD will perfect that which concerneth
me," and pray, pleading God's faithfulness,
"Forsake not the works of thine own hands"
(Ps. 138:8). If God

In patient length of days,
Elaborated into life
A people to His praise,[9]

he will not abandon his undertaking. W. B.
Yeats pictures him unceasingly toiling at that
which he is creating:

[He] stands before it modelling in the clay
And moulding there His image. Age by age
The clay wars with His fingers and pleads hard
For its old, heavy, dull, and shapeless ease.[1]

[9] John Henry Newman, *The Dream of Gerontius*,
Part V.
[1] *The Countess Kathleen*, scene 3, p. 65. Used by
permission of The Macmillan Co., publishers.

The series of descriptions, in which the
prophet speaks grandly of God's adequacy for
all situations, have in mind what the exiles were
confronting: (a) The peril that the renowned
hierarchy of Babylon's priests might lure them
from their faith. **Liars, diviners, wise men** are
named, and so famous were Babylon's astrologers, who read the planets and cast horoscopes,
that, as in Daniel, the word Chaldean came to
stand for fortuneteller and predictor. (b) The
ruined plight of the homeland where, even if
they reached it, nothing would be found as it
had been before the Babylonian conquest. The
rubble had to be got out of the way and building begun from the ground up. (c) The primeval chaos—the "deep," and the waters
thought of as flowing forth from it. This Babylonian conception of the cosmos resting on an
abyss may stand here for the anarchy of a world
going to pieces before the invading Persians
and the bewildering obstacles to be encountered
by those who, under God, were to help bring
the new and final order in the earth. (d) The
seemingly uncontrollable Cyrus, who was turn-

27 That saith to the deep, Be dry, and I will dry up thy rivers: | 27 who says to the deep, 'Be dry, I will dry up your rivers';

---

interesting shift in the second line of two members of the third triad (vss. 26c-28b) to the first person, an admirable stylistic feature, the purpose of which is not only to revert to the divine first person which dominates the strophe ("I am Yahweh") but also to prepare for the address to Cyrus.

27. The word צולה, **deep,** is a *hapax legomenon.* Various proposals have been offered to explain its meaning. Some scholars think of the Red Sea; others of a general figure for distress as in 43:2 and passages in the psalms (Duhm, Levy); others of the Euphrates and its channels (Rashi, Ziegler, Fischer); still others of the chaotic deep, the *tehôm rabbāh* of 51:10 (Kissane, Wade, Volz, Torrey). Second Isaiah is fond of mythological allusions, and such a climax as this would be a suitable context for a reference to the chaos-dragon motif. In that event cosmogony and history are superbly related. Volz goes so far as to say that Second Isaiah may be recalling the conversation between Marduk and Tiamat. The direct address to **the deep** and to Cyrus (vs. 28) is very effective and lends a dimension to the latter which is consonant with the eschatological matrix of the prophet's prevailing thought (cf. 51:9-10). Nature and history stand at the behest of their sovereign Lord.

---

ing things upside down and striking terror into all hearts.

One can match all these in our epoch after two vast wars: (a) Credulous folk in a troubled time lend an ear to quack religious teachers, and to dabblers in the occult who claim to read the future. (b) Our vaunted civilization is in ruins and must be painfully reconstructed. This is as true in lands untouched by the destructive hand of war as in those where physical ruin is everywhere visible. International, interracial, economic, and industrial relations must be re-thought and re-established on a more just basis. Communism seems a divine instrument to force us to this rethinking. (c) We are painfully aware of an anarchic factor in the fabric of things which, like the "deep" of Babylonian cosmogony, plunges mankind into disorder. (d) On the current scene are powers which know no ethical control, or whose ethics are opposite to those of Christendom.

Were what appear to us divine purposes our ideals merely, what assurance have we of their achievement? But if they are grounded in the structure of the universe, then we espouse them not solely as desirable, but as the only purpose which surely will come to pass.

Many modern men and women have thought an ethical imperative a sufficient religion. They believed in the supremacy of duty. That-which-ought-to-be claimed them, and they responded with devotion. But they were agnostic as to whether there is a God of the universe and whether that which they felt ought to be, had behind it his mind and will. Theirs was a survival faith from a more robust and intelligible religion. This remainder-piety seemed im-

potent to reproduce itself. In a history of an outstanding American family it is pointed out that something disappeared in the third generation. John Adams and John Quincy Adams had both the Puritan conscience and the Puritan faith; and in their times they were driving forces. Charles Francis Adams had the Puritan conscience without the Puritan conviction of God, and the family lost its moral energy.[2]

The prophet's emphasis upon God's redemption and creation of his people as the basis of assurance in the restoration of national unity is identical with our confidence in the reunion of the Christian church. This is no dream of man. It is God who, by the death of his Son and the gift of his Spirit, both redeemed a spiritual community for the achievement of the salvation of the world and has been fashioning it through the centuries. Every utterance concerning the church should begin, as does this prophecy, with an adequate statement of who the church's Lord is.

The distinction between prophecy and the reading of omens rests on the conviction of God's control of history. Omens are nonsense unrelated to the course of events, while God's consistent purpose enables those who know him to discern the meaning of occurrences and be sure that they fulfill a divine plan. He

confirms the word of his servant, and performs the counsel of his messengers.

They alone, who with eyes on God scan history, can read its meaning.

[2] James Truslow Adams, *The Adams Family* (Boston: Little, Brown & Co., 1930), p. 232 ff.

| 28 That saith of Cyrus, *He is* my shepherd, and shall perform all my pleasure: even saying to Jerusalem, Thou shalt be built; and to the temple, Thy foundation shall be laid. | 28 who says of Cyrus, 'He is my shepherd, and he shall fulfil all my purpose'; saying of Jerusalem, 'She shall be built,' and of the temple, 'Your foundation shall be laid.' " |

28. All the lines converge on Cyrus. The climax is reinforced by the reference to the deep which precedes it and by the fulfillment of the divine purpose which follows it. To press the effect even further, Yahweh addresses Cyrus, **my shepherd.** Kuenen, Stade, Oort prefer to read the same Hebrew consonants, רעי, "my friend" (cf. II Sam. 15:37; I Kings 4:5). G. R. Driver (in a review of Joseph Ziegler's *Untersuchungen zur Septuaginta des Buches Isaias, Journal of Theological Studies,* XXXVI [1935], 82) on the basis of the Syriac *r'ā* renders the word as "thought" (cf. LXX φρονεῖν "[who says to Cyrus] to be wise"). But this does not suit the context so well, despite the improved parallelism. The allusion to a **shepherd** has numerous analogies both within (II Sam. 5:2; Jer. 3:15; 23:1 ff.; Ezek. 34:23; Mic. 5:5) and outside the Bible. (The title is common among the Sumerians, Akkadians, and Egyptians; cf. also Homer *Iliad* II. 243, ποιμὴν λαῶν; see John A. Wilson, *The Burden of Egypt* [Chicago: University of Chicago Press, 1951], pp. 125-53, *et passim.*) The usual rendering of חפץ is **pleasure,** but Second Isaiah constantly uses the word to mean **purpose,** and this is the meaning needed here. No blind caprice or fortuitous succession of events; no hidden, mysterious force within the nature of things; no view of self-fulfilling history explains the coming of Cyrus, but only a divine government with a steadfast and consistent **purpose** (note the prophet's use of *çédheq* elsewhere).

The last two lines of the verse are usually deleted. They are attached awkwardly by the conjunction and the infinitive construct, which the LXX alters to conform with

---

George Bancroft, who has been called the foremost historian of the United States, "a man of the present, valuing justly the past," [3] in a letter to his wife, wrote:

Each page of history may begin and end with Great is God and marvellous are his doings among the children of men; and I defy a man to penetrate the secrets and laws of events without something of faith. He may look on and see as it were the twinkling of stars and planets and measure their distances and motions; but the life of history will escape him. He may pile a heap of stones, he will not get at the soul.[4]

44:28–45:4. *What God Does for His Agents.*— A signal instance of the penetration of current events by a man of faith is Second Isaiah's interpretation of Cyrus' significance for Israel in the concluding lines of 44:24-28 and in 45:1-9. It is not that he was unique in seeing divine power behind the startling military career of this king of a small realm who became the conqueror of his world. The Cyrus Cylinder ascribes his successes to Marduk, who, it is said, "beheld with joy the deeds of his vicegerent, who was righteous in hand and heart. To his city of Babylon he summoned his march; he bade him

also take the road to Babylon; like a friend and comrade he went at his side." [5] The difference between such heathen interpreters and our prophet lies in the characters of their deities. Marduk, god of Babylon, is called "the arch-magician of the gods," and his worship at its loftiest in the penitential confessions is a series of incantations.[6] The Lord of the prophet's faith is the righteous and redeeming God, not only of Israel, but also of the whole earth. His character and purpose stand out as unique.

Two points are stressed in the Lord's relationship to Cyrus: (*a*) Cyrus is his agent, **my shepherd, his anointed,** or "Messiah," whose **right hand I have grasped.** The career of Cyrus must have perplexed this prophet, as it did all his contemporaries. But his faith in God's sovereign control of all factors on the scene triumphed. This outsider to Israel was one of her own kings, God's **anointed.** (*b*) Cyrus does not know who is girding him. The prophet expects that eventually he will recognize the true God as his hitherto unsuspected benefactor; but for the present he is God's unwitting instrument.

[3] *Encyclopaedia Britannica,* 14th ed., III, 21.

[4] M. A. deWolfe Howe, *The Life and Letters of George Bancroft* (New York: Charles Scribner's Sons, 1908), II, 77.

[5] See J. B. Pritchard, ed., *Ancient Near Eastern Texts Relating to the Old Testament* (Princeton: Princeton University Press, 1950), p. 315.

[6] Cf. G. F. Moore, *History of Religions* (Edinburgh: T. & T. Clark, 1914-20), I, 225 ff.

45 Thus saith the LORD to his anointed, to Cyrus, whose right hand I have holden, to subdue nations before him; and I will loose the loins of kings, to open before him the two-leaved gates; and the gates shall not be shut;

45 Thus says the LORD to his anointed,
   to Cyrus,
   whose right hand I have grasped,
to subdue nations before him
   and ungird the loins of kings,
to open doors before him
   that gates may not be closed:

---

the participles of the preceding triad. They repeat vs. 26 in part and appear as an anticlimax, in view both of what has been said already and of what is to follow in 45:1 ff. The reference to **the temple** looks suspicious, appearing only here in Second Isaiah. On the other hand, the conclusion alludes to the building of the city. The balance of the argument favors the deletion of vs. 28cd. (Theophile J. Meek, "Some Passages Bearing on the Date of Second Isaiah," *Hebrew Union College Annual*, XXIII [1950-51] 177-78, takes vs. 28c as a variant of vs. 26c and transfers vs. 28d after vs. 26c to fill in the gap. This is possible, but the absence of any reference to the temple in the climax of 45:13 argues against it.)

2. SECOND STROPHE: COMMISSION OF CYRUS (45:1-7)

The new oracle continues the same universal perspectives as the first. The repetition of "I am Yahweh" (45:3c, 5a, 6c, 7c), the monotheistic emphasis (vss. 5ab, 6-7), the focus upon Israel, the servant (vs. 4), the imminence of redemption, the divine sovereignty in creation, revelation, and history, and the commission of Cyrus all bear witness that the oracles are to be understood in relation to each other. The only adequate explanation

---

In 41:2 we dwelt on God's control of men without their belief in him. We do not know anything about Cyrus' religious faith, whether it meant much or little to him. But, directing events and the careers of men, stands "at the wheel that unknown steersman whom we call God."[7] He has access to all minds whether or not they suspect who is entering. His providences remain secrets hid from us. In current events his footsteps move along uncharted ways. His paths are "in the great waters." The exiles thought this eruption of Persian invaders a calamity; the prophet saw in it God's rescuing presence. Emerson had a similar confession of faith in the divine direction of his country:

Our helm is given up to a better guidance than our own; the course of events is quite too strong for any helmsman, and our little wherry is taken in tow by the ship of the great Admiral which knows the way, and has the force to draw men and states and planets to their good.

Such and so potent is this high method by which the Divine Providence sends the chiefest benefits under the mask of calamities, that I do not think we shall by any perverse ingenuity prevent the blessing.[8]

God's control of events is both beyond our comprehension and often apart from any effort of ours. But Emerson adds that "seeing this guidance in events," he "could heartily wish that our will and endeavor were more active parties to the work." Second Isaiah, by his assurance of God's activity in current happenings, would rouse his scattered and downcast fellow exiles to expect release from Babylon, and to assume their places in the corporate life and mission of God's servant nation.

This section on the call of Cyrus sets forth God's prevenient work with his chosen instruments. He is "long beforehand" with their souls, and prepares them for their good works in his cause. He "girds" them for tasks they little suspect. At a crucial juncture in World War II Winston Churchill, recalling his own ancestry and the history of the English-speaking peoples, stood before the Congress of the United States, aware that he was part of an "appointed plan" that "should all work out this way."[9] Both Israel and Cyrus are predestined. Such election to roles in God's purposes is a practical doctrine of the utmost religious worth. If Cyrus is a foreordained instrument, the Lord will see to it that he has whatever is requisite to discharge his mission. And Israel can read in the means for further conquest which fell to him the assurance that the Lord will furnish her as abundantly for her yet vaster task.

45:1-2. The Priority of God.—God's prearrangement of circumstances for his servants is

[7] Graham Balfour, *The Life of Robert Louis Stevenson* (New York: Charles Scribner's Sons, 1901), I, 122.
[8] *Miscellanies*, "The Fortune of the Republic."

[9] *The Grand Alliance* (Boston: Houghton Mifflin Co., 1950), p. 671.

2 I will go before thee, and make the crooked places straight: I will break in pieces the gates of brass, and cut in sunder the bars of iron:	2 "I will go before you and level the mountains,*d* I will break in pieces the doors of bronze and cut asunder the bars of iron,

d One ancient Ms Gk: Heb *the swellings*

for these motifs is that the prophet is thinking in eschatological categories. The divine sovereignty within and above history gives the poem its urgency and significance.

45:1. His anointed: LXX, τῷ χριστῷ; Vulg., *christo meo,* "my messiah." The title follows immediately upon "my shepherd." The content of the terms is explained in 41:2-3, 25; 46:11; 48:14-15. Note, for example, "bird of prey" and "man of my counsel" (46:11) and "he whom the LORD loves" (48:14). Only here in the O.T. is the ascription applied to a foreign king or to anyone outside the covenant people. Elsewhere it is applied chiefly to kings like Saul and David (I Sam. 16:6; 24:6, 10; 26:9, 11, 23; II Sam. 1:14, 16; 19:22). It must be confessed that the expression seems surprising as applied to a non-Israelite, even a non-Semite. Yet it is important to bear several things clearly in mind. (*a*) The term does not have the more developed associations of a later time or of the N.T. (*b*) It is applied in the O.T. not only to the kings but also to prophets, priests, patriarchs (Ps. 105:15; I Chr. 16:22), and even to the community of Israel (Hab. 3:13). (*c*) Other foreign monarchs are the agents of God (the Assyrian monarch in 10:5 and the Babylonian monarch in Jer. 25:9; 27:6; cf. 43:10, where Nebuchadrezzar is referred to as "my servant"). (*d*) Finally, the passage must be read as an expression of the prophet's faith. Yahweh consecrates Cyrus as the mediator of his purpose and equips him as his instrument. **Whose right hand I have grasped:** Cf. 8:11; also 41:13; 42:6*c*. In the Cyrus Cylinder it is Marduk who scans and looks through all the countries searching for a righteous ruler to lead him in the annual procession (Pritchard, *Ancient Near Eastern Texts,* p. 315). Cyrus is called and led by Yahweh to perform a divine commission (44:28*b*; 46:11*b*). **To subdue nations before him:** Cf. 41:2; 48:14. The infinitive *leradh* does not occur elsewhere in this form, but is not impossible. The meaning of **ungird** here is to deprive of power or to disarm (cf. I Kings 20:11). **That gates may not be closed:** It is not likely that this is a reminiscence of the historical event (cf. Cyrus Cylinder, "Without battle and conflict he permitted him to enter Babylon"). The description is more general, and Babylon had not yet been taken.

2. I [myself] will go before you: The first person is emphatic. Yahweh leads, Cyrus follows (cf. Cyrus Cylinder, "He made him set out on the road to Babylon going at his side like a real friend" [*ibid.*]). **And level the mountains:** Cf. 40:5; the RSV follows the LXX and the Dead Sea Scroll in reading the difficult Hebrew word הדורים, lit., **swellings** or "protuberances" as **mountains** (ההרים). Others prefer to emend the word to "ways" (הדרכים; cf. vs. 13). The Vulg. has *gloriosos terrae.* In the new exodus as in the old, Yahweh is the leader and shows the way. The verb represents a double reading of the Piel and the Hiphil. The Piel should be read. **I will break in pieces the doors of**

a discovery which all Christians make—**I will go before you.** When we anticipate what we may encounter in coming situations, we need to remind ourselves that if we are on divine errands, God has gone ahead of us, and we shall find obstacles removed, resources provided, and much which in anticipation we dreaded entirely out of our way. In Cyrus' case the capture of Babylon proved most unexpectedly easy. This prophet and his fellow captives must often have scanned her fortifications and especially **the doors of bronze** of her hundred gates. Herodotus begins the paragraph which describes the taking of the city with the comment, "Cyrus was now reduced to great perplexity." [1] Then he goes on to tell how the Persians entered by the bed of a stream of the Euphrates which had been diverted into another channel, and were masters of the city without a fight. **I will break in pieces the doors of bronze** had an utterly unanticipated fulfillment. God's servants should never be "reduced to great perplexity." Perplexed we cannot help being, but he who goes before us has already devised means where we can discern none.

[1] *History* I. 191.

3 And I will give thee the treasures of darkness, and hidden riches of secret places, that thou mayest know that I, the LORD, which call *thee* by thy name, *am* the God of Israel.

4 For Jacob my servant's sake, and Israel mine elect, I have even called thee by thy name: I have surnamed thee, though thou hast not known me.

3 I will give you the treasures of darkness
  and the hoards in secret places,
that you may know that it is I, the LORD,
  the God of Israel, who call you by
  your name.

4 For the sake of my servant Jacob,
  and Israel my chosen,
I call you by your name,
  I surname you, though you do not
  know me.

---

bronze: See Ps. 107:16 for this and the following lines (cf. Herodotus *History* I. 179: "In the circuit of the wall are a hundred gates, all of brass, with brazen lintels and side-posts").

3. The treasures of darkness: Cf. Job 3:21; Prov. 2:4. Xenophon reports a conversation of Cyrus with Gobryas, in which he speaks of the enormous wealth of Babylon (*Cyropaedia* V. 2. 8), and another conversation with Croesus, in which he says that his soldiers are in possession of Sardis, "the richest city in Asia, next to Babylon" (*ibid.* VII. 2. 11). Pliny estimates the booty as "24,000 pounds weight of gold, in addition to vessels and other articles of wrought gold, . . ." (*Natural History* XXXIII. 15). **That you may know:** The clause is deleted by many but unnecessarily. Cyrus will learn through his victories that it was Yahweh, the God of Israel, who called and guided him and brought about his triumphs. **The God of Israel, who call you by your name:** Cf. the Cyrus Cylinder: "(Then) he [Marduk] pronounced the name of Cyrus . . . , king of Anshan, declared him (lit.: pronounced [his] name) to be(come) the ruler of all the world" (Pritchard, *op. cit.,* p. 315; contrast the boast of Cyrus: "I am Cyrus, King of the world, great king, legitimate king, king of Babylon, king of Sumer and Akkad, king of the four rims (of the earth) . . . whose rule Bel and Nebo love, whom they want as king to please their hearts" [*ibid.,* p. 316]). The many affinities between the Cylinder and Second Isaiah have been explained as indicating some relationship of the prophet to the court of Cyrus (so Haller, *et al.*). Others have explained them as due to the use of Babylonian court style. A common Semitic speech is reflected here.

4. Two primary titles express the election of Israel, **servant** and **chosen** one (41:8; 42:1; 43:10; 44:1-2; cf. 49:3-6). Not for Cyrus' own aggrandizement and power (contrast his own words in the Cylinder) but **for the sake** of the **chosen servant** Yahweh calls Cyrus. **I surname you:** Yahweh designates Cyrus with an honorable title (cf. 44:5). **Though you do not know me:** Cyrus is not aware that he is Yahweh's agent, that Yahweh has consecrated, called, equipped, empowered, and sent him on his great historical mission.

---

3. The Treasures of Darkness.—The booty which Cyrus accumulated from his conquests, especially from Croesus in Lydia, made possible the financing of further campaigns. He was to acquire much wealth from Babylon.

Secret hoards open up to God's servants as they carry out his will. Take the career of any leader in the Christian enterprise, and note the friends who are attached to him, the allies found in unsuspected quarters, etc. If "the earth is the LORD's, and the fulness thereof" (Ps. 24:1), it should not astonish us that the needs of his church and her servants are supplied beyond their calculations. When we wonder how some necessary enterprise is to be sustained, we must recall that there will be unforeseen and unforeseeable sources of aid. Every God-prompted undertaking has been prepared for by him, and his foresighted provision will be discovered as his servants advance in faith.

4-6. For the Sake of Jacob.—How startled would Cyrus have been, and how amazed all other contemporaries, had they been told that the world-shattering conquests of the Persians were for the benefit of some thousands of Jewish captives, hauled from their poor hilly land, and now through these changes to be returned to it! It was not for their sakes alone, but for mankind's sake, who through them were to

5 ¶ I *am* the LORD, and *there is* none else, *there is* no God besides me: I girded thee, though thou hast not known me;

6 That they may know from the rising of the sun, and from the west, that *there is* none besides me. I *am* the LORD, and *there is* none else.

7 I form the light, and create darkness: I make peace, and create evil: I the LORD do all these *things*.

---

5 I am the LORD, and there is no other,
  besides me there is no God;
  I gird you, though you do not know me,
6 that men may know, from the rising of the sun
  and from the west, that there is none besides me;
  I am the LORD, and there is no other.
7 I form light and create darkness,
  I make weal and create woe,
  I am the LORD, who do all these things.

---

5. History is under the control of but one God; therefore it has an ultimate unity. The problem of the divine sovereignty and human free will does not disturb the prophet. Cyrus is not a mere automaton whose own character and achievement are of no account. "The human volition is taken up into the divine, without thereby losing its human actuality" (H. Wheeler Robinson, *Redemption and Revelation* [New York: Harper & Bros., 1942], p. 186). The repetition in this verse has prompted several scholars to reorder the text. It is a mistaken procedure, for Second Isaiah is making here one of his strongest emphases.

6-7. **That men may know:** The third *lemá'an* (vss. 3c, 4a, 6a) is doubtless meant to serve as a climax, even though the phrase does not have the same meaning in vs. 4a. The repetition of "I am Yahweh" has the same rhetorical purpose. Not only for the sake of Israel, the chosen people, does God call Cyrus (vs. 4), but also that all men everywhere may know that there is but one God. History, like creation, witnesses to his oneness. Vss. 6-7 form a single sentence and gain their intended effect by being read as one. The Targ., Syriac, Symm., Theod., and other MSS have a *mappiq* in the closing *hē* of the phrase **from the west**, thus giving the translation "from the rising of the sun and to its setting." The repeated monotheistic asseveration at the close greatly augments the power of the divine self-disclosure. The participles of vs. 7 (translated here as finite verbs) reflect the hymn style (cf. 44:24-28). Note the effect: "form the light, . . . create darkness, . . . make peace, . . . create evil." The passage has often been understood as a polemic against Zoroastrian dualism. There the forces of Ormazd, the god of light, were arrayed against Ahriman, the god of darkness. But this view has been generally and properly discarded. The primary thought is the oneness of God. The evil which God creates is not moral but physical, like disaster (cf. Amos 3:6cd). Cf. 41:23, "Do

---

become aware of the one true God, **That men may know . . . I am the LORD.** How little any of us can make out the hidden purposes in current happenings! If the church is the bearer of God's redemptive message, and his instrument for the reconciliation of mankind to him, we may be confident that he makes all things work together for her good. In retrospect it became clear that Cyrus' victories achieved Israel's restoration and her liberation to a wider mission.

7. *God the Dominant Factor in History.*—God is the chief factor in everything that happens, favorable or unfavorable. Good and evil represent prosperity and adversity, success and disaster. The prophet is not denying the human factor in events; but the part men play is always subordinate. The conditions of welfare and distress, of brightness and gloom, are largely outside human control. **I the LORD do all these things.** The prophet constantly repeats this message for the comfort of his disheartened people. He centers their attention and their expectation on God alone.

One may contrast the view of Plato, greatest of Greek thinkers:

God, if he be good, is not the author of all things, as many assert, but he is the cause of a few things only, and not of most things that occur to men: for few are the goods of human life, and many are the evils, and the good only is to be attributed to him: of the evil other causes have to be discovered.[2]

[2] *The Republic* II. 379.

8 Drop down, ye heavens, from above, and let the skies pour down righteousness: let the earth open, and let them bring forth salvation, and let righteousness spring up together; I the LORD have created it.

8 "Shower, O heavens, from above,
and let the skies rain down righteousness;
let the earth open, that salvation may
sprout forth,*
and let it cause righteousness to spring
up also;
I the LORD have created it.

* One ancient Ms: Heb *that they may bring forth salva-tion*

good, or do evil." Instead of שָׁלוֹם, **peace,** the Dead Sea Scroll reads טוֹב, "good." **I the LORD do all these things:** Or "I am Yahweh, who does [or "is doing"] all these things." Another overpowering climax (cf. the almost precisely similar words at the opening of the poem).

3. LYRICAL INTERLUDE: LET THE HEAVENS AND EARTH BRING FORTH SALVATION (45:8)

8. This verse is not a separate literary unit. It is directly related to the preceding strophes and is a characteristic outburst after a most profound thought. The invocation of the **heavens** and **earth** to participate in the work of **salvation** expresses the psychic rapport between nature and history (cf. 1:2-4). God creates and maintains nature to serve his own ends (cf. 55:10-11; Hos. 2:21-22). **Shower, O heavens:** The causative verb, like its parallel in the second line, has **righteousness** for its object. The word *cédheq* is the same as in 41:2, where the meaning is "victory"; here the meaning is the divine activity which brings about the triumph of righteousness. **Let the earth open:** The Dead Sea Scroll reads האמר לארץ, "the one who says to the earth," which may be explained as a conjectural restoration of an illegible text. **That salvation may sprout forth:** Lit., "And they may be fruitful salvation." The plural has no adequate antecedent and has given rise to many conjectural emendations. The Dead Sea Scroll reads ויפרח, "let it blossom," anticipated by Torrey and Kissane and properly adopted by the RSV: **That salvation may sprout forth.** The noun *cédhāqāh,* **righteousness,** denotes not the divine activity but its result. Torrey emends the causative verb to the simple Qal. **Created:** I.e., "brought about," "caused to happen" (cf. 44:23, where the hymn has the same function as here, "Sing, O heavens, for Yahweh has done it . . ."). The gifts of salvation are universal (cf. vss. 6-7), and the heavens and the earth respond in joy and gladness to the universal redemption (cf. LXX, εὐφρανθήτω).

Second Isaiah emphatically proclaims God creator of both weal and woe. His conviction may seem to render those who hold it liable to torture by the moral riddles of existence. A devout Scot asked: "Is it not a mystery that God should be *omnipotent love,* and yet that the world should be just a vast cauldron boiling over with violence and pollution and misery?" [3] Tragedies always remain a cross to faith in the goodness of a sovereign God. There is no complete explanation possible to finite man of the presence and prevalence of evil. This prophet will offer a profound interpretation of suffering vicariously endured by the Lord's servant for the healing of the nations; but even with the fulfillment of this conception in the cross of

Christ, evils in the universe and in men's lives remain inexplicable. In fact, however, those who accept bitter cups at the Lord's hand are victors over the world. The strophe ends, as the poem begins, with a confession of God's active role in all that occurs, **I the LORD do all these things.**

8. All Creation Jubilant.—This lyrical interlude is prompted by the contemplation of the Lord's redemption of his people and the magnificent destiny before them. If, as the Exeg. makes plain, the prophet thinks of the restoration of Israel as the beginning of the consummation of all history, this call to heavens and earth to participate in the climax of God's purpose becomes plain. Nature above and below shares gladly in the setting up of the glorious order of God's righteous reign.

[3] H. F. Henderson, *Erskine of Linlathen* (Edinburgh: Oliphant, Anderson & Ferrier, 1899), p. 285.

9 Woe unto him that striveth with his Maker! *Let* the potsherd *strive* with the potsherds of the earth. Shall the clay say to him that fashioneth it, What makest thou? or thy work, He hath no hands?	9 "Woe to him who strives with his Maker, an earthen vessel with the potter!*f* Does the clay say to him who fashions it, 'What are you making'? or 'Your work has no handles'?
10 Woe unto him that saith unto *his* father, What begettest thou? or to the woman, What hast thou brought forth?	10 Woe to him who says to a father, 'What are you begetting?' or to a woman, 'With what are you in travail?' "

f Cn: Heb *potsherds* or *potters*

---

4. THIRD STROPHE: DIVINE SOVEREIGNTY OVER NATURE AND HISTORY (45:9-13)

The strophe is beautifully constructed. The first half is a twofold invective (vss. 9-10); the second, a prophetic oracle with an extended divine asseveration in the style of the oracle of salvation in which the major motifs of the poem are woven together.

The prophet's proclamation that Cyrus is the divine instrument of Israel's deliverance gives offense to his contemporaries. Is this new and greater exodus to be ushered in by a foreign conqueror? Is the second Moses to be a Persian prince? Has Yahweh indeed called Cyrus? Is Cyrus the Lord's "messiah" in whom the divine purpose is at work? The prophet answers in the figure of the potter (cf. Jer. 18).

9-10. These verses form the sole invective in Second Isaiah, in contrast to the pre-exilic prophets who use the form frequently. Here there is no real judgment at all, but only condemnation of Israel's caviling. The word **Maker** is the same as that used in Gen. 2 of man's creation, and appears at the beginning of the poem (44:24b). It means "former," "fashioner," "molder," **potter,** as in the third line. **An earthen vessel with the potter:** Torrey translates, "A potsherd with him who formed the earth." Both he and the RSV emend the difficult *ḥarśê,* **the potsherds of,** to the participle *ḥōrēsh,* **the potter.** The specific context favors the RSV. The Amer. Trans. preserves the play in the original: "A pot with the Potter!" **Does the clay say to him . . . ?** The Dead Sea Scroll reads, "Woe to him who says to his Potter," thus improving the parallelism with vss. 9a, 10a, forming a characteristic triad and strengthening the style. **Your work has no handles:** The Dead Sea Scroll reads strangely ופועלכם אין אדם ידים לו, "Your work, no man has hands to it" (cf. Rom. 9:20-21); cf. also the poem used in the synagogue on the eve of Yom Kippur: "For as the clay in the hands of the potter are we in thy hands"). **What are you begetting . . . ?** No child has the right to utter such words to his parents. No more has Israel the right to speak such words to her fashioner. The invective forms

---

9-13. *The Creator Beyond the Criticisms of His Creatures.*—The exiles wanted no foreign messiah. Good people are chronic grumblers, and can always find fault with God's most gracious acts. We forget our utter dependence, and presume to criticize God. **Woe to him who strives with his Maker.** Thomas Chalmers, at sixty, entered in his journal:

Think of my creatureship, but not habitually, not closely enough. What a revolution would it be if I had just an adequate and practical sense of the God who made me! The very sense of being made by another, how it should annihilate the sovereignty of self—how it should subordinate and keep in check the waywardness of one's own will. What hast thou, O man, that thou didst not receive?[4]

[4] Hanna, *Memoirs of Chalmers,* IV, 248.

Earlier generations, e.g., Lincoln's, spoke of God as their **Maker.** The expression has gone out of vogue, with consequent loss of reverent humility among the devout. The prophet's sarcasm in these lines is a wholesome reminder of who men are before the Maker of all. **Will you question me?** The prophet again gives a majestic description of what God is and does (vss. 12-13). This is he who has raised up Cyrus, and who prepares his way to the completion of his task for Israel.

One other critical remark is taken out of the mouths of the grumblers. They felt sure that Cyrus would demand his price for any service which he rendered the captives. But the prophet is confident that Cyrus is so completely an instrument in the Lord's hand that he will play no politics in this matter. Israel's restora-

11 Thus saith the LORD, the Holy One of Israel, and his Maker, Ask me of things to come concerning my sons, and concerning the work of my hands command ye me.

12 I have made the earth, and created man upon it: I, *even* my hands, have stretched out the heavens, and all their host have I commanded.

13 I have raised him up in righteousness, and I will direct all his ways: he shall build my city, and he shall let go my captives, not for price nor reward, saith the LORD of hosts.

---

11 Thus says the LORD,
    the Holy One of Israel, and his Maker:
    "Will you question me[g] about my children,
    or command me concerning the work of my hands?
12 I made the earth,
    and created man upon it;
    it was my hands that stretched out the heavens,
    and I commanded all their host.
13 I have aroused him in righteousness,
    and I will make straight all his ways;
    he shall build my city
    and set my exiles free,
    not for price or reward,"
    says the LORD of hosts.

g Cn: Heb *Ask me of things to come*

---

a fine climax. The father-son relationship is not to be understood in terms of procreation, but in the biblical terms of lord-servant. It is gross impiety for the child to rebel against his birth and the subsequent nurture which belongs to his parents (cf. Mal. 1:6).

11. The three invectives are followed by a prophetic oracle; Israel's caviling queries of her God lead to the divine query of Israel, which in turn is properly and impressively introduced by the oracular formula: **Thus saith the LORD, the Holy One of Israel, and his Maker.** The divine titles are especially appropriate here, emphasizing Israel's unique relationship to her God (cf. especially vs. 9; 44:24*b*). The Hebrew of vs. 11*c* is difficult and many restorations have been proposed. The Dead Sea Scroll probably preserves the original text: "Thus says the LORD, the Holy One of Israel, who fashions the future, 'Will you question me concerning my sons, and concerning the work [of my hands] command me.'" God has created the world. Creation is his and belongs to him; the life and destiny of his creatures are in his hands. The universality of the poem reaches a crescendo here. **My children** and **the work of my hands** refer to the Gentiles (cf. vss. 6-7, 12-13).

12. The emphatic first personal pronouns in vss. 12-13*a* emphasize again the divine sovereignty over all created things: **earth** and **man, heavens** and **their host.** As Lord of his creation he is Lord of history (40:12-31; 44:24).

13. The verse opens with the third emphatic divine I (אנכי). **I have aroused:** Cf. 41:2, 25. **In righteousness:** Cf. 42:6. The meaning here is "with a purpose firm and sure" (cf. 44:28*b*). Yahweh is at work in contemporary history; Cyrus is but the agent of his will. The threefold **I** accents the theocentricity of the passage, and indeed of the whole poem (cf. 44:24-28). God goes before Cyrus to show the way, God levels or makes straight the

---

tion will not be for **price** or bribe (**reward**). Their independence will not be purchased; they will owe it entirely to God's amazing grace, and be bound to him in lasting obligation.

This poem on the anointing of Cyrus illustrates both the prescience of the Hebrew prophets and their limitations. If the assumption is correct that this and the preceding poems were spoken while the Persian armies were sweeping westward, but before Babylon fell, the prophet's reading of events and his forecasts are amazingly accurate. In details, however, they are incorrect

and his outlook is foreshortened. It was not Cyrus who rebuilt Jerusalem and the temple: it was under Artaxerxes that in the following century Ezra and Nehemiah did their work. Nor was the final age of history so proximate. But in the breakup of the Babylonian world Second Isaiah's conviction that God was employing Cyrus, and that the issue would be an independent Israel with the chance to become the missionary people to mankind, has been abundantly justified. His faith that God, the Lord of the universe and of history, would

14 Thus saith the LORD, The labor of Egypt, and merchandise of Ethiopia and of the Sabeans, men of stature, shall come over unto thee, and they shall be thine: they shall come after thee; in chains they shall come over, and they shall fall down unto thee, they shall make supplication unto thee, *saying*, Surely God *is* in thee; and *there is* none else, *there is* no God.

14 Thus says the LORD:
"The wealth of Egypt and the merchandise of Ethiopia,
　　and the Sabe'ans, men of stature,
shall come over to you and be yours,
　　they shall follow you;
　　they shall come over in chains and bow down to you.
They will make supplication to you, saying:
　　'God is with you only, and there is no other,
　　no god besides him.'"

road (vs. 13*b*, cf. vs. 2), God gives him his successes. After the threefold first person comes the expressed third person pronoun **he**, referring to Cyrus. **Not for price or reward** . . . : Lit., "Not for hire and not for a bribe." Cyrus is not acting from any motive of expediency; no mundane *quid pro quo* of politics or power or international diplomacy is involved. He is achieving his world conquest at the command and under the leadership of the Lord God of Israel, Lord of creation and Lord of history.

L. The Conversion of the Nations (45:14-25)

That the horizons which the prophet views are in reality eschatological can no longer be doubted. He knows that an old age is passing away and a new age is about to dawn. It is his conviction that all the past is but prologue to this hour. The coming of the King is at hand; the new age is imminent. To appreciate the quality of the poet's thought it is necessary to cast aside all literalistic interpretations. To be sure, the prophet keeps his feet on the ground of history, no matter how high his imagination soars. He mentions the name of Cyrus and of the peoples and, above all, of the people of Israel, redeemed, called, chosen, and covenanted by Yahweh. He can speak only in the categories and images and allusions to which he has fallen heir as an ancient Oriental of the Semitic world and as a son of Israel. He does so with an enthusiasm and excitement unmatched anywhere in the whole of the ancient Oriental world.

Many scholars consider vss. 14-25 a continuation of 44:28–45:13. The critics of the school of form criticism (Begrich, Köhler, Mowinckel, *et al.*) begin a new unit here, but resolve the section into two separate poems: 45:14-17, 18-25. The first of these is described by Begrich and others as an oracle of salvation, the second as a dispute. The terminology and style of these forms have been fused into a larger literary whole, however. The poem has two series of three strophes each (vss. 14-15, 16-17, 18-19 and vss. 20-21, 22-23, 24-25), as indicated by the relation between the first (vss. 14-15) and last strophes (vss. 24-25), the continuity of thought, the repeated monotheistic asseverations (vss.

become recognized as the righteous Lord of all peoples is being realized in the missionary outreach of the Christian church.

14-24. Conversion of the Gentiles.—With his great successor, the Apostle to the Gentiles, this prophet believes that "we are saved by hope" (Rom. 8:24). The poem leaves the immediate moment in history, and revels in the glory that is to be. The world judgment upon the nations, in which Cyrus is God's instrument, is thought of as past. Only the **survivors** of the once proud nations remain along with vindicated and exalted Israel. The poem has affinities

with that which portrays the triumph of the suffering servant (52:13 ff.). The nations are pictured as confessing (cf. 53:1-12). They have been **startled** (52:15) to discover the one God of the whole earth with this conquered and captive people (45:15). **The offspring of Israel** (45:24) are apparently the "seed" (53:10) — not merely numerous physical descendants, but also a vaster spiritual progeny produced by the community's redeemed life with God.

14-15. Heathen Nations Acknowledge God.—God first announces the passing over to Israel of such representative wealthy and powerful peo-

15 Verily thou *art* a God that hidest thyself, O God of Israel, the Saviour.	15 Truly, thou art a God who hidest thyself, O God of Israel, the Savior.

14*hi*, 18*ch*, 21*efh*, 22*c*, 24*a*), and the presence of the same personae throughout the poem (cf. Kissane and Ziegler).

1. First Strophe: The Confession of the Nations (45:14-15)

14. Is Cyrus addressed here? (Cf. Jerome, Ibn Ezra, Grotius, Skinner, Mowinckel, *et al.*) It does not seem that the verbs **bow down** and **make supplication** (which is elsewhere used only of prayer) would refer to Cyrus; they might conceivably be used of the nations' veneration of the people of God (note the words of their confession in vs. 14*hi*). Ehrlich meets the difficulty by reading ואל אלהיך, "and to your God," instead of אליך, **to you**; thus referring to Yahweh as the God of Cyrus. The use of the feminine suffixes supports the view that Israel is meant (cf. 18:7; 23:18; 60:5 ff.).

Egypt, Ethiopia, the Sabeans are mentioned in 43:3 as the ransom paid by Yahweh to Cyrus in exchange for Israel. There is perhaps no particular historical reference here; more probably they are taken as wealthy peoples "from the ends of the earth," representative of all the nations who will go to Zion (cf. 2:2-4; Mic. 4:1-5). The meaning of the lines is that the wealth of the nations will flow to Israel. The tall **Sabeans** come as slaves into Israel's possession. It is likely that the clause **they shall come over in chains** (vs. 14*f*) is a gloss on **shall come over** (vs. 14*d*). The next two lines then form a good parallel in 2+2+2 meter. The foreigners (vs. 14*ab*) **shall . . . bow down** and **make supplication** to Israel and to Israel's God, to whom they shall attach themselves. They acknowledge God's people not merely as their leaders and benefactors (Torrey) but as the covenant people in whom and with whom God is present. The coming together of all the peoples of the world marks the hour of the monotheistic confession (vs. 14*hi*), The meaning is not that the oneness of the human community brings the recognition that there is but one God over all, but rather that the great redemptive work of God in history brings men to a recognition that he alone is God.

15. Duhm and others emend אתה, **thou**, to אתך, "with thee," and translate, "Truly, with thee is a hidden God." Who is the speaker here? The RSV and some scholars hold it to be the prophet; others, the nations. There is much to be said for either view, but on the whole it is more probable that the nations are here continuing their witness, both because of the similarity in style and form and the passionate mood. Note the striking

ples as Egypt, Ethiopia, and Seba. If the words **in chains** belong in the passage, these people are enslaved; but the emphasis is on their religious deference to the superior fellowship with God which Israel possesses. She draws them by the magnetism of her life with God, as the apostle pictures the heathen impressed by the worship of the Christians in Corinth (I Cor. 14:24-25). One thinks of the effect of the company of worshiping disciples upon Marius in Walter Pater's story.[5] It is not the devoutness or the moral superiority of the restored community of Israel which demonstrates the divine presence, but the miracle of their rescue from captivity and exaltation to a potent independence. **God is with you only, and there is no other, . . . O God of Israel, the Savior.**

It is worth noting that with the coming of Christ the thought of salvation was so deepened

that the pleaders for the faith in the early generations of the church dwelt on the quality of folk Christ produced. Athenagoras, a former Athenian philosopher, told Marcus Aurelius: "Among us you will find uneducated persons, and artisans, and old women, who, if they are unable in words to prove the benefit of our doctrine, yet by their deeds exhibit the benefit arising from their persuasion of its truth."[6] Closest perhaps to the situation described in this poem with its startling reversal in the condition of the captives, members of a dead nation now about to see her vigorously alive, is Clement's comment on the feelings of the Christians of his time: "He hath changed sunset into sunrise."[7] Believers are the Bible for outsiders, who read no other scripture, and there must be

[5] *Marius the Epicurean*, ch. xxiii.

[6] *A Plea for the Christians* XI; cf. Aristides *Apology* XV; Tertullian *Apology* III; Lactantius *Divine Institutes* III. 26.

[7] *Exhortation to the Heathen* XI.

16 They shall be ashamed, and also confounded, all of them: they shall go to confusion together *that are* makers of idols.	**16** All of them are put to shame and confounded, the makers of idols go in confusion together.
17 *But* Israel shall be saved in the Lord with an everlasting salvation: ye shall not be ashamed nor confounded world without end.	**17** But Israel is saved by the Lord with everlasting salvation; you shall not be put to shame or confounded to all eternity.

sequence in vss. 14-15: אל, **God** אלהים אפס עוד אין, **no god beside him;** מסתתר אל, **a God who hidest thyself;** ישראל אלהי, **God of Israel;** מושיע, **Savior.** The witness of the nations continues through vs. 17. They are momentous words, a great confessional, which follows logically upon vs. 14. With the recognition that Israel's God is God alone the idols must go. The only God is the God of Israel, a Savior. He who is *hidden* in the shroud of mystery is *known* by the salvation he has wrought for his people. "YHVH, according to their [the nations'] opinion, had hidden Himself on the other side of history, so to speak, but now He has shone forth as the liberator of Israel and all of them" (Buber, *Prophetic Faith,* p. 217). To be sure, Israel too knew of God's hiddenness (cf. 8:17; 40:27; Deut. 29:29; Jer. 14:7-9), but this is not the reference here. The whole utterance is the confession of the nations (cf. 53:1-9). The strophe ends magnificently on the word **Savior,** which introduces the theme for the following lines (for a good Egyptian parallel see the hymn to Amon in Pritchard, *Ancient Near Eastern Texts,* pp. 368-69).

2. SECOND STROPHE: CONFOUNDING OF IDOL MAKERS AND SALVATION OF ISRAEL (45:16-17)

The confession of the nations is followed by a judgment on the idol makers. The end of the age is marked by the collapse of idolatry. Second Isaiah sees the whole meaning of history revealed in an imminent eschatological event to which the campaigns of Cyrus are but the prelude. The ambiguities of history are resolved at the dawn of a new age. A distich is devoted to the idol makers, and a second to the salvation of Israel.

16. The word צירם, **idols,** is unusual. Many explain it by a late Hebrew word (צורא, ציור), meaning "form" or "figure" or "picture." Torrey believes it is simply the Hebrew word for "pangs" or "pains" and is a masoretic play on the word for images (צורות).

17. While the gods of the nations and especially of Babylon are brought to confusion, **Israel shall be saved** by her God for all time. As in the previous strophe, the accent falls on **salvation.** The two aspects of all eschatology, judgment and redemption, are perfectly reflected in the strophe. The prophet stresses the decisiveness of the event: it is not merely the outcome of the present world crisis but the beginning of a new time in which Israel will experience the divine salvation.

magnetic attraction in the lives of God's people, or mankind is uninfluenced.

The hidden God (vs. 15), however we read this difficult verse, remains the puzzle of men in general. It is not intentional concealment on his part, for he wishes to be known; but we look for him in the wrong places. When men ask what is God's part in a series of events such as the campaigns of Cyrus, it is not surprising that he remains unseen. Second Isaiah alone of his generation was aware of God's presence. It was the outcome in Israel's restoration which convinced his own people, and ultimately would

convince a wider circle of the discerning among the nations. Where is God in the bewildering international and industrial conflicts of the twentieth century? Not in the earthquake, wind, or fire, but in the still, small voice which persistently urges toward justice, fellowship, mutual consideration. Where else could we see One whose nature is love?

17. *Idol Worshipers Confounded.*—This verse is convincing evidence that the prophet is thinking of the consummation of history. Amid the ups and downs of its course no people can be

18 For thus saith the Lord that created the heavens; God himself that formed the earth and made it; he hath established it, he created it not in vain, he formed it to be inhabited: I *am* the Lord, and *there is* none else.	18 For thus says the Lord, who created the heavens (he is God!), who formed the earth and made it (he established it; he did not create it a chaos, he formed it to be inhabited!): "I am the Lord, and there is no other.

3. Third Strophe: Yahweh's Revelation in Israel (45:18-19)

The strophe again has two divisions: the expanded oracular formula of seven lines and the word of revelation of seven lines. It connects directly with the second strophe by the introductory *kî, for.* It is therefore precarious to make vss. 18-25 a separate literary unit. Indeed, the meaning of the prophet is susceptible of mistaken interpretation except for the lines that follow. The God who reveals himself in history is the God who is Lord of heaven and earth, for he created it (cf. 40:12-31). The Creation, to which the religions of the ancient East sought to do justice, must be subordinated to the unique revelation in Israel. Observe that the opening line, which is followed by the usual participial phrases (vs. 18*bd*), is preliminary to what is disclosed in the second half of the strophe.

18. The introduction culminates in the last line (vs. 18*g*). The relative clauses are better rendered as "Creator of the heavens" and "Former and Maker of the earth." The stress falls on the divine personal pronoun **he** in vss. 18*c* and 18*e*; the clause is an expression of the oneness of God. Yet it is not like the prophet to content himself with an assertion that is divorced from the divine activity. The two verbs (vs. 18*fg*) repeat the verbs of the previous lines and press the point to its conclusion. The word *tōhû,* chaos, is also used in Gen. 1:2. God did not leave the earth empty and unoccupied; he created it for the purpose of making it a home for men (לשבת יצרה). His will, therefore, is not to undo his creation so that it will revert to the primeval chaos once more (cf. Jer. 4:23-26). The monotheism of the verse is oriented to this practical end. **I am the Lord:** The covenant word combined with the monotheistic asseveration constitutes the ground of hope and comfort as well as the basis for the remarkable words which follow.

everlastingly secure. Israel as a nation still had a checkered career before her.

18-19. God, Purposeful and Dependable.— The third strophe insists on the purposefulness of God, and his consequent trustworthiness. This is the meaning of **righteousness** and **right.** The Lord's purposeful work is taken up (*a*) in creation: **He did not create it a chaos.** He fashioned it for the dwelling place of men, and will therefore not blot out the race, for all his creative work would then be futile. One does not need to go so far as the teleological argument went in stating the rationality and purposiveness of everything in existence. William James well said: "Everything makes strongly for the view that our world is incompletely unified teleologically and is still trying to get its unification better organized."[8] Second Isaiah in his portrayals of the future represents the world of nature remade (cf. 55:13). But it is a rationally planned creation, as all our science presupposes. Its Maker is reliable.

[8] *Pragmatism,* pp. 141-42.

(*b*) The Lord is as dependable in revelation. **I did not speak in secret.** The oracles of heathendom were cryptic utterances, so ambiguous that several meanings could often be got from them. The Lord's work through his prophets is intelligible, straightforward, frank. One has only to think of Amos and his successors—and they are assuredly candid speakers. John Skinner writes: "Jehovah's revelation has not been like a dark, trackless desert, but a light in which men might walk towards an assured goal."[9] **I said not, . . . Seek ye me in vain** [lit., **in chaos**]. There is nothing ambiguous about fellowship with God. In his light we see light. Our finite minds never comprehend him fully; for that matter we never understand one another completely, and yet we possess the unspeakable blessings of companionship. The cravings in man's soul for God would not exist were there not an answer provided. A modern instance of

[9] *The Book of the Prophet Isaiah,* Chs. XL-LXVI (Cambridge: Cambridge University Press, 1905; "Cambridge Bible"), p. 65; cf. Jer. 2:31.

19 I have not spoken in secret, in a dark place of the earth: I said not unto the seed of Jacob, Seek ye me in vain: I the LORD speak righteousness, I declare things that are right.

20 ¶ Assemble yourselves and come;

19 I did not speak in secret,
    in a land of darkness;
I did not say to the offspring of Jacob,
    'Seek me in chaos.'
I the LORD speak the truth,
    I declare what is right.

20 "Assemble yourselves and come,
    draw near together,
    you survivors of the nations!

---

19. The God of Israel does not reveal himself **in secret** mysteries, in cryptic symbolism, in the strange muttering of ambiguous oracles, or in esoteric knowledge, available only to the initiates or professional functionaries of the cult. His word to Israel is clear and direct and relevant to her actual historical situation (see Deut. 30:11-14). The JE accounts of the covenant and its demands are an effective commentary on the prophet's words, and the whole of Hebrew prophecy documents them. The narratives of the Yahwist were intelligible to all. One thinks also of Elijah, Amos, Hosea, Isaiah, Jeremiah, and the others. Their "words" are **not spoken in secret,** but openly, in the market place, in the temple court, before the thrones of kings. They are addressed to the people for all to hear. **In a land of darkness:** Some have thought that the reference is to the underworld (8:19; I Sam. 28:7 ff.) or to the desert (Skinner; cf. Jer. 2:31), but it is more likely that the reference is more general, in parallelism with the first line, though the underworld is not excluded. What is true of God's creation is true of his revelation. The world was not created a chaos, neither do men find God in chaos, e.g., in the "wind and chaos" of idol worship (cf. 41:29) or of meaningless and empty forms. On the contrary, Yahweh reveals himself in his word. He speaks *çédheq,* **righteousness,** i.e., words which are true and reliable, upon which men may rely (cf. 55:10-11).

4. Fourth Strophe: The Gods Cannot Save (45:20-21)

The second half of the poem, like the first half, is composed of three strophes. The movement of the prophet's eschatology is particularly clear: the gathering of the nations (vs. 20), the defeat of the idols and the victory of monotheism (vs. 21), Yahweh's invitation to all the world (vs. 22), the confession of the nations (vss. 24-25). The dominant theme of salvation controls the prophet's thought.

20. **Assemble yourselves and come:** Cf. 41:1; 43:9. The imagery of the court trial is apparent in vss. 20-21. The Dead Sea Scroll improves the parallelism by reading for

---

the persistence of the yearning in one who had intellectually parted with God is Gamaliel Bradford. He had written somewhat flippant lines, *"Exit God";* years later he set down in his journal:

Who will tell me something of God? I know nothing about him whatever. It is a mere name, a mere word to me, yet it clings. Why? Mere association brought down from my childhood and thousands of others'? Clouds and dreams and reveries, hopes and wonderings and fears? Or is there something deep and mysterious there that really takes hold of my soul? I cannot tell. But still the word clings to me, sometimes in the form of an oath, sometimes in that of an invocation or appeal, but still clings, and it seems to me that it grows.[1]

[1] Van Wyck Brooks, ed., *The Journal of Gamaliel Bradford* (Boston: Houghton Mifflin Co., 1933), p. 152.

I the LORD speak righteousness, I declare things that are right. It is the Lord's dependability and forthrightness in his revelation, as opposed to the confusion of the idols, which the prophet has in mind. This remains a permanent characteristic of his word. The test of revelation is always: Does it enable us to see life more clearly?

20-21. *The Heathen Nations at the Lord's Bar.*—For a final time now at the climax of history the folly of idolatry is exposed. And again the question is put to them which has been raised repeatedly of the meaning of Cyrus: **Who told this long ago? Was it not I, . . . a righteous God and a Savior?** The Lord is faithful to his covenant people and is their deliverer. In many doctrines of the Atonement, God's justice is contrasted with his mercy in saving

draw near together, ye *that are* escaped of
the nations: they have no knowledge that
set up the wood of their graven image, and
pray unto a god *that* cannot save.

21 Tell ye, and bring *them* near; yea, let
them take counsel together: who hath declared this from ancient time? *who* hath
told it from that time? *have* not I the LORD?
and *there is* no God else beside me; a just
God and a Saviour; *there is* none beside me.

22 Look unto me, and be ye saved, all the
ends of the earth: for I *am* God, and *there is*
none else.

They have no knowledge
  who carry about their wooden idols,
and keep on praying to a god
  that cannot save.

21 Declare and present your case;
  let them take counsel together!
Who told this long ago?
  Who declared it of old?
Was it not I, the LORD?
  And there is no other god besides me,
a righteous God and a Savior;
  there is none besides me.

22 "Turn to me and be saved,
  all the ends of the earth!
For I am God, and there is no other.

---

together the imperative verb "come" (a synonym of the word in the previous line).
The situation envisaged here is after the great world conquest. The **survivors** are those
who have "escaped" the judgment. Volz says that the phrase at the time of Second Isaiah
was a *terminus technicus* of eschatological speech developed from the earlier conception
of the remnant (cf. 4:2-3; 7:22). The next line refers (vs. 20 *de*) to religious processions
in which the images of the gods were borne through the streets ceremonially by the
priests and others. This reference is a characteristic anticipation of the following poem.
The prophet himself may have seen such a procession in the streets of Babylon in the
face of the impending crisis. Those who carry the images **have no knowledge** of what
they are doing; they do not realize that these images correspond to nothing in reality,
a god that cannot save, in contrast to Yahweh, who is a Savior (vs. 15*b*) and saves with
an everlasting salvation (vs. 17).

21. The prophet is returning again to his favorite judgment scene (41:1 ff., 26 ff.;
43:8-12; 48:14-16; 50:8-9; 53:8). **Who told this long ago?** Or, "Who announced this from
the beginning?" This interrogative is very common in Second Isaiah, but here, as in
41:2, 4, 26; 43:9*c*, it is an example of judicial speech. The Judge looks back on the world
events which he pictures as already completed, and inquires who it was who had proclaimed and predicted all this. **Was it not I?** Yahweh had spoken his word to the
prophets. The monotheistic declaration fittingly concludes the strophe (cf. Exeg. on
45:14-25, pp. 528-29). **A righteous God and a Savior:** Cf. vss. 15*b*, 17, 20*g*. The word
righteous here has been explained in the usual ethical sense (Torrey *et al.*), or as meaning
"truth-telling and constant" (Levy), "prospering" or "victorious" (Snaith), "trustworthy"
or "straight-forward" (Skinner), "saving" (Volz *et al.*). The idea of **a righteous God**
and yet **a Savior** is attractive, but this does not seem to be the meaning in this context.
The noun form צדיק, **a righteous God**, is not infrequently associated with salvation, and
this suggests the meaning of vindication, deliverance, or victory. Thus the way is prepared
for the momentous lines which follow.

5. Fifth Strophe: Yahweh Is Lord (45:22-23)

22. **Turn to me:** Cf. vss. 14-17. Since Yahweh alone can foretell and interpret the
course of history as revealed in his prophecies, he alone can save; therefore the nations

---

men. But such a conception is far from this
prophet. The Creator who made men has undertaken an obligation and will not fail to do his
full part to save them. He has demonstrated
both his trustworthiness and his salvation in
this historic episode of the conquests of Cyrus.

22-23. *All Nations Bidden to the One God.*—
As Jesus' "Come unto me" (Matt. 11:28) is the
gracious invitation of the N.T., this is the
gracious invitation of the O.T., and is as inclusive. The judgment under Cyrus is past; but
the **survivors** among the nations need to turn

23 I have sworn by myself, the word is gone out of my mouth *in* righteousness, and shall not return, That unto me every knee shall bow, every tongue shall swear.

24 Surely shall *one* say, In the LORD have I righteousness and strength: *even* to him shall *men* come; and all that are incensed against him shall be ashamed.

25 In the LORD shall all the seed of Israel be justified, and shall glory.

23 By myself I have sworn,
 from my mouth has gone forth in righteousness
 a word that shall not return:
'To me every knee shall bow,
 every tongue shall swear.'

24 "Only in the LORD, it shall be said of me,
 are righteousness and strength;
to him shall come and be ashamed,
 all who were incensed against him.
25 In the LORD all the offspring of Israel
 shall triumph and glory."

---

are invited to accept the gift of salvation which he offers out of his grace. Read in the light of the tradition which had its historical origins in the Mosaic covenant where the seeds of such an utterance were sown, the passage is epoch-making. Such a universal invitation is rooted in the reality and sovereignty of the one God: **For I am God, and there is no other.**

23. By myself I have sworn: Thus the prophet records the momentousness of the divine decision (cf. 62:8). For the oath of Yahweh cf. Gen. 22:16; Exod. 32:13; Amos 4:2; 6:8; Jer. 22:5, and especially Heb. 6:13-18. Here **righteousness** means the perfect correspondence between God's **word** and God's deed. The **word** in Second Isaiah not infrequently has a spacious and inclusive meaning tantamount to revelation (see 40:8; 55:10-11). It goes forth into the world filled with his energy and power. Not merely the peoples and nations, but every individual person will worship Yahweh and **bow** in homage before him (cf. I Kings 19:18). When they invoke the deity in their oaths, they will **swear** by the name of Yahweh (cf. Amos 8:14). The reference to the cultic acts reveals deep sensitiveness on the part of the prophet. A. B. Davidson pronounces this "the death-knell of all idolatry" (*The Theology of the Old Testament* [New York: Charles Scribner's Sons, 1904], p. 102; cf. Rom. 14:11; Phil. 2:10).

6. Sixth Strophe: The Universal Confession (45:24-25)

24. Only in the LORD: Cf. vs. 14*hi*. **It shall be said of me:** The Hebrew has "he [or "one"] said," but the RSV interprets the verb impersonally (cf. יאמר in the Dead Sea Scroll). **Righteousness:** The Hebrew has the plural. The meaning is similar to that in vs. 21, "Yahweh's saving and helping acts of deliverance" (Judg. 5:11; Mic. 6:5; Ps. 71:19). **To him shall come and be ashamed:** Cf. vs. 16.

25. Triumph: Lit., "be righteous" (יצדקו). Compare Jer. 23:6, "Jehovah our righteousness." It is only through Yahweh that men can be saved, only by his victorious acts of deliverance and his might.

---

to the Lord if they are to enjoy fellowship with him. **Saved** evidently means more than delivered from the catastrophes of the breakup of the Babylonian epoch. The essence of the new era is the life in friendship with God.

From my mouth has gone forth in righteousness a word that shall not return (cf. 55:11).

This is an assurance given to the nations. The particularism of Jewish religion is done away, and the kingdom is "opened to all believers." The former heathen show their faith in worship: **every knee shall bow;** and in their transaction

of daily obligations: **every tongue shall swear.** The turning to the Lord has wrought a complete inward transformation. One feels oneself here on the level of the N.T. That also represents Jesus as ushering in a new age, offering its hospitality to all who enter with repentance and faith. In this entire poem the grandeur of God and the universality of his purposes are emphasized. Almost every poem contains "great notions of God" and opens an outlook of grace for all nations.

24-25. All Nations Acknowledge that in God Alone Is Salvation.—The final strophe is an-

<table>
<tr><td>

46 Bel boweth down, Nebo stoopeth;
their idols were upon the beasts, and

</td><td>

46 Bel bows down, Nebo stoops,
their idols are on beasts and cattle;

</td></tr>
</table>

Volz considers only vs. 24ab as the confession of the nations (cf. vss. 14h-15), the rest (vss. 24c-25) a later addition from the hand of someone who took offense at the universality of the prophet's words. However, such sudden shifts are characteristic, especially at the end of poems. **The offspring of Israel:** Levy extends this term to include all "believers" (cf. the nations' confession in vss. 14h-15). The poem as a whole would perhaps give justification for such an interpretation. It is not likely that the lines are an addition.

M. THE COLLAPSE OF THE GODS AND YAHWEH'S SALVATION (46:1-13)

This poem is a splendid example of the combination of old and new elements. The same literary characteristics and the same ideas are present, but here, as elsewhere, the prophet does not repeat himself. His thought has centered upon Cyrus and his deliverance; now he contemplates the imminent overthrow of Babylon and its gods. This theme carries him on through ch. 48. Cyrus is not forgotten, to be sure, but his significance as the Lord's instrument is subordinated to the events before which he stands. The collapse of the Babylonian Empire and the consequent liberation of captive Israel are the dominant interests of ch. 46.

Five strophes outline the progress of the writer's thought (vss. 1-2, 3-4, 5-7, 8-11, 12-13). The poem opens *in medias res*. Without any formal introduction Second Isaiah presents us with a vivid picture of the exodus of Babylon's gods on the occasion of the imminent Persian conquest. Thereupon follows a strophe introduced with the characteristic imperative, "Listen to me," and a sharp contrast is drawn between the gods of Babylon and Israel's God. This strophe closes with a powerful self-asseveration in which the divine I (אני) is repeated five times. The last word, **I . . . will save,** provides the clue for the prophet's major thought: it reaches back to vs. 2b—in which the gods of Babylon are said to be unable to save their devotees—and prepares the way for the deliverance by Cyrus described in vss. 10-11 and the assurance of imminent salvation which rings through the closing lines. The third strophe (vss. 5-7) is considered by many scholars to be an intrusion, but close examination shows that the passage belongs here. If any one thought emerges out of the first two strophes, it is the uniqueness and incomparability of Israel's God over against all other gods. The gods have to be made at great cost both of material and effort; they have to be carried about on men's shoulders; they have to be set down so that they will not fall over. They make no response to men's cries; they cannot save their worshipers in the time of their distress. The fourth strophe (vss. 8-11) is as remarkable for its literary form as for its thought. An urgent imperative calling upon Israel to remember the former things from of old is fortified by the usual asseveration and the proclamation of the oneness of Israel's God as he is revealed in his activity from the beginning to the end of history. These significant lines are the illuminating expansion of Yahweh's intimate words to Israel in vss. 3c-4b. Here they are given a vastly extended historical expression (from beginning to end) in order to

---

other confession, this time from the lips of the nations who have found salvation in the Lord. **Only in the LORD . . . are righteousness and strength.** This is the experiential monotheism arrived at by the redeemed peoples. "To him shall come with shame all that were incensed against him." [2] This is the ultimate act in the Lord's salvation. The nations and all their inhabitants are shown in contrition, thus completing God's acts in creation and in revelation.

[2] Skinner, *op. cit.*, p. 68.

His purpose is achieved. **The offspring of Israel** —the vast throng of believers—are Israelites indeed in the thought of Paul. They share the Lord's **righteousness.** The prophet's climax agrees with the same apostle's final expectation, "That God may be everything to every one" (I Cor. 15:28).

46:1-13. The Carried Gods and the God Who Carries.—Here is another derisive poem on the deities of Babylon. **Bel** is another name for Marduk, its chief divinity, and **Nebo,** originally

upon the cattle: your carriages *were* heavy laden; *they are* a burden to the weary *beast.*

these things you carry are loaded as burdens on weary beasts.

---

prepare for the disclosure of Yahweh's action in Cyrus' conquest of Babylon. The asseverations of vs. 9 are expanded by three participial double lines: **declaring** (vs. 10a), **saying** (vs. 10c), and **calling** (vs. 11a). The first provides the total eschatological context, the second indicates the purpose which accounts for the movement of history, and the third announces the imminent appearance of Cyrus. Word and historical event (vs. 11c), purpose and fulfillment (vs. 11d) bring the strophe to a magnificent close and prepare the way for the triumphant lines which announce the nearness of the divine salvation.

The vivid description of the opening lines serves as the background for the rest of the poem. It is hardly a mocking song as some have supposed. The following strophes combine exhortations with the oracles of assurance or salvation. The meter is 3+2 and 3+3.

1. First Strophe: Impotence of Babylon's Gods (46:1-2)

Babylon is about to fall. The idols are being led from the city on the backs of beasts of burden. In imagination the prophet sees the events taking place before his eyes.

46:1. The gods who had brought Babylon to power and world empire now bend and bow precariously as they are drawn from the temples. **Bel,** originally the god of Nippur, the father of the gods and the god of heaven, later coalesced with Marduk, the great god of Babylon (cf. Jer. 50:2). The elevation of Bel-Marduk to the head of the pantheon is vividly described in the Babylonian creation myth. He was the tutelary divinity of the city and was worshiped with elaborate rituals and ceremonies by a zealous priesthood. **Nebo** (some LXX MSS read "Dagon"), son of Marduk, possessed the tablets of destiny on which the fates were written. His temple E-ur-imin-an-ki was located in neighboring Borsippa. The presence of his name in the theophorous names of the Babylonian kings (Nabopolassar, Nebuchadrezzar, Nabonidus) suggests his popularity. **Bel** and **Nebo** were carried through the streets in the New Year's procession. It is possible that we have such a procession here. The short sentences at the beginning of the poem are effective. The impotence of the gods is revealed at once: **Bel bows, Nebo stoops.** The first verb is perfect, the second a participle, "is stooping." The Ugaritic texts have a number of parallels; cf. Baal and Anath (tr. H. L. Ginsberg, in J. B. Pritchard, ed., *Ancient Near Eastern Texts Relating to the Old Testament* [Princeton: Princeton University Press, 1950], pp. 130-31; extracts used by permission):

> Yamm collapses,
>> He falls to the ground;
> His joints bend,
>> His frame breaks (III AB A).

> The gods do drop their heads
>> Down upon their knees
> And on the thrones of princeship (III AB B).

Their idols are on beasts and cattle: (See Hooke, ed., *The Labyrinth*, p. 230, Fig. 9.) It is better to follow Bewer (*The Book of Isaiah* [New York: Harper & Bros., 1950;

---

the city-god of Borsippa, a few miles from Babylon, was worshiped as his son. Together they were "the Jupiter and Mercury of the Babylonian pantheon," [3] the supreme divinities of the empire in our prophet's time. Their huge statues, often studded with jewels, were borne about on floats drawn by oxen or mules. The prophet may have seen them in a mag-

[3] *Ibid.*

nificent New Year's pageant. Now, thinking of the city's proximate capture, he pictures its inhabitants vainly attempting to cart off their sacred idols to some place of safety, finding themselves thwarted and their cherished images carried away as loot.

1-2. *Things You Carry.*—The poem is satirical. At the New Year's festival a promenade was prepared, along which the idols moved

2 They stoop, they bow down together; | 2 They stoop, they bow down together,
they could not deliver the burden, but | they cannot save the burden,
themselves are gone into captivity. | but themselves go into captivity.

3 ¶ Hearken unto me, O house of Jacob, |

| 3 "Hearken to me, O house of Jacob,
| all the remnant of the house of Israel,

"Harper's Annotated Bible"], p. 28) and to read "are consigned to beasts and cattle." Merodach-baladan also carried off the gods at the approach of Sennacherib: "That Merodach-Baladan on whom I in my first military expedition inflicted a defeat and whose force I had broken in pieces, dreaded the onset of my powerful weapons. . . . The gods, the protection (?) of his land, he gathered in their shrines, shipped them on vessels and took himself off to the city Nagití-Rakki, which is in the midst of the sea, like a bird." (Eberhard Schrader, *The Cuneiform Inscriptions and the Old Testament* [tr. O. C. Whitehouse; London: Williams & Norgate, 1885-88], II, 36.) **These things you carry are loaded . . . :** Lit., "your carried things . . . ." Read with Bewer (*loc. cit.*): "They that should carry you are loaded as a burden upon weary beasts." Some scholars complain that the line is overfull, but it is a mistake to delete any of the words, as is shown by the way they are employed in succeeding strophes. The Kittel text has 2+2+2 meter throughout the verse, and this is probably right. **To the weary beast:** Lit., "for the weary." This is a fine touch. For the last line ("a burden for the weary") the Dead Sea Scroll reads "their announcers," which may suggest quite another interpretation of the meaning of the text. But there is no support elsewhere for it.

2. The verbs appear in the reverse order to that of vs. 1. The repetition emphasizes the utter impotence of the gods. The Hebrew **together** may suggest other gods also, as many scholars think, but this is not certain since the prophet uses the word often as an expression of emphasis. If other gods are included, however, it would be a fine anticipation of the monotheistic asseveration which follows in the next strophe. **They cannot save the burden:** This is the point of the strophe. Gods should rescue men, not men, gods. Bel and Nebo cannot even save their own worshipers. In Akkadian mythology men are created for the purpose of performing such services for the gods as will make their existence less burdensome, "that they might have ease" (*Enûma eliš* VI, 1-40; see Pritchard, *op. cit.*, p. 68). **But themselves go into captivity:** Lit., "their very self." Second Isaiah characteristically identifies the gods with the images. (Cf. 41:5-7, 21-24, and contrast 46:8-13. The thought is similar here. See Yehezkel Kaufmann, "The Bible and Mythological Polytheism," *Journal of Biblical Literature*, LXX [1951] 179-97.) Actually the course of events did not substantiate the prophet's claims. Cyrus recognized the lordship of Bel-Marduk, as his own inscription shows.

2. Second Strophe: Yahweh Bears Up His People (46:3-4)

The opening imperative presses on to the point of contrast between the gods of Babylon and the God of Israel. In Babylon gods and men are involved in a common ruin, for the gods cannot save; in Israel Yahweh hears his people, supports them, and carries them to old age. Yahweh has always borne Israel as his burden, and he will never cease doing so.

3. Hearken to me: The exhortation is addressed to Israel. It is followed by an extended vocative emphasizing the unique relationship between Yahweh and Israel.

---

with stately dignity. Now in headlong flight, the carts are driven through rutted streets and roads, and the statues sway or bob about behind or on the backs of straining beasts. The prophet laughs at these gods as frightened: **Bel bows down, Nebo stoops.** Scornfully he dubs them **these things you carry,** in your religious processions, now **loaded as burdens on weary beasts.** He ridicules their impotence—cattle, gods, and worshipers together go into captivity.

3-4. *The Upholding God.*—The living God addresses the **house of Jacob** and the scattered exiles in many lands, recalling how he has car-

| and all the remnant of the house of Israel, which are borne *by me* from the belly, which are carried from the womb: | who have been borne by me from your birth, carried from the womb. |

The four lines of vs. 3 are introductory to the four lines of vs. 4, a strophic arrangement not uncommon to our poet. **Borne . . . from your birth, carried from the womb:** See 44:2, 24; 49:5; cf. Exod. 19:4. So Israel had understood her tradition. Yahweh had brought her into existence, sustained her in her earliest years, and provided for her throughout her history. The imagery is most likely that of a father bearing his child (Deut. 1:31; Hos. 11:3; Ps. 22:10; cf. especially Isa. 40:11; 63:9). The verbs are intentionally in reverse order to that in vs. 1. The picture of the gods on the backs of dumb beasts is contrasted with Yahweh's bearing of Israel, his son, as his burden.

---

ried them since their nation's birth. Heathen religions leave their devotees to look after and transport their gods; the Controller of history **will carry** and **will bear** his people, and will uphold them to the end.

This superb passage contrasts religion as a load with religion as a lift. The objects to which secular-minded men give their allegiance have this perennial defect. Speaking of moderns who see no personal God behind the universe, Irwin Edman writes:

It has been said endlessly and patiently that the discovery that the universe has no purpose need not prevent a human being from having one, or indeed many, as many as his own life, circumstances and impulses generate. But the fact remains that it is precisely the lack of purposes, either fixed or beckoning, that the overcivilized and sensitive feel most deeply. Enlightened common sense and resourceful technique can do much in indicating what can possibly be done and how to do it. But they cannot provide reasons why the things possible in our civilization should be done, a guarantee that they can be accomplished, or, what is more important, the passions and incitements by which powers can be called out and intelligence enlisted.[4]

Christian faith supplies life with meaning, purpose, and passion to achieve the end. In a final paragraph in his *Life of Wesley*, Robert Southey calls Wesley a "man of great views, great energies, and great virtues." [5] Such views, energies, and virtues flow spontaneously from faith in God revealed in Christ. It is this enlightening and vitalizing faith which jaded moderns need.

Religion unfortunately appears to many an added burden. Creeds seem cramping loads under which minds must be forced. The Bible is viewed as a heavy book, boring to read. Services of worship are looked on as burdensome conventions. At twenty-five, Stevenson confided to a correspondent, "I've been to

church, and am not depressed—a great step." [6] Whenever any of our relations with God have such an effect upon us, we may be sure that we are in touch with some false deity, not the living God. The O.T. is full of metaphors in which the devout report God bearing them on eagle's wings (Deut. 32:11) or on his arms (Deut. 1:31; Hos. 11:3). This prophet employs both metaphors in 40:11, 31. Christian experience multiplies instances of such divine upholding.

Coleridge justified his habit of praying every night by declaring that it left him with

A sense o'er all my soul imprest
That I am weak, yet not unblest,
Since in me, round me, everywhere
Eternal Strength and Wisdom are.[7]

In a book widely read during World War I, Donald Hankey tells of a young Englishman whose religion had been "a spasmodic loyalty to the Christ-man," lying wounded under the skies:

The stars gazed at him imperturbably. There was no sympathy there but only cold, unseeing tolerance. Yet after all, he had the advantage of them. For all his pygmy ineffectiveness he was of finer stuff than they. At least he could feel—suffer. He had only to try to move to verify that. At least he was aware of his own existence, and could even gauge his own insignificance. There was that in him which was not in them, unless—unless it was in everything. "God!" he whispered softly. "God everywhere!" Then into his tired brain came a new phrase—"Underneath are the everlasting arms." He sighed contentedly, as a tired child, and the phrase went on repeating itself in his brain in a kind of chant—"Underneath are the everlasting arms." [8]

So also it is with the Bible. There is no denying that it is not easy reading. In a sermon on

---

[4] *The Contemporary and His Soul* (New York: J. Cape & H. Smith, 1931), pp. 74-75. Used by permission of The Viking Press, Inc.

[5] New York: Harper & Bros., 1847, II, 336.

[6] Sidney Colvin, ed., *The Letters of Robert Louis Stevenson* (New York: Charles Scribner's Sons, 1911), I, 219.

[7] "The Pains of Sleep."

[8] From the book *A Student in Arms*, pp. 151-52. Copyright, 1916, by Andrew Melrose, Ltd.; 1917, by E. P. Dutton & Co., Inc. Used by permission.

4 And *even* to *your* old age I *am* he; and *even* to hoar hairs will I carry *you:* I have made, and I will bear; even I will carry, and will deliver *you.*

4 even to your old age I am He,
   and to gray hairs I will carry you,
I have made, and I will bear;
   I will carry and will save.

---

4. Even to your old age I am He: The monotheistic assertion is especially appropriate after the description of the impotence of the gods of Babylon and the contrasting picture of Yahweh's gracious undergirding of Israel's life. As Yahweh has guided and supported Israel hitherto, so he will be her God until she is old; from youth to old age he is her God (cf. Ps. 71:9, 18). Israel knows but one God because her whole history is a demonstration of his activity. Levy (*Deutero-Isaiah*, p. 199) aptly refers to the "Hymn of Glory" in the sabbath ritual.

> Laden (upon him) he carried them, with a crown he adorned them,
> Since they were precious in his sight he honoured them.

The fivefold emphatic **I** of Yahweh (in the Hebrew) and the fivefold verbs forms a superb climax, especially effective in a strophe which begins with the call **Hearken to me,** followed by the affectionate words of address to Israel. The gods are forgotten, only God remains. Rarely in scripture are the power and grace of God more eloquently affirmed. **I have made:** Many scholars emend עשיתי to **I will bear** (נשׂאתי), which might be more felicitous but lacks textual support. The contrasting tenses in the last two lines are effective. What Yahweh has done he will continue to do. The verbs echo the first strophe. A new verb is added, however, in vs. 4d, אסבל, **I will carry,** which Ehrlich says is used only of heavy burdens—a fine touch, especially in its position before the final verb **I . . . will save** (cf. the position of this verb in vs. 2b). The prophet's ability to bring his central thought to a focus amid all these spacious superlatives is remarkable. Only Yahweh has a revelation to proclaim: a historical appeal to what he has already done and a prophetic proclamation of what he will do.

---

the twentieth anniversary of his ordination. Horace Bushnell spoke of "the Scriptures bolting out their incautious oppositions [i.e., contradictions] regardless of all subtleties." One has to bring to their pages mental acuteness, spiritual insight, and above all a hunger for God. Then their sustaining power is felt. William James tells of a period when he underwent deep depression, "a horrible fear of my own existence. . . . The fear was so invasive and powerful that, if I had not clung to scripture-texts like *The eternal God is my refuge,* etc., *Come unto me all ye that labor and are heavy-laden,* etc., *I am the Resurrection and the Life,* etc., I think I should have grown really insane." [9]

And as for the burdens which Christian conscience piles upon us, they prove wings rather than weights. Obligations exhilarate those who try to discharge them in the spirit of Christ. Frances Elizabeth Willard, an indefatigable worker, declared, "The chief wonder of my life is that I dare to have so good a time, physically, mentally, and religiously." [10] And when dangers and difficulties must be encountered in enter-

prises undertaken for religious principle, the devout constantly rely on God's support. A striking instance is the Pilgrims in 1620 as they reached the bleak shores of New England.

For summer being done, all things stand upon them with a weather-beaten face; and the whole country, full of woods and thickets, represented a wild and savage hue. If they looked behind them, there was the mighty ocean. . . . Let it also be considered what weak hopes of supply and succor they left behind them that might bear up their minds in this sad condition and trials they were under; and they could not but be very small. . . . What could now sustain them but the Spirit of God and his grace? [1]

They and many others have proved that God does sustain his people.

The promise in vs. 4 was given to a nation, but generations have applied it to individuals. Those who live close to God seem not to grow old in spirit. Their physical organism decays, their activities are severely curtailed, their mental powers may diminish, but their souls remain buoyant. C. A. Sainte-Beuve, in his sketch of Fénelon, writes of the letters penned toward the close of Fénelon's life: "They have

[9] Henry James, ed., *Letters of William James,* I, 146-47.
[10] *Glimpses of Fifty Years* (Chicago: Women's Temperance Publication Association, 1889), p. 633.

[1] William Bradford, *History of Plymouth Plantation,* Bk. 1, ch. ix.

5 ¶ To whom will ye liken me, and make *me* equal, and compare me, that we may be like?

6 They lavish gold out of the bag, and weigh silver in the balance, *and* hire a goldsmith; and he maketh it a god: they fall down, yea, they worship.

7 They bear him upon the shoulder, they carry him, and set him in his place, and he standeth; from his place shall he not remove: yea, *one* shall cry unto him, yet can he not answer, nor save him out of his trouble.

5 "To whom will you liken me and make
     me equal,
     and compare me, that we may be alike?
6 Those who lavish gold from the purse,
     and weigh out silver in the scales,
     hire a goldsmith, and he makes it into a
     god;
     then they fall down and worship!
7 They lift it upon their shoulders, they
     carry it,
     they set it in its place, and it stands
     there;
     it cannot move from its place.
If one cries to it, it does not answer
     or save him from his trouble.

3. Third Strophe: Yahweh Not Like Other Gods (46:5-7)

The strophe seems at first to break the continuity, but actually it is in harmony with its context. The major idea of vss. 1-4 is the utter ineffectuality of the idols and the unique, personal, sustaining care of Yahweh (cf. also vs. 9*bc*). Moreover, 40:18-19; 41:6-7; 44:9-20 speak of the idols in much the same manner as here. Finally, 45:20, which probably refers to the New Year's procession, is an admirable preparation.

5. To whom will you liken me . . . : Note the continuation of the divine first person. In 40:18-19, 25, Yahweh's uniqueness stands in a context of his creative activity; here it is his providence and sustaining help throughout Israel's history.

6. Precious metals were used as plating for the wooden core of the idol (see 40:19). Some scholars emend the word **lavish** (הזלים) to "pay" (הסלים), but unnecessarily. The word for **scales** is, lit., "reed" (קנה), and is used for scales by metonymy. **Then they fall down:** The same word (סגד) occurs in 44:15, 17, 19. The sequence of verbs culminating in **fall down and worship** is in the style of Second Isaiah. The materials are costly and the expense of manufacture great, but the idol remains an idol, and the worship of it is as futile as the effort exerted for its creation.

7. The verbs echo the same two verbs of the first two strophes (vs. 1*c*; cf. the twofold *massā'* of vss. 1*d*, 2*b*, 3*d*, 4*b*, 4*c*, 4*d*). They **lift it, carry it, set it in its place, and it stands, it cannot move from its place.** But when **trouble** comes and **one cries to it, it does not answer.** In the hour of distress **it does not . . . save** (cf. 45:20). Note that the accent of the verse falls precisely where it does in the first two strophes, and more especially in the last strophe where the salvation of Yahweh receives its major emphasis.

---

the effect upon me of the last days of a mild winter, beyond which I feel the springtime."[2] One would not speak disparagingly of Christians who seem burdened by the woes of the world, or by the problems which they personally confront, but something must be lacking in their conception of God. No surer test can be found of the genuineness of fellowship with God as revealed in the Bible than his **upholding** amid circumstances that weigh upon the spirit.

5-7. *Idols Ridiculed*.—The images of the Babylonian deities were representations in human form of the overwhelming might of natural forces. They suggested the unfeeling and un-

[2] *Portraits of the Seventeenth Century*, tr. Katharine P. Wormeley (New York: G. P. Putnam's Sons, 1904), p. 383.

moral power of the subhuman in nature. All plastic art confines the mind and limits its flight into the higher spiritual realms of righteousness, grace, and truth. Image-making religions ascend from nature through man; the iconoclastic faith of the Hebrews descends from a self-disclosing God, who remains forever beyond man's grasp of mind, much more beyond his capacity to body forth in plastic art. It is God's spiritual transcendence which lifts men in aspiration. No devout art can be more than suggestive of something beyond. John Addington Symonds wrote of the Renaissance: "Piety, at the lure of art, folded her soaring wings and rested on the genial earth. . . . The religion it interpreted transcended the actual conditions of humanity,

8 Remember this, and show yourselves men: bring *it* again to mind, O ye transgressors.
 	
9 Remember the former things of old: for I *am* God, and *there is* none else; *I am* God, and *there is* none like me,
	8 "Remember this and consider,
	    recall it to mind, you transgressors,
	9 remember the former things of old;
	for I am God, and there is no other;
	    I am God, and there is none like me,

4. Fourth Strophe: The One Lord of History (46:8-11)

The true character of the one God as he has been revealed in Israel's covenantal life has been in the thought of the prophet from the beginning, but here it comes to clear and eloquent formulation. The strophe is a superb expression of the prophet's theology. Beginning with the command to remember, repeated for emphasis (**remember, consider . . . recall . . . remember**), he establishes at once the mentality which guides him in his thought of God. Israel's faith is authenticated and understood by the things that Yahweh has done for her, by the events he brought about and in which he made himself, his word and purpose and will, known. Israel appropriates these "deeds" in memory. Her sanctuaries are places where the tradition is remembered and transmitted; her rituals rehearse the ancient stories; her festivals re-enact and dramatize the holy events of the past; her prophets recall epochal moments like the Exodus and the sojourn and Conquest; her priests recite and listen to the recitations of the *tôrôth* (instructions") ; her myths are transformed by the covenant acts and words.

8. Remember this: I.e., what follows in the rest of the strophe. **Consider** is a *hapax legomenon* which some derive from the noun איש, "man" (cf. KJV, **show yourselves men**), but with little support. The LXX reads στενάξατε, "groan"; the Vulg., *confundamini* (cf. Hebrew התבוששו), which is accepted by Lagarde and others. Torrey takes it as an Aramaic loan word meaning "to found," hence, "put yourselves on a secure foundation" (cf. Arabic *assassa*, "to be well grounded"; cf. the Palestinian Syriac of Matt. 7:25) or "be assured." This is the best solution. The RSV follows the Syriac in rendering **consider** (*hithbônānû*) .

9. Remember the former things of old: Cf. 41:4, 22-29; 42:8-9; 43:9-12; 44:7-8; 45:21; 48:3, 5, 14. The twofold call to remember is connected by the particle *kî*, **for,** to the twofold declaration of monotheism, **I am God.** Thus historical memory and the oneness of God are joined. History's unity lies under the sovereignty of one God who works in history. But the monotheistic declaration is given further content and force by the participles of revelation, "declaring," "saying," "calling," which introduce the impressive lines of vss. 10-11.

---

while art is bound down by its nature to the limitations of the world we live in."[3]

In vss. 5-7 the prophet exposes in detail the construction of an idol—the purchase of the metal, the hiring of the goldsmith, the carrying and placing of the image, and finally its futile worship. Its immobility and helplessness form a foil to the God of Israel's faith. How absurd to **fall down and worship** this impotent thing!

8-11. *The Living God's Work Through Cyrus.*
—The prophet makes a direct appeal to the **transgressors** to recall what is transpiring at the moment: Cyrus, **a bird of prey,** is **the man of my counsel,** announced for some time and now about to achieve God's purpose by the capture of Babylon. The energetic movement of this

[3] *The Renaissance in Italy: III, The Fine Arts* (New York: Henry Holt & Son, 1882), pp. 32, 31.

conqueror, representing God's working, contrasts with the do-nothing idols.

Remember is a most important word in spiritual religion. God is revealed in history, and we establish present fellowship by recalling what he has done. "This do in remembrance of me" places repeatedly before his church his mighty act of redemption in Jesus. **Remember the former things of old:** in rowing a boat one looks at some object on the shore, and by aligning one's efforts with it, steers accurately for one's destination. In Christ we know God's **counsel** which stands, and his **purpose** which he will surely bring to pass.

Cyrus seemed to his contemporaries **a bird of prey.** Similar predatory powers fill our current scene. While we dare not say that God inspires their rapacity, none the less he is em-

10 Declaring the end from the beginning, and from ancient times *the things* that are not *yet* done, saying, My counsel shall stand, and I will do all my pleasure:

11 Calling a ravenous bird from the east, the man that executeth my counsel from a far country: yea, I have spoken *it,* I will also bring it to pass; I have purposed *it,* I will also do it.

12 ¶ Hearken unto me, ye stouthearted, that *are* far from righteousness:

---

10 declaring the end from the beginning
    and from ancient times things not yet done,
saying, 'My counsel shall stand,
    and I will accomplish all my purpose,'
11 calling a bird of prey from the east,
    the man of my counsel from a far country.
I have spoken, and I will bring it to pass;
    I have purposed, and I will do it.

12 "Hearken to me, you stubborn of heart,
    you who are far from deliverance:

---

10. Cf. Exeg. on vs. 9. The whole course of history **from beginning** to **end** is in the mind of God, but it does not lie dormant there. He declares it, tells it, makes it known. History is not only in the thought of God; it is the theater of his action and concern. History is under the control of the divine counsel, the divine intention and **purpose.** This gives it its unity and dynamic meaning (cf. 41:21; 44:26; 48:14).

11. The reference is to Cyrus. Torrey emends the word עיט, **a bird of prey,** to עבדי, "my servant," for which there is no justification. The expression describes admirably the character of the conqueror's meteoric career (cf. 41:2-3). Cf. similar descriptions of the eagle as applied to Nebuchadrezzar in Jer. 49:22; Ezek. 17:3. Some scholars see a reference here to the golden eagle emblazoned on the Persian royal ensigns (Xenophon *Cyropaedia* VII. 1. 4). **I have spoken, . . . I have purposed:** An admirable reinforcement of the foregoing lines as well as a powerful conclusion to them. The events follow from God's words and purpose, from revelation and sovereignty. All that is taking place must be recognized in the perspectives which the prophet outlines; the future lies under the same purpose and the same activity as the past.

5. Fifth Strophe: My Salvation Is Near (46:12-13)

The motif of deliverance and salvation has run through all the poem; here it reaches its culmination.

12. You stubborn of heart: Many commentators, following the LXX (ἀπολωλεκότες), read "fainthearted" or "you who lose heart," but the Hebrew makes good sense and is supported by the "rebels" of vs. 8. **Far from deliverance:** The KJV renders by **righteous-**

---

ploying them in his plans. We have to hold together his character as love, which sets the ethical standard for men and nations, and his sovereignty, which enables him to work through such diabolic instruments as brutally aggressive nations. Pascal wrote: "Grand it is to see by the eye of faith, Darius and Cyrus, Alexander, the Romans, Pompey and Herod working, though unconsciously, for the glory of the Gospel."[4] There is an inexplicable paradox here: the goodness of God and his employment of agents morally abhorrent to him.

12-13. The Stubborn of Heart Warned.— God's comforting message is always uncomfortable for those **who are far from righteousness.** Such folk are unresponsive and cannot be made members of a missionary community. The

[4] *The Thoughts of Blaise Pascal,* tr. C. Kegan Paul (London: George Bell & Sons, 1890), p. 145.

stubborn of heart scoffed at the news of the imminence of Babylon's overthrow and Israel's liberation. All the prophet could do was to repeat in God's name the assurance

I bring near my deliverance, it is not far off,
    and my salvation will not tarry.

We live at a similarly critical juncture in history. God has a justice—a righteous world order—which is near; if not in time, near in his gracious purpose for mankind. By the light of Christ we may discern its outlines and descry the quality of its life. We see it only dimly; but the searching question is, Do we really wish it to arrive? Would we fit into it? What of our prejudice, greeds, pride, hypocrisies? It is later in history than most of us are disposed to recognize. Ours is a time of prestige and prosperity for the United States. But such periods pass

13 I bring near my righteousness; it shall not be far off, and my salvation shall not tarry: and I will place salvation in Zion for Israel my glory.	13 I bring near my deliverance, it is not far off, and my salvation will not tarry; I will put salvation in Zion, for Israel my glory."
47 Come down, and sit in the dust, O virgin daughter of Babylon, sit on	47 Come down and sit in the dust, O virgin daughter of Babylon; sit on the ground without a throne,

ness both here and in vs. 13, but the meaning is more probably "victory," "triumph," or **deliverance**, as often in Second Isaiah and as the parallel with "salvation" (vs. 13) suggests. Those addressed are far from salvation because they are **stubborn** and rebellious of heart and will not respond to the revelation which the prophet has been proclaiming.

13. I bring near my deliverance. The Dead Sea Scroll reads "my triumph is near"; so also the Targ. While the stubborn of heart are far from deliverance (or righteousness), God's deliverance is near at hand. In the light of the opening imperative and the address to the stubbornhearted, the prophet seems to be saying, "The time is at hand; repent and believe." The gods cannot deliver or rescue or save (vss. 2b, 7de), but Yahweh is a righteous God and a Savior (cf. 45:21; observe there the same two words). The last two lines may be rendered, "I will give my salvation in Zion and my glory to Israel." Yahweh gives his **salvation** in Israel, where his saving activity has always been known; he gives Israel the gift of splendor, honor, or distinction by the salvation that he brings her before all the nations of the world. The word **glory** here does not mean his tabernacling presence (*kābhôdh*). According to the RSV, the meaning is that Yahweh's **glory** is revealed through **Israel**, his elected and covenanted people, to whom he has given salvation.

Thus the contrast between the fate of Israel and of her oppressors is brought to a superb finale.

N. A Mocking Song on the Virgin of Babylon (47:1-15)

This chapter follows closely upon its predecessor both in mood and content. Ch. 46 describes the fall of the gods of Babylon; ch. 47, the fall of the city itself. Both poems

rapidly. Does it expose us in state or church as individuals **far from righteousness** or prepared to enter God's reign?

In Second Isaiah's view the external consummation of history is ushered in by Cyrus; but there is a spiritual transformation of mankind, and this is the missionary task of his servant Israel.

> **I will put salvation in Zion**
> **for Israel my glory.**

This is the distinctive mission today of the church. In many lands pagan deities of the ethnic faiths have fallen; and modern idols, borrowed from the West, have been set up in their place—naïve faith in science, or education, or physical betterment, and nationalistic self-seeking, etc. These, however, are already discredited with us, and will be shortly everywhere. A religious vacuum remains, which must at once be filled, or man's naturally god-making propensity will fill it. When modern idols have been exposed as incapable of carrying mankind

to wished-for goals of justice, the church has its chance to bring in the gospel of God, who can carry those who trust and obey him to their fulfillment in his world-wide mission. How tragic the somnolence of the church seems in this critical time! How many Christians are judging themselves unworthy of citizenship in Zion, the mediator of God's grace to mankind!

Let us note well that God's plan is not conditioned upon the conversion of the **stubborn of heart** to become his fellow workers. Those of whom we think as his acknowledged agents may fail him; but his resourcefulness will discover other ways to fulfill his plan. Luther caught the prophet's assurance when he wrote to Spalatin: "The Lord, who knows I am a wicked sinner, will conduct His cause through me, or some one else." [5] There are few more reassuring expressions on the divine lips than this: "I have purposed, and I will do it" (vs. 11).

47:1-15. God's Judgment on a Self-sufficient Nation.—This ode on the destruction of Baby-

[5] Currie, *Letters of Martin Luther,* Letter XLIV.

| the ground: *there is* no throne, O daughter of the Chaldeans: for thou shalt no more be called tender and delicate. | O daughter of the Chalde'ans! For you shall no more be called tender and delicate. |

prepare the way for the triumphant cries of later poems (chs. 49; 50; 54). The taunt song on Babylon is a superb example of the prophet's craftsmanship. Indeed there are few poems which rival it in the degree to which rhetorical devices are employed; observe, for example, the poet's use of repetition as a literary device, the remarkable onomatopoeia of vs. 2a, suggesting the grinding of the mill, the abundant imperatives, the striking words of address (vss. 1b, 1d, 5b, 5d, 8a, 8b), introductions (vss. 1, 5, 12, 14) and conclusions (vss. 4ef, 7, 9cd, 15), quotations (vss. 7ab, 8def, 10b, 10f), contrast, and personification. Almost forty words occur here which are not present elsewhere in the poems (Christopher R. North, *The Suffering Servant in Deutero-Isaiah* [London: Oxford University Press, 1948], p. 169).

The poem has two divisions of three strophes each (vss. 1-4, 5-7, 8-9; 10-11, 12-13, 14-15), the third strophe in each case forming an impressive climax. The meter is unusually regular and provides a classical example of the *qînāh* or lamentation.

1. First Strophe: Babylon, Throneless, Enslaved, and Judged (47:1-4)

A well-wrought composition with appropriate opening and close and with staccato imperatives, separated by moving words of address. The second imperative is repeated for emphasis. Then comes the *kî* clause usual in compositions of this sort (vs. 1ef) followed by a continuing series of brief imperatives, culminating in vs. 3 and reinforced by the customary asseveration of vs. 4.

Babylon, pictured as seated regally and proudly on the throne of empire, is bidden descend to the dust of humiliation and degradation (cf. M. J. Lagrange, *Études sur les religions sémitiques* [12th ed.; Paris: Victor Lecoffre, 1905], p. 280). From her position of power and privilege she is ordered to take upon herself the harsh duties of the most menial slave. Her fall is not merely an exhibition of a historical cycle of decline and fall, after the manner of the cyclical philosophies of history, but the result of the divine intention of such a god as the God of Israel, a covenant God, a Redeemer, Yahweh of hosts, Israel's Holy One.

47:1. Babylon is **virgin** because she is as yet unravished, unconquered. The phrase is applied to Israel in Jer. 31:4, 21; to Egypt in Jer. 46:11. Chaldea and Babylon are used

---

lon differs somewhat from the other poems. Its meter is largely that of Hebrew lamentations. Pathos as much as triumph is in its tone. Unlike the ode on the king of Babylon in 14:4-21, which was doubtless its model, it does not breathe the spirit of exultant revenge. Nothing is said of Babylon's destruction of the temple at Jerusalem and her removal of its holy vessels. She had been God's instrument in disciplining his unfaithful people (vs. 6); but she had been guilty of arrogant self-assurance and of brutality in her treatment of captives. Her dealings with the elderly among the conquered had lacked elementary human kindness (vs. 6). She had vaunted her luxury and been proud of her scientific achievements. The prophet ridicules her elaborate hierarchy of astrologers and magicians. She was religiously bankrupt. She had forgotten that before God all things human are frail and fleeting, and had foolishly fancied

herself secure in her might and knowledge. Now in bitterness she is to know how undependable are the objects on which she had so confidently relied. She is to taste to the full what she inflicted on others. The poem dwells on the misery of her lot. Her downfall from splendid ease to abject wretchedness is pictured in detail. Her pride and her inhumanity are the causes of her doom. Self-sufficiency seems to this ardent believer in the all-wise, sovereign God the height of blasphemy.

Who say in your heart,
"I am, and there is no one besides me" (vs. 8).

For the benefit of God's own people the futility of the entire paraphernalia of astrology is exposed—evidence of its fascination and danger for them. To this prophet it was a menace to true religion, a tragic substitute for humble and obedient fellowship with the living God.

2 Take the millstones, and grind meal: uncover thy locks, make bare the leg, uncover the thigh, pass over the rivers.	2 Take the millstones and grind meal, put off your veil, strip off your robe, uncover your legs, pass through the rivers.

interchangeably as in Isa. 48:20. The LXX omits **without a throne,** and some MSS read "enter into the darkness" for **sit on the ground. Tender and delicate:** Cf. Deut. 28:56. The years of ease and luxury are over. Cf. the parallel in the Ugaritic text, Baal and Anath (Cyrus Gordon, *Ugaritic Literature* [Roma: Pontificium Institutum Biblicum, 1949], p. 42).

> Thereupon Ltpn, God of *Mercy,*
> Goes down from the throne
> Sits on the footstool
> And from the footstool sits on the earth.

2. The grinding of the grain was the task of female slaves (Exod. 11:5; Job 31:10; Matt. 24:41). The mill consisted of a lower stone (*pélah tahtith*) and an upper stone (*pélah rékhebh*), usually of basalt. In the lower stone a pin was fixed, around which the upper stone was made to revolve by a handle (Wade, *Isaiah,* p. 303; Kurt Galling, *Biblisches Reallexikon* [Tübingen: J. C. B. Mohr, 1937; "Handbuch zum Alten Testament"], pp. 386-87, where illustrations are given; cf. also Gustav Dalman, *Arbeit und Sitte in Palästina* [Gütersloh: C. Bertelsmann, 1928-39], III, 207-12). **Put off your veil:** Especially for women of privilege and position the veil was worn to hide the face from the vulgar gaze (cf. Song of S. 4:3; 6:7) and the glare of the sun. **Strip off your robe:** Better, "Strip off the train" (ASV). The LXX reads "gray hairs"; similarly the Peshitta; Vulg., *humerum.* G. R. Driver ("Difficult Words in the Hebrew Prophets" in H. H. Rowley, ed., *Studies in Old Testament Prophecy* [New York: Charles Scribner's Sons, 1950], p. 58) suggests "flowing tresses." It is possible that the figure of the slave grinding at the mill is forgotten, and the allusion is to the captive deported into an alien land (cf. 20:4; Nah. 3:5; Jer. 13:22, 26). If so, we have excellent archaeological illustration for our passage from the bronze doors of Balawat, which picture the women of Dabigi

Babylon and Zion are foils to each other. The one reduced from the soft and irresponsible life of a great lady of the harem to a hard-toiling captive slave, the other raised by God's grace from exiled bondage to be no longer a widow and childless, but a rapidly multiplying people in exalted holy partnership with him in the redemption of mankind. As Jerusalem has become in the prophet's thought a symbol of a nation dedicated to God, so Babylon becomes the symbol of a nation that was anti-God, a symbol employed by the seer on Patmos (Rev. 17-18) and fixed in Christian poetry.

1-4. *From Dainty Ease to Coarse Drudgery.*— The prophet is speaking to his own people and pointing out God's judgments in history.

> **I will take vengeance,**
> **and I will spare no man**

is an ironical reference to the assurance of the wealthy in the power of money to bargain in

diplomatic negotiations. Cyrus is on the march, and the time for bargaining is past.

The power of wealth often blinds its possessors; it is part of "the deceitfulness of riches." The wealth of the United States may easily prove its undoing. Wealth is no ultimate force in international affairs. It may lure greedy nations to attack. Without the social conscience under God to employ it, it constitutes grave peril.

How differently from the relative poverty of a small pioneering democracy does the American people now view world affairs! Individuals who rise in the world display a similar alteration of outlook. John Morley, as a Radical, comments on the British elections in 1869:

The man who began life as a beggar and a Chartist softens down into the Radical when he has got credit enough for a spinning-shed; a factory of his own mollifies him into what is called a sound Liberal; and by the time he owns a mansion and a piece of land he has a feeling as of blue blood

3 Thy nakedness shall be uncovered, yea, thy shame shall be seen: I will take vengeance, and I will not meet *thee as* a man.

4 *As for* our Redeemer, the LORD of hosts *is* his name, the Holy One of Israel.

5 Sit thou silent, and get thee into darkness, O daughter of the Chaldeans: for thou

3 Your nakedness shall be uncovered,
    and your shame shall be seen.
I will take vengeance,
    and I will spare no man.
4 Our Redeemer — the LORD of hosts is
    his name —
    is the Holy One of Israel.

5 Sit in silence, and go into darkness,
    O daughter of the Chalde′ans;

---

taken captive by Shalmanezer III raising their clothes (Alfred Jeremias, *Das Alte Testament im Licht des alten Orients* [4th ed.; Leipzig: J. C. Hinrichs, 1930], p. 689). The Dead Sea Scroll reads חשופי שוליך, "strip off your skirts"; cf. Jer. 13:26. **Pass through the rivers:** Note the effect of the short clauses and the climactic order culminating in vs. 3. Note the 2+2 rather than the *qînāh* meter.

3. It is a mistake to think that the poet is retaining the imagery of the slave girl at the mill throughout the strophe. The change in grammatical form is in keeping with O.T. literary style, especially in such climactic contexts. **Your nakedness:** Cf. Jer. 13:26; Hos. 2:12; Ezek. 16:37; also passages cited in Exeg. on vs. 2. Babylon is stripped like an adulteress. **I will take vengeance:** The fate of Babylon is in the hands of God. Yahweh is the speaker throughout. **And I will spare no man:** The line is difficult. The LXX reads οὐκέτι μὴ παραδῶ ἀνθρώποις, "I will no longer deliver thee to men"; Vulg., *et non resistet mihi homo.* Commentators render variously: "I will not meet a man" (cf. KJV); "and will accept no man" (cf. ASV); "will not refrain." Many scholars emend *'ādhām,* **man,** to *'āmar,* "says," and connect the word with vs. 4. The lines should then be read:

> I will take vengeance, and will not spare,
>   says our Redeemer;
> Yahweh of hosts is his name, the Holy One of Israel.

The RSV rightly interprets the verb פגע (**meet** KJV) as meaning **spare** (so also Strack *et al.*). The holiness of God includes both judgment and redemption.

2. SECOND STROPHE: DIVINE JUDGMENT ON BABYLON'S PRIDE (47:5-7)

This strophe has been widely misunderstood, and attempts to improve it have marred both form and content. It is patterned after the first strophe, beginning in the same way, continuing with the *kî* (**for**) sentence, and then, above all, in vs. 6 interpreting the climactic stichs in vs. 3*cd*. The poet puts his stress on **mistress** (vss. 5*d*, 7*a*); it is upon her that God's judgment is to fall (vss. 9, 11).

---

tingling in his veins, and thinks of a pedigree and a motto in old French.[6]

Religious teachers, and supremely our Lord, warn of the perils of riches. Wealth can dehumanize its possessors, as it did Babylon. It endangers men's spiritual outlook and sensitiveness. Despite our Lord's outspoken sayings, many of his followers, especially in these later centuries, have paid no heed to them. Coleridge has a striking paragraph:

[6] F. W. Hirst, *Early Life and Letters of John Morley* (London: Macmillan & Co., 1927), I, 147.

Often as the motley reflexes of my experience move in long procession of manifold groups before me, the distinguished and world-honored company of Christian Mammonists appears to the eye of my imagination as a drove of camels heavily laden, yet all at full speed, and each in the confident expectation of passing through the *eye of the needle,* without stop or halt, both beast and baggage.[7]

5-7. The Doom of Cruelty.—In God's providence nations become leaders in world affairs. They may not wish for such responsibility, as

[7] "A Lay Sermon," *Complete Works* (New York: Harper & Bros., 1875) VI, 198.

shalt no more be called, The lady of kingdoms.

6 ¶ I was wroth with my people, I have
polluted mine inheritance, and given them
into thine hand: thou didst show them no
mercy; upon the ancient hast thou very
heavily laid thy yoke.

7 ¶ And thou saidst, I shall be a lady for
ever: *so* that thou didst not lay these *things*
to thy heart, neither didst remember the
latter end of it.

for you shall no more be called
  the mistress of kingdoms.
6 I was angry with my people,
  I profaned my heritage;
I gave them into your hand,
  you showed them no mercy;
on the aged you made your yoke
  exceedingly heavy.
7 You said, "I shall be mistress for ever,"
  so that you did not lay these things to
  heart
  or remember their end.

---

5. A fine climax: "sit in the dust" (vs. 1*a*), "sit on the ground" (vs. 1*c*), **sit in silence**
(vs. 5*a*). No more the proud vaunting, the imperious commanding of subject peoples.
It is not a silence of grief, although the LXX seems to take it so, but of loss of power to
rule and command. **Go into darkness**; i.e., imprisonment (cf. 42:7; 49:9). **The mistress
of kingdoms**: LXX, "the strength of a kingdom"; Vulg., *domina regnorum*. Here as
elsewhere the taunt song assumes more the aspect of a dirge. The imperial lady is fallen
no more to rise (cf. Amos 5:2).

6. The first impression is that the lines break the context, but the verse is designed
to show how it was that Babylon was permitted to be so exalted among the nations and
why it was that Yahweh who brought her to empire rejected her and left her forsaken
(cf. vss. 3-4; see Jer. 27:6 ff.). The divine sovereignty of history is viewed in the context
of Israel's covenant God. **My people, . . . my heritage**: Cf. Zech. 1:15. The covenant
love of God has turned to anger against his people; the holy relationship between the
holy God and the holy people is profaned. Yahweh delivered his people to their enemies,
but Babylon corrupted her divine mission by her cruelty (cf. 51:13, 17-23). **On the aged**:
Cf. Lam. 5:12, 14. In many ways it appears that the Babylonian rule was neither tyrannical
nor oppressive, certainly not in comparison with the rule of Assyria. On the other hand,
it is likely that in many instances it was both repressive and cruel (49:26; 51:13, 17 ff.).
In a time of fear of conquest and domestic confusion the lot of the alien captives may
have been far from comfortable.

7. **I shall be mistress for ever**: Omit **so that**. In the time of her great prestige, the
defeat of her imperial competitors, and her universal sway, Babylon did not reckon
with the precariousness of power and history. She did not take **these things to heart**, i.e.,
that she was the agent and instrument of God and that her mission was restricted and
defined by his will and purpose. **Or remember their end**: Many MSS read "your end"
(cf. 46:10). The primary meaning of **end** is "issue" or "outcome." The Dead Sea Scroll
reads אחרונה, "afterward," "what was to follow."

---

certainly the American people did not, but it
comes in God's ordering of events and cannot
be declined. Nations are not punished because
of their power but because they use it ill. It is
no fault of the United States that in an impoverished world it has a prosperous economy
and vast resources. But woe to the nation if it
forgets the victims of want in many lands.
Monuments depict the cruelty meted out by the
Babylonians on their vanquished foes. Our
sinning is at long range, for the remoteness of
the impoverished places them out of sight. But

the awful contrast between self-indulgent plenty
and unrelieved want glares out from the pages
of history to condemn the unimaginative. In
God's justice retribution is inevitable.

The ill will of mankind mounts up with
appalling volume against those who bask in
prosperity unmindful of millions in penury.
In such embittered feeling disaster brews like a
hurricane. One recalls the French Revolution!
Nowadays our world is an economic unit; nations have no option but to share their resources
with those in necessitous plight.

8 Therefore hear now this, *thou that art* given to pleasures, that dwellest carelessly, that sayest in thine heart, I *am,* and none else besides me; I shall not sit *as* a widow, neither shall I know the loss of children:

9 But these two *things* shall come to thee in a moment in one day, the loss of children, and widowhood: they shall come upon thee in their perfection for the multitude of thy sorceries, *and* for the great abundance of thine enchantments.

8 Now therefore hear this, you lover of pleasures,
 who sit securely,
who say in your heart,
 "I am, and there is no one besides me;
I shall not sit as a widow
 or know the loss of children":
9 These two things shall come to you
 in a moment, in one day;
the loss of children and widowhood
 shall come upon you in full measure,
in spite of your many sorceries
 and the great power of your enchantments.

3. Third Strophe: Collapse of Babylon's Securities (47:8-9)

This strophe brings the foregoing to a climax: **Now therefore.** Babylon's self-deification is revealed in her making ultimate claims for herself. She says of herself what only God can say. Her transcendence in power she construes as absolute transcendence, and thus beguiles herself into an absolute self-security and confidence. She trusts in false wisdom and knowledge, but does not know that she is known.

8. Now therefore hear this: Introducing the prophetic oracle in the manner of the threat following the invective. The demonstrative is effective after the "these" of vs. 7. **You lover of pleasures:** Hebrew, *ʿadhînāh,* which Duhm explains as "living blissfully in Eden"; also "voluptuous" or "luxury-loving." Again at the beginning of a strophe the poet refers to Babylon's sitting, this time **securely,** her condition prior to her seat in the dust. Cf. the fifth stich: **I shall not sit as a widow.** Babylon's idolization of her existence is reflected by her innermost thought in which she ascribes to herself the theocentric self-asseveration, **I am, and there is no one besides me** (cf. 45:5, 21; 46:9). Thus there is no transcendent source of criticism upon her life. Second Isaiah is here carrying on a major feature of prophetic religion, a feature which lay deeply embedded in the meaning of the covenant as over against all historical structures and relativities. The flaw that had corrupted so superb an expression of covenant faith as the Deuteronomic Code was its nationalistic motivation and distortion. Elijah's criticism of Phoenician mercantilism (I Kings 21:1 ff.), Amos' invective against the house of Jeroboam (Amos 7:16-17), and the prophetic oracles of their successors undermined in a radical way all attempts to equate God and people. The judgment of God falls on all nations, the more terribly on the more powerful (chs. 13–23; Amos 1–2; Jer. 46–51; Ezek. 25–34). The ethical "norms" of prophetism are extended to include all nations (see Eichrodt, *Theologie des A.T.,* III, 53-54; Paul Heinisch, *Theology of the Old Testament* [Collegeville, Minn.: Liturgical Press, 1950], p. 273). Babylon, portrayed as the mother, boasts of her security in terms of the family; she has both husband and children. The family (*mishpāḥāh*) is united by a common psychic bond: the social order, the source of common life.

9. The extended words of address come to an end with this verse and the threat is pronounced (observe **hear this,** in vs. 8*a*). The two evils from which Babylon prided herself in being most secure are the ones which will befall her. Note the repeated **come**

8-9. *Calamity Impends on the Pleasure-loving.* —Nations and individuals have a fatal tendency to fancy themselves unique and exempt from the common doom. The long isolation of the Americas from troubled Europe has built up a sense of security no longer having any basis in fact. National feelings are slow to respond to the grim realities of changed conditions. Carelessness and love of pleasure go hand in hand, but in a dangerous day love of amusement has to be restrained, and people must learn to live on the alert. Catastrophe, pictured as widow-

10 ¶ For thou hast trusted in thy wickedness: thou hast said, None seeth me. Thy wisdom and thy knowledge, it hath perverted thee; and thou hast said in thine heart, I *am,* and none else besides me.	10 You felt secure in your wickedness, you said, "No one sees me"; your wisdom and your knowledge led you astray, and you said in your heart, "I am, and there is no one besides me."
11 ¶ Therefore shall evil come upon thee; thou shalt not know from whence it riseth: and mischief shall fall upon thee; thou shalt not be able to put it off: and desolation shall come upon thee suddenly, *which* thou shalt not know.	11 But evil shall come upon you, for which you cannot atone; disaster shall fall upon you, which you will not be able to expiate; and ruin shall come on you suddenly, of which you know nothing.

(vss. 9a, 9d, 11a, 11e, 13f; cf. vs. 11c), emphasizing the event upon which Babylon had not reckoned, the event of God's judgment upon her inordinate pride. **In a moment, in one day:** The phrases stress that what is unexpected and unsuspected by Babylon will be brought about at the very point of Yahweh's assertion of his own rule and sovereignty over her. כתמם: **In full measure** or **in their perfection.** Important MSS of the LXX, Syriac, and Vulg. read פתאם, "suddenly," a reading adopted by many scholars (cf. vs. 11e). Others read תאמים, "like twins" (cf. vs. 9a). **Sorceries . . . enchantments:** The Babylonians were known far and wide for their magical practices. These the prophet sets forth in illuminating detail here and in the following verses. They represented the source of Babylon's security. But magic is not religion, and a nation's security and power are not determined by any devices which function *ex opere operato* (see further vs. 11).

4. Fourth Strophe: From Security to Disaster (47:10-11)

10. Like its predecessor, this strophe is divided into two parts with exactly the same contrasts. Here the depth of Babylon's security is superbly stated. **In your wickedness:** The Dead Sea Scroll has "in your knowledge," reading ברעתך for ברעתך, but since **knowledge** appears in the third stich, it should be rejected here. **No one sees me:** Cf. Pss. 10:11; 94:7-11. Thus Babylon defends her self-sufficiency. There is no judge or sovereign over her life. **Your wisdom and your knowledge:** The prophet refers to her expertness in divination, astrology, and magic. The pretentious words of ultimate pride, **I am, . . .** form the final climax of Babylon's **wickedness.** Her wisdom and knowledge are the means of absolutizing her power.

11. Evil: The Hebrew word is the same as that for **wickedness** in the first stich of the verse, an intentional play. **For which you cannot atone:** Render "Which you will not know how to charm away." Cf. **from whence it riseth** (KJV) and "thou shalt not know the dawning thereof" (ASV). The LXX seems to have interpreted the meaning thus

hood and childlessness, had overtaken disobedient Israel. Now it is Babylon's lot in spite of the host of her sorceries and the potency of her incantations. The prophet laughs scornfully at the pagan man-made devices to avert the moral judgments of history. Dryden's lines on "God's pampered people" apply to Babylon: Gods they had tried of every shape and size That godsmiths could produce, or priests devise.[8] The suddenness of her disaster is stressed: in one moment, in one day. [8] "Absalom and Achitophel," Pt. I.	10-11. *God Out of Sight Out of Mind.*—Because God in the background stands "within the shadows," he is easily lost sight of. Safety lies in living in the "great Taskmaster's eye." The skill on which men pride themselves blinds their eyes. Babylon made no inconsiderable contributions to mathematics and astronomy. But this scientific knowledge had been debased in astrology, by means of which the future of king and kingdom were supposed to be calculable. Studying the stars to ascertain future events hinders the mind from penetrating a yet higher realm and having sight of the All-seeing. All concepts of luck and fortune were rightly judged

12 Stand now with thine enchantments, and with the multitude of thy sorceries, wherein thou hast labored from thy youth; if so be thou shalt be able to profit, if so be thou mayest prevail.	12 Stand fast in your enchantments and your many sorceries, with which you have labored from your youth; perhaps you may be able to succeed, perhaps you may inspire terror.

(βόθυνος; cf. Vulg., *ortum eius*). The sense would then be "origin" or "whence it came." But most scholars derive the word from a possibly cognate Arabic root *saḥara* and read "to charm away" (cf. 8:20). Others emend slightly to read *shaḥdah*, "to bribe away," i.e., by magical spells (cf. Prov. 6:35). Observe the parallelism of the alternate lines, the ascending climax of the parallel lines, and the final line, **of which you know nothing,** which undercuts all of Babylon's trust.

5. FIFTH STROPHE: SALVATION BY MAGIC (47:12-13)

With sharp satire mingled with pity (**you are wearied**) the prophet calls on Babylon to stand fast in her false security. The nature of Babylonian "wisdom and knowledge" is clearly set forth here. Ancient writers like Strabo, Aelian, Achilles Tatius, Berossus, and Diodorus Siculus witness to the reputation of the Chaldeans in the ancient world for magic, astrology, etc. "The astrologer or the prophet who could foretell fair things for the nation, or disasters and calamities for their enemies, was a man whose words were regarded with reverence and awe. . . . The soothsayer was as much a politician as the statesman, and he was not slow in using the indications of political changes to point the moral of his astrological observations. . . . Nothing was too great or too small to become the subject of an astrological forecast" (*The Reports of the Magicians and Astrologers of Nineveh and Babylon in the British Museum,* ed. R. Campbell Thompson [London: Luzac & Co., 1900], II, xv. This volume gives a large number of omens of the stars, sun, moon, etc. See also Thompson, *Semitic Magic* [London: Luzac & Co., 1908]; Alfred Guillaume, *Prophecy and Divination* [New York: Harper & Bros., 1938]; François Thureau-Dangin, *Rituels accadiens* [Paris: Ernest Leroux, 1921]; Pritchard, *Ancient Near Eastern Texts,* pp. 338-39, contains an interesting temple ritual).

12. Enchantments . . . sorceries: In characteristic reverse order to that of vs. 9. **With which you have labored . . . :** Many consider the line a gloss (cf. vs. 15a). For the last two lines of the verse the Dead Sea Scroll substitutes "and until today," which fits the context well. If this is the correct text, then vs. 12c is original and in the characteristic repetitive style of the prophet. It is possible that the lines omitted by the Dead Sea Scroll are a satirical gloss.

by the prophets as incompatible with a righteous and faithful God. G. F. Moore's verdict on Babylonian religion concludes: "They were great in demonology and divination, but showed no capacity for religious ideas." [9] Present-day confidence in science to solve all our problems is the foe of true religion—trust in the ultimate power of justice and love. Atom bombs, radar, etc., are oftener in contemporary thought than the living God. Atheism lies not in a theoretical rejection of God, but in forgetfulness of his activity, with his gaze upon our secret intents.

The prophet ironically scoffs at fortunetellers with their devices incapable of preparing their devotees for the oncoming disaster. It was the practice to avert calamities by expiatory sacrifices, but prophetic religion insists upon the

[9] *History of Religions,* I, 242.

moral order, in which "whatsoever a man soweth, that shall he also reap" (Gal. 6:7).

12-13. *Astrologers Seem Ridiculous.*—In sarcasm the prophet exposes the absurdity of stargazers who are a weariness to the nation and unable to warn her of what lies ahead. His humor in vs. 12 is grim. The burden of this hierarchy, with its spells upon both government and business, and its nuisance to all social activities, is terrific. The necessity of procuring a lucky day for every undertaking is an impediment to business activity and entails economic waste. The utter uselessness of all such will be shown up in ghastly fashion when the calamity strikes (vs. 13).

In Thornton Wilder's *The Ides of March* Julius Caesar grumbles at the hampering of his military campaign by the augurs, and of the

13 Thou art wearied in the multitude of thy counsels. Let now the astrologers, the stargazers, the monthly prognosticators, stand up, and save thee from *these things* that shall come upon thee.

14 Behold, they shall be as stubble; the

13 You are wearied with your many counsels;
   let them stand forth and save you,
those who divide the heavens,
   who gaze at the stars,
who at the new moons predict
   what[h] shall befall you.

14 Behold, they are like stubble,
   the fire consumes them;

[h] Gk Syr Compare Vg: Heb *from what*

---

13. With your many counsels: The Hebrew contains a double reading, and many scholars prefer to read "counselors" here. These are not the same as those mentioned in vss. 9, 11, but the class of **astrologers,** "those who divided the heavens," i.e., mapped (lit., "cut up"; cf. Arabic *ḥabara*) the heavens into fields or constellations in order to forecast future events (Alfred Jeremias, *Handbuch der altorientalischen Geisteskultur* [20th ed.; Berlin: Walter de Gruyter & Co., 1929], pp. 108 ff., 201 ff.; also *Das A.T. im Licht des alten Orients,* pp. 689-90). **Who at the new moons predict:** Monthly almanacs based on astrological observations and reckonings were compiled for the sake of recording lucky and unlucky days. The omen tablets give an excellent impression of the detailed nature of these distinctions (see Morris Jastrow, tr., *The Religion of Babylonia and Assyria* [Boston: Ginn & Co., 1898], pp. 328-406). **What shall befall you:** Israel's religion, with its faith in a historical revelation (cf. 41:1–42:4), could foretell and proclaim what was to befall Babylon (cf. 47:9, 11); Babylonian wisdom and astrology, according to our prophet, was helpless to deal with the actuality of events. The answer to the mystery of history lay not in the constellations or the movements of stars, but in the divine purpose revealed in history.

6. Sixth Strophe: Judgment by Fire (47:14-15)

The final judgment on Babylon is introduced by the characteristic **behold** (vs. 14: cf. 41:11, 24), and reinforced by the emphatic **thus** (vs. 15). The imagery of **fire** is strongly accented and is drawn from the vocabulary of judgment (cf. Amos 1–2; etc.). The third strophe of the second division of the poem contains the climax which has been anticipated from the beginning.

14. The **fire** is irresistible. It will consume Babylon and all her power and magic (cf. especially 50:11). This, the prophet comments grimly, is **no fire to sit before** (cf. 44:16).

---

damaging effect of the whole superstitious system on Roman character.

I govern innumerable men, but must acknowledge that I am governed by birds and thunderclaps. . . . One afternoon, in the Rhine Valley, the augurs of our headquarters forbade me to join battle with the enemy. It seems that our sacred chickens were eating fastidiously. . . . We generals are reduced to viewing the sky with a chicken's eyes. I acceded for one day, though in my capability of surprising the enemy lay one of my few advantages. . . . These observances attack and undermine the very spirit of life within the minds of men![1]

Almanacs based on similar mysterious observations still have a wide circulation. No large city in the world is without fortunetellers and pre-

[1] New York: Harper & Bros., 1948, pp. 5-6.

dictors of future happenings. Man is incurably superstitious. And superstitions are the foes of genuine religion; they can be extirpated only by vital personal fellowship with the living God.

14-15. Destruction in Babylon.—Her famed astrologers not only cannot protect the city from invaders, but cannot even save themselves. The fire of judgment catches them, and with savage irony the prophet remarks,

No coal for warming oneself is this,
   no fire to sit before!

Finally the merchants from many lands, with whom the Babylonians have built up a roaring trade, decide that the city's commercial career is at an end, and take their departure. Financial ties form no bonds of enduring friendship. A city with no more than utilitarian religion and

fire shall burn them; they shall not deliver themselves from the power of the flame: *there shall* not *be* a coal to warm at, *nor* fire to sit before it.

15 Thus shall they be unto thee with whom thou hast labored, *even* thy merchants, from thy youth: they shall wander every one to his quarter; none shall save thee.

they cannot deliver themselves
    from the power of the flame.
No coal for warming oneself is this,
    no fire to sit before!
15 Such to you are those with whom you
    have labored,
who have trafficked with you from your
    youth;
they wander about each in his own direction;
there is no one to save you.

48 Hear ye this, O house of Jacob, which are called by the name of Is-

48 Hear this, O house of Jacob,
    who are called by the name of Israel,

---

15. Who have trafficked with you (RSV), or **thy merchants** (KJV): Cf. Nah. 3:16-17. The Hebrew word comes strangely here since we expect some reference to sorcerers or astrologers. Many scholars (Duhm, Kittel, *et al.*) therefore emend to "charmers" or "magicians." The change is slight and has much to commend it, and yet to resort to it is precarious. The closing lines may indeed refer to the nations who carried on trade and commerce with Babylon, who were members of her far-flung empire. With the fall of the city they shall **wander about** [or stagger "in doddering helplessness and perplexity"— Levy] **each in his own direction.** In the time of Babylon's distress her former vassals leave her to her fate. **There is no one to save** her (cf. vs. 13*b*; 45:15; 46:2, 4, 7, 13).

O. HISTORY AND PROPHECY (48:1-22)

This poem constitutes the climax and conclusion of the first division of the prophecy. The prophet addresses himself again to the actual conditions which the exiles face and the attendant problems of the divine providence and judgment upon them. He sums

---

utilitarian associates is left utterly alone. Only ties which transcend self-interest—ties with God and man—endure when disaster falls. It is God to whom men cleave even when he appears to slay them, and men who are loyal when it is no longer to their financial interest, are the true and lasting friends.

We must recall that this ode was not addressed to Babylon, but was spoken by the prophet to his own people. He was insisting that God alone is Lord of history and judges those who disregard his sovereignty. His message is identical with that of the seer on Patmos: "She hath glorified herself. . . . Strong is the Lord God who judgeth her" (Rev. 18:7-8). Richard Burton has put the lesson into verse:

Once Babylon, by beauty tenanted,
  In pleasure palaces and walks of pride,
Like a great scarlet flower reared her head,
  Drank in the sun and laughed, and sinned and
    died.

.   .   .   .

The destiny of nations! They arise,
  Have their heyday of triumph, and in turn
Sink upon silence and the lidless eyes
  Of fate salute them from their final urn.

.   .   .   .

Must a majestic rhythm of rise and fall
  Conquer the peoples once so proud on earth?
Does man but march in circles, after all,
  Playing his curious game of death and birth?

Or shall an ultimate nation, God's own child,
  Arise and rule, nor ever conquered be;
Untouched of time because, all undefiled
  She makes His ways her ways eternally? [2]

The N.T., however, gives no assurance that a secular community—nation or city—will in its corporate life become God's servant. Individuals may be brought under Christ's sway and be light and leaven to their communities. Where their saltness is sufficient to season the whole, we may expect corporate righteousness; but such cities of God are not to be looked for in always sinful human history. In the N.T. such a city comes at the climax of history, and descends from God out of heaven.

48:1-21. Redemption by God's Grace Alone.—This prophecy, Paul Volz [3] thinks, may origi-

[2] "The Ultimate Nation." From *The Collected Poems of Richard Burton,* copyright 1931. Used by special permission of the publishers, The Bobbs-Merrill Company, Inc.

[3] *Jesaia II* (Leipzig: A. Deichert, 1932; "Kommentar zum Alten Testament"), *ad loc.*

rael, and are come forth out of the waters of Judah, which swear by the name of the LORD, and make mention of the God of Israel, *but* not in truth, nor in righteousness.	and who came forth from the loins[i] of Judah; who swear by the name of the LORD, and confess the God of Israel, but not in truth or right.

[i] Cn: Heb *waters*

up his major argument, especially from history and prophecy and the relation of the former things to the new. Begrich calls the chapter the problem child of criticism because of the signs of disunity and contradiction which he believes it betrays. Some scholars view much of the poem as interpolation; others like Duhm reconstruct an original poem out of vss. 1-11 (vss. 1a, 3, 5ab, 6-7b, 8ab, 11a, 11c); Begrich finds two poems in vss. 1-11 (vss. 4, 5, 6b, 7-10) and a fragment (vss. 3, 6a, 6b, 11). But the contradictions are more apparent than real.

A stylistic analysis provides a clue not only to the interpretation but also to the essential unity of the poem. One example, and an important one, will illustrate. It is the use of the verb "to hear," most obvious in the Hebrew (vss. 1a, 3b, 5b, 6a, 6c, 12a, 14a, 16a, 18a, 20d; cf. vss. 8b, 14aα, 18a). Such devices are not merely rhetorical, and must be read in the light of the significance of "the word" in biblical thought. They reveal the dynamic quality of the prophet's mind and message. Other repetitions corroborate our conclusion: **call** (vss. 1b, 2a, 8d, 12b, 13c, 15a), "speak" (vss. 15a, 16c), "declare," or "tell" (vss. 3a, 5a, 6b, 14ab, 20d), **Jacob** (vss. 1a, 12a, 20g), **name** (vss. 1b, 1d, 2d, 9a, 11b, 19c). The position of these words shows their importance. The poem has two major divisions (vss. 1-11, 12-21), with four strophes each (vss. 1-2, 3-5, 6-8, 9-11; 12-13, 14-15, 16-17, 18-19) and a closing lyrical finale (vss. 20-21). Vs. 22 is a later addition. The text is in good order and needs little change. The meter is prevailingly 3+3.

It is impossible to know the precise occasion in which the words were spoken or written. Theologically the poem is of the first importance. For a knowledge of the meaning of Israel, of the relation of prophecy to history, of the former and latter events, of judgment and redemption, of creation and consummation, of the nature of Israel's God, and above all, of unmotivated grace, the poem has scarcely a rival.

1. FIRST STROPHE: ADDRESS (48:1-2)

48:1-2. The strophe sets forth the unique relationship between Israel and Yahweh in the form of direct address following the succinct opening imperative, **Hear this,** which strikes a dominant note of the poem (see above). The noun phrases are significant: **house of Jacob,** i.e., all who belong to the lineage of Jacob and are characterized by their living continuity with him; **name of Israel,** i.e., the name which marked their

nally have been a sermon delivered to a congregation of exiles in one of their synagogues in Babylon on a day of penitence. This would account for the harsh denunciation of Israel's sin as obstinacy and rebellion, a denunciation more severe than this prophet of comfort elsewhere utters. It would explain the attribution of idolatry to the entire people when only some had succumbed to the practices of their pagan neighbors. A nation shares and must confess the guilt of any of its members. The discourse is not a summons to penitence, as we might have expected, but a proclamation of the astounding grace of God, of whom alone comes Israel's salvation. For this reason it is a most effective means of producing sorrow for sin, for God's goodness leads to repentance (Rom. 2:4).

Volz also pictures the prophet as a brooding thinker, puzzled by God's mysterious ways. Both he and his people are beset with obstinate questionings and blank misgivings. Why should some events be foretold long in advance of their occurrence, and others kept concealed almost to the last minute? To this enigma the prophet finds an answer in the perversity of those to whom he is ministering. They call themselves **by the name of Israel,** but they easily slip into the magic and idolatry of their Babylonian acquaintances, and ascribe to some deity of wood or metal what the one God of the universe brings to pass for his undeserving people. A startling prediction, progressively fulfilled, confounds their belief in deities who effect nothing on the current scene. Again a

2 For they call themselves of the holy city, and stay themselves upon the God of Israel: The LORD of hosts *is* his name.

3 I have declared the former things from the beginning; and they went forth out of my mouth, and I showed them; I did *them* suddenly, and they came to pass.

---

2 For they call themselves after the holy
　city,
　and stay themselves on the God of
　　Israel;
　the LORD of hosts is his name.

3 "The former things I declared of old,
　they went forth from my mouth and I
　　made them known;
　then suddenly I did them and they
　　came to pass.

---

distinctiveness (cf. 44:5 for both Jacob and Israel; also Gen. 32:22-28), and **loins** [Hebrew **waters**] **of Judah,** i.e., those whose origins come from the body of Judah and thus share his blessing and vitality. The verbs **swear by** and **confess** are drawn from the cult (cf. 65:16; Jer. 4:2; 12:16; Deut. 6:13; 10:20; Exod. 23:13; Ps. 20:7). Cheyne, Torrey, Kissane, and others make a break after vs. 1*f*: "It is not in truth nor by right that they called themselves." An alternative would be to render: "It was not by truth nor by right, even though they call themselves after the holy city." Observe the repetition of **God of Israel** and the theocentric concluding line; also **the name of the LORD** in relation to **the name of Israel.**

2. SECOND STROPHE: FORMER THINGS (48:3-5)

This strophe is about the former things (הראשנות) and the next one (vss. 6-8) about the new things (חדשות).

3. The former things: Cf. 41:22-23; 42:9; 43:9, 18; 46:9-10; also 44:6-8; 45:21. The meaning of the words is to be determined by the context. Here the reference is general. What was predicted in the past actually came to pass. That Second Isaiah includes the early conquests of Cyrus among the **former things** is possible but not certain. C. R. North attempts to show that the term **of old** (מאז) may refer to relatively recent events, and on this basis suggests that the prophecies were those of our prophet himself. But parallel passages hardly support this view ("The 'Former Things' and the 'New Things' in Deutero-Isaiah," in Rowley, ed., *Studies in Old Testament Prophecy*, pp. 111-26). God's powerful and wonderful word was spoken, and his intention was revealed to man; then suddenly, unexpectedly, he performed his deed. Behind this suddenness lies a keen insight

---

prediction, withheld until its fulfillment is about to break, overwhelms with surprise at God's potent presence and shames their conventional views of him.

1-2. Unreal Confession of God.—A host of nominal Christians in modern churches are described in these two verses. By inheritance they belong to the church. They take pride in devout ancestors. In fear, sorrow, or other crisis they **stay themselves on the God of Israel.** As sharers in the hope of God's people, they **call themselves after the holy city.** But they conform to the ways of their community when these are patently out of accord with God's justice and love. Edmund Gosse speaks of church folk who show "the same cautious affability towards God and towards the devil." [4] George Eliot has drawn Mrs. Bulstrode, "whose imitative piety

[4] Evan Charteris, *The Life and Letters of Edmund Gosse* (New York: Harper & Bros., 1931), p. 161.

---

and native worldliness were equally sincere." [5] An outstanding evangelical, Sir James Stephen, wrote:

I have never yet passed a day without praying for the spiritual weal of my children, since I had any to pray for, and if we err on the side of not pressing them to religious demonstrations, developments or early sensibility, may God forgive us, and compensate the loss to them! My daily and nightly terror is that they should be "patent Christians"—formalists, praters, cheats, without meaning or even knowing it. [6]

3-5. Complacent Believers.—It is those whose God, like the God of Kipling's Tomlinson, is taken at second hand who are hardest to rouse to the coming of the living God in current events. Traditional ideas conceal from them

[5] *Middlemarch*, Bk. VI, ch. lxi.

[6] F. W. Maitland, ed., *The Life and Letters of Sir Leslie Stephen* (London: Duckworth, 1906), p. 18.

4 Because I knew that thou *art* obstinate, and thy neck *is* an iron sinew, and thy brow brass;

5 I have even from the beginning declared *it* to thee; before it came to pass I showed *it* thee: lest thou shouldest say, Mine idol hath done them; and my graven image, and my molten image, hath commanded them.

6 Thou hast heard, see all this; and will not ye declare *it?* I have showed thee new things from this time, even hidden things, and thou didst not know them.

4 Because I know that you are obstinate,
   and your neck is an iron sinew
   and your forehead brass,
5 I declared them to you from of old,
   before they came to pass I announced
      them to you,
   lest you should say, 'My idol did them,
      my graven image and my molten image
      commanded them.'

6 "You have heard; now see all this;
   and will you not declare it?
From this time forth I make you hear
   new things,
   hidden things which you have not
      known.

---

into the strange ways of the divine activity. He reveals his word and men have the revelation, but the event comes in unique and unpredictable ways, like a thief in the night.

4. Because I know . . . : Lit., "from my knowing." The Dead Sea Scroll reads "since I knew" (מאשר ידעתי; cf. 43:4). This verse gives the reason for Israel's present plight. **Your neck is an iron sinew:** Cf. Exod. 32:9 (J), Deut. 9:6, 13. Ezekiel's influence is probably present here. The **neck** and the **forehead** are physical organs which have psychical functions.

5. Through the prophets God made known future events so that Israel could not ascribe them to the work of her idols (cf. 41:5-7). Yahweh, not the idols, did them and commanded them, and his deed confirmed his word. The reference to idolatry may be general, e.g., the pre-exilic period or the period of apostasy to foreign cults under Manasseh and even later (cf. Jer. 44:15-19). The prophet's polemic against idolatry more than suggests that even the exiles may have been attracted to their worship.

3. THIRD STROPHE: NEW THINGS (48:6-8)

After a superb transition (vs. 6*ac*) the prophet makes his great disclosure, parallel to vss. 3*ab*, 5*ab*, concerning the new things. As vs. 3*ab* is repeated in vs. 5*ab*, so vs. 6*ac* is echoed in vs. 8*ab*. Then follows the conclusion introduced by *ki*, for, which is parallel

---

his presence in judgment and redemption. They do not love him, but their notion of him. A Japanese legend runs: "Sekko loved dragons, painted them, and spent days and nights in admiration of his work. A living dragon thought, 'If Sekko so fancies painted dragons, how great will be his love for me!' But when he put his head through Sekko's window, the artist fled in panic." **My idol** with us moderns is the idea of God produced by our minds, with which we are pleasantly at ease, not the disturbing God revealed in Jesus, who renders us uncomfortable and goads us to loftier life. Much of the teaching about peace of mind, so popular in modern times, is based on a conception of deity remote from him who manifested himself in the Man of Nazareth. The prevalent desire to be rid of worries and fears is utterly foreign to him who willingly took on himself men's sicknesses and sins. Books and preachers cater

to it by offering a religion unlike his, although usually offered in his name. "My peace" (John 14:27) included vicarious suffering on Calvary.

The prophet had astonished the exiles by proclaiming the world-shattering Cyrus to be God's instrument. Their notions of deity had no place for this truth. The armies of Cyrus, sweeping westward, had upset traditional religious views, as the two world wars plowed up the easy optimism current at the outset of the twentieth century, with its doctrine of God's fatherhood divorced from his judgments.

> When half-gods go,
> The gods arrive.[7]

6-8. Will You Not Declare It?—With clearly fulfilled prophecies before them, the prophet feels his hearers are not sufficiently roused from

[7] Emerson, "Give All to Love."

7 They are created now, and not from the beginning; even before the day when thou heardest them not; lest thou shouldest say, Behold, I knew them.

8 Yea, thou heardest not; yea, thou knewest not; yea, from that time *that* thine ear was not opened: for I knew that thou wouldest deal very treacherously, and wast called a transgressor from the womb.

7 They are created now, not long ago;
   before today you have never heard of
     them,
   lest you should say, 'Behold, I knew
     them.'
8 You have never heard, you have never
     known,
   from of old your ear has not been
     opened.
For I knew that you would deal very
     treacherously,
   and that from birth you were called a
     rebel.

---

to vss. 4, 5cd. The newness of the events is stressed from beginning to end. This emphasis upon the emergence of the new is a major category of Israel's prophetic, historical, and revealed religion.

6. The motif of hearing which pervades the poem is given solemn emphasis at this crucial point. The reference is to the fulfillment of the divine predictions in the past. **Now see all this:** Perhaps read "you have seen" (חזיתה for חזה). Israel has heard the prophecies and seen their fulfillment. **And will you not declare it?** Lit., "And you, will you not declare it?" The first two words are emphatic and must not be emended. Such shifts are common in the prophets (12:1-4; Ezek. 45:20) and express admirably the fluidity of individual and community to the ancient mind. The verb תגידו, **declare,** is sometimes emended to תעידו, "bear witness," which is certainly attractive in view of the prophet's emphasis upon Israel as Yahweh's witnesses (cf. 43:8-10; 44:8-9). But in view of the emphasis upon Yahweh's declaring in vss. 3a, 5a (note their position) it is likely that the beginning of the strophe intentionally calls upon Israel to declare what she has both heard and seen. **From this time forth** (מעתה): The word is in contrast to **of old** (מאז) in vss. 3, 5, 8. Albert Condamin thinks the **new things** which Yahweh is to make Israel hear are about the servant (cf. 49:1-6), but this is not likely. Rather, the new things are the great events associated with Cyrus' campaigns, the liberation of Israel, and the new exodus. These are the events referred to throughout chs. 40–47. **Hidden things:** Lit., "guarded things," preserved within the divine knowledge and purpose, as yet undisclosed to man.

7. God creates (*bārā'*) historical events as he creates the world of nature. Israel has not known of these new events before. This verse is theologically illuminating as to the authorship and date of chs. 40–55, which is sometimes attributed to a period two centuries before the events described. Such foreknowledge would inspire Israel to pride: **lest you should say, "Behold, I knew them"** (cf. Matt. 16:1-4). The hidden things are known only to God, so Israel lives by trust in the divine revealing and by her dependence upon events with which she has not reckoned.

8. The style of the opening lines is reminiscent of 40:21, 24, 28. The castigation of Israel is especially strong here. The prophet, like Hosea and Jeremiah and Ezekiel before

---

pagan worldliness to bear witness to God's mighty work. Now an astonishingly new thing is proclaimed: the fall of Babylon and the chance of immediate release. Will this surprise wake the people to wholehearted confidence in God? "Unbelief dies hard; when it can no longer say, 'My idol did it,' it is apt to take refuge in another subterfuge and say, 'It is what I expected.' " [8]

[8] Skinner, *Isaiah, Chapters XL-LXVI*, p. 82.

Similar unbelief is as long-lived among ourselves. We have been visited in two world wars when God spoke in tones of thunder; but how few are holding themselves alert to listen to him? It seems not to enter their heads that God is speaking, **From of old your ear has not been opened.** The inattentiveness of his people is a trial to God. He speaks to us constantly—in the needs of men, in alarming occurrences, in doors opening before his church. But he finds us

9 ¶ For my name's sake will I defer mine anger, and for my praise will I refrain for thee, that I cut thee not off.

10 Behold, I have refined thee, but not with silver; I have chosen thee in the furnace of affliction.

9 "For my name's sake I defer my anger,
   for the sake of my praise I restrain it for you,
   that I may not cut you off.

10 Behold, I have refined you, but not like[j] silver;
   I have tried you in the furnace of affliction.

[j] Cn: Heb with

---

him, views his people in the light of its long history of infidelity and apostasy. Yahweh knew how treacherous his people were, that they were rebellious from birth (1:2-3; Ezek. 2:6-8; 3:9, 26; 12:2-3; 16:3, 45). As apostates they made the history of God the history of man. The **new** and **hidden things** are of his own sovereign doing.

4. Fourth Strophe: "For My Own Sake" (48:9-11)

Israel deserved to be destroyed for her treachery. The contractual interpretation of the covenant required that (Exod. 19:5). But the covenant was more than a purely legalistic *quid pro quo.* Behind it lay Yahweh's unmotivated election, and the covenant itself contained within it the reality of God's grace. Thus it was susceptible of becoming a new covenant. So God does not cut off his people, but for his **name's sake** preserves a continuing community. The loss of Israel from the world would cast reflection upon Israel's God (cf. Ezekiel's similar view, Ezek. 20:9, 22; etc.) .

9. For my name's sake: Note the emphatic repetition in vs. 11. **I defer, . . . restrain:** The verbs here, as in vs. 11, are in the imperfect, but should be translated as present, or perhaps better: "I have continually deferred my anger. . . ." The literal meaning of the verb is "to bridle" (see Torrey, *Second Isaiah,* p. 376) . The worship of Israel was to a great degree worship in **praise** and song (cf. the hymns of the Psalter; also Isa. 42:8-12; 43:21; 60:18; 61:3, 11; 64:11; Deut. 26:19; Jer. 13:11; 33:9) .

10. But not like silver: Lit., "but not in silver." The phrase is difficult. Torrey emends לא, "not," to לי, "for me," and translates, "for myself as silver." But the preposition in Hebrew is probably to be taken as *bêth essentiae,* "as silver," the meaning being that the refining process has not produced silver but much dross (cf. 1:22, 25; Ezek. 22:18-22; Mal. 3:3). **I have tried you:** The verb is the usual word for "choose," but may be an Aramaic root with the given meaning. The Dead Sea Scroll reads בחנתיכה, which is the usual Hebrew expression for "I have tried [tested] you." **The furnace of affliction:** The expression is usually employed of bondage in Egypt (Deut. 4:20; I Kings 8:51; Jer. 11:4) .

---

apathetic. We are not servants on watch, but truants. We are both inattentive and tongue-tied. The routine of our days absorbs us and prevents our listening to God or witnessing his doings. "An opium sky rains down soporifics." This is our treachery and rebellion.

9-11. For My Own Sake.—The upsurging anger of God, which he is pictured as restraining and deferring with great effort, voices the prophet's conviction that God cares intensely. God who is love cannot be indifferent to his children's disloyalty. When he curbs his anger, he reveals a forbearance essential to godship.

Alas, long-suffering and most patient God,
Thou need'st be surelier God to bear with us
Than even to have made us! [9]

[9] Elizabeth Barrett Browning, *Aurora Leigh,* Bk. VII.

Very genuinely we may "account that the long-suffering of our Lord is salvation" (II Pet. 3:15) . God has himself so completely in hand that, when his servants prove incapable of doing anything, he can control and dispose events. In their captivity he has **tried** his people **in the furnace of affliction,** and apparently without result. They are not **like silver.** So for his own reputation's sake, that his name as God be not despised, he will take drastic action, and show himself redeemer of even so unworthy a nation.

In a day when men's efforts are manifestly futile, when our attempts to create a just and friendly society are patently vain, there is comfort in the assurance that God works for his **own sake.** Indeed, what could be more hopeful than that the results which he will achieve, apart altogether from us or even through our

11 For mine own sake, *even* for mine own sake, will I do *it:* for how should *my name* be polluted? and I will not give my glory unto another.	11 For my own sake, for my own sake, I do it,
	    for how should my name[k] be profaned?
	    My glory I will not give to another.

12 ¶ Hearken unto me, O Jacob and Israel, my called; I *am* he; I *am* the first, I also *am* the last.	12 "Hearken to me, O Jacob,
	    and Israel, whom I called!
	I am he, I am the first,
	    and I am the last.

[k] Gk Old Latin: Heb lacks *my name*

---

11. An impressive climax. I do it: The Hebrew omits **it.** The verb is used absolutely: "I do" or "I act" (cf. 41:4; 44:2, 3; 46:4; also 43:13). Note the usage of the verb in vss. 3c, 5c, 14d. The word **my name** has fallen from the Hebrew text, but is essential here. Note the repetition of the word throughout the poem (vss. 1b, 1d; 2c; 9a; 19d). It is present in the LXX. The Dead Sea Scroll has "should I be profaned." On the profanation of the name, cf. Ezek. 20:9, 14, 22, 39; 36:21-23; etc. **My glory I will not give to another:** See 42:8. When God acts for his own sake only, then Israel is supported by an ultimate and certain confidence. Thus the harsh notes of the poem may be understood as a reflection of deserved judgment accounting for Israel's present precarious plight in history but also as an assurance that though her sins have laid her low, her hope and expectation lie solely and finally in the **glory** of God, to which it is her task to witness and which it is her privilege to praise and worship.

5. Fifth Strophe: "The First and the Last" (48:12-13)

The second division of the poem begins here, in a most characteristic prophetic manner. The opening lines obviously echo vs. 1. The strophe is framed in the word "call": Israel is called (vs. 12b), and the heavens and the earth respond to the divine call (vs. 13c). Thus history and creation are united, the covenant people and the cosmos. God alone is God, the first and the last, the beginning and the end, and the universe is created by him. The elements of invective have disappeared, for they have all been grasped and interpreted in the light of the glory and purpose of God.

12. My called: It is the way of Yahweh to call men to his service and to call them by name. He calls his name over those who belong to him (cf. 63:19), and pre-eminently

---

blunders, will befit his character and reveal his **name?** In our time repeatedly we are moved to exclaim, "As we are ourselves, what things are we!" [1]

David Cairns described in a letter his similar confidence: "The longer I live, the more value I put on God's sheer *Grace,* which I take simply to be what by our human standards we would call His *extravagant* goodness, the forthcomingness, initiative and persistence of His Love. It is our *sole* Hope." [2]

Nor can we be confident that the suffering through which mankind is passing will make us more religiously sensitive. The furnace of affliction did not open ears previously deaf. Samuel Johnson well said: "A man who has never had religion before, no more grows religious when he is sick, than a man who has never learned

figures can count when he has need of calculation." [3] Experiences may mature that which we already possess; they rarely create new capacities. A secular generation is unlikely to be rendered spiritual even by the terrors of war and the miseries of its aftermath. **The furnace of affliction** apparently was the school in which this prophet was disciplined to understand God, and in matchless sentences to exalt him; but it had no such effects on the mass of the prophet's fellow exiles. "To a great experience one thing is essential, an experiencing nature. It is not enough to have opportunity, it is essential to feel it." [4] Only from an experiencing nature can the furnace refine the silver of devout faith.

12-16. God First and Last.—The prophet does summon his hearers to repent, as one might have anticipated were it spoken on a day

[1] Shakespeare, *All's Well that Ends Well,* Act IV, scene 3.
[2] *Autobiography,* p. 204.

[3] James Boswell, *Life of Samuel Johnson,* Apr. 29, 1783.
[4] Walter Bagehot, "Shakespeare—The Man," *Literary Studies* (New York: Longmans, Green & Co., 1895), I, 38.

13 Mine hand also hath laid the foundation of the earth, and my right hand hath spanned the heavens: *when* I call unto them, they stand up together.	13 My hand laid the foundation of the earth, and my right hand spread out the heavens; when I call to them, they stand forth together.
14 All ye, assemble yourselves, and hear; which among them hath declared these *things?* The LORD hath loved him: he will do his pleasure on Babylon, and his arm *shall be on* the Chaldeans.	14 "Assemble, all of you, and hear! Who among them has declared these things? The LORD loves him; he shall perform his purpose on Babylon, and his arm shall be against the Chalde′ans.

over a people who bear his name (cf. 43:1; also Deut. 28:10; Jer. 14:9; Dan. 9:19; II Chr. 7:14). They are his called ones. God's name is called over those who belong to him, for according to the O.T., a man cannot exist without belonging. The O.T. knows nothing of autonomous man (see Ludwig Köhler, *Theologie des Alten Testaments* [Tübingen: J. C. B. Mohr, 1936], p. 15; "my chosen" [41:8; 42:1]).

> I am he, I am the first,
> and I am the last.

A characteristic triad, emphasizing the oneness, the uniqueness, and the eternity of God (cf. 43:10, 13, 25; 41:4; 46:4 for the first term; 41:4; 44:6 for the second and third).

13. Yahweh is not only eternal, he is also creator of the earth and heavens (40:12-31, especially vss. 27-28; 42:5; 44:24; 45:11-12, 17-18). In all these passages the relation of historical Israel and the creation of the world is stressed. Creation is not an act once for all but a divine activity which continues to the present. The created world of nature has its "history" under divine sovereignty.

6. SIXTH STROPHE: THE MISSION OF CYRUS (48:14-15)

Here as throughout the poem the prophet is summarizing and deepening the major categories of the preceding chapters. The sequence of the lines is characteristic but notable: imperative and address, direct question, the central disclosure (vs. 14*cde*), and the theocentric conclusion. The verbs are all of great significance (cf. the strophic division of the RSV).

14. The summons is addressed to Israel, not to the nations, as in 41:1. The great argument from history is introduced again. With almost forty MSS, **among them** should be read as "among you." On the verb cf. vs. 3*a*, 5*a*, 6*b*. Israel is the Lord's witness (43:9-13). **These things** refer to the historical events that follow, viz., the victories of Cyrus. **The LORD loves him:** Again the intimate note is sounded in relation to Cyrus (cf.

of penitence. The message abruptly turns from the sin of Israel to the eternity of God. He, the creator of earth and heaven, is now calling upon Cyrus to execute his sentence upon Babylon (vss. 13-14). It is as though God said: "I can expect nothing from my people; I, the first and the last, will do all."

There is comfort in this. If God's deliverance depended upon our penitence, we should have no certain assurance. Gigantic blunders, like wars, do put us out of conceit with ourselves.

Men may not be as cocky as they seemed; but how few are governed by a new mind! The prophet's trust is in God's utter difference from man, in his everlastingness over against man's feebleness, in his resolve to accomplish his people's liberation whatever their changeful mood.

The hymn "O God, our help in ages past" (Isaac Watts' version of Ps. 90), considered by many the noblest in our language, is entitled in the original edition "Man Frail and God Eternal." It contains verses, now generally

15 I, *even* I, have spoken; yea, I have called him: I have brought him, and he shall make his way prosperous.

16 ¶ Come ye near unto me, hear ye this; I have not spoken in secret from the beginning; from the time that it was, there *am* I: and now the Lord God, and his Spirit, hath sent me.

15 I, even I, have spoken and called him,
    I have brought him, and he will prosper in his way.
16 Draw near to me, hear this:
    from the beginning I have not spoken in secret,
    from the time it came to be I have been there."
And now the Lord God has sent me and his Spirit.

"my shepherd," "my anointed," "man of my counsel"), but here even more emphatically. **He shall perform his purpose on Babylon:** The line is rather awkward and should perhaps be read, "Yahweh-loves-him [i.e., Cyrus] will perform his purpose, on Babylon and the seed [so LXX] of the Chaldeans." Such compound titles were common in the Orient, especially for royal figures (cf. 62:2, 4, 12; 65:15; Rev. 2:17; 3:12; 19:12). This is possibly an example of Babylonian court style. See the Cyrus Cylinder (Pritchard, *Ancient Near Eastern Texts,* pp. 315-16), especially "I am Cyrus . . . whose rule Bel and Nebo love, whom they want as king to please their hearts." The Esarhaddon prism (Francis Rue Steele, "The University Museum Esarhaddon Prism," *Journal of the American Oriental Society,* LXXI [1951], 1-12) is stylistically similar to the Cyrus passages of Second Isaiah. Note the line " 'Builder of the temple' he called my name." See also A. M. Honeyman, "The Evidence for Regnal Names Among the Hebrews," *Journal of Biblical Literature,* LXVII (1948), 13-25. The consonants for **arm** and "seed" are the same in Hebrew.

15. The answer to the question of vs. 14*b* continues here in most emphatic terms; note the repetition of **I** and the four verbs, **I . . . have spoken, I have called, I have brought, he will prosper** (LXX, Targ., Syriac read first person). This is the history of Cyrus' work from the religious perspective of our prophet.

7. Seventh Strophe: The Leader in the Way (48:16-17)

The strophe is climactic, as is shown by the opening words (cf. vss. 12*ab,* 14*a*) and the content which centers on the oracle to Israel (vs. 17). The inclusive perspectives from beginning to the present and to the end are those of the whole poem. In the past God did not speak in secret (cf. 45:19); in the hour of his initiative he spoke, and he was present at the fulfillment (cf. vss. 3, 5). Vs. 16*d* is either misplaced or textually corrupt. Possibly something has fallen out of the text at this point; in that event vs. 17 would introduce a new strophe.

16. The motif of speaking and hearing achieves a new dimension of depth here as vs. 16*cd* seeks to express. The antecedent to **it** is obscure, but the reference is doubtless

---

omitted from hymnals, which after the manner of Second Isaiah stress this frailty in comparison with God's enduring might:

> The busy tribes of flesh and blood
>   With all their lives and cares
> Are carried downward by thy flood,
>   And lost in following years.
>
> .   .   .   .
>
> Like flowery fields the nations stand
>   Pleased with the morning light;
> The flowers, beneath the Mower's hand,
>   Lie withering ere 'tis night.[5]

[5] Original text in *The Oxford Book of Christian Verse,* ed. David Cecil (Oxford: Clarendon Press, 1940), p. 310.

When frightened and puzzled by menacing events, faith carries our thought afar from the fickle and frail doings and misdoings of men to him who is before all history and has the final word in its occurrences.

16. *I Was There.*—God in events both guides their course and interprets them. In the startling occurrence of that day—the rise to power of Cyrus—**from the time it came to be I have been there.** If God is omnipresent, it may seem foolish to speak of him as "here" or "there." But in moral crises his presence is felt. Jacob, fleeing from Haran, discovers him where he had not thought to encounter him (Gen. 28:16).

17 Thus saith the Lord, thy Redeemer, the Holy One of Israel; I *am* the Lord thy God which teacheth thee to profit, which leadeth thee by the way *that* thou shouldest go.

18 O that thou hadst hearkened to my commandments! then had thy peace been

17 Thus says the Lord,
> your Redeemer, the Holy One of Israel:
"I am the Lord your God,
> who teaches you to profit,
> who leads you in the way you should
> go.

18 O that you had hearkened to my commandments!
> Then your peace would have been like
> a river,

to what was spoken in **the beginning**. God revealed himself in the past in the words of his chosen servants (Moses and the prophets), not in vague and cryptic oracles but in language everyone could understand, and the fulfillment of the prophecies was his work—he was there. The thought of the former things and the new things is still present in Second Isaiah's mind. **And now the Lord God has sent me and his Spirit:** The line is a *crux interpretum*. One might expect an antithesis to what has preceded. But the first personal pronoun is most exceptional (see 40:6). Moreover, **and his Spirit** is awkward here, and devoid of good parallel in prophecy (61:1; Mic. 3:8 are not relevant here). Various emendations have been proposed. Volz emends to ועתה אשלחנו לארחו "and now I send him [Cyrus] on his way." Others emend ורוחו, **and his Spirit**, to בחורו, "his chosen one." The problem does not admit any solution. This line is probably a gloss.

17. The oracular opening, originally the beginning of a new strophe, with its familiar juxtaposition of **Redeemer** and **Holy One** (47:4; 49:7; 54:5) is followed by a solemn word of revelation in which Yahweh makes himself known as Israel's teacher and leader. From the beginning and at all times Yahweh had given his teaching (*tôrāh*) to his people, and had led them in the way they should walk. Here again we have the familiar use of **way** as mode of behavior and conduct. Israel's destiny was classically described by keeping of the commandments and by her way of life. Yahweh's leading of Israel is a major element of her history and piety (Exod. 13:18, 21; 15:13; Deut. 4:27; 29:5; Pss. 5:8; 23:2; 27:11; 43:3; 139:10, 24; cf. also Isa. 40:11; 55:12; 63:13). Here, of course, the meaning is primarily related to conduct, as often in the Deuteronomic history.

8. EIGHTH STROPHE: REWARDS OF OBEDIENCE (48:18-19)

Ps. 81:13-16 is a good parallel. The opening words, expressing the fervent wish (cf. 64:1) within God himself, provide the clue for the understanding of the strophe. The divine mood is compassionate and yearning.

18. If only Israel had listened to the commandment whereby her life in history was guided and directed! Then her **peace**, i.e., her well-being, welfare, prosperity, would have been like a river, not an unpredictable and unreliable wadi (cf. 66:12; Amos 5:24).

Ezekiel pictures Edom proposing to attack and conquer Israel and Judah, and finding an unsuspected factor on the scene: "These two nations and these two countries shall be mine, and we will possess it; whereas the Lord was there" (Ezek. 35:10). So God gripped consciences in the scene in Browning's poem where Pompilia lies dying; and the confessor Celestino declares:

> There's something here,
> Some presence in the room beside us all,
> Something that every lie expires before.[6]

[6] *The Ring and the Book,* "The Other Half-Rome."

In certain situations God's grip on consciences becomes coercive and his presence cannot be denied.

17-19. *What Might Have Been.*—While there is no appeal for repentance, there is poignant retrospect compelling the exiles to think. Had Israel been obedient her prosperity would have been like the perennial Euphrates—this in contrast to the deceitful brooks (Jer. 15:18) in the wadies of Palestine, whose waters disappear in the months of drought—and her decimated population would now have been as the sands of the sea.

It is fatal to be bound by what has been, and

as a river, and thy righteousness as the waves of the sea:

19 Thy seed also had been as the sand, and the offspring of thy bowels like the gravel thereof; his name should not have been cut off nor destroyed from before me.

20 ¶ Go ye forth of Babylon, flee ye from the Chaldeans, with a voice of singing declare ye, tell this, utter it *even* to the end of the earth; say ye, The Lord hath redeemed his servant Jacob.

and your righteousness like the waves of the sea;

19 your offspring would have been like the sand,
and your descendants like its grains;
their name would never be cut off
or destroyed from before me."

20 Go forth from Babylon, flee from Chalde'a,
declare this with a shout of joy, proclaim it,
send it forth to the end of the earth;
say, "The Lord has redeemed his servant Jacob!"

This verse does not contradict the representation of Yahweh's unmotivated work of grace and redemption in vss. 9-11. Rather, it speaks to the situation which called forth the whole poem. The reasons for judgment are clear, but Yahweh's final word is not determined by what Israel deserves but by his divine grace. This is superbly reflected in the passionate cry.

19. Like the sand: A reminiscence of God's promise to Abraham in the great crisis of his life (Gen. 22:17; see Isa. 51:2; cf. Gen. 32:12; Hos. 1:10; Jer. 33:22; I Kings 4:20). **And your descendants:** Lit., "the offspring of your loins." This may be an echo of the beginning of the poem, a most common literary device. **Like its grains:** A *hapax legomenon*. The LXX reads "like the dust of the earth," which is accepted by some scholars. The Vulg. has *ut lapilli eius*. The word is similar to the Aramaic מעה, "tiny weights." **Their name:** Read with the LXX "your name." **Would never be cut off:** The imperfect is used to express the idea that the destruction and cutting off still continue (cf. vss. 1-2).

9. Ninth Strophe: A Lyrical Song (48:20-22)

The imagery of this impassioned song is drawn from the Exodus. The meter is 2+2. The first half of the strophe is a succession of staccato imperative clauses; the second half recounts the story of the sojourn by selecting crucial episodes. The poet sees the events taking place before his vision (cf. 52:11-12; also 49:4*b*-13). The final line appears to be an editorial insertion (cf. 57:21).

20: Go forth . . . flee: The moment has finally arrived for the conquest of Babylon, and the poet urges his countrymen to flee before the disaster falls (cf. Jer. 50:8; 51:6,

---

as fatal not to learn from it. God teaches profitably through reflection on days gone by, even through reflection on the alternatives which we might have pursued. "Faithfulness to history is the beginning of creative wisdom." [7] Amid the difficulties which beset our world in the mid-twentieth century we may well look back to its opening decade and ask ourselves what as a race we might be enjoying had we not committed the blunders which brought on two world conflicts, consuming millions of promising lives and wasting incalculable resources. At a meeting of the academic senate at a leading Scots university to nominate a professor of economics, man after man said, "I thought we should turn

to so and so," naming one who had been killed or hopelessly injured. Impoverished nations can join in the confession of a brilliant man of letters who wrecked his career:

> Surely there was a time I might have trod
> The sunlit heights, and from life's dissonance
> Struck one clear chord to reach the ears of God.[8]

O that you had hearkened! The stupidity of war and of those courses which caused war has been proved up to the hilt. The painful recollection of lives and wealth lost is used to move men to present obedience.

20-21. Go Forth from Babylon.—The poem reaches a startling climax with this announcement that the hoped-for hour of liberation has

[7] Josiah Royce, *The Spirit of Modern Philosophy* (Boston: Houghton Mifflin Co., 1892), p. viii.

[8] Oscar Wilde, "Hélas."

21 And they thirsted not *when* he led them through the deserts: he caused the waters to flow out of the rock for them: he clave the rock also, and the waters gushed out.

22 *There is* no peace, saith the LORD, unto the wicked.

21 They thirsted not when he led them through the deserts;

he made water flow for them from the rock;

he cleft the rock and the water gushed out.

22 "There is no peace," says the LORD, "for the wicked."

---

which may, however, be dependent on Second Isaiah). The excision of the references to Babylon and Chaldea (Torrey) deprives the prophet's work of its historical concreteness and mars the literary style. The Dead Sea Scroll omits **send it forth** and reads, "and proclaim it to the ends of the earth." The series of clauses culminates in a climactic line and the thought of all the preceding chapters comes to an impressive focus.

21. As it was in the fateful days of the Exodus, so it will be in the new sojourn and return (cf. Exod. 17:6; 20:11; Ps. 105:41; see especially Isa. 41:17-20; 43:19-21; 44:3). In the third line the Dead Sea Scroll has another verb for **made . . . flow,** but the meaning is the same.

22. This verse is taken from 57:21 as a conclusion to this major division of the prophecies.

---

arrived. The prophet has been leading up to it. In vs. 14 he has spoken of Cyrus as God's loved one. From the outset of his victorious career God has been using him. "From the time it came to be I have been there. . . . And now!" (vs. 16). But if this poem is a sermon, we can fancy the astounding effect of the words **Go forth.** In this glad moment, as in their misery, the exiles are given a memory out of their past. Like their forefathers in the exodus from Egypt, they must confront perils and cross a desert. Moses and Miriam had sung triumphantly. A hymn of similar trust is put on the exiles' lips.

In a lecture on eighteenth-century hymn-writers George Sampson said:

Watts and the Wesleys, above all other English writers, seem to have a feeling for the special work a congregational hymn has to do; and that work may be called the creation of a sense of belonging to a continuing fellowship. A hymn is a mystical poem, full of symbols which give us a hold upon that continuity . . . from which we cannot be cut off without being lost in a world of other lost creatures. True community can only be found in that conviction of continuity.[9]

Declare this with a shout of joy. The prophet's uppermost aim for his people is that they should become God's missionary nation. They must consecrate their joy in their freedom from captivity in a proclamation to the nations of God's grace to them. Among musicians, Johann Sebastian Bach stands out pre-eminent in the types of composition with which he en-

[9] *Seven Essays* (Cambridge: Cambridge University Press, 1947), p. 230.

riched the world. For him art was for God's sake. Inscribed on his *Orgelbüchlein* are two lines:

Dem höchsten Gott allein zu Ehren,
Dem Nechsten, draus sich zu belehren.[1]

And among the rules and principles of accompaniment which he wrote for his pupils is included:

Figured-bass is the most perfect foundation of music, and is played with both hands in such a manner that the left hand plays the notes written down, while the right adds in consonances or dissonances, the result being an agreeable harmony to the glory of God and justifiable gratification of the senses; for the sole end aim of general-bass, like that of all music, should be nothing else than God's glory and pleasant recreation. Where this object is not kept in view there can be no true music, but an infernal scraping and bawling.[2]

The disease of our civilization has been its man-centeredness. Few indeed in providing directions for the rendition of a piece of music, the construction of a machine, or the framing of a constitution, would insist on keeping in mind the glory of God. Most moderns would laugh at this as unpractical. Perhaps this man-centered regard is the cause of the "infernal clamor" of current happenings. It is the direc-

[1] Philip Spitta, *Johann Sebastian Bach* (tr. Clara Bell and J. A. Fuller Maitland; New York: Novello, Ewer & Co., 1899), Vol. I, p. 598, n. 329:

"Inscribed in honour of the Lord Most High
And that my neighbour may be taught thereby."

[2] *Ibid.,* III, 318.

49 Listen, O isles, unto me; and hearken, ye people, from far; The

49 Listen to me, O coastlands, and hearken, you peoples from afar.

II. THE REDEMPTION OF ISRAEL (49:1–55:13)
A. THE SERVANT OF THE LORD: CALLED, COMMISSIONED, AND COMFORTED (49:1-25)

The understanding of this chapter and the following is beset with difficulties of a peculiarly acute kind. The issues involved are of the first importance, for upon their solution depends to a great degree one's interpretation of the prophet's thought. The problem of the extent of the literary units has usually been settled by reference to Duhm's theory of the servant songs. Vss. 1-6 have accordingly been isolated from their present context. Now it is generally recognized that a break occurs after ch. 48, though this has been exaggerated. There is, indeed, not a little in this poem which naturally evokes the kind of utterance that we find in vss. 1-6 (cf. "my called one" in 48:12b and 49:1c; 48:8d and 49:1c and the restored text of 48:1c; 48:17-19 and 49:1-6). Moreover, the language and style of vss. 1-6 have many affinities with the foregoing chapters. The opening imperatives and address, the influence of Jeremiah, the imagery of vs. 2 (cf., e.g., 51:16), the quotations and dialogical style, the climax on salvation, the theme of restoration, Yahweh's glorification in Israel, the association of "You are my servant" with Israel as in 44:21, the relation of vs. 4 with 40:27 and 40:10d, and other phenomena are all in the manner of Second Isaiah. Observe, too, that the literary relations of vss. 1-6 and vss. 7-26 are often the same. Again, it is by no means difficult to find a relation between vss. 1-6 and those which follow. This has prompted many scholars to extend the unit, some through vs. 7, others through vs. 9a or vs. 9d, others to vs. 13, still others to the end of the chapter. Vs. 13 forms a splendid finale, much in the fashion of 48:20-21. But vs. 14 with its conjunction is hardly an appropriate beginning of a new unit. Moreover, the plaintive style is like that of vss. 1-6 (cf. vss. 14, 21, 24; cf. also vs. 7cd). It seems probable therefore that vs. 14 introduces the second half of the poem. If this is so, then the chapter may form a unit of two divisions (vss. 1-13, 14-26) with six strophes each, a structure that is characteristic of the poet.

The strophic divisions are in general plainly marked by their introductory and closing lines. Yet vs. 5ef clearly breaks the continuity of the poem, and resort to parenthesis, while possible, cannot be considered felicitous. Therefore many scholars place it after vs. 3. But this spoils the climactic effect of the important disclosure of vs. 3. An alternative would be to place it after vs. 4. This not only provides a good context to the lines but also solves the problem of strophic length both for the second and third strophes. If this view is accepted, then the awkward introductory **he says** of vs. 6 will be explained as an attempt on the part of a redactor to overcome the difficulty caused by the insertion of vs. 5ef in the wrong place. The nature of the structural problem

---

tion of life, both national and individual, to the glory of God—the message of this prophet and of one of the world's foremost musicians—which gives harmony, health, beauty. Our industry and commerce, our laws and policies, our art and education, our science and discovery, our homes and personal plans, must aim to honor God. This will be revolutionary. It is not absurdly irrelevant, as many think; for honoring God is the surest path to human well-being. It is "man's chief end." It lifts all life to its utmost height and renders its quality divine.

If this poem is originally a sermon on a day of penitence, it is along uncommon lines. It does

not call for repentance but for praise. Men's salvation is by God's grace alone, and therefore to him only is due all glory. Could there be a subtler or more effective way of bringing men to repentance than by overwhelming them with God's startling graciousness and lifting them to his presence in jubilation? There in his radiant light they see themselves. When men face God, they abhor themselves, and repent in dust and ashes (Job 42:5-6).

49:1-26. The Lord's Colloquy with His Servant.—In this dialogue we have the questions which the more thoughtful in the devout community among the exiles were asking as they faced the summons to accept their liberation,

Lord hath called me from the womb; from the bowels of my mother hath he made mention of my name.	The Lord called me from the womb, from the body of my mother he named my name.

will be seen when one recognizes that vs. 3 must conclude a strophe and vs. 5 begin a new one. Furthermore, it is obvious that vss. 8-13 cannot be a single strophe. One does not expect strophes of equal length, but the Hebrew poet does not employ units of such divergence. The best break comes after vs. 9ab, where we have a fine climax, and the use of the brief quotations (**Come forth** and **Appear**) at the close conforms to the poet's practice elsewhere. Vs. 12 may be misplaced, but vs. 18 needs an addition, and vs. 12 with its twofold "Behold" (RSV, **Lo**) would serve excellently as a finale here. Note too that vs. 13 follows superbly upon vs. 11.

The literary forms are to be explained by the dialogue style. Vss. 1-6 are confession in the manner of Jeremiah (so too vs. 14). Much of the rest is in the style characterized by Begrich as oracle of salvation. "The theme common to those passages, 1-7 and 8-21, is the antithesis of despondency and promise. The servant-prophet-Israel in 1-7 is filled with discouragement when he sees that he has failed. Yahweh encourages him, and a glorious new prospect is set before him. In XLIX. 8 ff. the coming return of the exiles is described, then the despondency of Zion, and finally how Zion is to be given yet greater glory." (Lindblom, *Servant-Songs in Deutero-Isaiah*, p. 31.)

The supreme difficulty of this chapter is the identification of the **servant**. No solution can be more than tentative. The view here taken is that the identification with Israel raises the fewest obstacles, that it is in conformity with the prophet's mentality elsewhere, and that ancient Israelite conceptions of corporate personality, combined with the highly imaginative and Oriental quality of the prophet's mind, serve to provide an interpretation in keeping with the prophet's theology (see especially Pedersen, *Israel, Its Life and Culture, I-II*, pp. 52 ff., 285 ff., 474 ff.; H. Wheeler Robinson, "The Hebrew Conception of Corporate Personality," in *Werden und Wesen des Alten Testaments*, ed., Paul Volz [Berlin: A. Töpelmann, 1936], pp. 49-62; Otto Eissfeldt, "The Ebed-Jahwe in Isaiah xl-lv in the Light of the Israelite Conceptions of the Community and the Individual, the Ideal and the Real," *Expository Times*, XLIV [1932-33], 261-68; Aubrey R. Johnson, *The One and the Many in the Israelite Conception of God* [Cardiff: University of Wales Press, 1942], and *The Vitality of the Individual in the Thought of Ancient Israel* [Cardiff: University of Wales Press, 1949]). A crucial element in the problem is the presence of the word **Israel** in the heart of the poem (vs. 3). The word cannot be deleted on any defensible textual or metrical grounds. When this is admitted, then the argument of literary relations with chs. 40-55, the arguments associated with corporate personality or "extension of personality," and the argument of the prophetic understanding of Israel throughout the O.T. achieve a degree of cogency which alternative views have not yet achieved. At the same time, it must be admitted that vss. 5-6 constitute the most serious obstacle to the collective view.

The text is in general well preserved, although the ancient versions and the Dead Sea Scroll contain important divergences from the M.T. The meter, though by no means regular, is prevailingly 3+3.

1. First Strophe: Call, Mission, and Destiny of the Servant (49:1-3)

The direct address to the nations (vs. 1ab) is in the same manner as the opening of the trial of the nations in 41:1–42:4. Whereas Yahweh is the speaker in the earlier

now that Babylon had fallen. Probably these questions had troubled the prophet himself. We overhear the back-and-forth discussion in his own thoughts—doubts which occurred to him and the answering assurances of faith. This poem opens for us the mind of the most sensi-

tively religious at the hour when Babylon's downfall made possible their freedom to return.

1-4. The Servant Muses on His Mission.—It may seem strange that this intimate conversation between the servant and his Lord should begin with a summons to far-off peoples to

2 And he hath made my mouth like a sharp sword; in the shadow of his hand hath he hid me, and made me a polished shaft; in his quiver hath he hid me;	2 He made my mouth like a sharp sword, in the shadow of his hand he hid me; he made me a polished arrow, in his quiver he hid me away.

poem, here the servant addresses the nations. After the manner of the great prophets he introduces the story of his life *in nuce* with a profoundly inward description of his call (cf. Hos. 1:1-11; Jer. 1:4-10; Ezek. 1:1–3:27; and the original position of Isa. 6:1-13). The words are reminiscent of Jeremiah's call and confessions. Like Jeremiah, the servant is fashioned and known in the womb of his mother; his sphere of activity includes the peoples of the world (Jer. 1:10; 25:15 ff.), his message is of doom and felicity (Jer. 16:19-21; cf. Isa. 49:6), his call leads to suffering and persecution (Jer. 11:18 ff.; 12:1 ff.; 15:10 ff.; 20:7 ff.) and he is put to trial (Jer. 26:1-24; cf. Isa. 50:4 ff.). Both are led as a lamb to the slaughter (Jer. 11:19; cf. Isa. 53:7) and are taken from the land of the living (Jer. 11:1-23; cf. Isa. 53:8; see Otto Procksch, *Theologie des Alten Testaments* [Gütersloh: C. Bertelsmann, 1950], p. 288). The servant's prophetic mission (vs. 2) is described in military imagery in contrast to the judicial (42:1-4) and agricultural (41:15-16) imagery elsewhere. The clauses with their significant verbs culminate in the direct address of vs. 3, **Thou art my servant.**

49:1. By means of a characteristic prophetic appeal (cf. 46:3, 12; 51:1, 7; 55:3), the servant speaks as a missionary to the far-off isles and remote peoples. The whole world is to be called upon to hear what he has to say about his mission and destiny. **The LORD called me . . . :** In 44:2, 24; 46:3 very similar words are used of Israel (cf. also 51:1; Ezek. 16:3). God creates his chosen ones for a purpose; in **the womb** he fashions them for his service (Jer. 1:5; Pss. 22:10-11; 139:13-16). It is probable that the prophet is alluding to the call of Abraham (see 51:1-3; cf. Gal. 1:15). **He named:** Cf. 43:1; 45:3, 4. The **name** identifies the person. The prophet is referring either to the sacral name **Israel** (probably "God rules"; see Gen. 32:28) or the name "Ebed" (**servant**). The servant is called from the womb, and immediately is given a name.

2. The third great mark of the servant, after his unique birth and unique name, is his **mouth.** A man is known by his words, and the servant is the prophet who is chosen and called to speak the word of God. Second Isaiah here is summing up the whole prophetic character of Israel's life; he is profoundly influenced by the great prophets,

listen in. But the mission which the Lord has been preparing his people to fulfill and the charge he is now giving them concerns all nations. Here is spiritual autobiography which furnishes an explanation of the task now laid on Israel and validates her message to mankind.

Beginning with vs. 1*b* the servant offers a retrospect of God's dealing with him. Obviously the nation which speaks is only the spiritually alive and responsive part of the people. The rest would not be under this sense of commission. This prophetic community attaches itself to the earlier prophets whom God had providentially separated and educated from birth (cf. Jer. 1:5). **From the womb** looks back to the beginnings of Israel's history. In retrospect God's hand may be seen at work from the start. Much which at the time neither a people nor an individual understands becomes clear in the perspective of subsequent years. At eighty-seven, the philosopher George Herbert Palmer concluded a brief autobiographical statement: "As

I see these things rising behind me they do not seem of my doing. Some greater power than I has been using me as its glad instrument."[3]

2. He Made My Mouth.—Israel's distinctive calling was to be a prophetic people. Other nations had their contributions for mankind; hers was to communicate the word of God. It was not professional religious leaders, but an entire community of businessmen, artisans, doctors, and housewives, who were to testify the "word" to their neighbors and acquaintances, and be the cutting edge of the advance of God's reign. This word, a weapon against wickedness and false views of God, was a sharp sword and a polished arrow (cf. Eph. 6:17; Heb. 4:12). The piercing qualities of the message throw into relief the hardness of the crust of custom which enamels men's minds and consciences. In their thinking and their sense of obligation they are

[3] G. P. Adams and W. P. Montague, eds., *Contemporary American Philosophy* (New York: The Macmillan Co., 1930), I, 61-62.

3 And said unto me, Thou *art* my servant, O Israel, in whom I will be glorified.

3 And he said to me, "You are my servant,
Israel, in whom I will be glorified."

---

especially Jeremiah, for whom the word of God produced such shattering effects (Jer. 20:9; 23:29). He surpasses all the prophets in the depth and power of his interpretation of the divine word (see 40:8; 45:19; 55:10-11). To describe its force he resorts to military figures, the **sword** with its cutting power and the **arrow** which drives home to its mark (cf. Heb. 4:12; Eph. 6:17; Rev. 1:16; 19:15). **He hid me** (twice): The Hebrew uses two different words, "concealed" and **hid** (cf. 51:16). God protected his servant and hid him in secret until the time appointed for his service.

3. The two great offices of the divine intermediary are to serve God and to glorify him. Those who were most characteristically the chosen ones of God are his servants, and not only the psalmists but also the historians, prophets, and apocalyptists sang his praises and **glorified** him. The word **Israel** is held by many scholars to be a gloss and to be an addition of the same order as the Jacob-Israel of the LXX of 42:1. But the only textual support for this view is an inferior MS (Kennicott 96) which is full of lacunae and corruptions (Julius A. Bewer, "Two Notes on Isaiah 49.1-6." in Salo W. Baron and Alexander Marx, eds., *Jewish Studies in Memory of George A. Kohut* [New York: Alexander Kohut Memorial Foundation, 1935], pp. 86-90). The Dead Sea Scroll, our earliest witness, contains the word. Poetic parallelism, the witness of the versions, similar passages elsewhere (41:8; 43:10; 44:2, 21), and meter all argue for its retention. The Jewish commentators Ibn Ezra, Rashi, and Kimhi take the reference as applying to an individual, but the text as it stands forbids it. It is possible that the last line is naming the name by which Yahweh's agent is called (cf. vs. 1*d*). Thus the confession begins and ends on the same note. Yahweh designates Israel to be his Servant; Israel is called to

---

conditioned by their society. A thick cake of conventionality has to be broken through if any new truth or responsibility is to lay hold of them. In her *Conversation at Midnight*, Edna St. Vincent Millay pictures a communist saying to a stockbroker:

You, an individual?—you, you regimented mouse?
You Harvard Club, Union Club, white tie for the
    opera, black tie for the theatre,
Trouser legs a little wider this year, sir,

. . . .
Pumps are no longer worn, sir,
Mah-Johnng, cross-word, anagram, backgammon,
    whist, bridge, auction, contract, regimented
    mouse!
Why, you're so accustomed to being flanked to right
    and left by people just like yourself
That if they ever *should* step aside you couldn't
    stand up.[4]

Every social group, communist or stockbroker, develops a pattern of thought and morals which hardens into rigidity. This must be penetrated and cracked to bits if a new divine pattern is to govern mind and conscience.

He hid me away. Israel had been protected again and again from forces which would have impaired her serviceableness to God. Such concealment was God's secret providence. In a survey of their history, men and nations recog-

nize this unsuspected grace in their past. Emerson confessed:

How much, preventing God, how much I owe
To the defences thou hast round me set;
Example, custom, fear, occasion slow,—
These scorned bondmen were my parapet.
I dare not peep over this parapet
To gauge with glance the roaring gulf below,
The depths of sin to which I had descended,
Had not these me against myself defended.[5]

3. My Servant, Israel.—God is self-sufficient, but he must have a people through whom his glory can burst upon the sight of men. Israel's message and life, conspicuously her sufferings, are the mediums through which God has revealed himself. The prophetic community was vividly aware of its divine election. It is often said that such a sense of predestination detracts from moral responsibility. In Second Isaiah the reverse is true. The circles in Christendom where this doctrine has been emphasized have been those in which sensitive and stalwart consciences have been bred. Samuel Rutherford made strenuous moral effort the evidence of election: "Wrestle, fight, go forward, watch, fear, believe, pray; and then ye have all the infallible symptoms of one of the elect of Christ within you." [6]

---

[4] New York: Harper & Bros., 1937, pp. 116-17. Copyright 1937 by Edna St. Vincent Millay. Used by permission.

[5] "Grace."

[6] *Letters*, III, To Lady Kenmure, July 27, 1628.

4 Then I said, I have labored in vain, I have spent my strength for nought, and in vain: *yet* surely my judgment *is* with the LORD, and my work with my God.

5 ¶ And now, saith the LORD that formed me from the womb *to be* his servant, to bring Jacob again to him, Though Israel be not gathered, yet shall I be glorious in the eyes of the LORD, and my God shall be my strength.

4 But I said, "I have labored in vain,
I have spent my strength for nothing
   and vanity;
yet surely my right is with the LORD,
   and my recompense with my God."

5 And now the LORD says,
   who formed me from the womb to be
      his servant,
to bring Jacob back to him,
   and that Israel might be gathered to
      him,
for I am honored in the eyes of the LORD,
   and my God has become my strength —

---

serve him just as Amos (7:15) and Jeremiah (1:5) were designated and called to proclaim his word. **I will be glorified:** Cf. 44:23; 60:21; 61:3.

2. SECOND STROPHE: THE SERVANT RECOMPENSED AND HONORED (49:4, 5*ef*)

In reflecting upon his high calling, mission, and destiny, the servant is conscious of his failure. Like that of the prophets before him, Isaiah and Jeremiah and the others, his ministry seems to have been in vain. So far as his success with the people was concerned, his strength was spent for nothing. Yet with Yahweh his God he found his right and reward, his honor and his strength. The lines anticipate 52:12-15; 53:10-12. The witness of the servant is profoundly theocentric; observe the repetition of **the LORD** and **my God** (vss. 4*cd*, 5*ef*; cf. 50:4-9).

4. But I said: In strong contrast to "Yahweh said" (see vs. 14; cf. 40:27). The servant's words about himself are few; his thought is all centered on God. **I have labored in vain:** His words have fallen on deaf ears (cf. 6:9-11; Mark 4:12 and parallels; Matt. 11:15-17). **Yet surely:** Or "nevertheless," in sharp contrast to the servant's pessimistic estimate. **My right . . . my recompense:** Through the eyes of faith the servant sees his life completely under the rule and providence of God (cf. I Cor. 4:1-5, a profound commentary on the words). The servant gives his answer to 40:27 (cf. 40:10*d*).

5*ef*. For I am honored: The prophets were rejected and dishonored by their contemporaries, but in the eyes of God they were esteemed. **My God . . . my strength:** A superb resolution of the servant's words, **I have spent my strength** (כחי). In vs. 5*e* the Targ. and the Dead Sea Scroll read עזרי, "my help," which has much to commend it, but the context favors the M.T. (cf. vss. 8; 50:7, 9).

3. THIRD STROPHE: THE LIGHT OF THE NATIONS (49:5*abcd*, 6)

5*abcd*. In the prophet's characteristic literary style and manner, the first half of the strophe expands the oracular formula, **And now the LORD says:** the second half gives the

---

4. The Discouraged Reply.—Israel's spiritual effort throughout the generations, and especially in the Exile, seems to her futile. It is the most vital religious nucleus in the nation who feels this. Their fellow exiles had made no endeavors and knew none of this frustration. **I have spent my strength for nothing.** Such disheartenment is common among the most devoted. It is not their work which exhausts them, but the feeling that nothing comes of it. One may condemn such discouragement as pride in reverse. Mazzini called it "disenchanted egotism." It is common

to the saintliest in all centuries. Gregory of Nazianzen in the fourth wrote to a friend: "All that is honorable is perishing; evils are naked; our voyage is in the dark; there is a beacon nowhere; Christ is sleeping."[7] To contemporaries the church has usually seemed to be collapsing. Happy for them if, with this prophet, their faith makes them go on.

5-6. The Lord's Reply.—Here is an astonishing answer to give a discouraged servant—an additional load. The spiritual community's

[7] *Epistles* LXXX.

6 And he said, It is a light thing that thou shouldest be my servant to raise up the tribes of Jacob, and to restore the preserved of Israel: I will also give thee for a light to the Gentiles, that thou mayest be my salvation unto the end of the earth.

6 he says:
"It is too light a thing that you should be
    my servant
  to raise up the tribes of Jacob
  and to restore the preserved of Israel;
I will give you as a light to the nations,
  that my salvation may reach to the end
    of the earth."

oracle itself, culminating in the great revelation of vs. 6ef (cf. vs. 3). The first half describes the life and mission of the old Israel; the second half that of the new Israel. The strophe continues the servant's words to the nations (vs. 1). Vs. 5a presents a contrast to vss. 1-4 and prepares the way for God's words through his servant to the nations. The most natural reading of the infinitive (vs. 5c) would consider the **servant** (vs. 5b) as the subject. But how can the **servant** Israel **bring back . . . Jacob (Israel)?** The distinction has often been made between the ideal and empirical Israel, between the faithful covenant community and those who have gone the way of the world, yielding to the corrosive acids of syncretism and adopting the worship of alien cults. An alternative and perhaps a preferable view would be to take Yahweh as the subject of the infinitive. This is the procedure followed by Bewer, who renders the passage as follows: "And now Yhwh, who formed me from the womb to be his servant, has said that he would bring Jacob back to himself and that Israel should be gathered to him" ("Two Notes on Isaiah 49.1-6," p. 90; cf. also the same author's essay in Walter Baumgartner, et al., eds., *Festschrift Alfred Bertholet* [Tübingen: J. C. B. Mohr, 1950], pp. 67-68, and *Isaiah*, p. 33; this view was anticipated by Ferdinand Hitzig, *Der Prophet Jesaja* [Heidelberg: C. F. Winter, 1833], and Karl Budde, "The So-called 'Ebed-Yahweh Songs,' and the Meaning of the Term 'Servant of Yahweh' in Isaiah, chaps. 40-55," *American Journal of Theology*, III [1899], 521). As Bewer points out, it is always Yahweh who restores Israel in chs. 40-55. In vs. 5d the Hebrew has the negative לֹא, **not** (KJV), but the word has the same sound as לוֹ, **to him** (RSV), and this is the reading of the *Qerê*, Aq., the Targ., and of several Hebrew MSS, including the Dead Sea Scroll. **Who formed me . . . :** A summary of the first strophe (see 44:2). Note the relation of vss. 5b and 6b, 5cd and 6cd.

6. Israel's mission extends beyond the confines of her own people (vss. 1-5) to the nations of the world. "Here is an end, once and for all, to the idea that Israel's sole duty is his own salvation" (Levy, *Deutero-Isaiah*, p. 224). Here, as elsewhere, the prophet is viewing the meaning of Israel's life in the range of her whole history, beginning with Abraham (Gen. 12:1-3; 18:18; 22:18; 28:14; cf. Acts 3:25-26; Rom. 4:13; Gal. 3:8, 16). The lament of the servant in vs. 4ab is answered by a call to even greater responsibility (cf. Jer. 12:1-6; 15:10-21). The grace of subjective and inward solace comes later (vss. 14-16). The servant is confronted here with his destiny of being **a light to the nations** (cf. 42:6), **that my salvation may reach to the end of the earth** (cf. 44:5; 45:6, 14 ff.; see also vs. 8 below).

main obligation had been indifferent fellow Israelites, **to bring Jacob back to him.** Apparently the servant had not succeeded. Now the responsibility is **the nations, that my salvation may reach to the end of the earth.** This is sound psychology: lesser troubles are forgotten in facing a vaster undertaking. The task of which Israel had complained is tossed off as a trifle—**too light a thing.** Small anxieties vanish in the presence of a grave peril. Individual cares seem nothing when war menaces a nation. Let Israel take on her conscience the entire world, and the disheartenment of her past and present will seem negligible.

I am honored in the eyes of the LORD. The honor is a larger responsibility. But in assuming this divinely assigned duty, the servant is encouraged and discovers the reinforcement of the Lord's empowering companionship: **my God has become my strength.** It is under the strain of taxing effort that God's power is manifest. The missionary is always the effective defender of the faith. As he labors with as much as in him is, he is astonished to find an increment

7 Thus saith the Lord, the Redeemer of Israel, *and* his Holy One, to him whom man despiseth, to him whom the nation abhorreth, to a servant of rulers, Kings shall see and arise, princes also shall worship, because of the Lord that is faithful, *and* the Holy One of Israel, and he shall choose thee.

7 Thus says the Lord,
   the Redeemer of Israel and his Holy One,
to one deeply despised, abhorred by the nations,
   the servant of rulers:
"Kings shall see and arise;
   princes, and they shall prostrate themselves;
because of the Lord, who is faithful,
   the Holy One of Israel, who has chosen you."

4. Fourth Strophe: The Homage of the Nations (49:7)

The oracular formula after vss. 1-6 is very characteristic of the prophet's style. The verse certainly has the servant in mind, the same figure as in vss. 1-6. This is admitted by many who hold that the servant is an individual.

7. The Hebrew does not have the conjunction **and.** Here again we have the association of the two basic relationships of Yahweh and Israel: **the Redeemer of Israel** and the **Holy One** of Israel (see vs. 7*h*; cf. 41:14; 43:14-15; 47:4; 48:17; 54:5). Yahweh's holiness was revealed negatively in his judgment, positively in his redemption. Both terms are rooted in the Sinaitic revelation and interpreted in the book of Deuteronomy. The **one deeply despised:** G. R. Driver adds the third person pronominal suffix ("Linguistic and Textual Problems, Isaiah XL-LXVI," *Journal of Theological Studies,* XXXVI [1935], 401). The Dead Sea Scroll and many modern scholars read the passive participle לבזוי (see RSV). It is better to retain the Hebrew text but to point, with Kissane, *lebhōzeh,* and to translate, "self-despised" or "one who despises himself" (see Job 9:21; cf. Torrey, König, Lindblom). **The servant of rulers:** The whole line reflects the despondency of vs. 4*ab*. But suddenly without transition the scene changes, and the great reversal, so common a theme here and especially in chs. 56–66, is before us. The **kings** and **princes** are of course the representatives of their nations (52:13-15; cf. vs. 23). The object of **see** is the reversal of fortune. The conclusion repeats **Lord** and **Holy One** from the opening and adds **who is faithful** (נאמן) and **who has chosen you.** Throughout Israel's history Yahweh reveals himself as the **faithful,** covenant-keeping God on whom Israel may rely (cf. Deut. 7:9). The chosen men of Israel were faithful men: Moses (Num.

of strength. Many Christians never know God's power because they embark on no enterprises so much beyond their abilities as to afford him the chance to reveal his energy in them. The same nexus between command and promise is in the Great Commission: As the church goes making nations disciples she becomes aware of the divine presence working through her mightily. If God becomes incredible and unreal it is because we are not engaging in purposes in which he can attest his potent partnership. A church disheartened in its work for its immediate community needs the larger horizon of the world mission. It is the congregations with most intelligent dedication to this world mission who show most evangelistic fidelity for their own neighborhoods.

7. *Israel's Future Renown.*—This is the Lord's consolation of his discouraged servant. The tone

is tender, as in ch. 40. It anticipates the rise from deepest degradation to loftiest glory among the nations and their kings set forth in 52:13–53:12. Israel is assured of a position of supreme eminence in the opinion of mankind. At present she is **one deeply despised, abhorred by the nations, the servant of rulers** (i.e., tyrants). Her low estate in the eyes of the world reacted upon her thought of herself. She seemed a nonentity; cf. the report of the spies on their meeting with the sons of Anak (Num. 13:33). How could Israel think of herself as a missionary to the world? The disdainful attitude to the church on the part of clever and able leaders in secular life often induces an inferiority complex. Such low estimates of ourselves as God's servants dishonor him who chose us and lose sight of his faithfulness. It is not for inherent qualities in us that we should be con-

8 Thus saith the Lord, In an acceptable time have I heard thee, and in a day of salvation have I helped thee: and I will preserve thee, and give thee for a covenant of the people, to establish the earth, to cause to inherit the desolate heritages;

9 That thou mayest say to the prisoners, Go forth; to them that *are* in darkness,

8 Thus says the Lord:
"In a time of favor I have answered you,
in a day of salvation I have helped you;
I have kept you and given you
as a covenant to the people,
to establish the land,
to apportion the desolate heritages;
9 saying to the prisoners, 'Come forth,'
to those who are in darkness, 'Appear.'

12:7), Samuel (I Sam. 3:20), David (I Sam. 22:14); and Jerusalem was once a "faithful city" (Isa. 1:21, 26). The living tensions within Israel's life are summed up in the closing line.

5. Fifth Strophe: Restoration of Land and People (49:8-9b)

The words are addressed to Israel. The present is a time of bondage like the bondage in Egypt. But the day of salvation will dawn, and the prophet pictures it as already realized (perfect tense, which the Dead Sea Scroll changes into imperfect [future]). The reminiscences of 42:1-4, 5-17 show again how Second Isaiah is consciously turning to the beginning of the corpus where the servant is introduced.

8. In a time of favor I have answered you: Heretofore God seemed to be silent and it was difficult to comprehend his ways with his people, but the time of favor (see 61:2) will give his answer to Israel's perplexity and doubt. The **day of salvation** will bring his help, his intervention for their redemption. The **time of favor** becomes part of the characteristic phraseology of later Jewish apocalyptic (Paul Volz, *Jüdische Eschatologie von Daniel bis Akiba* [Tübingen: J. C. B. Mohr, 1903], p. 356; see also Luke 2:14 [εὐδοκία]; II Cor. 6:2, which quotes vs. 8). **I have kept you . . . :** Repeated verbally from 42:6, but "light to the nations" is omitted because it has been employed in vs. 6e and because only Israel's destiny is described here. **To establish . . . :** An important motif in the theology of the O.T. The **land** is given as a **heritage;** it is destroyed and abandoned by the exile, but restored again in the time of salvation.

9ab. To the prisoners . . . : See 42:7. If the previous lines allude to the settlement of Palestine, then these allude to the Exodus, especially in view of the following lines which are like the prophet's description of the new exodus, the return to the homeland.

---

fident of the issue of the divine enterprise. The fidelity of God is the basis of assurance in his people.

. . . On our utter weakness and the hush
Of hearts exhausted that can ache no more,
On such abeyance of self and swoon of soul
The Spirit hath lighted oft, and let men see
That all our vileness alters God no more
Than our dimmed eyes can quench the stars in
    heaven:—
From years ere years were told, through all the sins,
Unknown sins of innumerable men,
God is himself for ever, and shows to-day,
As erst in Eden, the eternal hope.[8]

8-13. The Lord's Restoration of His People.— The promises already made in 42:6 are repeated; but there seems a new urgency now that Babylon has fallen. The verbs in vs. 8 are

[8] F. W. H. Myers, "Saint John the Baptist."

in the perfect tense to indicate certainty, but may be rendered as presents:

In a time of favor I am answering you,
In a day of salvation I am helping you.

The time has arrived

**to establish [restore] the land,
to apportion the desolate heritages.**

Without the confident faith of this prophet it is questionable whether the downhearted exiles would have plucked up courage to attempt the return. Sir James Stephen said that "great men differ from other men chiefly in the power of self-multiplication."[9] Second Isaiah infects with his faith the loyal community and commits it to become the servant of the Lord. One feels the

[9] *Essays in Ecclesiastical Biography* (London: Longman, Brown, Green, & Longmans, 1849), p. 288.

Show yourselves. They shall feed in the ways, and their pastures *shall be* in all high places.	They shall feed along the ways, on all bare heights shall be their pasture;
10 They shall not hunger nor thirst; neither shall the heat nor sun smite them: for he that hath mercy on them shall lead them, even by the springs of water shall he guide them.	10 they shall not hunger or thirst, neither scorching wind nor sun shall smite them, for he who has pity on them will lead them, and by springs of water will guide them.

6. Sixth Strophe: New Exodus and Return From the Diaspora (49:9c-11)

The strophe describes the journey through the desert, and refers not to the Gentiles (contra Torrey) but the exiles (the **prisoners** and **those who are in darkness**).

9cd. As in 40:11, returning Israel is compared with the flock and Yahweh with the shepherd. The LXX reads "along all the ways"; the Dead Sea Scroll "on all the mountains"; this reading commends itself on account of the parallelism and the repetition of **all my mountains** in the conclusion to the strophe (vs. 11a).

10. God not only supplies abundant food for the return, but he protects his people against the fierce heat of the *shārābh*, which may refer to hot air or "burning surface of the desert sands" (Torrey, *Second Isaiah*, p. 385). The Arabic word *sarāb* means

immediacy of the task with which he confronts them in the lines:

> Saying to the prisoners, "Come forth,"
> to those who are in darkness, "Appear."

The captives have been so inured to bondage that they lack the initiative to venture forth, now that the gates of their prison are open.

Vss. 9b-11 repeat the assurance of God's providential care of the returning captives which had been given in the initial message of comfort (40:1-11), and use the same metaphor of a shepherd leading his flock. God as the sole and sufficient recourse of those who adventure in response to his summons has many illustrations in history. A striking one is recorded of the Pilgrims in William Bradford's vivid narrative:

> They had now no friends to welcome them, nor inns to entertain or refresh their weatherbeaten bodies, no houses or much less towns to repair to, to seek for succor. . . . And for the season it was winter, and they that know the winters of that country know them to be sharp and violent, and subject to cruel and fierce storms, dangerous to travel to known places, much more to search an unknown coast. Besides, what could they see but a hideous and desolate wilderness, full of wild beasts and wild men? . . . Which way soever they turned their eyes (save upward to the heavens) they could have little solace or content. . . . What could now sustain them but the spirit of God and his grace? [1]

Lo, these shall come from afar. Not only the company of exiles in Babylon, whom the prophet could personally address, but those

scattered over many and distant lands are included in this home-coming (vs. 12). A united Israel is demanded for the work of the Lord's servant. At the moment it was a mere fraction of the people who were spiritually responsive, and a larger fraction who were within immediate reach of the message; but the whole people is required to carry out the mission to mankind. Similarly, a reunited church today is essential to communicate the message and fulfill the missionary task to an entire world. It is only as the mission of the church becomes uppermost in her thought and masters her conscience that her members will overcome their insistence upon matters divisive. Men on fire to carry out God's commission to bring all nations under his sway are those who plead most urgently for unity. The aged John Wesley wrote to Henry Venn:

> I desire to have a league offensive and defensive with every soldier of Christ. We have not only one faith, one hope, one Lord, but are directly engaged in one warfare. We are carrying the war into the devil's own quarters, who therefore summons all his hosts to war. Come, then, ye that love Him, to the help of the Lord . . . against the mighty! I am now wellnigh *miles emeritus senex sexagenarius;* yet I trust to fight a little longer. Come and strengthen the hands till you supply the place of
> Your weak but affectionate brother.[2]

The prospect of Israel's return and ingathering prompts an outburst of exultation, **Sing for**

[1] *History of Plymouth Plantation*, Bk. I, ch. ix.

[2] *Letters*, ed. Telford, IV, 218. Letter dated June 22, 1763.

11 And I will make all my mountains a way, and my highways shall be exalted.

12 Behold, these shall come from far: and, lo, these from the north and from the west; and these from the land of Sinim.

13 ¶ Sing, O heavens; and be joyful, O earth; and break forth into singing, O mountains: for the LORD hath comforted his people, and will have mercy upon his afflicted.

14 But Zion said, The LORD hath forsaken me, and my Lord hath forgotten me.

11 And I will make all my mountains a way,
    and my highways shall be raised up.
12 Lo, these shall come from afar,
    and lo, these from the north and from
      the west,
    and these from the land of Syene."*l*

13 Sing for joy, O heavens, and exult, O
    earth;
    break forth, O mountains, into singing!
For the LORD has comforted his people,
    and will have compassion on his af-
      flicted.

14 But Zion said, "The LORD has forsaken
    me,
    my Lord has forgotten me."

l Cn: Heb *Sinim*

"mirage." The Merciful One **will lead them** and **guide them** to **springs of water** (41:18; 48:21).

11. All natural barriers will be transformed into **a way,** a favorite motif of the prophet (see 40:3). The expression **all my mountains** is striking. Levy explains it as a reference to Yahweh's sovereignty of the world. The LXX reads "every mountain." All the mountains are Yahweh's, therefore they yield to his bidding.

12. For Exeg. see p. 575.

7. HYMN OF THANKSGIVING: YAHWEH HAS COMFORTED HIS PEOPLE (49:13)

13. All nature is called upon to participate in exultant praise to Yahweh because of what he has done for his people (cf. 44:23; 52:9; 55:12-13). **Have compassion:** The word is the same as that rendered "has pity" in vs. 10c. Creation and history are under a common sovereignty. Creation rejoices in God's redemptive work.

8. SEVENTH STROPHE: THE LORD HAS NOT FORGOTTEN ZION (49:14-16)

Zion gives expression to her dejection (cf. vs. 4). The words are in sharp antithesis to the exuberant words of comfort and compassion with which the first half of the poem closes (vs. 13). The answer (as in vss. 5ab-6) comes at once. In the former case it emphasized the servant's mission and responsibility to the nations; here the words are

---

joy, O heavens—the ecstasy of the creative artist in transport of spirit, so that his imagination is kindled and his work made to live. Second Isaiah is one of the supreme poets who (to borrow Bacon's metaphor) wielded "the pencil of the Holy Ghost." His intense joy in God's redemption of his people exalted him to his poetic eminence. No amount of skillful craftsmanship alone—and he assuredly was a painstaking craftsman in words—could have infused into his message its perennial vitality. It is said that Galileo made his discovery of the moons of Jupiter *incredibili jocunditate animi.* So this prophet caught sight of God's working in the events which led to the capture of Babylon by the Persians, and descried their implications for Israel's national future. It was his rapturous

certainty which made his faith infectious then and continues to render it infectious for all time.

14-18. *Israel's Doubts and God's Assurances.* —The poem suddenly changes its tone. C. C. Torrey speaks of the modulation "from *forte* to *piano,* and from triumph to pathos." [3] The lovely poetry vibrates with tender feeling. The dialogue breaks abruptly into another phase: **But Zion said.** The nation is personified in her hallowed association with God. The long years of exile have given even the spiritually loyal group among the people a sense of being forgotten and forsaken. Such feelings of abandonment are not uncommon among those keenly aware of a divine mission. Christ on the

[3] *The Second Isaiah* (New York: Charles Scribner's Sons, 1928), p. 386.

15 Can a woman forget her sucking child, that she should not have compassion on the son of her womb? yea, they may forget, yet will I not forget thee.
 	
16 Behold, I have graven thee upon the palms of *my* hands; thy walls *are* continually before me.
	15 "Can a woman forget her sucking child,
	    that she should have no compassion on
	    the son of her womb?"
	Even these may forget,
	    yet I will not forget you.
	16 Behold, I have graven you on the palms
	    of my hands;
	    your walls are continually before me.

directed in a very personal way to Zion, the mother of children. The corrector of the Dead Sea Scroll changes **my Lord** to "my God."

15. God's love for his people comes to superb expression. It is deeper than the deepest human love, beyond all the bonds of nature. The supreme source of Israel's life is the love of God for her, and it is the source of all her consolation (cf. 43:4; 44:21; 46:3-4). Only Jer. 31:20 matches these lines in their moving quality, and yet the note sounds again and again in the O.T. (Hosea, Deuteronomy, Psalms; see also Matt. 23:37). Observe that this particularism appears in a universalistic context. **These** and **I** are strongly contrasted (vs. 15*cd*).

16. As the lover tattoos the name of his loved one on his hand so that he may always be reminded of her, so Yahweh (an extreme anthropomorphism) inscribes Jerusalem **on the palms of** [his] **hands** (LXX, "my palms"). The **walls** of the future city, the true Jerusalem, **are continually before** [him].

cross knew this abyss. The chorus in Milton's *Samson Agonistes* comments on that champion's wretched plight in his blindness:

> God of our fathers, what is Man!
> That thou towards him with hand so various,
> Or might I say contrarious,
> Temper'st thy providence through his short course,
> . . . .
>   such as thou hast solemnly elected,
> With gifts and graces eminently adorn'd
> To some great work, thy glory,
> And people's safety, which in part they effect,
> Yet toward these thus dignified, thou oft
> Amidst their heighth of noon,
> Changest thy countenance, and thy hand, with no
>   regard
> Of highest favours past
> From thee on them, or them to thee of service.[4]

The prophet's portrayal of God's unforgetting affection (vs. 15) reaches one of the loftiest levels in all scripture. He rises to more than a mother's tenderness and constancy in the divine heart. He anticipates our Lord's "how much more" (Luke 11:13). George Eliot makes Dolly Winthrop assure the lonely Silas Marner: "It comes into my head as Them above has got a deal tenderer heart nor what I've got—for I can't be anyways better nor Them as made me." [5] **These may forget, yet I will not.** God is not "man at his best," but man at his best is a faint reflection of him who is love (cf. Eph. 3:14-15).

[4] Ll. 667-86.
[5] *Silas Marner*, Part II, ch. xvi.

Thy walls are continually before me. Jerusalem's walls, whether as at the time in ruins, or as in their future glory, are in name tattooed on the divine hands as a perpetual reminder. We moderns think of individuals as composing a society, but the Hebrews thought of the society as preceding and "mothering" the individual. When their city was destroyed, its people felt themselves orphans. Its rebuilding would furnish them not only home but also status. Without the city they felt forgotten of God, for it, rather than its individual inhabitants, was beloved of God. Now Zion's **children** or her **builders** (either reading has good MS basis) are hastening back. The mother will adorn herself with inhabitants as a bride puts on jewels. One may well remind one's self that religion, which is inherently social, proceeds from the church to her individual members. She precedes them. That is the basis in spiritual fact for the administration of baptism to the children of believing parents. God gives them as a birthright a place among Zion's citizens.

Stress is not laid on the moral loveliness of the dwellers in rebuilt Jerusalem, although this may be implied; but the N.T.'s emphasis is on the charming quality of Christians (cf. Tit. 2:10). Paul insists upon Christians showing not alone the virtues of a good life, but showing them attractively (cf. Rom. 12:8-21). There is a happy and becoming way of being generous, steadfast, patient, hospitable, etc. Good people are not invariably winsome, and in such members the church lacks magnetism. Bunyan speaks

17 Thy children shall make haste; thy destroyers and they that made thee waste shall go forth of thee.

18 ¶ Lift up thine eyes round about, and behold: all these gather themselves together, *and* come to thee. *As* I live, saith the Lord, thou shalt surely clothe thee with them all, as with an ornament, and bind them *on thee,* as a bride *doeth.*

19 For thy waste and thy desolate places, and the land of thy destruction, shall even now be too narrow by reason of the inhabitants, and they that swallowed thee up shall be far away.

20 The children which thou shalt have,

17 Your builders outstrip your destroyers,
    and those who laid you waste go forth
    from you.

18 Lift up your eyes round about and see;
    they all gather, they come to you.
  As I live, says the Lord,
    you shall put them all on as an ornament,
    you shall bind them on as a bride does.

19 "Surely your waste and your desolate
    places
  and your devastated land —
  surely now you will be too narrow for
    your inhabitants,
    and those who swallowed you up will
    be far away.

20 The children born in the time of your
    bereavement

---

9. Eighth Strophe: Glorious Home-coming (49:18, 12)

The structure of the strophe is characteristic, the first half expanding **Lift up your eyes,** the second **Lo, these** (thrice). The prophet sees the exiles returning from every direction, all of them bound for Zion.

18. Lift up your eyes . . . : The words are repeated verbatim in 60:4. The city pitifully decimated by war and exile is to become congested with new inhabitants. **As I live:** Yahweh gives his most solemn oath (cf. 45:23; Deut. 32:40; Jer. 46:18). **An ornament:** The returning exiles are Yahweh's jewels. Yahweh will adorn himself with them **as a bride** (cf. 3:16 ff.) adorns herself.

12. The repeated **these** stress the widespread diffusion of the Dispersion (cf. 43:5-7). **Syene:** Hebrew סינים; the Dead Sea Scroll reads סוניים. Various identifications have been made, including China (cf. Arabic *Tsin*), the least probable, Sin or Pelusium in the extreme northeast of Egypt, which is too near, and the Sinites of Gen. 10:17. The best solution is offered by J. D. Michaelis, who emends the word to "Sewenim," i.e., the inhabitants of Syene (modern Aswân), where there existed a Jewish military colony. Important Aramaic papyri were discovered there and at Elephantine in 1907-8 (cf. Ezek. 29:10; 30:6).

10. Ninth Strophe: Zion Rebuilt and Repopulated (49:17, 19)

17, 19. These verses seem to have suffered both disarrangement and textual disfigurement. In vs. 17 *bānâyikh,* "your sons," should probably be vocalized *bōnāyikh,* **your builders** (cf. Vulg., Dead Sea Scroll; also Targ. and LXX). The text of vs. 19*ab* is defective. By revocalizing the words Torrey (*op. cit.,* p. 387) renders: "I devastated thee, laid thee waste, razed thee to the ground." Such a series of verbs is characteristic of the prophet. Two lines may have fallen out after vs. 19*b*.

11. Tenth Strophe: Whence Have These Come? (49:20-21)

The strophe opens with עוד, "yet," a word which often introduces oracles of this kind (Jer. 31:4, 5; 33:10; Zech. 1:17; 8:4), tantamount to "the time will yet come when"

---

of certain Christians with genuine graces: "These are the men that *sweeten* churches, and that bring glory to God and to religion." [6]

[6] *The Saints' Knowledge of Christ's Love.*

19-21. *The National Territory Inadequate.*— We must infer another complaint from the doubting people: "We are so few." The widowed nation is pictured as amazed at the

after thou hast lost the other, shall say again in thine ears, The place *is* too strait for me: give place to me that I may dwell.

21 Then shalt thou say in thine heart, Who hath begotten me these, seeing I have lost my children, and am desolate, a captive, and removing to and fro? and who hath brought up these? Behold, I was left alone; these, where *had* they *been?*

22 Thus saith the Lord God, Behold, I will lift up mine hand to the Gentiles, and set up my standard to the people: and they shall bring thy sons in *their* arms, and thy daughters shall be carried upon *their* shoulders.

will yet say in your ears:
'The place is too narrow for me;
  make room for me to dwell in.'

21 Then you will say in your heart:
'Who has borne me these?
I was bereaved and barren,
  exiled and put away,
but who has brought up these?
Behold, I was left alone;
  whence then have these come?' "

22 Thus says the Lord God:
"Behold, I will lift up my hand to the nations,
  and raise my signal to the peoples;
and they shall bring your sons in their bosom,
  and your daughters shall be carried on their shoulders.

(Franz Feldmann, *Das Buch Isaias* [Münster in Westfalen: Aschendorff, 1925-26; "Exegetisches Handbuch zum Alten Testament"], p. 135). The host of those who return is so great that they strive for room in which to live. Zion is overwhelmed at the sight. Barren, divorced, widowed, she is now faced with a vast number of those born in the time of her bereavement.

20. The children are those born in the Diaspora during the time of exile. The great increase of population becomes a common motif in later apocalyptic. The passage may also be a reflection of the size of·the Diaspora (cf. 54:1-3).

21. Zion expresses her astonishment by the three questions (vs. 21*b*, 21*e*, 21*g*); note the emphasis upon **these** (cf. vs. 12). The Exile was a time of barrenness for Zion, but in the Diaspora a population of **children** had meanwhile grown up. The words **exiled and put away** are absent from the LXX; they are possibly an explanatory gloss. The line violates the form and spoils the meter. **Behold, I was left alone:** Aloneness and separation aroused a special dread for the ancient Hebrew, so great was his sense of community. The sufferers bewail their loneliness: Hosea (e.g., 8:9), Jeremiah (e.g., 15:17), the psalmists (e.g., 102:7-10), Job (e.g., 19:13-22). It is a poignant lament (cf. vs. 14; also 60:15; Lam. 1:1). Note the climax: **Whence then have these come?**

12. Eleventh Strophe: The Ensign to the Nations (49:22-23)

The questions of the previous strophe are answered in very vivid language. The strophe performs the same function at the close that vs. 7 does at the beginning.

22. My signal: A favorite image of Isaiah (cf. 5:26; 11:10, 12; 13:2; 18:3; 30:17; 62:10). Second Isaiah has been called the first Zionist, and the beginnings of Zionism have often been attributed to him. Such interpretations are doubtful. The historical situation, the prophet's religious presuppositions, the eschatological context of his thought, and his universalism must be taken into consideration. The divine solicitude and providential care are constant features of the prophet's thought.

---

numbers of her people. Where have they come from? In days when the church is painfully aware of herself as a minority group, she needs a reminder that God prepares spiritually sensitive men and women whom he will gather into the household of faith: **Surely now you will be too narrow for your inhabitants.**

22-26. God Himself Repeoples the Restored Land.—Again it is implied that the dialogue continues. Zion asks whether tyrants ever release voluntarily captives whom they find useful workers (vs. 24). The astounding vision is presented of the rulers of the nations, among whom the dispersed exiles live, returning them

23 And kings shall be thy nursing fathers, and their queens thy nursing mothers: they shall bow down to thee with *their*
face toward the earth, and lick up the dust
of thy feet; and thou shalt know that I *am*
the LORD: for they shall not be ashamed
that wait for me.
24 ¶ Shall the prey be taken from the
mighty, or the lawful captive delivered?

23 Kings shall be your foster fathers,
   and their queens your nursing mothers.
With their faces to the ground they shall
   bow down to you,
   and lick the dust of your feet.
Then you will know that I am the LORD;
   those who wait for me shall not be put
   to shame."

24 Can the prey be taken from the mighty,
   or the captives of a tyrant[m] be rescued?

[m] One ancient Ms Syr Vg: Heb *righteous man*

23. **Kings** shall serve as the guardians of the children (cf. Num. 11:12; II Kings 10:1; Esth. 2:7). **With their faces to the ground . . .** : Taken literally, such descriptions (cf. 45:14) represent an unfortunate side of the prophet's mind. But it is by no means certain that they should be taken so. From the Tell el-Amarna letters to *The Arabian Nights,* such picturesque language is familiar. They are "an extravagant, but thoroughly Oriental metaphor for self-humiliation" (Skinner). Gesenius (quoted by Skinner, *Isaiah, ad loc.*) gives the following parallel from a Persian poem: "When I shall have the good fortune to kiss the dust of thy feet, then I shall believe that fortune flatters me." A literal interpretation must take account of the prophet's widehearted universalism elsewhere (e.g., ch. 55). **Those who wait for me:** See 40:31; cf. 51:5. Like Isaiah before him, our prophet speaks from the point of view of the waiting community. The passage should not be unduly spiritualized as the continual return of the soul to God (contra Volz). Rather, Second Isaiah is speaking directly to a situation of deep distress, and he gives voice to his faith that they who wait for God will not be disappointed. God will come and liberate Israel from captivity and bondage. This leads directly to the following strophe.

13. TWELFTH STROPHE: SAVIOR, REDEEMER, AND MIGHTY ONE OF JACOB
(49:24-26)

Israel enters a final expostulation (see vss. 4*ab*, 14; cf. vs. 21), which is followed, as in vss. 5-6, 15-16, 22-23, by a final oracle of assurance culminating in the universal theocentric conclusion of vs. 26*cde*—a fitting finale for such an extended poem as this.

24. The answer to the question of this verse is affirmative, and is expanded by the words of assurance of vs. 25*cd*. Vs. 24 is parallel to vs. 14, and vss. 25-26 are parallel to vss. 15-16. This return to the beginning of the second division of the poem is

with deferential homage to the glorified Jerusalem. The prophet does not predict how the
release is to come about. He sets forth the
mighty God able to cope with any resistance:

**I will contend with those who contend with you,
and I will save your children.**

Apart from any effort of his helpless people,
God acts:

**Behold, I will lift up my hand to the nations,
and raise my signal to the peoples.**

Every generation, especially ours, needs this
faith in God's unsuspected contemporary activity on behalf of his church. Current movements in history may be beyond our control,

but they are not beyond his. We cannot discern
his working, and our guesses will be wide of the
mark. In current events "his footsteps are not
known"; none the less he is always moving
everywhere for the accomplishment of his redemptive purpose made known in Christ, and
carried on through the fellowship of his followers. The rise and fall of governments, the ebb
and flow of commerce, the increases in men's
knowledge and skill, have their bearing upon
the life and growth of the church. The dominant factors on the secular scene, little though
they suspect it, bear **on their shoulders** those
whom God is adding to his people; and unwittingly they are **foster fathers** and **nursing mothers** of his faithful family. Believers discover that
they **who wait for the Lord shall not be put to**

25 But thus saith the Lord, Even the captives of the mighty shall be taken away, and the prey of the terrible shall be delivered: for I will contend with him that contendeth with thee, and I will save thy children.

26 And I will feed them that oppress thee with their own flesh; and they shall be drunken with their own blood, as with sweet wine: and all flesh shall know that I the Lord am thy Saviour and thy Redeemer, the Mighty One of Jacob.

50 Thus saith the Lord, Where is the bill of your mother's divorcement,

25 Surely, thus says the Lord:
"Even the captives of the mighty shall be taken,
and the prey of the tyrant be rescued,
for I will contend with those who contend with you,
and I will save your children.
26 I will make your oppressors eat their own flesh,
and they shall be drunk with their own blood as with wine.
Then all flesh shall know
that I am the Lord your Savior,
and your Redeemer, the Mighty One of Jacob."

50 Thus says the Lord:
"Where is your mother's bill of divorce,
with which I put her away?

---

characteristic of Hebrew literary manner. **A tyrant:** The Hebrew reads צדיק, "righteous one," but the Vulg., the Syriac, the Dead Sea Scroll, and possibly the LXX, properly favor עריץ, **tyrant** or "ruthless one." Interestingly, the Dead Sea Scroll reverses the words **prey** and **captives,** thus conforming with vs. 25cd, but the M.T. is in the manner of Second Isaiah throughout.

25. The first person pronouns are emphatic (cf. 41:12; Jer. 2:9). **I will save your children:** A characteristic compassionate note (cf. vss. 10, 13, 14-18) echoing the poem's emphasis upon Zion's children. The prophet's interest in children is discernible elsewhere (47:8-9; etc.).

26. Cf. 9:20; Zech. 11:9. The excessive fury of the passage reflects the passionate hatred of the Oriental. Whatever ethical judgment one may register, the poem comes to an end at a pitch of great intensity, yet not without a magnificent theocentric conclusion. Observe the same note of passionate comfort as in the climax of vs. 13 and in the introduction of vss. 14-16.

B. An Impenitent Nation and a Confessing Servant (50:1-11)

In order to determine the extent and character of the literary unit one must first of all discern the structure of the poem and the proper articulation of its lines and strophes. Numerous excisions have been proposed, the text has been rearranged, and many emendations have been suggested. As has been seen, some scholars attach 50:1-3 to the end of ch. 49, since the verses do not appear to bear any perceptible relation to the rest of the chapter. But vss. 10-11 have given rise to other problems. Many delete them altogether as a gloss; others delete only vs. 11 (from Third Isaiah). The followers of Duhm quite generally reject vss. 1-3, 10-11; others like Kissane, Engnell, and Bentzen

---

shame, and unbelievers at long last are led to acknowledge in **the Mighty One of Jacob,** their **Savior** and all men's.

50:1-11. Impenitent Nation and Confessing Servant.—The religiously minded among the exiles were questioning whether God had not made an end of his covenant with them and had cast the nation off. Our doubts often arise from faulty conditions in ourselves. These dis-

heartened folk were blaming God when the prophet knew they themselves were to blame.

The first strophe (vs. 1) poses the question: Where is the evidence for the annulment of the covenant? (On divorce and the selling of children into slavery for debt see Exeg.) To whom could God be indebted? Certainly not to a nation, Babylon or any other. While Babylon had been employed by him to punish his sinful

whom I have put away? or which of my creditors *is it* to whom I have sold you? Be-	Or which of my creditors is it to whom I have sold you?

accept vss. 10-11 but do not admit vss. 1-3. Gressmann and Staerk see a complete poem in vss. 4-10. Torrey takes the whole chapter as a unit. The interpretation of the relationship of the lines and strophes to each other varies widely, however. Repetitions in the poem are in the style of the lament and have a number of affinities with the final servant song (52:13–53:12). The poem is fashioned for the most part of question and answer (cf. 40:12-31). It opens and closes with a divine oracle (vss. 1:3, 11; cf. 52:13-15; 53:10-12). The first strophe is made up of two divisions, a characteristic feature of Hebrew poetry. Each is introduced by a double question (vss. 1*bcde*, 2*abcd*), and each concludes with an answer introduced by **behold** (vss. 1*f*, 1*g*, 2*e*-3; cf. 41:24, 29). Then follow the words of the servant in the form of an autobiographical confession, composed of two strophes (vss. 4-6, 7-9). Begrich sees the poem as a lament; Volz, as a psalm; Bentzen, as a prayer of complaint; Engnell, as a royal psalm of confidence; Lindblom, as a prophetic confession. The elements of the lament are present, as a comparison with other examples of the literary type reveal, but the style of the whole is that of a confession (see Exeg. on 49:1-6 for literary affinities; cf. the same passage as to form, style, and structure). As the confession sweeps to its culmination the speaker pictures himself in a judicial proceeding (vss. 8-9; cf. 42:1-4; 53:8), and it is here that we meet again the central phenomenon of the poem: two questions introduced by **who** and two answers introduced by **behold**. The profound importance of the servant's words is enhanced by other repetitions, a stylistic feature common to Semitic, especially Ugaritic, poetry. Most significant perhaps is that of "Lord Yahweh" (vss. 4*a*, 5*a*, 7*a*, 9*a*). Finally, the concluding oracle of Yahweh contains a question introduced by the interrogative **who** and concluded by the exclamation **behold.** Both of the strophes, like the opening and concluding oracles, have two divisions.

In view of these stylistic features it is well to consider the possibility of the unity of the poem. The point of the first strophe is that though Israel has broken the covenant bond by her sins and apostasy and has been carried into exile as a consequence, God has never abrogated it. There was separation but no divorce. Vss. 2*e*-3 emphasize the power of God by appealing to his activity in nature and the universe, a constant theme in Second Isaiah. Then follows the poignant confession of the servant, who in spite of persecution and mistreatment, has yet remained faithful, trusting that his Vindicator is near, that justice will be done, and that he will yet be declared innocent. The confession closes with an expression of trust and of judgment to come upon the unfaithful. The final strophe contains an exhortation and a threat.

A deeper question concerns the character and identity of the **servant** of the Lord. The poet portrays this lonely figure in all his humility and spiritual grandeur in precisely the same way as throughout his other poems, i.e., with sympathy, imagination, and insight (cf., e.g., Abraham, David). The language is no whit more individualistic than in the book of Lamentations, which contains striking parallels to Second Isaiah in form, thought, and diction (cf. also the laments of the Psalter, such as Pss. 22; 44; 79; 80;

people, he is under no obligations to her for serving as his agent. She has amply paid herself in the labor of her captives. The blame for the captivity lies on sinful Israel (vs. 1). The whole Bible insists that man cannot place God under obligations to him. How can one completely dependent, the recipient of life and of everything else he has, have claims on his Maker? "What have you that you did not receive?" (I Cor. 4:7.) God feels responsible for his people, the work of his hands and his redeemed, to	whom he has pledged himself in covenant; but this is his grace toward them. They have been faithless, and have forfeited any claims upon him. This renders impossible all criticism of God on man's part. When we question what has befallen us, we must always search out what we have done and been. There is no room for inquiries whether God has fulfilled his obligations to us. The first Timothy Dwight told Yale students: "Our true wisdom lies in willingly feeling, and cheerfully acknowledging, our de-

| hold, for your iniquities have ye sold your-selves, and for your transgressions is your mother put away. | Behold, for your iniquities you were sold, and for your transgressions your mother was put away. |

83; also Pss. 31:1-9; 109; 142). Semitic conceptions of "the individual" and community were not ours (see Intro., pp. 408-12; and especially Eissfeldt, "Ebed-Jahwe in Isaiah xl-lv in Light of Israelite Conceptions of Community and Individual" pp. 261-68; H. Wheeler Robinson, "The Hebrew Conception of Corporate Personality," in Volz, *Werden und Wesen des alten Testaments*, pp. 49-62; J. P. Hyatt, "The Sources of the Suffering Servant Idea," *Journal of Near Eastern Studies*, III [1944], 79-86; Pedersen, *Israel, Its Life and Culture I-II*, pp. 474-79).

1. First Strophe: God's Judgment and Covenant Faithfulness (50:1-3)

Like Hosea, Jeremiah, and Ezekiel, Second Isaiah describes the covenant relationship between Yahweh and his people as a marriage, and like them he is concerned with the breech of the bond and its consequences. The two questions contain two figures for Israel's present situation: divorce of the wife and selling of the children into slavery. Israel complains that the Exile shows she has been divorced, that her people have been sold. The questions imply the answers to this complaint: Yahweh has never issued a bill of divorce, and he is under no obligation of debt to anyone to sell his children. The Exile is due to Israel's iniquities. The passage is closely related in form and content to 42:18-25.

50:1. Your mother's bill of divorce: Cf. Deut. 24:1-4, where the husband must write such a bill and put it into his wife's hand. She may then marry another, but she cannot return to her first husband. Israel has indeed been unfaithful and there has been a separation, but no bill of divorce has been issued (cf. Jer. 3:8, 14; see Code of Hammurabi 141 ff., Pritchard, *Ancient Near Eastern Texts*, p. 172). The husband has the unlimited right to divorce, but Yahweh, Israel's husband, has not exercised it. **Or which of my creditors:** Here the figure is of the father who in dire economic straits is compelled to sell his children for his debts (cf. 52:3; Exod. 21:7; II Kings 4:1; Neh. 5:5). But Yahweh has no such creditors. He is under no obligation to Babylon; his sovereignty

---

pendence on God; and in committing ourselves with humble reliance to his care and direction." [7]

The prophet places his finger on the reason for the exiles' doubts of God's fidelity in their own lack of a sense of guilt. Now, as then, relatively few are oppressed with a feeling of the evil of their community and of their involvement in it. What Thackeray wrote of British society a century ago is as true of ours:

For my part I believe that remorse is the least active of all a man's moral senses—the very easiest to be deadened when wakened; and in some never wakened at all. We grieve at being found out, and at the idea of shame or punishment; but the mere sense of wrong makes very few people unhappy in Vanity Fair. [8]

R. H. Hutton in his essay on F. D. Maurice dwells on the surprisingly keen awareness which Maurice felt of his implication in a sinful

world. It is an unusual instance when it should be the general rule:

No man's thoughts ever fell more into the forms of a kind of litany than Mr. Maurice's. [They were the confessions] poured forth in the name of a human nature, the weakness and sinfulness of which he felt most keenly, most individually, most painfully, but which he felt at least as much in the character of the representative of a race by the infirmities of which he was overwhelmed, as on his own account, . . . a sort of self-reproachful complicity in every sinful tendency of his age, . . . a deep sense of the cruel burden of social infirmity and social sin. [9]

Second Isaiah was burdened with a similar sense of the guilt of his people and of his involvement in it. A striking expression of the contrary state of mind—a mood still frequent in many—is Goethe's: "I had believed from my youth upwards that I stood on very good terms with my God, nay, I even fancied to myself,

---

[7] *Theology Explained and Defended* (12th ed.; New York: Harper & Bros. 1851), I, 265.

[8] *Vanity Fair*, ch. xli.

[9] *Essays on Some of the Modern Guides of English Thought in Matters of Faith* (London: Macmillan & Co., 1900), pp. 320-22.

2 Wherefore, when I came, *was there* no man? when I called, *was there* none to answer? Is my hand shortened at all, that it cannot redeem? or have I no power to deliver? behold, at my rebuke I dry up the sea, I make the rivers a wilderness: their fish stinketh, because *there is* no water, and dieth for thirst.

2 Why, when I came, was there no man?
  When I called, was there no one to answer?
Is my hand shortened, that it cannot redeem?
  Or have I no power to deliver?
Behold, by my rebuke I dry up the sea,
  I make the rivers a desert;
their fish stink for lack of water,
  and die of thirst.

---

transcends political and human laws. **Behold, for your iniquities . . . :** Cf. 54:1; Hos. 2:4; Ezek. 5:12. The fault lies in Israel, not in God, that she is in exile (cf. 42:24-25).

2. The people of Israel cannot believe and respond to the word of the Lord through his prophet (40:27). They do not see that his grace is greater than his judgment, that in wrath he remembers mercy. But his redemptive power is revealed in his activity in history and nature (cf. 40:12-31). **Why, when I came, was there no man . . . ?** Why is it that when God comes to redeem his people and to usher in his kingdom (40:8-10) there is no one present; why is it that when through his prophet he proclaims his words of promise and hope (40:1-11) there is no one to answer? (Cf. 59:16; 63:5; also Targ., "Wherefore, when I sent my prophets, did they not repent? they prophesied, but they hearkened not.") **Is my hand shortened . . . ?** Cf. 61:1 and Num. 11:23. **Or have I no power to deliver?** Cf. 49:24. **Behold, by my rebuke . . . :** Cf. Pss. 104:7; 106:9; on the general thought of the verse cf. 42:15-16; 44:27; Ps. 107:33 ff.; contrast 41:18; 43:19. Skinner, Levy, Kissane, and others think the allusion here is to the wonders of the Exodus; Budde and Gunkel see an allusion to the chaos-dragon myth; König and Haller interpret the reference as purely future. The words are fairly general here, but it may be that both mythological and historical allusions are present (cf. 51:9 ff., where the ancient myth and the Exodus [Exod. 14:21 ff.] motifs are combined). As God creates the world by his word, so he sustains and conserves it. The forces of nature are under his constant rule. They respond instantly to his mighty word. By his rebuke the **sea** becomes **dry** and the **rivers** become a **desert** (cf. Jer. 4:23-26; see especially Job 34:13-15; Wisd. Sol. 11:25). **Their fish stink:** The LXX and the Dead Sea Scroll read, תיבש, "are dried up." Torrey sees here an Aramaic cognate verb meaning "to be in evil case" or "to be distressed," but the more usual sense is satisfactory (cf. Exod. 7:18, 21).

---

according to various experiences, that He might even be in arrears to me; and I was daring enough to think that I had something to forgive Him." [1] Such characteristic pretension was doubtless in many of these exiles. It is this which the prophet most deplores as hostile to a humble dependence upon their sovereign God.

Is my hand shortened? The Lord is astounded that his message of redemption, announced by the prophet, meets with no believing response: **Why . . . was there no man?** Do these exiles doubt his ability to deliver them? He reminds them of his mighty acts in the exodus from Egypt—a dry path in the Red Sea, water in the desert, the sky made black in Egypt with a darkness that could be felt (Exod. 10:21).

In the immense panorama of futility presented by current happenings, the church's

[1] *Truth and Poetry: From My Own Life*, tr. John Oxenford (London: Bell & Daldy, 1867), I, 291.

weakness lies in her distrust in God's present effective working. We cannot overcome this distrust either in ourselves or in others by saying, "Look about, and see God at work!" The welter of events is too bewildering. But God has manifested himself in history, and we can look back and see what he has wrought. It always takes time for his activity to work through to a result which is patently divine. In retrospect the acts of God become indisputable. It is undeniable fact that a company of runaway slaves was led through terrifying experiences and made a nation with a unique religious mission. It is undeniable fact that in the first century of our era One lived, taught, died and conquered, and left an impress of his character which cannot be effaced—an impress through which similar qualities are communicated age after age to multitudes, claimed and transformed by him. We may wish there were as inescapably con-

3 I clothe the heavens with blackness, and I make sackcloth their covering.

4 The Lord God hath given me the tongue of the learned, that I should know how to speak a word in season to *him that*

3 I clothe the heavens with blackness,
　　and make sackcloth their covering."

4 The Lord God has given me
　　the tongue of those who are taught,
　　that I may know how to sustain with a
　　word
　　him that is weary.

---

3. I clothe the heavens with blackness: The medieval Jewish commentators say that the reference is to black clouds or to the eclipse of the sun and moon. Volz suggests a sandstorm; Fischer and Feldmann, a storm cloud. But the eclipse is the most likely. The heavens are shrouded in the black garb of mourning (cf. Mal. 3:14). God's mighty works in the seas are contrasted by his mighty work in the heavens (Jer. 4:23; Joel 2:31; Heb. 3:4; Rev. 6:12). Many scholars feel that the strophe is incomplete, but it is possible that this dramatic picture was meant to serve as a climax. Expansion would weaken the effect (cf. 9*cd*, 11; also 51:6, 8). The response of the servant to God's words concerning the persistence of the covenant bond and the judgment upon the unfaithful is not surprising; it is a further development of the major theme running throughout the preceding poem. To the faithlessness of the blind and self-centered the faithful one makes his witness of trust and expectation.

2. Second Strophe: The Suffering of the Disciple of Yahweh (50:4-6)

The two divisions of the strophe are marked by the opening words "Adonai Yahweh." The first division is occupied with the primary imagery and psychic reality of revelation, speaking and hearing. Yahweh gives his disciple a **tongue** to speak and wakens the **ear** to listen. Here is Israel's history of revelation in its final anthropomorphic categories. Observe the climax **He wakens my ear to hear.** The force of the line is enhanced by the beginning of the next division, **The Lord God has opened my ear,** and the results of this

---

vincing signs of his activity in today: the past seems less real and cogent. But the reverse is true. Past events are more solid than anything in the fluid present.

. . . Underneath the surface of To-day,
　Lies yesterday, and what we call the Past,
The only thing which never can decay.

Things bygone are the only things that last:
　The Present is mere grass, quick-mown away;
The Past is stone, and stands for ever fast.[2]

It was from their unquestionable past that the prophet heard God appealing. Their forefathers, in circumstances as overwhelming, had known a deliverance in which they saw his mighty hand. Is that hand too short now to redeem? The church of our time must be fed a diet of spiritual history until the memory of God's redemptive acts gives new strength to her faith.

The depression of the Hebrew exiles engulfed by the pagan culture of Babylon is understood in an age familiar with the effects

[2] Eugene Lee-Hamilton, "Roman Baths."

of the Nazis upon the countries they occupied. A representative of the churches of Holland has written:

There was not only a military usurpation. The enemy brought with him the National-Socialist's total non-Christian view of the world. Slowly but surely the Netherlands, occupied by Germany, fell prey to heathen powers, which tried to destroy all spiritual and moral foundations.[3]

It must have been even worse for the despised captives in Babylon, with no visible symbols or accessories of their faith at hand—the temple, etc. It is proof of the vitality of Israel's religion that a steadfast minority in time provided synagogues, maintained public worship, carried on religious education, and continued the outward marks of loyalty such as circumcision and the sabbath. This devout group conserved the religious tradition and contributed some of the most enriching writings of the O.T. canon.

4-9. The True Israel Makes Its Confession.— A note of autobiography is sounded in this

[3] Henry Smith Leiper, ed., *Christianity Today* (New York: Morehouse-Gorham Co., 1947), p. 12.

is weary: he wakeneth morning by morning, | Morning by morning he wakens,
he wakeneth mine ear to hear as the | he wakens my ear
learned. | to hear as those who are taught.

---

relation are recounted in the lines immediately following. The references to the various bodily organs are quite remarkable, especially in view of modern recognition of the nature of psycho-physical relations in Semitic thought: **tongue, my ear, my back, my cheeks, the beard, my face** (for a discussion of these see Pedersen, *Israel, Its Life and Culture, I-II, III-IV, passim;* H. Wheeler Robinson, "Hebrew Psychology," in Peake, ed., *The People and the Book,* pp. 353-62; and especially Aubrey R. Johnson, *Vitality of the Individual in the Thought of Ancient Israel*). Finally there are affinities between the servant's "confession" and all the literature of lamentation. The individualism of the lines is striking, but no more so than many other O.T. passages where the community is most certainly present.

4. **The Lord God . . . the tongue of those who are taught:** Cf. 54:13. The servant is equipped with the gift of speech; cf. Moses (Exod. 4:10-12), Jeremiah (1:4-10). He is Yahweh's pupil or disciple (see 8:16). Observe the characteristic repetition at the close of the verse. In 49:2 Yahweh makes the servant's mouth like a sword, calling him to a prophetic service; in 42:2 he lays his Spirit upon him that he may establish justice (*mishpāṭ*), but he does not cry aloud; in 53:7 "he [opens] not his mouth." The stress in the servant's confession is upon his personal spiritual communion with God which is the gift of grace (see Matt. 10:20). **That I may know how to sustain . . . weary:** The word rendered **to sustain** (עות) is difficult. The worst solution is to delete it. Torrey's suggestion that we have a double reading (לדעת; לעות) is plausible; in that event it is the first infinitive ("to know") that requires deletion. The LXX evidently derives the verb from the Hebrew root עת, meaning "time": "to speak in season" (so also the Jewish interpreters). The Vulg. reads *sustenare* (so Aq.), which may be right since Arabic and Aramaic roots have this meaning (cf. Hebrew שוע). König derives the word from the Arabic *ghâtha,* "to refresh," "to quicken"; Duhm and Ehrlich emend to ענה, "to answer"; Cheyne emends to רעות, "to teach." The expression **him that is weary** probably designates fellow Israelites.

> **Morning by morning he wakens,**
> **he wakens . . . .**

The first verb is taken with the preceding line by some scholars, but this then requires a correction: Kissane emends יעיר to יעיל, "that avails." The repetition is effective and the text must not be altered. The expression is good Hebrew; such repetitions are not unique. Isaiah says that Yahweh of hosts was in his ear (5:9, literally). The ear with its

---

declaration because the prophet belonged in the fellowship and was leading his fellow believers. It is an intensely personalized utterance.

The tongue of those who are taught. God's gift to Israel was a disciple's ears and voice. In the midst of the community of downhearted Hebrews, adjusting themselves as best they might to an alien city in order to earn their livelihoods, there were those who listened not to the voices about them so much as to the voice from the unseen. This is the first duty of the servant church. "Receptiveness is a rare and massive power."[4] These attentive folk were the spiritual nucleus of their congregations. Inspired listeners are more essential than in-

[4] George Eliot, *Daniel Deronda,* Bk. V, ch. xl.

spired speakers, for they hear the word of God out of the nation's past and through current happenings, as well as in the teaching of living leaders. This alertness to and understanding of the divine message sets them apart. They are the Israel within Israel, the servant of the Lord.

Their second gift was a disciple's speech, **that I may know how to sustain with a word.** Much is said among contemporary Protestants of the overemphasis upon preaching. Israel's main role among the nations was that of bearer of the word of God. We must continue the prophetic succession. During World War II came accounts from Europe of the part played by preaching when tyranny had crushed and silenced other public utterance. Intelligent

5 ¶ The Lord God hath opened mine ear, and I was not rebellious, neither turned away back.

6 I gave my back to the smiters, and my cheeks to them that plucked off the hair: I hid not my face from shame and spitting.

5 The Lord God has opened my ear,
    and I was not rebellious,
    I turned not backward.
6 I gave my back to the smiters,
    and my cheeks to those who pulled out
      the beard;
  I hid not my face
    from shame and spitting.

---

function of hearing plays a major role in the psychology and anthropology of both O.T. and N.T. It was the organ par excellence whereby man responded to the divine revelation. The activity of God in his word is not only vast in its historical and cosmic dimensions (40:8; 55:10-11), but also profoundly inward in its penetration. Compare also 45:19. At the beginning of each day God wakens the servant's ear to receive his words.

5. The Lord God opens the ear so that it may be obedient (48:8; Ps. 40:6). Cf. the Hebrew expression "to uncover the ear" for a divine revelation (I Sam. 9:15; II Sam. 7:27; Job 36:10, 15). The servant is not rebellious (contrast Lam. 1:18), but yields patiently to what may befall him in the carrying out of his ministry. One is reminded constantly of Jeremiah's call and confessions (cf. Jer. 20:7 ff.). Bernhard Duhm (*Die Theologie der Propheten* [Bonn: A. Marcus, 1875], p. 289) suggests that Second Isaiah had before him a prophetic account of the life and activity of Jeremiah. Saadiah identified the servant with Jeremiah as did Grotius, Bunsen, and Duhm (originally). For a brief but excellent discussion see Sheldon H. Blank, "Studies in Deutero-Isaiah," pp. 27-30 (note especially the detailed comparisons on p. 28). Cf. also F. A. Farley, "Jeremiah and 'The Suffering Servant of Jehovah' in Deutero-Isaiah," *Expository Times*, XXXVIII (1926-27), 521-24. It can scarcely be doubted that Jeremiah exerted a profound influence on the prophet's thought, but the perspective reaches far beyond Jeremiah. Other prophets too had suffered insult and opposition—men like Amos (7:10-17) and Hosea (9:14). Cf. Lewis Bayles Paton, "The Problem of Suffering in the Pre-exilic Prophets," *Journal of Biblical Literature*, XLVI (1927), 111-31.

6. The disciple of Yahweh pursues his call amid severest opposition from his fellow countrymen. He is subjected to the harshest physical persecution and insult. Volz supposes that the Jews objected to his missionary activity beyond the confines of Israel.

---

faith must be wakened and nurtured by the spoken word. Religion may use many symbols which lay hold of already prepared hearts, but symbols without the word become empty of truth and impotent in quickening consciences. Edward Rowland Sill addressed those who disparaged words:

Words,—only words; yet, save for tongue or pen

Of those great givers of them unto men,
And burdens they still bear of grave or sweet,
This world were but for beasts, a darkling den.[5]

Second Isaiah, a pre-eminent poet, poured himself with supreme art into words alive with an enduring message from God.

Him that is weary. The prolonged strain of the Exile had brought on fatigue. Now that the hour for movement homeward had come, they needed renewal. And the yet more exhausting task ahead in the rebuilding of their cities with

[5] "Words, Words, Words."

their prostrate institutions made spirits flag. In both Europe and Asia the mid-twentieth century found hungry and impoverished peoples jaded by what they had been through, and in various countries the church, with hopes dashed by repeated setbacks and efforts to help achieving imperceptible results, seemed depleted of ardor and expectancy. As Second Isaiah stayed frustrated people with his message of comfort, so contemporary Christians must be upheld by God's word. When the aspect of current happenings is least heartening and the age is spiritually lean, then we must fetch supplies from God himself, with whom is the fountain of life.

Listening to and speaking for God renders the servant different from his fellows, and exposes him to criticism and antagonism. He is tempted to be **rebellious** and turn **backward.** We have seen in our time heroic groups in several lands hazard themselves in the face of apparently overpowering brute force. The

7 ¶ For the Lord God will help me; therefore shall I not be confounded: therefore have I set my face like a flint, and I know that I shall not be ashamed.

7 For the Lord God helps me; therefore I have not been confounded; therefore I have set my face like a flint, and I know that I shall not be put to shame;

He was surrendering the uniqueness of Israel's holy God, casting pearls before swine, and confiscating the major reality of Israel's faith—her election. He was a heretic, a blasphemer, and, one may add, a visionary enthusiast carried off into the raptures of eschatological fantasy. His tenderhearted compassion and profound sensitiveness to "all flesh" (expressing itself even in the inanimate world) possibly seemed too broad and vague and idealistic. The prophet in that case is identifying his own work with the missionary work of the servant (see II Cor. 11:23-25). For the description cf. Isa. 53:3 ff. **I have my back to the smiters:** Ps. 129:3 has a very similar portrayal of Israel. **My cheeks . . . :** Cf. Lam. 3:30; Neh. 13:25. The disfigurement caused by plucking out the hair, i.e., destroying the beard, was the deepest insult (cf. 7:20; 15:2; II Sam. 10:4; Jer. 7:29). "As shame, like honour, finds expression in the body, so one may cause shame by disturbing the latter" (Pedersen, *Israel, Its Life and Culture, I-II*, p. 241). For **those who pulled out the beard** (מרטים) the Dead Sea Scroll reads "rods of wrought iron" (מטלים); cf. LXX, μάστιγας, "scourges." **I hid not my face:** Cf. Num. 12:14; Deut. 25:9; Job 30:10; Matt. 26:67; 27:30. The Vulg. and the Dead Sea Scroll read "I did not turn aside" (i.e., *averti* and הסירותי).

3. Third Strophe: My Helper and Vindicator (50:7-9)

A superb example of the prophet's rhetoric and feeling for form. The introductory words (vs. 7a) are repeated in the conclusion (vs. 9a) and are followed by two lines, introduced by **therefore,** which summarize the previous strophe. The three questions are introduced with the emphatic interrogative **who** (*mî*) and the conclusion with the twofold emphatic **behold.** The final lines are especially characteristic of the prophet's style. Notable throughout is the use of legal terminology: **He who vindicates me** (מצדיקי, "declares me innocent"), **contend** (יריב, "enter into legal encounter"), **stand**

---

churches in lands under Nazi occupation were conspicuous instances, and far too little attention has been given to the spiritual Germany within the temporarily victorious Germany, a servant of righteousness which gave its back to the smiters. In his account of this underground opposed to the triumphant regime, H. B. Gisevius tells of the time when the company of officials, intellectuals, army officers, church leaders, attempting to shake off Hitler's control, found themselves baffled by the ineptitude of the allied leadership which was playing into his hands. Disheartened, they were sorely tempted to flee their country and carry on their campaign as refugees, but they saw how futile resistance from the outside was proving:

Therefore, we felt that we could leave only if we were ready to give up the struggle, but how did we have the right to do that? Was it the world's business to restore order, justice, and decency in Germany by a more or less sanguinary intervention, or was it not first of all the business of the Germans themselves? It struck us as a parody of all natural concepts of responsibility and morality for those who did not like tyranny to withdraw from the battle, saying *en passant* to the British, the Americans, or the French that unfortunately it was now up to them to issue forth and shed their blood for freedom.[6]

They resolutely remained, and most of them paid for their devotion with their lives. Gisevius concludes with this homage to these unheralded dead who withstood the despot:

Let us not forget, however, that long before the first foreigner was murdered by the SS killers, hundreds of thousands of Germans had died. Let us leave to those whose ashes have been scattered at least their undefiled faith in a better world. Let us leave to them their last despairing hope that the world would be startled out of its slumber by their lonely cries of agony and would not wait for the thunder of Hitler's cannon.[7]

[6] *To the Bitter End,* tr. Richard and Clark Winston (Boston: Houghton Mifflin Co., 1947), p. 329. Used by permission.
[7] *Ibid.,* p. 605.

8 *He is* near that justifieth me; who will contend with me? let us stand together: who *is* mine adversary? let him come near to me.

9 Behold, the Lord GOD will help me; who *is* he *that* shall condemn me? lo, they all shall wax old as a garment; the moth shall eat them up.

8 he who vindicates me is near. Who will contend with me? Let us stand up together. Who is my adversary? Let him come near to me.
9 Behold, the Lord GOD helps me; who will declare me guilty? Behold, all of them will wear out like a garment; the moth will eat them up.

---

up (נעמדה, a *terminus technicus*), **adversary** (בעל משפטי, lit., "lord of my right"), **declare me guilty** (ירשיענו).

7. **For the LORD GOD helps me:** Cf. 41:10, 13, 14; 44:2; 49:8, always of Israel; so also the Dead Sea Scroll of 49:5. **Confounded:** The root is the same as that for "shame" in vs. 6*d*. It should be translated identically in both verses, either "shame" or "insult." The disciple of Yahweh is supported and upheld by his unshakable faith. He sets his **face like a flint** (cf. Jer. 1:8, 18; 15:20; 20:11; Ezek. 3:8-9; Luke 9:51). He is sustained by his absolute assurance: **I know.**

8. The disciple's knowledge and faith are described in a way which fits the Hebraic view of time, **He who vindicates me is near,** in the sense of personal fellowship and communion but also of conviction that God will defend his cause and vindicate him soon (cf. 52:13; 53:11). God is his judge and his protagonist (cf. 41:1–42:4; cf. especially Jer. 17:17-18; 20:7 ff.; 26:7 ff.; Ps. 22; Lam. 3:58 ff.).

9. **Behold** introduces the result of the legal proceeding (cf. 41:11, 24, 29; 42:1). **Who will declare me guilty** [or **condemn**]? Cf. Rom. 8:33. The closing figure is familiar (cf. 51:6, 8; Hos. 5:12; Ps. 39:11; 102:26; Job 13:28).

These men set their faces **like a flint,** and while their efforts were unavailing their names belong among the noble army of martyrs. One of them, a general, from his prison cell wrote to his son:

To our last breath we all remain upstanding men, as we were taught to be from childhood and in our soldierly discipline. Come what may, we fear only the wrath of God that will fall upon us if we are not clean and decent and do our duty.

And Gisevius adds:

He remained firm within himself, and this firmness sprang from his unshakable trust in God.[8]

It is a church as centered upon God, and therefore able to stand for his will against all pressures, that alone can move our world toward his purpose. It must possess the indomitable assurance of the servant (vss. 7-9), and be ready

To go on forever and fail and go on again,
And be mauled to the earth and arise,
And contend for the shade of a word and a thing not seen with the eyes:
With the half of a broken hope for a pillow at night

[8] *Ibid.*, p. 422.

That somehow the right is the right
And the smooth shall bloom from the rough.[9]

The servant, like the German underground, accepted voluntarily his painful role (vs. 6). The church has paralleled this in missionaries and in her pastors and members who have remained under communist domination and continued to worship and unashamedly practice their faith. Under such courageous fidelity Christians may look not alone for future vindication but also for present support: **He who vindicates me is near. . . . Behold, the Lord GOD helps me.** When the cardinal legate in his colloquy with Luther asked "whether he thought that his sovereign would on his account risk his domain[,] Luther answered: 'That I do not want.' The other continued: 'Where will you stay then?' Luther: 'Under the heavens.' "[1] The prophet's favorite emphasis upon the evanescence of man in contrast to the everlasting God is in his words, **the moth will eat them up.** Frightened exiles needed the reminder that human opponents would speedily disappear.

[9] Robert Louis Stevenson, "If This Were Faith."
[1] Julius Köstlin, *The Life of Martin Luther* (tr. John G. Morris; Philadelphia: Lutheran Publication Society, 1883), p. 122.

10 ¶ Who *is* among you that feareth the Lord, that obeyeth the voice of his servant, that walketh *in* darkness, and hath no light? let him trust in the name of the Lord, and stay upon his God.

10 Who among you fears the Lord
  and obeys the voice of his servant,
who walks in darkness
  and has no light,
yet trusts in the name of the Lord
  and relies upon his God?

---

4. Fourth Strophe: The Light of Faith and the Fire of Judgment (50:10-11)

The strophe forms an admirable conclusion to the whole poem. Its unity lies in the contrast between the faithful servant (vss. 4-9) and those who are faithless (vss. 1-3). Both style and thought are characteristic of the prophet. The RSV gives the proper interpretation. Moreover, the speaker throughout is Yahweh; the shifts from third to first person are characteristic of prophetic style (Eduard König, *Stilistik, Rhetorik, Poetik* [Leipzig: Theodor Weicher, 1900], p. 249). Note the excellent transition from vs. 9cd to vss. 10-11. "The concluding message of hope in L. 4-11 corresponds very well to the encouraging message in L. 1-3" (Lindblom, *Servant-Songs in Deutero-Isaiah,* p. 36).

10. Here we are told that the speaker of vss. 4-9 is the **servant** of the Lord; he **walks in impenetrable darkness,** yet he **trusts in the name of the Lord,** and **relies upon his God. Who among you:** Cf. 42:23. It is clear that those addressed are fellow Israelites, the unfaithful and those who have lost their roots in the covenant people (cf. 51:1, 7).

10-11. *The Servant's Sympathizers and Despisers.*—Whether these verses belong originally to the preceding poem or not (see Exeg.), their present position links them with it. The responsive to God's word through his servant are not at once blessed. Though obedient, they walk in darkness. This is a frequent puzzle to believers: Why is their path wrapped in shadows and the face of God hid from them? Light may be "sown for the righteous," but the harvest is often long deferred. Nor is it easy to clear up the darkness about such depressed disciples. John Ker wrote:

I find it very hard to deal with such cases. There is no more meeting them directly than melting an iceberg in the frozen zone. They must be floated into a warmer atmosphere and left to the gradual air that God breathes in upon them. Reasoning is breath that freezes almost as it touches.[2]

The supreme instance of the obedient who are left in darkness is our Lord himself. Hawthorne describes Il Sodoma's *Christ at the Pillar* in Siena:

It is inexpressibly touching. So weary is the Saviour, and utterly worn out with agony, that his lips have fallen apart from mere exhaustion; his eyes seem to be set; he tries to lean his head against the pillar, but is kept from sinking down upon the ground only by the cords that bind him. One of the most striking effects produced is the sense of loneliness. You behold Christ deserted both in heaven and earth; that despair is in him which wrung forth the saddest utterance man ever made, "Why hast Thou forsaken me?"[3]

The prophet bids these darkness-shrouded faithful to keep on trusting in God. If vs. 10 is used as a text the KJV seems preferable to the RSV: **Let him trust in the name of the Lord, and stay upon his God.** Jesus did this when, though feeling abandoned, he still addressed himself to God. It is in such circumstances that the true character of faith becomes apparent. Bushnell defined it as "the trusting of one's being to *a being,* there to be rested, kept, guided, moulded, governed, and possessed forever."[4] Such faith, however, may remain long in the dark without the sense of being upheld.

The deriders of the servant community,

> all you who kindle a fire,
> who set brands alight,

may by their machinations against the devout seem gay. The "children of this world" often appear to be having the best of it. But in sarcasm the prophet bids them:

> Walk by the light of your fire,
> and by the brands which you have kindled!

The man-made sources of merriment prove in time meager indeed. This may be copiously illustrated from the various stimuli to which men resort—drink, gambling, excitements of various sorts. These all pall after a while. Or the phrase may be read (with Skinner[5]) "Walk in the flame of your fire, and in the sparks that ye have kindled." This would be an instance of evil recoiling upon its perpetrators. Deriders

---

[2] *Letters of the Rev. John Ker, D.D.* (2nd ed.; Edinburgh: David Douglas, 1890), pp. 30-31.

[3] *The Marble Faun,* ch. xxxvii.

[4] *Life and Letters of Horace Bushnell,* ed. Mary A. Cheney (New York: Harper & Bros., 1880), p. 193.

[5] *Isaiah, Chapters XL-LXVI,* p. 105.

11 Behold, all ye that kindle a fire, that compass *yourselves* about with sparks: walk in the light of your fire, and in the sparks *that* ye have kindled. This shall ye have of mine hand; ye shall lie down in sorrow.

11 Behold, all you who kindle a fire,
　　who set brands alight![n]
Walk by the light of your fire,
　　and by the brands which you have
　　　　kindled!
This shall you have from my hand:
　　you shall lie down in torment.

51 Hearken to me, ye that follow after righteousness, ye that seek the LORD:

51 "Hearken to me, you who pursue deliverance,
　　you who seek the LORD;
look to the rock from which you were
　　hewn,

[n] Syr: Heb *gird yourselves with brands*

Obeys: Better, "listens to" (cf. vs. 4). **Who walks in darkness . . . no light:** The servant walks in the darkness of rejection by his own people, of persecution and insult (cf. vs. 6; cf. also Lam. 3:2, 6). The last four lines summarize the autobiographical confession of vss. 4-9.

11. The **Behold** introduces the judgment upon the apostate and faithless who walk in the light of the fire of their own kindling. The conclusion returns to the opening strophe. Cf. the quality of imagery in vss. 2e-3 and vs. 11. **Who set brands alight:** The RSV follows a generally accepted emendation of מאזרי (gird yourselves) to מאירי (set . . . alight), which has the support of the Syriac. **This shall you have:** The Hebrew tense is perfect of certainty. **Torment:** There is no reference to a place here. Therefore one cannot easily assume that it alludes to Gehenna. Thus the contrast between the faithful and his faithless foes is brought to a climax.

C. The Coming Salvation (51:1-16)

Like all the poems in Second Isaiah this composition belongs to what De Quincey calls the literature of power. Its theme is an exalted one and is developed by an appeal to history, creation, and eschatology. Imagination is displayed in every line, but always the imagery is used to body forth the intensity of the prophetic faith. Profound emotion matches the grandeur and scope of the theme. The mood and temper of the ancient Semite kindles the language with a rare intensity. In style, composition, and conception this poem is like the others, yet it has its own distinctive character. The prophet is not merely repeating himself; all that he has had to say is fashioned in a fresh matrix. To grasp the uniqueness of this poem, as well as its epical and theological scope and range, one must view it in the light of the whole literature of ancient Israel: historical, prophetic, apocalyptic, and devotional.

---

of the loyal will find their gibes searing themselves. It is the familiar lesson that

> We still have judgment here; that we but teach
> Bloody instructions, which, being taught, return
> To plague the inventor.[6]

The contrast in these verses is between the obedient devout in darkness and their despisers in the blaze of their own clever diatribes. An "even-handed justice" sees to it that those who through darkness rely on God at length reach the brightness of day, while those who exult in their self-kindled brilliance are eventually con-

[6] Shakespeare, *Macbeth*, Act I, scene 7.

sumed by it. The prophet is a "justicer" (to borrow a word of Shakespeare's) who insists on the automatic and inevitable issues of godliness and its opposite. If these verses, as some think, are an editorial addition, they fit in with the thought of the writer to whom we owe ch. 66, who may also have appended the present closing line of ch. 48.

51:1-3. Encouragement from the Heartening Past.—Here is the first part of the message for the loyal nucleus—the obedient of 50:10, and the servant who speaks in 50:4-9. In critical times there is strength in the sense of belonging to a community which through many centuries

The present composition has close affinities with the preceding poems, as a careful analysis clearly reveals: Cf. 51:3b and 49:19ab; 51:4d and 49:6d; 51:5a and 50:8a; 51:5b, 6f and 49:6e; 51:6ac and 50:3; 51:7cd and 50:6; 51:8ab and 50:9cd; 51:10a and 50:2ef; 51:13a and 49:14a; 51:16a and 50:4; 51:16b and 49:2b; see also 51:1 and 50:10.

The unity of the poem, which is denied by the great majority of contemporary scholars, is shown by the persistence of its dominant theme throughout: the comforting of Zion by the repeated assurance that the time of her deliverance is at hand. The progress of the prophet's thought is marked by increasing fervor. The last line, **and saying to Zion, "You are my people,"** admirably summarizes the remarkable and pervasive emphasis on the unique relationship between Yahweh and his people. An examination of the prophet's diction strongly reinforces the impression gained by the unity of the theme: **deliverance** ("righteousness," "victory," etc.; vss. 1e, 5a, 7a, 8c); **salvation** (vss. 5a, 6f, 8d); **joy and gladness** (vss. 3e, 11cd), **comfort** (vss. 3ab, 12a).

Vss. 1-8 are an eschatological oracle of comfort developed by an appeal to past historical revelation and by a promise of future salvation. Vss. 9-16 are an apostrophe in the form of a prayer of lament (cf. 63:7–64:12) and an oracle of assurance that the prayer is answered (*Erhörungsorakel*). This combination is frequent in the prophets (26:8-14, 16-21; 33:7-12; 49:14-23, 24-25; Jer. 15:10, 15-21; Hos. 14:2-8; Mic. 7:9-20; cf. Isa. 40:27-31; see also Hermann Gunkel and Joachim Begrich, *Einleitung in die Psalmen* [Göttingen: Vandenhoeck & Ruprecht, 1933; "Göttinger Handkommentar zum Alten Testament"], pp. 137-38, 245 ff.). The association of the prayer of lament and the divine assurance is to be found in the Babylonian and Egyptian rituals (see *ibid.*, p. 137 for literature). The way in which these forms are fashioned into a literary unity is a good example of the nature of the literary development in the exilic and postexilic period.

The strophes are in general clearly marked. The first three (vss. 1-3, 4-6, 7-8) are constructed on the same lines: an urgent imperative to listen (vss. 1a, 4ab, 7a), an emphatic vocative (vss. 1ab, 4ab, 7ab), a word of the Lord (*hieros logos;* vss. 1c-3d, 4c-6e, 7c-8b), and a powerful conclusion (vss. 3ef, 6fg, 8cd). The climactic strophe with its climactic reference to salvation and deliverance (vss. 5ab, 6fg, 8cd) stirs the prophet to an apostrophe in the manner of the interlude (vss. 9-11). The oracle of assurance follows (vss. 12-14, 15-16).

Another striking feature of the poem is the strong emphasis on the divine first person. This is illustrated not only by such prepositional phrases as **to me** (vss. 1a, 4a, 4cd, 5c, 7a) and the emphatic first person (vss. 12a, 15a) but also by the possessive pronoun **my** (vss. 4ab, 4d, 5ab, 5d, 6a, 6g, 7b, 8cd, 16ab, 16e). These latter phrases are accentuated by the words of address to Israel (1ab, 4ab, 7ab) and by the great climactic lines which crystallize the thought at the close: **I, I am he that comforts you** (vs. 12a); **For I am the LORD your God** (vs. 15a); **I have put my words in your mouth** (vs. 16a); and **You are my people** (vs. 16e). Israel's faith is stirred and quickened by divine imperatives (vss. 1a, 1c, 2a, 4a, 6ab, 7a, 7cd). The writer is fond of repeating important words and phrases (vss. 1c and 2a, 3a and 3b, 4a and 4b, 4d and 5b, 9a and 9c, 9e and 10a, 12a [I, I], 13bc and 16cd). His poem abounds in allusions and comparisons (vss. 1cd, 3cd, 6cde, 8ab, 9a, 12c). He shows the same familiarity with the narratives of the Yahwist as we have observed before (vss. 1-2), makes magnificent use of the chaos-dragon mythological motif (vss. 9-10), and closes each strophe with impressive lines which serve to bring his thought to a focus. The eschatological character of his thought is reflected in many of these lines as well as in the powerful imagery of vs. 6. Again and again he draws on the literature of his tradition to adorn his expression (cf. vss. 11, 14, 15-16, and Exeg. below).

The text has suffered somewhat, especially in vss. 14 and 15-16. Vs. 13f, **And where is the fury of the oppressor,** reads like a gloss. The meter of vss. 1-8 is prevailingly 3+3, although it is possible that originally many of the lines were read as 3+2. The first lines of the interlude (vss. 9-10) are clearly 3+2, and the remaining verses sometimes have 3+3, at other times 3+2 (vss. 12-13d).

| look unto the rock *whence* ye are hewn, and to the hole of the pit *whence* ye are digged. | and to the quarry from which you were digged. |

1. First Strophe: The Comforting of Zion (51:1-3)

The first half of the strophe is historical reflection, the second half eschatological promise. Both are designed to encourage and comfort Zion (40:1, 27; 41:10; etc.). The repeated blows from the foreign conqueror, the decimation of the population, the small size of the Jerusalem community, and the condition of the exiles naturally gave rise to despair and hopelessness. The prophet appeals to the story of Abraham (Gen. 12:1-3; 13:14-15; 15:5; 22:17 [J]). As Yahweh had called Abraham, and had blessed and multiplied him according to his promise, so Israel in her present plight may look forward to a miraculous increase of her population. This was a major feature of classical Hebrew eschatology (cf. Hos. 1:10 [Hebrew 2:1]; Jer. 3:16; 30:19; Ezek. 36:10-11; Zech. 8:5; 10:8). Second Isaiah was one of the major contributors to its formulation (49:19-21; 54:1-3). The form of the strophe is noteworthy. The three imperatives (vss. 1*a*, 1*c*, 2*a*) converge upon Abraham, and the point of the appeal is introduced by the usual *kî* (vs. 2*c*). Then with a second and more emphatic *kî* (vs. 3*a*) the thought of the strophe and of the whole poem is succinctly stated, and this is elaborated into the characteristic eschatological motif of joy.

51:1. You who pursue deliverance: Cf. 50:10. The word *çédheq* bears either an ethical or an eschatological meaning here. The KJV and the ASV favor the former (**follow after righteousness**); the Amer. Trans. and the RSV favor the latter ("press after" or **pursue deliverance**). Since the poem as a whole is eschatological, it is better to translate **deliverance**, "vindication," or "salvation." **Look to the rock from which you were hewn:** In this and the following clauses the phrase **from which** is omitted in the Hebrew in accordance with the prophet's style (E. F. Kautzsch, *Gesenius' Hebrew Grammar*, tr. A. E. Cowley [2nd English ed.; Oxford: Clarendon Press, 1910], sec. 155*k*;

has been watched over by God, who is **the rock from which you were hewn**, and **the quarry from which you were digged.** In our day the Christian church receives new emphasis in the thought and speech of her members. We see her dignity in God's appointment of her to create a world community, and also we are inspired by her role in history. A convert to Protestantism, William L. Sullivan, tells of the impression which the church made on him as a young Roman Catholic:

> The church is his aristocracy and romantic love; his household, where he mingles with the holiest of all the ages, children, like himself, of a mother solicitous and majestic, nurse of saints, yet mindful of her sinners, and keeping in her heart memories incomparable, as far back as the age of martyrs and the missions of the Apostles. When she takes him to her embrace, he ceases to be a casual atom of humanity; he becomes an heir of the ages, a citizen in the commonwealth of God; his name thenceforward is entered in the vastest brotherhood ever known on earth, and written through this august mediation in the book of life above. . . . For the mind she has light, for the heart tenderness, for the imagination magnificence, for the soul sanctity, for death consolation and a ministration of an immortality of beatitude.[7]

[7] *Under Orders* (New York: Richard R. Smith, 1944), pp. 36-37. Used by permission.

This is the deliverance of the lonely who feel their insignificance and insufficiency, the deliverance of being enfolded in a venerable and earth-wide society. The church is an essential part of the gospel.

The particular point in citing **Abraham** and **Sarah** is to meet the feeling of this exiled community that they were too few to hope to restore Jerusalem and render her the center of God's purposes for mankind. Abraham **was but one** when God called him and made him the progenitor of the chosen race. Suppose they are a mere handful, who can foresee what God will make out of them and their children?

Those who care intensely for God's purpose are in every age a relatively small minority. Their fewness discourages them. But it has been God's way to initiate vast movements by laying his cause on the consciences of a tiny company, and in time marvelously multiplying them. One thinks of the evangelical movement of the eighteenth century originating in the "holy club" at Oxford, and the missionary advance of the nineteenth century starting in this country in a student prayer meeting at a haystack in Williamstown. We dare not despise the day of small things (Zech. 4:10). The genuinely vital church in our time appears a diminutive minority in the population of

2 Look unto Abraham your father, and unto Sarah *that* bare you: for I called him alone, and blessed him, and increased him.

3 For the LORD shall comfort Zion: he will comfort all her waste places; and he will make her wilderness like Eden, and her desert like the garden of the LORD; joy and gladness shall be found therein, thanksgiving, and the voice of melody.

2 Look to Abraham your father
and to Sarah who bore you;
for when he was but one I called him,
and I blessed him and made him many.
3 For the LORD will comfort Zion;
he will comfort all her waste places,
and will make her wilderness like Eden,
her desert like the garden of the LORD;
joy and gladness will be found in her,
thanksgiving and the voice of song.

cf. Job 21:17). The rock and the quarry symbolize the solidarity of Israel. All Israelites were hewn from the same rock. Many have suspected an allusion to some mythological or folk idea (e.g., the cave of Machpelah at Hebron) but this is far-fetched. **The quarry:** Lit., "excavation of the pit." The word מקבת occurs only here, but the root (נקב) appears elsewhere in the O.T. and in the Siloam inscription: e.g., וזה היה דבר הנקבה, "this was the manner of the boring" (see Pritchard, *Ancient Near Eastern Texts*, p. 321). The word **pit** is generally held to be an explanatory gloss (cf. vs. 17).

2. Look to Abraham your father: Cf. 41:8; 63:16. All Israelites are the sons of Abraham and share in the blessing or vitality of their progenitor. His life lives on in them. As God fulfilled his promise to Abraham, so he will fulfill it for Abraham's children. The birth of a people is the central theme of the Yahwist's account of the patriarch. There may be an implication here of Abraham's obedience (Gen. 12:4 [J]) and faith (Gen. 15:6 [E]). **Sarah who bore you:** This is the only mention of Sarah in the O.T. outside Genesis. The verb (Polel imperfect of חול) is unusual; we should expect a participle. But the highly elliptical style of the strophe probably accounts for it. **For when he was but one I called him:** Lit., "for one I called" (cf. Gen. 12:1-3). Ezekiel (33:24) implies the same allusion but makes quite different use of it (cf. Mal. 2:15). **And I blessed him and made him many:** Cf. 49:20-22. The M.T. reads "that I might bless him and multiply him." Many scholars, following the versions, repoint to read as in the RSV and thus obtain a superb summary of the Yahwist epic. But the M.T. emphasizes that Yahweh continued to bless Abraham in his descendants (see Arnold B. Ehrlich, *Randglossen zur hebräischen Bibel* [Leipzig: J. C. Hinrichs, 1912], IV, 183-84). The contrast between the one and the many in the representation of Abraham as an individual and as the community of Israel is a fine example of the patriarch as a corporate personality (observe the same contrast between the one and the many in Isa. 52:13–53:12). The fluidity of both figures is noteworthy. This serves as an excellent transition to the following lines. For ואברכהו, **I blessed him,** the Dead Sea Scroll reads ואפרהו, "I made him fruitful."

3. For the LORD will comfort Zion: The introductory particle and the repetition of the verb underline the central importance of this line. The verbs are perfects of certainty, here (cf. ASV) properly rendered as future. Not only the people (40:1) but Zion and the surrounding desert of Judah will be "comforted" by the complete trans-

most Christian nations. It is usually suffering from an "inferiority complex." Let it look to the rock whence it was hewn—the little circle of his disciples to whom the Lord did not hesitate to entrust a mission to the world.

The restoration of Israel to her homeland (vs. 3) is to Second Isaiah the consummation of human history. Hence he connects it with the outset of that history in **Eden.** We have to acknowledge that in part he was mistaken. No paradise awaited these returned exiles. Joy and

gladness were mixed with disillusionment and wrangling. But the prophet was not basically mistaken. In the devout community who rebuilt the temple the voice of praise was heard. Many of the most exultant psalms come from those who worshiped in it. The spiritual fellowship became a **garden of the LORD** to many devout folk.

It is falling to mid-twentieth-century Christians, after the devastations of war and revolution, to rebuild the enterprises of the church

4 ¶ Hearken unto me, my people; and give ear unto me, O my nation: for a law shall proceed from me, and I will make my judgment to rest for a light of the people.	4 "Listen to me, my people, and give ear to me, my nation; for a law will go forth from me, and my justice for a light to the peoples.

formation of nature. The coming age is the time of the consolation of Zion (see 40:1; also 61:2; 66:13; Jer. 31:13; Luke 2:25; II Cor. 1:3-7). **And will make her wilderness like Eden:** From the world of history the eschatologist turns to the realm of nature. The end will be like the beginning. Echatological time returns to primordial time. In Gen. 2:8 the Lord plants a garden in Eden; here and in Ezek. 28:13 (cf. Gen. 13:10) Eden is the garden of God (cf. Ezek. 31:8-9). **Joy and gladness . . . :** Cf. 35:1-2; 61:7; 66:14; Jer. 30:19; Zech. 10:7. The Dead Sea Scroll adds "sorrow and sighing shall flee away" (cf. vs. 11; 35:10).

2. Second Strophe: The Time of Salvation Is Near (51:4-6)

A strophe of remarkable intensity and power. The crisp, succinct style of the first strophe is even more apparent here since the content is so momentous. The first half sets forth the promises of God; the second, their realization. The imperatives are more urgent, the words of address more inward, the repetitions more impressive, and the imagery more vivid and sublime. The personal pronouns are emphatic. The conclusion envisages an everlasting salvation. The Hebrew poets were fond of bringing their strophes to a climax with such time-fulfilling expressions. The influence of the servant poems is apparent (42:1-4; 49:1-6). The reference to the **arm** (or **arms**) of the Lord admirably prepares the way for the apostrophe in vss. 9-10 and the succeeding poems. Many scholars hold that the section is not genuine or that it does not belong here. This is due in part to what is said to be the precarious state of the text, in part to the close affinities with the servant poems, in part to the thought expressed. None of these arguments is convincing however. The M.T. is in relatively good condition, the affinities with the servant poems are to be expected in view of the continuity of the poems, and the thought is explained by the movement and development of the eschatological picture. Every line has parallels in other poems, and the deletion of verses impairs the poem's structure.

4. Listen to me, my people: The LXX repeats the imperative. Several Hebrew MSS and the Syriac read the plural, "peoples," "nations." This is preferred by many scholars, but the other versions support the M.T.; moreover, the vocative here is similar to that in vs. 7, and the strophe refers to the nations in the third person. The oracle is addressed to the chosen people. The word translated **nation** is really another Hebrew word for

and plan anew her missionary undertakings. For that we must recapture this prophet's joyful assurance. The horizon may be black with menacing clouds; fresh disasters may be impending; but the source of the church's gladness is in God, who commits to her his work, confident that through her he can bless mankind. There may not appear outward signs of great growth; but wherever God is, there will be **thanksgiving and the voice of song.** Part of our thanksgiving will be for the noble succession in which we stand, for **the rock** whence we **were hewn** and the company of the faithful of many generations to which we belong. Emerson, recalling certain writers of "fragrant piety," and having read Eph. 3, set down in his diary: "And yet I see not very well how the rose of Sharon could bloom so freshly in our affection but for these ancient men, who, like great gardens with

banks of flowers, do send out their perfumed breath across the great tracts of time." [8]

4-6. Encouragement from the Enduring Future.—The Lord himself assumes the mission assigned to his servant in 42:1-4. He will make his law **a light to the peoples.** The entire physical universe **will vanish,** but God's purpose for his people abides **for ever.**

The God-centeredness of the prophet's hope is in sharp contrast to the almost limitless anticipations of man's control of the universe entertained in the earlier decades of the twentieth century. A typical instance may be found in the autobiography of a British colonial governor and novelist who confesses that from 1880 onward he no longer believed "the theological nonsense generally understood by the term 'Religion'"; but he believed in "the

[8] *Journals*, Mar. 21, 1833.

5 My righteousness *is* near; my salvation is gone forth, and mine arms shall judge the people; the isles shall wait upon me, and on mine arm shall they trust.

5 My deliverance draws near speedily,
  my salvation has gone forth,
  and my arms will rule the peoples;
the coastlands wait for me,
  and for my arm they hope.

---

people, but elsewhere is not used of Israel. The writer needed a parallel to '*am*, and of course refrained from using *gôy*. The LXX reads "kings" for **my nation.** Kissane reads "my messenger." The Hebrew word order forms a chiasmus. **For a law will go forth:** Cf. 2:3. The revelatory word is introduced by the emphatic *kî* (cf. vss. 2*c*, 3*a*). Not **a law,** but **law,** in the sense of revealed teaching. **My justice:** For the association of *tôrāh* and *mishpāṭ* see 42:1-4. **For a light to the peoples:** See 42:6; 49:6. The prophet obviously echoes the servant passages.

5. The last word of vs. 4 (ארגיע) is difficult. The ASV renders, "I will establish." It is better, however, to take it with the next verse, following the LXX. The Vulg. reads *requiescet,* and Kimhi, Rashi, and the KJV translate similarly. Perhaps it is best to take a clue from the LXX (ἐγγίζει ταχὺ), as the majority of scholars do, and to render the word as an adverb, "speedily [or "suddenly"] I will bring near my deliverance" (lit., "I will do quickly"; cf. 46:13). G. R. Driver ("Studies in the Vocabulary of the Old Testament, VIII," *Journal of Theological Studies,* XXXVI [1935], 298) reached similar results by rendering "in a moment." Later (*ibid.,* p. 401), he takes the word with vs. 4, preserving the traditional division, and derives it from an Arabic cognate meaning "flashed in quick succession": "And I will make my judgment to flash for a light of the peoples." Volz preserves a similar meaning on the basis of a more radical emendation. The sequence of the eschatological events, *tôrāh, mishpāṭ, çédheq,* and *yĕsha',* culminates in the assertion of the divine sovereignty: **My arms will rule the peoples** (see 40:10). The representation of 45:20-25 is similar. The outgoing divine activity of God in the world, with all its momentous effects, has as its counterpart the active waiting of the peoples for his coming (vs. 5*d*) and their hoping for the redemption that his victorious arm ushers in (vs. 5*e*; cf. 42:4). In 49:1-6 the servant's confession is set in a matrix of the message to the peoples (vss. 1, 6); here the message to the peoples is set in the matrix of the call to Israel, the servant of the Lord (cf. also 41:1–42:4).

---

human side of religion"—in man's devotion to man.

Unless Mankind as a mass sticks together, helps Mankind; all that is human in our race may well perish in the struggle against the blind forces of nature. Whereas there is just a hope, a faint struggling hope that Mankind, united in purpose striving to create and maintain better and better control over this Planet, over the fate and welfare of its own species, may stave off eventually annihilation, may even make itself (millions or billions of years ahead) master of the Solar system.[9]

Our present blundering management of human affairs hardly renders us eager to see the solar system under our direction. That system, to this prophet, is in any case only temporary,

for the heavens will vanish like smoke,
the earth will wear out like a garment.

[9] Harry H. Johnston, *The Story of My Life* (Indianapolis: Bobbs-Merrill Co., 1933), p. 460.

God endures: his **righteousness** is an everlasting standard, and his **salvation** is for ever. It is therefore inevitable that

the coastlands wait for me,
and for my arm they hope.

In the Grange Cemetery in Edinburgh there is a plot where a devout woman who lost her husband and both her sons in World War I placed a stone, bearing their names and the place and dates of their deaths, and these three words from Heb. 1:11, "But thou remainest." Both Second Isaiah and the N.T. writer regard the solid firmament as transient. Things seen are temporal; but things unseen—the realm of God and of life with him—are eternal. **Lift up your eyes to the heavens** (vs. 6) may be set beside "Lift up your eyes on high and see" (40:26). The latter look is to note the vastness and multitude of the starry host and recall the might of their Maker; the former look is to

6 Lift up your eyes to the heavens, and look upon the earth beneath: for the heavens shall vanish away like smoke, and the earth shall wax old like a garment, and they that dwell therein shall die in like manner: but my salvation shall be for ever, and my righteousness shall not be abolished.

7 ¶ Hearken unto me, ye that know righteousness, the people in whose heart is my law; fear ye not the reproach of men, neither be ye afraid of their revilings.

6 Lift up your eyes to the heavens,
    and look at the earth beneath;
for the heavens will vanish like smoke,
    the earth will wear out like a garment,
    and they who dwell in it will die like gnats;[o]
but my salvation will be for ever,
    and my deliverance will never be ended.

7 "Hearken to me, you who know righteousness,
    the people in whose heart is my law;
fear not the reproach of men,
    and be not dismayed at their revilings.

[o] Or in like manner

6. **Lift up your eyes:** Cf. 40:26. The Dead Sea Scroll omits vs. 6cd and substitutes "and see who created these" from 40:26. Heaven and earth will pass away, but God's salvation will abide forever. The poet never wearies of pointing to the transitoriness and evanescence of all things in order to emphasize the eternity of God (see 40:6-8). Heaven and earth were the most permanent and enduring of God's creation, but they are fleeting and temporary in comparison with his redemptive purpose (cf. Matt. 24:35). The thought is developed by three striking figures and a sharp contrast. **For the heavens will vanish like smoke:** Cf. Hos. 13:3; Pss. 68:2; 102:3 [Hebrew 102:4]. The meaning of the verb is uncertain. G. R. Driver takes it as a denominative from *mélah*, "salt," which because of its color acquired a secondary meaning, as in Arabic, "to become gray." Thus, "the heavens are murky with smoke" (*ibid.,* pp. 401-2). Jer. 38:11 and Arabic and Akkadian cognates suggest "torn in pieces," but this meaning can be accepted in relation to smoke only if we diffuse it into such a general term as **vanish. Like a garment:** Cf. 50:9; Ps. 102:26. **Like gnats:** Or **in like manner.** The LXX, Vulg., KJV, ASV, and some modern scholars (Ehrlich, Torrey) prefer the latter, but the context anticipates another simile; moreover "likewise" is decidedly inferior stylistically (cf. especially 40:22, where the inhabitants are compared to grasshoppers). **Be ended:** Lit., "be shattered." LXX, ἐκλίπῃ, Vulg., *deficiet,* and Targ., "will not fail." Oort, Duhm, and others needlessly emend to תחדל, "shall not cease." The KJV and ASV, **be abolished.** The verb can mean "fall to pieces," "cut off," "cease" (see Torrey, *Second Isaiah,* p. 398).

3. THIRD STROPHE: FEAR NOT, BE NOT DISMAYED (51:7-8)

Intimately dependent upon the two preceding strophes in form, wording, and content, this strophe has a very definite word of comfort which is introduced by the characteristic **Fear not.**

7. **You who know righteousness:** Cf. vs. 1. The change in meaning is characteristic of the prophet's literary manner. This and the following clauses illustrate the climactic character of the strophe. The exiles not merely pursue righteousness (*çédheq*), they have a knowledge of it, i.e., they establish a relationship to God's righteous ordinances,

remind one's self that this innumerable throng which fills the sky **will vanish,** but their Maker abides. To men beginning to taste liberation, but embarking on an enterprise of restoration whose issue could not be foreseen and whose difficulties seemed insuperable, it meant everything to be assured, **My deliverance will never be ended.**

7-8. *The Reproach of Men.*—The servant community was enduring contempt (cf. 50:6). It is not clear whether their scorners were fellow Israelites or heathen neighbors or both. In 50:4-9 the group of the loyal is spoken of collectively as one, here they are addressed individually. In every age and culture the godly encounter criticism and opposition be-

8 For the moth shall eat them up like a garment, and the worm shall eat them like wool: but my righteousness shall be for ever, and my salvation from generation to generation.

9 ¶ Awake, awake, put on strength, O

8 For the moth will eat them up like a
    garment,
  and the worm will eat them like wool;
  but my deliverance will be for ever,
    and my salvation to all generations."

9 Awake, awake, put on strength,
    O arm of the LORD;
  awake, as in days of old,

---

and live in conformity with them. **The people in whose heart is my law:** Jeremiah may have influenced the thought here; if so, the prophet is thinking of the new covenant with its *tôrāh* or revelation written on the heart (Jer. 31:33; cf also Isa. 29:13; Ps. 40:8; Ezek. 36:27). Since God is both righteous and sovereign, the exiles need not fear (cf. Ps. 46). Amidst the transitoriness of the world of nature and of history, Israel possesses the interior resources of knowing righteousness and having a concrete knowledge of a revealed righteousness. The two lines beginning with **Fear not** constitute the heart of the climactic strophe. This central thought is expanded in vss. 12-14.

8. The *hieros logos* of vs. 7cd is here developed by a moving comparison (vs. 8ab) and a climactic contrast (vs. 8cd), precisely as the central disclosure of the previous strophe is developed (cf. also the similarity of vss. 1-3). The influence of the servant song of 50:4-9 is very noticeable here, and it is likely that the whole strophe is written against that background. In this connection the absence of any stress on Israel's power and glory is to be observed. The transitoriness in vs. 6 is of nature, in vss. 7-8, of the great oppressing power who reviled the small people. In contrast to the decay and corruption of power, the salvation of God is everlasting. The climax of the last two lines (cf. vss. 5a, 6fg) is a superb illustration of the effect that repetition could achieve among the literary men of Israel. The profound emotion which accompanied the eschatological vision and faith of the prophet finds expression in the following interlude (vss. 9-11).

4. Eschatological Interlude: A Fervent Call for God's Intervention (51:9-11)

To the repeated divine assurance of imminent salvation the prophet breaks out in a fervent invocation of God's conquering **arm.** The urgent imperatives of the preceding

---

cause of their difference from the mass of folk about them.

> He hath a daily beauty in his life
> That makes me ugly.[1]

The godly may not have attained the beauty of holiness, but that for which they stand is a rebuke to those who repudiate it. The N.T. says with blunt realism: "Yea, and all that will live godly in Christ Jesus shall suffer persecution" (II Tim. 3:12). The antidote to man's reproach is to recall his fleeting mortality (cf. 40:6-8). **The moth** and **the worm** are frequent symbols in the writings of all thoughtful men.

> Think, in this battered Caravanserai
> Whose Portals are alternate Night and Day,
>   How Sultan after Sultan with his Pomp
> Abode his destined Hour and went his way.[2]

[1] Shakespeare, *Othello*, Act V, scene 1.
[2] *The Rubáiyát of Omar Khayyám*, st. xvii.

One need not be **dismayed** by the **revilings** by any sultan of a neighbor if one recalls that he is a creature of an hour.

The transiency of man stands forth against the background of God's everlastingness, whose **deliverance will be for ever.** The prophet almost reaches the conviction of eternal life for those linked with God; but it is the nation, not individuals, that is to be delivered and saved. The final age is about to dawn, with Zion at its center. A successor, whose prophecy is bound up with this prophecy, sees not immortality but full and long life for Zion's citizens (65:20). The **revilings** of men are endured not so much in the confidence that every man is pathetically short-lived, but in the assurance that God's justice abides forever and his vindication is **to all generations.**

9-11. *A Call for Divine Help.*—This may be the prophet's or the servant people's prayer. The metaphors come from the Babylonian myth

arm of the Lord; awake, as in the ancient days, in the generations of old. *Art* thou not it that hath cut Rahab, *and* wounded the dragon?

the generations of long ago. Was it not thou that didst cut Rahab in pieces, that didst pierce the dragon?

strophes in which the Lord calls upon his people evoke a passionate cry that the salvation may come now. The whole period from 586 B.C., or indeed from the very beginning of time, to the present, has been the time of God's restraint and silence (cf. Volz, *Jesaia II*, pp. 118-19; see 42:14; 64:12). The magnificent apostrophe to the **arm** of Yahweh is developed by reference to primeval time when the world was created and to Israel's most ancient time in which she was delivered through mighty wonders from the land of Egypt. Mythology and history meet, but the former is employed only to give force and effect to the latter. Vs. 11 is derived from 35:10 and constitutes a characteristic eschatological finale of which the poet is very fond.

The mythology of the interlude is interesting. The poet recalls the primeval combat of the chaos-dragon myth, which in one form or another was known throughout the ancient Near East (T. H. Gaster, *Thespis* [New York: Henry Schuman, 1950] pp. 140 ff.; most familiar is the Akkadian account in the *Enûma elish* [IV, 35 ff.]), in which Marduk slays Tiamat, the great dragon, and out of the two halves of her body forms the heavens and the earth. In recent years the Canaanite form of the myth, the combat of Baal and the Sea (*yām*), has been uncovered at Ras Shamra (for pertinent discussions, see Otto Eissfeldt, *Baal Zaphon, Zeus Kasios und der Durchzug der Israeliten durchs Meer* [Halle: Niemeyer, 1932]; W. F. Albright, *Archaeology and the Religion of Israel* [Baltimore: Johns Hopkins Press, 1942], pp. 148-50; G. R. Levy, "The Oriental Origin of Herakles," *Journal of Hellenic Studies*, LIV [1934], 40 ff.). Here we have a Hebraic version of the myth in which Yahweh is the hero of the primordial conflict. Many scholars in the past have interpreted the whole passage as referring to Egypt, for such terms as **Rahab**, etc., were so employed. It seems more likely, however, that the prophet is combining cosmological and historical elements as he does elsewhere in order to give scope and depth to the meaning of history. The return of the sacred images to their original home was a familiar practice in the history of antiquity. But Israel's religion was imageless, perhaps from the very beginning, and the Hebrew poets describe the return of Yahweh for the redemption of his people in the glowing colors of eschatological miracle (see Johannes Hempel, "The Contents of the Literature," in H. Wheeler Robinson, ed., *Record and Revelation* [Oxford: Clarendon Press, 1938], p. 61). Myth is never allowed its free range in the O.T.; it is characteristically historicized, but its employment gives to the historical revelation a new profundity.

9-11. Awake, awake: The apostrophe in the form of a lament (Begrich, *Studien zu Deuterojesaja*, pp. 167-70) opens with a fervent call for help (cf. 63:7–64:12; Pss. 38; 74; 77; 79; and the laments of Jeremiah). The **days of old** are the primeval days of the

of the creation, where Marduk cuts the dragon in two to form the heavens and the earth. **Rahab** and the **dragon** are also symbols of Egypt (cf. 30:6-7), recalling in this prayer God's deliverance of his people with a strong arm at the Exodus. There was a creation of the universe and of the nation of Israel; now the moral universe needs re-creating, for it has been disordered by the reign of brute force in the Babylonian era.

Our disordered day as urgently needs this faith in the **arm of the Lord**, awake and active in the melee of human affairs. The vast majority of contemporary Christians assume that

God is currently inactive. Our world is chaotic, and of ourselves we are incapable of producing "a new earth wherein dwelleth righteousness." Our primary need is the faith out of which this prayer was born, and a similar prayer centuries later:

Come forth out of thy royal chambers, O Prince of all the kings of the earth! put on the visible robes of thy imperial majesty; take up that unlimited sceptre which thy Almighty Father hath bequeathed thee; for now the voice of thy bride calls thee, and all creatures sigh to be renewed.[3]

[3] John Milton, *Animadversions upon the Remonstrant's Defence Against Smectymnuus*, sec. 2.

| 10 *Art* thou not it which hath dried the sea, the waters of the great deep; that hath made the depths of the sea a way for the ransomed to pass over? | 10 Was it not thou that didst dry up the sea, the waters of the great deep; that didst make the depths of the sea a way for the redeemed to pass over? |

beginnings of heaven and earth (cf. vs. 6). The invocation of the **arm of the LORD** (cf. vs. 5) brings this motif, first sounded in the prologue (40:10), to its highest point thus far and prepares the way for its remarkable development in the two following poems (52:10; 53:1; cf. Luke 1:51). The Lord girds himself for the battle with armor of his strength just as in the creation myths (cf. 59:17-18; Ps. 93:1). The four mythological names, **Rahab,** the **dragon** (*tannîn*), **the Sea** (*yām* without the article), and **the great deep** (*tᵉhôm rabbāh*) are used to designate the chaos before the creation of the world (cf. 27:1; Ps. 74:13). The wonders of Yahweh's primeval victory are thus portrayed with the classical materials of mythological imagery. In view of the parallels in other mythological contexts, the participle המחצבת in vs. 9e should probably be read המחצת. So the Dead Sea Scroll, Vulg. (*percussisti*): "smite through" (cf. Judg. 5:26; Pss. 18:39 [II Sam. 22:39]; 68:22; 110:5; Job 26:12; Hab. 3:18; the same word appears in vs. 1, however). It is significant that the period following the destruction of the nation in 586 B.C. resorted to such imagery. This is not merely an indication of general Near Eastern or Babylonian influence. A profound theological interest inspires the use of such mythology (see above). For parallels see Ezek. 29:3-5; 36:2-6; Pss. 74:13-14; 89:9-10; 93:1-5; Job 7:12; 9:13; 26:12-13; 38:8-11; Hab. 3:8. Remarkably, the mythological description culminates in a reference to the way of the Lord, the *dérekh Yahweh*. This is not mythological at all. Mythology has been accommodated to Hebrew tradition. The symbol of the **way** is a major motif in the poems of Second Isaiah (40:3; 42:16; 43:16, 19; 48:17; 49:11;

The mighty acts of God at the nation's birth are recalled in order to awaken faith in his similar working now in the nation's rebirth. History confirms the faith of Americans when they sing with Leonard Bacon:

> O God, beneath thy guiding hand
> Our exiled fathers crossed the sea.

The prophet was on tiptoe, for God's vindication was at hand. It is this expectancy which must be reborn in the church. God is always near with an outstretched arm. His better day is not remote, but within reach, not because of man's skill or goodness, but because of God's availability and eagerness. His church must be agog with glad anticipation of what he is about to do:

> For we are afar with the dawning
> And the suns that are not yet high,
> And out of the infinite morning
> Intrepid you hear us cry—
> How, spite of your human scorning,
> Once more God's future draws nigh.[4]

It may seem presumptuous to pray **Awake,** . . . **O arm of the LORD,** but God desires to hear such prayers. Our lack of avid impatience

[4] Arthur O'Shaughnessy, "Ode."

thwarts him. Jesus declared: "But now the Kingdom of God presses in, and men of determined purpose lay impatient hands upon it."[5] Men with a conviction of the proximate advent of God have opened doors for his coming to change an evil time. Martin Luther is reported saying:

The darkness grows thicker around us, and godly servants of the Most High become rarer and more rare. Impiety and licentiousness are rampant throughout the world, and we like pigs, like wild beasts, devoid of all reason. But a voice will soon be heard thundering forth: *Behold, the bridegroom cometh.*[6]

Lyman Beecher whose ministry was a morally transforming power in the early years of the nineteenth century said of his own mood:

I am sensible that the fifty years of my active life have been years of unparalleled interest . . . ,—the commencement of the punishment of the antichristian powers, with reference to the predicted victories of the church in the evangelization of the world.

It was in the view of such predictions and providential indications that I early consecrated my

[5] William Manson, *Jesus the Messiah* (London: Hodder & Stoughton, 1943), p. 65.
[6] *Table Talk*, tr. William Hazlitt (London: George Bell & Sons, 1902), No. XV.

11 Therefore the redeemed of the LORD shall return, and come with singing unto Zion; and everlasting joy *shall be* upon their head: they shall obtain gladness and joy; *and* sorrow and mourning shall flee away. 12 I, *even* I, *am* he that comforteth you: who *art* thou, that thou shouldest be afraid of a man *that* shall die, and of the son of man *which* shall be made *as* grass;	11 And the ransomed of the LORD shall return, 　and come with singing to Zion; everlasting joy shall be upon their heads; 　they shall obtain joy and gladness, 　and sorrow and sighing shall flee away. 12 "I, I am he that comforts you; 　who are you that you are afraid of man 　　who dies, 　of the son of man who is made like 　　grass,

cf. 57:14; 59:8; 62:10). The cosmic combat has been transformed into the history of the Exodus and the crossing of the Sea of Reeds. In vs. 10c the Dead Sea Scroll reads "in the depths of the sea."

The question of the originality of vs. 11 is difficult. It is rejected by many scholars because it is practically a word-for-word repetition of 35:10 and seems out of place after vss. 9-10. The employment may be explained by the allusion to the **way** in the previous lines and the striking emphasis on the **way** in 35:8. The lines form an eschatological climax similar to other strophes of the poem. Finally, they form the inevitable counterpart to the description of primeval time (cf. the association of beginning and end in vss. 1-3, 12-16). The mistake has been to interpret vss. 9-10 solely as a prayer; they are also an impassioned cry to the arm of Yahweh and are subordinated to the dominant eschatological interest of the writer. When this is understood, there is no serious difficulty. Nevertheless, they may be a later insertion. Instead of **ransomed** (פדויי) the Dead Sea Scroll reads "scattered" (פזורי; cf. Ps. 89:10 [Hebrew 89:11]).

5. Fourth Strophe: The Consolation of Israel (51:12-14)

The impassioned cry of the interlude evokes the immediate answer of the Lord, without the usual introductory appeals (vss. 1, 4, 7). The opening line with its emphatic pronouns and Piel participle connect very well with the main theme of the poem. The characteristic admonition not to fear returns to the climactic *hieros logos* of vs. 7. Man is mortal and transitory, but God is eternal; God is the creator of Israel, and will not

powers and time to Christ, with reference to these opening scenes. . . .

I have never laid out far-reaching plans of my own, but awaited and observed the apparent fulfillments of prophecy and the developments of providence.

Of course, from the beginning of my public life, the church of God, and my country and the world as given to Christ, have been the field of my observation, interest, motives, prayers, and efforts. It is this early providential chart of my labors that has extended them beyond the common sphere of mere pastoral labor.[7]

To be sure, it is not the time element which matters but the assurance that God is at hand and his arm active in current events. Such faith enables him to do "exceeding abundantly."

Vs. 11 is a characteristic lyric outburst, and as a conclusion of the prayer evidences the faith

[7] *Lectures on Political Atheism* (Boston: John P. Jewett & Co., 1852), pp. vi-vii.

in which it is offered. The prophet believed that he and his fellow exiles were facing an "awful moment" to which heaven had "joined great issues"[8] for all mankind. He would have them face it "happy as a lover," for despite perils and hardships, he saw the ransomed of the LORD coming with singing to Zion.

12-13. Forgetting God Brings Fear of Man.— I, I am he confronts men personally with God; it is a favorite phrase with this prophet. The Lord towers before his people, overtopping Babylonian officials and scornful fellow countrymen. Who are you that you are afraid of man who dies? Fear, most difficult of emotions to control, is here counteracted by a stronger fear —that of bullying man by the threat of Almighty God. In ordeals where men are menaced, whether by brute might or arrogant contempt, they feel helpless, but believers are attended

[8] Wordsworth, "Character of the Happy Warrior."

13 And forgettest the LORD thy Maker, that hath stretched forth the heavens, and laid the foundations of the earth; and hast feared continually every day because of the fury of the oppressor, as if he were ready to destroy? and where *is* the fury of the oppressor?	13 and have forgotten the LORD, your Maker, who stretched out the heavens and laid the foundations of the earth, and fear continually all the day because of the fury of the oppressor, when he sets himself to destroy? And where is the fury of the oppressor?

abandon her. He has the power to comfort her, for he created the heavens and the earth. The appeal to Yahweh's unique relationship to Israel and to the creation of the universe forms another connection with the interlude.

12. I, I am he that comforts you: See 40:1; 49:13; cf. Exeg. on 51:3. The object of the verb is masculine plural, but in the following line the pronoun is feminine singular. The shift is characteristic, emphasizing the directness of the address to the individual Israelite. The expression **who are you** is not contemptuous, meaning nothing more than "Why?" or "How is it that?" (cf. Exod. 3:11; Judg. 9:28). The oppressor is but mortal (cf. 40:6). The days of **man** are as **grass** (Ps. 90:5), but God is eternal. The time of the oppressor is short and fleeting; God's time outlasts the times of men.

13. The two main verbs, **have forgotten** and **fear** are parallel to and connect with the verb **are afraid of** in vs. 12. Israel's fear shows that she has forgotten her God. Israel's faithfulness was a remembering of her God; unfaithfulness was forgetting. God also remembers and forgets. There may be a conscious echo here of Israel's lament, "Yahweh has forgotten me" (49:14). God first appeals to the unique relationship between himself and Israel: **the LORD, your Maker.** This stresses the primary point of view of the entire poem from the beginning. Then in the characteristic participial phrase (vs. 13*bc*; cf. 40:22-23) the true significance of the Creation, to which the prophet had appealed in the interlude, is pointed out. That the Creator of Israel is the Creator of the universe, and that the two great works of God are indissolubly related, is a constant theme of Second Isaiah (40:22; 43:1; 44:24; 45:12). In view of these supreme realities, historical and cosmic, Israel has no grounds for her constant despair and anxiety. **When he sets himself:** The figure is of setting the arrow on the string of the bow (cf. Pss. 11:2; 7:13). The text of vss. 13*e*-14 is difficult. The rhetorical question, **Where is the fury of the oppressor?** is not unlike Second Isaiah, but it looks like a marginal comment and does not fit in well with the form. If the line is original, it points to the time of the complete destruction of the Babylonian oppressor whose power is transitory (cf. vs. 12).

by a fortifying Presence. This is the experience behind the scene in the fiery furnace in Dan. 3:25. Reverent awareness of God protects against both frightening oppressors and enticing allurements to evil. Francis Paget wrote of Richard William Church: "He seemed to bear about with him a certain hidden, isolating, constraining, and ennobling fear, which quenched the dazzling light of many things that attract most men; a fear which would have to be clean got rid of before time-serving or unreality could have a chance with him." [9] Lincoln had a similar awed reverence for his **Maker.** Salmon P. Chase has left an account of a cabinet meeting at which the president read his proposed Emancipation Proclamation. Lincoln knew that many

[9] *Life and Letters of Dean Church,* ed. Mary C. Church (London: Macmillan & Co., 1897), p. xxii.

of his advisers as well as hosts of his supporters opposed this step, and that it might complicate the public situation.

Gentlemen: I have, as you are aware, thought a great deal about the relation of this war to Slavery: and you all remember that, several weeks ago, I read to you an Order I had prepared on this subject, which, on account of objections made by some of you, was not issued. . . . When the rebel army was at Frederick, I determined, as soon as it should be driven out of Maryland, to issue a Proclamation of Emancipation such as I thought most likely to be useful. I said nothing to anyone; but I made the promise to myself, and (hesitating a little) —to my Maker. . . . I have got you together to hear what I have written down. I do not wish your advice about the main matter—for that I have determined for myself. This I say without intending anything but respect for any one of you. . . . I must do the

14 The captive exile hasteneth that he may be loosed, and that he should not die in the pit, nor that his bread should fail.

15 But I *am* the Lord thy God, that divided the sea, whose waves roared: The Lord of hosts *is* his name.

14 He who is bowed down shall speedily be released;

he shall not die and go down to the Pit, neither shall his bread fail.

15 For I am the Lord your God,

who stirs up the sea so that its waves roar —

the Lord of hosts is his name.

---

14. He who is bowed down shall speedily be released: The prisoner, crouching beneath the burden of his fetters, will be freed from his captivity. The expression "bowed one" (literally) is unusual (cf. 63:1 where it means "marching"), and the versions propose various renderings. The Dead Sea Scroll reads צרה, "distressed." The KJV gives the correct meaning, **the captive exile,** but its literal rendering of the line obscures the thought, which is better expressed by the RSV. The emphasis falls on "soon" or **speedily,** and admirably connects with the beginning of the strophe with its stress on the transitoriness of the oppressing power. **The pit:** Sheol (cf. Pss. 16:10; 74:7; 89:40; Job 33:22, 24; etc.). Duhm, Marti, and others comment on the cold comfort for the exiles here. We should certainly expect something more than this in the light of the rest of the poem. Perhaps it is a very realistic and direct address to the exiles in their situation in Babylon: they will not suffer violent death or starvation (cf. Pss. 34:10; 37:25). God will preserve them and care for them.

6. Fifth Strophe: The God of Creation Is Israel's Covenant Lord (51:15-16)

These verses are considered by many to be an addition. But there are strong arguments for their authenticity: (a) the strong emphasis upon creation, on the one hand, and Yahweh's peculiar relation to Israel, on the other, which pervades the whole poem; (b) the affinities with the servant passages which run through the poem; (c) the characteristic ideas and words of the prophet. Observe how the strophe begins and ends: **For I am the Lord, your God** and **You are my people.** The strophe is remarkable for its combination of cosmic-eschatological elements with others dealing with history and the covenant. Creation, revelation, and redemption are inextricably related.

15. For I am the Lord your God: The divine assurance of vs. 14 is supported by Yahweh's special relationship to his people. Characteristically, the prophet expands this central affirmation of biblical religion. The remainder of the verse is found in Jer. 31:35, which is dependent on Second Isaiah. **The Lord of hosts is his name:** Yahweh, Israel's God, is mighty in power and the sovereign Lord of the universe. Therefore Israel need not fear as she languishes in exile.

---

best I can, and bear the responsibility of taking the course which I feel I ought to take.[10]

14-16. The Fettered Soon to Be Freed.—Israel is pictured as a prisoner crouching in a cell in danger of death through starvation (cf. Jer. 38:9-10). The sovereign Lord of the universe, of the sea and its waves, in the annihilation of the cosmos (vs. 6) protects his servant and makes the servant's mission to mankind culminate in a new world.

The religious thought of recent times, con-

vinced that nature is morally ambiguous, has looked at man's development apart from it. Such humanism cannot long satisfy devout minds. Can spiritual ideals be maintained against the indifference or antagonism of the cosmos? William James spoke of "vast driftings of the cosmic weather," and in similar vein A. Seth Pringle-Pattison said, "It is hard to see what interest lies for God or man in the infinite shiftings of the cosmic dust."[1] Thomas Hardy called the universe "nonchalant," and Frank Harris, walking beside the Thames with Carlyle, reports him as saying: "There is healing in the

---

[10] *Diary and Correspondence of Salmon P. Chase* (Washington: Government Printing Office, 1903), pp. 87-88.

[1] *The Idea of God* (Oxford: Clarendon Press, 1917), p. 30.

16 And I have put my words in thy mouth, and I have covered thee in the shadow of mine hand, that I may plant the heavens, and lay the foundations of the earth, and say unto Zion, Thou *art* my people.

16 And I have put my words in your mouth,
and hid you in the shadow of my hand,
stretching out[p] the heavens
and laying the foundations of the earth,
and saying to Zion, 'You are my people.' "

[p] Syr: Heb *plant*

16. The two finite verbs of vs. 16*ab* are expanded by three infinitive phrases, an unusual construction (Kautzsch, *Gesenius' Hebrew Grammar,* sec. 114*c*), particularly in this context since the infinitives do not seem to follow naturally from the verb they modify. It is obvious, however, that there is a momentous disclosure here, something of unprecedented import. The words (vs. 16*ab*) center in the commission to Israel and are derived from the servant poems (49:2; 50:4; cf. Jer. 1:9). But how are the following infinitive phrases related to the commission? As the lines stand, the meaning seems to be that God has made Israel the agent of his revelation, putting his words in Israel's mouth, and has protected and preserved her in a unique way. But then follow three phrases, the first two of which are cosmic in character, the last covenantal. The issue is the significance of the two cosmic phrases. In the context both before and after, the only probable meaning is that God is about to create a new world of righteousness, a new heaven and a new earth in the place of the old which will vanish and wear out (vs. 6; cf. 65:17; 66:22). The association of historical and cosmic features which is so pronounced a feature of the poem reaches its climax here. Israel's mission in the world is stated in the most universal ranges of biblical eschatology. The new heaven and earth are set within a framework of the people of revelation. Israel as the servant of the Lord has a supreme obligation resting upon her. Her life in history had always been one of responsibility and accountability (cf. Exod. 19:3*b*-8). This was the meaning of her *tôrāh.* In this passage the servant of the Lord is addressed with an eschatological commission, the meaning and consequence of which involves a transformed universe. The final words set the seal on Israel's new covenant existence within this new world: **You are my people.** In the light of the disclosure of this strophe the whole poem assumes new importance, for we recognize the force of the imperatives, the extraordinary words of address, the very striking words of revelation, and the climactic conclusions. The meaning of the interlude (vss. 9-10), with its mythological allusion and historical memory, is evident. The association of beginning and end, of nature and history, of creation and the life of the covenant people is understood. Above all, the unique relationship between God and Israel becomes clear. The final word is the covenant word, but its content has been vastly deepened by its eschatological context. **Stretching out . . . laying . . . and**

air and sunshine; but the sun and air and water care nothing for man's dreams or desires; they have no part nor lot wi' us." [2] A confident monotheism sees God working all factors, in nature as well as in human affairs, together for the achievement of his redemptive purpose. It is a faith akin to Dante's in "the Love that moves the sun and the other stars."

God's redemptive purpose is entrusted to his servant Israel. At the moment Israel may seem like a condemned criminal, loaded with chains in a cell, well-nigh famished, but **he shall not die and go down to the Pit.** Neither physically

[2] *Contemporary Portraits,* 1st Series (New York: Brentano's, 1920), p. 4.

nor spiritually will Israel face extinction as its people often feared. She is the bearer of God's message and can depend on his protection. And best of all, the forces of the whole creation co-operate with the servant nation in the mission entrusted to it. The climax of the poem brings these thoughts into combination:

**stretching out the heavens
and laying the foundations of the earth,
and saying to Zion, "You are my people."**

This is the assurance which God gives his servant church. She has seemed, perhaps still seems, in danger of extinction in some lands. She has felt herself starving in others for lack

| 17 ¶ Awake, awake, stand up, O Jerusalem, which hast drunk at the hand of the LORD the cup of his fury; thou hast drunken | 17 Rouse yourself, rouse yourself, stand up, O Jerusalem, you who have drunk at the hand of the LORD the cup of his wrath, |

---

saying: Read as infinitives, either "to stretch out . . ." or "that I may stretch forth. . . ." The first infinitive involves a slight emendation. Hebrew has לנטע, **plant,** but in vs. 13, which is plainly the source of the lines in vs. 16, the verb is לנטה, "stretch out," and this is in conformity with the prophet's usage elsewhere. In vs. 13 the cosmic lines are similarly set in a framework of the covenant life of the chosen people.

D. The Lord Has Become King (51:17–52:12)

The exalted theme of the imminent coming of the King, first announced in the heavenly council of the prologue, is here brought to full and complete expression. With a great and outstretched arm Yahweh came to his people in the dark hours of Egyptian bondage in a mighty act of deliverance; he now bares his holy arm in the eyes of all nations. The heralds of the glad tidings of peace and salvation proclaim with an exultant shout: "Your God has become king." The days of mourning are past; the time of consolation and comfort has arrived. As the first Exodus was celebrated by Miriam's passionate hymn of redemption, so the new age is ushered in by a new song of redemption in which history and nature join in ecstatic jubilation. The conception of the new exodus is the most profound and most prominent of the motifs in the tradition which Second Isaiah employs to portray the eschatological finale (see A. Zillessen, "Der alte und der neue Exodus," *Archiv für Religionswissenschaft,* XXX [1903], 289 ff.; Johann Fischer, "Das Problem des neuen Exodus in Isaias c. 40-55," *Theologische Quartalschrift,* XXX [1929], 111 ff.). The poem occupies a unique position in the collection. It is the crown of the prophet's message. This is made clear by its position in the sequence of poems, by its literary style and form, and by its literary relationships. The poet gathers up the major emphases of the preceding poems as is seen by his use of 40:1-11; 47:1-15; 48:1-22; 49:1-26. He employs the materials of his literary predecessors (Nahum, Jeremiah, Ezekiel, Lamentations). The great historical traditions associated with the Exodus and the wandering are woven into a fresh eschatological context. Creative imagination and memory are focused upon a single event. Second Isaiah brings to a culmination the thought and aspiration of his people's past, and fashions the matrix of thought for succeeding centuries.

The relation of the poem to its literary context is of the first importance for the understanding of Second Isaiah's poetry and theology. The message of comfort, central in 51:1-16, is now continued (cf. 51:3, 13 with 51:19d, 52:9a). The reference to the fury of the oppressor (51:13) becomes a major motif in the description of the cup of destiny (51:17d, 20d). The imminence of deliverance (51:5, 6g, 8c) here becomes reality, and the emphatic "speedily" of vs. 14 prepares for the great event of 52:1 ff. The "arm of

---

of resources. But because she is the bearer of his gospel he will not only defend and preserve her, but also order the forces of the cosmos and the factors of history so that they shall be revealed as allies in a divine confederacy. Nature therefore becomes a fortifying symbol of the all-sufficient might and wisdom of God. With a believing poet Christians may affirm:

By so many roots as the marsh-grass sends in the sod
I will heartily lay me a-hold on the greatness of
God.[3]

[3] Sidney Lanier, "The Marshes of Glynn."

51:17–52:12. The Lord Has Become King.— In the previous poem the announcement had been made, "My deliverance is near, my salvation has gone forth." The present imaginative poem begins in tragedy, as the poet places himself in Jerusalem when the long-besieged city is falling, passes on to contemplate the Lord returning to restore her desolations, then with a swift survey of Israel's checkered history, back to Babylon, whence he summons the captives to set out on their triumphant journey home. His aim is to rouse the hesitant, low-spirited people to follow their God on his vic-

| the dregs of the cup of trembling, *and* wrung *them* out. | who have drunk to the dregs the bowl of staggering. |

Yahweh," a pervasive eschatological symbol of the poems, especially in our literary setting (51:5, 9; 53:1), finds its perfect interpretation in the event (52:10). The motifs of judgment and salvation constitute the two major divisions of the poem. The fervent mood of 51:9 ff. has its counterpart in 52:1 ff. Not least important is the connection of the final strophe of 51:1-16 with what follows in the next poem, for the relation of Yahweh and his people is everywhere in the foreground. Note the succinct line of 51:22: **Your God, who pleads the cause of his people** (cf. 51:16e).

The construction of the poem has been interpreted in various ways. Many scholars find three major strophes (51:17-23; 52:1-6, 7-12). The triadic form is certainly characteristic of several of Second Isaiah's poems, and it is possible that this is intended here. But this makes the strophes unusually long; moreover, within these units are found evidences of another organization. A more difficult problem is the character of 52:3-6, which disturbs the continuity and is reminiscent of later writers like Zechariah. The RSV puts it in prose. If 52:3-6 is omitted we have two triads (51:17-18, 19-20, 21-23; 52:1-2, 7-8, 9-10) with the climax on the third strophe of each, and a coda. The meter is 3+2 almost throughout.

1. First Strophe: The Cup of Divine Judgment (51:17-18)

Jerusalem, portrayed as a mother (vs. 18) and wife (52:1), lies prostrate under the heavy blows of divine judgment. She is bidden rise, for the time of her redemption is at hand. The judgment is symbolized by the figure of the fateful cup.

17. The double imperative is in the reflexive form (Hithpalel) in contrast to the simple Qal of 51:9 (cf. 64:6). After long years of stupor and lifelessness, Jerusalem must arouse herself and stand up. The double imperative of 52:1 picks up the call and interprets its meaning. **The cup of wrath** is a favorite symbol of prophetic eschatology (best illustrated by Jer. 25:15-31; see also Hab. 2:16; Ezek. 23:31-34; Lam. 4:21; Obad. 16; Zech. 12:2; Pss. 60:3; 75:8; Rev. 14:10; 16:19). **At the hand of the Lord:** Cf. 40:2. **The bowl of staggering:** I.e., which causes staggering. The word for **bowl** (קֻבַּעַת) appears only here and in vs. 22, but it is found in the Ugaritic inscriptions (1 Aqhat 216, 218; see Gordon, *Ugaritic Handbook,* p. 181), in parallelism, as here, with the word for **cup** (*kôs*). In vs. 17e, the word *kôs* is repeated after קֻבַּעַת, **bowl**, an obvious gloss (cf. Vulg., *ad fundum calicis soporis*). The word *tar'ēlāh*, **staggering**, appears only here, in vs.

---

torious march to establish a purified and jubilant Zion.

51:17-20. Captured Jerusalem.—The prophet had probably never seen that city; certainly he had not been alive when it fell; but with poetic self-identification he sets himself within it at the hour of its complete defeat and humiliation. (Instances of corresponding poetic sympathy may be found in Walt Whitman's "Song of Myself," Sec. 33, and Edna St. Vincent Millay's "Renascence," lines beginning "In infinite remorse of soul.") For the appalling plight of a fallen city one may read Euripides' *Trojan Women,* where the heart-breaking hour of separation is pictured and the bleak prospect of exile faced. Jerusalem in her lowest moment of misery forms the prelude to God's restoration of her to pre-eminent glory. The capacity of a sublime poem to lift an incident out of its time and render it changeless may be found

here. When Homer has put the sack of Troy into his verse, to readers in all generations

> Hector and Ajax will be there again;
> Helen will come upon the wall to see.[4]

The prophet, like his predecessors, never forgets the moral factor:

> **You who have drunk at the hand of the Lord the cup of his wrath.**

His people must not forget that national disaster was doom for sin. In his sympathy he does not permit himself any relaxation of the divine demand. **The bowl of staggering** she had mixed for herself.

None to guide her . . . ; none to take her by the hand. The lack of comforters among Israel's sons had moved the prophet and claimed him

[4] Matthew Arnold, "Palladium."

18 *There is* none to guide her among all the sons *whom* she hath brought forth; neither *is there any* that taketh her by the hand of all the sons *that* she hath brought up.

19 These two *things* are come unto thee; who shall be sorry for thee? desolation, and destruction, and the famine, and the sword: by whom shall I comfort thee?

18 There is none to guide her
  among all the sons she has borne;
there is none to take her by the hand
  among all the sons she has brought up.

19 These two things have befallen you —
  who will condole with you? —
devastation and destruction, famine and
  sword;
  who will comfort you?*q*

q One ancient Ms Gk Syr Vg: Heb *how may I comfort you*

22, and in Ps. 60:5 (Hebrew). **Drunk to the dregs:** Cf. 40:2. Lit., "You have drunk, you have drained."

18. In a characteristic change of mood the prophet contemplates Zion's abject condition. Lying there as a poor widow, she has no one—repetition accentuates the pathos—**to guide** [נהל] **her.** The Dead Sea Scroll has נחל, "inherit" or "possess"; the LXX reads נחם, "comfort." There is no one among all Zion's sons to undertake the restoration of the stricken city. The Dead Sea Scroll reads "you" for **her** in vs. 18*a*. A Ugaritic text (Aqht A, i; see Pritchard, *Ancient Near Eastern Texts,* p. 150) refers to the son

> Who takes him by the hand when he's drunk,
> Carries him when he's sated with wine.

Ivar Engnell (*Studies in the Divine Kingship in the Ancient Near East* [Uppsala: Almqvist & Wiksells, 1943], p. 210) sees 51:17 ff. as belonging to the royal passion ideology, but this is unlikely. Cf. vs. 20.

2. Second Strophe: Jerusalem's Abject and Helpless Condition (51:19-20)

The first quatrain interprets the figure of the first half of the previous strophe (vs. 17*cdef*), the second explains the latter half (vs. 18). The two questions express succinctly the writer's thought. The strophe summarizes the disaster which befell Jerusalem in 586 B.C.

19 The first line is consciously fashioned after 47:9 and is a good example of the poet's dependence upon previous materials. The poignant questions are in the style of Jeremiah, the classical poet of the lament (Jer. 15:5; cf. Nah. 3:7). **These two things:** I.e., the ruin of the land by devastation and destruction and of the people by famine and sword (cf. 47:9). The verb **condole** means, lit., "to shake the head to and fro in grief" (Jer. 16:45; 22:10; Nah. 3:7; Job 2:11). The verb **comfort** in the M.T. is in the first

---

for his mission (cf. 40:1). Israel's spiritual penury had been the grief of Jeremiah (23: 9 ff.). Her loneliness for want of encouragers is the burden of an exilic psalmist (Ps. 69:20-21). Does not contemporary society suffer from the same deficiency? How few, if any, among current novelists, poets, essayists, historians, are heartening! Comfort cannot be drawn from the earthly scene, and secular minds are bankrupt.

Who will condole with you? is a perennial question in desperate times. If we read "How shall I comfort you?" the prophet is confronting his own problem, "What shall I cry?" (40:6). Self-questioning in the face of social calamity induces the sense of inadequacy and leads to God for his word.

Jerusalem's inhabitants had the frightful sensation of being trapped like an antelope in a net. The metaphor vividly recalls the weeks of the appalling siege with their privations and terrors. It applies as well to the long years of captivity. So a modern generation also knows itself caught in overwhelming historical situations. Men struggle, and struggle vainly, like the poor creature snared. Such situations have moral causes. Nations and individuals are in the meshes of social guilt, and are full of the wrath of the Lord. Like Marley's ghost in Dickens' *Christmas Carol,* we drag behind us the impeding chain of past neglects and misdoings. It is this which requires a religious message, a gospel of forgiveness and spiritual release. Only a pardoned people, reconciled with God, will have

20 Thy sons have fainted, they lie at the head of all the streets, as a wild bull in a net: they are full of the fury of the LORD, the rebuke of thy God.

21 ¶ Therefore hear now this, thou afflicted, and drunken, but not with wine:

22 Thus saith thy Lord the LORD, and thy God *that* pleadeth the cause of his people, Behold, I have taken out of thine hand the cup of trembling, *even* the dregs of the cup of my fury; thou shalt no more drink it again:

20 Your sons have fainted,
   they lie at the head of every street
   like an antelope in a net;
they are full of the wrath of the LORD,
   the rebuke of your God.

21 Therefore hear this, you who are afflicted,
   who are drunk, but not with wine:
22 Thus says your Lord, the LORD,
   your God who pleads the cause of his
      people:
"Behold, I have taken from your hand
   the cup of staggering;
the bowl of my wrath
   you shall drink no more;

---

person, but the versions (LXX, Syriac, Targ., Vulg.) and the Dead Sea Scroll read the third (see RSV).

20. Fainted or "swooned" (see Lam. 2:11, 19): The phrase **at the head of all the streets** is metrically superfluous and out of place; it was probably inserted from Lam. 2:19 by a copyist. Read, "they lie down swooning." **Like an antelope in a net:** A figure of the city's siege. The city is exhausted by its vain efforts to free itself. Its citizens are **full of the wrath of the LORD.** The last lines bring the description of Jerusalem's plight to a conclusion, and reach back to the wrath of divine judgment in vs. 17. The theocentric stress is particularly effective and necessary here.

3. THIRD STROPHE: THE CUP OF WRATH (51:21-23)

The prophet employs every device to call attention to the importance of the event he is about to communicate: first, the climactic position of the strophe; second, the introductory **therefore,** so characteristic of the introductory word of the threat (but instead of threat a glowing promise); third, the emphatic **hear this** characteristic of prophetic oracles; fourth, the extended words of address, which summarize the foregoing lines; fifth, the oracular formula; sixth, the apposition containing the theocentric line (vs. 22b), and finally seventh, the word **Behold** which presents the great disclosure. The situation of Jerusalem and that of her oppressors are to be reversed. Thus the prophet portrays a major feature of his eschatology: the reversal of fortunes of those who suffer and those who cause the suffering (cf. Luke 6:21-26; Matt. 5:3-12).

21. Hear this, you who are afflicted: Another echo from the taunt song on Babylon (47:8). The word of address to Babylon is ʿadhînāh, "voluptuous one"; to Jerusalem, ʿaniyyāh, "afflicted one"—possibly an intended play on words (cf. 54:11). The second line of the verse is dependent upon 29:9.

22. The Lord enters into judgment in behalf of his own people against their enemies (cf. 41:1–42:4; 43:8-13; 44:6-8, 21-23; 45:20-25; 48:14-16; 50:8-9). The verb **I have taken** is a perfect of certainty; render, "I am taking." In the characteristic manner of Second

---

energy and courage to undertake the arduous march with him and the even more taxing enterprise of re-establishing the nation and setting forth on its mission to mankind (cf. 40:2). **Your sons have fainted:** The defeatism that overwhelms many in disasters, and for which God alone in his grace and greatness is the cure.

21-23. God Pleads the Cause of His People.— It is the paradox of faith that God who punishes

us is on our side. Wrath is love's reaction to evil, and love is inexorable. It never lets down its standards for its devoted. But it must and will do everything to enable them to achieve its loftiest purpose for them. God is both just and the justifier (Rom. 3:26).

The contemporary generation may have its spiritual unease. Even if men do not have a sense of personal guilt, they may know themselves implicated in the social breakdown.

23 But I will put it into the hand of them that afflict thee; which have said to thy soul, Bow down, that we may go over: and thou hast laid thy body as the ground, and as the street, to them that went over.

23 and I will put it into the hand of your tormentors,
who have said to you,
'Bow down, that we may pass over';
and you have made your back like the ground
and like the street for them to pass over."

52 Awake, awake, put on thy strength, O Zion; put on thy beautiful gar-

52 Awake, awake,
put on your strength, O Zion;
put on your beautiful garments,

Isaiah, the expressions of vs. 17 (RSV) are reversed: **cup of staggering** and **bowl of wrath** (for a historical parallel of such a reversal of situations see 10:5-15).

23. Your tormentors: The same word occurs not infrequently in Lamentations (1:4, 5, 12; 3:32). Both the LXX and the Dead Sea Scroll add "and of those who afflict you," which is probably the better text (cf. 49:26). The reference is to the Babylonians. Torrey aptly calls attention to what is said of the servant in 50:6; 53:5. The cruel custom described here was practiced in Oriental antiquity—Josh. 10:24; Ps. 110:1; and the monuments, e.g., the stele of Naram-Sin (see Alfred Jeremias, *Handbuch der altorientalischen Geisteskultur,* p. 68) and Anu-bânini (see Hugo Gressmann, *Altorientalische Texte und Bilder zum Alten Testament* [Tübingen: J. C. B. Mohr, 1909], II, 80). In this context the expression is probably employed as imagery. The closing lines finely recall the abasement of Jerusalem described at the beginning, thus forming a framework for the first half of the poem. It is especially impressive here in view of the opening of the next strophe.

4. FOURTH STROPHE: "AWAKE, O JERUSALEM" (52:1-2)

In sharp and sudden contrast to the picture of Zion's degradation, the poet takes up the call of 51:17 and begins his hymn of redemption, a song of Zion. The ringing

---

"Under the perpetual smile of modernity there is a grimace of disillusion and cynicism." [5] We cannot accept ourselves until God's forgiveness renders us at one with him. We have tasted his fury; we must be as sure of his grace.

The transfer of the chalice of God's indignation to Israel's foes is an instance of the retributions of history. It has been seen in the cases of Germany and Japan; and other nations, failing to repent and walk humbly with God, will likewise suffer judgment. "One lesson, and only one, history may be said to repeat with distinctness: that the world is built somehow on moral foundations; that, in the long run, it is well with the good; in the long run, it is ill with the wicked." [6]

The enforced humiliation of the inhabitants of Jerusalem is made vivid: **You have made your back . . . like the street for them to pass over.** The nation's sin had been arrogant self-suffi-

ciency, unmindful and independent of God. Her discipline is to correct this pride. Humility in men, especially in nations, is not easily come by. "The very *lowest* degree of it is a difficult *height* to climb." [7] And concededly it is the essential, the prerequisite, to all other virtues.

The only wisdom we can hope to acquire
Is the wisdom of humility: humility is endless. [8]

Humility is achieved by companying with One infinitely above us. After a visit with Tennyson, Edward Fitzgerald wrote: "Perhaps I have received some benefit in the now more distinct consciousness of my dwarfishness." [9] For a people or an individual to walk with God is to walk **humbly.**

52:1-2. *Awake, O Zion.*—The names, **O Zion, O Jerusalem,** the holy city, would stir the exiles.

[5] Reinhold Niebuhr, *The Nature and Destiny of Man* (New York: Charles Scribner's Sons, 1941), I, 122.

[6] J. A. Froude, *Short Studies in Great Subjects,* 1st Series (New York: Charles Scribner's Sons, 1905), pp. 22-23.

[7] F. W. Faber, *Spiritual Conferences* (New York: Murphy & Co., n.d.), p. 32.

[8] T. S. Eliot, *Four Quartets* (London: Faber & Faber; New York: Harcourt, Brace & Co., 1943), p. 14. Used by permission.

[9] A. M. Terhune, *Life of Edward Fitzgerald* (London: Oxford University Press, 1947), p. 81.

ments, O Jerusalem, the holy city: for henceforth there shall no more come into thee the uncircumcised and the unclean.	O Jerusalem, the holy city; for there shall no more come into you the uncircumcised and the unclean.

imperatives are given an almost ecstatic quality by the double repetition in vs. 1*ab*, **awake, awake, put on, . . . put on . . .** , and by the climactic arrangement in vs. 2, **shake yourself, . . . arise, . . . loose,** which is heightened by the words of address in chiastic form: **O Zion, . . . O Jerusalem, the holy city. O captive Jerusalem, . . . O captive daughter of Zion.** The verses form a characteristic hymnic introduction to what follows, though vs. 1*ef* presents in its form the usual opening of the body of the hymn. This literary form, almost invariably introduced by *kî*, **for,** is repeated throughout the poem (vss. 3, 8*cd*, 9*cd*) and reaches its superb climax in the repeated *kî* lines of vs. 12. The content of the prophet's thought corresponds to the beauty and power of the literary form and style (cf. 12:1-2, 4-6; 42:10-12; and the enthronement hymns, Pss. 47; 93; 96–99).

52:1. Logically vs. 2 should precede vs. 1, but as Volz points out, the Hebrew poet writes more according to his mood and feeling than according to the logical sequence. The description is in conscious contrast to the taunt song on Babylon (47:1 ff.). **Awake, awake:** Cf. 51:9, 17. Observe how the final strophe employs a similar repetition (vs. 11). In keeping with the great event, the radical transformation of the existing state of affairs, Zion must clothe herself with **strength,** in the beautiful **garments** which befit the unique occasion. Instead of עֻזֵּךְ, **your strength,** some have proposed עֶדְיֵךְ, "your ornaments," but the change is not necessary. The days of mourning and of servitude are over; Zion is no longer a slave. Here we are on the threshold of the conception of the new Jerusalem. It will be a **holy city** as never before (cf. 48:2; Joel 4:17; Rev. 21:2), holy in its purity and freedom from the corruptions of the past. As in the enthronement hymns the Lord is clothed in majesty and strength (Ps. 93:1) when he ascends his royal throne, so Zion must prepare for the coming of the King by adorning herself in fresh apparel. The garments worn next to the body are indissolubly connected with the character of the wearer. A holy person wears holy garments; a king wears royal robes and bears the scepter and crown; Jerusalem's new clothes correspond to her transformed status. Both historical and eschatological motifs are at work in this imagery, which in later apocalyptic was greatly developed (Rev. 3:3-4, 18; 4:4; etc.). **The uncircumcised and the unclean:** (Cf. Nah. 1:15; Rev. 21:27; 22:14-15.) Not merely a reference to freedom from foreign oppression (cf. 25:1, 10; 32:18; 33:18 ff.), but to the cultically unclean, revealing the inveterate syncretism which had corrupted Israel's faith, as vs. 11 makes clear. Kissane sees an allusion to the holy way of 35:8, over which the unclean may not pass.

The prophet had boldly bidden God "put on strength" (51:9); now he summons the downhearted people, as God's representatives to mankind, to do the same. As his commissioned nation, they can possess derived strength with which to attempt the task he sets them.

Beautiful garments are Zion's as the future seat of God's glory. This anticipation is a stimulus to present effort. They are "to borrow for poor today from rich tomorrow." In a letter Edward Rowland Sill asks: "Haven't you often been newly startled at the sudden realization of how much man owes to Hope?" [1] Stevenson, on a walk in Fife, meets a laborer, cleaning a byre (cow-shed):

[1] Parker, *Edward Rowland Sill, His Life and Work,* p. 65.

The man was to all appearances as heavy . . . as any English clodhopper; but I knew I was in Scotland, and launched out forthright into Education and Politics and the aim of one's life. [The man said:] "Him that has aye something ayont need never be weary." [2]

The holiness of the restored Zion is not again to be defiled by the uncircumcised. Living among pagans these Jews stressed the outward marks of their distinctive relationship with God. Circumcision set them apart from their heathen neighbors. Present-day Protestants lay little stress on outward symbols of their Christian loyalty—church attendance, the observance of the Lord's day, grace at meals, family worship,

[2] *Letters,* I, 71-72.

2 Shake thyself from the dust; arise, *and* sit down, O Jerusalem: loose thyself from the bands of thy neck, O captive daughter of Zion.

3 For thus saith the LORD, Ye have sold yourselves for nought; and ye shall be redeemed without money.

4 For thus saith the Lord GOD, My people went down aforetime into Egypt to sojourn there; and the Assyrian oppressed them without cause.

2 Shake yourself from the dust, arise;
    O captive[r] Jerusalem;
loose the bonds from your neck,
    O captive daughter of Zion.

3 For thus says the LORD: "You were sold for nothing, and you shall be redeemed without money. 4 For thus says the Lord GOD: My people went down at the first into Egypt to sojourn there, and the Assyrian

[r] Cn: Heb *sit*

2. For **captive** the Hebrew reads **sit** or "sit down," interpreted by many scholars to mean "sit on the throne as queen," a fine contrast to 47:1 (cf. Pss. 29:10; 99:1; 102:12; etc.). If the slight emendation of the RSV and many commentators is accepted, the parallelism with the fourth line is restored in a manner characteristic of Second Isaiah. **Loose the bonds from your neck:** The monuments picture captives bound together by a rope from neck to neck.

5. INSERTION: WITHOUT COMPENSATION (52:3-6)

The passage is beset with difficulties, since the meter is by no means clear. The RSV, Kittel, and other scholars render it as prose; Torrey, Kissane, *et al.* put it in poetic form. It has probably suffered in transmission. In support of its originality are the following considerations: (*a*) the verses attach themselves to vss. 2 ff. with its description of Zion as an enslaved captive; (*b*) the reference to the Babylonian captors suits the context; (*c*) the climax of vs. 6 may prepare the way for vss. 7 ff.; (*d*) the history of Israel's suffering under the Egyptians, the Assyrians, and the Babylonians in the eschatological framework is artistically effective and theologically profound; (*e*) the lines may anticipate the next poem. On the other hand, the style is not that of the context and actually mars the structure of the poem. It is best, therefore, to delete the verses as a later insertion.

3. Yahweh has punished his people for their sins, but Babylon had no right or claim over Israel. Therefore the Redeemer is under no requirement to pay the ransom money for the enslaved people. The Lord redeems them for his own sake. The emphasis falls on the phrases **for nothing** and **without money** as is shown both by the repetition and the striking emphasis in vs. 5.

4. As the prophet scans history, he thinks of the Egyptian bondage and the Assyrian oppression. These were the major exploiting powers in the tradition of his people. The Hebrews had gone to Egypt of their own volition as sojourners in a time of famine, and the Egyptians later made them slaves without any cause or right. The Assyrians were the instruments of the divine judgment (cf. 10:5-6), but were solely interested in their own power and without conscience pursued their imperialistic designs (cf. 10:7-11).

etc. But the life of the Spirit needs an outer structure, especially in a secular age. The symbols are not in themselves religion. Paul had to correct an overemphasis upon them: "In Christ Jesus neither circumcision availeth any thing, nor uncircumcision, but a new creature" (Gal. 6:15). Nevertheless, outward marks assist fidelity of soul.

No more: To the prophet the restored Zion is the final stage of history. This is akin to the N.T. expectation of the proximate advent of Jesus and the end of the world. Literally, neither hope was justified; but spiritually, in the Jewish and the Christian church a new stage was reached in God's achievement of his purpose.

3-6. God's Soliloquy on Israel's History.— God tells himself that he gained nothing by handing the nation to her enemies; now he asks nothing for redeeming her. He is not self-seeking in his dealings with men: all is of grace. The retrospect shows a record of suffering. Sold at the outset into Egyptian slavery, and later invaded by Assyrians without right; **now therefore**

5 Now therefore, what have I here, saith the LORD, that my people is taken away for nought? they that rule over them make them to howl, saith the LORD; and my name continually every day *is* blasphemed.

6 Therefore my people shall know my name: therefore *they shall know* in that day that I *am* he that doth speak: behold, *it is* I.

oppressed them for nothing. 5 Now therefore what have I here, says the LORD, seeing that my people are taken away for nothing? Their rulers wail, says the LORD, and continually all the day my name is despised. 6 Therefore my people shall know my name; therefore in that day they shall know that it is I who speak; here am I."

---

5. **Now therefore** introduces the major thought after the reference to Egypt and Assyria. **What have I here?** (*Qerê* and the Dead Sea Scroll) is interpreted variously: "What have I to do here?" (Volz); "What am I about?" (Wade); "What have I received?" (Cheyne); or "What do I find here?" (Skinner; Amer. Trans.). The last best expresses the true meaning. Yahweh is present among the exiles in Babylon, and reflects upon the situation there in contrast to the situation in Egypt and in Assyria. **Seeing that:** The Hebrew *kî* here serves the function of quotation marks. This gives the line its proper effect. **Their rulers wail, . . . and continually:** The phrase is difficult. Ehrlich and Skinner read, "For nought are its [Israel's] rulers profaned"; Volz, "My sons howl constantly because of oppression"; Torrey, "Their rulers mock" (Piel). The Dead Sea Scroll reads והוללו for יהילילו. Render "Their rulers deal presumptuously [or "boast"] continually" (cf. Rom. 2:24). The weakness of Israel occasioned mockery and derision among her enemies (Joel 2:17; Pss. 42:10 [Hebrew 42:11]; 79:10; 115:2). The Lord maintains the honor of his own **name,** however, and will not permit it to be profaned (48:11). The exile of his people and the profanation of his name are the reasons for his imminent intervention.

6. The verse is emphatic. It is questionable whether the second **therefore** should be retained. The LXX, Vulg., and Dead Sea Scroll omit it. The Hebrew does not contain the repetition of **they shall know.** In the great day of redemption (vs. 3) Yahweh's people who have been carried into exile will know the name which their rulers despise. Then, as in the time of the covenant (Exod. 20:1), they will be the people who know his name. But the words carry an added meaning. The people will know that their God is sovereign and omnipotent, that he is Lord of history, and that the destiny of Israel as of the nations is in his power. **They shall know** by the events of the day of the Lord that his words and deeds are one; in the events they will recognize the fulfillment of his words (cf. 45:19; 46:11; 48:15-16). The Piel participle of *dābhar* (**speak**) is used absolutely here. The closing words are independent: **here am I.** Thus the whole history of the past—Egyptian bondage, Assyrian oppression, and Babylonian captivity—is focused upon the day of the divine revelation and salvation.

---

what have I here? A more disastrous event than either, blotting out the nation, brings its Lord's name into contempt: **Continually all the day my name is despised.** God's reputation is bound up with his people's. As in Ezekiel, the motive for God's intervention is to let his own people and the world know him. **Therefore in that day they shall know that it is I who speak; here am I.**

If we believe that world justice and friendship are God's will, then the failure to achieve them brings God into disrepute. All nations have deserved their discipline because of their disobedience; but God's purpose must not suffer defeat. That would involve his impotence.

Men's hopes may collapse, but not God's aims for the race.

> So God shall uncreate,
> Be frustrate, do, undo, and labour lose,
> Not well conceiv'd of God.[3]

Our confidence in the church is similarly based on God's name. The church may appear to have no "beautiful garments"; her grace may seem shabby and tattered. But her members have been baptized into God's name; and God has begun his good work for mankind in her. His faithfulness continues. Her divisions,

[3] Milton, *Paradise Lost*, Bk. IX, ll. 943-45.

7 ¶ How beautiful upon the mountains are the feet of him that bringeth good tidings, that publisheth peace; that bringeth good tidings of good, that publisheth salvation; that saith unto Zion, Thy God reigneth!

7 How beautiful upon the mountains
    are the feet of him who brings good
      tidings,
who publishes peace, who brings good
      tidings of good,
who publishes salvation,
    who says to Zion, "Your God reigns."

6. Fifth Strophe: "Your God Has Become King" (52:7-8)

In three magnificent strophes (vss. 7-8, 9-10, 11-12) the poet describes the coming of Yahweh to the holy city of Zion. Behind his thought lies the ancient conception of the day of Yahweh. This great theme of Hebrew religion was expressed classically in the prophetic representations of Amos, Isaiah, and Zephaniah, and later in the enthronement psalms. On that day the Lord reveals himself in theophany, conquers his foes, asserts his sovereignty, and comes to judge his people in righteousness. Second Isaiah employs this familiar category but uses it for his own purposes and in his own way. The event which he celebrates is more than the defeat of a historical enemy, more than the coming of Cyrus or any single nation. The theophany is universal, world wide in its range, and it comes at the end, fulfilling the whole of Israel's history and tradition (40:5). The imagery is drawn from the field of battle. Yahweh comes as a conqueror (40:10), as a man of war (42:13), victorious over all who oppose him. His holy arm is laid bare in the sight of all the peoples (40:10), and his victory ushers in salvation and peace. The day of consolation—so striking a feature of the poems throughout—dawns upon the chosen people (40:1). Once more, at the end of her warfare (40:2), Israel knows her God as mighty Redeemer.

These three strophes contain the center and climax of the entire collection of poems. The prophet plumbs still greater depths, but the eschatological event which it is his prophetic function to proclaim (40:1-11) is here more powerfully and clearly portrayed than anywhere else. The vision of the coming of Israel's Lord and King (40:9-10) fills his mind with ecstatic excitement. His mood is exultant. Yet in characteristic fashion his closing lines are drawn from the heart of the great tradition of the Exodus. Contemplation of the end stirs his memory of the past, and no event in Israel's history was so central as the deliverance from the land of her bondage. The writer employs repetition, climax, and direct quotation with superb effect. His imperatives continue, but they are more glowing and joyous here than in vss. 1-2. He deals with the great superlatives of eschatology, yet the lines follow in sound order, and the final lines of each strophe (and half-strophe) enshrine the essence of his thought.

7. How beautiful upon the mountains: See Ps. 125:2. The prophet concentrates on the swift approach of the messenger, and watches his feet as they bring him nearer the city. Many times in Israel's history the people waited with anxiety and impatience for news from the field of battle. The expression following **feet** is a single word in Hebrew, *mebhassēr* (cf. 40:9; 41:27; 61:1). Cf. a similar scene in II Sam. 18:25-27, where David watches the approach of the messenger from the field of battle. The "herald" or "evangelist" is one of the dramatis personae. His function is to announce the advent of

her scanty faith, her halfhearted members, the huge obstacles in her path and her redoubtable antagonists may dismay us; but his assurance to these exiles holds: **My people shall know my name.** The church is indissolubly linked with him; and were she to go down in defeat, it would bring him into contempt. He has committed himself, and keeps saying to us, **Here am I.**

7-10. *The Lord Returns to Zion.*—This poem recalls the overture in 40:1-11. The bringer of good tidings, like the voices in 40:3-8, is one of this prophet's dramatis personae. He has a single function—to announce to Zion that her God has become king. The watchmen in Jerusalem look forth and see the Lord returning; their eyes meet his. It is not the company of exiles arriving which claims attention but, as in

8 Thy watchmen shall lift up the voice; with the voice together shall they sing: for they shall see eye to eye, when the LORD shall bring again Zion.

8 Hark, your watchmen lift up their voice, together they sing for joy; for eye to eye they see the return of the LORD to Zion.

---

the king. The figure is portrayed with great fluidity. Sometimes he seems to be a group, as in 40:9; here he is an individual. The apostle Paul quotes this passage in Rom. 10:15 and identifies the *mᵉbhassēr* with the heralds of the gospel. Second Isaiah is dependent upon Nah. 1:15 in the first three lines of the verse. **Who publishes peace . . . :** Observe the effect of the repetition in these lines. The words, **peace, good,** and **salvation** give the content of the event. The Dead Sea Scroll reads: מבשר מבשר שלום משמיע טוב מש . . . ישועה, "who brings good tidings, who brings good tidings of peace, who publishes good, who publishes (?) salvation." However, there is no necessity for rejecting the M.T. **Your God reigns:** Or "Your God has become king" or "Your God is king." Cf. 40:10; Pss. 47:8; 93:1; 97:1; 99:1; Rev. 19:6. The theme of Yahweh's kingship is ancient (Judg. 8:22-23; I Sam. 8:7) and receives its classical formulation in Isaiah's vision (6:5; cf. 24:23; 33:20; 43:15; 44:6). In Babylon at the celebration of the New Year's festival Marduk's accession to the throne was celebrated by a cultic procession amid the cultic cries of his devotees. At the high point of the festival the cry "Marduk has become king" rang out and the creator-god Marduk was enthroned (cf. Pss. 47; 93; 96–99). Second Isaiah is probably employing these Babylonian elements for the picture of the eschatological event of Yahweh's enthronement. The new age is introduced by the inauguration of Yahweh as King (Henri Frankfort, *Kingship and the Gods* [Chicago: University of Chicago Press, 1948], pp. 313-33; H. Zimmern, *Das babylonische Neujahrsfest* [Leipzig: J. C. Hinrichs, 1926; "Der alte Orient"]). See Hans-Joachim Kraus, *Die Königherrschaft Gottes im Alten Testament* (Tübingen: J. C. B. Mohr, 1951), for the view that an ancient royal festival of Zion is here filled with new content. The original festival associated with the election of David and of Zion as Yahweh's dwelling is now reformulated by Second Isaiah: (*a*) Zion is chosen again (Yahweh's return to Zion); and (*b*) Yahweh himself has become King of his people (not a member of the line of David). Thus the kingdom of God is ushered in.

8. The prophet's vision turns from the approaching herald on the mountains to the **watchmen** stationed on the ruined walls of Jerusalem (cf. 21:6-9; 62:6). As the watchmen hear the herald's tidings they break out into shouts of jubilation, just as Miriam broke forth into song when the Lord came to the deliverance of his people at the crossing of the Sea of Reeds (Exod. 15:21). The expression **eye to eye** does not refer to the dense throng of the watchers (Duhm), nor to the unity and harmony with which they greet the event, but rather to the clear view they have of Yahweh. The Lord had spoken to Moses "mouth to mouth" (Num. 12:8) and "face to face" (Exod. 33:11); and as here was seen by Israel "eye to eye" (Num. 14:14). The extreme anthropomorphism is explained by the momentous occasion. All flesh shall see the glory of God. **The return . . . to Zion** does not imply that he had been with the exiles in Babylon, but rather that with the restoration of the city the Lord comes to dwell in the abode of his glory (cf.

40:9-10, it is God who fills the horizon. No doubt he will be leading his people; but they are secondary; eyes fasten on him.

It is the function of ministers to make and keep God central in men's minds. Whatever their message may be in detail—and there is no phase of life to which his reign is irrelevant —it must always proclaim his redeeming sovereignty: "Your God has become king" (Amer. Trans.). The point of this passage is not **Thy God reigneth**—that is always true—but at long

last he is assuming his active rule. It is this which prompts the outburst of joy in vs. 9. As with Luther, there is something almost boisterous in the prophet's delight in God. "Christians are a blissful people, who can rejoice at heart and sing praises, stamp and dance and leap for joy. That is well pleasing to God, and doth our heart good, when we trust God and find in him our pride and joyfulness." [4] A missionary purpose rules the restoration of Israel (vs. 10). She

[4] Sermon preached on Oct. 18, 1529.

9 ¶ Break forth into joy, sing together, ye waste places of Jerusalem: for the LORD hath comforted his people, he hath redeemed Jerusalem.

10 The LORD hath made bare his holy arm in the eyes of all the nations; and all the ends of the earth shall see the salvation of our God.

11 ¶ Depart ye, depart ye, go ye out from thence, touch no unclean *thing;* go ye out of the midst of her; be ye clean, that bear the vessels of the LORD.

9 Break forth together into singing,
    you waste places of Jerusalem;
for the LORD has comforted his people,
    he has redeemed Jerusalem.

10 The LORD has bared his holy arm
    before the eyes of all the nations;
and all the ends of the earth shall see
    the salvation of our God.

11 Depart, depart, go out thence,
    touch no unclean thing;
go out from the midst of her, purify yourselves,
    you who bear the vessels of the LORD.

Ezek. 43:1-5). To the last line the Dead Sea Scroll adds "in mercy." The Targ. reads, "When he shall bring back his Shekinah to Zion."

7. SIXTH STROPHE: COMFORT, REDEMPTION, AND VICTORY (52:9-10)

9. The prophet now calls upon the ancient ruins to come alive and **break forth together into singing.** Lit., "Break forth, sing together." The Dead Sea Scroll has the noun (רינה) for the second verb. This eschatological singing is an authentic expression of Israel's piety (see 44:23; 49:13; 55:12). Music was an accompaniment of her religious life from the beginning of her history. When the stricken city rises from the ashes of her destruction she immediately expresses herself in song, and for two great reasons: the Lord has comforted (cf. 40:1; 49:13; 51:3, 12) and redeemed (43:1; 44:22-23; cf. 41:14; 43:14; 44:6, 24; Luke 2:30) his people. (Albright, *Archaeology and Religion of Israel,* pp. 14-16, 125-26, *et passim.* Albright emphasizes Israel's debt to the Canaanites for her music. See also Ovid Sellers, "Musical Instruments of Israel," *Biblical Archaeologist,* IV [1941], 33-47.) Praise, thankfulness, and joy sound throughout the O.T. Second Isaiah brings these deep stirrings of Israel's piety to a magnificent climax in their eschatological setting (cf. the hymns of the book of Revelation).

10. The Lord prepares for battle. The fervent petition of 51:9 here receives its answer and prepares for 53:1. Yahweh throws back his cloak from his right arm in order that it may not impede him. His **arm is holy** because it is engaged in a holy undertaking (cf. 40:10; 42:13; Ps. 98:1). **All the ends of the earth:** Cf. 40:5; 45:22-23; 48:20; Luke 2:30-31.

8. CODA: THE NEW EXODUS (52:11-12)

The lines follow at once after vs. 10 and form an excellent close (contra Volz). God has prepared the way for his people to return to Zion, and the prophet urgently bids them to depart.

11. Thence: From Babylon (cf. 48:20). The prophet has been placing himself imaginatively in Jerusalem and writes from the perspective of one who is witnessing the

---

is not an "imperial Salem" (as Pope pictured her). In this poem there is no glorification of the nation. She falls into the background, and in her liberation and re-establishment it is the Lord's **arm** which is **bared** in the sight of mankind.

The purposes of God for our race are wrought out through nations and individuals and supremely through his church. But they are instruments merely, and must not claim attention. There is no room for nationalism, egoism, ec-

clesiasticism. The prominence of nation or of man or of church may obscure God's activity. We have taught the self-effacement of individuals; there must also be a corporate self-effacement of nations and churches.

11-12. *Depart from Babylon Uncontaminated.* —The uprooting of a people who had settled in and found their livelihoods in this commercial city was no easy task. To prudent men of business it seemed a terrifying risk. They had accommodated themselves to the new en-

| 12 For ye shall not go out with haste, nor go by flight: for the LORD will go before you; and the God of Israel *will be* your rereward. | 12 For you shall not go out in haste, and you shall not go in flight, for the LORD will go before you, and the God of Israel will be your rear guard. |

event of Yahweh's return to the city. **Touch no unclean thing:** The people must sanctify themselves in keeping with the holy occasion. Yahweh is with them as their leader. They who follow must therefore be holy. The cultic emphasis is unusual, but must be understood in the light of the eschatological situation and historical reminiscence. As so often in Second Isaiah, the affinities with the priestly history are close. As in the Exodus, the priests led the procession with the ark and the cultic appurtenances. There is no suggestion that the Lord's armor-bearers are meant (contra Budde). Nor is it necessary to infer any reference to the edict of Cyrus, which still lies in the future. The passage must be read in the light of the total event described in the preceding verses.

12. In contrast to the time of the Exodus (Exod. 12:11; Deut. 16:3), the exiles will return in peace, for the Lord is their vanguard and **rear guard** (cf. Exod. 14:19-20 [J]). As the pillar of cloud and fire guided Israel in its desert march, so **the LORD will go before you** (cf. Exod. 13:21-22; 14:19). In such fashion the prophet combines the motifs of the Exodus with the return. The emphatic conclusion with the twofold *kî,* **for,** brings the poem to an impressive close. The Dead Sea Scroll adds, "The God of the whole earth he is called."

vironment and built up their enterprises. Under Cyrus, Babylon would continue a center of trade. Why hazard a lifetime's work?

Touch no unclean thing, . . . purify yourselves, you who bear the vessels of the LORD. The vessels are probably no more than poetic symbols, for there was no sacrificial worship during the Exile, and the original vessels could not be recovered. The point is that the devout community should cleanse itself of any taint of paganism, and be ready to set up the worship of the Lord in its purity in the restored city and temple.

Vs. 11 is often used for the singlehearted devotion of those who lead the church's work. George Herbert described a rural parson with "the purity of his mind breaking out, and dilating itself even to his body, clothes and habitation." [5] The soldiers at Scarborough spoke of George Fox as "stiff as a tree and as pure as a bell." The invasion by secular motives—professionalism, commercialism, etc.—of the aims with which men and women serve the church soils and spoils them. Singleness of purpose makes and keeps service pure. John Wesley wrote of himself: "I have one point in view —to promote, so far as I am able, vital, practical religion; and by the grace of God to beget, preserve, and increase the life of God in the souls of men!" [6]

A contrast is drawn in vs. 12 between the

haste in the flight from Egypt and the lack of it in the exodus from Babylon. There had been fear of Pharaoh's pursuit; now Cyrus, God's servant, will assure an orderly departure. There is no criticism of haste or commendation of leisureliness. The situations were different. But where there is no pressure, hurry is wasteful, and in this case, with God leading and protecting, it would evince unbelief.

It was a saying of Joseph Hall's that "moderate speed is a sure help in all proceedings." Among Bacon's *Apothegms* is this: "I knew a wise man, that had it for a by-word, when he saw men hasten to a conclusion, *Stay a little, that we may make an end the sooner.*" John Owen in 1681 commented: "The world is at present in a mighty hurry, and being in many places cast off from all foundations of steadfastness, it makes the minds of men giddy with its revolutions, or disorderly in the expectations of them." [7] The foundations of steadfastness were this prophet's main concern. He could assure them to his people in the promise:

the LORD will go before you,
    and the God of Israel will be your rear guard.

It is in such faith in times of change and peril that men find "shelter to grow ripe" and "leisure to grow wise." [8]

---

[5] *Country Parson,* ch. iii.

[6] *Letters,* ed. Telford, III, 192. Letter dated September 3, 1756.

[7] *The Grace and Duty of Being Spiritually Minded,* Preface.

[8] Matthew Arnold, "Stanzas in Memory of the Author of *Obermann,*" st. xviii.

13 ¶ Behold, my servant shall deal prudently, he shall be exalted and extolled,
and be very high.

13 Behold, my servant shall prosper,
    he shall be exalted and lifted up,
    and shall be very high.

E. THE SUFFERING SERVANT OF THE LORD (52:13-53:12)

The poem begins and ends with the words of Yahweh. The first strophe (52:13-15) introduces the servant of the Lord, describes his appearance and humiliation, and announces his exaltation and vindication. Directly following the divine oracle is a confessional lament by the nations represented perhaps by their kings (cf. 52:14). It has the usual three-strophe organization (53:1-3, 4-6, 7:9), and the divisions are plainly marked. The final strophe (53:10-12) returns to the first, describing the purpose of God in the life of the servant, the servant's atoning and intercessory mission, and his ultimate vindication. The middle section of the poem (53:1-9) has been described in many ways by different scholars. Haller sees in it a sacrificial hymn after the manner of the mysteries; Engnell, a prophetic remodeling of a liturgical composition belonging to the annual festival of the enthronement of Yahweh; Begrich, a psalm of thanksgiving; Mowinckel and Bentzen, a dirge echoing the penitential psalms. It is possible that the influences of Akkadian (Tammuz) liturgies are present, but the most apparent and nearest relationships are with the O.T.: Lamentations; the confessions of Jeremiah; the individual laments of the Psalter (such as Pss. 6; 22; 31; 33; 69; 88; 102); Isa. 38:9 ff.; and the laments of Job (3:3-26; 6:2-7, 21; 9:25-10:22; 29:1-31:37). Gunkel and Begrich (*Einleitung in die Psalmen,* pp. 172-265) give a detailed treatment of this literary type. Hans Schmidt isolates a considerable group of psalms of innocence (e.g., Pss. 3; 4; 5; 7; 27; 31; 140; 142; etc.; see his *Das Gebet der Angeklagten im Alten Testament* [Giessen: Alfred Töpelmann, 1928], and Gunkel's relevant criticism, *op. cit.,* pp. 252-54). Some scholars see the major affinities with the so-called royal-passion psalms (Pss. 18; 22; 49; 88; 89; 96; 102; 118).

The literary style of the poem should be carefully observed. Some forty-six words appear here which are not present elsewhere in Second Isaiah (see North, *Suffering Servant in Deutero-Isaiah,* p. 168), but this can be explained by the nature of the subject

---

52:13-53:12. The Exaltation and Suffering of the Lord's Sin-bearing Servant.—This is the most influential poem in any literature. Its insight that the suffering of the righteous may bring redemption to many is an answer to pain and grief which supplies courage and comfort. Its interpretation of the God-appointed role of Israel, his servant, furnished to the Christian church the explanation of the death of the Son of God which has formed a principal part of her gospel. It apparently caught the imagination of Jesus himself, and confirmed his conviction of his Father's will for him. Did ever poet's composition do more?

In its description of Israel's future glory this poem attached itself to those which precede. It meets its listeners' present plight by its sympathy with their humiliation and pain. It anticipates the tender address, "O afflicted one" (54:11), with its description of the abject condition forced upon the conquered by oppressors who

made your back like the ground
and like the street for them to pass over (51:23).

It adds a transforming meaning to all that Israel has undergone, and to the wretchedness of the exiles. The prophet had set before the nation an evangelist's mission to mankind. Now he comforts her by the message that already her sufferings are a sin offering and will make many righteous. In her degradation and misery, little as she suspects it, the Lord is baring "his holy arm before the eyes of all the nations." In her agonizing experience of national destruction and captivity "all the ends of the earth shall see the salvation of our God."

In form the poem is a dramatic dialogue in which the speakers are God, who begins and concludes (52:13-15; 53:10-12), and the heathen peoples, confessing through their kings their astounding discovery (53:1-9). The servant, as in previous poems, is Israel (41:8; 42:1; etc.), although it is mainly the spiritual community that is in the prophet's mind (cf. 49:6). The kings of the nations already have appeared (cf. 49:7). While this sublime poem may seem to differ from the prophet's other messages, it has been prepared for and fits in with his whole line of thought.

and the particular phase of it that is dealt with. The special character of the vocabulary does not prove diversity of authorship. The poem is notable for its remarkable assonance, above all the recurrence of the *û* sound (53:4-6). Thought and sound reinforce each other. The profound literary effect of the poem is largely due to the many repetitions. Observe, for example, **he was despised** (53:3*a*, 3*d*), **he opened not his mouth** (53:7*a*, 7*e*), "**all of us**" (*kullānû*, 53:6*a*, 6*d*), **we esteemed him not** (53:3*d*, 4*c*), **afflicted** (53:4*d*, 7*a*), **bruise** (53:5*b*, 10*a*), **griefs and . . . sorrows** (53:3*b*, 4*ab*), **many** (52:14*a*, 15*a*; 53:12*a*, 12*e*) **he bore** (53:4*a*, 12*e*), **he carried** (53:4*b*, 11*c*), **his appearance . . . his form** (52:14*bc*; 53:2*cd*); **the will of the LORD** (53:10*a*, 10*e*). Some of these appear in chiastic form and produce a very striking effect. The dramatic power of the poem as a whole is almost overwhelming. Note how the servant is introduced, how the speakers of 53:1-9 enter without any introduction and follow at once upon Yahweh's momentous disclosure, how the servant is intensely present but never named, how the lines succeed each other in short clauses, and how the whole poem is dominated by the contrast between humiliation and suffering on the one hand, and exaltation and triumph on the other. This contrast is developed by the "many" of the transgressors and the solitariness of the servant, by the "then" and "now" of the nations' reflections, by the revelation of Yahweh and the life of the servant and the observations of the nations. Finally, the pronouns in the confession produce an extremely poignant effect, e.g., the contrast between **he** and **we,** **him** and **us.** This contrast is accentuated by the assonance.

The poem as a whole is one of triumph, as the opening and closing strophes plainly show. Thus they suit the context very well. Indeed the major motif of the great reversal in 49:1–52:12 and 52:13–53:12 is the same, and is continued in ch. 54. Detailed study confirms the connection of our poem both with what precedes and with what follows. The stress on the arm of Yahweh, the purpose of Yahweh, the parallelism of nations and kings, the words **bare** and **carried,** the extraordinary emphasis on affliction (50:5-6; 51:17-23; 54:11; cf. 52:2-6), and many other similar phenomena argue strongly for Second Isaiah's authorship of the poem and for its present position in the collection.

1. First Strophe: Future Success and Exaltation of the Servant
(52:13-15)

The poem opens dramatically with the direct discourse of Yahweh, who introduces his servant by announcing his "success" and exaltation. The **many** who were **astonished** (better, "appalled") at his tragic disfigurement will be startled to learn of his true character. Many scholars transfer vs. 14*bc* after 53:2 because it appears awkward here and fits the context well at the later point, but this spoils the strophe; moreover, the words of the speakers in 53:1-9 are intimately attached to the introduction of the poem. Actually, the strophe is superbly constructed: introduction (vs. 13), protasis and apodosis (vss. 14-15*a*), and conclusion (vs. 15*bc*). Dramatically the words are addressed to the nations, but of course the whole poem is composed for Israel. Here at last is the answer to Israel's despair and blindness (cf. 40:2, 27; 49:4*ab*, 14, 21*c*, 21*g*; 42:16; 42:17–43:7; *et passim*). Such major motifs as the mission of Israel, the relation of Israel to the nations, the meaning of her suffering, and her eventual exaltation are present here.

13. Behold, my servant: Cf. 42:1, where the servant is similarly presented, and note its relation to 41:8 ff. Under no circumstances is **my servant** (עבדי; cf. vs. 11) to be altered

---

52:13-15. *The Servant's Surprising Elevation.* —The transformation of Israel's position, soon to occur, will open the eyes of the nations and convey to them a revelation of God's unexpected salvation of mankind. The consummation of history is again before the prophet's eyes, when Israel, restored to her land, **shall prosper, . . . be exalted and lifted up, and shall be very high.** This reversal of her fate amazes the world,

and especially the rulers who watch the public scene: **Many were astonished at him, . . . so shall he startle many nations.** Were the servant an individual merely, it is unlikely that he would claim the awe-struck gaze of peoples; but if the servant is a nation, political observers would be astonished by its unanticipated rise from depths to heights. It was an elevation without precedent, **that which they had not**

14 As many were astonished at thee; his visage was so marred more than any man, and his form more than the sons of men:

14 As many were astonished at him[s] —
  his appearance was so marred, beyond human semblance,
  and his form beyond that of the sons of men —

[s] Syr Tg: Heb *you*

---

to "the servant of the Lord" (עבד יהוה). The verb *yaskîl* is rendered **shall deal prudently** by the KJV, "shall deal wisely" by the ASV, which is the primary meaning. The LXX renders συνήσει; Vulg., *intelliget*. Undoubtedly it also bears the meaning of **prosper** (RSV) or "have success" (as in Josh. 1:8; I Sam. 18:5, 14-15; I Kings 2:3; II Kings 18:7; Jer. 10:21). The idea of insight here coalesces with that of "success." The servant's ultimate triumph is related to his wisdom (cf. Dan. 12:3; also Pss. 2:10; 94:8). He lives in such close fellowship with his God that he discerns his ways and purposes, knows something of the mysteries of his revelation, and sees the deeper meaning involved in his suffering (cf. 50:4-9). The root of the verb appears in various forms both in the wisdom literature and in the cultic liturgies. Jeremiah uses it in connection with the future Davidic messiah (Jer. 23:5). Torrey takes the word here as a proper name like Meshullam or Jeshurun. Marti, Budde, and the Moffatt translation emend ישכיל to ישראל, "Israel," an indefensible procedure. Ivan Engnell sees it as a *terminus technicus* drawn from the Tammuz liturgies, "to execute a maskil," i.e., an annual festival psalm ("The 'Ebed Yahweh Songs and the Suffering Messiah in 'Deutero-Isaiah,' " *Bulletin of the John Rylands Library*, XXXI [1948], pp. 54-93). Interestingly, the Targ. reads יצלח, **shall prosper** (cf. vs. 10). The closing strophe develops the meaning of the word. The task of the servant is the accomplishment of the purpose of Yahweh. Note also the servant's knowledge in vs. 11*b*.

> He shall be exalted and lifted up,
> and shall be very high.

A characteristic climactic triad in a single stich. The announcement of the servant's exaltation at the beginning is in the manner of other passages (63:9 ff.; Ps. 73:1; Job 1:1–2:13; cf. Ecclus. 39:14-20).

14. The text is not in perfect order. In the first line **at thee** must be emended to **at him** (RSV; Lindblom argues for the text, however, on the basis of prophetic style elsewhere). The verse is protasis to the apodosis of vs. 15. In the Hebrew vs. 14*b* opens with כן, **so,** which is out of place (cf. vs. 15*a*). Some scholars emend it to כי, **for;** others

---

heard. God's acts shock like thunderclaps. They stun observers and leave them bemused. That is a first step toward redemption. A saying of Jesus recorded in the Gospel to the Hebrews and mentioned by Clement of Alexandria, tells us that the seeker for truth, having found it in the Christian teaching, "shall wonder."[9] Men who are not wondering are not in sight of the mighty acts of God.

They shall understand. "Should heathen nations see the exaltation of diminutive Israel, would it have any meaning for them?" the exiles may have asked. Want of understanding was our Lord's frequent discouragement with his disciples (cf. Mark 7:18). Amazement would

[9] J. H. Ropes, "Agrapha," in James Hastings, ed., *Dictionary of the Bible* (New York: Charles Scribner's Sons, 1909), V, 345.

appear to have little to do with understanding. It might seem likelier to bewilder. But the things of God are apprehended with every element in our make-up—imagination, intellect, conscience, sentiment. A Latin apologist speaks of clinging to God "with all our senses, so to speak."[1] Our whole being must be roused by a startling self-disclosure of God.

From the servant's future glory the poet turns to his present miserable aspect (vs. 14). Volz calls him "suffering personified." A loathsome disease like leprosy seems to lie behind the sentence. Israel's land had been despoiled, its inhabitants dispersed and exiled to many places. It had not the look of a nation. Its own people scarcely recognized it. These lines sympathize

[1] Arnobius *Adversus Gentes* I. 25.

15 So shall he sprinkle many nations; the kings shall shut their mouths at him: for *that* which had not been told them shall they see; and *that* which they had not heard shall they consider.

15 so shall he startle[t] many nations;
  kings shall shut their mouths because
    of him;
for that which has not been told them
  they shall see,
and that which they have not heard
  they shall understand.

[t] The meaning of the Hebrew word is uncertain

(KJV, ASV, RSV) take it as an adverb modifying **marred** (better, "disfigured"). The latter, though precarious, is the best solution to the difficulty (see Brown, Driver, Briggs, *Lexicon, s.v.* כן, for possible analogies). The word **marred** represents a double reading in the Hebrew, the Niphal participle *nishḥāth* and the Hophal participle *moshḥāth* (so Syriac). The Dead Sea Scroll reads משׁחתי, which is hard to explain. The servant was so disfigured that he no longer looked like a man (cf. 49:7; 50:6). Engnell gives a long list of parallels to the description of the servant's sufferings from the Sumero-Akkadian Tammuz liturgies ("'Ebed Yahweh Songs and the Suffering Messiah," pp. 77-79; note also his parallels to the sufferings of Aliyan Baal in the Ugaritic texts). It is probable that these liturgies influenced the poet's portrait. The word **many** is strongly emphasized in the opening and closing strophes (note its usage in Dan. 12:3; Mark 10:45; Rom. 5:19). Volz thinks that it belongs to the vocabulary of teaching on vicarious suffering. The **many** are contrasted with the one, the solitary, righteous, suffering, and finally victorious servant, and prepare the way for the sharp contrasts between the singular and plural of the lament.

15. The great significance of the servant is indicated by the response of nations and kings. The Oriental describes the greatness of God by the subservience and the worship of the mighty rulers of the nations. Even kings are utterly subject to him and extol his greatness (cf. 49:23; Pss. 76:12; 102:15; 107:40; 138:4; 148:11; Job 12:21). The collocation of kings and nations appears elsewhere (41:2; 45:1; 49:7, 22-23; 60:3, 16). Before the servant the nations are aroused and stirred, and kings shut their mouths in awe and reverential silence. The verb יזה in vs. 15a is difficult, and many emendations have been proposed. The best known of these is G. F. Moore's emendation ("On יזה in Isaiah LII. 15," *Journal of Biblical Literature*, IX [1890], 216-22) to ירגזו, "were excited," "perturbed," or "agitated" (cf. 64:1; Jer. 33:9). Torrey accepts the emendation, but includes גוים, **nations,** as part of the corruption. The LXX renders θαυμάσονται, "shall wonder" (Fischer, Condamin). It is possible that we have an Arabic cognate here (cf. the Arabic *naza*) meaning to leap up in surprise or respect (see Brown, Driver, Briggs, *op. cit., s.v* נזה; Gesenius and Buhl, *Hebräisches und aramäisches Handwörterbuch, s.v.* נזה). H. S. Nyberg, on the basis of another meaning of the root, "to sprinkle," etc. (cf. Vulg.

with the exiles' downcast feelings and convince them of the prophet's realistic appreciation of their condition. So highly individualized is the servant's figure that a martyr like Jeremiah or a sufferer like Job may have been in the prophet's thought as representative of his people.

Commenting on the harsh experiences of Charlotte and Emily Brontë, Sir Leslie Stephen wrote: "Great art is produced by taking an exceptionally delicate nature and mangling it slowly under the grinding wheels of the world." [2] Israel is educated for her prophetic mission through a similar long agony. Like all

O.T. writers, the prophet does not raise the question why suffering is included in God's order. Believing in his sovereignty, he accepts the fact of suffering, and in this poem dwells on its blessed results in the case of the righteous servant.

One may note the two renderings of the first verb in vs. 13: **deal prudently** and **prosper.** The O.T. makes much of wisdom and success. In 11:2, four of the nouns speak of the intelligence of the Davidic ruler. Here the prophet is probably thinking of insight into the meaning of God's discipline. "By his knowledge" (53:11) the servant achieves his redemptive task. In the Bible God's servants, by their fellowship with

[2] *Hours in a Library* (New York: G. P. Putnam's Sons, 1904), III, 284.

53 Who hath believed our report? and to whom is the arm of the LORD revealed?

53 Who has believed what we have heard? And to whom has the arm of the LORD been revealed?

---

asperget), translates, "many peoples offer a purificatory sacrifice [for his sake]." For a thorough discussion of the problem see Edward J. Young, "The Interpretation of יזה in Isaiah 52:15," *Westminster Theological Journal,* III (1941), 125-32. Young supports "he will sprinkle" and interprets it in a priestly sense (see Lev. 4:6; 8:11; 14:7, 27, 51; Num. 8:7; etc.). In view of the obvious meaning of the verb *nāzāh* in all these passages where it is used in reference to the sprinkling of water, blood, and oil, and especially in view of the relation of the opening to the closing strophe (see vs. 10c), it is best to retain "sprinkle" here, and this interpretation is supported by the Manual of Discipline (iv. 21; cf. iii. 10). Lindblom derives the word from the root נזה, I (see the proper names "Jeziel" in I Chr. 12:3 and "Izziah" in Ezra 10:25), which has the meaning of "besprinkle." He translates as follows: "He (i.e. the servant) will (at some time in the future) besprinkle many peoples, i.e. purify many peoples from their sins" (see his important discussion in *Servant Songs in Deutero-Isaiah,* pp. 40-41). The conclusion gives the reason for the deep feelings of the nations and kings. The strophe as a whole is an excellent example of the motif of the great reversal especially common in eschatological contexts.

2. SECOND STROPHE: THE SERVANT'S LIFE OF SUFFERING (53:1-3)

The lament opens with the prophet's favorite question form (see 40:12; 50:8-10). It connects admirably with the final words of Yahweh's oracle (ראו, "they shall see," and לא־שמעו, "they had not heard"), and with the succeeding description of the servant (**for he grew up**). Similarly, vs. 2 echoes 52:14, which the RSV and other versions obscure: "appearance" and **form** are repeated chiastically. Note the effect of the succeeding clauses, each stroke producing its own telling effect. The repetition of **he was despised** (vss. 3a, 3d) is profoundly moving, and the final line **we esteemed him not** gives a magnificent climax which serves as a link to the succeeding strophe (vs. 4c).

53:1. The direct discourse opens without introduction as in 52:13-15. Everything centers on the servant. The words express the wonder and surprise of the speakers: "Who could have believed what we have heard?" The expected answer is "no one" (cf. 40:12 ff.; Kautzsch, *Gesenius' Hebrew Grammar,* sec. 151a). What is it that they have heard? Some scholars think the preaching of the great prophets; others, the servant songs or the prophet's previous message; still others like Engnell see the word (*shemû'āh*) as the central cult word of the myth as used in the Tammuz liturgies. But the most obvious explanation is the words which they have just heard from Yahweh. The close connection

---

him, wisely handle life's complicated situations. According to an early theory of Christ's death, he outsmarted the devil and robbed him of enslaved mankind. We do well to emphasize the wisdom of the Lord's servant (cf. Matt. 12:42). Calvary was derided as weakness and folly, but to Paul it was "the wisdom of God" (I Cor. 1:24). The reversals of history, like Israel's restoration from exile, and the Son of God's exaltation from a gibbet to a throne, display divine sagacity which makes human cleverness seem absurd. This is the *divina commedia.*

53:1-3. *Their Startled Surprise.*—The dumbfounded kings now take up the dialogue (vss. 1-9). God's purpose for Israel was incredible. **Who has believed?** He takes earth's "nothings"

(I Cor. 1:28) and uses them mightily. The supreme instance is One who is known as the child of a carpenter and his peasant wife, cradled in a manger and hung up on a cross— the Savior of the world. **The arm of the LORD** was mysteriously hid in the baffling history of his people. His footsteps with them were in secret paths (Ps. 77:19).

Israel's history was ill-omened (cf. 52:4). Perhaps the servant's growth is supposed to occur in the Exile. If so **the young plant** and **the root out of dry ground** refer to the starving spiritual environment. The growth throughout was "before God," in his all-seeing providence, but in the eyes of the nations this community in its abjectness and dispersion had nothing attractive

2 For he shall grow up before him as a tender plant, and as a root out of a dry ground: he hath no form nor comeliness; and when we shall see him, *there is* no beauty that we should desire him.

2 For he grew up before him like a young plant,
and like a root out of dry ground;
he had no form or comeliness that we should look at him,
and no beauty that we should desire him.

---

of the two strophes clearly suggests this. What was disclosed seemed absolutely incredible. The emphatic reference to **the arm** of Yahweh at the beginning of the lament connects superbly with the central and crucial contexts of the foregoing poems (40:10-11; 48:14; 51:5; 52:10) and the impassioned cry of 51:9 ff. It is clear from most of these passages that the nations are referred to here. The Hebrew reads, lit., "the arm of Yahweh upon [or "over"] whom has it been revealed." The Dead Sea Scroll has מי אל, "to whom."

2. Here begins the life story of suffering. See Job's piercing lament, also in narrative form (Job 19:7-20), and the similar autobiographical lament of Jerusalem in Lam. 3:1-20. The disfigured servant of 52:14 is portrayed in detail. Many scholars emend **before him**, most of them to "before us," i.e., the speakers of the lament; G. R. Driver and Volz emend to *lô yāpheh*, "uncomely" (Volz), "straight up" (Driver). But the text makes intelligible sense: viz., before Yahweh. It is unwise to make any change. The word *yônēq*, **young plant** or "sapling" or "shoot," literally means "sucking one" (cf. Job 14:7; Ezek. 17:22). Those who identify the servant with the messianic Davidic king find an allusion here to the "shoot" and "branch" of 11:1, and explicitly the **root** (*shōresh*) of 11:10. The text of Jer. 23:5 is interesting because it reveals several affinities with the present poem. But it does not prove that the servant is a scion of David. There may be a genuine messianic allusion here, however. A parallel from the Akkadian texts frequently adduced reads as follows:

> A tamarisk which in the garden has no water to drink,
> Whose foliage on the plain sends forth no twig.
> A plant which they water no more in the pot,
> Whose roots are torn away.
> An herb which in the garden has no water to drink,
> Among the garden flowers he slumbers, among the garden flowers he is cast away.

(Christopher R. North, *The Suffering Servant in Deutero-Isaiah* [London: Oxford University Press, 1948], pp. 220-21 [used by permission]; see also Max Haller's interesting characterization of the shoot in *Das Judentum* [Göttingen: Vandenhoeck & Ruprecht, 1914; "Die Schriften des Alten Testament"], pp. 55-56.) Engnell sees in the allusion "the tree or plant of life, a symbol of the king-Tammuz . . . in the suffering aspect" ("'Ebed

---

(vs. 2). The devoted patriot frankly admits that his people had no charm for neighboring peoples. With bald realism Israel's historians depict the national ancestor and prototype, Jacob, in unlovely colors. They were painfully aware that they appeared repulsive to others. When the tragedy of national disaster and the long years of captivity overtook them, they became even less winsome (vs. 3). Defeat and hardship embitter individuals and nations and bring out offensive qualities. "That's the worst of sorrow. It's always a vicious circle. It makes one tense and hard and disagreeable, and this means that one repels and antagonises people, and then they dislike and avoid one—and that means

more isolation and more sorrow." [3] Subject peoples in self-defense develop pushing characteristics, and along with them, cringing and ingratiating manners. The total effect is repellent. The metaphor of loathsome disease like leprosy conveys the impression.

A man of sorrows and acquainted with grief: These words have become part of our heritage of language, aptly describing in peerless literature Israel's preparation for her unique career as an interpreter of God. The effort for happy adjustment of life to society runs the peril of stultifying the growth of the spirit. A world

[3] Vera Brittain, *Testament of Youth* (New York: The Macmillan Co., 1933), p. 493.

3 He is despised and rejected of men; a man of sorrows, and acquainted with grief: and we hid as it were *our* faces from him; he was despised, and we esteemed him not.

3 He was despised and rejected[u] by men; a man of sorrows,[v] and acquainted with grief;[w]
and as one from whom men hide their faces
he was despised, and we esteemed him not.

[u] Or *forsaken*
[v] Or *pains*
[w] Or *sickness*

Yahweh Songs and the Suffering Messiah," p. 82). But this goes too far. We may grant that there may be an echo of Akkadian mythology. In the M.T. the clause **that we should look at him** goes with the following line (cf. KJV and ASV), but the parallelism certainly favors the placing of the accent (*athnaḥ*) before it (as in RSV). North and others feel that this makes the line too long, and therefore delete either *welô hādhār*, **or comeliness**, or the clause in question (*wenir'ēhû*). The metrical argument is not coercive, and the stylistic argument depends on personal taste. There are good grounds for retaining the text as it is. If the servant is understood collectively as corporate personality, as the Israelite indeed who is the true Israel from beginning to end, then the description can be taken in part, at least, as her historical existence as the nations observed it, and indeed as Israel herself experienced it.

3. Repulsive and revolting in appearance, the servant was **despised and rejected.** Loneliness and solitariness were bitter afflictions to the Oriental. To experience peace, security, or well-being (*shālôm*) he must have the support and company of his family and neighbors. It is not good for him to be alone. Cain's grievous punishment is that he is exiled from community. The cry of loneliness is one of the most common in the laments (Lam. 1:1-3; 3:7, 14, 17; Job 19:13-19; Pss. 22; 31; 38; 69; 88; 102). Jeremiah sits alone (15:17). **He was despised:** See 49:7; Ps. 22:6; Jer. 49:15; cf. Lam. 2:15-16. **And rejected of men:** The expression is unusual. Lit., "ceased of men." Job 19:14 uses the verb in a similar context, "My relatives and my close friends have failed [ceased] me." The form of the plural noun is unusual (אישים), but not unique (Ps. 141:4; Prov. 8:4) and is used here for reasons of assonance (the singular form איש occurs immediately following). **A man of sorrows:** More literally, **of pains;** Vulg., *virum dolorum*. **And acquainted with grief:** We should probably translate "humbled" or "disciplined" (G. R. Driver, "Linguistic and Textual Problems: Isaiah I-XXXIX," *Journal of Theological Studies,* XXXVIII [1937], 48-49; D. Winton Thomas, "More Notes on the Root ידע in Hebrew," *ibid.,* pp. 404-5). Grief is more literally **sickness,** but the terms **pains** and **sickness** are used generally to describe sufferings, as elsewhere in the Near East (cf. Jer. 6:7; etc.). If the prophet is employing the language descriptive of a leper, which

---

smoothly fitted to its dwellers and they to it would be neither "a vale of soul-making" nor a world of men and women who inspire the race. Creators in religion, in music, in literature, have been in a harsher school. Dante spoke of the Italy of his time as "a hostelry of woe," and Burns termed Johnson's *Lives of the Poets* the most rueful of martyrologies. Sorrow and pain do not automatically render men either devout or creative, but often they are spurs to both.

> . . . Yet there is something that doth seek,
> Crying, for God, when one of us hath woe.[4]

[4] Euripides, *Trojan Women,* tr. Gilbert Murray (New York: Oxford University Press, 1915), p. 35.

Second Isaiah is an outstanding instance of one whose soul was sharpened by his people's griefs to penetrate the secrets of God and body them forth in moving speech.

It would be a poor result of all our anguish and our wrestling, if we won nothing but our old selves at the end of it, . . . the same feeble sense of that Unknown towards which we have sent forth irrepressible cries in our loneliness. . . . It is at such periods that the sense of our lives having visible and invisible relations beyond any of which either our present or prospective self is the centre, grows like a muscle that we are obliged to lean on and exert.[5]

[5] George Eliot, *Adam Bede,* Bk. VI, ch. 1.

4 ¶ Surely he hath borne our griefs, and carried our sorrows: yet we did esteem him stricken, smitten of God, and afflicted.

4 Surely he has borne our griefs[x]
   and carried our sorrows;[y]
yet we esteemed him stricken
   smitten by God, and afflicted.

[x] Or *sicknesses*
[y] Or *pains*

is very possible, it is easy to see why **men hide their faces** from the sufferer in loathing and disgust or in superstitious dread. The servant is the sufferer par excellence. What disturbs the speakers above all is that they **esteemed him not.** They did not know who he was or what he was doing.

3. THIRD STROPHE: HE SUFFERED FOR US (53:4-6)

The strophe is confessional. It emphasizes the contrast between the servant and the speakers by strongly accenting the pronouns. The opening word expresses this contrast very well, probably best rendered by an emphatic "but." The poet seizes upon the three central words of the previous verse to relate the confession to them: **griefs, sorrows, and we esteemed him.** The strophe is rich in the vocabulary of pain and affliction, but the climax falls appropriately on the confession of sin (vs. 6). The assonance is particularly notable. The problem of the source of the prophet's symbolism is complicated. It is likely that he was himself unaware of the influences behind his words. That the Tammuz interpretation of the text is a decisive fact is overstating the case, although in view of the pervasive Akkadian influence in the poems, it is likely that the rituals of the Babylonian Tammuz liturgies were familiar to Second Isaiah and that his language reflects their influence. But priority must certainly be given to the native developments within the O.T. where Tammuz influences are not present at all. It may be true that "the king's vicarious suffering in the New Year Festival by means of which he atones for the sins of the whole people, is one of the cardinal items of the ideology of sacral kingship all over the Ancient Near East" (Engnell, " 'Ebed Yahweh Songs and the Suffering Messiah," p. 84) without claiming that the prophet simply took over the ritual drama en bloc. On the other hand, Engnell may be right in seeing a Hebraic

4-6. The Servant Suffers Vicariously.—The LORD has laid on him and he has borne . . . and carried are two aspects of the servant's suffering (a) received from the Lord and (b) voluntarily accepted. Israel's harsh lot came about through historical circumstances. The exiled community was involved with its forebears. Their humiliation was not of their choosing. But believing in God's sovereignty, the servant takes it as God's assignment. It is punishment for national sin, education for a mission, and now redemptive sin offering. The rulers of the nations in surprise see the association of their lands with this despised people. The emphasis is upon **our** and **he.** Handel's music in *The Messiah* brings out the amazement of their discovery.

> Surely it was our sicknesses that he bore,
> and our pains that he carried.[6]

The poet has risen to this sublime interpretation of his people's humiliation. Few if any of his fellow Israelites shared his conviction. He is attempting to inspire them with it. It had

[6] Skinner, *Isaiah, Chapters XL-LXVI*, p. 126.

lifted him, and would lift them to heartening fellowship with God in his redemptive purpose for mankind. A Hasidic saying runs: "There are three ways in which a man expresses his deep sorrow: the man on the lowest level cries; the man on the second level is silent; the man on the highest level knows how to turn his sorrow into song." [7] The acceptance of pain and the effort to transmute it is illustrated in the diary of a twentieth-century novelist:

> There is no limit to human suffering. When one thinks: "Now I have touched the bottom of the sea—now I can go no deeper," one goes deeper. [But] I do not want to die without leaving a record of my belief that suffering can be overcome. . . . What must one do? . . . One must *submit*. Do not resist. Take it. . . . I must put my agony into something, change it. . . . It is to lose oneself more utterly.[8]

A woman dying of cancer said: "I wish that I could gather up into my own pain all the

[7] Ascribed to Rabbi Solomon of Radomsk, in *Syah Sarfe Kodesh* (Lodz: 1927), IV, 92.
[8] *Journal of Katherine Mansfield*, ed. J. Middleton Murry (New York: A. A. Knopf, 1927), pp. 166-67.

5 But he *was* wounded for our transgressions, *he was* bruised for our iniquities: the chastisement of our peace *was* upon him; and with his stripes we are healed.

5 But he was wounded for our transgressions,
he was bruised for our iniquities;
upon him was the chastisement that made us whole,
and with his stripes we are healed.

---

prophetic adaptation of the Akkadian liturgies. It is better, however, to suggest that the writer may be influenced by current Akkadian liturgical speech.

4. The suffering of the servant is due to sin. This is the conviction of Israel, as also of other peoples of the ancient Near East. Deuteronomic theology and the wisdom theology of the friends of Job are notable instances of it. But for prophets like Habakkuk and Jeremiah, for many psalmists like the writer of Ps. 73, and for Job this orthodox view did not correspond to experience. For Second Isaiah the presence of sin in the situation was indisputable. But the sinner here is not the sufferer. The sufferer is bearing the consequences of the sins of others than himself. Our sins, so the speakers confess, have been transferred to him. He bears **our griefs** and carries **our sorrows.** Observe how Matthew employs this passage (Matt. 8:17). "As for ourselves, we esteemed him." The verb is an echo of vs. 3. But then follow the heavy strokes **stricken, smitten, . . . afflicted,** and the crucial phrase which goes with all three words, **by God.** The speakers are right in what they think, but wrong in their interpretation, for the purpose of Yahweh's act was the opposite of what they supposed (cf. vs. 10).

5. But he is in sharp contrast with **yet we** of vs. 4c. **Wounded . . . bruised:** The clause is circumstantial. Observe the change in imagery: **he was wounded** (better, "pierced through"), **he was bruised** (or "crushed"). Such shifts in the portrait, and indeed the wide diversity of terms used to describe the suffering, forbid any attempt to identify its precise nature. In a sense all suffering is here, all of the servant's suffering in the total context in which the speakers utter their confession and lament. The sufferings had a twofold effect: they were the penalty for sins (vs. 5ab), and they were the means of

---

world must suffer from cancer, and pay the whole sum as I go." An illustration of such assumption of punishment comes from the career of Shamil, a religious and military leader in the Caucasus in the mid-nineteenth centry, who struggled for thirty years to maintain the independence from Russia of the tribes of Dagestan. At one time defeatism was rife among his followers. He announced that anyone pleading for negotiations with the enemy would receive one hundred lashes. A culprit was caught and proved to be his own mother. Shamil shut himself up in the mosque, refusing food and drink, and gave himself to prayer. On the third day he gathered the people and, pale as death, ordered the executioner to inflict the punishment. At the fifth stroke he called "Halt," had his mother removed, bared his own back, and bade the official lay on him the remaining ninety-five strokes, with severe threats if he failed to put the full weight into every blow. The awestruck people were deeply moved, and all talk of asking terms of the Russians ceased.[9] The servant's voluntary submission to obloquy and blows has been stressed in 50:6. The exiles might have

[9] J. F. Baddeley, *The Russian Conquest of the Caucasus* (New York: Longmans, Green & Co., 1908), pp. 374-79.

escaped some of this had they been faithless to their religion and conformed to the ways of their oppressors. The prophet gives them a new incentive to fidelity—their divine mission of redemption.

The pagan kings give the orthodox Hebrew explanation of suffering—**stricken, smitten by God, and afflicted.** Eliphaz, Bildad, and Zophar set it forth in Job. Second Isaiah shared the other poet's protest against this doctrine, and cleverly placed it on heathen lips. Wickedness brings on disaster; but the corollary that suffering implies wickedness is a cruel conception. It meets the sick, the bereaved, the impoverished, when they most need comfort, with the brutal statement that they deserve it. This prophet introduces the far loftier doctrine.

In vs. 5 the emphasis is again on **he** and **our. He was wounded for our transgressions.** It is not the servant's acceptance of his fate, but the world's evil-doing, victimizing him, that is stressed. All nations, greedily scrambling for power, bring on the wars which doom smaller peoples to misery and establish the harsh custom of deporting the vanquished.

The chastisement of our peace was upon him. Chastisement implies disciplinary pain;

6 All we like sheep have gone astray; we have turned every one to his own way; and the LORD hath laid on him the iniquity of us all.	6 All we like sheep have gone astray; we have turned every one to his own way; and the LORD has laid on him the iniquity of us all.

reconciliation and restoration (vs. 5cd). The **chastisement** of the servant was for the well-being of the nations; the **stripes** (bruises, blows; cf. 1:6; Ps. 38:5) were for their healing. The punishment was borne vicariously, and the vicarious suffering was efficacious in the eyes of God. The chastisement which broke his body made us whole (*shelômēnû*); the blows and stripes which prostrated him healed us (cf. Kautzsch, *Gesenius' Hebrew Grammar*, sec. 128q for genitive of purpose). *Shālôm* is a very inclusive word in the Hebrew and here denotes both physical and spiritual well being.

6. A moving finale: "All of us" (*kullānû*) begins and ends the poignant confession. We were all involved in the servant's suffering. The transgressions and iniquities were a going astray from God, a turning away, each in his own self-centered course (*dérekh*). The image of the sheep prepares the way for the next strophe. The same phenomena in previous strophes are to be observed, a witness, despite corruptions here and there, to the remarkable care with which the poem was composed. The climax, however, falls

but Israel may transform her retribution into a means of healing for many. A sonnet depicts this process in modern days:

I watched her in the loud and shadowy lanes
Of life; and every face that passed her by
Grew calmly restful, smiling quietly,
As though she gave for all their griefs and pains
Largesse of comfort, soft as summer rains
And balsam tinctured with tranquillity.
Yet in her own eyes dwelt an agony.
"Oh, halcyon soul," I cried, "what sorrow reigns
In that calm heart, which knows such ways to heal?"
She said—"Where balms are made for human uses,
Great furnace fires, and wheel on grinding wheel
Must crush and purify the crude herb juices;
And in some hearts the conflict cannot cease:
They are the sick world's factories of peace." [1]

It was after the nations realized that Israel's woes were for them that they were moved to a confession of sin (vs. 6). When the consequences of our wrongdoing are seen in others' suffering, our consciences are smitten (cf. Rev. 1:7). The results of world wars in human misery and loss are a glass in which nations see themselves. The spirit of every people is exposed; none is guiltless.

I pity the man among us, the clever ones, the thinking ones, who has not known, in his hour, that he, and *he alone*, bore the guilt of war. It is we, who have had that knowledge, or a glimmering of it, who must be changed. We who have wrung our hands over the mud and blood of the muckheap of the world, and have had a sudden sight that it is we, and we alone, who were the muckheap—we who knew and felt, and did not act. There is no

one for us to blame but ourselves. *Nostra culpa, nostra maxima culpa.* [2]

This poem presents the insight of a universal guilt in nations who have **turned every one to his own way.** It anticipates Rom. 3:23. An entry in *Amiel's Journal* reads:

I have just been glancing over the affairs of the world in the newspaper. What a Babel it is! . . . We shall end by feeling the pulse of the race. . . . The earth will see herself. Then will be the time for her to blush for her disorders, her hideousness, her misery, her crime—and to throw herself at last with energy and perseverance into the pursuit of justice. . . . War, hatred, selfishness, fraud, the right of the stronger, will be held to be old-world barbarisms. . . . Men will be brothers, peoples will be friends, races will sympathise one with another, and mankind will draw from love a principle of emulation, of invention, and of zeal, as powerful as any furnished by the vulgar stimulant of interest. [3]

The consciences of poets are "nerves o'er which do creep the else unfelt oppressions of the earth"; and this prophet, picturing the shocked kings confessing the sin of all peoples, reaches the topmost point of social responsibility in the Bible.

**The LORD has laid on him
the iniquity of us all.**

Not that Israel felt this load; but the effects of sin are social, so that the guilt of all falls upon each, and that of each upon all. One may compare with this sensitive poet Whitman's lines in *Leaves of Grass*, beginning, "I sit and

[1] "A Factory of Peace," ascribed to Mary Webb, but according to her publishers, Jonathan Cape, not in any of her printed volumes.

[2] Murry, *Things to Come*, p. 108.
[3] Tr. Mrs. Humphrey Ward (London: Macmillan & Co., 1890), p. 293.

7 He was oppressed, and he was afflicted, yet he opened not his mouth: he is brought as a lamb to the slaughter, and as a sheep before her shearers is dumb, so he openeth not his mouth.	7 He was oppressed, and he was afflicted, yet he opened not his mouth; like a lamb that is led to the slaughter, and like a sheep that before its shearers is dumb, so he opened not his mouth.

on the act of God in this supreme epic of the world's pain (cf. vs. 10, where the account of suffering is developed and even deepened) :

> and the LORD has laid on him
> the iniquity of us all.

The only name mentioned in the lament is Yahweh. The repeated pointing to the dramatis personae by pronouns (climaxed by *kullānû*) is beyond comment.

4. FOURTH STROPHE: SILENT SUFFERING IN LIFE AND DEATH (53:7-9)

The account of the servant's suffering continues, but is deepened line by line through his death and burial. Throughout there is a contrast between what he bore and how he bore it. The first line summarizes the sufferings described in vss. 1-6, and then his fate is described. The last lines appropriately stress his innocence. The repetition of the clause **he opened not his mouth** is in the style of our poet, and the last line is perhaps an echo of it, thus giving the strophe a fine unity.

7. He was **oppressed** or treated harshly (cf. Exod. 3:7; 5:6 [J]) , and he (emphatic) was **afflicted** (cf. the climax of vs. 4*d*; also 51:21; 54:11). Yet he did not cry out in protest or vengeance against his enemies, or to God against the cruel injustice of his afflictions. Such patience is not characteristic of the O.T. sufferers. Habakkuk, Jeremiah, and Job are not patient; they raise loud laments before the mystery and apparent injustice of their fate. The laments of the Psalter witness to the same impatience. Loud crying, not silence, is characteristic of them (contrast, however, Pss. 38:14; 39:1-2, 4) . This was natural so long as the orthodox interpretation of suffering as the result of sin was in control. But the deeper understanding produced a completely different effect. Cf. W. F. Albright (*From the Stone Age to Christianity* [2nd ed.; Baltimore: Johns Hopkins Press, 1946], pp. 254-55) : "Humility, silence, and meekness became increasingly characteristic of ancient oriental piety after the late second millenium B.C. The inscriptions of the Neo-Babylonian kings (sixth century B.C.) often begin with the words

look out." The potent result of confession in national guilt was seen at a conference in Denmark shortly after World War II, where representatives of the evangelical churches of Austria, Czechoslovakia, Hungary, Poland, the Scandinavian countries, and Germany were present. The Germans owned the sin of their land in bringing war to Europe. The others acknowledged that their countries had a mind which returned evil for evil. Finally, the leader of the Germans declared that

they had not forgotten—how should they forget— the experiences that they themselves and their country had passed through; but they had overcome those experiences. . . . It was . . . the reality of our fellowship in Christ, in which guilt was confessed and forgiven [which brought us together], because this fellowship derived its life solely from the grace of our Lord.[4]

[4] *Christianity and Crisis*, Vol. VII, No. 22, p. 6.

7-9. The Servant Submissive Under His Fate. —It requires vast self-control to be silent under unjust treatment. And quiet endurance of wrong is impressive. In the Commonwealth Period, Sir Matthew Hale dismissed a jury which he thought illegally selected to favor the Lord Protector. Angry, Cromwell told him he was not fit to be a judge. "That is very true," he replied; and Cromwell was disarmed.[5]

In the Free-Soil fight for "bleeding" Kansas, citizens, resisting assaults of ruffians egged on by the slave powers, declared they could not endure the wrongs inflicted on them. The general in charge of the Federal force told them: "Be patient! Your wrongs are your very strength."

As to vs. 8, **By oppression and judgment he**

[5] Gilbert Burnet, "Life of Sir Matthew Hale," in *Lives, Characters, and an Address to Posterity*, ed. John Jebb (New York: H. M. Onderdonk, 1846), p. 96.

8 He was taken from prison and from judgment: and who shall declare his generation? for he was cut off out of the land of the living: for the transgression of my people was he stricken.	8 By oppression and judgment he was taken away; and as for his generation, who considered that he was cut off out of the land of the living, stricken for the transgression of my people?

(following the titulary), 'the meek and humble one.' . . . This concept can hardly antedate the Exile in its present form, and we may attribute its increasing popularity to the influence of Deutero-Isaiah and his followers." The servant's behavior here is consistent with 42:1-4; 50:4-9. **Like a lamb, . . . like a sheep:** The first line is reminiscent of Jer. 11:19, but in Jeremiah the emphasis is rather upon lack of suspicion and unawareness; here it is upon the silence of the sheep. The young **lamb . . . is led to the slaughter** (on genitive of purpose see Kautzsch, *loc. cit.*) ; the ewe mother (*rāḥēl*) is too valuable to be killed and is preserved for her wool. She suffers the harsh hand of the shearer. The third line of the verse is somewhat long in the M.T.; many therefore emend the verb "was dumb" (third feminine singular perfect in pause) to the masculine perfect or participle and connect it with what follows: he **is dumb, so he opened not his mouth.** Others follow the masoretic pointing and delete the last line as dittography. Stylistic arguments can be advanced for retaining the text as it is: the masoretic stich **he opened not his mouth** is paralleled in vs. 7*b*; moreover, one can expect the short line immediately after the long one. To say "he was dumb and opened not his mouth" cannot be considered to be felicitous. The designation of Christ as the Lamb of God is derived from this reference (John 1:29, 36) .

8. A notoriously difficult verse. **By oppression and judgment:** The RSV follows the ASV and the Amer. Trans. The KJV has **He was taken from prison and from judgment.** The LXX reads ἐν τῇ ταπεινώσει ἡ κρίσις αὐτοῦ ἤρθη, "in his humiliation his judgment was taken away"; the Vulg., *de angustia, et de judicio sublatus est.* Others read, "without hindrance [or stay] and without right he was taken away." Others translate, "through oppression and through judgment he was taken away," i.e., through a judicial procedure. The rendering of עצר by **oppression** is supported by Ps. 107:39. Another rendering is "from oppression and from judgment he was taken away." Engnell takes it as a hendiadys, "a judgment of violence"; Nyberg, "legal exclusion." Torrey translates, "from dominion and rule he was plucked down," and says that the prophet refers to "the glory of David and Solomon, and of the most powerful of their successors" (*Second Isaiah,* p. 419) . Rowley takes the *min* in four different senses in vs. 8 *ab* and renders vs. 8*a*, "By oppression and without justice was he taken." One must first settle the question of the meaning of עצר. The noun form occurs only three times, but the verb is frequent. In II Kings 17:4 the king of Assyria "shut up" Hoshea "and bound him in prison." In Jer. 33:1; 39:15 the prophet is "shut up [עצור] in the court of the guard." The second word sometimes has the meaning of "judicial sentence" (Deut. 17:9, 11;

was taken away, see Exeg. The servant is pictured as led to execution. Israel no longer existed as an independent nation (cf. the "dry bones" in Ezek. 37). The people is now a corpse, **cut off out of the land of the living.** The prophet's listeners would accede to this; it summed up the depth of their discouragement and woe. Each of the pagan rulers links Israel's death with the sin of his own people (cf. "who loved me" in Gal. 2:20). The prophet knows that only as a vicarious sacrifice is personally ap-

propriated does it avail. No nation took Israel's fate as such an offering; but Christ's sacrifice of himself fulfilled the prophet's ideal and is accepted in faith by each Christian. Israel's **grave is with the wicked;** She is "one with Nineveh and Tyre," an extinct people destroyed by divine judgment.

The prophet insists that Israel was free from the two sins most common among nations in their official acts—**violence and deceit.** He does not make his people sinless, but happily in

9 And he made his grave with the wicked, and with the rich in his death; because he had done no violence, neither *was any* deceit in his mouth.	9 And they made his grave with the wicked and with a rich man in his death, although he had done no violence, and there was no deceit in his mouth.

I Kings 20:40; Ezek. 23:45; North, *Suffering Servant in Deutero-Isaiah,* pp. 124-25). Translate, "from imprisonment and from sentence [or judgment] he was taken away." The verb **he was taken away** (i.e., to death) has this meaning in Prov. 24:11 (cf. also Gen. 5:24; II Kings 2:3). **And as for his generation, who considered:** The difficulty lies in the word דור, **generation.** The LXX and Vulg. translate it so, but the meaning is by no means clear. Many proposals have been made. Driver ("Linguistic and Textual Problems," pp. 48-49) suggests "his state," on the basis of the Akkadian *durum,* "lasting state," "permanent condition," and the Arabic *daurun,* "turn" or "change of fortune" (cf. 24:6). North renders, "And on his fate, who reflected?" H. H. Rowley (*The Biblical Doctrine of Election* [London: Lutterworth Press, 1950], p. 116), "And who gave a thought to his fate?" Torrey reads, "his line," and adduces cogent parallels (Pss. 73:15; 112:2; Deut. 32:19-20). Volz (*Jesaia II,* p. 170) translates, "generation" (*Geschlecht*), and interprets it as posterity, though he makes no reference to Torrey. This is attractive, for "it is the last and bitterest drop in the cup of the dying that no one takes any concern about his children" (*um den Seinen, ibid.,* p. 178). Moreover, this would accentuate the solitariness of the servant, so marked a feature of the poem from the beginning. The prophet's constant interest in children and offspring is to be observed. Another difficulty is the expression מפשע עמי, **the transgression of my people** (vs. 8d). The LXX has ἀπὸ τῶν ἀνομιῶν, "the rebellious." If the prophet is the speaker, there is no difficulty, but it is not easily explained if the nations are speaking. Many exegetes therefore emend the phrase to מפשענו, "our transgressions." Torrey explains it as each nation speaking for itself. Others refer the pronoun to God. An alternative is to transfer the final *yôdh* of עמי to the next word and read, "he was stricken for the transgression of the people," the singular being used in the universal sense of "peoples" as in 42:6 (cf. Rowley, *Biblical Doctrine of Election,* p. 116, n. 3). The Dead Sea Scroll reads "his people," an unfortunate implication. The closing words of the verse נגע למו (lit., "stricken to him") seem awkward. The LXX reads "led to death" (ἤχθη εἰς θάνατον). This suggests the emendation to הגע למות. It is a distinct improvement over the present Hebrew text, is supported by the parallelism, and fits the total context of the strophe. The servant was imprisoned, subjected to an unjust trial, and condemned to death. He was cut off from the land of the living, stricken to death for the transgression of others. To the very last he was persecuted and rejected.

9. **His grave** was appointed (the Hebrew is impersonal, "one appointed") with common criminals. The Dead Sea Scroll has the plural verb. **A rich man** (עשיר) is

exile a nation is not tempted, for the nation is dead. This poet rightly diagnoses the besetting sins of governments.

Who can reflect, unmoved, upon the round
Of smooth and solemnized complacencies,
By which, on Christian lands, from age to age
Profession mocks performance. Earth is sick,
And Heaven is weary of the hollow words
Which States and Kingdoms utter when they talk
Of truth and justice.[6]

One may instance more recently the shameful record of the United States with the Cherokees, and of Britain with the Matabele and their

king, Lo Bengula. A missionary reports the latter as saying:

Did you ever see a chameleon with a fly? The chameleon gets behind the fly and remains motionless for some time, then he advances very slowly and gently, first putting forward one leg and then another. At last, when well within reach, he darts out his tongue and the fly disappears. England is the chameleon and I am that fly.[7]

The kings know well the practices of governments, and Israel was not guilty of their diplomatic iniquities.

[7] Basil Williams, *Cecil Rhodes* (London: Constable & Co., 1921), p. 173.

[6] Wordsworth, *The Excursion,* Bk. V.

10 ¶ Yet it pleased the LORD to bruise him; he hath put *him* to grief: when thou

10 Yet it was the will of the LORD to bruise him;
he has put him to grief;[z]
when he makes himself[a] an offering for sin,

[z] Heb *made him sick*
[a] Vg: Heb *thou makest his soul*

---

generally emended to "evildoers" (עֹשֵׂי רַע), a simple solution to a manifest difficulty. The LXX has the plural, "the rich"; Targ., "those that are rich in possessions they have obtained by violence." It is possible, however, that the allusion to "the rich" is lost to us or that it is meant as synonymous with **the wicked**, as in the prophets (Mic. 6:12; Jer. 9:23; 17:11), the sages (Prov. 11:16; 28:11) and in the N.T. (Luke 6:24; 12:21; 16:19; Matt. 19:23). **In his death:** Lit., "in his deaths." The LXX, Vulg., and Targ. read the singular. The Dead Sea Scroll has בומתו, lit., "his high place or mound"—burial mound (?)—so Ibn Ezra, but the word *bâmāh* does not have this meaning elsewhere in the O.T. (Ezek. 43:7 is insecure). The meaning may be present in Ugaritic, however. In Baal and Anath (I AB, 1. 7) *bâmāh* appears and is rendered as "tomb" by H. L. Ginsberg. W. C. Graham and H. G. May (*Culture and Conscience* [Chicago: University of Chicago Press, 1936], p. 133) and Engnell (" 'Ebed Yahweh Songs and the Suffering Messiah," p. 86) go much further in their interpretation of the Ugaritic passage, but the latter is so obscure that no clear meaning may be derived from it. See also Albright (*Archaeology and Religion of Israel*, pp. 105-7 and notes) for important discussion of the linguistic associations and interpretations of *bâmāh*. Numerous emendations have been proposed. One's conclusion can be only tentative. Read, "his tomb." Lindblom takes the word in its form in the Dead Sea Scroll as the poetic plural of "day" (יוֹם), "earlier in his life he had been with rich men," but this is most unlikely. The Dead Sea Scroll וְעַמֹן for the sign of the object וְאֵת may be of importance, but defies explanation for the present. **Although he had done no violence:** The concessive is introduced by the preposition *'al* (Kautzsch, *op. cit.*, sec. 160c). The servant suffered all these ignominies and injustices although he was absolutely innocent. Neither in deed nor word did he merit such treatment.

5. FIFTH STROPHE: THE LORD'S PURPOSE AND THE SERVANT'S DESTINY (53:10-12)

The final strophe parallels the first and brings the poem to a climax. It includes a number of the motifs of the lament but adds features of supreme importance. The prophet's thought is incandescent in its intensity and concentration. Second Isaiah does not seek to give a universal explanation to the problem of theodicy or to inculcate the merits of vicarious suffering. Behind the story of the servant's tragic career—life, death, and burial—stands the purpose of God. Many scholars find difficulty with the abruptness of vss. 10-12, but they connect admirably with what precedes. There was no apparent reason for the servant's evil fate. He had not deserved it. The explanation for it lies in the divine purpose. God is the speaker throughout; the shift from third to first person is by no means unprecedented.

10. The prophet shifts the normal order of the words to emphasize Yahweh's activity in all the servant's sufferings. **Yet it was the will of the LORD:** The opening word is the

---

10-12. *The Lord Purposed Israel's Sin-bearing.* —God concludes the dialogue. Israel did not choose suffering, nor are her resurrection and exaltation a reward of obedience. God has graciously planned all. Both through Israel and through Christ God was "reconciling the world unto himself." This transforms events in history into eternal revelations of his grace. Luther wrote of the narrative of Calvary: "To me it is not simply an old song of an event that happened fifteen hundred years ago; it is something more than an event that happened once—for

shalt make his soul an offering for sin, he shall see *his* seed, he shall prolong *his* days, and the pleasure of the LORD shall prosper in his hand.

he shall see his offspring, he shall prolong his days; the will of the LORD shall prosper in his hand;

---

ordinary *waw* ("and") in Hebrew. Instead of **will** we should probably read "purpose," a major element in the prophet's theology (44:28; 46:10; 48:14; cf. 42:21; 55:11). The repetition at the end of the verse not only confirms this but underlines the importance of the thought. For **bruise him** the LXX reads "cleanse [or "purge"] him," an acceptable meaning in the Aramaic. **He has put him to grief:** The Masoretes point the word as an imperfect Hiphil of חלה on the order of the *lāmēdh-'āleph* verbs, the *'āleph* being dropped as quiescent (*ibid.*, secs. 74k, 75ii). The consonants mean "the sickness" (cf. RSV mg.). The Vulg. reads similarly, *in infirmitate;* the LXX has "with blows." Budde, Torrey, and others therefore read simply "with sickness." The Dead Sea Scroll reads ויחללהו, "that he might wound [or "pierce"] him" (cf. vs. 5; Pss. 77:10 [Hebrew 77:11]; 109:22; and especially Ezek. 28:9). This deserves serious consideration, but it is best to read "with sickness" or "grief." **When he makes himself an offering for sin:** Cf. the Vulg., *Si posuerit pro peccato animam suam.* The subject of the clause is *naphshô,* which can be rendered either by "himself" or "his life." To make *naphshô* an object requires emendation of the Hebrew verb to the masculine. A literal translation of the Hebrew is "When his life shall make an offering for sin." Observe the same relation between life (*néphesh*) and offspring in Pss. 22:29-30 (Hebrew 22:30-31) and 25:13, in which the psalmist contrasts the present and future generations. The clauses (vs. 10cd) should not be separated. Although the servant offers his life as a guilt offering, he shall yet have posterity he was denied in his lifetime (cf. vs. 8b). Cut off and isolated from everyone, solitary and rejected and spurned, without family and defendants, he now will have the joy and comfort of children. The divine justice and mercy meet in the servant: sin must be punished and righteousness rewarded. The sin was not the servant's, to be sure; all the more will his voluntary offering of himself as an atoning sacrifice be of great avail. The idea of substitutionary sacrifice is of great antiquity and dispersed among many peoples in the ancient Near East (see Albright, *From Stone Age to Christianity,* pp. 252-55; René Dussaud, *Les origines cananéennes du sacrifice israélite* [Paris: Ernest Leroux, 1921], p. 127; Theodor H. Gaster, "The Service of the Sanctuary: A Study in Hebrew Survivals,"

---

it is a gift and a bestowing that endures forever." [8]

When he makes himself an offering for sin, does not imply that Israel placates a hostile Deity. The KJV rightly stresses God's prompting of this sacrifice. So it is at Calvary. Calvin insists: "God the Father doth with his love precede and go before our reconciliation in Christ; yea, because he first loved us, therefore he afterwards doth reconcile us unto himself." [9]

He shall see his offspring, he shall prolong his days. This is the nation's resurrection. One servant becomes a community. "There is a budding morrow in midnight." [10] This is the morrow of Israel's exile, when the restored community becomes God's evangelist to the world.

He shall see of the travail of his soul. The line may be uncertain in the Hebrew but

[8] *Werke* (Erlangen: Carl Heyder, 1845), Vol. XX, Part I, p. 114.
[9] *Institutes* II. 16. 3.
[10] Keats, "To Homer."

satisfied expresses the content of the passage. With what would such a servant as is here depicted be satisfied? Or the crucified Lord be satisfied?

By his knowledge, i.e., his insight into God's purpose. An illustration is the startling act of Albert Schweitzer, who in 1904 gave up his career as an outstanding organist and theologian with a university chair at Strasbourg, to study medicine. With his Christian conscience he had become convinced that he must make reparation for European mistreatment of the primitive Africans. His dedication of himself as a missionary doctor in Lambaréné contributed more to his spiritual influence than did his former career. Vs. 11b may be used as the effect of Schweitzer's act on the white race. It is a vicarious sacrifice for sins.

A portion with the great. No small part of Israel's eminence is her interpretation through this prophet of the national fate. A sin-bearing people is unique in history. Our poet claimed

11 He shall see of the travail of his soul, *and* shall be satisfied: by his knowledge shall my righteous servant justify many; for he shall bear their iniquities.

11 he shall see the fruit of the travail of his soul and be satisfied;
by his knowledge shall the righteous one, my servant,
make many to be accounted righteous;
and he shall bear their iniquities.

Mélanges syriens [Paris: P. Geuthner, 1939], II, 577-82; J. J. Stamm, *Das Leiden des Unschuldigen in Babylon und Israel* [Zürich: Zwingli, 1946], pp. 26 ff., 68 ff.; S. H. Hooke, "The Theory and Practice of Substitution," *Vetus Testamentum*, II [1952], 2-17). What is extraordinary here is the transformation of ancient categories into the loftiest values of religion, especially the unique character of the sufferer. The servant lives in intimate fellowship and communion with God, his silence and patience and humility are the expression of his nearness to his covenant Lord. It is the nations who live a broken and unholy existence, who need reconciliation and restoration. Therefore their sin must be atoned for. Sacrifice is the means of effecting the relationship. The servant's nearness to God makes him an instrument for God's purpose. He offers himself as an *'āshām* or "guilt offering" (Lev. 5:1-19; 7:1-38; 14:1-57; I Sam. 6:3) for the sins of the nations. He gives himself as a substitute, suffers vicariously, and his offering is efficacious in achieving the removal of the guilt of others. **He shall prolong his days:** Long life was a sign of God's favor and blessing. The verse seems to express the idea of resurrection or restoration to life. If the servant is the community, we have ample precedent for the idea, but it would be most striking if Second Isaiah referred to the resurrection of an individual, since this represents a late development (26:19; Dan. 12:2; cf. R. H. Pfeiffer, *Introduction to the Old Testament* [New York: Harper & Bros., 1941], p. 479). The great surprise of the nations reflected in vs. 1 and 52:13 need not imply that an individual is meant; surely the elevation and "success" of Israel, conceived with great elasticity and fluidity, would occasion a similar reaction (cf. Ezek. 37:1-14).

11. The concentration of mood and thought and the repetition of words and phrases notable throughout the poem come to a climax here and in vs. 12. The meaning of **servant,** both the nature of his service and its consequences, is revealed in a succession of lines which have no parallel in the O.T. The verbs are especially noteworthy. The servant makes himself an offering for sin, makes many to be accounted righteous, pours out his soul to death, is numbered with the transgressors, bears the sin of many, and makes intercession for the transgressors.

He shall see the fruit of the travail of his soul: The Hebrew reads, lit., "Of the travail of his soul [life] he shall see." The preposition **of** (*min*) has been construed in

---

this painful height for his nation: In his first version of Hyperion Keats interprets the poetic calling as a sympathetic sharing of the woes of men:

None can usurp this height. . . .
But those to whom the miseries of the world
Are misery, and will not let them rest.

And he adds:

Only the dreamer venoms all his days,
Bearing more woe than all his sins deserve.[1]

This height our prophet attained. This is the dream he sought to set in the hearts of his fellow exiles. It requires daring to hold up such

an ideal to a nation. He believed God had a glorious future in store for Israel; but the road to it lay through this tragedy. Mazzini declared:

A people cannot be regenerated by teaching them the worship of enjoyment; they cannot be taught a spirit of sacrifice by speaking to them of material rewards. . . . Say to men, *Come, suffer; you will hunger and thirst . . . , be betrayed, cursed; but you have a great duty to accomplish:* they will be deaf, perhaps, for a long time, to the severe voice of virtue; but on the day that they do come to you, they will come as heroes, and will be invincible.[2]

This is rarely the appeal of the politician. His usual message addresses self-interest. But this proves shortsighted. We stand today in one

[1] Canto I.

[2] *Essays* (London: Walter Scott, 1887), pp. 289-90.

12 Therefore will I divide him *a portion* with the great, and he shall divide the spoil with the strong; because he hath poured out his soul unto death: and he was num-

12 Therefore I will divide him a portion
    with the great,
  and he shall divide the spoil with the
    strong;
because he poured out his soul to death,
  and was numbered with the transgres-
    sors;

---

many different ways: because of, as a result of, as object (so RSV), etc. It is best to take it temporally, however: "after the travail of his life" (König, Volz, North; cf. Eduard König, *Das Buch Jesaja* [Gütersloh: C. Bertelsmann, 1926], p. 441; Kautzsch, *op. cit.*, sec. 119*y*, n. 3). The LXX and the Dead Sea Scroll provide the object of the verb: "shall see light" (cf. 60:19-20; Ps. 36:9). **By his knowledge:** This phrase is often attached to the preceding verb: "Be satisfied with his knowledge" (so Aq., Symm., Theod.). Rhythm and parallelism require some such change. Instead of "with knowledge," one MS reads "his adversity" or "the evil done to him," which is accepted by several scholars, though they all attach it to the preceding verb: "through his suffering he shall be filled" (Kissane); "through his affliction shall my righteous servant" (Bewer). D. Winton Thomas derives the word from a root meaning "to humiliate": "He shall be sated with his humiliation" ("More Notes on the Root ידע," pp. 404-5). If the evidence of the LXX and the Dead Sea Scroll of vs. 11*a* is accepted, however, the usual meaning of knowledge suits the parallelism better. Many scholars delete **the righteous one** as dittography (Hebrew יצדיק צדיק) and enlist the support of several MSS. Torrey transposes the words and translates, "He will be satisfied with the knowledge that he is right; my servant will bring many to the right." It is doubtful whether *çaddiq* has this meaning in the context, however. It is possible that it is a dittograph, but the arguments against it are not decisive. It is better therefore to retain it (see Kautzsch, *op. cit.*, sec. 132*b*). Later writers seem to have read it in their text (e.g., the writer of the Parables of Enoch). The verb **to be accounted righteous** has a forensic connotation here. The primary meaning is of acquittal; the many are declared innocent even though they were in reality guilty. The servant has taken on him the guilt of "us all." Volz is right in seeing the significance of the alternation of the perfect and imperfect of the verbs as designating an act accomplished once for all and one that has continuing efficacy. The verb **he shall bear** (*şābhal* in vs. 11*d* and *nāsā'* in vs. 12*e*) is another echo from the lament (vs. 4*ab*).

12. The concluding **therefore** is hardly the apodosis of vs. 11 but rather anticipates the "because" of vs. 12*c*. The repeated *rabbîm* (cf. 52:14*a*, 15*b*) is here rendered as **great** and **many**. This is of course possible, especially in view of the literary practice of the prophet. But this hardly suits the astonishment of the kings at the glory of the servant

---

world with all nations. To bid Americans be kind out of our abundance, without curtailing comforts, will neither move them nor meet the situation. There must be an outpouring of soul. Each nation must take on its conscience the lacks and wrongs of all.

He was numbered with the transgressors, numbered by the world and by God. Also by himself—for it is fellowship in penitence for the sins of all which is implied. Nations and individuals are so bound together in the one bundle of life that none can live or die to self alone. The God-imposed duty on those who are spiritually alive, pre-eminently upon the Christian church, is to make **intercession for the transgressors.** Intercessory prayer is social

prayer, like the Lord's Prayer where "us" and "our" include the whole family of God. A people feeling itself caught with all nations in the appalling entanglements of history will possess the sympathy to understand the situation and to make its own adversity or prosperity a guilt offering. So doing, **the will of the LORD shall prosper in its hand.** No richer message than that of this sublime poem could be preached to one's own country now.

Christians have rightly seen in this poem a prophecy of our Lord's passion, death, and resurrection. It was never spiritually appropriated by the Jewish nation or by the devout community within it. The N.T. church saw its fulfillment in Jesus, and it supplied an inter-

| bered with the transgressors; and he bare the sin of many, and made intercession for the transgressors. | yet he bore the sin of many, and made intercession for the transgressors. |

(52:15), and the general context leads us to expect something more than that he will share the power of other potentates. It is more likely that *bârabbîm* should be taken as direct object, the *bêth* belonging to the verb (König, *op. cit.*, p. 442, n. 3; Kautzsch, *op. cit.*, sec. 119*k*): "Therefore I will divide to him the many as a portion, the countless he will share as booty" (for *'açûmîm* as "countless" cf. Prov. 7:26). The servant's reward is described as **spoil**, which is often interpreted as material possessions and worldly power. There may be an allusion here to 40:9-10, where the same symbolism is used (cf. Exod. 15:9). The whole tenor of the poem and the imaginative way in which the sufferings of the servant are described leads one to suspect that the term *shālāl* is employed more generally of recompense (cf. Prov. 31:11; 16:19). This seems to be confirmed by the following lines:

> He poured out his soul to death,
> and was numbered with the transgressors.

His life was sacrificed as an offering for sin, and he was counted among criminals. Yet the truth was that **he bore the sin of many**, and while he was considered a transgressor, he was interceding for the transgressors who were persecuting and destroying him. Thus the poem closes magnificently on the note of intercession. Like Abraham, Israel's "father"; Moses, the mediator of the covenant; the prophets, and psalmists (Gen. 18:22-32; Exod. 32:11-14, 32; Amos 7:1-6; Jer. 7:16; 11:14; 15:1; Ezek. 14:14-20; for a thorough and extended discussion see Johannsen, *Parakletoi*), the servant of the Lord intercedes for others. But his intercession is raised to a height unparalleled by the others. He prays for those who were the instruments of his unexampled suffering. That the last line of this particular poem with its vast range and profundity and its eschatological context should center on the servant's prayer not only reveals the depths of Israel's faith but also provides us with a glimpse into the character of the servant himself. Like Hosea and Jeremiah and the other tragic sufferers of Israel, the servant of the Lord finds his ultimate and intensely personal fellowship with the Lord whose servant he was (see Eichrodt's important comments in *Theologie des A.T.*, I, 75-76, 246, 259). Christians are inevitably reminded of the cry from the cross (cf. also Rom. 8:26-27; Heb. 7:25).

It is a matter of major importance to understand how the covenant community employed this poem, how it interpreted it, and when it made use of it. For the Christian community this passage has a supreme significance: it depicts the life history of the Lord. The church is not disturbed over discrepancies between the O.T. portrait and the N.T. reality (see Acts 8:30-35; etc.). The poem reaches back to the very beginnings of Israel, for all Israel—in its varying distances and guises, held succinct and understood in its maximum form as a person—is present.

pretation of his baffling fate. The apostles preached their Master's death and resurrection as the supreme disclosure of God's love in offering his Son to die, the righteous for the unrighteous, to reconcile a sinful world to its God. This gospel was verified in their experience of forgiven fellowship with their Father, and in their victory through Christ over the world, sin, and death. Paul tells us that he preached that "Christ died for our sins according to the Scriptures," and that he "was raised again for our justification" (I Cor. 15:3; Rom. 4:25). Both cross and victory found their meaning through this prophecy.

Scholars differ whether our Lord himself saw in it his role as God's servant. Admittedly it is difficult to go behind his interpreters and be confident that we reach his own mind. But if men of far less spiritual discernment saw its relevance to him, it seems incredible that he did not draw inspiration from it. If he did, it would explain in part the supreme decision of his

54 Sing, O barren, thou *that* didst not bear; break forth into singing, and

54 "Sing, O barren one, who did not bear;
break forth into singing and cry aloud,
you who have not been in travail!

F. The Consolation of Israel (54:1-17)

The pathos of the preceding chapter is broken by a cry of joy. The new poem takes up the theme of comfort, developed in previous chapters and given a tragic dimension in 52:13–53:12, and paves the way to the final outburst of ch. 55. In literary composition and thought it stands in close relation with 51:17–52:13. There the theme of the coming of the king in his glory to usher in the time of salvation occupies the center of the stage; here it is the inauguration of the new covenant.

The problem of the relation of this chapter to the poem on the suffering servant is difficult. In every other poem we have encountered transitional devices and echoes of preceding poems, but ch. 54 contains relatively few. It is possible, however, that 52:13–53:12 performs a very special function. Between the two very striking and similar poems (51:17–52:12 and 52:13–53:12), pitched in an exalted key of rhapsodic excitement, Second Isaiah may have felt the need of a poem which would do justice to the tragic dimensions of the historical situation which he viewed in all its distances and depths. We have instances of such sudden shifts elsewhere, e.g., in the juxtaposition of invective and oracle of salvation. The prophet never maintains the level of ecstasy over an extended period. Precisely at the juncture of the coming of the kingdom and the inauguration of the new covenant, he finds it necessary to place the poem on the suffering servant. The portrait of the servant's career from an eschatological perspective is certainly not alien to the context. Besides, it must be borne in mind that the major context of 52:13–53:12 is one of triumph and exaltation, so that a very real continuity is after all present. Indeed, the sharp contrasts and the motif of the great reversal bind the poems into a fairly well-knit unity. The connection of 52:13–53:12 is coming more and more to be recognized in the works of recent writers, e.g., Bentzen, Mowinckel, Engnell, and others (see Lindblom, *Servant Songs in Deutero-Isaiah*, p. 50). Again, when once the servant poems are recognized as the work of Second Isaiah, the whole problem, theological as well as literary, is changed, for 52:13–53:12 must then be read in the light of a literary whole, which includes within it the portrait of the servant as a major *dramatis persona,* and

career, when he abandoned his ministry of teaching and healing in Galilee and went up publicly to Jerusalem, courting death at the hands of the leaders of the Jewish church and their Roman masters. It would supply a basis for a number of his recorded sayings which patently echo its language.

What Israel, even in her most believing fellowship, failed to realize, Jesus gloriously achieved. Ten thousand times ten thousand out of all nations have found in him the Savior who has borne their sins, through whom they are accounted and made righteous, and who, their exalted Lord, continues his redemptive work in and for them.

54:1-17. The Everlasting Mercy.—This poem of tender encouragement fulfills the initial command to "speak to the heart of Jerusalem" (40:2). Its background was the sadness of the exiles over the fact that at best they might expect only a fraction of their fellow country-

men to return to the homeland. For economic reasons the Jews had settled down where they were living. By no means the whole of Israel would leave and go back to Zion. The prospect was for a sparsely inhabited land and a city far less populous than the former Jerusalem. The preceding poem on Israel as the sin-bearing servant of the Lord had predicted that the nation would be "exalted," "lifted up," and "very high." The servant would see "seed." This chapter describes the seed, who are not only far more numerous than anyone dared anticipate but also disciples of the Lord (vs. 13), inhabiting a city established in righteousness (vs. 14). It is appropriate that the posterity of the servant should also be servants of the Lord, and henceforward the servant is not mentioned: he lives on in the citizens of the nation, rewooed and rewed to its Lord.

1-5. Zion Extends Her Borders.—The blood of martyrs has often been the seed of the

cry aloud, thou *that* didst not travail with child: for more *are* the children of the desolate than the children of the married wife, saith the Lord.	For the children of the desolate one will be more than the children of her that is married, says the Lord.

an eschatology which infinitely deepens the function of the servant and infinitely extends the range of his activity.

The literary imagination and theological penetration which were responsible for the poems in their present order are apparent in ch. 54. The variety of mood, the richness of allusion, the literary structure, and the numerous devices of literary emphasis all suggest that the poet is seeking to reproduce in words the deep feelings which surge through his soul and the thoughts which stir him as he approaches the end. This is clear, above all, in his use of the particle *kî* (vss. 1*c*, 3*a*, 4*abc*, 5*a*, 6*a*, 6*c*, 9*a*, 10*a*, 14*bc*). Again, the poem has a large number of *formulae citandi* like says the Lord, etc. (1*d*, 5*b*, 8*d*, 10*e*, 17*e*), employed in sharp contrast to the manner of the prophet's postexilic successors. Further, the titles applied to God are abundant and impressive, sometimes, as in vs. 5, following one upon another: **Your Maker, your husband, the Holy One of Israel, the God of the whole earth, your God, the Lord your Redeemer, the Lord, who has compassion on you.** Imperatives, words of address, contrasts, paronomasia, introductions and conclusions to the strophes, and figures of speech are all employed with special effect. Not the least impressive is the way in which verbs are employed and the way that they carry the burden of the prophet's thought. The poem as a whole is in the manner of the oracle of salvation. The lyrical quality is present throughout.

The poem is composed of six strophes (vss. 1-3, 4-5, 6-8, 9-10, 11-15, 16-17). The meter is not regular, but 3+3 prevails.

1. First Strophe: Zion's Many Children and Her Spacious Dwelling (54:1-3)

The strophe is composed of two series of imperatives, each followed by a solemn asseveration (vss. 1*ab*, 2). The language of vss. 1-2 is figurative; vs. 3 interprets the figures in a tristich. With the destruction of the city, Zion had become **barren,** for her husband had left her. She lies solitary, desolate, and unloved. But now in the imminent future she is to have more children than in the days of her married life from the covenant on Sinai to the separation at the fall of the city. The prophet uses the favorite figure of Hosea, Jeremiah, and Ezekiel to describe Yahweh's relation to Israel. It is remarkable that the prophets were able to utilize the relationship which had been so corrupted in contemporary nature cults, purge it of all its debasing elements, and transform its significance into a profound expression of the holy and intimate relation between the covenant people with her covenant God. Israel is to experience a new life and a new covenant devotion in which her Lord takes the initiative.

54:1. The prophet employs the figure of Zion as the bereaved and widowed mother (cf. 49:14-21; 50:3). Jerusalem was destroyed by the Babylonians in 586 B.C. and Judah

church. It was Stephen's fidelity to Christ attested in death which sharpened the "goad" in the conscience of Saul of Tarsus. A community which has suffered for righteousness' sake possesses a mysterious power of self-multiplication. The church has emerged from epochs of persecution stronger both in spirit and in numbers than she was before (vs. 1). The metaphor of marriage joining the Lord to his people is frequent in both Hosea and Jeremiah as well as in this prophet, and is taken up again in the

N.T., where Christ is spoken of as the husband of his people (Eph. 5:23; Rev. 21:2, 9). One must think of the Jewish family where the husband is the wife's lord, rather than of the modern family where husband and wife are equal mates. The metaphor implies submission to authority on the church's part, and for both the Lord and the church mutual possession and comradeship. The Lord chooses and weds his bride. Her unfaithfulness breaks the bond but does not quench his amazing love. "He abideth

2 Enlarge the place of thy tent, and let them stretch forth the curtains of thine habitations: spare not, lengthen thy cords, and strengthen thy stakes;
 	
3 For thou shalt break forth on the right hand and on the left; and thy seed shall inherit the Gentiles, and make the desolate cities to be inhabited.
	2 Enlarge the place of your tent,
	  and let the curtains of your habitations
	    be stretched out;
	  hold not back, lengthen your cords
	    and strengthen your stakes.
	3 For you will spread abroad to the right
	    and to the left,
	  and your descendants will possess the
	    nations
	  and will people the desolate cities.

laid in ruins. The motif of the increased population was probably not original with Second Isaiah, but he represents one of the major stages in its development (cf. among others, Hos. 1:10–2:1; Zech. 2:5; 8:3 ff.). **Barren:** The figure of the barren wife is a favorite one in the traditions of Israel, recalling the wives of the patriarchs, of Hannah, etc. Birth was a wonder full of mystery and was considered to be the gift and act of God's gracious goodness. The destruction of Jerusalem was the divorce between Yahweh and his people (50:1); the Exile, the period of her barrenness. **The married wife:** Cf. 62:4. The wonder of the great event is accentuated: she who is barren and solitary, separated from her husband in Babylonian exile, is to have more children than in the time of her marriage before 586 B.C. The affliction of barrenness and the importance of having many children, so common in the Bible and in the Orient today, lies behind this figure (see Gal. 4:27).

2. So numerous will be the children that the tent of mother Zion must be enlarged. For the same allusion but with the opposite application see Jer. 10:20. The nomadic coloring is felicitous. **And let the curtains of your habitations . . . :** It is probably better to read the imperative with the versions, **stretch forth.** The tent covering is to be greatly extended. **Hold not back:** "Without limit" (Amer. Trans.). The M.T. attaches the words to vs. 2b, the RSV with the following clause. A large tent requires long ropes and strong tent pegs.

3. The following lines, impressive in themselves, receive special emphasis by their climactic position, their triadic form, and their eschatological coloring. It is possible that there is a reminiscence here of Gen. 28:17; if so, the whole passage takes on fresh significance, for the patriarchs are then in the background of the writer's thought. How extensively Israel will spread out is not entirely clear. Volz thinks only to the neighboring territory, but Haller sees an expansion throughout the earth. Duhm and Marti find an allusion here to the restoration of the Davidic monarchy. In the years following the fall of Jerusalem in 586 B.C. the neighboring peoples, especially Ammon and Edom, took advantage of Judah's plight. The prophet combines historical and eschatological language here, so it is difficult to tell which is uppermost in his mind.

faithful: he cannot deny himself" (II Tim. 2:13).

Enlarge the place of your tent. How heartening to faith and hope, with the homeland under aliens, to contemplate additions to its territory! Such an expectation of growth ought always to be before the church. She must keep the balance between the outreach of her mission and the depth of her life in God. In eighteenth-century Britain a devout soul like William Law strengthened her **stakes** by exposing the superficiality of the piety of her members, and John Wesley and his colleagues lengthened her **cords**

to embrace neglected masses in the population. In twentieth-century United States the church lengthened her cords to bring society in its every realm under the spirit of Christ, but during some decades there was no corresponding strengthening of her anchorage in God. The spiritual quality of her life became pitiably thin.

You will spread abroad to the right and to the left. By the disasters of 597 and 586 Judah had been reduced to a tiny territory. The prophet is not thinking of a conquest of her neighbors, but of a peaceful expansion beyond her contracted borders. Like the church,

4 Fear not; for thou shalt not be ashamed: neither be thou confounded; for thou shalt not be put to shame: for thou shalt forget the shame of thy youth, and shalt not remember the reproach of thy widowhood any more.

5 For thy Maker is thine husband; The Lord of hosts is his name; and thy Redeemer the Holy One of Israel; The God of the whole earth shall he be called.

---

4 "Fear not, for you will not be ashamed;
  be not confounded, for you will not be
    put to shame;
for you will forget the shame of your
    youth,
  and the reproach of your widowhood
    you will remember no more.
5 For your Maker is your husband,
  the Lord of hosts is his name;
and the Holy One of Israel is your Redeemer,
  the God of the whole earth he is called.

---

2. Second Strophe: The Lord Is the Husband of Israel (54:4-5)

Two emphatic imperatives, which express Israel's memory of her past and present, are followed by two *ki* clauses; these, in turn, are reinforced by a *ki* distich which emphasizes Israel's forgetting of her past and present, while the final tetrastich, again introduced by *ki*, forms a superb theocentric climax. This contains the essence of the prophet's thought, the grounds for the admonition and assurance of the first lines.

4. The decisive event which is to inaugurate a new period in Israel's life is matched with the characteristic **Fear not.** The covenant people need not fear the recurrence of the humiliation and disgrace of the past, for the coming of the Lord as king and as initiator of the new covenant will bring an end to past misfortunes. As the meaning of Israel's faith was enshrined in memory of the past, the command has peculiar force here. **The shame of your youth** may refer to the period of Egyptian bondage, but more likely to the whole pre-exilic period of infidelity (cf. Hos. 2:17; Jer. 2:2). The period of widowhood is the time of the Exile. Thus the prophet comprehends past, present, and future within his range of vision.

5. The reasons for the admonitions and assurances are stated here: **Your Maker is your husband, . . . the Holy One of Israel is your Redeemer.** Israel owes the origin of her life to God, her uniqueness to the covenant marriage. As Israel's **Holy One,** he is her protector and the guardian of her destiny, the *gō'ēl* or **Redeemer** who is responsible for her deliverance and liberation. As God of the whole earth, he is omnipotent to achieve his purposes. Therefore Israel must not fear. The juxtaposition of the divine titles is noteworthy. Yahweh is Israel's **Maker,** and he is her **Redeemer;** he is her **husband** and her **Holy One.** Israel's beginning and end are under his sovereignty; her covenant existence is with the holy God.

---

the Jewish religious community is no imperial aggressor. She embraces and shares with nearby peoples her spiritual treasures. Every vital congregation should be spreading abroad. It is not numerical growth alone, but the areas of life which she leavens, which God asks of her.

You will not be ashamed. Zion forgets the humiliation of her youth as a slave people and of her widowhood in her exile. The church has had her periods of bondage. We are emerging from "the tyranny of things" in a materialistic epoch. The church realizes that she must keep before herself standards other than those by which she has been measuring her usefulness. Her physical resources may diminish, as indeed those of a war-devastated earth have shrunk.

There must be greater emphasis on "being rich toward God." That is the essence of the marital tie stressed in this passage. The wealth in God is enumerated. He is **the Lord of hosts,** with all the forces of the universe at his beck. He is **the Holy One,** immeasurably above and other than man, and at the same time **the Holy One of Israel,** her **Maker** and her **husband,** who has chosen, educated, and is now redeeming his people. In covenant with them he will carry forward his purpose for mankind, **the God of the whole earth he is called.** Vs. 5 sums up the prophet's theology. God is Lord of the universe high above and different from man, graciously entering into fellowship with his chosen people for the redemption of the entire human race.

<table>
<tr><td>

6 For the LORD hath called thee as a woman forsaken and grieved in spirit, and a wife of youth, when thou wast refused, saith thy God.

7 For a small moment have I forsaken thee; but with great mercies will I gather thee.

8 In a little wrath I hid my face from thee for a moment; but with everlasting kindness will I have mercy on thee, saith the LORD thy Redeemer.

</td><td>

6 For the LORD has called you
  like a wife forsaken and grieved in spirit,
  like a wife of youth when she is cast off,
  says your God.
7 For a brief moment I forsook you,
  but with great compassion I will gather you.
8 In overflowing wrath for a moment
  I hid my face from you,
  but with everlasting love I will have compassion on you,
  says the LORD, your Redeemer.

</td></tr>
</table>

3. THIRD STROPHE: EVERLASTING COMPASSION AND EVERLASTING DEVOTION (54:6-8)

6. Now the Lord is to restore the ancient marriage relationship, but this time it will be deeper because of the experience of separation and the years of Israel's longing and grief. The strophe gains its effect by the continuation of the *kî* clauses which follow climactically one after another. In this strophe the activity of the Lord resulting from the unique relationship described in the preceding verse is set forth. **Forsaken:** "Outcast." **Like a wife of youth:** The Hebrew lacks the introductory preposition, but the RSV properly interprets as the LXX. God cannot cast off his people any more than Hosea could cast out Gomer (Hos. 2:19; 11:8-9). The mutuality of the relationship is finely expressed: Israel is **grieved in spirit** for her Lord, and God calls her by his irresistible love. The Dead Sea Scroll inserts "LORD" before **your God.**

7. For a brief moment: Driver ("Studies in Vocabulary of O.T., p. 299) renders the phrase "with little emotion," on the basis of another meaning of the same root. The separation was only temporary, a **brief moment** in God's view. Yahweh could not endure the separation for long. The contrast between the **brief moment** in which Israel was **forsaken** and the **great compassion** which moves God to **gather** his people to him again is poignant. For the **brief moment** cf. Ps. 30:5; for the reconciliation cf. Ps. 27:10. See II Cor. 4:17-18, where Paul contrasts the slight affliction of the temporal with the eternal weight of glory.

8. In overflowing wrath: The expression is a striking paronomasia: *sheçeph qéçeph.* The first word is unknown in the Hebrew, but should probably be read *sheṭeph,* "flood," "a flood of wrath." God abandoned Israel in the terrible wrath of his judgment, but again, it was only **for a moment** that he hid his face from her (cf. 8:17; Pss. 30:7;

6-8. The Lord's Affection for His People.—A polygamous background in which a wife is cast aside, as was Vashti in the harem of Ahasuerus, is in the prophet's mind. Israel seemed unvisited of God and left to her own lonely thoughts. But a wife wooed and won in youth holds a unique place in a husband's heart (cf. Prov. 5:18; Mal. 2:14-15). The prophet hopefully asserts that God's punishment is **for a brief moment.** He shares the psalmist's optimism (cf. Ps. 30:5). He holds together a historical and eternal perspective. One generation, or even three, is a short epoch in the career of a nation, and to the prophet the proximate restoration of Israel ushers in the final and abiding stage of history.

To Christians the verses speak of the contrast between the brief education of each generation of the church in the earth's hard schoolroom, and of the eternal fellowship and service of the church triumphant. In the church's experience in history and in the lives of her members there are times when God seems to withdraw himself. This may be, as in Israel's case, punishment for sin; or it may be due to various factors in the age, circumstances, or temperaments of men and women. Hugh Latimer, writing to encourage a fellow martyr, Nicholas Ridley, said that God "cometh and goeth." [3] And typical

[3] *The Cambridge History of English Literature,* ed. A. W. Ward and A. R. Waller (Cambridge: Cambridge University Press, 1908), III, 38.

9 For this *is as* the waters of Noah unto me: for *as* I have sworn that the waters of Noah should no more go over the earth; so have I sworn that I would not be wroth with thee, nor rebuke thee.

10 For the mountains shall depart, and the hills be removed; but my kindness shall not depart from thee, neither shall the covenant of my peace be removed, saith the LORD that hath mercy on thee.

9 "For this is like the days of Noah to me:
  as I swore that the waters of Noah
    should no more go over the earth,
  so I have sworn that I will not be angry with you
    and will not rebuke you.
10 For the mountains may depart
    and the hills be removed,
  but my steadfast love shall not depart from you,
    and my covenant of peace shall not be removed,
  says the LORD, who has compassion on you.

104:29; 143:7). From the perspective of those who wait, the time is very long; from the perspective of fulfillment, it is short (Volz). **But with everlasting love:** Dead Sea Scroll: "my everlasting love." The noun *ḥésedh* often has the meaning of devotion or **love** as here. The line prepares for the great climax of vs. 10*cd*. Observe how the stress also falls on the divine compassion in vss. 7*b*, 8*c* and reaches its culmination superbly in vs. 10*e*. **Your Redeemer:** The strophe presses the motif of redemption as in the conclusion of the preceding strophe (vs. 5*c*).

4. FOURTH STROPHE: THE EVERLASTING COVENANT (54:9-10)

As so frequently in Second Isaiah, and especially in this poem, the strophe is divided into two parts (vs. 9 and vs. 10; cf. vss. 1-2 with vs. 3; vs. 4 with vs. 5; vss. 6-7 with vs. 8). The introductory *ki* appears at the beginning of each division, and serves to bring the poem to its highest climax. Again the prophet employs the early traditions of Israel to develop his thought.

9. This refers to what has been said in vs. 8. Many MSS and some versions read **the waters of Noah** (KJV), but **the days of Noah** (RSV) is generally preferred. The Jacob ben Chayyim text has "for the waters," the Ben Asher text, "like the days of." The reference, then, is to the present juncture in history. **As I swore . . . :** Cf. Gen. 8:21-22 (J); 9:11-17 (P). The prophet is quite clearly familiar with the priestly tradition of the eternal covenant. Neither J nor P mentions an oath, but the expression simply records the solemnity of the divine promise. As God swore to Noah and fulfilled his promise, so he swears now that he will turn his wrath from his people forever. It is more than a happy figure which the prophet uses here: the imminent events are of essentially the same order as the promise to Noah after the universal flood. The one promise is the ground and guarantee of the other.

10. For the mountains may depart: Or "though the mountains should move" or "leave their place." The mountains are the most mighty and stable of created things (cf.

---

of many modern Christians is Henry Sidgwick's confession:

The revealing visions come and go: when they come we feel that we know: but in the intervals we must pass through states in which all is dark, and in which we can only struggle to hold the conviction that—
  Power is with us in the night
  Which made the darkness and the light
  And dwells not in the light alone.[4]

[4] Quoted in C. F. G. Masterman, *In Peril of Change* (London: T. Fisher Unwin, 1905), p. 56.

The same thought is in a stanza of Toplady's:

  Still on his plighted love
    At all events rely;
  The very hidings of his face
    Will train thee up to joy.

9-10. God Promises His People an Enduring Covenant.—This finality betokens the prophet's conviction that the return of the exiles marks the consummation of history and ushers in the eternal divine order. In history there could be no such assurance that Israel would not again

11 ¶ O thou afflicted, tossed with tempest, *and* not comforted, behold, I will lay thy stones with fair colors, and lay thy foundations with sapphires.

11 "O afflicted one, storm-tossed, and not comforted,
 behold, I will set your stones in antimony,
 and lay your foundations with sapphires.[b]

[b] Or *lapis lazuli*

Pss. 46:2-3; 114:4, 6; Hab. 3:6). The eternity of salvation is expressed by the prophets in such cosmic comparisons (Volz; cf. 51:6; Jer. 31:35-36; 33:20-21). **My steadfast love:** Or "covenant faithfulness"; cf. vs. 8, where the same word occurs. **My covenant of peace:** Cf. Ezek. 34:25; 37:26; also Num. 25:12; Mal. 2:5. **Covenant** (*berîth*) and **peace** (*shālôm*) are closely associated, and may even be used interchangeably (Gen. 26:28-31; Ps. 55:20). The latter connotes well-being, "the state prevailing in those united: the growth and full harmony of the soul" (Pedersen, *Israel, Its Life and Culture, I-II*, p. 285), and includes within it the richness and fullness of the word peace. It is doubtful whether there is any allusion here to 53:5 (cf. Feldmann, *Isaias*, p. 177), but it is possible that the servant of the Lord was considered by the prophet to be the mediator of the covenant, as in the servant passages (42:6; 49:8). For the intimate association of servant and covenant, see Lindhagen, *The Servant Motif in the O.T.*, pp. 82-106. **Says the Lord, who has compassion on you:** Cf. vss. 7*b*, 8*c*. A fitting climax to this section of the poem.

5. Fifth Strophe: The New Jerusalem (54:11-14)

A new section of the poem begins here, although it continues the thought of the preceding verses. Covenant language persists (vs. 13*ab*) and the motif of **fear not** (vs. 4*a*) is repeated (vs. 14). Moreover, vs. 11 returns characteristically to vs. 1, both in the person addressed and in the motif of reversal. The opening lines are a threefold address culminating appropriately in **not comforted,** and this is followed by an emphatic **Behold, I . . . ,** the characteristic introduction of similar eschatological promises.

11. O afflicted one: Cf. 51:21. Israel is bowed down in misery in her present enslaved condition. She is **storm-tossed,** i.e., disconcerted and troubled by the events she has

---

provoke God's judgment, as in fact the nation did. God links his promise with the most stable symbol in nature—the everlasting **hills.**

This promise to the spiritual community is echoed in Christ's assurance concerning the church, "The gates of hell shall not prevail against it." The words do not apply to any empirical church; it may suffer destruction or serious assault in the events of history. But God's purpose requires the church for its achievement. He must have a devoted community in and through which to work. Therefore the church is everlasting. So long as the church witnesses the truth of God, like truth she is indestructible. In such confidence, Horace Bushnell, publishing his *God in Christ*, wrote to Bartol:

I have a certain feeling, too, I will not deny, that if what I am about to say should be stifled and killed by an over-hasty judgment, it will yet rise again the third day. This feeling I have, not in exultation, it seems to me, not so much in the shape of defiance, as in the shape of consolation, a soft whisper that lingers round me in my studies, to

hold me firm, and smooth me into an even, uncaring spirit. Still, the best of all attitudes, I know, is this— Let me do the right, and let God take care of me. I want to be in no better hands."[5]

11-17. External Beauty and Inner Security.— **O afflicted one, storm-tossed, and not comforted.** This outburst of compassion unveils the prophet's heart and shows his fitness to be the spokesman of God's comfort. He himself had felt keenly the indignities and disheartenments endured in Babylon. Thackeray's remark holds here: "The Samaritan who rescued you, most likely, has been robbed and has bled in his day, and it is a wounded arm that bandages yours when bleeding."[6]

This lover of beauty, Second Isaiah, depicts the rebuilt city with foundations, walls, gates, and pinnacles of many-colored, flashing gems. The precious stones, blue, red, and crystal, are set in costly dark mortar to enhance their brilliance. These stones, with additions, appear

[5] Cheney, ed., *Life and Letters*, pp. 211-12.
[6] *The Adventures of Philip*, Part II, ch. ii.

12 And I will make thy windows of agates, and thy gates of carbuncles, and all thy borders of pleasant stones.	12 I will make your pinnacles of agate, your gates of carbuncles, and all your wall of precious stones.

experienced. Above all, she is **not comforted** (לא נחמה; cf. 40:1). Cf. Hosea's second child *Lô-ruḥāmāh,* "Unloved One" (Hos. 1:6). The vivid address stands in sharp contrast to the glowing assurances of a new Jerusalem which follow. The holy city is to be rebuilt. The absence of any reference to the temple is noteworthy (contrast Ezek. 40:1–48:35). For the motif of the new city cf. 26:1 ff.; Tob. 13:16-17; Rev. 21:18-21. Where did the prophet receive the inspiration for his description? It is possible that here, as elsewhere, he is influenced by what he sees about him in Babylon, but seeks to paint Jerusalem in colors even more glorious and radiant. **I will set your stones in antimony:** Many scholars emend אבניך, **your stones,** to אדניך, "your foundations," but the change is unnecessary. The LXX reads ἄνθρακα, "carbuncle" (Hebrew נפך) or malachite, a substance used by Oriental women as an eye powder to heighten the luster of their eyes (II Kings 9:30; Jer. 4:30). Edward J. Kissane suggests that here it takes the place of mortar "to set off the beauty of the stones (sapphires) of which the city wall will be built" (*The Book of Isaiah* [Dublin: Browne & Nolan, 1941-43], p. 198). The best alternative is to accept the reading of the LXX (Sidney Smith [*Isaiah XL-LV,* pp. 166-67] thinks that this is probably our earliest description of floor mosaics and that the prophet probably derived his picture from those he had seen). **Your foundation with sapphires: Lapis lazuli,** a vivid blue stone highly valued in the ancient world (cf. Pliny, *Natural History* XXXVII. 39). According to G. A. Cooke (*A Critical and Exegetical Commentary on the Book of Ezekiel* [New York: Charles Scribner's Sons, 1937; "International Critical Commentary"], I, 21), what is now known as sapphire "was almost unknown before the time of the Roman empire" (cf. Exod. 24:10; 28:18; Ezek. 1:26). Volz refers to Adolf Erman's statement (*Aegypten und Aegyptisches Leben* [Tübingen: H. Laupp, 1887], I, 259) that the building stones in the royal palace appeared like lapis lazuli and malachite (blue and green precious stones).

12. The word for **pinnacles** is derived from the same word as "sun," and probably suggests the parts of the building which gleam in the sun. Instead of **agate** read "rubies." The word (*kadhekōdh*) occurs elsewhere only in Ezek. 27:16, and appears to be derived from the root meaning "to sparkle." Cooke renders (Ezek. 27:16) "red jasper." It may have been the Carthaginian carbuncle to which Pliny refers (*op. cit.,* XXXVII. 25). At any rate, the picture is a most brilliant one. **Carbuncles:** The Hebrew word is drawn from the root meaning "to be kindled," and here probably means fiery or glowing stones.

in the holy city in Rev. 21. Bernard of Cluny's lines, inspired by that vision of the *Patria Splendida,* have an exquisite rendering in a verse of John Mason Neale's:

> Then all the halls of Syon
> For aye shall stand complete,
> And in the Land of Beauty
> All things of beauty meet.[7]

All your sons shall be taught by the LORD. Every inhabitant is a disciple. The servant's description of himself in 50:4-5 is repeated in this entire community. Teachableness is a prime requisite in God's people, for God is always an educator opening his mind to them. Meredith called an unteachable spirit "one of

the most tragic things in life." It precludes communication. The Manx poet, Thomas Edward Brown, declared his incapacity to open his thought to any who were smugly complacent in their knowledge:

> I have a faith as strong as steel,
> Whether it is old or new,
> Shall I to you its form reveal?
> Certainly not to you, my friend,
> Certainly not to you.

> .   .   .   .

> For you're so "well-informed," dear sir,
> That if my thoughts are due
> To any man, I do aver,
> It's certainly not to you, my friend,
> Certainly not to you.[8]

[7] *The Celestial Country* (New York: Anson D. F. Randolph, 1885), p. 15.

[8] "Credo," from *Selected Poems of T. E. Brown* (London: Macmillan & Co., 1912), pp. xx-xxi.

13 And all thy children *shall be* taught of the LORD; and great *shall be* the peace of thy children.	13 All your sons shall be taught by the LORD, and great shall be the prosperity of your sons.
14 In righteousness shalt thou be established: thou shalt be far from oppression; for thou shalt not fear: and from terror; for it shall not come near thee.	14 In righteousness you shall be established; you shall be far from oppression, for you shall not fear; and from terror, for it shall not come near you.

The LXX λίθους κρυστάλλου; Vulg. *lapides sculptos* (so also Aq., Symm., Theod.). **Thy borders:** Better, "encircling wall" (cf. LXX τὸν περιβολόν).

13. From the physical splendor of the new Jerusalem the prophet turns to her inward glory. The one is the counterpart of the other. The first line connects immediately without transition with the former, though it is not parallel with it. The words **your sons** begin and end the line to give them their due emphasis. Many scholars emend the first phrase to "your builders," which has much to commend it, for it would make an excellent transition, but the style of the prophet favors the M.T. The Dead Sea Scroll corrects the second **your sons** to "my builders." Jerusalem's sons will be **taught by the LORD,** or "disciples of the Lord" (cf. 8:16; 50:4). Comparison with Jer. 31:34 points to the new covenant. In John 6:45 the phrase is directed to the disciples of Jesus. It is possible that we have here another echo of the servant passages (cf. 50:4-11).

The intimate interrelationship between material prosperity and profound spiritual life is typically Hebraic and finds superb expression here. It is remarkable that Second Isaiah has so little to say of institutions and religious leaders. In this he is, as usual, in deep spiritual sympathy with his prophetic heritage. Throughout his prophetic career Jeremiah had subjected both institutions and leaders to trenchant criticism. In the eschatological age which our prophet here envisions the spiritual history of Israel enters into its final heritage (cf. Exod. 19:6).

14. Jerusalem will be secure because her foundations are laid **in righteousness,** i.e., in conformity to the righteous will of her Lord. The word carries ethical content, but includes more particularly in Second Isaiah the meaning of salvation and vindication. It means both the character of Jerusalem's citizens, who are taught by the Lord, and God's redemptive activity in her transformed life. The line is important, for all that follows is a development of it. **You shall be far from oppression:** Cf. 51:12-16. The verb is in the imperative: lit., "Do not be far from oppression," i.e., let it not enter your thoughts. The conclusions, introduced by *ki*, **for**, are to be interpreted objectively: "For you will have no need to fear," "for terror will not approach you."

In righteousness you shall be established, i.e., in right relations with God. Adjustment to him in fealty precedes and assures the adjustment of man to man in justice and kindness. John Newton stresses this in his familiar hymn:

On the Rock of Ages founded,
What can shake thy sure repose? [9]

This passage presents, not an aggressive nation with imperialistic aims, but one obedient to God, and so immune from attack (cf. the church in Matt. 16:18). Today a timid apprehensiveness is common among leaders and members of the church, fearful of the difficulties and of their own seeming inadequacy. Luther

once replied to an anxious letter from Melanchthon:

Let the matter be ever so great, great also is He who controls, and has begun it, for it is not our affair. . . . It is your human learning, and not your theology, that is the cause of your trouble. Just as if you with your needless anxieties could accomplish anything! What more can the devil do than strangle us? I adjure you, who in all other things are a master disputant, not to contend against yourself as your greatest enemy. [1]

The church of our time lacks the assurance Newton ascribed to her: "Thou may'st smile at all thy foes."

The prophet is looking forward to the final

[9] "Glorious things of thee are spoken," st. i.

[1] Köstlin, *Life of Luther*, p. 358.

15 Behold, they shall surely gather together, *but* not by me: whosoever shall gather together against thee shall fall for thy sake.

16 Behold, I have created the smith that bloweth the coals in the fire, and that bringeth forth an instrument for his work; and I have created the waster to destroy.

17 ¶ No weapon that is formed against thee shall prosper; and every tongue *that* shall rise against thee in judgment thou shalt condemn. This *is* the heritage of the servants of the LORD, and their righteousness *is* of me, saith the LORD.

15 If any one stirs up strife,
    it is not from me;
whoever stirs up strife with you
    shall fall because of you.
16 Behold, I have created the smith
    who blows the fire of coals,
    and produces a weapon for its purpose.
I have also created the ravager to destroy;
17   no weapon that is fashioned against
        you shall prosper,
    and you shall confute every tongue that
        rises against you in judgment.
This is the heritage of the servants of the
    LORD
    and their vindication from me, says the
    LORD."

15. The Hebrew of the verse is difficult (cf. Amer. Trans. and RSV). The RSV gives the most probable meaning. In the event that **strife** should come, it is not God's doing, as it was with Tiglath-pileser, Sennacherib, and Cyrus. When the conqueror threatens war, he will be destroyed. Vs. 15 stands in immediate sequence to vs. 14.

6. SIXTH STROPHE: THE LORD'S OMNIPOTENCE (54:16-17)

The strophe begins with the emphatic **Behold, I . . .** (cf. vs. 11*b*) and closes with an impressive climax (vs. 17*cd*). Observe the repetition of the verb **I have created** (בראתי) and its emphatic position and form.

16. God's omnipotence is shown by the fact that he creates both the forger of weapons and the **ravager** who uses them. The achievements of technology are subject to his sovereignty (cf. Amos 1:3–2:12). He is therefore powerful to control their use and to bring their effectiveness to nought. **Coals:** Cf. 44:12. **For its purpose:** Better, "For its work."

17. Jerusalem will be invulnerable against attack without and calumny within (cf. Job 5:20-21). **This is the heritage:** The demonstrative sums up the preceding lines. The word **heritage** has rich and far-ranging associations in Israel's covenant life. The inheritance of the Holy Land stamped itself as an indelible category of her thought, both of the past and of the future. **The servants of the LORD:** Cf. 63:17; 65:8-9, 13-15; 66:14. Feldmann sees a reference here to the posterity of the servant described in 53:10, which is possible but by no means certain. The immediate reference is more likely to the disciples of the Lord in vs. 13, but both texts may be echoes of the servant figure. **Their vindication:** The same word is rendered "righteousness" in vs. 14. Thus the second division of the poem is given a remarkable unity.

divine order; but he does not expect enemies and other causes of anxiety to wholly vanish (vs. 15). They remain, but are powerless to disturb the tranquillity of God's people. All skills, including those of the ironsmith, come from God (cf. Gen. 4:17-18). He oversees their use. This is not so patent to us who are painfully aware of men's tragic misuse of the advances in technical production. The prophet's insistence on God's complete sovereignty overlooks the disorder wrought by sinful men. But the underlying conviction of his ultimate control remains true. Israel has no reason to fear hostile forces or accusers threatening her standing with God.

This is the heritage of the servants of the LORD and their vindication from me, saith the LORD.

This confidence in God's unshakable control is echoed during the French Revolution and the upheavals on the Continent in a letter of Cowper's to John Newton: "The unmanageable prince and the no less unmanageable multitude, have each a mouth into which God can thrust a curb when he pleases, and kings shall reign and the people obey to the last moment of His appointment."[2]

[2] Thomas Wright, ed., *The Correspondence of William Cowper* (New York: Dodd, Mead & Co., 1904), IV, 169.

55 Ho, every one that thirsteth, come ye to the waters, and he that hath no money; come ye, buy, and eat; yea, come,

55 "Ho, every one who thirsts, come to the waters; and he who has no money, come, buy and eat!

G. Grace Abounding (55:1-13)

In this poem Second Isaiah brings his prophecy to a triumphant close. All its major features indicate that he is here speaking his last word: the elevated mood, the literary characteristics, the nature of the introductory and concluding lines, the relation of the content to the major emphases of the preceding poems, especially the prologue (40:1-11), the striking interior quality of the piety, and the expanded figure associated with the word of the Lord.

The poem is written for the consolation of Israel. The time of forgiveness has arrived (cf. 40:2), the exiles are to return to Zion (cf. 40:3-5, 9-11), and nature will participate in the event in an outburst of song (cf. 40:4). The word of God will effect its purpose in the world (cf. 40:8). The everlasting covenant once promised to David will be established, and the new exodus, reminiscent of the event with which Israel's history began, will take place. The prophet stands in a living, inward relationship to them. He proclaims their imminence, issues an urgent invitation to all who hunger and thirst to accept the proffered blessings, and calls his people to repentance.

The poem continues the major theme of ch. 54. The covenant with its bond of covenant faithfulness, the assurance of well-being and peace, and the appeal to compassion and everlasting devotion are common to both poems. The light and shadow of ch. 54 are present in ch. 55 also, though in the latter the light predominates.

The structure of the poem is apparent. It is composed of five strophes. The first three are dominated by urgent imperatives (cf. 51:1-2, 3-5, 6-9); the last two, by the asseverative *kî*, for. The early strophes show a growing profundity and come to a climax in the offer of forgiveness (vss. 6-9). The next to the last strophe is devoted to the word of God; the last, to the event of the new exodus.

1. First Strophe: The Invitation to the Hungry and Thirsty (55:1-2)

Employing the literary form of the wisdom writers of wisdom's invitation to a banquet (Prov. 9:5-6; Ecclus. 24:19-21; cf. Matt. 11:28-29), the poet symbolizes the gifts of the new covenant by the figure of food and drink which give life to all who partake of them (Prov. 3:18; 4:22; 8:35). These gifts are the blessings conferred by the covenant relation and membership in the kingdom of God. They are freely and gratuitously given. The symbolism must not be pressed too far, however, for they include material welfare and physical well-being as well as spiritual blessings. The association of eating and drinking with the covenant is interesting, for not only the original Sinaitic covenant (Exod. 24:11) but also the day of the Lord was the occasion of such a celebration.

It is the community's firmly established standing with God which is uppermost in the prophet's mind. God's people have accepted their role as a sin-bearing servant and borne the iniquities of the peoples in Israel's death as an independent nation. Now, risen from the dead, Israel shares with God her destiny as a light to mankind. God can be relied on to guarantee her continuance in peace.

A similar carefree devotion to do and bear God's will is demanded of the church in every age. His will must be her sole concern. Its achievement, as in Israel's case, is often through the blighted and broken purposes of her mem-

bers. In history the church is again and again under the cross, and she must endure it with no glimpse whither her toils and tears will issue. She must not "throw away" her confidence, "which has a great reward," for after bearing and doing God's will, she inherits the promise (Heb. 10:35-36).

55:1-2. All Spiritually Dissatisfied Summoned. —The inclusiveness of the appeal—everyone who thirsts—suggests that the prophet is already beginning Israel's message to mankind. But while a few of their pagan neighbors may have learned something of the exiles' ancestral faith, the language of this poem is plainly meant for

buy wine and milk without money and | Come, buy wine and milk
without price. | without money and without price.

It is possible that these were in the background of the writer's mind although he transforms them in his own characteristic manner.

55:1. The introductory exclamation immediately calls attention to the invitation, and the words of address establish the universal context of the poem. **Every one** is invited, none excluded. The catholicity of the prophet's gospel comes to full expression here. The use of the imagery of hungering and thirsting, of eating and drinking, to express spiritual attitudes is common in both the O.T. and N.T. (Deut. 8:3; Pss. 42:2; 63:1; Prov. 9:5-6; Matt. 4:4; 5:6; Luke 22:30; John 4:10 ff.; 7:37-38; Rev. 21:6; 22:17). In the Orient water was a highly prized possession. It was bought and sold, as it is in the streets of Oriental cities to this day. The cry may therefore be reminiscent of the water seller, though the wisdom provenance seems clear in view of the parallels (Begrich, *Studien zu Deuterojesaja,* pp. 53-54). **He who has no money:** The words are parallel to the first line. Driver ("Linguistic and Textual Problems," p. 404) derives the word *kĕṣeph,* here rendered **money,** from the Akkadian *kispu,* "food," "meal," which improves the parallelism. All who hunger and thirst are invited. But the use of another word for food (לחם) in the same context, the phrase **without money** in vs. 1*f,* and the absence of O.T. linguistic parallels support the traditional rendering. The Hebrew wording of the last lines of the verse is less clear than the RSV suggests. The words **come, buy** of vs. 1*e* are awkward in the Hebrew and look like dittography. They are absent from the LXX and Syriac. The Dead Sea Scroll omits in addition the preceding word **and eat,** though this may be simply a case of homoeoteleuton. If the words are deleted, we may render as follows: "Buy and eat without money, and without price, wine and milk." The preceding line should then read, "And he who has no money, come."

---

the prophet's fellow countrymen. They had settled into the life of Babylon, and in absorption in their business they were not much concerned with the religious hopes of their people. But the prophet was sure that in many souls there was discontent. To this **thirst** he makes his plea. **Waters, bread, wine, and milk** are symbols for the life with God. They infer its necessity. It is no mere luxury or extra. Commodities like water, bread, etc., had to be purchased. Water was sold by carriers, whose cry is echoed in the **Ho, every one who thirsts.** If the reference here is to the miraculously opened well (41:17-18), a price to be paid was usual for such a boon.

In every generation life apart from God proves unsatisfying. Instances abound in the increasingly secular second half of the nineteenth century. George John Romanes, brilliant disciple of Darwin, parted from his inherited faith, confessed:

I know from experience the intellectual distractions of scientific research, philosophical speculation, and artistic pleasures; but am also well aware that even when all are taken together and well sweetened to taste, in respect of consequent reputation, means, social position, etc., the whole concoction is but as high confectionery to a starving man.[3]

[3] *Thoughts on Religion* (Chicago: Open Court Publishing Co., 1895), pp. 150-51.

William James, when a student in Berlin, wrote to a friend in New York who had complained of falling into "inward deadness and listlessness,"- and had spoken of a "homesick yearning for a *Better,* somewhere." James granted that "we long for sympathy, for a purely *personal* communication, first with the soul of the world, and then with our fellows." The first he deemed impossible, so he proposed to his friend to become "an accomplice in a sort of 'Mankind its own God or Providence' scheme"; and he adds: "I don't mean, by any means, to affirm that we must come to that, I only say it is *a* mode of envisaging life; which is capable of affording moral support—and may at any rate help to bridge over the despair of skeptical intervals."[4]

H. G. Wells spoke of the "God-shaped blank" in men's hearts, and that "blank" appears in a letter of Sir Leslie Stephen, who when his wife died began a sentence with "I thank . . . ," and, recalling that as an agnostic he had no God to whom to be grateful, wrote: "I thank—something—that I loved her as heartily as I know how to love."[5] A century later, countless folk, far less educated most of them than these nineteenth-century leaders, are wistful for firsthand assurance of and intercourse with the living God.

[4] *Letters,* I, 127, 131-32.
[5] Maitland, *Life and Letters of Stephen,* p. 256.

2 Wherefore do ye spend money for *that which is* not bread? and your labor for *that which* satisfieth not? hearken diligently unto me, and eat ye *that which is* good, and let your soul delight itself in fatness.

3 Incline your ear, and come unto me:

2 Why do you spend your money for that which is not bread,
　and your labor for that which does not satisfy?
Hearken diligently to me, and eat what is good,
　and delight yourselves in fatness.
3 Incline your ear, and come to me;
　hear, that your soul may live;

---

2. Why do you spend your money? Lit., "weigh silver." Pieces or bars of silver and gold were the means of exchange. Coins were not minted until the Persian Age. While the words are not meant to be taken literally, they doubtless refer to the ways in which many of the exiles accommodated themselves to their surroundings in Babylon. Evidences are not wanting that some of them gained considerable wealth and prosperity. Engaging in commercial and other pursuits carried with it the danger that the exiles would adopt the practices and habits of their conquerors (cf. Jer. 29:6). Such getting and spending do not satisfy the hunger and thirst of the soul; the true bread and water are the invisible spiritual resources which proceed from God alone (Deut. 8:3; Matt. 4:4; John 4:10; 6:27). **And your labor:** Cf. 45:14. **And delight yourselves in fatness:** The pronoun is, lit., **your soul.** The soul (*néphesh*) in Hebrew psychology was the seat of the appetite. The Oriental is especially fond of fatty foods. For fat or oil as a spiritual food see Ps. 36:8. The figure here is of prosperity (cf. Jer. 31:14; Ps. 63:5). Water, bread, wine, milk, and fat are all symbolic of the covenant gifts and benefits. The parallelism of **hearken diligently to me** and **eat what is good** prepares the way admirably for the next strophe.

2. Second Strophe: The Everlasting Covenant of David (55:3-5)

The first two lines summarize and bring to a point the previous strophe, the next two present the central thought in the mind of the poet, the following double lines,

---

He who has no money. God's grace is utterly free. The prophet proclaims the gospel as graciously as any N.T. apostle. **Why do you . . . ?** The questions are designed to provoke men to think. "Consideration is half conversion," said Thomas Wilson.[6] A psalmist's return to God began with reflection upon his own life: "I thought on my ways, and turned my feet unto thy testimonies" (Ps. 119:59). A pointed question brings men up short. Very few mean to do wrong, or to waste themselves. They never think on their courses. Thomas Wilson, whose maxim has been quoted, concludes, "It is for want of thinking that we are undone."

That which is not bread, . . . that which does not satisfy. Men who are souls cannot find their business and their human associations sufficient. The industrious and often prosperous existence of the exiles in Babylon and the coastlands left them restless in spirit. God's enterprise for mankind is **that which is good.** His purpose supplies life with meaning and zest. John Donne said, " 'Tis such a full, and such a filling good."[7] John Newton put the conviction in the last lines of his hymn:

Solid joys and lasting treasure
None but Zion's children know.[8]

Spend money, . . . your labor. " 'Tis only God may be had for the asking." The prophet is completely beyond legalism. The messianic community is open to everybody and without payment. It is accessible to the most sinful. There is no question of worthiness. **He who has no money** is invited, and only he who is "poor in spirit" is likely to come.

Hearken diligently. The "hearing ear" is the prerequisite of entrance into life with God. It is a happy circumstance that today many, convinced of the unsatisfactoriness of other remedies for the world's tragedy, look for a spiritual renewal. Their gropings are vague, but their minds are open to a religious message. "There is a blessedness in being willing to hear that comes before the blessedness of actual hearing—as the *dawn* before the *sunrise*." [9]

3-5. *Israel Inherits the Sure Compact.*—Israel is the messianic community through which God will establish his reign in the world (cf. II Sam.

[6] *Maxims of Piety and Morality*, No. 301.
[7] "The Second Anniversary."
[8] "Glorious things of thee are spoken," st. iv.
[9] Donald Campbell, ed., *Memorials of John McLeod Campbell* (London: Macmillan & Co., 1877), II, 65.

hear, and your soul shall live; and I will make an everlasting covenant with you, *even* the sure mercies of David.

4 Behold, I have given him *for* a witness to the people, a leader and commander to the people.

and I will make with you an everlasting covenant,
my steadfast, sure love for David.
4 Behold, I made him a witness to the peoples,
a leader and commander for the peoples.

---

introduced by an emphatic **Behold,** develop the Davidic covenant (vss. 4-5*b*), and the last lines (vs. 5*cd*) contain the theocentric conclusion. The poet proceeds gradually from the imagery of the first strophe to the meaning which the figures are designed to represent.

3. The invitation to **come** and to **hear,** the first and last words of the previous strophe, are explained, but here precedence is given to the latter. To those who accept God's freely given grace the gift of new life is assured. **An everlasting covenant:** Cf. 54:10; also 61:8. It will be a new covenant, more enduring than the old (Jer. 31:31-34). God will initiate and institute it as an act of his unmotivated grace. **My steadfast, sure love for David:** In II Sam. 7:8-16 Nathan describes the content of this covenant love to David: God will establish the throne of David's kingdom forever, his covenant faithfulness will be with him, and Israel will rest secure from all her foes. The promises to David pass on not only to his sons but also to Israel. In the last words of David (II Sam. 23:5) the king speaks of the "everlasting covenant, ordered in all things and secure" which Yahweh has made with him (cf. Pss. 18:50; 89:28-36; Jer. 33:21-22; II Chr. 6:42). The covenant "loves" of David (חסדי דוד) are not like those promised to David; they are the realization and fulfillment of them. It is noteworthy that the prophet does not appeal to the Mosaic covenant here, any more than in ch. 54, where the eternity of the bond is compared to the Noachian covenant. The reason may be that he believed the old covenant to be superseded by the new, and that the messianic character of Nathan's prophecy more adequately expressed his thought.

David was chosen by Yahweh to be king over Israel. He was anointed with the holy oil by the prophet Samuel, and the Spirit of the Lord came upon him. The activity of the Spirit of God dominates the whole history of David's kingly career. To what degree he was considered sacrosanct it is difficult to say, but that he was considered to stand in a special relationship to Yahweh is certain. This relationship is best described as one of election, but precisely this election involved his relationship with Yahweh's people, Israel. He is responsible for them; he is their leader and helper in battle, their representative among the nations of the world, and in some sense at least a mediator between Yahweh and them. His good acts bring beneficent results; his sins, dire consequences. Yahweh's promises to him affect Israel; Israel's history is bound with these assurances. It is in this context that the words of our prophet are to be understood.

4. Vss. 4-5 are closely parallel and stand in the same relation as vs. 3*d* to vs. 3*c*. David's supremacy is described succinctly. God has made him **a witness** (*'ēdh*), **a leader**

23:5). It is the religious, not the political, leadership of David which is stressed, and the covenant is broadened to embrace mankind. **Behold, I made him a witness to the peoples.** Israel is to testify to God's grace in her history and his inclusive purpose for all men. **Witness** anticipates the N.T.; **leader and commander** (cf. II Sam. 7:8) are not to undo the connotation of "servant." The task is guidance, not dominion; Israel is the bearer of the prophetic word.

The church is the messianic community. Her function is witness. When she attempts coercion, e.g., the use of political pressure, she employs

a weapon less potent than the sword of the Spirit. In eternal and assured compact with God, she should show no timidity nor harbor any doubt. But her task is to appeal to consciences and convince minds, not to bring pressure on the unconvinced. It is a temptation in a democracy to marshal her forces to push men in public office to do what she considers desirable. It may seem a more rapid method, but the slower road of persuasion attains the goal more permanently. The divine community does not drive, but draws (vs. 5). The church is a city set upon a hill, and the elevation of her life

5 Behold, thou shalt call a nation *that* thou knowest not, and nations *that* knew not thee shall run unto thee, because of the LORD thy God, and for the Holy One of Israel; for he hath glorified thee.	5 Behold, you shall call nations that you know not, and nations that knew you not shall run to you, because of the LORD your God, and of the Holy One of Israel, for he has glorified you.

(*nāghîdh;* cf. II Sam. 7:8) , and a **commander** [*meçaweh*] **to the people.** Is this a reference to the Messiah, the messianic David (Jer. 30:9; Ezek. 34:23-24) ? Many scholars (Duhm, Haller, Skinner, Torrey) think so. But the construction of the strophe shows very clearly that the emphasis falls not primarily on David but upon the people of Israel. It is to them that the covenant love assured to David is granted. David, like Jacob and Abraham, lives on in the life of the people, a view characteristic of Israel's psychical mentality. The historical reality embodied in David as king and representative of Israel through the power and purpose of God is to be realized in David's people. This does justice to the major emphases of Nathan's prophecy. Ps. 18:43 supports this interpretation:

> Thou hast made me head of the nations;
> A people I have not known shall serve me.

See also Ps. 89:3-4, 15-37. To be sure, nothing is said in these passages of David as a witness, but it is not difficult to see how Second Isaiah could interpret his work in this way. David had been a witness to God's power and activity in history in his defeat of the nations and his establishment of Israel in the land. A further objection to seeing the Messiah in David is that it contradicts the mission of the servant of the Lord, not only in the so-called servant songs, but in other passages as well. The attempt to equate the Messiah with the servant is precarious, and the excision of the messianic reference to Cyrus impossible. Finally, it seems likely that our prophet is spiritualizing David's mission, although the national features are by no means absent. As David was **a witness to the people, a leader and commander to the people,** so Israel will perform the same functions in the world. Her task was to be Yahweh's witness (43:10; 44:8) , and she was to be exalted and established among the peoples.

5. The M.T. has **nations** in the singular (so KJV) , but the reference is general (cf. 42:6; 49:7 ff.) . Because of the singular form of the second personal pronoun, in contrast to the plural of vs. 3, Kissane thinks the words are addressed to David. He supports his view by appeal to Ps. 18:43. But this does not take account of the more abrupt shift of thought, on the basis of Kissane's position, between the third person and second person, nor of the general address to Israel in vss. 1-3. It will be the mission of Israel to gather the nations of the world. Nations of whom she has never heard will be attracted by her witness to the Holy One of Israel (cf. 44:5; 45:14; 49:7) . **He has glorified you:** Cf. 44:23; 49:3.

and teaching gives her effective publicity. Of the church in the Roman Empire it is said: The watchwords of the State were oppression, coercion, and persecution; the maxims of the Church were love, compassion, and consolation. The Church, and she alone among the different religious communities, offered not only spiritual comfort but also practical assistance amidst the miseries of present life, while the State oppressed and persecuted the comforters.[1] [1] M. Rostovzef, quoted in G. G. Coulton, *The Medieval Panorama* (New York: The Macmillan Co., 1938), p. 15.	No argument is more cogent than that from the aureole. The lives of saintly men and women point to an actually existent spiritual world, as the coloring of trees and flowers points to the existence of light. There is an inherent force in the message committed to the church. Matthew Arnold, who had felt and in part been overwhelmed by the skepticism of his day referred to above, wrote: "Jesus Christ and his precepts are found to hit the moral experience of mankind, to hit it in the critical points, to hit it lastingly; and, when doubts are thrown

6 ¶ Seek ye the LORD while he may be found, call ye upon him while he is near:

7 Let the wicked forsake his way, and the unrighteous man his thoughts: and let him return unto the LORD, and he will have mercy upon him; and to our God, for he will abundantly pardon.

6 "Seek the LORD while he may be found,
  call upon him while he is near;
7 let the wicked forsake his way,
  and the unrighteous man his thoughts;
let him return to the LORD, that he may
  have mercy on him,
  and to our God, for he will abundantly
  pardon.

---

3. THIRD STROPHE: REPENT, FOR THE TIME IS FULFILLED (55:6-9)

The time of salvation is at hand. Israel must return to the Lord in repentance, for he is ready to forgive her sins. The opening imperatives are connected with the imminence of the kingdom of God; the following extended cohortatives are an earnest call to repentance, and the final lines fortify the call by the transcendence of the divine thoughts and ways.

6. The third series of imperatives (cf. vss. 1, 3) gives the clause unusual force. Now, in this present time, when God is coming to deliver his people, Israel must seek him (cf. Amos 5:4; Jer. 29:12-14). He is found by those who seek him; he is near for those who call upon him. The meaning is eschatological: the time of salvation is at hand (49:8). Repentance is a prerequisite for admission to the kingdom (cf. Matt. 3:2; Mark 1:15).

7. Wicked conduct and unrighteous thoughts stand in the way of God's mercy and grace. Repentance is a matter of a radical change of conduct and thought, an inward reversal of life. Since this seems to be a contradiction to God's free and unconditional grace (vs. 1; cf. also 43:22-28; 48:10-12), the verse is excised by some scholars. But religious experience supports its retention. Moreover, the proffered blessings of the new

---

upon their really hitting it, then to come out stronger than ever." [2] In the beauty and power of her message, and in the gifts and graces conferred by the Spirit on her people, God has glorified the church. These are her sufficient "attractions."

6-9. *The Gospel of Repentance and Forgiveness.*—This deserves to stand by the gracious invitation in Matt. 11:28-30. It is as universal in its scope and as penetrating in its analysis of human need (cf. way and thoughts, return).

While he may be found, . . . while he is near. In the historical crisis the prophet is vividly aware of God's presence. Cyrus' victory was so decisive that the return of the exiles could begin forthwith. The chance to follow God's leading to the homeland opened wide before everyone. There is a sense in which God is always near; but there are "times of his visitation." Historic circumstances affect his accessibility.

Seek, . . . call upon. The prophet stresses God's activity, sometimes wholly apart from and even despite man's effort; but he knows that man must stir up himself to take hold of God (64:7). Man's part in prayer is subordinate but indispensable: "Ask, . . . seek, . . . knock" (Luke 11:9). Dean Rust, preaching the funeral sermon of Jeremy Taylor, spoke of "the emigrations of his soul after God." There has to be a movement Godward on man's side to make possible God's full response. A leader of the social interpretation of theology wrote:

God does not work without means. He does not thrust reforms upon the world before the world is ready to receive them. The desires and petitions of individual hearts and united congregations are the signs by which the Spirit recognizes the fulness of time for a spiritual and social advance. [3]

There must be a genuine turning toward God, or prayer becomes merely a strong affirmation of our desire, not a search for and acquiescence in his will. There cannot be communion with him on our level; that would degrade him. We have to place ourselves before him, let his light search us, and sincerely enter into his purpose.

Mine inmost soul, before Thee inly brought,
  Thy presence owns ineffable, divine;
Chastised each rebel self-encentered thought,
  My will adoreth Thine. [4]

Let the wicked forsake his way. A thoroughly evangelical statement of repentance and forgiveness expressed in terms inclusive of every man.

---

[2] *Last Essays on Church and Religion* (London: Smith, Elder, & Co., 1903), p. xviii.

[3] William DeWitt Hyde, *Outlines of Social Theology* (New York: The Macmillan Co., 1895), p. 131.

[4] Arthur Hugh Clough, "Qui Laborat, Orat."

8 ¶ For my thoughts *are* not your thoughts, neither *are* your ways my ways, saith the LORD.

9 For *as* the heavens are higher than the earth, so are my ways higher than your ways, and my thoughts than your thoughts.

8 For my thoughts are not your thoughts, neither are your ways my ways, says the LORD.

9 For as the heavens are higher than the earth,

so are my ways higher than your ways and my thoughts than your thoughts.

---

age will be granted only to those who appropriate them through repentance (cf. 65:8-25; 66:1-24). The next verse connects perfectly with this interpretation. **For he will abundantly pardon:** Lit., "For he will be great to pardon." As in Jer. 31:34, the final emphasis of the new covenant falls on forgiveness; cf. the words of the Egyptian psalm, cited by Volz (*Jesaia II*, p. 144): "If the servant is ready to sin, then the Lord is ready to be gracious."

8-9. The repetition of the introductory particle, the wonderful contrast between the divine and human **ways** and **thoughts,** the cosmic comparison of vs. 9, and the expansive character of the conclusion are a vivid reflection of the momentous importance the prophet attached to his message of repentance and forgiveness. The fact that the same motif occurs at the beginning (40:2) and at the close (55:6-7) and that his supreme composition (52:13–53:12) is devoted to the reconciliation of the nations through Israel's suffering, make our passage remarkably impressive. It is essential, then, to see that vss. 8-9 connect immediately and perfectly with vss. 6-7. To men these wonders of the divine grace seem impossible and the universality of salvation hard to understand, but God's ways and thoughts are different from men's (cf. 45:9-13). His range of vision is universal and

---

In the O.T. one may see that every time the words contrition or humility drop from the lips of prophet or psalmist, Christianity appears. Luther's first thesis nailed on the door of the castle church in Wittenberg reads: "Our Lord and Master, Jesus Christ, in saying *Penitentiam agite,* meant that the whole life of the faithful should be repentance." The expressions in vs. 7 seem purposely so universal as to take in Gentile listeners and begin the mission of Israel to the nations. None the less the prophet was concerned mainly with his own people. **The wicked** is the godless, the Israelite so immersed in his own affairs in Babylon that God's claims upon him are unthought of. **The unrighteous man** is a man of falsehood, faithless to his calling as a member of the chosen people. Men's relationship to God is uppermost in both expressions. In our time how numerous the company who live oblivious of their obligations to God and of their resources in him! They are not convinced atheists, but they are unmindful of God.

> . . . In this world of worldlings, where
> Souls rust in apathy, and ne'er
> A great emotion shakes the air,
>   And life flags tame,
> And rare is noble impulse, rare
>   The impassioned aim.[5]

[5] William Watson, "Shelley's Centenary," st. xiv, from *The Poems of Sir William Watson, 1878-1935* (London: George G. Harrap & Co., 1936). Used by permission.

Were these exiles guilty of gross iniquities, their break with them would be a decisive act; but to **forsake** so negative a mode of life as God-forgetfulness is no easy matter. There must be deliberate remembering of God. Hence the stress in subsequent chapters on outward acts of loyalty. In our day such remembering requires a revival of customs widely in disuse—public and private worship, grace at table, a restoration of the Lord's day to special religious purposes, etc.

A man's way is the routine of his life. The exiles, like so many among us today, were absorbed in the commercial life, and such absorption prevented their seeing God's vast purpose for mankind and Israel's role in it. **Thoughts,** and in part lack of thought, accounted for their **ways.** A new mind must be acquired. The inwardness of the N.T. is here. Probably in that day, as in this, it was the negative quality of men's religion which gave most difficulty. "The larger number of men seem to an outside observer to walk through life in a torpid sort of sleep."[6] Men's preoccupation with their own interests is God's serious obstacle. His cause does not suffer so much from obdurate antagonists as from the apathy of a mass of indifferent nobodies. Such folk do not vigorously oppose, but "sit upon" his plans, not wishing to be disturbed. Repentance involves an entrance

[6] Bagehot, "The Ignorance of Man," *Literary Studies,* III, 180.

10 For as the rain cometh down, and the snow from heaven, and returneth not thither, but watereth the earth, and maketh it bring forth and bud, that it may give seed to the sower, and bread to the eater:	10 "For as the rain and the snow come down from heaven, and return not thither but water the earth, making it bring forth and sprout, giving seed to the sower and bread to the eater,

includes all men. His understanding of the human heart is deeper than human understanding. His government and sovereignty are different from human ways. It is precisely because of this that the invitation to **seek** and to **call** and to **return** have such force, for God is "permitting himself to be found" and is drawing near. Similarly, the exhortations of vs. 7 express the wonder that if the wicked man returns, God will have mercy and forgive. God is transcendent and holy (40:22-24), yet he draws near to those who seek him and repent (cf. 57:15; Ps. 103:11; also Ps. 130:4; Jer. 29:11).

4. Fourth Strophe: The Activity and Mission of the Word of God (55:10-11)

The little parable admirably connects the unsearchable ways and thoughts of God in vss. 8-9 with the fulfillment of his purpose in the deliverance and redemption of vss. 12-13. It is perhaps the most extended figure in Second Isaiah's poems: two tetrastichs, the one containing the figure, the other the interpretation.

10. In the great nature religions of the Orient **rain** was considered to be the chief gift of the gods, the source of fertility and life. Second Isaiah employs it as a basis of comparison for a far greater reality. How the prophet understood the processes of nature

upon God's outlook; a break with customary and ancestral ways and thoughts (vs. 7). Men must acquiesce in his mercy on all men. They must become cordial comrades of his forgiveness and companions of his redemptive purpose. Isolationist thoughts unhappily still persist. Irresponsibility now, as then, must be turned from.

It was in mercifulness that the prophet saw the unlikeness of the devout to God: **My thoughts are not your thoughts.** God waits to be gracious, but his pardon cannot be released in us until our thoughts and ways accord with his forgivingness. Many an Israelite then, as many among us now, find God's inclusiveness a stumbling block.

When we come to deal with God about forgiveness, we hang in every brier of disputing, quarrelsome unbelief . . . measuring him by that line of our own imaginations, bringing him down unto our thoughts and ways. . . . If there be any pardon with God, it is such as becomes him to give. . . . Go with your half-forgiveness, limited, conditional pardons, with reserves and limitations unto the sons of men; it may be, it may become them, it is like themselves. That of God is absolute and perfect, before which our sins are as a cloud before the east wind, and the rising sun.[7]

[7] John Owen, *A Practical Exposition on the CXXXth Psalm*, "Properties of Forgiveness."

Much was said a generation ago of "the humanity of God"; only a superhuman God can lift men into a mercy and redemptive service which embraces all peoples, and overleaps every limit we incline to deem reasonable. At an incalculable elevation—**as the heavens are higher than the earth**—he thinks and acts, and there we must seek fellowship with him.

10-11. *God's Word Potent for His World Plans.*—Our consummate poet keeps the word used in vs. 2, **bread,** and repeats it here in the poem's climax, **bread to the eater.** The spiritually apathetic now, as then, must be convinced that God's fantastically (as they think) impossible purpose for mankind will come to pass. The **word** which communicates his mind has, like **rain** and **snow,** inherent powers of fruitfulness. Christian hopes for the world are not self-born; they have **come down from heaven.** They are not destined to return with purpose unfulfilled. Steadfast confidence in God's word is essential to sharing its victory. When the Protestant forces had been driven from Edinburgh at a dark moment in the Scots Reformation, John Knox, preaching to them at Stirling, from Ps. 80, said: "Whatsoever shall become of us and of our mortal carcasses, I doubt not but that this cause, in despite of Satan, shall prevail in the realm; for, as it is the eternal

11 So shall my word be that goeth forth out of my mouth: it shall not return unto me void, but it shall accomplish that which I please, and it shall prosper *in the thing* whereto I sent it.

12 For ye shall go out with joy, and be led forth with peace: the mountains and the hills shall break forth before you into singing, and all the trees of the field shall clap *their* hands.

11 so shall my word be that goes forth from
my mouth;
    it shall not return to me empty,
but it shall accomplish that which I purpose,
    and prosper in the thing for which I
    sent it.

12 "For you shall go out in joy,
    and be led forth in peace;
the mountains and the hills before you
    shall break forth into singing,
    and all the trees of the field shall clap
    their hands.

---

is not stated, but perhaps after the manner of Job 36:26-29. The word *kî 'im*, **but,** is emphatic; "except it water the earth," or "without watering." It is in parallelism to vs. 11c.

11. So shall my word be: Cf. 40:8; 45:19, 23; 50:4; also Matt. 24:35. The efficacy of the word (*dābhār*) of God achieves its highest expression here. Isaiah pictures it going forth into history to call into action a whole series of events (9:8-21; see Jer. 1:4-12; Ezek. 37:1-14; cf. also Pss. 33:6; 147:15, 18; Wisd. Sol. 16:12; 18:14-16). In Second Isaiah the power and range of the word is even greater: it is cosmic and universal. It is the divine revelation working through the whole of history and the life of nature (Oskar Grether, *Name und Wort Gottes im Alten Testament* [Giessen: A. Töpelmann, 1934], pp. 133-34, 137), the revelatory power which effects salvation and brings in the kingdom of God on earth. **That which I purpose:** Nowhere in the O.T. is the purpose of God so great a concern as with Second Isaiah (44:28; 46:10; 48:14; 53:10). God's purpose is in his **word** and will be realized in the event with which his word is indissolubly related. **And prosper in the thing . . . :** The word is the messenger of God. Like the servant of the Lord (52:13), it will succeed in its mission (cf. 44:27-28 concerning Cyrus).

5. Fifth Strophe: The New Exodus (55:12-13)

Magnificently the poem closes with the liberation from exile, which is the occasion and a dominant theme of all the poems. This is the event which evokes the prophet's deepest feeling and most lyrical expression (40:3-5; 41:17-20; 43:19-31; 49:9c-13; 51:9-10; 52:11-12). He conceives it as a new exodus and portrays it in all the glowing imagery of nature. The years of affliction and oppression are over; the return home will begin a new life. The exiles will depart **in joy, and be led forth in peace.** So the note of comfort

---

truth of the Eternal God, so shall it once prevail, howsoever for a time it be impugned." [8]

The fructifying character of God's word is evidenced in the fact that great ages in religion have preceded great ages in art and science, in industrial expansion and literature, and especially in humanitarian advance. They were attending to "the fertilization of the ground." [9] A national revival in faith was essential if this community was to build the old waste places and make Jerusalem under God the capital of a new earth. The church of our time needs

[8] Eustace Percy, *John Knox* (London: Hodder & Stoughton, 1937), p. 325.

[9] See W. E. Hocking, *The Meaning of God in Human Experience* (New Haven: Yale University Press, 1912), **Part VI.**

this confidence in the fruits which the word always produces. One is struck by the fruits seen on mission fields, both in changed lives and homes, and in the indirect results in changed society—loftier standards of respect for manhood and womanhood, a keener sense of justice, and more feeling of social obligation.

12-13. *Nature Rejoices with the Exiles.*—A transformation in the vegetation betokens God's wonder-working presence. This remains as a memorial of him forever. For the prophet, facing his people's emancipation and return,

Earth and heaven seem one,
Life a glad trembling on the outer edge
Of unknown rapture. [1]

[1] George Eliot, *The Spanish Gypsy,* Bk. I.

13 Instead of the thorn shall come up the fir tree, and instead of the brier shall come up the myrtle tree: and it shall be to the LORD for a name, for an everlasting sign *that* shall not be cut off.

13 Instead of the thorn shall come up the cypress;
   instead of the brier shall come up the myrtle;
   and it shall be to the LORD for a memorial,
    for an everlasting sign which shall not be cut off."

---

with which the poems begin sounds again. The particle *ki*, with which the strophe opens, introduces the supreme climax.

12. This is the realization and fulfillment of God's effective word, and the response of the people to the Lord's event. **Be led forth:** A fine subtle touch showing God's leading and care of his people (cf. 40:11; 49:10, 22; also Jer. 31:8-9). Observe the contrast to the exodus from Egypt (Exod. 12:11, 33; Deut. 16:3; cf. Isa. 52:11). The Dead Sea Scroll reads **go** (תלכו). **The mountains and the hills . . . :** The wonders of the old exodus are surpassed by the wonders of the new. All nature joins in the jubilation of the returning exiles (cf. 44:23; 49:13; also Ps. 96:11-13). The singing of Israel is a noteworthy feature of her religious life. The religious history of Israel is lived and written to the accompaniment of songs and praises. Here the mountains and hills do not simply echo her songs and praises; they themselves join in the triumphant chorus. The Hebrew view of the aliveness of nature gives the figure peculiar force (see H. Wheeler Robinson, *Inspiration and Revelation in O.T.*, pp. 1-48).

13. Even the desert will be transformed (41:18-20; 43:19-20; 49:9-10). Instead of the desert scrub, luxuriant trees—**the cypress** and **the myrtle**—will spring up to give shade and comfort (cf. 35:1-2). **For a memorial** [lit., **name**], **for an everlasting sign:** The Dead Sea Scroll reverses the nouns. Israel lived by the remembrance of the revelatory

---

For you shall go out in joy, in a new triumphant exodus. This is still another instance of the poet's gladness.

. . . True souls always are hilarious,
They see the way-marks on their exodus
From better unto better; still they say,
Lo, the new law, when old things pass away;
Still keep themselves well guarded, nothing swerve
From the great purposes to which they serve
Scarce knowingly; still smile and take delight
In arduous things, as brave men when they fight
Take joy in feeling one another's might.[2]

And be led forth in peace: A throng of unprotected refugees might easily be waylaid. But God himself leads them. In the troubled and warring seventeenth century in Scotland, Robert Leighton cheered disheartened ministers and people: "Courage, it shall be well; we follow a conquering general, yea, who hath conquered already; *et qui semel vicit pro nobis, semper vicit in nobis.*"[3]

The poet believes that all nature will be renewed and redeemed when Israel is free (vs. 13). It has been said that nature is like a bride whose bridegroom died on their wedding day,

and she has been in mourning ever since. A more recent writer, protesting against the romanticization of nature, declares that she is a Katherine to be tamed by the Petruchio of science, rather than a Juliet to be worshiped by a lovesick Romeo. Thomas Hardy makes Tess's brother, as they look up at the planets, ask her:

"Did you say that the stars were worlds, Tess?"
"Yes."
"All like ours?"
"I don't know; but I think so. They sometimes seem to be like the apples on our stubbard tree. Most of them splendid and sound—a few blighted."
"Which do we live on—a splendid one or a blighted one?"
"A blighted one."[4]

There is much in our world with its diseases of mind and body, its storms, earthquakes, extremes of cold and heat, deserts, floods, etc., which renders it a harsh place for human beings. It seems both blighted and incomplete. It is the goal of science to understand nature and to utilize its resources for human weal. Such substitution of useful for worthless trees is part of man's cultivation of the earth. But a devout poet like this prophet is thinking not in terms of arboriculture, but of mystic ties which link

[2] Richard Watson Dixon, "Love's Consolation."
[3] D. M. Butler, *The Life and Letters of Robert Leighton* (London: Hodder & Stroughton, 1903), p. 260.

[4] *Tess of the D'Urbervilles*, ch. iv.

56 Thus saith the Lord, Keep ye judgment, and do justice: for my salva-

56 Thus says the Lord: "Keep justice, and do righteousness,

---

events of history, the "righteous acts" of the Lord (Judg. 5:11; Mic. 6:5). At the time of the institution of the Yahweh cult Moses made an inscription of the event of Yahweh's victory over Amalek, which must be remembered (Exod. 17:15-16). The kings of the Orient left throughout their realms inscriptions calling attention to their great victories and monuments representing their authority over conquered lands. Yahweh's inscription is an everlasting memorial. It will record his deed of redemption and deliverance. Time and weather and the hands of men will not efface it. It will be a **sign** (*'ôth*), a significant mark or event, which will **not be cut off** (cf. 7:11, 14; 8:18; 20:3; Deut. 13:2-3).

The question of the fulfillment of the prophecy is to be answered in the context of the future development of Israel's faith. The writers of the N.T. found the source of their inspiration and authority in these poems more than in any other portion of O.T. scripture. Imagination and faith, the stuff out of which the prophet fashions his thought, persisted within the community and achieved new and living forms to body them forth in reality.

III. Admonition and Promises (56:1–66:24)

A. Prophetic Instructions (56:1-8)

The final division of Isaiah opens with a prophetic oracle of instruction or *tôrāh*. While it was primarily the priest in ancient Israel who "gave *tôrāh*" (Jer. 2:8; 18:18; Mal. 2:7; Joachim Begrich, "Die priesterliche Tora," in Volz, *Werden und Wesen des Alten Testaments,* pp. 63-88; note also the laws of Ezekiel 40–48), this function was by no means restricted to him. The prophet was not only concerned about the observance of the divine teaching or "law" (1:10; 2:3; 5:24; 8:16; Jer. 5:4), but shared with the priest the task of communicating it (Hag. 2:14 ff.; Zech. 7:2 ff.; for possible prophetic

---

sinful man to an accursed earth and will link redeemed man to a renewed soil. He thinks in such language as Christina Rossetti has employed:

> Yet earth was very good in days of old,
>   And earth is lovely still:
> Still for the sacred flock she spreads the fold,
>   For Sion rears the hill.
>
> Mother she is and cradle of our race,
>   A depth where treasures lie,
> The broad foundation of a holy place,
>   Man's step to scale the sky.
>
> She spreads the harvest-field which Angels reap,
>   And lo, the crop is white;
> She spreads God's Acre where the happy sleep
>   All night that is not night.
>
> Earth may not pass till heaven shall pass away,
>   Nor heaven may be renewed
> Except with earth: and once more in that day
>   Earth shall be very good.[5]

The invitation to join the messianic community is a plea for detachment from the life into which these exiles have settled. The N.T. insists on a similar detachment of Christians, whom

[5] "Sexagesima."

it calls "strangers and pilgrims" (I Pet. 2:11) and "a colony of heaven" (Phil. 3:20 Moffatt). It is the identification of the church with its environing society—politically, economically, etc.—which constitutes its perennial peril. In a feudal age its mind is feudal, in a capitalistic age, capitalist, and under a communist order it may well become communist. The mores of a Christian's class are not the mores of Christ. Many a Protestant congregation lives in a "bourgeois ghetto," and cuts itself off from presenting any Christian appeal to the mass of workers. It is its "class-boundedness" which is the present Babylonian captivity of the church. In a world where East and West are in conflict, and within the West where there are class divisions, the church must win a complete detachment in mind and conscience, that it may take the message of God, freed from worldly entanglements, to men of all nations and of every social status. It must be "separated unto the gospel of God" in order to apply that gospel in every form of society. This is the relevance of the prophet's message to twentieth-century Christians.

56:1-8. The Welcome to the Devout Community.—Granting that this poem has a background in the postexilic life in Jerusalem, it is plain

tion *is* near to come, and my righteousness to be revealed.	for soon my salvation will come, and my deliverance be revealed.

---

tôrôth see 1:10-17; Amos 5:21-24; Jer. 7:21 ff.). In fact, priest, prophet, psalmist, sage, and apocalyptist are one in their devotion to the law. Moreover, the prophet was associated with the priest in the life of the cult. In this small poem, therefore, we have, not a radical break with the past, but a development that has its origin as far back as the religion of Moses. The structure of the poem is clear. It opens with a divine oracle (vs. 1) and is followed by a strophe containing a blessing (vs. 2) and an exhortation (vs. 3) to the alien and the eunuch. The second and third strophes are devoted (chiastically) to these two groups (vss. 4-5, 6-7). The conclusion is in the oracular form of the introduction.

The poem as a whole is akin to Second Isaiah. Vs. 1*cd* belongs to the heart of the latter's thought (46:13; 51:5-8), and vs. 8 bears the same close relationship to it (43:5 *et passim*). Moreover, the prophet has not a little to say about aliens (cf. especially 44:5; 49:6; cf. also the close relationship between 55:13 and 56:3). The universalism of both writers is warmhearted. The form of the poem is like that of Second Isaiah (cf., e.g., 40:1-11), and the style has affinities with him (note, e.g., the quotations in vs. 3). Yet there are striking differences. The mood is not the same; there is not the same impassioned fervor here. Moreover, the strong emphasis on the cult, law, sabbath, temple, sacrifices, and prayer suggests that we are moving in a different world of thought. To understand the writer one must recognize where he borrows from his predecessor and where he is independent of him. It is possible that he is a disciple of Second Isaiah (so Sellin, Elliger). Harris Birkeland (*Zum hebräischen Traditionswesen* [Oslo: Jacob Dybwad, 1938], pp. 39-40), following the traditio-historical school, and especially the view of Mowinckel (*Jesaja-diseplene* [Oslo: H. Aschenoug, 1926]) that an Isaiah school developed from the prophetic activity of Isaiah (cf. 8:16-18), suggests that Third Isaiah, like his predecessor, perpetuated the Isaiah tradition.

The poem provides little certain evidence of date. The reference to the temple must not be pressed (Eissfeldt, Bentzen, Birkeland) since we are dealing with poetry in an eschatological context (vss. 1*b*, 8). But the thought suggests a stage of development later than Second Isaiah. There is no reason why the emphasis of the poem should not

---

why it has been placed immediately after ch. 55. That hospitable message had invited all spiritually wistful souls to enter the messianic community. Such inclusiveness evidently was not shared by all Israelites. Were proselytes as welcome as those born of the seed of Jacob? Would eunuchs, who could not increase the population of depleted Jerusalem, have full standing in this religious fellowship preoccupied with the multiplication of its numbers? (Cf. 51:2; 54:1 ff.) Judaism has been and still is divided between those who stress its religious message to be shared with mankind and those who stress its racial solidarity. The prophet is bent on reassuring hesitant groups and reminding advocates of exclusivism that

> . . . the love of God is broader
> Than the measure of man's mind.[6]

He bids proselytes and eunuchs share fully the fellowship of God's worshipers, only insisting on

[6] Frederick W. Faber, "There's a wideness in God's mercy."

their loyalty to the covenant evidenced by righteous life and observance of the sabbath. The stress on outward evidence of fidelity had grown during the Exile (cf. Ezek. 20), and is a characteristic of postexilic Judaism. Some have seen in it a declension from the spiritual emphasis of the great prophets; but the devout life cannot flourish long in secret without practices and usages which reinforce it. In troubled times, when many are indifferent, leaders find it necessary to lay stress on outward expressions of religion, which are also its framework and support. Our generation and its immediate predecessor have disparaged the maintenance of the Lord's day, church attendance, and similar signs which testify allegiance to the faith. It is tragically patent that the gospel suffers as a force in social life when such religious customs are neglected.

1. God's Reign.—The oracle opens with a general exhortation, based on the nearness of the Lord's deliverance. If those addressed are in their homeland, the deliverance is not from

2 Blessed *is* the man *that* doeth this, and
the son of man *that* layeth hold on it; that

2 Blessed is the man who does this,
    and the son of man who holds it fast,
    who keeps the sabbath, not profaning it,

---

have arisen within a few decades after the fall of Jerusalem and the years of exile and national degradation. Perhaps a time between 530 and 510 b.c. suits the evidence best.

The text is on the whole well preserved. The Dead Sea Scroll has some interesting variants. The meter is irregular, but not to a degree to suggest prose (see Hugo Odeberg, *Trito-Isaiah [Isaiah 56-66]: A Literary and Linguistic Analysis* [Uppsala: A.-B. Lundequistska, 1931], p. 7).

1. Proem: Obey the Law (56:1)

Torrey attaches vss. 1, 7-8 to ch. 55; Kissane, vss. 1-2. The Dead Sea Scroll gives some support to this by introducing the oracular formula with *kî*. The oracular formula (vs. 1a) is followed by a twofold imperative (vs. 1b), which is motivated by the imminence of the divine deliverance (vs. 1cd introduced by *kî*). The association of teaching (*tôrāh, didachē*) with "gospel" (cf. κήρυγμα), is noteworthy (see Exod. 20:2 and 3-17). The entire poem is governed by these two interests (cf. vss. 2-7, 8).

56:1. Justice is tantamount to "what is lawful" (cf. 58:2; Ezek. 18:5, 19, 21, 27; 33:14, 15, 19; and especially Ps. 106:3, which combines vss. 1 and 2). **Righteousness** means conduct in conformity to the divine teaching or law. The urgency of the requirements is motivated by the nearness of God's salvation (cf. Mark 1:15; Matt. 4:17). The Hebrew word rendered **righteousness** in vs. 1b appears in vs. 1d with the meaning of **deliverance** (cf. 45:8, 23; 46:13; 51:1, 6). The events following Cyrus' conquest of Babylon and centering about Zerubbabel did not correspond remotely to Second Isaiah's hopes (for a judicious appraisal of the situation see Albright, "The Biblical Period," in Louis Finkelstein, ed., *The Jews, Their History and Culture* [New York: Harper & Bros., 1946], I, 49, 62).

2. First Strophe: Blessing and Exhortation (56:2-3)

The strophe places its stress on the individual: **the man, . . . the son of man.** Even the proselyte and eunuch are included within the blessing and its accompanying demands. The citation of their words provides the basis for the rest of the poem.

2. The blessing is the response to the oracle of vs. 1. The Hebrew word אשרי means "happy," as in the Beatitudes. The blessing is one of the oldest as well as one of the most common of Hebrew literary forms (cf. Gunkel and Begrich, *Einleitung in die Psalmen,* pp. 293 ff.; Sigmund Mowinckel, *Psalmenstudien V,* "Segen und Fluch in Israels Kult und Psalmendichtung" [Oslo: Jacob Dybwad, 1923]; Johannes Hempel, "Die israelitischen Anschauungen von Segen und Fluch im Lichte altorientalischer Parallelen," *Zeitschrift der deutschen morgenländischen Gesellschaft,* LXXIX [1925], 20-110). The pronouns **this** and **it** reach backward to vs. 1b and forward to vs. 2cd as the participles

---

captivity. Doubtless their homeland, when they had reached it, proved a disillusionment: it fell far short of the glowing anticipations by which they had been sustained. This is a frequent experience of God's people. His reign is always "at hand"; but in history it is never fully here. He comes, but his dwelling with men lies beyond history (cf. Rev. 21:3). His **salvation** is never complete either in individuals or in society. We are saved in hope (Rom. 8:24). At once we are saved in the sense of being forgiven and restored to his fellowship; but there is an unfulfilled expectation of "something evermore

about to be." Every goal, when reached, points to another beyond it.

2. Sabbathkeeping.—It appears a confusion to place observance of sabbaths on the same level as refraining from evil-doing. But with a mixed population inhabiting the land, and many Israelites religiously careless, it was important to stress outward fidelity to God. The sabbath had been a humane provision guaranteeing rest to slaves, to other workers, and to work animals (Deut. 5:14-15). Earlier prophets had protected it against gain-seekers and cravers of amusement (Amos 8:5). The exiles regarded

| keepeth the sabbath from polluting it, and keepeth his hand from doing any evil. | and keeps his hand from doing any evil." |

show. Several scholars argue for the spuriousness of this section because of the strong emphasis upon **the sabbath**. Second Isaiah does not refer to it. In the priestly history (contemporary with Isa. 40:1–66:24) of Gen. 1:1–2:4a, however, God's sabbath rest appears as the culmination of the creation account. It therefore has a cosmic basis and becomes the supreme motive for man's observance of it (see Exod. 20:8-11). During the Exile "it was the only institution of the Mosaic law by which the people could pay homage to the true God; hence the keeping of the Sabbath became the mark of the true Israelite" (Kissane, *Isaiah*, p. 209; cf. 58:13; Deut. 5:12; Jer. 17:21-22; Ezek. 20:12 ff.; 22:8, 26; Neh. 13:17-18). **And keeps his hand from doing any evil:** An inclusive expression stated negatively, as so often in O.T. legal literature, but descriptive of life according to the precepts of vs. 1b (cf. 58:7-9). It is strange that no reference is made to circumcision either here or elsewhere in the poem (for a discussion of this important point see Julian Morgenstern, "The Book of the Covenant, Part III—The Ḥuqqim," *Hebrew Union College Annual*, VIII [1931], 49-50).

it also as a symbol of loyalty to the God of Israel (Ezek. 20:12; Exod. 31:13-14).

Our Lord returned to the earlier teaching that "the sabbath was made for man." Paul apparently did not consider it a Christian institution, but part of the Mosaic law abolished in Christ (Rom. 14:5; Col. 2:16). His view was recovered at the Reformation. William Tyndale wrote: "We be lords over the sabbath, and may yet change it into the Monday, or any other day, as we see need; or may make every tenth day holy day only, if we see a cause why. We may make two every week, if it were expedient, and one not enough to teach the people." [7] The early church maintained the principle of setting aside one day in seven to be safeguarded from labor and devoted to the worship and service of God, and chose the first day of the week to commemorate Christ's resurrection. The Lord's day is not a Jewish sabbath, but a day to be hallowed by whatever lifts the individual and the community into the life of the risen Christ. The religious custom of devoting one day in seven to rest from common toil and to the improvement of the spiritual life meets with general approval. The urbane Addison wrote: "[I] think, if keeping holy the seventh day were only a human institution, it would be the best method that could have been thought of for the polishing and civilizing of mankind." [8] In a religiously mixed society the community may enact it as a holiday to safeguard those whom greed or desire for pleasure expose to a "sore task" which "does not divide the Sunday from the week." [9] Then it is for Christians to dedicate the holiday for a holy day—to raise themselves

and the community to the life with Christ in God. Its Christian use should not be thought of negatively—what is not permitted on the day (cf. the positive content suggested in 66:23). It may be well to combat a popular notion that the sabbath is a Puritan custom. It long antedated Puritanism. Theodore of Tarsus, archbishop of Canterbury in 669, told Englishmen "that his fellow Greeks would neither sail nor ride (except to church) or bake or bathe or write any unnecessary letters on Sunday." [1] And one of the greatest of Puritan divines, John Owen, declared: "We have no bounds, under the gospel, for a Sabbath-day's journey, provided it be for Sabbath ends." [2] Historically the Christian church won the day both as a humane time of rest and for the purposes of religion. The Christian who neglects this hard-won heritage is faithless to the church and to his spiritual ancestors.

It is noteworthy that those who have abandoned Christian beliefs have often confessed how much they missed Christian practices. George Eliot "once expressed to a younger friend, who shared her opinions, her sense of the loss which they had in being unable to practice the old ordinances of family prayer." [3] The Lord's day was extolled by George Gissing after he no longer called himself a believer:

There was a time when it delighted me to flash my satire on the English Sunday; I could see nothing but antiquated foolishness and modern hypocrisy in this weekly pause from labour and from bustle. Now I prize it as an inestimable boon, and dread every encroachment upon its restful stillness. . . .

[7] *Answer to Sir Thomas More's Dialogue*, ch. xxv.
[8] *The Spectator*, No. 112.
[9] *Hamlet*, Act I, scene 1.

[1] Coulton, *Medieval Panorama*, p. 181.
[2] Moffatt, *Golden Book of John Owen*, p. 222.
[3] F. W. Hirst, *Early Life and Letters of John Morley* (London: Macmillan & Co., 1927), I, 325.

3 ¶ Neither let the son of the stranger, that hath joined himself to the Lord, speak, saying, The Lord hath utterly separated me from his people: neither let the eunuch say, Behold, I *am* a dry tree.

3 Let not the foreigner who has joined himself to the Lord say,
"The Lord will surely separate me from his people";
and let not the eunuch say,
"Behold, I am a dry tree."

---

3. Who has joined himself to the Lord: Duhm, Marti, Morgenstern, and others excise the relative clause because of the awkward repetition in the Hebrew of **say** and **saying.** Note also the contrast with the brief *formula citandi* of vs. 3c and the repetition of the clause in vs. 6a. But the construction is not unparalleled, and the literary structure of the poem explains the repetition. The writer is indebted to Second Isaiah for his universalistic point of view (see, above all, 44:5; but also 45:14, 23; 55:5). In such passages we may have the origins of Jewish proselytism (for fuller discussion see Alfred Bertholet, *Die Stellung der Israeliten und der Juden zu den Fremden* [Leipzig: J. C. B. Mohr, 1896]; A. Causse, *Du groupe ethnique à la communauté religieuse* [Paris: Félix Alcan, 1937], pp. 277-97; Millar Burrows, *Outline of Biblical Theology* [Philadelphia: Westminster Press, 1946], pp. 278 ff.; Herbert G. May, "Theological Universalism in the Old Testament," *The Journal of Bible and Religion*, XVI [1948], 100-7). Later the prophet Zechariah, also influenced by Second Isaiah, speaks of ten men from the nations laying hold of a Jew and saying, "Let us go with you, for we have heard that God is with you" (Zech. 8:23). The prayer of Solomon in I Kings 8 and the composition of the Deuteronomist share the same universalistic view. Even the apparently exclusivistic

---

The idea is surely as good a one as ever came to heavy-laden mortals; let one whole day in every week be removed from the common life of the world. . . . Sunday has always brought large good to the generality, and to a chosen number has been the very life of the soul. . . . If its ancient use perish from among us, so much the worse for our country.[4]

Edward Rowland Sill, another caught in nineteenth-century doubt, depicted the day:

Not a dread cavern, hoar with damp and mould,
Where I must creep and in the dark and cold,
  Offer some awful incense at a shrine
  That hath no more divine
Than that 'tis far from life, and stern, and old;

But a bright hilltop in the breezy air,
Full of the morning freshness high and clear,
  Where I may climb and drink the pure, new day,
  And see where winds away
The path that God would send me, shining fair.[5]

In face of the widespread recognition that man's physical development has outstripped his spiritual growth, and that catastrophe impends unless his soul is reinforced, the urgent duty is on the church to teach the obligation of outward expression for the increase of the inner life with God, and to restore in her members devout habits—the weekly religious festival,

churchgoing, grace at table, family worship, etc., which witness faith and strengthen it.

3c-5. The Status of Eunuchs in the Religious Community.—These were the unhappy victims of despotism in Oriental courts where polygamy prevailed. The law (Deut. 23:1) excluded them from the worshiping fellowship, because "the deliberate mutilation of the nature which God has given to man is inconsistent with the character of Jehovah's people."[6] During the Exile Israelites in various lands may have been forced into this degrading servitude. The prophet takes a kindlier position than the law. These unfortunates, deprived of contributing children to prolong their memories in Israel, may have memorials ("hands") like the childless Absalom's (II Sam. 18:18) upon the walls of the temple court, testifying the regard of the godly.

A modern counterpart of these unfortunates are the victims of our social vices and maladies—alcoholics, prostitutes, the feeble-minded, etc.—for whom the church has a special obligation to provide the inspirations of the gospel and a place in her fellowship. It sometimes seems that the mentally defective flock to churches; but these folk are shunned elsewhere or snubbed, and in the churches they should be sure of kindly welcome.

3ab, 6-8. The Proselytes.—This message meets the upsurging nationalism and racialism of the restored community. Its present-day equivalent is the church's responsibility, in neighborhoods

---

[4] *The Private Papers of Henry Ryecroft* (London: Constable & Co., 1903), pp. 85-87.

[5] "Sunday."

[6] Driver, *Deuteronomy*, p. 260.

4 For thus saith the LORD unto the eunuchs that keep my sabbaths, and choose *the things* that please me, and take hold of my covenant;

5 Even unto them will I give in mine house and within my walls a place and a name better than of sons and of daughters: I will give them an everlasting name, that shall not be cut off.

4 For thus says the LORD:
"To the eunuchs who keep my sabbaths,
who choose the things that please me
and hold fast my covenant,
5 I will give in my house and within my walls
a monument and a name
better than sons and daughters;
I will give them an everlasting name
which shall not be cut off.

---

writer of Deut. 23:2-9 (Hebrew 23:1-8) looks forward to the inclusion into the assembly of the Lord of Moabites and Ammonites after the tenth generation. The book of Ruth is an eloquent plea in behalf of the Moabite proselyte. Cf. also Jonah 1; Ps. 87. The *ben-hannēkhār*—foreigner—does not make his home in Palestine as does the *gēr*—resident alien. **The LORD will surely separate me:** The verb (Hiphil of *bādhal*) is a *terminus technicus* for the exclusion of the heathen from the worship of the cult (Lev. 20:24 [H]; Num. 16:9 [P]; Ezra 6:21; Neh. 13:3; cf. I Kings 8:53). According to Deut. 23:1 (Hebrew 23:2) **the eunuch** was to be excluded from the cultic community, but the prophet betrays no familiarity with this law. The complaint of the eunuch is not so much of his evil fate, but that he will not contribute offspring to the community of God (cf. Jer. 34:19; Dan. 1:3 ff.; Acts 8:27; see also Matt. 19:12). Intentional mutilation of the body—a practice widespread in the ancient Near East—is a defiance of God's holy creation.

3. SECOND STROPHE: EUNUCHS (56:4-5)

The divine assurance is introduced impressively: **For thus says the LORD.** What follows forms a single sentence: **To the eunuchs . . . I will give in my house. . . .** The climactic ordering of the lines is noteworthy in both verses. The eunuch who is faithful to his religion will find an honorable place within the sacred community.

4. The things that please me: See Heb. 11:25. **And hold fast my covenant:** Accept the responsibilities and fulfill the obligations of the Mosaic covenant. Observe the parallel line. It is repeated in the same climactic position in vs. 6.

5. In my house and within my walls: The emphasis upon the worship of the community is well and emphatically expressed. The final phrase is not to be deleted (contra Duhm, Marti, Box). **A monument and a name:** Not to be taken in the sense of an actual monument (Hebrew *yādh*, "hand") such as Absalom built to keep his name in remembrance (II Sam. 18:18, contra Skinner). The name of a man lives on in the lives of his children, as Abraham and Jacob lived on in Israel; a part of his nature is perpetuated in them (Gen. 48:16; Deut. 25:6-7; Num. 27:4). But God will give the eunuchs a name **better than sons and daughters,** one that is honored within the temple community. More than this, it will be an enduring name which will not be blotted out (cf. 55:13).

---

where the population is composed of several racial stocks, nationalities, and social classes, to keep her congregations hospitable to them all. A "segregated" or one-class congregation denies the N.T. ideal of the church (Eph. 2:14; Col. 3:11). Racial prejudice and social snobbery are sins which damage the church and frustrate God's purpose through her. The prophet accords proselytes a place not only in the lay fellowship of believers but also in the priesthood.

While sacrifices are spoken of with apparent approval, the temple is primarily a **house of prayer.** This is an aspect of public worship which came to the fore during the Exile, when the cultus had to be abandoned and synagogues arose. Our Lord quotes this passage when cleansing the temple of the traffickers (Mark 11:17). It appealed to him for two reasons: (*a*) Its universalism, **for all peoples.** He was denouncing the nationalism which compelled pilgrims to exchange their currencies for the shekel of the sanctuary. (*b*) Its emphasis on prayer rather than on ceremonies and sacrifices. It remains

6 Also the sons of the stranger, that join themselves to the Lord, to serve him, and to love the name of the Lord, to be his servants, every one that keepeth the sabbath from polluting it, and taketh hold of my covenant;

7 Even them will I bring to my holy mountain, and make them joyful in my house of prayer: their burnt offerings and their sacrifices *shall be* accepted upon mine altar; for mine house shall be called a house of prayer for all people.

6 "And the foreigners who join themselves
    to the Lord,
  to minister to him, to love the name
    of the Lord,
  and to be his servants,
  every one who keeps the sabbath, and
    does not profane it,
  and holds fast my covenant —
7 these I will bring to my holy mountain,
  and make them joyful in my house of
    prayer;
  their burnt offerings and their sacrifices
    will be accepted on my altar;
  for my house shall be called a house of
    prayer
  for all peoples.

4. Third Strophe: Foreigners (56:6-7)

The strophe is composed after the same fashion as the foregoing; vs. 6 describes the foreigners or proselytes, vs. 7 gives the promise. Vs. 6 (cf. vs. 3) sets forth the piety of the proselytes in clear detail; vs. 7 (cf. vs. 4) takes us within the temple (**my house**). The text of vs. 6 seems to be overfull, and the meter is difficult to make out. The Dead Sea Scroll omits vs. 6b, **to minister to him, to love the name of the Lord,** and adds after vs. 6c the words "to bless the name of the Lord." But this is hardly superior textually. The same MS has the plural participle for **every one who keeps.** Duhm, Marti, and others delete the last two lines as repetition of vs. 4, but the emphasis upon the sabbath in vs. 2 favors its retention for both the eunuchs and the proselytes.

6. Who join themselves to the Lord: Cf. vs. 3a. Some scholars take this as a reference to circumcision; through this sign the foreigner became a Jew. But the reference seems to be more general. The infinitive phrases give content to the line. Three inward acts characterize the piety of the proselyte. The word **minister** is often used of service, especially in connection with the priestly service in the sanctuary (Exod. 29:30; 30:20; 35:19; 39:1; cf. Isa. 60:7, 10; 61:6). **To love the name of the Lord:** Cf. Deut. 10:12 (parallel to "serve Yahweh"), 11:13, 22; 19:9. The true Israelites are God's **servants.** The proselyte who offers his whole life in worship and service to God belongs to Israel (cf. 54:17; also Lev. 25:42, 55 [H]; on the prophets as servants cf. Jer. 7:25; Ezek. 38:17; Ezra 9:11). For vs. 6bcd the Dead Sea Scroll reads, "To be his servants and to bless the name of the Lord and those who keep the sabbath."

7. The cultic relationship between God and his people is emphasized: **my holy mountain; my house of prayer; my altar; their burnt offerings; their sacrifices.** The proselytes will share in the joy of the festivals, their sacrifices will be accepted, and their prayers heard. Joy and gladness were especially characteristic of Israelite worship as it is reflected in Deuteronomy and the Psalms. The sound of joy rings throughout Second Isaiah also, but there it is in anticipation of the imminent redemption and deliverance. Here the joy is centered in temple worship. A verb is missing in the Hebrew of vs. 7cd. Torrey has suggested that the word "go up" (יעלו) has fallen out, and his position has been substantiated by the presence of the word in the Dead Sea Scroll. Vs. 7e is an impressive climax. The words are quoted by Jesus in Mark 11:17 (and parallels).

a challenge to every congregation. Public worship and congregational life must be scrutinized to see whether they have meaning and attraction for all elements in the surrounding population. The church age after age falls into the hands of one class or set, and unintentionally becomes remote from the interests and needs of others.

The oracle closes with a promise of the ingathering of proselytes (vs. 8). Here is a sig-

8 The Lord GOD which gathereth the outcasts of Israel saith, Yet will I gather *others* to him, besides those that are gathered unto him.

9 ¶ All ye beasts of the field, come to devour, *yea,* all ye beasts in the forest.

8 Thus says the Lord GOD,
　who gathers the outcasts of Israel,
I will gather yet others to him
　besides those already gathered."*c*

9 All you beasts of the field, come to devour —
　all you beasts in the forest.

c Heb *his gathered ones*

The house of God is pre-eminently **a house of prayer.** There prayers are offered and there they are heard and answered (cf. the fervent words of Solomon in behalf of the foreigner as reported by the Deuteronomist in I Kings 8:41-43). **For all peoples:** Cf. 2:2-4; 60:1-14; 66:18-19.

5. CONCLUSION: THE GATHERED COMMUNITY OF GOD (56:8)

The poem closes with a special word of revelation (8*cd*). The oracular formula (vs. 1*a*) is expanded by a participial phrase appropriate to the situation. The oracle itself is contained in the concluding couplet. The threefold repetition of **gather** is impressive.

8. Thus says the Lord GOD: The Hebrew נאם אדני יהוה is better rendered, "Oracle of the Lord Yahweh." The expression often appears at the conclusion of the divine disclosure, but not always (cf. 1:24; Ps. 110:1; Zech. 12:1). **Who gathers the outcasts of Israel:** The verbal root means "drive out," "expel," "banish" (Jer. 49:5; cf. also Isa. 11:12; Ps. 147:2). The line connects with vs. 7, **these I will bring.** The gathering of Israel is a characteristic feature of Israel's eschatology, and finds expression particularly in her devotional life (cf. the Shemoneh Esreh: "Blessed art thou, O Lord, who gatherest the outcasts of thy people Israel").

Israel longed fervently for the time when her children might be united at Zion's hill. **I will gather:** Lit., "I will yet gather to him, to his gathered ones." The last three words are not a gloss. To the exiles of Israel God **will gather yet others,** the proselytes who have joined themselves to Israel in the Dispersion (see John 10:16). The particularism and universalism of Second Isaiah are preserved, though here the thought centers in the temple community: one God, one people, one worship, one temple for all peoples.

B. BLIND LEADERS AND CORRUPT WORSHIP (56:9–57:13)

The primary interest of the poem lies in its reflection of religious conditions. Unfortunately, difference of opinion concerning its date has obscured its importance for an understanding of Israel's religious development. The extent of the poem, the wide variety of its contents, the abundance of allusion, the richness of imagery, the dependence upon other literary sources, and the picture of the alien cult provide us with exceptional opportunity for analysis and evaluation.

This section forms a clear literary unity. Because of the sharp shift in grammatical construction here and there, some scholars have dissected the material into several units, but invariably this is done at a sacrifice both of continuity and of literary form. Moreover, the grammatical shifts in number and gender can be explained by the change of point of

---

nificant name for God—the Lord GOD who gathers (cf. Ps. 147:2). His nature is the opposite of exclusive. Evidently some of **the outcasts of Israel** were already in the homeland. **Yet others** are those still in foreign lands and Gentile proselytes. The prophet is in the succession of the missionary-minded writer to whom we owe chs. 40–55. This conception of Judaism's

temple as a house of prayer for all peoples anticipates the missionary spirit of the Christian gospel (cf. John 10:16).

56:9–57:13. *Blind Leaders and an Idolatrous People.*—Under the Persian regime the leaders of the people, subordinate to the Persian officials, were priests and prophets. This might seem favorable to the spiritual life, but the

view and imagery. More can be said for extending the poem to the end of ch. 57 (so Kissane, Torrey, Feldmann, *et al.*). There is an excellent transition from 57:12-13 to 57:14-21. Furthermore, the latter verses take account of the righteous and of the wicked; indeed vss. 17-21 would make a fine conclusion to the whole. On the other hand, the structure of 56:9–57:13, composed as it is of nine strophes with the climax on the third strophe of each division and the final climax on the ninth, raises doubt. Moreover, the influence of Second Isaiah is strong in 57:14-21, but only slight elsewhere. Finally, while the appeal to style is elusive and uncertain, it seems to be somewhat different. It is possible, however, that 57:14-21 belongs to the poem. One cannot be certain. An alternative would be to consider it the work of another disciple of Second Isaiah, the two writers sharing loyalty to a common master. Observe the introduction to 57:14 ("and one said"), which may be the connecting device of a redactor.

The poem has been assigned to various periods from the eighth century to the time of Ezra and Nehemiah. Those who favor a pre-exilic date appeal to the description of the cultic practices, the reference to religious apostasy as adultery (Hos. 1:1–3:5; 4:12 ff.; Jer. 2:20 ff.; Ezek. 16:23 ff.), the affinity with pre-exilic prophets (5:8 ff.; Amos 6:1 ff.; Jer. 9:1-2; Zeph. 3:3; numerous references in Hosea), the presence of civil rulers in Jerusalem, and the invective style, reminiscent of the earlier prophets. Others, like Duhm, Marti, and their followers, have detected allusions to the apostate Samaritan cultus of the fifth century. Recent criticism (Elliger, Procksch) seems to have converged upon a date between 538 and 500. Elliger points out that the leaders referred to in 56:9 ff. are religious, not political, that the invective is directed throughout against cultic violations, that the summary given in 57:11 is religious in content, and that the connection between 57:9a and 57:9b favors a religious interpretation. A careful reading of the Hebrew text supports this view. It can be reinforced by other considerations: (*a*) the tendency to depend upon the work of prophetic predecessors is characteristic of the period after 538 B.C. (cf., e.g., Zechariah); (*b*) there is no reason to doubt that many of the religious practices of the time of Manasseh and later continued among the people of the land; (*c*) the affinities with Jeremiah, Ezekiel, and especially Zechariah, do not encourage a much later dating; and (*d*) the presence of a pre-exilic passage in a literary context generally agreed to be exilic or postexilic is strange. As to an exilic dating, the reference to valleys, clefts of the rocks, and mountains suits a Palestinian locale better than the Babylonian. The prophet stands on the shoulders of his great predecessor; he addresses himself to the same major concerns and discusses them in his own way while he borrows where it suits his need.

---

reverse was true. Seldom are ecclesiastics effective rulers, and their political activities have a disintegrating effect on their characters and influence. Vividly the prophet calls on **beasts of the field**, i.e., wild beasts, to fall on an unprotected flock. Spiritual leaders had been called **watchmen** by Ezekiel (33:2) and the metaphor recurs in the N.T. (Heb. 13:17). Ministers are charged with safeguarding their congregations and communities from perils which endanger souls. Vss. 10-11b set forth four qualities which make men unfit for this duty:

(*a*) Blindness. This prevents them from discerning the times and the condition of their people. The Chronicler, with an eye on his own day, speaks of the leaders of Issachar as "men that had understanding of the times, to know what Israel ought to do" (I Chr. 12:32).

(*b*) Cowardice. They must speak boldly as a dog barks. Courage is a prime requisite in

ambassadors of God. When Robert Bruce was preaching before King James in Edinburgh, the king talked to courtiers sitting near him. Twice Bruce ceased speaking, and looked full at the king. Finally, when the king conversed again, Bruce remarked:

"It's said to have been an expression of the wisest of kings, . . . When the lion roareth, all the beasts of the field are at ease; the Lion of the Tribe of Judah is now roaring, in the voice of his Gospel, and it becomes all the petty kings of the earth to be silent." [7]

A dog's **bark** is sharply clear. Lack of precision in thought and utterance is a ministerial vice. There is an "indigenous intellectual haziness" [8]

[7] Robert Wodrow, *Sermons by the Rev. Robert Bruce* (ed. William Cunningham; Edinburgh: Wodrow Society, 1843), p. 154.

[8] John Morley, *On Compromise* (London: Macmillan & Co., 1886), p. 32.

10 His watchmen *are* blind: they are all ignorant, they *are* all dumb dogs, they cannot bark; sleeping, lying down, loving to slumber.

10 His watchmen are blind,
    they are all without knowledge;
they are all dumb dogs,
    they cannot bark;
dreaming, lying down,
    loving to slumber.

The style of the poem is notable for the severity of its rebuke. The leaders are blind, dumb, indolent, insatiable in their greed, utterly self-centered, and completely heedless of the needs of the people. The apostate people are children of a sorceress, offspring of an adulteress, children of transgression, offspring of deceit, who burn with unrestrained lust, slay their children, and engage in all the licentious practices of unbridled sexuality. The climaxes are obvious (57:2, 8*fgh*, 13*de*). The repetition of key words is worthy of special note (**beasts, dogs, righteous man, bed**, etc.). While the poem is quite different from 56:1-8, there are connecting links: **the righteous** (cf. 56:1 and 57:1); "the gathered ones" (cf. 56:8 and 57:13); **my holy mountain** (cf. 56:7*a* and 57:13*e*). Moreover, both poems show some influence of Second Isaiah. The meter in 56:9-12 is irregular, though 3+3 predominates; in the rest of the poem the lamentation meter 3+2 appropriately prevails.

1. First Strophe: The Decadence and Corruption of Leaders (56:9-10)

Yahweh calls upon the nations to devour his flock. The leaders do not fulfill their vocation as watchmen. Instead of being alert, intent, and vigilant, they are blind; instead of warning the people by the urgency and passion of the spoken word, they are dumb; instead of feeling responsible for the fate and welfare of the people, they are drugged in sleep and illusion. The closing triad summarizes their condition.

9. The figure of the nations as **beasts of the field** is a familiar one (see Jer. 12:8-9; 19:7*d*; Ezek. 34:1-28; 39:17 ff.). The twofold apostrophe with the intervening imperative seems awkward. It is perhaps best, with Volz, to consider it a substitution from Jer. 12:9 for a defective text. Others add an imperative to the second line. The word חיתו, **beasts**, is archaic and poetic (König, *Stilistik, Rhetorik, Poetik*, p. 278); the Dead Sea Scroll reads the more normal form חית. The repetition of words is typical of our writer (*ibid.*, p. 300). König gives many examples of similarity in sound at the beginning and ending of a line or larger unity. Such repetitions are a common and illuminating characteristic of Hebrew literary style. The form of the verb '*āthāh* ("come") is noteworthy (Kautzsch, *Gesenius' Hebrew Grammar*, sec. 29*t*). That the figure is drawn from the ravages of Judah's territory by wild animals during the Exile is questionable. The imagery moves more in the eschatological direction.

10. The prophet plunges at once into the reasons for his appeal to the beasts to devour. They are to come as instruments of the divine judgment upon the spiritual leaders (56:10–57:2) and upon the devotees of a corrupt cult (57:3-14). The **watchmen** are most probably the prophets (Jer. 6:17; Ezek. 3:17; 33:7). They are the men of God

---

in most men, and this in ministers becomes a major hindrance to the declaration of God's will.

(*c*) Indolence. **Sleeping, lying down, loving to slumber.** Baxter, in his *Reformed Pastor*, writes of ministers who "slubber" over their work. If modern ministers give the impression of constant activity, they do well to recall that there is a *strenua . . . inertia*,[9] which keeps busy at all manner of trifling things while neglecting those of vaster importance. In the

ministerial make-up a concomitant of the capacity to meditate is the habit of wool-gathering. George Herbert confessed: "A slack and sleepie state of minde did oft possesse me."[10]

(*d*) Greed. **The dogs have a mighty appetite.** The contemporary ministry is not cursed with gainseekers. The meagerness of ministerial stipends, however, tempts to covetousness, and often engenders ambition for wealth in min-

[9] Horace *Epistles* I. 11. 28.

[10] George Herbert Palmer, ed., *The English Works of George Herbert* (Boston: Houghton Mifflin Co., 1905), I, 61.

| 11 Yea, *they are* greedy dogs *which* can never have enough, and they *are* shepherds *that* cannot understand: they all look to | 11 The dogs have a mighty appetite; they never have enough. The shepherds also have no understanding; |

who stand upon the watchtower to see what it is that Yahweh has to reveal (21:6 ff.; Hab. 2:1-3), quick to discern the signs of the times, i.e., what God is about to do in the world. When the Lord God speaks in mighty events, they can but prophesy (Amos 3:8). There is nothing new about the false prophets here; the pre-exilic prophets had to deal with them—prophets who would speak favorably for monetary reward (Mic. 3:5-8), prophets like Hananiah, who predicted what the people wished to hear (Jer. 28:1 ff.; see also Jer. 14:14-18; Zech. 13:1-6). The true watchman is on the lookout for the people. It is possible, perhaps probable, that the priests are included among the watchmen (cf. Jer. 2:8; 14:18). **His watchmen are blind:** The Hebrew contains a double reading: a verbal form (so LXX, "see how they are all blinded") and a noun form, **his watchmen** (so also Dead Sea Scroll). The pronominal suffix refers to the people. Some scholars emend to "my watchmen," referring to God. The present leaders do not see impending events; so they cannot warn their people. **They are all dumb dogs:** The expression is one of extreme contempt (or servility), as in the Tell el-Amarna letters and the O.T. (I Sam. 17:43; 24:14; II Kings 8:13). Some see an allusion to the watchdog whose duty it is to guard the flock (Job 30:1). **Without knowledge:** Lit., "they do not know." Many critics supply an infinitive, usually "to understand" or "to have insight" from vs. 11c (*hābhîn*), which they believe to be misplaced. But the passage gives good sense without the change. **Dreaming:** The root הזים occurs only here in the O.T.; therefore some change ה to ח, and read חזים, "seers." The Arabic cognate of the word means "to talk nonsense [or deliriously]." The reference is not to the false dreams of the false prophets (Jer. 23:16-17, 25); the picture here is rather one of utter indolence and sloth.

2. SECOND STROPHE: THE GREEDY DOGS (56:11-12)

11. The strophe continues the description of the spiritual leaders. It is not a separate class of officials (contra Kissane *et al.*; cf. vs. 10c). **The dogs have a mighty appetite:** The Hebrew is "strong of life," *néphesh*, a natural collocation. The prophets and

isters' children. There is however, **a mighty appetite** for praise. Many a pastor laps up the flattery of certain of his parishioners. "Even a little flattery is a very heady kind of incense if you allow it to be a desire you sniff up like the wild ass."[1]

The sins of these spiritual leaders have recurred again and again in the church through the centuries. Milton condemned the Laudian clergy:

Enow of such as for their bellies' sake
Creep, and intrude, and climb into the fold!
Of other care they little reckoning make,
Than how to scramble at the shearers' feast,
And shove away the worthy bidden guest;
Blind mouths! that scarce themselves know how to hold
A sheep-hook, or have learn'd aught else the least
That to the faithful herdman's art belongs![2]

The striking metaphor "blind mouths" corresponds to the charges that the leaders are both undiscerning and gainseeking.

Vss. 11c-12 picture the leaders as carousers. Fifty-eight years before Milton penned *Lycidas,* Edmund Spenser brought the indictment of reveling against the Elizabethan clergy:

These faytours [hypocrites] little regarden their charge,
While they, letting their sheepe runne at large,
Passen their time, that should be sparely spent,
In lustihede and wanton meryment.[3]

In our day such gross sins are happily rare among evangelical ministers. An Elmer Gantry is felt to be a caricature; but well-meaning worldlings continue common. Thomas Hardy insisted that ministers should be "souls unreconciled with life";[4] and Edmund Gosse

---

[1] John Oman, *Concerning the Ministry* (New York: Harper & Bros. 1937), p. 44.

[2] *Lycidas,* ll. 114-21.

[3] *The Shepheard's Calender,* May Eclogue.

[4] Florence Emily Hardy, *The Early Life of Thomas Hardy* (London: Macmillan & Co., 1928), p. 315.

their own way, every one for his gain, from his quarter.

12 Come ye, *say they,* I will fetch wine, and we will fill ourselves with strong drink; and to-morrow shall be as this day, *and* much more abundant.

57 The righteous perisheth, and no man layeth *it* to heart: and merciful men *are* taken away, none considering that the righteous is taken away from the evil *to come.*

they have all turned to their own way, each to his own gain, one and all.

12 "Come," they say, "let us[d] get wine, let us fill ourselves with strong drink; and tomorrow will be like this day, great beyond measure."

57 The righteous man perishes, and no one lays it to heart; devout men are taken away, while no one understands. For the righteous man is taken away from calamity,

[d] One ancient Ms Syr Vg Tg: Heb *me*

---

priests are insatiable (cf. Mic. 3:5 ff. and Amaziah's implication in Amos 7:12). For **they never have enough** (lit., "they do not know satiety") the Dead Sea Scroll has "they do not know hearing." **The shepherds also have no understanding:** Lit., "and these are the shepherds; they cannot understand" (cf. KJV, RSV). The line is probably a marginal gloss, as is suggested by the form of the expression, the irregularity it causes in the arrangement of the lines, and by the irregularity of the meter. Fischer and others seek to improve the line by inserting "evil" (the letters רעים may mean either **shepherds** or "evil ones"; cf. Symm. and Targ.). The purpose of the glossator was to identify the leaders with the rulers, contrary to vs. 10c (cf. Jer. 10:21; 12:10; Ezek. 34:1-31; Zech. 11:4-17). **They have all turned to their own way:** Cf. 53:6. **One and all:** Lit., "from his end," but meaning "from one end to the other" (cf. Ezek. 25:9; 33:2; Jer. 51:31), i.e., all without exception. The word is not in the LXX.

12. A fragment from a drinking song (cf. 22:13; I Cor. 15:32 [cf. Luke 12:19], Wisd. Sol. 2:1-9). The poet without any introduction quotes the heedless song of the dissolute revelers. There is no thought for the morrow, still less of the imminence of the divine judgment. **Let us get wine** (RSV, Dead Sea Scroll): The Hebrew reads **let me get wine** (see RSV mg.). The verse is completely absent from the LXX. For the third line the Dead Sea Scroll reads, "Today and tomorrow will be like this."

3. Third Strophe: The Fate of the Righteous (57:1-2)

While the spiritual leaders sleep the hours away, gorge themselves with food, and intoxicate themselves with drink, the righteous pass away without notice. The generation which had listened to the words of Second Isaiah and been stirred and comforted by his proclamation of an imminent redemption were gradually disappearing, while another generation arose which gave no heed to their ancestral faith.

57:1. The LXX and Syriac introduce the climactic strophe with "Behold." The decadence of the time revealed in the moral and spiritual indifference and callousness

---

satirized clergymen with "the same cautious affability towards God and towards the devil." [5] With such defective religious leadership, it is not surprising that the situation in the nation was deplorable. As the devout of a former generation passed away, there were no comparable successors.

57:1-2. Men of Piety Are Dying Off.—It is not said that the devout are banished or slain. John Wesley did not hesitate to call a lifeless

[5] Charteris, *Life and Letters of Edmund Gosse,* p. 161.

unconverting parson "the murderer general of his parish." The prophet notes that no one seems to notice the increasing religious poverty, **no one lays it to heart.** It is perhaps as well for the upright, **taken away from calamity.** But their passing is an irreparable loss, for they are not succeeded by others of like faith and conscience.

The historian of a New England family recorded "something lacking" in the spiritual atmosphere of Boston when Theodore Parker,

| 2 He shall enter into peace: they shall rest in their beds, *each one* walking *in* his uprightness.

3 ¶ But draw near hither, ye sons of the sorceress, the seed of the adulterer and the whore. | 2 he enters into peace;
　they rest in their beds
　who walk in their uprightness.
3 But you, draw near hither,
　sons of the sorceress,
　offspring of the adulterer and the harlot. |

of the prophets and priests is seen in the fate of the **righteous man** who goes to his death without anyone being concerned about his passing (cf. Ps. 12:1; Mic. 7:2). The words **righteous man** are emphatic, as is shown by their position in the strophe as well as by the word order. They are parallel to "devout men," men of *ḥeṣedh*, i.e., those who have been faithful to the covenant. These are not the forerunners of the Hasidim of Maccabean times (cf. Neh. 13:14; II Chr. 32:32), but the faithful, godly men of Israel (cf. Hos. 4:1; 6:4; 10:12; Mic. 6:8; Jer. 2:2; Zech. 7:9). They fear God, remember him, and have him in their thoughts (cf. the conclusion in vs. 11). They are such men as are described in 58:7 (cf. 59:4, 14-15). **From calamity:** The righteous is taken away by God before the impending judgment, but the wicked do not understand this at all, so impervious are they to God's righteous rule in history.

2. The verse is grammatically awkward with its confusion of singular and plural. **He enters into peace:** Torrey says there is no reference to death here. "The upright man leaves Jerusalem, without looking behind him, because he would feel more at home somewhere else" (*Second Isaiah*, p. 433). But the context makes this view unlikely. On the other hand, the writer is not thinking of immortality, although the words suggest an adumbration of it (cf. Wisd. Sol. 4:7-17). So dismal are conditions that death is a release after life's fitful fever (cf. Job 3:13-19). **They rest in their beds:** Meaning "in their graves"; cf. the Eshmun'azar inscription, where the same expression is used (G. A. Cooke, *A Text-Book of North-Semitic Inscriptions* [Oxford: Clarendon Press, 1903], p. 31).

4. Fourth Strophe: Rebuke to the Apostates (57:3-4)

A finely organized strophe introducing a scene of judgment (vss. 3-13; see 41:1). The poet turns suddenly to a new group, **but you.** He calls upon them to draw near for judgment (cf. 41:1), castigates them with stern words of address, confronts them with a scathing challenge, and clinches his invective by calling them **children of transgression, offspring of deceit.**

3. But you: A contrast to the righteous of vss. 1-2. They are not the Samaritans (Duhm, Marti, Skinner), or the pre-exilic community (Ewald, Volz, *et al.*), or the godless in exile (Feldmann), but the inhabitants of Jerusalem who had yielded to the attraction

Octavius Frothingham, and Ralph Waldo Emerson had become its high priests. In John Quincy Adams faith had been the energizing force which had kept him singlehanded the undismayed proponent of the antislavery cause in Congress. His son, Charles Francis, disapproved of his father's unpopular course. "However more justifiable intellectually a mild deism may be, it is no substitute as a driving force . . . for the stronger religious feeling of the earlier generation." [6] Catherine Mumford wrote to her fiancé, William Booth, then a young Wesleyan preacher: "Talk of a stiff formal people, a cold

do-nothing people, a worldly, proud people; where there is a devoted, faithful, *holy* minister, I don't believe it; there never was such an anomaly lasted long." [7] In every generation there are spiritual survivors from a more devout past. The incapacity of their present religious guides does not ruin, although it grieves them. When, however, they pass from the scene, they leave a religious vacuum. It is this void which the prophet feels acutely in this postexilic period.

3-5. A Bitter Invective Against the Idolaters.
—It is thought that those denounced are the

[6] Adams, *The Adams Family*, pp. 232-33.

[7] Harold Begbie, *The Life of William Booth* (New York: The Macmillan Co., 1920), I, 180.

4 Against whom do ye sport yourselves? against whom make ye a wide mouth, *and* draw out the tongue? *are* ye not children of transgression, a seed of falsehood,
 	
5 Inflaming yourselves with idols under every green tree, slaying the children in the valleys under the clefts of the rocks?
	4 Of whom are you making sport?
	  Against whom do you open your mouth wide
	  and put out your tongue?
	Are you not children of transgression,
	  the offspring of deceit,
	5 you who burn with lust among the oaks,
	  under every green tree;
	who slay your children in the valleys,
	  under the clefts of the rocks?

of the Canaanite cult. It is the prophet's function to expose the guilt of his people; our writer is a worthy successor to the great prophets who came before him. **Sons of the sorceress:** Nothing could be more cutting and insulting to an Oriental than to revile his mother; cf. the popular proverb, "Like mother, like daughter" (Ezek. 16:44); also Ezekiel's sharp rebuke, "Your birth and nativity is of the land of the Canaanite; the Amorite was your father, and your mother was a Hittite" (16:3, 45). For the characterization of apostasy as adultery see Hos. 1:1–3:5; Jer. 3:1-20; Ezek. 16:1-63.

4. Making sport: "Making merry." The prophet refers to the derision and mocking scorn of the unfaithful (cf. 28:9-10). The last two lines return to the opening: the first words are emphatic as there: **children of transgression:** "Rebellious children" (cf. 1:2; 46:8; 48:8; Hos. 14:19; Amos 4:4; also Mic. 1:5, 13; Ezek. 18:22, 28). **Offspring of deceit:** "A brood of lies," i.e., "faithless brood." They deride the righteous who are faithful to God's covenant (cf. vs. 11).

5. Fifth Strophe: Devotees of the Nature Cult (57:5-6)

Vs. 5 is generally taken with the foregoing strophe (as in RSV), but it is more likely, in view of the literary form and strophic structure, to attach it to the following. It is to be understood as an extended vocative, as frequently in Second Isaiah. There is no reason to excise it with Duhm, Marti, Cheyne, Volz, and others.

5. You who burn with lust among the oaks: The same verb is used in the Ugaritic texts in connection with the divine amours (J. A. Montgomery, "The New Sources of Knowledge," in Robinson, ed., *Record and Revelation*, p. 22; Montgomery translates the phrase "are concupiscent with the Els"). Cf. Vulg., *in diis*; LXX, τὰ εἴδωλα, idols. If the word means terebinths, it is written defectively in Hebrew. **Under every green tree:** Cf. Deut. 12:2; 3:6; 17:12; Ezek. 6:13; II Kings 17:10. There is no coercive reason for believing that the attraction of the Canaanite and other nature cults ceased after the fall of Jerusalem. Child sacrifice was condemned by many of the prophets (Jer. 7:31; 19:5; Ezek. 20:28, 31; 23:39; Mic. 6:7; cf. also II Kings 23:10). It is usually associated with Topheth in the valley of Hinnom, south of the city.

Samaritans. Their mixed origin is derided in **offspring of the adulterer and the harlot.** Intermarriage with outsiders was considered a form of apostasy. A galling Oriental insult is to revile a man's mother—**sons of the sorceress.** The contemptuous attitude of Samaritans toward Jews is dealt with in Neh. 4:1-4. In this blazing denunciation of Samaritans, deemed a peril to Israel's faith, we have the origin of the N.T. aloofness—"Jews have no dealings with Samaritans" (John 4:9). It had justification at a time when the dilution of Israel's religion was threatening.

There may be warrant for religious isolation. We would not expose the immature to corrupting influences. Even among the mature, religious syncretism is a temptation. The "jealousy of the Lord" in the O.T. evidences prophetic fear of the people's compromising their faith by adopting current pagan practices. The insistence upon total devotion to Yahweh anticipates the emphasis of Jesus, "Thou shalt love the Lord thy God with all . . . ." Sidney Lanier wrote of the "almost-folk that hurt our hope," [8]

[8] Lanier, "Acknowledgment."

6 Among the smooth *stones* of the stream *is* thy portion; they, they *are* thy lot: even to them hast thou poured a drink offering, thou hast offered a meat offering. Should I receive comfort in these?

7 Upon a lofty and high mountain hast thou set thy bed: even thither wentest thou up to offer sacrifice.

8 Behind the doors also and the posts

6 Among the smooth stones of the valley is
　　your portion;
　they, they, are your lot;
　to them you have poured out a drink
　　offering,
　you have brought a cereal offering.
　Shall I be appeased for these things?
7 Upon a high and lofty mountain
　　you have set your bed,
　　and thither you went up to offer sac-
　　rifice.
8 Behind the door and the doorpost
　　you have set up your symbol;
　for, deserting me, you have uncovered
　　your bed,
　you have gone up to it,

6. **Among the smooth stones:** The Hebrew does not have **stones,** but this is probably the correct interpretation. Haller and Volz think the reference is to serpents, which were often venerated in the cults. The word **smooth** is doubtless a play upon the very similar word "portion," the consonants being the same in Hebrew. H. L. Ginsberg ("Some Emendations in Isaiah," *Journal of Biblical Literature,* LXIX [1950], 59) emends to בחלקם נחלות, "in their portion hast thou inherited thy portion," or as an alternative "in their portion is thy portion fallen [נפל]," which requires a too radical change of the text in view of the lack of any versional support. See Torrey's judicious comment, *Second Isaiah, ad loc.* The various *'ēlîm,* "gods" (vs. 5a), are described in the following verses: gods of the valleys (vs. 6); gods of the mountains (vs. 7); gods of the house (vs. 8); gods of the foreign shrines (vss. 9-10). **Your portion . . . your lot:** When Israel became the people of Yahweh in the covenant relation, he became their portion and lot (Deut. 4:19-20; 9:26; Jer. 10:16; 51:19; Pss. 16:5; 73:26; 142:5); but now the fertility deities have taken his rightful place. Sacrifices are offered to them, not to Yahweh. For the repeated **they** the Dead Sea Scroll reads שמה המה. Many scholars delete the last line of the verse as a gloss, but it actually forms the climax of the strophe. Many of the difficulties that have been found with vss. 5-6 are due to an erroneous view of the strophic structure.

6. SIXTH STROPHE: THE ADULTERIES OF NATURE WORSHIP (57:7-8)

The strophe opens very similarly to 40:9. Its unity is seen in the threefold repetition of **bed** (vss. 7b, 8c, 8g). The succession of lines in vs. 8 is unusually effective. They culminate in the increasingly realistic expression of vs. 8fgh. The illicit syncretistic practices of the faithless majority are condemned.

7. The prophet turns from the valleys to the mountains. The mountains were often the seat of famous sanctuaries (Hermon, Baal Zaphon, Carmel, Gerizim, Zion, etc.). For the adulterous worship at these shrines cf. Hos. 4:13; Jer. 2:20-25; 3:2; Ezek. 16:25. **You have set your bed:** Skinner inquires whether Gerizim is meant here. It is not likely. It is precarious to view the language here and in vs. 8 as merely symbolic or figurative of idolatry. The practices of the immoral sex cult are quite clearly in the mind of the writer.

8. The verse is usually interpreted as describing the household cult, but there is much to be said for Volz's view that the description continues vs. 7. In that event it is part

and George Eliot shrewdly describes "the creeping paralysis apt to seize an enthusiasm which is out of adjustment to a constant portion of our lives." [9]

[9] *Middlemarch,* Bk. VI, ch. lviii.

6-8. *Those Who Consort with Samaritans Denounced.*—To share pagan rites is to desert the God of their fathers. **Shall I be appeased for these things?** God's demand is always for total devotion: "Ye cannot serve God and . . . ."

hast thou set up thy remembrance: for thou hast discovered *thyself to another* than me, and art gone up; thou hast enlarged thy bed, and made thee *a covenant* with them; thou lovedst their bed where thou sawest *it*.

9 And thou wentest to the king with ointment, and didst increase thy perfumes, and didst send thy messengers far off, and didst debase *thyself even* unto hell.

you have made it wide;
and you have made a bargain for yourself with them,
you have loved their bed,
you have looked on nakedness.[e]

9 You journeyed to Molech[f] with oil
and multiplied your perfumes;
you sent your envoys far off,
and sent down even to Sheol.

[e] The meaning of the Hebrew is uncertain
[f] Or *the king*

---

of the public cult that is set forth here. Many think of the memorial as household gods, the local penates, or ancestor gods. But the context suggests sexual imagery. The word rendered **remembrance** (KJV), **symbol** (RSV) or "memorial" has the same consonants as the Hebrew word for "male." Ezekiel, in a chapter with which our poem has numerous affinities, speaks of Jerusalem taking fair jewels of gold and silver and making of them "images of men" (cf. the Priapean hermae in Europe). There are, of course, numerous parallels for this (see Volz, *Jesaia II*, p. 214, n.; also literature there referred to, especially Otto Weinreich, "Antike Heiligungswunder," *Religionsgeschichtliche Versuche und Vorarbeiten*, VIII [1909], 18-22). **Deserting me:** Lit., "from me." The KJV makes no sense. The lure of the fertility cults took Israel from her covenant Lord (cf. Hos. 2:5; Jer. 2:20-23). H. L. Ginsberg emends to "with them." The closing lines seem to be corrupt or incomplete. The LXX gives quite another rendering for this whole context. Many scholars insert the words from the LXX, "thou didst multiply thy whoredoms with them" before the last line of our verse. Ginsberg has proposed another solution: he reads ותכרי, "and thou didst buy," for ותכרת with Kittel and many other scholars (cf. Hos. 3:2), and renders the line as follows: "And thou didst buy thee from them lying love, crouching lust." He vocalizes *'ahbath mishkābhîm*, **you have loved their bed**, with which cf. Ezek. 23:17, an excellent parallel. The Ugaritic contains the parallelism of *'hbt* and *yd* (from the root *ydd;* see II AB Tablet 4-5, ll. 38-39; V AB, Tablet C, ll. 3-4). Aside from the precise English translation of the word, this commends itself as the proper line of interpretation.

7. Seventh Strophe: Endless Cultic Exertions (57:9-10)

9. The strophe is without any formal elements and continues the thought of the preceding one. The chief difficulty lies in the meaning of vs. 9a. Many commentators believe the allusion is political, i.e., the dispatch of emissaries to a foreign king, usually the king of Babylon. For the support of this view such passages as 30:6; 31:1; Hos. 5:13; 10:6; II Kings 16:7 ff. are adduced. But the only support in the context is vs. 9c, which is susceptible of quite another meaning. To be sure, the translation of the KJV is possible: **Thou wentest to the king with ointment.** But the word **king** is more likely the Canaanite god Melek or the Ammonite god **Molech** (RSV). The verb *shûr* ordinarily

---

9-10. The Climax of Apostasy.—Molech may not have been distant geographically, but the people's pilgrimage was to a far country of heathenism, **far off, . . . even to Sheol.** It is characteristic of the prophet's realism that he concedes that in this false religious worship they **found new life for their strength.** Devotees of odd cults testify to "the good" they derive from them. There is no reason to deny the genuineness of the relief or comfort or exhilaration which they experience. Such experi-ences, however, are no valid criteria of the correctness of the faith. Men have found religious satisfaction in all manner of cults from the lowest to the loftiest. This may indicate, as William James thought, "something there" not to be "poohpoohed away." [1] But as James realized, the experience does not validate any particular theory of the reality worshiped. Feelings are untrustworthy guides to fact. Men

[1] *The Varieties of Religious Experience* (New York: Longmans, Green & Co., 1902), p. 58; *Letters*, II, 214.

10 Thou art wearied in the greatness of thy way; *yet* saidst thou not, There is no hope: thou hast found the life of thine hand; therefore thou wast not grieved.

11 And of whom hast thou been afraid or feared, that thou hast lied, and hast not

---

10 You were wearied with the length of your way,
     but you did not say, "It is hopeless";
     you found new life for your strength,
     and so you were not faint.

11 Whom did you dread and fear,
     so that you lied,
     and did not remember me,
     did not give me a thought?

---

means "journey" or "travel." Driver ("Difficult Words in the Hebrew Prophets," in Rowley, ed., *Studies in Old Testament Prophecy*, p. 58) derives it (partly on the basis of the LXX) from the Arabic *tarra* and translates the line: "And thou wast drenched with oil (= in honour of) the king." Torrey derives it from a noun meaning "gift" (I Sam. 9:7), but the meaning of the word is purely conjectural (see Brown, Driver, Briggs, *Lexicon, s.v.* שׁור). The Vulg. reads *et ornasti te regi unguento.* Many follow Cheyne in emending to "and thou anointest thyself." Perhaps the best solution is to follow Driver in part (pointing the verb *tōserî*) and render "Thou didst drench [anoint] thyself with oil for Melek." This fits the immediate context very well (cf. Ezek. 16:18). **And sent your envoys far off:** Emissaries were sent to the sanctuaries (or gods) even of foreign nations. **And sent down even to Sheol:** The Hebrew verb is, lit., "and thou didst make deep." Volz takes the expression as meaning abject subservience, but this is most improbable. The line implies that **envoys** were sent to consult the gods of the underworld. Feldmann (*Isaias*, p. 209) says this interpretation goes back as far as Cyril of Alexandria (cf. Vulg., *et humiliata es usque ad inferos*).

10. Although the way was long and the envoys became weary, nothing deterred them from reaching their goal. Driven by their infatuation, they do not see how vain and hopeless their undertaking is (cf. Jer. 2:25). **You found new life for your strength.** The Hebrew reads, lit., **thou hast found the life of thy hand** (KJV). An obscure line. Ginsberg reads, perhaps correctly, "Thou hast gotten thy crouching lust" (cf. Exeg. on vs. 8).

8. Eighth Strophe: The Lord's Indictment (57:11)

Yahweh's case against Jerusalem comes to its close (see the introduction in vs. 3a and cf. the form of the indictment in vs. 4). The interpretation of this verse is difficult, but its climactic character and its clear reminiscence of the opening words of the indictment provide helpful clues.

11. **Whom did you dread and fear:** The expression is elliptical: "Who are these gods and idols, these pagan divinities whom you seek far and wide, of whom you are in such craven fear? Who are they that you should be treacherous and faithless to me?" (Cf. vss. 3-4, especially vs. 4e.) The question is by no means rhetorical, expecting the answer "You were not at all afraid" (contra Duhm, Marti, Box). In vs. 11c the RSV carries over the pronoun from the previous line, but the Dead Sea Scroll adds "these":

---

must be religious with all their faculties, intellect as well as feelings. The truth of the conception of deity has to square with the total impression of the universe grasped by our minds. Even then our idea of God will be far short of the actuality. Men may be **wearied,** but so long as they do not feel **faint,** they refuse to admit their quest **hopeless.** Only when the true God breaks in his fullness on their sight do the half-gods seem false.

11-13. *What Reason for Israel's Disloyalty?*— The pathos of these lines lies in the outraged husband of his people standing in silence and veiling his eyes while they dishonor him (cf. Ps. 50:21; Hos. 1:1–3:5). Part of God's suffering is his inability in some situations to do anything. He must endure his people's sins. This is his age-old cross. There are times when to remain still requires vastly more strength than to speak out. Swinburne, dedicating to Mazzini his *Songs*

remembered me, nor laid *it* to thy heart? have not I held my peace even of old, and thou fearest me not?

12 I will declare thy righteousness, and thy works; for they shall not profit thee.

13 ¶ When thou criest, let thy companies deliver thee; but the wind shall carry them all away; vanity shall take *them:* but he that putteth his trust in me shall possess the land, and shall inherit my holy mountain;

Have I not held my peace, even for a
    long time,
  and so you do not fear me?
12 I will tell of your righteousness and your
    doings,
  but they will not help you.
13 When you cry out, let your collection of
    idols deliver you!
  The wind will carry them off,
  a breath will take them away.
But he who takes refuge in me shall
    possess the land,
  and shall inherit my holy mountain.

"You did not give a thought to [lit., "take to heart"] these things." **Have I not held my peace:** Cf. 42:14. On the basis of the LXX, Vulg. (*quia ego tacens, et quasi non videns*) and Syriac many scholars read "was I not keeping silent and hiding myself" (reading *ûma'lim* for *ûmē'ōlām*). This is a permissible rendering of the C.T., but the parallel to 42:14 argues for the RSV. **And so you do not fear me:** Misunderstanding the silence of God, they ceased to fear him. Torrey takes the verb from *rā'āh*, "to see"—"while thou sawest me not." But the **fear** of Yahweh is related (though with different connotation) to the fear of the divinities of vs. 11*a*. This literary characteristic is common in the O.T. and in Arabic (König, *Stilistik, Rhetorik, Poetik*, p. 300; cf. 59:9).

9. Ninth Strophe: The Fate of the Gods and the Grace of God (57:12-13)

The former strophe compared the cringing fear and fanatical attachment of the unfaithful to the alien divinities and their want of fear of Yahweh in the face of his long-continued silence. But in this final strophe God speaks out in judgment (note the emphatic **I**). The rabble of gods will perish before a breath of air, but God will be the refuge and inheritance of his people. Nothing could make more clear than this final strophe that the emphasis throughout the poem is religious, not political or secular. From the distraught infatuation for the gods (cf. vs. 5) they will find security and peace in Yahweh's holy hill.

12. I will tell of your righteousness: The meaning is: "I will reveal," etc. For the second line the Dead Sea Scroll reads, "they will not gather [M.T., lit., "profit"] you." The construction of the strophe suggests that the words of promise and grace first begin with vs. 13*d*; the rest is judgment. This is exactly what we should expect not only from the present poem as a whole but also from parallels in Second Isaiah (e.g., 41:11-13, 14-16; also 41:28-29; 42:1-4). **Righteousness**, then, is meant ironically, and is parallel to **doings.** They will not avail in the day of judgment.

13. Your collection of idols: The Hebrew word translated **collection** means, lit., "your gathered [things]" or "your heaps [of divinities]." This continues the mood of scornful irony. But many scholars by a change of the first letter read שׁקוצים, "abominations." Torrey is probably right in seeing the word as a special creation with the

---

Before Sunrise, spoke of them as wrought "in the patience of passion." [2]

In vs. 12 the Lord breaks silence and proceeds to judgment. Israel's devices will avail her nothing, and her **collection of idols** cannot save her. A breath of wind will take them off. But for those who trust in the Lord the land remains a sure possession. Man-made religious satisfactions prove evanescent; but faith in the real

[2] London: W. Heinemann, 1917, p. vi.

God, faith born of him, brings lasting steadfastness. Adolf Harnack writes of Luther:

> Rising above all anxieties and terrors, above all ascetic devices, above all directions of theology, above all interventions of hierarchy and Sacraments, he ventured to lay hold of God, Himself in Christ, and in this act of his faith, which he recognised as God's work, his whole being obtained stability and firmness. [3]

[3] *History of Dogma,* VII, 184.

14 And shall say, Cast ye up, cast ye up, prepare the way, take up the stumbling-block out of the way of my people.	14 And it shall be said, "Build up, build up, prepare the way, remove every obstruction from my people's way."

vocalization drawn from abominations; cf. 54:7, where the verbal root occurs and Yahweh "gathers" Israel; also 56:8d. Is this a possible echo? Cf. also 56:7, "These I will bring to my holy mountain," and the closing words of 57:13. Those who take refuge in Yahweh will **possess the land,** which belongs to the covenanted holy people, and they **shall inherit** [the] **holy mountain** of Zion, where faithful Israelites offer a true and holy worship.

C. Persisting Grace (57:14-21)

The poem attaches itself immediately to the closing words of 56:9–57:13. In style, language, and thought it is closely allied with Second Isaiah. There are differences, to be sure, but these might be explained by a change in occasion. It is possible that the poem is Second Isaiah's, and that some disciple inserted it in this propitious place. Or it may be the work of some disciple who had entered intimately into his master's sphere of speaking and thinking. Like all the work of Second Isaiah, it rewards careful literary scrutiny. Observe, for example, the introduction (vs. 14), the oracle in the divine first person (vss. 15-18), introduced by the awe-inspiring lines of vs. 15, and the conclusion comparable in its brevity to the introduction (vs. 19). Vss. 20-21 are either a later addition or a kind of coda to the whole (56:9–57:21). Most noteworthy is the repetition of important words: **build up** (cf. the **peace, peace** of the conclusion), **way, dwell** (vss. 14b, 15c, the verb being the same in Hebrew), **holy, contrite, humble spirit, revive, be angry.** The theme of the poem is the transformation that God will effect for his people in the coming age. The mood of the writer is one of profound inwardness, but it is not divorced from the actualities of the people's condition. The text is not always well preserved, but the LXX is a precarious guide to its restoration. The Dead Sea Scroll contains a number of interesting variants. Not least significant is the obvious dependence of the writer on the work of his predecessors, above all, of course, on Second Isaiah, in the event that he is not himself its author. The 3+3 meter prevails. After vs. 16 the parallelism of the lines is difficult and obscure.

The poem is of theological importance. The conceptions of the divine holiness and mercy, transcendence and immanence, eternity and universality, judgment and grace, the way, and comfort are expressed in memorable words.

1. Proem: Prepare for the Time of Salvation (57:14)

14. The opening words serve to unite the two passages. The Hebrew reads, lit., "and he said" (cf. 40:6b; 65:8b). The Vulg. has dicam, "I shall say," the Greek and

The apparent inactivity of God may lose him shallow worshipers—**so you do not fear me?**—but in the end it separates the discerning from the obtuse, and steadies genuine believers in their faith.

14-16. The Lofty and Holy One Commands Grace to His People.—The third brief poem (vss. 14-21) both in thought and style contrasts with the two preceding poems, and returns to convictions and rhythm of chs. 40–55. But it has contrasts with the thought of the earlier poet. **And it shall be said** is reminiscent of the voices in ch. 40. It is the Lord who is speaking. Yet it is not of his coming, but of his people's

future advance that he speaks. **Build up . . .** is probably addressed to celestial forces, as in ch. 40; but here the words might be spoken to the leaders of the people. More likely it is a repetition of the call to the forces of history, for the **obstruction** is within men's minds as well as in their outward circumstances. **Every obstruction** includes the sins which have been denounced in the two preceding poems. Only God can alter the hearts of men, and even he finds himself often blocked.

We may compare this call to our current plight in the church, when factors in her own life and on the world scene hinder her advance in mis-

15 For thus saith the high and lofty One that inhabiteth eternity, whose name *is*

15 For thus says the high and lofty One who inhabits eternity, whose name is Holy:

Syriac have the third person plural, and the Dead Sea Scroll has the third person imperfect (ויואמר). The speaker is not named, though it is most probably God (note **my people's way**). The summons is dependent on 40:3 (cf. 62:10). It is possible that the writer is employing these words as a kind of text which he seeks to develop and interpret in his own way; cf. 58:1, where it is certainly the case. **Build up, build up**: Better, **Cast ... up.** The repetition is typical of Second Isaiah's style. The Dead Sea Scroll reads, "Cast up, cast up the highway," which has much to commend it. The LXX has "purge [καθαρίσατε] the ways before him"; the Vulg. has *viam facite*. The content of the poem suggests that the words are not used in the same way as in 40:1-11. It is an inward preparation of the heart that is in the writer's mind (cf. vs. 18a). It is precisely in this way that Second Isaiah's words are employed in the Gospels (Mark 1:3; Matt. 3:3; Luke 3:4; John 1:23). The people must **remove every obstruction** within themselves, every stone of stumbling, every moral and spiritual offense.

2. First Strophe: The Divine Dwelling Place (57:15)

15. The impressive oracular formula (vs. 15*ab*) prepares the way for all that is to follow. The strophe is notable for the strong tensions between the transcendence and immanence of God, his remoteness and nearness. Indeed, it is in some ways a remarkable summary of biblical piety. (This tension between the feeling of God's remoteness [*Abstandsgefühl*] and the feeling of being bound to him [*Verbundenheitsgefühl*] is the

---

sionary expansion, in growth into more complete fellowship with God and with fellow Christians, in the application of the gospel to social conditions. There are impeding factors in contemporary conditions in the world, in trends of thought and feeling, in the divided loyalties of Christians—in the poet's phrase, "almost Christians," with "names half entered in the book of life." If we can hear God's voice commanding, **remove every obstruction from my people's way,** our confidence rises to believe that his word will not prove futile.

And this is strengthened by the magnificent self-disclosure God makes in vs. 15, a supreme text in the Bible. It combines his loftiness—his distance and difference from man—and his tender condescension to the crushed and abased in spirit. It sums up the thought of God in 40:12-31. God's immeasurable greatness meets man's frailty and need. George Herbert voices a similar conviction:

Thousands of things do Thee employ
    In ruling all
This spacious globe: Angels must have their joy,
    Devils their rod, the sea his shore,
The winds their stint. And yet when I did call,
    Thou heardst my call, and more.[4]

The impression conveyed in vs. 15 of **the high and lofty One . . . , whose name is Holy** may be

compared with the impression Hawthorne derived from a Gothic cathedral:

Not that I felt, or was worthy to feel, an unmingled enjoyment in gazing at this wonder. I could not elevate myself to its spiritual height, any more than I could have climbed from the ground to the summit of one of its pinnacles. Ascending but a little way, I continually fell back and lay in a kind of despair, conscious that a flood of uncomprehended beauty was pouring down upon me, of which I could appropriate only the minutest portion. After a hundred years, incalculably as my higher sympathies might be invigorated by so divine an employment, I should still be a gazer from below and at an awful distance, as yet remotely excluded from the interior mystery. But it was something gained, even to have that painful sense of my own limitations, and that half-smothered yearning to soar beyond them. The cathedral showed me how earthly I was, but yet whispered deeply of immortality.[5]

Who inhabits eternity is an O.T. equivalent of the N.T. "King of ages" (I Tim. 1:17), and of an address to Christ in Matthew Bridges' well-known hymn:

. . . the Lord of years,
    The Potentate of time.[6]

In the Bible eternity is not qualitatively different from time, but sums up time completely—

[5] *Our Old Home*, "Lichfield and Uttoexeter."
[6] "Crown him with many crowns."

[4] "Praise."

Holy; I dwell in the high and holy *place,* with him also *that is* of a contrite and humble spirit, to revive the spirit of the humble, and to revive the heart of the contrite ones.	"I dwell in the high and holy place, and also with him who is of a contrite and humble spirit, to revive the spirit of the humble, and to revive the heart of the contrite.

major thesis of Hempel's *Gott und Mensch im A.T.*) The whole N.T. provides a running commentary on these words (cf. II Cor. 4:6; John 1:1-18). **The high and lofty One:** The words are titles and are drawn from 6:1 (cf. also 2:12-19). God sits enthroned as king in the heavens, his eternal dwelling; his **name is Holy** or "Holy One," another Isaianic influence (see 40:25). Some read, "In the height as Holy One I sit enthroned," but the RSV presents the more probable rendering. The Dead Sea Scroll reads very clearly, "In the height and in the holy place" (במרום ובקודש). The last three lines are in surprising contrast to the first three, although it is often contended that no contrast is meant; because he sits enthroned on high, he can see all that happens below on earth. König feels that the idea of the Holy One dwelling among men is contrary to O.T. thought, but he is compelled to render the Hebrew in a most awkward and unlikely fashion (cf. Pss. 113:4-9; 138:6). **Contrite and humble spirit:** Lit., "Crushed and lowly in spirit." It is not likely that the reference is historical, i.e., to the disinherited minority of the fifth century B.C. The crushed and lowly in spirit are those who have indeed experienced affliction, all the cares and disappointments and sorrows of life, the disdain and contumely of men, but without any pretensions for themselves live in the silent awareness that there is a God in heaven who is present among them, the sovereign, eternal, Holy One. Observe the absence of any personal words like Israel, Jacob, etc. (Volz). It is the great mystery and wonder that such a God should come down and dwell (the same verb as in **inhabits eternity**) among the lowly and meek. Yet it is not only his presence among them that is emphasized; much rather, the two infinitive phrases carry the active stress of the thought:

> **to revive the spirit of the humble,**
> **and to revive the heart of the contrite.**

The repetition of the infinitive and of the objects (from the previous line) is effective. Where the pulse of life beats low, God quickens with his life-giving spirit. The Dead Sea Scroll reads the Qal instead of the Hiphil infinitive of the M.T.

past, present, future. "From everlasting to everlasting, thou art God" (Ps. 90:2). Man the creature of a day, fractionally familiar with a tiny perspective of the past and wholly ignorant of time to come, looks reverently to One who knows beginning and end and appoints the times and seasons (Acts 1:7). "The Eternal One is in control of the entire time line in its endless extension."[7] This familiarity with what has been, what is, what is to be, makes God at home in eternity and differentiates him from mortal men.

This difference and distance between God and man was forgotten in nineteenth- and early twentieth-century Christian thought. But without it his gracious coming to dwell with weak and dependent men loses its meaning. Skinner comments on vs. 15:

It is the paradox of religion that Jehovah's holiness, which places Him at an infinite distance from human pride and greatness, brings Him near to the humble in spirit. . . . Through the discipline of the Exile Israel had come to know God in both characters—as infinitely exalted and infinitely condescending; it had learned that peace with God, the high and lofty One, is reached through humility, which is the recognition of His holiness and majesty.[8]

The humble and the contrite are the self-distrusting, made such by the afflictions through which they had passed and the frustrations of the postexilic years (cf. Neh. 1:3). Today men are in similar mood because of their inability to attain social harmony, and because they dread the forces they can unleash but cannot control. When the two parts of vs. 15 are viewed together, it is the lofty holiness of God which

[7] Oscar Cullmann, *Christ and Time* (tr. F. V. Filson; Philadelphia: Westminster Press, 1950), p. 72.

[8] *Isaiah, Chapters XL-LXVI,* p. 160.

16 For I will not contend for ever, neither will I be always wroth: for the spirit should fail before me, and the souls *which* I have made.	16 For I will not contend for ever, nor will I always be angry; for from me proceeds the spirit, and I have made the breath of life.

3. Second Strophe: The Time of Judgment Is Ended (57:16-17)

16. The strophe connects admirably with the foregoing, the two introductory words (*kî*, vs. 16a, 16c) giving content to the infinitives of vs. 15. The transition is to the period of judgment through which the people have passed. **For I will not contend for ever:** Cf. especially 54:7-9; also Gen. 6:3; Jer. 3:5, 12; Ps. 103:9. The motive for the end of the divine anger (punishment, judgment) is not the bond of election or the covenantal bond, but rather that man is the creation of God, his spirit proceeds from him, and the breath of life is his work. For God to destroy his own people would be for him to destroy his own special creation (cf. Gen. 6:1-8). **For from me proceeds the spirit:** Cf. KJV, **For the spirit should fail before me.** Most scholars interpret the verb as **fail** or "faint," but this is difficult. The LXX reads, "go forth" (ἐξελεύσεται); Vulg., *egredietur;* Syriac, *nafqa.* On the basis of this evidence, especially the Syriac root meaning "return"

---

induces lowliness in man. "If we think we are something," wrote Calvin, "we have only to turn our eyes to God, and immediately we are nothing." Humility is never a virtue easily obtained. But those who live in sight of God inevitably become humble. "In heaven an angel is nobody in particular." [9]

I dwell . . . with him. Such fellowship with man is the crown of O.T. religion, and anticipates John 14:23. Newman described a devout man as "one who has a ruling sense of God's presence." To be sure, our sense of his presence must not be stressed; it is affected by so many factors beyond our control—health, circumstances, etc. The truly religious do not question the fact of God's presence, whether or not they are sensible of it. Edward Burne-Jones declared: "I never doubt for a moment the real presence of God, I should never debate about it any more than I should argue about Beauty, and the things I most love." [1]

God's dwelling with his humble ones is to revive the spirit of the lowly and to restore the courage of the depressed. This repeats and follows up the message in 40:1. An instance of such renewal of courage in modern times is found in the diary of the Earl of Shaftesbury, a stalwart warrior for social justice and for the protection of the crushed. When beaten or blocked, he sought reinforcement of purpose in God. Typical entries run:

Great anxiety about Bill for relief of Chimney Sweepers. Have suffered actual tortures through solicitude for prevention of these horrid cruelties. . . .

The Government in the House of Commons

threw out the Chimney-Sweepers Bill, and said not a word of sympathy for the wretched children, nor of desire to amend the law . . . .

Very sad and low about the loss of the Sweeps Bill. . . . I must persevere, and by God's help so I will; for however dark the view, however contrary to all argument the attempt, however painful and revolting the labour, I see no Scripture reason for desisting; and the issue of every toil is in the hands of the Almighty. [2]

The strophe concludes (vs. 16) with a declaration of God's compassion for his frail creatures. He has made the souls of men, and the breath of their life proceeds from him. He will not unmake what he has been at such pains to create (cf. Psalms, *passim*). The N.T. speaks of God as "a faithful Creator" (I Pet. 4:19). In one of his hymns Frederick W. Faber wrote:

> Thou owest me no duties, Lord!
> Thy Being hath no ties. [3]

But the Bible depicts God as responsible for the work of his hands. A creator has obligations to his creatures, as has a father to his children.

> It were as tho' the Maker made a star,
> Lit it, and for an hour bade it afar
> Flash splendours forth: then struck it out and cried,
> "Go now, and lie where dark and dead things are!"
>
> . . . .
>
> O verily, verily, this is not God's plan,
> To spend eternities in making man,
> And then for all His skill to end in naught,
> To end at that same point where it began. [4]

[2] Edwin Hodder, *The Life and Work of the Seventh Earl of Shaftesbury* (London: Cassell & Co., 1887), pp. 493-94.

[3] "Father and God! my endless doom," st. viii.

[4] William J. Dawson, "Epilogue" from *The House of Dreams* (London: John Lane the Bodley Head; New York: Dodd, Mead & Co., 1897). Used by permission.

[9] G. B. Shaw, *Maxims for Revolutionists*, p. 223.

[1] Georgiana Burne-Jones, *Memorials of Edward Burne-Jones* (London: Macmillan & Co., 1906), II, 325.

17 For the iniquity of his covetousness was I wroth, and smote him: I hid me, and was wroth, and he went on frowardly in the way of his heart.

18 I have seen his ways, and will heal him: I will lead him also, and restore comforts unto him and to his mourners.

17 Because of the iniquity of his covetousness I was angry,
     I smote him, I hid my face and was angry;
     but he went on backsliding in the way of his own heart.

18 I have seen his ways, but I will heal him;
     I will lead him and requite him with comfort,
     creating for his mourners the fruit of the lips.

---

or "turn away," Torrey reads **proceeds**, which is accepted by the RSV. **I have made the breath of life:** See Gen. 2:7. He who breathed **the breath of life** into man will revive him with his life-giving spirit. **Breath** is an inclusive term for all animated life (cf. Deut. 20:16; Ps. 150:6).

17. Because of the iniquity of his covetousness I was angry: Or "Because of the guilt of his avarice I was angry." Odeberg and Torrey see another root instead of covetousness, meaning "little," "small," and shift the pronominal suffix to the second Hebrew word: "Because of his guilt I was wroth for a moment" (cf. LXX βραχύ τι; cf. 54:7-8). This may be accepted, though with reservation. Others emend more radically to produce a similar result. **I hid my face:** The words **my face** are not in the Hebrew. The Dead Sea Scroll reads, אהסתר (sic, doubtless the ה is error for ת): "I hid myself." God hides his face as a sign of anger (cf. 54:8; Pss. 22:24; 27:9; 88:14; 104:29). Note the effect of the succession of verbs and how **was angry** begins and ends the series. **But he went on backsliding:** Divine judgment brought no change of heart or conduct; he walked as an apostate in the direction that his perverted heart led him.

4. Third Strophe: Healing, Comfort, and the Gift of Praise (57:18-19)

The strophe of judgment with its series of verbs is paralleled by a strophe of restoration with another series of contrasting verbs.

18-19. The divine judgment did not heal the people, so God of his unmotivated grace heals (forgives) them. He becomes their physician (cf. 6:10; 53:5; Exod. 15:22-26; Hos. 5:13; 6:1; 7:1; 14:2 ff.; Jer. 3:22 ff.). **I will lead him:** Some scholars revocalize to "I will give him rest," or emend to ואנחמהו, "I will comfort him" (cf. LXX and Syriac). The Dead Sea Scroll has a different text. It omits **I will lead him** and reads the rest of the line, ואשלם לוא תנחומים לוא, "I will not reward them comforts." The verse in the

---

17-21. God's Reason for Judgment.—Because of the iniquity of his covetousness: Gainseeking had been a theme of the pre-exilic prophets; now it was prevalent in the postexilic nation (cf. 58:1-14; Neh. 5:1-19; Zech. 7:9-12). This, rather than the religious apostasies in vss. 5-9, is the cause of the Lord's wrath. In the N.T., covetousness is listed as idolatry (Col. 3:5), the worship of wealth for the power or comfort it confers. Despite divine disfavor, Israel had persisted in ruthless grasping. God had watched its sinful ways (vs. 18) in order to study their cure. Volz translates, "I will be his physician."[5] His strange remedy is comfort. Sin is sickness. While it is moral illness and cannot be excused, it is illness and requires treatment. Milton pleaded for such handling of it in his *Areopagitica:*

[5] *Jesaia II*, p. 216.

They are not skilful considerers of human things, who imagine to remove sins by removing the matter of sin. . . . Though ye take from a covetous man all his treasure, he has yet one jewel left, ye cannot bereave him of his covetousness. Banish all objects of lust, shut up all youth into the severest discipline that can be exercised in any hermitage, ye cannot make them chaste, that came not thither so: such great care and wisdom is required to the right managing of this point.

To the far and to the near: Those already home, and those still in exile. The prophet keeps the unity of Israel in mind. But no cure works infallibly. Some grieve over their own and their nation's sin, and respond to God's lovingkindness with confession, **the fruit of the lips.** Others go on in their perverse ways, and their lives continue restless and roiled like the sea.

19 I create the fruit of the lips; Peace, peace to *him that is* far off, and to *him that is* near, saith the LORD; and I will heal him. 20 But the wicked *are* like the troubled sea, when it cannot rest, whose waters cast up mire and dirt.	19 Peace, peace, to the far and to the near, says the LORD; and I will heal him. 20 But the wicked are like the tossing sea; for it cannot rest, and its waters toss up mire and dirt.

LXX reads: "His ways I have seen, and healed him, and comforted him, and given him true comfort." Nevertheless, we should follow the M.T. The idea of leading is certainly not infelicitous and the preceding line favors it. God requites his people not with the judgment they deserve but with the free grace of his comfort they do not deserve (cf. 40:1; 49:13; 52:9). This thought leads to the gift to the **mourners** of joy and thanksgiving, **the fruit of the lips** (Hos. 14:2 [Hebrew 14:3], LXX, Syriac; Heb. 13:15). But Kissane makes the point that the expression means only "words" (Prov. 12:14; 18:20), and the following clause (vs. 19*a*) suggests this. They still depend on "creating" and are Yahweh's message. **I will heal him** is certainly awkward here and may be an addition. It is probable that the text is corrupt. Instead of the usual explanation that the repeated **Peace, peace** is merely a promise of well-being to the near and far, one is tempted to view this as Yahweh's greeting (*shālôm, shālôm!*) to all who enter the city of Zion. In that event the conclusion is a superb finale to the repeated call of vs. 14. Eph. 2:17 alludes to this verse. **To the far and to the near:** The term is general and includes those in Jerusalem and all the exiles. It is equivalent to "all" (cf. 33:13).

5. CODA: THE WICKED (57:20-21)

20. Such conclusions appear in Second Isaiah. In view of this it is probably best to retain the words, possibly as a conclusion to 56:9–57:19. The lines begin and end with **the wicked,** and thus form a complete contrast to "the mourners," the crushed and broken in spirit. The godless have no rest, they know no healing. They are like troubled Cain, a vagrant and a vagabond, like tortured Saul, and guilty David (cf. Ps. 34:4-5; Job 15:20-21; Deut. 28:66-67). They are like the turbulent sea, ever tossing in the distraught and distracted misery of sin, bringing up mire and dirt from the bottom of the sea. They never know the comfort and peace of those who know they have been forgiven and restored by the grace of God. James A. Montgomery ("Ras Shamra Notes IV: The Conflict of Baal and the Waters," *Journal of the American Oriental Society,* LV [1935], 270) has called attention to the remarkable alliterative correspondence between this verse and a passage in the Ugaritic texts where the same verbal root *grs* appears.

The double result of God's winsome dealing anticipates Matt. 25:31-46. The penitent restored to fellowship exclaim exultantly, **Peace, peace;** the impenitent are self-doomed to continuing turbulence. In Ibsen's *Peer Gynt* the madhouse doctor describes his unhappy patients, counterparts of these self-willed Israelites:

Each one shuts himself up in the barrel of self,
In the self-fermentation he dives to the bottom,—
With the self-bung he seals it hermetically.[6]

We might wish that the final distinction were obliterated, and the poem brought to a happy conclusion. William R. Inge, in one of his essays, shows that such shallow optimism brings its

own nemesis, and quotes from W. Macneile Dixon's Gifford Lecture:

The kind-hearted humanitarians of the nineteenth century decided to improve upon Christianity. The thought of hell offended their susceptibilities. They closed it, and to their surprise the gates of heaven closed also with a melancholy clang. The malignant countenance of Satan distressed them. They dispensed with him, and at the same time God took his departure. . . . In yes and no all things consist.[7]

58:1-14. God's Judgment Concerning Religious Practices.—Along with the observance of the sabbath (cf. 56:2), fasting had received a new emphasis during the Exile. In addition to

[6] Act 4, scene 3. Tr. William and Charles Archer (New York: Charles Scribner's Sons, 1911). Used by permission.

[7] *The End of an Age* (New York: The Macmillan Co., 1949), pp. 238-39.

21 *There is* no peace, saith my God, to the wicked.	21 There is no peace, says my God, for the wicked."
58 Cry aloud, spare not, lift up thy voice like a trumpet, and show my	**58** "Cry aloud, spare not, lift up your voice like a trumpet;

21. The verse is original here (cf. 48:22, which is almost verbally identical). **No peace** is contrasted with the "peace, peace" of vs. 19.

D. The Service Pleasing to God (58:1-14)

From ancient times Israel celebrated the great historical events in which God had revealed himself to her. The exodus from Egypt, the sojourn in the desert, the covenant at Sinai were recalled in liturgies. In these priest and people participated, and through their recital the ancient events became present realities of faith and experience (see Artur Weiser, *Glaube und Geschichte im Alten Testament* [Stuttgart: W. Kohlhammer, 1931], pp. 38-42). In times of national crisis also the people would gather to hold fasts (Josh. 7:6; Judg. 20:26 ff.; 21:2 ff.; I Sam. 7:6; II Sam. 12:16; I Kings 21:12; Jer. 36:9; Joel 1:1–2:27; Ps. 35:13; I Macc. 3:47). The destruction of the temple at Yeb in Egypt, recounted in the Elephantine papyri, was followed by a fast in which mourning apparel was put on, and the people "prayed to Yaho the Lord of Heaven" (Pritchard, *Ancient Near Eastern Texts*, p. 492). Jer. 36 deserves special attention because it is on a fast day that the scroll is read by Baruch before the assembled people. The words of the book should have induced deeper repentance and sorrow because of their severe judgments, but the people do not apprehend the true nature of the fast any more than the countrymen of Third Isaiah. The greatest tragedy of Israel's national life was the fall of Jerusalem and the destruction of the temple in 586 B.C. This event called forth the day of mourning, but the period evoked many similar days, as we see in a developed form in Zech. 7:4 ff.; 8:19, in which four fast days are described for the fourth, fifth, seventh, and tenth months. On such days the community reflected earnestly upon the judgment that had befallen it. It was a time of contrition, repentance, and prayer. While the passage from Zechariah represents a somewhat later stage of development than does our present poem, it is illuminating both for the information it gives concerning the fasts themselves and for the prophetic response (Zech. 7:8 ff.). Both passages show the intimate relation of the prophet to the cult. It is clear that the prophet was consulted concerning a purely cultic question: "Why does God take no notice of our fasts? We observe the appropriate rites, but there is no answer." (Vs. 3.)

The prophet is dependent upon his predecessors. He cites their words (vss. 1, 8cd) and continues their cry for social righteousness. But he does not merely parrot their words and ideas. Rather, they serve as a kind of text from which he takes his start. He speaks directly to the situation, and the urgency and passion of his message are his own. Indeed, the inwardness of the prophetic mind is seldom surpassed (cf. 1:10-20; Amos 5:1-27; Mic. 6:1-8; cf. also Job 31:1-40), and the words are not an unworthy parallel to the words of Jesus in Matt. 25:31 ff. The chapter is rightly understood when it is placed in the context of this motif of fasting throughout scripture and in early Christianity (see the use of the chapter in Barn. 3; cf. Matt. 6:16-18; 9:14-15; Luke 5:33-35; 18:11-12; also Matt. 4:2).

The literary character of the chapter is notable. After a stirring introduction culminating in the words of the people addressed to God (vss. 1-3*b*) the prophet, as

the traditional fast on the day of Atonement, four anniversaries of days of bitter remembrance connected with the fall of Jerusalem were commemorated with fasts—the commencement of the siege, the capture of the city, its destruction, and the murder of Gedaliah, governor of the remnant of survivors. After the return the question was raised whether these fasts should be continued (cf. Zech. 7:2-3). This discussion gave prophets occasion to preach on the quality of fast pleasing to God (cf. similar teaching in Zech. 7). Like their predecessors, the prophets

people their transgression, and the house of Jacob their sins.	declare to my people their transgression, to the house of Jacob their sins.

God's representative, answers in vigorous language (note the repetition of **fast**, and **behold**, the three piercing questions which culminate in the crucial words of vs. 5, "Will you call this a fast, and a day acceptable to Yahweh?"). The next strophe (vss. 6-9b) describes by contrast the kind of fast that is really acceptable to God. The externalism of the fasts is completely deflated by a profoundly inward interpretation. Vss. 9c-12 continue the same style in more elaborate fashion. The conclusion of the poem has been generally misunderstood. Far from being an unworthy addition by a mind shackled by formalism, it places the whole poem in the context of the worship pleasing to God, occupying something of the relation of Gen. 2:1-4a to the rest of the creation story. The relation of vss. 13-14 to the introduction, the literary form, and the thought all support their originality. Without them the poem remains a torso. One obvious stylistic characteristic deserves emphasis: the relation of protasis to apodosis, especially vss. 9b-12 and vss. 13-14, but also vs. 3ab, and vss. 6-8 (assuming that the text has been transmitted correctly). Special attention should be paid to the relation of vs. 2b (**delight to know my ways**) and vs. 2f (**they delight to draw near to God**) to vs. 13b (**from doing your pleasure** —the Hebrew word is the same as **delight**), vs. 13c (where another word is used in Hebrew), vs. 13f, and the climactic vs. 14a (cf. especially the relation of vs. 3c and vs. 13b, 13f).

The date of the passage cannot be fixed with certainty. But there is no indication that the temple has been built or that sacrifices are being offered, for they would certainly have been mentioned in this context. The literary character of the poem stands midway between Second Isaiah and Zechariah. The style is not Second Isaiah's, but the writer clearly knows him and is probably a disciple. The dialogue style of Zechariah and Malachi is present only in a very incipient form (vss. 3cd, 4-12), and suggests that our prophet came before them. This is borne out by the stage of development of his thought: he stands in a living relation to the classical prophetic tradition, but the situation is quite different from that of his predecessors. On the other hand, the thought is not so developed as either Zechariah or Malachi. Again, the **ruins** referred to in vs. 12 point to a relatively early period. Finally, the great stress on **fasting**, while not so detailed and concrete as Zechariah's, suggests a period some time after 586 B.C. In the light of these and other considerations a date between 538 and 520 B.C. seems probable.

The poem is liturgical throughout, and the exhortations are given in response to the plea of the cultic community (cf. Ps. 50). The meter is quite regularly 3+3; most exceptions can be construed as anacrusis in which introductory words fall outside the rhythm.

1. First Strophe: God's Call to the Prophet (58:1-3b)

The strophe contains the call to the prophet to address his fellow worshipers in the cult, a description of the cultic life, and the complaint or lament of the people (cf. Hab. 1:2; Ps. 22:1 ff.; Job 3:11-23). The transitions are very abrupt. The closing lines

of the years following the return from exile insisted on God's supreme concern for justice and kindness. They also stressed the worth of formal religious usages as witnessing to and reminding of devotion to God. This last was necessary in a confused day when it was easy to fall away from the highest religious loyalty.

1. The People's Sin.—George Adam Smith points out that no subject provokes sneers more readily than the combination of formal religion with an unloved life; but there is not

a sneer (i.e., a nasal tone) in this entire sermon. **Declare to my people their transgression.** The prophet is specific in describing sins.

I'm willin' a man should go tollable strong
Agin wrong in the abstract, fer thet kind o' wrong
Is ollers unpop'lar an' never gits pitied,
Because it's a crime no one ever committed;
But he mus'n't be hard on partickler sins,
Coz then he'll be kickin' the people's own shins.[8]

[8] James Russell Lowell, *Biglow Papers*, 1st Series, No. 4.

2 Yet they seek me daily, and delight to know my ways, as a nation that did righteousness, and forsook not the ordinance of their God: they ask of me the ordinances of justice; they take delight in approaching to God.

3 ¶ Wherefore have we fasted, *say they,* and thou seest not? *wherefore* have we af-

2 Yet they seek me daily,
　　and delight to know my ways,
　as if they were a nation that did righteousness
　　and did not forsake the ordinance of
　　　their God;
they ask of me righteous judgments,
　　they delight to draw near to God.
3 'Why have we fasted, and thou seest it
　　not?
　Why have we humbled ourselves, and
　　thou takest no knowledge of it?'

(vs. *3ab*) prepare for the exhortation to follow both in content (**Why have we fasted?**) and in form (a question concerning the cultic act and the ineffectual result).

58:1. The urgency of the situation is reflected in the commands. Vs. 1*b* is not unlike Hos. 8:1 (cf. also Isa. 18:3; Jer. 4:5; Ezek. 33:6-20), and vs. 1*cd* is probably drawn from Mic. 3:8. Pre-exilic prophets were influenced by each other also (e.g., Amos and Isaiah; Isaiah and Micah; Hosea and Jeremiah), but they seldom if ever borrow in this way. It is instructive to observe the want of verbal exactness. **Cry aloud:** Lit., "Call with the throat," i.e., with vehemence and passion. "Those who have never heard an angry Oriental speak, have no idea of what power of denunciation lies in the human throat" (George Adam Smith, *The Book of Isaiah* [rev. ed.; London: Hodder & Stoughton, 1927], II, 447).

2. The words do not imply any reference to the temple. The people are faithful in their religious practices, they seek God every day, they delight to know his ways, how they may enter into relationship with him and what he requires. Ostensibly they are a righteous nation. They inquire from priest or prophet what they should do (cf. Ezek. 20:3). The thought is not that they ask when the time of salvation will come; they profess to be pious men for whom worship is an inspiration and a refuge, **they delight to draw near to God** (lit., "they delight in the nearness of God"). The clause should not be translated "they desire the coming of God" (contra Kissane *et al.*).

3ab. Through the prophet the people inquire of God why their fasts have been of so little avail. They have fasted, but God gives no heed to them. It is not stated whether a particular fast is meant (e.g., the day of Atonement; cf. Lev. 16). It is probable, however, that the fasts connected with the fall of Jerusalem are referred to (cf. Zech. 7:3; 8:19). Kissane refers to four such occasions: the tenth of the tenth month (beginning of the siege of the city), the ninth of the fourth month (capture of the city), the tenth of the fifth month (burning of the city and temple), and the third of the seventh month (murder of Gedaliah). It was an occasion for mourning and repentance for the sins that had brought about the divine judgment, but by this time it had obviously become

---

2-3b. The Element of Devoutness.—The sincerity of the godly is often denied when they are unscrupulous in business dealings; but human nature is complex. The immoral may be genuinely attached in heart to God. Samuel Pepys in his *Diary* seems to be among the most pious and the most lecherous of men. Shakespeare has Slender declare: "If I be drunk, I'll be drunk with those that have the fear of God." [9] The prophet's contemporaries were eager for directions how to serve God: It is this satisfaction in formal religion which at times

[9] *Merry Wives of Windsor,* Act I, scene 1.

renders it an obstacle to social conscientiousness. Gladstone, habitually a "twicer" and frequently a "thricer" in attending church on Sunday, wrote a friend: "There is one proposition which the experience of life burns into my soul; it is this, that man should beware of letting his religion spoil his morality. In a thousand ways, some great, some small, but all subtle, we are daily tempted to that great sin." [1]

But the religiosity of the people had not brought the divine favor, and they were

[1] John Morley, *William Ewart Gladstone* (London: Macmillan & Co., 1903), II, 185.

flicted our soul, and thou takest no knowledge? Behold, in the day of your fast ye find pleasure, and exact all your labors.

4 Behold, ye fast for strife and debate, and to smite with the fist of wickedness: ye shall not fast as *ye do this* day, to make your voice to be heard on high.

Behold, in the day of your fast you seek
    your own pleasure,*g*
    and oppress all your workers.
4 Behold, you fast only to quarrel and to
    fight
    and to hit with wicked fist.
Fasting like yours this day
    will not make your voice to be heard
      on high.

g Or pursue your own business

---

a purely external form. **Why have we humbled ourselves:** Lit., **wherefore have we afflicted our soul** (KJV; cf. Lev. 16:29, 31; 23:23, 32; Ps. 35:13). It is an expression from the cult referring to acts of self-denial and self-mortification. The questions suggest a purely formal attitude, a religious *quid pro quo*.

2. Second Strophe: Do You Call This a Fast? (58:3c-5)

3c. The strophe has two parts (vss. 3c-4, 5), the first reaching its climax in vs. 4cd, the second in vs. 5ef. It is throughout in sharp contrast with the preceding lines: note the repeated **behold** and the harsh questions of vs. 5. "This fasting of yours to which you appeal is not fasting at all. You are not really concerned with pursuing God's ways and learning his righteous judgments." **You seek your own pleasure:** Better, **you pursue your own business,** but the literal rendering should be kept in mind in connection with the poem as a whole in which **pleasure (delight)** is a strong motif: what pleases God and what pleases men. **And oppress all your workers:** It is better perhaps to translate, "You press your occupations" (i.e., business affairs). It is doubtful whether the couplet has any concrete reference; the idea is more general. Only in vs. 4 does it become concrete, and it is here that the emphasis falls.

4. They profane the day of fast by quarrels and contentions. It has been suggested that fasting made them unduly sensitive and quarrelsome. It seems more likely in this context that it is the strife in business transactions. The LXX apparently reads רש, "poor" or "lowly," for רשע, **wicked.** For **fist** the Dead Sea Scroll has another word derived from the same root (גורף). The thoughts of the worshipers are in reality not the thoughts of

---

troubled. Their disillusionment betrays the selfish element in their relations with God. They were not serving God "for nought." Hence they questioned whether he were living up to his part of the covenant. Any religion which implies that man's devoutness merits God's gratitude is poisonous. The common teaching that prayer for specific blessings assures their granting inevitably leads to doubt of God's reliability: **Why have we fasted, and thou seest it not?**

3c-4a. Fasting Accompanied by Hard Dealing.—According to the law (Lev. 16:29), a fast meant a universal cessation from labor; but these men made it a class affair—for employers only.

Behold, in the day of your fast you seek your own
    pleasure,
    and oppress all your workers.

A similar condition of affairs in our Lord's day made observance of the Torah possible only for

the leisure class. The poor and uneducated were not expected to keep it (John 7:49). In every age social status affects susceptibility to current religious stimuli. In modern times those at the top and those at the bottom are least likely to be appealed to by the church, the former because of their self-indulgent life and social snobbishness, the latter because of the pressures of poverty and of their bitterness toward the well to do. Thus the church's membership is composed largely of the middle class.

Fasting renders those accustomed to high living fretful and irritable, so that a fast is apt to be attended with quarreling and may end in blows (vs. 4). Commenting on Bulstrode, George Eliot speaks of those "whose celestial intimacies seemed not to improve their domestic manners." [2]

4b-5. Self-abasement of Itself Is Futile.—Has God any pleasure in a man's rendering himself uncomfortable? Many have considered the

[2] *Middlemarch*, Bk. II, ch. xviii.

5 Is it such a fast that I have chosen? a day for a man to afflict his soul? *is it* to bow down his head as a bulrush, and to spread sackcloth and ashes *under him*? wilt thou call this a fast, and an acceptable day to the LORD?

6 *Is* not this the fast that I have chosen? to loose the bands of wickedness, to undo the heavy burdens, and to let the oppressed go free, and that ye break every yoke ?

5 Is such the fast that I choose,
  a day for a man to humble himself?
Is it to bow down his head like a rush,
  and to spread sackcloth and ashes
  under him?
Will you call this a fast,
  and a day acceptable to the LORD?

6 "Is not this the fast that I choose:
  to loose the bonds of wickedness,
  to undo the thongs of the yoke,
to let the oppressed go free,
  and to break every yoke?

prayer at all; they are occupied with personal gain and profit, and so the formal prayers of the fast day are never heard (cf. Amos 5:23-24; Hos. 6:4-6; Isa. 1:15-17; Zech. 7:8 ff.) .

5. The verse reaches back to the people's plaint (vs. 3*ab*) ; the mere motions connected with the fast are meaningless in themselves. All this bowing down **like a rush,** the prophet says in biting satire, this spreading of **sackcloth and ashes** is external form. If it is not an expression of the heart and the deepest thought of the mind, it is not **an acceptable day** to God. The last line serves as an excellent transition to what follows.

3. THIRD STROPHE: THE RICH REWARDS OF THE TRUE FAST (58:6-9*b*)

Here the prophet stands in the true succession of the great prophets. He is of the same spiritual lineage as Amos, Hosea, Micah, Isaiah, and Jeremiah. The people ask for righteous judgments, and they desire the nearness of God. Here is the prophet's answer to their "desires." Observe the impressive questions with their succession of phrases in vss. 6-7, and the extensive consequences described in vss. 8-9*b* (cf. vs. 3*ab*) . Fasting may be self-indulgence, luxuriating in one's own feelings, or it may be purely magical in its mentality. Over against this the prophet strikes at the conscience and presses upon his hearers the inexorable demands of social justice, of sympathy and compassion, of love of neighbor and inward self-identification with him (cf. Hos. 6:4-6; Mic. 6:1-8; Isa. 1:10-20; Jer. 3:4 ff.; Ezek. 18:5-9, 14-18; Zech. 7:8 ff.; Job 31:13 ff.; Matt. 25:35-40) .

6-7. These verses describe the fast God chooses. The introduction is emphatic and impressive, giving exceptional force to the ethical requirements of Yahweh in the place of the purely formal and external practices of the cult. The LXX adds "says the Lord." **The bonds of wickedness:** All four verbs express the idea of liberation. The interrogative

voluntary assumption of the painful meritorious. George Whitefield as a young minister thought Christianity required him "to go nasty." [3] John of the Cross counseled: "Whatever you find pleasant to soul or body abandon; whatever is painful embrace it." There is value in disciplining self to endure hardness; but God has no satisfaction in our discomfort any more than he dislikes our happiness. Macaulay wrote that "the Puritan hated bear-baiting, not because it gave pain to the bear, but because it gave pleasure to the spectators." [4] Such fear of the pleasant is far removed from the appreciative enjoyment of the Son of man.

[3] See Southey, *Life of Wesley,* I, 142-44.
[4] *The History of England from the Accession of James II,* Vol. I, ch. ii.

6-7. *Not Self-denial but Loving Service.*—The metaphors deserve attention: **to loose the bonds of wickedness,** i.e., oppressive practices such as the harsh treatment of debtors; **to undo the thongs of the yoke,** i.e., to lift burdensome exactions; **to let the oppressed go free,** i.e., liberate the bankrupt whose families and themselves might be sold into slavery (Neh. 5:5) . During the Chaldean siege of Jerusalem slaves of Israelitish descent were declared emancipated, doubtless to gain divine favor; but when the Chaldeans withdrew, their masters claimed them again (Jer. 34:18-22) . **The homeless poor** refers to vagrants and political refugees, of whom a troubled time produces a vast number, like the displaced persons in mid-twentieth-century Europe. **Not to hide yourself from your**

7 *Is it* not to deal thy bread to the hungry, and that thou bring the poor that are cast out to thy house? when thou seest the naked, that thou cover him; and that thou hide not thyself from thine own flesh?

8 ¶ Then shall thy light break forth as the morning, and thine health shall spring forth speedily: and thy righteousness shall go before thee; the glory of the LORD shall be thy rearward.

7 Is it not to share your bread with the
    hungry,
  and bring the homeless poor into your
    house;
when you see the naked, to cover him,
  and not to hide yourself from your own
    flesh?
8 Then shall your light break forth like
    the dawn,
  and your healing shall spring up
    speedily;
your righteousness shall go before you,
  the glory of the LORD shall be your
    rear guard.

"is it not" (הלוא) takes up the formula of vs. 6a and presses the content to new dimensions of social compassion. The prophet here is lifting his voice like a trumpet in judgment against his fellow worshipers and in support of the poor. The last line summarizes the whole (cf. Deut. 22:1, 3-4 for similar idea). The fine section in Job 31 is an interesting parallel to the whole, especially vs. 15: "Did not he who made me in the womb make him? And did not one fashion us in the womb?" **The homeless poor** (RSV), **the poor that are cast out** (KJV): Lit., "the poor and the wandering [or "straying"]"; cf. LXX; Vulg., *vagos*. In no circumstances must one emend to "downtrodden" (from רדד). To vs. 7c the Dead Sea Scroll adds "with a garment."

8-9b. Here are described the rewards which come to him who observes the fast Yahweh chooses. Each verse begins with an emphatic **then** (אז), in contrast to the interrogatives of vss. 6-7. The imagery reflects the contrast to present conditions: **light . . . like the dawn, healing** like a fountain. The flight of imagination prompts the recollection of 52:12, clearly an allusion to the coming of salvation. **Your light:** Cf. 60:1, 3; Lam. 3:2. Skinner refers to the phrase in the Mesha stele, "from the splitting of the dawn." **Your healing:** An alternative is "your recovery," the literal meaning being the growth of fresh skin over a raw wound (cf. Jer. 8:22; 30:17).

In vs. 9ab the lines clearly refer to vs. 3ab (cf. also vs. 4d). Throughout it is obvious that the prophet attaches great importance to prayer, and his climax here at the close of the third strophe brings this out clearly. When the "true fast" of God is observed, men will **call**, and he will **answer**; they will cry, and he will be "very present": **Here I am** (cf. vss. 2-3). Volz and others find vss. 9c-10 particularly awkward in their present position and follow vs. 9b with vss. 11-12. This improves the order, but it is possible that

---

own flesh: The sin of the priest and Levite in Jesus' parable of the good Samaritan, the neglect satirized in Arthur Hugh Clough's lines:

> Thou shalt not kill; but need'st not strive
> Officiously to keep alive.[5]

The prophet assumes that all men, partakers of the same human nature, **flesh,** "constitute an indivisible unity, and a brotherhood pledged to mutual love."[6] He is as specific in delineating social duties as he has been in itemizing sins.

[5] "The Latest Decalogue."

[6] Franz Delitzsch, *Commentar über das Buch Jesaia* (4th ed.; Leipzig: Dörffling & Franke, 1889; "Biblischer Commentar über das Alten Testament"), *ad loc.*

Many Christian teachers fail to grip consciences because they deal in generalities. Obligations must be as detailed as transgressions.

8-9b. Religious Results of Social Conscientiousness.—Israel's path since her return had seemed wrapped in black darkness. Now dawn breaks. Her national life had been sorely crippled; her institutions were barely alive. Now recovery comes speedily. A people engaged in social justice and considerateness is like a caravan on the march: righteousness leads the way, God's glory defends the rear, gathers and keeps in the column scattered folk, so that none is missing.

Now fellowship with God is restored, so that

9 Then shalt thou call, and the LORD shall answer; thou shalt cry, and he shall say, Here I *am*. If thou take away from the midst of thee the yoke, the putting forth of the finger, and speaking vanity;

10 And *if* thou draw out thy soul to the hungry, and satisfy the afflicted soul; then shall thy light rise in obscurity, and thy darkness *be* as the noonday:

9 Then you shall call, and the LORD will answer;
    you shall cry, and he will say, Here I am.

"If you take away from the midst of you the yoke,
    the pointing of the finger, and speaking wickedness,
10 if you pour yourself out for the hungry
    and satisfy the desire of the afflicted,
then shall your light rise in the darkness
    and your gloom be as the noonday.

---

we have a literary device here (König, *Stilistik, Rhetorik, Poetik*, p. 171). This phenomenon, of which König gives numerous examples, is called palindrome (see his *Das Buch Jesaja,* p. 500; cf. also 52:6; 65:1).

4. FOURTH STROPHE: GLOWING PROMISES (58:9c-12)

In the previous strophe the introductory questions occupy the greater part of the prophet's thought, but here the conditions for the divine favor are briefer, while the expanded conclusion (vss. 10c-12) is of much greater length. The prophet is inspiring his people with the promise of a glorious future and holding before them the hope of a radical change. Much of the strophe is repetition, but the promises are greatly deepened.

9c. The pointing of the finger: A gesture of contempt and scorn (cf. Prov. 6:13). Among the Arabs this sign was a means of bringing misfortune upon people, and it is possible that some such association is present here (Ignacz Goldziher, *Abhandlungen zur arabischen Philologie* [Leiden: E. J. Brill, 1896-99], I, 56; cited by König, *Jesaja, loc. cit.*). **Speaking wickedness:** König thinks false prophecy is meant; Feldmann, quarreling and contention (vs. 4); Volz, slander. Volz's suggestion fits the context best.

10. The LXX reads, "And if you give bread to the hungry from your soul"; the Peshitta also has "bread." The primary meaning of the verbal root here is "to bring out," "to furnish," "to produce" (cf. Ps. 144:13). The word **yourself** (lit., **soul** or "life") may be a slip (the same word follows in Hebrew). In this case read, "furnish bread to the

---

prayer is answered. The answer to prayer is significant:

> **Then you shall call, and the LORD will answer;
>   you shall cry, and he will say, Here I am.**

God is himself the essential response to prayer. The accounts of a saying of Christ's concerning prayer differ in Matthew and Luke. In Matt. 7:11 God gives "good things" to those who pray; in Luke 11:13 he gives "the Holy Spirit." The Spirit is God himself in intimate and empowering fellowship. The specific requests which men make may or may not be granted. God always answers with his presence, his own thought and love. A parent's refusal or assent to a child's request contains his affection and judgment for the child, a refusal as truly as an assent. Whatever we pray for, the unfailing response is God—Here I am. God may always be "had for the asking." Other results of prayer are by-products of this invariable reply.

9c-12. What Is an Acceptable Fast?—The pointing of the finger, i.e., in contempt. The religious attitude toward fellow men is reverence for them as children of God (cf. I Pet. 2:17, "Honor all men"). **Speaking wickedness:** Torrey translates "slander" (see Exeg.). It may mean "idle words," "chatter," as in vs. 13 (cf. Matt. 12:36). A fast turned into a holiday for the well to do might easily breed gossip, a deadly antisocial sin. "Gossip is a beast of prey that does not wait for the death of the victim it devours." Such "vain speaking" is a temptation of the leisure classes whom the prophet has in mind. John Galsworthy pictures Forsyte 'Change, the home of Uncle Timothy and the aunts: "The homes of neutral persons of the secure classes, who are out of the battle themselves, and must find their reason for existing, in the battles of others."[7] **If you pour out**

[7] *The Forsyte Saga* (New York: Charles Scribner's Sons, 1929), p. 123.

11 And the Lord shall guide thee continually, and satisfy thy soul in drought,
and make fat thy bones: and thou shalt be
like a watered garden, and like a spring of
water, whose waters fail not.

11 And the Lord will guide you continually,
    and satisfy your desire with good
        things,ʰ
    and make your bones strong;
    and you shall be like a watered garden,
        like a spring of water,
        whose waters fail not.

ʰ The meaning of the Hebrew word is uncertain

---

hungry." **Satisfy the desire** [*néphesh*]: The noun might also be rendered "appetite."
Then shall your light: Cf. vs. 8a. Here the contrast is clearly stated.

11. Vss. 11-12 bring the prophetic oracle to a climax. God will no longer seem
remote and unresponsive (see vs. 3ab), but his righteous judgments and nearness (vs.
2ef) will be a living and continuing reality: **And the Lord will guide** [or "lead"] **you
continually.** So they will know his ways and walk by them. When they pray, he will
answer. Observe how the line connects with vs. 10ab. It is not likely that the prophet is
thinking of the new exodus (40:11; 42:16; 52:12). Rather, we have a characteristic
transformation of one of the major ideas of Second Isaiah (cf. also 57:18). **And satisfy
your desire with good things:** The closing phrase is usually rendered "in desert places."
König reads "in sunburnt regions" (cf. KJV **in drought**). The RSV follows Torrey in
deriving this word צחצחות (only here in the O.T.) from an Arabic root *ṣaḥ*, "good,"
"sound," "healthful." The LXX seems to paraphrase this idea, "according as your soul
desires"; Vulg., *splendoribus;* Targ. and Syriac, "delicacies." This suits the context.
Make your bones strong: The primary meaning of the root is one of strength and vigor,
therefore "invigorate." The **bones** represented the basic stability of the self. Psychological
disturbances such as despair or distress, etc., caused the bones to dry up, decay, or shake,
while good news, etc., gave strength to the bones, another vivid illustration of the Hebrew
view of man as a psycho-physical organism (cf. Aubrey Johnson, *Vitality of the Individual
in the Thought of Ancient Israel,* especially pp. 69-71; Eichrodt, *Theologie des A.T.,*
II, 74; see Pss. 6:2 [Hebrew 6:3]; 31:10 [Hebrew 31:11]; 32:3; 38:3; 51:8; 102:3, 5
[Hebrew 102:4, 6]; see also Isa. 66:14; Prov. 15:30; Job 21:24). The promise answers
the depressed and confused state of the community. The second tristich seizes upon the
favorite Oriental allusion to **water,** expressing life and joy and abundant blessing. As
the result of Yahweh's guidance, the life of the community will be **like a watered garden**
(cf. Jer. 31:12), **like a spring of water** (lit., "gushing forth of water"), whose waters
do not fail (lit., "do not deceive"; cf. Jer. 15:18; Mic. 1:14). Kittel suggests, in view of
the shortness of the line, that a word has fallen out, perhaps "of life." The addition is
not necessary. Cheyne *et al.* render "channel of water" and adduce Assyrian parallels.
The last clause is a splendid figure for the vitality of the community's continuing life
under the guidance of God (vs. 11a).

---

yourself for the hungry—"The gift without the
giver is bare."⁸

The consequences first repeat vs. 8 and then
amplify. The prophet has in mind national
recovery and health. Isaiah's blessings, as
Delitsch points out, are both receptive, **a watered garden,** and inherent, **a spring of water,
whose waters fail not.** This is the prosperity of

a nation
Made free by love, a mighty brotherhood
Linked by a jealous interchange of good.⁹

⁸ James Russell Lowell, *The Vision of Sir Launfal,*
Part II, st. viii.

⁹ Shelley, *Revolt of Islam,* Canto V, st. xiv.

Vs. 12 reveals the major concern of these
returned exiles in their devastated homeland.
**Your ancient ruins shall be rebuilt. Founda-
tions of many generations** suggests buildings of
which the basement walls alone are standing.
The restoration of walls and streets renders a
city or countryside habitable. **Streets** implies
populous places now deserted. This is a text
which readily applies to the untouched or less
touched lands in a postwar world. Such more
prosperous nations will not assume the role of
repairer and **restorer** unless ruled by the spirit
which the prophet is inculcating. A people must
pour out itself **for the hungry,** must reverence

12 And *they that shall be* of thee shall build the old waste places: thou shalt raise up the foundations of many generations; and thou shalt be called, The repairer of the breach, The restorer of paths to dwell in.

13 ¶ If thou turn away thy foot from the sabbath, *from* doing thy pleasure on my holy day; and call the sabbath a delight, the holy of the LORD, honorable; and shalt honor him, not doing thine own ways, nor finding thine own pleasure, nor speaking *thine own* words:

12 And your ancient ruins shall be rebuilt;
   you shall raise up the foundations of
      many generations;
you shall be called the repairer of the
      breach,
   the restorer of streets to dwell in.

13 "If you turn back your foot from the
      sabbath,
   from doing your pleasure[i] on my holy
      day,
and call the sabbath a delight
   and the holy day of the LORD honor-
      able;
if you honor it, not going your own ways,
   or seeking your own pleasure,[j] or talk-
      ing idly;

[i] Or *business*
[j] Or *pursuing your own business*

12. This verse is a valuable clue to the conditions prevailing in Jerusalem and Judah. It certainly does not suggest that the temple had been rebuilt. The land will be restored. The **ruins** caused by the Babylonian invasion will be **rebuilt** (44:26, 28, "she shall be built"; 45:13; 54:11; 61:4; cf. also 49:8). Skinner's comment that this verse shows that the prophet is thinking chiefly of physical and political prosperity is contradicted by the preceding verses and the general context of the poem. The idea of physical restoration is clearly in the writer's mind, but spiritual regeneration significantly precedes it (vss. 8-9*b*, 10*c*-11). **And your ancient ruins shall be rebuilt:** The Hebrew seems awkward (see KJV). The second word (lit., "from you") has been emended in various ways, e.g., Cheyne, "thy children" (or "sons"); Duhm, "thy people." Torrey argues for the present text on the basis of the Arabic. The RSV follows him here. The verb, however, should be read in the Niphal (ונבנו) with König, Elliger, and Volz. The new situation will be recognized in the new name, **Repairer of the breach** (cf. 60:14; 61:3, 6; 62:2, 4, 12). **The restorer of streets to dwell in:** The word for **streets** (*nethibhôth*) should probably be emended to **ruins** (*nethiçôth;* so Kittel, *Biblia Hebraica,* 3rd ed.; *ad. loc.;* Johannes Hempel, *Hebräisches Wörterbuch zu Jesaja* [Giessen: A. Töpelmann, 1924]; Torrey, *et al.;* cf. König, *Jesaja,* p. 501). G. R. Driver sees the difficulty in the infinitive **to dwell** and derives it from an Akkadian root *sabatu,* "to clear ground"—"who restores paths by clearing them" ("Linguistic and Textual Problems," p. 405).

5. FIFTH STROPHE: KEEP THE SABBATH (58:13-14)

The **sabbath** was an ancient Israelite institution founded by Moses himself (Exod. 20:8; 23:12; 31:15; 34:21; see also Isa. 56:2). Volz calls it the grandest institution of O.T. religion. It was celebrated in pre-exilic times (1:13; Amos 8:5; cf. Hos. 2:11 [Hebrew 2:13]). The Deuteronomic decalogue (Deut. 5:15) associates it with Israel's bondage in

the nations it is called to serve, and must avoid thoughtless speech which might wound their sensibilities.

13-14. *The Sabbath and Fasting.*—The emphasis upon the holy day of the LORD is a product of the Exile. Ezekiel in his desire to stress the separateness of Israel had said much of sabbaths, "I gave them my sabbaths, as a sign between me and them" (Ezek. 20:12; etc.).

Ezekiel does not stress the humanitarian benefits of a labor-free day. Its humane aspect drops out in his emphasis upon its holiness, a symbol of national dedication to God. This is not the more attractive aspect of the sabbath. But here, where the prophet places it side by side with his moving appeal for social kindness, it seems to recapture the more generous purpose of its institution.

14 Then shalt thou delight thyself in the Lord; and I will cause thee to ride upon the high places of the earth, and feed thee with the heritage of Jacob thy father: for the mouth of the Lord hath spoken *it*.

14 then you shall take delight in the Lord,
    and I will make you ride upon the
        heights of the earth;
I will feed you with the heritage of Jacob
    your father,
        for the mouth of the Lord has spoken."

Egypt, and the original Elohist decalogue (Exod. 20:11) is expanded in the light of the priestly account of the Creation (Gen. 2:1-4*a*). During the Exile it achieved great prominence because it was an institution that could be celebrated on foreign soil. It was for Israel a confession of her faith and a witness to the nations of Israel's loyalty to her covenant Lord. The Babylonians also celebrated the seventh day which involved a cessation of all ordinary activities (W. W. Cannon, "The Weekly Sabbath," *Zeitschrift für die Alttestamentliche Wissenschaft*, XLIX [1931], 325). Volz finds the origins of the synagogue in its celebration, and this is indeed possible. There is no contradiction between vss. 1-12 and vss. 13-14 of our poem. The sabbath here is tantamount to worship of the God of Israel (cf. Gen. 2:1-4*a*). The special value of these verses is that they place the whole poem in a profoundly theocentric context.

13. The **sabbath** is holy ground (cf. Exod. 3:5). As the Lord's day, it is a holy time, and a holy time must be observed by cessation of all secular preoccupations and by worship of the holy God. **From doing your pleasure:** Cf. vss. 2*b*, 2*e*, 3*c*. Perhaps we should read, "from carrying on your business" (cf. vs. 3*d*). Not for man's profit but for the glory and praise of God the sabbath was instituted. Cf. vs. 13*e*, where the phrase should be rendered as in vss. 3*c*, 13*b*. The repetitions in this strophe are notable. **And the holy day of the Lord:** The Hebrew has **the holy of the Lord,** a most interesting phrase, emphasizing the unique place of the sabbath as holy. **Honorable:** Vulg., *gloriosum*. **Or talking idly:** Lit., "speaking a word." The LXX, "Not speaking a word in anger from your mouth," is perhaps a paraphrase of the supposed meaning. The words are probably a warning against idle talk that might desecrate the holiness of the day.

14. This concluding verse is the apodosis of vs. 13. The lines are impressive and obviously climactic, and the last line crowns the entire poem. **Then you shall take delight in the Lord:** Cf. vs. 2*b*, 2*e*. **And I will make you ride upon the heights of the earth:** Cf. Deut. 32:13; 33:29; Ps. 18:33; Hab. 3:19. **The heritage of Jacob your father:** Cf.

Not a few commentators regard these verses on the sabbath as irrelevant in this chapter, and delete them. But in the confused days which followed the return from the Exile it was essential to restore fidelity to the God of Israel; the sabbath was a symbol of such loyalty. In the Maccabean period, with a similarly confused background, a thousand loyal Jews allowed themselves to be slaughtered rather than engage in battle in self-defense on the sabbath (I Macc. 2:36-38). But "Time makes ancient good uncouth," and Jesus scandalized his contemporaries by his treatment of the sabbath. This was one of the reasons which led devout churchmen to demand his execution. That which martyrs died for in 168 B.C. two centuries later became a chief cause of the death of the Son of God. Thus does time alter the relevance of the most sacred institutions.

The plea here is for the recognition of the sabbath as **the holy day of the Lord.** One could wish that the prophet had been as specific in his teaching on how the day is to be honored as he was in his teaching of the right observance of a fast. During the Exile the synagogue and its services had sprung up, and these were brought back to the homeland. Corporate worship of God and instruction in his word are unquestionably included in honoring the sabbath. The emphasis throughout this chapter is upon **delight in the Lord.** This is the mood of many of the psalms (cf. Pss. 37; 42; 119). To "enjoy God" is considered "man's chief end." Much current religion stops short of this. Augustine Birrell has spoken of Charlotte Brontë's religion as "robust Church of Englandism, made up of cleanliness, good works and hatred of humbug—all admirable things certainly, but not specially religious." Of the three brilliant daughters in the Yorkshire rectory, he says that "alone amongst the sisters Anne had enough religion to give her pleasure."[1] The elderly Franz Josef

[1] *Life of Charlotte Brontë* (London: W. Scott, 1887), pp. 59, 65.

59 Behold, the LORD's hand is not shortened, that it cannot save; neither his ear heavy, that it cannot hear:

59 Behold, the LORD's hand is not shortened, that it cannot save, or his ear dull, that it cannot hear;

"the house of Jacob" in vs. 1d, probably an intentional literary reminiscence. Yahweh will give his people the holy land as a possession. Palestine is the land of Yahweh, and he feeds his people with the heritage of their father Jacob (cf. Gen. 28:13-14).

E. GOD'S INTERVENTION (59:1-21)

Ch. 58 and ch. 59 are so similar in style and content that many scholars consider them a single literary unit. They describe a living encounter between Yahweh and the worshiping community. They center upon the transgressions of the community and the remoteness of God, the long delay in his coming to redeem and save, which Second Isaiah had proclaimed in such moving and powerful words. They contain both invective and promise. The prophet appears as a preacher of repentance and calls his people to a life of righteousness and worship. The events associated with 586 B.C. and the succeeding years, conditions existing in the Jerusalem community, and the lack of religious vitality among its members, constitute the background of both chapters. Nevertheless, they form two separate units, as is clear from an analysis of their literary structure and style.

The poem in ch. 59 appears upon first reading to contain three separate sections (vss. 1-8, 9-15a, 15b-20). There are sudden shifts in literary form, in content, in speaker, and in grammatical constructions. Therefore some scholars detect several independent literary units. But such a disintegration of the materials does violence to the meaning of the poem and to the literary structure. The situation described in vss. 1-2 is not resolved until the close. Only in the conclusion does Yahweh intervene to save, only there does he lend an ear to the pleadings of the people, overcome the separation, and no longer hide his face. His glory is from the rising sun, his coming like a rushing stream. He comes to redeem those who turn from their transgressions. The central words of the poem are present in all three sections, above all the words which describe Israel's sins. Few chapters in the Bible are so rich and diverse in their vocabulary of sin (cf. Ps. 51). Indeed, so rich is this language that English translation fails to do justice to it. Observe the following words: **iniquities, sins, lies, blood, wickedness,** "chaos" (RSV, **empty pleas**), "trouble" (RSV, **iniquity**), **deeds of violence, transgressions, denying the LORD, turning away from following our God,** etc. These are the barriers which separate God and man. The coming of God as **Redeemer** and Savior to those who repent is the single event upon which the prophet's eyes are fixed from the very beginning. The literary form which explains the diversity of the materials—structure, content, and diction— is the liturgy. Another support for this view is its use of traditional materials (for an interpretation of the liturgical character of the poem see Procksch, *Theologie des A.T.,* p. 294; cf. also Haller, *Das Judentum,* pp. 131-32). Observe how vss. 9 ff. connect with the closing words of vss. 1-8 (especially **justice**) and the motif of **the way** (or **paths**). The sequence of lament (vss. 9-15b) and response (vss. 15c-20) is employed by Second Isaiah (e.g., 49:14 and 49:15 ff.), and other prophets (e.g., 33:7-9 and 33:10-12; Mic. 7:7-10

Haydn told Carpani that "at the thought of God his heart leaped for joy, and he could not help his music doing the same." [2] A whole devout community, such as the prophet envisages, exalted by joy in God, would ride upon the high places of the earth, overcoming life's obstacles, and possess the heritage of its loftiest spiritual forefathers.

[2] Giuseppe Carpani, *The Life of Haydn* (tr. from the French of L. A. C. Bombet; Providence: Miller & Hutchens & Samuel Avery, 1820).

59:1-21. Sin and Confession: Judgment and Redemption.—This sermon-poem has the same background as those which immediately precede it. There is gloom over national conditions, and there are glaring social sins to which the people are blind. Torrey calls it *De Profundis.* [3] That certainly is the mood in which it begins. The community feels itself deserted of God.

1-4. God-forsakenness and the Real Cause— Sin.—God is charged with indifference and

[3] *Second Isaiah,* p. 439.

2 But your iniquities have separated be-tween you and your God, and your sins have hid *his* face from you, that he will not hear.	2 but your iniquities have made a separation between you and your God, and your sins have hid his face from you so that he does not hear.

and 7:11-13) and is paralleled in the Babylonian and Egyptian liturgies (see also 63:7–64:12). Vss. 1-8 contain the prophet's preaching of repentance, vss. 9-15*b* the *Confiteor* of the congregation, vss. 15*c*-20 the *Absolutio*. In the call to repentance and confession our prophet stands close to Hosea and Jeremiah.

Each division of the liturgy contains two strophes (vss. 1-4, 5-8; 9-11, 12-15*b*; 15*c*-17, 18-20). Vs. 21 is an addition.

1. First Strophe: The Separation Between God and the Community (59:1-4)

The poet taxes his resources to describe the separation between God and the people. He begins with a reply to the implied lament of the community that God is remote, that he does not intervene to save or respond to its prayers. The prophets of Israel from the beginning had asserted that Israel had broken the covenant, but years of exile and darkness and the distressing conditions in Palestine had done much to arouse the deeper levels of her conscience. The relation between the events of history and the faith of the community finds expression here. The strophe is thus a reflection of one of the major directions in which the thought of the time turned. Note the strong anthropomorphisms: **the Lord's hand, his ear, his face.** The language is drawn from the cult.

59:1. The liturgy opens with a prophetic "word" (vss. 1-8). In his customary manner the writer recalls a prophetic passage (50:1-2); the words of his great master who had proclaimed the imminent coming of God in glorious redemption serve as the basis for his message (cf. also vss. 19-20). But the return to Palestine did not correspond with Second Isaiah's rhapsodic expectations, and the people are plunged into an abyss of doubt (cf. 40:27). God does not act and prayers are not heard. **His ear dull:** Lit., **His ear heavy** (cf. 6:10).

2. God is not limited in power (50:2) or unable to hear the prayers of his people. The true reason for the separation between God and Israel is that sin has erected a barrier between them. In the covenant relationship Israel became a holy and separated people, holy and separate to Yahweh her God (Lev. 17:1–26:46; I Kings 8:23). But the relationship was a contingent one, based on obligation and responsibility, upon obedience and holiness of life. Now, the prophet says, Israel's sins have separated her from God: **Your sins have hid his face.** Men went to the sanctuaries and the divine services to seek Yahweh's **face,** a *terminus technicus* for worship. But the sins of the people have turned God's face away (cf. 8:17; 57:17; Job 34:29). Interestingly, the prophet says "so that he does not hear." The presence of God in Israel was recognized not so much by "seeing" as by hearing what he had to say. The Hebrew has simply **face** without

impotence—his hand is shortened that it cannot save, his ear dull. The Hebrews were never atheists in the sense of believing God nonexistent. But they had moods, like that of Luther when he cried, "O my God, thou art dead"; or like Thomas Hardy, where he describes mankind as a company of dejected folk:

"O we are waiting for one called God," said they,
. . . .
"Waiting for him to see us before we are clay:
  Yes; waiting, waiting, for God *to know it.*" . . .

"To know what?" questioned I.
"To know how things have been going on earth and
  below it." [4]

The prophet sharply turns their minds from God to themselves: "'Tis your sins are separating you, barring you from your God." Augustine represents man when he falls from God as be-

[4] "Fragment," *Collected Poems* (London: Macmillan & Co.; New York: The Macmillan Co., 1923), p. 482. Used by permission of the Hardy Estate and of the publishers.

3 For your hands are defiled with blood, and your fingers with iniquity; your lips have spoken lies, your tongue hath muttered perverseness.

4 None calleth for justice, nor *any* pleadeth for truth: they trust in vanity, and speak lies; they conceive mischief, and bring forth iniquity.

5 They hatch cockatrice' eggs, and weave

3 For your hands are defiled with blood
  and your fingers with iniquity;
your lips have spoken lies,
  your tongue mutters wickedness.
4 No one enters suit justly,
  no one goes to law honestly;
they rely on empty pleas, they speak lies,
  they conceive mischief and bring forth
    iniquity.
5 They hatch adders' eggs,
  they weave the spider's web;

the pronoun, but it is doubtful whether the word is used in any absolute sense as in the later development of Judaism (cf. also Shekinah, Name, etc.). The word simply signifies the divine presence.

3. The first two lines still speak of sins in a general way. When men stretch forth hands stained with **blood** (cf. vs. 7), God gives no heed (1:15). **Your lips have spoken lies:** The Dead Sea Scroll omits. Observe the four parts of the body (**hands, fingers, lips, tongue**) and the sins which are associated with each. The first two are associated with deeds, the last two with words. The former were fashioned to perform such good deeds as are described in ch. 58; the latter to speak the truth, to pray in sincerity, and to praise God. But Israel uses her members for just the opposite functions. Such sins have separated her from her covenant Lord. With vs. *3c* the prophet begins his enumeration of specific sins. Both the N.T. and later Judaism elaborate such lists of sins (e.g., Mark 7:21-23; Matt. 15:19; Rom. 3:10-18; Gal. 5:19-21; II Cor. 12:20; I Pet. 2:10-19; Barn. 19-20; Did. 3-5). See especially the Dead Sea "Manual of Discipline."

4. The first two lines and possibly all of them should be understood forensically. **No one enters suit justly:** Lit., "no one calls in righteousness." The RSV gives the right meaning (cf. Job 9:16). Here again our prophet is close to his pre-exilic predecessors (1:17; 10:1-2; 29:21; Amos 5:10, 13; Jer. 5:28). It is an insensate and callous community that knows neither the ways of God nor the rights of the neighbor. **They rely on empty pleas:** Lit., "Trusting in chaos" (*tōhû*). The verbs are infinitive absolutes: "relying," "speaking," "conceiving," "bringing forth" (cf. Jer. 7:9). The Dead Sea Scroll has the finite verb for the first and last. **They speak lies:** Cf. vss. *3c, 13d.* **They conceive mischief:** This is a favorite figure: they are pregnant with wrong or violence (cf. 33:11; Ps. 7:14 [Hebrew 7:15]; Job 15:35). Note again the Semitic way of developing the thought by a succession of brief units.

2. Second Strophe: The Crooked Roads of the Evil (59:5-8)

The shift from the second to the third person is explained by the transition provided by the repeated "no one" in vs. *4ab.* The mildly figurative language of vs. *4cd* leads to

coming not quite but almost a nonentity: "[Not] absolutely nothing, but being turned toward himself, his being became more contracted than it was when he clave to Him who supremely is."[5] Sin-dwarfed men lack capacity to discern God's presence. Whittier employs another metaphor for it:

> We turn us from the light, and find
>   Our spectral shapes before us thrown,
> As they who leave the sun behind
> Walk in the shadows of themselves alone.[6]

[5] *The City of God* XIV. 13.
[6] "The Shadow and the Light."

The instance of social sin is chosen from the courts of law, where litigants are brazen in their falsehood and dishonesty. There is no effort to achieve justice (vs. 4). **They rely on empty pleas,** lit., "on chaos." There is a total collapse of ethical standards. Such moral nihilism we saw in Nazism, and sometimes see in our own political and industrial life. **They conceive mischief,** i.e., chicanery; to tamper with veracity is to open the floodgates to all manner of tricky devices.

5-8. The Disastrous Effects of Falsehood.— The reference in vs. 5 is to current folklore.

the spider's web: he that eateth of their eggs dieth, and that which is crushed breaketh out into a viper.	he who eats their eggs dies, and from one which is crushed a viper is hatched.

6 Their webs shall not become garments, neither shall they cover themselves with their works: their works *are* works of iniquity, and the act of violence *is* in their hands.

7 Their feet run to evil, and they make haste to shed innocent blood: their thoughts *are* thoughts of iniquity; wasting and destruction *are* in their paths.

6 Their webs will not serve as clothing;
    men will not cover themselves with
        what they make.
Their works are works of iniquity,
    and deeds of violence are in their
        hands.
7 Their feet run to evil,
    and they make haste to shed innocent
        blood;
their thoughts are thoughts of iniquity,
    desolation and destruction are in their
        highways.

---

the more elaborate imagery of vss. 5-6. Vs. 5a is expanded by vs. 5cd, vs. 5b by vs. 6ab. The succeeding lines return to the more general language of vss. 2-3b.

5. The evildoers transmit the deadly poison of their deeds to others as an adder transmits its poison through its eggs. Their evil begets evil, as a viper is hatched from the broken egg. **They hatch adders' eggs:** König describes the tense as aorist gnomicus: "They are accustomed to hatch." The adder referred to here is a poisonous snake, but it does not lay eggs (Brown, Driver, Briggs, *Lexicon, s.v.,* צֶפַע; cf. Isa. 11:8; Prov. 23:32). The **viper,** which is hatched, is the poisonous *echis colorata* (Köhler and Baumgartner, *Lexicon,* p. 78; cf. 30:6; Job 20:16). The second figure of **the spider's web** may refer to the way the spider seeks to capture the insect within its web and bring it to destruction, but primarily the figure seeks to show the utter futility of its efforts (vs. 6ab).

6. "The profits arising from injustice are as unsubstantial as a spider's web" (Kissane, *Isaiah,* p. 247; cf. Job 8:14-15).

7. The evildoers are swift to carry out their sinister deeds. The first two lines appear in Prov. 1:16. Parts of this verse and vs. 8 occur in the LXX^A version of Ps. 14 and are cited by Paul in Rom. 3:14-17. The repetition of **thoughts** in vs. 7c (cf. vs. 6c) is paralleled by the alliteration of desolation and destruction (*shōdh washébher*) of vs. 7d; **highways** has the sense of plans (Kissane) or designs, and forms a transition to the important climax in vs. 8. The Dead Sea Scroll adds "and violence" after **destruction.**

The serpent, particularly the species mentioned, was credited with superhuman cunning. The spider with its web of gossamer threads is the symbol of the entangler. The point of the first illustration is that cleverly contrived projects of wicked men are "almost equally fatal to those who acquiesce in them and to those who oppose them." [7] The point of the second comparison is the social futility of such schemes (vs. 6). The conclusion, like many in Proverbs, insists that sorrow follows wrong. Sins which begin in **thoughts** (vs. 7) are soon seen in **highways.** Our Lord taught that all evil comes "from within" (Mark 7:14-23). The Bible believes that outer circumstances respond to secret motives. Those who "devise iniquity . . . upon their beds" discover that in the morning "it is in the power of their hand" (Mic. 2:1). Lady Macbeth urges upon her hesitant husband

[7] Skinner, *Isaiah, Chapters XL-LXVI,* p. 170.

When you durst do it, . . . nor time nor place
Did then adhere, and yet you would make both;
They have made themselves.[8]

In the final line of vs. 8 the poet turns completely preacher. He gives the familiar warning that once involved in wickedness, all hope of peace disappears. A modern dramatist repeats it:

Dimly I dread lest having struck this blow
Of my freewill, I by this very act
Have signed and pledged me to a second blow
Against my will. What if the powers permit
The doing of that deed which serves us now;
Then of that very deed do make a spur
To drive us to some act that we abhor?
The first step is with us; then all the road,
The long road is with Fate.[9]

[8] Shakespeare, *Macbeth,* Act I, scene 7.
[9] Stephen Phillips, *Herod* (London: John Lane the Bodley Head, 1901), Act I, p. 35. Used by permission.

8 The way of peace they know not; and *there is* no judgment in their goings: they have made them crooked paths; whosoever goeth therein shall not know peace.

9 ¶ Therefore is judgment far from us, neither doth justice overtake us: we wait for light, but behold obscurity; for brightness, *but* we walk in darkness.

10 We grope for the wall like the blind, and we grope as if *we had* no eyes: we

8 The way of peace they know not,
　　and there is no justice in their paths;
　　they have made their roads crooked,
　　no one who goes in them knows peace.

9 Therefore justice is far from us,
　　and righteousness does not overtake us;
　we look for light, and behold, darkness,
　　and for brightness, but we walk in
　　　gloom.

10 We grope for the wall like the blind,
　　we grope like those who have no eyes;
　　we stumble at noon as in the twilight,

8. Vss. 7-8 contain four words for road: **highways** (*meṣillôth* 7d), **way** (*dérekh*), **paths** (*ma'gelôth*, "tracks"), **roads** (*nethîbhôth*, "paths"). The writer of the poem is fond of using synonyms. **The way of peace** [שׁלוֹם] **they know not:** Observe the repetition in vs. 8d (the finale of the prophet's "word"). It is the way of well-being, security, and prosperity, but the godless have no experience of walking in it. **There is no justice** [or "right," *mishpāṭ*] **in their paths.** The straight paths of right they make **crooked.** The figure of the way is the central symbol of biblical ethics (Jer. 2:17, 19; 4:18; 6:16; 21:8; Prov. 4:26; 5:21; 10:9). Walking or going expressed the course of one's life. Observe its usage in describing biblical piety ("Enoch walked with God," Gen. 5:22, 24), the course of history, and eschatology.

3. Third Strophe: The Community's Lament (59:9-11)

The prophetic word is followed by the prayer of the community: vss. 9-11 are a lament, vss. 12-15b a confession of sins. The strophe is notable for its firm construction, its rich imagery, its diction, and the effect produced by the succession of clauses. Observe how the conclusion repeats the introduction (vss. 9ab, 11bc), how contrasts are accentuated, words repeated (**justice, grope, far from us**—cf. "separation" in vs. 2—**we look for**), and above all, how the motif of salvation brings the lament to a climax (cf. vs. 1a).

9. Because of her iniquities and sins God's justice delays, his deliverance does not come (cf. vs. 2). **We look for light** or **We wait for light.** Cf. Jer. 8:15; 13:16; 14:19; Job 3:9; 6:19; Lam. 2:16; also Isa. 50:10; 58:8, 10. With the long delay of the promises proclaimed by Second Isaiah the community's consciousness of guilt deepens (cf. 64:5 ff.; Pss. 130; 143; Neh. 9). The contrast of **light** and **darkness** which dominates the strophe is characteristic of Israel's reflection about beginning and end (13:10; 50:3; Jer. 4:23, 28; Joel 2:31); the description here, however, is of present conditions.

10. The LXX has the third person instead of the first. With no deliverance in sight and no beacon of light to guide its course, the community gropes blindly for its way and staggers step by step, not knowing where it is or whither it is going. For **we**

9-12. The Wretched Plight of the People.—The lines are in the form of a confession—**we** and **us. Therefore** is the acknowledgment that not God's remissness or inability causes Israel's troubles, but their own wicked minds. The prophet identifies himself with the better mind of the community in this confession. When individual or nation becomes thus aware of wrongdoing, the hour of deliverance is at hand. Self-criticism, and that means self-detachment, renders possible attachment to the holy and saving God.

The individual, so far as he suffers from his wrongness and criticises it, is to that extent consciously beyond it, and in at least possible touch with something higher, if anything higher exist. . . . *He becomes conscious that this higher part is conterminous and continuous with a* MORE *of the same quality, which is operative in the universe outside of him, and which he can keep in working touch with.*[1]

It was the lack of deliverance (vs. 9) from the social chaos which had made the people think

[1] James, *Varieties of Religious Experience*, p. 508.

stumble at noonday as in the night; *we are* in desolate places as dead *men.*

11 We roar all like bears, and mourn sore like doves: we look for judgment, but *there is* none; for salvation, *but* it is far off from us.

among those in full vigor we are like dead men.

11 We all growl like bears, we moan and moan like doves; we look for justice, but there is none; for salvation, but it is far from us.

---

stumble at noon, the LXX reads "we stumble as in midnight." **Among those in full vigor:** The meaning of the word אשמנים is uncertain (cf. Köhler and Baumgartner, *op. cit., s.v.*). Many emendations have been suggested. Torrey proposes מאשים נעים (cf. Deut. 28:29; Job 5:14), "groping," "reeling"; Volz, נשב נשמים, "we sit appalled" (cf. Symm.); others, נשב במחשכים, "we sit in darkness"; still others, באמשים, "in dusk," which gives good parallelism. Kissane emends to שכבנו שאפים, "we lie gasping." The ASV and the RSV derive the word from a root meaning "to be fat or robust," hence "robust," "strong," "vigorous." Certainty as to the original text and meaning is precluded; it is best therefore to accept the RSV here, construing the form as an elative (see Kautzsch, *Gesenius' Hebrew Grammar,* secs. 85*b*, 133*a* and note, also secs. 20*a* and 93*ee* on the medial *nûn*).

11. The figure changes suddenly and sharply. In their distress and perplexity they **growl like bears** filled with ominous dread and fear. There is no thought here of bears in captivity (Volz). They **moan like doves** (cf. 38:14; Nah. 2:7 [Hebrew 2:8]; Ezek. 7:16) in plaintive sense of foreboding. The fundamental thought in the figures of vss. 10-11 is the same. This gives the climax of vs. 11*bc* its special force. The Babylonian prayers of repentance contain many interesting parallels (e.g., to the moaning of the doves; see Friedrich Stummer, "Einige keilschriftliche Parallelen zu Jes. 40–66," *Journal of Biblical Literature* XLV [1926], 186. For an excellent discussion of the Hebrew prayer of

---

God apathetic and which now stings their own consciences. The harsh conditions of the far country are part of God's merciful awakening of souls. His hand was working when they least realized it. If this prophecy is postexilic, it was the disillusionment of the restored community that was educating it for truer fellowship with God. "Do you not see how necessary a world of pains and troubles is to school an intelligence and make it a soul?" [2]

We grope. Bafflement may not necessarily betoken sinfulness. Life is always bewildering, and sometimes the dawn of new light confuses. Physicists state a law of the interference of light: under some circumstances additional light means darkness, for the light rays interfere with one another. But it is also true that sincere motives brighten an obscure situation. A very conscientious statesman wrote: "In old days men had visions and dreams to guide them in difficult times. I am afraid I cannot expect them, but if I try to decide rightly, it may be accepted." [3]

We stumble at noon. The return to the homeland had been a morning after a dark

night. Now, as the years had elapsed, it was noon in the national restoration, and the people stumbled along **as in the twilight.** This stumbling along when we should be walking confidently is a common experience for individuals, churches, and nations. The darkness is partly in ourselves, partly in others with whom we are joined in human society, partly in the bewildering circumstances of a shifting world. In Bunyan's allegory the pilgrims, after they leave the Valley of Humiliation, pass into the Valley of the Shadow, "a doleful place." "Over that Valley hung the discouraging clouds of confusion. . . . In a word, it is every whit dreadful, being utterly without order." [4]

The growling **bears** and moaning **doves** (vs. 11) are metaphors for the low-spirited people. They began by mourning over the wretched condition of the nation. Now they lament over its sin. In modern times grieving over sin, personal or corporate, has been deemed unhealthy. "The Christian's soul which has freed itself from sin is in most cases ruined by the hatred against sin. Look at the faces of great Christians. They are the faces of great haters." [5] Some psychia-

[2] *The Letters of John Keats,* ed. Sidney Colvin (London: Macmillan & Co., 1891), p. 256.

[3] George M. Trevelyan, *The Life of John Bright* (London: Constable & Co., 1913), p. 397.

[4] Mary Patricia Willcocks, *Bunyan Calling* (London: G. Allen & Unwin, 1944), p. 178.

[5] Nietzsche, quoted in Arthur Symons, *William Blake* (London: A. Constable & Co., 1907), pp. 2-3.

12 For our transgressions are multiplied before thee, and our sins testify against us: for our transgressions *are* with us; and *as for* our iniquities, we know them;

13 In transgressing and lying against the Lord, and departing away from our God,

12 For our transgressions are multiplied before thee,
  and our sins testify against us;
for our transgressions are with us,
  and we know our iniquities:
13 transgressing, and denying the Lord,
  and turning away from following our God,

---

repentance, together with many Babylonian parallels, see Johannes Hempel, *Gott und Mensch im A.T.*, pp. 253 ff. *et passim;* A. H. Edelkoort, *Het zondebesef in de babylonische boetepsalmen* [Utrecht: Oosthock, 1918]; A. van Selms, *De babylonische termini voor zonde* [Wageningen: H. Veenman, 1933]).

4. Fourth Strophe: The Community's Confession (59:12-15*b*)

The lines are drawn from the hidden depths of the community's conscience. Every kind of evil now emerges into the clear light of confession. In the presence of God (note **before thee** in vs. 12*a*, which must not be emended) transgressions of the past confront them in ever-increasing number. Vs. 12 is general like vss. 2-3*b*; vs. 13 is specific like vss. 3*c*-8; vss. 14-15*b* describe the consequence like vss. 9-11. The strophe is a veritable lexicon of Hebrew ethical terms (cf. Ps. 51).

12. For our transgressions are multiplied before thee: The reasons for the grievous situation described in vss. 9-11 are **our transgressions** (note the *kî*), or "rebellions," repeated in vs. 12*c*. This is paralleled by **sins** (vs. 12*b*) and **iniquities** (vs. 12*d*; cf. vs. 2). Kissane makes a tempting proposal to read "accuse" (*rābhû*, from the root ריב) for

---

trists regard consciousness of guilt as pathological. C. A. Sainte-Beuve, however, pure naturalist and incapable of sharing the Christian faith in redemption, wrote of the Jansenists:

Let those who cannot accept the remedies proposed by these mournful believers respect them at least and pity as fellow creatures for having felt so deeply on certain days the nothingness and wretchedness of human nature, that ocean of vices and pains, and its murmur, its fury, its eternal plaint.[6]

Deeper Christians are persuaded that sorrow for sin is an essential part of the process of salvation. Lancelot Andrewes prays for the grace of tears;[7] Jeremy Taylor commends "a pungent, afflictive sorrow";[8] and Christina Rossetti wrote:

Whoso hath anguish is not dead in sin,
  Whoso hath pangs of utterless desire.
Like as in smouldering flax which harbors fire,—
Red heat of conflagration may begin,

[6] *Port Royal* (8th ed.; Paris: Librairie Hachette & Cie, 1912), II, 115.
[7] *Lancelot Andrewes and His Private Devotions*, tr. John Henry Newman (New York and Nashville: Abingdon-Cokesbury Press, 1950), p. 137.
[8] *The Rule and Exercises of Holy Living* (Cambridge: E. P. Dutton & Co., 1876), ch. iv, sec. 9, p. 365.

Melt that hard heart, burn out the dross within,
  Permeate with glory the new man entire,
  Crown him with fire, mould for his hands a lyre
Of fiery strings to sound with those who win.
Anguish is anguish, yet potential bliss,
  Pangs of desire are birth-throes of delight.[9]

Vs. 12 places the penitents in the presence of God against whom they have sinned. Social iniquities, such as those in the law courts, are wrongs against fellow men; but their true character is seen in the light of God as sins against him (Ps. 51). **Our transgressions are with us.** "So long as men are very imperfect, the sense of great imperfection should cleave to them." [1] In Dante's vision of purgatory a group of spirits in the seventh cornice advance toward him, but are careful "not to step forth where they would not be burned." [2] They know their sin, and are resolved to be purified.

13-15*b*. *Their Sins with Their Consequences Set Forth.*—First are placed sins of apostasy from God: **transgressing, denying, turning away from.** Disloyalty to him is the root of the antisocial conduct which has reduced the nation morally to chaos. With God is "the fountain of life," and to be sundered from him by neglect

[9] "Gifts and Graces."
[1] Bagehot, "Bishop Butler," *Literary Studies*, III, 123.
[2] *Purgatory*, Canto XXVI.

speaking oppression and revolt, conceiving and uttering from the heart words of falsehood. 14 And judgment is turned away backward, and justice standeth afar off: for truth is fallen in the street, and equity cannot enter. 15 Yea, truth faileth; and he *that* departeth from evil maketh himself a prey:	speaking oppression and revolt, 　conceiving and uttering from the heart 　lying words. 14 Justice is turned back, 　and righteousness stands afar off; for truth has fallen in the public squares, 　and uprightness cannot enter. 15 Truth is lacking, 　and he who departs from evil makes 　himself a prey.

are multiplied (*rabbû*), but since it involves the change of the following phrase to "before him," it probably should be rejected. It is generally recognized that this section is a prayer of the community. **And our sins testify against us:** So the Hebrew reads literally.

13. The general confession of vs. 12 is developed by infinitive absolutes detailing the specific sins (cf. the same grammatical situation in vs. 4). Two groups of sins are enumerated: against God (vs. 13*ab*), against man (vs. 13*cd*). **Transgressing, and denying the LORD, and turning away:** The people confess their rebellion, faithlessness, and disobedience. Apostasy or idolatry or worship of pagan gods is hardly meant. The sins exposed in chs. 58–59 are obviously referred to. **Speaking oppression:** Lagarde and many after him emend עשׁק, **oppression,** to עקשׁ, "deceit," an easily explicable metathesis, which improves the meaning decidedly. **Conceiving and uttering from the heart lying words:** Cf. vss. 3*c*, 4. The Dead Sea Scroll omits **and uttering,** a probable dittography in the Hebrew. The word **conceiving** does not mean intellectual activity but "making pregnant" or "begetting" (as in vs. 4*d*).

14. The result was complete corruption of social relationships and an undermining of the structure of the community. The ethical norms of justice, righteousness, truth, honesty are antonyms to the parallel words of vs. 13. Where personal integrity cannot be depended upon, law loses its force, judicial proceedings lose their purpose, and communal life loses its stability.

15*ab*. "Thus truth is missing" (Torrey); it is no longer present (cf. Hos. 4:1). The last word (משׁתולל) has been questioned. Torrey emends it to השׂכל, "piety," reading, "piety has fled because of evil." The literal meaning is "one despoiled" or "plundered" (cf. Ps. 76:5 [Hebrew 76:6]). The expression is a little unusual, but it is precarious to emend it. It makes an effective concluding line.

of his worship is to block the divine flow of social inspirations. This is the reason for the insistence upon the sabbath in chs. 56; 58. Then follow **speaking oppression and revolt, conceiving and uttering . . . words of falsehood.** The prophet has in mind business dealings, the law courts, and other social relations. Jesus placed two O.T. commandments side by side—not that loving one's neighbor is not also loving God. If we give him all—heart, soul, mind, and strength—there would seem no remainder with which to love our neighbor. But loving the neighbor is part of loving God. The order of our duties which places God first is essential. Henry Sidgwick, thinking out a modern system of ethics, began with duty to man, but said: "All my apparent knowledge of duty falls into chaos if my belief in the moral government of the world is conceived to be withdrawn." [3]

In vss. 14-15*b* the social virtues are personified: **justice, righteousness, truth, uprightness.** Where they ought to be is in the public market place where people assemble, business is transacted, children play, and courts are held; but they have been driven off or lie prostrate. Anyone who avoids evil makes himself **a prey,** i.e., "an easy mark." For a society to turn its back on God leads to "Only infinite jumble and mess and dislocation." [4] The scene suggests the moral nihilism of the mid-twentieth century apparent in many lands.

[3] Murry, quoted in *Things to Come*, p. 35.
[4] Arthur Hugh Clough, "The Bothie of Tober-na-Vuolich," Part IX.

and the Lord saw *it,* and it displeased him that *there was* no judgment.

16 ¶ And he saw that *there was* no man, and wondered that *there was* no intercessor: therefore his arm brought salvation unto him; and his righteousness, it sustained him.

17 For he put on righteousness as a breastplate, and a helmet of salvation upon his head; and he put on the garments of vengeance *for* clothing, and was clad with zeal as a cloak.

The Lord saw it, and it displeased him that there was no justice.

16 He saw that there was no man, and wondered that there was no one to intervene; then his own arm brought him victory, and his righteousness upheld him.

17 He put on righteousness as a breastplate, and a helmet of salvation upon his head; he put on garments of vengeance for clothing, and wrapped himself in fury as a mantle.

---

5. Fifth Strophe: God Prepares to Intervene (59:15c-17)

In the last section of the liturgy the sudden shift perplexes many scholars who do not recognize a liturgical form. But it is precisely the function of the liturgy to give such support and hope as is described. The people have gathered to hear the reasons for the divine judgment upon them. They acknowledge their sins, confess their guilt, and express their grief. The function of the lines is similar to the priestly oracle of assurance so common in the Psalter.

15cd. The words connect very well with the foregoing (cf. vss. 4, 8-9). Vss. 15c-16 are similar to 41:28; 42:13; 63:5. The situation is so hopeless that the community of itself cannot change matters. The only possibility is God's coming to help and to save.

16. God sees that there is no human agent **to intervene** in the existing conditions. There is certainly no allusion to Cyrus here, as some have thought. God is astonished, even appalled (ישתומם; Brown, Driver, Briggs, *Lexicon, s.v.,* שׁמם), **that there was no man** on whom he could count. But he needs no helper or counselor (40:12-14; 41:28; etc.). **His own** mighty **arm** alone brings in the victory (cf. 40:10; 51:5, 9; 52:10; 53:1; and especially 63:5). The verb **brought victory** is the Hiphil imperfect of the verb "to save" (cf. vss. 1*a,* 11*c*). The coming salvation is the exclusive manifestation of his purpose and power. While the verbs of vss. 16-17 are in the past, the thought is of a future deliverance. The prophet frequently employs this prophetic perfect of certainty.

17. God arms himself as a warrior to engage in battle in behalf of his community (cf. 42:13; 49:25; 52:10; Exod. 15:3). The armor has symbolical meaning. **Righteousness** is his body armor or coat of mail. On his head he puts **a helmet of salvation.** He clothes

---

15c-17. *The Lord Comes to Judge and Redeem.*—In chs. 41 ff. where the exiles are helpless under the Babylonian domination, God raises up Cyrus. Now there is **no one to intervene.** So the Lord himself interposes. Where sin enslaves, no human help can suffice, either in the individual's soul or on the social scene. One of the most influential thinkers of the nineteenth century wrote:

When I began in earnest to seek God for myself, the feeling that I needed a deliverer from an overwhelming weight of selfishness was the predominant one in my mind. Then I found it more and more impossible to trust in any Being who did not hate selfishness, and who did not desire to raise His creatures out of it.[5]

---

[5] *Life of Frederick Denison Maurice,* II, 15-16.

The Lord's displeasure is his hatred of injustice. Love and wrath in him are not incompatible. George MacDonald prayed:

Give me thine indignation—which is love
Turned on the evil that would part love's throng;
Thy anger scathes because it needs must bless,
Gathering into union calm and strong
All things on earth, and under, and above.[6]

The conception of the Lord as a warrior is frequent in Isaiah (cf. 42:13; 49:24-26; 52:10), and the elaboration here of his armor may well have suggested I Thess. 5:8; Eph. 6:10-17. The Lord's advent in judgment is usually associated with the climax of history, as in the

[6] *Diary of an Old Soul* (New York: Longmans, Green & Co., 1898), June 25.

18 According to *their* deeds, accordingly he will repay, fury to his adversaries, recompense to his enemies; to the islands he will repay recompense.

19 So shall they fear the name of the LORD from the west, and his glory from the rising of the sun. When the enemy shall come in like a flood, the Spirit of the LORD shall lift up a standard against him.

18 According to their deeds, so will he repay,
    wrath to his adversaries, requital to his
    enemies;
to the coastlands he will render re-
    quital.
19 So they shall fear the name of the LORD
    from the west,
  and his glory from the rising of the
    sun;
for he will come like a rushing stream,
    which the wind of the LORD drives.

---

himself with **vengeance**, and wraps himself completely with the **mantle** of **fury**. The word **clothing** is deleted by many (cf. LXX, Vulg.) but the reasons for its deletion are not compelling. The imagery is related to the great conflict and triumph of the day of Yahweh. Here he is completely enveloped in the armor of help and redemption. The anthropomorphism is of course extreme (cf. vss. 1-2). The final line gives an impressive climax. Yahweh wraps himself in his **fury** or **zeal** or ardor (קנאה). This terrible inner drive of the holiness of God has its roots in Mosaic religion and expresses one of its primary characteristics (42:13; 63:15; Exod. 20:5 [E]; 34:14 [J]; Deut. 5:9; Zech. 8:2). The passage exerted a wide influence (cf. Wisd. Sol. 5:17-23; Eph. 6:14-16; I Thess. 5:8).

6. SIXTH STROPHE: GOD COMES AS REDEEMER (59:18-20[21?])

The strophe is dominated by the thought of God's active intervention. He will bring judgment upon his adversaries. Who the enemies are remains unclear. External foes are suggested by vss. 18c, 19, but vs. 20b may suggest the foes within Israel. The former is more probable. To those who turn from their transgressions Yahweh comes in mighty power and zeal as Redeemer. The oracle of salvation closes appropriately with the usual formula, **says the LORD.**

18. The first line is rendered literally by the KJV. The LXX either paraphrases or has a different text. Many emendations have been proposed, but Torrey is doubtless right in interpreting the second *ke'al* as a temporal adverb meaning "now" (cf. the Syriac *kel*): **according to their deeds** [even now] **he will repay.** The words **repay** and "render" are the same in Hebrew (ישלם), so too **deeds** and **requital** (twice) (גמול). The third line is considered by several scholars to be a gloss because the **coastlands** are usually the object of God's salvation and deliverance.

19. God appears in a mighty and universal theophany (cf. 40:5; 60:1-2; 66:18-19). Clothed in his mantle of awful fury and the intensity of his zeal (vs. 17), he comes in judgment like a pent-up **stream** that breaks through its channels and is driven on by the mighty **wind** of Yahweh. A parallel may be found in 30:27-28 which may serve as a guide to its interpretation. The opening verb **they shall fear** may be pointed to read "they shall see," which is found in some MSS and is adopted by many modern scholars. It is tempting to accept the latter since the coming of Yahweh in theophany (cf. 40:5; 60:1-2; 66:18-19) would be expressed well by "they shall see his glory." On the other hand, the immediate context is one of mighty judgment in which the wrath of God is revealed against his foes. The influence of Second Isaiah is certainly present

---

earlier chapters of this book; but here it may be an advent within history, particularly if vs. 21 is connected with this scene. The divine armor is made up of spiritual qualities. The combination of **righteousness** with might assures the certain victory of God.

18-20. *The Results of the Lord's Coming.*—The sins listed had been Israel's, but the judgment is on a world scale. It begins "at the house of God," but (unless one adopts the LXX reading) it includes the entire earth. The outcome is a manifestation of God to all mankind.

20 ¶ And the Redeemer shall come to Zion, and unto them that turn from transgression in Jacob, saith the LORD.

21 As for me, this *is* my covenant with them, saith the LORD; My Spirit that *is* upon thee, and my words which I have put in thy mouth, shall not depart out of thy mouth, nor out of the mouth of thy seed, nor out of the mouth of thy seed's seed, saith the LORD, from henceforth and for ever.

20 "And he will come to Zion as Redeemer, to those in Jacob who turn from transgression, says the LORD.

21 "And as for me, this is my covenant with them, says the LORD: my spirit which is upon you, and my words which I have put in your mouth, shall not depart out of your mouth, or out of the mouth of your children, or out of the mouth of your children's children, says the LORD, from this time forth and for evermore."

---

here, and the twofold **he will come** in vss. 19c, 20a gives force to the theolphanic context. Either interpretation is possible, **shall fear** or "shall see." The latter is perhaps preferable.

20. The manifestation of the glory of God brings judgment and redemption. **To Zion** he comes **as Redeemer** (cf. 41:14). Paul interprets this passage messianically in Rom. 11:26, after the LXX, which renders the text freely. The closing words, **says the LORD**, are lacking in the LXX. Many scholars delete them, but they give a good conclusion to the liturgy. The argument that it violates the meter is pointless.

21. This verse has been added to the liturgy either by a compiler of the Isaianic prophecies or by another disciple of Second Isaiah, possibly as the conclusion to a collection of prophecies. The emphatic subject, **and as for me** (ואני), is explained by the Hebrew composition of the compound sentence (Kautzsch, *Gesenius' Hebrew Grammar*, sec. 143a). **This is my covenant with them:** Cf. Gen. 9:9; 17:4 (P). The **covenant** is with the people (contra Volz). It is to be realized by the presence of the **Spirit** of God in their midst (cf. 42:1) and by the gift of the prophetic word (cf. 49:2; Jer. 1:9). God is present in the community through the gift of the Spirit, which manifests itself in all sorts of wonderful powers. In the midst of the darkness and discouragement of the times its presence gave assurance that the time of salvation was not remote (Hag. 2:4-5; Zech. 4:6; 6:1-8). Conspicuous here is the association of the **Spirit** of God and **words** of God. Among the early ecstatic prophets the Spirit was the organ of inspiration, but the pre-exilic writing prophets seem to avoid it (the reference to the spirit in Mic. 3:8 is probably a gloss). After 586 B.C. the Spirit again assumes an important role, e.g., in the prophet Ezekiel (cf. Pss. 51:11 [Hebrew 51:13]; 143:10; Job 32:8 ff.). In the future (usually the messianic age) the Spirit will inspire the community (cf. 4:4; 32:15-20; 44:3-5; Ezek. 37:1-14; Zech. 12:10; etc.). To the gift of the **Spirit** is added the gift of Yahweh's **words.** The meaning of Yahweh's words for Israel had become greatly deepened by the experience of exile when the services of temple and sacrifice were impossible. The revelation to Moses and the patriarchs, the word of God to the prophets, and indeed the whole covenant history from the beginning had come to have enormous significance in the services of worship. The verse therefore forms a wonderful climax. It is one of those verses which summarize the religious life of a people and an age. The Dead Sea Scroll omits **says the LORD,** but the expression should be retained since it is probably the device of the editor to attach it to the foregoing.

He comes in resistless might, **like a rushing stream, which the wind of the LORD drives.** He comes with impartial justice (vs. 18), but with grace for his own peoples (vs. 20). This links the poem's conclusion with its beginning. He comes as **Redeemer to those in Jacob who turn from transgression.** Judgment, while terrifying to all confronted with the holy God, becomes the welcome purification of his faithful people. It is this certain assurance of cleansing from all evil which makes a Christian sing

> Thy justice is the gladdest thing
> Creation can behold.[7]

21. *The Lord's Promise to the Spiritual Community.*—This is the company in Israel in

[7] Frederick W. Faber, "O God! Thy power is wonderful," st., ii.

60
Arise, shine; for thy light is come, and the glory of the LORD is risen upon thee.

60
Arise, shine; for your light has come, and the glory of the LORD has risen upon you.

F. The Coming Glory of the Lord (60:1-22)

The theme of this poem is expressed in 40:5: "The glory of the LORD shall be revealed, and all flesh shall see it." In the midst of a world shrouded in gloom the day of the Lord's epiphany dawns in all the splendor of an Oriental morning. Zion is flooded with the radiance of the rising sun. Glory (kābhôdh) is the central term of the divine epiphany (4:4-6; Exod. 24:16 ff.; Num. 14:10; Deut. 5:23-27; I Kings 8:11; Hab. 2:14; Ezek. 1:1-28; Luke 2:9).

The poem is a superb example of Hebrew literary style. The rhetorical devices, the imagery, and the key words are not unlike Second Isaiah. The structure is clearly defined. The opening strophe (vss. 1-3) summarizes the thought. Three major divisions (vss. 4-9, 10-16, 17-22), of three strophes each, follow the introduction. Each division is marked by a stirring climax (vss. 9efg, 16cd, 22cd). An interesting feature of the poem is the repetition of the word come and "causing to come" (vss. 1a, 4bc, 5d, 6c, 9c, 11c, 13a, 17ab), and this word is made emphatic by concrete synonyms. The world is coming to Zion's hill.

The poem is intimately connected with those that follow (chs. 61–62). But it is also related to the preceding poem to which it forms a striking contrast. There the emphasis is upon judgment, darkness, and unrighteousness; here the stress falls on redemption, light, and righteousness. The words of 58:8, 10 anticipate the contrast between light and darkness, and ch. 59 presses the contrast (e.g., 59:9-10, 19). The closing verses (59:19-20) strike the keynote for the present poem.

In theme, language, mood, and thought the writer is dependent upon Second Isaiah. He is obviously familiar with such passages as 47:1-15; 52:1-2; and 54:1–55:13. It is possible that Second Isaiah is the writer of 60:1–62:12, but it is better to think of the author as his disciple. His employment of his master's words is in the manner of an Oriental disciple. He is kindled by the same great thought of the imminent theophany; he remembers his master's ipsissima verba and seeks to instill the same rapturous faith and enthusiasm in the hearts of his contemporaries that he himself felt in hearing or reading his master's words.

The central word of the poem is glory, the theophanic word par excellence. Its original associations are with the revelation on Sinai. There Yahweh appeared to Israel in the midst of the cloud in fire (Exod. 19:16 ff.; 24:16 ff.; Deut. 5:22-27). The great theophanic revelations of the O.T. are revelations of Yahweh in fire and dazzling light (6:1-30; Ps. 18:8 ff. [II Sam. 22:8 ff.]; Hab. 3:1-17; Ezek. 1:1-28; etc.). Moses' face

---

covenant with God—the church, who receive his Spirit and word, and hold it in trust to minister to mankind. No matter how faithless the people of God, there will always be a remnant to carry on his gracious purpose. This is the indestructible church of Matt. 16:18. The word of the Lord is given to his church for evermore.

60:1-22. Jerusalem Glorified.—This poem, as Torrey puts it, is "one blaze of light." [8] The gloom of ch. 59 makes its brightness stand out by contrast. **Light** and **darkness** are spiritual symbols: light is fellowship with the holy God; darkness is life apart from him. God's nature is light, "in whom is no darkness at all," and his

glory is the manifestation of himself. When the nations come to Jerusalem's **light**, they arrive at the knowledge of the Lord and his righteousness. The present application of this chapter is to the glory of the church in faithful companionship with her God, and to human society in obedience to his righteous will. Details must not be allegorized; the basic truth is the transforming and irradiating effect of life in God's presence.

1-3. Upon Shadowed Jerusalem the Dawn Breaks.—"In the East the sun leaps above the horizon." [9] While the entire earth lies black, Jerusalem becomes suddenly a single point of clear shining. She glitters with God's pres-

[8] Second Isaiah, p. 443.

[9] G. A. Smith, Isaiah, II, 465.

reflects the intensity of the holy light so that Israel cannot look upon him. Before it the prophet Ezekiel falls prostrate. Where God is present, there is no need of sun, moon, and stars. Yet fire and light are also more than their external manifestations. They reveal the majesty and power and holiness of God.

This coalescence of the external and physical manifestation with spiritual revelation is a central feature of the poet's eschatological representation. We see the sun rising over Jerusalem, kindling the whole city in a flame of light; the city becomes a new Jerusalem where his glory dwells. The nations bear their gifts of gold, silver, and precious wood, and the gifts are designed for the worship of God in his holy temple. The Hebrews never wearied of concrete physical detail, but the distinction between physical and spiritual or psychical did not occur to them. The physical contained an interior or psychical association: their language was rich in connotations. It is a mistake, therefore, to divorce the literal and material from the symbolic and spiritual. The external and internal manifestations of Yahweh's presence and his eschatological and redemptive deeds belong together. Imagination must be allowed free course in such pictures as these.

Volz has suggested the New Year's celebration as the occasion for the poem. Both theme and imagery are consistent with such a view. Yet it is perhaps sufficient to stress its eschatological character. The date cannot be fixed with certainty, but a time shortly after 538 B.C. is probable.

1. First Strophe: The Dawn of the Glory (60:1-3)

The new age is about to dawn. Zion, "the city of our God," the city of David and of the temple, is addressed with urgent imperatives to rise and reflect the brightness of the divine glory. The world lies plunged in the darkness of the former age, but from afar the nations behold the light of the new age. The poet employs all the resources of terminology, repetition, word order, and grammatical construction to portray the glory of the Lord's self-manifestation.

60:1. Arise: Zion is pictured as a woman lying prostrate on the ground (cf. 50:1; 51:17-23; 52:1-2; 54:1). The imperative carries with it the fulfillment of the event. The LXX omits this verb but repeats the following: **shine, shine** (cf. 40:1; 51:9, 17; also 57:14; 62:10; 65:1). The LXX, Targ., and Vulg. add "Jerusalem." **Shine:** Zion is bidden to "reflect light" or "become light" in response to the light that has been shed upon her (cf. Exod. 34:29-35; II Cor. 4:3-6). It is not impossible that the poet has in mind the deep darkness before the Creation, when God said, "Let there be light"; the end of time is then a repetition of the beginning of time (cf. Gunkel, "Endzeit gleicht Urzeit"). The strong imperative verbs are followed by the particle kî, which communicates the central disclosure: **for your light has come** (cf. 58:8, 10; 59:9, 19). The verbs here and in the following line are prophetic perfects; the prophet sees the eschatological event as having already occurred. **The glory of the LORD:** The phrase is parallel to **your light.** The kābhôdh of God is his self-manifestation. In 6:3; Pss. 57:5, 11; 72:19, the kābhôdh extends over all the earth. Here it is upon Jerusalem, the holy city, that the glory appears. **Upon you** is emphatic, as is shown by its repetition in vs. 2c, 2d and by the Hebrew word order. **Has risen:** Cf. the Arabic "bright" (red); Syriac "scarlet." Perhaps a better rendering would be "dawns" or "shines forth" (Gen. 32:31; Exod. 22:3, and especially Deut. 33:2, where, as here, the association is theophanic).

---

ence. This is God's doing, but his people must respond to his self-manifestation by rising from their dejection and letting his radiance stream forth from them.

Today **darkness** [covers] **the earth, and thick darkness the peoples.** After the disasters of the first half of the twentieth century, ours is pre-eminently a time of gloom, of a "darkness which may be felt" (Exod. 10:21). Only in the Christian church is assured confidence found. Secular writers are pessimistic, and the horizon on which they look is black. One feels the difference between secular verse and the hymns sung in church. Faith faces a tragic world, but faces it with hope in God. In the early centuries, as today, the pagan soul was bleak and gray, but within the church life was vibrant. "Holding festival . . . in our whole life, persuaded

2 For, behold, the darkness shall cover the earth, and gross darkness the people: but the Lord shall arise upon thee, and his glory shall be seen upon thee.

3 And the Gentiles shall come to thy light, and kings to the brightness of thy rising.

4 Lift up thine eyes round about, and see: all they gather themselves together, they come to thee: thy sons shall come from far, and thy daughters shall be nursed at *thy* side.

2 For behold, darkness shall cover the earth,
and thick darkness the peoples;
but the Lord will arise upon you,
and his glory will be seen upon you.
3 And nations shall come to your light,
and kings to the brightness of your rising.

4 Lift up your eyes round about, and see;
they all gather together, they come to you;
your sons shall come from far,
and your daughters shall be carried in the arms.

2. **For behold** introduces the striking contrast between **darkness** and **light**, between the earth with its peoples and the dawning kingdom of God (cf. 45:14). God sheds forth his light first of all upon Zion. The whole verse accentuates the contrast between Zion and the world.

3. **And nations shall come to your light:** Attracted by the effulgence of the new Jerusalem, the nations stream to the holy city (cf. 2:2-4; Mic. 4:1-5, where, however, the nations go to Zion in the messianic age to receive the divine teaching; cf. also the messianic passage of Isa. 9:1-2). **And kings:** Kings belong to the nations of this pre-eschatological age (cf. 52:15; 62:2). **The brightness of your rising:** An alternative rendering is "the effulgence of thy dawn." A splendid climax to a strophe flooded with light (cf. 10:17; Ps. 104:2; Mic. 7:8). The Dead Sea Scroll reads לנגר, "to tell," for לנגה, **to the brightness.**

2. Second Strophe: The Wealth of the Nations (60:4-5)

4. Zion is again addressed with a double imperative: **Lift up your eyes round about, and see.** A wonderful view greets the eyes of the mother: her children are returning home! The first and second lines are a repetition of 49:18ab, the third and fourth a virtual repetition of 49:22de. **Your sons shall come:** The sons walk, but the daughters are borne on the hips. The verb can also be rendered "supported" or "held firm," in the fashion of nurses. This manner of carrying a child is still followed in the Near East (cf. 66:12).

that God is altogether on every side present, we cultivate our fields, praising; we sail the sea, hymning." [1]

In the preceding poem men are groping in moral anarchy. Now the reign of God has arrived, the citizens of Jerusalem can move with clear vision, and the nations come to share their noonday. This is the difference between human society apart from and in the will of God. Our century has seen the moral nihilism of Fascist and Communist orders. Some human norm was made an absolute, and the light of God was blotted out. But the church is the bearer of his self-revelation. When that light springs up, like the leaping morning, she must arise and shine. To a people with as much to

[1] Clement of Alexandria *Miscellanies* VII. 7.

dishearten them as the preceding poems dwell upon, this assurance that the hour of salvation has dawned would of itself be uplifting. The prophet is saying to them: "Be what by God's presence you are—a brilliant light to mankind." This is no small part of the church's task—to be what she is.

4-5. *Lift Up Your Eyes Round About, and See.*—Jerusalem lies upon the central ridge of the country. From the landward side she can see caravans streaming in; from the west over the Mediterranean ships are sailing in like flocks of pigeons. Along with this vast commerce come her returning exiled children.

Congregations need this summons to turn their eyes abroad. In their immediate neighborhoods there may appear little movement toward

5 Then thou shalt see, and flow together, and thine heart shall fear, and be enlarged; because the abundance of the sea shall be converted unto thee, the forces of the Gentiles shall come unto thee.	5 Then you shall see and be radiant, your heart shall thrill and rejoice;*k* because the abundance of the sea shall be turned to you, the wealth of the nations shall come to you.

k Heb be enlarged

5. Then you shall see and be radiant: The adverb is emphatic. Many MSS read "you will fear" for the first verb. Budde suggests that Zion fears a hostile attack, but this is perhaps fanciful. When Zion beholds the coming of the nations with the returning exiles, she will be radiant with joy (cf. Ps. 34:5). For the second verb the LXX reads "fear"; the Vulg., *afflues,* flow (cf. KJV). **Your heart shall thrill:** The verb usually means **fear,** but here and in Jer. 33:9; Hos. 3:5, it is associated with joy. Zion is deeply agitated and stirred after her night of sorrow and distress. Her heart throbs with excitement. **And rejoice:** The Hebrew means **be enlarged,** a vivid expression for profound emotion (cf. Ps. 119:32). **The abundance of the sea:** The word המון, **abundance,** is the usual term for "multitude" or "tumult." In late usage it has the sense of wealth; here it refers to the sea-borne **wealth of the nations.** The glory of Yahweh manifesting itself in such external ways is not alien to the word; glory sometimes has the meaning of wealth or riches (Gen. 13:2; 45:13; cf. Ps. 49:17; Nah. 2:9).

the church. In any case, the familiar community does not catch our attention. God's purposes include all nations, and an earth-wide survey discloses companies of souls thronging toward her. Part of a minister's obligation, and of the obligation of all spiritual leaders and teachers, is to keep posted on what is occurring on many fields, and share encouraging sights with fellow churchmen. In 1723 the young Jonathan Edwards, then ministering in New York, read avidly the newsletters as they were published:

I had great longings for the advancement of Christ's kingdom in the world; and my secret prayer used to be, in great part, taken up in praying for it. If I heard the least hint of anything that happened, in any part of the world, that appeared, in some respect or other, to have a favorable aspect on the interest of Christ's kingdom, my soul eagerly catched at it; and it would much animate and refresh me.[2]

Then you shall see and be radiant. This is Edwards' experience, animated and refreshed. **Your heart shall thrill and rejoice**—Torrey translates, "Startled, thy vision shall widen" [3] —surely the best blessing a congregation can receive. Jerusalem is awaiting on tiptoe the ingathering of her dispersed people. Some of them are described as little children carried "on the hip." They are brought by the nations now attracted to Jerusalem's radiant glory. Applied to the church, these details may symbolize the influx of those who, Christians at heart, are in far lands because of the church's half-dead con-

dition, her captivity to the ways of the world, or because of their blindness to her faith and purpose when her light is so dull, or because of their failure to discern their obligation to seek her fellowship. Current trends in thought, and the bankruptcy and peril of life without Christian inspirations, are carrying many thoughtful persons toward the church. And since this vision of glorified Jerusalem is part of the ultimate reign of God in the consummation of history, these verses suggest the heavenly city. Zwingli depicts it as

the assembly of all the saintly, the heroic, the faithful and the virtuous, where Abel and Enoch, Noah and Abraham, Isaac and Jacob, will mingle with Socrates, Aristides and Antigonus, with Numa and Camillus, Hercules and Theseus, the Scipios and the Catos, and where every upright and holy man who has ever lived will be present with his Lord.[4]

The abundance of the sea, . . . the wealth of the nations. This is the commercial prosperity of the glorified city. Material riches are a legitimate economic goal; but in applying these expressions to the church, we must bear in mind that material wealth is by no means always a blessing to her. There are, however, immaterial resources in the world's thought and art, in its scholarship and skills, which may be of great worth in her service. They can never be received without careful scrutiny, lest her distinctive gospel be distorted or obscured. Whatever she takes from the contemporary culture must be thoroughly subjected and assimilated to the mind

[2] *Memoirs,* ch. ii, sec. 3.
[3] *Op. cit.,* p. 264.

[4] *Exposition of the Christian Faith,* ch. x.

6 The multitude of camels shall cover thee, the dromedaries of Midian and Ephah; all they from Sheba shall come: they shall bring gold and incense; and they shall show forth the praises of the LORD.

7 All the flocks of Kedar shall be gathered together unto thee, the rams of Ne-ba-ioth shall minister unto thee: they shall come up with acceptance on mine altar, and I will glorify the house of my glory.

6 A multitude of camels shall cover you,
   the young camels of Mid′ian and
      Ephah;
   all those from Sheba shall come.
They shall bring gold and frankincense,
   and shall proclaim the praise of the
      LORD.
7 All the flocks of Kedar shall be gathered
      to you,
   the rams of Nebai′oth shall minister
      to you;
   they shall come up with acceptance on
      my altar,
   and I will glorify my glorious house.

3. THIRD STROPHE: THE HOMAGE AND TRIBUTE OF THE EAST (60:6-7)

The scene is highly imaginative. The poet describes the eschatological pageant which unfolds before his vision in the most characteristic imagery of his own Oriental world. Camels lead the procession by traveling of their own volition to bear gifts to the temple, and the flocks follow by offering themselves willingly for the altar. The names of places are of venerable association; they are used poetically, almost as we should speak of fair Ilion or Cathay.

6. **A multitude of camels shall cover you:** The word for **multitude** is used of horses in II Kings 9:17; of waters in Job 22:11. The verb stresses the vast number; it might almost be rendered "overwhelm" (cf. Exod. 8:2; 16:13). **Midian:** A tribe of camel Bedouins (Judg. 6:5) originally located east of the Gulf of Aqabah. In Gen. 25:4 it is associated, as here, with **Ephah. Sheba:** As the queen of Sheba came to Jerusalem in the time of Solomon "with camels bearing spices, and very much gold, and precious stones" (I Kings 10:2), so now the caravans come from afar with their costly gifts of **gold and frankincense** (cf. Jer. 6:20; Ezek. 27:22; Ps. 72:15). **Shall proclaim the praise of the LORD:** Cf. vs. 18. A more literal and perhaps better translation would be, "They shall tell the good news of his praiseworthy deeds" (lit., "praises," but see Brown, Driver, Briggs, *Lexicon, s.v.*, תהלה). This is a climax in the manner of Second Isaiah.

7. **Flocks** from the pastoral tribes of north Arabia follow the caravans. As the camels bear gifts of treasures, so the flocks gather together to go to the **altar. Kedar** and **Nebaioth** are associated in the Assyrian inscriptions of Ashurbanipal (Schrader, *Cuneiform Inscriptions and O.T.*, I, 133-34; cf. Gen. 25:13) and in Pliny (*Natural History* V. 12). The latter are probably the Nabateans (cf. Nelson Glueck, *The Other Side of the Jordan* [New Haven: American Schools of Oriental Research, 1940], pp. 13, 40-41). **Minister:** The word is often emended, but unnecessarily. The LXX reads simply "come." The following lines support the interpretation that the flocks offer themselves as sacrificial victims (cf. vs. 10). **Come up:** A better translation is "go up," used in the liturgical sense of going up to a sanctuary (cf., e.g., the psalms of ascent). **They shall come up with acceptance on my altar:** The text of the line has been questioned. Observe that the Dead Sea Scroll reads ויעלו לרצון על מזבחי, "they shall go up for acceptance upon my altar." This is probably the right wording. **I will glorify:** An alternative rendering is "I will beautify my beautiful house." These words do not necessarily imply that the temple had already been rebuilt. In the new age the temple will be restored as the dwelling of God's glory (cf. 63:15b; 64:11a).

of Christ. She would, however, be immeasurably poorer had she not utilized the gains of secular advance and employed them in her theology, her worship, and her work.

6-7. *Caravans with Gifts, and Sacrifices.*—This is the outlook to be seen eastward. The emphasis is upon the supply for the cultus in the temple. Jerusalem is the capital of the

8 Who *are* these *that* fly as a cloud, and as the doves to their windows?

9 Surely the isles shall wait for me, and the ships of Tarshish first, to bring thy sons from far, their silver and their gold with them, unto the name of the LORD thy God, and to the Holy One of Israel, because he hath glorified thee.

10 And the sons of strangers shall build up thy walls, and their kings shall minister unto thee: for in my wrath I smote thee, but in my favor have I had mercy on thee.

8 Who are these that fly like a cloud,
and like doves to their windows?
9 For the coastlands shall wait for me,
the ships of Tarshish first,
to bring your sons from far,
their silver and gold with them,
for the name of the LORD your God,
and for the Holy One of Israel,
because he has glorified you.

10 Foreigners shall build up your walls,
and their kings shall minister to you;
for in my wrath I smote you,
but in my favor I have had mercy on you.

4. FOURTH STROPHE: FLEETS OF EXILES FROM THE WEST (60:8-9)

From camel caravans and flocks of sheep from the East the poet turns his vision to the West, to see the ships of the Mediterranean bearing their cargoes of returning exiles.

8. Who are these? Cf. 63:1; also Song of S. 3:6; 8:5. In the remote distance the tiny white-masted vessels converge upon the holy city. The vivid imagery must not obscure the speed of the exiles' return.

9. For the coastlands shall wait for me: Cf. 43:5-7, 14; 49:18; 51:5. The first two lines do not cohere well, and the first line is especially awkward in the immediate context. Perhaps we should emend **coastlands** (איים) to "vessels" (עיים) and, with Torrey (*Second Isaiah*, p. 449), render the verb as "gather." Translate, "Surely to me the vessels shall gather." **The ships of Tarshish first:** Tarshish (Tartessus) was a Phoenician colony in southern Spain (cf. Jonah 1:3). They lead the fleet because they are the high-masted ocean-going vessels (cf. 2:16; see Albright's discussion of the name, "New Light on the Early History of the Phoenician Colonization," *Bulletin of the American Schools of Oriental Research*, No. 83 [1941], pp. 21-22). They transport not only the Diaspora but also **silver and gold** for the temple. Hence the strophe ends in the same fashion as the two preceding ones, by a reference to the worship of Yahweh.

5. FIFTH STROPHE: THE RESTORATION OF THE WALLS AND THE WEALTH OF NATIONS (60:10-11[12?])

The prophet continues his dominant theme of the coming glory of the Lord. As once foreigners destroyed the city, foreigners will rebuild it, but it will be the new

worship of mankind. **They shall proclaim the praise of the LORD, . . . they shall come up with acceptance on my altar.**

8-9. *Fleets of Ships Approach from the West.* —The emphasis is upon commerce which brings with it Israel's returning dispersion from the **coastlands.** The inference is that the exiles in Babylon are already at home, and now those scattered all over the Mediterranean seaboard are being transported back. All this which is described in vss. 6-9 occurs for a religious reason, for the name of the LORD your God. Jerusalem's glory assists the missionary work of Israel and brings this response from the nations. The seer on Patmos draws on these pictures when he represents the kings of the earth bring-

ing their glory and honor into the holy city (Rev. 21:24).

Arnold Toynbee, discussing possible progress in civilization, concludes that "there is no reason to expect any change in unredeemed human nature"; but he places his hope in the church's conveying to mankind her revelation of God and man's true end, and her inspirations to live by this light, thus increasing the opportunity of souls for change and development in their passage through earth to the life beyond.[5]

10-12. *The Rebuilt Walls with Open Gates.* —Invading aliens had been the agents of God's judgment; the rebuilding of the walls by for-

[5] *Christianity and Civilisation* (Wallingford, Pa.: Pendle Hill, 1947), pp. 46-52.

11 Therefore thy gates shall be open continually; they shall not be shut day nor night; that *men* may bring unto thee the forces of the Gentiles, and *that* their kings *may be* brought.	11 Your gates shall be open continually; day and night they shall not be shut; that men may bring to you the wealth of the nations, with their kings led in procession.
12 For the nation and kingdom that will not serve thee shall perish; yea, *those* nations shall be utterly wasted.	12 For the nation and kingdom that will not serve you shall perish; those nations shall be utterly laid waste.
13 The glory of Lebanon shall come unto thee, the fir tree, the pine tree, and the box together, to beautify the place of my sanctuary; and I will make the place of my feet glorious.	13 The glory of Lebanon shall come to you, the cypress, the plane, and the pine, to beautify the place of my sanctuary; and I will make the place of my feet glorious.

Jerusalem, the center of the earth, to which the nations will come with their tribute of devotion and homage. Historical questions must not be pressed. The poet's perspective is the time of felicity when the gates will be open continually. It is the time of God's favor.

10. In the time of salvation the foreign nations will rebuild the holy city, and **kings shall minister** to the holy people (cf. 49:23).

11. The **gates** will be open **day and night** that the nations, led by their kings, may have ready and constant access to the city. **The wealth of the nations:** Cf. vs. 5. Torrey renders, "That the host of the nations may be brought to thee." The writer of Revelation (21:24-27) is dependent upon this poem and provides a good commentary to its meaning (cf. Zech. 14:14).

12. This is a prosaic addition by a writer who misunderstood and misinterpreted the poet's mood and thought. He was probably led astray by interpreting the closing participle of the previous verse as meaning "led into captivity."

6. SIXTH STROPHE: THE TEMPLE WILL BE REBUILT (60:13-14)

Here the poem reaches its second great climax. The points of emphasis in the preceding strophes and the prevailingly cultic language converge upon the sanctuary, the place of God's tabernacling presence, and upon **Zion, the city of the LORD, the Holy One of Israel.** The wealth of nations (vss. 5-6, 8-9) and the altar offerings (vs. 7) come to Jerusalem and its temple. Here the forests of **Lebanon** offer their **glory** of precious wood for the construction of the sanctuary. The glory of the Lord has dawned upon the holy city, and from this supreme event of the divine epiphany everything else flows. The temple and the holy city, where his glory dwells, is to be made **glorious,** and the nations will come bending low to express their allegiance and fealty (cf. 4:4-6; 12:1-6; 35:1-10; Ezek. 1:1-28; 10:4-5; 11:22-23; 43:1-7; Hag. 2:6-7; Zech. 2:10-11; 8:3, 20-22).

13. The glory of Lebanon: Cf. 35:2. As Lebanon had yielded her gifts for the building of Solomon's temple (I Kings 5:8-10), so now she will come with her glorious

eigners is a sign of his forgiveness. Converted nations are no longer a menace, so the city's gates remain open to them continually. The interpolated vs. 12 does not fit the poetic pattern, and adds nothing to the content of the poem.

13-14. *Forest Trees Embellish the City of the Lord.*—The trees are probably to be used for building but possibly they were planted in the squares of the city. If the latter, the barrenness of the Judean highlands would throw this landscaping into prominence. The descendants of its destroyers are now attracted by its beauty, enter it reverently and speak of it as **the Zion of the holy One of Israel.** The N.T. wished the citizens of the church, even those who were slaves, to "adorn the teaching of God." The edifices in which we worship, the language and music we employ, above all the lives and service of Christians, should be lovely. Paul stresses doing Christian acts in fitting ways: doing "acts of mercy, with cheerfulness" (Rom. 12:8); "love . . . is not irritable or resentful" (I Cor. 13:5). The Christian hope is to be de-

14 The sons also of them that afflicted thee shall come bending unto thee; and all they that despised thee shall bow themselves down at the soles of thy feet; and they shall call thee, The city of the LORD, The Zion of the Holy One of Israel.	14 The sons of those who oppressed you 　　shall come bending low to you; and all who despised you 　　shall bow down at your feet; they shall call you the City of the LORD, 　　the Zion of the Holy One of Israel.
15 Whereas thou hast been forsaken and hated, so that no man went through *thee,* I will make thee an eternal excellency, a joy of many generations.	15 Whereas you have been forsaken and 　　hated, 　　with no one passing through, I will make you majestic for ever, 　　a joy from age to age.
16 Thou shalt also suck the milk of the Gentiles, and shalt suck the breast of kings: and thou shalt know that I the LORD *am* thy Saviour and thy Redeemer, the Mighty One of Jacob.	16 You shall suck the milk of nations, 　　you shall suck the breast of kings; and you shall know that I, the LORD, am 　　your Savior and your Redeemer, the Mighty One of 　　Jacob.

forests for the new sanctuary of the new age. The same trees are referred to in 41:19. **To beautify the place of my sanctuary:** Cf. vs. 7; Jer. 17:12. **The place of my feet:** Cf. Ezek. 43:7; Ps. 132:7; Lam. 2:1; I Chr. 28:2; also Targ., "And the place where my Shekinah dwells I will make glorious." The LXX omits the clause.

14. With the opening lines cf. 49:26. The last two lines bring the prophet's thought to a focus. The verse should be read in the spacious context of Jerusalem throughout the O.T.—the city of David, of Isaiah, of the Deuteronomist, of Ezekiel, of the Chronicler, of the psalmists and apocalyptists. Such a perspective is particularly valuable in view of the eschatological character of this poem. The Dead Sea Scroll has "all" before **sons.**

7. SEVENTH STROPHE: THE ETERNAL CITY (60:15-16)

Zion now confronts the turn of the ages. Once despised and rejected, she is now to be restored to be the pride and joy of all the earth for all time. The time of judgment is over and the new age is at hand. In this great reversal she will know Yahweh as her **Savior, Redeemer,** and **Mighty One.**

15. **Forsaken and hated:** Cf. 49:14-15; 54:6-7; 62:4. Ezek. 16:1-63 forms an extended narrative commentary on the forsaken Zion, restored and made **majestic for ever. With no one passing through:** This is a characteristic motif of the new age (cf. 34:10; Ezek. 14:15; 33:28; Zeph. 3:6). **A joy from age to age:** Zion enters the age of her felicity. The biblical motif of religious joy comes to a climax here.

16. The **nations** and their **kings** will be the nursing mothers of Zion (cf. 49:23; Ezek. 16:1-63). **And you shall know:** The last two lines repeat 49:26. This is another

fended "with gentleness and reverence." God's presence is seen chiefly in his devoted servants. **The place of my feet** when God walked among men was beautiful in all that Jesus was, said, and did. Followers of his, in whom is God's contemporary temple, must take thought for the charm of his Spirit's dwelling. Bunyan has recorded that it was the attractiveness of lowly Christians, which turned him toward their faith: "I fell into company with one poor man that made profession of religion; who, as I then thought, did talk pleasantly of the Scriptures and of religion. Wherefore, what he said, I betook me to my Bible, and began to take great	pleasure in reading." And when in Bedford he met "three or four poor women sitting at a door in the sun," and listened to their conversation, "Methought they spake as if joy did make them speak; they spake with such pleasantness." [6] 15-16. *The City Once Desolate Now Majestic Forever.*—A vast volume of commerce supplies all her wants. This material prosperity is hailed as evidence that the Lord is her Savior. The prophet's position is intelligible in the light of the experiences through which Jerusalem had <hr>[6] *Grace Abounding to the Chief of Sinners,* pars. 29, 37, 38.

17 For brass I will bring gold, and for iron I will bring silver, and for wood brass, and for stones iron: I will also make thy officers peace, and thine exactors righteousness.
 	
18 Violence shall no more be heard in thy land, wasting nor destruction within thy borders; but thou shalt call thy walls Salvation, and thy gates Praise.
	17 Instead of bronze I will bring gold,
	  and instead of iron I will bring silver;
	instead of wood, bronze,
	  instead of stones, iron.
	I will make your overseers peace
	  and your taskmasters righteousness.
	18 Violence shall no more be heard in your land,
	  devastation or destruction within your borders;
	you shall call your walls Salvation,
	  and your gates Praise.

characteristic climax of a poem in which all the strophes culminate in theocentric asseverations. The order of the great theologoumena is important: **Savior, Redeemer, and Mighty One of Jacob.** Such lines show how intimately related the poet is to the writer of chs. 40–55.

8. EIGHTH STROPHE: THE PROSPERITY AND PEACE OF THE NEW JERUSALEM (60:17-18)

The age of millennial felicity will see a transformation of Zion's outward and inward life. Here again the poet seems to recall the age of Solomon (I Kings 10:14, 17, 22, 27). The new Jerusalem will be infinitely more beautiful and noble than Solomon's city. The juxtaposition of the material and the spiritual is both Oriental and Hebraic in conception. Yet the accent falls upon **peace, righteousness, Salvation,** and, climactically, **Praise** (cf. vs. 6e). Second Isaiah has influenced both thought and expression (cf. 49:26; 54:11-12).

17. **Instead of:** The repetition emphasizes the reversal of conditions. Many scholars remove vs. 17cd as secondary, but the evidence for doing so is insufficient. **I will bring:** Lit., "I will cause to come." Throughout the poem the writer seems to be playing on the coming of various gifts and treasures to Jerusalem, and Yahweh's "causing them to come." **Overseers . . . taskmasters:** External authority and rule will be transformed to the reign of **peace** and **righteousness.**

18. The **violence** and **destruction** of war and conquest which had marked Israel's history will be no more. The picture is a vivid contrast to 59:9 ff. In Zechariah's Jerusalem there will be no need of walls (Zech. 2:2-3). Our poet uses the characteristic physical imagery of the historical city and transforms and deepens it into eschatological equivalents: the **walls** will be **Salvation;** the **gates** will be **Praise** (for the former cf. 26:1; for the latter 60:6c; on the messianic conception cf. 9:1-7; 11:1-9). The absence of a Messiah is notable.

passed and was still passing. Her startling restoration was miraculous—a manifest act of God. From the Christian point of view, "roaring trade" or any other success is no criterion of divine favor. The Cross gives us another measure of God's approval, but the Cross must not be viewed without the brightness of the Resurrection.

17-18. The City's Splendor Rests on Its Moral Order.—Its buildings are of metal, both for shining brilliance and for durability. **Peace** and **righteousness,** in contrast with its past and present condition, are its political and industrial rulers. Misrule and anarchy had been denounced

in immediately preceding poems; the restored city has government of another spiritual fiber. Milton asserted that "to govern a nation piously and justly, which only is to say happily, is for a spirit of the greatest size and divinest mettle." [7] To obtain such spirits the prophet personifies **peace** and **righteousness,** and lodges authority with them. Since God is sovereign, they are his subordinates. Under such rule the ills which had cursed the city—**violence, devastation,** and **destruction**—are unheard of. God's **Salvation** forms her walls, and **Praise** (i.e., fame attracting whole peoples) her gates.

[7] *Of Reformation in England,* Bk. II.

19 The sun shall be no more thy light by day; neither for brightness shall the moon give light unto thee: but the LORD shall be unto thee an everlasting light, and thy God thy glory.

20 Thy sun shall no more go down; neither shall thy moon withdraw itself: for the LORD shall be thine everlasting light,

19 The sun shall be no more
　　your light by day,
nor for brightness shall the moon
　　give light to you by night;[l]
but the LORD will be your everlasting light,
　　and your God will be your glory.
20 Your sun shall no more go down,
　　nor your moon withdraw itself;
for the LORD will be your everlasting light,

[l] One ancient Ms Gk Old Latin Tg: Heb lacks *by night*

9. NINTH STROPHE: GOD, THE EVERLASTING LIGHT AND GLORY OF ZION
(60:19-20)

The end of the poem returns to the theme announced at the beginning (vss. 1-3). In the introduction the **glory** sheds its supernal light throughout the world; here it is an **everlasting light.** There is no need for sun and moon, for Yahweh is Israel's light. It is possible that the writer is thinking of the first creative act of God (Gen. 1:3-5), the creation of light. Sun and moon and stars were created "for signs and for seasons and for days and years" (Gen. 1:14-19), but light appeared at the very beginning. So with the eschatological dawn there will be the light of God again. Peculiarly, sun and moon still remain, in the fashion of the poet throughout, but they are not needed (cf. Ps. 139:11-12). The theophany will be permanent, not a temporary revelation as to Moses and Israel on the mount or to Isaiah in the temple. Yahweh manifests himself as an eternal God (Gen. 21:23; Deut. 32:40; 33:27; Jer. 10:10; Dan. 7:9, 13, 22; 12:7). The repetition is effective, especially vss. 19e, 20c. The new element in the last line is reminiscent of the style of Second Isaiah.

19. By night: The phrase is absent from the M.T. but present in the LXX, O.L., Targ., and the Dead Sea Scroll. Actually there will be no night (cf. Rev. 21:23-25), and if it were not for the fact that the phrase **by night** is needed for metrical reasons, one could understand how the poet would omit any reference to it. Perhaps it was intentionally omitted by some copyist because of the palpable contradiction.

20. Your days of mourning shall be ended: It will be a time of perpetual joy (35:10; 51:11; 65:18-19; 66:10; also Rev. 21:4).

The first of these expressions is noteworthy. The church has too often thought it necessary to safeguard God's salvation. Books have been written and societies formed to "defend" the Bible, or evangelical doctrines, etc. Such "defenses" betray lack of faith in God. His saving ways with men are themselves defenses for all who accept them. One does not think that sunlight needs protection; it needs to be lived in and walked by, and it demonstrates its inestimable worth.

19-20. The Lord Himself Is Sun and Moon. —Evidently we are beyond earthly history. **Sun** and **moon** are symbols, and God himself is lightgiver to the restored city. This links the conclusion of this sublime poem with its beginning. Jerusalem's light has dawned upon her because her God lifts his face in favor.

The **light** of **God** as the source of wise government was the theme of almost the last utterance of the venerable Benjamin Franklin. In the Constitutional Convention in Philadelphia in 1787, he made a moving appeal for prayer:

In this situation of this assembly, groping, as it were, in the dark to find political truth, and scarce able to distinguish it when presented to us, how has it happened, Sir, that we have not hitherto once thought of humbly applying to the Father of Lights to illuminate our understandings? . . . I have lived, Sir, a long time; and the longer I live, the more convincing proofs I see of this truth, *that* GOD *governs in the affairs of men.* And, if a sparrow cannot fall to the ground without his notice, is it probable that an empire can rise without his aid? [8]

[8] John Bigelow, ed., *The Life of Franklin Written by Himself* (Philadelphia: J. B. Lippincott, 1879) III, 388.

and the days of thy mourning shall be ended.	and your days of mourning shall be ended.
21 Thy people also *shall be* all righteous: they shall inherit the land for ever, the branch of my planting, the work of my hands, that I may be glorified.	21 Your people shall all be righteous; they shall possess the land for ever, the shoot of my planting, the work of my hands, that I might be glorified.
22 A little one shall become a thousand, and a small one a strong nation: I the LORD will hasten it in his time.	22 The least one shall become a clan, and the smallest one a mighty nation; I am the LORD; in its time I will hasten it.

10. TENTH STROPHE: THE NEW PEOPLE OF THE NEW TIME (60:21-22)

21. All the people of the new Jerusalem will be **righteous** (*çaddîqîm*), but Volz is probably right in saying that the meaning here is "participating in salvation." This suits the context much better and forms a good sequence to the preceding verses. **They shall possess the land for ever:** The inheritance of the land forms a major and constant motif of the entire Bible, and it constitutes a central element in the eschatological hope. To the people who share in the salvation belongs the blessed land (cf. 49:8; 57:13; 58:14; 61:7; 65:9; Amos 9:15; Pss. 25:13; 37:9, 11; etc.). Redemption, election, call, covenant, and inheritance are indissolubly related. **The shoot of my planting, the work of my hands:** The words are in apposition with **people.** Yahweh planted his people (cf. 5:1-7; 61:3) and fashioned them that they might achieve his purpose and perform their supreme function by glorifying him in the world. It is to be observed how this poem on God's glory constantly strikes the note of glorifying and praising him.

22. Cf. 54:1 ff. This is another characteristic eschatological motif. The literal meaning of the word rendered **clan** is **thousand,** but the meaning is extended to clan or tribe. **I am the LORD:** The covenant formula, so frequent in Second Isaiah, here introduces the eschatological word which dominates the entire poem: **in its time I will hasten it.** At the same time it must be read as the climax of all the other climaxes of the poem (vss. 3-7cd, 9e, 9g, 14ef, 16cd, 18cd, 20cd). For a similar ending cf. 9:7.

In God's clear shining, Jerusalem's trials—her sunsets and eclipses—are forever over. The prophet is not foreseeing another world, but this world delivered by God's presence from its shadows and unwelcome changes. Emily Dickinson, as a lovely summer drew to its close, wrote to a friend:

> If roses had not faded, and frosts had never come, and one had not fallen here and there whom I could not waken, there were no need of other Heaven than the one below—and if God had been here this summer, and seen the things that *I* have seen—I guess that He would think His Paradise superfluous. Don't tell Him, for the world, though, for after all He's said about it, I should like to see what He *was* building for us.[9]

21-22. *Jerusalem's Inhabitants All Righteous.* —**Righteous,** i.e., in true accord with God and one another. Their godliness and fellowship

attest them as God's planting. The climax of the poem takes us to a deeper level than the emphasis upon commercial prosperity and civic magnificence. There is a similar progression in the vision of the New Jerusalem in Revelation, where the climax is the reign of the God revealed in Christ, and the usefulness, companionability, and characters of the citizens (Rev. 22:3-4). It is the city's spiritual quality which assures permanence, **I shall possess the land for ever.** Plato believed that "no state can be happy which is not designed by artists who imitate the heavenly pattern."[1] Israel had always been a small people at the mercy of great powers, Egypt, Assyria, Babylonia, and Persia. Now in God's reign the tiniest tribe becomes **a clan,** and this **smallest** people **a mighty nation.** Here is nationalism, but nationalism under God for the enlightenment of all peoples. A similar combination is found in John's vision where "they bring the glory and honor of the nations" into the holy city (Rev. 21:26). Mazzini de-

[9] Martha Dickinson Bianchi, *The Life and Letters of Emily Dickinson* (Boston: Houghton Mifflin Co., 1924), pp. 199-200.

[1] *The Republic* VI. 500 E.

61 The Spirit of the Lord God *is* upon me; because the LORD hath anointed me to preach good tidings unto the meek; he hath sent me to bind up the broken-

61 The Spirit of the Lord God is upon me,
because the LORD has anointed me
to bring good tidings to the afflicted;*m*
he has sent me to bind up the brokenhearted,

m Or *poor*

G. GLAD TIDINGS OF SALVATION TO ZION (61:1-11)

A poem such as this is not of an age but for all time. It is a superb product of the Oriental imagination at its best. The mood and temperament of the ancient Semite, the glowing imagery of an intensely poetic mind, the impressive feeling for the significance of words pervade the poem, more particularly, of course, at the beginning and the end. To the Christian its immortality is assured by the use made of the opening lines by Jesus at the beginning of his prophetic ministry. Like so many of the poems in chs. 40–66, this one has its own distinctiveness, and yet it is related not only to the other poems of the collection but also to the rest of the Bible.

The construction of the poem is similar to many other biblical compositions. The opening strophe (vss. 1-3) is paralleled by the close (vss. 10-11) much in the fashion of 40:1-11; 52:13–53:12, and other poems. The central section contains three strophes (vss. 4-5, 6-7, 8-9), which are to be read in the light of the framework in which they stand (so also 40:1-11; 52:13–53:12). The influence of Second Isaiah is apparent not only in the literary construction but in the content. In the opening lines we are reminded at once of the servant poems, especially 49:1-6; 50:4-5, which have the same monologue style. There are a number of verbal parallels to chs. 40–55, and the imagery is much like Second Isaiah's. On the other hand, there are differences too, and the affinities with chs. 56–66 are such as to argue for diversity of authorship; e.g., the poem has a close relation to its predecessor (ch. 60). The theme and the eschatological mood and outlook are the same. There is the same interpenetration of external and internal realities, and the same emphasis upon reversal of conditions. The same motifs occur: salvation and praise, joy and jubilation, the glorification of God, the righteous people, the everlasting salvation, sowing and planting, the foreign nations, and Zion. The words and phrases of one chapter are repeated in the other, and the same stylistic devices are present. The most striking difference is the intensely personal character of the monologue, but this is not sufficient to detach the poem from the others in chs. 60–62 (contra Volz).

1. FIRST STROPHE: THE PROPHETIC GOSPEL OF THE HERALD (61:1-3)

In the Gospel of Luke (4:16-20) Jesus begins his ministry in the synagogue at Nazareth with these words. The passage is notable for its personal tone. Its affinities

---

clared: "Nationality and humanity are . . . equally sacred. To forget humanity is to suppress the *aim* of our labours; to cancel the nation is to suppress the instrument by which to achieve the aim." [2]

The prophecy concludes with the emphatic divine assurance:

I am the LORD;
in its time I will hasten it.

Jerusalem's glory will startle men when it breaks upon them, and its dawning is in God's secret

[2] *The Holy Alliance of the Peoples* (London: Smith, Elder, & Co., 1891), p. 274.

purposes. He, not men, brings it to pass. This is the faith preached to men in evil days. Significantly, Plato proclaimed a similar trust in God as the one hope of even usually self-assured Athenians. He puts on Socrates' lips the words: "I would not have you ignorant that, in the present evil state of governments, whatever is saved and comes to good is saved by the power of God, as we may truly say." [3]

61:1-9. The Bringer of Good Tidings.—The sequence of thought in chs. 60–62 is reminiscent of that in 52:13–53:12. The future exaltation of the servant is first pictured, then his painful mission, and finally God's reward in the success of his mission. In both series of poems the serv-

[3] *Op. cit.* VI. 492.

hearted, to proclaim liberty to the captives, and the opening of the prison to *them that are* bound;

to proclaim liberty to the captives, and the opening of the prison[n] to those who are bound;

[n] Or *the opening of the eyes:* Heb *the opening*

---

with the servant passages have naturally suggested that the servant is speaking. Cannon ("Isaiah 61, 1-3 as Ebed-Jahweh Poem," *Zeitschrift für die alttestamentliche Wissenschaft,* LX [1929], 284-88), Procksch (*Theologie des A.T.,* p. 290), and others take the passage as an independent utterance belonging with the other servant poems. Torrey takes the whole chapter as a servant poem "messianically conceived." Orelli takes vss. 1-3, 10-11, the monologue section, as a servant poem; van Hoonacker so takes vss. 1-6. It must be admitted that there is not a little in the poem to remind us of the servant. But it is strange that the word itself, so frequent in Second Isaiah, is absent (cf. 50:4-9 where it is also absent). The glad tidings and the interest in Zion might easily apply to the servant, but the form and content of the strophe are not quite the same as in Second Isaiah. It is perhaps best to think of the prophet as the speaker here. It is surely a profound and impressive mission that is given to him; he is the eschatological prophet in a superlative degree. It is little wonder that some scholars have seen the hand of Third Isaiah in 52:13–53:12.

The first strophe is closely related to the last in its emphasis on righteousness, salvation, praise, and joy. If Third Isaiah is a literary unity (Elliger), then it would make an admirable opening. Observe how the speaker begins *in medias res.* The first person account of the prophetic call is stirring. Observe that the words **anointed** and **sent** stand in parallelism: the anointing is followed significantly by a single infinitive, **to preach good tidings** (the gospel), the sending, by six impressive infinitive phrases. The threefold use of **proclaim** (קרא, 1e, 2a, 3e) is reminiscent of Second Isaiah, but the usage is not the same. The eschatological stress on **the year of the Lord's favor,** the **day of vengeance** is unmistakable (vs. 2).

61:1. The Spirit of the Lord God is upon me: Cf. 42:1; 59:21; cf. also 11:2; Num. 24:2; Mic. 3:8; Zech. 7:12. In general the pre-exilic literary prophets avoid the use of the Spirit as the mediator of their inspiration, perhaps in opposition to the ecstasy of the early *nebhî'îm* (I Sam. 10:9-13). In Ezekiel the spirit plays a central role. Observe that the divine name here is the same as in 50:4-9. The Hebrew is "Lord Yahweh." The Dead Sea Scroll omits **Lord. Because the Lord has anointed me:** The association of anointing and spirit is significant. See especially the anointing of David in I Sam. 16:14-23, and above all the remarkable last words of David in II Sam. 23:1-7. Kissane thinks that "anoint" here means no more than "designate" or "appoint," but the way in which it is related to the Spirit and the charismatic proclamation of the gospel

---

ant is so individualized that he appears a prophetic man; but in both it is the nation as a spiritual community that is primarily in mind. The bringer of salvation recalls the address in the initial vision in 40:9.

The speaker in ch. 61 does not call himself the servant, but the mission he sets before himself recalls that of the servant in 42:1; 48:16; 50:4. He is an evangelist, consecrated and endowed of the Lord, to declare the coming of the year of divine favor and a day of judgment. He is sent primarily to the distressed and downhearted people of God. They are described as **the afflicted** (akin to our "underprivileged"), **the brokenhearted, the captives,** and **the bound** (probably not those in prison or captivity but

those caught in a confining and oppressive social situation; cf. 58:6). The confused and chaotic years which followed the return from exile brought misgovernment, poverty, and moral disintegration to those who had come back buoyed with lofty hopes. The people, both physically and spiritually wretched, needed **good tidings** as sorely as had the exiles in Babylon. Hopes unfulfilled had brought frustration of soul. Those who mourned **in Zion** were the spiritual successors of Ezekiel's conscientious citizens who sighed over its abominations (Ezek. 9:4).

1-3. *The Evangelist's Prospectus of His Task.* —The words are hallowed for Christians by their use by Jesus at Nazareth to outline his

2 To proclaim the acceptable year of the LORD, and the day of vengeance of our God; to comfort all that mourn;	2 to proclaim the year of the LORD's favor, and the day of vengeance of our God; to comfort all who mourn;

surely stresses the solemnity and divine origin of the prophet's task in an almost unique way. Yet cf. I Kings 19:16; Ps. 105:15; also "sanctify" or "consecrate" in Jer. 1:5 (הקדשתי). The Targ. reads, "The prophet said, 'The spirit of prophecy before the Lord God [Yahweh Elohim] is upon me.'" **He has sent me:** The whole strophe forms a single sentence; the third verb is elaborated at great length. When Yahweh calls his servants—the patriarchs, Moses, Amos, Isaiah, and Israel herself—he sends them and they go. They all know that they bear a commission. **To bring good tidings:** See 40:9; 41:27; 52:7. The word **afflicted** may also be rendered **poor** and **meek,** which later suggested "pious" and "humble." The LXX has **poor** (cf. Luke 4:18-19). **To bind up the brokenhearted:** The words **afflicted** and **brokenhearted** are parallel; the prophet must heal their wounds (cf. Ps. 147:3). **To proclaim liberty to the captives:** The expression is used frequently in connection with the liberation of the year of Jubilee (Lev. 25:10 [H]) or the manumission of slaves (Jer. 34:8, 15, 17; cf. also Isa. 42:22; 45:13; 49:9; 51:14. **The opening of the prison to those who are bound:** Torrey follows the Greek in reading "blind"; cf. 42:7; and especially Luke 4:18 "recovering of sight to the blind"). The phrase **of the prison** is not in the Hebrew.

2. **To proclaim the year of the LORD's favor:** Cf. 49:8. In Luke 4:18-19 Jesus closes his quotation with this line. **The day of vengeance** ["requital"]: The rendering **vengeance** (cf. 59:16 ff.) is dubious (see George E. Mendenhall, "God of Vengeance, Shine Forth," *Wittenberg Bulletin* XLV [1948], 37-42; Mendenhall adduces a number of important

mission (Luke 4:17-19). They set forth the work of the spiritual community in Israel and that of the Christian church, its ministers and members.

(a) The mission is assigned by God. No one would take it upon himself. With the divine call goes the equipment with the **Spirit.** The Spirit is God personally present and active in his appointed agents. No task is ever given without the supply of wisdom and power to discharge it. Ignorance or forgetfulness of her divine force is the church's and Christians' most hampering weakness. On the arch of an old Saxon church in England is a hand reaching up in supplication; above the hand is the word "God"; at one side are the words "I will"; and at the other the words "I can." When his people devote themselves to work God lays upon them, they may be confident of ability through him to accomplish it (II Cor. 3:5).

(b) **To bring good tidings, . . . to proclaim.** Here is the evangel. It is tidings from and of God (cf. Mark 1:14). One may recall the news of the armistice to war-weary peoples in 1918, and of the surrender of Germany, then of Japan, in 1945. The gospel is never advice, or explanation of current events; it is tidings of what God has done with consequent liberation of men's spirits.

(c) In this instance it was tidings of **the year of the LORD's favor** and **the day** of [his] **vengeance.** The contrast between **year** and **day** is

important: grace is God's constant attitude toward men; vengeance is an occasional judgment necessary to remove obstacles to his grace. The restoration to their homeland had been a year of grace; now another was needed to bring deliverance to these politically, economically, and spiritually bound people. It is often pointed out that in quoting this passage our Lord stopped with **the year of the LORD's favor.** He came "to seek and to save." But social and religious conditions in postexilic Israel demanded the cleansing of judgment. The N.T. church, looking back upon Christ's coming and out upon his Spirit's work, saw both salvation and judgment (Luke 2:34; II Cor. 2:15-16; John 9:39). It is always a critical juncture when the good tidings of God is heard; one is either the better or the worse, never the same, after being confronted with it.

(d) Those to whom this evangelist was sent were discontented with their own and their nation's condition. They were those **who mourn in Zion.** In the late nineteenth century Bagehot summed up the social order: "By dull care, by stupid industry, a certain social fabric somehow exists; people contrive to go out to their work, and to find work to employ them actually until the evening; body and soul are kept together,—and this is what mankind have to show for their six thousand years of toil and trouble."[4]

[4] *Letters on the French Coup d'Etat,* Letter II, Jan. 15, 1852.

| 3 To appoint unto them that mourn in Zion, to give unto them beauty for ashes, the oil of joy for mourning, the garment of praise for the spirit of heaviness; that they might be called Trees of righteousness, The planting of the LORD, that he might be glorified. | 3 to grant to those who mourn in Zion — to give them a garland instead of ashes, the oil of gladness instead of mourning, the mantle of praise instead of a faint spirit; that they may be called oaks of righteousness, the planting of the LORD, that he may be glorified. |

Ugaritic usages of the term where the plain meaning is "rescue" or "requite"). The line is not included in Jesus' citation. Redemption and deliverance are the indissoluble elements of eschatological time. **To comfort all who mourn:** Second Isaiah's great message of comfort is echoed here in the poet's own way.

3. To grant to those who mourn: The line may be a marginal variant. It disturbs the meter. The mourners could be either **those who mourn in Zion** or those who mourn for her. The words **garland instead of ashes** are a paronomasia (פְּאֵר אֵפֶר). The word for **garland** is from the same root as "beautify" or "glorify" (cf. 60:7, 9, 19), a symbol of joy, festivity, and dignity. Perhaps we should translate "turban" (cf. vs. 10). **The oil of joy:** Cf. vss. 10-12. Aromatic unguents of fine quality were used at the festivals (cf. Pss. 23:5; 45:7; Luke 7:46). **The mantle of praise . . . a faint spirit:** Observe how in this poem, as in the preceding, the accent falls on **praise. A faint spirit** signifies discouragement. **That they may be called oaks of righteousness:** For the relative clause the Hebrew has the active participle, "calling." The **oaks of righteousness** recall 60:21, and the meaning is paraphrased in the closing strophe (cf. Pss. 1:3; 52:8; Jer. 17:8). The citizens of Zion

---

After the passage of the Fugitive Slave Law, Emerson, in an address at Concord, declared:

There is infamy in the air. I have a new experience. I wake in the morning with a painful sensation, which I carry about all day, and which, when traced home, is the odious remembrance of that ignominy . . . , which robs the landscape of beauty, and takes the sunshine out of every hour.[5]

Mazzini, at sixteen, "childishly determined to dress always in black, as in mourning for his country."[6] Such a social conscience, sad for one's community "in the clutch of circumstance," was in Jesus' mind when he said, "Blessed are they that mourn" (Matt. 5:4).

The classes pictured in this poem are all represented in our mid-twentieth century. Millions have been made abjectly poor; millions more are brokenhearted over the meager achievements of men's sacrifices for liberty and justice; sensitive spirits feel themselves to be captives of dominant political and social forces. Like the postexilic dwellers in Jerusalem, men are wistful for an emancipating jubilee, proclaiming liberty from oppressions to mind and spirit.

(e) In the church, as in the world at large, there is a **spirit of heaviness** ("a failing spirit";

the adjective is the same as in 42:3, "dimly burning"). The twentieth century began in high hopes; when it was half spent, men grew very sober. Many, like Hamlet, have felt our world "a sterile promontory," from which man seems bent on hurling himself in mass suicide. The good tidings of God brought rapturous change of mood (vs. 3). Modern pessimism is essentially atheistic. Where Christian faith is vigorous, there is gaiety of soul. In the second century the angel said to Hermas: "Put away sorrow from thyself, for she is the sister of doubtful-mindedness. . . . Clothe thyself with cheerfulness, which hath favor with God always. . . . For every cheerful man worketh good, and thinketh good, and despiseth sadness; but the sad man is always committing sin" (Herm. Mand. X. 1.1; 3.1). Wilhelm Herrmann, in his seminar in Marburg in May, 1899, said that Paul's "rejoice in the Lord" is the carrying out of Jesus' first commandment to love God, for it means "to have one's heart's true joy in him." Such jubilant servants of God are like evergreen trees, **oaks of righteousness.** The oak or terebinth has a sturdy trunk and permanent foliage. It stands out in the landscape which for most of the year is dry and brown. It is a symbol of a spirit linked with God, his **planting** (cf. 60:21). Writing from a very different region, the Yosemite Valley, John Muir said: "Miles and miles of tree scripture along the sky,

[5] O. W. Firkins, *Ralph Waldo Emerson* (Boston: Houghton Mifflin Co., 1915), p. 136.
[6] *Essays*, p. viii.

4 ¶ And they shall build the old wastes, they shall raise up the former desolations, and they shall repair the waste cities, the desolations of many generations.

5 And strangers shall stand and feed your flocks, and the sons of the alien *shall be* your plowmen and your vinedressers.

6 But ye shall be named The priests of the LORD: *men* shall call you The ministers of our God: ye shall eat the riches of the Gentiles, and in their glory shall ye boast yourselves.

4 They shall build up the ancient ruins,
　　they shall raise up the former devasta-
　　　tions;
　　they shall repair the ruined cities,
　　　the devastations of many generations.

5 Aliens shall stand and feed your flocks,
　　foreigners shall be your plowmen and
　　　vine-dressers;
6 but you shall be called the priests of the
　　LORD,
　　men shall speak of you as the ministers
　　　of our God;
　　you shall eat the wealth of the nations,
　　　and in their riches you shall glory.

---

will be splendid and mighty in their stature of righteousnes. They are the Lord's planting **that he may be glorified** (cf. 44:23; 49:5).

2. SECOND STROPHE: RESTORATION AND PROSPERITY (61:4-5)

4-5. Here begin the "good tidings." The cities long since laid waste will rise again (cf. 49:8; 58:12; 60:10). The **devastations of many generations** reach far back into the past, how far the poet does not tell us; perhaps he is thinking of the long history of Israel's "warfare." The words **ancient** (*'ôlām*) and **many generations** (*dôr wādhôr*) suggest "from time immemorial." All the past will be undone. Foreigners, now aware of the divine plan of salvation, will shepherd the flocks and serve as plowmen and vine-dressers. Torrey deletes vs. 5 since he thinks it is contrary to the prophet's characteristic kindly attitude, and Volz deletes both vs. 5 and vs. 6 as an intrusion into the structure of the poem. But their absence would create a gap and mar the structure. It is possible that two lines of vs. 5 have fallen out since the strophe does not have the characteristic conclusion of the others.

3. THIRD STROPHE: ZION'S SPIRITUAL PRE-EMINENCE AND MATERIAL PROSPERITY (61:6-7)

A continuation of the description of the new age. The strophe is a counterpart to vss. 4-5. The deletion of the introductory word (Torrey) and the change of the second person to the third is unnecessary. The emphasis is upon the second person. The strophe begins, as frequently in Hebrew, with the sudden shift of address.

6. Priests, . . . ministers of our God: Zion's unique status will be recognized; among the peoples of the world she will serve as **priests** just as the Aaronids did in Israel (cf. Exod. 19:6; I Pet. 2:9); she will perform the priestly functions of instruction and intercession (cf. 45:14-15; 60:14; also 66:21). Note the universality implied in **our God. The wealth of the nations:** Cf. 60:5, 11, 16. **And in their riches you shall glory:** The word for

---

a bible that will one day be read! The beauty of its letters and sentences have burned me like fire through all these Sierra seasons. Yet I cannot interpret their hidden thoughts. They are terrestrial expressions of the sun." [7]

4-6. Zion's Citizens Become Priests to Mankind.—The background is the city in ruins. The prophet is sure of renovation (cf. 58:12). In a note to *Hellas*, Shelley wrote: "Prophecies

of wars, and rumours of wars, &c. may safely be made by poet or prophet in any age, but to anticipate however darkly a period of regeneration and happiness is a more hazardous exercise of the faculty which bards possess or feign." [8]

6-7. Zion's Spiritual Function and Material Glory.—Priests of the LORD. A new turn to the earlier teaching of the universal mission

[7] W. F. Badè, *The Life and Letters of John Muir* (Boston: Houghton Mifflin Co., 1924), II, 24.

[8] *Poetical Works*, ed. H. B. Forman (London: Reeves & Turner, 1880), III, 97.

7 ¶ For your shame *ye shall have* double; and *for* confusion they shall rejoice in their portion: therefore in their land they shall possess the double: everlasting joy shall be unto them.

8 For I the LORD love judgment, I hate robbery for burnt offering; and I will direct

7 Instead of your shame you shall have a
      double portion,
   instead of dishonor you*o* shall rejoice
      in your*p* lot;
   therefore in your*p* land you*o* shall possess
      a double portion;
   yours*q* shall be everlasting joy.

8 For I the LORD love justice,
   I hate robbery and wrong;*r*
   I will faithfully give them their recom-
      pense,

o Heb *they*
p Heb *their*
q Heb *theirs*
r Or *robbery with a burnt offering*

riches is the same as that for **glory** (*kābhôdh;* cf. 60:13). The verb תתימרו is difficult. The Dead Sea Scroll and some versions (Vulg., *superbietis,* Syriac, Targ.) derive it from the root אמר, which in the Hithpael (see Ps. 94:4) may mean "act proudly," **boast,** or **glory** (Gesenius and Buhl, *Hebräisches und aramäisches Handwörterbuch, s.v* ימר). The LXX has θαυμασθήσεσθε. Torrey emends to תתיקרו, and renders, "and with their splendor shall be glorified." Others emend to תתפארו, "array or beautify yourselves" (Köhler, Kissane); still others take the verb as a variant, meaning "exchange," and render, "to their glory [riches] you shall succeed" (cf. ASV mg.). It is best perhaps to follow the versions and render **glory** (so RSV). A good alternative is the ASV's "you shall succeed."

7. The Hebrew text is out of order. The LXX reproduces only the last two lines. The Hebrew for the first line reads, "Instead of your double shame and dishonor, they shall rejoice in their lot." One is reminded at once of 40:2, and possibly an allusion is concealed here. The usual but not satisfactory solution is to read, "For their shame was double, disgrace and insult their portion." It is unduly harsh in the general context, and does not prepare the way for the following line. One might perhaps construe the line as highly elliptical and render as in the RSV, where the third person of the Hebrew is emended to the second person (so the Dead Sea Scroll). **Everlasting joy:** Cf. vss. *3c,* 10; a characteristic strophic conclusion.

4. FOURTH STROPHE: THE BLESSED PEOPLE OF THE EVERLASTING COVENANT (61:8-9)

Yahweh, who loves **justice** and hates **wrong,** recompenses his people with an ever-lasting covenant. All the nations will acknowledge Israel as the people blessed of the Lord.

in 42:1, 4, etc. Israel had been called to be "a kingdom of priests" (Exod. 19:6). Now the emphasis is on her exercising this priesthood for mankind. In return the nations serve her by performing life's ordinary labor. Roles are reversed: rich and powerful peoples minister to Israel, and this despised people ministers to them in the things of God. This general priesthood, independent of the lineage of Aaron and Levi, suggests an eloquent tribute paid to Dissenting Ministers:

They were true Priests. They set up an image in their own minds, it was truth: they worshiped an idol there, it was justice. They looked on man as

their brother, and only bowed the knee to the Highest. Separate from the world, they walked humbly with their God, and lived in thought with those who had borne testimony of a good conscience, with the spirits of just men in all ages.*9*

The N.T. sees the church a kingdom of priests, and every Christian called to mediate God's fellowship with men (I Pet. 2:5, 9; Rev. 1:6, etc.). The perquisites of Jewish nationalism stressed in this passage are of course omitted.

8-9. *The Blessed People of the Everlasting Covenant.*—The present wretched background

9 William Hazlitt, *Political Essays,* "On Court Influence."

their work in truth, and I will make an everlasting covenant with them.

9 And their seed shall be known among the Gentiles, and their offspring among the people: all that see them shall acknowledge them, that they *are* the seed *which* the Lord hath blessed.

10 I will greatly rejoice in the Lord, my soul shall be joyful in my God; for he hath clothed me with the garments of sal-

and I will make an everlasting covenant with them.

9 Their descendants shall be known among the nations,
   and their offspring in the midst of the peoples;
all who see them shall acknowledge them,
   that they are a people whom the Lord has blessed.

10 I will greatly rejoice in the Lord,
   my soul shall exult in my God;
for he has clothed me with the garments of salvation,
   he has covered me with the robe of righteousness,

---

8. For I the Lord, etc: "I am Yahweh who loves justice." The reversal of conditions, so constant a theme of both chs. 60 and 61, reaches its culmination here. **Robbery and wrong:** The Hebrew reads **robbery with a burnt offering.** But this is obviously not the writer's meaning. It is not the sin of Zion but of her oppressors that he has in mind. The word for **burnt offering** should be pointed to read "iniquity" (so several Hebrew MSS, LXX, Targ., and Syriac; cf. Ps. 37:28). **Faithfully:** Not only Yahweh's love of justice but also his faithfulness impels him to **recompense** his people. **Everlasting covenant:** Cf. 54:10; 55:3; 59:21; also Gen. 9:9-17 [P]; Jer. 32:40; Ezek. 16:60).

9. The everlasting covenant reflects itself in the children and children's children; the nations will recognize it, and those who see them shall acknowledge what they see, that **they are a people whom the Lord has blessed.**

5. Fifth Strophe: A Hymn of Thanksgiving and Praise (61:10-11)

An eschatological hymn follows the eschatological event (cf. 42:10-13; 45:8). The prophet speaks as usual from the standpoint of fulfillment. Language, literary form, imagery, and literary parallels are messianic. These lines should be read as the conclusion to the proclamation of glad tidings (vss. 1-3). The prophet speaks as the representative of Zion: her words are his words.

10. I will greatly rejoice: Cf. vss. 1-3, 7d; also 12:1-2; 25:1, 9; 41:16; 51:3; also Luke 1:46-55, 68-79. The Targ. introduces the song with "Jerusalem has said." **He has clothed me:** Cf. vs. 3; 49:18. The festal **garments of salvation** and the **robe of righteousness** are appropriate to the occasion of Yahweh's institution of an everlasting covenant and are worn by the people whom he has blessed. **He has covered:** "Wrapped" or "clad" (cf. 59:17; Ps. 104:2). **As a bridegroom decks himself with a garland:** The time of rejoicing

---

stands out in the words **robbery**—whether by fellow Israelites or the heathen—and **wrong.** "The prosperity of the future shall be a twofold recompense for the miseries of the past and the present."[1] Everlasting joy is theirs in **an everlasting covenant,** which forever assures their posterity a position of honor among the peoples. Israel's glory is part of her missionary equipment, capturing men's eyes and turning them Godward (cf. Matt. 5:16).

10-11. *A Hymn of Thanksgiving.*—Characteristic of these prophecies is this outburst of

[1] Skinner, *Isaiah, Chapters XL-LXVI,* p. 188.

gladness from the evangelist people. It is a crippling weakness of Christians that we do not think often enough of God and his goodness to us to be overwhelmed by his greatness and grace, and moved to ecstasy. The early church felt herself in a springtime of new life. A second-century Roman poet wrote: *Ver novum, ver jam canorum, ver renatus orbis est.*[2] Coventry Patmore tells us that as a boy of eleven, while reading a devotional book, "it struck me

[2] "New spring, singing spring, spring, the world reborn." Quoted in T. R. Glover, *The Christian Tradition* (London: Methuen & Co., 1913), p. 131.

vation, he hath covered me with the robe of righteousness, as a bridegroom decketh *himself* with ornaments, and as a bride adorneth *herself* with her jewels.

11 For as the earth bringeth forth her bud, and as the garden causeth the things

as a bridegroom decks himself with a garland,
and as a bride adorns herself with her jewels.

11 For as the earth brings forth its shoots, and as a garden causes what is sown in it to spring up,

---

is like a wedding feast. As in vs. 1 Yahweh clothes the prophet with his spirit and anoints him, so here the prophet as the mouthpiece of Zion is clothed with wedding garments for the day of salvation. The eschatological context of both passages accounts for the figure. The verb in the Hebrew means "to function as a priest," which gives no sense in the context. Perhaps the best reading is יכין, "prepare." **Garland:** Cf. vs. 3. To prepare one's turban is to wind it about the head. For wedding imagery, especially in an eschatological context, see Jer. 33:11; Matt. 22:2; Rev. 21:2.

11. The introductory word connects immediately with the foregoing verse and articulates its meaning (cf. the similar imagery of vs. 3). As surely as the earth puts forth

---

what an exceedingly fine thing it would be if there really was a God."[3] This exhilarating quality in religion is voiced by Bliss Carman:

> Lord of my heart's elation.
> Spirit of things unseen,
>
> .   .   .   .   .   .
>
> Be thou my exaltation
> Or fortitude of mien,
> Lord of the world's elation,
> Thou breath of things unseen![4]

Such rejoicing in God alters the spiritual climate, clears the atmosphere so that his face is more plain, and restores morale.

The metaphor of **bridegroom** and **bride** illustrates the mutual delight of God and his redeemed people. It is a metaphor employed for earth's loveliness in spring.

> What is so sweet and dear
> As a prosperous morn in May,
> The confident prime of the day,
> And the dauntless youth of the year,
> When nothing that asks for bliss,
> Asking aright, is denied,
> And half of the world a bridegroom is,
> And half of the world a bride?[5]

God's gracious presence shines upon his people as the spring sunlight on a garden, and **righteousness and praise** bloom like flowers. God's garden is lovely not alone for the delight of his people, but also as a witness to mankind. The church's supreme attraction is her people's lives. The soul of a saint points as cogently to

an existing spiritual world as the coloring of a flower points to the reality of sunlight. The early defenders of the Christian faith did not hesitate to adduce the characters of the members of the church as evidence:

> Among us you will find uneducated persons, and artisans, and old women, who, if they are unable in words to prove the benefit of our doctrine, yet by their deeds exhibit the benefit arising from their persuasion of its truth: they do not rehearse speeches, but exhibit good works; when struck, they do not strike again; when robbed, they do not go to law; they give to those that ask of them, and love their neighbours as themselves.[6]

This is "the argument from the aureole." When John Wesley was attacked by leaders of the Church of England, he wrote the bishop of London:

> What have been the consequences . . . of the doctrines I have preached for nine years last past? . . . The habitual drunkard that was is now temperate in all things; the whoremonger now flees fornication; he that stole, steals no more, but works with his hands; he that cursed or swore, perhaps at every sentence, has now learned to serve the Lord with fear and rejoice unto Him with reverence; those formerly enslaved to various habits of sin are now brought to uniform habits of holiness. These are demonstrable facts: I can name the men, with their places of abode.[7]

In the nineteenth century Charles Darwin reported: "The lesson of the missionary is the enchanter's wand. . . . The march of improvement consequent on the introduction of Christianity through the South Seas probably stands

---

[3] Edmund Gosse, *Coventry Patmore* (New York: Charles Scribner's Sons, 1905), p. 7.

[4] *"Veni Creator."* Used by permission of Dodd, Mead & Co. from *Bliss Carman's Poems.*

[5] "Ode in May," from *The Poems of Sir William Watson, 1878-1935* (London: George R. Harrap & Co., 1936). Used by permission.

[6] Athenagoras *A Plea for the Christians* XI.

[7] *Letters*, ed. Telford, II, 290. Letter dated June 11, 1747.

that are sown in it to spring forth; so the Lord God will cause righteousness and praise to spring forth before all the nations.

so the Lord God will cause righteousness and praise
to spring forth before all the nations.

62
For Zion's sake will I not hold my peace, and for Jerusalem's sake I

62
For Zion's sake I will not keep silent, and for Jerusalem's sake I will not rest,

---

its growth with unfailing certainty, so the Lord will cause his salvation to spring forth before all nations (cf. 42:9; 43:19; 45:8). The finale is reminiscent of 55:10 ff. To the very close the poet unites the physical and the spiritual, the world of nature and the time of salvation. He employs his maximum imagery to body forth the year of the Lord's favor to Zion.

H. The Messianic People (62:1-12)

The final poem in the trilogy centers in the messianic people. Its theme has been anticipated in the previous poems. Zion's distinctive titles (cf. 60:14ef; 61:3ef, 6ab, 9) express the new relationship between Yahweh and his people in the new age. The glory of God transforms the life and character of the people. In the day of his coming the people's fortunes will be reversed, and all nations will see Zion's vindication.

Like the other poems in this group, this poem is patterned both in thought and style after Second Isaiah. Yet there are sharp differences also. The poet weaves his materials from the supreme creations of his master (40:1-11; 52:1-12; 54:1-17). The structure of the poem corresponds exactly to 40:1-11; 61:1-11. The opening and closing strophes (vss. 1-3, 10-12) frame three strophes of approximately the same length (vss. 4-5, 6-7, 8-9). It is possible to cast the poem into three strophes (vss. 1-5, 6-9, 10-12), but close examination shows that the former analysis is more likely. The unity of each strophe and the closing lines of each reveal careful literary craftsmanship. The parallelism of the lines is especially striking. The meter of vss. 1-3 is 3+3, of vss. 4-12, 3+2. The

---

by itself in the records of history." [8] It hardly "stands by itself." That shrewd observer of men, Li Hung Chang, said of General Gordon: "It is a direct blessing from Heaven the coming of this British Gordon. . . . He is superior in manner and bearing to any of the foreigners whom I have come into contact with, and does not show outwardly that conceit which makes most of them repugnant in my sight." [9] A secretary of the president of China in 1916 spoke of reading the books of the religious teachers of his people; he asked, "What has Jesus which they seem to lack?" and answered his own query: "He seems to possess the capacity to create a more delicate conscience." This is the **righteousness** which the Lord God causes **to spring forth before all the nations.**

The Isaianic "gospeler" or bringer of good tidings claimed our Lord's attention. He is referred to in the sermon at Nazareth (Luke 4:16-27), and in the message sent to the Baptist as corroboration of the arrival of the messianic

kingdom (Matt. 11:2-6). Jesus was wary of accepting the title of Messiah; it had acquired meanings alien to his conviction of what God's representative should be. But this evangelist of God's gracious reign was congenial with his conviction of his mission. "The year of the Lord's favor" became fundamental in Christian thought to describe the new era. "Grace is goodness that triumphs over all reasons to the contrary." [1] To the frustrated people of the prophet's time and to us today it is the aspect of God which is "good tidings." It is not a summons "to build the kingdom of God"—a concept frequently stressed in the early twentieth century—but to proclaim that "the kingdom of heaven is pressing in" (the verb in Matt. 11:12 may be a middle as well as a passive), for the initiative and power are God's, but we may "with resolute purpose" lay hold upon it.

62:1-3. The Prophet's Prayer for Zion's Vindication.—The speaker is no longer the community but the evangelist of ch. 61. Zion is wrapped in night; but her triumph will arrive like morning **brightness** and like **a burning**

[8] *The Voyage of the Beagle* (New York: P. F. Collier & Son, 1909), p. 449.

[9] Lytton Strachey, *Eminent Victorians* (New York: G. P. Putnam's Sons, 1918), p. 253.

[1] P. Carnegie Simpson, *Life of Principal Rainy*, I, 423.

| will not rest, until the righteousness thereof go forth as brightness, and the salvation thereof as a lamp *that* burneth. | until her vindication goes forth as brightness, and her salvation as a burning torch. |

imagery is messianic, as is shown not only by the figures themselves but by their affinity to other messianic passages.

1. First Strophe: A Crown of Beauty (62:1-3)

The poem opens in the personal vein of ch. 61. The prophet's task is to proclaim unremittingly the coming of the day of vindication and salvation, which will be signalized by the new name.

62:1. It is the prophet who speaks in these lines, not the Lord. In view of his commission (61:1-3) and his vision of the great theophany with its attendant blessings (60:1 ff.), he will not refrain from proclaiming unceasingly the year of the Lord's favor and interceding for its coming (cf. vss. 6-7). He will preach and pray until the promise of salvation is fulfilled. **For Zion's sake . . . and for Jerusalem's sake:** The accent of the prophet's thought is finely expressed in the opening phrases. The thought of the whole poem flows from them. **I will not keep silent:** Elsewhere it is the silence of Yahweh that is spoken of (42:14; 57:11; 64:12; 65:6); this change in point of view is characteristic of our poet throughout. He uses the old materials but puts them in new settings. He will not be silent until God breaks his silence at his coming. It is often supposed that a long interval elapsed between these words and the former poem, but the situation is quite the contrary. The mood of urgency and joy and praise continues to stir the prophet. **I will not rest:** Cf. vs. 7a. The LXX reads "relax" and the Dead Sea Scroll has another verb meaning "to be silent," possibly because it was written from memory. **Until her vindication:** Cf. 61:11. The preposition is important (cf. vs. 7b). The prophet will proclaim and intercede until the dawn of the day of **salvation.** The word çedhāqāh, usually **righteousness** (KJV, ASV), is properly rendered **vindication.** As frequently in Second Isaiah, it bears this active connotation. The prophet is all absorbed in his intense expectancy. **Brightness** and **burning torch** are reminiscent of the glory of the Lord in ch.

torch. The church often feels her present condition shrouded. Men look down on her with contempt or ignore her. She longs to have her role as God's agent in the salvation of mankind made patent to all. This happens, however, only occasionally. Her steadfast resistance of tyranny under Hitler's regime is an instance. Walter Lippmann, who had disparaged her as negligible in human affairs,[2] a few years later—when in Germany, Holland, Norway, etc., she almost alone stood up and refused to be cowed by Nazi despotism—paid her this tribute:

It is no accident that the only open challenge to the totalitarian state has come from men of deep religious faith. For in their faith they are vindicated as immortal souls, and from this enhancement of their dignity they find the reason why they must offer a perpetual challenge to the dominion of men over men.[3]

Such vindication is rarely patent, for, like her Lord, the church is in the midst of men as one

that serves, and her service is not of the kind to command publicity and claim attention. She loses herself in her unassuming labors; but such ministry is the supreme attestation of her fellowship with the Most High God.

You shall be called by a new name. This name is mysterious, a secret known only to God (cf. 65:15; Rev. 2:17; 3:12). It is the symbol of closer intimacy with him, and a consequent holier character. It may be hinted at in the names in vss. 4 and 12, but is not necessarily any of these. He who makes his people glorious alone can say what Zion's nature will be. We do not know what we shall be (I John 3:2). God's gifts outdistance man's loftiest expectations. In the heavenly Jerusalem his name is upon his servants' foreheads (Rev. 22:4).

I will not keep silent. This is the prophet's commitment to persistent prayer for the vindication of his people. He is an insistent soul, like Simeon Stylites, "Battering the gates of heaven with storms of prayer."[4] The Lord has promised to rebuild Jerusalem in glory, but his servant is irked by the long delay. God appears "slack

[2] *A Preface to Morals* (New York: The Macmillan Co., 1929).
[3] *The Good Society*, p. 382.
[4] Tennyson, "St. Simeon Stylites," st. vii.

2 And the Gentiles shall see thy right-eousness, and all kings thy glory: and thou shalt be called by a new name, which the mouth of the LORD shall name.

3 Thou shalt also be a crown of glory in the hand of the LORD, and a royal diadem in the hand of thy God.

2 The nations shall see your vindication,
and all the kings your glory;
and you shall be called by a new name
which the mouth of the LORD will give.

3 You shall be a crown of beauty in the hand of the LORD,
and a royal diadem in the hand of your God.

---

60. Zion is still plunged in darkness (cf. 50:10; also 59:9-10), but the light is about to dawn (58:8).

2. The nations . . . and all the kings: Cf. 60:3; 61:11. In 40:5 all flesh will see the **glory** of the Lord. The glory reveals itself in action: the vindication and salvation of Zion, which all the nations will behold. The kings with their power and glory will now see the glory of Zion. **A new name:** According to the ancients, the name contains within it the interior character and being of the people; a new name means a new people (cf. 1:26; 56:5; 58:12; 60:14, 18). In Jer. 33:16 the new name of Jerusalem in the messianic age is "Yahweh is our Vindication" (or "Righteousness"). As Israel's progenitors Abram and Jacob received the new names of Abraham and Israel to correspond to their new status, so Zion will receive a new name in the coming age. Hosea's children, too, will have new names in the new age (Hos. 2:22-23; cf. Rev. 2:17; 3:12). **Will give:** Better, "designate." The primary meaning of the verb is "pierce," "bore," "prick." The name distinguishes the person (Num. 1:17; II Chr. 28:15; 31:19).

3. A crown of beauty: Cf. 28:1 ff., which has been proposed as the source of the figure here. More likely it is derived from the ancient custom of representing the tutelary deity of a city as crowned with the city walls. So the deity appears on ancient coins and in a Babylonian Marduk inscription referring to Bel: "Borsippa is thy tiara" (Stummer, "Einige keilschriftliche Parallelen zu Jes. 40–66," p. 186). The prophet shrinks from saying that Zion will be worn as a **crown** or **royal diadem** on the head of Yahweh; rather, Yahweh holds it in his **hand**. The crown is a visual representation of Israel's glory. It expresses the close relationship between Yahweh and Zion. Zion is very precious to him (cf. 60:21; 61:3, where the verb is a cognate of the noun **glory** [KJV]).

---

concerning his promise"; so the prophet constantly reminds him, and soon will associate with himself other "remembrancers."

Our Lord commended importunity in prayer (Luke 11:5-8), and showed his appreciation of it (Matt. 15:22-28). Richard Hooker in a sermon on the command to ask, seek, knock (Matt. 7:7-8) dwells on the last word:

There is always in every good thing which we ask, and which we seek, some main wall, some barred gate, some strong impediment or other objecting itself in the way. . . . As therefore asking hath relation to the want of good things desired, and seeking to the natural ordinary means of attainment thereunto; so knocking is required in regard of hindrances, lets, or impediments, which are doors shut up against us, till such time as it please the goodness of Almighty God to set them open: in the meanwhile our duty here required is to "knock." [5]

[5] "A Sermon Found Among the Papers of Bishop Andrews," in *Works*, arr. John Keble (Oxford: Clarendon Press, 1888), III, 704.

In a world where many obstacles frustrate the advance of the church, resolute souls, like this prophet, must keep unwearied in prayer. They may grow discouraged, but they cannot tell what their constancy in prayer achieves.

Be not afraid to pray; to pray is right.
Pray, if thou canst, with hope, but ever pray,
Though hope be weak, or sick with long delay:
Pray in the darkness if there is no light.
Far is the time, remote from human sight,
When war and discord on the earth shall cease;
Yet every prayer for universal peace
Avails the blessed time to expedite.[6]

You shall be a crown of beauty . . . and a royal diadem. This regal headdress, symbol of God's kingship, is not yet on his head, but in his **hand**. He is winning his sovereignty by the redemption of his people; and the nations, seeing them vindicated, acknowledge his kingship. Our Lord's cross is his crown: "He reigns

[6] Hartley Coleridge, "Prayer."

4 Thou shalt no more be termed Forsaken; neither shall thy land any more be termed Desolate: but thou shalt be called Hephzi-bah, and thy land Beulah: for the LORD delighteth in thee, and thy land shall be married.

5 ¶ For *as* a young man marrieth a virgin, *so* shall thy sons marry thee: and *as* the bridegroom rejoiceth over the bride, *so* shall thy God rejoice over thee.

4 You shall no more be termed Forsaken,[s]
and your land shall no more be termed Desolate;[t]
but you shall be called My delight is in her,[u]
and your land Married;[v]
for the LORD delights in you,
and your land shall be married.
5 For as a young man marries a virgin,
so shall your sons marry you,
and as the bridegroom rejoices over the bride,
so shall your God rejoice over you.

[s] Heb *Azubah*
[t] Heb *Shemamah*
[u] Heb *Hephzibah*
[v] Heb *Beulah*

---

2. SECOND STROPHE: THE NEW COVENANTAL MARRIAGE (62:4-5)

4. The names which best described Zion's past existence are **Forsaken** and **Desolate**, but these old names will give place to new, **My Delight is in her** and **Married** (cf. 54:6). The close relationship between people and land is to be observed (cf. Hos. 2; etc.). Our poet employs the marriage figure to describe the relationship between Yahweh and his people, much as his predecessors, Hosea, Jeremiah, Ezekiel, and Second Isaiah, had done. The rejected, forsaken wife will be restored to a new relationship, and her Husband will signalize the event by the name **Hephzibah** (חפצי־בה), **My Delight is in her** and **Beulah** (בעולה), **Married**. According to commentators, these are not the messianic names referred to in vs. 2, but this is by no means certain. It is likely that the poet in this strophe communicates in the name of Yahweh what the new name is to be. The prophetic confusion between the words of Yahweh and of the prophet himself is noticeable in this poem, and the names are peculiarly appropriate for messianic titles. **Hephzibah** was the name of Manasseh's mother (II Kings 21:1; cf. Azubah, "Forsaken," the name of the mother of Jehoshaphat in I Kings 22:42). **Desolate:** Cf. 54:1 for the proper pointing of the word (*shômēmāh*); so also the Dead Sea Scroll in this passage. In vs. 4b the words **shall no more be termed** should probably be stricken out for the sake of the meter of vss. 4-14. The new relationship is a revelation of Yahweh's love.

5. Vss. 4c and 4e are introduced by *kî*, rendered **but** and **for.** The third *kî* (vs. 5a) crystallizes the prophet's thought. The comparison is lost in the Hebrew, but the LXX and the Dead Sea Scroll, confirming proposed emendations, read as in the RSV, כי כבעול.

---

from the wood." "Lifted up," he draws all men to him.

4-5. *The Desolate City Becomes God's Delight.*—We see the forlorn present, a land **Forsaken, Desolate.** Behind these poems of future magnificence is a devastated and hungry city, exposed to the ravages of foes. This particular poem does not stress the righteous life of the redeemed Israel or her missionary role. It hardly attains the religious elevation of other prophecies in this collection. The poet is depressed by his surroundings in a ruined land to which only a handful of its exiled inhabitants have returned. Under such circumstances the emphasis upon the rebuilding of its walls, upon its assured food and drink, upon the throngs of

its homecoming dwellers, and upon its reputation as a sought after city is understandable.

The restoration is the happy remarriage of the Lord to his people. The N.T. pictures the church as the Lord's bride (Eph. 5:23-27), but in this present age it is never a perfect marriage of mind and heart. That awaits the heavenly order (Rev. 21:9 ff.), where Christ and his followers are comrades in thought and partners in effort. The emphasis in the Bible is on God's relationship to his people rather than on theirs to him. The emendation "thy builder" for **thy sons** fits with the parallel **thy God** (for the metaphor cf. Ps. 147:2).

We rightly make much of our possession of God, but the Bible lays more stress on his pos-

6 I have set watchmen upon thy walls, O Jerusalem, *which* shall never hold their peace day nor night: ye that make mention of the LORD, keep not silence,

7 And give him no rest, till he establish, and till he make Jerusalem a praise in the earth.

---

6 Upon your walls, O Jerusalem,
  I have set watchmen;
all the day and all the night
  they shall never be silent.
You who put the LORD in remembrance,
  take no rest,
7 and give him no rest
  until he establishes Jerusalem
  and makes it a praise in the earth.

Your sons: By a very slight emendation read "your Builder" (בֹּנֵךְ); otherwise the meaning is difficult or absurd (cf. Ps. 147:2). For the husband-wife relationship between Yahweh and Israel see 49:14 ff.; 54:1 ff. The strophe closes with the divine rejoicing over Zion (cf. 61:3, 7, 10).

3. THIRD STROPHE: THE WATCHMEN ON ZION'S WALLS (62:6-7)

The first quatrain is spoken by the Lord, the second by the prophet. Such shifts are characteristic of O.T. prophecy, and it is not likely that it is the prophet who stations the prophets on the walls. The passage is reminiscent of the watchman of 21:12-13, who gives an enigmatic response to the people's cry "What hour of the night is it?" Here the watchmen intercede unceasingly for the time when Yahweh will establish the messianic city. These messianic watchmen are authentic representatives of Israel, whose God from the beginning to the end of her existence raised up intercessors in her behalf (cf. Moses, Elijah, Amos, Habakkuk, Jeremiah, Ezekiel, Second Isaiah, and Daniel; cf. Rom. 8:26-27; Heb. 7:25). But who are these watchers? Are they divine beings (cf. 40:1-11), pious Israelites, poetic symbols, or prophets? What is clear is that their function is to pray unremittingly for the fulfillment of the divine promises. Perhaps the best solution is to view them as prophets. In this event there is a fine parallelism between the prophet's own sense of urgency in vs. 1 and his response to God's commission. Note the wording. The strophe hinges upon the preposition **until** in vs. 7 as in vs. 1.

6-7. Upon your walls: The lines of 49:16 are clearly in the poet's mind here (cf. 60:10). Zion is graven on Yahweh's hands; her walls are continually before him. The walls now lie in ruins; the watchers pray that they be raised. Torrey believes that here the walls are thought of as actually existing. **I have set watchmen:** The verb is translated

---

session of us (Deut. 4:20; I Pet. 2:9; Eph. 1:18). A willing church is essential for the achievement of his purposes. That which he invests in the training of his people is accumulated capital. **Hephzibah** expresses his gratification in a loyal partner, and **Beulah** the new relationship of the people to their Lord.

6-7. The Watchmen on the Walls.—The first four lines in vs. 6 are spoken by the Lord, who alone could appoint these watchers. They may be celestial beings, but as the Exeg. suggests, are more likely prophets. One thinks of the intercessors from Abraham and Moses down who besought God for Israel. This prophet had declared his determination to keep pleading with God (vs. 1). But that would prove a lonely picket duty. The Lord graciously provides him with companions in watching and prayer. Their supplication becomes corporate, and each strengthens his neighbor in intercession. The company of **remembrancers** has the

fervor and force which accompany common prayer. Explorers of group psychology discover the many times multiplied warmth and constancy that attend collective effort.

Take no rest, and give him no rest. In the following lines it is the prophet who is speaking. Such importunity seems irreverent to most moderns. Is man justified in thus urging God as though he were less eager and ready for good than mortals? Most of us are in danger of succumbing to the temptation which a profound diagnostician of the devout life described a century ago: "I am very fearful of giving place to the temptation to wait upon the evolution of a Benevolent Fate, rather than to deal with God as the Hearer and Answerer of prayer."[7] Those with genuinely personal relations with God cannot depersonalize him into a cosmic purpose, however benign. Hence they may

[7] Donald Campbell, *Memorials of John McLeod Campbell,* II, 39.

8 The LORD hath sworn by his right hand, and by the arm of his strength, Surely I will no more give thy corn *to be* meat for thine enemies; and the sons of the stranger shall not drink thy wine, for the which thou hast labored:

8 The LORD has sworn by his right hand and by his mighty arm:
"I will not again give your grain to be food for your enemies,
and foreigners shall not drink your wine for which you have labored;

more accurately "appointed" or "stationed." The Dead Sea Scroll in the fourth line has simply "not" for "never." **You who put the LORD in remembrance:** The Lord's remembrancers constantly remind him of his promises; cf. the palace official in the court of the king (the *mazkîr* of II Sam. 8:16). The official was represented in other Near Eastern courts although his functions were greatly varied, as, for example, in Egypt.

Take no rest (vs. 6*f*), **and give him no rest** (vs. 7*a*): The prophet continues his response to the words of Yahweh in vs. 6*d*, **They shall never be silent.** It is not likely that the prophet would so address heavenly beings. The word **Jerusalem** in vs. 7*b* (RSV) is transferred here from vs. 7*c* (KJV). In vs. 7*b* a word, such as "his word" or "Zion," may have fallen out. The Dead Sea Scroll reads עד יכין ועד יכונן, "until he establish and found." The verbs are two forms of the same Hebrew root. **And makes it a praise in the earth:** The strophe ends on a note of joy (see 60:15; 61:11). The holy city will be the praise of the whole earth.

4. Fourth Strophe: The Felicity of Zion (62:8-9)

The third strophe of the body of the poem is introduced by Yahweh's solemn oath that the years of Zion's economic plight will be ended. Hostile invaders will no more reap the crops that Israel has sown; Israel will enjoy the fruits of her own labors, and celebrate in song and thanksgiving the favors of her God.

8. The LORD has sworn: Yahweh's oath expresses the great power of the word, the certainty of its realization as well as the intensity of the prophet's faith (cf. 45:23; 54:9). **By his right hand and by his mighty arm:** Cf. 40:10; 41:10; 51:9; 52:10; 53:1. The arm of

justifiably plead with him, as do the men of the Bible, for what they feel to be his revealed will. The prophet, to whom God has said that he will set watchers on Jerusalem's walls, on the basis of this assurance speaks to those remembrancers, summoning them to uninterrupted pleas that God's promise for Zion be accomplished. It must be confessed that the number of those in the modern church who **put the LORD in remembrance** is very small. This is an area of fellowship with him which needs to be entered and understood. All prayer is mysterious; and to attempt to rid it of the humanly puzzling is to destroy its richness. The few in every age who have been remembrancers have discovered elements of communion with God hidden from the majority of their less believing fellow Christians. They know that ours is no mechanistic universe in which God is "cabin'd, cribb'd, confin'd," [8] but his realm in which he lives, speaks, and acts freely. He makes promises to his servants, as these prophets firmly believed he had made to them. To urge insistently their fulfillment was to live and pray in accord with his will.

[8] Shakespeare, *Macbeth*, Act III, scene 4.

Until he establishes Jerusalem. Recently man's part, rather than God's, in building the holy city has been accented. Few lines have been oftener quoted than Blake's

Till we have built Jerusalem
In England's green and pleasant land.[9]

But our designs for an ideal order are always faulty. This prophet, hoping for an enduring city which wins the praise of mankind, knows that its architect and builder must be God.

8-9. Zion's Harvests and Festival.—The LORD has sworn by his right hand, i.e., by his limitless power. In two striking lines Isaac Watts places all the resources of the universe behind God's purposes:

The Voice that rolls the stars along
Speaks all the promises.[10]

Security from attack is much in the prophet's mind. The prospect of undisturbed peace leads to thanksgiving and the transformation of all meals into festive rejoicing before God. A feast

[9] "Milton."
[10] "Begin, my tongue, some heavenly theme," st. iii.

9 But they that have gathered it shall eat it, and praise the Lord; and they that have brought it together shall drink it in the courts of my holiness.

10 ¶ Go through, go through the gates; prepare ye the way of the people; cast up, cast up the highway; gather out the stones; lift up a standard for the people.

9 but those who garner it shall eat it
　　and praise the Lord,
and those who gather it shall drink it
　　in the courts of my sanctuary."

10 Go through, go through the gates,
　　prepare the way for the people;
build up, build up the highway,
　　clear it of stones,
　　lift up an ensign over the peoples.

Yahweh which had wrought so mightily in the past (Exod. 6:6 [P]; Deut. 4:34; 5:15; 7:19; etc.) expresses his power to do what he has promised. His oath is as mighty as his power to fulfill it. **Foreigners:** It is often suggested that the reference is to the requisitions of Persian officials or to the incursions of hostile Samaritans; it is just as likely that the Edomites and other neighboring peoples are meant. In the decades following 586 B.C. they had taken advantage of Judah's dire plight. The age of felicity will be free from economic deprivation (cf. 65:21-22). There is no necessary allusion to the rebuilt walls, though it is not excluded.

9. The quatrain matches the quatrain of vs. 8: the first two lines are a contrast to vs. 8cd, the last two to vs. 8ef. The accent of the strophe falls on the praise of God in the temple courts (cf. the conclusions to the two previous strophes). The reference may be to the feast of Tabernacles. According to Deuteronomy, the first fruits of the grain and wine and oil were to be enjoyed in the sanctuary (Deut. 12:17 ff.; 14:23 ff.; and especially 16:13 ff.). The Dead Sea Scroll has "name" before **the Lord,** and adds "says your God" at the close.

5. Fifth Strophe: The Messianic People (62:10-12)

The strophe is almost a catena of quotations from Second Isaiah. The eschatological thought of the prophet is drawn from 40:1-11; 52:1-12; etc. The word **behold** is used three times, as in the final strophe of the opening poem (cf. the threefold *ki* in vss. 4-5 and of 40:2). But the climax of the strophe, as of the whole poem, falls on the people. The experience of the celebrations of the feast of Tabernacles had quickened within the prophets the longing for the return of the Diaspora (Fischer, *Isaias*, II, *ad loc.*). The sight of thousands of festival pilgrims celebrating the feast in joyful thanksgiving inspires the prophet to contemplate the great return of all the Diaspora to the holy city.

10. **Go through, go through:** For the double imperative cf. 40:1; 51:9, 17; 52:1; 57:14; 65:1. Both the LXX and the Dead Sea Scroll have but one imperative here. **Build up, build up:** With the KJV and the ASV, read **cast up, cast up.** The third and fourth lines parallel the first two, and the fifth line provides the characteristic climax of

---

of Tabernacles may be in the poet's mind in vs. 9b, but in the perfected society all meals become sacred occasions (vs. 9a).

Christians live in God's redeemed Jerusalem. Our Lord habitually gave thanks before eating (Mark 6:41; 8:6; 14:23), and Christians have followed his example (Acts 2:46-47). This devout custom reminds us of our dependence upon God and transforms a common meal into a communion eaten with him. Cavilers may ask, "Why give thanks before eating rather than before washing or dressing or any other act?" To acknowledge God in one often repeated action is symbolic. The thanksgiving before

food is a time-honored devout habit, hallowed by many generations. Its omission, due to false shyness in expressing faith or to sheer forgetfulness of God, weakens our sense of relationship to him and our testimony to his goodness. It is part of the secularization of life, and frustrates the hope of this prophet in the priesthood of all God's people.

10-12. *Prepare the Way for the Returning People.*—The inhabitants of the city, already returned, are to make ready the route for the throng of the dispersed Israelites who presently are to appear. As the Exeg. suggests, the passage is reminiscent of phrases in passages in Second

11 Behold, the LORD hath proclaimed unto the end of the world, Say ye to the daughter of Zion, Behold, thy salvation cometh; behold, his reward *is* with him, and his work before him.

12 And they shall call them, The holy people, The redeemed of the LORD: and thou shalt be called, Sought out, A city not forsaken.

11 Behold, the LORD has proclaimed
    to the end of the earth:
Say to the daughter of Zion,
    "Behold, your salvation comes;
behold, his reward is with him,
    and his recompense before him."
12 And they shall be called The holy people,
    The redeemed of the LORD;
and you shall be called Sought out,
    a city not forsaken.

---

the whole. But to whom are these words addressed? Many have supposed that the Jews of the Diaspora are in the poet's mind. The reference to **the way of the people** makes this difficult, however, though not impossible. Others have proposed the angelic beings of 40:1-11, but this, while not inconsistent with the tenor of the prophet's thought, does not seem likely. Perhaps it is best, with Duhm and others, to think of the present inhabitants of Jerusalem. The **gates** are the gates of Jerusalem, not of Babylon. **Lift up an ensign over the peoples:** Cf. 49:22. The time has come for the nations to return the sons and daughters of Israel to the hill of Zion where the ensign is raised. The reading of the Dead Sea Scroll is not clear (contra Burrows).

11. Say to the daughter of Zion: Those addressed are the same as in 40:9-11, not the nations. **Behold, your salvation comes:** Cf. 40:9-10a; also 52:8. The rest of the verse is drawn entirely from 40:10. Both the LXX and the Vulg. read "your Savior."

12. The members of the community are called **The holy people** (cf. 61:6, "priests of Yahweh"; 63:18; Exod. 19:6; etc.) —the holy people of the holy God. **The redeemed of the LORD:** Cf. 35:10; 48:20; 51:10. **Sought out:** The name is in contrast to **forsaken** (cf. vs. 4; see also 54:6; 60:15; 62:4). With such words the prophet returns to his major theme of the new people.

Isaiah. It is not now the nations but the scattered people of God, for whom the **ensign** is raised. This is a text for church unity. Zion is inadequate for the mission assigned her until all her members are together within her walls. The church cannot give her witness with complete cogency until all followers of Christ are manifestly one (John 17:21). There is a sense in which in our time we may

> **Say to the daughter of Zion,**
> **"Behold, your salvation comes."**

Most of the divisive barriers which have sundered Christians have become relatively unessential and subordinate in believers' minds. The perilously hostile forces of the twentieth century demand a united witness and a co-ordinated strategy. Inertia is the most serious impediment to unification, as it was to the return of dispersed Israel. Hence the rousing call to action, **Go through, go through the gates, prepare the road, . . . lift up an ensign.** There is much planning and tactful effort demanded on the part of leaders, and hearty co-operation from all churchmen in large-minded endeavor to do away with the impeding **stones.** To **clear** the way in any community demands the removal of

a host of small objections and large ignorances. God's **reward** will consist of the increased spiritual power which will be the united church's possession.

In ecumenical assemblies men and women from many diverse traditions know the moving of God's Spirit in their common worship and in their united witness to his will for the church. Any who were present in St. Giles' Cathedral, Edinburgh, in October, 1929, when elements in the national church which had been sundered for generations came together in the reunited Kirk of Scotland, will recall the singing of Ps. 147:

> God doth build up Jerusalem;
>   And he it is alone
> That the dispersed of Israel
>   Doth gather into one.

The reunion of the church has to be God's doing, but his servants always have many exhausting tasks to do away with obstacles which block the consummation.

The order of the words in vs. 12 should be noted. When the church is patently **holy,** dedicated to her task as bearer of God's word, when she is **the redeemed of the LORD,** freed from

63 Who *is* this that cometh from Edom, with dyed garments from Bozrah? this *that is* glorious in his apparel, traveling in the greatness of his strength? I that speak in righteousness, mighty to save.

63 Who is this that comes from Edom,
in crimsoned garments from Bozrah,
he that is glorious in his apparel,
    marching in the greatness of his strength?
"It is I, announcing vindication,
    mighty to save."

J. THE YEAR OF REDEMPTION (63:1-6)

This little poem belongs to the literature of eschatological judgment. It describes the coming of a mighty Conqueror on the day of the Lord. At first sight it does not seem to bear any immediate relation to what precedes or follows. Upon closer scrutiny, however, it is apparent that its affinities are twofold: with 59:15c-20 and with 61:2 (the acceptable year of the Lord and the day of vengeance). It is likely, then, that chs. 60–62 were inserted after ch. 59, and that 63:1-6 was written to create a unity between the two sections.

Divine judgment was an indissoluble part of Israel's understanding of her relationship to God. To him she owed her historical life and character, but precisely for this reason she was peculiarly accountable and responsible (cf. Exod. 19:3-8). Where this responsibility was related to a historical revelation and a historical covenant, the eschatological character of the judgment was bound to emerge. Moreover, the history of Israel was related from the beginning to other nations and peoples, and her own existence and destiny were constantly threatened by their incursions into her land. Living in the midst of the world of peoples, she could not extricate herself from them. Classical eschatology naturally reflects this international character of Israel's situation in history, and the foreign nations therefore play a decisive role in its formulation. The sources of eschatological thought lie in the earliest period of Israel's history—in the exodus from Egypt and

worldly entanglements of race, class, political interest, etc., then she exerts her attraction on wistful souls. Here fellowship with God will populate her with those eager for life with him. Others only cumber her membership rolls and lower her standards. Much is said about rendering the church attractive. But to whom? And by what magnetism? Let her exercise under God the priesthood of all her members, and God will see to it that she is **Sought out, a city not forsaken.**

63:1-6. The Conqueror from Edom.—In chs. 60–66 the prophet or prophets picture the climax of history. Beside the glorification of Israel is presented the annihilation of an envious and hostile people. Babylon (ch. 47) stands for an enslaving despotism, spiritually the foe of everything which Israel represents. Edom, a people akin to Israel in origin and speech, devoid of her religious mission and jealous of her attainments, symbolizes a most bitter rival. The Christian church in our time has a similar competitor in Marxian communism, a philosophy and ethic from the same O.T. roots with a messianic community (the proletarian class), basically at variance with O.T. faith. The judgment in these verses is linked with the consummation of history, but

seems also an event in history. In 62:8 "enemies" are still present, and while the prophet comforts the people with visions of the glorious future, he reassures them against menacing foes by this figure of the warrior God. Amid the struggles of our time with a materialistic and secular view of life, however forward to proclaim justice and brotherhood, this militant Judge is a message for us.

The metaphors in this sublime poem have been often drawn on by later poets. An instance is Francis Thompson's "The Veteran of Heaven," whose first stanza runs:

O Captain of the wars, whence won Ye so great scars?
  In what fight did Ye smite, and what manner was the foe?
Was it on a day of rout they compassed Thee about,
  Or gat Ye these adornings when Ye wrought their overthrow? [11]

The poem is certainly not a prophecy of the passion of Christ. It portrays an advent of God in judgment, a battling Deity who takes the field on behalf of his people. His figure stands

[11] From *Collected Works*, ed. Wilfred Meynell. Used by permission of Burns, Oates & Washbourne, Ltd., and the Newman Press, publishers.

the period of the conquest—and the literary prophets from Amos to Second Isaiah deepen and develop the tradition. Third Isaiah, like his master, is heir to this great prophetic heritage. In this little poem we have a superb expression of his ability to transform and elevate the message of judgment into new imaginative dimensions.

The most striking feature of the poem is its remarkable dramatic character. By the employment of dialogue without any indication of the speakers, and by vivid imagery, repetition, and emphasis the poet succeeds in producing one of the supremely dramatic scenes of ancient literature. The portrait of the Victor in bloodstained garments, the figure of the wine press and its terrible Treader, the repeated emphasis on the awful fury of the swiftly approaching Warrior, culminate in the day of Vengeance, the year of redemption. The awesome portraiture reveals a poet of supreme imagination; the theme was one to exact all his powers of speech. The universal judgment is historical in the sense that it is a profoundly authentic expression of Israel's historical life throughout the centuries and of the prophetic response to the invasions of foreign nations. But it is no specific event that is clearly remembered, although the writer was surely familiar with such remarkable scenes as Judg. 5:1-31; Deut. 32:1-52 (cf. Isa. 42:13-17). The writer is using the pre-eminently congenial category of poetry, raised to eschatological and universal proportions, to describe his vision.

---

out in contrast to the aloof and imperturbable deities of pagan faiths—the Assyrian divinities or those of Egypt and Babylon, usually part animal. The prophet's God has a conscience and a heart, and shares in the brutal melee of human affairs. This vision prepares the way for One willing to become incarnate for man's deliverance. During World War I, G. A. Studdert-Kennedy wrote:

How can it be that God can reign in glory,
    Calmly content with what His Love has done,
Reading unmoved the piteous shameful story,
    All the vile deeds men do beneath the sun?

Are there no tears in the heart of the Eternal?
    Is there no pain to pierce the soul of God?
Then must He be a fiend of Hell infernal,
    Beating the earth to pieces with his rod.

. . . .

Passionately fierce the voice of God is pleading,
    Pleading with men to arm them for the fight;
See how those hands, majestically bleeding,
    Call us to rout the armies of the night.[1]

One of the supreme products of poetry, the *Divine Comedy*, was born of a great love and a blazing indignation.

    Dante, who loved well because he hated,
    Hated wickedness that hinders loving.[2]

Similarly, this poem depicts the love of God manifest as a consuming fire to cleanse his world of unbrotherliness. Opposition brings love to expression, as obstructing rocks along the shore cause incoming waves to break into spray.

The splendent sun no splendour can display
Till on gross things he dash his broken ray.

. . . .

Stay is heat's cradle, it is rocked therein,
And by check's hand is burnished into light.

. . . .

God's Fair were guessed scarce but for opposite sin;
Yea, and His Mercy, I do think it well,
Is flashed back from the brazen gates of Hell.[3]

Such a conception of God, entering the rough and tumble of history, hazarding blows and pain, is the progenitor of the N.T. portrait of the Son of God, made man for our salvation, enduring the cross and triumphing over the world, sin, and death.

In this poem we have again the contrast between the **year** of the divine favor and the **day** of wrath. This dialogue is concerned with such a day. Thunderstorms are not a lasting state of weather; but when the atmosphere is oppressive, an electrical disturbance, violent and possibly destructive, clears the air for men to breathe freely. Days of divine fury occur in history, frightfully devastating, and they rid the earth of factors malignantly hostile to God and his people. This poem does not raise the question of the damnation of individuals in the final judgment; that question had not yet arisen. It deals with a nation which in conscienceless unkindness obstructs God's will by cruelty to its neighbor. Grace is God's enduring attitude toward mankind; but grace is manifest in indignation toward those who thwart it.

1. The Marching Conqueror from Edom.— To the prophet's challenging **Who is this?** comes

---

[1] "The Suffering God," from *The Sorrows of God and Other Poems* (New York: G. H. Doran, 1924). Used by permission.

[2] Browning, "One Word More," st. v.

[3] Francis Thompson, *Sister Songs*, Part the Second. From *Collected Works*, ed. Wilfred Meynell. Used by permission of Burns, Oates & Washbourne, Ltd., and the Newman Press, publishers.

| 2 Wherefore *art thou* red in thine apparel, and thy garments like him that treadeth in the winevat? | 2 Why is thy apparel red, and thy garments like his that treads in the wine press? |

It was only to be expected that later thought would seize upon this passage. Church fathers like Tertullian, Origen, Jerome, and their successors have interpreted it messianically. Theology and poetry have joined in recasting and reinterpreting the thought in ways which, while foreign to the original meaning, have nevertheless done some justice to its sublimity. The meter is prevailingly 3+3.

1. First Strophe: The Conqueror from Edom (63:1)

The seer or watchman, stationed on his watch tower or on the wall of Jerusalem, sees the swift approach of a mighty Conqueror from the South, and inquires who it is. The reply comes forthwith in word and event:

> It is I, announcing vindication,
> mighty to save.

Cf. "The Burden of Edom" in 21:11-12 for form and style.

63:1. Who is this that comes from Edom? The first words strike the theme of the whole (for the introductory question cf. Song of S. 3:6; 8:5; Ps. 24:8, 10). Many scholars, beginning with Lagarde, have by a very slight and ingenious emendation read "stained with red" (*me'oddām*, Pual of אדם; cf. Nah. 2:4 [Hebrew]). But there is no good reason why Edom should not be used, for it represented, or came to represent, the very embodiment of the nations' hostility to God (cf. 21:11-12; 34:1-17; Obad. 1-21; Amos 1:11-12; Jer. 49:7-22; Ezek. 25:12-14; Mal. 1:2-5; Joel 4:19; Ps. 137:7; Lam. 4:21-22). The similarity of the two words in Hebrew evoked the paronomasia. So also with the parallel word **Bozrah,** which has been similarly emended to "vintager." Both are played upon in vs. 2. **Bozrah** was the chief city of Edom (cf. Amos 1:12; Jer. 49:13). **In crimsoned garments:** Or, "in brightly colored garments." **Marching:** The Hebrew word is ço'eh, "bowed down," but should be emended to ço'ēdh as in the RSV (cf. Vulg., *gradiens*). **Announcing vindication:** Cf. KJV, ASV. Yahweh brings his word into effect in the vindication of his people. **Mighty to save:** The LXX has "with saving judgment"; the Vulg., *propugnator sum ad salvandum,* "I am a champion to save." The occasion is, of course, the day of Yahweh.

2. Second Strophe: The Treader of the Wine Press (63:2-3)

To the seer's query about the red garments the answer comes that the Conqueror is in reality the Treader of the wine press. The figure is grandiose in its eschatological perspectives (cf. 59:15c-20).

2. Why is thy apparel red? The word **red** has the same consonants as Edom in its shortened form. The Hebrew reads, "Why is there red to thy apparel?" but the removal

the reply, **It is I, announcing vindication, mighty to save.** This Figure, with gory stains of struggle upon him, is a wholesome corrective of doctrines of the Father's role in man's redemption which remove him from personal participation in the conflict with evil and exempt him from its cost in suffering. In Italy one may see representations of the Crucifixion which show the nails going through the hands of Jesus and through the wooden beam on which he hangs into the hands of the Father, dimly visible in the background.

Marching in the greatness of his strength: God's activity is not effortless, though he is never exhausted. He puts forth his power to bring his purposes to pass. This Figure "swaying along" would catch the attention of people familiar with the seated deities of contemporary paganism. A fourteenth-century poet, Richard Rolle, declared, "Love cannot be lazy," and Walter Hylton coined the term "a busy rest" for God's peace.[4]

2-3. *The Treader of the Wine Press Declares Himself.*—The solitariness of God is stressed. No nation felt obliged to frustrate malice and maintain brotherhood. This is the sin of isola-

[4] Wingfield-Stratford, *History of British Civilization,* p. 258.

3 I have trodden the winepress alone; and of the people *there was* none with me: for I will tread them in mine anger, and trample them in my fury; and their blood shall be sprinkled upon my garments, and I will stain all my raiment.

4 For the day of vengeance *is* in mine heart, and the year of my redeemed is come.

5 And I looked, and *there was* none to help; and I wondered that *there was* none to uphold: therefore mine own arm brought salvation unto me; and my fury, it upheld me.

3 "I have trodden the wine press alone,
  and from the peoples no one was with
    me;
I trod them in my anger
  and trampled them in my wrath;
their lifeblood is sprinkled upon my gar-
    ments,
  and I have stained all my raiment.
4 For the day of vengeance was in my heart,
  and my year of redemption*w* has come.
5 I looked, but there was no one to help;
  I was appalled, but there was no one
    to uphold;
so my own arm brought me victory,
  and my wrath upheld me.

w Or *the year of my redeemed*

of the preposition is supported by the versions. It is the prophet's comparison to the **wine press** which gives the key to the answer.

3. The reply is that the Conqueror has indeed **trodden the wine press**, and the **peoples** of the world are the grapes that are crushed by his treading. The picture is exceedingly realistic. The **blood** of the grapes is the blood of the peoples flowing from the wine press (for the figure cf. Joel 4:13; Rev. 14:19-20; 19:15). **And from the peoples:** The Dead Sea Scroll reads interestingly, "and from my people," i.e., Yahweh was not aided by his own people. Yahweh alone, mighty in power and salvation, brings the judgment on the nations. As usual, the events are described as having already taken place. Vs. *3cde* is lacking in the Dead Sea Scroll.

3. THIRD STROPHE: THE DAY OF VENGEANCE (63:4-6)

The climax falls here, and the point of the poem is introduced with the characteristic *kî*. The day of Yahweh is a day of universal judgment.

4. For the **day of vengeance . . . and my year of redemption:** For the conception cf. 49:8-9; 59:17 ff.; for terminology cf. 34:8; 35:4; 61:2. Kissane suggests that there is probably an allusion in the **year of redemption** to the year of Jubilee, when Hebrew slaves were set free (cf. Lev. 25:39-40; Exod. 21:2 ff.; Deut. 15:12 ff.). The Hebrew reads **my redeemed**, which Budde emends to *gemûlî*, "my recompense." **The day** was in Yahweh's **heart**, i.e., in his will. It is the realization of his purpose.

5. Cf. 59:16. Yahweh's mighty **arm** brought about the great **victory**; lit., **brought salvation** (cf. vss. 1-2). There was no mediator like the Assyrians or Babylonians or Medes, like Nebuchadrezzar, "my servant," or Sennacherib, or Cyrus, "my anointed." The word **to help** is a military term; no one supported Yahweh in his conflict against the nations. The Dead Sea Scroll uses another word with the same meaning for **uphold**.

tionism. So the Lord took all upon himself. The richer a personality the more ties it has with others and the more it craves companionship. The loneliness of Jesus is brought out in the evangelists' narratives—misunderstood, misrepresented, denied, betrayed, deserted, finally seemingly abandoned by God himself. His isolation mirrors the awful solitariness of his Father throughout long ages, with none to whom he can communicate his thoughts, and none capable of sharing his conscience. Alone he shoulders the responsibility of his world; alone he frames

his plans; alone he enters into the turmoil of human history and single-handed wins the fray.

4-6. The Day of Vengeance.—**I was appalled, but there was no one to uphold.** The vivid portrayal of God's pained surprise at man's indifference to moral wrongs and cruelties is a much needed religious insight. Renaissance painters sometimes placed such crises as the Crucifixion and the Resurrection against a placid background, where under a smiling sun men are seen plowing, fishing, etc., taking life "as usual." When conversation turned on in-

6 And I will tread down the people in mine anger, and make them drunk in my fury, and I will bring down their strength to the earth. 7 ¶ I will mention the loving-kindnesses of the LORD, *and* the praises of the LORD,	6 I trod down the peoples in my anger, I made them drunk in my wrath, and I poured out their lifeblood on the earth." 7 I will recount the steadfast love of the LORD, the praises of the LORD, according to all that the LORD has granted us,

6. This verse is a tristich where the first two lines practically repeat vs. *3cd,* though the verbs are not the same. The LXX omits the second line. The Targ. reads "trample" for the M.T. **made them drunk,** and some Hebrew MSS have a *kaph* instead of a *bêth* in the latter word, "shattered them" (cf. ASV mg.). But the imagery is not unparalleled (cf. 49:26; 51:17, 21-22). **Their strength** (KJV) is better rendered **their lifeblood** as in the RSV and most modern versions (cf. vs. *3e*). A more literal translation would be "I let their lifeblood run down upon the earth" (so Bewer).

K. A Prophet's Intercessory Prayer (63:7–64:12)

The role of intercessor belonged to the interior life of ancient Israel. Not only the priest but also the prophet represented the people before God. Like Abraham (Gen.

difference toward high-minded men, a visitor reported that Carlyle remarked: "If Jesus Christ were to come today, people would not even crucify him. They would ask him to dinner, and hear what he had to say, and make fun of it." [5] A brilliant young Englishman, who laid down his life in World War I, wrote:

> We do not see the vital point
> That 'tis the eighth, most deadly, sin
> To wail, "The world is out of joint"—
> And not attempt to put it in.[6]

A penetrating diagnostician of the spirit, Frederick W. Faber, called lukewarmness "often nothing more than a clogging up of the avenues of the soul with sins of omission, so that the cool and salutary inundations of grace are hindered." [7] It is the "hangers-back" who break the divine heart.

My anger: A nineteenth-century economist spoke of "the supine placidity of civilisation." [8] We in the twentieth have had our sympathies hardened by the frequency of cruelties in our sorrowful generation. A rebirth of fury at wrong is imperative. It evidences a conscience alive.

A friend reported of F. W. Robertson that he had "seen him grind his teeth and clench his fist when passing a man who, he knew, was bent on destroying an innocent girl." And Robertson says of himself, "My blood was running liquid fire." [9] A blazing wrath at the deceitful mishandling of truth by the Jesuits carried Pascal through his long and painstaking toil in penning his *Provincial Letters,* with their annihilating irony. Fury is not the antithesis of compassion, but one of its manifestations. Harriet Martineau wrote of Carlyle: "[His] savageness is, in my opinion, a mere expression of his intolerable sympathy with the suffering." [1]

My wrath upheld me: Some of the greatest saints have witnessed to the power of indignation to inspire and sustain them.[2] Writers know how, when moved to a white heat, they find ideas and language flowing readily.

No other passage in scripture more poignantly sets forth the intensity of the conflict in history where God is on the field against unbrotherliness. His righteousness agonizes. His is a bitter solitary ordeal century after century, and especially in the years of his grace. And faith is confident that the issue is sure: he strides on **in the greatness of his strength, . . . mighty to save.**

63:7–64:12. *An Appeal to the Lord's Fatherly Faithfulness.*—This is one of the sublimest

[5] D. A. Wilson, *Carlyle at His Zenith* (London: Kegan Paul, 1927), p. 238.

[6] C. H. Sorley, "A Call to Action," from *Marlborough and Other Poems* (Cambridge: Cambridge University Press, 1919), p. 46. Used by permission.

[7] *Growth in Holiness* (4th ed.; New York: H. H. Richardson & Co., 1872), p. 298.

[8] Walter Bagehot, *Biographical Studies,* ed. Richard Holt Hutton (London: Longmans, Green & Co., 1914), p. 61.

[9] Brooke, *Life and Letters of F. W. Robertson,* I, 186.

[1] D. A. Wilson, *Carlyle on Cromwell and Others* (New York: E. P. Dutton & Co., 1925), p. 22.

[2] Cf. Luther, *Table Talk,* No. CCCXIX.

according to all that the LORD hath bestowed on us, and the great goodness toward the house of Israel, which he hath bestowed on them according to his mercies,	and the great goodness to the house of Israel which he has granted them according to his mercy,

---

18:22-32), Moses (Num. 14:13-19), Amos (7:1-6), Jeremiah (14:1-9), the psalmists, Ezra (9:6-15), and Daniel (9:4-19), our prophet identifies himself with the life and fate of his people. He is not the preacher of oracles but, like the priest, the intercessor in behalf of the people to God. Perhaps there is no utterance of similar scope in the Bible which portrays so profoundly and elaborately the nature of the relationship between Israel and God. The words are born in the agony and travail of the prophet for his people and in the great historical tradition in which God had made himself known to Israel. They are Israel's autobiography in man's loftiest and deepest language.

The body of the prayer is contained in 63:15–64:12. But it is preceded by 63:7-14, in which the impassioned historical retrospect clearly anticipates the fervent cry which follows (cf., e.g., 63:10). Moreover, the prayer cannot begin in the manner of 63:15. The literary parallels such as 26:7-21, 33; Lam. 1:1–5:22; and Pss. 36; 74; 77; 79 support this view. The characteristic style and terminology of the lament pervade the entire poem, and the key words (e.g., **my people,** vs. 8; **remembered,** vs. 11; **thy name,** vs. 19) serve to give it continuity. It is possible that the poem is a liturgy, and it may indeed extend beyond the limits of ch. 64 (Kissane, Bentzen). It opens in hymnic fashion (63:7), but the crucial verse which follows strikes the note of the entire poem and constitutes its necessary background (cf. 63:8b, 10). This is followed by a historical retrospect (63:9-14), a petition (63:15–64:5b), a confession of sin (64:5c-7), and a final supplication (64:8-12) incorporating the major motifs of the entire prayer. The structure falls into seven strophes, the first two (63:7-10, 11-14) containing the historical retrospect, the next three (63:15-16, 17-19; 64:1-5b) the petition, the sixth (64:5c-7) the confession, and the seventh (64:8-12) the closing appeal.

It is probable that the prayer was composed for a special occasion, most likely a day of prayer for the people. The strong corporate consciousness, the appeal to the Exodus, the spiritual elevation of the language, and the composition of the prayer suggest some such occasion. The references to the city of Jerusalem lying in ruins and to the destruction of the temple seem relatively fresh in the writer's mind. The description of the temple as

> Our holy and beautiful house,
> where our fathers praised thee (64:11)

most naturally suggests the Solomonic temple (see Exeg. for the difficulty raised by vs. 18). The strong sense of national guilt is not unlike that of the writers of Lamentations. On the other hand, the poem has little relation to Second Isaiah either in its form or content. It should be observed that there is no appeal to a historical deliverer like Cyrus. It is a time of despair in which the devastation of Judah and the ruined temple have daunted the hopes of the people. No date is without its difficulties, but a period between 560 and

---

prayers in the Bible, lofty in poetic form, and profound in its revelation of the richness of God's fellowship with his people. It probably stands at this point in the collection of prophecies as an instance of the prayers of the remembrancers (62:6).

7-10. Israel's Ungrateful Response to God's Acts.—Words descriptive of God's graciousness are heaped one on another: steadfast love, praises, great goodness (Ps. 145:7), compassion (Ps. 51:1), the abundance of his steadfast love.

Many biblical prayers commence with reminders of God's surprising grace in the past (Neh. 9:5 ff.; Pss. 78; 89; 105; 106), and Paul's prayers for his correspondents start by thanking God for them (cf. Rom. 1:8, "First, I thank my God"). The initial step in intercourse with God is to set him before us as he has disclosed himself. Commemoration of his loving-kindness inspires expectant faith. This prayer is uttered *de profundis,* from people whose land and temple were in ruins, their fellow believers scat-

| and according to the multitude of his loving-kindnesses. | according to the abundance of his steadfast love. |

550 B.C. seems to present the fewest problems. The meter of 63:7-14 is 3+2; of the rest of the poem, prevailingly 3+3.

1. First Strophe: The Election and Judgment of Israel (63:7-10)

Observe how vs. 7 begins and ends with **steadfast love** (in Hebrew), the threefold repetition of Lord, the repetition of the verb *gāmal* (**has granted**), the threefold **according to,** the twofold בׇ—God's **great goodness** and **the abundance of his steadfast love.** Following this general exordium the words of Yahweh are introduced, words of election and fidelity. So he became the **Savior** of Israel. He entered into their historic life in all their afflictions; his angel **saved them, he redeemed them, lifted them up and carried them.** The phrase **all the days of old** prepares the way admirably for the next strophe and runs like a musical strain throughout the prayer. Vs. 10 belongs with this strophe, not with the following, as in the RSV. The thought is similar to 1:2-3. It strikes the note of lament which sounds throughout the following lines. So God the Savior and Redeemer becomes the **enemy** in judgment.

7. The whole verse is fashioned in a framework of the divine faithfulness (vss. 7a, 7f). The prophet begins in the style of a hymn, passing imperceptibly from the singular first person to the plural. Israel's conception of herself as corporate personality and the prophet's intimate identification of himself with the life and destiny of the people made such transitions easy. **I will recount:** Cf. Pss. 51:1; 89:1; 145:7 (for this and similar introductions cf. Gunkel and Begrich, *Einleitung in die Psalmen,* pp. 33 ff.). The word may be rendered "bring to mind," "commemorate"; lit., "cause to remember." The festival days in ancient Israel were occasions of recollection of events of the past: the Exodus, the wilderness sojourn, the giving of the covenant, etc. The word "remember" is employed with changing nuances throughout the poem (vss. 11a; 64:5b, 9b; cf. Pss. 77:11; 87:4). A better rendering for **steadfast love** here is "faithfulness" (cf. Ps. 89:1). **Praises:** The meaning is praiseworthy deeds (as in 60:6e). These were recounted at the

---

tered afar, their nation sorely discouraged, and the devout depressed with a feeling of God-abandonment while their hearts reach up toward him. It was keen insight which led the prophet to begin by recalling God's gracious acts in his people's history.

Thomas Halyburton testified: "I observe, then, when I was at the lowest ebb . . . , without finding the Lord, or any sense of his love, I have often found him in the duty of thankfulness."[3] Wordsworth pays a similar tribute to gratitude as a basis for faith:

Theologians may puzzle their heads about dogmas as they will, the religion of gratitude cannot mislead us. Of that we are sure, and gratitude is the handmaid to hope, and hope the harbinger of faith. I look abroad upon Nature, I think of the best part of our species, I lean upon my friends, I meditate upon the Scriptures, especially the Gospel of St. John; and my creed rises up of itself with the ease of an exhalation, yet a fabric of adamant.[4]

[3] *Memoirs* (London: Thomas Tegg & Sons, 1835), p. 743.

[4] *Letters of the Wordsworth Family,* ed. William Knight (Boston: Ginn & Co., 1907), II, 257-58.

This prayer is what the Germans call *Andacht,* "devout thinking." Such thinking needs kindling. Luther declared: "Prayer is cold, listless and difficult unless the heart be already inflamed with the coals of blessing."[5] Such coals of blessing are the wealth of God's remembered loving-kindnesses. **He said, Surely they are my people, sons who will not deal falsely,** an unusual statement of God's faith in man. He chose his people in the confidence that they would not disappoint him. If we love because he first loved us, we trust because he first trusted us. His faith in us is a potent stimulus. In the eighteen-nineties the Gordon Highlanders were campaigning against tribesmen in Baluchistan on the frontier of India. One task assigned them was the storming of the steep height at Dargai in the face of guns pointing down at them from its summit. In giving the order to charge, their commanding officer called out: "The Gordons will do it," and they did.

In all their affliction he was afflicted: A phrase embedded in the hearts of English-speaking Christians as a crowning expression of God's

[5] *Werke,* VII, 130.

8 For he said, Surely they *are* my people, children *that* will not lie: so he was their Saviour.

9 In all their affliction he was afflicted, and the Angel of his presence saved them:

8 For he said, Surely they are my people, sons who will not deal falsely; and he became their Savior.

9 In all their affliction he was afflicted,ˣ and the angel of his presence saved them;
in his love and in his pity he redeemed them;

ˣ Another reading is he did not afflict

---

festivals and were the theme of many of the psalmists (Pss. 77; 78; 105; 135; 136; also Deut. 32; Neh. 9:6 ff.). **According to all that the LORD has granted us:** The verb גמל also means "render to" or "deal out." **And the great goodness to the house of Israel:** Many scholars emend slightly to *kerōbh ṭûbhô,* "according to the abundance of his goodness." Many also delete **to the house of Israel.** But the words are not metrically excessive (the line is 3+2); moreover, they are admirably suited to the context. Deut. 32; Hos. 8 ff. contain similar retrospects of the sacred history.

8. The first event which the prophet "calls to mind" is the election of Israel. Yahweh himself speaks the emphatic election words in the succinct fashion of such revelatory speech (only six words in the Hebrew): "Surely my people are they, sons, etc." Quotation marks should precede "surely" and follow "falsely." Then comes the prophet's impressive succession of verbs which develop the election utterance: **he became their Savior, he redeemed them, he lifted them up, and carried them.** The word of election made Israel the chosen people. As a chosen people, God expected to fulfill his purpose in them; he expected that they would be loyal and faithful, **sons who will not deal falsely** (faithlessly; cf. 1:2). For Israelites as the sons of God cf. further Exod. 4:22; Deut. 14:1; 32:6, 19; Hos. 1:10 (Hebrew 2:15); 11:1; Mal. 1:6; 2:10; also Isa. 43:6; 45:11. These election words provide the background for the relation between the Lord and Israel which dominates the poem. Trusting in Israel's filial relation to him, Yahweh became their Savior in all their affliction.

9. The opening phrase probably belongs with the previous verse: **He became their Savior in all their affliction.** The C.T. is difficult and obscure. The older commentators therefore read the *Qerê:* **In all their affliction** [lit., "affliction to them"] **he was afflicted.** The thought is surely one of the most lofty and inspiring in the whole O.T., expressing God's presence in human suffering. But it is likely that the LXXᴮ has preserved the better text. Translate vs. 9*bc:* "Neither envoy nor messenger—but his own Presence [lit., "his face"]—saved them." The word צר is read ציר, meaning "envoy" or "messenger." In the O.T. the word is never used of an angelic being, but the close association with

---

sympathy. It is probably a mistranslation of a difficult line of Hebrew verse, but it renders the poet's thought, for he is insisting that God sent no substitute to guide and deliver his people. His own presence saved them (Exod. 33:14-15). The God of the Bible is never remote from his children's experiences, and sharing them, he must share their painfulness. A. T. Quiller-Couch has phrased it: "There is no suffering in the world but ultimately comes to be endured by God." [6] Edward Wilson, physician on Captain Scott's fatal expedition to the Antarctic, set down the conviction:

[6] Quoted in *A Little Book of Life and Death,* ed. Elizabeth Waterhouse (London: Methuen & Co., 1902), p. 84.

This I know is God's own truth, that pain and trouble and trials and sorrows and disappointments are either one thing or another. To all who love God they are love tokens from Him. To all who do not love God and do not want to love Him they are merely a nuisance. Every single pain that we feel is known to God because it is the most loving . . . touch of His hand.[7]

In his love and in his pity ("forgiving gentleness" [8]): Additional words to those in vs. 7 to portray God as revealed in his dealings with Israel. He takes the rough and tumble of

[7] George Seaver, *Edward Wilson of the Antarctic* (London: John Murray, 1933), p. 71.

[8] Delitzsch, *Jesaia, ad loc.*

| in his love and in his pity he redeemed them; and he bare them, and carried them all the days of old. | he lifted them up and carried them all the days of old. |
| **10** ¶ But they rebelled, and vexed his Holy Spirit: therefore he was turned to be their enemy, *and* he fought against them. | **10** But they rebelled and grieved his holy Spirit; therefore he turned to be their enemy, and himself fought against them. |

mal'ākh, the contrast to the *pānim* (presence) of God, and the general thought and context seem to support such an interpretation (cf. Zech. 1:12-14; Mal. 3:1). Messengers and angels were closely related to Yahweh; they belonged to his heavenly entourage, but they were independent beings. In the great days of the Exodus, when God wrought mighty works of redemption for his people, it was not an angel or envoy whom he sent; he himself (lit., "his face") saved them (see, however, the words of the Covenant Code in Exod. 23:20-23 [E] and Exod. 32:34 [P]; in the former passage Yahweh promises to send an angel before Israel to keep her by the way and to bring her to the Promised Land). "Face of Baal" was a title for the goddess Tanit among the Phoenicians (see the votive tablet unearthed in Carthage, published in G. A. Cooke, *Text-Book of North-Semitic Inscriptions,* pp. 131-32). The face of God is, of course, his self-manifestation (Aubrey Johnson, "Aspects of the Use of the Term פנים in the Old Testament," in J. Fück, ed., *Festschrift Otto Eissfeldt* [Halle: M. Niemeyer, 1947], pp. 155-59; cf. especially Exod. 33:14-15; Deut. 4:37). In the earliest days the relationship between Israel and Yahweh was close and intimate. His "face" went with them, though Moses was not permitted to view it (Exod. 33:17-23). But as our passage makes clear, Israel did not merely live in the consciousness of his presence among them; rather, **his presence saved them; his love** and **his pity . . . redeemed them.** Moreover, it was not only at the beginning of Israel's life that he was present; rather, **he bare them, and carried them all the days of old** (cf. 46:3-4; Deut. 32:7, 11-12).

10. The opening words **but they** are emphatic (cf. the same emphatic pronoun in vs. 8*a*, "My people are they"). The climax of the verse falls here. Israel was an elect and covenanted people, **but they rebelled** (1:2) against God, **and grieved his holy spirit** (cf. Acts 7:51; Eph. 4:30). In the O.T. this expression appears only in this context and in Ps. 51:11 (Hebrew 51:13). There is here no reference to the third person of the Trinity, but a personification which moves in the direction of a hypostasis. The word *rûaḥ* is frequently employed to describe various moods and emotions (Johnson, *Vitality*

---

human events—slavery in Egypt, the passage of the Red Sea, the wilderness wanderings, etc.— and through them discloses his inmost nature in his works for man. There is an outside and an inside view of redemptive events; the Cross to casual observers was a brutal execution, to the redeemed church, "God so loved."

He bare them, and carried them: A metaphor often used of God's tender care for his people (cf. Exod. 19:4; Deut. 1:31; 32:11; Hos. 11:3). According to one reading of Acts 13:18, Paul says, "As a nursing father bare he them in the wilderness." Israel confesses that the Lord is both her home and her support (Deut. 33:27). Religion is often viewed as burdensome, a series of obligations to be fulfilled. Genuine believers, however, discover that God upholds. After his wife's death, Calvin wrote to his friend, William Farel, of the affecting scene at the bedside,

adding that he went to a secret place to pray. And the letter goes on:

I at present control my sorrow so that my duties may not be interfered with. . . . May the Lord Jesus strengthen you by His Spirit; and may He support me also under this heavy affliction, which would certainly have overcome me, had not He, who raises up the prostrate, strengthens the weak, and refreshes the weary, stretched forth His hand from heaven to me.[9]

Israel's response to God's grace had been rebellion (vs. 10). They had **grieved his holy Spirit.** The Spirit is a national endowment residing in the chosen people, and **holy** like God himself, recoiling from sin. In this passage we have a disclosure of God's relation to his

[9] *The Letters of John Calvin,* comp. Jules Bonnet (Boston: Little, Brown & Co., 1857), II, 205.

11 Then he remembered the days of old, Moses, *and* his people, *saying,* Where *is* he that brought them up out of the sea with the shepherd of his flock? where *is* he that put his Holy Spirit within him?

11 Then he remembered the days of old, of Moses his servant.
Where is he who brought up out of the sea
the shepherds of his flock?
Where is he who put in the midst of them
his holy Spirit,

---

of the Individual in the Thought of Ancient Israel, pp. 26-39). To grieve Yahweh's spirit is to grieve him. The personification is not carried so far as that of wisdom in the Wisdom of Solomon. Because Israel rebelled against him who had made them a chosen people and had named them sons, he became **their enemy.**

2. SECOND STROPHE: THE WONDERS OF THE DAYS OF OLD (63:11-14)

The strophe is not simply a retrospect of the heroic days of Israel's beginning. Rather, the dominant mood is of lament that these days are gone and that the situation of the present is so completely different. The first stich combines two major elements of the preceding strophe, and there follow the stirring events associated with Moses and the Exodus: the passage through the Red Sea, the desert march, and the realization of the goal. The repetitions in this strophe are as common and as effective as in the preceding. More interesting is the hymnic style (cf. the participles in vss. 11c, 11e, 12a, 12c, 13a).

11. Then he remembered: The questions which follow are clearly the words of Israel, so we should read the plural "they remembered" (cf. 46:8-9). Volz suggests the first person, parallel to vs. 1, but this is less natural (cf. vs. 10). In their deep distress the people remember the time of grace when Yahweh wrought wonders among them. **Of Moses his servant:** The M.T. reads "Moses, his people." The words are lacking in the LXX but the Vulg. has **Moses, and his people** (so KJV). The Syriac reads "Moses,

---

people which prepares the way for his self-revelation in the Christian church, set forth by her in the doctrine of the Trinity-in-Unity. We have Yahweh, his presence, and his holy Spirit. The experience of the devout community in Israel (as they interpreted it) is analogous to the fellowship of God in Christ in the Spirit with the church. The Holy Spirit may be **grieved** (cf. Eph. 4:30), or "resisted" (Acts 7:51), or "quenched" (I Thess. 5:19): this is the inevitable suffering of God dwelling with and in his sinful people. If one may illustrate the divine by a lowly human experience, when G. H. Lewes, the future husband of George Eliot, had reviewed some of Charlotte Brontë's books, to her exasperation analyzing the feminine elements in her writing, she wrote him:

I will tell you why I was so hurt by that review in the *Edinburgh*— . . . because after I had said earnestly that I wished critics would judge me as an *author,* not as a woman, you so roughly—I even thought so cruelly—handled the question of sex. I dare say you meant no harm, and perhaps you will not now be able to understand why I was so grieved at what you will probably deem such a trifle; but grieved I was, and indignant too. . . . I know what your nature is: it is not a bad or unkind

one, though you would often jar terribly on some feelings with whose recoil and quiver you could not possibly sympathise.[1]

It is the "recoil and quiver" of the Holy Spirit in proximity to man's intended, but usually unconscious, wickedness which gives him constant pain in dwelling with us.

He turned to be their enemy. This was the sorry conclusion of those offering this prayer. How else explain their devastated land and dispersed people? But in ancient days God's seeming antagonism had been his discipline, not his abandonment, of his people. Theirs would prove an experience like that of the man of Uz (Job 19:6-22; 42:5-6). **Himself fought against them:** An echo of the same thought which is behind Gen. 32:24-30. The antagonist becomes the source of blessing.

11-14. *The Wonders of Ancient Times.*—Repeatedly leaders in crises fortify themselves by recollections of historic deliverances in their peoples' past: **Then he remembered the days of old.** As Israel recalled Moses, so our statesmen go back to Washington or Lincoln. In World War II pressure had to be exerted to attempt

[1] Shorter, *The Brontës, Life and Letters,* II, 106-7.

12 That led *them* by the right hand of Moses with his glorious arm, dividing the water before them, to make himself an everlasting name?

13 That led them through the deep, as a horse in the wilderness, *that* they should not stumble?

---

12 who caused his glorious arm
    to go at the right hand of Moses,
who divided the waters before them
    to make for himself an everlasting
    name,
13   who led them through the depths?
Like a horse in the desert,
    they did not stumble.

---

his servant." Torrey emends to מושיע עמו, "savior of his people," which is attractive, but since Moses is obviously referred to, it is best to read with the Syriac, עבדו, **his servant**, for עמו, "his people" (cf. Ps. 77:20). Moses is not frequently mentioned in the prophets (cf. Jer. 15:1; Mic. 6:4). **Where is he who brought up:** Several MSS of the Greek and Syriac and the Dead Sea Scroll read *ma'aleh*, without the pronominal suffix "them." **The shepherds of his flock:** Cf. Heb. 13:20. The LXX and the Targ. read **shepherd** (so KJV and most modern scholars). Does the writer refer to Moses or to the people at the Red Sea? The versions seem to support the former alternative (but cf. Vulg., *pastoribus*); the M.T. supports the latter. The verb **brought up**, and the reference to **the sea**, as Volz has pointed out, go better with the crossing of the Red Sea than with the rescue of Moses. The thought that dominates throughout is the great deliverance of Israel (vss. 11*c*, 12*c*, 13*a*). The fervent and anxious repetition **Where is he?**, the length of the sentence with its five participial phrases (vss 11*e*-13*a*), and the repeated allusion to the crossing of the sea reveal the intensity of the writer's mood. Jeremiah castigates the leaders of his day for not asking these central questions of Israel's historical life, and the psalmists represent Israel's enemies as asking in scorn "Where is your God?" (Pss. 42:3, 10; 79:10). **In the midst of them his holy Spirit:** See vs. 10*b*. The days of Israel's beginnings saw great signs and wonders in which the spirit of God was active among them (cf. especially Num. 11:17, 24-30; Hag. 2:5; Neh. 9:20); in the present situation God seems absent and silent.

12. His glorious arm: Cf. the frequent references in Deuteronomy to God's mighty and stretched out arm; also vs. 5; 40:10; 51:9; 52:10; 53:1; 59:16; 62:8. The allusion is again to the crossing of the Red Sea. The arm of God is personified here much in the manner of the spirit in the preceding verse; it symbolizes the mighty power of God which accompanied the work of Moses.

13. Who led them through the depths? The final participial phrase of the series: "bringing up," "putting," "causing to go," "dividing," "leading" (cf. 64:3-5). The motif of Yahweh as leader is one of the most pronounced in the story of the Exodus. The **depths** (*tehōmôth*) refer poetically to the Red Sea (cf. Exod. 15:5, 8; Ps. 77:16; and Isa. 51:10, where it also refers to the primeval chaos waters). The text seems to be in

---

the invasion of Europe across the English Channel. On Aug. 10, 1943, Secretary of War Henry L. Stimson handed President Roosevelt a memorandum urging that the hour for attack was coming and that an American commander should be offered for the assault. He reminded the President of Abraham Lincoln:

We are facing a difficult year at home with timid and hostile hearts ready to seize and exploit any wavering on the part of our war leadership. A firm resolute leadership, on the other hand, will go far to silence such voices. The American people showed this in the terrible year of 1864, when the firm unfaltering tactics of the Virginia campaign were endorsed by the people of the United States in spite

of the hideous losses of the Wilderness, Spottsylvania and Cold Harbor.

Finally, I believe that the time has come when we must put our most commanding soldier in charge of this critical operation at this critical time. You are far more fortunate than was Mr. Lincoln or Mr. Wilson in the ease with which that selection can be made.[2]

It is such a historical retrospect which this prayer employs to raise faith to expectancy.

Who caused his glorious arm to go at the right hand of Moses. A striking metaphor of

[2] Henry L. Stimson and McGeorge Bundy, *On Active Service in Peace and War* (New York: Harper & Bros., 1947), p. 437. Used by permission.

14 As a beast goeth down into the valley, the Spirit of the LORD caused him to rest; so didst thou lead thy people, to make thyself a glorious name.	14 Like cattle that go down into the valley, the Spirit of the LORD gave them rest. So thou didst lead thy people, to make for thyself a glorious name.

disorder. Vs. 13a is obviously parallel to vs. 12a, 12c and should come to the margin, and vs. 12d forms the obvious climax to the section (cf. vs. 14d). Perhaps the simplest solution is to place vs. 12d after vs. 13a and to assume that a line has fallen out after vs. 12c. Budde and Volz, however, propose to attach **like a horse in the desert** (vs. 13b) to the preceding line, reading: "who led them through the floods like horses, through the desert without stumbling." Torrey, Feldmann, and others think the clause **they did not stumble** is a gloss. But vss. 13b-14 seem to form a close-knit unity, reaching a climax after the two comparisons (vss. 13cd, 14ab) in the reference to God's guidance of his people. The attachment of the phrase **like a horse in the desert** to the preceding line is possible, but the effect is less felicitous than the transfer of vs. 12d and vs. 13a suggested above.

14. The third reference to the **Spirit** is effective in this climactic context: **The Spirit of the LORD gave them rest** (cf. vss. 10b, 11e). Many commentators, following the versions, derive the verb (נוח) from another root meaning "to lead" (נחה; cf. Vulg., *spiritus Domini ductor eius fuit*). The emendation is slight and the context is decidedly favorable to the change. The thought of Yahweh's leading dominates this whole section and comes to its splendid culmination in the last two lines. As **cattle** go into the **valley** to seek pasture, so **the Spirit of the LORD** brings Israel to Canaan; it leads them all the way from Egypt to Palestine; cf. Jeremiah's vivid comparison to the homing instinct of the birds (8:7). **So thou didst lead:** The prophet shifts suddenly to the second person of direct address and prepares the way for the prayer which follows. **To make for thyself a glorious name.** This is another of the many repetitions with which this poem abounds (cf. vs. 12d) and a characteristic theocentric climax; note especially "glorious habitation" in vs. 15.

comradeship in struggle. In Milton's poem on the fateful day when Adam and Eve separate to their tasks, Adam says to her: "For God towards thee hath done his part, do thine."[3] But God's work for and with us is never in the past. His arm goes at our right hand in unfailing partnership. Had Eve been mindful of that, she might more steadfastly have withstood the tempter.

In vss. 13-14 are two descriptions of God's leading: in the depths of the Red Sea,

Like a horse in the desert,
 they did not stumble [cf. Ps. 160:9].
Like cattle that go down into the valley,
 the Spirit of the LORD gave them rest.

He led his people securely and restfully. How differently events appear in retrospect from the sensations of those who are passing through them! It requires the perspective of time to discern God's hand in occurrences. The crucifixion and resurrection of our Lord were not immediately understood. It took a generation or

longer for their effects to become felt. Then the redeemed saw God's revelation in them. God is ever our contemporary, but in fact he is recognized only when the event recedes and its consequences become an enriching memory.

> Not "Revelation" 'tis that waits,
> But our unfurnished eyes.[4]

The event in which God manifests himself redeemingly quickens the soul to perceive him. The abiding self-revelation of God lies in a historic yesterday. It is in memory that we discern God's "great goodness" (Ps. 145:7). The "monitory touch o' the tether" is

>   named by none
> At the moment, only recognized aright
> I' the fulness of the days, for God's.[5]

God's glorious name remains fixed in the national and racial memory. By a heartening retrospect the prophet leads up to the prayer which his people wish to offer.

[4] *Letters of Emily Dickinson*, ed. Mabel L. Todd (New York: Harper & Bros., 1931), p. 279. Used by permission.
[5] Browning, *The Ring and the Book*, "The Pope."

[3] *Paradise Lost*, Bk. IX, l. 375.

15 ¶ Look down from heaven, and behold from the habitation of thy holiness and of thy glory: where *is* thy zeal and thy strength, the sounding of thy bowels and of thy mercies toward me? are they restrained?

16 Doubtless thou *art* our Father, though Abraham be ignorant of us, and Israel acknowledge us not: thou, O Lord, *art* our Father, our Redeemer; thy name *is* from everlasting.

15 Look down from heaven and see,
    from thy holy and glorious habitation.
Where are thy zeal and thy might?
    The yearning of thy heart and thy compassion
are withheld from me.
16 For thou art our Father,
    though Abraham does not know us
and Israel does not acknowledge us;
thou, O Lord, art our Father,
    our Redeemer from of old is thy name.

3. Third Strophe: Thou Art Our Father and Redeemer (63:15-16)

From retrospect of the glorious past, from the Exodus to the entrance into the Holy Land, the prophet turns suddenly to the tragic conditions of the present. His petition falls into three strophes, each dominated by an urgent imperative (vss. 15*a*, 17*c*; 64:1). The prophet appeals to God's revelation of his character in the past and to the sorrowful conditions of the present, and finally begs for a new theophany. The contemplation of the past inspires the urgency of the prayer.

15. **Look down from heaven and see:** Cf. Ps. 80:14 for the same words. The prophet envisages God remote in his heaven, indifferent to what is happening to his people. He implores him to **look down . . . and see. Where are thy zeal and thy might?** Cf. vs. 11. The word for **zeal** (קנאה) expresses deep emotion, like ardor or jealousy. The word **might** is in the plural but should be pointed to read in the singular, following the versions. Together the words describe the nature of Yahweh. But the prophet follows the appeal to power by an appeal to God's great love, **the yearning of thy heart** (RSV), lit., **the sounding of thy bowels** (KJV), a vigorous anthropomorphism expressing profound feeling. Emotions have their physical counterpart with organs of the body. Similarly, the word for **compassion**, usually in the plural, is derived from the word for womb (cf. 16:11; Jer. 31:20). The question mark should follow **compassion**, not **might. Are withheld from me:** Read, "Restrain not thyself," by a slight emendation (the omission of a *yôdh*). The imperative should be connected with vs. 16 (cf. 64:12).

16. **For thou art our Father:** Observe how the thought of the strophe centers and culminates in this O.T. affirmation (cf. 64:8). It is derived from Yahweh's election word in vs. 8—"Surely they are my people, sons"—and has precisely the same position in the prayer (63:15–64:12) as there. Note the parallels in vs. 8 and cf. also Jer. 3:4, 19. **Though Abraham does not know us . . . :** Cf. 51:1-2; also Matt. 8:11-12; John 8:39-42; Rom. 2:28-29. Abraham and Jacob lie dead in Sheol and belong to the dim past, but God is Israel's Father for all time. **And Israel does not acknowledge us:** An alternative rendering is, "does not recognize us" (cf. Deut. 33:9). There is no polemic against

15-16. *A Piteous Plea for God's Fellowship.*— The meter changes into that used in lamentations, heightening the effect of the plea. **Look down from heaven and see.** Israel felt that God had withdrawn to his heavenly palace. Luther had similar moods: "When we seek him, he often locks himself up, as it were, in a private chamber." [6] This prayer deals with God at firsthand: **Where are thy zeal and thy might?** Here is an appeal from their present doubt of God's friendliness to their long experience of his active concern for them in the past. Israel had known his mighty acts. They knew he had a heart, al-

[6] *Table Talk*, No. CCCXXXIX.

though it now seemed closed to them. They cling to him despite appearance. They belong to the

> . . . strenuous souls for belief and prayer,
> . . . .
> That stand in the dark on the lowest stair,
> While affirming of God, "He is certainly *there!*" [7]

Thou art our Father, i.e., Father of the nation; an idea not yet extended to individuals. **Abraham** and **Israel** had been potent figures in their day, but centuries sundered them from these their needy descendants. God, however, con-

[7] Elizabeth Barrett Browning, "The North and the South."

17 ¶ O Lord, why hast thou made us to err from thy ways, *and* hardened our heart from thy fear? Return for thy servants' sake, the tribes of thine inheritance.	17 O Lord, why dost thou make us err from thy ways and harden our heart, so that we fear thee not? Return for the sake of thy servants, the tribes of thy heritage.

necromancy here or any implication concerning personal survival. There is, however, an implication of the relationship of Israel to her progenitors with whom her life and character were bound; yet the prophet does not appeal for help through them, but from God alone. This is brought out in the closing lines. Yahweh is Israel's **Father** and **Redeemer**; at the time of the Exodus he adopted Israel as his son (Exod. 4:22-23) and signalized the adoption by the redemption of his people from slavery. The redeemer as the nearest relative had the right of purchase or redemption. This strophe, like the preceding, refers to Yahweh's unique and immemorial **name**.

4. Fourth Strophe: Return! (63:17-19)

The earnest supplication moves into pure lament in this strophe. The prophet grieves over the deepening sin of his people, the loss of the holy sanctuary, and the absence of all evidence of the divine sovereignty.

17. Why? The characteristic cry of the lament (cf. Job 3:11-12, 20, 23; Hab. 1:3). The verse contains a profound mystery and paradox. Israel is responsible and accountable to God for her conduct, and yet the source of sin is traced to him; cf. Yahweh's hardening of Pharaoh's heart (Exod. 7:3). The effect of sin is more sin, callousness, and irreligion. But the converse is also stated by Jeremiah (31:18) when Ephraim cries, "Turn to me, and I shall be turned." Cf. also Second Isaiah (44:22): "Return to me, for I have redeemed you." Sin and grace are both conceived as originating in God. The only answer to this perplexity is in the experience of the soul whose life is everywhere rooted in the consciousness of God. God is the originator, creator, and sovereign Lord of all. The problem is understood in the context of bitter lament and in the profound religious faith of the petitioner. The terrible consequence of sin is the hardening of the heart, **so that we fear thee not**. God is not blamed for injustice here; rather, the mystery of his divine providence and sovereignty over every area of human life is recognized (cf. Paul's confession in Rom. 7:7-25). **Return for the sake of thy servants:** Return and

tinued—still their **Redeemer**, a present help. His fatherhood is a continuing relationship with his people, to be recalled in the blackest hour when his face seems hid from them.

17-19. An Expostulation with God.—Had he not withdrawn his face in anger, they had not wandered so far. One recalls the gloomy questioning of the Persian poet:

O Thou, who didst with pitfall and with gin
Beset the Road I was to wander in,
    Thou wilt not with Predestined Evil round
Enmesh, and then impute my Fall to Sin! [8]

God's relation to sin is an insoluble mystery. This devout O.T. poet knew that God's abandonment of Israel had led them to further sinning. God's grace provides a climate in which righteousness flourishes, his wrath a climate in which all good withers and dies. The religious intuition which raises the problem is correct.

If God's presence brings life, his turning away means death. The tragedy of Israel's situation lay in evidences of his continuing displeasure in a ruined land, a scattered people, a profaned sanctuary. Evil's results are cumulative. Sin hardens hearts, and hardened hearts sin more terribly. *Peccatum peccati est poena* is Luther's comment on this verse. In nations and men sin deteriorates character. In George Eliot's delineation of Tito she notes "that change which comes from the final departure of moral youthfulness —from the distinct self-conscious adoption of a part in life. The lines of the face were as soft as ever . . . ; but something was gone—something as indefinable as the changes in the morning twilight." [9] God has so made us that good and evil grow in us, the good becoming better, the evil worse. He is therefore, as this poet felt, chargeable with the progressive hardening which follows sin.

[8] *The Rubáiyát of Omar Khayyám*, st. lxxx.

[9] *Romola*, Bk. II, ch. xxii.

18 The people of thy holiness have possessed *it* but a little while: our adversaries have trodden down thy sanctuary.

19 We are *thine:* thou never barest rule over them; they were not called by thy name.

18 Thy holy people possessed thy sanctuary
     a little while;
     our adversaries have trodden it down.

19 We have become like those over whom
     thou hast never ruled,
     like those who are not called by thy
     name.

---

become to us our Father and Redeemer, as in the days of old (cf. vs. 16). The prophet never ceases his emphasis upon the unique relationship between God and Israel. All that is characteristic of God and all that Israel became through the act of his grace meet in the election and the covenant bond. Therefore the words

> for the sake of thy servants,
> the tribes of thy heritage.

18. Israel had been made a **holy people** by the act of grace of her holy God; she was holy, consecrated, sanctified by Yahweh. To the holy people belonged a holy place, the great **sanctuary** of Solomon, where the glory dwelt, the tabernacling presence signifying God's reality in the midst of his people. **Thy holy people, . . . a little while:** A very difficult line since it does not seem applicable to Solomon's temple. Sellin and Volz believe, however, that the second temple was destroyed (they date this destruction shortly after the erection; Morgenstern and Buttenwieser date it 485 B.C.). The text is certainly insecure, as the LXX and the Vulg. show. Many emendations have been proposed: Bewer, "It is only a short time ago that our enemies dispossessed thy holy people"; Kissane, "Why did the tyrant possess Thy holy city?"; Fischer, "Why should the godless tread the holy mountain?" (cf. LXX); Marti and Torrey, "Why did evil men desecrate thy sanctuary?" Bewer's rendering is closest to the M.T. and is therefore to be preferred.

19. Yahweh was the king of Israel (6:5; 33:22; 41:21; 43:15; 44:6; the enthronement psalms such as Pss. 47; 93; 96–99), but there is no vestige of his ancient sovereignty evident; he had named his **name** over Israel (Deut. 28:10; Jer. 14:9), but it is as though his name was lost from them. The prophet plumbs the deepest depth of his grief. Observe that the strophe, like the two foregoing (vss. 14*d*, 16*d*), closes with a reference to the divine **name**.

Return is uttered with passionate vehemence. It is the essence of the prayer. Israel's genius was her occupation with God. The prayer does not mention her oppressors. It contains no plea for deliverance from them or for the restoration of Jerusalem. It is concerned only with God's favoring presence. If he returns, all will be well. An incident in the career of an outstanding Scots divine, Robert Bruce, reveals a like concern:

> When he preached at Larbert Kirk, there was near by a chamber, where he used to go in betwixt sermons. One day, some noblemen and gentlemen, who had been hearing him, wearied betwixt sermons, when he stayed longer than he used. They having a good way to ride after sermon, they called for the bellman, and desired him to go to him in this little room, where he was retired, and knock softly at the door, and, if he opened, to acquaint him, they desired he might begin as soon as conveniently he could, because some of them had far to ride. The bellman did as he was commanded; but Mr. Bruce was taken up so in wrestling that he did not hear him. However, the bellman, while at the door, heard some of Mr. Bruce's words, which, poor

man, he did not understand; and so he came back to those that sent him, and told them that he did not know when the minister would come out. He believed there was somebody with him, for he heard him many times say, with the greatest seriousness, "That he would not,—he could not go,—unless He came with him; and that he would not go alone;" adding, that he never heard the other answer him a word. When he came out in a little, he was singularly assisted.[1]

This may be paralleled by the vision of Thomas Aquinas, to whom a Presence said, "Thomas, thou hast served me well: what wouldst thou have?" Thomas replied, *Nihil nisi te, Domine.*

For the sake of thy servants: Knowing that they longed for nought but God himself, they were confident that there was some mysterious quality in them which had originally led to his choice of them, and which, despite their sin, still held his affection. True religion is a personal relationship in which believers love God for his own sake, and he loves them for their sakes. There is no explaining why persons "take

[1] Wodrow, *Sermons by Bruce,* pp. 150-51.

64 Oh that thou wouldest rend the heavens, that thou wouldest come down, that the mountains might flow down at thy presence,
 	
2 As *when* the melting fire burneth, the fire causeth the waters to boil, to make thy
	64 O that thou wouldst rend the heavens and come down,
	    that the mountains might quake at thy presence —
	2ʸ as when fire kindles brushwood
	    and the fire causes water to boil —
	to make thy name known to thy adversaries,
	
	ʸ Heb Ch 64. 1

5. Fifth Strophe: Prayer for a Universal Theophany (64:1-5b [Hebrew 63:19b–64:4a])

Out of the *de profundis* of the lament the prayer breaks into its most impassioned and earnest petition. God's utter remoteness, apparent indifference, and silence must end. The prophet prays with intense longing for a theophany even greater than that at Sinai (Exod. 19) and the waters of Megiddo (Judg. 5). He implores God not only to "look down from heaven and see" (63:15), but to rend the adamantine heavens and reveal himself to his people so that its adversaries (cf. 63:18) may know that he alone is God, who works great and terrible wonders, who responds actively to those who wait for him, and meets those who repent and remember his ways. Observe the pervasive theophanic emphasis in the threefold **at thy presence** (vss. 1b, 2d, 3c), the twofold **come down** (vss. 1a, 3a), and the twofold "quaking of the mountains," the characteristic element in the classical theophanies in which the mighty bulwarks of the world are shaken and threatened (vss. 2b, 3c).

64:1. The Hebrew chapter division between vs. 1 and vs. 2 is most unfortunate. **O that thou wouldst rend:** The particle **O that** governs the two verbs (cf. the similar plea of Ps. 144:5). The description recalls the theophanies of Exod. 19:16-18; Deut. 32:22; Judg. 5:4-5; Mic. 1:3-4; Nah. 1:4-6; Hab. 3:3-15; Ps. 18:8-16. They represent the classical formulations for the divine appearing. The verbs are in the pluperfect: "hadst rent," "hadst come down," "had quaked." The fervent wish is contemplated as already realized. **Quake:** So the Hebrew from *zālal*, but many read with the LXX and Vulg., **flow down,** which represents a different pointing (cf. Judg. 5:5) and derives from the root *nāzal.* The omission of the conjunction before **come down** in the Hebrew, and the repetition in vs. *3c*, leads Torrey to delete the words here as a scribal error, but such repetition is in the style of the writer, especially at the beginning and end of a predication.

2. As when fire: Fire is the characteristic element in most, if not all, theophanies (cf. Exod. 19:18; Deut. 5:4; Heb. 12:18; etc.) and is frequently associated with the divine

to one another." On the human level a poet's sonnet concludes:

> So why I love thee well I cannot tell:
> Only it is that when thou speak'st to me,
> 'Tis thy voice speaks, and when thy face I see
> It is thy face I see; and it befell
> Thou wert, and I was, and I love thee well.[2]

Israel could give no more reason for God's love of her: "The LORD did not set his love upon you . . . because . . . , but because the LORD loved you" (Deut. 7:7-8).

In this frank prayer the poet puts the people's feelings candidly. They asked, "Why have our adversaries trodden down thy sanctuary?" It seemed to them that the Lord had been remiss in not protecting his own temple. It was the

same also with them, his holy people: **We have become like those over whom thou hast never ruled.** Honesty in prayer is a criterion of genuine religion. Dr. Johnson told Boswell: "I do not approve of figurative expressions in addressing the Supreme Being; and I never use them. Taylor gives a very good advice: 'Never lie in your prayers; never confess more than you really believe; never promise more than you mean to perform.' "[3] He might have added, "If you feel critical of God, tell him so."

64:1-5b. A Vehement Supplication for an Advent of God.—This is a plea for a dramatic appearance as in Judg. 5:5, etc. Such a theophany, shaking mountains and causing water to boil, would confound Israel's foes. They long for a repetition of the marvels of the Exodus,

[2] Edward Rowland Sill, "The Mystery."

[3] Boswell, *Life of Johnson,* June 11, 1784.

name known to thine adversaries, *that* the nations may tremble at thy presence!	and that the nations might tremble at thy presence!
3 When thou didst terrible things *which* we looked not for, thou camest down, the mountains flowed down at thy presence.	3 When thou didst terrible things which we looked not for, thou camest down, the mountains quaked at thy presence.
4 For since the beginning of the world *men* have not heard, nor perceived by the ear, neither hath the eye seen, O God, besides thee, *what* he hath prepared for him that waiteth for him.	4 From of old no one has heard or perceived by the ear, no eye has seen a God besides thee, who works for those who wait for him.

judgment. Israel's God is a consuming fire (Heb. 12:29). It must be admitted that the comparison in vs. 2*b* is not very effective. Some scholars seek to emend with the help of the LXX: "They will melt like wax in the fire, like water the wood devours." Torrey believes that the word "thunder" (המון) has dropped out after **brushwood,** and renders the phrase, "water which fire boils by the thunder of boiling waters." "In our passage the 'fire' which causes the celestial seas to boil is the lightning; they then 'thunder' like the waves of the ocean" (*Second Isaiah,* p. 465). This is surely the kind of comparison that is needed in the context, but the parallel in vs. 2*a* favors the RSV, though the latter is not felicitous. **To make thy name known:** Cf. vss. 12*d*, 14*d*, 16*e*, 19*e*. Revelation is the purpose of all theophanies. **Adversaries . . . nations:** Cf. vs. 18. The revelation involves judgment upon Yahweh's and Israel's foes (cf. 30:27).

3. When thou didst terrible things: The reference is to the momentous events at the time of the Exodus and the wilderness wanderings (cf. Deut. 10:21; II Sam. 7:13; Ps. 106:22). They were beyond anything Israel had expected or hoped for. **The mountains quaked . . . :** It is possible, though by no means certain, that the line represents a scribal error copied from vs. 1. Some scholars read: "O that thou wouldst come down that the mountains might quake."

4. From of old: Not "from eternity" but from the ancient time referred to throughout the poem. No one has ever heard of or seen any other **god** like the God who performs wonders **for those who wait for him** (reading the plural with the versions). The line recapitulates vs. 3*a*. Reflection upon the ancient wonders and the fervor of prayer evoke faith and expectation. Paul quotes the verse in I Cor. 2:9. There is a strong note of courage and hope in the final lines of the strophe.

Many scholars read vss. 1-4*b* as a single sentence. There is more to be said for reading vss. 1-3 in one predication. Observe the repetition of vss. 1*b*, 2*d*, 3*c*, and especially the context of each. To the climactic repetition of vs. 3*bc* (if original) vs. 4 attaches itself effectively.

with Sinai ablaze. This passage may be used as a Christmas text, for while the startling physical accompaniments are absent, Christ came both as Judge and Savior (cf. John 9:39; 12:31-32).

A God . . . who works for those who wait for him is almost the opposite of the conception of God current in the mid-twentieth century. Men have thought of God as waiting—waiting to be explored by man's faith, waiting to have his purposes achieved by man's scientific devices and increasing good will. Few have thought that a devout man is one who waits for God. In the Bible's faith God takes the initiative and labors beyond the utmost reach of man's imaginings. We must not be bustling interferers but patient subordinates, quietly looking for his signals to come into his plans. Of his mightiest acts, the birth and death of his Son, Ignatius writes: "The which were wrought in the silence of God" (Ign. Eph. 19:1). This unceasing activity of God on behalf of his people is unique, altogether unlike the deities of the heathen. His people therefore must not take the initiative. He is always "long beforehand" with us, and meets the man who **works righteousness. Thou meetest**—it is an unexpected surprise. We go out to tasks burdened with their difficulty and feeling alone in responsibility. But God was occupied in them before we started, and he encounters us. We shall miss the satisfaction of recognizing him unless we **remember** him in his **ways.** To be thankful for past mercies and seeking grace for what faces us is to **remember** him and discover his presence.

5 Thou meetest him that rejoiceth and worketh righteousness, *those that* remember thee in thy ways: behold, thou art wroth; for we have sinned: in those is continuance, and we shall be saved.

5 Thou meetest him that joyfully works righteousness,
those that remember thee in thy ways.
Behold, thou wast angry, and we sinned;
in our sins we have been a long time,
and shall we be saved?[z]

[z] Hebrew obscure

5*ab*. Thou meetest him that joyfully works righteousness: "Thou hast met him who rejoices and does righteousness." The LXX reads, "He will meet those who do righteousness," a rendering followed by several scholars. The verb "meet" has the sense here of entering into friendly encounter. The reference to rejoicing (שׂשׂ) seems strangely out of place. Ehrlich emends the word to שׁב, "repent." Moreover, the sentence should be introduced by the particle *lû*, which has been dropped through haplography. Render: "O that thou wouldst meet him who repents and does righteousness." **Those that remember thee:** This is perhaps an echo of vss. 7*a*, 11*a*, peculiarly appropriate in this climactic context. Read with the LXX, "those who remember thy ways" (cf. 26:8; 63:17).

6. Sixth Strophe: A Confession of Guilt (64:5*c*-7)

The strophe has a character of its own. From the mood of faith and hope the prophet turns to penitence and confession. The thought is summarized in the words **we have sinned.** What follows is a vivid description of deterioration and demoralization. From the introduction **Behold, thou** to the climactic close introduced by *kî*, we follow stroke by stroke the growing corruption which marks the career of evil (cf. Hos. 13:2).

5*cd*. Behold, thou wast angry, and we sinned: Perhaps the poet is simply saying that God's wrath drove the people to greater sin (cf. 63:17). **In our sins we have been a long time:** The Hebrew is certainly corrupt. Lit., "in them of old, and we shall be saved." The LXX reads simply διὰ τοῦτο ἐπλανήθημεν, "therefore we have erred"; Vulg., *in ipsis fuimus semper, et salvabimur;* Targ., "by the deeds of our righteous fathers who are from of old were we delivered." Among the many emendations that have been proposed perhaps the least violent is Volz's בהצלמך ונרשע, "when thou hidst thyself we became guilty" (cf. 57:17). The RSV interprets the supposed meaning by reading **in our sins** for "in them."

5*c*-7. A Confession of Sinfulness.—There is a strange sequence in **Thou wast angry, and we sinned.** We should have anticipated "We sinned, and thou wast angry." This prayer comes from those who had tasted the bitter punishment of God and, when his face was turned from them, had found their whole people sinking into worse sin. Devout souls know the darkness of God's withdrawal. Pascal wrote: "If [God] interrupts [the] flow [of his mercy] ever so little, drought will necessarily set in."[4] The strophe pictures the entire people sinning—**all** is thrice repeated. It is a tragic picture of a whole nation in spiritual disintegration. Inwardly they are unclean; outwardly they appear withered and swept away by the wind. **There is no one . . . that bestirs himself to take hold of thee** is a significant description of the effort required in faith. Faith is response

to God's gracious approach, and demands a rousing of the whole self to cleave to him. Walt Whitman has described the soul's outreaching for the perfect Comrade:

A noiseless, patient spider,
I mark'd where on a little promontory it stood isolated,
Mark'd how to explore the vacant vast surrounding,
It launch'd forth filament, filament, filament, out of itself,
Ever unreeling them, ever tirelessly speeding them.

And you O my soul where you stand,
Surrounded, detached, in measureless oceans of space,
Ceaselessly musing, venturing, throwing, seeking the spheres to connect them,
Till the bridge you will need be form'd, till the ductile anchor hold,
Till the gossamer thread you fling catch somewhere, O my soul.[5]

[5] From *Whispers of Heavenly Death.*

[4] Blaise Pascal, Letter to Madame Perier, his sister, Nov. 5, 1648. See *Great Shorter Works of Pascal,* tr. Emile Caillet and John E. Blankenagel (Philadelphia: Westminster Press, 1948), p. 81.

6 But we are all as an unclean *thing,* and all our righteousnesses *are* as filthy rags; and we all do fade as a leaf; and our iniquities, like the wind, have taken us away.

7 And *there is* none that calleth upon thy name, that stirreth up himself to take hold of thee: for thou hast hid thy face from us, and hast consumed us, because of our iniquities.

8 But now, O Lord, thou *art* our Father; we *are* the clay, and thou our potter; and we all *are* the work of thy hand.

6 We have all become like one who is unclean,
   and all our righteous deeds are like a polluted garment.
We all fade like a leaf,
   and our iniquities, like the wind, take us away.
7 There is no one that calls upon thy name,
   that bestirs himself to take hold of thee;
for thou hast hid thy face from us,
   and hast delivered[a] us into the hand of our iniquities.

8 Yet, O Lord, thou art our Father;
   we are the clay, and thou art our potter;
   we are all the work of thy hand.

[a] Gk Syr Old Latin Tg: Heb *melted*

---

6. We have all become . . . unclean: Sin grew like a deadly infection until everyone was seized with it. The word **unclean** is drawn from cultic usage (Hag. 2:13-14). **All our righteous deeds:** Even the best deeds of men are contaminated with evil. **Like a polluted garment:** Cf. Lev. 15:19-24. **We all fade like a leaf:** Sin takes away the vitality of the people so that they lose not only their sense of responsibility but their will and desire to resist it. They wither like autumn leaves, and are driven away before the wind (cf. 40:24; 41:16; 57:13; Job 27:21; Ps. 1:3).

7. No one makes any effort to avail himself of God's help, so desperate is the people's condition. **For thou hast hid thy face from us:** Cf. vss. 1*b*, 2*d*, 3*c*, emended text of vs. 5*d*; Exeg. on 63:9*b*. Sin had so dulled the conscience and sensibilities that the reality of God's presence was completely lost. In worship they could seek his **face;** in the degradation of their sin they no longer sought him, and he **hid** his **face** from them. **And hast delivered us:** Lit., **hast melted us.** The RSV is supported by the LXX, Syriac, and Targ. This dark picture of Israel's guilt explains the impassioned petition for a theophany.

7. Seventh Strophe: Final Supplication (64:8-12)

Out of the deep distress of confession the poet breaks into a final appeal to the Lord in which the major motifs of the prayer appear. The strophe begins with a strong

---

Faith, however, is response, and when God withdraws himself there is no energy in men's spirits to attempt such outreaches. When God hides his face, men lack the impulse to venture toward him. The climax of this piteous confession is the declaration of the people's bondage, not to their adversaries, but to their own sins. **Thou hast . . . delivered us into the hand of our iniquities** (the reading of LXX, Peshitta, and Targ.). This is the slavery of which Paul wrote in Rom. 6:16, and which Augustine acknowledged:

Bound as I was not with another man's irons, but with mine own iron will. But the enemy held my will, and thence had made a chain for me, and bound me. For of a froward will was a lust made; and a lust served became custom; and custom not resisted became necessity. By which links, as it were,

joined together (whence I called it a chain) a hard bondage held me enthralled.[6]

No profounder religious insight into sin meets us in the O.T. The poet saw his people conquered, not by the Babylonians or other foes, but by their own wickednesses. This prayer for another Exodus is primarily a petition for God's rescue of them from themselves. With nations and individuals their most tyrannical despot is their own ego:

Myself, arch-traitor to myself;
My hollowest friend, my deadliest foe,
My clog whatever road I go.[7]

8-12. *A Final Plea to Father and Maker.*—Again it is the nation which God has borne and

[6] *Confessions* VIII. 5.
[7] Christina Rossetti, "Who Shall Deliver Me?"

9 ¶ Be not wroth very sore, O LORD, neither remember iniquity for ever: behold, see, we beseech thee, we *are* all thy people.

10 Thy holy cities are a wilderness, Zion is a wilderness, Jerusalem a desolation.

11 Our holy and our beautiful house, where our fathers praised thee, is burned up with fire: and all our pleasant things are laid waste.

9 Be not exceedingly angry, O LORD,
and remember not iniquity for ever.
Behold, consider, we are all thy people.
10 Thy holy cities have become a wilderness,
Zion has become a wilderness,
Jerusalem a desolation.
11 Our holy and beautiful house,
where our fathers praised thee,
has been burned by fire,
and all our pleasant places have become ruins.

transition, **But now, O LORD**, and closes effectively with two pathetic questions. As is customary with the poet, the strongest words appear in the opening and closing lines.

8. Yet, O LORD: The Hebrew, "And [yet] now, O LORD," expresses transition better (cf. 63:16). The poet refrains from saying "and we are thy sons," although this was involved in the election (63:8). The pronouns are emphatic: **thou** (vs. 8*ab*) and **we** and "all of us" (literally). **Thou art our potter:** See Exeg. on 45:9. The appeal in Job 10:9 is much the same as here (cf. also 29:16; Jer. 18:4 ff.; Rom. 9:19 ff.). In 63:16 the appeal is to the Lord as Father and Redeemer (cf. 44:6, 24; 49:5-7); here it is to the Lord as **Father** and creator. **We are all the work of thy hand:** In contrast to the universal corruption of the confession (vs. 6), the appeal here is to the common creaturehood. Will the Lord destroy what he has made? (Cf. 60:21; especially Jer. 18:5-6.)

9. Be not exceedingly angry: Cf. vs. 5; 63:10. **Remember not . . . for ever:** Cf. Ps. 79:8. That God remembers is characteristic of Israel's historical mentality. The toll of past guilt seemed endless. **Behold, consider, we are all thy people:** An important line, summarizing the relationship between the Lord and Israel, and returning to the beginning (63:8). The word **consider** hardly renders the Hebrew, lit., "look," as in 63:15; cf. Vulg., *Ecce, respice;* the German expresses the sense: *schau doch her.* The prophet maintains the solidarity of the people throughout.

10. Thy holy cities: It is **Jerusalem** that is the holy city above all others, but as all of Palestine was the Holy Land, so all its cities are considered holy. The land is holy because it belongs to the holy God. The description would not apply to the period after the second temple.

11. This verse confirms the impression of the preceding. The clause **where our fathers praised thee** most naturally suggests Solomon's temple. **Our holy and beautiful house:**

fashioned. It would be the height of unreason for the potter to cast away the utensil he has shaped:

And He that with his hand the Vessel made
Will surely not in after Wrath destroy.[8]

There is a note of exhaustion in the cry **remember not iniquity for ever.** If the Exile lay behind, now the keen disappointment of the continuing struggle in a devastated land, with most of its inhabitants still in exile and the temple only a ruin, drove the people to despair. **We all** occurs again. There had been a confession of the involvement of the entire nation in sin; now the plea is for the restoration of the whole nation, even as it was a whole nation in the liberation at the Exodus. It is upon the

fatherhood and creatorship of God that Christians too base their inclusive hopes for mankind.

The assurance that the righteous Creator can never cease to desire and urge the righteousness of His creature is the eternal hope for man. . . . If this be His purpose for one, it must be His purpose for all. I believe that it is His purpose for all, and that He will persevere in it until it is accomplished in all.[9]

The description of the desolated land and burned temple is touching. All the cherished implements connected with worship were gone. Congregations which have lost a venerable, or at least a loved, edifice can enter into the feeling in the phrase **Our holy and beautiful house,**

[9] Thomas Erskine, *The Spiritual Order, and Other Papers* (Edinburgh: Edmonston & Douglas, 1876), pp. 54-55.

[8] *The Rubáiyát of Omar Khayyám*, st. lxxxv.

| 12 Wilt thou refrain thyself for these *things,* O Lord? wilt thou hold thy peace, and afflict us very sore? | 12 Wilt thou restrain thyself at these things, O Lord? Wilt thou keep silent, and afflict us sorely? |
| 65 I am sought of *them that* asked not *for me;* I am found of *them that* | 65 I was ready to be sought by those who did not ask for me; I was ready to be found by those who did not seek me. |

Lit., "The house of our holiness and our beauty [or "glory"]." **Our fathers:** The perspective of the prayer suggests not the immediately preceding generation but the many generations of the past. **All our pleasant places:** The Hebrew has simply **pleasant** or "desirable" in the plural. The phrase more likely refers to the precious objects of Solomon's temple: its altar, brazen sea, etc.; hence KJV **things.**

12. How can the Lord **refrain** from intervening in this dark situation? The anthropomorphism is striking but not unusual (cf. 42:14; 62:1). In view of the afflictions of his holy and elected people, the destruction of his holy cities and the holy city of Zion, and above all, the desolation of the sanctuary where his glory dwelt and where the fathers worshiped him, how can he refrain from acting now? (Cf. 63:15.) The prophet is borne down by God's silence. His loud and passionate outcry, his confession and penitence, his many pleas, and his appeals to the memory of the past are designed to move God to reveal himself in word and deed.

L. Judgment and Salvation (65:1-25)

This chapter is so similar to ch. 66 in style, thought, and implied historical background that common authorship is often assumed. But opinion diverges sharply concerning its connection with the preceding poem.

It is sufficiently clear that God is the speaker throughout. But are the words an answer to the prayer of 63:7–64:12? Many scholars think not. That it is not the kind of answer one might expect should not blind us to the fact that in reality it does constitute an answer to the insistent cries of the suppliant. Both poems refer to the people, although in ch. 65 they are sharply divided into two groups. Yet in 63:7–64:12 the prophet speaks in behalf of the people (see Exeg. *ad loc.*), and while he identifies himself in his sense of guilt and contrition with the whole people, nothing is more evident than that he represents a substantial group within the community who share the same attitude and concern as he. It is only with 65:8 that the division within the people becomes apparent, and a special point is made of this. As men say at the vintage season, "Do not destroy it, for the blessing is in it," so the Lord says he will not destroy the whole people, but will bring forth descendants from Jacob. This important verse answers as clearly as possible the contentions of those who see no connection with 63:7–64:12. But a careful scrutiny of the whole poem shows numerous small relationships with its predecessor. To the repeated "Where is he?" (63:11; cf. vs. 15) the Lord replies, **Here am I, here am I**

where our fathers praised thee. Birds line a nest with feathers plucked from their breasts, and men fill a building with associations from their hearts. A church gathers sacred sentiments which aid worship, for memory uplifts, and when the building goes, something irreplaceable is lost.

With hearts breaking, so that tears cannot be held back, the prayer ends with a direct question, **Wilt thou restrain thyself at these things, O Lord?** This is an argument from man at his tenderest to the most loving God. It is the plea of heartbroken sinners to One whom they believe a heartbroken God. Calvin, who shared their feeling of the inward filthiness, the total ruination, and the iron slavery of sin, paraphrases with approval the publican's prayer: "Lord, let the bottomless depth of thy mercy swallow up the bottomless depth of my sin." [10]

65:1-25. Threats to the Faithless, Promises to the Loyal.—In Chs. 65–66 two sharply separated groups in the nation are addressed. One is com-

[10] *Institutes* III. 4. 18.

sought me not: I said, Behold me, behold me, unto a nation *that* was not called by my name.	I said, "Here am I, here am I," to a nation that did not call on my name.

(65:1-2; cf. vss. 12, 24). He is not remote in the heavens, indifferent and deaf to the call of his suppliants, but ready to be sought and found by them. Note also the following: **that did not call on my name** (vs. 1*d*; cf. 64:7; or, if the passive is read in vs. 1*d* as in the M.T., cf. 63:19*b*); **to a rebellious people** (vs. 2*b*; cf. 63:10*a*); **who walk in a way** (vs. 2*c*; cf. 63:17*a*; 64:5*b*); **I will not keep silent** (vs. 6; cf. 64:12*b*); **iniquities** (vs. 7; cf. 64:6*d*, 7*d*, 9*e*); **my servants** (vss. 8, 9, 13 [thrice], 14; cf. 63:17*c*); **all of you** (vs. 12*b*; cf. vs. 8; 64:6 [twice], 9). Note especially the reference to the anger of God (vss. 3*a*, 5*cd*; cf. 64:5*c*, 9*a*). No one of these alone may be important, but all of them together should at least inspire caution against denying a real connection between the poems. Observe also the threefold reference to **the former things** or **troubles** (vss. 7*g*, 16*e*, 17*c*). Gunkel and others have noted the relation between lament and oracular response in the O.T. prophecy. It is easy to see, therefore, why Bentzen and others take 63:7–65:25 as a national liturgy.

Another difficult problem faces us in connection with the date and historical background. There has been a strong tendency to place the poem in the age of Ezra and Nehemiah and to explain the division within the community by the hostility between the cultic community at Jerusalem and the Samaritans. But such a sharp cleavage is nowhere made clear; besides, the division exists within the Jewish community, not outside it (cf. vs. 8). Ezra and Nehemiah do not suggest any attempt to attract the Samaritans (cf. Ezra 4:2 ff.). Volz (*Jesaia II, ad loc.*) explains the religious practices of vss. 3-5 by Hellenistic influence (cf. the picture described in 56:9–57:13). In view of the fact that the temple had not yet been built (66:1), combined with the foregoing considerations, we may tentatively date these chapters 538-520 B.C., and understand them as following 63:7–64:10.

The eschatology of the poem deepens with the progress of its thought. The literary forms of threat and promise emerge naturally from the two dominant emphases of eschatology: judgment and felicity. The relation of vss. 1-2, 12, and 24 illustrates the unity of the prophet's thought, and the divine first person is maintained throughout. The quotation at the close is in the manner of much exilic and postexilic literature. The strophic divisions in vss. 8-20 are clearly marked, less so in vss. 1-7, 21-25. The writer is fond of striking contrasts (vss. 11-15), rhetorical series (vss. 13-14), repetition (e.g., **my servants** in vss. 13-15), and climax. Frequently the parallelism is effective (vss. 1, 13-14, 19-20). The meter is not easy to determine, but in general it varies between 3+3 and 3+2. The text is not always certain. The Dead Sea Scroll has several interesting divergences from the M.T. Vs. 20 is a gloss.

1. First Strophe: The Lord Is Accessible (65:1-2)

Far from being aloof and silent in the face of the people's misery and despair, God replies that he was always available and accessible. To their cry "Where is he?" and their longing for a miraculous theophany, he answers, **Here am I.** It was in reality the people who were silent; they did not seek Yahweh or call on his name.

65:1. I was ready to be sought . . . to be found: The verbs are in the tolerative Niphal and express emotions which react upon the mind (Kautzsch, *Gesenius' Hebrew*

posed of those who combine pagan practices with their worship of the God of Israel; the other, of the faithful remnant of the people. Hitherto we have seen the nation considered as a unit in relation to its God; but now this discrimination between apostates and faithful is insisted on. The prayer in 63:7–64:12 had pleaded for the Lord's return to his people. If that prayer is answered here, it is a return to the steadfast remnant.

These chapters are relevant to modern situations where the church finds herself made up of members imperfectly familiar with the Christian faith and combining it with questionable

2 I have spread out my hands all the day unto a rebellious people, which walketh in a way *that was* not good, after their own thoughts;	2 I spread out my hands all the day to a rebellious people, who walk in a way that is not good, following their own devices;

Grammar, sec. 51*c*): "I let [or "permitted"] myself to be sought [or "consulted"]." Cf. Ezek. 14:3; 20:3, 31; 36:37. **To be found:** Cf. 55:6; Deut. 4:7. The Hebrew omits the **me** in the first line but the Dead Sea Scroll, LXX, and Vulg. have it. **I said:** Note how Yahweh's words are similarly introduced in the same position in the previous poem (63:8). Such succinct quotations in the divine first person contain the heart of the prophet's thought. **Here am I, here am I** and **Behold me, behold me:** Such repetitions are frequent in both Second and Third Isaiah (see 66:1-24; cf. 63:11*c*, 11*e*, 15*c*). **That did not call on my name:** The M.T. reads the passive. It is better to read as here with the ancient versions and the ASV mg. (cf. 64:7*a*).

2. **I spread out my hands:** Cf. Prov. 1:24. In Isa. 1:15, the people spread out their hands to God; here he spreads out his hands in eager invitation. **To a rebellious people:** The LXX reads, πρὸς λαὸν ἀπειθοῦντα καὶ ἀντιλέγοντα, which may be a conflation of the M.T. סורר and the Dead Sea Scroll סורה. The meter favors the LXX, "A disobedient and contrary people." **A way that is not good:** Cf. Ps. 36:4; Prov. 16:29. The **way** (*dérekh*) is used primarily with reference to the cult as the following lines show. It represents the devices of the people themselves (*mahshebhôth*), not the divinely instituted ordinances (cf. 63:17). The expression is a litotes (as in Ezek. 38:10). Vss. 1-2 reveal the same divine characteristics of love and pity and infinite longing as does 63:9. The apostle Paul, following the LXX, quotes these verses in Rom. 10:20-21, but applies vs. 1 to the Gentiles, vs. 2 to Israel.

---

beliefs and habits, and of a minority who understand more clearly their Lord's will and attempt to live in fidelity to him. Religious syncretism is not confined to foreign mission fields and to recent converts from heathenism. Many Christians worship the God of the N.T. and nationalism, or social position, or wealth, or various private divinities which enlist their devotion. Christian convictions are mixed with ideas and practices which distort and contradict them.

1-2. *God Eager to Be Found.*—The prayer has complained of God's withdrawal. His remoteness and seeming silence troubled his people. Now he assures them that on the contrary it is he, not they, who waits to enter fellowship with them: **I was ready to be sought by those who did not ask for me.** This is an O.T. anticipation of "Behold, I stand at the door" (Rev. 3:20). The superstitious practices mentioned in the following verses were onerous devices to reach and influence God; but all the while he was accessible to trustful and obedient worshipers. True intercourse with God presupposes his prior approach to us. We do not overcome his reluctance but lay hold on his eagerness. The contrivances men invent for successful access to the Deity betray their fear of him and their misunderstanding of his fatherly nature. The sublime prayer in 63:7–64:12 is in sharp contrast to the weird usages described in 65:3-5. Here are two basically different religions:

I said, "Here am I, here am I,"
to a nation that did not call on my name.

God's initiative is disclosed again and again throughout both the O.T. and the N.T. He is at hand, but is forgotten and disregarded.

In the autumn of 1652, John Owen preached a straight sermon to Parliament on a day of humiliation in the naval war with Holland:

You take counsel with your own hearts, you advise with one another, hearken unto men under a repute of wisdom; and all this doth but increase your trouble, you do but more and more entangle and disquiet your own spirits. God stands by and says, *I am wise also,* and little notice is taken of him.[1]

I spread out my hands all the day—the yearning gesture of one who would have his people run to him and be embraced; cf. our Lord's saying to Philip, "Have I been so long time with you, and yet . . ." (John 14:9). Here is the patience of unwearying divine love. A tragedy of human history is the burdensome ceremonial and complicated set of practices devised by men's troubled consciences to put themselves right with God, while he "waits to be gracious" and asks only the confiding and obedient affection of his children. In these opening

[1] Sermon XXXIX, "Christ's Kingdom and the Magistrate's Power."

<table>
<tr><td>

3 A people that provoketh me to anger continually to my face; that sacrificeth in gardens, and burneth incense upon altars of brick;

4 Which remain among the graves, and lodge in the monuments; which eat swine's flesh, and broth of abominable *things is in* their vessels;

</td><td>

3 a people who provoke me
   to my face continually,
sacrificing in gardens
   and burning incense upon bricks;
4 who sit in tombs,
   and spend the night in secret places;
who eat swine's flesh,
   and broth of abominable things is in
      their vessels;

</td></tr>
</table>

2. SECOND STROPHE: THE CORRUPT AND SUPERSTITIOUS CULT (65:3-5)

The prophet details the cultic sins of the people, the "way that is not good." The strophe opens and closes with the divine provocation and wrath: **continually** (vs. 3*b*), **all the day** (vs. 5*d*). Beginning with the **people,** the thought is developed by a series of participial phrases: "provoking," "sacrificing," "burning incense," "sitting," "eating," and "saying" (cf. 63:11-13). The cultic practices are not always clear, though the LXX gives us some help. Despite the continuity between vss. 1-2 and vss. 3-5, it is better to begin a new strophe here (so Kittel).

3. A people who provoke me: Lit., "The people provoking me against my face." There may be an echo here of the repeated reference to Yahweh's **face** in the preceding poem. **To my face:** Brazenly, without fear or shame. The verb is in the Hiphil, "causing me to be provoked" or "angry." It is frequently used in Deuteronomy, Jeremiah, and Kings in reference to the worship of other gods. **Sacrificing in gardens:** Cf. 1:29; 57:5; 66:17. The gardens point to the widespread nature cult. **And burning incense upon bricks:** Many commentators read "on the roofs" (cf. II Kings 23:12; Jer. 19:13), but this is by no means clear. There is nowhere such a prohibition in the O.T., but it has been suggested that incense jars made of baked clay, such as those found at Bethshean and Taanach, may be meant. The Dead Sea Scroll has a completely different reading, which is far from clear: וינקו ידים על האבנים.

4. Who sit in tombs: They go to the tombs for the purpose of consulting the dead (cf. 8:19; 29:4). **And spend the night:** The LXX interprets correctly, διὰ ἐνύπνια, "for the sake of dreams." The practice of incubation was widespread in the ancient world, as in the cult of Asclepius at Epidaurus (Vergil *Aeneid* VII. 88-91; also Horace *Satires* I. 8. 23-29; see Lowth and Wade, *ad loc.*). For O.T. parallels cf. Gen. 28:11 ff.; I Kings 3:4-15. Ehrlich emends **in secret places** to "between the rocks," but the Hebrew is hardly obscure. To the Hebrews **graves** were unclean. **Who eat swine's flesh:** Specifically prohibited in the Mosaic law (Lev. 11:7; Deut. 14:4; cf. Isa. 66:17). According to the common view set forth in W. Robertson Smith (*Lectures on the Religion of the Semites* [3rd ed.; London: A. & C. Black, 1927], pp. 218, 290-91), the prohibition was inspired by the fact that swine was either sacred to the god or a totemistic animal. In Babylon it was sacred to the god Ninurta. It could be eaten only in certain exceptional situations in the celebration of the cult. **Broth of abominable things:** For **broth** the Hebrew *Kethîbh* (ופרק) reads "piece" or "fragment," but the *Qerê*, LXX, Vulg., and Dead Sea Scroll all read "broth" (ומרק). The word rendered **abominable things** (פלנים) is a *terminus technicus* for unclean sacrificial flesh (Kissane, *Isaiah*, p. 303; cf. Lev. 7:18; 19:7). The allusion is doubtless to sacrificial meals.

---

verses we have an O.T. version of the invitation in Matt. 11:28.

3-5. Superstitious Cults.—Whenever religion deteriorates to conventional worship, the door opens wide for the entrance of superstition. Lord Byron had given up whatever Christian faith had possessed him, but he believed that ill luck came from Fridays, from spilling salt, from breaking mirrors, etc. In our time, when thousands have no vital faith in the God and Father of Jesus Christ, fortunetellers, mediums, "healers," etc., and many quack religionists flourish among us. Nor is superstition confined to the uneducated.

5 Which say, Stand by thyself, come not near to me; for I am holier than thou. These *are* a smoke in my nose, a fire that burneth all the day.	5 who say, "Keep to yourself, do not come near me, for I am set apart from you." These are a smoke in my nostrils, a fire that burns all the day.
6 Behold, *it is* written before me: I will not keep silence, but will recompense, even recompense into their bosom,	6 Behold, it is written before me: "I will not keep silent, but I will repay, yea, I will repay into their bosom

5. Who say, "Keep to yourself": As a result of the sacred rites which have rendered the communicant holy (*qādhôsh*), he must not be profaned by contact with the unholy; therefore he says, **Keep to yourself,** lit., "draw near to you." **Do not come near me:** The Dead Sea Scroll reads, "Do not touch me," which is excellent here, but has no versional support and is against the parallelism. **For I am set apart from you:** Lit., "So that I do not make you holy" or "taboo" (reading the Piel; cf. Ezek. 44:19; 46:20). Some commentators see in this verse the words of the mystagogue to the initiate, who is not to be made taboo because of the danger involved in contact with common things. It is not necessary to appeal to Hellenistic influence, however. The mysteries were not confined to Greece. The passage is not dissimilar to Ezek. 8. Nor do we need to invoke the hypothesis of Samaritan provenance. The rites may best be explained by conditions obtaining in Jerusalem at the time. The clause **who say** modifies "the people" (vs. 3*a*) and refers to those who have through these mysterious cultic practices rendered themselves holy (cf. Hag. 2:10 ff.). The source of the practices may be Assyrian or Babylonian, such as we see reflected in Deuteronomy, Jeremiah, Zephaniah, and II Kings; or it may be the popular folk religion, which, influenced by widely diffused Semitic practice, experienced a recrudescence in the chaotic years following the destruction of Jerusalem. Volz's resort to Hellenistic influence encounters the difficulty that some, if not most, of the practices referred to were familiar throughout the ancient world. Wade's citations from Greek sources are interesting, but they can be paralleled by Semitic sources. **These are a smoke in my nose, a fire:** A climactic and summarizing statement. The cultic rites are **smoke** arousing God's wrath (cf. Ps. 18:8), **a fire** burning **all the day** (cf. Deut. 32:22; Jer. 17:4; see vs. 3*ab*; 64:5*c*, 9*a*). In Hebraic psycho-physical anthropology, the **nose** was the seat of anger. The word for "anger" and **nose** or **nostrils** is the same in Hebrew. The strophe ends in an effective climax after the long series of participial phrases.

3. THIRD STROPHE: THE TOLL OF DIVINE JUDGMENT (65:6-7)

6. Behold, it is written: The divine sentence has been determined. The idea of the divine accounting in a heavenly register was familiar to the Babylonians; the god

Which of those who say they disbelieve,
Your clever people, but has dreamed his dream,
Caught his coincidence, stumbled on his fact
He can't explain.[2]

The only safeguard against superstition is a warm and intelligent trust in God. Thomas Erskine defined the mature character as "a cordial, and delighted, and intelligent sympathy with the whole will of God."[3] Such only are proof against superstition. There is a stern judgment here against these distrustful and disloyal folk who are **a smoke in [God's] nostrils.**

[2] Robert Browning, "Mr. Sludge, 'The Medium.'"
[3] *Unconditional Freeness of the Gospel*, p. 204.

6. The Toll of Divine Judgment.—Iniquity accumulates. So judgment is meted out to **their iniquities and their fathers' iniquities together.** Groups of apostates perpetuate themselves in a nation. Pagan practices capture imaginations and pass themselves on as a tradition. This is as true with social immoralities as with religious defections. There may be periods when these do not seem to be a serious force; but like a reservoir, there is a gradual filling up, until one day it bursts in a devastating torrent. In the chaotic years in Palestine during the Exile and immediately thereafter, pagan syncretism had mounted into a flood. The prophet feels that the hour of recompense has arrived.

7 Your iniquities, and the iniquities of your fathers together, saith the LORD, which have burned incense upon the mountains, and blasphemed me upon the hills: therefore will I measure their former work into their bosom.

8 ¶ Thus saith the LORD, As the new wine is found in the cluster, and *one* saith, Destroy it not; for a blessing *is* in it: so

7 their[b] iniquities and their[b] fathers'
    iniquities together,
                says the LORD;
because they burned incense upon the
    mountains
    and reviled me upon the hills,
I will measure into their bosom
    payment for their former doings."

8 Thus says the LORD:
"As the wine is found in the cluster,
    and they say, 'Do not destroy it,
    for there is a blessing in it,'

[b] Gk Syr: Heb *your*

Nebo wrote down the destinies of men in a book (cf. Volz, *Jesaia II*, p. 283; cf. also 4:3; Exod. 32:32; Mal. 3:16; Ps. 69:28; Dan. 7:10; Rev. 20:12; also Deut. 32:34; Pss. 130:3; 139:16). The same idea is present both in later Jewish apocalyptic (Enoch 81:4; etc.) and in Zarathustran eschatology (*ibid.*). **I will not keep silent:** Cf. 62:1; 64:12. **Into their bosom:** The reference is to the fold above the belt in which the ancient Oriental carried his money and personal possessions (cf. Jer. 32:18; Ps. 79:12; Luke 6:38).

7. Their iniquities and their fathers' iniquities: The RSV follows the LXX and the Syriac in the use of the third person pronoun. God will repay the accumulated guilt of the fathers, together with the guilt of the prophet's contemporaries. **Says the LORD:** Probably a gloss. **Because they burned incense:** The constant plaint of the prophets against Israel (cf. 57:5, 7; Hos. 4:13; Ezek. 6:13). **For their former doings:** It is questionable whether the Hebrew can be so rendered. The implication seems to be that God will recompense only the earlier sins, but this is surely not the meaning. The LXX omits **former.** Literally the word is "first." Some scholars, following the very similar passage in Jer. 16:18, read the word as an adverb: "So I will measure their recompense first into their bosom." The corruption of the line seems deeper, however. Torrey's explanation (*Second Isaiah*, p. 468) that ראשנה על is a text-critical note on vs. 6*b* which has been inserted into the text, is convincing, and his translation is certainly correct, "I will measure out their payment in their lap."

4. FOURTH STROPHE: GOD WILL NOT DESTROY THE WHOLE PEOPLE (65:8-10)

The strophe opens with the oracular formula, continues with an important figure containing the essence of the thought, and closes with a most important line, recalling vs. 1*a* and perhaps the faithful Israel who "sought" the Lord in 63:7–64:12.

8. The writer begins a new stage in his thought, as is suggested by the opening words. Heretofore he has pronounced a judgment of doom upon the people, but now he proceeds, by a figure drawn from the vintage, to assure Israel of a remnant who will

The pervasion of the minds of men by secularism in modern times is a corresponding influence. It invades religious beliefs and chills them. One thinks of teachers and preachers who have told men how little they must believe in order to be Christians. It penetrates individual and corporate conduct. In national policies, in legislation, in business practices, even in friendly and family relations, where is there clear recognition of the sovereignty and presence of the God revealed in Jesus Christ? It is this appalling omission which is repaid in judgment.

8-10. *The Entire People Will Not Be Destroyed.*—Here is the heart of the answer to the prayer in ch. 64. In 64:6 stress had been laid upon the sin of all; but the divine response is that a remnant will be found worthy of preservation. A cluster of grapes becomes in the wine press a mass of stuff which is of no use for wine, but there is also the "must," the unfermented juice from the crushed grapes. So in Israel, along with these disloyal folk are the faithful—**my people who have sought me.** Much is made throughout the O.T. of a

will I do for my servants' sake, that I may not destroy them all.	so I will do for my servants' sake, and not destroy them all.
9 And I will bring forth a seed out of Jacob, and out of Judah an inheritor of my mountains: and mine elect shall inherit it, and my servants shall dwell there.	9 I will bring forth descendants from Jacob, and from Judah inheritors of my mountains; my chosen shall inherit it, and my servants shall dwell there.

be spared. When men gather grapes from the vineyard and sort them, they say of the good cluster,

> Do not destroy it,
> for there is a blessing in it.

So the Lord will not destroy all the clusters, but will preserve those with good juice in them. Many scholars think that there are good and bad grapes on the cluster and that the whole is saved for the sake of the good grapes. But this can only be inferred, and it is doubtful whether the grammar of the lines permits such an interpretation. The definite article before **wine, cluster,** and **all** rather points to the view that the whole cluster is good and is therefore spared. **As the wine is found:** The word *tîrôsh* means the must or new wine, here the juice of the grapes. **And they say, "Do not destroy it":** It is possible, though by no means certain, that a vintage song is quoted here, similar to those in 5:1-7 and 27:2-6. If this is true, then the melody may be alluded to in the superscriptions to Pss. 57; 58; 59; 75. **Blessing:** The life-power or vitality in the grape. "It is the blessing of the grape to contain juice, just as it is the blessing of the kneading-trough to be full of dough" (Pedersen, *Israel, Its Life and Culture,* I-II, p. 183). **So I will do for my servants' sake:** Cf. 63:17c; also the substance of 64:4-5b. **And not destroy them all:** The Hebrew has "the whole." This is the great disclosure of the new section of the poem. The elect community represented by the pious Israel of 63:7—64:12 is to be separated from the other clusters, for in it too there is **a blessing,** a *berākhāh*. It is this group, how large we cannot say, of which the Lord speaks. The meaning is not the same as in Gen. 18:23-33 (contra Wade), but rather that of the good and bad figs in Jer. 24. If our understanding is correct, then we have here a development of the doctrine of the remnant to which both Isaiah and Second Isaiah had made their contribution (cf. 1:8-9; 6:11-13; 17:4-6; 30:17-18; 51:1 ff.; also 57:13; 66:5 ff.).

9. Faithful Israel will occupy the Promised and Holy Land (cf. 57:13; 60:21). Observe the words used in reference to the people: **descendants from Jacob, inheritors of my mountains, my chosen, my servants.** The possession of the sacred soil became a fixed

saving remnant. God would have spared Sodom could he have found ten righteous men in it (Gen. 18:32), and he reduced Gideon's forces to three hundred of resolute initiative (Judg. 7:1-7). It is his method to start and carry forward his purposes by minorities, often by a minority of one. In his sonnet on W. L. Garrison, James Russell Lowell speaks of God's employment of such pioneering figures as Luther and Columbus and this clamant reformer:

> Men of a thousand shifts and wiles, look here!
> 　See one straightforward conscience put in pawn
> To win a world; see the obedient sphere
> 　By bravery's simple gravitation drawn! [6]
> 　　　[6] St. viii.

The entire land is to be peopled by servants of God. **Sharon** and **Achor** are mentioned as its extreme limits, as Americans speak of their country "from Maine to Florida." In the quotation from the vintage song, **Do not destroy it, for there is a blessing in it,** is a suggestion of the worth of the true Israelites for the entire nation. Through them God's purpose for the whole land is fulfilled. The Lord's land is for his true servants only. What a perversion of this prophetic hope may be that element in modern Zionism which would give to this religious ideal a merely nationalistic realization! When Christians use the prophetic promise, we must be careful not to empty it of its exacting demand. Only the spiritually faithful can rightly claim to be the **blessing in the cluster.**

10 And Sharon shall be a fold of flocks, and the valley of Achor a place for the herds to lie down in, for my people that have sought me.

11 ¶ But ye *are* they that forsake the LORD, that forget my holy mountain, that prepare a table for that troop, and that furnish the drink offering unto that number.

10 Sharon shall become a pasture for flocks, and the Valley of Achor a place for herds to lie down, for my people who have sought me.

11 But you who forsake the LORD, who forget my holy mountain, who set a table for Fortune and fill cups of mixed wine for Destiny;

---

feature of classical eschatology. **Inheritors of my mountains:** The reference is to those who will possess Palestine (cf. 57:13; also 14:25; 49:11; Ezek. 38:21). **My chosen shall inherit it:** The land will be for the **elect** only.

10. The whole land of Palestine, from the Mediterranean in the east to the descent of the Jordan in the west, will be inherited by the elect servants of the Lord. The word השרון, **Sharon,** designates the region of the Maritime Plain from Mount Carmel to Joppa (see George Adam Smith, *The Historical Geography of the Holy Land* [25th ed.; London: Hodder & Stoughton, 1931], pp. 147-64). Since the transformation of Sharon to a pasture would mean a transformation for the worse, many scholars emend it to ישמון, "Jeshimon." But this is to mistake the writer's meaning. The passage describes the idyllic state of peace and contentment of the new age; a place where shepherds feed their flocks. The **Valley of Achor** is probably the Wadi Kelt, near Jericho (Josh. 7:24; 15:7; Hos. 2:15). The closing line **for my people who have sought me** is not a gloss, as has been supposed, but an important climax pointing to the contrast between vss. 1-7 (see vs. 1) and vss. 8-10.

5. FIFTH STROPHE: THE DESTRUCTION OF THE APOSTATES (65:11-12)

The heart of the strophe is the word of judgment in vs. 12ab. It is preceded by an emphatic vocative, **but you,** modified by a quatrain of participial phrases (cf. vss. 3-5b), and followed by another quatrain describing the reason for the terrible judgment (cf. vss. 1, 7).

11. **But you who forsake the LORD:** The apostates are those who practice the cultic rites described in vss. 1-7 and the end of this verse. **Who forget my holy mountain:** Those who neglect and ignore the faith and worship associated with the temple mount. There may be no allusion here to actual abstention from the temple ritual, however. **Fortune** and **Destiny:** It is better to preserve the proper names, Gad and Meni. They were probably gods of fate; cf. the LXX, τῷ δαιμονίῳ; the Vulg. renders the former by *Fortuna.* Gad is a Syrian divinity (Friedrich, Baethgen, *Beiträge zur semitischen Religionsgeschichte* [Berlin: H. Reuther, 1888], pp. 76-80), whose name is preserved in such place names as Baal-gad (Josh. 11:17; 12:7; 13:5) and Migdal-gad (Josh. 15:37). The name appears frequently in Greek inscriptions in the region of the Hauran, near the area originally occupied by the tribe by that name, where there may have been temples for his worship. It is also preserved in Phoenician and Palmyrene inscriptions. J. H. Mordtmann ("Mythologische Miscellen," *Zeitschrift der deutschen morgenlän-*

11-12. The Destruction of the Disloyal.—Gad and Meni, translated **Fortune** and **Destiny,** were ancient symbols of good and ill luck, much as we speak of "heads and tails" in the flip of a coin. These disloyal Israelites trusted to chance more than to their God. They did not desert him altogether, but they combined his worship with this cult of luck. Deities of fortune were a menace to true religion because they insisted on no standards of personal or social righteous-

ness in their devotees. There may be an element of chance in this apparently law-abiding universe, but the Bible never speaks of "luck" because it introduces an irreligious and unethical factor into men's outlooks. Events are under God's control and must be received at his hand. The essence of religion is such fidelity to him and his will as leaves no place for chance in men's calculations. One of John Galsworthy's characters remarks: "I don't know whether I

12 Therefore will I number you to the sword, and ye shall all bow down to the slaughter: because when I called, ye did not answer; when I spake, ye did not hear; but did evil before mine eyes, and did choose *that* wherein I delighted not.

13 Therefore thus saith the Lord GOD, Behold, my servants shall eat, but ye shall be hungry: behold, my servants shall drink,

12 I will destine you to the sword,
    and all of you shall bow down to the
        slaughter;
because, when I called, you did not an-
        swer,
    when I spoke, you did not listen,
but you did what was evil in my eyes,
    and chose what I did not delight in."

13 Therefore thus says the Lord GOD:
"Behold, my servants shall eat,
    but you shall be hungry;
behold, my servants shall drink,
    but you shall be thirsty;

---

dischen Gesellschaft, XXXIX [1885], 44-46) quotes a Latin inscription where the names Gad and Meni appear together. The Syriac and later Jewish literature also preserve the name. Skinner (*Isaiah, ad loc.*) mentions a Syriac writer of the fifth century who refers to the *lectisternia* prepared for Gad. Gressmann claims that the name Meni also appears in the Egyptian inscriptions as a female deity. It is probable that the two divinities were astral gods. The LXX suggests that they bore opposite functions, favorable and evil destinies, as in Arabic astrology. Our text seems to allude to sacred meals in which communion was established between the gods and their communicants (cf. I Cor. 11:27). The names have not been found among the gods of the Babylonian pantheon (cf. Skinner and Volz, *ad loc.*).

12. I will destine you: The verb *mānāh* is a play on Meni. **Because, when I called, . . . when I spoke:** Cf. vss. 1-2. There may be in these lines an implied answer to the plaint concerning the Lord's silence in 63:7–64:12. **But you did:** The people did not respond to the divine call to turn and repent, but chose **evil** instead. The last four lines of this verse are practically repeated in 66:4.

6. SIXTH STROPHE: THE LORD'S SERVANTS AND THE APOSTATES (65:13-14)

13-14. The oracle of eschatological judgment is introduced with great solemnity as a climax to the two preceding strophes (cf. vss. 6-7). The judgment is four times preceded

---

understand what loyalty is. Loyalty to what? To whom? Nothing's fixed in this world; everything's relative. Loyalty's the mark of the static mind, or else just a superstition, and anyway the negation of curiosity." [5] In biblical religion there is one "fixed" fact—God—and everything is "relative" to him and his purpose. Hence to speak of "my luck" is to suggest some control other than his. Gad and Meni are serious rivals to the righteous Lord revealed in Jesus. And so far from being the negation of curiosity, loyalty to truth and confidence in its dependability underlie all scientific investigation. Gad and Meni are as inimical to science as they are to genuine religion. In the life with God one takes chances; Abram went out not knowing whither he went, and our Lord in Gethsemane did not see the exact outcome of his Father's will; but both knew whom they believed, and were per-

[5] *Flowering Wilderness* (New York: Charles Scribner's Sons, 1932, p. 26.

suaded that obedience to him would be best for them and the world.

In vs. 12 the verb is a play upon Meni, **Destiny:** Men chose a deity of chance, but God said, **I will destine you to the sword.** And the strophe concludes with a splendid reaffirmation of the indispensableness of obedience: **When I spoke, you did not listen.** Men have the fatal gift of choice. That may seem to intrude a large factor of chance into God's universe. He cannot predetermine precisely their decisions. But to choose what God does not delight in carries with it destructive consequences. Evil is self-defeating. That assures the permanence of God's kingdom and his righteousness. His sovereignty is never in question. We may willingly espouse it, and become his fellow workers. We may flout it, and seal our own doom.

13-14. *The Lord's Servants and the Apostates.* —This solemn oracle takes up the conception of lucky and unlucky destinies. It may seem

but ye shall be thirsty: behold, my servants shall rejoice, but ye shall be ashamed:	behold, my servants shall rejoice, but you shall be put to shame;
14 Behold, my servants shall sing for joy of heart, but ye shall cry for sorrow of heart, and shall howl for vexation of spirit.	14 behold, my servants shall sing for gladness of heart, but you shall cry out for pain of heart, and shall wail for anguish of spirit.
15 And ye shall leave your name for a curse unto my chosen: for the Lord God shall slay thee, and call his servants by another name:	15 You shall leave your name to my chosen for a curse, and the Lord God will slay you; but his servants he will call by a different name.

by **behold** in the manner of eschatological oracles. The emphatic vocative (ואתם) of vs. 11 is four times repeated, each time with renewed stress. The reference to the two gods of destiny, good and evil, in vs. 11, may have evoked these powerful lines in which the fates of the servants and the apostates are set forth. While it is not expressly stated, the inference seems to be present that the judgment will involve a complete reversal of existing conditions: they who hunger will be satisfied; they who weep will rejoice. The first two judgments refer to economic conditions; the last two refer to psychological transformation. The meter is 3+2.

7. Seventh Strophe: The New Name and the New Blessing (65:15-16)

The elect, the **servants** of the Lord, will be called by **another name;** their character will be completely transformed and will express itself in the new blessing and oath by the God of truth. The time of affliction is forgotten. The strophe forms a link between the eschatological judgment of vss. 13-14 and the new age of vss. 17-18.

15. You shall leave your name: All that is remembered of the apostates is the use of their name in a **curse.** We should expect some such formula as "May God requite you as he requited them!" or "May their fate befall you!" **And the Lord God will slay you:** The line is very awkward here. Many see in it the substance of the curse: "May the Lord God slay you" (cf. Jer. 29:22). But the introductory conjunction before the verb, the future tense instead of the expected jussive, and the absence of any comparison to the apostates argue against it. Torrey recasts the line to read: "But my chosen I will hold fast, saith Yahweh." The emendation is perhaps too radical. The simplest solution is to consider the line as a marginal gloss with Marti, Skinner, and others (cf. vs. 12). The parallelism is thus effectively restored. The Dead Sea Scroll suffers a substantial gap

that the disloyal to God are enjoying a fortunate lot at present. But the future contains a reversal of fortunes dependent solely on men's spiritual relations with God. The old evangelistic summons, "Get right with God," echoes this prophetic message. Economic and psychological well-being, emphasized in the fourfold **behold,** depend ultimately upon a man's standing with God. To seek first to be under his rule is to find all outward and inward satisfactions added. Much is made today of "adjustment"; but adjustment to whom? If to God as revealed in Christ, then—whatever maladjustment may seem the immediate issue in this sinful earth— in God's ultimate judgment blessings of possessions and of emotional peace and joy are assured.

15-16. *The New Name and the New Blessing.* —All that will remain of the apostates is their name in a curse (cf. Jer. 29:21-23). **His servants he will call by a different name.** As the Exeg. suggests, this name may be "trustworthy" or "dependable." This is the vindication of their fidelity. They are the authentic servants and representatives of One who is **the God of truth,** i.e., the faithful God (cf. 62:2-4, where it is not the name "Israel" which is discarded, but the names "Forsaken," "Desolate"). This conception of the new name is taken up in Rev. 3:12. To be called by God's name is so manifestly to belong to him that his fellowship is at once suggested. There are those with whom one cannot be for long without a sense of the divine presence. They have ties with him who is invisible, and they bind those who are their companions to God. The relationship of men with the reliable God informs the life of the land with this trustworthiness. Oaths become trust-

16 That he who blesseth himself in the earth shall bless himself in the God of truth; and he that sweareth in the earth shall swear by the God of truth; because the former troubles are forgotten, and because they are hid from mine eyes.

17 ¶ For, behold, I create new heavens and a new earth: and the former shall not be remembered, nor come into mind.

---

16 So that he who blesses himself in the land
　shall bless himself by the God of truth,
and he who takes an oath in the land
　shall swear by the God of truth;
because the former troubles are forgotten
　and are hid from my eyes.

17 "For behold, I create new heavens
　and a new earth;
and the former things shall not be remembered
　or come into mind.

---

in the text. After vs. 15b it has the word "continually," followed by a long space. It omits all the words of the text beginning with vs. 15c and ending with **bless himself** in vs. 16b (from אדני יהוה to באלהי), and substitutes והיה הנשבע, "and it shall be that he who swears."

16. Volz deletes the whole verse as an intrusion occasioned by the word for **curse** (oath) in vs. 15a. It is true that the verse attaches itself somewhat unnaturally (note the awkwardness of the אשר, **so that**), but in the absence of any textual support (the Dead Sea Scroll simply has a blank space between vs. 16 and vs. 17) it is precarious to remove it. **He who blesses himself:** "Invokes a blessing." **The God of truth:** The Hebrew has "the God of Amen," which may be a liturgical accommodation (cf. Rev. 3:14). Torrey explains that the "new name" of vs. 15 is here given, "true, faithful, dependable," and cites the parallel of the name given Mohammed in Mecca, "al-Amin, the trustworthy." The omission of the article constitutes no difficulty. The usual explanation that God's faithful performance of his threats and promises will inspire men to call on him in blessing and oath is not apparent on the surface. **Because the former troubles:** Cf. 63:9. The time of distress and despair will be no more. When it is **forgotten,** it does not exist.

8. Eighth Strophe: The New Creation and the New Age (65:17-19)

The third main section of the poem (vss. 17-25) is devoted to the life of the new age. It will be a time of joy and peace (cf. vss. 9-10 and vs. 25). The radical character of the eschatological turning point is expressed in the words **for behold** (vs. 18c). Against the background of the creation of **new heavens and a new earth** the life of the community is described. The significant word **create** (ברא) is used three times (vss. 17a, 18bc) at the points of greatest emphasis. It is within this context that the joy and gladness of the new age are to be understood. The poet not only repeats the verbs **be glad** and **rejoice** (vss. 18a, 18cd, 19ab) but places them in new contexts and different grammatical forms.

17. New heavens and a new earth: Throughout the O.T., especially among the prophets, the redemptive acts of God are reflected in the natural world. The modern conception of nature is absent from such passages; the forces of nature are subject to

---

worthy and corporate life is rid of hypocrisy and deception.

**He who blesses himself in the land
　shall bless himself by the God of truth.**

The land is blessed with sincerity and candor. Life is under the all-seeing eye of the Holy One. This feature of heaven is suggested in the chorus of Frederick W. Faber's hymn, "O Paradise, O Paradise":

Where loyal hearts, and true,
Stand ever in the light.

The brightness of the new age eclipses all prior suffering. **The former troubles are forgotten;** they have ceased to exist even as memories which might shadow the glorious present.

17-19. The New Creation and the Messianic Age.—Behold, I create emphasizes God's activity. This is a new beginning. The present world

18 But be ye glad and rejoice for ever *in that* which I create: for, behold, I create Jerusalem a rejoicing, and her people a joy.

19 And I will rejoice in Jerusalem, and joy in my people: and the voice of weeping shall be no more heard in her, nor the voice of crying.

20 There shall be no more thence an infant of days, nor an old man that hath not filled his days: for the child shall die a hundred years old; but the sinner *being* a hundred years old shall be accursed.

18 But be glad and rejoice for ever
in that which I create;
for behold, I create Jerusalem a rejoicing,
and her people a joy.

19 I will rejoice in Jerusalem,
and be glad in my people;
no more shall be heard in it the sound of weeping
and the cry of distress.

20 No more shall there be in it
an infant that lives but a few days,
or an old man who does not fill out his days,
for the child shall die a hundred years old,
and the sinner a hundred years old shall be accursed.

the divine will and respond to his command (cf. 1:2; 11:6-9; 34:1–35:10; Jer. 4:23-28). The sovereignty of God over nature, classically expressed in Gen. 1, is here applied to the new age. The time of salvation for the elect community is ushered in by a new creation. To a new age belong **new heavens and a new earth.** The meaning is not that the present world will be completely destroyed (cf. 51:6) and a new world created (cf. Rev. 21:1; II Pet. 3:13), but rather that the present world will be completely transformed. It should be observed that there is no cosmological speculation here; like Gen. 1:1–2:4a, creation provides the background for history, here the new history of the new age. **The former things . . . remembered:** Cf. vs. 16; also 42:9; 43:18-19; II Cor. 5:17; Rev. 21:4. **Or come to mind:** "Come on the heart" (cf. Jer. 3:16).

18. But be glad and rejoice for ever: The LXX reads, "they shall find in her joy and gladness." Torrey emends עֲדֵי עַד, **for ever,** to עָרֵי עַד, "eternal cities," but the word suits the context perfectly (for the same usage cf. 26:4; Pss. 83:17 [Hebrew 83:18]; 92:8; 132:12, 14). **Jerusalem a rejoicing:** The contrast is to the sorrow of the former age, the subject of the preceding poem (see 64:10; cf. 51:3; 60:15; 61:2-3). Messianic Jerusalem is the city of joy and gladness.

19. The new relationship established by the new creation unites Jerusalem and God in a common joy. God rejoices in the community of his elect (62:5; Deut. 30:9; Zeph. 3:17). The time of mourning is over (cf. 25:8; 30:19; 35:10 [=51:11]; Rev. 21:4).

9. Ninth Strophe: Life in the Messianic Community (65:[20]21-23)

20. This verse is probably a late gloss (Torrey, Kissane). Not only does it overload the strophe, but the style is not like that of the rest of the poem. Skinner rightly describes the thought as "unaccountably labored and obscure." The language is reminiscent of late Jewish apocalyptic. **An infant that lives but a few days:** The Hebrew is **an infant of days.** Premature death was often interpreted as due to divine displeasure; a long life, like the lives of the patriarchs, was due to God's blessing and approval. **And the sinner**

is to be entirely renovated and transformed as the setting for the new redeemed community. The Bible regards the physical creation as the background for the history of men and women under God. A new stage in history, the final stage, requires a new setting. The "newness" consists primarily in God's closeness to his people. Irenaeus writes of the coming of Christ: "Learn that he brought every new thing by

bringing himself." [6] He brought a new covenant, a new man, a new hope, a new Jerusalem. Here it is God's joy in his people which alters the face of heaven and earth. Christians have found the world remade for them by the renewal of their spirits in Christ (cf. the experience of Saul Kane in John Masefield's *The Everlasting Mercy*).

[6] *Against the Heresies* IV. 34. 50.

21 And they shall build houses, and inhabit *them;* and they shall plant vineyards, and eat the fruit of them.	21 They shall build houses and inhabit them;
	they shall plant vineyards and eat their fruit.
22 They shall not build, and another inhabit; they shall not plant, and another eat: for as the days of a tree *are* the days of my people, and mine elect shall long enjoy the work of their hands.	22 They shall not build and another inhabit;
	they shall not plant and another eat;
	for like the days of a tree shall the days of my people be,
	and my chosen shall long enjoy the work of their hands.
23 They shall not labor in vain, nor bring forth for trouble; for they *are* the seed of the blessed of the LORD, and their offspring with them.	23 They shall not labor in vain,
	or bear children for calamity;[c]
	for they shall be the offspring of the blessed of the LORD,
	and their children with them.

[c] Or *sudden terror*

a hundred years old: Better, "He who comes short of a hundred years." The death of one who lives only a hundred years will be due to the divine anger.

21. Men will enjoy the **fruit** of their own labors. The messianic description is in sharp contrast to the judgment of prophetic oracles (Amos 5:11; Mic. 6:15; Zeph. 1:13; cf. 62:8-9; Deut. 32:39 ff.).

22. **Like the days of a tree:** Cf. 61:3. The ancient Hebrew was impressed with the life and long duration of trees (cf. Job 14:7 ff.; Pss. 1:3; 92:12-13; Jer. 17:8; Ezek. 19:10). The LXX and Targ. read interestingly "the tree of life." **My chosen shall long enjoy:** The thought of the **elect** people runs through the entire poem. The verb means literally "to wear out" (cf. Job 21:13).

23. **They shall not labor in vain:** Throughout the strophe there are traces of the idyllic existence in paradise, yet there is a realism here which is in striking contrast to the more developed descriptions of later apocalyptic eschatology in which the soil yields a hundredfold. Men will labor, but their labor will yield plenty (cf. Hab. 3:13). **Or bear children for calamity:** The calamity may be some sudden stroke of misfortune, as in sickness or catastrophe (cf. Lev. 26:16; Jer. 15:8; Ps. 78:33; Vulg. reads *in conturbatione*). **For they shall be the offspring:** Cf. 61:9; Job 21:8. They with the generations following will have God's blessing upon them. The Dead Sea Scroll reads the active for the passive participle **blessed.**

21-23. *The Messianic Community's Life.*— Men will enjoy the fruit of their labors, something which our war-scarred age can appreciate. Think of unhappy peasants whose crops are destroyed on the eve of harvest, and whose homes are leveled by artillery or bombing! **Like the days of a tree shall the days of my people be.** Immortality was not yet on the religious horizon, but unusually long life is set before the people (vs. 20, usually considered an addition, enlarges on this thought). This extension of life enables men to realize their plans and enjoy the results of their work. Trees were the most enduring living things these Hebrews knew (cf. Ps. 92:12). They outlive several human generations. The length of days made possible the continuance of family and neighborly relations for a century or longer. It is a vain speculation whether this would be an improvement or not in human affairs. The movement of thought and life is aided by the rapidity with which dominant figures disappear and others have their day of opportunity. Mature minds are sorely missed, but their passing opens doors for their followers to become leaders. We can scarcely conceive the tempo of a society where the elderly live on indefinitely with the next three, four, or five generations (**their children with them**). But this and incredibly more is implied in the Christian expectation of heaven. It should be a spur to open-mindedness and to the mutual regard of older and younger in order that we may be fit citizens of that city whence none goes forth forever.

24 And it shall come to pass, that before they call, I will answer; and while they are yet speaking, I will hear.

25 The wolf and the lamb shall feed together, and the lion shall eat straw like the bullock: and dust *shall be* the serpent's meat. They shall not hurt nor destroy in all my holy mountain, saith the LORD.

66 Thus saith the LORD, The heaven *is* my throne, and the earth *is* my footstool: where *is* the house that ye build unto me? and where *is* the place of my rest?

24 Before they call I will answer,
    while they are yet speaking I will hear.
25 The wolf and the lamb shall feed together,
    the lion shall eat straw like the ox;
    and dust shall be the serpent's food.
They shall not hurt or destroy
    in all my holy mountain,
           says the LORD."

66 Thus says the LORD:
    "Heaven is my throne
    and the earth is my footstool;
what is the house which you would build for me,
    and what is the place of my rest?

10. TENTH STROPHE: AN AGE OF PEACE (65:24-25)

The silence of God, which tried the soul of the suppliant in 63:7—64:12, will be broken. The poet at vs. 24 reaches back to vss. 1-2, but the picture of felicity is deeper here. God will know men's thoughts, and **before they call . . . will answer.** His blessing extends even into their interior consciousness (cf. 58:9; also 30:19; Jer. 29:12).

25. The poet draws his closing picture of the new age from the messianic description in 11:6-9. The third line, **and dust shall be the serpent's food,** is an allusion to Gen. 3:14 (cf. Mic. 7:17). Duhm and others reject it as a gloss. It is more likely that reflection upon the new age following the new creation inspired this reminiscence. **They shall not hurt:** They shall do no harm. The Jerusalem of the messianic era will be the city of peace (cf. Hos. 2:18; Ezek. 34:25, 28; for classical and other parallels see 11:6-9).

M. THE NEW BIRTH OF ZION AND THE FIRE OF JUDGMENT (66:1-16)

Three questions present themselves in the interpretation of this chapter. What is its relation to the preceding chapter? Is it a literary unit or a mosaic of disparate fragments? To what historical situation does the writer address himself? Commentators

24-25. God's Communion with His People.— In the prayer in ch. 64 the climax of Israel's sorrow had been the Lord's unresponsiveness. "Wilt thou keep silent?" (64:12.) Now—and this is an additional evidence that ch. 65 contains the answer to the prayer in 63:7—64:12— God anticipates his children's pleas: **Before they call I will answer.** This takes up in the conclusion the thought in the opening line of the poem and brings all to a unity. It is a rich disclosure of God's eagerness to fulfill his people's needs, and to give himself—the one supreme need of man—to complete their blessedness. This is the crowning glory of the new Jerusalem in Revelation: God himself shall be with them. This phrase of the prophet's—**before they call I will answer**—is an important contribution to the conception of prayer. God knows our secret thought and our phrasing of it is always clumsy. He answers the unexpressed longing of souls. To be sure, our attempt to utter that longing accurately aids him in his response.

The description of the ultimate peace is drawn from 11:6-9. Religious thought has often seen man's sin as introducing discord into an otherwise harmonious creation. One thinker put it that nature is like a bride, adorned in her wedding garments, whose bridegroom died on their wedding day, leaving her in tears ever since. Modern man has been impressed with her cruelty—"red in tooth and claw"[7]—and the biblical writers, too, saw this aspect of her. The "new earth" would be different. Paul cherished the hope that redeemed men would make possible God's redemption of the groaning creation (Rom. 8:21-23). When man's salvation is complete, he will find himself in surroundings matching his spiritual nature. "In Christ" he will be surrounded by a world also "in Christ," from which strife and the law of prey are gone, and in which God is "all in all" (I Cor. 15:28).

66:1-24. The New Birth of Zion and the Fire of Judgment.—The temple was apparently in

[7] Tennyson, *In Memoriam,* st. lvi.

differ greatly in their answers. It is perhaps impossible to arrive at any great degree of certainty. Yet the first question seems to admit of a fairly probable solution. Affinities between the two chapters are clearly present. The repetition of the same words (cf., e.g., 66:4cdef, 22ab and 65:12cdef, 17) indicates that the writer was familiar with ch. 65. The eschatological point of view, imagery, and mood persist through both chapters. The division of the community into the pious faithful and the rebellious apostates, the description of the syncretistic practices, and verbal affinities suggest a similar provenance and authorship. It is true that there are striking differences, but they are not so pronounced as to demand literary independence.

The question of literary integrity is more difficult. Certainly the initial impression is of discontinuity and compositeness. The transitional devices so marked in other poems are almost absent here. The meter appears more irregular, and vss. 18-21, 24 are so prosaic that they require considerable textual alteration before they can be put into poetic form. Most scholars today see in the chapter a series of loosely connected poems or a collection of completely separate fragments. Duhm divides the chapter into five independent units (vss. 1-4, 5-11, 12-17, 18-22, 23-24); Haller into three (vss. 1-4, 5-16, 17-24), Volz into three (vss. 1-2; 3-4, 17, 5-6; 7-16, 18-24). Volz dates vss. 1-2 ca. 520 B.C.; vss. 3-4, 17, 5-6 in the Hellenistic age, and vss. 7-16, 18-24 somewhat later. The writer of the commentary in *La Sainte Bible* (Paris: Société Biblique de Paris, 1947), II, 445, believes that an editor has gathered together a group of fragments to form a summary for Third Isaiah. Torrey sees the chapter as a single poem; Kissane finds a complete unit in vss. 1-16, Fischer in vss. 1-17. Kissane's view seems most convincing although the strophes are to be divided somewhat differently.

The two major eschatological emphases of judgment and felicity pervade the poem. They are made concrete in the two groups of the Jewish community. The persistent contrast between true and false worship connects what seem like *disjecta membra* into a fairly intelligible unity. Stylistic elements reinforce this impression to some degree. Throughout, the poet has a tendency to use key words twice: vs. 1, **where** (אי זה); vs. 2, **all these** (כל אלה); vss. 3e, 4a (גם); vs. 6, **hark** or **voice** (קול; thrice); vs. 7, **before** (בטרם); vs. 8, **who** (מי); vs. 9, the emphatic **I** (אני); vs. 11, **that** (למען); vs. 12, **like a river** (כנהר).

The crux of the historical problem which the poem raises centers in the allusion to the temple in vs. 1. Is the allusion historical or ideal? Various answers have been given to this question.

(a) Hitzig and Knobel believe that the verse refers to a project contemplated by the Jews in Babylon to build a house of worship to Yahweh there, as the Jews in Leontopolis actually did in Egypt some time later.

---

process of rebuilding. The prophets Haggai and Zechariah had been urging the people to rebuild it. The community at Jerusalem seemed to this prophet too absorbed in the reconstruction of the material shrine. Many of them were in addition practicing the pagan rites dealt with in ch. 65. Like earlier prophets, this poet cares little for the cultus, and demands obedience to the word of the Lord. During the Exile synagogues had become the places of worship where the reading and preaching of the law were the major element in the service. Third Isaiah eyes askance the zeal for the rebuilding of the temple, the re-establishment of the cultus, etc. The righteous Lord of the universe cares most for righteousness.

This final chapter gives unity to the entire book of Isaiah. The book begins with a people sedulous for ceremonies and lacking in social conscience (1:10-17); it concludes with a plea for the service of God in obedience to his word. The editor of the miscellaneous prophecies, now combined in this rich collection and combined with careful attention to their sequence, has evidently seen to it that their commencement and their climax coincide in their message. The book contains various appraisals of the temple, sacrifices, the sabbath, etc. One cannot say that any poem is utterly hostile to outward forms of religion. But throughout the insistence is upon thoughtful and loyal fellowship with God in response to his righteous word.

1-2. Worship in Humility and Penitence.— Over against the current zeal for the rebuilding of the temple, this poet repeats earlier messages of prophets and teachers upon the impossibility of localizing him who fills the universe. The Exeg. gives these passages. He does not de-

(b) Duhm, Marti, Skinner, and others hold that the oracle is directed against the schismatic Samaritans who, after their request to co-operate in the building of Zerubbabel's temple had been rejected, threatened to build their own temple in rivalry to the temple and cult at Jerusalem. The returning exiles who preserved the inherited faith of the fathers could not tolerate the admission of such a heretical group. Skinner refers to the construction of a temple on Mount Gerizim either ca. 430 B.C. on the basis of Neh. 13:28-29 or ca. 330 B.C. on the basis of Josephus. Feldmann (Isaias, p. 284) has summarized the objections to this view: (i) The contrast in vss. 1-4 is not to the place but to the manner of worship. (ii) There is no support in the books of Ezra and Nehemiah for the view that the Jews considered the Samaritans their "brothers." The reverse seems to have been the case. (iii) The threat of a new temple on the part of the Samaritans would not have had the desired effect upon the faithful adherents of Yahweh. (iv) There is no evidence whatsoever that in the period under discussion the Samaritans ever contemplated the building of a temple.

(c) Sellin and Elliger hold that the reference is to the temple of Zerubbabel. Here it is the Jews living in Palestine who represent the syncretistic apostates; their request to join in building the temple was denied by the returning exiles. We have no real evidence anywhere of such a situation; cf. also (a) above.

(d) The most widely held view, however, is that the passage is a complete rejection of the temple as such (Wellhausen, Budde, Gressmann, Hans Schmidt, Rudolph, Volz, Torrey, et al.). The prophet, standing in the great succession of his pre-exilic forebears, contends for a purely spiritual worship. Volz argues forcefully that such a lofty view was already implicit in Mosaic religion with its rejection of all visual imagery. The supreme assertion of a religion of the spirit in John 4:24 reaches back to the beginning and persists through the O.T. among the prophets, historians (cf. II Sam. 7:5 ff.), and the psalmists (Pss. 40; 50; 51; 69). There were those in ancient Israel who looked upon the destruction of the temple in 586 B.C. as a judgment against the temple (cf. Jer. 29:5 ff.). The movement represented in 520 B.C. by such prophets as Haggai was opposed by men of deeper prophetic faith who asserted that Yahweh needed no temple at all.

(e) Other scholars (Kissane, Fischer, Feldmann, etc.), recognizing the force of (d) above, nevertheless hold that the passage does not reject all external forms of worship. It is not the temple as such that is condemned but the corrupt religious practices of those who wish to perpetuate debased and pagan syncretism. As the pre-exilic prophets did not condemn the institution of sacrifice as such, so, it is said, God does not reject the building of a house for himself. Just as sacrifice must be the expression of a sincere heart and a holy life, so the temple is acceptable if it corresponds to a pure and undefiled

---

nounce the temple, but insists on its relative unimportance. The same cast of mind which stressed outward form loved the semipagan rites which were a menace to the true worship of the invisible Lord of heaven and earth. The prophet will have no substitute for a conscience sensitive to the righteous will of God. It is of course possible to combine some ritual with spiritual fellowship with One who transcends all forms man may devise; e.g., George Herbert in his poem "Sunday" extols the glories of that hallowed day, but adds:

> there is no place so alone
> The which He doth not fill.

Coleridge, in the Hartz Forest, turns homesick thoughts toward his loved native England, and patriotically sings her praises, but at once goes on:

> Nor will I profane,
> With hasty judgment or injurious doubt,
> That man's sublimer spirit, who can feel
> That God is everywhere! the God who framed
> Mankind to be one mighty family,
> Himself our Father, and the World our Home.[8]

This chapter, at first reading apparently composite, finds unity in a noble strophe on God's omnipresence, a unity enforced in the concluding proclamation of the God of Israel as God of the entire earth who will gather multitudes to his people. The insistence that God has regard to the man of humble heart removes national and local barriers and renders him accessible to the spiritually minded everywhere.

And trembles at my word: The function of

[8] "Lines written in the Album at Elbingerode."

2 For all those *things* hath mine hand	2 All these things my hand has made, and so all these things are mine,[d] says the LORD.

[d] Gk Syr: Heb *came to be*

worship. The construction of a material temple will not of itself alter the hard conditions under which the people are living (cf. Hag. 1:7 ff.). Isa. 66 is a condemnation of those who engage in a corrupt and false worship and a proclamation of comfort and hope to the true followers of the Lord. The prophet calls for a spiritual and condemns an external worship, whether it is reliance on the temple building or on sacrifice, but he nowhere suggests that these external forms are necessarily incompatible with a profoundly ethical religion (cf. II Sam. 7:4-13; I Kings 8:27-29).

The present chapter belongs to Third Isaiah and comes from the period between 538 and 520 B.C. There is nothing in it which forbids an exilic date. The two parties within the community are the same as those in 63:7–64:12 and 65:1-25. James D. Smart ("A New Interpretation of Isaiah lxvi, 1-6," *Expository Times,* XLVI [1934-35], 420-24) makes a good case for allocating vss. 1-6 to the time of the rebuilding of the temple under Haggai. Third Isaiah rejects Haggai's appeal to the people and also Haggai's assurance that the rebuilt temple will bring better days as a false hope. This position is exposed to fewer objections than any alternative view, especially any view which is dependent upon a historical situation for which we have no creditable evidence.

1. First Strophe: Worship in Spirit and in Truth (66:1-2)

God's dwelling is in heaven, and no earthly sanctuary can contain him. II Sam. 7:4-14 and I Kings 8:27 ff. are closely parallel; cf. I Kings 8:27: "But will God indeed dwell on the earth? Behold, heaven and the highest heaven cannot contain thee; how much less this house which I have built!" The prophet continues the protest of his prophetic predecessors against an external cult (cf. 1:11-17; Amos 5:21-25; Hos. 6:6; Jer. 3:16-17; 7:21 ff.; 29:5 ff.). He does not reject all temples made with human hands, as in Stephen's polemic (Acts 7:49-50), nor does he proclaim a religion of the spirit as in John 4:24, but he moves in this direction. He addresses his words to those who in the decades following the destruction of Jerusalem and its temple put their confidence and hope in the rebuilding of a temple. Not the practices of the cult, but humility, a contrite heart, and faith in God's revealing word were the requirements of worship. Jeremiah had his successors, and our prophet is one of them.

66:1. Heaven is my throne: Cf. Pss. 11:4; 103:19. **And the earth is my footstool:** Cf. 60:13; Ps. 132:7; Ezek. 43:7; Lam. 2:1. In Matt. 5:34-35 Jesus alludes to this verse. In I Chr. 28:2 the ark is the Lord's footstool; in Ezek. 43:7; Lam. 2:1; and Isa. 60:13, the temple. **What:** The Hebrew is, lit., "Where this?" The LXX reads ποῖον, "what kind of," a rendering followed by most exegetes but for which there is little support in O.T. usage. The Vulg. reads *quae est ista Domus . . . et quis est iste locus.* The KJV reads **where . . . where.** The ASV combines the LXX and Vulg. renderings: "what manner of . . . what place." The emphatic phrase is repeated. It contrasts God's throne in the heavens and his footstool on earth with the material earthly temple which men wish to build for him. **The place of my rest:** With the LXX the word **place** should be read in the construct.

2. All these things: The reference is to the heavens and the earth, not the temple buildings on Zion, as Duhm and others suppose (cf. 44:24). **Are mine:** Cf. Ps. 50:9-12.

---

a temple is to inspire reverence in those who worship in it the high and lofty One who fills the universe. But a temple may be profane to any who do not feel abased at every touch of the divine upon the soul, and to any who seem also to desire superstitious rites to induce the feeling of the divine presence. A building however impressive, and rites however awesome, are contrasted with the word, which commands rational as well as emotional response. The

made, and all those *things* have been, saith the LORD: but to this *man* will I look, *even* to *him that is* poor and of a contrite spirit, and trembleth at my word.

3 He that killeth an ox *is as if* he slew a man; he that sacrificeth a lamb, *as if* he

---

But this is the man to whom I will look, he that is humble and contrite in spirit, and trembles at my word.

3 "He who slaughters an ox is like him who kills a man;
he who sacrifices a lamb, like him who breaks a dog's neck;
he who presents a cereal offering, like him who offers swine's blood;

The לי has dropped out, but the LXX and the Syriac have it (so RSV). The Vulg. reads, *et facta sunt universa ista*. **But this is the man:** The contrast (cf. אי־זה and אל־זה) brings the strophe to its climax. **Contrite:** Lit., "smitten." For the Hebrew ונכה the Dead Sea Scroll reads ונכאי, "stricken," as was conjectured by Kittel (cf. Prov. 15:13; 17:22; 18:14; Ps. 109:16). **And trembles at my word:** The true servants of God, knowing their own unworthiness in the presence of the righteous and holy God, nevertheless wait with expectation and fear for the revelation of his will (cf. Ezra 9:4; 10:3).

2. SECOND STROPHE: THE CORRUPTION OF THE SACRIFICIAL CULT (66:3-4)

The first half of the strophe describes the syncretistic practices of those who have chosen their own ways; the second half gives the reasons for the divine judgment. The last four lines are taken from 65:12. It is possible that they have been inserted by a redactor. They do not have quite the same character as the rest of the strophe, and vss. 3e-4b form an excellent close. Whereas the first strophe is a protest against a trust in the material temple structure, the second is directed against a debased and corrupt sacrificial cult.

3. Four pairs of participial phrases describe the sacrificial practices of those who are hostile to the faithful who tremble at the Lord's word. Rendered in relative clauses the passage would read:

> Who slaughters an ox, who kills a man,
> Who sacrifices a lamb, who breaks a dog's neck,
> Who presents a cereal offering, who offers swine's blood,
> Who makes a memorial offering, who blesses an idol.

Bible throughout claims for God man's whole being. This is always a reverent response of the creature to the Creator. There is no true worship without "that stoop of the soul which in bending upraises it too."[9] The setting forth of God's vastness, incapable of inclusion in any structure of man's erection, inspires such humility. These verses take up the teaching of 40:12-31. Goethe put on Faust's lips the line: "The thrill of awe is man's best quality."[1] Unhappily, that thrill is infrequent among moderns, epecially among Americans. Worse yet, awe is scarcely felt in our worshiping congregations. This hampers, if not blocks, our approach to God and cheapens our intercourse with him. Many erroneously fancy that awe holds us at a remove from God revealed in Jesus Christ. John Owen, however, declares: "We are never nearer Christ than

when we find ourselves lost in a holy amazement at his unspeakable love."[2] Cotton Mather wrote of Thomas Shepard, the first minister of the church at Cambridge, Massachusetts: "The character of his daily conversation was *a trembling walk with God.*"[3] Perhaps the sheer terribleness of events in the first half of the twentieth century is intended to break through the cake of convention which encases men's minds and expose whatever is sensitive in us to the impact of the God of righteousness.

3-4. *The Corruption of the Sacrificial Cult.* —The Exeg. gives an interpretation to this passage not found in the RSV. The point is that the same persons who so scrupulously attend the temple rites also indulge as earnestly in horrible pagan practices. This is a repetition of

9 Browning, "Saul," st. xvii.
1 Part II, Act I, scene 5.
2 From *The Glory of Christ.*
3 In his *Magnalia Christi Americana,* Vol. I, Bk. III, ch. vi, sec. 17.

cut off a dog's neck; he that offereth an oblation, *as if he offered* swine's blood; he that burneth incense, *as if* he blessed an idol. Yea, they have chosen their own ways, and their soul delighteth in their abominations.

he who makes a memorial offering of frankincense, like him who blesses an idol.
These have chosen their own ways,
and their soul delights in their abominations;

But what is the relation between the first and second members of each pair? The KJV, RSV, and ASV agree in linking them by a word of comparison. This interpretation implies a condemnation of the regular sacrifices beyond anything else in the whole O.T. It has the support of the LXX (ὡς), the Vulg. (*quasi*), and, interestingly, the first member of the series of the Dead Sea Scroll (כמכה). But it is not unlikely that all of these represent interpretations. An alternative solution is to connect the phrases as follows: "He who slaughters an ox also kills a man," i.e., they who offer the regular sacrifices of the first series also offer the unlawful sacrifice of the second. What is condemned is not sacrifice root and branch, but a sacrificial practice which has been debased by syncretism with corrupt pagan practices. The writer's thought is similar to 58:3-14; 59:12-21; cf. also the confession of 64:5-7; 65:3-5. If this view is correct, then we should read: "He who slaughters an ox also kills a man, etc." The first series should be taken as subjects, the second as predicates. **Like him who kills a man:** The reference is to human sacrifice, not murder or human violence, as the other members in the series plainly suggest. Jeremiah (7:31; 19:2-6) and Ezekiel (23:39) refer to the practice of child sacrifice in their day. It seems to have been widely prevalent among the ancient Semitic peoples (cf. 57:5). **Who breaks a dog's neck:** According to Justin (*History of the World* XIX. 1. 10), Darius forbade the Carthaginians to offer human victims in sacrifice or to eat the flesh of dogs. The latter practice was also common among the Semites (Robertson Smith, *Religion of the Semites,* p. 291), as among the Romans in the festivals of the Robigalia and Lupercalia (W. W. Fowler, *The Roman Festivals of the Period of the Republic* [London: Macmillan & Co., 1908], pp. 89, 311). **Who offers swine's blood:** The Hebrew has simply "the blood of swine." One would expect a verb, and many scholars insert a participle, נוסך, "pour out." It is possible, however, that the expression is elliptical (cf. vs. 17; 65:4). **He who makes a memorial offering:** The *'azkārāh*, described in Lev. 2:2; 24:7, also associates the memorial offering with incense. **Who blesses an idol:** The series reaches its climax here. The Hebrew uses the word און, which has the connotation of evil, magical power and "therefore . . . has all the characteristics of sin" (Pedersen, *Israel, Its Life and Culture, I-II,* p. 431). The whole expression here is cultic and probably denotes the use of magic words in homage or "blessing" to the god (cf. Köhler

---

what has been said of the apostates in ch. 65. It is an attempt to shock thoughtless folk into a realization of their ambiguous relation to the God of truth. Such dramatic preaching might be resented, but seems needed to startle our complacent half-Christians into an appreciation of their folly. **These have chosen their own ways.** Self-will is the essence of sin. **I also will choose.** With the capricious, God shows himself capricious; if they **choose,** so will he. For both nations and individuals life contains welcome and unwelcome happenings. The pagan rites were attempts to banish or control the unwelcome. But to try to render life's happenings always favorable to our judgment and pleasure is to banish God. "Not as I will" is an essential element of our intercourse with him. Thomas

Browne concludes his *Religio Medici* with the prayer: "Dispose of me according to the wisdom of thy pleasure; thy will be done, though in my own undoing." General ("Chinese") Gordon wrote to his sister:

For some wise design God turns events one way or another, whether man likes it or not, as a man driving a horse turns it to right or left without consideration as to whether the horse likes that way or not. To be happy, a man must be like a well-broken, willing horse, ready for anything.[4]

Self-abandonment to the will of God is the essence of true faith. To will to do or bear God's will is loftier than merely doing it, for such willingness accepts his will when there is noth-

[4] Strachey, *Eminent Victorians,* p. 261.

4 I also will choose their delusions, and will bring their fears upon them; because when I called, none did answer; when I spake, they did not hear: but they did evil before mine eyes, and chose *that* in which I delighted not.

5 ¶ Hear the word of the LORD, ye that

4 I also will choose affliction for them,
  and bring their fears upon them;
because, when I called, no one answered,
  when I spoke they did not listen;
but they did what was evil in my eyes,
  and chose that in which I did not delight."

5 Hear the word of the LORD,
  you who tremble at his word:
"Your brethren who hate you
  and cast you out for my name's sake

---

and Baumgartner, *Lexicon,* p. 20; cf. also 41:29; Hos. 4:15; 10:8; Amos 5:5). **These have chosen their own ways:** [As] **These have chosen** . . . [so] **I also will choose.** The contrast is emphatic: גם־המה and גם־אני. The syncretistic practices are **abominations;** they are the ways the apostates have chosen themselves, not the ways ordained by Yahweh for his people.

4. Affliction: The word connotes caprice or capricious dealing (cf. 3:4). For those who have chosen capriciously in their celebration of alien rites God will choose, not the rewards of the faithful who tremble at his word, but capricious and wanton dealings. What they feared most and sought to avert is what will come upon them by their self-chosen ways.

3. THIRD STROPHE: THE VOICE OF JUDGMENT FROM THE CITY (66:5-6)

The strophe contrasts those who **tremble** at God's **word** (vs. 2*cd*) and the **brethren who hate** their fellow Jews (vs. 4*ef*). It is a promise of deliverance and salvation for the former, of judgment for the latter. The strophe ends dramatically with the threefold voice (קול) of judgment (so the Hebrew).

5. You who tremble at his word: Cf. vss. 2-3. The faithful in Israel receive an oracle from the Lord through the prophet. Volz interprets the words eschatologically: they who tremble at God's word wait for an eschatological utterance on the day of

---

ing to be done. Faith always involves choice. Wilhelm Herrmann made the indispensable element in being a Christian a decision for Christ:

He claims to be the Saviour of the world, and the nearer we approach Him the clearer does it become that He is different from ourselves and from all other men. When we thus feel His spiritual power upon us, the question arises, "Are we willing to yield to this power . . . ?" No one can be spared this decision . . . wherein we choose our side for good or evil in the great history of humanity.[5]

5-6. The Voice of Judgment from the City.—The faithful in Israel are addressed as **you who tremble at his word,** an indication of the poet's emphasis upon that obeisance of spirit which Browning calls "The submission of man's nothing-perfect to God's all-complete." [6] His

[5] *The Communion of the Christian with God,* tr. J. S. Stanyon (London: Williams & Norgate, 1895), pp. 67-68.
[6] *Loc. cit.*

word here is probably the message of judgment. Life is always confused and confusing, with good and evil intermixed, and we are never certain that in our sincerest efforts we are not mistaking and thwarting the will of God. This prompts Paul to bid Christians work out their salvation "with fear and trembling" (Phil. 2:12). But such a mood has been conspicuously lacking in modern churchmen. In his old age, Robert W. Dale remarked to his successor at Carr's Lane Chapel, Birmingham: "Ah, Berry, no one is afraid of God now." Diagnosticians of the good life recognize a wholesome function in it for fear:

Experience has abundantly shown that men who are wholly insensible to the beauty and dignity of virtue, can be convulsed by the fear of judgment, can be even awakened to such a genuine remorse for sin as to reverse the current of their dispositions, detach them from the most inveterate habits, and renew the whole tenor of their lives.[7]

[7] W. E. H. Lecky, *History of European Morals* (New York: D. Appleton & Co., 1887), II, 4.

tremble at his word; Your brethren that hated you, that cast you out for my name's sake, said, Let the LORD be glorified: but he shall appear to your joy, and they shall be ashamed.

6 A voice of noise from the city, a voice from the temple, a voice of the LORD that rendereth recompense to his enemies.

have said, 'Let the LORD be glorified,
   that we may see your joy';
but it is they who shall be put to
   shame.

6 "Hark, an uproar from the city!
   A voice from the temple!
The voice of the LORD,
   rendering recompense to his enemies!

Yahweh. In fear and trembling (cf. Phil. 2:12) they look for the time of God's final revelation. But the expression here rather emphasizes the piety of the faithful. To be sure, it is a piety born in an eschatological climate of expectation and hope, but **the word** (Dead Sea Scroll, "his words") is rather the will of God as expressed in his law and in the words of the prophets. **Your brethren:** The words apply to those who had debased and corrupted the worship of Yahweh. The implication seems to be that the enemies are in control, for they are powerful enough to cast out the faithful followers of Yahweh. The word **cast out** (נדה) in later Talmudic usage acquired the technical meaning of excommunicate in reference to expulsion from the synagogue. **Let the LORD be glorified:** The pious faithful await the day in which the Lord will reveal his glory and bring deliverance. They are mocked and derided by their fellow Jews:

> Let the LORD be glorified,
>   that we may see your joy.

The two groups are sharply separated: the one lives by faith and hope and trust in the word spoken through the prophets; the other relies on the efficacy of a material temple and a syncretistic sacrificial system. The emphasis on **joy**, which the faithful Israel expected, is pronounced in Third Isaiah; the time of salvation is a time of great rejoicing (56:7; 60:15; 61:3, 7, 10; 65:13, 14, 18, 19; cf. 35:1, 10; 51:3). **But it is they . . . put to shame:** While the joy and expectation of the righteous, which their enemies deride, are realized, doom and judgment befall those who depend upon the efficacy of their own religious acts and anticipate no divine intervention.

6. Hark, an uproar or "the sound [voice] of uproar from Zion": Cf. Joel 3:9-17, especially vs. 16 (=Amos 1:2). The great theophany on the day of the Lord is implied. **From the temple:** That Yahweh would appear in glory from his holy dwelling is a feature of such eschatological pictures (Mic. 1:2; Rev. 11:19; 16:1, 17; cf. Joel 3:16).

Calvin describes the role he thinks Paul meant fear to play in the Christian life:

> By the name of fear Paul meaneth that trembling that is stricken into our minds so oft as we think both what we have deserved, and how horrible is the severity of God's wrath against sinners. For we must then be vexed with a marvellous unquietness which both instructeth us to humility, and maketh us more wary against the time to come.[8]

Teachers in the church need carefully to observe the distinction between wholesome and unwholesome fear, for in the effort to banish the latter the former has seemingly vanished, much to our loss.

   Your brethren who hate you. In every religious community differences of conviction

arouse keen feelings. In a day when enthusiasm for the temple and its cultus had been stimulated, those who made light of it and laid their emphasis on ethical religion were cordially disliked. One thinks of the hostility to the Puritans, to the followers of Wesley, etc. Violators of popular conventions are suspect and often persecuted. The stress on inward reverence for the word is not easily communicated and is open to mockery. We apparently have the very gibes of the scorners

> Let the LORD be glorified,
>   that we may see your joy.

The emphasis upon imminent judgment would be bitterly resented in a community just attempting to repair the ravages of its sorest judgment in centuries and to set up its devas-

8 *Institutes* III. 3. 15.

7 Before she travailed, she brought forth; before her pain came, she was delivered of a man child.
 	
8 Who hath heard such a thing? who hath seen such things? Shall the earth be made to bring forth in one day? *or* shall a nation be born at once? for as soon as Zion travailed, she brought forth her children.
	7 "Before she was in labor
	    she gave birth;
	before her pain came upon her
	    she was delivered of a son.
	8 Who has heard such a thing?
	    Who has seen such things?
	Shall a land be born in one day?
	    Shall a nation be brought forth in one
	      moment?
	For as soon as Zion was in labor
	    she brought forth her sons.

James Smart insists, however, that Yahweh is not associated with the temple here, but that the thunderous sound is of God taking vengeance in the city and in the temple. In any case the eschatological context is clear. **Rendering recompense to his enemies:** Cf. 59:18.

4. Fourth Strophe: The Wonderful Birth of the New People (66:7-9)

Suddenly, miraculously, Zion is transformed. The great eschatological act, introduced by the return of the glory of God to his holy temple, whence he comes forth to judge the earth, now makes of Zion an entirely new city with a new people. The imagery of **birth** was natural to Israel. From the loins of Abraham a child was to be born who would be Israel, the people of God; Abraham was but one, yet he became a great people (51:1-5). So now in the great day of his manifestation, the Lord brings about a great wonder. Before the pangs come on her Zion brings forth a son. Torrey believes the son is the Messiah, but vs. 8 makes it clear that it is the people (or the land). Such an event was unprecedented; no one had ever witnessed such a wonder. In this very moment, so it seems to be implied, the child is about to be born, and God will bring the birth to completion (cf. 49:17-21; 54:1-8; 60:1-22).

The thought is eschatological throughout. If historical allusions are present, they are obscure and secondary. The chief thought appears to be the bringing of joy and comfort (vss. 5-6, 10-14) to Zion.

7. Before she was in labor: Salvation comes as unexpectedly and swiftly as judgment. The style of vss. 7-8 is mysterious, as is characteristic of such oracles; we are not told who the mother is until vs. 8e.

8. The mood is not of derision and contempt (contra Kissane) but of astonishment.

tated sanctuary. If the prophet's message in vs. 6 were taken up by his followers, one can fancy the reaction of a community engrossed in the effort to rebuild the national shrine. Here is the stuff for a blazing religious conflict. We seem to be overhearing the combatants in this controversy, and can understand the background in which the poet delivered his message. From the sacred edifice of the people's devout pride comes this strident denunciation of doom upon those whose piety is superficial. How infuriating to the zealous proponents of the rebuilding of the temple to have this prophet picture it as the scene where the Lord will pronounce judgment upon those who make so much of outward religious forms while lacking the devout spirit of obedience to righteousness!

7-9. The Miraculous Birth of the New People. —Only a small minority of the people had left their places of exile and returned; only a small minority of them were among those who trembled at the Lord's word and loyally strove for a messianic missionary people. It was disheartening to belong to a mere remnant of a remnant. Now an astounding creative act of God is promised. Zion will give birth to a new people. The fires and terrors of judgment prove the birth pangs of a new nation. History has many analogies of nations born out of the destruction of an old order; but this is no human event. It is a miracle which accompanies the final events of human history. **Who has heard such a thing? . . . Shall a nation be brought forth in one moment?** Those who listened to the prophet must have seen no reason to expect any such event. To anticipate it confidently demanded sheer faith in a wonder-working God. And such faith was required in so desperate a

9 Shall I bring to the birth, and not cause to bring forth? saith the LORD: shall I cause to bring forth, and shut *the womb?* saith thy God.

10 Rejoice ye with Jerusalem, and be glad with her, all ye that love her: rejoice for joy with her, all ye that mourn for her:

9 Shall I bring to the birth and not cause
    to bring forth?
  says the LORD;
shall I, who cause to bring forth, shut the
    womb?
  says your God.

10 "Rejoice with Jerusalem, and be glad for
    her,
    all you who love her;
rejoice with her in joy,
    all you who mourn over her;

---

9. Shall I bring to the birth: Cf. 37:3: "children have come to the birth, and there is no strength to bring them forth." In a word of Yahweh, the people are told that he will carry through his purpose. The time of the Lord's coming is the time of new birth, and God will bring to completion what he has begun. The solemnity of his assurance is marked by the repetition of vss. 9*b*, 9*d*, the twofold emphatic **I**, and the direct questions.

5. FIFTH STROPHE: THE JOY AND PLENTY OF THE MESSIANIC AGE (66:10-11)

The glowing promise and assurance of the preceding lines prompts the poet to break out in a lyrical song of joy.

10. Rejoice with Jerusalem: The LXX reads "Rejoice thou, O Jerusalem," which the Hebrew consonants permit, but the preceding lines and the parallel phrase **with her** in vs. 10*c* favor the M.T. The Hebrew has three different verbs for **rejoice** in this verse besides the noun **joy**. **All you who love her, . . . all you who mourn over her:** The address is in the exultant mood of the prophet's vision of the new age (cf. 57:18; 60:20; 61:2-3).

---

time. No appeal is made to signs of a renaissance; the appeal is to God's creative power and to his faithfulness in achieving that which he commences. **Shall I bring to the birth and not cause to bring forth?**

There are periods when we look about us in vain to discover evidences of a new and better order of justice and peace in the earth. The twentieth century is such a period. One can see hardly any bright prospects on the immediate horizon. We need this faith in a miracle-working God. He is not limited to the resources which we can itemize. It is the altogether unprecedented, the wholly unheard-of, that he creates.

These are Thy wonders, Lord of power,
Killing and quickening, bringing down to Hell
  And up to Heaven in an hour;
Making a chiming of a passing-bell.
    We say amiss,
    This or that is;
Thy word is all, if we could spell.[9]

The ability of the Christian message to make men over completely was what its early advocates pointed to as evidence of God's marvelous work through it. "Behold the might of the new song! It has made men out of stones, men out

[9] George Herbert, "The Flower."

of beasts!" [10] George Whitefield wrote a tactful letter to Benjamin Franklin, asking him to investigate this extraordinary phenomenon:

I find you grow more and more famous in the learned world. As you have made a pretty considerable progress in the mysteries of electricity I would now honestly recommend to your diligent unprejudiced pursuit and study the mysteries of the new birth. It is a most important and interesting study, and, when mastered, will richly answer and repay you for all your pains.[11]

Nor is God's re-creating power confined to the changing of individuals. It is untrue to fancy that corporate life cannot be as radically altered. One has only to reflect what Nazism did to Germany and communism to Soviet Russia. "There is not an existing institution in the world of civilized humanity which cannot be profoundly modified or altered, or abolished in a generation." [1] Here is solid basis for hope for believers in an active God.

10-11. Exultation over the Messianic Age.— This outburst of rejoicing is characteristic of

[10] Clement of Alexandria, *Exhortation to the Heathen,* ch. i.
[11] A. D. Belden, *George Whitefield* (London: Sampson, Low, Marston & Co., 1930), p. 182.
[1] Benjamin Kidd, *The Science of Power* (New York: G. P. Putnam's Sons, 1918), p. 126.

11 That ye may suck, and be satisfied with the breasts of her consolations; that ye may milk out, and be delighted with the abundance of her glory.

12 For thus saith the Lord, Behold, I will extend peace to her like a river, and the glory of the Gentiles like a flowing stream: then shall ye suck, ye shall be borne upon *her* sides, and be dandled upon *her* knees.

11 that you may suck and be satisfied
    with her consoling breasts;
that you may drink deeply with delight
    from the abundance of her glory."

12 For thus says the Lord:
"Behold, I will extend prosperity to her
    like a river,
and the wealth of the nations like an
    overflowing stream;
and you shall suck, you shall be carried
    upon her hip,
and dandled upon her knees.

---

11. That you may suck: Cf. 60:16. The thought of Zion as the mother of many children (cf. 49:17-21; 54:1-6) inspires the imagery of the nursing child. Zion's economic prosperity is compared to the precious milk of the mother (cf. I Pet. 2:2). **From the abundance of her glory:** A cognate of the word rendered **abundance** (מזיז) occurs in Pss. 50:11; 80:13 (Hebrew 80:14), but with a completely different meaning, coming from another root. Ugaritic *zd* (*td*) means "breast," Akkadian *zizu*, "udder," and the vulgar Arabic *zizah*, "udder." Ewald, Cheyne, and others suggested some such meaning long ago. The phrase should be rendered "from her bountiful breast." Note the improved parallelism.

6. Sixth Strophe: Prosperity and Comfort (66:12-14)

The description continues, but the writer explains the character of the age less figuratively. His words are drawn from other similar passages. **Prosperity** and **comfort** are the foundations of Zion.

12. The oracle of salvation opens in the usual manner. **Behold, I will extend:** Cf. Gen. 39:21 for the same usage of the verb. **Prosperity like a river:** Cf. 48:18. The Hebrew word *shālôm*, often rendered **peace** (KJV, ASV), here means **prosperity.** Similarly, the Hebrew word *kābhôdh*, usually translated **glory** (KJV, ASV) has the meaning of **wealth** (cf. 60:5; 61:6). **You shall suck:** The text seems to be in disorder. The LXX reads for the verb, τὰ παιδία αὐτῶν, "their children," probably translating "sucklings." The first part of the word is missing from the Dead Sea Scroll, which is torn at this point, but the remaining letters (ותיהמה) suggest that the original reading was similar to the LXX,

---

the poems in chs. 40–66. The poet contemplates the proximate glory about to supplant the dispirited condition of the community in Jerusalem, and his soul rises and gives voice to a triumphant cry. Recalling the circumstances about him, we appreciate how his faith and hope lift him. The immediate situation is depressing; but God is about to bring into being a new people. Such exultant gladness would be contagious, and infuse in the prophet's listeners new confidence and enthusiasm. Men of God

can borrow
For poor today from rich tomorrow.[2]

12-14. Prosperity and Comfort.—As the Exeg. indicates, the poet draws on predecessors for his metaphors—prosperity . . . like a river, and

[2] Shelley, "Love, Hope, Desire and Fear."

Zion's children nursed and carried. Christians employ the latter conception in such phrases as "O mother dear, Jerusalem." Protestants have not made as much of "mother church" as have our Roman Catholic brethren; but it is none the less a spiritual fact that we are **satisfied with her consoling breasts.** Timothy Dwight's hymn, "I love thy kingdom, Lord," is true to our experience. This chapter combines nationalism and universalism. Patriotic pride sets Zion at the center and brings the wealth of nations to her; but a broader outlook succeeds, and in vs. 18 all peoples see the Lord's glory.

As one whom his mother comforts. The poet has been comparing Zion's children to infants sucking the breasts and carried and dandled. But now in speaking of God's dealing with the nation, it is no baby but an oldster, experienced in wounds and sorrow, returning for consola-

13 As one whom his mother comforteth, so will I comfort you; and ye shall be comforted in Jerusalem.

14 And when ye see *this,* your heart shall rejoice, and your bones shall flourish like an herb: and the hand of the LORD shall be known toward his servants, and *his* indignation toward his enemies.

15 For, behold, the LORD will come with fire, and with his chariots like a whirlwind,

---

13 As one whom his mother comforts,
  so I will comfort you;
  you shall be comforted in Jerusalem.

14 You shall see, and your heart shall rejoice;
  your bones shall flourish like the grass;
  and it shall be known that the hand of the LORD is with his servants,
  and his indignation is against his enemies.

15 "For behold, the LORD will come in fire,
  and his chariots like the stormwind,

"their sucklings." Render, "Their sucklings shall be carried on the side [or **hip**]." Cf. 49:22; 60:4. **And dandled:** The verb is the Palpel imperfect of שעשע. In Ps. 119:16, 70 the verb in different forms has the meaning of "delight oneself in" and "take delight in" (cf. also Isa. 11:3; Amos 5:21).

13. The image of the nurslings recalls the consoling and bountiful breasts of vs. 12. Third Isaiah, like his master, thinks of the consolation of Israel as a major feature of the messianic age. Several scholars delete the third line as a later insertion. It looks like a marginal gloss. It does not prove that the writer is in Babylon, as some have thought; the poet's perspective is that of a new Zion, the messianic community.

14. The psycho-physical character of Hebraic thought is illustrated in this verse. The experience of Zion's happy state will put new life and vigor into the bodies of her citizens (cf. Pss. 32:3; 42:10; 84:2; 102:3; Job 21:24; Prov. 15:30). The reference to the Lord's **servants** and his **enemies** provides another indication of the relation of the poem to its context.

7. Seventh Strophe: The Lord Comes to Judge the Earth (66:15-16)

The Lord appears in a theophany of **fire.** Not only is the fervent prayer of 64:1-3 answered, but the movement of the poems reaches its great culmination. The strophe,

---

tion. This is one of the Bible's most cherished expressions for God's grace to men. It is the acme of tenderness. After his mother's death Carlyle entered in his diary:

O pious mother! kind, good, brave, and truthful soul as I have ever found, and more than I have ever elsewhere found in this world, your poor Tom, long out of his school-days now, has fallen very lonely, very lame and broken in this pilgrimage of his; and you cannot help him or cheer him by a kind word any more. From your grave in Ecclefechan kirkyard yonder you bid him trust in God, and that also he will try if he can understand, and *do.*[3]

The hand of the Lord is with his servants. The prayer in ch. 64 had voiced the frequent complaint of the devout at the absence of God from the scene of their struggles and sufferings.

He hides Himself so wondrously,
  As though there were no God;
He is least seen when all the powers
  Of ill are most abroad.

[3] D. A. Wilson, *Carlyle to Threescore-and-Ten* (London: Kegan Paul, Trench, Trubner & Co., 1929), p. 85.

Or He deserts us at the hour
  The fight is all but lost;
And seems to leave us to ourselves
  Just when we need Him most.[4]

Henry Churchill King, a theological teacher of the last generation, aptly entitled a book, *The Seeming Unreality of the Spiritual Life.*[5] He was voicing the feelings expressed centuries before by Augustine: "Thou wert not any solid or substantial thing unto me, when in those days I thought upon thee."[6] But believers know also times when God's hand is manifestly with them in the outcome of a puzzling train of events. **You shall see**—in an experience of judgment when **his indignation is against his enemies,** and those who have served him know his favor.

15-16. *The Lord's Coming in Fiery Judgment.* —This too is an answer to Israel's prayer (64: 1-3). It is a judgment **upon all flesh,** and espe-

[4] Frederick W. Faber, "Oh it is hard to work for God," sts. ii-iii.

[5] New York: The Macmillan Co., 1908.

[6] *Confessions* IV. 7.

to render his anger with fury, and his rebuke with flames of fire.

16 For by fire and by his sword will the
LORD plead with all flesh: and the slain of
the LORD shall be many.

17 They that sanctify themselves, and

to render his anger in fury,
and his rebuke with flames of fire.

16 For by fire will the LORD execute judgment,
and by his sword, upon all flesh;
and those slain by the LORD shall be
many.

17 "Those who sanctify and purify themselves to go into the gardens, following one

---

introduced in characteristic manner (כי־הנה יהוה) is dominated by the symbolism of fire,
and its thought is succinctly stated in the line: **For by fire will the LORD execute judgment.**

15. For behold, the LORD will come in fire: Similar theophanies of judgment are
described in 10:17-18; 29:6; 30:27-28; 64:1-3; Pss. 50:3-4; 97:1-5. The Sinaitic theophany
is doubtless the major, though not necessarily the exclusive, influence in such descriptions
(cf. Exod. 19:18 [J]; Deut. 5:22 ff.; Exod. 24:17 where, as often elsewhere, fire and the
glory [*kābhôdh*] are associated). **And his chariots like the stormwind:** In the Ugaritic
poems Baal is "the Rider of the Clouds," as in Baal and Anath (Pritchard, *Ancient
Near Eastern Texts,* pp. 132, 134, 136, and especially 137). Yahweh is also "the Rider
of the Clouds" (19:1; Pss. 18:10; 68:33; 104:3; Deut. 33:26). He rides upon the
stormwind as his swift chariot—an expression which has theophanic associations (Hab.
3:8; Ps. 68:18; cf. Ezek. 1:15 ff.). Jeremiah uses a similar vivid description in his portrait
of the coming foe from the north (Jer. 4:13).

16. God appears **in fire, and by fire will** [he] **execute judgment** (נשפט)). The Dead
Sea Scroll reads, "He will come to judge." The LXX renders, "For in the fire of the Lord
all the earth will be judged." **And by his sword:** For Yahweh as warrior cf. 27:1; 42:13;
52:10; 59:17; Exod. 15:3. God comes not only in fire; he comes also as warrior with his
sword to execute judgment (cf. 27:1; 31:8; 34:5; Deut. 32:41-42; Jer. 46:10; Ezek. 21:3-5;
38:21). **Upon all flesh:** The judgment will be universal as the theophany will be
universal (40:5; cf. 60:12; 63:6). **Slain by the LORD:** Cf. Zeph. 2:12; Jer. 25:33.

N. AN ESCHATOLOGICAL SUMMARY (66:17-24)

A redactor has added vss. 17-24 as a conclusion to chs. 56–66. Vs. 17 is composed as
a link between vss. 1-16 and vss. 18-24. Volz and others transfer it to vss. 3-6, but form and
style are against this procedure.

17. Those who sanctify . . . into the gardens: The redactor takes up the theme of
the syncretistic cult (65:3-5, 11; 66:3-5) and presses it to its eschatological climax: **shall
come to an end together.** The Hebrew has simply "for the gardens," where the RSV
interprets **to go into the gardens.** The allusion is doubtless to the lustrations preliminary
to the cultic practices in the gardens. The latter term may actually have borne a technical

---

cially upon the apostates among his own nation.
This may seem excessive fury in dealing with
those whose offense had been the addition of
pagan rites to their worship according to the
law. But eclecticism which picks and chooses
elements to combine with the divinely prescribed religion betrays unbelief. "All Eclectics
are essentially and at bottom sceptics; the more
comprehensive, the more sceptical." [7] Modern
folk who indulge in various cults—spiritualism,
devices for discovering the future, etc.—are
invariably those who do not give all their heart

to the service of Christ. In Henry Drummond's
interleaved testament a biographer came on the
entry: "Receipt for Misery—Be a half-hearted
Christian." [8] Sidney Lanier denounced his age
for the numbers of its "almost-folk":

Yea, if the Christ (called thine) now paced yon
street,
Thy halfness hot with His rebuke would swell;
Legions of scribes would rise and run and beat
His fair intolerable Wholeness twice to hell. [9]

[8] J. Y. Simpson, *Henry Drummond* (Edinburgh: Oliphant, Anderson & Ferrier, 1902), p. 42, n. 1.

[7] Novalis, quoted in Carlyle, "Essay on Novalis."

[9] "Acknowledgment."

purify themselves in the gardens behind one *tree* in the midst, eating swine's flesh, and the abomination, and the mouse, shall be consumed together, saith the LORD.

18 For I *know* their works and their thoughts: it shall come, that I will gather all nations and tongues; and they shall come, and see my glory.

in the midst, eating swine's flesh and the abomination and mice, shall come to an end together, says the LORD.

18 "For I know*e* their works and their thoughts, and I am*f* coming to gather all nations and tongues; and they shall come

e Gk Syr: Heb lacks *know*
f Gk Syr Vg Tg: Heb *it is*

---

meaning (see 65:3). **Following one in the midst:** The text is obscure and possibly corrupt. The Hebrew אחר אחד בתוך, is, lit., "behind one in the midst" (ASV). The *Qerê* of **one** is feminine, so also the Dead Sea Scroll and many MSS. Volz finds strong support in the line for his view that the alien cult represents the Greek mysteries. "This recalls the mystagogue of the Eleusinian mysteries or the *pater patrum* of the Mithras circle, through which the participants of the community were initiated into all the secrets" (*Jesaia II*, 292; cf. Franz Cumont, *Die Mysterien des Mithra* [3rd ed.; Leipzig: B. G. Teubner, 1923], p. 142). Others suggest that the phrase describes the procession behind the image of the god, either Tammuz (see 17:10) or Ishtar. Wade (*Isaiah*, p. 418) thinks the phrase should be read "after one in the midst," a description of the imitation by a group of novices "of the ritual acts of the priest (or a priestess) who is initiating them into mysteries (cf. Ezek. viii. 11)." In this connection it is interesting that several scholars, in dependence on Macrobius (*Saturnalia* I. 23), find the name of the god Hadad in the word **one** (Lagarde). The Targ. reads "one company after another," but this does not account for **in the midst** and requires a change in the text. The Syriac reads similarly (cf. Symm.; also *alter post alterum*). The LXX reads ἐν τοῖς προθύροις, "in the porches," an interesting parallelism to **in the gardens**, but it is not easy to discover the text behind the reading (cf. also Vulg., *post januam intrinsecus*). Kissane emends the Hebrew to אחר אחד יכרתו, "one by one shall be cut off." The RSV is a satisfactory rendering of the C.T. and may be explained in the light of Ezek. 8:11 (Ezek. 8 is a valuable parallel to the description of the debased cult described in Isa. 65–66): "And before them stood seventy men of the elders of the house of Israel; with Jaazaniah the son of Shaphan standing among them. Each had his censer in his hand, and the smoke of the cloud of incense went up"; cf. further, vs. 12: "What the elders of the house of Israel are doing in the dark, every man in his room of pictures" (for other interpretations see Kissane and Feldmann, *ad loc.*). **Swine's flesh:** Cf. 65:4. **And the abomination:** Many scholars (Fischer, Kissane, Torrey) read והשרץ, "and creeping things" or "vermin" for והשקץ. If the Hebrew text is retained, Lev. 7:21; 11:10, 41, would explain the meaning, but it is better to accept the emendation. **Mice:** Hebrew, **the mouse,** which the RSV takes as a collective. In Levitical law the mouse was forbidden as unclean (Lev. 11:29). It was probably regarded as sacred in the apostate group and eaten sacramentally. The word is used as a proper name in Gen. 36:38; II Kings 22:12, 14. Among the Phoenicians and the Edomites the name is given to persons.

18. The new age is ushered in by the coming of the **glory** and the setting of the **sign** of the Lord among the nations of the world. The opening of the verse is corrupt, and many conjectures have been proposed. The Hebrew reads, lit., "I their works and their

---

This announcement of the Lord's advent in judgment may be the conclusion, as the Exeg. suggests, of the prophecies, and what follows are editorial additions.

18-21. *The Coming of the Glory.*—Survivors from the judgment in vs. 16 are sent to the

people living on the periphery of Israel's world, **that have not heard my fame or seen my glory.** Nationalistic and universalistic motives appear mingled. This is a mission to distant peoples, it fulfills the expectation often set forth as Israel's task in chs. 40–66. But the interest is

19 And I will set a sign among them, and I will send those that escape of them unto the nations, *to* Tarshish, Pul, and Lud, that draw the bow, *to* Tubal and Javan, *to* the isles afar off, that have not heard my fame, neither have seen my glory; and they shall declare my glory among the Gentiles.

20 And they shall bring all your brethren *for* an offering unto the LORD out of all nations upon horses, and in chariots, and in litters, and upon mules, and upon swift beasts, to my holy mountain Jerusalem, saith the LORD, as the children of Israel bring an offering in a clean vessel into the house of the LORD.

and shall see my glory, 19 and I will set a sign among them. And from them I will send survivors to the nations, to Tarshish, Put,*g* and Lud, who draw the bow, to Tubal and Javan, to the coastlands afar off, that have not heard my fame or seen my glory; and they shall declare my glory among the nations. 20 And they shall bring all your brethren from all the nations as an offering to the LORD, upon horses, and in chariots, and in litters, and upon mules, and upon dromedaries, to my holy mountain Jerusalem, says the LORD, just as the Israelites bring their cereal offering in a clean vessel

g Gk: Heb *Pul*

thoughts has come to gather." Many scholars, following Duhm, transfer **their works and their thoughts** to the preceding line and make it the subject of **shall come to an end.** Others insert the verb "know" after the pronoun "I" and emend "has come" to the first person (באתי), a procedure followed by the RSV. **All nations and tongues:** The phrase is characteristic of later apocalypse and the N.T. (cf. Zech. 8:23; Dan. 3:4, 7; 4:1; 6:25). **My glory:** The nations of the world will come to Zion and its temple, where they will see the **glory** of Yahweh (cf. 60:1 ff.) denied even to Moses (Exod. 33:18-23; cf. Ezek. 43:1-4). The influence of Ezekiel is apparent throughout this section.

19. Not only will the **glory** (*kābhôdh*) be revealed from the sanctuary, but the miraculous **sign** (*'ôth*) will accompany the revelation of his glory: **I will set a sign among them.** The Dead Sea Scroll has the plural "signs." The beginning of the new age is initiated by the Lord's presence and his revealing work (cf. 7:11; 55:13; 49:22; 62:10; Exod. 7:3; 10:2). What the sign is, or among whom it is set, is not clearly stated. The glory of God is not a static but a dynamic, active reality. It works destruction upon some, salvation upon others. The list of places is drawn from Ezekiel. **Tarshish** or Tartessus is a Phoenician mercantile city in Spain (cf. 2:16; 60:9; Ezek. 27:12). **Put** (so LXX; Hebrew, **Pul**) and **Lud** are African peoples (cf. Gen. 10:6, 13; Ezek. 27:10; 30:5). **Who draw the bow:** Hebrew, *môshekhê qésheth;* LXX, Μόσοχ. Torrey explains the addition of *qésheth* by influence from Jer. 46:9; Duhm and others propose another place name, "Rosh." Rosh, Meshech, and **Tubal** appear together in Ezekiel (38:2; 39:1). The two latter probably represent the Moschi and Tibareni mentioned by Herodotus (*History* III. 94; VII. 78) and the Muski and Tabal of the Assyrian monuments (Schrader, *Cuneiform Inscriptions and O.T.*, I, 64, 66). All three lay in the region south or southeast of the Black Sea. **Javan:** The Ionians of Asia Minor or Greece (Ezek. 27:13, 19; Joel 3:6; Zech. 9:13; Dan. 8:21; 10:20). **To the coastlands afar off:** The mission of the survivors to the most remote regions is a characteristic feature of the prophet's eschatology (cf. 42:1-7; 49:1-6; 51:4).

20. And they shall bring all your brethren: The nations, hearing the great news from the survivors of the glory of God in the temple at Zion, will bring the Diaspora

apparently not so much in the conversion of strangers to the God of Israel as in inducing them to send home the scattered Israelites. Here again, as the Exeg. comments, the prophet is using the metaphors and summarizing the teaching of the preceding poems from ch. 40 on.

And some of them also I will take for priests and for Levites. If, as the Exeg. indicates is possible, the allusion may be not merely to the returned Israelites but to the heathen peoples, it must correspond to the satisfaction felt by missionaries and converts alike when a native

21 And I will also take of them for priests *and* for Levites, saith the Lord.

22 For as the new heavens and the new earth, which I will make, shall remain before me, saith the Lord, so shall your seed and your name remain.

23 And it shall come to pass, *that* from one new moon to another, and from one sabbath to another, shall all flesh come to worship before me, saith the Lord.

to the house of the Lord. 21 And some of them also I will take for priests and for Levites, says the Lord.

22 "For as the new heaven and the new earth
which I will make
shall remain before me, says the Lord;
so shall your descendants and your
name remain.
23 From new moon to new moon,
and from sabbath to sabbath,
all flesh shall come to worship before me,
says the Lord.

---

back home. The detailed enumeration is in the style of later apocalypse, and expresses both the characteristic mode of transportation of the various peoples throughout the world and the fact that all the Diaspora will return, old and young, infirm and strong. The journey is a triumphant procession to the holy mountain of Jerusalem. God has set his sign in the world, and the nations stream to Zion with their cereal offering to the Lord. In this description the writer is again summarizing the eschatology of all the poems of Second Isaiah (43:6; 49:22) as well as of Third Isaiah (60:1-22).

21. And some of them: Whether of the Diaspora or of the nations is not clear; 56:6-7 and 61:6 are said to argue for the former, and this would seem to be the more natural interpretation. On the other hand, the whole context describes exceedingly momentous events. The sacrificial offering of the peoples (vs. 20) and the worship of all flesh (vs. 23) make the more universal application to the nations congenial. It would not contradict 56:6-7 and 61:6, but go beyond it.

22. The stability and permanence of the new people of the new age are as sure as **the new heaven and the new earth** (cf. 65:17). Both are the creation of God. Cosmological and historical events are under the same purposeful sovereignty. Again the prophet weaves familiar motifs into a new pattern (51:8, 11; 60:20-21; 62:7; 65:18 ff.). In Jer. 31:35-36; 33:25-26 the permanence of Israel is similarly related to the natural order.

23. As the original creation was a preparation for worship on the seventh day (Gen. 2:1-3; cf. Exod. 20:10-11), so the new provides the setting for worship. **From new moon to new moon:** Lit., "And it shall come to pass that as often as the new moon [month] is on the new moon, and as often as the sabbath is on the sabbath" (cf. Num. 28:10, 14). The phraseology shows the solemnity of the eschatological climax. The description surpasses Zech. 14:16.

---

ministry is raised up and can take over the leadership of the church.

22-23. *All Mankind to Worship God.*—These verses link the climax of the chapter with its beginning. God, who cannot be confined in any one place or building, is worshiped by all men the earth over. The traditional festive seasons, new moons and sabbaths, continue the framework of this universal worship. These two verses form a fitting conclusion to a great prophetic book, with the missionary outlook of chs. 40–55 and of many of the subsequent poems. Particularism is left behind. Israel is the nation of priests, but chosen that along with her all

flesh may pay homage to the God of the whole earth. It is in worship that the unity of the nations is realized—**before me.**

'Tis but as men draw nigh to thee, my Lord,
They can draw nigh each other and not hurt.[1]

Worship is an act which enlists the entire personality and lays hold of more in man than his opinions. As Martineau once put it: "The blending affections are more than the dissevering thoughts." Our loyalties lie far deeper than our views.

[1] George Macdonald, *Diary of an Old Soul*, Nov. 10.

24 And they shall go forth, and look upon the carcasses of the men that have transgressed against me: for their worm shall not die, neither shall their fire be quenched; and they shall be an abhorring unto all flesh.

24 "And they shall go forth and look on the dead bodies of the men that have rebelled against me; for their worm shall not die, their fire shall not be quenched, and they shall be an abhorrence to all flesh."

---

24. Vss. 22-23 are a magnificent climax not only to chs. 56–66 but to chs. 40–55 as well. Vs. 24, however, has a different spirit. It is true that judgment upon the apostates is predicted again and again, but not in these terms. The verse may conceivably be the work of our redactor, but it is possible that there is another hand here. **And they shall go forth:** The worshipers of Zion will go forth to look upon the **dead bodies** of the apostate rebels. The place is doubtless the valley of Hinnom (Gehenna) at the foot of Mount Zion, where the contemporaries of Jeremiah built the high places of Topheth for human sacrifice (Jer. 7:31). In the future, says Jeremiah (7:32), it will be called "the valley of Slaughter: for they will bury in Topheth, because there is no room elsewhere." In later times it was used as a place for the refuse of the city, and according to rabbinical tradition, corpses of criminals, etc., were cast there to be burned or allowed to decompose (see Enoch 26–27 for the apocalyptist's description of the place). The proximity of the place of blessedness to the place of suffering and torment is encountered in later apocalyptic also (cf. Luke 16:23-26). **For their worm shall not die:** Cf. Judith 16:17; Mark 9:47-49. Worms continue eternally to eat the bodies, but they are never devoured. The bodies are burned by an eternal **fire,** but are never consumed. The mutilation and destruction of the body was particularly offensive to the ancient Hebrew. **And they shall be an abhorrence:** The noun דראון occurs here and in Dan. 12:2. The LXX reads, "a spectacle" (εἰς ὅρασιν); Vulg., *ad satietatem visionis.*

The masoretic scholars directed that when this chapter was read in the synagogue, part of vs. 23 must be repeated after vs. 24, so that the final words are of comfort. Similar instructions are placed at the close of the minor prophets, Lamentations, and Ecclesiastes.

---

24. *The Damnation of the Rebellious Apostates.*—Christian readers of the book of Isaiah wish that vs. 23, rather than vs. 24, had been its conclusion. It seems horrible to picture devout worshipers going out from communion with God and looking on the corpses of God's enemies. But the parables of our Lord contemplate a similar ultimate separation: wheat garnered and tares cast into the fire; the spiritually fit entering with the bridegroom and the door shut upon the unready; faithful servants sharing their Lord's joy while the unprofitable is cast into outer darkness; the Judge dividing sheep from goats, with his "Come ye" and his "Depart ye." If we may think of chs. 40–55 with their exalted and moving gospel of God circulating in the devout community, their message must have been known to some extent by all Israelites. Those who indulged in the heathen rites in gardens behind a leader of the cult, and partook of swine's flesh, the broth of abominable things, and the mouse (vs. 17), were sinning against the light from the face of the God of redeeming comfort and of victorious righteousness. "[It is] a terrible ending, but only too conceivable. For though God is love, man is free . . . ; free to be as though he had never felt it; free to put from himself the highest, clearest, most urgent grace that God can show." [2] Men judge themselves "unworthy of eternal life" (Acts 13:46) and become **an abhorrence to all flesh.**

An outstanding mid-twentieth century poet, T. S. Eliot, sees the choice before his contemporaries to be "fire or fire"—the fire of our divisive motives and diabolical ingenuity, or the fire of divine love to consume the other malignant fire and transfigure whatever it touches to generous and noble ends.

> The only hope, or else despair
> Lies in the choice of pyre or pyre—
> To be redeemed from fire by fire. [3]

The book of Isaiah ends by facing its readers with this momentous and inevitable choice.

[2] G. A. Smith, *Isaiah,* II, 512.

[3] *Four Quartets* (London: Faber & Faber; New York: Harcourt, Brace & Co., 1943), p. 37. Used by permission.

The Book of

JEREMIAH

Introduction and Exegesis by JAMES PHILIP HYATT
Exposition by STANLEY ROMAINE HOPPER

LYDIA
(LUDIM?)

ARARAT

ASSYRIA

Carchemish

Nineveh

ASHKENAZ

MINNI

MEDIA

To Caphtor
To Tarshish KITTIM

Arpad
Hamath
Riblah
Damascus

R. Euphrates

ELAM

KEDAR

Babylon
BABYLON
(CHALDEA)

Tahpanhes

To Put
Memphis On

Migdol
Teman
Sela

Thebes
(No)

PATHROS

EGYPT

ARABIA

Tema
Dedan

Sidon

Mt. Lebanon

Mt. Hermon (Sirion)

Damascus

SYRIA

ETHIOPIA
(CUSH)

R. Nile

RED SEA

OPHIR

UPHAZ

SHEBA

Tyre

Dan

MAACAH

BASHAN

SEA OF
CHINNERETH

THE GREAT SEA

Mt. Carmel

Mt. Tabor

Megiddo

[ISRAEL]
(EPHRAIM)

Samaria
Shechem

SAMARIA
HILLS OF
EPHRAIM
[Shiloh]

GILEAD

R. Jabbok

AMMON
[GAD]

Rabbah

Bethel
Mizpah
Gibeon
Ekron
Kiriath-jearim
Beth-haccherem
Libnah
Azekah
Ashdod
Ashkelon

Ramah
Anathoth
Jerusalem
Bethlehem
Netophah
Tekoa

Jericho

Elealeh
Mephaath
Heshbon
Sibmah
Nebo
Jahaz
Bezer (Bozrah)
Beth-meon
Beth-diblathaim

Moresheth
Lachish

JUDAH

SHEPHELAH
(THE LOWLAND)

HILL
COUNTRY

Gaza

PHILISTIA

NEGEB

(THE SOUTH)

SALT SEA

ARABAH

The Jordan

Kiriathaim
Dibon
Aroer
Beth-gamul

R. Arnon

Madmen

MOAB

[Gomorrah?]

[Sodom?]

Kir-heres
(Kir-hareseth)

Waters of
Nimrin

Zoar?
Br. Zered

EDOM

Bozrah

PALESTINE

JEREMIAH

MILES
KILOMETERS

0 10 20 30 40 50
0 10 20 30 40 50 60 70 80

JEROME S. KATES, *Cartographer*
HERBERT G. MAY, PH.D., *Research Editor*
COPYRIGHT 1949, THOMAS NELSON AND SONS

JEREMIAH

INTRODUCTION

Jeremiah lived in an important transitional period in Near Eastern history. He witnessed the fall of the Assyrian Empire, and the rise of the Neo-Babylonian Empire under a Chaldean dynasty. He saw his own country lose its political independence and become a Babylonian province.

Though not recognized as such at the time, Jeremiah was the outstanding personality of his age. He helped his fellow countrymen to survive the crises through which they had to pass, and to find new foundations on which to build their faith. In doing this he became one of the dominant figures of O.T. history.

I. Historical Background

The Assyrian Empire had been founded in the middle of the eighth century by Tiglath-pileser III, but its last strong king was Ashurbanipal (669-ca. 633 B.C.). Assyria was weakened by prolonged wars, internal intrigues, and invasion by barbarians from the north, the Cimmerians and the Scythians. The decisive blow came from the Medes and Chaldeans. In 614 B.C. the Medes captured the city of Asshur and made an alliance with the Chaldeans. Under the attack of these allies Nineveh, the Assyrian capital, fell two years later and the fate of the Assyrian Empire was sealed. Some of the Assyrian leaders fled to Harran and there attempted to maintain a kingdom under a man who assumed the name of Ashur-uballit. The final defeat was delivered by the Chaldeans in the battle of Carchemish (605 B.C.) to the fragments of the Assyrians and to their allies from Egypt under Pharaoh Neco.

Control of the countries which had been in the Assyrian orbit now passed to the Babylonians under a Chaldean dynasty. Chaldea was a province situated in the southern part of Babylonia. The people there had revolted several times against Assyria; one of the revolts had been led by Marduk-apal-iddina II, called Merodach-baladan in the Bible (II Kings 20:12; Isa. 39:1). The Chaldean Nabopolassar made himself independent ruler of Babylonia by the year 626 B.C. He led the successful attack on Nineveh. Nabopolassar died shortly after the battle of Carchemish, in the summer of 605, and was succeeded by his son, Nebuchadrezzar II, who ruled for forty-three years.

Nebuchadrezzar is the most famous of the Babylonian monarchs; his name appears not only in the book of Jeremiah, but also in II Kings and Daniel. Little is known of political events of his reign outside of the information given in the Old Testament. Inscriptions from his time are abundant, but they deal largely with commercial matters or building operations. He rebuilt the city of Babylon, which has been excavated in modern times by a German expedition. The most famous construction was the temple tower of Marduk, called *Etemenanki*, "House of the Foundation of Heaven and Earth." The boundaries of his empire were virtually those of the old Assyrian empire; Judah was a tributary. He invaded Egypt late in his reign but did not succeed in establishing his power there.

The history of Judah was, as usual, deeply affected by these international events. Jeremiah was probably born during the reign of Josiah (640-609). That king is most noted for the religious reforms which he instituted in the year 621, as the result of the finding of the original edition of Deuteronomy. These reforms had an important political aspect: they involved the throwing off of the Assyrian yoke, for Josiah extended his power into the old Assyrian province of Samaria and centralized all political control in Jerusalem. Little is known of Josiah's reign apart from the Deuteronomic reforms; he died in 609 at the hands of Pharaoh Neco of Egypt as the latter was on his way to give aid to the Assyrians at the Euphrates River. The information in II Kings 23:29 is cryptic, but the account in II Chr. 35:20-24 says that Josiah attacked Neco at Megiddo and was killed in battle. It is difficult to determine whether the Chronicles account is historical; it is possible that Josiah was summoned to an interview by Neco and, when he refused to promise aid to the Egyptians, was put to death.

Josiah's son, Jehoahaz, was placed on the throne of Judah by popular consent, but ruled for only three months. As the Egyptians returned from their expedition into Mesopotamia, they deposed Jehoahaz and placed Jehoiakim, another son of Josiah, on the throne.

Jehoiakim was king of Judah during eleven of the most active years of Jeremiah's life (609-598), and succeeded in arousing the bitter opposition of the prophet. Jehoiakim used oppressive measures in dealing with his own people; he was pompous and proud, and he probably reversed many of the religious reforms which had been instituted by his father. Jehoiakim was subservient to the Egyptians, who had placed him on his throne, until shortly after the battle of Carchemish when he transferred his loyalty to the Babylonians, who were then clearly the dominant power. His vacillation in paying tribute to the Babylonians brought on two invasions of Judah: in about 602 B.C., when marauding bands of Chaldeans, Syrians, Moabites, and Ammonites invaded the land (II Kings 24:2; see Jer. 9:10-22; 12:7-13); and again in 598, when a more formal invasion took place and Jerusalem was besieged. Jehoiakim himself died during the siege.

Upon the death of Jehoiakim his son, Jehoiachin, succeeded to the throne. After a brief reign of three months he surrendered to the Babylonians who were besieging Jerusalem. He himself, many members of his court, and many of the people of Jerusalem were taken into exile to Babylonia. He was apparently kept in prison throughout the reign of Nebuchadrezzar, but was released from prison and given preferential treatment at the royal court by that monarch's successor, Awel-Marduk, or Evil-merodach, as he is known in the Old Testament (52:31-34).

Upon the surrender of Jerusalem Nebuchadrezzar did not take away the independence of Judah, but appointed as king another son of Josiah, Zedekiah, who ruled for eleven years. The character of Zedekiah was quite different from that of Jehoiakim. He was friendly to Jeremiah and followed a pro-Babylonian policy for ten years. But he finally gave in to the pro-Egyptian faction in Jerusalem and withheld tribute from Babylonia. This brought the Babylonian army to Judah again. This time many of the towns were devastated, and Jerusalem itself was besieged. After besieging the city for a year and a half (during which the siege was lifted once upon the approach of an Egyptian army), the Babylonians finally captured Jerusalem in August, 587. Much of the city was burned, including the temple and royal palace; the king was taken into captivity; and many Jews were exiled. This time Judah was made a province of the Babylonian Empire, with a governor rather than an independent king. The governor appointed by the Babylonians was Gedaliah, of a highly respected Jewish family. After ruling for about five years (see Exeg. on 40:7–41:18), Gedaliah was assassinated by Ishmael, a member of the royal family, under the goading of the Ammonites. Some of the Jews, fearing Babylonian reprisal, fled to Egypt, taking Jeremiah with them. Little is known in detail of the history of the Babylonian province of Judah after the death of Gedaliah.

II. Life and Message of Jeremiah

We are in the fortunate position of having more authentic information about Jeremiah than about any other Hebrew prophet, perhaps than any other character in the Old Testament. His book is one of the longest in the Old Testament. It contains not only a considerable amount of biographical information, perhaps preserved by his scribe and disciple Baruch, but also a number of passages, often called Jeremiah's "confessions," which reveal much about the prophet's inner life. This section will deal with the events of his life and the main emphases of his messages to the people of his time; the next section will consider his personality.

Jeremiah was born and grew up at Anathoth, a small village two miles northeast of Jerusalem, now marked by the site called Râs el-Kharrûbeh. He was born into a priestly family, the members of which may have served in the local sanctuary of Anathoth, or they may have served—at least after the Deuteronomic reformation of 621 B.C. —in the temple of Jerusalem, only an hour's walk distant. Jeremiah never served as priest; in fact, in his prophetic career he came into frequent conflict with the priests, even members of his own family (12:6).

Jeremiah's poems contain many allusions to nature, reflecting the experiences of his childhood in a rural village. He must have become acquainted early with the capital city of Jerusalem, for it was very close, and it was in the capital that he spent his adult years. He probably came to know in his childhood the preserved messages of former prophets, especially of Hosea. His early messages show the deep influence of that prophet, both in his thought and in the figures in which he clothed it.

While still a young man Jeremiah received a call to prophesy, now preserved in 1:4-10. The two visions in 1:11-16 apparently came soon after his call, but this is not definitely stated and may not be correct. The call of Jeremiah reflects his sense of predestination to the office of prophet, his timidity in accepting the call, and his confidence in the presence of God in his life.

According to the traditional interpretation of Jeremiah's life, the prophet was born about 650 B.C. and received the call to prophesy in the thirteenth year of Josiah, 626 B.C. (1:2). In his second vision he is represented as seeing "a boiling pot, facing away from the north" (1:13), and this is interpreted to mean that evil is about to break forth upon the land out of the north. Several of the poems in the early chapters of the book (4:5-8, 13-22, 27-31; 5:15-17; 6:1-8, 22-26; 8:14-17) describe in vivid language the sudden onslaught of a foe from the north, causing great destruction in Palestine. These poems are usually interpreted as depicting the coming of the Scythians, a nomadic people, depending on horses rather than sheep or cattle, who invaded western Asia, apparently from the Caucasian steppes, early in the seventh century. According to an account of Herodotus,[1] the Scythians invaded Palestine and tried to enter Egypt, but were bought off by Psamtik, king of Egypt. Some of the Scythians then sacked a temple at Ascalon. Herodotus says that the Scythians ruled Asia for twenty-eight years, but he does not record any invasion of Judah or Jerusalem, the only city in Palestine he mentions being Ascalon.

When the threat from the Scythians failed to materialize, at least on the scale prophesied by Jeremiah, the young prophet was discredited. But he continued to prophesy, uttering messages now preserved largely in chs. 2–6.

At the time of the reforms instituted by Josiah in 621 B.C., not Jeremiah but a prophetess named Huldah was consulted (II Kings 22:14-20). However, many scholars believe that Jeremiah ardently supported the reforms and even traveled around the villages of Judah calling upon the people to accept them (11:1-8). Later he became disillusioned, seeing that the reformers dealt only with externals rather

than with the inner spirit and moral behavior of the people.

The view which is adopted in the Exegesis differs from the traditional interpretation of the early life of Jeremiah, the principal points of difference being: (a) The date 626 B.C. is taken to be the probable date of Jeremiah's birth, rather than of his call. (b) The foe from the north was not the Scythians, but the Babylonians, and the poems which describe the coming of that foe were uttered in the time of Jehoiakim. (c) Jeremiah did not advocate the Deuteronomic reforms, but in fact opposed some of their basic tenets. (d) No passages in the book can with confidence be attributed to the reign of Josiah; hence, Jeremiah's career begins in the reign of Jehoiakim. The prophet's favorable view of Josiah is given in 22:15-16. Some scholars believe that portions of the "book of comfort" in chs. 30–31, or the oracles against foreign nations in chs. 46–51, were composed in the time of Josiah. For refutation of such views see the Exegesis.

The theory which interprets the foe from the north as the Scythian hordes rests upon very insecure foundations and has been abandoned by many scholars. There is no valid evidence for a Scythian invasion of Judah around 625 B.C. The account of Herodotus contains several improbable statements; but even it does not connect the Scythians with Judah. While some of the poems could fit the Scythians, several characteristics of the foe from the north do not fit them at all: that they were "an ancient nation" (5:15), that they used chariots (4:13), that they besieged cities (4:16; 6:6), that they fought in regular ranks (6:23), and that they were the "lovers" of Jerusalem (4:30). The supposition that poems originally dealing with the Scythians were subsequently revised to fit the Chaldeans hardly does justice to the poems themselves or to the methods of the prophet. All the poems can be understood as describing the Babylonians, and it is certain that the enemies "from the north" are the Babylonians in 13:20; 25:9 (cf. 46:24). If Jeremiah predicted in these poems the coming of the Babylonians, his vision was clear, and his prophecy was ultimately fulfilled, though his attitude toward the Babylonians later changed when he counseled submission to Babylonia rather than continued resistance. Jeremiah did not as a young prophet become greatly exercised over a Scythian invasion that failed to materialize, and then have to suffer criticism and temporary retirement because of his mistake.

The theory which maintains that Jeremiah for a time actively supported the Deuteronomic reforms likewise rests on insecure foundations. There is not a single passage among the genuine oracles of Jeremiah which can be adduced to support this theory (for 11:1-8 see Exeg.). On the other hand, several passages indicate that Jeremiah held views at variance with fundamental principles of the Deuteronomic reforms. The Deuteronomists sought to centralize all sacrificial worship in the Jerusalem temple, but Jeremiah in his temple sermon (7:1-15; 26:1-6) predicted the destruction of the temple if the people did not show true moral reform. In several passages he expresses opposition to the need for sacrifice (6:20; 7:21-24; 11:15). In two passages—2:8; 8:8-13—he seems to have expressed opposition to some of the methods and ideas of the Deuteronomists. The prophet indeed must have felt sympathy with some of the purposes of the Deuteronomists, particularly those which aimed at the correction of social injustices and corrupt business practices, but it is difficult to believe that he ever was concerned with such matters as the centralization of sacrificial worship in the Jerusalem temple and the reform of ritual. Because the book of Jeremiah has been edited by Deuteronomists (see pp. 788-89), the affinities between the prophet and Deuteronomy appear closer than they actually were.

The earliest messages of Jeremiah were delivered in the reign of Jehoiakim (609-598). Apart from the brief lament over the exile of Jehoahaz by the Egyptians, the earliest public utterance of any length may have been the famous temple "sermon" (7:1-15; 26:1-6), delivered at the beginning of the reign of Jehoiakim, possibly at the time of his coronation. This sermon led to the immediate arrest of Jeremiah on a capital charge. The priests and the temple prophets were arrayed against him, but the princes and common people were on his side. Jeremiah's life was saved by his own courage, the recalling of a precedent from the life of Micah, and the fact that the officials, especially Shaphan, championed his cause. This sermon must have made a great impression, and thereafter Jeremiah must have been listened to with care.

Early in the reign of Jehoiakim, Jeremiah delivered those oracles which are now preserved in 2:1–6:30 and possibly in 8:4–9:1. Recalling to the Hebrews their original devotion to Yahweh in the Mosaic period, he condemns them for their participation in the syncretistic worship of the day, which he terms harlotry or adultery, following Hosea. Several times he calls on the people to repent and return to Yahweh, as in 3:22–4:4, in which 4:3 quotes from Hos. 10:12. As the result of their continued sinfulness, Yahweh is about to bring upon them punishment, the foe from the north, who is described in most vivid terms. Whoever the foe may have been, humanly speaking, Jeremiah

was certain that it was Yahweh who was sending him against the Hebrews in punishment for sin. For the most part he condemns in these oracles the false worship and idolatry of the Hebrews, but on occasion he condemns social injustice as vividly as Amos had (5:26-28). For the dating of these chapters see especially the Exegesis on 2:14-19, 36-37.

Near the time of the battle of Carchemish in 605 B.C. Jeremiah delivered the oracle in 46:3-12, directed against Egypt, the nation that suffered defeat along with the Assyrians. The result of that battle, and the accession of Nebuchadrezzar to the throne of Babylonia soon afterward, produced a great change in the international situation. Within a short time Jeremiah, in order to bring to the attention of the people and their leaders the seriousness of the situation, dictated his messages to Baruch, as related in ch. 36. The scroll was read in the temple on a fast day, then to the princes, and finally to King Jehoiakim, who burned it. Subsequently Jeremiah and Baruch went into hiding, and Jeremiah redictated his messages, making additions to them.

The period between the writing of the scroll and the fall of Jerusalem seven years later was one of the busiest in the life of the prophet, though he must have been in hiding for part of the time. To this period we should probably assign his "confessions" (see p. 782). At the time of the invasion by marauding bands of Chaldeans, Syrians, Moabites, and Ammonites in 602 B.C. he uttered the lament in 12:7-13 and probably that in 9:10-11, 17-22. The incident in which Jeremiah used the Rechabites as an object lesson to the Hebrews belongs to the same time (35:1-19). Sometime in the latter part of the reign of Jehoiakim, Jeremiah was arrested by Pashhur for prophesying the destruction of Jerusalem, was beaten, and was placed in stocks overnight (20:1-6).

When Jehoiakim withheld tribute from Nebuchadrezzar, Jeremiah became very active in warning the Hebrews of the destruction which would overtake Judah at the hands of those who had previously been their friends, the Babylonians (13:20-27; 17:1-4; 22:6-7; 25:8-13). Though previously he had called upon his fellow countrymen to repent, he now felt that they were too accustomed to doing evil to learn how to do good (13:23). In spite of his warnings the Hebrews persisted in their resistance to Babylonia, and the first siege of the city took place. Jeremiah mourned over the sufferings of the people at this time (10:17-22; 15:5-9). King Jehoiakim died during the siege, but Jeremiah hardly wept over him, for in 22:13-19 he condemns him in the strongest language he uses for any king of Judah.

Jehoiachin reigned for only three months before capitulating to the Babylonians. Jeremiah lamented the exile of the king in 13:15-19; 22:24-30. But he was not among those who continued to consider Jehoiachin the legitimate king and expect his return soon, as the latter passage shows.

Zedekiah was more favorably disposed toward Jeremiah than Jehoiakim had been, and the prophet had closer relations with that king. Early in the reign of Zedekiah, the prophet sent a letter to the exiles in Babylonia to warn them against expecting an immediate return to their homeland, as false prophets were encouraging them to do. Jeremiah directed them to build houses, plant gardens, marry, and in general seek the welfare of the place to which they had been exiled, praying to Yahweh on its behalf (29:4-9). This letter to the exiles is very important for understanding the religion of Jeremiah.

In the fourth year of Zedekiah's reign emissaries came to Judah from Edom, Moab, Ammon, Tyre, and Sidon, to try to enlist the support of Judah in a rebellion against Babylonia, probably in alliance with Egypt, where a new Pharaoh, Psamtik II, had just come to the throne. Jeremiah performed a symbolic action by placing a yoke on his own neck, and told those emissaries and the king of Judah that it was the will of Yahweh that they should submit to the yoke of the king of Babylon, who was in reality the servant of Yahweh (27:1-22). This led to a conflict with a false prophet, Hananiah from Gibeon, who proclaimed that Yahweh had broken the yoke of the king of Babylon, and would in two years bring back the exiles from Babylonia. Jeremiah at first expressed the wish that Hananiah's words might come true, but declared that the earlier prophets had for the most part prophesied the coming of evil rather than of peace (28:8-9). Later Jeremiah returned to say that Yahweh had broken the wooden bars but made in their place bars of iron, indicating that it was still God's will that the Hebrews should serve Nebuchadrezzar; and he predicted the death of Hananiah, who died within a year. The counsel of Jeremiah—submission to the yoke of Babylonia—continued to be his point of view down to the very moment of Jerusalem's destruction.

Zedekiah apparently did not join in revolt against Babylonia at this time (594 B.C.), and he seems to have wished to follow the prophetic counsel of Jeremiah and continue to pay tribute to Babylonia. But there was in Jerusalem a strong faction that advocated rebellion against Babylonia and alliance with Egypt. The civil strife in the city is reflected in the parable of the jars (13:12-14). This pro-Egyptian faction eventually gained the upper hand, and the Hebrews withheld tribute. Again the Babylonian army came to Palestine, and this time, as we have seen, Jerusalem was captured.

The book of Jeremiah contains an unusually full account of the prophecies and actions of the prophet during the time of this Babylonian invasion, probably from the pen of Baruch. Because the material is not now arranged in proper time sequence in the book, it may be useful to the reader if the sections are set down in their chronological order, with a brief summary of each.

(a) 34:1-7: Jeremiah warns Zedekiah that Yahweh will give Jerusalem into the hand of Nebuchadrezzar, but promises the king a peaceful death and honorable burial, probably on the condition that he surrender the city to the Babylonian monarch. This may have been in the summer or fall of 589 B.C., before the siege of Jerusalem began.

(b) 37:1-10: During an interval when the Babylonians lifted the siege of Jerusalem, upon the approach of an Egyptian army (probably the spring of 588 B.C.), Zedekiah sent a deputation to Jeremiah asking him to pray for the city. Jeremiah sent back word that the Babylonians would return to the city and capture it. (A variant account of this is preserved in 21:1-10, but it has no independent value.)

(c) 34:8-22: After the siege of Jerusalem began, Zedekiah had issued a royal proclamation that Hebrew slaves should be set free; but when the siege was lifted upon the approach of an Egyptian army, the slaveowners took back their former slaves. Jeremiah rebukes them for their hypocrisy at this time, and again affirms that the Babylonian army will return and carry out Yahweh's judgment upon those who have sinned in this manner.

(d) 37:11-15: Shortly afterward Jeremiah set out from Jerusalem to go to the land of Benjamin (probably to Anathoth), and was arrested by a sentry on a charge of deserting to the enemy. The prophet was brought to the princes, who beat him and imprisoned him in the house of Jonathan the secretary. Jeremiah remained in prison until the fall of Jerusalem.

(e) 37:16-21: King Zedekiah sent for Jeremiah to come to the royal palace for a secret interview. He inquired of him: "Is there any word from the Lord?" Jeremiah replied that it was still the will of God that he be delivered into the hand of the king of Babylon. The prophet requested that he not be returned to the house of Jonathan, and he was committed to the court of the guard, probably an open court in the palace compound, less confining than his former place of imprisonment.

(f) 32:1-15: While in this prison, and after the return of the Babylonian army to the siege of Jerusalem, Jeremiah purchased a field in Anathoth from his cousin Hanamel, to redeem it for the family. After going through the redemption procedure he declared, "Thus says the LORD of hosts, the God of Israel: Houses and fields and vineyards shall again be bought in this land" (32:15).

(g) 38:1-13: In the court of the guard Jeremiah continued to advise the people of Jerusalem to surrender to the Babylonians. A group of princes appealed to the king to put him to death, on the charge that he was weakening the hands of the soldiers defending the city. Zedekiah gave them permission to do with the prophet as they wished, and they placed him in a cistern. Since there was no water but only mire in the cistern, they thought he would soon die. The prophet was rescued by an Ethiopian eunuch in the royal service, Ebed-melech, and returned to the court of the guard.

(h) 38:14-28: King Zedekiah sent to Jeremiah for a second secret interview, this time in the third entrance of the temple. Again the prophet advised the king to surrender to Babylonia and promised that his life would be spared and the city not be burned. Zedekiah replied that he was afraid of the Jews who had deserted to the Chaldeans, and did not follow the prophet's counsel.

(j) 39:1-40:6: Upon the fall of Jerusalem, Jeremiah was taken out of prison and entrusted to Gedaliah, the new governor of the province of Judah. It may be that he was offered safe conduct to Babylonia, but the prophet preferred to remain with his own people.

Little is known concerning the activities of Jeremiah during the governorship of Gedaliah. He probably supported Gedaliah in his attempts to rebuild the land, and continued to combat those who wished to rebel against Babylonia. The beautiful poems now preserved in 31:2-6, 15-22 may come from this period; they express great hope for the future, based on the continuing love of Yahweh for his people.

After the assassination of Gedaliah, some of the Jews wished to flee to Egypt and they asked Jeremiah to pray to Yahweh to discover his will for them. After ten days Jeremiah told them that it was the will of Yahweh that they should remain in Judah rather than flee to Egypt. They refused to believe him, saying that Baruch had set Jeremiah against them in order that they might be delivered into the hand of the Babylonians. So they went to Egypt anyhow, taking the unwilling prophet with them.

In Egypt Jeremiah continued to rebuke his fellow countrymen. On one occasion he carried out a symbolic action designed to show them that even in Egypt they were not safe from Nebuchadrezzar, for that monarch would come

to Egypt and set up his throne (43:8-13). He condemned the Hebrews, especially the women, for worshiping the queen of heaven rather than Yahweh. We do not know how long Jeremiah continued to live in Egypt; if 44:29-30 is authentic (see Exeg.), he was still alive about 570 B.C.

According to tradition, Jeremiah was stoned to death in Egypt by his exasperated fellow countrymen.

III. Jeremiah's Personality

Jeremiah's own personality constitutes one of his most important contributions to the history of Hebrew religion. He was the most subjective of the prophets; his personal experiences and inmost feelings are more vividly reflected in his words than is the case with any other prophet. It may be that Jeremiah's life is not wholly typical, but it shows one important aspect of Hebrew prophecy: as a messenger of God to the people of his time, the prophet was not a mechanical puppet but a strong individual. The prophets did not lose their individuality and personality in performing their office. They were not mystics who became absorbed in the Divine, but retained a vivid consciousness of self over against the Divine.

The book of Jeremiah has preserved a group of passages which give us unusual insight into his inner feelings: 10:23-24; 11:18-12:6; 15:10-21; 17:9-10, 14-18; 18:18-23; 20:7-12, 14-18. They are usually called his "confessions," but the term is not very appropriate. Some of the passages have the form of a monologue or, rather, outcry of the prophet, such as 15:10; 20:14-18. Most of them are prayers to God, and in three sections we have not only the prayer of the prophet but the answer of Yahweh: 11:18-23; 12:1-6; 15:15-21. These passages may have been composed approximately in their present order, since the last represents the climax of Jeremiah's bitterness; they probably come from the latter half of Jehoiakim's reign before Jeremiah became deeply involved in national and international crises. For the study of the prophet's personality most of his messages are revealing, but special attention should be given also to 1:4-10; 6:27-30; 8:18-9:1; 16:1-13.

Jeremiah's inner life was marked by a strong tension between his natural desires and inclinations on the one hand and his deep sense of vocation on the other. He was by nature sensitive, reticent, and introspective, and like most men wanted the good will of his fellow men. But he had a very deep sense of his commission as a prophet, and his loyalty to that commission caused him to be hated and even persecuted, since his message was usually one of violence and destruction (20:8). He was denied partici-

JEREMIAH

pation in the ordinary joys and sorrows of his fellows, and was forbidden to marry (16:1-13). He thus felt that he must live alone, with the hand of God upon him (15:17).

This inner tension made Jeremiah a man of fluctuating, sometimes violent, moods. In his most despondent times he wished that he had never been born (15:10; 20:14-18), or he wanted to run away from his people and from his prophetic commission, to live alone in the desert (9:2). He even reached the point of shaking his fist at God, calling him "a deceitful brook, . . . waters that fail" (15:18), the same God he had on another occasion termed a "fountain of living waters" (2:13). In his most despondent and bitter moment he even accused God of deceiving him, overpowering him, and making of him a perpetual laughingstock (20:7).

Yet Jeremiah had his periods of exaltation, when he had great faith in God and pleasure in his task. He could say, "Thy words became to me a joy and the delight of my heart" (15:16), and he could speak of God as "a dread warrior" fighting on his side against all opposition (20:11). If there were times when he wanted to run away from his prophetic task and speak no more in the name of Yahweh, he felt the word of God in his heart "as it were a burning fire shut up in [his] bones," which he could not contain or control (20:9). Even when he cried out against God and his own fate, Jeremiah did not doubt the existence of God or the reality of his prophetic call.

On account of his deep faith in God, and because he did not hesitate to give vent to his feelings of despair and bitterness, the tension of his inner life did not cause him to break down. The characteristic quality of his outer life was courage, with complete fidelity to his prophetic office. He was in reality "a fortified wall of bronze" (15:20). His prophecies usually predicted doom and destruction to the nation unless it repented. He did not hesitate to condemn all the people around him: priests and prophets, the common people, the princes, and even the ruling kings. In the latter days of the kingdom of Judah he had to espouse a very unpopular course of action: surrender to Babylonia. For this he suffered great indignities and imprisonment. Yet even when he was summoned from the confinement of prison to an interview with King Zedekiah, he did not hesitate to continue to counsel surrender, when a little compromise might have secured his release.

Jeremiah was thus far from being merely a "weeping prophet," as popular tradition has often made him. He did on occasion weep and lament, sometimes for himself, but more often— like Jesus—for the people around him: "For the wound of my people my heart is wounded" (8:21). His reputation as a weeping prophet comes in part from the ascription of Lamentations to him, but it is probable that he did not write that book. His book does contain poems of lamentation (e.g., 8:18–9:1; 9:10-11, 17-22; 10:19-21; 14:2-6), but the prophet never lacked courage when it was needed.

Jeremiah's personality was not without traces of impatience and quickness of temper. He was emotional and sensitive. The very qualities which made him a great poet and faithful prophet must have made him unpopular with his fellow men. His impatience can be seen at its worst in his attitude toward his enemies. He often called upon Yahweh to take vengeance upon his persecutors (see 11:20; 12:3; 15:15; 17:18); on one occasion he even prayed that God might afflict the wives and children of his personal enemies (18:21-23). We should not seek to eliminate such an attitude on the part of the prophet by pronouncing the passages in which it occurs secondary. It was a fault in his character or, we might better say, a defect in the religious level which he and others of his time had attained. Yet one or two things may be said in extenuation of Jeremiah's attitude. For one, he found it easy to identify his personal enemies with the enemies of God, since he was so fully persuaded that his message represented the will of God. For another, we must note that Jeremiah protested in his prayers that he had in truth prayed on behalf of his enemies and sought their welfare, but they had spurned him (15:11; 17:16; 18:20). Furthermore, Jeremiah had little outward success during his lifetime. He may have made a few disciples who preserved his messages, but for the most part his voice went unheeded by all to whom he spoke— common people, religious leaders, princes, and kings. It is small wonder, then, that he sometimes lost patience.

One of the "confessions" contains a reply from Yahweh in which there is a rebuke to the prophet for his impatience with men and even with God:

> If you return, I will restore you,
>   and you shall stand before me.
> If you utter what is precious, and not what is
>   worthless,
>   you shall be as my mouth.
> They shall turn to you,
>   but you shall not turn to them (15:19).

It is significant that these words have been preserved. The prophet could not claim perfection of character, but he had need, as other men did, to return to God—that is, to repent. He was not called to perfection of character, but to faithfulness; Jeremiah did not fail in his response to this call.

IV. Jeremiah's Theology

Like all the Hebrew prophets, Jeremiah was not a theologian or a systematic thinker. He was a spokesman for Yahweh to the people of his time. Yet he necessarily dealt with many problems that were basically theological, and his whole message had a theological foundation. Hence we may speak of the "implied theology" of the prophet. Such theology, embodied in the messages of prophets and preachers through the centuries, has probably had more influence on the popular mind than the writings of systematic thinkers.

The sections below are an attempt to outline Jeremiah's theology under four topics, but it will readily be seen that there is much overlapping in these topics, and that his thoughts are here put into a system which is never set down as such in his book.

A. God.—Jeremiah had an unusual, almost unique, experience with God, as we have seen in discussing his personality. He believed in the majesty and transcendence of Yahweh, but this did not leave him adoring God in awe, as it did Isaiah and Ezekiel; rather, we see him wrestling and struggling with God, perplexed and sometimes even defiant. But his faith in the power and goodness of Yahweh won in the end, and it was this which gave him the courage that characterized his life.

Jeremiah uses a number of vivid figures to describe God. Two are of special significance. In 2:13 he speaks of Yahweh as a "fountain of living waters"—that is, one who is ever available, always invigorating and creative. (Yet we have seen that in 15:18 he could also speak of Yahweh as "like a deceitful brook, like waters that fail.") The other significant figure is that of the "potter" (18:1-12), a figure which he did not originate (cf. Isa. 29:16) but which he established in the thinking of the Hebrews. This is a splendid figure with which to describe the sovereignty of God as a free Person over men who are likewise free persons.

Jeremiah believed that Yahweh was the creator of the world and the natural order (5:22; 8:7; 27:5; other passages more elaborately describing Yahweh as creator are secondary: 10:12-13; 31:35-36). Yahweh is the controller of history. He has controlled the history of the Hebrew people from the time of their election, and it was Yahweh who commissioned Nebuchadrezzar to rule over Judah and the surrounding nations. When Jeremiah speaks of Nebuchadrezzar as a "servant" of Yahweh (27:6), he does not suggest that the king worshiped Yahweh, but rather that he carried out the commission given him by Yahweh. Jeremiah emphasizes the fact that Yahweh tries and knows the hearts of men, rewarding them according to their merit (11:20; 16:17; 17:10; 20:12; 29:23). He thought of Yahweh as being both "a God at hand" and "a God afar off" (23:23), that is, both immanent and transcendent.

Jeremiah believed Yahweh to be a God of love as well as of justice and power. He speaks of him under the figure of the husband of Israel (2:2) or the father of the nation (3:19). An especially striking verse describes Yahweh as being *ḥāṣîdh,* translated "merciful" in both the Revised Standard Version and the King James Version (3:12). This word is used of God only here and in Ps. 145:17. It is frequently applied in the psalms to men—as in Pss. 4:3; 30:4; 32:6; 86:2, with the English translation "godly," "saint," or "holy." George Adam Smith renders it "Loyal-in-Love." [2] It describes Yahweh as exercising *ḥéṣedh,* which the Revised Standard Version often translates "steadfast love" when it refers to God. The love of God is seen also in the passages in which the prophet speaks as if the sin of Israel both amazed and pained Yahweh (2:5, 31-32). The love of Yahweh for Israel is most clearly expressed in a passage which comes from near the end of Jeremiah's career:

I have loved you with an everlasting love;
  therefore I have continued my faithfulness to
  you (31:3).

It must not be forgotten, however, that Jeremiah sometimes experienced in his own life the overpowering, almost demonic, side of Yahweh's nature (see 15:18; 20:7, also pp. 782-83).

Jeremiah believed that Yahweh required of men not sacrifice and ritual (6:20; 7:22-23; 11:15), as the priests and temple prophets taught, but rather repentance and obedience to his moral laws, which would issue in righteous living. His conception of Yahweh's nature and requirement is neatly summarized in 9:24: "Let him who glories glory in this, that he understands and knows me, that I am the LORD who practice kindness [*ḥéṣedh*], justice, and righteousness in the earth; for in these things I delight, says the LORD."

Jeremiah was a monotheist. Other gods are described in various terms which indicate he thought of them as having no power or real existence: they are "worthlessness" (2:5), "no gods" (2:11), and "broken cisterns, that can hold no water" (2:13), and are completely unable to help men in time of trouble (2:28). On the other hand, Yahweh really governs the destiny of nations such as Babylonia and the nations surrounding Judah, even if they do not recognize him. We do not find in Jeremiah the fully articulated monotheism of Second

[2] *Jeremiah* (4th ed.; Garden City: Doubleday, Doran & Co., 1929), p. 364.

Isaiah, but his thought leaves no place for deities other than Yahweh.

B. The Nation and the Individual.—Though Jeremiah is rightly considered the prophet of personal religion and of individualism, we must not forget that he ministered to his nation in a period of unparalleled crisis, and had much to say to and regarding the nation.

Jeremiah believed that Israel was the chosen people of Yahweh. He describes the nation as "the first fruits of [God's] harvest" (2:3), "a choice vine" planted by Yahweh (2:21), the "beloved" of Yahweh (11:15; 12:7), Yahweh's own "heritage" (12:7-9), "vineyard" (12:10), and "flock" (13:17). The word "covenant" occurs rarely in Jeremiah's own words, but the covenant idea underlies his attitude toward the relationship between Yahweh and Israel.

Like Hosea he saw the history of the nation as beginning with a period of faithfulness in the Mosaic age, but issuing in a long era of faithlessness when Israel came into Canaan (ch. 2). Israel was like "a restive young camel" or "a wild ass used to the wilderness" (2:23-24). In Canaan the people worshiped either false gods or Yahweh with pagan rites; following Hosea, Jeremiah depicts such worship under the figure of adultery or harlotry. Yahweh had continually called upon Israel, through the prophets, to return to him, and he had sent upon them many afflictions as chastisement or correction (*mûṣār*, 2:30; 5:3; 7:28; etc.), but they had refused to return or obey. Now Yahweh was about to destroy them for their repeated rebellions against him. In the future, however, he would establish his "new covenant with the house of Israel and the house of Judah" (31:31).

Yet the individual within the nation is very important. It is possible that as Jeremiah preached to the nation and had less and less success he turned more and more to individuals. He may have had a body of disciples, as Isaiah had (Isa. 8:16). It is difficult to prove either statement from his own words. The individual is emphasized in the messages of Jeremiah more by implication than by explicit statement.

Jeremiah's own experience with God was such that it must have led him to see the great significance of the individual person in God's sight. Then he stresses, as no other prophet before him had, the importance of the "heart" of man, which in Hebrew psychology is the seat of the mind as well as the emotions. We have seen that he emphasized the fact that Yahweh sees and tries the heart; and we shall see that he saw the source of evil as being in man's heart.

Jeremiah promoted the ideal of personal religion in various ways. He saw that true obedience to Yahweh was not dependent upon the existence of the Jerusalem temple and its sacrifices (7:1-15; 26:1-24); or upon residence in the land of Palestine (29:1-14); or upon the rite of circumcision (9:25-26; see Exeg. of this obscure passage; cf. 4:4). Whenever men seek God with the whole heart they will find him (29:13-14). The new covenant is made with the nation, but its implications are such as to heighten the importance of the individual, his motives, and his relationship to God.

Jeremiah's messages were delivered to ancient Israel, and were cast within the molds of ancient Hebrew thought, which necessarily emphasized the nation and its election; but many of the implications of Jeremiah's words were worked out later in Judaism and Christianity. They had great influence in helping Judaism to survive the loss of its land and nationhood.

C. Sin and Repentance.—Like the other prophets, Jeremiah condemned the sins of Israel. While he may have given special attention to the sins of false worship, he did not fail to condemn social injustices and all forms of iniquity. But Jeremiah shows more interest than former prophets in analyzing the source of sin in the life of the people; he finds it in the weakness and corruption of the hearts of men. The following quotations will give examples of his thought:

O Jerusalem, wash your heart from wickedness,
  that you may be saved.
How long shall your evil thoughts
  lodge within you? (4:14.)

But this people has a stubborn and rebellious heart;
  they have turned aside and gone away (5:23).

The sin of Judah is written with a pen of iron; with a point of diamond it is engraved on the tablet of their heart (17:1).

  The heart is deceitful above all things,
    and desperately weak;
    who can understand it? (17:9.)

Jeremiah frequently uses a phrase to describe the source of sin: "the stubbornness of the [evil] heart" (*sherîrûth hallēbh* [*hārā'*] mistakenly translated by the King James Version as "imagination of the heart": 7:24; 13:10; 23:17; etc.).

Yet Jeremiah apparently did not believe that man is born with an evil and corrupt heart; it becomes corrupt through willful disobedience and the hardening influence of habit. The latter is especially emphasized in 13:23. Instead of treating or seeing sin as the natural state of man or the nation, several passages emphasize its very unnaturalness. In 2:10-11 Jeremiah contrasts Israel's forsaking her God with the practice of pagan nations in remaining loyal to their deities, even though in his eyes they are "no gods." In 5:22-23; 8:7 and 18:13-16 he contrasts the sinfulness of Israel with the obedience of birds, animals, and forces of nature to what we would call "the law of nature." The attitude of Jeremiah toward Israel's sin, reflecting what he believes to be the attitude of Yahweh, is constantly one of bewilderment and pain rather than acceptance of it as natural.

The remedy for Israel's sin is repentance, issuing in a life of obedience to Yahweh. Jeremiah says more about repentance than any other prophet. His messages are obscured, however, by his terminology. The Hebrew word most often rendered "repent," *nāḥam*, is used of man's repentance in two passages (8:6; 31:19). It is more frequently used of Yahweh's "repenting"—that is, of his change of purpose in view of the response of men to his original intent (4:28; 15:6; 18:8, 10; 20:16; 26:3, 13, 19; 42:10). The Hebrew word most often used by Jeremiah (as well as by other prophets) for repentance is *shûbh,* usually translated "return" or "turn" in English versions, including the Revised Standard and the King James. It is significant, however, that the former renders it as "repent" in 5:3; 9:5; 34:15; this could appropriately be the rendering elsewhere. Good examples of Jeremiah's summons to repentance or of statements he makes concerning it may be seen in 3:12-14; 4:1-4; 18:11; 31:18-19. For Jeremiah repentance meant a conscious turning away from evil and a turning toward God in such a way that one might live obediently and righteously, and—in the phrase of John the Baptist—"bear fruit that befits repentance" (Matt. 3:8). Even the prophet himself was rebuked by God and ordered to repent (15:19).

Jeremiah was much more hopeful of repentance in the early part of his career than he was later. The famous passage, 13:23, which compares Israel's chances of learning to "do good" with the possibility of an Ethiopian's changing his skin or of a leopard's changing his spots, expresses the prophet's pessimism. Yet this pessimism is not based upon lack of faith in Yahweh's ability to forgive; it is based rather on Jeremiah's knowledge of the force of habit and custom: it is "you . . . who are accustomed to do evil" who find it so difficult to repent and learn to obey Yahweh (cf. the phrase "skilled in doing evil" in 4:22).

The book of Jeremiah contains three passages, 3:22-25; 14:7-10, 19-22, which may be described as "confessions of sin" of the type which the prophet believed the people should make (see Exeg. and cf. Hos. 6:1-3; 14:2-3).

D. Eschatology.—Jeremiah was concerned with the future of his nation, but we do not find in his genuine prophecies any highly apocalyptic imagery, with vivid portrayals of cosmic cataclysms and of the glorification and elevation of Israel. His eschatology is on the whole sober and realistic.

The book, however, contains numerous eschatological passages that are in all probability secondary: 3:15-18; 4:9-10, 23-26; 12:14-17; 16:14-15 (=23:7-8); 23:3-4; 25:30-38; 30:8-11, 16-24; 31:1, 7-14, 23-28, 35-40; 33:6-26. Here we find elements familiar in other prophetic passages of exilic or postexilic origin: the day of the Lord as a time of judgment, cosmic disturbances, the destruction of foreign nations (30:11, 16) or their conversion to the worship of Yahweh (12:14-17; cf. 16:19-21), the rebuilding and glorification of Jerusalem, the union of Israel and Judah, and the establishment of ideal conditions for the Israelites.

Any discussion of Jeremiah's eschatology—in the broad sense of his hope for the future—must begin with two important passages: the account of his purchase of a field at Anathoth (32:1-15), and his letter to the exiles (29:1-14). In the former we are told that the prophet, at a time when he was in prison and the Babylonians were besieging Jerusalem, purchased by redemption a field at Anathoth from his cousin Hanamel, and then explained what he had done as follows: "Thus says the LORD of hosts, the God of Israel: Houses and fields and vineyards shall again be bought in this land" (32:15). By this action Jeremiah expressed a very great faith and hope in the future of his land and people at a time when he had many reasons for deep discouragement, both for himself and his nation.

In the letter to the exiles he seeks to combat false hopes of an immediate return from Babylonia, and encourages the exiles to settle down as good citizens in the land of their exile, even to pray for it, saying that in the welfare of Babylonia they will find their own. While the promise contained in 29:10-14 may not be in the very words of Jeremiah, it gives the substance of his thoughts: he promises an ultimate restoration to their homeland, but in the meantime the exiles can truly find Yahweh if they seek him with their whole heart.

To these two important passages we must add consideration of a few others that are probably authentic. If 31:2-6, 15-22 are genuine poems from the time of Gedaliah, they portray in splendid poetic imagery the rebuilding of the land and the restoration of the happiness of the people after the destruction wrought by the Babylonians. Jeremiah apparently had grounds for his hope that this could be accomplished under Gedaliah, until the senseless assassination of the governor by Ishmael. Here his faith in the restoration rests upon his belief in the continuing love of Yahweh for Israel.

The new covenant passage, 31:31-34, is essentially eschatological in its language and content (see Exeg.). We may note here that it promises, not a new law, but a new inward motivation and power to fulfill the law already known. While the new covenant is to be with the nation, the emphasis which it places on the writing of the law on the hearts of men has important implications for personal religion and personal fellowship with God.

We cannot be certain whether Jeremiah's hopes for the future included a messianic expectation. The only "messianic" passage which has any serious claim to Jeremianic origin is 23:5-6, repeated with slight variation in 33:15-16 (30:9; 33:17, 21, 26 are secondary). Here there is a prediction of the raising up of "a righteous Branch" for David, a king who will deal wisely, executing justice and righteousness in the land. He is to be called "The Lord is our righteousness," which in Hebrew plays on the name of Zedekiah. The righteous "Branch"—which in later times was a messianic title, but may not have been in Jeremiah's day—is not a world-conquering hero or a supernatural figure, but an earthly king from the Davidic dynasty who is to reign wisely. If this prediction is from Jeremiah, it is an example of the fact that his eschatology was not highly speculative and imaginary but realistic and sober. In any event, messianism did not play for him an important role.

In summary, Jeremiah's eschatology envisaged the restoration, and so the continuation, of the people of Israel in their own land, under a good government and with faithful worship of Yahweh. He says nothing of the restoration of the temple and cultus and the familiar trappings of national glory, but says much which involves the regeneration and purification of the hearts of the people.

V. Composition of the Book

The reader who approaches the book of Jeremiah for the first time is likely to feel that there is much confusion in its arrangement. Ch. 1 does, to be sure, tell of the call of the prophet, and chs. 2–6 seem to be largely appropriate to the opening years of his career. But as one reads on, one finds various types of arrangement and sometimes no discernible pattern at all. Sometimes the material is in excellent chronological order, as in chs. 37–44. Elsewhere it is in topical order, as in chs. 21–23; 30–31; 46–51, so that if the reader wishes to follow the prophet's life step by step, or make a specific study of areas of thought, he must skip about from chapter to chapter and passage to passage.

This seeming lack of order arises from the fact that this book, like many others in the Old Testament, is not the product of one person, or of a small group of persons. It is the product of growth over a long period of time, to which many contributed. Yet the book contains a larger amount of authentic material from and concerning the prophet himself than some of the others, such as Isaiah.

Though the subject has long been studied, there is no consensus among scholars as to the stages in the composition of the book of Jeremiah, or the process of growth by which it arrived at its present state.

A. Baruch's Scroll.—Ch. 36 is an immensely valuable account of how Jeremiah dictated a scroll containing his messages to Baruch, his secretary and disciple, and how this scroll was subsequently read in the temple to the hosts of people assembled there, then in a chamber of the palace to a group of royal officials, and finally to King Jehoiakim, who was so angered by it that he cut it up and burned it. He ordered that the prophet and his disciple be arrested; but they escaped by hiding, and Jeremiah redictated the scroll, with additions. The reading of the first scroll took place in the month of December, 605 b.c., on a great fast day, called as the result of a prolonged drought or some other calamity. The second scroll dictated to Baruch apparently constituted the "first edition" of our book of Jeremiah. We cannot recover this edition with certainty, but it probably was relatively short, since the scroll was apparently read three times in a single day; it must have consisted primarily or exclusively of warnings and threats directed against Jerusalem, Judah, and the nations (36:2 LXX).

We may conjecture that Baruch's scroll contained the following passages in our present book: 1:4-14, 17; 2:1-37; 3:1-5, 19-25; 4:1-8, 11-22, 27-31; 5:1-17, 20-31; 6:1-30, and possibly 8:4–9:1. The final section of this group, 8:18–9:1, would form an excellent conclusion to a scroll read on a fast day called as the result of drought.

B. Second Collection.—Beginning with 9:2 and continuing into ch. 23, the book of Jeremiah contains messages of the prophet that are clearly or probably later than 605, as well as materials which do not fit the category of threats and warnings. Some come from as late as the reign of Zedekiah, and a few oracles may be associated with the downfall of Jerusalem in 587 b.c. It seems therefore that someone made a collection of these materials after the fall of Jerusalem, and added them to Baruch's scroll. The person most likely to have done this was Baruch himself. He survived the fall of the city and went with Jeremiah to Egypt (43:6). We have surprisingly few oracles of Jeremiah that can be dated from the governorship of Gedaliah, and the record of the happenings of that period in 40:7–41:18 contains no mention of the prophet. Perhaps Baruch was at this time busy making the collection of Jeremiah's prophecies (with the aid of the prophet). He seems to have added this collection to his first scroll, and he may have combined both collections with his own memoirs (see below).

This second collection may have contained the following passages, here arranged according to literary types; in some cases the date (certain or probable) of a passage is given directly after the passage itself, but many cannot be satisfactorily dated.

1. "Confessions" of Jeremiah: 10:23-24; 11:18–12:6; 15:10-21; 17:9-10, 14-18; 18:18-23; 20:7-12, 14-18 (all probably from the latter part of Jehoiakim's reign).

2. Oracles of condemnation and warning: 9:2-9, 25-26; 13:15-17 (598 B.C.), 20-27 (604-598 B.C.); 17:1-4; 18:13-17; 21:11-14; 23:9-33. The genuine oracles in 22:1–23:6 may have been in this collection, but are more likely to have been first gathered by the Deuteronomic editor.

3. Laments over national or personal sorrow: 9:10-11, 17-22 (both 602 B.C.); 10:17-22 (598 B.C.); 12:7-13 (602 B.C.); 13:18-19 (598 B.C.); 14:1–15:4 (in part); 15:5-9 (598 B.C.).

4. Parables, acted or only spoken: 13:1-10 (604-598 B.C.), 12-14 (Zedekiah's reign); 18:1-6.

5. Proverblike saying: 9:23-24.

C. Baruch's Memoirs.—The book of Jeremiah contains a long series of passages, mainly in the last half of the book, which give detailed information concerning some of the activities of the prophet as well as reports of his words. These are all in prose, and the very detailed nature of some of them suggests that they come from an eyewitness of the events reported. It has long seemed to most interpreters that these passages were written by Baruch, the scribe, disciple, and confidant of Jeremiah.

These passages have been called "Baruch's biography of Jeremiah," but they do not cover a sufficient portion of Jeremiah's life to be termed a biography. Baruch was concerned largely to record Jeremiah's conflicts with priests and false prophets (as in chs. 26–29) and to record his last days, from the time of the Babylonian invasion to the flight into Egypt. Volz has called the latter a "passion narrative" (*Leidensgeschichte*), and has compared it in fullness of detail with the passion narratives of the Gospels. As now preserved, the memoirs of Baruch are not in chronological order; they contain material extending from Jeremiah's temple "sermon" at the beginning of Jehoiakim's reign (which, as we have seen, may have been his first important public utterance), down to the time when Jeremiah and Baruch were in Egypt.

Baruch's memoirs consisted of materials now found within the following passages (which have in some instances been extensively revised by the Deuteronomic editor; see below): 19:1-2a, 10-11a, 14-15; 20:1-6; 26:1–29:32; 32:1-15; 33:4-5; 34:1–36:32; 37:3-21; 38:1-28; 39:3, 14; 42:1–44:30. Baruch apparently did not write 40:7–41:18 (see Exeg.). As suggested above, he may have combined his memoirs with the original scroll and his second collection. If this is correct, his memoirs at first included only material to the fall of Jerusalem, chs. 42–44 being his subsequent addition. He prefixed 1:1-3 as the heading for his original memoirs and the two collections of oracles.

D. The Deuteronomic Edition.—Numerous passages in the book of Jeremiah are similar in style and thought to Deuteronomy and the historical books which were edited by the Deuteronomic school—Joshua, Judges, I and II Samuel, and I and II Kings. So marked is the similarity that in the nineteenth century John W. Colenso advanced the theory that Jeremiah was the author of Deuteronomy and editor of many of the historical books of the Old Testament.[3] This theory is extreme, for there is a great difference between the poetry of Jeremiah and the prose sections which are similar to the writing of the Deuteronomists. The similarities can best be explained by the theory that an edition of the book of Jeremiah was prepared by a Deuteronomist. We may use the symbol "D" for this Deuteronomist or the school of writers we call the Deuteronomists. It is not likely that the whole of Deuteronomy, the historical books (Joshua through II Kings), and the edition of Jeremiah were all prepared by one individual; the work of the Deuteronomists was done in at least two stages. But it exhibits a remarkable uniformity of style and thought. D has a tendency to use repeatedly certain words and phrases, and the general tone is homiletical. The style sometimes has great beauty but is frequently monotonous.

The D edition of Jeremiah was made about 550 B.C. The man (or group) who made it may have lived in Egypt. D made use of the three preceding collections, adding his own work to them or revising them at some points. D's main theme in the book of Jeremiah is that all of history is under the control of Yahweh. He led Israel out of Egypt into the land of Canaan, but there they fell into the worship of false gods. Yahweh gave them repeated opportunities to repent, sending them many prophets (Jeremiah among them). But Israel persisted in sin, and Yahweh gave them into the hand of Nebu-

[3] *The Pentateuch and Book of Joshua Critically Examined* (London: Longman Green Longmans, Roberts & Green, 1879), VII, 12, 225-27, 259-69, and Appendix 149.

chadrezzar. Yet Yahweh's ultimate plans for Israel are good rather than evil, and he will finally restore them to their land. Writing in the mid-exilic period, his hopes for the future are positive, though vaguely expressed. D shows in his edition of Jeremiah a special predilection for composing long "sermons" and prayers, a characteristic that may be observed in other works from the Deuteronomic school.

D sometimes preserves genuine prophecies of Jeremiah in the prophet's words; sometimes he gives the gist of Jeremiah's prophecies in his own words; and sometimes he composes freely and departs from Jeremiah's thoughts. Examples of these three methods will be noted in the Exegesis.[4] The work of D in preparing an edition of Jeremiah may be summarized as follows:

In ch. 1, D has added vss. 15-16, 18-19. They are the counterpart of 25:1-13a and reflect the Babylonian siege of Jerusalem and Jeremiah's bold courage throughout his career. In ch. 3, vss. 6-14 are from D, incorporating a genuine oracle of the prophet, vss. 12b-14a, from an independent source (or Baruch's scroll?).

D is responsible for 5:18-19; 9:12-16; 16:10-13; 22:8-9, giving a convenient explanation of the Exile in question-and-answer form, similar to Deut. 29:22-28; I Kings 9:8-9.

In 7:1–8:3, D has collected various teachings of Jeremiah dealing with cultic places and practices, preserving the general attitude but not the actual words of the prophet, except in 7:29, which is in poetic form. If it is surprising that a Deuteronomic editor has preserved the words of a prophet concerning the destruction of the Jerusalem temple, so dear to the heart of his school, we must remember that he wrote in 550 B.C., after the temple had been destroyed, and that Jeremiah's words made such a lasting impression that they could not be suppressed.

There is a brief gloss by D in 8:19b, which is inappropriate to the context.

D wrote 11:1-17, but 11:15-16 (which is poetry) represents the actual words of the prophet, probably taken from a source other than the collections discussed above. Otherwise the section is largely a free composition of D. In ch. 13, D has appended vs. 11 to the parable of the waistcloth, making an unnecessary application of a single detail of the parable. In 14:1–15:4, where analysis is very difficult, 14:11-12 and 15:1-4 may be from D.

In ch. 16, vss. 1-13, 16-18 are from D, incorporating a genuine poem, vss. 16-17. A brief

[4] For a more detailed discussion of D's edition see J. Philip Hyatt, "The Deuteronomic Edition of Jeremiah," R. C. Beatty, et al., Vanderbilt Studies in the Humanities (Nashville: Vanderbilt University Press, 1951), I 71-95. Cf. Sigmund Mowinckel, Zur Komposition des Buches Jeremia (Kristiania: J. Dybwad, 1914).

gloss by D in 17:2b-3a is intended to convey the idea that certain specific objects in the cultus are sinful.

The section 17:19-27, a long passage on sabbath observance, is a free composition by D, which departs widely from the thought of Jeremiah. The prophet may have had some interest in sabbath observance, but he did not put the extreme emphasis on it that this section does. In ch. 18, D has added his own interpretation to the parable of the potter, vss. 7-12. His interpretation shifts the underlying thought of the parable from the intention and plan of Yahweh to the action of the people.

In 19:1–20:6, D has inserted his "sermon" on Topheth, 19:2b-9, 11b-13, into an account of a symbolic action which was reported in Baruch's memoirs. The section 21:1-10 is D's version of the incident reported in 37:3-10 (in Baruch's memoirs); it has no value independent of the account in ch. 37.

D has provided an introduction (22:1-5) to the group of oracles concerning the rulers of Judah in 22:1–23:6. It was probably D who first collected these oracles as we now have them (apart from 23:3-4, which is later), though it is possible that they were in Baruch's second collection. Within this group, 22:8-9, 11-12, 24-27 are prose sections by D.

Ch. 24, written by D, expresses an attitude toward the exiles and the people left in Judah which does not accord with Jeremiah's own attitude. The mention of the exiles in Egypt (24:8) suggests that the Egyptian exile chronicled in chs. 43–44 was of recent occurrence, and that the residence of D may have been in Egypt. It is worthy of notice that D frequently displays a friendly attitude toward Babylonia and her rulers.

In ch. 25, vss. 1-13a in their original form were written by D to provide the conclusion to what he believed was Baruch's scroll of 604 B.C. The words "this book" in 25:13 refer backward rather than forward. The Septuagint form of 25:1-13 is closer to the original, as written by D, than the Masoretic Text. It does not have the references to Babylon and Nebuchadrezzar, and makes clear that the condemnation was originally directed against Judah and Jerusalem.

In ch. 26, D has revised the report of the sermon in vss. 4-6, but has left the remainder largely as it stood in Baruch's memoirs. He has also expanded ch. 27 at several points. In ch. 29, vss. 10-20 were written by D, or considerably revised by him.

In ch. 32, vss. 16-44, containing a long prayer and long "word of the Lord," were added by D to Baruch's account. These verses give an excellent summary of D's interpretation of history.

In ch. 34, D has rewritten vss. 8-22 to make it appear that the release of the slaves was the sabbatical release according to the law of Deut. 15. In ch. 35, D has rewritten and expanded the speech of Jeremiah in vss. 12-19. In ch. 36, vss. 28-31 are D's rewriting of the word of the Lord instructing Jeremiah to dictate a second scroll. In ch. 37, vss. 1-2 may be a historical note by D, giving a general estimate of Zedekiah's reign of the type familiar in I and II Kings. In ch. 38, vss. 2, 23 are from D.

In the account of the fall of Jerusalem and Jeremiah's release in chs. 39-40, only 39:3, 14 are from Baruch; the rest is from D. The section 39:1-2, 4-10 is a shortened account of the events narrated in 52:4-16 (=II Kings 25:1-12). The two sections, 39:11-13; 40:1-6, are D's legendary account of the prophet's release which justifies the Babylonians' actions. In 40:2-3 the Babylonian general is made to expound the Deuteronomic doctrine of divine retribution.

D revised 42:7-22; the kernel of the prophet's own words is in 42:9-14. Ch. 44 has been rewritten by D; it probably rests upon authentic words of Jeremiah preserved in Baruch's memoirs, but they cannot now be recovered.

Finally, D wrote ch. 45 in order to pay tribute to Baruch and show that the faithful secretary received his reward.

E. Later Additions.—A number of additions were made to the book, after it left the hands of D, by different authors or editors and at various times. We cannot date them with precision; most of them, however, were made in postexilic times. In some instances these additions preserve genuine poems of the prophet, while others were composed after his death. We cannot identify the authors, but in some of the additions we can see the influence of Second Isaiah or similarity to portions of other prophetic books. These additions to the book may be conveniently classified as follows:

1. Chs. 30-31 constitute a small "book of comfort," giving glimpses into the future restoration of Israel and Judah. This is a collection of materials of varied origin made by an editor who lived after the time of Second Isaiah (whose influence is discernible in 30:10; 31:7-14) and possibly as late as the time of Nehemiah (see 31:38-40). The following are genuine poems of Jeremiah: 30:5-7, 12-15; 31:2-6, 15-22. The new covenant passage, 31:31-34, gives the substance of Jeremiah's thought, but not in his words. The remaining passages are largely eschatological, dealing with the future restoration.

2. Closely related to this collection is ch. 33. Only vss. 4-5 are genuine, but they are obscure and difficult to interpret; they may have once stood in Baruch's memoirs. The rest of the chapter deals with the restoration of Jerusalem, the Davidic dynasty, the Levitical priesthood, and the like. The section 33:15-16 is a quotation of 23:5-6, with slight change.

3. Numerous eschatological predictions, similar in some respects to those found in chs. 30-31; 33, occur in various parts of the book: 3:15-18; 4:9-10, 23-26; 12:14-17; 16:14-15 (=23: 7-8); 23:3-4; 25:30-38. These are not uniform in attitude, hence are not all from the same hand (cf. the discussion of Jeremiah's eschatology on pp. 786-87).

4. Several psalms and psalmlike compositions occur in the book, apparently inserted at appropriate points by later editors: 10:25 (=Ps. 79:6-7); 16:19-21; 17:5-8, 12-13; 20:13.

5. The long passage which contrasts the worship of idols and the true worship of Yahweh, 10:1-16, shows the influence of Second Isaiah, and must have been written in or after his time.

6. The "confessions of sin" in 14:7-9, 19-22, seem to be secondary because of the presence of phrases and ideas of later times, but it is not impossible that they originated with Jeremiah.

7. The proverbial saying in 17:11, in form and substance like other sayings of the sages, is a secondary addition.

8. The long discussion of the phrase, "burden of the LORD" (23:34-40), is a late addition, perhaps one of the latest in the whole book.

9. The oracles against foreign nations in chs. 46-51 constitute a separate collection, made sometime after the fall of Babylon; 25:15-29 was originally the introduction to the collection. Only the first of these oracles, 46:2-12, is clearly from Jeremiah; several of the others, most notably those against Babylon, are not his work. In the Exegesis a number of passages are pointed out which may be from him, but there can be no certainty as to their authorship.

10. Two historical sections are late additions: 40:7-41:18; 52:1-34. Both of these were probably taken from a source used by the editor of II Kings 24-25. The former of these, apparently not written by Baruch, is an extended account of information contained in II Kings 25:22-26. Ch. 52 is almost identical with II Kings 24:18-25:30. It omits the account of Gedaliah's governorship just referred to; Jer. 52:28-30, which seems to be authentic, is not found in II Kings. Ch. 52 is an appendix to the book of Jeremiah added in order to show how some of his prophecies were fulfilled; it ends on a note of hope with the account of the release of King Jehoiachin and the favorable treatment shown him by the Babylonian king.

This survey of the growth of the book of Jeremiah through numerous stages will account in some measure for the present arrangement of the material. We have noted that sometimes a chronological principle is employed, sometimes a topical. A third type of arrangement is by "catchwords." A single word in two or more passages may serve to account for their having been placed together, as in other prophetic books and in the Gospels (for examples see Exeg. on 3:1–4:4; 8:8-13; 19:1–20:6). Yet it must be admitted that an adequate explanation cannot be given for the present position of every passage in the book.

VI. The Septuagint Version

The Septuagint version of the book of Jeremiah is of special interest because it differs in a number of respects from the Hebrew text as transmitted by the Masoretes. It is approximately one eighth shorter than the Hebrew text, and contains a number of omissions, a few minor additions, and several variations in the order of the material. The longest omissions are 29:16-20; 33:14-26; 39:4-13; 52:28-30. The most striking difference is that in the Septuagint the oracles against the foreign nations, which constitute chs. 46–51 of the Hebrew (and English) arrangement, follow immediately after 25:13a, and the oracles themselves are in a different order (see Exeg. on 46:1–51:64).

Generalizations regarding the superiority of the Septuagint over the Hebrew text, or of the latter over the Septuagint, are dangerous. Every instance of variation between the two must be carefully considered on its own merits. In the Exegesis some of these variations are pointed out; in a few cases a judgment is expressed as to the superiority of the Septuagint and in some cases it is possible to explain the Septuagint variation without considering it as superior.[5]

VII. Outline of Contents

---

[5] The LXX and M.T. have been conveniently printed side by side in Eberhard Nestle, ed., *Das Buch Jeremia griechisch und hebräisch* (2nd ed.; Stuttgart: Württembergische Bibelanstalt, 1934).

VIII. Selected Bibliography

CONDAMIN, ALBERT. Le livre de Jérémie ("Études bibliques") . 3rd ed. Paris: J. Gabalda, 1936.

CORNILL, C. H. Das Buch Jeremia. Leipzig: B. Tauchnitz, 1905.

DUHM, BERNHARD. Das Buch Jeremia ("Kurzer Hand-Commentar zum Alten Testament") . Tübingen: J. C. B. Mohr, 1901.

ERBT, WILHELM. Jeremia und seine Zeit. Göttingen: Vandenhoeck & Ruprecht, 1902.

GIESEBRECHT, FRIEDRICH. Das Buch Jeremia ("Handkommentar zum Alten Testament"). 2nd ed. Göttingen: Vandenhoeck & Ruprecht, 1907.

PEAKE, A. S., ed. Jeremiah and Lamentations ("The New-Century Bible"). Edinburgh: T. C. & E. C. Jack, 1910-12.

RUDOLPH, WILHELM. Jeremia ("Handbuch zum Alten Testament"). Tübingen: J. C. B. Mohr, 1947.

SKINNER, JOHN. Prophecy and Religion. Cambridge: Cambridge University Press, 1922.

SMITH, GEORGE ADAM. Jeremiah. 4th ed. Garden City: Doubleday, Doran & Co., 1929.

VOLZ, PAUL. Der Prophet Jeremia ("Kommentar zum Alten Testament"). 2nd ed. Leipzig: A. Deichert, 1928.

JEREMIAH

TEXT, EXEGESIS, AND EXPOSITION

1 The words of Jeremiah the son of Hilkiah, of the priests that *were* in Anathoth in the land of Benjamin:	1 The words of Jeremiah, the son of Hilki′ah, of the priests who were in

I. SUPERSCRIPTION (1:1-3)

1:1. Like several other prophetic books, Jeremiah opens with a superscription which gives the name of the prophet, his date, and brief information concerning his family background.

The words: The Hebrew (*dibhrê*) can also mean "acts" or "history"; e.g., in 5:28 it is translated "deeds," and it appears frequently in the sense of "chronicle" or "history" in Kings and Chronicles. Since the book of Jeremiah includes both words of the prophet and records of events in his life, it may have the meaning "history" here; Moffatt renders "The story of Jeremiah." In the LXX the book opens, "The word of the LORD which came to Jeremiah."

Jeremiah was a fairly familiar name among the Hebrews; it is borne by other individuals mentioned in 35:3; 52:1. It occurs also in other O.T. books and outside the Bible, e.g., in Lachish Letter No. I (Harry Torczyner, *et al., The Lachish Letters* [London: Oxford University Press, 1938], p. 27) and on a seal found at the site of ancient Beth Shemesh (Elihu Grant and G. Ernest Wright, *Ain Shems Excavations V* [Haverford: Haverford College, 1939], p. 80). The meaning of the name has been much disputed. It must have been applicable at the birth of the child, and not necessarily to the whole career of the prophet. Hebrew names usually expressed gratitude to God for the child

1:1-3. *Jeremiah: "Yahweh Hurls!"*—Jeremiah belongs with that class of man described by Unamuno as "men of flesh and bone." [1] He was, like these, an "agonistic" soul, one whose burden is wisdom rather than knowledge, and who, through compassion, suffering, and love, moves unflinchingly into the deepest defile of his time's predicament. He looked into his time's abyss, and though there were moments when he recoiled from its terrors, he returned again and again to gaze more deeply until, beyond and beneath every anguish of his age, he discovered a new transcendent ground of hope.

The three introductory verses, flat and unimaginative as they seem, are singularly appropriate, as though the editors of Jeremiah's book (see Intro., p. 787) had sensed how utterly impossible it would be to "introduce" either

[1] Miguel de Unamuno, *The Tragic Sense of Life* (London: Macmillan & Co., 1921), pp. 1 ff.

the prophet or his book. Overtures to his "greatness," while paying him conventional praise, would fail to adduce him. The man Jeremiah, the man "of flesh and bone," the man who was rejected by his family and local community, the man who was obliged to oppose priests, kings, prophets, and people, the man who stood at the last altogether alone, a coerced exile with the poor remnant of his people in Egypt, the man whose entire life was prolonged martyrdom to the integrity of his faith, the man whom Yahweh "hurled" into the most crucial and most tragic period in the entire history of Israel—this is the man who is too easily lost behind the protective barriers of the scholar's praise, or behind our unconscious resistance (though epochs removed) to the uncomfortably true.

Into what kind of situation was Jeremiah hurled? He was hurled into the time of Judah's last catastrophe. This was the period of the

or a pious prayer from the parents on behalf of the child. The usual explanation is "Yahweh shoots" or "Yahweh hurls"; the applicability of this at the child's birth, however, is obscure. A more probable meaning is "Yahweh loosens [the womb]," if the verb is derived from a root רמה; or "Yahweh exalts," if the verb is from a root רום.

Hilkiah, Jeremiah's father, has sometimes been identified with the high priest in the time of Josiah who found the "book of the law" in the temple in 621 B.C. (II Kings 22). While this cannot be categorically denied, it is improbable; had the father been a person of such prominence, the fact would likely have been mentioned or have been reflected in Jeremiah's life.

Of the priests is the only phrase in the whole book which suggests that Jeremiah was from a priestly line. The usual explanation of this awkward phrase (rather than simply "Jeremiah the priest") is that Jeremiah was from a priestly family but never functioned as a priest. T. J. Meek ("Was Jeremiah a Priest?" *The Expositor,* Ser. 8, XXV [1923], 215-22) has forcefully argued that Jeremiah was not of a priestly family at all, this phrase being originally a marginal gloss of a scribe to explain that **Anathoth** was one of the priestly cities, as indicated in Josh. 21:18. In any event, Jeremiah's outlook was wholly prophetic rather than priestly; he was often in opposition to, as well as opposed by, the priests of his day (5:31; 6:13; 23:11; 26:8, 11; 29:26).

The prophet's birthplace was **Anathoth in the land of Benjamin,** a town mentioned also in 11:21, 23; 29:27; 32:7-9. It has usually been identified with the modern village of 'Anâtā, two and a half miles northeast of Jerusalem. However, archaeological soundings conducted at that site in 1937 proved that it was not occupied in Jeremiah's time (E. P. Blair, "Soundings at 'Anâtā (Roman Anathoth)," *Bulletin of the American Schools of Oriental Research,* No. 62 [Apr., 1936], pp. 18-21; and A. Bergman, "Soundings at the Supposed Site of Old Testament Anathoth," *ibid.,* pp. 22-25; cf. Bergman, "Anathoth?" *ibid.,* No. 63 [Oct., 1936], pp. 22-23; the new identification was first proposed by Albrecht Alt, "Das Institut im Jahre 1925," *Palästinajahrbuch,* XXII [1926], 23-24). No remains were found of Iron I and Iron II periods, so that the earliest possible date of its settlement is about 600 B.C. Soundings were conducted also at Râs el-Kharrûbeh, a hill which is now deserted, approximately half a mile south-southwest of 'Anâtā. The settlement at this site reached its peak in the period between 800 and 600 B.C. and lasted until Byzantine

---

decline and fall of the little kingdom. He was hurled into the time of great contention between competing world powers, and, with his people, stood in the midst of their vast collision. Not only was Judah a political bauble in the contending play of the great states but she was, as Toynbee says, "pounded on their native threshing-floor by an Assyrian flail."[2] It is perhaps even more important to see beyond and behind and underneath this great agitation of the time that Jeremiah was also hurled into what Karl Jaspers has called a great "axial age" of world history. "The spiritual process which took place between 800 and 200 B.C. seems to constitute . . . an axis. It was then that the man with whom we live today came into being."[3] This was the age of Confucius and Lao

[2] Arnold J. Toynbee, *A Study of History,* Abridgement of Vols. I-VI by D. C. Somervell (New York: Oxford University Press, 1947), p. 386.

[3] *Way to Wisdom,* tr. Ralph Manheim (New Haven: Yale University Press, 1951), p. 99. For Jaspers' definitive elaboration of his views of history see his *Vom Ursprung und Ziel der Geschichte* (Zurich: Artemis, 1949), especially pp. 18 ff.

Tse, of Mo Tse, Chuang Tse, Liädsi, and others in China; of the Upanishads and of Buddha in India; of Zoroaster in Persia; of Elijah, Isaiah, Jeremiah, the Prophet of the Exile (Second Isaiah) in Palestine; of "Homer," Parmenides, Heraclitus, Plato, the great tragedians, Thucydides, and Archimedes in Greece.

Man everywhere became aware of being as a whole, of himself and his limits. He experienced the horror of the world and his own helplessness. He raised radical questions, approached the abyss in his drive for liberation and redemption. And in consciously apprehending his limits he set himself the highest aims. He experienced the absolute in the depth of selfhood and in the clarity of transcendence.[4]

We note here simply that the Hebrew prophets of this age, and Jeremiah particularly, are hurled into the tensions of extreme political clash; that in their highest moments of insight they see through these tensions, recognizing

[4] *Way to Wisdom,* p. 100; cf. *Vom Ursprung und Ziel der Geschichte,* p. 20.

| 2 To whom the word of the LORD came in the days of Josiah the son of Amon king of Judah, in the thirteenth year of his reign. | An'athoth in the land of Benjamin, 2 to whom the word of the LORD came in the days of Josi'ah the son of Amon, king of Judah, in the thirteenth year of his reign. |

---

times. It is probable that the Anathoth of Jeremiah's day is to be identified with this latter site; the ancient name was apparently transferred at some time (probably in the Roman period) to what is now known as 'Anâtâ.

Anathoth was the town to which Abiathar, the priest of David, was banished by Solomon when the latter came to the throne (I Kings 2:26). There is no objective evidence for the oft-repeated view that Jeremiah was descended from him. If the prophet's family was indeed priestly, they may have officiated either at the local sanctuary of Anathoth (before the time of the Deuteronomic reforms, 621 B.C.) or in the Jerusalem temple. Some of the priests apparently lived in villages outside Jerusalem and went to the capital to perform their official duties (see Neh. 11:20; Luke 1:39-40).

2. Josiah the son of Amon reigned 640-609 B.C., his **thirteenth year** being 627-626 B.C. He is referred to in 3:6; 25:3; 36:2. Jeremiah gives a very favorable opinion of him in 22:15-16, contrasting him with his wicked son Jehoiakim.

---

them as fortuitous results of deeper causes— symptoms of an underlying shift in the racial consciousness. They see through the surface tensions to the real limits and polarities of the human situation where the consciousness of God as the real being takes hold. Their message will break through (1:10) the structures by which the truth has heretofore been channeled and which have now become oppressive. It will be resisted by the people and all the vested interests; by all

Who fear the blessing of God, the loneliness of the night of God, the surrender required, the deprivation inflicted,
Who fear the injustice of men less than the justice of God.[5]

Into this "loneliness of the night of God" Jeremiah also was hurled.

He could hardly have sustained such pressures as these had his sense of call been less profound. This we shall discover in the following pages. In the interpretations here set forth the reader will note certain discrepancies between the points of view expressed by the exegete and the expositor. Since they are not mainly of a technical kind, the majority more than likely will not be noticed. On the critical side the chief difference is that the Expos. does not conform to the exegete's thesis of the later date for Jeremiah's birth. The evidence for this does not appear to be conclusive; it seems to create, from the standpoint of exposition, as many problems as it solves. This difference will affect certain local perspectives on the oracles and

[5] T. S. Eliot, *Murder in the Cathedral* (London: Faber & Faber; New York: Harcourt, Brace & Co., 1935), Part II, p. 86. Used by permission.

other matters under consideration, such as the placing and the date of the so-called "Scythian" poems. Also some recognition of the principle of growth and development in the prophetic consciousness of Jeremiah seems, on literary grounds, to be essential to an understanding of the deeper implications of the book.

The Expos. has attempted to supplement the literary-critical approach by many of the disclosures of the historical-traditional school. The latter view releases us at many points from the limitations of a one-way theory of time—that is, from the view that all that is "late" (the Deuteronomist's editing) must on that account be "secondary" and foreign to Jeremiah's aims. Secondly, it releases us into a recognition of the larger aesthetic unities, forms, and strategies which the literary-critical approach may sometimes overlook. The poetic strategies of the biblical prophets and their aesthetic forms are much more nearly akin to the strategies of contemporary poetry than to any other literature. Affinities may be found with the strategies of the "metaphysical" poets, Elizabethan drama, or in such double-pointed symbolizations as appear in the second part of Goethe's *Faust*. There would also be some points of contact with the Greek tragedies, particularly with those of Aeschylus.

The remaining difference ties in with this. It has to do with the logic and the *theologic* with which we try to classify and appraise the book's content. The Hebrew mind is not the Western mind. Its "thought" does not assimilate to our Western hierarchical forms. It is what we should today call "existential." Its concern is not for accuracy of place and date, but for the large symbolic use of these as evocative

3 It came also in the days of Jehoiakim the son of Josiah king of Judah, unto the end of the eleventh year of Zedekiah the son of Josiah king of Judah, unto the carrying away of Jerusalem captive in the fifth month.

3 It came also in the days of Jehoi′akim the son of Josi′ah, king of Judah, and until the end of the eleventh year of Zedeki′ah, the son of Josi′ah, king of Judah, until the captivity of Jerusalem in the fifth month.

---

3. Jehoiakim reigned 609-598 B.C., and **Zedekiah,** 598-587 B.C. The **captivity of Jerusalem in the fifth month** refers to the destruction of the city and the exiling of many of its inhabitants in 587 (cf. 39:1 ff.; 52:12 ff.; II Kings 25:8 ff.) .

The superscription makes the career of Jeremiah end with the fall of Jerusalem, but the latter part of the book (chs. 40–44) records events which transpired during a period of several years after the fall of that city. It seems probable therefore that vss. 1-3 originally stood at the head of a collection of material which did not include the whole of the book. That collection is most likely to have been Baruch's memoirs, with which were joined his scroll and the second collection of Jeremiah's prophecies. Baruch's memoirs originally ended with 39:14; his material in chs. 42–44 was added later (see Intro., p. 788; Exeg. on 39:1-14; 40:7–41:18) .

The date in vs. 2, equivalent to 627-626 B.C., is usually interpreted as the year in which Jeremiah received his call and began to prophesy. It is very difficult, however, to assign any of the messages of the prophet to the reign of Josiah (see Intro., p. 779) . T. C. Gordon ("A New Date for Jeremiah," *Expository Times,* XLIV [1932-33], 562-65; he is followed by Hans Bardtke, "Jeremiah der Fremdvölkerprophet," *Zeitschrift für die alttestamentliche Wissenschaft,* LIII [1935], 218-19) has suggested that the **thirteenth**

---

of decision and response. Theologically, the Exeg. (see Intro.) and Expos. are not formally in disagreement; but again, the dynamic elements in Jeremiah's context of the covenant-relation are not adduced in the formal summation of his ideas about God, sin, eschatology, and the like. The Expos. attempts, therefore, to supplement these necessary formal statements by setting them within the vital context of Jeremiah's passion which everywhere impinges upon the universal human need.

This identification, in our time, is fairly easy to arrive at. Stefan Zweig tells how, when he was caught up in the frenzy of World War I, he

sought for a symbol to express these problems: of solitude in the midst of hypnotized masses, of tragic forebodings and painful presentiments. My first sketches were meant for a "Cassandra." But soon it was the character of Jeremiah that forced itself upon me, for, being Biblical, it was closer to me and closer also for being bound up with the people.[6]

"But soon it was the character of Jeremiah that forced itself upon me." This is the experience of every careful student of the book of Jeremiah. The effect of this on Zweig evoked with vividness the situation into which Jeremiah was hurled. In his drama Zweig shows the

hosts of Nebuchadrezzar encamped around Jerusalem, and two lone sentries standing in the white moonlight, keeping watch upon the ramparts of the city, conversing:

Second Sentry: Do you hear?
First Sentry: What?
Second Sentry: The sound is very faint, but the breeze bears it to us. When I was in Joppa, for the first time I heard in the night the distant murmur of the waves. Such a sound rises now from the plain. They are there in their thousands, moving quietly, but the air is stirred by the rolling wheels and the clashing arms. A whole nation must be afoot, falling upon Israel. The noise echoes from our walls like the noise of the sea. . . . Why does God hurl the nations against one another? There is room for all beneath the skies. There is still plenty of land unploughed; many forests still await the axe. Yet men turn their ploughshares into swords, and hew living flesh with their axes. I cannot understand.[7]

Habakkuk's question was the same. Perplexed by the way the Lord permits the faithless man to swallow up "the man more righteous than he" (Hab. 1:13) , and observing too how the successive conquerors are like fishermen dragging men into their nets from the sea of these contemporary troubles, he shrewdly observes how all these conquerors become drunk with their own achievements and turn to worship

[6] *Jeremiah,* tr. Eden and Cedar Paul (2nd ed.; New York: Viking Press, 1939), p. viii.

[7] *Ibid.,* scene 4, pp. 107-8. Used by permission.

| 4 Then the word of the Lord came unto me, saying, | 4 Now the word of the Lord came to me saying, |

year of Josiah is a mistake for an original "twenty-third year," the difference between the two figures being much less when they are written in Hebrew than in English (**thirteenth** is שלש עשרה and "twenty-third" is שלש ועשרים). If this suggestion is correct, Jeremiah began to prophesy in 617-616 B.C., near the time when Nabopolassar first attacked Assyria, and Babylonian power was becoming strong. While this is possible, we must note that the suggestion has no ancient versional support, and the date in 25:3 is the same as here. The corruption of the text is not likely to have occurred in two such widely separated passages.

A third interpretation of the date 627-626 B.C. is possible. It may be the date of Jeremiah's birth rather than of his call. If the superscription comes from Baruch, as has been suggested, it is not surprising that he knew the year of Jeremiah's birth. Furthermore, if Jeremiah's career began at the beginning of Jehoiakim's reign, 609 B.C., he would have been seventeen or eighteen years of age when called to prophesy—an age which is appropriate to the statement of vs. 6 that Jeremiah was "only a youth." Also, this interpretation is in agreement with the idea expressed in vs. 5 that Jeremiah was actually chosen and consecrated to be a prophet even within his mother's womb.

II. Inaugural Visions (1:4-19)
A. Call of Jeremiah (1:4-10)

Like many other prophets, Jeremiah received at the beginning of his career a call to perform the function of a prophet of the Lord. The account of his call is succinct and

their own power (Hab. 1:16). Then he asks the pertinent question:

Is he then to keep on emptying his net
    and mercilessly slaying nations for ever? (Hab. 1:17.)

Habakkuk's answer—contemporaneous with that of Jeremiah—comes with surprising clarity, for one who has been called the "skeptic-prophet"!

The vision has its own appointed hour,
it ripens, it will flower;
if it be long, then wait,
for it is sure, and it will not be late (Hab. 2:5 Moffatt).

Behold, he whose soul is not upright in him shall fail,
    but the righteous shall live by his faith (Hab. 2:4).

Habakkuk dimly divines what Jeremiah came to know. "Behold ye among the heathen," he wrote, "and regard, and wonder marvelously: for I will work a work in your days, which ye will not believe, though it be told you" (Hab. 1:5). So the words of the superscription of the book of Jeremiah, toneless as they are, take on an almost startling resonance when sounded within the acoustical setting of the history that was about to unfold. They are the inaugural for

a long record that grows continually more somber. Josiah ("whom Yahweh heals"), Jeremiah ("whom Yahweh hurls"), Jerusalem ("habitation of peace")—these simple names, which sound so flat to us, were names in ruin to those whose sad inheritance was heaped upon them.

4-10. The Divine Commission.—The first unit of the book of Jeremiah is in the form of a dialogue. The Lord speaks, Jeremiah replies, and the Lord responds to his reply. This is the poetic distillation of Jeremiah's years of reflection on his call: and though it is supplemented with the visions, it is significant that the consciousness of God as someone over against him —as a genuine and invincible otherness—is placed first in the order of his recollection.

The importance of this must not be minimized. It is what the contemporary theologian means by the "divine-human encounter." "The Biblical conception of truth is: truth as encounter. . . . Faith, which appropriates God's self-revelation in His Word, is an event, an act, and that a two-sided act—an act of God and an act of man. *An encounter takes place between God and man.*" [8]

For Jeremiah the central point of this encounter was **the word of the Lord which came**

[8] Emil Brunner, *The Divine-Human Encounter* (tr. A. W. Loos; Philadelphia: Westminster Press, 1943), pp. 7, 74.

vivid, comparing favorably with that of Isaiah (ch. 6); it probably was dictated by Jeremiah to Baruch. In this account several facts are emphasized: (a) Jeremiah had a strong sense of his predestination to his task. No other prophet felt so strong a sense of divine urgency to prophesy; this appears especially in the passages known as the "confessions" of Jeremiah (see Intro., p. 782). (b) Jeremiah was not, like Isaiah (6:8), immediately willing to respond to God's call. He protested that he was only a youth and, like Moses under similar circumstances (Exod. 4:10), that he was not eloquent. (c) Jeremiah was conscious at the outset of being sent to the nations (vs. 4) and of being set over nations and kingdoms (vs. 10); he was not merely a prophet to Israel. (d) His mission was to include both the negative task of destroying and overthrowing, plucking up and breaking down, and the positive task of building and planting (vs. 10).

---

to me saying. In the encounter the prophet "meets in faith the God who meets him in the Word."

In His Word, God does not deliver to me a course of lectures in dogmatic theology, He does not submit to me or interpret for me the content of a confession of faith, but He makes Himself accessible to me. . . . An exchange takes place here which is wholly without analogy in the sphere of thinking. The sole analogy is in the encounter between human beings, the meeting of person with person.[9]

It is useful to have this from a theologian. Brunner acknowledges here the peculiar embarrassment of the systematic thinker. He wishes on the one hand, as scientific thinker, to comprehend this relationship objectively; but he must at the same time (and his reader also) appropriate it subjectively, or it is not really comprehended, no matter how many fine words he has spoken. This "doubleness" is "the particular burden and difficulty of theology. The theologian is really a wanderer between two worlds." [1] Actually the problem should be put more sharply. He is not really such a wanderer. The two realms are existentially incommensurable. The theologian is really a *monologist* extrapolating (almost interminably at times in *Dogmatiks*) the infinitely divisible variables compounded in recollection from the lived moment of the *dialogue*. Here the "other" of the lived moment is no longer really met as the other, but merely as a projection of the monologic self. In dialogue we turn toward the other, whereas in monologue the self turns back upon itself. It is important to stress this when approaching Jeremiah.

At once, however, a contrary danger arises—from the side of mysticism. Berdyaev runs this risk.[2] And no doubt there is, as in Isaiah's vision

of the Lord in the temple, an authentic sense of the *mysterium tremendum* in every profound encounter with God. Nevertheless, Jeremiah's opening account permits us to draw a sharp difference between the prophetic experience of God and that of the metaphysical mystics.

It is difficult to say how deep the Israelite prophets' inner experience goes. But it is not as among the mystics an aim in itself, it is a means by which the prophet is inspired to outward action. [It] means a strengthening of the will, an incentive to action, in order that he may influence others by what has inspired him. Thus the experience of the prophet, despite much similarity, is different from that of the mystic. The world does not fade away from him, and he does not feel himself changed into God. Hence the prophets of Israel create no new idea of what God is. They experience the ancestral God as power and will.[3]

The mystic's experience frequently volatilizes toward the infinite, or toward identity or coalescence with the Godhead, whereas Jeremiah's experience guides him precisely into the boundary, into his finitude, his creatureliness, as over against God. Consequently, through the word he is called, he is commissioned, he is sent, he is made a watchman and an assayer of the people. There is in him none of that "heavenly transcendental selfishness" such as the philosopher assigns to the subjective mystic.[4]

Were one to compare the experiences of Jeremiah, Isaiah, and Pascal in this regard, one would find the sense of the otherness of the Living God the most prominent feature of the accounts. Jeremiah is the least "mystical" in the sense, say, of William James's *Varieties of Religious Experience*,[5] and Pascal the most.

James[6] quotes with approval William San-

[9] *Ibid.*, p. 85.

[1] *Ibid.*, p. 84.

[2] After seeing clearly the need for the prophetic dimension in faith and the shortcomings of traditional theological method, he says: "Cataphatic theology knows only the objective God. But apophatic theology or mysticism goes beyond this objectivization of God, [and]

releases (*débarrasse*) the conception of God from all anthropomorphic deformities." (*Dialectique existentielle du divin et de l'humain* [Paris: J. B. Janin, 1947]), p. 63.

[3] Johannes Pedersen, *Israel, Its Life and Culture,* III-IV (London: Oxford University Press, 1940), p. 494.

[4] Nicolas Berdyaev, *The Destiny of Man* (New York: Charles Scribner's Sons, 1937), p. 171.

[5] New York: Longmans, Green & Co., 1902.

[6] *Ibid.*, p. 480.

5 Before I formed thee in the belly I knew thee; and before thou camest forth out of the womb I sanctified thee, *and* I ordained thee a prophet unto the nations.	5 "Before I formed you in the womb I knew you, and before you were born I consecrated you; I appointed you a prophet to the nations."

5. Before I formed you in the womb: Cf. the similar words of the servant of the Lord in Isa. 49:1, 5, and of Paul in Gal. 1:15. The idea of predestination from the womb occurs in other religions—e.g., an ancient Sumerian royal hymn begins, "A king am I; from the womb I have been a hero" (*lugal-me-en šà-ta ur-sag-me-en,* in a self-laudatory hymn of Shulgi; see Samuel N. Kramer, "The Oldest Literary Catalogue," *Bulletin of the American Schools of Oriental Research,* No. 88 [Dec., 1942], p. 14). **I knew you** means

day's claim: "The personality of the prophet sinks entirely into the background; he feels himself for the time being the mouthpiece of the Almighty."[7] What is important in Jeremiah's witness is the persistent realism of his utterance and its content: especially so in this chapter, which recounts an experience "recollected in tranquillity" and marked by the highest degree of clarity and authenticity. The experience serves to clarify his creaturehood: but it clarifies it absolutely, as the philosopher would say. Instead of experiencing the diffusion of his spirit, the prophet's spirit is unified in his finitude as he becomes one with his "call." He neither "wraps himself in silence" nor "steps aside into the accustomed way"[8] nor ascends mystically to coalescence with the Godhead: rather he steps into the situation which has, so to speak, stepped into him. He responds to the moment, and becomes responsible to it; he answers for it. From that point he begins his speaking.

5. The Divine Election.—When we read vs. 5 it is important to bear in mind two things: (*a*) that this account was in all probability dictated by Jeremiah himself; and (*b*) that it was dictated some twenty-three years after the event itself (see ch. 36) and represents the prophet's careful crystallization of the crucial event of his youth. It is proper to note, therefore, with Gillies, the three things which Jeremiah specifies within the call: the foreknowledge —**I knew you;** the sanctification—**I consecrated you;** and the scope of his commission—**I appointed you a prophet to the nations.** The Hebraic hyperbole here is the most emphatic way of formulating his sense of "destiny," his "predestination," his sense of the inescapability of his being chosen: everything brought him to this moment of consciousness, and everything in

the years which follow confirms it as "the will of God." It is the power of God and not his fiat which Jeremiah is trying to communicate. "Necessity was laid upon him," as W. R. Thomson[9] says. The sense of being called is not strange, nor even exceptional; it is what ought to be experienced by every dedicated spirit.

Do we not recall utterances of Ptah Hotep, of Socrates, of Alexander, of Dante, Spinoza, Montesquieu, Hugo, Froebel, Pitt, Browning, Disraeli, sent out in the teeth of hostile circumstances, asserting a sense of invincibleness in their historic position? . . . We may assume that whenever a supreme type of experience is possible to human nature, it will have numerous analogues and anticipations scattered throughout our common experiences. If the prophetic consciousness is possible, it will not be left without a witness here.[1]

A simple and obvious analogue of this more common kind may be found ready to hand in a letter of the late Thomas Wolfe:

My vision of life is becoming stronger and more beautiful than I thought possible a few years ago—it is the fantasy, the miracle that really happens. For *me* at any rate. My life with its beginnings has been a strange and miraculous thing. I was a boy from the mountains, I came from a strange wild family, I went beyond the mountains and knew the state, I went beyond the state and knew the nation, . . . I went to the greatest city and met strange and beautiful people, good, bad, and ugly ones, I went beyond the seas alone and walked down the million streets of life. When I was hungry and penniless . . . all manner of strange folk came to my aid. In a thousand places the miracle has happened to me. . . . It may never come again, but I've had the magic—what Euripides calls "the apple tree, the singing, and the gold."[2]

[7] *The Oracles of God* (London: Longmans, Green & Co., 1891), p. 55.

[8] Cf. Martin Buber, *Between Man and Man* (New York: The Macmillan Co., 1948), pp. 16-17.

[9] *The Burden of the Lord* (London: James Clarke & Co., 1919), p. 41.

[1] William Ernest Hocking, *The Meaning of God in Human Experience* (New Haven: Yale University Press, 1912), pp. 504-5.

[2] "Writing Is My Life," *The Atlantic Monthly,* CLXXIX (1947), 41.

6 Then said I, Ah, Lord God! behold, I cannot speak: for I *am* a child.

6 Then I said, "Ah, Lord God! Behold, I do not know how to speak, for I am only a

"I chose you," the word "know" being the equivalent of "choose," as also in Hos. 13:5; Amos 3:2; Gen. 18:19; in the last-named passage the RSV translates the same Hebrew word used here, "I have chosen." Jeremiah was a **prophet to the nations** in the sense that his prophecies frequently dealt with international affairs and with the fate of nations other than his own. Also, though Jeremiah emphasized personal religion, he was constantly concerned with the nation as a whole as well as with individuals within it. This commission must not, however, be taken as authenticating all of the oracles against foreign nations in chs. 46–51.

6. I am only a youth: The Hebrew *na'ar* could be used of an infant, as of Moses in the ark of bulrushes (Exod. 2:6); at the other extreme, it was used of a young man

This is the temptation of the poet, to reduce the exalted consciousness to "magic"; and Jeremiah also was a poet. He was a boy from the country, from the little town of Anathoth, and he came from a priestly family steeped in the traditions of the meaningful past; but he went beyond the town, and beyond the little state of Judah, and beyond the nation, and he knew the nations. He went to his people's greatest city and met many strange and exacerbated people, good, bad, and ugly ones; and he went beyond their vision of things alone and walked the streets of a deep despair. In a thousand places the miracle happened to him, until, after many years, it became integral to his consciousness. But he never in the world would have said, as Wolfe did, "Isn't it glorious that this should have happened to me when I was still young and rapturous enough to be thrilled by it?"[3]

On the contrary, when this encounter with the word of the Lord is recollected in tranquillity, he still repeats the frightened cry of pathetic dismay, the lonely "Alas!"—the cry which again and again was upon his lips in the years when he was "rejected by men" (Isa. 53:3) and disesteemed.

6. The Dread Commission.—Moses also recoiled from his divine appointment. Before the flaming bush he "hid his face, for he was afraid to look at God" (Exod. 3:6). And, quite suddenly, he was eloquent with excuse (Exod. 4:1, 10). Augustine, who also had written poetry and was skilled in rhetoric, nonetheless put off the deep encounter: "I, convicted by the truth, had nothing at all to reply, but the drawling and drowsy words: 'Presently, lo, presently;' 'leave me a little while.' But 'presently, presently,' had no present; and my 'leave me a little while' went on a long, long while."[4] Everyone knows his famous prayer: "Grant me

chastity and continency, but not yet!"[5] Augustine also was afraid: "I was afraid lest Thou shouldest hear me soon, and soon deliver me."[6]

Between Augustine and Jeremiah, however, there lies a dimension of difference. While Augustine had experienced his "barren seedplots of sorrows," had been "anxious" and "full of alarms," and had become to himself "an unfruitful land," he had not yet encountered the prophet's God. He had encountered the philosopher's Universal and the mystic's Absolute; and while he knew that God somehow "opposed me unto myself" and that he had need "not to stagger and sway about this way and that, a changeable and half-wounded will, wrestling, with one part falling as another rose,"[7] he resolved the conflict in this initial phase by withdrawing his mind "from the crowds of contradictory phantasms" so that it might "find out that light by which it was besprinkled, when, without all doubting, it cried out, that the unchangeable was to be preferred before the changeable. . . . And thus, with the flash of a trembling glance, it arrived at that which is."[8]

The language of Plotinus here is far removed from Jeremiah's account of the Lord's reply. "Retreat from history," as Hocking notes, "is the mystic's temptation. And he who dwells in the universal alone becomes false."[9] The encounter with Reality is too much for the average soul to bear. Yet the mystic's encounter must be translated into prophetic power if it is to take hold upon the world. What is striking about the prophetic consciousness is that it is directed outward upon the world. The prophet becomes the bearer of a message having to do with "a uniquely living God."[1]

[5] *Ibid.*, VIII. 8. 17.
[6] *Ibid.*
[7] *Ibid.*, VIII. 8. 19.
[8] *Ibid.*, VII. 17. 23.
[9] *Op. cit.*, p. 512.
[1] Cf. Max Scheler, *Le saint, le génie, le héros* (tr. Émile Marmy; Fribourg: Egloff, 1944), p. 84.

[3] *Ibid.*
[4] *Confessions* VIII. 5. 12.

7 ¶ But the Lord said unto me, Say not, I *am* a child: for thou shalt go to all that I shall send thee, and whatsoever I command thee thou shalt speak.

8 Be not afraid of their faces: for I *am* with thee to deliver thee, saith the Lord.

youth." **7** But the Lord said to me,
"Do not say, 'I am only a youth';
for to all to whom I send you you shall go,
and whatever I command you you shall speak.
8 Be not afraid of them,
for I am with you to deliver you,
                 says the Lord."

---

of marriageable age, as of Absalom during his revolt against David (II Sam. 18:5; cf. Gen. 34:19). We cannot therefore derive from this verse the exact age of Jeremiah at the time of his call. The LXX renders, "I am too young."

This is not to deprive either the poet or the mystic of the authenticity of his witness. In Jeremiah the poet and the mystic are assimilated to his prophetic task. To poetize his calling, or to ascend mystically to another world of contemplation, would have been for Jeremiah (and for the Hebrew religious consciousness generally) a form of "the great refusal." [2]

Jeremiah's temptation is not of this kind. What makes him draw back are the intimations of terror which pertain to every encounter with the Absolute. He is nigh to the misery of Eliphaz:

> dread came upon me, and trembling,
>   which made all my bones shake.
> A spirit glided past my face;
>   the hair of my flesh stood up (Job 4:14-15).

He senses the proximity of the demonic threat:

> Through endless solitudes shalt thou be drifted.
> Hast thou through solitudes and deserts fared? [3]

He has reached the dread point of the summons, and vaguely knows that:

>   those who follow me are led
> On to that Glassy Mountain where are no
> Footholds for logic, to that Bridge of Dread
> Where knowledge but increases vertigo. [4]

Even more deeply he has begun to experience "the awful daring of a moment's surrender" [5] —when this surrender is absolute, and *to* the Absolute. He has felt what George Eliot once called "that thorn-pressure" of this peculiar crowning.

[2] Cf. Dante, *Inferno*, Canto III, 1. 60.
[3] Goethe, *Faust*, Part II, Act I, scene 5; tr. Bayard Taylor.
[4] W. H. Auden, "The Summons," Part I, from *For the Time Being, A Christmas Oratorio* (New York: Random House, 1944; London: Faber & Faber, 1945). Used by permission.
[5] T. S. Eliot, "What the Thunder Said," from *The Waste Land*, Part V.

Jeremiah protests his youth not merely because "in Oriental society a young man has no *rôle* to play," [6] but because he is overwhelmed and intimidated by the awful arrogance of setting aside princes, priests, and people (vs. 18), to become "a prophet to the nations" (vs. 5), and to proclaim a view of God which goes beyond the apprehension of his time. Warm-hearted, affectionate, not given to strife, a young man well trained in the learning and tradition of his people, timid in spirit with the sensibilities of a poet, he might well have felt something of the trepidation of Job when that man, or his author, "from the land of Uz" (Job 1:1), was forced to regard the traditional patterns as narrow and outgrown. It is for this reason that the Lord's reply is so significant.

7-8. The Divine Rebuke.—Young or old, learned or uninformed, handsome or crippled, none of this matters. All this pertains to that ego which to Pascal was so "hateable." This is that ego which must be "collapsed" in order that "the own self" may arise. All this pertains to *my* powers, to *my* status, to *my* will to have reality on *my* special terms. This is the mark of that primary defection of the self "curved in upon itself," the projected ego which would override its creaturehood and exalt itself in its own image. Jeremiah is not to go on his own terms: God will **send** him, and he will go on God's terms. God will **command** him and he shall speak; and his word shall be **to all to whom** he is sent, and it shall consist in **whatever** he is told to speak in the specific situations as they arise, whether agreeable to his youth, temperament, moods, or station in life.

To be sure, it is a shock to encounter the otherness of Reality in this form; but the whole of Reality is such an otherness, and demands this sort of subjective authenticity in some form from each of us. When the antennae of our self-interests (which are projected so far in ad-

[6] T. K. Cheyne, *Jeremiah, His Life and Times* (New York: Anson D. F. Randolph, 1888), p. 3.

9 Then the LORD put forth his hand, and touched my mouth. And the LORD said unto me, Behold, I have put my words in thy mouth.

9 Then the LORD put forth his hand and touched my mouth; and the LORD said to me,

"Behold, I have put my words in your mouth.

---

9. Touched my mouth: This symbolic action was very important, for the Hebrew prophet was believed to be himself a spokesman or mouthpiece for God. His mouth must be pure, and he must speak the words given to him. In 15:19 God says to Jeremiah, "Thou shalt be as my mouth." Cf. the similar action in the call of Isaiah (6:7).

---

vance of our dissembled self-seeking) touch ever so slightly upon the genuine, the Absolute, the real, they wince from the encounter with a shuddering recoil, and the "self" contracts into its protective shell.

For the vast majority of people this refuge is the crowded collective, the covering of anonymity. As Kierkegaard speculates: "It is most comfortable to stride unknown through the world, without being known to His Majesty the King. . . . To be known by God in time makes life so acutely strenuous. Wherever He is, there every half hour is of tremendous importance. But to live in that manner is not endurable for sixty years." [7] Surely it is not endurable to the self which does not wish to be an authentic self—which has not the courage, as Paul Tillich puts it, to "accept acceptance." [8]

As Tillich notes in his meditation on Ps. 139: "man *desires* to escape God. . . . Men of all kinds, prophets and reformers, saints and atheists, believers and unbelievers, have the same experience. It is safe to say that a man who has never tried to flee God has never experienced the God Who is really God." [1] Once it is made plain to Jeremiah that the point at issue has not to do with the sum of his powers or the excellence of his talent or any other ego concern, then the mask is removed from his reticence; and it is possible for him to become a messenger, one whose function is to deliver the message.

On behalf of the message, and in consideration of its Sender, he is not to be **afraid of them.** He goes not in his own strength, but in God's; he speaks not on his own authority, but on the authority of the Lord. **I am with you to deliver you, says the LORD.** The qualms of the egocentric consciousness may be set aside as the messenger assumes his proper vocation. The principle is the same as the Apostle's "Yet not

I, but Christ . . . in me" (Gal. 2:20) source of strength and power. Here the ego perishes (so long as it remains constant to its call).

This is probably the initial crisis point in Jeremiah's inner experience. Here "his own law" (as the psychologist would describe it [2]) and the law of the Lord become one. To be a prophet or an apostle on one's own terms would be arrogance; "Divine authority is the decisive factor." [3]

Jeremiah here learns the inner meaning of those words attributed to Luther: "the Word of God is a battle, a ruin, and a sword." What begins as a battle, and continues more often than not as a battle within, accomplishes the ruin of the private ego before it becomes a sword. But what is always miraculous in this most shattering of all individual experiences is that, given the ruin of the individual pretension, there comes the singular touch of the hand of God.

9-10. *The Divine Appointment.*—The word of the Lord is here visualized in keeping with the Hebrew habit of thinking concretely in metaphor and figure and hyperbole "which invests everything with bodily form." [4] Not only is the figure used elsewhere in scripture (cf. II Sam. 17:5; Isa. 51:16; 59:21), but it recurs in Jeremiah in unique and splendid expressions (cf. 5:14). He writes:

Thy words were found, and I ate them,
and thy words became to me a joy
and the delight of my heart (15:16).

What is here signified is that he is filled with the sense of the inward presence of God.

Two things are surprisingly absent from this

---

[7] *The Concluding Unscientific Postscript*, tr. David F. Swenson and Walter Lowrie (Princeton: Princeton University Press, 1941), p. 402.

[8] Cf. *The Courage to Be* (New Haven: Yale University Press, 1952), p. 171 *et passim*.

[1] *The Shaking of the Foundations* (New York: Charles Scribner's Sons, 1948), p. 42.

[2] Cf. Carl G. Jung, *The Integration of the Personality* (tr. Stanley Dell; New York: Farrar & Rinehart, 1939), p. 301: "In so far as a man is untrue to his own law and does not rise to personality, he has failed of the meaning of his life."

[3] Søren Kierkegaard, *The Present Age* (tr. Alexander Dru and Walter Lowrie; London: Oxford University Press, 1940), p. 144.

[4] Cf. C. J. Ball, *The Prophecies of Jeremiah* (New York: A. C. Armstrong, 1893; "The Expositor's Bible"), pp. 70-71.

10 See, I have this day set thee over the nations and over the kingdoms, to root out, and to pull down, and to destroy, and to throw down, to build, and to plant.	10 See, I have set you this day over **nations** and over kingdoms, to pluck up and to break down, to destroy and to overthrow, to build and to plant."

10. The prophet was even more than a spokesman for Yahweh, an utterer of the words which came from God. The word of God was filled with divine energy and accomplished the task for which God sent it, bringing its own fulfillment. Elsewhere Jeremiah describes the word of the Lord as being a fire to devour the people (5:14), or as a hammer that shatters the rock (23:29). The classic statement of the conception is found in Isa. 55:10-11.

account. In the first place, there are no expressions either of poetic or prophetic ecstasy. The verse quoted above shows clearly that Jeremiah knew the sweetness of this inner joy; but even here the restraint of the phraseology is significant. One may speak justifiably of Pascal's "night of religious ecstasy" [5] as depicted in his account of his midnight experience of November 23, 1654, with its testimony of "joy, joy, joy, tears of joy." [6] Or one may speak of the cultivation of ecstasies among the early Hebrew prophets. This held for the prophetic societies of the times of Saul and Samuel, and may be seen in the practices of Ezekiel. But to hold that "no one has given stronger expression to the ecstatic transports of prophets than Jeremiah and Ezekiel" is misleading as far as Jeremiah is concerned.[7]

The perspectives of depth psychology throw a much firmer light on Jeremiah's account of himself than has been recognized. Buttenwieser very likely puts the matter too strongly when he holds that "the inspiration of the great literary prophets has nothing in common with the ecstasy of the prophets of the older type." [8] But Gordon is clearly on sound ground when he recognizes that the development of prophecy evolved a higher and a lower type. "The lower prophets adhered to the ecstasy, which became in its mature form the trance or dream. To-day we should call it self-hypnotism, and this is indeed just the charge that Jeremiah levels against them (xxiii. 16)." [9] Gordon cites W. Robertson Smith: "The characteristic of the true prophet is that he retains his consciousness

[5] *Great Shorter Works of Pascal*, tr. Emile Cailliet and John C. Blankenagel (Philadelphia: Westminster Press, 1948), p. 11.

[6] Cf. Pascal's "Memorial" recorded on a parchment found sewn on the inner lining of his coat at the time of his death.

[7] Cf. Pedersen, *Israel, Its Life and Culture, III-IV,* pp. 107-11, *et passim.*

[8] Cited in T. Crouther Gordon, *The Rebel Prophet* (New York: Harper & Bros., 1932), p. 14.

[9] *Ibid.,* pp. 15, 16.

and self-control under revelation." [1] The scorn which Jeremiah heaps upon the prophets who "speak visions of their own minds" (23:16) and protest their prophetic authority by crying "I have dreamed, I have dreamed" (23:25) is itself ample witness to Jeremiah's rejection of the lower prophetic practices.

The second remarkable aspect of this touch of the hand of God is the singular absence of any guilt consciousness in Jeremiah's account of it. When Isaiah beheld the Lord high and lifted up, his first exclamation was a "Woe is me! For I am . . . a man of unclean lips" (Isa. 6:5). The truth of the Lord which he had doubtless proclaimed theretofore had been spoken in the name of a conception and experience of God so far below that which was now revealed to him that he was quick to perceive the gap of ungodliness which distance from the true word of God made plain. Augustine also, throughout the early portions of his *Confessions,* exposes a manifold guilt-consciousness. But these are not Jeremiah's problems. Once he had passed the basic shock of encounter in which, as Tillich says, "nobody wants to be *known,*" [2] he was ready for the definition of his task.

This task is twofold: he is to be a prophet to the nations; and its "burden" will consist in the necessary plucking up and breaking down of the false and the wicked in order that the true and the righteous may be planted and built. For this purpose the Lord says to him, **I have put my words in your mouth** (vs. 9). This is the proclaimed word; and it carries intrinsic power within itself. This is not, however, to be understood magically. To hold, as is sometimes done, that the Hebrew conception of prophecy regards the word "as effecting its own fulfillment" is a dangerous half-truth—as though the word uttered by the prophet were "filled with His divine energy" and "passed

[1] *The Old Testament in the Jewish Church* (2nd ed.; New York: D. Appleton, 1900), p. 289. For a full discussion of this problem, see Gordon, *op. cit.,* pp. 9-33.

[2] *The Shaking of the Foundations,* p. 43.

11 ¶ Moreover the word of the LORD came unto me, saying, Jeremiah, what seest thou? And I said I see a rod of an almond tree.	11 And the word of the LORD came to me, saying, "Jeremiah, what do you see?" And

B. VISION OF THE ALMOND ROD (1:11-12)

Hebrew prophets sometimes received the word of the Lord in a vision. A clear example of this among the early prophets is that of Micaiah ben Imlah in I Kings 22:19-22. Among the canonical prophets such visions came most frequently in connection with their call; this was true of Isaiah (ch. 6), Ezekiel (chs. 1–3), and probably Amos (7:1-9; 8:1-3; 9:1). The present position of these two visions in the book suggests that they probably came to Jeremiah at the time of his call or in the days which immediately

---

from the prophet's lips into an independent existence of its own." [3] To discount the poetic virtue of metaphorical speech in this fashion is to lose the intrinsic virtue of the prophetic power (see Isa. 55:10-11). The true word, the word of God, is the Living Word; it necessarily transfigures the inert forms. Such a word cannot return empty. As Martin Buber observes, the divine word "breaks into the whole order of the word world. . . . [It] suddenly descends into the human situation, unexpected and unwilled by man, is free and fresh like the lightning. And the man who has to make it heard is over and over again subdued by the word before He lets it be put in his mouth (1, 9; 20, 7)." [4] The language here is still poetic, which is true equally of Ezekiel's vision of the dry bones (Ezek. 37) and of Zechariah's vision of the flying roll (Zech. 5:1-4). But an attempt is made to formulate that dimension of transcendence which shatters the congealed forms of the conspiracies of our immanence: the prophet, caught between the nether millstone of his historical situation moving rapidly toward its catastrophe, and the upper millstone of the Absolute moving always into dialectical encounter through the Word, is himself plucked up and destroyed at this precise point of the Lord's planting.

It is the Word so derived that sets him, i.e., makes him an overseer, the Lord's deputy, over the nations. Even if Jeremiah never traveled, and spoke only to the people of Judah, his word, and the authority of his word, is clearly for the nations. It is for the historical hour as such. He experiences the matrix of his time's history from within, at its most sensitive point of inner awareness, where the clash of powers, the shaking of the foundations, evokes through

stress and suffering, through destruction and exile, a higher God-consciousness than his world had known. Jeremiah clearly grasps the magnitude of the collision of powers; but he sees in this God's action in history, with the inevitable judgment that sooner or later must befall the God-defiant, and the necessary overthrowing which must precede the world's renewal.

Hence the double metaphor—that of the pulling down if the Great Architect is to rebuild, and that of the plucking up if the Gardener is to replant. Here the ground-theme of the book of Jeremiah is first introduced. This people will, in Jeremiah's time, be plucked up and scattered far from this land; in due time, a remnant will return, that the land may be replanted by the purified faithful and become fruitful unto the Lord once more. So also this present building, from the great temple to the very walls of Jerusalem itself, shall, in Jeremiah's time, be overthrown and destroyed; then, after many years of remembering Zion by the waters of Babylon (Ps. 137), and sifting the memory while the great winnowing of the world powers is going on, a purified remnant shall return to build the new Jerusalem. The recurrence of this theme in 42:10 and in 45:1-5 gives a startling unity to the book as a whole.

God also is revealed as the sufferer who has been obliged to break down and to pluck up what he himself had attempted to build and to plant. Should it appear that the oracles against the nations, collected in chs. 46–51, are largely from Jeremiah's hand and come from the earliest period of his prophecy, as has been recently maintained, then Jeremiah's appointment as a prophet to the nations is clear. Regardless of this, it is necessary to say that in this hour of the world's destiny, the plight of the people is inevitably bound up with that of the colliding powers.

11-16. The Two Visions.—These visions must presuppose the long gestation of a deep concern. Jeremiah had clearly fled long since to his soli-

[3] A. S. Peake, ed., *Jeremiah and Lamentations* (Edinburgh: T. C. & E. C. Jack, 1910-12; "The New-Century Bible"), I, 82, 77-78.
[4] *The Prophetic Faith*, tr. Carlyle Witton Davies (New York: The Macmillan Co., 1949), p. 164.

12 Then said the LORD unto me, Thou hast well seen: for I will hasten my word to perform it.

I said, "I see a rod of almond."[a] 12 Then the LORD said to me, "You have seen well, for I am watching[b] over my word to perform it."

[a] Heb shaqed
[b] Heb shoqed

---

followed. They may have come when the prophet was in an ecstatic state, but the objects involved were objects which he had seen in his normal consciousness.

In their literary form these two visions are similar to those found in 24:3; Amos 7:7-9; 8:1-2; Zech. 4:2; 5:2. The question-and-answer pattern emphasizes the fact that God is present in the vision and that the separation between God and the prophet is maintained. Hebrew prophets never experienced complete mystical absorption in the divine nature.

11-12. A rod of almond: The name of the almond in Hebrew is shāqēdh; the word for watching is shōqēdh. The verse thus contains a wordplay or pun of the type frequently found in the O.T. (see especially Amos 8:1-2). The almond is said to receive its name from the fact that it is the earliest tree to "wake" after the winter is over. However, the text says nothing of a blossoming rod, and the Hebrew apparently does not mean "twig" or any part of the living tree.

Elsewhere in the O.T. the rod is usually a symbol of judgment, of the wrath of God. This is true of the rod of Aaron in Num. 17:1-11; of that in Ezek. 7:10; and perhaps of the rods in Zech. 11:7, 10, 14. Hence the rod here symbolizes the imminent judgment of God against his rebellious people (cf. Pearle Stone Wood, "Jeremiah's Figure of the Almond Rod," Journal of Biblical Literature, LXI [1942], 99-103). This interpretation is supported by the words of vs. 12, I am watching over my word to

---

tude, to learn there the troubled silence of the hidden self and the hard-won patience of long "waiting on the Lord." John Skinner's remark that the dialogue preceding these visions could not have been the beginning of Jeremiah's fellowship with Yahweh, but "is the consummation of a genuine religious experience, rooted probably in the pieties of home and early life, of a growing self-knowledge and knowledge of God, which now ripens into the consciousness of a special mission" must be assumed.[5] The symbols of the experience often precede by many years the conscious formulation of the what which they have now proposed in visionary form. In the instance of the almond branch—and in that of the caldron to follow—the vision symbols are not forgotten, but grow in implication. They become distillation points within that which was most nebulous in the prophet's inner life, drawing all his conflict steadily upon their forms.

The almond rod and the caldron are typical transformation symbols: the one masculine and phallic, with potential creativity super-aboundingly implied; the other, its feminine counterpart, pointing to the threatening evils of the subconscious. (The caldron was, for Freud, a frequent symbol of the subconscious.) Calkins

[5] Prophecy and Religion (Cambridge: Cambridge University Press, 1922), p. 27.

is right, here, in pointing to the contrast between the two visions, "the one simple, the other terrible," and in holding that in this contrast we see "at the very outset of [his] career the tragic contrast in [Jeremiah's] soul."[6]

These two visions belong together as symbolizing Jeremiah's own inner struggle when he begins to sense that he is called to become one against the world: a call that is bursting with the splendor of deliverance and renewal on the one hand, and fraught with dangers, desolation, and ruin on the other. "The inner voice," as Jung says, "is the voice of a fuller life, of a wider, more comprehensive consciousness." At the same time (and this is the point we must stress) "the inner voice brings to consciousness whatever the whole—whether the nation to which we belong or the humanity of which we are a part— suffers from."[7] When the vision of the almond branch and the vision of the boiling caldron are projected outward upon the world, they formulate wonderfully the positive and negative features of Jeremiah's prophecy.

11-12. The Almond Branch.—Anyone who has lived in some land of the almond will not fail to respond to the incomparable loveliness of this first vision. There is nothing quite like

[6] Raymond Calkins, Jeremiah the Prophet (New York: The Macmillan Co., 1930), p. 65.
[7] Integration of the Personality, pp. 302-3.

13 And the word of the LORD came unto me the second time, saying, What seest thou? And I said, I see a seething pot; and the face thereof *is* toward the north.

13 The word of the LORD came to me a second time, saying, "What do you see?" And I said, "I see a boiling pot, facing away

---

perform it (**will hasten** is a mistranslation which apparently arose from the fact that the word has a meaning close to this in postbiblical Hebrew). Here is an assurance that God will truly fulfill his word, but Jeremiah usually employs the expression "watch over" in an ominous sense. In 5:6 he uses it of a leopard "watching against" the cities of Judah to destroy those who go out from them. In 44:27 he employs it of God watching over the people "for evil, and not for good." In 31:28 (a passage which may not be from Jeremiah) it is used in a double sense. The present verse should be taken as a threat that Yahweh will carry out his judgment upon Israel rather than as a promise of mercy. This is consistent with Jeremiah's early message in general.

C. VISION OF THE SEETHING POT (1:13-16)

This vision is closely connected on the one hand with the call of Jeremiah, and on the other with the early prophecies which warn of the approach of an enemy from the north (4:6; 6:1; 10:22). It indicates primarily the direction or source from which the evil is to come. For the identification of the foe from the north see Intro., p. 779.

---

the almond tree, the first to waken in the spring. Its nearest rival is the cherry tree, which A. E. Housman has celebrated so beautifully:

> Loveliest of trees, the cherry now
> Is hung with bloom along the bough,
> And stands about the woodland ride
> Wearing white for Eastertide.[8]

The poetic leap from the cherry white to Eastertide is similar in kind to that which Jeremiah makes from the almond rod, the "wake-tree" (*shāqēdh*)—the first to waken in the spring—to the picture of God watching (*shōqēdh*) over his people. Housman, the poet, knew how images such as these set up "the strong tremor of unreasonable excitement . . . in some region deeper than the mind" where they will often "with sudden and unaccountable emotion" give rise to the unanticipated poem.[9] We may suppose, in Jeremiah's case, that, seeing the dry barren branch of winter break almost suddenly into bloom, he was moved, almost by the free association of the Hebrew words, from the *shāqēdh* (almond tree), meaning "wakeness" or "watchfulness" (the almond tree wakes into bloom as early as January), to the *shōqēdh,* and the sense that the Lord was "awake" and "watchful"—a difference of only one vowel!

[8] "Loveliest of Trees," from *The Collected Poems of A. E. Housman* (London: Jonathan Cape; New York: Henry Holt & Co., 1940). Used by permission of The Society of Authors as the Literary Representative of the Trustees of the Estate of A. E. Housman, and the publishers.

[9] Cf. *The Name and Nature of Poetry* (New York: The Macmillan Company, 1933), pp. 43, 48.

One of the most apt translations here is that of Earl B. Marlatt who, playing upon both words and image, touches the line with aesthetic splendor: "Thou hast well seen: for behold, I bloom through my word to perform it." [1] There is here no intrinsic violence, for the vision is laden with an infinite effulgence which is central and essential to Jeremiah's sense of God's relation to the world. The world may be spiritually dead, the people moribund, the winter of ungodliness upon them all; but the Word is ready to break through always, a living word, through which God's righteousness blooms as he performs it.

Many scholars hold that Jeremiah saw the almond branch and the caldron, as he saw the figs (24:6) and the potter's wheel (18:6), and formulated their special significations with rhetorical deliberateness. It would seem, on the contrary, that the branch and the caldron are dream-symbols, formulated by the unconscious out of Jeremiah's undoubted experience of the almond through recurring springtide seasons from his boyhood on, and precipitated into the conscious mind at that time when what was repressed in him came into conflict with that which he was called to become. As such, the symbols were mysterious and invincible, compelling the consciousness. The one was projected upon reality as the intuition and promise of God; and the other as the impending gloom, the threat of disaster, the divine warning.

13-16. *The Divine Warning.*—Skinner would seem to be psychologically sound when he in-

[1] *Lands Away* (New York and Nashville: Abingdon-Cokesbury Press, 1944), p. 150.

14 Then the LORD said unto me, Out of the north an evil shall break forth upon all the inhabitants of the land.

15 For, lo, I will call all the families of the kingdoms of the north, saith the LORD; and they shall come, and they shall set every one his throne at the entering of the gates of Jerusalem, and against all the walls thereof round about, and against all the cities of Judah.

16 And I will utter my judgments against them touching all their wickedness, who have forsaken me, and have burned incense unto other gods, and worshipped the works of their own hands.

from the north." 14 Then the LORD said to me, "Out of the north evil shall break forth upon all the inhabitants of the land. 15 For, lo, I am calling all the tribes of the kingdoms of the north, says the LORD; and they shall come and every one shall set his throne at the entrance of the gates of Jerusalem, against all its walls round about, and against all the cities of Judah. 16 And I will utter my judgments against them, for all their wickedness in forsaking me; they have burned incense to other gods, and wor-

13-14. The object seen in vision is **a boiling pot,** i.e., a wide-mouthed cooking pot, probably with two handles, examples of which have been found in Palestinian excavations (James L. Kelso, *The Ceramic Vocabulary of the Old Testament* [New Haven: American Schools of Oriental Research, 1948], pp. 27, 48, Fig. 16). The same word (*ṣîr*) could be used for a washbasin (cf. Ps. 60:8). It is not necessary to press the details of this vision; the meaning is simply that as the pot is **facing away from the north,** so the evil is about to come from that direction **upon all the inhabitants of the land.**

15-16. These verses are the addition of the Deuteronomic editor (see Intro., pp. 788-90). The original word of the Lord which explained the vision of the boiling pot was the single sentence of vs. 14, very short and pointed, like the similar explanation of the previous vision in vs. 12 and of other visions of this type. Vss. 15-16 are the

terprets the caldron symbolism as both magical and mysterious, like the witches in *Macbeth*— "Act IV, scene 1: A dark cave. In the middle, a Caldron Boiling"; or in *Faust*—"Part I, scene 6. Witches' Kitchen. Upon a low hearth stands a great caldron, under which a fire is burning. Various figures appear in the vapors which rise from the caldron." Here in Jeremiah's vision is "the image of a magic cauldron brewing in the mysterious north, and sending forth deadly fumes which will carry ruin and desolation over the world—an emblem of the sense of calamity which already haunted Jeremiah's mind, and was to find impassioned expression in his earliest poetic effusions." [2] This means that these visions reflect something of Jeremiah's inner struggle, but they also show how squarely and unflinchingly he looked at reality. Meanwhile we should note, with Jung, that the symbol of "fire is emotional excitement or sudden bursts of impulse, and if a pot is set upon the fire, then one knows that transformation is under way." [3]

This is what we have in this dream symbol. Its formulation toward the public fact is clear.

[2] *Prophecy and Religion,* pp. 31-32.

[3] Jung, *op. cit.,* p. 94; cf. Augustine *Confessions* III. 1. 1: "To Carthage I came, where a cauldron of unholy loves bubbled up all around me." Cf. T. S. Eliot's use of this figure in *The Waste Land.*

Out of the north evil shall break forth upon all the inhabitants of the land. This danger was apparent already in the fall of Israel to the Assyrians; the rise of the Babylonian power is coincident with Jeremiah's lifework. The unanticipated Scythian hordes which swept over the Asiatic world at this time in a succession of raids and in sufficient strength to extract gifts from the king of Egypt may also have served to make apparent "the northern peril." (But cf. Intro., p. 779.) Through the projection of these vision symbols upon the factual conflict of the time, Jeremiah's struggle with himself— the play of opposites in his personality—is in principle effectively resolved: the extent to which "the sense of vocation appealed only to one side of his nature" while the other side "cries out in protest against it" is here assuaged through acceptance of his high vocation.

The evil descending **out of the north** upon all of Judah is clearly foreseen by Jeremiah. The caldron itself is apparently situated in the north. And when the caldron is "blown upon," or the fire beneath it "fanned from the north" (Moffatt) the empires of the north will lay siege to Jerusalem. The manifold evils of this seething brew will **break forth upon all the inhabitants of the land.** The addition of vs. 15 by the Deuteronomic editor after the fall

17 ¶ Thou therefore gird up thy loins, and arise, and speak unto them all that I command thee: be not dismayed at their faces, lest I confound thee before them.

shiped the works of their own hands. 17 But you, gird up your loins; arise, and say to them everything that I command you. Do not be dismayed by them, lest I dismay you

---

counterpart of 25:1-13a, also from the hand of the Deuteronomic editor. They were written after the capture of Jerusalem by the Babylonians in 587 B.C. The best explanation of them is contained in 25:8-11. In vs. 16 the antecedent of **them** is **the cities of Judah,** not the kings of the northern countries, who are here pictured as the witnesses of Yahweh's judgment upon his people.

D. Encouragement to Jeremiah (1:17-19)

These verses have come to us through the hand of the Deuteronomic editor. Vs. 17 is original, but its proper position is perhaps immediately after vs. 14. Vss. 18-19 have been borrowed or imitated from 15:20, but the editor has expanded the figure in his characteristic style, and the enumeration of the various classes against which Jeremiah

---

of Jerusalem does not violate in principle the threat which Jeremiah sees quite clearly at the beginning of his work. And this may be said also of vs. 16 which assigns, as the inward cause of this calamity, the infidelity and the idolatries of the people. These are rooted in a wrong relation to God.

17-19. The Divine Power.—Here the call is imperative. The dialogue is ended, the command is given. By virtue of his faithfulness to this command, Jeremiah will be flung into "the storm center of conflict between God and the world, between faith and despair."[4] It is inevitable that suffering and dismay will arise where the perspectives of an unfaithful people are contradicted by the spokesman of God. He will stand, like Athanasius *contra mundum,* like Luther at Worms, against the whole land, against **kings, princes, priests, and people.** He will know "the separateness, the awful responsibility, the power, of the Single Soul."[5] Too soon also he will come to know the hard hostility of those thousands of "estrangèd faces" that "miss the many-splendoured thing."[6] Hence the injunction: **Do not be dismayed by them, lest I dismay you before them.** For Jeremiah's task will not be measured by the approval of the multitude or the plaudits of the crowd. He whose inner strength is not great enough to dispense with these will certainly feel the dismay of the sensitive soul when refused and rejected by the people, and also waver, quail, and be overborne by their callous stubbornness. The insight here is psychologically sound, though paradoxical. If Jeremiah exhibits fear and suffers himself to be intimidated by the

opposition of the officials or the people, God "will break him down before them"; i.e., the reflex of his evident timidity will but serve to elicit scorn and derision toward him on the part of those whom he must accuse.

It is misleading to say with Smith that this warning implies that Jeremiah was wanting in manly courage, that "his strength as a poet may have been his weakness as a man," that "God does not speak thus to a man unless He sees that he needs it"; and that "it was to his most impetuous and unstable disciple that Christ said, *Thou art Peter, and on this rock will I build.*"[7] It is not Jeremiah's weakness that is his temptation, but his strength. It is precisely because Jeremiah has had courage enough to think beyond the thoughts and practices of the people and the authorities, and because he is sensitive enough in spirit and candid enough to perceive the fatal limitations in public behavior and private pride, that he has dared to confront himself and his time with the dimension of the absolute—at once the most edifying and terrifying experience that can come to a sensitive soul.

The problem of fear here is paradoxical in the sense in which Pascal knew the identical paradox. "Fear not, provided you fear; but if you fear not, then fear."[8] What is meant by this is well known by the poet and prophet and saint. Yeats speaks of certain "personifying spirits" of the past who through their great dramatic power "bring our souls to crisis." "They have but one purpose," he says, "to bring their chosen man to the greatest obstacle he may confront without despair."[9] This is an

[4] Paul S. Minear, *Eyes of Faith* (Philadelphia: Westminster Press, 1946), p. 7.

[5] George Adam Smith, *Jeremiah* (4th ed.; New York: Harper & Bros., 1929), p. 88.

[6] Francis Thompson, "The Kingdom of God."

[7] *Op. cit.,* p. 333.

[8] *Thoughts,* No. 775.

[9] *Autobiographies: Reveries of Childhood and The Trembling of the Veil* (New York: The Macmillan Co., 1916), p. 337.

18 For, behold, I have made thee this day a defensed city, and an iron pillar, and brazen walls against the whole land, against the kings of Judah, against the princes thereof, against the priests thereof, and against the people of the land.

before them. 18 And I, behold, I make you this day a fortified city, an iron pillar, and bronze walls, against the whole land, against the kings of Judah, its princes, its

---

was to be arrayed is typical of his writing. The whole section is very appropriate in the place where it now stands, and it may be taken as a brief summary of the prophet's life. It emphasizes the fact that Jeremiah aroused the opposition of all classes of the people, but stood firm against them in his faith in God and in his own call to be God's prophet.

18. Its princes were not sons of the royal family, but officials of the government.

---

interesting reading of the problem of destiny, which is compounded in Yeats from many sources. And though his notion of these personifying spirits, or of the demon, remains as nebulous and uninformed as with the Greeks, his intuition in depth is remarkably clear.

> I think that all religious men have believed that there is a hand not ours in the events of life. . . . When I think of life as a struggle with the Daemon who would ever set us to the hardest work among those not impossible, I understand why there is a deep enmity between a man and his destiny, and why a man loves nothing but his destiny.[1]

The tension of this deep enmity is, in Jeremiah, expanded to the absolute, for his "Daemon" is the word of Yahweh. "There is such a thing," says Hocking, "as losing one's soul: and that is, rejecting one's call to prophesy." [2]

It is this which makes this third great metaphorical passage (vs. 18) so decisive, whether placed here as integral to this initial consciousness of call, or whether borrowed from the second religious crisis (15:20). Jeremiah is not to speak in his own strength. Nor will his strength be as the strength of ten because his heart is pure: he will speak in God's strength, because when the officials and the people lay siege to him, Yahweh will make him like **a fortified city**, and like **an iron pillar** and like **bronze walls**. The people will fight against him; **but they shall not prevail** (vs. 19; cf. vs. 8).

The metaphors are obvious and powerful. The vision of the almond branch to contain the wakefulness and watchfulness of God is here carried over to link the metaphors of his prophetic appointment. The decisive element in the experience is Jeremiah's persuasion that he is forced into this position; that, God helping him, he can do no other—and that it is precisely the power of God that is forcing him. "A man cannot in reason embark upon 'the voluntary' (the requirements of which are

higher than the universal requirements) unless he has an *immediate* certainty that it is required of him *in particular*." [3] Otherwise the pretension to speak the word of God would be presumptuous. But Jeremiah has this sense; and just for this reason the term "genius" (as the term "poet" or the term "mystic") does not apply here. A genius, as Samuel Johnson somewhere says, is a man of broad general powers accidentally determined to some particular end. Jeremiah is not "accidentally determined"; he feels he is "compelled."

By the same token the term "reformer" does not apply. "Those whom we call 'reformers,' " wrote Max Scheler, "such as Savonarola and Luther, distinguish themselves in this: that they never preach a new doctrine, but, on the contrary, preach a 'return' to the origins." [4] Jeremiah is not without a certain definite doctrine of "return," as we shall see; but he feels compelled to proclaim both the genuinely old and the radically new (see chs. 30; 31). Kierkegaard's distinction between the genius and the apostle applies in part:

> Just as a man, sent into the town with a letter, has nothing to do with its contents, but has only to deliver it . . . : so, too, an Apostle has really only to be faithful in his service, and to carry out his task. Therein lies the essence of an Apostle's life of self-sacrifice. . . . It is otherwise with genius; it has only an immanent teleology, it develops itself, and while developing itself this self-development projects itself as its work. . . . Genius lives in itself.[5]

One may point out, in the light of the evident and continuing agony of Jeremiah, that Kierkegaard's illustration of the letter is unfortunate and fails to existentialize the notions of "mission" and "authority": clearly what is "paradoxical" in the "prophet's" situation (however it may be with the "Apostle") is that Jeremiah

[3] *The Journals of Søren Kierkegaard*, ed. and tr. Alexander Dru (New York: Oxford University Press, 1938), pp. 413-14.
[4] *Le saint, le génie, le héros*, p. 75.
[5] *The Present Age*, pp. 160-61.

[1] *Essays* (New York: The Macmillan Co., 1924), p. 499.
[2] *Meaning of God in Human Experience*, p. 513.

19 And they shall fight against thee; but they shall not prevail against thee; for I *am* with thee, saith the LORD, to deliver thee.

2 Moreover the word of the LORD came to me, saying,

2 Go and cry in the ears of Jerusalem, saying, Thus saith the LORD; I remember

priests, and the people of the land. 19 They will fight against you; but they shall not prevail against you, for I am with you, says the LORD, to deliver you."

2 The word of the LORD came to me, saying, 2 "Go and proclaim in the hearing of Jerusalem, Thus says the LORD,

---

III. ORACLES OF THE EARLY MINISTRY (2:1–6:30)

A. ISRAEL'S FAITHLESSNESS TO YAHWEH (2:1-37)

2:1-37. With ch. 2 begins a series of oracles, extending through ch. 6, which seem to come largely, if not wholly, from the early part of Jeremiah's career, in the first few years after his call. Ch. 2 contains a group of messages which are fairly unified in theme, but they were not necessarily delivered all at the same time and on the same occasion. The prophets usually did not deliver long, well-prepared "sermons," but spoke brief "oracles" as the occasion demanded and as they received the word of the Lord.

The general theme of the chapter is that Israel's history, since she entered Canaan, has been one of continual faithlessness to Yahweh. The opening verses describe Israel's loyalty to Yahweh in the desert period, a time when she was holy to God (vss. 1-3). But when Israel entered Canaan she began to desert Yahweh in order to worship the false gods of Canaan (vss. 4-9). Such action, however, was entirely contrary to the practice of foreign nations; they do not exchange their gods (which are really no gods) for others (vss. 10-13). As a result of such faithlessness, the land of Israel has suffered, especially at the hand of Egypt; nevertheless the people continue to seek alliance with Egypt and Assyria (vss. 14-19). Israel's sin is of long standing and is very deep rooted; the prophet piles figure upon figure to depict her apostasy (vss. 20-29). Yahweh has sought through chastening and through loving care to bring her back, but he has not succeeded (vss. 30-37).

This chapter is usually dated in the period before the Deuteronomic reforms of 621 B.C. It is said to reflect conditions which prevailed at that time, but were corrected in part by those reforms. Yet most commentators recognize that vss. 16, 18, 36-37 do not fit that period, since we do not know of any destruction of the land by the Egyptians, or of alliances with Egypt and Assyria, at that time. Accordingly, many believe that those verses were added in the time of Jehoiakim, possibly by the prophet himself in his dictation of the scroll to Baruch (ch. 36). It is better to assign all of this chapter to the reign of Jehoiakim in the period between his accession (609) and the battle of Carchemish (605). Under Jehoiakim many of the religious practices which Josiah's reforms sought to abolish undoubtedly returned (for the historical situation see Exeg. on vss. 16, 18, 36-37).

I. ISRAEL'S EXCHANGE OF YAHWEH FOR OTHER DEITIES (2:1-13)

2. Through the prophet Yahweh recalls **the devotion of your youth.** The word rendered **devotion** is the Hebrew *ḥéṣedh,* a very rich word which primarily means faith-

---

has *everything* to do with the message, because the message has everything to do with him. Nevertheless, Kierkegaard comes nearest to describing the prophetic dimension when he notes that the Apostle is "absolutely, paradoxically, teleologically placed." [6] The categories of immanence focus absolutely in his confrontation with the Lord, whose word, paradoxically, cuts across the universal practice and opinion which nails him out in isolation, as the preten-

[6] *Ibid.,* p. 160.

tious exception—yet he is without presumption since his purposes are the purposes of God. He is the one whom Yahweh hurls; the one who stands at the conflux of the ages, holding eternity in his hands; in him we see those

Desperate tides of the whole great world's anguish
Forced thro' the channels of a single heart.[7]

2:1-3. The Remembrance of Things Past.— The "oracles" of Jeremiah which are now set

[7] F. W. H. Myers, *Saint Paul,* st. ix.

thee, the kindness of thy youth, the love of thine espousals, when thou wentest after me in the wilderness, in a land *that was* not sown.

3 Israel *was* holiness unto the LORD, *and* the firstfruits of his increase: all that devour him shall offend; evil shall come upon them, saith the LORD.

I remember the devotion of your youth,
   your love as a bride,
how you followed me in the wilderness,
   in a land not sown.
3 Israel was holy to the LORD,
   the first fruits of his harvest.
All who ate of it became guilty;
   evil came upon them,

               says the LORD."

---

fulness to the obligations imposed by the covenant, and which may be used either of God or of the people. Here it refers to the loyalty of Israel to her God during the life of Moses and the desert sojourn. Hosea believed that this was the ideal period in Israel's history (Hos. 2:15; 9:10; 11:1-2), and Jeremiah apparently derived the idea from him, for this chapter contains a number of verbal parallels with Hosea. Ezekiel denies that there was a honeymoon period of faithfulness (Ezek. 23), and the historical books hardly depict it as a time of complete fidelity (see, e.g., Num. 14–16).

3. **Israel was holy to the LORD**: The word **holy** has its root in the idea of being set apart, and that is the meaning here. Israel was a nation set apart and chosen by God.

---

before us (2:1–6:30) are generally held to belong to the earliest prophetic utterances of Jeremiah. It is felt by some that the easy and natural movement is from the vision of the seething caldron to the "Scythian poems" of ch. 4 through ch. 6. This would afford, without doubt, much chronological comfort to the reader; but it would bypass the all-important theological order in which the chapters now stand. What Jeremiah is told to **go and proclaim in the hearing of Jerusalem** is profoundly religious before it is either ethical or political. The deeper logic here is not from the caldron to the threatening "foe from the north"; it is, as in ch. 1, first the almond rod (the dialectic of the God-man relation) and *then* the caldron (the visible consequences of the human defection). Most important is the profoundly religious character of Jeremiah's starting point, set forth in ch. 2.

The prophet's Proustian search for his lost past is neither nostalgic nor superficial. It is central to Jeremiah's prophetic strategy and message. The initial movement in his approach to the people is a recollection—a recalling of the people to a former condition: **I remember**, says the Lord.

Neither is this "prophetic retrospect," as it has been called,[8] merely rhetorical in character. It is a recollection of a particular kind. It focuses upon those signs and events which the people have shared from the beginning as a people. These are the covenant signs and the covenant-making events which have formed the religious consciousness of the people, and which may therefore be held to inform the total con-

text of their behavior and understanding even in their defection from the covenants. Jeremiah attempts to recover the context of meanings which the people have forgotten or perverted.

Two similes are used in vs. 2, both of which revive the covenant dimension. The simile of the bride is powerful; it introduces here, in simplicity and disarming innocence, a first foundation image wherewith Jeremiah will accuse the people throughout the succeeding poems. The original purity of the relation with God, as of bride to the loyal husband, anticipates the degeneration of that relation into infidelity, adultery, harlotry. This is the more meaningful inasmuch as Jeremiah identifies this defection with the failure of Israel to maintain its religious purity as over against the cult practices of the Canaanites, into whose land they had come. Jeremiah exempts no one from this primary betrayal (see vs. 8).

The influence of Hosea upon the prophetic heart of Jeremiah is apparent here. Through suffering love for his own bride Gomer, and through her persistent unfaithfulness to him, Hosea had learned something very profound concerning the nature of the love of Yahweh for his people. Yahweh was, in his inmost essence (to employ a non-Hebraic thought-form), he who was Loyal-in-Love, whereas Israel, his bride, went after her lovers, made sacrifices to the baals, to the graven images, to Samaria's calf, on the assumption that these agricultural gods of the Canaanites which provided her with her bread, corn, and wine.

The second figure is the metaphor of a journey—a journey at once particular and more general. Its covenant sign is clearly with "him

[8] Cf. Minear, *Eyes of Faith*, pp. 201 ff.

4 Hear ye the word of the Lord, O house of Jacob, and all the families of the house of Israel:

5 ¶ Thus saith the Lord, What iniquity have your fathers found in me, that they are gone far from me, and have walked after vanity, and are become vain?

4 Hear the word of the Lord, O house of Jacob, and all the families of the house of Israel: 5 Thus says the Lord:

"What wrong did your fathers find in me
  that they went far from me,
and went after worthlessness, and became
  worthless?

The RSV correctly translates the verbs of vs. 3*b* as past tense; they are the imperfect of repeated action in the past.

5. The word rendered **worthlessness** is *hébhel,* and the verb is derived from it. It means, lit., "vanity," "nothingness," and is the favorite word of Ecclesiastes; Jeremiah thus designates the pagan gods of Canaan, who are called in vs. 11 "that which does not profit." Men become like that which they love and worship (cf. Hos. 9:10; II Kings 17:15).

---

who smote the first-born of Egypt . . . ; and brought Israel out from among them" and with "him who divided the Red Sea in sunder . . . ; and made Israel pass through the midst of it" and with "him who led his people through the wilderness" (Ps. 136:10-16). This people, chosen as a bride, had been faithful in that season; they had experienced a great deliverance, based upon a covenant made and promises given, which deliverance becomes typical in the life of the people as in the lives of individuals within that people. A covenant is again made with the tribes as they cross the Jordan and enter into the promised land (Josh. 24:1-33; Ps. 136:16-22). It is later confirmed under David, during a time of comparative faithfulness. **Israel was holy to the Lord.** For Jeremiah the turning from loyalty to Yahweh dates from the Davidic covenant. Hence the period of the wilderness wanderings represents for him, as for Amos and Hosea, a period of ideal piety before the long rebellion sets in. To the Deuteronomist, as well as to Isaiah, Ezekiel, and the J and E histories, this period was itself the period of the origins of sin. On the unsown land of the wilderness there had been, for Jeremiah, no rival gods; defection begins when the loyalty of the people is seduced by the agricultural gods of Canaan, with all their fertility rites and cult practices. This is the place where the long "detour," as Minear calls it, begins. We shall see below (6:16) how easily this metaphor of the journey is lifted by Jeremiah into a general principle.

A third simile now appears: **Israel was holy** [i.e., set apart] **to the Lord** [like] **the first fruits of his harvest.** Here again a strong figure is used: one which is calculated to lay firm hold upon the conscience of the people. For, as every Israelite knew, a portion of the first fruits of the harvest was especially set aside and consecrated to Yahweh; and no one was permitted

to eat thereof, save only the priests (Num. 18:12-13); even the priests were permitted only because they were Yahweh's representatives living on his bounty.[9] Those who trespassed upon this rule were subject to severe penalties: **All who ate of it became guilty.** The relationship with Yahweh is violated; the sacrilegious derogation to oneself of that which belongs exclusively to God is, for Jeremiah, the source of the guilt consciousness, which persistently bears witness to the corruption of the very ground of personal, as well as national, integrity.

The almost terrifying power of this comparison will be seen if the metaphor is carried back to the original in Hos. 9:10. For here in the finding of Israel in the Sinai desert the people truly come to know God. Cut off from all secondary securities, with nothing but flight and the wandering, the encounter with God is deep and real. But it is miraculous, as though one were to find ripe grapes growing in an unirrigated desert, so discovering what is luscious and rare where certainly one never expected to find it. Or again, it is as though God's fig tree, the tree of mankind, planted long since has produced fruit for the first time, and this first fruitage of the tree turns out to be the Israelite fugitives from Egypt, the **firstfruits of** [God's] **increase.**

Thus Jeremiah, with the swift concision of the poet's skill, has recalled to the people the period of purity, fidelity, and holiness founded upon the covenant of the wilderness, and, by implication, he has drawn the sobering contrast of a people impure, unfaithful, and corrupt. "He is infinitely tender," Gordon observes, "to the nation as a nation: he is terribly harsh on the individuals of the nation."[1]

4-13. The Encounter with Nothingness.—To Jeremiah this progressive deterioration in the

---

[9] Cf. Peake, *Jeremiah and Lamentations,* I, 88.
[1] *Rebel Prophet,* p. 60.

6 Neither said they, Where *is* the LORD that brought us up out of the land of Egypt, that led us through the wilderness, through a land of deserts and of pits, through a land of drought, and of the shadow of death, through a land that no man passed through, and where no man dwelt?

7 And I brought you into a plentiful country, to eat the fruit thereof and the goodness thereof; but when ye entered, ye defiled my land, and made mine heritage an abomination.

8 The priests said not, Where *is* the LORD? and they that handle the law knew me not: the pastors also transgressed against me, and the prophets prophesied by Baal, and walked after *things that* do not profit.

9 ¶ Wherefore I will yet plead with you, saith the LORD, and with your children's children will I plead.

10 For pass over the isles of Chittim, and see; and send unto Kedar, and consider diligently, and see if there be such a thing.

6 They did not say, 'Where is the LORD
    who brought us up from the land of
      Egypt,
  who led us in the wilderness,
    in a land of deserts and pits,
  in a land of drought and deep darkness,
    in a land that none passes through,
    where no man dwells?'
7 And I brought you into a plentiful land
    to enjoy its fruits and its good things.
  But when you came in you defiled my
      land,
    and made my heritage an abomination.
8 The priests did not say, 'Where is the
      LORD?'
  Those who handle the law did not
      know me;
  the rulers[c] transgressed against me;
    the prophets prophesied by Ba'al,
    and went after things that do not profit.

9 "Therefore I still contend with you,
                         says the LORD,
  and with your children's children I will
    contend.
10 For cross to the coasts of Cyprus and see,
    or send to Kedar and examine with
      care;
    see if there has been such a thing.

[c] Heb *shepherds*

---

8. This verse enumerates four groups of leaders who were faithless to Yahweh: (*a*) the priests; (*b*) they that handle the law, apparently those who were skilled in interpreting and administering the law, such as that in Deuteronomy, a subdivision of the priesthood and the predecessors of the later "'scribes" (for more detailed discussion see J. Philip Hyatt, "Torah in the Book of Jeremiah," *Journal of Biblical Literature,* LX [1941], 385-87); (*c*) the shepherds or rulers (KJV strangely renders the Hebrew for "shepherd" by the word pastors only in this book; see 3:15; 10:21; 12:10; 17:16; 22:22; 23:1-2); and (*d*) the prophets [who] prophesied by Baal, a Canaanite deity.

10. Chittim is the island of Cyprus, and possibly also some of the coast of the mainland opposite Cyprus, here chosen by the prophet as an example of a land in the west. Kedar was the name of an Arab tribe in the desert east of Palestine (cf. 49:28-29). The prophet thus says, "Go to the west, and go to the east."

---

land of promise is incredible. Living in the time when Israel has already fallen and when Judah is facing a like disaster, he is appalled and shocked by the blindness of the people. One can only "shudder" (Moffatt) in dismay and amazement. Instead of seeking the Lord they turned away from him, defiled [his] land when they entered into it, and made [his] heritage an abomination. Priests, interpreters of the law, rulers, and prophets have all gone after things that do not profit. The people too have ex-

changed the God who was their glory for that which does not profit. It is incredible.

> Only
> The fool, fixed in his folly, may think
> He can turn the wheel on which he turns.[2]

You may go either to the west, or to the east—either to the coasts of Cyprus or to Kedar—

[2] T. S. Eliot, *Murder in the Cathedral* (London: Faber & Faber; New York: Harcourt, Brace & Co., 1935), Part I, p. 24. Used by permission.

11 Hath a nation changed *their* gods, which *are* yet no gods? but my people have changed their glory for *that which* doth not profit.

12 Be astonished, O ye heavens, at this, and be horribly afraid, be ye very desolate, saith the LORD.

13 For my people have committed two evils; they have forsaken me the fountain of living waters, *and* hewed them out cisterns, broken cisterns, that can hold no water.

11 Has a nation changed its gods,
    even though they are no gods?
But my people have changed their glory
    for that which does not profit.

12 Be appalled, O heavens, at this,
    be shocked, be utterly desolate,
                says the LORD,

13 for my people have committed two evils:
    they have forsaken me,
the fountain of living waters,
    and hewed out cisterns for themselves,
broken cisterns,
    that can hold no water.

---

11. Their glory is Yahweh; the word has a meaning close to our word "majesty."

13. The figure here used was very vivid to those who lived in Palestine, where the rainfall is usually not very abundant and many people through the centuries have had to depend on **cisterns. Living waters** means the running water of a spring or fountain, as contrasted with the stagnant water of a cistern.

---

and no such behavior will be found. Even the peoples whose gods **are no gods** do not change their gods. They remain loyal to what they have even though they have nothing. But his people, says the Lord, have forsaken him.

13. The Fountain Perennial.—This verse is easily one of the most memorable in the whole of Jeremiah's writing. It is aesthetically complete, with singular and universal appeal. Its irony is purgative. It contains one of the few names for God which Jeremiah himself seems to have formed—God is **the fountain of living waters.** The springing fountain, filled with water cool and abundant, fed with countless hidden springs flowing into it secretly from the highlands, and long since offered to the people without labor and without price, suggested to Alexander Maclaren "the great thought of God's own loving will as the self-originated impulse by which He pours out all good." [3] Its image appeal is perennial, like that of the overflowing cup in the twenty-third psalm. How much more powerful is the image when it is considered that it is addressed to people who dwelt in a semi-arid land, where water was prized and thirst was common. How incredible, then, and how utterly absurd, the leaving of this constant and life-giving source in order to hew from the hard rock, through hard toil and great price, the artificial basin. Water collected in cisterns from the rains had to be carried in jars from distant places. It became hot and stagnant and often polluted. Such cisterns often cracked and the precious liquid seeped away.

[3] *The Books of Isaiah and Jeremiah* (New York: A. C. Armstrong & Son, 1906; "Expositions of Holy Scripture"), II, 250.

How great the dismay of the person athirst who, seeing the cistern afar off, should come to it eagerly only to find it broken and empty. Clearly the broken cisterns are the idols to whom the people have given themselves: they disappoint the wayfarer, they cannot sustain the worshiper.

This, however, is only half the story. It is not merely in the contrast between Yahweh and the idols that the power of Jeremiah's argument consists; nor in the fact that the idols are "no gods," or "that which does not profit" (vs. 11). The clue to this entire discourse, with its forensic contention with the people (vs. 9), is to be found in vs. 5. In turning from Yahweh, the people "went after worthlessness, and became worthless." The Exeg. (see above, p. 813) rightly calls attention to the root concept, meaning "vanity," or "nothingness"; and the recurrence of this term, together with the several modifications of its root throughout the oracles of Jeremiah, should underscore the dimension of meaning that is commonly lost. It is not merely that men become like that which they love and worship, as is frequently pointed out, as though vanity, or the idol, or the nothingness were static and inert. On the contrary, the nothingness of which Jeremiah speaks is extremely lively. It is as lively as we are, as powerful as our thirst is powerful, and as desperate as our hunger is desperate. For it is not anything outside of us; its root is within the soul. Where the individual spirit is not related to God as to the fountain of living waters, he is filled with a great emptiness, is deceived by all that he values; everything to which he puts his hand crumbles as he grasps

14 ¶ *Is* Israel a servant? *is* he a home-born *slave?* why is he spoiled?

15 The young lions roared upon him, *and* yelled, and they made his land waste: his cities are burned without inhabitant.

14 "Is Israel a slave? Is he a homeborn servant?
  Why then has he become a prey?
15 The lions have roared against him,
  they have roared loudly.
  They have made his land a waste,
  his cities are in ruins, without inhabitant.

2. Results of Israel's Apostasy (2:14-19)

These verses depict the suffering which came upon Israel as the result of forsaking the Lord. Some have taken vss. 15-16 to be a prophecy of the future, employing the "prophetic perfect" of Hebrew, but the general tenor of the section is that of a destruction which has just come upon the land. The verses date from the time which followed the death of Josiah at Megiddo at the hands of Neco, king of Egypt (II Kings 23:29-30). After his death the people of Judah proclaimed his son Jehoahaz king, but he remained on the throne for only three months. When Neco returned from Assyria he deposed Jehoahaz and placed Eliakim on the throne, changing his name to Jehoiakim (II Kings 23:31-35). Some destruction of the land may well have taken place during this period, and Judah remained subservient to Egypt until the defeat of that country in the battle of Carchemish (605 B.C.).

14. A **slave** might be one of two types: (*a*) purchased or secured as a war captive; or (*b*) born to parents who were in slavery, and thus a **homeborn servant** (see Exod. 21:2-4). The answer to the question is negative; Israel is not a slave at all, but a son, though its actions have made it appear to be a slave.

it; he "pursues nothingness," and by the desperate dialectic of his choosing, he "becomes nothing."

But this becoming nothing is a movement: it is a movement in which the false premise, on which the self is attempting to constitute itself, constantly reinstates itself with every effort which the spirit makes to be rid of its distress. It is, to employ a dubious neologism, an experience of nothingness *nothing-ing*. Desperation arises and feeds on itself; frustration frustrates itself; the pursuit of phantasms [4] becomes increasingly fantastic; self-affirmation achieves the negation of itself.

To turn away from **the fountain of living waters** is to experience the progressive breakdown of sustaining belief:

One is cut off from creative participation in a sphere of culture, one feels frustrated about something which one had passionately affirmed, one is driven from devotion to one object to devotion to another and again on to another, because the meaning of each of them vanishes and the creative eros is transformed into indifference or aversion. Everything is tried and nothing satisfies.[5]

Thus the people of Israel who, as Jeremiah says, not merely forsook the God who was the foun-

tain of living waters, but who committed the second evil of hewing out empty projections of their deepest concerns in the form of idols, were doubly deceived: as Skinner puts it, "they neither worshiped a real God, nor worshiped with their real selves." [6] They actually worshiped "Nothingness as the vacuum left by the [for them] nonexistent God." [7]

14-19. *Nothingness as Apostasy.*—Jeremiah's analysis takes another turn. He has used two terms for Israel's rebellion—"adultery" and "idolatry." He now uses a third—**apostasy.**

The appropriateness of the term, and its logical inclusion here as a dialectical extension of the argument already developed in the chapter, makes the technical question as to time of authorship and fitness to this immediate context a matter of secondary importance. The simple and obvious fact is that Israel has **become a prey** to the nations: **the lions** [Assyria] **have roared against** Israel, and the heaping misfortunes are plain to see. Jeremiah's question is, Why? Is it because Israel is a slave? Is it through having been conquered by an alien power? No. Or is it because Israel has been born into serfdom? Not at all. Israel's status

---

[4] Cf. Augustine *Confessions* VII. 1. 1.
[5] Tillich, *The Courage to Be*, pp. 47-48.

[6] *Prophecy and Religion*, p. 71.
[7] Cf. Helmut Kuhn, *The Encounter with Nothingness* (Chicago: Henry Regnery Co., 1949), p. xix; cf. p. xxii.

16 Also the children of Noph and Tahapanes have broken the crown of thy head.

17 Hast thou not procured this unto thyself, in that thou hast forsaken the LORD thy God, when he led thee by the way?

18 And now what hast thou to do in the way of Egypt, to drink the waters of Sihor? or what hast thou to do in the way of Assyria, to drink the waters of the river?

16 Moreover, the men of Memphis and Tah'panhes
have broken the crown of your head.

17 Have you not brought this upon yourself
by forsaking the LORD your God,
when he led you in the way?

18 And now what do you gain by going to Egypt,
to drink the waters of the Nile?
Or what do you gain by going to Assyria,
to drink the waters of the Eu-phra'tes?

---

16. Noph is **Memphis** in Egypt. **Tahpanhes** is Greek Daphnae, modern Tell Defenneh, on the eastern border of the Egyptian delta.

18. This verse refers to attempts to make alliances with, or secure favors from, Egypt and Assyria. Like Hosea (7:11-12) and Isaiah (30:1-5), Jeremiah opposed foreign alliances, partly because they usually brought with them religious influences from the other nation. Many have found it difficult to date this verse, but a brief review of the historical situation should enable us to place it with some measure of accuracy. Following the capture of Nineveh, the Assyrian capital, by the Babylonians and Medes in 612 B.C., Ashur-uballit II and some of his army fled to Harran, where they were able to continue a semblance of the old Assyrian kingdom for a time. Egypt was making a bid for renewed power, and was in alliance with Assyria (Babylonian Chronicle, ll. 61-75; see C. J. Gadd, *The Fall of Nineveh* [London: British Museum, 1923]). The Judean king, Jehoiakim, owed his throne to the Egyptians and was loyal to them as long as they remained powerful. We may place the events referred to here and in vss. 36-37 in the period between the death of Josiah in 609 and the battle of Carchemish in 605, when the Babylonians

---

was that of a favored son. No, says Jeremiah, you have clearly **brought this upon yourself by forsaking the LORD**, the fountain of living waters—by hewing out cisterns that are broken and empty.

The attempt to make up for this by going to the Nile (to Egypt) for water, or to the Euphrates (to Assyria), is fatuous. Hosea had already put this clearly (Hos. 7:11). Assuming that the verses are written sometime between the death of Josiah at Megiddo (609 B.C.) and the battle of Carchemish (605 B.C.) when Egypt was defeated, this fluttering first to one power and then to the other can at best be put down to political expediency. Jeremiah sees more deeply. A people that forsakes the Lord will know evil and bitterness. For the well-being of a people is founded upon its relationship with the living God; when the covenants of this relationship are broken, a necessary dialectic of decline sets in. When a desertion of the reality principle takes place, a loss of fullness will follow: all things suffer the perversion of the principles, and the people are set against themselves, both inwardly and outwardly.

No one, perhaps, has seen this principle so clearly as Athanasius who, in describing the condition of sin, pointed out that, intellectually,

the principle of understanding is lost and, morally, the principle of life is lost. A spiritual devitalization or wasting away of the life principle pervades all moral action. Like the branch cut off from the vine, it can only progressively wither away and die as the sap that is running within it is gradually used up and not replenished.

The same principle is apparent in Nicolas Berdyaev's comment on Dostoevski's novels:

Dostoievsky's Satan . . . is an empty spirit. . . . "Divided" people have a "devil." . . . This second self is the spirit of not-being, it represents the loss of the essence of personality and is the manifestation of an empty liberty, the freedom of nothingness. . . . Nothingness is immanent in evil.[8]

Much is involved here. It is this principle which accounts for the fact that evil overreaches itself and turns into its own opposite. At first, that is, one sees an immediate advantage in forsaking Yahweh in order to get help from Egypt; but the advantage is temporary. The moment of enhanced freedom and power quickly becomes vassalage and oppression. In the experience of the individual, the sense of freedom

[8] *Dostoievsky, An Interpretation* (tr. Donald Attwater; New York: Sheed & Ward, 1934), p. 110.

19 Thine own wickedness shall correct thee, and thy backslidings shall reprove thee: know therefore and see that *it is* an evil *thing* and bitter, that thou hast forsaken the Lord thy God, and that my fear *is* not in thee, saith the Lord God of hosts.

20 ¶ For of old time I have broken thy yoke, *and* burst thy bands; and thou saidst, I will not transgress; when upon every high hill and under every green tree thou wanderest, playing the harlot.

21 Yet I had planted thee a noble vine, wholly a right seed: how then art thou turned into the degenerate plant of a strange vine unto me?

19 Your wickedness will chasten you,
    and your apostasy will reprove you.
Know and see that it is evil and bitter
    for you to forsake the Lord your God;
the fear of me is not in you,
            says the Lord God of hosts.

20 "For long ago you broke your yoke
    and burst your bonds;
    and you said, 'I will not serve.'
Yea, upon every high hill
    and under every green tree
    you bowed down as a harlot.
21 Yet I planted you a choice vine,
    wholly of pure seed.
How then have you turned degenerate
    and become a wild vine?

administered a final defeat to the Egyptians and Assyrians (cf. Julius Lewy, *Forschungen zur alten Geschichte Vorderasiens* [Leipzig: J. C. Hinrichs, 1925; "Mitteilungen der Vorderasiatisch-Aegyptischen Gesellschaft"], especially p. 59, and W. F. Albright, "The Seal of Eliakim and the Latest Preëxilic History of Judah, with Some Observations on Ezekiel," *Journal of Biblical Literature,* LI [1932], 77-106; Lewy denies that there was a battle of Carchemish, but on insufficient grounds).

3. Depth of Israel's Sin (2:20-29)

This section emphasizes the fact that Israel's sin is of long standing and deep rooted, and it multiplies figures of speech in Oriental fashion to express the idea. Israel is

which comes with the rejection of the God-relation becomes self-assertion and self-will, and self-will leads to resistance, opposition, and strife. "Once man has set his foot upon the road of self-will and self-affirmation he must sacrifice the primacy of spirit and his original freedom and become the plaything of necessity and compulsion." [9] What begins as "freedom" ends as slavery.

It is precisely this that Jeremiah sees in his people's predicament. Apostasy is self-defeating. It carries within itself an implicit dialectic of contradiction. Therefore,

> Your wickedness will chasten you,
>   and your apostasy will reprove you.

Neither the person nor the people can successfully set themselves against God, just as one cannot successfully set oneself against the life principle without forfeiting life itself. There was a time when the people were faithful; but forgetfulness and rebellion set in. This way leads into punishment, correction, chastening, out of which comes a new remembering (in the Exile), followed by a return and new building and planting.

[9] *Ibid.,* p. 82.

To what extent Jeremiah grasps this total dialectic at this stage it is difficult to say. But it is not surprising that Irenaeus, when he sought to comprehend the mystery of the human condition, took his principle from these verses:

> It is impossible to live without the principle of life, but the means of life are found in fellowship with God. . . . God has shown His long-suffering during the apostasy of man, and man has been trained thereby, as the prophet says: "Thy apostasy shall reform thee" (Jer. ii. 19). For God arranged everything from the first with a view to the perfection of man, in order to edify him and reveal His own dispensations. . . . Thus man may eventually reach maturity, and, being ripened by such privileges, may see and comprehend God.[1]

There can be no doubt of Jeremiah's aim:

> See for yourself how sore it is for you
>   to abandon me,
> to have no reverence for me,
>   says the Lord (Moffatt).

20-29. The Seven Similes of Israel's Defection. —This section is possibly a poem written by Jeremiah at a later time. The appropriateness of its inclusion here is, however, apparent. It

[1] *Against the Heresies* IV. 20. 5; IV. 37. 7.

22 For though thou wash thee with nitre, and take thee much soap, *yet* thine iniquity is marked before me, saith the Lord GOD.

23 How canst thou say, I am not polluted, I have not gone after Baalim? See thy way in the valley, know what thou hast done: *thou art* a swift dromedary traversing her ways;

22 Though you wash yourself with lye
    and use much soap,
  the stain of your guilt is still before me,
                          says the Lord GOD.
23 How can you say, 'I am not defiled,
    I have not gone after the Ba'als'?
  Look at your way in the valley;
    know what you have done —
  a restive young camel interlacing her
    tracks,

---

compared to: an animal that has broken its yoke (vs. 20*a*); a **harlot** (vs. 20*b*); a vineyard that was planted with choice vines, but produced only wild ones (vs. 21; cf. Isa. 5:1-7); a person washing himself in vain with **lye** and **soap** (vs. 22); a **young camel** straying away from the herd, perhaps in heat (vs. 23); a **wild ass** in heat (vs. 24); and finally a **thief** (vs. 26).

23. The valley is probably the valley of Hinnom, in which child sacrifice and other abominable rites were practiced (7:31-32; 19:2-6; 32:35; II Kings 23:10).

---

exhibits the frequent tendency on the part of the Hebrew writer to crowd a number of similes together. Each of the figures of speech serves to reinforce the principle.

The rebellion of the people is likened (*a*) to the oxen that break their yoke and burst their thongs, asserting willfully that they **will not serve,** and (*b*) to a **harlot.** Being yoked to God is necessary to private and social well-being. Speaking as a Christian, it may be the source of both peace and power, inasmuch as this "fellowship" with the Eternal links the finite to the Infinite and the creature to his Creator. Yet even here, though the yoke may be easy (Matt. 11:30), there is work to be done and services to be rendered. There is obedience.

Here we may assume that the covenant signs and the covenant events comprise the yoke whereby the people had been united to Yahweh; and in the recurrence of this second figure the argument of the opening verses of this chapter is resumed. The capitulation of the Hebrews to the agricultural rites of the fertility cults of the Baals was for Jeremiah, as for the prophets who preceded him, a prostitution of true piety and a betrayal of the true God. It is this fundamental apostasy which has brought their miseries upon them; and, as Pedersen remarks, "by the apostasy Jeremiah means in the first place the sexual cult at the numerous sanctuaries in honour of the Baalim."[2] The two religions were, for the prophets, irreconcilable. For the covenantal relationship with Yahweh is substituted "a sensuous abandonment to the worship of nature."[3] No doubt some collision between the nomadic god, Yahweh, and the agricultural gods of the Canaanites

was inevitable; but the nominal assimilation of the Baals to Yahweh while capitulating in fact to the cult practices of the Baals was not the way. Not only primitive peoples, but many another culture and civilization has fallen prey to the seductions of "Nature" and the divinization of natural drives and desires. The peoples become **degenerate,** moral corruption saps the tegument of the community, a creeping guilt-consciousness perverts the forms. The extraordinary vividness of Jeremiah's phrase, **under every green tree,** derives from its intentional double-pointedness: the shrines and images were to be found on every hill and under every green tree, but the licentious rite evoked the licentious practice, already evident in the immoral and irresponsible delinquencies of the people. The similes become progressively sharp and scathing.

Once more the glance backward to the time when Yahweh had **planted** [them] **a choice vine,** when the seed was **pure,** enforces the figure (*c*) of **degeneration.** Few figures could be more apt than that of **a choice vine,** properly planted in the Lord's vineyard, which has become **wild.** Such intransigence is, at bottom, against nature, as the behavior of the people is against God. This same parable meant for Isaiah (5:1-7) that Israel had become estranged from the justice and righteousness of God. In Jeremiah's context it is a third form of rebellion: as such a vine is abnormal in the well-tended vineyard, so it is abnormal in the people.

"The dirty face that can't be washed clean"[4] indicates the depth of the apostasy. It is not something discoloring the surface life of the

[2] *Israel, Its Life and Culture, III-IV,* p. 560.
[3] Skinner, *op. cit.,* p. 67.

[4] Cf. Lawrence E. Toombs, *A Year with the Bible* (National Council of the Young Peoples' Unions of the United Church of Canada, 1953), p. 52.

24 A wild ass used to the wilderness, *that* snuffeth up the wind at her pleasure; in her occasion who can turn her away? all they that seek her will not weary themselves; in her month they shall find her.

25 Withhold thy foot from being unshod, and thy throat from thirst: but thou saidst, There is no hope: no; for I have loved strangers, and after them will I go.

26 As the thief is ashamed when he is found, so is the house of Israel ashamed; they, their kings, their princes, and their priests, and their prophets,

27 Saying to a stock, Thou *art* my father; and to a stone, Thou hast brought me

24 a wild ass used to the wilderness,
in her heat sniffing the wind!
　Who can restrain her lust?
None who seek her need weary themselves;
　in her month they will find her.
25 Keep your feet from going unshod
　and your throat from thirst.
But you said, 'It is hopeless,
　for I have loved strangers,
　and after them I will go.'

26 "As a thief is shamed when caught,
　so the house of Israel shall be shamed:
they, their kings, their princes,
　their priests, and their prophets,
27 who say to a tree, 'You are my father,'
　and to a stone, 'You gave me birth.'

27. This verse may refer to the ritualistic use of sacred standing stones (*maççēbhôth*) and wooden pillars (*'ashērîm*), the prophet ironically confusing the two, since the former were usually associated with the male deity and the latter with the female. Some scholars (e.g., Volz, Rudolph) believe that the reference is to even more primitive folk rites of worship of the numina in trees and stones.

people. The rebellion of the people is likened (*d*) to the stain of . . . guilt which cannot be washed away with soap or lye: the stain is too deep. The cleansing must come from within. "Sin," comments H. Wheeler Robinson, "springs from the inner attitude [whereby] the result of long continuance in the evil will is a hardening of the purpose, and indifference to the consequences, from which there is practically no hope of recovery in man himself." [5] The inward thrust of Jeremiah's religious thought is evident here; but Jeremiah begins to conceive of God in a new way, as we shall have frequent occasion to note, as a trier of the heart and kidneys (will and emotions) —similar to the depth perspective of the 139th psalm (vss. 1, 3, 23). "For the first time in Hebrew religion," holds Robinson, "we reach the declaration of this truth." [6] For the moment, however, the similes continue to dramatize the results of the apostasy, as we move from the wild vine and the stained flesh to the wandering camel.

The protest on the part of many that they have not [been] defiled, that they have not gone after the Baals, is disproved by a single glance at the valley of Hinnom, where child sacrifice was practiced. Such practices could prevail only in an environment of moral lassitude and religious indifference; but this itself is only symptomatic of a deeper problem—that of spiritual impotence and moral ambiguity. The people are (*e*) like a restive young camel interlacing her tracks. Without the driver the camel wanders hither and yon over the desert. "If you look at her tracks they are a crazy patchwork, going nowhere. So is a life which lacks the direction of God." [7]

This is a graphic figure, arising appositely enough from the peoples' own desert wanderings in the time when they were first found of God and guided into the promised land. Western literature substitutes the figure of the wood, or forest, for that of the desert.

　　In the midway of this our mortal life,
　　I found me in a gloomy wood, astray
　　Gone from the path direct. [8]

And Heidegger, recognizing the Nietzschean "death of God" in our time, describes our presence in the deep woods where the familiar trails to reality, which cross and recross each other, are swallowed up in thickets of confusion, and we are bound to seek today some fresh track, some new footprint of the gods, which may lead us out of our darkness. [9]

[7] Toombs, *op. cit.*, p. 52.
[8] Dante, *Inferno*, Canto I, ll. 1-3; tr. H. F. Cary. Cf. T. S. Eliot, "East Coker," from *Four Quartets*, Part II (London: Faber & Faber; New York: Harcourt, Brace & Co., 1943).
[9] Cf. *Holzwege* (Frankfurt a. M., V. Klostermann, 1950), epigraph, p. 3.

[5] *The Cross of Jeremiah* (London: Student Christian Movement Press, 1925), pp. 77-78.
[6] *Ibid.*, p. 78; cf. Jer. 17:10.

forth: for they have turned *their* back unto me, and not *their* face: but in the time of their trouble they will say, Arise, and save us.

28 But where *are* thy gods that thou hast made thee? let them arise, if they can save thee in the time of thy trouble: for *according to* the number of thy cities are thy gods, O Judah.

29 Wherefore will ye plead with me? ye all have transgressed against me, saith the LORD.

30 In vain have I smitten your children; they received no correction: your own sword hath devoured your prophets, like a destroying lion.

For they have turned their back to me,
    and not their face.
But in the time of their trouble they say,
    'Arise and save us!'
28 But where are your gods
        that you made for yourself?
    Let them arise, if they can save you,
        in your time of trouble;
    for as many as your cities
        are your gods, O Judah.

29 "Why do you complain against me?
    You have all rebelled against me,
                                    says the LORD.
30 In vain have I smitten your children,
        they took no correction;
    your own sword devoured your prophets
        like a ravening lion.

---

4. USELESSNESS OF YAHWEH'S CHASTENING (2:30-37)

Israel's sin is not due to any fault in her God, Yahweh, who has chastened Israel and has taken care of her, but in vain.

The predicament is the same. Israel experiences that double-mindedness, that vacillation, brought about by the attempt to mediate between irreconcilables. "Man has always," said Luther, "either God or an idol"; and the dialectic of the idols is invariably the same.

For this reason Jeremiah introduces, with merciless irony, the bitterest of his indictments. Judah has become (f) like **a wild ass or "a heifer running wild"** (Moffatt)—**in her heat sniffing the wind!** "Running wild," as Skinner describes it, "in the heat of sexual desire, utterly beyond the control of her owner, but easily approachable by the males who seek her."[1] So strong is Judah's idolatrous passion that she runs after her lovers, the false gods. "Do not run your feet bare," interjects Jeremiah, with fine irony, "or your throat dry" (Moffatt). But the people reply, to all these injunctions, "It is no use to talk; I am in love with foreign [strange] gods" (Moffatt), **and after them I will go.**

The pathos of this last protestation—**it is hopeless**—whereby the people are represented as having fallen so far into lustful passions that they cannot respond to the Lord's recall, serves merely to underscore once more, as in vs. 22, how locked in its own willfulness the will to self becomes when the relationship with God is broken. The projection of the self's absolute possibilities upon nothingness leads to the vicious involution of pursuing more and more desperately the absolute form of one's emptiness

[1] *Op. cit.,* p. 68, n. 1.

—"the shadow of the repudiated God."[2] Emptiness and guilt-consciousness will arise in the heart; and as the guilt feeling becomes increasingly acute the people will seek a scapegoat in the person of the one who most sharply opposes them—in this case, Jeremiah.

Meanwhile, their shame is (g) like that of **a thief** who, when caught, retains nothing of that which he stole and knows only the deepening chagrin of penalty, frustration, impotence, and shame. People, kings, princes, prophets, and priests—all who have worshiped either "a pole" or "a pillar" (Moffatt)—will be confounded like the thief when, in desperation **in the time of their trouble,** they appeal to Yahweh. The fatal ambiguity of their behavior is clear: they want to retain Yahweh as their national god, on whom they might count when the need should arise, but meanwhile they want to have gods in their own image. This attempt to turn **their back to God, but not their face,** will not do. If they make gods for themselves, these are the gods that should help them in the time of trouble. They have attempted to steal from God himself nothing less than his gifts and their own birthright. Yet despite all this, says Jeremiah, you still **complain against** him! "Godless, all, . . . rebels, all" (Moffatt). In the fine phrase of Moffatt's translation—"the Eternal protests."

29-37. The Eternal Protests.—The verses which follow do not greatly advance the argument. Yahweh submits, however, a bill of par-

[2] Kuhn, *Encounter with Nothingness,* p. xxii.

31 ¶ O generation, see ye the word of the LORD. Have I been a wilderness unto Israel? a land of darkness? wherefore say my people, We are lords; we will come no more unto thee?

32 Can a maid forget her ornaments, *or* a bride her attire? yet my people have forgotten me days without number.

33 Why trimmest thou thy way to seek love? therefore hast thou also taught the wicked ones thy ways.

34 Also in thy skirts is found the blood of the souls of the poor innocents: I have not found it by secret search, but upon all these.

35 Yet thou sayest, Because I am innocent, surely his anger shall turn from me. Behold, I will plead with thee, because thou sayest, I have not sinned.

36 Why gaddest thou about so much to change thy way? thou also shalt be ashamed of Egypt, as thou wast ashamed of Assyria.

37 Yea, thou shalt go forth from him, and thine hands upon thine head: for the LORD hath rejected thy confidences, and thou shalt not prosper in them.

---

31 And you, O generation, heed the word
　　of the LORD.
Have I been a wilderness to Israel,
　　or a land of thick darkness?
Why then do my people say, 'We are free,
　　we will come no more to thee'?
32 Can a maiden forget her ornaments,
　　or a bride her attire?
Yet my people have forgotten me
　　days without number.

33 "How well you direct your course
　　to seek lovers!
So that even to wicked women
　　you have taught your ways.
34 Also on your skirts is found
　　the lifeblood of guiltless poor;
you did not find them breaking in.
　　Yet in spite of all these things
35 you say, 'I am innocent;
　　surely his anger has turned from me.'
Behold, I will bring you to judgment
　　for saying, 'I have not sinned.'
36 How lightly you gad about,
　　changing your way!
You shall be put to shame by Egypt
　　as you were put to shame by Assyria.
37 From it too you will come away
　　with your hands upon your head,
for the LORD has rejected those in whom
　　you trust,
and you will not prosper by them.

---

34. The first half of this verse seems to refer to social injustice by which the poor were oppressed. The second half is very obscure in Hebrew, and the text may be corrupt. Volz emends אלה, **these things,** to ארח, "way," and renders vs. 34b: "Not by breaking in did I find it, but open upon every way"—i.e., Israel's sins were not committed in secret, but in the open where everyone might see. The emendation is plausible and gives a good sense to the verse.

36-37. For the circumstances on which these verses are based see Exeg. on vs. 18. The reference to **Assyria** here is probably to earlier alliances with that nation when she was at the height of her power following the accession of Tiglath-pileser III. The figure in vs. 37 is of people weeping in shame (cf. II Sam. 13:19).

---

ticulars with which to round out his pleading (vs. 29). Seeing the defection of Israel and Judah he had attempted to correct them through penalties and punishments. They would not be corrected. Prophets were slain, but they "would not heed" (Moffatt). Far from being a desert to them, he had brought them into a rich land; but the people chose to do as they pleased. How fickle and ironical is the people's behavior. A girl does not forget her **ornaments** and baubles, and **a bride** will take

infinite pains with **her attire;** but the bride of Yahweh, so attentive to herself, has forgotten him **days without number.** Not merely that, she has gone after other lovers. Her skirts have been found stained with the blood of the innocent poor. In spite of all this she continues to protest her innocence, which is itself a compounding of the sin, a refusal to be wrong, which Yahweh must condemn. The turning to Egypt for help is but a further sign of her fickleness; it can but lead to eventual shame

3 They say, If a man put away his wife, and she go from him, and become another man's, shall he return unto her again? shall not that land be greatly polluted? but thou hast played the harlot with many	3 "If[d] a man divorces his wife and she goes from him and becomes another man's wife, will he return to her? Would not that land be greatly polluted? You have played the harlot with many lovers;

[d] Gk Syr: Heb *Saying, If*

B. A Plea for Israel's Repentance (3:1–4:4)

This section continues the description of the sinfulness of Israel, but issues for the first time a plea for repentance and return to the Lord. It is widely recognized that 3:6-11, 15-18 break into the context and presuppose a different historical situation from the rest of the section. Some consider that these verses—or part of them—are from Jeremiah, but were spoken after the destruction of Jerusalem (especially vss. 15-18). It is more probable that they are entirely secondary (see below).

The general theme is the "return" of Israel. The various parts of the section are brought together because of the frequent occurrence of the verb שׁוּב, **turn, return,** and adjectives derived from it. It is the catchword by which editors made additions to the oracles of Jeremiah. But the word has several different meanings: (a) it is used of a husband's return to his wife in 3:1a, and of Israel's return to God in 3:1b, 7, 10, 12, 14a, 22; 4:1; (b) משבה, **faithless** or **backsliding** is used in 3:6, 8, 11-12, and שׁובבים with the same meaning in 3:14a; and (c) the idea of a return from exile occurs in 3:14, 18, with other Hebrew words, the editor having misunderstood the meaning of the word שׁוּב in previous verses. In the verses which are from Jeremiah a contrast is drawn between feigned or superficial repentance and true return to God.

The section should be divided according to subject matter as follows: (a) 3:1-5, 19-20—Israel as a faithless wife has committed harlotry and cannot expect to return to Yahweh with only facile repentance; (b) 3:6-11—Judah is worse than the Northern Kingdom, Israel, but has not learned from her punishment; (c) 3:14b-18—prediction of a future return to Jerusalem; and (d) 3:12-14a, 21–4:4—a plea for genuine repentance.

1. Israel, the Faithless Wife (3:1-5)

Israel is depicted as a wife who has been faithless to her husband. The figure of harlotry is used to describe the false, Canaanitish worship of the Hebrews, as in Hosea

---

and dismay, of which the hand on the head is the sign (vs. 37; cf. II Sam. 13:19). It is strange, if not pathetic, that the people should expect to be sustained by a power which the Lord has already rejected.

Harlotry, idolatry, apostasy—these three; but the foundational term of Judah's defection is apostasy.

3:1–4:4. *Nevertheless, Return!*—Jeremiah's appropriation from Hosea of what Emil Brunner has called "the most daring parable of the love of God"[3]—namely, Gomer's unfaithfulness as an analogue of the deep apostasy of Israel—illustrates as forcibly as any human analogy could that Hosea and Jeremiah regard God's covenant with Israel as "the outflow of His eternal Love."[4]

[3] *The Christian Doctrine of God,* tr. Olive Wyon (Philadelphia: Westminster Press, 1950), I, 184.
[4] *Ibid.*

I led them with cords of compassion,
with the bands of love (Hos. 11:4),

wrote Hosea. "Return, O Israel, to the Lord your God" (Hos. 14:1). Nothing shows more clearly the proximity of Jeremiah's early message to that of Hosea, not to say his indebtedness thereto, than the turn which Yahweh's plea (2:9) to the people now takes. In spite of all that they have done—their infidelities, their backslidings, their idolatries, their defections—they are now invited to return.

3:1-5. *Casual Repentance and the Harlot's Brow.*—Any turning, however, must be thorough and complete. The possibility of it in the case of Judah seems remote. Even under the circumstances of divorce, whereby the wife has married a second time, the woman is regarded as defiled so far as her former husband is concerned. It is hardly likely that he will return to

lovers; yet return again to me, saith the LORD.

2 Lift up thine eyes unto the high places, and see where thou hast not been lain with. In the ways hast thou sat for them, as the Arabian in the wilderness; and thou hast polluted the land with thy whoredoms and with thy wickedness.

3 Therefore the showers have been withholden, and there hath been no latter rain; and thou hadst a whore's forehead, thou refusedst to be ashamed.

and would you return to me?
                says the LORD.

2 Lift up your eyes to the bare heights, and see!
Where have you not been lain with?
By the waysides you have sat awaiting lovers
like an Arab in the wilderness.
You have polluted the land
with your vile harlotry.

3 Therefore the showers have been withheld,
and the spring rain has not come;
yet you have a harlot's brow,
you refuse to be ashamed.

and other prophets, partly because of the belief that Yahweh was the true "husband" of Israel and partly because the false worship frequently included licentious rites in which religious harlots (*qedhēshôth*) played a part.

3:1. This verse has its background in the law of Deut. 24:1-4, whereby a divorced woman who married a second time was not permitted to return to her first husband if the second husband also divorced her or died. Here Israel is pictured as a faithless wife who has committed harlotry with many lovers, but seeks a casual return to Yahweh. The LXX has a different reading in the latter part of this verse: "Will she return to him? Will not that woman be greatly polluted?" This may represent the original text, as it is more appropriate to the figure of divorce and remarriage than is the M.T.

And would you return to me? The Hebrew here uses an infinitive absolute, which can stand for various forms of the finite verb. The KJV translates as an imperative: **yet return again to me.** The context indicates, however, that this is a rebuke to Israel for seeking to return to Yahweh with only facile repentance, as elaborated in vss. 4-5. The invitation to return comes later (vs. 12) in what was originally a separate poem, or separate strophe of the same poem. The RSV correctly renders the Hebrew as a question.

3. The prophets believed that Yahweh sometimes withheld **rain** as a chastening for sin, seeking through punishment to bring Israel back; yet Israel has **a harlot's brow,** too hardened for shame (cf. Amos 4:6-12).

her. The case of Judah is far worse. She has never been divorced, but has **played the harlot with many lovers. Yet would you return to me?** exclaims Yahweh. Is it credible that Yahweh would receive her? Indeed, it is because of this adulterous behavior, this obsession with the Canaanite gods, this wanton harlotry upon the hills and **by the waysides** that has brought every kind of pollution upon the land, **that the showers have been withheld,** the people feel the drouth of spirit and the inner emptiness (cf. 5:24; Amos 4:7). Many a mystic has known this arid "dryness"; there are times of decomposition and decay when civilizations have known it too.

But Israel is not ashamed. She has the **harlot's brow,** which brazenly defies her accusers. Even now, while she pursues her overt practice of betrayal, she employs solicitous language, saying "Dear bridegroom of my youth!" (Moffatt)

and thinking "he will not be angry for ever" (Moffatt). So Judah says, it being kept in mind that the masses of the people, as well as their leaders, did not discriminate the fundamental religious differences between Yahweh and the Baals as sharply as the prophets did. This is what she says, but what she does "is vilest of the vile" (Moffatt). They want to have it both ways: in spite of their constant fears of military subjection, and in spite of inner anxiety and moral debilitation everywhere, they refuse to examine themselves to effect the wholehearted turning. The **harlot's brow** betrays not love but the hardened inability to love. And as for the spontaneous feel for love which children have, before the brow is hardened, how wistful is the thought of Yahweh who, in Jeremiah's terms, would have set his daughter, Judah, among his sons, to receive an equal portion of his heritage —"a pleasant land . . . most beauteous of all

4 Wilt thou not from this time cry unto me, My father, thou *art* the guide of my youth?

5 Will he reserve *his anger* for ever? will he keep *it* to the end? Behold, thou hast spoken and done evil things as thou couldest.

6 ¶ The Lord said also unto me in the days of Josiah the king, Hast thou seen *that* which backsliding Israel hath done? she is gone up upon every high mountain and under every green tree, and there hath played the harlot.

7 And I said after she had done all these *things,* Turn thou unto me. But she returned not. And her treacherous sister Judah saw *it.*

4 Have you not just now called to me,
    'My father, thou art the friend of my
        youth —
5 will he be angry for ever,
    will he be indignant to the end?'
Behold, you have spoken,
    but you have done all the evil that you
        could."

6 The Lord said to me in the days of King Josi'ah: "Have you seen what she did, that faithless one, Israel, how she went up on every high hill and under every green tree, and there played the harlot? 7 And I thought, 'After she has done all this she will return to me'; but she did not return,

4-5. These verses are an example of the facile and casual repentance of the people, relying upon God's good nature, spoken with the lips but involving no change of heart and action. The term **father** was sometimes used by a young wife of her husband (Volz).

2. Judah Worse than Israel (3:6-11)

6-11. These verses present a different subject from the preceding. **Israel** here means the Northern Kingdom which had suffered destruction in 721 b.c. Some scholars think that this passage shows Jeremiah's special interest in northern Israel, arising from his

nations" (vs. 19). Then the figure returns (vs. 20, though the context is uncertain) to the familiar picture of the faithless wife. J. R. Gillies' account is plausible: "The nation, as individuals, were Jahveh's apostate children; as a community, His faithless wife."[5]

6-11. *The Ambivalent Return.*—This section, frequently regarded as not written by Jeremiah at all because of its apparent similarity in theme to the verses preceding, is not without significance.[6] The comparison of Judah with Israel is very pertinent if vs. 10 may be taken as referring to the attempts at reform under King Josiah. It would appear that this is carefully pointed out: **in the days of King Josiah** the prophet is asked whether he has seen what Israel did. Jeremiah has seen quite well, as indeed have all the people of Judah. For approximately a hundred years have passed since Israel fell at the hands of Assyria. At that time she was sent away **with a decree of divorce.** Israel had turned her back on Yahweh. She had **played the harlot** in the places of the Baals—**on every high hill and under every green tree.** Yahweh had sent prophet after prophet to bring her back, and hoped she would return; but she

would not. All this her sister Judah witnessed. All this she saw, and all its consequences. And so she is doubly guilty. In spite of what she has seen, she herself, as Calvin says, has "surpassed by her levity and lustfulness the whoredoms of her sister."[7]

The ambivalence of Judah's attitude is implied. And if the **pretence** refers to the Deuteronomic reforms under Josiah, the passage is very strong. The turning of the reform, in which the leaders of the people joined, did not go deep enough. No doubt Josiah himself was sincere, and very many of the others; but for the bulk of the people the reform was too official, too designed, a fact which, no doubt, they piously dissimulated even from themselves. Through public espousal of the national movement they appeared to turn back to Yahweh, yet all the while their back was turned. The play upon words here has been noted by S. R. Driver.[8] The word translated "faithless" (vss. 6, 11), and sometimes rendered "backsliding," contains a play upon the two senses of the Hebrew root—implying both to turn the back on Yahweh and to turn back to him. This describes superbly the inner ambivalence at the

[5] *Jeremiah, the Man and His Message* (London: Hodder & Stoughton, 1907), p. 59.
[6] Cf. Sigmund Mowinckel, *Prophecy and Tradition* (Oslo: Jacob Dybwad, 1946), p. 63.

[7] *Commentaries on the Book of the Prophet Jeremiah,* tr. John Owen (Grand Rapids: Eerdmans, 1950), I, 168.
[8] *The Book of the Prophet Jeremiah* (New York: Hodder & Stoughton, 1906), p. 340, n. 6.

8 And I saw, when for all the causes whereby backsliding Israel committed adultery, I had put her away, and given her a bill of divorce; yet her treacherous sister Judah feared not, but went and played the harlot also.

9 And it came to pass through the lightness of her whoredom, that she defiled the land, and committed adultery with stones and with stocks.

10 And yet for all this her treacherous sister Judah hath not turned unto me with her whole heart, but feignedly, saith the LORD.

11 And the LORD said unto me, The backsliding Israel hath justified herself more than treacherous Judah.

12 ¶ Go and proclaim these words toward the north, and say, Return, thou back-

and her false sister Judah saw it. 8 She saw that for all the adulteries of that faithless one, Israel, I had sent her away with a decree of divorce; yet her false sister Judah did not fear, but she too went and played the harlot. 9 Because harlotry was so light to her, she polluted the land, committing adultery with stone and tree. 10 Yet for all this her false sister Judah did not return to me with her whole heart, but in pretence, says the LORD."

11 And the LORD said to me, "Faithless Israel has shown herself less guilty than false Judah. 12 Go, and proclaim these words toward the north, and say,

'Return, faithless Israel,

                says the LORD.

---

own residence in the land of Benjamin. Yet we are compelled to agree with Duhm, Erbt, Skinner, *et al.*, that the passage is non-Jeremianic because Jeremiah usually employs the word "Israel" to mean all the Hebrews, or Judah; because he nowhere else expresses the view that the Northern Kingdom was better than Judah; and because the whole passage shows close affinities with Ezek. 16:44-63; 23:1-49, to which it is indebted. These verses were written by an editor (probably the Deuteronomist) who compiled them as an introduction to the summons in vss. 12-14 for the northern tribes to return from their captivity. He is responsible also for the introductory lines in vs. 12 and perhaps also for vs. 14b.

3. CALL TO RETURN TO GOD (3:12-14a)

These verses are genuine, though the editor (just referred to above) has misunderstood the meaning of **Return**. Jeremiah meant it as a plea to all the Hebrews to return to God in true confession of sin and repentance; the editor understood it as a summons to the Northern Kingdom to return from exile (vs. 14b). The thought is continued in vss. 21-25.

12. Merciful is a translation of *ḥāṣidh*, which is used of God only here and in Ps. 145:17. It is used frequently of men in the psalms, where it may be translated "godly,"

---

heart of the people. It becomes also the deliberated strategy of the use of the term "return" throughout the rest of ch. 3 and in 4:1. With the example of Israel before her, this moral ambivalence but compounds the guilt of Judah. How far-reaching the effects of this duplicity have gone is indicated in vs. 9. Of course, says Calvin, "the land, we know, was in itself pure, and could contract no pollution from the vices of men." [9] But this is not altogether certain. There is a good deal of evidence to support the view that the Hebrew regarded the earth as being formed for man, who was to cultivate it and "serve" it, and the earth was dependent upon him. Thus man's intransigency brings a

curse upon the earth (Gen. 3:17) and it becomes "corrupted" (Gen. 6:11, 12) as man himself becomes corrupt. Thus the land may well "degenerate" under its inhabitants (Isa. 24:5; Num. 35:33; Ps. 106:38). The repetition of this phrase in Jeremiah may, therefore, be more than rhetorical. [10]

In any case, it carries through efficiently here to the double-entendre of soil pollution and the adultery with stone and tree (feminine and masculine idols); and thereby to the strong indictment: **Faithless Israel has shown herself less guilty than false Judah.**

12-14. Turn Again, O Turncoat Israel!— The efficacy of this wordplay appears in the

[9] *Loc. cit.*

[10] Cf. Buber, *The Prophetic Faith*, p. 90.

sliding Israel, saith the LORD; *and* I will not cause mine anger to fall upon you: for I *am* merciful, saith the LORD, *and* I will not keep *anger* for ever.

13 Only acknowledge thine iniquity, that thou hast transgressed against the LORD thy God, and hast scattered thy ways to the strangers under every green tree, and ye have not obeyed my voice, saith the LORD.

14 Turn, O backsliding children, saith the LORD; for I am married unto you: and I will take you one of a city, and two of a family, and I will bring you to Zion:

15 And I will give you pastors according to mine heart, which shall feed you with knowledge and understanding.

16 And it shall come to pass, when ye be multiplied and increased in the land, in those days, saith the LORD, they shall say no more, The ark of the covenant of the LORD: neither shall it come to mind; neither shall they remember it; neither shall they visit *it;* neither shall *that* be done any more.

I will not look on you in anger,
for I am merciful,
says the LORD;
I will not be angry for ever.
13 Only acknowledge your guilt,
that you rebelled against the LORD your God
and scattered your favors among strangers under every green tree,
and that you have not obeyed my voice,
says the LORD.
14 Return, O faithless children,
says the LORD;
for I am your master;
I will take you, one from a city and two from a family,
and I will bring you to Zion.

15 " 'And I will give you shepherds after my own heart, who will feed you with knowledge and understanding. 16 And when you have multiplied and increased in the land, in those days, says the LORD, they shall no more say, "The ark of the covenant of the LORD." It shall not come to mind, or be remembered, or missed; it shall not be

---

"saint," or "holy." Yahweh is *ḥaṣîdh* in that he manifests his "steadfast love" (*ḥeṣedh*) toward Israel.

14. I am married unto you is a more suitable translation in this context than **I am your master,** though one must remember that the husband was thought of as being master over his wife.

4. PREDICTION OF RETURN FROM EXILE (3:14b-18)

These verses are editorial, expressing ideas that are generally foreign to Jeremiah but are frequently found in exilic and postexilic apocalyptic passages (so Duhm, Cornill, Erbt, Skinner; Peake considers vss. 14-15, 17-18 secondary; Volz, vss. 16-18b; and Rudolph, vss. 17a-18).

15. Shepherds after my own heart (on **pastors** see Exeg. on 2:8) are rulers obedient to God (cf. Ezek. 34).

16. Nothing is known definitely concerning the time when **the ark of the covenant of the LORD** was removed from the temple in Jerusalem. If Lam. 2:1 means by "his

---

verses which follow (12-14): "Turn again, Oh, turncoat Israel"; [11] or again, "Turn back, ye back-turning sons." [12] While the redactor has interpreted this invitation to return as implying a return from exile (vs. 14b), Jeremiah's message went far deeper. Jeremiah's inherited affection for the tribes of Rachel—Anathoth having been located in the territory of Benjamin, though now in the kingdom of Judah—is sufficient to account, perhaps, for the proclamation of these words **toward the north.** More

[11] Gillies, *op. cit.,* p. 58.
[12] Ball, *Prophecies of Jeremiah,* p. 119.

than once he expressed his longing that their exiled children might return (cf. 9:15-20; 31:4-6). The meaning here is profounder. The invitation implies that the ten tribes had gone into exile through their own choosing. That, indeed, is essentially the case, from Jeremiah's standpoint—so closely is the external misfortune of the people tied in with the pivotal turning away from God.

15-18. *The Promise of After Days.*—Gillies remarks, at the close of his discussion of the preceding verses, that "what the people needed in Jeremiah's day was, not the urgency either

17 At that time they shall call Jerusalem the throne of the LORD; and all the nations shall be gathered unto it, to the name of the LORD, to Jerusalem: neither shall they walk any more after the imagination of their evil heart.

18 In those days the house of Judah shall walk with the house of Israel, and they shall come together out of the land of

made again. 17 At that time Jerusalem shall be called the throne of the LORD, and all nations shall gather to it, to the presence of the LORD in Jerusalem, and they shall no more stubbornly follow their own evil heart. 18 In those days the house of Judah shall join the house of Israel, and together they shall come from the land of the north

---

footstool" the ark of the covenant (cf. Ps. 132:7; I Chr. 28:2), then it apparently was taken to Babylon by Nebuchadrezzar in 587 B.C. This verse could have been written by Jeremiah, but it probably dates from a later time, along with the rest of the passage, vss. 15-18.

17. For **Jerusalem** (or the temple) as **the throne of the LORD**, cf. 14:21; 17:12; and for the idea of this verse cf. Isa. 2:2-4; Mic. 4:1-4. **Stubbornly follow their own evil heart** is a favorite expression of Jeremiah, but he applies it to Israel rather than the foreign nations.

18. The union of Judah and Israel was a frequent theme of later apocalyptists (cf. Ezek. 37:16-28; Isa. 11:12-14).

---

of patriot or of prophet, but some new and more spiritual conception of Jahveh." [1] This is undoubtedly true. One may go further and say that this is precisely what was moving in the heart of Jeremiah, compelling and driving him on despite opposition, rejection, and abuse, even as it would later drive Job. And while these immediate verses are generally regarded as stemming from a later period, they are relevant as forecasting the actual movement of Jeremiah's thought. If the catastrophe through which the people were passing should become profound enough, it was conceivable on Jeremiah's grounds that a new universal hope could grow out of it.

The factor to focus upon, therefore, is not the historical question of return from the Exile (vs. 18), or the prediction of the same, but the profile of the promise. Four things are promised. First, they will be given **shepherds**, i.e., rulers of the Davidic line of shepherd kings, **who will feed** [them] **with knowledge and understanding.** Second, they will multiply and increase (cf. Gen. 1:28). Third, the ark of the covenant will be forgotten and Jerusalem will become the throne of God for all the nations. And fourth, the people **shall no more stubbornly follow their own evil heart.**

The **knowledge and understanding** implied here would seem to be a dimension deeper than instruction and "sense" (Moffatt). It is again knowledge within the context of the covenant idea, and within the context of the dialogue between God and men. Return to the knowledge of the mercy and righteousness of

God (must we not say "love" in Hosea's sense?) is necessary to the promise. Once they are known of God, and have the understanding of their calling before him, the early promises will be renewed (in this case, that of Gen. 1:28). Then shall men "no longer speak of 'the ark'"; it "shall never enter their minds, . . . they shall never miss it" (Moffatt). For they will have outgrown the localized God-idea. The magical influence of the visible symbol will no more be necessary to sustain the sense of the presence of God. Jerusalem will become the universal symbol of Yahweh's throne to which all the nations shall respond.

The anticipation here of Jeremiah's proclamation of the new covenant (cf. 23:1-8; 31:31-34), with its sense that "no longer shall each man teach his neighbor and each his brother, saying, 'Know the LORD,' for they shall all know me" (31:34), supports the view of Peake that vs. 16, at least, is from the hand or dictation of Jeremiah.

The fall of Jerusalem and the destruction of the Temple had been prophetic certainties to Jeremiah long before they happened, and he must have meditated on the future relations between Yahweh and His people. The popular religion identified the ark with the presence of Yahweh. Such a conception must have been utterly repulsive to Jeremiah, with his spiritual view of religion. The blessed future to which he looked forward was the era of the New Covenant, the ark was the ark of the old covenant; how natural for the dissolution of the covenant to be associated with that of its material embodiment! [2]

[1] Op. cit., pp. 58-59.

[2] Jeremiah and Lamentations, I, 109.

the north to the land that I have given for an inheritance unto your fathers.

19 But I said, How shall I put thee among the children, and give thee a pleasant land, a goodly heritage of the hosts of nations? and I said, Thou shalt call me, My father; and shalt not turn away from me.

20 ¶ Surely *as* a wife treacherously departeth from her husband, so have ye dealt treacherously with me, O house of Israel, saith the LORD.

21 A voice was heard upon the high places, weeping *and* supplications of the

to the land that I gave your fathers for a heritage.

19 " 'I thought
how I would set you among my sons,
and give you a pleasant land,
a heritage most beauteous of all nations.
And I thought you would call me, My Father,
and would not turn from following me.
20 Surely, as a faithless wife leaves her husband,
so have you been faithless to me, O house of Israel,

says the LORD.' "

21 A voice on the bare heights is heard,
the weeping and pleading of Israel's sons,

---

5. ISRAEL'S INFIDELITY (3:19-20)

This section, which continues the thought of vss. 1-5, originally formed a single poem (or strophe of a poem) with those verses; it ended, as it began (3:1), with the picture of Israel as a faithless wife.

19. I would set you among my sons: The pronoun **you** is feminine in Hebrew. Israel is here considered as a daughter to whom Yahweh wished to give an inheritance like that of sons, contrary to Hebrew practice (Num. 27:1-8; however, cf. Job 42:15). The **heritage** is the land of Palestine, **a pleasant land,** . . . **most beauteous of all nations.**

6. SUMMONS TO GENUINE REPENTANCE (3:21–4:4)

The section closes with a plea. Israel is called to return to the Lord in heartfelt penitence (continuing the thought of 3:12-14*a*). The Israelites **on the bare heights,** where their false worship of pagan gods took place, are invited to return to Yahweh,

---

This last observation has to do with the disappearance of the ark. No one knows how or when it disappeared. According to Pss. 24 and 68 it was there until comparatively late times, as late as King Josiah, if the account in II Chr. 35:3 can be accepted. It is not mentioned among the spoils taken from the temple by Nebuzaradan (52:17-23); nor is it listed in the treasure taken by Nebuchadrezzar at the time of Jehoiachin's surrender. It evidently disappeared in Jeremiah's days, and was missed by the people. But the people's repetition of **the ark of the covenant of the LORD** receives from Jeremiah the same scornful irony as the pious clamor of that other phrase, "The temple of the LORD, the temple of the LORD" (7:4).

The implications here are unmistakable: Jeremiah grows, and he looks forward to the day when the people also will have grown, to a conception of God and his relation with men which does not depend upon the tangible forms of mediation, but upon a "direct and first-hand

knowledge of God." [3] When this day arrives the ark, and the reactionary forms of religion symbolized by it, will have become obsolete (cf. Heb. 8:13). It is one of those astonishing ironies of literary history which led the anonymous but Pharisaic author of II Maccabees to relate (2:4) how Jeremiah himself took both the tabernacle and the ark and the altar of incense and hid them away in a cave on the mountain which Moses had climbed to catch his glimpse of the promised land. "Legend had no scruple," comments Moffatt, "in transforming a prophet who was radically indifferent, if not hostile, to the ritual of the temple into a pious conservative." [4]

3:21–4:4. *Conditions of the Return.*—As we now move into the climax of the pleading with the people which began in ch. 2, we are able to

[3] *Ibid.*, p. 110.
[4] In R. H. Charles, ed., *The Apocrypha and Pseudepigrapha of the Old Testament in English* (Oxford: Clarendon Press, 1913), I, 133.

children of Israel: for they have perverted their way, *and* they have forgotten the Lord their God.

22 Return, ye backsliding children, *and* I will heal your backslidings. Behold, we come unto thee; for thou *art* the Lord our God.

23 Truly in vain *is salvation hoped for* from the hills, *and from* the multitude of mountains: truly in the Lord our God *is* the salvation of Israel.

24 For shame hath devoured the labor of our fathers from our youth; their flocks and their herds, their sons and their daughters.

25 We lie down in our shame, and our confusion covereth us: for we have sinned against the Lord our God, we and our fathers, from our youth even unto this day, and have not obeyed the voice of the Lord our God.

---

because they have perverted their way,
    they have forgotten the Lord their
      God.
22 "Return, O faithless sons,
    I will heal your faithlessness."
  "Behold, we come to thee;
    for thou art the Lord our God.
23 Truly the hills are a delusion,
    the orgies on the mountains.
Truly in the Lord our God
    is the salvation of Israel.
24 "But from our youth the shameful thing has devoured all for which our fathers labored, their flocks and their herds, their sons and their daughters. 25 Let us lie down in our shame, and let our dishonor cover us; for we have sinned against the Lord our God, we and our fathers, from our youth even to this day; and we have not obeyed the voice of the Lord our God."

---

their true husband and true father. Then follow the words (3:22*b*-25) which the Israelites should say as they acknowledge their sin and return to Yahweh (for the form cf. Hos. 6:1-3; 14:2-3). The divine answer is contained in 4:1-4, which describes in detail the nature of true repentance. The prophet believed that the people could not return to God with the expectation of being received by him, unless they should remove their idols (4:1), learn to swear their oaths only by Yahweh, thus recognizing him as the only God (4:2), and experience a genuine conversion of the heart, expressed by two figures derived from the farmer's plowing and the rite of circumcision (4:3).

23. **The hills are a delusion:** The reference is to the pagan rites which usually took place on the heights and often included veritable **orgies.**

---

appreciate the insight of the French critic, Jean Jacques Joubert: "With God it is necessary to be neither a scholar nor a philosopher, but child, slave, pupil, and above all, a poet." [5] This section opens with a very moving poem in which Jeremiah projects a vision of the repentance of the people, whereby both Israel and Judah might be recovered into the well-being and bounty of the Lord. It is in dialogue form. The answer to the people is found in 4:3-4, one of the great passages in the book of Jeremiah.

3:21-25. The Colloquy with God.—Several things should be noted here. The sober movement of the poem, with its tone of deep sorrow, indicates that it is intentionally composed in such a way as to exhibit authentic repentance as over against those shallow and faithless avowals already indicated above. The suggestion that Jeremiah adopts the form of the temple liturgy in order to achieve this is a further witness to

his great poetic skill. In his capacity to exploit the associational virtues of that which the people know (as, for example, in T. S. Eliot's use of the *Book of Common Prayer,* or of the *terza rima* in the Dante section of his "Little Gidding") the mark of true craftsmanship is seen. The same should be noted of the poet's intentional borrowing from Hos. 14:1-4; 6:1, a device so universally employed as to have led T. S. Eliot to say, "One of the surest of tests is the way in which a poet borrows." [6] Especially is this important in a disintegrating age, when the quotational component, whether in poetry or music, is woven into a new unity, thus recollecting (or "recalling," Jer. 2:2) the significant or relevant past.

The picture that we have, then, is that of the people weeping. The voice from the bare heights, with its sobs and muffled cries, is evoked by a twofold recognition: (*a*) that **they** [the people who have gone after the strange gods]

---

[5] *Pensées*, Titre I, No. xciii (Edition Complete; Paris: Perrin et Cie, 1928), p. 27.

[6] *The Sacred Wood, Essays on Poetry and Criticism* (3rd ed.; London: Methuen & Co., 1932), p. 125.

4 If thou wilt return, O Israel, saith the Lord, return unto me: and if thou wilt put away thine abominations out of my sight, then shalt thou not remove.

2 And thou shalt swear, The Lord liveth, in truth, in judgment, and in righteousness; and the nations shall bless themselves in him, and in him shall they glory.

4 "If you return, O Israel,
                    says the Lord,
   to me you should return.
If you remove your abominations from
      my presence,
   and do not waver,
2 and if you swear, 'As the Lord lives,'
   in truth, in justice, and in uprightness,
   then nations shall bless themselves in
      him,
   and in him shall they glory."

4:1. The prophet had begun in 3:1 with the thought of a facile and superficial "return" which was not acceptable to God; he now comes to speak of the nature of a true **return**. It must be far more than mere lip service to Yahweh (3:4-5); it must affect the actions and the heart.

2. Among the Hebrews an oath was considered a very powerful thing; to swear by a deity was to recognize its existence and to invoke its power. The Israelites had been swearing by deities other than Yahweh; now they must take their oaths by Yahweh alone, and do so **in truth, in justice, and in uprightness.**

---

have perverted their way, by which perversion they have set themselves against both the true God and themselves; and (b) **they have forgotten . . . their God,** whereby they depart progressively from him. The consciousness of this twofold character of their defection has produced at last, after Yahweh's long pleading, the godly sorrow. Remorse has passed over into repentance.

The depth of this movement must not be underestimated. What we recognize in these opening verses is sorrow, the awakened conscience, and supplication. The divine answer, which follows, would seem to be an instantaneous response. It is, says Alexander Maclaren,

like the action of the father in the parable of the prodigal son. . . . We see here how God meets the penitent with a love that recognizes all his sin and yet is love. It is not rebuke or reproach that lies in that designation, "backsliding children." It is tenderest mercy that lets us see that He knows exactly what we are, and yet promises His love and forgiveness. He loves us sinners with a love that beckons us back to Himself, with a love that promises healing.[7]

The quotation employed by Jeremiah for the response of the Lord is, of course, from Hos. 14:1-4. This is important; for in it Jeremiah reiterates once more the line of prophetic development in which he stands. The divine promise of Hosea, "I will heal their faithlessness" (Hos. 14:4), is not to be found in Amos. It is to be found under the sign of the God who is Loyal-in-Love, and not elsewhere.

[7] *Isaiah and Jeremiah,* II, 256.

4:1-2. The Conditions of the Unconditioned. —"The sins which man commits," the Rabbi Bunam is reported to have said, "—those are not his great crime. Temptation is powerful and his strength is slight! The great crime of man is that he can turn at every moment, and does not do so."[8]

This is the pathos of Israel's condition. The suffering and sorrow and compassion and hope of the prophet Hosea preside like a beneficent but inescapable presence over these early and penetrating utterances of the young Jeremiah. It is Hosea whose own experience has guided him into a sure sense of the unfathomable mercy and tenderness of God. The outflowing love of God, for Jeremiah as for Hosea, is not based upon any special merit in the people of Israel, nor upon anything which they have done to deserve it.

What is deeply anticipated here is that inner secret of the new covenant to come: "In this is love, not that we loved God but that he loved us" (I John 4:10). God is the unconditioned; he gives of himself by virtue of the fact that he is that which he does.[9] At the same time it is clear that the creature is not compelled to return. If he would return the first condition is quite simply that he should return. He should turn himself to the healer. This does not mean, of course, that he is not moved by God to re-

[8] Martin Buber, *Tales of the Hasidim* (tr. Olga Marx; New York: Schocken Books, 1948), II, 257.
[9] Cf. Norman H. Snaith, *The Distinctive Ideas of the Old Testament* (London: Epworth Press, 1944), p. 48. "The Hebrew verb *hayah* does not mean 'to be,' so much as 'to come to be.' Hebrew has no real verb of 'being,' but one of 'becoming.' The verb is active and not static."

3 ¶ For thus saith the LORD to the men of Judah and Jerusalem, Break up your fallow ground, and sow not among thorns.

4 Circumcise yourselves to the LORD, and take away the foreskins of your heart, ye men of Judah and inhabitants of Jerusalem; lest my fury come forth like fire, and burn that none can quench *it,* because of the evil of your doings.

3 For thus says the LORD to the men of Judah and to the inhabitants of Jerusalem:
"Break up your fallow ground,
    and sow not among thorns.
4 Circumcise yourselves to the LORD,
    remove the foreskin of your hearts,
O men of Judah and inhabitants of Jerusalem;
lest my wrath go forth like fire,
    and burn with none to quench it,
        because of the evil of your doings."

---

3. The latter part of this verse is probably quoted directly from Hos. 10:12. Repentance must be as thoroughgoing as the plowing up of fallow ground, which removes the thorns and prepares the way for new seed.

4. Through physical circumcision (as a rite of initiation, probably in very early times at puberty) an individual became a member of the people of Israel; but only a real change of heart can make him acceptable to God (cf. 9:26; Rom. 2:25).

---

turn. But this God does, as Irenaeus held, "not with violence, . . . but by moral force, as it became God, by persuasion."[1] This persuasion is, for Irenaeus, the kind represented by Hosea and Jeremiah in their pleadings with the people: it is the persuasion of the divine love.

However, the turning which is a return must be real and not halfhearted; and it must begin where the people are. They must remove [their] abominations from [his] presence: the swearing, the devotion and new direction of the heart, must be in the truth, the justice, and the righteousness of the living God. When these three conditions are met, then they shall come again to know the blessings and the glory. These are the conditions—the three ungolden but disciplinary "ifs"—as inserted by a later writer; but underneath these is the inner pivot, the existential condition, upon which these conditions turn.

3-4. The Condition of the Conditions.—Vss. 3-4 "are among the grandest in the prophetic literature and comprise Jeremiah's whole theology in a couple of brief sentences."[2] Here again two powerful figures of speech are used, both shearing through the surface solutions to the problem and cutting into the inmost core of the human condition. These verses form a fitting climax to what has gone before. They are a call to a deeper repentance than the peoples of the world, let alone Judah, are prone to. The influence of Hosea is plain (Hos. 10:11b-12). Jeremiah's adroit quotation here brings with it a context of exceeding richness. The object of the plowing is clear. The soil that has been left untilled, that has been hard-

ened under the dry heat and packed solid by being repeatedly trod upon, this ground must be broken up and turned; it must be prepared for the reviving and fructifying rain of the Lord's grace. The callous and hardened hearts will have to feel the discipline of the plow; the rigid and implacable egos of the people, stiffened under the incessant treading of the heavy soled feet of pride, will have to be turned over, so that the repressed hunger for seed is exposed and the whole self loosened into responsiveness. Every tiller of the soil understood.

The parable of the sower is anticipated here. This turning of the soil, of the inside out, will hurt. The weeding will hurt. The plucking which precedes the planting will hurt. What Judah—the kings and the priests and the prophets and the people—has pretended to be and was not; her infidelities under every green tree; all this will have to be unmasked, and confessed, to let the heart lie open to the quickening rain. But the defection is deep, deeper than Judah knows, and the share of iron will pierce to her very life before she is turned open into the deeper paradox of joy.

The analogical depth of Jeremiah's insight becomes plain the moment we move to his second metaphor, the circumcision of the heart. For while it is true, as George Adam Smith points out,[3] that the breaking up of the fallow ground of the moral disposition implies that human nature has depths which, if thoroughly plowed, will be receptive to the good seed, Jeremiah does not permit us to conclude to anything less than the radical renewal of the heart. The recurrent use of the figure by Jere-

[1] *Against the Heresies* V. 1. 1.
[2] Peake, *Jeremiah and Lamentations,* I, 115.

[3] *Jeremiah,* p. 109.

5 Declare ye in Judah, and publish in Jerusalem; and say, Blow ye the trumpet in the land: cry, gather together, and say, As-

5 Declare in Judah, and proclaim in Jerusalem, and say,
"Blow the trumpet through the land;
cry aloud and say,

C. The Foe from the North (4:5-31)

This section presents a vivid description of the coming of the foe from the north, about which the prophet had received warning in the vision of 1:13-14. The heart of the section (vss. 5-8, 13-17, 19-21, 29-31) is a series of lyrical poems which portray with great feeling the coming of the foe upon the land of Judah. Though they probably were composed over a period of time, they seem to have been selected and arranged in their present position to form a complete cycle. They begin with the first warning blast of the trumpet, describe the onrush of the foe and the reaction of the people, and reach a climax in the death shriek of the destroyed capital. They have been put together by an editor who has supplied introductory formulas and interspersed warnings and reflections, some of them from Jeremiah and some from secondary sources.

These poems are filled with vivid description and highly emotional outbursts. So far as we know the history of Israel, the only actual situation to which they could apply in Jeremiah's time is the advance of the army of Nebuchadrezzar in 598 B.C. or

---

miah (9:26; 33:7-9) and its appearance in Deuteronomy (10:16; 30:6), together with the particular uses made of it by Ezekiel (36:24-36; cf. also 11:19-20) and the apostle Paul (particularly Rom. 2:25-29; Gal. 5:6; Col. 2:11) shows clearly the force of its appeal to the Jewish mind. In its more primitive origins it appears remotely as a part of the ritual of death and resurrection.[4] It may easily have been at one time also a form of sacrifice to the goddess of fertility among the Semitic peoples.[5]

For the people of Judah circumcision had come to represent the covenant made by Yahweh with Abraham—a rite of initiation or dedication whereby impurity should be removed and singleness of devotion pledged. Wesley therefore is analogically justified in regarding circumcision as the seal of the covenant, and suggesting that it bore the same relation to the old covenant as baptism bears to the new.[6]

Since the people were prone to glory in being thus chosen through Abraham, they were tempted also to accept the outward sign as sufficient. But it is precisely this externality of religious rite, cultism, or legal rectitude which is, for Jeremiah, the root of the betrayal. It is not the outer part, the outer form of sacrifice, but the **foreskin of the heart** which must be

[4] Cf. Sir James George Frazer: *The Golden Bough* (abridged ed.; New York: The Macmillan Co., 1940), pp. 694 ff.

[5] Cf. George A. Barton, "Circumcision (Semitic)," in James Hastings, ed., *Encyclopaedia of Religion and Ethics* (New York: Charles Scribner's Sons, 1911), III, 680.

[6] John Wesley, *Treatise on Baptism*. See *The Works of John Wesley*, ed. John Emory (New York: Carlton & Porter, 1856), VI, 17.

removed if the heart is to be open to God and genuinely humble and responsive to his will.

It was very likely held by Jeremiah's contemporaries that circumcision would serve as a protective shield against God's wrath, that he "will do nothing" (5:12). But Jeremiah will not allow this. Nothing happens until the people change radically within, until their hardness of heart is overcome. Hence Jeremiah's warning in these verses. Once the wrath of the Lord breaks upon the land, there will be no extinguishing it. There will be none to quench it.

It will be impossible not to note the recurrence of the symbol of fire in the poems of Jeremiah. It has long stood as the symbol of the spirit, and may appear as a refining fire, a baptismal fire, a pentecostal fire; in Rev. 1:14 the eyes of the Son of man are "like a flame of fire." Its meaning in vs. 4 would seem to be obvious; yet it should be noted that this symbol, as well as others, must be held in the dynamic context of Jeremiah's general perspective. As such, it cannot be interpreted as being simply vengeful or punitive, but contains as its presupposition the perversion of power and spirit brought about by man's own propulsion of the accumulating evils. It is also impossible not to see in this particular fire the threat of destruction and devastation which the "foe from the north" seems everywhere about to bring. From such wrath going forth like fire one is redeemed only by the new heart, by the baptism Jeremiah came to know so well.

5-31. The Foe from the North.—Skinner has performed a genuine aesthetic service in calling attention to the fact that the seven primary poems of this section are so arranged as to form

| semble yourselves, and let us go into the defensed cities. | 'Assemble, and let us go into the fortified cities!' |

ten years later. Yet this is too late in the prophet's career for them to have originated, especially if they are related to the vision of 1:13-14, and if they were included in Baruch's scroll. We must conclude then that they are based upon vision experiences or that they are the product of a very fertile imagination. However, since only vss. 23-26 have the form of a vision (see below), we cannot affirm with certainty that vision experiences lie back of these poems.

The problem of the identity of the foe from the north has been dealt with in the Intro., p. 779. In a number of particulars the description here hardly fits the Scythians of traditional theory. They are not known to have employed **chariots** (vs. 13); they did not have the means to besiege cities (vs. 16, though **besiegers** may be too specific a translation of *nôçerîm*); and it is not likely that the Scythians would be spoken of as the **lovers** of Jerusalem (vs. 30; see below).

a complete dramatic cycle. They begin with the shrill blast of the trumpet accompanied by the watchman's warning cry; the storm gathers; the foe approaches; the tumult of the assault is followed by the prophet's vision of chaos; thence panic and flight; and, finally, the "overpowering climax in the death-shriek of the doomed capital."[7]

While the dramatic theme of the cycle is that of the all-desolating invasion and overthrow of Judah by the "foe from the north," it is the function of these summary units to orient the lesser images of the poem to its general truth: a truth stated quite plainly in vs. 18.

Once it is clearly grasped that the entire cycle is a brilliant imaginative construction designed to awaken its hearers in the temple to some realization of the gravity of the nation's peril, the question as to who the "foe" was (whether Scythian, Assyrian, or Chaldean), or the question as to the precise historical events which it purports to describe, becomes secondary if not irrelevant. It has been fashionable since Eichhorn (until fairly recently) to see in the Scythian invasion of Palestine the probable "foe" to which these verses allude.

The text, however, gives practically no detailed description of the northern foe. **Chariots,** which the Scythians never used, are mentioned (vs. 13); but **horses . . . swifter than eagles** could certainly apply to them. They are called **destroyers, besiegers,** "a nation from afar" (5:15)—terms which could apply to any considerable foe. The mention of "sword" (5:17) and "quiver" (5:16) and "bow and spear" (6:23) could also be applied generally, and the same is true of the terms "enduring nation," "ancient nation" (5:15), and "great nation" (6:22), though the Scythian "nation" would hardly be spoken of in this wise. The casting up of "a siege mound" (6:6) would certainly not apply

[7] *Prophecy and Religion*, p. 38.

to the Scythian hordes, while the "lion from the forest," the "wolf from the desert," and the "leopard . . . watching against their cities" suggests, in accordance with its symbolism, the Assyrians, the Scythians, and the Ethiopians (5:6). In short, the vivid sense of the approaching "foe" is conveyed by the most artful suggestion which achieves the maximum of effect with a minimum of specific reference. It will be found that the substance of the poem is given not to a description of the "foe" but to the indictment of the people.

All this is commensurate with the view that Jeremiah was "one who might have been . . . the greatest poet of his people";[8] though it should be added at once that there is nothing of the aesthete nor of the escapist in Jeremiah's work; his poetry is never informed with the categories of immanence, but with the prophetic dialectic of the God-man relation (the divine-human encounter). It is at once a species of divination (as we shall note later) and proclamation. Jeremiah knew what the twentieth-century poet has come to know through much distress of alienation and return: namely, that

> we must earn through dull dim suffering,
> Through ignorance and darkened hope, and hope
> Risen again, and clouded over again, and dead
>   despair,
> And many little deaths, hardly observed,
> The early morning light we have deserved.[9]

Poetry, in short, is in its greatest moments a solemn engagement with reality, undertaken as a means of absolute clarification at the precise point where the frailty and fraud of human doing come into conflict with whatever is ulti-

[8] George Adam Smith, *Jeremiah*, p. 71.
[9] Delmore Schwartz, "True Recognition Often Is Refused," from *Vaudeville for a Princess and Other Poems* (New York: New Directions Books, 1950). Copyright 1950 by New Directions; used by permission.

6 Set up the standard toward Zion: retire, stay not; for I will bring evil from the
north, and a great destruction.

7 The lion is come up from his thicket,
and the destroyer of the Gentiles is on his
way; he is gone forth from his place to make
thy land desolate; *and* thy cities shall be
laid waste, without an inhabitant.

8 For this gird you with sackcloth, lament and howl: for the fierce anger of the
LORD is not turned back from us.

9 And it shall come to pass at that day,
saith the LORD, *that* the heart of the king
shall perish, and the heart of the princes;
and the priests shall be astonished, and the
prophets shall wonder.

10 Then said I, Ah, Lord GOD! surely

---

6 Raise a standard toward Zion,
  flee for safety, stay not,
for I bring evil from the north,
  and great destruction.

7 A lion has gone up from his thicket,
  a destroyer of nations has set out;
he has gone forth from his place
to make your land a waste;
  your cities will be ruins
  without inhabitant.

8 For this gird you with sackcloth,
  lament and wail;
for the fierce anger of the LORD
  has not turned back from us."

9 "In that day, says the LORD, courage shall
fail both king and princes; the priests shall
be appalled and the prophets astounded."
10 Then I said, "Ah, Lord GOD, surely thou
hast utterly deceived this people and Jerusalem, saying, 'It shall be well with you';

Whoever the actual foe from the north may have been, Jeremiah emphasizes the
fact that he is but an agent of Yahweh, who is sending him to punish the Israelites for
their sins.

1. THE ALARM (4:5-8)

5-8. These verses form a general introduction to the series, the "overture" in which
the coming of the foe is announced.

2. FAILURE OF COURAGE (4:9-10)

9-10. These verses are in a different mood and style and probably secondary. **In
that day** is an eschatological formula, and vs. 10 expresses the viewpoint of false prophets
rather than that of Jeremiah.

---

mate in the human situation and in the orders
of creation.

5-8. *The Alarm.*—The blowing of the
trumpet throughout the land is the signal of
alarm. The watchman calls, summoning the
people into the protection of the fortified cities.
The danger flag is hoisted. The **lion** (the Assyrians or the Chaldeans?) will lay waste the
land and ruin the cities; it is on its way. This
would appear to be the point of the imperative.
It has been on its way for a hundred years.
Israel has already succumbed. Judah is in the
line of the historical inevitability of the clash
of world powers. Jeremiah reads clearly the
ascendancy of the northern powers. The seething caldron begins to boil over, more surely
than ever.

The world-hour brings upon Judah her last
hour. It is the time of the pulling down and the
rooting out. The trouble begins to form like a
storm about to break (vs. 13). Lament for
this, cries the poet, since Yahweh's anger against

you is not turned away. This is the first part of
the divine demand implied in the historical
situation. Yahweh is using the nations to effect
a change in the people, an axial change in the
religious consciousness of the world.

4:8, 18, 22, 28, 31. *Yahweh's Plangent Plea.*—
We have suggested above (pp. 833-34) that
these verses, whether regarded as secondary or
not, fulfill a summary function for the poems
of this cycle, somewhat like the *parabasis* in a
Greek play, in which the chorus comes forward
from the masks of the drama and speaks the
poet's message directly to the people. Vs. 8,
which follows the trumpet of alarm, summons
the people to repentance,

> **for the fierce anger of the LORD
> has not turned back from us.**

Vs. 18, on which we have commented elsewhere,
assigns the cause to the **ways** and **doings** of the
people, reinforcing Jeremiah's general recognition of the dialectical nature of wickedness. Vs.

thou hast greatly deceived this people and Jerusalem, saying, Ye shall have peace; whereas the sword reacheth unto the soul.

11 At that time shall it be said to this people and to Jerusalem, A dry wind of the high places in the wilderness toward the daughter of my people, not to fan, nor to cleanse,

12 *Even* a full wind from those *places* shall come unto me: now also will I give sentence against them.

13 Behold, he shall come up as clouds, and his chariots *shall be* as a whirlwind: his horses are swifter than eagles. Woe unto us! for we are spoiled.

14 O Jerusalem, wash thine heart from wickedness, that thou mayest be saved. How long shall thy vain thoughts lodge within thee?

15 For a voice declareth from Dan, and publisheth affliction from mount Ephraim.

16 Make ye mention to the nations; behold, publish against Jerusalem, *that* watchers come from a far country, and give out their voice against the cities of Judah.

17 As keepers of a field, are they against her round about; because she hath been rebellious against me, saith the LORD.

18 Thy way and thy doings have procured these *things* unto thee; this *is* thy wickedness, because it is bitter, because it reacheth unto thine heart.

whereas the sword has reached their very life."

11 At that time it will be said to this people and to Jerusalem, "A hot wind from the bare heights in the desert toward the daughter of my people, not to winnow or cleanse, 12 a wind too full for this comes for me. Now it is I who speak in judgment upon them."

13 Behold, he comes up like clouds,
    his chariots like the whirlwind;
his horses are swifter than eagles —
    woe to us, for we are ruined!

14 O Jerusalem, wash your heart from wickedness,
    that you may be saved.
How long shall your evil thoughts
    lodge within you?

15 For a voice declares from Dan
    and proclaims evil from Mount E'phraim.

16 Warn the nations that he is coming;
    announce to Jerusalem,
"Besiegers come from a distant land;
    they shout against the cities of Judah.

17 Like keepers of a field are they against
    her round about,
because she has rebelled against me,
                    says the LORD.

18 Your ways and your doings
    have brought this upon you.
This is your doom, and it is bitter;
    it has reached your very heart."

---

3. WIND OF JUDGMENT (4:11-12)

11. The **hot wind** is the sirocco, a dry wind from the eastern desert which brings suffocating heat into Palestine. **The daughter of my people** is the people of Judah personified as a woman (cf. vs. 31).

4. CALL TO REPENT (4:13-18)

18. This is a reflection, possibly of an editor, but fully within the spirit of Jeremiah.

---

22 specifies these ways and doings as foolishness and stupidity, as not knowing the Lord, and consequently being without understanding. The anticipation here of the existential principle inherent in the medieval formula *Credo ut intelligam* is reinforced negatively by the ironic praise of their skill in doing evil. Vs. 28 reiterates vs. 8, Yahweh's **I have not relented nor will I turn back**, which carries the moral theme, quite as directly as the other verses carry the descriptive theme, directly into vs. 31, where the two themes join in the historical and moral

dialectic of woe—the ultimate consequence of rebellion against God.

13-18. *The Gathering Storm.*—Here the movement of Jeremiah's images is clear cut and precise. As Gordon observes, Hebrew poetry "is probably the 'pithiest' poetry in existence. . . . There are no wasted words in this poetry."[1] The storm clouds are gathering. The chariots of the "foe" are like a **whirlwind,** and "his horses swifter than a vulture's swoop" (Mof-

[1] *Rebel Prophet,* pp. 168-69. This is also the aim of much modern poetry.

19 ¶ My bowels, my bowels! I am pained at my very heart; my heart maketh a noise

19 My anguish, my anguish! I writhe in
   pain!
Oh, the walls of my heart!
My heart is beating wildly;

5. The Prophet's Suffering (4:19-22)

19-21. Here the poet seems to personify the land, as in 10:19-21, though he identifies himself so closely with his people that he would make no sharp distinction in his own feelings between their sorrows and his own.

My bowels, my bowels! The Hebrews considered the bowels to be the seat of emotion.

fatt). Information concerning the approaching enemy is reported **from Dan**, the northern limit of Judah; then word comes from **Mount Ephraim**, just ten miles north of the city. And now, notes Gordon, "the rhythm changes as if to imitate the padding gait of the leopard, the classical symbol for Babylon." [2] Doom hangs also over Jerusalem.

> **Your ways and your doings**
> **have brought this upon you.**
> **This is your doom, and it is bitter;**
> **it has reached your very heart.**

This is the second occurrence of the term **bitter** (cf. 2:19), the bitterness which comes to people who forsake their God; and Jeremiah has pointed out that such a doom is brought by people on themselves (2:17). Bitterness of heart arises from within when all the masks of unreality are stripped away; or whenever a people is drawn

> Into the snarl of the abyss
> That always lies just underneath
> Our jolly picnic on the heath
> Of the agreeable, where we bask,
> Agreed on what we will not ask,
> Bland, sunny and adjusted by
> The light of the accepted lie. . . .[3]

The refusal of the people to be faithful to the covenant foreshortens the vision; the self-concern of the introverted mind and will ("heart") perverts the judgment; the just community is lost and each one seeks his own. One need not wonder that Jeremiah knew this bitterness. It is a common knowledge in times of calamity, when great massed powers, overwhelming and depersonalized, pillage the little peoples, leaving devastation and waste, destruction and death, in their wake, only to fall upon each other in the massed and fratricidal folly of the nations' will to power, hacking out on one another the inner pains and conflicts of the introverted heart. *Cor incurvatum in se!* [4]

[2] *Ibid.*, p. 171.

[3] "New Year Letter," Part II, from *The Collected Poetry of W. H. Auden* (London: Faber & Faber; New York: Random House, 1945). Used by permission.

[4] Martin Luther, *Römerbrief*, II, 184.

What frustrates and agonizes the prophet's heart is that he perceives in all this the vast stupidity (vs. 22) of the people propelling the folly by their perpetual and blind return upon the causes that give rise to it. Stephen Crane has described this perennial bitterness in an unforgettable dialogue:

> In the desert
> I saw a creature, naked, bestial,
> Who, squatting upon the ground,
> Held his heart in his hands,
> And ate of it.
> I said, "Is it good, friend?"
> "It is bitter—bitter," he answered;
> "But I like it
> Because it is bitter,
> And because it is my heart." [5]

The irony in this verse is both apparent and profound. With Jeremiah the plight of his people is, as a rule, too profound for irony, though there are instances in which the ironical turn is unavoidable. As a rule, however, the situation and behavior of the people call forth the injunction

> **O Jerusalem, wash your heart from wickedness,**
> **that you may be saved.**

And when no response to this appeal is forthcoming the bitterness shifts, not to irony, but to the deepest anguish.

19-22. O Pain, Pain, the Toils of My Heart!— The cycle of poems reaches now its twofold crest—the private (vss. 19-22) and the public (vss. 23-26) intensity of crisis and panic as the innumerable foe falls in wave after wave upon

[5] "The Black Riders." Reprinted from *The Collected Poems of Stephen Crane*, by permission of Alfred A. Knopf. Copyright 1895, 1922 by W. H. Crane. The persistence of this figure in literature is worth noting. In Dante (*La Vita Nuova*, Part III) it is a heart aflame—"in one of his hands methought he held a thing that was all aflame; and methought he said to me these words: *Vide cor tuum.*" In William Beckford's *Vathek* "the Caliph discerned through his bosom, which was transparent as a crystal, his heart enveloped in flames." But in the contemporary cartoon of Abner Dean, it is again the heart being eaten—this time in an empty restaurant, by an unclothed man, his heart unwound as from a pince-nez spring, and lying on his plate where he feeds upon it with knife and fork in our "civilized" fashion.

in me; I cannot hold my peace, because thou hast heard, O my soul, the sound of the trumpet, the alarm of war.

20 Destruction upon destruction is cried; for the whole land is spoiled: suddenly are my tents spoiled, *and* my curtains in a moment.

21 How long shall I see the standard, *and* hear the sound of the trumpet?

22 For my people *is* foolish, they have not known me; they *are* sottish children, and they have none understanding: they *are* wise to do evil, but to do good they have no knowledge.

I cannot keep silent;
for I hear the sound of the trumpet,
    the alarm of war.
20 Disaster follows hard on disaster,
    the whole land is laid waste.
Suddenly my tents are destroyed,
    my curtains in a moment.
21 How long must I see the standard,
    and hear the sound of the trumpet?
22 "For my people are foolish,
    they know me not;
they are stupid children,
    they have no understanding.
They are skilled in doing evil,
    but how to do good they know not."

---

22. This is another reflection, in which Yahweh speaks. The language is that of the wisdom writers, but the passage may well be from Jeremiah; Duhm considers it secondary.

---

the city. The skill of the poet is here at its peak. The pitch of feeling is such that the anguish of suffering and defeat is at once that of the prophet who identifies himself with the suffering of Yahweh's people, of the poet who foresees so vividly the oncoming disaster, and of the people who experience the assault in the poem. The anguish which he feels, and which assaults the walls of his heart as the enemy will assault the walls of the city, is already too deep to be withheld—**I cannot hold my peace.** This irrepressible anguish will arise again and again in the heart of Jeremiah, and almost always with the accent of "the stricken deer." But the pathetic and deep-seated hurt turns quickly to the situation of the people (vs. 19 KJV).

> Crash upon crash it comes—
>   the whole land is ravaged!
> In a moment my tents are ruined.
> In an instant my curtains are torn.[6]

The double-pointedness of the image must again be stressed. The tents are undoubtedly the tents of the people, of those stationed for battle as well as those in the temporary dwellings within the walls through which the breaches are made.[7] No more pathetic image of rout and defeat could be chosen than that of the collapsed tents with their colorful curtains disheveled and torn. But the recurrence of this image in 10:19-22 suggests that it is not merely the tents of the personified Judah that are ruined, but something in Jeremiah too is fallen or collapsed. The reader (or the hearer) is

made to feel at once the inner consternation and panic in conjunction with the outer confusion of the enemy pouring through the walls —the noise of battle, the waving of the pennons, the blare of the trumpets, which go on echoing in the mind after the words have ceased, putting in efficient poise the question

> **How long must I see the standard,
>   and hear the sound of the trumpet?**

Why is this happening to us? And Yahweh's answer is supplied again: because of the foolishness and stupidity of the people.

> **They are skilled in doing evil,
>   but how to do good they know not.**

This poem has been reckoned as "among the best descriptions of a vision in the Old Testament, nay in all literature." [8] Continued and careful study of the passage will go far to confirm this. But the term "vision" should not lead us away from the specifically literary feature of this achievement; it should lead, on the contrary, more firmly into it. The greatness of Jeremiah as a poet-prophet will become more evident when it is seen that Hebrew poetry, and that of Jeremiah in particular, was a leap of images, a juxtaposition of metaphors with no apparent affinity for one another, a play upon words and meanings, an exploitation of the strategies of parallelism, and a use of the precise image and the "direct treatment" that are being relearned in the poetry of today. It has been truly said that "art never plays; it is sober, even when it laughs, even when it dances. It must be repeated that in art whatever is not

---

[6] Skinner, *Prophecy and Religion*, p. 36.

[7] Peake suggests that the opening line of vs. 20 may mean "breach meeteth breach," implying that one breach follows upon another (*Jeremiah and Lamentations*, I, 123).

[8] Hans Schmidt, *Die grossen Propheten und ihre Zeit*, p. 205; quoted in Skinner, *op. cit.*, p. 49.

| 23 I beheld the earth, and, lo, *it was* without form, and void; and the heavens, and they *had* no light. | 23 I looked on the earth, and lo, it was waste and void; and to the heavens, and they had no light. |

6. Vision of Cosmic Destruction (4:23-26)

23-26. These verses are in a different meter from the surrounding verses (four lines in 4+3, closing with one line in 2+2). The earth is represented as returning to its primeval condition; the words used to describe it in vs. 23a, **waste and void** (*tōhû wābhōhû*), are the same used in Gen. 1:2. It is very difficult to decide whether this

necessary is useless; and whatever is useless is bad." [9] Jeremiah's art never plays; and while it never laughs and never dances, it sometimes weeps and often pleads. For his art is altogether the instrument of his message; and his message is altogether the words which the Lord has put into his mouth (1:9) —that highest source of all high seriousness. Thus, when his anguish flows over into the full shock of the land's oncoming disaster and he envisions its ruin and chaos, his art is able to contain it as his spirit is able to sustain it, though his world falls apart and the dark of death's terrors comes.

23-26. *The Shaking of the Foundations.*— This passage is a poem of unique power, wrought with exquisite finesse. In the cycle of poems which includes it it stands clear like the prime jewel in a ring of lustrous splendors. It is the peak point of feeling, where the soul of the panic-stricken victim is overwhelmed with the onslaught, and his consciousness floods, and his little cosmos of false securities, projected so stubbornly upon his narrow world, topples over into disorder, rampage, and ruin.

Three things will be noted at once in the structure of the poem. The shift in the meter, as in the earlier shift to capture the leopard's tread (vss. 16b-17), is commensurate with the shift to the absolute shock of ruin. The strong and regular repetition of the beautiful Hebrew word *rā'ithî* (variously translated "I scanned," **I looked,** "I look out" [Moffatt], **I beheld,** etc.) secures its primary order and control over the parts of the poem by the formula, four times uttered, of **I looked . . . and lo**—an order nevertheless counteracted by the superimposed effect of an intentionally broken (therefore disordered) Qinah rhythm (3+2). Finally, there are the deliberately placed parallelisms in a descending order: **earth—heavens; mountains—hills; man—birds** (animate life) **; fruitful land . . . a desert—cities razed.** This may appear, at first sight, to reverse the logical order of climax; but the moment the reader acquiesces in the

poem's strategy—i.e., becomes the "I" who looks—he will see that the movement is precisely from the largest term to the smallest, to the progressive and rapid intensification of the lone individual's sense of isolation and utter desolateness.

Paul Tillich in the title sermon of his book, *The Shaking of the Foundations,* in which he brings this poem into conjunction with two passages from Isaiah (54:10; 24:18-20), writes:

There was a time when we could listen to such words without much feeling and without understanding. There were decades and even centuries when we did not take them seriously. Those days are gone. Today we must take them seriously. For they describe with visionary power what the majority of human beings in our period have experienced, and what, perhaps in a not too distant future, all mankind will experience abundantly: "The foundations of the earth do shake." [1]

For us it is no longer "merely a poetic metaphor" to say that the "earth is split in pieces" (Isa. 24:19 Moffatt). It is an ugly fact. But this fact, so new to us, is not new to scripture, which always speaks within the context of the beginning and the end. The O.T. perpetually protests against presumptuousness, whereby man presumes to be God—"and whenever he has claimed to be like God, he has been rebuked and brought to self-destruction and despair. . . . All the foundations of his personal, natural and cultural life have been shaken." [2] It has always been so. Whenever either the poetic or the prophetic consciousness is forced so absolutely into the time's concussion as Jeremiah knew it and as our more sensitive contemporary voices know it, "only two alternatives remain—despair, which is the certainty of eternal destruction, or faith, which is the certainty of eternal salvation." [3]

The prophets, of course, stood for the latter. They saw beyond the rise and fall of the na-

[1] New York: Charles Scribner's Sons; London: Student Christian Movement Press, 1948, pp. 2-3. Used by permission.
[2] *Ibid.,* p. 6.
[3] *Ibid.,* p. 10.

[9] De Gourmont, *Jehan Rictus;* quoted in Ezra Pound, *Make It New* (New Haven: Yale University Press, 1935), p. 323.

24 I beheld the mountains, and, lo, they trembled, and all the hills moved lightly.	24 I looked on the mountains, and lo, they were quaking, and all the hills moved to and fro.
25 I beheld, and, lo, *there was* no man, and all the birds of the heavens were fled.	25 I looked, and lo, there was no man, and all the birds of the air had fled.
26 I beheld, and, lo, the fruitful place *was* a wilderness, and all the cities thereof were broken down at the presence of the Lord, *and* by his fierce anger.	26 I looked, and lo, the fruitful land was a desert, and all its cities were laid in ruins before the Lord, before his fierce anger.

passage is from Jeremiah or not. Duhm, who is very free in pronouncing passages secondary, accepts it as genuine, and Cornill declares it one of the most powerful pieces in the whole of prophetic literature. On the other hand, Giesebrecht and Volz deny it to Jeremiah, the latter quoting with approval Skinner's dictum that Jeremiah was the least eschatological of the prophets. Because of the absence of other portrayals of cosmic

tions, looking to "the city which has foundations, whose builder and maker is God" (Heb. 11:10). Clearly the shaking of the nations (Hag. 2:7) would continue "yet once more" (Heb. 12:26) until there is brought about "the removal of what is shaken . . . in order that what cannot be shaken may remain" (Heb. 12:27). Only the person who has such a hope can gaze directly into the whirling gyres of destruction. Tillich writes:

All others are compelled to escape, to turn away. How much of our lives consists in nothing but attempts to look away from the end! . . . But ultimately we fail; for we always carry the end with us in our bodies and our souls. And often whole nations and cultures succeed in forgetting the end. But ultimately they fail too, for in their lives and growth they always carry the end with them. . . . We happen to live in a time when very few of us, very few nations . . . will succeed in forgetting the end. For in these days the foundations of the earth *do* shake.[4]

This is well said, and puts us in a position to note more sharply two aspects of Jeremiah's "vision."

First of all, the poem contains practically no "apocalyptic coloring" in the biblical critic's sense of the term; at the same time it must be said that the poem is highly apocalyptic, or eschatological, in the poetic sense, or in the sense in which the terms are used in current philosophical theology. The poet's vision brings the reader into a total confrontation with the ultimate terms of the human predicament, such that the dimensions of the human situation are laid bare and the awareness of the "end" is radical and absolute. The poem is "apocalyptic" in the same profound sense in which our most effective contemporary poetry is apocalyptic. It is more than an accidental coincidence that

[4] *Ibid.*, p. 11.

a climactic chapter in a recent book dealing with modern poetry should be entitled "The Shaking of the Foundations."[5] It holds that in a period of common disintegration "the paradox arises that peoples can understand each other in terms of a common disorder and a common language of disorder. . . . The disorder [today] is of such a general kind that the man's deeper nature is involved in it, that which he shares with all men and all times."[6] Just as Dante said "my subject is man, not a man" so the subject of contemporary poetry is the situation of man. The historical and international dimensions arise, precluding regional narrowness or local themes; the sense of existential crisis becomes pervasive, and the arts are shaped by it.

What we have said about the present crisis and its characteristic art helps us again to answer the questions that many men have with regard to traditional poetry. Is it really any wonder that writers like Masefield and Bridges, Alfred Noyes, Vachel Lindsay, Edwin Markham and a host of others do not speak to the modern soul? Is it surprising that Tennyson and Browning, Emerson and Whitman, are not for this place or for this hour? Is it any wonder that we go back rather to Herman Melville and his white whale, to Hawthorne and his symbolism of evil, to Blake, to the French symbolists, Rimbaud, Baudelaire, to John Donne, and indeed, to Dante, to Ezekiel, to the flood, the Fall of Man, and to the original myths of creation and chaos?[7]

A group of younger British poets accepted as the designation for their work "The New Apocalypse."[8]

[5] Amos N. Wilder, *Modern Poetry and the Christian Tradition* (New York: Charles Scribner's Sons, 1952), pp. 205-30.

[6] *Ibid.*, pp. 205-6.

[7] *Ibid.*, p. 211.

[8] Cf. *The New Apocalypse: An Anthology of Criticism, Poems and Stories* (London: Fortune Press, n.d.), containing work by Dylan Thomas, Alex Comfort, Henry Treece, J. F. Hendry, *et al.*

27 For thus hath the LORD said, The whole land shall be desolate; yet will I not make a full end.

28 For this shall the earth mourn, and the heavens above be black: because I have spoken *it*, I have purposed *it*, and will not repent, neither will I turn back from it.

27 For thus says the LORD, "The whole land shall be a desolation; yet I will not make a full end.

28 For this the earth shall mourn,
    and the heavens above be black;
for I have spoken, I have purposed;
    I have not relented nor will I turn back."

---

destruction in the genuine words of Jeremiah, it is wise to share the skepticism of Giesebrecht and Volz.

7. DESOLATION OF THE LAND (4:27-29)

27. Yet I will not make a full end is unsuited to the context, and should be considered as "a mitigating gloss" (Peake), influenced by 5:10, 18. Cf. 30:11.

Nathaniel Micklem suggests that "the vaticinations of the prophets of weal" (the false prophets) were the outcome "of the imagination working upon *the material presented by the desires*" (their wishful thinking) whereas "the prophecies of Amos, Hosea, Isaiah, Jeremiah . . . always express the result of profound meditation into *the meaning and order of the actual world*—in other words, they are not mere fancies; they are interpretations; in particular, these visions are based upon insight into the moral order." [9]

Jeremiah's experience was different [from Coleridge and his *Kubla Khan*]. He did not fall into a sleep induced by opium in which he dreamed of mysterious caverns, of damsels and dulcimers, as Coleridge did. He heard the voice of God; believed that he had learned the mind of God. That this experience should have excited him, as our poets have been excited before they have produced their great creative work, is what would be expected.[1]

The struggle of the Hellenic mind with the cosmic powers and with human destiny and fate is not as penetrating in depth as are the probings and insights of the contemporary eschatological sense. It is relevant to note, however, Plato's use of materials from the Orphic cosmological myths, and to note that "they impressed him so deeply because he felt as an artist that a proper transcendental background was needed for the heroic loneliness of Socrates' fighting soul." [2] If such a background is required for the loneliness of Socrates it is easy to see how inevitably the poetic-prophetic mind is driven to eschatological concepts and settings in order to depict the utter desolation of Judah.

Tillich has suggested that just as the eschatological dimension of awareness in Jeremiah's poem is precipitated by the dooms of Samaria and Damascus, so our own eschatological awareness has been evoked by recent world wars and by a specific event—the effective splitting of the atom and the explosion of the atom bomb. For the apocalyptic appearance of this contemporary event within our poetry and the mood it induces, two examples will suffice. In Stephen Spender, the desperate cry—

Oh save me in this day, when Now
Is a towering pillar of dust which sucks
The ruin of a world into its column.
When to perceive is to be part of that cloud
Whose castle changes into dragon.[3]

And in Edith Sitwell, the lament—

We did not heed the Cloud in the Heavens shaped like the hand
Of Man. . . . But there came a roar as if the Sun and Earth had come together—
The Sun descending and the Earth ascending
To take its place above . . . the Primal Matter
Was broken, the womb from which all life began.
Then to the murdered Sun a totem pole of dust arose in memory of Man.[4]

It should by now be apparent (*a*) that the poets' figures of cosmic destruction are not intended to be taken literally: they are plainly figures "for an apocalypse"; that is, metaphors, the purpose of which is (*b*) to expand the consciousness, the imaginative grasp of the predicament, to its absolute conditions. To say that "Yahweh, who made the world a cosmos,

[9] Nathaniel Micklem, *Prophecy and Eschatology* (London: George Allen & Unwin, 1926), p. 44.

[1] Alfred Guillaume, *Prophecy and Divination* (London: Hodder & Stoughton, 1938), p. 341.

[2] Werner Jaeger, *Paideia* (New York: Oxford University Press, 1943), II, 151.

[3] "Time in Our Time," from *The Edge of Being*. Copyright 1949 by Stephen Spender. Used by permission of Faber & Faber and Random House, publishers.

[4] "The Shadow of Cain," from *The Canticle of the Rose*. Copyright 1949 by Edith Sitwell. Published by Vanguard Press. Used by permission.

29 The whole city shall flee for the noise of the horsemen and bowmen; they shall go into thickets, and climb up upon the rocks: every city *shall be* forsaken, and not a man dwell therein.

30 And *when* thou *art* spoiled, what wilt thou do? Though thou clothest thyself with crimson, though thou deckest thee with ornaments of gold, though thou rentest thy face with painting, in vain shalt thou make thyself fair; *thy* lovers will despise thee, they will seek thy life.

29 At the noise of horseman and archer
    every city takes to flight;
  they enter thickets; they climb among
    rocks;
  all the cities are forsaken,
    and no man dwells in them.
30 And you, O desolate one,
  what do you mean that you dress in scar-
    let,
  that you deck yourself with ornaments
    of gold,
  that you enlarge your eyes with paint?
In vain you beautify yourself.
  Your lovers despise you;
  they seek your life.

8. The Harlot's Murder (4:30-31)

30. Jerusalem is addressed as a harlot who decks herself to impress her lovers, but meets death at their hands. It is a bold figure, but is used elsewhere by the prophets (cf. 13:20-27; Isa. 1:21-23). **Enlarge your eyes with paint,** by the use of a black mineral powder, antimony, in the manner of the Egyptian women in ancient times and of the Arabs today (cf. II Kings 9:30; Ezek. 23:40). The word translated **lovers** is not the ordinary Hebrew word, but *'ôghebhîm.* The verb means "to lust," and occurs only here and in Ezek. 23:5, 7, 9, 12, 16, 20, where Samaria and Jerusalem are personified as harlots. The **lovers** are foreign nations, or the people of one foreign nation, rather than pagan

was about to reduce it to the condition from which He brought it" [5] is to literalize the poet's attempt to liberate the mind and soul from literalism; it is to betray the message at the precise point where one insists upon it. The pious device whereby the "day of the Lord" was, and continues to be, translated from present fact to a future cataclysmic quash of the created order is one of those most bathetic ironies of religious history. One must say, however, in the same breath that the poems are based, as Micklem put it, upon insight into the moral order; or, in Tillich's view, upon the prophetic perspectives of beginning and end in which these terms are themselves metaphors which are the only adequate language for the communication of such "facts." The position is put very well by Harold Knight:

The presupposition of this peculiar prophetic awareness of the divine is not the validity of logical concepts, but the validity of man's total life-experience, and the ever-present possibility of a numinous confrontation by God on the plane of historical reality. [6]

[5] Adam C. Welch, *Jeremiah: His Time and His Work* (New York: The Macmillan Co., 1951), p. 110.

[6] *The Hebrew Prophetic Consciousness* (London: Lutterworth Press, 1947), p. 173; cf. Abraham Heschel, *Die Prophetie* (Krakow: Polnischen Akademie der Wissenschaften, 1936), pp. 1-5, 140.

Such a confrontation may be absolute, a "fullness of time" (*kairos*), a moment of decisive significance, in which the issues of time and eternity intersect in that unpredictable but inevitable tryst between God and the soul. It is to this consciousness that the prophet would awaken the people.

29-31. Panic, Flight, and the Cry.—The cycle of vivid lyrics has mounted to its climax. The trumpet of alarm, the gathering of the storm, the terrible burst of the enemy's power in crash after crash upon the city walls, the collapse, devastation, and ruin of a proudly garnered little world; and now, panic. The game is up. [7] The pretense is over. The heavens are black (vs. 28). Here again Jeremiah secures to the vividness of his portrayal of the peoples' plight the very highest pitch of implication by retaining the quotational overtones of Isa. 2:19. In Isaiah the context is general, predicting doom "against all that is proud and lofty—For the LORD of hosts has a day!" (Isa. 2:12.) Here again the apocalyptic lift is apparent, without the poem's losing its own dramatic momentum or compromising its realistic drive. The Lord's day is still the moment when his patience would be at its end, when the reckoning with his righteousness must come, when he could no longer

[7] Cf. George Adam Smith's rendering, *Jeremiah*, p. 117: "All is up!"

31 For I have heard a voice as of a woman in travail, *and* the anguish as of her that bringeth forth her first child, the voice of the daughter of Zion, *that* bewaileth herself, *that* spreadeth her hands, *saying,* Woe *is* me now! for my soul is wearied because of murderers.	31 For I heard a cry as of a woman in travail, anguish as of one bringing forth her first child, the cry of the daughter of Zion gasping for breath, stretching out her hands, "Woe is me! I am fainting before murderers."
5 Run ye to and fro through the streets of Jerusalem, and see now, and know, and seek in the broad places thereof, if ye	5 Run to and fro through the streets of Jerusalem, look and take note! Search her squares to see if you can find a man,

gods, and it is hard to see how the term could be applied to the Scythians. They are much more likely to be the same as "those whom you yourself have taught to be friends to you" of 13:21, where the reference is to the Chaldeans. The thought of vss. 30-31 is very close to that of 13:20-27. In 30:14 the "lovers" are probably the Egyptians (see Exeg. on 22:20).

31. The daughter of Zion is Jerusalem personified as a woman; cf. "the daughter of my people," vs. 11.

D. ISRAEL'S UTTER SINFULNESS (5:1-31)

The theme of this chapter as a whole is the utter sinfulness of the Israelites which makes it impossible for them to receive the Lord's forgiveness. Vss. 1-14 are a unified account of Jeremiah's vain search for even a single upright man in Jerusalem. Vss. 15-17 apparently refer to the coming of the foe from the north. Vss. 18-19 are a Deuteronomic addition explaining the Exile. The remaining verses depict the sinfulness of various groups in Israel.

1. JEREMIAH'S VAIN SEARCH FOR AN UPRIGHT MAN (5:1-14)

The conjecture of Duhm that between the composition of ch. 4 and ch. 5 Jeremiah moved from Anathoth to Jerusalem in order to prophesy there is unnecessary. Many of Jeremiah's previous words were directed to Jerusalem (see 2:2; 4:3, 4, 14, 30-31), and

forbear; the "day" had not yet reached its postexilic inflation into otherworldly pyrotechnics.

The Lord's vexation appears through the instrumentality of the invaders. The imagery of the first poems (ch. 2) is recovered in the personification of Judah as the Lord's unfaithful bride. That she should even now, thinking still to avert the enemy, bedeck herself with ornaments, wear scarlet and seductive clothes, enticing the invaders with painted eyes, is ironical in the extreme. She has not learned that

> A dress has the sound
> Of Reality, reverberates like thunder.
> And ghosts of aeons and of equinoxes
>
> .   .   .   .
>
> Take on the forms of fashionable women
> With veils that hide a new Catastrophe, and under
> Is the fall of a world that was a heart.[8]

[8] Edith Sitwell, "The Coat of Fire," from *The Canticle of the Rose.* Copyright 1949 by Edith Sitwell. Published by Vanguard Press. Used by permission.

The pathetic figure is extended. Her "lovers" despise her—those nations with whom she sought in political and religious fickleness to make alliances (2:33-34), and with whom she had behaved adulterously, since Yahweh was her proper husband (3:1). They seek her life. They overtake her. And the poem ends with dramatic and pitiful consistency, with the beloved of Yahweh spreading out her hands in desperate appeal, fainting before her murderers, and emitting that piercing cry to be heard again and again in these poems—the cry of anguish, **as of a woman in travail.** It is the death-shriek. The city has fallen.

5:1-31. Searching the City.—We shall not expect from chs. 5 and 6 the same dramatic unity which we found in the cycle of poems in the preceding chapter. The order of these poems is clearly not dictated by the dramatic imperative which governs the order in ch. 4. They are much more loosely placed. Some would appear

can find a man, if there be *any* that executeth judgment, that seeketh the truth; and I will pardon it.
 	
2 And though they say, The LORD liveth; surely they swear falsely.
 	
3 O LORD, *are* not thine eyes upon the truth? thou hast stricken them, but they have not grieved; thou hast consumed them, *but* they have refused to receive correction: they have made their faces harder than a rock; they have refused to return.
	one who does justice
	  and seeks truth;
	that I may pardon her.
	2 Though they say, "As the LORD lives,"
	  yet they swear falsely.
	3 O LORD, do not thy eyes look for truth?
	Thou hast smitten them,
	  but they felt no anguish;
	thou hast consumed them,
	  but they refused to take correction.
	They have made their faces harder than
	  rock;
	  they have refused to repent.

in any case Anathoth was less than three miles from the capital city, an easy walking distance. As there are several shifts of speakers in this section, it is important to note carefully who is speaking and to whom the words are spoken. The Exeg. below points out these shifts.

5:1-2. Yahweh speaks to Jeremiah, directing him to search the streets and public squares of Jerusalem for a man who **does justice and seeks truth.** He must be one who is just in his dealings and true in his heart. The thought of the passage is similar to that of Gen. 18:23-33, in which God agrees to spare Sodom if ten righteous men can be found in it. For the importance of swearing by Yahweh see Exeg. on 4:2.

3. Jeremiah prays to the Lord, protesting that the people have not profited by God's chastening, and so **have refused to repent.** Giesebrecht conjectures that the reference

to have been inserted at a later time; others may well have been modified by Jeremiah himself at the time of the preparation of Baruch's roll. Nevertheless a certain unity is discoverable as governing the poems in the two chapters.

The unifying theme is that of Jeremiah's searching the streets of Jerusalem and of his taking plain and candid account of what he finds there. Once more he indicts the people in an effort to make them aware of their condition. This condition is comprised of two things: the need for repentance within, and the threat of alien powers without. These reflections evoke some important clarifications of Jeremiah's function as a prophet. The easy dramatic transition from his office as a searcher of the streets of the city (5:1) to that of assayer and tester of the people (6:27) is effective and provides a unifying climax of the poems as a whole.

1-14. The First Diogenes.—On reading these verses the Western reader will think of Diogenes—who reputedly went through the streets of Athens, candle in hand, looking for a man. The initial difference is that whereas Diogenes' search was ironical, Jeremiah's was serious. Also, for Diogenes, finding a man was qualitatively different from Jeremiah's similar pursuit. For Diogenes a "man" would be one whose conduct fulfilled the requirements of a prudential wisdom as measured by moderation, sagacity, and aristocratic contempt for the general

ways of man; whereas, for Jeremiah, the terms **justice** and **truth** would imply constant and faithful response to the will of God. This will was in no wise conditioned either by *anangkē* ("necessity") or *dikē* ("justice"), but God was himself the lord of his creation. His righteousness (*çédheq*), therefore, was characterized by a concern for the people, especially as Yahweh's nature was understood by Hosea and Jeremiah (4:3-4).

The prophet Zephaniah uses a similar figure (Zeph. 1:12). Here also the Diogenes dimension is present. "At that time I will search Jerusalem with lamps," he writes. This figure in Zephaniah is the more interesting in view of the fact that he was Jeremiah's contemporary. It is also probable that the verses of this first chapter of Zephaniah's book were written either during or shortly after the reign of Josiah. The comparison is, therefore, the more startling in view of the repetition in Zeph. 1:12b of an attitude similar to that expressed in Jer. 5:12. Zephaniah's words are addressed to

> "those who say in their hearts,
> 'The LORD will not do good,
> nor will he do ill.' "

Jeremiah speaks of those who

> ". . . have spoken falsely of the LORD,
> and [who] have said, 'He will do nothing.' "

4 Therefore I said, Surely these *are* poor; they are foolish: for they know not the way of the Lord, *nor* the judgment of their God.

5 I will get me unto the great men, and will speak unto them; for they have known the way of the Lord, *and* the judgment of their God: but these have altogether broken the yoke, *and* burst the bonds.

6 Wherefore a lion out of the forest shall slay them, *and* a wolf of the evenings shall spoil them, a leopard shall watch over their cities: every one that goeth out thence shall be torn in pieces: because their transgressions are many, *and* their backslidings are increased.

4 Then I said, "These are only the poor,
they have no sense;
for they do not know the way of the Lord,
the law of their God.
5 I will go to the great,
and will speak to them;
for they know the way of the Lord,
the law of their God."
But they all alike had broken the yoke,
they had burst the bonds.

6 Therefore a lion from the forest shall slay
them,
a wolf from the desert shall destroy
them.
A leopard is watching against their cities,
every one who goes out of them shall
be torn in pieces;
because their transgressions are many,
their apostasies are great.

---

is to the suffering in the battle of Megiddo, in which Neco killed Josiah. It may well be more general than that.

4-6. Jeremiah reports to the Lord after his first search of Jerusalem: he is not successful, but the people among whom he has searched **are only the poor,** who could not be expected to know God's **law.** The group included those known in later times as the ʿam hāʾāreç, people without the leisure and learning to understand God's requirements, day laborers, shopkeepers, etc. Of the word here translated **law** (mishpāṭ), S. R. Driver (*The Book of the Prophet Jeremiah* [2nd ed.; London: Hodder & Stoughton, 1908], p. 344) says: "The right way of worshipping God . . . *a prescribed system of ordinances.* . . . The word thus becomes virtually equivalent to *religion.*"

Undoubtedly the indifference of the people is, to both prophets, a very striking feature of the people's behavior during this period of crisis. Both prophets wished to startle the people out of their complacency. One significant difference, however, may be observed. Zephaniah's poem places the words of vs. 12 in the mouth of Yahweh. It is Yahweh who will search Jerusalem with lamps and he is to do it on "that day," for "the day of the Lord is at hand"; it is on this day, according to Zephaniah, that Yahweh "will utterly sweep away everything from the face of the earth." Here is further evidence of the extent to which the apocalyptic flavor pervades the work of Zephaniah as over against the much milder use of such figures by Jeremiah. It is not Yahweh who searches the streets of Jerusalem in the book of Jeremiah, but it is the prophet himself who is instructed to **run to and fro.**

Jeremiah is told to move through the streets of Jerusalem and to **look and take note.** Clearly his intention here is not that of the ironically acted parable of Diogenes, nor is it that of the apocalyptically heightened judgment of Zephaniah. It is far more like that of the poet described by Robert Browning:

I only knew one poet in my life:
. . . .
He walked and tapped the pavement with his cane,
Scenting the world, looking it full in face,
An old dog, bald and blindish, at his heels.
. . . .
He stood and watched the cobbler at his trade,
The man who slices lemons into drink,
. . . .
If any beat a horse, you felt he saw;
If any cursed a woman, he took note;
. . . .
We had among us, not so much a spy,
As a recording chief-inquisitor,
The town's true master if the town but knew! [9]

That is to say, Jeremiah's movement into the town was at this point like that of "a recording chief-inquisitor," a sort of *corrector errarum,* his function exceeding that of Browning's poet by virtue of the divine intention which in-

[9] "How It Strikes a Contemporary."

7 ¶ How shall I pardon thee for this? thy children have forsaken me, and sworn by *them that are* no gods: when I had fed them to the full, they then committed adultery, and assembled themselves by troops in the harlots' houses.

8 They were *as* fed horses in the morning: every one neighed after his neighbor's wife.

9 Shall I not visit for these *things?* saith the Lord: and shall not my soul be avenged on such a nation as this?

7 "How can I pardon you?
    Your children have forsaken me,
    and have sworn by those who are no gods.
When I fed them to the full,
    they committed adultery
    and trooped to the houses of harlots.

8 They were well-fed lusty stallions,
    each neighing for his neighbor's wife.

9 Shall I not punish them for these things?
               says the Lord;
and shall I not avenge myself
    on a nation such as this?

After this failure Jeremiah determined to **go to the great,** the officials, priests, prophets, and others who might be expected to know God's requirements. But he found that they too had thrown off God's yoke. The punishment in vs. 6 may refer to the coming of the foe from the north (cf. 4:7, with its figure of the lion for this foe).

7-9. Yahweh speaks to the people (through the prophet): how can he forgive those who swear by false gods and commit adultery? He must **punish them.**

The word יתגדדו, translated **trooped** or **assembled themselves by troops,** may also mean "lacerated themselves," as in Canaanite cultic practices (cf. I Kings 18:28; Deut. 14:1). If this is the correct rendering, the verse has to do with false religious practices.

---

formed his search, what Skinner calls "his work as a moral censor." [1]

But Jeremiah's searching of the streets of Jerusalem is not merely that of a moral censor. He is motivated by a divine purpose. He undertakes to find a man, one who does justice and seeks truth in order that Yahweh may pardon the city.

This is reminiscent of Abraham's bargaining with God (Gen. 18:22-33) to obtain his mercy and leniency for the people of Sodom. The principle here, however, is more profound. It anticipates the subsequent theological recognition of the fact that the mercy and forgiveness of God run in advance of the behavior of men. Yahweh is already seeking out the penitent man before man is aware of it!

The degree and depth of Jeremiah's disillusionment is indicated in his reply to Yahweh (vss. 2-3). Recognizing that the Lord is constantly looking for faithful men in order that he may deal bountifully with them, Jeremiah goes on to point out that the Lord has already chastened them. But the people have **felt no anguish** and **they refused to take correction.** It is possible that there is a reference here to the battle of Megiddo, in which Josiah had been slain. Or the reference may be to misfortunes accumulated through the past hundred years. The unhappy fact is that the people **have made their faces harder than rock** and **have refused to repent.**

[1] *Prophecy and Religion,* p. 141.

Though this stubbornness seemed universal, Jeremiah apparently argued to himself that the stubborn were **only the poor.** These were the common people, those in the shops, the workers, the planters, the shepherds, people who **have no sense;** they were not sufficiently trained to **know the way of the Lord.** Since their plight could not be healed from below, Jeremiah decided to go to **the great,** the leaders. But neither did these **know the way of the Lord.** Perhaps there is nothing quite so shattering as the disillusionment of a young man who, having discovered the shortcomings and delinquencies of the people in general, turns with eagerness to the men in high position—the men of learning, the men of influence, the men of power—only to find that these too are willful, self-seeking, and blind to the people's real predicament. The statement attributed to Sir Robert Walpole in the House of Commons, that he knew the price of every man in that house except three, is pathetic in the extreme. Since his own political integrity was not beyond reproach, it is easy to see how political corruption can so pervade a society as to make it vulnerable to every sort of moral compromise. Even this, however, falls short of Jeremiah's insight. For he had come upon one of the very great mysteries of the human condition. He was forced to recognize that

     they all alike had broken the yoke,
     they had burst the bonds.

10 ¶ Go ye up upon her walls, and destroy; but make not a full end: take away
her battlements; for they *are* not the LORD's.

11 For the house of Israel and the house
of Judah have dealt very treacherously
against me, saith the LORD.

10 "Go up through her vine-rows and destroy,
but make not a full end;
strip away her branches,
for they are not the LORD's.

11 For the house of Israel and the house of
Judah
have been utterly faithless to me,
says the LORD.

Some read, with two Hebrew MSS, the LXX, and O.L., יתגוררו, "they became guests in harlots' houses."

10-11. The Lord commands destroyers to go up and ravage the vineyard of Israel. The rendering of the RSV is correct rather than that of the KJV. Israel is spoken of as a vineyard, as in 2:21; Isa. 5, *et al.* In 10$a\beta$ the word **not** is probably a mitigating gloss (cf. vs. 18; 4:27).

He had discovered what T. S. Eliot has called "the Mystery of Iniquity"—"a pit too deep for mortal eyes to plumb." [2]

More than likely vs. 6 does not belong here. It appears to be thrown in by the editor whose disposition it is to supply a poem of judgment after every poetic indictment, just as ch. 4 does on a much larger scale for chs. 2 and 3. Nevertheless the placing of the fragment in this position is sound in principle, for Jeremiah sees a moral equivalence between the moral corruption of a people and the disasters which overtake it. This principle is again tied in with the notion of the apostasy of the people.

Also worth noting is the recurrence of the animal symbols (cf. 4:7, 16*b*-17). The lion, the wolf, and the leopard again symbolize dangers appropriate to the continuation of the metaphor in vs. 5 where, as above (2:20), the people like oxen had **broken the yoke** and **burst the bonds.** Thus, morally, they wander from the protection of spiritual integrity and, in their aimless movements, fall within reach of the lion from the jungle and the wolf from the steppes, to say nothing of the stealthy leopard. In any case the animals are to be taken as metaphors, and it is possible even that they imply once again the Assyrians, the Scythians, and the Ethiopians.[3] Dante, in appropriating this verse for the purposes of his *Divine Comedy,* has extended the allegory even further. In Canto I of the *Inferno* he encounters

> . . . a panther, nimble, light,
> And cover'd with a speckled skin. . . .

The panther or leopard so described stands for pleasure or luxury. The lion and the she-wolf

which next confront him stand respectively for pride, or ambition, and avarice. Rossetti, interpreting Dante's meaning here, is persuaded that Dante's leopard is used to denote in addition the city of Florence, while his lion denotes the king of France and his wolf the court of Rome. Multiple implications in a poetic symbol are frequently employed in the poetry of many periods, including our own. The leopard is particularly effective in this context, as it may lie in wait a great while outside the walls of the city until such time as the stupidity of the people leads them too far (like wandering oxen) and then it will be too late.

The return to vs. 7 is abrupt unless it is held to resume the argument from the close of vs. 5. In the light of the people's behavior Yahweh asks how he can possibly pardon them; and here the familiar metaphors of Jeremiah—idolatry, adultery, and harlotry—reappear with cumulative power. The three terms are tied in, however, with a fresh metaphor, that of the **lusty stallions.** The skill with which this metaphor is introduced (vs. 7) is indicated by the phrase, **when I fed them to the full,** anticipating the climax of the metaphor in vs. 8, where the people who have been fed are specified as **lusty stallions, each neighing for his neighbor's wife.** This powerful metaphor tends both to literalize and to generalize the behavior of the people at one and the same time. Harry Freedman points to the Talmudic proverb: " 'The lion does not growl over a heap of straw, but over a heap of flesh' (Ber. 32a), i.e., satiety produces haughtiness. The prosperity which God granted to them, instead of making them grateful, led to depravity (cf. Deut. xxxii. 15)." [4] Freedman also suggests that in addition to the fine pun in the English line **each neighing for his neighbor's wife** the Hebrew for

[2] "You have seen the house built, you have seen it adorned," Chorus No. X, from *The Rock* (London: Faber & Faber; New York: Harcourt, Brace & Co., 1934).

[3] Cf. Herodotus *History* VII. 62-79.

[4] *Jeremiah* (London: Soncino Press, 1949), p. 36.

12 They have belied the LORD, and said, *It is* not he; neither shall evil come upon us; neither shall we see sword nor famine:
 	
 13 And the prophets shall become wind, and the word *is* not in them: thus shall it be done unto them.
	12 They have spoken falsely of the LORD,
	    and have said, 'He will do nothing;
	no evil will come upon us,
	    nor shall we see sword or famine.
	13 The prophets will become wind;
	    the word is not in them.
	Thus shall it be done to them!' "

12-14. Yahweh speaks to Jeremiah: because the people deny God's power and the inspiration of the prophets, he will make his word **a fire** in the mouth of Jeremiah to destroy the people. The quotation of the saying of the people continues through vs. 13. Their attitude is a "practical atheism," which denies God's power though not his

lusty stallions is an abbreviated form for a denominative of the male organ of generation. The apostasy of the people is thus heightened to the extreme, and the Lord's punishment appears to be inevitable.

Jeremiah's persuasion that the people, through their iniquities, betrayals, and corrupt behavior, bring their punishment upon themselves (cf. 4:18) is made apparent in the following metaphor in which Yahweh commands the "foe" to come up against Judah to punish and destroy. Anyone who has lived in a country of vineyards will be impressed with the power of this metaphor. He is certain to be struck by the accuracy with which it is employed (cf. also 2:21; 6:9; 8:13). The ravaging of the vine-rows by the approaching foe bears a greater significance for the understanding of Jeremiah's attitude than at first appears. For Yahweh instructs the ravagers to **make not a full end of** Judah but to **go up through her vine-rows** and **strip away her branches.** The stump of the vine is not to be destroyed. The season's growth, its branches, must be destroyed because **they are not the LORD's.** The trunk is sound (but see Exeg.). When the people remember their original covenant with Yahweh the vineyard may once again become fruitful and its fruit be pleasing in the sight of the Lord.

This hope, however, is concealed in the vigor of the indictment which follows. The reason for the stripping away of the branches of the Lord's vineyard is clear: **the house of Israel and the house of Judah** have been unfaithful. The people have been unfaithful because of the false leadership which they have had. Those persons responsible for the mediation of the word of the Lord, and for the instruction of the people, have **spoken falsely.** A fatal complacency has overtaken the people. They have been lulled into apathy and a sense of false security by the unrealistic optimists who were saying, "It can't happen here." These were the men who, according to Zephaniah,

were "thickening upon their lees," becoming stagnant in spirit and consoling themselves with the thought that nothing would happen to them:

> "The Lord will not do good,
>   nor will he do ill" (Zeph. 1:12).

The prophets of doom, according to these people, were nothing but windbags. Their words were empty.

The introduction of the term *rûah* in this passage indicates again the rhetorical and poetic skill of the author. For the term *rûah*, here employed to signify wind, nevertheless carries with it always a sense of "power, violent, strong, overwhelming and controlling in its nature." As such it is a term that is big with implication. It is a term which carries over in other contexts to "the life-giving-spirit-wind-breath" of Ezek. 37:5-14. It may also be applied to the spirit of the Lord: "the *ruach-adonai* is the manifestation in human experience of the life-giving, energy-creating power of God." [5]

Once this is noted it is impossible not to see how the movement of the poem carries forward into the powerful climax of vs. 14. Having set out at the command of Yahweh to search the streets of Jerusalem for a man who would be just and a genuine seeker for the truth, Jeremiah had the fact forced upon him that people were universally rebellious. He had found this true both of the poor and of people of higher estate. **All alike . . . had burst the bonds** and had sworn themselves by the idols which were no gods. Thus were they both adulterous and faithless. They had reached a point of callous indifference to the integrity of their election under the covenant with the Lord. The essence of this election, as Brunner has pointed out, consists in the fact that its

[5] Norman H. Snaith, "The Spirit of God in Jewish Thought," in Snaith *et al., The Doctrine of the Holy Spirit* (London: Epworth Press, 1937), p. 11.

14 Wherefore thus saith the LORD God of hosts, Because ye speak this word, behold, I will make my words in thy mouth fire, and this people wood, and it shall devour them.

15 Lo, I will bring a nation upon you from far, O house of Israel, saith the LORD: it *is* a mighty nation, it *is* an ancient nation, a nation whose language thou knowest not, neither understandest what they say.

16 Their quiver *is* as an open sepulchre, they *are* all mighty men.

14 Therefore thus says the LORD, the God of hosts:
"Because they[e] have spoken this word,
behold, I am making my words in your mouth a fire,
and this people wood, and the fire shall devour them.
15 Behold, I am bringing upon you
a nation from afar, O house of Israel,
says the LORD.
It is an enduring nation,
it is an ancient nation,
a nation whose language you do not know,
nor can you understand what they say.
16 Their quiver is like an open tomb,
they are all mighty men.

[e] Heb *you*

---

existence (cf. Ps. 14:1; Zeph. 1:12). In vs. 13 there is a play on the word *rûaḥ,* which can mean either "spirit" or **wind:** the prophets think they have the spirit of God, but the people think they have only **wind.** The people deny that prophets like Jeremiah are truly inspired. But that which the people thought was mere wind will have the power of fire (on vs. 14 cf. Exeg. on 1:10).

2. THE COMING OF A FOE (5:15-17)

15-17. Though this passage does not mention the north, it probably has reference to the foe from the north of ch. 4. The description is so general that it might fit a number of nations. But the adjectives **enduring** and **ancient** would not fit the Scythians. Herodotus

---

basis "never lies in the one who is chosen, but exclusively in the one who chooses. Election means precisely this: that Israel knows itself to be wholly dependent upon the grace of the One who has chosen her, and that she ought to live in this attitude of continual dependence."[6] Once the people have turned aside from their allegiance to the Lord and walked in other ways they lose the benefits of his grace, and the desert of emptiness opens before them, just as the abyss of non-being opens beneath them. Therefore Jeremiah's sense of his prophetic vocation is borne in upon him invincibly. Because of the indifference of the people and of their teachers the Lord says to him

behold, I am making my words in your mouth a fire,
and this people wood, and the fire shall devour them.

The *rûaḥ* or empty wind now fans the Lord's words into a fire. It is perhaps stretching the internal consistency of the poem too far to

[6] *The Christian Doctrine of God,* I, 310.

suggest that the branches of the vineyard which were stripped away soon wither and are fit only to be burned. For while the people of vs. 14 are not yet the people whose vine-rows have been ravaged, the N.T. principle is nonetheless clearly operative: "If a man does not abide in me, he is cast forth as a branch and withers; and the branches are gathered, thrown into the fire and burned" (John 15:6). Jeremiah knows that the people's complacency is such that honeyed speech and soothing metaphors will not bring about the repentance which they need. They must be awakened, startled, flogged by his prophetic word into a consciousness of their condition; and if, in their hearts, they have become dull and unresponsive wood, then he must devour them in his prophetic fire.

15-17. *Their Quiver Is Like an Open Tomb.* —Here is another of the so-called Scythian poems, a fragment interjected very much as vs. 6 into the predominantly moral tone and purpose of the poems in the two chapters. Thus are conserved the dramatic effects of ch. 4 which evoked the sense of impending doom; and the sense of external threat is permitted to preside over

17 And they shall eat up thine harvest and thy bread, *which* thy sons and thy daughters should eat: they shall eat up thy flocks and thine herds: they shall eat up thy vines and thy fig trees: they shall impoverish thy fenced cities, wherein thou trustedst, with the sword.

18 Nevertheless in those days, saith the LORD, I will not make a full end with you.

19 ¶ And it shall come to pass, when ye shall say, Wherefore doeth the LORD our God all these *things* unto us? then shalt thou answer them, Like as ye have forsaken me, and served strange gods in your land, so shall ye serve strangers in a land *that is* not yours.

17 They shall eat up your harvest and your food;
    they shall eat up your sons and your daughters;
    they shall eat up your flocks and your herds;
    they shall eat up your vines and your fig trees;
your fortified cities in which you trust
    they shall destroy with the sword."

18 "But even in those days, says the LORD, I will not make a full end of you. 19 And when your people say, 'Why has the LORD our God done all these things to us?' you shall say to them, 'As you have forsaken me and served foreign gods in your land, so you shall serve strangers in a land that is not yours.'"

(*History* IV. 5) reports, "The Scythians say that theirs is the youngest of all nations"; the Hebrews could hardly have considered them to be an ancient nation. This passage is very similar to Deut. 28:49-51; for this reason, and because of its apocalyptic tone, Volz denies that it is from Jeremiah. The dependence, however, is more likely to be of Deut. 28:49-51 upon this passage (Rudolph; see further J. Philip Hyatt, "Jeremiah and Deuteronomy," *Journal of Near Eastern Studies,* I [1942], 172-73). On the identity of the foe see Intro., p. 779.

Their quiver: Volz (followed by Rudolph) emends אשפתו to אשר פיהו, "whose mouth"; this is more appropriate to the figure involved here.

3. EXPLANATION OF THE EXILE (5:18-19)

18-19. These verses are widely recognized as editorial. They are from the Deuteronomic editor who here furnishes a ready answer to the question raised by the destruction of Jerusalem and the exile of some of the people to Babylonia in 587 B.C. The passage is very similar in form and content to 9:12-14; 16:10-13; 22:8-9; Deut. 29:22-28; and I Kings 9:8-9. Vs. 18 shows D's awareness that the land was not fully destroyed in 587; from this verse glosses have been added to 4:27; 5:10.

---

the moral indictment and moral instruction as a whole. **An enduring nation** and **an ancient nation** do not necessarily apply either to Assyria or to Babylonia (cf. Exeg.). The Scythian nation was doubtless to Jeremiah a primitive people. The poem is built, as a matter of fact, around a single compound metaphor (vs. 16). **Their quiver is like an open tomb** is one of the finest of Jeremiah's figures. It contains that freshness and audacity so much admired by the Elizabethans and the seventeenth-century metaphysical poets, as well as by our moderns. It falls within Dr. Samuel Johnson's definition of wit-writing as "a kind of *discordia concors;* a combination of dissimilar images, or discovery of occult resemblances in things apparently unlike." Nothing could set forth more vividly

than this metaphor the sense of the deadliness of the enemies' arrows. They are shot so rapidly that the enemies' quivers are empty, and their emptiness is the emptiness of death.

By this death they shall be devoured. The movement from the **open tomb** to the open, devouring mouth is a further poetic achievement. The **food,** the **sons,** the **daughters,** the **flocks,** the **herds,** the **vines,** the **fig trees,** shall all fall and be devoured by the onslaught of the foe. Their **fortified cities** shall fall. And the whole of this fine metaphorical *perçu* is aesthetically enhanced by the term **mighty** (vs. 16), a term customarily applied to a never-failing or perennial stream. So shall the enemy come, in a great flowing tide, the arrows leaping in the splashing turbulence of death and ruin.

20 Declare this in the house of Jacob, and publish it in Judah, saying,

21 Hear now this, O foolish people, and without understanding; which have eyes, and see not; which have ears, and hear not:

22 Fear ye not me? saith the LORD: will ye not tremble at my presence, which have placed the sand *for* the bound of the sea by a perpetual decree, that it cannot pass it: and though the waves thereof toss themselves, yet can they not prevail; though they roar, yet can they not pass over it?

20 Declare this in the house of Jacob,
    proclaim it in Judah:
21 "Hear this, O foolish and senseless people,
    who have eyes, but see not,
    who have ears, but hear not.
22 Do you not fear me? says the LORD;
    Do you not tremble before me?
I placed the sand as the bound for the sea,
    a perpetual barrier which it cannot pass;
though the waves toss, they cannot prevail,
    though they roar, they cannot pass over it.

4. DENIAL OF YAHWEH'S POWER IN NATURE (5:20-25)

20-25. Duhm declares that all of this chapter after vs. 17 is secondary, and Volz rejects vss. 15-25. Several other scholars reject vss. 20-22 because of the similarity in style and content to the wisdom literature and to Second Isaiah. Yet the idea of God's

20-25. The Unnaturalness of Sin.—Jeremiah has already pointed out (4:22) how the people in their foolishness and stupidity have brought upon themselves (4:18) the political disasters which are about to overtake them (5:5-6). He has also shown how their refusal "to take correction" (vs. 3) has already brought upon them certain punishments. He is now about to make a third appeal. Not only is their behavior **foolish** and stubborn (vs. 3*b*), but it is also unnatural in the extreme. Immanuel Kant was filled with awe when he beheld the starry heavens above and the moral law within. But the people of Judah are not moved when they behold the greatness of God.

Something of this same sense of wonder and awe pervades the speech of Augustine when, in *The City of God*, he contemplates "the rich and countless blessings with which the goodness of God, . . . has filled this very misery of the human race." His style becomes almost lyrical when he says

How can I tell of the rest of creation, with all its beauty and utility, which the Divine Goodness has given to man to please his eye and serve his purposes? . . . Shall I speak of the sea, which itself is so grand a spectacle, when it arrays itself as it were, in vestures of various colors, now running through every shade of green, and again becoming purple or blue? [7]

Augustine's purpose here is not altogether unlike that of Jeremiah. He seeks to raise the eye of his reader from these earthly harmonies to more ultimate ones. Jeremiah too complains

[7] XXII. 24.

that the people **have eyes, but see not.** But Jeremiah is more realistic here than Augustine. What the people do not see is not some ethereal or metaphysical citizenship in heaven, but the overwhelming and ordering power of God. This is that primitive power described by the modern poet as that "dolphin-torn, that gong-tormented sea." [8] But for Jeremiah it is that primitive power as it has been subdued by the ordering and ordaining power of God. For here is a picture of the creative power of God setting "the sands to bound the deep" and making thereby "a barrier that no breakers shall o'erleap" (Moffatt).

Now it is frequently pointed out, in exposition of this section, that Jeremiah is emphasizing the fact that nature is everywhere obedient to the ordinances of God, whereas man is disobedient.[9] Spurgeon, in his powerful sermon on these verses, puts this quite clearly:

I can scarcely conceive a heart so callous that it feels no awe, or a human mind so dull and destitute of understanding, as fairly to view the tokens of God's omnipotent power, and then turn aside without some sense of the fitness of obedience. [But, he continues,] Is it not, my brethren, a marvelous thing, that the whole earth is obedient to God, save man? . . . On earth man makes the base exception, he is continually revolting and rebelling against his Maker.[1]

[8] W. B. Yeats, "Byzantium," in *The Collected Poems of W. B. Yeats* (New York: The Macmillan Co., 1935), p. 286.

[9] Cf. T. K. Cheyne and W. F. Adeney, et al., *Jeremiah* (London: Kegan Paul Trench Trübner & Co., n.d.; "The Pulpit Commentary"), I, 115, 118.

[1] C. H. Spurgeon, *Sermons, Fifth Series* (New York: Sheldon & Co., 1859), pp. 180-83.

23 But this people hath a revolting and a rebellious heart; they are revolted and gone.

24 Neither say they in their heart, Let us now fear the LORD our God, that giveth rain, both the former and the latter, in his season: he reserveth unto us the appointed weeks of the harvest.

25 ¶ Your iniquities have turned away these *things,* and your sins have withholden good *things* from you.

23 But this people has a stubborn and rebellious heart;
they have turned aside and gone away.

24 They do not say in their hearts,
'Let us fear the LORD our God,
who gives the rain in its season,
the autumn rain and the spring rain,
and keeps for us
the weeks appointed for the harvest.'

25 Your iniquities have turned these away,
and your sins have kept good from you.

---

creation of the world is certainly older than Second Isaiah and Job; cf. Gen. 14:19, 22, where we should translate "creator of heaven and earth," giving קנה the meaning it has in Ugaritic and in Prov. 8:22. The myth of the deity's conquest of the rebellious ocean is very early. Also we should note that the parallels in wording with Second Isaiah are not close. The thought of vss. 20-25 seems to be entirely in agreement with Jeremiah's thinking. With vss. 24-25 cf. 3:3.

Nothing could point out more clearly the unnaturalness of the people's rebellious behavior than to observe how the whole of nature is ordered by natural law. Byron saw the irony of this contrast when in his famous "Apostrophe" he wrote

Roll on, thou deep and dark-blue Ocean—roll!
Ten thousand fleets sweep over thee in vain;
Man marks the earth with ruin—his control
Stops with the shore; . . .[2]

There is, however, a much deeper implication here. The poet is building upon the ancient Babylonian mythology, according to which Marduk, the sun god, created the world out of primeval chaos by overcoming the demon of chaos under the leadership of the monster Tiamat. The detail of this struggle has dropped away under the development of Hebrew speculation. The world picture of the prophets still works, however, within this cosmological setting. It is by way of this earlier mythological cosmology that water, the ocean, and the leviathan of the sea symbolize chaos in all Semitic poetry. Numerous passages—in Second Isaiah (Isa. 40–66), in the opening chapter of Genesis, in Proverbs (8:22-31), and in the Psalms (8; 19:1-6; 29; 104; 147; 148)—when compared with this passage, will show the retention of this cosmological setting, together with the obvious fading away of the earlier mythology as the concept of Yahweh acquired clear form.[3]

Job 38 is perhaps an amplification of this verse in Jeremiah.

[2] *Childe Harold's Pilgrimage,* Canto IV, st. clxxix.
[3] Cf. Herbert E. Ryle, *The Book of Genesis* (Cambridge: Cambridge University Press, 1921; "Cambridge Bible"); also Intro. to Genesis, Vol. I, and Exeg. on Gen. 1:1-2.

"Where were you when I laid the foundation of the earth?" (Vs. 4.)

"Or who shut in the sea with doors,
when it burst forth from the womb?" (Vs. 8.)

Here, as in several other places, there is a clear reference to the activity of God, to a time when he "prescribed bounds for it" (Job 38:10). Or, as Jeremiah says, placed the sand as the bound for the sea.[4] In spite of the tremendous power whereby God did set bounds for the sea, and subdued chaos, this foolish and senseless people do not fear him.

They do not say in their hearts,
"Let us fear the LORD our God."

But because of their stubborn and rebellious heart, they have turned aside. They are not even grateful for the gifts of God who gives the rain in its season and so prepares the time of the harvest. "Man," said Dostoevski, "is the creature without a sense of gratitude."[5]

But we must go one step further to reach the final implication of Jeremiah's comparison. It is to be found in the fact that

though the waves toss, they cannot prevail,
though they roar, they cannot pass over

the perpetual barrier of sand wherewith God has bound the rebellious seas. So also is Israel rebellious, and Judah, too, is beginning to toss. But just as the ocean cannot prevail against the ordinance of God, so the people cannot prevail against his higher purposes.

[4] Cf. Job 26:12; also Albion Roy King, *The Problem of Evil* (New York: Ronald Press Co., 1952), pp. 38-39.
[5] *Letters from the Underworld,* tr. C. J. Hogarth (New York: E. P. Dutton Co., 1929), p. 35.

26 For among my people are found wicked *men:* they lay wait, as he that setteth snares; they set a trap, they catch men.	26 For wicked men are found among my people;
	    they lurk like fowlers lying in wait.*f*
	They set a trap;
	    they catch men.

27 As a cage is full of birds, so *are* their houses full of deceit: therefore they are become great, and waxen rich.	27 Like a basket full of birds, their houses are full of treachery; therefore they have become great and rich,

28 They are waxen fat, they shine: yea, they overpass the deeds of the wicked: they judge not the cause, the cause of the fatherless, yet they prosper; and the right of the needy do they not judge.	28 they have grown fat and sleek.
	They know no bounds in deeds of wickedness;
	    they judge not with justice
	the cause of the fatherless, to make it prosper,
	    and they do not defend the rights of the needy.

f Heb uncertain

5. Wickedness of the Wealthy (5:26-29)

26-29. The Hebrew of vss. 26-28 is difficult and perhaps corrupt, and the LXX differs at a number of points. The sense, however, is given by the RSV. The wealthy are compared with **fowlers** who catch birds in traps. The **trap** was apparently a clapnet of the type pictured on Egyptian monuments: a large net with cords attached, the cords being held by men lying in wait who used them to close the net when a bird came into it. The birds were then placed in a **basket** (a better rendering of *kelûbh* than **cage,** vs. 27;

They will soon begin to feel the restrictive power of God whose ordinances cannot be so easily overleaped. Thus Jeremiah returns to his consistent teaching. "Your apostasy will reprove you" (2:19).

    Your ways and your doings
      have brought this upon you (4:18).

One cannot emphasize too strongly this basic dialectical feature of Jeremiah's view of the futility of rebellion against God, in all of its pathetic, ironical, and, at the last, tragic senselessness (vs. 21).

26-29. *The Wicked . . . Like Fowlers.*—Again we have one of Jeremiah's vivid metaphors, and a further specification of the moral and spiritual callousness which he found when he searched the city (vs. 1). This was the people with whom God had made a covenant. This was

    the people of his pasture,
      and the sheep of his hand (Ps. 95:7).

Here, if anywhere, should be found a people both upright and faithful. Such, however, is not the case. Wickedness abounds. As the terms of the covenant with God are ignored, so are the relations of man to man perverted. Wicked

men, rogues, employ their talents in wiles and stratagems in order to deceive their fellows. As fowlers set traps to catch birds, so these set traps to catch men. Their gains, therefore, are ill-gotten,

like cages filled with birds,
    their houses are full of swindling gains (Moffatt).

Three things mark the "prosperity" of such people. First, they grow **fat and sleek**—a figure used elsewhere in scripture (Deut. 32:15; Job 15:27; Ps. 73:7). Especially vivid is the description in Ps. 73:7, where the condition with its moral consequence is reduced to the pithiness of a proverb:

    their eyes swell out with fatness,
      their hearts overflow with follies.

It is interesting to note how the terms "sleekness" and "fatness" have become attached to this social type through all the ages and in all the peoples, persisting today most vividly in the cartooning caricatures of the plutocratic capitalist.

Second, it is characteristic of these people that

    they go to any length in crime,
      but make no move for justice (Moffatt).

| 29 Shall I not visit for these *things?* saith the LORD: shall not my soul be avenged on such a nation as this? | 29 Shall I not punish them for these things?
      says the LORD,
and shall I not avenge myself
  on a nation such as this?" |
| 30 ¶ A wonderful and horrible thing is committed in the land; | 30 An appalling and horrible thing
  has happened in the land: |

cf. Gillis Gerleman, *Contributions to the Old Testament Terminology of the Chase* [Lund: C. W. K. Gleerup, 1946]). This is a strong figure for social injustice, a subject which is not touched on by Jeremiah as often as false worship.

6. SINS OF PROPHETS AND PRIESTS (5:30-31)

30-31. The chapter closes with a picture of the corruption of the religious leaders and the apathy of the people. Jeremiah frequently speaks of the false **prophets** and **priests** (see especially 6:13-15; 23:9 ff.). The close association of the two here is probably an indication that the prophets were connected with the temples as professionals who consulted oracles.

The priests rule at their direction: This line is unusually difficult to render because both the verb and the phrase which follows can bear more than one meaning. The verb

---

The crimes, of course, are covert, and technically within the law. But their self-centeredness is revealed in the fact that, third,

> they never champion an orphan's cause
> or rally to a poor man's rights (Moffatt).

The passage in Mic. 7:2-3 may be, in some respects, a more vivid description of this type of social injustice; but it is not more incisive. Once the basic motivation of covert deceit, as exemplified in the fowler's traps, is disclosed, the indictment takes hold with fearful power, and the ruthless overriding of the people's justice and the poor man's rights becomes plain. **Shall I not punish them for these things?** the Eternal asks. For Jeremiah the punishment is already implicit in the deed; for it is unthinkable that the ordinances of God should be violated indefinitely.

30-31. *Prophets, Priests, and People.*—A glance back over the movement of this chapter will indicate that Jeremiah, when he entered the city to "look and take note" (5:1) and to search the streets for a man, went first to the poor and then to the great and finally to the people of influence—the wealthy and the magistrates (vs. 28) —only to find that

> they all alike had broken the yoke
> [and] had burst the bonds (5:5*b*).

To this "appalling and disgusting situation" (5:30 tr. Aubrey Johnson) he now adds the prophets and the priests.

A great deal of work has been done in recent years to show that the prophet as well as the

priest was a cult functionary in the life of Judah.[6] Associated with the king in the administration and maintenance of the community were the chiefs, the judging magnates, the soothsaying prophets, the teaching priests, and the elders. The functions of the chiefs had primarily to do with war against external enemies, though in early times the chief as well as the prophet "experienced that expansion of psychic power which meant that they were filled with the divine soul."[7] The prophet, on the other hand, not having the chief's responsibility for the community, cultivated his inward experiences as "something of independent value." This undoubtedly accounts, as Aubrey R. Johnson suggests, for the fact that the priests are ready, according to the present verses, to accept the direction of the prophets.[8]

In view of the fact that the divine knowledge of the prophet was so essentially different from that of the priests in that it was derived from personal contact with Yahweh, such a position may be readily understood. In fact, one may say that it was almost inevitable.[9]

As subsequent references by Jeremiah to the prophets and the priests will indicate, the position of the priests could not have been very subordinate to that of the prophets. Nonetheless Jeremiah is pointing out the appalling and

---

[6] Cf. Alfred O. Haldar, *Associations of Cult Prophets Among the Ancient Semites* (Uppsala: Almqvist & Wiksells, 1945), p. 113.

[7] Pedersen, *Israel, Its Life and Culture*, III-IV, p. 107.

[8] *The Cultic Prophet in Ancient Israel* (Cardiff: University of Wales Press Board, 1944), pp. 54 ff.

[9] *Ibid.*, p. 54.

| 31 The prophets prophesy falsely, and the priests bear rule by their means; and my people love *to have it* so: and what will ye do in the end thereof? | 31 the prophets prophesy falsely,
    and the priests rule at their direction;
my people love to have it so,
    but what will you do when the end comes? |

ירדו can mean either "they rule" or "they scrape out"; Cornill, Rudolph, and Peake emend to יורו or הורו, "they teach [or give oracles]." The remaining phrase, 'al yedhêhem, can be translated literally "into their hands," or figuratively "by their [the prophets' or their own] authority," **at their** [the prophets'] **direction,** or "at their [the prophets'] side." The simplest solution is perhaps to follow Duhm and read, "they scrape into their own hands," the figure of which can be readily understood. A very similar phrase occurs in Judg. 14:9, of Samson scraping honey into his hands from the carcass of the lion he had killed. The Amer. Trans. renders, "the priests make profit through them."

The worst aspect of the situation pictured here is that **my people love to have it so,** preferring to those religious leaders who are true those who are false to their office.

---

horrible thing which has happened in the land, namely that

> **the prophets prophesy falsely,**
> **and the priests rule at their direction.**

But what is appalling and horrible beyond words is the fact that the **people love to have it so!** This is the disconcerting mystery of human behavior. The rebellion against God distorts all the orders, perverts all the values, and the astonishing thing is that people not only persist in these ways but seem to prefer them. Jean Cocteau has put this with almost prophetic irony in his remark that "If it is necessary to choose one to be crucified the crowd always saves Barabbas."[1] No doubt this is a part of that "Mystery of Iniquity" which T. S. Eliot calls "a pit too deep for mortal eyes to plumb." Luther put it bluntly: "the world wills to belong to the devil."[2]

Jeremiah, however, is neither content to permit the problem to dissolve into its mystery, nor will he escape from it prophetically by projecting its solution apocalyptically into the indefinite future. He sees quite well that in proportion as the people default at the point of their covenantal integrity (i.e., in their relationship to God), "things fall apart. The center cannot hold."[3] In like manner, as the prophets and others who are chiefly responsible for the spiritual instruction and heritage of the people compromise the authenticity of the God-man relationship, so the community is corrupted from its very core.

One thinks inevitably of Julien Benda's vigorous and prophetic polemic against the intellectuals of France in the late twenties, a work which was given, in its English translation, the title of *The Great Betrayal*. As an epigraph for his indictment of *les clercs* of France, the author chose a passage from Renouvier: "The world suffers for the want of faith in a transcendent truth."[4]

For Jeremiah the world was suffering from a lack of constancy and faithfulness to the divine word. The truth of the covenant was a relational truth. Once the relation was broken the negative evils of manifold disorder and perversion would inevitably set in. This would give rise to what Kierkegaard called "the negative unity of the negative reciprocity of all individuals."[5] But this negative unity is anxiety-ridden, escapist, and inwardly frustrating. Its unconscious emotional component builds up what Nietzsche termed *Ressentiment*—a "sort of rumination," as Max Scheler expounded it, which gradually expands into "a whole world of negation and animosity." It produces a "hidden, continuously grumbling exasperation which is independent of the activity of the self and which little by little engenders a ruminative hate, or an animosity without any definite object towards which it is hostile, but big with an infinite number of hostile intentions."[6] This unconscious conspiracy of the negative unity of a people, which flies from whatever is increasingly threatening and perilous in its predicament and thereby refuses to come to terms with itself, breeds that stubbornness of heart

---

[1] "Le coq et l'arlequin." *Le rappel à l'ordre* (Paris: Librarie Stock, 1926), p. 39.

[2] *Colloquia*, ed. H. E. Bindseil (Detmold: Meyer, 1863), I, 173.

[3] W. B. Yeats, "The Second Coming," in *The Collected Poems of W. B. Yeats* (New York: The Macmillan Co., 1935), p. 215.

[4] *La trahison des clercs* (Paris: Bernard Grasset, 1927), pp. 7, 10, *et passim*.

[5] *The Present Age*, p. 28.

[6] Max Scheler, *L'homme du ressentiment* (Paris: Gallimard, 1933), p. 9; quoted in Kierkegaard, *The Present Age*, pp. 23-24, n. 1.

| 6 O ye children of Benjamin, gather yourselves to flee out of the midst of Jerusalem, and blow the trumpet in Tekoa, and set up a sign of fire in Beth-haccerem: for evil appeareth out of the north, and great destruction. | 6 Flee for safety, O people of Benjamin, from the midst of Jerusalem! Blow the trumpet in Teko′a, and raise a signal on Beth-hacche′rem; for evil looms out of the north, and great destruction. |

E. Threats and Warnings (6:1-30)

This chapter contains two additional poems describing the foe from the north, who is represented as besieging Jerusalem (vss. 1-8, 22-26). Jeremiah finds the people still unrepentant and wholly corrupt (vss. 9-15). They have refused to follow **the ancient paths** or to heed the warnings of **watchmen**, trusting rather in ritual (vss. 16-21). In a closing section the prophet is represented as an assayer of the people (vss. 27-30).

1. Jerusalem Threatened with Siege (6:1-8)

In the first poem which dealt with the foe from the north, Jeremiah summoned the Judeans to flee into the fortified cities, especially Jerusalem, for safety (4:5-6). But now Jerusalem is unsafe, being itself threatened with siege, and he summons the people to leave that city and flee to other towns, such as Tekoa and Beth-haccherem.

6:1. It is difficult to understand why the prophet summons the **people of Benjamin** to leave Jerusalem. After its conquest by David, Jerusalem was sometimes reckoned to

which Jeremiah perceived on every hand. Sooner or later it will vent its hostility upon the man who seeks to set it right, meanwhile applauding those who offer easy solutions, upon whom it can project its own unrealistic illusions. Luther has reminded us that, if Jeremiah appears to be negative in his persistent chastisement of the people, it is because the conditions of the time permit him no other vocational alternative.[7]

Under these conditions it is not surprising that Jeremiah should attempt to bring the people up short with the question, **What will you do when the end comes?** for the people, like those described by Pascal, run carelessly to the precipice, after having covered their eyes to prevent their seeing it.[8]

The temptation to give this reference to the end an apocalyptic coloring is very great. Luther himself did so, in a very similar situation. "The darkness grows thicker around us. . . . Impiety and licentiousness are rampant throughout the world. . . . God will not be able to bear this wicked world much longer, but will come, with the dreadful day."[9] Luther recognizes the same cause, to wit, "the great unthankfulness, contempt of God's word, and [the] wilfulness of the world."[1] It is easy to see that this is not what Jeremiah intends. The dangers which threaten

the life of the people are imminent and apparent from where he stands. And the dangers are more appalling because they come from the folly of the people who look at evil and **love to have it so.**

6:1-30. The People's Assayer.—It is impossible not to observe in this chapter how the several themes of chs. 4-5 have been progressively reduced to three: how the one which was most prominent in ch. 4 is least so here, and how what was incidental at the beginning becomes climactic at the end. The brilliant cycle of the city's siege by the foe from the north set forth in ch. 4 and made to undergird the indictment of the people in ch. 5 is reiterated in ch. 6; but while it may still be said to occupy in some sense the foreground of the argument, the dramatic interest of the three chapters taken as a whole has been transferred from the external aspects of the people's predicament to the terms of inner defection whereby they bring this doom upon themselves. This could imply that the urgency which impelled the highly charged utterances of ch. 4 has passed (as, e.g., in the hypothesis that the Scythian hordes had come, passed by, and receded into the northland); or it could mean that the editorial work in chs. 5-6 has not the aesthetic excellences of that in ch. 4; or it could mean that the interest of the three chapters taken as a whole intentionally begins with the trumpet of alarm in terms of the practical predicament of the people and passes to the prophet's real concern, viz., the corruption and defection of the people; or, if it be granted that

[7] "Vorrede über den Propheten Jeremia," *Sämmtliche Werke* (Frankfurt a. M.: Hender & Zimmer, 1854), LXIII, 59 ff.

[8] *Thoughts*, No. 183.

[9] *Table Talk*, tr. William Hazlitt (Philadelphia: United Lutheran Publication House) No. XV, p. 9.

[1] *Ibid.*, p. 8.

2 I have likened the daughter of Zion to a comely and delicate *woman*.

3 The shepherds with their flocks shall come unto her; they shall pitch *their* tents against her round about; they shall feed every one in his place.

4 Prepare ye war against her; arise, and let us go up at noon. Woe unto us! for the day goeth away, for the shadows of the evening are stretched out.

5 Arise, and let us go by night, and let us destroy her palaces.

2 The comely and delicately bred I will
　destroy,
　　the daughter of Zion.
3 Shepherds with their flocks shall come
　against her;
　they shall pitch their tents around her,
　they shall pasture, each in his place.
4 "Prepare war against her;
　up, and let us attack at noon!"
"Woe to us, for the day declines,
　for the shadows of evening lengthen!"
5 "Up, and let us attack by night,
　and destroy her palaces!"

Judah and sometimes to Benjamin (George Adam Smith, *Jerusalem* [New York: A. C. Armstrong & Son, 1907], II, 35; F. M. Abel, *Géographie de la Palestine* [Paris: J. Gabalda, 1938], II, 54). Perhaps Jeremiah considered Jerusalem as being in Benjaminite territory; the phrase would thus include all the inhabitants. This is more probable than the view that he was concerned only with the safety of his fellow tribesmen of Benjamin who had settled in the capital.

Tekoa was twelve miles south of Jerusalem, the native town of Amos. The Hebrew has a play on words in the line, *bitheqôaʿ tiqeʿû shôphār*. The identification of **Beth-haccherem** is uncertain; some identify it with ʿAin Kârim, west of Jerusalem; others with Frank Mountain, three miles northeast of Tekoa. Neh. 3:14 is the only other verse in which it occurs. To **raise a signal** was to build a fire and make a smoke signal, as in Judg. 20:38-40 (described in detail for later times in the Mishnah, Rosh Ha-shanah 2:2-3). The word משאת occurs also in Lachish Letter No. IV, l. 10 (Torczyner, *et al.*, *Lachish Letters*, p. 79); see Exeg. on 34:7.

2. The daughter of Zion is Jerusalem personified as a woman, **comely and delicately bred.** The Hebrew, however, is difficult, and it is probable that the word here translated **comely** should be pointed so as to mean "meadow," with a rendering such as, "Has the

---

these poems were prepared over a considerable period of time, it could be that the prophet's message and insight matures in such a way as that after the moment of initial excitement he proceeds (ch. 5) to evaluate the behavior and practice of the people, and, in the course of doing so, defines gradually the real nature of his own prophetic call. In any case, the sense that the Lord had touched his mouth (1:9) is greatly enhanced (5:14) by the increasing awareness that the words of the Lord are in his mouth as a fire which increasingly he cannot contain (6:11), and which imposes upon him the office of people's assayer and tester (6:27-30) whereby he must "know and assay their ways." This is consistent with the dramatic perspective of ch. 5, wherein he is instructed to move through the streets of Jerusalem, to "look and take note" (5:1). It was the external threat of the foe from the north which was prominent at the beginning of ch. 4; it is the increasing maturation of his prophetic consciousness which is dominant and inescapable at the end of ch. 6.

1-8. Vignettes of the Siege.—Again the trumpet is sounded, the people are in flight, and the signal fire is lighted on the highest hill. A personification of the impending doom, "evil looks athwart from the north" (ERV) is a more vivid reading. So also is Moffatt's rendering of vss. 2-5:

Is it a meadow fair,
　the higher slopes of Sion?
Yet shepherds grim are bringing flocks,
　and pitching tents around,
　as though they owned the ground.
"Open the campaign," they cry;
　"come on, let us attack at noon!"—
"Pity the day is declining,
　the shadows are lengthening!"
"Come on, let us attack by night,
　and wreck her palaces!"

In this rendering the metaphor of the shepherds which is so confused in the original and seems to be uncharacteristically weak as a poetic metaphor takes on pictorial power in its portrayal of the oncoming foe as grim shepherds being in number like flocks of sheep.

6 ¶ For this hath the LORD of hosts said, Hew ye down trees, and cast a mount against Jerusalem: this *is* the city to be visited; she *is* wholly oppression in the midst of her.	6 For thus says the LORD of hosts: "Hew down her trees; cast up a siege mound against Jerusalem. This is the city which must be punished; there is nothing but oppression within her.
7 As a fountain casteth out her waters, so she casteth out her wickedness: violence and spoil is heard in her; before me continually *is* grief and wounds.	7 As a well keeps its water fresh, so she keeps fresh her wickedness; violence and destruction are heard within her; sickness and wounds are ever before me.
8 Be thou instructed, O Jerusalem, lest my soul depart from thee; lest I make thee desolate, a land not inhabited.	8 Be warned, O Jerusalem, lest I be alienated from you; lest I make you a desolation, an uninhabited land."

daughter of Zion become a lovely meadow?" (Cf. Cornill, Volz, Rudolph.) Such a translation is more appropriate to the figure of vs. 3.

6. Jerusalem is to be placed under **siege**; the verse would not fit the Scythians, who did not have the engines for besieging cities, but would be appropriate to the Chaldeans.

Similarly, the snatches of conversation from the foe are graphic. They appear to propose an initial attack at midday, when most of the people would be "taking their siesta"; [2] but the occasion for this surprise attack having passed they decide to attack by night.

In the verses which follow, the cutting down of trees to assist in the setting up of mounds, from which the battering-rams of assault could be operated to better advantage, is indicated vividly. This was a common practice of the Assyrian and Babylonian expeditions (cf. Deut. 20:20; Hab. 1:10).

There are two aspects of the description of **the city which must be punished** which stand out prominently. The first is the simile of the **well** [which] **keeps its water fresh** even as the city **keeps fresh her wickedness**. The second is the series of terms used to describe the nature of the city's wickedness and the condition which results from it.

The power of the simile is derived from the fact that the well is obviously self-fed. As such it is commonly employed in a constructive or affirmative sense—as in John 4:14: "the water that I shall give him will become in him a spring of water welling up to eternal life." But here, in Jeremiah, it is used negatively, to describe the mysterious and all-pervasive depth of Israel's wickedness; which makes it clear that Israel's wickedness is not thought of by Jeremiah as having to do merely with specific acts, but with the deepest and most elemental orien-

[2] Peake, *Jeremiah and Lamentations*, I, 138.

tation of the soul. This is consistent with his notion, already noted (2:19), of sin as apostasy, and with the successive metaphors of Israel's defection already described. Some translators prefer to read "a cistern" for "a well" and insist upon the importance of the distinction between a well which is self-fed and a cistern which has its water poured into it for storage from without. But this distinction does not arise for Jeremiah. For him one's "moral" orientation is conditioned by his antecedent relationship with God. He is not harassed by the syllogistic bifurcations of either Aristotelian or Scholastic logic. He is neither Augustinian nor Pelagian, for these alternatives do not arise in his universe of discourse. These are a people who have already been chosen of GOD. They stand in a covenantal relation with him, with promises and obligations mutually given and received. They respond freely to the conditions of this covenant. If they do not, or if they reject it, they stand immediately in the position of infidelity and betrayal. All the consequences of this condition infect their behavior. Oppression, wickedness, violence, destruction, and sickness well up, as it were, from within, and the sickness of the people is **ever before me.** The sickness is a sickness of the soul, resulting from its alienation of itself from God; and the violence is the indescribable succession of interweaving hostilities which souls so conditioned work perpetually upon one another.

Once more the prophet's poem concludes with a warning to the Lord's people. To be

9 ¶ Thus saith the LORD of hosts, They shall thoroughly glean the remnant of Israel as a vine: turn back thine hand as a grape gatherer into the baskets.

10 To whom shall I speak, and give warning, that they may hear? Behold, their ear *is* uncircumcised, and they cannot hearken: behold, the word of the LORD is unto them a reproach; they have no delight in it.

9 Thus says the LORD of hosts:
   "Glean*ᵍ* thoroughly as a vine
      the remnant of Israel;
   like a grape-gatherer pass your hand
      again
      over its branches."
10 To whom shall I speak and give warning,
      that they may hear?
   Behold, their ears are closed,[h]
      they cannot listen;
   behold, the word of the LORD is to them
      an object of scorn,
      they take no pleasure in it.

ᵍ Cn: Heb *they shall glean*
[h] Heb *uncircumcised*

2. THE PEOPLE'S TOTAL CORRUPTION (6:9-15)

9. This verse has been given various interpretations. It is best to consider it as a sequence to the thought expressed in 5:1. The prophet is to continue his search for an upright man. Like a gleaner who carefully passes his hand over all the branches of a vineyard seeking good grapes, the prophet is to continue to seek one who is upright. Vs. 9 is thus spoken by Yahweh to Jeremiah. The succeeding verses show that he still searches in vain.

10. This is the reply of the prophet to Yahweh, continuing through vs. 11*a* (through *holding it in*). We have here the first hint of Jeremiah's personal disappointment and bitterness over the cold response of the people which reaches its climax in 20:7-18.

alienated is, literally, to be "pulled out" as of something being pulled out by the roots, or as of someone's heart being torn or wrenched away. Yahweh's concern and care for his people is all-pervasive of their well-being; but the effect of the people's disorientation is such that all the positive benefits of his presence are being violently pulled out or wrenched away. Only desolation can follow. "For there is a joy which is not granted to the 'wicked,' but to those who worship Thee thankfully, whose joy Thou Thyself art. And the happy life is this,— to rejoice unto Thee, in Thee, and for Thee; this it is, and there is no other." [3]

9-15. *The Gleaning of the Vine.*—This opening verse stands in clear apposition with the first verse of ch. 5. There Jeremiah was told to search the squares of Jerusalem to see if he could find a man, one whose interest was focused in justice and truth. Now, in a parallel sense, he is told to

> **Glean thoroughly as a vine
> the remnant of Israel.**

Again, as in 5:10, the figure will strike with singular vividness anyone who has had any experience of grape picking. The grapes hang concealed beneath the thick leafage of the vine.

After the pickers have gone through the vineyards, reaching under the leaves to detach the heavy bunches, it is often possible to lift the branches and find bunches which the pickers have missed. Just as it was hoped that a man of integrity might be found in the city, so now it is hoped that in the remnant vines of Israel some evidence, heretofore overlooked, of good fruit may be found.

But Jeremiah protests. To whom could he speak, or give warning? The people were so far gone in the induration of their wills and hearts that they could no longer heed the word even if it were spoken. Just as they were uncircumcised of heart (4:4), so also were they uncircumcised of ear. Says H. Wheeler Robinson:

> The ear itself must be consecrated, if there is to be responsive hearing. . . . There is a certain momentum in moral evil, which carries on the will through what we should call the law of habit to a definite hardening, which is part of the penalty. The very phrase "stubbornness of the will" denotes its firmness or fixity in evil purpose.[4]

Yet there is in all of this a certain paradoxicality which Augustine knew quite well, whereby the person whose heart and mind has

[3] Augustine *Confessions* X. 22. 32.

[4] *The Cross of Jeremiah*, pp. 76-77.

11 Therefore I am full of the fury of the LORD; I am weary with holding in: I will pour it out upon the children abroad, and upon the assembly of young men together: for even the husband with the wife shall be taken, the aged with *him that is* full of days.

12 And their houses shall be turned unto others, *with their* fields and wives together: for I will stretch out my hand upon the inhabitants of the land, saith the LORD.

13 For from the least of them even unto the greatest of them every one *is* given to covetousness; and from the prophet even unto the priest every one dealeth falsely.

---

11 Therefore I am full of the wrath of the LORD;
　I am weary of holding it in.
"Pour it out upon the children in the street,
　and upon the gatherings of young men, also;
both husband and wife shall be taken,
　the old folk and the very aged.
12 Their houses shall be turned over to others,
　their fields and wives together;
for I will stretch out my hand
　against the inhabitants of the land,"
　　　　　　　　　says the LORD.
13 "For from the least to the greatest of them,
　every one is greedy for unjust gain;
and from prophet to priest,
　every one deals falsely.

---

11. Yahweh begins to speak with **Pour it out,** and continues through vs. 15. Vss. 12-15 are found in slightly different form in 8:10-12, but their original place was here, for they are more appropriate to the context here than in ch. 8.

---

turned from God both initiates his own hardness and flies from it.

I it was who willed, I who was unwilling. It was I, even I myself. I neither willed entirely nor was entirely unwilling. Therefore was I at war with myself, and destroyed by myself. And this destruction overtook me against my will, and yet showed not the presence of another mind, but the punishment of mine own.[5]

Thus, in our complicity with evil we willingly turn aside from the word of God, but at the same time piously seek him where he is certain not to be found. The ear is conditioned by the antecedent attitude to hear only what it wishes to hear and to be scornful of that which is unpleasant to it. "He is Thy best servant," says Augustine again, "who does not so much look to hear that from Thee which he himself wisheth, as to wish that which he heareth from Thee."[6] Jeremiah found no such servants in Jerusalem. He begins to exhibit a rising bitterness over the resistance of the people and their refusal to listen. This callousness and indifference on the part of the people, not to say their scorn, was undoubtedly disconcertingly frustrating to a young man of Jeremiah's sensibilities and prophetic temper. He begins to feel **the wrath of the LORD** arising within him. The longer he holds it in, and does not vent it upon

[5] *Confessions* VIII. 10. 22.
[6] *Ibid.* X. 26. 37.

the people, the more pent up and explosive within him it becomes. He reaches the psychological bursting point in 20:9; but already he finds a partial answer in the reply of Yahweh: **"Pour it out upon the children, . . . young men, . . . husband and wife, . . . old folk,**

　For from the least to the greatest of them,
　·　　·　　·　　·　　·　　·　　·
　and from prophet to priest,
　　every one deals falsely."

Here is the first anticipation of the graphic figure in 25:15 of the cup of the Lord's wrath.

No one is exempt from the acid accusation. From the least to the greatest, from prophet to priest, "every one acteth the fraud."[7] The lines which follow have become almost proverbial for describing sham counsel in times of trouble. Micah described the condition before Jeremiah, and Ezekiel makes the same charge after him. But its formulation here carries the restraint of genius and the power—indelible and fixed— of prophecy. Micah held that the prophets were perverting their function for private gain (Mic. 3:5-6). They gave out oracles and promises of "peace" to those who put food in their mouths, but made trouble for those who did not. Ezekiel held that the prophets attempted to whitewash the real difficulties, like people who whitewash a wall to conceal its defects (Ezek. 13:15).

[7] Johnson, *Cultic Prophet in Ancient Israel*, p. 45.

14 They have healed also the hurt of the daughter of my people slightly, saying, Peace, peace; when *there is* no peace.

15 Were they ashamed when they had committed abomination? nay, they were not at all ashamed, neither could they blush: therefore they shall fall among them that fall: at the time *that* I visit them they shall be cast down, saith the Lord.

14 They have healed the wound of my people lightly,
Saying, 'Peace, peace,'
when there is no peace.
15 Were they ashamed when they committed abomination?
No, they were not at all ashamed;
they did not know how to blush.
Therefore they shall fall among those who fall;
at the time that I punish them, they shall be overthrown,"

says the Lord.

---

14. This verse describes the false optimism of the religious leaders who deceive the people by their shallow prophesying of **peace.** For Jeremiah's view of the attitude of the true prophet see 28:8-9. The Hebrew word for **peace** (*shālôm*) means far more than absence of war; it is used to describe an ideal condition of material and spiritual prosperity.

This they did while "observing" vainly and "divining" falsely (Ezek. 22:28; cf. also Lam. 2:14). Jeremiah's figure, **they have healed the wound of my people lightly,** is at once more pathetic and more incisive. The deep seriousness of the people's wound—its "sickness unto death"—is minimized. Instead of skilled and honest surgery by which the malicious growth of infidelity and wickedness might be cut away, the cult prophets, like faithless physicians, are treating the wound superficially, soothing the patient with false assurances of essential well-being.

The prophets to whom Jeremiah here alludes are not scattered individuals who arise fortuitously here and there within the larger Israelite community, and who speak because they feel they are moved by the spirit of the Lord; they are definite groups fulfilling specified functions in the cultus of the people—in particular at the temple in Jerusalem. It should be noted in passing that Jeremiah (as well as Micah and Ezekiel) does not level his attack upon the function of the prophets as such, but upon the abuse of the office and the accommodation of the word to the wishful thinking of the people. On the other hand, the fact that the function of the cult prophets dies out in the course of time, and ceases to be after the period of Nehemiah, is doubtless to be accounted for in part by their failure at precisely this point of deepest integrity.[8] In any case, the author of the book of Lamentations sees clearly that the "false and deceptive visions" of the cultic prophets have failed to expose the people's "iniquity," and that such exposure is prerequisite to a restoration of their fortunes (Lam. 2:14).

Aubrey Johnson points out that the term

[8] *Ibid.,* p. 29, *et passim.*

"peace" used in this connection is not to be understood in a passive sense. "The Hebrew term has a more active meaning, and is thus more forceful; it denotes an ordered or harmonious functioning of the whole personality, individual or collective, and may be rendered more appropriately by 'welfare.'"[9]

The fact that this term "peace" may be applied equally to the individual or to what H. Wheeler Robinson called "the corporate personality" no doubt justifies George Whitefield's accommodation of this text to a highly evangelical sermon addressed to the individual on "The Method of Grace." In his heightened rhetoric Whitefield holds that "the greatest curse that God can possibly send upon a people in this world, is to give them over to blind, unregenerate, carnal, lukewarm, and unskillful guides. . . . None spake more," says he, "against such ministers, than Jeremiah." Jeremiah therefore delivered his "thundering message" against the false prophets for "daubing over the wound" and "stifling people's convictions." And since, holds Whitefield, "religion is everywhere represented in scripture, as the work of God in the heart," it is necessary, if people are to experience the peace of which Jeremiah speaks, that they "be made to see, made to feel, made to weep over, made to bewail [their] actual transgressions against the law of God." From the standpoint of God even "our best duties are so many splendid sins." Until people are convicted of their own self-righteousness no genuine peace can come. "It is the last idol that is taken out of our heart." Jeremiah's people are far from this sense of self-conviction. **Were they ashamed,** asks Yahweh, **when they committed abomination? No,** he answers, **they**

[9] *Ibid.,* p. 44, n. 1.

16 Thus saith the LORD, Stand ye in the ways, and see, and ask for the old paths, where *is* the good way, and walk therein, and ye shall find rest for your souls. But they said, We will not walk *therein*.

16 Thus says the LORD:
"Stand by the roads, and look,
 and ask for the ancient paths,
where the good way is; and walk in it,
 and find rest for your souls.
But they said, 'We will not walk in it.'

3. REJECTION OF THE ANCIENT PATHS (6:16-21)

16. By **the ancient paths** Jeremiah means the ways pointed out in ancient times, especially in the time of Moses. The words are addressed to the people, whose reply is given in the last line. The phrase **rest for your souls** occurs in Matt. 11:29, but in a deeper spiritual sense than here.

were not at all ashamed; in fact they could not even **blush.** And this is the reason, from Jeremiah's day until our own, that **they shall fall.** Things fall apart, as Yeats has said, when the center cannot hold.

16-21. *The Parting of the Ways.*—The concluding verses of this poem (vss. 18-21) make its general argument plain. Two things the people ought to have done if they wished the blessings of the "peace" alluded to in vs. 14. They ought to have walked in the good way, the way of the *tôrāh;* but they said, **"We will not walk in it."** Secondly, the Lord had provided them with the words of the prophets (watchmen) to whom they ought to have given heed; but they said, **"We will not give heed."** It now appears that the people have tried to compensate for these failures by introducing substitute forms of devotion. The "old paths" are contrasted, as Skinner notes, with "newfangled costly refinements in cultus—'frankincense that comes from Sheba' and 'fine calamus from a far-off land' (v. 20)—through which their new spiritual guides held out the delusive promise of peace of mind." [1] It is quite possible, as Skinner holds, that we have in these verses a reflection of Jeremiah's attitude toward the Josian reform. He may have seen "the whole reform movement degenerating into a superstitious trust in the Temple and its worship." [2] He might therefore be holding the Deuteronomic code itself up to the test of its faithfulness in principles to the **ancient paths.** If this is true, it is probably also accurate to hold that Jeremiah himself stood in a sense at the parting of the ways. This is quite conceivable inasmuch as, in any case, a man stands *always,* in Jeremiah's view, at the parting of the ways. For we have in this poem, particularly in vs. 16, a profound statement of principle, which not only points up the depth of inwardness in Jeremiah's own religious consciousness, but underscores once more the

dialectical fulcrum of his entire understanding of the God-man relation.

Two things make this passage—particularly vs. 16—one of the most significant in the whole of the book of Jeremiah. (*a*) First is the obvious renewal here of the metaphor of the journey, with all its implications, as already noted above (2:2-3). Unquestionably the people are at the crossroads. The **ancient paths,** for which they were told to ask in order to discover once again **where the good way is,** refer not so much to the Mosaic code as to the days of Israel's "youth" when Israel followed Yahweh "as a bride . . . in the wilderness" (2:2). This was the time when "Israel was holy to the LORD." Here the covenantal relationship was established, subsequently confirmed when Israel crossed the Jordan, and reformulated in dignity and completeness under David. For Jeremiah, as for Amos and Hosea, this was the period of ideal piety before the long rebellion had set in. This remains, for Jeremiah, **the good way;** all other ways are but "byways" (cf. 18:15*b*) of the spirit, which breed anxiety, instability, doublemindedness, fickleness, and ultimately induration and hardness of the heart.

The presumption of man under these circumstances has also been acutely, if ironically, described by Stephen Crane:

A learned man came to me once.
He said, "I know the way—come."
And I was overjoyed at this.
Together we hastened.
Soon, too soon, were we
Where my eyes were useless,
And I knew not the ways of my feet.
I clung to the hand of my friend;
But at last he cried, "I am lost." [3]

The pursuit of the truth, when the truth is conceived as a way, is always for Jeremiah a deceptive way if that truth (or that way) does not stand within the covenantal relationship

[1] *Prophecy and Religion,* p. 116.
[2] *Ibid.,* p. 119.

[3] "Black Riders." Reprinted from *The Collected Poems of Stephen Crane* by permission of Alfred A. Knopf. Copyright 1895, 1922 by W. H. Crane.

| 17 Also I set watchmen over you, *saying,* Hearken to the sound of the trumpet. But they said, We will not hearken.
 18 ¶ Therefore hear, ye nations, and know, O congregation, what *is* among them. | 17 I set watchmen over you, saying,
    'Give heed to the sound of the trumpet!'
 But they said, 'We will not give heed.'
 18 Therefore hear, O nations,
    and know, O congregation, what will happen to them. |

17. The **watchmen** were prophets, as in Ezek. 3:17; 33:2; Hab. 2:1; Mic. 7:4. It was the duty of a watchman on a city wall to warn of approaching danger.

with God. Such "blind leaders of the blind" always lead to the condition of lostness. One thinks of John Oxenham's "Way, and Ways, and a Way." [4] But for Jeremiah there is no middle ground. Any man who does not travel in the right way goes, in fact, another way. He does not walk in the good way, and he does not find rest for his soul.

According to Martin Buber—building upon the words of the saddik—God calls to every man as he called to Adam, "Where art thou?" or "Where are you in your world?" and just as Adam hid himself to

avoid rendering accounts, [or] to escape responsibility for his way of living [, so] every man hides [and in seeking] to escape responsibility for his life, he turns existence into a system of hideouts. . . . This is the situation into which God's question falls. This question is designed to awaken man and destroy his system of hideouts; it is to show man to what pass he has come and to awake in him the great will to get out of it.

Everything now depends on whether man faces the question.[5]

The question may come in a variety of ways, just as it came to Jeremiah in the form of the visions in his call. It leads to that "decisive heart searching" which is "the beginning of the way."

This is the movement traced unerringly by many of our contemporary poets, poets who know quite well that

> Fresh addenda are published every day
> To the encyclopaedia of the Way.[6]

W. H. Auden describes with ruthless irony "the alternative routes, the facial glad-handed highway or the virtuous averted track, by which the human effort to make its own fortune arrives all eager at its abruptly dreadful end." [7] This is a lively description of Kierkegaard's

[4] "The Ways," from *The Pilgrim Way.*
[5] *The Way of Man* (London: Routledge & Kegan Paul, 1950; Greenwich, Conn.: Seabury Press, 1954), pp. 12-13.
[6] "The Way," from *The Collected Poetry of W. H. Auden* (London: Faber & Faber; New York: Random House, 1945). Used by permission.
[7] "The Sea and the Mirror," *ibid.,* p. 399.

category of "despair," or of Jeremiah's soul as a broken cistern which can hold no water (2:13). But it is precisely this despair which will bring a man to that seriousness whereby the "sickness unto death" may become a "sickness unto life." [8] For Kierkegaard recognized that when we compare life to a way what matters is not so much the question where the way is as how it is traveled; for under God the "way" is the same for all. When we read in the Gospel about the Good Samaritan, the way in question is the one between Jericho and Jerusalem. But the material highway makes no difference; of the five people who go "on the same way," for one it is a law-abiding way, for the second it is a way of lawlessness, for the third a way of thoughtlessness, for the fourth a way of hard-heartedness, and for the fifth a way of mercy. It is the spiritual fact, says Kierkegaard, of how one travels on the way of life which makes the difference. We tend, as did the Israelites of Jeremiah's day, to divert our attention from the real question by converting it into another, namely, the question as to where the way is.[9]

At bottom it is the same for Jeremiah: the **good way** is the way of the covenant with Yahweh. Kierkegaard notes that this way is, in this world, a way of tribulation; and Jeremiah experiences this in manifold forms. Such a person will be accused of misleading the people; and he will be abused by them by reason of the fact that he will bring upon them, with all the inner distress of the requirement to make an absolute decision, the very question which they seek to avoid. The responsibility for this decision the people—whether individual or corporate—would avoid by making a scapegoat of the one who most sharply confronts them with it.[1]

[8] Søren Kierkegaard, *The Sickness Unto Death* (tr. Walter Lowrie; Princeton: Princeton University Press, 1941).
[9] Cf. Søren Kierkegaard, *The Gospel of Suffering and the Lilies of the Field* (tr. David F. and Lillian Marvin Swenson; Minneapolis: Augsburg Publishing House, 1948), pp. 97 ff.
[1] Cf. Denis de Rougemont, *The Devil's Share* (tr. Haakon Chevalier; New York: Pantheon Books, 1944), pp. 57 ff.

19 Hear, O earth: behold, I will bring evil upon this people, *even* the fruit of their thoughts, because they have not hearkened unto my words, nor to my law, but rejected it.

20 To what purpose cometh there to me incense from Sheba, and the sweet cane from a far country? your burnt offerings *are* not acceptable, nor your sacrifices sweet unto me.

19 Hear, O earth; behold, I am bringing evil upon this people,
    the fruit of their devices,
because they have not given heed to my words;
    and as for my law, they have rejected it.
20 To what purpose does frankincense come to me from Sheba,
    or sweet cane from a distant land?
Your burnt offerings are not acceptable,
    nor your sacrifices pleasing to me.

---

19. By **my words** Jeremiah means the words of God given through the prophets, and by **my law** he means primarily the ethical law given in the time of Moses (see Hyatt, "Torah in the Book of Jeremiah," pp. 381-96).

20. The people have depended upon offerings and sacrifices to secure the favor of God, but these are not acceptable to him; for Jeremiah's attitude toward the sacrificial system see Exeg. on 7:21-28. **Sheba** was a tribe in southwest Arabia, noted as traders.

Since the way is in any case a narrow way (for it leads through the defile of one's own self-discovery, and between the manifold ways of flight and departure from one's self), and since it is a way of tribulation (both because the way to one's self is painful, and because the people account it as a betrayal that one should come to himself), it is only natural that one's thoughts should run forward to the promise of the New Covenant, where tribulation is not an obstacle, but precisely the way—the way which leadeth unto life. "I have said this to you, that in me you may have peace. In the world you have tribulation; but be of good cheer, I have overcome the world" (John 16:33).

(*b*) Secondly, one should not minimize the subjective agony of this tribulation. It is often a way of solitariness, of rejection by one's community, of being misunderstood by those nearest to one. It is, as Friedrich Nietzsche quite rightly says, the way of the Creating One. It is a call into responsible disclosure beyond the forms of the people's present awareness. It is a call into a comprehension of God's new word for the people. It is a call into the open and into the inner solitariness of the dialogue with God, in which the prophet cannot always be certain (as we shall see below) that God is there. "Thou lonesome one, thou goest the way to thyself! . . . Ready must thou be to burn thyself in thy own flame!"[2] No doubt this is the reason that men prefer, as John Henry Newman says, "themselves" and "the certainty of time" to God and the "chance of eternity."[3] Though its supports may be based not upon

truth but upon falsehoods, the ego prefers its apparent securities; the very thought of abandoning these fills the soul with panic, albeit they should be, as Augustine says, "fictions of my misery, not the supports of Thy blessedness."[4]

This is, to Jeremiah, a mysterious contradiction in human nature. This strange forgetfulness of the ordinances of the Lord he cannot understand. Even a maiden, he has said (2:32), cannot forget her ornaments. Even the wild waves of the sea cannot pass over the bound of the sand wherewith it is girt (5:22). The very birds of the air remember the times of their coming (8:7). But the Lord's chosen people continue to walk in the ways which "bring forth briars and thorns to them."[5] It is, therefore, not surprising to find in Augustine a passage very like that of Jeremiah:

Behold, there is He wherever truth is known. He is within the very heart, but yet hath the heart wandered from Him. Return to your heart, O ye transgressors, and cleave fast unto Him that made you. Stand with Him and you shall stand fast. Rest in Him, and you shall be at rest. . . . Why, then, will ye wander farther and farther in these difficult and toilsome ways? . . . Seek what ye seek; but it is not there where ye seek. Ye seek a blessed life in the land of death; it is not there. For could a blessed life be where life itself is not?[6]

Here again, one's thoughts run forward to the consoling words of the New Covenant: "Come to me, all who labor and are heavy-laden, . . . and you will find rest for your souls" (Matt. 11:28-29).

---

[2] *Thus Spake Zarathustra*, Part I, ch. vii, "The Way of the Creating One."

[3] *Parochial and Plain Sermons* (London: Rivingtons, 1875), IV, 238.

[4] *Confessions* IV. 16. 29.

[5] *Ibid.*

[6] *Ibid.* IV. 12. 18.

21 Therefore thus saith the Lord, Behold, I will lay stumblingblocks before this people, and the fathers and the sons together shall fall upon them; the neighbor and his friend shall perish.

22 Thus saith the Lord, Behold, a people cometh from the north country, and a great nation shall be raised from the sides of the earth.

23 They shall lay hold on bow and spear; they *are* cruel, and have no mercy; their voice roareth like the sea; and they ride upon horses, set in array as men for war against thee, O daughter of Zion.

24 We have heard the fame thereof: our hands wax feeble: anguish hath taken hold of us, *and* pain, as of a woman in travail.

25 Go not forth into the field, nor walk by the way; for the sword of the enemy *and* fear *is* on every side.

26 ¶ O daughter of my people, gird *thee* with sackcloth, and wallow thyself in ashes: make thee mourning, *as for* an only son, most bitter lamentation: for the spoiler shall suddenly come upon us.

---

21 Therefore thus says the Lord:
'Behold, I will lay before this people
stumbling blocks against which they
shall stumble;
fathers and sons together,
neighbor and friend shall perish.'"

22 Thus says the Lord:
"Behold, a people is coming from the
north country,
a great nation is stirring from the
farthest parts of the earth.
23 They lay hold on bow and spear,
they are cruel and have no mercy,
the sound of them is like the roaring
sea;
they ride upon horses,
set in array as a man for battle,
against you, O daughter of Zion!"
24 We have heard the report of it,
our hands fall helpless;
anguish has taken hold of us,
pain as of a woman in travail.
25 Go not forth into the field,
nor walk on the road;
for the enemy has a sword,
terror is on every side.
26 O daughter of my people, gird on sackcloth,
and roll in ashes;
make mourning as for an only son,
most bitter lamentation;
for suddenly the destroyer
will come upon us.

---

4. Terror Aroused by the Foe from the North (6:22-26)

22-26. This poem on the foe from the north vividly portrays the terror aroused in Judah by the approach of the enemy. The description is such that it could fit many peoples; however, if the phrase **set in array as a man for battle** (vs. 23) refers to an army marching in closed ranks, it would not apply to the barbaric Scythians.

Jeremiah's idea of "rest" is polemic against any taint either of legalism or of sacerdotalism. And while it is true (vs. 19) that the Lord is bringing evil upon this people because they have paid no heed either to the law or to the words of the prophets, the real point is that this neglect is the outer evidence of the inner failure—the failure to ask where the good way is and to walk in it. It is for this reason that the evil is **the fruit of their [own] devices.** External adherence to formal command would never satisfy the righteousness (*çédheq*) of God. This is why Jeremiah's principle is so near to that of Augustine: "Thou hast made

us for Thyself, and our hearts are restless till they find their rest in Thee." [7]

22-26. *Once More—the Foe!*—The introduction here of a last vivid description of the enemy from the north serves to maintain the external pressure of impending disaster. It serves to point up and heighten not merely the danger, but the manifold follies of the people. The description is vivid. The phrase **the farthest parts of the earth** is subsequently used of Babylon (31:8). Once again the anguish of

[7] *Ibid.* I. 1. 1; cf. Clement of Alexandria *Miscellanies* V. 1. Clement interprets the passage as "walking . . . without turning till we attain to what we desire."

27 I have set thee *for* a tower *and* a fortress among my people, that thou mayest know and try their way.

28 They *are* all grievous revolters, walking with slanders: *they are* brass and iron; they *are* all corrupters.

27 "I have made you an assayer and tester
    among my people,
  that you may know and assay their
    ways.

28 They are all stubbornly rebellious,
  going about with slanders;
  they are bronze and iron,
    all of them act corruptly.

5. THE PROPHET AS ASSAYER (6:27-30)

This section contains several difficulties of translation, but the theme is the role of the prophet as **an assayer and tester among my people**, not **a tower and a fortress**. We see here an important aspect of the prophet's function, and another example of the power of the word of the Lord in the mouth of his prophet. As **an assayer** the prophet was not merely to test the ways of the people that he might report to God, but he was to attempt to refine them. The word of the Lord was like **fire** in his mouth, to destroy the wickedness of the people (5:14). Yet Jeremiah discovered that he could not refine them; they were therefore to be cast away like **refuse silver.**

27. Yahweh speaks to the prophet in this verse, and the prophet replies in vss. 28-30. The translation **tester** is based upon a repointing of the Hebrew word to make it

the people is described as being like the pain **of a woman in travail** (cf. 4:31), and the people are bidden to **make mourning as for an only son**—which is the severest loss that a Hebrew could suffer. Something of this **terror . . . on every side** has been felt by countless people throughout the world:

Heavy upon the heart the world's great wrong
Grinds night and day a grim goose-stepping boot;
We set our mouths for singing, but the song
Sickens against the tongue like Dead Sea fruit.[8]

27-30. A Tester by Fire.—This brief poem brings to a climax the poems and oracles of the chapters which precede it, especially chs. 5–6. It gathers together all that has gone before in a singular metaphor of extraordinary power and completeness. But there is also a sense in which it brings to a focus *all* that has gone before. For the careful reader is certain to note, in the modified tension and subject matter of chs. 4–6, a slow shift in Jeremiah's attitude toward his call, as though, after the first blush of prophetic excitement when he perceived the gravity of the international situation and warned the people with all the power of eloquence and passion at his command, he was then shocked and disillusioned by their callousness and indifference. From his initial call as a "prophet to the nation" (1:5) his prophetic consciousness steadily matures. He enters the city to observe with care the actual defections of the people. From the humblest to the great-

est, even to the priests and prophets in the temple, he probes with meticulous care. He begins to strip off the trappings of the masquerade, in order to disclose the genuine that lies beneath. He has also gone back through the lost domain of truth and, quite clearly, has begun to revise it possessively.[9] He has been filled increasingly with indignation at what he sees. He experiences the terrible psychical enervation of keeping his wrath pent up in himself. It becomes like a fire which he cannot contain (20:9). But as he pours it out in these first poems and oracles, while becoming at the same time increasingly aware of the depth of the people's corruption, the real nature of his prophetic vocation is steadily borne in upon him. "A new conception of the divine purpose"[1] begins to emerge. He becomes to the people **an assayer and tester** by fire.

H. Wheeler Robinson notes that

the intensity of the inner experience . . . marks the limits of possible revelation through that experience. . . . The fire that tested Judah was the fire of moral and spiritual conviction, the conviction which both commissioned the messenger and supplied his message. Behind the fire there was an invisible hand, feeding the flame, as in Bunyan's vision of the Interpreter's House. . . . Not only did the revelation of God come *through* [Jeremiah's] experience, but in a unique way, not equalled by any other prophet, the fact of that experience *itself* became the supreme revelation. He revealed the meaning of personal religion through the struggles

[8] Joseph Auslander, "Appeal to Our Poets," from *The Unconquerables.* Copyright, 1943, by Joseph Auslander. Used by permission of Simon & Schuster, publishers.

[9] Cf. Karl Jaspers, *Man in the Modern Age* (New York: Henry Holt & Co., 1933), pp. 89-90.

[1] Skinner, *Prophecy and Religion*, p. 159.

29 The bellows are burned, the lead is consumed of the fire; the founder melteth in vain: for the wicked are not plucked away.

30 Reprobate silver shall *men* call them, because the Lord hath rejected them.

7 The word that came to Jeremiah from the Lord, saying,

2 Stand in the gate of the Lord's house,

29 The bellows blow fiercely,
the lead is consumed by the fire;
in vain the refining goes on,
for the wicked are not removed.

30 Refuse silver they are called,
for the Lord has rejected them."

7 The word that came to Jeremiah from the Lord: 2 "Stand in the gate of the

---

mebhaççēr (Duhm) ; but this form is not found elsewhere, and it is not certain that the verb has this meaning. It may be a scribal gloss, with the meaning **fortress,** to explain בחון, which was misunderstood as **tower,** as in Isa. 23:13 (Jeremiah is called a "fortified city" in 1:18).

29. In ancient practice **lead** was placed with the silver ore in a crucible. When heated the lead would oxidize and carry off the alloys, leaving the pure silver. Here it is supposed that the ore is so impure that the lead does not succeed in carrying off the alloys. Since lead could not actually be **consumed** by the fire (lead being nonvolatile), we should translate the second line, "From the fire the lead comes out whole," i.e., untouched by the alloys.

IV. The Vanity of the Cultus (7:1–8:3)

This section is the product of the Deuteronomic editor, the first large section from his hand. That it is his product is shown by (*a*) the prose style so characteristic of his

---

of his soul against his hard destiny. In him we begin to learn that a *life* is the fullest revelation of truth—which is one of the secrets of the Incarnation.[2]

All this is apparent in Jeremiah's indictment of the people that they are **all stubbornly rebellious,** as well as in the double-edged metaphor that their hardness is like that of **bronze and iron.** Like these metals they are equally corrupt. He will test them, therefore, as these metals are tested, in the smelting furnace. He will see whether in the refining fire of God's word there be any who "shall come forth as gold" (Job 23:10).

The description which follows rehearses the ancient metallurgical processes whereby, as Driver describes it,

the alloy containing the gold or silver is mixed with lead, and fused in a furnace on a vessel of earth or bone-ash: a current of air is turned upon the molten mass (not upon the *fire*); the lead then oxidizes, and acting as a flux, carries away the alloy, leaving the gold or silver pure (J. Napier, *The Ancient Workers in Metal,* 1856, pp. 20, 23).[3]

But what has Jeremiah discovered by this refining process? It is that his efforts are vain. So

corrupt are the people, so thoroughly is the silver mixed with the impure alloy, that, in spite of the fierce blowing of the bellows, the refining goes on in vain; for though the lead is oxidized, the baser metals (the wicked) are not carried away, and only the impure silver remains.

Follows then the superb play upon words, the clinching and unforgettable summary of the whole:

"Refuse silver," are they called,
For the Lord has refused them (Amer. Trans.).

Gillies suggests the possibility that Jeremiah ended the first draft of his roll with this powerful and pathetic charge—"which met with so ungracious a reception at royal hands."[4] This is a powerful supposition, for the official function of the prophet (let alone the particular prophetic genius of Jeremiah) was well known; it would be understood both by king and court that that which the prophet Jeremiah had rejected in Israel's life had already been rejected by Yahweh.[5]

7:1-15. The Temple Sermon.—The sensitive reader will recognize a definite break between the poems in chs. 4–6 which we have just passed

---

[2] *The Cross of Jeremiah* (London: Student Christian Movement Press, 1925), pp. 65-66. Used by permission.

[3] S. R. Driver, *The Book of the Prophet Jeremiah,* p. 39, note *b.*

[4] *Jeremiah, the Man and His Message,* p. 85.

[5] Cf. Welch, *Jeremiah: His Time and His Work,* pp. 44 ff.

work, (b) the presence of numerous Deuteronomic words and phrases, and (c) the fact that it contains several verses which are duplicates of, or closely parallel to, other Deuteronomic passages in the book; e.g., 7:16=11:14 (cf. 14:11-12) ; 7:24 (cf. 11:8) ; 7:30-33 (cf. 32:34-35; 19:6-7) ; 7:34 (cf. 16:9; 25:10). The Deuteronomic editor has collected here various teachings of Jeremiah dealing with cultic places and practices—the Jerusalem temple, the worship of the queen of heaven, sacrifice in general, and the rites carried on in the valley of Hinnom. Mowinckel has aptly compared the section with Matthew's Sermon on the Mount. It is a collection of teachings which were not given at one place and one time, but they constitute some of the most important messages of the prophet. We do not have here his actual words, since the Deuteronomic style pervades the whole section, but for the most part we do have the substance of his teachings, for the passage largely agrees with his sayings elsewhere in the book (a few divergences will be pointed out).

The so-called "temple sermon" probably extends only through vs. 15, the rest being from other occasions. It is not impossible that vss. 21-26 were spoken on the same occasion, but neither is it probable. The parallel account of the temple sermon in 26:4-6 includes

under review and those in chs. 7–10 which now follow. It is suggested (see Exeg.) that the present address is supplied from the hand of the Deuteronomic editor. Its recurrence in ch. 26 dates the sermon as having been given in the reign of Jehoiakim. Thus the reader must adjust himself to a shift from the early period of Jeremiah's prophetic career to its middle period. This he must effect by supplying several factors which do not appear in the immediate unfolding of the narrative.

Clearly the main shift is from the conditions in the time of Josiah to those under Jehoiakim. We may suppose, with the majority of critics, that the initial phase of Jeremiah's prophetic activity was begun under Josiah; that he assessed the conditions of his time and people, beheld with extraordinary clearsightedness the precariousness of their very existence as a nation, and prepared his oracles of warning; that, after beginning his prophecy, he was for some reason driven into silence—either (a) because the prophecies of doom which he had announced did not come quickly to pass, or (b) because of some event which persuaded him to withhold his prophecies for a time. That event (see Exeg.) is generally supposed to have been the discovery in the temple of the book which is usually identified with the main portions of the present book of Deuteronomy. This book was undoubtedly prepared much earlier than Josiah's time, very likely in the days of Hezekiah, when a collection and adaptation of great traditional writings was formulated under the influence of Hosea's prophecies and the school of Isaiah, with a view to implementing Hezekiah's reform. Unfortunately, however, this movement fell under dark days with the accession of Manasseh, who, capitulating to superstition and syncretism, restored the remnants of star worship, magic, and the pagan cults. It

would appear that the book was carefully hidden in order to avoid its total destruction at the ruthless hands of the king, and was subsequently discovered in the days of Josiah. Once the discovery was made, the book was taken to the young king, and it received the support of both the priests (Hilkiah) and the prophetic party (Huldah, a prophetess).

Martin Buber speaks of the book as "this great attempt at a practical synthesis." For it attempted to fuse into a single legal tradition "the spirit of the first writing prophets, a priestly organizational tendency and a preaching style, schooled on great examples." [6] It was enthusiastically espoused by Josiah, who undertook with all sincerity the radical reform of the religious cult. "The heart of Deuteronomic law is not legal enactment, but a pleading for the generous heart." [7] It aimed at purification of the religious practices of the people. It sought to bring this about through centralization of worship in the temple at Jerusalem. In this way the corruptions which had entered into religious practice through compromise with the Canaanitish cults of Baal could be brought under control and purified. It is easy to understand how Jeremiah could have suspended his polemic against Judah while waiting to see to what extent this program of reform would take hold.

Such a view, however, is not sufficient. It is not conceivable that Jeremiah's "waiting" would be of a passive kind, or that he would stand aloof as a spectator merely observing. So also the hypothesis of Jeremiah's "silent years" is a biographical resort that is much too simple, however plausible, to bridge the chasm between

[6] *The Prophetic Faith*, pp. 159-60.

[7] Herbert Cunliffe-Jones, *Deuteronomy* (London: Student Christian Movement Press, 1951; "Torch Bible Commentaries"), p. 23.

only the substance of 7:2-15. The words of the prophet reach their climax in 7:14-15 (cf. 26:6), and it is likely that the religious leaders would not allow him to continue, but arrested him immediately, as is reported in 26:8 ff. Furthermore, 7:21-26 is separated from 7:1-15 by words which could hardly form part of the temple sermon. We may therefore conclude that only vss. 1-15 report the temple sermon, though it is highly probable that vss. 21-26 were spoken in the temple area at another time.

---

the conclusion to ch. 6 and the beginning of ch. 7. One is bound to sense that the poems of these first chapters are presided over by a certain subjectivity, an unconscious but mildly inhibiting self-consciousness, together with a tendency to prophesy in general rather than in the terms of concrete events. In ch. 7 Jeremiah stands forth from the shadow of these reticences. He stands in the gate of the temple in a deliberately chosen hour of crisis in the life of the people. His words cut across the occasion as Luther cuts across the papacy. With infinite courage he flings down his challenge before the king, the priests, the prophets, and the people. As Skinner says: "Jeremiah must have known that he took his life in his hand when he went up to deliver this tremendous message." [8] It has been remarked of Lincoln that he went forward steadily, "slowly maturing his way." It is possible to say of Jeremiah that he held aloof, in his early period of prophetic labor, from political action "while maturing in secret those conceptions of the essential nature of religion which were to be his guiding light in the stormy years that lay before him." [9]

In the case of Jeremiah, however, it would appear that something more fundamental took place. Something far more like the prophetic withdrawal and return would seem to have occurred. It has frequently been observed of the very greatest of prophets that after their initial sally upon the world, and the experienced rebuff of indifference and disillusionment, they move into the "wilderness" for indefinite periods, there to revise in depth the fuller implications of their protests, and to work through the inner agony of a deeper integration of the self at a level of perception which is new in the world and in which the prophet walks alone with his God.[1] W. H. Auden writes:

He is the Way.
Follow Him through the Land of Unlikeness;
You will see rare beasts, and have unique adventures.[2]

[8] *Prophecy and Religion*, pp. 171-72.
[9] *Ibid.*, p. 231.
[1] Cf. A. J. Toynbee, *A Study of History*, pp. 217-30.
[2] "The Flight into Egypt," Part IV, from *For the Time Being, a Christmas Oratorio* (New York: Random House, 1944; London: Faber & Faber, 1945). Used by permission.

Since we live, however, in an age no longer integrated either by cult practice, ritual acceptance, or sustaining religious beliefs, our contemporary man is cut off from the usual systems of protection against such terrors. With our general impoverishment of symbols and the loss of dogmatic archetypes, which in orthodox times absorb the life of the unconscious and so protect people against themselves, the creative and searching soul is thrown upon these terrors in the raw. He has no longer either the queen of heaven of the Canaanites, or the goddesses of Greek mythology, or the image of the virgin of medieval times to cushion him against himself: that is, to protect him against his call to become under God what he is able to become. The experience of the creative or deeply searching soul in our time is, therefore, more realistically expressed by W. H. Auden in another passage:

All those who follow me are led
On to that Glassy Mountain where are no
Footholds for logic, to that Bridge of Dread
Where knowledge but increases vertigo:
Those who pursue me take a twisting lane
To find themselves immediately alone
With savage water or unfeeling stone,
In labyrinths where they must entertain
Confusion, cripples, tigers, thunder, pain.[3]

Since we wish to apply this experience to the inner life of Jeremiah, it is interesting to compare the following statements by Carl G. Jung and Paul Tillich. Writes Jung:

This confrontation [of the self with itself] is the first test of courage on the inner way, a test sufficient to frighten off most people, for the meeting with ourselves belongs to the more unpleasant things that may be avoided as long as we possess living symbol-figures in which all that is inner and unknown is projected.[4]

Tillich also calls attention to our use of pretexts to avoid this encounter. "It is not because it is too profound, but rather because it is too uncomfortable, that [we] shy away from the truth." However, no soul can really avoid or evade these tests, since everyone has to face the deep things of life sooner or later.

[3] "The Summons," Part I, *ibid.* Used by permission.
[4] *Integration of the Personality*, p. 69.

It must be remembered that the Deuteronomic editor wrote about 550 B.C. (see Intro., pp. 788-89), when some of the predictions of this chapter had been fulfilled. That fact helps to explain why he was willing to have Jeremiah express ideas which run counter to ideas usually held by the Deuteronomists.

A. The Temple Sermon (7:1-15)

This was one of the most important events in Jeremiah's life. It is an outstanding example of his unflinching courage, it raised against him strong opposition, and it shows his attitude toward the Jerusalem temple.

Volz has pointed out that the central question with which this passage deals is: What gives men protection and safety? The question was especially acute in view of the political events which had only recently occurred in Israel (on the date, see Exeg. on 26:1). The priests and prophets replied to the question: The temple and its sacrifices give protection. The people generally followed the opinion of these leaders. But Jeremiah said: Only moral living is the source of genuine protection.

The wisdom of all ages and of all continents speaks about the road to our depth. It has been described in innumerably different ways. But all those who have been concerned—mystics and priests, poets and philosophers, simple people and educated people—with that road through confession, lonely self-scrutiny, internal or external catastrophes, prayer, contemplation, have witnessed to the same experience. They have found that they were not what they believed themselves to be, even after a deeper level had appeared to them below the vanishing surface. That deeper level itself became surface, when a still deeper level was discovered, this happening again and again, as long as their very lives, as long as they kept on the road to their depth.[5]

It is interesting also to compare Jung's references to the symbol of fire in the fragments of Heraclitus, for whom the soul at the highest level was fiery and dry, and for whom also an "eternally living fire" was at the very center of reality, with Paul Tillich's metaphorical remark: "And who can really bear the ultimate depth, the burning fire in the ground of all being, without saying with the prophet, 'Woe unto me! For I am undone. For mine eyes have seen the Lord of Hosts!' "[6] The Jeremiah parallel is even closer than that of Isaiah, when he speaks of the word of God as an irrepressible fire within him. And Jung quotes more than once "an uncanonical saying of the Master" which reads "Who is near unto Me is near unto the fire."[7]

[5] *The Shaking of the Foundations* (London: Student Christian Movement Press; New York: Charles Scribner's Sons, 1948), p. 56 (used by permission); cf. pp. 60-61. Cf. also *The Courage to Be, passim*, especially pp. 155 ff. Robert Browning's "Childe Roland to the Dark Tower Came" also applies here.

[6] Jung, *op. cit.*, pp. 75, 188; Tillich, *The Shaking of the Foundations*, p. 60.

[7] *Ait autem ipse salvator: Qui iuxta me est, iuxta ignem est, qui longe est a me, longe est a regno.* From Origen, *Jerem. Hom.* XX. 3, cited from Erwin Preuschen,

What the reader must bear in mind as he passes from the end of ch. 6 to the beginning of ch. 7 is that Jeremiah has passed through some such experience. The early part of his prophetic ministry was based upon an indictment of the people's wickedness. This could be managed with comparative safety to the self through a warning against the present and an appeal to the past. But as Jeremiah watched the Deuteronomic reforms under Josiah he became increasingly and acutely aware that he was not only called to place himself over against the people's wickedness, but that he was obliged also to stand over against their righteousness. When it is recognized that this righteousness represents the highest corporate achievement in the history of the people, it is easy to see that the courage which Jeremiah required was a courage based upon nothing less than "being itself" (Tillich). This was a penetration in depth deeper than that attained by anyone who preceded him. It meant that he was thrust out of the usual protections of the self against itself. Like Job he must experience the agonies of this adventure. It is our persuasion that the record of this movement and of these agonies is to be found in the collection of poems usually described as "The Confessions of Jeremiah," comprising roughly chs. 12-20. There we shall see Jeremiah in the inner toils of exploration and acceptance, together with the various facets of expostulation and reply evoked by his struggle with his age and with himself. After that, the political career of Jeremiah begins. "He certainly becomes one of the outstanding public figures of the time, and plays an active part as an adviser in public and national affairs."[8]

The wrestle with himself is largely at an end. His acts are bold and open; they are directed at

Antilegomena (Giessen: A. Topelmann, 1901), p. 44. Quoted in Jung, *op. cit.*, p. 188.

[8] Skinner, *op. cit.*, p. 231.

and proclaim there this word, and say, Hear the word of the Lord, all *ye of* Judah, that enter in at these gates to worship the Lord.

3 Thus saith the Lord of hosts, the God of Israel, Amend your ways and your doings, and I will cause you to dwell in this place.

4 Trust ye not in lying words, saying, The temple of the Lord, The temple of the Lord, The temple of the Lord, *are* these.

5 For if ye thoroughly amend your ways and your doings; if ye thoroughly execute judgment between a man and his neighbor;

6 *If* ye oppress not the stranger, the fatherless, and the widow, and shed not in-

Lord's house, and proclaim there this word, and say, Hear the word of the Lord, all you men of Judah who enter these gates to worship the Lord. 3 Thus says the Lord of hosts, the God of Israel, Amend your ways and your doings, and I will let you dwell in this place. 4 Do not trust in these deceptive words: 'This is the temple of the Lord, the temple of the Lord, the temple of the Lord.'

5 "For if you truly amend your ways and your doings, if you truly execute justice one with another, 6 if you do not oppress the alien, the fatherless or the widow, or shed

---

The boldness of Jeremiah on this occasion can be realized only as one recalls the central place given to the Jerusalem temple by the reforms of Josiah in 621 B.C. They made it the sole place of sacrificial worship of Yahweh for all Jews. The temple and its personnel thus had acquired by this time greater importance than ever before. In the name of Yahweh, Jeremiah issued a challenge which struck at the very existence of the temple. It is not surprising that he was arrested and tried, as reported in ch. 26.

7:2. Stand in the gate of the Lord's house: According to 26:2, Jeremiah stood "in the court" of the temple. Since the gate was probably one of those which separated the

---

specific persons and events. He moves with incredible consistency and courage through the balance of his years, and works through to that amazing proclamation of the newer Covenant which reaches its fulfillment at a later day.

1-15. The Sermon in the Temple Gate.—This sermon may well have been the earliest public utterance of Jeremiah (see Intro., p. 780). Martin Buber suggests that it was spoken approximately three months after the death of Josiah.[9] Josiah had been slain at the battle of Megiddo (608 B.C.), when he had foolishly gone out to challenge the power of Pharaoh Neco. The popular election of Jehoahaz to fill the vacant throne was promptly vetoed by the Pharaoh, and Jehoiakim, the eldest son of Josiah, was placed upon the vacant throne.

It was a time of crisis for the nation. When Josiah fell, his dream of a new Davidic kingdom free from the corroding taint of foreign cultic elements fell with him. "All . . . Judah" came pressing into the temple to petition their God for protection (26:2). This may either have been ordered by the authorities, enjoining a public fast and appropriate expressions of humiliation, arising out of the national emergency,[1] or it may have been a celebration at the coronation time of Jehoiakim (Duhm; see also Intro., p. 780). In either case, the people's

dependence upon the protection of the temple is made plain.

Jeremiah stood where the prophets customarily stood: in the gate between the inner and the outer courts. Here the people were assembled.

The opening paragraphs of the address are marked by a tone of controlled earnestness, by an unadorned plainness of statement, without passion, without exclamation, apostrophe, or rhetorical device of any kind; which betokens the presence of a danger which spoke too audibly to the general ear to require artificial heightening in the statement of it. The position of affairs spoke for itself.[2]

Clearly the sermon is an open and scathing attack on the supposition that Yahweh can be appeased by any sort of temple worship or ritual sacrifice. **Amend your ways and your doings,** said Jeremiah; *then* will the Lord permit them to dwell in the land. He exposes their behavior by his superb and cutting irony: they have put their trust in **deceptive words. This is the temple of the Lord, the temple of the Lord, the temple of the Lord.** As though the very repetition of the phrase had some magical property wherewith their safety was assured.

But the house of the Lord provided the people with *no* unmerited safety, and particularly not when it was impounded into a formula for

[9] *The Prophetic Faith*, p. 159.
[1] Ball, *Prophecies of Jeremiah*, p. 150.

[2] Ferdinand Hitzig, quoted in Ball, *ibid.*

nocent blood in this place, neither walk after other gods to your hurt;

7 Then will I cause you to dwell in this place, in the land that I gave to your fathers, for ever and ever.

8 ¶ Behold, ye trust in lying words, that cannot profit.

9 Will ye steal, murder, and commit adultery, and swear falsely, and burn incense unto Baal, and walk after other gods whom ye know not;

10 And come and stand before me in this house, which is called by my name, and say, We are delivered to do all these abominations?

11 Is this house, which is called by my name, become a den of robbers in your eyes? Behold, even I have seen *it,* saith the LORD.

12 But go ye now unto my place which *was* in Shiloh, where I set my name at the first, and see what I did to it for the wickedness of my people Israel.

innocent blood in this place, and if you do not go after other gods to your own hurt, 7 then I will let you dwell in this place, in the land that I gave of old to your fathers for ever.

8 "Behold, you trust in deceptive words to no avail. 9 Will you steal, murder, commit adultery, swear falsely, burn incense to Ba′al, and go after other gods that you have not known, 10 and then come and stand before me in this house, which is called by my name, and say, 'We are delivered!' — only to go on doing all these abominations? 11 Has this house, which is called by my name, become a den of robbers in your eyes? Behold, I myself have seen it, says the LORD. 12 Go now to my place that was in Shiloh, where I made my name dwell at first, and see what I did to it for the wicked-

---

courts of the temple, there is no discrepancy in the two accounts; 26:10 reports that the trial of the prophet took place in the New Gate; his message may have been delivered there.

9. The similarity to five of the Ten Commandments (Exod. 20; Deut. 5) has often been noted.

11. Jesus quoted the phrase **a den of robbers** when he cleansed the temple (Matt. 21:13), combining with it a quotation from Isa. 56:7. In the present context the emphasis is not as much upon "the robbers" as in Jesus' words. The robbers' den was usually a cave in which they could find refuge and have a feeling of safety.

12. Shiloh, eighteen miles north of Jerusalem, was the site of a very important sanctuary in the early days of Israel. The house of Eli served as priests there, and Samuel grew up in its temple (Josh. 18:1; I Sam. 1:1–4:22). The O.T. nowhere tells of the

---

magical incantation. Jeremiah had reached the point where he saw clearly that nothing short of a radical change within could bring about the real safety of the people (cf. Mic. 3:11; also Isa. 28:16). When the people genuinely amend their ways and authentically achieve the practice of the moral virtues, **then** shall they be permitted to **dwell in this place** (vss. 5-7). Their **trust in deceptive words** is sheer vanity. That they should go about breaking the commandments (five are mentioned) **and then come and stand before me** [Yahweh] **in this house** exclaiming **"We are delivered!"** is incredible. As though the mere fact of their presence in the temple should cancel out the manifold abominations of their behavior! The temple has virtually become **a den of robbers** (vss. 8-11).

The astounding temerity of this "sermon" will be felt when it is recognized that Jeremiah

sets himself with one sweeping metaphor against the false prophets, the people, and the priests; just as, at a later time, Jesus heightens the power of his own castigation of the temple practice by saying, "It is written, 'My house shall be called a house of prayer' [cf. Isa. 56:7]; but you make it a den of robbers" (Matt. 21:13).

But Jeremiah is not through. Moses Buttenwieser remarks that "every utterance falls like the blow of a sledge-hammer." [3] He draws a parallel between the fate of the temple at Shiloh and the impending doom of Jerusalem's temple. No account remains to us of the fall of Shiloh (*ca.* 1050 B.C.), but the sanctuary there had been pre-eminent in its possession of the ark. Just as Shiloh, which had once been the commanding shrine of Israel, had fallen, so now

[3] *The Prophets of Israel* (New York: The Macmillan Co., 1914), p. 23.

13 And now, because ye have done all these works, saith the LORD, and I spake unto you, rising up early and speaking, but ye heard not; and I called you, but ye answered not;

14 Therefore will I do unto *this* house, which is called by my name, wherein ye trust, and unto the place which I gave to you and to your fathers, as I have done to Shiloh.

15 And I will cast you out of my sight, as I have cast out all your brethren, *even* the whole seed of Ephraim.

16 Therefore pray not thou for this people, neither lift up cry nor prayer for them, neither make intercession to me: for I will not hear thee.

ness of my people Israel. 13 And now, because you have done all these things, says the LORD, and when I spoke to you persistently you did not listen, and when I called you, you did not answer, 14 therefore I will do to the house which is called by my name, and in which you trust, and to the place which I gave to you and to your fathers, as I did to Shiloh. 15 And I will cast you out of my sight, as I cast out all your kinsmen, all the offspring of E'phraim.

16 "As for you, do not pray for this people, or lift up cry or prayer for them, and do not intercede with me, for I do not hear

---

destruction of Shiloh and its sanctuary, but the excavations carried on by the Danish Palestine Expedition at the site, modern Seilûn, showed that Shiloh was destroyed about 1050 B.C., apparently by the Philistines at the time they captured the ark of the covenant from the Israelites (I Sam. 4:11). The ruins were probably still visible in Jeremiah's day, for the site was not reoccupied until the Hellenistic period, *ca.* 300 B.C. (Hans Kjaer, "The Excavation of Shiloh 1929," *Journal of the Palestine Oriental Society,* X [1930], 87-174).

B. No Intercession for the People (7:16-20)

These words are addressed by Yahweh to the prophet, and are closely paralleled in 11:14; 14:11-12. One of the functions of the prophet was to intercede with God for the people; an excellent example is provided by Amos 7:2, 5. Jeremiah is here forbidden to intercede because the people are so sinful that God will not hear him. As an example of their sinfulness is cited the worship of the **queen of heaven** (vs. 18), probably the

---

the Lord will bring about the fall of Jerusalem. It was a shocking conclusion. It was, as Gordon says, "blasphemy most foul, sacrilege insufferable, pure and unrelieved rebellion." [4]

We shall defer our discussion of the consequences of this sermon to its appropriate place in ch. 26, where we shall see Jeremiah on trial for his life; but it is easy to see why Buttenwieser should regard this sermon at the temple gate as the outstanding event and turning point in the career of Jeremiah. Pascal classifies the verses of ch. 7 under the title "Reprobation of the Temple," and notes, after the reference to Shiloh, the finality of God's promise—"For I have rejected it, and made myself a temple elsewhere"; then, after the final pronouncement—I will cast you out of my sight, as I cast out all your kinsmen—he notes pathetically, "rejected forever." Therefore (he adds) pray not for this people.[5] So deeply sounds the prophet's knell upon Jerusalem.

[4] *Rebel Prophet,* p. 112.
[5] *Thoughts,* No. 712.

16-20. *A False Reliance.*—These verses, inserted here by editorial design, either depict the condition of the people as Jeremiah observed it in the earlier period of his ministry, or one must suppose that the people reverted with incredible swiftness to the corrupt forms of alien worship immediately after the death of Josiah. The latter movement is not impossible; for history shows how quickly and how violently reaction may set in after a legislated moral reform, and how quickly moral degeneration appears when virtuous leadership is gone.

It is possible that the editor intends, as Gillies suggests,[6] a dramatic movement from the scene at the temple courts to this flash-back of the city's streets and thence out through the city's gates (7:1–8:3). In any case, the vignette provided of the children running about the streets gathering sticks of wood, of their fathers preparing and kindling the fire, and of the mothers kneading the dough **to make cakes for the queen of heaven,** is almost as vivid as those

[6] *Jeremiah, the Man and His Message,* pp. 93-94.

17 ¶ Seest thou not what they do in the cities of Judah and in the streets of Jerusalem?

18 The children gather wood, and the fathers kindle the fire, and the women knead *their* dough, to make cakes to the queen of heaven, and to pour out drink offerings unto other gods, that they may provoke me to anger.

19 Do they provoke me to anger? saith the LORD: *do they* not *provoke* themselves to the confusion of their own faces?

20 Therefore thus saith the Lord GOD; Behold, mine anger and my fury shall be poured out upon this place, upon man, and upon beast, and upon the trees of the field, and upon the fruit of the ground; and it shall burn, and shall not be quenched.

21 ¶ Thus saith the LORD of hosts, the God of Israel; Put your burnt offerings unto your sacrifices, and eat flesh.

you. 17 Do you not see what they are doing in the cities of Judah and in the streets of Jerusalem? 18 The children gather wood, the fathers kindle fire, and the women knead dough, to make cakes for the queen of heaven; and they pour out drink offerings to other gods, to provoke me to anger. 19 Is it I whom they provoke? says the LORD. Is it not themselves, to their own confusion? 20 Therefore thus says the Lord GOD: Behold, my anger and my wrath will be poured out on this place, upon man and beast, upon the trees of the field and the fruit of the ground; it will burn and not be quenched."

21 Thus says the LORD of hosts, the God of Israel: "Add your burnt offerings to your

---

Assyro-Babylonian goddess Ishtar, who was known by that title (*sharrat shāmê*); she was the goddess of the planet Venus. Her worship is also described in 44:17-25, where it is indicated that the women especially participated in her rites. It was probably under Manasseh, when Assyrian influence was at its height, that Ishtar worship flourished most; though put down by Josiah, it must have been revived after his death.

Because of the pessimistic attitude expressed in this passage, we may suppose that it represents the attitude of Jeremiah in the latter part of his career rather than at the time of the temple sermon.

18. The **cakes for the queen of heaven** were probably in the form of the goddess or of her symbol, a star; in 44:19 they are described as "cakes for her bearing her image."

C. MORAL OBEDIENCE REQUIRED, NOT SACRIFICE (7:21-28)

These words were probably spoken in the temple area at the time of some great festival when sacrifices were being offered in abundance, but not at the same time as the temple sermon (see above). They express Jeremiah's basic conception of religion: God requires of men moral obedience, not sacrifice. Many interpreters have tried to escape

---

glimpses of the city which Jeremiah provided when he was told to search the squares (5:1). The queen of heaven has appeared in history under many forms—Queen Venus, Goethe's Helen, Ishtar.

The reference here is dramatically important, for it has the effect, in the protest which follows against burnt offerings and sacrifices (21:2-28), of reducing these to the same level as the idolatrous worship of the queen of heaven, in connection with which they **pour out drink offering to other gods, to provoke me to anger.** The principle is identical with Jeremiah's argument from the beginning: **Is it I whom they provoke? says the LORD. Is it not themselves, to their own confusion?** The idols are always

empty, and the people deliver themselves into emptiness.

For this reason Jeremiah is advised that he must **not pray for this people,** or lift up cry for them, nor intercede with the Lord on their behalf (things which Jeremiah wished from his very heart to do); for the people's persistence in this rebellious pattern, with its myriad forms, brings down God's wrath on them, inasmuch as it is only through the visitation upon them of the consequences of their own behavior that this people will be made to see wherein the truth lies. The adulterous and idolatrous people has alienated itself from the Lord.

21-28. *Hearken unto the Voice.*—Franz Werfel's spokesman, in a novel based on the

22 For I spake not unto your fathers, nor commanded them in the day that I brought them out of the land of Egypt, concerning burnt offerings or sacrifices:

sacrifices, and eat the flesh. 22 For in the day that I brought them out of the land of Egypt, I did not speak to your fathers or command them concerning burnt offerings

---

the plain meaning of vss. 22-23 by saying that moral obedience was the primary demand of God and sacrifice the secondary demand, or that the prophet was calling for the purification or the moralization of the sacrificial system. Such views often rest upon the dogmatic assumption that in ancient times religion could not exist without some form of sacrifice. Yet it is best to take Jeremiah's words here at their face value and see in them his belief that the sacrificial system was man-made and not willed by Yahweh (for his view cf. 6:20; for that of other prophets cf. Amos 5:21-25; Hos. 6:6; Isa. 1:10-17; Mic. 6:6-8; on the subject in general see the commentaries of Volz and Rudolph, *ad loc.*, and J. Philip Hyatt, *Prophetic Religion* [New York and Nashville: Abingdon-Cokesbury Press, 1947], pp. 118-32).

21. Burnt offerings were entirely consumed on the altar, but many of the other types of sacrifice were eaten in part by the worshipers. Jeremiah says that they may as well eat their burnt offerings as they do the others, for in God's sight they are all mere **flesh.**

22. Jeremiah plainly says that in the time of Moses God did not lay down any requirements of sacrifice but only of moral obedience; he perhaps had in mind specifically

---

life of Jeremiah, concluded "that greatness is consistent only with running counter to the world and never with acceptance of it; that the eternally defeated are the eternally victorious; and that the Voice is more real than the clamour that seeks to drown it." [7]

Certain it is that Jeremiah sets the unmediated voice of God, together with the practice of justice, righteousness, and mercy, over against the systems of sacrifice and the semi-magical contrivances of the priesthood. One must say quite simply, with Nathaniel Micklem, that "there is no escape from Jeremiah vi. 20, vii. 22. It is here emphatically and explicitly stated that ceremony and sacrifice have nothing to do with the religion of Moses and the true worship of Israel." [8] Heap up your burnt offerings as high as you like, says Jeremiah, both those that are meant to be eaten and those that are not, and eat them all. It is a matter of indifference to Yahweh. This was not a part of Yahweh's covenant with Israel when he brought them out of the land of Egypt.

Two things are to be noted here: the uncompromising character of Jeremiah's rejection of the sacrificial system; and the clear-cut primacy given to the voice of Yahweh over all other authoritative claims.

With regard to the first it is often claimed that Jeremiah did not intend that his words should be interpreted in any such thoroughgoing manner: that his declaration was either heightened by the polemical stress of the occa-

sion (Welch), or that the structure of Jeremiah's statement is based upon a familiar idiom in which the first portion of the sentence containing the denial is not intended as a negation, but is supposed to be subsumed within the affirmation in the second clause, as when Hosea says

I desire steadfast love and not sacrifice,
  the knowledge of God, rather than burnt offerings (6:6).

Here it is held that Hosea does not say that sacrifice is in itself undesirable, but rather that mercy and knowledge are fundamental and that sacrifice is not to be substituted for them (Guillaume). The passage in I Sam. 15:22 would be similar:

  To obey is better than sacrifice,
    and to hearken than the fat of rams.

To collate the several passages which bear upon this problem, however, merely serves to strengthen the impression that the prophetic protest against the priestly compromise is growing steadily, and that, in Jeremiah, in a time (i.e., a *kairos*) when every claim is being pushed upon the absolute conditions, this rising consciousness bursts through with the unmistakable clarity that breaks the bonds of compromise. Amos, Hosea, Micah, Isaiah, and certain of the Psalms (notably 50:13-14; 51:16-17) all witness to the clarity of the prophetic insight. Nothing could be stronger, for example, than Amos' statement in 5:21-24. Hosea's emphasis upon "steadfast love and not sacrifice,"

---

[7] *Hearken unto the Voice,* tr. Moray Firth (New York: Viking Press, 1938), p. 779.

[8] *Prophecy and Eschatology,* p. 200.

23 But this thing commanded I them, saying, Obey my voice, and I will be your God, and ye shall be my people: and walk ye in all the ways that I have commanded you, that it may be well unto you.

24 But they hearkened not, nor inclined their ear, but walked in the counsels *and* in the imagination of their evil heart, and went backward, and not forward.

25 Since the day that your fathers came forth out of the land of Egypt unto this day, I have even sent unto you all my servants the prophets, daily rising up early and sending *them:*

and sacrifices. 23 But this command I gave them, 'Obey my voice, and I will be your God, and you shall be my people; and walk in all the way that I command you, that it may be well with you.' 24 But they did not obey or incline their ear, but walked in their own counsels and the stubbornness of their evil hearts, and went backward and not forward. 25 From the day that your fathers came out of the land of Egypt to this day, I have persistently sent all my servants

---

the ethical decalogue. This verse should not be used (as by Graf, *et al.*) to prove that the priestly code was not in existence in Jeremiah's time. Certainly many sacrifices were offered in his day, and Jeremiah may well have known the original Deuteronomy and historical narratives (J, E) which told of sacrifice being offered in the Mosaic period (e.g., Exod. 24:1-8). He deliberately sets himself against the prevalent view that Moses commanded sacrifice (cf. Amos 5:25). Modern research has shown that much of the sacrificial system was of Canaanite origin, but a few sacrifices may have been offered in the time of Moses.

24. This verse is contrary to the view expressed in 2:2-3, and probably represents the view of the Deuteronomic editor rather than that of Jeremiah.

---

upon "knowledge of God, rather than burnt offerings" (Hos. 6:16), may be less severe and possibly less absolute, but its intentional juxtaposition of what it approves as over against the people's practice is sufficient to subordinate the latter to the level of the disapproved. (Compare carefully the following passages: Mic. 6:6-8; Isa. 1:11-17; Pss. 40:6, 8; 50:10-14; 51:16-17.)

In Jeremiah's view, when the right spirit comes, the sacrificial system is irrelevant, if not idolatrous. Nor is it merely that there is an ineradicable ambiguity in sacrifices and symbols as such. It is not merely that the symbol or the sacrifice might be, for one person, "an aid to worship," whereas for another person it would be a barrier if not an image substituted for the genuine encounter with God. It is rather that the ambiguity is in the worshiper; that this ambiguity is itself a result of an antecedent rejection of the God-man relationship, and that whatever is done outside this relationship, or whatever substitutes itself for the relationship, is necessarily polemically and dialectically in retreat from the relationship. The only right way is the way which is necessarily tied in with the primacy of the voice. Vss. 24-26 are therefore a genuine continuation of the prophet's argument. When the people refused to listen to the voice in the wilderness and consequently **walked in their own counsels and the stubbornness of their evil hearts,** they went back-

ward and not forward, spiritually speaking. They could not advance in the knowledge of the love of God, but steadily slipped backward, becoming increasingly corrupt until in Jeremiah's time they appear to be beyond correction.

Welch's contention that these verses cannot be ascribed to the prophet because they contradict directly the idea of the innocence of the wilderness period is based, therefore, upon a misunderstanding of Jeremiah's total viewpoint.[9] It is precisely Jeremiah's initial viewpoint (2:2) that is made explicit here. It is the dialectical aspect of departure from the primary relationship with God that Jeremiah dramatizes. This is made even more plain when he points out that **I have persistently sent all my servants the prophets to them, day after day.** The true mediators between God and his people have been not the priests but the prophets. It is the prophets who have attempted to recall the people to the purity of their original faithful relationship with God. It is the priests, on the other hand, who, instead of going to the root of the relationship, have tried to secure the people by offering them "religion" as a substitute.

Jeremiah is being driven steadily forward upon his concept of the New Covenant, when God's word shall be written upon Israel's heart,

[9] *Jeremiah: His Time and His Work,* pp. 142-43.

26 Yet they hearkened not unto me, nor inclined their ear, but hardened their neck: they did worse than their fathers.

27 Therefore thou shalt speak all these words unto them; but they will not hearken to thee: thou shalt also call unto them; but they will not answer thee.

28 But thou shalt say unto them, This *is* a nation that obeyeth not the voice of the LORD their God, nor receiveth correction: truth is perished, and is cut off from their mouth.

29 ¶ Cut off thine hair, *O Jerusalem*, and cast *it* away, and take up a lamentation

the prophets to them, day after day; 26 yet they did not listen to me, or incline their ear, but stiffened their neck. They did worse than their fathers.

27 "So you shall speak all these words to them, but they will not listen to you. You shall call to them, but they will not answer you. 28 And you shall say to them, 'This is the nation that did not obey the voice of the LORD their God, and did not accept discipline; truth has perished; it is cut off from their lips.

29 Cut off your hair and cast it away;
    raise a lamentation on the bare heights,

D. SINFUL RITES IN THE VALLEY OF HINNOM (7:29–8:3)

This entire passage is a prediction of the evils that are to come, mainly because of the abominable practices, including child sacrifice, in the valley of Hinnom. It contains more eschatological details than are usually found in Jeremiah; it has several parallels in other passages from the Deuteronomic editor (19:6-7; 32:34-35; 25:10; 16:9); and 8:3 presupposes the Exile. There are thus many traces of the Deuteronomic editing, but the general spirit is not untrue to Jeremiah.

wherein each man shall stand before his Maker without tablets, with no ark, and without any intermediaries. Thus the prophets become the harbingers of the New Covenant; and, though the new community may be far in the future, Jeremiah has learned that the way to it is not by way of the illusory structures of temple, sacrifice, and priestcraft, but by way of the people becoming open to that singular touch of God which he himself had known.

Franz Werfel comes very close to this insight when he has Jeremiah explain to one of the characters, "the greatest gift that we can offer Him is to accept His gift, the commandments." [1] But there is something deeper still. The commandments, taken alone, are sterile. As Jeremiah stands beyond the priest, and beyond the false prophets of his day, so he also stands beyond the scribes. George Adam Smith would appear, therefore, to be right when he says:

Whether from Jeremiah or not, this is one of the most critical texts of the Old Testament because while repeating what the Prophet has already fervently accepted, that the terms of the deuteronomic Covenant were simply obedience to the ethical demands of God, it contradicts Deuteronomy and even more strongly Leviticus, in their repeated statements that in the wilderness God also commanded sacrifices. The issue is so grave that there have been attempts to evade it. None, however, can be regarded as successful. [2]

[1] *Hearken unto the Voice*, p. 303.
[2] *Jeremiah*, p. 156.

It is we ourselves, no doubt, who are still intimidated by the cult, and who continue to hear only what we are conditioned to hear. Perhaps Jeremiah himself saw the futility of his pronouncements. **So you shall speak all these words to them, but they will not listen to you.** But because they would not answer and because they did not obey the voice of the Lord their God and did not accept his discipline, Jeremiah sees clearly that **truth has perished.** Therefore the concluding lament: in which, as Gillies notes, the cutting of the hair is taken as an omen of death. [3] The cutting of the hair implies that Judah's life is forfeit. Jeremiah's dialectic is the same:

Not where the wheeling systems darken,
And our benumbed conceiving soars!—
The drift of pinions, would we hearken,
Beats at our own clay-shuttered doors.

The angels keep their ancient places;—
Turn but a stone, and start a wing!
'Tis ye, 'tis your estrangèd faces,
That miss the many-splendoured thing. [4]

7:29–8:3. *The Valley of Slaughter.*—W. R. Thomson has remarked on "the maturity, depth, and range of the Temple Address. . . .

[3] *Jeremiah, the Man and His Message*, p. 95.
[4] Francis Thompson, "The Kingdom of God," from *Collected Works*, ed. Wilfred Meynell. Used by permission of the publisher, Burns Oates & Washbourne, London.

on high places; for the LORD hath rejected and forsaken the generation of his wrath.

30 For the children of Judah have done evil in my sight, saith the LORD: they have set their abominations in the house which is called by my name, to pollute it.

31 And they have built the high places of Tophet, which *is* in the valley of the son of Hinnom, to burn their sons and their daughters in the fire; which I commanded *them* not, neither came it into my heart.

32 ¶ Therefore, behold, the days come, saith the LORD, that it shall no more be called Tophet, nor The valley of the son of Hinnom, but The valley of slaughter: for they shall bury in Tophet, till there be no place.

for the LORD has rejected and forsaken
  the generation of his wrath.'

30 "For the sons of Judah have done evil in my sight, says the LORD; they have set their abominations in the house which is called by my name, to defile it. **31** And they have built the high place*ⁱ* of To'pheth, which is in the valley of the son of Hinnom, to burn their sons and their daughters in the fire; which I did not command, nor did it come into my mind. **32** Therefore, behold, the days are coming, says the LORD, when it will no more be called To'pheth, or the valley of the son of Hinnom, but the valley of Slaughter: for they will bury in To'pheth, because there is no room elsewhere.

ⁱ Gk Tg: Heb *high places*

---

29. This verse is poetry and is apparently a direct quotation of the prophet's words. They are addressed to the nation or to Jerusalem personified as a woman; note that the KJV supplies **O Jerusalem,** which is not in the Hebrew.

31. The high place of Topheth, which is in the valley of the son of Hinnom was apparently an altar on which children were sacrificed. Little is definitely known concerning this cult practice. Child sacrifices may have been offered in very early Hebrew religion (Exod. 22:29), but provision was soon made for animal substitutes (Exod. 34: 20). The rite was revived by Ahaz and Manasseh, apparently under foreign influence (Syrian rather than Assyrian), but was stamped out by Josiah (II Kings 16:3; 21:6; 23:10). The references in Jeremiah show that it reappeared after the death of Josiah. **Topheth** may have originally meant "fireplace," but the word was pointed by the Hebrews with the vowels of *bôsheth,* "shame" (W. Robertson Smith, *Lectures on the Religion of the Semites* [3rd ed.; New York: The Macmillan Co., 1927], p. 377). The **valley of the**

It is clear from the address that not only had the reformation failed to touch the deeper springs of conduct, it had failed to eradicate the desire for heathenish practices in worship."[5] Nothing could have brought this factor into sharper relief, nor have penetrated more deeply into the nature and consequences of the people's condition, than this closing focus upon child sacrifice in the valley of Hinnom. Not only have they **set their abominations** in the temple, but **they have built the high place of Topheth . . . to burn their sons and their daughters in the fire.** Not only did Yahweh never issue such a command but, argues Jeremiah, it would never have entered his mind. Nothing exhibits so clearly the extent to which the spiritual life of the people has become degraded. Then comes that thunderous word **therefore**—which again and again occurs (as we have seen) when Jeremiah is about to draw the consequences of the people's behavior. The valley of Hinnom becomes typical. It is so placed in relation to Jeremiah's whole polemic

[5] *The Burden of the Lord,* pp. 80-81.

as to draw the full force of all the abuses upon it, as though this last scandalous outrage against the God of mercy and love concentrates the whole and precipitates the principle. The supposed high place of worship evokes the depth of their apostasy: the valley of Hinnom shall become **the valley of Slaughter.** In the place where they have slaughtered their children they shall themselves be slaughtered. So thoroughgoing shall be their destruction that the valley itself will have to be used for their burial because all other burial places will be full. Even the valley of Hinnom will not have room for them, and their bodies will lie exposed upon the ground.

This dramatic reversal of fortunes is continued into the next chapter. The depredations of the enemy will be so great that the bones of the kings, the princes, the priests, the prophets, and the people (all of whom have participated in the refusal to obey the Voice) shall be exposed, and spread before the idolatrous objects to which they were heretofore so sanguine and devoted. Thus the action of the enemy becomes

33 And the carcasses of this people shall be meat for the fowls of the heaven, and for the beasts of the earth; and none shall fray *them* away.

34 Then will I cause to cease from the cities of Judah, and from the streets of Jerusalem, the voice of mirth, and the voice of gladness, the voice of the bridegroom, and the voice of the bride: for the land shall be desolate.

8 At that time, saith the LORD, they shall bring out the bones of the kings of Judah, and the bones of his princes, and the bones of the priests, and the bones of the prophets, and the bones of the inhabitants of Jerusalem, out of their graves:

2 And they shall spread them before the sun, and the moon, and all the host of heaven, whom they have loved, and whom they have served, and after whom they have walked, and whom they have sought, and whom they have worshipped: they shall not be gathered, nor be buried; they shall be for dung upon the face of the earth.

33 And the dead bodies of this people will be food for the birds of the air, and for the beasts of the earth; and none will frighten them away. 34 And I will make to cease from the cities of Judah and from the streets of Jerusalem the voice of mirth and the voice of gladness, the voice of the bridegroom and the voice of the bride; for the land shall become a waste.

8 "At that time, says the LORD, the bones of the kings of Judah, the bones of its princes, the bones of the priests, the bones of the prophets, and the bones of the inhabitants of Jerusalem shall be brought out of their tombs; 2 and they shall be spread before the sun and the moon and all the host of heaven, which they have loved and served, which they have gone after, and which they have sought and worshiped; and they shall not be gathered or buried; they shall be as dung on the surface of the

---

son of Hinnom, or the valley of Hinnom, as it sometimes occurs, located south of Jerusalem, gave its name to the N.T. word for "hell," *Gehenna,* γέεννα.

33. The Hebrews considered that one of the worst possible curses was for **dead bodies** to be violated and not to receive proper burial. In 8:1-2 it is said that even the bodies of the leaders will be dishonored.

---

the instrument of the extreme irony of God, for the people dreaded nothing more than to be left unburied after death.

The reader who is venturing through Jeremiah for the first time will undoubtedly experience a sense of shock at the unrestrained assault of Jeremiah's words upon the nation; but it is probably something more fortuitous than chance which converted the valley of Hinnom into the N.T. word for "hell" (Gehenna). The bitterness here poured out (6:11), because of the unresponsiveness of the people, is due to the fact that Jeremiah sees that such indifference is, in fact, a complicity with evil. No sooner had Dante followed Vergil through the gate of hell than he beheld an interminably "long train of spirits" who had spent their lives in a state of apathy and indifference both to good and evil—wretches, who fled naked through the doleful stretches of the Inferno, "sorely stung by wasps and hornets." Astonished that there should be so many, Dante exclaims:

I should ne'er
Have thought that death so many had despoil'd—[6]

[6] *Inferno,* Canto III, ll. 53 ff.

a phrase which Eliot, in his *Waste Land,* applied to the crowd which, in our contemporary world, "flowed over London Bridge, so many."[7]

Jeremiah saw that a purgation in depth was essential to the people's return, and that they were now so far advanced along the way of self-deception that nothing short of the great calamity would work the inner chastening.

Through such Purgatory pain, it is appointed us to pass; first must the dead Letter of Religion own itself dead, and drop piecemeal into dust, if the living Spirit of Religion, freed from this its charnel-house, is to arise on us, newborn of Heaven, and with new healing under its wings.[8]

It would be a mistake, however, to conclude this section of "the temple sermon" without noting how Jeremiah's bitterness is shot through with suffering and pathos. The sufferings of the people are more intimately his than they are those even of the people themselves: for he has gone through the valley before them and has already been nailed out in isolation at the pre-

[7] Part I, "The Burial of the Dead" (New York: Boni & Liveright, 1922).
[8] *Sartor Resartus,* Bk. II, ch. iii.

3 And death shall be chosen rather than life by all the residue of them that remain of this evil family, which remain in all the places whither I have driven them, saith the LORD of hosts.

4 ¶ Moreover thou shalt say unto them, Thus saith the LORD; Shall they fall, and not arise? shall he turn away, and not return?

ground. 3 Death shall be preferred to life by all the remnant that remains of this evil family in all the places where I have driven them, says the LORD of hosts.

4 "You shall say to them, Thus says the LORD:
When men fall, do they not rise again?
If one turns away, does he not return?

V. MISCELLANEOUS MATERIALS (8:4–10:25)

This section contains a group of prophetic oracles which have no common theme. It is impossible now to determine why some of the individual oracles have been placed in their present position. The section, 8:4–9:1, probably stood originally in Baruch's scroll. If that scroll was read on a fast day proclaimed to mourn a prolonged drought, as suggested in the Exeg. on 36:6, the final oracle, 8:18–9:1, formed an appropriate ending to Baruch's scroll. The genuine oracles after 9:1 apparently originated after 604 B.C.

A. UNNATURALNESS OF ISRAEL'S BACKSLIDING (8:4-7)

The prophet here contrasts Israel's perpetual backsliding with "nature," i.e., with the actions of men in everyday life (vs. 4) and with the life of birds (vs. 7). Elsewhere Jeremiah emphasizes the unnaturalness of sin (see 2:10-11; 5:22-23; 18:13-17).

8:4. This verse presents a well-known truth: if a man falls down, he rises up as soon as possible; or if one turns away from the right path, he returns to it as soon as possible. The last line uses the two contrasted meanings of the verb *shûbh*; the same verbal root occurs three times in vs. 5: **turned away, backsliding,** and **return** (on this Hebrew word see Exeg. on 3:1–4:4).

---

cise point where the alienation of the people has driven the deepest wound into the heart of God. Vs. 34 betrays his bruise "for our iniquities," and it is written to "the still, sad music of humanity." It anticipates at once the peroration of *Ecclesiastes* and Vergil's "sense of tears in mortal things." For Jeremiah knows that the day will come quite soon when Yahweh will make to cease from the cities of Judah and from the streets of Jerusalem the voice of mirth and the voice of gladness, the voice of the bridegroom and the voice of the bride; for the land shall become a waste.

This passage, with its singular loveliness, becomes antiphonal for the book of Jeremiah (16:9; 25:10; 33:11).

8:4-7. *The Migratory Birds.*—We have just seen how Jeremiah

. . . The bold spirit, like an eagle
Before the tempests, flies prophesying
In the path of his advancing gods.[9]

Between the lightning flashes and the tempest cloud, we come now upon the brooding and the speculating stillness in which the troubled soul of Jeremiah probes persistently the deeper

mysteries. In all of this he is, as we should say today, the greatest of the O.T. psychologists. The mystery with which he now concerns himself arises both before and after his pronouncement to the people. Underneath their manifold defections he writes the troubled question, "Why?" It is the problem which the poet notes in every time, the mystery that

We would rather be ruined than changed,
We would rather die in our dread
Than climb the cross of the moment
And let our illusions die.[1]

Why then, asks Jeremiah, **has this people turned away in perpetual backsliding?** Why do they **hold fast to deceit,** and **refuse to return?** What is more, not one of them regrets his wickedness. And, like horses **plunging headlong into battle, every one turns to his own course,** oblivious of, or captivated by, the clash and ruin towards which they run.

Jeremiah, of course, is not the only poet to have experienced this mystery. From Prometheus to Hölderlin men have somehow felt that "the flame was put in our hands." Poets and prophets alike have felt that we are here

---

[9] Friedrich Hölderlin, *Empedocles*, IV, 135; quoted in Martin Heidegger, *Existence and Being* (tr. Douglas Scott; Chicago: Henry Regnery, 1949), p. 311.

[1] W. H. Auden, *The Age of Anxiety* (London: Faber & Faber; New York: Random House, 1946), p. 134. Used by permission.

5 Why *then* is this people of Jerusalem slidden back by a perpetual backsliding? they hold fast deceit, they refuse to return.

6 I hearkened and heard, *but* they spake not aright: no man repented him of his wickedness, saying, What have I done? every one turned to his course, as the horse rusheth into the battle.

7 Yea, the stork in the heaven knoweth her appointed times; and the turtle and the crane and the swallow observe the time of their coming; but my people know not the judgment of the LORD.

5 Why then has this people turned away
   in perpetual backsliding?
They hold fast to deceit,
   they refuse to return.
6 I have given heed and listened,
   but they have not spoken aright;
no man repents of his wickedness,
   saying, 'What have I done?'
Every one turns to his own course,
   like a horse plunging headlong into
     battle.
7 Even the stork in the heavens
   knows her times;
and the turtledove, swallow, and crane*j*
   keep the time of their coming;
but my people know not
   the ordinance of the LORD.

j The meaning of the Hebrew word is uncertain

---

7. Here the life of the people is contrasted with the life of birds, apparently in migration. While we would say that birds follow "instinct" or "natural law," the Hebrews conceived of them as obeying the direct commands of Yahweh (though it must be said that the conception here is close to our idea of "natural law"). The word translated **ordinance** (*mishpaṭ*) is rendered **law** in 5:4-5 (see Exeg., *ad loc.*).

---

to be tested, to be tried, to be dipped in fire: and that this is not altogether a bad thing, that in this way one's "true metal" comes clean.

> Ripe are, dipped in fire, cooked
> The fruit and sifted on the earth, and it is law
> That all goes in, like serpents,
> Prophetic, dreaming on
> The hills of heaven.[2]

But Hölderlin, whose lines these are, also knew that

> . . . evil are
> The paths. For wrongly,
> Like horses, go the imprisoned
> Elements . . .
>   . . . And always
> There is a yearning into the unbound.[3]

The persistence of this theme through Jeremiah's early and middle poems makes plain to what extent his troubled spirit was preoccupied with it. As tester of the people he was both heeding and listening, but nowhere did the people speak aright. Already it had puzzled him that they would prefer a broken cistern to a fountain of living waters (2:13). That a choice vine planted of pure seed should turn degenerate and become wild was to him an unnatural

[2] "Ripe are, dipped in fire . . . ," from *Poems of Hölderlin,* tr. Michael Hamburger (London: Harvill Press; New York: Pantheon Books, 1952). Used by permission.

[3] *Ibid.*

and abortive thing (2:21). Even a maiden could not forget her ornaments, but the people had forgotten God (2:32). The waves of the sea observe the bounds of sand that are set for them, but the people "have turned aside and gone away" (5:22-23). They have been told where the good way is and that by walking therein they should find rest for their souls, "but they said, 'We will not walk in it'" (6:16) —which to Jeremiah was incredible. If a man should fall down, he would certainly get up again. And if a man turns away out of the tried and proper path to his destiny and finds himself perplexed, alone and moving into a manifestly alien ground, he naturally returns to the way that he has left. When Jeremiah beholds the senseless plunge of people into destruction and perceives how essentially unnatural it is, he cannot forbear contrasting, in one of his most exquisite metaphors, the reckless plunging of humanity with the steadfast, simple order of the birds:

> Even the stork in the heavens
>   knows her times;
> and the turtledove, swallow, and crane
>   keep the time of their coming;
> but my people know not
>   the ordinance of the LORD.

There is almost infinite pathos in these lines. The movements of the migratory birds, so straightway healing to the distraught soul, and

8 How do ye say, We *are* wise, and the law of the LORD *is* with us? Lo, certainly in vain made he *it;* the pen of the scribes *is* in vain.

8 "How can you say, 'We are wise,
    and the law of the LORD is with us'?
But, behold, the false pen of the scribes
    has made it into a lie.

B. FALSE CLAIM TO WISDOM (8:8-13)

This oracle has no direct connection with the preceding one but was probably placed here by an editor because of the similarity in meaning of **ordinance** (vs. 7) and **law** (vs. 8). The central thought is the contrast between a written **law** (*tôrāh*), which to Jeremiah is false, and the living **word of the LORD,** the word given through the prophet. Many scholars (e.g., Marti, Wellhausen, Duhm, Cornill, *et al.*) have thought that this passage is a polemic against the book of Deuteronomy as it was known in Jeremiah's day. Deuteronomy was known as "the book of the law" (II Kings 22:8, 11; Deut. 30:10), and it is hard to imagine that any other book in Jeremiah's time could have been the object of such confidence as is implied here. Yet Jeremiah may well have been opposing the tendency to consider Deuteronomy and other books as "scripture"; he was perhaps objecting to the very idea that God's will can be crystallized in a book, especially if that book demands sacrifice and glorifies the temple, and if those who use it become proud and reject the living, oral word of the Lord through the prophet. "It is truly the tragedy of religion that the dead prophet kills the living" (Bernhard Duhm, *Das Buch Jeremia* [Tübingen: J. C. B. Mohr, 1901; "Kurzer Hand-Commentar zum Alten Testament"], p. 90).

8. The scribes were similar to "those who handle the law" of 2:8; they were not merely copyists, but men who interpreted and applied the law, the predecessors of the

---

so effective a contrast to the violence of the plunging battle horse, have an almost irresistible appeal.

The thesis of return is so persistent in Jeremiah that we shall meet with it yet again; but for the moment, let us note simply how this strangely moving word calls out to us across the ages:

> When I was a child
> Down in the land of Awa,
> I wondered that the swallows,
> Year after year,
> Came back to their same nests again;
> Just as Jeremiah wondered
> At God's guidance of the swallows,
> And wept,
> As he thundered,
> "My people Israel
> Will not return!"
>
> . . . .
>
> O Brothers,
> Coming back
> Empty handed,
> Desolate,
> From your sojourn
> Beyond the seven seas,
> Look up,
> Behold the birds . . . .
> And are ye not much better
> Than are these? [4]

[4] Toyohiko Kagawa, "I Call the Sparrows," from Kagawa, *et al., Songs from the Land of Dawn* (New York: Friendship Press, Inc., 1949). Used by permission.

There is an exile implicit in every turning away from God. But that men should "love to have it so" (5:31), that they should "stick fast to their falsehood" (vs. 5 Moffatt), and that they should, as Augustine would remark, "be willing to be deceived" and "unwilling to be convinced that they are so" [5] when the whole of nature cries out against it—all this is both purblind and presumptuous. "Only the fresh impact of his purpose can recall a man to his appointed time (Jer. 8:7) and his immediate vocation." [6]

But this "repetition of God's creative act" can be brought about only by the radical movement from presumptuousness to confession, from obstinacy to repentance: and between the two lies a chasm as deep as a man's self will. But consider the **stork in the heavens,** the **turtledove,** the **swallow,** the **crane:** these keep **the time of their coming.** Behold the birds of the air which accept quite simply the ordinances of God for their moment in time: to seek first the kingdom and his righteousness is the simple ordinance of God for men in eternity.

8-13. *"Nothing . . . but Leaves."*—It is important to note how easily one moves from the reflections of the preceding section to the opening verses and the last of the passage now before us. When Jeremiah holds that "my people know not the ordinance of the Lord" (vs. 7), one easily imagines the protest which must

[5] *Confessions* X. 23. 34.
[6] Minear, *Eyes of Faith,* p. 54.

9 The wise *men* are ashamed, they are dismayed and taken: lo, they have rejected the word of the Lord; and what wisdom *is* in them?

10 Therefore will I give their wives unto others, *and* their fields to them that shall inherit *them:* for every one from the least even unto the greatest is given to covetousness, from the prophet even unto the priest every one dealeth falsely.

11 For they have healed the hurt of the daughter of my people slightly, saying, Peace, peace; when *there is* no peace.

9 The wise men shall be put to shame,
they shall be dismayed and taken;
lo, they have rejected the word of the
Lord,
and what wisdom is in them?
10 Therefore I will give their wives to others
and their fields to conquerors,
because from the least to the greatest
every one is greedy for unjust gain;
from prophet to priest
every one deals falsely.
11 They have healed the wound of my people lightly,
saying, 'Peace, peace,'
when there is no peace.

---

scribes of postexilic Judaism. The exact translation of vs. 8*b* is difficult; the RSV is more nearly accurate than the KJV, but it involves reading a *mappîq* in the final letter of עשה (**made it**). In Jeremiah *shéqer* means **lie** rather than "vanity." The reading of the RSV suggests that the scribes had falsified the law; Jeremiah could well have approved of the ethical prescription of Deuteronomy but not its ritualistic prescriptions and the writing down of the whole as the law of Yahweh.

10-12. These verses are out of place here, and may have originally followed 6:12-15. The LXX omits vss. 10*b*-12.

---

have arisen many times, namely, that the ordinances of Yahweh are precisely that which they do know; they are written in a book, or in the instructions (*tôrāh*) of the prophets and the priests. It is probably not important here whether the verse refers to Deuteronomy, though many critics preoccupy themselves with this question. Nor does the deeper meaning of the verse hinge upon his simply meaning the "instruction" or "direction" given orally by the priests (Deut. 17:11) and the prophets to those who came to counsel with them. What matters is the specious claim to wisdom based upon the assumption that **the law of the Lord is with us.** In either case Jeremiah's charge is clear: **the false pen of the scribes has made it into a lie.** The deeper question follows (and it contains the nub and burden of Jeremiah's continuing critique) : **lo, they have rejected the word of the Lord,** "so what 'wisdom' have they?" (Moffatt). Jeremiah is trying to say, quite simply, there is no wisdom apart from that which is founded upon a knowledge of God.

The falsification which Jeremiah sees is not confined to deliberate misrepresentation of the law, but rather to that inevitable falsification of meanings and values which must arise from the "wisdom" of any teacher whose wisdom constructs and construes itself outside the living relationship with God. The conversion of the living ordinances of God into legalistic counters of barter and exchange, or into codes to be in-

terpreted by scholastic skills, will, in the nature of the case, bend the spirit to the letter. Doubtless something of this kind was in A. B. Davidson's mind when he wrote that "Pharisaism and Deuteronomy came into the world the same day." [7] And what is difficult in all such cases is, as Emil Brunner says, that the Pharisee is at once the person who is nearest to, and at the same time the farthest from, God. [8]

This deeper betrayal may be illustrated from one of Martin Buber's *Tales of the Hasidim.* For thirty years a certain man lived in seclusion and devoted himself to the *tôrāh.* When he returned from his years of study he sought out a certain saddik (Rabbi Vitzhak of Vorki) ; but he grew embarrassed when the saddik said to him, "You are so learned a man [that] surely you know what God says?" He attempted several replies, at which the saddik only laughed. "You do not understand my question," he said. When, after many days, he was about to take his leave, the saddik asked him, "What are you taking home with you, since you don't know what God says!" In bewilderment and trouble the man asked the saddik to enlighten him. "It is written in Jeremiah," said the saddik, " 'Can any hide himself in secret places,'—that means,

[7] "Jeremiah," in James Hastings, ed., *Dictionary of the Bible* (New York: Charles Scribner's Sons, 1899), II, 577.
[8] *The Divine Imperative*, tr. Olive Wyon (Philadelphia: Westminster Press, 1947), p. 64.

12 Were they ashamed when they had committed abomination? nay, they were not at all ashamed, neither could they blush; therefore shall they fall among them that fall: in the time of their visitation they shall be cast down, saith the LORD.

13 ¶ I will surely consume them, saith the LORD: *there shall be* no grapes on the vine, nor figs on the fig tree, and the leaf shall fade; and *the things that* I have given them shall pass away from them.

12 Were they ashamed when they committed
   abomination?
   No, they were not at all ashamed;
     they did not know how to blush.
Therefore they shall fall among the
   fallen;
   when I punish them, they shall be
     overthrown,
                    says the LORD.
13 When I would gather them, says the
   LORD,
   there are no grapes on the vine,
     nor figs on the fig tree;
   even the leaves are withered,
     and what I gave them has passed away
       from them."[k]

[k] Heb uncertain

---

13. This verse continues the thought of vs. 9. The "wise" have no fruit, being like a barren vine or fig tree. The last line is very obscure; various emendations have been suggested, but none carries conviction.

---

anyone who locks himself into his room for thirty years and studies the Torah; 'that I shall not see him?'—that means, I may not want to see such a man; 'saith the Lord'—that is what God says." The man was deeply moved, and, given permission to ask a question, he said, "What is the prescribed thing to do, when scraps of a holy book which has been torn fall to the ground?" "They should be picked up," said the saddik, "lest they be destroyed." Whereupon the man threw himself on the floor crying, "Rabbi, rabbi, a vessel filled with scraps of the Holy Scriptures lies before you. Do not let them be destroyed!"[9]

If, on the other hand, Jeremiah *is* referring to Deuteronomy, or to Deutoronomy and other books of Scripture, his appraisal of the false pretensions of the wise is all the more incisive. We should be justified in thinking that the clause **they have rejected the word of the LORD** refers to their rejection of the word of the prophet, inasmuch as it is through the true prophet that the word of the Lord is mediated. The quotation from Duhm (see Exeg.) is most appropriate. "It is a law of spiritual history," said Paul Volz, "that the preachers of new religious systems have their hardest battles with the contemporary religious leaders."[1] (The mounting tide of opposition to the word of the Lord as conveyed by Jeremiah will be seen increasingly in the passages which follow.)

Moffatt skips over vss. 10-12, inasmuch as they are a repetition of 6:12-15. Vs. 13 follows

[9] Vol. II, pp. 293-94.
[1] *Der Prophet Jeremia* (Leipzig: A. Deichert, 1928), p. xxxi.

normally here. Because the wise **have rejected the word of the LORD, . . . what wisdom is in them?** asks the prophet. When the Lord comes to gather the fruit of their wisdom,

    there are no grapes on the vine,
      nor figs on the fig tree;
    even the leaves are withered.

Just as in the preceding passage (8:4-7) the mind runs forward to the lilies and the birds of the Sermon on the Mount, so here the description of the fig tree will suggest the "hypocrite fig" of Matt. 21:19. Jesus came over the hill looking down upon Jerusalem and saw the fig tree in full leaf (as Jerusalem in all her magnificence was in full leaf). He would naturally expect to find fruit upon the tree, inasmuch as the fruit of the fig matures simultaneously with the leaves. The tree was therefore a hypocrite tree since it had no figs, just as Jerusalem was a hypocrite city because (in full leaf) it contained no fruits of the Spirit. Hence his cursing of the fig tree was parabolic of his indictment of the spiritually barren city.

As for the concluding sentence—**and what I gave them has passed away from them**—there seems to be no legitimate reason to speculate as to whether this gift was their inheritance or their land or their teaching, etc. Once the principle involved is grasped (and it runs, as we see, throughout Jeremiah), it is clear that the spiritual inheritance of Israel is that which is passing from them. This is increasingly apparent as one collates parallel passages below (e.g., 10:16; 12:7-17; 16:18; 17:4). The principle is that of Athanasius' "moral phthisis," in

14 Why do we sit still? assemble yourselves, and let us enter into the defensed cities, and let us be silent there: for the LORD our God hath put us to silence, and given us water of gall to drink, because we have sinned against the LORD.	14 Why do we sit still? Gather together, let us go into the fortified cities and perish there; for the LORD our God has doomed us to perish, and has given us poisoned water to drink, because we have sinned against the LORD.
15 We looked for peace, but no good *came; and* for a time of health, and behold trouble!	15 We looked for peace, but no good came, for a time of healing, but behold, terror.
16 The snorting of his horses was heard from Dan: the whole land trembled at the sound of the neighing of his strong ones; for they are come, and have devoured the land, and all that is in it; the city, and those that dwell therein.	16 "The snorting of their horses is heard from Dan; at the sound of the neighing of their stallions the whole land quakes. They come and devour the land and all that fills it, the city and those who dwell in it.

C. DESPAIR OVER FOREIGN INVASION (8:14-17)

This poem is similar to the poems about the foe from the north, and may belong with them. Vs. 14 contains a quotation from 4:5, and **Dan** (vs. 16) was in the extreme north of Palestine. But the poem is not well unified, and its mood is one of utter despair, much more so than the other poems about the foe from the north. Emphasis is laid on the fact

which the moral life can do nothing but waste and wither away once it is severed from its source of vitality. For Jeremiah this source is the content of the lived relationship with Yahweh, and the fruits of that relationship are the fruits of the Covenant. The principle, therefore, of gain and of loss is similar to that of Matt. 13:12: "For to him who has will more be given, and he will have abundance; but from him who has not, even what he has will be taken away." (Cf. also Matt. 25:29; Mark 4:25; Luke 8:18.) For this is the law of the spiritual life: the one way is the way of life, and the other the way of death.

14-17. Adders That Cannot Be Charmed.—Despite the quotation from 4:5 in the opening lines of this poem, its mood of helplessness would seem to place it in a later period. But in any case it serves once more to bring the people up short against the immediacy of the threat from the north. The rhetorical verve of the opening line is something we know quite well in the more familiar phraseology, "Why sit we here idle!" The people, clearly stupefied by the news of impending disaster from the north **(from Dan),** are summoned to get them hence quickly into the fortified cities. Not that there is any hope there, for the wickedness of the

people has doomed them to defeat and punishment. "There are," says Gordon, "two poles in the prophet's thinking, one the oncoming disaster and the other the vileness of public morality." [2] This is very largely true, especially at the beginning of Jeremiah's ministry; but we should not neglect Luther's warning that the predominance of negative features in Jeremiah's message is due to the time and situation in which he was called to speak.[3] The main point is that the people, who had been insulating themselves unrealistically against the danger, recognized suddenly that, whereas they had looked for peace and for a time of healing, nothing has come but terror. The foe from the north has already reached Dan. Though Dan is located in the extreme north of Palestine it is near enough for the snorting and neighing of the horses to be heard. It is already well known what type of treatment the people will receive at the hands of the invader. Already they begin to know the bitterness of gall (poisoned water); but the full force of Jeremiah's poetic invective is not felt until we reach the concluding line. Here, as in our conventional sonnet form, is the whip line of the poem:

[2] *Rebel Prophet,* p. 174.
[3] "Vorrede über den Propheten Jeremia," pp. 59-60.

17 For, behold, I will send serpents, cockatrices, among you, which *will* not *be* charmed, and they shall bite you, saith the LORD.

18 ¶ *When* I would comfort myself against sorrow, my heart *is* faint in me.

17 For behold, I am sending among you
    serpents,
adders which cannot be charmed,
and they shall bite you,"
                  says the LORD.

18 My grief is beyond healing,*
    my heart is sick within me.

Cn Compare Gk: Heb uncertain

---

that the invasion is a punishment from Yahweh for Israel's sin; the **poisoned water** of vs. 14 (cf. 9:15; 23:15), and the **serpents** and **adders which cannot be charmed** of vs. 17 indicate the extreme bitterness and inescapability of the punishment.

17. On the charming of snakes cf. Eccl. 10:11; Ps. 58:4-5.

D. SYMPATHY WITH THE STRICKEN PEOPLE (8:18–9:1)

This poem poignantly expresses the prophet's grief over some great calamity that has befallen the people. The occasion is probably a drought, as vs. 20 suggests; the **slain** of 9:1 could be those slain by famine, as in Lam. 4:9. The situation may thus be similar to that of ch. 14. Some scholars think the calamity was the invasion which lies back of vss. 14-17, but this seems improbable. An unusual feature of this passage is that it contains

---

For behold, I am sending among you serpents, adders which cannot be charmed.

Two things may be supposed here. The first is that the imagery employed represents a conscious carry-over on the part of the poet from the well-known description by Jacob of his son, Dan:

A serpent on the road is Dan.
  a snake upon the path,
that bites the horse's hoof,
    till the rider tumbles backward (Gen. 49:17
    Moffatt).

Secondly, snake-charming was not an uncommon practice in Israel. (Cf. Eccl. 10:11; Ps. 58: 4-5.) Some serpents were susceptible of being charmed, and others not. Heretofore the public policy had been that of charming the several serpents contending for world power. By such guileful practices the people had been lulled into a sense of false security. But now the time has passed. The serpents which are now coming among them are of a more deadly kind: they are **adders which cannot be charmed!**

These verses, and possibly the next (8:18–9:1), would appear to have been written under the sign of some great disaster. In spite of the verse overlappings with the poems of chs. 4–6 (cf. vs. 14 with 4:5; vs. 16 with 4:15; and vss. 18 ff. with 4:19 ff.), the mood is so different from those early poems as to throw it into a later time. Skinner argues quite convincingly that both poems belong to the period immediately following the battle of Megiddo in which Josiah was slain.

There is but one situation known to us which would enable us in some measure to combine [the poems'] varied allusions; and that is the time of consternation and dismay which must have followed the disastrous battle of Megiddo. It closed the period of mingled optimism and anxiety which had been initiated by the Deuteronomic covenant, and lasted till the death of Josiah. It shattered the illusory hopes based on the formal acceptance of the Covenant, and must have plunged the nation into the depth of gloom which is the ground-note of these verses.[4]

Their false optimisms are shattered. Their dejection and despondency break suddenly into a sense of panic, and they flee to **the fortified cities,** there to await the return of the Egyptian armies and the final crushing blow.

8:18–9:1. Elegy to a Wound.—Gordon says truly that Jeremiah "is the master *par excellence* of the elegy [and] the master of the elegy was the master of his people's heart."[5] Nor is it surprising that there should be more poems written in the elegiac mood than in any other form. The "incomparable elegy which follows"[6] is one of the most moving pieces in all literature. The prophet's identification with the sorrows of his people is complete. Here we touch not merely "the sense of tears in mortal things" but the cry of the daughter of his people. The prophet is heartsick and grief ridden.

There is a parallel dramatic structure between this elegy and the poem which precedes it. As the people are broken by the event of

[4] *Prophecy and Religion,* p. 127.
[5] *Op. cit.,* pp. 177-78.
[6] Smith, *Jeremiah,* p. 197.

19 Behold the voice of the cry of the daughter of my people because of them that dwell in a far country: *Is* not the Lord in Zion? *is* not her king in her? Why have they provoked me to anger with their graven images, *and* with strange vanities?

20 The harvest is past, the summer is ended, and we are not saved.

19 Hark, the cry of the daughter of my people
from the length and breadth of the land:
"Is the Lord not in Zion?
Is her King not in her?"
"Why have they provoked me to anger with their graven images,
and with their foreign idols?"
20 "The harvest is past, the summer is ended,
and we are not saved."

---

no suggestion that the calamity is a punishment for sin (vs. 19c is secondary) ; it is purely an expression of the prophet's grief, and shows his deep sympathy with the people whom he often had to denounce.

19. Daughter of my people: See Exeg. on 4:11. **From the length and breadth of the land** is the correct translation; the Hebrew has the same meaning in Isa. 33:17. **Why have they . . . foreign idols** (vs. 19c) is widely recognized to be an insertion, breaking into the context very abruptly. It is a gloss by the Deuteronomic editor, who emphasized the sin of idolatry.

---

the disaster, so is the prophet broken within. As their wound is incurable, so is his grief. As the time for civic hope is past, so the season is past when he might have hoped that the people would turn. Nothing, in this moment, is left but the strong lament for the wound of his people. The images of this lament are among the finest in poetry.

**The harvest is passed, the summer is ended,
and we are not saved.**

Peake reminds us that

to understand this famous verse we must remember that "the harvest" and "the summer" were quite distinct seasons in Palestine. The harvest lasted from April to June; "summer" was . . . the "ingathering of summer fruits." If the harvest failed the people might still look forward to the fruit, but if the fruit also failed famine stared them in the face.[7]

This is difficult to understand in a country where the fruits of the season all ripen at the same time. But figs and grapes, for example, ripen in some climates as late as September; whereas other produce, certain vegetables, fruits, and grains, ripen much earlier. No eschatological significance is to be attached to the term "saved"; but the passage, as touching the human spirit, is singularly moving. Soon, all too soon, we become aware that the season of the harvest is past and our summer is ending. And much that we ought to have prepared for godly fruition we have neglected. Too many talents

have been buried, too many "thought-balls" (Ibsen) were never woven into fabric of exchange. Thus has the passage slipped into common use quite easily and become a proverb.

As for the famous **balm in Gilead,** Calkins suggests that "the resin of the mastic tree is meant, which was used as a remedy."[8] Charles E. Jefferson wrote with eloquence:

He saw that sin is a cancer, a malignant disease which goes down to the very roots of our being. He saw that there is no physician this side of God who can do anything for it. Did you ever feel the pathos of his piercing question—"Is there no balm in Gilead? Is there no physician there?" Gilead was a region which lay on the prophet's eastern horizon. It was over Gilead that the sun rose every morning to illumine little Anathoth and big Jerusalem. It was the land which symbolized hope. In Gilead grew the herbs and trees and flowers from which balsams were made to supply the physicians of that Eastern world. Is there no balm even in Gilead? Is there no physician, no prophet, no priest, no healer, no teacher who can cure a sick heart? And the answer is "No." There is no remedy on earth for a heart which is desperately sick.[9]

Were there an easy answer to this rhetorical question, Jeremiah would not be obliged to reply with another question implying a negative:

Then, why does not close
My dear people's wound?[1]

[8] Calkins, *Jeremiah the Prophet,* p. 117.
[9] *Cardinal Ideas of Jeremiah* (New York: The Macmillan Co., 1928), p. 141. Used by permission.
[1] Gordon, *op. cit.,* p. 178.

[7] *Jeremiah and Lamentations,* I, 163.

21 For the hurt of the daughter of my people am I hurt; I am black; astonishment hath taken hold on me.

22 *Is there* no balm in Gilead? *is there* no physician there? why then is not the health of the daughter of my people recovered?

9 Oh that my head were waters, and mine eyes a fountain of tears, that I might weep day and night for the slain of the daughter of my people!

2 Oh that I had in the wilderness a lodging place of wayfaring men; that I might leave my people, and go from them! for they *be* all adulterers, an assembly of treacherous men.

21 For the wound of the daughter of my
    people is my heart wounded,
  I mourn, and dismay has taken hold on
    me.

22 Is there no balm in Gilead?
    Is there no physician there?
  Why then has the health of the daughter
    of my people
    not been restored?

9 *m* O that my head were waters,
  and my eyes a fountain of tears,
  that I might weep day and night
    for the slain of the daughter of my
    people!

2 *n* O that I had in the desert
  a wayfarers' lodging place,
  that I might leave my people
  and go away from them!
  For they are all adulterers,
  a company of treacherous men.

m Heb Ch 8. 23
n Heb Ch 9. 1

---

22. Balm in Gilead was resin from the Styrax tree, for which Gilead in Trans-Jordan was famous; it was used medicinally, and was exported (46:11; 51:8; Ezek. 27:17; Gen. 37:25).

E. Lament over the People's Treachery (9:2-9)

This passage is somewhat similar to 8:18–9:1, and the similarity accounts for its present position; but the tone of the two passages is entirely different. There Jeremiah was sympathizing with the stricken people; here he is so disgusted with their treachery that he wishes to get away from them. Great emphasis is placed upon their sins of the tongue: slander, deceit, lying, double-dealing, etc. The poem ends with a threat of punishment (vss. 7, 9).

9:2. A wayfarers' lodging place, with its bare comforts and isolation, would be preferable to life with such treacherous people.

Follow then the incomparable elegiac lines which close the poem:

> O that my head were waters,
>   and my eyes a fountain of tears,
> that I might weep day and night
>   for the slain of the daughter of my people!

Thus, alone, as Rilke would say, Jeremiah climbs to his mountains of Primal Pain.

Perhaps there are no passages in the whole of scripture that are quite so moving, except for David's cry, "O Absalom, my son, my son!" (II Sam. 18:33) and Jesus' highly prophetic lament, "O Jerusalem, Jerusalem! slaying the prophets and stoning those who have been sent to you! How often I would fain have gathered your children as a fowl gathers her brood under

her wings! But you would not have it!" (Matt. 23:37; Luke 13:34 Moffatt).

9:2-9. *Ah, Wilderness!*—While it is quite impossible to date this poem, one must agree on the whole with Peake, who is persuaded that it cannot belong to Jeremiah's early period for "a good deal of unhappy experience lies behind it." [2] One is certain to feel, in these opening lines, the depth to which the heart of Jeremiah has already been pierced by the sword of sorrow. His position here is perhaps on that account justified, as he has clearly felt "the wound of the daughter of my people" (8:21). But, overwhelmed with a sense of revulsion, as he contemplates the entrenched foolhardiness of the people, this outburst is not inconsistent with his feeling of grief. Perceiving

[2] *Op. cit.*, I, 164.

3 And they bend their tongues *like* their bow *for* lies: but they are not valiant for the truth upon the earth; for they proceed from evil to evil, and they know not me, saith the LORD.

4 Take ye heed every one of his neighbor, and trust ye not in any brother: for every brother will utterly supplant, and every neighbor will walk with slanders.

5 And they will deceive every one his neighbor, and will not speak the truth: they

3 They bend their tongue like a bow;
  falsehood and not truth has grown
    strong[o] in the land;
for they proceed from evil to evil,
  and they do not know me, says the
    LORD.

4 Let every one beware of his neighbor,
  and put no trust in any brother;
for every brother is a supplanter,
  and every neighbor goes about as a
    slanderer.
5 Every one deceives his neighbor,
  and no one speaks the truth;
they have taught their tongue to speak
  lies;

[o] Gk: Heb *and not for truth they have grown strong*

3. The RSV emends the Hebrew slightly with the help of the LXX; the result is better poetry.

4. **Is a supplanter:** The Hebrew is *'āqōbh ya'qōbh,* using the verbal root that occurs in the name "Jacob," which is explained in Gen. 27:36. Moffatt renders, "For a brother will cheat like a Jacob."

5-6. The RSV presents a better translation of the end of vs. 5 and the beginning of vs. 6, partly by following the LXX and partly by redividing and revocalizing the

everywhere the moral duplicity of the people and their obstinate refusal to recognize how their compounded treacheries bring their evils upon themselves, he is filled with indignation and chagrin. Hence the authenticity and force of this initial outcry, so like the cry we often hear: "If I could only get away from it all!"

> O that I had in the desert
> a wayfarers' lodging place,
> that I might leave my people
> and go away from them!

Two comparisons may be drawn here. The first is with William Cowper, when, in his most significant poem, he clearly paraphrases from Jeremiah:

> Oh for a lodge in some vast wilderness,
> Some boundless contiguity of shade,
> Where rumour of oppression and deceit,
> Of unsuccessful or successful war,
> Might never reach me more.[3]

The poem goes on to specify in more contemporary language the treacheries of man upon man and brother upon brother which Cowper saw about him in eighteenth-century England. Jeremiah specifies adultery, treachery, and falsehood; whereas Cowper inveighs against racial tyranny, petty nationalisms, and slavery. Cow-

per's claim that "man devotes his brother, and destroys"[4] is not unlike Jeremiah's claim that every brother is a Jacob, intent on deceiving his brother. Superficially it may appear that Cowper's charge is stronger than Jeremiah's. But with Jeremiah it is not enough merely to catalog the several sins of the tongue—slander, deceit, lying, double-dealing, etc. All this must be thrown back upon the fact that **they do not know me, says the LORD.** The word, to the Hebrew, "is more than a word; it is a bearer of power, a projection of the authority and purpose of him who speaks."[5] And the kind of power or authority or purpose which a man exercises is defined when his speech and deeds are pushed back upon and assessed within the context of the covenant relation. The man who does not know his God sets himself in opposition to himself and in contradiction to his world and other people.

A comparison with Ps. 55, the first verses of which are frequently attributed to Jeremiah, reinforces what has been said. Here the city is revealed as being full of "violence and strife" and "mischief and trouble" and "ruin . . . oppression and fraud." But all these things are clearly in connivance against the author of the psalm. "They bring trouble upon me, . . . they cherish enmity against me." Because of this his

[3] *The Task,* Bk. II.

[4] *Ibid.*

[5] Minear, *Eyes of Faith,* p. 53.

have taught their tongue to speak lies, *and*
weary themselves to commit iniquity.
6 Thine habitation *is* in the midst of
deceit; through deceit they refuse to know
me, saith the LORD.
7 Therefore thus saith the LORD of hosts,
Behold, I will melt them, and try them; for
how shall I do for the daughter of my
people?
8 Their tongue *is as* an arrow shot out; it
speaketh deceit: *one* speaketh peaceably to
his neighbor with his mouth, but in heart
he layeth his wait.
9 ¶ Shall I not visit them for these
things? saith the LORD: shall not my soul be
avenged on such a nation as this?
10 For the mountains will I take up a

they commit iniquity and are too weary
to repent.[p]
6 Heaping oppression upon oppression,
and deceit upon deceit,
they refuse to know me, says the LORD.

7 Therefore thus says the LORD of hosts:
"Behold, I will refine them and test them,
for what else can I do, because of my
people?
8 Their tongue is a deadly arrow;
it speaks deceitfully;
with his mouth each speaks peaceably to
his neighbor,
but in his heart he plans an ambush
for him.
9 Shall I not punish them for these things?
says the LORD;
and shall I not avenge myself
on a nation such as this?

10 "Take up[q] weeping and wailing for the
mountains,

[p] Cn Compare Gk: Heb *your dwelling*
[q] Gk Syr: Heb *I will take up*

---

consonants of the Hebrew text. The M.T. gives little sense without such a change; **thine habitation** has no connection with the preceding or the following, and the reference of **thine** is obscure. The text translated by the RSV as the last line of vs. 5 and the first line of vs. 6 is as follows:

העוו נלאו שב
תך בתוך מרמה במרמה

7. For the thought cf. 6:27-30.

F. Wail for the Destruction of Judah (9:10-22)

This whole passage deals with the destruction of Jerusalem and Judah, especially of the former. When it is recognized that vss. 12-16 are an insertion, the remaining verses

---

"heart is in anguish" within him (cf. Jeremiah 8:18). He experiences "fear and trembling," "horror," and "the terrors of death." Thus to his feeling of revulsion at the wickedness of the people there is added his own experience of their treachery and double dealing.

> And I say, "O that I had wings like a dove!
> I would fly away and be at rest;
> yea, I would wander afar,
> I would lodge in the wilderness" (Ps. 55:6-7).

It is important to note that these expostulations, whether arising out of revulsion against the people's wickedness or from the increasing trouble and treachery to which the psalmist is exposed, are not to be interpreted as temptations to flee. They are, indeed, precisely the reverse. Though, rhetorically, he could wish to flee, the terms of his commitment and commission are such that if he could he would not, and if he would he could not. For he knows that it is only through the fresh word-deed of Yahweh, delivered through the Lord's appointed mouthpiece, that the words of the people may be made whole again. Through him (i.e., the prophet) the Lord **will refine them and test them** until they are brought forth pure again.

10-11. ***Lament for the Land Laid Waste.***—This brief lament is not without its special power. It appears to be more than a vision of desolation: it bears witness to the depredations

weeping and wailing, and for the habitations of the wilderness a lamentation, because they are burned up, so that none can
pass through *them;* neither can *men* hear
the voice of the cattle: both the fowl of the
heavens and the beast are fled; they are
gone.

11 And I will make Jerusalem heaps, *and*
a den of dragons; and I will make the cities
of Judah desolate, without an inhabitant.

12 ¶ Who *is* the wise man, that may
understand this? and *who is he* to whom the
mouth of the LORD hath spoken, that he
may declare it, for what the land perisheth
and is burned up like a wilderness, that
none passeth through?

13 And the LORD saith, Because they
have forsaken my law which I set before
them, and have not obeyed my voice,
neither walked therein;

14 But have walked after the imagination of their own heart, and after Baalim,
which their fathers taught them:

and a lamentation for the pastures of
the wilderness,
because they are laid waste so that no one
passes through,
and the lowing of cattle is not heard;
both the birds of the air and the beasts
have fled and are gone.

11 I will make Jerusalem a heap of ruins,
a lair of jackals;
and I will make the cities of Judah a
desolation,
without inhabitant."

12 Who is the man so wise that he can
understand this? To whom has the mouth
of the LORD spoken, that he may declare it?
Why is the land ruined and laid waste like
a wilderness, so that no one passes through?
13 And the LORD says: "Because they have
forsaken my law which I set before them,
and have not obeyed my voice, or walked
in accord with it, 14 but have stubbornly
followed their own hearts and have gone
after the Ba'als, as their fathers taught

show unity of theme. In vs. 10 Yahweh calls upon the people to mourn because of the
desolation, and in vs. 11 he declares his intention to destroy Jerusalem and the cities of
Judah. Then vss. 17-22 are concerned largely with an appeal to professional mourning
women to wail over the city.

The date of this passage is probably the Chaldean invasion of Judah in 602 B.C.,
described in II Kings 24:1-2.

10. The RSV follows the LXX, O.L., and Syriac in reading as imperative (plural)
rather than as the first person of the M.T.

12-16. These verses are an addition by the Deuteronomic editor, designed to explain
the desolation of Jerusalem in 587 B.C. and the subsequent Exile, similar in form and
content to 5:18-19 (see Exeg., *ad loc.*). It is possible that vs. 12 is genuine, if it is to be
taken with what precedes rather than what follows.

of the invader. The passage tempts comparison
with 4:23-26, particularly at the point of its
description of the silence of emptiness which
has settled down over the land. So wasted are
the pastures that no one passes through, the
lowing of cattle is not heard, and the birds of
the air and the beasts of the field have fled.
The absence of the birds is a particularly powerful image. In our own time a poet gives this
argument a similar form: in his "Autumn
1940" W. H. Auden writes

There are no birds; the predatory
Glaciers glitter in the chilly evening;

And death is probable. . . .[6]

The unbearable oppressiveness of silence and
solitariness has been well expressed by Cowper:

Oh, solitude! where are the charms
That sages have seen in thy face?
Better dwell in the midst of alarms,
Than reign in this horrible place.[7]

Yahweh's threat that he **will make Jerusalem
a heap of ruins** is the unavoidable inference
drawn from the moral condition of the people
and the events which have already occurred.

12-16. *Challenge to the Wise Men.*—This
editorial insertion formulates a question of considerable pertinence. It takes the form, in fact,
of a challenge to the popular wise men (8:8-9).

[6] From *The Collected Poetry of W. H. Auden* (London:
Faber & Faber; New York: Random House, 1945). Used
by permission.

[7] "Verses supposed to be written by Alexander Selkirk,
during his solitary abode in the island of Juan Fernan-
dez."

15 Therefore thus saith the LORD of hosts, the God of Israel; Behold, I will feed them, *even* this people, with wormwood, and give them water of gall to drink.

16 I will scatter them also among the heathen, whom neither they nor their fathers have known: and I will send a sword after them, till I have consumed them.

17 ¶ Thus saith the LORD of hosts, Consider ye, and call for the mourning women, that they may come; and send for cunning *women*, that they may come:

18 And let them make haste, and take up a wailing for us, that our eyes may run down with tears, and our eyelids gush out with waters.

19 For a voice of wailing is heard out of Zion, How are we spoiled! we are greatly confounded, because we have forsaken the land, because our dwellings have cast *us* out.

them. 15 Therefore thus says the LORD of hosts, the God of Israel: Behold, I will feed this people with wormwood, and give them poisonous water to drink. 16 I will scatter them among the nations whom neither they nor their fathers have known; and I will send the sword after them, until I have consumed them."

17 Thus says the LORD of hosts:
"Consider, and call for the mourning
women to come;
send for the skilful women to come;
18 let them make haste and raise a wailing
over us,
that our eyes may run down with tears,
and our eyelids gush with water.
19 For a sound of wailing is heard from
Zion:
'How we are ruined!
We are utterly shamed,
because we have left the land,
because they have cast down our dwellings.'"

---

17. The mourning women were professional mourners employed to sing dirges and to stimulate grief in others.

The predicament of the people and the conditions of the wasted territory having been described, the question as to who the truly wise man is, that he can understand and explain what has happened to the people (cf. Hos. 14:9), is more than rhetorical. It really asks the question as to whether the popular leaders of the people can explain, on the basis of their principles and assumptions, why the land is ruined and laid waste. No doubt the people themselves are asking this question. Since hitherto these prophets and priests and wise men had been giving comfortable answers, healing the wound of their people lightly, it was tacitly impossible for them to give a satisfactory explanation. This having been made clear, Yahweh points out, as he has done again and again through Jeremiah, that all this has happened because the people have forsaken his law and have not hearkened unto his voice. They have obstinately followed their own desires and **gone after the Baals, as their fathers taught them.** The persistence with which the corrupting and demoralizing influence of the Baals is presented and re-presented shows with what persistence the prophetic tradition attempted to "purify the source" and keep their faithfulness free of compromise. Because of this compromise bitterness, dispersion, and the sword will overtake them. The sense of doom is heightened by the suggestion that the nations through which the people will be scattered are so remote that **neither they nor their fathers have known** them. This would seem to suggest the extreme isolation of Israel, politically and commercially speaking, prior to the time of the exile.[8]

17-22. Death the Reaper.—It has been said of this poem that "it is perhaps the most brilliant example of the prophetic elegy which the Old Testament contains."[9] Moschus' "lament for Bion":

Raise, raise the dirge, ye Muse of Sicily,
Who now shall play the pipe since Bion's dead[1]

is not so fine as vss. 21-22. The figure of death as the Reaper has long since become commonplace. It apparently originated with Jeremiah; and, once formulated, it took permanent hold upon the imaginations of men everywhere. Indeed, once the movement of this poem, with its mood and images, has taken hold upon the reader, its overtones will persist and its tones continue echoing like the *qînāh* rhythm itself.

The poem opens with a summons to the professional mourners to come (vs. 17); but

[8] Cf. Ball, *Prophecies of Jeremiah*, p. 201.
[9] Skinner, *Prophecy and Religion*, p. 124.
[1] *Idylls* III.

20 Yet hear the word of the Lord, O ye women, and let your ear receive the word of his mouth, and teach your daughters wailing, and every one her neighbor lamentation.

21 For death is come up into our windows, *and* is entered into our palaces, to cut off the children from without, *and* the young men from the streets.

22 Speak, Thus saith the Lord, Even the carcasses of men shall fall as dung upon the field, and as the handful after the harvestman, and none shall gather *them*.

23 ¶ Thus saith the Lord, Let not the wise *man* glory in his wisdom, neither let the mighty *man* glory in his might, let not the rich *man* glory in his riches:

20 Hear, O women, the word of the Lord,
   and let your ear receive the word of
   his mouth;
teach to your daughters a lament,
   and each to her neighbor a dirge.
21 For death has come up into our windows,
   it has entered our palaces,
cutting off the children from the streets
   and the young men from the squares.
22 Speak, "Thus says the Lord:
'The dead bodies of men shall fall
   like dung upon the open field,
like sheaves after the reaper,
   and none shall gather them.' "

23 Thus says the Lord: "Let not the wise man glory in his wisdom, let not the mighty man glory in his might, let not the

---

21. Death has come up into our windows: In one of the Canaanite epics found at Ras Shamra it is implied that Baal did not wish to have a window in his palace because he feared that the god Death (Mot) would steal in through the window and abduct his wives (H. L. Ginsberg, "The Ugaritic Texts and Textual Criticism," *Journal of Biblical Literature,* LXII [1943], 113-14). In the present passage there is at least a personification of death, and perhaps the reflection of some belief in a god (or demon) Death.

G. The Only True Ground for Boasting (9:23-24)

This passage may have its present position because of a slight similarity in subject matter to 8:8-13. Some commentators deny its authenticity. Volz does so because, he says, "knowledge of God" here is not meant as a practical relationship with God and fellowship

---

the conventional dirge will not suffice. The mourning women are instructed to teach the lament to their daughters and beyond them to the neighboring women. And this is the burden of the people's tears:

Death has come up through our windows—
   Has entered our halls,
Cutting off the child from the street—
   The youths from the square.

And the corpses of men lie prone
   On the open field,
Like sheaves behind the reaper,
   With none to gather.[2]

The last line tolls like a bell on a desolate and wind-swept waste.[3]

23-24. The Way to Wisdom.—Concerning this passage Peake argues: "There is no reason to deny its Jeremianic authorship, with Duhm

[2] Skinner, *loc. cit.*

[3] Cf. Stanley Romaine Hopper, "The Spiritual Implications of Modern Poetry," *Religion in Life,* XX (1951), 555, where these verses have been interwoven with passages from Edith Sitwell and Stephen Spender to show the contemporaneity of their images and their pure poetic power.

and Schmidt. The thought is quite in accord with what Jeremiah says elsewhere." [4] While conceding that the utterance appears in the text without any evident relation to what precedes it, we must, as against Volz (cf. Exeg.), place ourselves wholeheartedly with our Exeg. here. The distinction contained in these verses lies at the very heart of the prophetic viewpoint.

Ball's suggestion that the occasion of the verses might well have been in the period prior to Nebuchadrezzar's coming is as good as any. For two or three years, while a vassal to Egypt, the people enjoyed a brief respite under Jehoiakim, without foreseeing that Nebuchadrezzar would lay siege to Jerusalem as soon as Pharaoh Neco had been overcome. During this period the wise leaders and politicians may have congratulated themselves on having handled affairs so well, the military leaders may have boasted of their strategies and skill wherewith the safety of the people had been purchased, and the men of wealth may, like Croesus, have felt themselves the happiest mortals in the world because their properties and possessions were increased. Against this inordinate pride, so insubstantially

[4] *Jeremiah and Lamentations,* I, 169.

with him, but is meant in an abstract theological sense. This reads a good deal into the passage. It could well be genuine, for it agrees fully with Jeremiah's thought, though being somewhat proverbial in nature it differs from his usual style. At any rate, it presents in a fine manner the prophetic point of view. Man must not boast of wisdom, power, or wealth—the things of which men usually boast—but of the knowledge that Yahweh is a moral being who practices faithfulness, justice, and righteousness, and delights in men who practice these virtues.

---

founded, Jeremiah hurls his rebuke: **Let not the wise man glory in his wisdom, nor the mighty man . . . in his might, nor the rich man . . . in his riches**—the increase is temporary, and the advantage is slight.

More probably we have here a crystallization of prophetic teaching which, while not formulated "in an abstract theological sense" (Volz), yet has reached a level of particularity at which a practical generalization may be drawn.

This generalization *begins* at the point of Cowper's famous distinction, in which—

Knowledge and wisdom, far from being one,
Have oft-times no connexion.

. . . .

Knowledge is proud that he has learn'd so much;
Wisdom is humble that he knows no more.[5]

The element of pride here, as an untutored boastfulness in *our own* achievements, has been put more ironically by Miguel de Unamuno, who, seeing Culture as our modern substitute for godly wisdom, complains that today "the end of man is to create science, to catalogue the Universe, so that it may be handed back to God in order. . . . And at the end of all, the human race will fall exhausted at the foot of a pile of libraries." [6] The point is, of course, that we ought not to "glory" in this "wisdom" (culture, science): it is not wisdom, in the profounder sense. It is the practical fallacy against which Ecclesiastes warns: "Alas, the wise man dies like the fool!" (2:16 Moffatt).

There is, however, a deeper implication here. Two wisdoms are opposed: the wisdom "of the world," of "experience," of "reason" (what we should today call "humanism"), and the wisdom based upon the covenantal relationship, upon understanding and knowing God. These are two ways which have the same starting-point —the human condition—but which lead in opposite directions. The one way glories in God, the other in the greatness and misery of man.

To mark off Jeremiah's way even more sharply, one has only to set his covenantal view over against the Hellenic, or even the Christian-Hellenistic, view of "wisdom"—as we see it, e.g., in Solon and Aeschylus, Clement of Alexandria and Boethius. The following passage, to

[5] *The Task*, Bk. VI.
[6] *The Tragic Sense of Life*, p. 308.

choose at random, sounds very like the trepidations of Jeremiah:

Wandering from house to house you see the common disaster,
No barricading of doors will keep your dwellings exempt.
Scaling the highest wall, it will penetrate the interior,
Though you may anxiously flee into the hiddenest nook.

This is not, however, the "foe from the north" approaching; it is *dikē*, the vengeance of Necessity, rectifying the whole, punishing city and citizens when "we the citizens doom it by our folly and greed." [7] This is a profound penetration into the human condition, and should in no wise be minimized. But the way out, the way of overcoming these assaults of rectifying vengeance, is the way of righteousness—the way of the good law and right balance. This leads to Solon's view of justice, derived by way of reason, which informs the Greek view generally, and, through it, the West.

Jeremiah's terms for righteousness (*çédheq*) and justice (*mishpāṭ*) we have alluded to above (4:3-4; 5:1-14). They are both based upon the knowledge of God: they are not rationally and ethically derived. "There is to the Hebrew no *Ananke* (Necessity) and no *Dike* (Justice) to which both gods and men must conform. God is His own necessity. Justice is what God wills because such is His Nature. . . . God knows that justice is not enough." [8] For Jeremiah, both terms rest upon God's living being, the LORD who practice[s] kindness (*hésedh;* this is one of four passages in Scripture in which *hésedh* is linked with *çedhāqāh* [fem.] and *mishpāṭ* [9]). Tillich is attempting to recover what is implicit in Jeremiah's perspective when he writes: "Justice means more than propor-

[7] Solon, quoted in Karl Jaspers, *Existentialism and Humanism* (ed. Hanns E. Fischer; tr. E. B. Ashton; New York: Russell F. Moore, 1952), p. 27; cf. Jaeger, *Paideia*, Vol. I.
[8] Snaith, *Distinctive Ideas of the O.T.*, p. 77. Cf. his full discussion of these terms, pp. 51-78, 94-130.
[9] Hos. 12:6 (Hebrew 12:7); Prov. 21:21; Ps. 101:1; Jer. 9:24 (Hebrew 9:23). For a complete tabulation of the forty-three combining forms of the word, see *ibid.*, p. 100. We shall note below that the majority of these (twenty-three) are with the terms "fidelity," "firmness," "truth"; seven are directly with the covenant (*berith*).

24 But let him that glorieth glory in this, that he understandeth and knoweth me,

rich man glory in his riches; 24 but let him who glories glory in this, that he under-

---

24. The word rendered **kindness** or **loving-kindness** is the Hebrew *ḥeṣedh* (see Exeg. on 2:2).

---

tional justice. It means creative justice and is expressed in the divine grace which forgives in order to reunite. . . . Creative justice is the form of reuniting love. . . . Love reunites; justice preserves what is to be united."[1] For Jeremiah all men are separated from each other and from true values whenever they are separated from the knowledge of God; indeed, as we shall see (10:23), they are even separated from themselves.

Aeschylus is much nearer to Jeremiah than is Solon—nearer perhaps than any of the "ancients" other than Second Isaiah and Job. He shifted the ground of penetration into justice and wisdom from reason to suffering:

Justice doth wait to teach
Wisdom by suffering.

Few things in literature are finer than the following:

. . . (Zeus) hath ruled,
Men shall learn wisdom, by affliction schooled.

In visions of the night, like dropping rain,
Descend the many memories of pain
Before the spirit's sight: through tears and dole
Comes wisdom o'er the unwilling soul—
A boon, I wot, of all Divinity,
That holds its sacred throne in strength, above the sky![2]

This comes nigh to the solitariness which Jeremiah knew. It probes the human situation at the point where all the ultimate questions turn inward and require answers which make for life, not death nor speculation. It is impressive to note how this pursuit in depth led Aeschylus to a recognition of the "wild and reinless" treachery of man (cf. Jer. 9:2-9) and to the lack of an adequate balm for their healing (cf. Jer. 8:22):

Stalks o'er the Earth each murtherous plan.
Friend to friend his loss deploreth,
Lawless rapine, treacherous wound,
But in vain his plaint he poureth;
To his bruises
Earth refuses
Balm; no balm on Earth is found.[3]

[1] Paul Tillich, *Love, Power, and Justice* (New York: Oxford University Press, 1954), pp. 66, 71.
[2] *Agamemnon* (tr. John Stuart Blackie; New York: E. P. Dutton & Co., Inc., 1936), p. 50.
[3] *The Eumenides*, ed. cit., p. 157.

Aeschylus' sense of suffering carries him forward into recognition of a "Holy Justice"; but his "solution" seems to lie in a godlike domestication of both the Furies (*The Eumenides*) and of Zeus (*Prometheus*) by way of (*a*) what Robert Bridges called "masterful administration of the unforeseen,"[4] and (*b*) the gradual and eventual emergence of the Hero (Hercules, the man-god)—mankind suffering its way victoriously into a wise sense of the ultimate meanings of things.

Jeremiah does more. He suffers more deeply, inasmuch as tragedy for him is, at bottom, pathos—the beloved children (the bride of God) in alienation stray from all well-being. "Lo, all things fly thee, for thou fliest Me"[5] is Jeremiah's paradox. True glorying, therefore, is in that justice and righteousness which knows that God is the One who is Loyal-in-Love. It is to come to know what Marcel has called the "constant element" in things.[6] This constant element, however, must be understood "as a demand rather than a law": which means that it is relational, and supposes a self that hallows or profanes, and a wisdom founded on fidelity or deception. The latter destroys; but fidelity creates. We come near, then, to Tillich's remarks on Justice; for Marcel concludes: "Creative when it is genuine, it is so fundamentally and in every way, for it possesses the mysterious power of renewing not only the person who practises it, but the recipient, however unworthy he may have been of it to start with."[7]

It is easy to see how Jeremiah's **kindness, justice, and righteousness in the earth** in which the Lord "delights" runs back to Micah; but these things are "known" to the one who stands within and is faithful to the covenant relation whereby **the Lord who practice[s] these things** has made himself known and continues to do so. For Jeremiah there is no "kindness" or "justice" or "righteousness" outside this relationship; whatsoever (wisdom, power, riches) is outside the relationship contains "the destructive element." The "constant element," in which alone we may glory, is in the knowing of

[4] *The Testament of Beauty* (New York: Oxford University Press, 1930), Bk. I, 1. 7.
[5] Francis Thompson, "The Hound of Heaven."
[6] Gabriel Marcel, *Homo Viator, Introduction to a Metaphysic of Hope* (tr. Emma Craufurd; Chicago: Henry Regnery, 1951), p. 99.
[7] *Ibid.*, p. 134.

that I *am* the LORD which exercise loving-kindness, judgment, and righteousness, in the earth: for in these *things* I delight, saith the LORD.

25 ¶ Behold, the days come, saith the LORD, that I will punish all *them which are* circumcised with the uncircumcised;

26 Egypt, and Judah, and Edom, and the children of Ammon, and Moab, and all *that are* in the utmost corners, that dwell in the wilderness: for all *these* nations *are* uncircumcised, and all the house of Israel *are* uncircumcised in the heart.

stands and knows me, that I am the LORD who practice kindness, justice, and righteousness in the earth; for in these things I delight, says the LORD."

25 "Behold, the days are coming, says the LORD, when I will punish all those who are circumcised but yet uncircumcised —
26 Egypt, Judah, Edom, the sons of Ammon, Moab, and all who dwell in the desert that cut the corners of their hair; for all these nations are uncircumcised, and all the house of Israel is uncircumcised in heart."

H. Punishment of the Uncircumcised (9:25-26)

This passage is difficult to translate and interpret; it is impossible to see why it occupies its present position. The RSV perhaps gives the sense, though it is slightly paraphrastic. The meaning is probably that Judah cannot rely for salvation upon a rite such as circumcision which she shares with foreign nations, especially when she lacks the inward circumcision of the heart (demanded in 4:4) as much as they do. Jeremiah thus puts as little value upon circumcision as upon sacrifice, the temple, and other outward forms.

26. That circumcision was practiced in **Egypt** is implied by Josh. 5:9 and mentioned by Herodotus (*History* II. 104). Those who **cut the corners of their hair** (KJV misses the meaning) are Arab tribes, mentioned also in 25:23; 49:32. Their custom of cutting the hair, apparently as a religious rite, is noted by Herodotus (*ibid.* III. 8); the fact that foreigners also followed it probably accounts for the prohibition in Lev. 19:27. Circumcision of Arabs is implied by the story of the circumcision of Ishmael, their ancestor (Gen. 17:23; cf. Josephus *Antiquities* I. 12. 2). **For all these nations are uncircumcised:** The LXX and Targ. interpret this to mean "in the flesh," but that contradicts the preceding verse; the meaning is that they, as well as Israel, are uncircumcised in heart.

God. This is the insight which leads, long after Jeremiah's voice is silent, to

> that unbelievable adventure
> By which I, God, have tied my arms for my eternity,
> That adventure by which my Son tied my arms,
> For eternally tying the arms of my justice, for eternally untying the arms of my mercy,
> And against my justice inventing a new justice,
> A justice of love, a justice of Hope. All was over.
> That which was necessary. In the way that was necessary in the way my prophets had announced it.[8]

25-26. *The Outward Sign Versus the Inward and Spiritual Grace.*—This second detached oracle, like the one preceding (vss. 23-24), has been placed by Moffatt at the close of ch. 10, where it forms a much more consistent position in the argument and an effective transition to ch. 11. However, it is not without its uses in the present context. It forms a significant

[8] Charles Péguy, "Night," from *God Speaks* (tr. Julian Green; New York: Pantheon Books, 1945). Used by permission.

extension of the argument by emphasizing again (cf. 4:4) the need for inwardness—Jeremiah's persistent claim that the people must be changed from within. Just as they are not to glory in their supposed self-achievements, so also he will not allow them to suppose that outer conformity to traditional practice will suffice as a guarantee of righteousness. **All the house of Israel is uncircumcised in heart.** Therefore they are in no wise superior to the heathen peoples round about them. Jeremiah puts them on precisely the same level with the people of Egypt, Edom, Ammon and Moab and the desert Arabs. Before God they are all alike uncircumcised. The apostle Paul's position is the same as that of Jeremiah (I Cor. 7:19; cf. also Rom. 2:25). Jeremiah clearly anticipates Paul's letter to the Galatians, in which Paul indicates that what is needed is "a new creation" and "faith working through love" (Gal. 6:15; 5:6).

In defense of the position which these verses occupy in the present book of Jeremiah, it can be said that they do have the effect of returning

10 Hear ye the word which the LORD speaketh unto you, O house of Israel:
2 Thus saith the LORD, Learn not the way of the heathen, and be not dismayed at the signs of heaven; for the heathen are dismayed at them.

10 Hear the word which the LORD speaks to you, O house of Israel.
2 Thus says the LORD:
"Learn not the way of the nations,
nor be dismayed at the signs of the heavens
because the nations are dismayed at them,

J. CONTRAST BETWEEN IDOLS AND YAHWEH (10:1-16)

This passage is almost universally admitted to be secondary, even by conservative commentators. It presupposes a situation in which the people addressed are living among the heathen and need to be warned against idolatry. Jeremiah himself did speak against the worship of idols, but it was of those known in Palestine; and if it is maintained that this passage could come from late in Jeremiah's life after the first exile of the Jews (598 B.C.), it must be said that the tone of his letter to the exiles in ch. 29 is far different from the tone of this passage. Furthermore, both the ideas expressed and the terminology used are very close to those of Second Isaiah and other writers of a later time (see especially Isa. 40:19-22; 41:7, 29; 44:9-20; 46:5-7; Deut. 4:28; Pss. 115:3-8; 135:15-18). A favorite theme of Second Isaiah was the great contrast between the worthless heathen idols, mere wood and metal, the work of men's hands, and Yahweh, the creator of the world and the redeemer of Israel.

The present text is not in good order, and the passage probably was not all composed at one time. Vs. 8 seems fragmentary, and vss. 9, 11 seem out of place where they now stand. The LXX omits vss. 6-8, 10, and part of vs. 16; and it places vs. 9 within vs. 5. It is very probable that an original poem, composed during the time of the Exile, has been added to by editors and glossators.

10:2. The signs of the heavens were unusual celestial phenomena such as eclipses and comets, which gave rise to ancient astrology.

the argument (and thereby the emphasis) to the point where it began in ch. 7. There Jeremiah, standing "in the gate of the LORD's house" (7:2), warned the people against trafficking in "deceptive words," for so the familiar cry, "This is the temple of the LORD, the temple of the LORD, the temple of the LORD!" (7:4), became a hypnotic talisman, lulling the people into a false sense of security whereby they both disguised and hid their true condition from themselves.

10:1-16. The Hollow Men.—Man has always, said Luther, either God or an idol. And Pascal, noting how persistently we hide the truth from ourselves, added "we make an idol of truth itself." [9]

The technical matters governing these verses are admirably covered in the Exeg. It has been suggested that we have here the insert of some unknown prophet, and that his words are addressed to Israel, already in exile in Chaldea.[1] However this may be, we must call attention to the similarity between these verses and Jeremiah's initial polemic against idols (2:1-37).

The presuppositions are the same. And if we find parallel or near parallel passages in Second Isaiah it only goes to show how incisively Jeremiah has penetrated to the root of this particular species of human defection.

The merits of idols are here placed over against the glory of the living God. The astrological superstitions of the nations are pronounced false and their idols nothing. The irony is superb. They are like scarecrows in a cucumber field! They can't speak, they can't walk, they cannot do evil, nor can they do good; they can't move, they have to be carried. In short, they are nothing. The woodsman cuts the tree; the carpenter fashions it with the ax; and the goldsmith decks it with silver and gold.

The argument in vss. 14-15 is still more penetrating. Beside the awful power and glory of the living God as manifested in his wondrous works (vss. 12-13) **every goldsmith is put to shame by his idols; for his images are . . . worthless, a work of delusion.** For, as Ball translates, "every founder blushes for the image, because his molten figure is a lie, and there is no breath in them." [2]

[9] *Thoughts*, No. 581.
[1] *Prophecies of Jeremiah*, p. 218.
[2] *Ibid.*, p. 237.

3 For the customs of the people *are* vain: for *one* cutteth a tree out of the forest, the work of the hands of the workman, with the axe.

4 They deck it with silver and with gold; they fasten it with nails and with hammers, that it move not.

5 They *are* upright as the palm tree, but speak not: they must needs be borne, because they cannot go. Be not afraid of them; for they cannot do evil, neither also *is it* in them to do good.

6 Forasmuch as *there is* none like unto thee, O Lord; thou *art* great, and thy name *is* great in might.

7 Who would not fear thee, O King of nations? for to thee doth it appertain: forasmuch as among all the wise *men* of the nations, and in all their kingdoms, *there is* none like unto thee.

8 But they are altogether brutish and foolish: the stock *is* a doctrine of vanities.

9 Silver spread into plates is brought from Tarshish, and gold from Uphaz, the work of the workman, and of the hands of

3 for the customs of the peoples are false.
A tree from the forest is cut down,
> and worked with an axe by the hands
> of a craftsman.

4 Men deck it with silver and gold;
> they fasten it with hammer and nails
> so that it cannot move.

5 Their idols[r] are like scarecrows in a cucumber field,
> and they cannot speak;
they have to be carried,
> for they cannot walk.
Be not afraid of them,
> for they cannot do evil,
> neither is it in them to do good."

6 There is none like thee, O Lord;
> thou art great, and thy name is great
> in might.

7 Who would not fear thee, O King of the nations?
For this is thy due;
for among all the wise ones of the nations
and in all their kingdoms
> there is none like thee.

8 They are both stupid and foolish;
> the instruction of idols is but wood!

9 Beaten silver is brought from Tarshish,
> and gold from Uphaz.
They are the work of the craftsman and
> of the hands of the goldsmith;

[r] Heb *They*

---

5. Cf. Isa. 41:23; 46:7.

9. Tarshish was in southern Spain or the island of Sardinia. The location of **Uphaz** is not known; the name occurs elsewhere only in Dan. 10:5. The Targ., Syriac, and

---

It is better, however, to adhere to the terms of the present text, for the absence of the breath of God (*rûᵃh*) means that the images are empty. (As in 2:5 the people "went after worthlessness [nothingness], and became worthless [nothing]"; so here nothing can be expected of them.) The term "false" in vss. 3, 14 is the same as "vanity," and is similar to the "vain hopes" held out by the false prophets in 23:16—hopes which come from "their own minds" and do not come "from the mouth of the Lord." The terms "brutish," "foolish," "vanity" (8, 14-15 ERV), "stupid" (vss. 8, 14 RSV) partake of the same root as the nothingness of the "lying vision" of the false prophets in 14:14. The comparisons with Isaiah alluded to in the Exeg. (especially with Isa. 41:7, 29) while altogether apt, are even less striking than the comparison with Isa. 41:24, 29:

Behold, you are nothing,
> and your work is nought;

. . . .

Behold, they are all a delusion;
> their works are nothing;
> their molten images are empty wind.

What is missing from this passage is that which Jeremiah sees persistently: namely, the dialectical implications of a commitment to nothingness. The Francis Thompson principle —"Lo, all things fly thee, for thou flyest Me!" [3] —again applies. The deception of the idol is a deception of emptiness, experienced within, and leading inevitably to dismay and dread.

The Lord of the house of Israel is great and mighty and incomparable: **he is the living God and the everlasting King.** He is also the creator

[3] "The Hound of Heaven."

the founder: blue and purple *is* their clothing: they *are* all the work of cunning *men*.

10 But the LORD *is* the true God, he *is* the living God, and an everlasting King: at his wrath the earth shall tremble, and the nations shall not be able to abide his indignation.

11 Thus shall ye say unto them, The gods that have not made the heavens and the earth, *even* they shall perish from the earth, and from under these heavens.

their clothing is violet and purple;
they are all the work of skilled men.
10 But the LORD is the true God;
he is the living God and the everlasting
King.
At his wrath the earth quakes,
and the nations cannot endure his indignation.

11 Thus shall you say to them: "The gods who did not make the heavens and the earth shall perish from the earth and from under the heavens."[s]

[s] This verse is in Aramaic

---

some other ancient versions read "Ophir," but this is probably a substitution of a well-known place for one whose location was unknown.

11. This verse is in Aramaic, the only verse in that language in the book of Jeremiah. It is out of place in its present position, belonging rather with vs. 9 or one of the earlier verses dealing with idols. It was perhaps originally a gloss, written on the margin, which was designed as a formula to be used in exorcizing heathen idols and demons, or as a ready answer for Jews to give in reply to the claims of heathen idolaters. The presence of internal rhyme and of careful chiastic arrangement supports the former view. The form of the Aramaic (use of both ארקא and ארעא, and the form להום) suggests a date in the fifth century B.C. for its original addition to the passage.

(vs. 12) who **by his power** and **wisdom** and **understanding stretched out the heavens.** In all the earth **There is none like thee, O LORD.** Puny godhoods of little men are dwarfed to inconsequence by the waters, the mists, the lightnings, and the rain. As over against this awful and presiding Power, "a scarecrow in a garden of cucumbers that keepeth nothing, so are their gods of wood, and overlaid with gold and with silver" (Baruch 6:70; cf. vs. 5).

Something of this sort must have been in the mind of T. S. Eliot when he surmised that

> Those who have crossed
> With direct eyes, to death's other Kingdom
> Remember us—if at all—not as lost
> Violent souls, but only
> As the hollow men
> The stuffed men.

This is a powerful irony impounded to dramatize our loss of spirit. Without the animating dimension of the breath of God, we are like scarecrows:

> We are the hollow men
> We are the stuffed men
> Leaning together
> Headpiece filled with straw. Alas!
> Our dried voices, when
> We whisper together
> Are quiet and meaningless.

And the reason for this is that

> The eyes are not here
> There are no eyes here
> In this valley of dying stars
> In this hollow valley
> This broken jaw of our lost kingdoms.

Our world of values and meanings and devotions lies about us in formless fragmentation, and because the world of spiritual significances is lost, our world ends "not with a bang but a whimper." [4]

Eliot's poem illustrates again how the idol is not a mere nothing, but contains an active negating element that is projected upon it, so that it is in fact a nothing nothing*ing*. It is a wood that woodens—**the instruction of idols is but wood!** "What idols teach is wooden like themselves!" as Moffatt translates it. The idol diminishes the sense of awe, contracts our sense of dread, brings the Divine into finitude by means of the wooden symbol. Upon it we project our call into the open, as well as our courage for Transcendence, and thus feel ourselves released from and protected from the threat of Nothing. Very likely this is what Heidegger means when he says that the true philosopher must possess the courage of "let-

[4] "The Hollow Men," from *Complete Poems and Plays* (London: Faber & Faber; New York: Harcourt, Brace & Co., 1953). Used by permission.

12 He hath made the earth by his power, he hath established the world by his wisdom, and hath stretched out the heavens by his discretion.

13 When he uttereth his voice, *there is* a multitude of waters in the heavens, and he causeth the vapors to ascend from the ends of the earth; he maketh lightnings with rain, and bringeth forth the wind out of his treasures.

14 Every man is brutish in *his* knowledge: every founder is confounded by the graven image: for his molten image *is* falsehood, and *there is* no breath in them.

15 They *are* vanity, *and* the work of errors: in the time of their visitation they shall perish.

16 The portion of Jacob *is* not like them: for he *is* the former of all *things;* and Israel *is* the rod of his inheritance: The Lord of hosts *is* his name.

12 It is he who made the earth by his power,
who established the world by his wisdom,
and by his understanding stretched out the heavens.

13 When he utters his voice there is a tumult of waters in the heavens,
and he makes the mist rise from the ends of the earth.
He makes lightnings for the rain,
and he brings forth the wind from his storehouses.

14 Every man is stupid and without knowledge;
every goldsmith is put to shame by his idols;
for his images are false,
and there is no breath in them.

15 They are worthless, a work of delusion;
at the time of their punishment they shall perish.

16 Not like these is he who is the portion of Jacob,
for he is the one who formed all things,
and Israel is the tribe of his inheritance;
the Lord of hosts is his name.

12-16. These verses are reproduced in 51:15-19.

16. The portion of Jacob is Yahweh. For the idea cf. Lam. 3:24; Pss. 73:26; 119:57; for the idea that Israel was Yahweh's **portion** see Deut. 32:9.

---

ting oneself go into Nothing, that is to say, freeing oneself from the idols we all have and to which we are wont to go cringing." [5] But the call to the open is the way to life. The idol protects us from our dread of Nothing (which is in fact our dread of our call to true Being) by finitizing and localizing our awe and wonder; but it does so at the expense of annihilating both the call and the relation which the call provides. The idol, though wooden, has in it all the dynamics of the self's will to escape from itself—i.e., the way of death.

Man, according to Paul Valéry, is "a hollow which is always future" (*Un creux toujours futur*).[6] If so, it is because man is a viator.[7] Man is a creature who goes a way. But the way which he goes is either into fullness or into emptiness. Either he knows reality as a "fountain of living waters" or as "broken cisterns

that can hold no water" (2:13). The "hollowness" of his futurity, therefore, consists in his capacity to take his present "fullness" as a point of departure for a further creative summons into the "open," or it is his capacity to decline the fullness of communion and to try desperately to fill his hollowness by deifying it as an infinite, and then projecting it infinitely upon things that are finite. But the things are "wooden": that is, they neither receive nor respond, they do not "satisfy"; and, as Irving Babbitt was fond of saying, "There is nothing that so resembles a hollow as a swelling." But **not like these is he who is the portion of Jacob**; as Alexander Maclaren points out "a reciprocal possession" is set forth here. "We possess God, He possesses us. We are His inheritance, He is our portion. . . . This mutual ownership is the very living centre of all religion. Without it there is no relation of any depth between God and us." It is a relation maintained through "continuous acts of communion and consecration." [8] In the context of this communion it is possible to speak of possessing and being

[5] *Existence and Being*, p. 380.

[6] Quoted in Alfred Stern, *Sartre, His Philosophy and Psychoanalysis* (New York: Liberal Arts Press, 1953), p. 40.

[7] Cf. Stanley Romaine Hopper, *The Crisis of Faith* (New York and Nashville: Abingdon-Cokesbury Press, 1944), pp. 248, 250, 301; also Marcel, *Homo Viator.*

[8] *Isaiah and Jeremiah*, II, 268, 270.

17 ¶ Gather up thy wares out of the land, O inhabitant of the fortress.	**17** Gather up your bundle from the ground, O you who dwell under siege!
18 For thus saith the LORD, Behold, I will sling out the inhabitants of the land at this once, and will distress them, that they may find *it so*.	**18** For thus says the LORD: "Behold, I am slinging out the inhabitants of the land at this time, and I will bring distress on them, that they may feel it."
19 ¶ Woe is me for my hurt! my wound is grievous: but I said, Truly this *is* a grief, and I must bear it.	**19** Woe is me because of my hurt! My wound is grievous. But I said, "Truly this is an affliction, and I must bear it."
20 My tabernacle is spoiled, and all my cords are broken: my children are gone forth of me, and they *are* not: *there is* none to stretch forth my tent any more, and to set up my curtains.	**20** My tent is destroyed, and all my cords are broken; my children have gone from me, and they are not; there is no one to spread my tent again, and to set up my curtains.
21 For the pastors are become brutish, and have not sought the LORD: therefore they shall not prosper, and all their flocks shall be scattered.	**21** For the shepherds are stupid, and do not inquire of the LORD; therefore they have not prospered, and all their flock is scattered.

K. The Coming of Destruction and Exile (10:17-22)

This passage continues somewhat the thought of 9:10-22, but it must come from a later time when Jerusalem was under siege. The date is probably 598 B.C., during the first siege of Jerusalem by the Chaldeans.

In form the passage is a dialogue between Jeremiah and personified Jerusalem. The prophet speaks in vss. 17-18; the city speaks in vss. 19-21; then the prophet speaks again in vs. 22. According to Condamin, the second speech of the prophet is vss. 21-22, and vss. 23-24 constitute a final "speech"—really a prayer—by the city. This is a possible division, but the word **For** at the beginning of vs. 21 connects it with vss. 19-20 rather than with vs. 22, and vss. 23-24 are too different in tone to be a part of the "dialogue."

17. The word rendered **bundle** or **wares**, Hebrew *kin'āh*, occurs only here, and its meaning is uncertain. An Arabic root (*kn'*) supports the conjectured meaning **bundle**.

19-21. "Mother Zion" speaks as one who lives in a **tent** and has **children**. For the figure cf. Isa. 49:14-23; 54:1-3. Jer. 4:20 is somewhat similar. **The shepherds** are the rulers (for **pastors**, see Exeg. on 2:8).

---

possessed (Maclaren): but with idols we are both obsessed and (demonically) possessed.

17-22. *Exile at Hand!*—This passage easily continues the prophecy interrupted at the end of 9:22. The city is besieged, the women have sung their lament, and nothing now remains but to take up their bundles and depart: for the Lord is **slinging** them out of the land.

The Exeg. calls attention to the dialogue form of this section. The reply of the people is deep and moving. The woe and hurt which they express carries within it the overtones of Jeremiah's own deep wound. Metaphors of the collapsed tent and its broken cords are remi-

niscent of Jeremiah's earlier use of this figure (4:20). It is the land which has been destroyed, the children (sheep) have been dispersed, and there is no adequate leadership to restore the country's well-being. Once again the failure of the leaders properly to **inquire of the LORD** is emphasized.

The depth of the personal tone in vs. 19, with the undeniable realism of its cry—

**Truly this is an affliction,
and I must bear it—**

persuades Skinner that Jeremiah is speaking here within the context of "an experience of

22 Behold, the noise of the bruit is come, and a great commotion out of the north country, to make the cities of Judah desolate, *and* a den of dragons.

23 ¶ O Lord, I know that the way of man *is* not in himself: *it is* not in man that walketh to direct his steps.

22 Hark, a rumor! Behold, it comes! —
    a great commotion out of the north
      country
  to make the cities of Judah a desolation,
    a lair of jackals.

23 I know, O Lord, that the way of man is
    not in himself,
      that it is not in man who walks to
      direct his steps.

---

22. This verse seems to be a fragment from the poems dealing with the foe from the north, or to be modeled after them. In the present context the foe could only be the Chaldeans.

L. Prayer for Self-correction and Foreign Retribution (10:23-25)

23-24. This is a prayer uttered by Jeremiah on behalf of the people (Cornill) or himself, or uttered by the people for themselves (Condamin). In the light of 15:19, it is perhaps best to interpret the verses as a prayer of the prophet for himself, but its date

---

which he himself is the subject."[9] The similarity of this passage in tone to the depth-penetrations of the confessional poems makes it impossible not to share in this recognition, however the question as to the allegorical character of the passage is resolved. The way of conflict, whether in prophet or people, is a way of suffering; and it is quite true that

One cannot tread it at once, but must learn it, stone
   by stone:
Upon it the foot may slip, though the heart goes on
   alone.[1]

23-25. The Way of Man Is Not in Himself.— In considering this passage, two suggestions may be offered. First of all, we are here given our first clear glimpse into the prayers of Jeremiah, a series of most remarkable utterances which would merit a study in themselves. (The more personal poems in which Jeremiah pours out his grief are Jer. 11:18-23; 12:1-6; 17:12-18; 18:18-23; 20:7-18. To these we should add 32:17-25 as belonging to the prayers of Jeremiah. Vss. 23-24 are eminently of this kind.) As Charles E. Jefferson has noted,

All of the prayers are interesting, and some of them are surprising. . . . Prayer became to [Jeremiah] conversation, an intimate intercourse with God. In his loneliness and suffering he discovered that true prayer is intimate fellowship with God. . . . He has taught the whole human race that prayer is talking with God.[2]

[9] *Prophecy and Religion*, p. 50, n. 1.
[1] Paul Claudel, "The Way of the Cross," from *Coronal* (tr. Sister Mary David; New York: Pantheon Books, 1943), p. 227.
[2] *Cardinal Ideas of Jeremiah*, pp. 149, 153-54.

But there is something deeper here. **I know, O Lord, that the way of man is not in himself.** The translation is superb, bringing out that which otherwise lies concealed. Ps. 37:23 (pre-exilic in Gunkel's classification) is proximate:

The steps of a man are from the Lord,
   and he establishes him in whose way he delights.

Even this, however, fails to grasp the inwardness of the statement. One should probably look forward to Job, where Job's entire drama is, at bottom, an agonistic way into this discovery. Job's attempt to live from himself, or from the standpoint of conventional piety, was but a way to "heart turmoil" and to a knowledge of himself as "a heap of ruins" (cf. Job 30:27, 24).

The closest parallel, however, in any literature, is Augustine's wonderful statement in his *Confessions*: "Too late did I love Thee! For behold, Thou wert within, and I without, and there did I seek Thee; I, unlovely, rushed heedlessly among the things of beauty Thou madest. Thou wert with me, but I was not with Thee."[3] This contains the heart of the human paradox, religiously considered. As in Jeremiah, it places the *relationship* with God first. It belongs by its psychological penetration to that "radical empiricism" in Augustine whereby he moved from the Neoplatonism of his early thought to the biblical realism of his mature religious consciousness. As a definitive insight it is preceded by a succession of utterances which point to it and anticipate it.

[3] *Confessions* X. 27. 38.

24 O Lord, correct me, but with judg- | 24 Correct me, O Lord, but in just measure;
ment; not in thine anger, lest thou bring | not in thy anger, lest thou bring me
me to nothing. | to nothing.

---

is unknown. In form and content it should be classified with the "confessions" of Jeremiah. For the thought of vs. 23 cf. Prov. 20:24; for vs. 24 cf. Pss. 6:1; 38:1.

He is within the very heart, but yet hath the heart wandered from Him. Return to your heart, O ye transgressors, and cleave fast unto Him that made you. Stand with Him and you shall stand fast. Rest in Him, and you shall be at rest. . . . Thou wert before me, but I had gone away even from myself; nor did I find myself, much less Thee! . . . It is good, then, for me to cleave unto God, for if I remain not in Him, neither shall I in myself . . ." [4]

In more recent times this paradox of the human condition has been grasped by men like Pascal, Dostoevski, Kierkegaard, Hölderlin, and Rilke; and negatively by Montaigne and Nietzsche. Pascal's insight is striking, if one understands by "self" the self-sufficient "ego" which he found so "hateable": "It is in vain, O men, that you seek within yourselves the remedy for your ills. All your light can only reach the knowledge that not in yourselves will you find truth or good." [5]

Kierkegaard's *Sickness Unto Death*, in which it is held that the self is a relation and can only become a true self through grounding itself upon the power that created it, is an amplification of this theme; as also his fine quotation elsewhere from Hamann:

We see how necessarily our Self is rooted and grounded in Him who created it, so that the knowledge of our Self does not lie within our own power, but that in order to measure the extent of the same, we must press forward into the very heart of God Himself, who alone can determine and resolve the whole mystery of our nature. [6]

This passage by one who also wrote commentaries on Jeremiah is strikingly similar to Jeremiah's insight above.

Contemporary depth-psychology, as well as some forms of existentialism, is clearly moving on this same terrain. The depth-psychologist tends, however, to confine his analysis to a dynamic empiricism, without regard to the particular "religious" features of "Reality." "In so far as a man is untrue to his own law and does not rise to personality, he has failed of

the meaning of his life." [7] Jung's "personality" here is the self that has already discovered that **the way of man is not in himself**—that is, in his individuality, or projected ego. At the same time, this being true to "his own law" courts disaster of the kind both Jeremiah and Jung seek to avoid, through the ambiguity of its terms. Jung also knows that "whoever is unable to lose his life by the same token will never gain it"; but he affirms it in such a way as that this demand is innate in things, like the "watercourse that resistlessly moves toward its goal" (or like the migratory birds?), and the

hero, leader, and saviour is also the one who discovers a new way to greater certainty. Everything could be left as it was if this new way did not absolutely demand to be discovered, and did not visit humanity with all the plagues of Egypt until it is found. [8]

It must be borne in mind that Jeremiah is in precisely this position: he must grow through the inadequacies of his contemporary religious practices and consciousness. This is an agonistic way, which will plague him with inner pain until he discovers the inner terms of a newer covenant. But this newer way will be founded upon a conception of God (Reality) which personalizes the experience, and so converts the *telos,* the purpose and end involved, into creative integrity and love—an awareness which lies beyond the river's coiling gravitation to the sea.

A more significant description of the personal *telos* involved, therefore, and one much nearer to Jeremiah, will be found in the following from Gabriel Marcel:

It is . . . well to remember that contrary to what might have been expected, my self-presence (*présence à moi-même*) is not a fact which we can take for granted. The truth is rather that it is liable to be eclipsed and must constantly be reconquered. You may ask what this presence is, and what is the self to which it is so difficult to remain faithful. The reply would have to be that it is the particle of creation which is in me, the gift which from all eternity has been granted to me of participating in the universal drama, of working, for instance, to humanise the earth, or on the contrary to make it more uninhabitable. But when all is said and done,

---

[4] *Ibid.* IV. 12. 18; V. 2. 2; VII. 11. 17.

[5] *Thoughts*, No. 430. Cf. Hopper, *The Crisis of Faith,* pp. 233-43, and p. 278, where this citation from Pascal is placed alongside Jer. 6:16.

[6] Quoted in Emil Brunner, *Man in Revolt* (tr. Olive Wyon; New York: Charles Scribner's Sons, 1939), Epigraph, p. 1.

[7] *Integration of the Personality*, p. 301.

[8] *Ibid.*, pp. 304-5.

| 25 Pour out thy fury upon the heathen that know thee not, and upon the families that call not on thy name: for they have eaten up Jacob, and devoured him, and consumed him, and have made his habitation desolate. | 25 Pour out thy wrath upon the nations that know thee not, and upon the peoples that call not on thy name; for they have devoured Jacob; they have devoured him and consumed him, and have laid waste his habitation. |

25. This verse is virtually equivalent to Ps. 79:6-7, and probably was taken by an editor from that psalm and placed here. It is not from Jeremiah, who would never have uttered a prayer filled with such narrow nationalism. Yet he often prayed for revenge against his personal enemies (see 11:20; 17:18; 18:23; 20:11).

such definitions are bound to be fallacious; whoever has loved knows well that what he loved in the other cannot be reduced to describable qualities—and in exactly the same way the mystery of what I am in myself is the very thing about me which is only revealed to love.[9]

This teleological factor, this swing of the emphasis from my*self* to the end which my life and I are called to subserve, is the real reason why **it is not in man who walks to direct his steps.** "Not knowing his own heart, [man] acts as though he does, and is progressively deceived," as Minear very trenchantly puts it.[1] This is not due, however, as Minear holds, to an ignorance inherent in man's status as creature (as though we were quite uncertain as to what a self is, but quite clear as to the nature of a creature); nor does it arise from "the recognition of that distinction [between God's knowledge and man's ignorance] as ineradicable"[2] (a rationalistic and scholastic perspective which deprives Jeremiah's context of rebellion and obstinacy of its purely existential character). It is rather that man's refusal of vocation perverts the knowledge (the knowing and being known of God): but, willfully refusing to acknowledge this, and acting as though he were searching for that from which he flees, he progressively deceives himself. The passage in Proverbs suggested by Duhm and Driver is apposite, then, only within this context: "A man's mind plans his way, but the Lord directs his steps" (Prov. 16:9; cf. "Man proposes, God disposes!"). Therefore Jeremiah prays, **Correct me, O LORD, but in just measure**—or, as Moffatt translates it, "but not too hard." In other words, the **just measure,** which sounds like Aeschylus and the Greek view generally, is

something very different: it is not "just measure" in the sense of a calculus of equivalent punishment for weighable wickedness, but rather punishment in terms of what I can take rather than what I deserve. When we read, "So correct us, O Eternal One, but not too hard" (Moffatt), we think, of course, of Augustine's "Grant me chastity and continency, *but not yet!*" But it is here precisely that the difference lies. Augustine was "afraid lest Thou shouldest hear me soon, [whereas] I desired to have [my concupiscence] satisfied rather than extinguished."[3] With Jeremiah, the correction is desired but mitigated, as he hopes, by the mercy of the Lord, **lest thou bring me to nothing.**

It is at this point that commentators have been tempted to convert the prayer into a plea for the people, or into a prayer by the people for themselves: "So correct us, O Eternal One, . . . lest thou make our numbers few" (Moffatt); and have argued that the strange language of bringing them to nothing implied their fear lest Judah should be reduced to a mere political shadow of its former greatness. This seems a desperate diversion from the plain psychological preciseness of the personal witness of one who knows that if the Lord "shuts a man in, none can open" (Job 12:14). Being "hedged in" by the Lord (Job 3:23) is painful and it is bitter, as Jeremiah well knew; one is easily overborne by it and reduced to nothing. The commitment of the self to a negative way—the way of the self's self-centered search for itself—is the way in which the self progressively negates itself. Since the self is antecedently sustained by the spirit in this flight from itself (in the God-relation) it is progressively deceived, and experiences that most baffling of all the inner contradictions—that of nothing nothing*ing,* or of emptiness emptying.

[9] *Homo Viator, Introduction to a Metaphysic of Hope* (tr. Emma Craufurd; Chicago: Henry Regnery, 1951), p. 132. Used by permission.

[1] *Eyes of Faith,* pp. 134-35 (on Jer. 17:9).

[2] *Ibid.,* p. 134.

[3] *Op. cit.,* VIII. 7. 17.

11 The word that came to Jeremiah from the Lord, saying, 2 Hear ye the words of this covenant,

11 The word that came to Jeremiah from the Lord: 2 "Hear the words

VI. EVENTS IN JEREMIAH'S LIFE (11:1–12:6)

This section consists of three parts: (a) a long passage (11:1-14) in which Jeremiah advocates the keeping of **this covenant** and pronounces judgment upon those who fail to do so; (b) a poem (11:15-16) dealing with the inadequacy of sacrifices, with a prose addition (11:17); and (c) a passage (11:18–12:6) which tells of a plot against Jeremiah by the men of Anathoth and of the prophet's subsequent raising of the question with God: Why do the wicked prosper?

A. JEREMIAH AND THE COVENANT (11:1-14)

This is an important passage for the interpretation of Jeremiah's attitude toward the Deuteronomic reforms, but it is difficult to interpret correctly.

Many scholars (e.g., George Adam Smith, Skinner, and Peake) accept this passage as a historically accurate account of Jeremiah's advocacy of the Deuteronomic reforms. They believe that in 621 B.C., or soon thereafter, Jeremiah became an itinerant prophet, going around in the streets of Jerusalem and the cities of Judah urging the people to follow the reforms of Josiah. Subsequently, however, Jeremiah became disillusioned and saw that the reforms were only superficial and materialistic, not striking at the real evils of the time.

This view has been questioned by other scholars. They have asked why it should have been necessary for Jeremiah, an obscure prophet from Anathoth, to go about advocating reforms which had the full weight of the royal house and of the Jerusalem priesthood behind them. And is it probable that Jeremiah would have supported reforms which, however praiseworthy they may have been in many respects, placed great emphasis on sacrifice and temple worship? Furthermore, this section is permeated with the style and the diction of the Deuteronomic editor, whose work is known elsewhere in this book. This fact has been shown by Mowinckel, *et al.*; detailed evidence for it will be given below.

Rudolph recognizes the presence here of Deuteronomic elements, but thinks that the editor has made use of a trustworthy tradition. **This covenant** does not refer to the Deuteronomic law, but to the covenant made at Sinai, as related in Exod. 24, with its strong emphasis on the moral law. Volz presents a similar interpretation, concluding

11:1-14. Amen, Yahweh!—The Exeg. justifiably calls our attention both to the difficulty and to the importance of this passage. Questions both as to its composition and its content are rife; and, in the present state of critical scholarship, the answers are very moot. The average reader, indeed, must frequently feel as J. E. McFadyen felt many years ago: "Everywhere uncertainties abound, and, like the dove after the Deluge, we seem to find no solid ground anywhere for the sole of our foot." [4] Some inkling of the complexity of the subject is supplied in the Exeg. by its indication of the work of Smith, Skinner, and Peake as over against the somewhat different interpretations of Mowinckel, Rudolph, and Volz. As every biblical student knows, this barely scratches the

[4] "The Present Position of Old Testament Criticism" in A. S. Peake, ed., *The People and the Book* (Oxford: Clarendon Press, 1925), p. 218.

surface of the very extensive biblical research now moving about these themes; for not only is the reading of Jeremiah itself concerned, but the entire complexity of Pentateuchal criticism on its own account cuts sharply athwart our interpretations here. The names of Hölscher, Welch, Eissfeldt, von Rad, Gunkel, H. S. Nyberg, Engnell, Noth, and Pedersen, to mention a few, will serve to indicate its many-sidedness. These developments represent in part a criticism and rejection of the methodologies of literary and source criticism of the Wellhausen type. Some scholars would also press beyond the Form type of literary criticism, of which Gunkel may be taken as a prime representative.

Out of the welter of crosscurrents and counterclaims, which Christopher R. North reviews so ably, little comfort is offered the non-technical reader except, perhaps, the consolation to

and speak unto the men of Judah, and to the inhabitants of Jerusalem;	of this covenant, and speak to the men of Judah and the inhabitants of Jerusalem.
3 And say thou unto them, Thus saith the LORD God of Israel; Cursed *be* the man that obeyeth not the words of this covenant,	3 You shall say to them, Thus says the LORD, the God of Israel: Cursed be the man who does not heed the words of this cove-

from vss. 9-10 that Jeremiah spoke these words in the time of Jehoiakim, who had made a public renewal of the Josianic reforms, but did not attempt to enforce them.

To others, however, it seems that these views do not take sufficient account of the pervasiveness of Deuteronomic phraseology and ideas in this whole section. It was written during the time of the Exile, *ca.* 550 B.C., and had a twofold purpose: (*a*) to show that Jeremiah was one of a line of prophets who had called upon Israel to obey **the words of this covenant** as the Deuteronomists understood them (the Decalogue in Deut. 4:13; 9:9, 11, 15 and the Deuteronomic Code itself in Deut. 29:1, 9, 21—but between these two there was no contradiction in their mind) ; and (*b*) to say that because the people had not obeyed the covenant, the evils pronounced for disobedience (as in Deut. 28:15-68) had come upon them. To some extent, then, this section is "prophecy after the event." It is largely a free composition of the Deuteronomic editor, and we cannot recover a Jeremianic kernel from it with any certainty. If Jeremiah spoke of obeying a covenant in words similar to those found here, he meant not the Deuteronomic law, but the Sinai covenant with special emphasis on the ethical Decalogue.

11:2. The words of this covenant: Cf. Deut. 29:1, 9; II Kings 23:3, 21.

3. Cursed . . . covenant: Cf. Deut. 27:26.

which North himself appeals at the close of his fine chapter:

During the period we have had under review the contrast between the Theology of the Old Testament and the History of Israel's Religion has been so sharp and stubborn that the task of writing a Theology has seemed well-nigh impossible. But if we must now, perforce, be less dogmatic about the History than we used to be, we may perhaps essay to write the Theology with fewer misgivings.[5]

To all of this it should be added that J. Philip Hyatt[6] has made a very important contribution, in which he holds that Jeremiah did not begin his ministry till 615 B.C., which obviates the embarrassment of this chapter by making it clearly impossible for Jeremiah to have supported the Josian reform inaugurated some six years earlier. "But all such arguments," comments Otto Eissfeldt, "fall to the ground in face of the case made out by H. H. Rowley,"[7] who, after a re-examination of the relevant passages (Jer. 44:34; 3:1; and 11:1-14) came to the conclusion that these passages "support the view that Jeremiah at first welcomed the

[5] "Pentateuchal Criticism," in H. H. Rowley, ed., *The Old Testament and Modern Study* (Oxford: Clarendon Press, 1951), p. 82.

[6] "Jeremiah and Deuteronomy," *Journal of Near Eastern Studies*, I (1942), 156-73.

[7] "The Prophet Jeremiah and the Book of Deuteronomy," in H. H. Rowley, ed., *Studies in Old Testament Prophecy* (New York: Charles Scribner's Sons, 1950), pp. 157-74.

Josianic reform instigated by the book of Deuteronomy, and supported it, but that later he took exception to its dangerous developments."[8] Inasmuch as our own exposition follows a somewhat different line (though nearer, perhaps, to that of Rowley than to that of Hyatt) we shall do well to take a little more pains with this passage than it might otherwise seem to warrant.

It is commonly agreed that the passage under discussion involves a Deuteronomic editing; but it is also recognized that it could not be a pure invention, and is therefore based upon some tangible event. It is also recognized that the verses do not *name* the Deuteronomic code but refer throughout to **this covenant.** There are numerous reasons, however, why **this covenant** would normally be assumed to apply to the document which was found in the renovation of the temple and which King Josiah accepted and made the basis for extensive religious reforms throughout the land.

In the first place the central ideas of Deuteronomy do not stand in sharp opposition to those of Jeremiah. The book holds for circumcision of the heart, for purification within, and for the suppression and extinction of idols. Conversely, it would appear that the Deuteronomists of a later time approved of Jeremiah's prophecies to the extent of preserving them and editing them with the clear supposition that Jeremiah or his position was favorable to the

[8] Eissfeldt, "The Prophetic Literature," *ibid.*, p. 153.

4 Which I commanded your fathers in the day *that* I brought them forth out of the land of Egypt, from the iron furnace, saying, Obey my voice, and do them, according to all which I command you: so shall ye be my people, and I will be your God:

5 That I may perform the oath which I have sworn unto your fathers, to give them a land flowing with milk and honey, as *it is* this day. Then answered I, and said, So be it, O LORD.

nant 4 which I commanded your fathers when I brought them out of the land of Egypt, from the iron furnace, saying, Listen to my voice, and do all that I command you. So shall you be my people, and I will be your God, 5 that I may perform the oath which I swore to your fathers to give them a land flowing with milk and honey, as at this day." Then I answered, "So be it, LORD."

---

4. When . . . furnace: Cf. Deut. 4:20; I Kings 8:51.
5. Perform the oath . . . fathers: Cf. Deut. 7:8; 8:18; 9:5. **A land . . . honey:** Cf. Deut. 6:3; 11:9; 26:9, 15; 27:3; 31:20. **As at this day:** Cf. Deut. 2:30; 4:20, 38; 6:24; 8:18, *et al.* **Then I answered, "So be it, LORD":** Cf. Deut. 27:15-26.

---

general postulates of the Deuteronomic reformation. Jeremiah's favorable opinion of Josiah was such that he does not appear to have stood in opposition to him. More impressive still is the close relationship which obtained between Jeremiah and the house of Shaphan. Micklem summarizes these relationships most effectively:

Shaphan, the chancellor, was closely connected with the finding of the law-book; it was in the chamber of his son Gemariah that Jeremiah's roll was first read; Ahikam, Shaphan's son, saved Jeremiah's life; it was in Ahikam's son's house that Jeremiah was received when he was delivered from prison by the Chaldeans; it was by another of Shaphan's house that Jeremiah sent his letter to the exiles. In view of the friendship of Jeremiah with the house of Shaphan, and, indeed, in view of the friendly hearing given by the princes to the roll, it is almost incredible that Jeremiah should have spoken of Deuteronomy as a work botched together by lying scribes, and we are bound to assume a real understanding between the prophet and at least the more spiritually minded of those behind the reformation movement.[9]

To assume that Jeremiah had co-operated with the reform movement would not only make it easy to account for his mission to the cities of Judah (vs. 6), but it would also help to account, as Peake puts it, for "the murderous hostility of the men of Anathoth described in this section of the book"[1] (vss. 18-23). Already sensitive over having been excluded from service at the central sanctuary at Jerusalem by King Solomon, the house of Abiathar (Jeremiah's priestly family at Anathoth) would re-

sent even more the concentration of power in the rival priesthood of Zadok which the reformation now proposed; and to have Jeremiah, the descendant of Abiathar, supporting such a program, would doubtless have excited extreme hostility on the part both of Jeremiah's family and his community.

As over against this there is the persistent and undeniable sense that Jeremiah could not have supported the Deuteronomic reform without reservation at any time. There is the entire sacrificial and ceremonial legislation of the book, so contrary to Jeremiah's interest; and the entire ritual element of the law, as well as the tendency to secure religious fidelity by way of legal requirements, which is so foreign to Jeremiah's religious sense. There is, in short, something in A. B. Davidson's observation that "Pharisaism and Deuteronomy came into the world the same day."[2] Either the book or its protagonists disclosed soon what Skinner calls "the insidious error of regarding external obedience to the law, irrespective of the inner disposition of the heart, as a satisfactory response to the will of Yahweh."[3]

Clearly these approaches are too narrow and preclusive, and some fresh approach to the problem must be made.

We return, therefore, to our initial observation regarding these verses, namely, that the Deuteronomic code is not specified by **the word that came to Jeremiah from the LORD** (vs. 1). What **this covenant** refers to is immediately specified (vs. 4) as that **which I commanded your fathers when I brought them out of the land of Egypt;** it is further specified as that covenant which contains the specific covenant formula: **so shall you be my people, and I will**

[9] Nathaniel Micklem, *Prophecy and Eschatology* (London: George Allen & Unwin, 1926), p. 201; used by permission. Cf. II Kings 23:3 and II Chr. 34:15; Jer. 26:24; 29:3; 36:10; 36:16 ff.; 39:14.
[1] *Jeremiah and Lamentations*, I, 13.

[2] Quoted in Skinner, *Prophecy and Religion*, p. 96.
[3] *Ibid.*

6 Then the Lord said unto me, Proclaim all these words in the cities of Judah, and in the streets of Jerusalem, saying, Hear ye the words of this covenant, and do them.

7 For I earnestly protested unto your fathers in the day *that* I brought them up out of the land of Egypt, *even* unto this day, rising early and protesting, saying, Obey my voice.

8 Yet they obeyed not, nor inclined their ear, but walked every one in the imagination of their evil heart: therefore I will bring upon them all the words of this covenant, which I commanded *them* to do; but they did *them* not.

6 And the Lord said to me, "Proclaim all these words in the cities of Judah, and in the streets of Jerusalem: Hear the words of this covenant and do them. **7** For I solemnly warned your fathers when I brought them up out of the land of Egypt, warning them persistently, even to this day, saying, Obey my voice. **8** Yet they did not obey or incline their ear, but every one walked in the stubbornness of his evil heart. Therefore I brought upon them all the words of this covenant, which I commanded them to do, but they did not."

7-8. These verses are omitted by the LXX, except for the last clause, **but they did not.** The omission is probably accidental, by partial homoeoteleuton.

---

be your God. And to the Lord's command to proclaim **this covenant** to all the people Jeremiah answered boldly and heartily: "Amen, Yahweh!" (vs. 5).

This is the point at which our appraisal of this passage must begin: with the assumption, that is, that Jeremiah is affirming, clearly and emphatically, his own starting point. This starting point embodied, as we noted above (2:2-3), a prophetic retrospect, a looking back to the covenant signs and the covenant-making events by which the people became the chosen of the Lord. Jeremiah's thinking focuses here upon the honeymoon period in the wilderness, when, as he believed, the devotion of the people to their Lord was constant and whole. We emphasize the influence of Hosea upon Jeremiah's thinking, which informed his understanding and interpretation of the covenant relation with the understanding that God was loyal in love (*ḥesedh*). It is apparently to this covenant that Jeremiah is referring now. It was this covenant which he had been instructed to speak **to the men of Judah and the inhabitants of Jerusalem** (vs. 2), in an attempt to induce in them that depth of repentance which would initiate a return. Only in such a repentance and return could he see any hope for Judah. The metaphor of the journey which this passage contains, and its subsequent conversion into a general principle (6:16) shows how intrinsic to Jeremiah's view are the existential features of this covenant relation with Yahweh. So emphatically is this the case that one is tempted to raise the question at once as to whether there is not, as between Jeremiah and the Deuteronomic code, an essential difference in principle, which, not apparent on the surface, becomes increasingly explicit as the differences

between the priestly-legal religious orientation are translated into the experiences of the people.

Adam Welch advances the view that the Deuteronomic reform must be understood in the context of the political-religious activities of the time. The attempt to restore the unity of the whole of Israel under one political head made it highly desirable that there should also be one religious center. Therefore, in his reversal of the policies of Manasseh, Josiah had not only supported a stringent Yahwism, but in destroying heathen altars on his visit to Samaria had destroyed a Yahweh altar also. To bring the remaining people of Israel into political unity with Judah it was necessary to centralize worship at the capital in Jerusalem, very much as David had once brought the ark, the emblem of Ephraim, into the new city. Secondly, in order to further the consolidation of the life and worship of the two kingdoms, an effort was made by the religious leaders in Jerusalem to bring together and harmonize the sacred literature and traditions of the north with those of the south.

The incorporation of the sacred literature of Israel was deliberately carried out in order to win over Northern Israel to the surrender of their local shrine or shrines, and to make easier for them the recognition of the primacy of Jerusalem and its priesthood. There was to be again one nation with a single religious and political center and one set of sacred books to guide its religious life.[4]

Welch never argues that the code of Deuteronomy was originally the law of northern Israel

[4] Adam C. Welch, *Jeremiah: His Time and His Work* (Oxford: Clarendon Press, 1928; New York: The Macmillan Co., 1951), p. 28. Used by permission.

9 And the LORD said unto me, A conspiracy is found among the men of Judah, and among the inhabitants of Jerusalem.

10 They are turned back to the iniquities of their forefathers, which refused to hear my words; and they went after other gods to serve them: the house of Israel and the house of Judah have broken my covenant which I made with their fathers.

11 ¶ Therefore thus saith the LORD, Behold, I will bring evil upon them, which they shall not be able to escape; and though they shall cry unto me, I will not hearken unto them.

12 Then shall the cities of Judah and inhabitants of Jerusalem go, and cry unto the

9 Again the LORD said to me, "There is revolt among the men of Judah and the inhabitants of Jerusalem. 10 They have turned back to the iniquities of their forefathers, who refused to hear my words; they have gone after other gods to serve them; the house of Israel and the house of Judah have broken my covenant which I made with their fathers. 11 Therefore, thus says the LORD, Behold, I am bringing evil upon them which they cannot escape; though they cry to me, I will not listen to them. 12 Then the cities of Judah and the in-

---

9. **Revolt** is better than **conspiracy**. The latter suggests political action, whereas the reference is to revolt against the commands of God.

---

and that a copy of this code was brought to Jerusalem along with other religious literature and deposited in the temple. When they ran across it at the time of the temple repairs it was adopted as part of the Judean law. Now comes the important point:

But, just as the reformers have retouched the other documents by adding to the records of the history and to the book of Hosea evidence of their interest in the question of centralization, so, before issuing the Code of Deuteronomy, they countersigned it by the addition of the little section 12:1-7, the one section in the book which demands the unique sacredness of their temple.[5]

Now it is this action which Welch conceives to have been the target for Jeremiah's protest. The following statement, therefore, may be said to summarize his interpretation:

The original Code of Deuteronomy was not only one of the finest efforts ever made by any nation to bring the great commanding principles of a national religion into contact with the actual life of common men, it was also the law of Yahweh which had commanded [Jeremiah's] allegiance and worthily guided his thought in his youth. It was the law of Northern Israel to which he belonged.

The priesthood of Jerusalem have taken it over and acknowledged its validity for the whole nation. But in the process they have perverted it. The pen of the scribe has superinduced upon it, either as its only legitimate interpretation or as a novel and unwarranted addition to its regulations, something which has no authority. Jeremiah rejected this in the plainest terms, and called the men's act mere falsification.[6]

This hypothesis is persuasive not merely because it harmonizes the most salient points at issue, but also because it interprets from within the context of political as well as religious factors of the time. It has also the merit of not foreclosing the question of the composition of Deuteronomy, permitting the development of that book to continue from the fall of Samaria until its final formulation in the postexilic period. Better still, it permits us to return to the position from which we started: namely, that Jeremiah is pointing away from the negative features of the Deuteronomic reform and back to the terms of the original covenant with Yahweh, to which he could heartily say, "Amen, Yahweh!" Thus, as Davidson held, "Jeremiah may have sought to impress on men the general idea of Deuteronomy, that of the covenant between Yahweh and Israel, for this was his own idea in another form, but a formal championship of Deuteronomy would have been very unlike him."[7] Skinner interprets this to mean that

what Jeremiah means by covenant is just the fundamental principle of Old Testament religion, that Yahwe is Israel's God and Israel Yahwe's people, and that this relation is maintained on the condition of obedience to the will of Yahwe in whatever way it may be revealed.[8]

We have suggested, however, that Jeremiah's view of this fundamental principle of O.T. religion was quite specific, that it is informed with the theological orientation of Hosea's view of God and with Jeremiah's deep person-

[5] *Ibid.*, p. 32; cf. pp. 16-32.
[6] *Ibid.*, p. 92.
[7] "Jeremiah," in Hastings, ed., *Dictionary of the Bible*, II, 570b.
[8] *Prophecy and Religion*, p. 100.

gods unto whom they offer incense: but they shall not save them at all in the time of their trouble.

13 For *according to* the number of thy cities were thy gods, O Judah; and *according to* the number of the streets of Jerusalem have ye set up altars to *that* shameful thing, *even* altars to burn incense unto Baal.

14 Therefore pray not thou for this people, neither lift up a cry or prayer for them: for I will not hear *them* in the time that they cry unto me for their trouble.

15 What hath my beloved to do in mine house, *seeing* she hath wrought lewdness with many, and the holy flesh is passed from thee? when thou doest evil, then thou rejoicest.

habitants of Jerusalem will go and cry to the gods to whom they burn incense, but they cannot save them in the time of their trouble. 13 For your gods have become as many as your cities, O Judah; and as many as the streets of Jerusalem are the altars you have set up to shame, altars to burn incense to Ba'al.

14 "Therefore do not pray for this people, or lift up a cry or prayer on their behalf, for I will not listen when they call to me in the time of their trouble. 15 What right has my beloved in my house, when she has done vile deeds? Can vows[t] and sacrificial flesh avert your doom? Can you

[t] Gk: Heb *many*

---

13. For the idea cf. 2:28.

14. This verse is similar to 7:16 (in a Deuteronomic section; see Exeg. on 7:16-20).

B. Doom Not Averted by Sacrifices (11:15-17)

Vss. 15-16 constitute a poem which is very poorly preserved in the M.T. The versions give some aid in its restoration. It was probably spoken in one of the courts of the temple, where there were apparently olive trees (Ps. 52:8). The theme is the inadequacy of the temple cultus to avert the doom which is coming upon Israel for her moral failures (cf. 6:20; 7:1-15, 21-23). Vs. 17 is a prose addition, made by the Deuteronomic editor; the thought is similar to that of vss. 8, 12, 14. Taking vss. 1-17 as a whole, we can see that the Deuteronomic editor has incorporated a genuine poem by Jeremiah in a long section of his own.

15-16. With some emendation these verses may be translated as follows, in poetic form and in perfect 3+2 meter:

---

alization of the God-man relationship. The passage under discussion recognizes (vs. 4) the centrality of the covenant idea as the point of living contact between God and his people. The pressure of the Josianic reforms may well have been one of the factors which propelled Jeremiah's thinking, with increasing clarity and conviction, toward the anticipation of a new covenant based upon a profounder inwardness and a deeper devotion.

Two concluding observations may be made. We may remark again, with Minear, that "the retrospect of the Deuteronomic literature is different [from that of Jeremiah] at a number of points." [9] Jeremiah feels that the people's apostasy begins with their defection from the covenant with David, which leads him to a prediction of national disaster and exile and locates his essential hope in the re-establishment of a higher and purified Davidic kingdom. The Deuteronomist, however, locates the origi-

[9] *Eyes of Faith*, p. 217.

nal defection in a defiance of the Mosaic covenant in the wilderness; disloyalty to the commandments appeared to be the contemporary form of disloyalty, and so drew the reform of the people into priestly and legalistic patterns.

So also the repetition (vs. 7) of the phrase, "hearken unto my voice" (vs. 4; cf. 7:23), permits us to emphasize again, with Buber, the importance of the primacy of the prophetic word—"this living, ever new, unforeseen, unforeseeable" word—which the people have rejected; and "without the rousing and renovating life of the word even the book does not live." [1] It was to this word that the people had refused obedience. They had refused to listen, and **every one walked in the stubbornness of his evil heart** (vs. 8). Without the listening ear, there could be no renewing and revitalizing Voice.

15-17. *Prelude to Protest.*—In the light of the foregoing, it is easy to see how effectively

[1] *The Prophetic Faith*, p. 169.

16 The LORD called thy name, A green olive tree, fair, *and* of goodly fruit: with the noise of a great tumult he hath kindled fire upon it, and the branches of it are broken.

17 For the LORD of hosts, that planted thee, hath pronounced evil against thee, for the evil of the house of Israel and of the house of Judah, which they have done against themselves to provoke me to anger in offering incense unto Baal.

18 ¶ And the LORD hath given me knowledge *of it,* and I know *it:* then thou showedst me their doings.

then exult? **16** The LORD once called you, 'A green olive tree, fair with goodly fruit'; but with the roar of a great tempest he will set fire to it, and its branches will be consumed. **17** The LORD of hosts, who planted you, has pronounced evil against you, because of the evil which the house of Israel and the house of Judah have done, provoking me to anger by burning incense to Ba'al."

18 The LORD made it known to me and I knew;
   then thou didst show me their evil deeds.

What right has my beloved in my house?
   She has done vile deeds!
Can fatlings and holy flesh avert
   from you your doom?
"A spreading olive tree, beautiful in form"
   was your name called.
Fire was kindled against it;
   its branches were consumed.

(For the details of this reconstruction see J. Philip Hyatt, "The Original Text of Jeremiah 11₁₅₋₁₆," *Journal of Biblical Literature,* LX [1941], 57-60.) The principal changes from the M.T. are the following: vs. 15, read הברים for הרבים, the error arising by metathesis and haplography; אז תעלזי is a marginal gloss, overloading the meter; in vs. 16 read יפיפה־תאר for the strange יפה פרי־תאר, and excise as marginal glosses יהוה (because Yahweh is the speaker throughout the poem) and לקול המולה גדלה (cf. Ezek. 1:24).

My beloved is Israel, as in 12:7; Isa. 5:1. **My house** is the temple in Jerusalem.

C. PLOT AGAINST JEREMIAH'S LIFE (11:18–12:6)

In this section we are told of a plot against Jeremiah's life by his kinsmen of Anathoth, and of the prophet's reaction. In ch. 12 he raises the difficult question: Why

this little poetic fragment reveals the movement of Jeremiah's thinking. Whether encouraged by the Deuteronomic reform or not, the people's faith in the inviolability of the temple increased. It had had its origin in the faith of Isaiah, to whom the reforming party stood in line of direct descent. Jeremiah, observing the increase of sacrificial practices in the temple, expresses in this poem two moods.

The first is a mood of astonishment, or rather, incredulity, that the people—the beloved of God—could so misconstrue their relationship with him as to think that "scraps of fat and sacred flesh" [2] could in any wise represent the true content of that relationship. The mood of exaltation which seems to accompany these sacrifices has led Cornill to point out the possible proximity of these reflections to the coronation of Jehoiakim, whose appointment to the throne

[2] Skinner, *op. cit.,* p. 168.

seemed to encourage the people in their belief in the inviolability of the temple.

This first reflection is followed by a second which takes the form of an exclamation of high indignation. The people—the beloved of God—are compared to the open loveliness of an olive tree. Such had Judah once been. But suddenly Jeremiah sees the flash of lightning whereby the tree is blasted and its branches consumed.

Something of this tempestuous indignation seems to be gathering in Jeremiah's soul, especially if it is true that these verses depict the behavior of the people at the time of Jehoiakim's coronation. This would mean that these verses are but the prelude to the rhetorical storm and lightning crash of Jeremiah's sermon in the temple (chs. 7; 26).

11:18-21; 12:6. *Expostulation and Reply (I).* —"Test yourself on humanity. It makes the

do the wicked prosper? The whole passage is very revealing of Jeremiah's nature, and is properly placed among his "confessions."

The Hebrew text connects 12:1-6 with 11:18-23 by stating in 12:6 that it was Jeremiah's own kinsmen who were plotting against him, and many commentators believe that the questioning of Jeremiah in ch. 12 arose as a result of the plot of ch. 11. This may well be true, but only in part. His question was not an intellectual or academic one, but came as the result of his personal fortunes. However, the experiences that lay behind his questioning may well have been more than the plot reported in 11:18-23, although this plot may have brought his questioning to a climax.

The present text of this section seems to be disarranged, and many suggestions have been made for the purpose of securing a more logical sequence. (In addition to the commentaries, see especially H. H. Rowley, "The Text and Interpretation of Jer. 11:18-12:6," *American Journal of Semitic Languages and Literatures,* XLII [1925-26], 217-27.) It is best to read 12:6 between 11:18 and 11:19, as the words of Yahweh which recount what he made known to the prophet. Also, 12:4 (except for the last line) is out of place in the present passage, and belongs in a context such as that of ch. 14 or 9:10. Possibly we should go further (with Volz and Rudolph) and place 12:3 between 11:20a and 11:20b, but that is not wholly necessary.

The theory is widely held that this plot against Jeremiah's life arose as the result of his advocating the Deuteronomic reforms. According to this theory Jeremiah's relatives, who were priests in Anathoth, lost their positions upon the destruction of the local sanctuaries decreed by Deuteronomy; then they vented their wrath upon their renegade kinsman, Jeremiah, for supporting Josiah's reformation. This theory is improbable. Cornill rightly points out that such a plot as related here would hardly have been made against a young man just taking his first timid steps in public, but would rather be

---

doubtful doubt, the believer believe." So wrote Franz Kafka in his *Aphorisms.*[3] Jeremiah, in the passage before us, has reached this difficult point. He is about to be tested on humanity. He finds the experience shocking, then sobering, and at the last miraculously sustaining.

Jeremiah's account of his innocence, as he returned from Jerusalem to Anathoth after scrutinizing the city's squares (5:1), suggests that the full power of the prophetic position which he assumed was still in its rhetorical stages, not having felt as yet the counterpressures of resistance which the vested interests of prophets, priests, and people were certain to present. To take his stand on the wilderness covenant, and so to cut the ground from under both the ceremonial systems of the priests and the prudential compromises of the prophets, was to incur "the hatred of priests against a priest who attacks his own order, [and] the hatred of prophets against a prophet who ventures to have a voice and will of his own."[4] To do this with such candor and cutting directness was bad enough:

> the prophets prophesy falsely,
> and the priests rule at their direction;
> [and] my people love to have it so (5:31)!

[3] *The Great Wall of China,* tr. Willa and Edwin Muir (London: Secker & Warburg, 1933), p. 152.

[4] Quoted from Stanley, by S. Conway, in Cheyne and Adeney, *et al., Jeremiah,* I, 309.

But to do it in the name of the Lord was intolerable!

In other words, when Jeremiah returns to Anathoth he returns with his message thought through in both its positive and negative aspects. Whereas in the city the deeper implications of this message might be easily absorbed and deflected until some such event as the coronation of Jehoiakim and Jeremiah's sermon in the temple gate would dramatize and crystallize his meaning absolutely, in the little town of Anathoth these implications would be quickly detected. In this setting he would be told, **Do not prophesy in the name of the LORD, or you will die by our hand** (vs. 21).

At the beginning, however, of his collision with the people, Jeremiah's innocence is to be noted: he was, as we say, as innocent as a lamb (vs. 19). He **did not know,** had no inkling, of the schemes that were being devised against him; but they became clear to him, we are not told how, and he saw the people's evil intent toward him.

If we were to suppose that vss. 15-17 were spoken to the people of Anathoth, it is easy to see how their deep hostility would be excited. If we were to assume that the charges of making heathenish vows and practicing rituals of sacrifice were being leveled at the proud sanctuary at Anathoth, it is easy to see how the prophetic ardor of Jeremiah would take hold. The ques-

19 But I *was* like a lamb *or* an ox *that* is brought to the slaughter; and I knew not that they had devised devices against me, *saying,* Let us destroy the tree with the fruit thereof, and let us cut him off from the land of the living, that his name may be no more remembered.	19 But I was like a gentle lamb
	  led to the slaughter.
	I did not know it was against me
	  they devised schemes, saying,
	"Let us destroy the tree with its fruit,
	  let us cut him off from the land of the living,
	  that his name be remembered no more."

directed against one who had prophesied long enough to gain some authority and to arouse bitter enmity. Furthermore, it is very improbable that Jeremiah was ever an advocate of the Deuteronomic reforms (see Exeg. on 11:1-14, and Intro., pp. 779-80). Volz may be much nearer the truth when he conjectures that the Jerusalem priesthood was back of the plot against Jeremiah's life. They had been foiled in their attempt to get rid of him immediately after the temple sermon (7:1-15; 26), and so sought to have him murdered by some of their colleagues, the priests of Anathoth, who may themselves have served in the Jerusalem temple (see Exeg. on 1:1). Jeremiah's relatives must have opposed him for his many attacks upon those whom he considered false priests and prophets, and upon the institutions which they held dear.

In 12:1-5 we have the earliest literary evidence in the O.T. for the raising of the question: Why do the wicked prosper? That Jeremiah was one of the first, if not actually the first, to criticize the generally accepted doctrine of divine retribution, and question even God himself, arose from several factors: his own bitter experiences, which made the doctrine seem false; his independence of mind; his strong sense of the worth of the individual; and his feeling of closeness to God. In 12:1-5 ideas and terminology borrowed from the law court are employed: Yahweh is considered as a righteous judge, before whom the prophet pleads his case against his adversaries, the wicked and treacherous men. He receives his verdict from God in 12:5 (cf. Sheldon H. Blank, "The Confessions of Jeremiah and the Meaning of Prayer," *Hebrew Union College Annual*, XXI [1948], 331-54).

19. The word לחמו, translated **its fruit,** is properly rendered "its bread." Because it is not certain that this word can have the meaning **fruit,** many scholars adopt the suggestion of Hitzig to read לחו, "its sap." This may be correct.

tion, "What right has my beloved in my house, when she has done vile deeds?" (vs. 15) would no longer be rhetorical. It would strike at the very heart of the sanctuary and the house of Abiathar. The question, "Can you then exult?" (vs. 15) would then be leveled at the pride of the house of Abiathar. If the house of Abiathar had once been called "a green olive tree, fair with goodly fruit" (vs. 16) and a son of that house, to wit, Jeremiah, was now telling them that a lightning flash of the wrath of God would shortly blast it beyond recognition, it is easy to see how this prophet would be without honor in his own country! Should the indictment, finally, be climaxed by the charge that Yahweh, who had planted them, had now pronounced evil against them because they had been "burning incense to Baal" (vs. 17), clearly the prophet would be tempting fate in much the same way that he would shortly do in Jerusalem (cf. ch. 7).

The reader will bear in mind that this interpretation is, like other interpretations of this event, mere conjecture. As Skinner remarks of his own interpretation that the threats at Anathoth were a consequence of Jeremiah's advocacy of the Deuteronomic reform, "We may admit at once that it cannot be proved to be true." He goes on to say that "in considering a passage of uncertain *provenance* there can be no objection to placing it at what may be called the point of maximum illumination." [5] The common resort to the Deuteronomic hypothesis would not seem to provide this illumination: it is not sufficient, on psychological grounds, to call forth the depth of hostility to which this account bears witness. C. J. Ball comes nearer when he suggests a possible connection between vs. 16 and vs. 20. When Jeremiah spoke of the green olive tree, someone in the company may have given the sarcastic retort,

[5] *Op. cit.,* pp. 109-10.

20 But, O LORD of hosts, that judgest righteously, that triest the reins and the heart, let me see thy vengeance on them: for unto thee have I revealed my cause.

21 Therefore thus saith the LORD of the men of Anathoth, that seek thy life, saying, Prophesy not in the name of the LORD, that thou die not by our hand:

22 Therefore thus saith the LORD of hosts, Behold, I will punish them: the young men shall die by the sword; their sons and their daughters shall die by famine:

23 And there shall be no remnant of them: for I will bring evil upon the men of Anathoth, *even* the year of their visitation.

20 But, O LORD of hosts, who judgest righteously,
who triest the heart and the mind,
let me see thy vengeance upon them,
for to thee have I committed my cause.

21 Therefore thus says the LORD concerning the men of An'athoth, who seek your life, and say, "Do not prophesy in the name of the LORD, or you will die by our hand" — 22 therefore thus says the LORD of hosts: "Behold, I will punish them; the young men shall die by the sword; their sons and their daughters shall die by famine; 23 and none of them shall be left. For I will bring evil upon the men of An'athoth, the year of their punishment."

---

20. Let me see thy vengeance upon them: Jeremiah not infrequently prayed God to destroy his personal enemies (cf. 17:18; 18:23; 20:11). This was in part a natural sequence from his belief that his own enemies were God's enemies too. But it must be recognized as a defect in the religion of one who had not learned to pray for his enemies: "Father, forgive them, for they know not what they do."

21. Anathoth: See Exeg. on 1:1.

22-23. These verses contain the judgment of God upon Jeremiah's enemies, who are to be visited with the punishment they sought to inflict upon him.

Let us destroy the tree with its fruit,
let us cut him off from the land of the living.

Such a remark may have revealed to Jeremiah the animosity directed toward him. Vs. 20 then might be taken to contain Jeremiah's reply, "in the form of an unexpressed thought, or a hurried ejaculation upon discovering their deadly malice."[6] Yea, but it is Yahweh who will judge between us. He judges righteously: he tries the heart and the mind. Under the divine justice his own kin as well as the people of Anathoth were certain to come, sooner or later, under the same condemnation of disaster which was about to overtake all the other unfaithful people of the land.

It was this conviction, rather than personal resentment, however excusable under the circumstances that feeling would have been, which led Jeremiah to exclaim: "I shall see Thy vengeance on them, for unto Thee have I laid bare my cause." . . . Looked at in this light, his words are a confident assertion of the Divine justice, not a cry for vengeance.[7]

A more common view, however, accepts them in the full spirit of resentment and vindictiveness which they display. To Gordon, for example, this is a "harsh" and "unbeautiful element" in Jeremiah's character—an element

made more apparent by the fact that "we are dealing with one of the gentlest spirits of all times"—a character "shy, sensitive, imaginative. . . ." Gordon continues:

But have we not seen already that Jeremiah is a man of extremes, scorning the dull, mediocre levels of life, with a spirit too passionate for common achievements? If, on the one hand, we find him a man of intense tenderness of heart, . . . we can hardly express surprise that when his mighty purpose is thwarted by pride and prejudice he should vent a righteous indignation against the enemies of Jehovah.[8]

Without doubt there is abundant evidence to support this point of view. It appears to have been a characteristic of Jeremiah, just as it was a characteristic of Yahweh of whom Jeremiah was the mouthpiece. But more than likely it was a characteristic of Yahweh because it was a trait projected upon him by a people of whom it was characteristic. One has only to glance at Ps. 137 to note how the most plaintive song to come from the literature of the exiles concludes with the harshest and most terrible of imprecations. Hosea's recognition that the justice and power of Yahweh were to be understood in terms of the reconciling wisdom of suffering love was but a very recent insight to the Hebrew religious consciousness.

[6] C. J. Ball, *Prophecies of Jeremiah*, pp. 262-63.
[7] *Ibid.*, p. 263.
[8] *Rebel Prophet*, pp. 59-60.

12 Righteous *art* thou, O Lord, when I plead with thee: yet let me talk with thee of *thy* judgments: Wherefore doth the way of the wicked prosper? *wherefore* are all they happy that deal very treacherously?

2 Thou hast planted them, yea, they have taken root: they grow, yea, they bring forth fruit: thou *art* near in their mouth, and far from their reins.

3 But thou, O Lord, knowest me: thou hast seen me, and tried mine heart toward thee: pull them out like sheep for the slaughter, and prepare them for the day of slaughter.

---

12 Righteous art thou, O Lord,
   when I complain to thee;
   yet I would plead my case before thee.
Why does the way of the wicked prosper?
   Why do all who are treacherous thrive?
2 Thou plantest them, and they take root;
   they grow and bring forth fruit;
thou art near in their mouth
   and far from their heart.
3 But thou, O Lord, knowest me;
   thou seest me, and triest my mind toward thee.
Pull them out like sheep for the slaughter,
   and set them apart for the day of slaughter.

That Jeremiah, in the first shock of his collision with his brethren at Anathoth, should have seen in this affront a defiance of Yahweh's own cause and so have invoked Yahweh's vengeance upon them is not unthinkable. This was an accepted and proper aspect of the true prophet's function, just as it was his proper function "to deliver what was the burden of all prophecy from the beginning," as over against the accommodated perspectives of the Josian reform.[9] Indeed, it would appear that these prophetic forms and manners were not confined to the prophets of Israel.[1] And while the oracle in vss. 21-23 is typical of the "messenger" type of utterance, and therefore a deliberated word under prophetic inspiration, what is more remarkable in this incident is the sobering afterthought of Jeremiah.

Being tested by humanity is sobering enough in general, but when one's enemies become "those of his own household" (Matt. 10:36) it may well induce long, long thoughts even in a prophet as zealous as Jeremiah. **Even your brothers . . . even they have dealt treacherously with you** is the melancholy reflection (vs. 6) of Jeremiah after the event. This is the point at which the testing will be most severe. Here the doubtful will doubt and the believer believe. Nevertheless it is a melancholy, if necessary, lesson to learn: "If any man come to me, and hate not his father, and mother, and wife, and children, and brethren, and sisters, yea, and his own life also, he cannot be my disciple" (Luke 14:26). Yet it is probably not too much to say that it was precisely this experience of collision and rejection by his own household and in his home town which delivered Jeremiah, psycho-

logically, from dependence upon his formative conditioning patterns and tossed him out faithfully upon his "seventy thousand fathoms" (Kierkegaard) where his dependence was solely upon the Lord. Whatever unrealistic idealisms he may have held up to this time are now shattered. Certainly his bold movement into his proclamation at the temple gate is unthinkable without some such thoroughgoing clarification within. It is more than likely this experience of shock which informs his "retrospective meditation" (12:1-5), written, as even Skinner holds, "when he was driven from his native village to find a refuge in the crowded streets of the capital."[2]

12:1-5. Expostulation and Reply (II).—"Men must be lifted from one cleave of being to another," wrote Gerard Manley Hopkins, who, in his "Terrible Sonnets" reveals an inner ordeal not unlike that which Jeremiah discloses in his confessions. The "confessions of Jeremiah" are made up of "a unique series of devotional poems" of which the two under consideration are regarded by many as being the first. They unfold, writes Skinner, "the secret of his best life, the converse of his soul with God through which the true nature of religion was disclosed to him." Skinner then makes this significant comment:

It would throw great light on his spiritual history if we could ascertain that this strain of subjective piety dates from the crisis in his life when he first tasted the bitterness of the man whose foes are they of his own household.[3]

With the security patterns of his youth now permanently cut from under him, Jeremiah must learn that faith is a risk, and, in a sense more profound than most people suppose, he

---

[9] Cf. Welch, *Jeremiah: His Time and His Work*, p. 96; cf. also Jer. 26:16.

[1] Cf. Haldar, *Associations of Cult Prophets*, p. 73, *et passim*, also Geo Widengren, *Literary and Psychological Aspects of the Hebrew Prophets* (Uppsala: Lundeqvist, 1948), especially pp. 11-56.

[2] *Op. cit.*, p. 112.
[3] *Ibid.*, p. 114.

4 How long shall the land mourn, and the herbs of every field wither, for the wickedness of them that dwell therein? the beasts are consumed, and the birds; because they said, He shall not see our last end.

4 How long will the land mourn,
    and the grass of every field wither?
For the wickedness of those who dwell
    in it
    the beasts and the birds are swept away,
    because men said, "He will not see our
      latter end."

12:4. The verse is probably out of place (see above), though the last line, **because men said, "He will not see our latter end,"** probably is original, to be read immediately after vs. 2 (or possibly vs. 3). The LXX reads, "God will not see our ways." The use of the subject "God" is only interpretation (yet a valid one), but "our ways" may be derived from a text that read ארחותינו rather than אחריתנו. This is adopted by some as the original reading, but the M.T. makes good sense. The line expresses the attitude of "practical atheism" (see Exeg. on 5:12-14).

must be prepared to revise his beliefs as his personality matures—even should this amount to nothing more than coming to understand what he has all along been proclaiming. Since, with Jeremiah, this understanding goes both to the roots of his heritage and to the roots of his own being, it places him, probably for a period of years, upon the knife-edge of struggle and doubt. He has been confronted with the real threat of death, and with the fact of essential conflict. Death stepped out from behind her masks:

Believe them not,
    though they speak fair words to you (vs. 6).

Essential conflict came out into the open: "Do not prophesy . . . , or you will die" (vs. 21). He experiences the first throes of suffering. All "happiness," all temporizing with destiny (his call), has been pushed upon the boundaries of his "limit-situation": the suffering through which he passes will either win him into Transcendence ("leap, then, into the arms of God") or remand him to conflicts and terrors and so, imperceptibly, to death. This passage makes plain which way he will go; but meanwhile, as with Augustine, he will become to himself "an unfruitful land."[4]

First comes the formulation of his case, the presentation of his brief (vs. 1). Once before he had used the legal form, only that time it was Yahweh as plaintiff pleading against the people as defendants: "wherefore I will yet plead with you, saith the LORD, and with your children's children will I plead" (2:9 E.R.V.).

He presents the evidence succinctly.

Thou [Yahweh] plantest them and they take root,
    they flourish, yes, and they bear fruit! (Vs. 2
    Moffatt.)

[4] *Confessions* II. 10. 18.

But though they give the appearance of piety and observe all the forms, the true spirit of God is not in their hearts. How long will Yahweh tolerate this condition? "How long is the land to lie woe-begone" (Moffatt), impoverished and demoralized "by the wickedness [of those who add insult to injury by saying], 'God never sees [pays any attention to] what we do [anyway]!' " (Moffatt).

Then he formulates his own initial vindictiveness. The Lord knows what happened to him in Anathoth; he has also tried him and proved his sincerity; why not, therefore, "drag them away like sheep to the slaughter" (Moffatt) — had *he* not been innocent "like a gentle lamb led to the slaughter"? (11:19) —and set them apart for their doom! This is included here, it would appear, as a confession and as an exposure of the full gamut of his feeling. For it already anticipates the Lord's rebuke in vs. 5. It therefore signifies that Jeremiah has moved through the sobering and maturing aftereffects of the shock of his initial encounter; and it has thrown him, for the time at least, more firmly upon the transcendence of God.

As is so often true of Christ's answers to his questioners, the Lord does not answer the speculative question which Jeremiah has raised; but he reproves his impatience, and confronts him with the deeper implications of his vocation. Anathoth is only the beginning. This was a trifle compared with the risks ahead (cf. Exeg. on vs. 5). Jerusalem is more than Anathoth, and the prophets and priests and princes and kings are far more formidable than his brethren in the country town. As Demosthenes put it: "If they cannot face the candle, what will they do when they see the sun?"[5]

Jeremiah has already chosen. He is back in Jerusalem. He has won his first great victory,

[5] Quoted in Ferdinand Hitzig, *Der prophet Jeremia* (2nd ed.; Leipzig, 1866), p. 95.

5 ¶ If thou hast run with the footmen, and they have wearied thee, then how canst thou contend with horses? and *if* in the land of peace, *wherein* thou trustedst, *they wearied thee*, then how wilt thou do in the swelling of Jordan?

5 "If you have raced with men on foot,
and they have wearied you,
how will you compete with horses?
And if in a safe land you fall down,
how will you do in the jungle of the
Jordan?

---

5. This verse is the reply of Yahweh to Jeremiah's question. It is not an abstract "answer" to his problem, but a challenge to him to have greater faith and courage for even more trying contests with evil men in the future.

Vs. 5*b* has given much trouble to translators. The KJV makes sense of it only by inserting words not in the Hebrew (perhaps depending upon Rashi), as the use of italics indicates. Many scholars follow the suggestion of Hitzig and emend בוטח to בורח, "if in a land of peace you flee," but the figure is unnatural, especially with the preposition **in**, and the emendation has no versional support. Others follow Codex Vaticanus of the LXX and insert "not" before "you trust"; but this was an attempt of that text to make sense of a difficult passage. The RSV has correctly rendered by ascribing to the Hebrew verb בטח the meaning **fall down**, which is the meaning of a cognate Arabic verb *baṭaḥa*. This suggestion was made long ago by the Karaite philologist David ben Abraham al-Fāsī (tenth century), and has been adopted by a few modern scholars. (For a full discussion

---

has experienced an initial release from conventional and empirical bondage, and has found it miraculously sustaining.

The parallelism of the metaphors confirms this. The first applies more to the steady pressures of a vocational commitment, the increasing challenge of the race, which accelerates in direct ratio to the absoluteness of our vocation experienced by others as a threat. First it will be, "even his brothers did not believe in him" (John 7:5); then it will be, "and when his friends heard it, they went out to seize him, for they said, 'He is beside himself'" (Mark 3:21); and then it will be the Cross. There is a sense in which none of us is exempt from this. As Kafka learned out of his own suffering: "What each of us possesses is not a body but a process of growth, and it conducts us through every pain, in this form or that." [6]

The second metaphor is different. Here the crises of life, the unanticipated threats and dangers which spring upon us without warning, are like the denizens of the jungle or like the ancient Sphinx, propounding the ultimate riddles. The older translation—**then how wilt thou do in the swelling of Jordan?**—is equally vivid. In arid countries the still, steady flow of a stream may swell suddenly into a treacherous swirling torrent after a heavy rain. If the quiet stream is too much for us, how shall we fare when the floods come? The first teaches us of Yeats's sense of life as "a struggle with the daemon who would ever set us to the hardest work among those not impossible" [7] (see Expos. on 1:13-16, pp. 807-9); the other teaches us of the pain of

the power by which the man of the spirit is "nailed out in isolation" [8] (see Expos. on 1:13-16, pp. 807-9).

The book of Job moves over the same terrain. In him also "the arrows of the Almighty" are fixed; he too "drinks their poison" and feels "the terrors of God . . . arrayed against [him]" (Job 6:4). He too cries out in bitterness and in exasperation,

Why do the wicked live,
reach old age, and grow mighty in power? (Job 21:7.)

Out of his vexation of spirit Job also addresses his complaint to God (see Job 31:35-37).

Neither did Job receive a direct or theoretical answer to his pleading. He learned the great awe, the depth of power beyond and behind chaos; he learned that

When half-gods go,
The gods arrive; [9]

he learned that God is great, unsearchable, that his aims are larger than ours, that he moves

Whether for correction, or for his land,
or for his love (Job 37:13).

And Job was able, at last, to rest in this—in Transcendence, in "the God beyond God"—in the belief that "when he has tried me, I shall come forth as gold" (Job 23:10; cf. Jer. 6:27-30).

But there is an indescribable pathos at the other extreme, where the call into the open

---

[6] *Great Wall of China*, p. 157.
[7] *Essays*, p. 499.

[8] Søren Kierkegaard, *Journals*, p. 407.
[9] Emerson, "Give All to Love."

6 For even thy brethren, and the house of thy father, even they have dealt treacherously with thee; yea, they have called a multitude after thee: believe them not, though they speak fair words unto thee.

7 ¶ I have forsaken mine house, I have left mine heritage; I have given the dearly beloved of my soul into the hand of her enemies.

6 For even your brothers and the house of your father,
even they have dealt treacherously with you;
they are in full cry after you;
believe them not,
though they speak fair words to you."

7 "I have forsaken my house,
I have abandoned my heritage;
I have given the beloved of my soul
into the hands of her enemies.

---

see Solomon L. Skoss, "The Root בטח in Jeremiah 12.5, Psalms 22.10, Proverbs 14.16, and Job 40.23," in S. W. Baron and Alexander Marx, eds., *Jewish Studies in Memory of George A. Kohut* [New York: The Alexander Kohut Memorial Foundation, 1935], pp. 549-53; cf. G. R. Driver, "Linguistic and Textual Problems: Jeremiah," *Jewish Quarterly Review*, XXVIII [1937-38], 111-12.) The Targ. reads, מתבטח ונפיל, "you feel secure and fall down." The verb may have the same meaning in Prov. 14:16.

By the jungle [lit., "the pride"] of the Jordan is meant the land immediately adjoining the river Jordan, which was filled with bushes and thick undergrowth, and was inhabited by wild animals. That it was the haunt of lions is shown by 49:19; 50:44; Zech. 11:3.

VII. Israel and Her Neighbors (12:7-17)

This section, which has no connection with the preceding, has as its common theme the relationship between Israel and her neighbors. In vss. 7-13 Yahweh laments the desolation of the land of Israel caused by her neighbors; vss. 14-17 describe how Yahweh will exile these "evil neighbors" but later restore them to their own land if they learn to worship him. Since the two parts have different origins, they will be treated separately.

A. Yahweh's Lament over Israel's Desolation (12:7-13)

This passage is unusual in several respects. It is a lamentation by Yahweh, not by the prophet, over the destruction caused in the land of Israel by enemies. It is lyric poetry of a type not frequently found in Jeremiah. It contains an abundance of figures to describe Israel: she is the heritage of Yahweh, the beloved of his soul (vs. 7) ; she is like a lion (vs. 8), or a speckled bird (vs. 9) ; she is Yahweh's vineyard (vs. 10) .

The poem seems to have originated in a specific situation when Israel was devastated by some of the neighboring peoples. Most commentators have followed Hitzig in supposing that it was composed after the invasion described in II Kings 24:2, when Nebuchadrezzar sent against Jehoiakim, as punishment for his rebellion, bands of Chaldeans, Arameans

---

fails: as in the opening lines of the fiftieth sonnet of Gerard Manley Hopkins' "Terrible Sonnets":

Thou art indeed just, Lord, if I contend
With thee; but, sir, so what I plead is just.
Why do sinners' ways prosper? and why must
Disappointment all I endeavour end? [1]

Again and again, in both Hopkins and Jeremiah, "we hear our hearts grate on themselves." Both were poets. Both were priests. But Hop-

kins was a Jesuit, and tried to sacrifice the word for the discipline, to forfeit the tangibilities of the one for the world-withdrawal of the other; whereas Jeremiah was a prophet, and found no conflict between the word of the poet and the Word of God, learning to sacrifice himself for both of them. The anguish of the one (Hopkins) left him "a lonely began"; the loneliness of the other (Jeremiah) brought him through anguish into fellowship with God.

7-17. *Yahweh's Heritage.*—The Exeg. traces here the prevailing view concerning this passage. It seems strange, however, that the carefully deliberated and construed poetic form

8 Mine heritage is unto me as a lion in the forest; it crieth out against me: therefore have I hated it.

9 Mine heritage *is* unto me *as* a speckled bird, the birds round about *are* against her; come ye, assemble all the beasts of the field, come to devour.

10 Many pastors have destroyed my vineyard, they have trodden my portion under foot, they have made my pleasant portion a desolate wilderness.

11 They have made it desolate, *and being* desolate it mourneth unto me; the

8 My heritage has become to me
    like a lion in the forest,
she has lifted up her voice against me;
    therefore I hate her.
9 Is my heritage to me like a speckled bird
    of prey?
Are the birds of prey against her round
    about?
Go, assemble all the wild beasts;
    bring them to devour.
10 Many shepherds have destroyed my vineyard,
    they have trampled down my portion,
they have made my pleasant portion
    a desolate wilderness.
11 They have made it a desolation;
    desolate, it mourns to me.

(or Edomites, if one emends ארם to אדם), Moabites, and Ammonites. The description of the marauders as **birds of prey** and **many shepherds** would fit such an invasion better than that of the Scythians, or that of the Chaldeans at a later time. The date was *ca.* 602 B.C. The prophet makes it clear, however, that the invaders were sent by Yahweh to punish Israel for her sins (vss. 8, 13).

7. **My house** is either the temple, as in 11:15, *et al.*, or the house of Israel, as in Hos. 8:1; 9:15. In the present context the latter is more probable. **My heritage** is the land of Israel (cf. I Sam. 10:1; I Kings 8:53; II Kings 21:14; *et al.*). The idea is especially frequent in literature of Deuteronomic origin. For Israel as **the beloved of my soul,** cf. 11:15; Isa. 5:1.

9. Israel is **like a speckled bird** that is attacked by other **birds of prey** because of its brightly colored plumage. The last half of the verse is similar to Isa. 56:9; it may be taken as the words of the birds of prey to one another (so Volz).

10. **Many shepherds** are kings of foreign nations that trample upon Yahweh's **vineyard** (for **pastors** see Exeg. on 2:8). For the idea of Israel as Yahweh's vineyard cf. 2:21; 5:10; Isa. 5:1-7; *et al.*

(vss. 7-13) should be recognized and that the clear literary dependence of this section upon what immediately precedes it should be ignored. Clearly the imagery upon which it is based (especially vss. 7-8) is carried over from Jeremiah's experience at Anathoth. The results of his encounter and rejection there are now employed to dramatize Yahweh's experience with his people. When Jeremiah uses such phrases as **I have forsaken my house, . . . abandoned my heritage,** and given up **the beloved of my soul,** the conscious or unconscious overtones of his personal experience are too apparent to be set aside. Similarly when Yahweh remarks

    My heritage has become to me
    like a lion in the forest,

the poetic carry-over from Jeremiah's rebuke in vs. 5 is obvious. So also the expression of Yahweh's hate because **she has lifted up her voice against me** is too plain a projection on

Jeremiah's part to pass without remark. As the perspective moves out, in the next verses, to the beleaguered conditions of the people in general, it is not necessary to petition the Chaldeans as a necessary historical explanation. The heritage, which could include Israel as well as Judah, has indeed become like a **bird of prey,** and the wild beasts are assembled all about her ready to devour. Meanwhile depredations have been wrought, the vineyards trampled down, and the people driven increasingly into the fortified towns. Either that, or, like the so-called "Scythian poems," the description may easily be a prediction of what is shortly to befall. The people shall be **ashamed of their harvests:** the wheat which they have sown is trampled down and wild thorns have grown up instead. The **destroyers** have made the land a desolation: **desolate, it mourns to me.** In any case, the main point is that once more the people have brought destruction upon them-

whole land is made desolate, because no man layeth *it* to heart.

12 The spoilers are come upon all high places through the wilderness: for the sword of the LORD shall devour from the *one* end of the land even to the *other* end of the land: no flesh shall have peace.

13 They have sown wheat, but shall reap thorns: they have put themselves to pain, *but* shall not profit: and they shall be ashamed of your revenues because of the fierce anger of the LORD.

14 ¶ Thus saith the LORD against all mine evil neighbors, that touch the inheritance which I have caused my people Israel to inherit; Behold, I will pluck them out of their land, and pluck out the house of Judah from among them.

15 And it shall come to pass, after that I have plucked them out I will return, and have compassion on them, and will bring them again, every man to his heritage, and every man to his land.

The whole land is made desolate,
  but no man lays it to heart.
12 Upon all the bare heights in the desert
  destroyers have come;
for the sword of the LORD devours
  from one end of the land to the other;
  no flesh has peace.
13 They have sown wheat and have reaped
    thorns,
  they have tired themselves out but
    profit nothing.
They shall be ashamed of their[u] harvests
  because of the fierce anger of the
    LORD."

14 Thus says the LORD concerning all my evil neighbors who touch the heritage which I have given my people Israel to inherit: "Behold, I will pluck them up from their land, and I will pluck up the house of Judah from among them. 15 And after I have plucked them up, I will again have compassion on them, and I will bring them again each to his heritage and each to his

[u] Heb *your*

---

13. This verse must refer to the Israelites, not the enemies; it gives the prophet's reason for the desolation of the land of Israel.

B. EXILE AND RESTORATION OF ISRAEL'S NEIGHBORS (12:14-17)

This is a prose passage which has been added to the above poem, partly in order to soften the strong feeling against the Israelites expressed in the poem, especially in vss. 8, 13. Though it is not wholly out of harmony with Jeremiah's teaching, the entire passage is probably editorial for the following reasons: (*a*) in the poem Yahweh sends Israel's neighbors to punish her, but here they are **my evil neighbors;** (*b*) in the poem Israel is in Palestine, but here in exile (vs. 14*b*); (*c*) the idea that foreign nations must learn **the ways of my people** (vs. 16) is alien to Jeremiah's thinking (see his condemnation of their ways in 2:23, 33; 3:21; 4:18); and (*d*) the passage is like others which come from later writers who anticipate the conversion of foreigners: see 3:17 (editorial); Isa. 2:2-4; 19:19-22; 56:6-7. The passage is considered secondary by Stade, Duhm, Volz, *et al.;* Rudolph considers only vs. 14 genuine; Giesebrecht and Cornill think it has a Jeremianic kernel which has been expanded by later writers.

15. For the idea of a restoration of foreign nations, cf. 48:47 (Moab); 49:6 (Ammon).

---

selves, not by being abandoned of God, but by having abandoned him. Their labors of spirit make the heart weary and nothing profits.

The oracle which follows (vss. 14-17) is interesting in that there is no precise historical parallel for the things here predicted. It is interesting, therefore, as throwing some light on Jeremiah's view of history, if the verses are indeed of Jeremiah's authorship. The repetition of the words "pluck up" and "build up," reminiscent of Jeremiah's commission (1:10),

is possibly too studied to be genuine. What is important to note, however, is the alternation between the punishment of the nations (**neighbors**) and the subsequent relenting to those peoples who will learn the way of Yahweh and live as devotedly by him as they have formerly done by Baal. This gives considerable scope to the prediction. The exile of the peoples round about Judah becomes a part of the divine plan. And the summoning of the peoples to the worship of Yahweh is an expansion of the

16 And it shall come to pass, if they will diligently learn the ways of my people, to swear by my name, The LORD liveth; as they taught my people to swear by Baal; then shall they be built in the midst of my people.

17 But if they will not obey, I will utterly pluck up and destroy that nation, saith the LORD.

13 Thus saith the LORD unto me, Go and get thee a linen girdle, and put it upon thy loins, and put it not in water.

land. 16 And it shall come to pass, if they will diligently learn the ways of my people, to swear by my name, 'As the LORD lives,' even as they taught my people to swear by Ba'al, then they shall be built up in the midst of my people. 17 But if any nation will not listen, then I will utterly pluck it up and destroy it, says the LORD."

13 Thus said the LORD to me, "Go and buy a linen waistcloth, and put it on your loins, and do not dip it in water."

17. The author has drawn upon 1:10; Volz speaks of the passage as a homily on that verse.

VIII. PARABLES AND WARNINGS (13:1-27)

This chapter contains five passages which do not have any common theme. All are somewhat pessimistic in tone, and come from the latter part of Jehoiakim's reign, or even later.

A. PARABLE OF THE WAISTCLOTH (13:1-11)

Few passages in Jeremiah are as puzzling to the interpreter as this. Duhm thought that even to raise the question whether Jeremiah wrote it was to disparage the prophet; only one who considered the prophets as marionettes could think of him as carrying out the symbolic action here described. Duhm therefore considered it as secondary and late. But this is to apply modern criteria to the prophets, rather than ancient ones, and to suppose that the story is necessarily historical.

There are indeed great difficulties in accepting the passage as a record of a series of acts by Jeremiah. The distance from Judah to the Euphrates River was at least four hundred miles; at a later time Ezra required four months for the trip from Babylon to Jerusalem (Ezra 7:9). Jeremiah would have had to make two round trips to the Euphrates. The real difficulty, however, is in seeing how such trips could have been given meaning to the people living in Judah. Some scholars have sought to obviate this difficulty by supposing that the place to which he went was not the Euphrates River but a small town named Parah, mentioned in Josh. 18:23, modern Khirbet el-Fârah, about four miles northeast of Anathoth (an interpretation first proposed by Schick in 1867, and accepted by Driver, et al.). This, however, is a very doubtful expedient. The Hebrew *perâth* elsewhere always refers to the Euphrates (though it is usually preceded by נהר, "river"); and there would be no significance in the place if it referred only to a small town in Palestine.

It is best therefore to interpret the passage as a spoken parable (Volz, Cornill, et al.), or possibly as the report of a vision experience (Rudolph). The most likely meaning is that Judah is corrupted by its political and religious alliances with Mesopotamia, or specifically with Babylonia. This interpretation is supported by 2:18, with its condemnation of the people for drinking the waters of the Euphrates (see Exeg., ad loc.). The

covenantal hope beyond the preclusive interests of the Hebrew people. This would imply that the nature of God as Jeremiah understands it, and of his ordinances and communications toward the world, is universal; and if any nation will not listen then it will be utterly plucked up and eventually destroyed, whereas those peoples who diligently learn shall come to know his compassion and shall once more be established.

13:1-11. The Parable of the Loincloth.—We have remarked above (5:1) on the ironic strategy employed by Diogenes in Athens. When begging from a statue, he was asked, "What are you doing, Diogenes?" To which he replied, "I am learning to be refused." Again, when he was observed entering a theater when all the people were leaving, he explained that this had always been his custom. And when he began trampling up and down on Plato's costly rugs,

2 So I got a girdle according to the word of the Lord, and put *it* on my loins.

3 And the word of the Lord came unto me the second time, saying,

4 Take the girdle that thou hast got, which *is* upon thy loins, and arise, go to Euphrates, and hide it there in a hole of the rock.

5 So I went, and hid it by Euphrates, as the Lord commanded me.

6 And it came to pass after many days, that the Lord said unto me, Arise, go to Euphrates, and take the girdle from thence, which I commanded thee to hide there.

7 Then I went to Euphrates, and digged, and took the girdle from the place where I had hid it: and, behold, the girdle was marred, it was profitable for nothing.

8 Then the word of the Lord came unto me, saying,

9 Thus saith the Lord, After this manner will I mar the pride of Judah, and the great pride of Jerusalem.

2 So I bought a waistcloth according to the word of the Lord, and put it on my loins.

3 And the word of the Lord came to me a second time, 4 "Take the waistcloth which you have bought, which is upon your loins, and arise, go to the Eu·phra'tes, and hide it there in a cleft of the rock." 5 So I went, and hid it by the Eu·phra'tes, as the Lord commanded me. 6 And after many days the Lord said to me, "Arise, go to the Eu·phra'tes, and take from there the waistcloth which I commanded you to hide there." 7 Then I went to the Eu·phra'tes, and dug, and I took the waistcloth from the place where I had hidden it. And behold, the waistcloth was spoiled; it was good for nothing.

8 Then the word of the Lord came to me: 9 "Thus says the Lord: Even so will I spoil the pride of Judah and the great pride

date, then, is probably in the reign of Jehoiakim, after the battle of Carchemish (605 B.C.), when that king turned his allegiance to Nebuchadrezzar.

Volz's interpretation of the passage as referring to the corruption of Judah in the Babylonian exile is not satisfactory. Jeremiah did not think of the Exile as necessarily corrupting to Judah (see ch. 29); rather, it came as the result of their corruption. If Volz presses the point that the waistcloth was taken to the Euphrates, then we must remember that it was also brought back from the Euphrates to Judah. The parable has only one main point, and it is dangerous to strain the meaning of all its details.

Vs. 11 is to be recognized by its terminology as a Deuteronomic addition, making an unnecessary application of one of the details of the parable (cf. Deut. 26:19, and the use of the verb "cleave" in Deut. 10:20; 11:22; 13:4; 30:20; Josh. 22:5; 23:8; II Kings 18:6).

13:1. The object was a **waistcloth** or loincloth, not a **girdle** (or sash, as we might now say). It was a garment such as that worn by Elijah, his being made of skin (II Kings

to the consternation of Plato's guests, he explained, "I am trampling on Plato's pride!" Plato's reply on this occasion was particularly keen: "But with what pride of your own, Diogenes!" [2] In all of these instances, these "acted parables" of Diogenes were for a particular purpose; their design was ironical, intending through this extraordinary behavior to guide the people into ways of sounder sense or sanity.

The acted parables or symbolic actions of the prophets were altogether different. Behind both the prophetic oracle and the symbolic act there is a long tradition of Semitic divination and magic as a formative element informing the consciousness of the prophets and that of the people as well. "Both the prophet and his con-

temporaries believe the declared Word of prophecy to be a mysterious entity which cannot fail to fulfill itself in the outward embodiment of event. It not only reveals but effectually determines the shape of things to come. Hence, it excites awe and fear in the hearers." [3] To be sure, these formative elements have undergone development. The prophetic symbolism has "ceased to be magic and [become] religion," as H. Wheeler Robinson [4] holds. Moreover the devices employed by the magician were employed to coerce the mysterious powers to the magician's special ends, whereas the prophets' practices are in the interests of the Lord. It is doubtless true that "the prophets work with the

[2] Diogenes Laërtius, *The Lives and Opinions of Eminent Philosophers*, Bk. VI.

[3] Knight, *Hebrew Prophetic Consciousness*, p. 48.

[4] *Redemption and Revelation* (New York: Harper & Bros., 1942), p. 250.

10 This evil people, which refuse to hear my words, which walk in the imagination of their heart, and walk after other gods, to serve them, and to worship them, shall even be as this girdle, which is good for nothing.

11 For as the girdle cleaveth to the loins of a man, so have I caused to cleave unto me the whole house of Israel and the whole house of Judah, saith the LORD; that they might be unto me for a people, and for a name, and for a praise, and for a glory: but they would not hear.

12 ¶ Therefore thou shalt speak unto them this word; Thus saith the LORD God

of Jerusalem. **10** This evil people, who refuse to hear my words, who stubbornly follow their own heart and have gone after other gods to serve them and worship them, shall be like this waistcloth, which is good for nothing. **11** For as the waistcloth clings to the loins of a man, so I made the whole house of Israel and the whole house of Judah cling to me, says the LORD, that they might be for me a people, a name, a praise, and a glory, but they would not listen.

12 "You shall speak to them this word:

1:8; cf. Isa. 5:27; 11:5). Possibly it was thought of as being of **linen** because priests wore garments of that material (Lev: 16:4), and Judah was a priestly nation; but that detail may have no significance apart from the fact that linen would easily rot, and skin or leather would not.

B. PARABLE OF THE JARS (13:12-14)

In this brief passage Jeremiah takes up a popular proverb, or a common tippler's saying, and uses it as the basis of a warning to the people. The saying may seem to us quite

---

ancient quasi-magical conception of the Word as an unquenchable independent energy which must produce the effects proper to it." [5] But magic, meanwhile, has passed over into religion, and religion has reached its highest and most perceptive expression in the qualitative leap of the prophetic consciousness. Yet, as we approach the several symbolic actions of the prophet Jeremiah, we must recognize that, for him and for the people, "to speak a word, . . . is to introduce a new potentiality into the stream of historical events." [6] And, as Guillaume puts it, "The preaching of the word of Yahweh might only enrage: the presence of a sign could terrify." [7] In other words, the prophetic oracle carries with it the authority of mysterious powers, enhanced by the more formidable aspects of Yahweh's character as understood by the people; this is much more the case with the symbolic actions which, as actualizations of the word *in parvo*, already have the effect of putting in motion what they are meant to symbolize.

In the present instance, therefore, there is no point in complaining, with Duhm, that Jeremiah's journeys to the "Euphrates" are ridiculous suppositions. From our contemporary point of view, yes; but they were neither quaint nor nonsensical to the people for whose instruction they were performed. Similarly, to

treat them as dramatic illustrations calculated, like those of Diogenes, to attract and capture the imagination and fancy of the people, is to miss their point. For they are examples with power, as the oracles were pronouncements with power. And the people understood them as such.

In like manner it is unnecessary to take the term "Euphrates" literally. A journey of 400 miles, twice repeated, is not necessary to the prophet's symbolization. But a symbolic journey of some sort would be in keeping with the divinitory form.

The message of the journey falls strictly within Jeremiah's covenantal consciousness. Israel, in her early days, was like the unsoiled linen wherewith the Lord had sought to adorn himself. This people had been chosen to ornament his person in the world; and he bound it to him in the covenant relation. But the cloth was unfaithful, seeking to secure itself secretly with Assyria and Babylon. Dealings of this sort usually carried with them recognition of the foreign people's gods. By exposure to the river's damp the linen had become corrupt, just as Judah, through becoming idolatrous and obstinate, had become corrupt and **good for nothing.** And once more, as in so many cases heretofore, the passage closes with the prophetic phrase, **but they would not listen.**

12-14. The Parable of the Jars.—This second parable is perhaps not as dramatic as

[5] Knight, *op. cit.*, p. 49.
[6] *Ibid.*
[7] *Prophecy and Divination*, p. 150.

of Israel, Every bottle shall be filled with wine: and they shall say unto thee, Do we not certainly know that every bottle shall be filled with wine?

13 Then shalt thou say unto them, Thus saith the LORD, Behold, I will fill all the inhabitants of this land, even the kings that sit upon David's throne, and the priests, and the prophets, and all the inhabitants of Jerusalem, with drunkenness.

14 And I will dash them one against another, even the fathers and the sons together, saith the LORD: I will not pity, nor spare, nor have mercy, but destroy them.

15 ¶ Hear ye, and give ear; be not proud: for the LORD hath spoken.

'Thus says the LORD, the God of Israel, "Every jar shall be filled with wine."' And they will say to you, 'Do we not indeed know that every jar will be filled with wine?' 13 Then you shall say to them, 'Thus says the LORD: Behold, I will fill with drunkenness all the inhabitants of this land: the kings who sit on David's throne, the priests, the prophets, and all the inhabitants of Jerusalem. 14 And I will dash them one against another, fathers and sons together, says the LORD. I will not pity or spare or have compassion, that I should not destroy them.'"

15 Hear and give ear; be not proud,
　　for the LORD has spoken.

---

banal, but the prophet was capable of using a banal proverb for his purposes. Possibly he spoke at some sacrificial feast when much wine was being consumed. In the application (vs. 13), the drunkenness coming from Yahweh is symbolic of the divine judgment, as in 25:15-28; Ezek. 23:31-34; Isa. 51:17; Ps. 60:3. Vs. 14 may have reference to civil strife or the clash of opposing political parties in Judah, such as existed especially in the reign of Zedekiah.

12. The translation **jar** is preferable to **bottle**. The *nēbhel* was a large storage jar used for oil and grain as well as wine. The largest found in excavations hold nearly ten gallons and measure about twenty-five inches in height and sixteen inches in diameter. The same word is used for wineskins, but that would not be appropriate here (Kelso, *Ceramic Vocabulary of the O.T.*, pp. 25-26).

C. WARNING AGAINST PRIDE (13:15-17)

15-17. This poem is marked by a tone different from the preceding pronouncements of judgment. Here the prophet earnestly pleads with the people to give up their pride

---

the first, but its accusation is more direct. Jeremiah may have been near the potter's gate, much as we see him on a later occasion watching the earthen vessels there as they came from the potter's wheel. Or it may be that he was present at some festival and standing near the empty jars. He begins, in any case, with a truism: **every jar shall be filled with wine.** Quoting this familiar proverb, or "toper's witticism," [8] with his hand, perhaps, upon the jar, he would easily have gained the attention of the people about him. Being already apprehensive of the prophet's messages, and seeing in his word and gesture the prelude to some oracle, they might well have replied derisively, "Of course, everybody knows that!" Whereupon the prophet turns upon them—"then you must tell them straight" (Moffatt) that, as every jar shall be filled with wine, so shall all the people be filled with drunkenness: the kings (Jehoiachin and the queen mother?), the priests, the proph-

[8] Peake, *Jeremiah and Lamentations*, I, 195.

ets, and all the people. The symbol of the wine is doubtless anticipatory of the wine of the wrath of God (Jer. 25:15; 51:7; cf. Ps. 75:8; Isa. 19:14-15; Rev. 16:19). Since this wrath is taking the forms which we already know, the symbol of intoxication serves well to exhibit the behavior of the people in their panic-stricken, fumbling stupidities, unable to make decisions in principle because of their moral corruption and confusion, helpless for want of leadership and inwardly defeated for want of faith. Hence they will fall upon one another, **fathers and sons together**, destroying themselves from within and being destroyed from without. The figure is harsh; but not more harsh than the people's need to be shaken out of their purblind lethargy, and not more harsh than the realities of the punishment when it came.

15-17. *A Secret Weeping.*—Concerning this poem the commentators have practically nothing to say. Yet it remains one of the priceless jewels of Hebrew literature. Gordon speaks of

16 Give glory to the Lord your God, before he cause darkness, and before your feet stumble upon the dark mountains, and, while ye look for light, he turn it into the shadow of death, *and* make *it* gross darkness.

16 Give glory to the Lord your God
before he brings darkness,
before your feet stumble
on the twilight mountains,
and while you look for light
he turns it into gloom
and makes it deep darkness.

and turn to God before it is too late. Vs. 17 shows his deep sympathy with the sorrows of the people, brought on by their failure to listen to him.

The poem is difficult to date because of its general nature, and because we do not know whether the last line of vs. 17 is prophecy or statement of fact. If it is the latter, the date is probably the first deportation of the Jews to Babylonia in 598 B.C. This is made more likely by the proximity to vss. 18-19, which can be dated.

it as "one of the loveliest and most pathetic cameos in his whole poetic output." [9] George Adam Smith speaks of its "sombre . . . vague and far-looming" premonitions of doom.[1] There may be a "gleam" of hope from one of Jehoiakim's ill-advised alliances, or perhaps even from the hypnotic belief in the inviolability of Jerusalem. But it is already very late. *Der Untergang des Abendlandes* has already been written (Zephaniah, *ca.* 626); the "patriot" prophet, Nahum, has rejoiced too soon (*ca.* 605) over Nineveh's fall. Jehoiakim had made his blunders and his fatal compromises. The twilight of Judaic civilization was at hand. The "darkness" was a *kairos* darkness: the kind of lowering storm cloud which appeared at times in connection with theophanies (Exod. 20:21; I Kings 8:12), but which, on the other hand, was ominous like the shadow of death. The hour was dark: the drops, the ledges, the "cliffs of fall" (Hopkins), were everywhere about them. One very slender hope remained—a hope against hope, so callous had the people been to Yahweh's word.

No one who loves poetry could remain insensible of the pathos of vss. 15-17. They have that power to move which only the finest poetry has. And they speak to the heart of the hurt of the world, where the most secret wound lies open to tears. No one who has loved, or suffered loss, or been ashamed, or been disillusioned or betrayed, or been lost with himself in the valley of shadows, or who has stood helpless before the hurt of a child (with learning of earthly achievement filling both his hands) but will know something of this secret weeping.

But if he is not destroyed by the very depth of pathos, and if he is mastered by creative innocence, it is because he is upheld in the way that Thomas à Kempis knew: *Si crucem*

portas, portabit te, "he who carries his cross, his cross will carry." [2]

But there is a further dimension in this pathetic identification with the world's plight in any given time. It is not easy; and the prophet must become one with the suffering at the heart of the world. There was a secret weeping in Gethsemane. "My soul is ringed round with sorrow!" (Matt. 26:38) is the pathetic word (περίλυπός) spoken there: and by one who had said, a brief hour before, "Be of good cheer, I have overcome the world" (John 16:33). The three who saw Christ's agony in the Garden were so little moved that they slept! Was there not, perhaps, a pathetic note of bitterness, together with acceptance and compassion, in the words, "Could you not watch with me one hour" (Matt. 26:40)? But the mystery of this moment (this divine *kairos*, or fullness of time) consists in that which Pascal saw: "Jesus will be in agony even to the end of the world." The divine pathos is implied; and Pascal's warning continues to apply: "Do not be caught asleep then!" [3]

This is not unlike Jeremiah's **But if you will not listen.** And the ways of sleeping, or of refusing to listen, remain the same: by pursuing the several proliferations of flight from the meeting place between God and ourselves, through idolatries as manifest as "people" or "party" or Baal, or as subtle as the soft core of contemporary sophistication; through harlotries of compromise and infidelities of fear; through indifference to the "heritage" or through "action" and "reform" at secondary levels. "A man was astonished how easily he went the eternal way," wrote Kafka. "He happened to be rushing backwards along it." [4]

In Jeremiah's time the Word had been spoken. He himself had spoken in the temple

[9] *Rebel Prophet*, p. 180.
[1] *Jeremiah*, p. 59.

[2] *The Imitation of Christ* II. 12.
[3] *Thoughts*, No. 552, "The Mystery of Jesus."
[4] *Great Wall of China*, p. 286.

17 But if ye will not hear it, my soul shall weep in secret places for *your* pride; and mine eye shall weep sore, and run down with tears, because the LORD's flock is carried away captive.

18 Say unto the king and to the queen, Humble yourselves, sit down: for your principalities shall come down, *even* the crown of your glory.

17 But if you will not listen,
  my soul will weep in secret for your pride;
my eyes will weep bitterly and run down with tears,
  because the LORD's flock has been taken captive.

18 Say to the king and the queen mother:
  "Take a lowly seat,
for your beautiful crown
  has come down from your head."*v*

v Gk Syr Vg: Heb obscure

D. LAMENT OVER THE KING AND QUEEN MOTHER (13:18-19)

In all probability **the king** here referred to is Jehoiachin and **the queen mother** is Nehushta. He was the son of Jehoiakim who died during the first siege of Jerusalem by the Babylonians. Jehoiachin then succeeded to the throne, but after only three months surrendered to the Babylonians and was taken into exile (598 B.C.). His mother is prominently mentioned in connection with him; since he was only eighteen years of age

---

gate. He had prepared his "book"; the "foe from the north" poems had been included, the "foe" at last identified as the Chaldeans. It is possible, according to some, that this very poem may have been a part of the "roll" read before Jehoiakim and cut and burned by him in the brazier. Or could it have been written immediately thereafter, when, still in hiding,[5] Jeremiah received the news of the proud action of the king? If so, there is more sorrow than bitterness in Jeremiah's word to this pathetic king: "Be not too proud to hearken" (Moffatt). **Give glory to the LORD** before it is too late. Being wise in one's own conceits is always pathetic: it always "goes before destruction, [as] a haughty spirit before a fall" (Prov. 16:18). In the universal scorn and contempt for the prophetic word Jeremiah has already come to know what it means to be "despised and rejected by men" (Isa. 53:3).

This is not merely the prophet's pathos: it is the divine pathos as well. Here the prophet's sorrow is one with the divine sorrow. God, for the Hebrew, does not stand beyond or "outside the range of human . . . suffering. He is the greatest sufferer of all, because He alone can realize the true spiritual repercussions of the drama of human history."[6] For the same reason —but extended into the heart of God—the prophet becomes a hearer and a mouthpiece of the Lord. The Unmoved Mover is no part of the theological consciousness of the Hebrew prophet.

[5] Duhm, *Das Buch Jeremia*, pp. 122-23.
[6] Knight, *Hebrew Prophetic Consciousness*, p. 138. Cf. pp. 138-50. Cf. also Heschel, *op. cit.*, pp. 164-65, *et passim*.

The central truth of the theology implicit in the prophetic consciousness is just this *Erlebbarkeit* for God of human life and experience. Since God is perfect goodness, He is the one Being who is capable of feeling to the full the tragedy of the world's evil. He is the One whom everything concerns, because He lives in and with the created universe, gathering it up into the heart of His eternal life.[7]

The powerful proclamation in Isa. 46:4b supports this:

  I have made, and I will bear;
  I will carry and will save.

By this we perceive that we are already entrained, as the French would say, in a movement of ideas that runs from Hosea through Jeremiah to the Suffering Servant passages of Second Isaiah and so to the Cross.

Jeremiah reads many ciphers within the perspective of ruin—the almond branch, the caldron, the loincloth, the jars, the potter's wheel, the yoke, the packet of earth at Anathoth. He has also discovered, like Job, that the Eternal speaks in the tempest. But in the shock of pathos God speaks more deeply still. For here, at the point of silence, we perceive the secret weeping, where God and his prophet shed bitter tears "for the Eternal's flock borne off to exile" (Moffatt; cf. Ps. 119:136). Thus Jeremiah read the cipher of the God who loved and cared—and who loves and cares forever.

18-19. *Alas! For the Crown Hath Fallen!*— The lament which follows undoubtedly carries us forward to the brief reign of Jehoiachin, to

[7] *Ibid.*, pp. 138-39. Cf. Heschel, *op. cit.*, pp. 56, 67, 70, 130-31.

19 The cities of the south shall be shut up, and none shall open *them:* Judah shall be carried away captive all of it, it shall be wholly carried away captive.

20 Lift up your eyes, and behold them that come from the north: where *is* the

19 The cities of the Negeb are shut up,
 with none to open them;
all Judah is taken into exile,
 wholly taken into exile.

20 "Lift up your eyes and see
 those who come from the north.

---

at his accession, he was probably strongly under her influence (see 22:24-30; 29:2; II Kings 24:6-17).

18. The KJV has taken the obscure word מראשותיכם to mean **your principalities;** the RSV follows the LXX, Vulg., and Syriac in reading as if it were *mērā'shēkhem,* **from your head,** which is doubtless correct.

19. The Negeb was the southern part of Judah. In the first Babylonian invasion of 599-98 B.C. some of the cities of this region were probably attacked, but not separated from Judah. **Are shut up, with none to open them:** The gates of the cities were closed as protection against the enemy. The towns of the Negeb had to defend themselves, since Jerusalem could not aid them. The last half of this verse is prophetic hyperbole.

E. The Shame of Jerusalem (13:20-27)

Here Jerusalem is addressed under the personification of a woman. She is a shepherdess who has forsaken her flock, and is now about to be dishonored by those whom she has previously known as friends. The date is after the battle of Carchemish (605 B.C.), perhaps close to the time of the first Chaldean invasion (599-98). Since the reign of Hezekiah the Judeans had at intervals been friendly with the Chaldeans (II Kings 20:12-19), and after the battle of Carchemish Jehoiakim paid tribute to Nebuchadrezzar (II Kings 24:1); when later he withheld tribute, Nebuchadrezzar attacked him.

Vss. 23-24 are probably out of order. Vs. 23*b* uses the second person plural pronoun, and vs. 24, the third person plural, whereas the rest of the poem employs the second person feminine singular, addressing the personified Jerusalem. Vss. 23-24 may originally have stood after vs. 27 and have been composed as a reply to the question raised in that verse.

20-21. The LXX adds "Jerusalem" after **your eyes;** this may have been in the Hebrew text used by the LXX, or may simply have been added by the translators to make the

---

the time when the preceding prophecy was fulfilled. When Jehoiachin succeeded to the throne (see Exeg.) he was but eighteen years of age and, apparently, well thought of by the people (cf. 22:24-27). It is possible that this oracle, addressed to the king and the queen mother, might well have influenced his surrender to Nebuchadrezzar.

The pathos of vs. 18 is very moving. The nation with its people is humbled. From its head the golden crown has fallen. There is nothing that the king or the queen mother can do but to accept in abject humility the realities of the situation. As Bunyan says:

He that is down, need fear no fall;
 He that is low, no Pride;
He that is humble, ever shall
 Have God to be his Guide.[8]

[8] *The Pilgrim's Progress,* Part II, Song in the Valley of Humiliation.

Here the pathos is that humility passes over into humiliation.

Because of Jerusalem's situation, the strategy of the attackers always began by cutting off the southern cities of the Negeb. Once these are cut away the final fact is as good as accomplished: **all Judah is taken into exile.** Shortly hereafter the eighteen-year-old king, with the elite of his community, is carried away to Babylon.

20-27. Jerusalem, How Long?—This warning of the approaching foe from the north contains something of the spirit of the early "Scythian poems." It is, however, much later, and is typical of the open warnings with which Jeremiah warned the people and flayed the rulers during the period of Jehoiakim. The verses gain much in power when surrounded with the struggle and turmoil, opposition and clash, which characterized the turbulent career of the prophet during this reign.

flock *that* was given thee, thy beautiful flock?

21 What wilt thou say when he shall punish thee? for thou hast taught them *to be* captains, *and* as chief over thee: shall not sorrows take thee, as a woman in travail?

22 ¶ And if thou say in thine heart, Wherefore come these things upon me? For the greatness of thine iniquity are thy skirts discovered, *and* thy heels made bare.

23 Can the Ethiopian change his skin, or the leopard his spots? *then* may ye also do good, that are accustomed to do evil.

Where is the flock that was given you,
    your beautiful flock?
21 What will you say when they set as head
    over you
    those whom you yourself have taught
    to be friends to you?
Will not pangs take hold of you,
    like those of a woman in travail?
22 And if you say in your heart,
    'Why have these things come upon me?'
    it is for the greatness of your iniquity
    that your skirts are lifted up,
    and you suffer violence.
23 Can the Ethiopian change his skin
    or the leopard his spots?
Then also you can do good
    who are accustomed to do evil.

---

object of address clear (cf. vs. 27*b*). **The flock:** The inhabitants of Jerusalem, and perhaps of Judah, who were under the care of the capital city.

Vs. 21*a* is difficult to translate, but the RSV is more nearly correct than the KJV. The reference is to the Chaldeans; cf. "your lovers" in 4:30, also a reference to the Chaldeans.

22. The last line reads, lit., "your heels be made to suffer violence"; "your heels" is a euphemism for the secret parts, like "feet" in Deut. 28:57; Ezek. 16:25. The RSV paraphrases.

23. This famous verse is not intended to deny the freedom of the will, or to deny absolutely the possibility of repentance. It is a recognition of the force in human life of custom or habit and of training. The last line is, lit., "who are learned in evil." Man is born with freedom of the will, but through habit his will may become virtually unfree. The verse expresses the truth of John 8:34, "Every one who commits sin is a slave to sin." **The Ethiopian** was dark-skinned. It was an Ethiopian, Ebed-melech, who later rescued Jeremiah from certain death (38:7-13).

Their message is clear. Jeremiah has seen and properly read the meaning of the battle of Carchemish. The balance of world power has shifted from the Assyrians to the Chaldeans. These are they who are certainly coming to overwhelm Jerusalem.

> What will you say when you feel the sway
> of those you trained as allies? (Moffatt.)

The illicit relations which Jerusalem, the shepherdess, has held both religiously and politically with these "lovers" are now about to turn upon her: her "lovers" are about to become her tyrants. And should Jerusalem wonder why,

> it is for a host of sins
> that you are exposed and stripped (Moffatt).

So inured in this corrupt behavior have the people become that they are hopelessly fixed in it. They are no more capable of changing their ways than an Ethiopian could change his skin

or a leopard his spots. Therefore they will be scattered, because they forgot the Lord and "relied on what was false" (Moffatt).

It is hardly necessary to point out that Jeremiah is not speaking in vs. 23 of "natural evil" or of any "radical defect in human nature." He is not saying that men are so necessarily sinners that they are like the Ethiopian or the leopard and can do nothing about it. He is, however, saying that whether totally black or only spotted the perspective of evil in the people is so fixed that they *will* do nothing about it. The cause of it is the foundation cause: they have forgotten the Lord. Therefore the disasters come. "How long," he had asked before, "shall your evil thoughts lodge within you?" (4:14) and how often he had said,

> Be warned, O Jerusalem,
> lest I be alienated from you (6:8).

Even now, he repeats the pathetic hope (vs. 27*b*).

24 Therefore will I scatter them as the stubble that passeth away by the wind of the wilderness.

25 This *is* thy lot, the portion of thy measures from me, saith the Lord; because thou hast forgotten me, and trusted in falsehood.

26 Therefore will I discover thy skirts upon thy face, that thy shame may appear.

27 I have seen thine adulteries, and thy neighings, the lewdness of thy whoredom, *and* thine abominations on the hills in the fields. Woe unto thee, O Jerusalem! wilt thou not be made clean? when *shall it* once *be?*

14 The word of the Lord that came to Jeremiah concerning the dearth.

---

24 I will scatter you[w] like chaff
    driven by the wind from the desert.
25 This is your lot,
    the portion I have measured out to
        you, says the Lord,
because you have forgotten me
    and trusted in lies.
26 I myself will lift up your skirts over your
        face,
    and your shame will be seen.
27 I have seen your abominations,
    your adulteries and neighings, your
        lewd harlotries,
    on the hills in the field.
Woe to you, O Jerusalem!
    How long will it be
    before you are made clean?"

14 The word of the Lord which came to Jeremiah concerning the drought:

[w] Heb *them*

---

27. **Neighings** is a figure for illicit love, derived from the neighing of the mare to the stallion (cf. 5:8; 50:11).

IX. A Drought and Other Catastrophes (14:1–15:4)

This section contains both genuine and secondary material that has been put in its present form by an editor. The heading in 14:1 indicates that it has to do with a drought. While some parts of the section fit this description (14:1-6, 22), others speak of catastrophes brought on by the sword, pestilence, etc. (14:16, 18; 15:2-3). Some of the material is genuine, but there are passages which show the influence of Deuteronomy and Second Isaiah.

The most clearly Jeremianic passage is 14:13-18. The opening verses (14:1-6) could be from the prophet, but have little of the prophetic note in them. Also, 14:7-9, 19-22, containing confessions of sin, may be from the prophet; but they are more likely secondary, since they contain phrases associated with later writers (see Exeg. below). An editor has artfully combined the genuine material with matter derived from other sources, and arranged the whole, partly in the form of dialogue. The editor lived after the time of the deportation in 587 B.C., and so could consider the sins of the people as beyond forgiveness. If he prefixed the title in 14:1, he was one of the latest editors of the book; the title has an unusual form in Hebrew, occurring elsewhere only in 1:2; 46:1; 47:1; 49:34.

The section divides itself into seven parts, according to subject matter and speaker; cf. the shift of speakers in 5:1-14.

A. Description of the Drought (14:1-6)

In Palestine the failure of rainfall has often caused much suffering, since the rainfall is not abundant at best. This is an artistic and vivid description of the suffering brought on by a drought: first in the cities (vss. 2-3), then in the countryside among the farmers (vs. 4), and finally even among the animals (vss. 5-6).

14:1-18. *Jeremiah's "Waste Land."*—Since there is slight agreement among the exegetes as to theme and date of these passages, or as to what is "from the hand of Jeremiah" and what is not, we shall do well to approach them from the standpoint of their aesthetic or dramatic structure. Hitzig, as exegete, breaks the chapters up into some eight isolated and disconnected pieces; Ball, as expositor, sees clear connections of a logical kind uniting the parts

2 Judah mourneth, and the gates thereof languish; they are black unto the ground; and the cry of Jerusalem is gone up.

3 And their nobles have sent their little ones to the waters: they came to the pits, *and* found no water; they returned with their vessels empty; they were ashamed and confounded, and covered their heads.

4 Because the ground is chapped, for there was no rain in the earth, the plowmen were ashamed, they covered their heads.

5 Yea, the hind also calved in the field, and forsook *it,* because there was no grass.

6 And the wild asses did stand in the high places, they snuffed up the wind like dragons; their eyes did fail, because *there was* no grass.

2 "Judah mourns
     and her gates languish;
   her people lament on the ground,
     and the cry of Jerusalem goes up.
3 Her nobles send their servants for water;
     they come to the cisterns,
   they find no water,
     they return with their vessels empty;
   they are ashamed and confounded
     and cover their heads.
4 Because of the ground which is dismayed,
     since there is no rain on the land,
   the farmers are ashamed,
     they cover their heads.
5 Even the hind in the field forsakes her
     newborn calf
   because there is no grass.
6 The wild asses stand on the bare heights,
     they pant for air like jackals;
   their eyes fail
     because there is no herbage.

14:2. The **gates** of Judah are personified, because at them the people frequently assembled, and at them cases at law were sometimes decided. The subject of **lament** (lit., **are black**) may be either **her people,** as supplied by the RSV, or the gates themselves, the personification being continued.

5-6. The poet selects as examples of the wild animals that suffer under the drought **the hind,** noted for its tender solicitude for its young, that now **forsakes her newborn calf** because of the lack of grass; and **the wild asses,** the hardiest of wild animals that would be among the last to suffer for lack of food and water.

into something approaching "a well-organized whole." [9] The advantage is with the expositor, though the connections are less of a logical than of an aesthetic kind.

The unifying perspective is to be sought somewhat along the analogy of chs. 5-6. There we see Jeremiah searching the squares of Jerusalem and reporting what he sees; here it is the conditions of drought and defeat which provide the observer's perspective. When and by whom this unifying factor was supplied we can only surmise. There remains open to us, from the standpoint of exposition, the recognition of its organizing principle conceived poetically or dramatically. This means that interpretative passages such as this should be read less like Gibbon's *Decline and Fall of the Roman Empire* and more like T. S. Eliot's *The Waste Land,* which owes much more to biblical antecedents than critics have conceded. One may note quickly that both poems are episodic in structure, comprised of units with no apparent connection, seemingly without meaning. Both poems unify their disjunct parts against

[9] Cf. *Prophecies of Jeremiah,* p. 300.

the background of drought—mystical and spiritual, not to say cultural, for Eliot; actual and spiritual for Jeremiah.

The plots of the two dramatic poems differ, though basic parallels remain. The major difference lies in the fact that Jeremiah's poem is elaborated against the background of the real absence of a real God, whereas Eliot's poem exploits the nondescript cultural and moral emptiness which results from the absence either of his presence *or* absence—that is, from not knowing whether there is or can be any God at all.

This is clear in the development of Jeremiah's poem. First the plight of the people from the drought (14:1-6), then the people's confessional prayer and Yahweh's answer to the prophet (14:7-10); then Jeremiah throws the blame on the false leadership of the prophets and priests, whom Yahweh condemns (14:11-19). Follows then the second confessional prayer of the people, with Yahweh's answer (14:19–15:4) and a review of the military disaster which he has already sent to punish them (15:5-9). This throws the prophet back

7 ¶ O Lord, though our iniquities testify against us, do thou *it* for thy name's sake: for our backslidings are many; we have sinned against thee.	7 "Though our iniquities testify against us, act, O Lord, for thy name's sake; for our backslidings are many, we have sinned against thee.

B. Confession of Sin (14:7-9)

The people confess their sins and cry to the Lord for help. Since the Hebrews believed that an affliction such as drought was sent as punishment for sin, they thought that relief could come only if they repented of their sins and cried to Yahweh for deliverance. These verses represent either an actual confession of the people, probably in a temple ceremony, or an ideal confession which the prophet believed they should make (as in 3:22-25; Hos. 14:2-3).

7. For thy name's sake: For the sake of God's reputation, and because of his nature as a God of mercy. The phrase is especially frequent in Psalms (23:3; 25:11; 31:3; 79:9; 106:8; 109:21; 143:11) and Ezekiel (20:9, 14, 22, 44).

upon himself. He confesses his sense of isolation and conflict and his sense of the absence of God (15:10-18); to which the Lord replies with the same advice which the prophet has previously given to the people (3:12-14, 22; 4:1-2) and lays down the conditions on which his sense of vocation may be resumed and maintained (15:19–16:9). And when the people repeat the question, "Why?" he is told what he must say to them (16:10-13, 16-18; 17:1-4). The poem ends, as does Eliot's, with a desideratum of moral inferences—four in the case of Jeremiah (17:5-13), three in the case of Eliot (give, sympathize, control)—and concludes with a reflective "postcript," as does Eliot's ("Shall I at least set my lands in order?").

7-9, 19-22. *The Antiphonal Prayers.*—The first prayer follows immediately upon the vivid description of the drought, as the second follows immediately upon the graphic picture of disaster on the battlefield. Aesthetically, they are like the choruses in Aeschylus—at once naïve and accurate, bordering upon ritual confession and collective petition, but speaking the playwright's more direct message to the people; or again, they are like the choral chants in Eliot's *Murder in the Cathedral:*

Forgive us, O Lord, we acknowledge ourselves as type of the common man,

. . . .

Who fear the blessing of God, the loneliness of the night of God, the surrender required, the deprivation inflicted,
Who fear the injustice of men less than the justice of God,
Who fear the hand at the window.[1]

The ritual and collect movement of this, with snatches and overtones from the prayer book,

is apparent. Something of the same *memoriter* movement clings to the framework of Jeremiah's first prayer (vss. 7, 9b; cf. 15:16).

The verses would appear to be an intentional paraphrase of the temple ritual. "How beautiful both plaint and prayer!" Ball exclaims.[2] Maclaren, who compares the drought poem to Dante—"in its realism, in its tenderness, and in its terror"—finds the prayer no less impressive because of its "wonderful fulness and richness." [3] Vss. 8, 9a, however, have led other critics to appraise the passage differently (cf. 15:18b).

Duhm regards the putting of such a prayer in the people's mouths as a bitter irony upon the people's unrealistic way of praying. Wilhelm Erbt supposes that Jeremiah himself appeared at the temple on a humiliation day and uttered the prayer as a parody of the people's prayer, in order the better to enforce his prophecy that the Lord would not save them. And Skinner, while holding that such a mocking parody by Jeremiah "is almost inconceivable," is nevertheless puzzled by the fact that the prayer "contains nothing which rises above the popular religion of the time." [4]

But these are perplexities which arise only when the prayer is detached from its dramatic context. Within that context, as it stands, its balance is perfect—naïveté, formal repetition of deep confession, and the unconscious irony of pathetic seeking. The balance of these factors is very delicate; the irony is soft, being contained within the contradictory naïveté of the people's bland and unthinking piety, whereby in one breath they confess their faults and in the next lay the blame on Yahweh. He comes like a wayfarer passing through the land, stop-

[1] London: Faber & Faber; New York: Harcourt, Brace & Co., 1935, Part II, pp. 86-87. Used by permission.

[2] *Op. cit.*, p. 304.

[3] *Isaiah and Jeremiah*, II, 281, 282.

[4] *Prophecy and Religion*, p. 130; for Duhm and Erbt, cf. Peake, *Jeremiah and Lamentations*, I, 201-2.

8 O the hope of Israel, the Saviour thereof in time of trouble, why shouldest thou be as a stranger in the land, and as a wayfaring man *that* turneth aside to tarry for a night?

9 Why shouldest thou be as a man astonished, as a mighty man *that* cannot save? yet thou, O LORD, *art* in the midst of us, and we are called by thy name; leave us not.

10 ¶ Thus saith the LORD unto this people, Thus have they loved to wander, they have not refrained their feet, therefore the LORD doth not accept them; he will now remember their iniquity, and visit their sins.

8 O thou hope of Israel,
    its savior in time of trouble,
why shouldst thou be like a stranger in
    the land,
    like a wayfarer who turns aside to
      tarry for a night?
9 Why shouldst thou be like a man confused,
    like a mighty man who cannot save?
Yet thou, O LORD, art in the midst of us,
    and we are called by thy name;
    leave us not."

10 Thus says the LORD concerning this people:
"They have loved to wander thus,
    they have not restrained their feet;
therefore the LORD does not accept them,
    now he will remember their iniquity
    and punish their sins."

C. YAHWEH'S REPLY (14:10-12)

Yahweh's answer concerns the people (vs. 10) and Jeremiah's role (vss. 11-12). The answer concerning the people emphasizes their continual sinfulness. Perhaps it implies that their repentance is insincere or ephemeral, but vs. 10 perhaps did not originally stand immediately after vss. 7-9; it owes its present position to an editor.

ping for the night only; or like some powerful Samson, shorn of his locks, now impotent and confused. The term "blasphemous" is out of place here: it is a question rather as to the adequacy of the representation. Its merit will be seen at once if the passage is placed alongside a somewhat similar one from T. S. Eliot:

A Cry from the North, from the West and from the
   South
Whence thousands travel daily to the timekept
   City;
Where My Word is unspoken,
In the land of lobelias and tennis flannels
The rabbit shall burrow and the thorn revisit,
The nettle shall flourish on the gravel court,
And the wind shall say: "Here were decent godless
   people:
Their only monument the asphalt road
And a thousand lost golf balls." [5]

Here again the irony is contained until the last three lines, where it seems to break over into the author's irony at our expense (a move from humility within the predicament to the critic's superiority *to* the predicament); although, even here, if the *ruᵃh*-property of "the

[5] "The Word of the Lord Came unto Me Saying," Chorus No. III from *The Rock* (London: Faber & Faber; New York: Harcourt, Brace & Co., 1934). Used by permission.

wind" be recognized, the irony is not too strong.

But Eliot's chorus leaves us at the level of the ironic reduction, whereas that of Jeremiah succeeds not only in doing this but in resuming *at the same time* the perspective of the early Covenant. Yahweh is petitioned to act, if not for the people, then for his name's sake: the name whereby he reiterates perpetually his creative and sustaining work. Secondly, despite the unworthiness of the people, he *is* their hope: he is bound by what he is, and bound by the people's expectation in the covenant. And thirdly, although their **backslidings are many,** the people are called by his name: they belong to him, and therefore he must not leave them. The Lord's answer is quite plain (vs. 10). It is what Jeremiah has been saying repeatedly (cf. 5:31; 8:6*b*).

The second prayer follows the passage on the prophets (see Expos. on vss. 19-22, p. 935).

10-18. Concerning the False Prophets.—Vss. 11-12 are doubtless an insertion (see Exeg.). Skinner, however, regards their recurrence (7:16; 11:14) as indication that they have some foundation in Jeremiah's experience. That he should have reached the point where he felt that the people were beyond healing, beyond intercession, is not surprising. At the same time,

11 Then said the LORD unto me, Pray not for this people for *their* good.

12 When they fast, I will not hear their cry; and when they offer burnt offering and an oblation, I will not accept them: but I will consume them by the sword, and by the famine, and by the pestilence.

13 ¶ Then said I, Ah, Lord GOD! behold, the prophets say unto them, Ye shall not see the sword, neither shall ye have famine; but I will give you assured peace in this place.

11 The LORD said to me: "Do not pray for the welfare of this people. **12** Though they fast, I will not hear their cry, and though they offer burnt offering and cereal offering, I will not accept them; but I will consume them by the sword, by famine, and by pestilence."

13 Then I said: "Ah, Lord GOD, behold, the prophets say to them, 'You shall not see the sword, nor shall you have famine, but I will give you assured peace in this place.' "

The words of Yahweh to the prophet in vs. 11 have close parallels in 7:16; 11:14. In all three passages Deuteronomic phraseology and ideas are present. It is therefore very probable that vss. 11-12 are by the Deuteronomic editor, though it is not impossible that Jeremiah himself, late in his career, came to believe that intercession was useless (cf. 15:1).

D. JUDGMENT ON THE FALSE PROPHETS (14:13-16)

13-16. Though this passage also has Deuteronomic phraseology, it may well represent the attitude of Jeremiah toward the prophets who misled the people by predicting continual peace rather than doom. Jeremiah frequently came into conflict with the false prophets of his day, and he did not mince words in denouncing them; see especially 6:13-14 (=8:10-11); 23:9-33; and the encounter with Hananiah, ch. 28. The present passage predicts that they will suffer from the **sword and famine** which they have denied

---

what the verses really point out is that Jeremiah was praying for and pleading for his people all the time. This negative assertion of his inner conflict merely underscores the depth of his concern.

The people blunder pathetically; but the prophets and priests, the spiritual leaders of the people, blunder too, and they should be held to answer for their betrayal of the people (cf. Benda's *La trahison des clercs*).

We shall defer a full consideration of this problem until Jeremiah's case is presented more fully (see Expos. on 23:9-40); but already the reader will have become aware of the steadily mounting and inevitable collision between Jeremiah and the temple prophets (cf. 4:10; 5:13, 31; 6:13-14; 8:10*b*-11). At the same time we must recognize that

such a record [as vss. 13 ff.] is of the first importance; for it reveals Jeremiah as standing in opposition to a company of prophets (how numerous it is impossible to say) who are characterized by the fact not simply that they give oracles of "Peace!", but that they do so with a claim to authority equal to his own—that of speaking in the Name of Yahweh.[6]

This means that the collision between Jeremiah and prophetic voices which differ from his own

[6] Johnson, *Cultic Prophet in Ancient Israel*, p. 45.

must raise the question as to criteria between the true and the false. How is Jeremiah to know that his word of Yahweh is the true one and all the others, also "words of Yahweh," false? And if he finds himself *Jeremias contra mundum* he will be driven far, far in upon himself to be certain of his calling.

We must note, therefore, the terms of Jeremiah's accusation: these prophets are prophesying falsely because (*a*) their words are based upon **a lying vision**, itself rooted in magical practice (**worthless divination**). "The practice of divination (*qesem*)," as Guillaume remarks, "he regards as contemptible. . . . The diviners were not always prophets, but they were always in league with the false prophets and agreed with their prophecies of peace in opposition to Jeremiah."[7] Their words are thus a **deceit of their own minds**—"things of nought."

We may note also (*b*) that such falsification was due to the fact that Yahweh **did not send them;** he neither commanded them, nor spoke to them (vs. 14); their call is not rooted in the encounter with God.

Finally (*c*), they blindly or deceitfully prophesy what the people wish to hear: "peace and permanence in this place" (vs. 13). And though this has a traditional appeal, basing itself upon the great teaching of Isaiah, so nobly vindicated

[7] *Prophecy and Divination*, p. 353.

14 Then the LORD said unto me, The prophets prophesy lies in my name: I sent them not, neither have I commanded them, neither spake unto them: they prophesy unto you a false vision and divination, and a thing of nought, and the deceit of their heart.

15 Therefore thus saith the LORD concerning the prophets that prophesy in my name, and I sent them not, yet they say, Sword and famine shall not be in this land; By sword and famine shall those prophets be consumed.

16 And the people to whom they prophesy shall be cast out in the streets of Jerusalem, because of the famine and the sword; and they shall have none to bury them, them, their wives, nor their sons, nor their daughters: for I will pour their wickedness upon them.

17 ¶ Therefore thou shalt say this word unto them; Let mine eyes run down with tears night and day, and let them not cease: for the virgin daughter of my people is broken with a great breach, with a very grievous blow.

18 If I go forth into the field, then behold the slain with the sword! and if I enter

14 And the LORD said to me: "The prophets are prophesying lies in my name; I did not send them, nor did I command them or speak to them. They are prophesying to you a lying vision, worthless divination, and the deceit of their own minds. 15 Therefore thus says the LORD concerning the prophets who prophesy in my name although I did not send them, and who say, 'Sword and famine shall not come on this land': By sword and famine those prophets shall be consumed. 16 And the people to whom they prophesy shall be cast out in the streets of Jerusalem, victims of famine and sword, with none to bury them — them, their wives, their sons, and their daughters. For I will pour out their wickedness upon them.

17 "You shall say to them this word:
'Let my eyes run down with tears night
　　and day,
　　and let them not cease,
for the virgin daughter of my people is
　　smitten with a great wound,
　　with a very grievous blow.
18 If I go out into the field,
　　behold, those slain by the sword!
And if I enter the city,
　　behold, the diseases of famine!

would come upon the people of Judah. It is difficult to agree with Volz and Rudolph that this passage comes from the early career of Jeremiah because his judgment on the false prophets was not at that time critical. The passage has nothing to do with the drought, but presupposes the invasion of the land by an enemy, and probably comes from the time of one of the Babylonian invasions.

E. JEREMIAH'S LAMENT OVER THE PEOPLE'S SORROWS (14:17-18)

This passage is undoubtedly genuine, showing Jeremiah's deep sympathy with the people and his sorrow over their misfortunes (cf. 8:18–9:1; 13:17).

17. The virgin daughter of my people: See Exeg. on 4:11.

18. Both prophet and priest ply their trade through the land, and have no knowledge: The RSV is preferable to the KJV, which predicts the exile of the religious leaders into a foreign land. The verb סחרו is ordinarily used of merchants carrying on their trade, as in Gen. 34:10, 21; 42:34; the participle *ṣōḥēr* means "merchant." Jeremiah uses the

in his time, Jeremiah sees clearly that "that which had been a vital act of faith in Isaiah's day had sunk to the level of a dead dogma" [8] a hundred years after. Not only that, but despite the open wound of the people and the calamitous conditions of drought and defeat (vss. 17-18; cf. 9:18; 8:21; and 9:22), **both prophet and priest ply their trade** [go about like pedlars

hawking their wares] **through the land,** commercializing, as it were, their very office, **and have no knowledge** of Yahweh, with life-giving power in it (cf. 8:9). The Exeg. notes pointedly the irony here; and there appears to be no adequate reason for assuming, as does Peake, that the last phrase, **and have no knowledge** (understanding), indicates the beginning of a fresh sentence, the balance of which has been lost. For "to know God" is big with the con-

[8] John Paterson, *The Goodly Fellowship of the Prophets* (New York: Charles Scribner's Sons, 1948), pp. 150-51.

into the city, then behold them that are sick with famine! yea, both the prophet and the priest go about into a land that they know not.

19 Hast thou utterly rejected Judah? hath thy soul loathed Zion? why hast thou smitten us, and *there is* no healing for us? we looked for peace, and *there is* no good; and for the time of healing, and behold trouble!

20 We acknowledge, O LORD, our wickedness, *and* the iniquity of our fathers: for we have sinned against thee.

21 Do not abhor *us,* for thy name's sake; do not disgrace the throne of thy glory: remember, break not thy covenant with us.

22 Are their *any* among the vanities of the Gentiles that can cause rain? or can the heavens give showers? *Art* not thou he, O LORD our God? therefore we will wait upon thee: for thou hast made all these *things.*

> For both prophet and priest ply their
>   trade through the land,
>   and have no knowledge.' "

19 Hast thou utterly rejected Judah?
    Does thy soul loathe Zion?
Why hast thou smitten us
    so that there is no healing for us?
We looked for peace, but no good came;
    for a time of healing, but behold, ter-
    ror.
20 We acknowledge our wickedness, O
    LORD,
    and the iniquity of our fathers,
    for we have sinned against thee.
21 Do not spurn us, for thy name's sake;
    do not dishonor thy glorious throne;
    remember and do not break thy cove-
    nant with us.
22 Are there any among the false gods of
    the nations that can bring rain?
Or can the heavens give showers?
Art thou not he, O LORD our God?
    We set our hope on thee,
    for thou doest all these things.

---

word ironically of the venal priests and prophets who carry on their business as usual in a time of great distress. Some scholars emend סחרו to נסחבו and omit **and** in the last line, but this spoils a vivid figure. It has nothing to do with exile to a foreign land.

F. RENEWED LAMENT OF THE PEOPLE (14:19-22)

These verses are more impetuous and filled with more anguish than vss. 7-9, also spoken by the people. Israel confesses her sin (vs. 20) and calls upon Yahweh not to bring dishonor upon his own temple and not to break his own covenant (vs. 21). The background is a time of drought, as vs. 22 indicates.

21. Thy glorious throne is Zion, or more specifically the temple in which Yahweh was believed to dwell, enthroned on the cherubim within the holy of holies (cf. I Sam. 4:4; II Sam. 6:2; II Kings 19:15; Pss. 80:1; 99:1). For the phrase cf. 3:17; 17:12; Ezek. 43:7. Cornill rightly says that such a phrase is impossible in the mouth of Jeremiah, but the people themselves would not hesitate to use it.

22. The false gods: Lit., **the vanities.** The word הבלים is used also in 2:5; 8:19; 10:8, 15; 16:19 for heathen gods or their idols.

---

tent of the personal encounter, and Jeremiah has indicated already (vs. 14) that it is just this intimate communion with God which the false prophet or professional priest lacks. The lament (vs. 17), therefore, though "characteristic" and though a recurrence (9:18; 8:21), is appropriate here; there is nothing more lamentable than the picture of the people lying slain in the field from battle, and lying diseased in the city from famine, with prophet and priest trafficking a pseudo holiness throughout the land at their expense. It is indeed **a very grievous blow.**

19-22. *The Second Chant Prayer of the People.*—As the first prayer (vss. 7-9) followed the vivid description of the drought—3:3 would place this in Josiah's reign—so the second appeal to Yahweh follows the equally vivid picture of defeat on the field of battle, perhaps the battle of Megiddo. Here again the ambiguities of collective utterance as in the ritual confession, together with naïveté and earnestness, petition and complaint, are admirably blended. The ambivalent mood of the people is deftly drawn. The half-prayer, in which we

15 Then said the LORD unto me, Though Moses and Samuel stood before me, *yet* my mind *could* not *be* toward this people: cast *them* out of my sight, and let them go forth.

2 And it shall come to pass, if they say unto thee, Whither shall we go forth? then thou shalt tell them, Thus saith the LORD; Such as *are* for death, to death; and such as *are* for the sword, to the sword; and such as *are* for the famine, to the famine; and such as *are* for the captivity, to the captivity.

3 And I will appoint over them four kinds, saith the LORD: the sword to slay, and the dogs to tear, and the fowls of the heaven, and the beasts of the earth, to devour and destroy.

4 And I will cause them to be removed into all kingdoms of the earth, because of Manasseh the son of Hezekiah king of Judah, for *that* which he did in Jerusalem.

15 Then the LORD said to me, "Though Moses and Samuel stood before me, yet my heart would not turn toward this people. Send them out of my sight, and let them go! 2 And when they ask you, 'Where shall we go?' you shall say to them, 'Thus says the LORD:

"Those who are for pestilence, to pestilence,
and those who are for the sword, to the sword;
those who are for famine, to famine,
and those who are for captivity, to captivity."'

3 "I will appoint over them four kinds of destroyers, says the LORD: the sword to slay, the dogs to tear, and the birds of the air and the beasts of the earth to devour and destroy. 4 And I will make them a horror to all the kingdoms of the earth because of what Manas'seh the son of Hezeki'ah, king of Judah, did in Jerusalem.

G. YAHWEH'S FINAL REPLY (15:1-4)

The repentance of the people and the intercession of the prophet are completely unavailing; doom is certain to come. In its present form this passage is from the Deuteronomic editor, whose style and ideas pervade all the verses.

15:1. For **Moses** as intercessor see Exod. 32:11-14, 31-34; Num. 14:13-25; for **Samuel,** see I Sam. 7:5-11; 12:19; Ps. 99:6.

4. The idea that destruction comes because of the sins of Manasseh is found also in II Kings 23:26; 24:3. The idea is Deuteronomic, certainly not Jeremiah's, for he believed that the destruction came because of the sins of the people themselves.

---

the people **acknowledge our wickedness** while at the same time accusing God—**Why hast thou smitten us?**—reveals with the subtlest irony the contradictory consciousness of the people. The retention of the drought symbol in vs. 21—"Cause not Thy glorious throne to wither" [9]—ties it in with the thematic symbols of the entire unit. It also anticipates the diminished sense of the proper meaning of the God-relationship in the movement to the remembrance of the Covenant and Yahweh's usefulness as a rain maker. For Jeremiah the remembrance of the Covenant goes back to the loving and obedient time of the wilderness when "Israel was holy to the LORD" (2:3). But now the people would recall Yahweh to his agreement with them because of the benefits which will accrue to them. He alone among the gods can bring rain (vs. 22). Widengren would appear to miss the point here when he remarks that "we find Jeremiah in the corresponding rôle [of the rain maker] of the man of God praying for rain (Jer. 14)—an important action in the Ancient Near East." [1] This overlooks the fact that the prayer is a prayer of the people, and that the force of the ironic issue here exhibits the decline of genuine piety toward magic and expedient propitiation.

15:1-4. Yahweh's Reply and the Four Fatalities.—As in Yahweh's reply to the first prayer (14:10), the people's ambivalent plea is refused. Indeed, it is this very ambivalence, both in heart and behavior, which makes any other reply impossible. **Though Moses and Samuel**—both famous as intercessors before the Lord for the people (cf. Exeg. for references; also Deut. 9:18-20)—should stand before him, the Lord could not turn to them. For the people have not repented in their hearts, as Israel had done *before* either Moses or Samuel had interceded on her behalf.

Hence, the sharpness with which the prophet confronts them with the realistic consequences of their deep moral and spiritual vacillations. When they ask at last, in naïveté and helpless

[9] Gillies, *Jeremiah, the Man and His Message,* p. 134.

[1] *Literary and Psychological Aspects of the Hebrew Prophets,* p. 111.

5 For who shall have pity upon thee, O Jerusalem? or who shall bemoan thee? or who shall go aside to ask how thou doest?	5 "Who will have pity on you, O Jerusalem, or who will bemoan you? Who will turn aside to ask about your welfare?
6 Thou hast forsaken me, saith the Lord, thou art gone backward: therefore will I stretch out my hand against thee, and destroy thee; I am weary with repenting.	6 You have rejected me, says the Lord, you keep going backward; so I have stretched out my hand against you and destroyed you; — I am weary of relenting.
7 And I will fan them with a fan in the gates of the land; I will bereave *them* of children, I will destroy my people, *since* they return not from their ways.	7 I have winnowed them with a winnowing fork in the gates of the land; I have bereaved them, I have destroyed my people; they did not turn from their ways.

If our analysis of 14:1–15:4 is correct, we cannot assign it to any specific period of Jeremiah's life. The editor here has combined materials from various times in the prophet's career with secondary materials.

X. Lamentations of Jeremiah (15:5-21)
A. Lamentation over Destruction in the Land (15:5-9)

This poem is considered by many commentators to be the continuation of 15:1-4, and is interpreted as a prediction of the future (so Duhm, Giesebrecht, Cornill, Peake). But the verbs are all perfects in Hebrew, except that in vs. 9c. The RSV correctly translates the Hebrew perfects by the English perfect or past tense; the KJV does not translate consistently, using the future tense in vss. 6-7 and the past in vss. 8-9. It is best to consider the poem as a description of the destruction wrought in Judah by one of the Babylonian invasions. Volz assigns it to the time of the invasion of 602 b.c., described in II Kings 24:2, Rudolph to that of 598, and Skinner to that of 588-587. The details are not sufficiently clear for us to decide definitely, but the invasion of 598 seems the most probable. Little is known of that of 602, and the final destruction and capture of Jerusalem in 588-587 would have been described by the prophet in even stronger terms than used here.

This genuine poem of Jeremiah has been joined by an editor to the Deuteronomic passage, 15:1-4, with the word **For** (כִּי).

6. Yahweh is represented as being **weary of relenting** in his determination to punish Judah for her sins. The word translated **relenting** means, lit., **repenting**, but it is here God's own change of purpose that is referred to, not that of the people.

desperation, "**Where shall we go** (if not to Yahweh)?" the answer is made incredibly plain: to pestilence, sword, famine, and captivity—the four catastrophes implicit in their refusals to return. In forsaking the way of Yahweh, these are the gods to which they have in fact already turned. And, as if to fix the fateful element indelibly in the minds of his hearers, the prophet adds to these four fatalities **four kinds of destroyers, . . . the sword to slay, the dogs to tear, the birds . . . and beasts . . . to devour and destroy.** Even after they are slain their bodies shall suffer the extreme humiliation of being preyed upon by ravenous beasts and ruth-

less fowls. But the cause of these catastrophes is wholly within themselves, as Yahweh's reply to the first prayer makes plain (14:10); the Deuteronomist (vs. 4) shifts the entire axis of Jeremiah's dialectic by carrying the cause of the horror back to Manasseh (see Exeg.).

5-9. *The Brutal Winnowing*.—The ambivalent petitions of the people (14:7-10; 14:19–15:1) having now been twice refused, the bitter plight of Jerusalem is brought into full focus. Jeremiah, throughout the scroll, does not allow the attention of his hearers (cf. 36:2 ff.) to stray very far from the impending crisis, portrayed here once more in a passage which

8 Their widows are increased to me above the sand of the seas: I have brought upon them against the mother of the young men a spoiler at noonday: I have caused *him* to fall upon it suddenly, and terrors upon the city.

9 She that hath borne seven languisheth: she hath given up the ghost; her sun is gone down while *it was* yet day: she hath been ashamed and confounded: and the residue of them will I deliver to the sword before their enemies, saith the LORD.

10 ¶ Woe is me, my mother, that thou hast borne me a man of strife and a man of contention to the whole earth! I have neither lent on usury, nor men have lent to me on usury; *yet* every one of them doth curse me.

8 I have made their widows more in number
  than the sand of the seas;
I have brought against the mothers of
    young men
  a destroyer at noonday;
I have made anguish and terror
  fall upon them suddenly.
9 She who bore seven has languished;
  she has swooned away;
her sun went down while it was yet day;
  she has been shamed and disgraced.
And the rest of them I will give to the
    sword
  before their enemies,
                    says the LORD."

10 Woe is me, my mother, that you bore me, a man of strife and contention to the whole land! I have not lent, nor have I

---

8. The RSV correctly translates the last third of this verse. The word עִיר, rendered **city** by the KJV, usually has that meaning, but here means **anguish,** agitation, or the like.

9. She hath given up the ghost: The reference is not to dying, but to fainting or swooning, as the RSV indicates. The Hebrew is, lit., "she breathed out her soul [*néphesh*]."

B. LAMENTATION OVER HIMSELF, AND YAHWEH'S REPLY (15:10-21)

Within this section vss. 13-14 are virtually a duplicate of 17:3-4. Their proper place is in ch. 17. When these verses are removed, we are left with two distinct and related parts: (*a*) a bitter lament of the prophet over the suffering he has had to bear in prophesying the word of the Lord, a protestation of his own faithfulness, a cry for vengeance on his persecutors, and a strong accusation against God that approaches

---

evokes both the vivid recollection of disasters which have already overtaken the people (Megiddo? the Babylonian invasions?) and the steady movement of things toward the last calamity. The poem's images are at once historical and figurative.

I have winnowed them with a winnowing fork
  in the gates [the borders] of the land;
I have bereaved them, I have destroyed my people.

And again:

    She that bare seven doth languish,
      She breathes out her soul;
    Her sun has gone down while it was day.[2]

This "darkness at noon" which falls so suddenly, smiting the mother (Jerusalem? "an idiom implying everybody"?[3]) through the sudden loss of her seven sons (the ideal number, and the flower of familial pride) achieves the poet's

dramatic aim. It concentrates the disaster in the concrete particular, in a symbol most moving and pitiable, evoking by its pathetic appeal the sense of the entire disaster. Behind the figure of the stricken mother lies the symbol of the winnowing (cf. Ps. 1:4) —the sons and the people overborne and scattered by the violent wind (the *rûaḥ* from the north); just as behind this is the persistent message of the prophet:

You have rejected me, says the LORD,
  you keep going backward;
[therefore] I have stretched out my hand against
    you.

The sense of the condition must be fastened upon the people, until the question "Why?" is wrung from them out of **anguish and terror,** and *not* from within the unconscious ambivalence of a compromised and temporizing refusal to see and take the blame for their apostasy.

10-21. *Alas, My Mother!*—That Jeremiah knew well the depth and anguish of this win-

[2] Skinner, *Prophecy and Religion,* p. 271.
[3] Freedman, *Jeremiah,* p. 107.

11 The LORD said, Verily it shall be well with thy remnant; verily I will cause the enemy to entreat thee *well* in the time of evil and in the time of affliction.

borrowed, yet all of them curse me. 11 So let it be, O LORD,[x] if I have not entreated[y] thee for their good, if I have not pleaded with thee on behalf of the enemy in the time of trouble and in the time of distress!

[x] Gk Old Latin: Heb *the* LORD *said*
[y] Cn: Heb obscure

---

blasphemy (vss. 10-12, 15-18) ; and (*b*) Yahweh's reply, in which the prophet is rebuked with a command to repent and is assured that when he does repent God will be with him to strengthen him in his prophetic career and to save him from his enemies (vss. 19-21) .

This section belongs among the "confessions" of Jeremiah, and constitutes one of the bitterest outcries in the prophet's whole life. The Lord's reply shows that the prophet himself needed to repent of his mood and to be careful to speak only what was true. But he experienced what Duhm has called self-purification (*Selbstreinigung*) . Few passages in the O.T. are as revealing as this one for the personality of Jeremiah, and for the nature and function of the Hebrew prophet.

We do not know the occasion of this lament, but it may well have been one similar to that of 11:18–12:6. The time was probably the latter part of Jehoiakim's reign, when the prophet met a great deal of opposition.

10. This outcry is the result of Jeremiah's experience in preaching God's word and meeting only unpopularity and persecution from the people. The second half of the verse does not have to do with lending or borrowing **on usury** only, but with any kind of borrowing and lending (in the time of KJV usury did not necessarily mean exorbitant or illegal interest, as today) . Deuteronomy forbids all lending on interest to a fellow Hebrew (Deut. 23:19) . Such financial transactions, whether legal or not, have always been likely to arouse animosity. Jeremiah may here be using a popular saying or proverb.

11. This verse is difficult. The M.T. makes it a word of the Lord to the prophet (for a literal translation see ASV; KJV gives a very strange rendering) . But such a word of

---

nowing is now made apparent. After the descriptions of drought and disaster, the people's ambivalent prayers and Yahweh's refusals and rebukes, which leave no one to pity Jerusalem (vs. 5), the prophet is thrown severely back upon himself, feeling inwardly both the tragic failure and dereliction of his people and the sharp frustration of his message. His word is refused (they will not listen) ; his friends reject him (11:18 ff.; 20:10) ; his office is resented—he **is a man of strife and contention to the whole land.** Without a doubt he feels "the slings and arrows of outrageous fortune";[4] as in Job, the "arrows of the Almighty" are in him (Job 6:4) . Like Hamlet, he knows "the time is out of joint"; is, indeed, at radical odds with itself. And he begins to mutter

> O cursed spite,
> That ever I was born to set it right![5]

Like Job, he is "not at ease" (Job 3:26) and he begins to "complain in the bitterness of [his] soul" (Job 7:11) .

But Dante is, perhaps, a happier transitional point:

[4] Shakespeare, *Hamlet*, Act III, scene 1.
[5] Act I, scene 5.

All ye that pass along Love's trodden way,
Pause ye awhile and say
If there be any grief like unto mine:
I pray you that you hearken a short space
Patiently, if my case
Be not a piteous marvel and a sign.

This passage from the *Vita Nuova*[6] is deliberately based on Jeremiah. Dante's city, now that Beatrice has departed from it, was desolate to him as he perceived Jerusalem was desolate to Jeremiah since Yahweh had departed from it. Interestingly, though, the passage attributed by Dante to "Jeremiah" comes from the book of Lamentations (1:12) . It breaks through the sharp lament for Jerusalem, a passage also much admired by Dante:

Ah, how lonely lies the city,
once so full of folk,
once a power among the nations,
now like a poor widow! (Lam. 1:1 Moffatt.)

It is impossible not to note in Lamentations the carry-over of the movement of Jeremiah's argument: first, the lament for Jerusalem— "Who will have pity on you, O Jerusalem"

[6] Part VII. Tr. Dante Gabriel Rossetti.

12 Shall iron break the northern iron and the steel? | 12 Can one break iron, iron from the north, and bronze?

---

comfort is out of place at this point, coming much too early. The LXX presupposes a different Hebrew text, and is followed by most commentators. The RSV emends, partly on the basis of the LXX and partly by conjecture, to give what is probably the original meaning of the verse. The text translated by the RSV is: אמן יהוה אם־לא שרתיך לטוב. Jeremiah thus protests that he does not deserve the curses of his enemies (vs. 10), for he has sought only their welfare, pleading with Yahweh on their behalf in their time of distress (for the thought cf. 17:16; 18:20).

12. This verse is also difficult, and some scholars (e.g., Condamin) give it up as impossible to translate and interpret. Perhaps the most natural translation of the Hebrew is, "Can iron break iron from the north and bronze?" An interpretation of this, which goes back to Rashi, is as follows: the prophet himself is **iron** (1:18), and the people are **iron** and **bronze** (cf. 6:28; **iron from the north** may be unusually hard iron from the Black Sea region). The prophet is protesting that he is not strong enough to stand against the hardness and the stubbornness of the people to whom he must prophesy. This interpretation is probably the best one can make of the present text, though obviously it is far-fetched. Duhm offers an ingenious emendation to read, "Is an arm of iron on my shoulders, is my brow bronze?" (הזרע ברזל באצלי קצחי נחשת). For the thought he compares Job 6:12. This suggestion is apparently adopted by the Amer. Trans. Others are proposed by Erbt and Volz. Rudolph considers the verse a corruption of 17:1, but this is improbable, since the thought is apparently referred to in vs. 20.

(15:5) —in which Jerusalem is compared to the desolate widow; then the woe and outcry—

> my groans are many
> and my heart is faint (Lam 1:22b).

Jeremiah's lament, though highly personal, should not be deprived of its symbolic and typical uses. It is Jeremiah, yes; but it is Jeremiah who as poet and prophet is also the city. His cry, which cuts to the core, is every man's cry. "We understand deep within us this ultimate protest against being born as we were born, born to be the kind of persons we are, with all our peculiar moods and drives and dispositions and tempers. *Alas, my mother!* says Jeremiah, and in that cry he echoes every man's final cry." [7]

With this in mind, the most haunting and reverberating line (like an outdoor bell, "sent out of tune" [Hölderlin] by a light snow covering it) is vs. 17—the climax, indeed, of desolation: **I sat alone because of thy hand.** Everything leads to this, and into it, and through it once more to the divine conditions. Jeremiah is doubly alone. He is alone as Jerusalem is desolate; and he is alone within Jerusalem, within the desolation of his isolation and rejection by the people. Clearly he has not computed the resentment and hostility which his blunt and scathing words were certain to arouse; and in his bitterness he comes very near to that most

[7] James Muilenburg, "A Confession of Jeremiah," *Union Seminary Quarterly Review*, IV (1949), 17.

terrible of all desolations, that of feeling God-forsaken.

He is therefore disconcerted and dismayed to find himself **a man of strife . . . to the whole land.** He has observed the rules of the common life, having been neither a borrower nor a lender. He has done more: he has even prayed for them who hated him and who despitefully used him. **Yet all of them curse me,** he exclaims.

The obscurities of vs. 12 (see Exeg.) admit of two readings. Jeremiah may be alluding to the overwhelming and conquering power (the **iron**) from the north, against which resistance is foolhardy and vain, and the fact that as prophet he has no alternative but to try to get the people to see this. Or, it may mean that he himself is overborne by the threats and hostilities of his enemies and before such odds is only human:

> Have I an arm of iron,
> Or a brow of bronze?

Therefore the Lord should succor him and avenge him on his persecutors. For after all, it is for the Lord's sake that he has borne **reproach.** He had been, moreover, attentive to God's word: it had been to him **a joy and the delight of** [his] **heart**—"my very soul thrills at thy word" (Moffatt). He has even shunned the customary pleasures, forgoing the social rounds of pleasantness and merrymaking in order the better to devote himself wholly and singly to God's call. **For I am called by thy name** [cf.

13 Thy substance and thy treasures will I give to the spoil without price, and *that* for all thy sins, even in all thy borders.

14 And I will make *thee* to pass with thine enemies into a land *which* thou knowest not: for a fire is kindled in mine anger, *which* shall burn upon you.

15 ¶ O Lord, thou knowest: remember me, and visit me, and revenge me of my persecutors; take me not away in thy long-

13 "Your wealth and your treasures I will give as spoil, without price, for all your sins, throughout all your territory. 14 I will make you serve your enemies in a land which you do not know, for in my anger a fire is kindled which shall burn for ever."

15 O Lord, thou knowest;
    remember me and visit me,
    and take vengeance for me on my persecutors.

13-14. These verses are repeated in 17:3b-4, which is their proper place.

15. For the desire of the prophet that God should take vengeance on his enemies cf. 11:20; 12:3; 17:18; 18:23; 20:11.

14:9], O Lord God of hosts. . . . I sat alone because of thy hand.

There are two dimensions in this loneliness—and the one is a dimension beneath the other. "The penalty of leadership is loneliness," notes H. Wheeler Robinson.[8] This is the first dimension:

When he tried to arrest the course of a nation, only to be thrown down and trampled underfoot, when he cried out in bitterness of heart against the inexorable Will that compelled a poet to become a prophet, and a lover of men to be counted their enemy, he little knew that the development and record of his own lonely experience of failure was to be a success of the highest rank and influence. For if we want to know the meaning of personal religion at its finest and highest in the Old Testament, we must become, like Baruch, disciples of Jeremiah. In this respect there is no figure comparable with his, nor any of whom the revelation is so intimate and full.[9]

This dimension has yet to pass over into solitariness, as in "The Ancient Mariner":

Alone, alone, all, all alone,
Alone on a wide, wide sea!
And never a saint took pity on
My soul in agony.[1]

Nor has it yet learned the wistful longing of the trapped soul:

I never saw a man who looked
With such a wistful eye
Upon that little tent of blue
Which prisoners call the sky.[2]

In Jeremiah's loneliness there is a far deeper dimension. Frederick W. Robertson held that

"there are two kinds of solitude; the first consisting of insulation in space, the other of isolation of the spirit. The first is simply separation by distance. . . . The other is loneliness of soul." It is the latter that he speaks of as "the loneliness of Christ."[3] "Behold, the hour cometh, yea, is now come, that ye shall be scattered, every man to his own, and shall leave me alone: and yet I am not alone, because the Father is with me" (John 16:32). It is to this dimension of loneliness that Jeremiah is now pressed. Nothing stays for him. The sense of power which came from the first prophetic utterances was unsound; the dismay which he experiences at the hostility and resistance which family, friends, and people have directed toward him precipitates in the form of fervid complaint the last-ditch stand of his ego-consciousness. He is alone as Job was alone. "Frightful is the solitude of the soul which is without God in the world. . . . Chill, houseless, fatherless, aimless Cain, the man who hears only the sound of his own footsteps in God's resplendent creation. To him, it is no creation. . . . To him, heaven and earth have lost their beauty."[4] The very intensity of his spirit, together with the astringent preclusiveness of his piety, has estranged him from God. At last he stands, as Muilenburg puts it,

on the abyss of *the everlasting nay.* He has focussed his fierce emotion upon himself with such intensity that finally God is called to the board and is accused of treachery and deception. "Art thou like a spring torrent, like a wadi which gushes with water in the springtime and then becomes a dry river bed the rest of the year? Art thou only a fantastic vision which comes now and then, a deceitful mirage?"[5]

---

[8] *The Cross of Jeremiah* (London: Student Christian Movement Press, 1925), p. 2. Used by permission.

[9] *Ibid.*, p. 1.

[1] Coleridge, "The Rime of the Ancient Mariner," Part IV, st. iii.

[2] Oscar Wilde, "The Ballad of Reading Gaol," st. iii.

[3] "The Loneliness of Christ," in *Sermons Preached at Brighton* (new ed.; New York: E. P. Dutton & Co., 1882), Sermon No. XV, p. 168.

[4] Emerson, *Lectures and Biographical Sketches*, "The Preacher."

[5] *Op. cit.*, pp. 17-18.

suffering: know that for thy sake I have suffered rebuke.

16 Thy words were found, and I did eat them; and thy word was unto me the joy and rejoicing of mine heart: for I am called by thy name, O LORD God of hosts.

17 I sat not in the assembly of the mockers, nor rejoiced; I sat alone because of thy hand: for thou hast filled me with indignation.

In thy forbearance take me not away;
   know that for thy sake I bear reproach.
16 Thy words were found, and I ate them,
   and thy words became to me a joy
   and the delight of my heart;
for I am called by thy name,
   O LORD, God of hosts.
17 I did not sit in the company of merry-makers,
   nor did I rejoice;
I sat alone, because thy hand was upon me,
   for thou hadst filled me with indignation.

---

16. The opening words remind one of the experience of Ezekiel (2:8–3:3) and of Rev. 10:9-10. The idea, however, is without parallel in Jeremiah, who usually thought of the **word** of the Lord as a source of pain and suffering. The LXX connects this verse with vs. 15, and so provides a somewhat different reading. The LXX text may be translated:

Know that for thy sake I bear reproach
   from those who despise thy words.
Consume them, and thy word will be
   the joy and delight of my heart.

This is considered the original text (wholly or in part) by Condamin, Duhm, Cornill, Amer. Trans., *et al.* The Hebrew which it presupposes differs only slightly from the M.T., principally מנאצי for נמצאו, and כלם for ואכלם. Since the M.T. expresses an idea somewhat foreign to Jeremiah, and the LXX reading is consonant with his thought, the latter may represent the original text.

17. Thy hand was upon me: The **hand** of God represents the coming of the divine inspiration; the idea is especially frequent in Ezekiel (1:3; 3:14, 22; 37:1; 40:1; cf. I Kings 18:46; II Kings 3:15; Isa. 8:11). Here the hand of God is thought of as being oppressive to the prophet.

But it must always be borne in mind that it is Jeremiah who confesses this; and that invariably, after his intimate confession of excess, he records Yahweh's chastening and correcting word to him. In this instance the Lord's rebuke is doubly remarkable, showing Jeremiah's profound grasp upon the nature of the God-relation. It shows also the maturity of his religious consciousness, of his prophetic office, at the time of the preparation of the Scroll.

First of all, he not only confesses his sense of God's withdrawal from himself and his people; not less vivid and forthright is his confession of inner distress—his unceasing pain, his wound incurable. His conflict is intense, whether viewed in terms of his office, or in terms of his personal calling. He was, as Knight reminds us, "both the representative of God before the people and the representative of the people before God. Hence, he feels to a degree shared by no other the tragic poignancy of the

estrangement between God and his chosen people."[6] Thus in applying to him the category of corporate personality, with the people on the one hand and with God on the other, we merely intensify in one man, the prophet chosen as the mouth of Yahweh, the deep conflict, the rift, between Yahweh and his people. This cleft would have been unbearable after Copernicus (as, e.g., in a Pascal), to anyone for whom God was the Infinite. It is supportable in Jeremiah only because Yahweh remains so awfully personal and present, even in his absence!

But Jeremiah's conflict arises also out of the fact that he is the prophet in whom the category of corporate personality both reaches its highest pitch of identification, with the twofold pathos of God and the people, and its shattering collapse in the prophetic upthrust of the individual's responsibility before God. Alone for the

[6] Knight, *Hebrew Prophetic Consciousness*, p. 140. Cf. Heschel, *op. cit.*, pp. 68-70.

18 Why is my pain perpetual, and my wound incurable, *which* refuseth to be healed? wilt thou be altogether unto me as a liar, *and as* waters *that* fail?

19 ¶ Therefore thus saith the Lord, If thou return, then will I bring thee again, *and* thou shalt stand before me: and if thou take forth the precious from the vile, thou shalt be as my mouth: let them return unto thee; but return not thou unto them.

18 Why is my pain unceasing,
　　my wound incurable,
　　refusing to be healed?
Wilt thou be to me like a deceitful brook,
　　like waters that fail?

19 Therefore thus says the Lord:
"If you return, I will restore you,
　　and you shall stand before me.
If you utter what is precious, and not
　　　what is worthless,
　　you shall be as my mouth.
They shall turn to you,
　　but you shall not turn to them.

---

18. This is the climax of Jeremiah's lament, in which he accuses even God of failing him. For the thought of the second half of the verse cf. Job 6:15-20. In Palestine there are many brooks that contain water only after heavy rainfalls; if a traveler goes to one expecting to find water he may be disappointed. In 2:13 Jeremiah had compared Yahweh to a never-failing fountain of living water, but now he accuses God of disappointing him.

19. The prophet had often called upon men to repent and return to God. Now he is told that he must repent of his self-pity and of his accusation against Yahweh if he would be a true prophet. He must **utter what is precious, and not what is worthless**

people; but alone also before the people: alone for God (because of thine hand); but alone also before God! This is the terrible point to which Jeremiah's religious passion has brought him.

The notion of religion as "what the individual does with his own solitariness" takes hold here. Even Whitehead, who has been quoted too glibly on this point, recognized three stages in the individual's encounter with solitariness as well as the fact that it begins after the emergence of the individual consciousness from the collective consciousness. "All collective emotions leave untouched the awful ultimate fact, which is the human being, consciously alone with itself, for its own sake."[7] This is the point to which Jeremiah has come. And he is experiencing in this and the other confessions "the transition from God the void to God the enemy" and he has yet to move "from God the enemy to God the companion."[8]

We must underscore here the painful emergence of Jeremiah's religious sense from its original and conditioning collective life. With this break with his past, his family, his society, his cult pattern, with tradition—of which the priests are representative of the collective view—his pain becomes unceasing. The traditional view of God is voided in the light of his private sense of call. He begins to question, out of his insecurity, just as Hopkins did:

[7] Alfred North Whitehead, *Religion in the Making* (New York: The Macmillan Co., 1930), p. 16.

[8] *Ibid.*, pp. 16-17.

Wert thou my enemy, O thou my friend,
How wouldst thou worse, I wonder, than thou dost
Defeat, thwart me?[9]

Or just as Job exclaimed:

Why dost thou hide thy face
　　and count me as thy enemy? (Job 13:24.)

The primitive "cake of custom," as Toynbee calls it, is broken. This is the crucial moment. In the period of struggle, between letting go of the collective demands with their compromising security patterns and the courageous venturing forward in faith to the new awareness, God will seem to be withdrawn; Hopkins will pray, "send my roots rain";[1] Job will cry, "Oh, that I had one to hear me!" (Job 31:35); and Jeremiah will exclaim, **Why is . . . my wound incurable?** (Cf. Job 34:6.)

The answer which comes is not only profound in its understanding of the human spirit as it stands alone before God but it is an answer which could come only to one who has worked through his pain incurable, one who has come to know God not merely by the hearing of the ear but because "now my eye sees thee" (Job 42:5).

Here again two dimensions in depth may be noted. The first concentrates attention upon

[9] Sonnet No. 50. From *Poems of Gerard Manley Hopkins*, ed. Robert Bridges (2nd ed.; London: Oxford University Press, 1935). Used by permission.

[1] *Ibid.*

20 And I will make thee unto this people a fenced brazen wall: and they shall
fight against thee, but they shall not prevail
against thee: for I *am* with thee to save thee
and to deliver thee, saith the Lord.

21 And I will deliver thee out of the
hand of the wicked, and I will redeem thee
out of the hand of the terrible.

20 And I will make you to this people
    a fortified wall of bronze;
they will fight against you,
    but they shall not prevail over you,
for I am with you
    to save you and deliver you,
                 says the Lord.

21 I will deliver you out of the hand of the
    wicked,
    and redeem you from the grasp of the
    ruthless."

---

if he is to be God's **mouth** (cf. Exod. 4:16). The end of the verse has a wordplay on
return and **turn** (שׁוּב).

20-21. These verses are the promise that God will strengthen the prophet against
his enemies; they are used by the Deuteronomic editor in 1:18-19. The reply of Yahweh
to Jeremiah should be compared with 12:5, and with the reply of Yahweh to Job (Job
38:1–41:34). "Unshrinking obedience, rendered without hesitation or complaint, that is
the condition imposed by God on those who aspire to the high dignity of His service.
And the reward of service faithfully rendered is, as in the Parable of the Pounds, more
service." (A. S. Peake, ed., *Jeremiah and Lamentations* [Edinburgh: T. C. & E. C. Jack,
1910-12; "The New-Century Bible"], I, 213.)

---

the second of the Lord's requirements. Jeremiah "has hardly given us anything more illuminating than the words addressed to him by
Yahweh: 'If thou wilt bring out the precious
from the worthless, as my mouth shalt thou
be.' The prophetic consciousness is here virtually analysed as a spiritual value-judgment,"
according to H. Wheeler Robinson.[2] "If thou
separate the precious from the common within
thee" is Peake's reading of the text.[3] Jeremiah
has actually felt the mystic's "dryness"; he has
felt the withdrawal of God **like a deceitful
brook, like waters that fail** (cf. 14:8*b*). The
source has gone dry. If he is to **be as** [the
Lord's] **mouth**, this condition must be amended.
When the Lord is withdrawn he can utter only
what is worthless. What is uttered from himself
alone (from his ego-pretension) is arrogant and
vain. And now comes what Muilenburg describes as "the amazing shift."

Precisely because [Jeremiah] is so intensely religious,
so intensely near to God, he is most in need of
repenting. His intensely religious mood has actually
separated him from the men to whom he ministered, and, more astonishing, it has actually separated him from God.[4]

This is well said. It is what Hopeful had to
learn from Faithful in *The Pilgrim's Progress*—
that he could never be saved either by his own
righteousness or by that of the rest of the

world: "but now, since I see my own infirmity,
and the sin [of presumption?] that cleaves to
my best performance, I have been forced to
be of [that] opinion."[5] Jeremiah's "repentance"
contains this insight into his own defection.
For at the climax of his distress he turns
upon himself the full and self-convicted impact
of the message and plea he has been proclaiming to the people: "Return, O faithless sons, I
will heal your faithlessness" (3:22). "Turn
again, O turncoat Israel. . . . Only acknowledge your guilt" (3:12-13). Precisely this is
the Lord's word to Jeremiah: **If you return,
I will restore you** (will make you return).
Then and only then, as Jeremiah understands
it, can one be as [his] **mouth**; and then and
only then shall the people turn to the prophet
without his turning, in some sense, to them.
On this basis alone can he stand against the
time as **a fortified wall of bronze** and hope
to prevail against those who will certainly fight
against him. Not in his own strength will he
be able to stand; but the Lord will be with
him to save and deliver him.

This is a salient victory for Jeremiah. It is
victory over himself at the point of the prophet's greatest vulnerability—the temptation to
glory in his office and so to be exempt from both
the pathos of the people and the pathos of God.
Here again Bunyan was right. It was Vain-
confidence who got both Christian and Hopeful
into the byway which led to Doubting Castle
and Giant Despair. And it is appropriate that,

[2] *Redemption and Revelation*, pp. 152-53.
[3] *Jeremiah and Lamentations*, I, 213.
[4] *Op. cit.*, p. 18.
[5] Part I.

16 The word of the LORD came also unto me, saying,

2 Thou shalt not take thee a wife, neither shalt thou have sons nor daughters in this place.

3 For thus saith the LORD concerning the sons and concerning the daughters that are born in this place, and concerning their mothers that bare them, and concerning their fathers that begat them in this land;

4 They shall die of grievous deaths; they shall not be lamented; neither shall they be buried; *but* they shall be as dung upon the face of the earth: and they shall be consumed by the sword, and by famine; and

16 The word of the LORD came to me: 2 "You shall not take a wife, nor shall you have sons or daughters in this place. 3 For thus says the LORD concerning the sons and daughters who are born in this place, and concerning the mothers who bore them and the fathers who begot them in this land: 4 They shall die of deadly diseases. They shall not be lamented, nor shall they be buried; they shall be as dung on the surface of the ground. They shall perish by the sword and by famine, and their dead

XI. THREATS AND PROMISES (16:1-21)

This chapter contains a great deal of secondary material, vss. 16-17 being the only ones that are unquestionably from Jeremiah. The first section (vss. 1-13) is Deuteronomic and tells how Jeremiah was forbidden to marry and to join in the joys and sorrows of his fellow countrymen, for his manner of living was to be a warning of the approaching destruction. This is followed by a prediction of restoration from exile (vss. 14-15). Then comes a promise of double recompense for the iniquity the Israelites have committed (vss. 16-18). At the close is a poem in which the heathen nations are represented as recognizing the power of Yahweh (vss. 19-21). The chapter thus contains two passages of doom which alternate with two passages predicting a bright future.

A. JEREMIAH'S LIFE A WARNING (16:1-13)

These verses occupy their present position because they are a detailed illustration of 15:17. As a whole the treatment is prosaic and diffuse. Commentators have usually considered certain parts as secondary, but Rudolph (against Mowinckel) has rightly recognized that it is of Deuteronomic origin. Deuteronomic phraseology is especially evident in vss. 4, 9, 10-13. Since the Deuteronomic editor lived about 550 B.C., he could look back upon the events which culminated in the Babylonian exile and interpret the prophet's celibacy and austerity as a sign to the people of the coming destruction. It is doubtful that this was the prophet's own motive for his manner of living. The true explanation is perhaps that Jeremiah's wholehearted devotion to his prophetic mission did not leave him room for devotion to wife and family, and for participation in all the joys and sorrows of his fellow men.

16:2. Since it was considered most important for a Hebrew to have children to carry on the family name and property, celibacy was very rare, among the prophets as well as others. Some of the prophets used experiences in their married life to reinforce their prophetic message (see, e.g., Hos. 1:2-9; Isa. 8:3-4; Ezek. 24:15-27).

when Christian and Hopeful debated as to who should lead the other as they sought to return to the way, "for their encouragement, they heard the voice of one saying, 'Set thine heart toward the highway, even the way which thou wentest, turn again.' " [6] This is pure Jeremiah (31:21).

Jeremiah himself has become, through his own confession and through the confession's return upon the twofold pathos of the covenant

predicament, a type of the form of the deliverance needed, of the only deliverance possible to a people so far estranged from the God who is Loyal-in-Love. "We can scarcely be wrong in thinking," writes Skinner, "that this illumination, which comes to Jeremiah in answer to prayer, marks a turning-point in his life." [7]

16:1-21. *A Parenthesis of Pain.*—The contents of this chapter bear little relation to the drought poem into which they have been in-

[6] *Pilgrim's Progress*, Part I, ch. xv.   [7] *Prophecy and Religion*, p. 214.

their carcasses shall be meat for the fowls of heaven, and for the beasts of the earth.

5 For thus saith the Lord, Enter not into the house of mourning, neither go to lament nor bemoan them: for I have taken away my peace from this people, saith the Lord, *even* loving-kindness and mercies.

6 Both the great and the small shall die in this land: they shall not be buried, neither shall *men* lament for them, nor cut themselves, nor make themselves bald for them:

7 Neither shall *men* tear *themselves* for them in mourning, to comfort them for the dead; neither shall *men* give them the cup of consolation to drink for their father or for their mother.

8 Thou shalt not also go into the house of feasting, to sit with them to eat and to drink.

9 For thus saith the Lord of hosts, the God of Israel; Behold, I will cause to cease out of this place in your eyes, and in your days, the voice of mirth, and the voice of gladness, the voice of the bridegroom, and the voice of the bride.

10 ¶ And it shall come to pass, when thou shalt show this people all these words, and they shall say unto thee, Wherefore hath the Lord pronounced all this great

bodies shall be food for the birds of the air and for the beasts of the earth.

5 "For thus says the Lord: Do not enter the house of mourning, or go to lament, or bemoan them; for I have taken away my peace from this people, says the Lord, my steadfast love and mercy. 6 Both great and small shall die in this land; they shall not be buried, and no one shall lament for them or cut himself or make himself bald for them. 7 No one shall break bread for the mourner, to comfort him for the dead; nor shall any one give him the cup of consolation to drink for his father or his mother. 8 You shall not go into the house of feasting to sit with them, to eat and drink. 9 For thus says the Lord of hosts, the God of Israel: Behold, I will make to cease from this place, before your eyes and in your days, the voice of mirth and the voice of gladness, the voice of the bridegroom and the voice of the bride.

10 "And when you tell this people all these words, and they say to you, 'Why has

---

6-7. These verses give an interesting insight into popular mourning customs. Self-laceration and shaving of the head were forbidden by Deuteronomy (14:1; cf. Lev. 19:28), but many of the Hebrews apparently practiced such rites (41:5; 47:5; Isa. 22:12; Amos 8:10; Mic. 1:16; Ezek. 7:18). They are mentioned here without either approval or disapproval. The RSV correctly renders **break bread for the mourner** rather than **tear themselves for them in mourning**, reading לחם instead of להם, with two Hebrew MSS and the LXX. It was apparently customary for a mourner to fast until the evening of the day of burial (cf. II Sam. 1:12; 3:35); his friends would then persuade him to eat and to be comforted. The food of mourners was considered unclean (Hos. 9:4; cf. Deut. 26:14). **The cup of consolation** is not elsewhere mentioned, but was probably a cup of wine presented to the mourner when his fast was over.

10-13. These verses should be compared with 5:18-19 and the other passages of Deuteronomic origin listed in the Exeg., *ad loc.* They were designed to furnish a ready answer to anyone who wanted to know the reason for the Babylonian exile.

---

serted. They break its movement and obscure its themes. They form an awkward parenthesis depriving 17:1-18 of its poetic purpose and power. Since its contents are amply covered by the Exeg. we shall pass over it with but slight comment.

Vss. 1-9 clearly document the prophet's loneliness, here spelled out in biographical detail. Like Paul, Jeremiah refrains from marriage "for

the present distress" (I Cor. 7:26). So assured is Jeremiah of the coming catastrophe and of his prophetic mission that he forgoes the desirable and normal pleasures of family and home. So universal is the calamity bearing down upon the people that he will not bear children to suffer its outrages. Similarly he is forbidden both to mourn and to rejoice: so many shall fall that no time shall be had for burial rites or

evil against us? or what *is* our iniquity? or what *is* our sin that we have committed against the Lord our God?

11 Then shalt thou say unto them, Because your fathers have forsaken me, saith the Lord, and have walked after other gods, and have served them, and have worshipped them, and have forsaken me, and have not kept my law;

12 And ye have done worse than your fathers; for, behold, ye walk every one after the imagination of his evil heart, that they may not hearken unto me:

13 Therefore will I cast you out of this land into a land that ye know not, *neither* ye nor your fathers; and there shall ye serve other gods day and night; where I will not show you favor.

14 ¶ Therefore, behold, the days come, saith the Lord, that it shall no more be said, The Lord liveth, that brought up the children of Israel out of the land of Egypt;

15 But, The Lord liveth, that brought up the children of Israel from the land of the north, and from all the lands whither he had driven them: and I will bring them again into their land that I gave unto their fathers.

16 ¶ Behold, I will send for many fishers, saith the Lord, and they shall fish them; and after will I send for many hunters, and they shall hunt them from every mountain, and from every hill, and out of the holes of the rocks.

the Lord pronounced all this great evil against us? What is our iniquity? What is the sin that we have committed against the Lord our God?' **11** then you shall say to them: 'Because your fathers have forsaken me, says the Lord, and have gone after other gods and have served and worshiped them, and have forsaken me and have not kept my law, **12** and because you have done worse than your fathers, for behold, every one of you follows his stubborn evil will, refusing to listen to me; **13** therefore I will hurl you out of this land into a land which neither you nor your fathers have known, and there you shall serve other gods day and night, for I will show you no favor.'

14 "Therefore, behold, the days are coming, says the Lord, when it shall no longer be said, 'As the Lord lives who brought up the people of Israel out of the land of Egypt,' **15** but 'As the Lord lives who brought up the people of Israel out of the north country and out of all the countries where he had driven them.' For I will bring them back to their own land which I gave to their fathers.

16 "Behold, I am sending for many fishers, says the Lord, and they shall catch them; and afterwards I will send for many hunters, and they shall hunt them from every mountain and every hill, and out of

---

B. Promise of Return from the Diaspora (16:14-15)

14-15. These verses are virtually a duplicate of 23:7-8, where they have a more appropriate place. The passage is of late origin (see Exeg. on 23:7-8), and was inserted here in order to soften to some degree the preceding prediction of exile.

C. Retribution for Israel's Iniquity (16:16-18)

These verses originally stood immediately after vs. 13, and were a continuation of the threat uttered there. The figures of hunting and fishing are used to describe the total punishment of the people for their sins and do not necessarily describe two periods of destruction—in 598 and 587 b.c. For the idea cf. especially Amos 9:2-4.

---

customs; nor is it meet to feast irresponsibly when **the voice of mirth and the voice of gladness** is about to cease from the land. The Lord is sending **many fishers** who shall take the masses of the people in their nets; and so thorough will be the work of the enemy that they are likened to hunters, who will hunt the people out from all places of hiding so that none shall escape. **For my eyes are upon all their**

ways; they are not hid from me, nor is their iniquity concealed from my eyes, says the Lord. This is a deft turn, for God also is a hunter, from whom we cannot hide, and who tracks us down even in those recesses of betrayal whereby we would hide even from ourselves.

Vss. 10-13 are not as sharp as vs. 17. The "Why?" that is asked here is not as deep as that of 14:8 or 14:19, and is almost superficial after

17 For mine eyes *are* upon all their ways: they are not hid from my face, neither is their iniquity hid from mine eyes.

18 And first I will recompense their iniquity and their sin double; because they have defiled my land, they have filled mine inheritance with the carcasses of their detestable and abominable things.

19 O LORD, my strength, and my fortress, and my refuge in the day of affliction, the Gentiles shall come unto thee from the ends of the earth, and shall say, Surely our fathers have inherited lies, vanity, and *things* wherein *there is* no profit.

20 Shall a man make gods unto himself, and they *are* no gods?

21 Therefore, behold, I will this once cause them to know, I will cause them to

the clefts of the rocks. 17 For my eyes are upon all their ways; they are not hid from me, nor is their iniquity concealed from my eyes. 18 And[z] I will doubly recompense their iniquity and their sin, because they have polluted my land with the carcasses of their detestable idols, and have filled my inheritance with their abominations."

19 O LORD, my strength and my stronghold,
   my refuge in the day of trouble,
to thee shall the nations come
   from the ends of the earth and say:
"Our fathers have inherited nought but lies,
   worthless things in which there is no profit.
20 Can man make for himself gods?
   Such are no gods!"

21 "Therefore, behold, I will make them know, this once I will make them know my

[z] Gk: Heb *And first*

18. The Hebrew has **first**. Though this is omitted by the LXX (which the RSV follows), it probably was in the text used by the LXX, and was perhaps inserted by the editor who placed vss. 14-15 in their present position. He apparently interpreted vss. 16-17 as a promise of restoration rather than as a threat of doom. For the idea of double recompense cf. Isa. 40:2. There is no need, however, to suppose dependence of this passage upon Second Isaiah; vss. 16-17 bear every mark of genuineness.

Rudolph has rightly pointed out that vs. 18 is of Deuteronomic origin. It originally closed the section, vss. 1-13, 16-18, in which the Deuteronomic editor included a genuine oracle (vss. 16-17) along with material of his own composition. The situation here is thus similar to 11:1-17, where the Deuteronomic editor has included a genuine oracle (vss. 15-16) within his own composition.

D. CONVERSION OF THE NATIONS TO YAHWEH (16:19-21)

This poem concludes the chapter on a note of hope. However, it is in all likelihood not from Jeremiah but from a writer of postexilic times who expected the conversion of the other nations, probably under the influence of Second Isaiah. The poem is very loosely constructed, consisting of (a) the prayer of a pious individual in liturgical phrases; (b) the words of the heathen who come to Yahweh; (c) a reflection by the author; and (d) a word of the Lord. The author has made use of phrases drawn from other parts of the book of Jeremiah, especially from 2:5, 8, 11; 3:23-24; 17:17; his ideas and phrases should be compared with Isa. 45:20-24; Ezek. 36:23. Similar passages in the present book are 3:17; 12:16.

21. This verse is connected by some commentators with vs. 18 rather than with vs. 20. However, it is appropriate in its present position and can be applied to the foreign nations as well as to the Israelites, as would be the case if it were transferred to a position

15:18. The placing of the blame upon the fathers is counter to the trend of Jeremiah's thinking. Only in vs. 13—**therefore I will hurl you**—do we have the Jeremian touch, the play upon his name—Yahweh hurls!—being highly

apposite and also retrieving an authentic overtone from 10:18.

The promises of vss. 14-15, 19-20 are doubtless late (cf. 23:7-8), though due recognition should be given to Cornill's argument that such an

know mine hand and my might; and they shall know that my name *is* The LORD.

17 The sin of Judah *is* written with a pen of iron, *and* with the point of a diamond: *it is* graven upon the table of their heart, and upon the horns of your altars;

power and my might, and they shall know that my name is the LORD."

17 "The sin of Judah is written with a pen of iron; with a point of diamond it is engraved on the tablet of their heart,

---

after vs. 18. Perhaps it implies that the heathen nations will recognize the power of Yahweh and the impotence of their own deities when the Israelites are returned from the Diaspora. In that case, vss. 19-21 may have been added at the same time as vss. 14-15.

XII. MISCELLANEOUS MATERIALS (17:1-27)

The contents of this chapter are miscellaneous in character, having no central theme. Some parts are clearly secondary, others very probably so.

The chapter may be analyzed as follows: (*a*) a statement of the prophet that because Judah's sin is engraved on the hearts of her people and in the cultus, she must go into exile and lose her treasures (vss. 1-4); (*b*) a psalm contrasting trust in flesh and trust in God (vss. 5-8); (*c*) a proverb on the deceitfulness of the heart and God's knowledge of it (vss. 9-10, possibly the introduction to vss. 14-18); (*d*) a proverb on the transitoriness of ill-gotten wealth (vs. 11); (*e*) a fragment on the sanctuary (vs. 12); (*f*) a brief prayer on the fate of those who forsake the Lord (vs. 13); (*g*) one of the "confessions" of Jeremiah (vss. 14-18); (*h*) a Deuteronomic passage on sabbath observance (vss. 19-27).

We can be certain of the genuineness of vss. 1-4 (except for the gloss, vss. 2*b*-3*a*), 9-10, 14-18, and of the non-Jeremianic origin of vss. 12-13, 19-27; the remaining verses are probably secondary, but their Jeremianic origin cannot be entirely ruled out.

A. JUDAH'S HARDENED SIN (17:1-4)

The prophet says that Judah has become so hardened in her sin that she must be punished by exile and the loss of her treasures. The text is difficult, especially in vs. 2 and the beginning of vs. 3. We can, however, restore some order if we adopt the emendation suggested by Volz at the beginning of vs. 2, כזכרון בהם, and join these words with the end of vs. 1. We then have as the last two lines of a genuine poem the following:

> And on the horns of their altars,
> as a memorial against them.

The words which follow, **their altars . . . open country**, should then be considered a gloss (Volz, Rudolph), probably by the Deuteronomic editor, who here lists a series of specific details in the cultic system which he considered to be sinful.

Jeremiah is saying that Judah's sin is written in two places: (*a*) in their hearts, which have strayed away from Yahweh, and (*b*) in the cultus, which is symbolized by the horns of the altar. Possibly the words were spoken, as Volz suggests, on a great day of atonement, when the people were lightheartedly seeking to atone for their sins through the making of sacrifices. The prophet rebukes them, seeing the sacrificial system itself as

---

expectation as we see in vs. 19 is implicit in Jeremiah's theological outlook. The notion that one day all the nations of the earth shall come as suppliants to Israel is based upon Jeremiah's initial recognition that all ways which lie outside the true way must be byways, that all gods who are other than the living God must be no-gods, and that it is in the nature of things (of the ordinances of Yahweh) that this will

eventually become plain. Certainly this is implicit in the dialectic nature of Jeremiah's view of the God relation, and justifies Peake in referring to vss. 19-20 as "this great utterance." [8]

17:1-18. *End of the Drought Poem.*—The concluding movement of Jeremiah's poem is strikingly similar to that of Eliot's *Waste Land*. The similarities are observable both in strategy

[8] *Op. cit.,* I, 219.

2 Whilst their children remember their altars and their groves by the green trees upon the high hills.

3 O my mountain in the field, I will give thy substance *and* all thy treasures to the spoil, *and* thy high places for sin, throughout all thy borders.

4 And thou, even thyself, shalt discontinue from thine heritage that I gave thee; and I will cause thee to serve thine enemies in the land which thou knowest not: for ye have kindled a fire in mine anger, *which* shall burn for ever.

5 ¶ Thus saith the LORD; Cursed *be* the man that trusteth in man, and maketh flesh his arm, and whose heart departeth from the LORD.

and on the horns of their altars, 2 while their children remember their altars and their Ashe'rim, beside every green tree, and on the high hills, 3 on the mountains in the open country. Your wealth and all your treasures I will give for spoil as the price of your sin*ᵃ* throughout all your territory. 4 You shall loosen your hand*ᵇ* from your heritage which I gave to you, and I will make you serve your enemies in a land which you do not know, for in my anger a fire is kindled which shall burn for ever."

5 Thus says the LORD:
"Cursed is the man who trusts in man
    and makes flesh his arm,
  whose heart turns away from the LORD.

ᵃ Cn: Heb *your high places for sin*
ᵇ Cn: Heb *and in you*

---

part of Judah's sin (cf. 6:20; 7:21-23; 11:15). As a result, their treasures must be despoiled and the people must go into exile.

17:1. A pen of iron was a stylus made of iron (cf. Job 19:24) which had a **point of diamond** with which letters could be cut in a very hard surface such as rock. Diamond has not been found in excavations in Palestine, but we know from Pliny (*Natural History* XXXVII. 15) that it was used for purposes such as are described here. The emphasis upon sin as being written **on the tablet of their heart** prepares the way for the new covenant passage in which it is promised that the law will be written in the hearts of the people (31:33).

Blood was smeared **on the horns of their altars** in some of the sacrifices (Lev. 4:7; 16:18; etc.); in an earlier time refuge could be found in the sanctuaries by those who grasped the horns of the altar (I Kings 1:50-51; 2:28). In the present passage they are a symbol of the sacrificial system.

3-4. These verses are virtually a duplicate of 15:13-14, but their original place is here. Volz considers this a separate oracle directed against the owning class, but it is better connected with the preceding, as the statement of the punishment of the sins just described.

B. A PSALM OF CONTRASTS (17:5-8)

5-8. This is a psalm contrasting the fates of those who trust in man and of those who trust in God. The similarity of this poem to Ps. 1 has often been noted. It is almost certain that the present passage is earlier than Ps. 1, and that the dependence is of Ps. 1

---

and dramatic structure. The factors of drought and military disaster having been graphically drawn, the people have twice asked the question "Why?"—why is this happening to us? They have been twice answered and rebuffed by Yahweh. The prophet also, having been driven into a sense of extreme isolation and of separation from God, has asked "Why?"—why is this happening to me?—and has been admonished to return. Now, in a climax passage, Yahweh spells out both the sin and the doom of the people: the prostitution of the covenant relation to the manifold idolatries which the children "remember" (cf. Jer. 2:20; 3:2, 23;

etc.) is but the outward sign of the inner defection—defection in the cultus (the **horns of their altars**) and defection in the heart—where it is **written with a pen of iron** and engraved **with a point of diamond**. So hard is the heart of Judah, and so deeply engrained her betrayal, that the guilt cannot be removed. Exile must follow.

5-8. *The Two Ways.*⁹—This is the first of three wisdom passages and of four moral inferences. The established functions of the priests, the wise men, and the prophets are plainly recognized in Jeremiah's time (18:18). The

⁹ Cf. Expos. on 6:16-21, pp. 862-65.

6 For he shall be like the heath in the desert, and shall not see when good cometh; but shall inhabit the parched places in the wilderness, *in* a salt land and not inhabited.

7 Blessed *is* the man that trusteth in the LORD, and whose hope the LORD is.

8 For he shall be as a tree planted by the waters, and *that* spreadeth out her roots by the river, and shall not see when heat cometh, but her leaf shall be green; and shall not be careful in the year of drought, neither shall cease from yielding fruit.

6 He is like a shrub in the desert,
  and shall not see any good come.
He shall dwell in the parched places of
    the wilderness,
  in an uninhabited salt land.

7 "Blessed is the man who trusts in the
    LORD,
  whose trust is the LORD.
8 He is like a tree planted by water,
  that sends out its roots by the stream,
and does not fear when heat comes,
  for its leaves remain green,
and is not anxious in the year of drought,
  for it does not cease to bear fruit."

---

upon our passage rather than vice versa. Ps. 1 is one of the very latest of the psalms, probably being composed as an introduction to the whole Psalter. Furthermore, the poem here is more original and more spiritual than Ps. 1 (cf. Hermann Gunkel, *Die Psalmen* [Göttingen: Vandenhoeck & Ruprecht, 1926; "Göttinger Handkommentar zum Alten Testament"], p. 3; for an Egyptian parallel from the Wisdom of Amenemope see J. H. Breasted, *The Dawn of Conscience* [New York: Charles Scribner's Sons, 1933], pp. 364-65).

Some scholars have denied that the poem was composed by Jeremiah, while others have affirmed its Jeremianic authorship. Aside from the fact that its form has few if any parallels in the genuine portions, we must note that its general outlook is contradictory to the prophet's own experience. He trusted in the Lord, but found himself constantly

---

wise man, giving guidance mainly to individuals, was a phenomenon common not only to Semitic cultures but to Egypt and Babylonia as well. This particular comparison—of the wicked to the stunted desert shrub and the righteous to the well-watered tree—may be paralleled from the writings of Ámen-em-ápt, who wrote about 1000 B.C.[1] There, as here, a comparison is made with Ps. 1, the psalm being generally regarded as later in composition than the verses from Jeremiah. What is significant about the appearance of this wisdom teaching in Jeremiah's poem is the form it is given, the position in which it is placed, and the new accent it derives from the Jeremiah context.

By its inclusion here it ceases to be wisdom and becomes prophecy. It is no longer a detached moral saying; but it takes on existential implication. The either/or of the soul's decisive orientation under God is its burden. Either a man trusts in his "flesh," the self-centered "flesh-substance common to men and beasts,"[2] or he stands within the spirit-filled dynamism of his

relationship with God. Either he stands trustfully in this relationship, or his **heart turns away from the LORD.** Either he **does not cease to bear fruit** by virtue of this relationship, or he feels the mystic's "dryness" as of **the parched places** and the **salt land.** Either he lives in the "quiet desperation" (Kierkegaard) of a mounting anxiety in which he is "unable to see the coming of good" or he achieves victory over fear and anxiety "and lives serene" (Moffatt). Either he is like the scrub dwarf juniper, eking out in parched rocky places the dried-up life of the soul, or he knows the fullness of the tree planted by the waters **that sends out its roots by the stream.** The moral wisdom is given the dialectic depth of the profound anthropology of Jeremiah's doctrine of man.

Once this dialectic feature is seen, one recognizes easily that it presents "a nobler and wider conception of personal religion" than is found in the contexts of the several wisdom literatures, and also wider than that found in Ps. 1, "which defines it within the limits of Jewish legalism, the observance of the Law."[3] Robinson also holds that "the figure of growth may suggest a certain inevitability in the working out of life, for good or for evil."[4] One may go farther, and suggest the prophet's anticipations of

---

[1] *Ger Maa*, the Silent True One. "The man of God is like a large leafy tree planted in fertile ground. . . ." Grace Turnbull (*Tongues of Fire* [New York: The Macmillan Co., 1929], p. 24) gives the date as after 1555 B.C. Cf. E. A. Wallis Budge, *The Teaching of Ámen-em-ápt* (London: Martin Hopkinson & Co., 1924).

[2] John A. T. Robinson, *The Body, A Study in Pauline Theology* (Chicago: Henry Regnery Co., 1952), p. 17.

[3] H. Wheeler Robinson, *The Cross of Jeremiah*, p. 79.
[4] *Ibid.*, p. 80.

9 ¶ The heart *is* deceitful above all *things,* and desperately wicked: who can know it?

9 The heart is deceitful above all things,
  and desperately corrupt;
  who can understand it?

---

hated and persecuted. It is more likely, therefore, to have been composed by a poet of the wisdom school who held the orthodox doctrine of divine retribution.

The psalm was probably placed here because it enunciates the principle on which the doom predicted in vs. 4 was based. Cornill suggests that the one whom the author had in mind as having flagrantly trusted in man rather than in God was Zedekiah, whose alliance with the Egyptians was responsible for the Babylonian invasion, 589-587 B.C.

C. A Wisdom Saying (17:9-10)

The first of these verses is a proverblike statement of the deceitfulness and weakness of the human heart; the second is a word of the Lord stating that he—and, by implication, he alone—searches the human heart and rewards men according to their actions. These verses may be only the reflections of a late wisdom writer (Volz). The ideas expressed, however, are quite true to Jeremiah's thought (cf. 11:20; 16:17; 20:12). Duhm has made the happy suggestion that vss. 9-10 form the introduction to vss. 14-18. In that case, vs. 9 is a complaint of Jeremiah; vs. 10 is the reply of Yahweh; and vss. 14-18 are a prayer of the prophet.

9. "Weak" is a better rendering of 'ānúsh than either **wicked** or **corrupt**. The root אנש usually denotes weakness or sickness rather than wickedness.

Paul and Pascal.[5] The principle invoked here is that employed by Pascal to demarcate the two movements of his projected Apology for the Christian Faith: the misery of man without God, and the happiness of man with God.[6] The first of these orientations, for Pascal, signifies the "natural" man: he is characterized by self-love and contradictions. His condition is one of inconstancy, weariness, unrest.[7]

9-10. O Desperately Sick the Heart!—It is clear from the foregoing that this second moral inference is neither "an isolated proverb" nor "detached" nor "without apparent connection" with the poem's argument. On the contrary, we are forced upon some such reflection by what precedes. Clearly something is radically wrong with man; and Jeremiah, with his uncanny penetration into the hidden secret, puts his finger unerringly upon the spot. Much more truly than it was said of Goethe might it be said of him:

> He took the suffering human race,
> He read each wound, each weakness clear;
> And struck his finger on the place,
> And said: *Thou ailest here, and here!* [8]

For Jeremiah, all the "places" led to one place, the central defection of the human heart.

The argument moves in Jeremiah precisely

as it later moves in Augustine and Pascal. Beneath and behind all forms of human betrayal is the unacknowledged treachery of the heart. "The heart is treacherous above all things, and desperately sick—who can understand it?" The contemporaneity of this utterance is more than striking: Jeremiah's realistic psychological penetration into man's existential predicament is. in contexts such as this, not less than astonishing. Here he lays bare in a single sentence the fact of human ambivalence and contradiction.

Pascal knew this condition well. "We are only falsehood, duplicity, contradiction; we both conceal and disguise ourselves from ourselves." And the fault lies in the heart's commitments: "the heart naturally loves the Universal Being, and also itself naturally, according as it gives itself to them; and it hardens itself against one or the other at its will. You have rejected the one, and kept the other." When the choice is for self, as against God, the self becomes *le moi haïssable* (the hateable ego); and one begins to feel "his nothingness, his forlornness, his insufficiency, his dependence, his weakness, his emptiness." What emerges is "man in contradiction." "We perceive an image of truth, and possess only a lie." [9]

It is interesting that we should have waited until our own time to come into possession of this perspective—in Dostoevski and Kierkegaard, our contemporary poets and existentialist philosophers, in depth psychology and Protestant theology. Emil Brunner, to take a single example, gathers up the total argument:

---

[5] For Paul's use of the term "flesh" (*bāsar*) see John A. T. Robinson, *op. cit.*, pp. 13, 16.

[6] *Thoughts*, No. 60.

[7] *Ibid.*, Nos. 94, 100, 127. Cf. also, Augustine's use of Jer. 17:5 ff. in his "conversation with a heathen inquirer," in his *Reply to Faustus the Manichaean* XIII. 7-8.

[8] Matthew Arnold, "Memorial Verses, (April, 1850)."

[9] *Op. cit.*, Nos. 377, 277, 455, 131, 434.

10 I the LORD search the heart, *I* try the reins, even to give every man according to his ways, *and* according to the fruit of his doings.

11 *As* the partridge sitteth *on eggs,* and hatcheth *them* not; *so* he that getteth riches, and not by right, shall leave them in the midst of his days, and at his end shall be a fool.

10 "I the LORD search the mind
    and try the heart,
  to give to every man according to his
    ways,
  according to the fruit of his doings."

11 Like the partridge that gathers a brood
    which she did not hatch,
  so is he who gets riches but not by
    right;
  in the midst of his days they will leave
    him,
  and at his end he will be a fool.

D. THE TRANSITORINESS OF ILL-GOTTEN WEALTH (17:11)

11. Here is a proverb which could be from Jeremiah, but it is more likely to be a secondary insertion by a wisdom writer, since it has the form and the language typical of the Hebrew proverb (*māshāl*). It has been placed here apparently because it illustrates

Even "flesh" in the New Testament is not a natural but a personal definition: the permanent act of being turned away from God. . . . In the Bible—not only in the Old Testament, but also in the New . . . —there is nothing said about sin which means anything other than the act of turning away from God. But . . . this act is conceived as one which determines man's *whole* existence. [By this act of turning man] sets himself in opposition to his constitution. . . . Because man is in opposition to his divine origin in the Creation . . . he lives in opposition to his own God-given nature; therefore his present nature itself is: contradiction.[10]

This being the condition of the heart of man, one may well ask **who can understand it?** It will not be understood from within its contradictions. From the divine side alone will it be understood.

**I the LORD search the mind
and try the heart—**

a testing which goes on constantly: the most inward psychical evidence of which is well attested; for he gives **to every man according to his ways,** and **according to the fruit of his doings.** Wherever this dimension is not acknowledged the result is easily measured:

The note, my son, is loneliness.
Over all the world
Men move unhoming, and eternally
Concerned: a swarm of bees who have lost their
    queen.
Nothing else is so ill at ease.[1]

[10] *Man in Revolt,* pp. 148, 152, 204.
[1] Christopher Fry, *Venus Observed* (New York and London: Oxford University Press, 1949), Act II, p. 52. Copyright 1949 by Christopher Fry. Used by permission of the publishers.

11. *The Partridge and the Fool.*—It may be readily conceded that the whimsical wisdom piece (*māshāl*) of this verse is not altogether apposite to what precedes and follows. It stands apart more sharply from the whole, possessing as it does a complete dramatic integrity in its own aesthetic kind. Because of this it does not so easily receive the dialectic dimension of the whole. Nevertheless it is a useful specification of the principle already set forth in the two units preceding. Like a kaleidoscope when shaken, each of the four moral inferences, though differing greatly in color detail and surface statement, shows a design leading everything to the same controlling center. The device of employing the popular proverb to draw its wisdom and the people who prize it into a context of deeper implication is a sound tactic. Just as in the first unit the folly of the man who makes flesh his arm is specified, so here the folly of ill-gotten gains is exposed. And just as we are led, in the Sermon on the Mount, from the proverbial advice "Do not lay up for yourselves treasures upon earth" (Matt. 6:19) to the controlling principle "but seek first his kingdom and his righteousness, and all these things shall be yours as well" (Matt. 6:33), so here we should focus attention upon the fact that **riches illegitimately procured by anyone in the midst of his days . . . will leave him.**

In other words this passage is not merely another instance of what Samuel Johnson, following Juvenal, called *The Vanity of Human Wishes,* a purely Stoical wisdom. It is much nearer to Pascal's insight, that "even if we should see ourselves sufficiently sheltered on all sides, weariness [*l'ennui*] of its own accord would not fail to arise from the depths of the heart

12 ¶ A glorious high throne from the beginning *is* the place of our sanctuary.	12 A glorious throne set on high from the beginning is the place of our sanctuary.

how one who gets his wealth unjustly is rewarded "according to the fruit of his doings" (vs. 10) .

The figure is that of a mother bird that gathers young birds she has not hatched and attempts to raise them; they cling to her while they are young, but when they grow up and their true nature asserts itself they desert the foster mother. The point is that ill-gotten wealth can be only transitory; the owner can in the end only **be a fool**. For the rendering of דגר by **gathers a brood**, cf. Isa. 34:15, the only other occurrence of the word.

E. The Greatness of the Temple (17:12)

12. This statement is entirely out of harmony with Jeremiah's attitude toward temple worship (cf. 7:1-15; 26:1-6) and it must be secondary. It is probably placed here to

wherein it has its natural roots, and to fill the mind with its poison." [2]

It has been suggested that whoever wrote vss. 5-8 may have had Zedekiah in mind (see Exeg.) or Jehoiakim's confidence in Egypt (as C. J. Ball), which led to the ill-fated alliance which in turn led to the revolt from Nebuchadrezzar, and so to the country's final catastrophe. The verses might also refer to Jehoiakim's self-aggrandizing extravagances, such as the building of the sumptuous palace on Mount Zion, employing forced labor and alien patterns and styles (cf. 22:13-17). Jeremiah's "woe to him who builds his house by unrighteousness" (22:13) is not unlike the present protest against him who **gets riches but not by right**. Considering the hardened hostility of Jehoiakim toward the prophet, as well as the fact that the scroll was prepared to be read before this king, it seems more than likely that the irony of the *māshāl* points directly to Jehoiakim. To compare him with a partridge gathering a brood which she did not hatch is a superb touch, especially in its comic reduction of the king's tyrannical and unwarranted pretensions to the level of the stupid sobriety of the silly, interloping partridge. From the moment that Peisthetaerus, in Aristophanes' *The Birds*, exclaims "Apollo the Deliverer! what an enormous beak!" it is impossible for the pompous struttings of the birds to appear otherwise than fantastic and absurd. Few of the pomps of human pretension, whether of open power or covert pride, can withstand the comic reduction to the absurd; the tyrants triumph when the people have lost the comic dimension for themselves and their rulers. But the Hebrew mind as revealed in the O.T. is essentially serious and concerned. The prophetic consciousness of Jeremiah alights but briefly upon the wisdom of

comic displacement and carries it over immediately into pathos and denunciation. If Jehoiakim was in his mind—and it must be remembered that Jehoahaz had been the people's choice upon Josiah's death, and that Jehoahaz was removed by the Egyptians and Jehoiakim made king in his stead (II Kings 23:31 ff.) —one must recognize with Skinner that Jehoiakim's palace building "symbolized a conception of royalty which Jeremiah repudiated with his whole heart." [3] **At his end** such a man **will be a fool**.

This leads to a final possibility that Judah herself, by virtue of her capitulation to these betrayals of her heritage, has become like the partridge gathering a brood which she did not hatch—a brood of false gods, false mores, and false commitments. And **in the midst of** [her] **days** these will certainly leave her, as Jeremiah has been proclaiming from the beginning. For all such pretensions are false in their essence, as Israel herself is false and pretentious save in so far as she moves constantly and perpetually into a land which "the Lord thy God giveth thee" (Deut. 27:3) . For Jeremiah, all activity arising from motivation which lies outside the covenant relationship is in its essence false, for there is "a glorious throne set on high from the beginning" which is the one true "place of our sanctuary" (vs. 12) . This is clearly a transcendent appeal. It is the one abiding source of all authenticity: all else is a pathetic playing of the partridge while the earthly sanctuaries fall. Whatever fails to take its origin from the ultimate throne "shall be written in the earth [dust]" (vss. 12-13) .

12-13. The Dust and the Fountain.—Here there must be disagreement with the exegete, for we come to what seems to the present writer to be the poem's climax in one of the purest and

² *Op. cit.*, No. 139.
³ *Prophecy and Religion*, p. 247.

contrast the eternal temple of Yahweh with the false altars and other cultic objects of
vss. 1-2. Some commentators (e.g., Condamin) join the verse with vs. 13, and consider
all of vs. 12 as vocative—the temple itself is addressed, as is Yahweh in the first line of vs.
13. This is possible but awkward.

---

most elevated passages in Jeremiah. The apostrophes of its opening movement, together with the recapitulating figures which follow, make it one of the finest summations both of Jeremiah's faith and of his principle to be found in this middle period of his work. It is depressing to find a textual critic so generally astute as Peake making the usual comment that these verses are "not connected with their context" and regarding vs. 12 as setting a "value on Jerusalem as Yahweh's throne" which is "surprising" in Jeremiah.[4] Textual criticism, with its syntactical methodology, assumes that what is disjunct is therefore "not connected"; when not connected, vs. 12 stands apart from the context; apart from the context it seems to laud the temple in Jerusalem; since this is out of harmony with Jeremiah's general attitude it must imply another authorship and therefore late insertion by someone with another point of view. Seldom could the *non sequitur* of the textual critic seem so plain, nor the limitations of the critic as interpreter so apparent. Not only is the utterance altogether central to Jeremiah's attitude, but it, together with vs. 13, may very well be one of the pivotal utterances of his book.

Following as it does the depth penetrations of the preceding verses—the empty man and the blessed man, the deceitful heart with its desperate sickness, and the naïve pretentiousness of a people who would usurp the gifts of God without observing the integrities of the God-relationship—and climaxing as it does a thematic context which has presented, in Gillies' fine summary, "Drought on the land, Defeat on the field, Desolation in the heart,"[5] the apostrophes announce with clarion clarity the one hope of Israel:

Thou throne of glory, on high from the beginning,
Thou place of our sanctuary,
Thou hope of Israel, the Lord![6]

These exclamations of adoration and praise are based, without doubt, upon the presence of the temple in Jerusalem and upon the place which the temple held in the minds of the people; but precisely not as fixing the greatness of God within the temple, but as being infinitely beyond it. It is beyond it as the real is beyond the symbol, and as the substance is beyond the shadow. "All things" (vs. 9), for Jeremiah, which are less than "trust in the LORD" (vs. 7) must be **written in the earth.**

Thus, what we have here is what Maclaren calls "a wonderful vision of what God is."[7] What we are to behold here is not "a glorious throne" but a throne of glory, a much more exalted thing. Maclaren, who compares this use of the term "glory" to the light which was afterward called the "Shekinah," goes on to comment: "This, then, is the first of Jeremiah's great thoughts of God, and it means—'The Lord God omnipotent reigneth,' there is none else but He, and His will runs authoritative and supreme into all corners of the universe."[8] Similarly, as over against the little hill upon which the temple sat, the Lord was **high from the beginning.** And it is this God who is the true **place** of **our sanctuary.** He is the true place of safety, of asylum, of security. When earthly temples fall, he remains "our dwelling place in all generations" (Ps. 90:1): the oriental guest rights are perpetually available in him. He is finally the one true **hope of Israel.** When all other resources fail he is still **the LORD.**

There is a tendency among some critics to discount so enlightened a view of God in Jeremiah on the ground that the age and its people had nowhere reached so high a level of transcendent generalization, and therefore Jeremiah could not have reached it either. Therefore such notions as his being "a prophet to the nations," his dialectical view of apostasy, his penetration into the limitations of the Deuteronomic code, his proclamation of the New Covenant, etc.—all these must somehow be diminished or assigned to a later development of the religious consciousness. The temptation to accept a foreshortened vision on these points must be resisted on behalf of the possibility that Jeremiah was greater than the hypotheses of the critics and the methodology of textual criticism will permit him to be. It must also be resisted on behalf of the fact that it was precisely in this bracket of years that the religious consciousness of the race achieved this leap of religious generalization all over the known world—in Confucius and Lao-tse, in Buddha and the Upanishads, in Zoroaster, in Homer and the Greek philosophers, in Isaiah, Jeremiah, and Second Isaiah. In Jeremiah the hard bud of the tribal God-consciousness is burst open, and the spirit opens for a moment like an almond bloom.

---

[4] *Jeremiah and Lamentations*, I, 224.
[5] *Jeremiah, the Man and His Message*, p. 146.
[6] Freedman, *Jeremiah*, p. 120.

[7] *Isaiah and Jeremiah*, II, 312.
[8] *Ibid.*, p. 313.

13 O Lord, the hope of Israel, all that forsake thee shall be ashamed, *and* they that depart from me shall be written in the earth, because they have forsaken the Lord, the fountain of living waters.

13 O Lord, the hope of Israel,
> all who forsake thee shall be put to shame;
> those who turn away from thee[c] shall be written in the earth,
> for they have forsaken the Lord, the fountain of living water.

[c] Heb *me*

F. A Prayer for Healing (17:13)

This prayer is really a declaration regarding the fate of those who forsake Yahweh. It makes use of phrases from other parts of Jeremiah (e.g., 14:8; 2:13), but is probably secondary.

Written in the earth: In the ground or dust, rather than written forever in the "book of life" (cf. Exod. 32:32; Isa. 4:3; *et al.*). A contrast is implied with the eternal existence of the temple (vs. 12).

But the lifelong pain of this unfolding must be admitted. It is, indeed, the core of Jeremiah's inner distress. For Jeremiah's psychical trouble is not accounted for on the familiar grounds of temperamental conflict between his sensitivity as poet and his call to prophesy. Like that of Job, his agony arises from the fact that his consciousness of God must shatter all the forms; he finds himself standing beyond family, people, kings, priests, prophets, scribes, seers, temples, and laws—an isolation of spirit that is as frightening, in its initial phases of conflict with every conditioning form of security, as was Pascal's abyss of the infinite and the dark void over the bridge when his carriage hung suspended there in the awful poise between life and death. The "independence" which Jeremiah achieves, from this mid-point on, is that described by Karl Jaspers:

> This he gains by establishing a relation to authentic being. He gains independence of everything that happens in the world by the depth of his attachment to transcendence. What Lao Tse found in the Tao, Socrates in the divine mission and in knowledge, Jeremiah in Yahweh who revealed himself to him . . . : that was what made them independent.[9]

To which it must be added that this enhanced consciousness is gained through a clear-cut awareness of the real polarities in any given situation. In Jeremiah's time these polarities are declared at the extreme limits of the human situation: it is at once a crisis of the people as a community and of the images of the community. Jeremiah experiences these polarities agonistically and at their extremes. He approaches the truth through them. *Les extrêmes*

[9] *The Perennial Scope of Philosophy*, tr. Ralph Manheim (New York: Philosophical Library, 1949), p. 166.

se touchent (the extremes touch in him),[1] but at a deeper level of God-consciousness than the age or his people have known. Much may be known of Jeremiah's book; but until this deeper mystery is grasped, Jeremiah himself—and what is finally significant about him—is not recognized.

Given the transcendence of God, the corollaries follow:

> All that forsake Thee come to shame.
> They that turn from Thee are writ in dust.[2]

The characteristic Hebraic parallelism is apparent here. The term "dust" not only recovers the drought theme of the poem as a whole but more accurately renders the term "earth," which does not mean particularly the soil but that which passes away as over against that which endures. Thus those who depart from God write their names in the impermanent earth which passes, as over against those who "rejoice" because their "names are written in heaven" (Luke 10:20). The recurrence of this metaphor throughout the Scriptures—in Moses, the Psalms, Isaiah, Ezekiel, the Revelation—is significant. But the main thrust here is upon the cause. The man who "makes flesh his arm" (vs. 5) is accursed, the man "who gets riches but not by right" (vs. 11) is a fool, and the man who turns away from God is put to shame and his name is written in the dust **because they have forsaken the Lord, the fountain of living waters.** All else is drought, desperation, and dust.

This is not the first time that this metaphor occurs (cf. 2:13). We have already seen that

[1] Pascal, *Thoughts*, No. 72: "These extremes meet and reunite by force of distance, and find each other in God, and in God alone."
[2] Gillies, *op. cit.*, p. 145.

14 Heal me, O Lord, and I shall be healed; save me, and I shall be saved: for thou *art* my praise.

15 ¶ Behold, they say unto me, Where *is* the word of the Lord? let it come now.

16 As for me, I have not hastened from *being* a pastor to follow thee: neither have I desired the woeful day; thou knowest: that which came out of my lips was *right* before thee.

17 Be not a terror unto me: thou *art* my hope in the day of evil.

14 Heal me, O Lord, and I shall be healed;
   save me, and I shall be saved;
   for thou art my praise.

15 Behold, they say to me,
   "Where is the word of the Lord?
   Let it come!"

16 I have not pressed thee to send evil,
   nor have I desired the day of disaster,
   thou knowest;
   that which came out of my lips
   was before thy face.

17 Be not a terror to me;
   thou art my refuge in the day of evil.

G. Jeremiah's Lament and Prayer (17:14-18)

This section, to which vss. 9-10 probably are an introduction (see above), is a part of the "confessions" of Jeremiah. In a prayer the prophet complains of those who mock him, and asks God to take vengeance upon his enemies. His opponents have been mocking him because his prophecies of doom had not been fulfilled (vs. 15), and have been accusing him of personally desiring that misfortune should come upon them (vs. 16). The prophet has faith that the Lord knows his motives and will be his refuge.

16. The RSV changes slightly the vocalization of the M.T. in the first part of this verse: *mērā'āh* instead of *mērō'eh;* the resultant translation is superior to the KJV. For the idea cf. 15:11; 18:20.

this is the vital and fulfilling *rûaḥ* which stands over against the empty, and self-emptying, *rûaḥ* of the broken cistern (cf. 2:13). There, as here, whatever men undertake apart from the God-relation is, as Isaiah said a hundred years before,

    a delusion;
  their works are nothing;
their molten images are empty wind (Isa. 41:29).

So also the streams may fail, like the deceitful wadi (15:18), when the self turns in upon itself; but the fountain springs eternally. God himself is both the Breath of the Spirit and the Fountain of Living Water: apart from which we are like the acrobats of Picasso who repeat the spot

          where the pure too-little
  incomprehensibly changes,—springs round
  into that empty too-much! [3]

14-18. *Let Me Not Be Dismayed.*—After proclamations as bold and profound as the verses we have just reviewed, this brief postscript of prayer is appropriate, both religiously and aesthetically. Once again, one is reminded of Pascal's closing remark at the end of his discourse on the "wager": "If this discourse pleases you and seems impressive, know that it is made

by a man who has knelt, both before and after it, in prayer." [4]

**Heal me, O Lord, and I shall be healed;
save me, and I shall be saved.**

It is not necessary to link these words to vss. 9-10. Though there is much to be said for this suggestion, a grasp of the movement of the whole makes them follow more penetratingly from the verses which immediately precede. It is not merely the taunts of his enemies (vs. 15) which have driven him to thoughts which have "revealed to him the deceitfulness of his heart and the weakness of his self-restraint." [5] It is also in the mood induced by the grandeur of his vision of God. On both accounts humility is induced—both the prayer for healing and the petition that God be not a terror to him (vs. 17). His response to the taunts of the people, and to the opposition generally, is not as vindictive as appears at the first reading. He has not desired the day of disaster; he has no choice but to proclaim it. It is in the nature of the situation and the choices of the rulers and their people. And it must be borne in mind that those whose opposition to him has reached the obsessive point of persecution are also the enemies of Yahweh who is identified with his prophet; they would actually prevent his prophetic message to the people. For the people,

[3] Rainer Maria Rilke, *Duino Elegies* (tr. J. B. Leishman and Stephen Spender; New York: W. W. Norton & Co., 1939), 5th Elegy, ll. 84-87. Used by permission.

[4] *Op. cit.*, No. 233.

[5] Peake, *Jeremiah and Lamentations*, I, 225.

18 Let them be confounded that persecute me, but let not me be confounded: let them be dismayed, but let not me be dismayed: bring upon them the day of evil, and destroy them with double destruction.

19 ¶ Thus said the LORD unto me; Go and stand in the gate of the children of the people, whereby the kings of Judah come in, and by the which they go out, and in all the gates of Jerusalem;

20 And say unto them, Hear ye the word of the LORD, ye kings of Judah, and all Judah, and all the inhabitants of Jerusalem, that enter in by these gates:

21 Thus saith the LORD; Take heed to yourselves, and bear no burden on the sabbath day, nor bring *it* in by the gates of Jerusalem;

18 Let those be put to shame who persecute me,
   but let me not be put to shame;
let them be dismayed,
   but let me not be dismayed;
bring upon them the day of evil;
   destroy them with double destruction!

19 Thus said the LORD to me: "Go and stand in the Benjamin*d* Gate, by which the kings of Judah enter and by which they go out, and in all the gates of Jerusalem, 20 and say: 'Hear the word of the LORD, you kings of Judah, and all Judah, and all the inhabitants of Jerusalem, who enter by these gates. 21 Thus says the LORD: Take heed for the sake of your lives, and do not bear a burden on the sabbath day or bring it in

d Cn: Heb *sons of people*

18. This is not really contradictory to vs. 16, as many commentators have maintained. In vs. 16 Jeremiah says that he has not pressed God to send evil upon the people in general; here he prays God to bring evil upon his persecutors. The two groups are not identical. For the idea of vs. 18 cf. 11:20; 12:3; 15:15; 18:23; 20:11. The verse should not be separated from the preceding verses as secondary or as coming from a different time in the life of the prophet.

H. SABBATH OBSERVANCE (17:19-27)

19-27. This section is all but unanimously considered secondary by critical scholars; only Condamin and a few others maintain that it is from Jeremiah. The style is prosaic and repetitious, and very different from the genuine work of the prophet. The author loves the cult in detail (vs. 26), and he makes the continued existence of the nation dependent upon proper observance of **the sabbath**. Jeremiah may well have favored

though wayward, Jeremiah's compassion is again and again evident; toward these, who are the primary betrayers of the people, he can have none.

19-27. Keep the Sabbath Day Holy.—Clearly we begin here a section which "neither formally nor factually has . . . the least connection with the poetical prophecies of evil that preceded it."[6] Also it contains an emphasis on ritual observance "out of harmony with Jeremiah's thought."[7] This is the usual view (see Exeg.), and one against which we need not contend. At the same time it must also be said that even those "hostile to Jeremiah's authorship must admit that the writer has imitated the prophet's style with abundant success."[8] There is, in short, the possibility that it is Jeremiah's.

If so, it must apparently be regarded differ-

[6] Mowinckel, *Prophecy and Tradition,* p. 38.
[7] Calkins, *Jeremiah the Prophet,* p. 161, n. 4.
[8] Guillaume, *Prophecy and Divination,* p. 379.

ently; that is, it must be seen as the first of three episodes which are one in strategy—the strategy of symbolic action: actions which take place in the Benjamin Gate, at the potter's house, and in the valley of Ben-hinnom.

In the first of these the action is that of the people, which is given symbolic meaning by the words which the prophet addresses to them. As the inhabitants of the city and its "kings" go in and out through the Benjamin Gate, he warns them to **take heed for the sake of** [their] **lives,** for they are bearing burdens on the Sabbath, the day which they have been enjoined from the beginning to keep holy. But **they** [their fathers] **did not listen . . . , but stiffened their neck, that they might not hear.** It is this behavior that becomes the symbolic action.

What is at stake is the people's holiness. What Jeremiah would dramatize is their defection from it. Their violation of sabbath holiness is typical of their violation of general holiness.

22 Neither carry forth a burden out of your houses on the sabbath day, neither do ye any work, but hallow ye the sabbath day, as I commanded your fathers.

23 But they obeyed not, neither inclined their ear, but made their neck stiff, that they might not hear, nor receive instruction.

24 And it shall come to pass, if ye diligently hearken unto me, saith the LORD, to bring in no burden through the gates of this city on the sabbath day, but hallow the sabbath day, to do no work therein;

25 Then shall there enter into the gates of this city kings and princes sitting upon the throne of David, riding in chariots and on horses, they, and their princes, the men of Judah, and the inhabitants of Jerusalem: and this city shall remain for ever.

26 And they shall come from the cities of Judah, and from the places about Jerusalem, and from the land of Benjamin, and from the plain, and from the mountains, and from the south, bringing burnt offerings, and sacrifices, and meat offerings, and incense, and bringing sacrifices of praise, unto the house of the LORD.

27 But if ye will not hearken unto me to hallow the sabbath day, and not to bear a burden, even entering in at the gates of Jerusalem on the sabbath day; then will I kindle a fire in the gates thereof, and it shall devour the palaces of Jerusalem, and it shall not be quenched.

by the gates of Jerusalem. **22** And do not carry a burden out of your houses on the sabbath or do any work, but keep the sabbath day holy, as I commanded your fathers. **23** Yet they did not listen or incline their ear, but stiffened their neck, that they might not hear and receive instruction.

24 " 'But if you listen to me, says the LORD, and bring in no burden by the gates of this city on the sabbath day, but keep the sabbath day holy and do no work on it, **25** then there shall enter by the gates of this city kings[e] who sit on the throne of David, riding in chariots and on horses, they and their princes, the men of Judah and the inhabitants of Jerusalem; and this city shall be inhabited for ever. **26** And people shall come from the cities of Judah and the places round about Jerusalem, from the land of Benjamin, from the Shephe'lah, from the hill country, and from the Negeb, bringing burnt offerings and sacrifices, cereal offerings and frankincense, and bringing thank offerings to the house of the LORD. **27** But if you do not listen to me, to keep the sabbath day holy, and not to bear a burden and enter by the gates of Jerusalem on the sabbath day, then I will kindle a fire in its gates, and it shall devour the palaces of Jerusalem and shall not be quenched.' "

[e] Cn: Heb *kings and princes*

---

proper sabbath observance, but he would surely not have made as much depend upon it as these verses imply. Rudolph (against Mowinckel) has correctly recognized that the passage is of Deuteronomic origin. It has the diffuseness and repetitiousness of the Deuteronomic editor, and his phrases frequently occur. One should compare its phraseology with other Deuteronomic passages such as 7:2, 24, 26; 11:8; 22:2, 4-5.

Many commentators date this section in the postexilic period in or near the time of Nehemiah, for Neh. 13:15-22 shows a similar concern for sabbath observance. It is not impossible, however, that such a concern arose at an earlier time and was one of the important interests of the Deuteronomic editor of 550 B.C. A similar emphasis on the

---

"So great is the holiness of the sabbath," notes Pedersen, "that it has its root in remote antiquity." It is the only law which finds its justification in a myth (Gen. 2:2b-3). "Breaking the sabbath is a breach of what is holy." [9]

Perhaps it should be added that, as C. J. Ball observes, the Sabbath "was originally a joyous festival and day of rest" before it developed

[9] *Israel, Its Life and Culture, III-IV*, pp. 290, 289.

into "an intolerable interlude of joyless restraint" under the Pharisees such that Jesus had to remind them that the Sabbath was made for man, and not man for the Sabbath (Mark 2:27).[1]

But the main point is that kings and people illustrate by their secularization of the holy day the deep inward failure of fidelity which is the

[1] *Prophecies of Jeremiah*, p. 372.

18 The word which came to Jeremiah from the Lord, saying,

2 Arise, and go down to the potter's house, and there I will cause thee to hear my words.

18 The word that came to Jeremiah from the Lord: 2 "Arise, and go down to the potter's house, and there I

---

sabbath may be seen in Isa. 56:2-6; 58:13-14. The date of these passages has been much disputed, but W. S. McCullough ("A Re-examination of Isaiah 56–66," *Journal of Biblical Literature,* LXVII [1948], 27-36) has suggested that Isa. 56–66 comes from the period 587-562 B.C. If 17:19-27 are not from the Deuteronomic editor, they are from another who closely imitated his style.

XIII. Parable and Plot (18:1-23)

The chapter consists of three parts which are only loosely bound together: (a) a message received by Jeremiah at the potter's house (vss. 1-12); (b) a poem emphasizing the fact that Israel's sin is contrary to nature (vss. 13-17); and (c) a record of a plot against Jeremiah, and the prophet's prayer for vengeance against his enemies (vss. 18-23).

A. Parable of the Potter (18:1-12)

This parable has come to us through the hands of the Deuteronomic editor, as recognized by Mowinckel and Rudolph. The editor has used a genuine event and saying of Jeremiah's, and expanded it in his own way. Deuteronomic phraseology and ideas are evident especially in vss. 7-12. Cf. vs. 8 with 35:17; vs. 11 with 7:3; 25:5; 35:15; vs. 12 with 11:8; 16:12.

Jeremiah here employs what has become "the classical illustration of the divine sovereignty" and "the fitting emblem for the highest conception man can form of the divine sovereignty in relation to human freedom" (John Skinner, *Prophecy and Religion* [Cambridge: Cambridge University Press, 1922], pp. 162, 164). He probably did not originate the figure, for it occurs earlier in Isa. 29:16. It is used many times later: Isa. 45:9; 64:8; Wisd. Sol. 15:7; Ecclus. 33:13; Rom. 9:21.

The figure of the potter stresses the sovereignty of God over Israel, a sovereignty that is exercised by a free Person over other persons who have freedom of will. It is difficult to determine whether Jeremiah originally employed the figure to give a message of hope to the people, emphasizing the idea that a potter intends to make only good vessels, and can remake spoiled ones according to his own design (Cornill, Skinner); or whether he employed it as a threat of the coming doom of the nation, as vss. 11-12 imply (Erbt, Giesebrecht). As the section has come to us through the Deuteronomic editor, who wrote after the destruction of Jerusalem in 587 B.C., the message is pessimistic, but it clearly recognizes that the will of God is conditioned by the repentance or rebellion of men. The prophet himself may have originally used the figure as the basis for his hope that Israel would ultimately become what God wants her to be. As George Adam Smith

---

root of all their distress. It is not improbable that Jeremiah's words were spoken on the sabbath as the people passed, taking them, as it were, in the act. Therefore the warning to keep the sabbath day holy. But if you do not listen [cf. 13:17], then I will kindle a fire in [the city's] gates. When holiness is lost the fire, a devouring fire, rages within and consumes, at the very entryways of the spirit, all things that would go either in or out. Either the fire of the spirit warms from within and is a creative and refining flame, or it devours and destroys:

We only live, only suspire
Consumed by either fire or fire.[2]

18:1-12. The Potter and the Clay.—The second episode is more dramatic. Here Jeremiah adapts to his purpose a figure which long before had become, and was long after to prove, the "classical illustration" of God's sovereignty. Its

[2] T. S. Eliot, "Little Gidding," Part IV. From *Four Quartets.* Copyright 1943 by T. S. Eliot. Used by permission of Harcourt, Brace & Co. and Faber & Faber, publishers.

3 Then I went down to the potter's house, and, behold, he wrought a work on the wheels.

4 And the vessel that he made of clay was marred in the hand of the potter: so he made it again another vessel, as seemed good to the potter to make *it*.

5 Then the word of the LORD came to me, saying,

6 O house of Israel, cannot I do with you as this potter? saith the LORD. Behold, as the clay *is* in the potter's hand, so *are* ye in mine hand, O house of Israel.

7 *At what* instant I shall speak concerning a nation, and concerning a kingdom, to pluck up, and to pull down, and to destroy *it;*

8 If that nation, against whom I have pronounced, turn from their evil, I will repent of the evil that I thought to do unto them.

9 And *at what* instant I shall speak concerning a nation, and concerning a kingdom, to build and to plant *it;*

will let you hear my words." 3 So I went down to the potter's house, and there he was working at his wheel. 4 And the vessel he was making of clay was spoiled in the potter's hand, and he reworked it into another vessel, as it seemed good to the potter to do.

5 Then the word of the LORD came to me: 6 "O house of Israel, can I not do with you as this potter has done? says the LORD. Behold, like the clay in the potter's hand, so are you in my hand, O house of Israel. 7 If at any time I declare concerning a nation or a kingdom, that I will pluck up and break down and destroy it, 8 and if that nation, concerning which I have spoken, turns from its evil, I will repent of the evil that I intended to do to it. 9 And if at any time I declare concerning a nation or a kingdom that I will build and plant it,

---

recognized, the section teaches the divine patience as well as the divine sovereignty and freedom.

18:1. The potter's house was the workshop or factory in which the potter made vessels. It was probably located in the Hinnom Valley, south of Jerusalem, with access to the drainage of the valley and to the pools of Siloam. The industry probably gave its name to one of the nearby city gates, the Potsherd Gate (19:2). A factory would have included the potter's workshop, a field for storing and treading clay, a kiln for vessels, and a dump for discards.

3. The potter's wheel, in Hebrew a dual form, *'obhnáyim,* probably consisted of two (stone?) discs, a heavier one below to give momentum, and a lighter one above for the shaping of the clay. (For details on the manufacture of pottery vessels, see Kelso, *Ceramic Vocabulary of the O.T.,* pp. 9-10.) Ecclus. 38:29-30 describes the work of a potter using a wheel turned by the foot.

7-10. In Deuteronomic phraseology these verses apply the lesson of the potter to all nations; the application was probably originally only to Israel (vss. 6, 11-12).

---

plot is simple in the beginning, like that of Omar—

> For I remember stopping by the way
> To watch a Potter thumping his wet Clay:
> And with its all-obliterated Tongue
> It murmur'd—"Gently, Brother, gently, pray!" [3]

Jeremiah also goes out to the valley of the potteries. But his going is not so casual; he goes with prophetic intent. And what he sees is something far more profound than what Carlyle ironically termed the "Pot-theism" of Omar's

[3] *The Rubáiyát of Omar Khayyám,* 5th ed., st. xxxvii.

and John Sterling's pantheisms. He observes the way of the potter as maker. When the first design of the vessel turns out misshapen and spoiled, he remolds it into another form. So Yahweh does with his people. If the clay is rebellious and will not respond to the design of the Maker, it must be broken up and reformed. If the clay is still malleable, if it repents and turns from its evil, the Maker can still fashion it into a vessel of usefulness; but if the clay has already hardened and set, then Judah must fall. The fingers of the Maker have been pressing upon Judah more and more firmly.

10 If it do evil in my sight, that it obey not my voice, then I will repent of the good, wherewith I said I would benefit them.

11 ¶ Now therefore go to, speak to the men of Judah, and to the inhabitants of Jerusalem, saying, Thus saith the LORD; Behold, I frame evil against you, and devise a device against you: return ye now every one from his evil way, and make your ways and your doings good.

12 And they said, There is no hope: but we will walk after our own devices, and we will every one do the imagination of his evil heart.

10 and if it does evil in my sight, not listening to my voice, then I will repent of the good which I had intended to do to it. 11 Now, therefore, say to the men of Judah and the inhabitants of Jerusalem: 'Thus says the LORD, Behold, I am shaping evil against you and devising a plan against you. Return, every one from his evil way, and amend your ways and your doings.'

12 "But they say, 'That is in vain! We will follow our own plans, and will every one act according to the stubbornness of his evil heart.'

Behold, I am shaping evil against you and devising a plan against you. Return . . . and amend your ways.

It will be noted with what skill Jeremiah weaves into this analogy the first terms of his prophetic call (1:10). Here again, the solemn alternative is presented, but in a fresh form which gathers up these grand polarities into the context of God's dealings with men and their destinies: "so that it is not too much to say that this remarkable utterance is one of the keys to the comprehension of Hebrew prophecy." [4] It touches what we should today call "philosophy of history."

Two comparisons should be drawn. First, the passage in which the prophet asks,

Shall the potter be regarded as the clay;
that the thing made should say of its maker,
"He did not make me" (Isa. 29:16),

is not unlike Jeremiah's starting point. For Isaiah is accusing those who hide their counsels from the Lord of inverting the orders: "You turn things upside down!" This inversion corrupts everything since it corrupts the principle. Instead of beginning from God they would begin from themselves. Which is Jeremiah's rebellious clay. But Jeremiah goes farther. God is the Potter who is in the course of fashioning; and the stresses exerted by the tensions of the competing world powers are devisings of the Almighty whereby the rebellious vessel may be constrained to the pattern of its intended usefulness.

Secondly, Jeremiah's focus differs from that of Second Isaiah (45:9) and Paul (Rom. 9:20) in that he is not concerned here with the formal problem of God's sovereignty and that of election, or predestination. One commentator quotes Paul:

[4] Ball, op. cit., p. 382.

"Nay but, O man, who art thou," he says, "that repliest against God? Hath not the potter power over the clay, of the same lump to make one vessel unto honour, and another unto dishonour?" To which the vessel might reply: "O Paul, he may have the power, but if this clay be the sentient souls of men, hath he the right?" No, this metaphor of the potter is one of the most heart-sickening shifts of a false theology. I would not presume to question the design of Providence, for God's ways are not as our ways; but to ask me to believe that a just and omnipotent Deity chooses to fashion human beings to the end of dishonour is to quench the only light I have in this dark world and to make a mockery of my moral sense. . . . I would rather waive the omnipotence than the goodness of God.[5]

But it is clear that Jeremiah waives neither the one nor the other. He was not plagued by this dilemma of Lactantius' Epicurean, which More here deploys so well.[6] The integrity of Jeremiah's analogy, as applied to the individual, is best contained in the following passage from Irenaeus—a passage obviously building upon this of Jeremiah as its original:

If, then, thou art the work of God, await the hand of thy Maker [Artist], who fashions everything in due course. . . . Keep thy heart soft and pliable for Him; retain the form in which the Artist fashioned thee, having moisture in thyself, lest, becoming hard, thou shouldst lose the marks of His fingers. . . . But shouldst thou prove hardened and reject His artistic work and prove ingrate for being made man, with thy ingratitude thou hast also lost His art and thy life. For to make is the property of God, but to be made that of men.[7]

[5] Paul Elmer More, The Christ of the New Testament (Princeton: Princeton University Press, 1924), pp. 198-99. Used by permission.
[6] Cf. Lactantius On the Anger of God 12; also Irenaeus, Against the Heresies II. 5. 2; for a fuller discussion see also Hopper, "The Anti-Manichean Writings of Saint Augustine" in Roy Battenhouse, ed., Companion Study to the Writings of Saint Augustine (New York: Oxford University Press, 1955), pp. 164 ff.
[7] Op. cit. IV. 39. 2.

13 Therefore thus saith the LORD; Ask ye now among the heathen, who hath heard such things: the virgin of Israel hath done a very horrible thing.

14 Will *a man* leave the snow of Lebanon *which cometh* from the rock of the field? *or* shall the cold flowing waters that come from another place be forsaken?

13 "Therefore thus says the LORD:
Ask among the nations,
    who has heard the like of this?
The virgin Israel
    has done a very horrible thing.
14 Does the snow of Lebanon leave
    the crags of Sirion?*f*
Do the mountain*g* waters run dry,*h*
    the cold flowing streams?

f Cn: Heb *the field*
g Cn: Heb *foreign*
h Cn: Heb *Are . . . plucked up?*

B. UNNATURALNESS OF ISRAEL'S SIN (18:13-17)

A vigorous poem of Jeremiah's is placed here by a redactor as an example of the rebelliousness and lack of repentance referred to in vs. 12. The idea expressed is similar to that found in 2:10-11, 32; 8:7. Israel's forsaking of Yahweh in order to worship false gods is unlike the practice of other nations (vs. 13; cf. 2:10-11) and unlike the order of nature (vs. 14; cf. 8:7). For her rebellion Israel must suffer exile and desertion by God.

The poem is difficult to translate on account of corruptions in the Hebrew. The RSV emends the text at several points, giving much better sense than the KJV.

14. The crags of Sirion: Read שריון for the M.T. שדי (the field) following Cornill (so Rudolph, Peake, *et al.*). **Sirion** is the Phoenician name for Mount Hermon, as explained in Deut. 3:9; the name occurs in Ps. 29:6 and in Ugaritic, II AB VI:19,21 (Cyrus H. Gordon, *Ugaritic Handbook, II, Texts in Transliteration* [Rome: Pontificium Institutum Biblicum, 1947], p. 142). The top of Mount Hermon, 9,100 feet above sea level, is usually covered with snow the year around.

Do the mountain waters run dry? Read ינשתו מי הרים for the M.T. ינתשו מים זרים, lit., **Are the foreign waters plucked up?** The reference is to the perennial streams on the mountain peaks.

This principle is again illustrated in the following section.

13-17. The Snows of Lebanon.—The appeal of this passage, like that of the migratory birds (8:7), turns upon the singular mystery and pathos of its dominant image—the snows of Lebanon. It is made the more poignant by the response to God's pleading to return which Jeremiah sees already in the people's faces. What these faces say (vs. 12) is plainly that all his pleading is in vain: they will follow obstinately the stubbornness of their own hearts—which to Jeremiah is not merely ironical but is both outrageous and pathetic and fills him again and again, as, indeed, we have already seen, with wonder and vexation at their willful persistence in this incredible folly. Such behavior is in the deepest sense unnatural and perverse. It contradicts the primary instinct of the soul for God (cf. 8:7). Here again, the people turn their backs upon the eternal and unfailing source of the very waters of life, going **into bypaths** of their own (cf. 6:16), stumbling blindly, **making their land a horror,** reducing the spirit to an arid waste as the dry, hot sirocco wind blows in from the east. Gillies' suggestion

that vs. 14*b* should read "the wet winds from the sea" [8] would form a fine poetic counterpoint here; for the west wind, cool and laden with moisture, would perpetually bring its relief to the spirit and showers for the arid land. But it is the image of the snows which dominates the whole.

Why this appeal? "One of the master-songs of the world" is the appraisal given by D. B. Wyndham Lewis to a ballad of Villon's. He speaks of "the exquisite ache of its music." [9] The poem itself is lovely. It brings before the reader the procession of great heroines, famous queens, illustrious beauties, and asks, "Where are they now?"—and replies only with one poignant question: "But where are the snows of yester-year?" [1] Sainte-Beuve points out that this "pearl of Villon" derives its magic power from that single line. [2]

There is another instance of the power of a single sentence, as related to another sufferer.

[8] *Jeremiah, the Man and His Message,* p. 188.
[9] *François Villon* (London: P. Davies, 1928), p. 306.
[1] "Ballade des dames du temps jadis."
[2] *Causeries du Lundi* (3rd ed.; Paris: Garnier Frères, n.d.), XIV, 298.

15 Because my people hath forgotten me, they have burned incense to vanity, and they have caused them to stumble in their ways *from* the ancient paths, to walk in paths, *in* a way not cast up;
16 To make their land desolate, *and* a perpetual hissing; every one that passeth thereby shall be astonished, and wag his head.
17 I will scatter them as with an east wind before the enemy; I will show them the back, and not the face, in the day of their calamity.
18 ¶ Then said they, Come, and let us devise devices against Jeremiah; for the law shall not perish from the priest, nor counsel from the wise, nor the word from the prophet. Come, and let us smite him with the tongue, and let us not give heed to any of his words.

15 But my people have forgotten me,
    they burn incense to false gods;
they have stumbled[i] in their ways,
    in the ancient roads,
and have gone into bypaths,
    not the highway,
16 making their land a horror,
    a thing to be hissed at for ever.
Every one who passes by it is horrified
    and shakes his head.
17 Like the east wind I will scatter them
    before the enemy.
I will show them my back, not my face,
    in the day of their calamity."

18 Then they said, "Come, let us make plots against Jeremiah, for the law shall not perish from the priest, nor counsel from the wise, nor the word from the prophet. Come, let us smite him with the tongue, and let us not heed any of his words."

[i] Gk Syr Vg: Heb *they made them stumble*

C. A Plot Against Jeremiah (18:18-23)

The opening verse suggests a plot against Jeremiah's life similar to that of 11:18–12:6, and to that implied by 15:15-21. The date and other details are unknown. It was apparently initiated against the prophet by the religious leaders, who believed that he was undermining their authority. The occasion for this scheming was not simply the oracle of vss. 13-17, as the present position of the section implies. The plot must have been the climax of a long period of struggle between Jeremiah and his adversaries.

Vs. 18 is of special interest as revealing the three groups of religious leaders of the time, and the special prerogatives claimed by each: (*a*) the priests, who gave *tôrāh* (law); (*b*) the wise men, or sages, who gave counsel; and (*c*) the prophets, who mediated the word of the Lord. Jeremiah was critical of all these groups, and did not hesitate to express his opinion of them (see particularly 2:8; 8:8-9; 14:13-16; 23:9-40; 26:1-24).

Jeremiah's prayer for vengeance should be compared with 11:20; 12:3; 15:15; 17:14-18. This is the bitterest prayer for vengeance in the book, and some interpreters (e.g.,

Abraham Lincoln had learned the deep humility of the human condition when he used to quote: "O why should the spirit of mortal be proud?"[3] He had

> The pity of the snow that hides all scars;
> The secrecy of streams that make their way
> Under the mountain to the rifted rock.[4]

The lines are Edwin Markham's: they are startlingly reminiscent of vs. 14. And if we may note, without impiety, how acceptably the words of Isa. 53 ("a man of sorrows and acquainted

[3] William Knox, "Mortality," from *Songs of Israel*.
[4] "Lincoln, the Man of the People," from *Poems of Edwin Markham*, selected and arranged by Charles Wallis (New York: Harper & Bros.). Copyright 1950 by Virgil Markham. Used by permission.

with grief, . . .") may be applied to the character of Lincoln, and then reflect that Jeremiah may have been the portrait source for these reflections on the Suffering Servant, it is easy to see how secretly these hidden springs of healing come together; and how Jeremiah, through his early toils, was learning to rest upon the eternal Source—a source "high from the beginning" (17:12)—from which the streams of reconciling life forever flow. It is this growing knowledge of the Most High which helps him, in the difficult but less ambivalent years ahead, to reach a degree of transcendence and insight scarcely achieved by any other Hebrew figure.

18-23. *Well, Then, Let It Come!*—The obduracy of the people is now further revealed. It is not merely that they "will follow [their]

19 Give heed to me, O LORD, and hearken to the voice of them that contend with me.

20 Shall evil be recompensed for good? for they have digged a pit for my soul. Remember that I stood before thee to speak good for them, *and* to turn away thy wrath from them.

19 Give heed to me, O LORD,
      and hearken to my plea.*j*
20 Is evil a recompense for good?
      Yet they have dug a pit for my life.
   Remember how I stood before thee
      to speak good for them,
      to turn away thy wrath from them.

j Gk Compare Syr Tg: Heb *my adversaries*

Duhm, Cornill, Peake) have thought that vss. 21-23 must be secondary because they are unworthy of Jeremiah. While we would like to think that he did not pray for vengeance to come upon the wives and children of his enemies, we must remember that he was after all a child of his own age and that he was capable of strong emotion. Furthermore, we must note that he is here asking vengeance upon the spiritual leaders, the men from whom he expected the greatest aid and sympathy, but from whom he experienced the greatest animosity (Volz compares Jesus' attitude toward the Pharisees in Matt. 23 and Paul's attitude toward the Judaizers in Gal. 5:12).

The event which lies back of this section probably occurred in the latter part of Jehoiakim's reign, when opposition to Jeremiah reached a great height.

18. For the association of the priests with the **law** (*tôrāh*) see Deut. 17:11; 33:10; Hos. 4:6; Zeph. 3:4 (cf. Joachim Begrich, "Die priesterliche Tora," in Paul Volz, ed., *Werden und Wesen des Alten Testaments* [Berlin: A. Töpelmann, 1936; "Beihefte zur Zeitschrift für die alttestamentliche Wissenschaft"], pp. 63-88). The priestly *tôrāh* was probably concerned primarily with making proper distinctions between the holy and the profane, the clean and the unclean—chiefly, therefore, with matters of the cult and very little with ethical principles.

The **wise,** or the sages, became especially prominent in the postexilic period, but by the time of Jeremiah they must have been recognized as a separate class of spiritual leaders.

Smite him with the tongue means to slander him. For the last clause the LXX reads "let us listen to all his words," i.e., "let us try to trap him and secure the basis for a charge against him." This may represent the original text (Giesebrecht, Rudolph, Peake).

20. Jeremiah feels especially bitter because he had entreated God to be merciful to his opponents (cf. 15:11; 17:16).

---

own plans" (vs. 12); but now, as at Anathoth, the warnings and pleadings of Yahweh through his prophet Jeremiah are met by plots against his life. The priests, the prophets, and the wise men of the temple now join together to trump up charges against him. The LXX reads "let us give heed to all his words"—watch his pronouncements in order to catch him either in blasphemy or treasonable utterances. Which raises the interesting question as to what in Jeremiah's teaching was so radical in its challenge to the prevailing religious orthodoxies as to arouse so determined a resistance to him on the part of the official parties. The mounting hostility toward him which began in Anathoth, and reached to the temple and the king, implies either a dimension in depth of a religiously revolutionary kind or a dimension in personal power which the organized and vested interests could not evade. But it clearly filled Jeremiah

with a righteous indignation which in this middle period of his own development spilled over into bitter imprecation.

The personal accents of this seemingly vengeful utterance are somewhat mitigated, however, if it is borne in mind (*a*) that it is written in poetic form, and so becomes a formal recognition of the doom implicit in their failure to respond; (*b*) that the acceptance of the convention of poetic form used by the professional prophets identifies its pronouncements with the prophetic office as such; and (*c*) that the burden of its argument falls upon the fact that Jeremiah had repeatedly spoken both to the people and on behalf of the people **to turn away** [the Lord's] **wrath from them,** but they had persistently returned evil for good: therefore, let the inevitable come—**let their wives become childless . . . their men meet death by pestilence, their youths be slain . . . in battle.**

21 Therefore deliver up their children to the famine, and pour out their *blood* by the force of the sword; and let their wives be bereaved of their children, and *be* widows; and let their men be put to death; *let* their young men *be* slain by the sword in battle.

22 Let a cry be heard from their houses, when thou shalt bring a troop suddenly upon them: for they have digged a pit to take me, and hid snares for my feet.

23 Yet, Lord, thou knowest all their counsel against me to slay *me*: forgive not their iniquity, neither blot out their sin from thy sight, but let them be overthrown before thee; deal *thus* with them in the time of thine anger.

19 Thus saith the Lord, Go and get a potter's earthen bottle, and *take* of the ancients of the people, and of the ancients of the priests;

---

21 Therefore deliver up their children to famine;
　　give them over to the power of the sword,
　let their wives become childless and widowed.
　　May their men meet death by pestilence,
　　their youths be slain by the sword in battle.
22 May a cry be heard from their houses,
　　when thou bringest the marauder suddenly upon them!
　For they have dug a pit to take me,
　　and laid snares for my feet.
23 Yet, thou, O Lord, knowest
　　all their plotting to slay me.
　Forgive not their iniquity,
　　nor blot out their sin from thy sight.
　Let them be overthrown before thee;
　　deal with them in the time of thine anger.

19 Thus said the Lord, "Go, buy a potter's earthen flask, and take some of the elders of the people and some of the

---

XIV. Symbolic Actions and Imprisonment (19:1–20:18)

This section is placed immediately after ch. 18 because of the similarity in subject matter, and because of the catchword **potter**. It is apparent, however, that it is not well unified. In 19:1-2 the prophet is commanded to buy a pottery flask and go to the entry of the Potsherd Gate, taking with him some of the elders of the people and priests. But he is immediately told to proclaim certain words to the kings of Judah and inhabitants of Jerusalem regarding Topheth and the valley of Hinnom. Not until 19:10 does he break the flask and speak words which interpret the symbolic action. Then 19:11*b*-13 reverts to the subject of **Topheth**. It is most likely that we have here two different events which have been combined by an editor, or one event which has been expanded by editorial additions.

The most natural division of the material is as follows: (*a*) 19:1, 2*a* (reading "go out to the entry of the Potsherd Gate"), 10-11*a*, 14-15; 20:1-6, which relates the symbolic action with the flask, Jeremiah's address to the people in the temple court, and his imprisonment; (*b*) 19:2*b*-9, 11*b*-13, which records the "sermon" on Topheth and Hinnom.

. . . **Let them be overthrown . . . in the time of thine anger.** He rehearses once more, in other words, the nature of the calamities about to befall them, and in precisely the forms which do befall them. It is another way of putting the inevitable "if you will not listen" the calamities will come. It seems to stand in almost deliberate apposition to his earlier prayer, where Jeremiah said,

> Behold, they say to me,
> "Where is the word of the Lord?
> Let it come!" (17:15.)

Now, having met with their refusals and threats once more, it is as though he were saying, "Very well, then, since you *will* have it so, let it come!"

19:1–20:6. The Parable of the Broken Bottle. —The third episode enforces this view. Here the symbolic action carries out what is implicit in the people's refusal to return (18:11). It is clear that the clay has hardened: it is no longer malleable and subject to the Maker's remolding pressure. It has firmly set in its stubbornness. So—the alternative remains. It must

2 And go forth unto the valley of the | senior priests, 2 and go out to the Valley of
son of Hinnom, which *is* by the entry of | Ben-hinnom at the entry of the Potsherd
the east gate, and proclaim there the words | Gate, and proclaim there the words that I
that I shall tell thee:

The (*b*) material is a characteristic sermon by the Deuteronomic editor. His influence
may be clearly seen if the following comparisons are made: vs. 3 with II Kings 21:12;
vss. 5-6 with Jer. 7:31-32; vs. 7 with Deut. 28:26; and vs. 9 with Deut. 28:53. He has
inserted into the (*a*) material his own long speech about Topheth and Hinnom, and has
slightly worked over the account of Jeremiah's arrest and punishment (his phraseology
being evident in 19:15; 20:4-6). The same editor refers in 7:31-34; 32:35 to abominations
committed at Topheth.

This is the first record of a symbolic action by the prophet (unless 13:1-11 is
interpreted as such), and also the first account of bodily harm to Jeremiah. The breaking
of the flask symbolized the breaking of Jerusalem and its people by Yahweh, as 19:11
explains; cf. the Egyptian practice of writing on clay vessels the names of enemy princes
or rebels and then breaking them at a sacred place; such an action was supposed to have
the effect of bringing about their destruction. Perhaps the action of the prophet here
should be interpreted as more than symbolic: it may have been thought to effect the
destruction of the city. That would explain the extreme opposition provoked by his
action and subsequent message in the temple court.

The original (*a*) material is apparently the first in the book from Baruch's memoirs,
which dealt largely with Jeremiah's conflict with his enemies and with his personal
sufferings. It is not necessarily the earliest chronologically.

These events probably occurred near the time of the battle of Carchemish (605 b.c.),
when it became clear that Babylon was the great world power. They may have taken
place before the events of ch. 36, since Jeremiah was at that time denied access to the
temple (36:5). If the prohibition of 36:5 was only temporary, the events here described
may have come in the latter part of the reign of Jehoiakim.

A. Symbolic Actions (19:1-15)

19:1. A potter's earthen flask: The *baqbûq* was a water decanter, the name being
derived from the gurgling sound made as water was poured out. Those found in
excavations range in height from four to ten inches. "It is the most artistic and expensive
member of the pitcher family. It was thus well fitted to typify Jerusalem in Jeremiah's
illustrated sermon (19:1-15). Its use was doubly significant since it had the narrowest
neck of all pitchers and therefore could never be mended (19:11)." (Kelso, *Ceramic
Vocabulary of the O.T.*, p. 17.)

The senior priests, lit., "elders of the priests," are mentioned also in II Kings 19:2,
but nothing is known of their special position or authority.

2. In the original account this verse probably read simply, "and go out to the entry
of the Potsherd Gate," the rest being added by the Deuteronomic editor to make the

---

be broken up and destroyed. Even though the
vessel were a precious and a costly one (see
Exeg.), if it has been marred in the making or
fails of the maker's design, it is broken up and
the potter makes another.

Of course it is true in one sense that for
Jeremiah to purchase a costly bottle, carry it
into the valley of the potteries, and break it in
the sight of certain of the elders and the priests
was as simple and as "trivial" as it was possible
for it to be, as Duhm has held.[5] It is far from

[5] *Das Buch Jeremia*, pp. 159 ff.

trivial, however, if the following factors are
kept in mind: (*a*) that such symbolic acts were
filled, in the minds of the people, with mysterious power and almost magical implication (see
Expos. on 13:1-11); (*b*) that cumulative interest had already been established by way of the
parable of the jars (see Expos. on 13:12-14),
the sabbath day lesson (see Expos. on 17:19-27),
and the analogy of the potter and the clay (see
Expos. on 18:1-12)—particularly the last; and
(*c*) that the carrying of the message to the
priests and elders (vs. 1) and then to the temple

3 And say, Hear ye the word of the Lord, O kings of Judah, and inhabitants of Jerusalem; Thus saith the Lord of hosts, the God of Israel; Behold, I will bring evil upon this place, the which whosoever heareth, his ears shall tingle.

4 Because they have forsaken me, and have estranged this place, and have burned incense in it unto other gods, whom neither they nor their fathers have known, nor the kings of Judah, and have filled this place with the blood of innocents;

5 They have built also the high places of Baal, to burn their sons with fire *for* burnt offerings unto Baal, which I commanded not, nor spake *it*, neither came *it* into my mind:

6 Therefore, behold, the days come, saith the Lord, that this place shall no more be called Tophet, nor The valley of the son of Hinnom, but The valley of slaughter.

7 And I will make void the counsel of Judah and Jerusalem in this place; and I will cause them to fall by the sword before their enemies, and by the hands of them that seek their lives: and their carcasses will I give to be meat for the fowls of the heaven, and for the beasts of the earth.

tell you. 3 You shall say, 'Hear the word of the Lord, O kings of Judah and inhabitants of Jerusalem. Thus says the Lord of hosts, the God of Israel, Behold, I am bringing such evil upon this place that the ears of every one who hears of it will tingle. 4 Because the people have forsaken me, and have profaned this place by burning incense in it to other gods whom neither they nor their fathers nor the kings of Judah have known; and because they have filled this place with the blood of innocents, 5 and have built the high places of Ba'al to burn their sons in the fire as burnt offerings to Ba'al, which I did not command or decree, nor did it come into my mind; 6 therefore, behold, days are coming, says the Lord, when this place shall no more be called To'pheth, or the Valley of Ben-hinnom, but the Valley of Slaughter. 7 And in this place I will make void the plans of Judah and Jerusalem, and will cause their people to fall by the sword before their enemies, and by the hand of those who seek their life. I will give their dead bodies for food to the birds of the air and to the beasts

---

transition to his sermon on Hinnom and Topheth. **The Valley of Ben-hinnom** was south of Jerusalem. **The Potsherd Gate** is otherwise unknown; the Targ. calls it "the Dung Gate." It may be identical with the gate of that name in Neh. 2:13; 3:13-14; 12:31. The name used here probably was derived from the great number of potsherds lying nearby, thrown out by the potters who may have had their workshops in the valley of Hinnom (see Exeg. on 18:1). The translation **east gate** derives the word *ḥarṣîth* from *ḥéreṣ*, "the sun."

4-6. On the rites practiced at **Topheth** see Exeg. on 7:31.

7. **I will make void:** The Hebrew is *baqqōthî*, the editor making a play on the word *baqbûq* (**flask**) in vs. 1. This is part of the evidence that the section recognized as (*b*) material did not have a separate existence but was added to the (*a*) narrative by the Deuteronomic editor (see further Wilhelm Rudolph, *Jeremia* [Tübingen: J. C. B. Mohr,

---

itself (vs. 14) brings the entire prophecy to bear upon the priestly dogma of the supposed inviolability of the temple. This last had been a vital and saving belief in Isaiah's time; but like the hearts of the people, it had hardened into an unrealistic dogma in Jehoiakim's time. To break the costly bottle at the Potsherd Gate, where the persons with him could look down into that valley where idolatry and child sacrifice had been practiced, and then to return to the temple to repeat the message of Yahweh's doom upon Jerusalem, was to hurl defiance in the teeth of orthodoxy and officialdom. The

suggestion of vs. 7, that Yahweh would **make void** [i.e., "empty out," the word being deliberately chosen as a cognate carry-over from "bottle" in vs. 1] **the plans of Judah and Jerusalem,** very likely carried with it greater offense than the dooms which follow, the consequence of which is seen in the sequel.

The action of Pashhur, the priest and chief officer of the temple, is of considerable significance. Probably it was his duty to maintain order in the temple (cf. II Kings 25:18; and Jer. 29:26, where Zephaniah, the priest, has "charge in the house of the Lord over every

8 And I will make this city desolate, and a hissing; every one that passeth thereby shall be astonished and hiss, because of all the plagues thereof.

9 And I will cause them to eat the flesh of their sons and the flesh of their daughters, and they shall eat every one the flesh of his friend in the siege and straitness, wherewith their enemies, and they that seek their lives, shall straiten them.

10 Then shalt thou break the bottle in the sight of the men that go with thee,

11 And shalt say unto them, Thus saith the LORD of hosts; Even so will I break this people and this city, as *one* breaketh a potter's vessel, that cannot be made whole again: and they shall bury *them* in Tophet, till *there be* no place to bury.

12 Thus will I do unto this place, saith the LORD, and to the inhabitants thereof, and *even* make this city as Tophet:

13 And the houses of Jerusalem, and the houses of the kings of Judah, shall be defiled as the place of Tophet, because of all the houses upon whose roofs they have burned incense unto all the host of heaven, and have poured out drink offerings unto other gods.

14 Then came Jeremiah from Tophet, whither the LORD had sent him to prophesy; and he stood in the court of the LORD's house, and said to all the people,

15 Thus saith the LORD of hosts, the God of Israel; Behold, I will bring upon this

of the earth. 8 And I will make this city a horror, a thing to be hissed at; every one who passes by it will be horrified and will hiss because of all its disasters. 9 And I will make them eat the flesh of their sons and their daughters, and every one shall eat the flesh of his neighbor in the siege and in the distress, with which their enemies and those who seek their life afflict them.'

10 "Then you shall break the flask in the sight of the men who go with you, 11 and shall say to them, 'Thus says the LORD of hosts: So will I break this people and this city, as one breaks a potter's vessel, so that it can never be mended. Men shall bury in To'pheth because there will be no place else to bury. 12 Thus will I do to this place, says the LORD, and to its inhabitants, making this city like To'pheth. 13 The houses of Jerusalem and the houses of the kings of Judah — all the houses upon whose roofs incense has been burned to all the host of heaven, and drink offerings have been poured out to other gods — shall be defiled like the place of To'pheth.' "

14 Then Jeremiah came from To'pheth, where the LORD had sent him to prophesy, and he stood in the court of the LORD's house, and said to all the people: 15 "Thus says the LORD of hosts, the God of Israel, Behold, I am bringing upon this city and

---

1947; "Handbuch zum Alten Testament"], p. 109, though he does not recognize the editor here as the Deuteronomist).

14. The beginning of the verse may well have read originally, "Then Jeremiah came from the entry [of the gate]," reading מהפתח instead of the M.T. מהתפת (Volz, Rudolph). The present reading arose after the editorial addition in 19:11b-13, with its mention of Topheth.

---

madman who prophesies, to put him in the stocks and collar"). But the fact that he both struck Jeremiah and confined him overnight in the stocks signifies that opposition to the prophet had at last lost patience and broken out into overt opposition. As in a drama, certain well-defined developments of the antagonistic forces may be observed: first the entrenched powers are indifferent to the challenger; then they are restively tolerant; then at some moment entirely unforeseen, and frequently around some incident otherwise of no great importance, the mounting irritation and uneasy

concern of the challenged interests declares its hand through some passionate and ill-considered act, thus dignifying and defining the ultimate symbolic significance of the protagonist; thereafter these contending forces clash as principles, and demand a reconciliation and catharsis at a higher, and a deeper, level than either, taken by itself, foresees. Jeremiah now has thrust upon him all the reflex power of these national and religious policies catapulting to a fall. And Pashhur—a name obscure and otherwise unknown—acquires a place in history, because he materializes, and henceforth

city and upon all her towns all the evil
that I have pronounced against it, because
they have hardened their necks, that they
might not hear my words.

20 Now Pashur the son of Immer the
priest, who *was* also chief governor
in the house of the LORD, heard that Jeremiah prophesied these things.

2 Then Pashur smote Jeremiah the
prophet, and put him in the stocks that
were in the high gate of Benjamin, which
was by the house of the LORD.

3 And it came to pass on the morrow,
that Pashur brought forth Jeremiah out of
the stocks. Then said Jeremiah unto him,
The LORD hath not called thy name Pashur,
but Magor-missabib.

upon all its towns all the evil that I have
pronounced against it, because they have
stiffened their neck, refusing to hear my
words."

20 Now Pashhur the priest, the son of
Immer, who was chief officer in the
house of the LORD, heard Jeremiah prophesying these things. 2 Then Pashhur beat
Jeremiah the prophet, and put him in the
stocks that were in the upper Benjamin
Gate of the house of the LORD. 3 On the
morrow, when Pashhur released Jeremiah
from the stocks, Jeremiah said to him, "The
LORD does not call your name Pashhur, but

B. IMPRISONMENT OF JEREMIAH (20:1-6)

20:1. Pashhur, as **chief officer** in the temple, was probably the head of the temple
police, with the duty of seeing that nothing untoward took place in the temple area
and that no unauthorized person entered it. His position must have been similar to that
of Amaziah at Bethel (Amos 7:10-17), or the later "captain of the temple" (Luke 22:52;
Acts 4:1; 5:24).

2. The upper Benjamin Gate must have been on the north side of the temple area,
serving as a gate of the temple area rather than of the city, toward the land of Benjamin;
it had been built by King Jotham (II Kings 15:35; cf. Ezek. 9:2). The Jerusalem Talmud
says that "the upper gate" was one of the seven names of the eastern gate of the temple
(the "Golden Gate" as it was later called; cf. Julian Morgenstern, "The Gates of
Righteousness," *Hebrew Union College Annual,* VI [1929], 19, n. 42). The name
Benjamin, however, indicates that it was on the north side.

3. The name **Pashhur** is of Egyptian origin, *Pš-Ḥr* (Wilhelm Spiegelberg, "Eine
Vermutung über den Ursprung des Namens יהוה," *Zeitschrift der Deutschen Morgenländischen Gesellschaft,* LIII [1899], 635). Since the words **on every side** (*miṣṣābhîbh*)
do not occur in the LXX (which translates the new name as Μέτοικος), and are not
used in vs. 4, it is probable that the Hebrew originally had only *māghôr* (**Terror**) and
that *miṣṣābhîbh* (**on every side**) has been added under the influence of vs. 10 (cf. 6:25).
The new name is not a play on the meaning of Pashhur, which was probably unknown
to Jeremiah, but an expression of Jeremiah's attitude toward the man.

---

typifies, the animus of the official orthodoxy of
the temple against the word of God proclaimed
by Yahweh's prophet.

Jeremiah sees this—in itself an indication of
his very remarkable and realistic powers. After
a terrible night of pain and suffering, both of
body and spirit, in which he apparently
wrestles, like Jacob, to know both God's name
and his own, he emerges triumphantly and fixes
indelibly the public meaning of this event—a
meaning heretofore hidden and undefined, now
open and formulated. When Pashhur releases
him from the stocks, his first word is, **The
LORD does not call your name Pashhur, but
Terror on every side. . . . Behold, I will make**

you a terror to yourself and to all your friends.
Henceforth, where Pashhur goes he will be a
walking symbol of the advancing catastrophe.
It is even possible that Jeremiah perceived that
the distempered violence of Pashhur's impulsive
act was a symptom of a deeper insecurity which
would develop into dread and panic as the
tensions increased, making him more and more
a terror to his friends and those about him, and
so a manifest embodiment of the unacknowledged insecurity behind the hardening of the
religious consciousness of the official powers
generally. So confident is Jeremiah on the morning after the stocks, that, at last, he even names
the foe from the north! **To Babylon you shall**

4 For thus saith the Lord, Behold, I will make thee a terror to thyself, and to all thy friends: and they shall fall by the sword of their enemies, and thine eyes shall behold *it:* and I will give all Judah into the hand of the king of Babylon, and he shall carry them captive into Babylon, and shall slay them with the sword.

5 Moreover I will deliver all the strength of this city, and all the labors thereof, and all the precious things thereof, and all the treasures of the kings of Judah will I give into the hand of their enemies, which shall spoil them, and take them, and carry them to Babylon.

6 And thou, Pashur, and all that dwell in thine house, shall go into captivity: and thou shalt come to Babylon, and there thou shalt die, and shalt be buried there, thou, and all thy friends, to whom thou hast prophesied lies.

7 ¶ O Lord, thou hast deceived me, and I was deceived: thou art stronger than I, and hast prevailed: I am in derision daily, every one mocketh me.

Terror on every side. 4 For thus says the Lord: Behold, I will make you a terror to yourself and to all your friends. They shall fall by the sword of their enemies while you look on. And I will give all Judah into the hand of the king of Babylon; he shall carry them captive to Babylon, and shall slay them with the sword. 5 Moreover, I will give all the wealth of the city, all its gains, all its prized belongings, and all the treasures of the kings of Judah into the hand of their enemies, who shall plunder them, and seize them, and carry them to Babylon. 6 And you, Pashhur, and all who dwell in your house, shall go into captivity; to Babylon you shall go; and there you shall die, and there you shall be buried, you and all your friends, to whom you have prophesied falsely."

7 O Lord, thou hast deceived me,
  and I was deceived;
thou art stronger than I,
  and thou hast prevailed.
I have become a laughingstock all the day;
  every one mocks me.

4-6. These verses are considered secondary by Cornill and Giesebrecht. They are an expansion by the Deuteronomic editor, written *ca.* 550 B.C., after the Babylonian exile had begun. Therefore we cannot be certain that the mention of **Babylon** (vs. 4) goes back to Jeremiah himself. Pashhur was probably among the officials deported in 598 B.C., for his position was occupied by one Zephaniah the son of Maaseiah in the period immediately following that date (29:25-26).

C. Jeremiah's Bitterest Complaint (20:7-18)

Here we have the bitterest and saddest laments of Jeremiah in all the series of his "confessions." It is the last of the series and one of the most important for the study of the prophet's personality, especially of his strong sense of divine compulsion to a prophetic career.

The section is now placed immediately after the account of Jeremiah's mistreatment by Pashhur, with the implication that the latter was the immediate occasion of his complaint. While this is possible, it is more likely that the present position is due to an

---

go, he tells Pashhur. This would place the incident very near to the battle of Carchemish (605 B.C.), which meant the fall of the Egyptian power which had placed Jehoiakim on the throne, and the necessity of coming to terms with the new world power. (But see Exeg.)

The above account gains considerably if it is allowed that the name Pashhur is compounded of words meaning "glad" (*pāsh*) and "free" (*hōr*); and still more if it should be a quadrilateral form compounded from Hebrew,

"to leap," "prance," Ethiopic, "to be glad," Assyrian, "to be at ease," "to rest," and Arabic, "free from distress or narrowness of mind."[6] To make such a one a fear to himself and others would mean a psychical conversion of all this into its opposite. (Yet see Exeg.)

20:7-18. *As It Were a Burning Fire!*—Vss. 7-13 have been described as "one of the most powerful and impressive passages in the whole of the prophetic literature. [They take us] not

[6] See Ball, *Prophecies of Jeremiah*, p. 413, n. 1.

8 For since I spake, I cried out, I cried violence and spoil; because the word of the Lord was made a reproach unto me, and a derision, daily.

9 Then I said, I will not make mention of him, nor speak any more in his name. But *his word* was in mine heart as a burning fire shut up in my bones, and I was

8 For whenever I speak, I cry out,
  I shout, "Violence and destruction!"
For the word of the Lord has become for
  me
  a reproach and derision all day long.
9 If I say, "I will not mention him,
  or speak any more in his name,"
there is in my heart as it were a burning
  fire
  shut up in my bones,

---

editor, and that the occasion of the prophet's complaint was a series of events rather than the single incident with Pashhur.

There are three divisions: (*a*) Jeremiah's struggle with God and his sense of God's overpowering mastery which compels him to prophesy (vss. 7-9); (*b*) Jeremiah's conviction that God is with him, and will punish his persecutors (vss. 10-13; vs. 12 [=11:20] probably does not belong here; on the authenticity of vs. 13, see below); (*c*) Jeremiah's curse upon the day of his birth (vss. 14-18). It is not certain that these divisions represent a single experience of the prophet, and were therefore composed at one time. The first two are more closely related to each other than they are to the third. In the first God is the primary antagonist of the prophet, whereas in the second God is his protagonist against his human enemies; but his human enemies are referred to in the first (vs. 7). The third is a bitter outcry which does not follow logically the vivid expression of trust in God in vss. 10-11 (and vs. 13, if genuine). It is probable therefore that vss. 14-18 originated at a different time from the preceding verses.

7-9. No other passage in all the prophetic literature of the O.T. expresses so clearly as this the prophet's sense of divine compulsion to his task. The closest passages of similar nature are Amos 3:8 and I Cor. 9:16. Jeremiah here gives utterance to his conviction that he has been deceived or enticed by the "demonic" in God, made the

---

only into the depths of the prophet's soul, but into the secrets of the prophetic consciousness. For the psychology of prophecy there is nothing which is so instructive."[7] So much is this the case that one is tempted to regard these verses and vss. 14-18 as Jeremiah's "dark night of the soul." Such a view is even the more tempting by virtue of their position here, having been editorially placed immediately after the encounter with Pashhur and the night of pain and humiliation in the stocks and collar. For, from a psychological point of view, it is precisely some such crisis of violence, with its humiliating outcome, which would plunge the young prophet into despondency and bitterness. The poems depict extremely well what must have been the mood of the mouthpiece of the Lord—whose face had been struck and whose feet had been beaten—as he struggled with his feelings through the dark night of pain and discomfort. Such an inner struggle was essential to the bold denunciation of Pashhur which came with the morning. The pattern is similar in the later encounter with Hananiah, when Jeremiah retreats for a time before returning to denounce the false prophet (28:10-16).

[7] Peake, *Jeremiah and Lamentations*, I, 241.

The incident is in any case typical, in its psychological aspects, of what John of the Cross called "the purgative way."

For in this state . . . the flame does not burn brightly, but is darksome, and if it gives forth any light at all it is only to show to the soul and make it feel all its miseries and defects; neither is it sweet, but painful. . . . It is not a refreshing and peaceful fire, but a consuming and searching one that makes the soul faint away and grieve at the sight of Self; not a glorious brightness, for it embitters the soul and makes it miserable, owing to the spiritual light it throws on Self.

At this juncture, the soul suffers in the understanding from deep darkness, in the will from aridity and conflict, and in the memory from the consciousness of its miseries. . . .

Suffering all these things together, the soul undergoes, as it were, its Purgatory.[8]

Nevertheless, despite the psychological resemblance, we must repeat that Jeremiah never identifies himself with God after the Neoplatonic patterns of the medieval mystic. He does

[8] From "The Living Flame of Love," in *The Mystical Doctrine of St. John of the Cross* (abridged ed.; intro. by R. H. J. Steuart; New York: Sheed & Ward, 1936), pp. 142-43. Used by permission.

weary with forbearing, and I could not *stay*.

10 ¶ For I heard the defaming of many, fear on every side. Report, *say they,* and we will report it. All my familiars watched for my halting, *saying,* Peradventure he will be enticed, and we shall prevail against him, and we shall take our revenge on him.

and I am weary with holding it in,
and I cannot.
10 For I hear many whispering.
Terror is on every side!
"Denounce him! Let us denounce him!"
say all my familiar friends,
watching for my fall.
"Perhaps he will be deceived,
then we can overcome him,
and take our revenge on him."

---

laughingstock of all men, and compelled to preach only doom; but when his nature rebelled and he determined to remain silent, he found that he could do no other than prophesy, for the word of the Lord was like a burning fire within him.

It is significant that Jeremiah's inner struggles and his persecutions never led him to doubt the reality of his divine commission, and the sense of being overpowered by God never made him lose his own personality. The Hebrew prophets did not experience mystic absorption in the divine. The prophet with the most vigorous personality has the strongest sense of being mastered by God.

Thou hast deceived me: The verb פתה is a strong one; in the Piel (the form used here) it means to "seduce" (a virgin) in Exod. 22:16; it is used of the lying spirit that deceives Ahab in I Kings 22:20-22. For the idea expressed here, the only comparable passage in Jeremiah is 15:18.

The first half of vs. 8 means that Jeremiah's message is constantly one of doom and destruction (cf. 28:8).

10-13. Jeremiah had to contend with persecution even at the hands of his own friends (cf. 12:6; 18:18). The present passage expresses the prophet's faith that God is his champion against such enemies; vs. 11 is an affirmation rather than a prayer, as are 11:20; 12:3; 15:15; 17:18; 18:21-23. Vs. 12 is a duplicate of 11:20. It is somewhat out of place here, since it is more a prayer than an affirmation. Interpreters generally consider it secondary.

The genuineness of vs. 13 has been debated. It is in a quite different mood from the context, and is more like one of the psalms than the material known to be from

---

not approximate even the pitch of psychic disruption recounted by the author of the oracles of Isa. 21, where "the sense of being gripped by an overpowering, invading, presence becomes so intense that the prophet experiences a violent disruption of his personality," [9] and in which he staggers, reels, trembles, and is filled with anguish. There is a threatened disruption here, but it is due to a different cause.

O LORD, thou hast deceived me,
and I was deceived.

He has felt the divine *rûah* compelling him invincibly from within; but the word that he has spoken has failed to come true. He has been repulsed and repudiated all along the line. He begins to fear lest the divine *rûah* should be a demonic spirit within him; or that he is an "enticed" prophet, trapped by Yahweh and humiliated and laughed at by men. Everyone

[9] Knight, *Hebrew Prophetic Consciousness,* p. 61.

mocks him; he has become a laughingstock. He is torn by the impossibility of going on and by the impossibility of not going on. For though he resolves to proclaim the word no more

**there is in my heart as it were a burning fire
shut up in my bones,
and I am weary with holding it in,
and I cannot.**

The passage appears to combine two earlier passages: "my words in your mouth a fire" (5:14), and

I am full of the wrath of the LORD:
I am weary of holding it in (6:11).

Once again he is full of the Lord's fury. It is the intensity of his indignation which is paramount in his conflict, together with that last protest of the ego against the Lord's failure to uphold the prophet's arm on his terms instead of on God's terms. (See Expos. on vss. 14-18.)

11 But the LORD *is* with me as a mighty terrible one: therefore my persecutors shall stumble, and they shall not prevail: they shall be greatly ashamed; for they shall not prosper: *their* everlasting confusion shall never be forgotten.

12 But, O LORD of hosts, that triest the righteous, *and* seest the reins and the heart, let me see thy vengeance on them: for unto thee have I opened my cause.

13 Sing unto the LORD, praise ye the LORD: for he hath delivered the soul of the poor from the hand of evildoers.

14 ¶ Cursed *be* the day wherein I was

---

11 But the LORD is with me as a dread warrior;
    therefore my persecutors will stumble,
    they will not overcome me.
They will be greatly shamed,
    for they will not succeed.
Their eternal dishonor
    will never be forgotten.
12 O LORD of hosts, who triest the righteous,
    who seest the heart and the mind,
let me see thy vengeance upon them,
    for to thee have I committed my cause.

13 Sing to the LORD;
    praise the LORD!
For he has delivered the life of the needy
    from the hand of evildoers.

14 Cursed be the day
    on which I was born!

Jeremiah; the mention of **the needy** (אביון) is characteristic of many psalms. It is considered secondary by Cornill, Giesebrecht, Duhm, Volz, and Peake. Other scholars interpret it as indicative of a sudden change of mood, from despondency to elation (Rudolph, who refers to Baumgartner and Köberle).

14-18. This is the prophet's saddest complaint against his unhappy lot as a prophet of doom. It is not prayer so much as lamentation couched in the form of a curse upon

---

He is still importunate and vexed with having to run with horses; he still does not accept the painful mystery of his own refining; he still does not glimpse beyond his succession of little Gethsemanes the plateau of patience and prayer wherein, as God's instrument, he carries within himself the divine catharsis for the people in the larger strategies of the Lord. He has yet to learn the acceptance that John Henry Newman learned, and expressed for himself and countless others in "Lead, kindly light." Or better still, he has not yet answered with the assent of his total being, Newman's deeper question: "Why didst thou kneel beneath His hand, but that He might leave on thee the print of His wounds?"[1] Just as one sorrow does not buy off the next so one suffering does not obviate another; it but prepares the soul for a deeper penetration into the matrix of all human suffering and guilt.

At the same time, the open, and literary, formulation of these sufferings, which are thereby tantamount to the prophet's open confession, is the very clearest mark of Jeremiah's progress toward the dawn of a higher and fuller religious consciousness—of the Jacob struggle "till the dawn" when the Adversary of his inner recalcitrance is pinned and gives his blessing. For does he not convert the very

[1] *Parochial and Plain Sermons*, V, 296.

whisperings of the many into a symbolic either/ or for the people? **Terror is on every side!** "Denounce him!" Either the terror that is Pashhur, or the terror that is Jeremiah (whom Yahweh hurls)! It may well be a terrible choice:

The times are nightfall, look, their light grows less;
The times are winter, watch, a world undone;
. . . .
Or what is else? There is your world within.
There rid the dragons, root out there the sin.[2]

Is there not even a note of exultation in the closing verses of this strophe (vss. 11-12)? For **the LORD is with me as a dread warrior!** There is even a kind of exhilaration in it, as though the sword of the Word which pierces him springs into his hand as his own blade. The power of God the adversary passes over into the self which, having been tried, accepts its mission. The paragraph of praise, the burst of exultation (vs. 13), is not wholly out of place if it bears witness to this rising consciousness in Jeremiah.

14-18. O Cursed Spite!—There is something irresistibly poignant in Shakespeare's lines:

[2] Sonnet No. 60. From *Poems of Gerard Manley Hopkins*, ed. Robert Bridges (2nd ed.; London: Oxford University Press, 1935). Used by permission.

| born: let not the day wherein my mother bare me be blessed. | The day when my mother bore me, let it not be blessed! |

15 Cursed *be* the man who brought tidings to my father, saying, A man child is born unto thee; making him very glad.

16 And let that man be as the cities which the LORD overthrew, and repented not: and let him hear the cry in the morning, and the shouting at noontide;

15 Cursed be the man
who brought the news to my father,
"A son is born to you,"
making him very glad.

16 Let that man be like the cities
which the LORD overthrew without
pity;
let him hear a cry in the morning
and an alarm at noon,

---

the day of his birth and upon the man who brought the news of his birth. Job 3 is a similar lament, probably later than (and dependent upon) the present passage.

Duhm points out that Jeremiah spoke so strongly against his life because he could not view it *sub specie aeternitatis* or consider it as only one short step in his eternal existence. He further remarks that Jeremiah in all his bitterness never did contemplate suicide; suicide was extremely rare among the ancient Semites.

14. The Hebrew could think of each **day** as being a separate entity, having objective existence; cf. the personification of days and nights in Ps. 19:2-4.

15. "It is usual in the East to reward the messenger who brings tidings of a son's birth" (Peake, *Jeremiah and Lamentations,* I, 245). Instead, Jeremiah pronounces a curse upon him. He could not, of course, pronounce a curse upon his own father and mother.

16. **The cities which the LORD overthrew** were Sodom and Gomorrah (Gen. 19).

I will not think but [curses] ascend the sky,
And there awake God's gentle sleeping peace.[3]

But no one supposes that Yahweh was a gentle-sleeping God, however curses might be held to ascend the sky! A curse in Jeremiah's time carried with it more power, both magical and religious, than it did in Hamlet's. And though the Hamlet comparison arises inevitably—

The time is out of joint: O cursed spite,
That ever I was born to set it right! [4]—

the two are really far apart. Nevertheless, Gordon's comparison is apt:

[Jeremiah] is the nearest figure of all the ancient world to the classical creation of Hamlet, and he is this just because his sensitive heart took all the "slings and arrows of outrageous fortune" so seriously that he could not look past them and view them and view the world from an impersonal and dispassionate standpoint. He is ever and again on the verge of life, and dares to peep over into the black abyss that men call madness.[5]

It is true that both were sensitive; both absorbed the slings and arrows of an outrageous fortune; both were far from viewing their worlds dispassionately, though both their worlds

and their passionate concerns were far, far different; both walked quite near the edge of the abyss; and Hamlet, certainly, along with Lear and possibly Macbeth, peeped over into it. But here the likeness ends, and the differences become of greater moment than the similarities.

Much nearer to Jeremiah than Hamlet's painful struggle for self-justification is the incident on the Jutland heath (also in Denmark) which Kierkegaard, with his extraordinary literary adroitness, has manipulated into a sustaining myth of himself—the incident about the man, his father, who as a boy herding sheep on the heaths of Jutland, and suffering through hunger and want, stood upon the hillock and cursed God, and was unable to forget it at the age of eighty-two.[6] But here again an important difference is to be noted. Jeremiah does not curse God. His imprecation does not even fall upon his own parents, but upon the day of his birth and upon "the man" who brought the tidings to his father, obviously no man in particular, but a simple rhetorical device for expanding and extending the hyperbole of the opening line of the poem. At the same time, the expansion gains in power by reason of the fact that it was customary in the East to reward the messenger who should bring tidings of the birth of a son.

To fall back upon Job 3:1-26, so clearly based

[3] *King Richard III,* Act I, scene 3.
[4] Act I, scene 5.
[5] *Rebel Prophet,* p. 55.

[6] *Journals,* p. 150.

17 Because he slew me not from the womb; or that my mother might have been my grave, and her womb *to be* always great *with me.*

18 Wherefore came I forth out of the womb to see labor and sorrow, that my days should be consumed with shame?

17 because he did not kill me in the womb; so my mother would have been my grave, and her womb for ever great.

18 Why did I come forth from the womb to see toil and sorrow, and spend my days in shame?

21 The word which came unto Jeremiah from the Lord, when king Zedekiah sent unto him Pashur the son of Mel-

21 This is the word which came to Jeremiah from the Lord, when King

---

XV. Oracles Concerning Kings of Judah (21:1–23:8)

This section is concerned largely with messages delivered by the prophet to or concerning kings of Judah. Some of the passages are directed to reigning kings who are named or can easily be identified: **Zedekiah** (21:3-7), **Shallum** (22:10-12), **Jehoiakim** (22:13-19), Jehoiachin (**Coniah,** 22:24-30). Others are directed to the **house of the king** (21:11-12; 22:1-7) or to the rulers of the people (23:1-2). Still others predict the raising up of ideal rulers or a messianic king (23:4-6). The remaining passages are of miscellaneous character (see Exeg.). This collection of oracles was made by the Deuteronomic editors, but it includes genuine poems by Jeremiah.

A. Reply to a Deputation from Zedekiah (21:1-10)

This passage is not in chronological order, but was apparently placed in its present position by an editor because it involves an individual named **Pashhur,** the name borne also by the official who placed Jeremiah in stocks (20:1-6). The date is during the siege of Jerusalem by Nebuchadrezzar—589-587 B.C.—probably sometime in the early stages of that siege.

---

upon this passage from Jeremiah, also points up a difference. Whereas Job's outburst is a dramatic prologue to the drama of soul transition through which Job himself must pass, Jeremiah's outburst is preliminary to the powerful whip line with which the poem ends:

Why did I come forth from the womb
to see toil and sorrow,
and spend my days in shame?

There may well be bitterness in this; for the mounting resistance to the word of the Lord and the refusal to listen now taking the objective form of evasion through ridding the land of its accuser were certain to be felt with increasing chagrin and vexation by one so sensitive and, at the same time, so outspoken as Jeremiah. His very office formulates the real nature of this resistance as it draws the people's guilt upon him; and it unmasks the hidden motive, heretofore concealed—which unmasking, in direct ratio to the prophet's candor, offends the people and their leaders and makes them heap increasing abuses upon him. Therefore, as George Adam Smith expresses it, "whomever he touched he singed, whomever he struck he broke" [7]—though it is probably more important

[7] *Jeremiah,* p. 321.

to note that whoever touched him was singed and whoever struck him was stricken. For it was in this wise that Jeremiah became "a man of strife and contention to the whole land . . . yet all of them curse me" (15:10).

What was agonizing about this was that Jeremiah, as prophet, could not do otherwise. It was his task to be to the people as the Lord's mouth. Therefore the bitterness—that he should have to be the bearer of this word in this day of Israel's catastrophe; that he must see and know the toil, the sorrow, and the shame, not merely of Israel's betrayal of both Yahweh and themselves, but that he, of all people, should be the one who must declare this to the people. To curse the day of his birth, therefore, was neither to curse those who bore him nor even the fact of his being born, but rather it points once more to the curse of Israel's betrayal of her heritage by which both leaders and people are marching hourly nearer and nearer to the great catastrophe. The whiplash of the poem falls not upon Jeremiah, as the anguished and confessing prophet, but upon the people and their stubborn will.

21:1-14. *The Two Ways.*—The sudden shift in this chapter from Pashhur who became "Terror on every side" to **Pashhur the son of Mal-**

chiah, and Zephaniah the son of Maaseiah the priest, saying,

2 Inquire, I pray thee, of the LORD for us; for Nebuchadrezzar king of Babylon maketh war against us; if so be that the LORD will deal with us according to all his wondrous works, that he may go up from us.

3 ¶ Then said Jeremiah unto them, Thus shall ye say to Zedekiah:

4 Thus saith the LORD God of Israel; Behold, I will turn back the weapons of war that *are* in your hands, wherewith ye fight against the king of Babylon, and *against* the Chaldeans, which besiege you without the walls, and I will assemble them into the midst of this city.

5 And I myself will fight against you with an outstretched hand and with a strong arm, even in anger, and in fury, and in great wrath.

6 And I will smite the inhabitants of this city, both man and beast: they shall die of a great pestilence.

Zedeki'ah sent to him Pashhur the son of Malchi'ah and Zephani'ah the priest, the son of Ma-asei'ah, saying, 2 "Inquire of the LORD for us, for Nebuchadrez'zar king of Babylon is making war against us; perhaps the LORD will deal with us according to all his wonderful deeds, and will make him withdraw from us."

3 Then Jeremiah said to them: 4 "Thus you shall say to Zedeki'ah, 'Thus says the LORD, the God of Israel: Behold, I will turn back the weapons of war which are in your hands and with which you are fighting against the king of Babylon and against the Chalde'ans who are besieging you outside the walls; and I will bring them together into the midst of this city. 5 I myself will fight against you with outstretched hand and strong arm, in anger, and in fury, and in great wrath. 6 And I will smite the inhabitants of this city, both man and beast; they shall die of a great pestilence.

The relationship of this event to the very similar one recorded in 37:3-10 has been the subject of debate among scholars. Bernhard Stade believed that both refer to the same episode, and he combined parts of both to secure a complete account ("Bemerkungen zum Buche Jeremiah," *Zeitschrift für die alttestamentliche Wissenschaft*, XII [1892], 276-308; see especially pp. 277-87). Duhm thought the account in 37:3-10 was legendary midrash and the present account a free composition by a later editor on the basis of that passage and of 38:1 ff. Erbt took 37:3-10 to be historical, but regarded the present account as largely a free composition. Cornill, Giesebrecht, Volz, and Peake accept both as basically historical, referring to two separate missions from Zedekiah to the prophet.

The correct interpretation must be based on recognition of the Deuteronomic phraseology of the passage as a whole, as pointed out by Mowinckel and Rudolph. Whereas 37:3-10 is precisely dated, the time of this deputation is vague, and the account is artificially constructed: vss. 3-7 are addressed to the king through the envoys, and vss. 8-10 to the people of Jerusalem in general. For the Deuteronomic phraseology cf. vs. 5a with Deut. 4:34; 5:15; etc.; vs. 5b with Deut. 29:27; Jer. 32:37; and vs. 8b with Deut. 11:26, 30:15. Rudolph has noted that the message to Zedekiah here is inconsistent with that of 34:2-7, in which the possibility of salvation is held out to the king (as also in 38:14-28). We may therefore consider 21:1-10 as the Deuteronomic editor's rewriting of the event of 37:3-10, without any independent historical value.

21:1. Pashhur the son of Malchiah is otherwise unknown. **Zephaniah the priest, the son of Maaseiah,** appears also in 29:25, 29; 37:3; 52:24.

chiah and Zephaniah the priest (cf. Exeg.) serves to underscore two things: (a) the dramatic reversal of Jeremiah's status, so far as official recognition is concerned, and (b) the shift within his own consciousness. As to the reversal of his status, he is no longer being humiliated by an underofficer of the temple, but is actually being petitioned by the king to

intercede with Yahweh on Jerusalem's behalf. The pathos of this appeal is doubtless apparent in that faltering word **perhaps**—as though the shaken king already knows in his heart what the "eagle-sighted Prophet" (Donne) would say (for Jeremiah has proved to be the one single-eyed and unswerving statesman of the time's condition and agony from the beginning), and

7 And afterward, saith the LORD, I will deliver Zedekiah king of Judah, and his servants, and the people, and such as are left in this city from the pestilence, from the sword, and from the famine, into the hand of Nebuchadrezzar king of Babylon, and into the hand of their enemies, and into the hand of those that seek their life: and he shall smite them with the edge of the sword; he shall not spare them, neither have pity, nor have mercy.

8 ¶ And unto this people thou shalt say, Thus saith the LORD; Behold, I set before you the way of life, and the way of death.

9 He that abideth in this city shall die by the sword, and by the famine, and by the pestilence: but he that goeth out, and falleth to the Chaldeans that besiege you, he shall live, and his life shall be unto him for a prey.

10 For I have set my face against this city for evil, and not for good, saith the LORD: it shall be given into the hand of the king of Babylon, and he shall burn it with fire.

11 ¶ And touching the house of the king of Judah, *say,* Hear ye the word of the LORD;

7 Afterward, says the LORD, I will deliver Zedeki′ah king of Judah, and his servants, and the people in this city who survive the pestilence, sword, and famine, into the hand of Nebuchadrez′zar king of Babylon and into the hand of their enemies, into the hand of those who seek their lives. He shall smite them with the edge of the sword; he shall not pity them, or spare them, or have compassion.'

8 "And to this people you shall say: 'Thus says the LORD: Behold, I set before you the way of life and the way of death. 9 He who stays in this city shall die by the sword, by famine, and by pestilence; but he who goes out and surrenders to the Chalde′ans who are besieging you shall live and shall have his life as a prize of war. 10 For I have set my face against this city for evil and not for good, says the LORD: it shall be given into the hand of the king of Babylon, and he shall burn it with fire.'

11 "And to the house of the king of Judah say, 'Hear the word of the LORD,

8-10. Although in Deuteronomic language, these verses are not inconsistent with the attitude of Jeremiah during the Babylonian siege. The prophet advised the king to surrender to the Babylonians as the only avenue of safety (38:17-18), and the prophet himself was arrested on a charge of desertion to the enemy (37:13-14). Yet it is clear that he took such a position because he believed that Nebuchadrezzar was an agent of Yahweh's will (cf. 27:6). Jeremiah proved that he was not a traitor to his country by choosing to remain in Palestine after the Babylonian capture of Jerusalem (40:6).

B. THE HOUSE OF THE KING OF JUDAH (21:11-12)

11-12. This is a very general admonition to the royal house of Judah, fully within the prophetic tradition. Because of its general nature it might have been delivered during

as though he knew quite well that the deliverance of Jerusalem in the time of Hezekiah was certain *not* to be repeated at this "end of the times." The king cuts a pathetic figure in these closing episodes of his vacillating reign. As to the shift within Jeremiah's consciousness, there is no longer any evidence of vocational strife within; his speech is straightforward, direct, and as clear cut as it is possible to be. It is as though his dark night in the stocks had precipitated his final acceptance of the dimension of suffering and abuse which must accompany his function as "the mouth of the Lord" in these terrible days of the spiritual and political collapse of his people.

As the complete moral breakdown of Judah's statesmanship in these latter days is borne in upon the reader, the thoroughgoing and uncompromising sharpness of Jeremiah's response to the king's messengers is easier to understand. For at the time of the king's question there are literally but two ways open: death in the city through futile persistence in resisting the Chaldeans who are without the gates, or life through surrender. There is the way of life (and that is about all), and the way of death.

The proper question at this point is not, Was Jeremiah a traitor? or, Was he guilty of treason? These questions may be raised in due course. It is rather to note carefully (a) that Jeremiah's

12 O house of David, thus saith the Lord; Execute judgment in the morning, and deliver *him that is* spoiled out of the hand of the oppressor, lest my fury go out like fire, and burn that none can quench *it,* because of the evil of your doings.

13 Behold, I *am* against thee, O inhabitant of the valley, *and* rock of the plain, saith the Lord; which say, Who shall come down against us? or who shall enter into our habitations?

14 But I will punish you according to the fruit of your doings, saith the Lord: and I will kindle a fire in the forest thereof, and it shall devour all things round about it.

---

12 O house of David! Thus says the Lord:
" 'Execute justice in the morning,
and deliver from the hand of the oppressor
him who has been robbed,
lest my wrath go forth like fire,
and burn with none to quench it,
because of your evil doings.' "

13 "Behold, I am against you, O inhabitant of the valley,
O rock of the plain,
says the Lord;
you who say, 'Who shall come down against us,
or who shall enter our habitations?'
14 I will punish you according to the fruit of your doings,
says the Lord;
I will kindle a fire in her forest,
and it shall devour all that is round about her."

---

the reign of any of the kings, but it would have been especially appropriate for Jehoiakim, whom Jeremiah condemned for acting unjustly toward his subjects (22:13-17).

Rudolph has taken the opening words of vs. 11, "Concerning the house of the king of Judah" (reading לבית for ולבית) as the superscription of the collection of oracles in 21:11–23:8, comparable to the superscription in 23:9 to the collection concerning the prophets.

C. Oracle Against Jerusalem (21:13-14)

13-14. This brief oracle is obscure, and may be only a fragment of a longer one. Most interpreters believe that it is directed against Jerusalem, since the word for **inhabitant** is feminine (ישבת; cf. Mic. 1:11-13, 15). It is thus a condemnation of that city and its inhabitants for their belief in the impregnability of Jerusalem because of its location on easily defended hills.

But the description of Jerusalem as situated in a **valley** and a **plain** is very strange. Cornill interprets the valley as the lower city of Jerusalem (perhaps the Tyropoeon Valley), and the **rock of the plain** as the upper city, especially Mount Zion. This is a forced interpretation. The word for **plain,** מישר, is usually applied to the plateau of Trans-Jordan. The LXX apparently took צור as a reference to Tyre (Σορ; Aq. has Τύρος). Peake suggests that the verses are a quotation from a different context in which another city was originally referred to; this seems probable, but we cannot now determine its original reference. Rudolph and Volz resort to conjectural emendations to make the oracle fit Jerusalem.

---

pronouncement is consistent with his prophetic warnings over the past thirty years, consistent, indeed, with his prophetic vision from the beginning; (*b*) that it is based upon a view of history (see Exeg.) which finds God on the side of the enemy, turning back the weapons of war that were in the Hebrew hands and fighting against them (vss. 4-5); (*c*) that the *two ways* appointed here are based firmly upon, and are

but the specific application of, the two ways of the covenantal consciousness (6:16-21); and (*d*) that the king is himself aware of this, anticipates the negative answer, and, indeed, stands in need paradoxically of the rebuke of Yahweh to assuage his guilt consciousness for having permitted his policies to be dominated by the nobles, princes, and the fanatic party. His attitude toward Jeremiah, in this and sub-

22 Thus saith the LORD; Go down to the house of the king of Judah, and speak there this word,

2 And say, Hear the word of the LORD, O king of Judah, that sittest upon the throne of David, thou, and thy servants, and thy people that enter in by these gates:

3 Thus saith the LORD; Execute ye judgment and righteousness, and deliver the spoiled out of the hand of the oppressor: and do no wrong, do no violence to the stranger, the fatherless, nor the widow, neither shed innocent blood in this place.

4 For if ye do this thing indeed, then shall there enter in by the gates of this house kings sitting upon the throne of David, riding in chariots and on horses, he, and his servants, and his people.

5 But if ye will not hear these words, I swear by myself, saith the LORD, that this house shall become a desolation.

6 For thus saith the LORD unto the king's house of Judah; Thou *art* Gilead unto me, *and* the head of Lebanon: *yet* surely I will make thee a wilderness, *and* cities *which* are not inhabited.

22 Thus says the LORD: "Go down to the house of the king of Judah, and speak there this word, 2 and say, 'Hear the word of the LORD, O King of Judah, who sit on the throne of David, you, and your servants, and your people who enter these gates. 3 Thus says the LORD: Do justice and righteousness, and deliver from the hand of the oppressor him who has been robbed. And do no wrong or violence to the alien, the fatherless, and the widow, nor shed innocent blood in this place. 4 For if you will indeed obey this word, then there shall enter the gates of this house kings who sit on the throne of David, riding in chariots and on horses, they, and their servants, and their people. 5 But if you will not heed these words, I swear by myself, says the LORD, that this house shall become a desolation. 6 For thus says the LORD concerning the house of the king of Judah:

"'You are as Gilead to me,
    as the summit of Lebanon,
yet surely I will make you a desert,
    an uninhabited city.[k]

[k] Cn: Heb *cities*

D. THE ROYAL PALACE AND CITY (22:1-9)

This section is a composition of the Deuteronomic editor—except vss. 6-7, which constitute a genuine poem of Jeremiah—and was probably intended by that editor as a general introduction to the oracles against specific kings in vss. 10-30. The Deuteronomic origin is proved by the conventional and general tone of the admonitions in vss. 2-5, and by the presence of Deuteronomic terminology (cf. vs. 2 with 7:2-3; 17:20; cf. vs. 3 with 7:5-6; 21:12; cf. vs. 4 with 17:25; cf. vs. 5 with 17:27; for the Deuteronomic origin of vss. 8-9 see Exeg. on 5:18-19).

22:1. Go down to the house of the king of Judah: The prophet is thought of as being in the temple area, from which he goes down to the palace of the king, which adjoined the temple but was on a somewhat lower level (cf. Jer. 26:10; 36:11-12; II Kings 19:14; 23:2).

6-7. This poem in *qînāh* meter is in the style of Jeremiah. In all probability it is addressed to the king's palace (Volz, Rudolph) rather than to the royal dynasty. The phrase **an uninhabited city** (a rendering required by the Hebrew נושבה, which is

sequent passages, shows that he dimly perceives that not Jeremiah, but he himself (and Israel) is the real betrayer of Judah.

The fragments which follow confirm this. The wrath of Yahweh is due to their **evil doings;** he is against those who still take refuge in escapist orthodoxy, in the superstition of the inviolability of Jerusalem. He will punish them also **according to the fruit of** [their] **doings.**

22:1-23:8. The Pageant of Unable Kings.— It has been remarked that these words of Jeremiah (see Exeg. on their edited form) are "un-

paralleled in the literature of the ancient Orient for their liberty of spirit."[8] Here, in a few brief oracles, is the full sum of Jeremiah's running battle with the kings. He is pictured as going down from the temple to the palace of the king to deliver his message. Just when this event may have taken place is difficult to say (see Exeg.); but the introductory scene (vss. 1-5; cf. 21:11-12) is useful in that it presents the principle which Carlyle set forth so grandiloquently: "This is the history of all rebellions,

[8] Buber, *The Prophetic Faith*, p. 174.

7 And I will prepare destroyers against thee, every one with his weapons: and they shall cut down thy choice cedars, and cast *them* into the fire.

8 And many nations shall pass by this city, and they shall say every man to his neighbor, Wherefore hath the Lord done thus unto this great city?

9 Then they shall answer, Because they have forsaken the covenant of the Lord their God, and worshipped other gods, and served them.

10 ¶ Weep ye not for the dead, neither bemoan him; *but* weep sore for him that goeth away: for he shall return no more, nor see his native country.

11 For thus saith the Lord touching Shallum the son of Josiah king of Judah, which reigned instead of Josiah his father, which went forth out of this place; He shall not return thither any more:

12 But he shall die in the place whither they have led him captive, and shall see this land no more.

7 I will prepare[l] destroyers against you,
  each with his weapons;
and they shall cut down your choicest
    cedars,
  and cast them into the fire.

8 " 'And many nations will pass by this city, and every man will say to his neighbor, "Why has the Lord dealt thus with this great city?" 9 And they will answer, "Because they forsook the covenant of the Lord their God, and worshiped other gods and served them." ' "

10 Weep not for him who is dead,
  nor bemoan him;
but weep bitterly for him who goes away,
  for he shall return no more
  to see his native land.

11 For thus says the Lord concerning Shallum the son of Josi'ah, king of Judah, who reigned instead of Josi'ah his father, and who went away from this place: "He shall return here no more, 12 but in the place where they have carried him captive, there shall he die, and he shall never see this land again."

[l] Heb *sanctify*

feminine) is metaphorical rather than literal. **Gilead** and **the summit of Lebanon** were noted for their trees. The temple complex included the House of the Forest of Lebanon (I Kings 7:2-5), and much cedar from Lebanon was used in the building of the palace and other royal buildings (I Kings 5:6, 8-10; 10:27). Jeremiah here boldly predicts the destruction of the royal palace as he had earlier predicted that of the temple of Jerusalem (7:1-15).

E. Oracle Against Shallum (22:10-12)

The historical background of these verses is given in II Kings 23:29-35. After the death of King Josiah at Megiddo at the hands of Pharaoh Neco, Josiah's son Jehoahaz (Shallum) was placed on the throne by the people of Judah. Following a brief reign of three months he was deposed by the Pharaoh and taken in exile to Egypt. The Pharaoh then placed on the Judean throne Jehoiakim, another son of Josiah, who was apparently more pliable in the Egyptian king's service. Josiah was **him who is dead,** and Jehoahaz **him who goes away** into Egypt, where he died.

11-12. These verses are a prose explanation, probably by the Deuteronomic editor. Such an explanation would have been unnecessary at the time Jeremiah spoke the poem, when the people were lamenting the death of Josiah and the exile of Jehoahaz.

French Revolutions, social explosions in ancient or modern times. You have put the too *Unable* Man at the head of affairs!" [9] This is true also of the collapse of nations through forfeit of integrity by default of faith. Jeremiah calls for justice and righteousness, protection for the op-

[9] "The Hero as King," *On Heroes, Hero Worship, and the Heroic in History.*

pressed, and obedience to God's word. We behold here the pageant of unable kings who did not heed the prophet's word; a sad spectacle, indeed, as they are brought before us in review —Josiah, Jehoahaz, Jehoiakim, Jehoiachin, and Zedekiah.

How quickly Jeremiah's thinking turns to lamentation. Like **Gilead** (cf. 8:22), like **Leba-**

13 ¶ Woe unto him that buildeth his house by unrighteousness, and his chambers by wrong; *that* useth his neighbor's service without wages, and giveth him not for his work;

14 That saith, I will build me a wide house and large chambers, and cutteth him out windows; and *it is* ceiled with cedar, and painted with vermilion.

15 Shalt thou reign, because thou closest *thyself* in cedar? did not thy father eat and drink, and do judgment and justice, *and* then *it was* well with him?

16 He judged the cause of the poor and needy; then *it was* well *with him: was* not this to know me? saith the LORD.

13 "Woe to him who builds his house by
   unrighteousness,
   and his upper rooms by injustice;
who makes his neighbor serve him for
   nothing,
   and does not give him his wages;
14 who says, 'I will build myself a great
   house
   with spacious upper rooms,'
and cuts out windows for it,
   paneling it with cedar,
   and painting it with vermilion.
15 Do you think you are a king
   because you compete in cedar?
Did not your father eat and drink
   and do justice and righteousness?
   Then it was well with him.
16 He judged the cause of the poor and
   needy;
   then it was well.
Is not this to know me?
               says the LORD.

Shallum was the private name (see I Chr. 3:15) of the king whose regnal name was Jehoahaz (for details of the practice involved here see A. M. Honeyman, "The Evidence for Regnal Names Among the Hebrews," *Journal of Biblical Literature,* LXVII [1948], 13-25).

F. ORACLE AGAINST JEHOIAKIM (22:13-19)

Here is the strongest condemnation the prophet uttered against any of the Judean kings. He pronounces judgment upon Jehoiakim (609-598) because of his selfishness and injustice in enlarging and beautifying his own palace at a critical time in the nation's history. In the early part of his reign Jehoiakim was subservient to the Egyptians, who had placed him on the throne, and he had to tax his people in order to pay tribute to Egypt (II Kings 23:35). In addition, he forced his subjects to work on his palace without pay. Jeremiah saw a strong contrast between the policy and character of Jehoiakim and those of his father Josiah.

13. The prophet significantly refers to the king's subject as **his neighbor** from whom he had no right to exact labor without compensation. Though several Hebrew kings acted like Oriental despots, the prophets did not sanction their actions.

15-16. Your father: Josiah, not Ahaz (as LXX mistranslates) or some other remote ancestor of the king. Josiah was not an ascetic, nor did he revel in luxury. He lived simply and justly, showing an interest in **the cause of the poor and needy.** Thus he had

---

non (cf. 18:14), is the land of Judah to the Lord; but though Judah is to him like the land of the choicest cedars it will be made like a desert, and travelers from **many nations** passing by will pause and wonder **"Why?"** (Cf. Deut. 29:24-25.) The answer will be clear: **they forsook the covenant of the LORD their God.** As though to leave no least shadow of a doubt the editor of the opening verses (see Exeg.) has made the Lord swear by himself, the full import of which may be gleaned from Heb. 6:13-18.

The first lament for Jehoahaz (22:10-12) is brief but poignant. When Josiah was killed "the people of the land" (II Kings 23:30) chose Jehoahaz for king over Jehoiakim (Eliakim), his elder brother. But he was soon deposed by Pharaoh Neco and taken off to Egypt, where he died. The present lament was evidently written after his exile and while Josiah's death was still mourned by the people. But Josiah, though cut off in the midst of his reign, had nevertheless ruled long, and had been a right-

17 But thine eyes and thine heart *are* not but for thy covetousness, and for to shed innocent blood, and for oppression, and for violence, to do *it*.

18 Therefore thus saith the LORD concerning Jehoiakim the son of Josiah king of Judah; They shall not lament for him, *saying*, Ah my brother! or, Ah sister! they shall not lament for him, *saying*, Ah lord! or, Ah his glory!

19 He shall be buried with the burial of an ass, drawn and cast forth beyond the gates of Jerusalem.

17 But you have eyes and heart
   only for your dishonest gain,
  for shedding innocent blood,
   and for practicing oppression and violence."

18 Therefore thus says the LORD concerning Jehoi'akim the son of Josi'ah, king of Judah:
  "They shall not lament for him, saying,
   'Ah my brother!' or 'Ah sister!'
  They shall not lament for him, saying,
   'Ah lord!' or 'Ah his majesty!'

19 With the burial of an ass he shall be buried,
   dragged and cast forth beyond the gates of Jerusalem."

---

true knowledge of God, which to the prophets was primarily a moral rather than an intellectual matter.

17. II Kings 24:4 also informs us that Jehoiakim **shed innocent blood**—by which is meant the pronouncement of unjust decisions in his role as supreme judge in the land, or possibly persecution of innocent persons such as the prophets.

18-19. These verses present a difficult problem as to whether Jeremiah's prediction was fulfilled or not. II Kings 24:6 says that "Jehoiakim slept with his fathers," a phrase which ordinarily means that the person named was buried in his ancestral tomb. The LXX[B] of II Chr. 36:8 contains the additional information that Jehoiakim "was buried in the garden of Uzza [Γαναζαε=אזע ןג] with his fathers." The garden of Uzza is named as the burial place of Manasseh and Amon in the Hebrew text of II Kings 21:18, 26; it was probably situated in the grounds of the royal palace in Jerusalem (S. Yeivin, "The Sepulchers of the Kings of the House of David," *Journal of Near Eastern Studies,* VII [1948], 34-35).

It is possible that Jehoiakim did receive proper burial, but that later his body was disinterred and dishonored, either by the Chaldeans or by his own subjects (so Cornill). Or it may be that the LXX[B] text of II Chr. 36:8 is of late origin, and that Jehoiakim received no funeral, his body being thrown outside the gates of Jerusalem, possibly following a palace revolt, as suggested by Albright ("Seal of Eliakim and Latest Preëxilic History of Judah," pp. 90-91). On the other hand, it is not impossible

---

eous king; therefore weep not for him. For these were misplaced tears. Weep rather for the one **who goes away.** Why? **For he shall return no more.** Jeremiah's love of homeland, of his native soil, illumines this passage like a lantern in the night; at the same time it is a quiet warning lest a like deprivation should overtake the ones who remain.

In startling and almost terrible contrast with the prophetic sympathy of the first lament are the two "impassioned philippics" [10] against Jehoiakim (22:13-17, 18-19). It is clear from the foregoing lament that Jeremiah stood in opposition to Jehoiakim from the very beginning of the latter's reign. The opening verses of this chapter quite possibly describe his going down to the palace of Jehoiakim. In any case the

[10] Skinner, *Prophecy and Religion,* p. 247.

powerful temple sermon (chs. 7; 26) brings the opposition sharply and unavoidably into the open, and is later confirmed by the publication of the roll (ch. 36), the main contents of which we have already examined. The present polemic focuses very shrewdly upon an object plainly visible to everyone—Jehoiakim's sumptuous palace built by forced labor on Mount Zion. The polemic consists of two very incisive arguments. The first underscores the king's injustice and his vanity. **Woe to him who builds his house by unrighteousness,** who employs forced labor, and **makes his neighbor** [note how shrewdly Jeremiah establishes the God-given parity between the Hebrew kings and those to whom Yahweh has set them to minister] **serve him for nothing;** and who thinks only of building himself **a great house,** with many-

20 ¶ Go up to Lebanon, and cry; and lift up thy voice in Bashan, and cry from the passages: for all thy lovers are destroyed.	20 "Go up to Lebanon, and cry out,
	    and lift up your voice in Bashan;
	cry from Ab′arim,
	    for all your lovers are destroyed.

21 I spake unto thee in thy prosperity; but thou saidst, I will not hear. This hath been thy manner from thy youth, that thou obeyedst not my voice.	21 I spoke to you in your prosperity,
	    but you said, 'I will not listen.'
	This has been your way from your youth,
	    that you have not obeyed my voice.

22 The wind shall eat up all thy pastors, and thy lovers shall go into captivity: surely then shalt thou be ashamed and confounded for all thy wickedness.	22 The wind shall shepherd all your shepherds,
	    and your lovers shall go into captivity;
	then you will be ashamed and confounded
	    because of all your wickedness.

23 O inhabitant of Lebanon, that makest thy nest in the cedars, how gracious shalt thou be when pangs come upon thee, the pain as of a woman in travail!	23 O inhabitant of Lebanon,
	    nested among the cedars,
	how you will groan when pangs come upon you,
	    pain as of a woman in travail!"

that the prediction of Jeremiah actually was unfulfilled. The lack of literal fulfillment would not have disturbed the prophet; and it is by no means certain that ancient scribes and editors were careful to include in the prophetic books only predictions that were known to have been fulfilled. To suppose this is to attribute to ancient scribes and editors modern editorial methods.

G. Wail over Jerusalem! (22:20-23)

This poem is directed against Jerusalem, personified as a woman (the feminine gender being used in Hebrew). The date is probably 598, near the time of Jehoiachin's surrender to the Babylonians and the exile of many of the leaders of Jerusalem (II Kings 24:11-16). The position of this poem between oracles concerning Jehoiakim and Jehoiachin is thus appropriate.

20. The prophet imaginatively summons Jerusalem to wail over her own fate on three high mountains: **Lebanon** in Syria, to the north; **Bashan** in upper Trans-Jordan, to the northeast; and **Abarim** in Moab, to the southeast (where Moses died, Num. 27:12; Deut. 32:48; identical with or including Mount Nebo).

Your lovers here and in vs. 22 are probably the leaders of Jerusalem; note in vs. 22 the parallel with **your shepherds.** The same figure is applied to the leaders of Jerusalem in Lam. 1:19. It was in fact the leaders who were exiled to Babylon, according to II Kings 24:12-16. Elsewhere the term or its equivalent means false gods (3:1; 2:25; Hos. 2:5, 7, 10, 12, 13) or foreign allies (4:30; 13:21; probably 30:14; Ezek. 16:33, 36-37; 23:5, 9, 22).

21. **Your way from your youth** was one of disobedience. This does not contradict 2:2, which refers to the Israelites in the wilderness; here the reference is to Jerusalem. A similar judgment on Jerusalem's history is expressed in Ezek. 16.

23. **O inhabitant of Lebanon:** For the use of Lebanon as a figure for Jerusalem, or specifically Mount Zion, cf. vss. 6-7. With the last half of the verse cf. 4:31; 6:24; 13:21.

windowed rooms, cedar paneling, decor of bright **vermilion** (the word occurs again only in Ezek. 23:14). Then comes the second movement, the shattering contrast drawn between the vanity and injustice of the oppressor son and the faithful practices of the righteous father. With what incredibly trenchant irony Jeremiah describes the former:	**Do you think you are a king because you compete in cedar?** And how adequately and how exactly he grounds the greatness of the latter upon the greatness of God! The passage is apposite enough if it simply means that Josiah enjoyed the material comforts of his kingly office and

24 *As* I live, saith the Lord, though Coniah the son of Jehoiakim king of Judah were the signet upon my right hand, yet would I pluck thee thence;

25 And I will give thee into the hand of them that seek thy life, and into the hand *of them* whose face thou fearest, even into the hand of Nebuchadrezzar king of Babylon, and into the hand of the Chaldeans.

26 And I will cast thee out, and thy mother that bare thee, into another country, where ye were not born; and there shall ye die.

27 But to the land whereunto they desire to return, thither shall they not return.

24 "As I live, says the Lord, though Coni'ah the son of Jehoi'akim, king of Judah, were the signet ring on my right hand, yet I would tear you off 25 and give you into the hand of those who seek your life, into the hand of those of whom you are afraid, even into the hand of Nebuchadrez'zar king of Babylon and into the hand of the Chalde'ans. 26 I will hurl you and the mother who bore you into another country, where you were not born, and there you shall die. 27 But to the land to which they will long to return, there they shall not return."

H. Oracles Against Jehoiachin (22:24-30)

Jehoiachin was the son of Jehoiakim. When the latter died, during (or immediately preceding) the Babylonian siege of Jerusalem, Jehoiachin succeeded to the throne at the age of eighteen. After a reign of three months he surrendered to Nebuchadrezzar and was taken captive to Babylon, from which he never returned (II Kings 24:8-17; 25:27-30). Many of the Judeans continued to consider him the legitimate king, even in exile, rather than his uncle Zedekiah, whom Nebuchadrezzar had placed on the Jerusalem throne; they expected the return of Jehoiachin to Jerusalem in the near future (28:1-4; Ezek. 17:22; for detailed discussion see Albright, "Seal of Eliakim and Latest Preëxilic History of Judah," pp. 92-103). Jeremiah opposed the expectation of an immediate return of the exiles to Judah (29:1-14), and did not consider the exiled Jehoiachin as legitimate king; he apparently supported Zedekiah. Another oracle concerning Jehoiachin may be found in 13:18-19.

24-27. These verses are in their present form from the Deuteronomic editor; his phraseology is especially evident in vss. 25-27 (which have been considered editorial by Cornill, Duhm, *et al.*). Vs. 24 can be scanned as poetry with the omission of **the son of Jehoiakim, king of Judah**; it may well be a genuine poem of the prophet, expressing his attitude toward Jehoiachin, here called by a shortened form of his name, **Coniah**. The Deuteronomic editor has made a prose addition to this poem; the whole is prophecy after the event. The figure of the **signet ring**, a very valuable personal possession, was applied to Jehoiachin's grandson Zerubbabel (Hag. 2:23).

---

at the same time was a king of justice, righteousness, and holy concern for the poor and the needy; but knowing something of the poetic skill wherewith Jeremiah gives to his comparisons the highest possible pitch of implication, it seems probable that "eating and drinking" refers here to the king's participation in the holy covenant meal whereby he enters the covenant with Yahweh and fulfills the same by observing the practical virtues here detailed by Jeremiah. (Josiah also reintroduced the feast of the Passover [II Kings 23:21-23] and the feast of Unleavened Bread, not celebrated in so lavish a way [II Chr. 35:1-19] since the days of Samuel.) [1]

But more significantly, Josiah's concern for the people would make plain the true nature of his knowledge of God. **Is not this to know me?** asks Yahweh through his prophet after Josiah's practices reveal the inner tie: for these are the evidences of Hosea's equation—"steadfast love" as the "knowledge of God" (Hos. 6:6). Martin Buber puts it well: "The most sublime conception in the teaching of his master Jeremiah sees realized in the life of the king." [2]

The contrast is not too sharp, for subsequent ages placed David, Hezekiah, and Josiah among the holier kings who built upon the greatness of God. [3] It was insight into the same principle which led the great French pulpit orator, Bos-

[1] Cf. Pedersen, *Israel, Its Life and Culture, III-IV*, pp. 389 ff.

[2] *Op. cit.*, p. 163.
[3] Cf. Ecclus. 49:1-3.

28 *Is* this man Coniah a despised broken idol? *is he* a vessel wherein *is* no pleasure? wherefore are they cast out, he and his seed, and are cast into a land which they know not?

29 O earth, earth, earth, hear the word of the LORD.

30 Thus saith the LORD, Write ye this man childless, a man *that* shall not prosper in his days: for no man of his seed shall prosper, sitting upon the throne of David, and ruling any more in Judah.

28 Is this man Coni'ah a despised, broken pot,
    a vessel no one cares for?
Why are he and his children hurled and cast
    into a land which they do not know?
29 O land, land, land,
    hear the word of the LORD!
30 Thus says the LORD:
"Write this man down as childless,
    a man who shall not succeed in his days;
for none of his offspring shall succeed
    in sitting on the throne of David,
    and ruling again in Judah."

---

28. This verse should be interpreted as a quotation, spoken by the people of Judah, or specifically by the party favorable to Jehoiachin. It expresses their feeling—not Jeremiah's—toward the exiled king.

29-30. The attitude of Jeremiah is reflected in an oracle of the Lord. Jehoiachin was not childless. I Chr. 3:17 lists the names of his seven sons. Cuneiform tablets found at Babylon list rations of oil provided for *Yaukin* (i.e., Jehoiachin) king of Judah and his five sons (see J. B. Pritchard, ed., *Ancient Near Eastern Texts Relating to the Old Testament* [Princeton: Princeton University Press, 1950], p. 308; for discussion see W. F. Albright, "King Joiachin in Exile," *Biblical Archaeologist*, V [1942], 49-55). Though his grandson Zerubbabel was governor of Judah ca. 520 B.C., and was involved in an abortive attempt to establish Jewish independence, it is literally true that none of Jehoiachin's descendants

---

suet, in his famous eulogy on the death of the Prince de Condé, to appeal from human glory to the glory of God, and to recognize that "God has revealed to us that He alone creates conquerors, and that He alone makes them serve his designs." [4]

In the sharpest contrast possible to his praise of Josiah stands Jeremiah's pronouncement upon Jehoiakim (22:19). Regardless of the actual form of his death (see Exeg.) it is this picture of the carcass of an animal left to rot in the field which remains to sum the perfidies of the faithless king.

After so strong an oracle the more general lament of the following fragment concerning the fate of Jerusalem's rulers is exceedingly well placed. It is also addressed to the community (as the feminine pronouns show). It both softens the bitterness of the foregoing and ties the peoples' fate to that of their leaders. Again the people are reminded how Yahweh's messengers came with frequent warnings: and again Jeremiah repeats his antiphonal refrain—**but you said, "I will not listen."** There is nothing now but lamentation, and that from the highest places (at other times the places for proclaiming glad tidings—Isa. 40:9). These are the mountains which the Chaldeans will pass by on their

[4] *Oraisons Funèbres* (Paris: E. Plon Cⁱᵉ, 1875), p. 324.

movement south; and one (O soft but pathetic irony) the mountain, Abarim, from which Moses viewed the Promised Land. The easy play on words—**the wind [*rûaḥ*] shall shepherd all your shepherds**—shows gently how the purposes of God preside unseen above the overconfident designs of men: how, though the leaders shepherded the people, they themselves are being shepherded into exile. Then comes the climax line of unimpeachable beauty and singular sadness:

O inhabitant of Lebanon,
    nested among the cedars,
how you will groan when pangs come upon you.

For though Judah had been confident of her safety, like a bird far away in the high branches of the cedars on the heights of Lebanon, her agony is about to fall. Seeking a false and escapist refuge, Judah had not learned the humbler certainty:

As the marsh-hen secretly builds on the watery sod,
Behold I will build me a nest on the greatness of God:

        .   .   .   .

By so many roots as the marsh-grass sends in the sod
I will heartily lay me a-hold on the greatness of God.[5]

[5] Sidney Lanier, "The Marshes of Glynn."

23 Woe be unto the pastors that destroy and scatter the sheep of my pasture! saith the LORD.

2 Therefore thus saith the LORD God of Israel against the pastors that feed my people; Ye have scattered my flock, and driven them away, and have not visited them: behold, I will visit upon you the evil of your doings, saith the LORD.

23 "Woe to the shepherds who destroy and scatter the sheep of my pasture!" says the LORD. 2 Therefore thus says the LORD, the God of Israel, concerning the shepherds who care for my people: "You have scattered my flock, and have driven them away, and you have not attended to them. Behold, I will attend to you for your

---

did **succeed in sitting on the throne of David.** The translation in the RSV is correct; it is a permissible rendering of the Hebrew and conforms better to the historical situation.

J. Restoration and Ideal Rule (23:1-8)

In this section, which closes the collection of oracles dealing with the kings of Israel, 22:1–23:8, four oracles are presented: (*a*) a pronouncement of woe on the false shepherds (vss. 1-2); (*b*) promise of the return of the flock of Israel to its own land, with good shepherds to rule over them (vss. 3-4); (*c*) promise of a righteous branch from the line of David (vss. 5-6); (*d*) promise of return to the land of Israel (vss. 7-8). The first and third are probably genuine, but not the second and fourth.

23:1-2. These verses pronounce **woe** upon the **shepherds** who are false to their duty. The shepherd is a standing figure in the O.T. for ruler; frequently it refers only to the king, but in the plural the word may refer to ruling officials in general. The date of the passage is probably the time of Zedekiah. That king was not the object of violent condemnation by the prophet, who merely considered him weak and vacillating and too much given to following the counsel of his officials who wanted to rebel against

---

When Jehoiakim died, the people apparently hoped that the accession of Jehoiachin would release them from the oppressions and disastrous policies of his father; but Jeremiah's realism cuts through these hopes. In the first of these oracles on Jehoiachin (22:24-27) he says bluntly, almost unfeelingly, that though Jehoiachin **were the signet ring on** [Yahweh's] **right hand,** he would nonetheless tear him off and deliver the people into the hand of the Chaldeans. Jehoiachin's actual fate is indicated (see Exeg.): **I will hurl you and the mother who bore you into another country.** The retention of the phrase "I will hurl" renews the thought of Jeremiah's call: Jeremiah—Yahweh hurls! Within three months, when Nebuchadrezzar's armies appeared before the city's gates, Jehoiachin surrendered and was carried into exile, never to return to the land from which the golden crown had fallen (13:18).

The second oracle (22:28-30) is later, while Jehoiachin is in exile, and the people are asking "Why?" Why was Jehoiachin thrown aside like a broken image or useless vessel? Does Yahweh care so little for **this man Coniah?** Again Jeremiah cuts short any hopes placed in the young king. Neither Jehoiachin nor his seed will ever come to sit on David's throne (see Exeg.). The oracle thus cut two ways: it clarified the situation to the people at home;

and it aimed to cut short agitation among the exiles in Babylonia, where unrealistic leaders were instigating a movement of revolt centered in the exiled king, whereby they hoped to restore the Jewish kingdom and their own positions of power (ch. 29).

The section on the kings of Judah now moves (23:1-8) with a fine crescendo to its surprising and powerful climax. We now have an oracle on Zedekiah, though not at first apparent. Jeremiah never strikes him openly with the lash and sting of God's rebuke as he repeatedly had to do with Jehoiakim, for Zedekiah is well-meaning but ineffective, trapped by the policies of the controlling princes. Nebuchadrezzar put Zedekiah in power and even named him "Yahweh is my salvation"—as though to remind him constantly, as did Jeremiah, of his primary function: to reign as the servant of Yahweh. But the very indirection of Jeremiah's oracle is eloquent with judgment. The initial **Woe to the shepherds who destroy and scatter the sheep of my pasture** falls upon both the king and the princes, upon the leaders who have been responsible for the ruin of Judah. This is the negative but logical consequence of all that has gone before.

It is important to note, now, against this background of lamentation and defeat, the quick reversal into hope—as though, when the

3 And I will gather the remnant of my flock out of all countries whither I have driven them, and will bring them again to their folds; and they shall be fruitful and increase.

4 And I will set up shepherds over them which shall feed them: and they shall fear no more, nor be dismayed, neither shall they be lacking, saith the LORD.

5 ¶ Behold, the days come, saith the LORD, that I will raise unto David a righteous Branch, and a King shall reign and prosper, and shall execute judgment and justice in the earth.

evil doings, says the LORD. 3 Then I will gather the remnant of my flock out of all the countries where I have driven them, and I will bring them back to their fold, and they shall be fruitful and multiply. 4 I will set shepherds over them who will care for them, and they shall fear no more, nor be dismayed, neither shall any be missing, says the LORD.

5 "Behold, the days are coming, says the LORD, when I will raise up for David a righteous Branch, and he shall reign as king and deal wisely, and shall execute

---

Babylonia. The oracle may therefore be directed more against such officials than against the king himself. Its position here, following the oracle concerning Jehoiachin (22:24-30), is appropriate.

3-4. These verses predict the return of the **flock** of Israel from the lands to which they have been driven, with good **shepherds** to rule them. The verses presuppose the dispersion of the Jews, and are probably from the same editor who wrote 3:15-18 (see references in Exeg., *ad loc.*, especially Ezek. 34). Such a prediction is hardly appropriate to Jeremiah (Cornill; Rudolph considers only vs. 3 secondary).

5-6. The authenticity of this messianic oracle, repeated in 33:15-16, has been much debated by scholars. It is maintained, for example, by Cornill, Giesebrecht, Peake, and Rudolph, but denied by Duhm, Volz, Erbt, and (very hesitantly) Skinner. Favoring its genuineness are the following arguments: (*a*) The prediction here is not of a world-conquering military hero (as in some eschatological passages), but rather of a just and righteous king of the Davidic dynasty; it includes nothing of which we would expect Jeremiah to disapprove. (*b*) The name **The LORD is our righteousness** is in Hebrew *YHWH-çidhqēnû*, and can be interpreted as a play on the name of King Zedekiah, which in Hebrew is *çidhqiyyāhû*, meaning "Yahweh is my righteousness." His name had been changed from Mattaniah by Nebuchadrezzar (II Kings 24:17). Jeremiah did not oppose Zedekiah as he had Jehoiakim, and he may well have suggested that a future king

---

broken nation has reached the nadir of despondency, Jeremiah, almost alone, is able to translate its ruin into its transcendent meaning. For Jeremiah, as for Job, it is precisely out of the tempest that the Eternal speaks. At last the people have a foothold on the real. The ciphers of their history may now be read in the light of the divine intention. It is in this sense that Jeremiah's "eschatology" is to be understood.

In three assurances he swiftly makes these transcendent meanings plain. Each of the three promises (see Exeg.) converts a familiar term into ultimate significance. The first fixes Isaiah's floating formula—"a remnant shall return"—upon **the remnant of my flock** in exile. **I will bring them back to their fold.** The third sees that the old exodus from Egypt shall be supplanted by a newer exodus out of the north. So glorious will be this new deliverance that the old will be forgotten. And the second, which is the master stroke of the three, and the one

most authentically Jeremianic (see Exeg.), is the appearance of the ideal king, whose name (how deft the play on Zedekiah's name!) shall be **"The LORD is our righteousness"** (or "our salvation," "deliverance"). The messianic interest here may wisely be minimized. The emergence of such a king is implicit in Jeremiah's understanding of the covenant relationship realized inwardly in the heart. When this fresh "shoot" comes

> all shall be well and
> All manner of thing shall be well
> By the purification of the motive
> In the ground of our beseeching.[6]

He shall be out of David (the Davidic covenant); he shall **deal wisely** (cf. Isa. 52:13, where

[6] T. S. Eliot, "Little Gidding," Part III. From *Four Quartets.* Copyright 1943 by T. S. Eliot. Used by permission of Harcourt, Brace & Co. and Faber & Faber, publishers.

6 In his days Judah shall be saved, and Israel shall dwell safely: and this *is* his name whereby he shall be called, THE LORD OUR RIGHTEOUSNESS.

7 Therefore, behold, the days come, saith the LORD, that they shall no more say, The LORD liveth, which brought up the children of Israel out of the land of Egypt;

8 But, The LORD liveth, which brought up and which led the seed of the house of Israel out of the north country, and from all countries whither I had driven them; and they shall dwell in their own land.

9 ¶ Mine heart within me is broken because of the prophets; all my bones shake:

justice and righteousness in the land. **6** In his days Judah will be saved, and Israel will dwell securely. And this is the name by which he will be called: 'The LORD is our righteousness.'

7 "Therefore, behold, the days are coming, says the LORD, when men shall no longer say, 'As the LORD lives who brought up the people of Israel out of the land of Egypt,' **8** but 'As the LORD lives who brought up and led the descendants of the house of Israel out of the north country and out of all the countries where he*ᵐ* had driven them.' Then they shall dwell in their own land."

9 Concerning the prophets:
My heart is broken within me,
    all my bones shake;

ᵐ Gk: Heb *I*

---

would fulfill the promise of Zedekiah's name. (*c*) The epithet **Branch** is a messianic title in Zech. 3:8; 6:12 (cf. Isa. 11:1, where a different Hebrew word is used). It is argued by some scholars that the word must have acquired a messianic meaning before the time of Zechariah (520-516 B.C.), and hence must go back to the time of Jeremiah. This third argument is not strong. There was a long enough period between Jeremiah and Zechariah for the word to have acquired such significance.

It seems best to consider this passage as Jeremianic, but it must be admitted that messianism did not play an important or decisive role in Jeremiah's thought; outside the present passage, only 30:8-9 and 33:17 are possibly messianic, and their authenticity is open to question. Rudolph may be entirely correct in arguing that the present passage is not properly eschatological, and therefore not truly messianic. It may only envisage the rise of a just and righteous king of David's line in the normal course of events. We cannot be certain that the term **Branch** had genuinely messianic significance at this time.

In the name **The LORD is our righteousness** the word צדק has the double meaning of **righteousness** and "salvation" or "deliverance" as it (and צדקה) has in Second Isaiah (e.g., 46:13; 51:1, 6, 8).

7-8. These verses are found also in 16:14-15, where they are out of place. The LXX omits the passage here but inserts it inappropriately after 23:40. It is undoubtedly an exilic or postexilic addition, predicting return from all the lands of the Dispersion, like vs. 3 (cf. 3:14, 18).

XVI. ORACLES CONCERNING THE PROPHETS (23:9-40)

In this section is collected a series of Jeremianic messages concerning the prophets. The collection was made very early, possibly by Baruch, and shows no evidence of

---

the same phrase is used of the servant of Yahweh), and **shall execute justice and righteousness in the land**—and, implicit in Jeremiah's message from the beginning, both Judah and Israel shall live securely. Outside this relationship with Yahweh there is neither security nor justice nor righteousness. Their ruin has made this plain. The name which Zedekiah received on his accession to the throne—a name

so helplessly collapsed in him—is precisely the name of hope when, out of the heart's exile from God, the transcendent awareness comes.

23:9-40. *Concerning the Prophets.*—The difference between Jeremiah and the official prophets is radical. It is a difference in vision, in historical, moral, and spiritual perspectives. The clue to this axis of difference is stated clearly in vs. 10: **Their might is not right.**

I am like a drunken man, and like a man whom wine hath overcome, because of the LORD, and because of the words of his holiness.	I am like a drunken man,
	    like a man overcome by wine,
	because of the LORD
	    and because of his holy words.

10 For the land is full of adulterers; for because of swearing the land mourneth; the pleasant places of the wilderness are dried up, and their course is evil, and their force *is* not right.	10 For the land is full of adulterers;
	    because of the curse the land mourns,
	    and the pastures of the wilderness are
	      dried up.
	Their course is evil,
	    and their might is not right.

11 For both prophet and priest are profane; yea, in my house have I found their wickedness, saith the LORD.	11 "Both prophet and priest are ungodly;
	    even in my house I have found their
	      wickedness,
	                 says the LORD.

Deuteronomic editing. It was placed immediately after the collection concerning the rulers, because both prophets and rulers were considered to be important in their respective realms.

The book of Jeremiah more than any other refers to "false" prophets (2:8; 5:30-31; 6:13-14; 8:10-11; 14:13-15; 18:18-23; 26:8, 11, 16; 27:1–28:16; and the present section). It is probable that prophets were unusually numerous in Jerusalem during Jeremiah's career, since the Deuteronomic reform of 621 B.C. involved the removal of many cultic prophets and priests from the local sanctuaries to the capital. A strong sense of prophetic calling made Jeremiah sensitive to what he considered the hypocrisies and failings of other prophets.

Jeremiah's indictment of these prophets may be summarized under four heads: (*a*) Some of them prophesied by Baal rather than by Yahweh; this charge is made specifically against the prophets of Samaria (23:13), but is not frequent. The implication is that most of them prophesied by Yahweh, but in a false manner. (*b*) They were men of low moral character and therefore were incapable of giving moral leadership. (*c*) They prophesied peace and prosperity rather than doom, and thus instilled vain hopes within the people (see especially 28:8-9). (*d*) Because of all these facts Jeremiah was convinced that they did not speak the word of Yahweh, which they could receive only in the "council of the Lord," but only words derived from their own minds or stolen from one another. He considered them to be "false" prophets, not because they made unfulfilled predictions, but because they were utterly faithless to their prophetic calling. They were a burden to the Lord, who would punish them with destruction when he destroyed the sinful people.

The messages here collected come from various periods in Jeremiah's life and cannot be precisely dated. The collection is almost wholly authentic, except vss. 34-40, and consists of five separate oracles.

A. GENERAL WICKEDNESS IN THE LAND (23:9-12)

9-12. This section describes the prophet's great sorrow over the general wickedness in which both prophets and priests share. It serves as an introduction to the series because

Something very similar has been said in our own time: "Where there is no vision . . . , the people perish; but where there is sham vision, they perish even faster."[7] What makes Jeremiah's bones shake, and makes him reel like a drunken man, is simply that he sees clearly the sanctified shams on which official religion in his time is based, and he is staggered at the consequences. What breaks his heart is that this has

occurred at the core of the community, with the prophets. This is a matter which might be viewed with indifference, as with the general run of the people, were it not for the words of the Lord which cut across this fatal compromise and reveal to Jeremiah what is horrible in it (23:9, 14).

Their might is not right. In three ways it is wrong or perverted. It is adulterous (23:10). This does not mean, as is so often pointed out, that the cult prophets were men of bad morals

[7] Irving Babbitt, *Democracy and Leadership* (Boston: Houghton-Mifflin Co., 1924), p. 16.

12 Wherefore their way shall be unto them as slippery *ways* in the darkness: they shall be driven on, and fall therein: for I will bring evil upon them, *even* the year of their visitation, saith the LORD.

13 And I have seen folly in the prophets of Samaria; they prophesied in Baal, and caused my people Israel to err.

14 I have seen also in the prophets of Jerusalem a horrible thing: they commit adultery, and walk in lies: they strengthen also the hands of evildoers, that none doth return from his wickedness: they are all of them unto me as Sodom, and the inhabitants thereof as Gomorrah.

15 Therefore thus saith the LORD of hosts concerning the prophets; Behold, I will feed them with wormwood, and make them drink the water of gall: for from the prophets of Jerusalem is profaneness gone forth into all the land.

12 Therefore their way shall be to them
　　like slippery paths in the darkness,
　　into which they shall be driven and
　　　fall;
　for I will bring evil upon them
　　in the year of their punishment,
　　　　　　　　　　says the LORD.
13 In the prophets of Samar'ia
　　I saw an unsavoury thing:
　they prophesied by Ba'al
　　and led my people Israel astray.
14 But in the prophets of Jerusalem
　　I have seen a horrible thing:
　they commit adultery and walk in lies;
　　they strengthen the hands of evildoers,
　so that no one turns from his wicked-
　　　ness;
　all of them have become like Sodom to
　　me,
　　and its inhabitants like Gomor'rah."
15 Therefore thus says the LORD of hosts
　concerning the prophets:
　　"Behold, I will feed them with worm-
　　　wood,
　　and give them poisoned water to drink;
　for from the prophets of Jerusalem
　　ungodliness has gone forth into all the
　　　land."

of the mention of **both prophet and priest** (vs. 11), who are guilty of ungodliness even within the temple (**my house**). For **slippery paths** as a mode of punishment cf. Pss. 35:6; 73:18.

B. EVIL-DOING OF THE JERUSALEM PROPHETS (23:13-15)

13-15. The sin of the Jerusalem prophets is greater than that of the Samaritan prophets. The latter prophesied by a false god; the former prophesy by Yahweh and yet **commit adultery and walk in lies,** and even **strengthen the hands of evildoers** by their own moral failures.

and that Jeremiah is moralistically outraged; it means rather that Judah, as the faithful bride of Yahweh (2:2), has become faithless through the words of these prophets, who are betraying her. Secondly, their power is profane. "Both prophet and priest are *profane;* even in my *fane* I come upon their crimes." [8] The use of the Latin *fane* (*fanum,* "temple") retains the sense of the play upon ideas which Jeremiah intends. Here again it is not intended primarily that the prophets of the temple should be denounced because of particular transgressions of the law, but rather because all that they do or say profanes God's word: **Their**

[8] Vs. 11. Cf. Johnson, *Cultic Prophet in Ancient Israel,* p. 52; also Moffatt's tr. For a fuller discussion of this play upon words see Expos. on 49:1-39, pp. 1117-23.

might is not right. The immediate dialectical consequence of this, to the temple prophets, is that their way is into spiritual darkness. They are progressively deprived of the sense of security and move as on slippery paths. They are driven from within by the anxious propulsions of ever-increasing introversion, or by the compulsions of unconscious evasion and aggressiveness. Sooner or later they will **fall** (23:12). Thirdly, since their power is not of God, they speak from themselves (23:21). These are prophets whom God did not send—**yet they ran!** They are prophets to whom Yahweh did not speak—**yet they prophesied!** And thus the great damage is done.

The consequences are twofold; to the prophets, and to the people. The consequences to the

16 Thus saith the LORD of hosts, Hearken not unto the words of the prophets that prophesy unto you; they make you vain: they speak a vision of their own heart, *and* not out of the mouth of the LORD.

17 They say still unto them that despise me, The LORD hath said, Ye shall have peace; and they say unto every one that walketh after the imagination of his own heart, No evil shall come upon you.

18 For who hath stood in the counsel of the LORD, and hath perceived and heard his word? who hath marked his word, and heard *it?*

16 Thus says the LORD of hosts: "Do not listen to the words of the prophets who prophesy to you, filling you with vain hopes; they speak visions of their own minds, not from the mouth of the LORD. 17 They say continually to those who despise the word of the LORD, 'It shall be well with you'; and to every one who stubbornly follows his own heart, they say, 'No evil shall come upon you.'"

18 For who among them has stood in the council of the LORD
to perceive and to hear his word,
or who has given heed to his word and listened?

C. NATURE OF THE FALSE PROPHETS' MESSAGE (23:16-22)

The false prophets prophesy welfare and peace rather than doom, because they have not **stood in the council of the LORD** and have not been sent by him (cf. 6:14; 8:11; 14:13-14). This accords with the principle expressed in 28:8-9, which is an almost categorical statement that the true prophet prophesies war, famine, and pestilence rather than peace. The prophet who proclaims peace and prosperity gives no moral challenge to evildoers and fills men with **vain hopes.**

18. **The council of the LORD** (cf. vs. 22) is the place where the true prophet receives the word of Yahweh. The Hebrew *ṣôdh,* here translated **council** (RSV), is used in 6:11 of "the gatherings of young men" (RSV), and in 15:17 of "the company of merrymakers" (RSV). In Amos 3:7 the same word may be rendered "counsel" of Yahweh, revealed to the prophets. The Hebrews believed in the existence of a council or assembly of supernatural beings, presided over by Yahweh. The lower beings are known variously as "holy ones," "spirits," "sons of God," etc.; their existence is no denial of monotheism, since they were thought of as rendering homage to Yahweh and under his power. Ps. 89:7 speaks of "the council of the holy ones" (*ṣôdh qedhôshîm*); and the idea, usually with different words, is found in Ps. 82; I Kings 22:19-22; Job 1:1–2:13; 15:8; Isa. 6:1-13; Ecclus. 24:2; *et al.* The same general idea, within a polytheistic system, occurs in Mesopotamian and Canaanite religion, from which it was ultimately derived. Jeremiah believed that in some manner the true prophet was actually admitted to such a council, where he received the "word of Yahweh," but that the privilege was denied to the false

---

prophets we have just signified. Jeremiah adds (vs. 15) that they will have **wormwood** to eat and **poisoned water to drink.** Wormwood is the biblical symbol for bitter calamity and sorrow; and water, so often a symbol for the spirit, is poisoned from the first by their perverted righteousness.

It is this last principle, which entails the consequences to the people, that appalls Jeremiah. The corruption moves from the prophets to the priests to the people, and **ungodliness has gone forth into all the land** (23:15). That the prophets of Samaria should have prophesied by Baal was unsavory enough (23:13); but the deterioration of the prophetic spirit in Jerusalem, whereby all their words are adulterous and false, makes them like Sódom and

Gomorrah. The people, meanwhile, are the victims; they are filled with **vain hopes,** nothingness. Their counsels are unrealistic, superficially optimistic, and based only on pious fancies of their own minds (23:16). **Behold,** [therefore,] **the storm of the LORD!** There is no escape from the dialectical consequences of perverted behavior based upon the perversion of spirit.

What Jeremiah means by the true prophet is now beginning to emerge. To be a prophet whose might is right, he must have **stood in the council of the LORD;** he must have learned **to perceive** the word; he must have learned how **to hear** it; and he must be ready to give heed to it faithfully (23:18). "To prophesy," as Pascal says, "is to speak of God, not from out-

19 Behold, a whirlwind of the LORD is gone forth in fury, even a grievous whirlwind: it shall fall grievously upon the head of the wicked.

20 The anger of the LORD shall not return, until he have executed, and till he have performed the thoughts of his heart: in the latter days ye shall consider it perfectly.

21 I have not sent these prophets, yet they ran: I have not spoken to them, yet they prophesied.

22 But if they had stood in my counsel, and had caused my people to hear my words, then they should have turned them from their evil way, and from the evil of their doings.

23 *Am* I a God at hand, saith the LORD, and not a God afar off?

24 Can any hide himself in secret places that I shall not see him? saith the LORD. Do not I fill heaven and earth? saith the LORD.

19 Behold, the storm of the LORD!
    Wrath has gone forth,
  a whirling tempest;
    it will burst upon the head of the
      wicked.
20 The anger of the LORD will not turn
      back
    until he has executed and accomplished
    the intents of his mind.
  In the latter days you will understand it
    clearly.

21 "I did not send the prophets,
    yet they ran;
  I did not speak to them,
    yet they prophesied.
22 But if they had stood in my council,
    then they would have proclaimed my
      words to my people,
  and they would have turned them from
    their evil way,
  and from the evil of their doings.

23 "Am I a God at hand, says the LORD, and not a God afar off? 24 Can a man hide himself in secret places so that I cannot see him? says the LORD. Do I not fill heaven

prophet (cf. H. Wheeler Robinson, "The Council of Yahweh," *Journal of Theological Studies,* XLV [1944], 151-57).

19-20. These verses duplicate 30:23-24, with only minor variations. Here they seem to break the connection between vs. 18 and vs. 21. Most commentators consider them an insertion from 30:23-24. It is possible, however, that they belong here and that they should be interpreted as the content of the true word of the Lord as Jeremiah understood it (cf. Rudolph). The passage has a closer connection with the context here than in ch. 30.

D. THE FALSE PROPHETS' LYING DREAMS (23:23-32)

The content of this oracle is more miscellaneous and prolix than the preceding. Jeremiah is not necessarily condemning the belief that dreams may be a medium of God's revelation (he himself experienced visions; cf. 1:11-14), but he sees that the false prophets proclaim as God's word what is only the product of their own dreams, a medium easily abused.

23-24. The most obvious meaning here is that Yahweh is not a merely localized deity whom the prophets can easily escape, but an omnipresent and transcendent God

ward proofs, but from an inward and immediate feeling." [9]

But Jeremiah drives his distinction further. In 23:23-40 three sharp contrasts are drawn. The first has to do with the nature of God and the God-relation; the second deals with the intrinsic power of the Word; the third dramatizes the consequences of perverting the vision.

[9] *Thoughts,* No. 731.

The first is a contrast between the far and the near; the second between the dream and the reality; and the third between falsehood and actuality.

In the first of these the attitude of the cult prophets is sharply drawn. When they run about saying, **"I have dreamed, I have dreamed!"** (23:25), they unwittingly reveal the unconscious self-satisfaction which they

25 I have heard what the prophets said, that prophesy lies in my name, saying, I have dreamed, I have dreamed.

26 How long shall *this* be in the heart of the prophets that prophesy lies? yea, *they are* prophets of the deceit of their own heart;

27 Which think to cause my people to forget my name by their dreams, which they tell every man to his neighbor, as their fathers have forgotten my name for Baal.

28 The prophet that hath a dream, let him tell a dream; and he that hath my word, let him speak my word faithfully. What *is* the chaff to the wheat? saith the Lord.

29 *Is* not my word like as a fire? saith the Lord; and like a hammer *that* breaketh the rock in pieces?

30 Therefore, behold, I *am* against the prophets, saith the Lord, that steal my words every one from his neighbor.

31 Behold, I *am* against the prophets, saith the Lord, that use their tongues, and say, He saith.

and earth? says the Lord. 25 I have heard what the prophets have said who prophesy lies in my name, saying, 'I have dreamed, I have dreamed!' 26 How long shall there be lies[n] in the heart of the prophets who prophesy lies, and who prophesy the deceit of their own heart, 2 who think to make my people forget my name by their dreams which they tell one another, even as their fathers forgot my name for Ba'al? 28 Let the prophet who has a dream tell the dream, but let him who has my word speak my word faithfully. What has straw in common with wheat? says the Lord. 29 Is not my word like fire, says the Lord, and like a hammer which breaks the rock in pieces? 30 Therefore, behold, I am against the prophets, says the Lord, who steal my words from one another. 31 Behold, I am against the prophets, says the Lord, who use their

[n] Cn Compare Syr: Heb obscure

---

who will punish the lying prophets (cf. Amos 9:1-4; Ps. 139:7-12). In theological language, he is both immanent and transcendent.

Cornill ingeniously offers a variant interpretation that makes a close connection with the context. He believes that Jeremiah here denies that Yahweh is a Deity with whom one can be on such easy, familiar terms as the prophets think; he is not their next-door neighbor whose door always stands open. It is a high dignity to stand in the council of the almighty God. One cannot elect himself to the office of prophet; even less can one escape God's summons if he is called. Such an interpretation is not untrue to Jeremiah's experience and thinking, but is perhaps strained for the present passage.

28-29. These verses draw a sharp contrast between the dream of the false prophet and the true word of God. **Let the prophet who has a dream tell the dream,** but not as the true word of Yahweh. Such a dream is mere **straw,** having nothing **in common with wheat,** the **word** of the Lord. His **word** is very powerful, not being merely prediction, but having great force to accomplish its end; it is **like fire** or **like a hammer** (cf. the thought in 5:14; Isa. 55:10-11).

---

take in their vocation, as also the false center about which it turns. The unconscious self-deification which takes place in this is revealed in the description of them as men who try to make God's people forget his name (23:27). This is a strong comparison, in which it is asserted that their dreams become a God-substitute even as the images for Baal were substituted for the God-relation by their fathers. The covert idolatry of the practice is thus revealed. Finally, the progressive deterioration of the prophets' calling is revealed in 23:30-32. They secure their interpretations not from the unmediated word of God, or from standing

within the dynamic vitality of the God-relation, but at second hand. Thus their "messages" are stolen from one another, or from those who have gone before, or (as Gillies describes it) from books and professors and seminaries and the published sermons of other preachers.[1] To this they become accustomed, and, though they use the familiar prophetic phrase, **says the Lord,** they do so in the false acoustic setting of their own proclamations. The false prophet "hears his own voice, till he can hear no other."[2] Thus such supposed prophets become

[1] Cf. *Jeremiah, the Man and His Message,* pp. 181-83.
[2] *Ibid.,* p. 182.

32 Behold, I *am* against them that prophesy false dreams, saith the Lord, and do tell them, and cause my people to err by their lies, and by their lightness; yet I sent them not, nor commanded them: therefore they shall not profit this people at all, saith the Lord.

33 ¶ And when this people, or the prophet, or a priest, shall ask thee, saying, What *is* the burden of the Lord? thou shalt then say unto them, What burden? I will even forsake you, saith the Lord.

34 And *as for* the prophet, and the priest, and the people, that shall say, The burden of the Lord, I will even punish that man and his house.

35 Thus shall ye say every one to his neighbor, and every one to his brother, What hath the Lord answered? and, What hath the Lord spoken?

36 And the burden of the Lord shall ye mention no more; for every man's word shall be his burden: for ye have perverted the words of the living God, of the Lord of hosts our God.

tongues and say, 'Says the Lord.' **32** Behold, I am against those who prophesy lying dreams, says the Lord, and who tell them and lead my people astray by their lies and their recklessness, when I did not send them or charge them; so they do not profit this people at all, says the Lord.

33 "When one of this people, or a prophet, or a priest asks you, 'What is the burden of the Lord?' you shall say to them, 'You are the burden,*º* and I will cast you off, says the Lord.' **34** And as for the prophet, priest, or one of the people who says, 'The burden of the Lord,' I will punish that man and his household. **35** Thus shall you say, every one to his neighbor and every one to his brother, 'What has the Lord answered?' or 'What has the Lord spoken?' **36** But 'the burden of the Lord' you shall mention no more, for the burden is every man's own word, and you pervert the words of the living God, the Lord of hosts, our

º Gk Vg: Heb *What burden*

E. Discourse on the Burden of the Lord (23:33-40)

33-40. Critical scholars are almost unanimous in the opinion that only vs. 33 is from Jeremiah, the rest being a late editorial addition. Vs. 33 (properly translated by RSV) is entirely in accord with Jeremiah's thought, but vss. 34-40 are foreign to his thinking. The latter are from the late scribe or rabbi who considered it improper to use the term **the burden of the Lord** to refer to God's word.

The word translated **burden** is *massā'*, from a root meaning "to lift up." It frequently has the literal meaning "a burden," as in vs. 33*b*: **You are the burden** [of the Lord],

---

"peddlers" of the word of God, plying a trade throughout the land, but without any godly knowledge (14:18).

Now Jeremiah notes in all this an impious familiarity with the word of God which breeds in him a profound contempt and scorn. This presumptuous intimacy whereby we suppose that the inner understanding with God is so easy to come by, this casual impertinence whereby we assume that God is our private possession, this unacknowledged arrogance wherewith we would force his kingdom, excites even Yahweh's sovereign disdain. **Am I a God at hand, says the Lord, and not a God afar off?** God keeps his divine distance, and the more we presume upon his nearness the farther away he becomes.

But at the same time, God's infinite nearness is such that a man cannot hide his true motives in a way that God will not see them. Between God and ourselves there are no secret places in which a man, though a prophet, may hide

himself. Be sure your ego-assumptions will find you out, says Jeremiah. We also perceive that when we serve him falsely, though we implore his name, he is infinitely far; when we serve him faithfully, though his ways of trying us be strange, he is infinitely near. In the latter case, there is nothing in our experience which cannot be seen as the cipher and sign of his intending presence; in the case of the former, there is nothing we do which fails to betray the sign of our ego-centeredness, from which he is infinitely far.

The same argument makes plain the distinction between the dream and reality: **What has straw in common with wheat?** The word of the Lord, when spoken faithfully, contains in itself the power that is right. It is like fire which consumes the chaff of non-godly prophecy; it contains in itself the self-revealing power which, like a hammer, breaks the rocks of our protests into pieces. When the obscure monk in the

37 Thus shalt thou say to the prophet, What hath the LORD answered thee? and, What hath the LORD spoken?

38 But since ye say, The burden of the LORD; therefore thus saith the LORD; Because ye say this word, The burden of the LORD, and I have sent unto you, saying, Ye shall not say, The burden of the LORD;

39 Therefore, behold, I, even I, will utterly forget you, and I will forsake you, and the city that I gave you and your fathers, *and cast you* out of my presence:

40 And I will bring an everlasting reproach upon you, and a perpetual shame, which shall not be forgotten.

24 The LORD showed me, and, behold, two baskets of figs *were* set before the temple of the LORD, after that Nebuchad-

God. **37** Thus you shall say to the prophet, 'What has the LORD answered you?' or 'What has the LORD spoken?' **38** But if you say, 'The burden of the LORD,' thus says the LORD, 'Because you have said these words, "The burden of the LORD," when I sent to you, saying, "You shall not say, 'The burden of the LORD,'" **39** therefore, behold, I will surely lift you up and cast you away from my presence, you and the city which I gave to you and your fathers. **40** And I will bring upon you everlasting reproach and perpetual shame, which shall not be forgotten.'"

24 After Nebuchadrez'zar king of Babylon had taken into exile from Jerusalem Jeconi'ah the son of Jehoi'akim, king

---

which he finds difficult to bear. It was also a technical term for a message or oracle of God, as in Nah. 1:1; Hab. 1:1; Mal. 1:1; *et al.* The usage may have originated in the idea that the message of the prophet was a burden placed by God upon the prophet, which he in turn was expected to place on the nation or individual. It was most often used of messages foretelling catastrophe and doom (cf. H. S. Gehman, "The 'Burden' of the Prophets," *Jewish Quarterly Review*, XXXI [1940-41], 107-21).

XVII. VISION OF GOOD AND BAD FIGS (24:1-10)

1-10. This account of a prophetic vision should be compared for its form with the visions in 1:11-19; Amos 7:7-9; 8:1-3. The date (if it is historical) is after the deportation of Jehoiachin (here called **Jeconiah**) in 598 B.C. For the historical background see II Kings 24:10-17.

The interpretation of this chapter is easy since the meaning of the vision is clearly stated in vss. 4-10. But its origin is less easy to explain. The attitude here expressed is inconsistent with attitudes and actions of the prophet Jeremiah on other occasions, such

---

monastery at Wittenberg discovers the phrase "the just shall live by faith," it is the self-evidencing power of the word which breaks open the epoch, and Luther knows that the word of God "is a battle, a ruin, and a sword!"

Finally, Jeremiah brings the teaching home by adducing, as he so frequently does, a trifle that is known to everyone. But he converts the trifle into the sign of the Infinite. **What is the burden of the LORD?** contains the word *massā'* which originally meant simply a burden or a weight to be carried (see Exeg.). But it came easily to mean, as it has in all languages, a message or a burden on one's heart. Since the prophets were carriers of such burdens, the term soon became attached to the prophetic oracle. Jeremiah's oracles had been mostly of a negative and doomful kind. These are doubtless heavy for the people to carry and such as they would willingly avoid. It would appear, then, that the term was used mockingly by some

of these and addressed to Jeremiah as a taunt to indicate the excessive gloom of his oracles. So when, from the perspectives of the false optimisms engendered by the unfaithful prophets, the question was addressed to Jeremiah in mockery, **What is the burden of the LORD?** he replied with telling effect: **You are the burden!** It is precisely their misplaced levity which is the real burden on God. They are the burden and the Lord will certainly cast them off. This is the eventual fate of those who mistake the superficial for the real, the false for the actual—and sadly so, for they have missed "the many-splendour'd thing." [3]

24:1-10. *Two Baskets of Figs.*—The whole point of Jeremiah's vision of the two baskets of figs is contained in the second of its primary symbols. The all-important feature is that the two baskets were **placed before the temple of the LORD.** The distinction here is not a moral

[3] Francis Thompson, "The Kingdom of God."

rezzar king of Babylon had carried away captive Jeconiah the son of Jehoiakim king of Judah, and the princes of Judah, with the carpenters and smiths, from Jerusalem, and had brought them to Babylon.

2 One basket *had* very good figs, *even* like the figs *that are* first ripe: and the other basket *had* very naughty figs, which could not be eaten, they were so bad.

3 Then said the LORD unto me, What seest thou, Jeremiah? And I said, Figs; the good figs, very good; and the evil, very evil, that cannot be eaten, they are so evil.

4 ¶ Again the word of the LORD came unto me, saying,

5 Thus saith the LORD, the God of Israel; Like these good figs, so will I acknowledge them that are carried away captive of Judah, whom I have sent out of this place into the land of the Chaldeans for *their* good.

of Judah, together with the princes of Judah, the craftsmen, and the smiths, and had brought them to Babylon, the LORD showed me this vision: Behold, two baskets of figs placed before the temple of the LORD. 2 One basket had very good figs, like first-ripe figs, but the other basket had very bad figs, so bad that they could not be eaten. 3 And the LORD said to me, "What do you see, Jeremiah?" I said, "Figs, the good figs very good, and the bad figs very bad, so bad that they cannot be eaten."

4 Then the word of the LORD came to me: 5 "Thus says the LORD, the God of Israel: Like these good figs, so I will regard as good the exiles from Judah, whom I have sent away from this place to the land

---

as the following: (*a*) the view expressed in ch. 5 that *all* groups and classes in Jerusalem are sinful; (*b*) the viewpoint expressed in ch. 29 toward the impatient exiles in Babylonia; (*c*) Jeremiah's opinion of Jehoiachin, as one whom Yahweh had rejected (see especially 22:24-30); (*d*) the general attitude of Jeremiah toward King Zedekiah, who was weak and vacillating rather than evil (see chs. 37–38); and (*e*) Jeremiah's decision, upon the fall of Jerusalem in 587 B.C., to remain in Palestine rather than go to Babylonia (39:13-14; 40:1-6). It is hard to believe that Jeremiah thought God's favor depended on whether or not a man had been exiled, rather than upon his repentance and obedience.

The view here attributed to Jeremiah is similar to that of those Jews who considered the exiled Jehoiachin as the legitimate king and opposed King Zedekiah's claims to the throne (see Exeg. on 22:24-30); and to the attitude, especially prevalent in the time of Ezra and Nehemiah (Ezra 2; 8–10), that the true Israelites were those Jews who had been taken to Babylon and later returned, rather than those who remained in Judah and

---

one, as though some classes were sinful and some were not; nor is it a matter of cultural preference, concerned with the fact that the elite were taken away in the first exile and the social scum allowed to remain behind. The entire argument turns upon a religious issue, and this chapter should be read, therefore, in conjunction with ch. 29: here we have the message to the people in Jerusalem, and there the message to the exiles. The moment this is done both the logical and theological consistency of Jeremiah's thought will appear. (The argument in the Exeg., that the chapter is Deuteronomic and not a true vision of Jeremiah's because it does not represent his own thought, seems unwarranted.)

Jeremiah is telling the people that the exiles in Babylon are nearer to Yahweh than those who have remained at home beside the temple, for those who have remained at home worship

him wrongly. They are still constrained by the Josian reformation and its doctrine of the inviolability of the temple. Thus the conventions of orthodoxy, and the temple itself, are substituted for the direct relation with Yahweh. Their false center of worship corrupts their images and falsifies their lives. They are thus the bad figs. Nothing corrupts like a false conception of a true religion.

Those who have been carried off into exile, on the other hand, have suffered shipwreck. The illusory securities of the narrow nationalist religion of the temple are shattered. They are therefore one step nearer to the liberation of their souls since they are liberated from the hypnotizing powers of their false hopes. They are on the verge of learning what Jeremiah has already perceived, that the focus of life in the tangible temple and its city is not essential to a genuine relationship with God. Therefore the

6 For I will set mine eyes upon them for good, and I will bring them again to this land: and I will build them, and not pull *them* down; and I will plant them, and not pluck *them* up.

7 And I will give them a heart to know me, that I *am* the Lord; and they shall be my people, and I will be their God: for they shall return unto me with their whole heart.

8 ¶ And as the evil figs, which cannot be eaten, they are so evil; surely thus saith the Lord, So will I give Zedekiah the king of Judah, and his princes, and the residue of Jerusalem, that remain in this land, and them that dwell in the land of Egypt:

9 And I will deliver them to be removed into all the kingdoms of the earth for *their* hurt, *to be* a reproach and a proverb, a taunt and a curse, in all places whither I shall drive them.

10 And I will send the sword, the famine, and the pestilence, among them, till they be consumed from off the land that I gave unto them and to their fathers.

25 The word that came to Jeremiah concerning all the people of Judah,

---

of the Chalde′ans. 6 I will set my eyes upon them for good, and I will bring them back to this land. I will build them up, and not tear them down; I will plant them, and not uproot them. 7 I will give them a heart to know that I am the Lord; and they shall be my people and I will be their God, for they shall return to me with their whole heart.

8 "But thus says the Lord: Like the bad figs which are so bad they cannot be eaten, so will I treat Zedeki′ah the king of Judah, his princes, the remnant of Jerusalem who remain in this land, and those who dwell in the land of Egypt. 9 I will make them a horror[p] to all the kingdoms of the earth, to be a reproach, a byword, a taunt, and a curse in all the places where I shall drive them. 10 And I will send sword, famine, and pestilence upon them, until they shall be utterly destroyed from the land which I gave to them and their fathers."

25 The word that came to Jeremiah concerning all the people of Judah,

[p] Compare Gk: Heb *horror for evil*

---

intermarried with the surrounding peoples. Furthermore, the phraseology of the Deuteronomic editor is very evident, most noticeably in vss. 6-7, 9-10. The mention in vs. 8 of the exiles (**those who dwell in the land of Egypt**) suggests that the flight to Egypt recorded in chs. 43–44 was of recent occurrence, and the general tone suggests that opposition to King Zedekiah was of vivid memory.

We must conclude that this chapter is of Deuteronomic origin (*ca.* 550 B.C.) and wholly a literary product, not a true account of a vision experienced by Jeremiah, for it does not represent his own thought (cf. Duhm; H. G. May, "Towards an Objective Approach to the Book of Jeremiah: The Biographer," *Journal of Biblical Literature,* LXI [1942], 148-49) .

XVIII. Summary Warning to Judah (25:1-14)

This section was written by the Deuteronomic editor to warn the people of Judah that, as the result of their constant refusal to heed the prophets sent by Yahweh, they

---

exiles are the potential good figs. Jeremiah sees in this exile all the aspects of an act of Providence. He perceives that Yahweh's eyes are **upon them for good**; that by virtue of this realistic crisis he **will give them a heart to know** who their Lord is. He will be able to **plant them,** and to **build them up;** and this is possible because, through their suffering, they will return to him **with their whole heart.**

This is the way of every profound religious growth. It is the way of the journey and return.

One must be driven out from under the possessive features of the false security systems, attached as they are to whatever tangible images our unrealistic thoughts evoke. There must follow the exile into silence and abandonment until we learn to hear the newer word from God. Only by abandonment of the images, and by the movement into holy emptiness, can one learn to wait until the Joyous comes.

25:1-38. So I Took the Cup from the Lord's Hand.—Gillies has described this chapter as the

in the fourth year of Jehoiakim the son of Josiah king of Judah, that *was* the first year of Nebuchadrezzar king of Babylon;

2 The which Jeremiah the prophet spake unto all the people of Judah, and to all the inhabitants of Jerusalem, saying,

3 From the thirteenth year of Josiah the son of Amon king of Judah, even unto this day, that *is* the three and twentieth year, the word of the LORD hath come unto me, and I have spoken unto you, rising early and speaking; but ye have not hearkened.

in the fourth year of Jehoi'akim the son of Josi'ah, king of Judah (that was the first year of Nebuchadrez'zar king of Babylon), **2** which Jeremiah the prophet spoke to all the people of Judah and all the inhabitants of Jerusalem: **3** "For twenty-three years, from the thirteenth year of Josi'ah the son of Amon, king of Judah, to this day, the word of the LORD has come to me, and I have spoken persistently to you, but you

---

were about to be destroyed by an enemy from the north. In its original form it may have been written by D as a conclusion to what he believed was the scroll of Baruch written at Jeremiah's dictation, as described in ch. 36. Its ideas are not wholly foreign to Jeremiah, but the phraseology is not his.

The text of these verses in the LXX is much shorter than the Hebrew, on which the English is based. The LXX omits the chronological note in vs. 1*b*, and the references to Nebuchadrezzar, Babylon, and the land of the Chaldeans in vss. 9, 11-12. In vs. 9 the LXX reads: "Behold I will send and take a family [πατριὰν] from the north, and I will bring them against this land," etc. The LXX omits vss. 13*b*-14, closing with **everything written in this book.** It seems most probable that the LXX represents the original form of this section; or it may have been even shorter, e.g., as printed by Skinner (*Prophecy and Religion*, pp. 240-41).

The Deuteronomic editor also wrote 1:15-16, which is similar in content to the present section. Originally 25:1-14 was a threat of destruction upon Judah, without mention of the precise agent of destruction. The additions, which are contained in the M.T. but not in the LXX, were made after the Babylonian exile was over, or near the end of the Exile. The purpose was to connect 25:1-14 more closely with 25:15-38, and to soften the threat against Judah.

A. JUDAH'S CONTINUAL DISOBEDIENCE (25:1-7)

25:1. The fourth year of Jehoiakim was 606-605 B.C., mentioned also in 36:1; 45:1; 46:2. **The first year of Nebuchadrezzar king of Babylon:** Nebuchadrezzar became king in July or August, 605, upon the death of his father. The Babylonians counted the period from this date to the next New Year's Day in April, 604, as his accession year (*rêsh sharrûti*), and the period from April, 604, to April, 603, as his **first** year. The Hebrew writer apparently here means the former, 605-604 B.C. However, since this is an editorial addition (see above), it may not be completely accurate. The Hebrews may have called the accession year "the beginning of the reign" (*rē'shîth mamlekhûth*) as in 26:1. For the historical situation see Exeg. on 36:1-32.

3. The date here given agrees with 1:2, from which it was probably derived. There was a period of **twenty-three years** from 626 B.C., which was **the thirteenth year of Josiah,** to 605-604 B.C.

---

turning point.[4] In one obvious sense this was true. First came the decline of Assyria and the fall of the great city Nineveh. Then came the victory of Nebuchadrezzar over Egypt at Carchemish (605 B.C.). From this point on the destiny of Judah was linked with that of Babylon. "Like a flash of lightning," says A. B. Davidson, "Carchemish lighted up to [Jere-

miah] the whole line of God's purposes with His people right on to the end."[5] The Chaldeans become now the obvious "foe from the north."

All of which makes the opening summary of Jeremiah's prophetic activity peculiarly apropos. The summary of twenty-three years of prophetic

[4] *Op. cit.*, p. 190.

[5] *Exile and Restoration;* quoted in Thomson, *Burden of the Lord*, p. 101.

4 And the LORD hath sent unto you all his servants the prophets, rising early and sending *them;* but ye have not hearkened, nor inclined your ear to hear.

5 They said, Turn ye again now every one from his evil way, and from the evil of your doings, and dwell in the land that the LORD hath given unto you and to your fathers for ever and ever:

6 And go not after other gods to serve them, and to worship them, and provoke me not to anger with the works of your hands; and I will do you no hurt.

7 Yet ye have not hearkened unto me, saith the LORD; that ye might provoke me to anger with the works of your hands to your own hurt.

8 ¶ Therefore thus saith the LORD of hosts; Because ye have not heard my words,

9 Behold, I will send and take all the families of the north, saith the LORD, and Nebuchadrezzar the king of Babylon, my servant, and will bring them against this land, and against the inhabitants thereof, and against all these nations round about, and will utterly destroy them, and make them an astonishment, and a hissing, and perpetual desolations.

10 Moreover I will take from them the voice of mirth, and the voice of gladness, the voice of the bridegroom, and the voice of the bride, the sound of the millstones, and the light of the candle.

11 And this whole land shall be a desolation, *and* an astonishment; and these nations shall serve the king of Babylon seventy years.

have not listened. 4 You have neither listened nor inclined your ears to hear, although the LORD persistently sent to you all his servants the prophets, 5 saying, 'Turn now, every one of you, from his evil way and wrong doings, and dwell upon the land which the LORD has given to you and your fathers from of old and for ever; 6 do not go after other gods to serve and worship them, or provoke me to anger with the work of your hands. Then I will do you no harm.' 7 Yet you have not listened to me, says the LORD, that you might provoke me to anger with the work of your hands to your own harm.

8 "Therefore thus says the LORD of hosts: Because you have not obeyed my words, 9 behold, I will send for all the tribes of the north, says the LORD, and for Nebuchadrez'zar the king of Babylon, my servant, and I will bring them against this land and its inhabitants, and against all these nations round about; I will utterly destroy them, and make them a horror, a hissing, and an everlasting reproach.q 10 Moreover, I will banish from them the voice of mirth and the voice of gladness, the voice of the bridegroom and the voice of the bride, the grinding of the millstones and the light of the lamp. 11 This whole land shall become a ruin and a waste, and these nations shall serve the king of Babylon seventy years.

q Gk Compare Syr: Heb *desolations*

B. IMMINENT DESTRUCTION (25:8-14)

As noted above, this section originally contained no specific threat against the Babylonians, but was directed against Judah.

11-12. **Seventy years** constitute the period during which the Jews were to serve Babylonia, at the end of which Babylon itself was to be punished. The same figure occurs in 29:10. The number was not intended to be taken literally, but rather as a round or "perfect" number, perhaps the length of a man's lifetime (Ps. 90:10). The use

activity in the familiar refrain, **I have spoken persistently to you, but you have not listened** (vs. 3), is underscored dramatically by the swift turn of world-shaking events. The people had been warned persistently to turn from their evil ways and to refrain from worshiping other gods; but to their own hurt they have not listened. It is because of this that Nebuchadrezzar is coming up against them.

Against this background there are two passages of singular appeal within this chapter. The first is the prophetic eloquence contained in vs. 10, apparently of authentic Jeremianic origin. The verse foresees the end of mirth and gladness. No more the open joys of the marriage celebrations, nor the comforting sounds of the millstones by the homes at eventide, nor the inviting lamps of domestic comfort shining in

12 ¶ And it shall come to pass, when seventy years are accomplished, *that* I will punish the king of Babylon, and that nation, saith the LORD, for their iniquity, and the land of the Chaldeans, and will make it perpetual desolations.

13 And I will bring upon that land all my words which I have pronounced against it, *even* all that is written in this book, which Jeremiah hath prophesied against all the nations.

14 For many nations and great kings shall serve themselves of them also: and I will recompense them according to their deeds, and according to the works of their own hands.

15 ¶ For thus saith the LORD God of Israel unto me; Take the winecup of this

12 Then after seventy years are completed, I will punish the king of Babylon and that nation, the land of the Chalde'ans, for their iniquity, says the LORD, making the land an everlasting waste. 13 I will bring upon that land all the words which I have uttered against it, everything written in this book, which Jeremiah prophesied against all the nations. 14 For many nations and great kings shall make slaves even of them; and I will recompense them according to their deeds and the work of their hands."

15 Thus the LORD, the God of Israel, said to me: "Take from my hand this cup

---

of the figure could not give much comfort to those who were taken into exile, for they could not expect to live to see the punishment of Babylonia. It is somewhat difficult to reconcile this figure with the adjective **everlasting** used in vs. 9.

These verses and 29:10 have influenced Zech. 1:12; II Chr. 36:21; Dan. 9:2. The Babylonian exile actually lasted from 598 (or 587) to 538 B.C. If the view expressed above is correct, the figure comes from the Deuteronomic editor writing *ca.* 550 B.C., during the time of the Exile. The LXX of vss. 11-12 contains this figure but the verses are somewhat shorter.

13. That land was, in the original form of this section, Judah, not Babylonia (cf. vss. 9, 11). The words **this book** refer backward, not forward (cf. 51:60, where "a book" refers to the oracles against Babylonia in chs. 50–51). The Deuteronomic editor intended vss. 1-13*a* to be the conclusion of Baruch's scroll written in the fourth year of Jehoiakim (ch. 36). The LXX of this section does not contain vss. 13*b*-14.

XIX. THE CUP OF YAHWEH'S WRATH (25:15-38)

This section was composed at least in part to serve as the introduction (or possibly the conclusion) of the oracles against the foreign nations, chs. 46–51. In the LXX, 25:13*a* is immediately followed by the oracles against foreign nations in an order different from the M.T., and these are followed by the present passage (32:1-24 in LXX). Most modern scholars believe that 25:15-38 (or 25:15-29 only) formed the introduction to the foreign oracles, which originally followed immediately, i.e., in the middle of the book of Jeremiah (like the position of similar oracles in the books of Isaiah and Ezekiel), rather than near the end.

The nations listed in vss. 19-26 correspond roughly to the nations against which oracles are now found in chs. 46–51. There is no oracle against **Uz**, the nations of vss. 23-24, and **Zimri**, but the oracle against Kedar and the kingdoms of Hazor in 49:28-33 deals with Arab tribes (LXX omits Uz and Zimri here). There is no oracle against the Medes, but they are mentioned in 51:11, 28. **Tyre** and **Sidon** are not treated in a separate oracle, but are mentioned in 47:4. There is an oracle against Damascus (49:23-27) which is not named in the present list.

---

the windows after dark. **This whole land shall become a ruin and a waste** (vs. 11).

The second figure is that of the cup of the wine of God's fury, and Jeremiah's commission **to make all the nations to whom I send you**

drink it (vs. 15). It is probable that the passages which follow are not from the hand of Jeremiah; but there is no reason to suppose that Jeremiah's vision and prophetic consciousness did not apply the purposes of God as he knew

fury at my hand, and cause all the nations, to whom I send thee, to drink it.

16 And they shall drink, and be moved, and be mad, because of the sword that I will send among them.

17 Then took I the cup at the LORD's hand, and made all the nations to drink, unto whom the LORD had sent me:

18 *To wit,* Jerusalem, and the cities of Judah, and the kings thereof, and the princes thereof, to make them a desolation, an astonishment, a hissing, and a curse; as *it is* this day;

19 Pharaoh king of Egypt, and his servants, and his princes, and all his people;

20 And all the mingled people, and all the kings of the land of Uz, and all the kings of the land of the Philistines, and Ashkelon, and Azzah, and Ekron, and the remnant of Ashdod,

21 Edom, and Moab, and the children of Ammon,

22 And all the kings of Tyrus, and all the kings of Zidon, and the kings of the isles which *are* beyond the sea,

23 Dedan, and Tema, and Buz, and all *that are* in the utmost corners,

24 And all the kings of Arabia, and all the kings of the mingled people that dwell in the desert,

of the wine of wrath, and make all the nations to whom I send you drink it. **16** They shall drink and stagger and be crazed because of the sword which I am sending among them."

17 So I took the cup from the LORD's hand, and made all the nations to whom the Lord sent me drink it: **18** Jerusalem and the cities of Judah, its kings and princes, to make them a desolation and a waste, a hissing and a curse, as at this day; **19** Pharaoh king of Egypt, his servants, his princes, all his people, **20** and all the foreign folk among them; the kings of the land of Uz and all the kings of the land of the Philistines (Ash'kelon, Gaza, Ekron, and the remnant of Ashdod); **21** Edom, Moab, and the sons of Ammon; **22** all the kings of Tyre, all the kings of Sidon, and the kings of the coastland across the sea; **23** Dedan, Tema, Buz, and all who cut the corners of their hair; **24** all the kings of Arabia and all the kings of the mixed tribes that dwell in

---

This section must be in large part secondary, for the foreign oracles are largely secondary (see Exeg. on 46:1–51:64). There may be a nucleus from the prophet Jeremiah—perhaps 25:15-16. If these verses are genuine they derive from a vision experienced by the prophet. The poem, vss. 30-31, 34-38, has more claim to authenticity than the prose of vss. 17-29, but it is more highly apocalyptic than we expect from Jeremiah, and is somewhat imitative. The authenticity of vss. 30-38 must be questioned.

A. NATIONS THAT MUST DRINK THE CUP (25:15-29)

15. The figure of the **cup of the wine of wrath** may have originated with Jeremiah. A similar figure, "the cup of the LORD's right hand," occurs in Hab. 2:16, which is perhaps contemporaneous with our passage. The **cup** as a symbol of God's wrath is frequently used in later O.T. literature (49:12; 51:7; Ezek. 23:33; Isa. 51:17, 22; Lam. 4:21; Pss. 11:6; 75:8). The cup is a symbol of God's blessing in Pss. 16:5; 23:5.

18. This verse was apparently inserted when chs. 1–25 (in whole or part) were joined with the foreign oracles. The latter part imitates Deuteronomic phraseology, but the insertion was not by the Deuteronomic editor.

20. Uz is the land where Job lived (Job 1:1). It was east of Palestine, probably in Edomite territory (cf. Gen. 10:23; 22:21; 36:28; I Chr. 1:17; Lam. 4:21). **The remnant of Ashdod:** According to Herodotus (*History* II. 157), Ashdod was destroyed by Psamtik I (663-609 B.C.), after a siege of twenty-nine years; it was rebuilt by Nehemiah's time (Neh. 13:23).

23. Dedan and Tema were in northwest Arabia; for the former cf. Gen. 10:7; Jer. 49:8; for the latter, Isa. 21:14; Job 6:19. The location of Buz is unknown; it must have

25 And all the kings of Zimri, and all the kings of Elam, and all the kings of the Medes,

26 And all the kings of the north, far and near, one with another, and all the kingdoms of the world, which *are* upon the face of the earth: and the king of Sheshach shall drink after them.

27 Therefore thou shalt say unto them, Thus saith the LORD of hosts, the God of Israel; Drink ye, and be drunken, and spew, and fall, and rise no more, because of the sword which I will send among you.

28 And it shall be, if they refuse to take the cup at thine hand to drink, then shalt thou say unto them, Thus saith the LORD of hosts; Ye shall certainly drink.

29 For, lo, I begin to bring evil on the city which is called by my name, and should ye be utterly unpunished? Ye shall not be unpunished: for I will call for a sword upon all the inhabitants of the earth, saith the LORD of hosts.

the desert; 25 all the kings of Zimri, all the kings of Elam, and all the kings of Media; 26 all the kings of the north, far and near, one after another, and all the kingdoms of the world which are on the face of the earth. And after them the king of Babylon[r] shall drink.

27 "Then you shall say to them, 'Thus says the LORD of hosts, the God of Israel: Drink, be drunk and vomit, fall and rise no more, because of the sword which I am sending among you.'

28 "And if they refuse to accept the cup from your hand to drink, then you shall say to them, 'Thus says the LORD of hosts: You must drink! 29 For behold, I begin to work evil at the city which is called by my name, and shall you go unpunished? You shall not go unpunished, for I am summoning a sword against all the inhabitants of the earth, says the LORD of hosts.'

[r] Heb *Sheshach,* a cipher for Babylon

been in the same general region. In Gen. 22:21 Buz is the name of a brother of Uz, son of Nahor. **All who cut the corners of their hair:** See Exeg. on 9:26.

25. The location of **Zimri** is quite unknown; the LXX omits.

26. Sheshach (also in 51:41) stands for **Babylon** by the form of cipher known as "athbash": the first letter of the Hebrew alphabet (א) stands for the last letter (ת) or vice versa; the second (ב) stands for the next to last (ש); etc. In Hebrew the consonants of Babylon are בבל, represented by "athbash" as ששך. Some believe that the use of the name Babylon was dangerous, yet it is found often in chs. 50–51. The clause containing the name in 25:26 is omitted by the LXX.

Another theory of the origin of **Sheshach** is that it was derived from the name of a dynasty of the second millennium B.C., called by R. P. Dougherty (*The Sealand of Ancient Arabia* [New Haven: Yale University Press, 1932], pp. 11-18) the "First Sealand Dynasty," which was written in cuneiform characters read in Sumerian, SHESH-KU-[ki] (or SHESH-KU₆). While this dynasty may be from the same region as the Chaldean, such an explanation is most improbable, for it is unlikely that this name was known to Hebrew scribes of a later time (even if the name of the dynasty was actually read according to the Sumerian values).

them to the other nations of his world. There is no question whatever but that Jeremiah's vision was from the beginning upon the greater tensions of the world predicament and the failure of Judah's leaders to read the obvious signs of the times. So he took the cup from the Lord's hand and conveyed it through his prophecy to all the nations immediately concerned.

Again and again we are in the position of taking the cup from the Lord's hand. At times the cup is bitter, and we, like the nations, would willingly refuse the cup; but, as the text makes plain, our moral attitude entails always

an existential imperative—**you must drink!** The cup of the consequences of our moral actions is always being pressed against our lips. This is true of nations as of individuals. In relation both to ultimate reality and to our own integrity, we do not occupy the wishful neutrality of the speculative or hypothetical suspension of choice. "But you must wager!" exclaimed Pascal. Indeed, we have already wagered, because "we are already embarked!"[6] Doubtless again and again we would refuse the cup, for we gradually discover that the cup of the wine of God's fury

[6] *Thoughts,* No. 233.

30 Therefore prophesy thou against them all these words, and say unto them, The LORD shall roar from on high, and utter his voice from his holy habitation; he shall mightily roar upon his habitation; he shall give a shout, as they that tread *the grapes,* against all the inhabitants of the earth.

31 A noise shall come *even* to the ends of the earth; for the LORD hath a controversy with the nations: he will plead with all flesh; he will give them *that are* wicked to the sword, saith the LORD.

32 Thus saith the LORD of hosts, Behold, evil shall go forth from nation to nation, and a great whirlwind shall be raised up from the coasts of the earth.

33 And the slain of the LORD shall be at that day from *one* end of the earth even unto the *other* end of the earth: they shall not be lamented, neither gathered, nor buried; they shall be dung upon the ground.

34 ¶ Howl, ye shepherds, and cry; and wallow yourselves *in the ashes,* ye principal of the flock: for the days of your slaughter and of your dispersions are accomplished; and ye shall fall like a pleasant vessel.

---

30 "You, therefore, shall prophesy against them all these words, and say to them:

'The LORD will roar from on high,
   and from his holy habitation utter his voice;
he will roar mightily against his fold,
   and shout, like those who tread grapes,
   against all the inhabitants of the earth.
31 The clamor will resound to the ends of
   the earth,
   for the LORD has an indictment against
   the nations;
he is entering into judgment with all
   flesh,
   and the wicked he will put to the
   sword,
             says the LORD.'

32 "Thus says the LORD of hosts:
Behold, evil is going forth
   from nation to nation,
and a great tempest is stirring
   from the farthest parts of the earth!
33 "And those slain by the LORD on that day shall extend from one end of the earth to the other. They shall not be lamented, or gathered, or buried; they shall be dung on the surface of the ground.
34 "Wail, you shepherds, and cry,
   and roll in ashes, you lords of the flock,
for the days of your slaughter and dispersion have come,
   and you shall fall like choice rams.[s]

[s] Gk: Heb *a choice vessel*

B. The Coming of Yahweh in Judgment (25:30-38)

Vss. 30-31, 34-38 may be taken as a single poem, with vss. 32-33 as an insertion. While the poem is rather vigorous and vivid, and could possibly be from Jeremiah, it is more likely to be secondary because the language is more apocalyptic than one usually finds in the genuine work of Jeremiah, the poetry is somewhat imitative, and its closest parallels are with later literature (cf. especially Joel 3:16; Lam. 1:15; Isa. 63:1-6; Nah. 3:18; Zech. 11:2-3).

30*a.* Almost a direct quotation from Amos 1:2.

32*b.* Very similar to 6:22.

34-36. Shepherds and lords of the flock: Leaders and rulers of the nations.

---

is but the outer dialectic of the inner movement toward Gethsemane. It is for this reason that we know so well the words of Jesus, "Let this cup pass from me." But for this reason also we know quite well that the only way is the way of "nevertheless not my will, but thine, be done."

The eschatological passages with which the

chapter concludes extend his dialectic farther than Jeremiah ever did. But they contain the vintage **shout** as Yahweh goes "trampling out the vintage where the grapes of wrath are stored,"[7] while Babylon comes marching on; and, though it may be insight after the event, it is certainly true that a **great tempest** was

[7] Julia Ward Howe, "Battle Hymn of the Republic."

35 And the shepherds shall have no way to flee, nor the principal of the flock to escape.

36 A voice of the cry of the shepherds, and a howling of the principal of the flock, *shall be heard:* for the Lord hath spoiled their pasture.

37 And the peaceable habitations are cut down because of the fierce anger of the Lord.

38 He hath forsaken his covert, as the lion: for their land is desolate because of the fierceness of the oppressor, and because of his fierce anger.

26 In the beginning of the reign of Jehoiakim the son of Josiah king of Judah came this word from the Lord, saying,

---

35 No refuge will remain for the shepherds, nor escape for the lords of the flock.

36 Hark, the cry of the shepherds, and the wail of the lords of the flock! For the Lord is despoiling their pasture,

37 and the peaceful folds are devastated, because of the fierce anger of the Lord.

38 Like a lion he has left his covert, for their land has become a waste because of the sword of the Lord,[t] and because of his fierce anger."

[t] Syr: Heb *the dove*

26 In the beginning of the reign of Jehoi'akim the son of Josi'ah, king of Judah, this word came from the Lord,

---

XX. Conflicts with Religious Leaders (26:1–29:32)

These chapters, which recount three important incidents in the life of Jeremiah, have a common theme: his conflict with Judean religious leaders—the priests and prophets, especially the latter. It is this common theme which has brought these chapters together in spite of the fact that the events they record are of different dates. In addition, chs. 27–29 have three stylistic peculiarities which they share with each other, but not with the rest of the book: (*a*) the name of the Babylonian king is usually Nebuchadnezzar, rather than Nebuchadrezzar; (*b*) personal names compounded with the name of Yahweh usually end in *-yāh* rather than *-yāhú;* and (*c*) Jeremiah is usually designated as "Jeremiah the prophet" and the title is given to Hananiah also. The LXX here has a number of striking variations from the M.T., some of which will be pointed out below. The basis of the chapters was Baruch's memoirs, which have been revised by the Deuteronomic editor.

A. The Temple Sermon and Jeremiah's Arrest (26:1-24)

Ch. 26 tells of the preaching of the temple sermon, the contents of which are given more fully in 7:1-15. A brief summary of the sermon itself is followed by details of the arrest and trial of the prophet, with an appendix relating how a prophet who spoke as Jeremiah had spoken was put to death. Both 7:1-15 and ch. 26 come from the Deuteronomic editor; here that editor has used Baruch's memoirs, confining himself largely to a rewriting of the summary of the sermon in vss. 4-6. Baruch probably witnessed the events recorded.

1. Preaching of the Sermon (26:1-6)

26:1. The date of this sermon was **the beginning of the reign of Jehoiakim.** The king was placed on the throne by the Egyptians in 609, following the three-month rule by his brother Jehoahaz (II Kings 23:31-37). The Hebrew phrase *rē'shith mamlekhúth,* **beginning of the reign,** is possibly equivalent to the Babylonian *rēsh sharrúti,* meaning "accession year" (see Exeg. on 25:1). If Jehoiakim was crowned in Tishri (September-

---

stirring from the farthest parts of the earth (vs. 32). It is in Jeremiah's grasp upon the relation of man to God and of God to his world that we find these stirrings in the tempest most clearly and most adequately revealed.

26:1-24. *The Sermon in the Temple Gate (II).* —We have already noted above (ch. 7) the contents and uncompromising power of this sermon. Delivered shortly after the accession of Jehoiakim to the throne, it does unquestion-

2 Thus saith the LORD; Stand in the court of the LORD's house, and speak unto all the cities of Judah, which come to worship in the LORD's house, all the words that I command thee to speak unto them; diminish not a word:

3 If so be they will hearken, and turn every man from his evil way, that I may repent me of the evil, which I purpose to do unto them because of the evil of their doings.

4 And thou shalt say unto them, Thus saith the LORD; If ye will not hearken to me, to walk in my law, which I have set before you,

5 To hearken to the words of my servants the prophets, whom I sent unto you, both rising up early, and sending *them,* but ye have not hearkened;

6 Then will I make this house like Shiloh, and will make this city a curse to all the nations of the earth.

7 So the priests and the prophets and all the people heard Jeremiah speaking these words in the house of the LORD.

8 ¶ Now it came to pass, when Jeremiah had made an end of speaking all that the LORD had commanded *him* to speak unto all the people, that the priests and the prophets and all the people took him, saying, Thou shalt surely die.

2 "Thus says the LORD: Stand in the court of the LORD's house, and speak to all the cities of Judah which come to worship in the house of the LORD all the words that I command you to speak to them; do not hold back a word. 3 It may be they will listen, and every one turn from his evil way, that I may repent of the evil which I intend to do to them because of their evil doings. 4 You shall say to them, 'Thus says the LORD: If you will not listen to me, to walk in my law which I have set before you, 5 and to heed the words of my servants the prophets whom I send to you urgently, though you have not heeded, 6 then I will make this house like Shiloh, and I will make this city a curse for all the nations of the earth.' "

7 The priests and the prophets and all the people heard Jeremiah speaking these words in the house of the LORD. 8 And when Jeremiah had finished speaking all that the LORD had commanded him to speak to all the people, then the priests and the prophets and all the people laid hold of him, say-

---

October), 609, he probably had come to the throne only a few weeks before. It has been suggested that Jeremiah delivered his temple sermon at the time of Jehoiakim's coronation on New Year's Day (so Duhm and Volz; see especially Morgenstern, "The Gates of Righteousness," pp. 20-22), when great crowds would be flocking to the temple area. While this is possible, we cannot be certain, since we do not know the precise meaning of the phrase just discussed, and we have little knowledge of the coronation ceremonies of the Hebrews.

2. Jeremiah preached the sermon in the court of the LORD's house (cf. 7:2).

6. I will make this house like Shiloh: See Exeg. on 7:12.

2. ARREST AND TRIAL OF JEREMIAH (26:7-19)

Not surprisingly, Jeremiah's words arouse immediate antagonism, especially among the priests and prophets of Jerusalem. In the account of the arrest and trial it is they who attempt to have Jeremiah condemned to death, while the princes and many of the common people apparently take his side. The religious leaders would have suffered greatly if the temple had been destroyed as Jeremiah predicted. The prophets who are involved in the present account are doubtless cult prophets attached to the Jerusalem

---

ably represent the precipitation of Jeremiah's prophetic activity into its political form. All the vestiges of doubt and hesitation which mark the early years fall sharply away; his word is no longer veiled by the indirection of poetic symbols. There is no least suggestion here of

what Kierkegaard liked to call "indirect communication"! Jeremiah achieves here, in the address and in the events which follow, what the world has admired so greatly in the bravery at Thermopylae and the godly courage at the Diet at Worms. It was in fact a challenge

9 Why hast thou prophesied in the name of the LORD, saying, This house shall be like Shiloh, and this city shall be desolate without an inhabitant? And all the people were gathered against Jeremiah in the house of the LORD.

10 ¶ When the princes of Judah heard these things, then they came up from the king's house unto the house of the LORD, and sat down in the entry of the new gate of the LORD's *house.*

11 Then spake the priests and the prophets unto the princes and to all the people, saying, This man *is* worthy to die; for he hath prophesied against this city, as ye have heard with your ears.

12 ¶ Then spake Jeremiah unto all the princes and to all the people, saying, The LORD sent me to prophesy against this house and against this city all the words that ye have heard.

13 Therefore now amend your ways and your doings, and obey the voice of the LORD your God; and the LORD will repent him of the evil that he hath pronounced against you.

14 As for me, behold, I *am* in your hand: do with me as seemeth good and meet unto you.

15 But know ye for certain, that if ye put me to death, ye shall surely bring innocent blood upon yourselves, and upon this city, and upon the inhabitants thereof: for of a

ing, "You shall die! 9 Why have you prophesied in the name of the LORD, saying, 'This house shall be like Shiloh, and this city shall be desolate, without inhabitant'?" And all the people gathered about Jeremiah in the house of the LORD.

10 When the princes of Judah heard these things, they came up from the king's house to the house of the LORD and took their seat in the entry of the New Gate of the house of the LORD. 11 Then the priests and the prophets said to the princes and to all the people, "This man deserves the sentence of death, because he has prophesied against this city, as you have heard with your own ears."

12 Then Jeremiah spoke to all the princes and all the people, saying, "The LORD sent me to prophesy against this house and this city all the words you have heard. 13 Now therefore amend your ways and your doings, and obey the voice of the LORD your God, and the LORD will repent of the evil which he has pronounced against you. 14 But as for me, behold, I am in your hands. Do with me as seems good and right to you. 15 Only know for certain that if you put me to death, you will bring innocent blood upon yourselves and upon this city and its inhabitants, for in truth the

temple (see Exeg. on 23:9-40). It is significant that the LXX in vss. 7-8, 11, 16, calls them "false prophets" (ψευδοπροφῆται).

9. The RSV about in the second sentence is correct, since the context does not suggest that all the people were gathered **against** Jeremiah, as the KJV indicates.

10. The people designated as **princes of Judah** were not members of the royal family, but officials of the king's court, such as those who are mentioned by name in ch. 36. The location of the **New Gate** is unknown; it is mentioned also in 36:10.

13-15. The dignity and assurance with which Jeremiah replied to his accusers are worthy of note. His own bearing on this occasion must account in large part for his winning the support of the princes and many of the people, and for his subsequent release.

thrown passionately and boldly before Jehoiakim, **the priests and the prophets and all the people.** It is for this reason that "from the twenty-sixth chapter onwards . . . the story of the prophet becomes that of a Passion, interwoven with the fortunes of Jerusalem itself." [8] Jeremiah's words define the issue in its bedrock, or absolute, form. By thus translating into event what heretofore had lain smothered and ill de-

[8] H. Wheeler Robinson, *The Cross of Jeremiah,* p. 6.

fined, he draws upon himself the forms of enmity and hostility evoked by his words when felt as an ultimate and impassable threat. **The priests and the prophets said to the princes . . . , "This man deserves the sentence of death"**—a pattern of reaction not infrequent in human affairs.

The defense of Jeremiah quite possibly should be regarded as one of the great pivotal moments in man's fight for holy freedom, quite

truth the Lord hath sent me unto you to speak all these words in your ears.

16 ¶ Then said the princes and all the people unto the priests and to the prophets; This man is not worthy to die: for he hath spoken to us in the name of the Lord our God.

17 Then rose up certain of the elders of the land, and spake to all the assembly of the people, saying,

18 Micah the Morasthite prophesied in the days of Hezekiah king of Judah, and spake to all the people of Judah, saying, Thus saith the Lord of hosts; Zion shall be plowed like a field, and Jerusalem shall become heaps, and the mountain of the house as the high places of a forest.

19 Did Hezekiah king of Judah and all Judah put him at all to death? did he not fear the Lord, and besought the Lord, and the Lord repented him of the evil which he had pronounced against them? Thus might we procure great evil against our souls.

20 And there was also a man that prophesied in the name of the Lord, Urijah the son of Shemaiah of Kirjath-jearim, who prophesied against this city and against this land according to all the words of Jeremiah:

Lord sent me to you to speak all these words in your ears."

16 Then the princes and all the people said to the priests and the prophets, "This man does not deserve the sentence of death, for he has spoken to us in the name of the Lord our God." 17 And certain of the elders of the land arose and spoke to all the assembled people, saying, 18 "Micah of More'sheth prophesied in the days of Hezeki'ah king of Judah, and said to all the people of Judah: 'Thus says the Lord of hosts,

Zion shall be plowed as a field;

    Jerusalem shall become a heap of ruins,
      and the mountain of the house a
      wooded height.'

19 Did Hezeki'ah king of Judah and all Judah put him to death? Did he not fear the Lord and entreat the favor of the Lord, and did not the Lord repent of the evil which he had pronounced against them? But we are about to bring great evil upon ourselves."

20 There was another man who prophesied in the name of the Lord, Uri'ah the son of Shemai'ah from Kir'iath-je'arim. He prophesied against this city and against this

---

18. The quotation is from Mic. 3:12. It is most unusual for a prophet to be quoted by name in another prophetic book. The fact that Micah's words were remembered approximately a century after they were uttered is evidence of the strong impression he made upon his hearers. The quotation of Mic. 3:12, not Mic. 4:1-5, has a bearing on the question of the authenticity of the latter passage. If Mic. 4:1-5 had been regarded as authentic, it is most probable that it would have been quoted by the enemies of Jeremiah on this occasion.

19. This information is not contained elsewhere, but we are told in II Kings 18:3-6 that King Hezekiah made certain religious reforms.

3. Arrest and Execution of Uriah (26:20-24)

This section is added as an appendix to the story of the arrest and trial of Jeremiah to show in what grave danger he lay as the result of his temple sermon. Vss. 20-23 probably

---

as fine in its way as Joshua before the tribes of Israel, Socrates before the Athenians, or the forcing of the Magna Charta, or the passion of Patrick Henry before the colonists. Without doubt it was Jeremiah's bearing and confidence through his arrest and trial that inspired the princes, as with Luther at Worms, to stand in his behalf. It is splendid to see how all self-consciousness has dropped away, and how the prophet stands powerful within the power of

God. Amend your ways and your doings, and obey the voice of the Lord. . . . But as for me, behold, I am in your hands. Do with me as seems good and right to you. When the princes and the people defended him, certain of the elders adduced the incident of Micah, and so established precedent for Jeremiah's release. The inclusion of the case of Uriah at the close of this incident shows how narrowly Jeremiah escaped a like fate.

21 And when Jehoiakim the king, with all his mighty men, and all the princes, heard his words, the king sought to put him to death: but when Urijah heard it, he was afraid, and fled, and went into Egypt;

22 And Jehoiakim the king sent men into Egypt, *namely*, Elnathan the son of Achbor, and *certain* men with him into Egypt.

23 And they fetched forth Urijah out of Egypt, and brought him unto Jehoiakim the king; who slew him with the sword, and cast his dead body into the graves of the common people.

24 Nevertheless, the hand of Ahikam the son of Shaphan was with Jeremiah, that they should not give him into the hand of the people to put him to death.

27 In the beginning of the reign of Jehoiakim the son of Josiah king of Judah came this word unto Jeremiah from the LORD, saying,

land in words like those of Jeremiah. 21 And when King Jehoi′akim, with all his warriors and all the princes, heard his words, the king sought to put him to death; but when Uri′ah heard of it, he was afraid and fled and escaped to Egypt. 22 Then King Jehoi′akim sent to Egypt certain men, Elna′than the son of Achbor and others with him, 23 and they fetched Uri′ah from Egypt and brought him to King Jehoi′akim, who slew him with the sword and cast his dead body into the burial place of the common people.

24 But the hand of Ahi′kam the son of Shaphan was with Jeremiah so that he was not given over to the people to be put to death.

27 In the beginning of the reign of Zedeki′ah[u] the son of Josi′ah, king of Judah, this word came to Jeremiah from

[u] Another reading is *Jehoiakim*

---

were not spoken by the elders of vs. 17; nor is it necessary to suppose that the death of Uriah took place near the time of Jeremiah's arrest. The addition was suggested by the fact that Uriah's message had been very similar to that of Jeremiah (vs. 20*b*). Uriah's flight to Egypt was in great contrast to Jeremiah's boldness in replying to his accusers (vss. 12-15).

22. Elnathan the son of Achbor is mentioned in 36:12, 25.

23. The execution of a prophet was a most unusual occurrence in ancient Israel. A prophet was usually permitted to speak in the name of the Lord, and his person was respected even if his words were unpopular. The only other record in the O.T. of such an execution is that of Zechariah in II Chr. 24:20-22. In the course of time legends arose that many of the prophets met martyrdom (cf. Matt. 23:29-31; Luke 11:47-51; see C. C. Torrey, *The Lives of the Prophets* [Philadelphia: Society of Biblical Literature and Exegesis, 1946]).

24. Ahikam the son of Shaphan was a "prince" who had served under Josiah (II Kings 22:12, 14) and now was one of the officials of Jehoiakim. His son Gedaliah was appointed governor of Judah by Nebuchadrezzar after the fall of Jerusalem (II Kings 25:22). The support of so prominent a personality was one of the reasons for Jeremiah's release.

B. THE YOKE OF BABYLON (27:1–28:17)

These chapters record Jeremiah's attitude in a situation when King Zedekiah and the kings of surrounding nations were considering or planning rebellion against Nebu-

---

Doubtless more dramatic parallels could be drawn; but inasmuch as it is the priests and the prophets who oppose the true prophet of God in this chapter, it is useful to recall here the lofty spiritual independence of the Abbé de Saint-Cyran and how he incurred thereby the enmity of Cardinal Richelieu. On the evening of Ascension Day, at Port-Royal in 1638, Saint-Cyran requested that a scripture passage be

read to him. The passage selected was Jer. 26 and when vss. 14-15, **as for me, behold, I am in your hands . . .** , were read, the Abbé exclaimed: "That's for me!" Shortly thereafter he was arrested and imprisoned in the Donjon of Vincennes, where he remained for the next five years.

27:1-22. *Parable of the Yoke Bars.*—In T. Crouther Gordon's work on Jeremiah, *The*

2 Thus saith the Lord to me; Make thee bonds and yokes, and put them upon thy neck,

---

the Lord. **2** Thus the Lord said to me: "Make yourself thongs and yoke-bars, and

---

chadrezzar, king of Babylonia. In 598 B.C. Zedekiah had been placed on the throne of Judah by Nebuchadrezzar (II Kings 24:17), but four years later he was ready to consider revolt against Babylonia. As 27:3 implies, the kings of Edom, Moab, Ammon, Tyre, and Sidon sent envoys to Jerusalem for conference with Zedekiah, either to persuade him to rebel or, if he had already consented to rebel, to plan their strategy. To the envoys, to Zedekiah, and to the people of Judah Jeremiah made his position crystal clear: These nations ought to submit to the yoke of Babylonia, for Yahweh has given all of them into the hand of Nebuchadrezzar, who is really Yahweh's servant. Strange as this attitude may seem, it is thoroughly consistent with Jeremiah's attitude elsewhere (cf. 21:1-10; 32:3-5; 34:2-5; 37:7-10; 38:17-23). While Jeremiah may have sensed that rebellion against Nebuchadrezzar would be unsuccessful (as indeed it later proved to be), his reason for this attitude was basically religious. We have no information from any other source regarding the events of chs. 27–28. It seems probable that the rebellion was not carried out; Jeremiah's counsel may have been one of the factors in preventing it. His attitude should be compared with that of Isaiah in a similar situation (Isa. 20). It was probably the pro-Egyptian party in Jerusalem which favored rebellion at this time, encouraged by the accession of Psamtik II as Pharaoh of Egypt in 594 B.C. Later they secured the upper hand with Zedekiah and brought about the revolt which resulted in the destruction of Jerusalem in 587.

These chapters are based on Baruch's memoirs as revised by the Deuteronomic editor. The latter's diction is evident especially in 27:5, 8, 13; ch. 28 has little trace of his editing. He may be responsible for the repetitiousness in ch. 27, and for the careless interchange of first and third persons. The LXX of ch. 27 differs markedly from the M.T. It does not contain vss. 1, 7, 13-14a, or most of vss. 21-22. Some of the material omitted has to do with the return of the Jews from exile, together with the temple objects. It seems probable that the LXX represents on the whole the earlier text, and that the additions now in the M.T. were made near the end of the Babylonian exile or after it was over. It should be remembered that the Deuteronomic editor lived *ca.* 550 B.C. Some details of the LXX text will be noted in the Exeg.

1. Message to the Foreign Kings (27:1-11)

27:1. This verse is not in the LXX. Most Hebrew MSS have **In the beginning of the reign of Jehoiakim,** but this must be erroneous. The events of chs. 27–28 took place in the fourth year of Zedekiah (28:1; cf. 27:3, 12, 20), which was 594-593 B.C. Whatever may be the precise meaning of **the beginning of the reign** (see Exeg. on 26:1), it is unlikely that Zedekiah and his allies planned rebellion in his first year. The verse was erroneously copied by a Hebrew scribe from 26:1 (cf. Exeg. on 28:1).

2. The yoke which the prophet is instructed to make and use in his symbolic action was like those used on an ox, made up of a wooden yoke-bar (or **yoke-bars**), with leather

---

Rebel Prophet, there is an obscure but important footnote regarding this chapter. Gordon remarks that "the strongest proof of Jeremiah's statesmanship lies in the fact that although Moab and Ammon lay near to him, he saw that the conflict lay not between them, but between the two farthest off powers, namely Egypt and Babylon." [9] Apropos of this and Jeremiah's capacity to exploit a public situation in which to communicate his message, Gordon's

[9] P. 67.

footnote adds, "Chap. xxvii . . . practically proves this quality of statesmanship in the prophet." [1]

This is indeed the most impressive feature of this chapter. The gathering of envoys at Jerusalem to consider the possibilities of revolt against Babylonia provides Jeremiah with the occasion for his acted parable. The battle of Carchemish in 605 B.C. had already awakened in Jeremiah the sense of the growing power of

[1] *Ibid.,* n. 1.

3 And send them to the king of Edom, and to the king of Moab, and to the king of the Ammonites, and to the king of Tyrus, and to the king of Zidon, by the hand of the messengers which come to Jerusalem unto Zedekiah king of Judah;

4 And command them to say unto their masters, Thus saith the LORD of hosts, the God of Israel; Thus shall ye say unto your masters;

5 I have made the earth, the man and the beast that *are* upon the ground, by my great power and by my outstretched arm, and have given it unto whom it seemed meet unto me.

6 And now have I given all these lands into the hand of Nebuchadnezzar the king of Babylon, my servant; and the beasts of the field have I given him also to serve him.

7 And all nations shall serve him, and his son, and his son's son, until the very time of his land come: and then many nations and great kings shall serve themselves of him.

put them on your neck. 3 Send word[v] to the king of Edom, the king of Moab, the king of the sons of Ammon, the king of Tyre, and the king of Sidon by the hand of the envoys who have come to Jerusalem to Zedeki'ah king of Judah. 4 Give them this charge for their masters: 'Thus says the LORD of hosts, the God of Israel: This is what you shall say to your masters: 5 "It is I who by my great power and my outstretched arm have made the earth, with the men and animals that are on the earth, and I give it to whomever it seems right to me. 6 Now I have given all these lands into the hand of Nebuchadnez'zar, the king of Babylon, my servant, and I have given him also the beasts of the field to serve him. 7 All the nations shall serve him and his son and his grandson, until the time of his own land comes; then many nations and great kings shall make him their slave.

[v] Cn: Heb *send them*

thongs which came down under the neck. Apparently only one yoke was made. The RSV is correct in translating מוטות as yoke-bars (27:2; 28:10, 12, 13), and על as yoke (27:8, 11, 12; 28:2, 4, 11, 14). The KJV renders both words by yoke(s).

3. The kings of the small nations of Syria-Palestine frequently rebelled against their overlord in Mesopotamia, usually in league with Egypt, but they were seldom successful. An outstanding example is the revolt which was put down by Sennacherib in 701 B.C. (see II Kings 18:13–19:37 and the Assyrian record in Pritchard, *Ancient Near Eastern Texts,* pp. 287-88).

6. When Jeremiah speaks of Nebuchadrezzar as the servant of Yahweh, he means not that the Babylonian king is a worshiper of Yahweh, but that he is one who serves as an agent of and receives his authority from Yahweh; cf. Second Isaiah's designation of Cyrus the Persian monarch as the one who is "anointed" by Yahweh (Isa. 45:1). This is a bold thought, but it is in accord with Jeremiah's conception of Yahweh as a world deity who controls the history of nations.

7. This verse is missing in the LXX. It may be an addition to the original text, made in the latter part of the Exile; or it may have been omitted by the LXX because it was not literally fulfilled. The last king of the Neo-Babylonian Empire was Nabonidus (556-539 B.C.), who was the fourth king in succession after Nebuchadrezzar, not a blood relative of Nebuchadrezzar.

Babylon (cf. ch. 46; also Gordon's quotation in ch. 25, above). The world-wide vision of his prophetic perspectives has been apparent from the moment of his call. It pervades his prophetic messages throughout. Hence, the device of dramatizing the message for the sake of Zedekiah and the conspirators against the Babylonian rule was a very adroit method for getting his message carried back to the little countries from which the envoys had come. The message

which accompanies it is also plain. It is the present will of God that Nebuchadrezzar should dominate the nations of the world until the time of his own land comes. The only sensible course, therefore, is for Zedekiah and all the other little nations to put their necks under the yoke of the king of Babylon. The deftness with which the prophets are included with the diviners, dreamers, soothsayers, and sorcerers, will hardly be missed by the astute reader of Jere-

8 And it shall come to pass, *that* the nation and kingdom which will not serve the same Nebuchadnezzar the king of Babylon, and that will not put their neck under the yoke of the king of Babylon, that nation will I punish, saith the LORD, with the sword, and with the famine, and with the pestilence, until I have consumed them by his hand.

9 Therefore hearken not ye to your prophets, not to your diviners, nor to your dreamers, nor to your enchanters, nor to your sorcerers, which speak unto you, saying, Ye shall not serve the king of Babylon:

10 For they prophesy a lie unto you, to remove you far from your land; and that I should drive you out, and ye should perish.

11 But the nations that bring their neck under the yoke of the king of Babylon, and serve him, those will I let remain still in their own land, saith the LORD; and they shall till it, and dwell therein.

12 ¶ I spake also to Zedekiah king of Judah according to all these words, saying, Bring your necks under the yoke of the king of Babylon, and serve him and his people, and live.

13 Why will ye die, thou and thy people, by the sword, by the famine, and by the pestilence, as the LORD hath spoken against the nation that will not serve the king of Babylon?

14 Therefore hearken not unto the words of the prophets that speak unto you, saying, Ye shall not serve the king of Babylon: for they prophesy a lie unto you.

15 For I have not sent them, saith the LORD, yet they prophesy a lie in my name; that I might drive you out, and that ye might perish, ye, and the prophets that prophesy unto you.

8 " ' "But if any nation or kingdom will not serve this Nebuchadnez'zar king of Babylon, and put its neck under the yoke of the king of Babylon, I will punish that nation with the sword, with famine, and with pestilence, says the LORD, until I have consumed it by his hand. 9 So do not listen to your prophets, your diviners, your dreamers,[w] your soothsayers, or your sorcerers, who are saying to you, 'You shall not serve the king of Babylon.' 10 For it is a lie which they are prophesying to you, with the result that you will be removed far from your land, and I will drive you out, and you will perish. 11 But any nation which will bring its neck under the yoke of the king of Babylon and serve him, I will leave on its own land, to till it and dwell there, says the LORD." ' "

12 To Zedeki'ah king of Judah I spoke in like manner: "Bring your necks under the yoke of the king of Babylon, and serve him and his people, and live. 13 Why will you and your people die by the sword, by famine, and by pestilence, as the LORD has spoken concerning any nation which will not serve the king of Babylon? 14 Do not listen to the words of the prophets who are saying to you, 'You shall not serve the king of Babylon,' for it is a lie which they are prophesying to you. 15 I have not sent them, says the LORD, but they are prophesying falsely in my name, with the result that I will drive you out and you will perish, you and the prophets who are prophesying to you."

[w] Gk Syr Vg: Heb *dreams*

2. MESSAGE TO ZEDEKIAH (27:12-15)

12-15. The message to **Zedekiah king of Judah** is very similar to that given to the envoys of the foreign kings. Zedekiah appears in the biblical records as a weak, vacillating king who was willing to listen to counsels of revolt; later he did revolt unsuccessfully against Babylonia (589-587 B.C.).

miah's message. It is clear that their prophecies seek their own advantage, and are not spoken within the context of a philosophy of history whose scope includes the purposes of God. The same policy addressed to Zedekiah evidently had its effect. The conspiracy was, for the time at least, postponed. The specious optimism of the false prophets again is broken through. What must be noted here is the pivotal significance of Jeremiah's philosophy of history. This means that the submission which Jeremiah enjoins under the symbol of the yoke bars is submission,

16 Also I spake to the priests and to all this people, saying, Thus saith the Lord; Hearken not to the words of your prophets that prophesy unto you, saying, Behold, the vessels of the Lord's house shall now shortly be brought again from Babylon: for they prophesy a lie unto you.

17 Hearken not unto them; serve the king of Babylon, and live: wherefore should this city be laid waste?

18 But if they *be* prophets, and if the word of the Lord be with them, let them now make intercession to the Lord of hosts, that the vessels which are left in the house of the Lord, and *in* the house of the king of Judah, and at Jerusalem, go not to Babylon.

19 ¶ For thus saith the Lord of hosts concerning the pillars, and concerning the sea, and concerning the bases, and concerning the residue of the vessels that remain in this city,

20 Which Nebuchadnezzar king of Babylon took not, when he carried away captive Jeconiah the son of Jehoiakim king of Judah from Jerusalem to Babylon, and all the nobles of Judah and Jerusalem;

21 Yea, thus saith the Lord of hosts, the God of Israel, concerning the vessels that remain *in* the house of the Lord, and *in* the house of the king of Judah and of Jerusalem;

22 They shall be carried to Babylon, and there shall they be until the day that I visit them, saith the Lord; then will I bring them up, and restore them to this place.

16 Then I spoke to the priests and to all this people, saying, "Thus says the Lord: Do not listen to the words of your prophets who are prophesying to you, saying, 'Behold, the vessels of the Lord's house will now shortly be brought back from Babylon,' for it is a lie which they are prophesying to you. 17 Do not listen to them; serve the king of Babylon and live. Why should this city become a desolation? 18 If they are prophets, and if the word of the Lord is with them, then let them intercede with the Lord of hosts, that the vessels which are left in the house of the Lord, in the house of the king of Judah, and in Jerusalem may not go to Babylon. 19 For thus says the Lord of hosts concerning the pillars, the sea, the stands, and the rest of the vessels which are left in this city, 20 which Nebuchadnez'zar king of Babylon did not take away, when he took into exile from Jerusalem to Babylon Jeconi'ah the son of Jehoi'akim, king of Judah, and all the nobles of Judah and Jerusalem — 21 thus says the Lord of hosts, the God of Israel, concerning the vessels which are left in the house of the Lord, in the house of the king of Judah, and in Jerusalem: 22 They shall be carried to Babylon and remain there until the day when I give attention to them, says the Lord. Then I will bring them back and restore them to this place."

3. Message to the Priests and People (27:16-22)

16. This message is delivered to the priests because they had a special interest in the return of the temple objects (here translated infelicitously **vessels**) which had been carried away by the Babylonian king.

19. The LXX contains no references to **the pillars, the sea, the stands.** The three are mentioned together in II Kings 25:13=Jer. 52:17. **The pillars,** made of bronze, stood in front of the Jerusalem temple (I Kings 7:15); **the sea** was a great bronze basin in the temple court (I Kings 7:23-26); and **the stands** were the objects on wheels described in I Kings 7:27-37. The Babylonians valued all these objects for their metal.

21-22. Vs. 21 and most of vs. 22 are missing in the LXX, which refers only to the taking of the temple vessels to Babylon.

not so much to Nebuchadrezzar, the conqueror, as to Nebuchadrezzar, the instrument of God. Nebuchadrezzar's time will also come. This is the distinction so difficult to see, especially by the people who are chafing under the yoke. To them the prophet will doubtless appear "unpatriotic," as indeed he must appear to anyone who does not see behind the rise and fall of temporal powers the moving chastisements of God.

28 And it came to pass the same year, in the beginning of the reign of Zedekiah king of Judah, in the fourth year, *and* in the fifth month, *that* Hananiah the son of Azur the prophet, which *was* of Gibeon, spake unto me in the house of the LORD, in the presence of the priests and of all the people, saying,

2 Thus speaketh the LORD of hosts, the God of Israel, saying, I have broken the yoke of the king of Babylon.

3 Within two full years will I bring again into this place all the vessels of the LORD's house, that Nebuchadnezzar king of Babylon took away from this place, and carried them to Babylon:

4 And I will bring again to this place Jeconiah the son of Jehoiakim king of Judah, with all the captives of Judah, that went into Babylon, saith the LORD: for I will break the yoke of the king of Babylon.

5 ¶ Then the prophet Jeremiah said unto the prophet Hananiah in the presence of the priests, and in the presence of all the people that stood in the house of the LORD,

6 Even the prophet Jeremiah said, Amen: the LORD do so: the LORD perform thy words which thou hast prophesied, to bring again the vessels of the LORD's house,

28 In that same year, at the beginning of the reign of Zedeki'ah king of Judah, in the fifth month of the fourth year, Hanani'ah the son of Azzur, the prophet from Gib'eon, spoke to me in the house of the LORD, in the presence of the priests and all the people, saying, 2 "Thus says the LORD of hosts, the God of Israel: I have broken the yoke of the king of Babylon. 3 Within two years I will bring back to this place all the vessels of the LORD's house, which Nebuchadnez'zar king of Babylon took away from this place and carried to Babylon. 4 I will also bring back to this place Jeconi'ah the son of Jehoi'akim, king of Judah, and all the exiles from Judah who went to Babylon, says the LORD, for I will break the yoke of the king of Babylon."

5 Then the prophet Jeremiah spoke to Hanani'ah the prophet in the presence of the priests and all the people who were standing in the house of the LORD; 6 and the prophet Jeremiah said, "Amen! May the LORD do so; may the LORD make the words which you have prophesied come

---

4. CONFLICT WITH HANANIAH (28:1-17)

This chapter tells of the encounter of Jeremiah with Hananiah, who is designated by the LXX as a "false prophet" (ψευδοπροφήτης). The encounter must have taken place very shortly after the events of ch. 27, for the symbol of the yoke is used in both chapters. Hananiah was a representative of the "prophets of weal" who continually prophesied peace (vs. 9). He predicted that the exiles would return from Babylonia within two years, but subsequent events proved him wrong and Jeremiah correct.

28:1. The LXX here has only "in the fourth year of Zedekiah king of Judah, in the fifth month," which must be correct. It cannot be reconciled with the Hebrew, at the beginning of the reign of Zedekiah, which has been erroneously influenced by 26:1; 27:1. The fourth year of Zedekiah was 594-593 B.C., the fifth month being Tebet (December-January).

6. Jeremiah uttered these words because of his sympathy with the people. He would have been willing to have Hananiah's prophecy come true. Note that he did not immediately receive a counter oracle from Yahweh. The prophecy which he later uttered (vs. 12) must have come to him not in ecstatic experience but as the result of further reflection.

28:1-17. *Yokes of Wood or Yokes of Iron.*—It was inevitable that Jeremiah's symbolic act should be opposed. Considering that by his acted parable he (*a*) classified the official prophets with the dreamers and soothsayers, and (*b*) identified, by the assumption of the yoke, his

mantic power with the prophetic action, and so exhibited the divine energy as already moving toward its implied fulfillment, it is not surprising that one of the temple prophets should have risen with a counter-prophecy. This was Hananiah. There is no reason to question

and all that is carried away captive, from Babylon into this place.

7 Nevertheless, hear thou now this word that I speak in thine ears, and in the ears of all the people;

8 The prophets that have been before me and before thee of old prophesied both against many countries, and against great kingdoms, of war, and of evil, and of pestilence.

9 The prophet which prophesieth of peace, when the word of the prophet shall come to pass, *then* shall the prophet be known, that the LORD hath truly sent him.

10 ¶ Then Hananiah the prophet took the yoke from off the prophet Jeremiah's neck, and brake it.

11 And Hananiah spake in the presence of all the people, saying, Thus saith the LORD; Even so will I break the yoke of Nebuchadnezzar king of Babylon from the neck of all nations within the space of two full years. And the prophet Jeremiah went his way.

12 ¶ Then the word of the LORD came unto Jeremiah *the prophet,* after that Hananiah the prophet had broken the yoke from off the neck of the prophet Jeremiah, saying,

true, and bring back to this place from Babylon the vessels of the house of the LORD, and all the exiles. **7** Yet hear now this word which I speak in your hearing and in the hearing of all the people. **8** The prophets who preceded you and me from ancient times prophesied war, famine, and pestilence against many countries and great kingdoms. **9** As for the prophet who prophesies peace, when the word of that prophet comes to pass, then it will be known that the LORD has truly sent the prophet."

10 Then the prophet Hanani'ah took the yoke-bars from the neck of Jeremiah the prophet, and broke them. **11** And Hanani'ah spoke in the presence of all the people, saying, "Thus says the LORD: Even so will I break the yoke of Nebuchadnez'zar king of Babylon from the neck of all the nations within two years." But Jeremiah the prophet went his way.

12 Sometime after the prophet Hanani'ah had broken the yoke-bars from off the neck of Jeremiah the prophet, the word of

---

8-9. These verses should not be interpreted to mean that the entire message of all prophets before Jeremiah had been one of unrelieved doom. It is not correct to use these words as an indication that all hopeful passages in earlier prophets are secondary. Jeremiah says only that the usual message of earlier prophets included threats of punishment; in prophesying doom he is more in the line of the earlier prophets than those like Hananiah, who could prophesy only welfare and prosperity (cf. Deut. 18:20-22).

Hananiah's sincerity. As W. Robertson Smith has put it,

The prophets who opposed Jeremiah took their stand on the ground of Josiah's reformation, and plainly regarded themselves as conservators of the prophetic traditions of Isaiah, whose doctrine of the inviolability of Jehovah's seat on Zion was the starting point of their opposition to Jeremiah's predictions of captivity.[2]

Hananiah also begins his oracular pronouncement with the customary prophetic formula, **Thus says the LORD of hosts.** To Hananiah the symbol of the yoke represented the tyrannous alien power which should be broken by the word of the Lord; to Jeremiah it symbolized the captivity about to come. Hananiah stood within

a context of foreshortened perspectives. He was doubtless unconsciously responsive to the wishful thinking of the court and the people. It is not difficult, therefore, to understand his passionate words and action. At the same time it is easy to see how Hananiah's action falls within the cryptic statement of Ezekiel (14:9): "If the prophet be deceived and speak a word, I, the LORD, have deceived that prophet." In other words, if the prophet allows the voice of the people, or the voice of convention, or the voice of orthodoxy, to become identified with the voice of God, he is certain to distort the voice, and Yahweh must permit him to be deceived.

Jeremiah was bound to reply, and his reply contains a penetrating and far-reaching principle. To put off the wooden yoke with which the people presently are bound would mean

[2] "Prophet," *Encyclopaedia Britannica* (9th ed.), XIX, 817.

13 Go and tell Hananiah, saying, Thus saith the LORD; Thou hast broken the yokes of wood; but thou shalt make for them yokes of iron.

14 For thus saith the LORD of hosts, the God of Israel; I have put a yoke of iron upon the neck of all these nations, that they may serve Nebuchadnezzar king of Babylon; and they shall serve him: and I have given him the beasts of the field also.

15 ¶ Then said the prophet Jeremiah unto Hananiah the prophet, Hear now, Hananiah; The LORD hath not sent thee; but thou makest this people to trust in a lie.

16 Therefore thus saith the LORD; Behold, I will cast thee from off the face of the earth: this year thou shalt die, because thou hast taught rebellion against the LORD.

17 So Hananiah the prophet died the same year in the seventh month.

29 Now these *are* the words of the letter that Jeremiah the prophet sent from Jerusalem unto the residue of the elders which were carried away captives, and to the priests, and to the prophets, and

the LORD came to Jeremiah: 13 "Go, tell Hanani'ah, 'Thus says the LORD: You have broken wooden bars, but I* will make in their place bars of iron. 14 For thus says the LORD of hosts, the God of Israel: I have put upon the neck of all these nations an iron yoke of servitude to Nebuchadnez'zar king of Babylon, and they shall serve him, for I have given to him even the beasts of the field.'" 15 And Jeremiah the prophet said to the prophet Hanani'ah, "Listen, Hanani'ah, the LORD has not sent you, and you have made this people trust in a lie. 16 Therefore thus says the LORD: 'Behold, I will remove you from the face of the earth. This very year you shall die, because you have uttered rebellion against the LORD.'"

17 In the same year, in the seventh month, the prophet Hanani'ah died.

29 These are the words of the letter which Jeremiah the prophet sent from Jerusalem to the elders^y of the exiles,

* Gk: Heb *you*

^y Gk: Heb *the rest of the elders*

---

17. The verse should not be considered unhistorical, nor is there any value in attempting to give a rational explanation of Hananiah's death.

C. LETTERS TO THE EXILES IN BABYLONIA (29:1-32)

The situation in which Jeremiah is involved here is similar to that of chs. 27–28; but in the present passage the prophet is concerned primarily with the exiles in Babylonia and their false religious leaders who were promising that they would soon return to Judah, whereas in chs. 27–28 he was concerned with those left in Jerusalem. This chapter is not dated, but we may surmise that the letter was written within a few years after the beginning of the Babylonian exile in 598 B.C. The Babylonian exiles were influenced by their leaders, prophets, and priests to expect an immediate return to their homeland; two of their prophets were named Ahab and Zedekiah (vss. 21-22). Jeremiah wrote a

---

simply that they would bring upon themselves heavier servitude. This is perennially true. No man lives as an island unto himself, as John Donne said. We live under the yoke of solemn engagements with ourselves, our fellow men, and ultimate reality. To throw aside these easy yokes is but to bring upon ourselves the more oppressive and constricting yokes of iron. Similarly, Christ's yoke is easy because its wearer is yoked to the power of God. And here again the Thomas à Kempis principle applies: "He who carries his cross, his cross will carry." [3] Nothing is to be gained, as Jeremiah has shown (27:12-13), by breaking the yoke of the king of Babylon. For Nebuchadrezzar is, for the time being, God's instrument. It is Hananiah's fail-

[3] *The Imitation of Christ* II. 12.

ure to discern this that makes him rebellious, not against Nebuchadrezzar but against Yahweh. He thus perverts the word of the Lord and makes **this people trust in a lie** (vs. 15). Hence the severity of Jeremiah's prophecy: Hananiah will die because he has **uttered rebellion against the LORD** (vs. 17). Jeremiah evidently penetrated very deeply into Hananiah's unconscious motives. He was responding more to the prestige of his office and the wishful hopes of the people than he was consciously aware. Jeremiah brought these concealed motivations into the open, and Hananiah's ambitious earnestness produced a guilt consciousness unto death.

29:1-32. The Letter to the Exiles.—This letter has been called very justly "one of the most

to all the people whom Nebuchadnezzar had carried away captive from Jerusalem to Babylon;

2 (After that Jeconiah the king, and the queen, and the eunuchs, the princes of Judah and Jerusalem, and the carpenters, and the smiths, were departed from Jerusalem;)

3 By the hand of Elasah the son of Shaphan, and Gemariah the son of Hilkiah, (whom Zedekiah king of Judah sent unto Babylon to Nebuchadnezzar king of Babylon) saying,

and to the priests, the prophets, and all the people, whom Nebuchadnez'zar had taken into exile from Jerusalem to Babylon. 2 This was after King Jeconi'ah, and the queen mother, the eunuchs, the princes of Judah and Jerusalem, the craftsmen, and the smiths had departed from Jerusalem. 3 The letter was sent by the hand of Ela'sah the son of Shaphan and Gemari'ah the son of Hilki'ah, whom Zedeki'ah king of Judah sent to Babylon to Nebuchadnez'zar king of

---

letter to the exiles in order to counteract this false hope, and to pronounce judgment on Ahab and Zedekiah. Subsequently he wrote another letter (vss. 24-32) to pronounce judgment on Shemaiah of Nehelam, who had written to the temple overseer in Jerusalem in order to try to silence Jeremiah and prevent him from giving counsel such as the previous letter had contained. Ch. 29 is joined with chs. 26-28 because, like them, it deals with conflicts between Jeremiah and religious leaders of his time.

The basis of this chapter is Baruch's memoirs, but it has been revised by the Deuteronomic editor. Vss. 4-9, the heart of Jeremiah's letter, are apparently quite genuine, but vss. 10-20 show much evidence of Deuteronomic editing, particularly vss. 16-20. There is some confusion in the order of the verses (see Exeg.). In spite of the editing this chapter has received, it gives us very important insight into some of Jeremiah's basic beliefs.

1. General Letter to the Exiles (29:1-23)

29:3. The letter was sent by the hand of envoys whom King Zedekiah sent to Babylonia in order to take tribute to the Babylonian king, or to assure the king of Zedekiah's loyalty after Nebuchadrezzar heard of the projected revolt implied by ch. 27, or for some other purpose. **Elasah the son of Shaphan** was probably the brother of Ahikam, who had taken Jeremiah's part at the time of his arrest after the temple sermon (26:24), and also of that Gemariah in whose temple chamber Baruch had read the scroll (36:10). Nothing else is known of **Gemariah the son of Hilkiah**; he was hardly the brother of Jeremiah, whose father also was named Hilkiah.

---

significant documents in the Old Testament."[4] It was evidently sent at a somewhat earlier time than the events recorded in chs. 27–28.[5] It forms the logical counterpart of ch. 24. Directed as it is against the restlessness of the people in exile, and against any false hopes being aroused by prophets who may be deceiving them with illusions of an early return, it is characterized by soundness and sense, shows a clear penetration into the mood and development of the people in exile, and rises to the highest pitch of religious consciousness to be found in the religious history of mankind up to this time.

There are three parts to his message which are of perennial value. First, says Jeremiah, **build . . . plant . . . pray.** This is the beginning

[4] John Paterson, *Goodly Fellowship of the Prophets,* p. 156.

[5] Peake, *Jeremiah and Lamentations,* II, 55.

of all sound religious practice. It was all the more imperative in the circumstances of the exiles. Jeremiah makes it clear to them that their exile is to be of long duration. Therefore, they must **seek the welfare of the city** (vs. 7). Second, they must not permit themselves to be deceived by diviners who dream dreams; for their unrealistic wishes are father to their misleading thoughts. And third, when they have learned the patience and the capacity to let their unsound dreams volatilize with the unsound notions on which they are based, they will discover that the Lord has **plans** for them and will hold out to them **a future and a hope** (vs. 11). Jeremiah wisely refrains from specifying either the form or pattern of this hope. Indeed, only when it is realized that the hope consists neither in form nor pattern is one in a position to discover the real nature of the Lord's gift of hope.

4 Thus saith the LORD of hosts, the God of Israel, unto all that are carried away captives, whom I have caused to be carried away from Jerusalem unto Babylon;

5 Build ye houses, and dwell *in them;* and plant gardens, and eat the fruit of them;

6 Take ye wives, and beget sons and daughters; and take wives for your sons, and give your daughters to husbands, that they may bear sons and daughters; that ye may be increased there, and not diminished.

7 And seek the peace of the city whither I have caused you to be carried away captives, and pray unto the LORD for it: for in the peace thereof shall ye have peace.

8 ¶ For thus saith the LORD of hosts, the God of Israel; Let not your prophets and your diviners, that *be* in the midst of you, deceive you, neither hearken to your dreams which ye cause to be dreamed.

9 For they prophesy falsely unto you in my name: I have not sent them, saith the LORD.

10 ¶ For thus saith the LORD, That after seventy years be accomplished at Babylon I will visit you, and perform my good word toward you, in causing you to return to this place.

Babylon. It said: 4 "Thus says the LORD of hosts, the God of Israel, to all the exiles whom I have sent into exile from Jerusalem to Babylon: 5 Build houses and live in them; plant gardens and eat their produce. 6 Take wives and have sons and daughters; take wives for your sons, and give your daughters in marriage, that they may bear sons and daughters; multiply there, and do not decrease. 7 But seek the welfare of the city where I have sent you into exile, and pray to the LORD on its behalf, for in its welfare you will find your welfare. 8 For thus says the LORD of hosts, the God of Israel: Do not let your prophets and your diviners who are among you deceive you, and do not listen to the dreams which they dream,[z] 9 for it is a lie which they are prophesying to you in my name; I did not send them, says the LORD.

10 "For thus says the LORD: When seventy years are completed for Babylon, I will visit you, and I will fulfil to you my promise and bring you back to this place.

[z] Cn: Heb *your dreams which you cause to dream*

4-7. This passage contains the essence of Jeremiah's counsel to the exiles. They must not expect immediate return to Judah but plan to live normal lives in Babylonia. They must even **seek the welfare of the city** in which they may be living, **and pray to the LORD on its behalf.** This viewpoint is revolutionary. Jeremiah here shows the Jews that their religion does not depend on residence in the land of Palestine, as previously he had shown it did not depend on the existence of the temple or offering of sacrifices (7:1-15, 21-22).

These verses show us that the Babylonian exile did not mean imprisonment for the Jews. Most of them were allowed considerable freedom in the cities in which they were settled.

10-11. Scholars like Duhm and Volz consider vs. 10—sometimes vss. 10-11—as secondary. It is difficult to determine whether Jeremiah himself is responsible for the idea of a return after **seventy years.** In any event, the prediction is not precise, and gives little hope to those who were in exile at the time the letter was written (see Exeg. on 25:11-12).

Only when the pseudo-hopes have failed, and localized resemblances to God have proved their falsity, can one be said to enter truly into prayer. Then comes the climax line—a line which contains the distilled essence of Jeremiah's religious insight: **You will seek me and find me; when you seek me with all your heart, I will be found by you, says the LORD.** Herein is contained the paradox of all religion, learned by Jeremiah out of the toils and sufferings of his own religious quest, through the midst of which he had learned, to use his oft-repeated simile, that anguished "pain as of a woman in travail."

The phrasing of this insight as it appears in Deut. 4:29 was caught up by Mendelssohn, in his *Elijah,* wrested from all local contexts, and flung with unforgettable and uncannily haunt-

11 For I know the thoughts that I think toward you, saith the LORD, thoughts of peace, and not of evil, to give you an expected end.

12 Then shall ye call upon me, and ye shall go and pray unto me, and I will hearken unto you.

13 And ye shall seek me, and find *me*, when ye shall search for me with all your heart.

14 And I will be found of you, saith the LORD: and I will turn away your captivity, and I will gather you from all the nations, and from all the places whither I have driven you, saith the LORD; and I will bring you again into the place whence I caused you to be carried away captive.

15 ¶ Because ye have said, The LORD hath raised us up prophets in Babylon;

16 *Know* that thus saith the LORD of the king that sitteth upon the throne of David, and of all the people that dwelleth in this city, *and* of your brethren that are not gone forth with you into captivity;

17 Thus saith the LORD of hosts; Behold, I will send upon them the sword, the famine, and the pestilence, and will make them like vile figs, that cannot be eaten, they are so evil.

18 And I will persecute them with the sword, with the famine, and with the pestilence, and will deliver them to be removed to all the kingdoms of the earth, to be a curse, and an astonishment, and a hissing, and a reproach, among all the nations whither I have driven them:

11 For I know the plans I have for you, says the LORD, plans for welfare and not for evil, to give you a future and a hope. **12** Then you will call upon me and come and pray to me, and I will hear you. **13** You will seek me and find me; when you seek me with all your heart, **14** I will be found by you, says the LORD, and I will restore your fortunes and gather you from all the nations and all the places where I have driven you, says the LORD, and I will bring you back to the place from which I sent you into exile.

15 "Because you have said, 'The LORD has raised up prophets for us in Babylon,' — **16** Thus says the LORD concerning the king who sits on the throne of David, and concerning all the people who dwell in this city, your kinsmen who did not go out with you into exile: **17** 'Thus says the LORD of hosts, Behold, I am sending on them sword, famine, and pestilence, and I will make them like vile figs which are so bad they cannot be eaten. **18** I will pursue them with sword, famine, and pestilence, and will make them a horror to all the kingdoms of the earth, to be a curse, a terror, a hissing, and a reproach among all the nations where

13-14. These verses are in the phraseology of the Deuteronomic editor (cf. vs. 13 with Deut. 4:29; I Kings 8:48; cf. vs. 14 with Deut. 30:3, 5). We cannot dogmatically say, however, that the ideas expressed are foreign to Jeremiah the prophet. The LXX has only the first clause of vs. 14. It is possible that the rest of the verse, which concerns a return from the whole Diaspora, is from the latter part of the Exile or the postexilic period. It is hardly a part of the original letter to the Babylonian exiles.

16-20. This section, considered by most modern critics secondary, is out of place, since vs. 15 is naturally continued by vss. 21-23, not by vs. 16. The passage deals with the Jews left in Judah rather than with the exiles in Babylonia. Its Deuteronomic phraseology is reminiscent of ch. 24. It was probably written by the Deuteronomic editor—or by

ing melody into the innermost depths of the soul—"If with all your heart ye truly seek me, ye shall surely find me." Inasmuch as the introductory chapters of Deuteronomy were written, not by the early Deuteronomists, but by the later ones, it is probable that "this passage was written after the historical experience of the

exile." [6] It thereby carries the authentic imprint of Jeremiah's inspiration. The oft-cited passage from Pascal, "console yourself, thou wouldst not be seeking me hadst thou not already found me," contains the same undefinable appeal. [7]

[6] Cunliffe-Jones, *Deuteronomy*, p. 46.

[7] *Thoughts*, No. 552, "The Mystery of Jesus."

19 Because they have not hearkened to my words, saith the LORD, which I sent unto them by my servants the prophets, rising up early and sending *them;* but ye would not hear, saith the LORD.

20 ¶ Hear ye therefore the word of the LORD, all ye of the captivity, whom I have sent from Jerusalem to Babylon.

21 Thus saith the LORD of hosts, the God of Israel, of Ahab the son of Kolaiah, and of Zedekiah the son of Maaseiah, which prophesy a lie unto you in my name; Behold, I will deliver them into the hand of Nebuchadrezzar king of Babylon; and he shall slay them before your eyes;

22 And of them shall be taken up a curse by all the captivity of Judah which *are* in Babylon, saying, The LORD make thee like Zedekiah and like Ahab, whom the king of Babylon roasted in the fire;

23 Because they have committed villainy in Israel, and have committed adultery with their neighbors' wives, and have spoken lying words in my name, which I have not commanded them; even I know, and *am* a witness, saith the LORD.

24 ¶ *Thus* shalt thou also speak to Shemaiah the Nehelamite, saying,

I have driven them, **19** because they did not heed my words, says the LORD, which I persistently sent to you by my servants the prophets, but you would not listen, says the LORD.'— **20** Hear the word of the LORD, all you exiles whom I sent away from Jerusalem to Babylon: **21** 'Thus says the LORD of hosts, the God of Israel, concerning Ahab the son of Kola'iah and Zedeki'ah the son of Ma-asei'ah, who are prophesying a lie to you in my name: Behold, I will deliver them into the hand of Nebuchadrez'zar king of Babylon, and he shall slay them before your eyes. **22** Because of them this curse shall be used by all the exiles from Judah in Babylon: "The LORD make you like Zedeki'ah and Ahab, whom the king of Babylon roasted in the fire," **23** because they have committed folly in Israel, they have committed adultery with their neighbors' wives, and they have spoken in my name lying words which I did not command them. I am the one who knows, and I am witness, says the LORD.' "

24 To Shemai'ah of Nehel'am you shall

---

some later editor who knew ch. 24 well—and does not represent Jeremiah's attitude. Vss. 16-20 are omitted in the LXX, but the omission is probably an error of a scribe, whose eye skipped from **Babylon** at the end of vs. 15 to the same word at the end of **vs. 20,** and who thus inadvertently omitted the intervening words.

2. LETTER CONCERNING SHEMAIAH (29:24-32)

This was not a part of the general letter to the exiles. It concerns the actions of Shemaiah of Nehelam, a leader in Babylonia, who had written to Zephaniah the son of Maaseiah in Jerusalem, appointing him overseer of the temple in Jerusalem and rebuking him for not imprisoning Jeremiah for writing as he had to the exiles in Babylonia. Jeremiah pronounces judgment on Shemaiah for his opposition.

24. There is some confusion here, for we do not have a complete letter **to Shemaiah.** When Jeremiah learns of Shemaiah's action, he writes a letter to the exiles condemning Shemaiah (vss. 31-32). Probably the beginning of this verse should read "concerning Shemaiah" (ASV), since *'el* is often equivalent to *'al.*

The same is true of Hölderlin: "That which thou seekest is near, and already coming to meet thee."[8] The paradox is that the finding is in the seeking—when that which is sought is ultimate reality and the seeking is conducted with all our heart. But better still is Jeremiah's recognition that the truth is in the relationship, and that which is attested by the heart is the

content of the relationship with God. **I will be found by you.** Jeremiah's insight contains not merely the simple paradox of the Sermon on the Mount, "Seek, and ye shall find," but also the anticipation of the Fourth Gospel: "Ye shall neither in this mountain, nor yet at Jerusalem, worship. . . . But the hour cometh . . . when the true worshipers shall worship . . . in spirit and in truth" (John 4:21-23).

In short, Jeremiah is telling the people in

[8] *Heimkunft* ("Homecoming"), IV, from *Das Meisterwerk* (Stuttgart: W. Kohlhammer, 1952), p. 357.

25 Thus speaketh the LORD of hosts, the God of Israel, saying, Because thou hast sent letters in thy name unto all the people that *are* at Jerusalem, and to Zephaniah the son of Maaseiah the priest, and to all the priests, saying,

26 The LORD hath made thee priest in the stead of Jehoiada the priest, that ye should be officers in the house of the LORD, for every man *that is* mad, and maketh himself a prophet, that thou shouldest put him in prison, and in the stocks.

27 Now therefore why hast thou not reproved Jeremiah of Anathoth, which maketh himself a prophet to you?

28 For therefore he sent unto us *in* Babylon, saying, This *captivity is* long: build ye houses, and dwell *in them;* and plant gardens, and eat the fruit of them.

29 And Zephaniah the priest read this letter in the ears of Jeremiah the prophet.

30 ¶ Then came the word of the LORD unto Jeremiah, saying,

31 Send to all them of the captivity, saying, Thus saith the LORD concerning Shemaiah the Nehelamite; Because that Shemaiah hath prophesied unto you, and I sent him not, and he caused you to trust in a lie:

say: 25 "Thus says the LORD of hosts, the God of Israel: You have sent letters in your name to all the people who are in Jerusalem, and to Zephani'ah the son of Ma-asei'ah the priest, and to all the priests, saying, 26 'The LORD has made you priest instead of Jehoi'ada the priest, to have charge in the house of the LORD over every madman who prophesies, to put him in the stocks and collar. 27 Now why have you not rebuked Jeremiah of An'athoth who is prophesying to you? 28 For he has sent to us in Babylon, saying, "Your exile will be long; build houses and live in them, and plant gardens and eat their produce." ' "

29 Zephani'ah the priest read this letter in the hearing of Jeremiah the prophet. 30 Then the word of the LORD came to Jeremiah: 31 "Send to all the exiles, saying, 'Thus says the LORD concerning Shemai'ah of Nehel'am: Because Shemai'ah has prophesied to you when I did not send him, and

---

25. Zephaniah the son of Maaseiah is named as a member of the deputation sent by King Zedekiah to Jeremiah in 21:1; 37:3. He is probably the same Zephaniah who is called "the second priest" in 52:24 (=II Kings 25:18) and was among those executed after the capture of Jerusalem in 587 B.C. In the present situation he is overseer of the temple (vs. 26), occupying the position which had been held earlier by Pashhur, who had put Jeremiah in stocks (20:1-6).

26. The use of the phrase **every madman who prophesies** cannot be taken to prove that Jeremiah was an ecstatic prophet. Because of the nature of his message he was considered by his opponents as **mad**. Peake (*Jeremiah and Lamentations*, II, 67) rightly says: "The sanity of the prophet was never more apparent than when he administered this cold douche of common sense to their fevered enthusiasm."

29. Zephaniah the priest was apparently friendly to Jeremiah, since he read to him Shemaiah's letter and did not follow the latter's instruction to imprison the prophet.

---

exile that, as Heidegger puts it, "Homecoming is the return into the proximity of the source" [9] —not a return to Jerusalem; and that exile is the journey into far countries of the self-centered mind, not a long sojourn in Babylon. The question is the same today: "You shall not cease, O clamour, until upon the sands I shall have sloughed off every human allegiance. (Who knows his birthplace still?)" [1] Jeremiah's

message extended to a condemnation of the false prophecies of Ahab and Zedekiah, the son of Maaseiah. The irony of vs. 22, which pronounces upon them, contains a very grim word-play: Ahab is the son of "Koliah"; he and his companions shall be a "curse" (qᵉlālāh) to their countrymen; because of their misdeeds Nebuchadrezzar shall "roast" them (qālām). Here again Jeremiah condemns them, not because of the specific follies they have committed, which clearly outraged the Babylonians, but because they were perverting the true word of the Lord.

[9] *Existence and Being*, pp. 278-79.
[1] St.-John Perse, *Exile and Other Poems* (tr. Denis Devlin; New York: Pantheon Books, 1949), p. 82.

32 Therefore thus saith the LORD; Behold, I will punish Shemaiah the Nehelamite, and his seed: he shall not have a man to dwell among this people; neither shall he behold the good that I will do for my people, saith the LORD; because he hath taught rebellion against the LORD.

30 The word that came to Jeremiah from the LORD, saying,
2 Thus speaketh the LORD God of Israel, saying, Write thee all the words that I have spoken unto thee in a book.

has made you trust in a lie, 32 therefore thus says the LORD: Behold, I will punish Shemai'ah of Nehel'am and his descendants; he shall not have any one living among this people to see[a] the good that I will do to my people, says the LORD, for he has talked rebellion against the LORD.' "

30 The word that came to Jeremiah from the LORD: 2 "Thus says the LORD, the God of Israel: Write in a book all

[a] Gk: Heb and he shall not see

XXI. The Book of Comfort (30:1–31:40)

These two chapters, which break into the prose narrative that began with ch. 26, constitute a miniature "book of comfort," giving glimpses into the future restoration of Israel and Judah. They were placed immediately after ch. 29 because that chapter itself deals in part with restoration (see 29:10-14). In its present form this collection of materials was made by an editor who lived after the time of Second Isaiah (whose influence is discernible especially in 30:10; 31:7-14), possibly as late as the time of Ezra and Nehemiah.

Chs. 30–31 have been the subject of the most varied interpretation by scholars, both as to their authenticity and as to their date. Rudolf Smend (*Lehrbuch der alttestamentlichen Religionsgeschichte* [2nd ed.; Freiburg i. B.: J. C. B. Mohr, 1899], pp. 249-51) rejected the whole, but most critical scholars have seen some genuine oracles of the prophet Jeremiah here. There is fairly general agreement on the authenticity of 31:2-6, 15-20 (or 15-22). The genuine oracles have been considered by some scholars (e.g., Cornill, Duhm, Peake, Rudolph) as having been uttered, as a whole or in large part, in the early period of Jeremiah's ministry under Josiah, but by others (e.g., Condamin, Skinner, Erbt) as having been spoken after the fall of Jerusalem.

Volz has sought to show that a large number of the oracles here were concerned with the restoration of the Northern Kingdom only, and that they were uttered by Jeremiah in the period between 594 and 588 B.C. He considers the following as genuine: 30:1-7, 10-15, 18-21a; 31:2-13, 15-22, 27b, 31-37. Rudolph's interpretation is very similar, but he dates the genuine oracles in the period between 621 and 609 B.C. While this is an attractive theory, it does not sufficiently take into account the influence of Second Isaiah on some of the oracles, and it requires us to consider certain references to Judah and Zion as glosses (e.g., 30:3-4, 17; 31:12, 31). Further, it is difficult to prove that Jeremiah had a special interest in the restoration of the Northern Kingdom; 3:6-11 is largely secondary (see Exeg., *ad loc.*). The references to the Northern Kingdom (or northern tribes) and places situated in the north are better explained by the theory that some of the oracles were spoken by Jeremiah during Gedaliah's governorship when the capital was at Mizpah, where the prophet himself may have been living (see especially Skinner, *Prophecy and Religion*, pp. 298-309). This dating is supported by the fact that the

---

Jeremiah was regarded as an impostor, **madman,** to be put **in the stocks and collar** (vs. 26). But Passhur was no longer priest in the temple. Shemaiah's protest was therefore left unheeded by Zephaniah the priest; and Jeremiah's pronouncement also falls on Shemaiah because **he** [also] **has talked rebellion against the LORD** (vs. 32).

30:1-24. *The Great Reversal.*—It is desirable now to dramatize as far as possible the difference between this present **book** (vs. 1) and the book of oracles previously prepared for Jehoiakim (see ch. 36). The earlier scroll has been called the "book of doom." This one has been called the "book of consolation" (Ewald), the "book of hope," the "book of comfort" (see

3 For, lo, the days come, saith the Lord, that I will bring again the captivity of my people Israel and Judah, saith the Lord: and I will cause them to return to the land that I gave to their fathers, and they shall possess it.

4 ¶ And these *are* the words that the Lord spake concerning Israel and concerning Judah.

5 For thus saith the Lord; We have heard a voice of trembling, of fear, and not of peace.

6 Ask ye now, and see whether a man doth travail with child? wherefore do I see every man with his hands on his loins, as a woman in travail, and all faces are turned into paleness?

7 Alas! for that day *is* great, so that none *is* like it: it *is* even the time of Jacob's trouble; but he shall be saved out of it.

8 For it shall come to pass in that day, saith the Lord of hosts, *that* I will break his yoke from off thy neck, and will burst thy bonds, and strangers shall no more serve themselves of him:

the words that I have spoken to you. 3 For behold, days are coming, says the Lord, when I will restore the fortunes of my people, Israel and Judah, says the Lord, and I will bring them back to the land which I gave to their fathers, and they shall take possession of it."

4 These are the words which the Lord spoke concerning Israel and Judah:

5 "Thus says the Lord:
    We have heard a cry of panic,
      of terror, and no peace.
6 Ask now, and see,
    can a man bear a child?
  Why then do I see every man
    with his hands on his loins like a
      woman in labor?
  Why has every face turned pale?
7 Alas! that day is so great
    there is none like it;
  it is a time of distress for Jacob;
    yet he shall be saved out of it.
8 "And it shall come to pass in that day, says the Lord of hosts, that I will break the yoke from off their[b] neck, and I will burst their[b] bonds, and strangers shall no more

[b] Gk Old Latin: Heb *your*

genuine oracles in chs. 30–31 were not included in the second collection of Jeremiah's prophecies, probably made by Baruch soon after the fall of Jerusalem in 587 b.c. (see Intro., pp. 787-88).

Within this "book of comfort" the following seem to be genuine oracles from Jeremiah: 30:5-7, 12-15; 31:2-6, 15-22, and possibly 31:9c.

A. Introduction (30:1-3)

30:1-3. These verses serve as an introduction to the two chapters which constitute the **book**, giving the theme as that of the restoration of Israel and Judah and the return of the people to their land. They come from the hand of the editor who made the collection of oracles.

B. Terror of the Day of Yahweh (30:4-9)

This section consists of a vivid poetic description of the terror of the day of Yahweh (**that day**) and a prose description of the coming salvation from the foreign yoke. It is possible that vss. 5-7 (with the exception of the last line which forms the transition to vss. 8-9) are from Jeremiah, probably only a fragment of a longer poem. The description

Exeg.), and "a hymn of praise" (Gillies). In his meditation on chs. 30–33, Charles E. Jefferson wrote of "Jeremiah as a prophet of hope. . . . All the artists have painted him with hopeless eyes, and the popular imagination has long pictured him as a man with a desponding heart. Few men have been so widely misunderstood." [2] He concedes that the book is a somber book;

[2] *Cardinal Ideas of Jeremiah*, p. 194.

but this is because it is "a long-drawn tragedy. A storm rages from the first page to the last, a storm more furious and more pitiless than the storm in King Lear." [3] It is out of this storm that Jeremiah wrests his proclamation of hope. The people have heard the **cry of panic** [and] **terror** (vs. 5); they shall one day join in hymns of praise (33:11). Their houses and dwellings

[3] *Ibid.*, p. 196.

9 But they shall serve the Lord their God, and David their king, whom I will raise up unto them.

10 ¶ Therefore fear thou not, O my servant Jacob, saith the Lord; neither be dismayed, O Israel: for, lo, I will save thee from afar, and thy seed from the land of their captivity; and Jacob shall return, and shall be in rest, and be quiet, and none shall make *him* afraid.

11 For I *am* with thee, saith the Lord, to save thee: though I make a full end of all nations whither I have scattered thee, yet will I not make a full end of thee; but I will correct thee in measure, and will not leave thee altogether unpunished.

make servants of them.[c] 9 But they shall serve the Lord their God and David their king, whom I will raise up for them.

10 "Then fear not, O Jacob my servant, says the Lord,
   nor be dismayed, O Israel;
for lo, I will save you from afar,
   and your offspring from the land of their captivity.
Jacob shall return and have quiet and ease,
   and none shall make him afraid.
11 For I am with you to save you,
               says the Lord;
I will make a full end of all the nations
   among whom I scattered you,
   but of you I will not make a full end.
I will chasten you in just measure,
   and I will by no means leave you unpunished.

[c] Heb *make a servant of him*

of the day of Yahweh is not unlike that in other pre-exilic prophets (cf. Amos 5:18-20; Isa. 2:12-21; Zeph. 1:14-18). The date may be during the final siege of Jerusalem. Vss. 8-9 are hardly from Jeremiah. They are prosaic and show strong dependence on other passages, particularly Isa. 10:27; Hos. 3:5; Ezek. 34:23. Vs. 8 has in mind the reversal of the condition depicted in 25:14; 27:1–28:16.

9. **David their king, whom I will raise up for them:** The promise is hardly that Yahweh will resurrect King David from the dead, but that he will raise up an ideal king of the line of David (cf. Hos. 3:5; Ezek. 34:23). Jeremiah himself placed little emphasis on the expectation of a Davidic Messiah (see Exeg. on 23:5-6).

C. The Salvation of Israel, Yahweh's Servant (30:10-11)

The promise of salvation to Israel is continued in this poem, but it has a different origin from vss. 8-9. It is not from Jeremiah, for vs. 10 shows strongly the influence of Second Isaiah, and vs. 11 is made up largely of lines taken from other parts of the book of Jeremiah. The verses are found with very slight change also in 46:27-28. They are omitted by the LXX here, but not from ch. 46. The present position, however, seems more appropriate for them; in ch. 46 they are an appendix to an oracle against Egypt.

10. The phraseology of this verse should be compared with Isa. 41:8-10, 13-14; 43:1, 5; 44:1-2. **Jacob my servant** is an especially characteristic expression and idea in Second Isaiah.

11. **For I am with you to save you:** Cf. 1:8, 19. **But of you I will not make a full end:** Cf. 4:27; 5:10, 18. Is the same editor responsible for all these passages, which indicate that Judah was not completely destroyed in 587 b.c.? **I will chasten you in just measure:** Cf. 10:24. **I will by no means leave you unpunished:** Cf. 25:29; 49:12.

have been destroyed; Yahweh will restore them. The city is burned; it shall be rebuilt. The stones of the palace have been strewn about the city; it **shall stand where it used to be** (vs. 18). For Jeremiah, argues Jefferson, "there is always light ahead!" [4]

[4] *Ibid.*, p. 199.

Jeremiah's principle, however, is deeper. It comes nearer to the N.T. realization that "all things are become new" (II Cor. 5:17). The reversal of fortunes which Jeremiah's drama reveals goes straight to the root of the human condition and proposes the deepest change. When all is apparently lost, and all of Jere-

12 For thus saith the LORD, Thy bruise *is* incurable, *and* thy wound *is* grievous.

13 *There is* none to plead thy cause, that thou mayest be bound up: thou hast no healing medicines.

14 All thy lovers have forgotten thee; they seek thee not; for I have wounded thee with the wound of an enemy, with the chastisement of a cruel one, for the multitude of thine iniquity; *because* thy sins were increased.

15 Why criest thou for thine affliction? thy sorrow *is* incurable for the multitude of thine iniquity: *because* thy sins were increased, I have done these things unto thee.

16 Therefore all they that devour thee shall be devoured; and all thine adversaries,

12 "For thus says the LORD:
Your hurt is incurable,
  and your wound is grievous.
13 There is none to uphold your cause,
  no medicine for your wound,
  no healing for you.
14 All your lovers have forgotten you;
  they care nothing for you;
for I have dealt you the blow of an enemy,
  the punishment of a merciless foe,
because your guilt is great,
  because your sins are flagrant.
15 Why do you cry out over your hurt?
  Your pain is incurable.
Because your guilt is great,
  because your sins are flagrant,
  I have done these things to you.
16 Therefore all who devour you shall be devoured,
  and all your foes, every one of them,
  shall go into captivity;

D. HEALING OF ZION'S WOUNDS (30:12-17)

The two parts of this poem do not fit well together. In the first part, vss. 12-15, it is said that Zion's wound or hurt is incurable, and that God has brought upon the city deserved punishment. But in the second part, vss. 16-17, Zion is promised health and healing, with punishment to be visited upon its enemies. The second part is joined to the first by **therefore,** but the connection is awkward and illogical. Duhm has suggested that vss. 12-15, being in the poetic meter which he believes was commonly used by Jeremiah and employing the prophet's ideas, are genuine, but vss. 16-17 are an addition by an editor. This opinion is probably correct. The date of vss. 12-15 may well be immediately after the fall of Jerusalem in 587 B.C. or shortly before, if the words are prediction rather than explanation of the fall of the city.

12. Your hurt is incurable: Jeremiah used similar language of his own sufferings in 15:18.

14. All your lovers have forgotten you: The reference is probably to the allies of the Hebrews, in this case the Egyptians, who had come to the aid of Jerusalem under siege but subsequently had to retire before the Babylonians (37:5; cf. especially 4:30; 13:21; 22:20, 22, and see Exeg. on 22:20).

---

miah's prophecies have literally been fulfilled, the message to the people takes on this different form.

Four characteristics of this reversal are indicated. The panic and terror and wholesale agony are described in the first poem (vss. 5-7). It is a day of calamity and world ordeal. There has been no day like it. Nevertheless, despite this "hour of anguish for Jacob" (Moffatt) the people shall yet be **saved.** In the second section (vss. 8-11) indication is given not only that they shall be saved but that they shall be saved **from afar.** Out of exile they shall return to their lands, and have **quiet and ease.** The third

unit (vss. 12-17) indicates that not only will they be saved from afar but they will also be saved *from within.* Their hurt incurable will be healed. And in the final section (vss. 18-22) —a unit superbly conceived—they will be saved *unto God.* We see here four forms of deliverance: deliverance from outer pain, deliverance from captivity, deliverance from themselves, and deliverance from their pseudo-faiths.

It is to be noted with care, however, that though deliverance is the corollary of this historical judgment, the judgment is also the corollary of forgiveness. The people are not exempt from the severity of this chastening.

every one of them, shall go into captivity; and they that spoil thee shall be a spoil, and all that prey upon thee will I give for a prey.

17 For I will restore health unto thee, and I will heal thee of thy wounds, saith the LORD; because they called thee an Outcast, *saying,* This *is* Zion, whom no man seeketh after.

18 ¶ Thus saith the LORD; Behold, I will bring again the captivity of Jacob's tents, and have mercy on his dwelling places; and the city shall be builded upon her own heap, and the palace shall remain after the manner thereof.

19 And out of them shall proceed thanksgiving and the voice of them that make merry: and I will multiply them, and they shall not be few; I will also glorify them, and they shall not be small.

those who despoil you shall become a
    spoil,
  and all who prey on you I will make a
    prey.
17 For I will restore health to you,
  and your wounds I will heal,
                says the LORD,
because they have called you an outcast:
  'It is Zion, for whom no one cares!'

18 "Thus says the LORD:
Behold, I will restore the fortunes of the
  tents of Jacob,
  and have compassion on his dwellings;
the city shall be rebuilt upon its mound,
  and the palace shall stand where it
  used to be.
19 Out of them shall come songs of thanksgiving,
  and the voices of those who make
  merry.
I will multiply them, and they shall not
  be few;
  I will make them honored, and they
  shall not be small.

E. RESTORATION OF THE FORTUNES OF JACOB (30:18-22)

This poem depicts the restoration of the land of the Israelites, the renewed joy of the people, and the establishment of an independent state with an Israelite ruler. Several elements suggest that it is from the pen of a later writer rather than from Jeremiah. Vs. 21*a* suggests prolonged experience with a foreign oppression which made the people desire a ruler of their own nation; and vs. 21*b* implies that this ruler will also be a priest. The word **congregation** ('*ēdhāh*) is a favorite word of the priestly writers (P). The emphasis on political restoration and priestly rule is not characteristic of the thought of Jeremiah. It seems best therefore to assign this poem to a writer later than Jeremiah.

18. The city and **the palace** are probably used here in a collective sense, meaning the cities and the palaces of the land. Or the reference may be to Jerusalem and her palace, or to Samaria and her palace.

I will by no means leave you unpunished (vs. 11). Similarly, there is no relaxing of the realism of the people's hurt. Not only is the wound grievous, but the people are without defense, and their **guilt is great** (vs. 15). It is precisely the experience and recognition of these extremities that open the way for their deliverance.

The vision of the new theocratic state drawn in vss. 18-22 is one of the remarkable projections of the social structure of a godly people in ancient literature. Not only are the physical features of the community restored, and songs of praise resounding with the people's happiness, but **their children shall be as they were of old**

—that is, shall be as they were when they were led by the hand of God. The people will have become, moreover, a congregation. It is out of this congregation that their rulers shall come, and shall be as one of themselves. These leaders, as the representatives of the people, shall themselves draw near to the sanctuary. There will be no need for priestly mediation, for the line between the civil and the ecclesiastical offices will have been broken away. The nation as a whole will have become a priestly nation, being sanctified from within their God relation. That this is a radical departure from their past is recognized in vs. 21, **for who would dare of himself to approach me?** When King Uzziah

20 Their children also shall be as afore-time, and their congregation shall be established before me, and I will punish all that oppress them.

21 And their nobles shall be of themselves, and their governor shall proceed from the midst of them; and I will cause him to draw near, and he shall approach unto me: for who *is* this that engaged his heart to approach unto me? saith the LORD.

22 And ye shall be my people, and I will be your God.

23 Behold, the whirlwind of the LORD goeth forth with fury, a continuing whirlwind: it shall fall with pain upon the head of the wicked.

24 The fierce anger of the LORD shall not return, until he have done *it,* and until he have performed the intents of his heart: in the latter days ye shall consider it.

20 Their children shall be as they were of
      old,
    and their congregation shall be established before me;
    and I will punish all who oppress them.
21 Their prince shall be one of themselves,
    their ruler shall come forth from their
      midst;
  I will make him draw near, and he shall
      approach me,
    for who would dare of himself to approach me?
                            says the LORD.
22 And you shall be my people,
    and I will be your God."

23 Behold the storm of the LORD!
    Wrath has gone forth,
  a whirling tempest;
    it will burst upon the head of the
      wicked.
24 The fierce anger of the LORD will not
      turn back
    until he has executed and accomplished
    the intents of his mind.
  In the latter days you will understand
      this.

20. **Their congregation:** The word *'ēdhāh* is used 115 times by the priestly writers, and occurs only very rarely in pre-exilic literature—I Kings 8:5; 12:20; and Hos. 7:12, where the text is obscure and should be emended (as in RSV).

21. By the use of the words **prince** (*'addîr;* see 14:3; 25:34-36) and **ruler** the writer consciously avoids the use of "king." Emphasis is placed on the fact that the new ruler is to be an Israelite, not a foreigner, but the passage is not messianic. The second half of the verse implies that the ruler should also be a priest, one who will approach God not rashly but only as God **will make him draw near.** Duhm thinks that the passage comes from the Maccabean period, when some of the rulers were also high priests. But the poem is hardly that late.

22. The verse is not in the LXX, and probably has been added under the influence of 31:1. The change of person is very awkward here (cf. 7:23; 11:4; 24:7; 31:33; 32:38).

F. The Storm of Yahweh (30:23–31:1)

The section 30:23-24 is to be found also in 23:19-20 (see Exeg., *ad loc.*). The editor of chs. 30–31 has taken over those verses and added to them 31:1, to give an eschatological tone to the predictions of restoration, a tone which is generally lacking in chs. 30–31.

presumed to invade the sanctuary it was at peril of his life. But now the peril is withdrawn, for **you shall be my people, and I will be your God.**

Jeremiah's "book of hope" is based, therefore, upon a sense of reversal as shattering and renewing as his own experience. He had himself moved into an aeon of deep catastrophe and change. His conversion of a people's "great refusal" into a recognition that at the depths of change there lies the secret of a "great reversal," and that this reversal takes place in the heart (but also between the heart of man and the heart of God), brings his vision near to the region of theophany from which new life and visions spring.

31 At the same time, saith the Lord, will I be the God of all the families of Israel, and they shall be my people.

2 Thus saith the Lord, The people *which were* left of the sword found grace in the wilderness; *even* Israel, when I went to cause him to rest.

3 The Lord hath appeared of old unto me, *saying*, Yea, I have loved thee with an everlasting love: therefore with loving-kindness have I drawn thee.

4 Again I will build thee, and thou shalt be built, O virgin of Israel: thou shalt again be adorned with thy tabrets, and shalt go forth in the dances of them that make merry.

31 "At that time, says the Lord, I will be the God of all the families of Israel, and they shall be my people."

2 Thus says the Lord:
"The people who survived the sword
    found grace in the wilderness;
when Israel sought for rest,
3   the Lord appeared to him[d] from afar.
I have loved you with an everlasting love;
    therefore I have continued my faithfulness to you.
4 Again I will build you, and you shall be built,
    O virgin Israel!
Again you shall adorn yourself with timbrels,
    and shall go forth in the dance of the merrymakers.

[d] Gk: Heb *me*

31:1. See Exeg. on 30:22.

G. Yahweh's Everlasting Love (31:2-6)

This is one of the poems in chs. 30–31 which most scholars agree must come from Jeremiah. It is one of the finest in the whole book, both in its beauty of expression and in its religious content. The date, however, is a matter of dispute. Many scholars (e.g., Duhm, Cornill, Peake, Rudolph) assign it to the earliest part of Jeremiah's ministry, and think it shows his special concern with the restoration of the Northern Kingdom. Others (e.g., Erbt, Skinner) assign it to the latest phase of Jeremiah's career in Palestine, during the governorship of Gedaliah. The references to **the mountains of Samaria** (vs. 5), and **the hill country of Ephraim** (vs. 6) indicate that the poem originated in the Northern Kingdom. These are just as appropriate to Gedaliah's governorship, when the capital was at Mizpah, as to the reign of Josiah; and the general tone of hope and cheerfulness seems more appropriate to the time of Gedaliah than to that of Josiah (if indeed Jeremiah was prophesying in the reign of that king; see Intro., p. 779.

2. Found grace in the wilderness: In the period of the wilderness wanderings, following the escape from the army of Pharaoh at the Red Sea.

3. The Lord appeared to him from afar: The reference is probably to the appearances on Mount Sinai. **I have loved you with an everlasting love:** Cf. 2:1-7. The word translated **faithfulness** is *ḥésedh,* frequently rendered in the RSV by "steadfast love" when it is used of Yahweh's attitude toward men. It is significant that *ḥésedh* is here in parallelism with **everlasting love.**

4. O virgin Israel: Israel is personified as a virgin; the reference is to the whole nation, not just to the Northern Kingdom (cf. Amos 5:2). The second half of this verse

31:1-6. *The Vocation of the Poet.*—The deeply searching poems of this great chapter are about a homecoming, built around the Jeremianic symbols of return. Recapitulated here are Jeremiah's essential themes, recollected partially, perhaps, in the comparative tranquillity of Ramah and Mizpah, when he had joined himself to Gedaliah; but recollected also by the ever-deepening gyre of suffering, now turning from the vortex of pity and fear to the rising axis of the eternal promises. This means that, throughout these verses, the symbols of the exile and return are happily ambiguous. Skinner can say, "We observe, then, throughout the series a fixed expectation of a return of exiled Israelites";[5] whereas Micklem can say, "On the contrary, we seem to have come to a point of very considerable uncertainty and doubt as to whether the prophet has really a

[5] *Prophecy and Religion,* p. 306.

5 Thou shalt yet plant vines upon the mountains of Samaria: the planters shall plant, and shall eat *them* as common things.

6 For there shall be a day, *that* the watchmen upon the mount Ephraim shall cry, Arise ye, and let us go up to Zion unto the Lord our God.

7 For thus saith the Lord; Sing with gladness for Jacob, and shout among the

5 Again you shall plant vineyards
  upon the mountains of Samar'ia;
the planters shall plant,
  and shall enjoy the fruit.
6 For there shall be a day when watchmen
    will call
  in the hill country of E'phraim:
'Arise, and let us go up to Zion,
  to the Lord our God.' "

7 For thus says the Lord:
"Sing aloud with gladness for Jacob,
  and raise shouts for the chief of the
    nations;

---

and vs. 5 show that Jeremiah was not always gloomy, and that he was not opposed to merriment as such (cf. 16:1-9).

6. Cornill believed that this verse was not suitable to Jeremiah, who condemned the temple worship (7:1-15; 26:1-6) and emphasized the inwardness of true religion. But the verse does not say that Yahweh can be found only in the Jerusalem temple, and possibly Jeremiah would not have opposed a purified temple worship by a regenerate people. Yet Cornill's objection is weighty, and the verse may be an addition to the original poem (vss. 2-5). In 41:5 there is an account of eighty men who came from northern towns to present offerings in the Jerusalem temple during Gedaliah's rule (see Exeg.).

H. Return of the Exiles from All Nations (31:7-14)

This section predicts the immediate return of the people from the many lands to which they have been exiled. The close similarity to the ideas and phrases of Second Isaiah, the concern with return from the whole Diaspora, and the presence of ideas foreign to Jeremiah, all indicate that it is later than Jeremiah, from a writer who lived in the early postexilic age. Only vs. 9c can be considered as Jeremianic; vs. 14 is so foreign to the prophet's thought that even Volz and Rudolph, who consider vss. 7-13 as genuine, deny its authenticity.

7. For the chief of the nations: We should adopt the suggestion of Duhm and emend הגוים to הרים, and read "on the top of the mountains" (cf. Isa. 42:11). **The Lord has saved his people:** This is the reading of the LXX, Targ., and one Babylonian Hebrew MS (Eb 10).

---

word to say about a literal return from exile." [6] They are happily ambiguous, because such ambiguity is the very breath of life of poetry; and because we are thereby released into the poet-prophet's larger meaning. There is exile and captivity and longing for return in the outer world, whence thousands from the Northern and the Southern Kingdoms had been carried; there is exile and captivity and longing for return in the breast of every man, whether in those who were carried away or in those who are left behind.

The initial verses, therefore, resume Jeremiah's first proclamation (2:2)—its metaphor of the journey, its covenant sign, its picture of the ideal piety in the wilderness when the people were as a faithful bride to Yahweh. The

[6] *Prophecy and Eschatology*, p. 187.

Hosean starting-point is evident. It acquires new meaning in Jeremiah, where vs. 3 (cf. Hos. 11:1-14) may be translated

With a love everlasting I love thee;
Therefore with kindness I draw thee.

This is the one stability in a broken world. It is because of this, and this alone, that Israel shall again be built. The compounding of the metaphors of marriage and the journey gives the soul's infidelity a double meaning—we wander from the ways which are true; we are unfaithful to the love that is true. By the former we are lost in far countries; by the latter we corrupt the core of every relationship.

7-14. *The Proximity to the Source.*—In the light of the foregoing the intrusion of the Deutero-Isaianic passages is not amiss here.

chief of the nations: publish ye, praise ye, and say, O LORD, save thy people, the remnant of Israel.

8 Behold, I will bring them from the north country, and gather them from the coasts of the earth, *and* with them the blind and the lame, the woman with child and her that travaileth with child together: a great company shall return thither.

9 They shall come with weeping, and with supplications will I lead them: I will cause them to walk by the rivers of waters in a straight way, wherein they shall not stumble: for I am a father to Israel, and Ephraim *is* my firstborn.

10 ¶ Hear the word of the LORD, O ye nations, and declare *it* in the isles afar off, and say, He that scattered Israel will gather him, and keep him, as a shepherd *doth* his flock.

11 For the LORD hath redeemed Jacob, and ransomed him from the hand of *him that was* stronger than he.

proclaim, give praise, and say,
'The LORD has saved his people,
   the remnant of Israel.'

8 Behold, I will bring them from the north country,
   and gather them from the farthest parts of the earth,
among them the blind and the lame,
   the woman with child and her who is in travail, together;
a great company, they shall return here.
9 With weeping they shall come,
   and with consolations[e] I will lead them back,
I will make them walk by brooks of water,
   in a straight path in which they shall not stumble;
for I am a father to Israel,
   and E'phraim is my first-born.

10 "Hear the word of the LORD, O nations,
   and declare it in the coastlands afar off;
say, 'He who scattered Israel will gather him,
   and will keep him as a shepherd keeps his flock.'
11 For the LORD has ransomed Jacob,
   and has redeemed him from hands too strong for him.

e Gk Compare Vg Tg: Heb *supplications*

8-9. On the general thought of these verses, the return of the Jews from all the lands of the Dispersion, cf. Isa. 35:5-6; 40:11; 42:16; 43:6. **Walk by brooks of water:** Cf. Isa. 41:18; 43:20; 48:21; 49:10. **In a straight path:** Cf. Isa. 35:8-10; 40:4; 42:16; 45:2.

I am a father to Israel, and Ephraim is my firstborn may be from Jeremiah (cf. vs. 20; 3:19). It is unlikely that a postexilic writer would have considered Ephraim rather than Judah as the **firstborn**. Peake has suggested that the most appropriate place for these lines is after vs. 20.

10. The coastlands: A favorite word of Second Isaiah (cf. 41:1; 42:10; 49:1). **Will keep him as a shepherd keeps his flock:** Cf. Isa. 40:11.

11. Cf. Isa. 44:23; 48:20. Second Isaiah frequently uses the words "ransom" and "redeem" in the sense which they have here, i.e., the return of the Jews from the lands of the Dispersion to their homeland, which is to be rebuilt. **Hands too strong for him:** Cf. Isa. 49:24-25.

What is Deutero-Isaiah, if not the expanded hope of the prophet-soul in whom the fire of the Lord made pure the covenant-vision?

But the home, as Hölderlin knew, is difficult to win. Perhaps, indeed, it must be lost before one can know the "hallowed gateway" of return. Then may come the moment when "the valleys amicably open" and the paths are luminous and all is familiar. "To be sure! It is the native land. . . ." Suddenly the poet sees that

"That which thou seekest is near, and already coming to meet thee." [7] This is the return into the straight paths (vs. 9), by "streams of water" (Moffatt) into the realms of song and radiance (vs. 12), where their lives are like "a saturated garden," [8] and their mourning is turned into joy (vs. 13). Always we are very near to this: we are almost led by compassion (vs. 9). For

[7] Hölderlin, *Heimkunft*, IV, 2.
[8] Peake, *Jeremiah and Lamentations*, II, 90.

12 Therefore they shall come and sing in the height of Zion, and shall flow together to the goodness of the Lord, for wheat, and for wine, and for oil, and for the young of the flock and of the herd: and their soul shall be as a watered garden; and they shall not sorrow any more at all.

13 Then shall the virgin rejoice in the dance, both young men and old together: for I will turn their mourning into joy, and will comfort them, and make them rejoice from their sorrow.

14 And I will satiate the soul of the priests with fatness, and my people shall be satisfied with my goodness, saith the Lord.

15 ¶ Thus saith the Lord; A voice was

12 They shall come and sing aloud on the height of Zion,
  and they shall be radiant over the goodness of the Lord,
over the grain, the wine, and the oil,
  and over the young of the flock and the herd;
their life shall be like a watered garden,
  and they shall languish no more.
13 Then shall the maidens rejoice in the dance,
  and the young men and the old shall be merry.
I will turn their mourning into joy,
  I will comfort them, and give them gladness for sorrow.
14 I will feast the soul of the priests with abundance,
  and my people shall be satisfied with my goodness,
                        says the Lord."

15 Thus says the Lord:
"A voice is heard in Ramah,
  lamentation and bitter weeping.
Rachel is weeping for her children;

---

12. The goodness of the Lord is primarily the material things which God supplies, such as those mentioned in the following lines. **Like a watered garden:** The figure is probably derived from Isa. 58:11. It is especially appropriate to a land such as Palestine, where the rainfall is limited and often uncertain.

14. I will feast the soul of the priests with abundance: These words hardly come from Jeremiah, who often was in conflict with the priests of his day. The meaning is that the priests will have plenty to eat because sacrifices will be abundant in the new age.

J. Rachel's Weeping and the Return of Her Children (31:15-22)

Rachel, the mother of Joseph and Benjamin and hence the ancestress of the northern tribes, is here represented as weeping over the loss of her children, i.e., over the exile of the northern tribes. The prophet comforts her with the promise that after their repentance they will be returned and restored to their land.

This section (or at least vss. 15-20) is believed by most scholars to be from Jeremiah; it is comparable in its poetic beauty and religious depth to vss. 2-6. The date is the same as that of vss. 2-6, most likely the period of the governorship of Gedaliah. The exile of the northern tribes is either that of 721 b.c. or that of 587 b.c., or it may indeed include both.

15. Ramah is the modern er-Râm, about five miles north of Jerusalem. According to Gen. 35:16-20; 48:7, at the birth of Benjamin Rachel died and was buried on the way from Bethel to Ephrath. I Sam. 10:2 indicates clearly that Rachel's sepulcher was in

---

"homecoming really consists solely in the people of the country becoming at home in the still-withheld essence of home." [9] "Build houses . . . ; plant gardens . . . ; take wives. . . . You will seek me and find me; when you seek me with all your heart." (29:5-6, 13.)

[9] Heidegger, *Existence and Being*, p. 264.

15-22. The Secret Weeping (II).—A voice is heard in Ramah . . . weeping. This is the deepest secret. Though the home is nigh, we are somehow far from it. Our lives are not fed by the spirit "like a saturated garden." Our faces are not radiant with the glow of the Lord's goodness. Between us is the desert of

heard in Ramah, lamentation, *and* bitter weeping; Rachel weeping for her children refused to be comforted for her children, because they *were* not.

16 Thus saith the Lord; Refrain thy voice from weeping, and thine eyes from tears: for thy work shall be rewarded, saith the Lord; and they shall come again from the land of the enemy.

17 And there is hope in thine end, saith the Lord, that thy children shall come again to their own border.

18 ¶ I have surely heard Ephraim bemoaning himself *thus;* Thou hast chastised me, and I was chastised, as a bullock unaccustomed *to the yoke:* turn thou me, and I shall be turned; for thou *art* the Lord my God.

she refuses to be comforted for her
  children,
because they are not."

16 Thus says the Lord:
"Keep your voice from weeping,
  and your eyes from tears;
for your work shall be rewarded,
              says the Lord,
  and they shall come back from the land
    of the enemy.
17 There is hope for your future,
              says the Lord,
  and your children shall come back to
    their own country.
18 I have heard E'phraim bemoaning,
'Thou hast chastened me, and I was
    chastened,
  like an untrained calf;
bring me back that I may be restored,
  for thou art the Lord my God.

---

the territory of Benjamin. Ephrath must have been north of Jerusalem, and not identical with Bethlehem, as the gloss in Gen. 35:19; 48:7 indicates (probably confusing it with Ephrathah of Ruth 4:11; Mic. 5:2). Since early Christian times, however, the tomb of Rachel has been located on the road between Jerusalem and Bethlehem, about a mile north of the latter. The identification is based on the gloss just mentioned and Matt. 2:18. **Rachel is weeping for her children:** Following popular belief, the prophet may have thought of Rachel's spirit as returning to her grave and weeping over the loss of her children; on the other hand, he may only be using a poetic figure to represent the nation's sorrow over the exiling of the northern tribes.

18. Bring me back that I may be restored: The Hebrew is, lit., "cause me to return [or turn] in order that I may return." If the word "return" is used in the sense of

---

exile. Within us is the abyss of emptiness. We taste at our lips the cup of God's fury which the errant nations are drinking.

A voice is heard in Ramah . . . weeping. This is the bitterest secret. For the weeping is bitter. **Rachel is weeping for her children.** She refuses, like Jacob, to be consoled. The blood-stained cloak of Joseph is brought by the envious nations to show that he is dead. But this is not so. He has only been sold as captive into Egypt. Now comes the second captivity into Babylon. The spirit of Rachel by the ancient grave near Bethel, and Ephrath, in the land of Ephraim, wails and will not be consoled.

> The Babylonian starlight brought
> A fabulous, formless darkness in.[10]

When a thing happens that is contrary to the promises of God it cannot permanently succeed.

It may run its course; but its course is ever farther and farther into the contradiction. But this brings folly and destruction and waste, and struggle and suffering and guilt. It brings also great sorrow to the heart of God. This is the consoling secret. The voice heard weeping in Ramah is the voice of the heart of God who, like Rachel, is not consoled for the loss of the tribes. Rachel becomes a type of Yahweh, weeping for his children.[1] Therefore his promise: **they shall come back.** He opens a way of return.

18-22. The Prodigal Ephraim.—"Vers. 18-20," writes Micklem, "are a poem almost built on the idea of 'return,' but it does not necessarily, or even probably, refer to a literal return."[2] (Yet see Exeg.) The secret is found in the double paradox of the poem. For here,

---

[10] William Butler Yeats, "Two Songs from a Play," from *Collected Poems.* Copyright 1940 by Bertha Georgie Yeats. Used by permission of The Macmillan Co., publishers.

[1] Cf. Matt. 2:17-18 and Chrysostom, *Homilies on Matthew, ad loc.*
[2] *Op. cit.,* p. 186.

19 Surely after that I was turned, I repented; and after that I was instructed, I
smote upon *my* thigh: I was ashamed, yea,
even confounded, because I did bear the
reproach of my youth.

20 *Is* Ephraim my dear son? *is he* a pleasant child? for since I spake against him, I
do earnestly remember him still: therefore
my bowels are troubled for him; I will
surely have mercy upon him, saith the
Lord.

21 Set thee up waymarks, make thee high

---

19 For after I had turned away I repented;
     and after I was instructed, I smote
       upon my thigh;
I was ashamed, and I was confounded,
     because I bore the disgrace of my
       youth.'
20 Is E'phraim my dear son?
     Is he my darling child?
For as often as I speak against him,
     I do remember him still.
Therefore my heart yearns for him;
     I will surely have mercy on him,
                              says the Lord.

21 "Set up waymarks for yourself,
     make yourself guideposts;

"repent," the prayer here uttered emphasizes the divine initiative in repentance: God
must initiate the repentance by which men return to him. But vs. 19 seems to imply that
the repentance has already taken place; hence the word "return" probably means in this
place return from exile.

19. This verse shows the emphasis which the prophet placed upon repentance as
a prerequisite for the restoration of the people. Vss. 18-19 are best interpreted as expressing
the ideal repentance which the people must make before they can be restored, not the
actual condition of the Ephraimites (cf. 3:22*b*-25; Hos. 6:1-3; 14:2-3, for examples of
"liturgies of repentance" placed in the mouth of the penitent people).

After I was instructed is perhaps better read, "after I was made submissive," taking
the Hebrew root ידע in the sense of the cognate Arabic, "to become quiet," "submissive"
(cf. D. Winton Thomas, "The Root ידע in Hebrew," *Journal of Theological Studies,*
XXXV [1934], 304). This fits the parallelism with the preceding line. **I smote upon my
thigh:** An action designed to express extreme grief (cf. Ezek. 21:12).

21-22. These words are probably spoken by the prophet rather than by Yahweh.
He admonishes **virgin Israel** (cf. vs. 4) to give careful attention to the road by which

---

at the peak of O.T. prophecy, is unfolded the
dialectic of the prodigal son.

The son is Ephraim. He is in a far country,
whether in Babylon or in Ephraim. He has
been carried captive, whether by the invading
powers or by the dialectic of inner rebellion,

> out into the much-promising distance,
> There, where wonders are, there, where the divine
> quarry runs.[3]

Behind the externality of capture lie the inner
betrayal, rebellion, and flight. Which Ephraim
knows! "Cause me to turn . . . that I may return!" is the initial paradox (cf. Exeg. on vs. 18).
Chastened (vs. 18) and **ashamed** (vs. 19) by
the disgrace of [his] **youth,** he cries out, **bring
me back that I may be restored.** Ephraim's
prayer is as deep as Thompson's "Hound of
Heaven," "All things betray thee, who betrayest Me."

[3] Hölderlin, *Heimkunft,* IV.

We should have to combine all three—
Hölderlin, the "Hound of Heaven," and the
prodigal son—together with Jeremiah's own
fondness for the northern tribes, to reach the
pathos of the second paradox.

> **For as often as I speak against him,
> I do remember him still** (vs. 20).

For here again it is the God whose **heart yearns
for him,** whose forgiveness is eager, whom Jeremiah knows. The Yahweh who chastens is instructing us into his mercies:

> Ah, fondest, blindest, weakest,
> I am He Whom thou seekest!
> Thou dravest love from thee, who dravest Me.[4]

Therefore, **set up waymarks for yourself,**
whithersoever you have wandered or have been

[4] Francis Thompson, "The Hound of Heaven," from
Collected Works, ed. Wilfred Meynell. Used by permis-
sion of the publisher, Burns Oates & Washbourne,
London.

heaps: set thine heart toward the highway, *even* the way *which* thou wentest: turn again, O virgin of Israel, turn again to these thy cities.

22 ¶ How long wilt thou go about, O thou backsliding daughter? for the LORD hath created a new thing in the earth, A woman shall compass a man.

23 Thus saith the LORD of hosts, the God

consider well the highway,
    the road by which you went.
Return, O virgin Israel,
    return to these your cities.
22 How long will you waver,
    O faithless daughter?
For the LORD has created a new thing on
    the earth:
    a woman protects a man."

23 Thus says the LORD of hosts, the God of Israel: "Once more they shall use these

---

she goes into exile, in order that she may return. The first two lines are difficult to interpret literally, for it is unlikely that the exiles themselves could **set up waymarks** and **guideposts.** Perhaps the lines are to be given a figurative interpretation: the exiles should remember the difficulties of the road to exile, that they may have the greater ambition to repent and return.

The second half of vs. 22 is one of the most difficult sentences in the whole of the book of Jeremiah to understand; it has given rise to the most varied interpretations. The difficulty comes in part from the translation of the verb *teṣōbhēbh,* rendered by the RSV as **protects** and by the KJV as **shall compass.** Further difficulty arises from the question whether **woman** and **man** are to be taken in a generic sense, or whether they refer figuratively to Israel and Yahweh.

If the translation of the RSV is correct, the best interpretation is that in the future the land will become so peaceful that a woman will not need protection, but indeed will be able to protect a man. In that case, however, one might ask: If a woman does not need protection in the era of peace, why does the man?

The verb **compass** (the literal meaning of the Hebrew) has been taken by some interpreters as implying that the usual relationship is reversed, so that the woman embraces the man, or even "the woman woos the man" (Amer. Trans.). If this is correct, it should be taken as applying to Israel's relationship to Yahweh, as suggested by the immediate context.

In view of the difficulty of interpretation, several scholars have proposed emending the verb. Duhm suggests *tiṣṣōbh,* and translates, "the woman is turned into a man." He interprets the sentence as the witty gloss of a reader who here points out that Israel, who had earlier been referred to as a man, is now referred to as a woman. This reader was an early critic of the poetry! Another suggestion is that Israel, who has been a timid, weak woman, is now to become a strong, resolute man.

Condamin has suggested emending the last two words to *tāshûbh leghébher,* and translating, "the woman returns to the man." This would be interpreted, in the light of 3:1, as describing the return of the virgin Israel to Yahweh, and is perhaps the best interpretation that can be given.

K. RESTORATION OF THE LAND OF JUDAH (31:23-26)

As the preceding section was concerned with the restoration of Ephraim, so vss. 23-25 predict the restoration of the land of Judah. It is unlikely that this section is from Jeremiah, for he would hardly have used the words **habitation of righteousness** and

---

driven: mark **well the highway, the road by which you went,** and learn from God to

    stand by the roads, and look,
    .   .   .   .
    where the good way is; and walk in it,
    and find rest for your souls **(6:16).**

23-30. *I Wake Through My Word to Perform It.*—So far Ephraim. But what of Judah? Do we not all yearn for the homeland? Is there not in every soul the hunger for specific soil? How universal is the word of John of Gaunt, when he extols

of Israel, As yet they shall use this speech in the land of Judah and in the cities thereof, when I shall bring again their captivity; The LORD bless thee, O habitation of justice, *and* mountain of holiness.

24 And there shall dwell in Judah itself, and in all the cities thereof together, husbandmen, and they *that* go forth with flocks.

25 For I have satiated the weary soul, and I have replenished every sorrowful soul.

26 Upon this I awaked, and beheld; and my sleep was sweet unto me.

words in the land of Judah and in its cities, when I restore their fortunes:

'The LORD bless you, O habitation of righteousness,
O holy hill!'

24 And Judah and all its cities shall dwell there together, and the farmers and those who wander*f* with their flocks. 25 For I will satisfy the weary soul, and every languishing soul I will replenish."

26 Thereupon I awoke and looked, and my sleep was pleasant to me.

f Cn Compare Syr Vg Tg: Heb *and they shall wander*

---

holy hill in referring to Judah and to the temple hill in Jerusalem (cf. 17:12, which is also secondary). The verses are from a Judean writer who was interested in the restoration of the land of Judah, not only of its cities but also of its farmers and shepherds.

26. Thereupon I awoke and looked, and my sleep was pleasant to me: The words are very puzzling. The speaker is not the people or Yahweh, but the prophet himself or some editor or glossator. The Targ. prefixes the words "The prophet said." Duhm thinks that the verse marks the end of the book which began with 30:4; he interprets vs. 26 as the remark of the same reader who wrote vs. 22*b*. It has in it good-natured mockery, with a little skepticism. Cornill interprets it as the sigh of a reader, its original place being after vs. 22. Volz considers it as a marginal gloss by one who had received comfort from what he read in the preceding verses, and compares Ps. 126:1. Others have thought it was written by an editor who wished to indicate that the preceding oracles had been received in a dream. In any case, the verse is hardly from Jeremiah, who did

---

> This happy breed of men, this little world,
> This precious stone set in the silver sea,
> .   .   .   .
> This blessed plot, this earth, this realm, this England.[5]

To understand the power and the yearning in these lines concerning the land of Judah, we must multiply this consciousness immeasurably. For Judah's land was the gift of God! Yahweh, taking them by the hand, as little children, had brought them into it. There they should dwell together. But when the breach of faithfulness came, the hill was no longer holy, and righteousness as their habitation was no more.

Now comes the important turn. Yahweh's love for Ephraim has been movingly expressed. Yahweh's love for Judah has been revealed by the prophet from the beginning, though in its first movement it took necessarily a negative form. Jeremiah was set over the nations

> to pluck up and to break down,
> to destroy and to overthrow,
> to build and to plant (1:10).

Now at the end of his work, Jeremiah reverses—on behalf of the Lord's promises—the commission's emphasis. As the Lord had been wakeful over his word through Jeremiah **to pluck up**

[5] Shakespeare, *King Richard II*, Act II, scene 1.

and break down, so now he **will watch over them to build and to plant.**

Seldom does a man in his lifetime succeed, as Jeremiah does, in uniting the end of his work with its beginning; but here, in this oracle, this is achieved. But it is achieved in principle, and with one radical ethical change. The return is by way of individual renewal, in which each of himself undertakes the choice absolutely before God. This is the first essential in any depth change in the personality. Regardless of how the critical debate as to editorship and composition of the book turns out, Jeremiah's entire prophecy is missed if it is not seen that this personalization of the God-relationship is implicit in his work from the beginning. To be sure, vs. 30 must not be read or understood in a "moralistic" sense. Nor should it be read within the context of an Adamic theology, with which Jeremiah's teaching has nothing to do. The "corporate personality" thesis is also broken through in the spiritualization of images which is the climax of Jeremiah's maturest prophecies. **Each man** must assume responsibility for his action: which is to say, for his freedom. He is not to blame his fathers, nor anyone else, nor anything. And he must assume it absolutely, at the realistic limits of the human conditions, and at the depth implication of his

27 ¶ Behold, the days come, saith the LORD, that I will sow the house of Israel and the house of Judah with the seed of man, and with the seed of beast.	27 "Behold, the days are coming, says the LORD, when I will sow the house of Israel and the house of Judah with the seed of man and the seed of beast. 28 And it shall come to pass that as I have watched over them to pluck up and break down, to overthrow, destroy, and bring evil, so I will watch over them to build and to plant, says the LORD. 29 In those days they shall no longer say:
28 And it shall come to pass, *that* like as I have watched over them, to pluck up, and to break down, and to throw down, and to destroy, and to afflict; so will I watch over them, to build, and to plant, saith the LORD.	
29 In those days they shall say no more, The fathers have eaten a sour grape, and the children's teeth are set on edge.	'The fathers have eaten sour grapes, and the children's teeth are set on edge.'
30 But every one shall die for his own iniquity: every man that eateth the sour grape, his teeth shall be set on edge.	30 But every one shall die for his own sin; each man who eats sour grapes, his teeth shall be set on edge.

not value dreams highly (see 23:25-28). It is probably from a scribe who wrote the verse in a margin to indicate that he found a great gulf between the words he was reading and the reality he saw about him. Duhm's theory that it marks the end of the book, beginning in 30:4, is not convincing, since the collection of oracles extends through ch. 31.

L. REPOPULATION OF ISRAEL AND JUDAH (31:27-28)

These verses come from a time, after the fall of Jerusalem in 587 B.C., when the population of Judah and Israel was sparse. They predict that the land will be repeopled and the nation will be built up. On the repopulation of the land cf. Ezek. 36:9-11; Hos. 1:10; 2:23; on the union of Israel and Judah cf. 3:18; 50:4; Isa. 11:11-14; Ezek. 37:15-24; Hos. 1:11.

28. This verse is modeled after 1:10 (cf. 18:7, 9; 24:6). The terminology is characteristic of the Deuteronomic editor, but he is not necessarily responsible for the passage.

M. INDIVIDUAL RETRIBUTION (31:29-30)

29-30. The popular proverb quoted here is also quoted in Ezek. 18:2, and its spirit is found in Lam. 5:7. Ezekiel sought to disprove the truth of the proverb completely (see Ezek. 14:13-20; 18:1-32). Here it seems to be assumed that the proverb applies to the present situation, but will not apply **in those days,** i.e., in the future which is predicted in the context. The saying expresses vividly the ancient Hebrew belief in collective responsibility and retribution, and must have been widely used as an explanation of the tragedy of the Babylonian exile. It is not probable that vss. 29-30 are from Jeremiah. They presuppose the discussion by Ezekiel. Jeremiah himself usually held to the doctrine of collective responsibility and it is not likely that he would have made such a great distinction between the present and the future. This passage, furthermore, conflicts with the hope for the future expressed in vs. 34.

"ultimate concern" (Tillich). For, as Judah has been brought to the crisis of its destiny, its historical meanings through which it has interpreted itself have reached a crisis—"a crisis of images," as Austin Farrer splendidly describes it.[6]

This means that Jeremiah was the prophet of a new religious consciousness. "The appearance of a new religion, and the trans-

formation of basic images, are not simply connected things: they are one and the same thing."[7] It was this, at bottom, and not his "sensitivity of temperament" that caused him (as also Job) his inner agony; but it was this also which brought him to the greatest turning point in Hebrew religion—the proclamation of a new covenant, "the gospel before Christ."[8]

[6] *The Glass of Vision* (Westminster: Dacre Press, 1948), p. 134.

[7] *Ibid.*

[8] See T. K. Cheyne, "Jeremiah," *Encyclopaedia Britannica* (9th ed.), XIII, 627.

31 ¶ Behold, the days come, saith the LORD, that I will make a new covenant with the house of Israel, and with the house of Judah:	31 "Behold, the days are coming, says the LORD, when I will make a new covenant with the house of Israel and the house of

N. THE NEW COVENANT (31:31-34)

This passage presents the most important single teaching of Jeremiah, where his religious thought reaches its climax. It is one of the mountain peaks of the O.T. and came to have great importance in the N.T. It is quoted in full in Heb. 8:8-12, and in part in Heb. 10:16-17. It lies behind the words used at the Last Supper: "This cup is the new covenant in my blood" (I Cor. 11:25; cf. Luke 22:20). It is referred to in other N.T. passages, and is responsible for the distinction which was eventually made between "The Old Testament" and "The New Testament." Such a distinction between the two covenants, or testaments, was adumbrated in II Cor. 3:5-14, and was in general use in the church by the end of the second century A.D.

A few scholars have denied that this great passage originated with Jeremiah. The most vigorous opponent of its authenticity was Duhm. He declared with reluctance that he could "find in it only the effusion of a scribe who holds as the highest ideal that everyone among the Jewish people shall know by heart and understand the Law, that all Jews shall be scribes" (*Das Buch Jeremia*, p. 255). He complained that it did not promise a new law, and did not advance a new conception of religion. It did not promise for the individual any more than Deuteronomy had already considered desirable and possible (Deut. 6:6-8; 30:11 ff.). Duhm described the style of the passage as poor, drawling, and imprecise.

Few scholars have followed him in his low estimate of the new covenant passage and his theory that it is postexilic in origin. Refutations of this view were made by C. H. Cornill (*Das Buch Jeremia* [Leipzig: B. Tauchnitz, 1905]) and W. J. Moulton ("The New Covenant in Jeremiah," *The Expositor*, Ser. 7, I [1906], 370-82).

The new covenant does not involve the giving of a new law; that is unnecessary. For Jeremiah the first covenant was the covenant made at Sinai, and the law was the moral law, perhaps primarily the ethical decalogue, certainly not the ceremonial prescriptions (see especially 6:16-21; 7:5-10, 22-23; 26:4-6; cf. Hyatt, "Torah in the Book

---

31-34. The Gospel Before the Gospel.— Isaiah indicates the need for eyes and ears in man, if God's wonders are to be known:

Behold, I am doing a new thing;
  [Even] now it springs forth, do you not perceive it? (Isa. 43:19.)

Or, as Moffatt translates it, "have you no eyes for it?" But the new thing springing to light in the time of Second Isaiah had its origin in the struggle of Jeremiah. The images of "return" are not a return to that which has been; they are a return to the Source of that which has been. The path to the new covenant must be seen if the covenant itself is to be seen in its radical newness. As there are three provisions in the new covenant, so there are three steps leading to it, which we may note briefly.

The first is often a desperate move, for it is the way to the deeper homecoming: that is, to the Source. It means that the old gods die, and their forms, and their doctrines. God is not bound by our definitions: for these arise within the contexts of our limited insights—insights based upon the finite prejudice of our partial experience, and the temptation we are under to universalize the insight and bind it upon God as the measure of his infinite mystery. Before Job saw (Job 42:5), it was this presumption that had to be dwarfed by the grandeur of God. But between the god that is passing and the God that is coming there is a moment of terror, when the man to whom the "new thing" is discovered stands alone before God. Jeremiah knew this. It is the moment of "God's failure." And what is terrible is that "without fear of the appearance of godlessness he must remain near the failure of the god, and wait long enough in the prepared proximity of the failure, until out of the proximity of the failing god the initial word is granted, which names the High One." [9] For Jeremiah the word held a double image—the caldron of failure and the branch of the budding promise. And the first provision of the new covenant is that it

[9] Heidegger, *Existence and Being*, pp. 285-86.

32 Not according to the covenant that I made with their fathers, in the day *that* I took them by the hand to bring them out of the land of Egypt; which my covenant they brake, although I was a husband unto them, saith the LORD:

Judah, **32** not like the covenant which I made with their fathers when I took them by the hand to bring them out of the land of Egypt, my covenant which they broke, though I was their husband, says the LORD.

---

of Jeremiah," pp. 381-96). The covenant is to be new in the sense that it will confer a new, inward motivation and power for fulfilling the law already known. The promised forgiveness of sin and the knowledge of Yahweh will give to men a new incentive for obeying Yahweh and his law.

Note also that while the new covenant is to be with the nation—Jeremiah does not wholly overcome the old sense of national solidarity—it yet carries weighty implications for personal religion, since the law must be written upon the hearts of individual men.

It is entirely possible that the wording of vss. 31-34 is not Jeremiah's. The style is more prolix than his, and in some places is a bit awkward, especially in vs. 32. Nevertheless the thought is essentially his. We cannot now identify with precision the disciple or editor who may be responsible for the present form. He may have been Baruch. He probably was not the Deuteronomic editor, in spite of the presence of some Deuteronomic phrases. Had that editor been responsible for the new covenant passage, or for other considerable portions of chs. 30–31, his style and phraseology would be prominent and unmistakable.

The idea of a covenant was basic to Hebrew religion. For discussions of this idea and its history see Vol. I, pp. 299-300, 354-57.

31. Behold, the days are coming is an eschatological formula. The new covenant is an eschatological promise. It is possible that the phrase **and the house of Judah** is an insertion. In vs. 33 it does not appear, but the phrase **house of Israel** includes both Judah and Israel.

32. The former covenant, **the covenant which I made with their fathers when I took them by the hand to bring them out of the land of Egypt,** was undoubtedly the covenant made at Sinai, not the Deuteronomic covenant on the plains of Moab, or any of the other covenants described in the O.T. (cf. 7:22; Hos. 11:1-4). **Though I was their**

---

shall be **not like the covenant which I made with their fathers** (vs. 32). It shall not be finitized like the tables of stone when they came out of Egypt. Moses opened up a new epoch in history; it is over, a newer epoch begins. There was a deliverance from Egypt; it is over, a second and newer deliverance must come.

The second move is not desperate, but it is difficult. It consists in not remembering the former things: neither must we "consider the things of old" (Isa. 43:18). "The new is created not out of the old, not out of the best of the old, but out of the *death* of the old. It is not the old which creates the new. That which creates the new is that which is beyond old and beyond new, the Eternal." [1] Nevertheless the past is with us though behind us. What matters then is our form of remembrance. If not Moses, then the bridal covenant in the wilderness (2:2), and Hosea and his God who cared, and

[1] Tillich, *The Shaking of the Foundations*, pp. 181-82.

Rachel weeping for Ephraim; not the moralistic development of the Torah, not the sacrifices, not the temple, not the inviolability of Jerusalem, not the priests, not the prophets who had never shared in the counsels of the secret heart of God (23:22). Judah, alas, had already gone into captivity before Nebuchadrezzar ever came. And God was already excluded, because they would not listen.

Already the new is arising, but where? It did not arise when we attempted to force it—by the code discovered in the temple, by trying to keep silent when the word was within like a mighty fire. Where then? Where, indeed, but from within ourselves? Suddenly the new comes, not only when we least expect it, but when we least believe in it, as Tillich says. Suddenly, as the old fails to take hold, or continues to take hold with increasing viciousness, depths of meaning open out within us which we had not heretofore known or even believed possible. What was stifled begins suddenly to breathe. The ways

33 But this *shall be* the covenant that I will make with the house of Israel; After those days, saith the LORD, I will put my law in their inward parts, and write it in their hearts; and will be their God, and they shall be my people.

34 And they shall teach no more every man his neighbor, and every man his brother, saying, Know the LORD: for they shall all know me, from the least of them unto the greatest of them, saith the LORD: for I will forgive their iniquity, and I will remember their sin no more.

33 But this is the covenant which I will make with the house of Israel after those days, says the LORD: I will put my law within them, and I will write it upon their hearts; and I will be their God, and they shall be my people. **34** And no longer shall each man teach his neighbor and each his brother, saying, 'Know the LORD,' for they shall all know me, from the least of them to the greatest, says the LORD; for I will forgive their iniquity, and I will remember their sin no more."

---

husband: The Hebrew verb is *bāʻaltî,* which occurs also in 3:14. Yahweh is here conceived of as the husband of the nation. On the basis of the LXX, Peshitta, and O.L. many scholars emend to *gāʻaltî* and render, "so that I rejected [or "abhorred"] them" (cf. 14:19). If correct, the reference is probably to the Babylonian exile. The emendation is not wholly necessary since the M.T. can be satisfactorily translated.

33. The verb used here, as in vss. 31-32, translated **I will make,** means, lit., "to cut" (*kārath*). It is the verb used to describe covenant-making by J, E, and D, but not by P (see Moulton, *op. cit.,* p. 373). **I will put my law within them, and I will write it upon their hearts:** Jeremiah had much to say about the stubbornness of the evil heart (3:17; 7:24; 9:14; 11:8; 13:10; 16:12; 18:12; 23:17; many of these verses belong to editorial sections); and about the wickedness and weakness of the heart (4:14; 5:23; 17:9). In 17:1 he said, "The sin of Judah is written with a pen of iron; with a point of diamond it is engraved on the tablet of their heart." Therefore the law, in order to be effective, must be written **upon their hearts,** rather than on tables of stone, as the Ten Commandments had been at Sinai. The prophet's thought here comes very close to Ezekiel's doctrine of the new heart (Ezek. 11:19; 18:31; 36:26), and the Johannine doctrine of regeneration. **I will be their God, and they shall be my people** is a basic formula of the covenant: Yahweh is the covenant God of Israel, and Israel is the chosen people of Yahweh (cf. 7:23; 11:4; 24:7; 30:22; 31:1; 32:38; Lev. 26:12; Ezek. 11:20; 14:11; 36:28; 37:23, 27; Zech. 8:8). The formula is found in Jeremiah especially in passages by the Deuteronomic editor.

34. They shall all know me: Hosea had put great emphasis on the knowledge of Yahweh (Hos. 2:20; 4:1, 6; 5:4; 6:6), and it was emphasized by Jeremiah (2:8; 4:22;

---

that were closed lie suddenly open. "In the moment when the old becomes visible *as the old and tragic and dying,* and when no way out is seen"[2]—it is then that the almond bursts along the branch of promises. In those days, **I will put my law within them, and I will write it upon their hearts** (vs. 33). This is the eternal mystery of grace which is not understood by those who would deny the new covenant to Jeremiah on the ground that it must have developed through countless hands over a long period of time and hence must be postexilic! It is precisely in this way that the leap never comes. The formulation may exhibit such marking (to the detriment, perhaps, of its original poetic form); but whoever does not see in this epochal utterance of the spirit the inevitable

but unpredictable jewel of Jeremiah's agony knows little of the spirit's ordeal or of the ways of grace.

The third thing, of course, is forgiveness (vs. 34); and behind forgiveness is love. It is this which is new, which is always new, and eternally new. **They shall all know me, from the least ... to the greatest, says the LORD.** It is hardly necessary to observe here that this "knowledge" is nothing external or esoteric or formal; it is the knowledge of the experience of the God of the yearning heart (vs. 20). "The law demands what it cannot give. Grace gives what it demands."[3] The new life in the almond's petals of promise has here in principle and in vision burst the chrysalis of winter's hardened branch: the old will pass away (II Cor. 5:17).

[2] *Ibid.,* p. 183.

[3] Pascal, *Thoughts,* No. 521.

35 ¶ Thus saith the LORD, which giveth the sun for a light by day, *and* the ordinances of the moon and of the stars for a light by night, which divideth the sea when the waves thereof roar; The LORD of hosts *is* his name:

36 If those ordinances depart from before me, saith the LORD, *then* the seed of Israel also shall cease from being a nation before me for ever.

35 Thus says the LORD,
who gives the sun for light by day
and the fixed order of the moon and
the stars for light by night,
who stirs up the sea so that its waves
roar —
the LORD of hosts is his name:
36 "If this fixed order departs
from before me, says the LORD,
then shall the descendants of Israel cease
from being a nation before me for
ever."

9:3, 6, 24; 22:16). The passage which most clearly shows his definition of it is 22:15-16, in the description of Josiah. The new covenant promise is that all men will know Yahweh as the prophets had known him, directly and intimately. Far from being the ideal of a scribe, the new covenant expresses the ideal of a prophet, implying the multiplication of the experience and the consciousness of the prophet. **I will forgive their iniquity:** The promise of the new covenant is not of sinlessness, but rather of forgiveness of sin. This brings restoration of the fellowship with God, which was broken when the old covenant was broken.

O. ETERNAL DURATION OF THE NATION (31:35-37)

This passage promises that the nation Israel will last as long as the order of nature, which Yahweh has created; a similar idea is expressed in 33:20, 25. It is not probable that the section is from Jeremiah; it is more strongly nationalistic than is characteristic of his thought, and the ideas are similar to later ideas of creation, found especially in Second Isaiah (cf. 40:12, 26; 42:5; 44:24; 45:7, 18; 54:10). A few genuine verses in Jeremiah suggest the idea of "natural law," but not to the extent here developed (see 5:22; 8:7; 18:14).

35. Who stirs up the sea so that its waves roar: The same words are found in Isa. 51:15, followed as here by **the LORD of hosts is his name.**

In II Cor. we note that the believer is a living epistle, "written not with ink but with the Spirit of the living God, not on tablets of stone but on tablets of human hearts" (II Cor. 3:3). Christ's spirit in our hearts confirms this, "for all the promises of God find their Yes in him" (II Cor. 1:20). In him "the new has come" (II Cor. 5:17). This is the first word of the covenant.

When William Manson in *The Epistle to the Hebrews* presents "the charter-passage for the New Covenant," [4] he cites Jer. 31:31-34 entire (Heb. 8:8-12). This is the covenant which Christ mediates; it dispenses with the old because it is "enacted on better promises" (Heb. 8:6). By way of this covenant he "treats the first as obsolete. And what is becoming obsolete and growing old is ready to vanish away" (Heb. 8:13). This is the second word of Jeremiah's covenant.

In the Gospels we read: "Now as they were eating, Jesus took bread, and blessed, and broke

[4] London: Hodder & Stoughton, 1951, p. 127.

it, and gave it to his disciples and said, 'Take, eat; this is my body.' And he took a cup, and when he had given thanks he gave it to them, saying, 'Drink of it , all of you; for this is my blood of the covenant, which is poured out for many for the forgiveness of sins.' " (Matt. 26: 26-28.) This is the third word of Jeremiah's covenant—which becomes the first and the last and the source and the home and the cup of God's love forever.

35-40. The Two Seals.—The "great charter" having now been drawn up and its promises defined, it lies before us, poetically speaking, as though awaiting its signatures of validation. The two units remaining, vss. 35-37, 38-40, appear like the two seals which attest its ratification by the parties involved. The one is the seal from the hand of God; the other is the seal from the hand of man.

The first is as permanent as sun and moon and all the stars. Nay, more! It is as enduring as the dear might of him who fixed their paths and set the orders of their glory. The infinite

37 Thus saith the LORD; If heaven above can be measured, and the foundations of the earth searched out beneath, I will also cast off all the seed of Israel for all that they have done, saith the LORD.

38 ¶ Behold, the days come, saith the LORD, that the city shall be built to the LORD from the tower of Hananeel unto the gate of the corner.

39 And the measuring line shall yet go forth over against it upon the hill Gareb, and shall compass about to Goath.

40 And the whole valley of the dead bodies, and of the ashes, and all the fields unto the brook of Kidron, unto the corner of the horse gate toward the east, *shall be* holy unto the LORD; it shall not be plucked up, nor thrown down any more for ever.

37 Thus says the LORD:

"If the heavens above can be measured,
     and the foundations of the earth below
          can be explored,
then I will cast off all the descendants of
     Israel
     for all that they have done,
                              says the LORD."

38 "Behold, the days are coming, says the LORD, when the city shall be rebuilt for the LORD from the tower of Hanan'el to the Corner Gate. **39** And the measuring line shall go out farther, straight to the hill Gareb, and shall then turn to Go'ah. **40** The whole valley of the dead bodies and the ashes, and all the fields as far as the brook Kidron, to the corner of the Horse Gate toward the east, shall be sacred to the LORD. It shall not be uprooted or overthrown any more for ever."

P. REBUILDING OF JERUSALEM (31:38-40)

The "book of comfort" closes with a detailed description of the rebuilding and enlargement of Jerusalem, the holy city. It is indeed an anticlimax after the great new covenant passage of vss. 31-34, and can hardly be from Jeremiah. While he expected the continuation of the city of Jerusalem, he would hardly have interested himself in the geographical details here set down. The passage is from the postexilic period when there was expectation of the rebuilding of Jerusalem, probably before the time of Nehemiah. The closest parallel is Zech. 14:10-11.

38. The tower of Hananel was at the northeast corner of Jerusalem (cf. Neh. 3:1; 12:39; Zech. 14:10). **The Corner Gate** was probably at or near the northwest corner of the city (cf. II Kings 14:13; II Chr. 26:9).

39. The hill Gareb and **Goah** are not elsewhere named; the former was probably southwest of the city, and the latter southeast, but whether Goah was the name of a hill or some other geographical feature is not known.

40. The whole valley of the dead bodies and the ashes must be the valley of Hinnom, south of Jerusalem, where child sacrifice had been practiced (7:31-32; 19:2, 6; 32:35; II Kings 23:10; II Chr. 28:3; 33:6), in spite of the fact that the word for valley, ʿēmeq,

reaches of its unfathomable depths suggest the inexhaustibility of his forgiving love. The sublime and incredible beauty of its mystery—that vast tiara of mild, blazing stars—is but the symbol of his long-suffering patience while he awaits our long-anticipated return. The abyss of grandeur stays and at the last consoles our abyss of solitude. Behind the seal is the God who is beyond and behind and within every finite form of his signature. Until this God fails this covenant will stand.

The second seal has yet to be subscribed. It is based at once upon the divine promises and the conditions of human freedom: "You will come to a great city that has expected your

return for years." [5] The march is long, from man's side; but by the promises we are enabled to

> Strengthen the wavering line,
> Stablish, continue our march,
> On, to the bound of the waste,
> On, to the City of God! [6]

But this effort, as we know now, is the paradox: "That which thou seekest is near, and already coming to meet thee." [7] "And I saw the holy

[5] W. H. Auden, "The Flight into Egypt," Part IV, from *For the Time Being, a Christmas Oratorio.*
[6] Matthew Arnold, "Rugby Chapel," closing lines.
[7] Hölderlin, *Heimkunft* ("Homecoming"), IV, from *Das Meisterwerk,* p. 357.

32 The word that came to Jeremiah from the LORD in the tenth year of Zedekiah king of Judah, which *was* the eighteenth year of Nebuchadrezzar.

32 The word that came to Jeremiah from the LORD in the tenth year of Zedeki'ah king of Judah, which was the

is not elsewhere used of the valley of Hinnom. **The brook Kidron** is east of Jerusalem, joining the valley of Hinnom to the southeast of the city. **The Horse Gate** must have been at or near the southeast corner of Jerusalem (Neh. 3:28; cf. II Kings 11:16).

XXII. PURCHASE OF A FIELD IN ANATHOTH (32:1-44)

This chapter is very important for the study of Jeremiah's attitude toward the future of Judah. Through the act of purchasing a field in Anathoth at the very time when Jerusalem was under siege and he himself was in prison, the prophet showed unmistakably and dramatically his belief that the land had a future and would not be completely destroyed. It is also important as an example of the application of the law of redemption contained in Lev. 25.

The account is apparently placed here because of its subject matter, not because of any chronological considerations. As chs. 30–31 treat especially of the future of Israel (the Northern Kingdom), so this chapter is concerned with the future of Judah. Chronologically it belongs near the end of the period of Judah's independence, and might have been placed between ch. 37 and ch. 38.

There is in it a great amount of secondary material. Vss. 1-5 (more accurately, vss. 2-6) are widely recognized as editorial; because the chapter is not in chronological order these verses were inserted to give the setting for the event. Vss. 16-44 are considered as editorial, either in whole or in part, even by conservative commentators. The long prayer and Yahweh's reply contain material which is not relevant to the situation here described, and are filled with phrases and ideas which occur elsewhere in the O.T., especially in parts which come from the Deuteronomists. Some commentators believe that a Jeremianic kernel has here been expanded; e.g., Volz considers as genuine the following: vss. 16, 17aα, 24-29, 36aα, 42-44. Others (e.g., Duhm, Cornill, Kent) consider the whole of vss. 16-44 as secondary. Probably the entire section is of Deuteronomic origin, inasmuch as Deuteronomic phraseology and ideas pervade it. Indeed it provides almost a summary of the theology and the conception of Hebrew history held by the Deuteronomists. Perhaps vss. 16, 24-27 are original, but even these may be Deuteronomic, the editor making use in them (and in vss. 43-44) of the genuine word of the Lord in vs. 15. If this view is correct, we have here a good example of the work of the Deuteronomic editor: he found in Baruch's memoirs an account of the redemption of the field, which had a brief word of the Lord appended to give it significance, and has added a long prayer of the prophet and Yahweh's reply. Both the prayer and the reply are actually inappropriate, since vs. 15 contains all that is needed to give the significance of this semipublic action carried out by Jeremiah. Vss. 2-6 may likewise be from the Deuteronomic editor, but are more probably from a later redactor who arranged the chapters in their present order.

A parallel in Roman history has frequently been referred to (first apparently by Grotius). When Hannibal was encamped against Rome, he was told by a prisoner that the land on which his camp stood had just been sold, with no reduction in price (Livy XXVI. 11. 6).

---

city, new Jerusalem, coming down. . . . 'Behold, the dwelling of God is with men'" (Rev. 21:2-3).

32:1-44. The Packet of Earth.—Men react differently to enforced confinement. Boethius, accused of treason and imprisoned without trial in the time of King Theodoric, wrote his *Con-*

solation of Philosophy. Communing with Wisdom he sought to know himself. He learned that "all things must find their own peculiar course again, and each rejoices in his own return."[8] We know how Bunyan spent his time in prison at the restoration of Charles II in

[8] III. 2.

2 For then the king of Babylon's army besieged Jerusalem: and Jeremiah the prophet was shut up in the court of the prison, which *was* in the king of Judah's house.

3 For Zedekiah king of Judah had shut him up, saying, Wherefore dost thou prophesy, and say, Thus saith the LORD, Behold, I will give this city into the hand of the king of Babylon, and he shall take it;

4 And Zedekiah king of Judah shall not escape out of the hand of the Chaldeans, but shall surely be delivered into the hand of the king of Babylon, and shall speak with him mouth to mouth, and his eyes shall behold his eyes;

5 And he shall lead Zedekiah to Babylon, and there shall he be until I visit him, saith the LORD: though ye fight with the Chaldeans, ye shall not prosper?

eighteenth year of Nebuchadrez'zar. 2 At that time the army of the king of Babylon was besieging Jerusalem, and Jeremiah the prophet was shut up in the court of the guard which was in the palace of the king of Judah. 3 For Zedeki'ah king of Judah had imprisoned him, saying, "Why do you prophesy and say, 'Thus says the LORD: Behold I am giving this city into the hand of the king of Babylon, and he shall take it; 4 Zedeki'ah king of Judah shall not escape out of the hand of the Chalde'ans, but shall surely be given into the hand of the king of Babylon, and shall speak with him face to face and see him eye to eye; 5 and he shall take Zedeki'ah to Babylon, and there he shall remain until I visit him, says the LORD; though you fight against the Chalde'ans, you shall not succeed'?"

The action of Jeremiah on this occasion, separated from the secondary material, must be taken as the basis of his conception of the future. Nothing is said here about exile and return from exile, and nothing of a glorious future for a triumphant nation; he says nothing of his own fate. But this action, which he believed was prompted by God, expresses eloquently his fundamental faith in the future of the people of Judah in their own land.

A. COMMAND OF YAHWEH (32:1-8)

32:1. The date was within the year 588 B.C., probably the summer or early fall. The siege of Jerusalem had begun in January of that year, and the city fell in August, 587 B.C.

2. Jeremiah had been arrested during an interval when the Babylonians had lifted the siege for fear of an approaching Egyptian army, as he sought to leave the city to go to Anathoth. He was first placed in prison in the house of Jonathan the scribe, but upon petition to the king he was removed to the **court of the guard,** where he remained until the city fell (37:11-21). If vs. 24 is correct, this could hardly have taken place during the interval when the siege was lifted. The court of the guard, an open court in the palace complex, was used for the detention of prisoners who did not require strict confinement. The event here recorded was obviously witnessed by many people.

3-5. These verses are not strictly accurate. Jeremiah was put in prison because of his attempt to leave the city. He was quite naturally charged with treason. His real opponents were the officials who said that he was weakening the hands of the defenders of the city; Zedekiah was actually friendly to the prophet and wished to release him (see ch. 38). The editor has probably taken these verses from 34:2-4 or 21:4-7. **Until I visit him:** The

---

1660. We also know how the apostle Paul, imprisoned at Rome, wrote his Epistle to the Colossians. He explored there the profoundest dimension of the Christian life: "For you have died, and your life is hid with Christ in God" (Col. 3:3). Concerning this epistle Adoph Deissmann remarked: "When I open the chapel door of the Epistle to the Colossians it is to me as if Johann Sebastian [Bach] himself sat at the

organ." [9] It would appear that something similar took place in the thought of Jeremiah while he was shut up in the court of the guard in a palace of the king. He had written his "book of doom" during the reign of Jehoiakim. It would appear that now, as the great catastrophe came

[9] *Paul: A Study in Social and Religious History,* tr. by William E. Wilson (New York: G. H. Doran Co., 1926), p. 107.

6 ¶ And Jeremiah said, The word of the Lord came unto me, saying,

7 Behold, Hanameel the son of Shallum thine uncle shall come unto thee, saying, Buy thee my field that *is* in Anathoth: for the right of redemption *is* thine to buy *it*.

8 So Hanameel mine uncle's son came to me in the court of the prison according to the word of the Lord, and said unto me, Buy my field, I pray thee, that *is* in Anathoth, which *is* in the country of Benjamin: for the right of inheritance *is* thine, and the redemption *is* thine; buy *it* for thyself. Then I knew that this *was* the word of the Lord.

9 And I bought the field of Hanameel my uncle's son, that *was* in Anathoth, and weighed him the money, *even* seventeen shekels of silver.

10 And I subscribed the evidence, and sealed *it,* and took witnesses, and weighed *him* the money in the balances.

11 So I took the evidence of the purchase, *both* that which was sealed *according* to the law and custom, and that which was open:

6 Jeremiah said, "The word of the Lord came to me: 7 Behold, Han'amel the son of Shallum your uncle will come to you and say, 'Buy my field which is at An'athoth, for the right of redemption by purchase is yours.' 8 Then Han'amel my cousin came to me in the court of the guard, in accordance with the word of the Lord, and said to me, 'Buy my field which is at An'athoth in the land of Benjamin, for the right of possession and redemption is yours; buy it for yourself. Then I knew that this was the word of the Lord.'

9 "And I bought the field at An'athoth from Han'amel my cousin, and weighed out the money to him, seventeen shekels of silver. 10 I signed the deed, sealed it, got witnesses, and weighed the money on scales. 11 Then I took the sealed deed of purchase, containing the terms and conditions, and

editor has probably confused Zedekiah with Jehoiachin (see 52:31-34). Zedekiah was blinded by the Babylonians and taken to Babylon, where he died in prison (52:11). The LXX omits all of the verse after **he shall remain.**

7. **The right of redemption by purchase:** The purpose of the law of redemption, found in Lev. 25:25 ff. (P), was to keep property within the family so that it might not be alienated; the bond between the family and its property would thus be maintained. Hanamel had probably fallen into straits because of the siege of the city and the attendant suffering. Jeremiah apparently bought the property to prevent its being taken by a creditor or sold outside the family; it is not strictly a case of buying property back. Jeremiah must have had an income from some source, but we do not know what it was.

B. Act of Purchase (32:9-15)

9-12. These verses are especially instructive as an example of the method by which such transactions were carried out, the only occurrence in the O.T. where such details are given. Inasmuch as the Hebrews did not at this time use coined money, the silver was **weighed out. Seventeen shekels of silver** weighed approximately seven ounces, but since we do not know the size of the field or the purchasing power of silver at that time, it is idle to attempt to make an equation with modern values. **The sealed deed . . . and the open copy:** Some scholars have interpreted this as referring to a clay tablet inscribed with cuneiform characters, placed within an inscribed "envelope," many examples of which have been found in Mesopotamia. It is most improbable that cuneiform writing

nearer, he experienced a great reversal, and composed his "book of consolation."

The event which crystallized this reversal of his mood came to him as a premonition that his cousin Hanamel would come to sell him a field at Anathoth. When Hanamel actually came and asked him to buy his field because the right

of redemption by purchase was his (vs. 8), Jeremiah, ever alert for the ciphers of the divine communication, perceived suddenly the deep significance of this petition. The redemption of the field at Anathoth became symbolic of the Lord's redemption of Israel. Not merely was the purchase of the field an evidence of

12 And I gave the evidence of the purchase unto Baruch the son of Neriah, the son of Maaseiah, in the sight of Hanameel mine uncle's *son*, and in the presence of the witnesses that subscribed the book of the purchase, before all the Jews that sat in the court of the prison.

13 ¶ And I charged Baruch before them, saying,

14 Thus saith the LORD of hosts, the God of Israel; Take these evidences, this evidence of the purchase, both which is sealed, and this evidence which is open; and put them in an earthen vessel, that they may continue many days.

15 For thus saith the LORD of hosts, the God of Israel; Houses and fields and vineyards shall be possessed again in this land.

16 ¶ Now when I had delivered the evidence of the purchase unto Baruch the son of Neriah, I prayed unto the LORD, saying,

the open copy; 12 and I gave the deed of purchase to Baruch the son of Neri'ah son of Mahsei'ah, in the presence of Han'amel my cousin, in the presence of the witnesses who signed the deed of purchase, and in the presence of all the Jews who were sitting in the court of the guard. 13 I charged Baruch in their presence, saying, 14 'Thus says the LORD of hosts, the God of Israel: Take these deeds, both this sealed deed of purchase and this open deed, and put them in an earthenware vessel, that they may last for a long time. 15 For thus says the LORD of hosts, the God of Israel: Houses and fields and vineyards shall again be bought in this land.'

16 "After I had given the deed of purchase to Baruch the son of Neri'ah, I

---

was used in Judah for such purposes at that time. The material was probably papyrus, and the writing was in cursive Hebrew such as is known from the contemporaneous Lachish letters (which were written on pieces of broken pottery; see Torczyner, *et al.*, *The Lachish Letters*). From archaeological discoveries and later references in the Talmud, we may assume that the procedure was as follows (see especially Leopold Fischer, "Die Urkunden in Jer 32₁₁₋₁₄ nach den Ausgrabungen und dem Talmud," *Zeitschrift für die alttestamentliche Wissenschaft*, XXX [1910], 136-42): The text of the deed was written twice on a single sheet of papyrus, with a small space left blank between the two copies. The sheet was then cut through the blank space to half its width. Then the upper half was rolled, folded over itself, and tied with thin strips of papyrus (holes being made in the middle of the sheet to receive them), and a seal was placed on the strips. This was **the sealed deed**, to be preserved as a permanent record. The lower half of the papyrus sheet was then rolled up, and this roll was bent under the sealed copy and left attached to it. This was **the open copy** which could be consulted at any time without breaking the seal. In some cases no cut was made in the middle of the papyrus sheet, but the upper half was rolled and sealed, and the lower half left unrolled. **Containing the terms and conditions:** The phrase is obscure; it may be that the KJV is correct in translating it **according to the law and custom**, as the Targ. evidently understood it. The Hebrew has nothing which corresponds to either **containing** or **according to**.

14. Since the deed was made in duplicate, it could be referred to as **these deeds**, or in the singular as in vs. 12. **An earthenware vessel:** Papyrus documents have been found preserved in pottery jars at Elephantine (Egypt) and elsewhere.

C. PRAYER OF JEREMIAH (32:16-25)

16-25. This passage is in the main, if not wholly, secondary; only vss. 24-25 have any claim to being original (see above). The prayer is largely irrelevant to the situation, and

---

his own ultimate optimism and faith in the future of his people, but it was also his belief that Yahweh would again plant his people and build them in the land. So he **bought the field at Anathoth** (vs. 9) at the time when Jerusalem itself was under siege! With meticulous care he

observed all the details of the transaction, signing the deed before witnesses, and placing the deed in the care of Baruch. Baruch was charged to seal the deed in an earthenware vessel where it might be protected for a long time to come. For there should come a time when **houses**

17 Ah Lord God! behold, thou hast made the heaven and the earth by thy great power and stretched out arm, *and* there is nothing too hard for thee:

18 Thou showest loving-kindness unto thousands, and recompensest the iniquity of the fathers into the bosom of their children after them: The Great, The Mighty God, The Lord of hosts, *is* his name;

19 Great in counsel, and mighty in work: for thine eyes *are* open upon all the ways of the sons of men, to give every one according to his ways, and according to the fruit of his doings:

20 Which hast set signs and wonders in the land of Egypt, *even* unto this day, and in Israel, and among *other* men; and hast made thee a name, as at this day;

21 And hast brought forth thy people Israel out of the land of Egypt with signs, and with wonders, and with a strong hand, and with a stretched out arm, and with great terror;

22 And hast given them this land, which thou didst swear to their fathers to give them, a land flowing with milk and honey;

23 And they came in, and possessed it; but they obeyed not thy voice, neither walked in thy law; they have done nothing of all that thou commandest them to do: therefore thou hast caused all this evil to come upon them.

24 Behold the mounts, they are come unto the city to take it; and the city is given into the hand of the Chaldeans that fight against it, because of the sword, and of the famine, and of the pestilence: and what thou hast spoken is come to pass; and, behold, thou seest *it*.

25 And thou hast said unto me, O Lord God, Buy thee the field for money, and take witnesses; for the city is given into the hand of the Chaldeans.

26 ¶ Then came the word of the Lord unto Jeremiah, saying,

27 Behold, I *am* the Lord, the God of all flesh: is there any thing too hard for me?

28 Therefore thus saith the Lord; Behold, I will give this city into the hand of

prayed to the Lord, saying: 17 'Ah Lord God! It is thou who hast made the heavens and the earth by thy great power and by thy outstretched arm! Nothing is too hard for thee, 18 who showest steadfast love to thousands, but dost requite the guilt of fathers to their children after them, O great and mighty God whose name is the Lord of hosts, 19 great in counsel and mighty in deed; whose eyes are open to all the ways of men, rewarding every man according to his ways and according to the fruit of his doings; 20 who hast shown signs and wonders in the land of Egypt, and to this day in Israel and among all mankind, and hast made thee a name, as at this day. 21 Thou didst bring thy people Israel out of the land of Egypt with signs and wonders, with a strong hand and outstretched arm, and with great terror; 22 and thou gavest them this land, which thou didst swear to their fathers to give them, a land flowing with milk and honey; 23 and they entered and took possession of it. But they did not obey thy voice or walk in thy law; they did nothing of all thou didst command them to do. Therefore thou hast made all this evil come upon them. 24 Behold, the siege mounds have come up to the city to take it, and because of sword and famine and pestilence the city is given into the hands of the Chaldeans who are fighting against it. What thou didst speak has come to pass, and behold, thou seest it. 25 Yet thou, O Lord God, hast said to me, "Buy the field for money and get witnesses"— though the city is given into the hands of the Chaldeans.' "

26 The word of the Lord came to Jeremiah: 27 "Behold, I am the Lord, the God of all flesh; is anything too hard for me? 28 Therefore, thus says the Lord: Behold, I am giving this city into the hands of the

---

is more like a prayer for use in a public service of worship by a group than the prayer of an individual (Volz). It is mostly taken up with a long descriptive address to Yahweh, in the style of the hymns of the O.T. (such as Ps. 103). The similarity to the longer prayer in Neh. 9:6-38 has often been pointed out. The terminology and ideas are Deuteronomic.

the Chaldeans, and into the hand of Nebuchadrezzar king of Babylon, and he shall take it:

29 And the Chaldeans, that fight against this city, shall come and set fire on this city, and burn it with the houses, upon whose roofs they have offered incense unto Baal, and poured out drink offerings unto other gods, to provoke me to anger.

30 For the children of Israel and the children of Judah have only done evil before me from their youth: for the children of Israel have only provoked me to anger with the work of their hands, saith the LORD.

31 For this city hath been to me *as a* provocation of mine anger and of my fury from the day that they built it even unto this day, that I should remove it from before my face;

32 Because of all the evil of the children of Israel and of the children of Judah, which they have done to provoke me to anger, they, their kings, their princes, their priests, and their prophets, and the men of Judah, and the inhabitants of Jerusalem.

33 And they have turned unto me the back, and not the face: though I taught them, rising up early and teaching *them,* yet they have not hearkened to receive instruction.

34 But they set their abominations in the house, which is called by my name, to defile it.

35 And they built the high places of Baal, which *are* in the valley of the son of Hinnom, to cause their sons and their daughters to pass through *the fire* unto Molech; which I commanded them not, neither came it into my mind, that they should do this abomination, to cause Judah to sin.

Chalde'ans and into the hand of Nebuchadrez'zar king of Babylon, and he shall take it. **29** The Chalde'ans who are fighting against this city shall come and set this city on fire, and burn it, with the houses on whose roofs incense has been offered to Ba'al and drink offerings have been poured out to other gods, to provoke me to anger. **30** For the sons of Israel and the sons of Judah have done nothing but evil in my sight from their youth; the sons of Israel have done nothing but provoke me to anger by the work of their hands, says the LORD. **31** This city has aroused my anger and wrath, from the day it was built to this day, so that I will remove it from my sight **32** because of all the evil of the sons of Israel and the sons of Judah which they did to provoke me to anger — their kings and their princes, their priests and their prophets, the men of Judah and the inhabitants of Jerusalem. **33** They have turned to me their back and not their face; and though I have taught them persistently they have not listened to receive instruction. **34** They set up their abominations in the house which is called by my name, to defile it. **35** They built the high places of Ba'al in the valley of the son of Hinnom, to offer up their sons and daughters to Molech, though I did not command them, nor did it enter into my mind, that they should do this abomination, to cause Judah to sin.

D. REPLY OF YAHWEH (32:26-44)

Only vss. 26-27 and just possibly vss. 42-44 have any claim to being original. The substance of the passage is the Deuteronomic conception of the history of Israel and the future return from exile.

35. See Exeg. on 7:31.

---

and fields and vineyards [should] again be bought in this land.

The prayer which follows focuses upon the apparent contradiction in Jeremiah's action. The city virtually is given into the hands of the Chaldeans, yet God has instructed him to buy the field before witnesses. The answer to this

prayer, though of later origin (see Exeg.), gives to Jeremiah's act its proper pitch of promise.

Two views of the human predicament are here juxtaposed. The one is the average, disillusioned view of man's behavior which frequently appears in times when the altruistic bottom has dropped out of things:

36 ¶ And now therefore thus saith the Lord, the God of Israel, concerning this city, whereof ye say, It shall be delivered into the hand of the king of Babylon by the sword, and by the famine, and by the pestilence;

37 Behold, I will gather them out of all countries, whither I have driven them in mine anger, and in my fury, and in great wrath; and I will bring them again unto this place, and I will cause them to dwell safely:

38 And they shall be my people, and I will be their God:

39 And I will give them one heart, and one way, that they may fear me for ever, for the good of them, and of their children after them:

40 And I will make an everlasting covenant with them, that I will not turn away from them, to do them good; but I will put my fear in their hearts, that they shall not depart from me.

41 Yea, I will rejoice over them to do them good, and I will plant them in this land assuredly with my whole heart and with my whole soul.

42 For thus saith the Lord; Like as I have brought all this great evil upon this people, so will I bring upon them all the good that I have promised them.

43 And fields shall be bought in this land, whereof ye say, *It is* desolate without man or beast; it is given into the hand of the Chaldeans.

44 Men shall buy fields for money, and subscribe evidences, and seal *them,* and take witnesses in the land of Benjamin, and in the places about Jerusalem, and in the cities of Judah, and in the cities of the mountains, and in the cities of the valley, and in the cities of the south: for I will

36 "Now therefore thus says the Lord, the God of Israel, concerning this city of which you say, 'It is given into the hand of the king of Babylon by sword, by famine, and by pestilence': **37** Behold, I will gather them from all the countries to which I drove them in my anger and my wrath and in great indignation; I will bring them back to this place, and I will make them dwell in safety. **38** And they shall be my people, and I will be their God. **39** I will give them one heart and one way, that they may fear me for ever, for their own good and the good of their children after them. **40** I will make with them an everlasting covenant, that I will not turn away from doing good to them; and I will put the fear of me in their hearts, that they may not turn from me. **41** I will rejoice in doing them good, and I will plant them in this land in faithfulness, with all my heart and all my soul.

42 "For thus says the Lord: Just as I have brought all this great evil upon this people, so I will bring upon them all the good that I promise them. **43** Fields shall be bought in this land of which you are saying, It is a desolation, without man or beast; it is given into the hands of the Chalde'ans. **44** Fields shall be bought for money, and deeds shall be signed and sealed and witnessed, in the land of Benjamin, in the places about Jerusalem, and in the cities of Judah, in the cities of the hill country, in the cities of the Shephe'lah, and in the

---

[This is] man: . . . He gets children, buys and sells small packets of everlasting earth, intrigues against his rivals, is exultant when he cheats them. He wastes his little three score years and ten in spendthrift and inglorious living; from his cradle to his grave he scarcely sees the sun or moon or stars; he is unconscious of the immortal sea and earth.[1]

Over against this stands the covenantal consciousness that breaks into triumphant expres-

[1] Thomas Wolfe, *You Can't Go Home Again* (New York: Harper & Bros., 1940), p. 433.

sion in vss. 37-41. It was the sense of these promises which gave Jeremiah the knowledge that God regards himself as bound by the declarations he has made, that Jeremiah and the people could rest secure within the knowledge of these intentions. Men buy and sell their little packets of everlasting earth, largely unconscious of the immortal earth and sky: but Jeremiah knew that a little packet of earth, when once redeemed, filled all the space between Anathoth and the covenantal stars.

cause their captivity to return, saith the
Lord.

33 Moreover the word of the Lord
came unto Jeremiah the second time,
while he was yet shut up in the court of
the prison, saying,

2 Thus saith the Lord the maker thereof,
the Lord that formed it, to establish it;
the Lord is his name;

3 Call unto me, and I will answer thee,
and show thee great and mighty things,
which thou knowest not.

4 For thus saith the Lord, the God of
Israel, concerning the houses of this city,
and concerning the houses of the kings of
Judah, which are thrown down by the
mounts, and by the sword;

5 They come to fight with the Chaldeans,
but it is to fill them with the dead bodies of

cities of the Negeb; for I will restore their
fortunes, says the Lord."

33 The word of the Lord came to Jeremiah a second time, while he was
still shut up in the court of the guard:
2 "Thus says the Lord who made the earth,*g*
the Lord who formed it to establish it —
the Lord is his name: 3 Call to me and I
will answer you, and will tell you great and
hidden things which you have not known.
4 For thus says the Lord, the God of Israel,
concerning the houses of this city and the
houses of the kings of Judah which were
torn down to make a defense against the
siege mounds and before the sword:*h* 5 The
Chalde'ans are coming in to fight*i* and to

g Gk: Heb *it*
h Heb obscure
i Cn: Heb *They are coming in to fight against the Chaldeans*

XXIII. Promises of Restoration (33:1-26)

The general theme of chs. 30–32 continues, promising health and restoration to
Jerusalem, the return of joy to the nation, and the eternal duration of the Davidic
kingship and the Levitical priesthood. Many of the ideas presented are found in chs.
30–31. There is very little material here from Jeremiah. Vss. 14-26 are certainly not his;
in the first half of the chapter vss. 4-5 are a genuine historical fragment, but the rest is
secondary. Vss. 1-13 contain some phrases reminiscent of the Deuteronomic editor, but
the section as a whole is probably from a later editor.

A. Rebuilding of Jerusalem (33:1-9)

This section is connected with ch. 32 by the phrase **a second time** (cf. 32:2). Vss. 4-5
appear to be genuine, preserving a genuine remembrance of measures taken to defend
Jerusalem against the Chaldeans, but the rest is editorial.

33:2-3. These verses are filled with ideas and phrases of Second Isaiah (cf. especially
45:18; 47:4; 48:6). The artificiality of the invitation to prayer in vs. 3 appears when
comparison is made with the genuine prayers of the prophet, as in 12:1-6; 15:15-21.

4-5. The translation is difficult; the Hebrew of vss. 4b-5a is corrupt and obscure.
The KJV gives a fairly literal translation but does not make sense; the RSV is based upon
a slight emendation of the Hebrew, primarily the omission of 'eth- before hakkasdîm,
which is then taken to be the subject of the verb bā'îm rather than the object of lehillāhēm.
Vs. 4 implies that some of the houses inside Jerusalem, probably near the wall, were torn

33:1-26. The Name of Joy.—Probably we
should take into account from the very outset
that these verses are a late collection about the
future, with virtually none assignable to Jeremiah (see Exeg.). The section may nevertheless be intended to give a certain climax and
completeness to the "book of consolation." The
opening movement assigns to Jeremiah, while
still imprisoned, a vision of the future based
upon the elements in the siege. The tearing
down of the houses to repair the defenses
against the siege mounds of the Chaldeans, the

conditions of pestilence, of famine, and of death
are suddenly reversed by a vision of health and
healing, together with abundance and security.

Vs. 8 suggests a triple cleansing—from **guilt,**
from **sin,** and from **rebellion.** These are three
interlocking aspects of the human condition,
and must be changed if ever we are to know
the **name of joy** (cf. Ezek. 36:25). "Guilt" means
something that is twisted or warped. The mainspring of guilt is always the twisting of a man's
central integrity from its proper course. The
experience to which it leads is that of Jeremiah's

men, whom I have slain in mine anger and in my fury, and for all whose wickedness I have hid my face from this city.

6 Behold, I will bring it health and cure, and I will cure them, and will reveal unto them the abundance of peace and truth.

7 And I will cause the captivity of Judah and the captivity of Israel to return, and will build them, as at the first.

8 And I will cleanse them from all their iniquity, whereby they have sinned against me; and I will pardon all their iniquities, whereby they have sinned, and whereby they have transgressed against me.

9 ¶ And it shall be to me a name of joy, a praise and an honor before all the nations of the earth, which shall hear all the good that I do unto them: and they shall fear and tremble for all the goodness and for all the prosperity that I procure unto it.

10 Thus saith the LORD; Again there shall be heard in this place, which ye say *shall be* desolate without man and without beast, *even* in the cities of Judah, and in the streets of Jerusalem, that are desolate, without man, and without inhabitant, and without beast,

fill them with the dead bodies of men whom I shall smite in my anger and my wrath, for I have hidden my face from this city because of all their wickedness. 6 Behold, I will bring to it health and healing, and I will heal them and reveal to them abundance*j* of prosperity and security. 7 I will restore the fortunes of Judah and the fortunes of Israel, and rebuild them as they were at first. 8 I will cleanse them from all the guilt of their sin against me, and I will forgive all the guilt of their sin and rebellion against me. 9 And this city*k* shall be to me a name of joy, a praise and a glory before all the nations of the earth who shall hear of all the good that I do for them; they shall fear and tremble because of all the good and all the prosperity I provide for it.

10 "Thus says the LORD: In this place of which you say, 'It is a waste without man or beast,' in the cities of Judah and the streets of Jerusalem that are desolate, without man

j Heb uncertain
k Heb *and it*

down in order to strengthen the defense of the city by making it possible for soldiers to maneuver near the wall (for a similar situation see Isa. 22:10). Vs. 5*b* expresses the same attitude toward the destruction of Jerusalem as 21:4-7; 34:2-3; 37:7-10, and is doubtless genuine.

6-9. This promise of **health and healing** and **abundance of prosperity and security** is too vague and optimistic to be from Jeremiah, especially coming immediately after vs. 5*b* (cf. 30:17).

B. RETURN OF JOY (33:10-11)

This is clearly from a time after the destruction of Jerusalem in 587 B.C., as vs. 10 indicates, though the degree of destruction is exaggerated. The return of joy to the city is depicted, as in 30:19; 31:4, 5, 12-14.

young camel interlacing her tracks in the wilderness (2:23), aimlessly wandering in a deepening maze of anxiety and discontent. The second term, "sin," means that which misses its mark. In the realm of the spirit, the arrow which misses its target not only misses its aim but endlessly flies in the infinite projection of introverted deviation from fidelity to God. The third term, "rebellion," contains the willful element in all of this. This is, in fact, the self's denial of its relationship to God, or its attempt to have reality upon its own terms. Since the self properly cannot become a self without relating itself positively to reality it

can never, by the courses of rebellion, genuinely become a self. Consequently joy is forbidden it, and the obverse of joy is all that it knows.

There is something very basic, therefore, in the movement which the chapter takes. If the people are cleansed from within **there shall be heard again the voice of mirth and . . . of gladness, . . . of the bridegroom and . . . of the bride, the voices of those who sing** (vs. 11). This is a dramatic reversal of Jeremiah's pathetic metaphors of that which had passed out of the life of Judah. Not only is this reversal appropriate but the sense of renewal and hope is caught up in a hymn of praise. The hymn

11 The voice of joy, and the voice of gladness, the voice of the bridegroom, and the voice of the bride, the voice of them that shall say, Praise the LORD of hosts: for the LORD *is* good; for his mercy *endureth* for ever: *and* of them that shall bring the sacrifice of praise into the house of the LORD. For I will cause to return the captivity of the land, as at first, saith the LORD.

12 Thus saith the LORD of hosts; Again in this place, which is desolate without man and without beast, and in all the cities thereof, shall be a habitation of shepherds causing *their* flocks to lie down.

13 In the cities of the mountains, in the cities of the vale, and in the cities of the south, and in the land of Benjamin, and in the places about Jerusalem, and in the cities of Judah, shall the flocks pass again under the hands of him that telleth *them*, saith the LORD.

14 Behold, the days come, saith the LORD, that I will perform that good thing which I have promised unto the house of Israel and to the house of Judah.

or inhabitant or beast, 11 there shall be heard again the voice of mirth and the voice of gladness, the voice of the bridegroom and the voice of the bride, the voices of those who sing, as they bring thank offerings to the house of the LORD:

'Give thanks to the LORD of hosts,
for the LORD is good,
for his steadfast love endures for ever!'
For I will restore the fortunes of the land as at first, says the LORD.

12 "Thus says the LORD of hosts: In this place which is waste, without man or beast, and in all of its cities, there shall again be habitations of shepherds resting their flocks. 13 In the cities of the hill country, in the cities of the Shephe'lah, and in the cities of the Negeb, in the land of Benjamin, the places about Jerusalem, and in the cities of Judah, flocks shall again pass under the hands of the one who counts them, says the LORD.

14 "Behold, the days are coming, says the LORD, when I will fulfil the promise I made to the house of Israel and the house of

11. This verse imitates the phraseology of 7:34; 16:9; 25:10 (all from the Deuteronomic editor), with reversal of the conditions described in those verses. The poetic quotation in vs. 11b is virtually the equivalent of Ps. 136:1 and probably is intended to stand for a whole hymn.

C. RESTORATION OF THE FLOCKS (33:12-13)

These verses promise restoration of conditions which will make possible sheep raising again in the countryside of southern Palestine (cf. 31:24b).

13. The phraseology imitates that of 17:26; 32:44, listing the parts of southern Palestine. The Targ. gives a messianic interpretation by substituting the word "Messiah" (*meshîḥā'*) for the one who counts them.

D. DAVIDIC KINGS AND LEVITICAL PRIESTS (33:14-26)

This passage quotes 23:5-6 and then makes a long commentary on it, promising the continuance of the Jewish state with a king from the line of David and a priesthood from the tribe of Levi. The whole section is lacking in the LXX. Rudolph has suggested that vss. 14-26 may have existed for a long time as an independent composition, designed to promise the continuation of the Davidic kingship and the Levitical priesthood. Then at a late date this composition was added to Jeremiah because it contained a quotation from that book. It is possible therefore that these verses were not a part of the book when the LXX was made, but were added subsequent to the making of that version.

is an old cult hymn; it nevertheless gives thanks to the Lord of hosts and recognizes that his **steadfast love endures for ever!** Then comes the symbol of the shepherds and the flocks. Considering the pervasiveness of this symbol, not only throughout Jeremiah but throughout Hebraic literature generally, it is difficult to

imagine a finer touch wherewith to symbolize the restoration of **the fortunes of the land** (vs. 11) than is contained in the phrase **flocks shall again pass under the hands of the one who counts them** (vs. 13).

Vss. 14-16 give a startling turn to Jeremiah's anticipation of the future coming of the right-

15 ¶ In those days, and at that time, will I cause the Branch of righteousness to grow up unto David; and he shall execute judgment and righteousness in the land.

16 In those days shall Judah be saved, and Jerusalem shall dwell safely: and this *is the name* wherewith she shall be called, The LORD our righteousness.

17 ¶ For thus saith the LORD; David shall never want a man to sit upon the throne of the house of Israel;

18 Neither shall the priests the Levites want a man before me to offer burnt offerings, and to kindle meat offerings, and to do sacrifice continually.

19 ¶ And the word of the LORD came unto Jeremiah, saying,

20 Thus saith the LORD; If ye can break my covenant of the day, and my covenant of the night, and that there should not be day and night in their season;

21 *Then* may also my covenant be broken with David my servant, that he should not have a son to reign upon his throne; and with the Levites the priests, my ministers.

Judah. **15** In those days and at that time I will cause a righteous Branch to spring forth for David; and he shall execute justice and righteousness in the land. **16** In those days Judah will be saved and Jerusalem will dwell securely. And this is the name by which it will be called: 'The LORD is our righteousness.'

17 "For thus says the LORD: David shall never lack a man to sit on the throne of the house of Israel, **18** and the Levitical priests shall never lack a man in my presence to offer burnt offerings, to burn cereal offerings, and to make sacrifices for ever."

19 The word of the LORD came to Jeremiah: **20** "Thus says the LORD: If you can break my covenant with the day and my covenant with the night, so that day and night will not come at their appointed time, **21** then also my covenant with David my servant may be broken, so that he shall not have a son to reign on his throne, and my covenant with the Levitical priests my min-

The passage must have originated in the postexilic period when there was need to encourage the Jewish people in the belief in the continuation of the Jewish state under a Davidic kingship and Levitical priesthood. It may be as early as the time of Haggai and Zechariah, *ca.* 520 B.C., when Zerubbabel, a descendant of David, was Persian governor and Joshua was high priest, and there was an abortive attempt to set up an independent kingdom (see Hag. 1:1; 2:23; Zech. 4:11-14; 6:9-13). Or it may be from a later time, such as that of Malachi, *ca.* 500 B.C., when there were discouragement and dissension such as are depicted in vs. 24 (cf. Mal. 2:4, 8, 17; 3:14-15).

It is not at all probable that Jeremiah would have had an interest in the continuation of the Levitical priesthood in such strong terms as occur here.

15-16. See Exeg. on 23:5-6. The significant variation from that passage is that **Jerusalem** is substituted for "Israel," and the name is applied to the city rather than to the righteous king.

18. The Levitical priests: A favorite phrase of Deuteronomy (17:9; 18:1; 24:8; 27:9; Josh. 3:3; 8:33; cf. Deut. 21:5; 31:9).

20. My covenant with the day and my covenant with the night: This is the equivalent of our idea of "natural law," according to which day and night are regulated (cf. the idea in 31:35-37).

eous king (see 23:5-6). The righteous shoot out of David is shifted from the king to the city. It is Jerusalem that shall **be called "The LORD is our righteousness."**

The new covenant now is sealed. It is established in the intention of God as are the ordinances of heaven and earth. Yahweh does not break his **covenant with the day** or his **covenant with the night** (cf. 31:35-36). This is very

like Jeremiah's perception of the great stabilities of the creation. We are not permitted to break the covenant of the day or the night. This is the all-inclusive ordinance of God. In literature generally the night has become a destructive symbol, whereas the day has come to stand for order and clarity. They nevertheless are ordained of God, and we somehow know that even the road to destruction can lead as

22 As the host of heaven cannot be numbered, neither the sand of the sea measured; so will I multiply the seed of David my servant, and the Levites that minister unto me.

23 Moreover the word of the LORD came to Jeremiah, saying,

24 Considerest thou not what this people have spoken, saying, The two families which the LORD hath chosen, he hath even cast them off? thus they have despised my people, that they should be no more a nation before them.

25 Thus saith the LORD; If my covenant *be* not with day and night, *and if* I have not appointed the ordinances of heaven and earth;

26 Then will I cast away the seed of Jacob, and David my servant, *so* that I will not take *any* of his seed *to be* rulers over the seed of Abraham, Isaac, and Jacob: for I will cause their captivity to return, and have mercy on them.

34 The word which came unto Jeremiah from the LORD, when Nebuchadnezzar king of Babylon, and all his army, and all the kingdoms of the earth of his dominion, and all the people, fought against Jerusalem, and against all the cities thereof, saying,

isters. **22** As the host of heaven cannot be numbered and the sands of the sea cannot be measured, so I will multiply the descendants of David my servant, and the Levitical priests who minister to me."

23 The word of the LORD came to Jeremiah: **24** "Have you not observed what these people are saying, 'The LORD has rejected the two families which he chose'? Thus they have despised my people so that they are no longer a nation in their sight. **25** Thus says the LORD: If I have not established my covenant with day and night and the ordinances of heaven and earth, **26** then I will reject the descendants of Jacob and David my servant and will not choose one of his descendants to rule over the seed of Abraham, Isaac, and Jacob. For I will restore their fortunes, and will have mercy upon them."

34 The word which came to Jeremiah from the LORD, when Nebuchadrez'zar king of Babylon and all his army and all the kingdoms of the earth under his dominion and all the peoples were fighting against Jerusalem and all of its cities:

---

24. The two families are probably Israel and Judah, not the families of David and Levi. The verse indicates that some of the Jewish people themselves (**these people**) were becoming discouraged and thinking that Yahweh had actually rejected the Israelites. The passage was written to overcome such discouragement.

25. See Exeg. on vs. 20; 31:35-37.

XXIV. A WARNING TO KING ZEDEKIAH (34:1-7)

The date of this passage is suggested by vs. 7, which says that only Lachish and Azekah remained of the fortified cities of Judah that were being attacked by the Babylonians. This must have been early in the invasion of Palestine, possibly even before the siege of Jerusalem itself (see Exeg. on vs. 7). Jeremiah was not yet in prison. The message he delivers to the king is similar to that which was given later according to 21:1-10; 32:3-5; 37:8-10, 17; 38:17-23 (not all of which are genuine; see Exeg., *ad loc.*). The unusual feature here is the promise in vss. 4-5 that the king will die an honorable death and be lamented by his people. Actually Zedekiah was captured by the Babylonians,

---

well to the presence of God. It is often under the sign of the darkness that we come to ourselves, as the mystics and psychologists know. We can get lost equally by day. Whether lost or found, however, we cannot break God's covenant with the day and the night. This is the vast stability of things which Jeremiah knew. It is within this covenant, this large continuum of

our limit-situations, that God proposes another covenant with man. For man he ordains a distinctive plan to the end that man should come to know the very **name of joy**, to live in fellowship with the God who is loyal in love.

34:1-7. Message to Zedekiah (I).—We have already noted (ch. 21) something of Jeremiah's advice to King Zedekiah. The one in this chap-

2 Thus saith the LORD, the God of Israel; Go and speak to Zedekiah king of Judah, and tell him, Thus saith the LORD; Behold, I will give this city into the hand of the king of Babylon, and he shall burn it with fire:

3 And thou shalt not escape out of his hand, but shalt surely be taken, and delivered into his hand; and thine eyes shall behold the eyes of the king of Babylon, and he shall speak with thee mouth to mouth, and thou shalt go to Babylon.

4 Yet hear the word of the LORD, O Zedekiah king of Judah; Thus saith the LORD of thee, Thou shalt not die by the sword;

5 *But* thou shalt die in peace: and with the burnings of thy fathers, the former kings which were before thee, so shall they burn *odors* for thee; and they will lament thee, *saying*, Ah lord! for I have pronounced the word, saith the LORD.

2 "Thus says the LORD, the God of Israel: Go and speak to Zedeki'ah king of Judah and say to him, 'Thus says the LORD: Behold, I am giving this city into the hand of the king of Babylon, and he shall burn it with fire. 3 You shall not escape from his hand, but shall surely be captured and delivered into his hand; you shall see the king of Babylon eye to eye and speak with him face to face; and you shall go to Babylon.' 4 Yet hear the word of the LORD, O Zedeki'ah king of Judah! Thus says the LORD concerning you: 'You shall not die by the sword. 5 You shall die in peace. And as spices were burned for your fathers, the former kings who were before you, so men shall burn spices for you and lament for you, saying, "Alas, lord!"' For I have spoken the word, says the LORD."

who put out his eyes and took him to Babylon, where he died in prison (39:7; 52:8-11; II Kings 25:5-7; cf. Ezek. 12:13). There is no good reason to doubt (with Duhm) the records which tell of this treatment of the king. We must then interpret the present passage either as an unconditional promise which was not fulfilled, or as a conditional promise that was unfulfilled because the king did not follow its condition—which probably was that he must surrender to the Babylonians. The latter is more probable, and we may suppose that some words containing the condition have fallen out in vs. 4. Rudolph believes that in vs. 2, **and he shall burn it with fire,** and vs. 3, **and you shall go to Babylon,** are editorial additions, as prophecies after the event; and that vs. 5 originally had "in Jerusalem" after **peace** (the phrase now being found by mistake in vs. 6). Thus the promise made by Jeremiah was to the effect that Zedekiah would not be exiled but would be allowed to live out his life in Jerusalem if he surrendered. This is quite possible; yet we should remember that Jehoiachin earlier had surrendered but had been exiled to Babylon, where subsequently he was removed from prison and given a favored position (52:31-33). Zedekiah, who had rebelled against Nebuchadrezzar, would hardly have been given better treatment than Jehoiachin.

This passage is not from the Deuteronomic editor (contra Mowinckel); it shows no trace of his editing (except possibly vs. 1), and is on the whole quite authentic, coming apparently from Baruch's memoirs. Since the promise to Zedekiah was not fulfilled, we can hardly view it as a secondary addition. Vs. 1, with its rather bombastic phraseology, is probably editorial (Rudolph).

34:5. The reference is not to cremation of the body, which was not practiced by the Hebrews, but to ceremonies performed after the death of a king (see II Chr. 16:14; 21:19). **Alas, lord!** was a phrase used in lamentation over a deceased king (cf. 22:18).

ter is apparently earlier than that of ch. 21. Egypt's overtures to Judah on the accession of Hophra (successor to Psamtik) appear to have seduced the ambitious princes of Jerusalem once again. The Ammonites also joined in the alliance against Nebuchadrezzar, whose forces were then tied up with the siege of Tyre. It appeared for a moment that this resistance

might succeed. Jeremiah was not deceived (37:6-10). In far-off Babylon the prophet Ezekiel also warns against "the rebellious house" which is "sending ambassadors to Egypt" (Ezek. 17:11, 15). When Nebuchadrezzar turns to deal with the threat from the south, Ezekiel envisions his armies as they reach the "two ways"—the one marking the road toward the Ammonites,

6 Then Jeremiah the prophet spake all these words unto Zedekiah king of Judah in Jerusalem,

7 When the king of Babylon's army fought against Jerusalem, and against all the cities of Judah that were left, against Lachish, and against Azekah: for these defensed cities remained of the cities of Judah.

8 ¶ *This is* the word that came unto Jeremiah from the LORD, after that the king Zedekiah had made a covenant with all the

6 Then Jeremiah the prophet spoke all these words to Zedeki'ah king of Judah, in Jerusalem, 7 when the army of the king of Babylon was fighting against Jerusalem and against all the cities of Judah that were left, Lachish and Aze'kah; for these were the only fortified cities of Judah that remained.

8 The word which came to Jeremiah from the LORD, after King Zedeki'ah had

---

7. Lachish was in the Shephelah, twenty-three miles southwest of Jerusalem, the modern Tell ed-Duweir. The site was excavated between 1932 and 1938 by the Wellcome archaeological research expedition to the Near East with results that support, if they do not actually prove, the identification. **Azekah** is modern Tell ez-Zakarîyeh, eleven miles north of Lachish, and eighteen miles west-southwest of Jerusalem. One of the letters found at Lachish (written in Hebrew on broken pieces of pottery) provides remarkable confirmation of this verse (Torczyner, *Lachish Letters,* pp. 79, 83-84). Letter No. IV, ll. 10-13, contains these words: "We are watching for the smoke-signals of Lachish, according to all the indications which my lord gave, because we do not see Azekah." The letter was written by the captain of a Hebrew outpost, probably between Azekah and Lachish, to the commander in Lachish; it must have been written shortly after the fall of Azekah to the Babylonians and before the fall of Lachish. Nebuchadrezzar had attacked and captured many of the **fortified cities of Judah,** as archaeological discoveries have verified; Lachish and Azekah were the strongest and held out the longest.

If the Babylonians followed the Assyrian practice of taking the smaller towns of a country before laying siege to the capital, the event here described may have occurred before the siege of Jerusalem itself began in January, 588 B.C. W. F. Albright ("A Supplement to Jeremiah: The Lachish Ostraca," *Bulletin of the American Schools of Oriental Research,* No. 61 [Feb., 1936], pp. 15-16; "A Reëxamination of the Lachish Letters," *ibid.,* No. 73 [Feb., 1939], p. 16) thinks that the Lachish letters reflect conditions in the summer of 589 B.C., Lachish itself being captured in the fall.

XXV. THE BROKEN PLEDGE TO RELEASED SLAVES (34:8-22)

Some time after the Babylonian siege of Jerusalem began in January, 588 B.C., the people of that city made a solemn covenant to release their slaves, hoping thereby to gain the favor of Yahweh. But after a time (probably in the spring of 588), the Egyptians

---

the other the road to Jerusalem. And when the lot fell toward Jerusalem, the allies of Judah melted away; according to Obadiah these petty neighbors

> rejoiced over the people of Judah
> in the day of their ruin;
> [they] boasted
> in the day of distress (vs. 12).

Vss. 1-7 contain a message for Zedekiah delivered at a time when there was still some chance that by judicious action the king might save himself and Jerusalem. Should he surrender (see Exeg.) he might still escape with his life. Jeremiah does not relax for a moment his persuasion that Jerusalem will fall. This has been his conviction for two decades. But

there was still a possible leniency for the king: he would be carried into exile, but he would be accorded such honors as might pertain to a captive king. Lachish and Azekah have not yet fallen: something might still be done for king and people if Zedekiah would but act. But, though Jeremiah's messages told quite clearly on the king, Zedekiah had not the strength, either in himself or in his circle, to oppose himself to the princes in power or to sacrifice his present safety (it *might* be that his city would survive) for the dubious chance of easy exile.

8-22. *The Great Equivocation.*—The disappointment which one must feel in the vacillating king is as nothing compared with the open treachery of the equivocating nation. Later than the incident above, when the siege was pressed,

people which *were* at Jerusalem, to proclaim liberty unto them;

9 That every man should let his manservant, and every man his maidservant, *being* a Hebrew or a Hebrewess, go free; that none should serve himself of them, *to wit,* of a Jew his brother.

10 Now when all the princes, and all the people, which had entered into the covenant, heard that every one should let his manservant, and every one his maidservant, go free, that none should serve themselves of them any more; then they obeyed, and let *them* go.

11 But afterwards they turned, and caused the servants and the handmaids, whom they had let go free, to return, and

made a covenant with all the people in Jerusalem to make a proclamation of liberty to them, 9 that every one should set free his Hebrew slaves, male and female, so that no one should enslave a Jew, his brother. 10 And they obeyed, all the princes and all the people who had entered into the covenant that every one would set free his slave, male or female, so that they would not be enslaved again; they obeyed and set them free. 11 But afterward they turned around

---

sent an army into Judah to give aid to the Hebrews, and the Babylonians lifted the siege for a period (37:6-11). Thereupon the former slaveowners, thinking the danger was past, broke their covenant and took their former slaves back. This hypocritical action was rebuked by Jeremiah, who promised that the Babylonians would return and capture the city.

This passage, which probably rests upon a section of Baruch's memoirs, has been reworked by the Deuteronomic editor. His hand is especially evident in vss. 13-15, 17, but he has largely rewritten the whole account. He has made the release of the slaves appear to be in obedience to the law contained in Deut. 15:1, 12-15 (Exod. 21:2), but it is most improbable that this was the case. The Deuteronomic law provides for the release of a slave after he has been in servitude for six years; since the term of so many slaves could not have expired at the same time, the action described here must have been a release by special proclamation of the king under an emergency situation. Aside from this detail, however, the account is largely authentic.

A. Action of the Owners (34:8-12)

The motives of the slaveowners in releasing their slaves were not unmixed. With Jerusalem under siege, many of the slaves were economic liabilities rather than assets. Those who were employed in working farms that lay outside the city would be useless, and at a time when food was scarce owners must have been hard pressed to feed their slaves as well as their families. Furthermore, the freeing of the slaves made more men available for the defense of the city. The people cloaked their action in religious motives, but the prophet must have seen through it and rebuked them both for their hypocrisy and for their perfidy in breaking a solemn covenant. Peake (*Jeremiah and Lamentations,* II, 139) speaks of the incident as "a death-bed repentance, with the usual sequel on recovery."

11. The time of the re-enslavement is made clear by vs. 21.

---

it appears that the nation sought to propitiate its Lord by a belated stratagem of high moral idealism. They freed their slaves! Men were still trying to do this in the day when Emerson wrote: "What proof of infidelity like the toleration and propagandism of slavery?" [2] But to guarantee their purpose and to proclaim their

purity of motive, the royal proclamation was conveyed in covenantal form, with sacrifices and all the rites of solemn religious engagement. Then the forces of Babylon withdrew! They fell away to meet the armies of Egypt coming from the south! No sooner was the siege of Jerusalem thus temporarily lifted than the bondsmen, just freed, were forced into serfdom once again. For Jeremiah, the

[2] *Conduct of Life,* "Worship."

brought them into subjection for servants and for handmaids.

12 ¶ Therefore the word of the LORD came to Jeremiah from the LORD, saying,

13 Thus saith the LORD, the God of Israel; I made a covenant with your fathers in the day that I brought them forth out of the land of Egypt, out of the house of bondmen, saying,

14 At the end of seven years let ye go every man his brother a Hebrew, which hath been sold unto thee; and when he hath served thee six years, thou shalt let him go free from thee: but your fathers hearkened not unto me, neither inclined their ear.

15 And ye were now turned, and had done right in my sight, in proclaiming liberty every man to his neighbor; and ye had made a covenant before me in the house which is called by my name:

16 But ye turned and polluted my name, and caused every man his servant, and every man his handmaid, whom he had set at liberty at their pleasure, to return, and brought them into subjection, to be unto you for servants and for handmaids.

17 Therefore thus saith the LORD; Ye have not hearkened unto me, in proclaiming liberty, every one to his brother, and every man to his neighbor: behold, I proclaim a liberty for you, saith the LORD, to the sword, to the pestilence, and to the famine; and I will make you to be removed into all the kingdoms of the earth.

18 And I will give the men that have transgressed my covenant, which have not performed the words of the covenant which

and took back the male and female slaves they had set free, and brought them into subjection as slaves. **12** The word of the LORD came to Jeremiah from the LORD: **13** "Thus says the LORD, the God of Israel: I made a covenant with your fathers when I brought them out of the land of Egypt, out of the house of bondage, saying, **14** 'At the end of six[l] years each of you must set free the fellow Hebrew who has been sold to you and has served you six years; you must set him free from your service.' But your fathers did not listen to me or incline their ears to me. **15** You recently repented and did what was right in my eyes by proclaiming liberty, each to his neighbor, and you made a covenant before me in the house which is called by my name; **16** but then you turned around and profaned my name when each of you took back his male and female slaves, whom you had set free according to their desire, and you brought them into subjection to be your slaves. **17** Therefore, thus says the LORD: You have not obeyed me by proclaiming liberty, every one to his brother and to his neighbor; behold, I proclaim to you liberty to the sword, to pestilence, and to famine, says the LORD. I will make you a horror to all the kingdoms of the earth. **18** And the men who transgressed my covenant and did not

[l] Gk: Heb *seven*

B. JEREMIAH'S REBUKE (34:13-22)

14. This verse is largely quoted from Deut. 15:1, 12, rather than Exod. 21:2; it is interesting that this law is considered as having been given at the time of the exodus from Egypt (vs. 13), though the laws of Deuteronomy were supposed to have been spoken by Moses in Moab shortly before his death.

18-19. These verses shed interesting light on the manner in which a covenant was made among the Hebrews. The RSV gives what is probably the correct reading of vs. 18

---

people of Israel have no excuse. **You made a covenant before me in the house which is called by my name** [their action was as sacred as it could be]; **but then you turned around and profaned my name when each of you took back his male and female slaves.** Comes then the thunderous and outraged **Therefore** of the prophet, who speaks from the integrity of the Lord's word and covenant, **behold, I proclaim**

to you liberty—even as they have treated their slaves, so now is a like liberty granted to them **—to the sword, to pestilence, and to famine.** They shall become **a horror** to all nations of the earth. For the king of Babylon will return and destroy the city.

One can easily sense the indignation of the prophet in this message. The passion of outrage is in his words. Nothing betrays the deeper

they had made before me, when they cut the calf in twain, and passed between the parts thereof,

19 The princes of Judah, and the princes of Jerusalem, the eunuchs, and the priests, and all the people of the land, which passed between the parts of the calf;

20 I will even give them into the hand of their enemies, and into the hand of them that seek their life: and their dead bodies shall be for meat unto the fowls of the heaven, and to the beasts of the earth.

21 And Zedekiah king of Judah and his princes will I give into the hand of their enemies, and into the hand of them that seek their life, and into the hand of the king of Babylon's army, which are gone up from you.

22 Behold, I will command, saith the LORD, and cause them to return to this city; and they shall fight against it, and take it, and burn it with fire: and I will make the cities of Judah a desolation without an inhabitant.

keep the terms of the covenant which they made before me, I will make like[m] the calf which they cut in two and passed between its parts — **19** the princes of Judah, the princes of Jerusalem, the eunuchs, the priests, and all the people of the land who passed between the parts of the calf; **20** and I will give them into the hand of their enemies and into the hand of those who seek their lives. Their dead bodies shall be food for the birds of the air and the beasts of the earth. **21** And Zedeki′ah king of Judah, and his princes I will give into the hand of their enemies and into the hand of those who seek their lives, into the hand of the army of the king of Babylon which has withdrawn from you. **22** Behold, I will command, says the LORD, and will bring them back to this city; and they will fight against it, and take it, and burn it with fire. I will make the cities of Judah a desolation without inhabitant."

[m] Cn: Heb lacks *like*

by emending העגל to כעגל, **like the calf.** For the ceremony which lies back of these words cf. Gen. 15:9-17, which is similar but not completely parallel. Some exegetes emphasize the fact that the calf was killed, and suppose that the ceremony involved a kind of self-imprecation. The parties to the rite are thought to have taken upon themselves a curse, either spoken or implied, such as the following: "May Yahweh do to me as has been done to this calf, if I break the terms of this covenant." This explanation has a parallel in a treaty between Ashurnirari V king of Assyria, and Mati-ilu of Bit-Agusi. A ram was beheaded, and the treaty says: "This head is not the head of a ram, but it is the head of Mati-ilu. . . . If Mati-ilu sins against this oath, then as the head of this ram was cut off, so will the head of Mati-ilu be cut off." (Quoted by Rudolph, *Jeremiah*, p. 190, and by Quell, "Der alttestamentliche Begriff ברית," in Gerhard Kittel, ed., *Theologisches Wörterbuch zum Neuen Testament* [Stuttgart: W. Kohlhammer, 1935], II, 118, n. 49.) Other interpreters emphasize the fact that the parties to the covenant passed between the two parts of the calf, which in this manner were bound together in a union not to be lightly broken; likewise, among Arabs and other peoples, parties to a covenant were sometimes bound together by partaking of each other's blood or by being smeared with the blood of a slain animal (W. Robertson Smith, *Religion of the Semites*, pp. 314-17, 479-81, 691-92). In the present context the former explanation is preferable. In any event, a rite such as this probably accounts for the fact that in Hebrew the verb usually employed for making a covenant means, lit., to **cut** the covenant.

equivocation of the heart of the people more than this outer offense against their kind. During the siege the slaves were a burden on the state. The moment the siege was lifted they were once more needed in the fields outside the city. They were forced back into bondage before they had tasted the sweets of freedom. But the all-important point to Jeremiah was the double breach of faith—to their own kind,

and to their covenant commitment with Yahweh. This is but the manifest violation of faith already implicit in the nation's infidelity to their primary Davidic covenant perceived by Jeremiah almost from the beginning of his work (cf. 2:2).

There is a fine saying of Emerson's: "There are Scriptures written invisibly on men's hearts, whose letters do not come out until they are

35 The word which came unto Jeremiah from the Lord, in the days of Jehoiakim the son of Josiah king of Judah, saying,

35 The word which came to Jeremiah from the Lord in the days of Jehoi'a-

XXVI. Example of the Rechabites (35:1-19)

Jeremiah brings into a chamber of the temple a group of Rechabites and offers them wine to drink. When they refuse, observing the prohibition laid down by their founder, the prophet uses them as an example to the people of Jerusalem. The Rechabites apparently had been founded by Jonadab the son of Rechab in the time of Jehu king of Israel (842-815 B.C.). Jonadab was a fanatic for the worship of Yahweh, the God of the desert, and supported Jehu in his bloody slaughter of the house of Ahab and of the worshipers of Baal (II Kings 10:15-28). The Rechabites were a puritan group, somewhat like the Nazirites (Num. 6:1-21). They protested against the Canaanite corruptions of the pure religion of Yahweh of the desert days, refusing to live in houses, to till the soil, or to drink wine. Their refusal to drink wine was not based on considerations like those of the modern teetotaler, but wine made from grapes symbolized to them Canaanite corruption. Wine was unknown to the Hebrews in their desert period. (I Chr. 2:55 speaks of Kenites that came of Hammath, the father of the house of Rechab, but this verse is too obscure to be used for historical purposes.)

Jeremiah here commends the Rechabites for their fidelity to the rules of their order, but it is not to be thought that he approved of their rules as such. The problem of the relationship between religion and culture was met in different ways by the Rechabites and the prophets. The Rechabites believed that religion stood against culture, and their cry was "Return to the desert life!" The prophets believed that religion stood above culture as critic, and protested against the sins of the civilization which the Israelites adopted from the Canaanites. Their cry was "Repent and return to the Lord!" The prophets did not believe that the hands of the clock can be turned back, but many of them did believe that Israel had been more faithful to Yahweh in the days of the desert than in Palestine (2:2-3; Hos. 2:15; 9:10; 11:1-2; et al.). Amos was sympathetic with the Nazirites (Amos 2:11-12), as Jeremiah is here with the Rechabites.

The date of this incident is a matter of dispute. Vs. 11 indicates that it took place when the Chaldeans and Syrians (Arameans) were invading Judah. This may have been the invasion of 602 B.C., when bands of Chaldeans, Syrians, and others invaded the land (II Kings 24:2); or it may have been the later invasion of 598, although at that time there is no mention of Syrians allied with the Chaldeans. The former date is thus more probable. The fact that the Rechabites took refuge within the walls of Jerusalem (though even there they may have continued to live in tents) shows the dilemma an absolutist group sometimes faces; in time of danger the Rechabites were forced to seek protection provided by those who lived contrary to the type of life which they professed.

There is genuine material in the chapter (probably from Baruch's memoirs), but it has been rewritten by the Deuteronomic editor. His hand is evident especially in

---

enraged." [3] Clearly Jeremiah's anger is of this fundamental kind, deepened and enhanced as it is by his profoundly probing covenantal consciousness.

35:1-19. Jeremiah and the Rechabites.—It would appear that Jeremiah missed no opportunity to dramatize his message and bring its import home. No sooner had the nomadic Rechabites come to Jerusalem in fear of the ravaging Chaldeans than Jeremiah exploited

[3] *Miscellanies,* "American Civilization."

their peculiar appearance, converting it into an object lesson wherewith to convict the people of Judah. The Rechabites notoriously lived in tents, did not sow seeds nor plant vineyards, and refrained from drinking wine. All this they did because of their ancestral law. For two hundred years the sect had strictly maintained its regimen. Not even the word of a prophet could tempt them to compromise it. Jeremiah was well aware that this was so, and it clarified at once his course of action. He took the Rechabites into the temple, where his

2 Go unto the house of the Rechabites, and speak unto them, and bring them into the house of the LORD, into one of the chambers, and give them wine to drink.

3 Then I took Jaazaniah the son of Jeremiah, the son of Habaziniah, and his brethren, and all his sons, and the whole house of the Rechabites;

4 And I brought them into the house of the LORD, into the chamber of the sons of Hanan, the son of Igdaliah, a man of God, which *was* by the chamber of the princes, which *was* above the chamber of Maaseiah the son of Shallum, the keeper of the door:

5 And I set before the sons of the house of the Rechabites pots full of wine, and cups; and I said unto them, Drink ye wine.

6 But they said, We will drink no wine: for Jonadab the son of Rechab our father commanded us, saying, Ye shall drink no wine, *neither* ye, nor your sons for ever:

7 Neither shall ye build houses, nor sow seed, nor plant vineyard, nor have *any:* but all your days ye shall dwell in tents; that ye may live many days in the land where ye *be* strangers.

8 Thus have we obeyed the voice of Jonadab the son of Rechab our father in all that

kim the son of Josi'ah, king of Judah: 2 "Go to the house of the Re'chabites, and speak with them, and bring them to the house of the LORD, into one of the chambers; then offer them wine to drink." 3 So I took Jaazani'ah the son of Jeremiah, son of Habazzini'ah, and his brothers, and all his sons, and the whole house of the Re'chabites. 4 I brought them to the house of the LORD into the chamber of the sons of Hanan the son of Igdali'ah, the man of God, which was near the chamber of the princes, above the chamber of Ma-asei'ah the son of Shallum, keeper of the threshold. 5 Then I set before the Re'chabites pitchers full of wine, and cups; and I said to them, "Drink wine." 6 But they answered, "We will drink no wine, for Jon'adab the son of Rechab, our father, commanded us, 'You shall not drink wine, neither you nor your sons for ever; 7 you shall not build a house; you shall not sow seed; you shall not plant or have a vineyard; but you shall live in tents all your days, that you may live many days in the land where you sojourn.' 8 We have obeyed the voice of Jon'adab the son of

Jeremiah's speech (vss. 12-19). Many Deuteronomic phrases and ideas occur; vss. 16, 18-19 probably contain the original nucleus, later expanded by the editor. He has also expanded parts of vss. 1-11, which are now very repetitious.

A. The Offer of Wine to the Rechabites (35:1-5)

35:2. "Clan" is a better translation of the Hebrew *bêth* than **house**, since the reference is not to the place where they lived, but to the group. **Bring them . . . chambers:** Surrounding the temple proper and within the temple courts were a number of chambers which were used as storerooms, residences, rooms for sacrificial feasts, etc. The chamber used here was apparently somewhat open to the public.

3-4. The individuals named are otherwise unknown, except that **Maaseiah** may be the father of the priest Zephaniah mentioned in 21:1; 29:25; 37:3.

5. Pitchers is a better rendering than **pots**. Though *gābhîa'* is used in Gen. 44 for Joseph's cup, here it is probably the common pitcher used by the Israelites for either wine or water, ordinarily measuring eight to ten inches in height (Kelso, *Ceramic Vocabulary of the O.T.*, p. 17).

B. The Rechabites' Refusal (35:6-17)

6-7. Jonadab is called **father** in the sense that he was the founder and spiritual ancestor of the Rechabites, not their physical ancestor (cf. the use of the word for Elisha

action would be widely noticed, and where maximum significance would attach to it. He offered the Rechabites wine which they refused. The moral was clear: the Rechabites were faithful to the command of a single ancestor. For

two hundred years they had observed faithfully and literally the command of Jonadab ben Rechab.

But this people has not obeyed me, exclaimed Jeremiah, thrusting the moral home. **I have**

he hath charged us, to drink no wine all our days, we, our wives, our sons, nor our daughters;

9 Nor to build houses for us to dwell in; neither have we vineyard, nor field, nor seed:

10 But we have dwelt in tents, and have obeyed, and done according to all that Jonadab our father commanded us.

11 But it came to pass, when Nebuchadrezzar king of Babylon came up into the land, that we said, Come, and let us go to Jerusalem for fear of the army of the Chaldeans, and for fear of the army of the Syrians: so we dwell at Jerusalem.

12 ¶ Then came the word of the LORD unto Jeremiah, saying,

13 Thus saith the LORD of hosts, the God of Israel; Go and tell the men of Judah and the inhabitants of Jerusalem, Will ye not receive instruction to hearken to my words? saith the LORD.

14 The words of Jonadab the son of Rechab, that he commanded his sons not to drink wine, are performed; for unto this day they drink none, but obey their father's commandment: notwithstanding I have spoken unto you, rising early and speaking; but ye hearkened not unto me.

15 I have sent also unto you all my servants the prophets, rising up early and sending *them,* saying, Return ye now every man from his evil way, and amend your doings, and go not after other gods to serve them, and ye shall dwell in the land which I have given to you and to your fathers: but ye have not inclined your ear, nor hearkened unto me.

16 Because the sons of Jonadab the son of Rechab have performed the commandment of their father, which he commanded

Rechab, our father, in all that he commanded us, to drink no wine all our days, ourselves, our wives, our sons, or our daughters, **9** and not to build houses to dwell in. We have no vineyard or field or seed; **10** but we have lived in tents, and have obeyed and done all that Jon'adab our father commanded us. **11** But when Nebuchadrez'zar king of Babylon came up against the land, we said, 'Come, and let us go to Jerusalem for fear of the army of the Chalde'ans and the army of the Syrians.' So we are living in Jerusalem."

12 Then the word of the LORD came to Jeremiah: **13** "Thus says the LORD of hosts, the God of Israel: Go and say to the men of Judah and the inhabitants of Jerusalem, Will you not receive instruction and listen to my words? says the LORD. **14** The command which Jon'adab the son of Rechab gave to his sons, to drink no wine, has been kept; and they drink none to this day, for they have obeyed their father's command. I have spoken to you persistently, but you have not listened to me. **15** I have sent to you all my servants the prophets, sending them persistently, saying, 'Turn now every one of you from his evil way, and amend your doings, and do not go after other gods to serve them, and then you shall dwell in the land which I gave to you and your fathers.' But you did not incline your ear or listen to me. **16** The sons of Jon'adab the

---

in II Kings 6:21; 13:14). The prohibitions laid upon this group are similar to those which Diodorus Siculus (XIX. 94) says the Nabataeans observed (first century B.C.), not, however, for religious reasons but on account of their nomadic life.

---

spoken to you persistently, says the Lord, **but you have not listened to me.** The contrast was emphatic, the rebuke deserved. **Therefore, . . . says the LORD . . . I am bringing on Judah and all the inhabitants of Jerusalem all the evil that I have pronounced against them.**

It is important to note two things which Jeremiah does not say. In his approval of the Rechabites he focuses upon the single fact of

their fidelity. He does not approve their practices. The Rechabite return to the practices of the wilderness is in no way comparable with Jeremiah's insistence on the primacy of the wilderness covenant relation. The two are dimensions apart. The Rechabite movement was narrow and reactionary, that of Jeremiah dynamic and open to the future.

Again, though he commends them for their

them; but this people hath not hearkened unto me:

17 Therefore thus saith the LORD God of hosts, the God of Israel; Behold, I will bring upon Judah and upon all the inhabitants of Jerusalem all the evil that I have pronounced against them: because I have spoken unto them, but they have not heard; and I have called unto them, but they have not answered.

18 ¶ And Jeremiah said unto the house of the Rechabites, Thus saith the LORD of hosts, the God of Israel; Because ye have obeyed the commandment of Jonadab your father, and kept all his precepts, and done according unto all that he hath commanded you;

19 Therefore thus saith the LORD of hosts, the God of Israel; Jonadab the son of Rechab shall not want a man to stand before me for ever.

son of Rechab have kept the command which their father gave them, but this people has not obeyed me. 17 Therefore, thus says the LORD, the God of hosts, the God of Israel: Behold, I am bringing on Judah and all the inhabitants of Jerusalem all the evil that I have pronounced against them; because I have spoken to them and they have not listened, I have called to them and they have not answered."

18 But to the house of the Re'chabites Jeremiah said, "Thus says the LORD of hosts, the God of Israel: Because you have obeyed the command of Jon'adab your father, and kept all his precepts, and done all that he commanded you, 19 therefore thus says the LORD of hosts, the God of Israel: Jon'adab the son of Rechab shall never lack a man to stand before me."

C. THE PROMISE (35:18-19)

19. **Stand before me** sometimes has the sense of interceding before the Lord (15:1; 18:20), but it is a mistake to suppose that the Rechabites served in a priestly capacity. Jeremiah recognizes their life as a form of service before the Lord.

Neh. 3:14 refers to one "Malchijah the son of Rechab, ruler of the district of Beth-haccherem"; whether he was a descendant of the Rechabites here mentioned is not known, but from the type of work he was doing it is natural to conclude he was not.

Eusebius (*Church History* II. 23. 17), quoting Hegesippus, refers to "one of the priests of the sons of Rechab, the son of Rechabim," who protested the martyrdom of James the Just. In medieval and modern times travelers in Syria and Arabia have found tribes that claimed to be Rechabites and to follow the rules of Jonadab. In all of these instances we probably have to do with groups that followed one or more of the Rechabite rules, not lineal descendants of the Rechabites of this chapter. All faithful Moslems refuse to drink wine.

---

faithfulness, he does not in the same breath commend them for their asceticism. The reason the Rechabites drank no wine was not that they were opposed to intoxication, but because their ancestor believed that the planting of vines would attach them to the land and bind them to a permanent residence. There is little of the ascetic in Jeremiah. Indeed, as one thinks of his sensitivity to all the grandeurs of nature and his obvious hunger for "the voice of mirth and the voice of gladness, the voice of the bridegroom and the voice of the bride, the voices of those who sing" (33:11), it is clear that he is far removed in spirit from legalistic disciplines. One is reminded of the words of St. Francis of Sales:

I have never been able to approve the method of those who in order to reform mankind begin from

the outside. . . . It seems to me, on the contrary, that it is necessary to begin from within. Return to me, says God, with all your heart. . . . After you do this your life, which opens from your heart like an almond tree from its stone, will produce all its actions, which are its fruits, already inscribed and engraved with the same word of salvation. . . . Whoever gains the heart of man gains the man entire.[4]

This is not far from the spirit of Jeremiah. We may also observe in passing that, if the Rechabites could remain faithful in their nomadic life to the command of an ancestor for two hundred years, it should be possible for the people of Judah to remain faithful to Yahweh during their impending journey into exile and their uprooted life there pending their return.

[4] *Introduction to the Devout Life* III. 23.

36 And it came to pass in the fourth year of Jehoiakim the son of Josiah king of Judah, *that* this word came unto Jeremiah from the LORD, saying,

2 Take thee a roll of a book, and write therein all the words that I have spoken unto thee against Israel, and against Judah, and against all the nations, from the day I spake unto thee, from the days of Josiah, even unto this day.

36 In the fourth year of Jehoi'akim the son of Josi'ah, king of Judah, this word came to Jeremiah from the LORD: 2 "Take a scroll and write on it all the words that I have spoken to you against Israel and Judah and all the nations, from the day I spoke to you, from the days of

---

XXVII. Two Scrolls of Jeremiah's Prophecies (36:1-32)

This chapter is unique in that it is the only detailed description in the O.T. of the writing of a prophetic "book." It gives valuable information concerning the physical process involved in the writing. Furthermore, it marks an important turning point in the career of Jeremiah, being the first time his words were written to be read in public.

The dictation of the book took place in 605 B.C., and its reading in the month of December of that year. Jeremiah was probably impelled to reduce his words to writing partly by the momentous events which were taking place in the international scene. In the spring or summer of 605, Nebuchadrezzar defeated the Egyptians and the remnant of the Assyrians in the battle of Carchemish (46:2-12); in July or August his father Nabopolassar died, and Nebuchadrezzar ascended the throne of Babylon. The Babylonians were now the dominant power and Judah, which had been dependent upon Egypt, was in danger. Jeremiah sought through the reading of his words to bring the people of Judah to a realization of the seriousness of their situation. It was now very clear who the "foe from the north" was. Jeremiah may also have been influenced by the fact that he himself was prevented from going to the temple to deliver his message in person (vs. 5; see Exeg.). His book was read before the people in the temple on a great fast day, again before the officials, and finally before the king. The king contemptuously cut up and burned the book, but a new one was prepared, with additional words.

The present account comes in all probability from Baruch, who played a prominent role in the events here recorded, though he does not exaggerate his own part. Vss. 27-32 bear marks of the style of the Deuteronomic editor; he has apparently rewritten the account of the dictation of the second scroll, though there is no reason to doubt the fundamental accuracy of the whole chapter.

It has usually been assumed that the second scroll described here formed the "first edition" of the book of Jeremiah, and many attempts have been made to discover within our present book the passages which were contained in it. Our book of Jeremiah is very probably an expansion of that scroll, and we can make conjectures concerning the passages it contained, but we cannot have full confidence in such conjectures (this subject is discussed more fully in the Intro., pp. 787-91; for a detailed discussion of the nature of writing and of writing materials in O.T. times see J. Philip Hyatt, "The Writing of an Old Testament Book," *Biblical Archaeologist*, VI [1943], 71-80).

A. Dictation to Baruch (36:1-7)

36:1. The fourth year of Jehoiakim was 606-605 B.C. (see Exeg. on vs. 9).

2-3. Take a scroll: The Hebrew *meghillath ṣēpher* is used for a scroll of sufficient size to make a "book." The codex (the modern book form) did not come into use until

---

36:1-32. The Penknife Versus the Pen.— There came a point in Kierkegaard's stormy career when he said, "I must make them strike me!" If he was to succeed in bringing the issue between Christianity and Christendom into

sharper definition, he knew that something had to be done to define the issue. Jeremiah's aims were more authentic than those of Kierkegaard, but he also knew that the issue must be brought out into the open and focused at the very core

1063

3 It may be that the house of Judah will hear all the evil which I purpose to do unto them; that they may return every man from his evil way; that I may forgive their iniquity and their sin.

4 Then Jeremiah called Baruch the son of Neriah: and Baruch wrote from the mouth of Jeremiah all the words of the LORD, which he had spoken unto him, upon a roll of a book.

5 And Jeremiah commanded Baruch, saying, I *am* shut up; I cannot go into the house of the LORD:

6 Therefore go thou, and read in the roll, which thou hast written from my mouth, the words of the LORD in the ears of the people in the LORD's house upon the fasting day: and also thou shalt read them in the ears of all Judah that come out of their cities.

Josi'ah until today. 3 It may be that the house of Judah will hear all the evil which I intend to do to them, so that every one may turn from his evil way, and that I may forgive their iniquity and their sin."

4 Then Jeremiah called Baruch the son of Neri'ah, and Baruch wrote upon a scroll at the dictation of Jeremiah all the words of the LORD which he had spoken to him. 5 And Jeremiah ordered Baruch, saying, "I am debarred from going to the house of the LORD; 6 so you are to go, and on a fast day in the hearing of all the people in the LORD's house you shall read the words of the LORD from the scroll which you have written at my dictation. You shall read them also in the hearing of all the men of

---

later, probably the first century A.D. The material used by Baruch was doubtless papyrus, which was widely used at this time. Any writing material made of animal skins (leather or vellum) would have been difficult to cut with a penknife, and would have made an intolerable stench when burned. A scroll was made by pasting together a number of single sheets of papyrus.

The LXX has "against Jerusalem" instead of **against Israel,** and this may be the original reading, since Jeremiah's words of condemnation were addressed to Jerusalem and Judah rather than the old Northern Kingdom of Israel. Note that vs. 3 has only **house of Judah.**

4. Baruch the son of Neriah has already been mentioned in 32:12-13, 16. He was apparently from a prominent family, his brother Seraiah being an important official under Zedekiah (51:59). Josephus (*Antiquities* X. 9. 1) describes him as being "from a very distinguished family and exceptionally well instructed in his native tongue."

5. I am debarred from going to the house of the LORD is a better translation than **I am shut up,** though we do not know why Jeremiah was prevented from going to the temple at this time. He was not in prison (see vs. 19). Some scholars believe that the events of 20:1-6 lie back of the prohibition, but those events must have been later. It is possible that the prophet had not been allowed to go into the temple area since the preaching of his "temple sermon" (7:1-15; 26:1-6). Or it may be that he was debarred because of some religious impurity, the nature of which we do not know.

6. The reading of the scroll in the temple took place **on a fast day.** The ancient Hebrews had very few fixed days of fasting, but they were proclaimed on special occasions in times of national distress. One was proclaimed at this time because either of the approaching danger from the Babylonians or of drought. The former explanation is

---

of the life of the people. His sermon at the temple gate had gone far toward crystallizing the issue. His object lessons, his parables, his opposition to the false prophets, his denunciation of Jehoiakim's extravagant palace building —all had served to make his position increasingly plain. We must allow for the possibility that Jehoiakim had already heard that "with

the burial of an ass he [should] be buried" (22:19). Now, on the occasion of the great fast, Jeremiah strikes again. He prepares the scroll, with its dramatic summation of all his prophecies, from the time of Josiah to the crisis brought about by the battle of Carchemish. Since he himself was under surveillance of the king's police, and debarred from entering the

7 It may be they will present their supplication before the LORD, and will return every one from his evil way: for great is the anger and the fury that the LORD hath pronounced against this people.

8 And Baruch the son of Neriah did according to all that Jeremiah the prophet commanded him, reading in the book the words of the LORD in the LORD's house.

9 And it came to pass in the fifth year of Jehoiakim the son of Josiah king of Judah, in the ninth month, that they proclaimed a fast before the LORD to all the people in Jerusalem, and to all the people that came from the cities of Judah unto Jerusalem.

10 Then read Baruch in the book the words of Jeremiah in the house of the LORD, in the chamber of Gemariah the son of Shaphan the scribe, in the higher court, at the entry of the new gate of the LORD's house, in the ears of all the people.

Judah who come out of their cities. 7 It may be that their supplication will come before the LORD, and that every one will turn from his evil way, for great is the anger and wrath that the LORD has pronounced against this people." 8 And Baruch the son of Neri'ah did all that Jeremiah the prophet ordered him about reading from the scroll the words of the LORD in the LORD's house.

9 In the fifth year of Jehoi'akim the son of Josi'ah, king of Judah, in the ninth month, all the people in Jerusalem and all the people who came from the cities of Judah to Jerusalem proclaimed a fast before the LORD. 10 Then, in the hearing of all the people, Baruch read the words of Jeremiah from the scroll, in the house of the LORD, in the chamber of Gemari'ah the son of Shaphan the secretary, which was in the upper court, at the entry of the New Gate of the LORD's house.

improbable; it is unlikely that the king would have treated the scroll of Jeremiah so lightly if a fast had been called because of the Babylonian danger, for the scroll must have contained some of the warnings concerning the foe from the north. According to the Mishnah (Taanith 1:5), if no rain had fallen on the first day of Kislev (November-December), three days of fasting were to be observed; this practice may go back to early times. At any rate, Jeremiah chose an occasion for the reading when many people were assembled in the temple courts.

B. Reading in the Temple (36:8-10)

9. **The fifth year of Jehoiakim** was 605-604 B.C. **The ninth month** was Kislev. According to the computations of R. A. Parker and W. H. Dubberstein (*Babylonian Chronology 626 B.C.—A.D. 45* [Chicago: University of Chicago Press, 1942], p. 25) the ninth month in 605 began on December 4. If the beginning of the king's regnal year was dated from the fall (with the seventh month) rather than from the spring, as seems likely, there was not necessarily a long interval between the writing of the scroll and its reading. The fourth year of Jehoiakim ended in approximately September, 605. Though the regnal year probably began in the fall, the calendar year began with Nisan, roughly March-April (cf. Julian Morgenstern, "The New Year for Kings," in Bruno Schindler, ed., *Gaster Anniversary Volume* [London: Taylor's Foreign Press, 1936], pp. 439-56).

10. **In the chamber of Gemariah:** See Exeg. on 35:2.

temple, the reading of the scroll was entrusted to his secretary, Baruch, from whose hand it is supposed we have the present account. The scroll is first read to the people, then to the officials, and finally it is brought to the king himself.

Eduard Nielsen has rightly called attention to the excellent narrative art with which the chapter is composed.[5] This literary skill is exhibited in the clear division of the account

[5] *Oral Tradition* (Chicago: Alec R. Allenson, 1954), pp. 64-79.

into three sections: vss. 1-8, vss. 9-26, and vss. 27-32. Each of these sections is a complete unit in itself, yet they are also linked together. In the first unit we are told of the preparation of the scroll, and Jeremiah's hope that the people on hearing it would turn from their evil way and repent in order that God's anger might be stayed. In the second unit we learn that Baruch read the scroll **in the hearing of all the people** (vs. 10). Micaiah, grandson of Shaphan, was deeply impressed, and carried the word to the princes. The princes sent for Baruch and the

11 ¶ When Michaiah the son of Gemariah, the son of Shaphan, had heard out of the book all the words of the LORD,

12 Then he went down into the king's house, into the scribe's chamber: and, lo, all the princes sat there, *even* Elishama the scribe, and Delaiah the son of Shemaiah, and Elnathan the son of Achbor, and Gemariah the son of Shaphan, and Zedekiah the son of Hananiah, and all the princes.

13 Then Michaiah declared unto them all the words that he had heard, when Baruch read the book in the ears of the people.

14 Therefore all the princes sent Jehudi the son of Nethaniah, the son of Shelemiah, the son of Cushi, unto Baruch, saying, Take in thine hand the roll wherein thou hast read in the ears of the people, and come. So Baruch the son of Neriah took the roll in his hand, and came unto them.

15 And they said unto him, Sit down now, and read it in our ears. So Baruch read *it* in their ears.

16 Now it came to pass, when they had heard all the words, they were afraid both one and other, and said unto Baruch, We will surely tell the king of all these words.

17 And they asked Baruch, saying, Tell us now, How didst thou write all these words at his mouth?

11 When Micai'ah the son of Gemari'ah, son of Shaphan, heard all the words of the LORD from the scroll, 12 he went down to the king's house, into the secretary's chamber; and all the princes were sitting there: Eli'shama the secretary, Delai'ah the son of Shemai'ah, Elna'than the son of Achbor, Gemari'ah the son of Shaphan, Zedeki'ah the son of Hanani'ah, and all the princes. 13 And Micai'ah told them all the words that he had heard, when Baruch read the scroll in the hearing of the people. 14 Then all the princes sent Jehu'di the son of Nethani'ah, son of Shelemi'ah, son of Cushi, to say to Baruch, "Take in your hand the scroll that you read in the hearing of the people, and come." So Baruch the son of Neri'ah took the scroll in his hand and came to them. 15 And they said to him, "Sit down and read it." So Baruch read it to them. 16 When they heard all the words, they turned one to another in fear; and they said to Baruch, "We must report all these words to the king." 17 Then they asked Baruch, "Tell us, how did you write all these words? Was it at his dictation?"

C. READING BEFORE THE PRINCES (36:11-19)

12. The princes were not members of the royal family but administrative officials of Judah. Note that these officials treat Baruch with respect and seem to be somewhat friendly to the prophet; in vs. 25, they seek to prevent the king from burning the scroll.

14. It is very unusual for a name to be given, as here, with the ancestors of three generations listed. Accordingly, Cornill, Rudolph, *et al.*, read, "the officials sent Jehudi the son of Nethaniah and Shelemiah the son of Cushi," supposing that an original ואת has become בן. This may be correct.

scroll was read to them. When the princes heard the scroll, **they turned one to another in fear** (vs. 16).

> But all sat mute,
> Pondering the danger with deep thoughts; and each
> In other's countenance read his own dismay,
> Astonished.[6]

They agree that the words must be reported to the king; but before this is done, Baruch is instructed to take Jeremiah and **go and hide.** Follows then the highly dramatic scene with Jehudi, the usher, reading the scroll to the king

[6] Milton, *Paradise Lost*, Bk. II, l. 420.

while the princes stand nearby. Since it was winter the king was sitting beside a fire burning in a brazier. As Jehudi read, the king reached out and, with his penknife, cut away the columns of writing and threw them into the fire until the entire scroll was consumed. Three of the princes protested, but the king ignored them. It is carefully noted that **neither the king, nor any of his servants** betrayed either fear or other signs of repentance (vs. 24). At the conclusion of the episode Jehoiakim commanded that Baruch and Jeremiah be seized.

Two important comparisons will be noted in the narrative. Its construction is deliberately

18 Then Baruch answered them, He pronounced all these words unto me with his mouth, and I wrote *them* with ink in the book.

19 Then said the princes unto Baruch, Go, hide thee, thou and Jeremiah; and let no man know where ye be.

20 ¶ And they went in to the king into the court, but they laid up the roll in the chamber of Elishama the scribe, and told all the words in the ears of the king.

21 So the king sent Jehudi to fetch the roll; and he took it out of Elishama the scribe's chamber. And Jehudi read it in the ears of the king, and in the ears of all the princes which stood beside the king.

22 Now the king sat in the winter house in the ninth month: and *there was a fire* on the hearth burning before him.

23 And it came to pass, *that* when Jehudi had read three or four leaves, he cut it with the penknife, and cast *it* into the fire that *was* on the hearth, until all the roll was consumed in the fire that *was* on the hearth.

24 Yet they were not afraid, nor rent their garments, *neither* the king, nor any of his servants that heard all these words.

18 Baruch answered them, "He dictated all these words to me, while I wrote them with ink on the scroll." 19 Then the princes said to Baruch, "Go and hide, you and Jeremiah, and let no one know where you are."

20 So they went into the court to the king, having put the scroll in the chamber of Eli'shama the secretary; and they reported all the words to the king. 21 Then the king sent Jehu'di to get the scroll, and he took it from the chamber of Eli'shama the secretary; and Jehu'di read it to the king and all the princes who stood beside the king. 22 It was the ninth month, and the king was sitting in the winter house and there was a fire burning in the brazier before him. 23 As Jehu'di read three or four columns, the king would cut them off with a penknife and throw them into the fire in the brazier, until the entire scroll was consumed in the fire that was in the brazier. 24 Yet neither the king, nor any of his servants who heard all these words, was afraid, nor did they rend their garments.

18. A Hebrew scribe made **ink** by mixing soot or lampblack with an aqueous solution of gum. The chief ingredient was apparently carbon. Chemical tests made on the Lachish letters showed the possible presence also of iron (Torczyner, *Lachish Letters,* pp. 188-95). It is thought that oak galls and copperas may have been used in making the ink on those letters.

D. Reading Before King Jehoiakim (36:20-26)

22. This verse indicates clearly that the calendar year began with the month Nisan in the spring, our March-April (see Exeg. on vs. 9). **The winter house** was probably not a special edifice, but a part of the palace exposed to the winter sun and used in the winter because of its warmth. **The brazier** was probably made of metal. In modern times the natives of Palestine use braziers commonly made of clay. The Hebrew אח is of Egyptian origin, indicating that the use of the brazier was derived from Egypt.

23. The RSV translation is correct. The Hebrew imperfect and perfect with waw-consecutive are here used to express repeated action in the past. The scroll was cut with a **penknife**, lit., "a scribe's knife," used by the scribe for cutting papyrus and for sharpening the reed pen after the split point type came into use.

reminiscent of the reading of the scroll of the book of the law before Josiah. In II Kings 22:11 we are told that "when the king [Josiah] heard the words of the book of the law, he rent his clothes." Jehoiakim's reaction is precisely the opposite. Instead of instituting reform, as his father had done, he seeks Jeremiah to put him to death. Secondly, the religious significance of this confrontation of the king by the words

of the prophet is suggested by the obvious parallel with Elijah (I Kings 17:2-4): as the Lord hid Elijah from Ahab, so here he hides Jeremiah from the king.

It might appear that the action had reached its climax. Clearly the scroll is an absolute challenge to the king. The king's action in cutting the scroll symbolizes his view that Yahweh does not stand behind the prophecy. The scroll is the

25 Nevertheless Elnathan and Delaiah and Gemariah had made intercession to the king that he would not burn the roll; but he would not hear them.

26 But the king commanded Jerahmeel the son of Hammelech, and Seraiah the son of Azriel, and Shelemiah the son of Abdeel, to take Baruch the scribe and Jeremiah the prophet: but the LORD hid them.

27 ¶ Then the word of the LORD came to Jeremiah, after that the king had burned the roll, and the words which Baruch wrote at the mouth of Jeremiah, saying,

28 Take thee again another roll, and write in it all the former words that were in the first roll, which Jehoiakim the king of Judah hath burned.

29 And thou shalt say to Jehoiakim king of Judah, Thus saith the LORD; Thou hast burned this roll, saying, Why hast thou written therein, saying, The king of Babylon shall certainly come and destroy this land, and shall cause to cease from thence man and beast?

30 Therefore thus saith the LORD of Jehoiakim king of Judah; He shall have none to sit upon the throne of David: and his dead body shall be cast out in the day to the heat, and in the night to the frost.

31 And I will punish him and his seed and his servants for their iniquity; and I will bring upon them, and upon the in-

25 Even when Elna'than and Delai'ah and Gemari'ah urged the king not to burn the scroll, he would not listen to them. 26 And the king commanded Jerah'meel the king's son and Serai'ah the son of Az'ri-el and Shelemi'ah the son of Abdeel to seize Baruch the secretary and Jeremiah the prophet, but the LORD hid them.

27 Now, after the king had burned the scroll with the words which Baruch wrote at Jeremiah's dictation, the word of the LORD came to Jeremiah: 28 "Take another scroll and write on it all the former words that were in the first scroll, which Jehoi'akim the king of Judah has burned. 29 And concerning Jehoi'akim king of Judah you shall say, 'Thus says the LORD, You have burned this scroll, saying, "Why have you written in it that the king of Babylon will certainly come and destroy this land, and will cut off from it man and beast?" 30 Therefore thus says the LORD concerning Jehoi'akim king of Judah, He shall have none to sit upon the throne of David, and his dead body shall be cast out to the heat by day and the frost by night. 31 And I will punish him and his offspring and his servants for their iniquity; I will bring upon

---

26. Jerahmeel the king's son was probably not the son of Jehoiakim, who was only thirty years of age at this time (see II Kings 23:36); he may have been a related member of the royal family. **Hammelech** is Hebrew for "the king," and should be so translated (as in RSV), not be considered a personal name.

E. The Second Scroll (36:27-32)

30. The prediction contained in this verse was not literally fulfilled (see Exeg. on 22:18-19). Jehoiakim was succeeded by his son Jehoiachin, who reigned for only three months before he surrendered to the Babylonians and was exiled (II Kings 24:6-15). The whole section shows marks of Deuteronomic editing; the editor may have overlooked the short reign of Jehoiachin, or the prediction may be genuine.

---

visible symbol of Yahweh's judgment upon Judah; Jehoiakim destroys it to neutralize its meaning. The cutting of the roll implies, by extension, the cutting off of Jeremiah and his secretary. The reason for Jehoiakim's action is given in vs. 29: **Why have you written in [the scroll] that the king of Babylon will certainly come and destroy this land?**

There comes now the third movement in the drama (vss. 27-32). Yahweh hides the prophet

and instructs him to prepare another scroll, with a fresh oracle concerning the fate of Jehoiakim added to it. The pattern of the action here is very similar to that in the case of Hananiah (28:1-17). There Jeremiah appears with the yoke; Hananiah appears with a counter-prophecy, and rebuffs the prophet by breaking the yoke. Then Jeremiah returns with the fresh word of Yahweh that he will replace the broken wooden bars with bars of iron. So here,

habitants of Jerusalem, and upon the men of Judah, all the evil that I have pronounced against them; but they hearkened not.

32 ¶ Then took Jeremiah another roll, and gave it to Baruch the scribe, the son of Neriah; who wrote therein from the mouth of Jeremiah all the words of the book which Jehoiakim king of Judah had burned in the fire: and there were added besides unto them many like words.

37 And king Zedekiah the son of Josiah reigned instead of Coniah the son of Jehoiakim, whom Nebuchadrezzar king of Babylon made king in the land of Judah.

2 But neither he, nor his servants, nor the people of the land, did hearken unto the words of the LORD, which he spake by the prophet Jeremiah.

3 And Zedekiah the king sent Jehucal the son of Shelemiah and Zephaniah the son

them, and upon the inhabitants of Jerusalem, and upon the men of Judah, all the evil that I have pronounced against them, but they would not hear.' "

32 Then Jeremiah took another scroll and gave it to Baruch the scribe, the son of Neri′ah, who wrote on it at the dictation of Jeremiah all the words of the scroll which Jehoi′akim king of Judah had burned in the fire; and many similar words were added to them.

37 Zedeki′ah the son of Josi′ah, whom Nebuchadrez′zar king of Babylon made king in the land of Judah, reigned instead of Coni′ah the son of Jehoi′akim. **2** But neither he nor his servants nor the people of the land listened to the words of the LORD which he spoke through Jeremiah the prophet.

3 King Zedeki′ah sent Jehu′cal the son

XXVIII. SIEGE AND FALL OF JERUSALEM (37:1–40:6)

With ch. 37 begins a series of events which includes the fall of Jerusalem and ends with Jeremiah prophesying in Egypt (chs. 37–44). For the most part the material is authentic and in chronological order. The events of these chapters, together with certain of those in earlier chapters, are chronologically summarized in the Intro., p. 781.

A. JEREMIAH JAILED (37:1-21)
1. EDITORIAL INTRODUCTION (37:1-2)

These verses are intended to furnish the transition from the events of ch. 36 (which took place under Jehoiakim in 605 B.C.) to those of 37:3-21 (which occurred near the end of Zedekiah's reign, 598-587 B.C., following his rebellion against Nebuchadrezzar; cf. II Kings 24:20–25:2).

37:1. The RSV rendering is correct. It was **Zedekiah, not Coniah, whom Nebuchadrezzar king of Babylon made king in the land of Judah** (see II Kings 24:17). **Coniah** is a shortened form of Jehoiachin, used also in 22:24, 28.

2. PREDICTION OF THE CHALDEANS' RETURN (37:3-10)

This passage is a highly authentic record, whereas its parallel, 21:1-10, is an artificial account by the Deuteronomic editor. There was probably only one deputation from the king to the prophet (see Exeg. on 21:1-10).

3. Jehucal the son of Shelemiah appears as Jucal in 38:1. **Zephaniah the priest, the son of Maaseiah** is named also in 21:1; 29:25, 29; 52:24.

---

the word is given; it is destroyed; then is reasserted with compounded mantic power and the seal of the people's doom. "It was now open war between the pen and the penknife. But the pen was to triumph. Jehoiakim . . . might destroy a book. But he could not still the living word." [7]

[7] Thomson, *Burden of the Lord*, p. 111.

37:1-10. *Message to Zedekiah (II).*—Reference has already been made to the temporary lifting of the siege of Jerusalem (34:1-7) at the time of Pharaoh Hophra's approach from the south, and to the unrealistic hope of king and counselors that once again events might prove the indestructibility of Jerusalem. The editorial attempt (vss. 1-2) to link the events of this

of Maaseiah the priest to the prophet Jeremiah, saying, Pray now unto the LORD our God for us.

4 Now Jeremiah came in and went out among the people: for they had not put him into prison.

5 Then Pharaoh's army was come forth out of Egypt: and when the Chaldeans that besieged Jerusalem heard tidings of them, they departed from Jerusalem.

6 ¶ Then came the word of the LORD unto the prophet Jeremiah, saying,

7 Thus saith the LORD, the God of Israel; Thus shall ye say to the king of Judah, that sent you unto me to inquire of me; Behold, Pharaoh's army, which is come forth to help you, shall return to Egypt into their own land.

8 And the Chaldeans shall come again, and fight against this city, and take it, and burn it with fire.

9 Thus saith the LORD; Deceive not yourselves, saying, The Chaldeans shall surely depart from us: for they shall not depart.

10 For though ye had smitten the whole army of the Chaldeans that fight against you, and there remained *but* wounded men among them, *yet* should they rise up every man in his tent, and burn this city with fire.

of Shelemi'ah, and Zephani'ah the priest, the son of Ma-asei'ah, to Jeremiah the prophet, saying, "Pray for us to the LORD our God." **4** Now Jeremiah was still going in and out among the people, for he had not yet been put in prison. **5** The army of Pharaoh had come out of Egypt; and when the Chalde'ans who were besieging Jerusalem heard news of them, they withdrew from Jerusalem.

6 Then the word of the LORD came to Jeremiah the prophet: **7** "Thus says the LORD, God of Israel: Thus shall you say to the king of Judah who sent you to me to inquire of me, 'Behold, Pharaoh's army which came to help you is about to return to Egypt, to its own land. **8** And the Chalde'ans shall come back and fight against this city; they shall take it and burn it with fire. **9** Thus says the LORD, Do not deceive yourselves, saying, "The Chalde'ans will surely stay away from us," for they will not stay away. **10** For even if you should defeat the whole army of Chalde'ans who are fighting against you, and there remained of them only wounded men, every man in his tent, they would rise up and burn this city with fire.'"

---

5. The **Pharaoh** was Hophra king of Egypt (588-569 B.C.), mentioned by name in 44:30. It was doubtless the alliance with the Egyptians that led Zedekiah to rebel against Nebuchadrezzar. Inasmuch as they usually waited until the end of the rainy season in Palestine to put an army in the field, they probably came to the aid of Jerusalem in the spring of 588 B.C. Their advance caused the Chaldeans to lift for a time the siege of Jerusalem (cf. 34:21); but they later returned, probably with a much larger force.

10. This verse expresses unmistakably the view of Jeremiah that the capture of Jerusalem by **the Chaldeans** was the will of Yahweh which must be fulfilled if the Judeans persisted in their rebellion against the Chaldeans.

---

chapter with those of ch. 36 is, in at least one respect, a very perceptive achievement. For the historical statement of vs. 1 is followed by the efficient and summary appraisal of Zedekiah's reign: **Neither he nor his servants nor the people of the land listened** to the prophet's words of warning. How this phrase brings back the pathos of Jeremiah's early pleading (13: 17)! But the time for pleading is now past. Jeremiah knew well that "This is the day of fire when much can burn."[8] Jeremiah knew that speech must be direct and plain: it must

also be unmistakable. Therefore, when the king's messengers come, he first makes plain the real factors in the political conflict. Pharaoh's army will soon run back to Egypt; Nebuchadrezzar's army will soon return to the siege of the city. Be not deceived! Or, more penetratingly and more powerfully: **Do not deceive yourselves!** So certain it is, as Jeremiah has been pointing out for twenty years, that Jerusalem will fall that, even though the Chaldeans should be defeated and have nothing but their wounded left, these would still rise up and overwhelm the city!

[8] Leonard Bacon, *Day of Fire* (New York: Oxford University Press, 1943), p. 3.

11 ¶ And it came to pass, that when the army of the Chaldeans was broken up from Jerusalem for fear of Pharaoh's army,

12 Then Jeremiah went forth out of Jerusalem to go into the land of Benjamin, to separate himself thence in the midst of the people.

13 And when he was in the gate of Benjamin, a captain of the ward *was* there, whose name *was* Irijah, the son of Shelemiah, the son of Hananiah; and he took Jeremiah the prophet, saying, Thou fallest away to the Chaldeans.

14 Then said Jeremiah, *It is* false; I fall not away to the Chaldeans. But he hearkened not to him: so Irijah took Jeremiah, and brought him to the princes.

11 Now when the Chalde'an army had withdrawn from Jerusalem at the approach of Pharaoh's army, 12 Jeremiah set out from Jerusalem to go to the land of Benjamin to receive his portion[n] there among the people. 13 When he was at the Benjamin Gate, a sentry there named Iri'jah the son of Shelemi'ah, son of Hanani'ah, seized Jeremiah the prophet, saying, "You are deserting to the Chalde'ans." 14 And Jeremiah said, "It is false; I am not deserting to the Chalde'ans." But Iri'jah would not listen to him, and seized Jeremiah and

[n] Heb obscure

3. Arrest and Imprisonment of Jeremiah (37:11-15)

This passage tells how Jeremiah sought to leave Jerusalem during the interval when the siege was lifted, and was arrested on a charge of desertion. He naturally denied the charge, but the officials as naturally believed it, for he had persistently urged the king and the people to surrender to the Chaldeans. That some of them did so is indicated by 38:19; 39:9; 52:15. The officials belonged to the pro-Egyptian party in Jerusalem; they had everything to lose by surrender, and there was a possibility that the Jews and Egyptians together might defeat the Chaldeans.

12. **To receive his portion:** The Hebrew לחלק is very obscure (M.T. apparently intends it to be a Hiphil infinitive construct, with elision of ה). The LXX MSS took it to mean variously "to buy [bread]" ἀγοράσαι [ἄρτον]), "to sojourn" (παροικίσαι), or "to escape" (ἀποδρᾶσαι). The RSV may be correct, since the noun חלק means **portion;** this is roughly the rendering of the Targ., Aq., Theod., and Vulg. It is impossible, however, to connect this proposed trip to Anathoth with the redemption of the field in Anathoth recorded in ch. 32, for the redemption took place while Jeremiah was in prison in the guard court. **Among the people** may mean among his own people, his own family (Rudolph, comparing II Kings 4:13).

13. Jeremiah was arrested **at the Benjamin Gate,** which was apparently in the north wall of Jerusalem, leading to the land of Benjamin (cf. 20:2; 38:7; Zech. 14:10).

37:11-16. *Jeremiah's Arrest.*—The mounting hostility toward Jeremiah now breaks through. It is not difficult to see why. His consistent opposition to the pro-Egyptian parties; his denunciation of moral vacillation in high places; his counsel of what must have appeared to the party in power as desertion; his recent excoriation of the princes for their treatment of the slaves; his unflinching courage and authority as Yahweh's prophet, together with the guilty conscience, steadily growing, of all those in power responsible for the shortsighted and crumbling policies which had brought them to the verge of ruin and collapse—all this would make for increasing resentment which would certainly take overt form on the earliest pretext. This pretext was soon provided by Jeremiah

himself. Doubtless he was being closely watched for just such an indiscretion as he now committed. Taking advantage of the lifting of the siege he sought to leave the city to go to Anathoth on business. As he went out the north gate he was seized by the sentry and accused of desertion. It would add considerably to the dramatic interest of this episode if the sentry, Irijah, described as the grandson of Hananiah, could be attached to Hananiah, the prophet who formerly had sought to discredit Jeremiah (ch. 28); but Hananiah was apparently too young a man to have been grandfather to Irijah.

Jeremiah's response to the charge is reassuring: **It is false; I am not deserting to the Chaldeans.** Nevertheless, appearances could be

15 Wherefore the princes were wroth with Jeremiah, and smote him, and put him in prison in the house of Jonathan the scribe; for they had made that the prison.

16 ¶ When Jeremiah was entered into the dungeon, and into the cabins, and Jeremiah had remained there many days;

17 Then Zedekiah the king sent, and took him out; and the king asked him secretly in his house, and said, Is there *any* word from the Lord? And Jeremiah said, There is: for, said he, thou shalt be delivered into the hand of the king of Babylon.

18 Moreover Jeremiah said unto king Zedekiah, What have I offended against thee, or against thy servants, or against this people, that ye have put me in prison?

brought him to the princes. 15 And the princes were enraged at Jeremiah, and they beat him and imprisoned him in the house of Jonathan the secretary, for it had been made a prison.

16 When Jeremiah had come to the dungeon cells, and remained there many days, 17 King Zedeki'ah sent for him, and received him. The king questioned him secretly in his house, and said, "Is there any word from the Lord?" Jeremiah said, "There is." Then he said, "You shall be delivered into the hand of the king of Babylon." 18 Jeremiah also said to King Zedeki'ah, "What wrong have I done to you or your servants or this people, that

---

4. Secret Interview with King Zedekiah (37:16-21)

Here is revealed much concerning the nature both of the king and the prophet. Zedekiah shows his secret desire to follow Jeremiah (as he does more clearly in 38:16, 19), and Jeremiah shows his complete abandon to the proclamation of the word of the Lord without any personal fear. Duhm has written (*Das Buch Jeremia*, p. 301) on this interview:

> This scene is just as moving as it is historically interesting: on the one hand is the prophet, disfigured by mistreatment, the prison atmosphere and privations, but firm in his predictions, without any invective against his persecutors, without defiance, exaggeration or fanaticism, simple, physically mild and humble; on the other hand is the king, who obviously against his own will had been led by his officials into the war adventure, anxiously watching the lips of the martyr for a favorable word for himself, whispering secretly with the man whom his officials had imprisoned for treason, weak, a poor creature but not evil, a king but much more bound than the prisoner who stands before him.

so construed as to "gag" the man who had become so sharp a thorn in the political flesh of the controlling nobles. **The princes were enraged at Jeremiah** is a very revealing statement. It should be borne in mind that these "princes" were a very different group of men from those who supported Jeremiah in the time of Jehoiakim. That earlier group had been carried off in the first exile. They were the "first-ripe figs" of Jeremiah's vision; the present princes were the "very bad figs, so bad they could not be eaten" (24:2). So they beat Jeremiah and imprisoned him, and confined him in a dungeon, in "the house of the pit."

37:17-21. *The Secret Summons.*—The episode which follows is one of those rare events in which romancers and dramatists alike rejoice. The shy and sensitive young man from the obscure village of Anathoth who had protested "Ah, Lord God! . . . I am only a youth" (1:6), has become "a fortified city, an iron pillar . . . against the whole land, against the kings of Judah, its princes, its priests, and the people of

the land" (1:18). And the king who had just condoned his capture, after **many days** has the prophet brought before him **secretly in his house**—a dramatic summons from "the house of the pit" to the house of the king.

Jeremiah's attitude is one of respect, forthrightness, and quiet courage. He knows his danger: his life is plainly in the hands of the vacillating king. But he is so far master over the king who has rebelled against both God and Nebuchadrezzar that he is almost gentle, almost compassionate in what he says. The word from the Lord is precisely what it had always been: **You shall be delivered into the hand of the king of Babylon.** It is spoken quietly but unmistakably, yet without the open flaying of the pathetic king with whips and stings of prophetic indignation. The rebukes are of another kind: how have I wronged you **that you have put me in prison?** and, perhaps the deepest probe of all, **where are your prophets who prophesied** that the king of Babylon would not come up against you?

19 Where *are* now your prophets which prophesied unto you, saying, The king of Babylon shall not come against you, nor against this land?

20 Therefore hear now, I pray thee, O my lord the king: let my supplication, I pray thee, be accepted before thee; that thou cause me not to return to the house of Jonathan the scribe, lest I die there.

21 Then Zedekiah the king commanded that they should commit Jeremiah into the court of the prison, and that they should give him daily a piece of bread out of the bakers' street, until all the bread in the city were spent. Thus Jeremiah remained in the court of the prison.

38 Then Shephatiah the son of Mattan, and Gedaliah the son of Pashur, and Jucal the son of Shelemiah, and Pashur the son of Malchiah, heard the words that Jeremiah had spoken unto all the people, saying,

you have put me in prison? 19 Where are your prophets who prophesied to you, saying, 'The king of Babylon will not come against you and against this land'? 20 Now hear, I pray you, O my lord the king: let my humble plea come before you, and do not send me back to the house of Jonathan the secretary, lest I die there." 21 So King Zedeki'ah gave orders, and they committed Jeremiah to the court of the guard; and a loaf of bread was given him daily from the bakers' street, until all the bread of the city was gone. So Jeremiah remained in the court of the guard.

38 Now Shephati'ah the son of Mattan, Gedali'ah the son of Pashhur, Jucal the son of Shelemi'ah, and Pashhur the son of Malchi'ah heard the words that Jeremiah

21. The king's concern for the safety of Jeremiah is revealed. **The court of the guard** was not as confining as the house of Jonathan; according to 32:2, it was in the royal palace. **A loaf of bread** was a small round loaf, barely enough to keep Jeremiah alive. **The bakers' street:** In ancient Jerusalem, as in the modern city within the walls, certain streets were set aside for certain trades and professions (cf. I Kings 20:34).

B. The Prophet's Advice to Surrender (38:1-28)

The events of this chapter must have occurred during the last stages of the siege of Jerusalem. Jeremiah's enemies seek to put him to death by placing him in a cistern, where he would have died of suffocation and starvation if it had not been for the efforts of an Ethiopian eunuch (vss. 1-13). He has a final interview with Zedekiah in which he repeats his counsel to surrender to the Babylonians (vss. 14-28). The chapter is marked by fullness and intimacy of detail, especially in the account of Jeremiah's rescue from the cistern. The material is largely from Baruch's memoirs, with very little editing.

The pitiful plight of the king is thus indicated. All counsel has failed, has indeed proved false, save that of the prophet whose unswerving loyalty to God and to covenant have led the shortsighted but real betrayers of the nation to charge him with desertion. Zedekiah knows this inwardly; but he lacks the strength to face it outwardly—to oppose the princes, to guide the affairs of state, to shape the policy. He bargains therefore against himself, his conflict deepens, and in his shifting toils to shape his peace by having it both ways, he drifts pathetically into the tragic catastrophe prepared by his weakness for himself and his people. How ardently he hopes that the word of the Lord may have changed; but how well he knows, in unconscious awareness of his inner compromise, that this is not to be. "There is a Throne in every Man," says Blake: "it is the Throne of God." [9] But it is easily usurped, and men are tempted always to play king in his stead. Very much as Nicodemus, a ruler of the Jews, came to Jesus secretly by night, so Zedekiah summoned Jeremiah to him secretly, by night. And at bottom what each was seeking, though Zedekiah did not know it altogether, was very much the same.

Jeremiah was not remanded to his dungeon cell, but was committed, on his plea, to the court of the guard; **and a loaf of bread was given him daily from the bakers' street, until all the bread of the city was gone.**

38:1-28; 39:15-18. *A King's Fears, and a Heathen's Trust.*—We have spoken already (21:1-14) of the perspectives which the reader

[9] "Jerusalem," folio 34.

2 Thus saith the Lord, He that remaineth in this city shall die by the sword, by the famine, and by the pestilence: but he that goeth forth to the Chaldeans shall live; for he shall have his life for a prey, and shall live.

3 Thus saith the Lord, This city shall surely be given into the hand of the king of Babylon's army, which shall take it.

4 Therefore the princes said unto the king, We beseech thee, let this man be put to death: for thus he weakeneth the hands of the men of war that remain in this city, and the hands of all the people, in speaking such words unto them: for this man seeketh not the welfare of this people, but the hurt.

was saying to all the people, 2 "Thus says the Lord, He who stays in this city shall die by the sword, by famine, and by pestilence; but he who goes out to the Chalde'ans shall live; he shall have his life as a prize of war, and live. 3 Thus says the Lord, This city shall surely be given into the hand of the army of the king of Babylon and be taken." 4 Then the princes said to the king, "Let this man be put to death, for he is weakening the hands of the soldiers who are left in this city, and the hands of all the people, by speaking such words to them. For this man is not seeking the welfare of

1. Jeremiah's Rescue from a Cistern (38:1-13)

The officials who belong to the pro-Egyptian party and fear surrender to the Chaldeans receive the king's permission to throw Jeremiah into a cistern where they expect him to die. He is rescued by the quick action of Ebed-melech. The king's own weak and vacillating nature is clearly revealed in this episode.

38:1-3. Gedaliah the son of Pashhur may be the son of that Pashhur who earlier had beaten Jeremiah and put him in stocks (20:1-6). **Jucal the son of Shelemiah** appears as Jehucal in 37:3. **Pashhur the son of Malchiah** is named in 21:1. Vs. 2 is probably the work of the Deuteronomic editor, almost exactly the same words appearing in 21:9. The authentic word of the Lord is vs. 3.

4. He is weakening the hands of the soldiers: It is very interesting that almost precisely the same charge is made in one of the Lachish letters against certain officials in Jerusalem. The letter was written from the captain of an outpost to Ya'osh, the commander in Lachish: "Who is thy servant but a dog that my lord has sent the letter of the king and the letters of the officials, saying, 'Pray read them'? And behold the words of the officials are not good, but only to weaken your hands and to slacken the hands of the men who are informed about them." (No. VI, ll. 2-8; see Torczyner, *Lachish Letters,* pp. 104-5. The rendering given here follows closely that of W. F. Albright, "The Lachish Letters After Five Years," *Bulletin of the American Schools of Oriental Research,* No. 82 [Apr., 1941], p. 22, and is preferable to Torczyner's translation and interpretation. Ll. 7-8 are not well preserved.) This letter, from a period perhaps two years earlier than the events of ch. 38 (see Exeg. on 34:7), shows that the king and some of his officials were willing at the time the letter was written to surrender to Babylon (as the king himself was apparently willing to do later).

must bring to bear upon the **words that Jeremiah was saying to all the people.** It is clear from 37:14 that Jeremiah was no deserter. It is clear from this chapter that when the princes failed to remove his influence by arresting him at the Benjamin Gate, they brought a more serious charge—that of high treason against the government. This is a thorny problem, especially in a secular age when nations have forfeited their sense of election. Jeremiah's sense of the covenant election was not merely strong, it was the controlling axis of both his office and the people's destiny. His calling as a prophet

compelled him to give absolute primacy to this covenant consciousness: otherwise he should be traitor both to God and his calling. As a prophet "to the nations" (1:10) his perspectives were as wide as the struggle for power between the contending world powers—in which contention the political importance of Judah was of the slightest. Judah was long since betrayed. The failure of her rulers to trust in the wilderness covenant, to found themselves and their people upon the God-consciousness, left them without power as it left them without character. Reduced to the level of the world

5 Then Zedekiah the king said, Behold, he *is* in your hand: for the king *is* not *he that* can do *any* thing against you.

6 Then took they Jeremiah, and cast him into the dungeon of Malchiah the son of Hammelech, that *was* in the court of the prison: and they let down Jeremiah with cords. And in the dungeon *there was* no water, but mire: so Jeremiah sunk in the mire.

7 ¶ Now when Ebed-melech the Ethiopian, one of the eunuchs which was in the king's house, heard that they had put Jeremiah in the dungeon; the king then sitting in the gate of Benjamin;

8 Ebed-melech went forth out of the king's house, and spake to the king, saying,

9 My lord the king, these men have done evil in all that they have done to Jeremiah the prophet, whom they have cast into the dungeon; and he is like to die for hunger in the place where he is: for *there is* no more bread in the city.

10 Then the king commanded Ebed-melech the Ethiopian, saying, Take from hence thirty men with thee, and take up

this people, but their harm." 5 King Zedeki'ah said, "Behold, he is in your hands; for the king can do nothing against you." 6 So they took Jeremiah and cast him into the cistern of Malchi'ah, the king's son, which was in the court of the guard, letting Jeremiah down by ropes. And there was no water in the cistern, but only mire, and Jeremiah sank in the mire.

7 When E'bed-mel'ech the Ethiopian, a eunuch, who was in the king's house, heard that they had put Jeremiah into the cistern — the king was sitting in the Benjamin Gate — 8 E'bed-mel'ech went from the king's house and said to the king, 9 "My lord the king, these men have done evil in all that they did to Jeremiah the prophet by casting him into the cistern; and he will die there of hunger, for there is no bread left in the city." 10 Then the king commanded E'bed-mel'ech, the Ethiopian,

5. This verse reveals the weakness of Zedekiah. He was friendly to Jeremiah and often wished to follow his counsel, but he did not dare oppose the officials who insisted on resisting the Chaldeans and considered the prophet a traitor.

6. Jeremiah was placed in a **cistern,** not a **dungeon.** In ancient Jerusalem, as today, there were many cisterns for catching water during the rainy season of the winter, to be stored for use in the virtually rainless months from May to October. At this time **there was no water in the cistern, but only mire.** The time was shortly before the Babylonians made a breach in the wall of Jerusalem, August, 587 B.C. (52:5-7). **Malchiah, the king's son,** was a member of the royal family, but probably not the son of Zedekiah, who was only thirty-two years of age at this time (see II Kings 24:18). **Hammelech:** See Exeg. on 36:26.

7. The prophet was rescued through the efforts of **Ebed-melech the Ethiopian,** an important palace official (not necessarily a physical **eunuch,** since *ṣārîṣ* may mean simply "palace official," being derived from Akkadian *sha rêshi [sharri]*). He acts with much haste and efficiency to rescue the prophet before it is too late (see the promise made to Ebed-melech in 39:15-18). **The king was sitting in the Benjamin Gate,** which was in the north wall (see Exeg. on 37:13). He may have been there officiating as supreme judge, or observing the defense of the city.

10. The RSV follows one Hebrew MS in reading **take three men;** it was obviously unnecessary to secure **thirty men** (KJV) for the task of rescuing the prophet.

struggle for power they were helpless and adrift, awaiting merely the moment when they would be overturned by the gigantic tidal wave of power pouring down from the north. The shortsightedness of the rulers and the "lying visions" of the false prophets were not merely a betrayal of the people: they were part of a

policy which drove Jeremiah more and more firmly upon the one foundation stone of the nation's integrity—its calling (election) under God. When a nation forfeits its calling it is already yielding its usefulness to God and humanity to some other people. The effect of this may be seen in Zedekiah, who had received his

Jeremiah the prophet out of the dungeon, before he die.

11 So Ebed-melech took the men with him, and went into the house of the king under the treasury, and took thence old cast clouts and old rotten rags, and let them down by cords into the dungeon to Jeremiah.

12 And Ebed-melech the Ethiopian said unto Jeremiah, Put now *these* old cast clouts and rotten rags under thine armholes under the cords. And Jeremiah did so.

13 So they drew up Jeremiah with cords, and took him up out of the dungeon: and Jeremiah remained in the court of the prison.

14 ¶ Then Zedekiah the king sent, and took Jeremiah the prophet unto him into the third entry that *is* in the house of the LORD: and the king said unto Jeremiah, I will ask thee a thing; hide nothing from me.

15 Then Jeremiah said unto Zedekiah, If I declare *it* unto thee, wilt thou not surely put me to death? and if I give thee counsel, wilt thou not hearken unto me?

16 So Zedekiah the king sware secretly unto Jeremiah, saying, *As* the LORD liveth, that made us this soul, I will not put thee

"Take three men with you from here, and lift Jeremiah the prophet out of the cistern before he dies." 11 So E'bed-mel'ech took the men with him and went to the house of the king, to a wardrobe of*⁰* the storehouse, and took from there old rags and worn-out clothes, which he let down to Jeremiah in the cistern by ropes. 12 Then E'bed-mel'ech the Ethiopian said to Jeremiah, "Put the rags and clothes between your armpits and the ropes." Jeremiah did so. 13 Then they drew Jeremiah up with ropes and lifted him out of the cistern. And Jeremiah remained in the court of the guard.

14 King Zedeki'ah sent for Jeremiah the prophet and received him at the third entrance of the temple of the LORD. The king said to Jeremiah, "I will ask you a question; hide nothing from me." 15 Jeremiah said to Zedeki'ah, "If I tell you, will you not be sure to put me to death? And if I give you counsel, you will not listen to me." 16 Then King Zedeki'ah swore secretly to Jeremiah, "As the LORD lives, who made our souls, I will not put you to death or deliver you

⁰ Cn: Heb to under

11. A wardrobe of the storehouse: The RSV emends אל־תחת to מלתחת, which occurs in II Kings 10:22. This manifestly is superior to **under the treasury,** because of the nature of the objects secured by Ebed-melech. As a court official he was well acquainted with various parts of the palace.

2. FINAL INTERVIEW WITH KING ZEDEKIAH (38:14-28)

It is erroneous to consider this as merely a duplicate of 37:17-21, as Skinner does (following Steuernagel). The two accounts differ in important details, and it is not at all improbable that the king, in his nervous state, did summon the prophet twice.

14. Nothing is known of **the third entrance of the temple of the LORD,** as nothing is known of the first and second. If correct, it probably was a gate between the palace and the temple. Giesebrecht emends *mābhô' hashshelishi* to *mebhô' hashshālishim,* "entrance of the bodyguards" (for "bodyguard" or "captain" see II Kings 7:2, 17, 19; 9:25, *et al.*). Linguistically that may be preferable, but nothing is known of such an entrance.

15-16. The verses reflect Jeremiah's previous experiences with Zedekiah, but he is convinced of the king's sincerity by his oath (vs. 16).

appointment at the hands of Nebuchadrezzar, and had foolishly betrayed this allegiance at the instigation of the hotheaded "princes" who rose to power after the better leaders had been removed in the first deportation to Babylon.

Nothing could be more revealing than the king's helpless reply to the princes who demanded Jeremiah's death. **Behold, he is in your**

hands; for the king can do nothing against you. So they **cast him into the cistern** where he began to sink into the mire.

The story of his rescue by Ebed-melech the Ethiopian follows. The unhesitating action of the Ethiopian is striking. He acts swiftly, with the king's permission. He is a heathen. But the **word of the LORD** pronounced by Jeremiah

to death, neither will I give thee into the hand of these men that seek thy life.

17 Then said Jeremiah unto Zedekiah, Thus saith the LORD, the God of hosts, the God of Israel; If thou wilt assuredly go forth unto the king of Babylon's princes, then thy soul shall live, and this city shall not be burned with fire; and thou shalt live, and thine house:

18 But if thou wilt not go forth to the king of Babylon's princes, then shall this city be given into the hand of the Chaldeans, and they shall burn it with fire, and thou shalt not escape out of their hand.

19 And Zedekiah the king said unto Jeremiah, I am afraid of the Jews that are fallen to the Chaldeans, lest they deliver me into their hand, and they mock me.

20 But Jeremiah said, They shall not deliver *thee*. Obey, I beseech thee, the voice of the LORD, which I speak unto thee: so it shall be well unto thee, and thy soul shall live.

21 But if thou refuse to go forth, this *is* the word that the LORD hath showed me:

22 And, behold, all the women that are left in the king of Judah's house *shall be* brought forth to the king of Babylon's princes, and those *women* shall say, Thy friends have set thee on, and have prevailed against thee: thy feet are sunk in the mire, *and* they are turned away back.

23 So they shall bring out all thy wives and thy children to the Chaldeans: and thou shalt not escape out of their hand, but shalt be taken by the hand of the king of Babylon: and thou shalt cause this city to be burned with fire.

into the hand of these men who seek your life."

17 Then Jeremiah said to Zedeki'ah, "Thus says the LORD, the God of hosts, the God of Israel, If you will surrender to the princes of the king of Babylon, then your life shall be spared, and this city shall not be burned with fire, and you and your house shall live. **18** But if you do not surrender to the princes of the king of Babylon, then this city shall be given into the hand of the Chalde'ans, and they shall burn it with fire, and you shall not escape from their hand." **19** King Zedeki'ah said to Jeremiah, "I am afraid of the Jews who have deserted to the Chalde'ans, lest I be handed over to them and they abuse me." **20** Jeremiah said, "You shall not be given to them. Obey now the voice of the LORD in what I say to you, and it shall be well with you, and your life shall be spared. **21** But if you refuse to surrender, this is the vision which the LORD has shown to me: **22** Behold, all the women left in the house of the king of Judah were being led out to the princes of the king of Babylon and were saying,

'Your trusted friends have deceived you
    and prevailed against you;
now that your feet are sunk in the mire,
    they turn away from you.'

23 All your wives and your sons shall be led out to the Chalde'ans, and you yourself shall not escape from their hand, but shall be seized by the king of Babylon; and this city shall be burned with fire."

---

19. The surrender of some of the Jews is indicated also by 39:9; 52:15. The king's fear was certainly not an idle one.

21-22. The word of the Lord is here given to the prophet in a **vision** and an audition. The RSV correctly prints vs. 22*b* as poetry. It is in 3+2 meter, the type used especially for a lamentation (*qînāh*). Such a poem is appropriate to the situation. It recalls the fact that the king had just allowed Jeremiah to be placed in a cistern where his feet were **sunk in the mire.**

23. The verse is a prosaic addition, probably by the Deuteronomic editor; the prophet did not need to give such an explanation of the vision.

---

upon him (39:16-18) contains a very significant word: **you shall have your life as a prize of war, because you have put your trust in me.** The word "trust" in this passage is very similar to the N.T. use of "faith." The eunuch's trust is "counted unto him for righteousness" (Rom.

4:3). It is this trust which Zedekiah wanted, but which he did not have. (Cf. Rom. 2:13.)

Zedekiah again calls Jeremiah to him, and swears **secretly** that he will not punish Jeremiah regardless of the Lord's word to him. Clearly Jeremiah sees that he must speak the same

24 ¶ Then said Zedekiah unto Jeremiah, Let no man know of these words, and thou shalt not die.

25 But if the princes hear that I have talked with thee, and they come unto thee, and say unto thee, Declare unto us now what thou hast said unto the king, hide it not from us, and we will not put thee to death; also what the king said unto thee:

26 Then thou shalt say unto them, I presented my supplication before the king, that he would not cause me to return to Jonathan's house, to die there.

27 Then came all the princes unto Jeremiah, and asked him: and he told them according to all these words that the king had commanded. So they left off speaking with him; for the matter was not perceived.

28 So Jeremiah abode in the court of the prison until the day that Jerusalem was taken: and he was *there* when Jerusalem was taken.

39 In the ninth year of Zedekiah king of Judah, in the tenth month, came Nebuchadrezzar king of Babylon and all

24 Then Zedeki'ah said to Jeremiah, "Let no one know of these words and you shall not die. 25 If the princes hear that I have spoken with you and come to you and say to you, 'Tell us what you said to the king and what the king said to you; hide nothing from us and we will not put you to death,' 26 then you shall say to them, 'I made a humble plea to the king that he would not send me back to the house of Jonathan to die there.' " 27 Then all the princes came to Jeremiah and asked him, and he answered them as the king had instructed him. So they left off speaking with him, for the conversation had not been overheard. 28 And Jeremiah remained in the court of the guard until the day that Jerusalem was taken.

39 In the ninth year of Zedeki'ah king of Judah, in the tenth month, Nebu-

24-28. Volz is probably correct in his theory that these verses originally stood after the interview reported in 37:17-21. Vs. 26 would fit such a situation better (37:20). By the time of the events of ch. 38, the officials were so enraged against Jeremiah that they would hardly have been put off with so simple an explanation. Also, an interview which took place in the third entrance of the temple would have been much more likely to be overheard (vs. 27) than one which took place within the royal palace (37:17).

Jeremiah should not be condemned for the half-truth he tells here (a white lie if the verses are now in their correct position). He assented to the request of the king not for the sake of his own safety (he did not fear death), but in order to protect the life of the king and promote the welfare of the people of Jerusalem. The fanatical officials were in no mood at this time to listen to reason.

C. BABYLONIAN CAPTURE OF JERUSALEM (39:1-14)

This section records in summary fashion the siege and fall of Jerusalem, and gives special information regarding the fate of Jeremiah upon the fall of the city. Vss. 1-2, 4-10

message—the word pronounced seditious and traitorous by the princes. And when he advises Zedekiah to surrender for his own good and the safety of the people, Zedekiah answers, **I am afraid,** this time of the people who have already gone over to the Chaldeans, a further evidence that there were many in these desperate straits who thought as Jeremiah did.

In a **vision which the LORD has shown to me,** Jeremiah makes the alternative very clear: the king's **trusted friends** will deceive him, and dominate him, and will turn from him as they see his feet sinking **in the mire**—as Jeremiah's had just been doing; for it is indeed Zedekiah,

and not Jeremiah, who has been sinking in the mire of moral equivocation.

But Zedekiah's trepidation is still uppermost. It is again the princes whom he fears, lest they should learn of his interview with the prophet. He tells Jeremiah what to say, just in case. This Jeremiah does when the princes accost him—a humble plea that he not be returned to the cistern. Thus, thanks to the eunuch's faith and the king's fears, Jeremiah **remained in the court of the guard until the day that Jerusalem was taken.**

39:1-14. The Fateful End.—What follows is written at some distance from the foregoing

his army against Jerusalem, and they besieged it.

2 *And* in the eleventh year of Zedekiah,
in the fourth month, the ninth *day* of the
month, the city was broken up.

3 And all the princes of the king of Babylon came in, and sat in the middle gate,
even Nergal-sharezer, Samgar-nebo, Sarse-
chim, Rab-saris, Nergal-sharezer, Rab-mag,
with all the residue of the princes of the
king of Babylon.

chadrez'zar king of Babylon and all his
army came against Jerusalem and besieged
it; 2 in the eleventh year of Zedeki'ah, in
the fourth month, on the ninth day of the
month, a breach was made in the city.
3 When Jerusalem was taken,*p* all the
princes of the king of Babylon came and
sat in the middle gate: Ner'gal-share'zer,
Sam'gar-ne'bo, Sar'sechim the Rab'saris,
Ner'gal-share'zer the Rabmag, with all the
rest of the officers of the king of Babylon.

p This clause has been transposed from the end of Chapter 38

---

are a shortened form of the record in 52:4-16, which itself is virtually equivalent to
II Kings 25:1-12. Vss. 1-2 actually break into the middle of a Hebrew sentence which
begins in 38:28*b* and continues in 39:3. Vss. 3 and 14 have no parallel in ch. 52 and
the corresponding portion of II Kings. Doubtless from Baruch's memoirs, they give
us reliable information concerning the release of the prophet—in fact all that we need
to know regarding his release (cf. 40:1-6). It is most improbable that Nebuzaradan dealt
with Jeremiah as he is reported to have done, either in vss. 13-14 or 40:1-6, for
Nebuzaradan did not arrive in Jerusalem until one month and a day after the city wall
was breached, according to 52:12 (cf. II Kings 25:8, which varies by three days).

Vss. 1-2, 4-13 are from the Deuteronomic editor, who copied most of the material
from II Kings (itself a Deuteronomic work), or from the source used by II Kings. In vs.
13 some of the names of vs. 3 are repeated in order to connect vs. 12 with vs. 14. The
LXX omits vss. 4-13, either because most of the material is contained in ch. 52, or simply
by accident, the scribe's eye passing from **Babylon** at the end of vs. 3 to the same word
at the end of vs. 13 (cf. 29:16-20, where the same kind of error occurs in LXX).

For a detailed comment on vss. 1-2, 4-10 see Exeg. on II Kings 24:18–25:17.

39:3. The RSV is quite correct in transposing **When Jerusalem was taken** from the
end of 38:28*b*. The location of **the middle gate** is not certainly known; according to the
Jerusalem Talmud (Erubin V 22*c*), it was one of seven names given to the great eastern
gate of the temple which is now called the Golden Gate.

Nergal-sharezer is the Babylonian Nergalsharusur, the name borne by Nebuchadrezzar's son-in-law and second successor, who ruled 560-556 B.C. The common form of his
name is Neriglissar. **Samgar-nebo, Sar-sechim the Rabsaris:** The first two of these names
are not Babylonian formations. On a prism found at Babylon containing a list of officials
under Nebuchadrezzar, there appears the name "Nergalsharusur the *Sin-magir*" (*Nergal-
shar-uṣur* ^amêl^*Sin-māgir*), who is one of the "princes of the land of Akkad [i.e., Babylonia]"
(*rabûti sha* ^mât^*Akkadi*; Eckhard Unger, "Namen im Hofstaate Nebukadnezare II,"
Theologische Literaturzeitung, L [1925], 481-86; Pritchard, *Ancient Near Eastern Texts*,
pp. 307-8). The meaning and function of his title is unknown; it is written in another
Neo-Babylonian text as ^amêl^*si-im-ma-gir* (Alfred Pohl, *Neubabylonische Rechsturkunden
aus den Berliner staatlichen Museen* [Roma: Pontificio istituto biblico, 1933], Vol. I,
Text 56, ll. 7, 12, 14). **Samgar** is perhaps a corruption of this title, which was probably
pronounced by the Hebrews as *simmagir*. This leaves **-nebo Sar-sechim**, which is not a
recognizable Babylonian name. Many scholars believe that it is a corruption of the name
Nebushazban, which appears in vs. 13, and is a good Babylonian formation, Nabû-
shezibanni; he bears the title **the Rabsaris**. The latter is the equivalent of Babylonian
rabû sha rêshi (*sharri*), usually translated "chief eunuch," but more probably meaning
"chief court official." **Rabmag** is also a title, probably the Babylonian *rab-mugi*, though
the meaning and function are unknown (the usual translation "chief of the soothsayers"
is probably incorrect). Some scholars believe that the name **Nebuzaradan**, which is first
in the list in vs. 13, should be substituted for the first **Nergal-sharezer**. This is improbable,

4 ¶ And it came to pass, that when Zedekiah the king of Judah saw them, and all the men of war, then they fled, and went forth out of the city by night, by the way of the king's garden, by the gate betwixt the two walls: and he went out the way of the plain.

5 But the Chaldeans' army pursued after them, and overtook Zedekiah in the plains of Jericho: and when they had taken him, they brought him up to Nebuchadnezzar king of Babylon to Riblah in the land of Hamath, where he gave judgment upon him.

6 Then the king of Babylon slew the sons of Zedekiah in Riblah before his eyes: also the king of Babylon slew all the nobles of Judah.

7 Moreover he put out Zedekiah's eyes, and bound him with chains, to carry him to Babylon.

8 ¶ And the Chaldeans burned the king's house, and the houses of the people, with fire, and brake down the walls of Jerusalem.

9 Then Nebuzar-adan the captain of the guard carried away captive into Babylon the remnant of the people that remained in the city, and those that fell away, that fell to him, with the rest of the people that remained.

10 But Nebuzar-adan the captain of the guard left of the poor of the people, which had nothing, in the land of Judah, and gave them vineyards and fields at the same time.

4 When Zedekiah king of Judah and all the soldiers saw them, they fled, going out of the city at night by way of the king's garden through the gate between the two walls; and they went toward the Arabah. 5 But the army of the Chalde'ans pursued them, and overtook Zedeki'ah in the plains of Jericho; and when they had taken him, they brought him up to Nebuchadrez'zar king of Babylon, at Riblah, in the land of Hamath; and he passed sentence upon him. 6 The king of Babylon slew the sons of Zedeki'ah at Riblah before his eyes; and the king of Babylon slew all the nobles of Judah. 7 He put out the eyes of Zedeki'ah and bound him in fetters to take him to Babylon. 8 The Chalde'ans burned the king's house and the house of the people, and broke down the walls of Jerusalem. 9 Then Nebu'zarad'an, the captain of the guard, carried into exile to Babylon the rest of the people who were left in the city, those who had deserted to him, and the people who remained. 10 Nebu'zarad'an, the captain of the guard, left in the land of Judah some of the poor people who owned nothing, and gave them vineyards and fields at the same time.

for Nebuzaradan did not arrive in Jerusalem until a month after the breaching of the wall of the city (52:12). There may well have been two men with the name Nergal-sharezer, who were distinguished from each other by the designations given them in this verse. One of them may have been king of Babylon later. The name is fairly common in Neo-Babylonian texts.

In the light of the suggestions given above, it is proposed to read these names as follows: "Nergal-sharezer the Simmagir, Nebushazban the chief court official, Nergal-sharezer the Rabmag."

8. The corresponding account in 52:13 does not speak of **the house of the people.** It may have been a general assembly hall or council building, from which subsequently the Jewish synagogue developed; or it may have been a designation of the temple itself, as in Mandaic scriptures (cf. Franz Landsberger, "The House of the People," *Hebrew Union College Annual,* XXII [1949], 149-55) .

events, and reads as the sad aftermath of the calamitous policies of Zedekiah's reign. The breach in the wall, the flight of the king, his capture and terrible punishment, the burning of palace and temple, the destruction of the

walls, and the carrying away into exile of the people is a depressing and tragic end, inevitable but long deferred.

As for Jeremiah, it seems probable that Nebuchadrezzar's chiefs had learned about him

11 ¶ Now Nebuchadrezzar king of Babylon gave charge concerning Jeremiah to Nebuzar-adan the captain of the guard, saying,

12 Take him, and look well to him, and do him no harm; but do unto him even as he shall say unto thee.

13 So Nebuzar-adan the captain of the guard sent, and Nebushasban, Rab-saris, and Nergal-sharezer, Rab-mag, and all the king of Babylon's princes;

14 Even they sent, and took Jeremiah out of the court of the prison, and committed him unto Gedaliah the son of Ahikam the son of Shaphan, that he should carry him home: so he dwelt among the people.

15 ¶ Now the word of the LORD came unto Jeremiah, while he was shut up in the court of the prison, saying,

16 Go and speak to Ebed-melech the Ethiopian, saying, Thus saith the LORD of hosts, the God of Israel; Behold, I will bring my words upon this city for evil, and not for good; and they shall be *accomplished* in that day before thee.

11 Nebuchadrez'zar king of Babylon gave command concerning Jeremiah through Nebu'zarad'an, the captain of the guard, saying, 12 "Take him, look after him well and do him no harm, but deal with him as he tells you." 13 So Nebu'zarad'an the captain of the guard, Nebushaz'ban the Rab'-saris, Ner'gal-share'zer the Rabmag, and all the chief officers of the king of Babylon 14 sent and took Jeremiah from the court of the guard. They entrusted him to Gedali'ah the son of Ahi'kam, son of Shaphan, that he should take him home. So he dwelt among the people.

15 The word of the LORD came to Jeremiah while he was shut up in the court of the guard: 16 "Go, and say to E'bed-mel'ech the Ethiopian, 'Thus says the LORD of hosts, the God of Israel: Behold I will fulfil my words against this city for evil and not for good, and they shall be accomplished be-

---

11. The information here seems improbable, and is not necessary in the light of vs. 14. According to vs. 5, the Babylonian king was at Riblah in Syria. It is doubtful either that he knew of Jeremiah and his message, or that he would have taken so personal an interest in his release had he known of him. Vss. 11-13, as well as 40:1-6, are from the Deuteronomic editor.

Nebuzaradan, the captain of the guard: In the Babylonian prism referred to (Col. 3, 1. 35; see Unger, *loc. cit.;* Exeg. on vs. 3), there appears the name *Nabû-zêr-iddin rab nuḫtimmu,* "Nabu-zer-iddin the chief baker"; the same name and title appear in a letter published in A. T. Clay, *Neo-Babylonian Letters from Erech* (New Haven: Yale University Press, 1919), Letter 122, ll. 7-8. Since the name was common in Neo-Babylonian times, we cannot be certain that the biblical person was identical with this individual.

14. This verse continues vs. 3. Being from Baruch's memoirs, it is a reliable account of the release of Jeremiah **from the court of the guard,** where he had been imprisoned and where we are expressly told he remained until the fall of Jerusalem (38:28).

D. Oracle Concerning Ebed-melech (39:15-18)

15-18. Ebed-melech was the Ethiopian eunuch who took the initiative in rescuing Jeremiah from the cistern into which his enemies had placed him (38:7-13). Jeremiah may well have felt most grateful to him and believed that he merited special reward from Yahweh. However, the presence here of Deuteronomic phraseology, as Mowinckel has pointed out, and of the basic Deuteronomic notion of retribution, as well as the

---

from Gedaliah, who might plausibly have taken Jeremiah's advice and surrendered to the Chaldeans. It was Gedaliah's father, Ahikam, who had protected Jeremiah in the earlier part of Jehoiakim's reign (26:24); and it is to the son now that Jeremiah is entrusted, that **he should**

take him home. What is important is that, being free to choose, Jeremiah **dwelt among the people** with whom, from the beginning, he is identified in his heart as well as in his calling.

15-18. See Expos. on 38:1-28; 39:15-18, pp. 1073-78.

17 But I will deliver thee in that day, saith the LORD; and thou shalt not be given into the hand of the men of whom thou *art* afraid.

18 For I will surely deliver thee, and thou shalt not fall by the sword, but thy life shall be for a prey unto thee; because thou hast put thy trust in me, saith the LORD.

40 The word which came to Jeremiah from the LORD, after that Nebuzar-adan the captain of the guard had let him go from Ramah, when he had taken him being bound in chains among all that were carried away captive of Jerusalem and Judah, which were carried away captive unto Babylon.

2 And the captain of the guard took Jeremiah, and said unto him, The LORD thy God hath pronounced this evil upon this place.

fore you on that day. 17 But I will deliver you on that day, says the LORD, and you shall not be given into the hand of the men of whom you are afraid. 18 For I will surely save you, and you shall not fall by the sword; but you shall have your life as a prize of war, because you have put your trust in me, says the LORD.' "

40 The word that came to Jeremiah from the LORD after Nebu′zarad′an the captain of the guard had let him go from Ramah, when he took him bound in chains along with all the captives of Jerusalem and Judah who were being exiled to Babylon. 2 The captain of the guard took Jeremiah and said to him, "The LORD your God pronounced this evil against this place;

---

artificiality of the account and its present position, have led several scholars to doubt the genuineness of this oracle. It is probably from the Deuteronomic editor, who felt that Ebed-melech should not go unrewarded. In form and content this oracle should be compared with that on Baruch (45:1-5).

E. RELEASE OF JEREMIAH (40:1-6)

40:1-6. We have seen that 39:3, 14, based on Baruch's memoirs, give us all the information we need concerning the release of Jeremiah from his imprisonment in the court of the guard. The officers of the king of Babylon who are named in 39:3 had the prophet released from his prison and entrusted to Gedaliah the governor. That information cannot be reconciled with the statement here (vs. 1) that Jeremiah was found by Gedaliah at **Ramah . . . bound in chains** among **the captives of Jerusalem and Judah who were being exiled to Babylon.** Vss. 2-3 are most improbable on the lips of the Babylonian officer; he would hardly speak in such Deuteronomic language to the prophet. It is

---

40:1-6. *Jeremiah's Choice.*—It is interesting to speculate on the possible relations between Nebuchadrezzar and Jeremiah. The account in 39:11 is generally discredited by the critics. They are also reluctant to concede too much to the present passage, largely on the grounds that the composition comes from the hand of later Deuteronomist editors, who betray a desire to aggrandize the place and significance of the prophet. True it is that we like to adorn history and create the myths of real equivalence above the narrowness of fact. Nevertheless, on psychological grounds, it would be strange if Nebuchadrezzar did not know of the work and influence of Jeremiah. A statesman as acute as Nebuchadrezzar was clearly alert to every voice and every advantage which favored his cause. His genius for ordering the territories which came under his sway and his policies of clem-

ency and qualified dominion status to the conquered indicate his plan. The decision to make Gedaliah the governor of conquered Judah was surely reached before his actual appointment. It was also known that Gedaliah's and Jeremiah's policies and opinions coincided. When Jeremiah was discovered among the captives on the way to exile, he was quickly released by the captain of the guard, treated with courtesy, and given the choice of going to Babylon or of remaining with Gedaliah. (But see Exeg.)

We know, moreover, how greatness seeks its own. Alexander the Great sought the approval of Diogenes, the "tub philosopher." Frederick the Great was not content until the great Voltaire had come to ornament his court. We know also of Napoleon's admiration for Goethe, of their meeting at Erfurt, of Napoleon's concern years later when, in flight from Warsaw, at a

3 Now the LORD hath brought *it,* and done according as he hath said: because ye have sinned against the LORD, and have not obeyed his voice, therefore this thing is come upon you.

4 And now, behold, I loose thee this day from the chains which *were* upon thine hand. If it seem good unto thee to come with me into Babylon, come; and I will look well unto thee: but if it seem ill unto thee to come with me into Babylon, forbear: behold, all the land *is* before thee: whither it seemeth good and convenient for thee to go, thither go.

5 Now while he was not yet gone back, *he said,* Go back also to Gedaliah the son of Ahikam the son of Shaphan, whom the king of Babylon hath made governor over the cities of Judah, and dwell with him among the people: or go wheresoever it seemeth convenient unto thee to go. So the captain of the guard gave him victuals and a reward, and let him go.

6 Then went Jeremiah unto Gedaliah the son of Ahikam to Mizpah; and dwelt with him among the people that were left in the land.

7 ¶ Now when all the captains of the forces which *were* in the fields, *even* they and their men, heard that the king of

3 the LORD has brought it about, and has done as he said. Because you sinned against the LORD, and did not obey his voice, this thing has come upon you. **4** Now, behold, I release you today from the chains on your hands. If it seems good to you to come with me to Babylon, come, and I will look after you well; but if it seems wrong to you to come with me to Babylon, do not come. See, the whole land is before you; go wherever you think it good and right to go. **5** If you remain,*q* then return to Gedali′ah the son of Ahi′kam, son of Shaphan, whom the king of Babylon appointed governor of the cities of Judah, and dwell with him among the people; or go wherever you think it right to go." So the captain of the guard gave him an allowance of food and a present, and let him go. **6** Then Jeremiah went to Gedali′ah the son of Ahi′kam, at Mizpah, and dwelt with him among the people who were left in the land.

7 When all the captains of the forces in

q Syr: Heb obscure

possible, of course, that Nebuzaradan offered the prophet safe conduct to Babylon, but not probable. In any case, Jeremiah would not have been seduced by that offer for he knew that his position was with his own people (see 39:14).

We must conclude that this section is by the Deuteronomic editor, and that it has little independent historical value. It was designed to elevate the standing of the prophet and to justify the actions of the Babylonians in destroying Jerusalem.

XXIX. GOVERNORSHIP AND ASSASSINATION OF GEDALIAH (40:7–41:18)

With vs. 7 there begins a historical account, extending through 41:18, which is apparently very authentic. Untouched by the Deuteronomic editor, it is usually believed

change of horses in the middle of the night in Weimar, he thrust out his head and inquired, "And how is Herr Goethe?" Napoleon, the man of destiny, recognized in Goethe a greatness mysterious with a dimension other than his own. Now it was precisely Jeremiah who had recognized in Nebuchadrezzar "a man of destiny." Nebuchadrezzar and Jeremiah were easily the greatest men of their time. It is wrong to dwarf the greatness of Jeremiah because of the littleness of his people or the focus of biblical history upon the moral destiny of Judah. Nebuchadrezzar and Jeremiah are the two men of the time whose vision was world-wide; and though

their visions moved on separate planes they intersected when the destiny of the conqueror fell athwart that of Yahweh's people.

That Jeremiah chose to remain with Gedaliah will occasion no surprise. It is, however, of extreme importance, as showing his profound and basic faith in Israel. This he had attested already by the purchase of the plot of ground at Anathoth. He now attests it again in his decision to work with Gedaliah in the governor's task of reordering and rebuilding the land.

40:7–41:18. *The Rise and Fall of Local Autonomy.*—The appointment of Gedaliah to the

Babylon had made Gedaliah the son of Ahikam governor in the land, and had committed unto him men, and women, and children, and of the poor of the land, of them that were not carried away captive to Babylon;	the open country and their men heard that the king of Babylon had appointed Ged-ali'ah the son of Ahi'kam governor in the land, and had committed to him men, women, and children, those of the poorest of the land who had not been taken into

to have come from Baruch. However, it contains not a single word about Jeremiah, and it seems improbable that Baruch could have written so much material without even mentioning the prophet. We know that Baruch was alive after the fall of Jerusalem (43:3). It is possible that he prepared a collection of the oracles of Jeremiah and his own memoirs soon after the fall of the city. This work of Baruch's may be contained within chs. 1–39, its introduction being 1:1-3. These verses stood at the head of a work which brought the life and words of Jeremiah only down through the fall of Jerusalem, as 1:3 indicates (see Exeg., *ad loc.*). The present section, 40:7–41:18, may therefore not be from Baruch but from another source. II Kings 25:22-26 gives a brief summary of the events here recorded, partly in the same words (cf. II Kings 25:23-24 with 40:7-10; and II Kings 25:25-26 with 41:1-2, 16-18). The editors of II Kings and of the present passage may have used the same source, but the material is preserved here in more detail.

After the capture of Jerusalem the Babylonians appointed Gedaliah as governor of Palestine, which became a province of the Babylonian Empire. Gedaliah was no quisling, but a member of a prominent Jewish family. His father, Ahikam the son of Shaphan, had been an official in the court of Kings Josiah and Jehoiakim, and a friend and protector of Jeremiah (26:24; II Kings 22:12, 14). His grandfather Shaphan may have been the man of that name who was scribe in the court of King Josiah (II Kings 22:3 ff.). Gedaliah showed himself to be sympathetic and understanding toward the Jews; it was in fact his leniency that led to his own assassination.

It is not certain how long Gedaliah served as governor before he was put to death. Probably, however, it was nearly five years. According to 52:30, the Babylonians made a third deportation of Jews in the twenty-third year of Nebuchadrezzar, which was 582-581 B.C. This deportation was probably punishment for the disturbances in connection with the assassination of Gedaliah. If Gedaliah governed for a period of nearly five years, the present account is only a partial record of his governorship, containing details of the beginning and the end of his career.

While we have no direct information on the activity of Jeremiah in this period (cf. Exeg. on chs. 30–31), it is likely that he was friendly to Gedaliah and supported his policies. The governor was not one of those superpatriots who wanted to resist the Babylonians to the bitter end; indeed, he may have been influenced by the counsels of Jeremiah during the siege of Jerusalem.

A. GEDALIAH'S PROMISE (40:7-10)

7-9. Gedaliah attempts to pacify **the captains of the forces in the open country** who had led the Jewish resistance to the Babylonians. There is no recrimination in his words, but only counsel to **serve the Chaldeans,** and a promise that he will properly represent the interests of his fellow countrymen before their new rulers. The Babylonians were not unduly oppressive in their treatment of subject peoples, and Gedaliah succeeded in reassuring most of the Jews of his good intentions.

governorship was a stroke of constructive statesmanship. One has only to read Lam. 2 and 4 to see how thorough was the defeat and devastation. "For vast as the sea is your ruin" (Lam. 2:13). "Even the stones of the temple lay scattered at the head of every street" (Lam. 4:1).	Gedaliah's words to the people are almost identical with those of Jeremiah, whose interests Gedaliah's family had long served: **Do not be afraid to serve the Chaldeans. Dwell in the land, and serve the king of Babylon, and it shall be well with you.** (40:9.) The people begin to rally about him. It appeared for a time

8 Then they came to Gedaliah to Mizpah, even Ishmael the son of Nethaniah, and Johanan and Jonathan the sons of Kareah, and Seraiah the son of Tanhumeth, and the sons of Ephai the Netophathite, and Jezaniah the son of Maachathite, they and their men.

9 And Gedaliah the son of Ahikam the son of Shaphan sware unto them and to their men, saying, Fear not to serve the Chaldeans: dwell in the land, and serve the king of Babylon, and it shall be well with you.

10 As for me, behold, I will dwell at Mizpah, to serve the Chaldeans, which will come unto us: but ye, gather ye wine, and summer fruits, and oil, and put *them* in your vessels, and dwell in your cities that ye have taken.

11 Likewise when all the Jews that *were* in Moab, and among the Ammonites, and in Edom, and that *were* in all the countries, heard that the king of Babylon had left a remnant of Judah, and that he had set over them Gedaliah the son of Ahikam the son of Shaphan;

12 Even all the Jews returned out of all places whither they were driven, and came to the land of Judah, to Gedaliah, unto

exile to Babylon, **8** they went to Gedali'ah at Mizpah — Ish'mael the son of Nethani'ah, Joha'nan the son of Kare'ah, Serai'ah the son of Tan'humeth, the sons of Ephai the Netoph'athite, Jezani'ah the son of the Ma-ac'athite, they and their men. **9** Gedali'ah the son of Ahi'kam, son of Shaphan, swore to them and their men, saying, "Do not be afraid to serve the Chalde'ans. Dwell in the land, and serve the king of Babylon, and it shall be well with you. **10** As for me, I will dwell at Mizpah, to stand for you before the Chalde'ans who will come to us; but as for you, gather wine and summer fruits and oil, and store them in your vessels, and dwell in your cities that you have taken." **11** Likewise, when all the Jews who were in Moab and among the Ammonites and in Edom and in other lands heard that the king of Babylon had left a remnant in Judah and had appointed Gedali'ah the son of Ahi'kam, son of Shaphan, as governor over them, **12** then all the Jews returned from all the places to which they had been driven and came to the land of Judah, to

---

10. Mizpah, capital of the province under Gedaliah, was north of Jerusalem in the territory of Benjamin, either modern Tell en-Naṣbeh or Nebī Samwîl. The former, on the main road from Shechem to Jerusalem, is more suitable to the events related in 40:7–41:18. In the excavation of Tell en-Naṣbeh, W. F. Badè discovered in a tomb a seal bearing the inscription, "Belonging to Jaazaniah, official [*ébhedh*] of the king" (C. C. McCown, *Tell en-Naṣbeh, Archaeological and Historical Results,* I [Berkeley and New Haven: Palestine Institute of Pacific School of Religion and the American Schools of Oriental Research, 1947], Pl. LVII, Nos. 4-5). He may be the **Jezaniah** of vs. 8 (cf. II Kings 25:23), but since the name occurs elsewhere of other individuals, this is not certain (cf. 35:3; Ezek. 8:11; 11:1; Lachish Letter No. I, ll. 2-3).

B. FUGITIVES' RETURN TO JUDAH (40:11-12)

11-12. During the Babylonian invasion of Judah, which lasted a year and a half, many of the residents were driven out of their homes and fled to surrounding countries such as Moab, Ammon, and Edom. When Gedaliah established order they returned to their homes, thus indicating their confidence in the governor and their belief in the

---

that Gedaliah, with the help of Jeremiah, would succeed in the task of restoring order and unity and confidence among the scattered people.

It seems probable that this gave to Jeremiah a new hope. The advices he had given by letter to the exiles in Babylon he could now begin to realize at home. Here also the people could be

taught to "build houses and live in them; plant gardens and eat their produce" (29:5). It is possibly from this period that there came from Jeremiah's hand his "book of consolation" (chs. 30-31).

Even the response of the land was auspicious. There was promise of a plentiful harvest. The grapes and fruits were gathered in great abun-

Mizpah, and gathered wine and summer fruits very much.

13 ¶ Moreover Johanan the son of Kareah, and all the captains of the forces that *were* in the fields, came to Gedaliah to Mizpah,

14 And said unto him, Dost thou certainly know that Baalis the king of the Ammonites hath sent Ishmael the son of Nethaniah to slay thee? But Gedaliah the son of Ahikam believed them not.

15 Then Johanan the son of Kareah spake to Gedaliah in Mizpah secretly, saying, Let me go, I pray thee, and I will slay Ishmael the son of Nethaniah, and no man shall know *it:* wherefore should he slay thee, that all the Jews which are gathered unto thee should be scattered, and the remnant in Judah perish?

16 But Gedaliah the son of Ahikam said unto Johanan the son of Kareah, Thou shalt not do this thing: for thou speakest falsely of Ishmael.

41 Now it came to pass in the seventh month, *that* Ishmael the son of Nethaniah the son of Elishama, of the seed royal, and the princes of the king, even ten men with him, came unto Gedaliah the son of Ahikam to Mizpah; and there they did eat bread together in Mizpah.

Gedali'ah at Mizpah; and they gathered wine and summer fruits in great abundance.

13 Now Joha'nan the son of Kare'ah and all the leaders of the forces in the open country came to Gedali'ah at Mizpah 14 and said to him, "Do you know that Ba'alis the king of the Ammonites has sent Ish'mael the son of Nethani'ah to take your life?" But Gedali'ah the son of Ahi'kam would not believe them. 15 Then Joha'nan the son of Kare'ah spoke secretly to Gedali'ah at Mizpah, "Let me go and slay Ish'mael the son of Nethani'ah, and no one will know it. Why should he take your life, so that all the Jews who are gathered about you would be scattered, and the remnant of Judah would perish?" 16 But Gedali'ah the son of Ahi'kam said to Joha'nan the son of Kare'ah, "You shall not do this thing, for you are speaking falsely of Ish'mael."

41 In the seventh month, Ish'mael the son of Nethani'ah, son of Eli'shama, of the royal family, one of the chief officers of the king, came with ten men to Gedali'ah the son of Ahi'kam, at Mizpah. As they ate

---

possibility of restoring security in the land. The abundance of the crops (vs. 12) added to their confidence and prosperity.

C. WARNING TO GEDALIAH (40:13-16)

13-16. The leaders of the Jewish forces who had sworn allegiance to Gedaliah now discovered that one of their number, **Ishmael the son of Nethaniah,** was plotting the assassination of the governor. Gedaliah, unwilling to believe their report, failed to take special precaution to protect himself from the plotters. **Johanan the son of Kareah** shows his knowledge of the situation, and his belief in the indispensability of Gedaliah to the welfare of the Jewish province, by offering to murder Ishmael secretly. Gedaliah's own good nature and lack of suspicion will not permit such a deed. Perhaps one of his motives was to do nothing which would in any way arouse suspicion in the minds of the Babylonians he was seeking to serve.

D. ASSASSINATION OF GEDALIAH (41:1-3)

The assassination of the trusting governor by Ishmael may appear to us as an act of sheer madness, but it is not difficult to understand Ishmael's motives. He was probably one of the anti-Babylonian superpatriots who thought that Gedaliah was co-operating

---

dance (40:12); but before the olives could ripen the entire situation changed. Gedaliah was murdered.

It appears that Ishmael was the tool of the king of Ammon. Baalis of Ammon had no de-

sire to see a new kingdom arise between himself and the Mediterranean. Ishmael, a prince of the blood, was evidently jealous of Gedaliah's appointment and resented bitterly the humiliation of having someone inferior to himself elevated

2 Then arose Ishmael the son of Netha-niah, and the ten men that were with him, and smote Gedaliah the son of Ahikam the son of Shaphan with the sword, and slew him, whom the king of Babylon had made governor over the land.

3 Ishmael also slew all the Jews that were with him, *even* with Gedaliah, at Mizpah, and the Chaldeans that were found there, *and* the men of war.

4 And it came to pass the second day after he had slain Gedaliah, and no man knew *it*,

5 That there came certain from Shechem, from Shiloh, and from Samaria, *even* four-score men, having their beards shaven, and their clothes rent, and having cut them-selves, with offerings and incense in their hand, to bring *them* to the house of the LORD.

bread together there at Mizpah, **2** Ish'mael the son of Nethani'ah and the ten men with him rose up and struck down Geda-li'ah the son of Ahi'kam, son of Shaphan, with the sword, and killed him, whom the king of Babylon had appointed governor in the land. **3** Ish'mael also slew all the Jews who were with Gedali'ah at Mizpah, and the Chalde'an soldiers who happened to be there.

4 On the day after the murder of Geda-li'ah, before any one knew of it, **5** eighty men arrived from Shechem and Shiloh and Samar'ia, with their beards shaved and their clothes torn, and their bodies gashed, bring-ing cereal offerings and incense to present

---

too fully with the Babylonians. Furthermore, he was **of the royal family** and was jealous of Gedaliah, who was not a member of the royalty. Also, Ishmael may have wished to exact vengeance for the cruel act of Nebuchadrezzar in putting to death the sons of King Zedekiah at Riblah, and then blinding Zedekiah and taking him captive to Babylonia (39:6-7; II Kings 25:6-7). Ishmael was in league with King Baalis of Ammon, whose territory was in Trans-Jordan (40:14). Baalis did not wish to see a strong Judah rise again, and he hoped by sowing strife in Judah to be in position to take some of the Judean territory. His reasoning of course was defective, for he certainly did not profit from the subsequent events.

41:1. The murder of the governor took place **in the seventh month**, or Tishri (September-October). The year is not given; it was not necessarily 587 B.C. Ishmael was in a good position to carry out his plot, since he was **one of the chief officers of the king** and had sworn allegiance to Gedaliah (40:8).

3. This verse may be an exaggeration. The slaying of the governor appointed by the Babylonians, and of **the Chaldean soldiers who happened to be there,** was certain to bring on the Jews the vengeance of the Babylonians.

E. MURDER OF SEVENTY PILGRIMS (41:4-9)

It is difficult to understand the motive for Ishmael's slaying of these unarmed pilgrims. Perhaps it was an act of desperation in an attempt to keep the assassination of Gedaliah from becoming known; perhaps he wished to rob them, for ten of the men saved their lives by offering their stores of wheat, barley, oil, and honey (vs. 8). In any event, the cruel murder shows the irrationality of Ishmael and his followers.

5. The **eighty men** were coming from cities which formerly had been considered a part of the Northern Kingdom but had been taken into Judean territory in the time of King Josiah. The fact that they had **their beards shaved and their clothes torn, and their bodies gashed** indicates that they were in mourning. We do not know the reason; it may have been for the destruction of Jerusalem, but, if our estimate of the length of

---

to the position of chief control. When Gedaliah was warned that Ishmael was planning his death he refused to believe it. It was probably characteristic of Gedaliah that he refused to take the warning seriously. It was, in any case,

good sense to do everything possible to inspire confidence in the broken leaders who were gradually rallying to his leadership. Instead, therefore, of permitting Ishmael to be slain, he invited Ishmael with ten of his men to dine

6 And Ishmael the son of Nethaniah went forth from Mizpah to meet them, weeping all along as he went: and it came to pass, as he met them, he said unto them, Come to Gedaliah the son of Ahikam.

7 And it was so, when they came into the midst of the city, that Ishmael the son of Nethaniah slew them, *and cast them* into the midst of the pit, he, and the men that *were* with him.

8 But ten men were found among them that said unto Ishmael, Slay us not: for we have treasures in the field, of wheat, and of barley, and of oil, and of honey. So he forbare, and slew them not among their brethren.

9 Now the pit wherein Ishmael had cast all the dead bodies of the men, whom he had slain because of Gedaliah, *was* it which Asa the king had made for fear of Baasha king of Israel: *and* Ishmael the son of Nethaniah filled it with *them that were* slain.

10 Then Ishmael carried away captive all the residue of the people that *were* in Mizpah, *even* the king's daughters, and all the people that remained in Mizpah, whom Nebuzar-adan the captain of the guard had committed to Gedaliah the son of Ahikam: and Ishmael the son of Nethaniah

at the temple of the LORD. 6 And Ish'mael the son of Nethani'ah came out from Mizpah to meet them, weeping as he came. As he met them, he said to them, "Come in to Gedali'ah the son of Ahi'kam." 7 When they came into the city, Ish'mael the son of Nethani'ah and the men with him slew them, and cast them into a cistern. 8 But there were ten men among them who said to Ish'mael, "Do not kill us, for we have stores of wheat, barley, oil, and honey hidden in the fields." So he refrained and did not kill them with their companions.

9 Now the cistern into which Ish'mael cast all the bodies of the men whom he had slain was the large cistern[r] which King Asa had made for defense against Ba'asha king of Israel; Ish'mael the son of Nethani'ah filled it with the slain. 10 Then Ish'mael took captive all the rest of the people who were in Mizpah, the king's daughters and all the people who were left at Mizpah, whom Nebu'zarad'an, the captain of the guard, had committed to Gedali'ah the son of Ahi'kam. Ish'mael the son of Nethani'ah

[r] Gk: Heb *he had slain by the hand of Gedaliah*

Gedaliah's governorship is correct, that had taken place four or five years earlier. There can be no doubt they were going to present their gifts in **the temple of the LORD** in Jerusalem, not in a local sanctuary at Mizpah, for Ishmael had to induce them to turn aside to Mizpah. By this time the temple in Jerusalem had been sufficiently restored so that some offerings could be made there.

8. Ishmael may have planned to conduct guerrilla warfare against the Chaldeans and would therefore have been able to make good use of the **stores** here offered him.

9. The large cistern which King Asa had made for defense against Baasha king of Israel: I Kings 15:22 says that King Asa of Judah built Geba of Benjamin and Mizpah as protection against King Baasha of Israel. Such cisterns were for the storing of water, and are found in the excavation of many ancient Palestinian cities. At Tell en-Nașbeh no less than fifty-three were found, but none could clearly be identified with the one mentioned here (*ibid.*, pp. 129-39).

F. CAPTURE OF THE PEOPLE OF MIZPAH (41:10)

10. Ishmael took captive the remaining people of Mizpah and fled with them toward the land of the Ammonites in Trans-Jordan; he was in league with King Baalis of the Ammonites (40:14).

with him. In the middle of the night Ishmael and his men arose and murdered Gedaliah. The events which follow (see Exeg.) are depressing in the extreme. The single crime begets more, apparently lest the initial crime

should be found out. When the ten pilgrims who were not massacred effected their escape, the tidings of Ishmael's crime spread rapidly. Forced to flee, he was overtaken at Gibeon by Johanan; but he made good his escape and,

carried them away captive, and departed to go over to the Ammonites.

11 ¶ But when Johanan the son of Kareah, and all the captains of the forces that *were* with him, heard of all the evil that Ishmael the son of Nethaniah had done,

12 Then they took all the men, and went to fight with Ishmael the son of Nethaniah, and found him by the great waters that *are* in Gibeon.

13 Now it came to pass, *that* when all the people which *were* with Ishmael saw Johanan the son of Kareah, and all the captains of the forces that *were* with him, then they were glad.

14 So all the people that Ishmael had carried away captive from Mizpah cast about and returned, and went unto Johanan the son of Kareah.

15 But Ishmael the son of Nethaniah escaped from Johanan with eight men, and went to the Ammonites.

16 Then took Johanan the son of Kareah, and all the captains of the forces that *were* with him, all the remnant of the people whom he had recovered from Ishmael the son of Nethaniah, from Mizpah, after *that* he had slain Gedaliah the son of Ahikam, *even* mighty men of war, and the women, and the children, and the eunuchs, whom he had brought again from Gibeon:

17 And they departed, and dwelt in the habitation of Chimham, which is by Bethlehem, to go to enter into Egypt,

took them captive and set out to cross over to the Ammonites.

11 But when Joha'nan the son of Kare'ah and all the leaders of the forces with him heard of all the evil which Ish'mael the son of Nethani'ah had done, 12 they took all their men and went to fight against Ish'mael the son of Nethani'ah. They came upon him at the great pool which is in Gib'eon. 13 And when all the people who were with Ish'mael saw Joha'nan the son of Kare'ah and all the leaders of the forces with him, they rejoiced. 14 So all the people whom Ish'mael had carried away captive from Mizpah turned about and came back, and went to Joha'nan the son of Kare'ah. 15 But Ish'mael the son of Nethani'ah escaped from Joha'nan with eight men, and went to the Ammonites. 16 Then Joha'nan the son of Kare'ah and all the leaders of the forces with him took all the rest of the people whom Ish'mael the son of Nethani'ah had carried away captive[s] from Mizpah after he had slain Gedali'ah the son of Ahi'kam — soldiers, women, children, and eunuchs, whom Joha'nan brought back from Gib'eon. 17 And they went and stayed at Geruth Chimham near Bethlehem, intending to go

[s] Cn: Heb *whom he recovered from Ishmael*

G. RESCUE OF THE CAPTIVES (41:11-18)

The prompt action of **Johanan the son of Kareah** and the loyal leaders of the Jewish forces made possible the rescue of the captives of Mizpah.

12. The loyal leaders overtake Ishmael at **Gibeon,** usually identified with modern Ej-Jîb, about three miles southwest of Tell en-Naṣbeh. The fact that the route implied here is not the direct way to Ammon seems to favor the identification of Mizpah with Nebī Samwîl rather than with Tell en-Naṣbeh. But we know too little about the details of this event to press the point. Perhaps the forces under Johanan the son of Kareah were so disposed that Ishmael could not take the direct route to Ammon. II Sam. 2:13 mentions a pool of Gibeon which is probably identical with the **great waters** or **great pool** mentioned here.

17. The location of **Geruth Chimham** is unknown. The Hebrew *gĕrûth* hardly means simply **habitation**; it may mean "inn." If the second word is a personal name, we

as Gillies puts it, "disappeared from history, a right royal villain." [1]

Johanan was no Gedaliah. He was a man of action but not of wisdom. Fearing lest the

[1] *Jeremiah, the Man and His Message,* p. 325.

Chaldeans would blame him and his men for Gedaliah's assassination, Johanan and his leaders moved south toward Bethlehem—a little nearer to Egypt! Gedaliah was slain; Ishmael had achieved none of his aspired gains; Johanan

18 Because of the Chaldeans: for they were afraid of them, because Ishmael the son of Nethaniah had slain Gedaliah the son of Ahikam, whom the king of Babylon made governor in the land.

42 Then all the captains of the forces, and Johanan the son of Kareah, and Jezaniah the son of Hoshaiah, and all the people from the least even unto the greatest, came near,

2 And said unto Jeremiah the prophet, Let, we beseech thee, our supplication be accepted before thee, and pray for us unto the LORD thy God, *even* for all this remnant; (for we are left *but* a few of many, as thine eyes do behold us:)

3 That the LORD thy God may show us the way wherein we may walk, and the thing that we may do.

4 Then Jeremiah the prophet said unto them, I have heard *you;* behold, I will pray unto the LORD your God according to your words; and it shall come to pass, *that* whatsoever thing the LORD shall answer you, I will declare *it* unto you; I will keep nothing back from you.

to Egypt 18 because of the Chalde'ans; for they were afraid of them, because Ish'mael the son of Nethani'ah had slain Gedali'ah the son of Ahi'kam, whom the king of Babylon had made governor over the land.

42 Then all the commanders of the forces, and Joha'nan the son of Kare'ah and Azari'ah[t] the son of Hoshai'ah, and all the people from the least to the greatest, came near 2 and said to Jeremiah the prophet, "Let our supplication come before you, and pray to the LORD your God for us, for all this remnant (for we are left but a few of many, as your eyes see us), 3 that the LORD your God may show us the way we should go, and the thing that we should do." 4 Jeremiah the prophet said to them, "I have heard you; behold, I will pray to the LORD your God according to your request, and whatever the LORD answers you I will tell you; I will keep nothing

[t] Gk: Heb *Jezaniah*

may translate "Chimham's Inn" (Amer. Trans.) and suppose it was a lodging place near Bethlehem.

XXX. FLIGHT TO EGYPT (42:1–43:7)

We have noticed that Jeremiah does not appear at all in the events narrated in 40:7–41:18. In the present section he is consulted by those who are planning to flee to Egypt, and he remains the center of the narrative through 44:30. Chs. 42–44 show evidence of Deuteronomic editing, especially in 42:7-22; 44:1-14. It is usually believed that the basic work used by the Deuteronomic editor was a continuation of Baruch's memoirs. While that is possible, we may at least question whether Baruch would have reported the accusation made against him in 43:2-3.

A. CONSULTATION WITH JEREMIAH BY THE REMNANT (42:1-6)

42:1-6. The survivors of the city of Mizpah and their rescuers now consult Jeremiah so that through him they may receive the guidance of Yahweh regarding their proposed flight to Egypt. There is no need to doubt their sincerity and initial desire to obey the will of Yahweh as it should be revealed through the prophet. It was indeed a difficult decision to make. If they remained in Palestine, they were certain to be suspected by

and his leaders were thrown into a panic of fear. The last hope of Judah was broken under such circumstances as make

> Ridiculous the waste sad time
> Stretching before and after.[2]

[2] T. S. Eliot, "Burnt Norton," Part V. From *Four Quartets*. Copyright 1943 by T. S. Eliot. Used by permission of Harcourt, Brace & Co. and Faber & Faber, publishers.

42:1–43:7. We Will Hearken unto the Voice.
—These closing chapters show the last vestiges of political hope in Judah falling apart. Johanan and his leaders come to Jeremiah, hoping to secure through him divine approval on their unconscious but fixed intent to run away.

The fact that Jeremiah took ten days in which to think this problem through may be significant. It shows, in the first place, that the

5 Then they said to Jeremiah, The LORD be a true and faithful witness between us, if we do not even according to all things for the which the LORD thy God shall send thee to us.

6 Whether *it be* good, or whether *it be* evil, we will obey the voice of the LORD our God, to whom we send thee; that it may be well with us, when we obey the voice of the LORD our God.

7 ¶ And it came to pass after ten days, that the word of the LORD came unto Jeremiah.

8 Then called he Johanan the son of Kareah, and all the captains of the forces which *were* with him, and all the people from the least even to the greatest,

9 And said unto them, Thus saith the LORD, the God of Israel, unto whom ye sent me to present your supplication before him;

10 If ye will still abide in this land, then will I build you, and not pull *you* down; and I will plant you, and not pluck *you* up: for I repent me of the evil that I have done unto you.

11 Be not afraid of the king of Babylon, of whom ye are afraid; be not afraid of him, saith the LORD: for I *am* with you to save you, and to deliver you from his hand.

back from you." 5 Then they said to Jeremiah, "May the LORD be a true and faithful witness against us if we do not act according to all the word with which the LORD your God sends you to us. 6 Whether it is good or evil, we will obey the voice of the LORD our God to whom we are sending you, that it may be well with us when we obey the voice of the LORD our God."

7 At the end of ten days the word of the LORD came to Jeremiah. 8 Then he summoned Joha'nan the son of Kare'ah and all the commanders of the forces who were with him, and all the people from the least to the greatest, 9 and said to them, "Thus says the LORD, the God of Israel, to whom you sent me to present your supplication before him: 10 If you will remain in this land, then I will build you up and not pull you down; I will plant you, and not pluck you up; for I repent of the evil which I did to you. 11 Do not fear the king of Babylon, of whom you are afraid; do not fear him, says the LORD, for I am with you, to save you and to deliver you from his

---

the Babylonians of having participated in the rebellion of Ishmael, but they might have been given the opportunity to prove their own loyalty and to show that the rebellion had been engaged in by only a small group around Ishmael. If they fled to Egypt, they were open to the charge of thereby admitting their guilt, but they stood a chance of being safe from the vengeance to be exacted by the Babylonians.

Jeremiah and Baruch may have been among those who lived at Mizpah, and may thus have been captured by Ishmael and subsequently rescued by the forces of Johanan. We have no certain information as to Jeremiah's residence during Gedaliah's regime.

B. YAHWEH'S REPLY (42:7-22)

The account as given here is long and repetitious. It shows the hand of the Deuteronomic editor, especially in vss. 10-11, 13, 18, 22. The essence of the reply is in vss. 10-12, which Volz considers poetry; yet they are probably not the actual words of the prophet.

7. It is significant that Jeremiah received the word of Yahweh only **at the end of ten days.** It is likely not that he received the word suddenly in an ecstatic state, but rather that a period of **ten days** was required for him to be certain that he was correctly giving the will of Yahweh. We should not deny that the prophet's own reasoning may have entered into his quest for the will of Yahweh. As we have seen, the decision as to

---

prophet's sense of the authenticity of the word of God was often arrived at through hours of inner struggle and concern, the midnight wrestle with the threatening angel, until the blessings of the Lord should come. The irony

of such a return to Egypt would be extreme for all of Jeremiah's policies. But doubtless he discerned the unconscious mind of Johanan and the others and their will to flee. He doubtless felt keenly the loss of Gedaliah. He must easily

12 And I will show mercies unto you, that he may have mercy upon you, and cause you to return to your own land.

13 ¶ But if ye say, We will not dwell in this land, neither obey the voice of the LORD your God,

14 Saying, No; but we will go into the land of Egypt, where we shall see no war, nor hear the sound of the trumpet, nor have hunger of bread; and there will we dwell:

15 And now therefore hear the word of the LORD, ye remnant of Judah; Thus saith the LORD of hosts, the God of Israel; If ye wholly set your faces to enter into Egypt, and go to sojourn there;

16 Then it shall come to pass, *that* the sword, which ye feared, shall overtake you there in the land of Egypt; and the famine, whereof ye were afraid, shall follow close after you there in Egypt; and there ye shall die.

17 So shall it be with all the men that set their faces to go into Egypt to sojourn there; they shall die by the sword, by the famine, and by the pestilence: and none of them shall remain or escape from the evil that I will bring upon them.

18 For thus saith the LORD of hosts, the God of Israel; As mine anger and my fury hath been poured forth upon the inhabitants of Jerusalem; so shall my fury be poured forth upon you, when ye shall enter into Egypt: and ye shall be an execration, and an astonishment, and a curse, and a reproach; and ye shall see this place no more.

19 ¶ The LORD hath said concerning you, O ye remnant of Judah; Go ye not

hand. **12** I will grant you mercy, that he may have mercy on you and let you remain in your own land. **13** But if you say, 'We will not remain in this land,' disobeying the voice of the LORD your God **14** and saying, 'No, we will go to the land of Egypt, where we shall not see war, or hear the sound of the trumpet, or be hungry for bread, and we will dwell there,' **15** then hear the word of the LORD, O remnant of Judah. Thus says the LORD of hosts, the God of Israel: If you set your faces to enter Egypt and go to live there, **16** then the sword which you fear shall overtake you there in the land of Egypt; and the famine of which you are afraid shall follow hard after you to Egypt; and there you shall die. **17** All the men who set their faces to go to Egypt to live there shall die by the sword, by famine, and by pestilence; they shall have no remnant or survivor from the evil which I will bring upon them.

18 "For thus says the LORD of hosts, the God of Israel: As my anger and my wrath were poured out on the inhabitants of Jerusalem, so my wrath will be poured out on you when you go to Egypt. You shall become an execration, a horror, a curse, and a taunt. You shall see this place no more. **19** The LORD has said to you, O remnant of

whether or not flight to Egypt was advisable was not easy. Jeremiah himself had written to the exiles in Babylonia encouraging them to settle down, be good citizens, and worship Yahweh (29:1-14). He had not previously placed great emphasis on residence in Palestine, though he had expressed the belief that life could and would continue there (32:6-15). Now he finally comes to the conclusion that flight to Egypt is not the will of God, and advises those who had come to him to remain in Palestine.

13-22. These verses anticipate the reply of the survivors and must be largely editorial.

have perceived that there was none to take his place, that trustworthy leadership would have to be grown through unpredictable adversities of trial and error. He must have been searching long for a way to tell his people that the way of Yahweh was not in flight but in learning to accept him where they were. True, they had

promised ardently that they would obey his voice; but the vehemence of Jeremiah's word, when it comes, shows plainly that he knew this would not be. Therefore, perhaps, the sharpness wherewith he emphasizes the divine command. If they stay, the Lord will build them up and plant them. They will not have to fear

into Egypt: know certainly that I have admonished you this day.

20 For ye dissembled in your hearts, when ye sent me unto the LORD your God, saying, Pray for us unto the LORD our God; and according unto all that the LORD our God shall say, so declare unto us, and we will do *it*.

21 And *now* I have this day declared *it* to you; but ye have not obeyed the voice of the LORD your God, nor any *thing* for the which he hath sent me unto you.

22 Now therefore know certainly that ye shall die by the sword, by the famine, and by the pestilence, in the place whither ye desire to go *and* to sojourn.

43 And it came to pass, *that* when Jeremiah had made an end of speaking unto all the people all the words of the LORD their God, for which the LORD their God had sent him to them, *even* all these words,

2 Then spake Azariah the son of Hoshaiah, and Johanan the son of Kareah, and all the proud men, saying unto Jeremiah, Thou speakest falsely: the LORD our God hath not sent thee to say, Go not into Egypt to sojourn there:

3 But Baruch the son of Neriah setteth thee on against us, for to deliver us into the hand of the Chaldeans, that they might put us to death, and carry us away captives into Babylon.

Judah, 'Do not go to Egypt.' Know for a certainty that I have warned you this day **20** that you have gone astray at the cost of your lives. For you sent me to the LORD your God, saying, 'Pray for us to the LORD our God, and whatever the LORD our God says declare to us and we will do it.' **21** And I have this day declared it to you, but you have not obeyed the voice of the LORD your God in anything that he sent me to tell you. **22** Now therefore know for a certainty that you shall die by the sword, by famine, and by pestilence in the place where you desire to go to live."

43 When Jeremiah finished speaking to all the people all these words of the LORD their God, with which the LORD their God had sent him to them, **2** Azari'ah the son of Hoshai'ah and Joha'nan the son of Kare'ah and all the insolent men said to Jeremiah, "You are telling a lie. The LORD our God did not send you to say, 'Do not go to Egypt to live there'; **3** but Baruch the son of Neri'ah has set you against us, to deliver us into the hand of the Chalde'ans, that they may kill us or take us into exile in

---

C. RESPONSE OF THE PEOPLE (43:1-3)

When Jeremiah gives Yahweh's reply to the people, they refuse to believe that he is telling the truth and accuse him of listening to Baruch rather than to the Lord. Thus they place themselves in the position not of disobeying Yahweh's will, but of doubting the prophet's truthfulness.

It may be that during the period of ten days when Jeremiah was seeking the word of Yahweh, the people became impatient and restless, and those men among the remnant who believed in flight to Egypt gained the upper hand and were able to convince the others of the wisdom of such a course.

43:3. Baruch the son of Neriah was the amanuensis of Jeremiah, who wrote the scroll at the prophet's dictation (36:4). He was with Jeremiah when the prophet in prison purchased a field at Anathoth (32:1-16), and had probably been the companion

---

the Chaldeans, for the Lord will be with them to save them and deliver them. But if they refuse to obey the voice and go to the land of Egypt, the wrath of the Lord will pursue them even there. Thus, against the final adversity, Jeremiah's faith and confidence in the future of Israel remain the same. The future of Israel is not in Babylon, it is even less in

Egypt. It is in Judah, as his "book of consolation" had recently proclaimed.

The reaction of the leaders, as Jeremiah himself must have anticipated, was a rejection of his word. They tried to rationalize their behavior by asserting to themselves that Jeremiah, now old, had succumbed to the greater youth and vitality of his secretary, Baruch; that it was

4 So Johanan the son of Kareah, and all the captains of the forces, and all the people, obeyed not the voice of the LORD, to dwell in the land of Judah.

5 But Johanan the son of Kareah, and all the captains of the forces, took all the remnant of Judah, that were returned from all nations, whither they had been driven, to dwell in the land of Judah;

6 Even men, and women, and children, and the king's daughters, and every person that Nebuzar-adan the captain of the guard had left with Gedaliah the son of Ahikam the son of Shaphan, and Jeremiah the prophet, and Baruch the son of Neriah.

7 So they came into the land of Egypt: for they obeyed not the voice of the LORD: thus came they even to Tahpanhes.

8 ¶ Then came the word of the LORD unto Jeremiah in Tahpanhes, saying,

Babylon." 4 So Joha'nan the son of Kare'ah and all the commanders of the forces and all the people did not obey the voice of the LORD, to remain in the land of Judah. 5 But Joha'nan the son of Kare'ah and all the commanders of the forces took all the remnant of Judah who had returned to live in the land of Judah from all the nations to which they had been driven — 6 the men, the women, the children, the princesses, and every person whom Nebu'zarad'an the captain of the guard had left with Gedali'ah the son of Ahi'kam, son of Shaphan; also Jeremiah the prophet and Baruch the son of Neri'ah. 7 And they came into the land of Egypt, for they did not obey the voice of the LORD. And they arrived at Tah'panhes.

8 Then the word of the LORD came to

---

and confidant of Jeremiah for many years. The accusation made against Baruch shows that the people believed he had great influence over the prophet, and indicates that Baruch must have been far more than a mere amanuensis.

D. FLIGHT TO EGYPT (43:4-7)

The leaders, refusing to believe that Jeremiah was correctly speaking the word of Yahweh, fled to Egypt, taking with them the people and also Jeremiah and Baruch. Jeremiah must have been taken by force, for he would hardly have accompanied them willingly after counseling them to remain in Palestine.

5. This verse is perhaps an exaggeration. It is more likely that vs. 6 gives correctly the make-up of the group that fled to Egypt. The group consisted primarily of the leaders of the forces, who would have been accused of rebellion, together with the residents of Mizpah whom they had rescued from Ishmael.

6. On the question of the punishment of the Jews by the Babylonians for the assassination of Gedaliah, see Exeg. on 52:30.

7. Tahpanhes: A city on the Egyptian border in the eastern part of the delta (cf. 2:16).

XXXI. JEREMIAH IN EGYPT (43:8–44:30)

A. SYMBOLIC ACTION ON THE FATE OF EGYPT (43:8-13)

After arriving in Egypt, Jeremiah performs a symbolic action and declares an oracle of Yahweh, designed to show the Jews that they are not safe from Nebuchadrezzar even in Egypt. The Babylonian king will come and set up his throne in the land to which they have fled.

This account has been declared by Duhm to be a "midrash" wholly without historical value, designed to condemn the sanctuaries of the Egyptian gods, and based perhaps on Ezek. 29:10 ff. Admittedly the account presents difficulties, but it is not easy to see why

---

Baruch's influence that had deflected the pure word of God. Nevertheless, Jeremiah and Baruch represent for the people a security interest. They represent, unconsciously, the people's tie to the presence of God. Thus, with characteristic ambivalence, they force Jeremiah and

Baruch to go with them into the land of Egypt —seeking, by this means, to retain their hold on the divine approval even as they run in disobedience to his word.

43:8-13. The Stones in Pharaoh's Palace.— The narrative skill of the Deuteronomist editors

9 Take great stones in thine hand, and hide them in the clay in the brickkiln, which *is* at the entry of Pharaoh's house in Tahpanhes, in the sight of the men of Judah;

10 And say unto them, Thus saith the LORD of hosts, the God of Israel; Behold, I will send and take Nebuchadrezzar the king of Babylon, my servant, and will set his throne upon these stones that I have hid; and he shall spread his royal pavilion over them.

11 And when he cometh, he shall smite the land of Egypt, *and deliver* such *as are* for death to death; and such *as are* for captivity to captivity; and such *as are* for the sword to the sword.

Jeremiah in Tah'panhes: 9 "Take in your hands large stones, and hide them in the mortar in the pavement which is at the entrance to Pharaoh's palace in Tah'panhes, in the sight of the men of Judah, 10 and say to them, 'Thus says the LORD of hosts, the God of Israel: Behold, I will send and take Nebuchadrez'zar the king of Babylon, my servant, and he[u] will set his throne above these stones which I have hid, and he will spread his royal canopy over them. 11 He shall come and smite the land of Egypt, giving to the pestilence those who are doomed to the pestilence, to captivity those who are doomed to captivity, and to the sword those who are doomed to the

[u] Gk Syr: Heb *I*

a late author would make up the whole story without any historical foundation when the oracle was not literally fulfilled. It is best to accept the account as basically authentic.

The detailed history of the Neo-Babylonian Empire is not well known, since most of the surviving inscriptions record building activities rather than military campaigns. A very fragmentary text in the British Museum (see Pritchard, *Ancient Near Eastern Texts*, p. 308) tells of an invasion of Egypt by Nebuchadrezzar in his thirty-seventh year, 568-567 B.C., in which he engaged in battle with Pharaoh Amasis (Ahmose II). The text is so fragmentary that we do not know the outcome of the battle. However, it is certain that the Babylonian king did not really conquer Egypt, for that country remained independent until its conquest by Cambyses of Persia. It is unlikely that Nebuchadrezzar caused as much destruction as is here predicted. Josephus (*Antiquities* X. 9. 7) tells of an invasion of Egypt five years after the destruction of Jerusalem, in which Nebuchadrezzar killed the Egyptian king and appointed another, and took the Jews of Egypt captive to Babylonia. But this is probably not based on any extrabiblical source and cannot be reliable.

9-10. It is impossible to reconstruct precisely the action of Jeremiah since the meaning of some of the words is obscure, particularly those rendered in the RSV by **mortar, pavement,** and **royal canopy.** The symbolic action involves the making of a pedestal on which the Babylonian king is expected to come and set up his **throne. Pharaoh's palace** (or **Pharaoh's house**) probably was not actually the palace of the Egyptian king, since the capital was not at Tahpanhes, but at Sais, in the western half of the delta. The building was probably a government structure of some nature. The symbolic action must have been performed in the presence of a small group of Jewish leaders, hardly before the whole community.

The Babylonian king is here called **my servant** (cf. 27:6).

11. Cf. the latter part of this verse with 15:2. Volz considers vss. 10*b*, 12-13*a* as poetry, but this verse as a prose addition.

becomes increasingly clear. Two incidents of Jeremiah's life in Egypt are conserved. The teaching in each is skillfully directed and pointed so as to break through the two great illusions of the refugees in Egypt.

The first of these illusions was the supposition that they would be safe in Egypt. By means of a symbolic action, Jeremiah demonstrates that they are not. Taking large stones and hid-

ing them **in the pavement ... at the entrance to Pharaoh's palace in Tahpanhes,** and exciting thus the curiosity and wonder of the refugees, he says to them that Nebuchadrezzar will come even unto Egypt and set up his throne above the stones which they have buried. He will destroy the land as he has destroyed Judah. Even the obelisks of Heliopolis will be broken (see Exeg.).

12 And I will kindle a fire in the houses of the gods of Egypt; and he shall burn them, and carry them away captives: and he shall array himself with the land of Egypt, as a shepherd putteth on his garment; and he shall go forth from thence in peace.

13 He shall break also the images of Beth-shemesh, that *is* in the land of Egypt; and the houses of the gods of the Egyptians shall he burn with fire.

44 The word that came to Jeremiah concerning all the Jews which dwell in the land of Egypt, which dwell at Migdol, and at Tahpanhes, and at Noph, and in the country of Pathros, saying,

sword. 12 He[v] shall kindle a fire in the temples of the gods of Egypt; and he shall burn them and carry them away captive; and he shall clean the land of Egypt, as a shepherd cleans his cloak of vermin; and he shall go away from there in peace. 13 He shall break the obelisks of Heliop'olis which is in the land of Egypt; and the temples of the gods of Egypt he shall burn with fire.' "

44 The word that came to Jeremiah concerning all the Jews that dwelt in the land of Egypt, at Migdol, at Tah'panhes, at Memphis, and in the land of Pathros,

[v] Gk Syr Vg: Heb *I*

---

12. He shall clean the land of Egypt, as a shepherd cleans his cloak of vermin: This rendering is based upon the belief that the LXX properly translates עטה by φθειρίζω, lit., "to delouse." The vivid figure shows what a low opinion Jeremiah had of **the land of Egypt.**

13. Heliopolis, or **Beth-shemesh,** "House of the Sun," is the modern Tel Huṣn, about six miles northeast of Cairo. It was famous in ancient times as a center of the worship of the sun-god Re. The **obelisks** (*maççēbhôth*, the name for sacred standing pillars) were tall granite shafts with pyramidal tops erected in commemoration of outstanding events in a king's reign. Of the obelisks of Heliopolis, only one remains in place; two of them, each known as "Cleopatra's Needle," were erected by Thutmose III; one is now on the Thames Embankment in London, the other in Central Park, New York. The Hebrew writer adds **which is in the land of Egypt** to distinguish this Beth-shemesh from the Palestinian city of the same name.

B. Rebuke of the Jews (44:1-14)

This chapter is repetitious and prolix and filled with phraseology and ideas characteristic of the Deuteronomic editor (Mowinckel, Rudolph). Vss. 2-10, for example, are a Deuteronomic résumé of history, with an exaggerated statement of the destruction wrought in Judah and emphasis on the repeated warnings which had been sent through the prophets, ending with a general condemnation for disobedience and false worship. It is difficult to disentangle a genuine oracle which may come from the prophet Jeremiah, but it is possible that he did condemn the Jews in Egypt for specific practices, e.g., worship of **the queen of heaven** (vss. 17-18, 25). Yet we must recall that in his Palestinian career Jeremiah had devoted relatively little effort to condemnation of false cultic practices. On the whole this chapter is of greater value for the study of the Deuteronomic editor's point of view than for Jeremiah's. Its presence in the book indicates that D probably wrote in Egypt (so Rudolph).

44:1. The rebuke is addressed to **all the Jews that dwelt in the land of Egypt, at Migdol, at Tahpanhes, at Memphis, and in the land of Pathros.** By this time there probably were Jews scattered over various parts of Egypt, including those who had fled after the murder of Gedaliah and those who had been migrating to Egypt at various

---

44:1-30. *The Last Word!*—The second incident of Jeremiah's life in Egypt begins with a formal statement addressed to all the Jews in the land. It reviews the history of recent events, the warnings of the prophetic succession, and rebukes them for their moral

regression into idolatrous practices, pointing out to them that they have apparently learned nothing from their recent history. (But see Exeg.)

The words of Jeremiah are countered with a spirited defense on the part of the women who were burning incense to the queen of heaven.

2 Thus saith the LORD of hosts, the God of Israel; Ye have seen all the evil that I have brought upon Jerusalem, and upon all the cities of Judah; and, behold, this day they *are* a desolation, and no man dwelleth therein;

3 Because of their wickedness which they have committed to provoke me to anger, in that they went to burn incense, *and* to serve other gods, whom they knew not, *neither* they, ye, nor your fathers.

4 Howbeit I sent unto you all my servants the prophets, rising early and sending *them*, saying, Oh, do not this abominable thing that I hate.

5 But they hearkened not, nor inclined their ear to turn from their wickedness, to burn no incense unto other gods.

6 Wherefore my fury and mine anger was poured forth, and was kindled in the cities of Judah and in the streets of Jerusalem; and they are wasted *and* desolate, as at this day.

7 Therefore now thus saith the LORD, the God of hosts, the God of Israel; Wherefore commit ye *this* great evil against your souls, to cut off from you man and woman, child and suckling, out of Judah, to leave you none to remain;

8 In that ye provoke me unto wrath with the works of your hands, burning incense unto other gods in the land of Egypt, whither ye be gone to dwell, that ye might cut yourselves off, and that ye might be a curse and a reproach among all the nations of the earth?

9 Have ye forgotten the wickedness of your fathers, and the wickedness of the kings of Judah, and the wickedness of their wives, and your own wickedness, and the wickedness of your wives, which they have committed in the land of Judah, and in the streets of Jerusalem?

2 "Thus says the LORD of hosts, the God of Israel: You have seen all the evil that I brought upon Jerusalem and upon all the cities of Judah. Behold, this day they are a desolation, and no one dwells in them, 3 because of the wickedness which they committed, provoking me to anger, in that they went to burn incense and serve other gods that they knew not, neither they, nor you, nor your fathers. 4 Yet I persistently sent to you all my servants the prophets, saying, 'Oh, do not do this abominable thing that I hate!' 5 But they did not listen or incline their ear, to turn from their wickedness and burn no incense to other gods. 6 Therefore my wrath and my anger were poured forth and kindled in the cities of Judah and in the streets of Jerusalem; and they became a waste and a desolation, as at this day. 7 And now thus says the LORD God of hosts, the God of Israel: Why do you commit this great evil against yourselves, to cut off from you man and woman, infant and child, from the midst of Judah, leaving you no remnant? 8 Why do you provoke me to anger with the works of your hands, burning incense to other gods in the land of Egypt where you have come to live, that you may be cut off and become a curse and a taunt among all the nations of the earth? 9 Have you forgotten the wickedness of your fathers, the wickedness of the kings of Judah, the wickedness of their[w] wives, your own wickedness, and the wickedness of your wives, which they committed in the land of Judah and in the streets of Jerusa-

w Heb *his*

times since the fall of Samaria. But the prophet hardly had any method of addressing so many people, and such an artificial audience is characteristic of the Deuteronomic editor. **Migdol** was near the northeastern border of Egypt, probably modern Tell el-Heir. **Memphis** (Hebrew **Noph**) is modern Mît Rahneh, fourteen miles south of Cairo (cf.

With open insolence they reject the authority of the prophet, arguing that all the difficulties which have overtaken them were a result of the Josian reformation. Things were better in the days of Manasseh. The popular view of history is thus sharply juxtaposed to the prophetic interpretation. To Jeremiah, it was precisely because of the abominations of Manasseh and the corrupting influences from alien cult practices that all their misfortunes had come.

10 They are not humbled *even* unto this day, neither have they feared, nor walked in my law, nor in my statutes, that I set before you and before your fathers.

11 ¶ Therefore thus saith the Lord of hosts, the God of Israel; Behold, I will set my face against you for evil, and to cut off all Judah.

12 And I will take the remnant of Judah, that have set their faces to go into the land of Egypt to sojourn there, and they shall all be consumed, *and* fall in the land of Egypt; they shall *even* be consumed by the sword *and* by the famine: they shall die, from the least even unto the greatest, by the sword and by the famine: and they shall be an execration, *and* an astonishment, and a curse, and a reproach.

13 For I will punish them that dwell in the land of Egypt, as I have punished Jerusalem, by the sword, by the famine, and by the pestilence:

14 So that none of the remnant of Judah, which are gone into the land of Egypt to sojourn there, shall escape or remain, that they should return into the land of Judah, to the which they have a desire to return to dwell there: for none shall return but such as shall escape.

15 ¶ Then all the men which knew that their wives had burned incense unto other gods, and all the women that stood by, a great multitude, even all the people that dwelt in the land of Egypt, in Pathros, answered Jeremiah, saying,

lem? 10 They have not humbled themselves even to this day, nor have they feared, nor walked in my law and my statutes which I set before you and before your fathers.

11 "Therefore thus says the Lord of hosts, the God of Israel: Behold, I will set my face against you for evil, to cut off all Judah. 12 I will take the remnant of Judah who have set their faces to come to the land of Egypt to live, and they shall all be consumed; in the land of Egypt they shall fall; by the sword and by famine they shall be consumed; from the least to the greatest, they shall die by the sword and by famine; and they shall become an execration, a horror, a curse, and a taunt. 13 I will punish those who dwell in the land of Egypt, as I have punished Jerusalem, with the sword, with famine, and with pestilence, 14 so that none of the remnant of Judah who have come to live in the land of Egypt shall escape or survive or return to the land of Judah, to which they desire to return to dwell there; for they shall not return, except some fugitives."

15 Then all the men who knew that their wives had offered incense to other gods, and all the women who stood by, a great assembly, all the people who dwelt in Pathros in the land of Egypt, answered

2:16). **Pathros** was the name for Upper Egypt, the Egyptian word meaning "Land of the South." Hence in the first part of the verse **land of Egypt** may refer only to Lower (northern) Egypt.

14. **Except some fugitives** seems to be an editorial gloss, for it is quite inconsistent with vss. 14a, 27; it is probably from the same hand as vs. 28.

C. Response of the Jews (44:15-19)

This insolent reply has a ring of authenticity and may well reflect the attitude of the people who refused to listen to Jeremiah in Egypt as he condemned them for their worship of the queen of heaven with rites that were essentially pagan. They attribute their prosperity to the fact that they had worshiped her, and refuse to heed Jeremiah's admonition that they should worship only Yahweh.

15. **Pathros** is Upper Egypt (see Exeg. on vs. 1).

It was precisely **because** [they] **burned incense, and because** [they] **sinned against the Lord and did not obey the voice of the Lord or walk in his law** that their evils have befallen them (vs. 23). (But see Exeg.)

The distinction cuts through to the core of religious difference. It is clear to Jeremiah that the covenant images are corrupted at the root. Idolatry was the fatal compromise against which he first had complained (ch. 2). How ironical

16 *As for* the word that thou hast spoken unto us in the name of the LORD, we will not hearken unto thee.

17 But we will certainly do whatsoever thing goeth forth out of our own mouth, to burn incense unto the queen of heaven, and to pour out drink offerings unto her, as we have done, we, and our fathers, our kings, and our princes, in the cities of Judah, and in the streets of Jerusalem: for *then* had we plenty of victuals, and were well, and saw no evil.

18 But since we left off to burn incense to the queen of heaven, and to pour out drink offerings unto her, we have wanted all *things,* and have been consumed by the sword and by the famine.

19 And when we burned incense to the queen of heaven, and poured out drink offerings unto her, did we make her cakes to worship her, and pour out drink offerings unto her, without our men?

20 ¶ Then Jeremiah said unto all the people, to the men, and to the women, and to all the people which had given him *that* answer, saying,

21 The incense that ye burned in the cities of Judah, and in the streets of Jerusalem, ye and your fathers, your kings and your princes, and the people of the land, did not the LORD remember them, and came it *not* into his mind?

22 So that the LORD could no longer bear, because of the evil of your doings, *and* because of the abominations which ye have committed; therefore is your land a desolation, and an astonishment, and a curse, without an inhabitant, as at this day.

Jeremiah: **16** "As for the word which you have spoken to us in the name of the LORD, we will not listen to you. **17** But we will do everything that we have vowed, burn incense to the queen of heaven and pour out libations to her, as we did, both we and our fathers, our kings and our princes, in the cities of Judah and in the streets of Jerusalem; for then we had plenty of food, and prospered, and saw no evil. **18** But since we left off burning incense to the queen of heaven and pouring out libations to her, we have lacked everything and have been consumed by the sword and by famine." **19** And the women said,[x] "When we burned incense to the queen of heaven and poured out libations to her, was it without our husbands' approval that we made cakes for her bearing her image and poured out libations to her?"

20 Then Jeremiah said to all the people, men and women, all the people who had given him this answer: **21** "As for the incense that you burned in the cities of Judah and in the streets of Jerusalem, you and your fathers, your kings and your princes, and the people of the land, did not the LORD remember it?[y] Did it not come into his mind? **22** The LORD could no longer bear your evil doings and the abominations which you committed; therefore your land has become a desolation and a waste and a curse, without inhabitant, as it is this day.

[x] Compare Syr: Heb lacks *And the women said*
[y] Syr: Heb *them*

17-19. On the worship of **the queen of heaven,** probably the Assyro-Babylonian goddess Ishtar, see 7:16-20. In her role as a fertility goddess she was served with special devotion by the Jewish women, who worshiped her by **burning incense, . . . pouring out libations to her,** and making **cakes for her bearing her image.**

D. Further Rebuke of the Jews (44:20-28)

The rebuke is couched in general terms, except for vs. 25, which is likely to be authentic.

that, after all the toils and struggles and sufferings and agonies and pronouncements and prophesyings to prophets and priests and people and kings, the drama of his life and that of his people should have come full circle. Little wonder that the irony of his own pronouncement is so strong as he breaks the last illusion

of his people—the illusion that Yahweh can be worshiped alongside the corruption of his covenant. **I have sworn by my great name, says the LORD** [cf. Heb. 6:13-18], **that my name shall no more be invoked by the mouth of any man of Judah in all the land of Egypt** (vs. 26). Go ahead, says Jeremiah, and **perform all your**

23 Because ye have burned incense, and because ye have sinned against the LORD, and have not obeyed the voice of the LORD, nor walked in his law, nor in his statutes, nor in his testimonies; therefore this evil is happened unto you, as at this day.

24 Moreover Jeremiah said unto all the people, and to all the women, Hear the word of the LORD, all Judah that are in the land of Egypt:

25 Thus saith the LORD of hosts, the God of Israel, saying; Ye and your wives have both spoken with your mouths, and fulfilled with your hand, saying, We will surely perform our vows that we have vowed, to burn incense to the queen of heaven, and to pour out drink offerings unto her: ye will surely accomplish your vows, and surely perform your vows.

26 Therefore hear ye the word of the LORD, all Judah that dwell in the land of Egypt; Behold, I have sworn by my great name, saith the LORD, that my name shall no more be named in the mouth of any man of Judah in all the land of Egypt, saying, The Lord GOD liveth.

27 Behold, I will watch over them for evil, and not for good: and all the men of Judah that are in the land of Egypt shall be consumed by the sword and by the famine, until there be an end of them.

28 Yet a small number that escape the sword shall return out of the land of Egypt into the land of Judah; and all the remnant of Judah, that are gone into the land of Egypt to sojourn there, shall know whose words shall stand, mine, or theirs.

29 ¶ And this shall be a sign unto you, saith the LORD, that I will punish you in

23 It is because you burned incense, and because you sinned against the LORD and did not obey the voice of the LORD or walk in his law and in his statutes and in his testimonies, that this evil has befallen you, as at this day."

24 Jeremiah said to all the people and all the women, "Hear the word of the LORD, all you of Judah who are in the land of Egypt, 25 Thus says the LORD of hosts, the God of Israel: You and your wives have declared with your mouths, and have fulfilled it with your hands, saying, 'We will surely perform our vows that we have made, to burn incense to the queen of heaven and to pour out libations to her.' Then confirm your vows and perform your vows! 26 Therefore hear the word of the LORD, all you of Judah who dwell in the land of Egypt: Behold, I have sworn by my great name, says the LORD, that my name shall no more be invoked by the mouth of any man of Judah in all the land of Egypt, saying, 'As the Lord GOD lives.' 27 Behold, I am watching over them for evil and not for good; all the men of Judah who are in the land of Egypt shall be consumed by the sword and by famine, until there is an end of them. 28 And those who escape the sword shall return from the land of Egypt to the land of Judah, few in number; and all the remnant of Judah, who came to the land of Egypt to live, shall know whose word will stand, mine or theirs. 29 This shall be the sign to you, says the LORD, that I will

---

23. The verse is a good example of the Deuteronomic editor's style. Jeremiah hardly placed so much emphasis on the sin of burning **incense.**

28. This verse is inconsistent with vss. 14a, 27, and is probably an addition by an editor later than D, who knew that some of the Jews did return from Egypt.

E. SIGN CONCERNING PHARAOH HOPHRA (44:29-30)

29-30. The sign was intended to be in confirmation of the predictions which had been made regarding the destruction to be wrought in the land of Egypt (for signs of this type cf. especially the "Immanuel" sign of Isa. 7:11-17, and further Isa. 37:30; 38:7; Exod. 3:12; I Sam. 2:34; 10:7-9).

---

vows! When the trouble comes those who **escape the sword shall return . . . to . . . Judah** and they **shall know whose word will stand, mine or theirs** (vs. 28). This, in the long run, is the dialectical test: the ordinances of the Lord cannot be violated, nor is he constrained by empty images. By such ambivalent strivings we only succeed in violating ourselves

this place, that ye may know that my words shall surely stand against you for evil:

30 Thus saith the LORD; Behold, I will give Pharaoh-hophra king of Egypt into the hand of his enemies, and into the hand of them that seek his life; as I gave Zedekiah king of Judah into the hand of Nebuchadrezzar king of Babylon, his enemy, and that sought his life.

45 The word that Jeremiah the prophet spake unto Baruch the son of Neriah, when he had written these words in a book

punish you in this place, in order that you may know that my words will surely stand against you for evil: **30** Thus says the LORD, Behold I will give Pharaoh Hophra king of Egypt into the hand of his enemies and into the hand of those who seek his life, as I gave Zedeki'ah king of Judah into the hand of Nebuchadrez'zar king of Babylon, who was his enemy and sought his life."

45 The word that Jeremiah the prophet spoke to Baruch the son of Neri'ah,

---

Hophra was the Pharaoh of Egypt, generally known as Apries, who ruled 588-569 B.C. At the very beginning of his reign he was in alliance with King Zedekiah of Judah and gave him assistance in the rebellion against Nebuchadrezzar, at one time sending an Egyptian army to relieve the siege of Jerusalem (37:5). His reign was generally prosperous, but toward its end he had difficulties with his troops, both native and foreign. On one occasion he sent one of his court officials, Amasis, to quell a revolt of soldiers, who turned the tables by proclaiming Amasis king. Hophra and Amasis reigned as coregents for about three years; then a struggle between them developed and Hophra was put to death. Amasis gave him an honorable burial and continued to reign until 526 B.C.

The present sign has every appearance of being a prophecy after the event and is probably not from Jeremiah. The prophet nowhere else makes use of such a confirmatory sign, and the style of the present narrative is that of the Deuteronomic editor.

Of course if this is a genuine passage, it indicates that Jeremiah was still alive *ca.* 570 B.C. It seems improbable, in view of the small amount of genuine material preserved from his Egyptian residence, that he actually lived for some ten years after the flight to Egypt.

XXXII. ORACLE TO BARUCH (45:1-5)

A brief oracle concerning Baruch closes the long section of prose narrative which began with ch. 26 (interrupted by chs. 30-31, 33). It comprises a "confession of Baruch," similar to the confessions of Jeremiah, in which he complains to Yahweh of his sorrow, and then receives a reply which is somewhat similar in tone to the reply Jeremiah had received in 12:5; 15:19. Like Jeremiah, he is given not the reward he seeks, but a summons to bear more suffering.

The actual date of the oracle has been debated by scholars. Some (e.g., Cornill, Volz, Rudolph, Peake) accept the date in vs. 1 as correct, and believe that its present position is due to the modesty of Baruch rather than to chronological considerations. They point to vs. 4 as indicating that the destruction of Judah lies in the future. Others (e.g., Giesebrecht, Duhm, Skinner, Erbt) reject the date in vs. 1, and believe that the position of the oracle and the nature of its contents favor placing it after the fall of

---

and bringing the ruin of emptiness on all our designs.

45:1-5. The Ambitions of Baruch.—As H. Wheeler Robinson has written, "There is hardly a passage in the Old Testament which gives us a more impressive glimpse of the eternal cross in the heart of God, the bitterness of His disappointment with man." [3] We may well ask, Why?

[3] *The Cross of Jeremiah*, p. 84.

To this four answers may be given. First, it resumes the core of Jeremiah's message from the beginning. **Behold, what I have built I am breaking down, and what I have planted I am plucking up—that is, the whole land.** This was the message that, from the beginning, he was called to deliver. This was the message for the crisis of civilization into which he was born. Thus, as Martin Buber points out, the clause "I have set you this day over nations and over

at the mouth of Jeremiah, in the fourth year of Jehoiakim the son of Josiah king of Judah, saying,

2 Thus saith the Lord, the God of Israel, unto thee, O Baruch;

3 Thou didst say, Woe is me now! for the Lord hath added grief to my sorrow; I fainted in my sighing, and I find no rest.

when he wrote these words in a book at the dictation of Jeremiah, in the fourth year of Jehoi'akim the son of Josi'ah, king of Judah: 2 "Thus says the Lord, the God of Israel, to you, O Baruch: 3 You said, 'Woe is me! for the Lord has added sorrow to my pain; I am weary with my groaning, and I

Jerusalem, near the end of Jeremiah's life. Skinner says that it sounds like a farewell oracle or even a deathbed charge from the prophet 'to Baruch. According to Wilhelm Erbt (*Jeremia und seine Zeit* [Göttingen: Vandenhoeck & Ruprecht, 1902], pp. 83-86), these were the final words of the prophet to his companion and scribe before he sent Baruch to the exiles in Babylonia to continue to be his witness.

It should be recognized that, though this oracle is basically authentic, it has come to us through the Deuteronomic editor (so Mowinckel, though not Rudolph). His phraseology is evident especially in vss. 4, 5*b*. The contents of the oracle do seem to be more appropriate to the end of Jeremiah's life, after he and Baruch had undergone much suffering, than to the time of the writing of the scroll of ch. 36; the date in vs. 1 is from the Deuteronomic editor, who is responsible for a similar date in 25:1.

45:1. For the date and the writing of the **book** see 36:1-32.

3. Cornill says that the **sorrow** of Baruch was not over his own personal misfortunes, but rather over the sorrows and sufferings of the people of Judah, for whom at the dictation of Jeremiah he had written the oracles of 605 B.C. They were not words of comfort but oracles of condemnation (36:2-3). The **great things** (vs. 5) he seeks are not

---

kingdoms" (1:10) means "I authorize thee to declare my will for *this hour* in the history of the nations." [4] In this hour of history the divine activity consists in plucking up and breaking down—the necessary prelude to any possibility of building and planting. From that point on Jeremiah exhibits the work of God as the ultimate architect, pulling down and building up, and as the ultimate gardener, rooting out and planting again. The ground motif of exile, purgation, and return coincides with these announcements (chs. 3–4). Breaking up the fallow ground of the heart (4:3), stripping away the branches from the vine-rows (5:10), refining the base metal of the people's ways (6:27-30), burying the linen waist cloth (13: 1-7), the potter remolding his vessel (18:4-7), the parable of the figs (24:1-10) —all these, and many other images, declare the same essential message. "There is no other divine activity in Israel at this world hour but pulling down and rooting out, as it is too at this time in the world of nations." [5]

Perhaps at no point does this core proclamation appear in sharper relief than in Jeremiah's reply to Baruch's restlessness. **Do you seek great things for yourself? Seek them not;** for the time is one of disaster, it provides no occasions for private aspirations (vs. 5).

There is a second way in which this chapter proves the heart of the God-man relation. It contrasts the limited view of the disciple-at-secondhand from the prophet in whom God's word is incandescent like a flame. It is not merely that Baruch, as an amanuensis, was inferior to Jeremiah by talent. It is rather that Baruch is being tempted away from the context of the divine-human commission, to assume the more limited point of view of his own social self-expression. In Kierkegaardian terms he would swap the absolute, paradoxical teleology of the prophet for the immanent teleology of the genius. [6] More simply, he would exchange the Eternal's task for his own.

Jeremiah does not appeal to his own example. Baruch's sufferings and sacrifices were slight as compared with those of Jeremiah, who had experienced the open hostility of family, priests, prophets, peoples, and kings. He not only had sacrificed the simple pleasures of social enjoyments but had given up the comforts of marriage and family. It seems probable that Baruch too had accepted many of these same conditions, and exposed himself by association to many of these same encounters and denials. If he had not acquired, as Jeremiah had done, a sense of his vocation as derived from the purposes of God, it is easy to see that his task as associate to a prophet whose words had appar-

[4] *The Prophetic Faith*, p. 165.
[5] *Ibid.*, pp. 166-67.

[6] Cf. *The Present Age*, pp. 137-63.

4 ¶ Thus shalt thou say unto him, The Lord saith thus; Behold, *that* which I have built will I break down, and that which I have planted I will pluck up, even this whole land.

5 And seekest thou great things for thyself? seek *them* not: for, behold, I will bring evil upon all flesh, saith the Lord: but thy life will I give unto thee for a prey in all places whither thou goest.

find no rest.' 4 Thus shall you say to him, Thus says the Lord: Behold, what I have built I am breaking down, and what I have planted I am plucking up — that is, the whole land. 5 And do you seek great things for yourself? Seek them not; for, behold, I am bringing evil upon all flesh, says the Lord; but I will give you your life as a prize of war in all places to which you may go."

---

for himself, but for the people. While this may be inferred from the words of Baruch, the lament seems to arise mainly from personal sorrow, and there is a tone of rebuke in vs. 5 which is directed toward personal lamentation.

4. For the phraseology here cf. 1:10; 18:7-9; 24:6 (the last two in passages clearly edited by the Deuteronomist). The words **that is, the whole land** are not in the LXX, and therefore may be a late addition.

5. It is difficult to know just what **great things** Baruch sought for himself. Could it be that toward the end of his life he sought to influence Jeremiah, and to make himself more a colleague than a disciple of the prophet? The charge made against Baruch in 43:3 may point in that direction.

I will give you your life as a prize of war: This promise means that, though Baruch may suffer, his life will be spared (cf. 21:9; 38:2; 39:18).

---

ently failed might become a difficult ordeal. Weariness could creep into the heart of Baruch, whose dependence was on the prophet, yet be conquered by the prophet whose dependence was on God. What Jeremiah makes clear to Baruch is that Yahweh himself has been obliged to give up all his aims, to pull down all that he had built, and to uproot what he had planted. This was nothing less than **the whole land.** "In the face of such Divine surrender," says George Adam Smith, "both of purpose and achievement, what was the resignation by a mere man, or even by a whole nation, of their hopes or ambitions?"[7] In such times, and under such conditions, Baruch should be content that the Lord has given him his life.

In this advice, however, there is more than meets the eye. For Baruch's open confession and Jeremiah's oracular reply reveal to us the only true way to the foundations of hope. Both Baruch and Jeremiah had seen the ruin of practically everything for which they cared. Death itself had "come up into [their] windows" (9:21). They had "looked on the earth, and lo, it was waste and void" (4:21). The cities had been laid in ruins and the fruitful land was a desert, and the people would not listen. But in the face of all this it is enough, says Jeremiah, that God is. Israel has failed. Their prophecies have failed. Ordinary ambitions are empty, and **great things** are vain. Yet when everything has failed, Jeremiah still knows what Baruch had

yet to learn—that God is. Until one comes to this realization, and founds one's life and hope upon it, nothing prospers and everything fails.

Perhaps the fact that Baruch has included this confession at the end of his memoirs indicates that he came through this experience to know what it means fully to renounce oneself. Dying to oneself in order to live unto God is at once most simple and most difficult. The N.T. propositions—"except it die" (I Cor. 15:36), or "he who loses his life for my sake will find it" (Matt. 10:39), or "you must be born anew" (John 3:7)—all exhibit the full maturation of this spiritual principle. Nevertheless, let us note that the disclosure here has in it nothing of the Platonic aura of otherworldly reality. Jeremiah does not say, "If my bark sinks, 'tis to another sea,"[8] nor does he say,

I saw eternity the other night
Like a great ring of pure and endless light.[9]

The persuasion that God is lies beyond these insights too. Jeremiah's faith is founded upon a final acceptance of existence as it is. It is beyond total failure that he knows that Yahweh is.

But, fourth and finally, the passage removes one further veil from the God-man relation. Once more we perceive the importance of the prophetic pathos. It is precisely because Jeremiah has come to a realization of the sorrow

[7] *Jeremiah*, p. 229.

[8] William Ellery Channing, "A Poet's Hope," st. 13.

[9] Henry Vaughn, "The World," st. i.

46 The word of the LORD which came to Jeremiah the prophet against the Gentiles;

46 The word of the LORD which came to Jeremiah the prophet concerning the nations.

XXXIII. ORACLES AGAINST THE FOREIGN NATIONS (46:1–51:64)

These six chapters constitute a clearly defined collection of oracles against foreign nations, with its own superscription. In the Hebrew and English Bibles they stand near the end of the book of Jeremiah, but in the LXX they stand immediately after 25:13a, and in the following order: Elam, Egypt, Babylon, Philistia, Edom, Ammon, Kedar, Damascus, and Moab. The position in the LXX seems more appropriate than in the Hebrew; cf. the position of the oracles against foreign nations in Isa. 13–23; Ezek. 25–31. However, the order in the Hebrew is more likely to be original, since it corresponds more closely to the list of nations in 25:19-26 and roughly to the chronological order of the history of the nations treated.

The question of the authenticity of these oracles has been vigorously debated by scholars. There is fairly general agreement that the first oracle against Egypt, 46:3-12, is from Jeremiah, and that none of the oracles against Babylon in chs. 50–51 is genuine. There is no general agreement regarding the others.

In 1888 Friedrich Schwally published an article ("Die Reden des Buches Jeremia gegen die Heiden. XXV. XLVI–LI," *Zeitschrift für die alttestamentliche Wissenschaft*, VIII [1888], 177-217) in which he denied the authenticity of all of the oracles. Other scholars who deny that any are from Jeremiah are Wellhausen, Duhm, Volz, and Skinner.

However, some scholars maintain that these chapters contain a nucleus of materials from Jeremiah, which have been expanded by later editors; e.g., Hans Bardtke ("Jeremia der Fremdvölkerprophet," *ibid.*, LIII [1935], 209-39; LIV [1936], 240-62) has sought to prove that Jeremiah uttered the oracles against foreign nations during the reign of Josiah. He believes that Jeremiah began his ministry in 616 B.C. (the "thirteenth year" of the reign of Josiah in 1:2 having been originally the "twenty-third year"), and that he promoted the nationalistic expansion of Judah which took place under Josiah. Subsequently Jeremiah prepared a booklet of antiforeign oracles which consisted of: (a) the prophet's call, 1:2, 4-10; (b) the cup of wrath pericope, 25:15-17; (c) oracle against Philistia, 47:1-7; (d) oracle against Elam, 49:34-39; (e) oracles against Egypt, Moab, Ammon, Edom, Damascus, and Kedar, 46:18-24; 48:1-47; 49:1-8, 10, 11, 22-33; and (f) the pericope on the refusal of the cup of wrath, 25:27-29. While this theory is attractive, we must note that Jeremiah's activity under Josiah is imperfectly known (see Intro., p. 779); and it is doubtful that Jeremiah was as nationalistic as the theory makes him.

---

in the heart of God that comfort comes to him. It is in this suffering that Baruch is invited to share. "Are you able to drink the cup that I drink?" asked Jesus of his disciples (Mark 10:38). It is something similar to this, at bottom, which Jeremiah has said to Baruch. Jeremiah's sense of the divine pathos leads him to see, as H. Wheeler Robinson has said, that "behind [his] disappointment there is the infinite patience of God. . . . Yahweh will not again give an eternal law, which men will disobey as before; He will work from within and by a spiritual change inspire a new and effective knowledge of Himself in the hearts of men"[1] (31:31-34).

[1] *The Cross of Jeremiah*, pp. 84-85. Cf. also *Redemption and Revelation*, pp. 279-80.

Why, then, is this chapter so impressive? It resumes the core of Jeremiah's message. It points the contrast between the limited view of the disciple-at-secondhand and the prophet's glowing heart. It opens to all the one sure way to the foundation of hope. It expounds the real pathos of the Cross in the heart of God. Since Baruch includes this confession so appropriately at the end of his book, perhaps he had learned more profoundly than Blake that he was "only the secretary: the authors [were] in Eternity."[2]

46:1-12. Rhapsody on the Battle of Carchemish.—There is very little agreement among the critics as to the authenticity of these concluding chapters (see Exeg.). Nevertheless a

[2] Quoted in Abraham Heschel, *Die Prophetie* (Krakow: Polnischen Akademie der Wissenschaften, 1936), p. 45.

2 Against Egypt, against the army of Pharaoh-necho king of Egypt, which was by the river Euphrates in Carchemish, which Nebuchadrezzar king of Babylon smote in the fourth year of Jehoiakim the son of Josiah king of Judah. 3 Order ye the buckler and shield, and draw near to battle.	2 About Egypt. Concerning the army of Pharaoh Neco, king of Egypt, which was by the river Eu-phra'tes at Car'chemish and which Nebuchadrez'zar king of Babylon defeated in the fourth year of Jehoi'akim the son of Josi'ah, king of Judah: 3 "Prepare buckler and shield, and advance for battle!

Other scholars who maintain that these chapters contain a nucleus of materials from Jeremiah are Giesebrecht, Cornill, Peake, and Rudolph.

The principal arguments against the authenticity of these oracles are the following: (a) The conception of Yahweh is usually of a God of wrath and vengeance, and agrees little with Jeremiah's conception as found elsewhere; and there is no call for the nations to repent, such as we would expect from Jeremiah. (b) The oracles contain very few details regarding historical events, and no king is ever mentioned; this is in contrast with the general nature of Jeremiah's oracles against Judah and Israel. (c) In their literary character these oracles differ from the genuine oracles in the rest of the book: they are repetitious and often in confused order, and they contain many verses apparently borrowed from other O.T. books, especially from Isa. 15–16, Obadiah, and the work of Second Isaiah. (d) The attitude toward the Babylonians in chs. 50–51 is directly contrary to Jeremiah's own attitude during the reign of Zedekiah, when he constantly counseled submission to the Babylonians because Yahweh had appointed Nebuchadrezzar as his own servant (27:6). (e) The oracles show no evidence of the editorial activity of Baruch or the Deuteronomic editor; the collection was clearly made after their work was finished. It is strange that none of the antiforeign nations were included by either of them in his work, if they knew them, and that the oracles are all combined in a collection which bears unmistakable evidences of late composition or late editing.

While it is possible that these chapters contain some original Jeremianic material, we can at present have little confidence in our ability to recover it. When the history of the various nations here mentioned is better known, it may be possible to date the oracles with some precision.

A. Superscription (46:1)

46:1. This verse serves as the heading of the oracles collected in chs. 46–51, and comes from the editor who made the collection in the postexilic period. The form of the Hebrew is unusual, occurring elsewhere only in the superscriptions of 1:2; 14:1; 47:1; 49:34.

B. Oracles Against Egypt (46:2-28)
1. The Defeat at Carchemish (46:2-12)

This oracle has greater claim to authenticity than any other in the collection, and many modern scholars believe it was composed by Jeremiah. However, some of the ideas expressed (particularly in vs. 10) seem foreign to him.

place must be made for the sensitive reader's reactions, which, when the critics disagree, may still press through to the core of the prophecy. T. Crouther Gordon has said:

I would . . . claim that the messages to the nations, in sheer consistency, must be laid to the credit of the central figure himself, Jeremiah, for they betray his poetic touch and issue the challenge and announce the doom straight from the mouth of Jehovah. For each and every people of which he

knew, the prophet had a message and a policy, written out and ready, and now preserved for us in Chapters xlvi-li.[3]

There is also a vivid picture here of the thwarted power of Egypt rising **like the Nile, like rivers whose waters surge.** Her armies surged north to threaten Nebuchadrezzar; but there by the **river Euphrates** . . . **the Lord**

[3] *Rebel Prophet*, pp. 65-66.

4 Harness the horses; and get up, ye horsemen, and stand forth with *your* helmets; furbish the spears, *and* put on the brigandines.

5 Wherefore have I seen them dismayed *and* turned away back? and their mighty ones are beaten down, and are fled apace, and look not back: *for* fear *was* round about, saith the LORD.

6 Let not the swift flee away, nor the mighty man escape; they shall stumble, and fall toward the north by the river Euphrates.

7 Who *is* this *that* cometh up as a flood, whose waters are moved as the rivers?

8 Egypt riseth up like a flood, and *his* waters are moved like the rivers; and he saith, I will go up, *and* will cover the earth; I will destroy the city and the inhabitants thereof.

9 Come up, ye horses; and rage, ye chariots; and let the mighty men come forth; the Ethiopians and the Libyans, that handle the shield; and the Lydians, that handle *and* bend the bow.

---

4 Harness the horses;
   mount, O horsemen!
Take your stations with your helmets,
   polish your spears,
   put on your coats of mail!
5 Why have I seen it?
They are dismayed
   and have turned backward.
Their warriors are beaten down,
   and have fled in haste;
they look not back —
   terror on every side!
                   says the LORD.

6 The swift cannot flee away,
   nor the warrior escape;
in the north by the river Eu-phra'tes
   they have stumbled and fallen.

7 "Who is this, rising like the Nile,
   like rivers whose waters surge?
8 Egypt rises like the Nile,
   like rivers whose waters surge.
He said, I will rise, I will cover the earth,
   I will destroy cities and their inhabitants.
9 Advance, O horses,
   and rage, O chariots!
Let the warriors go forth:
   men of Ethiopia and Put who handle
   the shield,
   men of Lud, skilled in handling the
   bow.

The poem is supposed to have been written in connection with the battle of Carchemish in 605 B.C., either as prediction or in celebration of the victory. In that battle the Egyptian army, under Pharaoh Neco, was defeated by the Babylonian army under Nebuchadrezzar, who shortly afterward succeeded his father on the Babylonian throne. The battle seems to be referred to by Josephus (*Antiquities* X. 11. 1; *Against Apion* I. 19). British excavations at the site of Carchemish in Syria have shown that the town was destroyed *ca.* 600 B.C., and that it had been occupied a short time before its fall by an Egyptian army, in whose quarters the excavators found a large number of Egyptian objects, including some from Psamtik I and Neco (cf. Albright, "Seal of Eliakim and Latest Preëxilic History of Judah," pp. 87-89; some scholars deny there was a battle of Carchemish—see Lewy, *Forschungen zur alten Geschichte Vorderasiens*). This battle was a turning point in the history of the ancient Near East; thereafter Babylonia, under its Chaldean dynasty, was the leader in world affairs, and Egypt was in a secondary position.

6. With the first half of this verse cf. Amos 2:14.

GOD of hosts holds a sacrifice. In the clash of battle Egypt's power was sacrificed to that of the young commander. And now the nations hear great Egypt's retreating cry; and though she should **go up to Gilead** and seek some healing balm, the wound to her power is fatal. All the nations perceive and hear her long farewell to all her greatness.

10 For this *is* the day of the Lord God of hosts, a day of vengeance, that he may avenge him of his adversaries: and the sword shall devour, and it shall be satiate and made drunk with their blood: for the Lord God of hosts hath a sacrifice in the north country by the river Euphrates.

11 Go up into Gilead, and take balm, O virgin, the daughter of Egypt: in vain shalt thou use many medicines; *for* thou shalt not be cured.

12 The nations have heard of thy shame, and thy cry hath filled the land: for the mighty man hath stumbled against the mighty, *and* they are fallen both together.

13 ¶ The word that the Lord spake to Jeremiah the prophet, how Nebuchadrezzar king of Babylon should come *and* smite the land of Egypt.

14 Declare ye in Egypt, and publish in Migdol, and publish in Noph and in Tahpanhes: say ye, Stand fast, and prepare thee; for the sword shall devour round about thee.

15 Why are thy valiant *men* swept away? they stood not, because the Lord did drive them.

10 That day is the day of the Lord God of
  hosts,
    a day of vengeance,
    to avenge himself on his foes.
The sword shall devour and be sated,
    and drink its fill of their blood.
For the Lord God of hosts holds a sacrifice
    in the north country by the river Eu-
      phra'tes.
11 Go up to Gilead, and take balm,
    O virgin daughter of Egypt!
In vain you have used many medicines;
    there is no healing for you.
12 The nations have heard of your shame,
    and the earth is full of your cry;
for warrior has stumbled against warrior;
    they have both fallen together."

13 The word which the Lord spoke to Jeremiah the prophet about the coming of Nebuchadrez'zar king of Babylon to smite the land of Egypt:
14 "Declare in Egypt, and proclaim in Mig-
    dol;
    proclaim in Memphis and Tah'panhes;
Say, 'Stand ready and be prepared,
    for the sword shall devour round about
      you.'
15 Why has Apis fled?[z]
    Why did not your bull stand?
    Because the Lord thrust him down.

[z] Gk: Heb *Why was it swept away*

10. The verse is more highly apocalyptic and filled with a greater spirit of vengeance than one finds in the genuine work of Jeremiah. If the oracle is largely genuine, this verse is probably interpolated (for the ideas expressed here cf. 25:34; Zeph. 1:7; Isa. 34:5-7; 63:1-6; Ezek. 39:17-20).

2. The Coming of Nebuchadrezzar (46:13-26)

This oracle is based on the belief that Jeremiah predicted the invasion of Egypt by Nebuchadrezzar, either immediately after the battle of Carchemish or at a later time, perhaps when the prophet himself was in Egypt (see 43:8-13). In reality Nebuchadrezzar did not at any time conquer Egypt, though he did invade the country (for details see Exeg. on 43:8-13). The vagueness of the references and the fact that the Babylonians never conquered Egypt contribute to the impression that the oracle is wholly secondary.

14. For the location of the places named here see Exeg. on 43:7; 44:1.

15. **Apis** was the bull-god of Memphis, considered as the son or the living reincarnation of the god Ptah. In ancient times images were frequently carried into battle,

46:13-28. *Why Has Apis Fled?*—The second poem (vss. 14-24) would appear to be of later authorship. It may imply an invasion of Egypt itself. The primary images of this poem are

three, and all conspire to show how sadly is Egypt fallen. The wordplay on the first image reveals that Apis, the **bull** (vs. 15), turned out to be nothing but a **heifer** (vs. 20). The second

16 He made many to fall, yea, one fell upon another: and they said, Arise, and let us go again to our own people, and to the land of our nativity, from the oppressing sword.

17 They did cry there, Pharaoh king of Egypt *is but* a noise; he hath passed the time appointed.

18 *As* I live, saith the King, whose name *is* The LORD of hosts, Surely as Tabor *is* among the mountains, and as Carmel by the sea, *so* shall he come.

19 O thou daughter dwelling in Egypt, furnish thyself to go into captivity: for Noph shall be waste and desolate without an inhabitant.

20 Egypt *is like* a very fair heifer, *but* destruction cometh; it cometh out of the north.

21 Also her hired men *are* in the midst of her like fatted bullocks; for they also are turned back, *and* are fled away together: they did not stand, because the day of their calamity was come upon them, *and* the time of their visitation.

22 The voice thereof shall go like a serpent; for they shall march with an army, and come against her with axes, as hewers of wood.

23 They shall cut down her forest, saith the LORD, though it cannot be searched; because they are more than the grasshoppers, and *are* innumerable.

16 Your multitude stumbled[a] and fell,
    and they said one to another,
  'Arise, and let us go back to our own people
    and to the land of our birth,
    because of the sword of the oppressor.'
17 Call the name of Pharaoh, king of Egypt,
    'Noisy one who lets the hour go by.'

18 "As I live, says the King,
    whose name is the LORD of hosts,
  like Tabor among the mountains,
    and like Carmel by the sea, shall one come.
19 Prepare yourselves baggage for exile,
    O inhabitants of Egypt!
  For Memphis shall become a waste,
    a ruin, without inhabitant.

20 "A beautiful heifer is Egypt,
    but a gadfly from the north has come upon her.
21 Even her hired soldiers in her midst
    are like fatted calves;
  yea, they have turned and fled together,
    they did not stand;
  for the day of their calamity has come upon them,
    the time of their punishment.

22 "She makes a sound like a serpent gliding away;
    for her enemies march in force,
  and come against her with axes,
    like those who fell trees.
23 They shall cut down her forest,
                says the LORD,
    though it is impenetrable,
  because they are more numerous than locusts;
    they are without number.

[a] Gk: Heb *He made many stumble*

and the flight or capture of the image of a god symbolized the defeat of the people who worshiped that deity.

17. Noisy one who lets the hour go by: Cornill has suggested that the Hebrew of this, *shā'ôn he'ebhîr hammô'ēdh* (transliterated by the LXX, not translated), contains

wordplay shows that the powerful name of Pharaoh was nothing but an empty noise (vs. 17). Moffatt's translation is helpful:

Call the Pharaoh "Fatality,"
For he has let his chance go by!

The chance that he let go by may have been either an opportune time to engage the enemy, or the chance to secure God's favor through a timely moral reformation of his people. The third wordplay is more subtle. It is based upon the common knowledge that Pharaoh's ideo-

24 The daughter of Egypt shall be confounded; she shall be delivered into the hand of the people of the north.

25 The LORD of hosts, the God of Israel, saith; Behold, I will punish the multitude of No, and Pharaoh, and Egypt, with their gods, and their kings; even Pharaoh, and *all* them that trust in him:

26 And I will deliver them into the hand of those that seek their lives, and into the hand of Nebuchadrezzar king of Babylon, and into the hand of his servants: and afterward it shall be inhabited, as in the days of old, saith the LORD.

27 ¶ But fear not thou, O my servant Jacob, and be not dismayed, O Israel: for, behold, I will save thee from afar off, and thy seed from the land of their captivity; and Jacob shall return, and be in rest and at ease, and none shall make *him* afraid.

28 Fear thou not, O Jacob my servant, saith the LORD: for I *am* with thee; for I will make a full end of all the nations whither I have driven thee: but I will not make a full end of thee, but correct thee in measure; yet will I not leave thee wholly unpunished.

---

24 The daughter of Egypt shall be put to shame,
  she shall be delivered into the hand of a people from the north."

25 The LORD of hosts, the God of Israel, said: "Behold, I am bringing punishment upon Amon of Thebes, and Pharaoh, and Egypt and her gods and her kings, upon Pharaoh and those who trust in him. 26 I will deliver them into the hand of those who seek their life, into the hand of Nebuchadrez'zar king of Babylon and his officers. Afterward Egypt shall be inhabited as in the days of old, says the LORD.

27 "But fear not, O Jacob my servant,
  nor be dismayed, O Israel;
for lo, I will save you from afar,
  and your offspring from the land of their captivity.
Jacob shall return and have quiet and ease,
  and none shall make him afraid.
28 Fear not, O Jacob my servant,
                              says the LORD,
  for I am with you.
I will make a full end of all the nations
  to which I have driven you,
  but of you I will not make a full end.
I will chasten you in just measure,
  and I will by no means leave you unpunished."

---

in the second word a play on the name of the Pharaoh Hophra (588-569 B.C.), whose Egyptian name was *Ha'abre'*. He thinks that the poem was written in Egypt by Jeremiah and is the latest passage by the prophet which has been preserved. The wordplay, however, is not close.

25-26. These verses are in prose, probably an editorial addition designed to explain the poem.

3. THE SALVATION OF ISRAEL (46:27-28)

27-28. This passage is found also at 30:10-11 (see Exeg.), which seems to be the original position. The addition was made here in order to contrast the salvation of Israel with the destruction of Egypt.

---

graph consisted in a serpent encircling a globe. Now this all-powerful serpent turns out to be **like a serpent gliding away** (vs. 22), hissing as it flees. This is a very different sound from that of the thunderous march of victorious armies.

The description of the enemy is equally vivid. They come like woodcutters, felling the trees (the dense population of Egypt); **they are more numerous than locusts** (vs. 23), devouring

everything in their path and leaving it waste as they come. To the question

> **Why has Apis fled?**
> **Why did not your bull stand?**

there comes the answer **Because the LORD thrust him down** (vs. 15). This is the single cause, and this is the single message. The chapter

47 The word of the LORD that came to Jeremiah the prophet against the Philistines, before that Pharaoh smote Gaza.

2 Thus saith the LORD; Behold, waters rise up out of the north, and shall be an overflowing flood, and shall overflow the land, and all that is therein; the city, and them that dwell therein: then the men shall cry, and all the inhabitants of the land shall howl.

3 At the noise of the stamping of the hoofs of his strong *horses,* at the rushing of his chariots, *and at* the rumbling of his wheels, the fathers shall not look back to *their* children for feebleness of hands;

4 Because of the day that cometh to spoil all the Philistines, *and* to cut off from Tyrus

47 The word of the LORD that came to Jeremiah the prophet concerning the Philistines, before Pharaoh smote Gaza.

2 Thus says the LORD:
"Behold, waters are rising out of the north,
    and shall become an overflowing torrent;
they shall overflow the land and all that fills it,
    the city and those who dwell in it.
Men shall cry out,
    and every inhabitant of the land shall wail.
3 At the noise of the stamping of the hoofs of his stallions,
    at the rushing of his chariots, at the rumbling of their wheels,
the fathers look not back to their children,
    so feeble are their hands,
4 because of the day that is coming to destroy
    all the Philistines,
to cut off from Tyre and Sidon
    every helper that remains.

C. ORACLE AGAINST THE PHILISTINES (47:1-7)

Oracles against the Philistines are found also in Amos 1:6-8; Isa. 14:28-31; Ezek. 25:15-17; Zeph. 2:4-7. This one shows no literary dependence upon any of them, and the fact has been used by some scholars in support of its authenticity. Little is known of the history of the Philistine cities in the seventh and sixth centuries.

47:1. Before Pharaoh smote Gaza: Herodotus (*History* II. 159) says that after the battle of Megiddo, Pharaoh Neco overran Kadytis (usually identified with Gaza). This is possibly the historical occasion of the oracle, though we must note that the verse is probably editorial, and that these words are missing in the LXX.

4. The mention of **Tyre and Sidon** is surprising, since they are not Philistine cities, but Phoenician. The phrase **every helper that remains** suggests that they were allied with the Philistines. **Caphtor** is the island of Crete (cf. Amos 9:7; Deut. 2:23).

concludes with a post-exilic poem of comfort, promising the eventual return from the exile.

47:1-7. *Sword of the Lord!*—Jeremiah appears to stand, in these verses, whirling the sword of the Lord and pointing it first at this nation and then at that. It turns every way, whirling in ever-increasing radius as it turns.

It is particularly interesting to note its direction here. It falls upon Israel's nearest and bitterest foe, the **Philistines.** As he sees the Philistines inundated by **the waters . . . rising out of the north** he is moved to pity. Yet the fault, as ever, is within themselves: **how long will you gash yourselves?**

No one sees this principle, however. The people protest as always against the sword of the Lord. Instead of seeking the fault within themselves, or repenting of their unfaithfulness, they petition the sword of the spirit:

**Put yourself into your scabbard,
    rest and be still!**

But, exclaims the poet,

**How can it be quiet,
    when the LORD has given it a charge?**

Indeed it cannot be quiet, for the sword of the Lord is his righteousness which can no more be suspended or denied than the ordinances of the creation which Jeremiah knew so well. To

and Zidon every helper that remaineth: for the LORD will spoil the Philistines, the remnant of the country of Caphtor.

5 Baldness is come upon Gaza; Ashkelon is cut off *with* the remnant of their valley: how long wilt thou cut thyself?

6 O thou sword of the LORD, how long *will it be* ere thou be quiet? put up thyself into thy scabbard, rest, and be still.

7 How can it be quiet, seeing the LORD hath given it a charge against Ashkelon, and against the seashore? there hath he appointed it.

48 Against Moab thus saith the LORD of hosts, the God of Israel; Woe

---

For the LORD is destroying the Philistines,
  the remnant of the coastland of Caphtor.
5 Baldness has come upon Gaza,
  Ash'kelon has perished.
O remnant of the Anakim,[b]
  how long will you gash yourselves?
6 Ah, sword of the LORD!
  How long till you are quiet?
Put yourself into your scabbard,
  rest and be still!
7 How can it[c] be quiet,
  when the LORD has given it a charge?
Against Ash'kelon and against the seashore
  he has appointed it."

48 Concerning Moab.
Thus says the LORD of hosts, the God of Israel:
  "Woe to Nebo, for it is laid waste!

[b] Gk: Heb *their valley*
[c] Gk Vg: Heb *you*

---

5. For an explanation of the **remnant of the Anakim** see Josh. 11:21-22.
6. See the Exeg. on 46:10 and the references there cited.

D. ORACLE AGAINST MOAB (48:1-47)

This oracle, or series of oracles, against Moab is distinguished by three characteristics: (a) its great length as compared with the other oracles in chs. 46–49; (b) the

---

deny God's righteousness is, in spiritual fact, to run upon it as upon a sword. "We are lost children," says Jacques Maritain, "who run among thorns in search of our crucified love, and we do not even know what that is for which we seek!"[4]

This is a difficult lesson to learn. Intimations of our willfulness appear from time to time, when we are thwarted by circumstances, or have some dim foreboding, some deep anxiety, that reality somehow stands over against us barring our way. Like Balaam we perceive this dimly, but, like him, would wish the angel with the sword to stand out of our way.

More deeply still, the sword of the Lord is none other than that of the angel standing guard over paradise. Once thrust out of paradise we cannot return. The way is forward into exile and on to the New Jerusalem; upon which journey we must learn that the sword of the Lord is sheathed when it becomes a cross.

When this happens, however, and this deeper insight comes, the sword appears once more, in a much more subtle form. It appears as the

[4] *Réflexions sur l'intelligence* (3rd ed.; Paris: Desclée de Brouwer, 1931), p. 319.

sword of orthodoxy, excluding the communion of the God-relationship, much as sacrifice and the temple excluded Jeremiah's covenant return. William Blake's *Jerusalem* contains this deepest turn:

I stood among my valleys of the south,
And saw a flame of fire, even as a Wheel
Of fire surrounding all the heavens: . . .
. . . .
And I asked a Watcher and a Holy One
Its Name. He answer'd: "It is the Wheel of Religion."
I wept and said: "Is this the law of Jesus,
This terrible devouring sword turning every way?"
He answered: "Jesus died because he strove
Against the current of this Wheel: its Name
Is Caiaphas, the dark Preacher of Death,
Of sin, of sorrow, and of punishment:
Opposing Nature. It is Natural Religion,
But Jesus is the bright Preacher of Life,
Creating Nature from this fiery Law
By self-denial and forgiveness . . .
And some called him Jeremiah."[5]

48:1-47. Terror, Pit, and Snare: Concerning Moab.—The plight of Moab as pictured in the

[5] Folio 77.

unto Nebo! for it is spoiled: Kiriathaim is confounded *and* taken: Misgab is confounded and dismayed.

2 *There shall be* no more praise of Moab: in Heshbon they have devised evil against it; come, and let us cut it off from *being* a nation. Also thou shalt be cut down, O Madmen; the sword shall pursue thee.

3 A voice of crying *shall be* from Horonaim, spoiling and great destruction.

4 Moab is destroyed; her little ones have caused a cry to be heard.

5 For in the going up of Luhith continual weeping shall go up; for in the going down of Horonaim the enemies have heard a cry of destruction.

6 Flee, save your lives, and be like the heath in the wilderness.

Kiriatha′im is put to shame, it is taken;
  the fortress is put to shame and broken down;
2 the renown of Moab is no more.
In Heshbon they planned evil against her:
  'Come, let us cut her off from being a nation!'
You also, O Madmen, shall be brought to silence;
  the sword shall pursue you.

3 "Hark! a cry from Horona′im,
  'Desolation and great destruction!'
4 Moab is destroyed;
  a cry is heard as far as Zo′ar.[d]
5 For at the ascent of Luhith
  they go up weeping;[e]
for at the descent of Horona′im
  they have heard the cry[f] of destruction.
6 Flee! Save yourselves!
  Be like a wild ass[g] in the desert!

[d] Gk: Heb *her little ones*
[e] Cn: Heb *weeping goes up with weeping*
[f] Gk Compare Is 15. 5: Heb *the distress of the cry*
[g] Gk Aquila: Heb *like Aroer*

---

unusually large number of place names occurring here (for a detailed identification see Rudolph, *Jeremia,* pp. 245-47); and (c) the extensive borrowings, especially from Isa. 15–16. Many scholars who maintain that the antiforeign oracles are genuine recognize that this chapter has received editorial additions.

Two incidents in the lifetime of Jeremiah may have given rise to oracles against Moab. According to II Kings 24:2, when Jehoiakim rebelled against Nebuchadrezzar (probably in 602; see Exeg. on 12:7-13), Yahweh sent against Judah bands of Chaldeans, Syrians, Moabites, and Ammonites. If this is historical, the Moabites must have been allied with the Babylonians and thus have caused destruction in Judah. The other incident is that recorded in 27:1-11, where Moab is named among the nations seeking to rebel against Nebuchadrezzar. Jeremiah counsels their ambassadors against such action. Apparently they did not rebel at this time, but they probably did join in the later uprisings which led to Nebuchadrezzar's invasion of Palestine and the destruction of Jerusalem in 587 B.C. It is not impossible that Jeremiah uttered oracles against Moab, but we can have little confidence in our ability to extract from the present chapter a genuine kernel. The sections containing extensive borrowings from Isa. 15–16 are hardly genuine; some of the others may be, especially those which are poetic and condemn the pride and arrogance of Moab, e.g., vss. 1-4, 6-9, 11, 14-20, 28, 41b-42.

In its present form the chapter is a long collection of oracles condemning Moab, the individual oracles having originated at various times.

48:5. The verse is almost equivalent to Isa. 15:5b.

---

three terrible similes of vss. 43-44 is due not merely to the arrival of the overwhelming foe from the north but, as everywhere in Jeremiah, and in the prophets generally, the causes arise from defections within. Three such causes are given.

The first is the pride of Moab. This had long been an offense to Israel. "We have heard of the pride of Moab" (Isa. 16:6). Here are rehearsed once more his sins of **loftiness, pride, arrogance, haughtiness of . . .** heart, and **insolence** (vss. 29-30). The poem makes it emi-

7 ¶ For because thou hast trusted in thy works and in thy treasures, thou shalt also be taken: and Chemosh shall go forth into captivity *with* his priests and his princes together.

8 And the spoiler shall come upon every city, and no city shall escape: the valley also shall perish, and the plain shall be destroyed, as the Lord hath spoken.

9 Give wings unto Moab, that it may flee and get away: for the cities thereof shall be desolate, without any to dwell therein.

10 Cursed *be* he that doeth the work of the Lord deceitfully, and cursed *be* he that keepeth back his sword from blood.

11 ¶ Moab hath been at ease from his youth, and he hath settled on his lees, and hath not been emptied from vessel to vessel, neither hath he gone into captivity: therefore his taste remained in him, and his scent is not changed.

12 Therefore, behold, the days come, saith the Lord, that I will send unto him wanderers, that shall cause him to wander, and shall empty his vessels, and break their bottles.

13 And Moab shall be ashamed of Che-

7 For, because you trusted in your strongholds[h] and your treasures,
  you also shall be taken;
and Chemosh shall go forth into exile,
  with his priests and his princes.

8 The destroyer shall come upon every city,
  and no city shall escape;
the valley shall perish,
  and the plain shall be destroyed,
  as the Lord has spoken.

9 "Give wings to Moab,
  for she would fly away;
her cities shall become a desolation,
  with no inhabitant in them.

10 "Cursed is he who does the work of the Lord with slackness; and cursed is he who keeps back his sword from bloodshed.

11 "Moab has been at ease from his youth
  and has settled on his lees;
he has not been emptied from vessel to
    vessel,
  nor has he gone into exile;
so his taste remains in him,
  and his scent is not changed.

12 "Therefore, behold, the days are coming, says the Lord, when I shall send to him tilters who will tilt him, and empty his vessels, and break his[i] jars in pieces. 13 Then Moab shall be ashamed of Chemosh, as the

h Gk: Heb *works*
i Gk Aquila: Heb *their*

7. **Chemosh** was the national god of the Moabites (see vss. 13, 46; Num. 21:29; I Kings 11:7, 33; II Kings 23:13). The name occurs several times on the Moabite stone.

11. This verse is inscribed on a large clay seal, now in the Oriental Institute of the University of Chicago, which evidently had been used for stamping the bitumen with which wine jars were sealed. The seal comes from some time between the first and sixth centuries A.D. (see W. A. Irwin, "An Ancient Biblical Text," *American Journal of Semitic Languages and Literatures*, XLVIII [1931-32], 184-93).

13. **Bethel** may here be the name of a deity, just as **Chemosh** is the name of the Moabite god (see vs. 7). A West Semitic deity named Bethel was worshiped in Syria, in

nently clear how the mighty are fallen! The destroyer has fallen upon the vintage of its vines, which one time **passed over the sea** (vs. 32); the shouting now is no longer **the shout of joy** (vs. 33). Moab's strength is lopped off, **his arm is broken** (vs. 25). **How the mighty scepter is broken** (vs. 17). Therefore Moab must

  come down from [his] glory,
    and sit on the parched ground (vs. 18).

No longer can the Moabites say **we are heroes and mighty men of war** (vs. 14). The insertion of vss. 26-27 obviously building on ch. 25, clearly glories in this fall, exhibiting Moab as both disgusting and ridiculous in its drunkenness.

  Loud was Moab in derision;
    so let him be derided.
  For Israel you did deride;
    you tossed your head in scorn (Moffatt).

mosh, as the house of Israel was ashamed of Beth-el their confidence.

14 ¶ How say ye, We *are* mighty and strong men for the war?

15 Moab is spoiled, and gone up *out of* her cities, and his chosen young men are gone down to the slaughter, saith the King, whose name *is* The LORD of hosts.

16 The calamity of Moab *is* near to come, and his affliction hasteth fast.

17 All ye that are about him, bemoan him; and all ye that know his name, say, How is the strong staff broken, *and* the beautiful rod!

18 Thou daughter that dost inhabit Dibon, come down from *thy* glory, and sit in thirst; for the spoiler of Moab shall come upon thee, *and* he shall destroy thy strongholds.

19 O inhabitant of Aroer, stand by the way, and espy; ask him that fleeth, and her that escapeth, *and* say, What is done?

20 Moab is confounded; for it is broken down: howl and cry; tell ye it in Arnon, that Moab is spoiled,

21 And judgment is come upon the plain country; upon Holon, and upon Jahazah, and upon Mephaath,

22 And upon Dibon, and upon Nebo, and upon Beth-diblathaim,

23 And upon Kiriathaim, and upon Beth-gamul, and upon Beth-meon,

24 And upon Kerioth, and upon Bozrah, and upon all the cities of the land of Moab, far or near.

25 The horn of Moab is cut off, and his arm is broken, saith the LORD.

house of Israel was ashamed of Bethel, **their** confidence.

14 "How do you say, 'We are heroes
    and mighty men of war'?

15 The destroyer of Moab and his cities has
    come up,
    and the choicest of his young men have
      gone down to slaughter,
says the King, whose name is the LORD of
    hosts.

16 The calamity of Moab is near at hand
    and his affliction hastens apace.

17 Bemoan him, all you who are round
    about him,
    and all who know his name;
say, 'How the mighty scepter is broken,
    the glorious staff.'

18 "Come down from your glory,
    and sit on the parched ground,
    O inhabitant of Dibon!
For the destroyer of Moab has come up
    against you;
    he has destroyed your strongholds.

19 Stand by the way and watch,
    O inhabitant of Aro'er!
Ask him who flees and her who escapes;
    say, 'What has happened?'

20 Moab is put to shame, for it is broken;
    wail and cry!
Tell it by the Arnon,
    that Moab is laid waste.

21 "Judgment has come upon the tableland, upon Holon, and Jahzah, and Meph'-a-ath, **22** and Dibon, and Nebo, and Beth-diblatha'im, **23** and Kiriatha'im, and Beth-ga'mul, and Beth-me'on, **24** and Ker'i-oth, and Bozrah, and all the cities of the land of Moab, far and near. **25** The horn of Moab is cut off, and his arm is broken, says the LORD.

Babylonia in late times, and by the Jews of Elephantine in Egypt (see J. Philip Hyatt, "The Deity Bethel and the Old Testament," *Journal of the American Oriental Society,* LIX [1939], 81-98) .

Second, Moab is revealed as a self-satisfied, stagnant, and unprogressive nation, suffering the defects of its own security. Moab, from the beginning, had **settled on his lees** (vs. 11) . Its strength and character had not been enriched by openness to new experience. The defects of moral indolence had crept in from the first: the

flatness of the lees infected the wine, and the whole deteriorated through resting back upon itself. Now come the tilters from the north,

tilting him up and over,
    emptying out his casks,
    and breaking up his flasks (vs. 12 Moffatt) .

26 ¶ Make ye him drunken; for he magnified *himself* against the LORD: Moab also shall wallow in his vomit, and he also shall be in derision.

27 For was not Israel a derision unto thee? was he found among thieves? for since thou spakest of him, thou skippedst for joy.

28 O ye that dwell in Moab, leave the cities, and dwell in the rock, and be like the dove *that* maketh her nest in the sides of the hole's mouth.

29 We have heard the pride of Moab, (he is exceeding proud,) his loftiness, and his arrogancy, and his pride, and the haughtiness of his heart.

30 I know his wrath, saith the LORD; but *it shall* not *be* so; his lies shall not so effect *it*.

31 Therefore will I howl for Moab, and I will cry out for all Moab; *mine heart* shall mourn for the men of Kir-heres.

32 O vine of Sibmah, I will weep for thee with the weeping of Jazer: thy plants are gone over the sea, they reach *even* to the sea of Jazer: the spoiler is fallen upon thy summer fruits and upon thy vintage.

33 And joy and gladness is taken from the plentiful field, and from the land of Moab; and I have caused wine to fail from the winepresses: none shall tread with shouting; *their* shouting *shall be* no shouting.

34 From the cry of Heshbon *even* unto Elealeh, *and even* unto Jahaz, have they uttered their voice, from Zoar *even* unto Horonaim, *as* a heifer of three years old: for the waters also of Nimrim shall be desolate.

26 "Make him drunk, because he magnified himself against the LORD; so that Moab shall wallow in his vomit, and he too shall be held in derision. 27 Was not Israel a derision to you? Was he found among thieves, that whenever you spoke to him you wagged your head?

28 "Leave the cities, and dwell in the rock,
    O inhabitants of Moab!
Be like the dove that nests
    in the sides of the mouth of a gorge.
29 We have heard of the pride of Moab —
    he is very proud —
of his loftiness, his pride, and his arrogance,
    and the haughtiness of his heart.
30 I know his insolence, says the LORD;
    his boasts are false,
    his deeds are false.
31 Therefore I wail for Moab;
    I cry out for all Moab;
    for the men of Kir-he′res I mourn.
32 More than for Jazer I weep for you,
    O vine of Sibmah!
Your branches passed over the sea,
    reached as far as Jazer;*j*
upon your summer fruits and your vintage
    the destroyer has fallen.
33 Gladness and joy have been taken away
    from the fruitful land of Moab;
I have made the wine cease from the wine presses;
    no one treads them with shouts of joy;
    the shouting is not the shout of joy.

34 "Heshbon and Elea′leh cry out;*k* as far as Jahaz they utter their voice, from Zo′ar to Horona′im and Eg′lath-shelish′iyah. For the waters of Nimrim also have

j Cn: Heb *the sea of Jazer*
k Cn: Heb *From the cry of Heshbon to Elealeh*

29-46. This section is made up largely of passages borrowed from other O.T. books, especially from Isa. 15–16. The individual verses are borrowed as follows: vs. 29 from Isa. 16:6; vss. 31-33 from Isa. 16:7-10; vs. 34 from Isa. 15:4-6; vs. 36 from Isa. 16:11; 15:7;

It is felt by many that this powerful figure of Moab **settled on his lees** is of Jeremianic origin. The insight has become, in any case, a recognized maxim among men. For it contains the mysteries of indolence and perpetual perishing which troubled Plato as the unsolved mystery of evil, and it contains the contemporary recog-

nition that in order to be one's self one must constantly be in the course of becoming that which one is able to become. To settle on one's lees is to lose in fact the ground of spiritual discernment already won.

This brings us to the third cause for Moab's downfall. Moab has fallen because of the illu-

35 Moreover I will cause to cease in Moab, saith the Lord, him that offereth in the high places, and him that burneth incense to his gods.

36 Therefore mine heart shall sound for Moab like pipes, and mine heart shall sound like pipes for the men of Kir-heres: because the riches *that* he hath gotten are perished.

37 For every head *shall be* bald, and every beard clipped: upon all the hands *shall be* cuttings, and upon the loins sackcloth.

38 *There shall be* lamentation generally upon all the housetops of Moab, and in the streets thereof: for I have broken Moab like a vessel wherein *is* no pleasure, saith the Lord.

39 They shall howl, *saying,* How is it broken down! how hath Moab turned the back with shame! so shall Moab be a derision and a dismaying to all them about him.

40 For thus saith the Lord; Behold, he shall fly as an eagle, and shall spread his wings over Moab.

41 Kerioth is taken, and the strongholds are surprised, and the mighty men's hearts in Moab at that day shall be as the heart of a woman in her pangs.

42 And Moab shall be destroyed from *being* a people, because he hath magnified *himself* against the Lord.

43 Fear, and the pit, and the snare, *shall be* upon thee, O inhabitant of Moab, saith the Lord.

44 He that fleeth from the fear shall fall into the pit; and he that getteth up out of the pit shall be taken in the snare: for I will bring upon it, *even* upon Moab, the year of their visitation, saith the Lord.

become desolate. 35 And I will bring to an end in Moab, says the Lord, him who offers sacrifice in the high place and burns incense to his god. 36 Therefore my heart moans for Moab like a flute, and my heart moans like a flute for the men of Kir-he′res; therefore the riches they gained have perished.

37 "For every head is shaved and every beard cut off; upon all the hands are gashes, and on the loins is sackcloth. 38 On all the housetops of Moab and in the squares there is nothing but lamentation; for I have broken Moab like a vessel for which no one cares, says the Lord. 39 How it is broken! How they wail! How Moab has turned his back in shame! So Moab has become a derision and a horror to all that are round about him."

40 For thus says the Lord:
"Behold, one shall fly swiftly like an eagle,
    and spread his wings against Moab;
41 the cities shall be taken
    and the stronghold seized.
The heart of the warriors of Moab shall be in that day
    like the heart of a woman in her pangs;
42 Moab shall be destroyed and be no longer a people,
    because he magnified himself against the Lord.
43 Terror, pit, and snare
    are before you, O inhabitant of Moab!
                    says the Lord.
44 He who flees from the terror
    shall fall into the pit,
and he who climbs out of the pit
    shall be caught in the snare.
For I will bring these things[l] upon Moab
    in the year of their punishment,
                    says the Lord.

[l] Gk Syr: Heb *to her*

vss. 37-38 from Isa. 15:2-3; vss. 43-44 from Isa. 24:17-18; vss. 45-46 from Num. 21:28-29; 24:17; cf. vss. 40-41 with 49:22.

sory ground of its confidence—its false god. It is the **people of Chemosh** that is **undone** (vs. 46). It is of the false god Chemosh that Moab **shall be ashamed** even as the house of Israel **was ashamed of Bethel, their confidence** (vs. 12). Because Moab trusted in its own strength (**your strongholds**) and in a false god, the

Moabites, and Chemosh with them, **shall go forth into exile** (vs. 7). Trusting in our own strongholds or in our treasures, or in our projected gods, leads always into exile. It is for this deep and basic reason that the poet's heart **moans for Moab like a flute,** for all **the riches . . . have perished** (vs. 36). Through pride,

45 They that fled stood under the shadow of Heshbon because of the force: but a fire shall come forth out of Heshbon, and a flame from the midst of Sihon, and shall devour the corner of Moab, and the crown of the head of the tumultuous ones.

46 Woe be unto thee, O Moab! the people of Chemosh perisheth: for thy sons are taken captives, and thy daughters captives.

47 ¶ Yet will I bring again the captivity of Moab in the latter days, saith the LORD. Thus far *is* the judgment of Moab.

49 Concerning the Ammonites, thus saith the LORD; Hath Israel no sons? hath he no heir? why *then* doth their king inherit Gad, and his people dwell in his cities?

2 Therefore, behold, the days come, saith

---

45 "In the shadow of Heshbon
  fugitives stop without strength;
for a fire has gone forth from Heshbon,
  a flame from the house of Sihon;
it has destroyed the forehead of Moab,
  the crown of the sons of tumult.
46 Woe to you, O Moab!
  The people of Chemosh is undone;
for your sons have been taken captive,
  and your daughters into captivity.
47 Yet I will restore the fortunes of Moab
  in the latter days, says the LORD."
Thus far is the judgment on Moab.

49 Concerning the Ammonites.
  Thus says the LORD:
"Has Israel no sons?
  Has he no heir?
Why then has Milcom dispossessed Gad,
  and his people settled in its cities?
2 Therefore, behold, the days are coming,
  says the LORD,
when I will cause the battle cry to be
  heard
  against Rabbah of the Ammonites;
it shall become a desolate mound,

45-47. These verses are missing in the LXX. Cf. 49:6, 39; 12:15; 46:26*b*. All these passages may be additions by a single editor who had a compassionate attitude toward foreign nations.

E. ORACLE AGAINST THE AMMONITES (49:1-6)

This oracle lacks the spirit of vengefulness which is found in some of the antiforeign oracles in the collection, and seems almost to express sympathy for the Ammonites. While it may be from Jeremiah, it is difficult to date precisely. The Ammonites were involved in the invasion of Judah in 602 B.C. (II Kings 24:2), and are named in the list of states plotting rebellion against Babylonia (27:3; cf. Exeg. on 48:1-47). The present oracle does not name the source of the destruction of the Ammonites; probably it was thought to be Nebuchadrezzar.

49:1. At the time of the captivity of some of the Israelite tribes in 732 B.C. by the Assyrian king, Tiglath-pileser (II Kings 15:29), the Ammonites had probably moved into Israelite territory east of the Jordan, that of **Gad**, or Gilead. The prophet believed it still belonged to other Israelite tribes. **Milcom** was the national deity of the Ammonites (I Kings 11:5, 33; II Kings 23:13). The M.T. reads *malkām*, **their king**; the RSV rendering is supported by the LXX, Peshitta, and Vulg.

2. Then Israel shall dispossess those who dispossessed him is probably secondary, since the Israelites could hardly dispossess the Ammonites after they themselves had gone into captivity (cf. the phraseology of Zeph. 2:9; Ezek. 39:10).

---

through moral indolence, and through false absolutes the nation and its people fall.

49:1-39. Horror, Taunt, Waste, and Curse.— These terms are all applied (vs. 13) to Edom; but they could doubtless be extended to include the oracles concerning the Ammonites, Damas-cus, Kedar, and Hazor. In all of these pretty much the same terrors (vss. 5, 24, 29) are to be seen. It is the same cup that all must drink (vs. 12). It is against Edom that the poet's purest "syntax of lightning" [6] strikes. For here is re-

[6] Cf. Perse, *Exile and Other Poems*, p. 93.

the LORD, that I will cause an alarm of war to be heard in Rabbah of the Ammonites; and it shall be a desolate heap, and her daughters shall be burned with fire: then shall Israel be heir unto them that were his heirs, saith the LORD.

3 Howl, O Heshbon, for Ai is spoiled: cry, ye daughters of Rabbah, gird you with sackcloth; lament, and run to and fro by the hedges; for their king shall go into captivity, *and* his priests and his princes together.

4 Wherefore gloriest thou in the valleys, thy flowing valley, O backsliding daughter? that trusted in her treasures, *saying,* Who shall come unto me?

5 Behold, I will bring a fear upon thee, saith the Lord GOD of hosts, from all those that be about thee; and ye shall be driven out every man right forth; and none shall gather up him that wandereth.

6 And afterward I will bring again the captivity of the children of Ammon, saith the LORD.

7 ¶ Concerning Edom, thus saith the LORD of hosts; *Is* wisdom no more in Teman? is counsel perished from the prudent? is their wisdom vanished?

and its villages shall be burned with fire;
then Israel shall dispossess those who dispossessed him,
  says the LORD.

3 "Wail, O Heshbon, for Ai is laid waste!
  Cry, O daughters of Rabbah!
Gird yourselves with sackcloth,
  lament, and run to and fro among the hedges!
For Milcom shall go into exile,
  with his priests and his princes.
4 Why do you boast of your valleys,[m]
  O faithless daughter,
who trusted in her treasures, saying,
  'Who will come against me?'
5 Behold, I will bring terror upon you,
  says the Lord GOD of hosts,
from all who are round about you,
and you shall be driven out, every man straight before him,
  with none to gather the fugitives.
6 But afterward I will restore the fortunes of the Ammonites, says the LORD."

7 Concerning Edom.
  Thus says the LORD of hosts:
"Is wisdom no more in Teman?
  Has counsel perished from the prudent?
  Has their wisdom vanished?

[m] Heb *valleys, your valley flows*

---

6. This verse is not in the LXX (see Exeg. on 48:45-47).

F. ORACLE AGAINST EDOM (49:7-22)

The Edomites were the object of special hatred by the Jews after the fall of Jerusalem in 587 B.C. Though the relations between the two countries had often been friendly up to that time (Deut. 23:7-8), the Edomites took advantage of the situation and moved into southern Judah (Ps. 137:7; Lam. 4:21; Mal. 1:2-4; Joel 3:19; Isa. 34:5-7; 63:1-6; Ezek. 25:12-14; 35; Amos 9:12). The present oracle shows an especially close relationship to the book of Obadiah, which was written after 587. Vss. 14-16 are almost identical with Obad. 1-4, and vss. 9-10a with Obad. 5-6. It is probable that both Obadiah and the present oracle are based upon an earlier poem written after 587.

After one has listed all the verses which are borrowed from Obadiah and other O.T. passages, there is left a small nucleus that could possibly be from Jeremiah: vss. 7-8, 11, 22. It is not very probable, however, that these are from the prophet, for it is

---

vived an ancient quarrel. It is the ancient feud between Jacob and Esau (Edom). Biblical history is full of the contention between these two. They had been rivals for possession of the land. They had been rivals in trade. More recently Edom, ostensibly an ally of Judah, had

thrown in her lot with the Chaldeans when they came up against Jerusalem. Malachi's witness is eloquent: "I have loved Jacob but I have hated Esau" (Mal. 1:2-3). "In the Old Testament there are many denunciations . . . hurled upon Edom. For brother Esau and Edom, Israel

8 Flee ye, turn back, dwell deep, O inhabitants of Dedan; for I will bring the calamity of Esau upon him, the time *that* I will visit him.

9 If grape gatherers come to thee, would they not leave *some* gleaning grapes? if thieves by night, they will destroy till they have enough.

10 But I have made Esau bare, I have uncovered his secret places, and he shall not be able to hide himself: his seed is spoiled, and his brethren, and his neighbors, and he *is* not.

11 Leave thy fatherless children, I will preserve *them* alive; and let thy widows trust in me.

12 For thus saith the Lord; Behold, they whose judgment *was* not to drink of the cup have assuredly drunken; and *art* thou he *that* shall altogether go unpunished? thou shalt not go unpunished, but thou shalt surely drink *of it.*

13 For I have sworn by myself, saith the Lord, that Bozrah shall become a desolation, a reproach, a waste, and a curse; and all the cities thereof shall be perpetual wastes.

14 I have heard a rumor from the Lord, and an ambassador is sent unto the heathen, *saying,* Gather ye together, and come against her, and rise up to the battle.

15 For, lo, I will make thee small among the heathen, *and* despised among men.

16 Thy terribleness hath deceived thee, *and* the pride of thine heart, O thou that dwellest in the clefts of the rock, that hold-

8 Flee, turn back, dwell in the depths,
  O inhabitants of Dedan!
For I will bring the calamity of Esau
  upon him,
  the time when I punish him.
9 If grape-gatherers came to you,
  would they not leave gleanings?
If thieves came by night,
  would they not destroy only enough
    for themselves?
10 But I have stripped Esau bare,
  I have uncovered his hiding places,
  and he is not able to conceal himself.
His children are destroyed, and his
    brothers,
  and his neighbors; and he is no more.
11 Leave your fatherless children, I will
    keep them alive;
  and let your widows trust in me."

12 For thus says the Lord: "If those who did not deserve to drink the cup must drink it, will you go unpunished? You shall not go unpunished, but you must drink. **13** For I have sworn by myself, says the Lord, that Bozrah shall become a horror, a taunt, a waste, and a curse; and all her cities shall be perpetual wastes."
14 I have heard tidings from the Lord,
  and a messenger has been sent among
    the nations:
"Gather yourselves together and come
    against her,
  and rise up for battle!
15 For behold, I will make you small among
    the nations
  despised among men.
16 The horror you inspire has deceived you,
  and the pride of your heart,
  you who live in the clefts of the rock,[n]
  who hold the height of the hill.

[n] Or Sela

---

difficult to find a time when he would have concerned himself with the Edomites (unless at the very end of his life in Palestine), and the verses do not form a unit.

8. Esau was considered the ancestor of the Edomites.

12. This verse presupposes the situation in 25:28.

---

reserved her fiercest words. No feud in all her history was so bitter."[7] It is in the book of Obadiah, which Paterson has called "a hymn of hate," that this bitterness of feeling is given its most eloquent expression. In Obadiah also the calamity of Esau is brought down upon him.

[7] Paterson, *Goodly Fellowship of the Prophets,* pp. 184-85.

Once more he will be dispossessed of the blessing.

Though you make your nest as high as the eagle's, I will bring you down from there (vs. 16).

The religious dimension in this pronouncement is brought out sharply by Paterson, who notes how the N.T. describes the character of

est the height of the hill: though thou shouldest make thy nest as high as the eagle, I will bring thee down from thence, saith the Lord.

17 Also Edom shall be a desolation: every one that goeth by it shall be astonished, and shall hiss at all the plagues thereof.

18 As in the overthrow of Sodom and Gomorrah and the neighbor *cities* thereof, saith the Lord, no man shall abide there, neither shall a son of man dwell in it.

19 Behold, he shall come up like a lion from the swelling of Jordan against the habitation of the strong: but I will suddenly make him run away from her: and who *is* a chosen *man, that* I may appoint over her? for who *is* like me? and who will appoint me the time? and who *is* that shepherd that will stand before me?

20 Therefore hear the counsel of the Lord, that he hath taken against Edom; and his purposes, that he hath purposed against the inhabitants of Teman: Surely the least of the flock shall draw them out; surely he shall make their habitations desolate with them.

21 The earth is moved at the noise of their fall; at the cry the noise thereof was heard in the Red sea.

22 Behold, he shall come up and fly as the eagle, and spread his wings over Bozrah: and at that day shall the heart of the mighty men of Edom be as the heart of a woman in her pangs.

23 ¶ Concerning Damascus. Hamath is confounded, and Arpad; for they have heard evil tidings: they are fainthearted; *there is* sorrow on the sea; it cannot be quiet.

Though you make your nest as high as the eagle's,
I will bring you down from there,
           says the Lord.

17 "Edom shall become a horror; every one who passes by it will be horrified and will hiss because of all its disasters. 18 As when Sodom and Gomor′rah and their neighbor cities were overthrown, says the Lord, no man shall dwell there, no man shall sojourn in her. 19 Behold, like a lion coming up from the jungle of the Jordan against a strong sheepfold, I will suddenly make them*o* run away from her; and I will appoint over her whomever I choose. For who is like me? Who will summon me? 20 What shepherd can stand before me? Therefore hear the plan which the Lord has made against Edom and the purposes which he has formed against the inhabitants of Teman: Even the little ones of the flock shall be dragged away; surely their fold shall be appalled at their fate. 21 At the sound of their fall the earth shall tremble; the sound of their cry shall be heard at the Red Sea. 22 Behold, one shall mount up and fly swiftly like an eagle, and spread his wings against Bozrah, and the heart of the warriors of Edom shall be in that day like the heart of a woman in her pangs."

23 Concerning Damascus.
"Hamath and Arpad are confounded,
    for they have heard evil tidings;
they melt in fear, they are troubled like the sea*p*
    which cannot be quiet.

o Gk Syr: Heb *him*
p Cn: Heb *there is trouble in the sea*

19-21. Adapted from 50:44-46. In the latter passage the words refer to Babylon, where they are more appropriate; vs. 21 would be much more appropriate to the fall of Babylon than to the fall of Edom.

G. Oracle Against Damascus (49:23-27)

It is difficult to fit this oracle into any known event in which Damascus was involved during the lifetime of Jeremiah. Damascus fell to the Assyrian king, Tiglath-pileser, in 732 b.c. (cf. Isa. 17:1-3), and little is known of its history in the next few centuries. The oracle contains lines borrowed from other O.T. passages: vs. 24b is modeled after 6:24; 13:21; 49:22; vs. 26 is borrowed from 50:30 (where the word "therefore" is suitable, but not here); and vs. 27 is borrowed from Amos 1:4. Furthermore, Damascus is not named in the list of nations who are expected to drink the cup of wrath in 25:18-26 (originally the introduction to the collection of antiforeign oracles; see Exeg. on 25:15-38). It seems

24 Damascus is waxed feeble, *and* turneth herself to flee, and fear hath seized on *her:* anguish and sorrows have taken her, as a woman in travail.

25 How is the city of praise not left, the city of my joy!

26 Therefore her young men shall fall in her streets, and all the men of war shall be cut off in that day, saith the LORD of hosts.

27 And I will kindle a fire in the wall of Damascus, and it shall consume the palaces of Ben-hadad.

28 ¶ Concerning Kedar, and concerning the kingdoms of Hazor, which Nebuchad-

24 Damascus has become feeble, she turned to flee,
  and panic seized her;
anguish and sorrows have taken hold of her,
  as of a woman in travail.

25 How the famous city is forsaken,[q]
  the joyful city![r]

26 Therefore her young men shall fall in her squares,
  and all her soldiers shall be destroyed in that day,
        says the LORD of hosts.

27 And I will kindle a fire in the wall of Damascus,
  and it shall devour the palaces of Ben-ha'dad."

28 Concerning Kedar and the kingdoms of Hazor which Nebuchadrez'zar king of Babylon smote.

[q] Vg: Heb *not forsaken*
[r] Syr Vg Tg: Heb *city of my joy*

---

very probable therefore that this oracle is a late addition to the collection in chs. 46–51, written in the postexilic period as a deliberately archaic oracle. It is possible but not probable that vss. 23-24a, 25 are from Jeremiah.

23. Hamath and Arpad were cities in northern Syria. Here they are represented as melting in fear over the **evil tidings** of the fall of Damascus.

25. Even in ancient times Damascus was a **famous city** because of its situation at a large oasis in southern Syria and its importance in commerce (cf. Ezek. 27:18).

27. Ben-hadad: The name of several kings of Damascus (I Kings 15:18, 20; II Kings 13:24).

H. ORACLE AGAINST KEDAR AND HAZOR (49:28-33)

This is an oracle against Arab tribes. In the list of nations required to drink the cup of Yahweh's wrath, Kedar and Hazor are not named, but various Arab groups and towns are named: "Dedan, Tema, Buz, and all who cut the corners of their hair; all the kings of Arabia and all the kings of the mixed tribes that dwell in the desert" (25:23-24). Little is known of the early history of the Arabs. Josephus (*Against Apion* I. 19), quoting Berossus, refers in passing to a conquest of Arabia by Nebuchadrezzar. If historical, this may have given rise to the present oracle during Jeremiah's lifetime. Vss. 30-31 have been influenced by a late passage, Ezek. 38:10-11. It is possible therefore that an original oracle by Jeremiah (vss. 28b-29, 32-33) has been expanded by a later editor, but of this we cannot be certain.

28. Kedar: An Arab tribe living in the desert east of Palestine; in Gen. 25:13 it is the name of one of the sons of Ishmael, who was considered the ancestor of the Arabs.

Esau as that of "a fornicator, or profane person" (Heb. 12:16). The word "profane," he then reminds us, is "derived from the Latin *fanum,* a fane or temple, and *pro,* meaning 'in front of.' "[8] It was in the front of the temple that the marketing of beasts was conducted. It

[8] *Ibid.,* p. 187.

was here also that the money-changers did their work (John 2:13). Edom's interest was materialistic, and her culture mercantilistic. Her people were, consequently, both godless and arrogant. "At the center of Israel's life was a shrine and the vital thought of a sovereign God; at the center of Edom's life was a **market**

rezzar king of Babylon shall smite, thus saith the LORD; Arise ye, go up to Kedar, and spoil the men of the east.

29 Their tents and their flocks shall they take away: they shall take to themselves their curtains, and all their vessels, and their camels; and they shall cry unto them, Fear *is* on every side.

30 ¶ Flee, get you far off, dwell deep, O ye inhabitants of Hazor, saith the LORD; for Nebuchadrezzar king of Babylon hath taken counsel against you, and hath conceived a purpose against you.

31 Arise, get you up unto the wealthy nation, that dwelleth without care, saith the LORD, which have neither gates nor bars, *which* dwell alone.

32 And their camels shall be a booty, and the multitude of their cattle a spoil: and I will scatter into all winds them *that are* in the utmost corners; and I will bring their calamity from all sides thereof, saith the LORD.

33 And Hazor shall be a dwelling for dragons, *and* a desolation for ever: there shall no man abide there, nor *any* son of man dwell in it.

34 ¶ The word of the LORD that came to Jeremiah the prophet against Elam in the

Thus says the LORD:
"Rise up, advance against Kedar!
Destroy the people of the east!
29 Their tents and their flocks shall be taken,
their curtains and all their goods;
their camels shall be borne away from them,
and men shall cry to them: 'Terror on every side!'
30 Flee, wander far away, dwell in the depths,
O inhabitants of Hazor!
says the LORD.
For Nebuchadrez'zar king of Babylon
has made a plan against you,
and formed a purpose against you.

31 "Rise up, advance against a nation at ease,
that dwells securely,
says the LORD,
that has no gates or bars,
that dwells alone.
32 Their camels shall become booty,
their herds of cattle a spoil.
I will scatter to every wind
those who cut the corners of their hair,
and I will bring their calamity
from every side of them,
says the LORD.
33 Hazor shall become a haunt of jackals,
an everlasting waste;
no man shall dwell there,
no man shall sojourn in her."

34 The word of the LORD that came to Jeremiah the prophet concerning Elam, in

---

Hazor: The name of two or more towns in Palestine, but there is no other mention of a town in the desert by this name. It is possible that Hazor (*ḥāçôr*) was a collective name for the villages (*ḥaçērîm*, probably meaning villages of tents and rude huts) in which half-nomadic, half-settled Arabs lived. According to Isa. 42:11, Kedar occupied such villages. If this is correct, **the kingdoms of Hazor** may have included Kedar and the towns and groups named in 25:23.

29. Terror on every side occurs also in 6:25; 20:3, 10; 46:5.

30-31. These verses are similar in phraseology to Ezek. 38:10-11, probably a postexilic passage.

32. For the meaning of **those who cut the corners of their hair** see Exeg. on 9:26.

33. A prediction similar to this is made for Jerusalem in 9:11.

J. ORACLE AGAINST ELAM (49:34-39)

Elam was a country located east of Babylonia and north of the Persian Gulf. It is **difficult** to date the oracle because of its extremely vague character, no human agent of

beginning of the reign of Zedekiah king of Judah, saying,

35 Thus saith the LORD of hosts; Behold, I will break the bow of Elam, the chief of their might.

36 And upon Elam will I bring the four winds from the four quarters of heaven, and will scatter them toward all those winds; and there shall be no nation whither the outcasts of Elam shall not come.

37 For I will cause Elam to be dismayed before their enemies, and before them that seek their life: and I will bring evil upon them, *even* my fierce anger, saith the LORD; and I will send the sword after them, till I have consumed them:

38 And I will set my throne in Elam, and will destroy from thence the king and the princes, saith the LORD.

39 ¶ But it shall come to pass in the latter days, *that* I will bring again the captivity of Elam, saith the LORD.

50 The word that the LORD spake against Babylon *and* against the land of the Chaldeans by Jeremiah the prophet.

the beginning of the reign of Zedeki'ah king of Judah.

35 Thus says the LORD of hosts: "Behold, I will break the bow of Elam, the mainstay of their might; 36 and I will bring upon Elam the four winds from the four quarters of heaven; and I will scatter them to all those winds, and there shall be no nation to which those driven out of Elam shall not come. 37 I will terrify Elam before their enemies, and before those who seek their life; I will bring evil upon them, my fierce anger, says the LORD. I will send the sword after them, until I have consumed them; 38 and I will set my throne in Elam, and destroy their king and princes, says the LORD.

39 "But in the latter days I will restore the fortunes of Elam, says the LORD."

50 The word which the LORD spoke concerning Babylon, concerning the land of the Chalde'ans, by Jeremiah the prophet:

the destruction or reason for it being given, and because of the paucity of our information concerning the history of Elam during Jeremiah's lifetime. Elam had been an important empire but was conquered *ca.* 640 B.C., in the time of Ashurbanipal; it was later a part of the Persian Empire, after the time of Cyrus. The oracle assumes the destruction of Elam at a period when it had its own king and princes (vs. 38). It has been conjectured that at the time of this oracle (vs. 34) the Elamites threatened Babylon, and the Jewish exiles in Babylon were filled with the expectation that they would overthrow Babylon; but there is no record of this possibility. The oracle probably is not from Jeremiah but from the early postexilic period. It may be deliberately archaic, the author having in mind the devastation of 640 as a pattern of its future devastation.

34. The date, **in the beginning of the reign of Zedekiah,** was 598 B.C. (cf. Exeg. on 26:1; 27:1; 28:1).

35. The bow of Elam: The Elamites were famous as archers (cf. Isa. 22:6).

39. This verse is translated in the LXX, which does not contain 48:47; 49:6 (see Exeg., *ad loc.*).

K. ORACLES AGAINST BABYLON (50:1–51:64)

This long collection of oracles has two themes: the fall of Babylon, and the return of the Jewish exiles from Babylon to their homeland. It is unlikely that any part of the collection is from Jeremiah. The attitude toward Babylon is diametrically opposed to that of the prophet, who counseled his fellow countrymen to submit to the yoke of Babylonia,

place and beasts; the *fane* belonged to Israel but Edom was profane." [9] This distinction falls well within the perspectives of Jeremiah, when the temple is seen as a symbol of the vital relationship with Yahweh in the covenant.

[9] *Ibid.,* p. 188.

50:1–51:58. Babylon Was a Golden Cup.—These verses are for the most part propaganda for a return to Palestine. They would appear to be later than the opening chapters of Daniel, where we see Daniel a faithful citizen of Babylon, carrying into practical effect the advices

2 Declare ye among the nations, and publish, and set up a standard; publish, *and* conceal not: say, Babylon is taken, Bel is confounded, Merodach is broken in pieces; her idols are confounded, her images are broken in pieces.

3 For out of the north there cometh up a nation against her, which shall make her land desolate, and none shall dwell therein: they shall remove, they shall depart, both man and beast.

4 ¶ In those days, and in that time, saith the LORD, the children of Israel shall come, they and the children of Judah together, going and weeping: they shall go, and seek the LORD their God.

5 They shall ask the way to Zion with

2 "Declare among the nations and proclaim,
set up a banner and proclaim,
conceal it not, and say:
'Babylon is taken,
Bel is put to shame,
Mer'odach is dismayed.
Her images are put to shame,
her idols are dismayed.'

3 "For out of the north a nation has come up against her, which shall make her land a desolation, and none shall dwell in it; both man and beast shall flee away.

4 "In those days and in that time, says the LORD, the people of Israel and the people of Judah shall come together, weeping as they come; and they shall seek the LORD their God. 5 They shall ask the way to Zion, with faces turned toward it, saying, 'Come, let us join ourselves to the LORD in an ever-

referred to Nebuchadrezzar as the servant of Yahweh (27:6), and urged the exiles in Babylon to pray for the city's welfare (29:7). It contains many passages modeled on the words of Jeremiah and on other parts of the O.T. Some of the poems show the influence of Second Isaiah. The present collection was probably not composed by one man; it consists of poems and prose sections of varying quality, from several hands, brought together under the two common themes.

Babylon fell without a battle to the armies of the Persian king, Cyrus, under Gobryas in October, 539, and soon thereafter Cyrus himself entered the city in triumph. Cyrus adopted a mild policy toward Babylon and the Jews, allowing the latter to return to their homeland (Ezra 1:1-4). Some of the poems in the present collection seem to reflect the city's downfall, as prophecies after the event rather than predictions (50:2-3, 11-16, 21-27, 35-38; 51:1-4, 41-44, 54-58). Because of the references to the Medes (51:11, 28), it has been suggested that these chapters come from *ca.* 561-560 B.C., when there was widespread expectation that the Medes would attack Babylon in a period of civil war and weakness—an expectation which did not materialize (George G. Cameron, *History of Early Iran* [Chicago: University of Chicago Press, 1936], pp. 222-23; see also Paul Volz, *Der Prophet Jeremia* [Leipzig: A. Deichert, 1928; "Kommentar zum Alten Testament"], pp. 383-84). It is quite possible that some of the sections in this collection did originate in that period, but not the whole, for some of the poems reflect too vividly the actual fall of Babylon and the influence of Second Isaiah.

This collection of oracles is poorly organized, without progress of thought. The two basic themes are treated in various ways, with the constant emphasis that the fall of Babylon and the return of the Jews are wholly the work of Yahweh's will and power.

50:2. Bel and **Merodach** were Babylonian deities, the latter known as Marduk, the patron god of the capital and the empire (cf. Isa. 46:1).

which Jeremiah had given when he urged the exiles to build and plant and pray (29:5-7). The latter (and later) chapters of Daniel reveal, however, the increasing unrest and agitation for return. The prophecy of Babylon's approaching desolation, alluded to so many times throughout these verses, is well summa-

rized in 51:7. Babylon had been a golden cup in the Lord's hand, obliging the nations to drink her wine. But, now, **suddenly Babylon has fallen and been broken** (51:8).

Against this background the oracles conduct the agitation for return. The most persistent metaphor is that of Israel as the hunted sheep

their faces thitherward, *saying,* Come, and let us join ourselves to the L ORD in a perpetual covenant *that* shall not be forgotten.

6 My people hath been lost sheep: their shepherds have caused them to go astray, they have turned them away *on* the mountains: they have gone from mountain to hill, they have forgotten their resting place.

7 All that found them have devoured them: and their adversaries said, We offend not, because they have sinned against the L ORD, the habitation of justice, even the L ORD, the hope of their fathers.

8 Remove out of the midst of Babylon, and go forth out of the land of the Chaldeans, and be as the he goats before the flocks.

9 ¶ For, lo, I will raise and cause to come up against Babylon an assembly of great nations from the north country: and they shall set themselves in array against her; from thence she shall be taken: their arrows *shall be* as of a mighty expert man; none shall return in vain.

10 And Chaldea shall be a spoil: all that spoil her shall be satisfied, saith the L ORD.

11 Because ye were glad, because ye rejoiced, O ye destroyers of mine heritage, because ye are grown fat as the heifer at grass, and bellow as bulls;

12 Your mother shall be sore confounded; she that bare you shall be ashamed: behold, the hindermost of the nations *shall be* a wilderness, a dry land, and a desert.

13 Because of the wrath of the L ORD it shall not be inhabited, but it shall be wholly desolate: every one that goeth by Babylon shall be astonished, and hiss at all her plagues.

lasting covenant which will never be forgotten.'

6 "My people have been lost sheep; their shepherds have led them astray, turning them away on the mountains; from mountain to hill they have gone, they have forgotten their fold. **7** All who found them have devoured them, and their enemies have said, 'We are not guilty, for they have sinned against the L ORD, their true habitation, the L ORD, the hope of their fathers.'

8 "Flee from the midst of Babylon, and go out of the land of the Chalde′ans, and be as he-goats before the flock. **9** For behold, I am stirring up and bringing against Babylon a company of great nations, from the north country; and they shall array themselves against her; from there she shall be taken. Their arrows are like a skilled warrior who does not return empty-handed. **10** Chalde′a shall be plundered; all who plunder her shall be sated, says the L ORD.

11 "Though you rejoice, though you exult,
    O plunderers of my heritage,
though you are wanton as a heifer at
    grass,
    and neigh like stallions,
12 your mother shall be utterly shamed,
    and she who bore you shall be disgraced.
Lo, she shall be the last of the nations,
    a wilderness dry and desert.
13 Because of the wrath of the L ORD she
    shall not be inhabited,
    but shall be an utter desolation;
everyone who passes by Babylon shall be
    appalled,
    and hiss because of all her wounds.

---

8. Cf. 51:6; Isa. 48:20.

13. Similar words are spoken about Jerusalem or the land of Israel in 18:16; 19:8; 25:9, 11, and about Edom in 49:17. **Babylon** was not destroyed by the Persians, and did not fall into ruin until after the time of Alexander.

---

about to be restored to its former pasture (50:17, 19).

Three passages appear, reflecting a deeper and slowly maturing consciousness moving toward the perspectives of Second Isaiah. The first of these is 50:4-5, a passage beautiful within itself. It contains the accent of repentance and confession, the people being moved to tears as

they return (cf. 3:12, 13, 18, 21-25). They have learned at last to

Stand by the roads, and look,
    and ask for the ancient paths (6:16; cf. 5:4).

The covenant consciousness has taken hold (cf. 31:1, 9, 31-34; 33:7). Their experience is such

14 Put yourselves in array against Babylon round about: all ye that bend the bow, shoot at her, spare no arrows: for she hath sinned against the LORD.

15 Shout against her round about: she hath given her hand: her foundations are fallen, her walls are thrown down: for it is the vengeance of the LORD: take vengeance upon her; as she hath done, do unto her.

16 Cut off the sower from Babylon, and him that handleth the sickle in the time of harvest: for fear of the oppressing sword they shall turn every one to his people, and they shall flee every one to his own land.

17 ¶ Israel is a scattered sheep; the lions have driven him away: first the king of Assyria hath devoured him; and last this Nebuchadrezzar king of Babylon hath broken his bones.

18 Therefore thus saith the LORD of hosts, the God of Israel; Behold, I will punish the king of Babylon and his land, as I have punished the king of Assyria.

19 And I will bring Israel again to his habitation, and he shall feed on Carmel and Bashan, and his soul shall be satisfied upon mount Ephraim and Gilead.

20 In those days, and in that time, saith the LORD, the iniquity of Israel shall be sought for, and there shall be none; and the sins of Judah, and they shall not be found: for I will pardon them whom I reserve.

21 ¶ Go up against the land of Merathaim, even against it, and against the inhabitants of Pekod: waste and utterly destroy after them, saith the LORD, and do according to all that I have commanded thee.

14 Set yourselves in array against Babylon round about,
  all you that bend the bow;
shoot at her, spare no arrows,
  for she has sinned against the LORD.
15 Raise a shout against her round about,
  she has surrendered;
her bulwarks have fallen,
  her walls are thrown down.
For this is the vengeance of the LORD:
  take vengeance on her,
  do to her as she has done.
16 Cut off from Babylon the sower,
  and the one who handles the sickle in time of harvest;
because of the sword of the oppressor,
  every one shall turn to his own people,
  and every one shall flee to his own land.

17 "Israel is a hunted sheep driven away by lions. First the king of Assyria devoured him, and now at last Nebuchadrez'zar king of Babylon has gnawed his bones. 18 Therefore, thus says the LORD of hosts, the God of Israel: Behold, I am bringing punishment on the king of Babylon and his land, as I punished the king of Assyria. 19 I will restore Israel to his pasture, and he shall feed on Carmel and in Bashan, and his desire shall be satisfied on the hills of E'phraim and in Gilead. 20 In those days and in that time, says the LORD, iniquity shall be sought in Israel, and there shall be none; and sin in Judah, and none shall be found; for I will pardon those whom I leave as a remnant.

21 "Go up against the land of Meratha'im,s
  and against the inhabitants of Pekod.t
Slay, and utterly destroy after them,
  says the LORD,
  and do all that I have commanded you.

s Or Double Rebellion
t Or Punishment

21. **Merathaim** means **Double Rebellion** or "Double Bitterness." It is a play on a name applied to southern Babylonia, *mât marrâti*, "Land of the Bitter River." **Pekod** means **Punishment**, and is a play on the name of a tribe in eastern Babylonia, the *Puqûdu*. The names are here applied to the whole land to express judgment on Babylonia.

that this newer covenant—a covenant of alienation and return—shall never be forgotten.

The second passage is even more indicative. Here (50:33-34) a significant development of the Jewish law affecting the next of kin appears. A man's nearest living blood relation had the offices of the kinsman-redeemer. If a man should become poor and be obliged to sell some of

22 A sound of battle *is* in the land, and of great destruction.

23 How is the hammer of the whole earth cut asunder and broken! how is Babylon become a desolation among the nations!

24 I have laid a snare for thee, and thou art also taken, O Babylon, and thou wast not aware: thou art found, and also caught, because thou hast striven against the LORD.

25 The LORD hath opened his armory, and hath brought forth the weapons of his indignation: for this *is* the work of the Lord GOD of hosts in the land of the Chaldeans.

26 Come against her from the utmost border, open her storehouses: cast her up as heaps, and destroy her utterly: let nothing of her be left.

27 Slay all her bullocks; let them go down to the slaughter: woe unto them! for their day is come, the time of their visitation.

28 The voice of them that flee and escape out of the land of Babylon, to declare in Zion the vengeance of the LORD our God, the vengeance of his temple.

29 Call together the archers against Babylon: all ye that bend the bow, camp against it round about; let none thereof escape: recompense her according to her work; according to all that she hath done, do unto her: for she hath been proud against the LORD, against the Holy One of Israel.

30 Therefore shall her young men fall in the streets, and all her men of war shall be cut off in that day, saith the LORD.

31 Behold, I *am* against thee, *O thou most proud*, saith the Lord GOD of hosts: for thy day is come, the time *that* I will visit thee.

22 The noise of battle is in the land,
   and great destruction!
23 How the hammer of the whole earth
   is cut down and broken!
   How Babylon has become
   a horror among the nations!
24 I set a snare for you and you were taken,
      O Babylon,
   and you did not know it;
   you were found and caught,
      because you strove against the LORD.
25 The LORD has opened his armory,
   and brought out the weapons of his
      wrath,
   for the Lord GOD of hosts has a work to
      do
   in the land of the Chalde'ans.
26 Come against her from every quarter;
   open her granaries;
   pile her up like heaps of grain, and destroy her utterly;
   let nothing be left of her.
27 Slay all her bulls,
   let them go down to the slaughter.
   Woe to them, for their day has come,
   the time of their punishment.

28 "Hark! they flee and escape from the land of Babylon, to declare in Zion the vengeance of the LORD our God, vengeance for his temple.

29 "Summon archers against Babylon, all those who bend the bow. Encamp round about her; let no one escape. Requite her according to her deeds, do to her according to all that she has done; for she has proudly defied the LORD, the Holy One of Israel. 30 Therefore her young men shall fall in her squares, and all her soldiers shall be destroyed on that day, says the LORD.

31 "Behold, I am against you, O proud one,
   says the Lord GOD of hosts;
   for your day has come,
   the time when I will punish you.

---

his land, his next of kin should come to him and "redeem what his brother has sold" (Lev. 25:25). It was also his office to buy back a member of his family who had been sold or who had sold himself into slavery. Finally, he should avenge the slaying of a kinsman. In these verses we observe the transference and projection of these offices upon Yahweh. Yah-

weh becomes the kinsman-redeemer of the people of Judah who have been taken into slavery. It is God himself who will plead their cause and stand for them over against the power of Babylon. The development of this figure is obvious in Second Isaiah where it recurs many times. It is best known from the book of Job, where Job, when all the rest have turned against

32 And the most proud shall stumble and fall, and none shall raise him up: and I will kindle a fire in his cities, and it shall devour all round about him.

33 ¶ Thus saith the LORD of hosts; The children of Israel and the children of Judah *were* oppressed together: and all that took them captives held them fast; they refused to let them go.

34 Their Redeemer *is* strong; The LORD of hosts *is* his name: he shall thoroughly plead their cause, that he may give rest to the land, and disquiet the inhabitants of Babylon.

35 ¶ A sword *is* upon the Chaldeans, saith the LORD, and upon the inhabitants of Babylon, and upon her princes, and upon her wise *men*.

36 A sword *is* upon the liars; and they shall dote: a sword *is* upon her mighty men; and they shall be dismayed.

37 A sword *is* upon their horses, and upon their chariots, and upon all the mingled people that *are* in the midst of her; and they shall become as women: a sword *is* upon her treasures; and they shall be robbed.

38 A drought *is* upon her waters; and they shall be dried up: for it *is* the land of graven images, and they are mad upon *their* idols.

39 Therefore the wild beasts of the desert with the wild beasts of the islands shall dwell *there,* and the owls shall dwell therein: and it shall be no more inhabited for ever; neither shall it be dwelt in from generation to generation.

40 As God overthrew Sodom and Gomorrah and the neighbor *cities* thereof, saith the LORD; *so* shall no man abide there, neither shall any son of man dwell therein.

41 Behold, a people shall come from the north, and a great nation, and many kings

32 The proud one shall stumble and fall,
    with none to raise him up,
and I will kindle a fire in his cities,
    and it will devour all that is round
      about him.

33 "Thus says the LORD of hosts: The people of Israel are oppressed, and the people of Judah with them; all who took them captive have held them fast, they refuse to let them go. 34 Their Redeemer is strong; the LORD of hosts is his name. He will surely plead their cause, that he may give rest to the earth, but unrest to the inhabitants of Babylon.

35 "A sword upon the Chalde'ans, says the
    LORD,
    and upon the inhabitants of Babylon,
    and upon her princes and her wise
      men!
36 A sword upon the diviners,
    that they may become fools!
A sword upon her warriors,
    that they may be destroyed!
37 A sword upon her horses and upon her
    chariots,
    and upon all the foreign troops in her
      midst,
    that they may become women!
A sword upon all her treasures,
    that they may be plundered!
38 A drought upon her waters,
    that they may be dried up!
For it is a land of images,
    and they are mad over idols.

39 "Therefore wild beasts and jackals shall dwell in Babylon, and ostriches shall dwell in her; she shall be peopled no more for ever, nor inhabited for all generations. 40 As when God overthrew Sodom and Gomor'rah and their neighbor cities, says the LORD, so no man shall dwell there, and no son of man shall sojourn in her.

41 "Behold, a people comes from the north;
    a mighty nation and many kings

---

34. Redeemer is frequently used as a title of Yahweh in Second Isaiah (43:14; 44:6; 47:4; 48:17; 49:7; 54:5).

39-40. These verses are very similar in phraseology and content to Isa. 13:19-22; 34:11-17.

41-43. This passage is borrowed, with adaptations to Babylon, from 6:22-24.

shall be raised up from the coasts of the earth.

42 They shall hold the bow and the lance: they *are* cruel, and will not show mercy: their voice shall roar like the sea, and they shall ride upon horses, *every one* put in array, like a man to the battle, against thee, O daughter of Babylon.

43 The king of Babylon hath heard the report of them, and his hands waxed feeble: anguish took hold of him, *and* pangs as of a woman in travail.

44 Behold, he shall come up like a lion from the swelling of Jordan unto the habitation of the strong: but I will make them suddenly run away from her: and who *is* a chosen *man, that* I may appoint over her? for who *is* like me? and who will appoint me the time? and who *is* that shepherd that will stand before me?

45 Therefore hear ye the counsel of the LORD, that he hath taken against Babylon; and his purposes, that he hath purposed against the land of the Chaldeans: Surely the least of the flock shall draw them out: surely he shall make *their* habitation desolate with them.

46 At the noise of the taking of Babylon the earth is moved, and the cry is heard among the nations.

51 Thus saith the LORD; Behold, I will raise up against Babylon, and against them that dwell in the midst of them that rise up against me, a destroying wind;

2 And will send unto Babylon fanners,

are stirring from the farthest parts of the earth.

42 They lay hold of bow and spear;
  they are cruel, and have no mercy.
The sound of them is like the roaring of the sea;
  they ride upon horses,
arrayed as a man for battle
  against you, O daughter of Babylon!

43 "The king of Babylon heard the report of them,
  and his hands fell helpless;
anguish seized him,
  pain as of a woman in travail.

44 "Behold, like a lion coming up from the jungle of the Jordan against a strong sheepfold, I will suddenly make them run away from her; and I will appoint over her whomever I choose. For who is like me? Who will summon me? What shepherd can stand before me? 45 Therefore hear the plan which the LORD has made against Babylon, and the purposes which he has formed against the land of the Chalde'ans: Surely the little ones of their flock shall be dragged away; surely their fold shall be appalled at their fate. 46 At the sound of the capture of Babylon the earth shall tremble, and her cry shall be heard among the nations."

51 Thus says the LORD:
  "Behold, I will stir up the spirit of a destroyer against Babylon,
against the inhabitants of Chalde'a;[u]
2 and I will send to Babylon winnowers,
  and they shall winnow her,
  and they shall empty her land,

[u] Heb *Leb-qamai,* a cipher for Chaldea

44-46. These verses are found also in 49:19-21, with changes in wording to make the passage suitable to Edom. The original position is here, since vs. 46 is much more appropriate to the fall of Babylon than to the fall of Edom.

51:1. Chaldea is here written in Hebrew *lēbh-qāmāy* which stands, by the literary device known as athbash, for *kasdîm,* the Chaldeans. The Hebrew means, lit., "the heart of those who rise up against me." The same literary device is used in 25:26; 51:41.

---

him, exclaims, "I know that my Redeemer lives" (Job 19:25). The ultimate translation of this notion into its cosmic implications is realized, of course, in the redemptive work of Christ.

The third passage (51:15-19) is one which we have noted before, for it is an insertion of a

striking passage from an earlier prophecy (10: 12-16). Here is a paean of praise to the creative power of God, to his ordinances, and to the dependability of his wisdom. As against this vast creative power the idols of men appear stupid and empty. All things not of God are **worthless, a work of delusion** and in due course

that shall fan her, and shall empty her land: for in the day of trouble they shall be against her round about.

3 Against *him that* bendeth let the archer bend his bow, and against *him that* lifteth himself up in his brigandine: and spare ye not her young men; destroy ye utterly all her host.

4 Thus the slain shall fall in the land of the Chaldeans, and *they that are* thrust through in her streets.

5 For Israel *hath* not *been* forsaken, nor Judah of his God, of the Lord of hosts; though their land was filled with sin against the Holy One of Israel.

6 Flee out of the midst of Babylon, and deliver every man his soul: be not cut off in her iniquity; for this *is* the time of the Lord's vengeance; he will render unto her a recompense.

7 Babylon *hath been* a golden cup in the Lord's hand, that made all the earth drunken: the nations have drunken of her wine; therefore the nations are mad.

8 Babylon is suddenly fallen and destroyed: howl for her; take balm for her pain, if so be she may be healed.

9 We would have healed Babylon, but she is not healed: forsake her, and let us go every one into his own country: for her judgment reacheth unto heaven, and is lifted up *even* to the skies.

10 The Lord hath brought forth our righteousness: come, and let us declare in Zion the work of the Lord our God.

11 Make bright the arrows; gather the

when they come against her from every side
on the day of trouble.

3 Let not the archer bend his bow,
and let him not stand up in his coat of mail.
Spare not her young men;
utterly destroy all her host.

4 They shall fall down slain in the land of the Chalde'ans,
and wounded in her streets.

5 For Israel and Judah have not been forsaken
by their God, the Lord of hosts;
but the land of the Chalde'ans[v] is full of guilt
against the Holy One of Israel.

6 "Flee from the midst of Babylon,
let every man save his life!
Be not cut off in her punishment,
for this is the time of the Lord's vengeance,
the requital he is rendering her.

7 Babylon was a golden cup in the Lord's hand,
making all the earth drunken;
the nations drank of her wine,
therefore the nations went mad.

8 Suddenly Babylon has fallen and been broken;
wail for her!
Take balm for her pain;
perhaps she may be healed.

9 We would have healed Babylon,
but she was not healed.
Forsake her, and let us go
each to his own country;
for her judgment has reached up to heaven
and has been lifted up even to the skies.

10 The Lord has brought forth our vindication;
come, let us declare in Zion
the work of the Lord our God.

11 "Sharpen the arrows!
Take up the shields!

[v] Heb *their land*

---

11. The Medes were a people from the highlands east of Babylonia. They aided the Babylonians in conquering Nineveh, and in the sixth century established a large important kingdom east and north of that country. In the period *ca.* 560 B.C. there

shields: the LORD hath raised up the spirit of the kings of the Medes: for his device *is* against Babylon, to destroy it; because it *is* the vengeance of the LORD, the vengeance of his temple.

12 Set up the standard upon the walls of Babylon, make the watch strong, set up the watchmen, prepare the ambushes: for the LORD hath both devised and done that which he spake against the inhabitants of Babylon.

13 O thou that dwellest upon many waters, abundant in treasures, thine end is come, *and* the measure of thy covetousness.

14 The LORD of hosts hath sworn by himself, *saying*, Surely I will fill thee with men, as with caterpillars; and they shall lift up a shout against thee.

15 He hath made the earth by his power, he hath established the world by his wisdom, and hath stretched out the heaven by his understanding.

16 When he uttereth *his* voice, *there is* a multitude of waters in the heavens; and he causeth the vapors to ascend from the ends of the earth: he maketh lightnings with rain, and bringeth forth the wind out of his treasures.

17 Every man is brutish by *his* knowledge; every founder is confounded by the graven image: for his molten image *is* falsehood, and *there is* no breath in them.

18 They *are* vanity, the work of errors: in the time of their visitation they shall perish.

The LORD has stirred up the spirit of the kings of the Medes, because his purpose concerning Babylon is to destroy it, for that is the vengeance of the LORD, the vengeance for his temple.

12 Set up a standard against the walls of Babylon;
  make the watch strong;
set up watchmen;
  prepare the ambushes;
for the LORD has both planned and done
  what he spoke concerning the inhabitants of Babylon.

13 O you who dwell by many waters,
  rich in treasures,
your end has come,
  the thread of your life is cut.

14 The LORD of hosts has sworn by himself:
  Surely I will fill you with men, as many as locusts,
  and they shall raise the shout of victory over you.

15 "It is he who made the earth by his power,
  who established the world by his wisdom,
  and by his understanding stretched out the heavens.

16 When he utters his voice there is a tumult of waters in the heavens,
  and he makes the mist rise from the ends of the earth.
He makes lightnings for the rain,
  and he brings forth the wind from his storehouses.

17 Every man is stupid and without knowledge;
  every goldsmith is put to shame by his idols;
  for his images are false,
  and there is no breath in them.

18 They are worthless, a work of delusion;
  at the time of their punishment they shall perish.

---

was widespread expectation of an attack by the Medes upon Babylon (see Exeg. on 50:1–51:64).

15-19. These verses are found also at 10:12-16; see Exeg., where the influence of Second Isaiah is pointed out.

---

they shall perish. Clearly the inference is that Babylon also shall perish when its time has come. This is consistent with Jeremiah's point of view; for though he counseled submission to the yoke of Babylon, he also recognized that there would come a time when Babylon would pass away. They have built (cf. Dan. 4:26-27) not on righteousness but upon power.

19 The portion of Jacob *is* not like them; for he *is* the former of all things: and *Israel is* the rod of his inheritance: the LORD of hosts *is* his name.

20 Thou *art* my battle-axe *and* weapons of war: for with thee will I break in pieces the nations, and with thee will I destroy kingdoms;

21 And with thee will I break in pieces the horse and his rider; and with thee will I break in pieces the chariot and his rider;

22 With thee also will I break in pieces man and woman; and with thee will I break in pieces old and young; and with thee will I break in pieces the young man and the maid;

23 I will also break in pieces with thee the shepherd and his flock; and with thee will I break in pieces the husbandman and his yoke of oxen; and with thee will I break in pieces captains and rulers.

24 And I will render unto Babylon and to all the inhabitants of Chaldea all their evil that they have done in Zion in your sight, saith the LORD.

25 Behold, I *am* against thee, O destroying mountain, saith the LORD, which destroyest all the earth: and I will stretch out mine hand upon thee, and roll thee down from the rocks, and will make thee a burnt mountain.

26 And they shall not take of thee a stone for a corner, nor a stone for foundations; but thou shalt be desolate for ever, saith the LORD.

27 Set ye up a standard in the land, blow the trumpet among the nations, prepare the nations against her, call together against

19 Not like these is he who is the portion of Jacob,
for he is the one who formed all things,
and Israel is the tribe of his inheritance;
the LORD of hosts is his name.

20 "You are my hammer and weapon of war:
with you I break nations in pieces;
with you I destroy kingdoms;
21 with you I break in pieces the horse and his rider;
with you I break in pieces the chariot and the charioteer;
22 with you I break in pieces man and woman;
with you I break in pieces the old man and the youth;
with you I break in pieces the young man and the maiden;
23 with you I break in pieces the shepherd and his flock;
with you I break in pieces the farmer and his team;
with you I break in pieces governors and commanders.

24 "I will requite Babylon and all the inhabitants of Chalde'a before your very eyes for all the evil that they have done in Zion, says the LORD.

25 "Behold I am against you, O destroying mountain,
says the LORD,
which destroys the whole earth;
I will stretch out my hand against you,
and roll you down from the crags,
and make you a burnt mountain.
26 No stone shall be taken from you for a corner
and no stone for a foundation,
but you shall be a perpetual waste,
says the LORD.

27 "Set up a standard on the earth,
blow the trumpet among the nations;
prepare the nations for war against her,

20-23. The words here may be addressed to Cyrus, who conquered Babylon. The attitude toward Cyrus is similar to that found in Second Isaiah (41:2-4).

27. Ararat, Minni, and Ashkenaz are the names of peoples north of Babylonia who were conquered by the Medes early in the sixth century. **Ararat** is the Urartu of the Assyrian inscriptions, roughly the equivalent of Armenia, north of Lake Van. The **Minni** are the Mannaeans of the Assyrian inscriptions, who lived south of Lake Urmia.

her the kingdoms of Ararat, Minni, and Ashchenaz; appoint a captain against her; cause the horses to come up as rough caterpillars.

28 Prepare against her the nations with the kings of the Medes, the captains thereof, and all the rulers thereof, and all the land of his dominion.

29 And the land shall tremble and sorrow: for every purpose of the LORD shall be performed against Babylon, to make the land of Babylon a desolation without an inhabitant.

30 The mighty men of Babylon have forborne to fight, they have remained in *their* holds: their might hath failed; they became as women: they have burned her dwelling places; her bars are broken.

31 One post shall run to meet another, and one messenger to meet another, to show the king of Babylon that his city is taken at *one* end,

32 And that the passages are stopped, and the reeds they have burned with fire, and the men of war are affrighted.

33 For thus saith the LORD of hosts, the God of Israel; The daughter of Babylon *is* like a threshingfloor, *it is* time to thresh her: yet a little while, and the time of her harvest shall come.

34 Nebuchadrezzar the king of Babylon hath devoured me, he hath crushed me, he hath made me an empty vessel, he hath swallowed me up like a dragon, he hath filled his belly with my delicates, he hath cast me out.

35 The violence done to me and to my flesh *be* upon Babylon, shall the inhabitant of Zion say; and my blood upon the inhabitants of Chaldea, shall Jerusalem say.

---

summon against her the kingdoms,
  Ar'arat, Minni, and Ash'kenaz;
appoint a marshal against her,
  bring up horses like bristling locusts.
28 Prepare the nations for war against her,
  the kings of the Medes, with their governors and deputies,
and every land under their dominion.
29 The land trembles and writhes in pain,
  for the LORD's purposes against Babylon stand,
to make the land of Babylon a desolation,
  without inhabitant.
30 The warriors of Babylon have ceased fighting,
  they remain in their strongholds;
their strength has failed,
  they have become women;
her dwellings are on fire,
  her bars are broken.
31 One runner runs to meet another,
  and one messenger to meet another,
to tell the king of Babylon
  that his city is taken on every side;
32 the fords have been seized,
  the bulwarks are burned with fire,
  and the soldiers are in panic.
33 For thus says the LORD of hosts, the God of Israel:
  The daughter of Babylon is like a threshing floor
  at the time when it is trodden;
yet a little while
  and the time of her harvest will come."

34 "Nebuchadrez'zar the king of Babylon has devoured me,
  he has crushed me;
he has made me an empty vessel,
  he has swallowed me like a monster;
he has filled his belly with my delicacies,
  he has rinsed me out.
35 The violence done to me and to my kinsmen be upon Babylon,"
  let the inhabitant of Zion say.
"My blood be upon the inhabitants of Chalde'a,"
  let Jerusalem say.

Ashkenaz probably stands for the Scythians, the Ashguzai of Assyrian inscriptions, nomadic peoples living generally east of Lake Urmia (cf. Gen. 10:3). The word אשכנז (Ashkenaz) may be a scribal error for אשכוז (Ashkuz). These three peoples are here summoned to aid the Medes (vs. 28) in battle against Babylon.

36 Therefore thus saith the Lord; Behold, I will plead thy cause, and take vengeance for thee; and I will dry up her sea, and make her springs dry.

37 And Babylon shall become heaps, a dwelling place for dragons, an astonishment, and a hissing, without an inhabitant.

38 They shall roar together like lions: they shall yell as lions' whelps.

39 In their heat I will make their feasts, and I will make them drunken, that they may rejoice, and sleep a perpetual sleep, and not wake, saith the Lord.

40 I will bring them down like lambs to the slaughter, like rams with he goats.

41 How is Sheshach taken! and how is the praise of the whole earth surprised! how is Babylon become an astonishment among the nations!

42 The sea is come up upon Babylon: she is covered with the multitude of the waves thereof.

43 Her cities are a desolation, a dry land, and a wilderness, a land wherein no man dwelleth, neither doth *any* son of man pass thereby.

44 And I will punish Bel in Babylon, and I will bring forth out of his mouth that which he hath swallowed up: and the nations shall not flow together any more unto him; yea, the wall of Babylon shall fall.

45 My people, go ye out of the midst of her, and deliver ye every man his soul from the fierce anger of the Lord.

46 And lest your heart faint, and ye fear for the rumor that shall be heard in the land; a rumor shall both come *one* year, and after that in *another* year *shall come* a rumor, and violence in the land, ruler against ruler.

36 Therefore thus says the Lord:
"Behold, I will plead your cause
and take vengeance for you.
I will dry up her sea
and make her fountain dry;
37 and Babylon shall become a heap of
ruins,
the haunt of jackals,
a horror and a hissing,
without inhabitant.

38 "They shall roar together like lions;
they shall growl like lions' whelps.
39 While they are inflamed I will prepare
them a feast
and make them drunk, till they swoon
away[w]
and sleep a perpetual sleep
and not wake, says the Lord.
40 I will bring them down like lambs to the
slaughter,
like rams and he-goats.

41 "How Babylon[x] is taken,
the praise of the whole earth seized!
How Babylon has become
a horror among the nations!
42 The sea has come up on Babylon;
she is covered with its tumultuous
waves.
43 Her cities have become a horror,
a land of drought and a desert,
a land in which no one dwells,
and through which no son of man
passes.
44 And I will punish Bel in Babylon,
and take out of his mouth what he has
swallowed.
The nations shall no longer flow to him;
the wall of Babylon has fallen.

45 "Go out of the midst of her, my people!
Let every man save his life
from the fierce anger of the Lord!
46 Let not your heart faint, and be not fearful
at the report heard in the land,
when a report comes in one year
and afterward a report in another year,
and violence is in the land,
and ruler is against ruler.

[w] Gk Vg: Heb *rejoice*
[x] Heb *Sheshach*, a cipher for Babylon

---

41. Babylon: Here written *shēshakh* (see Exeg. on vs. 1; 25:26).

47 Therefore, behold, the days come, that I will do judgment upon the graven images of Babylon: and her whole land shall be confounded, and all her slain shall fall in the midst of her.

48 Then the heaven and the earth, and all that *is* therein, shall sing for Babylon: for the spoilers shall come unto her from the north, saith the LORD.

49 As Babylon *hath caused* the slain of Israel to fall, so at Babylon shall fall the slain of all the earth.

50 Ye that have escaped the sword, go away, stand not still: remember the LORD afar off, and let Jerusalem come into your mind.

51 We are confounded, because we have heard reproach: shame hath covered our faces; for strangers are come into the sanctuaries of the LORD's house.

52 Wherefore, behold, the days come, saith the LORD, that I will do judgment upon her graven images: and through all her land the wounded shall groan.

53 Though Babylon should mount up to heaven, and though she should fortify the height of her strength, *yet* from me shall spoilers come unto her, saith the LORD.

54 A sound of a cry *cometh* from Babylon, and great destruction from the land of the Chaldeans:

55 Because the LORD hath spoiled Babylon, and destroyed out of her the great voice; when her waves do roar like great waters, a noise of their voice is uttered:

56 Because the spoiler is come upon her, *even* upon Babylon, and her mighty men are taken, every one of their bows is broken: for the LORD God of recompenses shall surely requite.

47 "Therefore, behold, the days are coming
    when I will punish the images of
      Babylon;
her whole land shall be put to shame,
    and all her slain shall fall in the midst
      of her.
48 Then the heavens and the earth,
    and all that is in them,
shall sing for joy over Babylon;
    for the destroyers shall come against
      them out of the north, says the LORD.
49 Babylon must fall for the slain of Israel,
    as for Babylon have fallen the slain of
      all the earth.

50 "You that have escaped from the sword,
    go, stand not still!
Remember the LORD from afar,
    and let Jerusalem come into your
      mind:
51 'We are put to shame, for we have heard
    reproach;
    dishonor has covered our face,
for aliens have come
    into the holy places of the LORD's
      house.'

52 "Therefore, behold, the days are coming,
    says the LORD,
    when I will execute judgment upon
      her images,
and through all her land
    the wounded shall groan.
53 Though Babylon should mount up to
    heaven,
    and though she should fortify her
      strong height,
yet destroyers would come from me upon
    her,
    says the LORD.

54 "Hark! a cry from Babylon!
    The noise of great destruction from the
      land of the Chalde'ans!
55 For the LORD is laying Babylon waste,
    and stilling her mighty voice.
Their waves roar like many waters,
    the noise of their voice is raised;
56 for a destroyer has come upon her,
    upon Babylon;
her warriors are taken,
    their bows are broken in pieces;
for the LORD is a God of recompense,
    he will surely requite.

57 And I will make drunk her princes, and her wise *men,* her captains, and her rulers, and her mighty men: and they shall sleep a perpetual sleep, and not wake, saith the King, whose name *is* The LORD of hosts.

58 Thus saith the LORD of hosts; The broad walls of Babylon shall be utterly broken, and her high gates shall be burned with fire; and the people shall labor in vain, and the folk in the fire, and they shall be weary.

59 ¶ The word which Jeremiah the prophet commanded Seraiah the son of Neriah, the son of Maaseiah, when he went with Zedekiah the king of Judah into Babylon in the fourth year of his reign. And *this* Seraiah *was* a quiet prince.

60 So Jeremiah wrote in a book all the evil that should come upon Babylon, *even* all these words that are written against Babylon.

61 And Jeremiah said to Seraiah, When thou comest to Babylon, and shalt see, and shalt read all these words;

62 Then shalt thou say, O LORD, thou hast spoken against this place, to cut it off, that none shall remain in it, neither man nor beast, but that it shall be desolate for ever.

57 I will make drunk her princes and her wise men,
　her governors, her commanders, and her warriors;
they shall sleep a perpetual sleep and not wake,
　says the King, whose name is the LORD of hosts.

58 "Thus says the LORD of hosts:
The broad wall of Babylon
　shall be leveled to the ground
and her high gates
　shall be burned with fire.
The peoples labor for nought,
　and the nations weary themselves only for fire."

59 The word which Jeremiah the prophet commanded Serai'ah the son of Neri'ah, son of Mahsei'ah, when he went with Zedeki'ah king of Judah to Babylon, in the fourth year of his reign. Serai'ah was the quartermaster. 60 Jeremiah wrote in a book all the evil that should come upon Babylon, all these words that are written concerning Babylon. 61 And Jeremiah said to Serai'ah: "When you come to Babylon, see that you read all these words, 62 and say, 'O LORD, thou hast said concerning this place that thou wilt cut it off, so that nothing shall dwell in it, neither man nor beast, and it

59-64. An appendix to the oracle against Babylon, designed to show how, written in **a book** (vs. 60), it was taken **to Babylon.** Some scholars have maintained that Zedekiah went to Babylon in his **fourth year** (594-593 B.C.) to clear himself of suspicion in connection with the rebellion plotted at that time (see ch. 27). But there is no other record of such a visit by the king, and it is not even certain that a rebellion took place at that time. Since the oracles in chs. 50–51 are all secondary, it is most probable that this appendix is also wholly secondary, written by the editor who put the collection of oracles

51:59-64. The Book and the Stone.—It seems too bad to lose this symbolic action to the conflicting theories of biblical research. Whether construed as a literal account or regarded as a symbolic overture in a historical-traditional complex, it is a highly dramatic episode. "There is . . . no inconsistency in supposing Jeremiah to be [its] author," wrote Driver. "A simple, unimpassioned declaration of the future end of Babylon is not inconsistent with Jeremiah's attitude at the beginning of Zedekiah's reign." [1] It forms, as a matter of fact, a striking parallel with Jeremiah's purchase of the field (32:9; also 13:1-7; 17:2; 19:1, 10; 43:9). The motiva-

[1] *The Book of the Prophet Jeremiah,* p. 326.

tion is much the same. The prophetic action, thus carried through, does not merely warn against the future but already begins to bring that future to pass. The power of the pronouncement is already made effective; it is bound fast (by the stone) to Babylon's destiny (the Euphrates), and is at the same time conveyed (by the river) to all the parts of Babylon.

The central meaning, however, is to be seen in the symbolic action taken as a whole. Seraiah was Baruch's brother. It is altogether probable, therefore, that such a scroll containing oracles on Babylon should have been carried by him on his special mission. Just as the purchase of the field bore witness to Jeremiah's faith in the

63 And it shall be, when thou hast made an end of reading this book, *that* thou shalt bind a stone to it, and cast it into the midst of Euphrates:

64 And thou shalt say, Thus shall Babylon sink, and shall not rise from the evil that I will bring upon her: and they shall be weary. Thus far *are* the words of Jeremiah.

52 Zedekiah *was* one and twenty years old when he began to reign, and he reigned eleven years in Jerusalem. And his mother's name *was* Hamutal the daughter of Jeremiah of Libnah.

2 And he did *that which was* evil in the eyes of the LORD, according to all that Jehoiakim had done.

shall be desolate for ever.' **63** When you finish reading this book, bind a stone to it, and cast it into the midst of the Eu-phra'tes, **64** and say, 'Thus shall Babylon sink, to rise no more, because of the evil that I am bringing upon her.' "*y*

Thus far are the words of Jeremiah.

52 Zedeki'ah was twenty-one years old when he became king; and he reigned eleven years in Jerusalem. His mother's name was Hamu'tal the daughter of Jeremiah of Libnah. **2** And he did what was evil in the sight of the LORD, according to

y Gk: Heb *upon her. And they shall weary themselves*

---

together and perhaps invented this story of a visit to Babylon. **Seraiah the son of Neriah, son of Mahseiah** was apparently a brother of Baruch, Jeremiah's secretary and companion (32:12).

XXXIV. HISTORICAL APPENDIX (52:1-34)

This chapter is almost identical with II Kings 24:18–25:30. The principal omission is II Kings 25:22-26, covering the governorship of Gedaliah and his assassination, which are recorded more fully in 40:7–43:7. The principal addition is vss. 28-30. Ch. 52 is a historical appendix to the book of Jeremiah (note the last sentence of 51:64), taken from II Kings or from the same source as the corresponding portion of II Kings. Because vss. 18-23 are more complete than II Kings 25:13-17, and vss. 28-30 seem to be quite authentic, it is most likely that ch. 52 is from a common source, and represents that source more fully than II Kings 24–25; it is also possible that in the course of the transmission of the text parts of II Kings 24–25 have been omitted.

The appendix was added to the book of Jeremiah in order to show how some of the prophecies of Jeremiah were fulfilled in the fall of Jerusalem and the exile of many Jews; it ends, with the account of the favorable treatment of King Jehoiachin, on a note of hope.

For details see Exeg. on II Kings 24:18–25:30. The Exeg. below will note only the significant variations from the passage in II Kings.

A. SUMMARY OF ZEDEKIAH'S REIGN (52:1-3)

This section is almost completely identical with II Kings 24:18-20. It is a brief summary and evaluation of Zedekiah's reign, like those provided by the Deuteronomic editor of Kings for most of the Judean and Israelite monarchs.

---

perpetuity of Israel, so the carrying of this book with its prophecy of Babylon's eventual fall, conveyed to the exiles Jeremiah's belief in the ultimate decline of that great world power. For though Babylon was the present instrument of Yahweh, it was only his instrument and not his people. Only by founding itself upon the righteousness of Yahweh could it become so. Jeremiah knew that his warnings would be ignored, as the word of the Lord was ignored. Therefore his scroll, with the stone

tied to it, should be cast into the middle of the stream. Thus, as the word of the Lord sank to oblivion in the ceaseless flow of the Euphrates River, so Babylon would sink in the endless flow of the rivers of time.

52:1-34. *The Seat Above the Seats of Kings.*
—The addenda supplied to the book of Jeremiah in this last chapter are of the severely matter-of-fact kind. The recounting of Nebuchadrezzar's sack of Jerusalem, the despoiling of the temple, and the enumeration of people

3 For through the anger of the Lord it came to pass in Jerusalem and Judah, till he had cast them out from his presence, that Zedekiah rebelled against the king of Babylon.

4 ¶ And it came to pass in the ninth year of his reign, in the tenth month, in the tenth *day* of the month, *that* Nebuchadrezzar king of Babylon came, he and all his army, against Jerusalem, and pitched against it, and built forts against it round about.

5 So the city was besieged unto the eleventh year of king Zedekiah.

6 And in the fourth month, in the ninth *day* of the month, the famine was sore in the city, so that there was no bread for the people of the land.

7 Then the city was broken up, and all the men of war fled, and went forth out of the city by night by the way of the gate between the two walls, which *was* by the king's garden; (now the Chaldeans *were* by the city round about:) and they went by the way of the plain.

8 ¶ But the army of the Chaldeans pursued after the king, and overtook Zedekiah in the plains of Jericho; and all his army was scattered from him.

9 Then they took the king, and carried him up unto the king of Babylon to Riblah in the land of Hamath; where he gave judgment upon him.

10 And the king of Babylon slew the sons of Zedekiah before his eyes: he slew also all the princes of Judah in Riblah.

11 Then he put out the eyes of Zedekiah; and the king of Babylon bound him in chains, and carried him to Babylon, and put him in prison till the day of his death.

all that Jehoi'akim had done. 3 Surely because of the anger of the Lord things came to such a pass in Jerusalem and Judah that he cast them out from his presence.

And Zedeki'ah rebelled against the king of Babylon. 4 And in the ninth year of his reign, in the tenth month, on the tenth day of the month, Nebuchadrez'zar king of Babylon came with all his army against Jerusalem, and they laid siege to it and built siegeworks against it round about. 5 So the city was besieged till the eleventh year of King Zedeki'ah. 6 On the ninth day of the fourth month the famine was so severe in the city, that there was no food for the people of the land. 7 Then a breach was made in the city; and all the men of war fled and went out from the city by night by the way of a gate between the two walls, by the king's garden, while the Chalde'ans were round about the city. And they went in the direction of the Arabah. 8 But the army of the Chalde'ans pursued the king, and overtook Zedeki'ah in the plains of Jericho; and all his army was scattered from him. 9 Then they captured the king, and brought him up to the king of Babylon at Riblah in the land of Hamath, and he passed sentence upon him. 10 The king of Babylon slew the sons of Zedeki'ah before his eyes, and also slew all the princes of Judah at Riblah. 11 He put out the eyes of Zedeki'ah, and bound him in fetters, and the king of Babylon took him to Babylon, and put him in prison till the day of his death.

B. Siege and Fall of Jerusalem (52:4-27)

10. And also slew all the princes of Judah at Riblah: Not in II Kings 25:7.
11. And put him in prison till the day of his death: Not in II Kings 25:7.

---

carried away captive on three successive invasions are told in a flat, unemotional style. In this they stand in sharp contrast with the book of Lamentations which, recounting the same episodes, floats all its words on its unsearchable reservoir of tears. This is a strange conclusion to the book of Jeremiah. We do not even know the place or manner of Jeremiah's death. Legend has it that he was stoned to death in Egypt. Thus he would become a martyr. According to another narrative, when the fall of his city came, he took from the temple certain of its hallowed relics and hid them in a cave upon Mount Zion. Thus he became a conserver of traditions, a myth which cut strangely across the forward-looking vision of his work. Again, in the time of the Maccabees, he appeared in a vision holding a golden sword—an omen for the success of the rebellious enterprise. Thus was he uplifted as a divine warrior in a time

12 ¶ Now in the fifth month, in the tenth *day* of the month, which *was* the nineteenth year of Nebuchadrezzar king of Babylon, came Nebuzar-adan, captain of the guard, *which* served the king of Babylon, into Jerusalem,

13 And burned the house of the LORD, and the king's house; and all the houses of Jerusalem, and all the houses of the great *men,* burned he with fire:

14 And all the army of the Chaldeans, that *were* with the captain of the guard, brake down all the walls of Jerusalem round about.

15 Then Nebuzar-adan the captain of the guard carried away captive *certain* of the poor of the people, and the residue of the people that remained in the city, and those that fell away, that fell to the king of Babylon, and the rest of the multitude.

16 But Nebuzar-adan the captain of the guard left *certain* of the poor of the land for vinedressers and for husbandmen.

17 Also the pillars of brass that *were* in the house of the LORD, and the bases, and the brazen sea that *was* in the house of the LORD, the Chaldeans brake, and carried all the brass of them to Babylon.

18 The caldrons also, and the shovels, and the snuffers, and the bowls, and the spoons, and all the vessels of brass wherewith they ministered, took they away.

19 And the basins, and the firepans, and the bowls, and the caldrons, and the candlesticks, and the spoons, and the cups; *that* which *was* of gold *in* gold, and *that* which *was* of silver *in* silver, took the captain of the guard away.

20 The two pillars, one sea, and twelve brazen bulls that *were* under the bases, which king Solomon had made in the house

12 In the fifth month, on the tenth day of the month — which was the nineteenth year of King Nebuchadrez'zar, king of Babylon — Nebu'zarad'an the captain of the bodyguard who served the king of Babylon, entered Jerusalem. 13 And he burned the house of the LORD, and the king's house and all the houses of Jerusalem; every great house he burned down. 14 And all the army of the Chalde'ans, who were with the captain of the guard, broke down all the walls round about Jerusalem. 15 And Nebu'zarad'an the captain of the guard carried away captive some of the poorest of the people and the rest of the people who were left in the city and the deserters who had deserted to the king of Babylon, together with the rest of the artisans. 16 But Nebu'zarad'an the captain of the guard left some of the poorest of the land to be vinedressers and plowmen.

17 And the pillars of bronze that were in the house of the LORD, and the stands and the bronze sea that were in the house of the LORD, the Chalde'ans broke in pieces, and carried all the bronze to Babylon. 18 And they took away the pots, and the shovels, and the snuffers, and the basins, and the dishes for incense, and all the vessels of bronze used in the temple service; 19 also the small bowls, and the firepans, and the basins, and the pots, and the lampstands, and the dishes for incense, and the bowls for libation. What was of gold the captain of the guard took away as gold, and what was of silver, as silver. 20 As for the two pillars, the one sea, the twelve bronze bulls which were under the sea,ᶻ and the

ᶻ Heb lacks *the sea*

---

12. **On the tenth day of the month:** II Kings 25:8 has "seventh day."

18-23. This is fuller than the corresponding account in II Kings 25:13-17. The latter omits some of the temple objects listed here, notably: most of those in vs. 19; **the twelve bronze bulls which were under the sea** in vs. 20; the detailed description of the pillars in vs. 21; and all of vs. 23.

---

of heroic but desperate courage. We know how Jeremiah influenced the portrait of the suffering servant of Yahweh, and how he inspired a great portion of the book of Job. Best of all, when Jesus was compared with Elijah, others described him as another Jeremiah. Nebuchadrezzar, one of the great conquerors and states-

men of the ancient world, was succeeded by Evil-merodach. Though he was, perhaps, the sun and stars of his century, his greatness has fallen away like his empire. Jeremiah has acquired a seat above the seats of kings.

There is something almost equally symbolic, in a curious way, about the fate of Jehoiachin.

of the LORD: the brass of all these vessels was without weight.

21 And *concerning* the pillars, the height of one pillar *was* eighteen cubits; and a fillet of twelve cubits did compass it; and the thickness thereof *was* four fingers: *it was* hollow.

22 And a chapiter of brass *was* upon it; and the height of one chapiter *was* five cubits, with network and pomegranates upon the chapiters round about, all *of* brass. The second pillar also and the pomegranates *were* like unto these.

23 And there were ninety and six pomegranates on a side; *and* all the pomegranates upon the network *were* a hundred round about.

24 ¶ And the captain of the guard took Seraiah the chief priest, and Zephaniah the second priest, and the three keepers of the door:

25 He took also out of the city a eunuch, which had the charge of the men of war; and seven men of them that were near the king's person, which were found in the city; and the principal scribe of the host, who mustered the people of the land; and three-score men of the people of the land, that were found in the midst of the city.

26 So Nebuzar-adan the captain of the guard took them, and brought them to the king of Babylon to Riblah.

27 And the king of Babylon smote them, and put them to death in Riblah in the land of Hamath. Thus Judah was carried away captive out of his own land.

28 This *is* the people whom Nebuchadrezzar carried away captive: in the seventh year three thousand Jews and three and twenty:

stands, which Solomon the king had made for the house of the LORD, the bronze of all these things was beyond weight. 21 As for the pillars, the height of the one pillar was eighteen cubits, its circumference was twelve cubits, and its thickness was four fingers, and it was hollow. 22 Upon it was a capital of bronze; the height of the one capital was five cubits; a network and pomegranates, all of bronze, were upon the capital round about. And the second pillar had the like, with pomegranates. 23 There were ninety-six pomegranates on the sides; all the pomegranates were a hundred upon the network round about.

24 And the captain of the guard took Serai'ah the chief priest, and Zephani'ah the second priest, and the three keepers of the threshold; 25 and from the city he took an officer who had been in command of the men of war, and seven men of the king's council, who were found in the city; and the secretary of the commander of the army who mustered the people of the land; and sixty men of the people of the land, who were found in the midst of the city. 26 And Nebu'zarad'an the captain of the guard took them, and brought them to the king of Babylon at Riblah. 27 And the king of Babylon smote them, and put them to death at Riblah in the land of Hamath. So Judah was carried captive out of its land.

28 This is the number of the people whom Nebuchadrez'zar carried away captive: in the seventh year, three thousand

C. THE THREE DEPORTATIONS (52:28-30)

28-30. Although these three verses are not in II Kings, or in the LXX of Jeremiah, they seem to give us authentic historical information because of the precision of the dates recorded and the smallness of the numbers. They raise difficulties when comparison is made of the dates and figures here given with those elsewhere, but the very difficulties

The book of Jeremiah says tantalizingly little about Jehoiachin, who was king of Judah for three months after Jehoiakim. He was evidently unlike his father. He gave to the people a moment of hope: because he was so young, perhaps, and had a future before him. But the hope was short lived, and the pathos profound;

for the eighteen-year-old king was carried away, along with the queen mother, into exile. There was a movement to rally the exiles around the young king in Babylon, but this hope too died early. Nothing more is said of Jehoiachin until vss. 31-34, where we learn that Evil-merodach, on succeeding to the throne of King Nebuchad-

29 In the eighteenth year of Nebuchad-rezzar he carried away captive from Jerusalem eight hundred thirty and two persons:

30 In the three and twentieth year of Nebuchadrezzar, Nebuzar-adan the captain of the guard carried away captive of the Jews seven hundred forty and five persons: all the persons *were* four thousand and six hundred.

31 ¶ And it came to pass in the seven and thirtieth year of the captivity of Jehoiachin king of Judah, in the twelfth month, in the five and twentieth *day* of the month, *that*

and twenty-three Jews; 29 in the eighteenth year of Nebuchadrez'zar he carried away captive from Jerusalem eight hundred and thirty-two persons; 30 in the twenty-third year of Nebuchadrez'zar, Nebu'zarad'an the captain of the guard carried away captive of the Jews seven hundred and forty-five persons; all the persons were four thousand and six hundred.

31 And in the thirty-seventh year of the captivity of Jehoi'achin king of Judah, in

are in favor of their authenticity; had the facts here recorded been made up by an editor, they would be in closer accord with facts given elsewhere.

The three deportations may be set down in tabular form as follows, assuming that the dates follow the Babylonian system of chronology, which has an "accession year" before the "first year" in a king's reign (see Exeg. on 26:1) :

First Captivity:	598-597 B.C.	3,023	Jews
Second Captivity:	587-586 B.C.	832	Jerusalemites
Third Captivity:	582-581 B.C.	745	Jews
		Total	4,600

The first deportation should probably be associated with the surrender of Jehoiachin (II Kings 24:12-16) . Because the number given here does not agree with the "ten thousand" in II Kings 24:14, some scholars have proposed that vs. 28 ought to read "seventeenth" year of Nebuchadrezzar rather than **seventh,** and that the deportation was of Judeans outside of Jerusalem at the beginning of the siege of Jerusalem in 588 B.C. This seems improbable since there is no record elsewhere of such a deportation, unless 13:19 is an allusion to it.

The date for the second deportation, **the eighteenth year of Nebuchadrezzar,** seems inconsistent with the date in vs. 12, where the coming of Nebuzaradan is placed in the "nineteenth year." A possible explanation is that vs. 12 uses the nonaccession-year system of dating (antedating) , whereas vs. 29 uses the accession-year system (postdating) .

The third deportation was probably made by the Babylonians in punishment of the Jews for the disturbances in Palestine surrounding the assassination of Gedaliah (see Exeg. on 40:7–41:18) .

D. Release of Jehoiachin from Prison (52:31-34)

This section is virtually equivalent to II Kings 25:27-30. For Jeremiah's attitude toward Jehoiachin, and a statement concerning Babylonian records which confirm the release of that king from prison, see Exeg. on 22:24-30.

rezzar, brought Jehoiachin out of prison. **He spoke kindly to him, and gave him a seat above the seats of the kings who were with him in Babylon.** After thirty-seven years, Jehoiachin put aside his prison garments. He dined at the king's table, received a regular allowance and was highly esteemed until the day of his death.

Man, it has been said, is a god in ruins. Would it be better, perhaps, to call him an exiled king? For there is something about

Jehoiachin that makes him typical, perhaps a symbol, of something in the human condition. He must have been a lonely king, a king without a people; or, if a people, then a people in captivity—like himself. It has been suggested that Jehoiachin "died" at the age of eighteen; but clearly this was not the case. He evidently learned to accept the conditions of his exile, as Jeremiah had advised. He had come to merit the esteem of kings, and after thirty-seven years

Evil-merodach king of Babylon, in the *first* year of his reign, lifted up the head of Jehoiachin king of Judah, and brought him forth out of prison,

32 And spake kindly unto him, and set his throne above the throne of the kings that *were* with him in Babylon,

33 And changed his prison garments: and he did continually eat bread before him all the days of his life.

34 And *for* his diet, there was a continual diet given him of the king of Babylon, every day a portion until the day of his death, all the days of his life.

the twelfth month, on the twenty-fifth day of the month, E'vil-mer'odach king of Babylon, in the year that he became king, lifted up the head of Jehoi'achin king of Judah and brought him out of prison; 32 and he spoke kindly to him, and gave him a seat above the seats of the kings who were with him in Babylon. 33 So Jehoi'achin put off his prison garments. And every day of his life he dined regularly at the king's table; 34 as for his allowance, a regular allowance was given him by the king according to his daily need, until the day of his death as long as he lived.

---

31. Lifted up the head of Jehoiachin: A literal rendering of a Hebrew idiom, which the RSV paraphrases correctly in II Kings 25:27, "graciously freed Jehoiachin." The same idiom occurs in Gen. 40:13, 20.

---

he was given a seat above the seats of kings. In the tragedy of Jeremiah he emerges at the last with sudden character—very much like Horatio, disclosing sudden greatness when the hero, Hamlet, dies:

> Good night, sweet prince,
> And flights of angels sing thee to thy rest! [2]

Perhaps it is that once again deliverance has come after long and patient suffering.

Jehoiachin emerges as a symbol of promise. He is a symbol of the growth of the exiles toward that knowledge of Yahweh which will empower their return. Yet he is also the king who became a captive: but who as captive eventually took captive the admiring king. Thus, quite dimly (and it is this, perhaps, which makes us conjure with his name), Jehoiachin foreshadows the King who became the Servant,

[2] *Hamlet*, Act V, scene 2.

and who, when crucified, took our captivity captive, in order that, through him, all men might know the Seat which is above the seats of kings.

> King must lay gold circlets down
> In God's sepulchral ante-rooms,
> The wear of Heaven's the thorny crown:
> He paves His temples with their tombs.
>
> O our towered altitudes!
> O the lustres of our thrones!
> What! old Time shall have his moods
> Like Caesars and Napoleons;
>
> Have his towers and conquerors forth,
> Till he, weary of the toys,
> Put back Rameses in the earth
> And break his Ninevehs and Troys. [3]

[3] Francis Thompson, "An Echo of Victor Hugo," from *Collected Works*, ed. Wilfred Meynell. Used by permission of the publisher, Burns Oates & Washbourne, London.

Gaza

PLAIN OF SHARON

Beer-sheba

Samaria

Hebron

Mt. Gerizim   Mt. Ebal

Jerusalem

Jericho   Jordan River

SALT SEA

Mt. Nebo

Rabbath-ammon

PALESTINE
in Old Testament Times